Medieval Iberia

E. Michael Gerli, Editor

MEDIEVAL IBERIA

AN ENCYCLOPEDIA

Associate Editors

Samuel G. Armistead, University of California, Davis
Robert I. Burns, S. J., University of California, Los Angeles
Pedro M. Cátedra, Universidad de Salamanca
Alan Deyermond, Queen Mary-Westfield College, University of London
Ana Domínguez Rodríguez, Universidad Complutense, Madrid
Harold V. Livermore, University of British Columbia
Joseph F. O'Callaghan, Fordham University
Norman Roth, University of Wisconsin, Madison
Robert Stevenson, University of California, Los Angeles

Routledge
New York London

Editorial Staff
Project Editor: Mark O'Malley
Production Editor: Jeanne Shu
Production Manager: Anthony Mancini, Jr.
Production Director: Dennis Teston
Developmental Manager: Kate Aker
Publishing Director: Sylvia Miller

Published in 2003 by
Routledge
29 West 35th Street
New York, NY 10001
www.routledge-ny.com

Published in Great Britain by
Routledge
11 New Fetter Lane
London EC4P 4EE
www.routledge.co.uk

Routledge is an imprint of the Taylor & Francis Group.
Printed in the United States of America on acid-free paper.

10 9 8 7 6 5 4 3 2 1

Library of Congress Cataloging-in-Publication Data

Medieval Iberia : an encyclopedia / edited, with introductions, by E. Michael Gerli.
p. cm.
Includes bibliographical references and index.
ISBN 0-415-93918-6 (hardcover : alk. paper)
1. Spain—History—711-1516—Encyclopedias. I. Gerli, E. Michael.

DP99 .M33 2002
946′.02′03—dc21
2002012828

Contents

Introduction

Medieval Iberia: An Encyclopedia is conceived as a single-volume, English-language reference work for scholars, students, and the general public seeking reliable information on subjects concerning the Iberian Peninsula, the geographic area comprised by present-day Spain and Portugal, from the period from approximately 470 to 1500. It consists of over eight hundred alphabetically arranged entries that deal with persons, events, works, institutions, and topics that have a particular relevance to all of medieval Iberia—Muslim, Jewish, and Christian alike. Ranging in length from 250 to 3,000 words, the articles that comprise the book are written by expert contributors, and seek to provide a basic orientation on the various subjects for ready reference. In addition, each entry supplies a selected bibliography of between two and ten items, whenever possible mostly in English. The scope of the work is broad but not comprehensive, with an emphasis on history, literature, language, religion, science, folklore, and the arts, including selected Jewish and Muslim topics. To complement its content and facilitate its use, the book offers a comprehensive index.

Given its broad, multidisciplinary sweep, *Medieval Iberia* is directed at a diverse readership and provides a wide variety of information on a great number of subjects. Literary scholars, for example, will be able to readily consult dates and events of historical importance, while historians will be able to clarify questions dealing with literature. Similarly, someone seeking information on folklore—for example, the Sephardic ballad tradition—may consult an authoritative entry on the latter providing a basic orientation and a selected list of readings that will serve as an introduction to the topic. The undergraduate wishing to write a research paper on scientific, philosophical, and literary translations completed in medieval Iberia, as well as the grade school teacher in need of basic facts about Prince Henry the Navigator and the Portuguese voyages of discovery, will also find this encyclopedia useful. In short, though the majority of its users will doubtless consist of individuals with some prior knowledge of medieval Iberia, and though its principal purpose is to facilitate scholarly access to information not readily available in standard reference sources on the Middle Ages, this volume will also be consulted by members of the general public who simply wish to obtain a succinct summary of a subject along with basic facts about it. On the one hand, then, *Medieval Iberia* serves as a reference tool for scholars seeking to undertake advanced research in areas of the humanities with which they are unfamiliar; on the other, it functions as a medium for the dissemination of knowledge about medieval Iberian culture and civilization throughout the English-speaking world.

Several criteria govern the scope and the determination of the entries:

1. Entries are generally restricted to the years 470–1500. Hence, Bartolomé de Torres Naharro, whose major literary work was published in 1517, is not included, while Juan del Encina, who completed his first opus in 1493, has an entry. Exceptions to the chronology are made for overlapping subjects that continue to bear significance as well as exercise their influence. Hence, Gil Vicente, the bilingual Portuguese author whose work first appears in 1502 merits coverage based on the close relationship of his theater to that of his predecessor, Encina.
2. Because of the availability of good reference sources on certain well-known entries, coverage has been designed to emphasize the lesser-known aspects of the subject. Thus, for example, the entry on Castilian explorations devotes greater attention to the Canary Islands and the western Atlantic than to Christopher Columbus and America, for which there are useful essays in standard encyclopedias like the *Britannica* and the *Americana*. Similarly, subjects that recent research has reevaluated and whose entries in other sources are now outdated merit attention.
3. Topics are of broad significance. Those that had a wide influence in their own time; those that initiated change; and those that are relevant today outside narrow areas of specialization are all included here. Thus, in the area of literature, key authors, works, concepts, and movements are covered, while more specialized topics in prosody, bibliography, and the like, are not.
4. In general, the shorter entries (250–500 words) are more factually oriented and seek to lead the user to authoritative sources. The longer entries (500–3,000 words), without prejudicing essential facts, tend to be more interpretive and strive to synthesize and place the topic within medieval Iberia as a whole.

Medieval Iberia thus places less emphasis on subjects fully treated in standard reference works and strives to address those areas not adequately covered in the latter. The material is distributed approximately in the following proportions:

twenty-five percent history (includes biographies, events, politics, law, economics, and the like).
twenty-five percent literature, language, and culture (includes Arabic, Hebrew, and peninsular Romance languages; oral culture, and folklore).
twenty-five percent life and society (includes religion, education, agriculture, popular causes, and so on).
fifteen percent philosophy and science (includes Christian, Moslem, and Jewish topics).
ten percent arts (architecture, music, painting).

Since *Medieval Iberia* provides information about subjects not easily located in reference works addressing all of the Middle Ages or medieval history exclusively, sources like the *Dictionary of the Middle Ages*, and *The Middle Ages: A Concise Encyclopedia*, though they cover only some Iberian themes, may be viewed as complements to this volume.

The entries are arranged according to several criteria. In listing literary works, preference is given to the names of authors, whenever known, rather than to titles; thus, *Milagros de Nuestra Señora* will be found under Gonzalo de Berceo and *Proverbios morales* will appear under Shem Tov of Carrión. Anonymous works generally appear under the commonly used form of the title; thus the *Libro de Alexandre* will appear under *Libro* but at the same time has a cross-reference from Alexander of Macedonia. In cases where titles are significantly ambivalent, as in *Cantar* vs. *Poema de Mio Cid*, the placement for the entry was left to the author of the entry to decide, vouchsafed by a cross-reference from the form of the entry not chosen. The form used to alphabetize individual names has often proved problematical. Strictly speaking, Gil Alvarez Carrillo de Albornoz should appear under Alvarez Carrillo de Albornoz, yet he is generally known as Gil de Albornoz. He will thus be located under Albornoz, which we have chosen in order to respect general usage and avoid confusion. The Spanish forms of the names of kings and nobles most currently in use in historical and literary research has also been given preference over English. Hence, rather than Henry IV and Isabella I of Castile, and Alfonso V of Portugal, we use Enrique IV and Isabel I of Castile, and Afonso V of Portugal. The same is true of certain place- and saints' names. Thus, Zaragoza and Mallorca are preferred to the English Saragossa and Majorca, although Seville and Lisbon are used in place of Sevilla and Lisboa; and St. Dominic, the founder of the Order of Preachers, can be found under Domingo de Guzmán as opposed to Dominic of Guzman, or St. Dominic. Loconymns have proved especially difficult and we have tried to resolve confusion in the following fashion: In the case of individual nobles and royals, listing can be found under their first name. Thus, Constanza de Mallorca may be found under Constanza and not Mallorca or de Mallorca. Others, whose loconymns are currently used in research as if they were last names, appear under their loconymns. Hence the fifteenth-century *converso* (Christian convert) poet Antón de Montoro is located under Montoro and not Antón, and Alonso Fernández de Madrigal may be found under Madrigal, and not Fernández de Madrigal. Finally, to facilitate the book's use by a broad range of individuals, all dates are given according to the familiar Gregorian calendar. The norms for the transliteration of Arabic into the Latin alphabet are placed at the end of this introduction.

This volume includes illustrations, maps, genealogies, and lines of succession that seek visually to complement or clarify the subjects they accompany. The index at the end is intended to guide users to topics that are frequently cited in the volume but lack their own entries. The bibliographies accompanying the entries are organized alphabetically first by author and, in the case of edited works or numerous works by a single author, then by title. They are composed of selected items and are intended only to provide reference materials to enable the student or scholar to move confidently into the subject.

Given the substantial academic interest in medieval studies, the recognition of Iberia's increasing importance within medieval culture, and an increased general interest in Iberia and in Hispanic culture in the United States and Britain, this encyclopedia seems not only desirable but timely and necessary. It should be welcomed by Hispanists of all disciplines, academics interested in learning more about Spain's and Portugal's crucial contributions to one of the formative periods of Western civilization, and the lay reader wishing to find information concerning Iberia's fundamental role in the creation of world culture. There is no equivalent reference source to *Medieval Iberia* in either English or Spanish.

Under the direction of general editor E. Michael Gerli and the board of associate editors, *Medieval Iberia* has been completed with the advice and direction provided by of a group of internationally distinguished scholars: the historians Robert I. Burns, S.J., Joseph F. O'Callaghan, and Norman Roth; the musicologist Robert Stevenson; the literary and intellectual historians Alan D. Deyermond, Pedro M. Cátedra, and Harold

V. Livermore; the folklorist, medievalist, and ballad expert Samuel G. Armistead; and the art historian Ana Domínguez Rodríguez. In consultation with the associate editors, the general editor has been responsible for proposing and establishing the list of entries as well as identifying potential contributors with the necessary expertise to produce authoritative articles on each of the topics selected for inclusion. He and an expert team of reference editors at Routledge have overseen the final editing and production of the manuscript.

Acknowledgments

A volume like this could not have been produced without the cooperation of literally hundreds of individuals, who gave of their time, enthusiasm, energy, and good will over a number of years to see it to completion. The editors are especially grateful to the indefatigable Gary Kuris, who originally proposed the work more than a decade ago, when he was editor at Garland; to numerous graduate students at both Georgetown University and the University of Virginia—Mary Zampini, Christopher McDonald, Laura Labauve, Pedro Pérez Leal, Matthew Bentley, and others—who helped with correspondence, filing, translation, and in the day-to-day organization of the myriad tasks involved in gathering, compiling, and sorting the entries; and to the editorial team at Routledge Reference in New York, who saved the project from oblivion and supplied their astonishing professional acumen to see it to its final publication. Among the latter group, special credit is reserved for Marie-Claire Antoine, who provided the basic impetus for the work's resurrection after five years of uncertainty; for Mark O'Malley, who with good humor, a deep sense of duty, and a youthful, sturdy constitution literally ran up and down the spiral staircase in the last weeks of its production; and for Kate Aker, who with austere reminders and stern words kept an unbending schedule and unraveling sensibilities always intact. Finally, the greatest credit is due to the associate editors and the scholars on two continents who gave of their time, good will, deep knowledge, and profound love of Hispanism to compose, read, edit, and check the entries and the accompanying bibliographies that comprise this work. *Jubilate! Fortuna favet fortibus.*

Publisher's Note

The Routledge Encyclopedias of the Middle Ages

Formerly the Garland Encyclopedias of the Middle Ages, this comprehensive series began in 1993 with the publication of *Medieval Scandinavia.* A major enterprise in medieval scholarship, the series brings the expertise of scholars specializing in myriad aspects of the medieval world together in a reference source accessible to students and the general public as well as to historians and scholars in related fields. Each volume focuses on a geographical area or theme important to medieval studies and is edited by a specialist in that field, who has called upon a board of consulting editors to establish the article list and review the articles. Each article is contributed by a scholar and followed by a bibliography and cross-references to guide further research.

Routledge is proud to carry on the tradition established by the first volumes in this important series. As the series continues to grow, we hope that it will provide the most comprehensive and detailed view of the medieval world in all its aspects ever presented in encyclopedia form.

Vol. 1 *Medieval Scandinavia: An Encyclopedia.* Edited by Phillip Pulsiano.
Vol. 2 *Medieval France: An Encyclopedia.* Edited by William W. Kibler and Grover A. Zinn.
Vol. 3 *Medieval England: An Encyclopedia.* Edited by Paul E. Szarmach, M. Teresa Tavormin, and Joel T. Rosenthal.
Vol. 4 *Medieval Archaeology: An Encyclopedia.* Edited by Pamela Crabtree.
Vol. 5 *Trade, Travel, and Exploration in the Middle Ages.* Edited by John Block Friedman and Kristen Mossler Figg.
Vol. 6 *Medieval Germany: An Encyclopedia.* Edited by John M. Jeep.
Vol. 7 *Medieval Jewish Civilization: An Encyclopedia.* Edited by Norman Roth

The present volume, *Medieval Iberia: An Encyclopedia*, edited by Michael Gerli, is Volume 8 in the series.

Arabic Transliteration

TERMINAL	MEDIAL	INITIAL	ALONE	TRANSLITERATION
ـا	ـا	ا	ا	a
ـب	ـبـ	بـ	ب	b
ـت	ـتـ	تـ	ت	t
ـث	ـثـ	ثـ	ث	th
ـج	ـجـ	جـ	ج	j
ـح	ـحـ	حـ	ح	ḥ
ـخ	ـخـ	خـ	خ	kh
ـد	ـد	د	د	d
ـذ	ـذ	ذ	ذ	dh
ـر	ـر	ر	ر	r
ـز	ـز	ز	ز	z
ـس	ـسـ	سـ	س	s
ـش	ـشـ	شـ	ش	sh
ـص	ـصـ	صـ	ص	ṣ
ـض	ـضـ	ضـ	ض	ḍ
ـط	ـطـ	طـ	ط	ṭ
ـظ	ـظـ	ظـ	ظ	ẓ
ـع	ـعـ	عـ	ع	'
ـغ	ـغـ	غـ	غ	gh
ـف	ـفـ	فـ	ف	f
ـق	ـقـ	قـ	ق	q
ـك	ـكـ	كـ	ك	k
ـل	ـلـ	لـ	ل	l
ـم	ـمـ	مـ	م	m
ـن	ـنـ	نـ	ن	n
ـه	ـهـ	هـ	ه	h
ـو	ـو	و	و	w
ـي	ـيـ	يـ	ي	y

VOWELS: short a ـَ u ـُ i ـِ long a ـَا u ـُو i ـِي

DIPTHONGS: aw ـَوْ ay ـَيْ

Contributors

Omaima Abou-Bakr
Cairo University

David S. Abulafia
University of Cambridge

A. C.
Al-Mudayna

Samuel G. Armistead
University of California, Davis

Gorka Aulestia
Universidad de Deusto

Martí Aurell i Cardona
Paris, France

Reinaldo Ayerbe-Chaux
University of Illinois, Chicago

Eduardo Aznar Vallejo
Universidad de La Laguna

Clifford Backman
Boston University

Lola Badía
Universitat de Girona

Ana M. Balaguer
Sabadell, Barcelona, Spain

Spurgeon Baldwin
University of Alabama

Fernando Baños Vallejo
Universidad de Oviedo

Theodore S. Beardsley, Jr.
Hispanic Society of America

Rafael Beltrán
Universidad de Valencia

Vicenç Beltrán
Universitat de Barcelona

Stephen P. Bensch
Swarthmore College

Matthew T. Bentley
University of Virginia

José Bernáldez Montalvo
Archivo Municipal de Madrid

Carmen Bernís-Madrazo
Consejo Superior de Investigaciones Científicas, Madrid

C. Julian Bishko
University of Virginia

Thomas N. Bisson
Harvard University

Jonathan Bloom
Richmond, New Hampshire

Roger Boase
Queen Mary-Westfield College, University of London

Seeger A. Bonebakker
Zeist, The Netherlands

Anthony Bonner
Palma de Mallorca

Ross Brann
Cornell University

Vivana Brodey
University of Honolulu

James Brodman
University of Central Arkansas

Thomas Burman
University of Tennessee

Charles Burnett
Warburg Institute, London

Paul C. Burns
University of British Columbia

Robert I. Burns, S. J.
University of California, Los Angeles

Lluis Cabré
Universitat Autònoma de Barcelona

Pierre Cachia
Columbia Universtiy

Vicente Cantarino
Ohio State University

Anthony Cárdenas
University of New Mexico

Dwayne E. Carpenter
Boston College

Robert Chazan
New York University

Antonio Collantes de Terán Sánchez
Universidad de Sevilla

Roger Collins
St. George's School, Edinburgh

Jane E. Connolly
University of Miami

Olivia Remie Constable
University of Notre Dame

Carol Copenhagen
Orinda, California

Antonio Corfíjo
Ocaña

Ivy Corfis
University of Wisconsin, Madison

Dustin Cowell
University of Wisconsin

Jerry Craddock
University of California, Berkeley

Miquel Crusafont i Sabater
Sabadell, Barcelona, Spain

Michèle Cruz-Sáenz
Wallingford, Pennsylvania

Amanda Curry
Washington, D.C.

John Dagenais
University of California, Los Angeles

Alan Deyermond
Queen Mary-Westfield College, University of London

José Manuel Díaz de Bustamante
Universidad de Santiago de Compostela

Ana Domínguez Rodríguez
Universidad Complutense de Madrid

Francis A. Dutra
University of California, Santa Barbara

Steven N. Dworkin
University of Michigan

Theresa Earenfight
Seattle University

John Edwards
University of Oxford

Daniel Eisenberg
Regis College

Mikel Epalza
Universidad de Alicante

Juan Espadas
Ursinus College

Clara Estow
University of Massachusetts, Boston

Charles B. Faulhaber
University of California, Berkeley

Seymour Feldman
Rutgers University

Felipe Fernández-Armesto
Hakluyt Society

Alberto Ferreiro
Seattle Pacific University

Luis Adão da Fonseca
Universidade de Porto

Angela Franco-Mata
Museo Arqueológico Nacional, Madrid

Charles F. Fraker
University of Michigan

Paul H. Freedman
Yale University

Alan Friedlander
Southern Connecticut State University

Alvaro Galmés de Fuentes
Universidad Complutense de Madrid

Raquel García Arancón
Universidad de Navarra

Blanca García Escalona
Universidad de Madrid

Blanca García Vega
Universidad de Valladolid

Antonio García y García
Universidad Pontífica de Salamanca

Elena Gascón Vera
Wellesley College

John Geary
University of Colorado, Boulder

Philip O. Gericke
University of California, Riverside

E. Michael Gerli
University of Virginia

Thomas F. Glick
Boston University

Harriet Goldberg
Villanova University

María Jesús Gómez Bárcena
Universidad Complutense de Madrid

Maricarmen Gómez Muntané
Universitat Autònoma de Barcelona

Cristina González
University of California, Davis

Ramón Gonzálvez
Catedral de Toledo

Antony Goodman
University of Edinburgh

T. J. Gorton
Paris, France

George D. Greenia
College of William and Mary

Juan Gutiérrez Cuadrado

Eleazar Gutwirth
Tel Aviv University

Joseph J. Gwara
United States Naval Academy

Thomas R. Hart
University of Oregon

L. Patrick Harvey
King's College, University of London

Warren Zev Harvey
Hebrew University, Jerusalem

Peter Heath
Washington University, St. Luois

Daniel L. Heiple
Tulane University

María Teresa Herrera
Universidad de Salamanca

Marilyn Higbee Walker
Columbia University

Bennett D. Hill
Georgetown University

David Hook
University of Bristol

Thomas M. Izbicki
Eisenhower Library, Johns Hopkins University

Frede Jensen
University of Colorado

Donald Kagay
Albany State University

Henry Kamen
Consejo Superior de Investigaciones Científicas, Barcelona

Hanna E. Kassis
University of British Columbia

Israel J. Katz
Teaneck, N.J.

John E. Keller
University of Kentucky

Mary Jane Kelley
Ohio University

Richard P. Kinkade
University of Arizona

CONTRIBUTORS

Ewald Könsgen
Philipps Universität Marburg

María del Carmen Lacarra Ducay
Universidad de Zaragoza

María Jesús Lacarra
Universidad de Zaragoza

Miguel Angel Ladero Quesada
Universidad Complutense de Madrid

Y. Tzvi Langermann
Jewish National and University Library, Jerusalem

Eva LaPiedra
Universidad de Alicante

Aurora Lauzardo
Princeton University

Jeremy Lawrance
University of Manchester

Oliver Leaman
Liverpool University

Béatrice Leroy
Université de Bordeaux

Antonio Linage Conde
Universidad de Madrid

Peter Linehan
University of Cambridge

Peggy Liss
Washington, D.C.

H. V. Livermore
University of British Columbia

Paul M. Lloyd
University of Pennsylvania

Francisco López Estrada
Universidad Complutense de Madrid

Consuleo López-Morillas
Indiana University

Elena Lourie
Ben Gurion University

Sieglinde Lug
University of Denver

Robert A. MacDonald
University of Richmond

Angus MacKay
Edinburgh University

Nancy F. Marino
Michigan State University

María Luisa Martín Ansón
Universidad Autónoma de Madrid

José Luis Martín Martín
Universidad de Salamanca

Salvador Martínez
New York University

José Mattoso
Universidade de Lisboa

Lawrence J. McCrank
Ferris State University

Michael R. McVaugh
University of North Carolina, Chapel Hill

Faustino Menéndez Pidal de Navascués
Universidad de Madrid

Guido Mensching
Universität zu Köln

Walter Mettmann
Universität Münster

Mark Meyerson
University of Toronto

José Luis Mingote Calderón
Museo Arqueológico Nacional, Madrid

Carlos Miranda-García
Universidad de Madrid

James A. Monk
University of Virginia

Jesús Montoya Martínez
Universidad de Granada

Margherita Morreale
Università di Padova

Lynn H. Nelson
University of Kansas

Colbert I. Nepaulsingh
State University of New York, Albany

Malyn Newitt
University of Exeter

Robert Oakley
University of Birmingham

Joseph F. O'Callaghan
Fordham University

A.H. Oliveira Marques
Universidade de Lisboa

Marilyn Olsen
Mayfield Heights, Ohio

John B. Owens
Idaho State University

Mark Gregory Pegg
Princeton University

Antonio Pérez Martín
Universidad de Murcia

Lucy K. Pick
University of Chicago

Ermelindo Portela Silva
Universidad de Santiago de Compostela

Brian Powell
University of Hull

James Powers
College of the Holy Cross

Matthew Raden
Tulane University

David Raizman
Drexel University

Marjorie Ratcliffe
University of Western Ontario

Luis Rebelo
King's College, University of London

Stephen Reckertt
Lisbon, Portugal

José M. Regueiro
University of Pennsylvania

Bernard F. Reilly
Villanova University

Manuel Riu
Universitat de Barcelona

David Pattison
University of Oxford

Julio Rodríguez-Puértolas
Universidad Autónoma de Madrid

J. Rodríguez Velasco
University of California, Berkeley

Regula Rohland de Langbehn
Universidad de Buenos Aires

Philipp W. Rosemann
University of Dallas

Norman Roth
University of Wisconsin, Madison

Adeline Rucquoi
CNRS, Paris, France

D. Fairchild Ruggles
University of Illinois, Urbana-Champaign

Teófilo Ruiz
University of California, Los Angeles

Alan Ryder
University of Bristol

Angel Sáenz Badillos
Universidad Complutense de Madrid

Regina Sáinz de la Masa Lasoli
Consejo Superior de Investigaciones Científicas, Barcelona

Julio Samsó
Universidad de Barcelona

Raymond Scheindlin
Jewish Theological Seminary

Cristina Segura Graíño
Universidad de Madrid

Dennis P. Seniff
Michigan State University

Dorothy S. Severin
Liverpool University

Dorothy C. Clarke Shadi
University of California, Berkeley

Harvey L. Sharrer
University of California, Santa Barbara

John C. Shideler
Hood River, Oregon

Harry Sieber
Johns Hopkins University

Larry Simon
Western Michigan University

Colin Smith
University of Cambridge

Wendell Smith
Transylvania University

Joseph Snow
Michigan State University

Thomas Spaccarelli
University of the South

Charlotte Stern
Randolph Macon Women's College

Robert Stevenson
University of California, Los Angeles

Ronald E. Surtz
Princeton University

Joseph Szövérffy
University of Vienna

Robert B. Tate
University of Nottingham

Barry Taylor
The British Library
University of Liverpool

Jane Tillier
University of Oxford

James J. Todesca
Fordham University

Juan Torres Fontes
Universidad de Murcia

Pierre Tucoo-Chala
Pau, France

Isabel Uría-Maqua
Universidad de Oviedo

Julio Valdeón Baruque
Universidad de Valladolid

Theresa M. Vann
Hill Monastic Library

Mercedes Vaquero
Brown University

Thomas J. Walsh
Georgetown University

Ruth H. Webber
University of Chicago

Jill R. Webster
University of Toronto

Julian M. Weiss
King's College
University of London

Barbara F. Weissberger
University of Minnesota

Nicolás Wey-Gómez
Massachusetts Institute of Technology

Jane Whetnall
Queen Mary-Westfield College, University of London

G. A. Wiegers
Rijks Universiteit Leiden

Chad Wight

Constance Wilkins
Miami University

George D. Winius
College of Charleston

Kenneth B. Wolf
Pomona College

Roger Wright
University of Liverpool

David Wulstan
University College of Wales

John Zemke
University of Missouri, Columbia

Alphabetical List of Entries

A

Abbey of Poblet
Abbeys, Royal
ʿAbd Al-ʿAzīz ibn Mūṣā
ʿAbd Allāh, Emir of Córdoba
ʿAbdallāh ibn Bullugin, King of Granada
ʿAbd Al-Raḥmān I, Emir of Córdoba
ʿAbd Al-Raḥmān II, Emir of Córdoba
ʿAbd Al-Raḥmān III, Caliph of Córdoba
Abraham Bar Ḥiyya (Ḥayya)
Abraham El-Barchilon (Al-Barjiluni)
Abravanel, Isaac
Abū Zayd, Governor of Valencia
Abulafia, Meir
Abulafia, Todros
Abū-l-Qāsim
Acuña, Luis de
Adelantado
Adminstration, Central, Aragón-Catalonia
Administration, Central, Castile
Administration, Central, León
Administration, Central, Navarre
Administration, Central, Portugal
Administration, Financial, Crown of Aragón
Administration, Financial, Castile
Administration, Financial, León
Administration, Financial, Navarre
Administration, Financial, Portugal
Administration, Judicial
Administration, Territorial, Castile, Portugal, León, Aragón, Catalonia, Navarre
Administration, Territorial, Muslim
Afonso Henriques, or Afonso I
Afonso II, King of Portugal
Afonso III, King of Portugal
Afonso IV, King of Portugal
Afonso V
Afonso, Count of Barcelos and Duke of Bragança
Agriculture
Alarcos, Battle of
Albalat, Pere de
Albigensian Crusade, The
Albo, Joseph
Albornoz, Gil Alvarez Carrillo de
Alburquerque, Juan Alfonso, Lord of
Alcázovas, Treaties of
Alcalá de Henares, Ordenamiento of
Alcañices, Treaty of
Alchemy
Alfarrobeira, Battle of
Alfonso de la Cerda
Alfonso de Toledo
Alfonso I, King of Aragón
Alfonso II, King of Aragón
Alfonso III, King of Aragón
Alfonso III, King of Asturias
Alfonso IV, King of Aragón
Alfonso IX, King of León
Alfonso V, King of Aragón, The Magnanimous
Alfonso V, King of León
Alfonso VI, King of León-Castile
Alfonso VII, King of León-Castile
Alfonso VIII, King of Castile
Alfonso X, El Sabio, King of Castile and León, Artistic Patronage, Art, Miniatures, and Portraits
Alfonso X, El Sabio, King of Castile and León, Historical Works
Alfonso X, El Sabio, King of Castile and León, Law
Alfonso X, El Sabio, King of Castilean and León, Musical Instruments of Cantigas
Alfonso X, El Sabio, King of Castile and León, Music of Cantigas
Alfonso X, El Sabio, King of Castile and León, Poetry
Alfonso X, El Sabio, King of Castile and León, Political History
Alfonso X, El Sabio, King of Castile and León, Science
Alfonso XI, King of Castile and León
Alfonso, *Infante* of Castile
Alhambra
Alhandega, Battle of
Aljama
Aljamiado Literature
Aljubarrota, Battle of
Almada, Felipa de
Almizra (or Almirra), Treaty of
Almohads
Almojarife
Almoravids
Alvares Pereira, Nun'
Alvarez de Villasandino, Alfonso
Alvarez Gato, Juan
Alvaro, Pelayo
Alvarus, Paulus
Amadís de Gaula
Anagni, Treaty of
Anchieta, Juan de
Animal Fables
António of Lisbon, Saint
Antifeminist Literature
Antiphoner of León
Arabic Language
Aragón, Crown of
Aragonese Language
Archeology
Architecture
Arias Dávila Family
Arias, Mayor
Army, Castilian, Catalan, Muslim, Portuguese

A

ABBADIDS *See* BANU ABBAD

ABBEY OF POBLET

Royal abbey and the premier Cistercian house in the Iberian Peninsula. Ramón Berenguer IV, Count of Barcelona (1131–1162) and Prince of Aragón (1137–1162) in 1149, founded Poblet twenty miles northeast of Tarragona with monks from Fontfroide (near Narbonne), a daughter-house of Clairvaux. Royal and noble gifts of vast lands acquired from the reconquest; the strategy of using loans and tax exemptions to attract peasant tenants for the exploitation of these estates; sheep farming on a vast scale; the early-adopted policy of accepting mortgaged land protected by royal privilege from the claims of creditors; the acquisition of a monopoly of the milling industry along the upper Francal River; and the expectation of landed or cash dowries—these economic practices yielded prodigious wealth. By 1297 the abbey possessed 55,000 acres divided into granges, twenty-nine villages, thirty-eight castles, and other properties.

Much of this wealth was spent on the construction of the abbey church and conventual buildings. The classic expression of Cistercian architecture in Spain and sometimes called the "Escorial of Aragón," though an austere Romanesque enriched by Gothic ogive vaulting, the church extends 85 meters long, with the vaulting over the nave rising 28 meters. Because the monastery held a strategic position in a frontier region commanding the Tarragona-Lérida highway and successive princes considered it of major military importance, heavily fortified walls and bastions surround the church and domestic buildings; the massive royal palace to the east of the church bears comparison with the palace of the popes at Avignon. In 1194, Alfonso II (1162–1196) held his court at Poblet and was later buried there; Pedro IV (1336–1387) conceived of Poblet as a dynastic mausoleum.

Poblet further exploited its wealth by serving as banker to the crown and nobility of Aragón. The abbey financed wars against the Muslims, the expeditions of Jaime I (1213–1276) against Mallorca and Valencia; the defense of Pedro III (1276–1285) against French invasion. Because the abbey exercised a stabilizing influence in a frontier region, and because it had pastoral responsibilities over a steadily expanding rural population, Poblet sought, and Pope Honorius granted, the abbot episcopal status. In 1336–1337, the Cistercian Pope Benedict XII granted the abbot the right to wear full pontificalia—mitre, ring, and sandals. If these liturgical practices, these economic and political activities blatantly violated the Cistercian constitutions, they were justified on the grounds of service to the crown, especially in its struggle against the Muslims.

Throughout the Middle Ages the recruits of choir monks came primarily from the nobility. Although badly bit by the Black Death—in 1348 alone, 2 abbots, 59 choir monks, and 30 lay brothers succumbed—numbers remained stable through the fourteenth and fifteenth centuries, with about ninety choir monks, while the number of lay brothers grew from eighty-five in 1311 to 135 in 1493. Poblet made four foundations of sister houses in the late Middle Ages. In 1531–1533, numbers stood at 60 choir monks and 30 lay brothers.

The abbey underwent continual remodeling until the late eighteenth century. Although the Cistercian order was suppressed in Spain in 1835, the monastic buildings remained in such excellent condition that when Poblet was restored in 1940, a community soon flourished. Unlike most monastic houses in the late twentieth century, Poblet has suffered no dearth of recruits, and in 1967 it made a foundation, Solius, in the province of Girona.

BENNETT D. HILL

Bibliography

Altisent, A. *La descentralizacíon administrativa del Monasterio de Poblet en la Edad Media*. Abadia de Poblet, 1985.

ABBEYS, ROYAL

In the twelfth and thirteenth centuries, the period of the expansion of Latin Christendom into frontier regions such as the Iberian Peninsula, first the Cistercian monks, and later the military orders and the mendicant friars proved highly effective agents in the spread of a common culture. The Cistercians and the new orders, rather than the Benedictines, acquired lands and ecclesiastical powers; they were the great beneficiaries of the *reconquista* (Reconquest).

A distinctive feature of Iberian monasticism in this period of expansion was the conjunction or union of the monastery and the royal palace. Leaders of the Reconquest, the count-princes pushed backed Islam and established monasteries for the military, as well as the religious and cultural security and integrity of conquered areas. Kings built their residences at some monasteries and formed close associations with them during their lifetimes; the construction of royal tombs in the monastic churches represented monastic support for royal power. While not totally unique to the Iberian Peninsula—the histories of the imperial abbey of Farfa in central Italy; of the abbey of Saint Denis near Paris and the Capetian dynasty; of the abbey of Saint Peter at Westminster near London and the English monarchy; and of the German *Reichsabteien*—all bear comparison to Iberian counterparts. But in contrast to other parts of Europe, where the inspiration for a monastic foundation came from individuals considered outstanding for their piety, in Iberia the impulse for a new foundation came from princes who built and endowed abbeys as spiritual supports for their power, resided in them, and were buried in tombs attached to them. As agents of princely power, royal abbeys lacked the political and religious independence characteristic of monasticism in England and Germany. Probably the most famous royal abbeys in Iberia, all of them Cistercian, were Poblet (1149) and Santas Creus (1150) in Catalonian Aragón; Las Huelgas (1187) in Castile, the only house of women among the royal abbeys, whose abbess was always a royal princess and all the nuns recruited from the highest aristocracy; and Alcobaça (1158) located between Lisbon and Coimbra, the "mother house" of all twelve Cistercian abbeys in Portugal, a center of rich cultural activity, and sometimes described as "one of the greatest monastic establishments in Europe."

By the seventh century and throughout the Middle Ages, Spanish monasteries, like those in other parts of western Europe and on the basis of scriptural precedent (1 Sam. 1 and Luke 1:63–80) and conciliar decress (Fourth Council of Toledo, 633), accepted boys or girls as oblates, offerings given to the house by their parents. These children, overwhelmingly descended from the nobility since a dowry was required or at least expected, raised and educated by the monastic community, made monastic profession (public statement of the vows of obedience, stability in the house of profession, and conversion of life) at about age sixteen and were thereafter denied a return to lay society. In Castile and elsewhere the nobility, wishing to preserve family estates intact, entailed them on the eldest son. Apart from the knightly life, careers in monasteries or dioceses represented virtually the only socially acceptable profession. Although the twelfth and thirteenth centuries witnessed the highpoint of child oblation, perhaps the most economically viable and humane way of divesting a family of superfluous or awkward children, the practice continued at least into the seventeenth century.

As in observant houses everywhere, the *Opus Dei* (Work of God, the monastic office to which St. Benedict had said nothing should be preferred) constituted the major work of the royal abbeys. The proximity of the royal court meant that chanceries drew on the monks for clerks, secretaries, treasurers, diplomats, and other officials. As monasteries acquired properties, some monks were assigned the supervision of them and of the revenues they yielded. The schools and libraries of some houses, such as Alcobaça, enjoyed considerable reputations for scholarship. The bulk of the wealth of the royal abbeys seems to have been spent on the decoration and expansion of the abbey church and buildings, and on charitable services to the local poor.

In 1562, King Felipe II decided to build a monastery to memorialize the Spanish victory over the French at Saint Quentin (1557). The vast granite buildings of the abbey of Saint Lawrence in the village of El Escorial near Madrid (constructed 1563–1584) was intended to combine the functions of a Hieronymite monastery for 250 monks in which the king had his own cell, a royal residence, and center of imperial administration, and a mausoleum for the dynasty. The idea for the Escorial rested on a long tradition.

BENNETT D. HILL

Bibliography

Lekai, L. *The Cistercians: Ideals and Reality*. Kent, Ohio, 1977.

Braunfels, W. *Monasteries of Western Europe: The Architecture of the Orders*. Princeton, N.J., 1972.

ʿABD AL-ʿAZĪZ IBN MŪṢĀ

The son of Mūṣā Ibn Nusayr, who in 711 had sent Tāriq across the Straits of Gibraltar to conquer Iberia, ʿAbd al-ʿAzīz Ibn Mūṣā governed al-Andalus from 714 to 716. During his tenure, he proved a capable and imaginative administrator who established Seville as his capital, and from there directed the Muslim conquest of the Iberian Peninsula toward the east, west, and south, consolidating and extending his power to Portugal, Málaga, Granada, Orihuela, Girona, and Barcelona. He was the first Muslim governor to organize the financial and administrative affairs of the newly conquered territories of Iberia, and he sought to eliminate the ethnic distinctions in government service between Berbers and Arabs. ʿAbd al-ʿAziz encouraged intermarriage between the Islamic conquerors and the native Iberian population. While his political and administrative program for the period immediately after the Conquest was generally successful, as a result of his marriage to Egilona, who was either the sister or the widow of Rodrigo, the last Visigothic king, he was accused by both Arabs and Berbers alike of favoring the native Christian population and of having monarchical ambitions. ʿAbd al-ʿAzīz was said to have been urged by Egilona to wear a crown on his head and to adopt the manner of a western monarch. Tensions grew within the army just as his father, Mūṣā Ibn Nusayr, had been recalled from North Africa and was disgraced by the Caliph in Damascus. ʿAbd al-ʿAzīz Ibn Mūṣā was executed in 716 on the grounds that he was seeking to separate himself and al-Andalus from Damascus.

E. MICHAEL GERLI

Bibliography

Chejne, A. G. *Muslim Spain: Its History and Culture*. Minneapolis, 1974.

Vernet, J. *La cultura hispanoárabe en oriente y occidente*. Barcelona, 1978.

ʿABD ALLĀH, EMIR OF CÓRDOBA

ʿAbd Allāh Ibn Muḥammad I was the grandson of ʿAbd al-Raḥmān II and grandfather of ʿAbd al-Raḥmān III. He succeeded his brother, al-Mundhir, as emir of al-Andalus in 888 and ruled until 912.

ʿAbd Allāh, born in 844, was forty-four years old when his brother died fighting the rebel Ibn Hafṣūn (some have accused ʿAbd Allāh of Hafṣūn fratricide). ʿAbd Allāh's reign was characterized by violence and upheaval—at times, he controlled only the city of Córdoba, which itself was full of tensions between "old" and "new" (*muwallad*) Muslims.

Arab biographers describe ʿAbd Allāh as being particularly pious, yet they also note his cruelty in dealing with enemies. ʿAbd Allāh quickly alienated most segments of the population, especially his own family. He is said to have encouraged the stabbing death of his son Muḥammad at the hands of his other son, al-Muṭarrif. Al-Muṭarrif, in turn, was killed after being accused of conspiring with the leaders of Seville. Two of ʿAbd Allāh's brothers were killed when they became too powerful. These harsh measures only served to further weaken the prestige of the Umayyad family as a whole and reflected the disintegration of centralized power at this time.

With a weak and paranoid-reclusive authority in Córdoba, the administrative and tax structure established by ʿAbd al-Raḥmān II completely fell apart. Strong local families quickly removed any remaining Umayyad-appointed governors and kept the taxes for themselves to maintain standing armies. Of the many provincial revolts that took place during ʿAbd Allāh's reign, the most significant was the revolt of the muwallad Ibn Hafṣūn in Bobastro, in a mountain valley outside Córdoba. He had begun his revolt in 881 during the reign of Muḥammad I, and under ʿAbd Allāh's nose, Ibn Hafṣūn began conducting raids right up to the walls of Córdoba itself with impunity. Until he announced his conversion to Christianity in 899, Ibn Hafṣūn was the unofficial leader of the muwallad factions of the lower Guadalqivir valley; after 899, he slowly lost most of his Muslim supporters. Other strong muwallad rebels at this time were Daysam Ibn Isḥāq of Murcia and Ibrāhīm Ibn al-Ḥajjāj of Seville.

Without doubt the best decision ʿAbd Allāh made during his reign was selecting and training his grandson ʿAbd al-Raḥmān as heir. When ʿAbd Allāh died in 912, ʿAbd al-Raḥmān III peacefully ascended to the throne and began a reign that ultimately proved to be the high point of Umayyad power in Spain.

MARILYN HIGBEE WALKER

Bibliography

Kennedy, H. *Muslim Spain and Portugal: A Political History of al-Andalus*. London, 1996.

Lévi-Provençal, E. *Histoire de l'Espagne musulmane*, 3 vols. Leiden, 1950–53.

ʿABDALLĀH IBN BULLUGIN, KING OF GRANADA

The last Zīrid king of Granada. He reigned from 1073 to 1090. His memoirs, written after being exiled to Morocco, were discovered in the last century in a mosque and have been translated into Spanish under the title *El siglo XI en primera persona*. They reveal precious information concerning the interaction of the members of his family and other tawā'if (party) kingdoms as well as the internal political administration of Granada shortly before the advent of the Almoravid invasion. Of particular interest are the details concerning the rise to power of his kinsman and predecessor,

Badis, who was helped by the Jewish magnate Samuel Ibn Nagrillah, who was generously compensated by being named vizier and put in charge of the finances of the kingdom.

ʿAbdallāh was a minor when he acceded to the throne in 1073. During his minority his tutor, Sīmacha, an astute and able individual, grasped the power of the monarchy for himself and continued to exercise it well after his pupil had come of age. Pressed during his reign by incursions into Granadan territory by the ʿAbbādis of Seville and Alfonso VI of Castile, ʿAbdallāh's time on the throne of Granada was made even more difficult by rivalries among his lieutenants and dissent in the army. When Sīmacha was expelled from court, he fled the kingdom and sowed conflict from afar between ʿAbdallāh and his brother, Tamīm of Málaga. In his memoirs, ʿAbdallāh vividly recalls how Alfonso VI took advantage of this situation by extorting huge sums from him in order to guarantee his protection.

Faced with a deteriorating situation in the Iberian Peninsula, aggravated by mutual competition and conquest between Muslims, ʿAbdallāh finally joined other tawā'if kings in seeking protection against Alfonso from Muslims abroad. In the end, Yūsuf Ibn Tashfin, the emperor of the Almoravids who had been called in by his coreligionists from North Africa to save them from the Castilians and from themselves, arrogated all power in al-Andalus to himself, deposing ʿAbdallāh and exiling him across the straits, from where he wrote his illuminating memoirs.

E. MICHAEL GERLI

Bibliography

Ibn Bullugin, ʿA. *El siglo XI en primera persona*. Ed. and trans. E. García Gómez, et al., Madrid, 1979.

Chejne, A. G. *Muslim Spain: Its History and Culture*. Minneapolis, 1974.

Vernet, J. *La cultura hispanoárabe en oriente y occidente*. Barcelona, 1978.

ʿABD AL-RAḤMĀN I, EMIR OF CÓRDOBA

ʿAbd al-Raḥmān I Ibn Muʿāwiya Ibn Hishām Ibn ʿAbd al-Mālik Ibn Marwān was the founder of the Muslim Umayyad dynasty that ruled Spain from 756 to 1031. He was born in Damascus in 731 and is purported to be the only member of the Umayyad family who survived their overthrow in 750 by the ʿAbbasids. ʿAbd al-Raḥmān escaped first to Palestine, then to Egypt, and then on to Morocco, where he took refuge with the Nafza Berber tribe, of which his mother was a member. When his efforts to gain power among the Moroccan Berbers failed, he looked to Spain, where the lack of unity among the Muslim conquerors—Yemeni Arabs, Syrian Arabs, and recently converted Berbers and Iberians—made for an easy conquest. Because of this successful entry and establishment of a dynasty, ʿAbd al-Raḥmān is known as *al-Dākhil*, or "the Immigrant."

At the time of ʿAbd al-Raḥmān I's entry into Spain in 756, Yūsuf Ibn ʿAbd al-Raḥmān al-Fihrī was the local governor appointed by the Umayyad regional governor in Qayrawān (in Tunisia). Like the many provincial governors who had preceded him since the Muslim conquest of Spain in 711, Yūsuf struggled to manage the infighting between the Arabs and Berbers. The Berbers formed a vast majority and resented the pretension of racial and cultural superiority of the Arabs despite Islam's injunction of equality. Yūsuf also had to deal with the perennial feuding (which dated back to pre-Islamic Arabia) between the Yemeni and Syrian Arab tribes. A large Syrian army contingent had entered Spain in 742 after being defeated by the Berbers in North Africa, several years after the original Yemeni conquerors, and there were power struggles between the "new" and "old" invaders. ʿAbd al-Raḥmān I took advantage of this rivalry and the support of Umayyad clients already in the peninsula. He arrived in Seville in 756 and, gathering forces along the way, defeated Yūsuf al-Fihrī on the outskirts of Córdoba. ʿAbd al-Raḥmān I proclaimed himself emir of al-Andalus (the Arabic name for the portion of Iberia controlled by the Muslims), refusing allegiance to the ʿAbbasids but recognizing their caliphal claim.

ʿAbd al-Raḥmān I ruled al-Andalus for over thirty-three years and spent most of that time struggling with the same problems of unity that the governors before him had faced: Berbers who had been settled in the geographically familiar mountainous north and northwest regularly rebelled against the central Córdoban authority; the Arabs, who had settled along tribal lines in various towns in the south and southeast, continued to feud; the local converts, or muwallads, felt as unjustly treated as the Berbers and often rebelled; and in the east, a coalition of Arab tribal leaders went so far as to encourage Charlemagne to lay siege to Zaragoza in 778 (he withdrew when recalled to the Rhineland and from this episode emerged *The Song of Roland*). Any group that had established themselves in the provinces prior to 756 resented the Umayyad efforts at administrative and financial control.

However, through a relatively lengthy reign and with the prestige and legitimacy attached to the Umayyad name, ʿAbd al-Raḥmān I was able to slowly consolidate power in the province of Córdoba and at least keep most of the localized rebellions in check. As for the outlying provinces, if the provincial leaders were willing to recognize his nominal right to rule and to send Córdoba a percentage of their taxes, ʿAbd al-Raḥmān I permitted them to continue in relative autonomy. He established an administrative and military structure similar to the one he had known in Damascus, and when news of his accession spread, Umayyad supporters throughout the Islamic world began coming to Spain, which increased his power base but further antagonized the earlier invaders, who resented having to share the spoils.

With so many internal concerns, ʿAbd al-Raḥmān I was unable to make much headway against the Christians in the north and failed to regain many of the towns lost to them under the governors. A border system of "marches" had been established to maintain the fluid frontiers with the Christians, but by the time ʿAbd al-Raḥmān I gained control internally, the marches had receded to the following positions: the eastern march became centered in Zaragoza, the central march in Toledo, and the western march in Badajoz. Berbers often occupied these unstable, agriculturally less-productive areas, and it was not until the reign of ʿAbd al-Raḥmān III in the early tenth century that these areas came firmly under Muslim control.

In the last two years of his reign ʿAbd al-Raḥmān I built, on the site of the Church of St. Vincent, the Great Mosque of Córdoba, which his successors expanded in stages and which still stands today. ʿAbd al-Raḥmān I died in 788 without a clearly designated successor. His son Hishām I, who had been ruling as governor of Mérida, declared himself emir two months later after defeating another of ʿAbd al-Raḥmān's sons, Sulaymān.

Marilyn Higbee Walker

Bibliography

"ʿAbd al-Raḥmān," in *Encyclopedia of Islam*. 2d ed. Leiden.

Kennedy, H. *Muslim Spain and Portugal: A Political History of al-Andalus*. London, 1996.

Lévi-Provençal, E. *Histoire de l'Espagne musulmane*. 3 vols. Leiden, 1950–53.

ʿABD AL-RAḤMĀN II, EMIR OF CÓRDOBA

ʿAbd al-Raḥmān II Ibn al-Ḥakam I was the great-grandson and namesake of the emir ʿAbd al-Raḥmān I, and ruled Muslim Spain from 822 to 852. ʿAbd al-Raḥmān II was born in 792 in Toledo and his father, al-Ḥakam I, clearly designated him successor before his own death. Like his predecessors, ʿAbd al-Raḥmān II had to face both internal and external threats to his power. His father had been quite heavy-handed in his reign, and ʿAbd al-Raḥmān II's first challenges were to put down the subsequent and continuing internal rebellions.

One of ʿAbd al-Raḥmān II's first steps was to give more official support to Islam—for example, he executed the chief of the palace guard, who was a Christian, and began building several mosques in Córdoba. The cooperation and legitimation provided by the Muslim scholarly class was essential to maintaining power in the capital. ʿAbd al-Raḥmān II's next concern was to regain control in the Levantine territories and in Toledo. Other sources of internal rebellion were the muwallads (converts to Islam) and the Berbers (Muslim converts from North Africa). In the Ebro valley the muwallad Banū Qasī family regularly rebelled against ʿAbd al-Raḥmān II's central authority. In Mérida, the Berber leader Maḥmūd Ibn ʿAbd al-Djabbār revolted. By the end of his reign, ʿAbd al-Raḥmān II succeeded in placing Umayyad-loyal governors in the three frontier capitals of Mérida, Toledo, and Zaragoza.

What has come to be known as the "Córdoba martyrs movement" began in 850 and finally came to a close with the death of the priest Eulogius in 869. Eulogius was chronicler of the movement, along with Paulus Alvarus, and their Latin accounts are the only sources available. This movement involved the voluntary martyrdoms of Christians who, distressed at the increasing cultural, linguistic, and religious weakness of the Christian community, publicly denounced Islam and the prophet Muḥammad, a crime punishable by death. For the most part these men and women came from monasteries on the outskirts of Córdoba, but some were offspring of religiously mixed (one parent Muslim, the other Christian) families in the city. The martyrs' deaths did not stem the tide of Islamization that continued well into the tenth century; rather, they caused increased tension between the Christians and Muslims and within the Christian community itself.

On a somewhat irregular basis ʿAbd al-Raḥmān II sent summer military expeditions to fight the Christians in the north, particularly in the eastern march region of Asturias-León. The primary purpose does not seem to be the conquest of territory; the collection of booty, the punishment of impertinent Christian and Muslim vassals, the legitimation of the emir's role as defender of the faith and thus his right to rule, and the chance to conduct military exercises appear to be the reasons for such expeditions. In 844 ʿAbd al-Raḥmān II faced a very real external threat in the form of Norsemen who landed at Lisbon and followed the Gualdalquivir River all the way to Seville, which they sacked. ʿAbd al-Raḥmān II did rally to recapture Seville and drove the Norsemen out in the same year, but the threat always remained. As a result, ʿAbd al-Raḥmān II reinforced the navy and built shipyards at Seville and a naval base at Almería.

ʿAbd al-Raḥmān II was the first ruler of al-Andalus strong enough to pursue wide-ranging diplomacy. He maintained ties with several coastal kingdoms in Morocco but shunned the Aghlabids of Qayrawān, who were loyal to the ʿAbbasids of Baghdad. He opened diplomatic relations with Byzantium and received an embassy from Theophilus; in return, ʿAbd al-Raḥmān II sent a delegation to Constantinople headed by the poet Ghazāl.

Known to be a great poet himself, ʿAbd al-Raḥmān II was a patron of arts and letters and brought learned men from all over the Islamic world to Córdoba. One of these, Ziryāb, was a renowned musician and singer from Baghdad who also knew astronomy and geography. The increasingly large and cosmopolitan population of Córdoba was developing a taste for luxury and ostentation under the prosperous reign of ʿAbd al-Raḥmān II, and Ziryāb quickly became the dictator of fashion and culture along ʿAbbasid lines. Ziryāb apparently introduced a new hairstyle; the vegetable asparagus; and the use of underarm deodorant, among other things.

ʿAbd al-Raḥmān II was also known as a great builder and organizer. With the increase in the population of Córdoba, he enlarged the Great Mosque twice, in 833 and 848. He built many public works in Córdoba, but like virtually all his Umayyad predecessors and successors, did little of such things outside Córdoba. Following the ʿAbbasid administrative style, the focus was on the capital, with the various provinces enjoying a large measure of autonomy.

ʿAbd al-Raḥmān II died in Córdoba in 852 and was succeeded by his son, Muḥammad I.

MARILYN HIGBEE WALKER

Bibliography

Coope, J. *The Martyrs of Córdoba*. Lincoln, Nebr., 1995.

Kennedy, H. *Muslim Spain and Portugal: A Political History of al-Andalus*. London, 1996.

Lévi-Provençal, E. *Histoire de l'Espagne musulmane*. 3 vols. Leiden, 1950–53.

ʿABD AL-RAḤMĀN III, CALIPH OF CÓRDOBA

ʿAbd al-Raḥmān Ibn Muḥammad was the grandson and successor of the emir ʿAbd Allāh and was known as ʿAbd al-Raḥmān III. He ruled al-Andalus from 912 to 966 and achieved a measure of prosperity and success unparalleled by those who came before or after him.

ʿAbd al-Raḥmān III was born in 891. It is said that he had blue eyes and fair hair because of his Christian grandmother from Pamplona, and that he dyed that fair hair black to better fit the physical ideal of an Arab Muslim ruler. Although he was relatively young when he succeeded his grandfather, ʿAbd al-Raḥmān III was already well-known at court for his intelligence, political common sense, and leadership abilities. He came to power at a time when the control of the Umayyad emirs did not extend much beyond Córdoba. When his reign ended almost fifty years later, ʿAbd al-Raḥmān III could count on allegiance from Toledo on the north to Ceuta in the south; he received annual tribute payments from the Christian kingdoms to the north; and he regularly welcomed embassies from Constantinople, Baghdad, and beyond.

The first thing ʿAbd al-Raḥmān III did when he came to the throne in 912 was to systematically consolidate power within al-Andalus and quell the internal revolts. The most pressing and long lasting of these was led by the muwallad rebel Ibn Hafṣūn in Bobastro, a mountain fortress outside Córdoba, where he had been ruling virtually autonomously since 888. ʿAbd al-Raḥmān III put pressure on Ibn Hafṣūn until his death in 917, and after him on his sons until they surrendered in 928. The emir attacked the rebel provincial leaders of large cities like Seville, Badajoz, and Toledo, laying siege for years if necessary. Once a city or castle capitulated, ʿAbd al-Raḥmān III either left his own deputy in charge or demolished the fortifications. He acted consistently and powerfully, but also shrewdly: if the rebel leaders submitted to his authority, he often appointed them as Umayyad military leaders in regions far from their own. In this way, by the year 933, ʿAbd al-Raḥmān III had achieved the full unification of al-Andalus.

The second task ʿAbd al-Raḥmān III set for himself involved securing the borders against the increasingly powerful Christian kings to the north. This he pursued simultaneously with his efforts at internal control: his summer campaigns (*ṣāi'fa*) to secure Andalusian allegiance all included forays and shows of force deep into the territory of the Christians. ʿAbd al-Raḥmān III led campaigns in 920 and 924 against the Basques and Leonese—not necessarily to conquer new territory, but to demonstrate his power to both Muslims and non-Muslims. In 920 he stopped the advance of Ordoño III of Asturias-León at the Battle of Junquera. In 924, to revenge the raids made by Sancho García of Navarre, he sacked and burned Pamplona. This was the farthest north he ever ventured. The only significant defeat ʿAbd al-Raḥmān III suffered was in 939 at the hands of Ramiro II of León at the Battle of Alhandega (in Arabic, *al-khandāq*, or "the trench") near Simancas. This defeat was apparently due to resentment within the Muslim army toward ʿAbd al-Raḥmān III's increasing appointment of foreign slave soldiers (*ṣaqāli-*

bah) to leadership positions and resentment of the rebellious Muslim vassals of the Upper March, who were forced to join the campaign. ʿAbd al-Raḥmān III never campaigned in the north again.

The third item on the political agenda of ʿAbd al-Raḥmān III was checking the progress of the Shiite Fāṭimids in North Africa. The Fāṭimids had come to power in 909 and built a new capital on the coast of Tunisia called al-Mahdīyya. From there Fāṭimid power spread west and soon threatened the coastal towns that faced al-Andalus. ʿAbd al-Raḥmān III responded by strengthening his own coastal fortifications and establishing bases on the Moroccan coast at Melilla (927), Ceuta (931), and Tangier (951). From there he forged alliances with Berber chiefs and continued to recruit Berbers into his army. A year after a Fāṭimid force from Sicilly burned the Andalusian city of Almería in 955, the caliph built a new fleet. ʿAbd al-Raḥmān III's position throughout this period was primarily defensive. When the Fāṭimids could make no further progress in the west, they turned east, and in 969 they conquered Egypt.

It was in the year 929 that the emir ʿAbd al-Raḥmān III declared himself caliph of al-Andalus, *amīr al-mu'mamīn* (Commander of the Faithful), and adopted the throne name al-Nāṣir (the Victorius One). It cannot be a coincidence that the declaration took place within a year of the conquest of Bobastro and defeat of the sons of Ibn Hafṣūn. Nor is it coincidental that the Fāṭimids, who were Shiites, had already proclaimed themselves caliphs in 909. ʿAbd al-Raḥmān III appears to have been persuaded that the decadence of the ʿAbbasid caliphs in Baghdad and their inability to defend the holy sites of Mecca and Medina disqualified them from the title, which he believed should be held by a Sunni Muslim leader. Calling himself a caliph was a way to enhance his power and prestige in and outside of al-Andalus. Al-Nāṣir quickly appropriated the two traditional symbols of caliphal power: he had his name invoked as caliph instead of the ʿAbbasid al-Qāhir during the Friday congregational prayers (*khuṭba*), and he began a new issue of coinage (*sīkka*), including gold coins with his name and new titles.

Córdoba grew and flourished under the reign of ʿAbd al-Raḥmān III. He enlarged the Great Mosque and built a large, square minaret in the Syrian style. But his court and political administration increasingly imitated the ʿAbbasid and Persian styles, a process that had begun under the rule of his namesake. ʿAbd al-Raḥmān II. One of the things the Persian style entailed was increasing the distance between the ruler and his subjects. The building of a new palace complex on the foothills southwest of Córdoba was ʿAbd al-Raḥmān III's logical next step toward enhancing Umayyad prestige, further distancing himself physically and psychologically from his subjects along ʿAbbasid lines. He named the new palace Madīnat al-Zahrā after his favorite concubine, al-Zahrā. Construction began in 936 and continued throughout the reign of al-Ḥakam II. The complex contained a mosque, luxurious gardens, baths, housing for courtiers, a garrison for his personal guard, and an impressive audience hall. To impress and intimidate his visitors, ʿAbd al-Raḥmān III had a large bowl of mercury placed in the audience hall which could be made to cast lightning bolts across the ceiling. Although he was not particularly interested in the arts himself, ʿAbd al-Raḥmān III created a court at Madīnat al-Zahrā that attracted poets, scholars, and artisans from all over the Islamic world. Cosmopolitan Córdoba began to rival Constantinople in terms of population, and no other western European capital came close to Córdoba on any terms.

Another measure that contributed to the distance between the caliph and the people he ruled was ʿAbd al-Raḥmān III's practice of importing slave soldiers (*ṣaqālibah*) from the north to staff the army and his palace guard. This is often cited as the source of resentment and division within the Umayyad forces that led to the debacle of Alhandega. But this was not a new practice—al-Ḥakam I had begun buying eastern European slaves from Jewish traders a hundred years earlier. What occurred during ʿAbd al-Raḥmān III's reign was that the numbers of *ṣaqālibah* grew exponentially, as did their presence in military and political leadership positions. Ghalib, the general who fought the Fāṭimids for al-Nāṣir, was from their ranks and became al Ḥakam II's most trusted adviser. Many *ṣaqālibah* were castrated and served as officials of the harem, but others were not and established dynasties that within a few generations rivaled Arab and muwallad families for power and prestige. The Andalusian elite were understandably resentful, and the unification and loyalty ʿAbd al-Raḥmān III had worked so hard to achieve began to unravel.

But it took almost a century for things to completely come apart. ʿAbd al-Raḥmān III had begun with a splintered and anarchic state in 912 and within twenty-five years had forged unity, loyalty, and territorial integrity. He did this by going out on campaign himself, bringing rivals and discontents into his Córdoba circles, and cultivating loyalty to his person and dynasty. As his power grew, however, he began distancing himself from the people—he never went on a military campaign after 939 and in fact hardly left the Córdoba area; he spent increasing amounts of state revenue on displays of opulence and luxury; and, as mentioned above, he imported huge numbers of foreign soldiers. ʿAbd al-Raḥmān III died in 961 at Madīnat al-Zahrā, leaving his clearly designated successor, his son al-Ḥakam II, a strong and powerful state to rule but with the seeds of decline planted and growing.

MARILYN HIGBEE WALKER

Bibliography

"ʿAbd al-Raḥmān," in *Encyclopedia of Islam*, 2d ed. Leiden.

Fierro, M. I. "Sobre la adopción del título califal por ʿAbd al-Raḥmān III." *Sharq al-Andalus* 6 (1989), 33–42.

Kennedy, H. *Muslim Spain and Portugal: A Political History of al-Andalus*. London, 1996.

Lévi-Provençal, E. *Histoire de l'Espagne musulmane*. 3 vols. Leiden, 1950–53.

Vallvé Bermejo, J. *El Califato de Córdoba*. Madrid, 1992.

ABNER OF BURGOS *See* VALLADOLID, ALFONSO DE

ABRAHAM BAR ḤIYYA (ḤAYYA)

Mathematician, astronomer, surveyor, philosopher, astrologer and translator Abraham bar Ḥiyya (ca. 1070–1136) lived in Barcelona. He was known by the honorific titles Ha-Nasi (Hebrew: "the prince") and Savasorda (Latin corruption of the Arabic: *ṣāḥib al-shurṭa*, "master of the guard"), which indicate that he held high offices in both the Jewish and the Catalonian communities.

Nine works by him are known, all written in Hebrew. He was the first medieval author to write major philosophic and scientific works in Hebrew, and many of his *termina technica* are still used in modern Hebrew (e.g., *qeshet* = arc, *maʿalah* = degree, *merkaz* = center, *shoq* = side of an isoceles triangle). His works:

(1) *Ḥibbur ha-meshiḥah ve-ha-tishboret* (*On Measuring*), a comprehensive introduction to surveying. Translated into Latin (1145?) by Plato of Tivoli, it played an important role in transmitting Arabic geometry and trigonometry to the West. Hebrew text, ed. M. Guttmann, 1912–13, Catalan translation, J. M. Millás Vallicrosa, 1931.

(2) *Yesode ha-tebunah u-migdal ha-emunah* (*The Foundations of Reason and the Tower of Faith*), an encyclopedia of science; parts are lost. Hebrew text and Spanish translation, J. M. Millás Vallicrosa, 1952.

(3) *Sod ha-ʿibbur* (*The Secret of Intercalation*), a study of the Hebrew calendar, written in 1123. Maimonides praised it as by far the best book on the subject (Commentary on Mishnah, *ʿArakhin* 2:2). Hebrew text, ed. H. Filipowski, 1851.

(4) *Megillat ha-megalleh* (*Scroll of the Revealer*), an eschatological and astrological work, written during the 1120s. According to it, the messianic era might begin by 1136, and the resurrection would take place in 1448 or 1493. Hebrew text, ed. A. Poznanski, 1924; Catalan translation, J. M. Millás Vallicrosa, 1929.

(5) *Epistle to Rabbi Judah ben Barzillai*, a defense of astrology, written ca. 1120. Abraham bar Ḥiyya had advised a student to delay his wedding for one hour in order to avoid the unpropitious influence of Mars. Judah ben Barzillai, the eminent talmudist, protested that such deference to astrology would amount to sorcery and idolatry. The wedding was not delayed, but Abraham wrote this epistle in defense of his view, arguing that astrological considerations are analogous to medical ones. Hebrew text, ed. A. Z. Schwarz, 1917.

(6) *Hegyon ha-nefesh ha-ʿaṣubah* (*The Meditation of the Sad Soul*), a philosophic study of human nature, discussing the place of human beings in the creation, the good life, repentance (including an analysis of *Jonah*), and the future world. While often described as neo-Platonic, it also reflects Aristotelian, Kalamic, and other influences. Hebrew text, ed. E. Freimann, 1860; G. Wigoder, 1971. English translation, G. Wigoder, 1969.

(7) *Ṣurat ha-areṣ ve-tabnit ha-shamavim* (*The Form of the Earth and the Figure of the Heavens*), a work on cosmography, written in 1132; part 1 of *Ḥokhmat ha-ḥizzavon* (*Science of Astronomy*). Hebrew text, Basel 1546 (abridged), Offenbach 1720; Spanish translation, J. M. Millás Vallicrosa, 1956.

(8) *Ḥeshbon mahalekhot ha-kokhabim* (*The Calculation of Astral Motions*), a textbook on Ptolemaic astronomy, written in 1136; part 2 of *Ḥokhmat ha-ḥizzayon*. Hebrew text and Spanish translation, J. M. Millás Vallirosa, 1959; this edition includes Abraham bar Ḥiyya's astronomical tables, *Luḥot ha-Nasi* (*The Prince's Tables*).

In addition, Abraham bar Ḥiyya was active in translating scientific works from Arabic into Latin, mostly in collaboration with Plato of Tivoli.

WARREN ZEV HARVEY

Bibliography

Abraham bar Ḥayya. *The Meditation of the Sad Soul*. Trans. and with an intro. by G. Wigoder. London, 1969.

Millás Vallicrosa, J. M. *Estudios sobre historia de la ciencia española*. Barcelona, 1949. 219–62.

——— *Nuevos estudios sobre historia de la ciencia española*. Barcelona, 1969. 183–90.

Sarfatti, G. B. *Mathematical Terminology in Hebrew Scientific Literature of the Middle Ages* (Hebrew). Jerusalem, 1968. 61–129.
Sirat, C. *A History of Jewish Philosophy in the Middle Ages*. Cambridge, 1985. 94–104, 425.

ABRAHAM EL-BARCHILON (AL-BARJILUNI)

A member of a prominent ancient Jewish family of Toledo, Abraham el-Barchilon (or, more correctly, al-Barjiluni) is undoubtedly identified with Abu Ishaq (*sic*) Ibn Abu'l-Hasan Binyamin in the Arabic documents of Mozarabic Toledo (1269, 1273, and 1294, the latter date by which he was already deceased).

He was *arrendador* (collector) of taxes for Sancho IV, who in June of 1287, following the advice of Don Lope Díaz, count of Haro, and of the *infante* Juan, placed Abraham in charge of all the taxes of the entire kingdom, including those of the Mesta. Like most Jewish officials, he was not a mere tax officer. For example, in August of 1287 he was with the king in Haro and signed (in Hebrew) a royal reprimand to the prior of a monastery, and later yet another to a monastery of Segovia; the following year he signed a letter to the cathedral of Burgos, and to that of Zamora. In 1292, as a result of the peace treaty between Jaime II and Sancho IV, Abraham and another Jew were mentioned as having been captured and held for ransom by Aragónese nobles, and Jaime II ordered their release.

From at least 1288 on he was in fact in charge of the royal chancellery, and thus it is no exaggeration that for at least two years he "administered almost the totality of the Castilian royal domain." We last hear of him in 1294, as administrator of taxes together with Todros Abulafia.

NORMAN ROTH

Bibliography

Gaibrois de Ballesteros, M. *Historia del reinado de Sancho IV de Castilla*. 3 vols. Madrid, 1922–28. I (apendice): clxxxv–ix; III: nos. 172, 173, 185, 196, 202 and p. 112; I: pp. 161, 187, 188.
León Tello, P. *Los judíos de Toledo*. 2 vols. Madrid, 1979; docs. 841, 564, 572, 913, and vol. I: 89.

ABRAVANEL, ISAAC

Isaac Abravanel (1437–1508) was one of the most important Jewish writers and statesmen of his age. His grandfather Samuel was already prominent in the reign of Juan I, and was *contador mayor* of Enrique III and treasurer of the queen. He converted to Christianity, however (long before the pogroms of 1491), before attaining these high posts, and took the name Juan Sánchez de Sevilla. Eventually, he determined to return to Judaism, and in order to accomplish this had to flee to Portugal with some of his sons, while others remained as Christians in Castile. Isaac Abravanel thus grew up in Portugal, where he eventually became a wealthy merchant in Lisbon (together with his father), at least from 1463 on. Ultimately he became a confidant and financier of the Duke of Braganza (ca. 1480) and banker to the king of Portugal, Afonso V. The death of that king brought a change in attitude toward the Jews under his successor, and in 1483 Abravanel fled to Castile.

He was able to obtain a minor role as tax farmer, but in 1485 his position and influence increased greatly when he was placed in charge of all the taxes of Cardinal Pedro González de Mendoza, prelate of Spain and *canciller mayor* of the kingdom. Later, Abravanel became contador mayor of the powerful Iñígo López de Mendoza (it should be mentioned that the Mendoza family, many of whom were themselves of *converso* origin, were always intimately involved with Jews). He was able to make substantial loans to the Catholic Monarchs, and on one occasion (1491) acted as financial agent for the queen.

When the edict of expulsion of the Jews came in 1492, Abravanel apparently used his influence to annul or at least delay it, but to no avail. He chose to be among the minority of Jews who left the land, and like all the other exiles, he was permitted to collect outstanding debts and take with him money and personal property.

From Spain he went to Italy, where he again attained important political prominence, and where he did most of his writing. His son Judah (known as León Hebreo) was the author of the famous *Dialoghi d'amore*.

Never a rabbi, Abravanel was a deeply religious person, with a "fundamentalist" zeal for Jewish tradition. He wrote various treatises, including important commentaries on the Bible, all in Hebrew. In these, and even more in what may be called his "theological" treatises, he displayed his opposition to Aristotelian and Muslim philosophy, more than to Maimonides, whom he greatly revered while still disagreeing cautiously with some of his views. Contrary to the teachings, rather, of the more rationalist followers of Maimonides (Gerson and others), Abravanel believed literally in creation ex nihilo, and in a literal understanding of miracles. Though he showed himself ultimately opposed to any attempt to establish "fundamental principles" of faith in the Bible, since all of it is divine, these two ideas were bound up with his understanding of God as omnipotent. Unlike Maimonides, he believed that man is the "final cause," or purpose, of the Creation, and that man's purpose is the contemplation of God (perhaps under scholastic influence). Again unlike Maimonides, he was also a believer in astrology.

His political attitudes, while not systematic enough to be called (as they have been) a "political philosophy," are of interest.

Abravanel played an important role in the messianic expectations of the generation of the exiles, and had a lasting influence on Jewish thought, and no less on later Christian thinkers.

It is believed that the *Panels of St. Vincent* of the Portuguese artist Nuño Gonçalves (ca. 1481) present an actual portrait of Abravanel, one of only two known portraits of a medieval Spanish Jew.

NORMAN ROTH

Bibliography

Netanyahu, B. *Don Isaac Abravanel.* Philadelphia, 1972.

Kellner, M. *Gersonides and his Cultural Despisers: Arama and Abravanel.* Charlottesville, Va. 1976.

Gomes, P. A. *Filosofia hebraico-portuguesa.* Porto, 1981.

ABŪ ZAYD, GOVERNOR OF VALENCIA

Abū Zayd ʿAbd al-Raḥmān, *sayyid* (Çeit Aboçeyt, to the Christians), was the great grandson of the caliph ʿAbd al-Mu'min, the founder of the Almohad caliphate. As *wālī* or governor of the Sharq al-Andalus (eastern Islamic Spain) during the general collapse of the Almohad empire in the early thirteenth century, he found himself effectively sovereign of the Valencian regions, or "king of Valencia" to the Christians, but challenged by the rise of the anti-Almohad Ibn Hūd. Allying first with Fernando III of Castile as "vassal" in 1225, in violation of the zones of reconquest agreements between Arago-Catalonia and Castile, and then with Jaíme I of Arago-Catalonia in 1226, he lost his capital and kingdom to a local revolt by Zayyān Ibn Mardanīsh in 1229, falling back on the remnant Segorbe region. In desperation he had signaled the pope his willingness to convert and had conducted overtures with the cardinal legate Jean d'Abbeville in 1228. He had previously executed the Franciscan missionary "Martyrs of Teruel" at Valencia. A series of treaties with Jaime I in 1229, 1232, and 1236 progressively surrendered his income and sovereignty, until he became a puppet collaborator in the Christian conquest of the Valencian "kingdom."

By 1236 he had converted, taking the name Vicente and the status of amply landed baron. He married the Aragónese lady María Ferrándiç, not Zurita's Dominga López of Zaragoza, who gave him a son, Ferran Péreç (who died childless in 1262) and a daughter Alda Ferrándiç whose progeny became the Arenós noble dynasty. The number of his previous Muslim sons and their conversions (perhaps four) is disputed, but Ibn Khaldūn testifies to Jaime's patronage of his Muslim sons "on account of the conversion of their father." Abū Zayd rarely used his baptismal name Vicente, and only late in life a noble surname, Belvis, keeping his attested conversion a secret for reasons of state from at least 1236 until 1264 when a bull of Pope Urban IV hailed the occasion. His latter years are identified with the military order of Santiago, of which he was a devout patron. Abū Zayd called himself King of Valencia in Latin documents until 1238, though Jaime I also took that title from 1236. His eagle seal survives, along with sufficient documentation both in Islamic and Christian sources to follow the trajectory of his full career. He died between 1264 and 1268; his body is entombed in the Franciscans' Puritat convent at Valencia.

ROBERT I. BURNS, S. J.

Bibliography

Burns, R. I., S. J., "Daughter of Abū Zayd, Last Almohad Ruler of Valencia: The Family and Christian Seigniory of Alda Ferrándis 1236–1300." *Viator* 24 (1993), 143–87, with references to the Spanish works by M. T. Barceló Torres, R. Chabás, M. de Epalza, A. Huici, and E. Molina López.

ABULAFIA, MEIR

Meir ben Todros ha-Levy Abulafia (ca. 1165–1244) was an important talmudic scholar and rabbi (though hardly "chief rabbi," as sometimes claimed) of Castile, and a member of a distinguished family. His father, Todros ha-Nasi ("prince, leader") was head of the Burgos Jewish community, and Meir's brothers were also distinguished scholars. Todros, the son of Meir's brother Joseph, was an important rabbi and cabalist of Toledo, and related to him was the renowned poet Todros ben Judah. Meir's other brother, Samuel, produced a long line of descendants that included Samuel ha-Levy, the *tesorero mayor* of Pedro I. This family flourished at least to the end of the fourteenth century in Toledo.

Abulafia was a student of the renowned Moses ben Nahman (Nahmanides), and by 1204 he was already a member of an important Jewish court (*bet din*) in Toledo, together with Joseph Ibn Megash and Abraham ben Natan ha-Yarhi, two of the most important scholars of the age. We possess from his pen a number of legal responsa, as well as commentaries on portions of the Talmud. However, Abulafia is most famous (or infamous) for his crucial role in the "Maimonidean controversy." Moses ben Maimon (Maimonides) had expressed certain ideas both in his legal code, *Mishneh Torah,* and in his earlier commentary on the *mishnah,* which were concepts of Aristotelian rationalism and were viewed by the young rabbi as extremely dangerous to traditional Jewish views. He, as well as his colleague Abraham ha-Yarhi, correctly concluded that Maimonides did not accept the traditional Abulafia views about resurrection, for example. According to Maimonides, this is entirely allegorical and to be explained in accord with Aristotelian and Muslim philosophical interpretation. Abulafia penned a sharp critique of Maimonides, which he sent to rabbinical scholars in Provence. These scholars, however, sided completely with the great Maimonides and sharply rebuked the "young upstart" of Castile who dared to challenge his authority. He was similarly severely criticized by Sheshet Benvenist, lay leader of the Jewish community of Barcelona. Undaunted, Abulafia wrote a series of letters farther north, to the rabbis of France. Completely unfamiliar as they were with philosophy, much less with Maimonides' views (which they little knew or understood), they took Abulafia's side. Abulafia finally collected all this correspondence, which he issued with an Arabic introduction intended for Jewish readers in Andalucía. Although the controversy soon died down, it may well have resulted in the forged "Treatise on Resurrection" (*Ma'amar tehiyat ha-metim*) long attributed to Maimonides; as well, perhaps, as a treatise on this subject introduced into Abulafia's commentary on Sanhedrin.

The Maimonidean controversy was to continue for centuries, along different lines. Abulafia's importance today remains his responsa and talmudic commentary.

NORMAN ROTH

Bibliography

Septimus, B. *Hispano-Jewish Culture in Transition*. Cambridge, Mass., 1982 (with numerous errors and omissions; cf. Norman Roth, review in *American Historical Review* 89 [1984], 420–21, which deals with only some of the problems).

Goldfeld, L. N. *Moses Maimonides' Treatise on Resurrection: An Inquiry into its Authenticity*. New York, 1986.

ABULAFIA, TODROS

Todros b. Judah ha-Levi Abulafia (1247–1298?) was a Hebrew poet who also served at the court of Alfonso X. Born in Toledo to an illustrious family of apparently modest means, Abulafia was steeped in Arabic and Romance cultures as well as in Jewish tradition. After being drawn into the entourage of a royal official named Solomon Ibn Sadoq, Todros traveled widely in Spain at the side of Ibn Sadoq's son Isaac, singing his patron's praises and otherwise entertaining him. Abulafia was apparently among the dignitaries swept into prison in 1280–1281 during the second round of royal attacks upon Jewish economic and political influence at Alfonso X's court. During his incarceration Abulafia's literary tastes and cultural sensibilities seem to have undergone a radical transformation. The imprisoned poet appears to make amends for his hedonistic lifestyle and licentious behavior by producing a cycle of confessional poems in which he bemoans his fate and renounces his previously profligate ways. Following his release, Abulafia wandered in exile until he made his way to Barcelona, where he studied with that city's leading sages and devoted himself to devotional verse and the poetry of spiritual love. In 1289 and for sometime thereafter, Abulafia served in the financial administration of Sancho IV and used his various offices to pursue lucrative business ventures.

Abulafia's poetry freely combines the prosodic forms, manneristic tendencies, and genres characteristic of Andalusian Hebrew poetry with themes, motifs, and voices drawn from contemporary Romance. A large part of Abulafia's *dīwān* (poetic corpus) consists of manneristic exercises and highly coventional poems designed to flatter the rich and famous.

Todros's love poetry, by contrast, cultivates the persona of the dissolute poet in the tradition of Abū Nuwās and Ibn Quzmān; yet his poetry also shares the trend toward a more personal and "realistic" poetry evident in thirteenth-century Romance lyrics.

Abulafia seems to have composed little liturgical poetry, but his secular verse—especially the lyrics composed during and after his confinement—includes many poems in which the poet speaks directly to God about matters of personal significance. Although Abulafia is frequently referred to as a gifted epigone of the Andalusian school of Hebrew poets, an image the poet himself may have sought to cultivate, his poetry should be viewed as evidence of the vitality and innovative spirit of Hebrew poetry in Christian Spain.

ROSS BRANN

Bibliography

Doron, A. *Todros Ha-Levi Abulafiah: A Hebrew Poet in Christian Spain* (Hebrew). Tel Aviv, 1989.

Yellin, D. (ed.) *Gan ha-meshalim we-ha-hidot*. 3 vols. Jerusalem, 1934–37.

ABULCASIS *See* ABŪ-L-QĀSIM

ABŪ-L-QĀSIM

Abū-l-Qāsim Khalaf ibn ʿAbbās al-Zahrq was wellknown as Abulcasis in Latin translations (d. 1013). The *nisba* (nickname) al-Zahrq seems to refer to his birthplace Madīnat al-Zahrq, the city-palace built by ʿAbd al-Raḥmān III near Córdoba in 936 (a *terminus post quem* for his birthdate). No details about his life are known. His only extant work is the *al-Tarf li-man ʿajiza ʿan al-taq-lif (How to Practice [Medicine] for Those Who Wish to Avoid the Use of [Other] Compilations)*, written, after fifty years of medical practice, for his "sons" (probably his students). Divided into thirty books, it is the greatest medical encyclopedia ever written in al-Andalus. Although he had a thorough knowledge of both Greek and Eastern Arab medical works, the *Tarf* is often based on his own personal experience. Books 1–2 and 28 were translated into Latin via Hebrew and, the latter, dealing with pharmacology, was well-known in Europe under the title *Liber servitoris*. Book 30, on surgery, was translated in the twelfth century by Gerard of Cremona (*Liber Alsahravi de cirurgia*) and it established the reputation of Abulcasis as the greatest surgeon of the Middle Ages. It contains useful descriptions and drawings of surgical instruments, among which we find a vaginal speculum and an obstetric forceps that anticipates that of Chamberlen. We can read in the *Tarf* of one of the first known descriptions of hemophilia and leprosy, as well as new techniques for suturing including the use of catgut, and formulas for different kinds of plaster casings used to repair broken limbs.

JULIO SAMSÓ

Bibliography

Tabanelli, M. *Albucasi: Un chirurgo arabo dell'Alto Medio Evo*. Florence, 1961.

Hamarneh, S. Kh., and G. Sonnedecker *A Pharmaceutical View of Abulcasis al-Zahrq*. Leiden, 1963.

Spink, M. S., and G. L. Lewis. *Abulcasis on Surgery and Instruments: A Definitive Edition of the Arabic Text with English Translation and Commentary*. Berkeley, Calif., 1973.

Vernet, J., and J. Samsó (eds.) *El legado científico andalusí*. Madrid, 1992. 134–135 (remarks by M. Castells), and 274–86.

ACUÑA, LUIS DE

Acuña was one of the most prominent personalities of ecclesiastic life in Burgos during the latter half of the fifteenth century. He belonged to a well-known noble family, not only as the son of Juan Alvarez Osorio and María Manuel, but also because of his family ties to Archbishop Alfonso Carrillo and to the marquis of Villena. After the death of his wife, Aldonza de Guzmán, he entered the clergy. He was the archdeacon of Valpuesta (Burgos) and bishop of Segovia, after which he acceded to the bishopric of Burgos in 1456. He participated actively in various political happenings of the time: he helped organize Prince Alfonso's revolt against Enrique IV and also supported Juana la Beltraneja against the Catholic monarchs. Faced with Queen Isabel's arrival to the city, Acuña abandoned the diocese until a reconcilation was achieved. His leadership of the diocese was characterized by his active role in religious matters, often with intentions of reform. He attended the Council of Aranda in 1473 and the Synod of 1474.

Acuña was a notable patron of the arts during a period in which Burgos stood out as one of the most active hubs for accomplished artists such as Simón de Colonia and Gil de Siloé. During his term as bishop, the pinnacles of the cathedral towers were completed and construction on the chapel of the Condestables de Castilla was started. Acuña himself funded what would later be his funeral chapel, the Capilla de la Concepción, or Santa Ana, which he adorned with an exceptional tableau of the Tree of Jesse, made of multicolored wood by Gil de Siloé. Later, Acuña's tomb (sculpted by Diego de Siloé) was added to the chapel. Upon his death in 1495, Acuña left a fascinating library that attests to his humanist spirit.

MARÍA JESÚS GÓMEZ BÁRCENA

Bibliography

López Martínez, N. "Don Luis de Acuña, el Cabildo de Burgos y la Reforma (1456–1495)." *Burgense* 2 (1961), 185–317.

Serrano, L. *Los Reyes Católicos y la ciudad de Burgos (desde 1451 a 1492)*. Madrid, 1943.

ADELANTADO

First documented in the eleventh century, the term seems to have referred to an officer in charge of a frontier zone who also had judicial powers. As a royal office, the *adelantamiento mayor* was institutionalized no later than the reign of Alfonso X who, in royal charters of privilege, listed an *adelantado mayor* of the frontier (1253) and others to the same office in León, Castile, and Murcia (1258; at this time charters no longer list *merinos mayores* in Castile and Murcia). Early in 1261, contemporaneous with the war against Niebla, the *adelantamiento* of Andalusia was formed from the merger of Murcia and the frontier. Two years later Alfonso appointed an *adelantado mayor* in Galicia. Later (1268–1272), in circumstances most likely related to reaction against Alfonsine legislation, the *adelantados mayores* in León, Castile, and Galicia ceased to be listed; the merger in the south was dissolved; and only the *adelantamiento mayor* of Murcia and the newly created *adelantamiento* (*mayor* is not mentioned) in Alava and Guipúzcoa continued to appear during the final, troubled years of Alfonso's reign. Succeeding kings reestablished the lost *adelantamientos*, all of which continued to exist (some sporadically) through the rest of the Middle Ages. The Alfonsine *Espéculo* describes two types of *adelantado mayor*: the one whose jurisdiction covered a major territory, and the one serving as chief justice of the royal tribunal, who judged certain types of cases and heard appeals from the decisions made in all inferior courts. Each *adelantado* was a lay *ricohombre* whose authority derived directly and exclusively from his royal appointment and whose powers, aside from specified limitations, were equivalent to those of the king.

The *adelantado mayor* of a kingdom or *tierra* administered justice conducive to the maintenance of law and order, at times exercising military and economic, especially financial, authority, and enjoying supreme judicial powers. The administration of justice especially gave rise to conflict with other authorities, notably with constituencies under foral law, until lines of jurisdiction became more finely drawn. Lords also named *adelantados*, analogous in function to those appointed by the king, in their respective spheres; a well-known ecclesiastical example is the *adelantado* named (1332) by the archbishop of Toledo to his fief of Cazorla (Jaén). Fernando and Isabel replaced the *adelantados mayores* of Castile, León, Andalusia, Murcia, and Granada with *alcaldes mayores*.

ROBERT A. MACDONALD

Bibliography

Cerdá Ruiz-Funes, J. *Estudios sobre instituciones jurídicas medievales de Murcia y su reino*. Murcia, 1987.

García Marín, J. M. *El oficio público en Castilla durante la Baja Edad Media*. Sevilla, 1974.

ADMINISTRATION, CENTRAL, ARAGÓN-CATALONIA

As one of most deeply acculturated sections of the Roman Empire, Spain retained the imprint of imperial government long after it was conquered by the Visigoths in the fifth century. To maintain control over the ruined Iberian political landscape, Visigothic kings adapted Roman political norms to their own rule. Though Toledo emerged as the core of the Visigothic kingdom, the administration that ruled Spain was less territorial than it was personal. With the influence of the Church through its councils, the Visigothic monarch seems in some ways only a first among equals. The center of this rule was the royal court (*aula regia*), comprised of the personal servants as well as the clerical and lay retainers of the king. The evolving nature of the Visigothic court and the administration that emanated from it often transformed such servants into officials, and officials into servants. While the realm retained the bare outlines of the Roman provincial system, civil government of the periphery was entrusted to nobles who, bearing the titles of duke (*dux*) or count (*comes*), stood as guarantors of public peace and justice in their districts. Since their jurisdictions were far too large for one man to rule, these local governors delegated authority to a number of vicars (*vicarii*, *veguers*), who carried out much the same duties as their ducal or comital superiors but on a more local level. This loose mesh of regional and local government established an administrative blueprint followed with few emendations in all realms of Christian Spain until the twelfth century.

Despite its weaknesses, the Visigothic government was a centralized state in comparison with the tenuous political existence of the Christian realms of the Iberian Peninsula that came into being after the Muslim conquest in the eighth century. Along a ragged and ever-fluctuating frontier with Islam, Christian rulers were forced to think of military defense more than political dominance. As a result, landscapes as varied as Catalonia and León came to be covered with castles built by sovereigns and other great lords (*seniores*) and garrisoned by their vassals (*homines*, *milites*, *fideles*). In this regime of feudal relations royal power—and with it, royal administration—withered. The same fortresses, which stood as bulwarks against Islamic invasion, also blocked the full operation of royal government. Thus, judicial and fiscal functions once carried out by royal agents were now routinely, though intermittently, exercised by great lords (*principes*) and churchmen. With the disappearance of public structures of administration and adjudication, the Church fashioned such institutions as the peace and truce of God (*pax et treuga Dei*) to serve the public functions of the king and his officials. The pax et treuga formally came to Catalonia by 1027 and came to be utilized by civil ruler from 1064.

With the rebirth of central power in the eleventh century, the old Visigothic model of administration was adapted to the realities of the feudal world. With the reigns of Sancho III the Great, king of Navarre (1000–1035), and Ramón Berenguer I, count of Barcelona (1035–1076), the royal court (*curia regis*) and the comital court (*curia comitis*) reemerged as the center of an administration that grew more powerful, as did the office of sovereign itself. At the center of the *curia* was a corps of palatine servants that included the steward (*majordomo*), seneschal (*senescalus*), chamberlain (*cubicularii*), constable (*comes stabuli*), standard-bearer (*armiger*, *alférez*), butler (*botellerius*, *repostero*), treasurer (*thesaurarius*), cupbearer (*scanti-*

arius), carver (*taliator*), and schoolmaster (*caput schole*, *doctor*). Besides these servitors, a number of curial officials carried out regnal administration. The most important of these were the scribes (*scriptores*, *notarii*) and the judge of the palace (*judex palatii*). Owing to the decentralized nature of eastern Spain, territorial administration had to be shared with great lords in Aragón and counts in Catalonia who maintained their own courts and were served by their own officials. While eleventh- and twelfth-century sovereigns used such palatine officials as the seneschal and steward to administer their realms, they also depended on such agents as the *merino* and *sayón* in Aragón and the vicar in Catalonia to judge local suits, carry out judicial verdicts, collect taxes, and summon the royal host. In addition to such salaried royal officials, Catalan and Aragónese clergy were used as judges, overseers, and administrators. With the growth of towns in eastern Spain, the same hybrid clerical and lay administration shared power within urban limits with emerging municipal councils (*universitates*).

With the marriage of Ramón Berenguer IV to Petronella in 1137, the realms of Catalonia and Aragón were linked under the same ruler. Such an event could not help but complicate the administration of two states. With two different peoples to serve and three different languages to deal with—Latin, Aragónese, and Catalan—the chancery was divided into two departments, one serving the government of Aragón and the other the government of Catalonia. Though some calligraphical differences remained between the documents that emanated from the two divisions, these began to fade in the thirteenth century as the Catalan style attained dominance when the notarial organization came under the supervision of a single head, the chancellor (*cancillarius*, *canciller*). The birth of the Crown of Aragón (*Corona de Aragón*)—as the new federated state came to be called—was accompanied by other administrative changes, most especially in the training and status of the men entering royal service. Far from being drawn only from the region's monasteries and cathedral canons, royal administration from the twelfth century onward also began to attract laymen. Many of this new class of officials had received training in the two laws, Roman and canon, in such universities as Bologna and Montpellier. With this background in mind, it is not unusual that the officialdom of Ramón Berenguer IV and his son Alfonso II (1162–1196) became proponents of a regalist philosophy that sought to extend the crown's power at the expense of feudal privilege. One of the great curials of this era was Renallus, a poet, historian, and theologian who served as the head of the Catalan-Aragónese chancery in the mid-twelfth century. Significant juridical outgrowths of the activist administrative philosophy in eastern Spanish administration were the Catalan legal compilations of the last half of the twelfth century, the *Usatges de Barchinona* and *Liber Feudorum Maior*.

With the long and eventful reign of Jaime I (1213–1276), the old forms of Aragónese and Catalan administration were tested, and this largely redefined the pretension of expanded royal power. Older classes of officials, such as the Catalan vicar, still held sway in their traditional jurisdictional units, but as Jaime I expanded political control over his older realms and conquered new ones, he increasingly used old bureaucrats in novel ways. The vicar was thus given an expanded role in carrying out the statutes of the peace and truce, a legal norm that Jaime I and his predecessors used as the base for all legitimate royal legislation. Unlike the vicars of the twelfth century, those of the thirteenth often worked in partnership with "peacekeepers" (*paciarii*) from the town councils who acted as guarantors of public tranquillity as well as municipal rulers. Locked in a life-and-death struggle with his baronies, the sovereign increasingly found the old functionaries ineffective in extending his power over the great men. To counter baronial interference in Aragón, the king established such new officers as the *sobrejuntero* and *justicia*. The first began as liaison with the defensive leagues (*juntas*) of the Aragónese towns but eventually became a governor of a district centered on one of the realm's largest towns. The second began as an urban judge but also attained a broader official mandate.

Jaime I took an even bolder step in administrative reshuffling by asserting more personal control over the bureaucracies of his realms. With the great conquests of Mallorca and Valencia (1229–1244), the Conqueror was away from his realms for long periods and increasingly relied on his son Pedro and the other crown princes as lieutenants (*locum tenentes*) who represented the crown in all official matters. Jaime I argued that he and his sons in their representative capacity were "one conjoint [royal] person." In addition to this "family government," Jaime I promoted bureaucratic loyalty by rewarding talent even when displayed by men of other faiths. The most important of these, the Jewish brothers Jehuda and Solomon de Cavallería, served as bailiff (*baiulus*, *batlle*) for much of Jaime I's later life. Under their tenure, the office became the centerpiece of a much more efficient management of royal lands and local revenues. This utilization of Jewish servitors avoided royal dependence on Christian nobles for administration and thus brought firm baronial opposition. This dissent among the eastern Spanish baronies was deepened when Jaime I eschewed the use of nobles in most royal offices in favor of such professional advocates and jurists as Pere Albert in Catalonia and Vidal de Canyellas in Aragón, who left their Romanist mark on the important legislation of both realms.

To the nobilities of Aragón and Catalonia, Jaime I's administrative adaptations were dangerous "innovations" that had to be rolled back at all costs. In Catalonia, Roman law and lawyers learned in it were outlawed from court use on several occasions. In Aragón, the baronial revolt of the *Unión* (1265–1266) not only attacked the governmental changes that the king had put in place but attempted to co-opt them with the establishment of the *justicia mayor*—a "middle judge" who theoretically was to stand as an impartial mediator and justice between the crown and the Aragónese people. In time, this official was used by the Union to hamstring the expansion of royal government. During the reign of Jaime I's immediate predecessors down to that of his great-great-grandson Pedro IV (1336–1387), the Union increased its power at the expense of the crown by the establishment of a baronial council that oversaw royal domestic and foreign policies, using the Aragónese parliament (*Cortes*) to legitimize these private actions as national law. Even after the Union's demise in 1348, an expanded governmental role for the parliaments of both realms remained with the establishment of permanent agencies—the *Generalitat* in Catalonia and the *Diputación* in Aragón—that aided the sovereign in such matters as taxation and emergency military funding.

The trends of royal administration were altered in the sixty years after Jaime I by these waves of baronial unrest that attempted to redraw the official lines between ruler and ruled in a way reminiscent of the tenth and eleventh centuries. Nowhere was the Union's anachronistic view of royal power better expressed than in the spurious *Fuero de Sobrarbe*, which attempted to hem in not only the king but the royal administration with an impenetrable hedge of custom. With the reign of Jaime II (1291–1337), the crown began to reclaim power lost to the rebellious baronies of Aragón and Catalonia. Spending his youth as the sovereign of Sicily, Jaime II brought a more centralized view of administration to the Crown of Aragón. The supreme post in Jaime II's government, which had its roots in twelfth-century Sicily, was the *maestre racional*. This servitor, initially an overseer of palace accounts, emerged as the most important member in the eastern Spanish government, subsuming a number of the functions of the Aragónese steward and Catalan bailiff in the process. Despite such bureaucratic importations, Jaime I did not destroy the offices of his predecessors but assigned to them a more restricted agenda. In one case, however, the king experimented with the older offices, creating an "overvicar" (*supravicarius*, *sobreveguer*) to oversee blocks of Catalan vicarates. In regard to the chancery, Jaime II and his successors continued its development as a professional entity. A chancellor oversaw the operation and was assisted by a vice chancellor. The royal seals were maintained by the *protonotario* while the everyday functioning of the chancery came under the authority of a "manager" (*regente*) who was also responsible for document production and sealing as well as their reproduction in registers. All of the realms of the Crown of Aragón had similar chancery offices headed by a vice chancellor.

The most far-reaching trend that Jaime II continued was the use of his sons as procurators or lieutenants in his Iberian realms even when he was present in them. This office, which had originally been a temporary one, now became permanent, eventually overriding the bureaucratic dominance of the maestre racional. The office of procurator, which came to be called governor general (*gubernator general*) by the late fourteenth century, eventually came to be called viceroy (*virei*) in the fifteenth century. Though royal princes (*infantes*) initially held such lieutenancies, other family members, including queens, occasionally served in such posts. This power delegation was absolutely necessary during the reigns of such sovereigns as Alfonso V (1416–1458) who spent most of his life away from his Iberian realms in search of new Italian ones, routinely leaving Catalonia under the rule of his queen and lieutenant María of Castile. In the viceregal office of the crown of Aragón, then, we see one of the strands that would culminate in the sixteenth century with the office of viceroy. With the emergence of Spain as great international power, the viceroy would take his place at the head of an administration that would link places as distant as Sicily, the Netherlands, Mexico, and Peru to Madrid and its royal master. For eastern Spain, however, such power delegation had ominous overtones. It pointed forward to an era after 1516 when Aragón and Catalonia were not ruled by a native dynasty but instead received their government from Madrid. In the marriage to Castile, then, the old administrative ways of Catalonia were undermined and then discarded, eventually to be replaced with such foreign governmental norms as Felipe V's Decreto de Nueva Planta (1716). Catalonia would not regain even a measure of administrative autonomy until 1931 with the Catalan Statute. With Francisco Franco's victory in 1939, this short-lived freedom abruptly ceased, not to return until the 1970s when Catalan home rule become one of the cornerstones of the new Spanish Republic.

DONALD KAGAY

Bibliography

Bisson, Thomas N. *The Medieval Crown of Aragón*. Oxford, 1986.

Hillgarth, J. N. *The Spanish Kingdoms, 1250–1516*. 2 vols. Oxford, 1976, I.

ADMINISTRATION, CENTRAL, CASTILE

The central administration of Castile-León was based on the Visigothic court, which in turn was modeled on the Roman imperial court. A body of officials (*officium palatinum*) attended the Visigothic king on a daily basis. Several counts were responsible for the administration of the patrimony and the treasury, and the supervision of notaries, chamberlains, and the royal guard. Magnates (*seniores* or *maiores palatii*) specially commended to the king's service, together with bishops and territorial officials constituted a council (*aula regia*) assisting the king in executing his duties.

Emphasizing the continuity between the Visigothic and Asturian monarchies, Alfonso II (791–842) tried to restore in Oviedo the Visigothic order as it had once functioned at Toledo. Visigothic terms for the royal council reappeared. The chief officials were the standard-bearer (*armiger*), the *maiordomus* or superintendent of the household, the notary, treasurer, and chamberlains. The king occasionally gathered bishops, magnates, and palace officials in an extraordinary *concilium*, such as the council of León held by Alfonso V in 1017 to restore the kingdom after the destruction wrought by al-Manṣūr. In twelfth-century Castile and León the term *curía regis* came into use to designate the royal court or council, whether meeting in ordinary or extraordinary sessions. The duties of the standard-bearer, now called *alférez*, the *mayordomo*, and lesser officials remained essentially the same. Supervision of the royal writing office was assigned to the chancellor, ordinarily a cleric. The council advised the king in matters of legislation, justice, finance, diplomacy, and war. The king often stated that he acted "with the counsel of the chief men of my *curia*." The great men of the realm participated in extraordinary sessions (*curia plena*, *curia generalis*, *curia solemnis*), as on the occasion of Alfonso VII's coronation as emperor of Spain at León in 1135. The curia of León held in 1188 by Alfonso IX was significant because he summoned to participate not only prelates and nobles but also the "elected citizens of each city." That event heralded the future development of the *cortes*.

By the thirteenth century the business of government had become so complex that the responsibilities of those daily attending the king were differentiated and administrative departments emerged. Legists (*letrados*) trained in Roman and canon law gave a professional cast to the court. Still there was no administrative capital, as the court continued to travel with the king. Alfonso X described the organization of the court (*corte*, *casa del rey*) in the *Siete Partidas*. The council (*consejo del rey*) was composed of clerics and laymen sworn to give good and loyal advice, to guard the king's secrets, and to obey his commands. The alférez, a noble of high rank, carried the king's standard and served as his advocate in matters of justice. Next in rank was the *mayordomo mayor*, a noble charged with oversight of the household and especially of financial accounts. The *almojarife* (usually a Jew) was responsible for collecting revenues and paying stipends to the nobility and to others. The admiral (*almirante de la mar*) was the commander of the fleet.

The chancery, composed mainly of clerics, handled much of the secretarial work, but the title of chancellor was now an honorific one shared by the archbishops of Toledo (for Castile) and Compostela (for León). The chief notaries (*notarios mayores*) of Castile, León, and Andalucía directed the scribes to draft documents, checked their form and content, ordered copies inscribed in registers, and seals of wax or lead to be affixed to the originals. Royal documents, ranging from the most solemn *privilegio rodado* to a simple mandate, now became more stereotyped.

An army of domestic servants, including chaplains and physicians, also accompanied the king. The chamberlain (*camarero mayor*) had custody of the bedchamber and the king's personal effects; the butler (*repostero mayor*) was in charge of service at table; the steward (*despensero mayor*) purchased food supplies and other necessities; the lodging master (*posadero mayor*) arranged suitable housing for the king and the court. The *portero mayor* directed heralds or ushers, who admitted visitors to the king's presence and served as messengers. The bodyguard (*caballero de la mesnada del rey*) completed the royal entourage.

This structure remained more or less intact until the Trastámaran era in the late fourteenth and fifteenth centuries. Then the main innovation was the clear separation of the royal household (*casa real*), whose responsibilities were essentially domestic, from the royal council (*consejo real*), the chancery, and the judicial tribunal. Every aspect of administration came within the purview of the council, which now became the principal organ of government. In response to the petitions of the *cortes* Juan I in 1385 created a council including four persons representing each of the three estates. The towns hoped that this would give them a permanent voice in the council, but the king quickly replaced the municipal representatives with four legists who could be counted on to uphold royal authority. Thereafter membership constantly fluctuated. Perceiving that control of the council would ultimately mean greater power over all the instruments of government, the nobility strove to secure places in that body so that they could dominate it.

Fernando and Isabel transformed the council from a battleground of conflicting nobiliary factions into an instrument of the royal will, reorganizing it in 1480. The council now consisted of a prelate, three knights, and eight or nine legists. The royal secretary served as the intermediary between the ruler and the council and began to assume something of the character of a prime minister. As required, other specialized councils were created for the administration of the Military Orders (*Consejo de las Ordenes*, established in 1495), the Inquisition (*Consejo de la Suprema y General Inquisición*, 1483), and the Hermandad (*Consejo de la Santa Hermandad*), dissolved in 1498 after order had been restored to the kingdom. This medieval legacy underwent subsequent evolution and alteration as the needs of the modern era demanded.

JOSEPH F. O'CALLAGHAN

Bibliography

García de Valdeavellano, L. *Curso de historia de las instituciones españolas: De los orígenes al final de la Edad Media*. Madrid, 1968.

O'Callaghan, J. F. *A History of Medieval Spain*. Ithaca, N.Y., 1975.

ADMINISTRATION, CENTRAL, LEÓN

From the repopulation of the city of León by Ordoño I (850–866) to the incorporation of the kingdom of León into that of Castile on the death of Alfonso IX (1188–1230), the chief constant of its administration was the king in his *curia*. Throughout those four centuries kingship remained a peripatetic institution that brought its government to the various corners of the realm by visiting them periodically and personally. Its central method of operation was to bring the charisma of the crown to bear on political, religious, and judicial problems where they originated. Though the city of León itself always remained the *civitas regia* it was primarily a cult center in which the court took up residence for the celebration of the greatest feasts of the Christian and royal year, such as Christmas and Easter. It was in no sense a permanent administrative center.

The king never functioned simply by himself, but always with and in his *curia*, which was at once the essential advisory body and the executive instrument of the crown. Though no one individual or officer was indispensable to the makeup of the curia except for the king himself, its constituent parts were fairly stable. First and foremost among them was the royal dynasty. That is, the prime advisers of the king were the other living adult members of the royal house, from queen mother, uncles, and aunts to sisters and younger brothers, the *infantes* or the generation to come, present in the court.

Second to the dynasts of the curia were the great churchmen of the realm. Usually that meant the bishop of León above all, closely followed by the bishops of Astorga and Zamora, who traveled with the court for long periods of the year. The bishops of Galicia, especially of Santiago de Compostela, became curial figures when the court was actually in Galicia itself but the very geography of the kingdom usually relegated them to minor participation. During the great period of union with Castile between 1037 and 1157, the bishops of Palencia, Burgos, and Toledo rivaled in importance even those of León proper. As the Reconquest of the twelfth and thirteenth centuries progressed, the bishops of Salamanca became curial figures, too.

The third constant element was composed of members of the great magnate families of the realm. These had not the institutional regularity or permanence of the episcopacy, and their identity at any given time is harder to specify. Nevertheless, some members of some such families were always present at court, though their composition would change from month to month. Ordinarily, those of the district through which the court was then progressing were most heavily represented.

A delicate and dynamic mix of the influence and advice of members of all three of these powerful groups lay behind every royal decision whether that latter had to do with matters dynastic, military, legislative, administrative, or judicial. Distinct organs to treat these areas had not evolved, and the curia dealt with all of them. In that work it was assisted by a number of officers of the crown who began to appear, as such, in the eleventh century although the functions themselves had doubtless existed earlier. We are not sufficiently informed as to the day-to-day functioning of the curia to determine in what measure they were actually regarded as members of it or simply as important royal servants. Probably such a distinction was not regularly made, for institutional categories were largely foreign to the age.

These offices were three. One was the *mayordomus*, responsible for the order and supply of the court on its travels and of its principal residences. A second was the *armiger*, or *alférez*, who was the commander of the royal bodyguard, the nucleus of the army, and the bearer of the royal standard in battle. The third was the royal notary, called chancellor from the reign of Alfonso VII (1126–1157). The first two offices were held by nobles drawn from one or another of the great magnate families of the realm ordinarily and the relative frequency of the latters' appearances in them is a good gauge of their contemporary influence at court and in the kingdom. Since the third required literacy, it was held by ecclesiastics. From the reign of Fernando II (1157–1188) the chancellorship was titularly held by the archbishop of Santiago de Compostela but usually exercised through a delegate.

None of these offices were held for a fixed term, and there is no good evidence of a hierarchical staff to support them, except in the case of the chancellor, though all doubtless had assistants of some sort. In the case of the notary or chancellor we can see already in the reign of Alfonso VI (1065–1109) a function vested in a group of four or five clerics arranged in a rough hierarchy, some being known simply as *scriptor*, others *notarius*, and finally as chief officer or *cancellarius*. Also from the time of Alfonso VI there seemed to be a rough sort of *cursus honorem* that operated in relation to all three offices. Some clerics, at any rate, appear to have moved from scriptor, to notarius, and even to cancellarius, and then go on to appointment to an episcopal office. In the lay offices, some male children of the nobility seem to have been raised at court, as adults are entrusted first with the office of alférez, move on to become mayordomus, and subsequently appear as count in an area where their father or an uncle had preceded them.

At least from the time of Alfonso V (999–1028), the ordinary curia was purposely swollen from time to time for functions of special importance. These "general curias" to which people were especially summoned and to which contemporaries referred by a variety of terms, decided questions of royal succession, war, peace, and church reform. One such, summoned to León in April of 1188 by Alfonso IX to ratify his own succession, is the first known to have included representatives selected by some of the towns of the realm. Therefore, it is ordinarily thought of by modern historians as the first *cortes*—the first parliament in Iberia as well as in the medieval west. Burghers are known also to have been summoned to other, later curias of Alfonso IX but it would be too much to say that their attendance had already become customary.

Bernard F. Reilly

Bibliography

García de Valdeavellano, L. *Curso de historia de las instituciones Españolas*: *De los orígenes al final de la Edad Media*. Madrid, 1968.

———. *Historia de España*. Vol. 2, pt. 2., 2d ed. Madrid, 1955.

Procter, E. S. *Curia and Cortes in León and Castile, 1072–1295*. New York, 1980.

ADMINISTRATION, CENTRAL, NAVARRE

It is only at the end of the medieval era that a real administration came about in the kingdom of Navarre. During the epochs of Sancho the Great (1005–1035), of the kings of "Aragón and Pamplona" (eleventh and twelfth centuries), and then of the last sovereigns of the native dynasty (the thirteenth century), one chancellor alone seemed sufficient to the whole of affairs, at the side of the king, head of his troops and master of his castles. As the kingdom became a real state such as the great neighboring kingdoms, Navarre asked for an administration and a specialized staff. The kings of the French dynasties have seen, in these appointments and this management, an element of their sovereignty; the political and economical necessities required it. The examination of this administration is therefore the most fruitful in the last centuries of the Middle Ages. The king had a palace and a court, from where everything was issued and everything ended up. The king of Navarre, like his contemporaries, only acted with the advice of a council. Within its ranks appeared the princes of the family and all those that the king wanted to summon according to his own will. On several occasions, as the kings of Navarre lived in France as much as in their kingdom, a governor replaced the king. In the thirteenth and fourteenth centuries the governors were French noblemen, treating Navarre as a bailiwick of the Capetian lands. But Charles II (1349–1387), definitively and truly setting down his kingdom, no longer appointed governors. His brother Louis, then his son Charles and also queen Jeanne, periodically replaced him, each bearing the title "king's lieutenant" (this was especially true of Louis, until 1361).

Beside this high officer, the members of the council were the Navarrese noblemen or the sovereign's personal secretaries whose social backgrounds were various. The chancellor of Navarre played one of the first parts, but he was not always appointed and could be replaced by the keeper of the seals or even by a college of solicitors and *alcaldes*—the judges of the court—who often took charge of the administration. But under Charles III (1387–1425), the chancellor Francés de Villaespesa was one of the greatest actors in the life of the kingdom. The chancellery's seal and the king's seal alternated in diplomatic acts, according to their object and according to their author.

Lastly, at the king's side, the palace sometimes grouped together several hundred people. To manage this king's house, this king's hotel, "masters" and *chambriers* had officers, servants, equerries, and clerks, who were gathered in the departments of the stable, kitchen, *fruiterie*, *echansonnerie*, pound, *paneterie*, and chapel. Each department had its budget, each officer his wages.

The supplying of the court lay on the management of the province as the efficiency of the royal government. Since the thirteenth century the kingdom of Navarre was divided into *merindades* of the mountains, Estella, Sanguesa, the Ribera, and the Châtellenie of Saint-Jean for northern Navarre. Each county town of a merindad had its bayle, sitting in Pamplona, Estella, Sanguesa, Tudela, and Saint-Jean-Pied-de-Port. Divisions according the valleys, walled towns, and enclaves still separated these merindades. Then, in the fifteenth century, the merindad of Olite was created. The *merinos* were the king's representatives, judges, and administrators, especially in charge of the castles (which had *alcaytes* filled by the king) and the raising of the troops; they were generally French noblemen, or Navarrese in the fourteenth and fifteenth centuries, often simultaneously holding duties in the court and in the council. At their side, a collector and a judge were indispensable experts.

Another way of controlling the province was to make it take part in the central government. Following the usual custom of occidental kingdoms, the king of Navarre convened representative meetings, the very Iberian *cortes*. Members of the clergy, nobility, and the delegates of the "good towns" therefore sat on the royal request, in order to grant fiscal aid and to support the great acts of politics (the raising of an army, the legal recognition of an heir to the throne). But the management of the merinos and of their tax collectors had to be controlled by investigators—reformers created by the French kings in imitation of the *Capetian*'s investigators, who supervised the whole of judicial and fiscal life, and provincial as well as treasury officers.

Everything indeed ended up in a treasury. The general treasurer of the kingdom, a cleric or French or Navarrian bourgeois, supervised all the provincial collectors, domestic officers, and the military or miscellaneous expenses of the life of the state. Besides this very great official, a chamber of accounts was created in 1365. This was a special court that dissected all financial initiatives and expenses with clerks, solicitors, and auditors, most of the time Navarrese bourgeois. Finally, a court tribunal, entrusted to four *alcaldes* and four solicitors, a lawyer, an inland revenue prosecutor, and a crown prosecutor, represented a breeding ground of councillors and high-ranking officers and played both political and juridical roles. The staff of these administration charges, with its solidarity, its careers, its remunerations, its efficiency, and also its abuse and faults, reflected the whole political life of the kings of Navarre.

Béatrice Leroy

Bibliography

Leroy, B. "Autour de Charles le Mauvais, groupes et personalités." *La Revue Historique* 273, no. 1 (1985), 3–17.

Ostoloza Elizondo, M. I. "La administración del reino de Navarra durante el reinado de Carlos II." *VI Centenario de Carlos II de Navarra; Príncipe de Viana* 48, no. 182 (1987), 621–36.

Zabalo Zabalegui, J. *La administración del reino de Navarra en el Siglo XIV*. Pamplona, 1973.

ADMINISTRATION, CENTRAL, PORTUGAL

The central administration of the kingdom of Portugal was initially patterned on that of the neighboring kingdom of León-Castile, from which Portugal separated in the twelfth century. The *curia regis* consisted of prelates and nobles who counseled the king on major affairs and a body of functionaries who accompanied the king on his travels. The royal court at that time had no fixed residence, nor were the responsibilities of royal officials clearly differentiated. The principal officials were the *signifer* (later called *alferes-mor*), a high-ranking noble who bore the royal standard and commanded the king's armies. Next in rank was the *maiordomus curie* or *mordomo mor da corte* who supervised the affairs of the royal household and the public administration. Under Sancho II (1223–1248) the mordomo was known as the *maiorinus maior* (*meirinho mor*) of Portugal, but Afonso III (1248–1279) restored the older title. Assisting the maiordomus was the *dapifer curie*, but this office soon disappeared. A notarius or notary originally acted as a royal secretary, but Afonso I (1128–1185) established the office of chancellor. The *cancellarius* or *chanceler* was a cleric whose task was to draft and publish charters and diplomas and to guard the royal seal used to authenticate them, notaries and scribes assisted him. From the time of Afonso II (1211–1223) royal documents were recorded in registers for future reference. The office of *superiudex* (*sobrejuiz*) or superior judge was created by Sancho II to adjudicate litigation brought before the king.

From the time of Afonso III the central administration became more complex and required greater organization and differentiation of functions. Whereas Coimbra had been a favorite residence of his predecessors, Afonso III opted in favor of Lisbon, which was more centrally located. There the royal archives were deposited, but the chancellor and much of the rest of the court continued to accompany the king as he traveled extensively about his realm. In 1258, Afonso III published a *Regimento da Casa Real* that described the duties of palatine officials. Besides the mordomo mor, the alteres mor, the chancellor, and the sobrejuiz there were numerous other officials whose functions were often of a private nature. They included the *reposteiro mor* or butler, the *porteiro mor* or chief usher and messenger, the chaplain, the royal physicians, and other subordinates. A royal council (*conselho d'el-rei*) composed of the mordomo mor, alferes mor, the chancellor, the sobrejuiz, and other counselors chosen by the king assumed a more permanent character and was consulted regularly by the king on matters of great importance.

After the conclusion of the Reconquest the chancellor assumed the dominant role in the court, supervising an ever-growing bureaucracy of clerks, notaries, scribes, and other professionals or legists educated in the universities in civil and canon law. The functions of diverse groups of officials now became more specialized. In the reign of Pedro I (1357–1367) the chancellor was gradually supplanted as the most influential person in the royal court by the *escrivão da puridade*, the king's private secretary, who used the king's personal seal (*anel de camafeu*) to handle business much more expeditiously than the cumbersome machinery of the chancery. Also playing a role of the utmost importance were the *livradores de desembargos* or deliverers of dispatches. These legists received petitions and requests for royal action; after reviewing them and determining how these matters should be handled, they presented their recommendations to the chancellor or to the king.

During this time as the administration of justice became more complex, requiring highly specialized knowledge, the royal tribunal was separated from other elements of the central administration. The sobrejuizes of earlier times were replaced by *ouvidores* or auditors, men usually trained in Roman and canon law, who constituted a tribunal or *audiência* to adjudicate suits in the king's name. Under Afonso IV (1325–1357) one group of auditors sat in a fixed place while another accompanied the king. This eventually gave way to the establishment of two principal royal courts. The Casa do Cível, settled first in Santarém and then in Lisbon by João I (1385–1433), was constituted by sobrejuizes and two *ouvidores do crime* to hear both civil and criminal cases. The two *ouvidores do civil* and two *ouvidores do crime* who formed the Casa da Justiça da Corte traveling with the king also dealt with civil and criminal matters. A third group of judges, the *vedores da fazenda*, handled litigation concerning the king's revenues and financial administration. The *corregedor da corte*, exercising police functions, maintained order in the court.

Recognizing the importance of the royal council in the initiation and development of royal policy, the municipal procurators in the courts of 1385 hoped to secure permanent representation in the council along with prelates, nobles, and legists. In the fifteenth century the council consisted of twenty-seven members, divided into three groups each consisting of six councillors, a prelate, a noble, and a townsman, chosen every three years; each group would serve for four months. While service in this body was largely honorific, the chancellor, the escrivão da puridade, another royal secretary (*secretario d'el-rei*), two corregedores da corte, and the meirinho mor overseeing the administration of justice in noble estates constituted a small council that met regularly to advise the king.

JOSEPH F. O'CALLAGHAN

Bibliography

Gama Barros, H. da. *História da administração pública em Portugal nos séculos XII a XV*. 11 vols., 2d ed. Lisbon, 1945–1954.

Sánchez Albornoz, Cl. *La curia regia portuguesa: Siglos XII y XIII*. Madrid, 1920.

ADMINISTRATION, FINANCIAL, CROWN OF ARAGÓN

The resources available to the kings of Aragón depended upon a wide array of patrimonial assets, customary exactions, and subsidies that varied in importance according to historical circumstances and regional tradition. Each component of the dynastic federation known as the Crown of Aragón possessed fiscal assets and prerogatives providing the ruler with support but also limiting his prerogatives. In the upland kingdom of Aragón and the counties of Old Catalonia, the foundation stones of the dynastic confederation, rulers originally lived and governed from their domain and traditional fiscal exactions. The impulse for new territorial conquests in al-Andalus and ambitions in the Mediterranean created heavy new demands that outstripped traditional resources by the late twelfth century. As a result, the early count-kings instituted fiscal initiatives to improve the management and collection of their older resources and turned to new forms of taxation. The forcible addition of the new realms of Valencia, Mallorca, and Sicily in the thirteenth century and the later conquests of Sardinia and the kingdom of Naples each presented new challenges to fiscal control, not to mention the heavy expense of maintaining such far-flung interests. New forms of central financial control were instituted, but the monarchy also had to recognize the financial and political concerns of the individual regional components. The tensions between central and local fiscal supervision, delegated and direct fiscal management, and traditional and novel forms of revenue created the dynamic behind the administrative and political actions of the kings of Aragón.

Early Fiscal Initiatives

The surviving fiscal accounts in Catalonia, whose administrative records are far fuller than those of Aragón, provide a window on the nature of early fiscal supervision. From the mid-twelfth century the records of account demonstrate that scribes and clerks provided a literate professionalism essential to the development of government. While vicars and bailiffs, the local agents in charge of the fisc, no doubt had traditionally been subject to irregular review, the spread of militant lordship in Catalonia from the early eleventh century had made the count's men look upon their charges as patrimonial assets rather than as delegated responsibilities. To rein in his officials and gain firmer control of his assets, Ramón Berenguer IV commanded an ambitious survey of comital domains, executed by Ramón de Caldes and Guillem de Bassa in 1151. Although a traditional form of memorializing assets, the "Little Domesday" for Catalonia provided a basis for erecting a more ambitious structure of fiscal control. Under Ramón Berenguer IV's successor, Alfonso I (Alfonso II of Aragón, 1162–1196), court accountants began to update inventories and supervise periodic fiscal reviews of officials. Copies of audits were kept in a new fiscal archive and professional literacy began to overshadow personal loyalty as the foundation of patrimonial control. Because of growing indebtedness in the later years of Alfonso I and especially during the reign of his son, Pedro I (1196–1213), the assignation of revenues from bailiwicks and vicariates as pledges to meet financial demands became increasingly common. Credit long remained a critical feature of local Catalan administration. Royal finance was still dependent on supervision by courtiers, without budget or treasury. One must not overemphasize the effectiveness of these reforms, but they did point the way to firmer fiscal control. A handful of accountants and scribes helped organize and supervise local financial administration, but firm central institutions were still lacking.

Expanded political ambitions in the thirteenth century severally strained traditional sources of revenue. King Pedro I incurred massive debts to barons and court financiers; his death at the Battle of Muret provoked a financial crisis during the early years of his son Jaime I (1213–1276). Large parts of the royal domain were given over to barons in order to recover their loans, but under the financial supervision of the Knights Templar, the crown gradually regained direct administration of its domains. The conquests of Mallorca (1229) and Valencia (1238) provided important new sources of revenues that offered immediate relief for the financial pressures on the old heartlands of Catalonia and Aragón, yet other sources of revenue would also be required to support even more ambitious military and political designs. Close supervision of commercial tolls and urban utilities provided important supplements to traditional patrimonial assets as towns grew. In addition, King Jaime I asked for more tallages from individual cities and regions, imposed taxes on Jewish communities, exploited the newly subjected Muslim communities in Valencia, and requested general levies. In Catalonia, the *bovatge*, distantly related to a peace tax in Cerdanya, was levied throughout the land in 1173. Although it became a customary accession tax, thirteenth-century kings came to impose it in emergencies. In Aragón, a tax levied for the redemption of the coinage, the *monedatge*, served a similar function. Territorially based and levied by paid collectors, the bovatge and monedatge became the first public subsidies in the Crown of Aragón and prompted the kings to ask the *cortes* (general assemblies) for the aid.

The reign of Jaime I was marked by growing institutional maturity and expanding bureaucracies. Bailiffs continued to supervise fiscal administration locally in Catalonia and Valencia while *merinos* served the same function in Aragón, only both increasingly employed subordinates or farmed out parts of their charge to investor-administrators. Substantial elements of older patrimonial assets were assigned to creditors, whose advances were critical in keeping local administration running smoothly. The kings kept tighter control of their rights in their newly conquered territories of Valencia and the Balearic Islands. Until the 1280s Jews served frequently in the principal urban bailiwicks, and major parts of the domain were pledged to barons and urban financiers. Fiscal supervision, once charged to the Templars, became connected with the chancery, for the early royal registers, dating from the 1250s, contain accounts and audits. Because of baronial revolts and the conquest of Sicily in 1282, the later years of Jaime I and the reign of his son Pedro II (III of Aragón, 1276–1285) were again marked by mounting financial pressure. To help organize his scattered assets for urgent military needs, in 1283 Pedro II experimented with a new, centralized fiscal supervisor for the Crown of Aragón, the *mestre racional*.

Central Fiscal Control (1283–1419)

The creation of the mestre racional was part of a general movement toward administrative specialization and maturation throughout the Crown of Aragón. Mediterranean conquests and the political repercussions they brought strained the financial resources of the Aragónese kings as a long series of confrontations with France, Castile, Genoa, and Naples, as well as the difficulty of subduing Sardinia, required substantial military and naval expenditures throughout the fourteenth century. To meet these demands, the monarchy needed to tap its widely dispersed resources and turn to new forms of revenue. As the fiscal overseer of accounts throughout the Crown of Aragón, the mestre racional became the principal fiscal official with responsibility over the federation.

Pedro II instituted the office after a Sicilian model in 1283, the year after the Catalan conquest of the island. At first, the mestre racional served with three other court officials to supervise accounts from the realms directly subject to the king of Aragón with the exception of Sicily, where the office originated. Without clearly circumscribed functions among his three peers, the mestre racional was not able to consolidate his position at first and encountered opposition from local administrators, particularly in Aragón. The office was briefly abolished from 1288 to 1293. Jaime II (1291–1326), however, reinstituted it and now gave the supervision of fiscal audit to the mestre racional alone, assisted by his scribes and a lieutenant. Later administrative ordinances in 1344 and 1358 further clarified and strengthened the nature of the office. The mestre racional oversaw a complex network of fiscal administrators and creditors to the crown. He received and audited accounts from the three general bailiffs, instituted in 1282 in Catalonia, Aragón, and Valencia to supervise local vicars, bailiffs, and merinos. Accounts kept by royal creditors, collectors of extraordinary revenues, and members of the royal family also fell under his jurisdiction. With increased central control of finance, the king could now total and compare revenues from various peninsular realms in order to determine the degree to which his resources could support his policies.

Besides the mestre racional and his assistants, two other officials also participated in central financial administration: the treasurer and the *escrivá de ració*, with attendant scribes. The treasurer was of course responsible for the receipts and disbursements from the royal treasury, which remained itinerant. Associated with the treasurer was the escrivá de ració, who dealt with the royal household, including jewelry, clothing, and other valuables, and occasionally with royal ambassadors or procurators. The central financial administration thus involved fifteen or twenty individuals, with the mestre racional at its summit.

The centralization and stability of fiscal audit produced a splendid series of financial records from the end of the thirteenth century. Together with the accounts of the general bailiffs in Aragón, Catalonia, and Valencia, the records kept by the mestre racional provide a detailed account of the state of finance throughout the Crown of Aragón, with the exception of the kingdoms of Sicily and Mallorca (which had its own mestre racional during its period of independence). These records reveal a substantial growth in the revenues available to the king since the early thirteenth century. The increases, however, came principally from commercial tolls and extraordinary taxation rather than from the older lands and revenues of the fisc. These traditional sources of income had been assigned to meet the expenses of local administration and debt or alienated either for long periods or in perpetuity. In the early fourteenth century only 10 percent of income that came from the traditional royal patrimony in Catalonia made its way into the coffers of the treasurer, and the state of the fisc was surely little better in Aragón. King Jaime II already complained that debt was forcing him to alienate parts of the royal patrimony, and the problem worsened during the second half of the fourteenth century. Owing to the erosion of the fisc, Martín I (1396–1410) attempted to recover portions of the lost patrimony and further alienations were prohibited. In Catalonia, royal officials concentrated on the recovery of jurisdictional rights, while in Aragón the cortes were in charge of recovering royal rents. Although not completely successful, these reforms did help slow the hemorrhaging of traditional sources of revenue and rights to the crown. The attempts at recuperation, however, above all demonstrate the financial difficulties facing the monarchy in the fourteenth century and the need to look for new sources of revenue.

Although the kings of Aragón had sought and received general levies such as the monedatge and bovatge as well as local tallages from the twelfth century onward, customary limitations on their assessment did not allow these revenues to meet the expenses of the crown. In the early fourteenth century, nondomainal revenues constituted the lion's share of income to the royal treasury. Regular tribute and irregular subsidies demanded from Mudéjar and especially Jewish communities grew in importance. In the treasury receipts of 1335, for which one of the few detailed studies exists, Jews contributed 21 percent of the total; the *aljamas* of Catalonia paid almost twice as much as those of Aragón. In the same year 58 percent of income to the crown came from irregular subsidies, of which only 4 percent derived from the traditional sources of tallage, monedatge, and bovatge. In that year the primary source of income to the crown as a whole came from an *imposición* (subsidy) voted by the *cortes* of Valencia. In Catalonia and Aragón as well irregular aids and impositions granted by the *cortes* of the individual realms provided important new means of war subsidies that far exceeded renders from customary domains and revenues. With larger and increasingly regular subsidies came greater demands on the part of representative bodies for fiscal supervision. Permanent standing deputations of the *cortes* in the three realms supervised and audited the collectors of the revenues they approved. The autonomous powers of the Diputación del General in Aragón, Catalonia (where it was called the Generalitat), and Valencia, each a permanent commission voted by their respective *cortes*, were fully recognized by the early fifteenth century. As representative institutions consolidated their power and provided substantial revenues to supplement the income from the royal domain, regional concerns in each of the three realms heightened the practical difficulties of managing financial affairs centrally.

By the turn of the fifteenth century Valencia, jealous of Catalan domination of the federation, had attained a new financial and economic importance. In addition, the installation in 1412 of a new dynasty the Trastámaras, had come at the price of strengthening the constitutional prerogatives of each of the realms. These new circumstances induced Alfonso IV (Alfonso V in Aragón), who would spend most of his long reign in southern Italy, to establish a separate mestre racional in Valencia in 1419.

Debt, Regionalism, and Reform (1419–1516)

With the foundation of separate mestres racionals, the treasury remained the only central financial institution after 1419. Yet the movement toward decentralization also eroded the traditional responsibilities of the office. From the 1420s onward the general bailiffs in each realm and local bailiffs and merinos authorized expenditures directly from the revenues they collected without receiving specific letters of payment from the general treasurer. As a result, specialized local treasuries formed and kept separate registers of account. The general treasurer's receipts therefore no longer reflected the balance of income from throughout the crown since large portions of patrimonial revenues and expenditure were handled at a local or regional level. His duties became limited to supervising the reduced amounts that actually arrived at the coffers traveling with the king.

During the fifteenth century the kings of Aragón continued to face the same financial difficulties that had plagued their predecessors in the fourteenth. We still know little about the effects that heavy military expenditure had on the royal fisc and local officials. The majority of revenues from traditional patrimonial resources continued to be consumed in local administration, and parts of the fisc were pledged to meet expenses. Owing to the persecution of Jews and declining number of Mudéjars, taxes from religious minorities declined. Contributions to the king administered by the diputaciones of the three regional *cortes*, however, continued to be substantial, as did subsidies and loans from the towns. In Catalonia, private banks also provided substantial amounts. Unable to meet the immediate demands of their sovereign from their ordinary revenues, the diputaciones and towns came to rely on the sale of annual and life annuities (*censals* and *violaris*) to investors, secured upon their taxes and other rights. The amount of public debt grew substantially in Aragón and Valencia during the fifteenth century, but the crisis was deepest in Catalonia, which was wracked by civil war and economic hardship from 1462 to 1472. The advent of Fernando I in 1474 marked an important turning point in the financial well-being of the Crown of Aragón for he set out with urgency and determination to reduce public debt, decrease the interest paid on annuities, and recover alienated portions of the royal patrimony. His reign witnessed an amelioration in the finances of the Crown of Aragón, but the amounts his territories could provide seemed meager in comparison to the resources Isabel possessed in the expansive Crown of Castile.

Stephen P. Bensch

Bibliography

Bisson, T. N. *Fiscal Accounts of the Early Count-Kings (1151–1213).* 2 vols. Berkeley, Calif., 1984.

Guilleré, C. "Les finances royales à la fin du regne d'Alfonso IV el Benigno (1335–1336)." *Mélanges de la Casa de Velázquez* 18 (1982), 33–60.

Montagut i Estragués, T. *El mestre racional a la Corona d'Aragó.* 2 vols. Barcelona, 1987.

Sánchez Martínez, M. "La fiscalidad real en Cataluña (siglo XIV)." *Anuario de estudios medievales* 22 (1982), 341–76.

ADMINISTRATION, FINANCIAL, CASTILE

The rudiments of the financial administration of the Roman Empire survived in the Visigothic era. Recesvinth, at the Eighth Council of Toledo in 653, confirmed the distinction between state property and the personal holdings of the king, which were transmissible to his heirs. Nevertheless, the distinction between public property and the private estates of the king tended to blur very easily. Officials such as the count of the patrimony and the count of the treasury appear to have had responsibility for the royal domain and revenues and expenditures. Revenues, including a land tax, poll tax, tolls, and fines, tended to be customary and of fixed amounts and were collected by local officials.

The data for the kingdoms of Asturias-León-Castile prior to the thirteenth century is so scant as to make it difficult to speak of financial administration. The distinction between public and royal property disappeared altogether. No attempt at a budget seems to have been made, and revenues, whatever their source, were used by the king as he saw fit. The *maiordomus* apparently took charge of the collection and expenditure of royal revenues, while the treasurer (*thesaurarius*) guarded the king's jewels and other valuables. Local officials (*merinos*) were responsible for the collection of tributes and other moneys owed to the king. Royal revenue continued to be derived from the tribute payable by tenants on the land, labor services, tolls, fines, hospitality, and transportation.

As royal needs and responsibilities became more complex in the thirteenth century so did the financial administration. The *mayordomo mayor* had general charge of the king's accounts, but the *almojarife mayor*, often a Jew, directed the collection of taxes and the payment of stipends to the nobility, one of the major expenses of the crown. Ordinarily the king contracted with tax farmers who were authorized to collect specific taxes in return for payment of a fixed amount into the treasury every year; for example, in 1276–1277 several Jewish tax farmers contracted to pay 1,670,000 *maravedís* from the collection of taxes due since 1261. In 1280 Alfonso X executed Zag de la Maleha, the almojarife mayor, for diverting funds already collected to the king's son, Sancho. The *cortes* (parliament) often demanded that only Christians should be permitted to collect taxes, to the exclusion of Jews, nobles, and clerics. Tax collectors (*merinos, cogedores*) were required to render accounts annually; among the few records still extant are accounts for several years in the reign of Sancho IV (1284–1295). From time to time the *cortes* demanded an accounting of royal income and expenditures; an audit carried out at Burgos in 1308 revealed a deficit of 4,500,000 maravedís. Fernando IV promised the *cortes* in 1312 that he would balance the budget, but that was never effectively accomplished. An audit in 1317 indicated income of 1,600,000 and expenditures of 9,000,000 maravedís for maintenance of the royal court, custody of castles, and stipends for the nobility. As a basis for assessing taxes a *padrón* was drawn up in each locality listing taxpayers and estimating their wealth.

Confusion seems to have been the hallmark of financial administration into the late Middle Ages, when some effort at reform was undertaken. The role of the mayordomo mayor was now honorific, and the office of almojarife mayor disappeared in the late fourteenth century; the *despensero mayor* continued to pay the salaries of members of the royal household. Tax collection was in the hands of *recaudadores* named in each district or *partido*. The principal financial administrators were now divided between the *contaduría mayor de hacienda* and the *contaduría mayor de cuentas*. Two accountants, or *contadores mayores de hacienda*, saw to the collection and disbursement of the king's ordinary revenues, which were recorded in *libros de asiento*. They also kept books recording alienated income (*libros de lo salvado*). Two additional *contadores mayores de cuentas* reviewed royal accounts, prepared an annual summary of expected income and expenses, and had jurisdiction over litigation concerning any of these issues. After 1436 they were required to take up permanent residence at Valladolid in the Casa de las Cuentas. Fernando and Isabel refined various aspects of this system, making it a more effective means of collecting and controlling the expenditures of royal revenues. As a consequence they greatly increased the income of the crown.

JOSEPH F. O'CALLAGHAN

Bibliography

Ladero Quesada, M. A. *Fiscalidad y poder regio en Castilla (1252–1369)*. Madrid, 1993.

———. *La Hacienda Real de Castilla en el siglo XV*. La Laguna de Tenerife, 1973.

O'Callaghan, J. F. *A History of Medieval Spain*. Ithaca, N.Y., 1975.

ADMINISTRATION, FINANCIAL, LEÓN

The fundamental resource of the Leonese monarchy was the landed property of the dynasty. From it were derived the horses and oxen that furnished its means of locomotion; cattle, sheep, and grains, which gave it sustenance; rents, which provided for the sophisticated goods that must be purchased in the Islamic south in the early years; and the men who filled out its raiding parties and war bands. The administrator who was responsible for all of this wealth in its various forms was the *merino*. He was essentially an estate manager. Surely he was appointed but rarely was he of such rank as to leave much trace in the documents. The last century of the Leonese kingdom sometimes saw *merinos* of some personal prestige and family but these were the custodians of royal urban properties and so of a rather different type. Their prime concern would have been the collection of rents from bakeries, forges, and presses owned by the crown, along with the proceeds of justice that they, like their country cousins, administered.

One thinks that such local officials must have been responsible to the royal majordomo at court for their stewardship. Still, it is so far impossible to discern any mechanism that would have regularly connected the two. A later period will see the *merindad* emerge as a fundamental unit of local government and the *merino mayor* as a coordinating official, but these are hard to detect in the kingdom of León. During the reign of the last of its kings, Alfonso IX, there are some persons designated *merino* of much larger units—Galicia, for instance—but not much is known of their function.

The merino must also have been responsible for the collection of what was the major tax revenue of the realm, that is, the *fossataria*. This was a "shield tax" levied on those who elected not to perform the *fossata*, or obligatory military service in time of war. No particular machinery was necessary to collect it since the merino could simply bring it to the gathering of the royal host.

This same near absence of administration as such marked the entire range of royal revenue and its collection. The coinage was a royal prerogative but the actual mints were located in the episcopal towns and were operated by the bishop, with a share of the proceeds going to the crown. So too, the *portaticum* and the *mercatum*, levies on goods transported or sold, seem often to have been administered by those bishops or abbots who had been alloted a share in them by royal charter, but the collection of the former, especially in country districts, must simply have been leased to local magnates or royal castellans. Likely the procedure was the same with the royal share from the proceeds of mining operations, especially of salt.

Finally, as everywhere during the Middle Ages, the proceeds of the administration of justice belonged to the crown. In fact, as the charters make abundantly clear, everywhere the regular procedure was that they were to be divided, most frequently evenly, between the injured party and the crown. The position of judge became most visible in the documents, although judges were ordinarily the most humble of officials, and exclusively local. Most probably, the collection and forwarding of the royal share of the imposts arising from their work again fell on the merino, castellan, or bishop of the vicinity. There is no trace of alternative machinery either at the local or royal levels.

While all of these rents and customary revenues may have sufficed ordinarily in time of peace, they had to be supplemented in wartime, which was quite frequent. By the second half of the twelfth century a special revenue, the *petitum*, emerged, and its levy was occasional and general. Again, since it was a special impost no particular machinery seems to have been devised to collect it, and apparently the proceeds would have been borne to a royal *curia* or assembly of the host by those who attended.

At the beginning of the thirteenth century this tradition of royal entitlement to special "grants in aid" in times of emergency would be linked to the emergence of the new *cortes* in both León and Castile. Doubtless, such requests had ordinarily been made in the context of a royal curia. One such grant may have been made at the first cortes of León in 1188, but the documents are not clear. Certainly one was authorized at the cortes at Benavente in 1202, where it was linked to a royal promise not to tamper with the coinage for a period of seven years afterward. Such a linkage became common in both León and Castile, and suggests that the bulk of the revenue was to be derived from the merchant community. Before 1230 there is no evidence that special tax collectors were appointed for its collection.

BERNARD F. REILLY

Bibliography

García de Valdeavellano, L. *Curso de historia de las instituciones españolas: De los orígenes al final de la Edad Media*. Madrid, 1968.

O'Callaghan, J. F. *The Cortes of Castile-León: 1188–1350*. Philadelphia, 1989.

Procter, E. S. *Curia and Cortes in León and Castile, 1072–1295*. Cambridge, 1980.

Sinués Ruiz, A. *El merino*. Zaragoza, 1954.

ADMINISTRATION, FINANCIAL, NAVARRE

Every state with a foreign policy and managed by a king and a court needs a serious financial administration. In the thirteenth to fifteenth centuries, the kingdom of Navarre had its own treasury and experts. The treasurer of Navarre, whose yearly registers detailed the expenditure and receipts kept, was usually a French clerk (Simon Aubert in the beginning of the fourteenth century) or a Navarese middle-class person (Juan Caritat, a "Franco" from Tudela, in the end of the fourteenth century). Helped by a chamber of deniers which supervised the minting of money, and by a chamber of accounts, which managed and judged the fiscal cases, the treasurer's main function was to plan the state's expenditure (war, fortifications, troops' pay, military and civilian officers' wages, equipment work, amounts of money granted to the king's loyalists, and court's expenditure); and to attend to the coming in of the receipts (*pechas* of the taxable commoners and of the Moors and Jews—that is to say, taxes of quota raised by homesteads, indirect miscellaneous taxes on trade, bridges, markets and fairs, registering rights under the king's seal). Therefore, the treasurer controled the provincial tax collectors, as well as all the officers of the court charged of a specialized duty and entitled to certain spending necessary to their responsibilities.

In the thirteenth to fifteenth centuries, the claims for "exceptional help" periodically returned. The king or his representative then convoked the *cortes* (parliament) and the delegates of the prelates, nobility, and "good towns" accepted the amount of money requested by the treasury for war causes, royal events, princely weddings, fortifications, and the like.

Social categories that were usually tax free, such as the Church and nobility, collaborated most often to these exceptional levyings. The sovereign always had the ability to exempt his subjects in a personal capacity, with a seal charter. For this reason expenditures very quickly exceeded receipts (a merino received 2,000 pounds in yearly wages, for instance, causing the expenditure of the court to possibly exceed 50,000 pounds each year) that relied only on the demography and economic prosperity of Navarre. During the fourteenth and fifteenth centuries the treasury had to resort to short-term measures. By the mid-fourteenth century, the treasury regularly leased taxations, either directly or indirectly. For a fixed and yearly amount of money, the *arrendadores* managed for themselves the royal resources; they gathered in groups of six to twelve members, most often Navarrese and Jews from the kingdom; thus, in 1392, they gave 60,000 pounds to the treasury, and then had enough money come in to be paid back. These amounts paid in advance and in one payment were still not enough for the courts of Charles II and Charles III (1349–1425), who constantly borrowed from the nobility, middle-class, and Jews and reimbursed them by giving them a fraction of the royal incomes, or by making installments, interest and usury being wholly legal in Navarre around 1400.

BÉATRICE LEROY

Bibliography

Zabalo Zabalegui, J. "La alta administración del Reino de Navarra en el Siglo XIV, Tesoreros y Procuradores," in *Homenaje a Don José Esteban Uranga*. Pamplona, 1973. 137–53.

ADMINISTRATION, FINANCIAL, PORTUGAL

The financial administration of the kingdom of Portugal was based originally on that of the kingdom of León-Castile, from which Portugal separated in the twelfth century. At that time the personnel responsible for the collection of tributes owed to the crown was undifferentiated from that of other administrative offices. Moreover, as many royal officials were remunerated from local contributions, those moneys did not ordinarily enter the royal treasury. Initially the *maiordomus curie* or *mordomo mor*, as he was known, not only supervised the royal household but also had general responsibility for the administration of royal revenues. From the thirteenth century onward as awareness of the distinction between the king's private patrimony and the public patrimony of the state increased, the role of the mordomo mor was restricted to the finances of the household, and general supervision of the collection and disbursement of tributes was entrusted to *almoxarifes*. The collection of royal revenues was usually given over to tax farmers who promised to pay the crown a certain sum from the various tributes and taxes collected and of course to pocket a profit for themselves. Municipal councils preferred to collect their own tributes.

The sources of royal revenue were many and varied but of unequal importance. There were tributes in the form of rents and services (*pectum*, *peito*) owed by the tenants on royal estates. In addition, the king was entitled to pasturage fees (*montado*); tolls (*portagen*) collected at roads and bridges; market tolls (*açougagen*, *alcavala*, *sisa*); judicial fines (*coima*) imposed by his courts; payments made in place of personal military service (*Fossataria*); and lodging and hospitality (*colheita*), which became a regular payment in money whether he visited each locality or not. He could also call on local inhabitants for service in building and repairing bridges, roads, and castles (*fazendera*), and to provide transport for himself or his representatives. He was also entitled to a fifth of any booty, and a fifth of the income derived from the exploitation of mines.

In the thirteenth century the Portuguese kings began to feel the need for extraordinary taxes to meet their steadily increasing financial requirements. To some extent that need was met by convoking the *cortes* (parliament) and asking the representatives of the townspeople for subsidies (*pedidos*). An early example of this came during the reign of Afonso III (1248–1279) who tried to improve his financial resources by altering the coinage. The ensuing economic distress evoked strong protest and he had to negotiate a solution with the cortes. In return for the king's pledge not to debase the coinage for a period of seven years, the cortes granted him a subsidy called *monetágio* or *moeda foreira*. The kings also exacted forced loans (*emprestitos*) and levied customs duties of a tenth (*dizima*) of the value of imported goods. The *sisa*, a sales tax, appeared as a royal tribute in the reign of Fernando (1367–1383), though it may antedate him; it remained an extraordinary tribute until the reign of João I (1385–1433) when it became a permanent levy.

King Dinis (1279–1325) established the rudiments of a financial bureaucracy separate from the royal household. The royal treasurer (*tesoureiro*) assumed general oversight of royal finances and received accounts from *almoxarifes* and other subordinate officials. Extant today are four incomplete books (*libri de recabedo regni*) recording royal revenues in the thirteenth century as well as the accounts of the *almoxarife* in 1273. As the variety of royal revenues became more extensive so did the apparatus responsible for their collection and disbursement. In the fifteenth century two *veedores da fazenda* (overseers) of the treasury assumed responsibility for financial administration and also adjudicated litigation concerning royal revenues.

According to Fernão Lopes, King Pedro (1357–1367) was especially careful in the management of royal finances, so that when Fernando succeeded him he found a treasure in Lisbon Tower of 800,000 gold pieces, 400,000 marks of silver, as well as other coins. Excluding the customs of Lisbon and Oporto, the revenues of the crown amounted to 800,000 *libras*, or 200,000 *dobras*, a significant amount. The customs of Lisbon were reported to be 35,000 to 40,000 *dobras* annually. The first royal budget appeared in 1473, with revenues of 47,000,000 *reais* or 145,000 gold *cruzados*, and expenses of 37.6 million reais or 115,600 cruzados. The bulk of those revenues, 81 percent, was used for the maintenance of the king, his court, and his family, and for stipends given to members of the nobility. As the medieval centuries drew to a close the expenses of royal efforts to expand into Morocco and to exploit the newly emerging continent of Africa meant that expenses quickly outran income and forced the government to operate at a deficit.

Joseph F. O'Callaghan

Bibliography

Gama Barros, H. da. *História da administração pública em Portugal nos séculos XII a XV*. 11 vols. 2d ed. Lisbon, 1945–1954.

ADMINISTRATION, JUDICIAL

For the greater part of the Middle Ages the judicial system was inextricably linked to civil administration. Besides the monarch, there were ecclesiastical and secular lords who enjoyed the privilege of immunity, and the Church, which had its own canon law and its own judges; all of these exercised jurisdiction.

Judicial administration in the Visigothic era was complicated by the coexistence of both Roman and Visigothic laws. Hispano-Romans were ruled by the Theodosian Code of 438 and its later derivatives. The Visigoths lived according to custom, but efforts to codify their law and to establish a uniform law for all the inhabitants of the peninsula were made. This process culminated in the *Liber Iudiciorum*, completed during the reign of Reccesvinth (653–672). This was a systematic, comprehensive code of law, derived in large part from Roman law, and unparalleled elsewhere in the barbarian kingdoms of western Europe. Justice was administered by the king and provincial officials.

In the kingdom of Asturias-León the *Liber Iudiciorum* continued in use, but in Castile custom prevailed. In the eleventh and twelfth centuries the new municipalities received *fueros* or charters regulating the status of persons and property and their obligations to the crown. The *Fuero* of Cuenca, issued after the conquest of that town in 1177, was the most comprehensive of these texts. The *Usatges* of Barcelona, a compilation formed in the eleventh and twelfth centuries, became the foundation of the legal and judicial system in Catalonia.

The king's court dealt with cases involving the great men, and provincial governors were responsible for administering justice in their respective territories. As there was no hierarchy of courts, there was no system of appeals, though in León one could appeal to the judgment of the book—that is, the *Liber Iudiciorum*. Procedure was largely Germanic. Except in cases of violation of the king's peace, the plaintiff had to bring suit by accusation. Once summoned, the defendant had to give pledges as a guarantee of appearance in court. The process was oral as the parties or their spokespersons argued the case. Once the charge was clearly established, judges of proof determined whether it should be proved by an oath of purgation, the ordeal of hot water or hot iron, or the judicial duel. The judges declared whether the proof was successful, but execution of the judgment was left in private hands. Monetary compensation was possible in case of murder or physical injury. Penalties included fines, confiscation, exile, mutilation, and hanging.

The reception of Roman law in the twelfth and thirteenth centuries brought with it the idea that the king had the primary responsibility for declaring the law and administering justice. This principle was enunciated clearly in the *Siete Partidas*, a code of law drawn up by Alfonso X of Castile for use in his court, and in the *Fuero Real*, a code of municipal law. The *Partidas* were translated into Portuguese under the aegis of King Dinis, and both texts influenced the development of Portuguese law. Roman law was the basis for the

Fori regni Valentie promulgated by Jaime I in 1240 but the *Code of Huesca* published in 1247, was largely comprised of the traditional laws of Aragón. While officials responsible for public administration also dispensed justice, a clear hierarchy of jurisdiction descending from the king through the provincial governors (*adelantados*, *merinos*, *vequeres*) and the municipal *alcaldes* was recognized. In Castile, *alcaldes fijosdalgo* and in Aragón the *justicia* were appointed to adjudicate litigation involving the nobility. Alfonso IX of León affirmed the principle of due process of law in 1188, as did his successors. Although prelates and nobles continued to exercise jurisdiction in immune lands, the king reserved the right to intervene in crimes such as treason, theft, rape, and highway robbery.

Under Roman influence procedure was now written rather than oral and purgation and ordeals were abandoned as methods of proof. Litigants could be represented by procurators and by professional lawyers (*advocati*, *voceros*). The *inquisitio* or inquest involving the sworn testimony of witnesses came into frequent use as a means of resolving civil cases. On the basis of the inquest or documentary evidence, the judge pronounced judgment but one could then appeal to a higher court. The inquest was also used to identify criminals, who were then arrested and brought to trial. In that way injured parties were relieved of the danger of retaliation by bringing an accusation.

From time to time kings such as Alfonso X endeavored to restructure the royal tribunal to make it more efficient. In 1371 Enrique II established the *audiencia*, composed of a number of auditors that came to be known as the *chancilleria* because it often sat in chancery rooms. The audiencia continued to follow the king until 1442, when Juan II decided that it should have a permanent residence at Valladolid. João I of Portugal also established the Casa do Civel at Lisbon. The Casa da Justiça da Corte was reorganized as a supreme court of appeals. After the conquest of Granada, Fernando and Isabel entrusted the Chancillería of Valladolid with jurisdiction over cases north of the Tagus River and created a new Chancillería with jurisdiction south of the river at Ciudad Real; it was moved to Granada in 1505. With increasing frequency the crown appointed judges to administer justice in the towns.

In the fourteenth and fifteenth centuries significant efforts were made to record and codify the laws. In Castile, Alfonso XI promulgated the *Ordenamiento de Alcalá* in 1348 and gave juridical force to the *Siete Partidas*. The ordinances of the *cortes* (parliament) were another source of law. Fernando and Isabel promulgated in 1484 the *Ordenanzas reales de Castilla*, a collection of the fundamental laws of the realm compiled by the jurist Alfonso Diaz de Montalvo. Fernando also issued a new edition of the *Constitucions i altres drets de Cathalunya* in 1495 and of the *Fueros y observancias del reino de Aragón in* 1496. The *Ordenações Afonsinas* promulgated in Portugal in 1446 served as the basis for the *Ordenações Manuelinas*, promulgated by Manuel I in 1521.

JOSEPH F. O'CALLAGHAN

Bibliography

García de Valdeavellano, L. *Curso de historia de las instituciones españolas: De los orígenes al final de la Edad Media*. Madrid, 1968.

O'Callaghan, J.F. *A History of Medieval Spain*. Ithaca, N.Y., 1975.

ADMINISTRATION, TERRITORIAL, CASTILE, PORTUGAL, LEÓN, ARAGÓN-CATALONIA, NAVARRE

In Roman times Spain was initially formed into two provinces, Hispania Ulterior and Hispania Citerior (whence later references to "the Spains"). Under Diocletian (284–305) the peninsula was divided into five provinces, Tarraconensis (Tarragona, the capital), Carthaginensis (Cartagena), Lusitania (Mérida), Baetica (Seville), and Gallaetia (Braga). This system survived into the Visigothic era, when the provinces were governed by *rectores*, *iudices*, or *duces* with both civil and military authority. Provincial subdivisions called *territoria* consisted of a city and its dependent area. As cities decayed as commercial and industrial centers the municipal *curia* so typical of Roman administration disintegrated. Henceforth a city was important as the headquarters of a provincial governor.

The Muslim invasion disrupted all aspects of civil administration, but Islamic Spain was divided at first into five zones corresponding more or less to Andalucía, Galicia and Portugal, Castile and León, Aragón and Catalonia, and Septimania or Gallia Gothica. Under the rule of the caliphs of Córdoba a more effective provincial regime was instituted as the realm was divided into at least twenty-one provinces whose extent in some cases probably corresponded to those of the Visigothic era. Provincial governors with both civil and military responsibilities ordinarily resided in the chief cities. Military commanders governed the frontier, which was divided into three segments: the Upper Frontier, embracing Catalonia and Aragón, with headquarters at Zaragoza; the Middle Frontier, centered at Medinaceli and running along the borders of Castile and León; and the Lower Frontier, touching Galicia and Portugal and administered from Toledo. These frontier governors often enjoyed considerable autonomy given the great distance separating them from the capital. The towns of Islamic Spain were not endowed with rights of self-government, but were directly controlled by the ruler who appointed a *sāhib al-madina* to maintain law and order, a *qāḍi* or judge who dispensed justice according to the Koran, and the *muḥtasib* who inspected the market.

After the breakup of the caliphate of Córdoba many of the provinces, such as Seville, Córdoba, Jaén, Granada, Málaga, Murcia, Baza, Almería, Beja, Silves, Badajoz, Valencia, and Mallorca, were formed into petty kingdoms known as *tā'ifas*. The *tā'ifas* were displaced in the late eleventh and twelfth centuries by the Almoravids and Almohads of Morocco who successively subjugated Islamic Spain and governed it through members of the royal family acting as viceroys. Once Muslim rule was reduced to the kingdom of Granada in the thirteenth century the royal *wazīr* appointed provincial governors, but large areas were often held as lordships. The Ashqilula family, for example, controlled Guadix, Comares, and Málaga, and often acted in opposition to the king. As the price of military assistance the kings of Granada also yielded important places such as Gibraltar and Algeciras to the Benimerines who ruled Morocco in the thirteenth and fourteenth centuries.

The system developed in Christian Spain after the collapse of the Visigothic kingdom was essentially new. The tiny kingdom of Asturias-León was initially divided into small districts (*mandationes*, *commissa*) often governed by officials having the personal title of count. Counts and other officials served at the king's pleasure and ordinarily did not acquire a hereditary right to their office. Together with their subordinates (known as *maiorini* or *merinos*) they had full responsibility for dispensing justice, collecting taxes, and providing for defense. Castile, which originated as a frontier province of the kingdom of León, was administered by a count. In the tenth century Fernán González transformed this into a hereditary office and so the county of Castile became an independent entity. In the Pyrenees a series of counties were created as part of the Carolingian empire. By the tenth century the counts had secured a hereditary right to their offices and also achieved practical independence of the Capetian kings of France. Their subordinates were known as vicars or viscounts. What cities or towns there were existed principally as administrative centers, and there was no organized municipal government.

In the eleventh and twelfth centuries the concession of immunities and the emergence of municipalities resulted in the decline of counties as major territorial divisions. Tenancies of districts, towns, and fortresses were assigned to royal vassals variously called *tenentes*, *seniores*, or *alcaides*. Only in Aragón (from 1134) and Navarre did they hold their offices or *honores* by hereditary right. A *merino mayor*, aided by subordinate merinos, appeared as the chief administrative officer in Castile after 1180. The Catalan counts were assisted by vicars (*vicarii*) with civil and military responsibilities and bailiffs (*bajuli*) who collected tributes.

From time to time the king granted the privilege of immunity in perpetuity to lands held by hereditary right by bishops, monasteries, nobles, and military orders. The beneficiary had authority to maintain law and order, appoint judges, administer justice, collect tributes and fines, and require military service. The lands so privileged were immune from the intervention of royal officials except in case of negligence, or in cases of treason, rape, robbery, and destruction of highways. The most notable immunity was that enjoyed by the archbishop of Compostela over broad lands in Galicia. The *pertiguero mayor* was the archbishop's representative. In the second half of the twelfth century and the first half of the thirteenth, large areas south of the Tagus River in both Castile and Portugal were handed over as lordships to the military orders of Santiago, Calatrava, Alcántara, and Avis, who were responsible for all aspects of defense and administration.

The municipalities in the central regions between the Duero and the Tagus river valleys enjoyed self-government in direct dependence on the king, who granted charters or *fueros* spelling out their military and tributary obligations, and the rights of the citizens. Consisting of an urban nucleus and an extensive dependent rural area (*terminus*, *alfoz*), and often populated with villages, the municipalities were a major element in the defense and control of vast areas in the kingdoms of Castile, León, and Portugal abutting the Islamic frontier. While the king appointed a noble (*dominus ville*, *senior civitatis*, *alcaide*) to guard the citadel or *alcazar*, an assembly of neighbors (*concilium*, *concejo*) was responsible for general municipal administration. A *judex* or *juez* headed the town government and was aided in the administration of justice by several *alcaldes* chosen from the parishes of the community. Other officials were in charge of finances (*iurati*, *fieles*), the collection of fines and taxes (merinos), inspection of the market (*almotacén*, *zabazoque*), inscription of public documents (*notarios*, *escribanos*), and the maintenance of law and order (*sayones*, *alguaciles*). After the conquest of Andalucía, Murcia, and the Algarve in the thirteenth century this municipal regime was introduced into southern cities such as Seville, Córdoba, Cartagena, and others.

The reconquest of these southern provinces in the thirteenth century also resulted in the creation of new extensive territorial districts governed by officials with responsibility for maintaining law and order, dispensing justice, and collecting tributes and fines owed to the king. Each of the principal constituents of the crown of Castile-León after the union of 1230—namely, the *merindades* of Castile, León and Asturias, and Galicia—was administered by a merino mayor whose principal responsibility was the administration of justice. Under Alfonso X the title *merino mayor* was changed to *adelantado mayor*; in the fourteenth and fifteenth centuries these titles alternated at times, but generally in Castile, León, Asturias, and Galicia the principal representative of the crown was usually called *merino mayor*. On the southern frontier the *adelantado mayor de la frontera*, as the chief administrator of Andalucía was called, was charged mainly with military defense against the Muslims. Another adelantado mayor exercised a similar responsibility in the old Muslim kingdom of Murcia. These posts were usually held by leading members of the nobility who often abused their powers, prompting the *cortes* (parliament) to complain again and again that only those who loved justice should be given this responsibility.

Other *adelantados mayores* (later known as *merinos mayores*) were entrusted with the administration of the Basque provinces of Álava and Guipúzcoa. Guipúzcoa was incorporated into the kingdom of Castile in the reign of Alfonso VIII (1158–1214) while Alfonso XI added Álava in 1332. Vizcaya in the eleventh century was ruled by a count under Castilian suzerainty; in the twelfth century it became a lordship held by the López de Haro family. Juan I (1379–1390) finally annexed Vizcaya to the crown; henceforth the king's representative there was called a *prestamero mayor*. In the later medieval centuries an *hermandad* or association of cities, towns, and districts was organized in Vizcaya, Álava, and Guipúzcoa, whose customs the king or his representatives swore to uphold. From the fourteenth century the archbishop of Toledo was also represented by an adelantado mayor in the frontier lordship of Cazorla.

Portugal was also divided into zones, each governed by a *meirinho mor* and marked out by river boundaries—namely, Além Douro, Aquém Douro, Entre Douro e Minho, Entre Douro e Mondego, and Entre Douro e Tejo. The municipal regime in Portugal was comparable to that of Castile-León.

As the Crown of Aragón consisted of several distinct elements—namely, the kingdoms of Aragón, Mallorca, and Valencia—and the county of Barcelona—the territorial administration was complicated. The heir to the throne was usually named procurator general of all the kingdoms, or lieutenant general. In the fifteenth century the office of lieutenant general assumed relatively continuous existence as Alfonso V pursued his ambitions in Italy. During his lengthy absence his wife María or his brother Juan were empowered to act for him throughout his dominions, effectively exercising the authority of a viceroy. In each of the constituent realms a procurator general (later called a governor general) represented the king during his absence. In Valencia and Mallorca that post was more or less permanent. Catalonia was divided into a varying number of vicariates (Rousillon, Cerdanya, Pallars, Manresa, Osona, Girona, Barcelona, Vilafranca, Cervera, Tárrega, Lérida, Montblanch, Tarragona, and Tortosa), each under a vicar (*veguer*) entrusted with full authority in matters of administration, justice, and defense. There were two vicariates in Mallorca—one for the city of Palma and the other for the rest of the island. In Aragón and Valencia justiciars (*justicia*) fulfilled much the same role as the vicars. The king also appointed *sobrejunteros* to direct the activities of *juntas* or associations of Aragónese towns organized to preserve order, to suppress crime, punish criminals, and levy fines. In the fourteenth century sobrejunteros presided over six such administrative districts—namely, Zaragoza, Huesca, Teruel, Jaca, Tarazona, and the counties of Ribagorza and Sobrarbe; a century later Exea had replaced Teruel. In the fifteenth century Valencia was divided into four zones or *governacions* (Valencia, Játiva, Castellón, and Orihuela), each administered by a *portant-veus* representing the governor general. Side by side with the vicars and justiciars, there were other officials whose duties were primarily financial—namely, the *batlles* or *bayles mayores* of Catalonia, Valencia, and Mallorca, entrusted with the collection of royal revenues.

Given the frequent absence of the kings of Navarre of the French dynasty of Champagne, a governor general often had full responsibility for the administration of the kingdom. In the fourteenth century Navarre was divided into six *merindades* (Pamplona, Tudela, Estella, Sangüesa, Ultrapuertos, and Olite).

A major development in the later Middle Ages was the increase in the number and extent of lordships held by the nobility immune from the supervision of royal officials. The reason for this was the king's need to gain support and to keep it. Enrique II (1369–1379), the first of the Trastámaran kings of Castile, was notorious for his *mercedes* or favors granting lordships and other favors to his adherents. Not only were rural estates alienated, so also were towns that had long been directly under the rule of the king and had long enjoyed self-government as such. Typical of such concessions was Juan II's charter of 1453 conferring certain towns on the widow of Álvaro de Luna "in hereditary right, for ever and ever . . . with their fortresses, lands, justice, civil and criminal jurisdiction, high and low justice, *merum et mixtum imperium*, rents, tributes and rights belonging to the lordship of those places." The cortes from the thirteenth century onward consistently protested such alienations and demanded that the king recover domain lands already alienated or usurped by others. Afonso III of Portugal (1248–1279) conducted extensive inquests to determine whether royal lands were in private hands, but efforts to recover them were often unavailing. João I (1385–1433), the first representative of the house of Avis in Portugal, ceded to his constable Nun' Alvares Pereira the counties of Ourém, Barcelos, and Arrailos, as well as eighteen cities and towns. The king subsequently hoped to resume possession of alienated royal lands, but it was left to his son Duarte in 1433 to enact the so-called *lei mental*, the law his father had in mind; according to this estates granted by the king were heritable only by the firstborn male and could not be divided; in default of a male heir such lands would revert to the crown. In spite of that Duarte's son Afonso V was extraordinarily liberal, as was Enrique IV of Castile, in yielding towns, lands, and other royal rights in lordship.

From the thirteenth century onward urban oligarchies gained control of the cities and towns, eliminating the lower classes from any real participation in public affairs. At the same time factionalism within the ruling aristocracy increased to such a point that the crown had to intervene to maintain order. Alfonso X tried to subordinate municipal fueros to a common royal law known as the *fuero real* but encountered strong opposition. To curb factional disputes kings began to send royal officials (*jueces de salario*, *veedores*, *juizes da fora*) to supervise municipal affairs. From the reign of Alfonso XI these officials known as *corregidores* began to assume a permanent status in the towns of Castile and Portugal. Municipal autonomy was also restricted when the king began to appoint the *regidores* or members of a small council or *ayuntamiento* (usually numbering twenty-four), which came to exercise the role of the older general assembly of citizens. In the thirteenth century the cities and towns of the Crown of Aragón also developed the instruments of self-government, such as a small council that supplanted a larger council of all the citizens. In Barcélona, for example, five councilors chosen yearly were charged with the oversight of day-to-day affairs while a *consell de cent* or council of one hundred also chosen annually met when the need required. A council or *cabildo* in Aragón consisting of several *jurados* or sworn men was elected annually to manage affairs; in Valencia six *jurats* performed a similar function. In Catalonia the king's vicar often supervised and regulated the activities of the towns; the royal justicia or *zalmedina* did likewise in Aragón and Valencia. While the towns increasingly lost internal autonomy as a consequence of royal intervention, further losses were incurred in the fifteenth century as many towns were handed over in lordship to nobles whose favor the king wished to purchase or retain.

Fernando and Isabel, whose marriage united the kingdoms of Castile and Aragón, and João II of Portugal adopted several measures intended to give them greater control over the territorial administration of their respective kingdoms. The Catholic Kings replaced the *adelantados* and *merinos mayores* with *alcaldes mayores*, responsible for the major subdivisions of the crown of Castile—namely, Castile, León, Andalucía, Murcia, and Granada. Asturias and Galicia continued to be administered by merinos mayores and Cazorla by an adelantado mayor. The territorial administration of the Crown of Aragón remained substantially unchanged. In Álava the crown was now represented by a *diputado general* and in Vizcaya and Guipúzcoa by a *corregidor*. In addition, Fernando and Isabel deprived the municipalities of the last vestiges of autonomy by dispatching corregidores to them all after 1480. João II also sent corregidores to assume responsibility for the administration of the Portuguese towns. His successor, Manoel I (1495–1521) undertook a review of all municipal charters, with the purpose of standardizing their obligations.

One of the major accomplishments of both Fernando and Isabel and João II in restoring the power and prestige of the monarchy was the recovery of alienated crown lands and the subordination of lordships to royal authority. With papal approval Fernando and Isabel took control of the lordships of the military Orders of Calatrava (1489), Santiago (1493), and Alcántara (1494), placing their general administration in the hands of the Consejo de las Órdenes. The lands of the orders were divided into eighteen districts, each administered by a *gobernador* or alcalde. Similarly, João II and Manoel I administered the lordships of the military orders of Avis and Christ, which were incorporated into the crown in 1551. As the medieval era came to a close in both Spain and Portugal the crown was taking steps to gain more effective control of territorial and municipal administration.

JOSEPH F. O'CALLAGHAN

Bibliography

Gama Barros, H. da. *História de administração publica em Portugal nos séculos XII a XV*. 11 vols. 2d ed. Lisbon, 1945–54.

García de Valdeavellano, L. *Curso de historia de las instituciones Despañolas: De los orígenes al final de la Edad Media*. Madrid, 1968.

O'Callaghan, J. F. *A History of Medieval Spain*. Ithaca, N.Y., 1975.

Pérez Bustamante, R. *El gobierno y la administración territorial de Castilla (1230–1474)*. 2 vols. Madrid, 1976.

ADMINISTRATION, TERRITORIAL, MUSLIM

Al-Andalus was divided into ten "climates" (Arabic *aqālīm*, sing. *iqlīm*, does not translate the same as the English "climate"; rather, it designates areas or regions). There is some confusion as to the term, for in Andalusian Arabic the Berber term *kūra* (pl. *kuwar*) was used for "districts" and *rastāq* (pl. *rasātīq*) for "province." There were ten of these regions: Aljarafe (al-Sharaf), the present province of Huelva; Albuhera, the present province of Cádiz (apparently the district called *Tākurunnā* in some Arabic sources), including Gibraltar, Algeciras, Tarifa, Cádiz, Rota, Jerez, and Arcos de la Frontera; Sidonia, which is a problem, and may refer to the Seville region, according to Saavedra, but this is unlikely and seems instead to be Shadūna, or Medina Sidonia; Campania, the province of Córdoba, including Écija, Baena, Lucena, and others; Osuna, which included sections of Estepa, Osuna, and Morón; Reya, the present province of Málaga, except for Ronda, and including parts of Córdoba and Granada; Elvira, the present province of Granada, excluding Alhama, Baza, and Huéscar (this region is variously referred to also as *jabal shulayr* or *jabal al-thalj*; i.e., the Sierra Nevada); Pechina, which only Al-Idrīsī mentions as a region, including the area of Almería; and Ferreira, the present area of Baza, Huéscar, and others. (Idrīsī also mentions al-Busharrāt, as including the kingdom of Jaén.)

Some Muslim sources refer also to "marches" (*thughūr*; sing. *thaghr*) in the northern valleys of the Ebro and Tagus, with the upper capital at Zaragoza and the lower at Toledo, but this is as problematic as the so-called march in Christian geography. The Pyrenees were referred to romantically as the "temple of Venus" (*haykal al-zuhara*), or more prosaically as "mountains of the ports" (*jibāl al-burt*). Each of these kuwar, or provinces, was administered by a governor (*wālī*) who resided in the provincial capital.

The Muslim government in Spain was highly organized, becoming more bureaucratic during the established caliphal period. The primary official was the *hājib*, often unhelpfully translated as "chamberlain," who in fact was the prime minister and often the military commander (interestingly, the word derives from a root that means "veil, conceal"; cf. *hijāb*, a veil). Originally, it is true, his function was to guard the entrance to the caliph, but in fact the office was far more important. After the fall of the caliphate, the *tā'ifa* rulers often used the title *hājib* to refer to themselves. Under the Almohads, the title seemed no longer to be known.

The *wazīr*, next in importance, was usually in charge of a particular department of the *dīwān* (chancellery), but the title was also given to those who were privileged to sit in council with the ruler. If one of these was also an administrator or other kind of officer, he held the title *dhū-l-wazartayn* ("master of two offices"), such as we find for the Jew Samuel Ibn Naghrillah in the tā'ifa kingdom of Granada, who was prime minister and also commander-in-chief.

The *khātib* was a secretary; there were increasing numbers of these, and they had to be highly skilled in caligraphy and styles of Arabic correspondence. Some were high-ranking administrators, such as the *kātib al-rasā'il*, in charge of the whole chancellery. Next in importance was the *kitābat al-dhimām*, or "secretariat of protected minorities." Although al-Maqqarī makes it sound as if this office was literally concerned primarily with the "protection" of Christians and Jews, it is clear from what he writes that it was the equivalent of the *khātib al-jihbādhah*, or tax officer, in other Muslim lands, and that its primary purpose was the collection of taxes from the *dhimmis*.

Other minor officials included the *sāhib al-shurtah*, a magistrate of morality and other civil crimes in at least the major cities (several Jews had this title also, including the famous scholar Abraham bar Ḥiyya, known in Latin as Savasorda, and Moses Ibn Ezra, the renowned poet of Granada). Others were the *sāhib al-madīna*, an official responsible for municipal services, the *muḥtabib*, supervisor of markets, and others (including that of the very efficient mail service).

Administrative orders were issued to the provinces through the secretariat, and most importantly taxes were imposed on the provinces, particularly for the support of the army. The expenses of the latter must have been enormous, for the Muslim army was nearly as organized and bureaucratic as a modern one. Salaries and expenses had to be paid also for the military doctors, masons, carpenters, and builders of siege machines, as well as the maintenance of a vast array of weapons. Taxes for these came not only from the Muslims, but also the *dhimmis* (Christians and Jews) of the provinces.

The tā'ifa kingdoms, themselves roughly equivalent to the provinces, administered correspondingly smaller territories, of course (the kingdom of Granada being the largest) but maintained essentially the same type of government.

The Almoravids and the Almohads of the twelfth and early thirteenth centuries essentially appear to have maintained the original territorial or provincial divisions (or at least as many of them as applied to the lands they were able to hold) and utilized the basic government offices already long established in al-Andalus, with some changes in titles. Finally, the *naṣrī* dynasty of the last surviving Muslim kingdom, that of Granada, simply divided its kingdom into *kūwar* (no less than thirty-three of them) that were administered in much the same manner.

An important subject that remains to be studied is what influence, if any, Muslim government administration had upon the Christians in Spain.

NORMAN ROTH

Bibliography

Arié, R. *España musulmana.* Barcelona, 1982. 60–68, 84–88.

Al-Maqqarī. *Analectes sur l'histoire et la littérature des Arabes d'Espagne.* 2 vols., ed. R. P. Dozy et al. Leiden, 1855–61.

Al-Muqadasī. *Description de l'occident musulman au IVe–Xe siècle*, ed. and trans. Charles Pellat. Alger, 1950.

Saavedra, E. *La geografía de España del Edrisí.* Madrid, 1881; reprt. in A. Ubieto Arteta, ed., *Geografía de España.* Valencia, 1974.

Al-Maqqarī. *The History of the Mohammedan Dynasties in Spain.* 2 vols., trans. Pascual de Gayangos. London, 1840–43.

ADOPTIONISM *See* CHURCH; HERESY; THEOLOGY

AESOP *See* ANIMAL FABLES; *YSOPETE YSTORIADO*

AFONSO HENRIQUES, OR AFONSO I

Count of Portugal from 1128, king of the Portuguese from 1140, conqueror of Lisbon in 1147, and forebear of all three Portuguese dynasties, Burgundian, Avis, and Bragança. Afonso's mother was the illegitimate daughter of Emperor Alfonso VI of León and Ximena Moniz of the Bierzo. The emperor had awarded Portugal with Galicia to his heiress Urraca on her marriage to Count Raymond of Burgundy, but when Raymond failed before Lisbon in 1094, he detached Portugal and Coimbra and gave them to Teresa on her marriage to Count Henri, Raymond's cousin. They were installed at Guimarais, where their son Afonso was born, probably in 1109, the year of the emperor's death. Teresa used the title of "queen," despite Urraca's disapproval. Henry was killed while claiming Zamora in May 1112, leaving Afonso and two daughters. Teresa entrusted the defense of Coimbra to the Galician count Fernando Peres of Trava, and endured the attempts of Gelmírez, first archbishop of Santiago, to overthrow the ancient primacy of Braga. Afonso appears in her documents from 1120. He was educated by barons of the Douro, who in 1128 removed Teresa and Trava in the battle of São Mamede, near Guimarais. Urraca's son Alfonso VII had been knighted at Santiago, and Afonso Henriques armed himself knight at Zamora in 1126. He now defied his cousin, with varying success, but did not appear when Alfonso VII assumed the title of emperor in 1135. A clash at Cerneja was averted by a Muslim attack on Coimbra. Afonso assumed the title of king in 1140, probably following the death of the aged Gelmírez. The miraculous victory of Ourique, once considered a proof of divine approval, is undocumented. In 1143 he reached agreement with his cousin at Zamora, and obtained the consent of Rome. Afonso married Mafalda, daughter of the Count of Savoy and Maurtienlle, in 1145 or 1146 and in March 1147 recovered Santarém (lost in 1111) in a surprise attack. St. Bernard's preaching of the Second Crusade brought a large contingent of 164 ships from England, the Low Countries, and southern Germany that participated in the conquest of Lisbon. An English priest, Gilbert of Hastings, became the first bishop of the restored diocese. Sintra and Palmela also capitulated, almost doubling Afonso's territories. His own wealth and authority were greatly increased, rendering secure the continuity of his house. He installed the military orders in castles to defend the line of the Tagus, while the Cistercians undertook the cultivation and settlement of largely abandoned frontier areas, from their headquarters at Alcobaça, founded in 1153. His usual capital was Coimbra, where the monastery of Santa Cruz Alcobaça served as his scriptorium and treasury. Queen Mafalda died there in 1157, having given him three sons and four daughters.

Although Afonso's daughter Urraca married Fernando II of León, now separated from Castile, the frontier beyond the Tagus was disputed. Afonso supported the adventurer Geraldo Sem Pavor who from Evora seized Badajoz, where in 1169 Afonso was wounded and captured, peace was later made at Pontevedra. Afonso remained incapacitated, and shared his military responsibilities with his heir, Sancho, born at Coimbra in 1154. Although Alcácer do Sal was taken in 1158, much of the lower Alentejo was overrun in the great Almohad invasion of 1171. Afonso Henriques obtained full recognition as an independent monarch from Pope Alexander III in 1179. He died at Coimbra on 8 December 1185 and is buried at Santa Cruz, the present monument having been erected by King Manoel. Afonso's qualities of boldness, persistence, and astuteness firmly established the Portuguese monarchy, free from the entanglements that had frustrated his mother.

The documents of Afonso Henriques are excellently edited by R. P. de Azevedo; see the *Documentos medievais portugueses* (Lisbon, 1958).

H. V. LIVERMORE

Bibliography

Livermore, H. V. *A New History of Portugal.* Cambridge, U.K., 1976.

Marques, H. Oliveira. *A History of Portugal.* 2 vols. New York, 1972. I.

Searrão, Joaquim Verissimo. *História de Portugal.* 3rd ed. 2 vols. Lisbon, 1979–80. I.

AFONSO II, KING OF PORTUGAL

Afonso II, Portugal's third monarch, was born in Coimbra in 1185, son and successor of King Sancho I and his Aragónese wife, Queen Dulce. Rarely in good health, Afonso was obese and most probably died of advanced leprosy on 25 March 1223. In 1208 he married Urraca, daughter of Alfonso VIII of Castile. Afonso II took over the kingship of Portugal at the end of March 1211.

Though his reign was relatively short, it was far from uneventful. Afonso II did much to consolidate the various gains of his predecessors, particularly by seeking to augment royal power. In 1211 Afonso II promulgated the first corpus of Portuguese law. This legislation had four chief purposes: (1) to guarantee the rights of royal as well as private property, (2) to regularize the administration of civil justice, (3) to defend the material interests of the crown, and (4) to eliminate abuses by both the clergy and the nobility. Afonso II also developed two institutions to strengthen royal prerogatives: the *inquirições gerais* (general inquiries) to investigate the legitimacy of earlier grants, and the *confirmações* (confirmations). He sent teams of investigators out into the country to check on the legitimacy of claims and grants, and to take testimony. Sometimes the inquiries resulted in an annulment of grants and loss of property or privileges. Predictably, this action to improve public administration and to strengthen royal control caused some turmoil, resented as it was by the higher clergy and nobles, jealous of their prerogatives and immunities. Serious disruptions often limited the scope of the inquiries. However, the investigations did improve public administration and were a model for future kings of Portugal, especially Afonso III and Dinis.

In his will, Sancho I had left part of the royal patrimony to Afonso II's brothers and sisters. Afonso II deemed this a challenge to his sovereignty. He argued that the royal patrimony was indivisible and that he should have jurisdiction over all crown properties. Rather than face the restrictions that their brother, the king, was putting on their goods and persons, Afonso's brothers left the kingdom for voluntary exile. However, the king's sisters, two of whom (Teresa and Mafalda) had been queens in Castile, refused to accept Afonso II's authority over their grants. When Afonso applied force to get his way, the princesses protested to Pope Innocent III, who reacted in August 1212 by placing Portugal under an interdict that lasted for a year and a half. In the meantime, Afonso paid the pope the annual tribute, which had been in arrears since Sancho I's lump-sum payment late in the preceding century. Finally, a papal bull published by Innocent III in 1216 provided the foundations for a settlement to the quarrel. It asserted that Sancho I had intended that his daughters have the revenue from, but not jurisdiction over, the towns he had willed them. But because of a new conflict involving Afonso II—this time with the archbishop of Braga—that resulted in the king's excommunication, the issue of the royal patrimony was not definitively settled until the beginning of Sancho II's reign in 1223.

In the process of investigating the grants that were claimed by the Church in Portugal, Afonso II annulled a number of them. Estêvão Soares da Silva, the archbishop of Braga, convoked an assembly of clergy and condemned the actions of the king, accusing him not only of abuses against the Church, but of living an adulterous life. The king redoubled his efforts against the Church in northern Portugal. When the archbishop excommunicated Afonso and his chief advisers and put Portugal under interdict, the monarch ordered his forces to destroy the properties of the archbishop, including his granaries, vineyards, and orchards. The archbishop then appealed to Rome, and Pope Honorius III intervened. Afonso II, with an heir only twelve years old and faced with a papal threat of deposition, began negotiations with the archbishop of Braga. But before they were concluded, the king died, an excommunicate.

When Afonso II assumed power in 1211, Portugal's independence was fairly well established, although there still were occasional threats from neighboring Christian kingdoms. In 1212 Alfonso IX of León used the clash between the Portuguese king and his brothers and sisters as an excuse to invade northern Portugal. With help from some Portuguese nobles, including one of Afonso II's brothers, the Leonese defeated the supporters of Afonso II at the Battle of Valdevez. Fortunately for the Portuguese, the threat of hostilities with Alfonso VIII of Castile forced the Leonese king to withdraw from Portugal and Afonso II was able to recover the occupied territory.

There was relatively little fighting against the Muslims on Portugal's borders during the reign of Afonso II. The Portuguese monarch did, however, send troops to aid his father-in-law, Alfonso VIII of Castile, in the famous Battle of Las Navas de Tolosa in 1212, in which the Christians decisively defeated the Almohad forces. Las Navas de Tolosa was the gateway to Andalucía, and the Almohads never recovered from this defeat. The Portuguese distinguished themselves by their bravery in this encounter, the outcome of which is considered by many to be the greatest Christian victory of the Reconquest.

Five years later, when Afonso II was at Coimbra, the bishop of Lisbon convinced knights from the Fifth Crusade to aid the Portuguese in an attempt to regain the important stronghold of Alcácer do Sal. The crusaders, together with the Templars, Hospitalers, and knights of Santiago, captured Alcácer after a two-month siege. The victory opened up the Sado River basin to Portuguese settlement and commerce.

FRANCIS A. DUTRA

Bibliography

Livermore, H. V. *A History of Portugal*. Cambridge, U.K., 1947.

Serrão, J. V. *História de Portugal*. Lisbon, vol. 1. 1977.

AFONSO III, KING OF PORTUGAL

The second son of Afonso II and Uracca of Castile, Afonso III was born in Coimbra on 5 May 1210. The fifth king of Portugal, he succeeded his brother Sancho II and reigned from early in 1248 to his death on 16 February 1279.

Before becoming king, Afonso lived first in Denmark and then in France, where in 1238 or 1239 he married the wealthy widow Matilda, heiress of the Count of Boulogne. Afonso was influential at the court of his maternal aunt, Queen Blanche, widow of Louis VIII and mother of Louis IX. While in France he became involved in Portuguese internal affairs, where his older brother was under attack by clergy and nobles. Pope Innocent IV, in a bull of 24 July 1245, effectively deposed Sancho II by reducing him to king in name only and by turning over the government to his younger brother, Afonso, Count of Boulogne. Innocent IV instructed the Portuguese to receive and obey Afonso as soon as he arrived in Portugal and to ignore the orders of Sancho II. After the pope issued his bull, a delegation of Portuguese—a number of whom had testified against Sancho II at the Council of Lyons—visited Paris, where they swore obedience to Afonso. They also exacted a series of promises from the future monarch to respect the Church, to honor the privileges and customs of Portugal, and to promote justice.

Arriving in Portugal in early 1246, Afonso took part in the civil war against supporters of the king. After Sancho II died in Toledo in January 1248, Afonso III was crowned king. The new monarch renewed the policies of Portugal's earlier monarchs by asserting authority wherever possible and by taking a hard line with the privileged classes when their immunities and prerogatives interfered with the royal treasury or administration. Early in his reign, Afonso III took up the task of driving the Muslims from their isolated strongholds in southwestern Portugal. The time was propitious for such a move. Fernando III of Castile, with the aid of the Portuguese military orders and some Portuguese nobles, had been campaigning successfully against the Muslim kingdoms in Andalucía. Seville would fall to Christian forces in November 1248. Afonso II personally led the drive to oust the Muslims from the Algarve. In March 1249 he captured Faro. Soon, Albufeira and Silves, along with a number of lesser towns and fortresses, fell to the Portuguese. This completed the ouster of Muslim military forces from what was to be the limits of modern Portugal. In 1251 Afonso II continued his campaign—this time to the east of the Guadiana River in territory that the Castilians regarded as their preserve. Castile, in the meantime, claimed parts of the Algarve. Armed conflict soon broke out between Portugal and Castile over these disputed territories.

In 1252 Alfonso X "el Sabio" (the Wise) ascended the Castilian throne. A year later, a truce was arranged between the two kings. It was resolved that Afonso III would marry Beatriz of Castile, the illegitimate daughter of Alfonso X. The marriage took place in 1253. In addition, it was decided that the administration of the newly conquered kingdom of the Algarve and the lands east of the Guadiana would be Portugal's but the usufruct of these territories would remain in the hands of Alfonso X until the firstborn son of the marriage between Afonso III and Beatriz reached the age of seven.

Unfortunately, there were a number of difficulties in implementing this marriage arrangement. Beatriz was very young and was related to Afonso III within the fourth degree of consanguinity. But most importantly, Afonso III was already married to Matilda, Countess of Boulogne, who was living in France. Soon Matilda was complaining to the pope about her husband's bigamous marriage. Although Pope Alexander IV placed under interdict those parts of Portugal where the king was residing, he was unable to persuade Afonso III to leave his young bride.

Matilda's death in 1258 helped resolve some of the Portuguese monarch's difficulties. But papal opposition to the marriage continued, as did the interdict. The bishops and cathedral chapters of Portugal came to the king's defense. In 1260—by which time Beatriz had already borne two children to Afonso—they pleaded with Pope Urban IV to lift the interdict and legitimize the children. They argued that the abandonment of Beatriz by Afonso would lead to war with Castile, and they claimed that ecclesiastical penalties were causing spiritual harm and scandal in Portugal. Finally, in 1263, after a visit to Rome by a delegation of Portuguese bishops, and after much lobbying by European leaders such as Louis IX of France and the Duke of Anjou, the request for the necessary dispensations and legitimizations was granted.

The birth in 1261 of Dinis, Afonso III's third child by Beatriz (the first was a girl, the second a boy who died in infancy), provided the necessary ingredient for the resolution of the controversy between Castile and Portugal. By the Treaty of Badajoz in 1267 Alfonso X of Castile renounced his rights to the kingdom of the Algarve, while Afonso III gave up Portuguese claims to the territories between the Guadiana and Guadalquivir Rivers. Portugal, however, would have authority over the territory to the west of the mouth of the Guadiana and its confluence with the Caia River.

In addition to the reconquest of the Algarve and the resolution of Portugal's boundaries with Castile, several other major accomplishments marked Afonso III's reign. Afonso promoted greater participation by towns and their officials in Portuguese national life. At Leiria in 1254, for the first time in the nation's history, representatives of the cities participated in the *cortes* (parliament) along with the nobility and the higher clergy. Laws were also enacted to protect commoners from abuse at the hands of the privileged classes. Furthermore, Afonso III restructured the country's monetary system. Charters issued during his reign show that a moneyed economy was replacing barter. Fixed monetary taxes replaced the custom of paying in kind. At the *cortes* of Coimbra in 1261, Afonso III agreed to devalue the currency only once during a reign instead of every seven years, as was becoming the practice. The monarch favored Lisbon over Coimbra as the kingdom's chief commercial and administrative center, and he increased the royal treasury by promoting the country's economy.

Afonso III continued his predecessors' policy of strengthening royal prerogatives. This was accomplished chiefly through the use of the *inquiricões gerais* (general inquiries) and *confirmacões* (confirmations). In 1258, in response to complaints from royal officials as well as commoners, the crown sent investigative teams into the *comarcas* (districts) of Entre Douro e Minho, Trás-os-Montes, and Beira Alta to examine titles to lands claimed by nobility and clergy. Sworn testimony was taken to determine if the rights of the crown were being respected. Afonso III was anxious to curb the power of the old nobility and the higher clergy, especially those in the comarca of Entre Douro e Minho, the oldest and most populous region of Portugal. These investigations revealed a wide range of violations, including the usurpation of the royal patrimony, evasion of taxes, and abuses of commoners by the privileged estates, both secular and clerical. Laws were promulgated to deal with these infractions and they soon sparked fresh opposition from clergy and nobility.

In 1267 a number of Portuguese prelates traveled to Rome and presented Pope Clement IV with an extensive list of grievances. They accused Afonso III of condoning, even encouraging, violence in civil administration, of using unfair practices in his business dealings, and of infringing on ecclesiastical liberties. The Portuguese monarch answered these charges with testimonials from the towns of the kingdom that defended his actions and praised his administration. In addition, in 1273, during the meeting of the cortes at Santarém, Afonso III established a commission to investigate his acts and those of his officials. But the papacy was not impressed by the results of this investigation, which maintained that there had been little wrongdoing. In 1275 Pope Gregory X ordered that the king correct abuses and promise not to repeat them under pain of a series of penalties. These penalties would be invoked in stages, beginning in 1277, and would progress from local interdict, to excommunication, to a general interdict for the kingdom, to freeing the Portuguese from obedience to their king. And, indeed, by the end of 1277, Afonso III had been excommunicated and the kingdom placed under interdict. Soon, minor revolts broke out against the king in which Afonso III's son and successor, Dinis, took part. In January 1279, a month before his death, Afonso III made his peace with the Church and with his son.

Francis A. Dutra

Bibliography

Livermore, H. V. *A History of Portugal.* Cambridge, U.K., 1977.

Serrão, J. V. *História de Portugal.* Lisbon, vol. 1 1977.

Mattoso, J. (ed.) *História de Portugal*, Lisbon, vol. 2 1993.

AFONSO IV, KING OF PORTUGAL

The seventh king of Portugal, Afonso IV, was the only son of King Dinis and his Aragónese queen, Isabel (later St. Isabel of Aragón). Afonso was born in Lisbon on 8 February 1291 and died in the same city on 28

May 1357. In 1309 he married Beatriz of Castile; he reigned from 1325 to 1357.

An austere ruler, Afonso IV continued his father's policies of augmenting the crown's patrimony, strengthening royal authority, and promoting justice. His reign, however, was marked by numerous internal revolts, conflicts with Castile, and dislocations in the wake of the Black Death.

During the early part of his reign, Afonso IV was preoccupied with the struggle against his illegitimate half-brother, Afonso Sanches. After the latter's death in 1329, Portugal became embroiled in a conflict with Castile over Afonso IV's daughter Maria, wife of Alfonso XI of Castile (reigned 1312–1350). After Alfonso XI abandoned her, Portugal gave its support to Infante Juan Manuel, Alfonso XI's cousin and a perpetual thorn in the Castilian monarch's side, and to others who contested Alfonso XI's power. In fact, Afonso IV married off his son and heir, Pedro, to Constanza, daughter of Infante Juan Manuel. Alfonso XI then refused to allow Constanza to leave Castile; Portugal, in alliance with Aragón, invaded Castile in 1336.

These disputes among the Christian kingdoms gave the Muslims the opportunity to recover some of the territory they had earlier lost to the Christians. The Marīnids were in the ascendancy in North Africa and allied with the Muslims in Granada. Gibraltar was seized in 1333. In 1340 the Marīnids invaded the Iberian Peninsula after destroying an Aragónese and Castilian fleet in the Strait of Gibraltar. Castile and Portugal temporarily put their differences aside and signed a peace treaty at Seville in July 1340. A Portuguese, Genoese, and Castilian armada was organized near the Strait of Gibraltar, but storms scattered it. Portuguese forces, led by Afonso IV and accompanied by the archbishop of Braga, the bishop of Évora, and knights from the Portuguese military orders, however, played an important role in the victory at Salado (30 October 1340), a major event in the Christian reconquest of the Iberian Peninsula. In the 1340s Afonso IV sponsored voyages to the Canary Islands.

The Black Death struck Portugal late in September 1348 and continued its devastation for the remainder of the year. The pestilence claimed at least one-third of Portugal's population. Some villages and small towns completely disappeared, while others became greatly depopulated. There was an exodus to the cities by many of the survivors, which further aggravated the problem of rural depopulation. Because the epidemic often wiped out entire families, some shifts occurred within the social strata as distant relatives and the poor came into vast sums of money or substantial properties. The Church also benefited greatly from the many deathbed grants of estates and goods. A shortage of labor led to higher wages and prices. Famine and food shortages became regular occurrences in many parts of the kingdom as the Black Death was followed by new plagues and epidemics. There were frequent devaluations. Abandoned agricultural lands were turned into vineyards, olive groves, pasturage, or hunting preserves. Social instability and famine led to discontent, unrest, and an increasing number of riots. Afonso IV and his successors used iron-handed methods to try to control these upheavals. They fixed wages, cracked down on vagrancy, and bound workers to their traditional occupations. The *cortes* (parliament) was convened in 1352 and 1361 in hopes of solving some of the problems.

Meanwhile, Prince Pedro's wife, Constanza, who had arrived in Portugal in 1340, gave birth to three children, including Fernando, the future king of Portugal. Pedro, however, had fallen in love with Inés de Castro, his wife's lady-in-waiting and a member of a powerful Galician family. Although Afonso IV banished Inés from his kingdom, she returned to Portugal after Constanza's death in 1345 and gave birth to four illegitimate children by Pedro. Afonso IV believed that his son Pedro was setting a bad example, neglecting his royal duties and compromising Portugal's security by falling under the influence of Galician and Castilian nobles, headed by Inés's brothers. In 1355, apparently at Afonso IV's orders, Inés was murdered. Prince Pedro, aided by Castilian forces led by the brothers of Inés de Castro, mounted a full-scale revolt against his father, but in 1356 peace returned.

FRANCIS A. DUTRA

Bibliography

Livermore, H. V. *A History of Portugal*. Cambridge, U.K., 1977.

Serrão, J. V. *História de Portugal*, Lisbon, vol. 1. 1977.

AFONSO V

Twelfth king of Portugal and third of the house of Avis, 1438–1481, sometimes called "the African" because of his crusading expeditions in the Maghrib. He was born at Sintra on 15 January 1432, the eldest son of King Duarte and Queen Leonor, and acceded at the age of six. His father's will appointed his mother regent, but she was opposed as a woman and a foreigner (a Castilian, though called "of Aragón"), and lacking consent of the *cortes* (parliament). His father's younger brother Dom Pedro was backed by the towns, and after an unsuccessful dual regency, Leonor fled to Castile, apparently to her relatives. Pedro assumed the sole regency, and fended off threats of Castilian intervention, but formed an alliance with the warlord Álvaro de Luna. Pedro arranged the marriage of Afonso V to his daughter Isabel, and appointed his son, also Pedro, constable. Afonso came of age at fourteen, and prolonged Pedro's authority. Pedro's costly intervention in Castile lost him support, and the intrigues of the Duke of Bragança, who claimed that the constableship was hereditary in his family, forced Pedro to resign. He was provoked into rebellion and killed at Alfarrobeira. Afonso V refused to put away Isabel, but could do little to curb the Braganças. In 1455 his heir Prince João was born, Queen Isabel died, and there was a reconciliation. The Portuguese voyages of exploration to West Africa under Prince Henrique had been actively pursued under Pedro, but Afonso V responded to the loss of Constantinople and the appeals of Pope Calixtus III by organizing a large crusading expedition that took al-Qaṣr aṣ' aghir (Alcácer Seguer) on 23 October 1458. It was hoped it would relieve the isolation of Ceuta, but the new conquest suffered several sieges, and then Afonso returned to Africa in 1464; he was saved from capture only by the sacrifice of Duarte de Meneses.

These costly military campaigns delayed the voyages of discovery, which had reached Serra Leoa (Sierra Leone), when Prince Henrique died in November 1460. Afonso entrusted the voyages to his younger brother Fernando, but until 1468 the main activity was in trading, with little further exploration. In 1469 Afonso awarded a monopoly of trade to Diogo Gomes, a Lisbon merchant, with the obligation to pursue the discoveries, and after the death of Fernando in 1470, the enterprise passed under the control of Prince João. By 1474, the Cape Verde Islands, the Equatorial isles and the African coast almost as far as the mouth of the Congo were made known.

Afonso was a liberal patron moved by religious idealism and somewhat outmoded notions of chivalry. His African illusions were crowned in 1471 when he led a vast fleet to take Arçila, and Tangier was abandoned without a fight. These conquests had to be supplied by sea, at considerable expense, but contributed something to the security of the seaways. Madeira, with about one thousand settlers, provided cereals and initial sugar production. The Azores, settled with some contribution from Flanders (where Afonso's aunt had married Philip the Good), produced cereals and dyestuffs. Afonso's aristocracy, drawn mainly from families that had supported his grandfather João I, were his pensioners, drawing *moradias* at court according to rank. He resided at Lisbon, Sintra, Santarém, and Évora. He convened cortes on twenty occasions, usually at one of these places, never in the north or south of Évora. This centralizing system strengthened the class of *letrados* emerging from the single university at Lisbon.

The Cape Verde Islands were claimed, but not yet settled. Guinea gold was obtained from Gambia from about 1458, but the supply attained large proportions with the foundation of the factory at Mina in 1481.

Afonso's personal inclination was to emulate his great-grandfather João I, whose conquest of Ceuta he commissioned Azurara to narrate. His sister Leonor married Emperor Frederick III and was the mother of Maximilian. His brother-in-law Pedro claimed to be king of Aragón (1464–1466). In 1455 his youngest sister Joana became the wife of Enrique IV of Castile, she gave birth to a princess, also Joana, whose succession was contested upon the death of Enrique in 1474, by Fernando of Aragón on behalf of his wife Isabel, Henry's sister. Supporters of Joana appealed to Afonso V, who accepted the challenge, and prepared to marry his niece and lead her partisans. He occupied the towns of Zamora and Toro, claiming the throne of Castile. He informed Louis XI, his ally, also hostile to the Aragónese, and entrusted Portugal to his son, João II. Fernando took Zamora, and after the battle of Toro (2 March 1476), Afonso decided to go to France to appeal to Louis, who received him at Tours and put him off with words. Afonso visited Paris and mainly sought help in Lorraine. He then decided to abdicate and go to Palestine, but changed his mind and returned to Portugal just as his son had begun to govern. He resumed his reign, but left João to rule. Since Fernando and Isabel were now entrenched, João concluded the Treaty of Alcáçovas (4 September 1479), by which Joana's claim was canceled, and Afonso retired to Sintra, where he died on 15 August 1481.

H. V. LIVERMORE

Bibliography

Livermore, H. V. *A New History of Portugal.* Cambridge, U.K., 1976.

Marques, H. Oliveira. *A History of Portugal.* 2 vols. New York, 1972. I.

Searrão, Joaquim Verissimo. *História de Portugal.* 3rd ed. 2 vols. Lisbon, 1979–80. I.

AFONSO, COUNT OF BARCELOS AND DUKE OF BRAGANÇA

Illegitimate son of Dom João, master of Avis, who became king of Portugal (1385) as João I, and Inês Pires, was probably born in the castle of Veiros in Alentejo, southern Portugal (ca. 1380). He was brought up in Leiria and legitimized by his father on 20 October 1391. Dom Afonso fought alongside João I in the eighteen-year-old war against Castile. In the siege of Túy in Galicia, he was knighted by the king on 25 July 1398, after the town had surrendered. On 8 November 1401, he married Doña Beatriz Pereira de Alvim (1378–1412), the daughter of Nun' Alvares Pereira, the wealthiest nobleman in the realm, and Doña Leonor de Alvim. He received by his marriage large donations in land and property, which made up the foundation of the House of Bragança in 1442. He was the eighth Count of Barcelos and the first Duke of Bragança.

João I and the queen, Philippa of Lancaster, held him in high esteem. He visited the court frequently and was a member of the Privy Council, taking part in all affairs of state even when Duarte I succeeded his father João I to the throne. Afonso had great ambitions for his family, and though he was extremely rich and enjoyed great prestige at court, he craved political power. He believed his opportunity had come when Duarte died, leaving a six-year-old son, Afonso. But Duarte's brother, Pedro, was elected regent (1440–1446) by the *cortes* (parliament) held in Lisbon (1439), one year after the young Afonso V had been crowned. The Count of Barcelos in 1443 headed the aristocratic faction that wanted to strenghten personal privilege, and led a campaign against Pedro that led to his death at the battle of Alfarrobeira (1449). Afonso died in 1461.

LUIS REBELO

Bibliography

Montalvão Machado, J. T. *Dom Afonso, Primeiro Duque de Bragança, Sua Vida e Obra*. Lisbon, 1964.

AGRICULTURE

Introduction

Both Christians and Muslims practiced styles of agriculture that were distinctively Mediterranean in style and were equally based in the classical "Mediterranean triad" of wheat, olives, and grapes. On this foundation, the Arabs superimposed, particularly in the great periurban *huertas* of southern and eastern Spain, a roster of irrigated crops characteristic of "Indian agriculture" (*filāha hindiyya*) which had the effect of broadening the nutritional base of the urban Islamic population. As with all aspects of material culture in medieval Spain it is important to track continuity or change over the key cultural transitions: that of late Roman times to the early middle ages, both Christian and Islamic, and that of the eleventh through thirteenth centuries, from Islamic to Christian society.

Agriculture in medieval Iberia was strongly conditioned by its Mediterranean climate (except for the more "continental" peninsular northwest) and by a high degree of continuity with Roman agriculture. Archeological evidence from Islamic sites in Castellón reveals virtually no change in the pattern of cultivars from Roman through Islamic times. However, this evidence is from rural dry farming and microscale irrigated *huertas* (gardens) that do not reflect the more cosmopolitan "Indian"-style agriculture of the irrigated huertas of the major cities of al-Andalus.

Thus, Butzer has found that to the Roman repertory of spring wheat, millet, a dozen species of orchard trees, and a great variety of fodder and vegetable crops, the Arabs (in Castellón) added only sorghum, four fruit trees, and some crops that were important commercially but which had no influence on the practice of the majority of the peasantry.

The case for the Arabic "green revolution" is made by Watson, who stresses the other side of medieval agriculture: that of the great urban huertas where crops introduced from the east made an entrance, these were rice, sugarcane, cotton, a number of citrus varieties not cultivated by the Romans, the banana, watermelon, a number of important new vegetables (spinach, artichoke, and eggplant), and hard wheat. The heart of Watson's argument lies in his conception of how and when these crops were deployed, namely in the process of economic regionalization that resulted from the breakup of the caliphate into more economically coherent entities, reflected in the political organization of the "party kingdoms." The most precise cultural marker, in any case, is less the roster of crops grown by different cultural groups than the balance struck among cereal farming, irrigation, arboriculture, and stock herding.

Agriculture in Al-Andalus

The most salient aspect of Islamic irrigation in Spain was its association with the distinctive form of rural social organization, namely the complexes of castles and hamlets (*alquerías*), that had been established throughout many rural districts, especially Valencia, Murcia, Almería, and Málaga. Such systems were of Islamic foundation and (following Butzer's typology) were either microsystems (based on tanks fed from wells or small springs) or mesosystems (from large springs or small streams). The latter used a variety of water conduction techniques, including filtration galleries or surface canals. Both micro- and mesoscale irrigation were associated with terracing, an example of which is the terraced agriculture of Banyalbufar, Mallorca, a replication of the Arabian *ma'jil* regime whose introduction from Yemen in the tenth century is documented. The mesosystems of southeastern Spain and Granada are institutionally similar to oasis-style irrigation systems of southern Arabia and the Sahara. The periurban macrosystems of the huertas of Murcia and Valencia are most likely Islamic expansions of preexisting Roman canal systems, but their existence in Islamic times has not been precisely documented.

The agricultural heartland of al-Andalus, that is the *campiña* (open country) of Córdoba and the the Guadalquivir Valley generally, had in the past constituted the wheat-producing area of Roman Baetica, one of the three breadbaskets (along with Sicily and Tunisia) of Rome. Although the data is inferential at best, we can presume that the Muslims grew less wheat than the Roman occupants of the same area had. Even though the lower Guadalquivir was in general not irrigated in Islamic times, much of the unirrigated land was put into tree crops, notably olives. Nevertheless, the Córdoban campiña and various places with the name *Fahs* (plain), such as Fahs al-Ballut to the north of Córdoba and Fahs Qāmara, near Colmenar, were famous for their wheat. The Arabs introduced hard wheat (*Triticum durum*) into Europe: in al-Andalus it was called *dārmaq* (in Castilian, *adárgama*). Millet, which had been the staple of the Roman working classes, was replaced by sorghum (Arabic *dhura*; *aldora* in medieval Castilian) which the Berbers brought from the Sudan. Sorghum played the same social and dietary role as was played in Christian Spain (and Europe generally) by rye; the Muslims also cultivated rye, which they called by its Romance name, *shantiyya*. The Muslim reshuffling of the cards of cereal culture was no doubt climatically motivated: hard wheat is much more resistant to heat and drought than were the soft varieties it replaced, and sorghum was well suited to the Mediterranean climatic regime of spring rains, followed by a hot, dry summer.

Cereals and irrigated field crops were complemented by vineyards and orchards. The Quranic prohibition of wine drinking did little to stifle the growing of grapes, although some *repartimientos* (land grants) indicate that vineyards were not as widespread in areas of southern Spain, such as Seville, which were later known for their wines. The Christian and Jewish minorities, of course, constituted a continuing market for wine, and Muslims not only used grapes and raisins in their cuisine, but many drank wine as well. Malagan grapes were greatly admired, as was the *qanbanī* variety from the Córdoban campiña.

Roman Spain had been an exporter of olive oil, so the Muslims were by no means innovators in this area. But Andalusi cuisine was almost wholly dependent on olive oil, to the exclusion of animal fats, and the universality of the use of olive oil and olives no doubt explains why they are known by Arabisms—*aceite*, *aceituna*, from *al-zait* and *al-zaituna*—while the tree has a Romance name, *olivo*. The Aljarafe region to the west of Seville was so densely planted in olive and fig trees that it could be traversed in the shade, and repartimientos suggest that there were two and a half million olive trees in the present province of Seville at the time of the conquest from the Muslims and that it produced five million kilos of olives annually.

Figs were noteworthy for the great number of varieties grown in al-Andalus, including the *rayyī* or Málaga fig the *doñeqal*, the *qūtiya* (Gothic), and so forth. The repartimiento of Málaga records equal numbers of fig and pomegranate trees, then a second line grouping of plum, apple, quince, lemon, and apricot, and in fewer numbers, lime, orange, peach, and pear. Almonds were also widely grown, due to the universal use of their flour as a thickener in Andalusi cooking. (Andalusi cookbooks, incidentally, are a valuable source of information about what foodstuffs were available in markets; more recipes have survived from al-Andalus than from any other medieval society.)

We know few specifics of stock raising in al-Andalus. Berber mountaineers practiced a mainly pastoral economy, along with arboriculture, and Berbers introduced the merino sheep from Morocco sometime before the fourteenth century.

Early Christian Agriculture

Tenth-century colonization in the Christian kingdoms produced a network of *aldeas*, which became the characteristic unit of peasant settlement. These were organized in two roughly concentric circles, in common with the morphology of villages all over western Europe. The inner circle was comprised of houses and closed parcels (*solares*) for private domestic agricultural exploitation. Surrounding this nucleus was an outer circle of fields, forest, or pasture. With the passage of time, the primitive *aldeas* became compacted, due to economic or demographic pressure, with the houses more tightly packed together and the *huertas* between houses in many cases squeezed out. Surrounding cereal fields and vineyards were also pressed together and something resembling the western European "open field" system emerged, with communal two-course, biennial rotations (*año y vez*) alternating plantings of winter wheat with fallowness. In areas where local stock raising was particularly strong, a further adaptation was made in the form of *cultivo al tercio*, which freed more space for fallow grazing.

Three-course rotations, with a spring sowing, could not be introduced under conditions of semiaridity on light soils where the Roman plow was used. The heavy plow, said to have been introduced by the Suevi, was known only in Galicia. Cereal yields were accordingly very low, three to one and four to one for wheat and barley, respectively, which compares unfavorably with typical northern European yields of five to one and nine to one. Oats were planted increasingly in Catalonia from the first half of the eleventh century. Both the military and agricultural use of horses were directly linked to the incidence of oat cultivation.

Cereal cultivation was complemented by vineyards, arboriculture, and herding. The diffusion of the grape was linked to monasticism and demand for wine resulted in the progressive conversion of wasteland and cereal land into vineyards until the end of the twelfth century. Grapevines became ubiquitous and, in Catalonia, terraced vineyards invaded hill country at the expense of rough pasture. Fruit trees provided an important component of a diet based on inadequate cereal stores. The Basques were associated with the apple tree; as they migrated southward the apple went with them. Figs, pears, cherries, peaches, and plums were also widely grown and, where possible, irrigated. The olive was not widely grown in Christian Spain before the tenth century and only in climatically appropriate zones, such as Catalonia, thereafter.

Irrigation was also widely developed in the Christian kingdoms. Wherever water was diverted for the milling of grain—which was practically everywhere—the diversion channels could be pressed into service for irrigating small gardens. In the early phases of settlement of sparsely populated plains such as the Duero Valley or the Plain of Vic, water as well as land was available for appropriation (*presura*). In the great age of monastic expansion (the ninth through eleventh centuries), monasteries sought riparian land both for milling and for irrigating domestic gardens. In general, vegetables grown on irrigated parcels were not commercialized in the northern kingdoms to the extent they were in al-Andalus, although by the early eleventh century, Barcelona was surrounded by *hortos subreqaneos* that produced vegetables and fruits for the urban market.

As more land was cleared for grain fields, vineyards, or orchards, less was available for the grazing of local herds. Seignorial herds tended to become transhumant while villagers were increasingly excluded from this sector. Monasteries in particular owned large herds—including the Cistercians, who ate no meat. Full transhumance did not emerge until the twelfth century when Catalan monasteries established summer pastures in Cerdaña and when, after the capture of Toledo in 1085, the Tajo Valley was opened to northern herds.

The Later Middle Ages

The process by which a feudalized agricultural system replaced the existing Islamic regimes as the conquest of al-Andalus proceeded has been imperfectly understood until recently. In part this was because the social organization of rural al-Andalus had been so neglected by historians. Now that such organization has been conceptualized, it is possible to make some generalizations concerning the agricultural transition, particularly in the thirteenth century. First, Christian settlement and political control radically altered the alquería networks or destroyed them completely. In Islamic society, alquerías were minimally subdivided and were farmed by collectivities of individuals—extended families or their successors. Christians did not understand this kind of property regime. When *mudéjars* (Muslims living under Christian rule) remained in their alquerías there was pressure to establish metes and bounds and to reduce collective holds into individual ones. When Muslims were replaced by Christian settlers, a completely different tenure system was introduced. Peasant settlers were given an allotment, generally no more than nine hectares, which generally included a mixture of cereal land, huerta, and vineyard parcels. Given the extremely high mobility of frontier society and Christian inheritance rules, it took only a few decades to completely transform the agricultural landscape, giving rise to a regime characterized by dispersion of parcels. Cereal cultivation and vineyards were privileged. Feudal rents were typically collected in kind, in grain and in vine. The products of small *huertas* fell outside this fiscal system and perforce led to an expansion of grain production. That did not mean, however, that irrigation systems fell into desuetude. In general, in places like Valencia, Murcia, and Andalucía, the Muslim systems were kept going, care being taken to learn the distribution and allocation arrangements directly from Muslim irrigators. It was probably as a result of Christian settlement that the huerta macrosystems were formed by a process of the linking up of previously unconnected small alquería channels. This process is documented, for example, in the post-Conquest Ribera del Júcar. Prior to the Conquest *alquerías* at some distance from the river had been irrigated by springs and small streams. As the river was tapped (Acequia Real del Júcar of the late thirteenth century) and canals dug and extended, the new unified system encompassed the dispersed elements of older alquería systems. A similar process took place in the plain of Castellón, where, prior to the Conquest, only Borriana and a number of separate *alquerías* had been irrigated; it may also have taken place in Valencia and Murcia, at least insofar as the extension of those *huertas* was concerned.

It is interesting to note that, with irrigation, the Christian settlers did not much alter their habitual ways of farming. It became possible, in Valencia for example, to introduce a three-course rotation, with a course of spring crops (oats, peas, beans, and barley). With irrigation it was possible to increase yields of cereals so as to enhance consumption, as well as produce the surplus needed to pay feudal dues. (Once such a surplus was generated, commercialization of the crops in question was inevitably stimulated.) Grapevines were also irrigated in medieval Valencia for the same reasons.

What specific elements of Muslim agriculture did the Christians adopt? In general terms, both the repertory of cultivation techniques and the roster of crops were broadened. Examples of the former are the use in southern Spain of the Berber plow with moldboard (a variant of the standard Roman plow), and the diffusion of most elements of modern harnessing (except for the padded horse collar) from Tripolitania into Europe through Spain and Italy. An example of the latter is the rise of rice as a staple grain, which was only possible in climatically appropriate areas with extensive irrigation.

THOMAS F. GLICK

Bibliography

El agua en zonas áridas: Arqueología e historia. 3 vols. Almería, 1989.

Al-Mudayna. *Historia de los regadíos en España*. Madrid, 1991.

Baroeló, M., et al. *Les aigües cercades (Els qanats) de l'illa de Mallorca*. Palma, 1986.

Bulliet, R. W. *The Camel and the Wheel*. Cambridge, Mass., 1975.

Butzer, H., et al. "Irrigation Agrosystems in Eastern Spain: Roman or Islamic Origins?" *Annals of the Association of American Geographers* 75 (1985), 479–509.

García de Cortázar, J. A. (ed.) *Organización social del espacio en la España medieval*. Barcelona, 1985.

García Fernández, J. "Campos abiertos y campos cerados en Castilla La Vieja," in *Homenaje a Amando Melón y Ruiz de Gordejuela*. Zaragoza, 1966. 117–31.

Glick, T. F. *Irrigation and Society in Medieval Valencia*. Cambridge, Mass., 1970.

———. *Islamic and Christian Spain in the Early Middle Ages*. Princeton, N.J., 1979.

Watson, A. M. *Agricultural Innovation in the Early Islamic World*. New York, 1983.

ALANS *See* GERMANIC INVASIONS

ALARCOS, BATTLE OF

The battle of Alarcos (19 July 1195) was a decisive victory for the Almohad caliph Yaʿqūb al-Manṣūr over the Castilian king Alfonso VIII. Al-Manṣūr had mounted expeditions against Portugal in 1190 in retaliation for Portuguese expansion in the Algarve and Castilian expansion into al-Andalus. Castile then sought treaties with Al-Manṣūr, but after they expired the Castilians began campaigning around Seville. In retaliation, Al-Manṣūr crossed into Spain at Tarifa in June 1195 and took his army on the road to Toledo, camping in the lands around Calatrava.

Prior to the battle of Alarcos, Alfonso VIII had unfriendly relations with the neighboring kingdom of León and its king, his cousin Alfonso IX; in 1194, the Treaty of Tordehumos created an alliance between the two kingdoms. But when Alfonso VIII heard of Al-Manṣūr's advance, he decided not to wait for reinforcements from León. Instead, he rushed from Toledo to the fortress of Alarcos, an unfinished fortification in the vicinity of Calatrava, located to the west of the modern Ciudad Real.

Alfonso engaged the Almohad army prematurely, and the king and a portion of the army were forced to flee to Toledo. Diego López de Haro covered the king's retreat and surrendered the castle of Alarcos to Al-Manṣūr. The Almohads also captured the castle of Calatrava and other fortresses along the road to Toledo. After the battle, though, Al-Manṣūr returned to Seville and did not continue his advance toward Toledo. Contingents of the Almohad army raided around Toledo and its hinterlands; this stopped when Alfonso entered into a five-year treaty with Al-Manṣūr in 1197.

Battle losses are hard to estimate. Muslim sources provide figures ranging from 30,000 to 300,000 Christian dead versus 500 to 20,000 Muslim dead. The Order of Santiago lost nineteen friars, and numerous associates. The Order of Calatrava lost its home fortress. The bishops of Ávila, Segovia, and Sigüenza were killed.

The blame for the defeat has been assigned to various people: to Pedro Fernández de Castro for betraying Alfonso VIII by turning over his contingent to Al-Manṣūr; to Arabs within the Christian population; and even to divine retribution for a fictional affair between Alfonso VIII and a Jewish woman in Toledo. But it seems reasonable to assign the blame for the debacle to Alfonso VIII himself. Alfonso apparently seriously underestimated the number of troops he needed, as well as Al-Manṣūr's abilities, and he engaged Al-Manṣūr before the Leonese reinforcements arrived.

The battle of Alarcos was the last great Almohad victory in Spain, and marks the height of Almohad power in the Iberian Peninsula. Alarcos weakened Castile, and its relations with other Iberian kingdoms were damaged when León and Navarre temporarily allied with the Almohads. Al-Manṣūr, however, did not follow up on his opportunity to pursue Alfonso VIII and to recapture territory. Castile recovered, and Alfonso VIII reversed the defeat of Alarcos at the battle of Las Navas de Tolosa seventeen years later.

THERESA M. VANN

Bibliography

Huici Miranda, A. *Las grandes batallas de la reconquista durante las invasiones africanas*. Madrid, 1956.

Martinez Val, J. M. "La batalla de Alarcos." *Cuadernos de Estudios Manchegos* 12 (1962), 89–128.

ALBALAT, PERE DE

Albalat died July 1251. Bishop of Lérida 1236–1238, archbishop of Tarragona 1238–1251. A churchman notable for his dedication to the implementation in the Crown of Aragón of the reform program of the Fourth Lateran Council (1215), Albalat summoned eight provincial assemblies during his fourteen years as archbishop and caused diocesan synods to be held by his suffragans, at which attention was given to legislation concerning clerical concubinage and pluralism, the sacraments (especially matrimony), and the enforcement of monastic discipline. He collaborated with Ramón de Penyafort and was closely attached to the Cistercian house of Poblet. During his pontificate Cistercian and Dominican influences predominated in the Aragónese hierarchy (between 1243 and 1248 five mendicant bishops were appointed); his first provincial council ordered the solemn celebration of the feast days of St. Francis, St. Dominic, and St. Anthony of Padua. His other principal mentor was Cardinal Jean d'Abbeville, legate to the peninsula 1228–1229, with whom he maintained contact into the 1230s. The so-called *Summa septem sacramentorum*, which he compiled, was based on the statutes attributed to Eudes de Sully, bishop of Paris (d. 1208). First promulgated by him at Barcelona in 1241, the *Summa* was an unsophisticated work of practical guidance for the clergy that enjoyed considerable influence throughout the province for the remainder of the century. Another side of him was revealed in the course of the *Ordinatio ecclesie Valentine*, the bitter struggle in which he engaged with Archbishop Rodrigo of Toledo for jurisdiction over the recently restored church of Valencia, and in the sometimes uneasy relationship which he maintained with King Jaime I, the "Conqueror."

PETER LINEHAN

Bibliography

Linehan, P. "Pedro de Albalat, arzobispo de Tarragona, y su 'Summa septem sacramentorum.' " *Hispania Sacra* 11, no. 1 (1969), 9–30.

———. *The Spanish Church and the Papacy in the Thirteenth Century*. Cambridge, 1971.

ALBIGENSIAN CRUSADE, THE

On the morning of 14 January 1208, just north of Arles, where the Rhône River divides, Pierre of Castelnau—virulent Cistercian denouncer of the Cathar heresy and the papal legate who, less than a year earlier, had excommunicated Raymond VI, count of Toulouse—was brutally murdered by a swiftly thrown lance puncturing his back. The killer was an anonymous horseman who escaped to nearby Beaucaire. Pierre's quick death was the immediate cause of twenty-one years of intermittent warfare and bloody conquest known as the Albigensian Crusade.

Pope Innocent III immediately accused Raimond VI of Pierre of Castelnau's murder, and then authorized a crusade, with the same indulgences as an expedition to Palestine, against Raymond and the Cathar (or Albigensian) heretics the count was accused of supporting. Raymond may have been tolerant toward the Cathar holy men and women, known as *perfecti* and *perfectae*, and he may have expropriated some church property, but he was also intelligent enough not to jeopardize his power in Languedoc by the impetuous killing of an apostolic legate.

The king of France, Philip Augustus, displayed no apparent interest in the papal holy war—despite the personal entreaties of Innocent III. Philip did, nevertheless, allow five hundred knights to take the cross. Raymond VI endeavored to stop the crusaders by reconciling himself with the Church on 18 June 1209; unfortunately, the crusading army was already on its way, under the leadership of Arnau Amalric, abbot of Cîteaux and head of the Cistercian Order. Four days later Raymond took the cross himself and helped redirect the crusaders toward the lands of the Trencavels, vassals of Pedro II of Aragón. The town of Béziers was captured easily, and the entire population allegedly massacred. Apparently reflecting upon such indiscriminate killing, Arnau Amalric is reported to have said, "God will know his own." Carcassonne, the Trencavel capital, surrendered on 15 August and its viscount, Raymond-Roger, was imprisoned. The crusaders, ignoring the claims of Raymond-Roger's young son and the feudal authority of the Aragonese crown, appointed Simon de Montfort, a baron from the Ile-de-France and titular Earl of Leicester, as ruler of Carcassonne.

Raymond VI left the crusading army after Carcassonne, but his excommunication was renewed in a series of Church councils (1209–1211). The papal legates would not listen to any of Raymond's attempts to reconcile himself; the crusade could now continue into the territories of the Count of Toulouse. At this point, in 1212, Pedro II of Aragón, Raymond's brother-in-law and the recent victor over the Muslims at Las Navas de Tolosa, placed Toulouse under his protection. On 12 September 1213 the combined armies of Pedro and Raymond, as well as the counts of Foix and Comminges, met Simon de Montfort's little army outside the fortified village of Muret. Simon was victorious and Pedro died in the battle (with his five-year-old son son Jaime, the future king of Aragón, held captive by Simon until April 1214).

In 1215 the Fourth Lateran Council deprived Raimond VI of all his lands. The marquessate of Provence was held in trust for the future Raymond VII, while everything conquered by the crusaders was to be ruled by Simon de Montfort (including the county of Comminges). Despite all this, the war went on for another thirteen years as Raymond VI and his son struggled to regain their lost domains. Eventually, after Simon de Montfort died while besieging Toulouse in 1218—his head crushed by a stone from a catapult worked by young girls and married women—the two Raimonds slowly succeeded in their reconquest. Throughout these years, Philip Augustus remained indifferent to the plight of Simon's son, Amaury. However, after Raymond VII, Raymond-Roger of Foix, and Raymond Trencavel were all excommunicated in November 1225, Philip's son, Louis VIII, undertook a royal crusade into Languedoc. The king captured Avignon in 1226 and then proceeded to march toward Toulouse. Louis effortlessly occupied the possessions of the Trencavels along the Aude River, but before he could strengthen his position, the king died on 8 November 1226.

Raymond VII, in the lull after the death of Louis VIII, was offered the chance for peace and he gladly took it in 1229. On 12 April 1229 the Treaty of Paris officially ended the Albigensian Crusade. Yet the spiritual and secular conquest of Languedoc, unleashed so many years earlier by the murder of a papal legate, would continue for at least another four decades. The treaty's insistence on the pursuit of heresy led not only to the founding of the university in Toulouse but also to the formation of the medieval inquisition. The treaty also stressed that Raymond was now a vassal of the northern French king—emphasized by the obligation of the count's nine-year-old daughter and heir, Jeanne, to marry a brother of the king—and that the traditional territorial claims of the kings of Aragón within Languedoc, as well as the right to interfere in southern French affairs, would no longer be acceptable. The Aragonese crown finally renounced all ambitions beyond the Pyrennees with the Treaty of Corbeil in 1258 between the French king Louis IX and (the son of Pedro II captured by Simon de Montfort after the battle of Muret almost forty years earlier), Jaime I.

MARK GREGORY PEGG

Bibliography

Evans, A. P. "The Albigensian Crusade," in *A History of the Crusades II: The Later Crusades, 1189–1311*. Ed. K. M. Setton, R. L. Wolff, and H. W. Hazard. Philadelphia, 1962. 277–324.

Lambert, M. *Medieval Heresy: Popular Movements from the Gregorian Reform to the Reformation*. Oxford, 1992. 97–146.

Mundy, J. H. *The Repression of Catharism at Toulouse*. Toronto, 1985. 18–26.

Roquebert, M. *L'Epopée Cathare I: L'Invasion*. Toulouse, 1970.

Strayer, J. *The Albigensian Crusades*. Ann Arbor, Mich. 1992.

Sumption, J. *The Albigensian Crusade*. London, 1978.

Wakefield, W. L. *Heresy, Crusade and Inquisition in Southern France, 1100–1250* London, 1974.

ALBO, JOSEPH

Aragonese rabbi of the fifteenth century, Albo represented the Jewish community of Daroca at the famous Tortosa Disputation (1413–1414), although he played apparently a minor role and was somewhat inconsistent in his statements. He was a student of the renowned leader of Aragonese-Catalan Jewry, Hasdai Crescas, and as such was certainly greatly influenced by his philosophical magnum opus, *Or Adonai* (*Light of the Lord*) and also by his small polemical treatise against Christianity.

Taking his cue from these works, Albo wrote a large work, *Sefer ha-Ciqarim* (*Book of the Principles*) on the fundamentals of revealed religion, specifically, of the Jewish religion. Critical of Maimonides for not giving the basis for his own enumeration of thirteen principles of "faith," Albo reduced these to three: existence of God, belief in revelation, and the doctrine of divine retribution. Yet he similarly failed to prove a basis for these dogmas. Notably lacking is a belief in creation, especially ex nihilo, which Albo held to be a necessary religious belief but not a fundamental dogma. A lack of belief in "dogmas" as supposedly found in the Bible, or an incorrect interpretation of the Bible, did not render one a heretic (as, apparently, did denial of the three fundamentals).

The belief in the messiah, which at the Disputation he had appeared to question altogether, is not to be considered a fundamental principle but only a binding belief (which nevertheless could not logically be deduced from any of the fundamentals). A major thrust of his argument is anti-Christian polemic. While theoretically admitting the possibility of a plurality of revealed religions, he in fact limited such revelations to those pre-Mosaic figures such as Adam, Noah, and Abraham. Christianity could not be recognized as a legitimate revealed religion because of its denial of the essential unity of God.

Nevertheless, his position on divine attributes, acceptance of positive attributes (in contrast to Maimonides), was directly influenced by Thomas Aquinas. Thus, ironically, Aquinas, who was himself influenced by Maimonides on other matters, became a source for this later Jewish work attacking both Maimonides and Christianity.

In actuality, there is little either original or of profound interest in Albo's work.

NORMAN ROTH

Bibliography

Albo, J. *Sefer ha-ikkarim*. Ed. and trans. I. Huskik. Philadelphia, 1930.

Guttmann, J. *Philosophies of Judaism*. New York, 1964.

ALBORNOZ, GIL ALVAREZ CARRILLO DE

Gil de Albornoz was one of the most eminent Spanish churchmen of the fourteenth century. He was born at Cuenca (ca. 1295) and was the son of García de Albornoz and Teresa de Luna. Albornoz was educated in Zaragoza under the watchful eye of his influential uncle, Jimeno, who at the time was archbishop there, and under the tutelage of Pedro Egidio, who would later become a deacon at Cuenca and come to administer Albornoz's household. In 1316 to 1317, Gil de Albornoz enrolled at the University of Toulouse, where he remained for a decade and from where before 1325 he was awarded a doctorate in decretals and canon law. While at Toulouse, he doubtless came into contact with Stephan Aubert.

Gil de Albornoz's life can be divided into two phases, an early Iberian one and a later Italian period following the accession of Pedro I to the crown of Castile and Albornoz's voluntary departure from the Iberian Peninsula. Since Albornoz's exploits in Italy are more amply known and readily accessible in many sources, greater attention will be given here to his achievements in Spain.

Upon returning to Castile from Toulouse in 1327, Gil de Albornoz joined the circle of Alfonso XI and, in addition to his ecclesiastical benefices at Cuenca, held the title of counselor to the king and archdeacon of Calatrava. By 1335 he had participated in an embassy to the king of Aragón and was actively engaged in the political life of Castile. In 1338, he was named archbishop of Toledo to succeed his uncle Jimeno, who held that position when he died. Albornoz was subsequently given the secular title of canciller de Castilla. It is at this point that he began to intervene vigorously in reforming the kingdom's judicial administration and in the organization of the armed forces. His active participation in the *cortes* (parliament) of Castile show him to be a dynamic force in all manner of affairs concerning the governance of the realm. Although Albornoz's influence in the adoption of the Ordenamiento de Alcalá in 1348 has not been carefully studied, he was doubtless a major participant in drafting and promulgating the new legal code. At the same time, Albornoz is known to have been energetically engaged in Alfonso XI's military exploits against the Muslims in the south and was named comisario de la cruzada for his efforts. Albornoz was at Alfonso's side at the Battle of the Salado River (1340), at the siege and capture of Algeciras (1342–1344), and at the siege of Gibraltar until the king's untimely death from the plague in 1350.

Albornoz's activity in the Spanish Church was no less forceful than his involvement in secular government. The synods and councils of Toledo in 1339 and 1345 show him to have been especially preoccupied with the moral life of his diocese, attempting to impose order upon the disposition of ecclesiastical property and benefices, the *cura pastoralis* and administration of the sacraments by the rectors of churches and parishes, and the general reform of the clergy, which was deemed to be in a lamentable state of decadence. Clerical simony and concubinage were two lapses that especially caught Albornoz's attention, and orders against these practices went out under his name. It is because of this that Albornoz is often associated with Juan Ruiz, the putative author of the *Libro de buen amor*, whom the Salamanca manuscript of the latter attests was jailed by the bishop for his carnal failings. Quite aside from reputedly policing the celibacy of the clergy in the diocese of Toledo, Albornoz was deeply concerned with the level of their culture, learning, and education. He began his reign as archbishop by ensuring that the edicts of the Council of Valladolid (1322) be strictly observed and that one out of every ten clergymen in every deaconry be commissioned to study theology and canon law, prohibiting the ordination of all who could not demonstrate an adequate level of clerical education, "ut nullus nisi litteratus ad clericatum promovetur" (unless literate, do not make him a cleric), according to the Council of Toledo of 1339. Albornoz's own fidelity to his vows and the requirements of ordination were said by all to have been exemplary.

The death of Alfonso XI led Albornoz to fear disgrace at the hands of Pedro I, the king's successor. As a result, he withdrew to the papal court at Avignon, where he was made a cardinal in December 1350. His career in the curia was as successful as it had been at the Court of Castile. He was made papal legate and vicar general of the Papal States, helping Pope Innocent VI to control firmly their administration and dominate central Italy politically. Between 1353 and 1360 Albornoz attempted to revive the Angevin-Guelph alliance of the 1320s to counter the power of the lords of Lombardy but, after great sacrifice and expenditure, he failed to pacify the Italian peninsula because of French inability to provide continued support.

Throughout his life Albornoz remained firmly committed to the education of the clergy. He was especially concerned with their preparation in canon law and ecclesiastical administration. As a result, he founded the Collegio di San Clemente, known as the Spanish College, at the University of Bologna. In the will he signed in 1364, he created the foundation to establish the college as the universal heir to his fortune and, in a codicil added in 1368, again made provisions for the disposition of his inheritance, which was to go in its entirety to support twenty-four Spanish students in the course of their studies at the university. By 1369, two years after Albornoz's death at Viterbo, the College of San Clemente received its first group of students, many of whom went on to become distinguished jurists upon completion of their studies and their return to the Iberian Peninsula. Albornoz's foundation of the Spanish College at Bologna served as a model for the subsequent development of the *colegios mayores* in Spanish universities.

E. MICHAEL GERLI

Bibliography

Beneyto Pérez, J. *El cardenal Albornoz, canciller de Castilla y caudillo de Italia*. Madrid, 1950.

———. *El cardenal Albornoz: Hombre de iglesia y de estado en Castilla y en Italia*. Madrid, 1986.

Colliva, P. *Il cardinale Albornoz, lo Stato della Chiesa, le Constitutiones Aegidianae (1353–1357)*. Bologna, 1977.

Martí, B. M. *The Spanish College at Bologna in the Fourteenth Century*. New York, 1966.

Verdera y Tuells, E. *El cardenal Albornoz y el Colegio de España*. Bologna, 1972.

ALBURQUERQUE, JUAN ALFONSO, LORD OF

A Portuguese aristocrat, born to an illegitimate son of King Dinis (1325), Juan Alfonso de Alburquerque arrived in Castile in 1328 as chief chamberlain to María, his second cousin, the Portuguese princess who married Alfonso XI of Castile that same year. He spent most of the rest of his life in Castile. Because of his connections and a most suitable marriage to Isabel de Meneses, whose family was one of Castile's wealthiest and most influential, he became a formidable presence in the politics of the kingdom.

As chamberlain to Pedro, Alfonso XI's and María's only surviving child, Alburquerque oversaw the education of the heir and wielded considerable influence over the young prince. Alburquerque was appointed chief chancellor when Pedro, at sixteen, became king following his father's death from the plague in 1350 during the Castilian siege of Gibraltar. For the next two years, Alburquerque as first minister was the chief architect of the crown's policies, many of which contributed to the king's future reputation and his sobriquet "the Cruel."

One policy attributable to Alburquerque's influence was the imprisonment and death of Leonor de Guzmán, Alfonso XI's favorite and mother of the future Trastámara dynasty. The elimination of Leonor caused the enmity of her numerous children, among them Enrique de Trastámara, and marked the beginning of Pedro's difficulties that culminated in the Castilian civil war of 1366–1369. Alburquerque presided over the defeat of Alfonso Fernández Coronel, a former vassal of Alfonso XI who opposed Aburquerque's policies. When Coronel surrendered in 1353 after a two-year siege, he spoke to Alburquerque in words that foreshadowed the first minister's own fate: "This is Castile, Lord Juan Alfonso; it makes men only to waste them."

The most costly of his policies, however, was his decision, along with Queen María's, to negotiate the marriage between Pedro and the French princess, Blanche de Borbón. When Pedro abandoned her two days after the wedding in 1353, likely because of the princess' inability to pay the agreed-upon dowry, the first minister failed to persuade the king to return to her side. While the marriage was intended to promote good relations between Castile and France, Pedro's rejection of Blanche served to alienate the French crown, whose participation in Castilian affairs led to Pedro's eventual defeat by Enrique de Trastámara. It was also in Alburquerque's household that Pedro met and fell in love with María de Padilla in 1352, a lasting attachment that might also have contributed to Pedro's reluctance to cohabit with Blanche.

Pedro's behavior caused considerable turmoil and opposition and unified his enemies. Queen María and Alburquerque were unable to convince him to resume normal relations with Blanche, which served to alienate them from the king. At the same time, the minister's influence had begun to wane as María de Padilla's relatives gained ascendancy with Pedro. Alburquerque fled to Portugal and refused to return to Castile even after Pedro summoned him. When he returned, he did so as the ally of Enrique and Fadrique, Pedro's half-brothers who had temporarily made peace with the king and had been sent in pursuit of the minister. Alburquerque and his pursuers decided to make peace among themselves and march against Pedro instead. On 28 September 1354, Juan Alfonso de Alburquerque, while on campaign, died under mysterious circumstances; it was believed that he was poisoned by an Italian physician in Pedro's employ. Alburquerque's allies, who continued their rebellion against Pedro, added the minister's death to their list of grievances against the king and adopted his corpse as their standard, pledging to parade the body until they could proclaim victory. At this stage of his reign, however, Pedro was able to defeat the conspiracy against him and the rebels eventually disbanded.

Alburquerque and his wife Isabel de Meneses had one son, Martín Gil, whose death in 1365 marked the end of the family line.

CLARA ESTOW

Bibliography

López de Ayala, P. *Crónica del rey don Pedro*. Madrid, 1956.

Suárez Fernández, L. *Historia de España antigua y media*. Vol. 2. Madrid, 1976.

ALCÁZOVAS, TREATIES OF

When Enrique IV of Castile died (11 December 1474), his sister Isabel and her husband Fernando were proclaimed as rulers of Castile, but a faction among the nobility, with the help of Afonso V of Portugal, upheld the rights to the succession of Juana, the daughter of Enrique and Juana of Portugal. The adherence of the Castilian nobility and of the cities, as well as military victories (Toro, 1 March 1476, La Albufera, 24 February 1479), secured the throne for Isabel and Fernando. Afonso V, urged by his son and heir, João, and by the majority opinion among his courtiers, had to begin the negotiations for peace that culminated in the four Treaties of Alcázovas (4 September 1479). They confirmed the peace of Almeirim (27 January 1432) in all its clauses, promising the mutual restoration of conquests and prisoners and reserving zones of influence in the Atlantic: the Canary Islands for Castile, the Azores and Madeira for Portugal. The Portuguese would have the exclusive right to navigate and occupy lands south of Cape Bojador on the route to Guinea, and the right of conquest in the emirate of Fez, except on the sliver of coastline between Capes Nun and Bojador reserved for Castile. Juana's situation was also resolved, as she preferred to enter a convent, although during her novitiate year she could still choose another solution—namely, to marry Prince Juan of Castile, the son and heir of Isabel and Fernando; she did not do so. The future marriage of Infanta Isabel, a daughter of the Castilian monarchs, with Afonso, the son and heir of Prince João of Portugal was also proposed. The Infanta would have a dowry of 106,000 *doblas*. Both she and Juana would remain in the fortress of Moura for two years, as a guarantee that the treaties would be carried out. Juana then made her profession as a nun in the convent of Santa Clara of Coimbra (15 November 1480). Finally, those Castilians who still followed Afonso V were assured of pardon and restitution of property and offices. Thus the war was brought to an end and a very solid plan for friendly relations between Portugal and Castile was outlined.

MIGUEL-ANGEL LADERO QUESADA

Bibliography

Suárez Fernández, L. *Los Reyes Católicos: La conquista del trono*. Madrid, 1989.

ALCALÁ DE HENARES, ORDENAMIENTO OF

Alfonso XI determined to try to bring order to the legal chaos of his kingdom and to the widespread anarchy and outrages against justice being committed, and in 1348 at the *cortes* (parliament) of Alcalá de Henares the new *ordenamiento* (ordinance; legal compilation) was adopted for uniform use throughout the kingdom. Unlike the *Siete Partidas* composed by jurists for Alfonso X, the Ordenamiento de Alcalá de Henares was intended to be not a theoretical treatise on law but a practical application for the use of jurists. The code drew upon previous legislation: the Ordenamiento of Villa Real in 1346, and that of Segovia (still unpublished) in 1347, both of which determined primarily judicial procedures for civil and criminal matters, and included also the laws of Alfonso VIII at the cortes of Nájera in 1138, with regard to the rights and duties of the nobility, judges, treason, and so on. The ordenamiento was confirmed by all successive monarchs and continued to play a prominent role in the legislation of the Catholic Monarchs and even beyond.

Various unsatisfactory efforts have been made to identify the legal advisers responsible for the text, with Juan Manuel being a likely candidate and Cardinal Gil de Albornoz a less likely one.

The Ordenamiento is also important in the history of the Jews in Spain, for it was the first attempt in Castile to severely restrict their economic activity, not only with regard to lending money on interest (of importance here is also the so-called pseudo Ordenamiento of Alcalá, said to be merely the preliminary section of the Leyes Nuevas, but in fact it is not; rather, it purports to be a law of Alfonso XI concerning usury), but also in that while recognizing the right of Jews to buy and sell property in the kingdom it sought to impose geographic restrictions on such property as well as restrictions on its value. It may easily be shown that these efforts were without any significant or lasting result, however.

The text of the Ordenamiento has been frequently published; see, for example, *Cortes de los antiguos reinos de León y Castilla*, volume I, and *Códigos españoles*, volume 1.

NORMAN ROTH

Bibliography

González Herrero, M. "El Ordenamiento de Segovia de 1347," *Estudios segovianos* 18 (1966), 205–28.

Sánchez, G. "Sobre el Ordenamiento de Alcalá y sus fuentes," *Revista de derecho privado* 9 (1922), 353–68.

ALCAÑICES, TREATY OF

The Treaty of Alcañices (12 September 1297) established the border between Castile and Portugal. During the minority of Fernando IV of Castile (1295–1312), Dinis of Portugal (1279–1325) allied with Jaime II of Aragón (1291–1327) to invade León-Castile and to divide it between Infante Juan and Alfonso de la Cerda. Jaime II planned to take Murcia, and Dinis hoped to expand Portugal's frontiers into Castile. At the same time Muḥammad II of Granada (1273–1302) besieged Tarifa.

The invasion took place in 1296 and succeeded almost according to plan. Jaime successfully captured the major cities in Murcia, and both Juan and Alfonso were proclaimed kings, the former of León, the latter of Castile. However, Tarifa withstood the siege and Dinis, facing a rebellion by his younger brother Afonso, made a separate treaty with Castile in 1297. Under this treaty of Alcañices Castile ceded various villages and castles in the Riba Coa: Sabugal, Castelo Rodrigo, Vila Maior, Castelo Bom, Almeida, Castelo Melhor, Monforte, Olivença, Ouguela, Campo Maior, and San Félix, and received in return Aroche and Aracena. The treaty also arranged for the marriage of Fernando IV with Constança, daughter of Dinis, and of Dinis's son, the future Afonso IV (1325–1357), with Fernando's sister Beatriz. The signing of the treaty broke the coalition between Portugal and Aragón, permitting Castile to defeat Aragón and to establish Fernando on the throne. The delineation of the border between Castile and Portugal is considered one of the achievements of Dinis's reign.

THERESA M. VANN

Bibliography

Livermore, H. V. *A New History of Portugal.* Cambridge, 1976.

O'Callaghan, Joseph F. *A History of Medieval Spain.* Ithaca, N.Y., 1975.

ALCÁNTARA, ORDER OF *See* MILITARY ORDERS

ALCHEMY

The history of alchemy in medieval Spain parallels in many respects the development of alchemical theory and practices in the rest of Europe, with two notable differences: (1) alchemy was practiced in the Arabic cultures of al-Andalus long before its introduction into the rest of Europe, and (2) most of the alchemical texts were translated from Arabic to Latin in Toledo in the twelfth and thirteenth centuries. It is possible the translators had contact with known Arabic experts, and the medieval practitioners in Hispanic regions may have been influenced even later by direct contact with Muslim adepts native to the Iberian Peninsula. Toledo and Salamanca became well-known in medieval Europe as centers for the study of magic and occult arts.

Alchemical theory was developed by Hellenistic scholars who lived, wrote, and experimented mainly in Alexandria. Alchemical writings described a hodgepodge of attempts to create false metals, experiments with the properties of metals, and theories of transmutations of the metals that had been elaborated from various elements of Aristotelian science. The theory of the transmutations of the metals in a hierarchical scheme in which a metal of a lower order was transformed into one of higher order was an innovation of Alexandrian scientists, whose writings were, through the Arabic translations, to be the basis of chemical and alchemical ideas well into the eighteenth century. In contrast, Latin writers, such as Pliny and Isidore of Seville, assumed gold was simply a metal deposited in the earth.

Alchemy introduced an alternative idea by which the metals were conceived of in a biological metaphor of growth and decay through which in a natural process in the earth the metals grew slowly as plants from the basest metal (lead) through the other metals to the most precious (gold). The laboratory alchemist simply tried to accelerate this process in a chemical flask. Alchemy was not only a scheme for achieving great wealth quickly, but it also became the established scientific explanation for the formation of metals in the earth. Of lesser importance in the Middle Ages were the spiritual initiations and purifications that the adept needed to undergo for the completion of the great work.

The medical and scientific research of late Greek culture became the basis of Arabic scientific research. The translation of Greek texts into Arabic in the eighth and ninth centuries was followed by intense activity among adepts in Islamic nations, which has lasted until the present day. Records show alchemical practitioners flourished in al-Andalus during the reign of Al-Ḥakam II (961–967). Especially noteworthy among the writers in medieval Spain was the astronomer Maslamah Ibn Ahmad al-Majrītī (first half of eleventh century), to whom an alchemical treatise, *The Sage's Steps*, was attributed. His treatise on magic was translated in 1256 and circulated in Europe as *Picatrix*. His disciple Ibn Bishrūn also practiced alchemy.

In the twelfth and thirteenth centuries, Toledo became one of the most important centers for the translation and diffusion of Arabic scientific and medical writings to Christian Europe. Numerous scholars came from northern Europe to translate the texts from Arabic to Latin. This cultural bridge to the rest of Europe made Spain noteworthy as a center for the study of occult sciences.

The two names most often associated with alchemy in medieval Spain are the Catalans Raimon Llull (ca. 1232–1315) and Arnau de Vilanova (1235?–1313). That either of these prolific writers was the author of the symbolical alchemical treatises attributed them is still doubted. Llull, who in his authentic works denies the possibility of transforming one metal into another, is a specially difficult case, since his great works on science, designed to convert Arabs to Christianity, became the basis of magic and alchemical thought in the Renaissance and later. The most important treatises ascribed to Llull are the *Clavicula* (*Little Key*) and *Testamentum*. A host of treatises have been attributed to Arnau de Vilanova, the most influential being *Semita Semitae* (*The Path of Paths*) and *Rosarium philosophorum* (*The Rosary of the Philosophers*).

In Castile, important figures associated with alchemy were Alfonso el Sabio, and in the fifteenth century Enrique de Villena, and Alfonso Carrillo, Archbishop of Toledo. Attributed to Alfonso el Sabio is the *Libro del Tesoro* (*Book of Treasure*) and to Enrique de Villena the answer to the *Carta de los veinte sabios cordoveses* (*Letter from the Twenty Sages of Córdoba*); both texts in Luanco's *La Alquimia en España*. Alfonso Carrillo left no writings, but his obsession with alchemy was reported by Hernando de Pulgar.

Possibly writers ascribed their alchemical treatises to various famous medieval figures such as Llull, Alfonso el Sabio, Arnau de Vilanova, and St. Thomas Aquinas to avoid prosecution by the Church, which had taken an active role in prohibiting alchemical transmutations. Even though the attributions of many of the Spanish treatises are of doubtful authenticity, the treatises themselves were well read and very influential. The numerous medieval alchemical texts found in Spain describe the secret processes and recipes with the same types of highly symbolic and coded language typical of alchemical treatises in the rest of Europe.

DANIEL L. HEIPLE

Bibliography

García Font, J. *Historia de la alquimia en España*. Madrid, 1976.

Luanco, J. R. de. *La Alquimia en España*. 2 vols. Barcelona, 1889; rprt. Madrid, 1980.

ALEXANDER OF MACEDONIA *See* LIBRO DE ALEXANDRE

ALFAQUÍ *See* LAW, MUSLIM

ALFARROBEIRA, BATTLE OF

In which the former regent of Portugal, Dom Pedro, Duke of Coimbra, met his death at the hands of the royal army of the boy-king Afonso V, manipulated by Pedro's half-brother Afonso, Duke of Bragança. The Alfarrobeira is a stream near Alverca twenty miles north of Lisbon, and the battle was fought on 20 May 1449. Dom Pedro's brother King Duarte had died in September 1438, his heir Afonso V being only six years old. The regency of his widow was abrogated as a woman and a Castilian, and when Pedro replaced her with the consent of the *cortes* (parliament), she fled to Castile and appealed to her family. Pedro's costly intervention in Castile lost him the support of the towns, and the marriage of his daughter to the king and appointment of his son, also Pedro, to the constableship, which Bragança regarded as hereditary in his family, the most powerful in Portugal. When Afonso V reached his majority in January 1448, he prolonged his regency, but was at length obliged to relinquish it. When the crown demanded a review of rewards by and to Pedro, the former regent was faced with the choice between resistence and spoliation. His counselors, meeting at Coimbra, favored conciliation, but his long-time crony Alvaro Díaz de Almada, Count of Avranches, recommended a heroic defense of honor. They may have hoped for support from Lisbon, toward which they marched. They faced overwhelming odds, and Pedro was killed bv an arrow to the heart, Avranches dying soon after.

The case is analyzed in great detail by H. Vaquero Moreno in *A Batalha de Alfarrobeira*, which shows that Pedro's 480 known supporters were adherents from the duchy of Coimbra and his forty-five nobles, disposing of the supposition that he had remained the leader of the bourgeoisie. His tragic end arose from his chivalrous ideals and from the influence of Alvaro Díaz, who mistakenly thought that he could and should exercise the authority of his powerful father, Juan I.

H. V. LIVERMORE

Bibliography

Baquero Moreno, H. *A Batalha de Alfarrobeira*. Coimbira, 1979.

Livermore. H. V. *A New History of Portugal*. Cambridge, 1976.

O'Callaghan, Joseph F. *A History of Medieval Spain*. Ithaca, N.Y., 1975

ALFONSO DE LA CERDA

Alfonso de la Cerda, (1271–1334?) oldest son of Fernando de la Cerda and Blanche of France, grandson of Alfonso X (1252–1284), became Alfonso X's legal heir when his father died suddenly in August 1275. Alfonso X acknowledged his second son, Sancho, as his heir in the *cortes* (parliament) of 1276, but a faction led by Juan Núñez de Lara supported Alfonso de la Cerda's claim. In January 1277 Blanche and Queen Violante brought Alfonso and his younger brother Fernando, known as the Infantes de la Cerda, to Aragón for safety. Violante's brother, Pedro III of Aragón (1276–1285), later imprisoned the two boys at Sancho's request. Alfonso X disinherited Sancho in 1282 and recognized Alfonso de la Cerda as his heir, but Sancho seized the entire kingdom when the king died in 1284. Four years later Alfonso III of Aragón (1285–1291) released Alfonso de la Cerda and had him proclaimed king of Castile in Jaca. The Aragonese invaded Castile to support Alfonso and to obtain Murcia, but when this failed Alfonso went to France in a futile attempt to seek aid there. Not until Sancho died in 1295, leaving as king a technically illegitimate minor (Fernando IV, 1295–1312) did Alfonso's claim seem feasible to foreign monarchs. Alfonso invaded Castile with Aragonese help and was crowned king of Castile at Jaén in 1296, but the Aragonese withdrew and the papal declaration of Fernando's legitimacy in 1301 forced Alfonso to quit his claims. Alfonso unsuccessfully reasserted his rights again when Fernando IV died in 1312. He finally renounced his claims in 1331, when he took an oath of fealty to Alfonso XI of Castile (1312–1350) and received several lordships in return.

Alfonso de la Cerda married Mafalda de Narbona. Their children were Luis de la Cerda, Juan Alfonso de la Cerda, Alfonso de España, Margarita de la Cerda, Inés de la Cerda, and Maria de la Cerda. Alfonso's date of death is uncertain; it was either 1333 or 1334. He and his wife were buried in the monastery of Nuestra Señora del Cármen, which they founded in the town of Gibraleón.

THERESA M. VANN

Bibliography

Ballesteros Beretta, A. *Alfonso X, El Sabio*. Barcelona, 1984.

Benavides, A. *Memorias de D. Fernando IV de Castilla*. Madrid, 1860.

Benito Ruano, E. "El problema sucesorio de la corona de Castilla a la muerte de Don Fernando de la Cerda," in *VII Centenario del Infante Don Fernando de la Cerda: Jornadas de Estudio Ciudad Real, Abril 1975*. Madrid, 1976. 217–25.

Díaz-Madroñero, C., and López de Pablos. "El problema sucesorio a la muerte de Don Fernando de la Cerda," in *VII Centenario del infante Don Fernando de la Cerda. Jornadas de Estudio Ciudad Real, Abril 1975*. Madrid, 1976. 227–36.

Hillgarth, J. N. *The Spanish Kingdoms 1250–1516*. 2 vols. Oxford, 1976.

O'Callaghan, J. F. *A History of Medieval Spain*. Ithaca, N.Y., 1975.

ALFONSO DE TOLEDO

Mid-fifteenth-century author of the *Invencionario*, a catalog of discoverers finished around 1467 and dedicated to Alfonso Carrillo, Archbishop of Toledo. According to autobiographical references gleaned from the *Invencionaro*, the author was born in Toledo, resided in Cuenca, held the degree of *Bachiller en Decretos*, and had earlier compiled an *Espejo de las Historias* (now lost) for the Bishop of Cuenca.

The *Invencionario* is evidently the earliest example of *heuremata* literature in any of the medieval vernacular languages of western Europe. In two books of ten *titulos* each, Alfonso de Toledo purports to list the discoverers (*inventores*) of things necessary for humankind's well-being, temporal (book 1) as well as spiritual (book 2). Book 1 discusses the discoverers of letters; kingdoms and kings; laws; cities; marriage; bread, wine, and meat; clothing; arms and martial arts; music and games; medicine; astrology; and other arts. Book 2 deals with the remedies for original sin; faith; prayer; offerings; fasting; priests and sacrifices; feast days; martyrs and religions; places of worship; and penance. There are frequent (and often interesting) amplifications and digressions.

The *Invencionario* is written in the Latinate style widely cultivated in fifteenth-century Castilian prose.

In its intent and organizational plan it resembles the *Etymoloqiae* of Isidore of Seville (one of Alfonso's primary *auctoritates*). The author also drew extensively from the writings of church historians, biblical commentarists, and specialists in canon law, documenting his sources with particular care.

Though now nearly forgotten, the work must have circulated widely in its time; at least fourteen manuscript versions survived to the eighteenth century, and twelve are extant today.

PHILIP O. GERICKE

Bibliography

Alfonso de Toledo. *Invencionario*. Ed. P. O. Gericke. Spanish Series No. 75. Madison, Wisc., 1992.

Gericke, P. O. "El 'Invencionario' de Alfonso de Toledo," *Revista de Archivos, Bibliotecas y Museos* 74 (1967), 25–73.

Piero, R. A. del. "Sobre el autor y fecha del *Invencionario*," *Hispanic Review* 30 (1962), 12–20.

ALFONSO I, KING OF ARAGÓN

Alfonso I of Aragón, el Batallador, was born (ca. 1073) to Sancho Ramírez, king of Aragón (reigned 1064–1094), and Felicia of Roucy. He established a reputation for military prowess, commanding the Aragonese vanguard at the Battle of Alcoraz (1096) and fighting alongside El Cid in the Battle of Bairén (1097). After his brother's unexpected death without descent in 1104, he continued the Aragonese offensive against the Muslims with substantial success. When Alfonso VI of Castile, having lost his only son in battle, sought a husband for his daughter, the heiress Urraca, his choice fell upon Alfonso of Aragón as the most able candidate.

Alfonso VI of Castile died 30 June 1109, and Urraca and Alfonso of Aragón were married in the autumn of the same year. The marriage conditions provided for joint rule of the realms of each, and provided for the succession of their descent to the united realms. The arrangement might have led to an early unification of Christian Spain, but there were many opponents to the marriage and little compatibility between the royal couple. Alfonso fought to establish his authority both over the lands of León-Castile and his wife, but finally abandoned his efforts. In about 1114, he repudiated Urraca and turned his attention increasingly to Aragonese affairs and the work of reconquest.

Gathering many French friends and relatives to his cause, he laid siege to Zaragoza, which capitulated on 18 December 1118. Tudela followed in February 1119, and Tarazona shortly after. Alfonso then marched on Calatayud and decisively defeated the Muslims in the battle of Cutanda, 17 June 1120. He then devoted himself to the difficult task of organizing and populating the extensive territories he had acquired. From September 1124 to about May 1125, he undertook a massive raid through Valencia, Murcia, Córdoba, and Granada, and succeeded in leading a large number of Mozarabs back to Aragón. In June 1127, he concluded a treaty with Alfonso VII of León-Castile at Támara, recognizing the young king's hereditary rights and freeing himself for new conquests.

He conquered Molina in December 1128 and attacked Valencia in spring 1129, at which time he defeated the Muslims in the battle of Cullera. From October 1130 to October 1131, he engaged in an unexplained and unsuccessful siege of Bayonne, where he issued his testament, leaving his realms to the crusading orders of the Temple, Hospital, and Holy Sepulcher. He undertook the siege of Fraga in the summer of 1133, and suffered a disastrous defeat there on 17 July 1134. Alfonso survived the battle and attempted to regroup his forces, but to no avail. He fell ill, died on 7 September 1134, and was buried at Montearagón, near Huesca. His brother, Ramiro el Monje, was immediately proclaimed king, and the kingdom that Alfonso had built began to disintegrate.

Alfonso's accomplishments were many. He greatly increased Aragón's power, expanded its territories, populated its lands, and inspired its armies with the spirit of the Crusade. Many refused to believe that he had died, and legends soon sprang up that he would return someday to lead the Aragonese to victories again.

LYNN H. NELSON

Bibliography

Arco y Garay, R. del. "Notas biográficas del rey Alfonso I el Batallador," *Boletín de la Real Academia de la Historia* 133 (1953), 111–209.

Lacarra, J. M. *Vida de Alfonso el Batallador*. Zaragoza, 1971.

ALFONSO II, KING OF ARAGÓN

The future Alfonso II of Aragón (Alfons I of Catalonia) known as "el Casto," was born in March 1157 to Ramón Berenguer IV, Count of Barcelona (1131–1162), and Petronilla, heiress to the kingdom of Aragón. His father died on 7 August 1162, and Alfonso was proclaimed Count of Barcelona on 24 February 1163. Petronilla renounced her royal dignity in favor of her son on 18 June 1164, and Alfonso was crowned king of Aragón at Zaragoza on 11 November 1164. The Crown of Aragón was formally established with this union of Aragón and Catalonia. Although by the terms of his father's will Alfonso was under the guardianship of Henry II of England, effective administration of the realm was in the able hands of Guillem Ramón de Moncada and Guillem Torroja.

With the death of Ramón Berenguer III, Count of Provence, in 1166, the Aragonese leaders seized the opportunity to reclaim for the main branch of the House of Barcelona sovereignty over Provence. By so doing they entered into conflict with Raymond V, Count of Toulouse, husband of the heiress of Provence. Alfonso was to remain embroiled in the tumultuous politics of the Midi for the next thirty years. These concerns generally dictated Alfonso's peninsular policies, and some historians would argue that he sacrificed advantages in the peninsula in order to advance his trans-Pyrenean interests.

In late 1173, Guillem de Moncada and Petronilla died, and Alfonso began to rule directly. In January 1174, he married Sancha of Castile and began to contemplate the conquest of the Muslim kingdom of Valencia. This venture was frustrated by war with Sancho IV of Navarre, however, and Alfonso began to draw even closer to Castile. In March 1179, Alfonso of Aragón and Alfonso VIII of Castile met at Cazorla and entered into a treaty in which they allied against Navarre and in which Alfonso of Aragón agreed that Murcia should be part of the Castilian zone of reconquest. By 1185, his peninsular frontiers were reasonably secure, and he undertook the solidification of his position in the Midi. He took Provence under his direct rule, and brought Béarne, Béziers, Bigorre, and Carcassone into alliance or vassalage.

In 1189, his situation changed unfavorably. Alfonso of Castile entered into an alliance with Frederick Barbarossa, who contemplated returning the county of Provence to direct homage to the Holy Roman Empire, a policy that was to continue under Emperor Henry VI. Alfonso of Aragón broke with Castile and, by 1191, had brought Navarre, León, and Portugal into an anti-Castilian alliance. The Almohad invasion and the defeat of Castilian forces in the Battle of Alarcos (1195) prompted the pope to appeal for Christian unity in the face of this perceived new Muslim menace. During a celebrated pilgrimage to Santiago de Compostela (late 1195–early 1196), Alfonso brought about such unity and laid plans for a crusade against the invaders. His design failed, however. While traveling to his possessions in the Midi, he fell ill, and died at Perpignan 25 April 1096 at the age of forty.

During the reign of Alfonso II, the union of Aragón and Catalonia was established, and the institutions of the Crown of Aragón developed. At the time of his death, the Crown of Aragón was close to becoming a Pyrennean state, interposed between the great powers of France and Castile. In the Iberian Peninsula, it had begun to exercise a role of real leadership among the Christian states. These were substantial accomplishments, but they vanished in the aftermath of the intervention of Pedro II in the Albigensian Crusade and his defeat and death in the Battle of Muret (1213). The reputation of Alfonso II has suffered by the squandering of the opportunities he created.

LYNN H. NELSON

Bibliography

Cabestany, J. "Alfons el Cast," in *Els primers comtes-reis*. Barcelona, 1960. 55–99.

Ventura, J. *Alfons el Cast: El primer comte-rei*. Barcelona, 1961.

ALFONSO III, KING OF ARAGÓN

King of Aragón and Valencia (born, 1236; ruled 1285–1291), son of Pedro III "the Great" and Constanza of Hohenstaufen, Alfonso spent most of his short reign contending, largely successfully, with the political implications of the territorial expansion of the crown begun during the reign of his grandfather, Jaime I (1213–1276), and continued by his father. He inherited not only the peninsular Aragonese territories of Aragón, Catalonia, and Valencia but also papal censure resulting from the seizure of Sicily, his mother's legacy, which his brother and successor, Jaime, inherited and ruled. As if this were not enough, he also inherited disgruntled barons who complained that Pedro's royalist reforms had fundamentally changed the constitution of Aragonese government. Alfonso came to the throne at a moment of political instability. He was in Mallorca at his father's death, in the process of completing the annexation of Mallorca to the Aragonese crown (Ibiza and Minorca followed soon after), and immediately upon his return, in April 1286, was crowned in Zaragoza. His first concern was to pacify the coalition of nobles, newly united with key towns, who had received concessions from Pedro III in 1283 and were determined to negotiate a greater role in royal government. Rather than risk civil war, and believing that Mediterranean expansion mattered more than royal prerogatives, Alfonso made peace with his subjects. In 1287 he granted them the privilege of convoking an annual assembly and pledged to uphold certain key legal protections. He then turned his attention to the problem of Sicily and faced a formidable alliance of hostile Angevins—led by Charles of Valois, who had been deprived of Sicily and in retaliation was designated papal candidate for the Aragonese throne—and their allies, Pope Martin IV and King Philippe IV of France. The political situation, already complicated, worsened after 1288 when King Sancho IV of Castile allied with France against Alfonso; the Infantes de la Cerda (Castilian princes) from Sancho's first marriage, and Charles of Salerno, the king of Naples and son of Charles of Valois, were caught in the middle of the fracas and taken as hostages. Warfare erupted along the border between Castile and Aragón. Alfonso realized the necessity of detaching Aragonese interests from direct involvement in Sicily and agreed at Tarascón, mediated by Edward I of England, to make peace with the Angevins, the pope, and the French. Both sides compromised: the pope agreed to lift his censure and revoke his donation of the kingdom to Charles of Valois; in return, Alfonso agreed to withdraw all support for his brother in Sicily and pledge loyalty to the pope. As part of an alliance with England, Alfonso agreed to marry Edward's daughter Eleanor, but his death just a few months later, in June 1291, rendered both that marriage and the treaty inoperative. He left no heirs, although he may have had an illegitimate son, and it was therefore up to his resourceful brother and successor, Jaime II, to resolve the matter.

THERESA EARENFIGHT

Bibliography

Bisson, T. *The Medieval Crown of Aragon: A Short History*. Oxford, 1986.

Martínez F. J. E., S. Sobrequés i Vidal, and E. Bagué. *Els descendents de Pere el Gran: Alfons del Franc, Jaume II, Alfonso el Benigne*. Barcelona, 1957.

Muntaner, R. *The Chronicle of Muntaner*. 2 vols. Trans. Henrietta Goodenough. London, 1920–21.

Zurita, G. *Anales de la Corona de Aragón*. 8 vols. Ed. A. Canellas López. Books 4–6. Zaragoza, 1967–77.

ALFONSO III, KING OF ASTURIAS

The long reign of Alfonso III (866–910) marks the most brilliant period of the Asturian realm. Taking advantage of the contemporary weakness of Muslim Andalusia, Alfonso continued the work of his father, Ordoño I (850–866), in the repopulation of the northern half of the Duero River basin, founding Zamora and Toro on its banks. Farther east, Burgos was founded in 884 and control over Álava was maintained despite Basque revolts. On the western frontier, the Christian repopulation was pushed south from southern Galicia with foundations at Braga, Oporto, Viseu, and even Coimbra. The king raided as far south as the lands of Badajoz and Mérida.

All of this growth occurred despite serious internal stress at one time or another. At the very beginning of his reign Alfonso had had to take refuge in Castile when a Count Froila of Galicia had briefly claimed to succeed Ordoño. He also had to face a conspiracy of his brother, Vermudo, who was taken and blinded but nevertheless subsequently staged a rebellion in Astorga that endured for roughly seven years and attracted Muslim support.

In fact, Alfonso's successes were such that he seems to have inspired his own, official history. As we now have them, there are three chronicles of the cycle of Alfonso III. One of them derives from Oviedo and the other two from the Navarrese see of Roda and the Navarrese monastery of Albelda; all of them stand in the same tradition; that is, they make the monarchy of Asturias the lineal descendant of the vanished Visigothic kingdom of the sixth and seventh centuries whose destiny it is to reclaim Iberia from the Muslims. In fact, these chronicles are also quite closely associated with those materials jointly described as the *Prophetic Chronicle*. The latter predicted the complete expulsion of the Muslims to occur in 884. These traditions likely antedate the reign of Alfonso himself, but the extent of his achievement and recognition is indicated by their association with him.

Certainly the king himself promoted such traditions, if he did not actually compose the earliest version of the chronicles, as has been asserted. He took pains to reassociate the kingdom with the growing shrine church of Santiago at Compostela. There he had the old church of Alfonso II (791–842) razed and a more splendid one erected. He built a new palace in the royal city of Oviedo. The king also commissioned a distinctive art in architecture and jewelry, the latter being represented by the magnificent "Cross of Victory" of Oviedo.

BERNARD F. REILLY

Bibliography

Collins, R. *Early Medieval Spain*. New York, 1983.

Cotarelo Valledor, A. *Alfonso III el Magno*. Madrid, 1933.

Gil Fernández, J., J. L. Moralejo, and J. I. Ruiz de la Peña, eds. *Crónicas asturianas*. Oviedo, 1985.

ALFONSO IV, KING OF ARAGÓN

King Alfonso IV of Aragón and Valencia (born 1299; ruled 1327–1336), known as "the Benign," was the second son of Jaime II and Blanca of Naples. He was named his father's successor when his elder brother Jaime repudiated his bride on his wedding day, renounced his right to succession, and joined a monastic military order. Alfonso was an able replacement, however, and well suited for governance. In 1322, as a young prince, his father sent him to Sardinia with a force of roughly fifteen thousand Catalans and Aragonese to bring the island under Aragonese control. He successfully fended off opposition from the Genoese, but the threat continued for decades and thwarted his plans to annex Corsica. His personal reign began with abundant optimism and an opulent coronation on Easter Sunday 1328, and he gained his reputation for benevolence partly from his good sense in remaining outside the chaotic fray of politics on the Iberian Peninsula and focusing his attentions on protecting the frontiers, aiding Castile in the defense of the Strait of Gibraltar, and protecting Aragonese privileges in Sardinia. Nevertheless, all of this was overshadowed by his own ill health and the long-term consequences of the death of his first wife, Teresa d'Entença, just before the death of his father. In 1329 he married Leonor of Castile, the woman spurned by his elder brother Jaime. The marriage was intended to cement an alliance of Castile and Aragón in order to fight the Muslims in Granada, but it resulted in an intense and bitter rivalry between his eldest son and heir, Pedro (later Pedro IV, the Ceremonious), and Leonor over her desire to endow her own sons, Fernando and Juan, at the expense of Pedro. To please his wife, Alfonso was obliged to sidestep the act of union, enacted at the *cortes* (parliament) of Tarragona in 1319, that prohibited alienation of royal patrimony. He created the marquisate of Tortosa for Fernando, and later added Alicante, Elche, Orihuela, Albarracín, and other towns in Valencia, an action that enraged the Valencians, who vociferously protested the partition of the realms, arguing that it left them vulnerable to attack from Castile. He later revoked this act, noting that such royal highhandedness was not in keeping with Aragonese kingship and governance. Both the conflict with Castile and bitter antagonism between Leonor and Pedro continued beyond Alfonso's death in 1336, however, and ended with Pedro ordering the execution of Fernando in 1363.

THERESA EARENFIGHT

Bibliography

Bisson, T. *The Medieval Crown of Aragon: A Short History*. Oxford, 1986.

Hillgarth, M., and J. N. Hillgarth (trans.). *Chronicle of Pedro, King of Aragon*. Toronto, 1980.

Martínez Ferrando, J. E., S. Sobrequés i Vidal, and E. Bagué. *Els descendents de Pere el Gran: Alfons del Franc, Jaume II, Alfonso el Benigne*. Barcelona, 1954.

Muntaner, R. *The Chronicle of Muntaner*. 2 vols. Trans. H. Goodenough. London, 1920–21.

ALFONSO IX, KING OF LEÓN

Son of Fernando II and the Portuguese *infanta* (princess) Urraca, daughter of Afonso I Henriques, whose marriage had subsequently been annulled by papal authority. The seventeen-year-old heir acceded to the throne in January 1088. Threatened on the one side by the claims of his stepmother, Urraca López de Haro, for her own child, and on the other by the ambitions of his cousin, Alfonso VIII of Castile (1158–1214), Alfonso took the novel step of summoning to the royal curia in León in April 1188 not only the usual prelates and nobles but also men chosen by some of the towns of the kingdom to speak in their behalf. The *cortes* (parliament) of León that resulted are usually credited, therefore, as being the first known medieval parliament. In that meeting in return for its support, Alfonso agreed not to make war or peace without consultation and to himself obey the laws of the realm. In subsequent *cortes* at Benavente in 1202 he agreed not to issue a new coinage for a period of seven years in return for a grant in aid.

While immediately provoked by the succession crisis of 1188, the novel inclusion of burgher representatives of the towns in the cortes of the realm is a measure of the stature they had achieved in the course of the twelfth century. Overseas trade in important quantities was now reaching the northern coast of Iberia through Gijón and La Coruña. The new king would find almost constant occupation in the adjudication of conflicts between town councils and bishops or abbots in Sahagún, in Lugo, and in Túy. He was also to be kept busy reworking or granting *fueros* (priviliges) to town councils in Castroverde, Sanabria, Mansilla, Oviedo, Zamora, and Toro in the north and to Salamanca, Cáceres, and Alcántara in the south. In 1204 cortes at León made town councils responsible for the maintenance of public order in their surrounding countryside.

But despite the support of the cortes in 1188, Alfonso found himself forced to attend his uncle's curia at Carrión de los Condes in June 1188 where Alfonso VIII personally knighted his cousin and exacted his homage in return. The new king determined to escape from this subjection and in 1191 found an ally in Sancho I of Portugal (1185–1211) whose daughter, Teresa, he married that same year. The two kings then joined further with Alfonso II of Aragón-Barcelona (1162–1196) in a general anti-Castilian alliance, Alfonso IX going so far as to conclude a truce with the Muslim Muwāhhid. The papacy reacted strongly against the ensuing war of Christian against Christian in the Iberian Peninsula and the papal legate Cardinal Gregory forced Alfonso to separate from his cousin, Teresa of Portugal. The kings of Castile and León then agreed in 1194 to a treaty at Tordehumos by which León would be reunited with Castile if Alfonso IX should die without heirs.

When in July 1195 Alfonso VIII of Castile was defeated in a great battle at Alarcos by the Muwāhhid caliph, Abū Yūsuf Ya'qūb, Alfonso of León reacted in 1196 by invading Castile with the aid of some troops furnished by the Muslim. Pope Celestine III excommunicated him. Nevertheless, a solution was provided by Eleanor, wife of Alfonso VIII, who arranged the marriage of their daughter, Berenguela, to Alfonso IX of León in Valladolid in 1197. With the bride, as dowry, went the border territories in dispute between the two monarchs. However, this new marriage between cousins would also be declared null and the principals excommunicated by Pope Innocent III. Nevertheless, the royal match was maintained until 1204 in the face of papal objections. By that time it had produced four children, including the Fernando, who would succeed first to Castile (1217–1252) and then to León as well (1230–1252).

The dissolution of the marriage reopened the border question between León and Castile and kept bad feeling alive amid marching and countermarching interspersed with truces. The result was that León would remain aloof from the great Castilian victory that would lead to the eventual fall of the Muwāhhid Empire in Iberia at Las Navas de Tolosa in July 1212. Alfonso IX was busy on the Portuguese border, where he defeated the forces of their new king, Afonso II (1211–1223), at Valdevez in 1211. During the Castilian campaign itself the Leonese king seized several border fortresses while the Castilians were occupied in the south. Only in November 1212 did the kings of Castile, León, and Portugal sign a truce at Coimbra by which they agreed to cooperate against the Muslims. In the following year Alfonso IX proceeded to the definitive reconquest of Alcántara.

In 1214 Alfonso VIII died, leaving an eleven-year-old son, Enrique, as heir. The next three years saw a continuing struggle to manipulate his person and government in which the contestants were his older sister, Berenguela; Count Alvaro Núñez de Lara; and Alfonso IX of León. No faction managed to gain a decisive advantage, and then the young king died in a domestic accident in 1217. Before Alfonso IX could learn of Enrique's death, agents of Berenguela traveled to the court of the Leonese king and secured the latter's permission to allow his own son by Berenguela, Fernando, to travel to Castile to visit his mother and his cousin. Once Fernando reached Castile, Berenguela hastily arranged a *cortes* in Valladolid in July 1217, in which she ceded her own rights to the throne in favor of her son. Fernando III (1217–1252) was accepted there as the new king of Castile and a tardy invasion by Alfonso IX was unable to overturn that settlement. Nevertheless, skirmishes and conspiracies continued until definitive peace was established in 1220 between the Leonese and the Castilians. A peace was also agreed during that same year between León and Portugal, which had been struggling along the line of the Miño River.

Without threat or great prospects in the north, Alfonso IX was now to turn his attentions to the reconquest. There the Order of Alcántara took Valencia de Alcántara south of the Tajo in 1221, from which position in the northwest they could threaten the whole valley of the Middle Guadiana River from Mérida to Badajoz. Beginning in 1222 Alfonso IX began annual attacks on Cáceres, whose control led the approach from the northeast to those two cities. Each year he returned to the attack but failed to meet his objective. Then, in January 1224, the Muwāhhid caliph al-Mustanṣir died and Muslim power in al-Andalus became increasingly fragmented as one contender after another sought control in Iberia or Morocco. Finally, in 1227, Cáceres fell to Alfonso IX. By 1230 that king was ready for a siege of Mérida. That undertaking called forth a relief army led by Ibn Hūd, former governor of Murcia and then the leader of the Muslim south, but it was defeated soundly at Alange, southeast of the city, and Mérida surrendered in March. The victorious army now moved downstream, where Badajoz promptly surrendered to it as well.

The whole of the upper and middle valleys of the Guadiana was now in Christian hands, but Alfonso IX died on 24 September 1230 while on his way to Santiago de Compostela to offer thanks for his late victories. He was interred in that cathedral. When Fernando III of Castile heard of his father's death he asserted his claim to the kingdom of León. His two half-sisters, born of Alfonso's first marriage to Teresa of Portugal, contested his claim but again his sister Berenguela arranged a settlement with Teresa at Benavente (on 11 December 1230), in which the infantas surrendered their claims in return for generous pensions. As a result, León and Castile were permanently reunited.

BERNARD F. REILLY

Bibliography

Gautier Dalché, J. *Historia urbana de León y Castilla en la Edad Media: Siglos IX–XIII.* Madrid, 1979.

González, J. *Alfonso IX.* 2 vols. Madrid, 1944.

Lomax, D. W. *The Reconquest of Spain.* New York, 1978.

Procter, E. S. *Curia and Cortes in León and Castile, 1072–1295.* New York, 1980.

ALFONSO V, KING OF ARAGÓN, THE MAGNANIMOUS

Born 1396, the eldest son of Fernando of Antequera and Leonor de Alburquerque, Alfonso V passed much of his childhood in the court of his uncle, Enrique III of Castile. Fernando, Victor of Antequera (1410), coregent of Castile from 1406, and from 1412 (Compromise of Caspe) King of Aragón, became the boy's hero, a model of knightly prowess and kingly virtue. An abiding thirst for adventure, deep piety, and a passion for hunting all derived from that paternal source.

Fernando's brief reign in Aragón (1412–1416), besides grounding Alfonso in the arts of government, introduced him to the constitutional pretensions and Mediterranean concerns of his future subjects. Castile remained nonetheless a vital element in the family's dynastic and political calculations, as evidenced by his marriage to María of Castile (1415), a match that proved loveless and barren. Thrust by his father's fatal illness (1415–1416) into the center of affairs, Alfonso found himself confronting the antipope Benedict XIII and Sigismund, King of the Romans, in a meeting called at Perpignan to end the Schism. In this, his first great test of political judgment, he opted for the Council of Constance, yet took care to keep Benedict in reserve as a bargaining counter in dealings with the restored authority of Rome.

On 2 April 1416 Alfonso became King of Aragón. Looking around for warlike ventures that had hitherto eluded him, he saw Sicily and Sardinia restive under Aragonese domination, Genoa challenging Catalan aspirations in Corsica, and Castile chafing at the overweening Antequera presence. His subjects, however, especially the Catalans and Valencians, opposed all foreign projects for they mistrusted their new Castilian dynasty and were resolved to bind it in constitutional fetters. In the succeeding four-year contest of wills he won the upper hand thanks largely to clerical and Castilian subventions, then sailed in high spirits for Italian shores.

Touching first at Sardinia, he subdued that island without difficulty, but in his next objective—Corsica—encountered a desperate Genovese defense. Frustrated there, he moved on to Naples in the guise of champion and adopted heir of Giovanna II against Louis III of Anjou whom Pope Martin V, suzerain of the kingdom, planned to install as successor to the childless queen. Enthusiasm greeted his arrival (July 1421), but the war against Louis soon embroiled him in intrigues that within two years left him totally isolated. Rescued by a Catalan fleet, he embarked for Spain in October 1423, having first sacked Naples; on the homeward voyage he paused to burn Angevin Marseilles.

Spain presented its own problems: Catalan demands for curbs on royal authority, the consequences of a breach with Rome over the Neapolitan investiture, and turmoil in Castile provoked by blind rivalry between his brothers and Álvaro de Luna for control of that kingdom. Against his better judgment he allowed Juan and a party of Castilian nobles to maneuver him into an intervention (1425) that freed another brother, Enrique, from captivity and briefly restored Antequera dominance. Within two years the brothers were again at odds, and Alfonso found himself once more driven to invade Castile. Álvaro Luna countered devastatingly by throwing the Antequera estates to his wavering adherents; a mere handful stirred to support Alfonso, Catalonia denounced the operation, and rebellion threatened in Aragón. His frontiers menaced by vastly superior Castilian forces, Alfonso was compelled to seek a truce that left the Antequera hold upon Castile broken and his own reputation battered. Small wonder that he developed an aversion to further involvement in Castile and seized upon an invitation from the anti-Angevin faction in Naples to prepare another Italian expedition. It cost many substantial concessions to the ruling classes of Catalonia before he could sail again in 1432, leaving his wife and Juan as regents in that province and Aragón, respectively.

Uncertain how matters stood in Naples, he alighted first in Sicily, then essayed a punitive raid against Tunisia that demonstrated his naval power and crusading credentials but deepened the hostility of that Muslim state. An attempt to force the issue in Naples by a show of strength at Ischia (1435) having come to nothing, he had to retire once again to Sicily and wait for the unfolding of events. At this juncture pressure from his brothers threatened to draw him back to Spa, where renewed war loomed with Castile. Orders for return had already been given when news that first Louis of Anjou, then Giovanna, had died transformed his prospects. Supported by all his brothers, he made for the mainland to claim his inheritance.

Yet again, Genoa's fear of a Catalan stranglehold on the western Mediterranean snatched away apparently certain victory. In a battle off Ponza (5 August 1435) its fleet not only destroyed an overconfident enemy but took Alfonso, two brothers, and a host of nobles as prisoners. Hauled, albeit courteously, to Milan—Genoa's overlord—Alfonso looked to all the world a beaten man. Yet by a veritable coup de theatre he transformed his captor, the volatile Visconti duke, into a devoted ally. Together they plotted a condominium over Italy, and early in 1436 Alfonso was once more pursuing his conquest of Naples. Dogged opposition from the papacy, Genoa, and René of Anjou delayed victory for another six years until with the fall of the capital on 2 June 1442 all resistance crumbled. A great triumph had crowned decades of unremitting persistence.

Alfonso now faced a choice between exploiting his Italian victory and returning to Spain, where domestic problems and Castilian complications continued to fester. While always proclaiming his intention to return, he chose instead to spend the rest of his life in Italy, where he enjoyed more unfettered authority, alluring international opportunities, and a stimulating cultural environment. Already he had gathered there his three children—all illegitimate—and proclaimed his only son, Ferdinando, heir to Naples. Wholeheartedly he threw himself into the strife of Italy, seeking to establish a virtual protectorate over the papal states, reduce Genoa to subservience, make good his claim upon Corsica, and secure, despite Venice, a hold upon the eastern shores of the Adriatic. Failure to find a dependable ally frustrated all these ambitions in some measure. Most galling of all was the about-face of his former chancellor, Alfonso Borja, who, once planted on the papal throne as Calixtus III (1455), turned from servitor into implacable foe.

More successfully, Alfonso exploited the commercial potential of his conquest, encouraging Catalans and Valencians to follow royal example. From Flanders to Alexandria royal vessels plied their trade as he wove schemes to integrate his states into an economic community.

Art and learning also fascinated him. From early youth he developed a taste for music and books; later he cultivated interests in architecture, painting, and sculpture. In his maturity these resulted in a library, a musical establishment, and a royal palace (Castelnuovo, Naples) to rival any in Europe. Under his patronage Italian and Spanish men of arts and letters brought the Renaissance to life in southern Italy and sowed its seed in Spain.

Ambitious, inscrutable, politically shrewd, and an indefatigable administrator, Alfonso V devoted himself conscientiously to his duty in the conviction that royal authority divinely ordained better served the common good than did the play of private interest. In war he displayed tenacity, courage, and a sense of mission rather than brilliant generalship. Sobriety marked his behavior as man and king, save for the occasional display of magnificence, and his autumnal passion for Lucrezia d'Alagno, a young Neapolitan.

He died on 27 June 1458, leaving Naples to his son and his other dominions to his brother Juan.

Alan Ryder

Bibliography

Ametller y Vinyas, J. *Alfonso V de Aragón en Italia y la crisis religiosa del siglo XV*. 3 vols. Gerona, 1903–1928.

Beccadelli, A. *De dictis et factis Alphonsi regis Aragonum et Neapolis*. Basel, 1538.

Pontieri, E. *Alfonso il Magnanimo: Re di Napoli 1435–1458*. Naples, 1975.

Ryder, A. *Alfonso the Magnanimous, King of Aragón, Naples and Sicily, 1396–1458*. Oxford, 1990.

ALFONSO V, KING OF LEÓN

When Vermudo II died in 999 he left his five-year-old son, Alfonso V (999–1028), in most difficult circumstances. The great vizier of the Córdoban caliphate, Al-Manṣūr, was at the height of his power. He had taken and sacked Barcelona in 987, León and Zamora in 988, and most recently Santiago de Compostela in 997, destroying there the church built by Alfonso III and carrying off its bells to decorate the mosque in Córdoba. Vermudo II sought a five-year truce before he died, and Al-Manṣūr himself died in 1002 but his son, ʿAbd al-Malik (reigned 1002–1008) kept up the policy of raids against the north until his early death.

That latter event coincided with the beginning of the personal rule of Alfonso V in 1008. His mother, the queen mother Elvira, and the Galician count Menendo González had had to bear the brunt of the Muslim assault during his minority. The death of ʿAbd al-Malik also precipitated the abrupt decline of the caliphate and Muslim Andalusia so that the threat from that quarter was effectively removed. What would concern Alfonso V most was the growing ascendancy of Sancho García el mayor of Navarre (1000–1035).

Alfonso managed to maintain his own independence of action during his lifetime but found it politic to marry Urraca, the sister of the Navarrese King Sancho. Still, he was unable to forestall the increasing influence of Sancho in Castile, traditionally a county of the Leonese kingdom. The Navarrese contrived his own marriage with the sister of its count, García Sánchez (1017–1029), and would claim the county for himself after the murder of the count in 1029.

The Leonese monarch would be chiefly remembered for the council of the realm held at León in 1017, which took measures to restore the regular government of the kingdom and of that rebuilt city. He did prove as well to be quite capable in taking advantage of the contemporary Muslim weakness to restore the fortunes of León. In 1028 he was conducting a siege of Muslim Viseu in the north of Portugal when he was killed by an arrow.

His early death left an eleven-year-old son, Vermudo III (reigned 1028–1037), to succeed him in a realm actually ruled by the queen mother Urraca, Sancho of Navarre's sister.

Bernard F. Reilly

Bibliography

Sánchez Candeira, A. *El Regnum-Imperium leonés hasta 1037*. Madrid, 1951.

ALFONSO VI, KING OF LEÓN-CASTILE

The second son of Fernando I, King of León-Castile (1037–1065), he was born about 1037. On the death of Fernando I the kingdom was divided between Alfonso and his two brothers. Sancho, the eldest, received the kingdom of Castile and the overlordship of the tributary Christian kingdom of Navarre as well as that of the Muslim *tā'ifa* (party kingdom) of Zaragoza. García, the youngest, was awarded Galicia-Portugal and the tributary Muslim kingdom of Badajoz. To Alfonso went Asturias, León, parts of the Bierzo and the Sorian highlands, and the tributary tā'ifa of Toledo. The division did not last long. In 1071 Alfonso took control of the lands of García and in 1072 was himself defeated in battle and dispossessed briefly by his brother Sancho in 1072. After a short term of exile in Toledo, Alfonso returned after the assassination of Sancho, outside the walls of Zamora in September 1072, and now became the ruler of the reconstituted kingdom of his father. When García returned from exile in Badajoz in 1073, Alfonso had him imprisoned until the former's death in March 1090.

The kingdom of León-Castile grew under Alfonso VI to be the greatest realm of the peninsula, Christian or Muslim. The major step in this process was the conquest of the tā'ifa of Toledo, which formally surrendered on 25 May 1085. With that success, the southern boundary of the kingdom was carried from the north bank of the Duero River to the north bank of the Tajo River. It enabled Alfonso to carry out the repopulation of the northern *meseta* (plateau) between the Duero and the Guadarrama Mountains unhindered and to begin that of the southern meseta between the Guadarrama and the Tajo. For a brief time the kingdom even included the old Toledan lands south of the Tajo and north of the Sierra Morena. Moreover, on the assassination of the king of Navarre, his cousin Sancho García IV (1054–1076), Alfonso participated with the King of Aragón, his cousin Sancho Ramírez I (1063–1094), in the partition of Navarre. León-Castile's share was most of the upper Rioja along the Ebro River.

The surrender of Toledo to Alfonso VI in 1085 was followed by his installation of the former Muslim ruler there, Al-Qādir, in the tā'ifa of Valencia in the east as his tributary. Since the other Muslim kings in Iberia, from Zaragoza through Granada, Seville, and Badajoz, were also his tributaries, the Leonese was virtually master of the entire peninsula. Under the circumstances, the Muslim rulers of the south appealed to the Murābit emir, Yūsuf Ibn Tāshfīn of Morocco, for protection. The Murābit were a Berber fundamentalist sect who from midcentury had been gradually overrunning Morocco and by this date controlled an empire stretching from the southern Sahara to the Mediterranean with its capital at the newly built Marrakesh.

In 1086 in response to the appeal of the Muslims of Andalusia, the Murābit crossed the Strait of Gibraltar. They advanced to the neighborhood of Badajoz where, with their Andalusian allies, they defeated the army of Alfonso VI at Zallāqah on 23 October 1086. Although Alfonso and much of his army escaped, he was to spend the remainder of his life battling to defend his realm against the Murābit.

In the aftermath of Zallāqah, the fundamentalist Murābit were to depose, one by one, the rulers of the Iberian tā'ifas whom they considered unfaithful to the Qur'ān because of their imposition of illegal taxes on the faithful; their use of alcohol, music, and poetry; and their payment of tribute to Alfonso VI, an infidel, above all. Gradually Muslim Iberia became the province of a North African empire. Yūsuf annexed Granada in 1090, Seville in 1091, and Badajoz in 1094. Valencia eluded him until 1102 when it was conquered by the Castilian adventurer Rodrigo Díaz de Vivar, usually called El Cid, who held it until his death in 1099. Zaragoza remained independent until 1110, by which time both Alfonso VI and Yūsuf Ibn Tāshfīn were dead. The Leonese monarch was the major Murābit opponent in all of this and defended the independence of the tā'ifas as best he could. Yet by his death in 1109, he had been forced back to the line of the Tajo and it was unclear if even the north bank of that river and the city of Toledo itself could be held.

At the same time, León-Castile was entering into a much closer relationship with Europe north of the Pyrenees. Fernando I had sealed a pact of friendship with the great Burgundian monastery of Cluny and agreed to subsidize that house in the amount of 1,000 gold *dinars* per annum. Alfonso VI would double that census and, in addition, begin the process of granting possession and authority over Leonese royal monasteries to the French house. By the end of his reign the Cluniac province in his kingdom counted better than a half-dozen houses. This cooperation with Cluny was joined to a similar policy of close ties with the Roman church. At the urging of Pope Gregory VII, Alfonso agreed to see that the Roman liturgical ritual replaced the Mozarabic one. In return he received the support of Rome for the restoration of the metropolitan sees of Braga and Toledo, the bishoprics of Salamanca, Segovia, Osma, Burgos, and Coimbra, and the recognition of the older royal creation at Oviedo. The former Cluniac monk Bernard was recognized by Pope Urban II as archbishop of Toledo in 1088, and that archbishop and his king and patron would fill up most of the new sees created with reforming French Cluniac monks.

These processes were accompanied by a rapid growth of the pilgrimage to the shrine of St. James at Santiago de Compostela by the peoples of western Europe. This also meant the infusion of the new Romanesque art, the Carolingian script, a more rigorous Latin, and a variety of other French manners into León-Castile. The great Romanesque cathedral at Santiago de Compostela, begun in 1076, is the most monumental example of this phenomenon. Most larger towns, even Toledo in the extreme south, would come to have their *barrio* (quarter) of French artisans and merchants as a side effect of the pilgrimage but there was no significant immigration of French nobles such as would shortly take place in Aragón.

In that respect, the most significant development was the marriage by Alfonso VI to a succession of foreign brides for his queens as he sought both a male heir and the prestige of an international match for its effect in the peninsula. Inés of Aquitaine (1074–1077), Constance of Burgundy (1078–1093), Berta of Lombardy (1095–1100), Elizabeth of France (1100–1106), and Béatrice of France (1108–1109) were such brides. On the other hand, Alfonso's only known son, Sancho Alfónsez (1094?–1108), was the son of the Muslim concubine Zaida, who became his wife in 1106 and died shortly thereafter.

The Burgundian alliance was also to be reflected in the marriage of Alfonso's daughter by Constance, Urraca, to Count Raymond of Burgundy who became Count of Galicia-Portugal and probably heir apparent in 1088. That match was followed by a similar marriage of a daughter by the Asturian noblewoman Jimena Muñoz, Teresa, to Raymond's cousin, Count Henri of Burgundy in 1096. Henri thus became Count of Portugal. The son of Raymond and Urraca was to become Alfonso VII of León-Castile (1126–1157). The son of Henri and Teresa was to become Afonso I of Portugal (1128–1185). In the lifetime of Alfonso VI the two counts were to become chief figures at his court and administrators and defenders of the west during the campaigning season. Another daughter, Elvira, born of Jimena Muñoz, was married to Count Raymond of Toulouse by 1094 and subsequently bore him a son in the Holy Land, Alfonso Jordán, who himself later became count of Toulouse.

In the spring of 1108 Alfonso VI was still engrossed in defending his realm from the attacks of the Murābit emirs of Morocco. On 29 May 1108 at the fortress of Uclés, about thirty kilometers south of the Tajo, one of his armies was routed by the enemy and his only son, Sancho Alfónsez, was killed. To solve the succession crisis the king turned to his daughter, Urraca (1109–1126), whose husband Raymond of Burgundy had died in November 1107. But he also provided for her future marriage to her cousin, Alfonso I, el Batallador, of Aragón (1104–1134), so as to provide for the military safety of the kingdom. Alfonso VI himself was seeing to those defenses at Toledo when he died on 1 July 1109, at the age of seventy-two. He was buried at the royal monastery of Sahagún on 21 July 1109.

BERNARD F. REILLY

Bibliography

Fletcher, R. A. *The Quest for El Cid*. New York, 1990.

González, J. *Repoblación de Castilla la Nueva*. 2 vols. Madrid, 1975–76.

Lomax, D. W. *The Reconquest of Spain*. New York, 1978.

Reilly, B. F. *The Kingdom of León-Castilla under King Alfonso VI, 1065–1109*. Princeton, N.J., 1988.

ALFONSO VII, KING OF LEÓN-CASTILE

Born on 1 March 1105 to the Infanta Urraca and Count Henri of Burgundy, the child was early to have a political influence. After his mother's accession to the crown of León-Castile the boy became a pawn in the hands of his powerful guardians, Bishop Diego Gelmírez of Santiago de Compostela and Count Pedro Froílaz of Galicia, in their opposition to the queen's policies. That game was not ended until Urraca associated her young son with herself in 1116, made him the titular ruler of Toledo and the lands south of the Duero River, and largely separated him from his prior mentors.

Upon his mother's death on 8 March 1126, he became Alfonso VII but had to face a wide variety of problems in the early years of his reign. One of these was the emerging kingdom of Portugal. Once a frontier county of León-Castile, the territory had enjoyed practical independence since the death of his grandfather, Alfonso VI (1065–1109). By 1126 his aunt, Teresa, who ruled there had adopted the title "queen" from 1117. When Teresa's own son, Afonso Henriques, forced her into exile in 1128, he affected the title "Infans" initially but by 1140 had come to call himself "Rex Portugalensis." His Leonese cousin fought two border wars with him in 1137 and 1140–1141 to forestall what was happening, but after the second of them the latter had to recognize Afonso I of Portugal (1128–1185) as king, if a vassal of León-Castile.

A second problem was to establish himself at home against the nobility of the realm. The chief threat was furnished by the house of the Lara counts of Castile and Asturias de Santillana, under Pedro and Rodrigo González, respectively. Count Pedro had been the third husband of Queen Urraca and the father of at least two children by her. The Lara thus represented a real threat and the Lara counts fomented a series of conspiracies and finally a rebellion in 1130 before their power was broken in that year. The same year had also seen an independent revolt by the magnate Diego Peláez in Asturias de Oviedo that recurred intermittently until 1134, by which time all internal resistance was at an end.

While coping with these two as best he could, Alfonso VII also had to deal with the problem of another stepfather, Alfonso I of Aragón (1104–1134). The Aragonese monarch had been married to Queen Urraca between 1109 and 1112. The marriage was consanguinous, foundered on the opposition of the papacy, the nobility of the realm, and its inability to produce a child. But Alfonso I had fought a war with Urraca between 1113 and 1116 to retain his title to León-Castile and still in 1126 held the Rioja, the Sorian highlands, eastern Castile, and a salient reaching west into León as far as Carrión de los Condes. Between 1127 and 1131, Alfonso VII waged a series of campaigns against his stepfather that resulted in the liberation of all of this territory up to the borders of the Rioja.

Alfonso I of Aragón had largely been preoccupied by the consolidation of his hold on the lands of the *tā'ifa* (party) kingdom of Zaragoza, which had fallen to him in December 1118 and had roughly quadrupled his prior realm in size and population. Now a Murābit counterattack inflicted a crushing defeat on him at Fraga on 17 July 1134, and Alfonso died on 7 September 1134, probably of wounds suffered there. The makeshift kingdom of Aragón now began to disintegrate. Ramiro II of Aragón (1134–1137) never was able to make his authority felt everywhere. To the northeast, García Ramírez IV (1134–1150) resurrected the former kingdom of Navarre out of its ruins. Alfonso VII seized the opportunity to reclaim the Rioja and the Sorian highlands, and attempted to annex the district around Zaragoza and Tarazona on the Middle Ebro. A three-cornered war erupted that lasted until 1142.

By 1137 Alfonso VII was forced to allow Count Ramón Berenguer of Barcelona (1131–1162) to rule in Aragón and the territories of Zaragoza. The count had been his brother-in-law since 1127, and had become the son-in-law of Ramiro II of Aragón in 1137 by marriage to the latter's daughter, Petronilla. Now Ramón Berenguer became the ruler of the kingdom of Aragón-Catalonia, although he did homage to Alfonso VII for Zaragoza. The Leonese king had also made peace with García Ramírez of Navarre in 1140, and that king did homage as well. With these rulers as his vassals, Alfonso now arranged his own coronation as "emperor" in the city of León on Pentecost, 26 May 1135.

Although the details of his domestic policy are not well understood, he kept a firm hand on the church of the realm. In the Council of Carrión in February 1130, for instance, he had the bishops of León, Oviedo, and Salamanca deposed and replaced by his own candidates. Alfonso also actively pursued the repopulation of the valley of the Tajo River at the same time as he pushed its frontiers south against the weakening Muslim foe. From the time when peace had been achieved with Navarre and Portugal by 1142, Alfonso VII's policy was bent on securing a coalition of the Christian powers against the Murābit Empire in the Iberian Peninsula. That Muslim empire was already being cannibalized in North Africa by the growing successes of the new, fundamentalist Muwāhhid movement and was rife with revolt in Andalusia. In 1146, Alfonso laid siege to Córdoba itself and forced its ruler to become his vassal. The following year, at the head of a force that included a fleet from Genoa, the Aragonese under Ramón Berenguer, and the the Navarrese under García Ramírez, Alfonso captured the Mediterranean port of Almería in the southeast after overruning most of Upper Andalusia.

Meanwhile, Afonso I of Portugal had taken Santarém in a surprise attack that March and, joined by a Flemish and English fleet bound for Palestine and the Second Crusade there, that monarch captured Lisbon in October 1147. Portions of that crusading army joined Ramón Berenguer and the Genoese fleet in 1148 to take Tortosa. In 1149, the Aragonese king took Lérida. In short, the northern coalition had permanently freed the basin of the Tajo in Portugal, and that of the Ebro in Aragón-Catalonia from the grip of Islam.

In subsequent years, Alfonso VII was unable to keep his allies in the field against the growing power of the Muwāhhid Empire, which had now mastered all of Morocco and Algeria in North Africa and was increasingly active in Andalusia. While the Portuguese and the Aragonese-Catalonian kingdoms would retain their gains of the period, Alfonso VII himself would meet his death from exhaustion at Las Fresnedas just north of the Sierra Morena on 21 August 1157. He was returning from an unsuccessful attempt to force the lifting of a Muwāhhid siege of Almería. That town fell again into Muslim hands, as would all of Upper Andalusia eventually.

After his death, Alfonso's León-Castile was divided into two kingdoms. His oldest son, Sancho III (1157–1158), would rule Old and New Castile, the Rioja, and the Basque country. His younger son, Fernando II (1157–1188), obtained León, Galicia, and Estremadura.

BERNARD F. REILLY

Bibliography

González, J. *Repoblación de Castilla la Nueva.* 2 vols. Madrid, 1975.

Recuero Astray, M. *Alfonso VII, Emperador.* León, 1979.

Reilly, B. F. *The Contest of Christian and Muslim Spain: 1031–1157.* Oxford, 1991.

Sánchez Belda, L. (ed.) *Chrónica Adefonsi Imperatoris.* Madrid, 1950.

ALFONSO VIII, KING OF CASTILE

Alfonso VIII (1155–1214; king of Castile, 1158–1214) was the son of Sancho III of Castile and Blanche of Navarre, grandson of Alfonso VII of León-Castile. Among the main points of Alfonso's long reign are the battles of Alarcos (1195) and Las Navas de Tolosa (1212); the siege of Cuenca (1177) and the granting of its *fuero* (privileges); and, together with his consort, Eleanor, the foundation of the monastery of Las Huelgas.

Alfonso's Minority

Alfonso's reign began inauspiciously. Orphaned by the death of his father, Alfonso's minority was marked by unrest and civil war. In his will Sancho III had divided the regency and the tutelage of the king between the noble families of Lara and Castro. The Laras forced the Castros to surrender Alfonso to them, and a civil war broke out between the two families. The Castros invited Alfonso's uncle, Fernando II of León, to intervene in the matter. Fernando II garrisoned his troops in Toledo and collected its revenues until 1166. He acted as Alfonso's tutor, although he never gained custody of Alfonso himself. In 1166 the Castilian bishops intervened and threw their support behind Alfonso VIII and the Laras. Alfonso and his regent regained Toledo and defeated the Castros in a series of campaigns that lasted from 1166 until 1168.

Alfonso's Reign

The end of Alfonso's minority in 1169 was marked by a curia in Burgos, which reviewed Castile's alliances with the other peninsular kingdoms. Alfonso's relations with other kings in the Iberian Peninsula varied, depending upon the relative strengths and weaknesses of the peninsular kingdoms. He maintained peaceful relations with his uncle, Fernando II, and he established friendly relations with Alfonso II of Aragón, making a pact with him in Sahagún in 1168. Sancho VI of Navarre, however, had invaded the Rioja and issued fueros there in 1164. Seeking an alliance outside the peninsula in order to regain these territories, the young king held a curia in Burgos in 1169–1170 that selected Eleanor, daughter of Henry II and Eleanor of Aquitaine, as a prospective consort for the king. The marriage took place in 1170. Eleanor had been chosen as a prospective spouse in order to gain Henry II's support for the recovery of Castilian lands from Navarre; portions of Eleanor's dower consisted of the parts of Castile occupied by Sancho VI. Castile began to recover its lands in the Rioja in 1170–1179, and went to war with Navarre in 1173. Alfonso VIII and Sancho IV agreed to arbitration before Henry II in 1176–1179, who found in favor of Alfonso VIII.

Relations with the Almohads

The Almohads had occupied most of the towns of al-Andalus in the 1160s, and by 1172 they were campaigning in the vicinity of Toledo, harassing Huete and Talavera. During this period Alfonso VIII entrusted most of the defense and resettlement of the Toledo frontier to the military religious orders of Santiago and Calatrava. In 1177 Castile, León, and Aragón agreed to the Treaty of Tarazona, in which they planned their campaigns against the Muslims. As a consequence of this treaty, Alfonso undertook the siege of Cuenca, a naturally fortified city east of Toledo located on Castile's border with Valencia. Although no contemporary narrative account of the siege survives, other evidence suggests that the siege sapped the resources of both Alfonso and the Castilian nobility. Alfonso captured the city of Cuenca, marking his first major military victory. He established a bishopric there, and Cuenca formed Castile's nucleus of repopulation for the La Mancha area. The major legal development of Alfonso VIII's reign was the implementation and granting of the Fuero of Cuenca, a systematic municipal law that became a model for later fueros.

Prelude to Alarcos

With the Treaty of Cazorla (1179), Alfonso VIII and Alfonso II agreed upon a division of the Muslim territories in the peninsula between Castile and Aragón. Aragón would expand in the territories to its south: Valencia, Játiva, Biar, Denia, and Calpe; Castile had free play in all the lands beyond. But after Cazorla, relations cooled between Castile and Aragón, and in 1190 Alfonso II joined forces with Sancho VI of Navarre against Castile. Meanwhile, Fernando II of León died in 1188, and Alfonso VIII tried to gain ascendancy over the new king, his cousin Alfonso IX. At the Curia of Carrión (1188), Alfonso VIII knighted Alfonso IX, who in return paid him homage and fealty. This act ultimately caused Alfonso IX to resent Alfonso VIII. León joined with Aragón and Portugal in a pact against Alfonso VIII, although the Treaty of Tordehumos (1194) patched up a temporary peace between León and Castile.

Alarcos

Al-Manṣūr, the Almohad caliph, proclaimed a holy war in retaliation against the Christians in June 1195. That summer he arrived in the vicinity of Alarcos, where Alfonso VIII rushed to meet him. The fortress of Alarcos was still uncompleted, and Alfonso initiated the engagement before expected Leonese reinforcements arrived. His impetuosity lost the battle; Alarcos was a major victory for the Almohads. Alfonso VIII fled with the remnants of his army to Toledo, while Al-Manṣūr captured the fortresses on the road to Toledo, including Calatrava, and ravaged Toledo's hinterlands. He did not, however, pursue his victory, and returned to Seville. Alfonso VIII obtained a treaty from the Almohads in 1197.

Aftermath of Alarcos

The defeat at Alarcos caused a crisis in Christian Spain. Alfonso II of Aragón attempted to promote peace among the Christian kings against the Almohads, but he died in 1196. Sancho VII of Navarre resumed attacks upon the Rioja, and Alfonso IX continued to attack Castile, claiming certain castles on the Castilian-Leonese border. Alfonso VIII's wife, Eleanor, proposed a marriage alliance between Alfonso IX and her daughter, Berenguela. The marriage took place in 1197, and the disputed castles were settled on Berenguela. But since the couple were cousins the pope forced them to separate, and they did so in 1204. The Treaty of Cabreros (1206) ended the marriage between Alfonso IX and Berenguela but recognized their son, Fernando, as Alfonso IX's heir. Berenguela and her two sons returned to Alfonso VIII's court. The Treaty of Valladolid (1209) settled the property issues raised by the annulment of the marriage.

Northern Campaigns

The treaty with the Almohads and the alliance with León enabled Alfonso to concentrate on the Navarrese incursions and to campaign in the Basque provinces of Guipúzcoa and Álava. He sought assistance from his brother-in-law, John of England, in 1199, and in 1200 he and Eleanor agreed to the marriage of their second daughter, Blanche, to Philip Augustus's heir, the future Louis VIII, as part of the treaty between England and France. But John and Philip Augustus resumed their fight, and John made a treaty with Sancho VII of Navarre. In turn, Alfonso VIII and Philip Augustus entered into alliance. Eventually, the kings of Castile, Navarre, and Aragón entered into a concord in 1204, and Alfonso VIII obtained the lands disputed with Navarre by treaty in 1207.

Gascony

Though Part of Eleanor's dowry, John refused to surrender Gascony after the death of Eleanor of Aquitaine in 1204. At the risk of war with Navarre and England, Alfonso campaigned in Gascony, but despite some initial success he was unable to secure Bayonne. Castile did not drop its claims to Gascony until the marriage of Eleanor of Castile to Edward I in 1254.

Prelude to Las Navas

Meanwhile, Pope Innocent III urged the bishops of the Iberian Peninsula to encourage the monarchs there to patch up their quarrels and resume the Reconquest. Rodrigo Jiménez de Rada, archbishop of Toledo, took a leading role in urging Alfonso to wage a crusade against the Almohads. The treaty with the Almohads was running out, and Alfonso's settlement of Moya in 1209 helped precipitate matters. Pedro II of Aragón began capturing cities in Valencia, and Alfonso VIII's heir, Fernando, dedicated himself to crusade.

Las Navas

In response to Christian raids and incursions, the Almohad caliph, Al-Nāṣir (called Miramamolín by the Christians), entered the peninsula and took the road to Toledo in 1211. He besieged the castle of Salvatierra, the home of the Order of Calatrava after Alarcos. The castle did not surrender until the end of the summer, and Al-Nāṣir returned to Córdoba to resume his campaigns the following year. This gave the Christians time to assemble an army in Toledo, consisting of Castilians, Leonese, Navarrese, Aragonese, and French troops, who left after the recapture of Calatrava. When the army set out it was led by three kings, Alfonso VIII, Pedro II, and Sancho VII. The battle took place on 16 July 1212, and it marked a major victory for the Christian forces. Alfonso VIII and his daughter, Berenguela, sent reports of the battle to Innocent III and Blanche of Castile, and the trophies from the battle were distributed over Christian Spain. The victory of Las Navas destroyed Almohad power in Spain and enabled the advance of the Christians in the thirteenth century.

Succession

Alfonso and Eleanor had ten children: Berenguela (1180–1246), who was proclaimed Alfonso's heir at the curia of Carrión in 1188 and who was first betrothed to Conrad of Germany, but married her cousin, Alfonso IX of León; Sancho (1181); Sancha (1182–1184); Urraca (1186–1220), who married Alfonso II of Portugal in 1208; Blanche (1188–1252), who married Louis VIII of France in 1199; Fernando (1189–1211); Mafalda (?–1204); Leonor (?–?), who was briefly married to Jaime the Conqueror; Constanza (?–1243); and Enrique (1204–1215), later Enrique II. Despite his numerous progeny, Alfonso's succession was clouded by the death of his oldest surviving son, Fernando, during the campaigns prior to Las Navas. Fernando had been unmarried, and Alfonso's other surviving son, Enrique, was ten years old when Alfonso died. Queen Eleanor, who had been named in Alfonso's will as Enrique's regent, only survived her spouse by one month. Enrique II's minority, like his father's, was marred by civil war. But Enrique died in 1215, and the throne devolved to his sister, Alfonso's oldest daughter, Berenguela. Berenguela stood aside in favor of her son, Fernando III.

Burial

Alfonso VIII and Eleanor had jointly founded the Cistercian monastery of Las Huelgas in Burgos and endowed it with numerous privileges and properties. The complex included a hospital and convent. It also served as a royal necropolis, and the pair were buried there in a joint tomb.

Theresa M. Vann

Bibliography

González, J. *El reino de Castilla en la época de Alfonso VIII*. 3 vols. Madrid, 1960.

ALFONSO X, EL SABIO, KING OF CASTILE AND LEÓN, ARTISTIC PATRONAGE, ART, MINIATURES, AND PORTRAITS

Alfonso X's artistic patronage, well documented in the realm of the illuminated manuscript book, is more uncertain in other areas. The research of Rafael Cómez Ramos is the necessary starting point of departure for the study of Alfonso's patronage of architecture, sculpture, and metalwork.

In the field of architecture, Alfonso's patronage appears to have been extended to two great thirteenth-century cathedrals, at Burgos and León, but not to a well-documented degree. The king seems also to have played a decisive role in the construction of the more modest cathedral of Badajoz. His intervention in these projects cannot, however, be compared to that of the French monarchs who collaborated through their patronage in the construction of the great cathedrals in and around Paris. The kings of France were both anointed and buried in their immense cathedrals, such as Saint-Denis, the first Gothic building in history, and Reims, where they received the crown of the realm from princes of the Church. Alfonso, however, according to his two surviving wills and testaments, vacillated between being interred in the Capilla Real of the Cathedral of Córdoba (which he had constructed ca. 1263) and two other former mosques that had been converted into churches: Santa María la Real of Murcia, and the Cathedral of Seville, where his parents, Fernando II and Beatriz of Swabia, had been buried. This indecision proved disagreeable to the bishops of each locale, who later allied themselves with the cities and the aristocracy and threw their support to the Infante don Sancho when he rebelled against his father.

Sancho IV, in his eponymous *Privilegio rodado e historiado*, referred to himself as the vicar of Christ in his kingdoms and forged an agreement with the bishops who aided him in the usurpation of the throne to be buried in the Cathedral at Toledo, where he had been crowned. At the same time, Alfonso X's tendency toward autocracy and absolutism, which, according to Peter Linehan, compelled the Vatican to investigate, also does not sit well with the notion of a patron who looked kindly on the construction of great cathedrals, even though he may have made some tentative gestures in this direction at the beginning of his reign. This notwithstanding, a case may be made for an Alfonsine ecclesiastical architecture in Andalusia, in the parishes of Córdoba, Jerez, and Seville, as well as for evidence of patronage in civil works (palaces, some strongholds, and the Ataranzas of Seville).

The sculpture and images of the cathedrals of Burgos and León have been the subject of recent careful scrutiny. The putative likenesses of Alfonso X and Doña Violante at Burgos have been shown to be problematic: they have been identified by Yarza as portraits of Solomon and Queen Sab, in an iconographical scheme much more attune to French traditions. They are additionally complicated by the fact that in all extant Alfonsine miniatures the king never appears with his consort. Alfonso's supposed representation in a stained glass window at León has been identified by Domínguez Rodríguez as that of Sancho IV, who bears an orb and scepter in his hands, symbols that closely identify Sancho with his ecclesiastical consecration, evidence of which cannot be found for Alfonso from among all his known manuscript portraits.

It is in the field of manuscript portraiture and illumination that Alfonso X's artistic patronage excelled and cannot be doubted. Alfonso's greatest labor in this area are the *Cantigas de Santa María*, of which there are two manuscripts that contain miniatures. The first is the so-called *Códice rico* (Escorial T.I.1 and Biblioteca Nazionale, Firenze Ms. B.R.20) and the *Códice princeps*, also referred to as *de los músicos* (Escorial B.I.2). The latter embraces forty-one miniatures, and although it is a work of secondary artistic merit has great historical, archeological, and musicological value. The miniatures in it show musical instruments in great detail while the text offers musical annotations that have permitted the reconstruction of the instruments and the reproduction of the music in modern times.

In contrast to his contemporary French and English monarchs, Alfonso did not occupy himself with the decoration of religious and liturgical books and psalters with miniatures, although some attempts have been made to tie his work to the Parisian tradition. While St. Louis was entirely compatible with the Church, which heaped its blessings upon him, Alfonso was much less so. The iconography of the *Códice rico* of the *Cantigas* portrays the Spanish king in diverse guises and poses: as a troubadour, with Christ and the Virgin occupying in a manner unprecedented anywhere a space normally reserved for saints or members of the clergy, lecturing to followers, or reciting poetry in public. His scientific works (*Lapidario*, *Libros del saber de astronomía*, *Manuscrito astrológico vaticano*) all have ties to pagan astrology, under interdiction by both the Church and the papacy, while his *Libro de ajedrez* (Escorial T.I.6), which the king recommends in the prologue for both leisure and the sharpening of wits, was proscribed by St. Louis in France. When compared to St. Louis, who publicly praised the Bible Moralisé, or the Bolognese Bibles based on the Vulgate, all with moralized commentaries and interpretations, Alfonso sought a direct translation of the Bible even from Hebrew sources. He sought to carry out more literal interpretations of it, too, when he incorporated parts of it, along with classical and Arabic sources, into his *General estoria*.

The miniatures in Alfonso's works have been compared by Domínguez Rodríguez with *De arte venandi cum avibus* and *De balneis puteolanis* from the south of Italy by King Manfred, the successor of Frederick II of Sicily. Both Manfred and Alfonso most likely found common ground in Byzantine and Islamic sources and antecedents. Gonzalo Menéndez Pidal has also pointed out the similarity of many Alfonsine miniatures to those from the Latin kingdom of Jerusalem, an observation that surely deserves further investigation.

Alfonso's second greatest illuminated work after the *Cantigas* is his *Lapidario*. Each of these books was designed to be exhibited on a book stand and they are the only extant works comparable to the Bibles Moralisés and the Bolognese Bibles, the greatest works of miniatures of the thirteenth century in Europe. The miniatures in the remaining Alfonsine books are of lesser quality and are not independent of the text, having been placed at the end of chapters as illustrations of content. However, the *Estoria de España* (Escorial Y.I.2) is of note for its portrayal of the heros and monuments of antiquity, done with a distinct sensibility that eschews the traditional Gothic way of representing them. The manuscripts of Alfonso's *Primera partida* (British Library Ms. Add. 20,787) and the *Libro de los juegos de ajedrez, dados y tablas* (Escorial T.I.6) are also of note for the number of miniatures they contain. In contrast, the Vatican manuscript of the *General estoria* (Ms. Urb. Lat. 539), the fourth and only original Alfonsine part of this work to be preserved, contains only one miniature.

The sole surviving contemporary portraits of Alfonso are the ones that appear in his illuminated manuscripts, identified by their placement as frontispieces or in the narrative prologues of the works. At the same time, there are several portrayals of the king as a troubadour or as the recipient of a miracle in the *Cantigas*. He is recognizable in the latter by means of his clothing and the heraldic images on it. Later images contained in works such as the later fourteenth-century *Cartulario de Tojo Outos* (Arch. Hist. Nacional, Ms. 1.302), where he appears with Doña Violante, cannot be considered faithful images of the king. In the frontispieces of his works, Alfonso is generally portrayed as an author, sitting on his throne, right hand and index finger extended upright, dictating to his scribes who are sitting on the floor around him as courtiers listen and observe. These images imply the king's active participation in the creation of these works or their prologues. He is depicted in this way in the *Cantigas*, the *General estoria*, the *Estoria de España*, and the *Libro de los juegos*. Aristotle, who appears as a bearded sage in oriental garb surrounded by his disciples, is portrayed as the author of the *Lapidario*. In the latter, an image of Alfonso may be found in the first chapter receiving the book from its kneeling translator. Finally, the manuscript of the *Primera partida* offers three successive portraits of the king: one as the legislating sovereign with closed book in one hand and drawn sword in the other; another as a scholar dictating to his scribes; and a final one kneeling, looking up toward God in an act of reverence, with the book in his hands, an image that sustains Alfonso's absolutism and the notion that the king's legislative power comes from on high.

ANA DOMÍNGUEZ RODRÍGUEZ

Bibliography

Aita, N. "Miniature spagnole in un codie fiorentinol." *Rassegna d'Arte* 19 (1919), 149–55.

———. *0 codice fiorentino das Cantigas do Alfonso o sabio.* Rio de Janeiro, 1922.

Alfonso X el Sabio. *Cantigas de Santa Maria.* Facsimile ed. 2 vols. Madrid, 1979.

———. *Libros de ajedrez, dados y tablas.* Facsimile ed. Madrid, 1987.

———. *El Primer Lapidario de Alfonso X el Sabio.* Facsimile ed. 2 vols. Madrid, 1982.

Burns, R. I., et al. *Emperor of Culture: Alfonso X the Learned of Castile and His Thirteenth-Century Renaissance.* Baltimore, 1990.

Cómez Ramos, R. *Arquitectura alfonsí.* Seville, 1974.

———. *Las empresas artísticas de Alfonso X el Sabio.* Seville, 1979.

Domínguez Bardona, J. *Manuscritos con pinturas: Notas para un inventario des los conservados en colecciones públicas y particulares de España.* 2 vols. Madrid, 1933.

———. "Miniatura," *Ars Hispaniae* 17 (1962), 220–48.

———. *La miniatura Española.* 2 vols. Barcelona, 1930.

Dominguez Rodríguez, A. *Astrología y arte en el Lapidario de Alfonso X el Sabio.* Madrid, 1984.

———. "Errores en la Exposición de Alfonso X et Sabio," *El Pais* 27 (1984), 22.

———. "Hércules en la miniatura de Alfonso X el Sabio," *Anales de Historia del Arte* 1 (1989), 91–103.

———. "Iconografía evangélica en las *Cantigas de Santa Maria.*" *Reales Sitios* 80 (1984) 37–44.

———. "Imágenes de presentación de la miniatura alfonsí." *Goya* 131 (1976), 287–91.

———. "Imágenes de un rey trovador de Santa María (Alfonso X en las Cantigas)." In *24° Congreso Internacional de Historia del Arte (Bologna, 1979), Il Medio Oriente e l'Occidente nell'Arte del XIII secolo.* Bologna, 1982. 287–91.

———. "El *Libro de los Juegos* y la miniatura alfonsí." *Libros de ajederez, dados y tablas de Alfonso X el Sabio.* Madrid, 1987. 2: 31–121.

———. "El *Officium Salomonis* de Carlos V en El Escorial. Alfonso X y el planeta sol. Absolutismo monárquico y hermetismo," *Reales Sitios* 83 (1985), 11–28.

———. "Pervivencia de la astrología islámica en las cortes europeas de los siglos XIII al XVI." *25° Congreso Internacional de Historia del Arte, 4–1 de septiembre de 1983. Europa und die Kunst des Islam. 15. bis 18. Jahrhundert.* Ed. Oleg Grabar. Vienna, 1986. 109–92.

———. "Poder, ciencia y religiosidad en la miniatura de Alfonso X el Sabio. Una aproximación," *Fragmentos* 2 (1984), 33–46.

———. "El testamento de Alfonso X y la catedral de Toledo," *Reales Sitios* 82 (1984), 73–75.

Greenia, G. "University Book Production and Courtly Patronage in Thirteenth-Century France and Spain." In *Medieval Iberia: Essays on the Literature and History of Medieval Spain.* Ed. D. J. Kagay and J. T. Snow. New York, 1997. 103–28.

Guerrero Lovillo, J. *Las Cantigas. Estudio arqueológico de sus miniaturas.* Madrid, 1949.

Katz, I. J., and J. E. Keller (eds.) *Studies on the "Cantigas de Santa Maria": Art, Music, and Poetry. Proceedings of the International Symposium on the "Cantigas de Santa Maria" of Alfonso X et Sabio (1221–1284) in Commemoration of Its 700th Anniversary Year 1981.* Madison, Wisc., 1987.

Keller, J. E. "The Art of Illumination in the Books of Alfonso X (Primarily in the *Canticles of Holy Mary*)." *Thought* 60, no. 239 (1985), 388–406.

Keller, J. E., and R. P. Kinkade. *Iconography in Medieval Spanish Literature.* Lexington, Ky., 1984.

Linehan, P. *La iglesia española y el papado en el siglo XIII.* Salamanca, 1975.

———. "The Spanish Church Revisited: The Episcopal *Gravamina.*" In *Authority and Power.* Cambridge, 1980.

Menéndez-Pidal, G. *La España del siglo XIII leída en imágenes.* Madrid, 1986.

———. "Los manuscritos de las *Cantigas.* Cómo se elaboró la miniatura alfonsí." *Boletín de la Real Academia de la Historia* 150 (1962), 25–51.

Ramos, G. "Estudio complementario sobre las miniaturas." In *Primera Partida.* Ed. J. A. Arias Bonet. Valladolid, 1975.

Scarborough, C. L. "A Summary of Research on the Miniatures of the *CSM.*" *Bulletin of the Cantigueiros de Santa Maria* 1 (1987), 41–50.

Solalinde, A. G. "El códice florentino de las *Cantigas* y su relación con los demás manuscritos." *Revista de Filología Española* 5 (1918), 143–79.

Yarza, J. "La Edad Media." In *Historia del arte hispánico.* Vol. 2. Madrid, 1980.

ALFONSO X, EL SABIO, KING OF CASTILE AND LEÓN, HISTORICAL WORKS

In 1274 the Alfonsine scriptorium abandoned work on the *Estoria de España*, a project that had occupied it for some years. By 1280 the same group had resumed work on its other great historical project, the *General estoria*, and managed to carry the text to where it ends in the modern edition. Neither composition was ever completed. The narrative of the *General estoria* runs up through the life of the Virgin Mary, while that of the *Estoria de España*, in its definitive form, goes only to about the year 800, although certain drafts and fragments do cover more recent periods. The unfinished state of the Spanish history may have something to do with the fact that the royal patron, Alfonso, was obliged to abandon his claim to the imperial throne: there is evidence that as the work was originally planned, he was to appear as the heir to both the Gothic royal line and the imperial, and that when the claim failed, the king had little desire to see the project through. Both works are compilations, vast mosaics of texts from older authors. In this sense the *General estoria* and the *Estoria de España* are not greatly different from dozens of other historical productions of the Middle Ages, both in Latin and in vernaculars. What sets the Alfonsine histories apart from their fellows, however, is the fact that the compilers modified and manipulated their sources so as to give the definitive text a distinctive shape, and to make it yield themes and emphases that were alien to this older material. To all appearances, the compilers' work was done in three stages. First, the source texts were translated entirely, Orosius's *Histories*, Josephus's *Antiquities*. One such version has actually survived, a Castilian prose translation of Lucan's *Pharsalia*. Second came the cutting and pasting: long stretches of text were planned, and it was determined that one bit of Eutropius was to be placed here, and another of Orosius there. Finally, there was the polishing process. The prose style of the separate bits was made uniform, the pieces themselves were linked together logically, and incompatibilities between the source texts were in some cases resolved, but in others explained or simply pointed out. The translations themselves often wound up amplifying their originals heavily: this is a feature the two histories have in common with other vernacular compilations, like the French *Fet des romains* or the *Orose en français*.

The organizing principle of the *General estoria* is, of course, chronology; this ground plan comes to it from the *Chronici canones* of Eusebius and Jerome, a virtual calendar of past events that coordinates biblical history with the nonbiblical. *Chronici canones* constitutes the backbone of the *General estoria*, and the narratives from other sources make up its other members. The work's biblical history depends heavily on Flavius Josephus's *Antiquities of the Jews* and Comestor's *Historia scholastica* as well as the Bible itself, although certain Quʿrānic elements are not absent. Nonbiblical material comes from an astonishing variety of sources, ancient and medieval texts as unlike as Lucan's *Pharsalia*, covering the civil war, and a version of the *Historia de preliis* for the story of Alexander the Great. A curiously demythologized and Euhemerized version of Ovid's *Metamorphoses* gives us much of the early history of the race. One should emphasize that the compilers make little distinction between biblical history and nonbiblical: both seem to have the same status, and the pair join to form a master narrative that is uniformly authoritative.

The *General estoria* is a spectacular achievement, in many ways unique in the Middle Ages. Its scope is broad. Its early portions present a highly original account of the progress of the human species from barbarism to civilization, in civil life, in material culture, in learning, and even in religion. Many of its conceptions are built around two large themes that are by no means uniquely Alfonsine: the *translatio studii* and the *translatio imperii*. The first as presented by the *General estoria* tells of the patriarch Abraham, liberal artist, natural philosopher, and monotheist, who passes on his lore to the Egyptians, whence it in turn goes on to the Greeks, Romans, and Franks. The second theme involves a purely human Jupiter, first universal emperor. Once again, Greeks, Romans, and Franks are seen as his successors; Frederick II, Alfonso's immediate predecessor on the imperial throne, is mentioned explicitly in this connection. One should make it clear that in forming all of these large conceptions the compilers are not wholly disrespectful of their sources. Hints, so to speak, in Josephus and others flower into these astonishing patterns of thought in the new text.

The *Estoria de España* has its own characteristic layout, quite different from that of the *General estoria*. We are given in succession an account of each of the dynasties and nations that ruled the Iberian Peninsula: Hercules and his successors, the "Almujuces," barely identifiable; Carthaginians; Romans; various lesser Germanic tribes; and finally, the Goths. The Arab domination, curiously, is seen as simply an episode in the Gothic period. In this sense, the Alfonsines follow a long line of earlier historians who present the kings of the Reconquest as Goths, in the full and literal meaning of the word successors of Tulga and Reccesvinth. The sections of the *Estoria de España* that are most fully developed are the Roman, and as we have seen, the Gothic. The former is divided into two parts, before and after Julius Caesar's assumption of the office of emperor (medievals generally regarded him as the first in the line). The account of the Republican period consists largely of episodes in Roman history that bear directly on Spain and its fortunes. The Second Punic War, for example, is treated extensively. The climax of the whole section is the long sequence on the rivalry and bloody war between Pompey and Julius Caesar. This text, heavily dependent on Lucan, figures largely in the *Estoria de España* not only because of the large role played by Spain in the history of the time, but because in the mind of the compilers it offers a lesson in statecraft: the community will not survive for if there are two powerful leaders on the scene. One would add that moral and political lessons are an important feature of both Alfonsine histories. The second part of the Roman section is simply an imperial history, with little focus on Spain or Spanish things.

In 1906, Ramón Menéndez Pidal published a long text he called *Primera crónica general.* Something more than half of the work consists of the incomplete *Estoria de España* as I have described it. The rest is a narrative of Spanish history into the reign of Ferdando III of Castile. This curious production contains the provisional material mentioned above, the drafts and fragments that in one way or another are related to the original project of a general history of Spain. One feature of this text is that it includes prosified versions of Castilian *cantares de gesta.* Some of these are important for the whole narrative in that they recount episodes in the early history of Castile that do not appear in the Latin chronicles the compilers otherwise depend on. The story of the formation of this large unit is too complicated to set forth in any detail. The oldest portions consist of two long sections that date from 1289, that is to say, in the reign of Sancho IV. This is the closest in time of composition to that of the *Estoria de España,* but even in this material there are strains that are patently un-Alfonsine. But as it happens, there does exist an independent chronicle that is nowadays believed to be very early and to fairly well reflect the plans and intentions of the compilers of the *Estoria de España*—the *Crónica de veinte reyes,* a work that covers the long period from Fruela II to Fernando III. Different as it is (in varying degrees) from the *Primera crónica,* the general likeness of the two texts over long stretches assures us that the latter preserves no small amount of Alfonsine substance. *Primera crónica* does not do badly. Certain of its episodes are fashioned with an art and wit that can properly be called Alfonsine. One is the narrative of the division of the kingdom by Fernando I and the generation of warfare that follows. Another is the narrative of El Cid, down to the victory over the Count of Barcelona.

Long stretches of the *Estoria de España,* in both the completed part and the provisional, become traditional from its own time down to the sixteenth century. It survives in dozens of differing recensions, further *crónicas generales,* histories of the kings of Castile, and in particular chronicles of El Cid, Fernán González, and others.

Charles F. Fraker

Bibliography

Alfonso X el Sabio. *General estoria primera parte.* Ed. A. García Solalinde. Madrid, 1930.

———. *General estoria, segunda parte.* 2 vols. Ed. A. García Solalinde, L. Kasten, and V Oelschlager. Madrid, Vol. 1:1957; Vol. 2, 1961.

———. *Primera crónica de España.* 2 vols. Ed. R. Menéndez Pidal. Madrid, 1955.

Catalán, D. *De Alfonso X al conde de Barcelos: cuatro estudios sobre el nacimiento de la historiografía romance en Castilla y Portugal.* Madrid, 1962.

Fraker, C. F. *The Scope of History.* Ann Arbor, Mich., 1994.

Lida de Malkiel, M. R. "La *General estoria*: notas literarias y filológicas," *Romance Philology* 12 (1958–59), 111–42.

Rico, Francisco. *Alfonso el Sabio y la General estoria: tres lecciones.* Barcelona, 1972.

ALFONSO X, EL SABIO, KING OF CASTILE AND LEÓN, LAW

A major contribution to Hispanic civilization is the body of law given form and organization during the early years of Alfonso X's reign (1252–1284). The need for new codification became apparent following extensive territorial conquests under Alfonso VIII and Fernando III and attendant political, demographic, and economic dislocations. Finding inspirational models in the unitary character perceived in the kingdom of Toledo and in Visigothic law, in the increasing contact with new legal ideas from Italy (notably Bologna), in familiarity with Justinian's legislation, and in recent examples (Valencia and Aragón) of a European trend toward new codification, Fernando III and his son, Alfonso X, conceived of a legislative plan that the father's death left the son to complete and execute.

Royal legislation during Alfonso's reign consists of three codes of general legislation and categories of special legislation. Of the codes, the *Espéculo* (in five, possibly seven, books redacted 1252–1255) was addressed to royal judges throughout Castile and contains the first systematic, detailed Hispanic treatment of the royal administration of justice. The *Fuero Real* (in four books, 1252–1255) contained more simply stated dispositions and was granted to specific municipalities (*concejos*) to whose needs it was directed. The *Siete Partidas* (in seven books, 1256–1265) made up a comprehensive code and veritable juridical encyclopedia. (The *Setenario,* self-described as an ethical guide prepared for educating heirs to the throne, at times has been included, erroneously, among the codes.) No manuscript from the Alfonsine chancery containing the text of these codes is known to exist, and the present titles are post-Alfonsine. These facts have led commentators to raise questions about textual accuracy, dating, completion, promulgation, and juridical relationships. The *Espéculo* probably was operative from 1255 to 1272 (although some say it was never promulga-ted); as did the *Setenario,* it served in the preparation of the *Siete Partidas.* The *Fuero Real* was operative in those municipalities from the date in the period 1255–1272, when it was granted (in some cases petition produced its abrogation by the king before the last named date) and continued to be observed by some towns after 1272; in 1348 it became a part of general Castilian law. The *Siete Partidas* were first declared operative in 1348 as suppletory law, but the code's influence grew rapidly, given impetus by the appearance (1555) of the printed Gregorio López edition.

ROBERT A. MACDONALD

Bibliography

Craddock, J. R. *The Legislative Works of Alfonso X, el Sabio: A Critical Bibliography*. London, 1986.

MacDonald, R. A. "Laws and Politics: Alfonso's Program of Political Reform." In *The Worlds of Alfonso the Learned and James the Conqueror: Intellect and Force in the Middle Ages*. Ed. Robert I. Burns. Princeton, N.J., 1985.

Pérez Prendes, J. M. "Las leyes de Alfonso X." *Revista de Occidente* 43 (1984), 67–84.

ALFONSO X, EL SABIO, KING OF CASTILE AND LEÓN, MUSICAL INSTRUMENTS OF CANTIGAS

The Escorial Codex B.I.2 (or E[1]), also referred to as *Códice de los músicos*, contains the famous forty-one miniatures preceding the musical notations of each of alfonso's *cantigas de loor*. They depict a total of seventy-eight instrumentalists (*juglares*, shown mainly in pairs, six of whom perform alone [nos. 100, 180, 200, 290, 350, and 400]). Discounting duplications, the varied instruments they hold comprise thirty-five in number and represent but a sampling of the wind, stringed, and percussion instruments that were in use at the time. It is reasonable to assume that they were among the more popular instruments known to the court artists. About half are of Arabic origin (see below, preceded by an asterisk).

The largest group is the stringed instruments (chordophones), comprising fifteen distinct types from among the forty shown, drawn from (a) the lute family: *baldosa* (similar to the *vihuela de mano*; a seven-stringed long-necked lute)(120), *cítola* (two-stringed long-necked lute)(130), *guitarra latina* (four-stringed plucked) (1/r, 10/r, 150), **guitarra morisca* (20/r, 150), **laúd* (in Arabic, *al ud*)(30, 170/r), **rabé* or rebec (three-stringed *mandura* or plucked rebec) (90), **rabé morisco* or *rebab* (bowed two-stringed, Arabic *rabab*)(110, 170/l), *vihuela de arco* (*fidula*; bowed fiddle)(1/l, 10/l, 20/l, 100), *vihuela de péñola* (three-stringed long-necked lute, with plectrum) (140), **viola arábiga* (bowed oval-shaped fiddle, shown with three and four stringed its actual identity is problematic)(210), and *zanfona* (*cinfonia*, hurdy-gurdy; a three-stringed mechanically bowed fiddle) (160); (b) the zither family: **canon entero* (Arabic *qanūn*)(wing-shaped and rectangular (70 and 80, respectively), *cedra* or *cítara* (290), **medio canon* (trapezoidal)(50), and **rota medieval* (triangular-shaped)(40); and (c) the harp family: *arpa gótica* (380).

Next follow the winds (aerophones), representing thirteen distinct types among the thirty-two depicted. These include (a) a natural horn: *corneta curva* (with a mouthpiece; perhaps with finger holes)(270); (b) trumpets: **trompa árabe*, *añafil* or *trompeta recta* (Arabic, *al-nafir*)(320, 360); (c) single-reed instruments:

Cantiga de loor, no. 340: "Virgen madre groriosa," from the «Codice rico» de las Cantigas de Alfonso X el Sablo (Ms. T.I.1 from the Library at El Escorial, Spain, Fol. 304C.)

launeddas (from Sardinia; triple-piped, one pipe of which functions as a drone)(60); (d) double-reed: **albogón* (large shawm with extended bell)(300/l), *caramillo* (small shawm)(340/l), **albogue* (Arabic, *al-buq*) (shawm, forerunner of the *dulzaina*)(310, 330/l, 340/r, 390), *chorus* or *chorón* (bladder pipe with chanter, shown with and without drones (250 and 230, respectively), *gaita* or *cornamusa* (bagpipe with chanter and drone)(350), and *odrecillo* (small bagpipe with chanter, shown with and without drones)(280 and 260, respectively); (e) flutes: *flauta travesera* (transverse flute; it has been linked to the **axebaba morisca*); (Arabic *al-shabbaba*) (240) and *flautilla* (three-holed whistle-flageolet or pipe)(370); and (f) organ: *organo portátil* (portative organ with bellows)(200). The aerophones exhibited in *Cantigas de loor* 220 and 360 are enigmatic. The former, described by some as a *flauta doble* or *doble chirimía*, was studied by Torres, who linked it with the *launeddas* and suggested that its semicircular portion functions as a bellows. The latter, exhibiting two instrumentalists, each blowing two straight trumpets at the same time, appears somewhat questionable.

Finally the percussion instruments constitute four distinct types among the eight depicted: (a) struck idiophones: *campanas* or *carillón* (bell chimes, struck on rim and manipulated by internal clappers)(180 and 400, respectively), **címbalos* or *platillos* (cymbals) (190), and *tejoletas* (a precursor of the castanets)(330/r); (b) membranophones: **tambor de doble cono* (Arabic, *darabukka*; single-headed hour glass-shaped drum)(300/r), and *tamboril* or *tamborete* (small cylindrical drum), shown as played in conjunction with the *flautillo* (370). The combination of pipe and tabor can be traced to the thirteenth century.

Among the more recent studies concerning B.I.2, Álvarez suggests that the musical miniatures were drawn by seven distinct hands: (1) nos. 1–40; (2) 60–80, 360–400; (3) 120–70, 290, 300, and 340; (4) 210–250, 320, and 350; (5) 50, 90–110, 190–200, 280, and 330; (6) 180 and 310; and (7) 260 and 270. Martínez and Le Vot discuss the same miniatures from the standpoint of their visual presentations (symmetry, parallelism, etc.), which may account for the inaccurate manner certain instruments were shown to be played; notice, for example, the hand positions among the wind players. In terms of detail, one must also consider the artist's personal familiarity with the instruments he depicted, as well as his sense of perspective and proportion.

Escorial Codex T.I.1 (or E[2]) duplicates ten of the aforementioned instruments, among which the *vihuelas de arco* (*Prólogo*, *Cantigas* 8 and 14, and *Cantiga de loor* 120) and the *añafiles* (*Cantigas* 62, 165, and 185) play a prominent role. The **atabal* (Ar. *naqqara*) (kettledrum), a pair of which can be seen in *Cantiga* 165, is the only addition. A comparison of its *Prólogo* with *Cantiga de loor* 1 (in B.I.2), reveals distinct artistic versions of the king supervising a rehearsal in progress. In the former he is flanked on his right by a scribe and three *juglares*; on his left by a scribe and four choristers. In the latter, to his right are four choristers and two *juglares*; to his left a scribe, three choristers, and two *juglares*. The latter miniature is significant in that one of the choristers is holding a text, implying the role of soloist. The *juglares* employed at the court were indeed proficient musicians who not only provided heterophonic accompaniments but were also adept in adding improvised preludes, interludes, and postludes to the performances.

Codex T.I.1 also bears testimony to two other ensembles that were utilized for performance: the first, distinctly Arabic (*Cantiga de loor* 100), comprising a *rabé morisco*, *laúd*, *canon medio*, *rota medieval*, and *címbalos*, with what appears to be a chorus singing behind them; the second, consisting of a *vihuela de arco*, *albogue*, *rota medieval*, and two *canons* (*entero* and *medio*) includes dancers and possibly singers.

Many of the above instruments were included among the thirty-seven mentioned in the *Libro de buen amor*.

Israel J. Katz

Bibliography

Álvarez, R. "Los instrumentos musicales en los códices alfonsinos: su tipología, su uso y su origen. Algunos problemas iconográficas," *Revista de Musicología* 10 (1987), 67–95.

Martine, J., and G. Le Vot. "Notes sur la cohérence formelle des miniatures à sujet musical du manuscrit b.I.2 de l'/Escorial," *Revista de Musicología* 10 (1987), 105–16.

Perales de la Cal, R. "Organografía medieval en la obra del Arcipreste." In *El Arcipreste de Hita: El libro, el autor, la tierra, la época. Actas del I Congreso Internacional sobre el Arcipreste de Hita.* Ed. M. Criado de Val. Barcelona, 1973. 498–506.

Torres, J. "Interpretación organológica de la miniatura del folio 201-versus del códice b.I.2 escurialense," *Revista de Musicología* 10 (1987), 117–35.

ALFONSO X, EL SABIO, KING OF CASTILE AND LEÓN, MUSIC OF CANTIGAS

Higinio Anglés's monumental study and transcription of the *Cantigas de Santa Maria* (Barcelona, 1943–1964) provided, for the first time, easy access to the combined repertoires of the three musical codices (Toledo, T.I.1, and B.I.2), thus promoting worldwide interest in their performance. Despite its shortcomings, this indispensable guide must be consulted for subsequent research.

Of the various figures adduced by scholars for the total number of *cantigas* melodies (narratives and *loors* alike), 413 is accurate and includes 403 tunes from Codex B.I.2, plus ten additional tunes for the *Fiestas de Jesucristo* from the Toledo Codex. In Codex B.I.2, seven texts and tunes are repeated (165 = 395, 187 = 394, 192 = 397, 267 = 373, 289 = 396, 295 = 388, 349 = 397), while one *cantiga* and two *Fiestas de loor de Santa Maria* share their melodies with other *cantigas* (213 = 377, FSM 2 = 340 and FSM 6 = 210, respectively). Lacking music are *cantigas* 298, 365, 401 (*Piticon*), and 402. In the case of 401, its melody can be found in the Toledo and T.I.1 codices. Of the 193 *Cantigas* texts in Codex T.I.1, all but two (nos. 113 and 146) carry the same melodies as those in B.I.2. The Toledo Codex comprises 128 melodies, 104 and 118 of which are duplicated in T.I.1 and B.I.2, respectively. In the Toledo, only the refrains and single strophes bear musical notation, whereas additional strophes have been notated in the Escorial codices. The Florentine Codex, MS Banco Rari 20, was prepared to incorporate music, but unfortunately its musical staves remained bare.

Two melodic styles can be readily identified from the notation: syllabic (basically one tone per textual syllable) and neumatic (wherein compound and ligated neumes feature prominently, comprising two to five tones or more per textual syllable). The notational values (*longa–breve*) of the Escorial Codices were halved in the Toledo (*breve–semibreve*), considered by Anglés to be the least perfect of the three manuscripts. Whereas the neumes depict the melodic progressions of each tune with great precision, it is their rhythmic interpretation that has provoked much controversy, particularly those in the neumatic style. Anglés considered the Escorial Codices to be fully notated in mensural notation, reflecting both strict modal (particularly trochaic, iambic, and dactylic) and mixed modal rhythms. Among the nonmodal, he discovered that binary rhythms surpass the ternary, and that combinations of both exist. In his view, the single neumes of the Toledo Codex carried mensural values, while the compound and ligated neumes did not. With regard to Anglés's transcriptions, H. van der Werf found that he adhered as often to the medieval rules of mensural notation as he departed from them and that the Escorial Codices were decidedly nonmensural. Furthermore, van der Werf suggested that the *Cantigas* should be rendered in a declamatory rhythm to best reflect the textual accents that were not fully articulated in Anglés's transcriptions.

Among the forms in the *Cantigas* repertory, the rondel types (comprising the *formes-fixes*) of late medieval French poetry predominate. Of these the *virelai* is most conspicuous. Anglés listed its occurrence in 368 instances (88 percent of the collection) and recently G. V. Huseby extended the count to 382 (92 percent). The *ballade* and *rondeau* follow, with five occurrences each. Inasmuch as Anglés's analysis of the remaining forms were somewhat questionable, a more recent accounting includes such genres as *canciones* (songs) with refrain, hymns, sequences, and a *cantiga de amigo* (song of love).

The *virelai*'s primacy not only reflected the high esteem which it held at Alfonso's court, but shows that it was clearly intended as a vehicle for disseminating the Marian narratives and lyrical texts. Comprising an *estribillo* (refrain), *mudanza* (strophe), and *vuelta* (continuation of strophe sung to the melody of the refrain), the *virelai* aptly suits a rendition alternating between soloist and chorus, with the latter merely reiterating the refrain text. Although the *virelais* appear as tripartite melodies (wherein repetition and contrast can be depicted simply as *A*BA, and in such variant forms as *AA* BBAA, *AB* BBAB, *AB* CCAB, etc.), closer study reveals that common melodic formulas were shared by a number of them. Moreover, the *mudanza* was normally notated in a higher range than the estribillo, exhibiting an arch-like contour.

The predominance of the *zajal*'s (Sp. *zéjel*) metrical form in association with the virelai (about 360 occurrences) has led to two diametrically-opposed arguments concerning *virelai's* origin—either from the south (Andalusia), from whence the zajal influenced the northern form, or vice-versa. A mutually independent genesis has also been proposed. Still, the crucial factor is the lack of musical documentation from Muslim sources.

The following diagram illustrates a fundamental difference between the *virelai* and *zajal*, musically (upper case) and metrically (rhyme scheme, lower case):

	Virelai	*Zajal*	(*Cantiga* 86)
Estribillo	*A a*	*A a*	[Ar. *Matla*]
	A a	*B a*	
Mudanza	B b	A′ b	
	B b	A′ b	[Ar. *Gusn*]
Vuelta	A b	A″ b	
	A′ a	B a	[Ar. *Simt*]

a) Cantiga de loor 340: "Virgen madre groriosa" (Anglés 1943, 2: 371), b) Giraut de Bornelh "Reis glorios . . ." (Fernández de la Cuesta 1979, 169) and c) Cadenet "S'anc fui bèla ni presada" (Fernández de la Cuesta 1979, 548)

In the *Cantigas* corpus, musical counterparts for the *zajal* (like that in *Cantiga* 86, shown above) can also be found in Cantigas 61, 80, 96, 102, 111, 168, 299, and 320.

The melodic origins of the *Cantigas* have been traced to three traditions: court (troubadouresque), popular, and liturgical. Nearly thirty of the tunes have been partially linked to preexistent melodies. *Cantiga de loor* 340 (see fig. 1) furnishes an excellent example of a tune contrafact that can be traced to the famous *alba* "Reis glorios" by Giraut de Bornelh (ca. 1173–1220) and upon which Cadenet (fl. 1204–1235) based his "S'ans fue belha ni presada."

Other musicologists who have contributed significantly to *Cantigas* research are Ismael Fernández de la Cuesta, Manuel P. Ferreira, Gerardo V. Huseby, José María Llorens Cisteró, and Zoltán Falvy.

Israel J. Katz

Bibliography

Anglés, H. *La música de las Cantigas de Santa María del Rey Alfonso el Sabio*. 3 vols. Barcelona, 1943–64.

Fernández de la Cuesta, I. "Las Cantigas de Santa María. Replanteamiento musicológico de la cuestión," *Revista de Musicología* 10 (1987), 16–26.

Fernández de la Cuesta, I., and R. Lafont. *Las Cançons dels trobadors*. Tolosa, 1979.

Huseby, G. V. "Musical Analysis and Poetic Structure in the *Cantigas de Santa María*." In *Florilegium Hispanicum: Medieval and Golden Age Studies Presented to Dorothy Clotelle Clarke*. Ed. J. S. Geary et al. Madison, Wisc., 1983. 81–101.

Katz, I. J. "Higinio Anglés and the Melodic Origins of the *Cantigas de Santa Maria*." In *Alfonso of Castile the Learned King (1221–1284)*. Ed. F. Márquez-Villanueva and C. A. Vega. Cambridge, Mass. 1990. 46–75.

van der Werf, H. "Accentuation and Duration in the Music of the *Cantigas de Santa Maria*." In *Studies on the "Cantigas de Santa Maria": Art, Music, and Poetry*. Eds. I. J. Katz, J. E. Keller et al. Madison, Wisc. 1987. 223–34.

ALFONSO X, EL SABIO, KING OF CASTILE AND LEÓN, POETRY

Alfonso X (1221–1284) spent his early years, like his father before him, in Galicia before going to court. The dominant lyric voice in the western two-thirds of the Iberian Peninsula for poets of all languages was Galician-Portuguese from approximately 1180 to 1325. Alfonso's early years coincided with the Albigensian persecutions in France, which increased the presence of Occitan (or Provenzal) poets in the courts of Iberia. Thus, both Galician-Portuguese and Occitan poets (and members of their entourages) were frequently to be heard entertaining in the courts ruled over by Alfonso VII, Alfonso VIII, Jaime I (Alfonso's father-in-law), and Fernando III. Since Alfonso X was accustomed to singers and composers all his life, and praised his father for these talents in his *Setenario*, it is not surprising that this young prince, so drawn to letters in general, and remembered even now as an "emperor of culture," should have himself become a poet.

Alfonso is responsible, first, for a small body of profane poetry, some forty-six poems in all. From the main genres associated with Galician-Portuguese verse (*cantigas d'escarnho e de maldizer*; *cantigas d'amor*; *cantigas d'amigo*) almost all his production falls into the first category of mostly satirical verse: there is one composition ("Senhora, por amor Deus")—the only one in Castilian—that seems to be about love. The remaining poems present a gallery of types, rich and varied satires of cowards, prostitutes (he was one of many poets to extol the "virtues" of one María Balteira), fops, bad poets, lascivious prelates, promise breakers, and more. The language is direct, vivid, and unflinching in its realism. A small number of the compositions (four) are *tensons*, dialogues between two poetic personae, one created by Alfonso and one by another poet. The tone established is nearly always only semiserious; the ludic, mocking voice pokes holes in the facade of well-known types (often individuals are named) while offering, at the same time, a celebration of the poetic virtuosity on display in the medieval Galician-Portuguese *cancioneiros*.

Alfonso is best known, however, for his *Cantigas de Santa María*. These were composed in a span extending from about 1250 to 1280 and almost certainly involved poets other than Alfonso. An early form (the Toledo manuscript) contains a core of one hundred poems, arranged in decades of nine narrations of the Virgin Mary's miraculous interventions in human affairs plus one praise song or *loor*. There are two introductory poems, one with a third-person voice telling us that Alfonso was the maker of these poems, the second using a first-person approach and narrating how difficult is the task of ever praising Mary sufficiently. In this prologue poem, the tone is set by a poetic persona who, casting aside all other women, adopts the troubadour stance of supplicant before his Lady, promising to serve her alone. The voice of this poetic persona is then interwoven into the collection as it grows, in various stages, to comprise forty-two decades of miracle-plus-praise song, with small additional bodies of poems dedicated to the feasts of Mary and the feasts of her son.

Justly, the *Cantigas de Santa María* has been described as the aesthetic Bible of the thirteenth century. While the Toledo manuscript has one presentation miniature depicting Alfonso surrounded by scribes and musicians in the act of composition, as well as musical transcriptions of the melodies, two other expanded editions are more lavishly illustrated and musicated. One, in two parts (located in El Escorial and Florence) contains lavish miniatures, some sixteen hundred in all, that opens windows on virtually all aspects of Alfonso's world. The musical transcription is extensive but, as with the miniatures, begins to be more sporadic toward the end of what remains an incomplete undertaking. The remaining MS, also in El Escorial, contains forty-two miniatures of musicians of both sexes and, doubtless, the three religious groups (Christians, Moors, and Jews) present at court. A majority of the *cantigas* are variants of the *zéjel* with refrain (AA bbba AA ccca, etc.) but musically show an affinity with the French *virelai* form.

The *Cantigas* contain miracle narrations that were conscientiously culled from sources in both Latin and the vernaculars that circulated widely throughout Europe and other areas of the peninsula (Montserrat in Catalonia, Terena in Portugal, Puerto de Santa María in Andalusia). But perhaps more significant is the presence of Alfonso in the collection. Many miracle accounts tell of cures for his parents, of favors Mary performs for other family members, of special rewards that Alfonso's great devotion and loyalty to Mary bring (there are several cures, many favors granted in battle). In the end, the royal presence blends with the notion of the poetic persona in service to his liege lady, the service being—at least in part—this very compilation, intended also to foment the praises of Mary to others who have witnessed how she has rewarded his service. Alfonso also had himself depicted frequently, in the miniatures that accompany the *loores*, in various postures of praise of Mary, throughout the liturgical year. Alfonso, like all sinners that appear in this vast compilation, is equal in Mary's human-yet-divine presence. There is, ultimately, a sense, most marked in cantiga 409, of all humanity celebrating, hands joined, singing and dancing, the hope that Mary brings of salvation from sin. It may be inferred that the *Cantigas de Santa María* were intended not as yet one more Marian compilation, but as an unsurpassingly rich evocation of her universal presence as felt in the life of the peninsula and, especially, in the spiritual and political affairs of its compiler.

JOSEPH T. SNOW

Bibliography

Alfonso X. *Cantigas de Santa Maria*. 4 vols. Ed. W. Mettman. Coimbra, 1949–72; reprt., 2 vols., Vigo, 1981.

Keller, J. E. *Alfonso X, el Sabio*. Boston, 1967.

Lapa, M. Rodrigues. *Cantigas d'escanho e de mal dizer*. 2d ed. Vigo, 1970.

O'Callaghan, J. F. *Alfonso X and the Cantigas de Santa Maria: A Poetic Biography*. Leiden, 1998.

Snow, J. T. "The Central Role of the Troubadour Persona of Alfonso X in the *Cantigas de Santa Maria*," *Bulletin of Hispanic Studies* 56 (1979), 305–16.

———. *The Poetry of Alfonso X, el Sabio: A Critical Bibliography*. London, 1977.

ALFONSO X, EL SABIO, KING OF CASTILE AND LEÓN, POLITICAL HISTORY

Alfonso X, king of León-Castile (1252–1284), the son of Fernando III and Beatrice of Swabia, was born on 23 November 1221 in Toledo and is known as El Sabio, the wise or the learned. His first task was to complete the colonization of Seville and the recently reconquered territory in Andalusia. An ambitious ruler, he also tried to assert his supremacy over neighboring Christian territories. He quarreled with Afonso III of Portugal over lands east of the Guadiana River and the Algarve, but reached a preliminary settlement in 1253 by arranging the marriage of his illegitimate daughter, Beatriz, to the Portuguese ruler. When Alfonso X demanded that Thibault II, the new king of Navarre, become his vassal, the Navarrese appealed for help to Jaime I of Aragón. As a consequence, Alfonso X had to give up his attempt to subjugate Navarre in 1256. He also had alleged rights to Gascony, but yielded them in 1254 to his sister Leonor and her husband Edward, the son and heir of Henry III of England.

Advancing claims to the Holy Roman Empire derived from his mother Beatrice, daughter of Emperor Philip of Swabia, Alfonso X was elected in 1257 in opposition to Richard of Cornwall. He incurred great expenses in a vain effort to win recognition, but he was unable to persuade the majority of the Germans and several popes to acknowledge him.

Alfonso X also planned an invasion of Morocco to deprive the Moors of easy access to the peninsula, but his African crusade accomplished nothing more than the plundering of Sale, a town on the Atlantic coast, in 1260. In order to broaden Castilian access to the sea, he developed Cádiz and the nearby Puerto de Santa María and conquered Niebla in 1262. When he demanded the surrender of Gibraltar and Tarifa, his vassal, Ibn al-Aḥmar, King of Granada, refused, because he realized that this would make it difficult for Morocco to aid Granada against Castile.

Threatened by Castilian expansion, Ibn al-Aḥmar in the spring of 1264 stirred up rebellion among the Mudejars or Muslims subject to Castilian rule in Andalusia and Murcia. Alfonso X took steps to contain the revolt in Andalusia, while appealing for help to his father-in-law, Jaime I of Aragón, who subdued Murcia by early 1266. Jerez, the last rebel stronghold in Andalusia, capitulated in October. As a result of the rebellion, the king expelled the Muslims from the recaptured towns and brought in Christian settlers. The suppression of the revolt was completed when Ibn al-Aḥmar resumed payment of a yearly tribute to Castile in 1267. In that same year, Alfonso X, in return for Afonso III's assistance in crushing the revolt, yielded all rights in the Algarve and agreed to a delimitation of the frontier with Portugal along the Guadiana River to the Atlantic Ocean.

Although tranquility was restored, Alfonso X soon encountered strong domestic opposition because of his innovations in law and taxation. Intent on achieving greater juridical uniformity, he drew upon Roman law in preparing the *Espéculo de las Leyes* (known in its later redaction as the *Siete Partidas*), intended as the law of the royal court, and the *Fuero Real*, a code of municipal law. The nobles accused him of denying them the right to be judged by their peers in accordance with their customs, and the townsmen were distressed by frequent imposition of extraordinary taxes.

Under the leadership of the king's brother Felipe, the nobles confronted the king during the *cortes* (parliament) of Burgos in 1272. By confirming traditional customs, he modified his plan for a uniform body of law, but as compensation, the towns granted him a tax levy every year for "the affair of the empire." Despite his efforts at accommodation many of the nobles went into exile to Granada, but were finally persuaded to return to royal service in 1274. With his realm at peace, Alfonso X then journeyed to Beaucaire in southern France, where in May 1275 he vainly tried to convince Pope Gregory X to recognize him as Holy Roman Emperor. Thereafter Alfonso X could not realistically expect to satisfy his imperial ambitions.

During his absence, Abū Yūsuf, the Marīnid emir of Morocco, invaded Castile. The king's son and heir, Fernando de la Cerda, died suddenly en route to the frontier in 1275, and Abū Yūsuf routed the Castilian forces. At that point, Alfonso X's second son, Sancho, reorganized the defense, cutting Marīnid communications with Morocco. A truce was arrived at, but Abū Yūsuf invaded again in 1277. Avoiding a battlefield encounter, Alfonso X blockaded Algeciras in 1278, but had to give it up early in 1279. In spite of the Moroccan threat, Castile emerged from this crisis without a loss of territory.

Meanwhile, the death of his oldest son in 1275 presented Alfonso X with a serious juridical problem. Fernando de la Cerda's oldest child, Alfonso, could claim recognition as heir to the throne, but Sancho appealed to the older custom that gave preference to a king's surviving sons. After much debate, the king in the cortes of Burgos in 1276 acknowledged Sancho. Fearing for the safety of her two sons, Fernando de la Cerda's widow, Blanche, accompanied by Queen Violante, took them in 1278 to the court of Violante's brother, Pedro III of Aragón, who kept them in protective custody.

Philip III of France, the uncle of the two boys, pressured Alfonso X to partition his realm and to establish a vassal kingdom for Alfonso de la Cerda. During the cortes of Seville in 1281, while the people complained that they were being impoverished by the heavy taxes, Sancho, angered by the possibility of losing any portion of the kingdom broke with his father. A public assembly held at Valladolid in April 1282 transferred royal power to Sancho, leaving Alfonso X only the royal title. Abandoned by his family and many of his subjects, the king turned to Abū Yūsuf, the Marīnid emir, who invaded Castile again. As many of Sancho's supporters renewed their allegiance to the king, a vain attempt at reconciliation was made, but in his last will Alfonso X disinherited his son. The king died at Seville on 4 April 1284 and was buried in the cathedral.

Despite the unhappy end to his reign Alfonso X was one of the greatest medieval kings of Castile, and his impact on the development of Spanish law and institutions was lasting.

Joseph F. O'Callaghan

Bibliography

Ballesteros, A. *Alfonso X*. Barcelona and Madrid, 1963; reprt. Barcelona, 1984.

O'Callaghan, J. F. "Image and Reality: The King Creates his Kingdom." In *Emperor of Culture. Alfonso X the Learned of Castile and his Thirteenth-Century Renaissance*. Ed. R. I. Burns. Philadelphia, 1990. 14–32.

ALFONSO X, EL SABIO, KING OF CASTILE AND LEÓN, SCIENCE

Alfonso X had already begun his career as a great medieval Maecenas two years prior to ascending to the throne of Castile and León, if the date provided in his

Lapidario is accurate. Although date and form of this work pose some, as yet, unresolved problems, it is certain that the *Lapidario* incorporates one aspect of the medieval discipline that the learned monarch must have held most dearly—astronomy and astrology. To categorize Alfonso's interest in astrology as marginal is inaccurate and anachronistic since the two in Alfonsine usage were essentially, although not entirely, synonymous. When Alfonso did distinguish between the two, more often than not *astronomía* meant "astrology" and vice versa. Thus, to emphasize a distinction between what is today the science of astronomy and the art (at best) of astrology is counterproductive, for astrology was virtually applied astronomy. If astronomy enabled one to calculate the positions of heavenly bodies, astrology allowed one to interpret the significance of a particular configuration. Alfonso makes amply clear in the writings he sponsored that God had placed the stars and planets in the heavens so that the intelligent man, his "omne entendudo," might exploit them to attain his goals. A modern analogue to astrology is radar. Just as it would be foolish, if not suicidal, for a pilot to eschew its use, so was it for a medieval king to shun astrology.

Thus, it is not surprising that eight of thirteen different titles that Alfonso sponsored pertain exclusively to Alfonsine science. These are: *Lapidario* (ca. 1250), *Tablas alfonsíes* (1252), *Libro conplido en los iudizios de las estrellas* (1254), *Libro de las cruzes* (1259), the so-called *Picatrix* (ca. 1250s), *Canones de Albateni* (ca. 1250s), *Libro del saber de astrologia* (1276–1277; most commonly and erroneously known as *Libros del saber de astronomía*), and *Libro de las formas et de las ymagenes* (1276–1279). These eight titles expand to twenty-seven if we realize that two of these codices are anthologies. The *Canones de Albateni* in fact contains four treatises—*Canones de Albateni*, *Tablas de Albateni*, *Tablas de Azarquiel*, and *Tratado del quadrante sennero*. The *Libro del saber de astrologia* comprises sixteen titles: *Libro de las estrellas del ochauo cielo* (1256), *Libro de la espera* (1259), *Capitulo pora fazer armillas en la espera*, *Libro del astrolabio redondo*, *Libro del astrolabio llano*, *Libro de la lamina universal*, *Libro de la acafeha* (1255 second half, or 1256 first half), *Libro de las armillas*, *Libro de las siete planetas*, *Libro del quadrante*, *Libro de la piedra de la sombra*, *Libro del relogio del agua*, *Libro del relogio del argent vivo*, *Libro del relogio de la candela*, *Libro del palacio de las horas*, and *Libro del ataçir*. The three followed by parenthetical dates were originally commissioned as indicated.

Noteworthy is that only two of the works, *Libro del saber* and *Libro de las formas*, were compiled in the 1270s. Also noteworthy is that the remaining six titles hale from the 1250s and were predominantly astrological. The *Lapidario* treats the magico-medicinal properties of stones. The *Picatrix* concerns talismanic magic. The *Iudizios* and *Cruzes* treat judicial astrology, the latter specifically as it pertains to a king—providing information such as the most propitious time to wage war, for example. Even astronomical tables had an astrological function—ease of prediction, that is, knowing the arrangement of the heavenly configurations not only without having to actually sight them, but especially beforehand. Astrology, thus, while serving Alfonso's practical purposes, on a larger scale, provided a powerful motive for the very basis of empirical science—observation.

Alfonso may have conceived of his final two science treatises, the *Libro del saber* and the *Libro de las formas*, as complementary anthologies—the former on the construction and use of instruments of astronomical observation and mensuration, the latter on practical astrological applications. Judging from the limited information retrievable from the fourteen-folio fragment, all that remains of the *Formas*, it is safe to say that it, like the *Libro del saber*, incorporates versions, possibly revised, of works compiled originally in the 1250s.

Ironically, Alfonso X owes his recognition in science to his *Tablas alfonsíes*, a work whose translation into Latin greatly enhanced its diffusion, whose interest lies in its application to astrological reckonings, and whose text does not survive, as do all his other science treatises, in a codex produced in his royal scriptorium.

ANTHONY J. CÁRDENAS

Bibliography

Cárdenas, A. J. "A Study and Edition of the Royal Scriptorium Manuscript of *El* [*sic*] *Libro del saber de astrologia* by Alfonso X, el Sabio." 4 vols. Ph.D. diss. University of Wisconsin-Madison, 1974.

Procter, E. S. "Translations from the Arabic." In *Alfonso X of Castile, Patron of Literature and Learning*. Oxford, 1951. 7–23.

ALFONSO XI, KING OF CASTILE AND LEÓN

Alfonso XI, king of Castile and León (1312–1350), the son of Fernando IV and Constanza of Portugal, was born at Toro on 13 August 1311. On his father's untimely death he succeeded to the throne at the age of slightly more than one year. His minority, lasting thirteen years, was a time of terrible stress, as the king's relatives vied for control of the regency. As a measure of the disorder, the towns, anxious to defend their liberties and to uphold the king's authority, revived the associations or *hermandades* that they had formed in similar times of crisis in the late thirteenth century. When the *cortes* (parliament) of Palencia assembled in 1313 to determine who should act as regent, some members recognized the king's great-uncle, Juan, while others accepted the king's grandmother, María de Molina, and her son, Pedro. After the death of Queen Constanza, who had custody of her son, María de Molina emerged as the principal champion of royal authority and guardian of the king. The contending regents eventually agreed to a unified regency in the *cortes* of Burgos in 1315, in which the *hermandades* played an influential role. Confusion and turmoil continued, however, as discontented persons worked toward their own advantage. As some measure of tranquility was established, infantes Pedro and Juan planned a joint campaign against the kingdom of Granada, but in 1319 both men died suddenly. Immediately the struggle for the regency resumed.

Once again, various members of the royal family, including Juan, son of the deceased Infante Juan, Felipe, brother of Infante Pedro, and Juan Manuel, a grandson of Fernando III and a figure famous in the history of Castilian literature, demanded a place in the regency. María de Molina tried to maintain some degree of order, but her death in 1321 removed the last restraint. As the self-proclaimed regents effectively divided the realm among themselves, law and order broke down entirely.

When Alfonso XI reached the age of fourteen in 1325 he boldly declared his minority at an end and called for the resignation of the three regents. Though still inexperienced, he thwarted their ambitions to control him, executing his cousin, Juan, and breaking his engagement to the daughter of Juan Manuel, who had expected that the marriage would enable him to dominate the king. Instead, Alfonso XI in 1328 married María, daughter of Afonso IV of Portugal, who pledged to join him in war against the Moors. Juan Manuel, considering himself betrayed, fled to Aragón but renewed his allegiance in 1329; thereafter his relationship with the king was always uncertain. When Alfonso de la Cerda acknowledged the king, pledging homage and fealty in 1331, a chapter in the long dynastic dispute stemming from the reign of Alfonso X was closed.

With his realm comparatively at peace, Alfonso XI, aided by Aragón and Portugal, planned to resume the war of reconquest. He seized several fortresses on the western frontier of the kingdom of Granada in 1327 and 1330, prompting Muḥammad IV to appeal to the Marinids in Morocco for help. Responding with enthusiasm, the Moroccans laid siege to Gibraltar and captured it at the end of five months in June 1333. Alfonso XI vainly tried to relieve the garrison and to recover the fortress after it capitulated, but he was distracted by continued discontent among the nobility and tense relations with his Christian neighbors. By inviting the Marīnids into his kingdom, Muḥammad IV angered the Granadan nobility, who feared Moroccan domination; they assassinated their king and elevated his brother, Yūsuf I. Soon later, Castile, Morocco, and Granada agreed to a truce.

While Alfonso IV of Aragón was irritated by Alfonso XI's presumption in military affairs, Afonso IV of Portugal was becoming outright hostile and conspired with Juan Manuel against the king of Castile. The Portuguese monarch believed that Alfonso XI, by openly flaunting his relationship with Leonor de Guzmán, the mother of his several illegitimate children, was dishonoring the queen, Maria of Portugal. Desultory warfare between Castile and Portugal followed, but Portuguese efforts to persuade Alfonso IV of Aragón to enter an alliance against Alfonso XI were of no avail.

As the truce with the Moors drew to a close, the Christian rulers realized that they were all threatened by the possibility of a new Moroccan offensive, and decided to set their own quarrels aside for the time being as they planned for a common defense of the peninsula. Although the Castilian and Aragonese fleet won a victory over the Moroccans in the straits in 1339, they were unable to prevent the sultan, Abū-l-Ḥasan, from invading Spain with a substantial army in the spring of 1340. Aided by Yūsuf I of Granada, he began the siege of Tarifa in June. Gathering his forces, Alfonso XI appealed to the pope for crusading indulgences and financial assistance. Warriors from the other peninsular realms and from northern European countries, hoping to distinguish themselves in a crusade, came to lend their support. Once again, Pedro IV of Aragón sent a fleet, while Afonso IV personally commanded Portuguese troops who joined the host.

Warned of the advancing Christian army, the Moors abandoned the siege of Tarifa and prepared to give battle on the banks of the nearby River Salado. Blessing the Christian soldiers, Gil de Albornoz, the archbishop of Toledo, assured Alfonso XI that victory awaited him and urged him to go forth without fear. In the ensuing conflict, which took place on 30 October 1340, Afonso IV and the Portuguese drove the Granadan troops from the battlefield while Alfonso XI dispersed the Moroccans. The thorough Christian victory delivered a decisive blow to Moroccan aspirations to dominate the peninsula. Christian Spain was liberated once and for all from the threat of invasion from Morocco. The Christians had triumphed in the long battle to control the Strait of Gibraltar and to deprive the Marīnids of easy access to the peninsula. As the Moroccan menace was perceived to recede, the need to complete the peninsular reconquest was not felt so urgently and eventually was allowed to fall into abeyance.

For the moment, however, an exuberant Alfonso XI intended to continue the war. Sending the trophies of war to the pope, he pleaded for continued spiritual and financial support of his crusade. In 1341 he seized Alcalá de Benzayde, Rute, Priego, Benamejí, and Matrera to the northwest of Granada. Then, in August 1342, supported financially by the pope and the king of France, and with ships supplied by Portugal, Aragón, and Genoa, he began the siege of Algeciras, one of the principal points of entry into the peninsula. Once again, he was joined by foreign soldiers, including Philip d'Evreux, king of Navarre, who died in 1343, the count of Foix, and the Earls of Derby and Salisbury. In November 1343 Alfonso XI gained a decisive victory over the Moroccan and Granadan forces on the river Palmones, eliminating any possibility of relief for Algeciras. With the permission of the emir of Morocco, the defenders surrendered Algeciras on 26 March 1344.

The reaching of a truce gave the king an opportunity to replenish his treasury and to prepare for the resumption of hostilities. As the Marínids still held Gibraltar, the king lay siege to that fortress in August 1349. The Black Death, the great plague that devastated western Europe, ravaged his camp, however, and he fell victim to it, dying on 27 March 1350 at the age of thirty-nine.

Aside from his military labors, Alfonso XI took steps to strengthen the monarchy by imposing stricter and more direct control on the towns by sending *corregidores* or royal administrators to control their affairs. He also resolved much of the confusion in the administration of justice by the Ordinance of Alcalá enacted in the *cortes* of Alcalá de Henares in 1348. Fearful of the *cortes*, which met frequently during his minority, he convened that assembly in full only three times during his majority, but otherwise preferred to convene partial assemblies, thus effectively dividing the estates, while getting what he wanted in taxes. His principal innovation in taxation was the introduction in the years 1342–1345 of the *alcabala*, a sales tax that became the most important source of revenue for the crown thereafter.

Alfonso XI had two legitimate sons, Fernando, who died as an infant in 1333, and Pedro, born on 30 August 1334, who succeeded him. He also had ten illegitimate children by Leonor de Guzmán; the most important of them was Enrique of Trastámara, who after overthrowing Pedro gained the throne as Enrique II (1369–1379).

JOSEPH F. O'CALLAGHAN

Bibliography

Gran Crónica de Alfonso XI. Ed. D. Catalán. 2 vols. Madrid, 1977.

Poema de Alfonso XI. Ed. Yo Ten Cate. Madrid, 1955.

ALFONSO, *INFANTE* OF CASTILE

Born in 1453, Alfonso was the son of Juan II of Castile and his second wife, Isabel of Portugal, the brother of Isabel the Catholic, and the half-brother of Enrique IV. Since he died in 1468 at age fourteen, he remains a shadowy figure whose importance was due to the way in which he was used as a pawn in the political disturbances that plagued Castile. That rebellious nobles could manipulate him is to be explained by several factors. It was argued, for example, that as long as Enrique IV remained childless Alfonso was heir to the throne. And when Enrique IV's second wife, Juana of Portugal, did give birth to a daughter it was claimed that the child's father was not the king, but Beltrán de la Cueva (hence, she was often referred to as Juana la Beltraneja), and that Alfonso was still heir to the throne. Moreover, whatever the truth about the many accusations leveled against Enrique IV, the young Alfonso could be presented as an "honest" alternative to a king who was alleged to be morally, sexually, and religiously corrupt. Matters came to a head when the rebel nobility sent a list of grievances and demands for reform to the king in 1464. The latter at first accepted these, but then retracted. There followed the famous Sentencia of Medina del Campo of 1465, a purportedly "neutral" attempt at reform, and the infamous deposition in effigy of Enrique IV, known as the Farce of Avila, that took place on 5 June of the same year. A large platform was erected outside the walls of Avila and a wooden statue of Enrique IV, decked out with the symbols of royalty, was placed on a throne. The leading rebels, who included such powerful men as Alfonso Carrillo, Archbishop of Toledo; Juan Pacheco, Marquis of Villena, Alvaro de Stúñiga, Count of Plasencia; Gómez de Solís, Master of Alcántara; Rodrigo Pimentel. Count of Benavente; and Rodrigo Manrique, Count of Paredes, then proceeded to strip the statue of its symbols, and after the deposition in effigy had been carried out Alfonso was taken up on to the platform and proclaimed king. But of course Enrique IV and his supporters denounced the Farce of Avila, and the two rival kings plunged Castile into anarchy. Just over three years later Alfonso unexpectedly died on 5 July 1468 at Cardeñosa, a village near Avila.

Alfonso may have died of the plague or he may have been poisoned. There had been an epidemic in the region, but there was some cause to believe in the theory of poisoning. Although his supporters were said to be grief stricken, it was also noted that those who had been manipulating Alfonso were finding that he was less malleable than his half-brother: hence the suspicion that they "dispatched" Alfonso in order once again to control the kingdom through the pliant Enrique IV. There is some evidence that Alfonso had been starting to display qualities that were not those of a "pawn" but rather those that his sister Isabel would later display on the chessboard of Castilian politics as queen. Nevertheless he had been manipulated, and there were many who grieved the death of Alfonso "the Innocent."

ANGUS MACKAY

Bibliography

Val Valdivieso, M. I. del. *Isabel la Católica, Princesa (1468–1474).* Valladolid, 1974.

MacKay, A., "Ritual and Propaganda in Fifteenth-Century Castile," *Past and Present* 107 (1985), 3–43.

ALHAMBRA

Citadel and palace dominating Granada from the south and comprising the most extensive remains of a medieval Islamic palace anywhere. It contains a virtual encyclopedia of Naṣrid architecture and decoration in glazed tile, carved and painted stucco, and wood, and is particularly notable for a group of superb *mugarnas* (stalactite) vaults. As early as the nineth century a citadel on the site was called *al-hamrā'* (the red), probably because of the reddish color of its walls. In the eleventh century it was linked with the town's defenses to the north, and between 1052 and 1056 Yūsuf Ibn Naghrallah, the Jewish vizier to the Zirīd rulers of Granada, built his palace there. Two centuries later, the Naṣrid sultan Muḥammad I (r. 1230–1272) made the Alhambra his residence and over the next two centuries his descendants continued to enlarge and embellish it. Most of the Alhambra is due to Naṣrid patronage, particularly by Yūsuf I (r. 1333–1354) and Muḥammad V (r. 1354–1391, with interruptions), though Charles V (r. 1516–1556) added a palace in the Renaissance style, and Felipe V (r. 1700–1746) Italianized some rooms. The site subsequently fell into ruin, but it was rediscovered in the early nineteenth century by the Romantics, to whom are owed the names by which its parts are commonly known.

The Alhambra is contained with a walled enclosure (740 by 220 meters) punctuated with twenty-three towers and gates. At its western end is the Alcazaba (in Arabic *al-qaṣaba*, fortress); to the east are the remains of several palaces, a mosque, baths, and an industrial zone with a mint, tanneries, and ovens. Across a ravine to the east of the enclosure are the palace and gardens of the *generalife* (in Arabic, *jinan al-ʿarif*, gardens of the overseer). The alcazaba, the oldest part, is a double-walled fortress of solid and vaulted towers containing barracks, cisterns, baths, houses, storerooms, and a dungeon. Access from the north was controlled by the Armas gate; access from the south was controlled by the Gate of Justice (in Arabic, *sharīʿa*, erroneously for *shurayyaʿa*, esplanade), decorated with carved stone, cut brick, marble, and glazed tile. The Puerta del Vino, framed with ceramic spandrels and stucco panels, is a ceremonial portal to the main street of the royal quarter.

The core of the Alhambra, the so-called Casa Real Vieja (to distinguish it from the addition of Charles V), consists of several palaces arranged along the northern curtain wall and incorporating several of its towers. The palaces follow the traditions of palace design in the western Islamic world, with rooms arranged symmetrically around rectangular courts. One entered the Palace of the Myrtles from the large square facing the Alcazaba and passed through the first court, whose foundations indicate that it had an oratory and minaret, into the second, or Machuca, court. Only its northern portico and a tower survive; from it passages lead to a dwelling, another oratory, and the facade of the Mexuar (in Arabic, *mashwar*, place of the royal audience), the present public entrance. From the Mexuar, a rectangular room with a flat roof supported on six columns, one passes through a narrow doorway into the Cuarto Dorado, whose plain lateral walls emphasize and illuminate the splendid carved stucco facade at its south. This internal facade, crowned by windows allowing women to watch the activities unobserved and a mu-

Court of the Lions. 14th century. Naṣrid dynasty. Copyright © Adam Lubroth/Art Resource, NY Alhambra, Granada, Spain.

Court of the Myrtles. Built by Yūsuf I between 1333 and 1354. Marīnid dynasty. Copyright © Adam Lubroth/Art Resource, NY Alhambra, Granada, Spain.

garnas cornice supporting deep eaves, presents the visitor with two identical doors: that on the right leads back to the Mashwar, while the other leads to a bent passage to the Court of the Myrtles. The court (36.6 by 23.5 meters) contains a long pool bordered by low hedges. Doors along the long walls open to rooms for the sovereign's wives, service areas, and the palace bath. At either end porticoes of seven arches on slender marble columns protect lavish tile and stucco decoration on the walls. A door in the center of the the northern portico opens to the Sala de la Barca, with a magnificent joined wooden ceiling, which was once the sovereign's bed- and sitting room. Beyond is the Hall of the Ambassadors, a large (11.3-meter) square room contained within one of the massive towers of the enclosure walls. Deep alcoves in its walls overlook the city; the one opposite the entrance is the most richly decorated, and the poem inscribed on its walls indicates that it was the throne recess. The floor and walls are superbly decorated with tile and carved plaster; the ceiling, composed of many thousands of individual wooden elements joined into a pyramidal vault, depicts a starry sky and probably symbolizes the seven heavens of Paradise.

The area to the south of the Comares court was modified when Charles V constructed his palace there, but a street once led from the Mexuar past the royal mausoleum (*rawda*), a square building with a central lantern, to the Palace of the Lions. One passed from its entrance through a bent passage to the relatively intimate Court of the Lions (28.5 by 15.7 meters). An arcade supported on slender columns arranged singly or in groups of two, three, and four surrounds the court and the kiosks projecting at either end. At its center a fountain with twelve white marble lions (probably preserved from Yūsuf Ibn Naghrallah's palace) spout around an elevated polygonal basin inscribed with a poem by the Andalusian poet Ibn Zamrak (1333–ca. 1393). To the south is the square hall of the Abencerrajes; squinches support a stellate drum and superb mugarnas vault, which also represent the dome of heaven. On the east of the court is the Hall of the Kings: alternately square and rectangular spaces with subsidiary side chambers separated by elaborate mugarnas arches and covered with painted and mugarnas vaults. To the north of the court is the Hall of the Two Sisters, a square hall with alcoves on its ground and first floors. *Mugarnas* squinches support an octagonal drum with eight paired windows and another superb *mugarnas* vault. From the hall one passes through another vaulted room to the exquisitely decorated belvedere of Lindaraxa overlooking the gardens below. Other palatial remains within the walls but outside the Casa Real Vieja include the Peinador tower, the Torre de la Cautiva, and the Partal palace.

Jonathan M. Bloom

Bibliography

Grabar, O. *The Alhambra*. Cambridge, Mass, 1978.

Dickie, J. "The Alhambra: Some Reflections Prompted by a Recent Study by Oleg Grabar," *Studia Arabica et Islamica: Festschrift for Ihsan ʿAbbas on his Sixtieth Birthday*. Ed. W. al-Qadi. Beirut, 1981.

ALHANDEGA, BATTLE OF

In 939 the Leonese king, Ramiro II (930–951) had been harassing and threatening the frontier possession of the caliphate of Córdoba for seven years. In 939 the Caliph ʿAbd al-Raḥmān III (912–961) resolved that the Leonese monarch must be punished severely and himself undertook the leadership of a strong army that marched north, reaching the banks of the Duero River near Simancas. There it encountered the army of Ramiro II, who had been reinforced with troops furnished by the Navarrese and Count Fernán González of Castile (923–970).

On 1 September a battle ensued that resulted in a resounding victory for Ramiro II. A large portion of the Muslim army was cut down, its camp captured, and ʿAbd al-Raḥmān's official Qur'ān and the caliph's ceremonial gold coat of mail formed part of the booty. The caliph himself escaped along with a substantial portion of his troops and returned to Córdoba. There he is said to have crucified three hundred officers of his cavalry for their cowardice. ʿAbd al-Raḥmān did not himself subsequently campaign against Ramiro II.

The battle seemingly takes its name from a field fortification built and utilized successfully by the Leonese at Albendiego near Simancas.

BERNARD F. REILLY

Bibliography

Rodríguez, J. *Ramiro II, rey de León*. Madrid, 1972.

ALJAMA

Aljāma (rarely *alfama*) is a Spanish word derived from Arabic *al-jāmiʿa*, "community." Many writers erroneously assume it refers exclusively to a Jewish community, but this is not in fact correct, for it refers to either a Muslim or Jewish community, and must therefore be qualified by one or the other adjective. The term may be either abstract, "the (Muslim or Jewish) community," or specific, referring to a particular community in a town or city and its physical neighborhood (*judería*), in later medieval usage, or *morería*.

The Muslim *aljāma* was originally rather loosely organized, but became increasingly bureaucratic over the centuries. Officials included the judges (religious and secular; almost indistinguishably the *faqīh* or *qāḍí*), with various minor magistrates, and the *Ṣaḥib al-Shurṭa*, often erroneously translated as "chief of police" but in fact was a court administrator who also gave punishments (the term passed into medieval Spanish as *zavasorda*, merely a civil judge; Jews also held this post). There were also various market officials and supervisors of weights and measures, prices, and so on.

The Jewish *aljāma* was organized around an elected council, that could range from a simple "seven good men" to thirty or more. These were responsible for ordinances, tax assessments, and the like. *Adelantados*, or *muqaddamim*, were elected officials who carried out the actual daily administration. There were also special commissioners (*berurim*) to supervise and even adjudicate such matters as morals and the schools. There were also judges to handle all internal affairs of Jewish law.

Salaried officials sometimes included these judges, teachers of children, scribes, and sometimes the slaughterers of meat. Rabbis, generally, were not salaried until later. Many Jewish *aljamas* had hospitals and/or charitable houses for the poor and elderly (*almosnas*) that were supported by taxes imposed by the Jewish council.

NORMAN ROTH

Bibliography

Romano, D. "Aljama frente a judería, call y sus sinónimos," *Sefarad* 29 (1979), 347–54.

ALJAMIADO LITERATURE

Literature written in Spanish but employing the Arabic alphabet. The term derives from *aljamīa* (in Arabic, *al-ʿajamiyya*), meaning "foreign language", "Romance language" in Spanish Arabic. Examples are extant from the fourteenth to the early seventeenth centuries, showing that this literature was cultivated by both Mudéjares and Moriscos. Continued use of the Arabic alphabet even after knowledge of the language itself was forgotten testifies to the Muslims' reverence for any manifestation of a tongue they considered holy. Also conventionally included in Aljamiado are the writings, in the Latin alphabet, of Spanish Moriscos exiled to North Africa after 1609.

The language of Aljamiado is almost exclusively Castilian, though many texts show a greater or lesser admixture of Aragonese. (The existence of a true Portuguese Aljamiado has been disproved.) Texts in Catalan or Valencian dialects are very rare, because although those regions had a large Muslim population it was for the most part Arabic-speaking. The Muslims of Castile and Aragón, more thinly spread within a Christian-dominated society, lost their Arabic fairly early, as is attested by the many surviving laments of authors and scribes. Nonetheless the texts contain many Arabic elements in the form of syntactic and semantic calques: *la isla de al Andalus* (the Iberian Peninsula; in Arabic, *jazīra*, meaning both "peninsula" and "island"); *ensañóse ensañamiento grande*, in imitation of the Arabic cognate accusative: *ya es a ti en que creas con Allah?* ("Have you [the will] to believe in God?") Likewise, vocabulary is borrowed freely and often adjusted to Spanish morphology: *halegar* (to create), in Arabic, *khalaka*; *el alhichante* (the pilgrim [to Mecca]), in Arabic, *al-hājj*; *los almalaques* (the angels), in Arabic (singular), *al-malak*. (Not coincidentally, all these terms are of Islamic import.)

Over two hundred Aljamiado manuscripts survive today; many of these were discovered inside the walls of houses in former Morisco villages of northeastern Spain, where the inhabitants had concealed them before their deportation. The largest such cache came to light in Almonacid de la Sierra (Zaragoza) in 1884, the most recent in Urrea de Jalón (Zaragoza) in 1984. The principal library collections are those of the Escuela de Estudios Arabes, Biblioteca Nacional, and Real Academia de la Historia, all in Madrid.

Only a handful of names can be attached with certainty to Aljamiado works. The vast majority are anonymous, not only because *incipits* and *explicits* have been lost (although of course many have) but because it is a literature that has evolved along collective and traditional lines. The author, rather than making his presence known, submerges his personality into that of the community from which he came and which forms his audience. Some of the stylistic features of Aljamiado, such as the second-person address to the hearers (e.g., *y veos aquí que . . .*) recall oral and popular forms of transmission.

The Aljamiado corpus contains many items that do not, strictly speaking, fall under the heading of literature. Among these are works of devotion (translations of the Qur'ān, collections of prayers, etc.) and works of superstition (such as charms, amulets, and the casting of horoscopes). But the line between the didactic or pietistic and the literary is not so neatly drawn as in the West: almost all Aljamiado works of the imagination are marked by a strong Islamic cast. The story of the Prophet Joseph (Yūsuf), for instance, which exists in both poetic and prose versions, follows the account in Qur'ān chapter 12, with embellishments taken from exegetical commentaries on the Qur'ān. There are lyric poems in praise of the prophet Muḥammad, and a long narrative one describing a pilgrimage to Mecca. Heroic tales and legends almost always turn on the adventures of Islamic heroes, such as the prophet's early adherents and his son-in-law ʿAli. Even Alexander the Great appears in the role the Arabs assign him, as Dhū-al-Ḳarnayn, transformed into a Muslim champion.

As is also clear from the above, the inspiration for this literaṭure is overwhelmingly eastern. Its Mudéjar and Morisco authors did not originate, but continued and embellished, a relatively narrow range of themes. Only one important Aljamiado work has its roots in western Europe (see below).

Prose Narrative

Some of the more extensive works, and those of greatest literary worth, are *Rrekontamiento del rrey Ališandre*, the Islamic retelling of the Alexander legend; *Leyenda de Yūsuf*, of Qur'ānic inspiration; *Libro de las batallas*, heroic tales of the early days of Islam; and *Historia de los amores de Paris y Viana*, a version of a popular European novel of chivalry (and as such the only major Aljamiado tale of Western inspiration). The *Tafsira* of the Mancebo de Arévalo is at the same time a guide to Islamic practice and the spiritual autobiography of a Morisco. Many short legends have been edited collectively. Some relate the deeds of early Islamic heroes or of biblical characters, others describe the Muslim vision of the afterlife. Collections of moral precepts form another category, as do works of divining and superstition such as *Libro de las suertes*.

Poetry

The *Poema de Yúçuf* is a fine example of *cuaderna vía* in Aljamiado from the late thirteenth or early fourteenth centuries; of the same genre and period is *Almadḥa de alabanza al an-nabī Muḥammad*. Other poetry, though rising to no great literary heights, also celebrates the prophet and the religion of Islam. Only three or four poets are known by name, most of them from the very end of the period: Muḥammad Rabadán (*Discurso de la descendencia de Muḥammad*), Juan Alfonso Aragonés, and Ibrahīm de Bolfad.

It is curious that Aljamiado literature should coincide so precisely in time to the period of literary *maurofilia* in Spain that produced the *romancero morisco* and *El Abencerraje y la hermosa Jarifa*. The romanticized Moor of the latter works could hardly differ more profoundly from the Morisco who was striving to retain his culture in conditions of poverty, persecution, and clandestinity. What the Mudéjares and Moriscos did produce was a literature of preservation rather than of creation, and one closely tied to their feelings of ethnic and religious identity. It speaks in the authentic voice of one of the principal marginalized groups of *marginados* in the history of Spain.

CONSUELO LÓPEZ-MORILLAS

Bibliography

Colección de Literatura Española Aljamiado-Morisca. 9 vols. to date. Madrid, 1990–1998.

Galmés de Fuentes, A. "La literatura española aljamiado-morisca," *Grundriss der romanischen Literaturen des Mittelalters* 9, pt. 1, fasc. 4, 117–32; pt. 2, fasc. 4, 103–112.

Klenk, U. *La Leyenda de Yūsuf, ein Aljamiadotext*. Tübinger, 1972.

Kontzi, R. *Aljamiado Texte*. 2 vols. Wiesbaden, 1974.

Nykl, A. R. "Aljamiado literature. *El Rrekontamiento del Rrey Ališandre*," *Revue Hispanigue* 77 (1929), 409–611.

ALJUBARROTA, BATTLE OF

The Battle of Aljubarrota took place on 14 August 1385, and historians continue to regard it as the decisive battle in the political struggle for the kingdom of Portugal. Fernando I of Portugal had designs on the Castilian throne and schemed unsuccessfully to obtain it. He paid for these ambitions by suffering invasions and heavy military defeats at the hands of Pedro the Cruel's usurping half-brother Enrique II of Trastámara in 1371 and 1372. With thoughts of revenge, Fernando made secret alliance with England. An Anglo-Portuguese force jointly led by King Fernando and the Earl of Cambridge campaigned unsuccessfully (1381–1385) against the armies of Juan I, who had succeeded his father Enrique II on the throne of Castile. The now ailing Fernando ill-advisedly wedded his daughter Beatriz to Juan I by the terms of the ensuing peace treaty, before dying in October 1383. The interregnum that followed his sudden death encouraged the Trastámaran monarch to lay a serious claim to the Portuguese throne through his marriage to Fernando's daughter. He was further encouraged by the fact that the great nobles in Portugal showed little enthusiasm for the exiled illegitimate sons of King Fernando's father, Pedro I, while at the same time strongly supporting the person and policies of King Fernando's widow, Doña Leonor Telles. Despite the popular acclamation of Dom João, Master of the Military Order of Avis as, first regent and then king, Juan I was so encouraged by the confused situation in Portugal that he invaded in 1384. After a series of indecisive engagements he besieged Lisbon but was obliged to raise the siege when plague decimated his army. In August of the following year, tempted again by support among the Portuguese nobility and by his own superior military strength, he invaded a second time. As in the previous year, Juan I planned his main attack from the southeast; but meeting stiff resistance, he marched north to Ciudad Rodrigo and after some hesitation, invaded through the Beira, thus approaching Lisbon from the north. His forces numbered some 22,000 men, outnumbering those of the Master of Avis by more than three to one; and yet he suffered a crushing defeat. Chroniclers attribute the Castilian defeat at Aljubarrota principally to the tactics of the Master's constable, Nun' Alvares Pereira, who counselled strongly that Dom João's army, small though it was, should interpose itself between the advancing Castilians and the capital and fight them in a pitched battle; for, he argued, if Lisbon were lost so would the kingdom be. When the Earl of Cambridge's forces had aided King Fernando in 1381–1382, the Portuguese saw something of the tactics that had given the English the upper hand in France during the Hundred Years' War. The Portuguese constable adopted these tactics: a heavy reliance upon infantry; the deployment of an exceptionally strong contingent of archers; and the tactic of inducing the enemy's cavalry to attack a fixed position carefully chosen beforehand by its defenders. The adoption of the third of these tactics is the reason why the Avis army came to be stationed near the village of Aljubarrota on the morning of 14 August 1385.

Aljubarrota is located at 39.34 north latitude and 8.55 west longitude, twenty-four kilometers southwest of Leiria on the main Coimbra-Lisbon road between the towns of Batalha and Alcobaça. The area is situated on a spur of the Serra de Porto de Mós. The countryside is consequently an undulating one of hills and mountain streams. According to the Castilian chronicler López de Ayala, en eyewitness and participant, the Trastamaran line of attack lay along a stretch of ground between two brooks that effectively narrowed the Castilians' vanguard and made it impossible for the right and left flanks to engage the enemy when the two armies met. Moreover, when the Trastamaran forces attacked the Avis position they were thrown into confusion by the steadiness of the Portuguese pikemen and by the concentrated fire of the mixed force of Portuguese crossbowmen and English longbowmen. Sensing impending defeat, King Juan fled the field in the direction of Santarém while his demoralized army disintegrated soon after.

The battle had several long-term results. It put an end to a civil war in which two candidates for the Portuguese throne had fought for two years; one of them, Juan I of Castile, had by no means the weaker claim, which was supported by many Portuguese magnates, some of whom fought on the Trastamaran side throughout the civil war. The slaughter or exile of these Trastamaran Portuguese produced a social revolution in which an old Portuguese nobility was replaced by a new. The battle put an end to serious Castilian claims to the Portuguese throne, confirmed Portuguese independence, and consolidated the reign of João I as well as the dynasty of the House of Avis. Aljubarrota was to have an enormous symbolic value for later Portuguese romantic nationalism that is illustrated by the enormous Abbey of Batalha that was built to commemorate the victory. Finally, the participation of English archers at Aljubarrota gave impetus to the budding Anglo-Portuguese alliance that would be confirmed in the following year by the Treaty of Windsor.

ROBERT OAKLEY

Bibliography

Lopes, F. *Crónica del Rey Dom Joham I da boa memória, Primeira Parte e Segunda Parte*. 2 vols. Ed. A. B. Freire and W. J. Entwistle. Lisbon, 1977.

López de Ayala, P. *Crónica del rey don Juan, primero de Castilla e de León*. Biblioteca de Autores Españoles, 68. Madrid, 1953.

Russell, P. E. *The English Intervention in Spain and Portugal in the Time of Edward III and Richard II*. Oxford, 1955.

Suárez Fernández, L. *Historia del reinado de Juan I de Castilla*. 2 vols. Madrid, 1977–79.

ALMADA, FELIPA DE

Very little is known about Felipa de Almada, a fifteenth-century Portuguese poet who was a member of the court of João II. The king was a lover of the arts and endeavored to surround himself with talented people. As one of the most important social graces, poetry was cultivated by many members of his court, including some women. Garcia de Resende's *Cancioneiro Geral* (Lisboa, 1516) contains short, cryptic verses by women for men to gloss. In the ongoing court poetry competition, women propounded riddles, and men solved them. The only woman who wrote a lengthy poem, however, was Felipa de Almada.

Rather than propounding a riddle, she solves one by scorning her former lover mercilessly: "What I cannot recover, oh world of uneven order, makes me not wish you well nor desire you harm." All her feelings are gone, and her indifference is total: "I find more pleasure, thus, living in the limbo of your favor, than with the pain of your wretched love."

Interestingly, of all the women poets of the Iberian Peninsula, only Felipa de Almada assumes an unfamiliar role. Constança de Mallorca and Mayor Arias clearly follow the popular tradition of the Galician "*cantigas de amigo*" (songs of love and friendship). Florencia Pinar, another fifteenth-century *cancionero* poet, assumes an active role in the sense that she solves riddles rather than propounding them. However, she presents herself as the suffering party, the victim of love. Where Florencia speaks of her imprisonment and compares herself to a partridge in a cage, Felipa de Almada proclaims her liberation from love. Her poem is almost the reverse of a *cantiga de amigo*, and coming from a Portuguese woman poet could be read as the intertextual game of a writer who refuses to fit into the local mold. Of course, she does so by adopting a different literary role: that of the disdainful lady of courtly love.

CRISTINA GONZÁLEZ

Bibliography

Costa, A. da. *A mulher em Portugal*. Lisbon, 1892.

Salvado, A. *Antologia da poesia feminina portuguesa*. Lisbon, n.d.

ALMANZOR *See* MANṢŪR, AL-

ALMIZRA (OR ALMIRRA), TREATY OF

Peace agreement signed between Jaime I of Aragón-Catalonia and the future Alfonso X of Castile (in the name of his father Fernando III) on 26 March 1244 at the captured Islamic castle of that name, presently the Camp de Mirra or El Capet in southern Valencia. The pact did not annul the Cazorla Treaty of 1179 between the two countries, by which respective zones of conquest from the Moors had been finalized. Instead, it worked out discrepancies as to the actual southern border of Valencia, so hotly disputed that war was then imminent between Jaime and Alfonso. After each king had seized towns assigned to the other's conquest, and especially with both claiming Játiva (then under siege by Jaime) Alfonso asked for a meeting.

Jaime's party stayed at Almizra castle and town, Alfonso's in tents at the foot of the hill at Caudete. Stormy arguments nearly aborted this effort at peace until Jaime's Queen Violante and the Master of Santiago intervened. The two kings "amicably" redrew the border, from the confluence of the Júcar and Cabriol Rivers down through Ayora, Almansa, and Biar, out to sea above Aguas de Busot. The 1304 treaty of Torrella later annulled Almizra by moving the border south past Orihuela and Alicante; but the Almizra line remained a civil division interior to Valencia until 1707 and the diocesan border to 1957. King Jaime details the bellicose negotiations in seven chapters of his autobiography, and the treaty itself has often been reprinted.

ROBERT I. BURNS, S. J.

Bibliography

González, J. *Reinado y diplomas de Fernando III*. 3 vols. Córdoba, 1980.

Jaime I. *Llibre dels feits*, in F. Soldevila, *Les quatre grans cróniques*. Barcelona, 1971. chs. 343–49.

ALMOHADS

Following the Almoravids, al-Andalus in the second half of the twelfth century was threatened by a new sect that had emerged in North Africa: the Almohads (unifiers, that is, strict believers in the unity of God; in Arabic, *al-Muwahhidīn*). Ibn Tūmart, the founder of the sect, objected to the moral laxity of the Berbers of North Africa and declared war against the Almoravid Dynasty, then in control in the Maghrib (North Africa and Muslim Iberia). During these battles he became ill and died (1130). He was succeeded by ʿAbd-al-Mu'min, who by 1147 had managed to capture Fez and Marrakesh, the capital of the Almoravids. When Marrakesh was captured, according to one source, the Christian church there was destroyed and a great number of Jews and Christian militia were killed. When ʿAbd al-Mu'min conquered Ifrīqiyah (Tunisia) in 1151, he gave the Jews and Christians there the choice of conversion to Islam or death. In 1147 he also sent an expedition to al-Andalus, but the Almohads did not firmly establish themselves there until 1163. Abū Ya'qūb Yūsuf was the first Almohad caliph to rule al-Andalus (1163–1184), establishing a dynasty that was to last there until 1227. Almohad rule in al-Andalus, however, would prove difficult from the start.

The Almohad condemnation of the popular Mālikite theological-legal school in North Africa led to rebellion against them throughout southern Morocco and along the coast. Although the rebellion was crushed and thousands, even followers of ʿAbd al-Mu'min, were executed, it left the Almohads a legacy of bitter enemies and deep resentments. As a result of a difficult situation in Morocco, Almohad rule in al-Andalus would always be loose and precarious. Given the deep internal divisions in North Africa, the Almohad rulers of al-Andalus, like Ya'qūb I (1184–1199), Yūsuf's successor who had taken the title Al-Manṣūr (the Victorious), were often obliged to rush back and forth from al-Andalus to Morocco in order to protect their interests. In 1195 when Alfonso VIII of Castile attacked the region of Seville, since it was the nature of the Almohads that only the caliph could lead an expedition to counter a Christian offensive, Ya'qūb, who found himself in Marrakesh, was obliged to hurry to al-Andalus. He met Alfonso's army at Alarcos, dealing Alfonso what would prove the last great Muslim victory over the Christians in Iberia. Ya'qūb pushed his conquest north and was able to take Guadalajara, Salamanca, and other towns. However, he was unable to exploit his success and was called back to Marrakesh to put down yet another revolt.

Like the Almoravids, the Almohads failed in maintaining their influence in Iberia. Religious zeal could not cement a heterogenous society across a large space. After Ya'qūb's death in 1199, he was succeeded by weak and even incompetent rulers who could not face the all-too-common revolts and dissension that met their brand of fundamentalism. By 1212, the combined forces of Castile, León, Navarre, and Aragón, along with volunteers and mercenaries from other parts

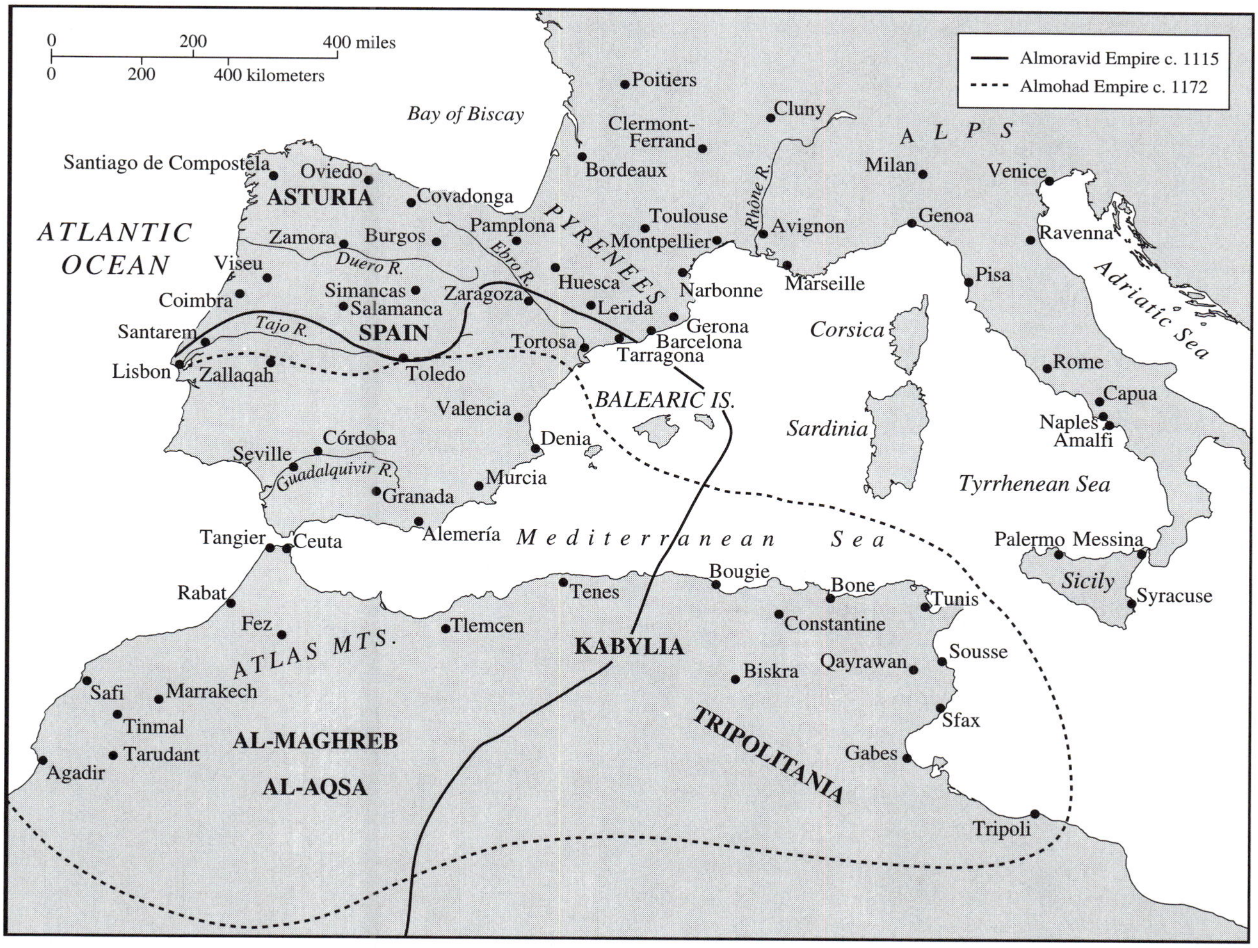

Almohads

of Europe, would deal a crushing defeat at Las Navas de Tolosa to Muḥammad (1199–1213), Ya'qūb's successor. Muḥammad had come to Iberia from Morocco with a large army and the hope of containing the revived territorial ambitions of Alfonso VIII. Barely escaping with his life at Las Navas, Muḥammad was forced to return back across the Straits of Morocco and leave al-Andalus to his adolescent son, Yūsuf II (1213–1223), who would witness the breakdown of Almohad power not only in al-Andalus but finally in the Maghrib as well.

E. Michael Gerli
Norman Roth

Bibliography

Chejne, A. G. *Muslim Spain: Its History and Culture*. Minneapolis, Minn., 1974.
Kennedy, H. *Muslim Spain and Portugal*. New York, 1996.

ALMOJARIFE

The term *almojarife* (correctly, in medieval texts or in Portugese, *almoxarife*) derives from Arabic *wazīr al-mushrif*, which is nevertheless found only in the Mozarabic documents of Toledo, and means, merely, "supervising minister." In those twelfth- and thirteenth-century documents, this was an official who not only collected taxes but who also served as a judge. However, in general use throughout medieval Spain in all kingdoms it refers to a "tax-farmer," one who either paid a lump fee for the privilege of collecting taxes or who paid a portion of the allocated taxes to the king in advance and then collected the entire sum, thus making a profit. Usually this post was held by Jews, and every king had several such Jewish *almoxarifes*, beginning at least with Alfonso VIII for Castile and Pedro I in Aragón-Catalonia (though the title in that kingdom was usually *baile*; *almoxarife* is, however, sometimes found).

Such officials were appointed, often for many years, for the taxes of the entire kingdom, but also on a local basis either by the king, the local overlord, and even church officials to administer their taxes. The title of *almoxarife mayor* (chief tax official of the kingdom) ceased to be used at the end of the fourteenth century; only Yuçaf de Ecija (under Alfonso XI), Samuel ha-Levy (Pedro I), and Joseph Pichó (Enrique II) held the title. While Jews continued to function as *almoxarifes* throughout the fifteenth century, the post was increasingly given to Christians.

Norman Roth

Bibliography

Baer, Y. *A History of the Jews in Christian Spain*. 2 vols. Philadelphia, 1966. See index to vol. 2, "Tax-farming."
Roth, N. "New Light on the Jews of Mozarabic Toledo," *AJS Review* 11 (1986), 189–220, especially 210 ff.

ALMORAVIDS

The Almoravid (*al-Murābitūn*) Dynasty was founded in North Africa in the early eleventh century. Unlike the later more extreme Almohads, they did not particularly single out Christians and Jews for persecution. However, the Almoravid ruler Yūsuf ibn Tāshfin was invited by the Muslims of al-Andalus to help defend against the invasion of the Castilian king Alfonso VI in 1086. On 23 October of that year, a major battle took place at Zallāqah (Sagrajas, near Badajoz), which turned the tide temporarily against the Christians in their efforts to conquer al-Andalus. Using the opportunity presented them, the Almoravids remained in al-Andalus and took it over from the weaker local rulers, many of whom were forced to flee.

While they were fierce warriors, they were hardly barbarians, as they have sometimes been described. They were often intolerant of philosophical ideas. ʿAlī ibn Yūsuf, who succeeded his father as ruler in 1106, ordered the burning of the works of the mystic philosopher Al-Ghazālī on religious grounds because he disagreed with his views. On the other hand, the Almoravids were not able to eradicate the strong hold of secular studies and literature among the Muslims of al-Andalus, and poetry especially continued to flourish.

While there is a lack of substantial sources, it appears that there was no persecution of Jews either in North Africa or in al-Andalus, at least not in the early years of the dynasty. According to Al-Idrīsī (d. 1162), the Jewish Barghawāta tribe in the region of Marrakesh had a sort of "capital of the South," the Jewish center of Agmat (Aghmāt). The Almoravids fought the "Judaized" Berbers there in 1059, and their decisive victory marked the decline of the Jewish Berber tribes. In the *Responsa* of Al-Fāsī, a couple of incidents of Muslim officials stealing property from Jews are reported and this was the period of some of the greatest Jewish scholars: Isaac al-Fāsī, Joseph ibn Saddiq, Judah ibn Ghiyāth and his son Isaac, and of such outstanding poets as Moses ibn Ezra and Judah ha-Levy. It is even possible that one of the poets wrote a poem commemorating the victory of the Almoravid armies against the Christian attacks in Lucena.

The oft-discussed "market regulations" (a manual of laws written by a Muslim judge responsible for the market) of Seville are somewhat misleading as a true indicator of relations between Jews and the Almoravid rulers, or certainly the Muslim population, at the time. According to those largely theoretical laws, Muslims could not massage Christians or Jews in the public baths, nor should a Muslim take care of an animal owned by a Jew or Christian. Jews were not allowed to slaughter meat for Muslims, although in fact we know they did. The clothing of lepers, libertines (sexually promiscuous people), Jews, or Christians could not be sold without indicating their origin. Christians and Jews were not to dress in the clothing of people of position nor greeted with the customary formula "peace be upon you," for "the devil has gained mastery over them and has made them forget the remembrance of God. They are the devil's party, and indeed the devil's party are the losers." Both Jews and Christians were to wear distinguishing insignia.

In fact, Jews and Muslims, including the rulers, were increasingly on good terms with each other in al-Andalus. It is thus hard to reconcile the statement of the great scholar, biblical commentator, and poet Abraham ibn Ezra that he was forced to flee Spain because of the "oppressors," when we have no evidence of any oppression. Indeed, it is possible that this statement refers to the Almohad invasion of 1145, although the Almohads were not firmly established in al-Andalus until at least 1163.

We hear of some isolated instances of Jews who converted to Islam during the Almoravid period in al-Andalus, but these were voluntary conversions. There are few studies of the Almoravid period in general.

NORMAN ROTH

Bibliography

Bosch Vilá, J. *Los Almorávides*. Tetuan, 1956.

Huici Miranda, A. "Contribución al estudio de la dinastía almorávide." *Études d'orientalisme dédiées a la mémoire de Lévi-Provençal*. Vol. 2. Paris, 1962. 605–21.

Kennedy, H. *Muslim Spain and Portugal*. New York, 1996.

Roth, N. *Jews, Visigoths, and Muslims in Medieval Spain*. Leiden, 1994, esp. 65–66, 113–16, 149–50.

ALVARES PEREIRA, NUN'

Son of Alvaro Gonçalves Pereira, Prior of the Hospitallers, and Iria Gonçalves do Carvalhal, born in Portugal, most probably at Sernache do Bonjardim, or Flor da Rosa in the Alentejo, in 1360. His life has become legend, and it is difficult to separate fact from fiction as the mythmaking process started in his own lifetime. Trained as a knight, he was a deeply religious man who lived up to the ideals of chivalry, inspired by the adventures of King Arthur and the Knights of the Round Table. In compliance with his father's wishes, he married Doña Leonor Alvim, a wealthy widow from northern Portugal, becoming a powerful landowner. He began to show his independence of character and his hatred of Castilian intervention in Portuguese affairs at the time of Fernando I's reign (1365–1383). During the crisis of the dynastic succession (1383–1385), he gave his support to Dom João, Master of Avis, distinguishing himself as a charismatic leader and a brilliant strategist. By fighting a war of movement at a time when laying siege to a town was the general rule, he changed the fortunes of war. The combined action of the infantry and bowmen proved an unbeatable match to cavalry charges. In this way were won in quick succession the battles that established firmly Portuguese independence. Nun' Alvares Pereira was made constable or chief general of the Portuguese armies, and granted large donations of land by João I. There was a serious friction between the two men, when Nun' Alvares distributed this property among officers who had served him well in the war. In 1423, he withdrew from the world, taking the Carmelite habit in the church of Carmo, which he had founded in Lisbon in 1389. Admired as a shining example of patriotism, he died in odor of sanctity in 1431 and was beatified by the Roman Catholic Church in 1918.

LUIS REBELO

Bibliography

Baião, A. *Biografia de Santo Condestável*. Lisbon, 1952.

Chronica do Condestabre de Portugal. Coimbra, 1911.

Lopes, F. *Crónica del Rei Dom Joham I*. 2 vols. Lisbon, 1968–73.

ALVAREZ DE VILLASANDINO, ALFONSO

A Castilian poet active from the early 1360s well into the reign of Juan II. Alfonso Alvarez de Villasandino was of petty noble birth, and therefore felt entitled to call himself *trovador*, poet for honor. But as his fortunes declined, he took on the character of a *juglar*, poet for pay. First and last, he was a man of the court: his writings testify that he was in royal company from the time of Enrique II to the early years of the majority of Juan. His production is large and varied. In the early Trastámara years he wrote in Galician, largely *cantigas de amor* love poems not greatly different from those of Macias or of the archdeacon of Toro. In later years he abandoned Galician for Castilian, composing along the way poems in a hybrid language, with elements of both. The themes, genres, and style of his production also changed. He continued to write both amorous and devout songs, though the former tended to be more elaborate and varied than his Gallego pieces. His later work is subtler in theme and more complicated in form. And song no longer monopolized his work. There appear *dezires* (narrative poems) of all sorts—allegorical, occasional, religious, and poems of petition, the last of which rank among his wittiest and most delightful. The changes that overtake Villasandino's production over time deserve special comment. The older manuals describe him globally as a member of the Galaico-Provençal school. The term is misleading. It fits perfectly the early Villasandino, the poet in Galician: at least one body of poetry in Galician or Portuguese is based generally on a set of rules and conventions inherited from those of Provençal song. Villasandino's later work is a response to social changes and to new currents in taste, but most importantly, it is a reflection of a second wave of Provençal influence in Castilian poetry, this time coming from the teachings of the Consistory of the Gay Science in Toulouse. The immediate source of the doctrine is almost certainly the copies or avatars of that institution, which existed in Barcelona and Valencia in his day. The formal complexity of his later verse, the elaborate metrical schemes, and the difficult rhyming patterns undoubtedly owe their existence to this neo-Provençal strain.

CHARLES F. FRAKER

Bibliography

Azáceta, J. M. (ed.) *Cancionero de Juan Alfonso de Baena*. 3 vols. Madrid, 1966.

Menéndez Pidal, R. *Poesia juglaresca y juglares*. 6th ed. Madrid, 1957.

ALVAREZ GATO, JUAN

Converso (Christian convert) poet born in Madrid ca. 1440. He served at the court of Enrique IV under the patronage of Beltrán de la Cueva. Later Alvarez Gato entered the service of two powerful Castilian converso families, the Arias Dávila and the Mendozas of Guadalajara. Toward the end of his career at court, he became the majordomo of Queen Isabel I. Alvarez Gato was close friends with Fray Hernando de Talavera, the queen's confessor and archbishop of Granada, with whom he shared a contemplative religious sensibility marked by a sense of doctrinal tolerance. Alvarez Gato died between 1510 and 1512.

Alvarez Gato's poetry is generally seen as developing in two periods: the first, dominated by profane, amorous verse characterized by hyperbolic religious metaphors and comparisons; and the second, whose tenor is religious and moral, marked by a deep spirituality that leads Alvarez Gato to appropriate and endow popular literary motifs with a religious sense (a style referred to as *a lo divino*).

E. MICHAEL GERLI

Bibliography

Márquez-Villanueva, F. *Investigaciones sobre Juan Alvarez Gato*. Madrid, 1960.

Scholberg, K. R. *Sátira e invectiva en la España medieval*. Madrid, 1971.

ALVARO, PELAYO

Alvaro Pelayo (Alvaro Pais) (d. 1353), a Portuguese Franciscan, after taking his doctorate in canon law at the University of Bologna and serving in the papal curia, was elevated to the bishopric of Silves in the Algarve in 1333. Conflict over ecclesiastical rights with Afonso IV of Portugal forced him to withdraw to Seville in 1349, where he later died.

A vigorous author, his principal work is the *De planctu ecclesiae*, written about 1330 at the request of Pope John XXII, as a defense of the absolute authority of the pope and a counterattack on Marsiglio of Padua, author of the *Defensor pacis*, and other champions of secular power. In order to achieve its spiritual purpose of leading all men to salvation, the church, in Alvaro's judgment, had need of a complex hierarchical structure, laws, and property. The pope, as the vicar of Christ, was godlike (*quasi Deus*) in the power and authority that he exercised subject to the constraints of no individual or institution. Endowed with a plenitude of power that included the temporal realm, the pope sanctioned and justified secular rulership. The Holy Roman Emperor was a papal delegate to whom other kings (excepting "the kings of Spain . . . because they have ripped their kingdoms out of the jaws of the enemy") were subordinated. While Alvaro effectively synthesized old arguments, the ideas that he espoused were coming under increasing challenge from royalist lawyers and even from canonists and theologians who believed that papal authority had been carried to extremes.

Besides his defense of the papal theocracy, Alvaro lamented the abuses that he perceived in all ranks in the church and in Christian society. Those who came under his lash included members of the papal curia; usurers; concubinary clerics; friars guilty of pride, idleness, incontinence, and ambition; and papal inquisitors who condemned victims in order to seize their money for themselves. Peasants, too, were a sinful lot who were unfaithful to their marriage vows and kept themselves from their wives so as not to have children they could not support. Although they attended church, they only entered during the elevation of the mass in order to see the Body of Christ, but not to receive it.

Alvaro also refuted various heresies in his *Collyrium fidei contra hereses*. His *Speculum regum*, a mirror for princes written between 1341 and 1344, was dedicated to Alfonso XI of Castile, whom he exhorted to defend the faith against the infidels, to expel the Moors from Spain, and to conquer Africa, because it pertained to the inheritance of the Visigothic kings. Ever the moralist, he castigated kings for failing to seek the counsel of their subjects, for manipulating the coinage to the detriment of the people, and for their oppression of the church. He argued that it was best to leave a tyrannical king to divine judgment, rather than bring about greater evil by seeking to dethrone him.

JOSEPH F. O'CALLAGHAN

Bibliography

Iung, N. *Un franciscain theologien du pouvoir pontifical au XIVe siècle. Alvaro Pelayo, Eveque et Penitencier de Jean XXII.* Paris, 1931.

ALVARUS, PAULUS

Córdoban laymen, author; mid-ninth century. Very little is known about his life. A reference in one of his letters hints at Jewish ancestry; another suggests Gothic blood. Either or both could, however, have been intended metaphorically given their contexts. His family owned enough land to allow them to use part of it to endow a monastery. Alvarus studied under Abbot Speraindeo at the church of St. Zoylus in Córdoba, where he met and befriended Eulogius. There, among other things, the two developed an interest in poetry, which Alvarus would pursue later in life, composing a number of poems that have survived. The preface to his *Vita Eulogii* suggests that Alvarus did not follow his friend into the priesthood. He appears to have married and to have lost three of his daughters, though the circumstances are unknown.

Letters to and from a variety of correspondents constitute the bulk of his extant writing. The earliest of these are the four directed to Bodo, a deacon in the Carolingian court who converted to Judaism, adopted the name Eleazar, and moved to Spain. Alvarus's letters to Bodo-Eleazar predictably attempt to prove that Jesus was the Messiah. Three responses survive, though in fragmentary form. Alvarus also wrote to his former teacher Speraindeo asking him to respond to an outbreak of some unnamed heresy. Alvarus directed another four letters to his friend (and perhaps brother-in-law) John of Seville, another layman, in which he explored the role of rhetoric in Christian education and delved into Christology.

Alvarus's role in the Córdoban Martyrs' Movement of the 850s was an auxiliary one. From his cell in the autumn of 851, Eulogius sent drafts of the *Memoriale sanctorum* and the *Documentum martyriale* to Alvarus for his comments. The letters that Alvarus wrote in response were subsequently appended to the treatises. We know from Eulogius that Alvarus advised at least one of the would-be martyrs who sought him out for advice. In 854 Alvarus wrote his *Indiculus luminosus*, the first half of which is a defense of the martyrs, and the second half a novel attempt to portray Muḥammad as a precursor of Antichrist by interpreting passages from Daniel, Job, and the Apocalypse in light of Alvarus's knowledge of Islam. Toward the end of the treatise, which seems not to have been completed, is the frequently quoted passage lamenting the fact that Christian youths of the day were more interested in studying Arabic than Latin literature. Finally, sometime after Eulogius's execution in 859, Alvarus wrote the *Vita Eulogii*.

The last of Alvarus's letters indicate that he had suffered from a serious illness and had received penance in anticipation of his death, only to recover. He solicited Bishop Saul of Córdoba to release him from his penitential obligation to refrain from participation in communion, a request that was denied. Alvarus's *Confessio*, a lengthy formal prayer for forgiveness of sins, probably also dates from this period. The fact that he is not mentioned in Samson's *Apologeticus* (864) and that Alvarus never referred to the controversies that elicited its composition suggests that he died in the early 860s.

KENNETH B. WOLF

Bibliography

Gil, J. (ed.) *Corpus scriptorum muzarabicorum.* 2 vols. Madrid, 1973. 1:143–361.

Sage, C. "Paul Albar of Córdoba: Studies on his Life and Writings." Washington, D.C., 1943.

AMADÍS DE GAULA

Amadís de Gaula is the Spanish book of chivalry par excellence. Historically, it is most likely the first among the Hispanic chivalric stories related to the *matière de Bretagne.* The plot is set in a time before Arthur's reign, since Arthur's world, after the discovery of the Grail, signified the apocalypse of chivalric adventures and of chivalry itself. It is impossible to summarize the number of interlaced plots and subplots that constitute the chivalric fable, *Amadís*, a veritable *roman fleuve* (river of romance). The main plot is based on what may be called the chivalric fable, which can be summarized as follows: the hero is removed by Providence from his royal family and heritage so that he can prove his virtue as a knight, win wealth, fame, and estate, and then recuperate his royal origins. Only after the hero has earned the latter are his origins revealed to him, and his royalty is publicly acknowledged. *Amadís* tells of Amadis's ancestry, birth, education, love, and adventures. He is the secret love child of King Perión and Princess Elisena. After his birth, he is set adrift in a basket (à la Moses) and rescued by a knight, Gandales, who educates him along with his own son, Gandalín. Amadís is introduced to King

Lisuarte of Britain and falls in love with Oriana, Lisuarte's daughter. Amadís dedicates his exploits and existence to Oriana, seeking to conquer her heart as well as la Ínsola Firme, a kingdom he wishes to vanquish and rule. Amadís's and Oriana's clandestine marriage in turn gives rise to a new plot based on the pattern of the chivalric fable. Oriana gives birth to their son, Esplandián, who is kidnapped by a lioness and then educated by Nacién the Hermit. Esplandián's destiny is to master the Empire of Constantinople. The romance narrates many more stories, all neatly interlaced through the use of rhetorical devices used in historiography and in Arthurian prose all over Europe. *Amadís de Gaula* is a microcosm of all the chivalric subjects that will be developed later in the sixteenth-century Spanish romances of chivalry.

The origins of *Amadís* remain uncertain. The only extant complete versions of the romance, all from the sixteenth century, differ from one another and ultimately prove reprints and transformations of the work, as it was originally planned and rewriten in four books by Garci Rodríguez de Montalvo at the beginning of the sixteenth century. There was in all likelihood an incunabulum first edition of *Amadís* that is now lost, probably printed in 1496. The first extant edition is the one published at Zaragoza by Jorge Coci in 1508. Printed editions notwithstanding, *Amadís de Gaula* had a long existence before its appearance in print. Antonio Rodríguez Moñino brought to light some manuscript fragments from a primitive *Amadís*, probably conceived in three books, in which Esplandián had already appeared. In these, Amadís was killed by his brother, Galaor, and Oriana committed suicide. Evidence indicates that tales and stories about Amadís were very popular from the middle of the fourteenth century on. Avalle Arce has speculated that the first Amadís story appeared circa 1290. Research by Cacho Blecua, however, shows that the first version of the story was probably composed during the reign of Alfonso XI, around 1330–1340.

One of the most interesting yet least studied features of the extant *Amadís* is the ideological tension that underlies the notions of chivalry, monarchy, and the discourses of power that accrued in the work during the century and a half of its circulation prior to finally appearing in print. Despite Garci Rodríguez de Montalvo's best efforts, he was unable to erase this tension, even as he tried to produce a text whose ethical and political principles reflected his own contemporary values.

J. Rodríguez-Velasco

Bibliography

Avalle Arce, J. B. *Amadís: el primitivo y el de Montalvo.* Mexico, 1990.

Ramos Nogales, R. "El *Amadís* y los nuevos libros de caballerías (1495–1530)," *Insula* 584–85 (1995), 13–15.

Rodríguez de Montalvo, G. *Amadís de Gaula.* 2 vols. Ed. J. M. Cacho Blecua. Madrid, 1986–87.

ʿĀMIRIDS *See* MANṢŪR, AL-

ANAGNI, TREATY OF

In 1295 a further attempt, with papal mediation, was made to put to an end the War of the Sicilian Vespers, which had been disrupting Italy and the Mediterranean since 1282. Pope Boniface VIII sought to strike an agreement that would strengthen his relations with King Charles II of Naples, for whom he had no great liking (Charles having been the principal support of his unhappy predecessor Celestine V), but whose influence in the Guelph factions throughout Italy made him an essential ally. Charles in the early months of 1295 showed his friendly disposition to the pope by investing Roffredo Caetani, Boniface's brother, with important estates in southern Italy. King Jaime II of Aragón also made attempts not to antagonize a pope who had already proved himself a figure not to be trifled with; he accepted Boniface's demand that he should avoid entering into marriage ties with France, which might lead to the creation of a Franco-Angevin access isolating the papacy. He was also keen to arrange the release of his sons, who were hostages in Aragónese hands. The French stabilized the situation further by renouncing all recent claims to the crown of Aragón. A third key figure was Jaime's lieutenant in Sicily, his younger brother Fadrique, who, although excommunicate, sought a meeting with the pope; Boniface was in a conciliatory enough mood to receive him away from public gaze, and to promise him the hand of Catherine de Courtenay, heiress to the Latin empire of Constantinople, in return for his abandonment of Sicily. Thus the stage was set for an agreement at Anagni, to be cemented by massive grants: a dowry of 75,000 marks when Bianca of Naples would marry Jaime II of Aragón; 6,000 florins for Jaime as the reward for an early cession of Sicily to the house of Anjou. The king of Aragón was, however, urged to recognize the rights of his uncle and namesake, Jaime II of Mallorca, in the lands from which the Aragónese had dislodged the Mallorcan king. Agreement was reached in stages during June 1295, and the treaty has been described as Boniface's first great diplomatic triumph. The problem that proved impossible to resolve was the cession of Sicily, because Fadrique of Aragón now emerged as the champion of Sicilian independence from the house of Anjou, with the backing of the Sicilian nobles and without the distraction of marrying Catherine de Courtenay (who is said to have argued that a princess without lands should not marry a prince without lands). The treaty resulted therefore in a breach between Fadrique and Jaime II of Aragón, and in new initiatives (including the grant of Sardinia to Jaime in lieu of Sicily).

DAVID S. ABULAFIA

Bibliography

T. S. R. Boase. *Boniface VIII.* London, 1933. 68–72.

S. Runciman. *The Sicilian Vespers* Cambridge, 1958. 294–95, citing primary sources.

ANCHIETA, JUAN DE

Spanish composer, born Urrestilla or Azpeitia, Guipúzcoa, 1462; died Azpeitia, 30 July 1523. His mother, Urtayzaga, was a close relative of the founder of the Society of Jesus. Queen Isabel on 6 February 1489 appointed him a singing chaplain in her court, which moved constantly (fifteen times between 1491 and 1503), and on 30 August 1493 raised his yearly salary to 30,000 maravedis. In 1495 he became *maestro de capilla* (music director) in the newly erected household of the crown prince, seventeen-year-old Don Juan (1478–1497). As such he frequently joined the music-loving prince and other selected youths in afternoons spent singing.

Queen Isabel died 26 November 1504, but Anchieta remained in her daughter Doña Juana's household. With such other court singers as Pierre de la Rue, Alexander Agricola, and Marbriano de Orto, he visited Flanders and from January to April 1506 was in southern England during the return voyage to Spain. After Felipe the Fair's death he remained Doña Juana's chaplain, at 45,000 maravedis salary. At age fifty-seven he was pensioned on 15 August 1519 by Charles V, who declared him too old to reside at court but allowed his high salary to continue to be paid until Fernando's, death, while Anchieta resided wherever he pleased. From 1500 to 1523 he was Rector of San Sebastián de Soreasu parish church in Azpeitia. He made a will, signed 19 February 1522 (codicil 26 July 1523) that itemizes rich holdings divided among blood-related heirs. From 1518 he also enjoyed large revenues from the abbacy of Arbas.

His earliest surviving work is the romance, *En memoria d'Alixandre*, composed in the summer of 1489. His *Missa ea iudios a enfardelar*, written in 1492, is lost, but in 1577 Francisco de Salinas quoted the popular song on which it was based. His villancico *Dos anades madre* continued being frequently sung as late as 1626, according to Francisco de Quevedo. Miguel de Cervantes mentioned the same work in *La ilustre fregona* (1614). In total, Anchieta's extant works include two masses for four voices (De Beata Virgine, Kyrie, Gloria, and Credo movements), *Quarti toni* (partially based on the ubiquitous *L'homme arme* song); two Magnificats; five motets; first verse __derum, for three voices; Libera me of the hymn *Conditor alme* responsory and *Salve Reqina* antiphon. His Latin works, although not scholarly, are always sonorous and graceful. His four charming songs with Spanish text are found at nos. 231, 404, 177, and 130 (*Con amores*, *Donsella*, *Dos anades*, *En memoria*) in the Palace Songbook (Madrid: Biblioteca del Palacio Real, MS 1335, formerly 2–I–5).

ROBERT STEVENSON

Bibliography

Stevenson, R. *Spanish Music in the Age of Columbus*. The Hague, 1960. 127–45, (with three complete music examples, a complete list of compositions, and sixty-nine bibliographical footnotes).

Rubio, S. *Obras completas de Juan de Anchieta*. San Sebastián, 1980. Contains also eight anonymous works attributed by the editor to Anchieta.

ANGLO-PORTUGUESE ALLIANCE *See* JOÃO I, KING OF PORTUGAL; JOHN OF GAUNT, DUKE OF LANCASTER

ANIMAL FABLES

St. Isidore explains that the behavior and speech of irrational animals in fables illustrate human behavior (*Etymologies* 1.40). Fables are narrative units customarily independent of moralization; they are heuristic, teaching by example, although in written versions promythia and epimythia are sometimes added. In discourse, fables, or allusions to them, usually explain or reinforce a statement of a cultural norm.

In remote times in India, Egypt, Syria, and in the Far East, the use of animals in illustrative tales is traceable to a belief in metempsychosis (See "The Rat Maiden," *Calila e Dimna* 4, motif B601.3). Animal tales told to illustrate an advice to princes form the five books of the Indian *Panchatantra* (third century of the Christian era). Ibn al-Muqaffa'''s eighth-century translation circulated widely in the Islamic world. In written form these tales came to the west through translation ordered in the thirteenth century by Alfonso X in *Calila e Dimna*.

In the Western tradition, a body of animal fables had accumulated around the figure of the fabulist Aesop. The first published collection by Demetrius of Phalerum (345–283 B.C.) has not survived. First-century A.D. collections available are: Latin verse by Phaedrus and slightly later Greek verse by Babrius. Avianus (late fourth–early fifth centuries) wrote forty-two fables in elegiac verse based on Babrius, and the various *Romulus* collections circulating in the Middle Ages relied on Phaedrus. (See *Ysopete ystoriado* for fifteenth-century Spanish translations.) Aesopic fables are the persuasive tools of the *Arcipreste*, *Don Amor*, *Trotaconventos*, and the various *dueñas* in the fourteenth-century *Libro de buen amor*. In the *Conde Lucanor*, out of a total of fifty-one exemplary tales, Patronio uses eleven animal fables, some drawn from Aesop and others from oriental sources, to counsel his master.

Allusions to animal fables in circulation in the oral tradition found their way into sermons. In the twelfth century, Petrus Alphonsi had alluded to three fables associated with the Arabic fabulist Loqman and included four others in the *Disciplina Clericalis*. The *Fabulae* or *Narratione* of Odo of Cheriton (thirteenth century) was the source of the fifteenth-century *Libro de los gatos*. However, a collection of over four hundred sermonic *exempla* includes only eighteen animal fables (see Clemente Sánchez de Vercial, *Libro de los exenplos por a.b.c*).

HARRIET GOLDBERG

Bibliography

Ysopete ystoriado (Toulouse 1488), Ed. V. Burrus and H. Goldberg. Madison, Wisc., 1990.

Lacarra, M. J. *Cuentística medieval en España: los orígenes*. Zaragoza, 1979.

Sánchez de Vercial, C. *Libro de los exemplos per a.b.c.* Ed. J. E. Keller, Madrid, 1961.

ANTÓNIO OF LISBON, SAINT

Fernando Martins, born in Lisbon ca. 1189, became known under the name of St. António of Lisbon. He attended the school of the Cathedral of Lisbon as acolyte and took religious vows at St. Vincent's Monastery of regular canons (ca. 1209). From there he moved to the Monastery of Santa Cruz of Coimbra (ca. 1212) where he completed his intellectual background studying patristic literature, later revealed in his sermons. He was ordained presbyter (ca. 1218) when a small group of Franciscans arrived in Coimbra and shortly after departed to Morocco, where they were martyrized. When their relics were taken back to Coimbra (1220), Fernando became a Franciscan friar and adopted the name of António. He wished to follow the martyrs' steps and went to Morocco, but he eventually settled down in Italy where he lived for some time with hermit friars. In 1222, having preached during the ordainment of several friars, he achieved so great success a that he was asked to give new sermons in places influenced by the Catharist and Albingensian heresies. He continued intensively with this activity in the north of Italy (1222–1224) and the south of France (1224–1227). He became master of the first Franciscan schools of theology in Bologna (1223), Montpellier (1223), and Toulouse (1225), and ran the Convent of Limoges (1226). The general minister João Parente appointed him visitor to the northern Italy convents (1227–1230) and itinerant preacher. Padova became the center of his preaching activity, and it was there that he wrote his *Sermones dominicales* and *Sermones festivales*. St. António mediated as peacemaker during the dissensions among the Franciscans and during the attacks led by the neighbor cities against Padova. He died on 13 June 1231 and was canonized on 30 May 1232.

JOSÉ MATTOSO

Bibliography

Gama Caeiro, F. da. *Santo António de Lisboa*. 2 vols. Lisbon, 1990.

Lopes, F. F. *Santo António de Lisboa, Doutor Evangélico*. 3rd. ed. Braga, 1980.

ANTIFEMINIST LITERATURE

With Lilith the evil succubus, and Eve the eternal temptress as models, medieval antifeminist literature portrayed woman as an inducement to sin. She was "confusión del ome e bestia syn fartura" (*Espéculo de los legos 62*). An ancient Aesopic tale compared the adulterous woman's insatiability to the hen's perpetual scratching for seed despite a barn full of grain (*Ysopete ystoriado*, motif J1908.4). Women dominated and destroyed great men: David, Aristotle, Vergil (*Libro de buen amor, Arcipreste de Talavera*).

Folktales about female adultery made their way into literature in translations from the Arabic in thirteenth-century Spain (*Libro de los engaños y assayamientos de las mugeres*; *Calila e Dimna*). Some had appeared earlier in the twelfth-century *Disciplina Clericalis* (motifs K1510 through K1544), and were subsequently recounted in the fifteenth century in the *Libro de los exemplos por a.b.c.*, *Ysopete ystoriado* (1488), and *Arcipreste de Talavera* (1438).

The audience for which antifemininist works were written is significant. Sermons and treatises intended to encourage and reinforce chastity or clerical celibacy were often explicitly antifeminist. The burned corpse of a woman hanging in a tree elicited the remark: "Oxalá llevasen todos los árbores tal fructo" (*Historia de Sequndo*).

However many sexual exempla about adultery in these treatises might have been told originally to mock their male protagonists rather than to attack women.

That humor inhered to the topic is evidenced by the seriocomic *Arcipreste de Talavera*, a work directed to both a clerical and a courtly audience. Alfonso Martínez de Toledo calls women avaricious, covetous, envious, inconstant, two-faced, disobedient, overproud, untruthful, garrulous, gossipy, and given to excessive drinking. His jocular retraction expressing mock fear of female retribution puts the lie to his serious intentions. Similarly, Pere Toroellas's vituperative *Maldezir de mujeres* (1440) ends with a graceful palinode: "Vos sois la que deshacéis lo que contienen mis versos." On the other hand, in Luis de Lucena's *Repetición de amores* (1497) the author takes seriously his censure of women and of worldly love. Not so in *Celestina*, where the servant Sempronio delivers a less-than-sincere vehement antifeminist speech as a ploy to deflate Calisto's courtly posturings about love.

HARRIET GOLDBERG

Bibliography

Goldberg, H. "Sexual Humor in Misogynist Medieval Exempla." In *Women in Hispanic Literature: Icons and Fallen Idols*. Ed. B. Miller. Berkeley, 1983. 67–83.

Lacarra, M. E. "Notes on Feminist Analysis of Medieval Spanish Literature and History," *Corónica* 17 (1988), 14–22.

ANTIPHONER OF LEÓN

The León Antiphoner is the most important document of Spanish music produced before the Reconquest of Toledo in 1085. A facsimile of the original manuscript was issued at Madrid in 1953. The manuscript, which reaches 306 folios, contains music over every page except those in the preface and calendar. The musical tradition of the León Antiphoner may be as old as King Wamba (662); Wamba's antiphoner is cited in the León (fol. 25vb) as its model. The main body was written circa 950, if the dedication to Abbat Ikilanus (917–960) is to be taken seriously. A miniature on the back of the first folio shows a scribe handing the completed antiphoner to the dedicatee. The manuscript contains eighteen other miniatures, that (at fol. 217^{v}) of royal consecration being one of the earliest of its class known. The preface, which includes 130 lines of inflated Latin poetry, bears a much later date: 1069.

This prefatory poem, like many of the chants in the León Antiphoner, is ascribed to a definite author: in this case Eugenius III of Toledo. According to our poet, no single individual endowed the Spanish Church with its numerous beautiful chants. On the contrary, many holy men inspired by God made up its dowry. Eugenius's poem notes that "In that former age many individuals, enjoying a common inspiration, composed chants in honor of the Almighty." The poet's testimony is confirmed by evidence scattered in the margins throughout the main body of the León Antiphoner. Marginal ascriptions mention such pre-Conquest fathers as Isidore, Ildephonsus, Julian of Toledo, Rogatus of Baeza, and Balduigius of Ercávica. The case for their authenticity is strengthened by the fact that the same scribe who jotted the ascriptions copied both text and neumes. However, several of the *plurimis sacris virorum* to whom chants in the León Antiphoner are ascribed were obscure persons, even by Spanish standards.

With his eye ever on the past, our Antiphoner poet complains not only that the threefold division of the choir has died out, but—worse still—that the whole body of singers *connexi nunc psallant exules a docmatu* (now stand together when singing praises, departing from right tradition). But he hopes for the return of better days, when singers who carefully meditate on every word they sing will win back many wandering minds from vain things.

Throughout the main body of the León Antiphoner such performance directions as the following appear: *Dicentes voces praeconias* (fol. 133); *Imponit arcediaconus voce clara hanc antiphonam* (fol. 153^{v}); *Imponit episcopus hanc antiphonam subtili voce decantando: Ecce venit hora ut dispergamini* (fol. 164^{v}); *Imponit episcopus voce tremula* (fol. 166^{v}). In the first rubric, the deacons giving instruction to an assembly of catechumens (not those to be confirmed, since confirmation in the Mozarabic rite was administered immediately after baptism, and by a priest, not a bishop) are required to sing in a loud town-crier's voice. In the second, the archdeacon is advised to sing a Palm Sunday antiphon in a clear voice. In the third, the bishop chants an antiphon with words from the Passion narrative—"Behold the hour cometh, yea is now come, that ye shall be scattered, every man to his own, and shall leave me alone" (John xvi. 32)—is enjoined to sing this particular text *sotto voce*, doubtless for dramatic effect. In the fourth, the bishop who sings *Populae meus* ("O my people, what have I done unto thee? and wherein have I wearied thee" [Micah vi. 3]) is directed to begin the *Improperia* with a tremolo in his voice—again, surely with deliberate dramatic intent.

Fortunately, the León Antiphoner is preserved in its entirety. Beginning with 17 November, the first day in the Mozarabic church year (St. Acisclus's Day), it carries through without interruption to the following 17 November, providing certain additional chants at the end for the dedication of a basilica, consecrations of bishops and kings, marriages, the ministry to the sick, and committals. Because it is not mutilated after the fashion of other Mozarabic monuments the liturgiologist can go through it, making a comparative study of "forms" in Mozarabic music. Such a study is the more necessary because certain Mozarabic chant types are uniquely Spanish while others, if not uniquely so, bear names that can cause confusion. For instance, *prolegendum* = introit; *psallendum* = gradual; *laudes* = alleluia; *sacrificium* = offertory; *trenos* = tract. The two uniquely Spanish chant types would seem to be the *preces* and the *sono*. But *sono*, like *selah* in the Hebrew psalms, is a term still too imperfectly understood to permit secure definition.

The León Antiphoner not only contains chants for the entire church year but (unlike modern antiphonaries) for the office as well as mass. Such ramifications of any chant type as the following can therefore be studied: (1) comparative position in the Hours and in the Sacrifice; (2) choice of text —different or the same in the Office and Mass; (3) syllabic versus melismatic treatments of the text; (4) formal structure of the melodies; (5) use of borrowed musical material.

The *laudes* are the one chant type that has been most exhaustively studied with just such criteria as the above in mind. As for their place in the eucharist laudes climactically closed the Mass of the Catechumens. They provided a musical coda to the homily expounding the Gospel for the Day. But if their position made of them an *Ite missa est* closing the Mass of the Catechumens, they also served as a transition into the Mass of the Faithful.

Though the word *alleluia* came after the scriptural verse in Office laudes it preceded the verse in Mass laudes. What is more, the scriptural texts of the Mass laudes—though still of a laudatory type—were not invariably chosen from Psalms 148 or 150, or even for that matter from any psalm. The jubilus in the alleluia, to make a further contrast with the Office laudes, came always on the last syllable, the *a*. In sixty-eight of the seventy-six Mass laudes, the luxuriant melisma on the final *a* in *alleluia* was again repeated on the final (or penultimate) syllable of the scriptural verse that follows the alleluia.

Mass laudes, outside Lent, can be grouped according to several well-defined musical types. One of these, the *Ecce servus* type of laudes melody, appears in masses honoring masculine saints: Andrew, Eugenius, Cucufatus (Cugat), Cyprian, Cosmas, and Damian. Another, the *Lauda filia* type, appears in masses honoring feminine saints: Eulalia. Justa, and Rufina. A third type, the *Lauda Hierusalem*, is again dedicated to masculine saints; John the Baptist, Columba, Emilianus. (Twenty-four laudes melodies cannot, however, be classified under types.)

If in the Visigothic liturgy the word *alleluia* dominates the Mass as well as Office laudes it appears even more frequently elsewhere in the liturgy as an interjection. A study of its use shows that the single word *alleluia* was considered equally appropriate in an Office for the Dead and in an Easter Mass. The alleluia outside laudes was always melismatically treated. Occasionally it stretched to spectacular lengths. Vocalisms in the León Antiphoner reaching such an extravagant number of notes as three-hundred are by no means rare. On the very first page of the facsimile (fol. 29) such a melisma can be seen. The scribe copied it in the outer margin, beginning the neumes at the bottom of the page and carrying them up to the top. In the first hundred leaves the margins of thirty-four pages have been so used.

Obviously neumes that can be written from bottom to top of a page lack any heightened implications; but patterns of neumes occur. In the marginal *alleluia* copied (at folio 60) the following musical structure can be easily enough detected: AA′, BB′, CC′, D (the vocalism appears here over the second syllable of the word). This same melody recurs elsewhere in the Antiphoner fitted syllabically to a text beginning *Sublimius diebus*. The melisma that served as a model for the sequence *Sublimius diebus* (fol. 1^v of the León Antiphoner) forms part of the "Sono" of the office *Ad matutinum* found at folio 60. Because long melismas of the AA′, BB′, CC′, DD′ type so frequently occur, it is not surprising to find that repeat signs were sometimes used to lighten the labor of copying. In the León Antiphoner a stylized letter *d* looking like a backward *6* with the ascender crossed (abbreviating *denuo* or *dupliciter*) is used 128 times as a repeat sign. The sequence was therefore an established form in Spain a century before Notker Balbulus.

Robert Stevenson

Bibliography

Anglés, H. "La música medieval en Toledo," *Gesammelte Aufsätze zur Kulturgeschichte Spaniens* 7 (1938), 11–12.

Antifonario visigotico mozárabe de la Cathedral de Leon. Edición facísimil. Madrid, 1953.

Brou, D. L. "L'Alleluia dans la liturgie mozarabe," *Anuario Musical* 6 (1951), 8, 11, 50.

———. "Le joyau des antiphonaires latins," *Archivos Leoneses* 8, no. 15 (1954), 32–34.

———. "Séquences et Tropes dans la liturgie mozarabe," *Hispania Sacra*, 4 (1951), 27–41.

Férotin, D. M. *Le Liber Mozarabicus Sacramentorum et les Manuscrits Mozarabes*. Paris, 1912.

Stevenson, R. *Spanish Music in the Age of Columbus*. Westport, Conn., 1979. 13–17.

Villada, Z. G. *Catálogo de los Códices y Documentos de la Catedral de León*. Madrid, 1919. 38–40.

APOLLONIUS OF TYRE *See* LIBRO DE APOLONIO

ARABIC LANGUAGE

The Muslim invasion of 711 had two broad linguistic consequences for the Ibero-Romance languages. First, it brought the Romance dialects of Hispania in contact with Arabic, thus creating an environment for substantial lexical borrowing and occasional morphological borrowing. Second, the dialectal map of Iberia was radically changed and importance was given to varieties of Romance that otherwise might have remained insignificant.

Against von Wartburg's claim that the Moors were responsible *per negationem* for the national and linguistic domains of Portuguese, Castilian, and Catalan, contemporary scholarship no longer sees the invaders and their language as passive onlookers to the development of the Ibero-Romance languages. Between 711 and 718 the Moors established control over approximately three-fourths of the Iberian Peninsula but allowed the survival of Christian enclaves in the north and northwest. The geographical unevenness of the Muslim presence on the peninsula is reflected today in the much weaker influence of Arabic on Galician and Eastern and Northern (French) Catalan than on Castilian, Portuguese, and Western Catalan.

Sociolinguistic tensions ran high among educated speakers of Arabic and Romance, with each side blaming the coexistence of languages for an erosion of native language abilities. Hillenbrand (Jayussi) cites Alvarus, bishop of Córdoba, who in 850 remarked of his coreligionists, ". . . hardly one can write a passable Latin letter to a friend, but innumerable are those who can express themselves in Arabic and can compose poetry in that language with greater ease than the Arabs themselves." As Harvey reports, toward the end of the cohabitation period, the fifteenth-century *muftī* (senior clerical exegete of the Qu'rān and the *sharī'a*) al-Wansharīshī lamented the loss of distinctive features of Muslim life as a consequence of bilingualism: "One has to be aware of the pervasive effect of their way of life, their language . . . as has occurred in the case of the inhabitants of Ávila and other places, for they have lost their Arabic, and when the Arabic language dies out, so does devotion in it, and there is consequential neglect of worship as expressed in world. . . ." Thus there is significant anxiety on both sides not just about losing language, but also about the inevitable loss of culture in a prolonged situation of bilingualism.

Across the north-central part of the peninsula, the Christian Reconquest seems to have had a devastating effect on the Arabic-speaking Muslim communities; little evidence is available to make strong conclusions about the status of Arabic in the everyday life of those areas. Yet in al-Andalus, the Arab-controlled southern portion of the peninsula, there is abundant evidence of more self-confident and self-assertive Muslim communities. It was to Valencia, for example, that Aragónese Muslims sent their young men who needed to be trained in Arabic. And though in the Arabic side to Mudéjar, where bilingual Muslims lived under Christian rule, Valencian historical documentation is sparse and suffused by the Romance speech of the incoming conquerors, there was no sign until the early fifteenth century that Arabic was in real danger of being replaced by Castilian there or in Naṣrid Granada (i.e., the line of kings, 1232–1492, descended from Yūsuf ibn Naṣr).

The multilingual nature of al-Andalus cannot by itself explain the host of Arabisms taken into Ibero-Romance, since the forms of Romance spoken bilingually with Arabic in Islamic Iberia (e.g., the Mozarabic dialects of Spain) were not forms of Portuguese, Castilian, or Catalan, but rather independent descendants of spoken Latin that became extinct in the later Middle Ages. Two important factors that motivated the substantial borrowing of Arabic words across Ibero-Romance are the need for names applicable to new concepts that reached north from al-Andalus and the high cultural prestige associated with Arabic in the early Middle Ages.

A very high percentage of Arabisms in Ibero-Romance are nouns. Lapesa's enthusiastic count of some four thousand Arabisms in Castilian has been reduced to around nine hundred (with derived forms accounting for the apparent total of four thousand. A comparable number is cited for Portuguese; Machado claims exactly 954 Arabisms. For Catalan, Badia and Moll give estimates of around two hundred borrowings. In his book-length study of four hundred Arabisms in Ibero-Romance and Italian, Kielser (1994) found eighty direct borrowings common to Portuguese, Castilian, and Catalan. The following semantic fields show examples of particularly frequent borrowings across Ibero-Romance: (1) plant life: in Portuguese, *albricoque*; in Castilian, *albaricoque*; in Catalan, *albercoc* (all meaning apricot); *alfarroba*; in Castilian, *algarroba*; in Catalan, *garrofa* (all meaning carob bean); in Portuguese *limão*; in Castilian, *limón*; in Catalan, *llimona* (all meaning lemon); (2) food preparations and seasonings: in Portuguese and Castilian, *escabeche* (meaning pickling brine); in Catalan, *escabetx* (meaning vinegar and oil sauce); in Portuguese and Catalan, *alcaravia* (more commonly in Catalan, *comi*); in Castilian, *alcaravea* (meaning caraway seeds); in Portuguese, *açúcar*; in Castilian, *azúcar*; in Catalan, *sucre* (all meaning sugar); (3) agriculture: in Portuguese, *alcaria*; Castilian, *alquería*; in Catalan, *alqueria* (all meaning farmstead); in Portuguese, *adua* (meaning common irrigation water); in Castilian and Catalan, *dula* (meaning common pasture); in Portuguese, *acéquiad*, in Castilian, *acequia*; in Catalan, *sèquia* (meaning irrigation ditch); (4) social organization: in Portuguese, *bairro*; in Castilian, *barrio*; in Catalan, *barri* (all meaning district, neighborhood); in Portuguese, *alfama* (meaning Jewish quarter); in Castilian, *aljama* (meaning gathering, quarter); and in Catalan, *aljama* (meaning Jewish or Arab quarter): in Castilian, *arrabal* (meaning poor neighborhood); (in Portuguese, *arrabalde*; and Catalan, *raval* (both meaning suburb); (5) in armed forces and weapons: in Portuguese, *adail* (meaning commander); in Castilian, *adalid* (meaning, champion); in Catalan, *adalil* (meaning captain, guide); in Portuguese and Catalan, *aljava*; in Castilian, *aljaba* (all meaning quiver); in Portuguese and Castilian, *almenara*; in Catalan, *alinara* (meaning beacon, signal fire); (6) mathematics and measurements: in Portuguese and Castilian, *cifra*; in Catalan, *xifra* (meaning figure, cipher); in Portuguese, *fânega*; Castilian, *fanega*; in Catalan, *faneca* (all meaning dry measurement [1.58 bushels]); in Portuguese, Castilian, and Catalan, *nadir* (all meaning nadir, lowest point).

Like many lexical borrowings, these Arabisms were rephonologized to meet the requirements of the various Ibero-Romance sound systems. Lloyd gives two good examples from Old Spanish: (1) the group of Arabic back fricatives—pharyngeal/ḫ/ ح, glottal/h/ ه, and dorsovelar /x/ خ —came into Old Spanish as labiodental fricative /f/; for example, *ḫatta* (in Old Spanish, *fa(s)ta*, meaning until), *al-hadiya* (in Old Spanish, *alfadía*, meaning bribe) *al-xumra* (in Old Spanish, *alfombra*, meaning carpet); (2) a few Arabic words beginning with voiceless palatal hushed fricative /š/ ش constitute a minor source for the same sibilant in Old Spanish, for example, *šah* (in Old Spanish, *xaque*, meaning king [in chess]) *šarab* (in Old Spanish, *xarabe*, meaning syrup). Note that these are not examples of Arabic phonemic interference in Romance—no Arabic phonemes were taken wholesale into Ibero-Romance—but rather of how Old Spanish, in these examples, used its existing sound inventory to render foreign sounds in loan words.

Arabic nouns are normally presented with the article *al-*, regardless of number and gender; this element has generally been incorporated into the lexeme across Ibero-Romance without the determiner value. The article appears less frequently in Catalan than in Castilian and Portuguese, for example, in Portuguese, *algodão*, in Castilian, *algodón*; in Catalan, *cotó*, (all meaning cotton); in Portuguese, and Castilian, *albacora*; in Catalan, *bacora* (meaning albacore, tuna). The Arabic relative adjective or *nisba* suffix /-i:/ was also borrowed by Castilian, especially for proper substantives related to Islam and Arabs, for example, in Castilian, *marroquí* (Moroccan), *iraní* (Iranian), *pakistaní* (Pakistani) but in Portuguese, *marroquiano*, *iraniano*, *paquistanense*, and in Catalan, *marroquí* (corresponding to the Castilian *marroquino*), *iranià*, *pakistanès*. Finally, the Arabic patronymic *ibn* was reanalyzed as prefix *ben-* in the formation of family names such as *Benavides* and *Benigómez*.

As for syntactic influences and semantic calques, Corriente (Jayussi 1994, 445–46) rejects widely accepted claims of Arabic influence in paronomastic expressions such as *burla burlando* (to get something unintentionally) and *calla callando* (to get something without making a fuss or being noticed), and in the semantic calques *infante* (son of the king), via Arabic, *walad* (child, son of the king) and *hidalgo* (noble), in Portuguese and Old Spanish, *fidalgo*, via Arabic, *ibn ad-dunya* (son of wealth).

Written sources of Arabic texts from Islamic Iberia include Díaz García's *Devocionario morisco en árabe dialectal hispánico* (1981) and Marugán's *El refranero andalusí de Ibn Asim Al-Garnati* (1994). Major dictionaries relevant to this topic are Corriente's *Diccionario de arabismos y voces afines en iberorromance* (1999) and *A Dictionary of Andalusi Arabic* (1997), and Machado's *Vocabulario português de origem árabe* (1991). A journal, *Estudios de dialectología norteafricana y andalusí* (1996–), is published by the University of Zaragoza.

James A. Monk

Bibliography

Corriente, F. *Árabe andalusí y lenguas romances*. Madrid, 1992.

———. *A Grammatical Sketch of the Spanish Arabic Dialect Bundle*. Madrid, 1977.

Galmés de Fuentes, A. *Influencias sintácticas y estilísticas del árabe en la prosa medieval castellana*. Madrid, 1956.

Harvey, L. P. *Islamic Spain, 1250 to 1500*. Chicago, 1990.

Jayussi, S. K. (ed.) *The Legacy of Muslim Spain*. 2 vols. New York, 1994.

Kiesler, R. *Kleines vergleichendes Wörterbuch der Arabismen im Iberoromanischen und Italienischen*. Tübingen, 1994.

Machado, J. P. *Ensaios arábico-portuguêses*. Lisbon, 1997.

Steiger, A. *Contribución a la fonética del hispano-árabe y de los arabismos en el ibero-románico y el siciliano*. Madrid, 1991 [1932].

Wasserstein, D. "The Language Situation in al-Andalus." In *The Formation of al-Andalus*. Ed. M. Fierro and J. Samsó. Aldershot, U.K., 1998. 2: 3–18.

Wright, R. "The End of Written Ladino in al-Andalus." In *The Formation of al-Andalus*. Ed. M. Fierro and J. Samsó, Aldershot, U.K., 1998. 2: 19–36.

ARAGÓN, CROWN OF

The Crown of Aragón was a dynastic union of Aragón and the county of Barcelona dating from the betrothal of Petronilla of Aragón and Ramón Berenguer IV of Barcelona in 1137. Their marriage took place in 1150, their son Alfonso was the first of their descendants to assume the title of king, and their dynasty ruled Aragón, Catalonia, and other lands added to the original nucleus until 1410. The term Crown of Aragón, however, dated only from the later Middle Ages. The union remained personal. The ruler was king in Aragón and count in Barcelona, an arrangement not without risk for the Catalans. But little attention was paid at first to constitutional niceties. Records of fiscal administration in Catalonia show that the ruler was "lord king" there, and not simply count, in the later twelfth century. But it is an even more striking fact that the early monarchs and their courtiers held tenaciously to the joint vision of Petronilla and her husband. The court of Alfonso II included Aragónese and Catalonian barons and clerks and the earliest conjoint assemblies of the two (or more) realms, ancestors of the *cortes* (parliament) of the Crown of Aragón, date from the second half of the twelfth century. In most respects, however, and most notably in the sphere of law and privilege, the monarchs were obliged to treat their peoples distinctly. Hence it is customary to speak of them as "count kings."

Under the early count-kings (Ramón Berenguer IV, 1131–1162, whose title was "prince" in Aragón; Alfonso II, 1162–1196; and Pedro II, 1196–1213) the union worked well. Neither Aragón nor Catalonia was neglected, both societies prospered and matured, and joint lordship promoted the expansive ambitions that fired later ages of conquest. Ramón Berenguer IV was the dynasty's first great conqueror. He opened up the frontiers of Catalonia and Aragón for Christian resettlement at the expense of the Moors, annexed Tortosa and Lérida (1148–1149), and encouraged ecclesiastical initiatives. The military Order of the Hospital and Temple were endowed in local commanderies, especially in frontier lands; Cistercian monks established their more austere form of the Benedictine Rule at Poblet and Santes Creus (1150–1153) in Catalonia and later at Veruela and (for nuns) Casbas in Aragón; while the archbishopric of Tarragona was reestablished (1154) with jurisdiction over the sees in both lands. Lay and religious lords encouraged immigration by granting liberal terms of settlements. The later twelfth century was a time of sustained demographic and economic growth and prosperity. There was movement toward frontier lands from the old uplands of Aragón and Catalonia, but settlers came also from north of the Pyrenees and even from England.

Under Alfonso II something of the expansionist fervor was lost. This ruler's marriage to Sancha of Castile confirmed the vision of a Christian Iberian Peninsula dominated by the two most advantaged crowns. Old understandings with Castile over prospective spheres of Muslim conquest were adjusted in favor of Aragón in the Treaties of Cazorla (1179). Valencia was to be Aragón's, a designation made just when this Moorish realm seemed an inviting prey. But Alfonso, a cultivated man with interests in southern France, had been brought up to distrust the barons and knights whose harsh lordships, especially in Catalonia, had been a cause of complaint for several decades. His programmatic effort to pacify his lands could only have succeeded if he had satisfied baronial demands for the spoils of aggressive conquest. Lacking the militancy of his father, Alfonso let pass the opportunity and it was characteristic that when in 1195 he responded to the threat posed by the Muslim victory at Alarcos it was in somewhat pretentious hopes of leading an all-peninsular crusade. Everywhere interests (they can hardly be called "policies") were more dynastic than territorial. Alliance with the Castilians and Angevins was deployed chiefly in southern France against the perceived threat of an expansionist Capetian monarchy allied with the count of Toulouse. But there was nothing imperialistic about Catalan-Aragónese interests across the Pyrenees. Provence might have remained under a cadet branch of the dynasty had Ramón Berenguer III not been killed (1166) without leaving a male heir; when the boy-king's advisers seized Provence, an old conflict between Barcelona and Toulouse was renewed. At the came of age Alfonso had to cultivate new allies in Béarn, Bigorre, and Foix to offset the disaffection of his old vassals in lower Occitania; but when the viscount Roger II of Béziers, having become vulnerable to the church's campaign against heretics, upset the Toulousan hegemony by commending himself to Alfonso, the count-king's influence in Occitania achieved its maximum success.

Pedro II (Pere I in Catalonia) succeeded his father in Aragón and Catalonia as well as in most of the Occitania suzerainties; his brother inherited Provence, Millau, and Razès. But while the concept of a solely peninsular union thus survived intact, Pedro was to be at once more ambitious and less successful across the Pyrenees than his father had been. He defied tradition by allying with Raymond VI of Toulouse, married the heiress María of Montpellier in 1204, and then had himself crowned at Rome by Pope Innocent III, to

Aragón Kings, 1213–1516

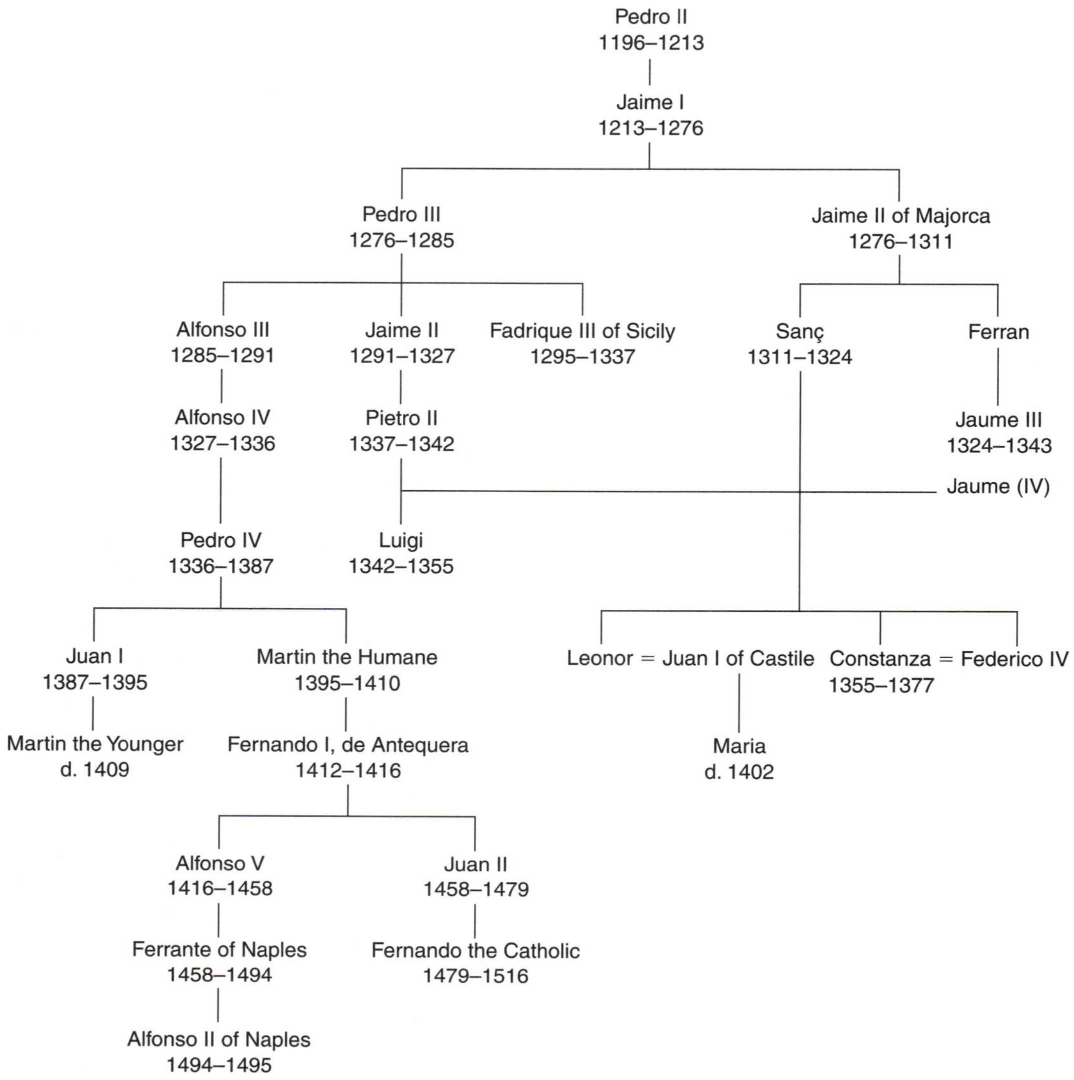

whom he engaged to pay a tribute of submission. The latter event was staged to enhance the count-king's prestige among Christian monarchs. It led Pedro's spectacular role in the united crusading army that crushed the Almohads at Las Navas de Tolosa in 1212. But the Aragónese-papal entente failed badly during the Albigensian crisis. Pedro tried to mediate, then worked to secure hegemony over the meridional lords opposed to the crusaders of Simon de Montfort. All these efforts collapsed in the Battle of Muret (12 September 1213). Pedro was killed and his suzerainties over Béziers, and Toulouse destroyed.

Historians have sometimes exaggerated the import of this disaster. In reality, the trans-Pyrennean lands had never formed part of the dynastic patrimony, which remained intact, so that disgruntled barons who remembered Ramón Berenguer IV may have been more relieved than upset when the Pyrennean distraction was removed. The child king, nurtured in a regency representing the pope, the Templars, and Aragónese and Catalan notables, learned early what power he had to gain by renewing the anti-Moorish conquest. Hardened by setbacks and factional opposition, Jaime I (1213–1276) led a well-financed and popular expedition against Mallorca in 1229. Catalans dominated in the conquest and resettlement, but townsmen of Italy and Provence joined in what was labeled a "crusade" and shared in the spoils. Gaining annulment of his marriage to Eleanor of Castile in 1229, Jaime waited until 1235 to marry Iolanda of Hungary with papal approval. Meanwhile, impatient Aragónese barons had forced the king's hand in Valencia, seizing Morella in 1232. A more urgent (and dangerous) motive for the Valencian conquest arose from the king's engagement to cede the Balearic Islands and Valencia to the sons of his second marriage.

The conquest of Valencia, projected in *cortes* at Monzón (1236), was achieved relentlessly in 1237–1238. The Moors were permitted to depart in peace, a guarantee made uneasy by Aragónese hopes for loot. The custom of Aragón had prevailed in charters granted in the early phases of conquest, but settlers from Aragón were far outnumbered by Catalans thereafter; and toward 1239 the king ordered a new territorial custom drawn up for Valencia (the *Furs*), eclectic and Romanist, first published in Latin and then (1261) in Catalan. Settlers coming chiefly from the plains of Lérida and Urgell remained the minority in a predominantly Mudéjar population. The conquest was virtually completed with the captures of Játiva (1244) and Biar (1245).

With the annexations of Mallorca and Valencia, Jaime I fulfilled the purpose of his forefathers. He had dramatically enlarged the Crown of Aragón in God's service. But he was no political expansionist, as his later conquest of Murcia on behalf of Castile (1266) was to prove; nor had any public concern for administrative unity overtaken the conception of the royal inheritance as a proprietary condominium. If he reserved the patrimonial realms for his firstborn, Alfonso, when he provided for his second son, Pedro (1241), Jaime seriously proposed, in a second partition occasioned by the birth of a third son (1243), to separate Aragón and Catalonia. This scheme reflected the king's estrangement from Alfonso, whose Castilian sympathies grew stronger as his ambitions were thwarted.

The conqueror's success in Spain was countered by setbacks in southern France. Dynastic hopes were dashed by the failure of the counts of Toulouse and Provence to bear male heirs, for the sons of Jaime I were too closely related to the heiresses to compete for their hands with Capetian princes. Despite urgent negotiations to prevent it, Jaime saw Provence pass to Charles of Anjou (1246) and Toulouse to Alphonse of Poitiers (1249). But while some lament was heard for the passing of native dynasties in the Midi, notably from the troubadours, there is no sign that the conqueror viewed the king of France as other than a fellow crusader. With the Treaty of Corbeil (1258) Jaime renounced all his rights in Occitania, save that over Montpellier, while Louis IX gave up his claim to counties of the former Spanish March. To complete the political reversal, which recognized Capetian expansion almost to the Pyrenees, Jaime engaged his daughter Isabel to Philip, the heir to France. On the other hand, his son Pedro's marriage to Constanza of Hohenstaufen was to open up a new prospect of Mediterranean expansion at the cost of renewed hostility with France.

Like his predecessrs, Jaime found it harder to rule in peace than in war. Thought by the Aragónese to favor Catalonia and by the Catalans to favor Castile, he spent his later years negotiating, organizing, and commemorating. No medieval king revealed himself so well to posterity; his *Book of Deeds* celebrated Jaime's peoples as well as himself in the glow of their most durable triumphs. The reign was marked by continued institutional growth. Registers of administrative correspondence were inaugurated while new forms of elite delegations pointed the way to the vice regencies of later times. The *cortes*, becoming an instrument of political influence in Aragón and Catalonia—and occasionally representing both lands, as in 1236—were instituted also in Valencia. Local administration and law were renovated, while religious life drew new sustenance from the spread of Franciscan and Dominican friars.

Pedro III (1276–1285) succeeded his father, as a grown and tried ruler. In dominating early rebellions and seizing dynastic opportunities, he achieved stunning triumphs while misunderstanding the political costs. He tried to neutralize Castile and France by seizing the Infantes de la Cerda, the disinherited grandsons of Alfonso X and the sons of Blanche of France. He arranged a truce with Granada and renewed a protectorate over Tunis. His Sicilian ambitious became clear when he prepared fleets for service on the Tunisian coasts in 1281 and 1282; his court had long harbored Hohenstaufen dissidents. When the Sicilians rose against the Angevins (30 March 1282), Pedro readied himself for their call and landed at Trapani to a warm welcome five months later. Having received the Sicilians' fealty and confirmed their privileges, he drove the Angevin fleet from Calabrian waters.

Never had a realm been so easily annexed to the Crown of Aragón. But it meant war on all fronts: against Charles of Anjou, who first challenged Pedro to single combat (with comically inconsequential results) and then proceeded to orchestrate a papal-Capetian crusade against Aragón; and against the estates of Aragón and Catalonia, which protested that they had not been consulted about the Sicilian business and that they were being taxed unlawfully. In stormy sessions with the Aragónese, Pedro was finally obliged to confirm a comprehensive definition of their privileges (October 1283). Thus originated the "Union" of Aragón, which was to be a constitutional force for decades thereafter; the office of *Justicia*, with power to mediate between the king and the Aragónese, dates also from this time. A similar settlement with the Catalans was reached in a great *cortes* of Barcelona in December 1283. But the hurt ran deep as war loomed with France. When Philip III invaded through the eastern Pyrenees in 1285, Pedro had difficulty mobilizing the defensive and naval forces, which prevailed to drive out the French (October 1285). Within weeks all the protagonists—Philip III, Charles of Anjou, Pope Martin IV, and Pedro himself—were dead.

Pedro III had won Sicily and pacified and defended his realm, but he had fundamentally altered the constitution by conceding baronial and municipal autonomy while allowing the power of the estates to be institutionalized. And it remained to be seen whether the Aragónese could be reconciled to an expansionist regime partial to Catalonian interests and whether Sicily could be secured against Angevins, Capetians, and popes.

These problems clouded the reigns of Alfonso III (1285–1291), Jaime II (1291–1327), and Alfonso IV (1327–1326). Alfonso III inherited all the realms except Sicily, which passed to his brother Jaime who in turn gave it as a lieutenancy to his younger brother Frederick when he (Jaime) succeeded in the main line in 1291. Settlement with France on terms of an eventual recovery of Sicily by the (Angevin) house of Naples was reached in 1302 but never effected. Jaime II acted with both energy and caution on all his frontiers, extending Catalan influence throughout the Mediterranean, and presiding over general prosperity and growth. In 1302 Catalan mercenaries idled by the end of the Sicilian wars agreed to aid the Byzantine emperor against the Turks in return for concessions that led to their settlement in Greece. After 1311 the Catalan duchies of Athens and Neopatria became dependent on Sicily with the customs of Catalonia; but these colonies were never more than a precarious outpost of the Crown of Aragón (1311–1388). As for Sardinia, which had been ceded by the pope in 1297 in compensation for the renunciation of Sicily, Jaime II entrusted its conquest to his son Alfonso, who carried it out in 1323–1324.

The Crown of Aragón attained its apogee as a federative state during the long reign of Pedro IV (Pere III in Catalonia, 1336–1387). He reintegrated Mallorca in the dynastic polity and imposed himself on the Aragónese by force, effectively undoing the union. He met his match in Castile, however, where Pedro the Cruel followed by Enrique of Trastámara proved worthy adversaries with superior resources. In 1375 Pedro IV settled on terms of the territorial integrity of Aragón while ceding his claims to Molina and Murcia. In a further agreement of unforeseen importance, the Infanta Leonora of Aragón was betrothed to Juan of Trastámara.

These events confirmed the federation's Mediterranean destiny, though it was not an easy one. Jaime IV made a desperate attempt to recover his ousted father's title to Mallorca in 1374. Sardinia remained turbulent, a prey to Genoese ambitions. The Sicilians for their part had come to think of the Catalan dynasty as foreign. Pedro failed to persuade his son to marry the heiress to Sicily, although she finally married the son of Pedro's second son, Martin, who in 1380 assumed viceregal powers in Sicily. When in the same year the Catalan duchies submitted to him, Pedro had achieved domination of a vastly extended Crown of Aragón, but at high cost, for the cortes of the old realms had wrung major concessions to their autonomy for their grants of subsidy. Moreover, the acquired lands remained restive: the duchies in Greece were lost in 1388, and Pedro's sons Juan I (1387–1395) and Martín I (1395–1410) were severely challenged in Mallorca, Sardinia, and Sicily.

Martín's death without heirs in 1410 brought the dynastic line to an end. Among contenders for the crown, the favorite in Catalonia was Jaime of Urgell, a direct descendant of Jaime II. But Jaime antagonized the Aragónese, opening the way for the candidacy of Fernando of Antequera, grandson of Pedro IV and uncle of the king of Castile. In 1412 electors chosen by parliaments in the peninsular realms met at Caspe and decided in favor of Fernando. Jaime rebelled, but was soon captured and imprisoned.

It was a fateful turning point, the dynastic ratification of Castile's demographic and military superiority. Fernando and his sons ruling after him—Alfonso V (Alfons IV in Catalonia), 1416–1458, and Juan II, 1458–1479—were Castilians in real and constant danger of losing touch with their subjects. Meeting resistence in Catalonia and Aragón, Alfonso V clung to power in Sicily and Sardinia and aspired to the succession in Naples, which he conquered only after years of negotiations and fighting in 1443. There he remained, leaving Catalonia to be ruled by his wife and other realms by viceroys. Seeking to create in Naples a dynastic preserve for his illegitimate son Fernando, Alfonso made some effort to revive Hohenstaufen administrative efficiency while patronizing literature, music, and theology and drawing heavily on revenues from Sicily and Catalonia.

Hopes for the best gave way to despair in the peninsula. Aragón bore the financial brunt of Prince Juan's self-serving yet futile conflicts in Castile. Mallorca was set back by renewed war with Genoa and agrarian disorder. Only Valencia seemed relatively free of the social unrest and economic dislocation that afflicted the other realms, Catalonia above all. Lacking firm direction, the *cortes* had fallen prey to searing antagonisms among the estates themselves and against royal agents trying to recover alienated patrimony. King Alfonso began by siding with the old aristocracy, but as their financial support dwindled he revived an old royal program of agrarian reform. This was to aggravate a smoldering conflict between landlords and peasants in Old Catalonia, where one of the most repressive modes of lordship in western Europe had survived. Moreover, royal efforts to undermine patrician dominations in the towns caused trouble from the 1440s, especially in Barcelona, where a party of "honored citizens" (the Biga) was opposed by merchants and artisans. (Existing tensions worsened under Juan II, whose insensitivity to all, including his popular son Prince Carlos, precipitated a revolt of the *remença* peasants. The Council of Catalonia raised an army to put down the rising, while Queen Juana tried to impose a settlement on the peasants and then allied with their leader. Meanwhile, the king's pledge of Roussillon and Cerdanya to Louis XI in return for French intervention fired a resurgence of antiroyalist patriotism. But the Catalonian cause so-called failed to elicit much response in the other realms, and its desperate bids to replace Juan with foreign rulers miscarried. In the end Juan prevailed through patient efforts. Girona and Barcelona returned to his fidelity in 1472, and the king confirmed Catalonian privileges. But the *remença* conflict continued, as did disorders in Aragón, Valencia, and Sardinia. Juan's son Fernando, having married Isabel of Castile in 1469, became king consort in Castile in 1474 and succeeded his father in the Crown of Aragón in 1479. The old dream of Hispanic hegemony was realized at last—in favor of a Castilian dynasty.

The Crown of Aragón had been an administrative state since the thirteenth century. It was not really an empire, nor were its institutions generated from some preconceived ideal of dynastic expansion. The viceroyalities and procuratorships of the later Middle Ages were descended from delegations of Provence in the twelfth century; they remained patrimonial lordships as well as offices to the end. Moreover, the insistence on privilege in each of the realms impeded the development of pan-regnal administration, although in various ways Jaime II, Pedro IV, and their successors promoted a community of interest. Federative impulses, such as the founding of a university at Lérida (1300) or the declaration that the realms be indivisible (1319), had little meaning outside the original nucleus of Aragón and Catalonia. The strength of the union, such as it was, lay in Catalonia's mercantile and maritime energies, with Aragón and Sicily cast in the role of agrarian suppliers. But the federation was vulnerable to social, technological, and demographic constraints. Everywhere the multiplied working masses were forced into harsh and resented dependencies, while communications, investment, and banking lagged behind real needs. Moreover, the peninsular realms lacked sufficient populations to compete with Castile in the long term. Totaling perhaps 1,500,000 people before the Black Death, Catalonia, Aragón, and Valencia struggled to rebuild even as their rulers pretended to lordships stretching from one end of the Mediterranean to the other. The federation's culture remained primarily Catalan. Whatever its limitations, the Crown of Aragón was one of the most durable dynastic polities of the Middle Ages. It was a major factor in Mediterranean history.

THOMAS N. BISSON

Bibliography

Bisson, T. N. *The Medieval Crown of Aragón*. Oxford, 1986.

Bonet y Navarro, A. *El justicia de Aragón: historia y derecho*. Estudio introductorio Angel Bonet Navarro, Esteban Sarasa Sánchez, Guillermo Redondo Veintemillas. Zaragoza, 1985.

Cortes de los antiguos reinos de Aragón y de Valencia y principado de Cataluña. Publicadas por la Real Academia de la Historia. 26 vols. Madrid, 1896–99.

González Antón, L. *Las Cortes de Aragón*. Zaragoza, 1978.

———. *Las uniones aragonesas y las Cortes del reino (1283–1301)*. Zaragoza, 1975.

El Privilegio general de Aragón: la defensa de las libertades aragonesas en la Edad Media. Ed. y estudio de Esteban Sarasa Sánchez. Zaragoza, 1984.

Ubieto Arteta, A. *Historia de Aragón: Creación y desarrollo de la Corona de Aragón*. Zaragoza, 1987.

ARAGÓN, KINGDOM OF *See* ARAGÓN, CROWN OF

ARAGONESE LANGUAGE

The county (later, kingdom) of Aragón originated in areas close to the Pyrenees Mountains, separating modern France and Spain, taking its name from the river Aragón. It was formed by the union of three counties: Aragón, Sobrarbe, and Ribagorza. The movement of colonists to the plains to the south led to the conquest of the Moorish city of Zaragoza in 1118, and eventually included Catalonia (1137) and other areas to the south such as Teruel, Valencia, Alicante, and the Balearic island Mallorca (in the thirteenth century).

The Ibero-Romance dialect of these areas reflects the position of Aragón between Catalonia to the east and Castile to the west. Castile came to exert an especially powerful influence, as its dialect began to impose itself as the standard language of the kingdom of Castile and León. The distinctive phonetic features of Castilian came to be considered standard and tended to overwhelm local features relegated to more isolated rural regions.

Aragonese shares with Castilian, Leonese, and the Mozarabic dialects of the south the diphthongization of Late Latin *e* and *o* in all tonic syllables, regardless of phonetic circumstances. Although the *e* for the most part gave the same result as in Castilian—namely, *ie* as in *tiempo* ("time," from *tempus*) or *miel* ("honey," from *mele*)—there was considerable fluctuation in the phonetic result, especially in the earliest years, with forms like *ia* also being found, as in *hiarba* ("grass," from *herba*) and *diande* ("tooth," from *dente*), in a limited area. Similar fluctuations appear in the form of the diphthong from *o*: *fuoro* ("municipal statute," from *foru*) vs. *cuallo* ("neck," from *collu*), *buano* ("good," from *bonu*), and *ue*: *pueio* ("hill," from *podiu*). The result, *ua*, is much more widespread than *ia*.

Diphthongization also is found before the yod, unlike Castilian, which maintains a single vowel, as in *fuella* ("leaf," from *folia*), *tiengo* ("I have," from *teneo*; cf. Cast. *hoja*, *tengo*). The final *-e* was frequently lost, as in Old Castilian; *fuent* ("fountain," from *fonte*); the final *-o* also tended to be lost, especially in the most mountainous areas and in eastern Aragonese, in consonance with this same feature in Catalan: *blan* ("soft, smooth," from *blandus*).

As for consonants, upper Aragonese retained the initial *f-*, in sharp contrast with its loss in the more southern dialects under the influence of Castilian: *fuyir* ("to flee," from *fugere*) and *fambre* ("hunger," from *famen*). The initial palatal fricative of Late Latin was kept as a hushing fricative, as in most of western Romance languages (excepting again Old Castilian): *germanos* ("brothers," from *germanos*), and *geitat* ("he throws," from *jactat* [z-]). Initial groups of consonant-plus-lateral are also retained: *plorar* ("to weep," from *plorare*), *clamar* ("to call," from *clamare*), and *flama* ("flame," from *flamma*). The palatal lateral of Late Latin (resulting from the yod) was generally retained: *güello* ("eye," from *oc(u)lu*), and *viello* ("old," from *vet(u)lu* [bek'lu]).

One of the most notable features of upper Aragonese phonetic development was the preservation of the intervocalic voiceless stops, which in almost all other dialects of western Romance became voiced: *arripa* ("bank of a stream," from *ripa*), *cuta* ("sharp," from *acuta*), and *paco* ("obscure," from *opacu*). The voiced intervocalic stops likewise tended to be preserved, in contrast with Castilian, where they were frequently lost, especially in contact with front vowels. Various explanations have been sought for this preservation, including the possible influence of Basque, but it seems more likely that it is simply a reflection of the isolated nature of upper Aragonese that escaped this particular phonetic innovation of late western Latin/Romance. Another distinctive feature of Aragonese was the voicing of voiceless stops after liquids and nasals: *planda* ("plant," from *planta*), *cambo* ("field," from *campu*), *aldo* ("tall," from *altu*), *ordiga* ("thistle," from *urtica*), and *bango* ("bench," from the Germanic *bank*). Directly related to the preceding change were assimilations of voiced stops to preceding liquids and nasals: *amos* ("both," from *ambos*; likewise found in Castilian), *fonno* ("base, depths," from *fundu*), and *retuno* (toponym, "round," from *rotundu*). Menéndez Pidal's theory attributing the preceding changes to the Latin brought by speakers from southern Italy who also spoke Oscan is well known but has been questioned.

One other distinctive feature of some Aragonese dialects is the occlusive pronunciation of the Latin *l*: as either *t*, *ts*, or *c*; for example: *(bielsa) betieco* ("calf," from *vitellu*), *estibieco* (toponym, *lanuza*, "summer pasturage," from *aestivella*), and many other toponyms. This change recalls similar occlusive pronunciations of the geminate *l*: in Gascon, as well as that found in some Sardinian and south Italian dialects. Loss of final vowels allowed for the existence of words ending in consonants and consonant groups that are characteristic of Catalan (and also during some centuries, Old Castilian): *-nt* as in *fuent* ("fountain," from *fonte*), and especially in the formation of plurals: *labradors* ("peasants"), *cochins* ("pigs"), and *arbols* ("trees").

In morphology the forms of the masculine definite article are *lo* and *o*, as well as forms reflecting the geminate lateral *l*: of earlier Latin: *ro* and *ra*, similar to the Gascon form *ero* and in some isolated areas *es* from *ipse*, used as a plural, as in *es arbres* ("the trees"). All compete with the Castilian *el*. Some adjectives tend to adopt the marked feminine ending *-a*, where other western Romance languages preserve the Latin third-declension common masculine/feminine ending: *berda* ("green," from *viridem*), *dolienta* ("suffering, aching," from *dolentem*), *jovena* ("young," from *iuvenem*), and *granda* ("large," from *grandem*). In verb morphology, the preservation of intervocalic voiced consonants left the *-er* and *-ir* conjugations with the *-b-* of the Latin imperfect are found, and a first- and third-person plural form based on the third singular: *-omos*, *ón*. The *-er* and *-ir* conjugations had a perfect in *-ié*: *vendié vendiés*, *vendié*, and so on.

In word formation, *-az(o)* appears as an augmentative more than in standard Castilian: *inocentaz*, *pobraz*, *narizaza* ("big nose"). The diminutive suffix *-ico* is often thought to be especially characteristic of Aragonese, although it is found all over the Iberian peninsula: *jovencico* ("young [one]").

Written sources of medieval Aragonese, in addition to Tomás's *Documentos*, are found in editions like Tilander's *Fueros de Aragón* (1937) and Cooper's *Liber regum* (1960).

PAUL M. LLOYD

Bibliography

Alvar, M. *El dialecto aragonés*. Madrid, 1953.

Cooper, L. Liber regum: *estudio lingüístico*. Zaragoza, 1960.

Elcock, W. D. *De quelques affinités phonétiques entre l'aragonais et le béarnais. I: La conservation des occlusives sourdes entre voyelles. II: La sonorisation des occlusives sourdes après nasal ou liquide*. Paris, 1938.

Kuhn, A. *Der Hocharagonesische Dialekt*. Leipzig, 1935.

Navarro T. *Documentos lingüísticos del Alto Aragón*. Syracuse, N.Y., 1957.

Tilander, G. *Fueros de Aragón*. Lund, 1937.

Umphrey, G. W. "The Aragónese Dialect," *Revue Hispanique* 24 (1911), 5–45; reprinted in *Archivo de Filología Aragónesa* 39. 163–201.

ARCHEOLOGY

Spanish medieval archeology as practiced in the 1930s and 1940s was politically conservative and designed in general to corroborate pan-Germanist hypotheses demonstrating medieval Iberian culture's linkages to a Germanic cultural zone. As in the rest of Europe, some work was done on ecclesiastical buildings and castles, mainly from the standpoint of artistic styles and motifs. Gómez-Moreno's study of Mozarabic churches (1919) is a model of the latter, though as much architectural as archeological in character. On the Islamic side, the journal *Al-Andalus*, from its inception in 1932, featured an archeological section conducted mainly by Leopoldo Torres Balbás and centered primarily on urban architecture and artifacts. During the 1930s, Torres was conservator of the Alhambra. Pan-Germanism was pushed during the Franco period, as was an abortive attempt to create a "Christian archeology."

In the late 1970s, under the stimulus of Pierre Toubert's 1978 Rome meeting on *incastellamento*, the process whereby in the early years of feudalism the landscape was reorganized in much of western Europe into "castral units" linking castle with dependent villages, a wave of extensive archeology ensued, mainly in Aragón, Valencia, Mallorca, and areas of Almería and Granada, broadly under the direction of archeologists and historians associated with the Casa de Velázquez. Extensive archeology consists mainly of broad-scale field surveys and site inspection, with only surface collection of ceramic remains. The key workers here were Pierre Guichard, André Bazzana, and Rafael Azuar working in the Valencian region; Patrice Cressier and Maryelle Bertrand in Almería; Antonio Malpica in Granada; and Philippe Sénac and Carlos Esco in Aragón. The picture of rural life in al-Andalus that emerged was a countryside organized in complexes of castles (*husun*; singular, *hisn*) and villages (*qura*; singular, *qarya*; in Spanish, *alquería*), the latter organized tribally, at least at the time of their initial settlement, and typically practicing irrigation agriculture. Clan settlement of villages explains the plethora of current and disappeared villages beginning with the particle Beni- "sons of," as in Benigazló, from the Nafza Berber Ghazlun clan or Benisanó from the Hawwara Berber Zannun clan, both in the province of Valencia. In addition to villages, castral units included private parcels called *rahals*, owned typically by persons who had held high state office.

In general, the husun were not permanently garrisoned but served as refuges for the villages and their beasts in times of insecurity. At such times, the state would dispatch a *qā'id* (captain) to oversee the castle, to the see to make sure that it was provisioned with wood and water (which appears to have been a peasant obligation), or else to collect taxes owed the state. That is, the model does not envision a feudalized castle, with a permanent garrison and castellan whose role is to control the peasantry.

The irrigation element has been studied by Cressier in the Sierra de Filabres and by Miquel Barceló and members of his group at the Autonomous University of Barcelona working at sites in Mallorca, Albacete, Andalusia, and Castellón de la Plana. In Mallorca and Albacete they found long canal systems broken down into segments, each terminating with a mill; it is supposed that each segment represents an original clan settlement unit. Barceló's hypothesis that Andalusi mills, typically terminate hydraulic systems in which the systems are secondary to irrigation can be contrasted with Catalan feudal mills heading systems. The idea that the latter in irrigation is an afterthought has both generated controversy and drawn attention to the hydraulic structuring of castral units. Barceló's team has also studied the distribution and use of small-scale *qanats*, or filtration galleries, particularly in Mallorca, where they were built by peasants using common technology.

A third team, headed by Karl Butzer and Joan Mateu, studied irrigation agriculture (but not in conjunction with castral units) in the Sierra de Espadán, Castellón. Butzer types irrigation systems by scale: macrosysems corresponding to the great periurban *huertas* (growing fields) of Valencia and Murcia; and meso- and microsystems corresponding to mountain villages and hamlets. The latter he believes to be of Islamic foundation, the former of Roman or pre-Roman base. Butzer, however, sees little innovation in what he describes as Mediterranean agro-irrigation systems of ancient provenance and notes that the same roster of crops were grown there by Romans and Muslims alike.

The study of pottery, in particular, by Juan Zozaya and Sonia Gutiérrez has allowed archeologists to define a paleo-Andalusi period extending from the Islamic conquest into the early tenth century and characterized by the persistence of late Roman pottery forms and ceramic techniques. This repertory is unglazed, typically made on turntables rather than kickwheels, and was limited to a few standard cookwares such as the *olla* and the *marmita*. Zozaya extends the concept of paleo-Andalusi culture to include such phenomena as the sharing of cemeteries and churches by Muslims and Christians, bilingual coinage, and certain architectural features; while Gutiérrez, Azuar, and Mateu have described early irrigation development in littoral marshes of the Lower Segura River basin dating to the eighth century, anteceding the development of the high medieval huertas.

On the Christian side some incastellamento studies have been carried out for Catalonia, and a great many ceramic studies document the diffusion and decline of Catalan greywares. Manuel Riu in particular has described this industry and its primitive firing techniques. Later, with the conquest of Valencia, the narrow roster of wares traditionally used by Catalans was vastly increased owing to contact with Mudéjar potters.

The Asociación Española de Arqueología Medieval, founded in 1985, edits a journal (*Boletín*) and holds biennial meetings with published acts.

THOMAS F. GLICK

Bibliography

Barceló, M. (ed.) *Arqueología medieval: En las afueras del "medievalismo."* Barcelona, 1988.

Bazzana, A., P. Cressier, and P. Guichard. *Les chateaux ruraux d'al-Andalus*. Madrid, 1988.

Glick, T. F. *From Muslim Fortress to Christian Castle: Dynamics of Cultural Change in Medieval Spain*. Manchester, 1995.

Gómez Moreno, M. *Iglesias mozárabes: arte español de los siglos IX al XI*. Madrid, 1919.

Guichard, P. *Les musulmans de Valence et la Reconquête (XIe–XIIIe siècles)*. 2 vols. Damascus, 1990–91.

Gutiérrez Lloret, S. *Cerámica común paleoandalusí del sur de Alicante (siglos* VII–X). Alicante, 1988.

ARCHITECTURE

Civil Architecture

Civil architecture includes both public and private buildings whose functions were not primarily related to religious life. Houses and palaces; government, commercial, and recreational buildings; as well as baths, hospital, and bridges, are among the numerous examples of civil architecture in medieval Iberia.

While substantial remains of Roman public and domestic architecture exist in Iberian cities like Mérida, evidence of civil structures from the earlier Middle Ages is scant. In some cases Roman civil structures were maintained during the Middle Ages, a good example being the so-called Alcántara bridge across the Tagus River at Toledo, which was rebuilt by the Muslims during the tenth century. The later St. Martín bridge in the city is an entirely thirteenth-century construction, built during the reign of Alfonso X and utilizing a series of pointed arches. Christian settlers in newly reconquered towns like Zaragoza (1118) or Cuenca (1177) acquired the formerly Muslim baths in those cities, and in Girona the Muslim baths were rebuilt using stone and date to the later thirteenth century.

The most prevalent form of civil architecture in medieval Iberia is the noble residence, whose primary development took place in urban settings beginning in the twelfth century. An example from the earlier Middle Ages is the two-story rectangular structure now known as Srenta. María de Naranco outside Oviedo, sometimes identified as the palace of Ramiro I (842–850). The upper story of this building is a barrel-vaulted rectangular room with carved capitals and porches extending on either side and an exterior staircase leading to the ground level below.

Though defensive elements occasionally remain a feature of the design (such as the towers in the early-thirteenth-century La Zuda Palace in Lérida), the noble residence is not primarily a military structure. A well-known twelfth-century example is the so-called Palace of the Dukes of Granada in Estella (Navarre). The ground level has a porticoed facade while the first story is pierced by a series of narrow, arched windows separated by thin colonnettes. In addition to the porticoed type, plain facades opened only by a single arched doorway are also a common design for the noble residence. This type is repeatedly illustrated in thirteenth-century miniatures of the *Cantigas* of Alfonso X, while an extant example exists in Tárrega (Lérida). The persistence of this design can be noted in the early-sixteenth-century Palacio de Ovando Solís in Cáceres, which also retains a fortified tower and machicolations above the entrance.

The majority of urban palaces date from the later fourteenth and fifteenth centuries. The palace at Tordesillas (León) was built for Alfonso XI beginning in 1340 and its Islamic-inspired exterior and interior decoration is entirely the work of Mudéjar craftsmen. Examples of later medieval noble houses survive in a number of Iberian towns including Cáceres, Avila, Salamanca, and Santiago de Compostela.

Many noble houses were designed around an interior patio surounded by an arcade or first-story gallery. Fourteenth-century examples are preserved at Tordesillas and the Episcopal Palace at Tortosa. Royal palaces also often contained larger meeting or assembly rooms (*salones*). One of the earliest preserved is located in the Episcopal Palace at Santiago de Compostela (mostly from the thirteenth century), consisting of a narrow rectangular space (31.9 by 8.3 meters) covered with low ribbed groin vaults springing from engaged piers on the lateral walls. Later examples include the much larger "Tinell" salon in the Episcopal Palace in Barcelona (1359–1370). This salon measures 33.7 by 17 meters and consists of a series of six grand transverse arches supporting a wooden roof. In other palaces interior columns or piers divided the space into a series of vaulted compartments, as seen in the ruins of the thirteenth-century palace at the monastery of Carrecedo, built for the sons of Alfonso IX. The construction techniques used for royal *salones* and patios are similar to those that appear earlier in chapter houses, refectories, cloisters, and dormitories associated with monastery and cathedral complexes.

Other forms of civil architecture in the later Middle Ages demanded large and open interior spaces. Economic and urban expansion in Catalonia during the later thirteenth and fourteenth centuries produced a number of novel administrative and commercial buildings. The Salon of the Council of the One Hundred in Barcelona was built toward the end of the fourteenth century to accommodate the assemblies of this municipal institution, which had previously met in local monasteries. The wooden ceiling of the rectangular salon is supported by a series of tranverse arches and the lateral walls are pierced with round windows embellished with tracery. The facade, dated at 1400–1402, follows the basic exterior form of the noble residence, but features smooth stonework and more elaborate and delicately carved Gothic ornament around the doorway and first-story windows.

The mercantile exchanges (*lonjas*) built in Catalonia were tall columned structures enclosing vast interior spaces. The Lonja in Barcelona dates to the second half of the fourteenth century. Its salon is a large rectangle measuring 33 by 21 meters, divided into three aisles by two series of tall arcades carried on piers supporting a wooden roof.

While the existence of hospitals is documented throughout the Middle Ages in Iberia, the late-twelfth-century Hospital del Rey in Burgos (now demolished), founded by Alfonso VIII, is among the earliest examples of a structure built expressly for the purpose of caring for the infirm. Constructed along the lines of a basilica, with a tall central nave supported by octagonal piers, the entrance to this structure was from one of the lateral sides, with beds probably located in the aisles. Other cities along the pilgrimage roads also had facilities for the sick, housed in monasteries or private residences. Hospitals built in Santiago de Compostela (Hospital Real) and in Toledo (Hospital de Santa Cruz) at the end of the fifteenth century followed a cruciform plan.

Despite some neglect and decay, the legacy of civil architecture in Medieval Iberia provides the basis for significant insights into secular life beyond the scope of castle, church, and monastery. The extant types and individual examples, dating predominantly to the thirteenth century and later, remain a viable record of the residential, mercantile, municipal, and infrastructural concerns of the men and women of the Middle Ages.

Ecclesiastical Architecture

The planning and construction of religious buildings demanded a significant measure of the economic, intellectual, and technical resources of the Middle Ages. The medieval church functioned variously to commemorate sacred sites, provide a setting for the ritual of mass and the veneration of relics, serve as the focus of monastic life, accomodate large numbers of pilgrims, and provide assurance of salvation for those whose donations paid for their expense. The history of medieval ecclesiastical architecture in Spain demonstrates the strength and continuity of native building traditions as well as their transformation by the individuals, events, and circumstances that affected the whole of Iberian culture.

The dominant type of church in Iberia and throughout western Europe during the Middle Ages was the basilica, rectangular in shape and directional in its focus upon an altar. The altar was located within a square or semicircular apse that projected from this simple rectangular form. During the Middle Ages this basic plan was modified to include a transept perpendicular to the nave and located in front of the apse often projecting laterally to form a Latin Cross; aisles flanking the central hall or nave and separated from it by series of cylindrical columns or square piers supporting arches; and an enlargement of the apse with additional chapels adjacent to it or radiating from a walkway (ambulatory) surrounding it. In addition to the dominant basilican plan, examples of equal-armed Greek Cross churches also exist, with central rather than longitudinal focus.

Most larger early medieval basilicas were timber roofed, but stone vaulting, especially in the apse or transept is not unknown even in earlier periods and becomes more general by the middle of the eleventh century. Basilican churches were also enriched through the construction of a gallery or triforium above the aisles and a more complex treatment of piers that occurs with the development of more intricate methods of vaulting.

The primary building material in ecclesiastical architecture is smoothly hewn stone, varied in color and texture depending upon region. Other materials include spolia (reused parts of Roman buildings), rubble and irregular stone for vaults (or interspersed with courses of cut stone), and brick, which occasionally appears above doorways and windows or is the dominant building material in some styles. Medieval churches were often embellished with relief sculpture or fresco decoration. Related buildings, particularly in a monastic setting, served varied aspects of religious life: these include cloisters, refectories, chapter houses, and dormitories.

Construction was often a protracted process, and the results are not always homogeneous: churches begun during one period were often completed or modified at a later time and under different circumstances. Wherever possible the dating of ecclesiastical buildings is made on the basis of documentary evidence in the form of inscriptions, charters, or chronicles, and relative chronologies are established on the basis of visual similarities with documented buildings; all dating is subject to revision stemming from the reexamination of documents and the uncertainty of later rebuildings and restorations. Also, the progression of styles generally used to designate medieval architecture is not always applied appropriately in Spain. Therefore the material is divided into periods corresponding to major events in Iberian Medieval history.

586–711: The Visigoths to the Muslim Invasion

From the period following the conversion of King Reccared to orthodoxy (589) until the Muslim invasions of 711, literary and archeological evidence reveal the existence of as many as sixty churches in the Iberian Peninsula, of which no fewer than six preserve substantial parts of their original construction. These survive mainly in areas north of the Duero River, but it is likely that important Visigothic churches also existed in major urban centers like Seville and Toledo.

The basilica is the most common plan adopted for churches of the sixth and seventh centuries, but there is great variety among individual monuments and examples of the Greek Cross plan also exist. The scale of these buildings is small, with few more than 25 or 30 meters in length. In some cases, such as that of Santa Comba de Bande, Orense, similarities have been noted with Late Roman buildings in Ravenna, such as the fifth-century Mausoleum of Galla Placidia. Also characteristic of Visigothic churches are the use of the horseshoe arch and the importance of relief sculpture in the form of capitals and friezes.

San Pedro de la Nave (late seventh century) is a well-preserved example located near Zamora. Although basilican in plan, it may best be described as a progression of longitudinal and square spaces with attention focused upon the tall groin-vaulted square tower near the center of the plan whose supporting piers are embellished with attached marble columns and carved capitals illustrating scenes from the Old Testament. San Pedro de la Nave is built of heavy blocks of stone, with brick and rubble used occasionally for vaults and the upper portions of walls. The interior tends to be dark with massive, solid walls and vaulted areas keeping direct illumination at a minimum.

Despite their modest size, the achievement of the Visigoths in ecclesiastical architecture is impressive and hardly less remarkable than the oeuvre of the Church Father, St. Isidore of Seville (d. 639) and the seventh-century compilation of law known as the *Liber Iudicorum*. San Pedro de la Nave and other surviving churches are admirable technically and in their preservation of Roman building traditions both in Spain and elsewhere in the Mediterranean World.

742–1031: The Asturian and Leonese Kingdoms to the Fall of the Caliphate of Córdoba

During the late eighth and ninth centuries, Christian architecture was confined almost exclusively to the extreme northeast region of Galicia, protected from Muslim raids by the rugged terrain of the Cantabrian mountains. With progress in the Reconquest and the shifting of the Christian capital to León, architectural activity in the tenth and early eleventh centuries extended south to the valley above the Duero River and east to Castile and Catalonia.

Located primarily around the successive strongholds and retreats of the Asturian kings, examples of late eighth and ninth century architecture are often ambitious in scale, inventive in their proportions, and striking in their often rich decoration. San Julián de los Prados (Santullano) on the outskirts of Oviedo is a spacious three-aisled (40 meters in length) basilica built toward the end of the long reign of Alfonso II (791–842). The nave arcade consists of piers supporting round arches, and there are three barrel-vaulted square apses. Although barely visible today, its arcades, walls, and vaults were decorated with fresco decoration from which both human and animal forms are conspicuously absent. San Miguel de Lillo on Monte Naranco just east of Oviedo (842–850) is a smaller basilica with a gallery above the entrance porch and a strong emphasis upon height in the tall central vaults (originally the church extended farther to the east). Building materials are primarily a combination of cut and rough stone with the occasional use of brick for the construction of arches.

The number of ninth-century ecclesiastical structures is small, but extant examples strive for dramatic effect in proportion and decoration, and mirror the aspirations of the nascent Asturian kingdom for legitimacy, recognition, and authority in Christian Spain. The architecture of this period (see also the preceding section, Civil Architecture) is contemporary with the first battles of the Reconquest and the compilation of exegetical texts on the Apocalypse by the monk Beatus of Liébana known as the *Beatus Commentary*.

A substantial number of ecclesiastical monuments from the tenth and early eleventh centuries were built in a region south and southwest of León and just north of the Duero River; other examples survive from Castile and Catalonia. The architecture from this period primarily served monastic communities who settled in areas of the Duero Valley claimed by the kings of León. These communities practiced their Hispanic rite and pursued a spiritual ideal amid the uncertain security of their isolated location on the frontier with Islam; indeed, Islamic military reprisals made at the end of the tenth century under al-Manṣūr destroyed many foundations such as Valeránica in Castile and Tabara in southern León. The term *Mozarabic* (literally Christians living under Muslim rule) is accurate only insofar as place names, dedications, and chronicles indicate that many of the monks were refugees from Muslim territories.

Among the largest and best preserved churches of the period (30 meters in length) is San Cebrián de Mazote (early tenth century) in southern León. Mazote is a three-aisled basilica with a horseshoe-shaped apse flanked by squares chambers covered with groin vaults. Melon-shaped domes cover the apse and three tall spaces of the transept. A series of five horseshoe arches supported by marble columns divide the nave from the aisles. A horseshoe-shaped apse is also located at the opposite end of the nave, while the entrance to the church is from the south aisle. The columns at Mazote are slender, the interior light and delicate owing to the smooth stonework, stucco surfaces, crisp contours of the horseshoe arcade, and the height attained in the domed areas. Islamic-inspired features on the exterior of the church include the framing of horseshoe arches (*alfiz*), the use of small double-arched windows (*ajima*), and the use of alternating orange and white stones above an arched doorway at the north transept (compare the Great Mosque at Córdoba). Tenth-century churches achieve a degree of sophistication and elegance not found earlier in the peninsula, and are contemporary with the flowering of the art of manuscript painting which produced some of the greatest masterpieces of early–Middle Age Apocalypse illustration to be found anywhere in Europe.

1031–1212: The Christian Kingdoms of Spain to the Battle of Las Navas de Tolosa

During the later eleventh and twelfth centuries, territorial expansion and settlement, economic growth, urbanization, and the zeal of monastic reform and the Roman Catholic Church supported an eruption of architectural activity in Catalonia, along the pilgrimage roads from Jaca to Compostela, and southward into the broad area between the Duero and Tagus Rivers. Churches of this period are characterized by stronger receptivity to building styles and influences beyond the Pyrenees, provisions for lay worship with a resulting augmentation of scale, ambitious vaulting techniques, and impressive programs of monumental relief sculpture. Contemporary with the buildings of this period are the fall of the caliphate of Córdoba (1031), the Christian Reconquest of Toledo (1085) and Zaragoza (1118), the introduction of the Roman rite into Spain (1080), the First and Second Crusades (1095 and 1147), and the influences of the French Monastic reform movements of Cluny and Cîteaux.

The churchman Oliba (d. 1046), bishop of Vich and abbot of Santa María de Ripoll and San Michel de Cuxá, sojourned to Italy and is usually regarded as the force behind the adoption of novel architectural forms in his native Catalonia. The five-aisled basilican plan of Ripoll (consecrated 1032) shows a wide transept with a series of semicircular chapels extending toward the rear, two square towers, and an overall length of 60 meters. The exterior is articulated with a series of round (not horseshoe) arches, in low relief below roof level, deriving from Lombardy. While Ripoll is not vaulted, other Catalan churches of this period employ barrel vaults and compound pier supports (e.g., San Vicentes de Cardona, 1040) in their naves, an ambitious feature in churches of this size.

Another major achievement of the period was the building of the Cathedral of Santiago de Compostela in Galicia, which housed the tomb of the Apostle James (Santiago), discovered in the ninth century. Construction began as early as 1075 and was completed during the years 1122–1128. The church is a monumental five-aisled barrel-vaulted basilica with gallery and transept; and ambulatory connects the transept with the main body of the church, and communicates with a series of radiating chapels. The overall length is 90 meters. The size and plan show strong similarities with the church of St. Sernin in Toulouse, built during the same period and located along the popular pilgrimage road to the tomb of St. James. Settlement and traffic along the road prompted cultural development across northern Spain. The construction of St. Sernin may have begun earlier than at Compostela, but the architecture of the pilgrimage roads is best seen as the result of interaction and exchange between Spanish and French masons and sculptors rather than as an importation. Aside from the Cathedral of Santiago de Compostela smaller pilgrimage road churches of the early twelfth century include the Cathedral of Jaca and the churches of San Isidoro in León and San Martín de Fromista. Many of these structures also included elaborate programs of relief sculpture for doorways and capitals.

Amid the progress of reconquest and repopulation of the Duero Valley, architectural activity in Iberia continued throughout the twelfth and thirteenth centuries, assimilating a wide range of elements both from trans-Pyrenean and Mediterranean cultures. Beginning in the third quarter of the twelfth century, pointed arches and ribbed groin vaulting, elements of the French Gothic style in architecture originating in the Ile de France, appear in Iberia first in the portal and porch added at the west front of Santiago de Compostela (Pórtico de la Gloria), as well as in a number of other monuments including the cathedrals of Avila, Zamora, Tarragona, and Lérida. In some cases the architect's name suggests a French origin (for example, Master "Fruchel" for the rebuilding of the cathedral of Avila) while in others the result suggests a synthesis of varied foreign elements by a native artist. Reasons for the incursion of this French style may be found in the success of Cistercian monasticism in Spain during the second half of the twelfth century and in the travels to France and impressions of influential prelates such as Martín de Finojosa, abbot of the Cistercian monastery of Huerta and adviser to Alfonso VIII. The early cathedrals built in the Gothic style in Spain, like those of Avila, are large-aisled basilicas with massive compound piers supporting the pointed arches and groin vaults of the nave. Avila includes a triforium above the aisles and an enlarged apse with tall arcade surrounding the main altar.

Despite its dominance in the later Middle Ages the Gothic style was only one source of inspiration in the buildings of the later twelfth and early thirteenth centuries. The carved ornament in the cathedrals of Lérida and Tarragona owes much to the persistence of Islamic artistic traditions following the Reconquest, as does the dome covering the octagonal church of Torress del Río in Navarre or the ornate crossing dome in the otherwise austere early Gothic interior of the cathedral of Zamora.

Yet another indication of this process is the existence both in Sahagún and in Toledo of a number of modest churches built in brick and *mampostería* (rubble amd mortar alternating with courses of brick) and based upon a tradition of architecture found in many urban centers of Muslim Spain. Sometimes called *mudéjar*, after the Muslim populations that remained following the reconquest of their cities, churches like the small Toledan basilica of Santa Cruz (ca. 1200) employ horseshoe arches and brickwork patterns of intersecting and polylobed arches on the exterior based upon the vocabulary of Islamic art. Examples of Mudéjar architecture from the early thirteenth century may be found near Madrid (San Martín de Valdilecha) and later in other areas formerly occupied by Muslims, such as Daroca and Teruel in southern Aragón. The originality of this period in Iberian ecclesiastical architecture seems to lie in its variety and creative assimilation of elements of both Mediterranean and trans-Pyrennean styles. These artistic developments are contemporary with other cultural achievements such as the founding of the University of Salamanca (early thirteenth century) and the emergence of Toledo as a center for the activities of scholars and translators.

1212–1492: The Christian Kingdoms of Spain from 1212 to the Fifteenth Century

Following the Battle of Las Navas de Tolosa and during the reconquest of the Muslim strongholds of Córdoba (1236), Seville (1248), and Valencia (1248), the Christian kingdoms of Spain embarked upon a period of ambitious ecclesiastical building throughout the thirteenth century under the guidance of influential bishops in the cities of Toledo, Burgos, and León. The grand cathedrals erected in the cities of Castile were built in a style based upon the major examples of Gothic architecture in northern France: the cathedral of Toledo had as its first architect a "Master Martín," perhaps called from France by its archbishop Rodrigo

Jiménez de Rada, who was educated in Paris. Toledo is a five-aisled basilica with (nonprojecting) transept and flying buttresses. It measures 120 meters in length and towers over the other buildings of the city. While grand in scale and spacious throughout, Spanish Gothic churches and cathedrals of the thirteenth century tend to achieve more balanced proportions as opposed to the preoccupation with height in their French counterparts. And there are striking examples of originality at Toledo, as in the Islamic decoration of the triforium arcades above the nave. The cathedrals of Toledo and Burgos were ongoing projects that outlasted the lifetimes of their founders and original architects: only León (ca. 1255–1300) achieves a homogeneity and suggests a closer relationship with a specific French Gothic model in plan, elevation, and proportions (Reims).

In the fourteenth century, building activity flourished in the Crown of Aragón, due in part to the kingdom's commercial interests in Mediterranean trade. The cathedral of Barcelona (begun 1298) rivals in size and follows in general disposition contemporary examples of Gothic architecture in southern French cities such as Narbonne, Toulouse, and Limoges. A three-aisled basilica more than 100 meters in length, the interior of the cathedral is dominated by a tall and wide nave arcade that opens the view and circulation to the narrow aisles. This unifying tendency in interior space occurs as well in other Catalan churches, such as the cathedral of Mallorca (begun circa 1320), whose nave reached a width of almost 20 meters and a vault height of 40 meters.

Despite constant political turmoil and civil disturbances in the fifteenth century, grandiose architectural projects, such as the cathedrals of Seville and the nave of the cathedral of Girona, were continued or undertaken. Progress was often slow, involving a sucession of architects both native and foreign, and energies were often directed more toward luxurious decoration and overwhelming size than innovations in design or structure. More manageable projects amid these periods of civil unrest were privately sponsored family tombs or chapels, built as independent structures or incorporated into the design of existing churches, usually as chapels entered from the aisles.

The cathedral of Seville is 145 meters long and 76 meters wide, with a height of more than 40 meters in the vaults of the ambulatory surrounding the apse. Construction began in 1402 but was not completed until a century later in 1519. During that time a number of architects were employed, including masters of Flemish and English origin. The influence, also seen in painting, manuscript illumination, and sculpture, and part of the rich decorative style known as "international Gothic," is apparent in the flamboyant carving of the moldings in the triforium openings and the starlike patterns of the vaults at Seville. Despite the preponderance of artisans from northern Europe, the team of craftsmen at the royally founded Franciscan monastery of San Juan de los Reyes in Toledo (ca. 1490–1500) also included at least two mudéjares, responsible for some of the most ornately carved surface decoration in the ensemble: their inclusion exemplifies the continued influence of Islamic traditions in the art of the later Middle Ages in Spain.

The Gothic style persisted in Spain well into the sixteenth century, with the building of the cathedrals of Salamanca, Segovia, and Zaragoza. At Salamanca the vocabulary and plan continue the legacy of early Gothic structures in the peninsula while the tall proportions and narrower nave virtually eliminate and deny any sense of weight or mass.

Military Architecture

Long centuries of armed conflicts arising from conquest, reconquest, and civil war resulted in numerous fortified structures throughout Iberia during the Middle Ages. Whether in ruins or restored form, castles and walls remain a significant part of the Iberian landscape.

In addition to the natural protection offered by rivers, mountains, and other natural barriers, many villages and cities were dominated by their castles or surrounded by heavily fortified walls. Due to their strategic location, fortifications often have a continuous history of building stretching from Roman settlement to Arab conquest to Christian reconquest and further rebuilding in the later middle ages.

13th century AD. City walls. 12th-13th c. Copyright © Giraudon/Art Resource, NY Avila, Spain.

Cities such as León and Mérida were fortified with walls in Roman times, parts of which remained and were augmented and strengthened in the Middle Ages. The most common building material in these examples was roughly cut stone of varying shapes and sizes, reinforced with square, polygonal, or round towers and interrupted by gateways. The Puerta de Bisagra (antigua) in Toledo is a tenth century gateway, primarily a Muslim construction with horsehoe arch, flanking square towers, large, heavily rusticated stones, and an imposing monolithic lintel. The crenellated superstructure of this gateway, however, was rebuilt in the later twelfth or thirteenth centuries long after the Christian reconquest of the city in 1085. Here the material employed is brick and mampostería (a mixture of stone and rubble). Another material used for walls and favored by the Muslims is tapia, a mortar held in place by wooden forms until dry. This material is still visible in the remains of the castles of Monteagudo in Murcia and Alcalá de Guadaira southeast of Seville. Later gateways, such as the Puerta de Cuarte in Valencia from the mid–fifteenth century, feature stone construction and strongly projecting cylindrical towers.

Other cities in Medieval Spain built their walls as the Reconquest extended Christian frontiers toward the south. Avila's walls in New Castile, reinforced with eighty-eight towers, were originally built sometime after 1090; those surrounding the cities of Daroca in southern Aragón and Santo Domingo de la Calzada (Castile) were erected sometime in the fourteenth century.

Castle plans vary according to site and the technology of siege and defense, but standard elements are walls, keep (*torre de homenaje*), and ward. Walls are reinforced with towers of varying shapes, capped with crenellations (merlons and embrasures) and sometimes outfitted with machicolations, portions of projecting wall supported by corbels through which pitch could be poured on would-be attackers. Behind the walls was a walkway, parts of which could be dismantled to isolate the keep. Walls were interrupted by gateways and posterns, small doorways usually hidden from direct view. Arrow slits were usually located in the towers: as a consequence of effective firearms in the fifteenth century, walls were built lower but more solidly to resist siege by cannon rather than by scaling. The keep was the noble residence and final line of the castle's defense. Recognizable by its great height (112 feet at Peñafiel in León), the keep was usually square and connected to the wall, but in some examples is located outside the walls (*torre de albarrana*) and accessible by a walkway. Until the fifteenth century the quarters of the keep were generally modest and not well lit, but in later examples they were embellished with decoration and amenities. Ceilings were vaulted rather than covered with timber to prevent entry from above. During the Reconquest, castles usually included chapels and churches for monks or members of military orders. Inside the walls the ward contained stables, living quarters for knights, cisterns, and storage areas for provisions. Many castles were fortified by outer (curtain) walls as well as dry moats to further stifle a siege.

In Spain as well as throughout western Europe, Christian castles built in stone were rare before the later twelfth century. After this time stone castles not only became more plentiful but also were built rapidly and at great expense. One striking early stone example is the castle/monastery of Loarre near Jaca in northern Aragón, a natural stronghold built in the later eleventh and twelfth centuries on a steep mountainous site. Its outer walls are articulated with round towers while the keep and church are protected by inners walls with square towers. The plan is irregular and compact with smoother stone and more sophisticated construction used for the basilican church within.

Zorita de los Canes, on the Tagus River near Guadalajara, is one of a few remaining castles built in the later twelfth and thirteenth centuries by the Order of Calatrava to protect the vast territories occupied during this active period of Reconquest. Originally a Muslim *alcazaba*, Zorita's expansive plan and extramural tower (torre de albarrana) parallel the large and complex forms of castles built in the Holy Land during the Crusades such as Krak des Chevaliers.

A number of later castles, like the well-preserved Torrelobatón near Valladolid, are square in plan, with three rounded corner towers and the fourth occupied by a tall square keep with sentry towers at its corners. Although built upon earlier foundations, Torrelobatón dates in its present form to the mid-fifteenth century and served as a stronghold for noble families vying for political power with the Castilian crown. The compact plan follows a general tendency throughout Europe during the fourteenth and fifteenth centuries.

Later castles, like Olite in Navarre (built by the French-born king Charles III) or Coca, near Segovia in Castile, were more luxurious in decoration and accomodations. Coca is essentially built of brick and mamposteria, with full exploitation of textural variety and relief patterns, while Olite employs Gothic-inspired stone construction with pointed arches and elegant proportions. Both have irregular plans, spacious living quarters, and patios. They served the dual purposes of defense and residence, and their form is dictated both by a desire for comfort and entertainment as well as protection.

DAVID RAIZMAN

Bibliography

Contamine, P. *War in the Middle Ages*. Trans. M. Jones. New York, 1984.

Fontaine, J. *L'art preroman hispanique I: L'art asturien*. La Pierre qui Vire, 1973.

———. *L'art preroman hispanique II: L'art mozarabe*. La Pierre qui Vire, 1977.

Gudiol, J., and J. Gaya Nuño. *Ars Hispaniae V: Arquitectura románica*. Madrid, 1948.

Lampérez y Romea, V. *Arquitectura civil española de los siglos I al XVIII*. 2 vols. Madrid, 1922.

Saez, E. (ed.) *Actas del I simposio internacional de mudejarismo*. Madrid, 1981

Sarthou-Carreres, C. *Castillos de España*. Madrid, 1963.

Schlunk, H. and Hauschild, T. *Die Denkmaler der fruhchristlichen und westgotischen Zeit*. Mainz am Rhein, 1978.

Torress Balbás, L. *Ars Hispaniae IV: Arte almohade arte nazari: arte mudejar*. Madrid, 1949.

———. *Ars Hispaniae VII: Arquitectura gótica*. Madrid, 1952.

Weissmuller, A. A. *Castles from the Heart of Spain*. London, 1967.

ARCHIVES *See* LIBRARIES

ARIANISM *See* CHURCH; HERESY; THEOLOGY

ARIAS DÁVILA FAMILY

The Arias Dávilas were an important dynasty of *converso* officials in fifteenth-century Castile. Diego Arias Dávila (d. 1466), who before his conversion to Christianity was named Ysaque (Isaac) Abenácar of Ávila, was apparently in Segovia where he converted during the preaching campaign of Vicente Ferrer in 1411 (when nearly the entire Jewish community was baptized). Shortly after his conversion he was known as Diego Bolante, or Volador, and he later became a protégé of Enrique IV (reigned 1454–1474). He married Juana Rodríguez (undoubtedly also a convert), who apparently died soon after, and then Elvira González of Ávila, also of Jewish background. As *contador mayor* of the kingdom (in charge of the finances), he was one of the most despised men in the realm. His considerable property was inherited by his two sons and one daughter.

His older son, Pedro, held the position of *contador mayor* after his father's death. Juan, the other son (ca. 1430–1497), became bishop of Segovia. Enemies of Pedro convinced Enrique, falsely, of Pedro's "treason," for which the king had him imprisoned. He was severely wounded while in prison. He was married to María Ortíz Cota, of an illustrious *converso* family; they had five sons and two daughters.

Pedro died during the siege of Madrid in 1476, and his eldest son, Diego, inherited the position of *contador mayor*. Diego also was named lord of Puñonrostro, lands created by his grandfather Diego. He married Marina de Mendoza, the illegitimate daughter of the *marqués* de Santillana (Iñigo López de Mendoza). Diego died about 1482. His brother Juan was the first count of Puñonrostro.

The most important member of this family, however, was another son of Pedro, Pedrarias (Pedro Arias) Dávila, born probably about 1440. He was known as the *gran justador*, an accomplished soldier who headed the forces of Segovia and Toledo in the conquest of Oran (in North Africa) in 1509. He also apparently participated in the conquest of Granada for Fernando and Isabel. In 1513 they sent him to "discover" and govern the "Tierra Firme" in the New World, recently discovered by Balboa but not effectively explored. He became the governor of Nicaragua and established the colony of Panama. Pedrarias married Isabel de Boabadilla y Peñalosa, granddaughter of the famous *marquesa* de Moya, an intimate of Queen Isabel. One of their daughters, María de Peñalosa, was promised in marriage to Balboa, but instead married Rodrigo de Contreras, also a governor of Nicaragua. Another daughter, Isabel, married the famous explorer Hernando de Soto.

A purported "blood libel" case in Segovia in 1468 (if it ever happened) involved charges that some Jews had captured and tortured a Christian boy in nearby Sepúlveda. Juan Arias Dávila, the bishop of Segovia, ordered the arrest of sixteen Jews supposedly guilty of this crime. However, according to one source, the bishop himself came under attack and was compelled to go to Rome to defend himself. The motive for this attack on the otherwise respected bishop (who gave both an important library and a hospital to his city) was no doubt due to the revenge he took for the unjust charges against, and imprisonment of, his brother Pedro. The bishop plotted to seize Segovia and turn it over to the rebel forces that supported Alfonso, his half brother. In Rome the bishop had to renounce his authority over the diocese, and he remained in Rome until his death in 1497. The bishop, his deceased father, his mother, and other members of the family were later accused of heresy by the Inquisition.

NORMAN ROTH

Bibliography

Cantera Burgos, F. *Pedrarias Dávila y Cota, capitán general y gobernador de Castilla del Oro y Nicaraqua: Sus antecedentes judíos*. Madrid, 1971.

Carrete Parrondo, C. *Proceso inquisitorial contra los Arias Dávila segovianos*. Salamanca, 1986.

Roth, N. *Conversos, Inquisition and the Expulsion of the Jews from Spain*. Madison, Wisc., 1995.

ARIAS, MAYOR

Mayor Arias was the wife of Ruy González de Clavijo, who was sent by Enrique III (1390–1406) on an embassy to Tamburlaine (Timur) in 1403 and afterward wrote an account of the expedition, the *Embajada a Tamorlán* (1943). She is also the author of the earliest Castilian poem that can be attributed to a woman. A manuscript miscellany in the Bibliothèque Nationale in Paris contains an exchange of poems between Mayor Arias and Ruy González, apparently written on the occasion of his voyage. Mayor Arias's thirteen-stanza poem, which carries the misleading rubric "Dezir de otro mensagero . . ." ("Poem of Another Messenger"), consists of an address to the sea pleading for the safe passage and return of her husband. The second is a simple, shorter poem of farewell from the husband to the wife, again with an unhelpful rubric. "Ay mar braba esquiba" ("Oh Fierce Cruel Sea) is by far the superior poem and, incidentally, of considerable historical and literary interest. The four-line *estribillo*, or refrain, allows us to identify it as a *contrafactum*, a remodeling, of an old song, "Alta mar esquiva," which is known, albeit imperfectly, from three later versions. The theme of a woman's complaint to the sea for carrying off her beloved at the behest of a king represents the earliest Castilian link with the *cantiga de amigo* (woman's song) of Galician-Portuguese tradition. As such it seems to provide unique evidence of continuity between the two main branches of Iberian lyric, otherwise undocumented during the Late Middle Ages. Whether or not Mayor Arias wrote it herself has to remain an open question. But precisely those features that distinguish it from the conventional court lyric of the period—the personal touches, vigorous language, positive outlook—constitute strong indications that it was composed by someone who did not feel bound by conventions: therefore, quite possibly, a woman.

JANE WHETNALL

Bibliography

López Estrada, F. "Las mujeres escritoras en la Edad Media castellana." In *La condición de la mujer en la Edad Media. Actas del Coloquio celebrado en la Casa de Velásquez del 5 al 7 de noviembre de 1984*. Madrid, 1986. 9–36.

Pèrez Priego M. A. (ed.) *Poesía femenina en los cancioneros*. Biblioteca de Escritoras 13. Madrid, 1989.

ARMY, CASTILIAN, CATALAN, MUSLIM, PORTUGUESE

Military forces underwent a remarkable evolution during the Middle Ages in the Iberian Peninsula. Starting with a fully professional army of long-term legionaries and auxiliaries that typify the Imperial Era, a series of invasions substantially altered the governmental systems and the armed forces they raised. The first of these incursions produced the Visigothic Kingdom, which was in the process of evolving from a migratory tribal kingship to an early form of territorial monarchy. Prior to the composition of the various codes of law promulgated by the Visigoths in Spain, we know little of their military organization beyond the fact that it consisted of tribal levies, assembled to fight under the king or leader designated by him. The system was apparently effective, capable of defeating a professional Roman army under Valens at Adrianople in 378. It proved sufficient over time to carry the Visigoths into the peninsula and defeat all of their adversaries there. Maintaining its primitive vigor was another story. By the sixth century, the Visigothic Code describes a military force raised by levies from each *civitas*, the old local Roman unit of government often converted into a county and placed under a Gothic *comes*, or count. These county levies were called *tiufa* and led by a *tiufadus*, the military count in command for military engagements, but occasionally subordinate to the city count in the event of any misconduct. Theoretically each tiufa numbered a thousand men, but it was levied primarily from the Visigothic populace, with only a small number of Hispano-Romans recruited. Therefore, the Goths raised such levies only where they had active garrisons and population settlements in Spain. The *hostis* or *expeditio* provided the occasion for the largest military levy, and all garrison commanders along with nobles sworn to the king were enjoined to assemble their retinues, including even 10 percent of their slaves, in order to serve the royal need. Their armies consisted of both infantry and cavalry, but we have no adequate information regarding their relative proportion or comparative employment in battle. The major military reform law ordered by King Wamba in 673 indicates that the military establishment had become a problem by the seventh century. The numerous punishments meted out for failure to appear for service or for desertion clearly point to a growing deficiency in the Gothic monarchy, whose ability to maintain order and defend the realm was absolutely central to its continued existence. Even after Wamba's enemies overthrew him, they continually endeavored to enforce modified forms of his military laws. However, the Goths seem never to have fully integrated the military structures into the Hispano-Roman society as a whole, a key to their collapse in the face of the Muslim invasion of 711–715.

The Islamic invasion brought combined armies of both Arabic and Berber North Africans into Spain. It was a Berber army under its chieftain Tāriq that achieved the initial victory at the Guadalete River in 711, while demonstrating its ability to operate independently. An Arab force joined them in 712, the combined troops subsequently routing all of the Visigothic garrisons in the Iberian Peninsula within four years. Again, little is known of the nature of Muslim military forces at this point, save that they were fired by the words of the prophet Muḥammad and possessed a conviction the Goths could not match in combat. Once ʿAbd al-Raḥmān I, last of the Umayyad dynasty that fled from Damascus in 750, crossed into Spain and began to organize a centralized emirate based in Córdoba, the outlines of a more formal military establishment began to take shape in the emerging state of unified Muslim Spain called al-Andalus. In addition to a succession of able emirs (after 929 known as caliphs), the real staying power of this empire lay in the bureaucratized state system evolved by these enterprising monarchs. Through the superior taxing system they introduced, the emir-caliphs maintained both a small standing force in Córdoba, along with a regional organization based in the local administrative units known as the *kūras*. These forces were placed under a vizier who took general charge of the military forces, yielding them to the monarch or his chief executive office, the *ḥājib*, when required. The kuras were often laid out along the lines of the former Roman civitates and Gothic counties. In these kuras, entire tribal or clannic groups called *junds* had been settled, and from the junds the local levies were raised and placed under the command of the royal officer or captain called the *alcaide*, directly responsible to the emir-caliph.

Down to the tenth century, al-Andalus fielded a centralized army from the kuras owing allegiance directly to the monarch. Against the emerging Christian states to the north, the caliphs organized frontier marches, an Upper March commanded from Zaragoza, a Middle March centered in Toledo, and a Lower March based in Mérida. As long as this system operated effectively under an able monarch, the armies of the Christian territories were no match for it in the field. Nevertheless, ʿAbd al-Raḥmān III shifted the basis for army recruitment in the mid-tenth century, depending increasingly on imported Slavic and Berber troops, less on the junds in the kuras. His successor in control of the military, the capable ḥājib general Al-Manṣūr, intensified these methods, placing decreasing dependence on the native kura levies. While such personnel offered Al-Manṣūr exceptional loyalty, enabling him to pursue many devastating campaigns deep into the Christian states with impunity, the system deteriorated under his successors. When the caliphate broke up into the smaller *ṭāʾifa* kingdoms after 1031, the overall effectiveness of the Muslim military establishment declined in the face of Islamic disunity. Increasingly the taifa states required the infusions of North African Berber reinforcements to stand up to the aggressive expansionism of the Christian north. This came at a time when these emerging states were forging armies and pressing fortified settlements well south of the Duero River.

While encased in the Cantabrian Mountains of the north, the nascent state of Asturias had need of a military force to control the lands on its flanks, especially Galicia and the northern fringes of Castile. Fortifications, garrisons, and raiding parties covered the basic concerns of offense and defense required to protect the state in this excellent defensive terrain. However, when the Asturian kings expanded onto the Meseta plateau and transformed Asturias into the Kingdom of León through the capture of that city in the tenth century, the entire picture changed. Both pressed against and threatened by the Middle and Lower Marches of the Caliphate, the stimulus to enhance the military capacity of the Leonese state became intense. The Asturo-Leonese monarchy recruited its traditional military forces from its magnates, who in turn gathered their forces from their retainers and bodyguards. As was true of much of the remainder of Europe at this time, an emphasis on mounted service was clearly present. Limited by economics and primitive state development to a comparatively small force, warriors on horseback covered a maximum of territory in a minimum amount of time, and were especially useful for lightning strikes and booty-gathering forays. The mounted aristocracy had foot soldiers among their retainers, who certainly made up the large majority of the forces for any extended campaign not exclusively intended as a raid. Certainly the movement onto the Meseta Plain opened the door to larger land holdings for the king, his nobility, and the Church, all of whom fielded military forces in time of need. Land revenues combined with enhanced booty opportunities enlarged the financial base necessary for expanded military needs. The royal tax base grew, especially given the ability to summon military expeditions (*fossato*, *fonsado*), and collecting fees (*fossataria*, *fonsadera*) from those who did not serve. But here seems to lie two important keys to the success of the Christian Reconquest. First, the Northerners' ability to settle in force in the open lands of the Duero Valley was neither matched nor resisted by an equal capability on the part of the Muslims. Second, at a time when the caliphate increasingly resorted to outside forces while cutting back on domestic recruiting from the kūras, the Leonese state began to consider methods for raising a larger military force from among the settlers on the Duero frontier.

There exists considerable debate among historians as to the degree we can trust the later tenth- and eleventh-century documents, but it would appear that this era began to produce the types of settlements we can describe as towns of a rudimentary sort. These fortified settlements begin to offer the possibility of military service, the first important statement of which is contained in the Fuero de León (1017–1020), a municipal charter that influenced a number of others in the eleventh century. From this beginning, the municipal settlements beginning to multiply both north and south of the Duero River increasingly found a military service obligation included in their settlement charters (*fueros*). Their obligation more often took the form of defense (*apellido*) rather than offense (*fonsado*), and was restricted in time and to their immediate locality in the later eleventh and early twelfth centuries. They nevertheless offered regional security and relieved the king of the total responsibility of their protection. This situation enabled Fernando I and Alfonso VI to add territories and tax revenues, equipping a larger army by the distribution of lands to a growing aristocracy. The kings also exploited the situation to bully the ṭāʾifa princes into granting them annual tributes (*parias*) that served to expand the Christian warmaking ability still further.

Weakened by all of these factors, the central Meseta town of Toledo fell to the Christians in 1085, compelling the ṭāʾifa states to resort to the older tenth-century practice of securing reinforcement from North Africa. The Almoravid Berbers responded with an expeditionary force that defeated the army of Alfonso VI at Zallāqah in 1086. For the Muslims, the older policy of relying on outside aid did not constitute a simple return to the circumstances of the tenth century. These Berber armies brought a new political and religious system in their wake, one that threatened to unify the Iberian Islamic states in the hands of often puritanical and unpopular outsiders. The recruitment of North African reserves also threatened the advantage gained by León-Castile earlier in the eleventh century, although these large-scale reinforcements would always be sporadic during the following decades. To deal with the possibility of this threat, the Leonese monarchy also called upon outside aid from France, especially, but here too support was occasional and particular to special campaigns. The Crusade movement in the Near East, ironically encouraged by the success of the Hispanic Reconquest, began to drain such forces away by the early twelfth century. It became clear that the Leonese-Castilian military machine must be geared to deal both with the ṭāʾifa states and the North African campaigning forces if it hoped to continue its expansionist pressure on the central Meseta. The problem was made no easier when the expansion generated during the reign of Alfonso VII (1126–1157) produced yet another reformist invasion, that of the Almohads after 1150.

With population resources available for settlement growing tighter, and the monarchy splitting into a separate León and Castile in 1157, creative skills in military recruitment reached a decisive point and took the form of two major responses. The first was gradually to encourage the settlement of larger towns by offering greater personal freedoms, while slowly expanding the reach of their militias. These town militias had played no role in distant campaigns in the south during the eleventh century, such as Alfonso VI's campaign against the Almoravids at Zallāqah. By the end of the twelfth century, they would be capable of campaigning for a month or longer with a striking range of two hundred miles or more, unparalleled for town forces at the time in Europe. Secondly, a new hybrid of monastic and military life, the military order, migrated from its place of origin in the Crusader Near East to appear on the Reconquest frontier in Iberia. Ideal for the garrisoning of castles and for initiating quick-striking raids (*cabalgadas*, *algaras*), the military orders could also enhance the campaigning forces of the king along with the municipal militias. The Templars and Hospitallers had appeared earlier in the twelfth century in Aragón, but the Leonese and Castilian states would generate their own domestic versions, starting with the Order of Calatrava (1158), followed by the Order of Santiago (1170) and the Order of Alcántara (1176), these being the most important among several others. While these forces were insufficient to avert the defeat of King Alfonso VIII at Alarcos in 1195 at the hands of the Almohads, their fuller combination at Las Navas de Tolosa in 1212 proved ample for the same king to win a decisive battle that turned the course of the Reconquest, in the face of both the Andalusian levies and expeditionary forces from Almohad North Africa.

The evolution of the Portuguese army followed a track similar to that of León-Castile. As the kingdom secured its independence in the 1140s under King Afonso I Henriques, serious military threats loomed to the east from Alfonso VII and the Leonese monarchy, and to the south, where the Almohad revival threatened from across the Tejo River. Afonso's greatest achievement, the capture of Lisbon in 1147, had only been accomplished with the assistance of troops from England and the Netherlands en route to the Second Crusade. But Portugal would respond to the stresses of the later twelfth century with an inventiveness equal to that of its Christian neighbors. The concept of military orders soon crossed to Portugal. The Templars arrived in the later twelfth century, and a domestic version appeared with the foundation of the Order of Évora in 1166, soon renamed the Order of Avis in 1211. The expanded role of the municipal militias to supplement the levies of aristocracy and church emerges in the kingdom, as well. The Portuguese municipal *forais* (analogous to the Castilian *fueros*) suggest the development of two kinds of charter pattern. The northern pattern, based on the charter of Trancoso, sought a defense of the frontiers against León, limiting the offensive range of the militia by a brief three-day span of service. To the south and east, charters patterned after the forais of Évora and Santarém were granted to the frontier towns, designed to enhance knightly forces in the expedition and to be able to reach into Leonese Extremadura and Andalusia in service time. In no case, however, do the Portuguese forais suggest the creation of municipal militias with the operating range and the month or more fighting time span known in León-Castile. Portugal possessed neither the vast territories of its eastern neighbor nor (after the mid-thirteenth century) a frontier against Granada that would have encouraged the monarchy to require an expeditionary capacity from its municipalities.

The military situation in the Crown of Aragón was somewhat more complex. The two political entities that came to make up the crown, the Crown of Aragón and the County of Barcelona, existed separately until the dynastic marriage of Petronilla of Aragón and Ramón Berenguer IV of Barcelona in 1137. The Crown of Aragón evolved a military system similar to that of Castile, including the development of municipal militias with an expeditionary capability. Domestic military orders gained no foothold here, but the Templars and the Hospitallers were very active. Feudal practices to secure a well-armed mounted force appear in all of the peninsular kingdoms, but were especially well-developed in Aragón, including a willingness to permit hereditary possession of fiefs, a practice not common in Castile. In the County of Barcelona, towns offered military levies to the count, but their militias did not indicate the long-range capabilities of those of the Reino de Aragón or of Castile. As was the case in Portugal, the territorial expansion was rather less extensive, and the counts were able to achieve their expansion with an army more centered on mounted feudal nobles. Alfonso II (Alfons I in Barcelona) was the first king to exploit the military establishment of both reino and county. With his Aragónese resources, Alfonso moved south to take Teruel, while his comitial forces enabled him to pursue his claims in southern France. After the trans-Pyrenean zone was closed by the disaster at Muret in 1213, the monarchy turned its attention toward the south and the ṭā'ifa of Valencia, and to the east toward the Balearic Islands. King Jaime I expertly combined his Catalan and Aragónese forces for the conquest of Mallorca and the assault on Valencia. Town forces from Lleida, Tarragona, and Barcelona, along with outstanding contributions from the Catalan nobles such as the Moncadas, accomplished the overseas conquest of the former, while the Aragónese nobility and the militias of Teruel and Zaragoza combined effectively in the latter campaign.

The victory attained at Las Navas de Tolosa in 1212 demonstrates the manner in which both Muslim and Hispanic Christian forces operated in combat in the thirteenth century. The Muslim army was a composite of both peninsular units and an Almohad expeditionary force from North Africa. The Christian army possessed contingents from Castile, Aragón, and Navarre, each led by the kings of their countries. French units had participated early in the campaign, but departed before the climactic confrontation in Andalusia. Having found a way to penetrate the Sierra Morena mountains, Alfonso VIII descended into the southern foothills on the Islamic flank. Muḥammad al-Naṣir, the Almohad king, promptly regrouped his forces at Navas de Tolosa, setting the stage for the grand conflict on 16 July. Both sides utilized a conventional arrangement of their troops along a line with a center and two wings, backed by a reserve force to be unleashed at the critical moment. The Muslims, who possessed the larger force, also added a line of light skirmishers at the front. On the opposing side, the Aragónese under Pedro II held the Christian right, the Navarrese under Sancho VII held the left, and the center disposed itself in triple layers, with a vanguard, the main body, and Alfonso himself directing the reserve. The Christian forces consisted of the royal standing army, the various aristocrats of the realm with their levies, the military orders of Calatrava and Santiago, and cavalry and foot soldiers of the municipal militias, of which Avila, Segovia, Medina del Campo and Toledo were specifically mentioned in the chronicles (with indications of many more townsmen mixed among the various components). The Almohad line of skirmishers, formed of arrow slingers and javelin hurlers, advanced toward the Christian vanguard, which responded to this provocation by rushing and scattering their tormentors on the way to attacking the Muslim center. The left, center, and right of each side promptly joined the conflict. As the struggle progressed, the Christians began to force the Muslims backward. Then Al-Naṣir dispatched a large portion of his reserve to brace the Muslim lines. In reaction to this, the Christian lines began to buckle, and a number of soldiers fled. Alfonso committed his reserve, including his best cavalry, to bring the infantry back into line, causing the momentum to swing back to the Christian army. Slowly the Muslim lines eroded, but the real breakthrough occurred when a part of the Christian army, probably the Navarrese left under King Sancho, penetrated to Al-Naṣir's camp and attacked his chained African guards. The Almohad caliph fled in panic on horseback, provoking his forces to break into flight. The battle had been comparatively even to this point, but the Andalusian, Berber, and Arabic forces exposed themselves to wholesale slaughter by a disorganized retreat. Only the Christians' pause to sack the Muslim camp slowed the general progress of the rout, but the carnage mounted steadily. The pursuit persisted until twilight forced a halt. The battle signaled the state of advance of Christian peninsular armies, evolved to a state of maturity that would henceforth never permit Muslims forces to win a major field conflict in the Reconquest.

The Later Middle Ages witnessed a slow evolution in the basic composition of the military establishment in Portugal, Castile, and Aragón. The monarchs of each kingdom sought at various times to restrain the development of the bellicose institutions that had advanced the Reconquest: the nobility, the military orders, and the towns. Both the orders and the municipal militias had developed less formidably in Portugal and the Crown of Aragón, but periodic social unrest between landlord and peasant and among the various classes in the towns gave these kings a continuing need for military forces. In Castile, towns and military orders had a major part in the politics of the fourteenth and fifteenth centuries. A frontier with Granada continued to exist. The armed nobility had divided into an upper stratum of *grandes*, *hidalgos*, and *caballeros de linaje*, who tended to ride in a long-stirrup, stiff-legged style that favored charges and contact with their enemies, while the lesser caballeros and *jinetes* favored speed and maneuver with a short-stirrup, bent-knee style. Some of these last two categories served with the towns, which formed into leagues (*hermandades*). Such forces threatened the royal efforts to consolidate national monarchies. In all three Christian kingdoms, kings sought to build independent military forces through the payment of money in lieu of service, using these revenues to pay for a growing standing army. Civil wars and succession crises delayed these endeavors until well into the Trastámara age. It would then be left to the Catholic Kings to bring these reforms to fruition, generating from the militarized heritage of the Reconquest and the organizational skills of Renaissance despotism the armies that would march across Europe and the New World in the sixteenth century. However, this society organized for war continued through its traditions to threaten even the Hapsburg monarch Carlos V in the Communero Revolt and the Germania of Valencia from 1519 to 1521.

James Powers

Bibliography

Ayres de Magalhães Sepúlveda, C. *Historia orgánica e politica do exêrcito português.* Vols. 2–4. Lisbon, 1898–1908.

Contamine, P. *War in the Middle Ages.* Trans. M. Jones. Oxford, 1984.

González Simancas, M. *España militar a principios de la Baja Edad Media.* Madrid, 1925.

Huici Miranda, A. *Las grandes batallas de la Reconquista durante las invasiones africanas.* Madrid, 1956.

Lomax, D. *The Reconquest of Spain.* New York, 1978.

Palomeque Torres, A. "Contribución al estudio del ejército en los estados de la Reconquista," *Anuario de Historia del Derecho Español* 14 (1944), 205–351.

Powers, J. F. *A Society Organized for War: The Iberian Municipal Militias in the Central Middle Ages, 1000–1284.* Berkeley, Calif., 1988.

Redondo Díaz, F. *Historia del ejército español.* Vol. 2, *Los ejércitos de la Reconquista.* Madrid, 1984.

Sánchez Albornoz, C. "El ejército y la guerra en el Reino Asturleonés, 718–1037," *Settimane di Studio del Centro Italiano de studi sull'alto medioevo* 15, no. 1 (1968), 293–428.

Wasserstein, D. *The Rise and Fall of the Party-Kings: Politics and Society in Islamic Spain, 1002–1086.* Princeton, N.J., 1985.

ART

See ARCHITECTURE; ART, JEWISH; ART, MUSLIM; MANUSCRIPT ILLUMINATION; SCULPTURE, GOTHIC, PORTUGUESE

ART, JEWISH

Jews have always practiced various forms of artistic expression, from biblical times to the present, in spite of the incorrect assumption that the second of the Ten Commandments prohibits art (it doesn't; it prohibits worship of images). It is known that there were mutual influences between the architecture and art of the Jews and of all peoples with whom they came in contact, including the early Greeks. Jewish art also had a direct and observable influence on early Christian art. From the medieval period the most frequent, and certainly best-known, form of Jewish art that has survived is manuscript illumination.

Illuminated Manuscripts

The earliest extant examples of illuminated Hebrew manuscripts come from Muslim lands, and no doubt this form of art was also practiced by Jews in Muslim Spain, though none has survived. Under Muslim influence the carpet page form of illumination evolved, full-page designs of intricate geometric or foliate patterns imitating the style of a carpet like those used in mosques and in synagogues. The most famous example from Spain comes from the Christian period, the *Damascus Keter* (Burgos, 1260), which has fourteen such pages. Also typical are the outlines of the forms done in micrographic script (minute Hebrew lettering). This manuscript probably was imitated in the Parma Bible (fourteenth century). Another interesting example is in the Lisbon Bible (1483). Far more important are the numerous elaborate carpet pages of the First Kennicott Bible (La Coruña, 1476), which also used as a model the Mudéjar style of carved wooden ceiling found in such structures as the Church of Santa Cruz in Toledo and the Alhambra (apparently authorities have not hitherto realized this source).

Whereas Castilian illumination drew heavily on Muslim as well as contemporary Christian influences, the numerous illuminated manuscripts of Aragón-Catalonia were inspired exclusively by the Gothic school of Provence and France, and later by the Italian school that dominated Catalan art of the fourteenth century. An important example of the latter is the Copenhagen *Moreh nevukhim* (1348) and its obvious relation to the Master of St. Mark. Another example, not hitherto noticed, is the borrowing of decorative elements (foliate designs, birds, flowers) in the Barcelona *Haggadah* from the Barcelona *Llibre verde* of the same period.

Hebrew manuscript illumination appears to have come to a virtual halt with the destruction of many communities in 1391, but strongly reemerged with new traditions in the fifteenth century, in places as far removed as La Coruña and Seville, but the main activity was in Portugal, where Bibles, prayer books, and at least one richly illuminated manuscript of Maimonides' *Mishneh Torah* were produced. These are profusely illuminated, in some cases every page, in a variety of rich colors and designs and with liberal use of gold.

In addition to the carpet pages and illuminations of scenes, Spanish Hebrew Bible manuscripts are unique for the illustration of Temple cult objects and vessels (the menorah, etc.), with many full-page illuminations. It has been demonstrated by Gutmann and others that these reflected a longing for the messianic return to Palestine and the rebuilding of the Temple. This was not a longing unique to Spanish Jews, but its symbolic portrayal in such illuminations is unique.

The most important illuminated Bibles are the Damascus *Keter* (Burgos, 1260), the Cervera Bible (Toledo?, 1300; of special importance is the magnificent full-page stylized menorah flanked by olive trees, in subtle blues and gold and strikingly "modern" in design), the Second Kennicott Bible (Soria, 1306), the Oxford Ibn Gaon Bible (Soria, ca. 1300), the Perpignan Bible (1299; Paris, Bibliothèque National, Ms. hébr. 7—the earliest to illustrate the cult utensils), the Parma Bible (Catalan, fourteenth century), the Duke of Sussex Bible (Catalan, fourteenth century), the King's Bible (Solsona, 1384), the Farhi Bible (1366–1382; richly illuminated, it took seventeen years to complete!), the First Kennicott Bible (La Coruña, 1476), and the various Portuguese Bibles of the fifteenth century.

In addition to their obvious importance for Jewish history, these volumes contain many details that are of interest for general Spanish history (coats of arms, illustrations of buildings, portraits of kings, soldiers, etc.). All of these deserve study.

Next in importance to Bibles are Passover *haggadot* (orders of the Passover meal and service), which usually are even more richly illuminated than Bibles, and also contain material of great historical interest. The rare Castilian (so-called Moresque) *Haggadah* (ca. 1300) should be pointed out, particularly for what may be a portrait of the king and for its architectural details, as should the famous Golden *Haggadah* (Barcelona, ca. 1300; available in facsimile edition), another mid-fourteenth-century Barcelona *Haggadah*, the magnificent Sarajevo *Haggadah*, the Kaufmann *Haggadah* (certainly not French or Italian, as has been argued; it has the coats of arms of León, Castile, and Aragón!). Both the Golden and Sarajevo *Haggadahs* have been published, as well as others.

Other illuminated Spanish manuscripts include the Oxford Catalan Maimonides (*Guide*) (Hebrew translation, fourteenth century); the Lisbon Maimonides (*Mishneh Torah*) (1472); the previously mentioned Copenhagen *Moreh* (*Guide*), unique for its important picture of a Jewish astronomer lecturing students; and various prayer books and other legal and philosophical works.

Other Artistic Forms

Jewish rings and seals existed from very early times (a ring was discovered in the Montjuich cemetery excavations in Barcelona), and were prevalent in Spain. The most sensational discovery purports to be the ring of Nahmanides, found at Acco in Israel, but the most famous and artistically important is that of Todros Abulafia, presumed to be the son of the famous Samuel ha-Levi, treasurer of Pedro I and builder of the El Tránsito synagogue of Toledo. The seal indeed reproduces the quatrefoil design, with a castle in the center, found over the window of that synagogue. The fleur-de-lis decoration is found also on other Jewish seals. Other seals include that of the Jewish community of Seville, various Passover seals for certifying unleavened bread, and signet rings.

Synagogue architecture is another artistic form. Important miscellaneous items include the famous key presented by the Jews of Seville to Fernado III (1248), with its Hebrew and Spanish lettering praising the king in the biblical language normally used for God, and an important picture of a ship, and the elaborate Hebrew eulogy and symbols of León and Castile on the same king's tomb in Seville.

Of interest is a unique Passover plate produced in Spain (Valencia, and specifically Manises, has been suggested) that may or may not have been done by a Jewish craftsman (the errors in the simple Hebrew words can easily be explained in view of many similar examples). It is of typical Majolican design, elegant but unremarkable save as an indication that undoubtedly other such plates once existed.

The subject of some debate is the Berlin rug that has been identified as a synagogue carpet (fourteenth century) with a design that, it is claimed (likely wrongly), represents a menorah, and with several stylized images of either a Torah ark or possibly the Temple. In any event we know of the existence of such rugs in synagogues, used as wall covers or even ark covers, from Jewish sources.

The names of various Jewish and/or *converso* artists of the fifteenth century (best known are Juan and Guillen de Levi) have survived. Jews did do work for Christians on cult objects and even prayer books. The fame of Jews as goldsmiths, jewelers, and dyers of fabrics is attested in numerous sources, particularly their employment by kings and the royal families.

NORMAN ROTH

Bibliography

Friedenberg, D. *Medieval Jewish Seals.* Detroit, 1987.

Gutmann, J. *Hebrew Manuscript Painting.* New York, 1978.

Meiss, M. "Italian Style in Catalonia." *Journal of the Walters Art Gallery* 4 (1941), 45–87.

Narkiss, B. *Hebrew Illuminated Manuscripts in the British Isles: Spanish and Portuguese Manuscripts.* 2 vols. Jerusalem, 1982.

ART, MUSLIM

For medieval Iberia, the term *Islamic art* refers to the arts made between the eighth century and the end of the fifteenth for Muslim patrons in the parts of the Iberian Peninsula where Islam was the religion of the rulers. Two other terms are also used to refer to related arts in the region. *Mozarabic*, from the Arabic *musta'rab* (Arabized), refers to the art of Christians living under Muslim domination, particularly in the tenth and eleventh centuries, and *Mudéjar*, from the Arabic *mudajjan* (permitted to remain), refers to the art of Muslims living under Christian rule from the eleventh through the fifteenth centuries. Although important works of art were produced throughout the nearly eight centuries of Muslim rule in the region, the two greatest periods of Islamic art are the tenth century at the Umayyad court at Córdoba and the thirteenth and fourteenth centuries at the Naṣrid court at Granada. In both periods, magnificent buildings—mosques, palaces, and citadels—were erected and furnished with fine silks, beautiful books, intricately carved objects of wood and ivory, precious metalwares, and glazed ceramics.

Al-Andalus, as the Islamic lands of medieval Iberia were known, entered into commercial and diplomatic relations with contemporary Muslim and Christian powers, but the relative geographical isolation of the region from artistic centers in the eastern Islamic lands gave its art a distinctively local character from an early date, as artists consequently looked back on and reinterpreted past achievements. The luxury and inventiveness of the Islamic arts of medieval Iberia gave them enormous prestige in the neighboring Muslim lands of northwest Africa as well as in the Christian kingdoms of Iberia. The value in which Islamic decorative arts were held by contemporary Christians is shown by the many examples preserved in church treasuries where they were often used to wrap and contain relics, regardless of the presence of Arabic inscriptions invoking God's blessing on a particular Muslim figure.

As elsewhere in the Islamic lands, architecture was the earliest and most important form of Islamic art in the peninsula, for the new Muslim community needed to have a congregational mosque in each town for communal prayer on Friday noon. Of these congregational mosques, the oldest and most important is that of Córdoba, begun in 786 and repeatedly embellished and enlarged. Like contemporary mosques elsewhere, this building consisted of a walled courtyard leading to a prayer hall in which the roof was supported by many columns. Assembled largely from materials taken from earlier buildings, the first mosque was distinguished by its unique solution for achieving the necessary height: two tiers of short columns were superposed and stabilized by arches assembled from red bricks and blocks of white stone. In subsequent enlargements during the ninth and tenth centuries—which graphically show the numerical growth of the Muslim community—such innovations as the two-tiered system of supports and the horseshoe shape and alternating materials of the arches were maintained. The mosque's square minaret (erected in 951 and later encased by the present bell tower) became the model for all minarets in the Muslim west, as well as many church towers after the Reconquest. The decorative and spatial culmination of the mosque was the *maqṣūra*, or area near the mihrab reserved for the caliph. Built on the orders of Al-Ḥakam, who reigned from 961 to 976, this part of the mosque was taken to unprecedented heights of decorative elaboration with the addition of marble capitals, cusped and intersecting arches, complex surface patterning with geometricized vegetal motifs, and Arabic inscriptions. The beautiful glass mosaics that cover the walls and central dome of the maqṣūra were executed in imitation of those that decorate the mosque of the Umayyads' ancestors in Damascus, for whom the Umayyads of Spain felt a special affinity.

None of the other congregational mosques that were erected in other cities of medieval Iberia survives, but such small mosques as that of Bab Mardum (Cristo de la Luz, 1000) in Toledo show that the architectural styles of the capital had wide currency. The ruins of Madinat al-Zahra, the splendid Umayyad palace-city built outside of Córdoba in 936, show that Umayyad styles of architectural decoration were not restricted to religious architecture. Córdoban features continued to be held in esteem after the fall of the Umayyads in 1031, as can be seen in such palaces as the Aljafería at Zaragoza, erected by a local tā'ifa ruler in the eleventh century, where cusped and intersecting arches were developed to an unusual degree. The integration of al-Andalus with northwest Africa under the Almoravid and Almohad Dynasties of Morocco in the eleventh, twelfth, and thirteenth centuries led to the creation of a hybrid architectural style, in which the exuberance of Umayyad decoration was rationalized and standardized. Only fragmentary remains survive from this period, such as the Giralda (1184–1198), once the minaret of the enormous congregational mosque erected in the Almohad capital at Seville.

Although Almohad power waned in Iberia after their disastrous defeat at Las Navas de Tolosa (1212), the Naṣrid sultans, who reigned from 1230 to 1492, emerged as major patrons of architecture for the remaining centuries of Islamic rule in Iberia. The Naṣrids are primarily remembered for the Alhambra at Granada, originally a palace-city overlooking the city itself, but remains of several other Naṣrid buildings—although no important religious ones—survive (e.g., Granada, Cuarto Real de Santo Domingo). Naṣrid architecture achieves its stupendous effects through the manipulation of exquisitely molded, carved, and painted surfaces of plaster, wood, and glazed tile applied to a rather indifferent armature constructed in brick, stone, and wood.

The primary role of the Qur'ān and of writing in Islam led to the development of the arts of the book—comprising calligraphy, illumination, illustration, and binding—in all regions of the Islamic world. Al-Andalus cannot have been an exception to the general rule, but the widespread destruction of Islamic books following the Christian Reconquest has skewed the picture, and only very few manuscripts survive to testify to the development of these arts in the region. Paper was made locally at Játiva beginning in the eleventh century, but—as elsewhere in the Islamic west—manuscripts of the Qur'ān continued to be copied on parchment in a distinctive *maghribi* (western Islamic) script, characterized by a watery brownish pen line of consistent width with looped descenders. Manuscript illumination was based on geometric motifs with vegetal fillers, executed in gold and several colors. The one illustrated manuscript known to have survived is a thirteenth-century copy of the romance of Bayad and Riyad (Rome, Vatican; Ar. 368). Its illustrations show some familiarity with contemporary work in northern Mesopotamia.

The finest work of the caliphal period is represented by a group of sumptuous carved ivory boxes made for members of the Umayyad court. Such masterpieces as the Mughira Casket (Paris, Louvre; 968) and the Pamplona Casket (Pamplona, Museo de Navarra, 1004–1005) are decorated with an extraordinary variety of figural motifs (the meaning of which have yet to be satisfactorily explained), as well as inscriptions specifying for whom they were made. Although the production of ivory caskets ceased as suddenly as the caliphate itself, workshops continued to produce exquisite wooden furnishings with carved and marquetry decoration in ivory and precious woods. The most important example to survive is an enormous minbar, or pulpit, made circa 1120 in Córdoba for the Almoravid mosque in Marrakesh, Morocco (Marrakesh, Badi' Palace Museum). The history of Iberian Islamic metalwork is known primarily from utilitarian objects cast from copper alloys as well as from scientific instruments, arms and armor. Many objects of precious metal must have been melted down for cash. One exception is a wooden box covered in hammered silver gilt and niello (Girona, cathedral) made in 976 for the Umayyad heir-apparent Hishām and clearly related to the group of ivory caskets.

The production of silk was introduced to Iberia by the Muslims, and sumptuous textiles, such as the so-called Veil of Hishām (Madrid, Real Academia de la Historia) display a mastery of tapestry weaving in colored silk and gold-wrapped thread. Drawloom weaving, which allowed the repetition of complex patterns, was introduced by the eleventh century. Early examples are based on Near Eastern models, but as in the other arts, a distinctive local idiom quickly emerged. An enormous crimson silk curtain (Cleveland, Museum of Art) dating from the fifteenth century represents the apogee of Naṣrid textiles. The art of knotting pile carpets was also introduced to Iberia from the eastern Islamic lands, and many fine examples have been preserved, including some woven in the fifteenth century with the armorial bearings of noble Castilian families. Early Iberian ceramics are rather mediocre earthenwares decorated with colored slips, but, from the early thirteenth century and particularly under Naṣrid patronage, workshops at Málaga and other centers produced some of the finest and largest examples of overglaze-painted lusterwares ever made, such as the Alhambra vases and the Fortuny tablet.

JONATHAN M. BLOOM

Bibliography

Balbás, L. T. *Arte Almohade, Arte Nazarí, Arte Mudéjar. Ars Hispaniae*, vol. 5 1947–81.

Barrucand, M., and A. Bednorz. *Moorish Architecture in Andalusia*. Cologne, 1992.

Blair, S. S., and J. M. Bloom. *The Art and Architecture of Islam: 1250–1800*. London, 1994. ch. 9.

Bloom, J. M. "The Revival of Early Islamic Architecture by the Umayyads of Spain." In *The Medieval Mediterranean: Cross-Cultural Contacts*. Ed. M. J. Chiat and K. L. Reyerson. St. Cloud, Minn., 1988, 35–41.

Dodds, J. D. (ed.) *Al-Andalus: The Art of Islamic Spain*. New York, 1992.

Ettinghausen, R., and O. Grabar. *The Art and Architecture of Islam: 600–1250*. Harmondsworth, U. K., 1987.

Gómez-Moreno, M. *El arte árabe español hasta los almohádes, Arte mozárab. Ars Hispaniae*, vol. 3 1947–81.

Kenesson, S. S. "Naṣrid Luster Pottery: The Alhambra Vases," *Muqarnas* 9 (1992), 93–115.

Mann, V. B., T. F. Glick, and J. D. Dodds (eds.) *Convivencia: Jews Muslims, and Christians in Medieval Spain*. New York, 1992.

ARTILLERY

Artillery is defined as hurling objects against enemy objectives by the use of machines that greatly exceed the capability of unassisted human muscle power. The Roman world had developed a variety of such hurling weapons, basically of two types: the arbalest and the catapult. The former took the shape of a large crossbow, placed on a stand or carriage, with each of its arms tightened separately by a windlass. The arbalest could hurl large pointed bolts or small stones on a flat trajectory against humans or lightly fortified objectives. The catapult existed in two varieties: the einarm, powered by wooden springs, and the larger mangonel, consisting of a lever arm with its base inserted in twisted fiber, often human hair. The crew twisted the fibers tightly together with twin windlasses while holding the throwing arm with a restraining device. When tightened fully, the object to be thrown was placed in a holding enclosure at the free end of the arm. Once released, the throwing arm swung, propelled by the tension of the twisted fibers at its base until stopped by the padded crossbar. Both the swing and the abrupt stop of the arm contributed to the velocity of the projectile, which traveled in a high, rounded trajectory. Projecting rocks of fifty pounds or more over two hundred yards, the mangonel could hit fortified walls from a safe distance. Catapults remained in wide use in the Middle Ages in Iberia and elsewhere, but damp or humid weather inhibited the building of tension in the fibers of the mangonel, making it less serviceable north of the Pyrenees.

A significant improvement, imported from the East, appeared in the twelfth century in the form of the traction trebuchet. In lieu of twisted fibers and torsion power, the traction trebuchet balanced the throwing end of the arm with the power of a crew of men pulling lines attached to the arm. By the thirteenth century an improved variety of this machine, the gravity trebuchet, replaced the crew of pullers with heavy counterweights. These consisted of containers filled with measured amounts of weights that could be adjusted to the weight of the projectile and the distance it had to travel.

Modern models have thrown three-hundred-pound stones over one hundred fifty yards, and potentially can hurl lighter objects to a maximum range of eight hundred yards. Both trebuchet models have more power, flexibility, and accuracy than a catapult, and are less affected by weather. The first European use of the traction trebuchet occured during the Christian siege of Lisbon in 1147, and its presence is noted in the Occitan-Catalan regions circa 1200. The gravity counterweight model appears to have been employed by King Jaime I of Aragón, noted in his chronicle of the assault on the regions north of Valencia. The contemporary Escorial manuscript of the *Cantigas de Santa María* depicts this model as well, and records of their use continue well into the fifteenth century. Cortés utilized one in his siege of México-Tenochtitlán in 1521. In addition to projectiles, these powerful machines were used to hurl dead humans, putrefying animal carcasses, and assorted forms of refuse into besieged castles and towns to encourage the outbreak of disease. Besieged areas often built trebuchets to destroy the machines of their attackers.

The last dramatic breakthrough followed the trebuchet rather closely in the thirteenth century; this was the use of gunpowder and the cannon. (Both remained highly experimental until the end of the fifteenth century.) Gunpowder was a blend of saltpeter, sulphur, and carbon, mixed in either a milled powder or in pellet form. It was initially used by Muslim Iberians, packed in vessels and hurled by trebuchets. By the early fourteenth century, gunpowder became itself the propulsive force for projectiles fired from a metal cannon. Again, the first recorded peninsular use was by the Moors, against Aragón in 1331. Some cannon were small-bore, fired bolts and pellets, and were employed against personnel. Others were larger bore, made of cast or beaten metal, and fired projectiles in a manner similar to the trebuchets. Once perfected by Italian casting methods in the later fifteenth century, cannon reached targets at distances of over two thousand yards. They were widely used in the armies of Fernando and Isabel, shattering the fortified places in Granada, and drastically shortening the final campaign against the Moors.

JAMES POWERS

Bibliography

Contamine, P. *War in the Middle Ages*. Trans. M. Jones. Oxford, 1984.

Reid, W. *Arms through the Ages*. New York, 1976.

ASCETICISM

Asceticism (in Greek, *askēsis*; training, exercise discipline) is the practice of austerity and self-denial; it is an ideal to which all Christians are called, but is usually associated with monks and other members of religious orders. The verb *askēin* (to strive, run) appears only once in the New Testament when St. Paul (1 Cor. 9: 24–25) compares the Christian life to the games of the amphitheater:

> You know that while all runners in the stadium take part in the race, the prize goes to one. . . . run so as to win. Athletes deny themselves. . . . They do this to win a crown of leaves that withers, but we a crown that is imperishable.

By the fourth century asceticism was a characteristic of Egyptian desert monasticism and the inspiration for the monastic life of western Europe, with famous female, as well as male, ascetics. Celibacy (complete abstinence from all sexual activity), fasting (especially rejecting meat), vigils (long hours of prayer, especially at night, thus reducing the hours of sleep and bodily rest) were typical ascetic practices; more extreme forms included wearing a shirt of rough animal hair next to the skin, and whipping the body with a cord of chains, itself later considered a discipline. *The Rule of St. Benedict* (ca. 529), subsequently the cornerstone of all institutional monasticism in Europe, emphasized moderation in all things, and rejected such extreme practices.

Asceticism had a negative side—self-denial—that saints, mystics and spiritual writers understood as a means of controlling pride and fighting bodily lusts. Fasting, for example, meant the control of one's circumstances, which strengthened the will; it also implied rejection of the values of a materialistic world. The positive side of asceticism aimed at the imitation of the sacrificial life of Jesus, the expiation of one's sins and those of the others, and thus the deeper following of Christ. Theoretically both the positive and the negative sides of asceticism sprang from the love of God and aimed at overcoming obstacles to that love. Asceticism was never an end in itself but a means and preparation for union with God through the development of interior tendencies to charity.

Ascetic monks served the Church as missionaries to pagan peoples: the activities of the Italian Augustine of Canterbury (d. 604) to England, those of the Englishman Winfrith/Boniface (ca. 675–754) in Frisia and Germany, and the missions of the French monk Ansgar (801–865) to Sweden, Norway, and Denmark serve as typical examples. But since the time of the early Church and throughout western Europe, the ideals of monastic asceticism had meant withdrawal from the broader secular society, lifelong stability in the monastery of profession, and the cultivation of both an inner spirituality and of the arts of peace. In Reconquest Iberia, however, a military and crusading spirit exemplified monastic asceticism. The Cistercian Order, which came to Spain within the wake of the Reconquest and was used by count-princes as a stabilizing influence in frontier regions, inspired a number of military religious orders. The Order of Calatrava, founded in 1158 by King Sancho III of Castile; the Order of Alcántara, founded in 1158 with the support of the Cistercian bishop Odo of Salamanca; and the Order of Christ, organized in 1319 by King Dinis of Portugal as replacement for the Knights Templar—all combined Cistercian spiritual ideals with the active military /missionary goal of wrestling land from the Muslims. The military values of an iron discipline, obedience, and devotion to duty represented the new ascetic values, and since conversion to Christianity was considered an indispensable part of becoming civilized, the sword and violence replaced prayer and piety as instruments of that conversion.

Christians in most parts of western Europe lived in relatively homogenous religious milieus. Christians in the Iberian Peninsula, however, because of the proximity of Muslims and Jews, perceived their religious faith as a cultural and racial difference. Just as their sense of identity stressed this difference, so too did their ascetic ideals.

BENNETT D. HILL

Bibliography

McGinn, B., and J. Meyendorff (eds.) *World Spirituality: An Encyclopedic History of the Religious Quest.* New York, 1985.

ASTROLOGY AND ASTRONOMY, CHRISTIAN

Few today realize that the modern clock, with its markers indicating twelve equal hours, is the direct descendant of the medieval horologe, on whose face were depicted the starts and planets of the heavens. Instead of using rotating hands, the entire face of the horologe rotated past a stationary marker representing the horizon, in an attempt to reflect simultaneously what was occurring in the sky above. The significance of this observation is that the rotation of the heavens, the alternation between day and night, unrelentlessly regulates the lives of plants, animals, and humans. This constant alternation with the regular appearance of the sun during the day and certain stellar patterns at night eventually came to serve as markers—predictors, in a way—for the somewhat regular patterns of nature. Heavenly patterns, associated with certain seasons, could in turn serve as predictors for following seasons.

Observation of the stars, then, has always contained, beyond the mere theoretical, a practical component. Medieval astronomy and its bedfellow, or perhaps its raison d'être, astrology, derived from the Greeks both directly and indirectly. The direct route, through the Romans, proved somewhat sterile. The indirect route, through the Arabs, on the other hand, provided an impetus over the stretch that eventually would lead to Nicolas Copernicus (1473–1543).

When Greek astronomy passed on to Rome, for myriad possible reasons—economics, war, plague, barbarian invasions—it degenerated to a low level and had little impact on medieval culture. The major Greek work passed on to the west was the outdated—by Ptolemaic standards—cosmology found in Plato's *Timaeus*. Isidore of Seville (ca. 560–636) reveals in his *Etymologies* the kinds of information arriving through this direct route. A major problem with information arriving directly from Rome was that it was unaccompanied by a theoretical background or the means to acquire it. Only a portion of Aristotle's writings came through this route. The fundamental interest of Christian astronomy, prior to the impetus it received from Arabic science in the tenth century, consisted essentially of explaining philosophically rather than empirically the composition of the universe—that is, of explaining cosmology as it was understood from the few Greek sources available.

Nestorian Christians fleeing persecution of the Byzantine Church (fifth century) brought to Persia much Greek knowledge. This, translated into Syriac, was passed on into Arabic, and subsequently into Latin and on to the Christian west.

Those who chide Arab astronomy for not advancing theoretically the Greek science passed on to them often fail to consider what the Arabs did achieve: accurate measurements, compilation of useful tables, refinement of instruments of astronomical observation, and a most important motive for pursuing all of this: astrology.

According to Pederson, Gerber of Aurillac (ca. 945–1003), later Pope Sylvester II, "introduced the abacus, the armillary sphere, and, apparently the astrolabe as teaching aids into the schools in which he taught." By 1277, King Alfonso X lists at least fourteen instruments of observation and mensuration including horologes in his *Libro del saber de astrología.* Such instruments enabled refining of astronomical science as the means to astrological prediction.

Astrology has always found proponents and opponents, yet the medieval church did not militate against it per se, providing it avoided any manner of determinism. The writings of the church fathers and the contents of Greek cosmology generally, although not always, found easy compromises. A major concern of Christianity was ensuring that empirical observation did not infringe upon the rights of a deity whose ways were considered infinite and inscrutable. When irreconcilable differences occurred, theology prevailed.

Medieval cosmology, never summarized or presented comprehensively in any one work, nevertheless manifests three major tenets: that the universe was geocentric, spherical, and finite. Heliocentric and geoheliocentric theories proposed earlier never took root. Geocentricity became so essential to western thought that attempts to displace the centrality of Earth met substantial resistance. One of the alleged reasons why the Inquisition burned Giordano Bruno at the stake (1600) was his support of heliocentrism; nearly half a century later, Galileo spent the final days of his life (d. 1642) under house arrest for his heliocentric theories. In the Ptolemaic view, with the Earth at center, the universe extended outward in a series of concentric spheres, each constituting a heaven inhabited by one of the seven planets (from Greek *planetes*, meaning "wanderer")—the Moon, Mercury, Venus, the Sun, Mars, Jupiter, and Saturn. The "Eighth Heaven" was the abode of the fixed stars—that is, the constellations, especially the twelve of the zodiac, which never varied in their appearance (hence the term *fixed*). The ninth, the Crystalline Sphere, followed as the locale of the Primum Mobile, an initiating force believed to set the rest of the circles into harmonious motion. The tenth and last sphere, the Empyrean, was the dwelling place of the Creator. The number of heavens fluctuated between eight and eleven in Christian astronomy, but ten seems to have constituted the standard conception of the universe.

In Aristotelian terms, perfect motion was circular, yet planets were long known to move irregularly across the sky, sometimes even in retrograde motion. Bound by the notion of the circle, Greek astronomers developed the theory of epicycles in an attempt to explain peculiar planetary motion. One planet, the moon, although regular in motion, varied constantly in appearance. Mutability and transience thus came to characterize the sublunary world, the domain of the four elements and their characteristics: water (moist), earth (dry), air (cold), and fire (hot). This portion of the cosmos was subject to change and *influence* (modern "influenza/flu" and "lunacy") from above. The medieval building blocks of the universe—the characteristics of the four elements—combined to form the four humors: sanguine (hot/moist), choleric (hot/dry), melancholic (cold/dry), and phlegmatic (cold/moist). The heavens—the macrocosmos—thus influenced all aspects of the earth below, the microcosmos. From the Christian viewpoint, of course, Divine Providence had established all of this.

Thus, with astrological prediction providing the motive, and astronomical observation providing the data, empirical science provided facts that increasingly challenged generally held notions of the cosmos—not all at once, but persistently and gradually. The heliocentrism of Copernicus, a theory that remained unacceptable for years to come, constitutes an adequate demarcation between medieval and modern astronomy/astrology.

ANTHONY J. CÁRDENAS

Bibliography

DeKosky, R. K. *Knowledge and Cosmos: Development and Decline of the Medieval Perspective*. Washington, D.C., 1979.

Grant, E. "Cosmology." In *Science in the Middle Ages*. Ed. D. C. Lindberg. Chicago, 1978. 265–302.

Lewis, C. S. *The Discarded Image: An Introduction to Medieval and Renaissance Literature*. Cambridge, 1964.

Pannekoek, A. *A History of Astronomy*. New York, 1969.

Pedersen, O. "Astronomy." In *Science in the Middle Ages*. Ed. D. C. Lindberg. Chicago, 1978. 303–37.

ASTRONOMY AND ASTROLOGY, JEWISH

Ḥasan ha-Dayyan (fl. ca. 950) and Isaac ben Baruch (1035–1094) are the earliest known Iberian Jews to have concerned themselves with astronomy. They wrote on calendarics, and their works are known only through extensive quotations by later writers. The earliest Iberian Jew to work on mathematical astronomy proper whose works have survived is Abraham bar Ḥiyya (d. ca.1136) of Barcelona. He wrote in Hebrew, employing a technical vocabulary of his own making, the following: *Ṣurat ha-Areṣ*., a nontechnical exposition in the tradition of the Arabic *hay'ah* literature; extensive tables (*Luhot ha-Nast*) and instructions for their use (*Ḥeshbon Mahalakhot ha-Kokhavim*); and some shorter items, including one on the differences between Ptolemy and Al-Battānī. Astronomical material is also included in Bar Ḥiyya's encyclopedia, *Yesodei ha-Tevunah*. Abraham ibn Ezra (1092–1167) wrote a treatise on the use of the astrolabe, *Kli ha-Neḥoshet*, and several sets of astronomical tables, all lost, and a number of other important works. Although Ibn Ezra was born and educated in Spain, and he has long been identified in Jewish tradition as the archetypical Spanish erudite, most of these works were actually written in Italy.

Several Jewish astronomers collaborated in writing and translating treatises for the corpus of astronomical works created under the patronage of Alfonso X of Castile. The most important of these was Isaac Ibn Sid, who is considered the outstanding Jewish astronomer of the thirteenth century. Unfortunately, hardly anything is known about Ibn Sid other than his name and the record of a few of his observations. We know he was the author (not translator) of ten of the Alfonsine treatises and served the king in the preparation of the Alfonsine Tables. His reputation in Toledo was as an astronomer (fl. 1263–1267). Yehudah b. Moses ha-Kohen (Mosca) was another famous translator of works for Alfonso, apparently related to the astronomer Yehudah b. Solomon Mosca, author of the astronomical *Misphatei kokavim: otot ha-shamayim*. He translated the famous *Lapidario* as well as Azarquiel (Al-Zarqālī), and together with Ibn Sid translated other works. The Toledan Judah ibn Mattka was, for all we know, not an astronomer, but he included in his encyclopedic *Midrash Ḥokhmah* extensive summaries of Ptolemy's *Almagest* and the nonconformist theories of al-Bitrūjī. Ibn Mattka presents some detailed criticisms of Ptolemy's computation of the planetary sizes and distances. Although it remains unpublished, it incorporates interesting astronomical discussions as well that are devoted ostensibly to religious matters; for example, in the section treating of the secrets of the letters of the Hebrew alphabet. *Midrash Ḥokhmah* was very influential in the diffusion of astronomical knowledge among Jews; it also preserves for the modern scholar fragments of the commentary to the *Almagest* written by one R. David, perhaps David ibn Naḥamias of Toledo.

Another Toledan, Isaac ben Joseph Israeli, produced in 1310 *Yesod ʿOlam*, on the face of it a practical handbook for computing the Jewish calendar but contained as necessary ancillary material exhaustive discussions of solar and lunar theory, and much other material as well. *Yesod ʿOlam* survives in over thirty manuscript copies; it and Bar Ḥiyya's *Surat ha-Ares* were undoubtedly the two most popular specimens of medieval Hebrew astronomical literature. In two other works, *Sha'ar ha-Shamayim* and *Sha'ar ha-Millu'im* (both of which are accompanied by tables), Israeli discusses those elements of astronomy, especially planetary theory, that were necessarily left out of his work on the Jewish calendar. Israeli's own son Joseph wrote a summary in Arabic of *Yesod ʿOlam*, which was then translated by another family member into Hebrew. *Yesod ʿOlam* was dedicated to Rabbeinu Asher (Ben Yehiel), a German rabbi who had just assumed the spiritual leadership of Spanish Jewry. Israeli wished to impress this presumably uncultured northerner with the achievements of Spanish Jewry and, it seems, he met with some success. Asher's son Judah (d. 1349) himself took up astronomy and produced a book, *Ḥuqqot Shamayim*, whose excellence was attested to by later astronomers. Judah's student Solomon Corcos, who may have worked at Avila, commented upon *Yesod ʿOlam*. Joseph ben Isaac ibn al-Waqār, yet another Toledan, drew extensive astronomical tables in Arabic (ca. 1357) and in Hebrew (ca. 1395); these have yet to be closely studied. Solomon Franco (fourteenth century) wrote an astronomical handbook of his own (including tables) and also a treatise on the astrolabe.

We know also of quite a number of Aragónese Jewish astronomers who flourished in the fourteenth century. Most important is Jacob ben Yem Tov Poʿel (Bonjorn), whose widely diffused tables were translated into Latin and Catalan. A number of Jews worked in the service of Pedro IV the Ceremonious (1336–1387), most notably the Mallorcan cartographer and instrument maker Isaac Nafuci, and Jacob Corsino, who was active in the preparation of Pedro's own astrological tables and also left us a treatise on the astrolabe. At the end of this century (1391) at least two copies of a complete and illuminated star catalog were prepared on vellum somewhere in central Iberia, close to the thirty-first parallel.

Judah ibn Verga, who worked at Lisbon in the middle of the fifteenth century, composed a number of astronomical treatises. By far the most accomplished Hispano-Jewish astronomer of that century is Abraham Zacut. Zacut taught at Salamanca, for whose meridian he drew up a set of tables; the Latin version, *Almanach perpetuus*, played no small role in the navigational feats of that great age of exploration.

Jewish thinkers shared in the deliberations of Hispano-Islamic savants concerning the true physical structure of the heavens. Maimonides notes his study of this issue with the students of Ibn Bājja; and the purportedly truer (in the philosophic sense) models of al-Biṭrūjī were available in Hebrew translation. Most worthy of scholarly attention are the detailed alternative models developed by Joseph ibn Nahamias in his *Nūr al-ʿālam*, which he himself translated into Hebrew as *Or ʿOlam*. The criticisms and innovations in more technical matters of two other Iberians, Al-Zarqālī and Jabir ibn Aflah, were translated into Hebrew and aroused considerable interest.

Astrology seems to have always been a matter of some controversy, though on the whole it probably was accepted by a majority of Jews. Abraham bar Ḥiyya offered a vigorous defense; two of his contemporaries, the mystic Bahya ibn Paqudah and the philosopher Judah ha-Levy, were both critical, as was Maimonides. It appears that, especially in the fourteenth century, astrology figured prominently in polemics with Christians, on account of its pertinence to the issue of freedom of action. The apostate Abner of Burgos (Alfonso de Valladolid) appealed to astrology in his attacks on Judaism, prompting a lengthy rebuttal of astrology from Isaac Polgar in his *ʿEzer ha-Dat*.

Few astrological texts were produced. Most interesting is Bar Ḥiyya's astrological history, *Megillat ha-Megalleh*. A small section of Ibn Mattka's encyclopedia is devoted to astrology. Joseph ben Abraham Ibn Waqār promulgated a synthesis of astrology, philosophy, and cabala. Astrology was also utilized in many biblical commentaries. The aforementioned Jacob Corsino, together with two Christians, composed *Tractat d'astrologia* for Pedro IV.

Finally we must take note of the deeper resonances of astronomy in Hispano-Jewish culture. Intellectuals in the main assimilated the notion that astronomy is the noblest of the sciences and a requisite stepping stone to further spiritual development. Solomon ibn Gabirol (ca. 1020–1057) devoted an entire section of his masterpiece *Keter Malkhut* to the science of the stars and, among other poets, most notably Isaac Ibn Ghiyat found inspiration in the stars for many verses.

TZVI LANGERMANN

Bibliography

Chabás, J. "Une période de récurrence de syzygies au XIVe siècle: Le cycle de Jacob ben David Bonjorn." *Archives Internationales d'Histoire des Sciences* 82 (1988), 243–51.

Corsino, Jacob. *Tractat d'astrologia*. Barcelona, 1890.

Goldstein, B. R. "The Hebrew Astronomical Tradition: New Sources," *Isis* 72 (1981), 237–51.
Langermann, Y. T., P. Kunitzsch, and K. A. F. Fischer. "The Hebrew Astronomical Codex Ms. Sassoon 823," *Jewish Quarterly Review* 78 (1988), 253–92.
Millás Vallicrosa, J. M. *Estudios sobre historia de la ciencia.* Barcelona, 1948.
———. (trans.) *Surat ha-Ares.* La obra *Forma de la tierra.* Barcelona, 1956.
Roth, N. "Jewish Collaborators in Alfonso's Scientific Work." In *Emperor of Culture.* Ed. R. T. Burns, S. J. Philadelphia, 1990. 59–71, 223–30.
Steinschneider, N. *Die Mathematik bei den Juden.* Hildesheim, 1964.

ASTROLOGY AND ASTRONOMY, MUSLIM

The Andalusian heritage is extremely rich in the fields of astronomy and astrology, two branches of knowledge that were closely related in the Middle Ages. Even, as hence, with a study of the development of astronomical instruments and the compilation of astronomical tables, one should bear in mind that the main purpose of most of the instruments was to simplify the tedious computations involved in the casting of a horoscope and that tables were compiled because planetary longitudes are an essential part of the same horoscope.

During the first century after the Muslim conquest, a Latin astrological, but also astronomical, tradition survived in al-Andalus. ʿAbd al-Wāḥid ibn Isḥāq al-Ḍabbī (fl. ca. 800), the first Andalusian astrologer who left a written work, composed an astrological *urjūza* (didactical poem in *rajaz* meter) of which only thirty-nine verses are extant and in which astrological predictions are based in the late Latin "system of the crosses" (*ṭarīqat aḥkām al-ṣulūb*). This Latin astrological tradition was much more crude than the standard Hellenistic one adopted by the eastern Arabs and introduced later into al-Andalus, and Al-Ḍabbī's *urjūza* was probably corrected, in the eleventh century, by a certain *Oueidalla* (ʿAbdallah ibn Aḥmad al-Ṭulayṭulī) and finally translated into Spanish (*Libro de las Cruzes*) by Yehudah ben Mosheh (fl. 1225–1276) for King Alfonso X. A second instance of such Latin influence is probably to be found in sundials. Qāsim ibn Muṭarrif al-Qattān (and many other sources after him) describes, toward the middle of the tenth century, a *balāṭa*, a very primitive kind of horizontal sundial in which the vertical gnomon is fixed in the center of a semicircle and the limits of the hours are determined by radii that divide the circle equally into fifteen-degree arcs. This instrument is very different from the standard Hellenistic horizontal sundial (in which the solar shadow in the solstices describes two arcs of a hyperbola, while in the equinoxes it describes a straight line) and I believe that it corresponds to a Latin tradition related to the kind of instruments that are often found in churches and that are called incised dials or mass clocks in England.

Andalusian astronomers seem to have been interested in designing astronomical instruments. The astrolabe, the standard analogue computer used to quickly solve problems of spherical astronomy and astrology, appears mentioned for the first time in an anecdote in which the characters involved are the emir ʿAbd al-Raḥmān II (821–852) and his astrologer, Ibn al-Shamir. This instrument attracted the attention of Maslama al-Majrīṭī (ca. 950–1007), who wrote a commentary on Ptolemy's *Planisphaerium*, the main treatise inherited from antiquity in which the theory of the instrument is analyzed. Maslama's disciples Aḥmad Ibn-al-Jaffār (d. 1035) and Abū-l-Qāsim Aṣbag ibn al-Samḥ (d. 1035) wrote books on the use of the astrolabe and the latter also on its construction. Ibn al-Samḥ's treatise on the use of the instrument was later adapted by the collaborators of Alfonso X in their treatise on the spherical astrolabe (*astrolabio redondo*).

The polar stereographic projection used in the astrolabe implies that the local horizon is projected as an arc of a circle and, therefore, the instrument requires a special plate for each latitude. If an adequate plate for the required latitude is not available, approximate

Astrolabe. From Córdoba. Moorish, 1154. Engraved with Latin text in Italy during the 14th c. Jagellon Library, Museum, Cracow, Poland. Copyright © Giraudon/Art Resource, NY.

methods that do not yield sufficiently accurate results need to be used. To avoid this inconvenience, two Toledan astronomers of the eleventh century, Abū Isḥāq Ibrāhīm ibn Yaḥyā al-Naqqāsh (d. 1100), called Ibn al-Zarqiyāl or Ibn al-Zarqālluh (also Azarquiel), and Abū-l-Ḥasan ʿAli ibn Khalaf al-Shajjār or al-Ṣaydalānī (fl. 1068–1072), designed the first universal astrolabes based on a meridian stereographic projection in which any horizon is projected as a radius of the instrument and a rotating ruler can easily become a movable horizon and be adapted to any required latitude. Ibn al-Zarqālluh seems to have been the first to design a universal instrument of this kind. The description of two varieties of the so-called azafea (*al-ṣafīḥa*) were dedicated by him to the ʿAbbādī prince and later king of Seville, Al-Muʿtamid (1069–1091). Unlike the standard astrolabe, Ibn al-Zarqālluh's instruments lacked a rete or spider, the rotation of which represents that of the celestial sphere around the earth. This is probably why ʿAli ibn Khalaf designed, in 1071 to 1072, a new instrument that he called *al-asṭurlāb al-ma'mūnī* and dedicated to King al-Ma'mūn of Toledo (1043–1074). This instrument was called, in the Alfonsine translation, *Lamina universal* and *Orizon universal*, and it superimposed a rotating rete on the standard grid of coordinates characteristic of Ibn al-Zarqālluh's azafeas. Finally, a last attempt to design a plate for all horizons, to be used with a conventional astrolabe, was done, in the thirteenth century, by the astronomer of Granada Ḥusayn ibn Aḥmad ibn Bāṣo. This new instrument bears the influence of the two aforementioned Toledan astronomers and of the characteristic Eastern "plate of horizons" usually ascribed to the Syrian astronomer Ḥabash al-Ḥāsib (d. ca. 864).

Both the standard and the universal astrolabe solved, quite easily, the problem of the division of the houses that was necessary to cast a horoscope; still, the computation of planetary longitudes using a set of astronomical tables (*zīj*) implied quite a long work. This is why *equatoria* (instruments consisting of Ptolemaic planetary models drawn to scale) were designed in order to offer graphical solutions to the problem. Although a possible Eastern origin has been suggested, it is a fact that the earliest descriptions of the equatorium appear in al-Andalus in the eleventh century. They were written by the aforementioned Ibn al-Samḥ and Ibn al-Zarqālluh, and by Abū-l-Ṣalt Umayya ibn Abī-l-Ṣalt (ca. 1067–1134). The two former treatises were the object of an Alfonsine Spanish translation that could be the starting point of the long tradition of Latin treatises on this instrument that appeared in Europe between the thirteenth and seventeenth centuries. Apart from its practical nature, the instrument described by Ibn al-Zarqālluh contains an important theorical development. The complexity of the Ptolemaic Mercury model led him to represent the planet's deferent as an oval (*bayḍī*) curve (called *figura pinnonada* in the Spanish translation), practically equivalent to an ellipse. Thus, he seems to have been the first astronomer with enough courage to cross the boundary of an astronomy based on circles and introduce a new astronomy of noncircular curves.

Astrolabes and equatoria are analogue computers, not observational instruments, the description of which is rare in the Andalusian tradition. Only two instruments of this latter kind appear documented: one of them is Ibn al-Zarqālluh's treatise on the construction of the armillary sphere extant only in the Alfonsine version (*Libro de las Armellas*). The second was designed by Jābir ibn Aflaḥ (fl. 1150). Conceived as a large-sized observational instrument (Jābir mentions a diameter of about six spans for the basic graduated circle) that can be mounted on any one of the three astronomical planes (horizon, equator, or ecliptic), it has been considered a predecessor of the *torquetum*, a European instrument described for the first time toward the end of the thirteenth century.

A third center of interest in Andalusian astronomy can be found in astronomical handbooks with tables (*zījes*). The first *zīj* was introduced in al-Andalus in the time of ʿAbd al-Raḥmān II (821–852), and it was probably a work of Indian descent, the *Sindhind* in the recension made by Muḥammad ibn Mūsā al-Khwārizmī (fl. 800–847), which, in the second half of the tenth century, was revised and adapted by Maslama al-Majrīṭī and his disciples. The time of Maslama was also that of the introduction, in al-Andalus, of the more elaborate Ptolemaic astronomy, but the Indian tradition was never completely forgotten in this country. A good example can be found in the *Tabulae Jahen* (an adaptation of Al-Khwārizmī's *Sindhind* to the coordinates of Jaén to which Ptolemaic or original materials were added) of Ibn Muʿādh (d. 1093), of which only the canons are extant in a Latin translation by Gerard of Cremona. Much more succesful were the *Toledan Tables*, only known through a Latin translation extant in an enormous number of manuscripts. These tables seem to have been the result of a hasty adaptation, done circa 1069, of all the available astronomical material (Al-Khwārizmī, Al-Battānī, and the *Almagest*) to the coordinates of Toledo. Its authors were a group of Toledan astronomers led by the famous *qāḍī* Abū-l-Qāsim Saʿīd ibn Aḥmad ibn ʿAbd al-Raḥmān ibn Muḥammad ibn Saʿīd (d. 1070). Among them we find Ibn Al-Zarqālluh and ʿAli ibn Khalaf as well as others. Even if the results achieved were not brilliant, the *Toledan Tables* incorporated the first results of a programme of observations that were continued by Ibn al-Zarqālluh until much later, as well as a set of trepidation tables that appear for the first time in al-Andalus. Trepidation theory—also called theory of accession and recession—which was later (ca. 1085) the object of further study by Ibn al-Zarqālluh in his book *On the Motion of Fixed Stars*, has an obscure Eastern origin but was mainly developed in al-Andalus. Its purpose is to design geometrical models that will justify the slow diminution of the obliquity of the ecliptic as well as the irregularities—based on inaccurate observations—in the velocity of the precession of the equinoxes. Ibn al-Zarqālluh's theorical work also includes a modification of the Ptolemaic lunar model as well as a book on the Sun in which he designed a solar model with variable eccentricity and established the solar apogee's own motion. These ideas became very influential in later Andalusian, Maghribī, and European astronomy.

After the *Toledan Tables* several Andalusian *zījes* were compiled. The first of these—although not properly a *zīj*—is Ibn al-Zarqālluh's own *Almanac* (extant in Arabic and in a Spanish Alfonsine translation), an adaptation of a Greek work computed by a certain Awmātiyūs (Humeniz) in the third or fourth century A.D. Its purpose is to furnish astrologers with astronomical tables allowing them to obtain planetary longitudes without all the computation involved in the use of a *zīj*, and it uses the Babylonian planetary cycles usually called "goal years." After the completion of one of these cycles, the longitudes of a given planet will be the same in the same dates of the year as in the beginning of the cycle. Ibn al-Zarqālluh's ideas (trepidation, new solar and lunar models) also influenced other conventional *zījes*, such as those computed by his disciple Abū Jaʿfar Ahmad ibn Yūsuf, known as (Ibn) al-Kammād (fl. beginning of the twelfth century), by Ibn al-Hā'im (fl. 1204–1205) and by Ibn al-Raqqām (d. 1315), the author of an important book on sundials. Furthermore, Ibn al-Zarqālluh's influence is also obvious in astronomers of the Maghrib, such as Ibn Ishāq al-Tūnisī (fl. beginning of the thirteenth century) and Ibn al-Bannā' al-Marrākushī (1256–1321).

Andalusian astronomy reached its peak with Ibn al-Zarqālluh and a period of decay starts immediately after when, in the twelfth century criticism of Ptolemaic astronomy started. This criticism had a mathematical basis in the case of Jābir ibn Aflaḥ (fl. ca. 1150), whose *Iṣlāḥ al-Majisṭī* (Correction of the Almagest) analyzed the inconsistencies and methodological defects of Ptolemy's work. A second kind of criticism was far more ambitious as well as dangerous: it was exerted by an important group of Aristotelian philosophers who rejected Ptolemy because of the mathematical (not physical) character of his planetary models that disagreed with Aristotelian physics. The *Almagest* was obviously useful for the computation of planetary positions but it just did not describe the real universe. Such criticisms appear, in very general terms, in the works of Ibn Bājjah (1070–1138), Ibn Tufayl (before 1110–1185), Ibn Rushd (Averroës) (1126–1198), and Maimonides (1135–1204), but it is only with Abū Isḥāq Nūr al-Dīn (ibn) al-Biṭrūjī, a disciple of Ibn Ṭufayl, that a complete cosmological system appears in his *Kitāb fī-l-hay'a*, probably composed between 1185 and 1192. With a limited knowledge of the astronomical literature available, he conceives a homocentric system that is purely qualitative, has too many defects and inconsistencies, and could never have been the base for the computation of a set of tables. It is, however, interesting to remark that, in order to explain the transmission of motion between the physical planetary spheres, he does not use Aristotelian but neoplatonic dynamics.

JULIO SAMSÓ

Bibliography

Comes, M., R. Puig, and J. Samsó. (eds.) *De Astronomia Alphonsi Regis*. Barcelona, 1987.

Comes, M., H. Mielgo, and J. Samsó. "*Ochava Espera*" y "*Astrofísica*." Barcelona, 1990.

Samsó, J. *Las Ciencias de los Antiguos en al-Andalus*. Madrid, 1992.

———. *The Exact Sciences in al-Andalus*. English summary. In *The Legacy of Muslim Spain*. Ed. S. K. Jayyusi. Leiden, 1992. 956–73.

Vernet, J. *Ce que la culture doit aux Arabes d'Espagne*. Paris, 1985.

———. *Estudios sobre historia de la ciencia medieval*. Barcelona, Bellaterra, 1979.

———. *Nuevos estudios sobre astronomía española en el siglo de Alfonso X*. Barcelona, 1983.

———. *Textos y estudios sobre astronomía española en el siglo XIII*. Barcelona, 1981.

———. (ed.) *Estudios sobre historia de la ciencia árabe*. Barcelona, 1980.

Vernet, J., and J. Samsó. (eds.) *El legado científico andalusí*. Madrid, 1992.

ASTURIAS, KINGDOM OF THE

The history of the kingdom of the Asturias (ca. 718 to 910) has to be reconstructed largely on the evidence of two brief chronicles first composed in the late ninth century, one of which, the *Chronicle of Alfonso III*, survives in two variant versions compiled early in the tenth century. The other chronicle, known as the *Chronicle of Albelda*, from the monastery in which a short continuation was added to it in 976, is much briefer than the Alfonsine texts, but is independent of them. To these chronicles can be added a few notices of the kingdom in the Arab historians of Umayyad Spain and in some of the contemporary Frankish annals. There also exists a body of charters relating to royal and other deeds of gift and sale, but many of the earliest of these are either forged or have been interpolated.

Although it is possible to reconstruct an outline history of the kings of the Asturias, it must be appreciated that this has to be done on the basis of a predominantly late-ninth-/early-tenth-century perspective. Thus, information concerning the creation of the kingdom and the first hundred years of its existence may be affected by the strong ideological preoccupations of the reign of Alfonso III (866–910). Particular care is needed in assessing the foundation legends of the kingdom and its royal dynasty.

In the Asturian historiographical tradition members of the family of the penultimate Visigothic king Wittiza (692/4–710) are cast consistently as the villains in the story of the fall of that kingdom and the ensuing foundation of the Asturian one. Wittiza himself is portrayed as an enemy of the father of Pelagius, who was to become the first king of the Asturias, and the cause of the latter's exile. When Pelagius subsequently led a revolt in the Asturias against the Arabs, one of Wittiza's sons, Oppas—who is made out to be either the bishop of Toledo or of Seville—accompanied the Arab army that was sent to crush him. In the two versions of the *Chronicle of Alfonso III* an elaborate but fictitious exchange of insults is made to take place between Pelagius and Oppas immediately prior to the battle fought at Covadonga, in which the Arabs are defeated and the independence of Pelagius's tiny kingdom is established.

In reality, very little is known of the causes and events of the Asturian revolt, or of the origins of Pelagius. Even the date of the battle of Covadonga is uncertain, though the traditional date of 718 is probably to be preferred to the more recent suggestion of 722. A local revolt, allied to a subsequent lack of interest on the part of the Arab governors in restoring their hold over the northern mountains of the Iberian Peninsula explains how the kingdom came into being, and why it was able to survive. In retrospect this was anachronistically seen as the beginning of the whole process of the Reconquest, and the crucial battle came to be associated with a miraculous appearance of the Virgin Mary.

After the Battle of Covadonga the chronicles record nothing of the reign of Pelagius beyond his burial at Cangas de Onís and the succession of his son Fáfila (737–739). That the kingdom he had created covered little more than the region of the eastern Asturias, centered on Cangas, is probable, and no further extension of its territory occurred until the accession of Pelagius's son-in-law Alfonso I (739–756) following the accidental death of Fáfila. Alfonso was the son of a duke of the region called Cantabria, the precise area of which in this context cannot be deduced. But his inheritance must have led to an eastward extension of the kingdom into Basque regions. Alfonso's son Fruela I the Cruel (756–768) faced what the chroniclers describe as a Basque revolt, and made a diplomatic marriage to a Basque wife after its suppression.

It is possible that the chronicle references to revolts on the part of both Galicians and Basques in this period are ideologically tainted, and that what was really at issue was resistance to Asturian conquest. Under both Alfonso I and Fruela I the western frontiers of the kingdom were expanding rapidly, first to the river Miño and then to the Atlantic coast. Although in the later perspective of the Reconquest this was a liberation, there are no good reasons to assume that in the eighth century the Basques or the Galicians wished to be ruled by the Asturias.

Warfare was also initiated on the southern frontiers in the reigns of these two kings. Various settlements in the northern Meseta were captured, and their Hispano-Gothic populations moved north into the Asturias. Rather than occupying the newly acquired territory on the Leonese Plateau, the kings were trying to create a deserted zone between themselves and the Arabs in the south and center of the peninsula. The Asturian chronicles attribute this activity to Alfonso, while Arab sources give the credit to Fruela.

Following the latter's murder in 768, the throne did not pass to his infant son Alfonso, but was taken in turn by a number of other members of the ruling family. This concern, not so much with primogeniture but with preserving a dynastic succession, is in marked contrast with the practices of the preceding Visigothic period. The first of these kings was Aurelius (768–774), a cousin of his predecessor and possibly implicated in his killing. After his death power passed to Fruela's brother-in-law Silo (774–783), and then to an illegitimate son of Alfonso I called Mauregatus (783–788). Of these kings hardly anything is known, and in general this was a period in which no further territorial expansion took place, and in which relations with the Arab south were generally pacific. Under Aurelius a servile revolt occurred and was crushed—a tantalizing episode about which no further details are preserved.

It was expected that Fruela's son Alfonso would obtain his father's throne on the death of Silo, when he was chosen by the Asturian court nobility. However, Mauregatus staged a coup, probably with Galician backing. On his death his supporters ensured the succession of Vermudo I (788–791; later known as "the Monk"), a brother of Aurelius. A defeat at the hands of an Arab army in 791 destroyed this king's credibility as a war leader, and he returned to or entered monastic life, leaving the way clear at last for Alfonso II (791–842), the son of Fruela I. Unlike his two predecessors, whose power base lay in Galicia, Alfonso's support derived primarily from the Basque eastern part of the Asturian kingdom.

Alfonso's accession coincided with, and indeed was caused by, a period of renewed conflict with the Umayyad Emirate of Córdoba. Under Hishām I (788–796) annual expeditions were launched from 791 onward against the Christian territories in the north. In 794 Alfonso II achieved a victory over one of these, but the Asturian chronicles make no mention of the other raids that did penetrate the kingdom, and which are recorded in the Arabic sources. In 797, in the period of disorder in the south following the premature death of Hishām I, Alfonso sent a raiding expedition down the western side of the peninsula; it reached as far as Lisbon. Some of the loot from this was sent to the Frankish king Charlemagne, who had been in diplomatic contact with the Asturias. A planned Frankish intervention in the peninsula in that year did not occur due to fighting in Saxony, and when the Frankish armies did move in 801 and take Barcelona, no comparable Asturian expedition was launched, probably because Alfonso had been briefly overthrown in a coup.

After his restoration to power in 802 little military action is reported in the Asturian sources, though Arab raids did occur in 823 and 838. Instead the chronicles record his building projects in Oviedo, the new capital he had founded following his accession. Of the extant buildings in the city, the Church of San Julián de los Prados, with its remarkable frescoes, is normally attributed to the reign of Alfonso II. However, it is possible that this should be redated to the time of Alfonso III (866–910). Other fragments of buildings, including the Camara Sancta, a reliquary chapel attached to the first cathedral of Oviedo, may be attributable to Alfonso II. For the chroniclers, Alfonso's work in the city marked a restoration of "the Gothic order," and from his reign dates the beginning of the self-presentation of the Asturian kingdom as the successor to and heir of that of the Visigoths, with consequential claims to a peninsula-wide authority.

Alfonso II's failure to marry, which later earned him the epithet "the Chaste," led to the throne passing to a nephew, called Nepotian, upon Alfonso's death in 842. However, the new ruler was instantly challenged and overthrown in a civil war with Ramiro I (842–850), son of Vermudo I the Monk. As with his father, Ramiro's backing came from Galicia. Although Nepotian is treated as a usurper in the chronicles of the time of Ramiro's grandson, there is little doubt that he was a legitimate, if unsuccessful, king.

Under Ramiro I Arab raids against the kingdom occurred in 846 and 849 or 850, but his son Ordoño I (850–866) was able to take a more active role in events in the south, and the Asturian kingdom entered a new phase of expansion for the first time in nearly a century. Some of the former settlements on the Meseta, such as León, were repopulated, and a number of others, including Talamanca and Coria, were looted, their Muslim garrisons massacred, and their inhabitants enslaved. An expedition sent in 854 to aid rebels in Toledo against the emir Muḥammad I (852–886) proved a disaster, but Ordoño was more successful in opposing the growing power on the eastern fringes of the kingdom of the local Muwallad potentates of the Banū Qāsi. In 859 the most powerful of these, Mūsā Ibn Mūsā was defeated at Albelda.

The kingdom was subjected to large-scale raiding by Umayyad armies in 863, 865, 866, and 867. Although the new king, Alfonso III (866–910), succeeded his father in a period of military difficulty, his reign was marked by more extensive and irrevocable expansion of the kingdom southward and repopulation of settlements on the Meseta and in Castile. Castile made its first appearance as a county at this time, and its principal town of Burgos was subsequently founded in 883. Alfonso's successes were in large measure due to the growing internal difficulties of the Umayyad regime, and the decline of its central power in the 880s. In 878 Alfonso won a significant victory over an Arab raiding army at Polvoraria, which gained him a three-year truce. After renewed raiding in 882 and 883 a peace was reached that lasted for the rest of the reign.

The peace with Córdoba and the growth of repopulation and the development of towns south of the Asturian mountains led to a shift in the political balance of the kingdom. Frontier settlements in the south, such as Zamora, grew in importance, and a southward move of the capital from the distant if secure Oviedo became necessary. The Kingdom's authority over the increasingly important frontier fortresses, together with Alfonso's son's impatience with their father's longevity, led to a coup in 910 in which Alfonso was deposed. He died the same year, and claims in twelfth-century sources that he did so while returning from a final expedition against the Arabs, which his sons let him lead, should be doubted. His eldest son García (910–914) moved the capital to León, and so with Alfonso III the kingdom of the Asturias came to an end.

ROGER COLLINS

Bibliography

Barrau-Dihigo, L. *Recherches sur l'histoire politique du royaume asturien (718–910).* Paris, 1921.

Collins, R. "Doubts and Certainties on the Churches of Early Medieval Spain." In *God and Man in Medieval Spain.* Ed. D. Lomax and D. Mackenzie. Warminster, 1989. 1–18.

———. *Early Medieval Spain.* Oxford, 1995.

Cortarelo Valledar, A. *Alfonso III el Magno; último rey de Oviedo y primero de Galicia.* Madrid, 1933.

Floriano, A. C. (ed.) *Diplomatica española del período astur.* 2 vols. Oviedo, 1949–51.

Gil Fernández, J., J. L. Moralejo, and J. I. Ruiz de la Peña. (eds.) *Crónicas Asturianas.* Oviedo, 1985.

Sánchez Albornoz, C. *Orígenes de la nación española: el Reino de Asturias.* 3 vols. Oviedo, 1972–75.

ATHANAGILD, LORD OF TUDMIR

Athanagild was the son of the Visigothic noble Theodemir, lord of a region in the southeast of the Iberian Peninsula that was known to Arab authors as Tudmir. This included seven towns, most of which have been identified, including Orihuela, Lorca, and possibly Valencia. Theodemir's status and the virtual independence of this region under his control was guaranteed by the treaty of capitulation he made with the Arab governor ʿAbd al-Aziz ibn Mūsa in 713. It is probable that by about 740 Athanagild had inherited his father's political authority, and the *Chronicle of 754,* which is the only source that refers to him, describes him as "the wealthiest lord of all." He was also notably generous, and this may explain the significance of the only episode in his career that the chronicler records. Around 743/4 the governor Abū al-Kattar (743–746) obliged Athanagild to pay a fine of 27,000 gold pieces, but this was paid for him by the Syrian army, which had entered Spain with Balj ibn Bishr in 742. This may imply that elements of this body were being settled in the region at this time, despite the terms of the treaty of 713. At the instigation of the Syrians, Athanagild was reconciled with the governor and was rewarded by him. Nothing more is known of his life, but the region of Tudmir had certainly lost its independent status by the 780s.

Roger Collins

Bibliography

López Pereira, J. E. (ed.) *Crónica mozárabe de 754.* Zaragoza, 1980. sec. 87; 2, pp. 112–15.

Collins, R. *The Arab Conquest of Spain,* Oxford, 1989.

ATAPUERCA, BATTLE OF

This battle in 1054 between Fernando of León-Castile and his brother García IV of Navarre can only be viewed through a Castillian historiographical tradition. Because García was killed in the course of the battle, which in consequence turned into a significant defeat for the Navarrese, his brother Fernando was anxious to avoid any accusation of fratricide. In the *Chronicle of Nájera,* and even more so in Rodrigo Jiménez de Rada's *De Rebus Hispaniae,* responsibility for initiating the conflict is placed firmly on the Navarrese and especially on the slain monarch. The battle was fought in the vicinity of Oña in northeastern Castile and was actually prompted by Fernando's ambition to make himself master of this region. In practice the battle was a vital one for the future of the Leonese-Castilian kingdom, as it put an end to nearly a century of Navarrese domination of eastern Castile, and enabled Fernando's kingdom to establish itself as the most powerful of the Christian states of northern Spain. In that the chronicles stress the role of two of his own knights in the killing of King García who in the Castillian tradition turned against their lord for his unjust prosecution of the conflict with his brother, it is even possible to suspect that treachery was involved, and that the death of the Navarrese ruler, which was crucial to the outcome, was the product of assassination under cover of battle.

Roger Collins

Bibliography

Crónica najerense. Estudio preliminar, edición crítica e índices por Antonio Ubieto Arteta. Valencia, 1966.

Jiménez de Rada, R. *Roderici Ximenii de Rada Historia de rebus Hispanie, sive, Historia Gothica.* Ed. Juan Fernández Valverde. Turnholt, 1987.

Lacarra, J. M. *Historia política del reino de Navarra desde sus orígenes hasta su incorporación a Castilla.* 3 vols. Pamplona, 1972–73.

———. "El lento predominio de Castilla," *Revista Portuguesa de Historia* 16 (1978), 63–81.

AUGUSTINIANS *See* MONASTICISM; RELIGIOUS ORDERS

AUTO DA FE

Literally an "act of faith," an auto da fe (de fe in Spanish) was a penance demanded by the Church from a person found guilty of religious error, in faith or doctrine. The Papal Inquisition, founded in the thirteenth century, normally held ceremonies for the reconciliation of penitents in churches, but the new Spanish Inquisition, after 1478, moved such ceremonies to public streets and squares. First in Castile, and soon afterward in the Crown of Aragón, convicted "heretics," after secret trial and sentencing, were processed through the streets of their native towns, barefoot, carrying candles, and clad in mitres and robes known as *sambenitos*, which detailed graphically the offences for which they had to do penance. A large crowd, including local ecclesiastical and secular authorities, would assemble to hear a sermon against heresy, and the reading of the penitents' sentences. Relapsed heretics, primarily "Judaizing" Christians up to about 1510, were then handed over to the secular authorities for burning at a separate site. In a dramatic early case, 750 were processed in an auto da fe in Toledo on 12 February 1486, while in both 1502 and 1504 over a hundred individuals were burned after autos da fe in Córdoba. Later in the sixteenth century, many other types of people, such as former Muslims, Protestants, and even gypsies and bigamists, were processed, but in decreasing numbers. Autos da fe in Spain, while losing none of their terror for those directly involved, became popular spectacles, but increasingly damaged the country's reputation abroad.

JOHN EDWARDS

Berruguete, Pedro (1450–1504). Auto da fe. Copyright © Scala/Art Resource, NY. Museo del Prado, Madrid, Spain.

Bibliography

Edwards, J. "Trial of an Inquisitor: the Trial of Diego Rodríguez Lucero, Inquisitor of Córdoba, in 1508," *Journal of Ecclesiastical History* 37 (1986), 240–57.

Hamilton, B. *The Medieval Inquisition*. London, 1981.

Kamen, H. *Inquisition and Society in Spain in the Sixteenth and Seventeenth Centuries*. London, 1985.

AUTOBIOGRAPHY

It is unusual for autobiography to be allowed its own entry in works of reference: users of the *Dictionary of the Middle Ages*, for instance, or of *Cassell's Encyclopaedia of World Literature* will look in vain for an entry. Yet autobiography is not merely one kind of biography, for it often has as much in common with other kinds of first-person expression as it does with most third-person narratives of a life.

There are classical and medieval Latin precedents—and sometimes direct sources—for most forms of biography in medieval Spanish: Berceo's *Vida de Santo Domingo de Silos*, or Gutierre Díez de Games's *El Victorial*, or Fernán Pérez de Guzmán's volume of biographical sketches, the *Generaciones y semblanzas*. The range of precedents for autobiographical writing is much more restricted, though they include two masterpieces, St. Augustine's *Confessiones* and Peter Abelard's *Historia calamitatum*. These, however, with their strongly confessional nature, seem to have had more influence on other genres than on autobiography.

The distinction often made between real and fictional autobiographies is hard to maintain in practice. Leonor López de Córdoba's *Memorias*, guaranteed by the author to be a truthful account, can now be seen to present a reordering and reinterpretation of events. At the other end of the spectrum, the *Libro de buen amor*, though clearly dependent on Latin and vernacular precedents for every episode, gives us a strong (though perhaps misleading) impression of the personality behind the narrative, and was at one time read as genuinely autobiographical. Other fictional constructs have always been recognized as such: Juan de Flores's *Grimalte y Gradisa*—in direct line of descent from two woman's-voice autobiographical narratives, Ovid's *Heroides* and Boccaccio's *Elegia di madonna Fiammetta*—and the brief but memorable snippets of recollection by several characters in *Celestina* (though we should recall that behind one of these there probably lies a memory of Fernando de Rojas's childhood).

Third-person biographies and first-person, more or less fictional, narratives converge in several forms of autobiographical writing in late medieval Spain. Some travel books take a personal approach to their subject; this is especially noticeable in Pero Tafur's

Andanças y viajes. Teresa de Cartagena's *Arboleda de los enfermos* gives us a memorable and convincing impression of the pain of growing deafness, and of life within a convent. Autobiographical vignettes may also be found in letters. The great majority of surviving medieval letters are more or less formulaic compositions, concerned with affairs of state or of business (that is why they have been preserved in archives), and some of those that do have a personal tone are concerned with other people, rather than with the writer's own life. Others, however, do speak of the writer's life and concerns. We have nothing in medieval Spanish comparable to the fifteenth-century letters of the Paston family, and for a collection of letters that open a window onto a woman's life we have to turn to Catalan, to the letters written by Sereneta de Tous to her husband, Ramon from 1374 to 1376. There is, however, a letter in Castilian by Constanza, wife of Juan Manuel, sent in 1327 to her father, Jaime II of Aragón, begging him to send Aragónese doctors to treat her worsening illness.

Most of the letters that can be regarded as autobiographical writing are from the fifteenth century. A particularly interesting collection preserves letters written between 1420 and 1431 by Fernando Díaz de Toledo, the converso archdeacon of Niebla, to the prior and other members of the monastery of Santa María de Guadalupe. These letters give a rounded picture of a life. They do deal with spiritual matters, but they are concerned more insistently with the archdeacon's worries about his health, his financial affairs, and such matters as a sheepskin coat that he had been promised.

When we turn from autobiographical letters to formally structured autobiography, two texts claim our attention. Both belong to an autobiographical subgenre, the memoir: Part 3 of Juan Manuel's *Libro de las tres razones* (ca. 1337–1342) and the *Memorias* of Leonor López de Córdoba (ca. 1400). The *Libro de las tres razones* is a blend of family history, personal memoir, and political advocacy. Juan Manuel, son of Prince Manuel and grandson of Fernando III, was obsessed by the belief that his father and he himself had been unjustly deprived of the right to rule, since Manuel had had the blessing of his parents, while Alfonso X was cursed by them. Part 3 of the *Libro* gives a vivid picture of Sancho IV's deathbed, when the tubercular king can only just find the strength to admit to the twelve-year-old Juan Manuel that he belongs to the blessed line, unlike the accursed line that holds the throne. The picture is compelling and moving, but what relation does it bear to reality? Is this a memoir or a well-crafted fiction?

The same question may to some extent be asked about Leonor López de Córdoba's *Memorias* (written a generation before what has been described as the first English autobiography, *The Book of Margery Kempe*). The narrative core is a broadly accurate account of the misfortunes of the author and of her family, though some of the incidents and a good deal of the interpretation have been viewed with skepticism. The family were on the losing side in the civil war that ravaged Castile in the 1360s and 1370s, and after their capture in 1371, Leonor's father was executed. She and the rest of the family were imprisoned for years, some dying from the plague. When she was released, she and her husband were penniless, so she was dependent on an aunt who had been on the winning side. Much of the book is taken up with the power struggles within the aunt's household—Leonor López against her cousins and the aunt's servants—and and eventually Leonor loses, being banished from the household, and the *Memorias* ends. From the moment she leaves prison, she lives in a gynocracy, a female microsociety that mirrors the patriarchal macrosociety of Castile. She tells us about herself without any barriers of artifice. We see her life as she sees it, and some of the scenes stay in our memory as they stayed in hers: her father being taken to execution, her young brother dying of the plague, her fury when the aunt's servants thwart her plans.

The harvest of autobiography in medieval Spanish is small, but the quality is exceptionally high. Part 3 of the *Libro de las tres razones* has long been acclaimed as a masterpiece of first-person narrative; Leonor López de Córdoba's memoir has, in the last thirty years, been recognized as a key text with an authentic personal voice, and similar recognition for the archdeacon of Niebla's letters will not be long delayed.

ALAN DEYERMOND

Bibliography

Ayerbe-Chaux, R. (ed.) "Las *Memorias* de doña Leonor López de Córdoba," *Journal of Hispanic Philology* 2 (1977–78), 11–33.

Connolly, J. E. *The Reception of Leonor López de Córdoba and of her Memorias. Papers of the Medieval Hispanic Research Seminar.* London, 2003.

Deyermond, A. "Spain's First Women Writers." In *Women in Hispanic Literature: Icons and Fallen Idols*. Ed. B. Miller. Berkeley, Calif., 1983. 27–52.

———. "The *Libro de las tres razones* Reconsidered." In *"Never-Ending Adventure": Studies in Medieval and Early Modern Spanish Literature in Honor of Peter N. Dunn*. Eds. E. H. Friedman and H. Sturm. Newark, Del., 2002. 86–113.

Mendia, L. (ed. and trans.) *Leonor López de Córdoba, Memorie*. Parma, 1992. 20.

AVERROËS, ABU 'L-WALĪD MUHAMMAD B. AHMAD B. RUSHD

Commentator on Aristotle, philosopher, physician and jurist; the greatest intellectual figure of Islamic Iberia. Averroës (the name is a corrupt Judaeo-Latin transcription of the Arabic name Ibn Rushd) was born in Córdoba in 1126, into a family of eminent judges. Little is known for certain about his early career, but he undoubtedly received the traditional Islamic education in Arabic literature and linguistics, jurisprudence and theology, together with instruction in medicine and philosophy. Of the great Muslim sages of medieval Iberia, Ibn Rushd can personally only have known Ibn Tufayl, who became his mentor at the court of the Almohad caliph Abū Ya'qūb Yūsuf. In an incident that Gauthier has described as being "of capital importance not only in the biography of Averroës, but in the development of European philosophy" Ibn Tufayl introduced Averroës to the learned sovereign, who was deeply impressed by his subject's thorough knowledge of the opinions of the "philosophers" (that is to say, the Arabic *falasifa* working in the tradition of Aristotle and the Neoplatonists). Abū Ya'qūb subsequently called upon Averroës to make Aristotle's hitherto all-too-obscure writings more perspicuous by means of commentaries. As a result of the caliph's favors, he was appointed cadi of Seville in 1169, chief qāḍī of Córdoba in 1171, and physician to the court of Marrakesh in 1182. The accession to the caliphate, in 1184, of Abū Yaq'ūb's son, Al-Manṣūr, did not at first change Ibn Rushd's fortunes. However, around 1194/5, al-Manṣūr found himself obliged to dissociate himself from him, yielding to the growing pressures of popular fundamentalism; Averroës's philosophical writings were burned, and the philosopher himself exiled to Lucena, southeast of Córdoba. This sentence, so obviously out of tune with the caliph's own intellectual leanings, was soon revoked, however and Averroës was allowed to return to Marrakesh, where he died on 10 December 1198. Averroës's cardinal legacy are his commentaries on Aristotle; they earned him the antonomastic title "the Commentator" among the Latin schoolmen, who kept relying on his translated commentaries after St. Thomas Aquinas had tried to supplant them with his own work and even after the great Averroistic crisis of the 1270s. Significantly, Aristotle's works continued to be accompanied by the elucidations of his commentator in the printed editions of the fifteenth and sixteenth centuries. Averroës composed two kinds of commentaries, "short" and "middle," on most of the writings of the Aristotelian corpus accessible to him; in addition, we have "long" commentaries" on the *Posterior Analytics*, *Physics*, *De Caelo*, *De Anima* and *Metaphysics*. The short commentaries or *epitomai* (in Arabic *jawāmi*) are manuals of Aristotelian philosophy, paraphrases written early in Averroës's career, and show the commentator under the influence of the Neoplatonizing Aristotelianism of his predecessors Al-Fārābī and Ibn Sīnā (Avicenna). In the later middle commentaries (Arabic, *talkhīs*), more detailed expositions of the philosopher's thought, we already witness a gradual emancipation from this older tradition of interpretation and see Averroës working toward an ideal of recovering Aristotle's thought in its original purity. Ibn Rushd's exegetical endeavors culminated in the long commentaries (Arabic *tafsīr*), scrupulous word-for-word commentaries of a rigorous literary form resembling that used in traditional Qur'ānic exegesis: and appropriately so, for the words of Aristotle had by that time gained almost divine authority for Averroës.

The long commentary on *De Anima*, fruit of a lifelong exploration of Aristotelian psychology, contains Averroës's final and most mature solution to the problems posed by Aristotle's notoriously difficult remarks on the nature of the "agent intellect." According to Aristotle, there is an active and a passive aspect to the human mind: the intellect, which is passive insofar as it receives the immaterial forms of sense percepts, is seen as active inasmuch as it must, prior to their reception, abstract these forms from the material conditions of sense perception. Averroës believed that both the active (or "agent") and the passive ("material," "possible") powers of the intellect were one for all human beings. The possible intellect, being the receptacle for the forms of material things, could not itself possess such a form; otherwise it would interfere with and distort the forms it received. But if it was immaterial, it had to be unique, for it is matter that causes plurality. The unicity of the agent intellect, on the other hand, safeguards the universal validity of human cognition in that the individuals' data of sense perception are abstracted and universalized by one faculty common to all. The activity of thought can on this interpretation only be ascribed to the individual inasmuch as his or her material organs of sense are necessary to furnish the transpersonal intellect with data to abstract. The thoughts themselves are no single person's possession; rather, the intellect is envisaged as a common pool of knowledge participated in by the individual according to each person's abilities. Full "conjunction" with the transcendent intellect, the possession of all possible knowledge, is the end and rare fulfillment of intellectual activity. Despite the denial of personal immortality that it implies, this theory of "monopsychism" exercised a deep and lasting influence on the development of philosophy in the Latin west. Its adoption by some Parisian masters in the latter half of the thirteenth century provoked the most profound intellectual crisis in the as yet young history of medieval Aristotelianism, but even the condemnations of 1270 and 1277 could not, in the long run, thwart its attraction. As Philip Merlan has brilliantly argued, the structures of Averroean psychology continue to be discernible in contemporary philosophy, especially in the Kantian tradition (compare with Kant's transcendental unity of apperception/*Bewußtsein überhaupt*).

Averroës never held the theory of "double truth" often falsely attributed to him: in his view, the truths of philosophy and religion were in perfect agreement. As he wrote in chapter 2 of the *Faṣl al-maqāl*, "truth does not oppose truth but accords with it and bears witness to it." Hence, contradictions between religious and demonstrative truth can only be apparent, caused by the fact that the Qur'an frequently uses symbols and rhetorical or dialectical arguments in order to reach the majority of the people. The superficial oppositions thus arising must be resolved by an allegorical interpretation (*tawīl*) of Scripture that penetrates from the level of its apparent (*zahir*) to that of its hidden (*batin*) meanings. But tawīl is only for the philosophers and should be taught esoterically, as it would endanger the faith of those untrained in demonstrative reasoning. With philosophy thus becoming the ultimate judge of the meaning of revealed truth, Averroës takes a rationalist stance toward religion: it has nothing to offer that reason cannot reach autonomously and without the veil of symbols. This attitude, while replacing faith with intellectual conviction, does not overtly challenge the truth of Islam (which does not contain any supernatural mystery in the Christan sense); however, it relegates it to the pragmatic role of teaching the "simple people" through symbols what the philosophers know with the clarity of reason.

As in the speculative branches of philosophy, Averroës also championed a resolute return to the principles of pure Aristotelianism in the natural sciences. In what has called the Andalusian revolt against Ptolemaic astronomy, Averroës and his contemporary Al-Bitrujī (Alpetragius) censured Ptolemy for departing from Aristotelian physics by postulating epicycles and eccentrics; but unlike Al-Bitrujī, Averroës's grasp of the Aristotelian alternative to epicycles and eccentrics remain unsatisfactory and vague. Averroës was not prepared to meet Ptolemy on the level of empirical observation; indeed he dismissed his computational evidence as "arrived at by the use of instruments" and "based on the senses," opposed to the empirical method "the true theories based on rational precepts" (especially on the *Metaphysics*). According to Averroës, Ptolemaic astronomy was in outright contradiction to these rational principles, mainly because it assumed circular movement not around the center of the universe and two contrary motions for one planet (nature would not employ two movements for what it could possibly achieve with one, Averroës claimed, for "nature does nothing in vain"). He hoped to account for the movement of the planets by positing, in Aristotelian fashion, simple homocentric spiral motions in one direction—without, however, checking the empirical viability of this proposition. It is interesting that Averroës's criticisms of Ptolemy, although almost exclusively negative in their failure to provide an alternative theory, later influenced Copernicus by convincing him of the shortcomings of traditional astronomy.

Similarly, the *Kullīyat fī-l-ṭibb* (*Generalities in Medicine in Seven Books*), or *Colliget*, imparted impulses toward a reform of medical science to Renaissance physicians, who appreciated Averroës's detached and apparently disinterested attitude vis-à-vis Galen without seeing the rather reactionary Aristotelianism underlying it. In a detailed analysis of the *Colliget* chapter on respiration, Bürgel has discovered general tendencies comparable to those also present in Averroës's astronomy: a preponderantly (albeit not exclusively) speculative approach rooted in Aristotelian natural philosophy, a preparedness to sacrifice scientific progress to defend the teachings of the master, and, to a lesser extent than in astronomy, resignation in the face of technical difficulties. In the *Colliget*, health is defined in the traditional manner as an equilibrium of the four humors; accordingly, the task of the physician consists in preserving this harmony or in restoring it when it has become disturbed through illness. The physician fights the cause of an illness with its opposite: an excess of moisture with dryness, a superabundance of heat with cold, amd so forth. In spite of interesting medical details, the *Colliget* is intended as a compilation of received medical wisdom rather than as an original work; but it has certainly not yet received the scholarly attention that it deserves.

The same could be said a fortiori of Averroës's handbook of Islamic law, the *Bidayat al-mujtahid wa-nihayat al-muqtasid* (*Beginning for Him Who Works Toward an Independent Judgment and End for Him who Contents Himself with Received Opinion*), a book that became a standard work of reference in the Islamic world (unlike Averroës's philosophical writings, which remained virtually unread by his fellow Muslims). The *Bidaya* aims at furnishing the reader with an exposition of the differences of opinion between the various juridicoreligious schools concerning the main points of the law. The objective is to enable the user of the *Bidaya* to come to an *ijtihād*, an independent legal judgment based on free choice among the orthodox traditions. The opinions taken into consideration are almost exclusively Sunnite, Averroës's acquaintance with the Malikite tradition (in which he was brought up) being most profound, but he is careful to be scrupulously objective and impartial in his presentation. Brunschvig has described the *Bidaya* as the "most accomplished example of the methodical application of the principles of Islamic law to the entirety of Sunnite jurisprudence." Together with Averroës's other writings, it testifies to the versatility and greatness of an encyclopedic mind.

PHILIPP W. ROSEMANN

Bibliography

Aristotelis Opera cum Averrois Commentariis. 9 vols. and 3 suppl. Venice, 1562; reprt, Frankfurt am Main, 1962.

Brunschvig, R. "Averroès juriste." In *Études d'Islamologie*. Vol. 2. Paris, 1976. 167–200.

Bürgel, J. C. "Averroes 'contra Galenum': Das Kapitel von der Atmung im Colliget des Averroes (. . .) eingeleitet, arabisch herausgegeben und übersetzt," *Nachrichten der Akademie der Wissenschaften in Göttingen* (1967). Philologisch-historische Klasse no. 9, 263–340.

Corpus Commentariorum Averrois in Aristotelem (in progress). Series Arabica: 9 vols.; Series Hebraica: 3 vols.; Series Latina: 3 vols.; Series Anglica: 3 vols. Published since 1949, variously in Cairo, Madrid, and Cambridge, Mass. More recently, several important editions have appeared in other series.

Gauthier, L. *Ibn Rochd (Averroès)*. Paris, 1948.

Rosemann, P. W. "Averroes: A Catalogue of Editions and Scholarly Writings from 1821 Onwards," *Bulletin de Philosophie Médiévale* 30 (1988), 153–221.

Urvoy, D. *Ibn Rushd (Averroes)*. Trans. O. Stewart. London, 1991.

AVIS, HOUSE OF

Founded by Dom João, Master of the order of Avis in Alentejo, Portugal. He was the illegitimate son of Pedro I and a Galician woman, Teresa Lourenço. Born probably in Lisbon (14 August 1357) he died in the same city (14 August 1433). He acceded to the throne via the revolution of 1383–1385. On 2 February 1387 he married in Oporto Philippa of Lancaster (1359–1415), sister of the future king of England, Henry IV. Philippa was the daughter of John Gaunt and his first wife, Blanche. By Philippa João I had eight children: Duarte (1391–1438), who succeeded João I; Pedro (1392–1449), Duke of Coimbra; Henrique (1394–1460); João (1400–1442), Fernando (1402–1403), who died in prison in Fez, following the disaster of Tangier (1437); and Isabel (1397–1471). The first two died at a very early age. In 1430 Isabel married Philip the Good, Duke of Burgundy. João married his niece, Isabel (1404–1465), daughter of the first duke of Bragança and his first wife, Beatriz. Before his marriage to Philippa of Lancaster, João I had two children by Inés Pires: Afonso, the first duke of Bragança, and Beatriz (1382–1439). She married Thomas Fitzalan, the Seventh Earl of Arundel, and moved to England. Duarte I married Leonor of Aragón in 1428. The firstborn, Afonso V (1432–1481), married Isabel, daughter of Pedro, Duke of Coimbra, and Isabel of Aragón. Afonso's sister, Joana, married (1455) Enrique IV of Castile. By Isabel, Afonso V had his successor João II (1455–95). João II married Leonor, daughter of Fernando, son of King Duarte, and Isabel, daughter of Afonso, Duke of Braganza. The accidental death of his legitimate son and heir to the throne, led Joâo II to pass the succession to Manuel, the queen's brother.

LUIS REBELO

Bibliography

Caetano de Sousa, A. *História Genealógica da Casa Real Portuguesa* 2d ed., vol. 2. Coimbra, 1946. Martins Zuquete, E. A. (ed.) *Nobreza de Portugal*. Lisbon, 1960.

AZARQUIEL

Abū Isḥāq Ibrāhīm ibn Yaḥyā al-Naqqāsh (d. 1100), known as Ibn al-Zarqālluh or Ibn al-Zarqiyāl, was the most important astronomer of the Middle Ages in the Iberian Peninsula. He worked in Toledo under King Al-Ma'mūn (1037–1074) and later in Córdoba, which then belonged to the ʿAbbādī kingdom of Seville. According to the *Yesod ʿOlam* of Isaac Israeli (fourteenth century), he started his career as an instrument maker who worked for the Toledan team of astronomers led by *qāḍī* Sā ʿid al-Andalusī (1029–1070). His interest in designing new astronomical instruments appears very early. In 1048–1049 he dedicated a treatise on the *azafea* (*al-ṣafīḥa*) to the ʿAbbādī prince of Seville, al-Mu'ayyad bi-Naṣr Allāh, who was then only eight or nine years old and later became king Al-Muʿtamid (1069–1091). The azafea, like the astrolabe, is an analogue computer used to solve graphically problems of spherical astronomy and astrology, but while the astrolable needs a specific plate for each latitude, the azafea is a universal instrument that can be used for any latitude. His description on the construction and use of the instrument is extant both in Arabic and in the Spanish Alfonsine translation (*Libro de la Açafeha*). At a later date, he seems to have dedicated a simplified version of the same instrument to the same Al-Muʿtamid. This variant became very popular in medieval Europe through Latin and Hebrew translations of the treatise on its use. He also dedicated to Al-Muʿtamid a treatise on the use of the *equatorium* (extant in Arabic), another analogue computer, the purpose of which is to calculate planetary longitudes. His descriptions of the construction of such an instrument (ca. 1080–1081) and of an armillary sphere are known to us only through Alfonsine translations (*Libros de las laminas de los siete planetas*, *Libro de las Armellas*).

Ibn al-Zarqālluh's collaboration with qāḍī Sāʿid and his team must have awakened his interest in observations astronomical tables, and astronomical theory. He made solar observations for twenty-five years, both in Toledo and in Seville, and he observed the moon for thirty-seven years, introducing a modification in Ptolemy's lunar model. His solar observations were incorporated to the solar mean motion tables extant in the *Toledan Tables* as well as to the solar tables of his perpetual *Almanac*. The former also include a set of "trepidation tables" (used to calculate the value of the precession of the equinoxes—then considered to be variable—for a given date), apparently related to the work of Ibn al-Zarqālluh, for he wrote, circa 1085, an important *Treatise on the Motion of the Fixed Stars* (extant in a Hebrew translation) in which he designed three different geometrical trepidation models. With them he tried to obtain results that would fit the observations made by Hipparchus (147 B.C.) and Ptolemy (139 A.D.), as well as those used by Thābit ibn Qūrra (831 A.D.) and, finally, Al-Battānī (883 A.D.) and Ibn al-Zarqālluh's own observations (ca. 1075). The same kind of historical preoccupations appears in his book on the Sun, written between 1075 and 1080 and known only through indirect sources. Its title was either *On the Solar Year* (*Fī sanat al-shams*) or *A Comprehensive Epistle on the Sun* (*al-Risāla al-jāmiʿa fī-l-shams*). In it Ibn al-Zarqālluh improved enormously on the corrections made, cira 830, by the astronomers of the ʿAbbāsid Caliph al-Ma'mūn, in Baghdad and Damascus, on Ptolemy's solar model, and established, very accurately, that the solar apogee has a characteristic motion of 1 degree in every 279 solar years. Furthermore, a study of the different values of the solar eccentricity established by the aforementioned Hipparchus, Thābit, al-Battānī, and himself led him to design a solar model with variable eccentricity that became extremely influential in later Andalusian and Maghribī astronomy and reached Europe, where it was mentioned by Copernicus.

JULIO SAMSÓ

Bibliography

Comes, M. *Los ecuatorios andalusíes*. Barcelona, 1991.

Millás-Vallicrosa, J. M. *Estudios sobre Azarquiel*. Madrid and Granada, 1943–50.

Pedersen, F. S. *Canones Azarchelis: Some Versions and a Text. Cahiers de l'Institut du Moyen Age Grec et Latin* 54 (1987), 129–218.

Puig, R. *Al-Šakkāziyya, Ibn al-Naqqāš al-Zarqālluh. Edición, traducción estudio*. Barcelona, 1986.

———. *Los tratados de construcción y uso de la azafea de Azarquiel*. Madrid, 1987.

Samsó, J. *Las Ciencias de los Antiguos en al-Andalus*. Madrid, 1992. 147–52, 166–240.

Toomer, G. J. "The Solar History of al-Zarqāl: A History of Errors," *Centaurus* 14 (1969), 306–36.

——— "A Survey of the Toledan Tables," *Osiris* 15 (1968), 5–174.

Vernet, J., and J. Samsó. (eds.) *El legado científico andalusí*. Madrid, 1992.

AZORES, THE

The Azores were likely the only great Atlantic archipelago adjacent to the Old World that was wholly unknown either to the ancients or to the medievals. The first of the group was found by the Portuguese around 1427, and the last in 1452. Their discovery, together with the (re-)discovery of the Madeiras a few years earlier, provides sure indication that by the first quarter of the fifteenth century, Portuguese navigators were able to operate hundreds of miles beyond sight of land; sailing thus was necessitated by return journeys from Africa, since the prevailing bands of northerly winds blowing down the African coast from Europe obliged navigators to turn far westward to sea in order to find southerly winds to carry them home.

The Azores were uninhabited when discovered, and the nearest, Santa Maria and São Miguel, are over seven hundred miles from the Portuguese coast. From these islands, prevailing winds blow toward the European continent; it is difficult to sail directly from Portugal toward them, as only an occasional wind blows from east to west. Hence, it is logical that their discovery should belong more to the activities involving African coastal exploration than to commerce with the northern countries of Europe itself.

The Valsequa map of 1439 is the first to show the archipelago (minus Flores and Corvo, not yet discovered) in its correct number and alignment from northeast to southwest. It bears the legend (though some maintain it was inserted later): "These islands were found by Diego de Silves, pilot of the king of Portugal, anno MCCCCXXVII." A different date is supplied by the German cartographer Martin Behaim, married to the daughter of the Captain-donatary of Fayal and Pico, in his globe of 1492: 1431. The problem is not solved by a donation of 1433 from King Duarte to his brother, the Infante Henrique, for it fails to mention the islands at all; rather, it is not until 1439 that they were included in a donation to Henrique from the regents of the young Afonso V.

This document provides the first indication of an attempt to colonize the group, for in it is stated that Henrique had already given orders to plant sheep on the seven islands then known, as a provision for eventual settlers. The first of these were next brought out to Santa Maria and São Miguel from the rural districts of central and southern Portugal by the man thought to have been the first Captain-donatary, Gonçalo Velho Cabral. In 1450, the peopling of Terceira began when the Flemish, Jacomé de Bruges brought families with him from Portugal. It is also interesting that after 1474, a number of Madeiran families emigrated to these islands. Meanwhile, around 1466, another Fleming, Jos de Utra (alias Jobst Hurter), future father-in-law of Behaim, was awarded the captaincy of the islands Pico and Fayal, and it is known that he enticed many of his countrymen to settle there. One of these, Guilherme de Silveira (alias Willem van der Haaghen), quarreled with him, and then endeavored to settle two of the remaining three islands of the group, São Jorge, and the outermost Flores. Graciosa was not settled until around 1510, through the offices of Pedro Correia and Vasco Gil Sodre. Little Corvo's settlement is not dated exactly, but seems to have occurred as a spillover from Flores. In addition to Flemish immigrants, it is also known that Spaniards, Italians, French, and even Englishmen settled the islands in smaller numbers, but all were later absorbed into the local Portuguese culture.

The islands were densely wooded when discovered, and naturally, their main industry was to provide timber for continental Portugal, and for naval construction along its littoral. But soon land began to be burned off and cleared for cereal production, the islands' first large-scale industry, which then began exporting large amounts to Portugal and to Africa. Wheat continued as the islands' main export commodity throughout the fifteenth and into the sixteenth centuries—unlike Madeira, which had already switched almost wholly to sugar by the third quarter of the fifteenth century. Sugar, incidentally, was also tried in the Azores, where the climate proved less than ideal, though there are no indications as to the quantity exported. In addition, the islands grew yams and sweet potatoes, fruits of all sorts, and even pine nuts. In the sixteenth century, dyestuffs were produced, and still later, citrus products and linen.

Throughout the fifteenth and sixteenth centuries, the Azores served as the jumping-off places and havens of returning exploration; Columbus stopped at Santa Maria, while the Corte Real brothers and João Fagundes Laborador all set sail for destinations in the New World from the islands, even ships returning from Brazil and India frequently called there.

George D. Winius

Bibliography

Cordeiro, P. A. *História Insulana.* Lisbon, 1717; reprt., 1981.

Martins da Silva Marques, J. *Descobrimentos Portugueses.* 5 vols. Lisbon, 1944–1971. Esp. 1 (1944) and its supplement.

Magalhâes Godinho, V. *A economia dos descobrimentos henriquinos.* Lisbon, 1962.

AZURARA, GOMES EANNES DE

Portuguese chronicler (ca. 1410–1473/4), the son of a cleric, Joan Eannes de Zurara, who succeeded Fernão Lopes (1380/90–ca. 1460), and had a long and distinguished career as the first official chronicler. King Duarte had created the post of *cronista-mor do reino* (chief chronicler of the kingdom) in 1434 and appointed Lopes, who had already been the keeper of the royal archives since 1418 or 1419. The decision of Duarte was motivated by his wish to have a record of the deeds of the Portuguese kings, continuing a literary tradition that dated from the fourteenth century. Fernão Lopes had worked for thirty years and was old and tired; by a decree of 6 June 1454, Afonso V appointed Azurara the keeper of the royal archives. But before the date of this appointment, probably in 1452, Lopes had already passed on to his successor the task of continuing the chronicles. Lopes seems to have rewritten a general chronicle of Portugal, beginning with the founder of the monarchy, before he produced the chronicles of Pedro I, João I, and Fernando, respectively the grandfather, father, and uncle of King Duarte. He had covered a large period of history that extended from 1357, when Pedro ascended the throne, to 1411, when João was still ruling, and had described the problems of the emergence of a national state in the throes of a conflict with Spain. Azurara was the chronicler of the Moroccan wars and of Portuguese maritime expansion. Yet whereas Lopes, writing about the past, could detach himself to a certain extent from the political questions of the day, Azurara had difficulty in avoiding his involvement in the contemporary events he was reporting.

Azurara's first work, the *Crónica da Tomada da Cidade de Ceuta* (1450), dealt with the conquest of the Moroccan city of Ceuta in 1415. It describes in detail how the idea of the Conquest was born in the courtly circle of João I. Initially the king wanted his sons to be knighted in a tournament in Portugal, but they objected to the idea and showed their interest in seeing real action in the service of God and in defense of the Christian faith, this, however, was not the only reason for his attack on the city. Azurara shows how commercial and strategic advantages were to be gained from the expedition given the wealth and the position of the city, and ascribes to João Afonso, royal treasurer, an important role in this project; it is the latter who convinced the princes to embrace the idea when their father seemed reluctant to accept it.

The secrecy of the military preparations, which raised fears in many European cities, and the clash of opinions that divided the royal council, are described by Azurara in great detail and in such an accomplished style that it is believed that a large part of this chronicle had already been written by Lopes, or that Azurara inherited the manuscript from him and later it shaped it in his own way. Committed as he was to the values of chivalry, Azurara was able nonetheless to paint a broad picture of the different motivations that led João I to attack Ceuta, going even so far as to express veiled criticism about the violence of the assault.

In the chronicles of *Conde Dom Pedro de Meneses* (1463) and *Conde Dom Duarte de Meneses* (1468), Azurara tells the history of the Portuguese in North Africa from 1415 to 1464. João Pedro de Meneses, Count of Viana, was the first governor of Ceuta (1415–1437) and Dom Duarte (1414–1464), his illegitimate son, ruled the city in his absence (1431–1437), becoming the governor of El-Qsar es-Seghir, or Alcácer-Seguer, in the autumn of 1458. Both were loyal subjects of Afonso V. Duarte lost his life to cover the retreat of the king in one of his expeditions into Muslim territory. Azurara reports meticulously in the Meneses chronicles, in a brilliant rhetorical style, successive military operations that are extolled as feats of chivalry, relying heavily on the oral testimony of the noblemen who participated in these actions. But for the chronicle of Duarte—Azurara's most accomplished piece of work—he went to North Africa to gather wider information, staying there from August 1467 to the summer of 1468.

With the capture of Ceuta, Muslim trade moved to other cities and the Portuguese adopted a dual policy: advance along the Moroccan seaboard and explore Africa's Atlantic coast. In his *Crónica dos Feitos da Guiné* (1453), based on the lost chronicle of Afonso de Cerveira, Azurara describes voyages along that coast and praises Prince Henrique for promoting them. He portrays also the arrival in Portugal in 1441 of the first African slaves, showing sympathy for their plight.

LUIS REBELO

Bibliography

Azurara, G. E. de. *Crónica do Conde D. Duarte de Meneses*. Lisbon, 1978.

———. *Crónica da Tomada da Cidade de Ceuta*. Coimbra, 1915.

———. *Crónica do Conde D. Pedro de Meneses*. In *Colecção de Livros Inéditos de História Portuguesa*. Vol. 2. Lisbon, 1972.

———. *Crónica do Descobrimento e Conquista da Guiné*. Porto, 1973.

Barradas de Carvalho, M. "L'idéologie religieuse dans la 'Crónica dos feitos de Guiné' de Gomes Eanes de Zurara," *Bulletin des Etudes Portugaises* 29 (1956), 5–34.

Costa Pimpão, A. J. da. *A "Crónica dos Feitos de Guiné" de Gomes Eanes de Zurara e o manuscrito Cortez-d'Estrées, Tentativa de revisão crítica*. Lisbon, 1939.

Saraiva, A. J. *O Crepusculo da Idade Média em Portugal*. Lisbon, 1988.

B

BADAJOZ, TĀʾIFA KINGDOM OF *See* TĀʾIFA KINGDOMS

BAENA, JUAN ALFONSO DE

Juan Alfonso de Baena was a Castilian poet active during the majority of Juan II (1406–1454). He describes himself as *escribano del rey* (in effect, "royal bureaucrat"); this office in turn suggests that Baena was from a family of burghers. A snide allusion to his baptism in the verses of one of his contemporaries hints strongly that he was originally a Jew. In a long poem full of references to his literary culture he declares that he has read "*le mosines*" and in fact, his poetic practice places him in the group of Castilian versifiers in the 1410s and 1420s who are most under the influence of the Consistory of the Gay Science of Toulouse and its peninsular imitators in Barcelona and Valencia. His fame nowadays rests less on his elegant writing than on the splendid collection that bears his name, a bulky anthology of more than five hundred pieces by poets active from the 1360s to perhaps as late as the 1440s. It is hardly a systematic collection, it is simply a broad selection of verse by Castilians from this period, but certain tendencies are visible nevertheless.

The *Cancicionero de Beana* contains a fair body of *cantigas de amor*, love songs in Galician, broadly on the model of the Provençal *canso*. These date from the last third of the fourteenth century, and are the work of poets such as the Archdeacon of Toro; Macías; and, eminently, the youthful Villasandino. The poetry written under the impact of Toulouse, Barcelona, and Valencia represents a very different strain of Provençal influence. Galician gives way to Castilian, and the relatively simple and uniform *cantiga de amor* gives way to a variety of verse forms and genres. Within this school, if we can call it that, there are several currents. One such is a bent toward technical virtuosity. Complicated verse and stanza patterns, difficult rhyme schemes and witty figures of speech mark this mode. Also, Provençal-Castilian, so to speak, are the poetic debates, the sets of and dialogues between two or more poets in which the respondent must follow the meters and rhymes of the initial poem. Some of these sequences are frivolous, some not. One group are of the virtuosic sort, in which the two poets put each other to the test, each obliging the other to repeat intricate stanza patterns and to find more and more obscure rhymes. The decorative tendency, within the debate poems and without, is represented by the later Villasandino, Baena himself, and to a certain extent, by Fernán Manuel de Lando. Debate may also take a serious turn and deal with subjects like predestination, or the influence of the stars, or even the very truth of Christianity: certain topics of Jewish anti-Christian polemic surface in some of these pieces. The contenders themselves are a striking lot. Some are learned friars, like Fray Diego de Valencia, who spar with lay poets like Lando, who claim the right to air their own views on grave subjects, scant theology notwithstanding. A third strain in Baena's collection is the moralizing text, full of reflections on mortality, fortune, and the fall of the great, and the vanity of human life apart from God. Fernán Sánchez Talavera represents this tendency in the days of Enrique III, and the brilliant and vehement Gonzalo Martinez de Medina in those of Juan II. Finally, there is the unique figure of Francisco Imperial—Genoese, but eloquent in Castilian—the most ambitious poet of the times, who combines solemn personification allegory with echoes of Dante, and who introduces elements of *dolce stil nuovo* into Castilian poetry. One may observe finally that Baena's epigraphs—analogous to Provençal *vidas* and *razos*—often head single poems and groups of them. These provide solid information about some of his contemporaries, blatant fiction about some others (notoriously, in the case of Macías), and sometimes odd critical remarks; of a very bad poet in the collection he says, kindly, "fizo esso que sopo" ("he did as best he could").

CHARLES FRAKER

Bibliography

Baena, J. A. de. *Cancionero de Juan Alfonso de Baena.* 3 vols. Ed. J. M. Azáceta. Madrid, 1966.

Piccus, J. "El dezir que fizo Juan Alfonso de Baena," *Nueva Revista de Filología Española* 12 (1958), 335–56.

BALEARIC ISLANDS *See* MALLORCA, KINGDOM OF

BALLADS

The chronological origins of the Hispanic *romance* roughly coincide with those of traditional ballad poetry elsewhere in Europe. The first extant ballad text dates from 1421, but historical evidence points to the composition of romances as early as the first third of the fourteenth century.

The typical meter of Hispanic ballads involves a sixteen-syllable verse divided into two eight-syllable hemistichs, with assonant rhyme in the second hemistich, though some narrative poems in other metrical schemes (parallel assonant octosyllabic couplets; six-syllable *romancillos*) are also admitted to the *romancero* (the Hispanic ballad corpus). The typical ballad verse is based on the anisosyllabic meter (usually six to nine syllables) of medieval Spanish epic poetry, a number of whose narratives are still fragmentarily represented in handwritten and printed ballad texts from the fifteenth and sixteenth centuries and, in some cases, continue to be known in the modern oral tradition. The first ballads undoubtedly started as fragments of medieval epic poems; non-epic historical events soon came to be narrated in the same verse as the newly independent epic fragments; early on, numerous ballad narratives from continental Europe, especially France, were retold in *romance* meter; the early Hispanic lyric also played an important role in the formation of the *romancero*. The genre's beginnings and later development are marked by its notable capacity to absorb and adapt narrative and poetic materials of the most diverse origins.

Typically, Hispanic ballads are relatively short, usually involving some twenty to one hundred verses, except certain early minstrel ballads (*romances juglarescos*), which may have as many as one thousand verses. The narrative is usually compact, well-structured (sometimes embodying ring composition), and frequently involves a dramatic confrontation between protagonist and antagonist. Sometimes, as a reflection of its origins as a fragment of an earlier epic, a ballad may be fragmentistic in character, beginning ex nihilo and ending before the action is resolved. Ballad style is allusive, rather than descriptive, calling upon our intuition to participate in the poetic process and supply details only hinted at by the ballad's minimalist approach. The oral tradition—of whatever epoch—involves a dynamic, creative process in which ballad texts are, over time, incessantly remodeled by their singers in accord with the developing value systems of a changing society.

The romance originated in Castile—also the homeland of the epic—but by the 1400s had already spread to the farthest reaches of the Iberian Peninsula, being sung in Galicia and in Catalonia. Ballads were first printed in broadsides (*pliegos sueltos*) in the early 1500s and by midcentury were being abundantly anthologized in *cancioneros* (song books) and *romanceros* (ballad collections). From the late 1400s on, ballad meter came to be used by learned as well as oral poets. Before 1580, the printed corpus is dominated by medieval narratives drawn from oral tradition (*romances viejos*); after that date, erudite compositions attest to the popularity of new ballads (*romances nuevos*) composed by learned authors. In the seventeenth century, the romances viejos, once known and sung at all levels of society, fell out of favor, were gradually relegated to peasant villages and mountain hamlets, and ultimately came to be unknown in learned circles. Only with the advent of Romanticism, with its interest in popular traditions and the distinctive character of national cultures, did the Hispanic traditional ballad come to emerge from its latent condition (*estado latente*) and be recognized as the heir to an oral tradition going back to medieval times.

Thanks to the initiatives of the great Spanish scholar Ramón Menéndez Pidal and his followers, Hispanic ballads have now been collected from essentially all areas where Spanish, Portuguese, Catalan, and Judeo-Spanish are spoken today, including some of the most isolated and "exotic" areas of the Hispanic world. This Pan-Hispanic character of the romancero is one of its essential features. It also leads to the inescapable conclusion that no study of Hispanic ballads can be considered complete without taking into account all known evidence from every modern geographic subtradition, together with the complex testimony of variegated early witnesses: not only manuscripts, pliegos sueltos, and cancioneros, but also early book lists, poetic medleys (*ensaladas*), glosses, guitar manuals (*vihuelistas*), literary allusions, proverbial expressions, pen trials, contrafact hymns and songs, religious adaptations (*romances a lo divino*), citations in Golden Age dramas and interludes (*comedias*; *entremeses*). The comparative study of such early evidence, together with texts recorded from modern oral tradition, obliges us to conclude that the latter are essentially independent from those texts that happened to have been copied or printed in the fifteenth and sixteenth centuries. What was written down reflects a highly selective, essentially distorted view of the early tradition. Though a few modern versions do derive directly (or indirectly) from early printed sources, the normal (now almost predictable) relationship between the tradition's two chronological segments is that the modern versions will often reflect lost medieval variants, which, in one or more essential features, may turn out to be quite different from those arbitrarily chosen by early copyists or sixteenth-century printers. The modern tradition is, then, an independent witness to the romancero's medieval origins and is essential to any comparative study and especially to the task of reconstructing the Hispanic ballad's earliest stages.

Space permits us to mention here only a few of the medieval narratives re-created in ballad form, excluding, in the case of epic and historical romances, secondary compositions based on historiographic sources. (For details concerning each title, see Armistead's *Catálogo-índice* and/or Menéndez Pidal's *Romancero hispánico*.) All the major national epics are reflected in the early ballad tradition: *Bernardo del Carpio*, *Fernán González*, *Infantes de Lara* (*Lords of Lara*), *Mocedades de Rodrigo* (*The Cid's Youthful Adventures*), *Partición de los reinos* (*Division of the Kingdom*), *Cerco de Zamora* (*Siege of Zamora*), *Jura de Santa Gadea* (*Oath at Santa Gadea*), and *Cantar de Mio Cid* (*Poem of the Cid*); of these, *Bernardo*, *Mocedades*, *Partición*, and *Mio Cid* can still be heard, at least fragmentarily, in the modern tradition. Many Old French epic poems were adapted by medieval Spanish minstrels (*juglares*) and eventually evolved into Hispanic ballads (here French titles are followed by those of related ballads): *Floovent*/*Floresvento*; *Mort Aymeri de Narbonne* (*Death of Aymeri*)/*Almerique de Narbona*; *Ogier le Danois*/*Roldán al pie de la torre* (*Roland at the Base of the Tower*); *Enfances de Charlemagne* (*Charlemagne's Youthful Adventures*)/*Galiana*; *Chanson de Roland*/*Roncesvalles*, *Guarinos*, *Don Beltrán*, *Sueño de doña Alda* (*Lady Alda's Dream*); *Aïol*/*Montesinos*; *Aye d'Avignon*/*Moriana y Galván*; *Beuve de Hantone*/*Celinos*. All themes mentioned here have survived somewhere in the modern tradition and, in the case of *Floresvento*, *Roldán al pie de la torre*, *Galiana*, and *Celinos*, the only surviving evidence comes from modern texts.

Some Hispanic ballads can be traced—ultimately—to Germanic origins: *Gaiferos y Melisenda* derives—doubtless through a lost Old French intermediary—from the same narrative represented by the medieval Germano-Latin *Waltharius* and the Anglo-Saxon *Waldere*, while *Don Bueso y su hermana* (*Bueso and his Sister*) agrees—down to some minor details—with the Middle High German *Kudrunslied*, though it undoubtedly does not derive directly, but through some lost balladic intermediary. Numerous events from medieval Spanish, Portuguese, and Catalan history were retold in ballad form, ranging from the earliest known historical narrative, *El prior de San Juan* (*The Prior of St. John*), probably composed around 1328, up to *La muerte del príncipe don Juan* (*The Death of Prince John*), which occurred on 6 October 1497. Of the latter, we knew only modern versions until 1991, when an early text was uncovered in a sixteenth-century manuscript. There are various classical narratives in medieval garb: *El juicio de Paris* (*Paris's Judgment*) and *El robo de Elena* (*Abduction of Helen*) are certainly based on medieval Troy narratives. *La muerte de Alejandro* (*The Death of Alexander*), already cited in 1492, reflects the Alexander legend. *Virgilios*, which sees Virgil as a womanizer, follows the medieval tendency to scandalize the author of the *Aeneid*. Some ballads are inspired by medieval adventure romances: *Espinelo* (*The Thorn Bush Foundling*) tells a story similar to Marie de France's *Lai del Freisne* (*Story of the Ash Tree*), while *Hermanas reina y cautiva* (*Two Sisters: Queen and Captive*) ultimately follows *Flore et Blanchefleur*. Arthurian stories are sparsely represented: In *Ferido está don Tristán* (*Tristan is Wounded*), known only in early texts, Iseult, weeping, goes to the hero's deathbed, with surprising results. *Lanzarote y el ciervo del pie blanco* (*Lancelot and the White-Footed Stag*), known in a sixteenth-century version, has been discovered in the oral tradition of Almería, Jaén, and the Canary Islands.

The earliest surviving ballad text is that of *La gentil dama y el rústico pastor* (*The Noble Lady and the Rustic Shepherd*), a sort of bawdy *pastourelle* in reverse, which was written down in a mixture of Castilian and Catalan, by a Mallorcan law student in Italy in 1421. The ballad is still sung by eastern Mediterranean and North African Jews, and in a form very close to that recalled by the fifteenth-century copyist. The Galician author, Juan Rodríguez del Padrón (d. 1450), transcribed and adapted to his courtly purposes three ballad texts taken from oral tradition: *El caballero burlado* (*The Baffled Knight*), *Rosaflorida y Montesinos*, and *Infante Arnaldos* plus *Conde Olinos* (*Prince Arnaldos*; *Count Olinos*), which are included in the *Cancionero de Londres*. All four themes have been collected from the modern tradition. *Blancaniña* (*The Unfaithful Wife*) is based, by way of a *chanson populaire*, on a medieval French *fabliau*: *Le chevalier à la robe vermeille* (*The Knight of the Red Cloak*). *La bella en misa* (*The Beauty in Church*) follows a medieval Greek ballad learned during the Catalan occupation of Athens (1311–1388) and thence taken back to Spain. *La vuelta del marido* (*é*) (*Husband's Return*: *é* assonance), sung today all over the Hispanic world, derives from a fifteenth-century French *chanson*. *Gritando va el caballero* (*The Weeping Knight*), still sung in Morocco and Extremadura, continues to echo a courtly, sentimental romance, composed in the late 1400s. The Hispanic ballad repertoire thus offers us a substantial and variegated corpus of medieval narratives that have survived and creatively evolved through seven centuries of living oral tradition.

SAMUEL G. ARMISTEAD

Bibliography

Armistead, S. G., J. H. Silverman, and I. J. Katz. *Folk Literature of the Sephardic Jews*. 3 vols. Berkeley, Calif., 1971–94 (ongoing).

Armistead, S. G., et al. *Judeo-Spanish Ballads in the Menéndez Pidal Archive*. 3 vols. Madrid, 1978.

Bénichou, P. *Creación poética en el romancero tradicional*. Madrid, 1968.

Catalán, D. *El Archivo del Romancero*. 2 vols. Madrid, 2001.

———, et al. *The Pan-Hispanic Ballad: General Descriptive Catalogue*. 4 vols. Madrid, 1982–88.

Costa Fontes, M. da. *O Romanceiro Portuguese Brasilerio*. 2 vols. Madison, Wisc., 1997.

Menéndez Pidal, R. *Romancero hispánico (hispano-portugués, americano y sefardí)*. 2 vols. Madrid, 1953.

———, and M. Goyri. *Romancero tradicional de las lenguas hispánicas (Español—portugués—catalán—sefardí)*. Ed. Diego Catalán et al. 12 vols. Madrid, 1957–85.

Rodríguez-Moñino, A., et al. *Nuevo diccionario de pliegos* sueltos poéticos (Siglo XVI). 2nd ed. Madrid, 1997.

———, with A. L.-F. Askins. *Manual bibliográfico de cancioneros y romanceros*. 4 vols. Madrid, 1973–78.

Webber, R. H. *The Hispanic Ballad Today*. New York, 1989.

BALLADS, MUSIC

Musically speaking, the Hispanic *romancero* ballad's hemistichs were sung to a reiterated melodic distich (AB) or to the more popular quatrain strophe (ABCD, less frequently AABB, ABCA), at times with added refrains or with interjections interpolated either between phrases or within lines. There are numerous examples of ballads representing different textual themes that share the same tune and ballads that share the same textual theme which are sung to different tunes. The tunes' medieval elements are reflected in the modes (mainly Dorian and Phrygian), together with their plagal forms, and in distich stophes comprising *ouvert* and *clos* cadences, respectively, which probably emanated from the Old French *chanson de geste*. Similar is the practice of *lexapren*, wherein the final verse of a quatrain strophe is repeated in the initial verse of the succeeding one. This was known in the Iberian Peninsula as *dexaprende, copla encadenada*, or *canción de coleo*.

It is generally agreed that ballads have been sung since the early fourteenth century. Yet, taking into account the thousands of romance texts that were subsequently printed in *pliegos sueltos* (chapbooks or broadsides) and in songbooks (*cancioneros*) dating from the sixteenth and early seventeenth centuries, it is unfortunate that their melodies were not included, particularly in those collections where specimens were probably taken directly from oral tradition.

Be that as it may, the anonymous four-part setting "Lealtat, o lealtat" from the *Crónica del Condestable Miquel Lucas de Iranzo* (1466; Madrid, Bib. Nac. MS 2092), which for long was thought to be the oldest notated romance, is nothing more than a praise song ("Versos fechos en loor del Condestable"), whose four textual strophes are written in ballad meter (see example 1).

Example 1: Lealtat, ¡O lealtat! (tiple of a4)
Madrid: Bibl. Nac. MS 2092 (olim G. 126), fols. 234v-235.

Also questionable is the so-called ballad "Olvida tu perdiçion" (fol. 71ᵛ), in the *Cancionero musical de la Biblioteca Colombina* (ca. 1490), whose two-verse fragment commemorating the fall of Granada in 1492 inspired a three-part setting by an anonymous composer that was added much later to the original compilation. Thus, one must turn to the *Cancionero musical de Palacio* (*CMP*) for the earliest ballad melodies.

The magnificent *CMP* (compiled c. 1490–1520) was discovered, in 1870, in the library of the Royal Palace (Madrid), by the bibliophile Gregorio Cruzada Villaamil. Two decades later, his friend Francisco Ansejo Barbieri published a critical edition. Though the original index listed forty-four romances among its 458 compositions, there are actually only thirty-three, including the ballad "Setenil, ay Setenil," which lacks music. Judging from their texts, thirteen are traditional and twenty are *culto*. Their composers, apart from the fifteen who remain unidentified, include Juan de Anchieta, Antonio de Contreras, Juan del Encina, Pedro de Lagarto, Lope Martines, Francisco Millán, Antonio de Ribera, and Francisco de la Torre. Whereas Barbieri advocated an entirely vocal rendering of the *CMP*'s ballad settings, Higinio Anglés, in his two-volume edition of the music (Barcelona 1947–1951), countered that the untexted vocal parts accompanying the *superius* (or *tiple*) were designated for instruments. Only in three instances does Anglés concur with Barbieri: "Dormiendo está el cavallero" "Mi libertad en sosiego" and "Por mayo era, por mayo" (see example 2), thus exhibiting the earliest examples that were sung a cappella. Barbieri did not follow the original order of the *CMP*'s compositions, whereas Anglés did. The ballad tunes (assigned to the *superius*) reveal such common features as strophic form (quatrain, ABCD), although "Por mayo era, por mayo" is, in reality, a distich (AB); balanced musical phrases, except for the more extensively ornamented cadences, ending on a sustained cadential tone (indicated by a fermata); restricted range (no less than a sixth, but not greater than an octave); melodic progressions are, for the most part, diatonic; meter is predominantly duple; and the tune-text relationship is basically syllabic, except for the cadences in the second and final phrases. The Dorian and Mixolydian modes prevail.

Example 2: Por Mayo era, por Mayo (Tiple I of a4)
Madrid: Bibl. Real, sign. 2-I-5, fols. 56v-57.

While the singing of ballads continued to be in vogue in court circles, it is surprising that, during the period of the *vihuelistas* (1536–1576), only twenty-two ballad texts were arranged for voice and *vihuela*, while the equally popular *villancico* is represented by eighty settings. With regard to ballads, Luis Milán contributed four, Luis de Narváez two, Alonso de Mudarra three, Enríquez de Valderrábano five, Diego Pisador five, Esteban Daza one, and Juan Bermudo one. Among them, Miguel de Fuenllana contributed three (two of which are intabulations of settings by Crístobal Morales and Francisco Bernal, while his own setting of "Paseábase el rey moro" was written for the guitar). In addition, Luis Venegas de Henestrosa included, in his collection of tunes, three ballad settings for voice, keyboard instrument, harp, and vihuela, two of which were attributed to Francisco Palero, and the third to an anonymous composer. Multiple settings can be found for such popular ballads as "A las armas moriscote" (Pisador, Fuenllana, the latter based on an intabulation of Bernal), "Paseábase el rey moro" (Narváez, Pisador, Fuenllana, and Palero), and "Mira, Nero de Tarpeya" (Bermudo [see example 3] and Palero).

Example 3: Mira, Nero de Tarpea
Juan Bermudo, Declaración de instrumentos musicales
(Osuna, 1555), Book IV, fol. 101,

The traditionality of the tune utilized by Valderrábano for "Los braços traigo cansados" *La muerte de don Beltrán* is confirmed in the settings of Millán (*CMP*), Francisco de Peñalosa (*Cancionero musical de Barcelona*), and in the singular ballad setting (a4) of Juan Vásquez in his *Recopilación de Sonetos y Villancicos* (see example 4).

Ex. 5: Los braços traigo cansados

The melody for "Durandarte, Durandarte" (in the *CMP*) was also used by Milán. Moreover, the famous "Conde Claros" tune adapted by Narváez as a *cantus firmus* for his *diferencias*, was subsequently taken up by Mudarra, Valderrábano, Pisador, and by an anonymous composer in the collection of Venegas de Henestrosa. The tune, notated as a trichordal (see example 5), was cited in Francisco Salinas's *De Musica Libri Septem* (Salamanca, 1577, libro VI, 342), along with four other ballad melodies ("Pensó el mal villano," "Yo me yua mi madre," "En la ciudad de Toledo," and "Retraída está la Infanta").

Example 4: Conde Claros
F. Salinas, De musica libri septem (Salamanca, 1577)
Book VI, p. 342

Conde Claros con amores no podía reposar.

Transcr. by I. Pope

Con-de Cla-ros con a - mo- res no po- dí - a re - po -sar.
* = modified

The *Cancionero de Sablonara*, which included settings of forty-seven ballad texts from the late sixteenth and early seventeenth centuries, marked the transition to a new stage in the development of Spanish balladry. Its texts comprise erudite poems in ballad meter written by learned Golden Age authors. This generic innovation, known as the *romancero nuevo*, lies outside the medieval purview of the present entry.

Although the Romantic movement of the nineteenth century revived national interest in the living oral tradition, manifesting particular interest in ballad text types of medieval origin, the tunes appearing in Romantic collections exhibit hardly any traces of medieval musical elements, save perhaps in formal structure and modality. Subsequent fieldwork by modern Spanish and American scholars has revealed that the romance is an essentially pan-Hispanic phenomenon that has survived from the Middle Ages down to the present, in practically all areas where Spanish, Portuguese, Catalán, and Judeo-Spanish are spoken today. The complex problem of the possible medieval antecedents of this vast musical repertoire remains to be explored.

Israel J. Katz

Bibliography

Anglés, H. *La Música en la corte de los Reyes Católicos: Cancionero Musical de Palacio (Siglos XV-XVI)*. 2 vols. Barcelona, 1947–51.

Barbieri, F. A. *Cancionero musical de los siglos XV y XVI*. Madrid, 1890.

Devoto, D. "Poésie et musique dans l' œuvre des vihuelistes." *Annales Musicologiques* 4 (1956), 85–111.

Katz, I. J. "The 'Myth' of the Sephardic Musical Legacy from Spain." In *Proceedings of the Fifth World Congress of Jewish Studies*. Vol. 4. Ed. A. Shinan. Jerusalem, 1973.

Menéndez Pidal, G. "Ilustraciones musicales." In *Romancero hispánico (hispano-portugués, americano y sefardí*. Madrid, 1988. 367–402.

Pope, I. "Notas sobre la melodía de Conde Claros." *Nueva Revista de Filología Hispánica* 15 (1961), 395–402.

Sage, J. "Romancero." *The New Grove Dictionary of Music and Musicians*. Vol. 16. London, 1980.

BANKING

From the eleventh century, there were money changers in the most active cities in Aragón (Jaca, Zaragoza), Catalonia (Barcelona), and Castile (villages on the way to Santiago de Compostela). In the twelfth century, the private banking in Catalonia evolved on Christian and Jewish money changers and moneylenders' hands, who invested their earnings in banking business, allowed deposits, opened current accounts with or without coverage, and earned interest at a rate of 12.5 to 25 percent. The count of Barcelona, Ramón Berenguer IV, perhaps counseled by the Templars, authorized (1150) his Christian subjects from Lérida to lend at interest. This privilege was confirmed by Jaime I in October 1217; but the development of trade in the kingdom of Aragón and the need of money caused the *tabelliones* (bankers) from Girona and Besalu to increase their interest rate to over 20 percent. The existing variety of coins, the fluctuating prices, and the search of a profit (*logro*) higher than what was allowed helped private banking to develop and impelled Barcelona to adopt its peculiar silver mark (*marca*; 327 gm.) in the first third of the thirteenth century.

In Castile, there were also public money changers, in fairgrounds such as Medina del Campo or in cities such as Cuenca or Seville, who were permitted to have their own wood bench, their balances to weigh gold and silver, and their account books. They could lend money on the condition that the interest did not double the loaned capital in a year; but the irresponsibility of many of them and speculation caused the first bankruptcies, fraudulent (by transferring the money to a third person by means of bills of exchange) or not, and gave rise to the first banking laws in the courts of Barcelona in February 1300 and in the courts of Lérida in March 1301, in which heavy penalties (exile, disqualification, loss of properties, and life sentence) were imposed on infractors, and changers and bankers were obliged to pay bail. In Barcelona, there were thirty-three private banks between 1301 and 1349.

After 1350, in all the Spanish kingdoms, the shortage of money and the bankruptcy of some money changers, with many debts, caused those who had surplus and were afraid of saving it at home to leave the money as a deposit in a solvent monastery or church on certain conditions, and some Castilian *conse* (councils or municipalities) controlled the profession of money changer by reducing the number of money changers authorized, but the king granted the practice of public money exchange to a privileged individual who sublet or transferred it to a professional (Jew or Christian), which roused social unrest.

From 1381 to 1383, there were spectacular bankruptcies of money changers, who had lent to the crown, in Barcelona, Girona, and Perpignan. In 1397 the municipality of Barcelona reorganized the profession of money changer–banker by obliging to deposit a high sum as an insurance, to rent a bank of credit in the exchange, where money changers were concentrated.

The municipality of Barcelona, on 25 January 1401, opened the first bank of deposit and public credit in the city warranted by the municipality, which was called *taula de canvi*. This bank became the executive agent of the Generalitat and was soon imitated in Palma de Mallorca (1401), Valencia (1407), Zaragoza, Girona (1443), Vic, Perpignan, Cervera (1559), and other cities, with varying luck because of the problems created by the large number of loans given to public organizations and the subsequent shortage of liquidity. In Barcelona, there are still private bankers forced to insure themselves to avoid fraudulent liquidations. The taula de canvi, which had 1,460 clients in 1433 and more than 600,000 pounds as a deposit in 1462, had to face the floating public debt and the interests of the consolidated public debt; whereupon, during the fifteenth century, it had to be restructured on several occasions. The banks of Barcelona produced half the finances of Catalonia.

The taula de canvi of Valencia operated from 1407 to 1416 and renovated its activities in 1519. The period from 1416 to 1519 was occupied by private banking. The cortes of Castile, in Madrid in 1445 and in Toledo in 1446, liberalized changes by allowing private banking to thrive again in the fundamental urban settlements in Castile and Andalusia (Jerez, Burgos, Baeza, Seville, Valladolid, Segovia, Madrid, Córdoba, Toledo, and Santiago de Compostela from 1450 to 1550. The new changers-bankers paid the deposits demanded by the city councils of the places where they were going to work. The rules about discounts or commissions were minimal (1488–1498), except for expressly forbidding foreigners to practice banking to save high-priced coins from going abroad. At the end of the fifteenth century, only twenty-four private banks operated in Barcelona besides the municipal taula.

Manuel Riu

Bibliography

Ruiz Martín, F. "La Banca en España hasta 1782." In *El Banco de España. Una historia*. Madrid, 1970. 1–196.

Usher, A. P. *The Early History of Deposit Banking in Mediterranean Europe*. Cambridge, Mass., 1943. Reprt. New York, 1967.

Riu, M. "Banking and Society in Late Medieval and Early Modern Aragón." In *The Dawn of Modern Banking*. New Haven, Conn., 1979. 131–68.

BANŪ ʿABBĀD

The Banū ʿAbbād clan traced its ancestral origins to Yemen via a progenitor who came to al-Andalus in the 740s. Lords of Seville, they were by far the most powerful of the dynasties that formed the tā'ifa kingdoms in eleventh-century Iberia. Ibn ʿAbī ʿĀmir (al-Manṣūr) had appointed his kinsman Ismāʿīl, a judge in the city during the latter part of the tenth century. Ismāʿīl was known as a man of probity who attempted to keep peace among the quarreling Berbers. In old age, Ismāʿīl passed down his office to his son, Muḥammad, who founded the ʿAbbādid Dynasty.

When Muḥammad inherited his father's office, he also inherited great wealth and vast tracts of land in and around Seville. At the time, he was said to be the wealthiest man in the region. He became governor of the city in 1023, when al-Qāsim was overthrown, and he formed part of a three-man council entrusted to oversee the city's administration. Shortly thereafter, he was asked to assume full power. During the nearly twenty years he ruled he was able to establish an autonomous state with a volunteer army composed of Arabs, Christians, and Berbers. During this period, he orchestrated an elaborate ruse by claiming that the deposed caliph, Hishām II, was alive and living in Seville, and that he was merely his servant. An impostor was clothed in caliphal robes and would conduct Friday prayers at the mosque while Muḥammad acted as his chamberlain. In 1035, Muḥammad asked all the provinces to swear an oath of allegiance to Hishām II, the legitimate caliph. Some cooperated, others ignored the request, and still others encountered problems with it. To castigate one of the dissenters, the Berber governor of Málaga, Muḥammad killed him and occupied Carmona. Afterward, Muḥammad attacked Almería, whose ruler sought an alliance with the Berbers of Granada. Muḥammad's son Ismāʿīl was killed in a military campaign against them.

When Muḥammad died in 1042, he was succeeded by his second son, Al-Muʿtaḍid. Al-Muʿtaḍid was an astute, determined, and often ruthless individual who was successful in extending his influence over fellow Mulims in Portugal, Huelva, Algeciras, Ronda, and Carmona. He was, however, compelled to pay large tributes to the Christians, who by 1056 had made significant advances in the south, particularly Fernando I, who attacked Seville in 1063. Dissatisfied with the title of chamberlain inherited from his father, in 1059 Al-Muʿtaḍid declared that Hishām II, the pseudo-caliph invented by Muḥammad, had died. He assumed full power as king. Full of contradictions, Al-Muʿtaḍid was capable of killing his own son for suspicion of treason and liquidating guests as they bathed in his palace as well as writing delicate poetry, appreciating music, and administering the state. Suspicious and greatly feared by his children, he chose carefully the one who would succeed him, the future Al-Muʿtamid, whom he appointed chamberlain, commander of the army, and governor of Silves.

Al-Muʿtamid assumed the throne in 1068. He was both tragic and magnificent, a man who would know both the heights of majesty and the depths of abjection during his life. When he assumed the governorship of Silves in 1063, Al-Muʿtamid was accompanied by his lifelong friend and close companion, Ibn ʿAmmār. When Ibn ʿAmmār later betrayed al-Muʿtamid and fled to Zaragoza, Al-Muʿtamid pursued him, seized him, imprisoned him, and then killed him with his own hands with an ax blow to the head. Although capable of exacting cruel vengeance, al-Muʿtamid is best known for his luxuriant poetry, especially the moving verses in which he records the love for his wife, Iʿtimīd al-Rumaykiyya, a former slave girl whom he encountered first on the banks of the Guadalquivir River. The worst chapter of his life, however, unfolded as a result of an error in his own judgment. Fearing the Christian inroads in the south, he succumbed to calling for aid from the Almoravids in North Africa. Instead of delivering him from his Christian enemies, however, the Almoravid emperor Ibn Ṭāsfīʾn would take his kingdom, and that of all the other ṭāʾifa kings, and lead al-Muʿtamid away from his beloved Seville into exile in Morocco, in chains and in humiliation.

The Banū ʿAbbād of Seville.

Muhammad (1023–1042)
al-Muʿtaḍid (1042–1068)
al-Muʿtamid (1068–1091)

E. Michael Gerli

Bibliography

Chejne, A. G. *Muslim Spain: Its History and Culture*. Minneapolis, Minn., 1974.

Jayyusi, S. K. (ed.) *The Legacy of Muslim Spain*. 2 vols. Boston, 1994. 1.

Kennedy, H. *Muslim Spain and Portugal: A Political History of al-Andalus*. New York, 1996.

BANŪ DHŪ-L-NŪN

The Banū Dhū-l-Nūn was a Berber clan that appeared in al-Andalus during the last years of the caliphate. The members of the clan established themselves near Toledo. Some of them held important positions in the army and the government during the regime of al-Manṣūr and his successors. Ismāʿīl, the first Dhū-l-Nūnid ruler of Toledo, seems to have been governor of the city and shared power with Abū Bakr al-Ḥadīdī at the time of the revolts during the first and second decades of the eleventh century in Córdoba, immediately following the unraveling of the caliphate. A well-respected citizen, Al-Ḥadīdī remained a close adviser to Ismāʿīl long after he became king in 1016 and continued in the same capacity under Yaḥyā, Ismāʿīl's son and successor. Yaḥyā proved a skilled diplomat who managed to play all external interests against each other and survive the perils presented by both his fellow Mulsims in al-Andalus and the encroaching Christians from the north. When menaced by the Banū Hūd of Zaragoza, Yaḥyā forged an alliance with Fernando I of Castile and León and, at one point, even offered refuge in Toledo to the future Alfonso VI, who would take the city from Yaḥyā's grandson and send the latter to Valencia in 1085. Yaḥyā allied himself closely with the ʿAbbādis of Seville and cooperated with Muḥammad I of that city by turning a blind eye to his ruse and recognizing the man Muḥammad said was Hishām II as the living caliph. The fate of Córdoba, however, soon put the Dhū-l-Nūnid at odds with the Banū ʿAbbād, just as they were at war with the Al-Afṭas of Badajoz. Despite these tensions, however, Yaḥyā's reign was distinguished by grandeur and abundance. It was only after his death in 1075 that the kingdom's circumstances began a steady decline. Yaḥyā was succeeded by his grandson, known as Yaḥyā "el Nieto," who lacked the maturity and finesse to deal with the difficult political situations arising from governing on the frontier. Yaḥyā el Nieto dismissed Al-Ḥadīdī, who had been a key adviser to both his grandfather and great grandfather, and other ministers who objected to Alfonso VI's extortionary demands for tribute. Tensions rose. Finally, amid internal rebellions in the city and pressure from the Banū Hūd of Zaragoza from the east, Alfonso VI from the north, and the Al-Afṭas of

Badajoz from the southwest, amid an insurrection that closed off nearly every exit from Toledo, Yaḥyā el Nieto was compelled to abandon the city when the Al-Afṭas attacked in 1079. Faced with an impossible situation, he turned to Alfonso, the lesser of the evils, who easily regained Toledo for him. In 1085, however, with the concurrence of Al-Muʿtamid of Seville, Alfonso decided the city was for him and himself alone, expelling Yaḥyā el Nieto and sending him to Valencia as its ruler. Alfonso's decision sealed Toledo's fate. It had fallen permanently into the hands of the Christians. The capitulation of Toledo sent a shockwave through al-Andalus and it would ultimately lead to the involvement of the Almoravids from North Africa in Iberia. The Almoravids would be called in at the instigation of Al-Muʿtamid of Seville and others to rescue them from the encroachments of Alfonso VI and the ambitious Christian rulers of the peninsula. Rather than provide redemption, however, the Almoravids took power for themselves, deposed the most assertive of the tā'ifa kings, and sent them packing into exile to Morocco in chains.

The Banū Dhul-Nun Dynasty of Toledo (1016–1085).

Ismāʿīl (1016–1043)
Yaḥyā (1043–1075)
Yaḥyā "El Nieto" (1075–1085)

E. Michael Gerli

Bibliography

Chejne, A. G. *Muslim Spain: Its History and Culture*. Minneapolis, Minn., 1974.

Jayyusi, S. K. (ed.) *The Legacy of Muslim Spain*. 2 vols. Boston, 1994. 1.

Kennedy, H. *Muslim Spain and Portugal: A Political History of al-Andalus*. New York, 1996.

BANŪ HŪD

The clan of the Hūd ruled Zaragoza from 1040 to 1142. They were the descendants of the Tjībids, a clan with Syrian Arab origins that had established itself in the region in the latter part of the ninth century. They became independent during the revolt in Córdoba following the dissolution of the caliphate. The founder of the dynasty was Sulaymān al-Musta'in, descendant of an Arab named Hūd who came to al-Andalus at the time of the Conquest. In 1039, taking advantage of the chaos in Córdoba, he took control of Lérida and Monzón and acquired jurisdiction over Huesca, Tudela, and Calatayud. At war with the Dhū-l-Nūn of Toledo in the 1040s, he sought alliances with the Christians. Sulaymān divided his kingdom among five sons, all of whom quarreled over their rightful share. Aḥmad al-Muqtadir, who emerged victorious, added Denia to the realm and became very powerful among the tāi'fa kings. Aḥmad was renowned as a builder and for many public works. Muḥammad, his son and successor, defended the integrity of the kingdom and challenged al-Mu'tamid of Seville by giving refuge to Ibn ʿAmmār, the king of Seville's enemy and former companion. At the same time, the Castilian Christian Rodrigo Díaz de Vivar, known as El Cid, served as a mercenary in Muḥammad's army and helped protect the kingdom against Christians and Muslims alike. Muḥammad's follower, Aḥmad II, failed to withstand Christian abuse and suffered a resounding defeat at Huesca in 1108, where he died. Despite this blow, the Banū Hūd preserved their independence until ʿAbd al-Malik allied himself with the Christians and provoked the Almoravids to occupy Zaragoza. The Almoravids, however, allowed Aḥmad III to continue as king until 1118, when Alfonso I and Ramiro II of Aragón entered the kingdom and deposed him.

The Banū Hūd of Zaragoza (1040–1142).

Sulaymān al-Musta'in (1040–1046)
Aḥmad I al-Muqtadir (1046–1082)
Muḥammad (1082–1085)
Aḥmad II (1085–1108)
ʿAbd al-Malik (1108–1110)
Aḥmad III (1110–1142)

E. Michael Gerli

Bibliography

Chejne, A. G. *Muslim Spain: Its History and Culture*. Minneapolis, Minn., 1974.

Fletcher, R. *The Quest for El Cid*. New York, 1990.

Kennedy, H. *Muslim Spain and Portugal*. New York, 1996.

BANŪ QASĪ

A turning point in the slow process of the Reconquest of the eighth and ninth centuries was the liberation of Barcelona in 801 by Christian forces (Visigoths and other Spanish Christian emigrants) under the orders of Louis the Pious of France. They continued south as far as Tarragona (808). These newly captured regions constituted the so-called (mostly fictitious) Marca Hispanica. However, the Muslims attacked Barcelona again in 813 and 815, and the rebellion of Mūṣa b. Mūṣa of Zaragoza against ʿAbd al-Raḥmān II (842) marked the emergence of the powerful Banū Qasī clan, supposedly descended from an early Christian count. Mūṣa's son Fortún succeeded him in Tudela (d. 874), and another son, Lubb, succeeded him in Zaragoza, where the dynasty continued until 929. The rebellion of Mūṣa was providential for Asturias, besieged by Muslim invaders and plagued by a quarrel of succession upon the death of Alfonso II. They apparently assisted Mūṣa, and he was able to withstand the attack of the Muslim ruler against him in Navarre, where he established an independent kingdom in 852.

According to Ibn Ḥazm, Fruela II (d. 925) of León, son of Alfonso III of Asturias, married a woman of the Banū Qasī named Urraca (apparently a convert to Christianity).

NORMAN ROTH

Bibliography

Cañada Juste, A. "El posible solar originario de los Banū Qasī." In *Homenaje á don José Maria Lacarra de Miguel*. Zaragoza, 1977.

Lévi-Provençal, E. *España musulmana hasta la caída del califato de Córdoba*. 2 vols. Trans. E. García Gómez. Madrid, 1950–1957.

BARBASTRO, CRUSADE OF

In 1064 a large army of Aquitanians, Burgundians, Normans, and Catalans laid siege to the Muslim fortress of Barbastro in the kingdom of Zaragoza. After forty days the city surrendered and there ensued a massacre of the Muslim inhabitants. In the short run it was of no great consequence, for in 1065, nine months after the siege, the Muslims reconquered the city after most of the foreign knights had departed.

The siege of Barbastro is, for several reasons, one of the most controversial battles of the early reconquest in Spain. Historians of the Crusades and the Reconquest have struggled with several problems, including the indulgence letter that Pope Alexander II allegedly granted to the soldiers at Barbastro, and whether this makes Barbastro the First Crusade, preceding the one called by Pope Urban II. In addition, the extent of involvement by Pope Alexander II, from 1061 to 1073, and the Cluniacs in propagating the Crusade has been debated, as has the identification of the leader of the Christian soldiers, among whom we find as candidates Duke William VIII of Aquitaine, William of Montreuil, the Norman Robert Crispin, and Armengol III, count of Urgel.

The controversy concerning the papacy is based upon a translation of a passage in the chronicle (1067–1076) of Ibn Ḥayyān, an eleventh-century Córdoban writer. Some have argued that Ibn Ḥayyān indirectly identified the leader of the armies at Barbastro when he referred to the "commander of ʿAr-Rum." Most scholars suggested that the leader of the Barbastro campaign was handpicked, so to speak, by Pope Alexander II. Recent scholarship demonstrates "ʿ*Ar-Rum*" was employed by the Muslims to identify Castilians, Galicians, Catalans, Aragónese, and even adversaries outside the peninsula; therefore, it does not refer specifically to a leader chosen by or coming from Rome.

There is no evidence to suggest that the peninsular kings ever needed or called upon the Cluniacs to invite foreign armies to Barbastro. The active participation of Pope Alexander II simply eludes us at every turn. The pope issued a bull allegedly directed to the knights at Barbastro, but it is addressed to the *clero Vulturensis*, whose exact identity is unclear. Neither the leaders nor the name of Barbastro are mentioned specifically in Alexander's bull. For these and other reasons, Barbastro cannot be called a bona fide "crusade," but it was indeed a "holy war." A major problem has been the identification of a single leader at Barbastro. Sources such as the *Chronica de Saint Maxentii*, *Historiae Francicae Fragmento*; Amato of Monte Cassino; *Gesta Comitum Barcinonensium*; Ibn Ḥayyān; and al-Bakri are governed by regional interests and personal bias. They each focused upon the specific roles of the various leaders, both foreign and domestic. At the "crusade" of Barbastro there were apparently multiple leaders, the most prominent being Duke William VIII of Aquitaine, Robert Crispin, and Armengol III, Count of Urgel. It has been decisively demonstrated that William of Montreuil did not participate at Barbastro.

In the long run, the role of foreign soldiers was of greater utility for the reconquest of the Iberian Peninsula. When the foreign knights returned to their own lands, they told of the fame and fortune to be had south of the Pyrenees. After Barbastro there is a marked increase of foreign soldiers, especially Normans, in the Iberian Peninsula. These later Normans were there for more than booty. Some even attempted to establish their own kingdoms in the peninsula. Although the soldiers at Barbastro could not know it, the battle would serve as a propaganda piece to lure others to seek fame and fortune in the Reconquest.

ALBERTO FERREIRO

Bibliography

Ferreiro, A. "The Siege of Barbastro, 1064–65: A Reassessment," *Journal of Medieval History* 9 (1983), 129–44.

Gayangos, P. de. (trans.) *Ahmed Ibn Mohammed Al-Makkari: The History of the Mohammedan Dynasties in Spain*. 2 vols. Reprint of 1840–43 edition. New York, 1964.

BARCELONA, CITY OF

Barcelona emerged as the political and economic capital of northeastern Iberia during the Middle Ages. Previously, the Greek city of Emporion (along the coast to the north of Barcelona) and Roman Tarragona had served as administrative centers. In the Roman period "Barcino" was important but secondary. Its growing significance after the collapse of Roman rule was due to its economic and military position given the circumstances of the Muslim-Christian military balance from 800 to 1150.

Barcelona would be a major port in the medieval and modern Mediterranean but its prominence in this regard cannot be attributed to natural advantage. Its harbor was neither sheltered nor convenient to moor boats. Guarded by hills on three sides, Barcelona was well-protected from a land attack and was further bolstered by the survival of its immense Roman walls. The military benefits of Barcelona's situation became especially important after the Carolingian reconquest in 801, which left Tarragona a deserted city between Christian and Muslim zones. Tarragona would not be reoccupied successfully until the twelfth century, although it remained the titular ecclesiastical metropolis. Barcelona was conveniently near the military frontier but usually safe from attack. A notable exception took place with the sack and burning of the city in 985. Muslim forces also overran Barcelona on two earlier occasions.

With the eclipse of direct Carolingian rule in the later ninth century, Barcelona became linked to the fortunes of its count, one among a related group of Pyrenean successors to Carolingian authority. The success of the count of Barcelona in dominating and ultimately annexing his neighbors paralleled the rise of the city.

The destruction of Barcelona in 985 by the troops of Al-Manṣūr proved a paradoxical disaster. It was the last gasp of the caliphate's power and ushered in a period of urban expansion. In the eleventh century the growth of Barcelona was based on agricultural prosperity and a local economy, not on overseas commerce. In the mid-eleventh century a system to channel water to the city from the Besos River was developed (the rec comtal), and mills were constructed along this waterway. Villages on the city's periphery engaged in intensive agricultural production that contributed to the development of local and regional trade. By the late eleventh century, according to Banks, the population of Barcelona was three or four thousand, compared with about one thousand in 900. The city remained centered on the area enclosed by the Roman walls but had expanded eastward toward the rec comtal. Within the city a Jewish quarter (the *Call*) emerged south and east of the cathedral before 1100.

The status of Barcelona as a Mediterranean port was achieved. After the growth of its regional agrciultural and political power, Barcelona in the twelfth century became a major port as it began to trade extensively with Italy. Banks estimates the population in 1200 at ten to twelve thousand. In the twelfth and thirteenth centuries the city expanded in every direction beyond the Roman walls and absorbed the port quarters and many of the once-rural villages on its former outskirts. Unlike Italy, where powerful families would dominate particular urban quarters, Barcelona's neighborhoods did not coalesce around particular magnate patrons. Prosperous and influential families were less prone to internecine violence than in Italy, and the count continued to dominate the city with little challenge to his rule.

Barcelona turned a considerable amount of aggressive energy outward, in Mediterranean expansion, beginning in the thirteenth century. These expeditions united military and commercial purposes and were supported by nobles and townsmen. Some conquests, such as that of Mallorca in 1229, proved permanent, while others, such as the Sardinia campaign (1323–1324), were ultimately unsuccessful. Barcelona attempted by these expeditions to offset the strength of its rivals (especially Genoa and Pisa), to impose its economic power on Muslim North Africa, to guarantee grain supplies, and of course to support the ambitions of the king. The Sicilian Vespers uprising against Angevin rule in 1282 led to the intervention of the king of Aragón and Catalan-Aragónese control of this strategic and grain-exporting territory. In part as a return on the financial investment of Barcelona's citizens in the Sicilian enterprise, the king granted what would become the fundamental charter of self-government to Barcelona, a document known as *Recognoverunt proceres* (1284). This assured property rights within the city and granted a degree of municipal autonomy. By this time Barcelona held an effective monopoly on Catalan long-distance trade, regulated the activities of foreign merchants, and had opened consular offices in other Mediterranean ports. The government of Barcelona was vested in a council of one hundred members (the Consell de Cent), established in 1265.

There is considerable debate about the nature and causes of the late medieval economic crisis in Barcelona. Certainly difficulties (famine in particular) were visible before the onslaught of the Black Death in 1348. As elsewhere, that epidemic had dramatic results, but how much of the subsequent decline of Barcelona can be directly attributed to it is in doubt. The population, which had been at 50,000 before 1348, sank to 38,000 by 1378 and would decline further in the fifteenth century. Yet the late fourteenth century also saw the construction of the shipyards (*drassanes*), the Hospital of Santa Creu, the exchange (*llonja*), and extensive building programs in parish churches. Barcelona's problems in the late fourteenth and fifteenth centuries were related to the overall European depression, but the city also fell behind its Italian competitors who also had to contend with the structural problems of the late Middle Ages. The difficulties of Barcelona are related not only to the superior economic power of Italy but to the internal crises of Catalonia, political factionalism, the unpopularity of the Trastámara rulers, and especially the low productivity of agriculture and the peasant discontent that culminated in war during the late fifteenth century.

Within the city the aftermath of the plague produced a sharpening of tension between artisans and patricians and an increased anti-Jewish sentiment. The riots of 1391 all but ended the Jewish presence in Barcelona. Economic decline became acute after 1425. Valencia prospered at Barcelona's expense while the king held his court in Naples as Barcelona vainly cajoled or demanded his return. Urban factions, the Biga and Busca fought each other in midcentury, the former identified with the higher patriciate, the latter with the middling groups. Their conflict formed part of the confusing civil war of 1462 to 1472, which appears to have completed the devastation of Barcelona's medieval economy.

PAUL H. FREEDMAN

Bibliography

Banks, P. "The Topography of Barcelona and its Urban Context in Eastern Catalonia from the Third to the Twelfth Centuries." 5 vols. Ph.D. diss., University of Nottingham, 1980.

Batlle y Gallart, C. *La crisis social y económica de Barcelona a mediados del siglo XV*. 2 vols. Barcelona, 1973.

Carreras y Candí, F. *La ciutat de Barcelona*. Barcelona, c. 1916; repr. 1980.

Carrère, C. *Barcelone, centre économique à l'époque des difficultés, 1380–1462*. 2 vols. Paris, 1967.

Ruiz Domènec, J. E. "The Urban Origins of Barcelona: Agricultural Revolution or Commercial Development?" *Speculum* 52 (1977), 265–86.

BARCELONA, COUNTS OF *See* BARCELONA, COUNTY OF

BARCELONA, COUNTY OF

The regions of the eastern Pyrenees later to be known as Catalonia were part of a vast territory organized by Charlemagne and his successors as a buffer against the Muslims in Spain. Toward the year 900 a number of counties were established, and in the tenth century the one centered at Barcelona assumed the precedence that followed naturally from its strategic location. But the early counts of Barcelona were the brothers and cousins of other counts descended from Guifré the Hairy (870–897), an energetic defender and colonizer, and it is a remarkable feature that the condominial solidarity he initiated persisted for many generations thereafter. Nevertheless, Borrell II, count of Barcelona and Urgell (947–992), was already the foremost count when renewed Muslim attacks in 985 and after forced a new destiny on Barcelona. Appealing unsuccessfully for aid from the king of France, Count Borrell and his successors not only drove off the Muslims but effectively reversed their aggressions in raiding expeditions that greatly enriched the prospering population of Barcelona and its hinterlands. Like the counties of Urgell, Cerdanya, and others, Barcelona remained nominally dependent on the king of France, although in later tradition the unaided defense of Barcelona was represented as marking a legal devolution of sovereignty to the counts of Barcelona.

The eleventh century was a great age of growth. Agrarian settlements expanded and multiplied, drawing on migration from the mountains; quickened commercial links with Spain and Occitania brought exchanges of slaves, weapons, horses and cloth; Muslim gold coins circulated and were minted in Barcelona by 1018. Clerical culture flourished in the old dynastic homeland, where Oliba (971–1046) was abbot of Ripoll and Cuixá from 1008 and bishop of Vic (1018–1046); he promoted monastic reform in touch with trans-Pyrenean influences, as well as liturgical and classical studies.

Traditional legal and institutional structures persisted. The law remained Visigothic, public and territorial; the administration, Carolingian. The count dominated his lands with the support of viscounts and vicars in well-spaced castles, drawing on the military and economic services of a mostly free population. But this social and institutional cohesion collapsed in the years after 1020. Count Berenguer Ramón I (1017–1035) was unable to maintain his predecessors' momentum against the Muslims, thereby depriving a fiercely ambitious military class of its cherished outlet. The castles of aggressive lineages, manned by mounted warriors ever more numerous and less disciplined, multiplied beyond the count's control. Castellans fought among themselves, ravaged peasant lands and requisitioned crops, and imposed upon helpless tenants an array of obligations that soon hardened into a custom of banal lordship. The old procedures of public courts gave way to private settlements. The principle of public order persisted in the Truce of God (1027 and after), proclaimed by bishops who imposed specific protections for clergymen and unarmed persons. The resulting statutes would later be appropriated by the count, but meanwhile the assault on his prerogatives continued.

It was Count Ramón Berenguer I (1035–1076) who finally prevailed and established a new political order. Regaining control of the principal castles, he progressively secured the alliance or fidelity of other counts and viscounts, as well as that of other lords of castles. He insisted on the sworn allegiance even of subordinate castellans and knights, together with the right of entry to castles. But little of the old order survived. Ties of personal fidelity proliferated throughout society, replacing the weakened sanctions of the law. Castellans and their enfeoffed knights formed a new aristocracy based on their exploitative lordship over peasants. The new regime was thus a feudal order dominated by the count of Barcelona, who now sought to expand his direct lordship even at the expense of his cousins in Besalú, Cerdanya, and other counties.

About 1060 dawned the great age of the county of Barcelona. Ramón Berenguer I and the Countess Almodis acted as independent "princes" to secure territorial order, reimposing the Peace and Truce (1064) and bringing the Visigothic law up to date. They and their successors cut great figures in the wider Mediterranean world. Ramón Berenguer II (r. 1076–1082) married a daughter of the Norman prince Robert Guiscard, and their son married first the Cid's daughter and later the heiress of Provence. Practices of the Gregorian reform were introduced in legatine councils (1077, 1078), while initiatives of Ramón Berenguer III (r. 1082–1131) in Muslim lands led Pope Urban II to proclaim the restoration of the archbishopric of Tarragona.

Arguably the greatest of the independent counts were Ramón Berenguer III and Ramón Berenguer IV (r. 1131–1162). They faced serious challenges from resurgent Muslim attacks, consolidated their power in the old counties, and set about instituting government. Ramón Berenguer III succeeded to the county of Besalú in 1111, a devolution carefully prepared, and to that of Cerdanya in 1118. Characteristically, the old counties were swallowed up in an expanded county of Barcelona, as were other counties thereafter: Roussillon (1172), Pallars Jussá (1192), Urgell (1314), and Empúries (1322). Interests in Occitania and Provence were cultivated at the price of enduring conflict with the counts of Toulouse, but the county of Barcelona as such was never conceived to extend north of the Pyrenees. Ramón Berenguer III was entitled count of Provence (in right of his wife) from 1113; Provence was a tremendous dynastic prize that his descendants would labor to secure and govern. He momentarily seized Mallorca (1114–1115) and began the effective restoration of the church of Tarragona.

His son Ramón Berenguer IV brought all these enterprises to triumphant fulfillment. Marrying the heiress to Aragón, he was count and prince from the year 1150. He led the ever restive barons on lucrative raiding expeditions as far as Almera before driving the Muslims out of Tortosa, Lérida, and Fraga (1148–1149). He renewed the effort to legislate for the expanded county, he tried to establish a territorial tribunal, and he encouraged the institution of a novel system of fiscal accountancy for his domains. He negotiated with Henry II and Alfonso VII as as if he were their equal. He encouraged new religious foundations, such as the Cistercians at Poblet and Santes Creus (1150–1153), and was celebrated by monks at Ripoll as a dynastic restorer and conqueror.

What he did not do was assume the title of king, either in Aragón or in Catalonia. His son (Alfons II, 1152–1196) would be Alfonso II in Aragón, the first of a dynastic series of kings; but they remained counts of Barcelona. So in a sense the county's history continues for centuries after 1162, but by the later twelfth century people were referring to the expanded county as Catalonia, whose history may be read elsewhere.

THOMAS N. BISSON

Bibliography

Bisson, T. N. *The Medieval Crown of Aragón*. Oxford, 1986.

Hillgarth, J. N. The Spanish Kingdoms 1250–1516. 2 vols. Oxford, 1976–1978.

Historia dels Catalans. Ed. F. Soldevila. 3 vols. Barcelona, 1962–1964.

BARRIENTOS, LOPE DE

Barrientos was a Dominican friar from a noble family born at Medina del Campo in 1382; he died at Cuenca, 30 May 1469. He was educated at the University of Salamanca and entered the OP at the convent of San Andrés at Medina. By 1415 he held a chair in theology at Salamanca. In 1434 he was named preceptor to Prince Enrique by Juan II of Castile. While at court, he intervened on the king's behalf in helping sort out the many intrigues aimed at weakening the monarchy and against the policies of the king's favorite, Don Álvaro de Luna.

When the intellectual and polymath Enrique de Villena died in 1434, it was Barrientos who carried out the king's order to burn Villena's library because Villena had fallen under suspicion of sorcery. In 1438 Barrientos became bishop of Segovia, a position that he exchanged with Juan de Cervantes for the diocese of Ávila in 1441 in his efforts to bring an end to the hostilities between Juan II and Prince Enrique in order to unite the kingdom against the designs of the Infantes de Aragón. By 1445 Barrientos was instrumental in the defeat of the nobility and the Infantes de Aragón at the battle of Olmedo. That same year he became bishop of Cuenca, whose defenses he organized in 1449 to repel repeated attacks by the partisans of the Aragónese and Navarrese interests in the realm. When don Álvaro de Luna was executed at Valladolid in 1453, Barrientos became Juan II's chief political adviser. After the king's death in 1454, he was named *canciller mayor del reino* by Enrique IV. Barrientos is buried in the Hospital de Piedad at Medina del Campo.

E. MICHAEL GERLI

Bibliography

Vaquero, Q. A., et al. (eds.) *Diccionario de historia eclesiástica de España*. 4 vols. Madrid, 1972. I.

Getino, L. A. *Vida y obras de Fray Lope de Barrientos*. Salamanca, 1927.

BASQUE LANGUAGE

Basque, or Euskara, the only non–Indo-European language of western Europe, is presently spoken by approximately 800,000 people in a community of less than three million inhabitants. It is probably the oldest European language. The Basque country (170 km east to west and 60 km north to south) extends on both sides of the French-Spanish border, in the western Pyreenes, by the Bay of Biscay.

The invasions of Indo-European peoples erased most of the indigenous languages. Basque survived due to its isolation. Later on, the Romans imposed Latin as the only official language in their empire, causing the disappearance of Indo-European and Iberian languages. Basque continued to survive even after the disappearance of Latin, while Romance languages developed and took root.

The Basque language is not part of any linguistic family, yet it is not a completely isolated language, as has often been said. Basque adopted the Latin alphabet, maintaining its five vowels (*a*, *e*, *i*, *o*, and *u*). There are twenty-two single letters plus seven compound letters (*dd*, *II*, *rr*, *ts*, *tt*, *tx*, and *tz*). Basque, while keeping its structure, adapted a number of words from Latin during the presence of the latter over five hundred years in the area. The first two sentences written in Basque date back to the tenth century. They appear in the manuscript "Glosas Emilianenses" (monastery of San Millán de la Cogolla, Rioja, Spain), written in Romance language.

An outstanding feature of the Basque language is its ergative form. Its morphology could be defined as being of an "agglutinating" kind, because verb forms include subject, direct and indirect objects, and plurals through prefixes, suffixes, and infixes. From the point of view of the syntax, the construction of the relative pronoun is one of the most original parts of its grammar. The relative particle is *-n* (after a vowel, or *-en*, after a consonant), and it always appears as a suffix to the auxiliary verb followed by the noun to which it refers.

Word order is also very different from English and the Romance languages. In Basque there is usually a focus or "element inquiry" that must immediately precede the verb.

The Basque language is divided into several dialects. L. L. Bonaparte (1813–1891) was the first writer to have elaborated a map of Basque dialects. According to him, from west to east and from south to north we encounter Biscayan, Guipuzcoan, High Navarrese (northern and southern), Labourdin, Low Navarrese (western and eastern), and Souletin or Zuberoan. In historical times the area in which the language is spoken has been slowly receding, particularly in the eastern and southern areas. Through the existence of toponimic names we know that Basque was spoken in the province of La Rioja and even in the north of the province of Burgos. However, during the last twenty years the number of Basque speakers has been steadily increasing, numbering over one hundred thousand new ones between 1982 and 1992.

Many scholars have tried to prove that Basque is related to other languages, such as Iberian or Georgian. However, these attempts have shed little light on the question of the origin of the Basque language and it is very likely that this question will remain unanswered.

GORKA AULESTIA

Bibliography

Saltarelli, M. *Basque*. New York, 1988.

Towards a History of the Basque Language. Ed. J. I. Hualde, J. A. Lakarra, and R. L. Trask. Amsterdam and Philadelphia, 1995.

BASQUE PROVINCES

Euskal Herria, or the Basque country, is composed of seven provinces situated in the western Pyrenees between Spain and France. Four of these provinces (Vizcaya, Guipúzcoa, Álava, and Navarra) lie in Spain and three (Labourd, Baja Navarra, and Zuberoa) in France. Euskadi covers 20,650 square kilometers and is inhabited by almost three million people.

This region dates back to antiquity, according to remains older than the Middle Paleolithic period. Some of these remains show the presence of Cro-Magnon man in Euskal Herria. The Basques are distinctly different from the peoples of the Mediterranean and Alpine regions.

In this small area, surprising for the diversity of its landscape, there exists and is preserved today an ethnic group that speaks a very particular language and has produced a culture with a customary judicial system. The Basque language has received various titles. From the language itself comes the name *Euskara*, and from a romanic perspective, the name Vascuence is derived. A geographically isolated language, it is clearly different from all surrounding Indo-European languages. This language has been the most effective transmitter of Basque culture and is today the fundamental element for its continued survival, as the language has been the most important element in the configuration of the Basque country. Euskara, defines the Basque as *Euskaldun*, or "possessor of Euskara."

The Basque language has conserved its ancient structures, original morphology, and syntax. The structure of the verb distinguishes it from Latin and the Romance languages. Euskara's verb forms are quite complex but at the same time very logical, and they have attracted the attention of many foreign linguists.

Today, Euskara is divided into six dialects, that demonstrate the necessity of a *kione* or common united language, especially for the media (press, radio, and television), written literature, and the Basque University. The first attempts to unify Euskara started at the end of the ninteenth century but were not finished until 1968, when the linguistic normalization of Euskara began. The number of speakers of Euskara is, today, some 800,000, unequally distributed throughout the Basque territory. In general, the highest densities of Basque speakers lie in the province of Guipúzcoa, the eastern part of Vizcaya, and the north of Navarra, with a higher incidence in rural rather than urban zones.

The Basque ethnic group also possesses distinct physical characteristics, Cranial morphology and hemotypology show unique characteristics among the Basques. For example, the incidence of blood type O is quite high, type A is in relatively low proportion, and type B is almost nonexistent. The frequency of the Rh-factor is higher in Basques than in other peoples.

Concerning the judicial system, Basque law is customary, popular, and natural, emanating from the social group that created its proper order of laws in conjunction with its necessities. Conceived by an agro-pastoral population, Basque law is essentially customary. The Basque houses, called *baserriak*, were the basic cells of the Basque social organization. Each one of these housed one family, uniting the house to the extent that each family took the name of its house. The judicial system was created to perpetuate this unity, and the Basques were able to conserve their identity through the centuries, even after their integration into the Spanish and French centralist monarchies.

Since the Middle Ages, the Basques preferred to group themselves in *hermandades* (brotherhoods) and thus secured their own protective armada. In this way, the majority of them avoided the feudal system, and if they had to suffer the guardianship of a monarch or powerful lord, they were always careful to pact with them. The Basques accepted feudal sovereignty, but under the condition that the king or feudal lords swore to respect the ancient *fueros* (codes of law) and old liberties. In this way, the king or feudal lord was not more than a military chief and supreme justice in criminal matters, and the people preserved their freedom and sovereignty. Even the powerful Catholic kings of Spain swore to respect the old Basque traditions under the sacred Tree of Gernika in Vizcaya. The king of Castile was recognized only as lord of Vizcaya and not as a Basque king. If this lord did not respect the old fueros, the Basques applied the saying, "Obey, but do not fulfill." Thus, they were able to maintain their institutions despite of the invasion of foreign concepts derived from Roman Law.

Each of the Basque territories, united with the crown, possessed a series of rights (exemption from military service and taxes, etc.) that the central powers—France as much as Spain—persisted in abolishing. In this way, the French Revolution (1789) attained the administrative assimilation of the three northern provinces, just as in the south, the First Carlist War (1833–1839) caused the destruction of the old liberties and the Second Carlist War (1872–1876) established their definite loss.

At the end of the ninteenth century and as a reaction against the loss of the aforementioned fueros, the new nationalism created by Sabino de Arana y Goiri (1865–1903) presented the problem of the independence of the Basque country, which culminated in the Spanish Civil War (1936–1939). The war abolished the autonomy of the Basque government, which sought refuge in exile after the bombing of Guernica and the fall of Bilbao under the troops of Franco, Hitler, and Mussolini. Exile did not diminish Basque nationalism, which was reborn more determined than ever. In modern times it represents two-thirds of the Basque electorate of the autonomous community of Euskadi (Guipúzcoa, Vizcaya, and Álava). Although the motto *Zazpiak Bat* (seven united Basque provinces) has resounded since the end of the ninteenth century, the Basque country continues to be politically divided into three parts: Euskadi; Navarra; and the French Basque country, with its three provinces.

The political unity and independent state so desired by many Basques is still very far away, but there does exist a certain cultural unity. On both sides of the border, many Basques conserve the very clear consciousness of belonging to a common ethnic group with the same cultural task. Euskal Herria is still far from attaining a real autonomy that includes political sovereignty, but the situation—cultural as much as political—is gradually improving. For the first time, Euskal Herria has a Basque University with 47,000 students, some Basque forms of communication (press, radio, and television), an official language that gives rise to a promising literature, and an ample network of *ikastolak*, or Basque schools for children.

GORKA AULESTIA

Bibliography

Collins, R. *The Basques*. Oxford, 1986

Medhurst, K. *The Basques*. London, 1975.

Ortzi (sic). *Los vascos: síntesis de su historia*. Donostia, 1998.

BATHS

Public bathhouses in Iberia were known in Roman times, as a number of archeological remains attest. While not on the scale of those in the imperial city of Rome, the bathhouses in Hispania contained the customary pattern of chambers, including a dressing room, steam room, hot water room, tepidarium for gradual cooling, and finally a cold water pool. The medieval Muslim bath, or *hāmmam*, varied from the Roman model in that it had fewer chambers and concentrated more on perspiration as a method of cleansing. The bather disrobed, stored garments, and received bathing materials. He or she then proceeded in turn to an unheated room, a warm room, and finally a hot steam room. The patron then returned to the warm room, where epidermal waste was removed by rubbing, scraping, lathering, and washing. When the expanding Christian kingdoms pushed southward, it was almost certainly the Muslim type of bathhouse the northerners encountered. While there is some evidence of public bathing in the Christian north during the eleventh and twelfth centuries, the evidence is scattered. More indicative, the great families of municipal charters (*fueros*), begun in the later twelfth and thirteenth centuries, demonstrated a concern for the operation of the bathhouses in the conquered Muslim towns, a concern that strongly suggests unfamiliarity.

In all probability, the initial amelioration of Christian apprehension with this established aspect of Muslim social life was begun in the wake of the conquest of Toledo in 1085. Little survives in the way of written evidence to reveal this process to us, but the *baños* (baths) law of the municipal charters and codes probably reflects a century or more of synthesis and absorption. Some have postulated bathhouses as an important source of *convivencia* (conviviality) given indications

Caldarium of the baths. Built by Yūsuf I (1334–1354), Naṣṣrid dynasty. Copyright © Scala/Art Resource, NY. Alhambra, Granada, Spain.

that men and women of Islamic, Jewish, and Christian faiths utilized this very personal facility. While Muslim and Jewish bathhouses continued to operate independently of Christian regulations and usage in larger cities such as Sevilla and Valencia, in the smaller towns like Cuenca, it was not likely that more than one public baño existed. Close reading of the charters and codes for such towns indicates some variety of practice with regard to religious segregation in these facilities. In the towns of Leonese Extremadura, Jews and Muslims were restricted from the bathhouses used by Christians. The Cuenca-influenced charters allowed Jewish use only two days a week, when Christians were not to bathe in them. Aragónese charters permitted Jewish and Muslim use but on one day of the week only. The longer codes of Tortosa and Valencia contain some ambiguity on the question, but seem to have been more liberal regarding use by individuals of mixed religious background. The fueros reveal great apprehension concerning *baño* use by women, segregating them strictly from men to avoid any question of their loss of honor. Punishments for mixing religions or sexes in these bathhouses were often severe.

The later fourteenth and fifteenth centuries witnessed a decline in the usage of baños, likely the result both of growing religious tensions in Iberia and of concern for the spread of disease in the wake of the Black Death. Arguably, their history suggests as much societal segregation as it does convivencia.

JAMES POWERS

Bibliography

Powers, J. F. "Frontier Municipal Baths and Social Interaction in Thirteenth-Century Spain," *American Historical Review* 84 (1979), 649–67.

Ruiz-Moreno, A. "Los baños públicos en los fueros municipales españoles," *Cuadernos de Historia de España* 3 (1945), 152–57.

BAZA, SIEGE OF

In the final period of the Nazarí (Naṣrid) kingdom, Baza was besieged by King Fernando the Catholic in the spring of 1489, and the town capitulated on 4 December 1489.

In connection with this historical event, the *romance* (ballad) "Sobre Baça estava el Rey . . ." was written. It was harmonized by the musicians of the Royal Chapel, and both text and musical notations have been preserved in the *Cancionero musical de Palacio* (ed. J. Romeu Figueras, Barcelona, 1965). The extant version is brief (26 octosyllabic verses); it may have been abridged for musical performance. The romance is in this version a characteristic sample of the primitive style of frontier ballads due to its use of rhetorical devices such as the anaphora, the enumeration, and the formula. The ballad does not relate the siege. Rather, it tells about the king looking at his own camp, the nearby orchards, and the walls surrounding the town. A Moor begs him to lift the siege, and thus the poem ends with an abrupt closure. The tense situation is handled in a way that relates to the point of view of the Moors, and it hardly corresponds to the actual development of events, since victory was achieved by the Christians. This ballad did not survive in oral tradition, except for a possible contamination detected in a few verses of the romance "El Mostadí" (see Armistead). Baza will be mentioned in some of the "new" or artistic Moorish ballads (almost always in ballads with an A–A rhyme scheme). There are two late ballads on the siege of Baza. "¡Arriba, gritaban todos . . ." (*Romancero General*, Madrid, 1947) is mainly fictional. Gabriel Lobo Lasso de la Vega is the author of "Confuso está y atajado . . ." (*Romancero y tragedias*, Alcalá de Henares, 1587), which has no connection with the frontier ballad mentioned above.

FRANCISCO LÓPEZ ESTRADA

Bibliography

Armistead, S. G. *El romancero judeo-español en el Archivo Menéndez Pidal*. Madrid, 1978.

"Cancionero Musical," facsimile ed. In R. Menéndez Pidal, *Estudios sobre el Romancero*. Madrid, 1973.

Menéndez Pidal, R. *Romancero hispánico*. 2 vols. Madrid, 1953.

BÉARN-ARAGÓN

It is well known that the kings of Aragón had dreamed of founding a vast state straddling the Pyrenees. However, historians often forget that such a state comprised, for almost two centuries, an area situated on the Atlantic side of the northern Pyrenees—the viscounty of Béarn. It was ruled from the middle of the twelfth century to the end of the thirteenth by a Catalan family from the north of Barcelona, the Moncade. That the viscounty of Béarn, born in the ninth and tenth centuries within the framework of the duchy of Gascony, left its influence to enter the orbit of the Aragón is due mainly to the Reconquest, the recapture of the valley of the Ebro River from the Moors by the Christians. Indeed, until the end of of the eleventh century Huesca, only fifty miles from Béarn, was a Muslim city. Only the small primitive kingdom of Aragón around Jaca stood between Béarn and the Moors. As a result, the viscounts of Béarn often found themselves fighting south of the Pyrenees on the Aragón side. They fought in all the important battles in the valley of the Ebro from the capture of Huesca (1096) to that of Palma de Mallorca (1229). One of the greatest victories was the capture of Zaragoza in 1118, thanks to the combined efforts of Alfonso I (el Batallador) of Aragón and the viscount of Béarn, Gaston IV the Crusader. However, after the Reconquest had been successfully concluded and Aragón had been united with Catalonia, the relationship between Béarn and Aragón changed: what had been an alliance of equals turned into a master-vassal relationship. Béarn had fallen to a woman who was forced to marry a Moncade; thereafter, the viscounts of Béarn had to pay homage to the kings of Aragón, and they remained their vassals even after the Aragónese had been defeated at Muret (1214). This political situation had long-lasting legal consequences. While under the control of Aragón, Béarn was granted a variety of complex charters of customs—directly modeled on the Spanish *fueros* (codes of law), and particularly those of Aragón—that were called the Fors of Béarn. At the end of the thirteenth century Béarn returned to the Gascony, which had itself passed under the control of the kings of England. Though Béarn had turned its back on Aragón, the two retained a close relationship in the fourteenth and fifteenth centuries. First, the viscounts of Béarn had also become counts of Foix (1290) and, as such, owned lands for which they owed allegiance to Catalonia; second, Béarnese merchants continued to trade on both sides of the Pyrenees.

PIERRE TUCOO-CHALA

Bibliography

Bordenave, N. de. *Histoire de Béarn et Navarre*. Paris, 1873.
Ubieto Arteta, A. *Historia de Aragón: la formación territorial*. Zaragoza, 1981.

BÉARN-NAVARRE

Lying on either side of the Pyrénees, the principalty of Béarn and the kingdom of Navarre shared a common border along the valleys of Baretous and Roncal. Thanks to their close links, over the course of time they developed a kind of good-neighbor diplomacy: the sanction in case of infringement of the treaties consisted of the guilty party paying a fine. This ritual is still enacted every year at the Pass of Pierre Saint-Martin. From the eleventh century, when they crossed into Navarre along the pilgrimage routes to Santiago, Béarnese merchants traded actively in Navarre; their activity reached its height in the fourteenth and fifteenth centuries. Thanks to their neutrality during the Hundred Years' War, they traded between Bayonne (where English goods were unloaded) and Pamplona and Tudela in Navarre. These routes also brought with them artistic influences, particularly after close relations had developed between the court of Béarn, at Orthez, and the court of Navarre. From the fourteenth century, when the viscounty of Béarn had become a sovereign principalty, the links with Navarre grew closer. Gaston III Fébus (1343–1391) had married Agnes, the sister of Charles II of Navarre. After cooperating for a number of years, however, the two brothers-in-law came into conflict with each other; Gaston repudiated Agnes and then tragically killed his own son at the court of Orthez.

The policy of union between Béarn and Navarre was resumed in the fifteenth century when economic relations between the two countries were strengthened by the founding of trading companies controlled by merchants from Béarn who had settled south of the Pyrenees and were supplying the court at Pamplona. The first marriage to take place between the two dynasties at the beginning of the fifteenth century failed to reached the desired conclusion: Jean of Foix Béarn and the infanta of Navarre died childless. In the end, Béarn fulfilled its ambition as the result of an incredibly complex crisis of succession that caused a civil war. The Viscount of Béarn, Gaston IV (1436–1470), married Eleonora, the daughter of Juan II, king of Aragón and Navarre. In a treaty signed at Barcelona, Juan II granted the right of succession of Navarre to Eleonora, to the detriment of her elder brother Don Carlos. As a result, part of Navarre rose up and Gaston IV died at Roncesvalles on his way to help his wife contain the rebellion. Nevertheless, the heirs of Eleonora and Gaston of Béarn retained the crown of Navarre. Thus, at the time when Castille and Aragón had united to form a single kingdom, another state, Béarn-Navarre, was being formed on both sides of the Pyrenees with control of the passes of Roncesvalles and Somport. However, Castillan pressure at the beginning of the sixteenth century put an end to the union of Béarn and Navarre. Thereafter, the western Pyrenees became a mere frontier between France and Spain.

PIERRE TUCOO-CHALA

Bibliography

Bordenave, N. *Histoire de Béarn et Navarre*. Paris, 1873.
Ubieto Arteta, A. *Historia de Aragón: la formacion territorial*. Zaragoza, 1981.

BEATRIZ OF SWABIA

See ALFONSO X, EL SABIO, KING OF CASTILE; FERNANDO III, KING OF CASTILE AND LEÓN

BEATRIZ

Wife of Afonso III (1210–1279), King of Portugal (r. 1248–1279). Beatriz was the illegitimate daughter of Alfonso X of Castile and León "the Wise," and María Guillén de Guzmán. The conditions of Beatriz's marriage were closely linked to the integration of the southern region of Algarve, into what was going to become part of the territory of Portugal. Afonso was a second son and, at the age of eighteenth, he left with his sister Leonor for Denmark, where she became the wife of Waldemar III. When the king died (1233), he moved to the French court of Louis VIII. Around 1238 he married Mathilde or Mahaut, Countess of Boulogne. Meanwhile, his brother Sancho II was deposed by the Church and Afonso was selected to be his successor. Sancho II had to interrupt his campaign against the Moors in the Algarve, and one of the main tasks of Afonso was to pursue the Reconquest. But Alfonso X, moved by a hegemonic ambition, wanted to expand his borders, and previous agreements with Sancho II were soon to be broken. Yet, as Alfonso X began to feel hard pressed on the borders of Aragón and Valencia, he sought a conciliation with Afonso III; Alfonso X arranged his marriage to Beatriz. Although she was too young and Afonso was still married, the contract was signed and sealed in 1253. It stipulated that before a son born out of that union reached the age of seven Alfonso X would be the beneficiary of those territories. This complex situation of bigamy raised serious problems, as Countess Mathilde complained to Pope Alexander IV, whose unsuccessful efforts to dissolve the marriage led him to excommunicate Afonso III. Mathilde's death in 1258 broke the impasse. Beatriz gave birth to twelve children, including Dinis, heir to the Portuguese throne.

Luis Rebelo

Bibliography

Herculano, A. *História de Portugal: Desde o começo da monarquia até o fim do reinado de Afonso III*. Lisbon, 1980.

Veríssimo, Serréo, J. *História de Portugal*. Lisbon, 1979. 129–40.

BEATUS OF LIÉBANA

Participant in the adoptionist controversy, commentator on the Apocalypse; very little is known about his life beyond his participation in the former. He appears to have been a priest or a monk in Liébana (Cantabria). In 785 he coauthored (with Eterius, who would later become bishop of Osma) a letter to Elipandus, the metropolitan of Toledo, that denounced the latter's belief that Christ had adopted his human nature at the time of the Incarnation. This letter was prompted by one written a short time before by Elipandus to an abbot Fidelis, asking him to reprimand Beatus and Eterius for an earlier challenge to his views on the Incarnation. At stake, at least from Elipandus' perspective, was not only doctrinal accuracy but the continued authority of the metropolitan see of Toledo over the greater Spanish church. Beatus was also attacked in two subsequent letters from the bishops of Spain to the bishops of Gaul and to Charlemagne, respectively, expressing their support for the adoptionist position. Charlemagne responded by convening the Council of Frankfurt in 794, at which the assembled bishops condemned adoptionism as heresy.

Beatus is better known today as the author of a commentary on the Apocalypse, though the evidence supporting this attribution is circumstantial. The first version of the commentary was finished in 776, with subsequent editions in 784 and 786. The commentary is little more than a compilation of the opinions of previous authorities on the subject, though the names of the sources from which the author drew reveal something of the range of materials available to a scholar in the early period of the Asturian monarchy. The conservatism of the author is interesting in light

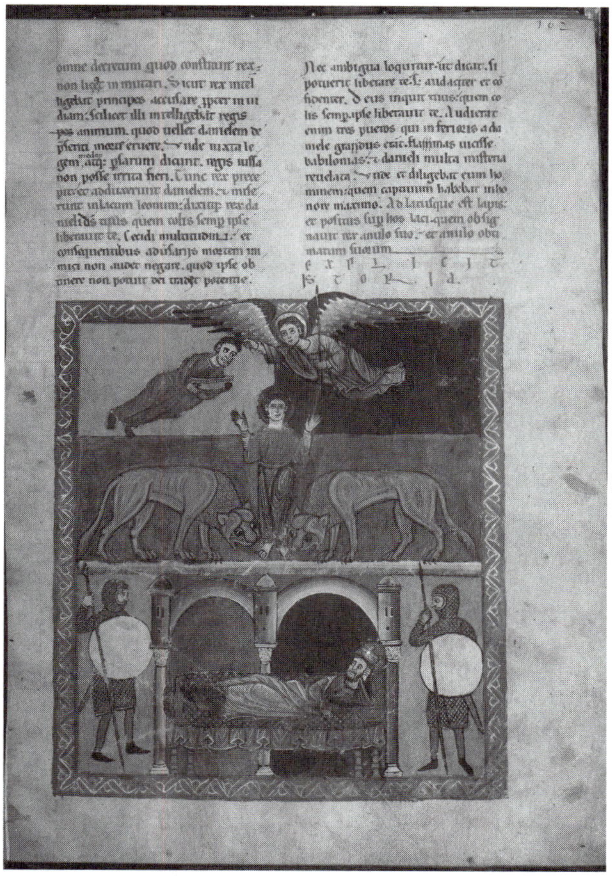

Beatus de Liébana (8th c.). Daniel in the lion's den, to whom Habakuk, lifted by an angel, is bringing food. Below, King Darius lying wakeful on his bed, is guarded by two soldiers. From Commentary on the Apocalypse, ca. 1220. Copyright © The Pierpont Morgan Library/Art Resource, NY. The Pierpont Morgan Library, New York, N.Y., U.S.A.

of the fact that he was writing more than fifty years after the Muslim invasion and thus was in a position to cast the invaders in an apocalyptic role, if he had been so inclined. The primary significance of the commentary lies not in the text but in the illuminations that accompany it in the many manuscripts of the work that have survived from the tenth through the twelfth centuries. These so-called "Beatos" contain some of the most impressive examples of the so-called Mozarabic artistic style.

Kenneth B. Wolf

Bibliography

"Beati et Eterii Adversus Elipandum." *Corpus Christianorum* 59 (1984), 320–22.

Colbert, E. "The Martyrs of Córdoba (850–859): A Study of the Sources." Ph.D. diss., Catholic University of America. Washington, D.C., 1962.

Collins, R. *The Arab Conquest of Spain, 710–797*. Oxford, 1989.
Saunders, H. (ed.) *Beati in Apocalypsim libri duodecim*. Rome, 1930.

BEHETRÍAS

In the fluid rural world of medieval northern Castile, the peculiar conditions of the Reconquest and of the early settlement of the land led to the emergence of distinctive forms of dependence and ties between peasant and lord. One of these bonds of reciprocity was the institution known as *behetría*. The behetrías have received a great deal of attention from Castilian institutional historians and have been the source of endless historiographical debates. In the simplest terms, the men and women of behetrías (*benefactoria*) had the right to choose their lords. They did this either from sea to sea (*de mar a mar*), that is, from any lord in the land—or, more often in the late Middle Ages, from a specific family, the so-called *behetrías de linaje* (of a specific lineage). According to Sánchez Albornoz, in theory the men and women of behetrías could change their lords as many as seven times in one day if the arrangements proved to be unsatisfactory. In reality, there is not yet any documentary evidence that these men and women could really exercise their theoretical right to change lords in the late Middle Ages.

The origins of these special agreements probably went back to the early centuries of the repopulation of the land, when the dispersion of agricultural settlements and the poverty of demographic resources in the northernmost part of Castile (the result of the occupation of the Duero River valley in the tenth and eleventh centuries) allowed these free peasants to enter into advantageous pacts of commendation (*encomendación*) with the lords in the region. These ties were hereditary, and by the mid-fourteenth century we find in the *Libro becerro de behetrías*—a census of royal, ecclesiastical and seignorial rights in most of the area north of the Duero River compiled in 1351—a large number of people of behetrías holding on, at least in theory, to the same privileges gained by their ancestors four centuries earlier. Free, yet owing certain seignorial dues to their lords, these men and women occupied a transitional stage between the free landholding peasants working royal lands and those free peasants who toiled in seignorial or monastic holdings under heavier fiscal and, at times, even semi-servile conditions. In fact, however, these distinctions often did not make a great deal of difference. As was the case in the lands held by the church, by noblemen, or by the crown, what the men and women of behetrías owed their lords changed from place to place and depended on local conditions. The late Middle Ages saw a progressive deterioration in the rights of the people of behetrías, to the point where there was little difference between them and those peasants holding land from secular lords, the so-called *solariegos*.

Although the figures vary from study to study, the number of behetrías listed in the *Libro becerro* ranges from 418 to 628 villages out of the about 2,400 places listed in the census. A good number of other villages were under mixed lordships: seignorial, royal, ecclesiastical. Regardless of the exact number of behetrías, it is clear that this type of arrangement between lord and peasant was of considerable importance as a pattern for relations between lord and peasant and between peasants and the land.

TEÓFILO RUIZ

Bibliography

Martínez Díez, G. (ed.) *Libro Becerro de Behetrías. Estudio y Texto Crítico*. 3 vols. León, 1981.
Sánchez Albornoz, C. "Las behetrías; La encomendación en Asturias, León y Castilla," *Anuario de historia del derecho español*, 1 (1924), 158–336.

BEHETRÍA DE LINAGE *See* BEHETRÍA

BELCHITE, CONFRATERNITY OF

Belchite, like Zaragoza, was reconquered from the Muslims in 1118. It was strategically placed south of the new capital, and in 1122 Alfonso I of Aragón made it the headquarters of a military confraternity, dedicated to permanent war against the infidel. Its privileges were confirmed in 1136, but it disappeared soon afterward. The confraternity was remarkable in possessing features characteristic both of a Christian military order and of an Islamic frontier *ribāt* (monastic fortress). Those who came to Belchite to fight in the service of Christ for the rest of their lives were compared to men entering the life of a monk or a hermit. But just as much attention was given to those who served for a term; one year's service earned the same remission of sins granted to those who marched to Jerusalem. One month's service was the equivalent of fasting on Fridays for a whole year. Any time spent fighting at Belchite earned double the merit to be gained for the same period spent on a pilgrimage. Moreover, propaganda on Belchite's behalf was as meritorious as service there—a principle long applied to the ribāt but only taken up into crusading ideology after 1122.

Belchite's combination of the Christian concept of a lifelong monastic vocation with the Islamic notion of spiritually meritorious stints of service in a ribāt constitutes firm evidence of Muslim influence on the emerging military orders. Consequently, the knights serving for a term in the temple were probably more important in the earliest days of that Order (1119–1128) than its subsequent rule suggests. Had Belchite survived to become a full-fledged religious house, it too would have had to confine its knights serving for a term to a marginal role, since a temporary vocation was alien to Christian monasticism. In the event, the complications created by Alfonso I's will greatly aided the confraternity's demise.

ELENA LOURIE

Bibliography

Rassow, P. "La cofradía de Belchite," *Anuario de Historia de España* 3 (1946), 220–26.

Lourie, E. "The Confraterity of Belchite, the *Ribāt* and the Temple," *Viator* 13 (1982), 159–176

BELTRÁN DE LA CUEVA

Beltrán de la Cueva owed his rapid political and social advancement to the fact that he was one of the favorites of Enrique IV of Castile. Shortly after joining the court in 1455, he was appointed *camarero mayor*, and then subsequently became a lord of Jimena, Count of Ledesma, master of the military order of Santiago (a position he was forced to give up in 1464), and Duke of Alburquerque. His rapid promotion provoked enormous hostility, especially among other competitors for the royal favor such as the marquis of Villena, Juan Pacheco. Married to a daughter of the second marquis of Santillana, rumor nevertheless associated his name with several scabrous sexual relationships, all of which are alluded to in the satirical verses of the contemporary *Coplas del Provincial*. It was alleged, for example, that he was not only the king's homosexual lover, but also the lover of the queen, Juana of Portugal.

Such allegations were to acquire enormous political importance in the context of the disputed succession to the throne after Enrique IV's death in 1474. For if the Infanta Juana was not the king's daughter but the illegitimate fruit of an adulterous relationship between Beltrán de la Cueva and the queen, then the succession could rightfully be claimed by Isabel the Catholic. The Infanta Juana, thus nicknamed "la Beltraneja," ended her days in exile in a convent in Portugal, and her putative father loyally served the Catholic Monarchs until his death in 1492.

ANGUS MACKAY

Bibliography

Bleiberg, G. (ed.) *Diccionario de Historia de España*. 3 vols. 2d ed. Madrid, 1968–69.

Rodríguez Puertolas, J. P. *Poesia de protesta en la Edad Media castellana*. Madrid, 1968.

BENEDICT XIII, ANTIPOPE

Pedro Martínez de Luna, a close relative of the Aragónese royal family, was elected Pope Benedict XIII in 1394 on the death of the Avignon antipope Clement VII in an attempt to settle the Great Schism that had divided the western Church since 1378. Instead of resolution, however, Benedict's papacy prolonged the schism and intensified the political polarization of western Europe.

Born in Illueca (Zaragoza) in 1328 or 1329, Martínez de Luna studied, obtained his doctorate, and taught canon law at Montpellier. He returned to Spain to serve as canon of Cuenca, archdeacon of the cathedral in Zaragoza, and provost of the cathedral in Valencia before joining the papal curia in Avignon in 1375; he was made cardinal deacon of Santa Maria in Cosmedin by Pope Gregory XI (papacy 1370–1378). Martinez de Luna voted for Urban VI (papacy 1378–1389) in the tumultuous papal elections of 1378, but later he concluded that the violent turmoil of the Romans prejudiced the election and rendered it invalid, and he threw his support instead to the French antipope Clement VII (papacy 1378–1394). The presence of the two popes—one in Rome and one in Avignon—divided the Church and initiated the Great Schism (1378–1422).

In 1378 Martínez de Luna was sent to Spain as papal legate, and secured for Clement VII political support from the Aragónese and Navarrese kings. His success in Spain prompted Clement to send Martínez de Luna as legate to Scotland, Ireland, England, France, and the Low Countries. It was in this capacity, while at a meeting at the University of Paris in search of solutions to the schism, that Martínez de Luna first advocated the *via cessionis*, whereby both rival popes would renounce the papal office so that a new pope could be elected.

When Clement VII died in 1394, Martínez de Luna was seen as the logical successor, someone who could be trusted to step down peacefully when the time came. He was anointed as Pope Benedict XIII despite the continued existence of the Roman Pope Boniface IX (papacy 1389–1404). Immediately after his election, however, Benedict XIII denouced the oath he had taken to abdicate and proposed a new solution to the schism, the *via declarationis justiciae*, or negotiated settlement. Fervent in his belief in his legitimacy as pope, obstinate in his refusal to compromise, and skillful in his ability to outmaneuver opponents, Benedict managed to prolong the frustrating stalemate for twenty-three years and to tarnish even further the reputation of the church.

Ecclesiastical affairs were thrown into disarray as each pope created new bishops and cardinals; European rulers took sides in the controversy prompting each pope to declare invalid all sacraments performed in rival kingdoms. England, the Roman Empire, and most of the Roman curia supported Boniface; France, Aragón, and Wales took Benedict's side. In 1398, the French, attempting to force a resolution in the matter, withdrew their obedience to Benedict, thus depriving him of substantial ecclesiastical revenues. Benedict's greatest support came from the Aragónese king Martin the Humane (r. 1396–1410) who literally saved Benedict from a French army that occupied Avignon in 1398. Benedict was nothing if not tenacious. He took refuge in Châteaurenard; by 1403, not only had he made peace with the French, but he had gained Castilian support as well.

Benedict made tentative moves toward a negotiated settlement in 1403, but Boniface IX died a year later and again the *via cessionis* was proposed as a means of settling the schism. The cardinals ignored Benedict's claims and elected Innocent VII (1404–1406) and later, Gregory XII (1406–1415), who pledged to work with Benedict to end the schism, but by then all attempts at negotiation were unsuccessful.

A general council was summoned at Pisa (1409), which both Benedict and Gregory refused to attend; they were condemned and deposed and a new pope, Alexander V (papacy 1409–1410), was elected. Benedict fled to Barcelona, where he maintained his legitimacy despite a second deposion in 1417 by the Council of Constance. He died in 1423 at Peñíscola, still styling himself as Pope Benedict XIII.

THERESA EARENFIGHT

Bibliography

Glasfurd, A. *The Antipope: Peter de Luna, 1342–1423*. London, 1965.

Puig y Puig, S. *Pedro de Luna, último Papa de Aviñón*. Barcelona, 1920.

Sesma Muñoz, J. Angel, J. A. Parrilla, J. A. Muñoz, and C. Caride. *Benedicto XIII: La vida y el tiempo del Papa Luna*. Zaragoza, 1987.

BENEDICTINE MONKS *See* MONASTICISM; RELIGIOUS ORDERS

BENJAMIN OF TUDELA

Benjamin of Tudela was a Jewish merchant renowned for his travels through various countries from about 1160 to about 1172, when he returned to Spain, dying shortly thereafter. He left a book in Hebrew (or more correctly his notes, which were turned into a book by an anonymous hand) concerning his travels, which became famous and in translation was one of the most widely read travel accounts of all time.

Muslim and Jewish travelers in the Mediterranean, and particularly from Spain, were numerous, and we have accounts of such voyages from many (among Jews, the most famous, besides Benjamin, were Ibrahīm ibn Yaʿqūb of the tenth century and Judah al-Harīzī of the thirteenth). Benjamin's account is particularly valuable because of its details on commerce, agriculture, manufacture, and so on, and for the information it gives concerning remote and exotic areas of the world (including China). True, he did not personally reach these lands, but at least some of the information he received from secondhand reports is of value. His own personal travels were limited to the coast of Provence; Italy; the Greek isles; Constantinople and Asia Minor; Syria and Mesopotamia (nearly to India); Palestine, and Egypt.

His primary goals were to investigate and report on commerce and agriculture and to report on the presence and condition of Jews in various parts of the world, as well as to visit "holy sites." His estimates of Jewish populations in various regions and towns are generally substantiated by other sources, and his work is an important source for Jewish history. For general history there is also much of great value, including his listing of some thirty Christian nations which had merchants in Alexandria, and certainly his information on agriculture and technology.

The first Hebrew edition appeared in 1543, based on a faulty manuscript, and was copied in subsequent editions and Latin and early English translations, in spite of the more accurate edition of 1556, which subsequently appeared. The edition, with English translation, of Asher is based on a much better manuscript reading. Most important are the extensive notes (English) in the second volume. Adler's edition, finally, is based on the most accurate extant manuscript. The Spanish Hebraist Benito Arias Montano made the first translation, in Latin (1575), from which Purchas's *Pilgrims* English translation and others in French were made. A second Latin translation by Constantin l'Empereur appeared in 1633. Among more modern translations, that in Spanish by the Hebraist Igancio González Llubera, *Viajes de Benjamín de Tudela* (Madrid, 1918), is of importance for its erudite notes and critical apparatus. The modern Spanish translation by Magdalena is generally excellent, but unfortunately he did not utilize the notes in Asher and thus there are several errors.

NORMAN ROTH

Bibliography

The Itinerary of Benjamin of Tudela. Ed. and trans. M. N. Adler. London, 1907; reprt. 1964.

The Itinerary of Benjamin of Tudela. Trans. A. Asher. 2 vols. London and Berlin, 1840.

Libro de Viajes de Benjamín de Tudela. Trans. J. R. Magdalena Nom de Déu. Barcelona, 1982.

BERBERS

An aboriginal people of northern Africa, they inhabit the area between the Sahara Desert and the Mediterranean Sea, from Egypt to the Atlantic coast and a substantial part of the population of present-day Libya, Algeria, and Morocco. The nomadic Tuareg distinguish themselves from other Berbers who live in villages and are loosely organized into tribes. Their native languages are classified as Hamitic, though many speak Arabic, the language of their religion, Sunni Islam. The Berbers were some of the earliest peoples to be Islamicized. Until their conquest by Muslim Arabs, many of them were Christians. Throughout their history, despite their shared religion, the Berbers have clashed with Arabs and risen up against them. At the beginning of the eighth century, they formed the rank and file of the Arab armies that conquered the Iberian Peninsula, which were generally directed by Arabs of Syrian or Arabian origin who fashioned themselves as elite and apart.

From the very beginning of the conquest of al-Andalus, the Berbers expressed their discontent, feeling that their just share of power and the spoils had been withheld from them. As a result, they often rebelled against the government, with whom they were frequently at odds. From the end of the ninth century on many were brought over to Iberia from North Africa by the caliphate to serve in its armies and to fill posts in the government. In this way, they later became a major presence in the civic life of al-Andalus in the eleventh century, influencing public affairs and the course of war and peace. In the years following the death of Al-Manṣūr, marked by political confusion and strife, the Berbers of al-Andalus succeeded in having one of their own briefly become caliph. At that point, they controlled all the territory from the northen frontier with the Christians to the Mediterranean in the south. During the reign of the tawā'if there were also small Berber kingdoms such as Albarracín in the lower Aragón ruled by the Razīn. Historically, however, the most important Berber clans proved to be the Dhū-l-Nūn of Toledo, later of Valencia, the Al-Afṭas of Badajoz, and the Zīrids of Granada. The mother of the first Umayyad ruler of al-Andalus, ʿAbd al-Raḥmān I, was a Berber.

Berber Tā'ifa Kings (1010–1094).

- The Dhū-l-Nūn of Toledo (1016–1085)
  - Ismāʿīl (1016–1043)
  - Yaḥyā (1043–1075)
  - Yaḥyā "El Nieto" (1075–1085)
- The Al-Afṭas of Badajoz (1022–1094)
  - ʿAbdallah (1022–1045)
  - Muḥammad (1045–1068)
  - Yaḥyā (1068)
  - ʿUmar (1068–1094)
- The Zīrids of Granada (1010–1090)
  - Zawi (1010–1018)
  - Maksan Habus (1018–1037)
  - Badis (1037–1073)
  - ʿAbdallah (1073–1093)

E. Michael Gerli

Bibliography

Chejne, A. G. *Muslim Spain: Its History and Culture*. Minneapolis, Minn., 1974.

Kennedy, H. *The Armies of the Caliphs: Military and Society in the Early Islamic State*. New York, 2001.

BERCEO, GONZALO DE

The first Castilian poet to identify himself by name, Gonzalo de Berceo (1196?–1264?) is considered by many to be the master of *cuaderna vía*. He was educated at the Benedictine monastery in San Millán (he reminds us of this in *Vida de San Millán*, is listed as a deacon in a document dating from 1221, and registered as a secular priest in Berceo and notary to Abbot Juan Sánchez in later manuscripts. Dutton suggests that, given his profession and his literary background, he was probably trained at the Estudio General at Palencia between 1221 and 1228.

Dutton and Kurlat de Weber have established the following chronology for Berceo's works:

1. *Vida de San Millán*
2. *Vida de Santo Domingo de Silos*
3. *Sacrificio de la Misa*
4. *Duelo que fizo la Virgen*
5. *Himnos*
6. *Loores de Nuestra Señora*
7. *Signos del Juicio Final*
8. *Milagros de Nuestra Señora*
9. *Vida de Santa Oria*
10. *Martirio de San Lorenzo*

Additionally, two lost works (*Historia de Valvanera, Traslación de los Mártires de Arlanza*) have been attributed to him. Berceo's poetry may be divided into three categories: hagiography (*San Millán, Santo Do-*

mingo, *Santa Oria*, *San Lorenzo*), Marian works (*Loores*, *Duelo*, *Milagros*), and liturgical/doctrinal works (*Sacrificio*, *Himnos*, *Signos*)

Dutton argues convincingly that, in addition to the two purposes traditionally ascribed to Berceo's works (instruction and entertainment), the hagiographic materials were designed to propagate the legends of saints related to San Millán in order to bolster the prosperity of the monastery, which had declined due to the rise of new pilgrimage centers. This goal is clearly reflected in Berceo's first work, dedicated to the patron saint of his monastery. *San Millán* derives from various sources (the *Vita Beati Emiliani* of Braulio, the writings of the monk Fernandus including the forged *Votos de San Millán*) and it follows the tripartite structure of a saint's life (biography, miracles performed in life, posthumous miracles). Berceo introduces the propagandistic element at the outset, promising his public that it will be happy to pay the tribute due to the monastery after hearing the life of San Millán (st. 2 cd). The climax of the poem (st. 362–481) recounts the origin of the tithe, justifies its continuance, and instructs the debtor towns (many of which he names) to pay the tribute owed to the saint for his miraculous intervention in battle.

Santo Domingo, based on the late eleventh-century *Vita Beati Dominici* by Grimaldus, narrates the life of another local saint. Once a hermit in San Millán de Suso as well as a monk and prior of its monastery, the saint became abbot of the monastery at Silos, which later (1190) signed a pact of mutual help and cooperation with San Millán; the renewal of this agreement in 1236 may have been the occasion for the composition of *Santo Domingo*. While there is no request for tributes such as that in *San Millán*, Berceo nonetheless reveals his desire to attract pilgrims to Silos by urging those who wish to know more of the saint's miracles to go to that monastery (st. 385–386).

Santa Oria, composed in his old age (st. 2 c), deals with a recluse unknown outside La Rioja but closely associated with San Millán de Suso; indeed, the poet gives directions to the saint's tomb near the monastery (st. 180–182). The most lyrical and allegorical of the hagiographic works, *Santa Oria* relates not the saint's miracles but three heavenly visions. While Berceo indicates that his poem is based on a narrative by Oria's confessor Muño, no source has yet been identified. Although most critics accept the theory of a lost eleventh-century *Vita Beatae Aureae*, Walsh, noting differences from the other hagiographic works, argues that *Santa Oria* draws heavily on otherworld literature as well as saints' legends and that it is primarily Berceo's own creation.

San Lorenzo, Berceo's only incomplete work, follows the structure of a *passio* rather than a *vita*. The poem breaks off in the middle of St. Lawrence's prayer during his martyrdom, suggesting that it was interrupted by the poet's own death. Dutton contends that there was a cult to the saint at San Millán related to a hermitage on nearby Pico de San Lorenzo, and he proposes that the missing portion would have made clear the connection between the monastery and the hermitage. Although the source is unknown, Pompilio Tesauro identifies the *Passio Polychroni* as the closest model.

Dutton believes that the Marian poems, like the saints' lives, are part of Berceo's propagandistic work, arguing that they do not reflect devotion to a universal figure of the Virgin but to the cult of Our Lady of March established in the tenth century at San Millán de Yuso. Dutton thinks that the Marian works, unlike the hagiographic poems, were not meant to attract pilgrims but to instruct and entertain them once they had arrived.

Some scholars have suggested that *Duelo*, because of its dramatic nature, is based on a lost French mystery or a Latin liturgical drama. Nonetheless, the most probable source of *Duelo* (a narrative of the Easter vigil of the Virgin as she tells her sorrows to St. Bernard of Clairvaux) is an apocryphal sermon of St. Bernard similar to the one found in Migne's *Patrologia latina*. The poem contains a song (*¡Eya velar!*) of the Jewish sentries ordered to guard the sepulchre. This early example of Castilian lyric, which is not composed in *cuaderna vía*, has been the subject of some debate: convinced that the verses are misordered, several scholars have tried to reconstruct the song based on parallel structure; others have rejected this reordering, arguing that the canticle is an imitation of a liturgical chant and that confusion may be eliminated if the stanzas are divided into antiphonal parts.

The content of *Loores* is diverse: lyrical exaltations of the Virgin at the beginning and end of the poem enclose a brief narrative of the life of Jesus as well as of various events from the Old and New Testaments. No source has been identified for the poem, and it seems likely that it is based on Berceo's knowledge of the Bible.

The source of *Milagros* is a lost collection of *miracula* similar to Royal Library of Copenhagen MS Thott 128. Berceo uses twenty four of the twenty eight miracles found there, adding one ("La iglesia robada") which occurs in Spain and may derive from oral traditions. The miracles fall into three categories (reward and punishment, forgiveness, conversion or spiritual crisis), and have as their premise devotion to the Virgin. The allegorical introduction, apparently an original composition based on common motifs, ties together the twenty-five miracles. As Michael Gerli confirms, the introduction traces the fall and salvation of mankind, while the miracles narrate the fall and salvation of individuals. Thus the introduction and miracles illustrate the redemptive role of the Virgin: through Her, original sin (introduction) and actual sin (miracles) are forgiven.

The first of the liturgical-doctrinal works, *Sacrificio*, is, with the exception of *Milagros*, Berceo's most allegorical poem. Dutton identifies the source of this poem as National Library of Madrid manuscript 298, which is a commentary on the mass solidly within the exegetic tradition. The three *Himnos*, each seven strophes long, are vernacular translations of *Veni Creator Spiritus*, *Ave Maris Stella*, and *Christe, qui lux est et dies*. *Signos*, a sermon in verse, treats the common medieval theme of the fifteen signs of the Apocalypse. The first twenty two strophes derive from a Latin poem in *cuaderna vía* by St. Jerónimo; the source of the remaining fifty five strophes is unknown, but Dutton suggests that they may be attributed to an extended version of the Latin poem used by Berceo.

Once portrayed in literary histories as a simple country priest, Berceo is now viewed as an educated and complex individual who, desiring to promote his monastery, skillfully transforms Latin texts (most of these of special interest to San Millán) into vernacular poetry intended for oral presentation. In order to reach a rural public accustomed to the *cantares*, Berceo uses rustic imagery and appropriates many techniques of the *juglar*'s (minstrel's) art. This strategy may be seen clearly in *San Millán* where he not only uses juglaresque formulae and epithets but portrays the saint as both a divine peasant and an epic hero; and, although Berceo occasionally criticizes juglares, he refers to himself in *Santo Domingo* as God's juglar and to his poem as a *gesta* (compilation of deeds).

JANE E. CONNOLLY

Bibliography

Artiles, J. *Los recursos literarios de Berceo*. Madrid, 1964.

Dutton, B. (ed.) *Gonzalo de Berceo: Obras Completas I–V*. London, 1967–1981.

Gariano, C. *Análisis estilístico de los "Milagros de Nuestra Señora" de Berceo*. Madrid, 1965.

Gerli, E. M. "La tipología bíblica y la introducción a los *Milagros de Nuestra Señora*." *Bulletin of Hispanic Studies* 62 (1985), 7–14.

Tesauro, P. (ed.) *Gonzalo de Berceo: "Martirio de San Lorenzo*." Romanica Neapolitana VI. Naples, 1971.

Walsh, J. K. "The Other World in Berceo's *Vida de Santa Oria*." In *Hispanic Studies in Honor of Alan D. Deyermond: A North American Tribute*. Ed. J. S. Miletich. Madison, Wisc., 1986. 291–307.

Kurlat de Weber, F. "Notas para la cronología y composición de las vidas de santos de Berceo." *Nueva Revista de Filología Hispánica* 15 (1961), 113–30.

BERENGUELA

Berenguela (1180–1246) was the firstborn child of Alfonso VIII and Eleanor of England. After the death in 1181 of a son, Sancho, and the subsequent births of more daughters, Alfonso VIII proclaimed Berenguela his heir at the *curía* at San Esteban de Gormaz in 1187. She was betrothed to Conrad, son of Frederick Barbarossa, at the curía of Carrión in 1188. There Alfonso VIII knighted Conrad and recognized Berenguela and Conrad as his heirs in the absence of male offspring. But in November 1189 a son, Fernando, was born to Alfonso and Eleanor. The birth of Fernando quashed Conrad's aspirations to the throne of Castile, and his betrothal to Berenguela was annulled.

Berenguela married Alfonso IX of León (1188–1230) in Valladolid in 1197. Her parents and Alfonso IX agreed to the match in order to end a state of war that had existed between Castile and León since Alfonso VIII's defeat at Alarcos in 1195. One of the issues in the peace negotiations were castles claimed by both Castile and León. The two sides reached a compromise by endowing Berenguela with the castles and lands under contention between Castile and León. At Palencia in 1199 Alfonso IX settled thirty-one castles on Berenguela: San Pelayo de Loyo, Aguilar de Mola, Alba de Bunel, Candrei, and Aguilar de Pedrayo in Galicia; Oviedo, Siero, Aguilar, Gozón, Corel, La Isla, Lugaz, Ventosa, Buanga, Miranda de Nieva, Burón, Peñafiel de Aler, and Santa Cruz de Tineo in Asturias; Colle, Portilla, Alión, and Peñafiel in Somoza; and Vega, Castro Gonzalo, Valencia, Cabreros, Castro de los Judíos de Mayorga, Villalugán, Castroverde, Mansilla, and Astorga in Campos. As part of the agreement, the castles would revert to León if Berenguela predeceased Alfonso; but if she had a son, he would inherit all his mother's property.

Although the marriage and the agreement ended the state of war between Castile and León, Pope Innocent III excommunicated Berenguela and Alfonso IX in 1198 because Berenguela was Alfonso IX's first cousin once removed; therefore, they were related within the prohibited degrees of consanguinity. Innocent remained adamant when the Leonese attempted to procure a dispensation for the marriage. Even though the pope had imposed an interdict on the married couple, the pair did not separate until 1204 when the papal excommunication was lifted. The lands and castles settled on Berenguela as part of the marriage treaty became the major issue in the separation. Innocent III insisted that since the castles were Berenguela's dowry and dower, they had to be returned because a marriage had not taken place. This stance revived the animosity between León and Castile, but the Treaty of Cabreros in 1206 endowed Berenguela's oldest son, Fernando, with the lands and castles she had received from her father and husband. Berenguela received an annual income of 8,000 *maravedís* and retained the title of queen of León. Alfonso IX made further provisions for her maintenance when he visited her in Burgos in 1207, and the treaty of Valladolid in 1209 between Castile and León bestowed more properties on her. These would go to Fernando upon her death, thus resolving the conflicts created by the annullment.

Berenguela's marriage with Alfonso IX produced four surviving children: Berenguela, Constanza, Fernando III of Castile-León (1201–1252), and Alfonso de Molina. Another daughter, Eleanor, died in 1202 and was buried in the church of San Isidro in León. Constanza became a nun in Las Huelgas and died in 1242. After Berenguela's marriage was annulled in 1204, the pope declared the offspring of the marriage illegitimate, but as part of the Treaty of Cabreros in 1206, Alfonso IX settled the succession to the Leonese throne first on Fernando and then on his younger brother Alfonso de Molina. After the separation, Berenguela and her children returned to Alfonso VIII's court in Castile, where she and her sons witnessed charters of the royal convent of Las Huelgas. Berenguela also wrote a letter to her sister Blanche of Castile describing Alfonso VIII's victory at Las Navas de Tolosa in 1212.

Upon the death of Alfonso VIII and Eleanor in 1214, Berenguela acted as regent for her younger brother Enrique I (r. 1214–1217), her brother Fernando having died in 1211. Alfonso VIII's will had initially named Eleanor as regent, but she had survived her husband only by a few weeks. Berenguela assumed her mother's place with the consent of the other regents named in Alfonso's will, taking custody of Enrique and the governance of the realm. But the Lara family, led by Count Alvaro Núñez de Lara, sought the custody of Enrique and forced Berenguela to surrender him to them in 1215. Berenguela, fearing a nobiliary rebellion, surrendered Enrique but named certain conditions. Count Alvaro did not heed Berenguela's restrictions, and a civil war broke out between Berenguela and the Laras. The Laras also alienated the Haro family and the Castilian church, which excommunicated Count Alvaro in 1215. As relations worsened, Berenguela sent her sons to their father's court in León.

In contravention of Berenguela's conditions, Count Alvaro planned to marry the twelve-year-old Enrique to a Portuguese princess, Doña Mafalda, aged twenty-one, in August of 1215. Berenguela used the Church to block the marriage by notifying Innocent III that the couple were related within the prohibited degrees. Berenguela tried to take Enrique from the Laras, but her attempts failed. Alvaro prepared to go to war against the queen and her followers in 1217

Enrique, however, died in an accident in June 1217. The count unsuccessfully tried to keep it a secret from Berenguela, who nevertheless found out about Enrique's death. She summoned her son Fernando to join her in Castile, keeping her intentions secret from Alfonso IX. The Castilians recognized Berenguela as the heir to the throne, but in an assembly at Valladolid she ceded her right to the throne to her son, Fernando III (r. 1217–1252). Berenguela then arranged his marriage to Beatrice, daughter of Philip of Swabia and a granddaughter of Frederick Barbarossa.

In order to obtain the throne of León for her son upon Alfonso's death in 1230, Berenguela negotiated with Alfonso IX's other surviving wife, Teresa of Portugal. Both of Alfonso IX's marriages ended in annullment, and upon his death he was survived by two sets of children: his two daughters with Teresa of Portugal and his four offspring with Berenguela. Berenguela and Teresa reached a settlement in Benavente on 11 December 1230. According to the terms of the settlement, Teresa's two daughters renounced their claim in return for a pension, enabling Fernando III to ascend to his father's throne. This agreement acheived the permanent union of the crowns of Castile and León.

Throughout the rest of her long life, Berenguela remained her son's chief adviser, retaining power and influence in the affairs of the kingdom. Berenguela's role in Fernando's reign is comparable to the part her sister, Blanche of Castile, played in France with her son Louis IX. The two differ, however, because unlike Blanche, Berenguela had a recognized claim to the throne her son occupied. The intitulation of Fernando's documents included Berenguela's formal assent to his alienation of royal properties and income. The *Chronica latina de los reyes de Castilla* and the *Historia* of Rodrigo Jiménez de Rada credit her with an active role in assisting Fernando's rule and facilitating his campaigns. Berenguela also commissioned Lucas, bishop of Túy, to write the *Chronicon mundi*. Berenguela died in 1246 and was buried in the convent of Las Huelgas.

THERESA M. VANN

Bibliography

González, J. *Reinado y diplomas de Fernando III*. Córdoba, 1980.

———. *El reino de Castilla en la época de Alfonso VIII*. Madrid, 1960.

BERGUEDÀ, GUILLEM DE

Guillem de Berguedà (1138–1192/96), a Catalan troubadour, was named after his father, the viscount of Berguedà. Guillem was not so much a professional poet as an important feudal lord who used poetry mainly for his personal benefit. Most of his thirty-one poems (another one is of dubious attribution), probably written from 1370 on, in a perfect Occitan, are *sirventes* (political or satirical song) closely related to his violent, itinerant life. They are sometimes a document of the everyday feudal struggle and, together with those written by his friend Bertran de Born, are among the best of the genre used as a political weapon. Among his enemies, we even find King Alfonso II (el Casto) and some of the most powerful noblemen of his age, such as the viscount Ramon Folc de Cardona, killed by Guillem in 1175. That also tells us something about the ferocity of Guillem's poetic attacks, in which he would introduce an element of personal cruelty, mocking his rivals' physical defects with deadly effect or accusing them of homosexuality or rape. Guillem had a great gift for caricature, as can especially be seen in the cycles addressed to Pere de Berga Bishop of Urgell, and to Ponç de Mataplana, but he was above all a brilliant poet, witty enough to popularize his satires by modeling them on popular songs, using, for example, a children's refrain to reinforce the humor. His moving *Consiros cant e planc e plor* for Ponç de Mataplana's death confirms Guillem's individuality: abhorring his past behavior, he substituted religious *planctus* conventionality for a personal courtly paradise. Guillem's medieval fame, though somehow related to a love legend, gave him status among the great troubadours, and the most copied of his four love poems (*Qan vei lo temps camjar e refrezir*) was still quoted by Jordi de Sant Jordi in the fifteenth century.

LLUIS CABRÉ

Bibliography

Riquer, M. (ed.) *Guillem de Berguedà*. 2 vols. Abadia de Poblet, 1971.

BERNÁLDEZ, ANDRÉS

Chronicler of the reign of the Catholic Monarchs. There are few known facts about Bernáldez's life. What little is known is recorded by Bernáldez himself in his work and is summarized in the introduction to Gómez Moreno's and Mata Carriazo's edition of Bernáldez's history, which the editors name *Memorias del reinado de los Reyes Católicos*. Known as *El cura de Los Palacios*, Bernáldez was chaplain to Diego de Deza, the archbishop of Seville who later became the inquisitor general of Castile. An "Old Christian" (*cristiano viejo*), Bernáldez was born in the province of León around 1454 and became curate of the town of Los Palacios near Seville in 1488, where he served until his death in 1516. His chronicle of the Catholic Kings, which Rodrigo Caro (1573–1647), the antiquarian from Seville, claimed was written as an eyewitness account, provides a particularly interesting description of the events leading up to the expulsion of the Jews. Bernáldez made extensive use of Fernando del Pulgar's work as a source, especially Pulgar's *Letras*, which circulated independently of Pulgar's *Crónica*.

E. MICHAEL GERLI

Bibliography

Bernáldez, A. *Memorias del reinado de los Reyes Católicos*. Ed. M. Gómez Moreno and J. de Mata Carriazo. Madrid, 1962.

Gerli, E. M. "Social Crisis and Conversion: Apostasy and Inquisition in the Chronicles of Fernando del Pulgar and Andrés Bernáldez." *Hispanic Review* 70.2 (2002), 72–93.

BERNARD DE SAUVETOT, ARCHBISHOP OF TOLEDO

The first archbishop of the primatial see of Iberia after the reconquest of Toledo by Alfonso VI of León-Castile in May of 1085, Bernard was chosen for that post by October 1086 and held it until his death in April 1125. He secured papal recognition for his own selection, for the restored primatial dignity of Toledo in the peninsula, and for a reconstituted archepiscopal province that included jurisdiction over all sees in Iberia whose proper metropolitan see still lay within Muslim-controlled territory. Bernard was, additionally, the chief counselor and usual companion of Alfonso VI of León-Castile (1065–1109) and of the latter's daughter and successor, Urraca I (1109–1126).

Bernard de Sauvetot was French by birth and had entered the Cluniac monastery of Orens about 1070, served at Cluny itself (becoming chamberlain there), and returned to St. Orens as prior about 1078. When Alfonso VI requested the assistance of the Cluniac abbot Hugh the Great, the latter dispatched Bernard to the peninsula and Alfonso VI made him abbot of the royal monastery and pantheon of Sahagún in 1080. As archbishop of Toledo, Bernard recruited Cluniac monks, from whom he fashioned the cathedral chapter of Toledo. Later he was to use his influence and that of the king to promote many of these Franch canons to the cathedral sees of Braga, Coimbra, Palencia, Segovia, Burgo de Osma, and Sigüenza. He himself was succeeded by one of them at Toledo.

BERNARD F. REILLY

Bibliography

Rivera Recio, J. F. *El arzobispo de Toledo Don Bernardo de Cluny*. Rome, 1962.

———. *La iglesia de Toledo en el siglo XII*. Rome, 1966.

BERNARDUS COMPOSTELLANUS ANTIQUUS

Bernardus's birthdate and birth place are unknown. Between 1183 and 1200 there are references to him in documents from Santiago de Compostela, where he was archdeacon. Around 1200 he left Santiago, heading to the Roman Curia. He studied in Bologna, and among his masters was the civil law expert Azzo. He was also a member of the Vicenza school, which existed only briefly from 1204 to 1209. His writings include: (1) the *Collectio Romana*, containing letters from the first ten years of Pope Innocence III's pontificate; (2) *Apparatus* to the Decree of Gratian; (3) appendices and annotations to Juan Teutónico's *Glossa Ordinaria* on the Decree of Gratian; (4) glosses on the *Compilatio prima antiqua*, written from 1205 to 1206 (glosses on the *Compilatio secunda antique* were attributed to him in the fourteenth century, though no evidence has been found that supports this claim); and (5) *Quaestiones disputatae*, possibly written in Vicenza. After 1217, there is no record of Bernardus's presence in Italy, or of his academic activity. Bernardus has been much more esteemed by modern scholars than he was by his contemporaries; this is surely due to the fact that the *Collectio Romana*, containing letters that the church leadership did not consider as precedents of canon law, was not to the Curia's liking.

ANTONIO GARCÍA Y GARCÍA

Bibliography

García y García, A. "Canonistas gallegos medievales," *Compostellanum* 16 (1971), 108–10.

Kuttner, S. "Bernardus Compostellanus Antiquus. A Study in the Glossators of Canon Law," *Traditio* 1 (1943), 277–340.

Weigand, R. "Mitteilungen aus Handschriften," *Traditio* 21 (1965), 482–85.

BESALÚ, RAMON VIDAL DE

Catalan troubadour named after a town in the province of Girona. Only his works give evidence of his professional links with some of the most important peninsular courts of the late twelfth century and the earlier thirteenth, such as those of Alfonso I and Pedro I of Aragón or Alfonso VIII of Castile. Vidal is well known for having written the earliest Romance language grammatical treatise (*Las rasos de trobar*, not after 1213), which, in fact, mainly deals with some aspects of Occitan as a poetic language to prevent his (Catalan) contemporaries from making mistakes, especially regarding the case system. Beyond some precious remarks on the use and the meaning of poetry (including folksongs), *Las rasos* somehow seems to be a reaction that nevertheless points to the decline of troubadour poetry, as is continued by Jofre de Foixà's *Regles de trobar* (1290) and other Catalan treatises. The same preoccupation is also to be found in the boastful erudition of Vidal's two didactic verse poems. Both of them show his interest in the art of *trobar* (make poetry) as well as in praising his favorite courts from the viewpoint of a *laudator temporis actii*, as in *Abrils issi'e mays intrava* (after 1199), where commonplace lament leads to a broad survey of the troubadour courtly environment in Vidal's time and to an *ensenhamen* (poetic lesson) on *joglaria* (minstrelsy) In *So fo el temps c'om era jais* (not after 1213), a conventional love judgment turns into a description of Huguet de Mataplana's court and a wide selection of troubadour quotations, including three of his own. The *Castia gilos* (after 1214), written in *novas* (a type of verse), is his only narrative, yet it has a similar framework. As though to prove the vitality of the troubadour tradition, Vidal succeeded in telling wittily a *fabliau* plot—the jealous husband deceived—adapted to his courtly audience.

LLUIS CABRÉ

Bibliography

Cluzel, I. *L'Ecole des Jaloux (Castia gilos), fabliau du XIIIe siècle par le troubadour catalan Raimon Vidal de Bezalu*. Paris, 1958.

Marshall, J. H. *The Razos de trobar of Raimon Vidal and Associated Texts*. London, 1972.

BESTIARY

Bestiary is a name given to popular medieval works of ancient provenance in which the physical and behavioral characteristics of animals, some real, some legendary, are related to Christian ethics, or to some basic theological concept such as the incarnation, salvation, or redemption. The visual impact of such allegory on the minds of the faithful is reflected in the most enduring examples of Christian iconography, such as the symbolism of the lion, the unicorn, the phoenix, the whale, and the pelican, which have their origin in these animal books.

While the ultimate source of the bestiary's animal lore is lost in antiquity, in the Christian era it takes definitive form in a book called *Physiologus*. The early history of this text is one of the most complicated imaginable, for certain details found in the Greek had also been picked up by Pliny himself, subsequently to be incorporated into authoritative natural history.

There are no extant manuscript versions of a *Physiologus* from an early date, but secondary evidence points to a second-century text in Greek and a fourth-century text in Latin; translations into Ethiopian and Armenian appeared in the fifth century; the oldest translation to a European vernacular is an Old English version of the eighth century. By this time, there is a tendency to treat the animals without the moralizations: Isidore himself uses the traditional descriptions from the *Physiologus*, but not the moralizations, and as early as the eighth century we have a Latin text of the *Physiologus* without the ethical and allegorical commentary.

In the encyclopedic age of the twelfth and thirteenth centuries, the natural history of the animals, as expanded by Isidore and further amplified by material from Pliny or from the traditional encyclopedic works of Cassiodorus or Martianus Capella, was incorporated into the collection: the forty-odd beasts in the *Physiologus* became as many as 150, and the common designation of the book came to be "bestiary." In this great century of the emerging vernaculars, translations were made into nearly every European language, with Old High German versions from the eleventh and twelfth centuries, and a proliferation of bestiaries in French during the same period. It was thus primarily a northern phenomenon: England, France, Germany.

Though secondary evidence gives testimony to its existence, due to the absence of manuscript witness the medieval Spanish bestiary has been characterized as "lost." However, while no autonomous text survives, the bestiary was in fact known in the Iberian Peninsula through its inclusion, intact, in Brunetto Latini's *Livre dou Tresor*. This work was written originally in French, but there are literally dozens of medieval manuscripts of translations into Castilian, Catalan, and Aragónese (complete editions of the medieval Castilian and Catalan versions of the *Livre dou Tresor* have been done by Spurgeon Baldwin and Curt Wittlin, respectively).

SPURGEON BALDWIN

Bibliography

Baldwin, S. (ed.) *The Medieval Castilian Bestiary*. Exeter, 1982.

McCulloch, F. *Medieval Latin and French Bestiaries*. Chapel Hill, N.C., 1960.

White, T. H. *The Bestiary*. New York, 1960.

BIBLE, JEWISH

Texts

Jews in Spain from the earliest time were very careful about the exactitude of their biblical texts. One of the earliest and most important manuscripts was known as the Hilleli (variously, Hillali) codex. Abraham Zacut, the famous astronomer and chronicler, relates that in the attack in León in 1196 (against the castle of the Jews), the Jews removed this manuscript, which was written some six hundred years earlier (596) by the scribe Moses b. Hillel. Zacut also mentions that he saw the section of the prophets of that codex, which was taken out by Jews expelled from Portugal and sold in Bougie (Bujaia, in Algeria). The same manuscript was cited already by Menahem b. Saruq in the tenth century, and frequently by scholars after that. In the thirteenth century or earlier, it was in Toledo, and from there copies were made in Burgos, Provence, and elsewhere. As late as the fifteenth century, it was still cited by a scholar of Toledo, as well (apparently) by a scribe in Zaragoza who made a copy from it.

Moses b. Maimon (Maimonides), after he left al-Andalus for Egypt, utilized the famous Aleppo Codex for his laws on the writing of Bible manuscripts (this is established by the Spanish edition and Oxford manuscript of his code).

Another important manuscript was the so-called Torah of Ezra of Burgos, cited by Jewish authorities. When Enrique II entered Burgos, he imposed a huge tax on the Jews (1366) and they had to sell all the Torah ornaments except for those of this scroll. In 1391, Jews of Burgos were asked to swear an oath on their *Tora* de *Yzra* not to sell arms.

Many individual Jews wrote their own copies of Bibles, and an interesting example is the extant Paris manuscript written in 1207 for the father of the famous Meir Abulafia, again in Burgos (Meir himself was instrumental in the diffusion of copies of the Codex Hilleli). The famous rabbi Nissim b. Reuben Gerundi inscribed important historical information on two Torah scrolls, one that he wrote in 1336 and gave to the community of Barcelona, and another that had belonged to his father and to which he appended a colophon in 1391.

While there are today many Hebrew biblical manuscripts in Spain, apparently there is only one that actually belonged to a Jewish *aljama* (community) that of Vitoria, and a small miniature scroll, as well as a few fragments. On the other hand, there are (or were—some may have been destroyed by the Nazis) several in various libraries of the world, including one written by the famous Shem Tov Ibn Gaon in Soria in 1313.

These manuscripts, as well as the early editions of Spanish Hebrew (and non-Hebrew translations) biblical texts, have obvious importance both for the history of the text as well as the eventual creation of a critical edition of the Bible.

Commentaries

Menahem b. Saruq in the tenth century apparently composed the first work in Spain dealing specifically with the Bible, although it was a dictionary rather than a commentary per se. This work, *Mahberet*, became famous due to its citation by Rashi (Solomon b. Isaac), famous commentator of France and Germany, and because it aroused the opposition of the important school of Hebrew grammarians centered around Córdoba and Lucena, and whose scientific investigation of Hebrew made possible the development of exegesis of the text. Both Samuel Ibn Naghrīllah the famous poet and prime minister of the Muslim kingdom of Granada, and the philosopher and poet Solomon Ibn Gabirol composed commentaries on parts of the Bible, which have been preserved only in citations by later authorities.

The most important commentator of the Spanish tradition—though he spent much of his life traveling outside Spain—was was Abraham Ibn Ezra. His commentaries exhibit a solid base of Hebrew grammar and good sense, replete with criticisms of some of his predecessors, from al-Andalus and other lands (Moses Ibn Chicatillah is particularly important), as well as a remarkably "modern" skepticism as to the divine origin of parts of the Torah and the traditional authorship of certain books of the Bible.

Bahya b. Asher of Zaragoza, a fourteenth-century author of a qabbalistic commentary on the Torah, claimed that Maimonides had also composed a commentary, but this is extremely doubtful since no one else mentions such a work (nevertheless, Maimonides' frequent analysis, allegorical and otherwise, of biblical statements made his legal and philosophical writings an important source for biblical interpretation in Spain).

Other important eleventh-century commentators include Judah Ibn Balcam (whose commentaries are in Judeo-Arabic) and Isaac Ibn Yashush, who also expressed skepticism about the Mosaic authorship of parts of Genesis.

In Aragón-Catalonia, under the influence of cabala, biblical commentary took mostly a homiletical-mystical direction. Most famous of these was Moses b. Naḥman (Naḥmanides), followed by the aforementioned Bahya b. Asher. However, Ibn Adret included some extremely important remarks on the Bible in his *responsa* and in scattered comments in his other writings. "Pietists" of the next generation, such as Nissim b. Reuben and Jonah b. Abraham Gerundi, tended to interpret the Bible along strictly homiletic lines.

In the thirteenth century in Castile, David Qimhi of Narbonne wrote several of his commentaries, there were marked by the careful grammatical analysis characteristic of Ibn Ezra (although with a good many flighty allegorical digressions and considerable anti-Christian polemic), The "pietistic" homiletical approach was firmly established in the fourteenth and fifteenth centuries. Jacob b. Asher of Toledo, son of the famous German scholar who became head rabbi there, typifies this in his Torah commentary, as does the far more important and interesting commentator Joseph Ibn Nahmias. By then, of course, the *Zohar*, composed chiefly or entirely by Moses de León, and qabbalistic works of that school also exercised a profound influence on biblical commentary. Finally, in the fifteenth and early sixteenth centurier, the work of allegorists like Isaac ʿArama and especially Isaac Abravanel (not composed until after the Expulsion) must be mentioned, of course. Rationalism had given way to homiletic flights of fancy.

NORMAN ROTH

Bibliography

Fernández Tejero, E. *La tradición española de la Biblia hebrea*. Madrid, 1976.

Reinhardt, K., and H. Santiago-Otero. *Biblioteca bíblica ibérica medieval*. Madrid, 1986.

Valle Rodríguez, C. del. *La escuela hebrea de Córdoba*. Madrid, 1981.

BIBLE IN SPAIN, THE MORALIZED

Moralized Bibles were an essentially French fashion that lasted from the thirteenth to the fifteenth centuries. Their highly selective and fragmentary scriptural texts, their popularizing interpretive glosses or "moralizations" based on the work of twelfth-century commentators like Hugh of St. Cher and the *Glossa Ordinaria*, and most conspicuously their vast programs of illuminations are what separate moralized Bibles from their more common cousins, the hundreds of medieval historiated Bibles and dozens of *Bibliae pauperum*. The most famous *Bibles moralisées* (of the fourteen now extant and distributed among eighteen codices) were executed in the Parisian style in the first half of the thirteenth century and linked to commissions by King Louis IX, his mother Blanche (Blanca) of Castile, and other members of his family. One distinguished *Biblia moralizada* was copied and translated into Castilian in Spain.

There are two preeminent three-volume sets of Latin moralized bibles copied in France and covering the entire Christian scriptures. One set is now divided between Oxford (Bodley 270b, reported as having been "acquired" by Sir Christopher Haydon during the sack of Cádiz in 1569), Paris (Bibliothéque Nationale Latin MS. 11560), and London (British Library, Harley 1526–1527).

Another complete three-volume set is still together in the treasury of the Cathedral of Toledo. The final quire of the last volume (one of the very few imperfections in the Toledo set) had already been detached from its binding by the beginning of the fifteenth century and currently forms part of the holdings of the Pierpont Morgan Library in New York. Since Louis IX and Blanche of Castile are shown in the closing illumination of the Morgan fragment as equals, the moralized Bible now in Toledo must have been executed during her regency while Louis was still a minor, between 1226 and 1236. The reasons for the loss of this *cuaderno* with the royal portraits are unknown, but since the French throne later supported the claims of the heirs of Fernando de la Cerda (1255–1275) to succeed their grandfather, Alfonso X (1221–1284), the almost surgical extraction of this quire could have been already performed during the reign of Sancho IV (1284–1294), Alfonso's second son who forcibly replaced his father as king.

Diplomatic and dynastic ties between Spain and France were especially strong in the early thirteenth century. Blanche of Castile was the daughter of Alfonso VIII of Castile and wife of Louis VIII of France, which made her son Louis IX cousin to Alfonso X. It is not unreasonable to suppose that the Toledo *bible moralisée* would have made a fitting coronation present for the young Spanish scholar and prince in 1252, or perhaps one of the dynastic exchange gifts when Alfonso's eldest son and heir betrothed Louis IX's daughter Blanca in 1266, or when he married her in 1269. Historians held that the common name of this bible, the *Biblia de San Luis*, arose from its association either with King Louis (r. 1236–1270) or with St. Louis of Anjou (1274–1297), bishop of Toulouse, onetime prisoner of Alfonso III of Aragón and later prisoner of Jaime II of Aragón. If these volumes acquired their name by passing through the hands of Bishop St. Louis, then the date of their arrival in Spain would have been considerably later, well after Alfonso's death, which would leave unexplained the avenues of physical transmission. The evidence from the testament of Alfonso X dated 21 January 1284 resolves this issue in favor of his personal ownership. The next undisputed mention of the great moralized French Bible is in an inventory of the cathedral of Toledo from 1539, although there are apparent witnesses as early as 1466 and perhaps earlier.

The great *Biblia de San Luis* contains an astonishing range of miniatures, some thirteen thousand in the three volumes, and was regarded by the learned king as both an important dynastic and devotional object. It is surprising therefore that this vast exemplar of high French Gothic manuscript illumination exercised little appreciable influence in terms of chromatic palette, composition, or theme on any the Alfonsine corpus of miniatures.

Finally, there is a Spanish *Biblia moralizada* (Biblioteca Nacional de Madrid 10232), also known as the *Biblia romanceada en latín y castellano* or the *Biblia de Osuna*, after a subsequent owner. It is a massive project, almost entirely without illuminations, that includes a vernacular translation of the allegorical interpretations of scriptural passages. The codex was executed in a three-column format in the late fourteenth or early fifteenth century for someone who knew this French source well and who also had authority over it for the time that it took to execute the bilingual manuscript—perhaps one of the archbishops of Toledo, as many of them well-known bibliophiles. The importance of this moralized Bible resides in its independent translation of sacred scriptures and glosses. The illuminations were omitted not by accident, but probably because executing them was beyond the means of the patron and the capabilities of the local craftsmen. There are occasional expansions and extrapolations on the Latin source material in the Spanish and a few incidences of brief descriptions of the pictures in the source text. The *Biblia de Osuna* was apparently meant as a companion or reader's copy to protect the great *Biblia de San Luis* from unnecessary use.

George D. Greenia

Bibliography

Daumet, G. "Les Testements d'Alphonse X le Savant, Roi de Castille," *Bibliothéque de l'École de Chartes* 67 (1906), 70–99.

Haussherr, R. "Drei Texthandschriften der Bible moralisée." In *Festschrift für Eduard Trier zum 60. Geburtstag*. Berlin, 1981. 35–65.

Laborde, Al. de. *La Bible Moralisée illustrée*. 4 vols. Paris, 1911–27.

Mezquita Mesa, T. "La Biblia moralizada de la catedral de Toledo," *Goya* 181–82 (1984), 17–20.

Morreale, M. "Vernacular Scriptures in Spain." In *The Cambridge History of the Bible*. Vol. 2. Cambridge, 1969.

———. "La 'Biblia moralizada' latino-castellana de la Biblioteca Nacional de Madrid (MS 10232)," *Spanische Forschungen der Görresgesellschaft* 29 (1975), 437–56.

Pérez de Guzmán, L., Marqués de Morbecq. "Un inventario del siglo XIV de la Catedral de Toledo. (La Biblia de San Luis)," *Boletín de la Real Academia de Historia* 90 (1926), 373–419.

Tormo, E. "La Biblia de San Luis de la Catedral de Toledo," *Boletín de la Real Academia de Historia* 82, no. 1 (1923), 11–17; no. 2 (1923), 121–32; no. 3 (1923), 198–201; and no. 4 (1923), 289–96.

BIBLE TRANSLATIONS

Castilian from Vulgate

The first known Castilian version of the Bible from the Vulgate goes back to the middle of the thirteenth century: as the oldest monument of literary prose, it proves that Castilian was no longer merely an oral medium between Arabic and Latin (as the vernacular had been in the "Toledo school of translators") but had come into its own as a written language. The manuscripts in which it has come down to us, though directly complementary and not complete, are Escorial I.1.8 (abbreviated E^8) and I.1.6 (E^6), transcribed, the latter in the original Castilian probably soon after composition (the New Testament possibly a few years later), the latter by a Navarro-Aragónese copyist of the early fifteenth century (the missing part of Genesis-Leviticus 6.7, is supplied in Castilian, by Escorial Y–1–6 as part of Alfonso X's *General Estoria* vide infra). Both E^8 and E^6 show some old readings from the earlier Hispanic tradition of the Latin Bible; nevertheless they stem substantially from the Vulgate in its thirteenth-century stage, known as the Parisian Bible because of the *librarii* of the Sorbonne who circulated it (collated by Wordsworth and White in their edition of the New Testament, and by the Benedictines of San Gerolamo in Rome in the yet unfinished edition of the Old Testament).

The Psalter in E^8 occupies a place apart as a version allegedly from Hebrew ("*según cuemos está en el ebraigo*"), attributed to Hermannus Alemannus, whom we know as the translator into Latin of Arabic (Averröan) commentaries on Aristotle's *Nicomachean Ethics* and *Rhetorics*. Whether the attribution is trustworthy or not, it is significant that we find a biblical version associated with a scholar whose activity is attested to in Toledo for the years 1240 and 1256. As to the original, on close scrutiny it proves to be a conflation of the Latin Psalter, especially the Jerominian *iuxta hebraeos*, and the Hebrew Massoretic text (Morreale, 1980). It is interspersed with moral glosses yet unidentified, none allegorical.

A second translation of several biblical books appears in the framework of the *General estoria* of Alfonso X of Castile, a history of mankind since Creation that the king planned along with his *Primera Crónica General* or *Estoria de España* (1270), in which the story of Moses was told in one brief chapter as the background for the settlement of Spain by Japhet's son Tubal. This universal history was to be built around the core of a paraphrased Bible on the pattern of Peter Comestor's *Historia Scholastica* (along with biblical glosses, Josephus, St. Augustine, Beda, Rabanus Maurus, and other sources), and combined with secular history, following the chronology of Eusebius' *Chronicle*. Literal renderings of Scripture were used for the canticles and the benedictions of Moses in Exodus 1: 15; and Deuteronomy 32, and 33:2–29, the Psalter, and Wisdom books. While in the paraphrased parts biblical matter is adapted to a more current style, avoiding parataxis and repetition, and often changing direct into indirect speech, the direct translations are a mixture of word-for-word renderings and circumlocutions, which make the Alphonsine version in many ways inferior to the preceding E^6-E^8 Bible. They point to a *Biblia romanceada* text that may have come earlier, and, in any case, ready for use. No traces of a non-Christian hand are found in these sections, in spite of the king's proverbial tolerance toward other religions, and the well-known part Muslims and Jews played in his works. The underlying text is of the same type as E^6-E^8 but not the same.

According to Alfonso's purpose (see the prologue of the *Crónica de España*), the authors of the *General estoria* did their best to explain the structure of sacred history by showing the unity of its parts. At the beginning of each book they took pains to translate Jerome's introductions and other prefatory matter, which give insights into various aspects of the biblical books and their early versions. The result was a monumental work, and much larger than the *Bible historiale* composed ten or twelve years later by Guyart des Moulins (as the largest of its kind produced in the Middle Ages, it assured the presence of the Old Testament in Castilian culture.

The biblical matter was thus distributed among the first four volumes of equal size: part 1, Pentateuch; part 2, Kings; part 3, Song of Songs, Proverbs, Wisdom, Ecclesiastes (in Salomon's alleged "autobiographical" order), and Psalms, Part 4 Joel and Isaiah, Hosea, Amos, Jonah, Tobit, Job, Ezekiel, and Chronicles with IV Kings intercalated at various points; part 4, Daniel, Obdiah, Zephaniah, Jeremiah, Lamentations, Baruch, Habakkuk, Judith, Ezra, Nehemiah, Haggai, Zechariah, Esther, and a literal translation of Ecclesiasticus. Parts 1 and 4 stem from the Alphonsine scriptorium (Madrid, Biblioteca Nacional, MS 816, and Vatican Library Latin MS 539, dated 1280). For part 5 we have to turn to Escorial I.1.2, which contains the same books as Vat. Library Latin MS 539, plus Maccabees, and a literal translation of the New Testament (Matt. 18 to Jude), taken over from E^6, and probably tacked on after the execution of the original plan had ceased. A part 6 is fragmentary and contains paraphrased allusions to the New Testament.

The desire to read Bible history uninterrupted by events alien to it caused some of the later copyists to omit portions of the nonbiblical content. Yet other copyists go back to the literal versions (Esc. Y-I–6, to E^8, Y–1–8, and I.1.2 to E^6; in the latter, the order of books of the New Testament are not the same as in the original: they are set in a sequence that we know from the ancient Visigothic manuscripts).

The fourteenth century produced versions of single books such as Job (Escorial b.II.7), whose anonymous author is identified by some as Chancellor Pero López de Ayala; undoubtedly his is a version (made between 1398 and 1407) of sayings from Pope Gregory's *Libri Moralium or Expositio in Job*, entitled *Las Flores de los Morales de Job* (Madrid, BN 10138; differences of biblical parts are pointed out by M. Morreale, *Hispanic Review* 34 1966).

In López de Ayala's *Rimado de Palacio* (with the second part based on Gregory's *Moralia*), the author bears witness to the Vulgate as a indirect or direct source of quotations (cf. M. M., 1983). Throughout the Middle Ages the Vulgate continued to be the fountainhead from which sprang all paraphrases, in prose and poetry, as well as quotations in doctrinal works such as *Los diez mandamientos*, *Castigos y documentos de Rey don Sancho*, *La Historia de los cuatro doctores*, the *Doctrina de discrición* of Pedro de Veragüe, *La doctrina que dieron a Sarra* by Fernán de Guzman and others, which with their renderings show the influence of the Latin on the Spanish language, first in more vernacular, later in Latinized forms. Nevertheless, some of the former reach present-day speech, such as *mandamiento* (commandment) or *Todopoderoso* (Almighty).

As for Bible translations as such, manuscript tradition takes us to the turn of the fourteenth and the first half of the fifteenth centuries, which is another period of fervent activity inspired not so much by the broad vision of universal history as by a zealous and somewhat indiscriminate erudition. In 1406 a great literary patron ascended to the throne of Castile: Juan II, who is said to have been fond of having Scripture read and its secrets declared to him. At the request of Alfonso de Guzmán, a Franciscan friar began in 1422 to translate the *Postillae* of Nicholas of Lyra. Another ponderous work is known as the *Osuna Bible* (Biblioteca Naclonal de Modrid ms. 10232), an adaptation of French *Bibles moralisées illustrées*, with its Latin and vernacular explanations alongside the biblibal text (the Castilian *Biblia moralizada* contains no illustrations, and the instructions for the illumination of the Psalter are mistaken by the copyist or translator for part of the text). Both found their way into the private library of the Marquis of Santillana). The devotion of Isabel I the Catholic and the zeal of the bibliophile Felipe II were responsible for the preservation of most of the biblical manuscripts, bequeathed by the monarch to the Escorial monastery.

The translations, committed by individual noblemen (as dedications and escutcheons show) and carried out presumably for a fee (cf. Bible translations from Hebrew), became more and more unreadable (and unreliable). This is the case of the deuterocanonical books of the early fifteenth-century Bible, contained in Escorial I.1.4 (E^4).

Royal and ecclesiastical prohibitions give an added insight into the history of translations—not so much the decree of 1233 by Jaime I of Aragón at the Council of Tarragona against all Bibles *in romancio*, since it reiterates a similar decision of the Council of Toulouse in 1229 against the Albigensians, but those of the Inquisition after its establishment in Castile (1478) and Valencia (1484), when vernacular Bibles became its concern, mainly because of the use converted Jews (*conversos*) could make of them.

At first, Psalters and liturgical Gospels and epistles escaped censure, along with the Little offices, containing psalms and biblical passages, and meditations on the Psalms—especially the Penitential Psalms and the Song of Songs. Martín de Lucenas' Gospels, translated at the request of Iñigo López de Mendoza (Biblioteca Nacional de Modrid ms. 9556; Schiff mentions Gospels and Epistles, both as "lost," p. 225), was followed in print by the Aragónese jurist Gonzalo García de Santa María's version of the liturgical Epistles and Gospels, with sermons drawn from the *Postilla super Epistolas et Evangelia* of Guillelmus Parisiensis, 1437 (Salamanca 1493), and the Franciscan Ambrosio Montesino's *Epístolas y Evangelios*, published a few years later upon request of Fernando the Catholic (Toledo, 1512), was reprinted many times, as was his successful *Vita Christi Cartuxano*, the Spanish version of the monumental *Meditationes Vitae Jesu Christi* by the Carthusian monk Ludolph of Saxony (Strasbourg, 1483), itself a harmony of the Gospels derived from the Latin version of Tatian's *Diatesseron*. These and previous *Vitae Christi*, such as that of Francesc Eiximenis, translated into Castilian, or Iñigo López de Mendoza's *Vita Christi por Coplas*, as well as other translations of Psalms and Gospels that fall outside our period, offer plentiful material to study the aftermath of the medieval *Biblia romanceada*.

In the sixteenth century Juan de Valdés marked a turn in his Italian period when he translated the Psalter "from Hebrew," the Pauline epistles (Romans and 1 Corintians extant) and the Gospels (Matthew extant) "from Greek" (but not without the help of Erasmus, *Novum Testamentum*, ed. 1527). In 1559 the exiled Casiodoro de Reina bequeathed his *Biblia* (through Cipriano de Valera's revision, 1602) to Spanish protestants.

They nevertheless fall in line to a certain extent with the oldest peninsular translations, while partial translations of single books and Felipe Scío de San Miguel's first full version of Scriptures in modern times (1791–94) are their natural heirs (as frequent quotations from medieval Bibles, especially E^6, in the footnotes also testify). The same holds true to a certain extent for J. M. Bover's and Cantera Burgos's Bible from Hebrew (1957). In 1975 the *Nueva biblia española* of Alonso Schökel and Mateos mark a breaking point, in accordance to the recent trend to make the Scriptures "accessible" (and acceptable) to the modern reader.

The intrinsic value of the *Biblia romanceada* as a vehicle of biblical Latin and as a source for the history of Spanish phonetics, morphology, syntax and style, and especially vocabulary has attracted the attention of scholars (L. Mourin and G. De Poerck, Baldwin, Morreale, J. Moreno Bernal).

At the University of Wisconsin-Madison the *Biblia romanceada* is being painstakingly transcribed down to the letter as a source for a planned *Old Spanish Dictionary*. For its edition other criteria have been worked out as regards script, parsing of words, and punctuation.

Since the number of extant texts is much less numerous than in neighboring France (189 signaled by Berger in the *langue d'oïl* alone), scholars would do well to agree on a way of publishing the *Biblia romanceada* in a way that would do justice to its meaning and sounds.

On the other hand, parts of the *General estoria* and works by other medieval authors have been scanned for traces of vocabulary and phraseology reminiscent of the Bible, and a corpus has been inaugurated by the Hebraist García de la Fuente, of the "biblical vocabulary" in medieval authors, but all too often it is as if there were no intermediate sources.

Abundant traces of the *Biblia romanceada* are found in Spanish dictionaries, many of which still subsist in the language, although they find less and less recognition in subsequent editions of the *Academy Dictionary*.

Whatever aspect of the *Biblia roamanceada* is examined, before the advent of the Sixto-Clementine edition of the Vulgate (1592–1593), care should be taken to reconstruct the stage of transmission of the underlying text, including extra-biblical elements (order of books, chapter division, glosses, and preliminaries). A tentative sample is given by the bilingual Latin-Castilian editions of former research assistants at Padua.

We do not know to what extent the *Biblia romanceada* reached the broader world of the uninitiated, but in any case it is an added testimony of how Spanish cultural and spiritual life was molded by the biblical message, and as such it should be studied in the first place.

Castilian from Hebrew

The extant Bibles translated from Hebrew by Castilian Jews are a scant representation of those actually in existence in medieval Spain, as contemporary references indicate: a contract between Aragónese Jews and the German printer Paul Hurus signed at Calatayud in 1478 mentions the commission of seventy nine large illuminated Castilian Bibles, four on parchment; interlinear glosses by Rabbi Arragel likewise refer to other translations unknown to us ("*otros romançan* . . .").

In E^8 we have seen a Psalter that is said to have been translated from Hebrew by a Christian author; an earlier version from Hebrew, of the first decades of the thirteenth century, is embedded in a guide to the Holy Land, known as the *Fazienda de Ultramar* (with approximately 2,100 verses in longer passages and single quotations, including Tobit and Maccabees.)

Part of the Old Testament, evidently translated from the Massoretic text, could be pieced together (including verbal elucidations) from disputations between Christians (mainly *cristianos nuevos*, or "New Christians") and Jews.

The same holds true even to a greater extent for translations of original works by Jews, as Maimonides' *More Nabuchim* (1190), by the Jewish convert Pedro de Toledo (1419–1432), since Maimonides intention was to "juntar e amigar la Santa escritura de Moisén e de los profetas con la muy altíssima escelente filosofía primera e moral e natural" (to join and make compatible the Holy Scripture of Moses, and the Prophets with the most excellent and high primary, moral, and natural philosophies).

As for the Jewish *Biblia romanceada* itself, extant manuscripts are relatively few. Most are found in Spain, at the Escorial Library; four in Madrid, two at the Biblioteca Nacional (BNM), one each at the Academia de la Historia (AC), and one in the Duke of Alba's private collection. Two are in Portugal. They are designated as follows: Escorial I.1.3, from the Hebrew with a paraphrase of Maccabees (abbreviated E^3), the Ajuda

(Lisbon), with Genesis through Judges plus a summary of Maccabees, Esc. 1.1.7 (E^7): Genesis 8:11–Kings (E^7), Esc. 1.1.5, (E^5): Isaiah-Chronicles, Esc. J-ii-19 (E^{19}): Genesis 25:17–2–Kings 23:4, Evora Public Library cxxi$^{1-2}$, fol. 348 to the end (Evora): Song of Songs, Proverbs, Wisdom, Ecclesiastes; Ac. n. 1: Major and Minor Prophets plus [Maccabees] (Ac^1), MBN ms 10288: Prophets and Lamentations, Chronicles, Psalms, Job, Song of Songs, Ecclesiastes, Proverbs, Lamentations (bis) plus deuterocanonical books from Vg (BN); Esc. I.1.4: OT [Ps and deuterocanonical books from Vg], (E^4), "Biblia de Alba": Palacio de Liria, Madrid: OT (Alba).

Of these, E^7 and E^5 are complementary; E^3 and Ajuda are closely related; part of E^5 coincides substantially with Evora, E^5 Judith is almost identical with E^{19}; Ac^1 belongs to the family of the Alba Bible as regards the Major Prophets, while the Minor Prophets, including the Prologue, bespeak common origin with Biblioteca Nacional, Daniel and its Prologue, with E^4; the latter in turn is related to Evora and Ac^1; in Biblioteca Nacional Lamentations is transcribed twice from different sources. Due to their composite quality, manuscripts should be collated thoroughly for mutual relations. The tendency, however, has been to publish manuscripts separately, without critical inquiry into the transmission of the texts (cf. eds. E^4, E^{19}).

E^3 belongs to the late fourteenth century, the others to the first half of the fifteenth. Only one, the Alba Bible, so called from the name of its present owners, bears the name of the translator, Rabbi Arragel of Gualajara, and the approximate dates 1422–1433; of the others, Evora only is dated 1429.

Only three Old Testaments have survived in their entirety (according to the Hebrew canon): E^3, E^4, and Alba; one represent a second volume, Ac^1, the first one being lost. None are entirely homogeneous, because of translations from the Vulgate or other Christian elements mixed in: Maccabees in E^3, Ac^1, E^4; deuterocanonical books in E^4 and BN, and even Vulgate Psalms in the former; Vulgate appears on parallel columns in Ac^1.

The service of noblemen, to which Jews were often assigned in the Middle Ages, explains the origin and preservation of the Alba Bible and probably of many of the other texts. Rabbi Arragel undertook the task imposed on him by Luis de Guzmán, Grand Master of the Military Order of Calatrava, who wanted a fresh translation, the older ones being outmoded. Of the Ajuda Bible we are told that it once belonged to a Portuguese king, Afonso II, and later to the Duke of Bragança; E^4 bears the escutcheon of Ribera, Luma, and Zúñiga; The manuscript of the Biblioteca Nacional de Madrid found its way into the Library of the Marqués de Santillana, who ordered or collected many biblical and patristic works along with translations of Josephus, Plutarch, Livy, and other historians and poets of antiquity. Most of the manuscripts were collected by the devotion of Isabel I the Catholic and the zeal of bibliophile Felipe II, who bequeathed them to the monastic Library of the Escorial.

The genesis of most of the manuscripts explains the large format and the illustrations, particularly varied and interesting in Alba, but also present in E^3, Ajuda, and E^4. This, however, does not exclude the perusal by Jewish readers who were no longer familiar with the Hebrew language. Even more significant for the pursuit of ancestral tradition and religious practice are the translations of prayer books and rituals, unfortunately preserved in even fewer numbers (cf. Yerushalmi).

No systematic study has been undertaken on the underlying Massoretic text and the Targumin. The presence of Targum of Onkelos has been ascertained piecemeal, especially in E^{19} (see Gen. 49:9, 12, but also in Gen. 49:25) and elsewhere; that of the Vulgate is detected in E^4 and Alba (where double translations are often included with the explicit purpose of satisfying readers of both religions).

As for the contents and "message" of Scripture, faithfulness to the letter is responsible for many of the valid interpretations confirmed by modern biblical scholarship (as well as for other readings dismissed today in favor of the old versions, including the Vulgate; see Ps. 17[18], "*quoniam iratus est eis*"). As could be expected, literal translation from Hebrew diminishes the messianic suggestions emphasized by *St. Jerome* (for example, in using the abstract *justicia* or *justedad* instead of *el justo* in Is. 12:3, 45:8, etc.) and does away with the basis for Mariological interpretations of verses such as Genesis 3:15; however, one passage must have been a touchstone for Christian inspection: in Isaiah 7:I4, E^3, E^5 and E^4 have *virgen*; Alba finally allowed *alma* to remain (the manuscript shows evidence of the deletion of *virgen* or *moça*).

As regards other extrabiblical elements, the Hebrew canon (Law and former and latter Prophets, hagiographs, with some divergences) is followed by E^3, E^{19}, E^7, Alba, and Ac^1. E^5 shows the chapter division introduced in the Vulgate since 1220. E^3 stands out for its commitment to Jewish religious practice; it is marked in the Pentateuch according to the synagogal readings of the *parashiot*, with Exodus 15:1–20 and Numbers 21:18 divided according to the Massoretic prescription (a feature that also appears in E^{19}).

Alba has an extensive marginal commentary and heterogeneous interlinear glosses and is abudantly illuminated, with extensive preliminaries explaining their circumstances. Ac^1 bears fragmentary glosses of Hebrew origin, starting with Ezelsiel 13:9, as does the Biblioteca Nacional Bible.

Translation is literal enough to make many Semitic syntactical and even morphological traits evident: more so in E^3, E^{19}, Ac^1, and Evora-E^5; somewhat less in E^4 and Alba. Without the interposition of the latinity of Jerome, clauses follow one another in paratactical order. They are continually punctuated by the interjection *ahe* (*hinneh*, i.e., "lo!, behold!"), undeterred by repetitions, and derive different words from the same root, with extraordinary license in word formation. Literalness is inspired by respect for the sacred text; but it also may be due to the sheer routine of rendering the text word by word, as in contemporary translations by Christians, which in the fifteenth century were at their worst; many an error is caused by the interpretation of a root in disregard of context.

A distinctive feature of the Jewish *Biblia romanceada*, on the other hand, is the use of expressions accessible to the Jewish readers, the sum of which is called *ladino* (in order to distinguish it from Judeo-Spanish or *judezmo*), and the sum of which varies, being larger in the more literal type.

The history of the Bible read and translated by Jews would not be complete unless we considered once more the quotations embedded in such works as Rabbi Santob de Carrión's *Proverbios morales*, and especially the parts of Genesis paraphrased in the versified History of Joseph and his brethren.

Since much textual evidence has been lost, in order to place the representatives of the Jewish *Biblia romanceada* in the right perspective within the Judeo-Spanish tradition, we could have started from the vernacular Bible as the Jews printed it as soon as they saw themselves relatively free to publish and circulate "the Book"; inverting the chronological order, we could have made make the most of the testimony of the Constantinople Pentateuch (1547, in Hebrew characters), and the Ferrara Bible (1553, in Latin, black-letter type), named after the towns in which they saw the light (Constantinople and Ferrara, via Venice, were not too far removed from each other in the sixteenth century; Eliezer Soncino, the editor of the Pentateuch, had himself come from Italy, where he had been an assistant of his father Gershom, the well-known printer of Italian, Latin, and Hebrew books).

The substantial identity of the two texts, compatible with clearly distinct interpretation of technical passages, and their editorial policies and partially different destination make them comparable with the two types we have seen in the *Biblia romanceada*. Constantinople was published explicitly for the benefit of Jews to help youth in the synagogal service; Ferrara, with an eye on Jews as well as on Christian patronage, as its two different dedicatory letters show, was addressed either to the Jewess Gracia Nasi (bearing a list of parashiots and haphtarots in some of the copies), or to Duque Hercules II of Ferrara. Constantinople is more slavishly literal and more definitely inclined to the use of ladino expressions; Ferrara allows a little more margin to make the text accessible; hence E^3 and E^{19} as antecedents of Constantinople, E^4 and Alba as an example of compromise—both groups, however, at a distance.

The authors of the Ferrara tell us that they had many versions, both ancient and modern, at their disposal; yet they call it a *new translation*. No "original" has been found among the manuscript Bibles circulated in the Iberian Peninsula, and none will be found with all the distinctive elements of the Constantinople and Ferrara: none that carries the word-for-word interlinear translation to such conscious extremes, none with the same proportion allowed to ladino, none following the editorial policies peculiar to BF—vernacular elements supplied in semicircles, asterisks to mark (irregularly) difficult or critical passages, abbreviation of the name of God *A*[*donay*]. All these fit into the Italian scholarly milieu of the first half of the sixteenth century (prior to the the diatribes over Scripture of the Reformation), when the call "back to the original languages" was headed by the Dominican Santes Pagnini, Cardinal Cayetan, and others, in an effort to correct or even substitute the Vulgate with a "more reliable" Latin translation. On the other hand, the translations represented by Constantinople and Ferrara hark back to the *phrasis* of peninsular ancestors in such a way that many have counted the text they represent to the medeival *Biblia romanceada*. The prayer books and rituals printed (in Ferrara 1552; two in Venice 1552) allow us to assume a tradition of long standing, probably oral, which explains the the similarity of the biblical texts. Thus "the venerable and sententious language" that was natural to the Jews of old was handed down to the Jewish diaspora, in the many editions of the Ferrara, or part of the same.

Catalan

The earliest testimony of biblical texts in Catalan are found in homilies; in fact, the history of Catalan prose opens with a short fragment of a collection of sermons, strongly influenced by Provençal, known as the *Homelies d'Organyá* (end of the twelfth century), in which the Gospels for several Sundays are explained mainly according to the moral meaning. Another series of homiletic materials is preserved in Barcelona (Biblioteca de Catalunya ms. 479); it is particularly interesting because of the fragmentary notes in Catalan, in which the scriptural theme is set forth in threefold rhymed phrases. Another manuscript that of the Marseilles Public Library (n. 1095), contains an extensive collection of homilies from the beginning of the fifteenth century or earlier, in which scriptural material is interwoven with Apocryphal narratives.

The history of Bible translations and adaptations in eastern Spain is divided between Catalan and Valencian (not always neatly distinguished or distinguishable). Both domains are difficult to assess because of lack of editions (the project of an integral 1908 edition of the Catalan Bible planned by Foulché Delbosc was never realized, and parts of the vernacular Bibles in these domains have appeared piecmeal or in bibliophile items difficult to locate).

One distinguishing feature is the relation of Catalonia with its northern neighbor, evident in the *Compendi Historial de la Bíblia* (1361), and in the Catalan versions preserved as such. Alfonso II of Catalonia is said to have translated a Bible from the French in 1287. We are told that the Apocalypse found in at least ten Italian manuscripts was the link between the French Bible and Italian translations.

There is a family of Catalan Bibles, one complete in three volumes, known as the Peiresc manuscript of the Bibliothèque Nationale in Paris (BNP), ms. esp. 2–4, and two others of one volume each (most of the Old Testament), to be found in London, British Library, Egerton 1526, dated in the colophon 1465, and (Gen. 2.21-Psalms) in BNP ms. esp. 5, likewise dated 1461. Berger points to certain similarities between a New Testament of the fourteenth century known as the Marmoutier New Testament (BNP esp. 486) and the Peiresc Bible (ms. BNP 4), as well as with French texts (BNP fr. 899, and fr. 398, ms. Bibliothèque Mazarine 684) but with significant differences as to the underlying Vulgate text and extrabiblical elements. In the Peiresc MS Old Testament the glosses are also reminiscent of those that belonged to the French Bible 398 and were appended to Guyart de Moulins's great *Bible historiale*, containing a direct translation that was circulated widely in fourteenth-century France.

A translation of the Psalms attributed to the Dominical Romero de Sabruguera, now in the Seville rhymed Bible, is what seems left from a complete Catalan Bible that existed in the Escorial Library, other Catalan Psalters are found in BNP ms. fr. 2434, of the fourteenth century and BNP fr. 2433, of the fourteenth century.

A summary of the Bible and apocryphal Gospels, apparently of the fourteenth century, translated from Provençal, is known as *Genesi de scritura*. The *Biblia rimada* of the Biblioteca Colombina at Seville is likewise a versified summary of the Bible combined with apocryphal material.

A Catalan translation of the whole Bible into Valencian was made by Bonifatius Ferrer (d. 1417) and printed in 1477–1478. This edition, however, was destroyed so thoroughly that only the last leaf has been found and is preserved in a manuscript of the Carthusian Order, now at the Hispanic Society in New York. It is hard to say whether Bonifatius Ferrer leaned on some earlier version, and which of the other partial manuscript texts, especially of Psalms and Gospels, are related to his translation. Revealing for the history of the exposition of the Bible in medieval preaching are the many sermons delivered by Vincent Ferrer, an ardent advocate of the study of the Bible, who preached in Valencian (hence the Valencian quotations from Scripture with which he started his sermons).

Adaptations in the vernacular of biblical matter or of short biblical texts were also found in catechetical works, such as the *Biblia parva*, which tradition attributes to Peter Pascasius (thirteenth century), with quotations from the Old Testament woven into a rather disorganized assemblage of heterogeneous matter, likewise expounded in Valencian.

A place apart belongs to Catalan prayer books from Hebrew, and further illustrations of Catalan biblical matter from Hebrew could be collected from disputations between Christians (*cristianos nuevos*) and Jews, such as Petrus Alfonsi, *Dialogus ex Judaeo Christiani et Moysi Judaei* (Migne PL 157, 5535–5672), of which there is a fragmentary Catalan translation, and the *Disputa contra los jueus*. (Rome, 1907).

Margherita Morreale

Bibliography

Avenoza, G. *La Biblia de Ajuda y la Meglililat en romance*. Madrid, 2001.

Morrale, Margherita, *La* Bibbia di Ferrara *450 anni doppo la sua Publicazione*. Rome, 1994.

BIOGRAPHY

The commemoration of the lives of famous people, lay or ecclesiastical, draws on a millenial tradition. Medieval Spain, like the rest of Europe, took its inspiration from two sources, classical and patristic literature. The earliest manifestations, lives of saints, can be found in Hispano-Latin writers from St. Isidore onward. From the thirteenth century, the Latin tradition is joined by romance narratives, often derived from Latin sources, like Gonzalo de Berceo's rhymed lives of Riojan saints or the anonymous *Vida de Santa María Egipciaca*. This vein continues in Castile through the fourteenth and fifteenth centuries from the *Vida de San Ildefonso* by the "Beneficiado de Ubeda" to the lives of St. Isidore and St. Ildefonso copied by Alfonso Martínez de Toledo. On the secular side, the Suetonian pattern is evident in the thirteenth-century *Liber illustrium personarum* by Gil de Zamora and numerous sketches of famous individuals scattered through the Alfonsine *Estoria de España*. The most powerful inspiration, however, issues from the military epic and its heroes, enshrined in the *Carmen campidoctoris* and the *Historia Roderici*, eulogistic portraits of Ruy Díaz de Bivar. Later, the prose romance and the elaboration of the chivaleresque ethic, fused with treatises on government and ethics, prepares the ground for the flowering of the secular biographical genre in the fifteenth century, in both Latin and the vernacular, but mainly in the latter. The practice of implanting individual profiles in the official regnal chronicles continues from López de Ayala onward, but Pulgar, looking back from the end of the fifteenth century, does not consider the tradition to be very rich: "no los leemos esten didamente en las corónicas como los fizieron, ni veo que ninguno los escrivió aparte, como fizo Valerio e los otros." Indeed, one must mention the impact of translations of the classics, like Plutarch, Caesar, Sallust, but above all Valerius Maximus, and other derivatives like Petrarch and Boccaccio anthologies of famous men and woman, together with contemporaneous humanist treatments of Alfonso V of Aragón by Beccadelli and Fazio.

In fifteenth-century Spain, there are over a half-dozen examples of varying extent and literary worth, all dealing with idealized concepts of man as knight, scholar, and priest, drawn from contemporary or near-contemporary history, either as single biographies or in collections of lives. The earliest, *El Victorial or La Crónica de don Pero Niño, conde de Buelna* (1379?–1458) is attributed to a Díez or Días de Games, *alférez* (lieutenant) to the count, and perhaps a royal scribe to Juan II of Castile. It deals with the education, career, and sentimental affairs of a wandering knight in Spain, France, the English Channel, and the Mediterranean. In contrast to this mélange of fantasy, legend, and diary jottings up to 1446, the *Crónica de don Miguel Lucas de Iranzo* records the deeds of the Constable of Castile during the dramatic years of the reign of Enrique IV. The chronicle stops short of his assassination in 1473. The narrative focuses on the daily patterns of life and the frontier exploits of a provincial noble by someone close to him, not clearly identified, but possibly Pedro de Escavias, *alcaide* of Andújar. The most compelling, most rhetorically elaborate account of a tragic life is the *Crónica de don Alvaro de Luna*, an earlier Constable of Castile (1388–1453), attributed to Gonzalo Chacón, *comendador* of Montiel, himself a figure of weight in the court of the Catholic kings. It was probably written in two drafts, one near the date of his execution and another later in the century by someone who wished to create a figure of dramatic proportions, dedicated to the common weal, who was sacrificed to it in the end. Two other incomplete biographies of minor aristocrats are set in the latter years of the century and possibly written in the early sixteenth. Alonso Maldonado's *Hechos de don Alonso de Monroy, clavero y maestre de la orden de Alcántara* is preserved as a prologue to a lost translation of Appian's *Civil Wars*. It recounts another frontier life, laced with siege, robbery, and assault, up to 1475. The anonymous *Historia de don Rodrigo Ponce de León, marqués de Cadiz* terminates in 1488 and limits its account to the part played by the marquis in the Granada campaign. Only one autobiography in Castilian survives, the emotional memoirs of Leonor López de Córdoba, daughter of a supporter of Pedro I. Two collections of biographies or semblanzas cover the century; the *Generaciones y semblanzas* by Fernán Pérez de Guzmán embraces the first half and ends on a somber note of stoic resistance to fortune's blows. The *Claros varones de Castilla* by Fernando del Pulgar takes in the next two generations and sets a similar selection of society in a more optimistic light, creating for Castile its own contemporary pantheon of heroes. The Crown of Aragón possesses some of the most remarkable monuments in this genre, particulary in the very personal chronicle of Jaime I (1213–1276), the *Libre dels feyts*, written in the first person with many epic resonances. Desclot structures his chronicle around the emergence of Pedro III (1276–1285), while that of Pedro IV the Ceremonious (1336–1387) is also autobiographical but much more refined and precisely organised. In fifteenth-century Catalonia there are two examples, in Latin, which illustrate the impact of humanism. Gonzalo García de Santa Maria's official biography of Juan II of Aragón (r. 1458–1439) draws its inspiration from Sallust to illustrate the triumph of fortitude over adversity, set against the Catalan Civil War (1462–1472). Miquel Carbonell's *De viris illustribus catalanis suae tempestatis libellus* concentrates on profiles of professional lawyers and notaries, taking as model Bartolommeo Fazio's portrait of Alfonso V. Finally, as an example of the expatriate scholar employed in the royal court, there is Lucio Marineo's *De Hispaniaie viris illustribus*, included as book 5 of *De laudibus Hispaniae* (printed 1495?). This ranges from classical to modern times and touches on all ranks of society. Marineo also wrote a biography of Juan II of Aragón, deriving from Gonzalo's, finished in 1508 and included in his *De rebus Hispaniae memorabilibus opus* (1530).

Robert B. Tate

Bibliography

de Riquer, M. *Historia de la literatura catalana.* Barcelona, 1964.

Sánchez Alonso, B. *Historia de la historiografía española.* Madrid, 1941.

Tate, R. B. *Ensayos sobre la historiografía peninsular del siglo XV.* Madrid, 1970.

BITRUJI, AL- (ALPETAGIUS)

See ASTROLOGY AND ASTRONOMY, MUSLIM

BLACK DEATH, THE

The Black Death, or bubonic plague, swept over most of western Europe during the two years between 1348 and 1350; it returned almost every generation afterward for the next two centuries. Although there is a consensus as to its course, there has long been a spirited debate among historians as to its long-term impact upon the economic, political, and social structures of medieval Europe. What was the overall impact of the plague? How lasting were its effects? How deeply did it transform medieval society? Although we have vivid firsthand accounts of the coming of the plague elsewhere and a plethora of documentary references to its onslaught for other parts of Europe, our knowledge of the nature and the impact of the plague in the Iberian Peninsula is negligible indeed.

Castile

We know that the plague killed Alfonso XI at the siege of Gibraltar in 1350, the only monarch to succumb to it in western Europe. There are also a few scattered references, in the ordinances of the *cortes* (parliament) and in the *Libro becerro de behetrías* to the *gran mortandad* (the large number of dead people), but beyond that, Castilian records are mute in their notice of the plague. We cannot really trace the course of the sickness through the peninsula, though common sense indicated that it must have spread from seaports and commercial thoroughfares into the interior—Gibraltar before Extremadura, the Crown of Aragón before Castile. We cannot pinpoint the first outbreak of the disease, nor can we date with any precise knowledge its ebbing away. Such questions as to how many people died and what percentage of the population the sickness vanquished remain more or less unanswered.

What is clear, however, is that the plague, coming as it did at the end of several decades of adverse weather, widespread nobiliary violence, and a high rate of inflation, had a catastrophic but short-term impact on Castilian society. The evidence is tangential but dramatic. For the ten to fifteen years after 1350, the number of documents in municipal and ecclesiastical archives is reduced to a mere trickle. Although there has been a decline in the number of royal charters, records of land and real estate transactions, donations and other such documents from the 1330s on, the drop in the number of such sources after 1350 is dramatic indeed, almost as if life had come suddenly to a full stop. Rents collected from mills and farms fell, in some cases, by half or as much as two-thirds. Such was the case in Burgos in 1350, when the cathedral chapter reduced its rental prices for mills by more than a half and still had difficulties finding tenants.

In 1351, the cortes of Castile enacted a statute of laborers. It was a response, as it was in England, to the scarcity of labor and the rapid increase in wages, signaling the desire of those in power to control the supply and cost of labor. Finally, the *Libro becerro de behetrías* (compiled in 1351–1352) reported that because of "the great death brought by the plague" one-fourth of the villages listed in the census (more than 2,000 altogether) were deserted. Although the collapse of northern Castilian rural life had begun much earlier than 1350, the plague must have accelerated this process.

We have further evidence for the psychological and spiritual impact of the plague in the somber and melancholy literature of the period. Rabbi Santob's *Proverbios morales* and the Castilian version of the "Dance of Death" bring us close to the pessimistic character of the age. At the same time, the Jews, who had enjoyed a fairly peaceful and prosperous existence in Castile throughout most of the thirteenth and early fourteenth centuries, became, once again, the targets for popular violence.

The Crown of Aragón

The history of the Black Death and of its impact on the lands of the Crown of Aragón is better known than for Castile. A number of local histories, as for example, that of Girona, allows for some estimates of the plague's effects. Overall mortality has been calculated to range between 25 to 35 percent, but in some areas, such as the Plain of Vic, as much as two-thirds of the population may have died from the pestilence. Other areas in Catalonia suffered mortality rates of 50 percent of the entire population. Recovery, as was the case throughout the west, was hampered by recurrent epidemics throughout the next two centuries. Most historians agree that the plague was the main cause of the Crown of Aragón's late medieval crisis. It sharply reduced the realm's demographic base and hurled it—above all the county of Barcelona—into an economic, social, and political crisis from which the eastern kingdoms would not fully recover for two hundred years.

While there are few objections to this assessment, its general conclusions do not apply to Castile. In the latter, the late medieval crisis had its origins in an earlier period and was the result of structural economic and political problems. There, the Black Death, for all of its impact, just added to serious problems that were already a century old. Castile, mostly through the beginnings of wool exports and of its political restructuring, recovered enough to claim hegemony in the peninsula within a short decades after 1350.

TEÓFILO RUIZ

Bibliography

Cabrillana, N. "La crisis del siglo XIV en Castilla: La Peste Negra en el obispado de Palencia," *Hispania* 28 (1968), 245–58.

López de Meneses, A. (ed.) "Documentos acerca de la peste negra en los dominios de la Corona de Aragón," *Estudios de la Edad Media de la Corona de Aragón* 6 (1956), 291–447.

BLANCHE OF CASTILE

Blanche of Castile (1188–1252: queen of France, 1223–1226), daughter of Alfonso VIII of Castile (1158–1214) and Leonor of England, was regent and chief adviser to Louis IX of France. In 1200, as part of a treaty between her uncle, King John of England, and King Philip Augustus of France, John's mother Eleanor of Aquitaine selected Blanche to marry Philip's heir, the future Louis VIII (1223–1226). Upon her husband's death, Blanche became regent for her minor son, Louis IX (1226–1270) under the terms of Louis VIII's will. As regent, Blanche sought to preserve the integrity of France by subduing baronial revolts and preventing English intervention in Normandy. Her actions strengthened the French monarchy. Throughout her life she exercised considerable influence over her son, even, according to Joinville, in his relations with his wife, Margaret of Provence. Against her wishes, Louis went on crusade (1248–1254), but he chose her as his regent. During his absence she successfully completed his program of administrative reform, raised money for his crusade, and dealt with the revolt of the Pastoureaux. Blanche died in November 1252 while Louis was still away, and a council of bishops assumed the regency. Blanche's instructions to Louis IX on piety are recorded in Joinville. Her daughter, Isabelle, chose a religious life in preference to a dynastic marriage arranged by Blanche and Frederick II. Her three other children were Robert of Artois, Alphonse of Poitiers, and Charles of Anjou.

THERESA M. VANN

Bibliography

Berger, É. *Histoire de Blanche de Castille, Reine de France*. Bibliothèque des Écoles Françaises d'Athènes et de Rome, Fascicule 70. Paris, 1895.

Joinville, J. de. *History of St. Louis*. Trans. Joan Evans. Oxford, 1938.

Jordan, W. C. *Louis IX and the Challenge of the Crusade*. Princeton, N.J., 1979.

Pernoud, R. *Blanche of Castile*. Trans. H. Noel, London, 1975 [1972].

BLANCA, QUEEN OF NAVARRE, WIFE OF ENRIQUE IV

Daughter of the Infante Juan of Castile (who was the son of Ferdnando of Antequera and played such a prominent role in the history of the Iberian kingdoms, becoming king of Navarre in 1425 and then king of the Crown of Aragón in 1458), the unfortunate Blanca consistently fell victim to the vagaries of political and dynastic intrigues.

Born in 1424, her first marriage to the Infante Enrique of Castile (the future Enrique IV) was arranged as a consequence of the peace treaty of Toledo of 1436 between Castile and Aragón-Navarre, the bethrothal conditions being drawn up early in 1437, and the marriage taking place in Valladolid in 1440 to the accompaniment of dazzling fiestas and elaborate *entremeses*, *juegos*, and *alegrías*.

The marriage, however, produced no children and was dissolved in 1453, the extraordinary reasons being set out in a lengthy canonical *sentencia*, or decision, delivered in a case presided over by the bishop of Segovia, Luis Vásquez de Acuña. According to this, the prince had never succeeded in having sexual intercourse with his wife, despite strenuous efforts, and two respectable and experienced women, probably midwives, testified that their physical examination of Blanca revealed that she was still a virgin. In addition, however, detailed evidence was accepted from certain women from Segovia that was designed to demonstrate beyond doubt that the prince frequently enjoyed perfectly normal sexual relations with them, evidence that of course was presented in order to provide conclusive proof of Enrique's virility. The essential point here is that all these salacious details made it possible for the case to be solemnly resolved on the grounds of an impotence that was specific rather than general, an impotence that applied only to Enrique's relationship with Blanca and that left both parties free to marry again after the annulment.

Yet such an extraordinary explanation amounted to a case of *maleficium*, with the clear implication that Blanca was the guilty party, and in addition she was obliged to leave Castile and return to Navarre. Her return posed fresh problems. Although her brother, Charles, prince of Viana, attempted to establish her rights as heiress to the throne, their father, Juan II of Aragón, retained effective control of Navarre. Indeed, Blanca never enjoyed any real freedom after her return. Charles of Viana died in 1461. Blanca, who had been kept virtually imprisoned in the castle of Olite, was subsequently handed over to the counts of Foix, the aim of Juan II almost certainly being to prevent her from marrying again, and thus vesting the right of succession in her sister, Leonor, Countess of Foix. Blanca died, allegedly of poison, in the castle at Orthez in 1464. Ironically, two years earlier she had relinquished her rights to the succession of Navarre to her ex-husband, Enrique IV. By this time, and equally ironically, rumors were already circulating at the Castilian court about both the latter's alleged homosexuality and his sexual impotence. The right of succession to Navarre passed to Blanca's sister, Leonor.

ANGUS MACKAY

Bibliography

Azcona, T. de. *Isabel la Católica: Estudio crítico de su vida y su reinado.* Madrid, 1964.

Marañón, G. *Ensayo biológico sobre Enrique IV de Castilla y su tiempo.* 14th ed. Madrid, 1997.

BLANCHE OF FRANCE

Blanche of France (1252–1320), daughter of Louis IX and Margaret of Provence, was wife to Fernando de la Cerda. Louis IX and Alfonso X of Castile (1252–1284) negotiated the marriage between Blanche and Fernando, Alfonso X's heir, when Blanche was fourteen and Fernando was eleven. According to the terms of the agreement, Blanche received a yearly income of 20,000 *maravedís*, a dowry of 10,000 *livres*, and retained the right to return to France and keep her income if her husband predeceased her. The wedding was celebrated in Burgos when Fernando came of age in 1269. The marriage ensured peace among Castile, France, and Navarre, although the display of the wedding feast and the guest list reflected Alfonso's European ambitions; later the Castilian nobles protested the sum that Alfonso spent on the celebrations. Blanche bore two sons, Alfonso and Fernando, later known as the Infantes de la Cerda. When Fernando de la Cerda predeceased his father in 1275, his younger brother Sancho was acknowledged as heir by the *cortes* (parliament) in 1276; the infantes were thus disinherited. Blanche's marriage contract left no provisions for her possible widowhood with disinherited minor children. The ensuing rupture with France reflected both concern over the payment of Blanche's Castilian income and the rights of the infantes to the throne. After the decision of the cortes, Blanche and her mother-in-law Queen Violante removed the infantes from Castile to Aragón. There they stayed in confinement while Blanche traveled to France and to Portugal, seeking supporters for her sons' rights. In France her brother, Philippe III, assumed the cause of the infantes to ensure his sister's income. Blanche sent representatives to Bayonne in 1290 where Philippe IV of France and Sancho IV of Castile (r. 1284–1295) decided her pension and possessions. She entered the Franciscan convent of Saint-Marcel of Paris, where she died 17 June 1320.

THERESA M. VANN

Bibliography

Ballesteros Beretta, A. *Alfonso X el Sabio.* Barcelona, 1984 [1963].

O'Callaghan, J. *A History of Medieval Spain.* Ithaca, N.Y., 1975.

BOABDIL, KING OF GRANADA *See* NASRID DYNASTY

BOBASTRO *See* IBN HAFSUN

BONIFAZ, RAMÓN

Of Italian or French descent, Ramón Bonifaz was one of those *francos* (people from beyond the Pyrenees) who settled in towns along the road to Compostela; in this particular case, the town was Burgos in the early thirteenth century. His fortune, derived mostly from mercantile activities, must have been substantial. In 1227, together with his cousin Arnalt Almarich, Bonifaz purchased a house in the neighborhood of Sanct Llorente, Burgos, for the unprecedented sum of 5,000 *maravedís*. He served as *alcalde* (mayor) of Burgos throughout most of the first half of the century, and in 1247 Ferdnando III, king of Castile and León, ordered Bonifaz to organize a fleet, drawn mostly from the Bay of Biscay ports, and to join the royal armies besieging Seville. Bonifaz's fleet, a motley combination of Cantabrian *naos* and *holops*, as well as some Mediterranean galleys, played a major role in the final capture of Seville in 1248, after breaking through a barge barricading the Guadalquivir River.

Although Burgalese historians have promoted Bonifaz as the first admiral of Castile, there is no convincing evidence that he ever held such title or that the fleet he gathered remained as a unit much longer beyond the Sevillian campaign. He was well rewarded by the king in the *repartimiento* of Seville and named a royal official in 1252.

Bonifaz's descendants dominated the social, economic, political and ecclesiastical life of Burgos for the next century and a half, holding important benefits (including the deanship of the cathedral chapter of Burgos) and municipal and royal positions. They also invested heavily in the land and real estate market in and around Burgos, a policy already initiated by the elderly Bonifaz.

TEÓFILO RUIZ

Bibliography

Avila y Díaz-Ubierna, G. *El primer almirante de Castilla: D. Ramón de Bonifaz y Camargo*. Burgos, n.d.

Ruiz, T. F. "Los Sarracín y los Bonifaz: Dos linajes patricios de Burgos, 1248–1350." In *Sociedad y poder real en Castilla*. Barcelona, 1981. 121–44.

BOOKS AND BOOKMAKING

The codicology of medieval Spanish books is still in its infancy. While there are good general studies available on the history of decorative bookbinding and manuscript illumination in Spain, monographic treatment of the archeology of the book is still wanting, and the difficulty results from many factors. Exemplars prior to the tenth and eleventh centuries are scarce, and many books were carelessly rebound in later centuries, including our own. Many fine examples of Spanish craft bindings were executed by and for Muslims and Jews whose works were destroyed by Islamic and Christian censors; our best information on practices among these Iberian connoisseurs of the book comes from witnesses elsewhere throughout the medieval Islamic (Tunisian, Moroccan) and Jewish worlds. As early as 531, prestigious Christian books were ravaged for their covers decorated with jewels, metalwork, and carved ivory or suppressed because of their contentious theological or liturgical content. Finally, the examination of the design, structures, and supports of books as integrated physical objects has commonly been subordinated to an interest in their decoration, whether on the illuminated page or on their tooled leather surfaces.

In terms of writing supports, Hispano-Romans probably employed the same materials as in the rest of Romania—namely, sheets of lead, papyrus, split wood, and wax tablets (still in use during the life of Gonzalo de Berceo). The long distance from Egypt and the disruption of sea lanes made the importation of papyrus to Iberia unreliable. Isidore of Seville records the availability of parchment from animal skins, and the same support later supplied the needs of the legendary libraries of the caliphate of Córdoba, which were reputed to boast 400,000 volumes. The adoption of parchment and the definitive adoption of the codex form date from the early Visigothic period. The classic Spanish codex, with gatherings of inscribed bifoliate leaves sewn across cords or parchment straps that were then attached to wood boards and covered with leather (sometimes with a Moorish-style flap that wraps around over the front cover), endured through the transition from parchment to paper and only saw serious modification with the advent of printing, when the leather-clad boards were replaced with cheaper limp covers.

Paper was introduced into al-Andalus by Islamic craftsmen in the twelfth century and grew into a highly advanced industry. Spanish paper, counted among the most prized in the Islamic world, was exported to sites as far away as Damascus and presumes a large number of local paper mills, mostly in the eastern half of the Iberian Peninsula but with several in the Guadalquivir valley below Córdoba. The most famous site of Moorish paper manufacture was in Játiva (Valencia), gradually incorporated into the kingdom of Aragón after 1244 by Jaime I, who inflated and nearly ruined the industry by optioning the entire output of its mills to stoke his paper-based bureaucracy, the first in Europe. Alfonso X included cautionary restrictions on the use of paper in the *Siete Partidas*, (Partida III.28.5), perhaps based on lingering prejudices against this Moorish artifact but also due to its still limited market as a taxable commodity within and beyond Iberia. The existence of a lively local trade in paper in southern Spain already in the mid-thirteenth century is suggested by the reams of blank script for sale in the miniature accompanying *cantiga* 173 in the *códice rico* (Escorial T.I.1). Paper established itself as the dominant book support in Spain by the early fourteenth century.

As elsewhere in premodern Europe, the production of books in Spain was a principally monastic affair until the start of the thirteenth century. Medieval Spanish universities, usually under royal rather than ecclesiastical patronage, never succeeded in sustaining a commercial infrastructure of parchmenters, stationers, book manufacturers, copyists, illuminators, and binders, as happened in Oxford and Paris. Interestingly, however, the visionary Alfonso X codified rules (Partida II.31.11) for maintaining stationers and certifying the reliability of the textbook chapters they rented out to students at the newly chartered universities in Salamanca (1254) and elsewhere. These rules antedate evidence of similar arrangements in Paris (1275) by a quarter of a century. Alfonso X can be credited with being the first true bibliophile of Spain—both commissioned books and treasured them as aesthetic objects—but noble patronage of the book arts did not flower as a by-product of class until the fifteenth century.

Romanesque and Gothic bookbindings manufactured in Spain, especially in the northeast, are much like their counterparts elsewhere in medieval Europe. One distinctively Spanish style of blind tooling on leather covers is commonly dubbed *hispano-árabe* or *mudéjar*, in not a few cases the creations of named Jewish and Moorish artisans working in the traditions of figured Cordovan goat skin. *Mudéjar* here refers to the fusion of Islamic decoration—precise interwoven plaitwork within sometimes complex geometric frames creating an interplay between areas of light and shadow—combined with the serial die stamping of transpyrenean decorative styles including straight lines and hatchwork with stamped rows of small figures of animals and other heraldic devices. Subsequent fifteenth-century styles incorporate effects of raised (*repujado*) covers with larger devices, in leather or applied metal work, sometimes set against or above rich cloth surfaces. Surviving bindings of this latter type include those made for the Marqués de Santillana and Queen Isabel I the Catholic, two of the earliest secular patrons of the book arts whose bindings survive in sufficient numbers for study. Toward the end of the fifteenth century, Flemish bindings (and the plastic arts in general) grew in influence in Spain, and a certain Antonio de Gavere of Bruges was court binder to Felipe el Hermoso. Full-cover stamping plates, decorating with patterning wheels, and mosaics of colored leather patches are all postmedieval phenomena, but tooling in gold leaf, a clearly Renaissance innovation in the rest of Europe, was already practiced by Muslim artisans in Spain in the thirteenth century and apparently spread, along with *mudéjar* decorative motifs, to the rest of the continent during Aragón's possession of Naples in the mid-fifteenth century.

New areas of study that focus on the medieval book in Spain are emerging in recent decades. There is fresh interest in the book as a symbolic object representing and bearing power within medieval society, and also as a nexus for the negotiation of meaning between writers and readers. The physical constraints of the medium enlighten studies of how books circulated and were reproduced, and also how they were used and shared by their consumers. The written page, with or without other decoration, is increasingly seen as an aesthetic unit worthy of examination, especially as it modulates the message of the text presented on it. The study of the evolution of the formal elements of Spanish books as cultural artifacts is also gaining greater regard as scholars explore their ties to the burgeoning market economy, the expansion of literacy, the diffusion of intellectual trends, the growth of private collections, the privatization of intellectual pursuits, and the interiorization of devotional practices.

George D. Greenia

Bibliography

Bohigas, P. *El libro español (ensayo histórico)*. Barcelona, 1962.

Brugalla, E. *El arte en el libro y en la encuadernación*. Bilbao, 1977.

Burns, R. I., S. J. "The Paper Revolution in Europe: Crusader Valencia's Paper Industry—A Technological and Behavioral Breakthrough," *Pacific Historical Review* 50, no. 1 (1980), 1–30.

Carrión Gútiez, M. "La encuadernación española en la Edad Media." In *Los manuscritos españoles*. Ed. Escolar Sobrino Hipólito. Madrid, 1993. 364–99.

Las edades del hombre. Libros y documentos en la iglesia de Castilla y León. Valladolid, 1990.

Encuadernaciones españolas en la Biblioteca Nacional. Ed. J. Ollero. Madrid, 1992.

Escolar, H. *Historia del libro*. Madrid, 1984.

Millares Carlo, A. *Introducción a la historia del libro y de las bibliotecas*. México City, 1971.

Ruiz, E. *Manual de codicología*. Madrid, 1988.

BOURGEOISIE

The development of the bourgeoisie in medieval Castile is closely related to the renewal of urban life in the region. The growth of towns in northern Castile, the conquest of great Muslim urban centers (Toledo, Córdoba, and Seville), and the foundation of new cities along conflicting frontiers led to the emergence of distinct patterns of economic development and social organization. If by *bourgeoisie* in the medieval context one understands as those urban middling groups who stood outside the so-called feudal relations and who, moreover, did not obtain their income from the land but from artisanal crafts, commerce, and financial transactions, then there was no bourgeoisie in Castile. It is doubtful that there were well-defined feudal ties between lords and vassals in the region, or, at least, in the manner in which those ties existed in France and England. There were a few cities and small towns in which the middling urban groups derived most of their income from long distance trade—Burgos, some of the ports on the Bay of Biscay (Bilbao, San Sebastián, etc.)—but even in such places, there is ample evidence that the bourgeoisie invested heavily in land and often lived a good part of the year in their rural estates. What types of social grouping, of social and economic organization can be thus described for medieval Castile?

The Revival of Urban Life

Most of the towns in the ancient kingdom of Asturias and later in its successor, the kingdom of León, were mere administrative centers or ecclesiastical sees. Urban centers such as Cangas de Onís and even Leóan in the period between the early eighth century and the beginning of the eleventh barely generated enough trade and artisanal activity to bring about the development of a fully formed bourgeoisie. North of the Duero River, in the area that in the eleventh century became the kingdom of Castile, the rise of the bourgeoisie was directly related to the popularity of the pilgrimage to Compostela. The large number of pilgrims who poured into the peninsula on the way to Compostela led to the emergence of towns and cities, convenient rest stops, along the road. Francos, people from beyond the Pyrenees, settled in Logroño, Vitoria, Burgos, Sahagún, and even in towns off the main pigrimage route, such as Santo Domingo de Silos. Merchants and artisans, these francos formed the core of an incipient bourgeoisie. They settled in the towns, and in less than a century they and their descendants married locally and set roots in their adopted cities. Together with a socially mobile local population, these groups, a mixture of foreign, foreign descendants, and native formed the bourgeoisie of northern Castile. Their ties with northern markets, above all with the textile centers of Flanders and northern Europe, gave them an advantage in the commercial competition that marked the opening of Castile and of Iberia to Cluniac and European-wide influence in the eleventh and twelfth centuries.

In many respects, the bourgeoisie of specific towns along the Road to Compostela behaved along patterns similar to those of their northern counterparts. In the twelfth century, these bourgeois groups challenged, in Sahagún, Compostela, and other towns, the authority of their ecclesiastical or lay lords. This period of bourgeois rebellions led, in spite of seignorial victories, to the political and social rise of bourgeois groups in most northern Castilian cities. Unlike their northern counterparts, the Castilian bourgeoisie played a significant military role from the very beginnings of its existence. Their wealth allowed them to serve on horseback, and this provided them with a clear superiority—military, social, economic, and political—against other social groups within the city. It also made the city militia an important component of the expansionist policies of the Iberian kings, as well as a formidable ally in the perennial struggle of the crown against nobiliary ambitions.

The Castilian Bourgeoisie South of the Duero River

The patterns of reconquest and settlement south of the Duero and the economic structure of the towns founded or resettled in the region dictated the emergence of urban groups quite distinct from those along the road to Compostela. Urban centers such as Avila, Segovia, Cuéllar, and Sepúveda developed a bourgeoisie that did not have the commercial orientation of the bourgeoisie along the road to Compostela. In the Duero basin, the ruling urban groups derived their income mostly from ranching and land rents. Artisanal and mercantile activities (mostly of a local nature) were often in the hands of Jews, Muslims, or foreigners. Patterns of inhabitation also indicate a flow from city to countryside and vice versa. Prominent members of the bourgeosie maintained country estates and farms in the towns' hinterlands. This was a pattern also present in the more commercially oriented cities of the north, but not to the extent to which it existed in places such as Avila. There, for example, the life of the bourgeoisie was decisively tied to the land. In very general terms, one can argue that the process of aristocratization of the bourgeoisie, a phenomenom that took place throughout Castile, was far more rapid and effective in those places without a strong mercantile orientation.

Urban Centers in Andalucía

The conquests of Córdoba (1236), Seville (1248), and other Andalusian cities marked the emergence of yet another stage in the development of the Castilian bourgeoisie. The original Muslim inhabitants were expelled from cities throughout Andalucía and repopulated with Christian inhabitants, mostly from the armies that had helped conquer the land. Foreigners, most notably Genoese and other Italians in Seville, soon came to dominate long distance trade and to profit, after the opening of the Strait of Gibraltar to Christian sailing, from the maritime linking of the Mediterranean and North Atlantic markets. Jews also played a significant role in the commercial life of the south and, after the massive conversions of 1391, *conversos* became an important and numerous component of Andalusian bourgeoisies. This was certainly the case at Seville, Jaén, and other towns in the region.

Economy, Society, and Culture

As indicated above, the Castilian bourgeoisie was engaged in a variety of economic pursuits and derived its income from different sources. The top echelon of the bourgeoisie of Burgos, probably the most dynamic and outward looking in northern Castile, gained its prominence from long distance trade. This meant, above all, the import of woolens and luxury textiles from Flanders and other manufacturing centers in northern Europe. It also exported horses, iron, hides, agricultural products, and, after 1350, immense amounts of wool. These bourgeois groups also benefited from the distribution of imported goods through the realm. Elsewhere in Castile, bourgeois elites gained their living from local trade, or more likely from rents and from ranching. In the south, patterns of trade and agricultural production were different. Seville drew into its orbit both Atlantic and Mediterranean products and exported olive oil and wine to local and foreign markets. Yet, regardless of location or of economic structure, the Castilian bourgeoisie uniformly invested its profits in land. Whether at Burgos, Avila, or Seville, the bourgoisie entered the market for land with a vengeance and, from the early thirteenth century on, built substantial landed estates. This seignorialization of the Castilian bourgeoisie represented an important stage in its development. Historians have argued for the structural weakness of the Castilian bourgeoisie and have held this responsible for the economic shortcomings of early modern Spain. This is accurate only in a very limited sense. In truth, because the import of luxury textiles from abroad and the export of wool proved to be so profitable for Castilian merchants and for the crown, there never was any serious or sustained effort to create a manufacturing economy. On the other hand, in its own terms, the Castilian bourgeoisie was extremely successful. By the mid-fourteenth century, it had moved boldly into the ranks of the lower nobility or enjoyed, through its military service, privileges usually reserved for the nobility elsewhere. It played an important role in the political life of the realm through its participation in the *cortes* and *hermandades* and through the monopoly, with the king's support, of municipal government. By the fifteenth century, the Castilian bourgeoisie (by this time most of them conversos) provided the bulk of the *letrado* (learned) group. Thus, they formed the core of royal administration and spearheaded the reception of the Renaissance in Castile.

Similarly, regardless of its economic orientation, the upper levels of the bourgeoisie, what one may describe as a patrician elite, also monopolized the most important urban ecclesiastical benefices. From the mid-thirteenth century on, important canonships, deanships, and even bishoprics were held by members of the bourgeoisie. This signaled an important transformation in the life of the church, for it meant the partial privatization of ecclesiastical resources. It also provided bourgeois groups with additional sources of income and social mobility.

Socially, the bourgeoisie established its distinctiveness from other social groups by the creation of exclusive brotherhoods and fraternities. Open only to members of the upper bourgeois groups, these religious and social organizations also brought together those sharing equal economic interests. Above all, these brotherhoods or fraternities reaffirmed social, economic, and political hierarchies and fostered the hegemonic policies of the bourgeoisie toward other social groups within their respective cities. How successful they were in establishing their control is clearly attested in the absence in Castile of any serious challenge to bourgeois control by less privileged urban groups. Although there are numerous reports of urban unrest throughout Castile, they never erupted into full-scale class conflicts, as they did elsewhere in the west. Moreover, the linking of patrician elites with important nobiliary houses through marriage and business also furthered the social, economic, and political hegemony of the Castilian patriciate.

TEÓFILO RUIZ

Bibliography

Gautier-Dalché, J. *Historia urbana de León y Castilla en la Edad Media (siglos IX–XIII).* Madrid, 1979.

García de Valdeavellano, L. *Orígenes de la burguesía en la España medieval.* Madrid, 1969.

Casado Soto, H. *Señores, mercaderes y campesinos: La comarca de Burgos a fines de la Edad Media.* Valladolid, 1987.

BRAGA

The archbishopric of Braga is one of the oldest centers of Christianity in the Iberian Peninsula. Under the rule of the Suevi in the sixth century, Galicia had embraced Arianism, but the arrival of Martin to its shores around 550 changed the entire situation. Martin, a monk and one of the most distinguished thelogians of his time, became the abbot of Dume and a bishop in 556. He took part in the first council of Braga in 561 and later became an archbishop, presiding at the second council of Braga in 572. From that year onward, his name appears in all records as Martin of Braga. He converted the Suevi kings to Christianity and worked hard to eradicate pagan practices, which were common among the peasants.

The church of Braga went through a very difficult period at the time of the Muslim domination. The bishop of Braga had to live for centuries in Asturias. Following the conquest of the city by Fernando the Great, the cathedral was restored in 1070. In 1121 Pope Calixtus II transferred the rights of the church of Mérida, which was under Muslim jurisdiction, to the cathedral of Compostela. But the archbishop of Compostela claimed also as its suffragan dioceses Lamego, Viseu, Guarda, Coimbra, Bisboa, and Evora. The archbishops of Braga and the kings of Portugal never accepted this claim and raised all sorts of obstacles to the prelates who wanted to fulfil their duties, sustaining the primacy of Braga in the peninsula. Braga had as its suffragan dioceses Oporto, Viseu, and Coimbra in Portugal, as well as Mondoñedo, Lugo, Orense, Túy, and Astorga in Castilian territory. Castilian intervention in Portuguese affairs between 1383 and 1385, followed by the war that gave Portugal its independence, led Boniface IX in his bull *In eminentissimae dignitatis* of 10 November 1393 to bring ecclesiastical frontiers in line with national boundaries.

In the fifteenth century the church had to face a serious conflict with the crown. Fernando da Guerra (1387–1467), archbishop of Braga (1417–1467), was a strenous upholder of the rights and privileges of the church. He reorganized the economy of the dioceses and fought vigorously the violences of the nobility against the church. On 10 January 1437, he recovered from King Duarte all the rights and privileges he had lost. Fernando da Guerra was the great-grandson of Pedro I and a nephew of João I.

Luis Rebelo

Bibliography

Almeida, F. de. *História da Igreja em Portugal.* 4 vols. Porto, 1967–71.

Marques, J. *A Arquidiocese de Braga no século XV.* Lisbon, 1988.

BRAGANZA, HOUSE OF

Founded in Portugal in the fifteenth century, the house of Braganza was established with the first duke of the same title, Dom Afonso (1377–1461). He was the illegitimate son of Dom João, Master of Avis, later João I, and Inés Pires. This relationship was dissolved before João I married Philippa of Lancaster, who welcomed Afonso at the court. On 1 November 1401 Afonso married Beatriz, the daughter of Nun'Alvares Pereira and Leonor Alvim. Nun'Alvares was the wealthiest nobleman of the realm and, as he had no other offspring, he made large donations of land and castles to Beatriz on her wedding. On the other hand, João I provided Afonso with more land and made him the count of Barcelos (1401). This property was further increased when Beatriz gave birth to Afonso (1402–1460), Fernando (1403–1478), and Isabel (1404–1465). Nun'Alvares granted Fernando large estates in the south and made him the count of Arraiolos. Through marriage alliances the family gained great power in the country. In 1424 Isabel married her uncle João (1400–1442), the son of João I, thus strenghtening the family ties with the crown. Her father Afonso was granted the title of first duke of Braganza in 1442 by the regent Dom Pedro on behalf of Afonso V. The vast estates owned by Afonso were secured in perpetuity in 1433 by King Duarte.

The first duke was an ambitious man and sought to increase his power and wealth even further. He opposed the policy of centralization pursued by the regent Pedro since 1443 and persuaded Afonso V to turn against him. His machinations led to a military confrontation between Afonso V and Pedro, who was killed in the Battle of Alfarrobeira (1449). The duke of Braganza gained materially from Pedro's defeat, being the undisputed leader of the interests of the high aristocracy. The duke's son, Fernando, became the second duke of Braganza, as his brother Afonso, count of Ourem, died one year before his father. Fernando had fought in Tangier and was appointed governor of Ceuta in 1445. He had tried unsuccessfully to dissuade his father and his brother from plotting the downfall of Pedro. In 1429 he married Joana de Castro, daughter of Dom João de Castro and Dona Leonor da Cunha. His son, Fernando II (1430–1483), became the third duke of Braganza (1475) and second duke of Guimarães. He married Isabel, daughter of Fernando, the son of Duarte I, and Beatriz, daughter of João, the fourth son of João I. Fernando, the third duke of Braganza, incurred the wrath of João II when he opposed the king in his struggle to curb the power of the great houses.

Fernando was tried for treason and executed in Evora in 1483. All his titles and estates were forfeited by the crown. These were restored by Manuel I (1469–1521) in his royal charter of 18 June 1496. Dom Jaime (1479–1532), Fernando's son, the fourth duke, returned to Portugal from Madrid in 1496.

Luis Rebelo

Bibliography

Caetano de Sousa, A. *História Genealógica da Casa Real Portuguesa.* 2d ed. Coimbra, 1948.

de Vilhena, M. de. *A Casa de Bragança, Memória Histórica.* Lisbon, 1886.

BRAULIO

Braulio came from a family deeply entrenched in the church in the northeast of the Iberian Peninsula. His father Gregorio was a bishop, probably of Osma, and one of his brothers, Fronimian, was abbot of the monastery founded on the site of the hermitage of St. Aemilian in the Rioja (later San Millan de la Cogolla), at least one of his sisters was an abbess. His other brother Juan held the bishopric of Zaragoza, to which Braulio succeeded on the latter's death in 631. Prior to this, Braulio had spent some time in Seville, where he studied with Isidore before returning to become Archdeacon of Zaragoza under John. For his brother

Fronimian he wrote a *Life of St. Aemilian* (ca. 636), and he drew up a list of the works of Isidore which that has been used to establish the authenticity and possible chronology of several of them. He carried out an editorial revision of Isidore's *Etymologiae* after the latter's death, and the present structuring of the work is probably that imposed by Braulio. His own most substantial literary inheritance is a corpus of forty-four letters, addressed to a wide variety of lay and clerical correspondents. These are among the most stylish literary products of the Visigothic period. After Isidore's death he seems to have been regarded as the foremost intellectual figure in the Visigothic Church, and he was entrusted by the bishops assembled at the Sixth Council of Toledo in 638 with the task of replying on their behalf to various criticisms that Pope Honorius I (papacy 625–638) had made of their failure to take sterner measures against the Jews.

One of Braulio's closest friends and disciples, Eugenius, who had previously been archdeacon of Zaragoza, became metropolitan bishop of Toledo in 636. By the time of Braulio's death in 651, intellectual leadership of the Spanish church had passed firmly into the hands of Toledo.

ROGER COLLINS

Bibliography

Lynch, C. H. *Saint Braulio, Bishop of Saragossa (631–651): His Life and Writings*. Washington, D.C., 1938.

Riesco Terrero, L. (ed.) *Epistolario de San Braulio*. Seville, 1975.

BREVIARY OF ALARIC

The Breviary of Alaric, also known as the *Lex Romana Visigothorum*, or "Roman Law of the Visigoths," was issued by the Visigothic king Alaric II (484–507) in the year 506. It consists of an abridged text of the Theodosian Code, to most of the laws of which are added what are called "interpretations." These are statements modifying the meaning or application of the law to which they are appended. Such a procedure for adapting Roman imperial law to local conditions had been employed by the Praetorian prefects of the Late Roman Empire, and Alaric and his advisers were thus following an established precedent. It is often thought that Alaric's Breviary was intended to apply only to his Roman subjects, while his Visigothic followers would be judged by the laws contained in the code of his father, King Euric (r. 466–484). This is probably mistaken, and both codes, which are neither mutually contradictory nor overlapping in their contents, should be seen as applying to all those subject to the Visigothic monarchs. The *Forum iudicum*, or *Lex Visigothorum*, the code of law issued by Recesvinth in 654, replaced all previous laws of the Visigothic kingdom, and thus put an end to the use of the Breviary.

ROGER COLLINS

Bibliography

Conrat, M. (ed.) *Breviarium Alaricanum*. Leipzig, 1903.

Collins, R. *Early Medieval Spain: Unity in Diversity, 300–1000*. London, 1983. 24–31.

BUREAUCRACY *See* ADMINISTRATION, CENTRAL

BURGOS, CITY OF

The medieval history of the city of Burgos is closely related to Castilian history, producing between the ninth and fifteenth centuries a perfect transition between the region's stages as a *condado* (territory ruled by a count) and as a kingdom. Christian repopulation in the time of Alfonso reached the banks of the Arlanzón River and resulted in the construction of a fortress around which several towns (*burgos*) were established. Diego Rodríguez Porcelos is commonly believed to have founded the city in 884. In the tenth century, Fernán González helped bring about the unification of Castile, and the existence of a primitive city wall is mentioned, which, along with the castle, would have been characteristic features of the city. The population would have been concentrated in the regions closest to the sides of the hill, and neighborhoods were organized around the churches—San Lorenzo, San Esteban—which played an important role in the configuration of the city.

The city's importance as headquarters of the Castilian monarchs brought the nobility's presence to Burgos. Other important moments in the evolution of the city were the relocation of the episcopal see of Oca to Burgos, and the construction of the Church of Santa María in the lower section of the city, which was built on land donated by Alfonso VI for a Romanesque cathedral. At the end of the eleventh century, San Lesmes created the Monasterio de San Juan outside the city walls. The building included a hospital, which became important due to the city's location on the route of Santiago. In the twelfth century the population in the lower river regions (la Llana) increased, and in 1187 Alfonso VIII established the Monasterio de las Huelgas, the Royal Pantheon, and the Hospital del Rey. The city also began to acquire an elongated shape stretching from east to west. The Jewish and Moorish quarters were located in the northwestern end of the city. These groups were important components of the population and participated actively in the city's economic activity, which was dominated by agriculture and craftsmanship. Beginning in the thirteenth century, Burgos (especially la Llana) was the commercial hub of northern Castile. The city's international economic activity was in the hands of a few families that acquired great wealth, power, and prestige, marking Burgos with a brief moment of glory in the fifteenth century.

The thirteenth-century construction of the Gothic cathedral (under the initiative of Bishop Mauritius and King Fernando III) was a decisive element of the city's urban configuration. Along with the parochial churches and the monasterios, which experienced a time of splendor at the end of the Middle Ages when the city reached its highest glory under the Catholic Monarchs, the cathedral was the most important religious center in Burgos. Other notable buildings are the palace known as "Casa del Cordón" and the Carthusian monastery of Miraflores, whose church contains extraordinary works of art, including the magnificent altarpiece and the tombs of Juan II and his wife Isabel.

MARÍA JESÚS GÓMEZ BÁRCENA

Bibliography

Estepa Diez, C., T. F. Ruiz, J. A. Bonachia Hernando, and H. Casado Alonso. *Burgos en la Edad Media*. Ed. and prologue Julio Valdeón. Junta de Castilla y León. Valladolid, 1984.

Montenegro Duque, A. (ed.) *Historia de Burgos*. Vol. 2, *Edad Media*. Burgos, 1986.

BURGOS, SOCIO-ECONOMIC HISTORY OF

Located on the banks of the Arlanzón River, on a strategic hill dominating ancient roads, the city of Burgos was founded in the early 880s (either 882 or 884) by Count Diego Porcelos, one of the rulers of the fledgling county of Castile. First as a strong place, a castle on the moving frontier with Islam in the ninth and tenth centuries, later as the see for the peripatetic diocese of Valpuesta-Oca, Gamonal, in the 1080s, the city became a bustling commercial center by the eleventh century and remained the most important distribution center for international and regional trade in northern Castile until the early modern period.

To a large extent, the development of commerce and of a bourgeoisie in the city was influenced by the pilgrimage to Compostela. Burgos, as one of the main stops on the road, it benefited from the pilgrimage trade and from the settlement within its walls of numerous foreign merchants, the *francos* of early castilian *fueros* (municipal charters). The city also became a favorite residence of the Castilian kings, a preferred site for the meetings of the *cortes* (parliament), the location of the royal chancery, and unofficial capital of the realm—or as its shield proudly proclaimed, *caput Castellae*.

Throughout the twelfth entury, foreign and native merchant families intermarried, and at the onset of the thirteenth century, these mercantile groups became a well-entrenched and powerful oligarchical elite. Deriving their income from long-distance trade—mostly the import of woolen cloth from Flanders—these merchants began to monopolize municipal offices and, by the thirteenth century, held tight control of the municipal council. The complex process by which a small group came to dominate the economic, social, and political life of Burgos and other Castilian cities is also directly related to the tax exemption granted by Alfonso X to the non-noble knights of Burgos and other cities after 1256.

Organized as a mounted militia, exempted from most taxes, enjoying a secure financial base and an almost complete monopoly of municipal and royal offices in Burgos, a few family groups, most notable the Sarracín and the Bonifaz, also invested heavily in the Burgalese hinterland, building sizable rural estates and binding the countryside to the city. In addition, they founded and/or joined exclusive brotherhoods and monopolized ecclesiastical benefices, turning Church income to their own benefit.

Institutionally, Burgos, a royal city, participated actively in the *hermandades* or leagues of cities organized in 1296 and 1315 to protect the crown from rapacious regents and unruly nobles. Its aspirations to autonomy, however, were short-lived indeed. By 1345, the imposition of the regimiento in Burgos and other Castilian cities, with the approval of the ruling oligarchy, signaled the beginning of direct royal control over municipal affairs.

Burgos's heyday, however, still lay in the future. After the upheavals of the mid-fourteenth century, the rise of the wool trade made the city the center for the profitable export of wool. The *consulado* of Burgos was the expression of this new commercial power, and by the late fifteenth and early sixteenth centuries Burgalese merchants appeared prominently in Flemish cities. Yet the long trend that moved the center of Iberian life southward and outward, the rise of Madrid as the capital of the kingdoms, and the economic disasters of the early modern period brought about the city's inexorable downfall.

TEÓFILO RUIZ

Bibliography

Estepa, C. et al. *Burgos en la Edad Media*. Valladolid, 1984.

BURGUNDY, HOUSE OF

The ducal and comital houses of Burgundy were two of the greatest lineages of the French kingdom, and both were much involved in the affairs of León-Castile in the eleventh and twelfth centuries. Duke Robert the

House of Burgundy

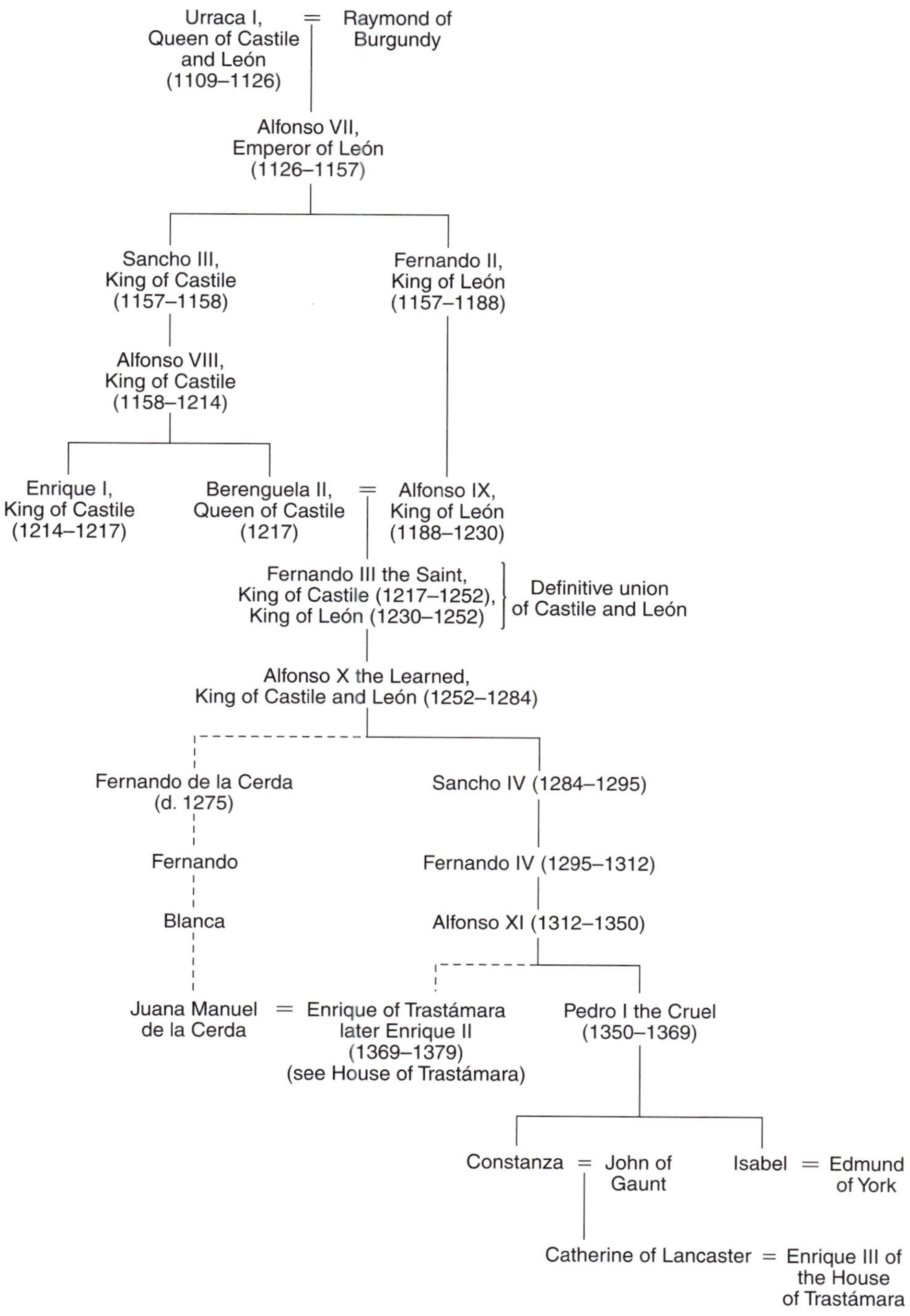

Old (r. 1032–1037) was the younger son of King Robert the Pious (996–1034) and the father of Constance, who became the second wife and queen of Alfonso VI of León-Castile (1065–1109) between 1079 and 1093. She thus became the mother of his future successor, Queen Urraca (1109–1126) but did not provide him with any other progeny who survived. One uncle of Constance was the great Abbot Hugh of Cluny (1049–1109), under whom that house came to receive an annual subsidy from Fernando I of León-Castile

(1037–1065), which was doubled by Alfonso VI in 1090. Both the latter and his daughter and successor also granted a number of monasteries in the realm to Cluny, which became the substance of a new Iberian province of the growing Benedictine order.

Count Guillaum the Great of Burgundy (1057–1087) was the grandson of Duke Richard II of Normandy and himself the father of Guy, Archbishop of Vienne and subsequently Pope Calixtus II (1119–1124), and Raymond, who was betrothed to Urraca of León-Castile about 1087. Raymond was named Count of Galicia about 1088, married Urraca about 1090, and became father of the future Alfonso VII of Leon-Castile (1126–1157) on 1 March 1105. He died on 20 September 1107.

However, the sister of Count Guillaum of Burgundy, Sybil, had married another son of Duke Robert the Old, Henri, and one product of this marriage was that Henri of Burgundy who was married to Teresa, the natural daughter of Alfonso VI of León-Castile, and appointed Count of Portugal in late 1096. He and his cousin, Count Raymond of Galicia, then controlled the entire western third of the kingdom. Count Henri remained the effective ruler of the province of Portugal during the civil war that erupted after the death of Alfonso VI on 1 July 1109, until his own death in that struggle at Astorga in May 1112.

His widow, Teresa, was the half-sister of Queen Urraca and vied with the latter for control of León-Castile after 1112, though unsuccessfully. From 1112 on Teresa was the independent ruler of Portugal and began to style herself queen after 1117. She remarried into the great Galician House of Trastámara and ruled in Portugal jointly with her new husband, Count Fernando Pérez of Traba, until their expulsion after their defeat by her own son, Afonso Henriques, at the battle of San Mamed on 24 June 1128. Teresa died in exile in Galicia in November of 1130, leaving a daughter, Sancha, by Fernando Pérez.

Her son by Count Henri of Burgundy, Afonso I (1128–1185), was the first king of an independent Portugal. Afonso initially styled himself merely "Infans" of the royal house of León-Castile, but from 1137 began to call himself "Portugalensis Princeps" and after 1140 "Portugalensium Rex." These changes were accompanied by warfare with his cousin, Alfonso VII of León-Castile, and resulted in the rule of two of the major Iberian kingdoms during much of the twelfth century by the sons of Burgundian counts.

BERNARD F. REILLY

Bibliography

Defourneaux, M. *Les français en Espagne aux XIe et XIIe siècles*. Paris, 1949.

Reilly, B. F. *The Kingdom of León-Castila under King Alfonso VI, 1065-1109*. Princeton, N.J., 1988.

———. *The Kingdom of León-Castilla under Queen Urraca, 1109–1126*. Princeton, N.J., 1982.

C

CABALA, CABALISM *See* MOSES DE LEÓN

CABALLERÍA FAMILY

One of the most promient Jewish dynasties of government officials in Aragón-Catalonia was that of the Caballerías (or Cavallerías, also known as Ibn Labi). Jahuda was the first important member, living in Zaragoza (as did most of the family for centuries), and in 1258 was already royal *baile* (bailiff) for Jaime I. The king borrowed money constantly from Jahuda, but also granted property and ever-increasing power to him. In 1260 he already was granted the power to receive all the taxes of the entire kingdom and was given virtual control over revenues. We do not hear of him after 1276, in which year (or shortly after) he probably died. The Caballerías were related to other powerful families (the Benvenistes and the Alcostantinís) and it was members of the latter family who rose to the highest ranks of government service under Pedro III and Jaime II.

In the fourteenth century we hear of prominent members of the family again in Zaragoza, including at least one doctor. The most important was Bienvenist de la Caballería, who for services to the archbishop was put in charge of all taxes for the region of Teruel (1396), having been an official of the royal treasury for Juan II since 1386. He was highly praised, and his power as an important government official was recognized in a Hebrew eulogy on his death (1414?). His son Juan, a *converso* (convert to Catholicism), became *comprador mayor* in 1414, and another son, Gonzalo (also a converso), reached even higher power as treasurer of certain taxes. Another member of the family, Bonafós, who also converted and took the name Fernando (in honor of the king, Fernando I), became that king's chief treasurer in 1414.

The son of this Fernando was Pedro de la Cavallería, a jurist and counselor of Alfonso V, as well as his *maestre racional* (essentially, in charge of the royal household). Like many conversos, he was a rabid anti-Semite and wrote a stinging denunciation of Judaism (*Zelus Christi*). He tried to convince the authorities he was not of Jewish descent, but failed. Under Juan II of Aragón Luis de Caballería was also an important converso treasurer.

In the reign of Fernando II, (ca. 1485 on), Alfonso, the son of Pedro, was vice-chancellor of Aragón-Catalonia. His grandson Francisco de la Caballería married Juana de Aragón, the great-granddaughter of Juan II (through his illegitimate son Alfonso, who also married a conversa).

There were also important members of the Ibn Labi/Benveniste–Caballería families in Castile, most of whom remained Jewish. One of these was an important rabbi, Vidal b. Benveniste de la Caballería, one of the last in Castile, who negotiated with the king of Portugal for the entry of Jews expelled from Castile in 1492.

NORMAN ROTH

Bibliography

Roth, N. *Conversos, Inquisition, and the Expulsion of the Jews from Spain*. Madison, Wisc., 1995.

Serrano y Sanz, M. *Orígenes de la dominación española en América*. Madrid, 1918.

Vendrell, F. "Aportaciones documentales para el estudio de la familia Caballería," *Sefarad* 3 (1943), 115–154.

CABALLEROS FIJOSDALGO, VILLANOS

In the simplest of definitions, a *caballero* is a man who fights on horseback—that is, a knight. In medieval Castile, the term *caballero* included a whole range of possibilities: from noble knights to non-noble knights living in the countryside or in towns, and to caballeros whose status and military service on horseback was directly related to income—the *caballeros de cuantía*. The definition of these different categories, of the duties and privileges concomitant with the rank depended, to a large extent, on location and on the period. Any attempt at providing a single definition must take into account all the variations in status, rights, and sources of income that were present in Castile from the tenth to the fifteenth centuries.

A *caballero fijodalgo* usually meant the lowest level of the nobility. They were noble knights, and most of them (except for those of Andalucía after 1250) lived in the countryside. Their income came from peasants' dues collected in their small estates or farms, from service to other more influential or powerful noblemen, and from booty or military service. The term *fijodalgo* (son of something) reveals that nobility was intrinsically linked, at least in Castile, to property. In a society in which almost everyone was liable for military duties, military service was not the monopoly of a social group. Thus, there was not in Castile the clear linking between fighting on horseback and noble status. Others who were not noble also fought on horseback and enjoyed, for all practical purposes, most of the benefits derived from such service. The condition of fijosdalgo, however, was hereditary and at the end, unlike that of the *caballero villano*, did not depend strictly on the performance of military duties and maintenance of horse and weapons.

Caballeros villanos, or non-noble urban knights, also served on horseback. Their privileges, above all exemption from most taxes, was directly related to their ownership of a house within the city walls, a horse, and appropriate weapons. This readiness to join the city militias in military campaigns was tested once a year. At the *alarde*, the parading in front of municipal officials with horse and weapons, the caballeros villanos showed that they had the necessary equipment for war. All their privileges derived from the fulfillment of the above conditions. Obviously, the status of caballero villano, if one were a Christian and a citizen of the town, depended strictly on income and was not, at least in the period before 1350, hereditary. Regardless of the dangers of warfare, the privileges granted to the caballeros villanos through the centuries, but especially by Alfonso X in the 1250s, allowed this group to gain a monopoly of the economic, political, and social life of Castilian cities. In the turbulent century and a half that followed the conquest of Seville in 1248, they provided valuable support for the crown. Often, as was the case in 1315, they joined the *fijosdalgo* in leagues, or *hermandades*, aimed at protecting the king from the ambitions of the high nobility.

In Andalucía, after the capture of the south by Fernando III and his son, Alfonso X, the kings of Castile sought to promote the development of the caballeria. In cities, such as Seville, we find fijosdalgo, caballeros villanos, and caballeros de cuantía sharing the same urban setting and martial responsibilities on the frontier. In the latter case, those with a certain income were commanded to maintain a horse and weapon and to render military service. What has been a privilege became an obligation. At the same time, however, the condition and status of caballero villano became, through the ordinances of the *cortes* and royal legislation, for all practical purposes hereditary. By the late thirteenth century and in the late Middle Ages, there was little difference between the two groups, a process of social mobility by which the upper echelons of the Castilian bourgeoisie entered the ranks of the lower nobility.

Teófilo Ruiz

Bibliography

García de Valdeavellano, L. *Curso de historia de las instituciones españolas: De los orígenes al final de la Edad Media*. Madrid, 1968.

Pescador, C. "La caballería popular en León y Castilla," *Cuadernos de historia de España* 33–34 (1961), 101–238; 35–36 (1962), 156–201; 37–38 (1963), 88–198; 39–40 (1964), 169–269.

CABESTANY, GUILLEM DE

(1175–1212) Knight and troubadour from the Catalan region of Rosselló who fought in the Battle of Las Navas de Tolosa (1212). According to the Provençal troubadours' biographies, which attributed a widely spread folk motif to Guillem's life, his romance with Saurimonda ended tragically: Ramon de Castell-Rosselló, the jealous husband, killed Guillem and made the adulteress eat her lover's heart; when Saurimonda realized the horror of it, she committed suicide. This fiction, containing characters who really existed, was the basis of Guillem's medieval fame as an archetype of the martyr of love, and even aroused the romantic interest of historians and writers, such as Stendhal. There are traces of Guillem's fame in Boccaccio's *Decameron* and Petrarch's *Trionfi* or in the Catalan verse vision *La glòria d'amor* of Bernat Hug de Rocabertí. All eight of Guillem's poems (one other is of dubious attribution), written in a perfect Occitan, are love songs that strictly follow the rhetorical pattern of the troubadour *canso*. One of them (*Ar vei qu'em vengut als jorns loncs*) points to Arnaut Daniel's style, because of the difficult rhymes and some unusual comparisons. However, Guillem is mainly a poet of the *trobar leu* who deals skilfully with the courtly love conventions by putting stress on the delicacy of the images (*Aissi cum cel que baissal fuoill*) and by subtle development of a wide range of love sentiments, like in *Lo doutz cossire*, to express the loyal memory of his beloved. This is his finest piece, remarkably written in short lines of four and six syllables, and it had a strong success, probably related to the legend. It is widely copied in the extant manuscripts; its verse pattern was followed by Cerverí de Girona, among other troubadours, and a fourteenth-century Catalan treatise mentions it twice as a model.

LLUIS CABRÉ

Bibliography

Cots, M. "Las poesías del trovador Guillem de Cabestany," *Boletín de la Real Academia de Buenas Letras de Barcelona* 40 (1985–86), 227–330.

Riquer, M. de. "Guillem de Cabestany." In *Història de la literatura catalana: Part antiga.* 4 vols. Barcelona, 1984–85. 1:95–101.

CABRERA, GUERAU DE

Catalan troubadour (1145–1159.) who has been identified as Guerau III de Cabrera, Viscount of Girona and Ager. His only extant poem, a *sirventes-ensenhamen*, (didactic, satirical, political poem) addressed to his jongleur Cabra, accounts for a family interest in letters, besides being reinforced by a chapter of Gervaise of Tilbury's *Otia imperialia* (*De equo Giraldi de Cabreriis*), though this refers to Guerau IV. Written in sextets (actually two stanzas of three lines), the ensenhamen provides us, above all, with a priceless amount of information about the earliest literary Romance culture in Catalonia. The troubadour starts with running down his servant in a comical way and, after making interesting remarks on the abilities required in Cabra's profession (which includes the lyric genres), boastfully lists a wide range of references to works, authors, passages, and characters that his jongleur should know. This rich survey mainly deals with the epic, but also covers the Arthurian field, the myth of Tristan, Romance versions of classical legends (Troy and Alexander), motifs coming from Ovid's *Metamorphoses*, and even some French *fabliaux*. There are, on the other hand, few mentions of the troubadours, all of them of the second generation, since the poem was probably written before 1165. It is remarkable that Marcabrun, included in the list and probably a friend of Guerau, used the same verse pattern echoing both the metrics (*versus tripartitus caudatus*) and the drama monologue that we find in the parodical *sermon joyeux*. Marcabrun's poem *D'aisso laus Deu* seems to be partly a source for Guerau's, but, all in all, the viscount, because of his rather pedantic intention, succeeded in making up a genre. Guiraut de Calanso's ensenhamen to his jongleur Fadet is the closest among those that followed Guerau's path and the one which clearly suggests that his model was thought an "ideal library" in his time.

LLUIS CABRÉ

Bibliography

Pirot, F. *Recherches sur les connaissances littéraires des troubadours occitans et catalans des XIIe et XIIIe siècles.* Memorias de la Real Academia de Buenas Letras de Barcelona XIV. Barcelona, 1972.

CADAMOSTO, ALVISE DA

Venetian merchant-navigator (1432–1488) in the service of the Infante Dom Henrique (Henry the Navigator), author, and discoverer of the Cape Verde Islands. After sailing extensively in Mediterranean and northern European waters, he was enroute to Flanders in 1454 when bad weather forced him to take shelter at Cape Saint Vincent, near the Vila do Infante of the prince, who sent a messenger to the Venetian fleet. The prince's relation of exotic lands to the south inspired Cadamosto to leave his countrymen's galley fleet and undertake the first significant Portuguese voyage of discovery authorized by the Infante Dom Henrique after a hiatus of eight years (during which, among other things, the Avis rulers were involved in rivalries with Castile over the Canaries and in an abortive assault on Tangiers).

In 1455 Cadamosto proceeded to Madeira and the Canaries, then crossed to Cape Blanco and the Senegal River in Africa, where he visited a chief of the Jalof tribe before going on to the Gambia River, where hostile natives prevented him from exploring it before returning to Portugal. The following year he made a second voyage to Africa, this time with three caravels and another Italian, the Genoese Antoniotto Usodimare. En route to the Gambia, he and Usodimare were blown off course and thereby discovered the Cape Verde Islands before proceeding to the river. This time, he was able to sail up the Gambia for about sixty miles, visit a native chief, and carry on a large barter trade with him and his subjects. Before turning back to Portugal, Cadamosto sailed on south to the Geba River, some 150 miles to the south.

Cadamosto remained in Portugal until 1563, three years after Henriques's death, though apparently as a trader, not as a navigator. But his interest in the African discoveries continued in a literary form; he composed a narrative that appeared posthumously in the Paesi *novamente retrovati*, published at Vicenza in 1507 and later in Ramusio. It contains not only his own vivid firsthand descriptions of what he personally saw and experienced, but an account of the last explorer's voyage who sailed under Prince Henrique, Pedro da Sintra. Cadamosto's is one of only two firsthand accounts of the classic voyages of discovery under the infante Henrique. The other, dictated by Diogo Gomes in his old age, describes voyaging in the same area, but is vague and of less value. It once led to Portuguese claims that Gomes, a Portuguese, had first discovered the Cape Verde Islands, but all parties now concede the primacy of Cadamosto.

GEORGE WINIUS

Bibliography

Crone, G. R. (ed. and trans.) *The Voyages of Cadamosto and Other Documents on Western Africa in the Second Half of the Sixteenth Century*. London, 1937.

Peres, D. *Descobrimentos Portugueses*. 2d ed. Coimbra, 1960.

CAESAR, ERA OF *See* CALENDAR

CALATRAVA, ORDER OF *See* MILITARY ORDERS

CALENDAR

The medieval Christian calendar in Spain was complicated, as it was everywhere in the Middle Ages. There was, in fact, no precise fixed calendar, but rather different "eras." The most important of these, for dating, was that simply known as era, which calculated the year from the birth of Christ. However, this was erroneously calculated as 38 B.C., and thus it is necessary to subtract 38 from the Spanish Era date in order to arrive at the actual Christian date A.D. This inaccurate system was replaced in the fourteenth century with the *año del nasçimiento* (year of Nativity), or Christian Era (as opposed to Spanish Era) dating. This was put into effect in Aragón in 1349; Valencia, 1358; Castile, 1383; Portugal, 1422. The beginning of the year had been 1 January under the old era, but now became 25 December (except that the Church calculated 11 January as the beginning of the year!). Thus, any date from 25–31 December *año del nasçimiento* must be reduced by 1 (e.g., 1455 = 1454 in our reckoning).

To further add to the confusion, there were other "eras" and means of calculation in use. Thus, eleventh-century Catalan documents often figure dates according to the reigns of Carolingian and French kings. In 1180 Catalonia (only) adopted the Christian Era (i.e., *año de la encarnación*). In addition, the old Latin forms of *ides*, *kalendes*, and *nones* are still used in many medieval documents of the kingdom of Aragón-Catalonia.

In the *crónicas* of the thirteenth- and fourteenth-century Castilian kings, one finds a vast additional reckoning of eras (Adam, or Creation; era of the Hebrews [Flood]; Nebuachadnezzar; Alexander the Great; Caesar; the Arabs; Persians; *era de galicianos y egipcianos* [i.e., Gracian's calendar]; etc.). Pero López de Ayala, in his *Crónica* of Pedro I, gives a detailed account of the various eras then in use.

In addition to the eras, there was also the liturgical calendar, very much in use, dating various saints' days, movable feasts, and so forth, which are often referred to in medieval documents. There are hundreds of these, but those of St. Michael and St. Martin were particularly important tax days. The Toledo church maintained its own separate Mozarabic calendar.

The Muslims had, of course, their own calendar and "era," dating from the Hijra, or migration of Muḥammad to Madīna in 622 A.D., and their own months. This Arab Era was also used in some Christian documents. The Jews, too, had their calendar, dating from the supposed creation of the world, and early Muslims in al-Andalus were quite familiar with this calendar. Jews, on the other hand, were very much at home with the Christian calendar, often citing it in Hebrew documents.

Astrological notions were common to all three communities, and there are various calendars that refer to propitious dates or to particular characteristics associated with each month.

NORMAN ROTH

Bibliography

Agustí y Casanovas, J., P. Voltes Bou, and J. Vives. *Manual de cronología española* y *universal*. Madrid, 1952.

Rivero, C. M. del "Indice de las personas, lugares y cosas notables que se mencionan en las *Tres Crónicas de los Reyes de Castilla*," *Hispania* 2 (1942), 357.

CALILA E DIMNA

A collection of short stories, *Calila e Dimna* was created in India by the sixth century (*Panchatandra*) and translated into Persian (sixth century), and Sirius, and Arabic (eighth century). The first Spanish version appeared by the middle of the thirteenth century. The Spanish text is kept in two manuscripts: one almost complete (A and B in the Library of El Escorial), and a much more rudimentary version coming from the Hebrew (manuscript P of the Library of Salamanca). At the end of manuscript A (H-III–9), it reads: "fue casado de aravigo en latin, et romancado por mandado del infante don Alfonso. . . ." J. Alemany was the first who discarded the use of an intermediate Latin version. The references that this manuscript makes with regard to dating are not very clear either, since it indicates that it was written in 1261 (1299 of the Spanish Era). By those dates, Alfonso X was already king, which has led some to scholars to consider that the translation was done just before Alfonso ascended to the throne

(1251), and thus it would have been one of the first works promoted by the king. Unfortunately, we do not have the codex from the royal scriptorium, though the above-mentioned manuscript, from the first third of the fifteenth century, has several good-quality illustrations. Given the continuous relationship between this work and the royal family, it has also been considered whether this illustrated manuscript would be the copy of the one belonging to Queen Isabel I the Catholic. By those dates, other stories were translated, such as the *Sendébar*, requested in 1253 by Don Fadrique, brother of Alfonso X, or books of sayings (*Poridat de las poridades, Bocados de oro*, etc.), which showed the same ideal of teaching the wise man.

The work is, therefore, included in a period of translation and assimilation of the eastern didactics. It is distributed in fifteen chapters plus three introductions, two of them assigned to explain the legendary transmission of the book from India through Persia, and the other serving as preface from the Arabic translator (there is no preliminary text that relates the work more directly to King Alfonso). In the first two introductions appears Berzebuey, a tireless traveler who will try to discover the knowledge later shown in the pages of the book. The Arabic translator, Ibn al-Muqaffa, explains in his introduction the didactic function of the book. According to what it is read, the beautiful words that hide sincere advice are very suitable for the education of the young, if they make an effort to get those doctrines, learn them, and put them into practice. Every other chapter usually works as a narrative model for other short stories, though it is preceded also by the dialogue between a king and a philosopher, lacking in literary character. The king starts the conversation, stating the subject of his concern, and the philosopher answers and teaches the case by means of a somehow extensive story, which often includes several fables belonging to the recourse called the "Chinese box." The stories, often with animals as the main characters, transmit a secular ethic, with the purpose of praising dignity and avoiding wrong opinions, which is easily assimilated within a Christian context. What can be considered as a basic story is in fact shortened to brief mention, significant for the tale. The brevity of the exposition contrasts with the systematic abundance of dialogues and monologues.

In the Spanish text, there are also structural and thematic differences according to the various creation stages. The first five chapters (with numbers 3, 5, 6, 7 and 8) are closer to the old Hindu collection *Panchatantra*. The series starts with the story that gives its name to the collection; the main characters are two jackals, Calila and Dimna; an ox, Señeba; and a lion. Dimna is a typical example of excessive political ambition, while the lion is a weakling who is influenced by inadequate advisers. From the beginning, the work suggests a relationship with the genre of "the mirror of princes." The following chapter, in which Dimna's death is narrated, was added by the Arabic translator, who was willing to punish the betrayer. From the tenth chapter on, the stories are much simpler, varying human beings with animals. The Spanish version of the *Calila* implies a literary experience that promotes the narrative art and shows a very important step in the development of fiction in a common language, despite its limited distribution. The circulation of the eastern collection through Europe was started when Juan de Capua made a Latin version. Following this translation, the text came back to Spain again, under the title of *Exemplario contra los engaños y peligros del mundo* (1493).

MARÍA JESÚS LACARRA

Bibliography

Cacho Blecua, J. M., and M. J. Lacarra. (eds.) *Calila e Dimna*. Madrid, 1984.

López Morillas, C. "A Broad View of *Calila e Dimna* on the Occasion of a New Edition," *Romance Philology*, 25 (1971), 85–95.

CALIPHATE OF CÓRDOBA *See* CÓRDOBA, EMIRATE AND CALIPHATE OF

CALIXTINUS CODEX

A manuscript of the Cathedral of Santiago de Compostela, the Codex Calixtinus was written in the middle of the twelfth century. The name derives from the spurious attribution of its authorship to Pope Calixtus II (papacy 1119–1124), who in equally false documents within the text figures as author. Its date, place, and true authorship have been much debated. A date of about 1140, perhaps 1139–43, is logical, at least for the putting of very diverse materials into final form, while the author, or rather, editor of received texts, may have been Aymeri Picaud, whose name figures in the work. As for location, it was at one time held that the Abbey of Cluny in southeast France was an obvious choice, but more recently the Abbey of Saint-Denis in Paris is indicated. The production was largely French, but certain elements show that clergy of Santiago, perhaps canons of the cathedral of French origin, collaborated or contributed. Santiago was certainly to benefit from the production, since the cult of the supposed tomb of St. James the Apostle, patron of Spain and, in his military aspect, heavenly leader in wars against the Muslims, was to benefit from this propaganda, and tens of thousands of pilgrims from all over Europe made the journey annually to this great cult center. *Codex* is the name of the manuscript; the text is the *Liber Sancti Jacobi*, the Book of St. James.

The text is divided into five books. Book 1 has thirty-two sermons on Jacobean themes, book 2 has twenty-two miracles of the Apostle, and book 3 narrates the translation of his remains from the Holy Land to Galicia and includes a papal authentication of this and an account of relevant feasts in the Church's calendar. Book 5 is the *Historia Turpini* or *Historia Karoli Magni et Rotholandi*, the spurious memoir of Turpin, Archbishop of Rheims, who fought beside Roland and the peers at Roncevaux in 778 during Charlemagne's campaign against the Muslims of Spain. Book 5 is the pilgrims' guide to routes to be followed through southwest France and across northern Spain, with notes on peoples to be encountered and shrines to be visited. There follow further hymns, epistles, miracles, and so forth. Book 4 has been much studied because of its importance for the French epic legends, and within the twelfth century it was being copied and circulated separately, its survival in hundreds of manuscripts and vernacular translations testifying to its influence in historiography up to the sixteenth century. The *Codex* as a whole has further importance in art and musical history.

COLIN SMITH

Bibliography

Jones, C. M. *Historia Karoli Magni et Rotholandi, ou Chronique du Pseudo-Turpin*. Paris, 1936, reprt. Geneva, 1972.

Whitehill, W. M. *Liber Sancti Jacobi (Codex Calixtinus)*. 3 vols. Santiago de Compostela, 1944.

CALLIS, JAUME

Catalan jurist and adviser to the Aragónese kings Joan I (r. 1387–95), Martin I (r. 1395–1410) and Fernando I (r. 1410–12), Jaume Callis was noted for his ability to blend juridical skills with a keen talent for political theory. Born in Vic in 1364, Callis studied canon and civil law in Lleída and Toulouse. After briefly working as assessor in the bishopric of Vic, he turned to a career first in municipal government and later in royal administration. He served as *procurador* at the *cortes* (parliament) of Valencia in 1393, was appointed legal counsel to the royal treasury in 1414, and five years later Alfonso IV (r. 1416–58) named him provisor of pleas to the cortes of Cucufate.

His most important contribution to Catalan jurisprudence is his gloss on the *Usatges* of Barcelona, a compilation of customs and laws for the province of Catalunya. In 1413 he was a member of the royal commission that was assigned with the revision and unification in a single volume the constitutions of the kings, the acts of the corts, and the *Usatges*.

THERESA EARENFIGHT

Bibliography

Beneyto-Pérez, J. "Jaime Callis y su 'Tratado de las Cortes,' " *Recueil de travaux d'histoire et de philologie* 3, no. 45 (1952), 55–65.

Callis, J. *Antiquiores Barchinomensium Leges, quas vulgas usaticos appellat cum commentariis supremorum Juris Consultorum Jacobi Calicii*. Barcelona, 1594.

Rius Serra, J. *Jaime Callis, Discurso*. Vic, 1944.

CALTABELLOTTA, TREATY OF

The effective end of the War of the Sicilian Vespers was only achieved after many false starts. By 1302 the combatants still in the field had been reduced to the Angevin king of Naples, Charles II (supported by the papacy), and Federico of Aragón, the master of Sicily. Seven years separate the Treaty of Anagni from that of Caltabellotta 1302, when Frederico of Aragón was at last recognized by Pope Boniface VIII and the Angevins as king of the island of Sicily for his lifetime, though his territory was renamed the kingdom of Trinacria to assuage Angevin and papal fears that their own title to the entire kingdom of Sicily, island and mainland, was being fatally undermined. In addition to the main island, Frederico was recognized as ruler over Malta, Pantelleria, and the other islands in the straits between Sicily and Tunisia, which had been battleground during the Vespers war, and over the Lipari islands to the north of Messina. More tricky was the question of who should exercise control over the straits of Messina, an important trade route, all the more so since northeastern Sicily traditionally received many supplies from Calabria, the toe of mainland Italy. A number of castles on the Calabrian side were thus left in Aragónese hands as a temporary measure, but otherwise troops were withdrawn and prisoners exchanged. The mood was certainly one in which to make peace: Charles II of Naples was short of funds, and his honor was to be salvaged by a marriage alliance with Frederico, who took his daughter Eleanor as wife. After Frederico's death the kingdom of Trinacria would be dissolved and reunited with the rest of the *regnum Siciliae*, which would retain loose suzerain rights over the island. But the future heir of Frederico was also promised aid in the acquisition of alternative rights elsewhere—for example, in Cyprus, which had throughout the war been regarded as a disposable territory (despite possessing its own Latin dynasty).

Church lands in Sicily, many now in noble hands, were to be returned to their rightful owners, assuming Frederico were capable of achieving this. The real difficulty lay in Frederic's own reluctance to accept the short-term nature of his kingdom; he refused to date his reign from the treaty, going back instead to his original coup d'etat, and within a few years he was again calling himself the king of Sicily; his eventual nomination of a successor quashed Angevin hopes of a peaceful transition. On the other hand, it has been suggested that the uncertainty over the succession acted as a brake on investment in economic enterprises; in addition, continuing differences with the Angevins made further war certain, despite vain attempts to persuade Frederico to take another kingdom such as Albania.

David S. Abulafia

Bibliography

Backman, C. *The Decline and Fall of Medieval Sicily*. Cambridge, 1995. 41–42, 66, 104.
Runciman, S. *The Sicilian Vespers*. Cambridge, 1958. 299.

CAMINO FRANCÉS *See* SANTIAGO DE COMPOSTELA

CANARY ISLANDS

The colonization of the Canary Islands during the Middle Ages meant the birth of a new historic reality. Three stages can be identified in the development of this process: Rediscovery (1336–1401); the age of lordship (1402–1477); and the age of the crown (1478–1526).

The name of the first stage is due to the fact that the Archipelago was known in classical times but fell into oblivion for most of the Middle Ages. During this same time period, European expansion did not seek to substitute the native (*guanche*) structures, but rather to mold them through commercial or evangelical contacts, which favored the continent's interests.

Despite its limited character, colonization will inherit some important elements from this period: first of all, geographical knowledge. This was obtained through a series of expeditions, the first of which were led by Mediterranean (Genovese, Catalonian, and Mallorcan) sailors, and later by Atlantic (Portuguese and Castilian) sailors. The second element is the economic contribution that is made: slaves, dragon-tree sap, archil, and leather. The third element is the issue of political sovereignty that was raised by the papal investiture of Luis de la Cerda as "prince of fortune." Lastly, it should be noted that during this stage the first contacts with the natives took place. We must aknowledge the important role of evangelizing efforts, which led to the establishment of the missionary episcopate of Telde. These contacts resulted in the first hint of material as well as ideological aculturation.

The so-called Age of Lordship implies the beginning of actual colonization, with an overall and substantial change from the previous reality. The first action taken to this end was the imposition of an actual sovereignty in the archipelago. This process occured within the framework of two characteristic phenomena of Europe at that time: the decline of "universal" powers in relation to the states, and the growing rise of the Atlantic countries. This explains why colonization had its origin in Castille, competing with Portugal, with only minor participation from the pope, who acted as an arbiter between different kingdoms.

The conquest of Lanzarote, Fuerteventura, and El Hierro was undertaken at this time. La Gomera was also incorporated, not through military action, but rather through the imposition of a superior power established with the backing of one of the aboriginal groups.

The lack of direct royal intervention that characterizes the Age of the Lordship may be observed in two periods: the Norman-French (1402–1418), and the Castilian-Andalusian (1418–1477). In the first period, Jean de Bethencourt's feudalization meant the creation of an immune lordship. In the second, the Castilian lords (Casas and Peraza) based their power on a jurisdictional delegation from the monarch, not in a feudal pact.

The Age of Lordship is characterized by low population levels. Since the occupied islands were those that were more open to attacks and had less agricultural potential, the indigenous population—which had lower population indexes—diminished even further. In addition, the restricted possibilities for agricultural exploitation hindered resettlement. The region of origin of possible resettlers was restricted to Castilians, French, and natives. Their social structure was simple, even though it had a few *hidalgos* (low nobility) as the top of the hierarchy and peasants at the bottom, with a progressive introduction of natives into the second.

The economy during this period is confined to a restricted level of production, based mainly on livestock and to a lesser extent on subsistence farming, which was complemented by the harvesting of natural products. Commerce provided products that were not produced locally, mainly wheat, wine, and manufactured items, while allowing for the export of raw materials such as archil and slaves and the surplus from local production of leather, tallow, and so forth.

Royal colonization involved direct intervention from the monarchy in three of the seven islands and a greater presence in the whole archipelago. This intervention lead to the creation of a monarchical legal framework in the islands, which can be observed in the norms of local organization (*fueros* and *ordenanzas*—i.e., jurisdiction, regulations) and in the composition of municipal councils, in which the presence of governors and other royal officials was permanent. State intervention was favored by the increasing military cost of the conquest, since the monarchy had greater human and economic resources than the lords. These resources supported the conquest of Gran Canaria, La Palma, and Tenerife.

The population rose significantly during this period as a consequence of three main factors: preservation of the most important indigenous communities; the attraction of a greater number of settlers due to the rise in Europe's population and better economic prospects; and a significant increase in the importance of slavery (blacks and Berbers) within the new economic order. Regarding the new settlers, they were more numerous and represented several social groups. The most notable aspects are the numerical importance of Portuguese settlers, who constitute, together with the Castilians, the majority of royal colonization; and the social importance of commercial colonies (Genovese, Flemish, Catalonian, etc.).

Social organization continued to be based, to a great extent, on land ownership, but money became increasingly important. Economic conditions led to this change. Significant investment was needed to put capitalist production schemes into practice. Due to this, the aristocracy had a twofold origin: on the one hand military, and on the other, commercial. Economic diversity became more difficult due to the differences in judicial statutes and the persistence of diverse mentalities within the various groups. All these factors led to greater difficulties in the aculturation process, such as those affecting indigenous communities.

The economy of this period was characterized by general growth, both with regard to the number of products involved and to the levels of production reached. Agriculture was based on the consolidation of subsistence crops (grain, grapes) and the introduction of cash crops (sugar, pastel). Livestock kept its privileged position, although it was no longer a priority, since it conflicted with the flourishing agriculture. The harvest of natural products also became important, although their relative significance within overall production decreased. Due to the greater demand for crafts products, the export of raw materials decreased. Thus, leather, cloth, metal, and clay crafts were born, whereas high quality products were imported. Commerce increased dramatically as a consequence of several circumstances: the privileged position of the islands on African and American routes, the existence of export products, and the settlement of commercial colonies.

Eduardo Aznar Vallejo

Bibliography

Aznar Vallejo, E. *La integración de las Islas Canarias en la Corona de Castilla (1478–1526): Aspectos administrativos, sociales y económicos*. La Laguna, 1983.

Marrero Rodríguez, M. *La esclavitud en Tenerife a raíz de la Conquista*. La Laguna, 1966.

Morales Padrón, F. *Canarias: Crónicas de su conquista*. Las Palmas de Gran Canaria, 1978.

Pérez Voituriez, A. *Problemas jurídicos internacionales de la Conquista de Canarias*. La Laguna, 1959.

Rumeu de Armas, A. *El Obispado de Telde*. 2d. ed. Madrid, 1986.

Serra Rafols, E., and A. Cioranescu. *Le Canarien: Crónicas francesas de la conquista de Canarias*. La Laguna, 1959–64.

Serra Rafols, E. *Los portugueses en Canarias*. La Laguna, 1941.

Tejera Gaspar, A. and Aznar Vallejo, E. *El asentamiento franco-normando de San Marcial del Rubicón (Yaiza-Lanzarote): Un modelo de arqueología de contacto*. Yaiza, 1989.

CANCIONEIROS

See POETRY, VERNACULAR, POPULAR AND LEARNED, CANCIONEIROS AND POETRY, VERNACULAR, POPULAR AND LEARNED, CANCIONEIROS

CANCIONEROS

See POETRY, VERNACULAR, POPULAR AND LEARNED, CANCIONEIROS AND POETRY, VERNACULAR, POPULAR AND LEARNED, CANCIONEIROS

CANELLAS, VIDAL DE

Thirteenth-century churchman who served as bishop of Huesca. From the sixteenth century on historians have praised both the work and special human qualities of Vidal de Canellas, yet little is known about his origins. In all likelihood, he was born in Barcelona. He studied at the University of Bologna in Italy, where his presence is documented in 1221. He died in 1252. Related by blood to Jaime I the Conqueror, King of Aragón, Vidal served as his counselor and confidant and was by the king's side during the Aragónese assault on Valencia in 1238. Vidal is said to have been the compiler of the *fueros* (municipal codes) of Aragón, assembled during the *cortes* (parliament) of Huesca in 1247. He most likely also intervened in the composition of the *furs* (fueras) of Valencia. The legal commentary *In excelsis Dei thesauris*, known commonly under the name of *Vidal mayor*, is also from his hand. Vidal was reputed to have been an excellent and impartial arbiter in legal disputes as well as a worthy trustee.

ANTONIO GARCÍA Y GARCÍA

Bibliography

Del Arco, R. "El jurisperto Vidal de Canellas, Obispo de Huesca." *Cuadernos de Historia Jerónimo Zurita* 1 (1951), 23–113.

Durán Gudiol, A. "Vidal de Canellas, obispo de Huesca." *Estudios de la Edad Media de la Corona de Aragón* 9 (1973), 267–369.

CANTAR DE LOS INFANTES DE LARA

One of the major narratives of the medieval Castilian epic, the *Cantar de los infantes de Lara* is known in three different versions partially prosified in Alfonsine and post-Alfonsine chronicles: Alfonso X's *Primera crónica general* (*Estoria de España* before 1289); Pedro Afonso, Count of Barcelos's *Crónica Geral de Espanha de 1344*; and the anonymous *Interpolación de la Tercera crónica general* (late fifteenth century). The narrative tells the following story: Seven brothers, the lords of Lara, sons of Gonzalo Gustioz, become involved in a violent altercation during the wedding celebrations of their uncle, Ruy Velázquez, who has married Doña Lambra, an impetuous, manipulative woman of fiery, unrestrained emotions (*lambra* < Latin *flamula*). The initial offenses, fomented by Doña Lambra, gradually escalate, until Ruy Velázquez, filled with implacable hatred, betrays his nephews on the field of battle, abandoning them—gravely outnumbered—to face an overwhelmingly superior army of Muslims. After fighting valiantly, the infantes are beheaded and their heads are taken as trophies to Córdoba and shown to the caliph, Almanzor (based on the historical Al-Manṣūr). Gonzalo Gustioz happens to be at Córdoba as a Christian emissary, sent there by Ruy Velázquez with a "Uriah letter," asking that the bearer be executed. Almanzor asks Gonzalo Gustioz to identify the Christian heads. Frantic with grief, the father seizes a sword and strikes down a Muslim guard. Almanzor, instead of having Gonzalo Gustioz killed, puts him in prison but, pitying his bereavement, sends a Muslim noblewoman to console him. She bears him a son, Mudarra (Arabic *mudharra*ʿ "of mixed ancestry"), who is educated at Almanzor's court and, years later, arrives in Castile with an army of followers, converts to Christianity, and wreaks bloody vengeance upon Ruy Velázquez and Doña Lambra.

The historical basis of the *Cantar* has gradually emerged from a meticulous exploration of notarial documents and Arabic historical sources. The epic accurately reflects the geography and the military and political circumstances of the late tenth-century Sorian *frontera*. Many of the major players are likewise attested in contemporary documents: Gonzalo Gustioz, Ruy Velázquez, Diego González (the eldest of the infantes), Count Garcí Fernández, and the Muslim frontier commander, Ghālib ibn ʿAbd al-Raḥmān (Galve). The epic's historical basis—aside from its many legendary components—is beyond dispute.

The *Estoria de España* records an early version of the narrative in which the second part—Mudarra's vengeance—is not developed in detail. Comparatively speaking, the *Estoria* version has been severely prosified, but even so a number of assonances and vestiges of formulaic verses still survive in the chronistic prose. The *Crónica de 1344* and the *Interpolación* both record two closely related traditional versions of a later *remaniement*, in which the second part is fully developed, achieving an aesthetically successful balance between the two segments of the narrative. Both chronicles combine historiographic and oral sources, supplementing the *Estoria de España* account with portions of fourteenth-century traditional texts. Where the Alfonsine narrative and the minstrel versions did not differ essentially, both histories copied the earlier chronicle, but when oral accounts diverged from the *Estoria de España*, the *Crónica de 1344* and the *Interpolación* chose minstrel texts, prosifying their sources very superficially, so that both works offer invaluable testimonies that preserve lengthy series of consecutive assonant verses. In numerous instances it is almost as if we had before us poetic fragments of the original *cantar de gesta*.

It is important to bear in mind that the *Crónica de 1344* and the *Interpolación* are not using identical texts of a fourteenth-century *Cantar de los infantes de Lara*. The chronicles reflect closely related versions, but in many instances one history will record one traditional formula while the other will use a different, though roughly equivalent, one: "la media poblada e la media por poblar" (*Crónica de 1344*, v. 94); "la media es çercada e la otra por çercare" (*Interpolación*) ("Half has been repopulated and the other half has not; Half has been fortified and the other half has not"). The two chronicles likewise offer mutually supplementary accounts, having chosen to record different segments of their epic sources. The *Crónica de 1344* and the *Interpolación* thus provide a unique opportunity to observe the process of oral variation in an Old Spanish epic poem, strikingly similar to what is seen in many Old French *chansons de geste* (songs of deeds) and also in modern Hispanic traditional ballads.

Though obviously many features of the original poetic texts have been obliterated in the process of chronistic prosification, the heroic narrative has been preserved well enough to offer invaluable evidence of its anonymous authors' poetic artistry. A sense of doom and fatal inevitability pervades the story. The young nobles' unreflective impetuousness (*desmesura*), Doña Lambra's manipulation and thirst for vengeance, Ruy Velázquez's implacable hatred and ultimate treachery will all lead inexorably to violence, betrayal, and death. The artistic structure, especially in the later *Refundición* recorded in the *Crónica de 1344* and the *Interpolación*, reveals a series of finely crafted parallelisms that show the poetic awareness of generations of *juglares* (minstrels) who gradually elaborated the *Cantar de los infantes de Lara* as we now see it in the medieval sources. The figures of Gonzalo Gustioz and Ruy Velázquez, who are present in both halves of the narrative; Mudarra, whose identical appearance will replicate, in the second part, the youngest *infante*, Gonzalo González, who was killed in the first part; the treacherous vengeance of Doña Lambra, at the beginning, balanced against the justified vengeance of Doña Sancha at the end; the gradual escalation of violent aggressions in the first part echoed in Mudarra's long delayed vengeance in the second part, as he pursues the traitor, Ruy Velázquez, from one town to another, always arriving too late to accomplish his purpose; the recurrent themes of blood, birds of prey, and fatal wedding festivities offer cogent parallelisms and ironic contrasts that strengthen the artistic unity of this admirable narrative.

The *Cantar de los infantes* did not disappear from oral tradition. In 1476 Lope García de Salazar summarized various features of yet another traditional account in his *Bienandanzas y fortunas*, and several *romances viejos* attest to the partial survival of late epic versions in ballad form. The horrendous scene of the seven heads is perpetuated down to modern times among eastern Mediterranean Sephardic Jews as a ballad of mourning (*endecha*), but this cannot count as a song of direct tradition, being based on a late and semi-learned reworking from the final years of the sixteenth century.

SAMUEL G. ARMISTEAD

Bibliography

Bluestine, C. "The Power of Blood in the *Siete Infantes de Lara*." *Hispanic Review* 50 (1982), 211–230.

Lathrop, T. A. *The Legend of the "Siete Infantes de Lara."* Chapel Hill, N.C., 1971.

Menéndez Pidal, R. *La leyenda de los infantes de Salas*. 3d ed. Madrid, 1971.

———. *Reliquias de la poesía épica española*. Edited by D. Catalán. 2d ed. Madrid, 1980.

———, and María Goyri. *Romancero tradicional de las lenguas hispánicas*. Vol. 2. Madrid, 1963.

CANTAR DE MIO CID

The *Cantar de Mio Cid* is the only Old Spanish epic to survive more or less complete. It was influential in its day and for some centuries, particularly when a prose version of it was incorporated into the national chronicles: the Cid became the national hero, and the poem about him, the earliest long text in Castilian verse that we have, is a cornerstone of Spanish literary culture. In recent times its poetic qualities and narrative and dramatic power have been amply appreciated.

The poem survives in a unique fourteenth-century manuscript long kept in a convent in Bivar, where the manor of the historical Cid was situated; after many vicissitudes since the late eighteenth century, the manuscript was acquired by the Spanish state in 1960 for the Biblioteca Nacional in Madrid. Closing lines of the text show that it was copied from, or derived in a series of copies from, an original of 1207, the work of copyist or author Per Abbat concluded in May of that year. In its present state the text has 3,730 lines plus its explicit, a few more lines in which a presenter takes leave of his public. Since the first folio and two in the interior are missing, and the scribe writes about fifty lines on each folio, the poem when complete had a little less than four thousand lines, thus corresponding closely (and perhaps not accidentally) to the prime version of the *Chanson de Roland*. The manuscript has some errors of copying and fails to record many line divisions correctly; diverse reasons for this have been suggested, among them that at some stage the work was written as lines of prose (as happened to other verse texts) and was inaccurately reconstituted later. Loss of the first folio prevents us from knowing if the poet gave his work a title, but he would certainly have announced his theme and addressed his audience, as in French epic. The word *cantar* appears within the text (line 2276) when defining one of the three sections into which the work is divided and is used in the chronicles about whole epics; *Poema de Mio Cid* is a common modern alternative, if anachronistic.

The origins and nature of the poem, as of the epic genre as a whole, are much debated. The *Cantar* may have been a member of a possibly large, age-old family of orally generated poems, evolving in an unbroken series of variant versions until (and of course after) being fixed in writing by a scribe who recorded a performance: such is the view of the "oralists." "Neo traditionalists," that is, Menéndez Pidal and his school believe similarly in the antiquity of the unbroken process, the close association of poetic creation with historical fact (thus dating the earliest version of the *Cantar* to within a few years of the Cid's death in 1099, and the present text to about 1140), and the force of the creative variant produced by the *autor-legión* working at popular level; they seem not wholly to exclude writing from both the original composition and transmission process, and hold that texts were memorized as well as extemporized for performance. In the "individualist" view, all such poems are relatively late compositions by authors of at least modest learning, in writing. Their sources included not only folk memory (in the case of the Cid, local knowledge and pride in Burgos, the home of the hero) but also written history, archival materials held in a city or monastery, French epics known from auditions and in writing, and in certain cases Latin texts known in extracts, the whole being moulded by the individual poetic imagination into a coherent literary construct. Facts of history that were known might be used but much adjusted for literary purposes. In this view, the poet was a responsible public figure who may well have had to please a royal or noble patron with an appropriate message about contemporary political and military concerns—in the case of the *Cantar*, perhaps legal reform, kingly duties, action against the Almohads, and relations with the Spanish Moors—while genealogical and monastic connections were relevant also. Many in consequence would now date the *Cantar* to the first years of the thirteenth century, perhaps to 1207. It is notable that Duggan, a convinced oralist, has original arguments in his 1989 book for a date very close to this, and very precise, too: "in the year 1199 or, more likely, 1200."

As for the place of composition, Medinaceli or elsewhere in the frontier region of southeast Castile, Burgos, and even Navarre, have been recently proposed. Smith is the only student to argue that the *Cantar* was the first work of its kind in Castilian, an effort (with features denoting a tentative or experimental composition, but masterly too) to provide Castile with a national poem to rival the best French *chansons de geste* he knew so well; and that he triumphantly succeeded and even outdid his models.

Discussion of the metrical structures of the *Cantar* is conditioned by the above views: the poet may have followed traditional practice, or invented a new system that was then followed in other epics. His lines are assonanced and grouped to form *laisses* (*tiradas*, *series*), as in French. Starting and ending a laisse obeys some observable but rather loose criteria, such as changing a speaker or a place. The line has a clear caesura. Line lengths vary greatly, continuing to do so even after adjustments (on which editors more or less agree) have been made to the manuscript readings. Probably no syllable count is applicable, the system having a basis of stresses, still variable but typically two or three to each hemistich. This accentual system obviously contrasts with the syllabic bases of French. Many of the poet's lines are pleasingly rhythmical, and many too have the extra force of internal assonances both "horizontal" and "vertical," enriched rhyme, and so on.

The poet's language is simple, direct, evocative, notably economical, with a special power in the direct speech that forms a high proportion of the text. The epic is essentially narrative, and we are occasionally reminded of the presence of the narrator, but analysis in terms of drama is very rewarding, especially when we bear the listening public in mind and assume the presenter's ability to vary his voice and reinforce diction with mime and gesture. Power of language is not much affected for moderns by the strongly formulaic nature of much of the rhetoric (proof for some that this and other poems were orally generated, for others adapted in part from French and then imitated in native ways, and equally useful in the written medium). Many stylistic features and much of the direct speech were preserved in the prose versions of the chronicles; any may thus have been influential in the very creation of Castilian prose discourse.

Those acquainted with the Cid of the ballads and Golden Age plays, with Corneille, and with the film, will be surprised to discover the unromantic, earthy, middle-aged hero of the *Cantar*. He enshrines virtues obviously thought important to the poet and his public and has a pleasing modernity in some ways, too. In the first *Cantar* he is unjustly exiled by his king and forced to make his way with a few followers into Moorish lands, where he starts to win wealth and local power. At first no more than a gentlemanly brigand, as his army grows he eventually defeats a semi-royal personage, the count of Barcelona, and the forces of his state, winning immense booty. He follows this at the start of the second *Cantar* by capturing Valencia and defeating the vast army of Almoravids sent to recover it, appointing a bishop and settling in the city with every sign of intended permanence, especially by sending for his family—Jimena, two daughters, and their entourage. The two young Infantes de Carrión are attracted by the Cid's wealth and, with direct approval and involvement from the crown, marry the Cid's daughters after the hero has been received back into royal favor. The Cantar ends on a triumphant note but with a hint of foreboding. In Cantar III the infantes disgrace themselves by cowardice when the domestic lion escapes and in battle against King Búcar's Moors. Having lost face, they resolve to avenge themselves by an outrage against their wives, whom they automatically repudiate, committed while journeying to their homeland. The collective dishonor caused to the Cid's family and men is washed away when the hero wins his action in the royal court assembled in Toledo (the high point of the poem's rhetoric) and when his men later defeat the Infantes and their brother in judicial duels. The daughters, recovered from the outrage, marry Iberian peninsular royalty, and the Cid dies peacefully in honor, assured that his line will continue royally (a claim amply justified in historical reality by the poet's time). At all points the author's precision in terms of geographical locale, routes, the seasons, even the time of day, convinces us of the essential truth of his tale. Some themes will be evident from the foregoing synopsis, but all are best followed up in the now immense bibliography, since emphasis has varied.

COLIN SMITH

Bibliography

Duggan, J. J. *The "Cantar de mio Cid": Poetic Creation in its Economic and Social Contexts.* Cambridge, 1989.

Menéndez Pidal, R. *Cantar de mio Cid.* 3 vols. Madrid, 1908–11.

Michael, I. *Poema de mio Cid.* 2d ed. Madrid, 1978.

Smith, C. *La creación del "Poema de mio Cid."* Barcelona, 1985.

———. *Poema de mio Cid.* 2d ed. Madrid, 1985.

CANTARES DE GESTA *See* POETRY, SPANISH, LYRIC, TRADITIONAL

CANTIGAS DE SANTA MARÍA *See* ALFONSO X, ELSABIO, KING OF CASTILE, POETRY AND PROSE WORKS

CANTAR DEL CERCO DE ZAMORA

Briefly summarized in the *Crónica Najerense* (1143–1157) and known in greater detail in partial prosifications absorbed by Alfonso X's *Primera Crónica General (Estoria de España)* (1289) and the anonymous *Crónica de los Reyes de Castilla* (ca. 1300), the epic poem of *El cerco de Zamora* (*The Siege of Zamora*) helps prepare the events of the *Cantar de Mio Cid* and, in its own right, is one of the most important *cantares de gesta* (epic songs).

The narrative concerns the following events: On his deathbed, Fernando I of Castile and León divides his kingdom among his three sons, giving Castile to Sancho, León to Alfonso, and Galicia to García, and leaving the city of Zamora to his daughter, Urraca. Sancho usurps his brothers' lands and imprisons García, while Alfonso flees into exile in Toledo. Sancho then lays siege to Zamora. Pretending to flee from the besieged city, a treacherous *zamorano*, Vellido Dolfos (Bellidus Ataulfus), ingratiates himself with the Castilian king and, promising to show him a secret door through which his troops can enter and capture the city, lures Sancho into going alone with him to inspect the city's walls, fatally stabs him in the back, and then flees back to Zamora. The Zamorans imprison Vellido, but a Castilian champion, Diego Ordóñez, challenges the city and its inhabitants to prove in single combat that they were not involved in Vellido's treason. By law, anyone challenging a city must fight against five consecutive champions. One after another, confident in the justice of their cause, three sons of the venerable Zamoran patriarch, Arias Gonzalo go out to meet the Castilian challenger and are killed, but the third Zamoran champion, Rodrigo Arias, seriously wounds Diego Ordóñez and mortally wounded himself, strikes Ordóñez's horse, which flees, carrying the Castilian challenger outside the legally prescribed battle area (*cerco*).

The judges (*fieles*) then declare there should be no more fighting and refuse to designate a winner. Vellido's punishment is left unspecified and Alfonso returns from exile in Toledo to take over a reunited kingdom, after swearing (perhaps equivocally) that he was not a party to his brother's death. The epic thus ends on an inconclusive, ambivalent note, but such an ending, which at first glance might seem to be a flaw, rather represents one of the lost poem's major achievements. At a time when the concept of a united Spain did not yet exist, the *Cerco de Zamora* achieves a supraregional perspective in which no one is totally to blame and no one is completely vindicated, instead, a complex human situation is evoked in all its conflictive ambivalence. Who is guilty, García, who first gave Sancho the excuse to usurp his brothers' lands? Sancho, for his impetuousness, greed, and ambition? Alfonso, who may somehow have plotted Sancho's death? Urraca, for having (unwittingly?) fomented Vellido's treachery? The Cid, who failed to advise the brothers, as he had promised the dying King Fernando? All share in the tragedy of this Hispanic *Iliad*.

The structure of the *Cerco de Zamora* is eminently familiar. Like the *Chanson de Roland*, the *Nibelungenlied*, and the *Infantes de Lara*, a family quarrel leads to a treacherous outrage, for which vengeance must later be exacted and order eventually restored. That here vengeance is avoided and judgment is withheld distinguishes the *Cerco* as a remarkably innovative poem. But the lost poem (or poems) consulted and partially prosified in the *Estoria de España* and in the *Crónica de Castilla* are not our only available witnesses. A number of late-fifteenth-century chronicles, undoubtedly reflecting contemporary oral tradition, do specify the traitor's punishment. Here, like Ganelon in the *Chanson de Roland*, Vellido Dolfos is tied hand and foot to four wild ponies and is torn apart. Two brief epic poems, *La partición de los reinos* (*The Division of the Kingdom*) and *La Jura de Santa Gadea* (*The Oath at Santa Gadea*) may well have functioned as prologue and epilogue to the *Cerco*. The sixteenth-century ballad *Rey don Sancho, rey don Sancho, no digas que no te aviso!* (*King Sancho, Never Say You Were Not Warned*) derives directly from an epic source. The *Estoria de España* attests to a few of the epic's *í-o-* assonances, while the *Crónica de Castilla*, independently reflecting a variant poetic text, includes many additional rhymes. Several episodes pertaining to the *Cerco de Zamora* have survived in ballad form down to the present day. Some may derive from epic sources, but most are clearly based on later retellings.

SAMUEL G. ARMISTEAD

Bibliography

Huber, V.A. *Chrónica del famoso cavallero Cid Ruydiez Campeador*. Stuttgart, 1853.

Menéndez Pidal, R. "Relatos poéticos en las Crónicas Generales." *Revista de Filología Española* 10 (1923).

Reig, C. *El Cantar de Sancho II y Cerco de Zamora*. Madrid, 1947.

Ubieto Arteta, A. (ed.) *Crónica Najerense*. Valencia, 1966.

Vaquero, M. *Tradiciones orales en la historiografia de fines de la Edad Media*. Madison, Wisc., 1990.

CÃO, DIOGO

Portuguese navigator in the service of João II who explored the African coast as far south as Cape Saint Catherine; his most memorable discovery was the Congo River. His itineraries and other accomplishments are unclear, as are the dates of his birth and death. He was descended from a Trasmontane family that had fought for Portuguese independence in the 1380s and, according to tradition, was born in Vila Real. The first mention of him is from 1480, as already being in the service of João II as a navigator; it is recorded that he returned from Africa with captured Spanish vessels.

In 1482 his career as an explorer seems to have begun on an expedition that stopped at San Jorge da Mina (Elmina) before proceeding south into the unknown seas beyond Cape Saint Catherine. It was on this voyage; that he discovered the Congo (Zaire) River and planted the stone pillar known as the Padraõ de San Jorge. He then proceeded south to Cape Santa Maria, where he erected another *padrão* before returning to Lisbon.

He brought with him four Sonyo nobles taken as hostages in return for the safety of Portuguese crew members, who had been sent on an embassy to the Manicongo but had not returned before the ship sailed. The nobles were treated well; according to the chronicler Barros, the intent was to teach them them the Portuguese language for future communication with natives of the region. João II was highly pleased with the results of the expedition and ennobled Cão, apparently believing, that his navigator had approached "the Arabian Gulf."

The outlines of Cão's second voyage of 1485 are much hazier, but it is known from Barros that he returned the hostages to their homeland; he then, planted a padrão at Cape Negro, Morocco, according to Martin Behaim's globe of 1492, and another at Cape Cross, before reaching Walvis Bay. During this voyage he seems to have visited the Manicongo, at least according to the chroniclers Rui de Pina and João de Barros. And, given the authenticity of inscriptions on the cliff at Ielala, he sailed his ships a hundred miles up the Congo River. Otherwise, reports on this second voyage are contradictory. A legend on the famous globe by the German cartographer Martin Behaim, *hic moritur*, has been taken to indicate Cão's death, proably in 1486, though Barros does not mention it in his *Decades*, (I, book 3, chapter 3) and speaks as if Cão returned safely home. Whether or not Cão actually returned from this second voyage, he fell into complete obscurity. The late Damião Peres suggests (based on the Soligo map) that Cão may have incurred the displeasure of João II (and subsequently fallen into obscurity) by asserting that he had found the terminal cape of Africa—which turned out to be only a deep, but blind, bay.

Two other confusions render even the briefest biography of Cão uncertain: the fact that one or more other voyages of Portuguese discovery somewhat overlap his and easily become confused with them, and the question of whether Martin Behaim accompanied Cão and labeled his maps in accordance with the explorer's discoveries.

GEORGE D. WINIUS

Bibliography

Barros, João de. *Décadas da Ásia*. Decade I, books 2 and 3. Lisbon, 1778.

Peres, D. *Descobrimentos portugueses*. 2d ed. Coimbra, 1960.

CAPE VERDE AND THE CAPE VERDE ISLANDS

The Cape Verde Islands were the last of the Atlantic Old World archipelagos to be discovered, and because they lie so close to Cape Verde (which gives them their name), their relationship with the mainland was intimate from the beginning. Though no copy of the original donation from Afonso V to his uncle, the Infante Henrique, survives, it was surely made soon after the return of Alvise da Cadamosto, its discoverer, and of Diogo Gomes, for Henrique left it in his will to the Infante Fernando in 1460. Its developmental pattern followed those of Madeira and the Azores, wherein the proprietor, in this case Fernando, divided the islands into captaincies and assigned their donatary contracts, in one instance to the Genoese, António de Noli, who may have visited the islands in the year after their discovery.

From all evidence, the captains had little trouble in finding colonists, if only because Henrique had created a *feitoria* (traiding post) up the coast at Arguin about the same time the islands were discovered; this must have suggested that a fairly proximate base of operations could yield rich benefits. In 1462 and 1466, they were given important rights to trade on the mainland opposite, and they seem to have been sufficiently influential by 1469 (when concessions were given Fernão Gomes to carry out further explorations southward) that their rights were specifically protected.

The settlers were primarily slave traders, and they would not have descended on the islands so swiftly if their motives had been agricultural. Even so, cotton growing soon became a possibility; cloth was one of the prime barter commodities for slaves, and the semiarid nature of the islands was well suited to cotton (being too dry for sugar). Slaves were already at hand, and it was but a simple step to convert their labor to the plants, the thread, and the cloth production itself. It was even discovered that the lichen urrzela would flourish there, and this yielded a purple dye that was used both for the textiles and for export. Afonso V even went so far as to make its export a monopoly, granting it in 1469 to two Spaniards, Juan and Pedro de Lugo. Another boon to the insular economy was the discovery that even a type of cowrie found in relative abundance on the island was worth money—in fact, it was money to the Africans on the mainland, where it was far rarer. In 1480, the crown even attempted to prevent their inflation by forbidding unlicensed persons from exporting them illegally.

Few Portuguese were eager to settle on the mainland opposite the islands, and in fact, this remained under their jurisdiction for centuries. The only European population there, in fact, were outcasts, the *lançados*, soon interbred with the native populations, plus some maroons or recluses of uncertain origin. These traded, usually clandestinely, with the inhabitants of the islands (to the annoyance of the crown) and served as intermediaries with the inland chieftains. Royal attempts to amnesty or repatriate them all seem to have failed.

GEORGE D. WINIUS

Bibliography

Albuquerque, L. de, and Maria Emília Madeira dos Santos. *História Geral de Cabo Verde*. Lisbon, 1988.

Crone, G. R. (ed. and trans.) *The Voyages of Cadamosto and Other Documents on Western Africa in the Second Half of the Sixteenth Century*. London, 1937.

CARBONELI, MIQUEL

Notary public, bibliophile, antiquarian and historian, (1434–1517), born in the Plaça Nova, Barcelona. He occupied the post of royal archivist from 1476 but his abiding passion was books and manuscripts, even to the detriment of his family. A self-taught dilettante in scholarship, he left a pedantic but picturesque image of himself in the marginalia of books and chancery registers. His library consisted of over sixty titles; there are no works in the vernacular nor any that do not relate to the humanities. The most attractive facet of his literary activity is his extensive Latin correspondence with his fellow lawyers; the Italian tutors at court, Antonio and Alessandro Geraldini; and his most learned cousin Geroni Pau, the first of the Catalan hellenists. His historical ideas were largely shaped by the advice of Pau and the knowledge drawn from his library. The influences are made explicit in his *De viris illustribus catalanis suae tempestatis libellus*, where he also claims that Bartolommeo Fazio was his model for this collection. The range of professions covered is not as wide as in Fazio's equivalent Italian work; the majority are lawyers whose main merit lies in the study of the humanities. His major work, the *Chròniques d'Espanya*, is a rather turgid exposition written over a long period and intended to expose the errors of an earlier chronicler, Pere Tomich. This is the only work he wrote in Catalan. Clearly intended as a eulogy of the Crown of Aragón, it ends in a climactic praise of the cultural patronage of Alfonso V, "which had awakened the nation from barbarity." The chronicle derives from such sources as that of San Juan de la Peña, of Pedro the Ceremonious, documents from the archives of the Crown of Aragón, a letter of Leonardo Bruni, and the biographies of Alfonso V written by Fazio and Beccadelli. It was not printed until 1547 in Barcelona.

ROBERT B. TATE

Bibliography

Balaguer, R. *La cultura catalana del renaixement a la decadencia*. Barcelona, 1964.

CARLOS, PRINCE OF VIANA

The political life of Spain at the end of the Middle Ages can be traced through the fortune of Carlos and his half-brother Fernando of Aragón. As heir first to the throne of Navarre (as his title of Prince of Viana indicated), then to the throne of Aragón-Catalonia, Don Carlos might have unified the lands of the Ebro River valley, whose people were strongly attached to their local privileges. His failure to do so allowed Fernando to unite Aragón and Castile by marrying Isabel the Catholic and to start a process of centralization that took little account of the regional *fueros* (municipal charters). The genealogical tree of the Trastámaras shows the two marriages of Juan II of Aragón, that created the complex family situation that, in turn, was to cause numerous family wars. Juan, the second son of Fernando I of Aragón, could not really expect to get a crown; however, his marriage to Blanche of Navarre made him the prince consort in her kingdom; then, when the elder brother Alfonso the Magnanimous died without heir, he also beacame King of Aragón. However, he decided by every means at his disposal to deprive his elder son, Carlos, of the throne in favor of his younger son, born of his second marriage to Juana Enríquez, the daughter of the admiral of Castile. When his mother Blanche died, Carlos should have inherited Navarre; but, as Blanche had, in her will, asked her son to get his father's consent, Juan took this opportunity to proclaim himself king, simply making Don Carlos his lieutenant general. Don Carlos was very respectful of the local *fueros* and thus made himself very popular. This led to a first war between the father and the son. There was a further crisis when Alfonso the Magnanimous died, making his brother Juan the king of Aragón, and Carlos the heir to the throne. His father, who had already dispossessed him of Navarre by giving his rights to the count of Foix-Béarn, maneuvered once again to deprive him of Aragón in favor of his half-brother Fernando. Again, there was fighting between father and son. As a result Don Carlos was again appointed lieutenant general in Catalonia. He displayed there the same qualities he had during his rule in Navarre. This prince was a scholar with a magnificent library, and he wrote a remarkable "Chronicle of Navarre." He died of tuberculosis in Barcelona in 1461. The Catalans gave him a royal burial and therefore venerated him as a saint. As he had no descendant, he left the way free for his half-brother Fernando, who then went on to unite Aragón and Castile, and for his sister Eleonor, who united Navarre with Foix-Béarn.

PIERRE TUCOO-CHALA

Bibliography

Bisson, T. N. *The Medieval Crown of Aragón*. Oxford, 1986.

Desdevises du Dezert, G. *Don Carlos d'Aragón, Prince de Viane. Etude Sur l'Espagne du nord au XV Siécle*. Paris, 1889.

Ruano Prieto, F. *Don Juan II de Aragón y el príncipe de Viana: guerras civiles eu los reinos de Aragón y Navarra durante el siglo XV*. Bilbao, 1897.

CARMELITES *See* RELIGIOUS ORDERS

CARMEN CAMPIDOCTORIS

The *Carmen* is a song of praise of the Cid. It survives in a unique copy in a manuscript of Ripoll and was composed by a monk of the house. The text is incomplete; it consists of 128 lines (and two words of 129) in four-line stanzas of rhythmic sapphics, and it was a kind of hymn designed to be sung. The best edition is that of Wright, with English version and full commentary. While most have thought it composed during the Cid' s lifetime, about 1083, Smith argues that it is of the later twelfth century, being based largely on the *Historia Roderici* written in the middle of that century.

The poem is a spirited evocation of aspects of the hero's fame, in simple but expressive Latin with biblical, Virgilian, and other resonances. After an invocation in which comparisons are drawn with classical heroes and Homer, there is a call to an assembled public and then rapid mention of the Cid's birth and early deeds. There follows a more detailed account of the Cid's relations with Alfonso VI and of the hero's exile. Finally the poet presents his subject splendidly arming for the battle of Almenar in 1082, the text breaking off at the point where the Cid prays for victory. Most have thought this the concluding episode, but Smith argues that the poem was more extensive and was to cover at least the Cid's conquest of Valencia in 1094, his greatest triumph.

COLIN SMITH

Bibliography

Carmen Campidoctoris, o poema latino del Campeador. Ed. A. Montaner Frutos and Angel Escobar. Madrid, 2001.

Smith, C. "The Dating and Relationship of the *Historia Roderici* and the *Carmen Campidoctoris*," *Olifant* 9 (1986), 99–112.

Wright, R. "The First Poem on the Cid: The *Carmen Campi Doctoris*," *Acta* 3 (1979), 213–48.

CARRILLO DE HUETE, PEDRO

Halconero mayor (Chief Falconer) of King Juan II (1406–1454), Pedro Carillo de Huete is best remembered for his *Crónica del halconero de Juan II*, an account of the events of the reign of that king, written largely from memory, ca. 1435–1454, but also supplemented with numerous important documents. The work exists in four manuscripts, which represent three different versions: the *Crónica del halconero* itself (Biblioteca Nacional Madrid, MS 9445, partially copied in that library's MS 12373); a *Refundición de la crónica del halconero* (Escorial MS X.II.13), expanded and emended by the famous bishop Lope de Barrientos (who would also purge the library of Enrique de Villena at the behest of Juan II, burning part of it), and a summary of the original, useful for filling its lacunae, the *Abreviación de la crónica del Halconero* (Biblioteca Universitaria de Santa Cruz de Valladolid. MS 225). Dedicated to Juan II and interested in documenting the historical events of his time from the Royal Court of Castile to the frontier of Granada, Pedro Carillo began his account around 1435 as a continuation of the official chronicle of Castile, 1406–1435, written by Alvar García de Santa María, and ended it before 1454 inasmuch as Juan II is referred to as having died. His successor as halconero mayor was Miguel Lucas de Iranzo, who began to serve Enrique IV in 1455.

Apparently a modest, uncomplicated man, Pedro Carillo had little interest in politics and maintains considerable impartiality throughout his narrative (see, for example, his equanimity in describing the powerful figure of Alvaro de Luna). However, such objectivity detracts from the artistic, belletristic quality of the work: it is essentially a diary of events—military expeditions, parties, and tournaments—although the chivalric aspects of a given situation (especially one in which he has participated directly) brings some emotion to his prose, such as the case of the extraordinary (and almost comic) taking of the castle of Montalbán on behalf of Juan II, virtually unguarded inasmuch as its *alcaide* (castellan) was outside hunting "de perdices con bueyes" (patridges with oxen). Leaving Diego López to secure the gate, Pedro Carrillo climbed unopposed to the tower (although the actual "taking" lasted "dos oras e media" (two and one-half hours) in order to call chivalrously to his king "Andad, señor, que vuestra es la fortaleza!" (Come forth, my lord, the fort is yours). The work contains an introduction and 387 chapters; some 200 documents have been used in preparing the *Crónica*, approximately forty transcribed in their entirety. "Cameos" of famous figures of the 1400s include, among others, Diego de Valera, Alvaro de Luna, the Marqués de Santillana, Fernán Pérez de Guzmán, and Enrique de Villena. Pedro de Carrillo's history is an excellent mirror of the life of its day.

Dennis P. Seniff

Bibliography

Barrientos, L. *Refundición de la "Crónica del halconero" [de Pedro Carrillo de Huete] por el obispo Don Lope Barrientos*. Ed. J. de Mata Carriazo. Madrid, 1946.

Carrillo de Huete, P. *Crónica del halconero de Juan II*. Ed. J. de Mata Carriazo. Madrid, 1946.

Hook, D. "Andar a caça de perdizes con bueyes," *Celestinesca* 8 (1984), 47–48.

CARRILLO, ALFONSO, ARCHBISHOP OF TOLEDO

Born in 1410, Alfonso Carrillo was regarded by some of his contemporaries as being typical of the kind of prelate whose promotion within the ecclesiastical hierarchy owed almost everything to his social background and political activities and virtually nothing to his religious merits. He was the son of Lope Vásquez de Acuña and nephew of Cardinal Carrillo de Albornoz who in turn had been closely related to Pedro de Luna, archbishop of Toledo, and also to Benedict XIII. In addition, Carrillo was the brother of Pedro de Acuña, count of Buendia, and the uncle of Luis de Acuña, bishop of Segovia and Burgos, and of Pedro Birón, master of the order of Calatrava. He succeeded his uncle as bishop of Sigüenza, and his promotion to the archbishopric of Toledo in 1447 was the reward for political and military support in favor of Juan II against the rebel nobility.

Aristocratic and politically minded, Carrillo could also be a formidable opponent on the battlefield. In his *Claros varones de Castilla*, Pulgar depicted him as bellicose and aggressive, always involved in assembling armies and participating in war. Pulgar also observes that Carrillo accumulated wealth not because he was greedy but in order to be generous and distribute largesse.

Carrillo played an important role during the confused political events of the reign of Enrique IV (1454–1474). Close to the king during the early years of the reign, he subsequently became involved in almost all the anti-royal conspiracies of discontented nobles, playing a substantial part in wrenching concessions from the crown, and as one of the leading participants in the curious deposition of an effigy of Enrique IV in the Farce of Avila of 1465. He supported the "antiking" Alfonso, Enrique IV's half-brother, during the ensuing civil war, and when Alfonso died in 1468 he threw his support behind the future Queen Isabel I the Catholic, being responsible for the falsification of the papal dispensation required for her marriage to Fernando of Aragón. On the accession of the Catholic kings in 1474, Carrillo took umbrage at the influence of the powerful Mendoza clan at court, retired to his estates, ingrigued in favor of the supporters of Enrique IV's putative daughter, Juana "la Beltraneja," and on the failure of these machinations allegedly spent his remaining days in fruitless attempts at trying to acquire more wealth by the study and practice of alchemy. He died in 1482.

Despite his capacity for political intrigue and his involvement in military campaigns, it may be that Carrillo's reputation was to some extent damaged by the hostility of chroniclers. The text of a letter of criticism and advice that he sent to Enrique IV, contained in the chronicle of Diego Enriquez del Castillo, suggests a sound grasp of the need to reform the political and socioeconomic ills of the kingdom. Moreover, when the rebellious Catalans invited Enrique IV to be their king, Carrillo resisted the costly schemes that would involve ruinous expenditure and war in Aragón, Catalonia, and Valencia. Above all, Carrillo's participation in the Farce of Avila in 1465 was not simply that of an unlettered thug. He had been the president of the Castilian embassy at the Council of Basel and was familiar with all the sophisticated arguments about papal and royal powers that had been advanced by such outstanding political thinkers as Juan of Segovia and John Turrecremato. Indeed, his awareness of the problems that had surfaced at Basel informed the precise nature of the grounds for the king's deposition at Avila; a charge of heresy, which would have allowed for direct papal intervention, was dropped and the king was instead charted with accusations that enabled the conspirators to maintain the traditional view that the kingdom was exempt from the jurisdiction of Rome in temporal matiers.

Angus MacKay

Bibliography

Azcona, T. *Isabel la Católica: estudio crítico de su vida y reinado*. Madrid, 1993.

Edwards, J. *The Spain of the Catholic Monarchs*. Cambridge, 2000.

CARTAGENA, ALFONSO DE

Alfonso García de Santa Maria (*Alphonsus Burgensis*, 1385/6–1456) was the second son of Shlomo ha-Levi, *rab de la corte* of the Jewish *aljama* of Burgos, who on 21 July 1390, before Alfonso had been taught Hebrew, converted to Christianity under the name Pablo de Santa María and was subsequently elected bishop of Cartagena (1402) and Burgos (1415). The Santa María became leading members of the Burgos patriciate, intermarrying with the noble houses of Manrique, Mendoza, Rojas, and others; on being granted a royal patent of nobility in 1440, the family changed its surname to Cartagena. Alfonso García read canon law at Salamanca (ca. 1400–1406) before entering the church and court bureaucracy. By 1415 he was dean of Santiago de Compostela (dean of Segovia and canon of Burgos, 1420) and judge in the royal *audiencia* of Castile; in 1419, on the majority of Juan II of Castile (1406–1454), he was appointed to the king's council. In 1421–1423 he was sent on the first of several diplomatic missions to the Portuguese court of João I, where in the summer of 1422, at the behest of Prince Duarte, he wrote the "first-born of all my writings," *Memoriale uirtutum*, a scholastic *compilatio* of Aristotle's *Nicomachean Ethics* with glosses from Aquinas written in rhythmical Latin prose; the prologue to Book II extols the delights of studious solitude, adducing the parallels of Scipio Africanus (Cicero, *De officiis*, III, 1) and Count Fernán González in Pelayo's cave on the banks of the Arlanza, while the *ultilogus* illustrates the effects of vice in public life with Tarquin's rape of Lucretia and King Roderick's of La Cava, while virtue is represented by the heroes of the Reconquest.

These *exempla* foreshadow a civic humanist ideal, based on the model of classical Roman culture and virtue but with a significant admixture of native elements, which it became Cartagena's life-long project to preach to the aristocracy. Within months he penned his first Castilian work, a completion of Pero López de Ayala's unfinished translation of Boccaccio, *De casibus illustrium uirorum (Caída de prínçipes de Juan Bocaçio*, 30 September 1422); this was followed by versions of Cicero's *De senectute* and *De officiis (Quatro libros de Tulio*, Montemór o Novo, 10 January 1422 o.s./1423 n.s.), *Pro Marcello (Oración de Tulio a Julio Çésar)*, and *De inuentione*, I (*Rethórica de Marco Tulio Çicerón*, 1425–27), whose prologues make explicit the program for educating knights in "lengua clara vulgar e maternal," steering a *via media* between the competing claims of classical rhetoric and scholastic philosophy.

Cartagena's next project was a cycle of vernacular translations from the Córdoban Stoic Seneca the Younger which, under the patronage of Juan II, was designed to show the antiquity and worth of Hispanic classical culture in defiance of the Italians (*Gran copilaçión del alphabeto de algunos dichos de Séneca*, from Fra Luca Manelli's fourteenth-century *Tabulatio et expositio Senecae*, 1428/9–30; *Cinco libros de Séneca*, from *De uita beata, Ep. ad Lucilium* 88, *De providentia*, the apocryphal *De institutis legalībus*, and Seneca the Elder's *Controuersiae*, 1431; *De constantia*; *De clementia*).

It was on a third Portuguese legation in 1427 that Cartagena experienced a first direct contact with Italian humanism, through a pair of Leonardo Bruni's Latin translations from the Greek brought back from Bologna by some Portuguese jurists. The result was his

Declinationes super noua quadam Ethicorum Aristotelis translatione, dedicated to Fernán Díaz de Toledo in 1431, a pamphlet criticizing Bruni's humanist version of Aristotle's *Ethics* as too rhetorical and unphilosophical. The *Declinationes* aroused European controversy when, in 1434, Cartagena took a copy to the General Council of Basel as a member of the Castilian delegation. There he also pronounced a number of public speeches, notably a disputation on *Lex Gallus de postumis instituendis uel exheredandis* (Avignon, 18 July 1434), sermons on the feasts of St. Thomas Aquinas (Juan II's birthday) and All Saints, and political briefs on the powers of the Council and the papal *plenitudo postestatis*, on the preeminence of the crown of Castile over that of England (*Propositio super altercatione preeminentie sedium inter reges Castelle et Anglie*, 14 September 1434), and on the Castilian right to the conquest of the Canaries (*Allegationes super conquesta insularum Canarie contra Portugalenses*, 27 August 1437). The latter are no less interesting for their Ciceronian rhetorical schemes than for their political ideology.

Aeneas Sylvius Piccolomini informs us that Cartagena's oratory so deeply impressed everyone that, when Pablo de Santa María died in 1435, Pope Eugenius IV immediately provided him to the vacant see; his election as bishop of Burgos was confirmed by Juan II's nomination. A further outcome of his stay in Basel was his Latin correspondence with Leonardo Bruni and Pier Candido Decembrio, in which he successfully requested translations from Greek (Porphyry, Homer, and Plato's *Republic*). In March 1438 Cartagena attended the imperial coronation of Albrecht III of Austria in Breslau, where he met Diego de Valera and Pero Tafur. He returned via Prague, Nuremburg, and Mainz, reaching Spain in December 1439, where his first act was to grant a canonry in Burgos to his protégé Rodrigo Sánchez de Arévalo; at the same time the young Alfonso de Palencia entered his retinue. In 1440 he was the chief negotiator in the marriage of Juan II's son Prince Enrique to Blanca of Navarre; it was during the princess's stay in his brother Pedro's palace in Burgos that the Bohemian traveler Rozmital met Cartagena, and it was probably also at this time that the latter formed his close friendships with Pedro Fernández de Velasco (*Epistola ad comitem de Haro*, ca. 1441, a Latin treatise on noble education which again propounds Cartagena's ideal of educated chivalry), with Íñigo López de Mendoza (*Respuesta a la questión fecha por el marqués de Santillana*, 1444, on Leonardo Bruni's *De militia*, a discussion of the classical origins of chivalry), and with Diego Gómez de Sandoval, Count of Castrojeriz (*Doctrinal de cavalleros*, ca. 1445, a compendium of laws and commentaries on chivalry). Cartagena formed a deeper friendship with Fernán Pérez de Guzmán, to whom he dedicated his *Duodenarium*, a set of Latin essays on political, moral, and linguistic questions sent to its addressee (unfinished) soon after 1442.

In the 1440s Cartagena wrote a number of juridical briefs on the rights and constitutions of his bishopric against the pretensions of Alfonso Carrillo, archbishop of Toledo (*Liber Mauricianus, Conflatorium*), and reorganized the cathedral archive; he was also responsible for major building works, including the cathedral's two famous openwork stone spires, designed by Johann von Köln, and the Chapel of the Visitation, which houses his own tomb, and the plaza and episcopal palace of El Sarmental. To these years belong his gloss on a devotional sermon of St. John Chrysostom and *Apologia super psalmum Judica me Deus*, a "*contemplación mezclada con oración*" on the Penitential Psalm 26, both written in Latin and subsequently translated by the author into Castilian; and the massive *Defensorium unitatis Christianae*, a reasoned impugnation of the anti-*converso* libels of Pero Sarmiento in the Rebellion of Toledo, addressed to Juan II in 1449, in which, once again, Cartagena brought his vast knowledge of history, theology, and oratory to bear on a subject which other writers had treated only in legal terms. The political situation in the wake of Sarmiento's rebellion was volatile, however, and, after Álvaro de Luna's arrest and imprisonment in his brother Pedro's Burgos palace in March 1453, Cartagena found himself in the invidious position of having to draw up the charges for the execution of the *privado* whose policy he had so loyally supported for twenty years.

Cartagena's last works were the *Oracional* (ca. 1455), a layman's treatise on prayer written in Castilian for Fernán Pérez de Guzmán, which lays stress on the inwardness of spiritual life in ways which point to the *Devotio moderna* and Illuminism rather than Italian humanism, while the Latin *Anacephaleosis regum Hispanie*, on which he was working in the months before his death and which he dedicated to Burgos cathedral chapter, develops the Neo-Gothic myth expounded in his father's *Coplas de las siete edades del mundo* on the Messianic imperial and crusading destiny of Hispania. In the summer 1456 Cartagena undertook a pilgrimage to Santiago for the jubilee, but he was already ill, and had to return before the feast of St. James, dying at Villasandino on 22 July. His decease is recounted in touching terms, with the obligatory deathbed miracle, in the contemporary *De actibus domini Alfonsi de Cartagena* (BNM 7432, fols. 89–92^{v}, attributed to his amanuensis Juan Sánchez de Nebreda). Other tributes were penned by Fernando de la Torre in a letter to Pedro de Cartagena; by Fernán Pérez de Guzmán in his *Coplas sobre el transitu del reverendo padre don*

Alfonso de Cartajena ("Aquel Séneca espiró | a quien yo era Luçilo"); and by his pupil and *camarero* Diego Rodríguez de Almela in a *semblanza* included in a work undertaken at Cartagena's behest, *Valerio de las estorias escolásticas e de España*, VIII, 6, 9 (completed March 1462, printed Murcia 1487). The most vivid portraits, however, are those by his fellow *conversos* (Catholic converts) Juan de Lucena (*Diálogo moral de vita felici*, 1463) and Fernando del Pulgar, whose *semblanza* shows Cartagena as a man of deep intelligence, pious modesty, and complete integrity (*Claros varones de Castilla*, ca. 1483–1486, published 1486).

JEREMY LAWRANCE

Bibliography

Birkenmajer, A. "Der Streit des Alonso von Cartagena mit Leonardo Bruni Aretino," *Beiträge zur Geschichte der Philosophie des Mittelalters* 20 (1917–22), Heft 5 (1922), 128–210, 226–35.

Cartagena, A. de *Defensorium unitatis Christianae*. Ed. M. Alonso. Madrid, 1943.

Espinosa Fernandez, Y. (ed.) *La Anacephaleosis de Alonso de Cartagena*. 3 vols. Madrid, 1989.

Gómez Moreno, A. "La *Qüestión* del Marqués de Santillana a don Alfonso de Cartagena," *El Crotalón: Ánuario de Filología Española* 2 (1985), 335–63.

González-Quevedo Alonso, S. (ed.) *El Oracional de Alonso de Cartagena*. Chapel Hill, N.C., 1983.

Lawrance, J. (ed.) *Un tratado de Alonso de Cartagena sobre la educación y los estudios literarios*. Bellaterra, 1979.

Morrás, M. (ed). *Texto y concordancias del* De officiis *de Cicerón, traducción castellana por Alfonso de Cartagena*. Madison, Wisc., 1989.

CARTAGENA, TERESA DE

Born between 1420 and 1425, Teresa de Cartagena was the author of two important pious prose works, the *Arboleda de los enfermos* (ca. 1450) and the *Admiración operum Dey* (of uncertain date but written out of self-justification to counter the surprise caused by the reception of the *Arboleda*). She was a member of the most illustrious *converso* family of fifteenth-century Castile, the Santa María-Cartagenas, whose members achieved great distinction in literature and the church. She was the grandaughter of Pablo de Santa María, successively the chief rabbi and bishop of Burgos as well as the author of an historical work, *Siete edades del mundo*, the niece of the humanist, statesman, and polemicist Alfonso de Cartagena, also bishop of Burgos, as well as his brother, the intellectual and chronicler Alvar García de Santa María. Teresa also corresponded with Gómez Manrique, one of the principal literary figures of the realm, and was urged by Manrique to continue her literary endeavors. Teresa lost her hearing at an early age and, educated at Salamanca, she became a Franciscan nun. Her deafness appears to have been instrumental in the development of both her spiritual sensibilities and her literary enterprise.

The *Arboleda de los enfermos* is a consolatory work couched in terms of an allegorical exposition and meditation on the spiritual benefits of illness, specifically her deafness, as a means of isolation from worldly distractions. In it, Teresa distinguishes between the physical and the spiritual ability to hear, concluding that deafness can be a defense against metaphysical blindness. Her aim in writing it was to teach others to cope with adversity. The work is rich with images and demonstrates an intimate spirituality that also places great value on human relationships, especially family. Its sources are complex, largely biblical and Patristic (Augustine, Boethius, Jerome, Gregory the Great, and St. Bernard, among them), and stand as a testimonial to Teresa's learning and erudition. At the same time, the *Arboleda* is notable for its authenticity and as a record of an intimate religious experience tempered by personal hardship.

The *Admiración*, although derived from largely the same sources as the *Arboleda*, was composed in response to her critics, whom she says disbelieved she could have written the *Arboleda* and chastised her for the audacity of pretending that a woman could have composed such a work. Although the *Admiración* is crafted in a tone framed by obligatory rhetorical modesty, there are at times murmurs of irony in Teresa's voice as she defends the *Arboleda*'s divine inspiration and fails to give ground on the fact that God may endow women with both strength and intelligence. The *Admiración* is notable because it constitutes an apology for female authorship as well as a series of reflections by Teresa on her own writing and its place in society and in the church.

Although there is no hint of heterodoxy in her works, Teresa's *converso* origins may have complicated her existence and helped shape the nature of her writing. Both her works were composed shortly after the anti-*converso* riots of 1449 in Toledo and appear to incorporate that experience into her choice of imagery. The traditional Augustinian allegory of the City of God is transformed by Teresa from a secure and ordered place into one of fear, suspicion, and isolation.

The date of her death is unknown.

E. MICHAEL GERLI

Bibliography

Cartagena, T. de. *The Writings of Teresa de Cartagena*. Trans. Dayle Seidenspinner-Núñez. Cambridge, U.K., 1998.

Deyermond, A. "Spain's First Women Writers." In *Women in Hispanic Literature*. Ed. Beth Miller. Berkeley, 1983.

CARTAS PUEBLAS *See* CHARTERS

CARTHUSIAN ORDER *See* MONASTICISM,

CARTOGRAPHY

Iberian cartography begins with St. Isidore of Seville who, codifying the knowledge of his day, sought to present a world picture. Isidore sought to explain the Creator's organization of the world by giving a Christian interpretation to the learning of antiquity that complemented the Bible. In order to depict the world created by God and maintained by his providence, he chose the infinite form of a circle, or *Orbis*, a reflection of the divine eternity and perfection of *Terra*—hence the name *Terrarum Orbis*—designated by a *T* within the circle formed by the letter *O*, to produce a tripartite division of the superimposed images. The three parts of the so-called *TO* map corresponds to the Trinity as well as to the tripartite division of the world (Europe, Asia, and Africa) populated by Noah's three sons, Shem, Ham, and Japheth, as described in Genesis 9: 19. The eschatological significance of this synthesis is completed by the similarity of the *T* to the *tau* of the cross of Christ and by the arrangement of the inhabited world around Jerusalem at its center, from which everything stems. This same theocentric, anthropocentric, and geocentric scheme seems to have inspired Western Christian cartography from the seventh century until the end of the thirteenth. Its archetype can be found in the work of the Iberian monk Beatus of Liébana, whose name has come to be applied to designate later versions of the *TO* scheme.

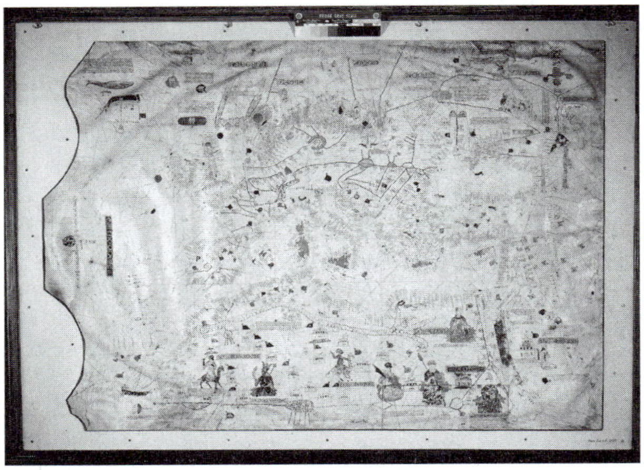

Catalan Portolano. Atlas of Charles V, map of Mecia de-Villadexte, 1413. Copyright © Giraudon/Art Resource, NY. Bibliotheque Nationale, Paris, France.

The regional map, whose mainly maritime use began toward the end of the thirteenth century, contrasts in almost every way with the traditional *TO mappa mundi*. In it, experience, empiricism, and observation prevail over the conceptual and the mystical. These charts are designated "portolan" maps and reveal the extent to which the aim, method, and focus of mapmaking had changed since the time of St. Isidore. Made from sheepskin, calfskin, or other animal skin, the material used is recognizable by its shape, which usually includes skin from the animal's neck. At first sight the image of a portolan map resembles a spider's web, which serves to organize a network of intricate interconnecting lines. Some of these lines (called rhumb lines and arranged in groups of sixteen radiate regularly within tangential circumferences to form compass roses, where their points of intersection with the circumference create sixteen nodal points and mark off sixteen compass divisions, each with a value of twenty-two degrees thirty minutes. Other lines join these nodal points together and make up a series of parallelograms, squares, and rectangles. The vertical lines seem to serve as meridians and the horizontal ones as parallels, yet they do not form a system of graduated coordinates and cannot be relied upon as such. The delineation of coast lines and the location of ports on the charts were made according to triangulation, according to the direction of the winds whose names are given in the vernacular (at first Tuscan) on the map. The use of this form of chart obviously required the ability to take bearings and estimate distances. Thus, portolans presuppose the existence of a corpus of knowledge and calculations vital for accuracy to mariners and cartographers. In order to manufacture and use them, ancient calculations transmitted through the so-called *Tablas toledanas*, replaced later by the *Tablas alfonsíes* of Alfonso X el Sabio, had to be used. At the same time, navigators availed themselves of *portolani*, or books that gave narrative descriptions of coasts and ports, listing the distances between the latter. The oldest and best known example of a portolan chart is the anonymous Italian *Carte pisane* (ca. 1290). Other early surviving examples are also Italian and were made by Petrus Vesconte (1313) and Angelino Dulcert (1325).

Late medieval mapmaking in Iberia is closely linked to political history. The first surviving Iberian portolan charts, for example, are from the so-called Catalan-Mallorcan school of cartography, which Hervé says derived from the Pisan and Genoese schools of mapmaking. The influence of Aragónese commercial expansion and subsequent political hegemony in the Mediterranean from the thirteenth century forward is responsible for this. The uniqueness of the

Mallorcan school's maps is alluded to by Ramón Llull and was doubtless affected by its emergence in Palma's multicultural society of Christians, Arabs, and Jews. Although the Mallorcan cartographers were doubtless influenced by their Italian colleagues, Mallorca became a focal point for the manufacture of charts and for instruction in their making that soon attracted cartographers even from Italy. By the middle of the thirteenth century, the Catalan maps were renowned for their precision, the wealth of their information, and their fine material composition.

The market for sea charts expanded proportionally to the development of navigation and progress in the use of portolans. In 1354, the king of Aragón issued a proclamation forbidding the master of any ship from setting sail without at least two charts on board. This explains not only the presence of many cartographic workshops in Mallorca but also in Barcelona and then later in the fifteenth century at Valencia. The arrangement of the Catalan charts, drawn on roughly dressed skin, conforms generally to the earlier Pisan charts of the Middle Ages. In these, a vertical distance scale is placed on the part of the chart corresponding to the neck of the animal from which the skin is taken. The wind directions are indicated by four medallions whose colors, often red and yellow, point to their Aragónese origins. These charts consist mainly of indications of natural features: rivers and their mouths, capes, bays, towns, and ports surrounded by walls decorated with armorial banners, and often include the delineation of inland mountain ridges and other physical features. Inland seas are represented by waves, and nomenclature is in the vernacular. In addition, certain decorative features mark the various workshops where they originated: the Virgin and Child, the Crucified Christ, St. Christopher, and so on. Mallorcan cartographic skill demonstrated a great deal of technical mastery and a refined artistic sense. The so-called Catalan Atlas, thought to be the work of Abraham Crescas (ca. 1375), is rightly considered the masterpiece of this type of mapmaking.

Few noteworthy Portuguese maps survive from before the beginning of the sixteenth century. From this, however, we should not assume that mapmaking was not an important activity in late medieval Portugal. The need for state secrecy (*sigillo*) may be the reason for their rarity. Portuguese voyages into the Atlantic are well documented from the end of the fourteenth century on, as is the Portuguese craving for maps. In 1428 Dom Pedro, Henry the Navigator's brother, for example, scoured Italy and brought back from Venice a *mappa mundi* whose extension to the Far East proved an incentive for Portuguese voyages and exploration. Henry's collection of cartographic information at Sagres, which he continued to compile throughout his life, is, of course, legendary and well documented as well. Cartography eventually became an official service in the households of the kings of both Portugal and Castile, who sought to attract foreign scholars as their mapmakers and cosmographers. Yehuda Crescas, son of Abraham, most likely worked at Sagres with Henry.

E. Michael Gerli

Bibliography

Bägrow, L., and R. A. Skelton. *A History of Cartography*. Cambridge, Mass. 1964.

Hervé, H. "Filiation des écoles hyrographiques." *Revue de Histoire Économique et Sociale* 45, no. 1 (1967)

Stevenson, E. L. *Portolan Charts: Their Origin and Characteristics with a Descriptive List of Those Belonging to the Hispanic Society of America*. New York, 1911.

CARVAJAL, JUAN DE

Juan de Carvajal (1399?–1469) was one of the papacy's most important diplomats in the mid-fifteenth century. Born at Trujillo in Extremadura, Carvajal studied law at Salamanca and became dean of Astoga in 1433. By 1438 he had attracted the notice of Pope Eugenius IV, becoming an auditor of the Rota. In 1440 Eugenius sent Carvajal to help sway the Holy Roman Empire from its policy of neutrality in the pope's struggle with the Council of Basel. Continuous labors in Germany between 1440 and 1447 earned Carvajal promotion to the episcopate and then to the cardinalate.

When Nicholas V (Tomasso Parentucelli) succeeded Eugenius in 1447, he dispatched Carvajal to Germany as his legate. The legate, aided by Aeneas Sylvius Piccolomini (later Pius II) won Frederick III, king of the Romans, to the pope's cause. Besides laboring for the dissolution of the Council of Basel, Carvajal promoted political peace between kingdoms threatened by the Turks. After spending the years 1450–1454 in Rome, Carvajal was dispatched to Hungary, where he served as a guardian to the new king, Ladislas Posthumous.

In 1456, as legate for Calixtus III, Carvajal helped save Belgrade from the Turks. The cardinal remained active in Hungary into the reign of Pius II seeing Matthias Corvinus succeed Ladislas. In 1461 Carvajal returned to Rome, becoming cardinal bishop of Porto. He remained active in the curia, serving as legate to Venice (1466–1467) and as chamberlain of the College of Cardinals (1468). Juan de Carvajal died in Rome in 1469 during the reign of Paul II, and he was buried at San Marcello al Corso. His writings were few, most of them being official documents.

Thomas M. Izbicki

Bibliography

Gómez Canedo, L., *Un español al servicio de la santa sede: Don Juan de Carvajal*. Madrid, 1947.

CASPE, COMPROMISE OF

The Compromise of Caspe in 1412 settled the four-way contest for the Crown of Aragón that had been left vacant in 1410 when King Martí the Humane died leaving neither a legitimate male heir nor any daughters, and not formally naming a successor. The prize in this dynastic sweepstakes was the prosperous and strategically important Mediterranean kingdom that included not only Aragón, Catalunya, and Valencia on the Iberian Peninsula but also the islands of Sicily, Sardinia, and Corsica.

Four candidates came forward to stake their claims for the crown. Count Jaime of Urgell, son-in-law of King Pedro IV (1336–1387) and great-grandson of Alfonso IV (1327–1336), appeared to have the strongest claim and was favored by influential Catalan nobles. In 1409 Urgell was appointed lieutenant, a position normally reserved for the heir, but he faced fierce opposition by the Aragónese, who feared Catalan dominance. Martí had favored his young grandson Federico, Count of Luna, the recently legitimized son of the late Marti the Younger, but he explicitly refused to come out in favor of Federico. The candidacy of Louis, duke of Calabria, the son of Louis of Anjou and Yolanda of Aragón, was advocated by the influential archbishop of Zaragoza. The fourth claimant, Fernando of Antequera, nephew of King Martí and uncle of Juan II of Castile, was a wealthy and powerful member of the Trastámara family, which had ruled Castile since 1369.

All parties agreed to settle the dispute through general deliberation in parliamentary sessions. The governor of Catalunya summoned the *cortes* (Parliament) to meet in Montblanch on 30 August 1410 but the meeting was moved to Barcelona and delayed until October. Early on, Federico of Luna was eliminated from the contest because his youth and inexperience would have necessitated papal tutelage. In the spring of 1411 Aragónese allies of Jaime of Urgell assassinated archbishop Heredía of Zaragoza because he refused to accept Urgell as a valid claimant. With him died the hopes not only of Louis but also those of Urgell, who, even though not directly connected with the murder was close enough to be seriously discredited. At this point the governor of Aragón threw his support to Fernando of Antequera, recent victor in a major battle against the Muslims of Granada and vigorous supporter of the antipope Benedict XIII as the legitimate pope.

Factional conflicts among the Aragónese and Valencian delegates threatened the meetings of those realms, prompting intervention by Benedict XIII. He proposed the formation of a representative commission composed of nine electors—three each from Aragón, Catalunya, and Valencia. The members of the commission included both the governor and the justicia of Aragón, the bishop of Huesca, the archbishop of Tarragona, and Friar Vicente Ferrer. The sessions met from 29 March to 29 June 1412 at Caspe, a location geographically central to all three realms.

Urgell's claim to the throne through the male line still made him a serious candidate, even though he was tainted by the murder of Heredia. In the end, it was the reluctance of the Catalan electors to declare solidly for Urgell that doomed his chances. By then, Fernando of Antequera, politically savvy and militarily successful, was the candidate viewed by many as the best hope for stability after the two year interregnum, despite Catalan objections to his "foreign" Castilian birth.

The decision in favor of Fernando I, who ruled from 1412 to 1416, was well received in Aragón, less so in Valencia, and not well at all in Catalunya. Nevertheless, the compromise was proof of the strength and vitality of a three-hundred-year-old parliamentary tradition in the Crown of Aragón.

The process by which the compromise was reached is just as important as the fact that the Trastámara family suddenly came to dominate the two most powerful kingdoms on the Iberian Peninsula, Castile and Aragón. At issue was more than just a legal fine point, but instead a political dilemma that forced the nine electors and their advisors to select the man who would make the best king, not simply the man with the best legal claim.

THERESA EARENFIGHT

Bibliography

Dualde Serrano, M., and C. M. Jos. *El compromiso de Caspe*. 2d ed. Zaragoza, 1976.

García Gallo, A. "El derecho de sucesión del trono en la Corona de Aragón," *Anuario de Historia del Derecho Español* 36 (1966), 5–178.

Sobreques i Vidal, S. *El compromis de Casp i le noblesa catalana*. Barcelona, 1973.

CASTIGOS E DOCUMENTOS PARA BIEN VIVIR

The title of this book does not appear in any manuscript but was so labeled for the library of the Count of Villaumbrosa.

Sancho IV, el Bravo (1284–1295), the son of Alfonso X, was, in spite of his nickname (which probably meant "the Fierce"), a man of excellent education and a patron of literature. This is made manifest by his *Los lucidarios*, a scientific work; by the translation he sponsored titled the *Libro de los tesoros*; by the completion during his reign of the *Primera crónica general*; by his founding of the Estudios generales de Alcalá; and, of course, his most valuable work, *Castigos*, which is the first complete dial of princes in Spanish, even though his father's *Siete Partidas* contains elements of this genre and surely served Sancho as a guide or model to be expanded upon. Sancho, who may have actually composed all or parts of *Castigos* and who certainly oversaw and corrected its composition, if he did not write the book himself, produced one of the most important works of the Spanish Middle Ages and, unfortunately, one of the most neglected to this day. Written in the first person and addressed to his son, to rule as Fernando IV, el Emplazado ("the Summoned" or "the Cited"), (1295–1310), the fifty chapters, some quite lengthy, were finished in 1293, when Fernando was only six. No doubt Sancho believed that as the boy matured he would benefit from the directives addressed to him, all of which set down the obligations a prince, and by extension every man, owed to God, to himself, and mankind. *Castigos*, finished while Alfonso's renaissance was still in flower, utilized many sources, some well known, some rare, and a few never included in any other book: Holy Writ, ancient philosophers, both eastern and western; Cicero; Seneca; stories from the classics, such as those of the Trojan War, and the seduction (by Aeneas) of Dido and her death (drawn from *General estoria*); the *Siete Partidas*; the *Cantigas de Santa Maria*; Peter Lombard; Gregory the Great's *Decretals*; St. the *Disciplina Clericalis*; possibly *Calila e Digna*; the *Bonium*; and the contemporary *Gran conquista de Ultramar*, to list some of the most important. More interesting are stories in which appear characters and places familiar to Sancho, which lend a very personal touch to *Castigos*.

While the style of the book is serious and sedate with a purpose primarily didactic, passages are nevertheless present in which there is obvious recreational intent.

Four manuscripts are extant, as are a few fragments. In the Biblioteca Nacional de Madrid can be found manuscripts A(6559) and B(6603), both of the fifteenth century, and C(3995) of the fourteenth; in the Biblioteca del Escorial can be found manuscript Ez III 4, of the late fourteenth or early fifteenth centuries. Manuscript A contains, in addition to the usual fifty chapters of *Castigos*, some forty chapters of gloss from the *Regimiento de principes* and other sources not always identifiable. Manuscript C is illuminated by twenty-two exceptionally artistic miniatures, revealing the development of book illustration of that period and the unusual artistic narrative techniques employed to depict events.

Two editions have been published: that of Gayangos, which is frequently reprinted unchanged, based upon manuscript B with additions and substitutions from manuscript A, but never explained or specified; and that of Rey.

JOHN E. KELLER

Bibliography

Foulché-Delbosc, R. "Les *Castigos e documentos* de Sancho IV," *Revue Hispanique* 15 (1906), 340–71.

Gayangos, P. de, (ed.) *Castigos et documentos para bien vivir del Rey Don Sancho IV*. Biblioteca de Antores Españoles, 51. Madrid, 1860. 78–228.

Rey, A., (ed.) *Castigos e documentos para bien vivir ordenados por el Rey Don Sancho IV*. Bloomington, Ind., 1952.

CASTILE, COUNTS OF

See CASTILE COUNTY KINGDOM

CASTILE, COUNTY AND KINGDOM

Castile, known in Roman times as Bardulia, first emerged as a separate political entity early in the ninth century in the upper reaches of the central Iberian meseta. Many of the early settlers there were mountaineers from the Cantabrian and Basque regions. Centered around the fortress town of Burgos, the *cabeza de Castilla*, Castile, governed by several counts appointed by the kings of León, was a frontier zone exposed to nearly annual raids by the Muslims of the emirate and the caliphate of Córdoba. The name Castile was derived from the numerous castles erected to guard against such incursions. In the tenth century Count Fernán González (923–970) gained control of the entire area and won renown as a champion of Castilian autonomy. In time the office of count became hereditary in his family. The thirteenth-century *Poema de Fernán González* celebrated his victories over the Muslims. At the same time distinctive language forms began to emerge, setting Castilian apart from the Romance tongue spoken in León. Moreover, the Castilians preferred to be ruled by customary law rather than by the *Forum judicum*, the old Visigothic Code that formed the basis of Leonese law.

Castile was transformed from a county into an independent kingdom early in the eleventh century. The dominant political figure at that time was Sancho the Great of Navarre (1000–1035), who took possession of Castile in 1029 and designated his son Fernando as heir to the county. After his father's death Fernando I (1035–1065) assumed the title of king of Castile and soon seized the kingdom of León as well. As a consequence Castile and León were now joined under the personal rule of one man. However, each kingdom continued to maintain its singular characteristics and at no time were they truly amalgamated into one realm. Before he died Fernando I divided his dominions among his three sons, Sancho II (1065–1072) of Castile, Alfonso VI (1065–1109) of León, and García of Galicia. The latter was soon driven from the Galician throne by his older brothers, but then Sancho II forced Alfonso VI into exile and thereby gained control of his father's entire patrimony. After Sancho II was murdered, perhaps with the complicity of his sister Urraca and his brother, Alfonso VI not only recovered possession of his own kingdom of León but also of Castile. In 1085 Alfonso VI achieved an even more significant advance southward when he seized Toledo on the Tagus River. During this time the Castilian noble Rodrigo Díaz de Vivar, known as the Cid, won fame as a warrior and was extolled as the epitome of Castilian chivalry by the thirteenth-century *Cantar de mío Cid*.

For many years the Duero River valley, which had not been populated by either Muslims or Christians, served as the southern extremity of Castile. Christian settlement there grew apace, however, and extended well south of the river into Extremadura. During the eleventh and twelfth centuries, the kingdom of Castile was organized around great municipal districts, such as Burgos, Valladolid, Palencia, Avila, Segovia, Soria, Logroño, and Santander, each dominating an extensive rural area dotted with tiny villages. *Fueros*, or charters of privileges granted by the king, defined the essential terms of municipal government. The militia forces of these municipalities came to play a significant role in the Reconquest and their mounted warriors (*caballeros villanos*) eventually came to dominate municipal government. The economy was generally agricultural and pastoral. As the frontier was pushed farther south the transhumance of sheep from the northernmost sectors of Castile became more and more prominent and in the thirteenth century led to the organization of the Mesta, a sheep-owners association. Important monastic houses such as Santo Domingo de Silos were established throughout the region. The thirteenth-century priest-poet, Gonzalo de Berceo, commemorated the lives of the saints and helped to forge the Castilian language as a poetic instrument.

The kingdoms of Castile and León were separated by Alfonso VII (1126–1157), who assigned León to his son Fernando II (1157–1188) and Castile to Sancho III (1157–1158). After the latter's untimely death his young son Alfonso VIII (1158–1214) successfully maintained his independence when his uncle attempted to dominate him and his realm. Alfonso VIII pushed the Castilian frontier well south of the Tagus River toward the Guadiana, although his initial efforts provoked the Almohads, a Muslim sect from Morocco, who inflicted a major defeat on him at Alarcos in 1195. Aided by a papal bull of crusade, Alfonso VIII triumphed over the Almohads at Las Navas de Tolosa in 1212, decisively tipping the balance of power in favor of the Christians. The southern frontier of the kingdom of Castile now extended southward toward the Guadalquivir River, and the road to Andalusia was opened.

After the brief reign of Alfonso VIII's son Enrique I (1214–1217), the Castilians proclaimed his sister Berenguela as queen, but she preferred that her son Fernando III (1217–1252) have the kingship. During his early years the Castilians began to move into the upper zone of the Guadalquivir. In 1230 he succeeded to the kingdom of León and from then on the two realms, while maintaining their different laws and institutions, remained conjoined for the rest of the Middle Ages. With the combined resources of both kingdoms at his disposal Fernando III captured Córdoba (1236), Jaén (1246), and Seville (1248), and reduced the Muslim kingdom of Granada to tributary status. In 1492 Fernando (1479–1516) and Isabel (1474–1504) finally conquered the kingdom of Granada.

Castile was the principal beneficiary of this expansion and always had first place in the royal intitulation. As the most extensive Christian kingdom in the Iberian Peninsula, Castile had a clear territorial preponderance, but the neighboring kingdoms of Portugal and Aragón through their maritime enterprise tended to enjoy greater prosperity. In the early modern era a geographic distinction between Old and New Castile gradually came into use. The lands north of the Sierra de Guadarrama were known as Old Castile and the former Muslim kingdom of Toledo extending southward to Andalusia and including Madrid, Guadalajara, Cuenca, and Ciudad Real, was called New Castile.

JOSEPH F. O'CALLAGHAN

Bibliography

Collins, R. *Early Medieval Spain: Unity in Diversity, 400–1000*. New York, 1983.

MacKay, A. *Spain in the Middle Ages: From Frontier to Empire, 1000–1500*. New York, 1977.

O'Callaghan, J. F. *A History of Medieval Spain*. Ithaca, N.Y., 1975.

CASTILIAN

Castilian (in Spanish, *castellano*) is a neo-Latin language. Like its Hispano-Romance congeners, Galician-Portuguese, Leonese, Navarro-Aragónese, and Catalan, it descends in a direct line from the spoken Latin brought to the Iberian Peninsula by the Romans, beginning in the late third century B.C. Its relatively archaic profile has been traced to this early colonization (as against later Romanization of such areas as Gaul and northern Italy).

Though vernacular features are often detectable as "errors" in early medieval Latin documents from Castile, it is customary to trace the origin of Castilian, the ancestor of modern Spanish, to the late tenth or early eleventh centuries, when certain scribes, especially in the monastery of San Millán de la Cogolla (La Rioja), began to insert vernacular glosses of Latin words no longer in spoken use into manuscripts containing religious texts. The so-called *Glosas Emilianenses* (see García Larragueta) also contain the earliest known continuous passage, a religious invocation running to forty-three words, in Castilian vernacular. It was not until almost two centuries later (c. 1200) that authors began intentionally to compose literary works in Castilian. The only surviving version of the great Castilian epic *Cantar de Mio Cid* appears to date from this period (see Smith).

Geography

Spoken at the time of the Muslim conquest in a small area of north/central Spain, specifically the region surrounding—and to the north of—the city of Burgos, Castilian was carried south as a result of the territorial expansion of the Christian kingdoms (traditionally labeled the Reconquest), in which Castilian warriors played the leading role from about the mid-tenth century. By the end of the Middle Ages, it was spoken in an area extending from a thin strip on the Cantabrian Sea in the north to a wide expanse of the Atlantic and Mediterranean coasts in the south (see Lapesa).

Periodization and Dialects

Like any language evolving spontaneously without the constraints imposed by an officially sanctioned prestige norm, Castilian, though confined at the outset of the literary period to a compact territory, exhibited considerable dialect differentiation, with western varieties merging smoothly into Leonese and eastern ones approximating neighboring Navarro-Aragónese. (Early literary works frequently evince a distinctly western or eastern flavor.) The mid-thirteenth century heralds a period of intense standardization, with King Alfonso X the Learned, through the activities of scribes and translators of the Royal Scriptorium at Toledo (a city returned to Christian control in 1085) shaping and imposing the Castilian literary standard (see Penny). That official prestige norm was based largely on Toledan usage, with certain nods to more northerly varieties.

Foreign Influences

Though at all times a mainstream member of the Romance family, Castilian has, at different stages of development, been strongly influenced, especially on the lexical level, by other languages with which it has come in contact (see Lapesa and Penny). While the spoken Latin from which Castilian derived had already appropriated many words from Greek as well as Germanic and Celtic languages, Castilian and Galician-Portuguese are unique in having absorbed thousands of Arabic words—mostly nouns belonging to such semantic spheres as agriculture (*berenjena*, "eggplant"), apparel (*albornoz*, "burnoose"), building and architecture (*alcoba* "alcove"), law and civic institutions (*alcalde*, "mayor"), mathematics (*cifra*, "zero, figure"), science (*auge*, "apogee"), and war (*adarga*, "leather shield"). Many peninsular toponyms, especially in Andalusia and the Levant, also betray Arabic origins, while others reflect the Arabicization of Latin names, the standard example being *Zaragoza* from *Caesarem Augustum.*

Words of French and Provençal origin percolated into Castilian throughout the Middle Ages. Many designated objects and institutions of feudal culture (*homenaje*, "homage"), but few corners of the Castilian lexicon were impervious to Gallicisms. Among factors promoting such lexical transfer were the presence of French quarters in many Castilian towns; the movement, from the tenth century, of vast numbers of French pilgrims across northern Spain to worship at the shrine of St. James in Compostela (Galicia); and the establishment of prominent French monastic outposts (e.g., Leyre, Sahagún) in northern Spain in the eleventh century.

While early Italianisms were chiefly nautical terms (*mesana*, "mizzenmast"), the closing century of the Middle Ages witnessed large-scale importation of Italian words belonging to many spheres of life, an influx favored in the conquest of Naples by Alfonso V of Aragón in 1443.

The incorporation of classical Latin words into written, then spoken, Castilian, which began at a modest pitch in the twelfth and early thirteenth centuries, assumed major proportions from the mid-thirteenth century through the end of the medieval period and beyond. These were often words that, having fallen into desuetude in the centuries separating classical Latin from early Castilian, were resuscitated and reincorporated first into the written and then the spoken language by scribes who altered their form slightly to make them compatible with Castilian phonotactics. These *cultismos* thus sidestepped phonetic changes, affecting such lexical material as was passed down from generation to generation through uninterrupted oral transmission.

Finally, a relatively small number of Castilian words came from Basque, among them such frequent personal names as *García*, *Javier*, *Jimeno* (> *Jiménez*), and *Sancho* (> *Sánchez*).

Pronunciation and Orthography

The pronunciation of medieval Castilian differed markedly from that of its modern offspring, Spanish (still often called *castellano* in the Spanish-speaking world). Though vowels have changed little over the centuries, consonants have undergone extensive transformations, some of which were already underway in the Middle Ages, perhaps only as local aberrations from the prestige standard (see Lloyd). Among features that distinguish medieval Castilian from modern Spanish are (1) preservation of a phonemic contrast between */b/* and */v/*, the latter sound a labial fricative as in modern French, Portuguese, or, indeed, English; (2) preservation of Latin *F-*, weakened to */h/* then effaced in many varieties, including ultimately the literary standard (Lat. farina, "flour" > /harina/ > /arina/); (3) a full array of sibilants, with *c* followed by *e* or *i* and *ç* = */ts/*, *s-* and *-ss* pronounced as in modern Spanish, *x* = */g/* (Eng. sh), *z* = */dz/*, *s* between vowels = */z/*, and *g* followed by *e* or *i* and *j* = */r/* (the medial consonant of Eng. "pleasure"); (4) *ll*, which in word-initial position often reflected Latin consonant clusters *CL*, *FL*, and *PL*, was invariably pronounced as a palatal */'/*, a sound restricted today to parts of northern Spain and the Andes. The *theta* characteristic of modern northern peninsular dialects and the *jota* common to all modern varieties were absent from the medieval phonemic inventory.

Orthography

A major problem for the earliest scribes attempting to write in a Romance language was the Latin alphabet's lack of symbols (i.e., letters) to designate sounds that, while nonexistent in the ancestral tongue, had evolved and achieved frequency in Romance. Experimentation was the order of the day, at least until Alfonso X the Learned imposed the system that, with periodic modifications, survives in modern Spanish. In addition to orthographic peculiarities described in the preceding paragraph, the reader of early Old Castilian texts should keep the following points in mind: (1) use of *ñ* for palatal /ɯ/ was far from universal; among other solutions tried out and ultimately rejected were *nn*, *ni*, *ng*, and *ny*; (2) *i* and *j*, originally variants of a single Latin letter, were frequently interchangeable; (3) likewise, *u* and *v* were not seen as distinct letters, with u often used as a consonant (*auer*, "to have", *uenir*, "to come"); (4) *lg*, *li*, or *ly* occasionally appear in place of *ll*; (5) *li* and *i* sometimes stand for *j* (i.e., /ɽ/); (6) /*m*/ is often written *n* before the labial consonants *p* and *b* (*canbiar*, "to change").

THOMAS J. WALSH

Bibliography

García-Larragueta, S. *Las Glosas Emilianenses: Edición y estudio*. Logroño, 1984.

Lapesa, R. *Historia de la lengua española*. Madrid, 1981.

Lloyd, P. M. *From Latin to Spanish*. Vol. I, *Historical Phonology and Morphology of the Spanish Language*. Philadelphia, 1987.

Penny, R. *A History of the Spanish Language*. Cambridge, 1991.

Smith, C. *Poema de Mio Cid*. Oxford, 1972.

CASTLES *See* ARCHITECTURE, MILITARY

CASTRO, INÉS DE

The date of Inés de Castro's birth is uncertain. She was born sometime at the beginning of the fourteenth century. Inés was the illegitimate daughter of Pedro Fernández de Castro, Lord of Galicia, and Aldonza Soares de Valladares. The Fernández de Castros were one of the most powerful and influential families in Iberia. Pedro's mother was the illegitimate daughter of Sancho IV el Bravo, King of Castile.

Inés de Castro was brought up at the home of an aunt, Teresa de Alburquerque, near the border with Portugal. Later, she was sent to be educated at the home of her cousin Don Juan Manuel, author of *El conde Lucanor* and one of the most prominent Castilian nobles of his day. In 1340 Inés accompanied Don Juan Manuel's daughter Constanza to Coimbra, where Costanza was to marry Pedro, the crown prince of Portugal. The marriage lasted for five years and produced three children. Constanza died on 13 November 1345. During the years of his marriage to Constanza, Pedro had fallen in love with Inés and had taken her as his mistress. Fearing the union, Afonso IV, the king, had banished Inés from Portugal and she was sent to live in the castle at Alburquerque. Disobeying his father's orders, Pedro brought Inés back to Portugal after Constanza's death in 1345. They lived together openly in Coimbra. One of the many contradictory accounts says that Pedro and Inés were married at Braganza by the bishop of Guarda in 1354. Although Pedro testified to this marriage in the third year of his reign, there is no documentary evidence of it, which makes it unlikely that it ever took place. Cristovão Rodrigues Acenheiro in his *Cronica dos Reis de Portugal*, citing an investigation of the matter in 1385, denies that the pair was ever married and adds that Pedro told his father that he was not married to Inés and would not marry her. Whether married or not, the union produced three children, who were viewed as a threat to the monarchy and to Portuguese independence. Alvaro Pires de Castro, Inés's brother, had become very influential and his power, along with that of Portugal's rival, the kingdom of Castile and León, threatened the realm if Pedro's successor were a son of Inés.

Pedro's relationship with Inés had become a problem of the state. Afonso IV was aware of the ambitions of the Castros and urged Pedro to proclaim himself a pretender to the crowns of both Castile and León. Three of the king's advisers, Coelho, Alvargonzález, and Pacheco, persuaded the king that Inés and her children should be assassinated to preserve the legitimate succession to the throne. It is said that the king himself went to destroy Inés but was moved by the pleas of her children. Later the king's three advisers persuaded the king that she should be removed and they murdered Inés. Overcome with grief and anger, Pedro led a rebellion against his father. Peace was restored and Pedro promised his father to forgive the murderers. However, when he became king in 1357, Pedro viciously murdered two of them; the third escaped. It is then that Pedro announced that he and Inés had been married and ordered two lavish tombs built at the monastery at Alcobaça depicting Inés's story. He and Inés are buried there. Legend has it that Pedro had Inés exhumed and before placing her remains in the tomb crowned her as queen of Portugal. The powerful story of Inés de Castro and Pedro I has been the object of many works of world literature.

E. MICHAEL GERLI

Bibliography

Asensio, E. "Inés de Castro: de la crónica al mito." In *Estudios portugueses*. Paris, 1957, 25–56.

Nozick, M. "The Inés de Castro Legend in European Literature," *Comparative Literature* 3 (1951), 330–41.

Vasconcelos, A. de. *Inés de Castro*. Barcelos, 1933.

CATALAN GRAND COMPANY

A mercenary soldier-republic gathered by the ex-Templar Roger de Flor on the Arago-Catalan side of the Sicilian Vespers War, at whose end in 1302 it contracted with Byzantium to recover Asia Minor from the Turks. The company's quartermaster/memoirist Ramon Muntaner documents 36 ships, 1,500 horses, and 4,000 *almogavers* or light-armed infantry irregulars from Arago-Catalonia's frontiers with Islam.

A corporation with its own seal, council, and rules, the Catalan Grand Company flew the banners of Arago-Catalonia, Catalan Sicily, and the papacy, as vaguely an overlord or protector. Its brilliantly successful campaigns throughout Asia Minor ended when Byzantine treachery provoked the "Catalan Vengeance"—destructive rampages out of Gallipoli—from 1305 to 1307 and then over Macedonia and Thessally. Aragón-Catalonia, Sicily, France, the Council of Vienne, and the Valois crusade unsuccessfully tried to co-opt them. In 1311 the company conquered Angevin Athens and set up its final state.

Rather than the isolated romantic episode enshrined in Catalan art and letters, the company's stormy passage was an essential part of contemporary Mediterranean diplomacy involving a dozen states, of the decline of Byzantium, of fourteenth-century crusading, and of the rise of effective infantry and of condottiere companies.

ROBERT I. BURNS, S. J.

Bibliography

Setton, Kenneth. *Catalan Domination of Athens 1311–1388*. 2d ed. London, 1975.

Burns, Robert I. "The Catalan Company and the European Powers, 1305–1311," *Speculum* 29 (1954), 751–71.

CATALAN LANGUAGE

Catalan is the Romance language that developed in the Carolingian counties of the Spanish March. Currently it is spoken in the areas corresponding to the principality of Catalonia, the valleys of Andorra, the French department of Pyrénées-Orientales, eastern Aragón, the majority of the former kingdom of Valencia, the Balearic Islands, and the city of Alghero on the northwest coast of Sardinia. Catalan dialects fall into two groups: Western Catalan, which includes Andorra, eastern Aragón, Lérida province, western Tarragona province, and Valencia; and Eastern Catalan, consisting of North (French) Catalan, Girona and Barcelona provinces, northeastern Tarragona province, the Balearics, and isolated *alguerès*. The boundary between the two groups runs just west of due south from Andorra.

The origins and formation of Catalan were the subject of a long debate featuring several prominent twentieth-century Romanists. A first grouping of Catalan with Provençal in the Gallo-Romance category was supported by Milà i Fontanals, Alcover, Meyer-Lübke, and Bourciez; the use of Provençal as the language of poetry in Catalonia until the fifteenth century was evoked to confirm that identity. That position was modified by Morf and Saroïhandy, who separated Catalan from the southern Gallo-Romance dialects and sketched an east-to-west dialectal blending in Ibero-Romance, from Catalan to Aragónese to Castilian. Diez and Wartburg presented Catalan as an independent language, rejecting the literary relation to Provençal but also denying a place for Catalan in Ibero-Romance based on the judgment that Catalan differs as much from Castilian as Castilian does from Portuguese. Alonso split the knot, fixing Catalan in Ibero-Romance and Provençal in Gallo-Romance. Catalan could not have been Provençal transplanted in the eighth century to Catalonia—specifically the Tarraconense province—as Meyer-Lübke had claimed in his book-length study on the question (*Das Katalanische*, 1925). The current taxonomy, offered by Baldinger and confirmed by Badia, is the *llengua pont* theory, which sees Catalan as a bridge language between Ibero- and Gallo-Romance.

The following historical data are relevant to the origins of Catalan: (1) Between 759 and 801 the Franks established the Spanish March, reconquering the French Septimania from the Arabs and entering Catalonia: Girona (785) and Barcelona (801) were liberated, and the region between the Pyrenees and the Llobregat River, currently known as *Catalunya Vella*, was subsequently incorporated into the archdiocese of Narbonne; (2) as Catalonia was consolidating politically, the independent counts of Barcelona, especially those of Ramón Berenguer III and IV, recovered all the current territory of Catalonia in the first half of the twelfth century. Those areas were partially repopulated with Catalan speakers; (3) Jaime I of Aragón conquered Mallorca (1230), Ibiza (1235), and Valencia (1238); his grandson, Alfonso III, conquered Menorca (1287). The island territories were repopulated more completely with Catalan speakers than had been the case on the mainland. Finally, Pedro the Ceremonious evacuated the Sardinians from Alghero (1372) and repopulated that city with Catalan speakers from south of the Llobregat.

Catalan participates in many of sound changes common to Western Romance, for example, the development of a seven tonic vowel system, syncope, lenition, and palatalization. In its atonic vocalism, Catalan shares with Gallo-Romance the apocope of Latin post-tonic /e/ and /o/, for example, CAELU (*cel*, "sky"), and FORTE (*fort*, "strong"). It develops post-tonic /a/ to /ə/ (Valencian /e/) before a consonant, for example, CASĀS (*cases*, "houses"), PAUSĀS (*poses*, "you [sing.] put"), and PORTANT (*porten*, "they bring").

A series of changes affecting the mid-front tonic vowels has made the outcome of /ɛ/ and /e/ (in Latin, Ĕ and Ē) less predictable than in Castilian and Portuguese. The pan-Catalan changes are: (1) /ɛ/—/e/ except before /ð/ in syllable codas (e.g., TĔMPUS, temps /tems/ "time", HĔRBA, herba /erba/ "grass"; but PĔDE, */pɛð/, *peu* "foot"; and (2) /e/—/ɛ/ before /l/, /r/ or /n'r/ (e.g., VĒLA, *vela* /vɛla/ "sail"; VĬRĬDE, *verd* /vɛrd/ "green"; CĬNĔRE, *cendra* /sɛndra/ "ash". Balearic adds another change, /e/ to /ə/ except as in (2) (e.g., CATĒNA, *cadena* [kəðənə] "chain", STRĬCTU [əstrət]). On the eastern mainland these are [kəðɛnə], [əstrɛt]. Finally, across Catalan dialects a yod /j/ can raise a preceding mid-open vowel (i.e., /ɛ/ and /ɔ/, two degrees to /i/ and /u/, e.g., FĔRIA, *fira* "fair"; ĔXIT, *ix* "he/she leaves"; FŎLIA, *fulla*; CŎLLIGIT, *cull* "he/she picks."

The following consonant changes are typical of Catalan: (1) palatalization of initial /l-/ to /ʎ-/ (e.g., LŪNA, *lluna* "moon"; LACU, *llac* "lake"; (2) assimilation and simplification of /-nd-/, /-nn-/, /-n-/ (e.g., MANDĀRE, *manar* "to order"; (3) loss of /-n/ in post-vocalic, word-final position (e.g., PĪNU, *pi* "pine" (but pl. *pins*); (4) neutralization of various syllable codas yielding diphthongs that end in velar semivowel [u]: IUGU, *jou* "yoke"; PEDE, *peu*; PUTEU, *pou* "well"; DICIT, *diu* "says"; NOVU, *nou* "new" (but fem. *nova*, NOVA) (Wheeler.).

In nominal morphology, one result of the historical development of post-tonic vowels is that masculine gender is unmarked. If a stem ends in a voiceless occlusive /p t k/, that sound is voiced in the feminine, for example, AMĪCU, AMĪCŌS, AMĪCA, AMĪCĀS: *amic, amics, amiga, amigues* "friend(s)" (msg, mpl, fsg, fpl); ACŪTU, ACŪTA: *agut, aguda* "sharp" (msg, fsg).

The Catalan pronoun system is among the more conservative in the Romance family. Each personal pronoun has a tonic subject form (1sg *jo*, 2sg *tu, vós*, 3sg *ell, ella*, 1pl *nosaltres*, 2pl *vosaltres*, 3pl *ells, elles*), an atonic, clitic, object form (1sg *-me*, 2sg *-te, -vos*, 3sg *-lo, -la*, 1pl *-nos*, 2pl *-vos*, 3pl *-los, -les*), and a possessive adjective-pronominal (1sg *meu*, 2sg *teu, vostre*, 3sg *seu*, 1pl *nostre*, 2pl *vostre*, 3pl *seu* ~ *llur*). Third person nonreflexive clitics also have distinct indirect object forms (3sg *-li*, 3pl *-los*), and first person singular and third person reflexive-reciprocal clitics have a separate prepositional object form (1sg *mi*, 3pl refl *si*). Just as Old Catalan 2sg *ti* gave way to *tu* in the modern language, so 1sg *mi* is being abandoned in favor of "subject" pronoun *jo*, which is used obligatorily with prepositions *malgrat* (despite), *llevat* (except), and *ultra* (beyond). There are also sets of contextual variants of the clitic pronouns that originally depended not on whether the elements were proclitic or enclitic to the verb, but rather if they preceded or followed consonants or vowels. Feminine possessives originally matched their Latin etyma, for example, in Old Catalan *mia*, *tua*, *sua*, MEA, TUA, SUA; but were later substituted by *meua teua*, *seua* in Valencia and *meva*, *teva*, *seva* in the principality. *Llur* (ILLŌRUM) has been relegated to literary usage, supplanted by *seu*.

The definite articles coming from ILLU, ILLŌS, ILLA, ILLĀS developed as expected in Old Catalan: *lo*, *los*, *la*, *les*. These forms have been retained generally in western Catalan; elsewhere, *lo*, *los* were replaced with *el*, *els*. Forms deriving from the IPSU series must have been used in Old Catalan and are current in the Balearics and the Costa Brava (*salat* dialect): masc. *es* before consonant, *ets* before vowel; fem. *sa*, *ses*. A third set of definite determiners used with proper names comes from DOMINU, DOMINA; the forms *en*, *na* (both *n'* before vowels) are used commonly in the Balearics, and in official styles elsewhere.

Verbs are organized in three conjugation classes by thematic vowel, for example, gerunds (I) *comprant* "(buying)", (IIa) *tement* (fearing), and (IIb) *perdent* (losing), (III) *dormint* (sleeping) and (IIIb) *oferint* (offering). Group IIb verbs lack the thematic vowel in the infinitive (*perdre*) and group IIIb shows the infix -*eix*- coming from Latin inchoative -ISC- in the present tense (*ofereix*, "he offers"). Historically the thematic vowel from group II extended to I, with a contribution from the group I present subjunctive, for example, pres indic 1pl *comprem* (we buy), *temem* (we fear); past subj 1sg and 3sg *comprés*, *temés* (cf. Sp. *compramos*, *tememos*; *comprase*, *temiese*).

Three other features of verbal morphology are characteristic of Catalan. First, for most of the group IIa verbs, plus *estar* (to be) and *eixir* (to leave), there is a velar consonant on the preterit stem, the 1sg present indicative and throughout the present subjunctive, for example, *deure* (to owe), perf indic 3sg *degué* (in Old Catalan, *dec*), pres indic 1sg *dec* (in Old Catalan, *deig*), pres subj 1sg *degui* (in Old Catalan, *dega*). The velar element is believed to have two sources: in the perfect from the Lat. perfect /-u-/ morpheme (POTUIT, in Old Catalan, *poc*), and in the present from Lat. stem-final /k/ or /g/ (DŪCŌ, *duc*; PLANGŌ, *planc*). Second, the *va*- formative (present of Latin VADĔRE) is used as a perfect auxiliary in analytical constructions, for example, 2sg perf *vas perdre* (you lost); cf. Fr. *tu vas perdre* (you are going to lose); 2sg past subj *vagis perdre*. Finally, an innovative /i/ morpheme appears in the singular and 3pl forms of the present subjunctive, in the plural and 2sg forms of the past subjunctive, and throughout the subjunctive of *va*- and *haver* (to have); for example, for *perdre*, 3pl pres subj *perdin* (in Old Catalan, *perden*); 3pl past subj *perdessin* (in Old Catalan, *perdessen*); 3pl past perf subj *vagin perdre* (Wheeler.).

Two important early documents in Catalan are a version of the *Forum judicum* and the *Homilies d'Organyà*, both from the late twelfth century. Anthologies of medieval Catalan texts include Badia's *Literatura catalana medieval: selecció de textos* (1985), Riquer's *Literatura catalana medieval* (1972), Rubio García's *Documentos lingüísticos catalanes, s. X–XII* (1979), and Russell-Gebbett's *Medieval Catalan Documents* (1965). Concheff has published a *Bibliography of Old Catalan Texts* (1985) for the Hispanic Seminar of Medieval Studies. The major historical dictionaries are Coromines's *Diccionari etimològic i complementari de la llengua catalana* (10 vols., 1980–) and Alcover's cross-dialectal *Diccionari català-valencià-balear* (10 vols., 1927–1962).

James A. Monk

Bibliography

Badia i, M., and M. Antoni. *Gramàtica històrica catalana*. Barcelona, 1951.

Baldinger, K. *La formación de los dominios lingüísticos en la Península Ibérica*. Madrid, 1963; reprt. 1972.

Duarte i Montserrat, C., and A. A. i Keith. *Gramàtica històrica del català, 1–3*. Barcelona, 1984–86.

Moll y Casanovas, F. *Gramática histórica catalana*. Madrid, 1952.

Nadal, J. M., and M. Prats. "Història de la llengua catalana," Barcelona, (1982).

Sanchis Guarner, M. *Introducción a la historia lingüística de Valencia*. Valencia, 1950.

Wheeler, M. W. *Catalan*. In *The Romance Languages*. Ed. M. Harris and N. Vincent. London, 1988, 170–208.

CATALINA DE LANCASTER

Reputedly one of the less attractive of medieval Castilian queens, and indeed of a masculine appearance, Catalina or Catherine, born in 1373, was the daughter of John of Gaunt, Duke of Lancaster, and Constance, daughter of Pedro I, the Cruel. As such, her importance to a large extent depended on what she represented in dynastic terms, her marriage to Enrique III of Castile being part of a more wide-ranging settlement of the civil wars that had plagued fourteenth-century Castile, pitting the supporters of Pedro against those of his half brother, Enrique of Trastámara (Enrique II) and subsequently involving Lancastrian claims to the throne.

But Catalina of Lancaster also played an important political role in her own right. Enrique III had never enjoyed robust health, and when he died in 1406 the heir to the throne, Juan II, was not yet two years old. By the terms of Enrique III's will the regency of the kingdom was to be jointly exercised by his wife, Catalina, and his brother Fernando. These two, however, were never on good terms, and it was decided to divide the regency geographically, the southern half of the kingdom being entrusted to Fernando and the northern half to Catalina. For his part Fernando dedicated his energies to campaigns against the Moors, taking Antequera in 1410, and subsequently being elected to the throne of Aragón by the Compromise of Caspe of 1412.

In the exercise of her share of the regency Catalina was perceived by contemporaries as being of a suspicious nature and possessive yet at the same time easily influenced by favorites, particularly Leonor López de Córdoba, Isabel Torres, and, to a lesser extent, Fernán Alfonso de Robles. After Fernando's death in 1416, Catalina became sole regent of Castile for a brief time before her death in 1418.

ANGUS MACKAY

Bibliography

Russel, P. E. *The English Intervention in Spain and Portugal in the Time of Edward III and Richard II.* Oxford, 1955.

CATALONIA

Catalonia coalesced into a distinctive linguistic and cultural region in northeastern Iberia under the pressures of invasion and the violent confrontation between Islam and Christianity. Later its people constituted a cohesive, self-conscious political community centered on the counts of Barcelona. Dominated by inward-looking, protective mountain valleys in the north and an urbanized, Mediterranean coastline to the south, the eastern Pyrenean area lacked a clear geographical unity. Although the balance between mountains and coastal areas was far from stable, the exchange between the two and the interdependence it fostered produced a stable society with a well-defined sense of its own historical identity. Catalonia was in all essentials a creation of the Middle Ages.

Invasion and Continuity (415–801)

The first part of Hispania settled by the Romans, northeastern Iberia, was thoroughly transformed by Latin civilization. Roman institutional and cultural foundations survived the installation of Germanic rulers, the Visigoths, and Islamic invaders. Both conquering peoples formed only a small minority among the local populations. First crossing the Pyrenees in 415, the Visigoths provided arms to maintain local Roman elites. Concentrated first in Aquitania and later in Castile, the Visigoths lightly governed the eastern Pyrenees and continued Roman administrative practices. King Alaric II issued a breviary of Roman law (506), later reworked into the *Liber iudiciorum.* It remained the basis of public order until the eleventh century.

Arriving in Spain in 711, Muslim raiders reached the Ebro by 714. Visigothic rule rapidly disintegrated. Tolerant masters, the Arab and Berber invaders allowed Christians to retain their churches and clergy in exchange for submission and tribute. Yet some Hispano-Gothic leaders resisted and sought refuge in the Pyrenees. The defensive militancy of the mountain valleys created a tough, cohesive Christian society capable of repelling Muslim advances from the plains. Linguistically the Islamic invasion accelerated the differentiation of Catalan from Aragónese and Castilian as the mountain population turned in upon itself.

The Spanish March (801–950)

The last of the early medieval conquerors, the Franks made the most lasting impression. Charlemagne ordered the campaigns culminating in the capture of Girona (785) and Barcelona (801), but Frankish armies failed to secure the Ebro as they had intended. The check proved decisive for it established a vibrant frontier society. In the Spanish March, the area subject to the Frankish protectorate extending just beyond Barcelona and including the eastern Pyrenees. Islamic influence disappeared; to the west, however, mass conversion produced a thriving Muslim culture centered on Tortosa and Lleida (Lérida). The Christian territory, later known as Old Catalonia bore the imprint of Carolingian order. Eventually divided into fourteen counties, the Spanish March adhered to Visigothic law administered in Carolingian courts. As the Frankish imperium weakened, local counts established hereditary rights to the territory they controlled. Descendants of Guifré the Hairy (r. 870–897) ruled several counties including Barcelona for more then five hundred years. Faced with a threatening frontier, the Pyrenean counties by the end of the early medieval conquests had emerged from the dislocation of the Roman world with a common language, institutions, and traditions. Political independence, dynastic consolidation, and territorial expansion still lay ahead.

Sovereignty and Social Change (950–1150)

Temporarily integrated into a non-Iberian realm by Frankish conquests, the Spanish March was an isolated, conservative region clinging to traditional forms of public order. Local comital dynasties, however, gradually asserted their sovereignty. The sack of Barcelona by the Islamic caudillo al-Manṣūr in 985 made clear that local leaders would have to look after their own needs since the Frankish king failed to heed the appeal of Count Borrell II for aid. To secure the frontier, lay and clerical lords encouraged and protected settlements in deserted regions. Repopulation was above all the work of small, independent freeholders many of whom came from the densely populated mountains. A demographic upsurge began around 950, accompanied by an increase in agricultural production and the creation of local markets. With prosperity came a new aggressiveness and openness. In 950 Count Borrell sent the first embassy to the caliph in Córdoba. Raids were later launched against al-Andalus. The expedition to Córdoba in 1010, involving warlords from throughout Catalonia confirmed the military ascendancy of the Christian north. Through pillage and regular tribute paid by Muslim princes (*parias*), gold, silver, and silks further stimulated an already thriving agricultural economy.

Rapid militarization and a scramble to control new wealth undermined the traditional order based on comital authority, public courts, and Gothic law. Lords with their armed bands built private castles, imposed new obligations on the peasantry, and defied counts and judges. The "feudal crisis" reached its peak during baronial insurrections from 1041 to 1059. Ramón Berenguer I (1035–1076), count of Barcelona, proved the most successful in restoring order, but the basis of power had shifted. Oaths of fealty, contracts of service (*convenientiae*), and castle command buttressed the shaky framework of public authority. The success and prestige attached to the dynasty of Barcelona allowed it to secure several counties in addition to Barcelona, Girona, and Osona. Through marital alliance Count Ramón Berenguer III (1096–1131) acquired Besalú and Vallespir in 1111; in 1117 he annexed Cerdanya, Conflent, and Bergà at the death of Bernat III of Besalú. More land was taken from the Muslims. Upon the arrival of the Almoravids from North Africa in the late eleventh century, Islamic resistance stiffened and the flow of tribute was dammed. A restive baronage turned from raiding to settling the frontier. Tarragona, definitively occupied in 1118, was made an archbishopric. The conquest of Tortosa in 1148 and Lleida in 1149 rounded out the territorial extension known as New Catalonia. A prosperous agrarian society anchored by its many castles, Catalonia remained a land of regional contrast even as its southwestern frontier stabilized. The name Catalonia first appears in an early twelfth-century Pisan work and probably derives from castellans (*castlàns*), the men who command local cells of power, the castles.

Consolidation and Expansion (1150–1333)

A period of internal stabilization and external expansion succeeded the turbulent transformations of the eleventh and early twelfth centuries. With the western frontier of Catalonia secured, in 1150 Count Ramón Berenguer IV of Barcelona (1131–1162) married Petronilla, heiress to the kingdom of Aragón. The match negotiated in 1137, brought the comital dynasty a crown and even greater ambitions. Alfonso I (1162–1196) and Pere I (1196–1213) aggressively pursued family interests in southern France, but the Albigensian Crusaders thwarted Catalan designs at the Battle of Muret (1213) and left Pere dead on the battlefield. Later count-kings, as Ramón Berenguer IV's descendants are called, consequently turned toward Iberian and Mediterranean expansion. The remarkable warrior-king Jaime I (1213–1276) conquered Mallorca (1229) and Valencia (1232–1245), his son Pedro II (1276–1285) subjugated Sicily (1282), and his grandson Jaime II (1291–1327) annexed Sardinia (1323). The brilliant phase of Catalan expansion depended on the rapid commercial and naval growth of the towns near the coast especially Barcelona, Tortosa, and Perpignan, and the restive energies of upland barons, knights, and soldiers. Each new conquest was treated as a separate state, but Catalonia remained the dominant member of the federative union known as the Crown of Aragón.

Internally the count-kings extended their control over independent counties and reestablished public order. Alfonso I obtained Roussillon (1172) and Lower Pallars (1192), and Jaime II completed the essential work of political unification with the annexation of Urgell (1314). Through the initiatives of Ramón Berenguer IV, legal experts produced the *Usatges de Barcelona*, a territorial code stressing regalian authority, and local officials called vicars and bailiffs moved toward routinized administration of the aggregate counties. These initiatives culminated in the creation of continuous royal registers by 1257 and a centralized fiscal overseer, the *mestre racional*, by 1283. Towns and villages obtained charters of liberty, fixing their obligations and internal organization. Economic prosperity, political consolidation, and military aggressiveness turned Catalonia into a Mediterranean power of the first rank.

Crisis and Decline (1333–1479)

Under Pedro III the Ceremonious (1336–1387) Catalonia reached the height of its influence, but signs of strain had already begun to appear. A severe famine struck in 1333, remembered as "the first bad year." The Black Death followed in 1348, taking away 25 to 35 percent of the population. Although mercantile prosperity continued well into the fifteenth century, the economy had been shaken. The vast scale of dynastic ambitions began to erode the fisc. By 1400 many royal assets had been alienated, and the count-kings relied so heavily on the *cortes* (general assemblies) that they lost the financial and political initiative. To obtain a subsidy Pedro ceded judicial supremacy to a deputation of the cortes called the *generalitat*, which evolved into a coordinate administration with the count-king's.

The difficulties of the fourteenth century led to decline by the end of the fifteenth. The lack of a direct male descendant provoked a constitutional crisis, resolved by the Compromise of Caspe (1412) in favor of a related Castilian family, the Trastámaras. The choice of a new dynasty proved a fateful acknowledgment of Castilian ascendancy. The new rulers tended to neglect Catalonia, which fell prey to bitter rivalries between aristocrats and lesser nobles, landlords and serfs, and urban factions. Increasing tensions led to a bitter civil war (1462–1472), accompanied by the revolt of unfree (*remença*) peasants. The war was an economic disaster and confirmed Catalan commercial decline. Before Juan II emerged the victor of the conflict, his son Fernando II had married Isabel of Castile in 1469. When Fernando succeeded his father in 1479, dynastic union brought about Castilian hegemony in Iberia and the eclipse of medieval Catalonia.

STEPHEN P. BENSCH

Bibliography

Bisson, T.N. *The Medieval Crown of Aragón: A Short History*. Oxford, 1986.

Hillgarth, J.C. *The Spanish Kingdoms, 1250–1516*. 2 vols. Oxford, 1976–78.

Nadal Farreras, J., and P. Wolff. (eds.), *Histoire de la Catalogne*. Toulouse, 1982.

Soldevila, F. *Història de Catalunya*. Barcelona, 1934.

Vilar, P. (ed.) *Història de Catalunya*. Vols. 2 and 3. Barcelona, 1987–90.

CATHAR HERESY

See ALBIGENSIAN CRUSADE; HERESY; WITCHCRAFT

CATHEDRALS

See ARCHITECTURE, ECCLESIASTICAL

CATHOLIC MONARCHS, ISABEL I OF CASTILE AND FERNANDO II OF ARAGÓN

Isabel I, Queen of Castile, known as Isabel la Católica, was born in the town of Madrigal de las Altas Torres, 22 April 1451. She died 26 November 1504, in the castle of La Mota at Medina del Campo (Valladolid). She was the daughter of Juan II, King of Castile, by his second wife, Isabel of Portugal. Only three when her father died, 1451, she was brought up piously by her mother at Arévalo. When she was thirteen, King Enrique IV, her older half-brother, took her and her younger brother, Alfonso, to court on the pretext of completing their education. Enrique's actual motive was to prevent the two royal children from serving as rallying points for the discontented nobles.

When she was already a grown woman Isabel devoted herself to the study of Latin, and became an eager collector of books. She was actively involved in the education of her five children (Isabel, Juan, Juana, María, and Catalina). To educate Prince Juan, she created a school at court similar to the Palatine School of the Carloingians. Her daughters, too, attained high degrees of education. A rather austere individual, Isabel exercised great moral influence on the nobility, discouraging inordinate luxury and vain pastimes. At the same time, she fostered learning not only in the universities and among the nobles but also among women. Some of the latter distinguished themselves through their intellectual attainments—e.g., Beatriz Galindo, called la Latina, Lucía Medrano, and Francisca Nebrija, the Princess Juana and the Princess Catalina (who later became queen of England), Isabel de Vergara, and others who attained proficiency in Latin, mathematics, read philosophy, and became qualified to fill chairs in the universities at Alcalá and Salamanca.

By 1464, when the teenage Isabel had been moved to court by Enrique IV, the Castilian nobility had gained great power by taking advantage of the minorities of succession of the kings Enrique II and Juan II. By the time of the minority of Juan II, they had almost completely stripped the crown of its authority. They availed themselves of Enrique IV's weak character and of the scandalous relations between Juana of Portugal, his second wife, and his favorite, Beltrán de la Cueva. Defeated at Olmedo and deprived of their leader the Infante Alfonso, who was probably poisoned on 5 July 1468, a group of nobles sought the crown for the Infanta Isabel, rejecting the king's presumptive daughter, Juana of Castile, who was called "La Beltraneja" on the supposition that Beltrán was her real father. On this occasion Isabel gave one of the earliest indications of her strength of character and intelligence, refusing the usurped crown offered to her, and declaring that she would never accept the title of queen while her brother lived. The king, on his part, recognized Isabel as his immediate heir, thus excluding Juana. Historians have generally been willing to interpret this act of Enrique IV as an implicit acknowledgment that Juana was not his daughter. However, even if Juana were his daughter, as she was by juridical presumption, he might have yielded to pressure from the nobles, who sought to give the crown immediately to Isabel. Enrique may thus have compromised with them by making Isabel his heir, as he did at Los Toros de Guisando on 19 September 1468. After the conclusion of the Pact of Los Toros de Guisando, Isabel was at odds with Enrique on account of his plans for her marriage.

As early as 1460 Enrique offered Isabel's hand to Carlos, Prince of Viana, eldest son of Juan II of Aragón and heir to the Kingdom of Navarre. Alienated from Don Carlos, Juan II, however, wished Isabel to marry his younger son, Fernando. Negotiations were protracted until the death of the prince of Viana. In 1465 Enrique made an attempt to arrange marriage between Isabel and Afonso V of Portugal, but the princess had already chosen Fernando of Aragón and was opposed to this alliance. For the same reason she subsequently refused to marry Pedro Girón, master of the Order of Calatrava and brother of Juan Pacheco, the powerful Marqués de Villena. Other aspirants for Isabel's hand were Richard, Duke of Gloucester, brother of Edward IV of England, and the Duke of Guyenne, brother of Louis XI of France. The *cortes* (parliaments) were assembled at Ocaña in 1469 to ratify the Pact of Guisando, when a Portuguese embassy arrived to renew Afonso V's suit for Isabel's hand. When she declined this alliance, Enrique threatened her with imprisonment in the alcázar of Madrid. Although fear of Isabel's partisans among the nobility prevented Enrique from carrying out his threat, he exacted a promise from his sister not to enter into any matrimonial negotiations during his absence in Andalusia. As soon as she was left alone, however, Isabel—with the aid of the archbishop of Toledo, Alfonso Carrillo, and the admiral of Castile, Fadrique Enríquez (the grandfather of her future husband)—fled to Madrigal and then on to Valladolid. From there she sent Gutierre de Cárdenas and Alfonso de Palencia in search of Fernando, who had been legitimized and proclaimed king of Sicily and heir of the Aragónese monarchy after the death of the prince of Viana. After his harrowing journey into Castile disguised as a muleteer, Fernando and Isabel were married in the palace of Juan de Vívero at Valladolid, on 19 October 1469.

Fernando, who shared a great-grandfather with Isabel, was a year younger than his wife. He was born 10 March 1452 at Sos in Aragón and led a peripatetic life from early childhood. He died at Madrigalejo in Extremadura on 23 January 1516. At the age of seventeen, when he married Isabel, he was already king of Sicily, the hero of two wars, and the father of an illegitimate child. He was raised under the tutelage of Francisco Vidal de Noya, a Latin master, but seems to have preferred the active over the scholarly life, acquiring early on the reputation of a rogue. Fernando's mother was the ambitious Doña Juana Enríquez, of the blood of Castile in collateral line, and like her he seemed very much in control of his destiny.

On 12 December 1474, the day after the death of Enrique IV, Isabel, who was at Segovia, was proclaimed queen of Castile. Doña Juana la Beltraneja had been betrothed to Afonso V of Portugal, and Enrique, revoking the Pact of Guisando, had proclaimed her heir to his dominions. The Archbishop of Toledo, the Marqués de Villena, and other nobles who in her father's lifetime had denied Doña Juana's legitimacy, now defended her claims. The conflict set off a five-year war between Castile and Portugal that ended in 1479, when Doña Juana abandoned her claims, retiring to the monastery of Santa Clara of Coimbra (1480). With this, Isabel's claim to the throne of Castile became unquestioned. Fernando meanwhile succeeded to the throne of Aragón, thus unifying the kingdoms of Castile and Aragón and laying the groundwork for the emergence of the Spanish nation. In the *capitulaciones*, the document governing their powers in the administration of their dominions, the monarchs agreed that they were to hold equal authority, a principle expressed in the motto "Tanto monta, monta tanto—Isabel como Fernando" (One counts as much as the other—Isabel as much as Fernando). On 19 December 1496 Pope Alexander VI, the Valencian nobleman Rodrigo Borja, conferred the title "Catholic Monarchs" upon them, a title that the kings of Spain still bear.

The union of the crowns of Castile and Aragón thus realized, it was necessary to reduce the power of the nobles, who had acquired a position almost independent of the monarchy, rendering government difficult. The monarchs directed their efforts toward various goals: (1) the establishment of the Santa Hermandad (Holy Brotherhood), a kind of permanent police force organized and supported by the municipal councils and intended for the protection of persons and property against the violence of the nobles; (2) improved administration of justice through the organization of tribunals, the establishment of a chancery at Valladolid, and the promulgation of a series of royal edicts known as the Edicts of Montalvo; (3) the abolition of the right to coin money, held by certain individuals, and the regulation of currency laws to facilitate commerce; (4) the revocation of *mercedes*, or extravagant grants, made to certain nobles during the reign of previous monarchs, the demolition of their castles, which were said to constitute a menace to public peace, and the vesting of the masterships of all the military orders in the crown. To preserve religious unity and orthodoxy, thought to be imperiled by rumors of heresy and Jewish apostasy in Andalusia, the monarchs in 1478 solicited the right to establish an inquisition in Castile from Pope Sixtus IV.

Once their hegemony had been established, the monarchs acted to bring to completion the conquest of Granada, the last Muslim stronghold in Europe, a project that had been at a virtual standstill since the time of Alfonso XI. The Muslim capture of Zahara afforded an occasion for renewing the war, which opened with the conquest of Alhama in March 1482. The Castilians were favored by internal dissension in Granada, which was largely due to quarreling between Emir Muley Hassan and his son Boabdil, and, after the death of the former, to the supporters of Boabdil's uncle ʿAbd-allah al Zagal. Fernando and Isabel prosecuted the war in spite of initial serious defeats at Ajarquía and Loja, subsequently taking Coín, Guadix, Almería, Loja, Vélez, Málaga, and Baza. Isabel played a prominent role in the war. Not only did she attend to the government of the kingdom and provide for the support of the army while Fernando was at the front, but she repeatedly visited the field to animate the troops, as during the sieges of Málaga and Baza. A final move to put an end to the hopes of the inhabitants of Granada and solve the logistical problems of the besieging Castilian army was made through the founding of the town of Santa Fe very near the city. As a result, Granada surrendered on 2 January 1492, and the territorial unity of the emerging Spanish monarchy was established. Invoking the need to protect religious purity and the security of the nation, the monarchs issued an edict three months later (31 March), expelling the Jews from Castile, a population estimated to comprise approximately 250,000 people.

At this time, Christopher Columbus, seeking patronage for a voyage of discovery, presented himself to the Catholic sovereigns at Santa Fe. Columbus was introduced to the queen by her confessor, Hernando Talavera, and Cardinal Pedro González de Mendoza. Columbus fitted out three caravels with the means provided by the monarchs and sailed on 3 August 1492 from the port of Palos to land in the Bahama Islands on 12 October. In 1503 the monarchs organized the Secretariate of Indian Affairs, which was the origin of the Supreme Council of the Indies. They were also the patrons of Cardinal Cisneros in his efforts to reform the monasteries of Spain, a work that Cisneros accomplished under the authority of Pope Alexander VI, a gesture that anticipated the reform executed throughout the entire church. During the 1490s the production of cloths and silk developed at Segovia, Medina, Granada, Valencia, and Toledo, the manufacture of glass and of steel weapons, leather, and silverware, and the wealth imported from the Indies ensured a sound economic footing for Spanish territorial ambitions and the campaigns against the French in Italy. Agriculture prospered as well, while navigation and commerce rose to an unprecedented height as a result of the great wealth from the Americas. The centralized government and stern absolutism of the Catholic Monarchs brought the power of Castile and Aragón to its apogee and augured the nation that would emerge under their grandson, the emperor Charles V, a nation whose influence would span the world and whose supremacy would remain unchallenged for nearly a century.

The Catholic Monarchs' children all suffered unhappy destinies. Prince Juan, the sole male heir, died in his late teens, full of brilliant promise; Catalina was eventually repudiated by her husband Henry VIII of England; Juana, heiress to the kingdom after the death of her brother, married Philip the Fair and lost her reason.

E. Michael Gerli

Bibliography

Azcona, T. *Isabel la Católica. Estudio crítico de su vida y su reinado*. Madrid, 1993.

Edwards, J. *The Spain of the Catholic Monarchs, 1474–1520*. Cambridge, 2000.

Fernández-Armesto, F. *Fernando and Isabel*. New York, 1975.

Liss, P. *Isabel the Queen*. New York, 1992.

Vicens Vives, J. *Historia crítica de la vida y reinado de Fernando II de Aragón*. Zaragoza, 1962.

CATTLE RANCHING

In medieval Iberia, as elsewhere in western Europe, the raising of all-purpose cattle for milk, meat, hides, and labor (oxen) in a mixed-crop farming animal husbandry agrosystem was widely disseminated. The bovine component was particularly prominent in the humid crescent lands of the north, extending from Galicia and Portuguese Minho and Tras-os-Montes and on through the Cantabrian valleys and uplands of Asturias, the proto-Reconquest areas of León and Old Castile, and into the western Pyrenees. Well known here is the ancient Asturian practice of driving large numbers of cattle up into summer pastures high in the mountains under guard by "highland cowboys" (*vaqueiros de alzada*). But the English term "cattle ranching", without strict equivalent in Iberian speech, connotes the rearing of relatively large numbers of cattle raised outside complementarity with agriculture—primarily for their beef, hides, and tallow. Between 1000 and 1500, as the Reconquest moved south beyond the Duero River and the Central Sierras, Castilian and Portuguese stockmen came to redevelop older and invent new methods and techniques of managing great herds of cows along lines that represent true ranching, the foundations of an industry and a special type of pastoral society important in the Iberian Peninsula and the direct antecedent of the far greater "cattle kingdoms" of Ibero-and Anglo-America.

The medieval sources for this rising new bovine industry include municipal *fueros* and *forais* (privileges), royal privileges and law codes, private charters of various kinds, acts of *concejo* governments where available, constitutional *ordenamientos* of the pastoralists' associations called *mestas*, and chronicle and literary notices. All of these require supplementation on actual practices and ancient customs that survived in later times in Spain and Ibero-America. Where they are not very helpful, apart from the surprising frequency of color details in early Asturo-Leonese diplomas, is on the cattle breeds basic to the rise of ranching. On the *meseta* (plateau), moving south in later centuries, the distribution is traditional: from the light-colored Gallegas, Minhotas, Tudancas, Asturianas, and Pirenaicas, we encounter differently shaped, differently colored, and above all differently usable species: dark-colored "orucha" around Salamanca, the brown, crimson or dark reds of Extremeñas and Berrendas, the white or yellowish Cacerenas, the blacks and reds of Andalusia. And among these often half wild and unruly breeds, descendants of *Bos taurus ibericus*, is the progenitor of the fighting bulls of the plazas already depicted in the *Cantigas* of Alfonso X. How far this distribution reflects Reconquest movements of raiding and settlement is obscure.

On the institutional side data is much more available. In all three customary forms characteristic of medieval Iberian seasonal movement of livestock between lowland winter pastures (*invernaderos*) and high summer grasslands (*agostaderos*) in the sierras—whether within the limits of a single municipality, the more extensive territories made available by intertown compact, or the long drives such as the mesta conducted on the royal *cañadas* linking León and Old Castile with Extremadura, New Castile, and Andalusia—the same imperatives imposed themselves. In contrast with small numbers of cattle penned in limited pastures, ranching involved far greater herds moving or grazing on the open ranges of the meseta. For this purpose, herdsmen (cowboys, *vaqueros*) were required now to be on horseback, a necessity eased by the comparative availablity of riding mounts to nonnobles in the Castilian kingdom. Armed with the long, pikelike *garrocha*, and assisted by fierce, capable dogs, and possessed of an expertise enabling them to round up or subdue their often resentful charges, these medieval Castilian cowboys, often themselves owners of cows, were the basis of the industry's successful operation. Whether they knew the lasso, found widely in early America, is obscure; that they were free men, working from San Juan to San Juan for themselves or wealthier stockmen, is certain; and much can be learned from the texts regarding their status as responsible *mayorales* (head shepherds), *rabadanes* (shepherds), or a common hands (*zagales*). The pastoral life for these men turned about the annual cycle of calving, branding, roundups (*rodeos*), and culling for drives to *carnicerías* and other urban markets. All their activities were closely regulated by town laws or those of the Mesta Real and other municipal mestas, which provided stiff fines for brand frauds, thefts, and general violations of the pastoral provisions of the *fueros* and *ordenamientos de mesta*. On these terms the ranching of cattle was widely pursued in medieval Spain and Portugal, much more than is reflected in the two often-relied-upon accounts and statistics of the modern era. While in most parts cattle ranching was subordinate to sheep ranching, in certain regions by 1500 it seems to have been the dominant pastoral form, specifically in large tracts of Extremadura and Andalusia in Spain and in the Alemtejo (more precisely Ribatejo) countryside of Portugal. Several North American geographers have argued that this essentially Castilian plains cattle system should be recognized as a different type from the one found in the great *marismas* or marshlands of the Gualquivir River delta. The medieval documentation supporting this thesis, however, has yet to be adduced.

One final question—that of access to grazing land by reason of municipal citizenship, royal concession or outright ownership, and of the complex of rents, taxes, and tolls imposed from outside upon bovine ranchers—can only be mentioned. Municipalities offered forage in town commons (*ejidos*) and mountain grasslands; royal concessions of pasture rights in the vast southern expanses of *realengo* (royal lands) were possible; and nobles, military orders, towns, and others exacted rents and other impost. The Late Middle Ages saw in Andalusia the rise of private grazings of some size, the early formation of the later important *estancia* of Ibero-American history.

C. Julian Bishko

Bibliography

Bishko, C.J. "The Peninsular Background of Latin American Cattle Ranching," *Hispanic American Historical Review* 32 (1956), 491–515.

Butzer, K.W. "Cattle and Sheep from Old to New Spain: Historical Antecedents," *Annals of the Association of American Geographers* 78 (1988), 39–56.

CAZOLA, TREATY OF

The Treaty of Cazola (20 March 1179) was an alliance between Alfonso VIII of Castile and Alfonso II of Aragón. Both kings pledged mutual aid to each other against all others, especially Sancho VI of Navarre. Alfonso VIII required help to recover the Castilian lands Sancho VI had seized during his minority, and he and Alfonso II had already entered into an alliance for the siege of Cuenca in 1177. The Treaty of Cazola also divided up future conquests in al-Andalus between Castile and Aragón. Aragón was allocated Valencia, Játiva, Biar, Denia, Calpe, Castellón, and the coast of Alicante, while Castile reserved for itself conquests in the rest of al-Andalus. This treaty is generally interpreted as being to the disadvantage of Aragón, but unlike the earlier Treaty of Tudellén (1155) Aragón held its future conquests free and clear, without owing vassalage to Castile for them. Alfonso VIII had already released Alfonso II from the vassalage for Zaragoza that Alfonso VII had imposed upon Ramón Berenguer IV in 1140. The treaty of Cazola thus represented one more step in Alfonso II's attempts to rid himself of Castile's overlordship, and it enabled Alfonso VIII to gain support against the king of Navarre.

THERESA M. VANN

Bibliography

González, J. *El reino de Castilla en la época de Alfonso VIII.* Madrid, 1960.

CELESTINA

Conceived in the university atmosphere of late-fifteenth-century Salamanca, the initial piece of the *Celestina* puzzle seems to have been an attempt to write a vernacular humanistic comedy with a happy resolution. This anonymous manuscript work fell into the hands of a young jurist, Fernando de Rojas, whose own literary and philosophical leanings resonated with its keen observations of human behavior; from it he fashioned a rather darker meditation on the failings of human love unaccompanied by higher values. This new work first saw print in Burgos, probably in 1499, and was titled *Comedia de Calisto y Melibea.* It contains the original piece—as a first act—and fifteen additional acts, all through a series of unmediated dialogues that are among the many formal excellences of the work.

It relates the passion of a young nobleman (Calisto) for the daughter (Melibea) of a wealthy entrepreneur (Pleberio) and his wife (Alisa). When in the work's opening scene Melibea summarily rejects Calisto, he seeks the solitude of his bedchamber to bemoan his cruel fate. When a servant, Sempronio, learns the true cause of this odd behavior, he seeks personally to benefit by enlisting the aid of a penurious go-between, Celestina, whose house of prostitution he frequents in order to visit his partner, Elicia. Celestina is also known to another of Calisto's servants, the younger Pármeno, whose mother (Claudina) was Celestina's mentor and who, on her death, left her young son in the bawd's care. Pármeno takes a strong negative tack with his master, attempting—unsuccessfully—to dissuade him from involving Celestina in the pursuit of Melibea. Calisto's treatment of Pármeno's well-intentioned admonitions opens avenues in which both Celestina and Sempronio are able to co-opt his loyalties.

What ensues is the entanglement of human emotions, the forming of alliances, and the betrayal of relationships, and in all this Celestina proves to be a masterful manipulator. Her superiority is bolstered by a rhetorical advantage obtained in long years of trafficking in clandestine love affairs, and an ironic, experienced eye for the profitability in the exploitation of others' weaknesses. It is through her that we come to focus on human frailty: we are able to see Calisto as a parody of the noble lover, Melibea, outwardly resisting, but all-too-willing to enter into a secret game of her own, and the servants and other members of the underclass as eagerly disloyal participants in a social fabric weakened by a lack of moral underpinnings. As Melibea prepares to indulge her newborn passion under the cover of darkness, and Calisto to violate the sanctity of Pleberio's home, Celestina is prevented from exulting in her professional triumphs or the spoils they bring her. Sempronio and Pármeno, having newly forged an alliance through shared cowardice, violently murder her over her refusal to keep their agreement to share all the profits and, moments later, are themselves executed for the crime. Subsequently, Calisto, in rushing from his initial tryst with Melibea, to aid another pair of servants, slips on the ladder that gave him access to her walled garden and falls to his death. Melibea, all her illusions and future thus dashed, makes a confession, from the turret of the house to a bewildered Pleberio below, and then leaps to her death in a willful suicide, a perverse imitation of Calisto's own fall. Pleberio, bereft of his only daughter and heir, is left to ponder the harsh world, in which cruel fortune and deceitful (carnal) love leave only chaos in their wake. The ensuing silence as the text ends is complete.

Not long after the three known printings of the *Comedia* appeared (1499–1501), Rojas was prevailed upon by readers to again take up his pen for the purpose of extending the lovers' tryst. The expanded version includes—grafted onto act 14 of the *Comedia*—the month of lovers' meetings but also a new subplot in which the surviving girlfriends of Sempronio and Pármeno devise a plan to avenge these deaths by conspiring with the ruffian, Centurio, to murder Calisto. This twenty-one-act version, the *Tragicomedia de Calisto y Melibea*, was almost immediately translated into Italian (1506); the expanded version is today better known as *Celestina*, a reflection of her crucial multiple roles in the plotting and unfolding of the action and in exposing the moral vacuum at its center. *Celestina* became very popular and continued to be popular well into the seventeenth century, with some eighty editions by 1634. It was also translated into German (1520, 1534), French (1527, 1578), English (c. 1530, 1598, 1631, 1707), Dutch (1550), Hebrew (mid-sixteenth century, no longer extant), and Latin (1624). In Spain, *Celestina* was revived in sequels (*Segunda Celestina*, *Tercera Celestina*) and imitated by other bawds in many works in prose (*Tragedia Policiana, Lisandro y Roselia, La Dorotea*) and dramatic works by, among others, Juan del Encina, Torres Naharro, and Lope de Vega. As early as 1510 a ballad circulated, with the work rendered into octosyllabic verse. In 1513 an eclogue by Pedro Manuel Ximénez de Urrea may possibly have been staged.

None of these works replicates the powerful literary language, probing insights into character, or social and moral vision that Rojas's *Celestina* possesses. Careful scholarship has revealed the debt Rojas contracted with previous authors (Terence, Petrarch, Seneca, Diego de San Pedro's *Cárcel de Amor*, etc.), has shown how the philosophical teachings in the Salamanca of his day are present in the work, and has brought to light how the text deals with the contemporary social issues of the early sixteenth century (the emerging bourgeoisie and the urbanization of the cities, the decay of and innovation in religious matters, the handling of public morality, and the like). It has shed light on the ways Rojas is both traditional (in his use of rhetorical models, for example) and highly original (in his development of fully three-dimensional characters who reveal themselves in pure dialogue). *Celestina*'s pessimism has been explored, as have its hedonism, its vitality, its ironies, its genre (dramatic or novelistic?), and its complicated textual history. As well, its presentation of magic, its celebration of the present, its confrontation with carnality, its existential nature, its didactic frame and its dialogue with readers have each been extensively scrutinized.

Celestina's continuing appeal, five hundred years after its first appearance, is evident in new editions, translations, adaptations (the theatrical stage, the operatic stage, ballet, film, and novelization) and its ongoing appeal to artists (Francisco de Goya and Pablo Picasso among them). Today *celestina* is a noun, *celestinear* a verb, and *celestinesca* an adjective in the Spanish language. And *Celestina* is considered to be Spain's second masterpiece, preceded only by Miguel de Cervantes's *Don Quijote*.

Joseph T. Snow

Biography

Berndt, E. R. *Amor, muerte y fortuna en "La Celestina"*. Madrid, 1963.

Corfis, I. A., and J. T. Snow (eds.) *Fernando de Rojas and "Celestina": Approaching the Fifth Centenary*. Madison, Wisc., 1993.

Dunn, P. N. *Fernando de Rojas*. New York, 1975.

Fraker, C. F. *"Celestina". Genre and Rhetoric*. London, 1990.

Gilman, S. *The Art of "La Celestina*." Madison, Wisc., 1956.

———. *The Spain of Fernando de Rojas*. Princeton, N.J., 1972.

Lida de Malkiel, M.R. *La originalidad artística de "La Celestina"*. Buenos Aires, 1970.

Menéndez y Pelayo, M. *La Celestina*. Madrid, 1979.

Severin, D. S. *Memory in "La Celestina"*. London, 1970.

Snow, J. T. *"Celestina" by Fernando de Rojas: An Annotated Bibliography of World Interest, 1930–1985*. Madison, Wisc., 1985; and continuing supplements in the journal *Celestinesca*.

CHANCERIES

The history of the writing offices of the Christian rulers of medieval Iberia has not been adequately studied. While the oldest charters date to the eighth century it is impossible to speak of a royal chancery, in the sense of a department of government hierarchically ordered, before the reign of Alfonso VI of León-Castile (1076–1109) or perhaps even of his daughter, Urraca (1109–1126), where the first such appeared on the Iberian Peninsula. Earlier documents were written by individual scribes who usually styled themselves royal notary or royal clerk.

The title of chancellor for the head of the royal writing office was used very sporadically under Queen Urraca but became regular under her son and successor, Alfonso VII (1126–1157). In Portugal the chancery was organized and the chancellorship appeared late in the reign of Afonso Henriques I (1128–1185). The title did not come into use in the kingdom of Aragón until the reign of Jaime I (1213–1276), delayed possibly because of the maintenance of separate writing offices for Aragón and for Catalunya even after the effectual combination of the two realms subsequent to 1137 during the reign of Ramón Berenguer IV (1131–1162).

The language of the chancery documents was Latin until the reign of Alfonso X (1252–1284) in Castile, then Castilian began to be employed, though Latin was still the language of international correspondence. In Portugal the vernacular replaced the classical language slightly later, in the time of King Dinis (1279–1325). Again, in the kingdom of Aragón the practical difficulties of a multitude of vernaculars militated to maintain Latin as the official language until well into the fourteenth century. The script of the documents was the peninsular Visigothic hand until the twelfth century when it was replaced everywhere by the Caroline, of French derivation. Subsequently Iberian script followed the general European development of the Caroline.

Dated documents followed the classical style of kalends, nones, and ides for the day and month until the modern method was introduced in the thirteenth century. At this time, Portugal, Castile, Aragón, and Navarre converted from the use of the "Iberian Era" calendar to use of the Christian Era calendar, thus setting back the chronology by thirty-eight years. Dating practice in Catalunya had rather followed the regnal year of the kings of France until 1180, when the use of the Christian Era calendar was adopted. The medium of the documents was parchment until the conquest of Muslim Játiva in 1244 by Jaime I of Aragón made paper more generally available; it became the standard everywhere for all but the most solemn documents by the middle of the fourteenth century.

Types of documents produced by the princely chanceries fall into four main categories prior to 1300. The most familiar and numerous of these is the charter, precisely because it ordinarily was the instrument for the conveyance of land and, subsequently functioning as title to real property, had a permanent value to the possessor. Probably during the course of the twelfth century the *fuero*, or grant of legal privilege to a town or village, became a gradually distinct type of document. The precise evolution is difficult to trace since *fueros* were subsequently emended and enlarged and their original documents seldom survived.

Both of these documentary genres were, in all likelihood, far outnumbered originally by the mandate. This was simply a royal order for obedience to or the accomplishment of a specific royal enactment or decision. One or more of these mandates probably accompanied each fuero and charter and alerted the persons affected to their new status or of a new superior. This ordinarily basic administrative and secondary character of the mandate made its preservation strictly haphazard. For the kingdom of León-Castile in the eleventh and twelfth centuries, for example, the known charters number more than two thousand but known mandates less than fifty.

Royal letters are quite poorly preserved in number for much the same reason. Their importance even to the principals vanished very quickly with the passage of time. Some survive in national archives but subsequent officialdom found them difficult to classify, particularly because they, like the mandate, were originally undated. Some of the more fortunate examples survive because of their incorporation into histories or chronicles.

Survival of the originals is crucial because the practice of copying a duplicate into a permanent official register was followed regularly nowhere in the Christian realms of the peninsula before the mid-thirteenth century. The earliest preserved series of such registers derive from the Kingdom of Aragón, starting about 1250.

Princes, prelates, and great nobles also developed chanceries, using the term in its broadest sense. That is, they sometimes came, at least by the late eleventh century, to boast an official called a notary rather than relying on a public notary of some sort. But the character of even such important persons was more particular and limited than that of the crown, of course, and the smaller volume of their official output of documents made the development of a true department infrequent. For the twelfth century a long series of charters exists of the Catalan counts of Urgell, but they seem to have been written mostly by their chaplain. For 1156 charters authorized by the Castilian Lara count, Manrique, exist and were written by the count's "chancellor" but there is no evidence that this person had subordinates. Archbishops and bishops more often had an official known as chancellor, for the latter title seems to have been intimately related to the appearance of cathedral chapters in the peninsula in the early twelfth century. But evidence for the appearance of an episcopal chancery, precisely as a department, must be investigated separately in every case.

BERNARD F. REILLY

Bibliography

Floriano Cumbreño, A.C. *Curso general de paleografía y diplomática españolas*. Oviedo, 1946.

Jesús de Costa, A. de. "La Chancellerie royale portugaise jusqu' au milieu du XIIIe siècle," *Revista Portuguesa de História* 15 (1975), 143–69.

Lucas Alvarez, M. *El reino de León en la Alta Edad Media: Las cancellerías reales (1109–1230).* León, 1993.

Millares Carlo, A. "La cancillería real en León y Castilla hasta fines del reinado de Fernando III." *Anuario de la Historia de Derecho Español* 3 (1926), 227–306.

Sevillano Colom, F. "De la cancillería de la Corona de Aragón." In *Martínez Ferrando, Archivero.* Barcelona, 1968. 451–80.

CHANCERY, LEÓN-CASTILE

While the chancery is the first of the offices of royal government to take shape, to speak of a chancery in León-Castile before the end of the eleventh century is misleading. As best we can tell, before that time the work of preparing the king's documents was entrusted to one or more scribes or notaries, presumably clerics. The documents are written on parchment, and the script is Visigothic. From the reign of Alfonso VI (1065–1109) the style and usage of the chancery become more regular. The documents it issues are charters, usually conveyances of property, mandates, or expressions of the royal will about some matter, and the *agnitio*, or record of a judicial decision. Some features of Caroline script are noticeable.

During the reign of Urraca (1109–1126) this characteristic becomes more pronounced and the title "chancellor" is occasionally employed. It is during the reign of her son, Alfonso VII (1126–1157) that the use of Caroline script becomes invariable until that script itself evolves into the Gothic after the mid-thirteenth century. Roughly nine hundred royal documents survive from Alfonso's reign. They depict the final adoption of the chancellor's title for the head of the royal writing office and a true department in which the ranks of scribe, notary, and chancellor are usual. The royal seal that appears on the documents is still ordinarily the drawn *signum*, but there is some disputable evidence for the utilization by Alfonso of a pendant seal as well.

In the separate chanceries of León and Castile after 1157 the *signum* continues to be employed but it has become the *rota*, or round design deriving from the papal design. It is also now supplemented by the use of a pendant seal. In the kingdom of León the title of chancellor has passed, of right, to the current archbishop of Santiago de Compostela while, in the kingdom of Castile, the archbishop of Toledo seems to have acquired something of the same prerogative but the title is less clear. However, the work of the chancery had become sufficiently demanding and professionalized so that the actual function was performed by a delegate in the case of León and perhaps also in Castile. Only after the unification of the two kingdoms under the aegis of Castile will the chancery adopt paper, the vernacular, and the Gothic script.

BERNARD F. REILLY

Bibliography

Floriano Cumbreño, A.C. *Curso general de paleografía y diplomática españolas.* 2 vols. Oviedo, 1946.

Fletcher, R. "Diplomatic and the Cid Revisited: The Seals and Mandates of Alfonso VII," *Journal of Medieval History* 2 (1976), 305–37.

CHARLEMAGNE

Charlemagne (Charles the Great), king of the Franks (768–814) and first of the Carolingian emperors (crowned 25 December 800), was interested in Spanish affairs throughout his reign, but enjoyed only limited success in his attempts to extend his influence into the Iberian Peninsula. In 777 he was persuaded by envoys sent from Zaragoza to launch an expedition into the Ebro River valley the following year. This was an area that earlier Frankish kings had coveted, and the threat of the northward extension of the newly developed power of the first Umayyad Amir of Córdoba made the local Arab and *muwallad* rulers in the valley initially anxious to cooperate with Charlemagne. In 778 one column of his army took Pamplona, while the other made its way around the eastern end of the Pyrenees. However, Charles's local allies deserted him, and both Barcelona and Zaragoza were held against the Franks. In the ensuing retreat across the mountains his rear guard was ambushed and destroyed by the Basques in the pass of Roncesvalles. Among other prominent members of the Frankish court killed there was Roland, the count of the Breton March, and from this episode developed the eleventh-century poetic epic *Chanson de Roland*. Its relationship to the historical realities of the battle is almost nonexistent. During his disastrous expedition the Saxons had revolted against Charlemagne, and he never led a Frankish army in person across the Pyrenees again. However, the Franks were able to make themselves masters of Girona in 785 with local support, and in 797 diplomatic contacts with the Asturian kingdom may have been part of an intended large-scale Frankish intervention in Spain. Huesca was then occupied, but another Saxon revolt seems to have led to the cancellation of any more extensive plans. In 801 the delayed offensive was resumed, and an army under Charlemagne's son Louis, King of Aquitaine (781–814) captured Barcelona. Between 801 and 810 Louis made various attempts to press farther south and take Tarragona and Tortosa, but these attempts were unsuccessful. A frontier was established roughly along the line of the Llobregat River. On the basis of these conquests a Frankish March was established, with its center in Barcelona. During Charlemagne's interventions in Spain a number of indigenous Christians entered his service. The most significant of these was Theodulf (778–821), who later became bishop of Orleans, and who was one of the emperor's closest ecclesiastical advisers. Spanish influences have been detected in the chapel he built at Germigny-des-Prés and in his theological writings, including the *Libri Carolini*.

ROGER COLLINS

Bibliography

Buckler, F.W. *Harunu'l-Rashid and Charles the Great*. Cambridge, Mass., 1931.

Collins, R. *The Arab Conquest of Spain: 710–797*. Oxford, 1989.

Freeman, A. "Theodulf of Orleans and the *Libri Carolini*," *Speculum* 32 (1957), 663–705.

Salrach, J. M. *El procés de formació nacional de Catalunya (segles VIII–IX)*. Vol. 1. Barcelona, 1978.

CHILDHOOD

Children appear frequently in Iberian literature, gainsaying twentieth-century ethnocentric assertions of medieval indifference to children and childhood. Seldom portrayed realistically, children are incarnations of certain topics: human innocence, the consequences of illicit sexuality, and potential greatness.

Innocent babies were abandoned: Isomberta's seven infants whimpered softly like a nest of animals in the *Gran conquista de Ultramar*. Unlike Tarsiana, of the *Libro de Apolonio* whose foster parents were chosen by her father, the tiny Amadís, protagonist of *Amadís de Gaula*, was set adrift. His designation *sin tiempo* (age unknown) might allude to the juridical status of an unbaptized infant less than twenty-four-hours old or of a child below the age of seven. Other innocent children were put at risk: "El niño judío" in Gonzalo de Berceo's *Milagros de Nuestra Señora*, and the *Cantigas de Santa María*; a little boy swept out to sea in Sánchez de Vercial's *Libro de los enxemplos*; a nine-year-old girl sent to confront the angry Cid by the frightened citizens of Burgos in the *Poema de Mío Cid*.

Evidence of parental sexuality, the children were disposed of (Amadís, Esplandián, and Florestán and the ballads *El hijo vengador* and *La infanta parida*). Multiple births were evidence of multiple sexual encounters as in the *Romance de Espinelo*, and Isomberta's brood in the *Gran conquista de Ultramar*. The fruits of incest were deformed either physically (Endriago in *Amadís de Gaula*) or spiritually (García in *La leyenda del Abad don Juan de Montemayor*).

Lost children found protection of either humans or beasts. During a peaceful family picnic little Garfín was carried off by a lioness in the *Libro del cavaillero Zifar*, and later his younger brother Roboán strayed from his parents' lodgings. Chance reunited them later in the care of a kindly family.

Some childish precocity prefigured future achievements, as in the *Libro de Alexandre* and the *Mocedades de Rodrigo*, or of a natural inclination: young Amadís's spirited defense of his little brother, or the piety of Santo Domingo de Silos and San Millán de la Cogolla in Berceo's accounts.

Books of instruction list the stages of childhood: *infancia* (birth to age seven), *mocedad* (ages seven to fourteen), and *adolescencia* o *mancebía* (ages fourteen to twenty eight). Rules for the care of children under seven dictated that they were to be fed milk or bland and tender foods; they were not to be given wine; they were to become accustomed to the cold; they were to take exercise; they were to be entertained by suitable tales and songs; they were not to cry because the soul escapes during sobs, and sobs were not be be stifled for fear that they become ill (*Glosa castellana al regimiento de príncipes*). Some royal children were sequestered to ward off their predicted destiny as in the *Sendébar*, *Barlaam e Josafat*, and *Libro de buen amor*. Finally many medieval Iberian folktales urge early moral training.

HARRIET GOLDBERG

Bibliography

Ariès, P. *Centuries of Childhood: A Social History of Family Life in Early Modern France*. Trans. Robert Baldick. New York, 1962.

Goldberg, H. "The Literary Portrait of the Child in Castilian Medieval Literature," *Kentucky Romance Quarterly* 27 (1980), 11–27.

CHIVALRY

Chivalry, or *caballería*, had many connotations within the political, cultural, and juridical framework of the Christian Middle Ages in the Iberian Peninsula. In the first place, it alluded to an institution that functioned as a nucleus for the defense of the borders of the realm, composed principally of groups of citizens and military professionals at the service of the king, the towns, the councils, and other entities that exercised political power. Over time, along with the pacification of the frontiers, individuals who practiced chivalry became established as local powers in the cities. They were constituted as groups of mounted military men referred to as the *caballería villana*, whose activities during peacetime were related to the guilds, the professions, and the working of the land. Through their ability to rehearse local power and influence, a strong sense of solidarity developed between the members of these groups in relation to the monarchy, which from time to time obliged them to display their skill at arms and horsemanship and to exhibit the authority of the crown through the array of the insignia that had been conferred upon them by the king. Additionally, they sought to define and consolidate their own power by organizing themselves in associations, chapters, or brotherhoods (e.g., el Cabildo de Caballeros Guisados de Caballo de Cuenca, la Cofradía de Caballeros de Santiago de Burgos, los Caballeros de Alarde de Jaén, etc.) that not only pursued royal sanction in order to make use of their power in the cities but also aspired to a rank that would confer social distinction on particular members. Both clerical and aristocratic authors during the Middle Ages refer to these individuals as *defensores non nobles* (Juan Manuel) or *omnes de cauallo* (Alonso de Cartagena) to distinguish them from a completely different manifestation of chivalry that reflected an *ordo* or estate.

The origin of chivalry as an estate, or *ordo*, in Castile may be traced to a specific chronological moment, when it was defined for the first time in Alfonso X el Sabio's (1251–1282) *Segunda Partida*. Chivalry in that context became an expression of the monarchy's desire to create a loyal aristocratic institution that could exist as an expression of solidarity with the crown and would recognize the latter's political and juridical supremacy. This institution—in both ethical and cultural terms—was essentially lay in nature. It was centered on the observance of what may perhaps have been its greatest interest: the strict affirmation of centralized monarchical power and the constitution of chivalry itself as a means toward achieving the highest expression of individual personal power, independent of lineage, through the practice of virtue. It is this last aspect that distinguishes the historical expression of chivalry in Castile from elsewhere in medieval Europe and marks, at the same time, both the public aspirations and critiques of the institution from the time of its first expression in the *Partidas* until the end of the fifteenth century.

Chivalry in late medieval Castile rests on a set of intertwined social beliefs and dependencies that comprise a *récit*, or narrative, that for the sake of discussion may be called the "chivalric fable," which in all of Europe, but especially in England and France, was tied to the development of the monarchy during the second half of the twelfth century. The chivalric fable embraced the public expression of a widely held aspiration: literary, and later political and legal, texts transmit the belief that the nature of humankind is not predetermined by its pedigree or ancestry, but rather by individual virtue, which has the power to alter radically all social destinies. In this scheme, the means for revealing individual virtue was principally through the exercise of chivalry. Fictional works like the *Libro del cavallero Zifar* and *Amadís de Gaula* reiterate the irrelevance of the chivalric hero's lineage, who must eschew family origins in order to prove his value in the world. Zifar, who labors under an ancestral curse, seeks to free himself from his origins; and Amadís, the son of a king and a princess, is cast to chance at birth upon the waters in a Moses basket. In both cases, each is obliged to remain blind to high-born privilege in order to earn through the personal exercise of arms and virtue society's highest ambitions. This central idea of the chivalric fable is also expressed in the juridical and political spheres of late medieval polity. The civic aspirations and personal statecraft of Alfonso X, for example, rested precisely upon the definition and propagation of a politics based on the interdependence of chivalry and monarchy. It is thus important to note that chivalry as a juridical institution was not driven merely by the higher social aspirations of the lower nobility but also by the centralizing political objectives of the monarchy. In this way, chivalry constituted a discourse of power that expressed a sense of unity between the crown and certain sectors of the nobility in the creation of the state whose ruling class was endowed with authority by the king through ritual investiture and, consequently, remained under his control.

Without the independent ability to interfere in the political and jurisdictional affairs of the kingdom, chivalry was thus a tool of monarchy used to counter the privileges and claims of the high nobility, whose interests were tied to the land, often at odds with the crown's, and were essentially feudal. The attempt to forge an alliance between the monarchy and the lower nobility was immediately recognized by the high nobility for what it was, a usurpation of their ancient territorial prerogatives. As in the case of Don Juan Manuel, the high nobility was obliged to accept the culture of chivalry and its forms of expression, but not the submission to the centralized political objectives of the monarchy that it implied. In contrast to the policies of Alfonso XI and the Orden de la Banda (a lay chivalric order that sought to constitute a political and administrative entity based on a deterritorialized notion of nobility), Don Juan Manuel proposed in many of his works a completely different hierarchy of power that made the institution of chivalry an honor pertaining to all noble men who were considered by him to be the real stalwarts of social, political, and juridical order, independent of their hereditary titles.

The duality espoused by Juan Manuel became the crux of a debate on chivalry that developed in Castile during the latter half of the late Middle Ages, particularly during the fifteenth century. By then, chivalry had acquired a well-defined legal status, which helped to radicalize the positions taken in the debate. Following the precedents set by the Italian jurist Bartolo de Sassoferrato, the Trastámaran monarchs of the fifteenth century established the possibility that chivalry could be defined as a noble distinction and thus confer nobilty upon all those who were invested in it, even individuals of nonnoble origin. The effects of chivalry were thus extended and opened and aspiration to it became more widely public since it offered everyone the possibility of elevation to noble rank, but especially to the members of the so-called *caballería villana*. Many among the high nobility, of course, abjured emphatically the notion that chivalric investiture denoted the conferral of noble status, and rejected even more strenuously the idea that the crown could create nobles from plebes by means of investiture in, or certification of, chivalric estate. On the other hand, some *caballeros* of noble lineage, especially those nobles of *converso* (Chistian convert) origin like Diego de Valera, defended the royal prerogative to confer nobility through chivalric investiture. For Valera this faculty constituted the highest expression of the crown's authority in the exercise of its power since it allowed the king to control, create, and define the nature of nobility ex nihilo, and thus to rule unquestionably the juridical and political life of the realm.

J. Rodríguez Velasco

Bibliography

Rodríguez Velasco, J.D. *El debate sobre la caballería en el siglo XV*. Valladolid, 1996.

Heusch, C. *La caballería castellana en la Baja Edad Media. Textos y contextos*. Montpellier, 2001.

Sánchez, M., et al. (ed.) *Libros de Caballerías (De "Amadís" al "Quijote"): Práctica, lectura, representación e identidad*. Salamanca, 2002.

THE CHURCH

One medieval tradition credited to St. Paul was the bringing of Christianity to Spain. It was based on the apostle's Epistle to the Romans, in which he told the Christians that, having finished his evangelization in the eastern Mediterranean, he intended first to visit them and then proceed to spread the word in Spain. (Rom. 15: 19, 28–29). There is no evidence, though, that such a visit ever took place. Equally spurious were later claims that it was one of Jesus's original disciples, St. James the Great, son of Zebedee, who brought the Gospel to Spain. This James, who was beheaded on the orders of Herod Agrippa in A.D. 44, seems never to have left Jerusalem. (Acts 12: 2) Nevertheless, a tradition developed in Spain in the seventh century that he had in fact been the first Christian evangelist there and, from the ninth century onward, it was claimed that James's body had been transported to Santiago de Compostela, in Galicia. In reality the earliest surviving information concerning the organization of the Spanish church is to be found in a letter of St. Cyprian (bishop of Carthage in North Africa, ca. 200–258), dated 254. There seems to be little doubt, though, that Christianity had, in some form, existed in the peninsula since the early days of the Church, as a result of the integration of Hispania into the Roman Empire. Testimony to its importance in the Spanish provinces is to be found in the martyrdoms that took place during the reign of Emperor Diocletian (245–313). Many of the Spanish martyrs of this period entered Christian tradition through the verse of the Latin poet and hymn-writer Prudentius (346–ca. 410) in his collection *Peristephanum*. At Elvira (later Granada) around 306, a council of the Spanish Church passed eighty-one canons, including severe disciplinary measures against apostates (to paganism or Judaism) and adulterers. Canon 33 ordered clerical continence on pain of removal from office, while many of the Elvira canons demanded lifelong excommunication of offenders, without the prospect of reconciliation to the Church even at death. Such official harshness was to be characteristic of the Spanish church during the centuries that followed the Roman withdrawal from the peninsula. During the fourth century, Hosius, bishop of Córdoba (ca. 256–357/8), and Gregory, bishop of Elvira (d. after 362), became active in the defense of Catholicism against the heresy known as Arianism. Hosius suffered persecution in Córdoba, took part in the Council of Elvira (ca. 306), and most famously, as adviser to Emperor Constantine, took a lead in the Council of Nicea in 325, which defined Catholic orthodoxy in the form of the "Nicene" creed, while Gregory urged harsh measures against Arianism at the Council of Ariminum (359). While Hosius and Gregory were defending orthodoxy on the international stage, a Hispano-Roman senator, Priscillian (d. 386), became bishop of Ávila and lost his life, supposedly for undermining clerical authority, encouraging even more severe ascetic practices than were currently orthodox, and allowing too great a public role in the Church to women.

During the fifth century, most of the peninsula fell under the rule of the Visigoths, who espoused the version of Christianity that became associated with the name of Arius (d. 336), in which, according to the Alexandrian's "Catholic" opponents, the humanity of Jesus, rather than his divinity, was held to be his dominant characteristic. It is not clear why the Visigoths adopted this fairly abstruse divergence from Catholicism, but Arianism remained a feature of the Visigothic Church until King Reccared (r. 586–601) announced his conversion at the third (Catholic) Council of Toledo in 589. Reccared, who since 573 had shared government with his Arian father, Leovigild, was probably converted by St. Leander, bishop of Seville, and the sometimes violent resistance of the Arians was quite soon repressed. Reccared was praised by St. Isidore of Seville as a founder of numerous monasteries and churches. What later became the Spanish primatial see of Toledo was the scene, in the Visigothic period, of about thirty church councils that legislated for the government of society in general, as well as the for the Church itself. A prominent feature of many of these councils was violent legislative hostility to Jews and Judaism. Bishop Leander (ca. 540–ca. 600), as well as championing Catholicism against the Arians, visited and influenced Pope Gregory the Great (ca. 540–604). He was surpassed, though, by his brother, St. Isidore (ca. 560–636), who was also bishop of Seville and metropolitan of Baetica (later Andalusia).

Through his writings on many subjects in addition to theology, including etymology, Isidore had a profound influence on the culture of medieval Europe, and forgers later exploited his name. During the remaining period of Visigothic rule, successive Toledan councils built up the collection of canon law known as the *Hispana*, monasticism spread widely, and the distinctive Spanish liturgy, later known as the Mozarabic rite, was developed. After the Berber and Arab invasions of 711 through 713, Iberia's new Muslim rulers tolerated Christianity as an inferior and subordinate faith, though persecution broke out from time to time. The most notable episodes occurred in Córdoba in the mid-ninth century, where Eulogio, Pedro Álvaro, and other believers, apparently in an attempt to halt Christian assimilation to Islam, attacked Islamic teaching and provoked the Muslim authorities to execute them. Although later dignified as pioneers of a systematic "reconquest" of the former Christian Spain, the fledgling northern Christian statelets moved only sporadically against the Muslim caliphate of Córdoba. Yet the story of the Córdoban martyrs paradoxically indicates the continuing vibrant presence of Catholic Christianity in al-Andalus, in the face of a slow large-scale conversion to Islam. Around 800, circles in the Iberian church and in its Gallic neighbor developed the last notable native-born heresy in the Spanish Middle Ages. Known as *Adoptionism*, the main distinctive claim of this doctrine was that, instead of coming from the Godhead, Jesus was "adopted" as Son of God at his baptism. Nevertheless, by about 1000 a large proportion of the Christian population of al-Andalus seems to have converted to Islam.

The conquest of Toledo by Alfonso VI of Castile in 1085 not only restored a historic center to Christian rule, but also opened up surviving Mozarabic Christianity to developments that had taken place in France and Rome during the intermediate period. After the Council of Burgos (1080), successful efforts were made to replace the Mozarabic liturgy with the Roman one, and to strengthen papal control over the whole Iberian church. After 1100 the idea of reconquest was increasingly incorporated into the developing concept of crusade as a divinely sanctioned war against non-Christians, which conferred spiritual benefits on Christians who took part in it. At the same time, reformed French Benedictine monasticism, as represented by the Cluniac and Cistercian orders, served further to integrate the Spanish church with developments beyond the Pyrenees. During the twelfth century, the new type of military order, which combined the religious with the crusading way of life, came to the peninsula, initially in the form of the existing Templar and Hospitaller orders, but soon in native orders, such as Santiago, Calatrava, and Alcántara. The next major steps in the Reconquest, in the early thirteenth century, completed the conquest of Portugal and western Andalusia, leaving the Naṣrid emirate of Granada to survive until 1492. At the same time, Spaniards became involved in the development of the new, primarily urban, ministry of friars, by far the most notable being Domingo de Guzmán (ca. 1172–1221), founder of the Order of Preachers. Dominican friars soon became involved in the work of the new papal inquisition, an engine for the identification and repression of heresy. A particular feature of the thirteenth-century Spanish church was the development of orders of friars, notably the Mercedarians and the Trinitarians, the latter of twelfth-century French origin, who specialized in negotiating the ransom of Christian captives in Muslim hands.

During the thirteenth century, a new diocesan structure was established in the southern half of Spain (excluding Granada), though some attempt was made to relate it to the organization of dioceses that existed before the Muslim invasion. Thereafter, the bishoprics of the Crowns of Castile and Aragón were organized into the provinces of Toledo, Santiago de Compostela, Seville, Zaragoza, Tarragona, and Valencia, while the Navarrese see of Pamplona came under Bayonne, and Braga remained the primatial see of Portugal. Only under Fernando and Isabel was this tangled ecclesiastical geography—which also included bishoprics such as Burgos and León, which were directly subject to the popes—to some extent rationalized. Notable among the diocesans of this period were Lucas, bishop of Tuy, and Rodrigo Jiménez de Rada (ca. 1170–1247), archbishop of Toledo. Lucas of Tuy (in fact mainly based in León) was the author of a world history (*Chronicon mundi*) and a treatise against the Albigensian, or Cathar dualist heresy, that affected Catalonia in the early thirteenth century. He was also a commentator on current affairs, and notably adopted the Greek philosopher Aristotle as a Spaniard, a claim still current around 1500. From his Leonese base, with its strong traditional links to the see of Seville, Lucas firmly resisted the primatial claims of his Toledan contemporary, Jiménez de Rada. Archbishop Rodrigo was the author of numerous works on Spanish history, and also chancellor of Castile under Alfonso VIII and Fernando III, being a powerful propagandist in the latter's cause. He was responsible for the decision to tear down the former main mosque of Toledo, to be replaced by a cathedral in the current Gothic style. Also in this period, some Spanish churchmen made notable contributions to the life of the wider Western Church, one of them being St. Raymond of Penyafort (ca. 1186–1275), a Catalan Dominican friar who was prominent both in attempts to convert Jews and Muslims to Christianity and particularly as a canonist. Also involved in missions to other faiths and in Christian mysticism was the eclectic Catalan Franciscan Ramón Llull (ca. 1235–ca. 1315).

A good example of a political prelate in the fourteenth century was Cardinal Gil Albornoz (ca. 1300–1367), who was active both in the Castilian court and also in the papal court, then at Avignon. In 1365, though, Albornoz made a significant and long-lasting contribution to the education of his country's clergy by founding the Spanish college, specializing in canon law, theology, and medicine in the papal *studium* (university) of Bologna. Despite the upheavals of the Avignon papacy (1309–1377), and the Great Schism of the Western Church (1378–1415), at least one bishop, Gutierre de Toledo (ca. 1330–1389) worked hard to govern his diocese of Oviedo in a manner that would eventually be mandated by the Council of Trent (1545–1563), holding regular synods and drawing up a catechism to assist his clergy in the instruction of the laity. Until nearly the end of the schism, Castile and Aragón, especially the latter, supported the antipopes in Avignon and later in Tortosa while Portugal retained allegiance to the popes in Rome, whose succession was declared legitimate at the Council of Constance in 1415. During these years, Spanish churchmen played an ever larger part in the affairs of Europe north of the Pyrenees, and foretold the arrival of Spain as a continental power.

In the turmoil of fifteenth-century Spain, bishops did not hesitate to intervene actively, even violently, in politics. In Castile, Alfonso Carrillo de Acuña (1412–1482), Archbishop of Toledo, played a major part in bringing Isabel to the throne, though they quarrelled both before and after her accession. The pugnacious prelate's tastes included diocesan reform and alchemy, as well as power politics. Carrillo's contemporary, Pedro González de Mendoza (1428–1495), was archbishop of Seville (1472–1485), and then of Toledo until his death. As a member of the upper noble Mendoza family, he was associated with the Castilian Renaissance while the new foundation of the Inquisition (1478) was introduced to Seville during his tenure of that see, once his efforts to evangelize the Judeoconversos were perceived to have failed. Cardinal Mendoza (of Santa Croce) entrusted this missionary task to Fray Hernando de Talavera (1430–1507), a member of the Jeronymite order of friars (founded in 1373), who was confessor to Isabel and from 1493 until his death was archbishop of the newly reconstituted see of Granada. Although an enforcer of Catholic orthodoxy in the face of Jewish belief and practice, Talavera seriously tried to comply with the terms of the 1492 surrender agreement, under which Muslims were granted religious freedom. He attempted to learn Arabic and gained a reputation among Muslims as a holy man, but his more gentle policies were undermined, firstly by the rebellions of 1499 to 1501, and secondly by the efforts of Cardinal Francisco Jiménez de Cisneros (1436–1517), who succeeded Mendoza in Toledo in 1495. This powerful and complex man, who effortlessly combined hard-nosed politics with a mystical and messianic Franciscan spirituality, had a highly varied career as prelate, inquisitor-general, patron of culture, founder of the theological and humanistic university of Alcalá de Henares (1499, 1508), and regent of Castile, in 1506 to 1507 and 1516 to 1517. Cisneros was an active supporter of printing in Spain, though not of scholastic works, his largest and most famous project being the multilingual translation of the Bible, known as the *Complutensian Polyglot*, produced at Alcalá (published 1520).

Two agencies dominated the life and work of the Spanish Church in the Middle Ages. One of them, the monarchy, had affected Christian life in the peninsula since the first century A.D. It had done so in various forms, first in the Roman emperors; then in the Visigothic kings; in the Muslim caliphs and the rulers of the small, revived Christian states of the north; in the consolidated kingdoms of the late Middle Ages, and finally in the dynastically united monarchies of Fernando and Isabel. The second essential, though external, force was the papacy, which claimed primacy for its see of Rome, on the basis that its first bishop, St. Peter, had apparently received authority over the whole Church from Jesus himself. (Matthew 16:18–19) As in other provinces of the Western Roman Empire, the Spanish Church inherited forms of government and territorial divisions from secular practice. While the first four centuries of Christian life in Spain saw many upheavals and much violence, at least up to the conversion of Constantine (ca. 312), the arrival of the Visigoths brought relative stability, though the conflict between Catholics and Arians lasted until about 600. Constantine, having become a Christian, was concerned about tying the Church to his own authority and control, even in doctrinal matters, Bishop Hosius of Córdoba (see above) being his righthand man. As part of their quest for at least external continuity with their Roman predecessors, the Visigothic kings took an equally active interest, before 589, in Arian councils, and in Catholic ones thereafter.

After 711 such authority moved to Muslim rulers, but as early as the tenth century, a strong attempt was made by the "kings" of Asturias to revive imperial authority, or at least its religious and architectural trappings, in their capital at Oviedo. Now, though, the explicit model was Charlemagne's Aachen (Aix-la-Chapelle), rather than Rome itself. By this time, the pretensions of the bishops of Rome had already begun to seem threatening to "national" churches. From the later eleventh century, the reformed papacy made inroads into the life of the Spanish Church, claiming to control the appointment of its leading bishops and abbots, but Spanish rulers, then and later, had one trump card to play in defense of monarchical rights. This was the Reconquest, the ongoing, but generally sporadic, war against the Muslims. It is sometimes suggested that the first military action to be called a crusade, in the sense that Christian participants "took the Cross" with a papal offer of spiritual benefits in return, was a minor campaign at Barbastro in 1064. In any case, crusading greatly benefited the military and the financial activities of late medieval Spanish monarchs. Not only did foreign crusaders join Castilian and Aragónese forces in direct action against Muslim armies, most notably in the battle of Las Navas de Tolosa (1212), which opened the way to western Andalusia, but successive popes granted to Spanish rulers two-ninths of the ecclesiastical tithe (*tercias reales*) and the income from papal bulls of indulgence (*bulas de la cruzada*), which noncombatants might buy as a substitute for military service. When the final, massive assault took place on the Naṣrid emirate of Granada (1481–1492), all these moral and financial benefits were exploited by Fernando and Isabel to their greatest effect, culminating in these rulers' being declared Catholic Monarchs by Pope Alexander VI Borja (Borgia) in 1496.

As well as repatriating powers over the appointment of senior churchmen and vesting in the king the masterships of the military orders of Santiago, Calatrava, and Alcántara, Isabel and Fernando actively supported reform in the Church. Their efforts to defeat Islam, to expel those Jews who refused to become Christians (after April 1492), and to use the new Spanish Inquisition (1478–1534) to enforce orthodoxy among Judeoconversos, were accompanied by attempts to purify the life of the clergy. They began at the top, using monarchical powers to improve the educational quality and zeal of bishops (Talavera, see above, being a model), and to support movements for reform in the Spanish provinces of the religious orders. Their twofold aim was always to improve discipline and to make traditional structures work properly. In the case of monks and friars, they supported the "observant" movement, which sought to restore the full rigor of founders' rules for religious orders, and also tended to favor spiritual zeal over academic activity. By all these means, the Spanish Church of 1474 to 1516 became more "national" in character, in a way that late Roman emperors and Visigothic and Asturian kings would have recognized. Such trends were to develop even further in the sixteenth century, under Habsburg rule.

The Catholic monarchs were also very interested in improving the religious and moral character of all their subjects, clergy and laity alike, and here the claims of their courtiers and supporters at the time, as well as those of later enthusiasts, from Diego Clemencín in the early nineteenth century to apologists for General Francisco Franco in the mid-twentieth century, were not totally wide of the mark. The whole Trastámaran Dynasty, in its Castilian and Aragónese branches (1368–1516), succeeded in combining religious zeal with a taste for royal absolutism, and actively patronized favored orders, in particular, the Jeronymite and Franciscan friars. This raises the question of the nature of Christian life in medieval Spain, especially in the centuries after 1200, when pressure against the Jewish and Muslim minorities began to increase once again. At the level of organization and official orthodoxy, the Hispanic Church, at least after the restoration of close organic links with the papacy in the late eleventh century, saw itself, and was generally perceived by outsiders, as a bastion of orthodoxy. Yet there is a paradox, in that, although Christianity was perpetually on the defense (and at times offense) against Islam, both within and beyond Spanish boundaries, and was therefore determined to remain strong and vibrant, modern historians have tended to regard most of the Christian population in this period as largely ignorant of the faith. It certainly seems to be true that Spanish Christianity, while following the same doctrinal formulae as the rest of the Western Church, preferred to define itself against the rival monotheistic faiths of Judaism and Islam, rather than in terms of the agonies of late medieval Christian scholasticism. In particular, there is virtually no evidence in Trastámaran Spain of internal doctrinal heresies to match those of the Lollard followers of John Wycliffe in England, or of the Czech Jan Hus in Bohemia, in which such matters as the process of salvation of individual Christians and the nature of the Mass were fiercely contested. Instead, as the work of the Inquisition demonstrated, especially in its new foundation after 1478, official Christianity tended to concentrate on ceremony and practical, external observance. In the case of those converts accused of reverting to Judaism and (after 1500) Islam, this generally meant such things as dietary laws, Jewish Sabbath observance, and Jewish and Muslim ritual bathing. Foreign commentators visiting Fernando and Isabel's Spain, such as the Florentine Francesco Guicciardini (1512), took a similar view of Christianity there, seeing the Church's "Old Christian" members as zealous in outward observance, but weaker in spiritual content. The truth of this is hard to measure, and modern scholars, like the inquisitors before them, are generally forced back on to externals.

Catholic Christianity was undoubtedly and evidently an integral part of the fabric of medieval Spain. The results of the past and current donations of the faithful, from king to peasant, were visible in a network of places of worship—cathedral and collegiate churches, monasteries and friaries, parish churches and (in the later period) chantries, as well as innumerable urban chapels and street images, rural hermitages, and wayside shrines. Much church building took place throughout the period, and over all loomed the mighty European pilgrim center of Santiago de Compostela in Galicia, and the influential Catalan Marian shrine at Montserrat.

It is not possible to calculate the proportion, for example, of Fernando and Isabel's subjects who took clerical orders, many of them minor, or entered religious orders, yet cathedrals were undoubtedly well staffed, as were collegiate and parish churches and the urban churches of the mendicant friars. Wherever possible, liturgical life was elaborate, and took place in churches decorated in a manner that seemed deliberately to defy Jewish and Muslim rejection of religious, and especially anthropomorphic, imagery. Much medieval religious painting still survives, and the treasures of the musical archives of the cathedrals, with their now largely lost choral tradition, are being steadily rediscovered. As elsewhere in western Europe, there was ample opportunity for the laity to participate in public devotion through confraternities, which provided religious and social services for their members. Although Holy Week processions, in their often elaborate modern form, were not to develop fully until later in the sixteenth century, the great summer Eucharistic feast of Corpus Christi was splendidly celebrated, from the late thirteenth century onward. The official liturgical processions, in which the Host, the Body of Christ, was carried in increasingly elaborate monstrances, were accompanied, not by guild mystery plays, as in late medieval England, but by "Moors" and Christians and, in Catalonia, by giants.

What, though, of the "inner" Christian life, with which so many believers north of the Pyrenees were becoming increasingly preoccupied as the year 1500 approached? The basic doctrinal and practical requirements of a lay Christian, in Spain as elsewhere, were limited and formulaic—knowledge, for example, of the Apostles' Creed, the Lord's Prayer, and the Marian *Salve Regina*. But the huge pastoral effort required after 1391, when tens of thousands of former Jews were baptized in a short period as Christians, exposed failings in the Church's efforts to teach its faith to the laity. Of course, knowledge of Christianity might be acquired by many methods other than reading, rote learning, or higher academic study. Paintings and sculpture, liturgy and music, and the indoor and outdoor celebrations of the liturgical year taught the faith, as well as provided social cohesion—and sometimes conflict—as in the anti-converso riots of 1473 in Córdoba, which arose out of a Marian processíon by an Old Christian confraternity. Internal discipline, as administered by the hierarchy, concentrated mainly on the clergy, for example in episcopal visitations in the archdiocese of Valencia in the fourteenth and fifteen centuries, but these, too, focused primarily on discipline and outward practice, as did the ecclesiastical courts, which attempted to police the morality of both clergy and laity. The work of the inquisitors (ca. 1480–1520) often purported to reveal both ignorance of Christianity and violent verbal hostility toward it. Yet outbursts of blasphemy, often expressed in religious terms, may have betokened fury or desperation rather than intellectual disbelief. Religious vocabulary and theological concepts were much readier currency in late medieval Spain than in the twenty-first century, even if they were commonly expressed outside the tortured intellectual frameworks that were favored by professional theologians. The Church of the Catholic Monarchs and Cisneros was a rich (in both a spiritual and a financial sense) but somewhat ramshackle affair. Its demands on lay people were legal and economic, as well as directly religious, in that many people paid their rent and other fees to bishops, churches, and monasteries, as well as supported the clergy (and the secular government) with their tithes and by helping the army along with their *bulas de cruzada*. Undoubtedly, these economic burdens caused popular resentment and tensions between municipal councils and cathedral and collegiate chapters, but religious devotion was nonetheless expressed in rich and diverse forms. All over western Europe, the unease about Christians' relationship with God, in terms of the salvation of their souls, might cause an overanxious preoccupation with physical works as a means of gaining spiritual security. In Spain, there were the additional perceived pressures of Jewish enmity "within" and Muslim enmity "without." In these circumstances, it is perhaps unsurprising that, as the year 1500 (the half-millennium) approached, many Spanish Christians, both "Old" and "New", took refuge in Messianic, and even Apocalyptic, belief and expectation. It was probably natural that Spanish Jews, faced in 1492 with the choice of expulsion or conversion, should have prayed for the arrival of their Messiah, and transportation to the Land of Israel. But Christians, too, from monarchs down to the humblest farm laborer, commonly believed at this time that the great events of conquest in Granada and "discoveries" in the Americas betokened a unique destiny for Spain in the culmination of world history. Belief in the imminent second coming of Christ thus escaped from the devotion of church and cloister, and directly affected Spanish policy at the highest level. In the event the sixteenth century was to bring different upheavals and demands, but without the preparation of the medieval period, the Spanish Church could not have occupied the prominent position, in Europe and the world, that it subsequently attained.

John Edwards

Bibliography

Azcona, T. de. *Isabel la Católica. Estudio crítico de su vida y su reinado*. 3d ed. Madrid, 1993.

Brodman, J. W. *Ransoming Captives in Crusader Spain: The Order of Merced on the Christian-Islamic Frontier*. Philadelphia, 1986.

Burrus, V. *The Making of a Heretic: Gender, Authority, and the Priscillianist Controversy*. Berkeley, 1995.

Cárcel Orti, M. M., and J. V. Boscá Codina. *Visitas pastorales de Valencia (siglos XIV–XV)*. Valencia, 1996.

Cavadini, J. C. *The Last Christology of the West: Adoptionism in Spain and Gaul, 785–820*. Philadelphia, 1993.

Collins, R. *Early Medieval Spain: Unity in Diversity, 400–1000*. London, 1983.

Coope, J. A. *The Martyrs of Córdoba: Community and Family Conflict in an Age of Mass Conversion*. Lincoln, Nebr., and London, 1995.

Cross, F. L, and E. A. Livingstone. (eds.) *Oxford Dictionary of the Christian Church*. 3d ed. Oxford, 1998.

Edwards, J. "Christian Mission in the Kingdom of Granada, 1492–1568," *Renaissance and Modern Studies* 31 (1987), 20–33. Repr. in his *Religion and Society in Spain, c. 1492*. Aldershot, 1996. Chap. 11.

———. "The 'Massacre' of Jewish Christians in Córdoba, 1473–1474." In *The Massacre in History*. Ed. M. Irvine and P. Roberts. New York, 1999. 55–68.

———. "Religious Faith and Doubt in Late Medieval Spain: Soria, *circa* 1450–1500," *Past and Present* 120 (1988), 3–25. Repr. in his *Religion and Society*. Chap. 3.

———. *The Spain of the Catholic Monarchs, 1474–1520*. Oxford, 2000.

Fernández-Armesto, F. "Cardinal Cisneros as a Patron of Printing." In *God and Man in Renaissance Spain: Essays in Honour of J. R. L. Highfield*. Ed. D. W. Lomax and D. Mackenzie. Warminster, England. 1989, 149–68.

Fernández Conde, F. J. *Gutierre de Toledo, obispo de Oviedo (1377–1389): Reforma eclesiástica en la Asturias bajomedieval*. Oviedo, 1978.

García-Villoslada, R. (ed.) *Historia de la Iglesia en España*. Vols. 1–3. Madrid, 1980–81.

Gil, J. *Los conversos y la inquisición sevillana*. Vol. 1. Seville, 2000.

Hillgarth, J.N. *The Mirror of Spain, 1500–1700: The Formation of a Myth*. Ann Arbor, Mich., 2000.

———. *The Spanish Kingdoms, 1250–1516*. 2 vols. Oxford, 1976, 1978.

Levi, A. *Renaissance and Reformation, the Intellectual Genesis*. New Haven, Conn., 2002.

Linehan, P. *History and the Historians of Medieval Spain*. Oxford, 1993.

———. *The Spanish Church and the Papacy in the Thirteenth Century*. Cambridge, 1971.

Nader, H. *The Mendoza Family in the Spanish Renaissance, 1350–1550*. New Brunswick, N.J., 1979.

Nieto, S., and J. M. *Iglesia y génesis del estado moderno en Castilla (1369–1480)*. Madrid, 1994.

Reilly, B. F. *The Contest of Christian and Muslim Spain, 1031–1157*. Cambridge, Mass., 1992.

———. *The Medieval Spains*. Cambridge, U.K. 1993.

Rummel, E. *Jiménez de Cisneros: On the Threshold of Spain's Golden Age*. Tempe, Ariz., 1999.

Valdeón Baruque, J. (ed.) *Isabel la Católica y la política*. Valladolid, 2001.

Wolf, K. B. *Christian Martyrs in Muslim Spain*. Cambridge, 1988.

———. "Muhammad as Antichrist in Ninth-Century Córdoba." In *Christians, Muslims, and Jews in Medieval and Early Modern Spain: Interaction and Cultural Change*. Notre Dame, Ind., 2000. 3–19.

CID, THE *See* *CANTAR DE MIO CID*; DÍAZ DE VIVAR, RODRIGO

CISTERCIANS *See* RELIGIOUS ORDERS

CITEAUX, BENEDICTINE ORDER OF *See* RELIGIOUS ORDERS

CITIES

The Celts and Iberians built fortified settlements in the Iberian Peninsula, and some preclassical urban sites such as Numantia (twenty-four hectares) were extensive. The Greeks added to these, usually coastal trade centers at natural ports, such as Rodes and Empurion (Ampurias, ca. 550 B.C.) in northeastern Spain; and a century later the Carthaginians did the same along the southeastern coast where Carthago Nova (228 B.C.) became the major base for the Punic Wars.

Systematic colonization, however, is most associated with the Romans who, after pushing the Carthaginians out of the peninsula, between 197 and 193 B.C. organized Hispania into two provinces. The largest, Citerior, was governed from Tarragona, ancient Tarraco (hence the Tarraconesis), which would develop port cities at Barcino (Barcelona) and Dentosa (Tortosa); inland cities at Gerunda (Girona), Osoa (Huesca), Illegerta (Lleida), Caesar Augusta (old Salduba, later Zaragoza), and Calagurri (Calahorra); take over Pampaelo (Pamplona); and create a corridor into the interior via Bilbilis (Calatayud), Segontia (Sigüenza), Compluto (Alcalá de Henares), and the border town that would become Segovia. The southern area of old Carthaginensis had port cities at Valentia, Dianium (Denia), and New Cartagena itself. The province of Ulterior, which was an extension of Baetica, made Corduba (Córdoba) a lasting governmental center. The latter province was the most densely populated, having ten indigenous cities that became Roman municipalities and another twenty-six that adopted Roman law but remained semi-autonomous. It included the port cities of Mallaca (Málaga) and Gades (Cádiz), inland Hispalis (Sevilla), and the interior cities of Toletum (Toledo) and Caesarobriga (Talavera). The least urbanized area, the remote frontier of Lusitania, was first controlled from Emerita (Mérida) and became a separate province in 27 B.C. The northern Cantabrians and Asturians were subdued from Legio (León) and Asturica (Asturias) by Agrippa for Octavian, who governed from Tarraco until 24 B.C. By Diocletian's time (the division of the empire in A.D. 284) Roman roads from Salamanca penetrated even Gallaecia to cities at Lucus Augusti (Lugo), Bracara (Braga), Conimbriga (Coimbra), Portucale (Oporto), Scallabi (Santarem), and Olispo (Lisbon), bringing the entire peninsula under the mythical *Pax Romana*.

Just as the concept of urbanization comes from *urbs*, the archetype being Rome itself, the term *municipality* is from the Latin root *munus*—that is, the combined obligation of military service and tribute. The Romans recognized cities both as places and as corporations of citizens having status, rights, and obligations: *foederati* were allies subject to taxes, military service, and Roman law; the *civitates deditatiae* were taxpaying neutrals that retained some autonomy within the burgeoning Roman Empire; and *stipenderiae*, which, like Numantia, had to be taken by force (in this case, a twenty-year campaign), were subjugated and exploited by a burdensome tribute.

The governance and law created by the Romans to assimilate cities into the empire remain the foundation of municipal law, even to this day. Municipal law coalesced into code, the *Ius latii munus*, in A.D. 73 under the emperor Vespasian. It was augmented from practices by the *Constitutio Antoniana* in A.D. 212 when Emperor Antoninus Caracalla imposed uniformity on municipalities as imperial cities. In the multicentury conversion of Roman hegemony from brute subjugation to federation and alliances, such law evolved to accommodate home rule through representative government: the municipal *curia*, modeled after the Roman senate; an executive usually composed of two magistrates (*duumviri*) or judges; and two police captains (*aediles*), who by the end of the empire evolved into *defensorses*. The *urbs* or urban core and a *territorium* comprised a city-state. Inhabitants included self-governing citizens (*cives*); colonists (*coloni*) subject to an external jurisdiction; guests (*hospites*); and slaves.

The late antique cities suffered from the post-Theodosian fragmentation of the empire, and after A.D. 407 civil war racked Hispania. Although many Roman cities were attacked and sacked by the various Germanic invasions after 415, they survived as Hispano-Roman enclaves—many reduced in size—while the nomadic tribes migrated through Spain or occupied outlying areas and the less densely populated highland plains that reminded them of their homeland steppes. Visigothic rule continued Roman municipal law and by the seventh century fused it with Germanic custom in the *Liber iudiciorum* of King Reccesvinth. County government grew at the expense of cities due to the rural preference of the overlords and elevation of the *comes civitatis*. Surviving cities, however, were often ruled by an oligarchy of *villici* or heads of major households. Whereas historians once claimed that the invasions had destroyed the network of Roman municipalities, revisionists see the decline in municipal government as a seventh century phenomenon and an essential continuity in the existence of the most important trade centers as functioning cities. Sánchez Albornoz, for example, has argued for the continuity between old curial government and local assemblies with later councils (*concejos* and *cortes*), which is seen as a tradition of Spanish freedoms (*fueros*), law, and representative government.

The Muslim conquest (711–718), after initially damaging cities such as Tarragona and Barcelona in what was to become a lasting frontier with the Christians where major fighting reoccurred, subsequently reinforced peninsular urbanization. Muslims resurrected the Roman territorial demarcations, identified regional capitals such as the Romano-Visigothic Toledo as their own, and rebuilt such cities as Zaragoza, Tortosa, and Lleida to defend the Upper March. New cities were founded, such as Murcia, built by ʿAbd al-Raḥmān III in 831, or Úbeda; and the Toledan outpost of Machrit founded by the Caliph Muḥammad (852–886) would eventually become Madrid. After an initial invasion by an estimated 35,000 Muslims, there were waves of immigration from the north Africa Maghrib, the Berbers, Slavs, Syrians, and later the Murābiṭ (Almoravid) and Muwāḥḥid (Almohad) invaders, augmented by the recruitment of mercenary armies, the medieval slave trade, and the welcoming of merchant Jews. The Muslims thus overlaid a base population of Hispano-Roman and Visigothic people who in time converted to Islam, the *muwalladūn* (*muladíes*), and tolerated both Jews and Christians, or Mozarabs.

Debate about Muslim urbanization often centers around estimates of city populations exaggerated partially because Christians of the rural north, largely composed of highland tribes and farm communities in the valleys, so marveled at southern cities and the sophistication of the Muslim Mediterranean and old world culture. The demographic research of Torres Balbás is still seminal to such debate. Based on the number of mosques, the enlargement of walled cities, the counting of adjacent gardens or *huertas* that often formed suburban clusters around cities proper, and other inferential data he estimated that during the height of the Umayyad caliphate during the last half of the tenth century, the largest Muslim city, Córdoba, reached slightly above 100,000 inhabitants (in contrast to the wild numbers—up to a half million—once bandied about); it was much greater than the next largest city, Toledo, with 37,000 residents maximum to the lower range of 28,000; Almería and Granada, with approximately 27,000 and 26,000, respectively; and Málaga, Jerez de la Frontera, and Badajoz, which were slightly smaller at 24,000, with the lower estimates for these cities at 20,000. Zaragoza is estimated at 17,000, followed by Valencia at 15,000. Torres Balbás thought that Sevilla's population could not be estimated, but others have ventured the plausible guess of 52,000 at its height. Moreover, these cities changed in size and importance across the centuries with two major African interventions and three periods of *ṭawāʾif ṭāʾifa* parochialism; the Christian Reconquest sent Muslim refugees south and conversely promoted emigration by Mozarabs to the north, as in the case of Alfonso I el Batallador's policy in repopulating lower Aragón after his conquest of Zaragoza in 1118 resulted in a major reduction in its populace. Such migrations from Lleida and Tortosa after 1148 swelled the Mediterranean coastal cities, especially Valencia. Only with Jaime I's conquest of the latter city in 1238, and perhaps earlier with Mallorca, did the Crown of Aragón absorb a large Mudéjar population. Sevilla and Toledo contained large, densely populated Jewish quarters, with perhaps 5,000 and 4,000 residents, respectively; but most Juderías were much smaller: Zaragoza held about 1,200 Jews, Tudela 1,000, and modest cities like Carmona only enclaves of about 200. Overall, the urban-to-rural ratio of population distribution in Muslim Spain before 1348 (i.e., the pre-plague years) has been estimated at 5 to 100 (5 percent).

Muslim city-states were even more centralized than Romano-Visigothic cities because of their large mosques in centers of learning and government, complete with the largest libraries in all Europe—especially that of the Great Mosque in Córdoba. Muslim cities were densely populated, walled enclosures that usually contained a central square, an open-air market, a mosque, a courtyard school, a government house, and a royal residence and court. Outside was the *alfoz* or *terminus*, similar to the Christian *comarca*—territory associated with the urban center. Most cities had extensive waterworks (repaired Roman aqueducts, cisterns and drains, sewers, etc.) and Muslims often maintained citadels (*alcázares*) and refuge castles on an historic Greco-Roman acropolis (e.g., La Zuda at both Lleida and Tortosa); subsidiary castles to protect the lower city and commercial districts; fortified main gates and bridges; and sometimes outlying blockades and earthworks along irrigation ditches, as well as stone terraces and the natural defense of rugged terrain. Throughout their territories,—strategically ringing the city itself—were dependent castles, watchtowers, and nonresident refuges for emergencies. Most of Spain's cities were as formidable to enemies as they were havens to their citizens.

An aristocracy of first-arrival families flourished inside each Muslim city, with an ever larger bureaucracy that tended to be open socially and therefore expanded to include lawyers and theologians loosely associated through various forms of patronage with the court. Urban mobility seems to have increased after 1031 in the absence of the controlling social influence of the caliphate. ʿAbd al-Raḥmān II reorganized municipal government based on the oriental model. Key officers included the *Ṣāḥib al-suq* or *Muḥtasib*, market overseers with extensive judicial authority in civil matters, who may have evolved into *dīwāns* or chief financial officers; the *Ṣāḥib al-madīna* or *Zalmedina* (*senior civitatis* or prefect), a top-ranking public magistrate; judges (*qāḍī*) of all kinds; and the *Ṣāḥib al shurtah* or chief of police who often formed special tribunals and came to control *ṭawā'if* mercenary armies. After the 1090s the Almoravids reverted back to military governorships (*wālī*, or *qā'id* in war zones) to control the *ṭawā'if* kingdoms, and the Almohads used viziers and an extensive network of couriers and inspectors working with local bureaucracies. The Naṣrids of Granada had these officials working in circuits or judicial districts called *kūra* (in, e.g., Guadix, Málaga, and Almería).

Christians brought their fortress mentality to bear on the idea of a city. The law code of the learned king Alfonso X, *Las Siete Partidas*, defined a city simply as a walled enclosure with buildings inside, nothing more. Muslim urbanity, both in size and quality of life, stood in sharp contrast to the predominant rurality of northern Spain, which during most of the Reconquest period could boast of no cities with populations over 2,000. The urban/rural ratio in the Christian population was no more than 1 to 100, meaning that Muslim Hispania was five times more urbanized than the Christian north, not counting the *despoblado* (deserted area) between them. The largest Christian cities of Compostela and Lugo in Galicia; Astorga and León in Castile-León (overlooking Burgos, which as its name implies, was merely a town); Oviedo in Asturias; Pamplona in Navarre; and Barcelona in Catalunya barely reached 1,500 inhabitants each during the eleventh century. The Reconquest was always hampered by a chronic manpower shortage until supplemented by major immigration across the Pyrenees, first through monastic connections and pilgrimage routes to Santiago de Compostela that helped Jaca, Pamplona, Estella, Logroño, Nájera, Burgos, León, Ponferrada, and Lugo as well as Santiago to grow; second, through the twelfth-century Crusades, which brought knights from as far north as Normandy and England who stayed in Spain because of the availability of land to substitute for estates most could never inherit in their homelands, and in cities like Lisbon, Tarragona, and Tortosa, where they benefitted from the spoils of war; and third, through the settlers attracted by the Cistercian monks and other colonizers, and an increasingly international middle-class of merchants and entrepreneurs lured south by the prospects of lucrative trade and fast profit along the war zone. They enlarged towns like Salamanca and Valladolid in the old Duero River frontier, which would become increasingly important cities by the late Middle Ages. Christian kings bestowed lands to a new frontier aristocracy and created new seignorial estates, but after the reconquest of Muslim cities such as Toledo they also offered attractive *fueros* to newcomers who replaced those residents they lost to the wars and emigration; they raided Muslim lands and coaxed Mozarabs there to return with them to Christian territory; they welcomed Andalusian Jews who fled the Almoravid and Almohad takeover of Al-Andalus; and they forged far-flung alliances both for military support and resettlement, as well as for long-term commerce. Rulers retained the Roman obligation of military service from townsmen. Warring kings relied on municipal militias to hold their cities and to operate in nearby territories, as backup for prolonged siege operations, and when attacking to swell their *huestes* with foot soldiers whose slower deployment and ability to dig in and hold ground so necessarily complimented the more rapid manueuvering of knights who initially took it.

When the Christians occupied former Muslim cities they usually rearranged things by rebuilding and taking over the central complex and outlying fortifications, creating military compounds in the cities and giving outposts to the military orders, and forcing inner-city dwellers to relocate to suburbs; but they were anxious to maintain public works, markets, and trade. The expulsion of entire Muslim populations was not preferred treatment; one may gain initially from confiscating the property of exiles, but property by itself does not generate ongoing revenues. Subjects were taxable. Along with Muslim emigration was certain assimilation. Mosques were converted to cathedrals, just as they had risen long before from Roman temples. True to their habit of defining the rural landscape with boundaries, Christians carved cities into seignorial districts and barrios that may have grown naturally as neighborhoods but became more officially delimited as *collationes* or tax collecting circuits that often coincided with tithing districts of *parroquias*. To free themselves of lay control, bishops insisted on their own ecclesiastical space—sometime whole cities, as in the cases of Santiago or Tarragona. In addition to Jews in their *aljamas*, and the Muslim *morerías* for the Moors, other people of like origin and language gathered together into localities within cities (as did the "Franks" in Toledo, whom Alfonso VI recognized as a separate "nation") often centered around their parish churches and linked together through intermarriage, social confraternities (*cofradías*), and trade guilds. Urban societies became more stratified and segregated as they expanded in the late Middle Ages.

In the tradition of Roman municipal law passed through both *fueros* or *franquicias*) and the *Liber iudiciorum*, Luso-Hispanic cities as early as 1020 (e.g., León) resurrected assemblies (the *conventus publicus vicinorum* or *concilium*) for popular representation in government and forums for public discussion, formed municipal councils (*concejos* or *cabildos*) with distinguished advisers (*boni* or *probi-homines*) by virtue of their social status and political delegates (*jurados* or *fieles*), headmen such as consuls (sometimes forming an executive committee or *consulado*), elected mayors (*alcaldes*, from the Arabic *al-qāḍī*, which really means "judge"), and also bred specialized offices such as bailiff with various titles (e.g., *batlle*, *veguer*, etc., in Catalan) and captains (equivalent of the *alférez*) of the local militia, but the administration of justice was often carried out by judges (*iusticia* or *judices*) appointed by counts. In Castile-León after the centralist reforms of Alfonso XI (1312–1350) introduced the *Regimiento*, elected magistrates were replaced by lieutenants appointed by the crown, *regidores* or two *corregidores*, one to keep check on the other. Townsmen usually resisted such royal encroachments, however, and taking their cases to the royal curia or cortes or gaining hearings by the *audiencia* they often bargained freedoms back or negotiated new privileges in exchange for taxes which the kings always needed to conduct their expensive wars.

Reconquest Castile-León grew from perhaps three million people in the eleventh century to a range of four to five million by the fourteenth century; and the Crown of Aragón perhaps grew to a million people. The largest cities in medieval Spain, however, continued to be those in the south. The year 1348, when waves of intermittent plagues first arrived, divides periods of urban development in Spain and Portugal as significantly as did the Reconquest. Catalunya, for example, lost a fourth of its population, and in all regions the cities were the hardest hit. The fifteenth-century census of Alonso de Quintanilla provides data for Granada's 1.5 million households and other sources, including tax records and those of the Inquisition, and telling detail about the impact of the plague, intermittent civil strife, tough economic times, popular religious movements, and social classes and mobility. In one case, for example, Lleida in 1359 is known to have had 5,459 residents after the first wave of plague; by 1497, just after the completion of the peninsular reconquest with the fall of Granada in 1492, this Arago-Catalan city was reduced to 3,362. It continued to decline to a low of 2,353 in the early 1700s, about the same size of Christian cities in the Middle Ages. The hinterland returned to a more rural state while coastal cities such as Barcelona or the Tarragona-Reus metropolitan complex expanded. The same happened along the Cantabrian, Atlantic, and southern Mediterranean coasts. The Catholic Monarchs ruled a united Spain of some nine million people that was still predominantly rural and agrarian, with regional trade centers mostly where they had been since Roman times, and the same cities dominating urban affairs of the peninsula as always, with the notable exception of Madrid.

LAWRENCE MCCRANK

Bibliography

Gutkind, E.A. *Urban Development in Southern Europe: Spain and Portugal*, New York, 1967.

Lacarra, J. M. "Panorama de la historia urbana en la península ibérica desde el siglo V al X." In *Estudios de Alta Edad media española*. Valencia, 1971. 25–65.

Powers, J.F. *A Society Organized for War. The Iberian Municipal Militias in the Central Middle Ages, 1000–1284*. Berkeley, 1988.

Sánchez Álbornoz, C. *Viejos y neuvos estudìos sobre las instituciones medievales españolas*. Madrid, 1976.

Torres Balbás, L. *Ciudades hispanomusulmanas*. 2 vols. Ed. H. Terrasse. Madrid, n.d.

———"Extensión y demografía de las ciudades hispano musulmanas," *Studia Islamica*, 3 (1955), 35–59.

Valdeavellano, L. *Sobre los burgos y los burgueses de la España medieval*. Madrid, 1960. Reprt. as *Orígenes de la burguesía en la España medieval*. Madrid, 1969.

CIVIL SERVICE *See* CENTRAL ADMINISTRATION

CLOTHING

At the beginning of the Middle Ages, the Visigoths introduced some Germanic elements into the classical costume of tunics and cloaks inherited from the Late Roman Empire, such as the *tuburcos*, and femoralia leg coverings.

In the tenth century, coincident with the splendor of the caliphate of Córdoba, Christian miniatures represent a surprising variety of tunics, cloaks and headgear without parallel in the rest of Europe, with Muslim influence evident in some of them.

During the eleventh and twelfth centuries links between Spain and the rest of Europe grew closer and, with the appearance of great Romanesque art and the resurgence of Christianity, a costume was born that was common to the whole western world. The Romanesque costume for both sexes consisted of one or two tunics and a cloak. The inner *brial* tunic was used as a long undergarment, while the outer *piel* or *pellizón* tunic was shorter and lined with fur. Typical of Romanesque costume were the ornamental additions on bodices and sleeves in the Byzantine manner, and a whole range of sleeves that later disappeared. Furs began to be used on a grand scale, and this was to continue. A special feature of Spanish costume were women's headdresses made of bands of entwined or plaited cloth.

Major changes occurred in the thirteenth century, coincident with the early Gothic era. Garments were characterized by their simplicity and comfort. There was no great difference in the clothes of men and women save in their length; men abandoned the down-to-the-heels costume of the previous period. Garments took on much more varied shapes. There was underwear for intimate or home use (*sayas* or *gonelas*), outer garments (*pellotes*), and outdoor clothes for cold weather (*garnachas*). The outer garments and outdoor clothes had a variety of sleeves, including cut-away and hanging sleeves with slits through which one put one's arms. The Romanesque cloaks, knotted on one shoulder, were now substituted by *capas con cuerda*, which allowed more freedom of movement. In headwear the chief novelty was the appearance of the *capirote* (hood), which went through various transformations in subsequent centuries. Although it had great similarities with that of other Christian countries, Spanish dress was remarkable for its originality. Typical Hispanic features were the pellotes, very deeply cut away from arm to hip and two-colored clothes *a metades* (both of these would pass to the rest of Europe during the fourteenth century); the *cosedizas* removable sleeves; cloaks and capes with side openings; feminine shirts embroidered with colored silks, and strangely shaped women's headgear with a parchment frame to which very large bands of plaited cloth were attached.

During the first thirty years of the fourteenth century, the fashions of the thirteenth century were maintained with only a few small novelties, such as the low neckline for dresses, which appeared for the first time. Thereafter, came a period of great change. The men's clothes, reflecting the changes in armour, were now lined with cotton and became gradually shorter and tighter, until a little before 1380 they reached the appearance of the *jaqueta* and the *jubón*. It was a revolution in the history of European dress, because the legs remained entirely uncovered for the first time. Men and women both wore higher necklines, and there was a profusion of small buttons and hanging elements from the elbows and hooded *capirotes*.

During the last years of the fourteenth century and the first years of the fifteenth, fashion seeks out everything that is complex and extravagant: sinuous outlines, and contrast between long and short or tight and loose. Tailoring became an expert art. From then on the variety of garments was such that is not possible to offer, in a short summary, even a brief list of them.

The fifteenth century brought gradual changes from a fashion common to all Christianity to one that was nationally distinctive. The man's costume in Spain followed very closely the fashion centered on the magnificent court of the dukes of Burgundy. The area of the Crown of Aragón also received some small Italian influences. As the century advanced it incorporated some Mauresque elements. Fashions followed one upon another. In the 1420s the masculine silhouette was of rounded and swollen forms, large heads and low waistlines, but around 1430 a new fashion appeared, coexisting for some time with the previous one: the waistline returned to its natural position. A little before midcentury the Burgundian court created a new style that was to impose itself on half of Europe until a little after 1477. In it the man emphasized, above all, slimness and contrast between the wide shoulders and the thin waist and hips; headgears rose, shoes became more pointed, the folds that had covered the costumes from top to bottom with perfect regularity now emphasized verticality. Most notable among outdoor garments was the closed *capuz*, with its hood; it was said to be for Spaniards what the toga had been for the Romans.

Women's dress, though it absorbed Franco-Flemish influences and more infrequently some Italian ones, always interpreted them very freely, and showed an increasing originality as the century progressed. We note as typical Hispanic features a great variety of cloaks of different cut—very short in the first half of the century and later longer; shirts with superimposed *listas* (ribbons) or embroidered *tiras* in the Mauresque manner; *cofia de tranzado* (headgear with a lining adorned with ribbons enveloping the platt); *chapines* (shoes with thick cork heels); and *verdugos* (hoops that filled out skirts). Several of these fashions passed on to other European countries during the Renaissance.

CARMEN BERNÍS-MADRAZO

Bibliography

Bernís, C. *Indumentaria medieval española*. Madrid, 1956.

———."La moda y las imágenes góticas de la Virgen. Claves para su fechación," *Archivo Español de Arte* 43 (1971), 193–218.

———. "Las pinturas de la Sala de los Reyes de la Alhambra. Los asuntos, los trajes, la fecha," *Cuadernos de la Alhambra* 18 (1982), 21–50.

———. *Trajes y modas en la España de los Reyes Católicos.* 2 vols. Madrid, 1978–79.

Menéndez-Pidal, G. "Traje, aderezo, afeites." In *La España del siglo XIII leída en imágenes*. Ed. Real Academia de la Historia. Madrid, 1986. 51–103.

COFRADÍA

The word *confraternity* or *cofradía* assumed diverse meanings during the medieval centuries. An association organized for fraternal and charitable purposes, a confraternity could also be intended to advance the economic and professional interests of its members. Confraternities begin to appear in important numbers from the twelfth century onward. Initially they were religious in origin, and were often composed of the residents of a parish or dependents of a monastery. The Cofradía de Frontarya y Lillet in Catalonia appeared at the end of the eleventh century, while in the twelfth the Cofradía de Santa Cristina of Tudela made its appearance. Also in the twelfth century Alfonso I of Aragón (1106–1134) organized the confraternity of Belchite for the defense of that newly recaptured position. A similar confraternity was organized at Uncastillo. To some extent the emergence of confraternities of this type anticipated the organization of the Spanish military orders in the second half of the twelfth century.

In the twelfth and thirteenth centuries, as industrial activity began to increase in volume, confraternities were organized in towns for economic and political purposes. These guilds or *gremios* were associations of workers and artisans interested in monopolizing their trade or craft and protecting themselves from external competition. The confraternity of muleteers (*recueros*) of Atienza and that of the shopkeepers (*tenderos*) of Soria were among the earliest to be established. Often members of a confraternity lived in the same street, as the street names in many older sections of Spanish cities still testify; and worshiped in the same parish church. That closeness enhanced their bonds of community and enabled them to carry out their activities more easily. The municipal *fueros* (statutes) of the eleventh and twelfth centuries often regulated the activities of working men and women, as did the later enactments of the *cortes* (parliament). Royal attitudes toward confraternities in Castile tended to be negative at first unless those associations existed only for religious and charitable purposes. Both Fernando III and Alfonso X condemned wicked associations (*cofradías malas* and *ayuntamientos malos*), that were seen as a detriment to royal authority. Alfonso X forbade merchants and artisans to fix prices and demanded that they sell their products on the open market. Also condemned was the tendency to reserve places in the craft to family members, as noted in the *Siete Partidas*.

In Aragón similar attempts were made to restrain the guilds, but in Catalonia, where the industrial middle class was more fully developed than elsewhere, guilds were more successful. The crown authorized their existence and in 1337 Pedro IV granted the towns the right to establish and to regulate guilds. Despite those strictures confraternities or guilds with a distinctly economic aim continued to appear, and by the close of the Middle Ages were found in most important towns. In the course of time they also endeavored to limit admission to their organization thereby effectively sharing the profits of their enterprise among fewer people. In 1389, for example, the artisans of Barcelona required that a prospective member demonstrate his fitness by proving that he had the necessary financial resources. He could either pay a substantial admissions fee or display a shop full of goods that he may have just acquired. Sons of masters were exempt from these obligations, and outsiders had to pay a doubled entrance fee. The apothecaries of Barcelona limited to two the number of new masters admitted each year and required an examination of their technical qualifications as well as payment of the fee. As happened elsewhere in Europe, an urban oligarchy gained control not only of municipal government but also of trade. Juan I of Aragón, for example, authorized the merchants of Barcelona to establish a council that would oversee trade and resolve commercial conflicts. As a consequence, the opportunity of the ordinary workingman to establish himself as an autonomous master craftsman with his own shop was greatly curtailed. The great divide between the urban oligarchs and ordinary workers often led to social upheavals in the towns.

Anyone seeking admission to a confraternity was first required to swear an oath to uphold the interests of the association. A general assembly or *cabildo general* brought all the brothers together to deliberate on rules and regulations, the appointment of inspectors who would guarantee good workmanship, and the election of officials. The principal officials, usually numbering one to three, were called *prebostes*, *mayordomos*, *mayorales*, or *priores*, and were ordinarily assisted by a committee of assessors. From time to time the confraternity might draw up ordinances regulating its affairs, as did the shoemakers' guild of Burgos in 1259. With the consent of the municipal council, ordinances were drafted providing for the taking of apprentices and the use of suitable materials under city inspection. These tended to become more detailed in the later medieval centuries. From time to time the king confirmed such ordinances, usages, and privileges, as Alfonso X did for the textile workers of Seville and Soria. The ordinances usually provided for the peaceful resolution of conflicts among the brothers and the imposition of fines on those who neglected to abide by the regulations of the guild. No matter what the varying purposes of confraternities may have been, each had a religious aim, each had a patron saint whose feast day was observed by solemn attendance at mass in the saint's honor, usually followed by a banquet. The brothers also were expected to take care of sick members, visiting them, observing the administration of the last rites of the church, attending the burial ceremonies, and commemorating the deceased in regular prayers. If a member was incapacitated, others would take his place at work and provide economic assistance for him and his family. Aged family members, widows, and orphans were all taken care of and dowries were provided for poor girls.

JOSEPH F. O'CALLAGHAN

Bibliography

Dufourcq, C.E., and J. Gautier-Dalché, *Historia económica y social de la España cristiana en la Edad Media*. Barcelona, 1983.

COINAGE AND CURRENCY, ARAGÓN

With monetary antecedents during the Iberian and Roman eras, the Visigoths established a few mints in the region, the mint of Zaragoza being the most productive.

After the Arabic invasion, Christian currencies were initiated by Sancho el Mayor (1000–1035), when Aragón was part of the Navarrese kingdom. Sancho's successor, García III (1035–1054), issued *vellón* coins with inscriptions reading "ARA-GON". These coins were minted in Jaca, giving them the name *dineros jaqueses*, a term that would continue even when production moved to Zaragoza. In the zone occupied by the Arabs, the mint of Zaragoza was especially active during the tā'ifa period (eleventh century).

Aragón regained independence in 1076, also gaining control of Navarre. The coins issued were exclusively the dineros jaqueses, although at the beginning of the twelfth century the gold *morabetín* of Almoravide origin was also used. King Sancho Ramírez (1063–1094) issued a gold coin called the *mancús de Jaca*, but it seems to have only been used in the payment of tributes to the pope.

The vellón coin, minted exceptionally in Monzón and Sarifiena, was the only legal circulating coin from the mid-thirteenth century to the early fifteenth century. Aragón's union with Catalonia in 1137 would not change this plan. Pedro III (1336–1387) did issue gold *florines* in Zaragoza during a period of three years, but production ceased because the Aragónese citizens rejected the florin, preferring their own coins. Weak commercial activity before the fifteenth century did not lead Aragón to adopt coins of a higher value; in addition, with one type of coin (the jaqués), speculation associated with trade and exchange was avoided.

From the mid-fifteenth century gold *ducados* and silver *reales* were issued in Aragón, but their influence was of little significance. In the Teruel region in the fifteenth century, Valencian coins circulated as a solution to the weak value of the Aragónese currency; contracts, however, were still stipulated in terms of the jaqués, which was the legal currency. Throughout the Middle Ages, payments in kind continued to be made, particularly for annual taxes.

M. CRUSAFONT i SABATER AND ANNA M. BALAGUER

Bibliography

Balaguer, A.M. "La moneda de oro del Reino de Aragón en las Edades Media y Moderna," *Acta Numismática* 13 (1983), 137–65.

Beltrán, P. *Obra Completa*. Vol. 2, *Numismática de la Edad Media y de los Reyes Católicos*. Zaragoza, 1972.

Crusafont i Sabater, M. "La circulación monetaria en el Aragón medieval a partir de las menciones documentales," *Gaceta Numismática* 114 (1994), 55–76.

———. *Numismática de la Corona Catalano-Aragónesa Medieval*. Madrid, 1982.

Crusafont i Sabater, M., and A.M. Balaguer. "La numismática navarro-aragonesa alto medieval: Nuevos hipótesis," *Gaceta Numismáatica* 81 (1986), 35–66.

COINAGE AND CURRENCY, CASTILE

There is no evidence that before the eleventh century the rulers of León and Castile coined money. Transactions that were made in money apparently utilized Islamic gold and silver coins. The first indisputable evidence for a royal coinage emerges during the reign of Alfonso VI (1065–1109), who minted billons (*vellónes*) of *denarii* of alloyed silver. Originating from the monetary reforms of Charlemagne, the billon *denarius* was the coin common throughout feudal Europe in this period. Because it was lower in value than the Islamic silver *dirhem*, it was more useful for common, daily transactions. This convenience, combined undoubtedly with royal insistence, helped the denarius eclipse the use of Islamic *dirhem*, in twelfth-century Castile-León, although Islamic gold continued to circulate. The Almoravids had introduced a reliable gold piece, the *morabetino*, which Castile adopted as a standard of value. While payment was made in either gold or its billon equivalent, prices were normally quoted in morabetinos.

In relation to the morabetino, the denarii, or dineros, of Castile-León gradually declined in value. True to their Carolingian heritage, dineros were counted in groups of twelve, called *solidii* or *sueldos*. By 1217, the morabetino in Castile was worth 7.5 *sueldos* of *dineros burgaleses* (90 coins) or 15 *sueldos* of the debased *dineros pepiones* (180 coins). In the then separate kingdom of León, it was worth 8 *sueldos* of *dineros leoneses* (96 coins). As the value of gold in terms of billon coins continued to rise, another method of counting emerged: the morabetino of account. Defined as 90 burgaleses or 96 leoneses, the morabetino of account was a fixed number of billon coins that did not fluctuate with the market price of the gold morabetino.

In the second half of the thirteenth century, a series of a billons of coins, each intrinsically weaker than its predecessor, drove older coins out of circulation and decreased the value of the morabetino of account. Between 1264 and 1268, Alfonso X (1252–1284) minted the *blanca*, or *moneda de la guerra*, a denarius with one-third less silver than the burgalés. He later issued the *prieto*, a coin declared to be worth 6 blancas but intrinsically equal to only 4. A second, weaker 6-denarius coin appeared by 1279. It was also called a blanca, so the original blanca came to be called a blanquilla. In theory, the morabetino of account in 1280 was made up of 90 blanquillas (or 96 of the same blanquillas in Leon), but it was usually composed of 15 *seisenes*, coins worth 6 denarii apiece.

The *cornado*, a 9-denarius piece or *noven*, appeared in the early years of Sancho IV (1284–1295). There were, then, 10 *cornados* counted to the *morabetino* but these contained less silver than 15 seisenes. Fernando IV (1295–1312), in turn, issued a new noven weaker than the cornado. To halt the disappearance of the old money, Fernando retariffed the coinage in 1303. Keeping his own coin fixed at 9 denarii, he raised the value of his father's noven, the cornado, to 15 denarii and the second blanca to 12. As a result of this reform, there were now 6 cornados to the theoretical morabetino of 90 denarii. Though repeatedly debased throughout the next 150 years, the noven and cornado remained the basic billon denominations of medieval Castile. In the fifteenth century, the morabetino was still defined as 6 cornados or 10 novenes, the latter often called simply dineros. Additionally, a new blanca appeared under Enrique II (1369–1379) with a value of 2 per morabetino, and continued to be minted by his successors.

The fourteenth century also saw the introduction of a new series of gold and silver coins. When the Islamic world ceased producing the morabetino, Alfonso VIII (1158–1214) prolonged its hegemony in Castile by minting his own gold *morabetino alfonsí*. At the same time, the Almohad gold piece, known as the *dobla*, was entering Castile. The Castilian crown probably ceased minting morabetinos by the 1260s and was regularly minting doblas by the reign of Alfonso XI (1312–1350). His successors continued to strike doblas and sometimes added larger denominations, such as the 10-dobla piece. Alfonso XI had originally fixed the full *dobla* at a value of 35 morabetinos of account. In 1435, however, the market price was between 85 and 96 morabetinos.

Pedro I (1350–1369) introduced the *real*, a coin of almost pure silver originally valued at 3 morabetinos. According to the documents, its weight and fineness were scrupulously maintained into the reign of Fernando and Isabel. Originally worth 3 morabetinos, the real commanded 8 morabetinos current billon in 1442. Though these silver and gold issues helped fulfill the demands of an economy increasingly involved in long-distance trade, the heart of the Castilian monetary system remained the morabetino of billon to which all other monetary values were tied.

James J. Todesca

Bibliography

Domingo Figueroa, L. and A. M. Balaguer. "Ordenación cronológica de las emisiones monetarias de Pedro I y de Enrique II," *Numisma* 28 (1978), 421–48.

MacKay, A. *Money, Prices and Politics in Fifteenth-Century Castile*. London, 1981.

Todesca, J. "The Monetary History of Castile-León (ca. 1100–1300) in Light of the Bourgey Hoard," *American Numismatic Society Museum Notes* 33 (1988), 129–203.

COINAGE AND CURRENCY, CATALONIA

Catalonia was the chief port of entry for money in the Iberian Peninsula. In the fourth century B.C., the Greeks minted coins in their colonies in Rhodes and Emporion; the coins of the Iberian tribes, who were later Romanized, were derived from these Greek coins. The official issuing of Roman money in the peninsular capital, Tarraco, marks a final point in the first century A.D.

The Visigoths issued their gold *trientes* in Roses, Girona, Barcelona, Tortosa, and Tarragona, but only the mint in Tarragona achieved any prominence.

The minting of coins, interrupted by the Arabic Conquest (714), was renewed around 800 with the French invasion of the northern half of the peninsula. Charlemagne issued silver money in Barcelona, Girona, Empúries, and Roses. His successor, Louis the Pious (814–840), would do the same in Barcelona,

Empúries, and Roses, while Charles the Bald (840–877) would only issue money in Barcelona. Throughout the tenth century, Carolingian territories were converted into *condados* (counties) and independent domains, with each region producing its own currency. These territories included Barcelona, Urgell, Empúries, Cerdanya, Rosselló, Besalú, and Pallars, as well as the dioceses of Vic and Girona and the viscountship of Cardona. This mosaic of territories was later annexed to Barcelona, the most active center, and the various coins soon disappeared, substituted by the Barcelona currency. This reunifying process was well underway in the twelfth century, though it did not conclude until the beginning of the fifteenth century.

From the tenth to the thirteenth centuries, circulating money consisted of coins of *vellón*, a silver-copper alloy, although in the eleventh and twelfth centuries gold Arabic coins also circulated: the *dinar* of the caliphate (tenth through eleventh centuries) and the *morabetín* of the Almoravide dynasty (twelfth century). The crisis that affected the issue of the Arabic gold coins during the tā'ifa period (eleventh century) was solved in Barcelona by minting imitations of the *dinar*—some coins even displayed part of the legend in Latin, displaying the name of the count, Raimundus Comes.

By the end of the thirteenth century the vellón coins of Barcelona were practically the only coins in circulation. The union with Aragón (1137) and the conquests of Mallorca (1229) and Valencia (1240) would lead to the creation of a political unit governed by only one sovereign, in which coins with several different engravings, but the same value, circulated. With Alfonso I (1162–1196) this currency was the *quatern* (33 percent silver) and with Jaime I (1213–1276), the *tern* (25 percent silver). This monetary correlation would also reach Provençe, then a territory of the Catalan monarchy.

Between the end of the thirteenth and the middle of the fourteenth century, the monetary system was broadened as a consequence of territorial expansion (the annexation of Sicily, Cerdeña, and later Naples) and rapid economic growth. The year 1285 saw the introduction of the *croat*, a silver coin with the value of twelve tern coins, followed by the 1340 appearance of the gold *florín* (a copy of the Florentine prototype worth eleven croat coins), which was stabilized at a moderate purity of eighteen carats (75 percent gold) in 1365. From then on, with the growing presence of the croat and the florín, the circulating currency was bimetallic, consisting of silver and gold coins.

With the Mediterranean expansion, the monetary system began to use one gold coin common to all countries, the florín, and a silver coin with different engravings and names (*ral, pirral, croat*), but with the same value as the croat of Barcelona. The vellón coin, the small change of everyday life, would, however, undergo different changes in each kingdom. Only Aragón, which was less developed commercially, would escape this general scheme; until the end of the fifteenth century it would continue using a system made up exclusively of a vellón coin called the *jaqués*.

In the fifteenth century several transformations took place: the florín of uniform marking and low purity would be replaced by the *ducado*, a Venetian-derived coin of high purity (98.97 percent gold) that adopted different markings in each kingdom. The silver coin continued to be used, following the croat model of Barcelona. A crisis originating in the fourteenth century prevented further minting of the vellón coin, though its value continued to be used as the reference for all payments that were made with the tern and its multiples: the *sueldo* (twelve tern) and the *libra* (twenty sueldos). The interest in maintaining the value of those payments made reducing the value of the tern undesireable, but the tendency to lower its value in other neighboring countries, along with the presence of other stronger coins (the florín and the croat), made the devaluation necessary. For a while the mints stopped producing the tern, which created a serious shortage of petty change that was resolved by the municipality's decision to mint coins locally. In the late fifteenth century, authorities decided to diminish the value of the vellón coin by half, but the shortage of small change and the recourse of minting local coins subsisted until the seventeenth century.

Despite these changes, Catalan money was characterized by great stability relative to the currency of many European countries and especially that of Castile, where the florín of the Catalan-Aragónese kingdom was at times used as a point of reference for establishing value. The croat was, nevertheless, the coin that experienced the most stability, and was Catalonia's preferred means of carrying out their extensive commercial activities in the Mediterranean.

Miguel Crusafont i Sabater and
Anna M. Balaguer

Bibliography

Balaguer, A.M. *Del mancús a la dobla. Or i paries d'Hispània.* Barcelona, 1993.

Botet i Sisó, J. *Les monedes catalanes.* 3 vols. Barcelona 1808–1811.

Crusafont i Sabater, M. *Barcelona i la moneda Catalana.* Barcelona, 1989.

———. "Del morabatín almorávide al florín. Continuidad o ruptura en la Cataluña medieval," in *I Jarique de Estudios Numismáticos Hispano-Arabes* (1988), 191–200.

———. *Numismática de la Corona Catalano-Aragónesa Medieval.* Madrid, 1982.

COINAGE AND CURRENCY, LEÓN

In the northwestern zone of the Iberian Peninsula, known in the Middle Ages as the kingdom of León, there was no ancient precedent for issuing currency, except for the presence of a roving Roman workshop in the Cantabrian-Asturian and Galician regions during the Cantabrian wars of the first century A.D.

The Suevi tribes that settled in the region (fifth century) were the first to mint money there. After the Visigothic Conquest (585), they continued to issue; money and open many new mints, with twenty-five within the Galician-Asturian-Leonese zone, including one each in León, Salamanca, Sanabria, Lugo, Túy, and Orense. These, however, were short-lived.

The entry of the Arabs marked the beginning of a long period without monetary issue. This continued even after the consolidation of the Asturian-Leonese monarchy, and we have no indication of the fabrication of money until the reign of Fernando I (1035–1065). There are various hypotheses as to how payments were made; the validity of a barter economy, however, can only explain in part the absence of currency in a society in which the concept of money is very much a reality, as documents show. One theory is that Visigothic, Swabian, and even Late Roman currencies survived, but it has been shown that Roman and Swabian coins did not last through the Visigothic era, and that Visigothic money was only used for fifty years at most. This all indicates that the term *solidos gallecanos* in Leonese documents of the eighth and ninth centuries does not refer to these monetary systems. Documents show that from the eighth century until the early eleventh century the only coins that circulated in León were gold and silver coins from al-Andalus.

The first uniquely Leonese money seems to have been issued during the reign of Fernando I, who united Castile and León; but until Alfonso VI (1073–1109), there is no completely reliable data concerning the production of money in these kingdoms. There are several known types of *vellón* coins that were issued by Alfonso in León and Toledo. He also granted the Cathedral of Santiago de Compostela a license to mint coins to fund the construction of its church. His successor, Urraca (1109–1126), would make similar concessions to various monasteries, including Sahagún and San Antolín de Palencia. The monetary issues continued with Alfonso VII (1126–1157). With his death the kingdom separated again, with Fernando II succeeding him in León (1157–1188); Fernando issued gold coins in the region for the first time, a significant event in a territory whose circulating money consisted exclusively of vellón coins and gold coins of Arabic origin. This new currency was the Leonese *maravedí*, with a pattern similar to the Arabic *morabetín* and to Castilian coins (the Alfonsine *maravedí*) that imitated the morabetín. The Leonese maravedí was exceptional in that it was the first gold coin of Christian appearance and Latin text minted in Western Europe; its Romanesque design is particularly notable. Alfonso IX (1188–1230) also issued the maravedí, and many new mints were established to issue vellón coins. In 1202 a coinage tax was introduced to compensate for the promise not to alter coin quality during a period of seven years. Alfonso IX was succeeded by Fernando III (1230–1252), who reunited the kingdoms of León and Castile definitively. From then on the uniqueness of the Leonese currency disappeared; a uniform Castilian-Leonese coin was introduced, whose only distinguishing mark was that of the mint, a few of which were located in the former kingdom of León.

The currency of León consisted basically of indigenous vellón coins and of Arabic gold coins. Several discoveries of coins originating from the other side of the Pyrenees show the importance of the pilgrim route of Santiago de Compostela throughout the Middle Ages.

ANNA M. BALAGUER

Bibliography

Balaguer, A. M. "Estudio de los hallazgos de la Vía Compostelana," *Gaceta Numismática*, forthcoming.

———. "Statutes Governing Coinage in Iberian Kingdoms during the Middle Ages." In *Problems of Medieval Coinage in the Iberian Area*. Santarem, 1984, 121–138.

Heiss, A. *Descripción de las monedas hispano-cristianas desde la invasión de los árabes*. Vol. I. Madrid, 1865.

Orol Pernas, A. *Acuñaciones de Alfonso IX*. Madrid, 1982.

COINAGE AND CURRENCY, MALLORCA

The only currency issued during the ancient era was the unique Punic coin on the island of Eivissa, which survived into the Roman age during Claudius I's reign (A.D. 41–54).

The medieval era begins with the issuing of Arabic coins during the tā'ifa period in Mallorca and Menorca, followed by Almoravide and Almohade currencies used until the Christian conquest of the islands.

After the conquest of Mallorca (1228), Jaime I introduced a coin of *tern* quality (25 percent silver), also used in Valencia. With the bequeathment of Mallorca to the king's son, Jaume II (1276–1311), an independent kingdom was created, incorporating in addition other territories like the *condados* of Rosselló and Cerdaña, where the kingdom's capital, Perpignan, was located. Although the independent kingdom had to recognize the supremacy of Catalonia-Aragón, it developed its own monetary system inspired by French models. This system was established between 1300 and 1310 with three basic currencies: the gold *real*, the silver *real*, and the *dobler*, made of *vellón*. An erroneous exchange rate between the silver real and the vellón coin caused the speculative emigration of the Mallorcan silver coin, with a foreign silver coin circulating in its place. The gold coin was minted in small quantities, making it almost of more symbolic worth than monetary.

The last monarch of the independent kingdom, Jaume III (1324–1343), moved the mint to Perpignan, where he issued coins modeled after Italian and French coins (the *florín* and the *gros tornés*, respectively), as well as exclusively Mallorcan models.

Pedro III (1336–1387) recovered the kingdom in 1343, maintaining the Mallorcan monetary system for a while. With Juan I (1387–1396) and Martín I (1396–1410), the currency was aligned with that of other territories in the Catalan-Aragónese kingdom, with the introduction of the gold *florín* and the reconciliation of the silver real's value. The indigenous vellón coin, however, continued to be used. With Fernando II (1479–1516) the gold *ducado* was adopted, as it was in the rest of the kingdom. To solve the problems with the silver real, coins of low monetary value were established to make their exportation more difficult.

MIGUEL CRUSAFONT I SABATER

Bibliography

Campaner, A. *Numismática Balear*, Palma de Mallorca, 1879.

Crusafont i Sabater, M. *Numismática de la Corona Catalano-Aragónesa Medieval*. Madrid, 1982.

———. "Jaume III de Mallorca (1324–1343), veritable creador del florí català," *Acta Numismatica* 15 (1985), 203–18.

———. "Problems of Chronology in the Coinages of the Catalan-Aragónese Crown: The Series of the Florins of Majorca Issued in the Name of Martí." In *Problems of Medieval Coinage in the Iberian Area*. Avilés, 1986. 103–40.

COINAGE AND CURRENCY, MUSLIM

No sooner had the Muslims begun their conquest of the Iberian Peninsula in 711 than they struck coins bearing the message of their faith. Depending on relations with the caliphate (Umayyad, 660–750, and Abbasid, 750–1258), as well as other factors, these coins vary, in legend and medium (gold, silver or, less frequently, copper), from age to age according to the following chronological schema:

1. The Emirate, 711–929
   a) The period of domination by the caliphate of Damascus, 711–750
      i) Latin-Muslim coins, 711–718 (gold);
      ii) Arabic coins (gold to 722, silver thereafter)
   b) The period of the independent emirate, 750–929 (silver)
2. The caliphate of Córdoba, 929–1031 (predominantly silver)
3. The *ṭā'ifa* rulers, 1031–1094 (predominantly silver, some gold)
4. The first Berber rule: the Almoravids, 1094–1143 (predominantly gold, some silver)
5. The second Berber rule: the Almohads, 1143–1212 (predominantly gold, some silver)
6. The Naṣrids of Granada, 1238–1492 (gold, silver, and copper)

It is obvious from this schema that as soon as the Muslims of the Iberian peninsula severed their relations with the caliphate of Baghdad shortly after 750, the supply of gold dried up and the autonomous rulers of al-Andalus had to depend on silver and copper as the metal of fiscal exchange. Gold returned to al-Andalus with the arrival of the Almoravids.

The standard weight of the golden *dinar* was 4.25 grams, although many pieces fell short of this ideal. The Almohads reduced the standard weight to 2.3 grams but struck a dinar double the weight, averaging 4.50 grams (known to modern numismatists as the *dobla*). This double dinar was also adopted by the Naṣrids.

With the exception of the coins of the Almohads and the Naṣrids, the distribution of the legends on the obverse and the reverse was more or less uniform: an inscription of several lines occupied the field and a circular legend was inscribed around the perimeter. On one side (the obverse) the legends (field and circle) were primarily religious in nature, while on the other side (the reverse) they appertained to details of state: the name or title of the ruler, in the field, and date and place of the mint, along the circular margin. Variations from this standard were employed as necessitated by the changing political scene.

The religious legends showed a great degree of minting conservatism. Passages were drawn from the Qur'ān to convey the basic tenets of the faith. The legends on the earliest coins known to us so far were in Latin and contained a condensed translation of some of the Arabic legends appearing on contemporary coins of the Muslim rulers in Syria, at that time the political heartland of Islam. The circular legend on the obverse of the earliest of these coins (dated A.H. 93/A.D. 712 and Indiction X) reads as follows: *INNDINN D SNSDSSLSNDSA* (*IN Nomine DominI NoN Deus NiSi DeuS SoLuS Non DeuS Alius*), condensing the translation of *bism Allāh lā ilāha illa Allāh waḥdaḥu lā ṣarīka lahu* ("In the Name of God. There is no deity other than God, alone, without compare"). The circular legend on the reverse identified the mint as *SPN* (Spania). Shortly thereafter (A.H. 98/A.D. 717), Arabic legends replaced the Latin and the name *Spania* was replaced by *Al-Andalus*. The circular legend on these Arabic coins affirmed the prophethood of Muḥammad, citing Qur'ānic passages that say "Muḥammad is the Apostle of God. He sent him with the guidance and the true religion despite the aversion of disbelievers." The religious legends were changed with the arrival of the Almoravids. The new legend in the field (on the obverse) contained the testimony of faith, "There is no deity other than God, Muhammad is the Apostle of God." Far more interesting, and inadvertently alarming to the Christians of the peninsula (the legend was initially directed against the Shiʿa Muslims of North Africa), was the circular legend in which the Qur'ānic verse was quoted, "Who so seeks a religion other than Islam, it shall not be accepted from him and in the Hereafter he shall be among the losers." The change in the distribution of the legends on the coins of the Almohads and Naṣrids led to an abandonment of earlier circular religious legends in favor of an occasional selection of other Qur'ānic statements or none at all.

The Muslim coinage of al-Andalus circulated throughout Christian Europe. This is particularly true of the period of the Almoravids and the Almohads, when gold was used extensively in minting coins. Having tapped the sources of gold in West Africa, these Berber dynasties minted coins that became the envy of their Christian enemies to the extent that Rome demanded that church dues owed by several European ecclesiastical provinces (including England, France, Germany, and Italy) were to be paid in *morabetinos*, the golden dinars minted by the Almoravids or their Spanish Christian imitators (Alfonso VIII), or in *doblas*, the double dinars of the Almohads.

HANNA E. KASSIS

Bibliography

Sáenz-Díez, J.I. (ed.) *I Jarique de numismática hispano-árabe*. Zaragoza, 1988.

———. *II Jarique de numismática hispano-árabe*. Lleida, 1990.

———. *III Jarique de numismática hispano-árabe*. Madrid, 1992.

Vives y Escudero, A. *Monedas de las dinastías Arábigo-Españolas*. Madrid, 1893; repr. 1978.

COINAGE AND CURRENCY, NAVARRE

Currency was introduced in Navarre by the ancient Iberians, who minted silver and gold; Roman currency was subsequently issued. During the Visigothic era, however, we do not encounter monetary workshops, perhaps because the region, populated by the Vascons, was involved in constant rebellion against the Visigothic monarchy.

The production of currency was renewed with Sancho el Mayor (1000–1035), who issued coins of *vellón* with inscriptions reading IMPERATOR and NAVARA. The region's domination of Aragón is manifest in the coins that existed during the reign of Sancho's son and successor, García (1035–1054), which include some coins reading NAVARA and others reading ARAGON. This dependency shifts with Sancho Ramírez de Aragón, who took over the Aragónese hegemony in 1076. With Sancho and his successors, Pedro (1094–1104) and Alfonso (1104–1134), we find some coins with the inscription NAVARA in the name of Sancho, and others with ARAGONENSIS that could easily have been produced in Navarre. The Arabs of the *ṭāʾifa* period (eleventh century) issued money in Tudela.

With García el Restaurador (1134–1150), Navarre regained independence, and the inscription NAVARA reappeared on the vellón coins.

The Navarrese coins came to be known as *sanchetes* because of the proliferation of kings named Sancho. The sanchete was circulated exclusively in Navarre, except during the period from 1120 to 1250 when the Almoravide *morabetín* circulated to some extent.

The French dynasty (1284–1349) introduced the *torneses* into Navarrese circulation; they were coins of a value inferior to the sanchete. The representative classes ended up agreeing to accept the torneses as comparable to the sanchete, explaining the expression "sanchetes y torneses mezclados" found in documents. The vellón coin was kept in circulation from 1250 until the second half of the fourteenth century, when the gold *florín* (initially the Aragónese version) began to gain prominence.

In this middle period, and despite the various monetary issues made by Carlos el Malo (1349–1387), there are no other species of coin detected other than the *vellón*, which was now called the *carlín*. Initially, the carlín was of high purity (*carlines blancos*), but was soon issued in a lower purity worth half the value of the sanchete (*carlines prietos/negros*).

In the fifteenth century the scope of the gold coin grows and is eventually used in almost half of all documented payments. During this period, indigenous gold coins began to be circulated; we also find the first references to silver carlines.

With Fernando II (1513–1516), the circulating currency would follow the model of the gold *ducado* and the silver *real*; the vellón, however, would conserve its own Navarrese design throughout the Modern Era.

MIGUEL CRUSAFONT I SABATER

Bibliography

Crusafont i Sabater, M. *Acuñaciones de la Corona Catalano-Aragónesa y de los Reinos de Aragón y Navarra.* Madrid, 1992.

———. "La circulación monetaria en la Navarra medieval," *Numisma* 230 (1992), 93–118.

Crusafont i Sabater, M., and A. M. Balaguer. "La numismática navarro-aragonesa alto medieval. Nuevos hipótesis," *Gaceta Numismática* 81 (1986), 35–66.

COINAGE AND CURRENCY, VALENCIA

Ancient currencies in Valencia consisted of Iberian issues, first with Punic influence, then Roman. After a considerable gap in monetary production, the Visigoths issued coins in Sagunto and Valencia, but in negligible quantities. Monetary production was renewed decisively with the Arabs, starting specifically with the age of the tā'ifa (eleventh century). The Muslims issued gold and silver coins in the city of Valencia and also minted coins in Denia, Alpont, Elda and Játiva.

After the conquest of Valencia, Jaime I of Catalonia-Aragón created the *reial de Valencia* (1246), shared by the kingdom of Mallorca. It was of the same purity as the *tern* (25 percent silver), with a value equivalent to the coins of Barcelona and of Aragón. With Jaime II (1291–1327), money was issued in Alicante, a former Castilian territory conquered by Murcia. When it was incorporated into the kingdom of Valencia, Alicante adopted the Valencian currency.

Pedro III (1336–1387) first issued the gold *florín* in Valencia, but until Juan I (1327–1396) there was no coin minted with a silver content higher than the *croat* of Barcelona. This difference would disappear with Martín I (1396–1410).

With Alfonso IV (1416–1458) the purity of the *vellón* was reduced to 12.5% silver. Alfonso also issued the short-lived *timbre d'or.*

Fernando III (1479–1516) minted *florines* in Valencia, but also introduced the *ducado* and kept the *real* and other coins in their previous metallic content. Valencia issued gold abundantly during his reign and during that of Carlos I, who abandoned the ducado model, opting instead for the *escudo.*

MIGUEL CRUSAFONT I SABATER

Bibliography

Mateu i Llopis, F. *La ceca de Valencia y las acuñaciones valencianas de los siglos XIII–XVIII.* Valencia, 1929.

——— Crusafonti Sabater, M. "Diners de València i diners d'Alacant," *Numisma* 165–167 (1980), 303–314.

———. *Numismática de la Corona Catalano-Aragónesa Medieval.* Madrid, 1982.

COLÓN *See* COLUMBUS, CHRISTOPHER

COLUMBUS, CHRISTOPHER

Christopher Columbus is seldom associated with late medieval European thought. Yet his written work and other written sources suggest that he was informed by an intellectual tradition resting more heavily on ancient, medieval, and scholastic authors than on the authority of experience one associates with the Modern Age. Columbus is in the company of scholastics who, between the twelfth and seventeenth centuries, strove to systematize knowledge by reconciling Aristotle and other pagan authors with Christian doctrine. If this literary influence is not explicit in his *Diario* or much of his early writing, it would become so in response to protests voiced by his enemies in the Spanish court for his administrative tactics in Hispaniola and for his

Ghirlandaio, Ridolfo (1483–1561). Portrait of Christopher Colombus. Copyright © Scala/Art Resource, NY. Museo Navale di Pegli, Genoa, Italy.

failure to meet the expectations fueled by the enterprise of the Indies. The list of authors directly or indirectly cited, or alluded to, by Columbus is too extensive to mention here, but striking examples of his reliance on the *auctores* sanctioned by scholastics may be found in his *Letter of the Third Voyage* (1498) and his *Libro de las profecías* (1501–1502), a compilation and commentary of mostly scriptural passages that he thought signified his discovery as the final stage in completing God's apocalyptic scheme. Columbus was strongly influenced by Franciscan eschatology, particularly by the ideas of the Calabrian Joachim of Fiore friar.

No record exists of Columbus's formal schooling except for the assertion, forwarded by the bibliophile Hernando Colón (Fernando Columbus) in the apologetic biography of his father, that Columbus had attended the university in Pavia. Columbus was probably an astute autodidact who absorbed the theology and philosophy of his time from the ecclesiastic and scientific communities in the courts of Portugal and Spain, and, particularly, from the important monastic learning centers of Santa María de la Rábida and Nuestra Señora Santa María de las Cuevas in Spain.

The earliest and most influential accounts of the admiral's learning are provided by Hernando and by the Dominican friar Bartolomé de las Casas, Columbus's most devoted early biographer, in his *Historia de las Indias* (completed in 1559). Both biographers—the latter follows Hernando's lead almost to the letter—offer a list of authors who appear to have kindled the admiral's wish to cross the ocean. According to Hernando and las Casas, Columbus's belief that the greater part of the globe had been circumnavigated and that only the space between Asia's eastern end and the Azores and Cape Verde Islands remained to be discovered comes from the Alexandrine astronomer Ptolemy, the Greek geographers Marinus of Tyre, and Strabo, the Greek physician and historian Ctesias, Onesicritus and Nearchus, respectively captain and admiral to Alexander the Great during the Macedonian campaign in India, the Roman historian Pliny the Elder, and the Arabic astronomer Alfraganus. Likewise, his belief that the distance between continents was small rests, in their view, on the works of Aristotle, the Córdoban astronomer Averröes, the Roman philosopher Lucius Annaeus Seneca, the Roman poet and grammarian Gaius Julius Solinus, the Venetian Marco Polo, the fictional author Sir John of Mandeville, the French theologian and natural philosopher Cardinal Peter Aliacus, and the Roman writer Julius Capitolinus. Las Casas, clearly more schooled than the discoverer, adds a list of Christian and pagan auctores from whom Columbus might have persuaded himself of the plausibility of his project. Whether Columbus was as learned as Hernando and las Casas claim is still the subject of debate. Columbus probably owes his acquaintance with many auctores in the scholastic tradition to encyclopedic works such as Peter Aliacus's widely read *Ymago mundi* (1410–1414) and Pliny the Elder's *Historia naturalis.*

The most concrete evidence of Columbus's learning are the incunabula he is known to have possessed. A few of these volumes, held in the Biblioteca Colombina of Seville, contain abundant postilles by his hand, a number of which betray firsthand knowledge of numerous other works. The following volumes have long been identified as his: an extensive geographical treatise by the humanist Aeneas Sylvius Piccolomini (Pope Pius II), *Historia rerum ubique gestarum* (1477); Peter Aliacus's *Ymago mundi* (1483); Francesco Pipino's Latin translation of Marco Polo's *Il milione*: *De consuetudinibus et conditionibus orientalium regionum* (1485); and the manuscript of the *Libro de las profecías* (dated 1504). Others identified in 1891 as Columbus's are the following: Christophoro Landino's Italian translation of Pliny the elder's work: *Historia naturale* (1489); Abraham Zacut's *Almanach perpetuum* (1496), which contained a tabulation of planetary aspects and may have helped Columbus predict an eclipse on Jamaica (1504); Alfonso de Palencia's Spanish translation of Plutarch's *Parallel Lives* (*Vidas de los ilustres varones*, 1491); a manuscript of the anonymous fifteenth-century *Concordiae Bibliae Cardinalis*, which may have furnished Columbus with quotes for his *Libro*. Albertus Magnus's *Philosophia naturalis* (Venice 1496), also known as *Philosophia pauperum*, containing the saint's commentaries to the works of Aristotle's cosmology: *Physics*, *On the Heavens*, *Metereology*, *On Generation and Corruption*, and *On the Soul*; St. Antoninus of Florence's confessional guide, the *Sumula confessionis* (1476); and a fifteenth-century palimpsest of Seneca's tragedies containing the *Medea*, from which Columbus extracted a passage foretelling the discovery of a new orb.

Las Casas judged the *Ymago mundi* to be the primary source for the enterprise of the Indies. Peter Aliacus wrote this series of treatises in preparation for the Council at Constance, which ended the Western Schism (1414). The *Ymago mundi*, essentially an astrological work, includes a systematic account of the geocentric world, incorporating ancient geoethnography into the theoretical frames of Aristotle's physics and Ptolemy's scientia stellarum. Although this work's influence on Columbus has been discussed primarily on the basis of its place in late medieval geoethnography, its central purpose was to describe the mechanics of the natural world and to chart out the motion of the *machina mundi* over time. (The "machine of the world" in motion represented apocalyptic time unfolding.) By this method, Peter Aliacus hoped to discern the historical status of the religious crisis at hand in relation to the rise of the Antichrist and the dawning of the end of time. This eschatological work illustrates the union of Christian theology and Aristotelian science, that characterized intellectual production in the Latin West between the twelfth and seventeenth centuries. Columbus owes much of his thought to this tradition.

NICOLÁS WEY-GÓMEZ

Bibliography

Casas, B. de las. *Historia de las Indias*. 3 vols. Ed. C. Agustín Millares. México, 1992.

Columbus, C. *The "Libro de las Profecías" of Christopher Columbus: An 'en face' Edition*. Ed. and trans. D. C. West. Gainesville, Fla., 1992.

Columbus, F. *The Life of the Admiral Christopher Columbus by his Son Fernando*. Ed. and trans. B. Keen. New Brunswick, N. J., 1959.

Flint, V.J. *The Imaginative Landscape of Christopher Columbus*. Princeton, N. J., 1992.

Milhou, A. *Cristóbal Colón y su mentalidad mesiánica en el ambiente franciscanista español*. Valladolid, 1983.

Rosa y López, S. de la. *Libros y autógrafos de Cristóbal Colón*. Sevilla, 1891.

COMEDIA DE CALISTO Y MELIBEA *See* CELESTINA

COMMUNICATION

In comparison to the Modern Age, the means of communication in Medieval Spain were quite simple. One communicated orally to a person in one's immediate vicinity, or in writing to someone at a distance. Oral communication, especially if it passed to several persons, was subject to considerable alteration and distortion. The transmission of news of the broader world to those living in the comparative isolation of rural villages was likely delayed by months or even years. Communications that were thought to embody permanent principles, concessions, rights, or privileges were often recorded in writing. A major obstacle to written communication was the illiteracy of the vast majority of the Iberian population. Written texts required someone, a cleric usually, to read them. More than likely, most people never communicated in writing to anyone. Written communication was restricted in practice to the cultural elite of kings, clergy, nobility, and the urban patriciate. The transmission of communications, whether oral or written, had to overcome both geographical and human obstacles such as inadequate roads and bridges, swollen rivers, mountains, foul weather, highwaymen, brigands, and grasping innkeepers.

The geographical considerations included the fact that the Pyrenees Mountains cut Spain off from northern Europe except by way of the western pass at Roncesvaux and the eastern pass at Le Perthus. On the other hand, the Mediterranean Sea, which bathed much of the eastern and southern coast of the Iberian Peninsula, served as a link with Italy and North Africa. The straits of Gibraltar facilitated travel and communication between Andalucía and Morocco. The Atlantic to the west gave Spain and Portugal access to the wider world of Asia and America in the closing century of the Middle Ages. Within the peninsula, mountain ranges running in an east-west direction intersected the central *meseta* (plateau), whose height restricted easy access from the coastal regions. The great rivers served as routes of travel and communication: the Duero (485 miles), the Tagus (565), the Guadiana (510), and the Guadalquivir (512) all flowed westward to the Atlantic while the Ebro (465 miles) proceeded eastward to the Mediterranean.

The Romans built a network of 13,000 miles of roads to facilitate the passage of troops, but these routes also served the needs of travelers and merchants. The Via Augusta, following the coast from Cádiz to Tarragona and thence to Gaul and Italy, was the principal highway. During the Visigothic era the road system began to deteriorate but the old roads continued to serve the needs of Muslim and Christian armies in succeeding centuries.

Aside from face-to-face interaction the means of communication were quite varied. In the caliphal epoch there was a regular postal service using carrier pigeons. In the Christian states *porteros* carried oral or written orders from the king. Merchants and soldiers in all ages, monks such as those of the French orders of Cluny and Cîteaux in the eleventh and twelfth centuries, Franciscan preachers and missionaries in the thirteenth century, and pilgrims to Santiago de Compostela especially from the eleventh century onward, as well as ransomers (*alfaqueques* or *exeas*) and escaped slaves all could carry verbal or written messages. Ambassadors from Constantinople and the Holy Roman Empire visited the court of the caliphs at Córdoba. The rulers of Christian Spain also sent envoys there and later to the *tā'ifas* or petty kings, and to the kings of Granada. From the eleventh century onward papal legates visited the peninsula with comparative regularity, while Spanish bishops often journeyed to France and to Italy. During the epoch of the crusades various Spaniards are known to have traveled to the Holy Land. The Christian rulers were extraordinarily peripatetic throughout the medieval era, so the movement of the royal court from one place to another was a major vehicle for the transmission of information and news of both a public and a private character.

Few written communications from the Visigothic and Islamic periods have survived, but the number from Christian Spain increased steadily from the tenth century onward. Among the extant documents are royal letters of different types, papal and episcopal letters, some private letters, and many private charters. In addition, stories and tales circulated orally and were then recorded in writing. These included the poems of Berceo (ca.1180–ca.1250), the *Cantar de Mío Cid*, and the *Cantigas de Santa María*, a treasure trove of miracles attributed to the Virgin Mary. Stories were also communicated in the sculptural programs of the great cathedrals.

Instantaneous communication over long distances was obviously not possible in Medieval Spain. Days, weeks, and months often passed before messages were delivered. The rapidity of communication depended on the urgency of the matter. Eulogius of Córdoba (c.859), for example, made a lengthy journey to Navarre in search of his brothers, who had gone on a commercial venture. The pilgrimage to Santiago took months because it was also an occasion for tourism and sightseeing. Preparing to challenge the Almohads, a Christian army departed from Toledo on 20 June 1212 and arrived at the battlefield of Las Navas de Tolosa on 13 July, covering a distance of about 112 miles in about twenty-three days, or at a rate of nearly 5 miles a day. On the other hand, Fernando III, contending with heavy rains and floods, made a forced march of nearly 300 miles from Benavente in León to Córdoba from mid-January to 7 February 1236. His rate of travel was about 14 miles per day. Jaime I of Aragón sailed to Mallorca on 5 September 1229, encountered storms, but arrived at Palma, about 140 miles away, on the night of 8–9 September. A fleet sent by Alfonso X from Cádiz to Salé on the Atlantic coast of Morocco arrived on 8 September 1260 about four days after its departure. Instructions issued by Pope Nicholas III to his legate on 23 March 1279 were delivered to the Castilian court in May. The itineraries of the Christian kings can be determined for the High and late Middle Ages and convey some idea of the pace of travel and communication.

Joseph F. O'Callaghan

Bibliography

Menache, S. *The Vox Dei: Communication in the Middle Ages*. New York, 1990.

COMPOSTELA, MUSIC RELATING TO

Discussions of music in the vast popular and scholarly literature dealing with the Jacobean pilgrimage have focused, to a greater or lesser extent, on its spiritual and recreational roles. Throughout the centuries, music provided not only spiritual sustenance during the arduous journey to Compostela, but also pleasurable diversions at particular stopovers, where the weary were entertained by *juglares* (minstrels), or where they observed and even participated in local musical festivities. In all, the pilgrims' exposure to a variety of regional traditions and intermingling with fellow itinerants from other countries, enriched their musical experiences along the principal routes of the *camino francés*, which, in Spain, converged at Puente la Reina and continued along the *Camino de Santiago*, passing through present day Huesca, Navarra, La Rioja, the uppermost part of Castilla la Vieja, and Galicia.

One of the earliest accounts concerning the musical activities of pilgrims upon their arrival in Santiago de Compostela can be found in book 1 (fol. 78) of the mid-twelfth-century *Liber Sancti Jacobi*. There a witness expresses his joy and wonderment upon observing the varied groups of pilgrims (Germans, French, Italians, et al.) who have gathered in the basilica bearing candles to maintain an all-night vigil before the altar of St. James. Among their instruments, he mentions citterns (*citharis*), lyres (*liris*), kettle drums (*timphanis*), flutes (*tibis*), small shawms (*fistulis*), trumpets (*tubis*), harps (*sambrecis*), fiddles (*violis*), and hurdy-gurdys (*rotis Brittanicis vel Gallicis*). Some sing to the accompaniment of psalteries (*psalteriis*), and others to diverse instruments (*diversa generibus musicorum*), and conversations and songs in languages "from all the climates of the world" could be heard.

One can imagine the countless number of personal accounts alluding to songs, dances, and musical instruments that were lost to oblivion, including, according to Anglés, thirteenth- and fourteenth-century collections of religious songs from the basilica in Santiago. We have a general idea of the vocal and instrumental genres that were familiar along the pilgrim routes from the twelfth through seventeenth centuries (ranging from the courtly and popular traditions of mainly French origin—*chansons de geste*, *cantilenas*, *rondeaux*, *virelais*, *cossantes*, songs with refrains, and so forth—to the secular and religious *romances* and *villancicos*, and other orally transmitted folk genres that continued in popularity through the Spanish Baroque). Yet, it was the vast hymn repertoire, together with the favorite *organa* and *conducti* from the liturgical tradition that sustained the journey's sacred character. Among the numerous song anthologies (*cancioneros*) from the aforementioned regions that were published since the early eighteenth century, one can find a wealth of tunes associated with the pilgrimage.

The earliest source for music at the cathedral is the *Liber Sancti Jacobi* or *Codex Calixtinus* (housed at the Archivo de la Catedral and falsely attributed to Pope Calixtus d. II, (d. 1124). It is also referred to as the *Liber Beati Jacobi*. Its five books were compiled primarily by French and Italian clerics about the year 1140, undoubtedly as a product of the Cluny reform. Surprisingly, only the first contains the liturgical texts and music (notated on fols. 101ᵛ through 193), about 90 percent of which is monodic, conforming to the Gregorian and comprising the "numerical" offices (seven of them, including antiphons and responds), masses, and processions for the feast of the apostle St. James, and hymns. There is also a votive mass titled "de los Peregrinos." Additional items include prosas and hymns and twenty-two two-part and one three-part *organa* (the renowned *Congaudeant catholici*, actually a Benadicamus trope), based upon Gregorian tenors, which are related stylistically to those from St. Martial. They are notated in Franco-Norman neumes on four-line staves. While their pitches are discernable, they lack rhythmic precision. A later copy, in Acquitanian nuemes, of the monophonic items was made in 1173 by Arnauld du Mont (Ripoll 99, housed at the Archivo de la Corona de Aragón).

In the *Liber* there are two monodic hymns bearing markedly popular traits: "Ad honorem Regis summi" (fol. 190ᵛ), attributed to Aymery Picaud, author of the Pilgrim's Guide (book 5), and "Dum Paterfamilias" (fol. 193ᵛ), more familiarly known as the *Canto de Ultreya*. According to López-Calo, the former is pronouncedly Galician in inspiration, while the latter, judging from its orthography and notation (Acquitanian), appears to predate the Codex and was probably incorporated in its initial binding. However, controversies abound concerning its transcription and the rendering of its supposed double refrain "*Primus ex Apostolis* . . ." and "*Herru Sanctiago* . . ." Among the numerous transcriptions, that of López-Calo bears considerable attention.

ISRAEL J. KATZ

Bibliography

Anglés, H. "La música sagrada y popular en el camino de Santiago y en Compostela." In *Historia de la música medieval en Navarra*. Pamplona, 1970. 131–64.

Echevarría Bravo, P. *Cancionero de los peregrinos de Santiago*. Madrid, 1967.

Fernández de la Cuesta, I. "La música litúrgica de la peregrinación a Santiago: El códice calixtino." In *Santiago, Camino de Euopa: Culto y Cultura en la Peregrinación a Compostela*. Santiago de Compostela, 1993. 37–53.

Filgueira Valverde, J. "Cantos y narraciones en el camino de la peregrinación." In *Historia de Compostela*. Santiago de Compostela, 1970. 3–21.

Helmer, P. *The Mass of St. James: Solemn Mass for the Feast of the Passion of St. James of Compostela according to the Codex Calixtinus*. Ottawa, 1988.

López-Calo, J. "Las peregrinaciones a Santiago y su música." In *La música medieval en Galicia*. La Coruña, 1982. 31–36.

CONGO, KINGDOM OF

An important Bantu kingdom and the first political entity of consequence encountered by the Portuguese in their explorations down the African coast during the fifteenth century. It also represented the first of Portugal's diplomatic and missionary successes and an important source of trade, primarily in slaves, because the region produced no precious metals, though it did provide some ivory in exchange for the desired metalwares, cloth and beads provided by the Portuguese. Its importance diminished as the Portuguese pressed on farther south and ultimately focussed their attention on Angola and India.

The first contact between the Portuguese and the Bantu kingdom took place in 1482 or 1483, when three caravels under command of Diogo Cão anchored off the Congo estuary in the Sonyo region. Although the population could not understand interpreters brought from the Guinea region, contacts were friendly and Cão dropped off an embassy bearing gifts to make its way inland to the sovereign of the region, the Mani Congo, while Cão continued his explorations down the coast. On his return, the emissaries had still not returned, and as a precaution, he took four hostages back to Portugal as a guarantee for his own men's safety; in Portugal, the hostages were feted, shown about, and taught some Portuguese.

Cão returned to the Congo the following year and liberated the Sonyo foursome; the Portuguese ambassadors also turned up and had been equally well treated. The Mani Congo, Nzinga Nkuwu I, then sent gifts to João II, accepted missionary priests and eventually was baptized (in 1491) as João I of the Congo. Along with priests, João II sent skilled workmen, such as blacksmiths and masons,—and even women to teach the domestic arts. Nzinga Nkuwu ruled until 1506 and was succeeded by his son, a devout Catholic. For a time, the two nations entertained cordial and fraternal relations.

But two circumstances militated against relations continuing on such an idyllic and cordial basis. One was the turning of Portuguese interests elsewhere—to Angola and to India. Repeated requests for more aid and embassies by Nzinga Nkuwu's successor, Nzinga Nvemba (ruling as Afonso I, 1506–c.1543), were ignored, while the Portuguese residents at court conducted themselves in an overbearing and un-Christian manner. Second, the economic relations between Portugal and the Congo were dependent wholly on the slave trade; even there the Portuguese found better sources of supply in Angola, to the south. Though Congolese kings remained nominal Christians until the seventeenth century, the once promising relationship steadily deteriorated from the reign of Manuel I.

GEORGE D. WINIUS

Bibliography

Brásio, António, *Monumenta missionaria Africana, Africa Ocidental.* 1st series, Vol. 1. 1952.
Jadin, L., and J. Cuvelier, *'Ancien Congo d'aprés les archives Romaines.* Brussels, 1954.

CONSEJO *See* TOWNS

CONSEJO DE ARAGÓN

The Consejo de Aragón, a seven-member royal council instituted in 1494 by Fernando and Isabel, administered the various realms that composed Fernando's personal patrimony, the medieval Crown of Aragón. Part of the bureaucratic evolution of Castile from a medieval monarchy into a modern state, the consejo de Aragón was one of several councils established to govern the vast Castilian territorial possessions in Europe and the New World during a period of rapid colonial expansion.

Conceived of as the administrative link between the territories of the former Crown of Aragón and a frequently absent king, the Consejo de Aragón was essentially a refurbishment of the former Aragónese Curia Regis. The Consejo's structure was based on delegation of royal authority in general and, in particular, the Aragónese institution of the viceroy, who was used to govern its Mediterranean territories. It was composed of a *vice-canciller* (vice-chancellor) and a *tesorero-general* (general treasurer) who presided over five regents, the viceroys of Aragón, Catalonia, Mallorca, Sicily, and Valencia. Located in Castile, the members of the consejo advised the king concerning matters relevant to its governance and transmitted his orders to the viceroys in charge of each realm.

The division of bureaucratic functions roughly paralleled the structure of Castilian government under Fernando and Isabel. Foreign affairs, taxation, fiscal policy, and military matters were handled by the Consejo Real (Royal Council) in Castile, while the Consejo de Aragón was responsible for coordinating the work of local and regional institutions. Although in theory the two kingdoms were unified, in fact no attempt was made to fuse the administration of the two crowns. The five viceroys were granted substantial freedom in their supervision of regional administration of justice and municipal government, which could vary widely from place to place. Thus, the veneer of a unified Castilian state was applied to what remained fundamentally a federation of regional and local governments.

The Consejo de Aragón illustrates the paradox of the government of Fernando and Isabel: a drive toward centralization offset by the preservation of traditional regional institutions. Owing to the representative character of the Aragónese institutions, the monarchy was limited by constitutional constraints in these five territories, unlike in Castile where it was more authoritarian. As a result, the Castilian monarchy ruled over a pluralistic state, an alliance of a series of separate patrimonies each governed in accordance with their own distinct laws.

THERESA EARENFIGHT

Bibliography

Elliott, J. H. *Imperial Spain, 1469–1716.* New York, 1963.
Font Rius, J. M. *Instituciones medievales españolas medievales.* Madrid, 1949.

CONSEJO DE LA SANTA HERMANDAD

The Consejo de la Santa Hermandad, formed in 1476 by Fernando and Isabel, was the unified central council in Castile that supervised the actions of the *santas hermandades* (holy brotherhoods), local militias that served as a combined police force and judicial tribunal. The consejo collected the taxes, maintained order among the militias, and mediated jurisdictional disputes. Presided over by the bishop of Cartagena, the consejo consisted of a supreme commander of the militias, a chief administrator, an attorney general, an advocate general, and the constable of Castile. Because the members of the consejo were direct representatives of the crown, and thus less likely to fall under the influence of a local magnate or town council, the local hermandades became a highly effective fighting force in the service of the monarchy.

The evolution of the Consejo de la Santa Hermandad is typical of how Fernando and Isabel strengthened a traditional medieval institution to meet their new needs. Local hermandades had existed since at least the mid-thirteenth century. Castilian towns were granted wide powers to form temporary militias composed of armed horsemen and *cuadrillas* (squads of archers) to patrol rural areas during periods of unrest. Each town provided a quota of troops and had its own cuadrilla to respond to the hue and cry and to pursue the malefactor to the limit of the town's jurisdiction, where the pursuit was taken up by the hermandad of the neighboring town. Their jurisdiction included all crime committed on the roads, including robbery, murder, arson, rape, burglary, blasphemy, counterfeiting, and acts of rebellion against the crown. An *alcalde* presided over the court of justice, pronounced justice, and assessed penalties. At first strictly ad hoc groups, by the late fourteenth century the hermandades had become a permanent fixture of the Castilian countryside.

The basic administrative structure of the hermandades was formalized and strengthened at the *cortes* (parliament) of Segovia in 1386, but during the civil strife of the fifteenth century, they fell prey to factionalism and lost much of their effectiveness. In 1467 Enrique IV, with the ordinances of Castronuño, organized the local militias into eight provinces under a supreme commander; he was, however, unable to effectively exert royal authority over them.

During the War of Succession (1474–1479) that followed Enrique's death, Fernando and Isabel turned to the hermandades for military support. Utilizing the hermandades as a temporary expedient to deal with an acute emergency, the monarchs transformed local militias into an army in the service of the crown. At the cortes of Madrigal in 1476 the Consejo de la Santa Hermandad was established, local jurisdiction was widened, and every city, village, and hamlet was ordered to join and to pay taxes to support them. During the Granada war (1483–1491) the consejo became a powerful semipermanent institution and the cuadrillas grew in number, forming an important component of the troops involved in the final battle of the reconquista.

After 1492 the Consejo's activities declined sharply and the militia never again saw combat. Nevertheless, the taxes continued to be collected and the consejo's mandate was renewed until 1498. By then, general peace prevailed and the consejo was dismantled. The rural police forces remained to provide justice and safety in the countryside, and the taxation for the archers and local administration continued long into the modern era.

THERESA EARENFIGHT

Bibliography

Elliott, J. H. *Imperial Spain, 1469–1716*. New York, 1963.

Lunenfeld, M. *The Council of the Santa Hermandad: A Study in the Pacification Forces of Fernando and Isabel*. Coral Gables, Fla., 1970.

Phillips, W. D. *Enrique IV and the Crisis of Fifteenth-Century Castile, 1425–1480*. Cambridge, Mass., 1978.

CONSEJO DE LA SUPREMA Y GENERAL INQUISICIÓN *See* INQUISISTION

CONSEJO DE LAS ÓRDENES

The Templars and Hospitallers, religious orders that became participants of the Spanish Reconquest by the early twelfth century, were joined at much the same time by a number of indigenous crusading orders in Castile, Aragón, and Portugal. The most important of these were the orders of Calatrava, Alcántara, and Santiago. In exchange for their role as the first line of defense for Christian Spain against Muslim Spain, the military orders attained legal autonomy and wealth which, by the thirteenth century, had caused the jealousy of sovereigns and commoners in all the Iberian realms. With the dissolution of the Templars in 1312, the ultimate fate of the Spanish crusading orders was sealed. As the Muslim threat to Spain fell back to the truncated kingdom of Granada, the military orders in Castile, thoroughly dominated by the kingdom's nobility, proved an even greater threat to royal autonomy. The first blow against aristocratic control of the Castilian orders took place in 1476 when Isabel I claimed the vacant mastership of the Order of Santiago and eventually granted it to her husband Fernando II of Aragón. Following the same procedure with the orders of Calatrava and Alcántara, Isabel's government had assumed administration of the three orders by 1495 with the creation of the Council of the Orders (*Consejo de las Ordenes*). This royal council, staffed with a president and five judges largely drawn from the orders' former leadership, administered the lands of the orders and adjudicated all suits that involved this property. The council survived as a royal agency until it was abrogated by the Constitution of 1812.

DONALD KAGAY

Bibliography

Edwards, J. *The Spain of the Catholic Monarchs, 1474–1520*. Cambridge, 2000.

CONSEJO REAL

The single most important governmental institution in Castilian government in the later Middle Ages and early modern period, the *Consejo Real* was a council separate and distinct from the royal bureaucracy normally in charge of governance. Members of the consejo routinely dealt with all aspects of government: they supervised the work of local government, administered law in their role as the supreme court of justice, and advised the king on whom to appoint to high office and whom to reward with royal favors.

Created in 1385 by Juan I (1379–1390), the Consejo Real was conceived originally as a permanent advisory body representing the *cortes* (parliament) and was composed of twelve members drawn from the three estates: nobility, clergy, and townspeople. Baronial interference, incompetence, and self-interest threatened the integrity of the consejo, prompting Enrique IV (1454–1474) in 1459 to reform the composition of the membership. Henceforth eight of the twelve members were to be *letrados* (legists) qualified in administration.

During the reign of Fernando and Isabel (1474–1516) the Consejo was transformed into a truly effective instrument of royal authority capable of acting independently on its own. In need of an institution to supervise the governance of their newly acquired territories in Europe and the New World, at the cortes of Toledo in 1480 Fernando and Isabel greatly expanded the power, functions, duties, and prerogatives of the Consejo Real so that many important matters previously handled personally by the monarchs fell under its jurisdiction. Five committees were established to implement royal policy concerning justice, foreign policy (after 1526, known as the Consejo de Estado, 1526), finance (after 1523, the Consejo de Hacienda), pacification of the countryside (the Consejo de la Santa Hermandad, dismantled in 1498), and the territories that composed Fernando's patrimony—the medieval Crown of Aragón (formalized as a distinct entity in 1494). In 1489 a president was appointed to act in place of the often-absent, itinerant monarchs.

The domination of the consejo by the legal profession was complete by 1493, when it was determined that all members be *letrados* with at least ten years' study of law at a university. The Consejo Real, once dominated by a military aristocracy armed with their own agenda, had been transformed into a modern institution, staffed by letrados who owed their jobs, and thus their loyalty, first and foremost to the monarchy.

THERESA EARENFIGHT

Bibliography

Edwards, J. *The Spain of the Catholic Monarchs, 1474–1520.* Cambridge, 2000.

Elliott, J. H. *Imperial Spain, 1469–1716.* New York, 1963.

Font Rius, J. M. *Instituciones medievales españoles medievales.* Madrid, 1949.

Phillips, W. D. *Enrique IV and the Crisis of Fifteenth-Century Castile, 1425–1480.* Cambridge, Mass., 1978.

CONTINUATIO HISPANA

See MOZARABIC CHRONICLE OF 754

CONVERSOS

Jews who converted to Christianity were called *conversos* ("converts", converted Muslims were referred to as *tornadizos*, or "renegades").

With the exception of individuals who converted entirely on their own at different periods (e.g., Pedro Alfonso), the conversion of Jews may be classified into four general periods.

The Visigothic Era

The first decree of compulsory baptism was issued by Sisebut in 613, a decree that it is often erroneously claimed met with the disapproval of Isidore of Seville. However, Swinthila permitted those Jews to return to their faith, but this was set aside by the next king, Sisenand, in 633. Once again, under Khintila (638), the Sixth Council of Toledo ordered the baptism or expulsion of all Jews. This seems not to have entirely worked, however, for Reccesvinth (653) had to renew the decree and again force baptized Jews to sign an agreement to abide by the Christian faith. Finally, in 681 Erwig renewed all the anti-Jewish measures, which again demonstrates their ineffectiveness, but the Jews were saved from total disappearance by the invasion of the Muslims in 711.

The "Pogroms" (1391)

Jewish life under both the Muslims and the Christians flourished with little or no hostile activity or attitudes until the disastrous Trastámara civil war brought new forces to power in Castile in the late fourteenth century. In spite of the general and official tolerance of Jews also in the Church, some elements of the minor clergy were nevertheless sometimes hostile. This was the case with Ferrán Martínez, an archdeacon of Seville, who in the summer of 1391 aroused mobs to riot against the Jews. Synagogues in Seville were burned and the Jews robbed, and this soon spread throughout all of Spain. Some Jews were actually killed, more were robbed and their synagogues destroyed. In spite of the most vigorous efforts of the kings to stop the attacks and to punish the perpetrators, the damage had been done. Thousands of Jews, apparently fearing yet worse to come, or acting in despair at this unprecedented attack, converted to Christianity. Some Jewish communities ceased to exist entirely, and others, including such notable ones as Barcelona and Seville, became so depleted and impoverished as to virtually cease functioning until the fifteenth century.

Even prior to these events, the sudden conversion of the rabbi of Burgos, Solomon ha-Levy, along with his sons and other relatives (his wife converted later), was an event of such magnitude that it sent shock waves throughout the entire Jewish population. Attaching himself to Benedict XIII, the anti-Jewish pope of Avignon recognized by Spain, Solomon received a thorough education in Christian theology and quickly became the bishop of Burgos as Pablo de Santa María. His son Alonso de Cartagena became first bishop of that see, and then succeeded his father in Burgos. The conversion of so prominent a family, all of whom then became illustrious writers and more or less virulent opponents of Judaism, made a tremendous impression. Joshua ha-Lorqi, an important Jewish scholar and protegé of the former rabbi, converted under his influence and became Jerónimo de Santa Fe, a major anti-Jewish polemicist. Other less prominent Jews were equally affected.

Vicente Ferrer and the Tortosa Disputation

The activities of the Dominicans and the Franciscans in attempting to convert the Jews date back to the thirteenth century. Having faced a temporary setback after the Barcelona Disputation, when their unfounded charges of "Jewish blasphemy" angered Jaime I, they saw their opportunity in the fourteenth century with renewed missionary efforts. However, it was the charismatic preaching and fanatical zeal of one man, Vicente Ferrer, that had the desired results. In the early years of the fifteenth century he marched throughout Spain, tirelessly exhorting the masses to religious reform and the Jews to conversion. Not content with that, he convinced the regents of Castile, Queen Catalina and Fernando de Antequera, to enact harsh anti-Jewish legislation (the Valladolid Ordinances of 1412). His attitudes no doubt strongly influenced Fernando, who soon became king of Aragón-Catalonia, and whose mercifully brief reign was marred by the harshest anti-Jewish decrees seen in that kingdom. His preaching alone had the desired effect, however, and thousands (possiby hundreds of thousands) of Jews converted all over Spain. Once again, entire Jewish communities, such as that of Segovia, were lost.

In 1413 Pope Benedict XIII, acting apparently with the encouragement of Pablo de Santa María, ordered a disputation at Tortosa to which were "invited" most of the outstanding Jewish scholars of Aragón-Catalonia. The result of this was once again the conversion of many rabbis and Jewish lay delegates, as well as a number of other prominent Jews in the kingdom.

To add to the disastrous state of Spanish Jewry, many of the most important rabbinical scholars had already fled Spain following the events of 1391, going to North Africa. An impoverished and demoralized Jewish population was hardly able to sustain the necessary schools to produce a new generation of scholars, and the effective rabbinical leadership that had always made Spanish Jewry prominent in the world came to an end.

The Inquisition and Expulsion

There is evidence that much of what remained of Spanish Jewry in the second part of the fifteenth century became zealous in religious devotion, if lacking in knowledge. The increasing hostility of certain of the nobility and, more particularly, the rising middle-class merchants, toward the conversos created the farce of the Inquisition, with its twin myths of *limpieza de sangre* ("purity of blood" of the so-called old Christians) and the infidelity of the conversos, falsely said to be "bad Christians." Thus their anti-Semitism was unleashed with official sanction under the guise of rooting out supposed "heresy," but with the real intent of destroying the conversos, and, once this was accomplished, removing the Jews who gave rise to them. This was behind the Edict of Expulsion, which the Catholic Monarchs were compelled to sign banishing the Jews in 1492. Given only a few months in which to sell their homes and businesses, collect debts, and so on, many Jews not surprisingly chose finally to convert rather than flee their ancestral home of centuries, not knowing what lay ahead or when they would end up. It is perhaps true, and ironic, that the motives of many of these conversos were not religiously pure, and thus that their enemies might to a degree have succeeded in creating the very class that their propaganda pretended to uncover: the lukewarm Christian convert.

The "Crypto-Jew" Myth

From the above account, it can readily be seen how little these conversos were "crypto-Jews," or secretly loyal to the Jewish tradition, as romantic legend maintained. Most were very sincere converts who became steadfast and even zealous in their Christian faith; all had chosen to convert and were not forced into doing so. This was an important distinction not lost on the rabbis of the age, who unanimously, from the fourteenth through the fifteenth centuries, decided that these converts were not *anusim* ("forced") but *meshumadim* ("apostates" who freely abandoned their faith and their people). The proof was that they had the opportunity to leave Spain, for Muslim Granada or North Africa, but did not do so.

Conversos entered the service of the Church in unprecedented numbers. Entire monastic orders, like the important one of San Jerónimo, became virtual *converso* enclaves. In addition to the Santa María-Cartagena family, numerous other *conversos* became bishops and archbishops, theologians and canonists.

Finally, the Inquisition itself did not permit even those few conversos who may have wished to maintain some ties with their Jewish past to do so. Watched constantly by spies, and required to educate their children by priests and to attend church constantly, the *conversos* had to be very devout Christians.

Cultural Activity

Converso writers and intellectuals soon gained a position of tremendous importance in late medieval

Spanish society. The majority of the Castilian chroniclers, for example, were *conversos* (Alfonso de Palencia, Diego de Valera, Fernando de Pulgar, and Gonzalo García de Santa María), as were many of the poets and literary figures: Juan Alvarez Gato, Juan Alfonso de Baena, Rodrigo Cota, Diego de Valencia, Diego de Valera, Juan del Encina, and many others. Important religious writers, and authors of anti-Jewish polemics, were Pablo de Santa María, his son Alonso de Cartagena, Pedro de la Caballería, and others.

Converso officials in service of the crown, both in Castile and later in Aragón-Catalonia, rose to levels at least as high as those formerly held by Jews. The Catholic Monarchs were served by at least three converso secretaries (of whom Fernando de Pulgar was the most important), and in Aragón-Catalonia almost all of Fernando's most important officials were conversos, including the famous Santángels and the de la Caballerías who were supporters of Christopher Columbus (who may himself have been a *converso*). Abraham Seneor of Castile, chief rabbi and important tax official, converted along with his family and his son-in-law Meir Melamed, and continued in the service of the queen in the sixteenth century. Fernando de Rojas, author of *Celestina*, and even St. Teresa of Avila were others who were of *converso* origin, as were Luis de León and many of the great families of Spanish nobility (including the king, Fernando himself).

NORMAN ROTH

Bibliography

Cantera Burgos, F. *Alvar García de Santa María. Historia de la juderia de Burgos y de sus conversos más egregios.* Madrid, 1952.

Netanyahu, B. *The Marranos of Spain.* New York, 1972.

———. *The Origins of the Inquisition in Fifteenth-century Spain.* 2d. ed. New York 2001.

Roth, N. "Jewish Conversos in Medieval Spain: Some Misconceptions and New Information." In *Marginated Groups in Spanish and Portuguese History.* Ed. W. D. Phillips and C. R. Phillips. Minneapolis, 1989. 23–52.

———. *Conversos Inquisition and the Expulsion of the Jews from Spain.* Madison, Wisc. 1995

COPLAS DE LA PANADERA

Through the popular ridicule of a ribald bread seller, dishonor came to Spain's most illustrious houses during the Battle of Olmedo, 19 May 1445. The forces of Alvaro de Luna—favorite of King Juan II of Castile—along with the king and his son, Prince Enrique, were arrayed against the forces of Juan I of Navarre and his brother, Prince Enrique of Aragón. The results were varied: victory went to Castile, Iñigo López de Mendoza was named the marqués of Santillana for his participation, the wounded Aragónese prince was one of the thirty-seven fatalities of the day, and there was an eyewitness, a *panadera* or bread seller. Her *coplas* in the earlier form of *¡Ay Panadera!* or the later *¡Di Panadera!* accuse the flower of Spanish nobility of cowardice in forty-six octaves with refrain. An introductory stanza, urging the *panadera* to tell all, and a venomous exchange between Juan de Mena and Iñigo de Estúñiga in two appended *coplas* complete the poem.

Few among the forty-two warring grandees escape the bread seller's razor-sharp tongue and scatological good humor: the Bishop of Sigüenza was so terrified that his undergarments needed laundering, Commander Rodrigo Manrique's heart seemed to be made of sugar candy, and Fernando de Rojas trembled like leaves. Pedro de Mendoza ran to hide in the well, the frightened Count of Haro broke wind so loudly that it was heard as far away as Talavera, and Pero Sarmiento who had an encounter with a wine flask, thought he was mortally wounded, and fled, spewing his recent dinner onto the road.

Speaking with the voice of a simple woman, the anonymous courtier-author identifies his peers, not by allusion or allegory, but by name or title and, in so doing, adds the realistic dimension of personalized satire to Spanish letters.

VIVANA BRODEY

Bibliography

"Coplas de la Panadera." In *Poesía de protesta en la Edad Media castellana.* Ed. J. Rodríguez-Puértolas. Madrid, 1968.

Guglielmi, N. "Los elementos satíricos en las *Coplas de la Panadera,*" *Filología* 14 (1970), 49–104.

COPLAS DE MINGO REVULGO

The thirty-five *coplas* of the *Coplas de Mingo Revulgo* conceal their meaning behind allegorical allusion in a rustic dialogue between two shepherds, Mingo Revulgo and Gil Arribato.

Mingo, who represents the people, complains that the head shepherd—King Enrique IV of Castile—neglects his flock, caring only for personal pleasure and solitude. The sheepcote, undefended by the four truant sheepdogs—the cardinal virtues—is invaded by the seven deadly sins. Even the clergy, disguised as guard mastiffs, are too corrupt to interfere, permitting the wolves—ministers, nobles, parvenus—to devour the sheep.

Gil, a prophet who represents a higher power, replies with an admonition: the Spanish people are equally to blame for the King's laxness; unless they embrace the three theological virtues, the North Wind—the devil—will bring famine, war, pestilence, and worse, spiritual death. Only through prayer, confession, contrition, and atonement can man avoid his inevitable doom—nothing less than the end of the world.

While the central theme of the *coplas* is the negligence of Enrique IV, present also is the veiled accusation of his possible homosexuality, as well as contempt for his allowing all three religions to commingle freely. This is political satire in the classical tradition, the idea that virtue may be promoted by exposing vice. The style is erudite and popular, the tone apocalyptic, the pastoral allegory analogous to biblical parable. The form is viewed as the precursor of the dramatic eclogue. Internal evidence suggests both the early date of 1456 and the authorship of Fernán Pérez de Guzmán, although other scholarly attributions have been proposed over the years.

At the heart of the poem lies Catholic doctrine, a religious solution to a political problem: through repentance and penance, the Spanish people may transform their indifferent monarch into a caring and conscientious king.

VIVANA BRODEY

Bibliography

Brodey, V. *Las Coplas de Mingo Revulgo. Edición, estudio preliminar y notas.* Madison, Wisc., 1986.

Ciceri, M. "Le 'Coplas de Mingo Revulgo,' " *Cultura Neolatina* 27 (1977), 75–149, 189–266.

COPLAS DE YÔSĒF

A lengthy Spanish-Jewish poem concerning the adventures of the biblical Joseph, from his initial dreams and the betrayal by his brothers, his slavery in Egypt, and subsequent empowerment, through to his death. (Compare Gene 37–48.) The *Coplas* consist of *cuaderna-vía*-like quatrains, having the peculiarity that every fourth verse ends with the name *Yôsēf*, regardless of the preceding three verses' consonant rhyme. Three Hebrew-letter manuscripts are known: A Paris fragment (in the Bibliothèque Nationale; now lost) consisting of sixteen quatrains; a Cambridge University fragment of fourty-two quatrains (ed. González Llubera); and an ample Vatican manuscript, recently discovered and edited by Lazar, that runs to 308 quatrains. The Cambridge fragment, reflecting a more archaic language than that of either the Paris or Vatican, can be dated to the first half of the fifteenth century. Since Cambridge represents the narrative's final segments and its quatrains are numbered (261–310), the poem, in an earlier form—supposing one missing leaf at the end—may have consisted of some 312 quatrains. The *Coplas*, like the Provençal *Esther* by Crescas del Caylar, probably were composed for reading or recitation during the Purim festival. The Vatican manuscript represents a major discovery, allowing us, for the first time, to see this important poem essentially in its entirety. With Shem Tov's *Proverbios morales*, the *Coplas* should rank as one of the most significant works of Hispano-Jewish literature written in Spanish. Together with the Hispano-Muslim *Poema de Yūçuf*, the *Coplas* characterize the *cuaderna vía* meter as a favorite vehicle for medieval Hispanic doctrinal poetry, regardless of the religious affiliation of the authors who used it.

SAMUEL G. ARMISTEAD

Bibliography

Armistead, S. G. "Three Jewish-Spanish Joseph Narratives," *Romance Philology* 49, no. 1 (1995), 34–52.

González Llubera, I. *Coplas de Yoçef.* Cambridge, 1935.

Lazar, M. *Joseph and His Brethren: Three Ladino Versions.* Culver City, Calif., 1990.

Schwab, M. "Quatrains judéo-espagnols." *Revue Hispanique* 23 (1910), 321–326.

COPLAS DEL PROVINCIAL

Although the complete text of the *Coplas del Provincial* has never been published in Spain, it has maintained its notoriety, figuring in litigations and finding its way into irreproachable genealogies. And in that sincerest form of flattery, a sequel—the *Provincial segundo*—appeared in the sixteenth century.

The satire begins with two introductory *coplas* heralding the arrival of the provincial, the church dignitary who has come to monitor his convent. But the convent turns out to be the court of Enrique IV of Castile. In the 147 *coplas* that follow in octosyllabic quatrains, the provincial calls the whole court to judgment, starting with the king himself. Each grandee is singled out by name or title. The accusations range from adultery, cuckoldry, fornication, homosexuality, incest, illegitimacy, sodomy, and sorcery to the most frequent slur of all, racial impurity. *Coplas* 3 through 97 are addressed to men, 98 through 149 to women. If it were not for the ingenious obscenity of the rhymes, combined with the seriousness of the calumny, the poem would border on monotony: there is no relief from the vulgarity of the language or the coarseness of the invective.

The *Coplas del Provincial* is the work of at least two court poets, its conjectured date 1465, its literary importance twofold. With regard to content, for the first time in Spanish letters the king himself is directly insulted: the provincial has heard that the king continually copulates with the courtier, who is copulating with the queen. With regard to style, the *Coplas* are the most flagrant example of the religious travesty of the erotic and the profanation of the sacred in all of Spanish literature. As such, they have never been surpassed. Today, even after more than five hundred years, the *Coplas del Provincial* seem no less scurrilous, and no less shocking.

VIVANA BRODEY

Bibliography

Ciceri, M. "Las Coplas del Provincial," *Cultura Neolatina* 35 (1975), 39–210.

"Coplas del Provincial," *Revue Hispanique* 5 (1898), 255–66.

CORBEIL, TREATY OF

In the years after the Battle of Muret (1213) Aragónese-Catalan interests in the south of what is now France proved hard to maintain. French rule was asserted in the county of Toulouse, which was placed in the hands of Louis IX's brother Alfonse of Poitiers, and another brother, Charles of Anjou, acquired Provence by marriage in 1243. Louis IX looked for a diplomatic solution that would confirm French ascendancy in the region without humiliating his rivals; the years 1258–1259 saw him come to terms with both the English rulers of Gascony (at the Treaty of Paris in 1259) and with Jaime I of Aragón, in the Treaty of Corbeil of 11 May 1258. The price was generous recognition that past French claims to suzerainty over Barcelona, Urgell, Besalù, Roussillon, Ampurias, Cerdagne, Conflent, Girona and other border areas must be allowed to lapse; the Aragónese reciprocated by renouncing any claim to interfere in Carcassonne, Rodez, Milhau, Béziers, Agde, Albi, Narbonne, Minerve, Nîmes, Toulouse and the highly autonomous county of Foix, as well as their dependent territories. The full list of places provides a reminder of how extensive Aragónese interference had been in the past. Yet the peace treaty also had strange omissions. The city of Montpellier does not appear, or rather the royal lieutenant appears as the emissary of Jaime I, without any concession being made in respect of Aragónese rights there, and the question of Montpellier would rumble on throughout the late thirteenth and early fourteenth centuries. The rural barony of Montpellier or Aumelas remained under Aragónese suzerainty. The small, remote enclave of Carladès was also left in Aragónese hands, for whatever obscure reason. To seal the alliance Louis and Jaime agreed to a marriage alliance whereby Philippe, heir to France, would take as his bride Isabel of Aragón, Jaime's daughter. This had limited effect because Isabel died in 1271. Jaime took the opportunity also to renounce any further claims in Provence. It is clear that a faction in Aragón-Catalonia was not prepared to accept the permanent annulment of Aragónese interests in southern France; even Jaime I continued to endow the monastery of Valmagne, beyond Montpellier; and the *Chronicle of San Juan de la Peña* shows that Pedro the Great attempted to resuscitate the Aragónese claim to Carcassonne and other lands in Languedoc in 1280. Yet from a Catalan perspective the treaty had great advantages, drawing a frontier to the north of Perpignan that was only broached by Louis XI and then, finally, by Louis XIV, though the acquisition of Navarre by the French in 1284 posed new threats. The status of Barcelona and the lesser Catalan counties remained for a time imprecise: they were not actually part of the Aragónese kingdom, or indeed any kingdom, though the blanket label "Principality of Catalonia" came into vogue in the fourteenth century as a way of solving this difficulty. Roussillon and Cerdagne were, however, assigned to the new Mallorcan kingdom in Jaime I's will of 1262. The treaty was thus a milestone in the creation of Aragónese-Catalan and French realms that possessed defined boundaries.

DAVID S. ABULAFIA

Bibliography

Abulafia, D. S. *A Mediterranean Emporium*. Cambridge, 1994. 38–39.

Chronicle of San Juan de la Peña. Trans. L. Nelson. Philadelphia, 1991. 71.

Layettes du Trésor des Chartes. Vol. 3. Ed. J. de Laborde. Paris, 1875. Docs. 4399, 4400, 4411–12, 4434–35.

Le Goff, J. *Saint Louis*. Paris, 1996.

Richard, J. *Saint Louis*. Trans. S. Lloyd. Cambridge, 1992. 204–5.

CÓRDOBA, CITY OF

The former capital of the Roman province of *Hispania Bætica* went through several periods of success and decline during the Middle Ages. It dominated the middle reaches of the river known later as the Guadalquivir, which were one of the main sources of olive oil for the entire empire, including Rome itself. There seems to have been little change to the political and economic infrastructure of the city under Visigothic rule, but the Muslim invasion of 711 was to have a very different effect. By 717, Córdoba was the capital of Muslim Spain (al-Andalus) under North African control, but between 726 and 929 the city ruled over an independent emirate. In the latter year, Al-Nāṣir li-dīn Allah (ʿAbd al-Raḥmān III) proclaimed himself "Prince of the Faithful," or caliph, thus severing Muslim Spain, politically and religiously, from the rest of Islam. Under the caliphate, the tensions that had brought about deaths of the "martyrs" of Córdoba between 850 and 859 were largely resolved, in the sense that the population became predominantly Muslim. Between 929 and the final collapse of the caliphate, in 1031, Córdoba reached its full splender. Not only was the city densely populated and wealthy in this period, but it spawned, under caliphal patronage, a circle of palaces, surrounded by satellite towns, of which the main, partially excavated, survivor is Madīnat al-Zahrā. The glory largely departed from Córdoba in the eleventh century, when al-Andalus divided into *tā'ifa* (party) kingdoms. In the late eleventh and twelfth centuries it once again became a dependency of North Africa, under Almoravid and Almohad rule. Once the Almohads had been defeated at Las Navas de Tolosa in 1212, a Christian conquest was just a matter of time.

The arrival in the city of Castilian troops in 1236 was a surprise as much to the besiegers as to the besieged, but surviving documentation clearly demonstrates that Fernando III's conquest led to a virtually complete demographic and social transformation in what became known as the "kingdom" of Córdoba. By 1264, nearly all the Muslim population had left the area, and a Spanish feudal system was introduced, complete with aristocracy, knighthood, urban crafts, a peasantry, and a parochial and monastic structure. From then until the end of the Middle Ages, Córdoba was never again a center of government, until Isabel and Fernando made it their base camp for the final Granada war. Nonetheless, the city retained the habit of turning up in the political, economic, and religious controversies that bedevilled Castile in the fourteenth and fifteenth centuries. Its Jews were among those attacked in the pogroms of 1391, and its resulting Jewish Christian (*converso*) community suffered, in 1473, one of the attacks that led the Catholic Monarchs to assert their authority forcefully over the towns of al-Andalus and elsewhere in the kingdom. In the 1480s, the wings of Córdoba's nobility were temporarily clipped, an inquisition was imposed to purge its converso community, and the city flooded with soldiers, courtiers, and traders from the rest of Spain. Its loyalty to the crown was rewarded by a decline in its manufacturing industry, and a series of natural disasters which outlasted Queen Isabel herself. It retained, however, a reputation for intellectual sharpness that ran from the Romans Seneca and Lucan, through Muslims Averröes and Avicenna and Maimonides the Jew, to the Christian Juan de Mena and the *converso* Antón de Montoro.

JOHN EDWARDS

Bibliography

Nieto Cumplido, M. *Historia de Córdoba.* Vol. 2, *Islam y Cristianismo.* Córdoba, 1984.

Edwards, J. *Christian Córdoba: The City and its Region in the Late Middle Ages.* Cambridge, 1982.

Escobar Camacho, J. M. *Córdoba en la Baja Edad Media. Evolución urbana de la ciudad.* Córdoba, 1989.

CÓRDOBA, EMIRATE AND CALIPHATE OF

The Córdoba emirate and caliphate ruled al-Andalus (the parts of the Iberian Peninsula under Muslim control) from 756 to 1031 and is sometimes known as the Umayyad dynasty or the Marwānid dynasty. Its zenith was reached during the reigns of the caliphs ʿAbd al-Raḥmān III and Al-Ḥakam II (912–976), when political control extended from the Ebro and Duero River valleys south to the Moroccan coastal towns of Ceuta and Melilla; when trade and cultural exchange flourished; and when Córdoba rivaled Constantinople in population, comfort, and beauty.

The emirate period encompasses the years 756 to 929, from the accession of ʿAbd al-Raḥmān I, "the Immigrant," to the declaration of a caliphate by ʿAbd al-Raḥmān III, "the Victorious One." *Emir* is an Arabic tribal title for prince or ruler, and as literal descendants of the Umayyad caliphs of Damascus, the Umayyads of Spain were certainly entitled to such a claim.

ʿAbd al-Raḥmān I was the apparent sole Umayyad survivor of the ʿAbbasid takeover of Damascus in 750; he fled across North Africa and took refuge with his mother's Berber relatives in Morocco. Governors appointed by the Umayyad representative in Qayrawān in Tunisia had been ruling al-Andalus since its Muslim conquest in 711, but their power had always been tenuous because of ethnic infighting between Berbers and

General view of the mosque at Córdoba. Copyright © Scala/Art Resource, NY. Mosque, Córdoba, Spain.

Arabs, and among the Arabs themselves. By 756 ʿAbd al-Raḥmān I was able to easily defeat the governor Yūsuf al-Fihrī with the help of discontents and Umayyad supporters. He ruled for thirty-two years as emir of al-Andalus, and his direct descendants continued to rule as emirs, and later as caliphs, for almost three centuries.

The caliphate period spans the years 929–1031, from the declaration of a caliphate by Al-Nāṣir to the "abolishment" of the caliphate by the citizens of Córdoba after a quarter century of complete political chaos. For this reason some give the date of the end of the caliphate as 1013, when the Berber Hammudids took the throne. The period immediately following the end of the caliphate is known as the rule of the *tā'ifa* ("party") kingdoms.

The caliphate as an Islamic institution began in Medina with the death of the prophet Muḥammad in 632. Since Muḥammad was the "seal of the prophets," no one could claim the same prophetic mantle of authority to lead the Muslim *umma* ("community"). Muḥammad had not left a clearly designated plan of succession, so it was decided by his earliest and most loyal followers, the *sahāba* ("companions"), that Abū Bakr should be named *khalīfa* (one who follows), or caliph. He led the Muslim community until his death in 634 and was followed by the caliphs ʿUmar (634–644), ʿUthmān (644–656), and ʿAlī (656–661). All four are known collectively as the *Rāshidūn* ("rightly guided caliphs"). With the murder of ʿAlī in 661, Mu'āwiyya, a member of Muḥammad's clan, moved the caliphate to Damascus, where he had been governor for twenty years, and established a short-lived dynasty. In 683 a man from another branch of the Umayyad clan, Marwān I, established a longer-lived dynasty in Damascus (thus, the use of the names Umayyad and Marwānid to later signify the dynasty in al-Andalus). The Marwānids continued ruling the Muslim *umma* as caliphs until the ʿAbbasids rebelled in 750 in northeastern Iran and claimed the caliphate for themselves in Baghdad.

The question remains why ʿAbd al-Raḥmān I did not claim the caliphate himself in the name of the Umayyads when he seized power in Córdoba. The other side of the question is why ʿAbd al-Raḥmān III did claim the caliphate almost two centuries later. The sources indicate that ʿAbd al-Raḥmān I had pretensions of regaining control of the *umma* and reclaiming the caliphate but had enough trouble just trying to consolidate power in al-Andalus. His few efforts to galvanize pro-Umayyad support in North Africa failed. Another explanation might also be related to geography: traditionally, the caliph's right to rule derived from his role as protector of the holy sites of Mecca and Medina. The ʿAbbasids definitely controlled those cities, as well as most of the Islamic world from the eighth to the tenth centuries. It is interesting to note that in the *khuṭba* (sermon) of the Friday congregational prayers, where a benediction on the name of the caliph traditionally was invoked by the imam, the ʿAbbasid caliph was mentioned in Córdoba from 750 to 757. After 757, however, the name of the Umayyad emir was given the blessing, and the name of the ʿAbbasid caliph received a malediction. From almost the beginning of his reign, then, ʿAbd al-Raḥmān I asserted his independence from and disdain of the ʿAbbasid caliphate, although he did not claim the title himself.

There are no concrete or documented explanations for ʿAbd al-Raḥmān III's later claim to the caliphate either. By the time ʿAbd al-Raḥmān III took over the emirate in al-Andalus in 912, the ʿAbbasids were growing weaker and more corrupt. Some detractors argued that they no longer merited the title of caliphs because they were no longer good Muslims. By the year 929, when ʿAbd al-Raḥmān III declared himself caliph, not only were the ʿAbbasids no longer able to aggressively pursue *jihād* ("holy war") on the borders of Islam, but they no longer controlled the holy sites in Arabia. Another explanation may lie in the fact that the possibility of more than one caliphal claim had been opened in 909 by the Fāṭimids in Tunisia, who were Ismāʿili Shiites. Others have argued that 929 was the year when ʿAbd al-Raḥmān III unquestionably gained internal political control, had pursued several successful campaigns against the Christians in the north, and felt confident enough to take a step he had long considered. Whatever his justifications were ʿAbd al-Raḥmān III faced no serious opposition to his caliphal claim in 929, and he easily appropriated the two main symbols of caliphal power-the right to have his name invoked in the Friday prayers (*khuṭba*) and the right to mint coins (*sikka*) under the title of commander of the faithful (*emīr al-mu'manīn*).

Córdoba became the capital of al-Andalus in 716 under the rule of the Umayyad governors, but did not become a real center of power and culture until the Umayyad emirate began in 756. At that time it also became a center of civil unrest, and the conflicts within its walls and suburbs often mirrored the ethnic tensions troubling al-Andalus as a whole.

In the last two years of his life, ʿAbd al-Raḥmān I began building a large mosque in Córdoba next door to the fortress on the Guadalqivir. Having a centralized and monumental mosque near the residence of the Umayyad emirs was a way to proclaim and enhance their prestige as well as to underscore the religious legitimacy of their rule. This mosque was completed by his son, Hishām I (788–796), and enlarged and remodeled successively by ʿAbd al-Raḥmān II

(822–852), Muḥammad I (852–886), ʿAbd al-Raḥmān III (912–961), and Al-Ḥakam II (961–976).

As the Umayyad court grew in wealth and power, Córdoba attracted increasing numbers of scholars, artisans, merchants, and opportunists from other parts of al-Andalus as well as the Islamic world. The Christian chronicler Eulogius, of the mid-ninth century, complained bitterly that Latin language and culture were being forgotten as talented young Christian men adopted Arabic language and manners to gain access to and favor in the Umayyad court. This process only accelerated when the caliph ʿAbd al-Raḥmān III built a new palace complex on the outskirts of Córdoba, Madīnat al-Zahrā, named after his favorite concubine. The palace was full of technological wonders and artistic splendors—no expense was spared—but it later came to symbolize the opulence of the Umayyad dynasty, as well as its distance from its subjects.

The political challenges of the emirate and caliphate in Córdoba remained virtually the same throughout their three centuries of power—ethnic infighting was the main internal challenge, and incursions by the Christian kingdoms to the north was the main external challenge. For the most part, until the first quarter of the eleventh century, succession within the Umayyad dynasty was straightforward and peaceful. A large part of the stability of the dynasty is due to a series of relatively lengthy reigns (some of thirty years or more) that gave the emirs and caliphs the opportunity to pursue long-range policies and to effectively train their successors.

From the beginning of the Muslim presence in Spain, internal politics was monopolized by ethnic infighting: after the initial conquest, the tension was between the Arabs and the newly converted Berbers from North Africa, and between the Arabs themselves, whose tribal rivalries went back to pre-Islamic times; as more native Iberians converted to Islam in the ninth century and later, tension between old and new Muslims emerged; as the emirs and caliphs began importing more Berber and *ṣaqāliba* (slave) troops, especially in the tenth century, tensions increased between the native military and political elite and the foreigners who were supplanting them. Some Umayyad rulers were better at managing these tensions than others, but such concerns were always foremost on the political agenda.

When rulers were able to consolidate power internally, like ʿAbd al-Raḥmān II and ʿAbd al-Raḥmān III, they could turn their energies to the Christian frontier to the north. The Muslim conquest had reached as far as Narbonne in the beginning, but by the time ʿAbd al-Raḥmān I took over in 756, a system of military frontiers, or marches (*thugūr*, in Arabic), had been established. The Upper March ran along the Ebro valley, was centered in Zaragoza, and was very rarely under direct Umayyad control—the Muwallad (converts to Islam) families of the Banū Qasī and later the Tujībīs were the autonomous rulers of the area, intermarrying with the royal families of Navarre and León and often enlisting their help militarily. The Middle March encompassed the lower Duero River valley, was centered in Toledo, and was often ruled by an Umayyad appointee, though Toledo was the site of several major rebellions. The Lower March was in the southwest of the peninsula, along the Guadiana River, and was centered first in Mérida, later in Badajoz, and ruled by a series of Muwallad dynasties. These marches were the sites of forays by both Muslims and Christians, neither making any lasting territorial gains.

The summer military expeditions (*ṣāʿifas*) of the emirs and caliphs to the marches were as much to discipline and impress unruly Muslim subjects as they were to pursue jihād against the Christians, to "protect" the Muslim community and legitimate the Umayyads' right to rule. An essential component of their political program was gaining the support of the religious scholars (*faqīhs*) based in Córdoba, who were virtually all from the conservative Malikite school of law. In Islam, religious legitimization of political power, especially if one claimed the caliphate, was necessary. The courting of the favor of the *faqīhs* began with Hishām I, and by the time of ʿAbd al-Raḥmān II, they had become fairly bureaucratized.

External threats to al-Andalus from outside the Iberian Peninsula came from the Vikings, who made a series of attacks in the ninth century, but more crucially from the Fāṭimids of North Africa. The Umayyads had always been interested in establishing a presence in North Africa but were usually too busy with internal concerns. The large number of Berber immigrants in al-Andalus, as well as the establishment of an Andalusi immigrant community in Fez, secured continuous and peaceful trade and communication. The Shiite Fāṭimids came to power in Tunisia in 909, and pursued a vigorous policy of expansion. Luckily for Al-Andalus, this coincided with the reign of ʿAbd al-Raḥmān III, its most capable and powerful ruler yet. By establishing a military presence in the coastal towns of Ceuta, Melilla, and Tangier, ʿAbd al-Raḥmān III was able to prevent the Fāṭimids from making much progress in Morocco. By the 950s they had turned eastward, and in 969 they conquered Egypt. The Umayyads continued to send troops to Morocco as well as to recruit soldiers from the Berber tribes there, but no lasting occupation occurred.

The political policy of the Umayyad emirs and caliphs toward Baghdad and the rest of the eastern

Islamic world was one mitigated by distance. They were too far away from each other to have much direct contact or conflict. Both were well aware of each other due to the continuous and extensive travel and trade throughout the Islamic world, most of it conducted by religious merchant-scholars, and cultural exchange did take place. ʿAbd al-Raḥmān II imported a poet-musician from the ʿAbbasid court, Ziryāb, who is said to have revolutionized the Umayyad court and Córdoban society. Increasingly the Umayyads imitated ʿAbbasid political and cultural forms. But al-Andalus also gained prestige among Eastern Muslims as an oasis of Muslim culture and Malikite orthodoxy and an active frontier of the jihād, and attracted many visitors for both reasons. Embassies were regularly sent to the courts of Constantinople and European capitals, usually headed by Andalusi Christians or Jews.

It is difficult to determine the date of the end of the caliphate but not difficult to trace the causes of its relatively quick decline. The caliph Al-Ḥakam II died in 976, leaving a large and powerful al-Andalus in the hands of his fifteen-year old son, Hishām II, who had virtually no political experience or training. There were several men in influential political and military positions, representing the various ethnic interests, who jockeyed for power under the weak caliph. Al-Manṣūr, the famous religious scholar turned politician and military leader, who had established power in the harem and as *qāḍī* (religious judge) of North Africa, won out. He methodically destroyed his rivals and established complete *de facto* political and military control while still claiming to be the supporter and defender of the Umayyad dynasty. (It is a situation parallel to that of the Buyids in Baghdad who kept the ʿAbbasid caliphs as puppet rulers for almost two centuries.) Al-Manṣūr was considered by many to be as effective a ruler as ʿAbd al-Raḥmān III, and even more so because of his piety, severity, and success militarily against the Christians.

But Al-Manṣūr was riding the cresting tide of divisive policies that had begun centuries before. The accelerated importation of slave soldiers (*ṣaqāliba*) from Eastern Europe (but also from the Christian parts of Spain) by ʿAbd al-Raḥmān III had led to their gaining great power in the political and military machinery of al-Andalus. Al-Ḥakam II had tried to counterbalance this presence by importing large numbers of Berber soldiers, who often came as intact tribes. Both groups antagonized the Andalusi and Umayyad elite, who were displaced. When Al-Manṣūr died in 1002, his sons, Al-Muẓaffar and Sanchuelo, successively came to power behind the figurehead of Hishām II. They did nothing but exacerbate the rivalries in the capital, and by 1009, all the ethnic groups were staging coups from provincial power bases and forwarding their own Umayyad pretenders to the throne. In 1013 Hishām II was murdered and the Hammudid Berber dynasty took over the caliphate. Power changed hands repeatedly until 1031, when the elites of Córdoba supposedly abolished the caliphate, making way for a splintering of power among the provinces.

MARILYN HIGBEE WALKER

Bibliography

Fierro, M. I. "Sobre la adopción del título califal por ʿAbd al-Raḥmān III," *Sharq al-Andalus* 6 (1989), 33–42.

Guichard, P. *Structures sociales "orientales" et "occidentales", dans l'Espagne musulmane*. Paris, 1977.

Kennedy, H. *Muslim Spain and Portugal: A Political History of al-Andalus*. London, 1996.

Lévi-Provençal, E. *Histoire de l'Espagne Musulmane*. 3 vols. Leiden, 1950–53.

Manzano Moreno, E. *La Frontera de Al-Andalus en época de los Omeyas*. Madrid, 1991.

Scales, P. C. *The Fall of the Caliphate of Córdoba*. Leiden, 1994.

Vallvé Bermejo, J. *El Califato de Córdoba*. Madrid, 1992.

Wasserstein, D. *The Caliphate in the West*. Oxford, 1993.

CÓRDOBA, MARTÍN DE

Fray Martín de Córdoba (d. 1476), an Augustinian friant trained at Toulouse held, among other posts, that of vicar general of the Augustinian convent at Salamanca, and conventual of the convent at Toulouse. Deeply involved in the conflict between those who thought the principal function of a convent was to be a spiritual retreat (*observantes*) and those who advocated an active role in study and teaching, he taught moral theology at the University of Salamanca. The *Jardín de nobles donzellas*—a praise of women and an advice to the then Princess Isabel (1468) just before she was to ascend to the Castilian throne—enjoyed two early printings. (Valladolid, 1500, and Medina del Campo, 1542). His other works circulated in manuscript, though three were edited in the twentieth century: the *Compendio de la fortuna* (1453) a work that deals with the mutability of fortune dedicated to Alvaro de Luna shortly before his beheading, and the *Tratado de la predestinación* (c. 1470–1476), printed unedited in 1917 by Fulgencio Riesco Bravo and subsequently edited by Sánchez Fraile and reprinted in 1956; and a brief essay on preaching, "Ars praedicandi."

Among works attributed to Fray Martín that have not yet come to light are *Exameron*, a treatment of the six days of Creation; *Comentarios sobre el Apocalipsis de San Juan*; another on the Epistles of Saint Paul, *Comentarios sobre las epístolas de San Pablo*; an advice to nuns, *Alabanza de la virginidad para religio-*

sas; a treatise on logic and philosophy, *Lógica et Philosophia*; an unspecified theological treatise, *De mistica et vera theologia*; and *Libro de diversas historias*, possibly a collection of *exempla*.

HARRIET GOLDBERG

Bibliography

Córdoba, Fray Martín de. "Ars praedicandi," ed. F. Rubio Alvarez, *La Ciudad de Dios* 172 (1959), 329–48.

———. *Compendio de la fortuna*. Ed. F. Rubio Alvarez. Madrid, 1958.

———. *Jardín de nobles donzellas: A Critical Edition and Study*. Chapel Hill, N. C., 1974.

———. *Tratado de la predestinación*. Ed. A. Sánchez Fraile. Salamanca, 1956.

CÓRDOBA, MARTYRS OF

The forty-eight Christians who were executed in Córdoba for religious offenses against Islam between 850 and 859 were known as the Martyrs of Córdoba. What we know about them comes almost exclusively from the martyrologies and apologetic treatises composed by Eulogius of Córdoba—who was himself executed in 859—and his friend Paulus Alvarus. Though the execution of the priest Perfectus in April 850 is the earliest recorded in the martyrology, the real beginning of the "movement" per se was the execution of Isaac on 3 June 851. Isaac had worked as a secretary in the Córdoban government prior to retiring to a monastery outside of Córdoba. Three years later, he returned to the city and spontaneously denounced Islam in the presence of a Muslim *qāḍī* (judge), and was decapitated as a blasphemer. Isaac's action inspired a number of other Christians, mostly from local monasteries, to follow his example, resulting in seven more executions over the next four days and three more by the end of July 851. By the end of the summer of 853, thirty-six Christians had been put to death, either for blasphemy or apostasy. Most of them actively sought their deaths, though some were, as Perfectus had been, victims of circumstances beyond their control. The executions became more and more sporadic as the decade wore on. The death of Eulogius himself in March 859 marks the traditional end of the "movement," though Arabic sources—which are silent about Eulogius's martyrs—indicate that there were occasional executions of Christians for religious offenses over the course of the next century. Though the incidence of executions between mid–851 and the end of 853 was no doubt unusually high, it was equally unusual that the victims should have someone like Eulogius to record their deeds. As a result, it is difficult to determine, outside of this two-year period, whether the victims were in fact linked to each other by more than their inclusion in Eulogius's martyrology.

The unusual concentration of Christian dissent in Córdoba in the early 850s was the cause of enough concern among the local Muslim authorities to prompt a variety of measures on their part to discourage would-be martyrs. In the summer of 851, the emir ʿAbd al-Raḥmōn II (822–1852) ordered the arrest of the Córdoban clergy and detained them for some months, hoping to impress upon them his impatience with the situation. His successor Muḥammad I (852–886) convened a council of Christian bishops to deal with the matter in the summer of 852.

The executions, and in particular the apparent willingness with which many of the victims embraced the sentence for blasphemy and apostasy, led to a deep rift within the Christian community of Córdoba. Some, like Eulogius and Alvarus, applauded the actions of these Christians, calling them martyrs and composing *passiones* that recorded the details of their martyrdoms. It is clear from the apologetic nature of these sources, however, that Eulogius and Alvarus were writing, at least in part, to convince a community of Christians that had by no means unanimously accepted Isaac and his like as legitimate martyrs. The arguments that Eulogius and Alvarus posed on behalf of the would-be martyrs reveal that many Christians did not regard the situation in Córdoba as persecutory and therefore had difficulty seeing their executed coreligionists as anything other than suicides. Others show that these same Christians saw the Muslims not as pagans bent on oppressing the church or as devotees of a false prophet but as fellow worshippers of God, with whom it was permissible for themselves as Christians to interact. These opposing views of Islam and the Muslims are perhaps best understood as a reflection of differences in levels of assimilation to Muslim society among the Christians in the area. Many, though certainly not all, of the executed Christians came from outlying monasteries and rural areas around Córdoba where their contact with Muslims was limited. Presumably the Christians who lived in Córdoba were more likely to come up with a workable modus vivendi with the Muslims that would allow all to participate in the local society and economy.

KENNETH B. WOLF

Bibliography

Gil, J. (ed.) *Corpus scriptorum muzarabicorum*. 2 vols. Madrid, 1973. 2:363–503.

Millet-Gérard, D. *Chrétiens mozarabes et culture islamique dans l'Espagne des VIIIe–IXe siècles*. Paris, 1984.

Wolf, K. *Christian Martyrs in Muslim Spain*. Cambridge, 1988.

CORNAGO, JOHANNES

Spanish composer, most noted from 1449 to 1475. Already a Franciscan friar, he received a bachelor of biblical studies degree from the University of Paris in 1449. No later than 1453 he was a member of Alfonso V el Magnánimo's court at Naples, where on 6 April his yearly salary was fixed at the equivalent of three hundred ducats. A papal bull drafted 29 June 1453 but not signed until 20 April 1455 by Pope Calixtus III, identified him as Alfonso V's chaplain—who despite his Franciscan vow of poverty was permitted to acquire any benefice secular or regular and to hold a canonry or other dignity in a cathedral or collegiate church. After Alfonso's death on 27 June 1458, Cornago became Don Ferrante's chief *almnoner* (dispenser of royal charity). On 3 April 1466 he received ten ducats and a tari to pay for the cost of altering certain garments in the royal wardrobe that Ferrante proposed giving away on Maundy Thursday to thirty-four poor persons. On the same day he took in trust twenty-five ducats to bestow as alms during the king's adoration of the true cross the following Good Friday. According to Higinio Anglés, Cornago, upon returning to Spain, became in 1475 a singer in Fernando V's court chapel.

Cornago was the first Spanish composer to write a complete extant polyphonic mass. Titled *Frater J. Cornago Missa Signum de lo mapa mundi Apud Neapolim est la missa de nostra donna Sancta Maria* (Trent Codex 88, fol. 276v), this mass includes a tune sung by the tenor, with the *Ayo visto lo mapa mundi / et la carta di naviga / re ma chichilie mi Pare la piu bella di questo mondo* [I have seen the map of the earth / and the mariner's chart, / but Sicily seems to me the most beautiful part of the world]. This popular song, inspired by Jan van Eyck's map painted about 1430 (and highly praised in 1456 by Bartolomeo Facio, resident at Alfonso's Neapolitan court 1444/5–December 1457), recurs with the tenor throughout the mass. Composed before 1460, Cornago's mass ranks with Guillaume Dufay's *Missa Se la face av pale* as one of the earliest masses based on a secular tune. Cornago's other Latin work, the four-voice fragment *Patres nostri peccaverunt* (Montecassino MS 871A, page 248), sets to music Lamentations 5:7.

Cornago's eleven surviving courtly songs, always for three voices, all express disappointment in love: the *Colombina cancionero* (1971) contains *Donde' stas que non te veo*, *Gentil dama non se gana*, *Porque mas sin duda creas*, *Qu'es mi vida Preguntays* (with a fourth voice added by Ockeghem), and *Señor qual soy venida* (= *Infante nos es nascido*). The *Cancionero de Palacio* (1947) also contains *Gentil dama non se gana* and *Señor qual soy venida*, and the Montecassino manuscript 871A adds *Moro perche non dai fede*, *Morte merce* (an Italian syllabic text in all voices), *Non gusto del male*, and *Sequn las penas me days*.

Robert Stevenson

Bibliography

Pope, I. "Cornago, Johannes." In *New Grove Dictionary*. Vol. 4.

Gerber, R. L. (ed.) *Johannes Cornago: Complete Works*. Madison, Wisc., 1984.

Stevenson, R. "Johannes Cornago," *Inter-American Music Review*, 8, no. 2 (1987), 52–66.

CORRAL, PEDRO DEL

Little is known about the life of the man who wrote the *Crónica sarracina* (or *Crónica del rey Rodrigo*) in the first half of the fifteenth century. Presumably he was the brother of Rodrigo de Viilandrando, Count of Ribadeo, with whom he participated in Juan II of Castile and León's campaign against Alfonso V of Aragón. It is possible that the brothers were involved in the incarceration of the bishop of Palencia and other Castilian noblemen, including Fernán Pérez de Guzmán, one of the most important historiographers of the Spanish Middle Ages and Corral's most severe critic. In the prologue to his *Generaciones y semblanzas*, which has been widely accepted as the first Castilian treatise on the rules of historical discourse and the duties of the historian, Pérez de Guzmán calls him "un liuiano e presuntooso onbre" (a light headed and presumptuous man) and his *Crónica* a "trufa o mentira paladina" (fraud or public lie). These words, written while Pérez de Guzmán was in jail, seem to have determined the fate of the *Crónica sarracina*, unfairly ignored, when not condemned, by historiographers who have looked mainly at its anachronisms, and later redeemed by literary critics who, focusing on the chivalric and courtly atmosphere that surrounds the events leading to the Moorish invasion of Spain, consider it an early historical novel.

Whether Corral's intention was to write a chronicle or a fictional text, the *Crónica sarracina* could be, and has been, read as both, because it incorporates medieval conventions of verisimilitude that were used in fictional as well as historical texts. Among these conventions are the fictitious authors, Eleastras and Alanzuri, who are introduced at the beginning of the story as the chroniclers commissioned by Rodrigo to write the history of his kingdom, and the forgery of letters and documents that are transcribed and quoted throughout the text. These fictitious authors and sources unveil the story of Rodrigo's haughtiness in Hercules' tower; his adulterous love affair with La

Cava; the treason plotted by her father, Count Julian, with the Moorish leaders Muça and Tarif; and the total defeat of the Christian army Eleastras's chronicle ends with his death in battle. An anonymous parchment containing the story of Rodrigo's repentance and penitence is found centuries later by a soldier called Carestes in the king's tomb and is incorporated into Eleastras's manuscript, which, according to the author, was found in a market.

Although these conventions could be considered fictional and were adopted by later authors like Miguel de Cervantes, textual and authorial forgery, rooted in the Christian apocryphal tradition, was largely used in the Middle Ages as a strategy to legitimize discourses that claimed historical truth, such as the *Privilegio de los votos de San Millán* attributed to Fernán González, in which the grateful hero imposes an annual tribute for the monastery of San Millán de la Cogolla, and many hagiographical texts. In a period when authority was based on antiquity, fame, and personal witness of events, it is not surprising to find that, in spite of Pérez de Guzmán's bitter judgment, the *Crónica sarracina* was followed by many historians, such as Diego Rodríguez de Almela, who quotes Eleastras as an *auctoritas* (authority) in his *Compendio histórico*, and was widely diffused during the fifteenth and sixteenth centuries, as proved by its many extant manuscripts and editions.

AURORA LAUZARDO

Bibliography

Crónica del rey don Rodrigo, prostrimero rey de los godos (Crónica sarracina). Ed. and intro. James Fogelquist. 2 vols. Madrid, 2001.

CORREGIDOR

The *corregidor* was a Castilian official appointed by the crown to direct the government of a city (or several neighboring cities), assuring that both the general laws of the kingdom and the local laws (*fueros*, *ordenanzas*) were obeyed, thereby also maintaining the supremacy of monarchical power over the municipal body. Alfonso XI increased royal control over local politics between 1326 and 1345 by substituting the general assembly of citizens (*consejo abierto*) with the smaller *cabildo de regidores*, consisting of twenty-four people named by the king from among the members of the *consejo abierto*. In addition, starting in 1348 he began to send corregidores with judicial and inspectorial functions to some cities. At the end of the fourteenth century, Enrique III renewed these appointments in order to fight disorder and abuse at the local level. Between 1406 and 1474 the monarchy appointed more corregidores, often against the wishes of local leaders, who protested the fact that this was always done previous to the city's request. The Catholic Monarchs (1474–1516) expanded the continual presence of the corregidores and regulated their functions (the *Capítulos* of 1480, 1493, and 1500): there were roughly eighty *corregimientos* throughout Castile. The corregidor depended on the *Consejo Real*, which appointed him and managed the coordination of the kingdom's governing bodies, but the city paid his salary. The term of appointment was one year, although occasionally this was extended. At the end of the term, the corregidor could be brought to trial (*juicio de residencia*) to determine if he had performed correctly his duties, which included exacting justice (he was the royal judge par excellence), presiding over the *cabildo de regidores*, and directing all municipal activity: local law reform, police activity, military citizen organizations, public works and services, control of the local finances, and the application of the kingdom's economic and ecclesiastic policy. The corregidor was, in short, the crown's "omnicompetent servant" in the city.

MIGUEL ANGEL LADERO QUESADA

Bibliography

Bermúdez Aznar, A. *El Corregidor en Castilla durante la Baja Edad Media (1348–1474).* Murcia, 1974.
Lunenfeld, M. *Keepers of the City: The Corregidores of Isabel I of Castile (1474–1504).* Cambridge, U.K. 1987.

CORTES, CROWN OF ARAGÓN

Parliamentary institutions in the Crown of Aragón developed, as elsewhere, from festive and consultative courts occasionally convoked by the greater counts and kings in Catalonia and Aragón. It is not clear whether there was anything specifically "feudal" about this experience. The early *cortes* (*corts* in Catalan) were obligations laid upon knights in the Pyrenees for attendance on great lords rather than for counsel. Moreover, as elsewhere, the conceptual association of counsel and aid was an ecclesiastical as well as a military legacy. Great courts throughout Christian Spain were solemn celebrations of lord-kingship, more nearly public than feudal in character; they were occasions on which protector-rulers often threatened by the Muslims habitually dominated proceedings in which the mode of action was passive and deferential, responsive to the lord-king but not political.

This situation prevailed until the thirteenth century. The great assemblies of Aragón and Catalonia, often termed *curia*, met to ratify statutes of territorial security and dynastic decisions; they sometimes coincided with ecclesiastical councils. As early as 1162 a plenary assembly at Huesca prefigured the future *cortes* of the Crown of Aragón. But that tradition never overcame the practice of convoking the magnates of one realm, as at Zaragoza (1164) for Aragón and at Fondarella (1173) for Catalonia. The latter assemblies, held in the early years of Alfonso II (r. 1162–1196), were both concerned with peace—that is, with sanctions against violators of what was then known as the "Peace and Truce" (*pax et treuga*). These were, so far as we can tell, characteristically celebratory occasions on which the lord-king's role as institutor of the peace was deferentially accepted.

However, the peace program in both lands, especially in Catalonia, was opposed by the barons, who saw it as threatening their habitually violent domination of peasants at a time when the lucrative Muslim wars had been interrupted. By the 1180s the program seems to have lapsed in both lands. Alfonso tried to reinstate it in great courts held at Huesca and Girona (1188), and whatever may have happened in Aragón, the reaction in Catalonia was explosive. At Girona the count-king was obliged to offer concessions to magnates who, in the end, refused to ratify the statutes. Then, in an assembly held at Barcelona (we do not know just when), the barons categorically rejected the whole peace program; that is, the king's prerogative to keep the peace. And in a series of assemblies from 1192 to 1205, Alfonso II and Pedro II (r. 1196–1213) struggled in vain to recover their lost initiative in consultation.

The Catalonian *corts* held from 1188 to 1205 mark the origins of parliamentary life in the Crown of Aragón. Here, for the first time, the barons can be seen to act politically—that is, to contest the ruler's prerogative in the ceremonial court or even to disrupt proceedings; here are the beginnings of debate between members of interested estates as distinct from passive deference to the lord-king. This politicized confrontation was the critical change, and it soon entailed another: the summons of towns and villages to be represented by their notables. Precedents for such enlarged summonses go back to the 1150s in the Pyrenees, but it was in the first quarter of the thirteenth century that they became common (if not yet quite customary) in Aragón and Catalonia. The people of both realms, including townsmen, were convoked at Lérida (in the borderland) to deal with the dynastic crisis in 1214. Great plenary assemblies met at Barcelona to prepare for the invasion of Mallorca in 1228 and at Monzón to prepare for that of Valencia in 1236.

By that time every significant attribute of the mature medieval *cortes* was in place. During the reign of Jaime I (1214–1276), the occasional summons of magnates was transformed into institutions of the estates, including that of the towns. And their experience in insisting on privilege was a cause of Jaime's reluctance in his later years to summon the *cort(e)s*. Moreover, an institutionalized procedure had already developed: the hortatory proposition by the king (or by a prelate speaking for him); responses by ad hoc delegates of clergy, barons, and towns, followed by discussion within the orders; and the public agreements and decisions: vote of taxes, setting of date of muster, promulgation of statutes. In 1264 at Zaragoza there was a demand for redress of grievances prior to deliberation on the king's request.

In 1283 King Pedro III's prolonged failure to confirm the privileges of Aragón and Catalonia, combined with his costly conquest of Sicily, resulted in tumultuous assemblies at Zaragoza and Barcelona. It is customary to date the *cortes* as a parliamentary institution in the Crown of Aragón from these meetings. This view is mistaken, for reasons that should be clear. With one exception, every element of these occasions, and indeed the combination of these elements, was traditional. Politicized confrontation over privilege, summons, representation of men from the several orders, procedure—none of this was new; and as for the demand in both assemblies that the *cortes* should henceforth be summoned periodically, this was so poorly observed thereafter that it must be disqualified as a test. It is true that Jaime II (r. 1291–1327) summoned *cortes* in his early years; by working through them before the estates were tempted to act on their own, this canny ruler defused political opposition.

In fact, as elsewhere, the *cortes* of the later medieval Crown of Aragón had a fitful history influenced by fiscal and political necessity. During his Castilian wars Pedro IV (r. 1336–1387) became so dependent on taxes voted by his *cortes* as to lose the initiative in policy and finance. The *diputació* of the Catalonian *corts* functioned from 1359 as a permanently standing commission of the assembly. Similar institutions developed in other realms (including Valencia); everywhere the *cortes* expressed the privileged aspirations of the powerful, being (in that sense) politically regressive. In Catalonia the exclusion of the lesser knights consolidated a formidable alliance of landed magnates and urban oligarchs through which a "pactist" program hostile to fiscal and agrarian reform was confirmed. The *cortes* of Aragón, constituted in four estates (that of the nobility being divided), supported Alfonso V (r. 1416–1458) in his Mediterranean ambitions better than the earlier *cortes*, but their interminable proceedings revealed the hollowness of their claim to represent power fairly.

THOMAS N. BISSON

Bibliography

Bisson, Thomas N. *The Medieval Crown of Aragón*. Oxford, 1986.

Bonet y Navarro, A. *El justicia de Aragón: historia y derecho.* Intro. Angel Bonet Navarro, Esteban Sarasa Sánchez, Guillermo Redondo Veintemillas. Zaragoza, 1985.

Cortes de los antiguos reinos de Aragón y de Valencia y principado de Cataluña. Publicadas por la Real Academia de la Historia. 26 vols. Madrid, 1896–99.

González Antón, L. *Las Cortes de Aragón.* Zaragoza, 1978.

———. *Las uniones aragonesas y las cortes del reino (1283–1301).* Zaragoza, 1975.

El Privilegio general de Aragón: la defensa de las libertades aragonesas en la Edad Media. Ed. Esteban Sarasa Sánchez. Zaragoza, 1984.

Ubieto Arteta, A. *Historia de Aragón; Creación y desarrollo de la Corona de Aragón.* Zaragoza, 1987.

CORTES, LEÓN, CASTILE, AND PORTUGAL

By the mid-thirteenth century the *corte* (plural, *cortes*), an example of the European parliamentary tradition, emerged in Castile, León, and Portugal. This reflected the growing importance of towns that controlled extensive territories and supplied substantial militia forces for the reconquest. The *corte* was a natural expansion of the royal council as kings summoned townsmen to assemble with bishops and magnates. The three estates gathered with the king constituted the fullness of the kingdom acting as one legal person. The king's need to ask consent before imposing new taxes or to alter the laws was the principal reason for summoning the *cortes*. The assembly gave the participants an opportunity to present their grievances to the king and to urge governmental reform.

Alfonso IX of León first summoned urban representatives to his council at León in 1188. The Castilian kings likely did so from the second quarter of the century. After the union of Castile and León in 1230, the *cortes* were convened jointly, though occasionally separate meetings were held in order to thwart opposition to royal policy. From the mid-fourteenth century the *cortes* were a joint assembly for both realms. Afonso III of Portugal convened the first *corte* at Leiria in 1254.

The *corte* consisted of three estates (later called *brazos*): prelates, nobles, and townsmen. Archbishops and bishops (about twenty) customarily attended, but abbots, priors, masters of military orders, and proctors of cathedral chapters were sometimes summoned. About twenty magnates (*ricos hombres*) and as many knights (*caballeros*) also participated. Prelates and nobles attended the Castilian *cortes* irregularly in the fifteenth century and not at all after 1538.

All towns directly subject to the crown were summoned, but not all of those summoned always sent representatives. Perhaps the largest assembly were the *corte* of Burgos in 1315, when 100 towns sent 201 representatives. The number of Castilian towns represented steadily decreased to a mere seventeen in 1480. Many towns were no longer summoned because they were held in lordship by bishops and magnates. Attendance was viewed as a burden. Whole regions had no representation at all, and representatives in attendance acted solely on behalf of the urban oligarchy.

Representatives, first described as *omnes bonos*, *los de la tierra*, or *personeros*, were by the early fourteenth century identified as procurators. This Roman legal term designated one empowered to represent an individual or a corporation in court. Urban procurators received letters giving them full power (*plena potestas*) to act in the name of the town and to bind it in advance by their actions. Royal insistence that representatives have full powers was intended to prevent a town from later repudiating its procurator. Representatives were probably elected in the same manner as other municipal officials. From the late fourteenth century they were designated by the town council, chosen by lot, or municipal officials who served in rotation. Despite protests by the *cortes*, in the fifteenth century Juan II and Enrique IV named procurators to represent Castilian towns. The Castilian *cortes* of 1430 prohibited persons of humble condition from serving as representatives. The number of representatives was usually two, who were remunerated by the towns, though in the fifteenth century they were paid by the crown. They were assured of royal protection when traveling to and from the *cortes*, and during the sessions.

Only the king or his regents could summon the *cortes*. His presence was essential to the legality of the assembly. Letters of summons indicated the purpose, place, and day of the meeting. The Castilian cortes met frequently in the late thirteenth and early fourteenth centuries, sometimes as often as every three or four years. Alfonso XI, however, convened the *cortes* at irregular intervals, and then usually in regional rather than plenary sessions. The Portuguese *cortes* of 1385 asked João I to hold annual parliaments, but these were found to be too burdensome. The Portuguese *cortes* met twenty-eight times between 1385 and 1491. Meetings, usually lasting a few weeks, were held in palaces or cathedral or monastic cloisters in centrally located towns such as Burgos, Valladolid, Madrid, Lisbon, Coimbra, and Santarém.

The king opened the assembly by declaring the reasons for convocation and perhaps requested a subsidy. Each estate then responded (in Castile and León, the archbishop of Toledo, the lord of Lara, and the representative of Burgos). Toledo persistently challenged Burgos's claims to speak for the Castilian towns, but in 1348 Alfonso XI declared that Burgos should speak for Toledo. Little is known of the deliberations of the estates as they met separately to consider the king's requests and to draw up petitions. Once the petitions were approved by the royal council and a subsidy was voted, the *corte* were dissolved. Texts (*cuadernos*) containing petitions and royal responses were given to the procurators as a record of the principal actions taken.

Few rules defined the competence of the *cortes*, but it could intervene in matters relating to the succession, the recognition of a new king or the heir to the throne or the regulation of a minority; legislation; taxation; and other aspects of foreign and domestic policy. The Portuguese estates assembled in 1385 elected João I as king, and in 1438 the *cortes* of Torres Novas declared that only the three estates could determine the regency for a minor heir. The Castilian *cortes* confirmed the authority of regents during several minorities and also recognized the rights of royal heirs.

The *cortes* participated in legislation chiefly by submitting petitions concerning most areas of government. Petitions were usually presented by the townsmen, but occasionally by nobles and prelates. The towns constantly demanded that the king guard their charters and privileges, guarantee justice to all, punish corrupt officials, curb the lending activities of Jews, control prices or wages, and restrict the alienation of the royal domain. Prelates petitioned the king to uphold ecclesiastical jurisdiction and immunities, and the nobles usually asked for confirmation of their traditional usages. Once the royal response was given, ordinances enacted these decisions into law. The king, with the counsel and consent of the *cortes*, also promulgated ordinances regulating the administration of justice, the chancery, military obligations, and the like.

More systematic legislation prepared by royal legists was also enacted in the *cortes*, such as the Ordinance of Alcalá, promulgated by Alfonso XI in the *cortes* of 1348. In 1305 and 1313 the principle was asserted that laws promulgated in the *cortes* could be repealed only by the *cortes*, but this was never strictly observed. Since the crown tended to issue charters contradicting enactments of the *cortes*, the *cortes* of 1379 protested, and in 1387 Juan I pledged that such charters were not legally binding. Nevertheless, in 1427 Juan II declared that his charter was to be obeyed as law "just as if it had been enacted in *cortes*." While acknowledging the legality of ordinances enacted in the *cortes*, he clearly believed that he could legislate without those bodies. The Portuguese *cortes* also protested against the derogation of ordinances enacted in them, but Afonso V declared in 1451 that he would alter the laws made in the *cortes* "whenever the case required it."

The most important function of the *cortes* and the principal reason for the frequency of their meetings was to consent to taxation. Requiring extraordinary funds to meet his increasing financial needs, the king had to ask his people for subsidies; he could not levy taxes arbitrarily. Since the clergy and nobility were exempt, his request was usually made to the townsmen. Prelates and magnates were sometimes asked to consent to the imposition of taxes on their dependents. Extraordinary taxes or *servicios* were often expressed in terms of *moneda forera*, a tribute paid in return for the king's pledge not to alter the coinage for seven years. Alfonso IX levied such a tribute in 1202, and Afonso III did so in the *cortes* of Leiria in 1254. The obligation to seek the consent of the *cortes* before levying taxes was affirmed in the Castilian *cortes* of 1307, 1315, 1329, and 1391. Taxes were usually imposed for a fixed term of a year or two, but there were exceptions. A specific purpose was often stated, as in 1407, when the Castilian *corte* asked that the subsidy would be expended only on the war against the Moors. Although the *cortes* often haggled over the amount requested, some kind of grant was always forthcoming. In 1308, 1315, 1317, 1386, and 1387 the Castilian *cortes* asked for an accounting of the king's revenues before giving consent. The *cortes* often demanded that taxes should be collected only by incorruptible citizens of towns and not by Jews, Muslims, nobles, churchmen, or high officials. The *cortes* of Segovia in 1386 appointed officials to receive and expend the subsidy voted to the crown, but this effort to control royal finance never developed further. Neither Juan II nor Enrique IV hesitated to collect taxes without consent or to spend money for purposes other than those stipulated by the *cortes*.

From the early thirteenth century until the middle of the fourteenth, the *cortes* passed through a time of vigorous growth and development. In times of crisis they could have a determining influence on public affairs and could effectively limit the power of the crown. At the same time it could be manipulated by the king to his own advantage. In the fifteenth century the *cortes* declined in importance, although Fernando and Isabel at first used them to bolster their reforms; from 1482 to 1498, however, they did not summon the *cortes* because they were not dependent on their subsidies. Thereafter they convoked *cortes* to obtain money for the conquest of Granada and the Italian wars. All told, they summoned *cortes* only nine times. João II of Portugal also used the *cortes* to undercut noble opposition, but he convened them only four times between 1481 and 1495; Manuel I summoned them four times between 1495 and 1521, and did not hesitate to levy taxes without consent. Thus, at the close of the Middle Ages, by infrequent convocation and careful manipulation, the *cortes* were subordinated to royal power.

JOSEPH F. O'CALLAGHAN

Bibliography

O'Callaghan, J. F. *The Cortes of Castile–León, 1188–1350.* Philadelphia, 1989.

Piskorski, W. *Las cortes de Castilla en el período de tránsito de la Edad Media a la moderna, 1188–1520.* Barcelona, 1930. Repr. Barcelona, 1977.

Procter, E. *Curia and Cortes in León and Castile, 1072–1295.* New York, 1980.

Sousa, A. de. *As cortes medievais portuguesas, 1385–1490.* 2 vols. Oporto, 1990.

COTA RODRIGO

Cota (also known as Ruy Sanches Cota, or de Toledo, "el Viejo" or "el Tío") was born between 1430 and 1440, to a family of *conversos* (Jewish converts to Christianity). The house of his father, the merchant Alfonso Cota, was burned in 1449 in the anti-*converso* riots that led to the formulation of the Toledan "purity of blood" statutes. The family background was one of comfortable merchants and financiers with landed estates who were involved in Toledo's municipal government and the kingdom's civil service. They were closely related to other *converso* families (e.g., Arias Dávila and Ciudad Real) by financial, marriage, and geographical ties. His marriages to Isabel de Sandoval (d. 1477) and to Isabel de Peralta, from noble Christian families, followed the pattern of other converso families. He died soon after August 1505 at Torrijos and was burried in Toledo at the family chapel in the parish of San Nicolás.

Cota's *Diálogo entre el Amor y un viejo*, first published anonymously in the *Cancionero general* of Hernando del Castillo (1511), probably was written between 1470 and 1480. The 630-line *Diálogo* is composed of seventy mixed *coplas* (stanzas). The strophes consist of a four-line *redondilla* followed by a five-line *quintilla*. It is written in octosyllabic verse that rhymes *cdccd*. Its dialogue form was common in medieval Castilian literature, and its theme has antecedents in the invective against *Frauendienst* and in the *cancionero* poetry (e.g., Pedro de Cartagena, Jorge Manrique, Juan Rodríguez del Padrón) in which male lovers confront the god of love. Similarly the setting—the garden or the house of love—is typical of the *cancioneros*. Yet clearly the work has an idiosyncratic character. Castro has explained it in vitalist terms and has spoken of a "*vivir amargo*," while Aragóne in the introduction to her edition has seen its particularity in the "biblical violence" of its heightened pessimism and in the "biblical dramatism" of the "Hispanic Semite."

Cota's other well-known work, the *Epitalmio burlesco*, is composed of forty-nine *redondillas* and nine *quintillas*, 241 lines in all. Its satire is directed against the "Judaizing" customs of a *converso* who marries a Christian (possibly, according to Cantera, Diegarias's marriage in the first half of the 1470s to Marina de Mendoza, bastard daughter of Diego Hurtado de Mendoza). The main problems of the text—the difficulty of the "vocablos semíticos" of a "texto oscurísimo," according to Cantera, and the allusions to what Menéndez y Pelayo termed "usos poco sabidos de la población israelita de España"—have not been solved by its many modern editions. It has been suggested that the "Jewish" element should be a main concern of *Epitalmio* research because it is the one addressed by its contemporary audience (e.g., the well-known comment of an early reader, Queen Isabel: "que bien parescia ladrón de casa" (he seemed like a house burglar). This has been attempted by trying to reconstruct the dynamics of ethnic humor within contexts of ethnic tensions, as well as by paying attention to the characteristics of representation of the ethnic "other." The main satire is directed against "Jewish" language (the lexical as well as the syntactic and morphologic components), names, and diet (i.e., against the prime themes of ethnological definition), and corresponds to the obsessions of Cota's audience and contemporaries, as revealed in Inquisition files that contain testimony from witnesses who lived in Segovia, Toledo, and Madrid at the time of the composition of the *Epitalmio*.

Francisco del Canto, the editor of the 1569 edition of the *Diálogo*, attributed to Cota the authorship of the *Egloga que dicen de Mingo Revulgo* and the first *auto* of *Celestina*. Though the first attribution seems to have been discarded, the second is still held by some scholars. In a poem Antón de Montoro attacks Cota for his anti-*converso* satire with the significant allusion to Cota's Jewish lineage in the line "vuestro agüelo, don Barú" (your grandfather, don Baru[ch]). Cota is also the author of an *esparza* in which he discovers the properties of love, and, of the "*Respuesta*" to Gómez Manrique's poetic question "sy ovo reyes primero/qué caualleros oviesse?" [If Kings were first, what knights would there be?]

ELEAZAR GUTWIRTH

Bibliography

Castro, A. *La realidad históricá de Espana.* México, 1954.

Menéndez y Pelayo, M. *Orígenes de la novela.* Madrid, 1910. II, XXIII–XXV.
Cota, R. *Dialogo entre el Amor y un viejo* Introduction, critical text, and commentary by E. Aragóne. Florence, 1961.
Gutwirth, E. "On the Background to Cota's 'Epitalamio Burlesco,' " *Romanische Forschungen* 97, no. 1 (1985): 1–14.

COURTLY LOVE

Courtly love (*amour courtois*), a term popularized in 1883 by Gaston Paris, is widely accepted by literary critics and cultural historians as a convenient description of a conception of love that informed a tradition of European literature from the twelfth century until the Renaissance. The Provençal troubadours used other expressions, such as *fin'amors*, *bon'amors*, and *vrai' amors*; similar terms (e.g., in Castilian *fin amor* and *buen amor*) are found in other Romance languages. Although the adjective *courtly* was rarely employed by medieval writers in this context, it is appropriate because it indicates the ethic of courtliness and draws attention to the aristocratic milieu in which this literary or poetic convention flourished. It thus establishes a link between Provençal poetry of the early twelfth century, northern French romances of the late twelfth century, German minnesinger poems, and romances of the thirteenth century, Galician-Portuguese lyrics of the same period, Italian literature of the early fourteenth century, English literature of the late fourteenth century, and Catalan and Castilian literature of the fifteenth century.

Whether it is treated seriously or satirically, this tradition is evident in the works of most major medieval authors, including Bernart de Ventadorn, Guillaume de Lorris, Chrétien de Troyes, Chaucer, John Gower, Dante, Petrarch, Marie de France, Charles d'Orléans, Gottfried von Strassburg, Thomas Malory, the Marqués de Santillana, Diego de San Pedro, and Fernando de Rojas. It is also of central importance in the works of Renaissance writers such as Gil Vicente and Garcilaso de la Vega. Although they have never been considered of major importance, partly because so little of their work has survived, twenty known women troubadours, at least a third of whom were patrons, were writing in Occitania in the late twelfth and early thirteenth centuries; their poetry, which is more varied and personal in tone than that of their male counterparts, sheds fresh light on the courtly love phenomenon.

The essential features of this conception of love are the beloved's superiority, love worship, voluntary commitment, secrecy, the interdependence of love and poetry, and the ennobling, yet potentially destructive, power of love. The beloved was invested with the sovereignty of a feudal overlord or the perfection of a goddess. The lover humbly pledged to serve her, demanding no more than a sign of recognition for deeds performed on her behalf. Since a public display of emotion might jeopardize the lady's honor, particularly if she was married, discretion was a fundamental precept and a condition of any sexual favor that she might confer. This explains why it was customary for the poet to conceal his beloved's identity and to express himself in a deliberately ambiguous manner. By endeavoring to make himself worthy of his beloved, the lover acquired a number of moral, courtly, and military virtues. If she was too easily accessible, love would cease to be arduous and ennobling; yet if she epitomized the archetypal *belle dame sans merci*, the traditional symptoms of love—emaciation, trembling, insomnia, fainting, and pallor—could deteriorate into a species of melancholia, leading ultimately to death.

Courtly love has been subjected to a variety of uses and definitions. Crypto-Cathar, Neoplatonic, Marian, Ovidian, and Freudian theories may all be discarded as untenable. More plausible are the arguments of those who suggest it was a game, a secular code of conduct, or a poetic convention. In fact few subjects offer such a fertile ground for speculation—on the relationship between men and women, life and literature, fact and fantasy, courtly and popular, personal and conventional, profane and sacred, sensual and spiritual, and so on. Ambiguity is inherent in *amour courtois* because it is founded on the tense coexistence of erotic desire and spiritual aspiration; critics who focus on one element at the expense of the other are falsifying the picture. It was neither a mere cover for extramarital relations nor a purely spiritual ideal.

Courtly love was not, as some have claimed, a distinctively European phenomenon. All the main features mentioned above are found in the Arab tradition of chaste love, *hubb al-ʿudhrā*, formulated in Ibn Ḥazm's *The Ring of the Dove*, which can be traced back to the poetry of the Banū ʿUdhrah (the Sons of Chastity), a seventh-century tribe renowned as martyrs of unrequited love, in particular to Jamāl al-ʿUdhrā (d. 701). We may infer that *hubb al-ʿudhrā* was imported from Muslim Spain into southern France by musicians, singers, captives, refugees, and slaves. Sicily was also a channel of communication between East and West. However, as a result of the analogy of feudalism and other social factors, courtly love acquired a deeper significance in Europe than it had ever possessed among the Arabs. Factors that created a demand for conventions of love outside marriage included a shortage of women in aristocratic circles because of the upward social mobility of men, the improved status of certain women whose crusading husbands left them in control of fiefs, and the existence of a "leisure class" with few military or material responsibilities. Thus courtly love did not remain confined to poetry and the world of the imagination; it not only left its mark on the values of polite society but eventually became the basis of marriage and gave rise to the modern concept of romantic love.

ROGER BOASE

Bibliography

Boase, R. *The Origin and Meaning of Courtly Love: A Critical Study of European Scholarship*. London, 1977.

Bogin, M. *The Women Troubadours*. New York and London, 1976.

Newman, F.X. (ed.) *The Meaning of Courtly Love*. Albany, N.Y.: 1968.

Paris, G. "Études sur les romans de la Table Ronde: Lancelot du Lac, II: Le conte de la charette," *Romania* 12 (1883), 459–534.

Parker, A.A. *The Philosophy of Love in Spanish Literature, 1480–1680*. Ed. T. O'Reilly. Edinburgh, 1985.

COVADONGA, BATTLE OF

A mountain cave in present-day Asturias near Cangas de Onís, Covadonga is roughly sixty-five kilometers east of Oviedo. According to the earliest preserved Asturian chronicles, it was the site (718/719) of the first battle between Muslim and Christian forces after the Muslim invasion of the Iberian Peninsula. The Christians emerged victorious, and it has thus been hailed as the beginning of the Spanish Reconquest.

The leader of the Christian forces is said to have been Pelayo, who through his success became the first king of Asturias (r.718/9–737). He is depicted as a refugee Visigothic noble who opposed a Muslim general named Alkhama. The chronicles, which draw on oral accounts, are highly dramatic. Pelayo, attempting to avoid a battle, took refuge on the edge of the Picos de Europa. There his force was discovered and surrounded by the Muslims. Christian bishop, Oppa of Seville, urged them to surrender, for resistance would be useless against the always victorious armies of Islam. Pelayo refused, placing his trust in divine aid, and claimed that the reconquest of Spain would begin there.

When the battle was joined, the spears and arrows of the Muslims, once they had reached the mouth of the cave that contained the chapel dedicated to the Virgin, were miraculously turned back against them. Great numbers of them were slain, and a sortie by Pelayo resulted in the death of Alkhama and the capture of Oppa. The remainder of the Muslim force attempted to retreat to safety over the mountains, but was caught in a divinely inspired earthquake, and perished.

BERNARD F. REILLY

Bibliography

Collins, R. *The Arab Conquest of Spain: 710–97*. Oxford, 1989.

Gil, J. F., (ed.) *Crónicas asturianas*. Oviedo, 1986.

COYANZA, COUNCIL OF

A meeting of the magnates and bishops of the realm of and Castile summoned by Fernando I (1035/37–1065) and his wife, Queen Sancha at what is today Valencia de San Juan, thirty kilometers south of the city of León, in 1055. It was attended by seven bishops of the kingdom as well as those of Pamplona and Calahorra, from the tributary kingdom of Navarre. The thirteen canons that resulted apparently were promulgated by the monarchs.

The stated purpose of the council was to reform the church and the realm. Reform was understood in a quite traditional sense, and the canons of the council are based upon ancient collections: the *Hispana*, the *Liber iudiciorum* (*Fuero juzgo*), the *Breviarium* and the *fuero* attributed to Alfonso V of León (r. 999–1027). The council was at pains to underscore the authority of bishops and abbots in the church, to maintain the proper independence of the church from lay authority, and to ensure the use of correct liturgical practice. So far as the council was concerned with secular administration, its attention was directed largely to the observance of proper legal practice and obedience to proper legal authorities.

The acts of the council are preserved in two textual traditions. The earliest is that of the twelfth century *Liber testamentorum* of the cathedral of Oviedo. The other is in the thirteenth century *Livro preto* of the cathedral of Coimbra.

BERNARD F. REILLY

Bibliography

El concilio de Coyanza: Miscelánea. León, 1951.

Martínez Díaz, G. "El concilio compostelano del reinado de Fernando I," *Anuario de estudios medievales* 1 (1964), 121–38.

CRESCAS, HASDAI

Even for a scholar as important as Hasdai Crescas, a major figure in fourteenth-century Aragón and Catalonia, dates (ca. 1326–ca. 1412) and data of his life are uncertain. He was descended from a long line of Jewish scholars of Barcelona, and both his grandfather (also named Hasdai) and his father, Abraham, are known from various sources.

Following in the footsteps of his grandfather, who was a government official in the service of Pedro IV (1326) and one of the six *adelantados* (secretaries) of the Jewish community of Barcelona, Crescas was an official of the same community. Sometime in 1370 or 1371 he, along with Nissim Gerundi, Isaac ben Sheshet, and other important Jewish scholars, was arrested by order of the king as a result of unspecified charges made against them by other Jews (probably angered at their strict interpretation of Jewish laws). Isaac ben Sheshet soon left Barcelona to become rabbi of Zaragoza, and Crescas succeeded him in that position (probably in 1385) when Isaac went to Valencia. Earlier, in 1359, Crescas had been in Perpignan, France, where he met Samuel Zarza, author of an important commentary on Ibn Ezra. It was probably while rabbi of Zaragoza, that he taught; among his students were Joseph Albo, Zerahyah ben Isaac ha-Levy (Ferrer Saladin), and Matityahu ha-Yishariy (all later participants in the famous Tortosa disputation of 1413). It should be noted that he was hardly the "chief rabbi" of Aragón—there never was such a position—but he was widely respected as one of the last great scholars of the kingdom. A letter purporting to be by Crescas, if authentic, is an important source for the events of the summer of 1391, when Jewish communities throughout Spain were attacked by mobs. We know that the king and queen took special measures to protect the Jews of Barcelona (and elsewhere), and particularly the family of Crescas, including his son and grandson. Therefore, the statement in the supposed letter of Crescas (somewhat difficult to understand) that his son and/or son-in-law was killed must either be rejected or understood to refer only to a son-in-law.

Crescas was the author of three works of which we know: *Or Adonai* (*Light of the Lord*), an anti-Aristotelian defense of the doctrines of Judaism completed in 1410; a work, possibly in Catalan, discussing and refuting ten "principles" of Christianity (this survived only in a Hebrew partial translation and synopsis); and a recently edited sermon on Passover.

It has been noted, however, that his theoretical work was composed both too late to make any impression on an already deteriorated and leaderless Jewish community, and too early for his more radical concepts to have been well received. The mass conversion of Jews to Christianity in the late fourteenth century and throughout the fifteenth century was in no way halted by his polemical writings or doctrinal defense. He was in fact, a leader who failed.

NORMAN ROTH

Bibliography

Crescas, H. *The Refutation of the Christian Principles*. Trans. D. Lasker. Albany, N.Y. 1992.

Roth, N. "The Arrest of the Catalan Rabbis," *Sefarad* 47 (1987): 163–72.

Wolfson, H. A. *Crescas' Critique of Aristotle*. Cambridge, Mass., 1929; repr. 1971.

CRÓNICA DE ALFONSO XI

The *Crónica de tres reyes* (Alfonso X, Sancho IV, and Fernando IV) and the *Crónica de Alfonso XI* (1344) are attributed to Fernán Sánchez de Valladolid, Alfonso XI's *notario mayor de Castilla y canciller del sello de la poridad* (Chief notary of Castile and Chancellor of the Privy Seal) This historical enterprise is the official continuation of the *Estoria de España* of Alfonso X and was sponsored by Alfonso XI toward the end of his reign.

The *Crónica de Alfonso XI* is considered to be of greater interest and quality than the *Crónica de tres reyes*. It draws on a variety of sources, the most important being its author's personal recollections. The chronicler witnessed many of the events he narrates, but also draws extensively on information gathered orally—expressions such as "él que escribió esta estoria oyó decir" (he who wrote this history heard it said), and "el Estoriador oyó decir" (the historian heard it said) are common. His main goal is not just to write a biography but, rather, "contar de las cosas que acaescieron en los regnos de Castiella et de León en el tiempo deste Rey Don Alfonso" (to recount the events that occurred in the kingdoms of Castile and León in the time of King Alfonso). However, the chronicler occasionally narrates events that occur outside the king's domains, such as truces in the Hundred Years' War and struggles of pretenders to the Holy Roman Empire and the papacy.

Some of his material comes from archival documents, including the genealogies of the Moorish kings of Granada and of the Almohads. Internal evidence demonstrates beyond doubt that he held an administrative position in the royal chancery. The detailed information he presents on internal and external political affairs strengthens the case for Fernán Sánchez de Valladolid as the author. For example, the author describes in detail the negotiation of the alliance between Alfonso XI and the king of France, in which the chancellor played a leading role as ambassador. The author was very close to, and a devout admirer of, the king. Alfonso XI is always presented favorably, without defects. If the royal chronicler had any goal beyond praising the reign of his lord, it was to portray Alfonso XI as a just monarch and to uphold the authority of the royal delegates who administered justice.

According to the chronicler the common people loved and admired the king; popular revolts were due to the ambition of the nobles. The king is also admired for his crusading spirit. At times of great difficulty God is always on his side, and miracles help him and the Christian troops. The chronicler tries to stay above personal infighting at the court, but occasionally there are glimpses of his personal preferences, as when he unfavorably presents Doña Leonor de Guzmán, the mother of the king's illegitimate children. Upon comparing this chronicle with the *Poema de Alfonso XI*—a text that was written by Rodrigo Yáñez in 1348 and covers many of the same events—one observes, for instance, the chronicler's dislike for Alvar Núñez de Osorio, an adviser to the king, and his sympathy for Pedro Fernández de Castro, "adelantado mayor de Castilla." Similarly he praises the Castilians and shows dislike for the subjects of other kingdoms, such as the Galicians.

Stylistically, although the *Crónica de Alfonso XI* is considered superior to the *Crónica de tres reyes*, it does not represent a great improvement in historiography. The chronicler prefers to describe rather than to explain. The order of the narration is chronological, and at times the author complains about his difficulties in properly narrating all the events that happened in different places at the same time. At one point, in an attempt to record every event of military importance, he organizes some of his entries by months. The only person who is described in detail is the king. This portrayal reveals the author as a man of letters. Among the most colorful descriptions, the knighting of the king in Santiago de Compostela and the coronation ceremony in the monastery of Las Huelgas stand out. Some other scenes of the king's life in periods of peace seem to have been influenced by the growing fashion for romances; for example, one sees the king hunting and participating anonymously in a tournament.

There are very few speeches in the text; most of them are short, and present the king's anger or his harangues to his troops. The chronicler asks his readers to bear with him and the length of his text. It seems that the chronicle was never completed, because it ends with the conquest of Algeciras (1344) and does not include the king's death (1350). This fact is quite striking, particularly because Fernán Sánchez de Valladolid survived his monarch by some ten years.

The anonymous author of the *Gran crónica de Alfonso XI* (written between 1376 and 1379) interpolated many sections from the *Crónica de Alfonso XI* and enriched his work with borrowings from the *Poema de Alfonso XI*, Arabic histories, and other sources.

MERCEDES VAQUERO

Bibliography

Gram crónica de Alfonso XI. Vol. 1. Ed. D. Catalán. Madrid, 1976. 15–24, 163–70.

Moxó, S. de. "La sociedad política castellana en la época de Alfonso XI," *Cuadernos de España, anejo* to *Hispania* 6 (1975), 187–326, at 282–83.

Rodgers, P. K. "José Pellicer and the Confusion over the Authorship of the *Cuatro Crónicas*," *La Corónica* 17 (1988), 41–51.

CRÓNICA DE DON PERO NIÑO, CONDE DE BUELNA (EL VICTORIAL) *See* DÍAZ DE GAMES, GUTIERRE

CUADERNA VÍA *See* MESTER DE CLERECÍA

CUARTE, BATTLE OF

On 15 June 1094 the great Muslim city of Valencia, capital of a prosperous kingdom (*tā'ifa*), surrendered to the Castilian warrior and adventurer Rodrigo Díaz de Vivar, better known as the el Cid. It was a major defeat for Islam, and the Almoravid emir, Yūsuf ibn Tāshfīn, decided that it must be reversed. From Morocco, he dispatched forces that were joined by others of Muslim Andalusia, the whole under the command of his nephew, Muḥammad.

Faced with a much superior force, el Cid appealed to his overlord, Alfonso VI of León-Castile, for assistance. The Almoravid army reached Valencia about September 1094 and set up siege lines around the city. Before any reinforcements of his own had arrived, el Cid noticed that the enemy was lax in discipline and that some units had actually left for home. In October he staged a sudden sally that concentrated on the enemy camp at Cuart de Poblet, rolled up the entire Almoravid force, end effectively lifted the siege.

The victory ensured that the city and territories of Valencia would remain in Christian hands until the death of El Cid in 1099 and, for that time, prevented the spread of Almoravid power on the eastern coast north of Murcia. In 1094 it gave Alfonso VI the opportunity to employ the army he had raised for the relief of Valencia to raid deep into Almoravid Andalusia at Granada. Following to the death of el Cid, Valencia proved impossible to defend; it was evacuated in 1102 and occupied by the Almoravids shortly thereafter.

BERNARD F. REILLY

Bibliography

Huici Miranda, A. *Historia musulmana de Valencia y su región*. Vol. 2. Valencia, 1970.

Reilly, B. F. *The Kingdom of León-Castilla Under King Alfonso VI, 1065–1109*. Princeton, N.J., 1988.

CURIA GENERALIS *See* CORTES

CURIA PLENA *See* ADMINISTRATION CENTRAL; CORTES

CURIA REGIS *See* CORTES

CURIA SOLEMNIS *See* CORTES

CURIAL E GÜELFA

Curial e Güelfa a fifteenth-century anonymous Catalan novel of chivalry. The first book relates how Curial, the son of a poor knight, gains the protection of the young widow Güelfa, the sister of his lord, the marquis of Monferrato. Some malicious *lausengiers* compel Curial to travel abroad. In Austria he overcomes the treacherous knights who had accused the duchess of adultery. Laquesis, the attractive sister of the duchess, is offered to Curial, who refuses her, although he cannot help falling in love. Güelfa feels offended even though Curial fights for her in a tournament held at Monferrato.

In the second book Curial is sent by Güelfa to Melun, in France, to fight against the greatest knights of the world. Curial easily overcomes them all, except for King Pere of Aragón. The hero once again meets the fair Laquesis and, confused by love and pride, forgets his fidelity to Güelfa. Thus Curial loses the protection of his beloved, who swears that she will never befriend him again until the whole French court gathered at the Puig de Nostra Dona pleads mercy for his sake.

In the third book the unhappy, fallen hero travels to the Holy Land and to Greece (in his dreams he even visits Mount Parnassus). On his way home Fortune decides to defeat him again: Curial's ship sinks and the young man is thrown onto Tunisian shores. For seven years Curial works as a slave on the farm of the Muslim Fàraig, whose pretty daughter, Càmar, falls in love with him. Curial avoids being seized by passion, and the girl, like Dido in Virgil's *Aeneid*, commits suicide after giving our hero a large treasure stolen from her father. Curial reaches Monferrato again, but Güelfa refuses to listen to the song he has written for her, *Atressi com l'aurifany* (which actually is the work of the twelfth-century troubadour Rigaut de Berbezilh). Finally Curial assembles an army to fight against the Turks, who have recently invaded Europe. In a successful battle he rescues the lord of Monferrato from the enemy; as a result he finally attains the highest glory, and the French court obtains Güelfa's mercy for him.

Whereas the first two books of the novel recount events from a realistic point of view, the last one includes a strange learned mythological background that enables the anonymous author to produce a moral interpretation of his hero's behavior.

LOLA BADÍA

Bibliography

Curial and Guelfa. Trans. by P. Waley. London, 1982.

Curial e Güelfa. Ed. by R. Aramon. 3 vols. Barcelona, 1930–33.

Espadaler, A. *Una reina per a Curial*. Barcelona, 1984.

D

DANCE

Although the tradition of dance had become well established in the Middle Ages, most of its repertoire has since been lost because it consisted mostly of instrumental music, which was not customarily written down until well into the fifteenth century. Nevertheless, chronicles and archival documents do make reference to specific dancers. The earliest reference concerns a master of Jewish dance, Rabbi Hacén ben Salomo, who in 1313 performed a circular dance in the Church of San Bartolomé in Tauste, Zaragoza. Quite different were the ten *dansas* (a type of troubador song) with vocal accompaniment that the *infante* Pedro composed and performed during a banquet celebrating the coronation of his brother, Alfonso IV of Aragón, in the Aljafería of Zaragoza in 1328. Ramón Muntaner, who chronicled the event, says that the city celebrated the event in the streets with "danses de dones e de donzelles e de molta bona gent" ["dances of young men and women and many good people"]. In the *Libro de Buen amor*, the Arcipreste de Hita claims to have written many dance compositions fit to be performed by different instruments ("muchas cantigas de dança e troteras,/ para judías e moras"). These might have resembled those heard in Burgos when Alfonso XI, King of Castile and León, was knighted: on that occasion, in the words of Rodrigo Yáñes, "ricas dueñas fasían dança/ a muy gran plaser cantando" ["Many fine ladies danced/and sang with pleasure"] (*Poema de Alfonso*).

The Aragónese monarchy showed constant fondness for dance. In Pedro IV's court there were at least two "trobadors de dances," Jacme Fluvia of Mallorca and Pere de Rius. Given Juan's exclusive interest in French music, it is quite possible that the dances performed for him followed French models; the manner of dancing "a la françessa," which Alfonso Alvarez de Villasandino mentions in a poem to the queen, Leonor de Navarra, would be characterized by the *rondel*, *virelai*, and *estampida*. Martín I of Aragón preferred a group of female Moorish dancers—*alfuleys*—that served in his court: the king describes one performer (Foix) wishing to join the troop in 1406 as "apta balladora." These women were from Valencia, as was Graciosa, the most famous Spanish *bailadora* of the era. In 1409 she was serving in the court of the Queen of France, but after traveling to Navarre and Castile, in 1417 Graciosa entered the service of Alfonso V ("the Magnanimous"), who paid her at the rate of two *sueldos* daily, just one less than he paid his marshals. In that same year, Alfonso ordered that twenty-five gold *florines* be sent to "Nutza la balladora, mora juglaressa de Valencia." In 1418 another group of "moros balladors" served in Alfonso's court: this troop consisted of the Valencian dancer Moratxo, his wife Uzey, their son Abdalla, and his wife Muzeys. The following year, the king sent for certain "moratelles balladores" who he wanted to see perform; later, in 1425, Alfonso requested that certain "moros e moras balladores de Xativa" join his court. The king's favorite performer, however, was Catherina "la Comare," a singer and dancer who was at Alfonso's service from 1417 to 1424, and who often danced dressed in Moorish costume despite the occasionally adverse reactions of the audience. She performed accompanied by her husband Johan de Muntpalau, a lutist and guitarist.

When the Aragónese royalty travelled to Valencia, it was welcomed by processions that always included musicians and "dançadores" from the city's guilds. The repertoire of these popular dances was probably quite different from the compositions contained in the *Llibre Vermell* de Montserrat, dating from about 1400. This collection of compositions, designed to entertain the pilgrims that visited the monastery at Montserrat, included four circular dances accompanied by lyrics with Marian themes: *Los set gotxs, Cuncti simus*, and *Polorum regina*, all performed "a ball redon" with one voice; and *Stella splendens*, a *virelai* performed "ad trepudium rotundum" with two voices. The choreography of the *Llibre Vermell* could very well be reflected in one of the miniatures of the T codex of the *Cantigas de Santa María* of Alfonso X; the illustration accompanies cantiga 5 and portrays a group of faithful dancers holding hands in a circle in front of an image of the Virgin. Another composition from the *Llibre Vermell* is *Ad mortem festinamus*, the oldest example of a dance of death whose music is preserved: subsequent versions of Spanish or Catalan *danzas de la muerte* are strictly literary. The Maundy Thursday procession celebrated in Verges (Girona) includes a dance—possibly with origins tracing back to the fourteenth century—in which Death takes part; it is performed by five individuals dressed as skeletons and consists of three rotating steps.

The first reference to the *baja danza* appears in Francesch de la Vía's poem *La senyora de valor* (1406). Both the *alta* and *baja* dances were fashionable in Spain throughout the fifteenth century. For example, in the descriptions in his *Crónica* of the parties given at the palace of Jaén, Miguel Lucas de Iranzo, Condestable of Castile, mentions several times that *chirimías* and other instruments played "baxas e altas" on a raised wooden platform at one end of the dance hall. While in Fuenterrabía in 1462, the ambassador of France danced "la baxa e la alta" with Doña Juana of Portugal, Enrique IV of Castile's wife; the hero of the anonymous novel *Curial e Güelfa* (c. 1450) performs the "baxa dança" at each of the parties he attends. The *Cancionero musical de Palacio* (c. 1500) includes one alta written for three voices by Francisco de la Torre in which the tenor voice coincides melodically with the famous *baja*, *La Spagna*. A dance manual printed in Toulouse around 1480 displays the choreography for *La Spagna* under the title *Casulle la novelle* [sic]; it also includes choreography for another *baja*, *La beauté de Castille*, whose melody was also incorporated in a collection of *bajas* compiled during the time of María de Borgoña, wife of Maximilian I of Austria. The same collection contains *La basse danse du roy d'Espaigne*, probably referring to Juan II of Castile, whose *Crónica* says that he danced very well ("danzaba muy bien"). A Catalan manuscript of 1496 reproduces the choreography of several dances dating from the second half of the fifteenth century, including *La Spagna* or *Baixa de Castilla*.

MARICARMEN GÓMEZ MUNTANÉ

Bibliography

Besseler, H. "Katalanische Cobla und Alta-Tanzkapelle." In *Kongressbericht Basel 1949*. Basel, 1949. 59–69.

Gómez, M. C. *El Llibre Vermell de Montserrat, Cantos y Danzas*. Sant Cugat del Vallés, 1990.

———. *La música en la casa real catalano-aragonesa durante los años 1336–1432*. Barcelona, 1979.

Mas, C. "La baixa dansa al regne de Catalunya i Aragó al segle XV," *Nassarre* 4 (1986), 145–59.

Pujol, F., and J. Amades. *Diccionari de la Dansa, dels Entremesos idels Instruments de Música i sonadors I. Dansa*. Barcelona, 1936.

Roca, J. *La processó de Verges*. Girona, 1986.

Sachs, C. *Eine Weltgeschichte des Tanzes*. Berlin, 1933.

DANTE ALIGHIERI

Along with Francesco Petrarca and Giovanni Boccaccio, Dante Alighieri (1265–1321) formed part of a triumvirate of Italian authors who provided the inspiration for new ways of writing and thinking about literature in later medieval Iberia. The earliest direct influence of the *Divina commedia* (Dante's other works left little or no impact) is to be found in the allegorical verse of Francisco Imperial, a member of the Genoese colony in Seville in the early fifteenth century. However, the close links between Aragón and Italy meant that admiration for Dante was at first more notable in authors connected with the Aragónese courts. The poet Andreu Febrer undertook the first complete translation of the *Divina commedia* into Catalan (1429), an accurate and fluid rendering with evident literary pretensions. An Aragónese nobleman, don Enrique de Aragón (Enrique de Villena), also attempted the first Castilian translation (1427–1428, *Inferno* only). Unlike Febrer, Villena conceived his version as a literal guide to the Italian original and had it transcribed in the margins of a manuscript of the *Commedia* owned by Iñigo López de Mendoza, the marqués de Santillana. The latter's marginalia indicate how Dante was plundered as a source of moral and political sententiae: a characteristic of medieval and early modern reading practice that is also found in a manuscript fragment of the *Inferno* with fifteenth-century Catalan glosses. But evidence for other modes of reading—at least on Santillana's part—comes from his copies of Castilian versions of the commentaries by Pietro Alighieri (anonymous) and Benvenuto da Imola (*Pùrgatorio* only, by Martín de Lucena). Santillana also owned an anonymous translation of the *Vite di Dante e Petrarca* by Leonardo Bruni. Although the commentaries by Jacobo de la Lana and Cristoforo Landino were known in Spain—the former is used by Villena, the latter by later translators (see below)—the commentary by Benvenuto da Imola seems to have been the most favored, being cited for example by Juan de Mena in the preface to his *Coronación*, and in the anonymous Castilian translation and gloss of first two cantos of the *Commedia*. Around 1500, Pedro Fernández de Villegas, archdeacon of Burgos, translated the *Inferno* for King Fernando's daughter, Juana de Aragón. Printed in Valladolid (1516), this verbose amplification into *arte mayor* stanzas was continued by an anonymous translator who experimented with octosyllabic verse (*quintillas* and *tercets*) to provide a more succinct version that would correspond more closely to Landino's commentary. Allusions to Dante are common in late medieval Catalan and Castilian poetry, though there is little substantive influence on a textual level. There are exceptions, such as the verse of Francisco Imperial, but for the most part, reminiscences of Dante are rhetorical or tonal in nature, as in the portentous allegorical verse of Mena (*Coronación, Laberinto de Fortuna*) and Santillana (e.g., *Infierno de los enamorados*). On the whole, the latter's comment that Imperial was not a *trobador* but a *poeta* is symptomatic: Dante provided a model for the new notions of vernacular authorship that were gaining ground in the later Middle Ages. Whether or not he was read outside fairly narrow circles of literati, the name Dante was part of the cultural baggage of lay poets who aspired to compose verse with transcendental pretensions.

JULIAN M. WEISS

Bibliography

Farinelli, A. *Dante in Spagna, Francia, Inghilterra, Germania*. Turin, 1922.

Pascual, J. A. *La traducción de la 'Divina comedia' atribuida a Don Enrique de Aragón*. Salamanca, 1974.

Penna, M. "Traducciones castellanas antiguas de la *Divina comedia*." *Revista de la Universidad de Madrid*, 14 (1965), 81–127.

DE REBUS HISPANIAE
See JIMÉNEZ DE RADA, RODRIGO

DECRETALS
See LAW, CANON

DESCLOT, BERNAT

Desclot is the author of the Catalan chronicle *Llibre del rei en Pere d'Aragó e dels seus antecessors passats*. Miquel Coll i Alentorn put forward the hypothesis that Desclot was an officer of the royal chancellery and a member of the Escrivá family from the Rosselló. Desclot's chronicle, written between 1283 and 1288, it is one of the oldest Catalan texts. The first eleven chapters include some dynastic legends (the establishment of the house of Barcelona in the Crown of Aragón, the birth of the great king Jaime I, Count Ramón Berenguer IV's rescue of the German empress, and the Aragónese rights to Provence). These episodes furnish the ideological background to a book conceived as a glorification of the Aragónese monarchs. Desclot narrates the life of Jaime I the Conqueror (r. 1214–1276), but his work is particularly centered on the reign of Pedro II the Great (r. 1276–1285). In this part of the chronicle, in spite of his enthusiasm for the chivalric nature of King Pedro, Desclot clearly used contemporary documents to compile his narrative (only once does he claim to be an eyewitness).

The most famous episode of Pedro II's life was his military expedition to Sicily, where he went to accept the crown offered to him as a result of the Sicilian Vespers (1282). Even though Charles I of Anjou, the deposed king of the island, persuaded the church to excommunicate the Catalan army, Pedro II's brave warriors (chiefly the *Almogávares*) managed to defeat the French. Desclot also narrates individual deeds of the king, such as his successful journey to Bordeaux in disguise to fight against the treacherous Charles of Anjou, and describes the invasion of Catalonia by the French crusading armies in their attempt to place Charles of Valois on the throne instead of Pedro II (1285). The chronicler does not avoid crude details in his descriptions of the bloody battles fought by the Aragónese navy, or the pursuit through the Pyrenees of the French army, which was suffering from a bad epidemic. Desclot's patriotism is best exemplified by the story of Pere II's Sicilian admiral, Roger de Llúria, who after the French defeat firmly refused an onerous treaty suggested by the Count of Foix. Llúria was sure of his strength because, he said, even the fish in the Mediterranean would now be wearing on their tails the red and golden stripes of the Aragónese flag.

LOLA BADÍA

Bibliography

Desclot, B. *Crónica*. Ed. by M. Coll i Alentorn. 5 vols. Barcelona, 1949–51.

Elliott, A. G. "The Historian as Artist: Manipulation of History in the Chronicle of Desclot," *Viator* 14 (1983): 195–209.

Rubió i Balaguer, J. *Història i historiografia*. Vol. 6, *Obres completes de J. Rubió Balaguer*. Barcelona, 1987.

DIAS, BARTOLOMEU

It is not known when or where this Portuguese navigator was born. Certainly he came from a family with some maritime tradition, for an ancestor was Dinis Dias e Fernandes who explored the North African shore in the 1440s and discovered Cape Verde in 1444.

Ptolemaic and medieval Italian conceptions of the disposition and shape of the Euro-African landmass had led cartographers to grossly underestimate the extent of the African continent. It was probably in the wake of the frustration felt by the Portuguese king João II, when the second expedition of Diogo Cão (1485–1486) revealed a seemingly unending coastline southward, that another expedition was immediately ordered, with Dias as its commander. His fleet consisted of two caravels and a supply ship captained by his brother Diogo.

The fleet left Lisbon in August 1487 and reached the farthest point attained by Diogo Cão (Cape Cross in modern Namibia) in early December. According to some accounts prolonged stormy weather then drove the fleet out of sight of land. In the event, Dias ran, heavily reefed, before the southeast trade winds and, then, at approximately forty degrees south latitude, encountered the Antarctic westerlies, which enabled him to turn to the northeast and make his first landfall, probably in Mossel Bay. He continued eastward as far as the Great Fish River, although his main stop was in Algoa Bay. Here, mindful of serious discontent among the half-starved crew, his fellow officers may have forced a reluctant Dias to turn for home.

On the return journey he discovered the southernmost tip of Africa, Cabo das Agulhas, where he experienced very bad weather. Thus, that when he reached False Bay, he named its promontory Cabo Tormentoso (Cape of Storms); he, or possibly King João, subsequently renamed it Cabo da Boa Esperança (Cape of Good Hope). He reached Lisbon in December 1488 but was received with none of the pomp and munificence enjoyed by his predecessor Diogo Cão or his successor Vasco da Gama. He later took part in Gama's voyage in 1497 and that of Pedro Alvares Cabral in 1500. He died on Cabral's expedition when his ship sank in heavy seas off the Cape of Good Hope.

Dias was the first European navigator to sail entirely out of sight of land in the southern hemisphere, discovering in the process the southeast trades winds and the westerlies; he confirmed that all existing maps of Africa were erroneous, and effectively opened up the sea route from Europe to Asia.

ROBERT OAKLEY

Bibliography

Barros, João de. *Décadas.* 4 vols. 6th ed. Lisbon, 1945.

Peres, Damião. *História dos descobrimentos portugueses.* Oporto, 1943.

DÍAZ DE GAMES, GUTIERRE (EL VICTORIAL)

Only one other fifteenth-century Castilian biography, that of Alvaro de Luna, is comparable in extension and importance to *El Victorial*, the only known work of Gutierre Díaz de Games. Written in an elegant, lively style, the work's lucid prose is enriched by rich nautical vocabulary, painting an expressive tableau composed of both real and imaginary scenes of chivalric life. This biography of Pero Niño, Count of Buelna, is historically authentic; but as a panegyric that exalts its subject to heroic levels, it also becomes a literary narration synthesizing the fifteenth-century European chivalric ideal of victory.

The author makes his presence known at the end of the *proemio*, manifesting not only his close, dependent relationship with Pero Niño but also his privileged position as a reliable witness of the "todas las más de las cavallerías" (*all the other forms of chivalry*) that will be narrated in the text. His position as naval lieutenant would not be incompatible with his career as notary; it seems probable, therefore, that he is the same Gutierre Díaz, notary to the king, who acted as diplomatic ambassador on various occasions during the regency of Fernando de Antequera and the reign of Juan II. The environment of the royal chancellery would have been favorable for the production of what Juan Marichal has called Gutierre Díaz's "voluntad de estilo."

It is commonly believed that Díaz started *El Victorial* in 1435, the year of Pero Niño's last will and testament, which contains a note about the work's commission and destination. However, the author may have begun the biography as early as 1431, when Pero Niño was named Count of Buelna. The work would likely have been finished (save perhaps some of the supplementary material) no later than 1436.

An extensive doctrinal and historical *proemio* opens the text as a means of justifying the novelty of the biographical story. Pero Niño's life will serve as a specific noble and Christian *exemplum* in a chivalric treatise ("tratado de caballería") that had universal appeal. The *tratado* itself, dedicated to narrating the count's life, is divided into three parts. The first relates Pero Niño's lineage, birth, childhood, education, the initiation of his career, and his first marriage.

Díaz shrouds Pero Niño's birth with an aura of legend facilitated by the fact that Enrique III was born around the same time and that Pero Niño's own mother served as the king's wet nurse. In this way the author infers a sort of "blood brotherhood" that is later ratified as the two boys are brought up together at court. To emphasize the count's education, the author incorporates a fragment of the *castigos* used by an anonymous master to indoctrinate the boy. The chapters dedicated to Pero Niño's initiation into knighthood continue incomplete scenes or add details that are absent from Ayala's chronicles; they also add new motifs to the chivalric biography genre, such as the precocity of the hero, the appearance of good omens, fights against animals, the petition of the king's weapons during first battle, or the comic challenge made to a foreign giant. The protagonist's physical and moral portrait precedes his marriage to his first wife, Constanza de Guevara, which is embellished with a curious discourse on the degrees of love.

The second part relates the expeditions that Pero Niño made to the Mediterranean and the Atlantic as captain of the Castilian fleet between 1404 and 1406. The essentially truthful nature of the historical events narrated in these sections is confirmed through the detail of some of the diary like episodes, that mark the passing of time day by day. Gutierre Díaz takes advantage of Pero Niño's arrival in England to introduce the fictitious "History of Bruto and Dorotea," pushing the chronicle once more into novelistic territory and seasoning the Pero Niño's already notable exoticism with shades of legend. The second part ends with a summary of the knight's participation in the first year of the War of Granada (1407).

The third part tells of the travails of the count's life up to his death. Of particular interest is the chapter on Pero Niño's "conquest" of Beatriz de Portugal, who would become his second wife. The author also includes an exonerative version of Pero Niño's participation in the sacking of Tordesillas, in which Juan II was retained by the *infante* Enrique and his men. The biography ends with a brief description of Pero Niño's exile to Aragón, a result of his support of Enrique's faction; his return and recuperation of the king's trust; a summary of the life of his ill-fated firstborn son, Juan; and passing references to the count's interventions in other military affairs.

Even though it is a fifteenth-century biography, the first representative of a genre associated with the dawn of the Renaissance, *El Victorial* does not display even the slightest humanist influence in its treatment of fame and the biographical subject, nor a trace of knowledge of or curiosity for the classics. Díaz constructs a perfect chivalric world, without fissures, that seems destined to ward off the political and ethical disorder of the real world. He makes use of the basic procedures of the chronicle narrative and the compositional organization of chivalric fiction. The unique characteristics of *El Victorial* arise precisely from the way in which the author attempts to assimilate the aristocratic conceptualization of life. Therefore, the work is as contradictory as it is harmonic, as disconcerting for the collector of objective past facts as it is attractive for the cultural and literary historian.

RAFAEL BELTRÁN

Bibliography

Beltrán, R. (ed.) *Gutierre Díaz de Games, "El Victorial."* Salamanca, 1996.

Carriazo, J. M. (ed.) *El Victorial. Crónica de Pero Niño, conde de Buelna. Por su alférez Gutierre Díaz de Games*. Madrid, 1940.

Circourt Puymaigre, C.E. (trans.) *Le Victorial. Chronique de Don Pedro Niño, comte de Buelna, par Gutierre Díaz de Gamez son alferez* (1379–1449). París, 1987.

Evans, J. (selec. and trans.) *The Unconquered Knight. A Chronicle of Deeds of Don Pero Niño, Count of Buelna, by his Standard-bearer Gutierre Díaz de Games* (1431–1449). London, 1928.

Ferrer Mallol, M.T. "Els corsaris castellans i la campanya de Pero Niño al Mediterrani (1404). Documents sobre *El Victorial*," *Anuario de Estudios Medievales* 5 (1968), 265–338.

Marichal, J. "Gutierre Díaz de Games y su *Victorial*" en *La voluntad de estilo. Teoría e historia del ensayismo hispánico*. Madrid, 1971, 51–67.

Pardo, M. "Un épisode du *mania Victorial*: biographie et élaboration romanesque," *Romania*, 85 (1964), 269–92.

———. "Pero Niño visto por Bernat Metge." In *Studia Philologica. Homenaje ofrecido a Dámaso Alonso*. Vol. III. Madrid, 1963. 215–23.

Riquer, M. de. "Las armas en *El Victorial*." In *Serta Philologica F. Lázaro Carrater*. Vol. I. Madrid, 1983. 159–78.

Scholberg, K. R. "Ingenuidad y escepticismo: nota sobre *El Victorial* de Gutierre Díaz de Games," *Hispania* 72 (1989), 890–94.

Surtz, R. E. "Díaz de Games' Deforming Mirror of Chivalry: the Prologue to the *Victorial*," *N* 65 (1981), 214–18.

Tate, Robert B. "The Literary *Persona* from Díaz de Games to Santa Teresa," *Romance Philology* 13 (1960), 298–304.

DÍAZ DE MONTALVO, ALFONSO

Born early in the fifteenth century in Arévalo (Segovia), Díaz de Montalvo as a child moved with his family to his permanent home in Huete (Cuenca). At the universities of Salamanca and Lérida he studied canon and civil law, obtaining his doctorate from Salamanca (1464/1672). Under Juan II he served as the king's representative (*corregidor*) in Baeza and Murcia (1444–1445), as delegate (*procurador*) from Huete to the *cortes* (parliament) of 1448, and in other judicial capacities both temporary (*pesquisidor*, *juez comisario*, in Madrid, 1453–1454) and permanent (*oidor*). Under Enrique IV, Díaz de Montalvo was named *asistente* of Toledo (1460–1461, 1463–1464), *gobernador* and *alcalde mayor* of the Order of Santiago, and member of the Royal Council. Fernando and Isabel commissioned him to produce a compilation of laws that would cover legislation from the time of Alfonso XI on. The result was the *Copilación de leyes* (1484), also known as the *Ordenamiento de Montalvo* and the *Ordenanzas reales de Castilla*. The work enjoyed wide diffusion (eight other incunabula editions are verified) and was used in legal studies through the first half of the sixteenth century. Modern scholars disagree on the authority and legitimacy of the work (both of which, on the weight of the evidence, seem most likely) and its promulgation (more improbable than not). The principal defect of the work lies in Díaz de Montalvo's personal selectivity and formulation of items according to unstated criteria, sometimes without regard to the validity of a particular disposition, let alone to full quotation.

Díaz de Montalvo also prepared glossed editions of the *Fuero real* (Seville, 1483, and at least eleven others, of which three are incunabula) and the *Siete Partidas* (Seville, October 1491, and at least six other verified editions, one from December 1491 and the rest from 1501 to 1550), both of which suffer from the same inadequacies as the *Copilación*. He also prepared two dictionaries: for canon law the *Repertorium quaestionum super Nicolaum de Tudeschis* (1477, and five more incunabula), and for civil law the *Repertorium seu secunda compilatio legum et ordinationum regni Castellae* (Salamanca, ca. 1485; two other verified incunabula editions; and at least two sixteenth-century editions). Additional works deal with the Royal Council (*De concilio regis*), glosses of the *Leyes del estilo* (Salamanca, 1497), and other legal topics. Díaz de Montalvo's will is dated 1496, and he is said to have died in 1499.

ROBERT A. MACDONALD

Bibliography

Caballero, F. *Noticias de la vida, cargos y escritos del Doctor Alonso Díaz de Montalvo*. Madrid, 1873.

Díaz de Montalvo, A. *Copilación de leyes del reino—Ordenamiento de Montalvo*. 2 vols. Valladolid, 1986. (Facsimile of Huete), 1484.

DÍAZ DE VIVAR, RODRIGO

Rodrigo Díaz was born at Vivar, near Burgos, in 1043, the son of the *infanzón* Diego Laínez. Because of his noble status and the protection of his maternal uncle, Nuño Alvarez, he was reared in the household of Infante Sancho, the son of Fernando I. He accompanied Sancho on his expeditions to protect the petty Muslim king (*tā'ifa*) of Zaragoza against the attacks of Ramiro I of Aragón, whom they defeated at Graus (1063). When Sancho II ascended the throne of Castile (1066), he named Rodrigo royal *alférez (armiger regis*, or standard bearer). As such he participated in quarrels with the neighboring kingdoms: a dispute with Navarre over the castle of Pazuengos, in which he gained the nickname *Campi doctor* or *Campeador*; an expedition against the *tā'ifa* of Zaragoza, who had stopped paying tributes (*parias*) to Castile (1067); the battles or "judgments of God" at Llantada (1068) and Golpejera (1072), fought by Sancho II and his brother, Alfonso VI of León, to determine to whom the thrones of Castile and León belonged. Sancho won both battles. Rodrigo's deeds during the siege of Zamora, which supported Alfonso, were extolled in legend. The assassination of Sancho II during the siege (October 1072) forced the Castilians to accept Alfonso as king, although Rodrigo and his followers required him first to swear an oath of purgation, in the Germanic fashion, that he had had no part in Sancho's death and had not plotted it. Rodrigo Díaz became a vassal of Alfonso but lost his important position at court.

In 1074 the king arranged a very advantageous marriage for him to Jimena Díaz, daughter of the Count of Oviedo and great-granddaughter of Alfonso V. At the end of 1079 he went to Seville to collect tribute owed by that *tā'ifa* to Alfonso VI. In 1081, as a consequence of an incursion that he made into the *tā'ifa* kingdom of Toledo, under Leonese protection, and the accusations made against him by Count García Ordóñez and other courtiers, Alfonso VI declared him subject to the *ira regia* (royal wrath), compelling him to go into exile.

Rodrigo's exile with his retinue interrupted his courtly career and launched him on enterprises in which he showed his capabilities and gained fame as well as the nickname El Cid (lord). He rendered military services to the *tā'ifa* of Zaragoza against King Sancho Ramírez of Aragón and Navarre (whom he routed in 1084) and against the Count of Barcelona and the *tā'ifa* of Lérida. After the African Almoravids' first invasion of al-Andalus and their rout of Alfonso VI at Zallāqah (1086), the king received Rodrigo again (in the spring of 1087) and entrusted him with the mission of protecting the *tā'ifa* of Valencia, al-Qādir, formerly king of Toledo. In 1089, when the *tā'ifa* of Zaragoza and the Count of Barcelona besieged Valencia, El Cid received from Alfonso VI all the lands that he might conquer in the eastern part of the peninsula, to be held by hereditary right. He lifted the siege of Valencia, using as a base of operations Albarracín, whose *tā'ifa* resumed payment of tribute to Castile.

The second Almoravid invasion (autumn of 1089) resulted in Rodrigo's disgrace once again because he was unable to relieve the advanced Castilian position at Aledo in the southeast. At the beginning of 1090 he consolidated his protectorate over Valencia when he routed and captured the count of Barcelona near Morella (Battle of the Pines of Tévar), dissolving his coalition with the *tā'ifas* of Lérída, Albarracín, and Zaragoza. The Almoravid conquest of al-Andalus after 1090 required Rodrigo, again in royal favor on various occasions, to strengthen his dominion in the east, thereby covering one of the flanks of the kingdom of Toledo and of all Castile, and blocking the coastal road to the Ebro valley. In the face of this danger, the *tā'ifa* of Zaragoza and Sancho Ramírez of Aragón allied against him. Alfonso VI, who tried to take Valencia in 1092, entrusted the defense of Christian interests in that zone to Rodrigo. Al-Qādir of Valencia was deposed and killed by the Valencian *qāḍī* Ibn Jahhaf, with Almoravid help. El Cid, with the aid of anti-African Muslims and of the Mozarabs, occupied Valencia and repelled the Almoravid relieving army (Battle of Cuarte, October 1094).

The Cid established himself as "lord of Valencia" and supreme judge, by hereditary right, maintaining his fidelity to Alfonso VI; he coined money and resided with his troops in the citadel of the city. He established a regime of coexistence, allowing the Muslims to keep their property, their system of taxation, and religious liberty, although they surrendered their arms. Former rebels were relocated to the suburb of Alcudia. After the Almoravid attack in January 1097, their defeat in the Battle of Bairén, and the capture of Murviedro (modern Sagunto) in 1098, Rodrigo converted the mosque into a cathedral (the first bishop was a Frenchman, Jerome of Perigord). To consolidate alliances he arranged the marriage of his daughters Cristina and María to Infante Ramiro of Navarre and Ramón Berenger III, Count of Barcelona, respectively. He died 10 July 1099 without a male heir, and Valencia fell to the Almoravids in 1102. Thus the route to the northeast was opened, and Castile's effort to consolidate its dominion in the east was nullified.

Rodrigo quickly became an epic personality, although the memory of his historical existence was not lost. He was a military genius, a hero formed by exile and adventure during the difficult years of the Almoravid invasion; he represented to perfection the values of chivalry and vassalage, the spirit of the frontier, and coexistence between Christians and Muslims, under the aegis of the king-emperor of León and Castile.

MIGUEL ANGEL LADERO QUESADA

Bibliography

Fletcher, R. *The Quest for El Cid.* Oxford, 1989.

Menéndez Pidal, R. *La España del Cid.* 7th ed. Madrid, 1969.

Lacarra, M. E. "*El poema de mío Cid. Realidad histórica e ideología.* Madrid, 1980.

DIDACTIC PROSE, CASTILIAN

Definition

There is no standard definition of didactic literature. It often suffers from being viewed as a miscellaneous genre, defined negatively as what remains of literature when narrative, lyric, and (possibly) the religious genres have been subtracted. In this view its postmedieval successors are the discursive genres, the essay, and belles-lettres, in which substance is poorly focused or subordinate to form.

For our purpose didactic literature is taken to be the literature that teaches either morals or facts. It includes wisdom literature, mirrors of princes, *exempla*, and didactic romances. In accordance with a modern critical tradition of doubtful validity, it excludes history, biography, and hagiography but includes a number of works, such as legal texts that, when they occur in postmedieval writing, are regarded by critics as subliterary or nonliterary. Some such works are so plain as to be artless, but they may also include, generally in an illustrative or corroborative capacity, elements such as anecdotes that would be regarded as literature.

Theory

The concept of didacticism is recognized in classical definitions of the function of literature. "Teaching" figures in the pair *docere ornare* (Quintilian, *Institutio oratia*, 9.4.127) and the triad *docere/delectare/movere* (Quintilian, *Institutio*, 3.5.2; 8 *prooem*, 7; hence Martianus Capella 5.473). "To teach" in these classical examples seems always to denote the conveyance of factual information; in medieval formulations "to teach" usually means to teach good ways.

Very often (given the medieval tendency to view the world in terms of issues rather than phenomena), the ethical and factual categories overlap. For example, Juan Manuel's *Libro de los estados* is notionally a sociological description of the estates of men, but is actually concerned with saving one's soul within one's estate. In the *Arte cisoria*, Enrique de Villena prescribes not only the professional but also the moral formation of the carver: one is reminded of Cato the Elder's description, picked up by Quintilian, of the orator as "a good man skilled in speaking" (*Ad filium*, 14). Similarly the mentality of the bestiary, reflected in Juan Manuel's *Libro del cavallero e del escudero*, or of the medieval historian gives moral interpretation a status equal or superior to that of the relation of facts.

The didactic frame of mind is also important in the reception of texts: the reading of literature as a source of facts or as the occasion for moral commentary, sometimes allegorical, was already established in the schools in antiquity, and encouraged by St. Paul's dictum, "All that is written is written for our doctrine" (Rom. 15:4, translated by Chaucer). The *Siete Partidas* is didactic in both senses: besides its practical intent, they it was used as material for moral works on chivalry. The double function of legal texts is encapsulated by the citation of the Horatian tag *Omne punctum tulit qui miscuit utile dulci* [Every point that combines the pleasing with the useful is well taken] (*Ars poetica*, 343) and the claim to benefit both body and soul in the prologue to the *Fueros de Aragón*. The popularity of such an attitude is shown by the use of the promise of moral teaching as a selling point on early title pages such as that of *Celestina*, and by the fact that, in surviving inventories of libraries and in the output of the early printers, didactic works outweigh lyric and romance works.

An essential feature of the genre is its seriousness; the unambiguous meaning is paramount. Juan Manuel insists on clarity as the basis of style: "Más de consentir et más aprovechoso para el que ha de aprender es en ser la scriptura más luenga et declarada que non abreviada et escura; ca el que aprende, entre todas las cosas que ha mester, es que aya vagar para aprender" [Clearly developed and openly declared writing is more beneficial and to be encouraged for those who are to learn, rather than tense, obscure writing; he who learns, must above all, have the space in which to do so] (*Libro de los estados*, I, 1xiv).

Prose

Isidore of Seville calls prose "an extended utterance free from metrical rules" ["producta oratio et a lege metri soluta"] (*Etymologies*, I.38.1). This is the ultimate source for the marqués de Santillana's reference in the *Prohemio e carta* to "la soluta prosa." Isidore goes on to give the etymology of prose as "extended and straight" and declares the chronological priority of prose over verse. This last point is generally accepted as regards Castilian literature. The earliest use of prose in its modern sense in Spanish may occur in the first translation of the *Consolation of Philosophy*.

Factual Works. Whereas factual verse is common in French, English, and other medieval languages, in Spanish factual material is largely in prose. The schema of the sciences that the Florentine Brunetto Latini (*Tesoretto*, I, 3–4) developed in the thirteenth century out of Aristotle and Isidore provides a background against which to place the various factual works. Philosophy is divided into theory, practice, and logic. Theory is divided into theology, physics, and mathematics, and mathematics is subdivided into arithmetic, music, geometry, and astronomy. Practice is divided into ethics, economics, and politics. Politics is subdivided into the mechanical arts and what in other schemes is called the trivium (grammar, dialectic, and rhetoric). Logic is divided into dialectic, physics, and sophistics. These topics are not evenly represented in Old Spanish, and while some subjects are present in the vernacular corpus from the beginnings, others are not found until the fifteenth century.

In theology there are plenty of religious texts, generally works of devotion meant for the layman rather than for the specialized religious reader. In physics there is a substantial corpus, not earlier than the fifteenth century, of medical works, including Villena's *Tratado de la lepra*. Although it concerns natural history, the *Lucidario* commissioned by Sancho IV proposes a religious interpretation of its material expressly in opposition to the rational sciences. There are some "natural questions" in *La Donzella Teodor*. In mathematics arithmetic, music, and geometry apparently have no Old Spanish texts. Astronomy is present in the vernacular as early as the Alfonsine corpus. (Ethics is discussed in "Books Teaching Morals," below.)

Economics (the art of running a household) is represented at the practical level by Villena's *Arte cisoria* and at the theoretical level by much of wisdom literature. Politics is covered by the mirrors of princes; Rodrigo Sánchez de Arévalo's *Suma de la política* is partly indebted to this genre.

Juan Manuel's claim (in the prologue to the *Libro de la caza*) that Alfonso X had translated all the liberal and mechanical arts is not borne out by the surviving Alfonsine corpus. There is nothing in Old Spanish on weaving, *armatura* (the plastic arts and architecture), or *theatrica*; perhaps travel books may be placed under navigation (which includes trade). Although there were Old Catalan treatises on agriculture, there apparently is nothing in Castilian. Hunting is well represented in Old Spanish from the beginnings. Medicine, which appears twice in Brunetto Latini's schema, is treated under physics. Villena includes his *Arte cisoria* among the mechanical arts.

Grammar seems not to be represented by vernacular works before the fifteenth century, when Villena's *Arte de trobar*, with some discussion of grammar, and Antonio de Nebrija's *Gramática* appeared. Rhetoric, according to Latini, includes preaching, Scripture, and law. Rhetoric proper and poetics are dealt with in Juan Alfonso de Baena's *Prologus baenensis*, Santillana's *Proemio*, Villena's *Arte de tro bar*, and Juan del Encina's *Arte de poesía castellana*. Vernacular works on sermonizing are lacking. Scripture is covered by works of exegesis, such as Villena on Psalm 8, *Quoniam videbo*; but the vast bulk of biblical scholarship, such as Alfonso Fernández de Madrigal's commentaries, is in Latin. Law, by contrast, was one of the first categories to be transferred to the vernacular (doubtless for practical reasons). On logic and its subdivisions there is nothing.

There is a considerable corpus of courtly material. To hunting may be added works on other courtly issues: chivalry is studied by a number of authors, among them Valera, indebted to the *Partidas*. There are works on heraldry by Juan Manuel (*Libro de las armas*), Juan Rodríguez del Padrón, Diego Valera, and Juan de Mena (*Tratado sobre el tītulo de duque*). Courtesy literature seems underrepresented in Spanish: a rare example is Villena's *Arte cisoria*. Chess is treated in Spanish as early as Alfonso X. Magic and alchemy are represented by the Alfonsine *Lapidario* and Villena's *Tratado del aojamiento*.

Spanning all these topics are the encyclopedias: the *Visión deleitable* of Alfonso de la Torre (a best-seller) and the much smaller scale *Libro del cavallero e del escudero* of Juan Manuel, as well as translations of Isidore, Latini, and Bartholomaeus Anglicus.

Why this uneven distribution? Some subjects may have been too technical for the vernacular; others may have been considered too lowly to be committed to writing and were transmitted orally. Thus, although in Italian there are such works as Cennino Cennini's late fourteenth-century manual for painters, in a less literate society such knowledge would have not been written down.

Books Teaching Morals. The difference between the exemplum and the didactic romance (*Barlaam* and *Josaphat*, *Zifar*) is not simply length. The characters in the exemplum are defined by wisdom or folly; in romances they are defined by a broader range of virtues and vices.

Although there were Castilian translations of John of Wales and the *Fiore di virtù*, summa on virtues and vices are rare in Spanish outside the mirrors of princes. The utilization of, for example, the *Moralium dogma philosophorum* in vernacular works shows that in at least this case Spaniards handled Latin manuals without the aid of translations. There is a body of preserved vernacular sermons; indebted to the sermon tradition is the *Corbacho* of Alfonso Martínez de Toledo. In the fifteenth century a variety of essayistic works on moral themes appeared: allegories (Villena's *Doze trabajos de Hércules*), dialogues (Juan de Lucena's *De vita beata*; *Diá logo de Cipión y Haníbal*), and Senecan epistle-essays (Hermando de Pulgar's *Letra* and Villena's *Tratado de la consolación*).

History and Stylistic Development

The earliest monuments of Spanish prose are, as elsewhere, paraliterary. The first examples of literary prose (thirteenth century) are didactic works translated from or modeled on Arabic or Hebrew at the Castilian court. The Alfonsine works were influential throughout the Middle Ages.

Broadly speaking, Whinnom was right to insist on the lack of a continuous tradition of Spanish prose. However, comparing the beginning of the vernacular period with the end of the Middle Ages, we might note a tendency away from Semitic parataxis and toward Latin periodicity, perhaps reflecting a movement away from oral to written culture. Indeed, some Alfonsine sentences are positively antiperiodic, with the strongest idea at the beginning, with the rest tailing away: "Fuerç nin premia non deuen fazer en ninguna manera a ningund judio por que se torne cristiano, mas con buenos exiemplos e con los dichos de las Santas escripturas e con falagos los deuen los cristianos conuertir a la fee de Nuestro Sennor Jhesu Christo, ca Nuestro sennor Dios non quiere nin ama seruicio quel sea fecho por premia" ["Force or coercion of any kind should not be brought to bear upon any Jew to turn Christian; rather he should be converted to the faith of Our Lord Jesus Christ through good examples and the sayings of Holy Scripture; Our Lord God does not love service rendered through force."] (*Partida* 7, xxiv. 6). In some cases authors use grammatically hypotactic structures in sentences that give equal status to all members in a way typical of parataxis: "El qual Anfiarao se escondio por non ir a conplir el su sacerdotal oficio en la batalla, enpero que non sopo otro ninguno de como se escondiera salvo su muger Erifile, la qual convencida por dones de oro mostro e descubrio el lugar donde Anfiarao estava escondido, al qual sacaron de alli e levaronlo a la batalla, segund convenia" ["The said Anfiarao hid in order not to carry out his sacerdotal duty in the battle, which was only known by his wife Erifile who, convinced by gifts of gold, revealed the place where Anfiarao was hiding, from where he was taken to the battle, as was necessary"]; Juan de Mena, Commentary on *Coronación*, (stanza viii). True Ciceronianism comes only with Luis de Granada in the sixteenth century.

One may also chart a growing use of Latin rhetoric. Although certain figures are always an option in Old Spanish, the repertoire expands as the Middle Ages wear on; the doublets of the early prosaists (often identified as an oral feature or a Semiticism) and *trias* of Baena's *Prologus* give way to classical *conduplicatio*. The style of the Old Spanish corpus can be highly mannered. Although prose was defined by its freedom from metrical rules, there is a minority current of metrical/numerical art prose. In such cases the passages or texts either take their style from their immediate source (as with certain passages in Alfonso or Juan Manuel, *Conde Lucanor*, II, 6) or belong to a readily identifiable tradition (as with the *Soliloquios* of Fernández Pecha, modeled on the suppositious works of St.

Augustine), or Juan Manuel's text on the Passion in *Libro de los estados*, I, 1vii).

It was difficult to accommodate the cadences of the Latin *cursus* (used in the liturgy and in chancery documents) to Spanish, partly because the *cursus* did not permit a stressed syllable at the end of the phrase, and valued the elegant proparoxytones common in Latin and Italian but rare in Castilian. The distinctive cadences of Villena rarely correspond to the *cursus* proper; they are generally the product of imitating "dovetailing" classical hyperbaton.

Translation afforded opportunities for imitating various Latin styles, such as the sample of Roman forensic rhetoric in Brunetto Latini's *Tesoretto* (III, xxxv). The higher of the two styles adopted by Martínez de Toledo in the *Corbacho* derives directly from his source, Andreas Capellanus.

BARRY TAYLOR

Bibliography

Bosch, S. "Les *Partides* i els textos catalans didáctics sobre cavalleria," *Estudis universitaris catalans* 22 (1936): 655–80.

Gallardo, A. "Alfabetismo en la oralidad (el escritor medieval y la cultura del idioma)," *Acta literaria* 10–11 (1985–1986): 133–43.

Lázaro Carreter, F. "La prosa de fray Antonio de Guevara." *Academia literaria renacentista* 5 (1988): 101–17.

Menéndez Pidal, R., ed. *Antología de prosistas españoles*. 5th ed. Madrid, 1928.

Whinnom, K. *Spanish Literary Historiography: Three Forms of Distortion*. Exeter, U.K., 1967.

DINIS, KING OF PORTUGAL

King Dinis, son of King Afonso III and Queen Beatriz of Castile, was born 9 October 1261 and died on 7 January 1325. The sixth king of Portugal, he ascended the throne on 16 February 1279.

During the long reign of Dinis, Portugal reached in many respects its high-water mark in the Middle Ages. The monarch's actions generated significant internal growth within his kingdom and also did much to ensure the viability of Portugal as an independent entity in the Iberian Peninsula. With the Muslim threat largely neutralized, Dinis was free to turn his attention to Portugal's boundaries with Castile. Towns, castles, and strongholds in three areas were of particular concern: (1) those on the east bank of the Guadiana River, (2) those of the Ribacoa district in the region of Boira Baixa, and (3) those near the Castilian border which were under the control of Dinis's younger brother Afonso.

Through shrewd alliances and the judicious use of military force, Dinis took advantage of the dynastic problems in Castile following the death of Sancho IV in 1295. The Portuguese monarch first gained undisputed authority over the towns of Moura, Serpa, and Mourão. Then, in the Treaty of Alcañices (1297), which definitively fixed Portugal's borders with Castile, Portugal gained the towns and fortresses it desired in the Ribacoa district. The treaty was sealed by marriage alliances between Fernando IV of Castile and Constança, Dinis' daughter, and between Fernando's sister Beatriz and Dinis' heir, the future Afonso IV.

Dinis also resolved the problems inherent in his younger brother's control of a number of towns on the Castilian border, which Prince Afonso used as staging points to intervene in Castilian affairs. Dinis was determined to bring Afonso's towns under royal authority and surrounded his brother's fortresses. In 1299 an accord was reached in which Afonso received privileges over Sintra, Ourém, and other places closer to Lisbon in exchange for his rights over the towns near Castile's borders. This action not only helped secure Dinis' borders, but also removed an irritant to Portugal's relations with Castile.

To further strengthen his kingdom's borders, Dinis undertook a large-scale program of renovation and repair, constructing forty-four new strongholds and castles and repairing many old ones. Also, because many of the border towns were underpopulated, Dinis promoted resettlement. The Ribacoa district and the east bank of the Guadiana River received the greatest attention. But the region north of the Duero River was not neglected. Walls were built to strengthen Guimarães and Braga, as well as several smaller towns. In addition, Dinis had a wall constructed along the banks of the Tagus River to protect Lisbon from attacks by sea.

Related to these activities were Dinis' efforts to separate from Castilian influence and authority the four clerico-military orders active in Portugal: the Templars, the Hospitalers, Santiago, and Avis. The first two were international orders with headquarters in the Holy Land and branches throughout Europe; the latter two had their origins in the Iberian Peninsula. All four had played important roles in driving out the Muslims, holding the frontiers, and reclaiming the newly won lands. For these activities, the orders had been given extensive spiritual and temporal privileges.

Portugal's conflicts with Castile, especially during the reigns of Sancho IV (1284–1295) and his son Fernando IV (1295–1312), convinced Dinis that his kingdom's security was threatened by the fact that the clericomilitary orders in Portugal were under the jurisdiction of non-Portuguese leaders. Castilian interference in the political and military life of the monk-knights living in Portugal was an ever-present danger, especially in the Order of Santiago. During the Portuguese Reconquest much land and many strongholds had been given to the order. As boundary disputes became more intense during the reign of Sancho IV, Dinis sought to obtain from the papacy a measure of independence for the order. But it was a long, drawn out struggle. However, by the time of Dinis' death, the Portuguese Order of Santiago was for all practical purposes under Portuguese control.

In the meantime the Templars had fallen on hard times. The loss of the Holy Land in 1291 was one of two main factors that led to the demise of the order. The other was the ultimately successful personal campaign of Philip IV the Fair of France and his advisers to destroy the order and gain control of its valuable and extensive holdings. In 1312 Pope Clement V suppressed the Templars and shortly afterward ordered their holdings to be distributed to their archrivals, the Knights Hospitalers. Dinis of Portugal, like a number of the other European monarchs, had sequestered all the Templar properties in his kingdom and put its knights under his protection. The Portuguese monarch's agents at the papal court argued that the annexation of the Templars' properties in Portugal by the Knights Hospitalers would be prejudicial to the Portuguese crown and the Portuguese people. As an alternative, they proposed the foundation of a new order of monk-knights that would incorporate the property of the Templars and, with headquarters in the Algarve, would protect the Portuguese frontier from the Muslims. Clement V's successor, John XXII, agreed with this proposal and on 14 March 1319 by the bull *Ad ca ex quibus* established the Military Order of Our Lord Jesus Christ, which would eventually, by the second half of the sixteenth century, become the premier order in Portugal.

During the reign of Dinis the economic foundations of Portugal were greatly strengthened. So energetic were the monarch's agricultural reforms that he was given the epithet "O Lavrador" (the farmer). Dinis cut back on large landholdings by the church and the higher nobility. He improved landholding patterns on a regional basis and affirmed the nobility of farming one's own land. He promoted the reclamation of marshes and swamps and ordered the planting of pine forests near Leiria to prevent the encroachment of coastal sand and salt as well as to provide needed timber. Dinis's agricultural reforms ranged from the division of uncultivated lands into groups of ten, twenty, or thirty *casais* with lifetime leases in Entre Douro e Minho; to cooperatives in Trás-os-Montes; to an emphasis on repopulating the Alentejo by founding towns, hampering the wealthy from unproductively monopolizing large tracts of property, and granting land to those who would cultivate it. In this way, Dinis increased the number of small proprietors and rural workers who paid rent to the crown. During the thirteenth century, Portugal's population probably numbered between 800,000 and 1,000,000 inhabitants.

Dinis also took note of Portugal's foreign trade. He encouraged the export of agricultural produce, salt, andfl salted fish to Flanders, England, and France in exchange for textiles and metals. He increased Portugal's foreign contacts as well and encouraged maritime development in the Algarve. In 1293 he supported the creation of a *bolsa de comércio* (commercial fund) by Portuguese merchants for their legal defense in foreign ports. The monarch promoted trade fairs and gave the towns that held them privileges and exemptions. Dinis also reformed the kingdom's coinage. Further, he promoted the mining industry by encouraging the extraction of silver, tin, sulphur, and iron.

Although Portuguese shipping had played a role in the kingdom's defense, as well as in the offensive against the Muslims, it was not until the reign of Dinis that a Portuguese navy was officially established. In 1317 the Portuguese monarch signed a contract with the Genoese Manuele Pessagno (Manuel Peçanha) that made him and his heirs admirals of Portugal and gave him many important rights and privileges. Pessagno was to provide twenty Genoese captains and build up the king's fleet. He was obliged to defend Portugal's coast, but at the same time was free to engage in commerce between his native Italy and England and Flanders.

Dinis ordered the exclusive use of Portuguese as the nation's language. Works of history and law were translated into Portuguese, including the *Siete Partidas* of Dinis's grandfather, Alfonso X of Castile and León. In 1290 papal approval was received for the University of Lisbon, which Dinis had founded several years earlier. In 1308 the university was transferred to Coimbra, where it remained until 1338. Between 1354 and 1377 it was again at Coimbra; then it returned to Lisbon and remained there until 1537.

By promoting royal justice and cracking down on the usurpation of royal prerogatives, Dinis also greatly increased royal authority. He reinstituted the *inquiricões* (general inquiries) of his predecessors, especially in the regions of Beira Baixa and Entre Douro e Minho. Further, he gradually resolved the kingdom's problems with the papacy, ending the twenty-two years struggle with Rome that had left his father and him excommunicates and Portugal under interdict. In 1289 a compromise, the Concordat of the Forty Articles, was signed. Although the church did not give up any of its ideas regarding the immunity of its holdings and its jurisdiction, it did agree to obey royal authority.

An important figure in Portugal during Dinis's reign was his wife, Isabel—the future St. Isabel—whom he married in 1288. The daughter of Pedro III of Aragón, the Portuguese queen played an important role as a mediator in the feuds between her husband and his brother Afonso, and between the king and his son, the future Afonso IV. In addition, her skill as a conciliator was of major significance in the negotiations leading to the Treaty of Alcañices, which fixed the definitive boundaries between Portugal and Castile.

FRANCIS A. DUTRA

Bibliography

Livermore, H.V.A *History of Portugal*. Cambridge, 1947.
Serrão, J.V. *História de Portugal*. Vol. 1. Lisbon, 1977.
Mattoso, J. (ed.) *História de Portugal*. Vol. 2. Lisbon, 1993.

DISPUTATIONS, RELIGIOUS

While there certainly were "debates" and disputes among Christians, and within and between various religious orders, when reference is made to religious disputations, it is preeminently to those between Jews and Christians. This is a topic with a history going back perhaps to the very early years of Christianity (although most scholars agree that the "disputation" in Justin Martyr, for example, is a literary fiction). Certainly in the fourth century Pope Sylvester I was involved in a disputation with a Jew that later was turned into a legend centered on the alleged conversion of Emperor Constantine. Real disputations were frequent in the Byzantine Empire, but we know of none in Visigothic Spain, which is all the more surprising, given the intensity of anti-Jewish polemic and legislation.

The upsurge of missionary zeal among the Dominicans and Franciscans in the thirteenth century, partly as a result of the Christian heresies that dominated Provence and parts of Spain, resulted in a new militancy with regard to Jews, and also Muslims, that had not been typical of church attitudes in prior centuries.

The most famous medieval disputation early in the thirteenth century was that at Paris (1239) between a Jewish convert to Christianity, Nicolas Donin, and rabbis such as Yehiel Ben Joseph of Paris, Moses ben Jacob of Coucy, and others. Another converted Jew, Pablo Christiani, who was preaching in France and Provence at that time, stirred up further animosity toward Jews.

This resulted in the first known disputation in Spain, the Barcelona Disputation. Actually, there were two of these. The first was between Pablo Christiani and Bonastrug de Porta, a well-known Jewish lay leader of Girona (whose son, Vidal, was condemned to death by the Jewish community as an informant). It also involved the bishop of Barcelona, Berengario (Berenguer de Palol), and others. Inasmuch as Berengario died in 1242 (not 1241, as sometimes claimed), this first disputation could not have taken place later than 1241, the date associated with other Christians who participated in it. Bonastrug wrote an account of his views, obviously in Catalan, which he gave to the bishop of Girona. This work was subsequently condemned for blasphemy, and Bonastrug was exiled from the kingdom of Aragón-Catalonia for two years.

The second, more famous, Barcelona disputation again involved Pablo Christiani, this time with Moses ben Naḥman (Nahmanides), who was not a rabbi but an important Jewish leader of Girona, and adviser to King Jaime I, in Barcelona. It disputation took place before the king, and again involved many prominent church leaders, the most important of whom was the notoriously anti-Jewish Ramón de Peñafort, head of the Dominicans and author of the *Decretals* and most of the *Siete Partidas*. Clearly he was the moving force behind this disputation. The debate centered mostly on the question of the Messiah in Jewish sources, and whether Jesus was or was not the expected Messiah. Obviously the Christians "won" the debate. There was no sermon in the synagogue by Jaime I, as Baer incorrectly states. Nahmanides, whom Baer and everyone following him has confused with Bonastrug de Porta, was not "banished" but apparently decided it would be prudent to leave Spain. He settled in Palestine, where he died. There is an official Latin record of the disputation and a Hebrew version that purports to be (but is not) the work of Nahmanides.

The result of the second Barcelona disputation was a disastrous investigation into the charges of anti-Christian polemic in one book of Maimonides' *Code of Jewish Law* (true; not "all" of Maimonides' books were ordered burned, nor were "any" Jews, contrary to the claims of some writers). A commission, composed of Peñafort and others, including Ramón Martí, later the author of an infamous anti-Jewish polemic, was set up to investigate all the books owned by Jews for evidence of blasphemy. However, the Jews convinced the king of the absurdity of this, and the order was rescinded.

Nevertheless, this investigation began a campaign of sermons, often compulsory (that is, Jews were forced to attend), preached by Dominican and Franciscan friars throughout Spain, especially in the kingdom of Aragón-Catalonia, from the thirteenth through the fifteenth centuries. Not all the monks were "anti-Semitic," and some, such as Ramón Llull, showed a remarkable spirit of tolerance and even understanding. The damage was done, however, and relations between

Jews and Christians in Spain were to some degree changed forever.

Some minor disputations continued. Jaime II, for example, ordered the Jews to permit and respond to disputations with Dominican preachers throughout the realm. In 1286 there was yet another disputation, this time in Mallorca, of less importance than those of Barcelona. In 1379 there was one involving Pedro de Luna, the cardinal who was to become Pope Benedict XIII.

When he became pope, Benedict at once demonstrated his strong hostility to Jews, which was to be manifested in many ways (his unsuccessful attempt to impose the wearing of the "badge" yet again, to condemn the study of the Talmud, etc.). In this he had the enthusiastic support of Vicente Ferrer, the dynamic Dominican preacher whose personal insistence had already convinced Queen Catalina of Castile and Fernando de Antequera, regents of the kingdom, to enact the anti-Jewish Ordinances of Valladolid (1412). Fernando then became king of Aragón, where the influence of Ferrer, as personal confessor of the king, led to more anti-Jewish measures during his short reign.

The recent conversion of important Jewish figures, such as Solomon ha-Levy (the rabbi of Burgos, also known as Pablo de Santa María), and Joshua aha-Lorqi (Jerónimo de Santa Fe), no doubt encouraged the pope in his plans to convene a major disputation at Tortosa in 1413. Letters were sent to all the Jewish communities of the kingdom of Aragón-Catalonia, ordering them to send representatives. Jerónimo took the leading role in presenting the Christian side of the debates, which again focused chiefly on messianic beliefs of the Jews. The debate dragged on for several days in February, was reconvened in the spring of 1413 and lasted at least to the end of August, and was resumed again in the fall, lasting until April 1414. This longest disputation in history involved the foremost Jewish scholars, rabbis, and lay leaders of the kingdom. Among these were famous scholars such as Zerahyah ha-Levy (Ferrer Saladin), Mattityahu ha-Yishari, and Joseph Albo. One of the important lay representatives was a Hebrew poet, Vidal Joseph ibn Labi (not de la Cavallería, as Baer incorrectly identified him), who converted to Christianity. His former teacher in poetry, the famous poet Solomon de Piera, did *not* "join him in going over to Christianity" (Baer), then or at any other time, but remained a loyal Jew and an official of the Zaragoza Jewish community. However, several other rabbis and prominent Jewish leaders did convert as a result of the disputation.

The devastating effects of these conversions, coupled with earlier ones of such important Jews as Solomon ha-Levy and his entire family, and Joshua al-Lorqi, both of whom now began writing anti-Jewish polemics, created a sense of despair throughout the Jewish communities of Spain. Vicente Ferrer thus found fertile ground for his missionary sermons, and entire Jewish communities converted.

The official Jewish response to the Tortosa disputation was weak and ineffective. Mattityahu ha-Yishari wrote a small and not very profound work that had limited readership. Joseph Albo composed a huge tome on the "principles" of the Jewish faith, but the arguments were weak and the work had little or no lasting effect upon the Jewish communities.

There were no more disputations between Jews and Christians in Spain, at least that we know about. This was undoubtedly due to the overwhelming success of the Tortosa disputation and, especially, of the preaching of Ferrer in converting thousands of Jews, and to the fact that there were no more rabbis or Jewish spokesmen capable of defending the Jewish position in Spain until the very end of the century. Thus, with some isolated exceptions, the Dominican and Franciscan campaigns among Jews diminished, and soon ceased altogether.

NORMAN ROTH

Bibliography

Baer, F. *A History of the Jews in Christian Spain*. Vol. 2. Trans. Louis Schoffman. Philadelphia, 1961. 170–210.

Chazan, R. "The Barcelona 'Disputation' of 1263," *Speculum* 52 (1977), 824–42.

———. *Daggers of Faith*. Berkeley, 1989.

Riera i Sans, J. *La crónica en hebreu de la disputa de Tortosa*. Barcelona, 1974.

DIPUTACIS DEL GENERAL DE CATALUNYA, *See* GENERALITAT

DISTICHA CATONIS

A collection of Latin proverbs, arranged in couplets, the *Disticha Catonis* was widely used as a school text in the Middle Ages, serving as both a handbook of moral education and a first Latin reader. The sayings provide bits of commonsense wisdom, such as the need to avoid excess and not to fear death, in addition to more mundane advice, such as to chew with one's mouth closed and not to be deceived by dishonest merchants. It was presumably the work's didactic value that motivated its translation into Castilian for the benefit of non-Latinists. The earliest translation is an anonymous *cuaderna vía* (monorhymed quatrain version) probably of the late thirteenth or early fourteenth centuries, but known only in sixteenth- and seventeenth-century imprints. There is also an eleven-stanza cuaderna vía gloss of a single distich that highlights the problem of free will. It is possibly part of a more extensive glossed version, and most likely dates from the late thirteenth or early fourteenth centuries. Later, other glossed translations were printed in Castilian verse: Martín Garòia Puyazuelo's *La traslatión del muy excellente doctor Chatón* (completed in 1467; printed ca. 1490) and Gonzalo García de Santa María's *El Catón en latín y en romance* (printed 1493/1494).

RONALD E. SURTZ

Bibliography

Pérez y Gómez, A. "Versiones castellanas del Pseudo-Catón. Noticias bibliográficas." In *El Catón en latín y en romance*. Ed. G. García de Santa María. *Incunables Poéticos Castellaños* Vol. 9. Valencia, 1964.

Surtz, R. E. "Fragmento de un *Catón glosado* en cuaderna vía," *Journal of Hispanic Philology* 6 (1982): 103–12.

DIVORCE *See* MARRIAGE AND DIVORCE

DOMINGO DE SILOS, ST.

Domingo Manso was born in 1000 in the Riojan village of Cañas (Logroño). From a very early age he was educated in the Scriptures, and he was ordained a priest before the age of twenty-five, then continued to live at his parents' house for a year and a half. Around 1027 he abandoned his home to become a hermit. After remaining in the wilderness for a year and a half, he decided to submit to the rule of obedience and traveled to the monastery of San Millán de la Cogolla. He lived there from 1030 to 1040 and was appointed *praepositus*. In 1040, as a consequence of friction with King García III Sánchez of Navarré, Domingo was forced to leave San Millán and move to Castile. There, in 1041, Fernando I appointed him abbot of the monastery of San Sebastián de Silos (in decay and ravaged by al-Manṣūr's raids) and charged him whith its restoration. Domingo reestablished monastic discipline, started the building of the romanesque cloister, and encouraged the work of scribes. In 1062 he was at the translation of the relics of the martyrs Vincent, Sabina, and Cristeta to the monastery of San Pedro de Arlanza in Burgos. He was also present, in 1063, at the translation of the relics of St. Isidore of Seville to the city of León.

Domingo was a distinguished figure at the Castilian court, and kings Fernando I, Sancho II, and Alfonso VI made important donations to the monastery. Domingo died on 20 December 1073. In 1076 the fame of his holiness caused the bishop of Burgos to order the translation of his body to an altar in the abbey church whose original name was replaced by that of the saint who had restored it. During his life he exorcised the possessed, healed many lame people, and liberated captives. The latter activity caused him to be called "Redeemer of the Captives."

ISABEL URÍA-MAQUA

Bibliography

Berceo, Gonzalo de. *La vida de Santo Domingo de Silos*. Ed. Brian Dutton. London, 1978.

Córtés, José. *El mundo poético de Gonzalo de Berceo en* la Vida de Santo Domingo de Silos. Montevideo, 1973.

Suszynski, Olivia C. *The Hagiographic-thaumaturgic art of Gonzalo de Berceo:* Vida de Santo Domingo de Silos. Barcelona, 1976.

DOMINICAN ORDER, OR ORDER OF PREACHERS

The Order of the Friars Preachers is the principal part of the Dominican Order. The order also includes two other parts: the Dominican Sisters (Second Order) and the Brothers of Penitence of St. Dominic (Third Order).

The thirteenth century is the classic age of the order, witness to its broad development and intense activity, especially in teaching and in the suppression of heresy. Through its preaching by word and book, it reached all classes of society, combated heterodoxy, schism, and paganism. The order's schools spread throughout the church and its doctors wrote monumental works in all branches of knowledge. Two of its most distinguished intellectuals were Albertus Magnus and Thomas Aquinas.

When Domingo de Guzmán (St. Dominic) asked the Vatican for official recognition of his order in 1216, the first preachers of his band of companions numbered only sixteen, seven of whom were of Iberian origin, including Domingo's brother Manés de Guzmán. Three of the Iberians, along with four others, were sent to Paris in 1217 to found a convent close to the university there. Miguel de Fabra, who was a member of the group, was the first Dominican to hold a chair at the University of Paris. Fabra later founded houses in Cataluña and Aragón and became the confessor of Jaime I of Aragón, accompanying the king on his conquests of Valencia and Mallorca. Fabra also organized the order's schools in Barcelona. The other four of Domingo's initial seven Hispanic companions were sent to Iberia to found convents in Madrid and Segovia. In 1218 Domingo came to Segovia in order to ensure the foundation of the convent there. During his visit to the peninsula, Domingo was instrumental in founding houses at Palencia, Burgos, Zamora, Zaragoza, Barcelona, and Santiago de Compostela. In 1219, his brother Manés was sent from Paris to Madrid to direct the convent of nuns recently established there.

By the time of the first general chapter in Bologna (1220), the order counted some sixty establishments, and was divided into eight provinces: the Spains (i.e., all the Iberian kingdoms), Provence, France, Lombardy, Rome, Teutonia, England, and Hungary. Aragón became a separate province in 1301. Each of the provinces was headed by a provincial under whom the conventual friars served. The order was headed by a master general who directed the provinces.

The spread of the order in the Iberian Peninsula was rapid. The first prior provincial of the Spains was Suero Gomes, a Portuguese who figured among Domingo's first group of companions. The first meeting of the chapters of the province (Toledo 1250) records twenty convents (Segovia, Palencia, Burgos, Zamora, Toledo, Salamanca, León, Pamplona, Santander, Lisbon, Coimbra, Porto, Santiago de Compostela, Zaragoza, Lérida, Valencia, Mallorca, Barcelona, Córdoba, and Seville). During that first meeting six conventual visitors were named to collaborate with the prior provincial to help oversee the work of the order in Iberia.

Several centers stand out in the thirteenth century, most notably Barcelona and Salamanca. The convent of San Esteban in Salamanca developed close ties to the university there and became an important focus for learning in the order. Barcelona saw the development of a center for specifically Dominican studies. The schools at Lisbon and Játiva are also important—especially the latter, which excelled in the teaching of Arabic and Hebrew for the purpose of evangelization. In 1225, the first Spanish Dominicans evangelized Morocco. Some years later they were already established at Tunis. In 1256 and the ensuing years Pope Alexander IV, at the instance of Raimundo of Peñafort, gave a strong impulse to this mission. Notable works by peninsular Dominicans of the thirteenth century include Raimundo of Peñafort's *Summa Poenitentialis* and Raimon Marti's *Pugio Fidei*. Raimundo also composed the first directory of inquisitorial law for trials of heresy and served as one of two Iberian master generals of the order during this time (1238–1240); the other was Munio of Zamora (1285–1291). Three fourteenth-century Iberian Dominicans were canonized: Domingo, the founder of the order, Raimundo of Peñafort, and Telmo. Manés de Guzmán was beatified.

Domingo did not write a rule for the Tertiaries. However, a large body of the laity, vowed to piety, grouped themselves around the rising Order of Preachers and constituted a third order. Munio de Zamora in 1285 wrote the rule for the Brothers and Sisters of Penitence of St. Dominic. The privilege for their constitution was granted on 28 January 1286 by Pope Honorius IV, thus giving the group a canonical existence. Munio's rule was not entirely original; some points were borrowed from the Rule of the Brothers of Penitence, whose origin dates back to St. Francis of Assisi. The Dominican Tertiaries were local and without any bond of union other than that of the preaching friars who governed them. After professing, however, they could not return to the world but could enter other religious orders.

During the first part of the fourteenth century the order came under royal patronage in Iberia and saw vigorous growth in personnel, houses, and influence. The plague years, however, witnessed a rapid decline in the order, which was obliged to relax standards for admission to the novitiate so as to fill the many vacancies created by disease and death. A reform of the order was initiated in Lombardy by both the master general, Raymond of Capua, and Catherine of Siena but did not reach Iberia until 1423, when it was begun at the instance of Alvaro de Córdoba. The Iberian reform was finished in 1504 under the direction of Diego Magdaleno.

Nicolau Eymerich, author of the *Tractatus de potesatate papae* written in defense of the papacy at Avignon, stands out as the most distinguished Iberian Dominican of the fourteenth century. Vicente Ferrer, achieved great notoriety through his preaching and became influential in politics in both Castile and Aragón, intervening in, among other things, the Compromise of Caspe (1411). Shortly after his death in 1412 Ferrer was canonized.

Alvaro de Córdoba, who had been confessor to Queen Catalina de Lancaster, in 1423 retired from the court to the convent of Santo Domingo de Scalaceli in Córdoba. From there he initiated the Iberian reform of the order begun in Lombardy at the end of the previous century. The reform was greatly aided by the efforts of Cardinal Juan de Torquemada who, with the aid of Fray Alonso de San Cebrián, arranged independence for the reform congregation of the order in the Iberian provinces. Torquemada was an eminent churchman and jurist who wrote extensive works on the *Decretals* of Gratian that were very influential in defense of pontifical rights.

The order's work in the suppression of heresy, in which it had been especially active, had diminished notably in the second half of the thirteenth century. The perception of the rise of heresy in and around Seville in the 1470s brought about the reestablishment of the Inquisition in Iberia with new duties for the inquisitor general. These were exercised from 1483 to 1498 by Tomás de Torquemada, nephew of Cardinal Juan de Torquemada, who reorganized the scheme of suppression. Tomás de Torquemada's efforts were followed by those of by Diego de Deza from 1498 to 1507. They were the first and last Dominican inquisitors general in Spain.

During the late fifteenth and early sixteenth centuries, the Dominicans established large colleges of higher education in the kingdom of Castile. Among the most famous of these were the Colegio de San Gregorio at Valladolid, founded in 1488 by Alonso de Burgos, and that of Santo Tomás at Seville, established in 1515 by Diego de Deza, who was then archbishop of that city.

E. MICHAEL GERLI

Bibliography

Arriaga, G. de. *Historia del Colegio de San Gregorio de Valladolid*. Ed. Manuel M. Hoyos. Valladolid, 1928.

Beltrán de Heredia, V. *Historia de la reforma de la provincia de España (1450–1550)*. Rome, 1939.

Hinnebusch, W.A. *The History of the Dominican Order*. Staten Island, N.Y., 1966.

Macías, J. M. *Santo Domingo de Guzmán: Fundador de la Orden de Predicadores*. Madrid, 1979.

Robles, L. *Escritores dominicos de la Corona de Aragón (Siglos XIII–XV)*. Salamanca, 1972.

Vaquero, Q. A., et al. (eds.) *Diccionario de historia eclesiástica de España*. Vol. 1 Madrid, 1972.

DRAMA

The rise of the theater in medieval Europe is connected with the Easter liturgy in the Catholic Church. Near the end of the tenth century the *Quem quaeritis*, one of the ceremonies that had developed as part of the celebration of Holy Week, became the focal point of liturgical drama. It depicted the dialogue between the angel and the three Marys at the sepulcher after the Resurrection, beginning with the words, "Quem quaeritis in sepulchro, o Christicolae?" (Whom do you seek in the sepulcher, o followers of Christ?). The addition to the *Quem quaeritis* of other scenes related to the Resurrection, such as the race of the Apostles Peter and John to the empty sepulcher and the three Marys purchasing ointments from the spice merchant, culminated in the *Visitatio sepulchri*, the oldest known complete liturgical play.

Though the earliest documented example of the *Quem quaeritis* dialogue in Spain is found in an eleventh-century breviary from Silos, the practice of presenting liturgical drama did not prosper in this region. The area to the east, however, displayed a vigorous and flourishing tradition. The Benedictine abbey of Ripoll in the province of Girona became a center of diffusion and innovation, and influenced the development of liturgical drama in both Spain and France. In addition to several examples of the *Quem quaeritis* dialogue, a fully developed twelfth-century *Visitatio sepulchri* is found in Ripoll. Although the manuscript does not contain representational rubrics, the dialogue is divided into two scenes requiring different staging locations, and for an early liturgical play it exhibits a highly developed sense of stage action. A singular aspect is that it contains the earliest recorded version in Europe of the spice merchant scene.

The Christmas season generated its own type of plays: the *Ordo prophetarum*, presented on Christmas Day, and the *Ordo stellae*, on Epiphany. The *Ordo prophetarum* derived from a sermon incorrectly attributed to St. Augustine. A long list of prophets from the Old Testament and several pagan ones, among them the sibyl, foretold the coming of Christ. The earliest recorded reference to the sibylline chant in Spain is found in a tenth-century manuscript from Ripoll. In Toledo the Erythraean Sibyl (there were several sibyls; the different names usually indicate the place of origin) appeared in the fourteenth century, and by the fifteenth she was chanting in Castilian and was dressed in oriental costume.

Toledo also claims one of the earliest dramatic texts in a romance vernacular, the *Auto de los reyes magos*. Composed in the twelfth century, it was discovered in 1789 by Felipe Fernández de Vallejo in a chapter library of the Toledo cathedral and was published in a modern edition by Ramón Menéndez Pidal in 1900. Unlike the *Ordo stellae*, the *Auto* seeks to delineate characterization in order to enhance dramatic conflict, and although the text lacks stage directions, it suggests dramatic movement. Versification is adjusted to the situation, and the action, developed in five scenes, is placed within designated spaces requiring separate locales.

Though Easter and Christmas gave rise to the earliest recorded forms of liturgical drama and to a large number of cyclical performances, the feast of Corpus Christi (then celebrated on the second Thursday after Pentecost) and the feast of the Assumption (celebrated on August 15) were the principal dates for religious performances in later centuries.

Unlike the Easter and Christmas cycles, which were normally performed indoors, the celebration of Corpus Christi took place during an open-air procession or pageant. It is not certain when plays were first acted in conjunction with this pageant, although references to the procession precede the first documented performances of plays by at least a hundred years. The feast of Corpus Christi was celebrated in Girona as early as 1360, and in Barcelona and Valencia by the end of the fourteenth century. In Valencia the procession had a spectacular splendor. The Host was carried through the streets accompanied by a large number of angels, virgins, prophets, saints, and other figures. The tableaux on floats or pageant carts, known as *roques*, represented episodes from the lives of saints, allegorical figures, or situations such as the creation of the world, Eden, Hell, and the salvation of the soul. This is in great contrast to the Easter and Christmas cycles, which dealt exclusively with events in the life of Christ. The city of Seville rivaled Valencia in the magnificence of its Corpus Christi festivities, but there is no evidence in either city of dialogue being used in an actual dramatic presentation until the sixteenth century. Textual evidence for the earlier period is found, however, in Toledo, where the account books detailing the expenses for the Corpus Christi procession for the years 1493–1510 include more than thirty titles of *autos* commissioned for performance in connection with the pageant. One of the pages contains a fragment of an *Auto de la Pasión* by Alfonso del Campo, written in the late fifteenth century.

The best-known Assumption play is the *Miste* or *Festa de Elche*, which has been performed more or less continuously since the fifteenth century. Today, as in earlier times, the *Miste* at Elche is normally acted by children and three priests. The latter impersonate St. Peter, the Father in the Holy Trinity, and the angel who carries the soul of the Virgin in the *araceli* (from the Latin *ara coeli*, heavenly altar); it refers to the platform that descends from the dome of the church over the transept. The play is presented in two acts on the afternoons of August 14 and 15; "La vespra," on the day preceding the celebration of the feast, and "La festa," on the feast day itself. In the first act the Virgin visits the Stations of the Cross placed along the columns of the nave as she proceeds slowly to the *cadaf* (platform) that has been erected in the transept. She climbs the *cadaf* and lies on the *llit* (her deathbed), surrounded by the apostles. The angel, carrying an image of the Virgin symbolizing her soul, ascends to heaven on the *araceli*, which is lifted to the dome. In the second act the angel returns from heaven and places the image of the Virgin on the body lying on the *llit*. Her body and soul having been reunited after death, the Virgin ascends triumphantly to heaven with the acclamation of the angels, the apostles, and the spectators.

Secular performances also were very important in the development of drama. Nonreligious festival performances and court spectacles reached considerable elaboration in the use of stage machinery and gave rise to new forms of drama. The term drama appeared as early as the fourteenth century and referred to the brief entertainment performed during a ceremonial banquet. The *momería* (mummery) represented one of the earliest forms of the court masque in Castile (early fifteenth century) where symbolic drama and lyric entertainment were joined. Gómez Manrique composed *momerías* for the young Princess Isabel of Castile. The secularization of drama was also evident in the pastoral plays and dialogues of political satire composed for court entertainment. The anonymous *Coplas de Mingo Revulgo* and Rodrigo de Cota's *Diálogo entre el Amor y un viejo* contain dramatic elements in dialogue form. In 1495 Francisco de Madrid composed an *égloga* in the form of a dramatic panegyric, and a year later in Salamanca, Juan del Encina published eight dramatic eclogues that mark the beginning of Renaissance drama in Spain.

José M. Regueiro

Bibliography

Donovan, R.B. *The Liturgical Drama in Medieval Spain.* Toronto 1958.

Hardison, O.B., Jr. *Christian Rite and Christian Drama in the Middle Ages: Essays in the Origin and Early History of Modern Drama.* Baltimore, 1965.

Llobregat, E.A. *La festa d'Elx.* Alicante, 1975.

Shergold, N.D. *A History of the Spanish Stage from Medieval Times until the End of the Seventeenth Century.* Oxford, 1967.

Stern, Charlotte. *The Medieval Theater in Castile.* Binghamton, N.Y., 1996.

Torroja Menéndez, C., and M. Rivas Palá. *Teatro en Toledo en el siglo XV: Auto Ide la Pasión de Alonso del Campo.* Madrid, 1977.

DUARTE, KING OF PORTUGAL

The son of João I and Philippa of Lancaster, Duarte was born at Viseu in 1391. He reigned from 1433 to 1438, but he had been in charge of the affairs of the state since 1431, when his aging father had delegated his powers to him. Duarte married Leonor of Aragón on 22 September 1428, and had ten children by her. He collaborated closely with his brothers, Henrique the Navigator and Pedro, Duke of Coimbra, in shaping the policy of the new Portugal that led to maritime expansion. At home he centralized political power by promulgating the *Le mental* (mental law) at the *corte* (Parliament) of Santarém (1434), so named because his father had it in mind. This law was designed to preserve and recover from previous donations the property of the crown. Duarte fully supported the voyages of exploration along the western coast of Africa to which Henrique was deeply committed. During his reign the dreaded Cape Bojador was rounded (1434) and one hundred leagues of coast were explored. He pursued the policy of conquering Morocco, which had begun in 1415, by attacking Tangier (1437). The expedition was a disaster and justified the reservations he had shared with Pedro and others about the effectiveness of this policy, strongly supported by Henrique. Duarte was also a writer and an intellectual. He produced the *Leal conselheiro* (1438), a compilation of his essays on human passions, morals, and society. He showed remarkable powers of self-analysis when he described the effects of melancholy and *saudade* (nostalgia), considered to be the expression of a national feeling. He has left a work on the art of riding (ca. 1433), the most complete on the techniques of jousting in the fifteenth century.

LUIS REBELO

Bibliography

Caetano de Sousa, A. *História genealógica da casa real portuguesa*. 2d ed. Vol. 2. Coimbra, 1946. 271–80.

———. *Livro da ensinança de bem cavalgar toda sela*. Lisbon, 1986.

Eanes de Zurara, G. *Crónica dos feitos da Guiné*. Oporto, 1973.

Duarte, D. *Leal conselheiro*. Lisbon, 1982.

Pina, R. de. *Chrónica de El-Rei D. Duarte*. Lisbon, 1901.

DUERO RIVER

From its source in Soria province, Spain, the Duero (Douro in Portuguese) flows for over 913 kilometers, then empties into the Atlantic Ocean near Oporto, Portugal. Its main tributaries from the east are the Pisuerga, Valderaduey, and Esla in Spain, and the Sabor, Tua, and Tamega in Portugal. Its tributaries from the west are the Eresma, and the Adaja. The Duero is the most important collector of the northern *meseta* (plateau), on which, after crossing rugged land, it runs over flat hills and fields down to the border with Portugal, where it narrows and flows through the peneplain (Arribes), then becomes navigable from Fregeneda (Salamanca) to the sea.

The barbarians seized the Duero basin, which was crossed by Roman roads, and divided it into four provinces. The Visigoths expanded into the northern and southern parts of the Duero basin, and their presence is witnessed in some medieval place names, such as Campos de los Godos (Gothic Fields) in Tierra de Campos, and in many campaigns against Cantabrians and Basques trying to advance toward the south. Arabs also followed the Roman roads in their advance to the north.

The reconquest of the Duero basin involved both the building of military strongholds and repopulation. Alfonso III of Asturias initiated the advance to León and then Oporto in 868, repopulating the lands between the Miño and Duero Rivers. In the east Castilian counts advanced as far as the Arlanza River and reached the Duero in 912 (Roa, San Estéban de Gormaz). However, to settle the Duero's northern lands it was necessary to introduce the *presura* system, which allowed the Galicians, Asturians, Cantabrians, Basques, and Mozarabic peoples coming from the south to claim land. Estate possession was determined by the monarchy or through a count, bishop, or abbot.

In the early-tenth century along the Duero, a line of fortifications—Soria, Almazán, San Esteban de Gormaz, Burgo de Osma, Aranda, Roa, Peñafiel, Tordesillas, Toro, and Zamora—protected the northern lands. ʿAbd al-Raḥmān III attacked the central Duero strongholds, and was defeated at Simancas in 934 (although his troops destroyed Roa). The victory allowed the Christians to cross the Duero and reach the Tormes River, and they resettled Salamanca and Sepúlveda. The occupation of the land between the Duero and the entral mountains—Castile-León-Estremadura—was fortified,and privileges were given to the cities of Salamanca, Avila, Segovia, and Sepúlveda. Al-Manṣūr attacked some cities of Castile-León and plundered Salamanca, Zamora, and Simancas, ending their tribute to Ramiro II. The many disputes among the Christian and Muslim kingdoms lessened the importance of the western Duero, and the making of the border at the central mountains was postponed until Fernando I of Castile and León advanced as far west as the Mondego River, regained the Duero valley strongholds, and subdued Toledo's *tāʾifa*. The city of Toledo was conquered by Alfonso VI in 1085, and the Christian-Muslim frontier was moved toward the Tagus River.

The political unification of the Duero basin depended on the distribution of patrimonies, which raised enmities between León and Castile. After Fernando I's death in 1065, Castile, León, Toro, and Zamora were divided, but were reunited by Alfonso VI, who gave Trás-os-Montes and Beira to his daughter Teresa. All of this area became Portuguese when his grandson was proclaimed king by King Alfonso VII in the Treaty of Zamora (1143). In the middle Duero, Tierra de Campos was incorporated by Fernando III. Therefore the Duero lost interest as a border. Its major cities became famous because of the Meseta's cattle trails, court celebrations in Toro and Zamora, the cities, privileges, and the magnificent buildings erected by the king and nobles in Tordesillas, Peñafiel, Almazán, and Berlanga.

BLANCA GARCÍA ESCALONA

Bibliography

Sánchez-Albornoz, Claudio. *Despoblación y repoblación del Valle del Duero*. Buenos Aires, 1966.

E

EBRO RIVER

The Ebro is the second longest Spanish river. First named the Iberus, for the Iberian Peninsula, it rises in the Cantabrian Mountains, where it is named Híjar. The river flows through gorges and flat hills down to La Rioja, where it forms a basin bounded on the north by the Pyrenees and on the south by the Iberian Mountains. The Ebro passes through a varied landscape of hills, flat expanses of arable land, and fertile lowland down to Mequinenza, carving gorges and canyons. Further on, the Ebro reaches Tortosa and flows into the Mediterranean. Its tributaries come from the Pyrenees: the Aragón, Gallego, Cinca, Noguera, and Segre Rivers. On the west the Jalón connects with the *Meseta* (plateau), and the Jiloca with Teruel province.

The Ebro valley, a major natural communications axis, connects the Cantabrian region with the Mediterranean coast and with Europe to the north through its Pyrenees tributaries. In the Middle Ages it was occupied by Muslims, Hispano-Visigoths, and Carolingians. The Ebro Valley was crossed by Roman roads, and boasted such important and prosperous cities as Zaragoza, Huesca, Tarragona, and Borja, which flourished until the fifth-century barbarian invasions. During the Visigothic period Euric (r. 466–484) seized Pamplona and Zaragoza, and in 631 the Franks arrived.

The Muslims invaded the Ebro valley and Musa seized Zaragoza in 714; Fraga and Monzón then capitulated. The Muslims' dominion was not onerous because they allowed the Christians to retain their property, religion, and local authorities. Thus they could control the whole territory from a few strategic strongholds. Muslims settled steadily along the Ebro—Calahorra was seized in 796 by Al Ḥakam I—and reached as far as eastern Castile. In the center of the valley Zaragoza, became one of the most important cities of the northern Muslim kingdom. Other major cities were Tudela, Lérida, and Tortosa. Christians in the Pyrenees were in contact with those living in the northern valleys, and through them the Carolingian invasion was made possible. Charlemagne seized Pamplona in 778 and neared Zaragoza but failed to consolidate the Spanish March in the Ebro valley.

Due to its strategic value, the northern stretch of the Ebro was disputed by Muslims and various Christian kingdoms. In the tenth century Sancho García I of Navarre seized Nájera and Tudela, but the Muslim counterattack reached Pamplona in 924. After Calahorra's seizure in 1045 by Navarre, that kingdom's border was established. Through this kingdom new European ideas arrived (Cluniac reform, Pilgrim's Way) and flourished in cities such as Logroño and Miranda de Ebro.

The central Ebro valley, from Tudela to Mequinenza, belonged to the Banū-Qāsi, *ṭāʾifa* of Zaragoza, who built the Aljafería Palace and seized Tortosa in 1061. From the Pyrenees the Christian refugees advanced and conquered Barbastro in 1064 with Norman support; Pedro I of Aragón conquered Huesca in 1096, and the Catalonian Christians advanced through the Cinca and Noguera River valleys.

In the twelfth century Alfonso I of Aragón, supported by Franks, Catalans, and Basques, conquered Zaragoza in 1118; two years later Tarazona, Borja, and Epila fell to him. After the victory over the Almoravids at Cutanda, they seized Calatayud and Daroca. In 1133, advancing along the Cinca and Segre rivers, they conquered Fraga. Once subdued, the Muslims capitulated and were allowed to remain as serf farmers (*exaricos*). However, with the arrival of great numbers of Mozarabs from the south, tension arose in the countryside. Muslims were forced to live in special quarters outside the towns (*morerías*), while the city centers were occupied by privileged Franks.

Once the valley of the Ebro had been reconquered, quarrels arose among the Christian kingdoms. Alfonso I's will led to the incursion as far as Zaragoza by Alfonso VII in 1136, and Tortosa's seizure by Ramón Berenguer IV in 1148. Once the Christian kingdoms' borders were established, the Ebro lost strategic value. However, its cities played important political roles (e.g., the Compromise of Caspe in 1412).

BLANCA GARCÍA ESCALONA

Bibliography

Documentos para el estudio de la reconquista y repoblación del Valle del Ebro. 2 vols. Ed. José Ma. Lacarra.: Zaragoza, 1982–1985.

Stalls, C. *Possessing the land: Aragón's Expansion into Islam's Ebro Frontier under Alfonso the Battler, 1104–1134*. New York, 1995.

EDUCATION, CHRISTIAN

The Roman-Visigothic schools of Iberia reached the height of their development at the time of St. Isidore of Seville and appear to have disintegrated almost immediately after the Muslim Conquest of 711. There exists little information about Christian education between this time and the first reliable recorded information from the eleventh century. A few oblique references exist for the period between 711 and the time of the redaction of the *Historia Silense*, composed by a monk at Silos in the twelfth century, but these appear to be anachronisms that reflect conditions contemporary to the *Historia*'s composition rather than actual circumstances. The paucity of specific documentation notwithstanding, wills, deeds, donations, and histories continued to be written between the time of the conquest and the earliest reliable information regarding the existence of a school in Christian Iberia in the eleventh century, a reference to the destruction of a *schola* at San Pedro Rocas in Galicia (set afire by its students!). This is followed by a reference from 1073 in which Bishop Pelayo of León writes that he was reared and educated in church doctrine at Santiago de Compostela. Later in the century, the first bishop of Santiago, Diego Gelmírez, speaks of reforming that same school, in which he had been a pupil. It is possible that the church councils of Coyanza (1055) and Compostela (1056) animated the development of schools, as well as the Cluniac reform in the Iberian Penisula during the same period. Specific recommendations for Christian education aimed at all Christendom were made during the Third and Fourth Lateran councils of the Catholic Church, in 1179 and 1215, respectively.

As Christianity moved south in the peninsula during the Reconquest, numerous decrees call for the establishment of cathedral schools. After the second quarter of the twelfth century, many witnesses who sign as *magistri scholae* begin to appear in canonical legal documents and legislation. This is the case with Salamanca (1131), Astorga (1154), Toledo (1172), Cuenca (1183), León and Segovia (1190), and Tuy (1203). By the thirteenth century similar documents had become too numerous to list.

Until the end of the twelfth century, parish schools seemed to prevail over centers of higher learning. The *Versus ad Pueros*, dated 1122, from the monastery of San Millán de la Cogolla offer the first glimpse of a curriculum, giving brief mention to Virgil and Cato. Generally, however, students in the parish schools of Iberia prior to the thirteenth century only learned certain subjects like the Pater Noster, the Psalms, the New Testament, hymns, and rudimentary Latin grammar. There were no intellectual centers in medieval Iberia comparable to St. Gall in Germany, Bobbio in Italy, or Fleury in France, prior to the foundation of the first university at Palencia, established by Alfonso VIII of Castile in 1212, followed by Salamanca in about 1218, when Alfonso IX of León officially established a *studium generale* there.

The thirteenth century saw the foundation of many schools that were not universities. Two of note are those founded by Alfonso X el Sabio at Seville for the study of Latin and Arabic (1254) and by his son, Sancho IV, at Alcalá de Henares (1293). After the thirteenth century, canonical legislation concerning the establishment of grammar schools appears to have taken effect. There is evidence of the existence of a number of grammar school masters, and by 1290 the synod of Calahorra ordered each of its archdeaconries to make provisions for two masters of grammar. The cathedral archives of Oviedo, Toledo, Santiago, Segovia, and Cuenca all contain documentation to the same effect that continues well up until the end of the fourteenth century, reflecting renewed ecclesiastical measures taken in 1322, when the council of Valladolid ordered each diocese, as well as monasteries, to establish two or three grammar schools and support masters of logic in the larger cities. At the same time, the council decreed that one of every ten clerics holding benefices should be sent to a university to study theology, canon law, or liberal arts. Clerics were sent not only to established university centers in the peninsula like Salamanca and Lérida, but abroad to places like Bologna, Montpellier, Toulouse, and Avignon. By the end of the fourteenth century, no diocese seems to have been without a school of some sort. The majority of them, however, continued to teach little more than grammar and liturgy, since the average cleric trained in them was required to possess only the bare rudiments of an education in order to celebrate mass.

E. MICHAEL GERLI

Bibliography

Beltrán de Heredia, V. "La formación intelectual del clero en España durante los siglos XII, XIII, y XIV," *Revista de Estudios Teológicos* 6 (1946), 313–47.

———. "La formación intelectual del clero en España según nuestra antigua legislación canónica (siglos XI–XIV)," *Escorial* 3 (1941), 289–98.

Fuente, V. de la. *Historia de las universidades, colegios, y demás establecimientos de enseñanza en España*. 4 vols. Madrid, 1884–1889.

EDUCATION, JEWISH

The tradition of learning among the Jews predates their coming to Spain, and goes back to the Bible itself, which commands study as a means (perhaps the ultimate means) of serving God. This tradition earned the Jews the title *ahl al-kitāb* (people of the book) among the Muslims.

The origins of Jewish education in Spain are lost in legend and myth, but clearly by the eleventh century outstanding scholars such as Judah ben Barzilai and Samuel ibn Naghrillah had established themselves, the former in Barcelona and the latter in Granada. Córdoba, Denia, and Lucena soon became other major centers of Jewish learning, the last with a yeshiva of international fame.

Scholars like Joseph ibn ʿAqnin (twelfth century) and others have left detailed programs for the education of children, beginning with Hebrew grammar and Bible, from the age of three, through the study of Midrash and Mishnah, from the age of ten. At age fifteen the study of Talmud could begin in earnest.

Along with this attention to religious studies, there was the pursuit of secular knowledge, for Jews shared with Muslims the conviction that all areas of knowledge led to the perfect apprehension of God. This meant mastery of Arabic as well as Hebrew, then of mathematics (including geometry, algebra, and more), physics and optics, poetry and music, logic and metaphysics, culminating in the study of medicine. All of this was accomplished before the age of eighteen, at the latest. Of course, in practice such an ideal was attained mostly by members of the aristocratic elite, unless a boy showed particular promise and would be supported by community funds. Jews studied these subjects, together with Muslim students, under outstanding Muslim scholars. Maimonides was one such; as a boy in al-Andalus he studied with some of the foremost Muslim scientists of his age.

The education of girls was not totally neglected, and while one rarely hears of Jewish girls attaining the high levels of sophisticated learning of some Muslims, there is evidence that many were skilled at least in Hebrew studies. Illiteracy practically did not exist among Spanish Jews of any age or either sex, as is evident in the numerous letters and other documents in the vernacular languages that have survived.

The Jews of Spain almost universally attained a knowledge of the entire Hebrew Bible that was unmatched elsewhere in the Jewish world. By the twelfth century, at least, Spain had become an international center for Jewish students, who came from France and Germany on a regular basis to study Talmud with the great masters there.

Support for Jewish education was one of the paramount obligations imposed by the law, and special taxes were established in many communities to hire teachers, support students, and maintain schools. Individual Jews, including important government officials of the kings, also gave private donations of money or houses for schools.

Sometimes the kings became involved with the support of Jewish schools, as when, in 1328, Alfonso IV of Aragón-Catalonia granted the petition of a Jew of Lérida that he be appointed administrator of a school for poor Jewish students. This school also had a dormitory where the students lived and probably ate. In 1338 Pedro IV of Aragón had to intervene to ensure that a Jewish teacher of Hebrew would be paid his salary. Again in 1357 he intervened to order the Jewish *aljama* of Exea to comply with the terms of a will providing for the establishment of a school and the salary for a teacher.

Secular education of the Jews in Spain, particularly in Muslim al-Andalus, enabled them to reach high levels of proficiency in science, mathematics, and philosophy. This knowledge was passed on in part to Christians, not only through translation but also through the composition of original works in Spanish. Similarly important was the contribution to Spanish of Bible translations and works of secular literature, such as that of Shem Tov de Carrión, and others, in Catalan.

Whether Jews were admitted to the universities of medieval Spain is unclear; certainly Jewish physicians were required, from at least the fourteenth century, to have received university training somewhere (perhaps at Montpellier). Some received degrees, including the doctorate in philosophy, from Spanish universities. The royal families sometimes used Jews as teachers, and in a famous letter Jaime II of Aragón wrote to his daughter Constanza that he hoped she would not employ Jewish tutors for her newborn daughter, as she had been "accustomed" to do with her other children.

After the widespread pogroms of 1391, Jewish education suffered a decline from which it only gradually recovered by the end of the fifteenth century.

Norman Roth

Bibliography

There are no articles, let alone monographs, on Jewish education in Spain. Some representative texts, often poorly edited, have been assembled.

See S. Assaf, (ed.) *Meqorot le-toldot ha-hinukh be-Yisrael.* Vol. 2. Tel Aviv, 1954.

EDUCATION, MUSLIM

The educational system for Muslims in al-Andalus consisted of three stages: elementary, advanced, and specialized. The first stage centered on the elementary school, the second on study in the mosque, and the third involved often lengthy apprenticeships with scholars in one's chosen field, frequently including extensive travel to study with famous scholars.

The first stage of education was the responsibility of parents. Wealthy parents hired private tutors or occasionally supervised their child's education themselves. Most parents, however, sent their children to private elementary schools, which were diverse in number of students, size, quality, and cost. Children began school when their parents saw fit, usually between the ages of five and eight, and there studied reading, writing, the Qur'ān, and basic levels of language, literature, history, the religious sciences, mathematics, and science. Students could stop their education at any time their parents deemed appropriate. Those taking the full course of elementary study completed it between the ages of thirteen and fifteen, at which time they entered their chosen profession or went on to take advanced training. There is little explicit reference to girls attending school, but educated women from the upper classes, perhaps taught mainly in their parents' homes, are mentioned frequently.

During the second stage, that of advanced education, the venue depended on the field of study. The most common site for study of the religious sciences or fields closely related to them, such as early Arabic literature and history, was the mosque. There students attended classes in individual subjects taught by masters, and progress proceeded book by book. After mastering a book or set of books in a field, a student received a certificate in which the teacher attested to mastery of the book or books and to competence to teach it or them to others. A student then moved to the next level of texts, either with the same teacher or with one qualified for a higher level of study. In this way students both completed their advanced general education and began to specialize in one or more specific areas: grammar, literature, Qur'ān, prophetic tradition, Islamic law, and so on.

Those who wished to specialize in nonreligious studies sought their teachers among recognized specialists in particular fields. Those desiring to enter government bureaucracy became apprentices in chancelleries or other government departments, where they received advanced, on-the-job training. Those interested in medicine, the exact sciences, and philosophy attached themselves to one or more recognized masters who guided them through the theory and practice of their discipline. Often fields became family specialties, so that sons of courtiers and officials entered governmental administration, while children of physicians, such as those of the famed Banū Zuhr family, were trained by their fathers and even replaced them when they retired.

The third stage of education, specialized study with the most famous scholars in a particular field, was optional but very prestigious. At this point students often traveled extensively to centers of learning in al-Andalus, North Africa, and the East. Such travel was essential for maintaining the quality and prestige of regional centers of education. Studying with and comparing one's level of education and expertise with masters and colleagues in other areas of the Islamic world boosted one's career and validated the quality of the education received in al-Andalus. For the religious scholar Mecca and Medina remained the most prominent centers, since there one could meet and measure oneself against students from throughout the Islamic world. For the secular scholar first Baghdad, and then post-Fāṭimid Cairo, were equally important. By this time the student had become a qualified teacher, and therefore could support himself by transmitting the learning he had acquired in al-Andalus.

In order to comprehend the rationale of the structure of Islamic education, it is essential to grasp the centrality given to the process of oral transmission of knowledge. This explains why traveling to study with diverse experts was so important. When scholars returned to al-Andalus after study in the East, or when prominent scholars from the East traveled to settle and teach in al-Andalus, their arrival signified the importation of new or recently renewed authentic lines of scholarly transmission that extended back to venerated founders and acknowledged masters of each field of specialization. Students traveling to obtain certificates were in fact accumulating scholarly pedigrees.

As is evident from the above, the general structure of premodern Islamic education was essentially private and personal rather than public and institutional. Teaching was done by individuals from one generation transmitting knowledge to those of the next on an oral, interactive basis. As a result the particular geographical or institutional venue of instruction mattered much less than it did in the university system that developed in Christian Europe. Although a city such as Córdoba became famous for its concentration of scholars, in theory the specific individuals with whom one studied and the students one later taught remained more important than the place where one received instruction.

Despite the ideals of oral transmission embedded in this educational system, learned individuals did value books as an important additional source of learning. Noted scholars at times accumulated extensive libraries in their area of specialization, and accounts exist of the extent to which wealthy individuals valued books as items of social prestige. Large libraries were crucial for the development or survival of certain fields. As a result of his bibliomania, caliph al-Ḥakam II (r. 961–976) amassed a library that reputedly encompassed over 400,000 volumes. These books, even after they were sold off, looted, and dispersed in the postcaliphate period, provided a basis for the development of philosophy and the sciences in al-Andalus. Libraries and bookstores were places where scholars and bibliophiles met informally to discuss subjects of mutual interest.

PETER HEATH

Bibliography

Makdisi, G. *The Rise of the Colleges: Institutions of Learning in Islam and the West*. Edinburgh, 1981.

Pedersen, J., and G. Makdisi. "Madrasa." In *The Encyclopedia of Islam*. 2d ed. Vol. 5. New York, 1993. 1123–34.

Vernet, J. *La cultura hispanoárabe en Oriente y Occidente*. Barcelona, 1978.

EGERIA

Egeria, whose *Peregrinatio* is the first travel book produced in the Christian West, is the most famous medieval woman writer from the Iberian Peninsula. Curiously, she is much better known beyond the borders of the peninsula, perhaps because for many years scholars believed her to be from France (and some still do).

Very little is known about her. Most scholars think that her name was Egeria, not Aetheria or Sylvia, and that she was a rich woman from Gallaecia (Gallcia) province who traveled to the Holy Land and wrote her work overseas in the late fourth century. However, some favor a French origin and an early fifth-century date. The name Egeria is unusual, but it has been found in a document from Oviedo, so the author of the *Peregrinatio* was not the only one with that name. Theories that she was a member of the nobility or an abbess have not been substantiated, nor has the theory that she was a middle-class laywoman. The consensus at present seems to be that, whatever her origin, Egeria was a nun or at least a member of a religious community. Her work obviously is addressed to a congregation of pious women to which she has strong emotional ties.

The *Peregrinatio* is a long letter to Egeria's fellow nuns that relates her activities and travel, over more than three years, in and around the Holy Land. Although Egeria based her work primarily on her own observations, she also used literary sources. Most of her quotations appear to be from the Bible and the *Onomasticon* of Eusebius of Caesarea. The text, which survives in one manuscript found in the nineteenth century in the library of the Brotherhood of St. Mary at Arezzo by Giovanni Gamurrini, is missing both the beginning and the end.

Through later references to her work by other authors, it is possible tentatively to reconstruct Egeria's trip. It apparently included an initial exploration of Jerusalem, and visits to Alexandria, the Thebaid, and Galilee, before her journey to Mount Sinai, as well as a visit to St. John of Ephesus after her arrival in Constantinople. The first twenty-three chapters narrate Egeria's ascent of Mount Sinai and her retracing of the route of the Exodus, a visit to the tomb of Job at Carneas, and the return trip to Constantinople, including a detour to the tomb of St. Thomas the Apostle at Edessa (modern Urfa) and the house of Abraham in Carrhae (modern Harrae), and another to the shrines of St. Thecla in Seleucia and St. Euphemia in Chalcedon. The last twenty-six chapters describe daily and weekly ceremonies, and the ceremonies of the major holidays from Epiphany through Pentecost and the feast of the dedication of the Basilica of the Holy Sepulchre.

Although there is a very extensive bibliography about Egeria's *Peregrinatio* (over three hundred titles), most studies deal with linguistic and liturgical issues. She is well known among students of Romance philology and church history because her work is an interesting example of Vulgar Latin and contains detailed information about Jerusalem rituals not found elsewhere. Her work has been studied as literature by only a few critics, who think the *Peregrinatio* is impersonal because it limits itself to describing the places visited from the point of view of whether or not they match the places in the Bible. These critics believe Egeria behaves like a Christian speaking to all Christians. Such a view has been questioned by critics who see Egeria's *Peregrinatio* as the work of a woman who writes for other women.

Egeria was not the first person to write about the Holy Land. Many others, before and after her, wrote itineraries (lists of places visited) giving the distance between places and describing each one in greater or lesser detail. The purpose of these itineraries was primarily to serve as guides for future pilgrims. They are written in the third person and contain little or no information about their authors or their experiences. Egeria's *Peregrinatio*, written in the first person, is a chronicle of her trip. Egeria could not write an itinerary because she was a woman, and women did not write guides addressed to the entire world. Women did not write very much at all. When they did, they wrote mainly things of a private nature, such as letters, often addressed to other women, and that is what Egeria did. Since her fellow nuns were not in a position to emulate her adventure, it was appropriate to justify and share such an uncommon deed by writing a letter. Had Egeria been a man, perhaps she and her peers would not have found her experience so remarkable, and she would not have written her work. Her overwhelming curiosity, scholarly abilities, social skills, and tremendous vitality come through clearly in the *Peregrinatio*, which was truly a woman's adventure.

CRISTINA GONZÁLEZ

Bibliography

Campbell, M. B. *The Witness and the Other World: Exotic European Travel Writing, 400–1600*. Ithaca, N.Y., 1988.

Franceschini, E., and R. Weber, eds. *Itinerarium Egeriae*. Corpus Christianarum, Series Latina, 175. Turhout, 1965.

Gingras, G. E., ed. *Egeria: Diary of a Pilgrimage*. New York, 1970.

Snyder, J. M. *The Woman and the Lyre: Women Writers in Classical Greece and Rome*. Carbondale: Ill., 1989.

EIXIMENIS, FRANCESC

A Catalan religious writer, Eiximenis, was born at Girona between 1330 and 1335. He entered the Franciscan order in his youth and studied in Italy, France, and England. In 1374, with the support of the king of Aragón, he obtained the *licentia docendi* at Toulouse University. He was highly esteemed by king Pedro III, while in whose entourage Eiximenis planned the *Crestià*, his ambitious Christian vernacular encyclopedia in thirteen large volumes. The first volume, *Primer del Crestià* (1381), was written in Barcelona and deals with the foundations of Christian dogma. The second, *Segon del Crestià*, which discusses temptation and divine grace, was finished in Valencia, where Eiximenis spent his mature years. In 1383 Eiximenis offered the citizens of Valencia a compendium of moral and political advice, the *Regiment de la cosa pública*, a vast treatise on the nature of human society and its government that was later included in the *Dotzè*. Meanwhile he finished another volume of the encyclopedia, the *Terç* (1384), an extensive description of the seven deadly sins, with theological explanations as well as all sorts of exempla and practical digressions. The *Dotzè* (1386, with an interpolation of 1391) is the twelfth, and the most popular, book of Eiximenis's encyclopedia. Titled *Regiment de prínceps i comunitats*, it is addressed to princes and kings, as well as to administrative officers with civil responsibilities. The two huge volumes of the *Dotzè* were kept in the city hall of Valencia for public consultation. Presumably Eiximenis did not complete the *Crestià* as planned. In 1392 he finished a very successful treatise on heavenly creatures, the *Llibre dels àngels*, and probably in 1396 a monograph on morals for women: the *Llibre de les dones*. Eiximenis also produced a *Vida de Jesucrist* (ca. 1400), which enjoyed great success and was designed to teach a personal approach to the human and divine figure of the Son of God, in the manner of Ludolph of Saxony and Ubertino of Casale's Latin *Vitae Christi*. Eiximenis's Latin works include an *Ars praedicandi*, a *Pastorale* giving advice to the bishop of Valencia, and a *Psalterium alias Laudatorium papae Benedicto XIII dedicatum*. The prayers of the latter were translated into Catalan in 1416.

Eiximenis supported Pope Benedict XIII, who in 1408 designated him patriarch of Jerusalem and bishop of Elna. He died at Perpignan, France, in April 1409. His books enjoyed a great success: There are many extant manuscripts of some of them; others were translated into Spanish and even into French; and some were printed in the fifteenth century. Eiximenis was a compiler deeply indebted to his sources (the great Franciscan writers of the thirteenth century, the treatises on vices and virtues), but he was also an extraordinarily talented vernacular prose writer and an acute observer of his times. His writings provided a fruitful bridge between the learned church traditions and the cultural needs of the inhabitants of the Catalan towns of the late Middle Ages.

LOLA BADÍA

Bibliography

Eiximenis, F. *Lo crestià*. Ed. by A. Hauf. In *Les millors obres de la literatura catalana*. Vol. 98. Barcelona, 1983.

Viera, D. *Bibliografia anotada de la vida i obra de Francesc Eiximenis*. Barcelona, 1980.

ELEANOR OF CASTILE

Eleanor (ca. 1161–1214) was the second daughter of Eleanor of Aquitaine and Henry II of England. She was born at Rouen in Domfront Castle and was married to Alfonso VIII of Castile in 1170. Her dowry included Gascony; in return Alfonso endowed her with holdings in the north of Castile, near the border with Navarre and Gascony. Both the marriage alliance and the location of Eleanor's lands may have influenced Henry II to decide in favor of Castile when he was asked to adjudicate a boundary dispute between Alfonso and Sancho VI of Navarre in 1177. However, the Castilians were never able to claim her dowry. Alfonso VIII tried to occupy Gascony in 1204–1206; Alfonso X renounced all claims to it in 1255 upon the marriage of his sister to the future Edward I of England.

Eleanor's first surviving child, Berenguela (born ca. 1180), married Alfonso IX of León; her other children were Urraca (born ca. 1186/1187), who married Afonso II of Portugal; Blanche (b. 4 March 1188), who married Louis VIII of France in 1200; Fernando (29 November 1189–1211); Constanza, abbess of Las Huelgas (d. 1243); and Enrique (b. 14 April 1204), who at her death became Enrique I.

Eleanor is thought to have followed her mother's lead and been a patron of troubadors in Castile. She established an altar to Thomas Becket at Toledo on 30 April 1179. With Alfonso she established the Cistercian convent of Las Huelgas at Burgos on 1 June 1187 (Rodrigo Jiménez de Rada gives her sole credit as the founder of the convent and the royal hospital there). Las Huelgas served many of the functions of Fontevrault for the Castilian royal family. According to Jiménez de Rada, Eleanor convinced Alfonso VIII to marry their daughter Berenguela to Alfonso IX of León in 1197. Eleanor had been named regent for Enrique, but she died within a month of Alfonso VIII in 1214, and was buried with her husband at Las Huelgas.

THERESA M. VANN

Bibliography

González, J. *El reino de Castilla en la época de Alfonso VIII.* 3 vols. Madrid, 1960.

ELVIRA

Elvira was the daughter of King Ramiro II of León and Urraca, the daughter of King García II Sánchez of Navarre. About 946, when she was roughly twelve years old, Elvira became a nun in the convent of San Salvador, which her father had established. From relative obscurity there she reemerged during the reign of her nephew, Ramiro III of León (966–984), who had acceded to the throne at the age of five. Despite her status as a religious, Elvira served as regent during his minority. Little is known of her responsibilities, except that she must have had to deal with a serious Viking invasion of Galicia in 968. Muslim sources inform us that she sent an embassy to the court of the caliph of Córdoba, Al-Ḥakam II, in November 973. They do not detail the substance of the negotiations, however. The last known notice establishes that she lived until at least 986.

BERNARD F. REILLY

Bibliography

Rodríguez, J. *Ramiro II. Rey de León.* Madrid, 1972.

ELVIRA (ILLIBERIS) COUNCIL OF

See CHURCH; WITCHCRAFT

ENACIADOS

As a marginal socioeconomic class, *enaciados* were an inevitable development of the peculiar circumstances on the medieval Hispanic frontier between Christians and Muslims. Guides, interpreters, messengers, or spies, *enaciados* were linguistically and culturally ambivalent, as at home in one ethnoreligious community as in the other. Although Alfonso X's *Estoria de España* alludes to "evil men, now called *enaziados*, who reveal to the Moors what Christians intend to do," the Christians gladly made use of their services. Thus Alfonso XI promised to maintain contact with Ruy Pavón, his spy in Granada, "by sending him men, called *enaciados*, who speak the language of the Moors." Probably based on a conflation of Arabic *naziʿ* (turncoat) and *nazih̤* (emigrant), the word also designated an individual who switched from one religion to another, to become, according to the *fueros*, a traitor and a criminal deserving the severest punishment. But the presence of communities of *enaciados* on the *frontera* substantiates their utility as a distinctive social group. The term survived in toponymy until recent times in Puebla de Naciados (Cáceres province).

SAMUEL G. ARMISTEAD

Bibliography

Corominas, J., and J.A. Pascual. *Diccionário crítico etimológico castellano e hispánico.* 6 vols. Madrid, 1980–91. Vol. 2, s.v.

Menéndez Pidal, R. *La España del Cid.* 4th ed. Vol. 1. Madrid, 1947. 188–89.

ENAMEL

Enamel is a glass powder composed of a basic mixture of lead and borax, to which are added metallic oxides like iron (producing a red color), antimony, lead, and silver (yellow), cobalt (blue), copper (green), and so forth. These oxides generally leave the powdered glass transparent, though if they contain zinc or arsenic, they can turn the enamel opaque. The powder is later applied to various substances, principally metal sheets (gold, silver, iron, and copper) coated with a flux to facilitate adhesion. Its temperature of fusion is 700–850 degrees Celsius (1300–1550 Farenheit).

The techniques employed in medieval enamelwork were:

Cloisonné [*alveolado*]. Of Byzantine origin, this process begins with the attachment of metal strips following the outline of a decorative pattern or drawing on the metal sheet. The cells formed by the metal walls are filled with enamel powders of different colors and then baked. This process is commonly used on sheets of gold or silver, and less often on copper.

Champlevé [*excavado*]. Characteristic of the Western Romanesque, this technique is executed on copper by gouging small grooves which are then filled with enamel powder and fused.

Basse-taille [*traslúcido*]. Typical of the Gothic era, this method is performed on gold or silver sheets engraved with bas-relief designs, or on round figures. The powders used in this technique are translucent, allowing the underlying low-relief composition to show through.

One example of the cloisonné technique is the enamelwork on the Cruz de Victoria of the Asturian period, a product of the royal workshop of Castillo de Gauzón in Avilés. In the latter part of the twelfth century, the abbey of Silos in Burgos was the major center of Iberian enamelwork. Works like the urn that adorned the tomb of Santo Domingo display the personality and exceptional quality of the Spanish enamels. The artwork on the altar of San Miguel de Aralar in Pamplona indicates the collaboration of craftsmen from both Spain and Limoges (France). During the Gothic era, the Catolonian and Levantine workshops take precedence, with works like the altarpiece of the Cathedral of Girona, or the Cross of Xátiva. In the Muslim world, the kingdom of fourteenth and fifteenth century Granada stands out. Decorative pins, belt buckles, necklaces, and sword sheaths/hilts were decorated with cloisonné enamels.

María Luisa Martín Ansón

Bibliography

Martín Anson, M. L. "Esmaltes," In *Historia de las artes aplicadas e industrales en España*. Madrid, 1982. 539–63.

———. *Esmaltes en España*. Madrid, 1984

ENCINA, JUAN DEL

A man of prodigious talent and driving ambition, Juan del Encina was born, in 1468, into the musically gifted family of a prosperous Salamancan cobbler. Under the tutelage of his older brothers, one a professor of music at the University of Salamanca and the other a chorister of the cathedral, Encina soon became an accomplished musician. His skill is evidenced by an extant corpus of sixty-two original works, the largest of any musician of the period. Several of his compositions are dedicated to Prince Juan, suggesting that he enjoyed favor at the Aragónese court of Fernando II.

As a student of the humanities at the University of Salamanca, Encina met two distinguished figures who would significantly influence his literary career: Antonio de Nebrija, who taught him Latin and rhetoric, and Gutierre de Toledo, chancellor of the university and brother of the second duke of Alba. In 1492 Encina became part of the duke's household, as creator of musical and theatrical entertainments. It was in this sumptuous, aristocratic milieu that Encina began his remarkable dramatic output and aggressive bid for professional advancement.

Encina's reputation rests primarily on the *Cancionero* of 1496, a collection of lyrics, long poems, original and translated prose works, and dramatic eclogues that he carefully prepared for publication. The volume contains a remarkable number of firsts in Spanish literary history: the first treatise on poetic theory (*Arte de poesía castellana*); the earliest rendering of Latin verse in Castilian meter (a paraphrase of Virgil's *Bucolics*); and the eight pastoral eclogues that have earned him the title "father of the Castilian theater."

The playlets that Encina produced and acted in at the ducal court were to have a lasting influence on Iberian drama throughout the sixteenth century. Their single greatest contribution was the character of the shepherd (*pastor*), the uncouth, unkempt, and ignorant rustic whose highly expressive stage language of *sayagués* Encina modeled on the rural dialect of his region. On one level the *pastor* was simply a comic figure intended to elicit laughter from a noble audience. In Encina's hands, however, he also gave voice to a variety of serious issues, such as social conflict, religious disharmony between Old and New Christians, and the difficulties of the artist-patron relationship. Last but not least, and aided by the fact that Encina often played the role himself, the shperherd became a vehicle for blatant self-promotion.

A notable lack of dramatic illusion often complements the multifarious role of the shepherd. In eclogues 1 and 2, for example, the shepherds are alternately contemporary Salamancan rustics guarding the duke of Alba's flocks, the four Evangelists, and biblical witnesses of the Nativity; one of them also represents the playwright and his anxieties about receiving adequate recognition from his patrons.

Another important influence on Encina's theater is clearly evinced in the final eclogues of the 1496 collection: the vast body of fifteenth-century love lyrics. In order to dramatize the power of love to transform lives and equalize social differences, eclogues 7 and 8 in particular draw heavily on the language and concepts of this amatory verse.

Social harmony becomes more elusive and love less benevolent in Encina's six remaining plays, probably written between 1493 and 1499. Eclogue 9, a Christmas play, deals only marginally with the Nativity, dwelling instead on the desolation wrought on town and country by the great rains of 1498 and the squabbling of four shepherds seeking shelter from the storm. The work seems to reflect a growing disillusionment, common to Encina's generation, with the possibility of peaceful coexistence between Old and New Christians in Spain.

It is believed that Encina's failure to secure ecclesiastical advancement and his continuing dissatisfaction with the Duke of Alba's patronage caused him to leave the latter's employ sometime around 1498. Shortly thereafter he left Spain for the first of three extended stays in Rome.

Encina's best-known works, eclogues 11–14, reflect his experience of the cultural wealth of Renaissance Rome, where his musical talents gained him the protection of three successive popes. The plays are noteworthy for their greater structural complexity, their borrowings from classical and Italian literature, and their increasing secularization, culminating in the sacrilegious suicide for love that occurs in eclogue 14, *Égloga de Plácida y Victoriano*. Eclogue 11, *Égloga de Cristino y Febea*, is generally regarded to be Encina's most accomplished. Although he had previously dramatized its theme of love's power to resolve conflicting values and lifestyles, here he achieves a more highly developed scenic structure.

Égloga de Plácida y Victoriano was performed in 1513. Some six years later Encina was ordained a priest and went on pilgrimage to Jerusalem. He spent the last ten years of his life (ca. 1520–ca. 1530) as prior of the cathedral of León. He had written the plays that determined the shape of Spain's secular theater before the age of thirty.

BARBARA F. WEISSBERGER

Bibliography

Andrews, J. R. *Juan del Encina: Prometheus in Search of Prestige*. Berkeley, 1959.

Encina, J. del. *Obras dramáticas*. Vol. 1. *Cancionero de 1496*. Ed. R. Gimeno. Madrid, 1975.

———. *Teatro (Segunda producción dramática)*. Ed. R. Gimeno. Madrid, 1977.

Sullivan, H. *Juan del Encina*. Boston, 1976.

ENGRAVING

Engraving was introduced in Spain with printing by German masters via Italy in the decade of the 1470s, as documented in the *Sinodal de Aguilafuente* (1472). The history of Spanish engraving begins with the consolidation of the printing industry in the period 1476–1480. The xylographic press was introduced immediately and anonymously created images engraved on wooden plates predominated during the early years of Spanish printing. The only Spanish metal engraving plate preserved from the period is that of *La Virgen del Rosario* by Domenech. Early Spanish engravings are distinguished by their decorative style, inspired by Venetian motifs enriched with elements of Islamic design. The images on the first Spanish xylographs are generally based on Italian and German sketches, which were either imported directly or copied from other sources. It is only during the last decade of the fifteenth century where one begins to see the emergence of an autocthonous style that could be referred to as uniquely Spanish.

In Zaragoza, the Hurus firm published important illustrated books during the first years of printing in the peninsula: the *Aurea Expositio Hymnorum* (1492), with plates closely related to Schongahuer; the *Thesoro de Passion* by Li (1494); and the *Viaje a Tierra Santa* by Breindenbach (1498). In Valencia, L. Palmer published the *Obres e Trobes* (1477). A clear example of Italian influence on engraving may be found in the edition of *Cárcel de Amor* by Diego de San Pedro (1493). Bartolomé Segura and Alfonso del Puerto produced the first illustrated book in the kingdom of Castile, the *Fasciculus Temporum* by Rolewinck (Seville, 1480), with both wood and metal engravings inspired by German models. Meynardo Ungut and Stanislao Polono established their engraving facility in Seville in 1490 and were instrumental in promoting the first printing press in Granada. *Los doze trabajos de Hércules* by Enrique de Villena (1483) is a work that contains the first engravings by a native Spanish artist, an anonymous master trained by German printers. Finally, the portrait of Prince Alfonso in the *Regimiento de príncipes* (1494) incorporates the courtly pictorial style of the fifteenth century. Many of the engravings produced at the end of that century reflect a Spanish-Flemish style that embodies a deep synthesis of both national and foreign elements.

BLANCA GARCÍA VEGA

Bibliography

Carrete, J., et al. *El grabado en España (siglos XV–XVIII)*. Madrid, 1987.

García Vega, B. *El grabado del libro español. Siglos XV–XVI y XVII*. 2 vols. Valladolid, 1984.

Gallego Gallego, A. *Historia del grabado en España*. Madrid, 1979.

Hind, A. *An Introduction to the History of the Woodcut*. New York, 1963.

Lyell, P. R. J. *Early Book Illustration in Spain*. London, 1926.

Thomas, H. "Cooperplate Engraving in Early Spanish Books." *The Library* (London), 2d ser., 21, no. 2 (1949), 81–96.

ENRIQUE DE ARAGÓN

Enrique de Aragón, also known as Enrique de Villena (1384–1434) was a fifteenth-century Castilian-Aragónese polymath intellectual reputed to be a sorcerer on the basis of his interest in the sciences and the preternatural. His father, Don Pedro, descended from the royal line of Aragón. His mother, Doña Juana, was the illegitimate daughter of Enrique II of Castile. Orphaned in infancy, he became a ward of his paternal grandfather Alfonso, Marqués de Villena, who took him to Aragón and attempted to educate him for a military career, which Enrique abandoned in order to pursue his intellectual curiosities. (Contrary to popular belief, Enrique never held the title of Marqués de Villena). Fernán Pérez de Guzmán includes an interesting portrait of Enrique in his *Generaciones y semblanzas*. Studious by nature, Enrique was drawn to the sciences, especially alchemy, astrology, and mathematics. Frustrated by life at court, he retired from society to pursue his academic interests. Upon his withdrawal from society, his reputation as a sorcerer and necromancer began to grow, while many acquaintances, on the basis of his renown, sought to flee his company. In an effort to engage him with the world, Enrique's grandfather arranged a marriage to María de Albornoz, a failed union that Enrique soon petitioned the king to dissolve.

In 1404 Enrique joined the military order of Calatrava without passing through the customary observances required of all novices. That same year, upon the death of Gonzalo Núñez de Guzmán, the grand master of the order, Enrique was elected to succeed him. Enrique's election produced deep dissent among many knights of the order, who voted to oppose his election on the basis of his notoriety as a magician and sorcerer. After years of litigation, the disputed election was resolved in 1414 by deposing Enrique, who had failed to get the necessary support of his uncle Enrique III, and could not count on help from Juan II that king's infant successor. Luis de Guzmán, son of the former head of the order of Calatrava, was elected grandmaster in don Enrique's place. At the same time, Enrique suffered another blow when the pope overturned the divorce from María de Albornoz granted to him by Enrique III. Disillusioned and economically pressed, Enrique retired to his estates at Iniesta to pursue a life of study.

As he withdrew more and more from the world, especially during the last decade of his life, Enrique de Aragón's reputation as a practitioner of the black arts grew considerably. The legend of his sorcery, necromancy, and magic spread throughout Castile and Aragón. As requested in his last will and testament, Enrique's works were examined for their orthodoxy and the ones found lacking were burned. Even then, after his death, his books were confiscated by order of Juan II and burned by Fray Lope de Barrientos, enlarging Don Enrique's legend to such an extent that his name became synonymous with the occult, medieval mystery, and witchcraft. This legend endured well into the nineteenth century, when Juan Eugenio Hartzenbusch made Don Enrique the protagonist of his play, *La redoma encantada*, about magic and the supernatural during the Middle Ages.

Although Enrique de Aragón's personal academic preferences tended toward the sciences and philosophy, his surviving scientific and philosophical works, although they show his fascination with arcane subjects, are highly derivative. Many of his theories are reformulations of Averröes and Avicena, when they do not reflect borrowings from Aranu de Vilanova. Don Enrique's intellectual distinction and his firm reputation as a humanist rest on his achievements in arts and letters. His Castilian translations of Homer, Dante, and Petrarch (the *Eneida*, *Divina comedia*, and a sonnet); his *Arte de trovar*, his *Los doze trabajos de Hércules*, and *Exposición del salmo "Quoniam video,"* plus his *Arte cisoria o tratado de cortar de cuchillo*, a treatise on culinary etiquette, reveal him, along with his friend, Iñigo López de Mendoza, Marqués de Santillana, as one of the two most agile and original humanistic intellects in late medieval Castile and Aragón.

E. MICHAEL GERLI

Bibliography

Carr, D. C. "A Fifteenth-Century Translation and Commentary of a Petrarchan Sonnet: Biblioteca Nacional MS. 10186, folios 196r–199r," *Revista Canadiense de Estudios Hispánicos* 5 (1980–81), 123–43.

Cátedra, P. M. "Algunas obras perdidas de Enrique de Villena con consideraciones sobre su obra y su bilblioteca," *El Crotalón. Anuario de Filología Española* 2 (1985), 53–75.

———. "Enrique de Villena y algunos humanistas," *Nebrija* 1 (1983), 187–203.

———. "Para la biografía de Enrique de Villena," *Estudi General* 1, no. 2 (1981), 29–33.

Gascón Vera, E. "La quema de los libros de Enrique de Villena: una maniobra política y antisemítica," *Bulletin of Hispanic Studies* (1979), 317–24.

Keightley, R.G. "Enrique de Villena's *Los doze trabajos de Hércules*: A Reappraisal," *Journal of Hispanic Phililogy* 3 (1978–79), 49–68.

Prendes, S.M. *El espejo y el piélago: la "Eneida" castellana de Enrique de Villena*. Kassel, 1998.

Weiss, Julian M. *The Poet's Art: Literary Theory in Castile c. 1400–60*. Oxford, 1990.

ENRIQUE DE VILLENA *See* ENRIQUE DE ARAGON

ENRIQUE I, KING OF CASTILE

Enrique I (b. 1204), the only surviving son of Alfonso VIII (r. 1158–1214), succeeded his father while still a minor. Alfonso VIII's will named Enrique's mother, Eleanor, as his regent, but she died less than a month after her husband. Berenguela. Enrique's oldest sister and former wife of Alfonso IX of León, took their mother's place and obtained custody of Enrique and of the realm. But by 1215 a group of nobles sought custody of Enrique, and Berenguela relinquished him to Count Álvaro Núñez de Lara, on the condition that he could not make war, grant property, or impose tribute without her consent. Despite these conditions Enrique's brief reign was marked by conflict between Álvaro Núñez and Berenguela. Berenguela accused Álvaro of endangering Enrique's health, and he claimed that Berenguela sent assassins after her brother. Either to diminish Berenguela's influence or to eliminate her from the government entirely, Álvaro negotiated a marriage between Enrique and Mafalda of Portugal in 1215, but Berenguela arranged to have the marriage annulled. Núñez's regency ended when Enrique died 6 June 1217 at Palencia, from a head wound received while playing. Álvaro Núñez tried to keep news of Enrique's death from Berenguela, but she found out and secretly summoned her son, Fernando, who was living with his father, Alfonso IX of León. She yielded her rights to the crown to Fernando in an assembly at Valladolid 2 July 1217. Enrique was buried at Las Huelgas Monastery in Burgos.

THERESA M. VANN

Bibliography

González, J. *El reino de Castilla en la época de Alfonso VIII*. Vol. 1. Madrid, 1960.

ENRIQUE II, KING OF CASTILE

Son of Alfonso XI, king of Castile, and his mistress, Leonor de Guzmán, Enrique II was born in Seville in 1333. He was adopted by the magnate Rodrigo Alvarez de las Asturias, from whom he received the *condado* of Trastámara, which provided the name of the dynasty initiated by Enrique. In 1350, he married Juana Manuel, daughter of the author and aristocrat, Juan Manuel. He died in Santo Domingo de la Calzada in May 1379 and was buried in the cathedral of Toledo.

From a very young age, Enrique opposed the kingship of his stepbrother, Pedro I of Castile, who had been accused of cruelty and of favoring the Jews. After the failure of the first uprisings against Pedro I in 1356 and 1360, Enrique, aspiring to crown himself king of Castile, sought strong military and diplomatic support before renewing the attacks. He found this support in two places: in the *Compañías Blancas* led by Beltrán Du Guesclin of Brittany in Aragón, who signed the Treaty of Monzón with Enrique in 1363, and in the pope, who consecrated the projected campaign as a crusade. In March 1366, Enrique invaded Castile, crowning himself king in Burgos the next month. As the illegitimate prince was waging his offensive, which reached as far as Seville, his stepbrother Pedro fled, seeking help from the English. But the defeat that Enrique suffered in Nájera (April 1367) at the hands of Pedro I and the English temporarily crippled his plans. He had to seek refuge in France, although he was able to return to Castile at the end of 1367. At that point a corrosive war between the brothers began, with Enrique increasingly gaining the upper hand, due to the economic travails of the time as well as the growing unpopularity of his rival. The assassination of Pedro I in Montiel (March, 1369) cleared Enrique's path to the Castilian throne.

The political outlook Enrique faced in the spring of 1369 was far from promising. In the Castilian interior, several regions maintained loyalty to Pedro I, including Carmona, Zamora, and a large part of Galicia, but an anti-Castilian coalition composed of the remaining Spanish kingdoms was forming. In 1371 the pockets of *petrista* support were crushed; at the same time, due to the signing of the treaty of Santarem with the Portuguese, its defensive strongholds along the frontiers of Aragón, Portugal, and Navarre crumbled. In 1375 the Treaty of Almazán made peace between Enrique II and Pedro IV of Aragón, who agreed to yield Molina to Castile, abandon his claims to Murcia, and consent to marriage between his daughter Leonor and Juan, the heir to the Castilian throne. Only the conflict with Navarre remained, though with the Treaty of Santo Domingo de la Calzada in 1379, this too was resolved. Clearly, between 1371 and 1379 the foundations were established for Castile's future hegemony in the Iberian Peninsula.

On the international front, Enrique II's rise to power produced a period of close alliance between

Castile and France, beginning with the Treaty of Toledo, signed in 1368 by the illegitimate prince and delegates sent by the king of France. As a result of this accord, Castile aided France in the Hundred Years War: its participation was particularly notable in the naval victory at La Rochelle (1372) and in the sacking of the Isle of Wight (1373). Accompanying the French alliance was Castile's hostility toward England; their economic rivalry acquired political motives as the duke of Lancaster laid claim to the Castilian throne due to his marriage to Constanza, daughter of Pedro I.

The generosity Enrique II displayed to the noblemen that helped him acquire the throne explains why he received the nickname "*el de las mercedes*" (he of the favors, or mercies). For the high Castilian nobility, Enrique II's ascent to the throne provided a prime solution for the problems created by the deep economic crisis of the time. For the crown, on the other hand, the *mercedes enriqueñas* produced a considerable decrease of royal property. Enrique's donations to his supporters consisted largely in seigneurial territories whose beneficiaries received revenues and possessed jurisdictional rights. Enrique II gave territories to captains of foreign troops such as Du Guesclin, who received but never occupied Soria and Molina, and Bernal de Béarne, who was awarded Medinaceli. The king's brothers, Sancho and Tello, were also beneficiaries of royal *mercedes*, as was his illegitimate son Alfonso Enríquez. But the majority of the donations were made to nobles, both from time-honored, traditionally powerful lineages (the Guzmán family, for example) and from social-climbing, newly powerful groups (like the Mendoza or Velasco families). Despite everything, Enrique II managed to slow down the negative impact these concessions had on the royal estates, establishing restrictive norms regulating their primogeniture succession.

In the political realm Enrique II strengthened the crown's power. In 1371 the seven-member *Audiencia* was established, serving as the kingdom's high court of justice. Also notable was the development of a system of estate administration, which by the end of the monarch's reign had taken the form of a *casa de cuentas* (billing house). Enrique II also called for frequent meetings of the *cortes* (parliament), which served as an essential instrument of dialogue with the kingdom and its cities. The principal sessions of the cortes occurred in Toro in 1369, when important legislation regarding price and salary regulation was approved, and in 1371. In conclusion, Enrique II lay the groundwork for the modern state in Castile.

In Enrique II's times, the tolerance that until then had prevailed between Christians and Jews began to crumble. Anti-Semitic propaganda, supported by the monarch during the war with his brother, led to violent attacks against numerous Jewish groups in Castile. Also supporting this trend were the intense criticisms made by the third estate of the cortes against the Jews. Once he had assured his place on the throne, Enrique II clearly changed his attitude, attempting to protect the Jews, even naming some to governmental positions, such as Yuçaf Pichon, *almojarife mayor* (chief tax collector) of the king's estate. But the anti-Semitic sentiments of the popular Christian sectors of Castile were already unstoppable.

Julio Valdeón Baruque

Bibliography

Suárez, L. "Política internacional de Enrique II," *Hispania*, 16 (1956), 16–129.

Valdeón, J. *Enrique II de Castilla: la guerra civil y la consolidación del régimen (1366–1371)*. Valladolid, 1966.

Suárez, L. "Castilla (1350–1406)." In *Historia de España*. Vol. 14. Ed. R. Menéndez Pidal. Madrid, 1966. 3–378.

Valdeón, J. *Los judíos de Castilla y la revolución Trastámara*. Valladolid, 1968.

———. "La victoria de Enrique II: Los Trastámaras en el poder." In *Génesis medieval del Estado Moderno: Castilla y Navarra (1250–1370)*. Ed. A. Rucquoi. Valladolid, 1988. 245–58.

ENRIQUE III, KING OF CASTILE

Enrique III was the son of Juan I of Castile and Leonor of Aragón. He was born in Burgos on 4 October 1379 and died in Toledo in 1406. He is often given the sobriquet *el Doliente* (the sufferer) because of his early death and the poor health he suffered from all his life. He was married to Catherine (Catalina), the daughter of John of Lancaster, who reigned as queen regent after his death.

Enrique was only eleven when in 1390, on his father's death, he acceded to the throne. After a controversy over his father's will and intention regarding his guardians, a regency council under the guidance of Pedro Tenorio, Archbishop of Toledo, was installed to direct the kingdom and watch over the boy during his minority. The arrangements lasted only into 1391, when deep divisions among the ambitious nobles who formed the membership emerged. The situation was immediately aggravated by a series of calamities that confronted the monarchy with a set of difficult decisions. Most important among those events was the anti-Semitic violence that broke out in Seville in the spring and spread throughout the kingdom during the rest of the summer. The council's internal divisions were resolved only by means of the actions of Enrique's aunt, Leonor, Queen of Navarra, who with the assistance of the papal legate, arranged for the disputing parties to accept with some modifications the original guardians Juan I had named for the boy in his will. The following year was followed by trouble with the kingdom of Granada, and the Portuguese with whom a truce was finally reached in 1393. Despite all earlier efforts, discord among the members of the regency council continued and, Don Pedro Tenorio, who threatened to resign, was taken prisoner and forced to turn over several fortifications under his protection. Deeply affected by the situation, yet still a minor, in August 1393 the young king declared his determination to govern and convene the *cortes* (parliament) in Madrid for October, the month he would turn fourteen and become legally of age. When the *cortes* convened at the appointed time, the king guaranteed the rights and privileges of his subjects and revoked all actions taken by the regency council during his minority to confer *mercedes* (grants of land, titles, privileges, and money). At the same time, he asked the *cortes* for moneys to shore up the kingdom's ailing finances.

Despite the young king's move to consolidate his authority, the contentious nobility remained a thorn in his side for the duration of his reign, fomenting discord with the king of Granada; his aunt, the queen of Navarra, who had been estranged from her husband Carlos *el Noble*, and the count of Gijón, Alfonso. In 1396, Portuguese troops crossed the border into Extremadura and took Badajoz by surprise, a move that was met by Castilian strikes that devastated the Lusitanian countryside and saw naval attacks along the Atlantic by Diego Hurtado de Mendoza, Admiral of Castile, that punished coastal cities. Hostilities ended when the Portuguese sued for peace. By 1398, Enrique was embroiled in papal politics, denying Castile's support, along with France, for Benedict XIII, the antipope Pedro de Luna. The last years of Enrique II's reign were marked by increased hostilities with the Muslims along the Granadan frontier. At the initiative of Muḥmmad VI belligerence intensified. Determined to take action against the new king of Granada, Enrique gathered an army to respond but died at Toledo before he could take the field.

Despite his promise and good intentions, Enrique III, like his son Juan II after him, would accomplish little to overcome the crippling effects of a contentious nobility that consistently confused the interests of the realm with their personal ambitions.

E. Michael Gerli

Bibliography

López de Ayala, P. *Corónica de Enrique III*. Ed. C.L. and H.M. Wilkins. Madison, Wisc. 1992.

Suárez Fernández, L. *Historia del reinado de Juan I de Castilla*. Madrid, 1977

Valdeón Baruque, J. *Los conflictos sociales en el Reino de Castilla en los siglos XIV y XV*. Madrid, 1975.

ENRIQUE IV, KING OF CASTILE

The son and heir of Juan II, Enrique was born at Valladolid on 25 January 1425. He did not take an interest in governance or politics until the last years of his father's reign, when he threw his support behind the nobles, whose efforts against Álvaro de Luna, Juan II's favorite, were led by Juan Pacheco, Marqués de Villena. When Juan II died in 1454, Enrique acceded to the throne of Castile. Irresolute and indecisive, however, he was incapable of exercising authority and left the work of governance largely to the energetic and ambitious Villena, his favorite, with whom he was rumored to have a homosexual liaison.

In 1440 Enrique had married Blanca of Navarra, the daughter of Juan II of that kingdom. By 1453, however, the marriage was dissolved amid rumors that Enrique was impotent and that the union had never been consummated. As a result, he is sometimes referred to as *el rey impotente*, or Enrique the Impotent. The consequences of the king's perceived impotence, linked with other events, would prove far reaching for monarchical succession in Castile during the second half of the fifteenth century.

In 1455 Enrique took a second wife, Juana of Portugal, who in 1462 gave birth to an heir, Juana of Castile, often referred to as *la Beltraneja*. This pejorative sobriquet reflected the belief that the princess's real father may not have been the king but rather Don Juan Beltrán, a high official at court reputed to have been her mother's lover.

Although on 9 May 1462 the *cortes* of Castile, attended by leading churchmen and the magnates of the realm, swore allegiance to Princess Juana as Enrique's rightful heir, and the king instructed all jurisdictions in the kingdom to do the same, rumors of the princess's illegitimacy began to circulate widely throughout Castile, amid a general malaise and dissatisfaction with the king. By 1465 Enrique was compelled by the nobles to recognize his adolescent half-brother, the Infante Alfonso, as his legitimate heir to the throne. Still dissatisfied, some of the nobles in June of that year, in the so-called Farce of Avila, deposed Enrique in effigy and proclaimed Alfonso King of Castile, leading to widespread civil unrest in the kingdom. Although the rebels were defeated at Olmedo in 1467, the mysterious death of the Infante in 1468 renewed and aggravated tensions. The allegations regarding Juana's illegitimacy endured at the center of controversy and continued to cloud Enrique's reign and the question of his succession. Pressure from the nobles persisted. They now favored the succession of Enrique's half-sister, Isabel of Castile, whom the king was then forced to recognize as his immediate heir at Los Toros de Guisando on 19 September 1468. Some historians have generally been willing to interpret this act as the king's implicit acknowledgment that Princess Juana was not his daughter. However, even if she were his daughter, as she was by juridical presumption, he might have yielded to the weight of the powerful nobles, who sought to give the crown immediately to Isabel. It is therefore possible that Enrique may have compromised with the nobles by making Isabel his heir.

After the conclusion of the Pact of Los Toros de Guisando, Isabel was at odds regarding Enrique's plans for her marriage. As early as 1460, the king had offered Isabel's hand to Carlos, Prince of Viana, eldest son of Juan II of Aragón and heir to the Kingdom of Navarre. Alienated from Carlos, Juan II, however, wished Isabel to marry his younger son, Fernando of Aragón. Negotiations were protracted until the death of the Prince of Viana. In 1465 Enrique made an attempt to arrange marriage between Isabel and Afonso V of Portugal, but the princess had already chosen Fernando of Aragón. For the same reason she also refused to marry Pedro Girón, master of the Order of Calatrava and brother of Juan Pacheco, the powerful Marqués de Villena. Other aspirants for Isabel's hand were Richard, Duke of Gloucester, brother of Edward IV of England, and the duke of Guyenne, brother of Louis XI of France. The *cortes* (parliament) assembled at Ocaña in 1469 to ratify the Pact of Guisando when a Portuguese embassy arrived to renew Afonso V's suit for Isabel's hand. When she declined this alliance, Enrique threatened her with imprisonment in the Alcázar of Madrid.

Although fear of Isabel's partisans among the nobility prevented the king from carrying out his threat, he exacted a promise from his sister not to enter into any matrimonial negotiations during his absence in Andalusia. As soon as she was left alone, however, Isabel—with the aid of the archbishop of Toledo, Alfonso Carrillo, and the admiral of Castile, Fadrique Enríquez (the grandfather of her future husband)—fled to Valladolid. From there she sent Gutierre de Cárdenas and Alfonso de Palencia in search of Fernando, who had been proclaimed King of Sicily, and heir of the Aragónese monarchy after the death of the prince of Viana. After Fernando's harrowing journey in disguise into Castile, Fernando and Isabel were married in Valladolid on 19 October 1469. The event created a tension that ceased only with the king's death on 11 December 1474, shortly after his return from Trujillo and the sudden, unexpected death of the Marqués de Villena. Isabel was proclaimed Queen of Castile the following day and Juana, who had in the interim become betrothed to Afonso V of Portugal and been reinstated as Enrique's heir when he revoked the Pact of Los Toros de Guisando, sought to press her claims via an alliance with the Portuguese. The archbishop of Toledo and other nobles who in Enrique's lifetime had denied Juana's legitimacy now defended her claims. The competing claims set off a five-year war between Castile and Portugal that ended in 1479, when Juana abandoned her case and retired to the monastery of Santa Clara of Coimbra (1480), from which she was never allowed to leave.

Research on the reign of Enrique IV has been hampered by the substantial lack of documentation, the disappearance of which can be traced to the diligence of Queen Isabel's loyal retainers. With few exceptions, most of the surviving testimonials of his reign are highly partisan, staunchly pro-Isabelline, and portray the king in an exceedingly negative light. In addition to the monumental problem of succession that hampered his reign, Enrique IV's time on the throne was marked by additional tensions and calamities. In 1455 and 1457, he was responsible for two disastrous campaigns against the Muslims of Granada that nearly ended with the revolt of the army. Not understanding economics, he later granted the privilege of coining money to private individuals, touching off devastating inflation. All the same, recent studies have indicated that many of the administrative reforms credited to Fernando and Isabel actually began under his initiative, and Enrique IV's role as a major patron of the arts is also beginning to emerge.

E. Michael Gerli

Bibliography

Calvo Poyato, J. *Enrique IV el Impotente y el final de una época*. Barcelona, 1993.

Phillips, W.D. *Enrique IV and the Crisis of Fifteenth-century Castile, 1425–1480*. Cambridge, Mass., 1978.

ENRIQUE, INFANTE OF ARAGÓN

Enrique was one of the younger sons of Fernando of Antequera and Leonor of Alburquerque. On the death of Enrique III of Castile in 1406, Fernando of Antequera became coregent during the minority of Juan II. Subsequently he became Fernando I of the Crown of Aragón after the Compromise of Caspe (1412), but he had used his regency in Castile to pursue his family's interests. Thus Enrique, who inherited the lands of his mother, devoted most of his ambitious life to the complicated politics of Castile. By 1409 Fernando had secured the mastership of the Order of Santiago for Enrique, and from then on, the latter was involved in almost every major political disturbance until his death in 1445.

When Juan II came of age in 1419, Enrique planned to secure a personal power base through the Order of Santiago. By criticizing abuses and the privileges that were being given to the followers of his powerful elder brother, the infante Juan, Enrique mounted a political offensive. Then, taking advantage of his elder brother's absence from the court, he engineered a coup d'état at Tordesillas on 24 July 1420. The king was captured; Enrique organized a sham *cortes* (parliament), married the king's sister Catalina, and secured the marquisate of Villena as part of her dowry.

Enrique's triumph was short-lived. The king and his favorite, Álvaro de Luna, managed to escape, and in 1422 Enrique was arrested and imprisoned. The internal politics of Castile were, however, subject to the intervention of Enrique's two brothers, Alfonso V of Aragón, and the infante Juan, who became King of Navarre late in 1425; between them they secured his release from prison in 1426.

At liberty Enrique devoted his efforts to undermining Luna, whom he clearly detested. Luna, however, was more than a match for him, and when Alfonso V threatened invasion in 1429, he converted what was in reality an internal crisis into a foreign war, crushed Enrique, and took control of the Order of Santiago. In July 1430 the Truce of Majano ended the war, and the infantes of Aragón were prohibited from living within the kingdom of Castile.

The vast increase in Luna's power provoked unrest, and when a revolt broke out in 1439, Enrique seized the opportunity to return to Castile, securing the restoration of all his lands and lordships shortly afterward. Royal government was to be controlled by the Royal Council, including Enrique and his brother Juan of Navarre, and in 1441 Luna was sentenced to six years of exile from the court.

However, government by the Royal Council was never more than a fiction, and by a coup d'état at Rámaga in July 1433, Juan of Navarre dropped all pretense of sharing power and purged the court and central administration. For two years Juan of Navarre and Enrique were the de facto rulers of the kingdom, but Juan II of Castile again escaped and joined Luna and other supporters. On 19 May 1445 a decisive royal victory was gained at Olmedo. Shortly after, Enrique died from a wound he received in the battle.

Like many of his noble contemporaries, Enrique was a devotee of chivalric spectacle and pageantry, and it may well be that Cervantes derived his idea for the famous episode of Don Quixote and the windmills from reading Carillo de Huete's description of an elaborate fiesta organized by Enrique at Valladolid in 1428. At one point during the joustings at this fiesta, the king of Navarre appeared in the company of twelve knights, all of them costumed as windmills.

Angus MacKay

Bibliography

Hillgarth, J.N. *The Spanish Kingdoms, 1250–1516.* 2 vols. Oxford, 1976–1978.

ENRÍQUEZ DEL CASTILLO, DIEGO

Enríquez, born in 1443, became a priest and subsequently was one of the chaplains to the king at the court of Enrique IV of Castile. A minor political figure, his importance lies in the fact that he was one of the official royal chroniclers and the author of the *Crónica de Enrique IV.*

The king aroused conflicting emotions among those who chronicled the events of his reign. Alonso de Palencia, another official and salaried chronicler, loathed him, and his account, full of vituperation, is a masterpiece of character assassination. Enríquez's chronicle provides a contrary view, ostensibly because he believed that the king was God's anointed and because "los corazones de los reyes están en las manos de Dios" (the hearts of kings are in God's hands). He repeatedly refers to the rebel nobles with such terms as *tiranos* and *tiranía*, and to the disaffected in general as *los pueblos ignorantes*. But he was far less subtle than Palencia, and at times almost naive. There was little of the humanist in Enríquez, despite the occasional classical reference, and in his prose he was much given to lengthy and conventional reflections, exclamations, invocations to God and the reader, and the reporting of rhetorical speeches that he attributed to the protagonists of the events he was describing.

Enríquez's chronicle must be assessed in the light of two specific contexts. The first relates to an unfortunate incident in which he was involved while at Segovia in 1467. According to Alonso de Palencia, Enríquez's papers and belongings were seized by royal opponents, and shortly afterward the unfortunate chronicler was taken before the archbishop of Toledo. The latter read extracts from Castillo's chronicle to members of the opposition nobility who were present, and only the chronicler's priestly status saved him from being condemned to death by King Alfonso V (Enrique IV's half brother and rival king). Enríquez himself briefly records this incident. With his material in the hands of the rebels, he had to start writing his version of events all over again, presumably mainly from memory, a fact that probably accounts for his confusion about the exact chronological details of certain events.

The second context involves a letter that Enríquez wrote to Queen Isabel the Catholic years later. In it he complained about the nonpayment of his salary of 37,000 *maravedís* as an official chronicler, and then went on to offer his pen in her service, proposing to write in her support if his pay were restored. Money, it would appear, could easily affect his opinions and his description of events.

Nevertheless, Enríquez's chronicle frequently contains valuable material that is missing or imperfectly recorded in other sources. Such is the case, for example, with his account of the virulent and inflammatory sermons against Jews and *conversos* (Jews who converted to Christianty) preached at the royal court in 1463 by the Franciscans Alonso de Espina and Fernando de la Plaza, to which the king reacted in a remarkably shrewd and rational way, and his account of the "republican" uprising and conspiracy in Seville of Archbishop Fonseca and the *comunidad* of the city in the same year and its consequences.

Although Enríquez disappeared from the political scene after Enrique IV's death in 1474, he was still alive in 1503, acting as a witness to a memorial concerning a dispute between the duke of Infantado and the marqués of Villena, and expressed the view that Álvaro de Luna had been a loyal and faithful servant to King Juan II.

ANGUS MACKAY

Bibliography

Enríquez del Castillo, D. *Crónica del rey don Enrique el Cuarto*. Madrid, 1878.

Paz y Meliá, A. *El cronista Alonso de Palencia. Su vida y sus obras: Sus Décadas y las crónicas contemporáneas*. Madrid, 1914.

EPIC *See* POETRY, EPIC

ERA, SPANISH *See* CALENDAR

ESCAVIAS, PEDRO DE

Castellan mayor (*alcaide*) of Andújar, Pedro de Escavias (ca. 1420–late 1490s) was identified by Juan de Mata Carriazo in his edition of *Hechos del condestable don Miguel Lucas de Iranzo* as the probable author of this chronicle about Enrique IV of Castile's favorite, Miguel Lucas de Iranzo. Mata Carriazo based his opinion on the internal evidence of the chronicle. He dismissed another possible candidate, Fernán Mexía, author of the *Nobiliario vero* (1492), on the grounds that the chronicle depicts him in a very poor light.

The chronicle is a priceless account of life on the frontier between Castile and Granada during the second half of the fifteenth century (ca. 1460–ca. 1471), a period characterized by alternating episodes of belligerence and remarkably tolerant episodes of *convivencia* (conviviality).

Miguel Lucas had voluntarily chosen exile from the royal court and in Jaén organized the town and its people in terms of Christian ideology (the feasts of the Christian calendar and problems of attack and defense on the frontier are remarkably recorded) and led a series of attacks on Muslim strong-holds along the frontier (described in panegyric terms). In Miguel Lucas's attacks on Granada, Pedro de Escavias is portrayed in the chronicle in a heroic light, very favorably. When, for example, Enrique IV (a worthless king, according to the account) wished to take Andújar, Escavias, replied in terms that totally debased royal power, addressing him as a king "if it is fitting to call someone king who is a slave."

The chronicle also records a *romance*, composed in honor of Miguel Lucas and his loyalty to the king. The spirit and the words probably express Escavias's own feelings rather than those of the former favorite of Enrique IV.

ANGUS MACKAY

Bibliography

Mata Carriazo, J., ed. *Hechos del condestable don Miguel Lucas de Iranzo*. Madrid, 1940.

ESCOBAR, PEDRO DE

Born at Oporto (ca. 1469) and therefore also known as Pedro del Puerto (do Porto), Escobar, may have been introduced to Isabel of Castile by the bishop of Oporto, João de Azevedo. While singing in her chapel choir from 1489 to 1499, Pedro—identified as Portuguese in a Simancas document—collaborated with Juan de Anchieta and Francisco de Peñalosa in composing two Lady Masses, extant in the Tarazona cathedral choirbook (vol. 3). On 19 May 1507 the Seville cathedral chapter dispatched a messenger to Portugal with an invitation to "come take charge of the choirboys." During his seven years at Seville, Escobar endured financial problems that the chapter attempted to alleviate. On 13 August 1514 Pedro Fernández was named his successor. On his return to Portugal he was chapel master (*mestre da capela*) for Cardinal Alfonso (Manuel I's son), continuing in that post from no later than

1521 to 1535. In the latter year he was living in poor circumstances at Évora.

Gil Vicente alludes to Escobar in his *Cortes de Júpiter* (August 1521); in that year he led a band of *tiples*, *contras altas*, *tenores*, and *contrabaxas* who performed at a royal prenuptial celebration. He was survived by two daughters who continued to receive royal pensions in 1554.

Escobar's eighteen pieces with Spanish text in the *Cancionero musical de palacio* include three trios that also appear in the *Elvas cancionero* (Em 11973): "*Lo que* es lo sequro" (lyrics by Garci Sánchez de Badajoz, ca. 1460–ca.1526); "*Pásame por Dios varquero*"; and "*Secáronme los pesares*" (lyrics by Sánchez de Badajoz). His *Quedaos adios* (in *Cancionero*, fol. 95v) appears with sacred text in the twenty-four-leaf *Consueta* of 1709, the oldest source of Mystery of Elche music. His motet *Clamabat autem mulier Cananea* (four voices), the most famous of his smaller Latin works (seven motets, four antiphons, two alleluias, eight hymns), circulated as far as Guatemala, and in 1546 was intabulated for *vihuela* by Alonso Mudarra. João de Barros praised it as the "prince of motets" in his "*Libro das antiquidades*" (Lisbon, Biblioteca Nacional, 216).

Robert Stevenson

Bibliography

Monumenta de la música española; Vol. 4 (1941) contains Pedro's Tone VIII Mass for four voices and his Tone VI four-voice Sanctus and Agnus Dei of a Lady Mass written with Juan de Anchiata. *Monumenta*; Vols. 5 (1947) and 10 (1951), contain his eighteen *villancicos* in the *Cancionero musical de palacio*. See also *Monumenta*, vols. 1 (1941), 5, and 7 (1949).

"Escobar, Pedro de." In *New Grove Dictionary of Music and Musicians*. Vol. 6, 243–44.

"Pedro de Escobar: Earliest Portuguese Composer in New World Colonial Music Manuscripts." *Inter-American Music Review* 11 (Fall-Winter 1990): 3–24. With three complete music examples and bibliography.

Stevenson, R. *Spanish Music in the Age of Columbus*. Westport, Conn., 1979. Pp. 167–74 With list of compositions.

ESPÁREC, ARCHBISHOP OF TARRAGONA

Espárec (also Aspareg, or Sparago) de la Barca, perhaps a native of Montpellier, where he studied law, entered ecclesiastical service in 1212 as bishop of Pamplona. He rose to prominence as a counselor of the royal family, and after the *cortes* of Lleida in 1215 he became archbishop of Tarragona, overseeing an ecclesiastical province, the Tarraconensis, largely coterminous with the Crown of Aragón's territory. In this capacity he was named by Pope Honorius III as one of the four regents during the minority of King Jaime I, having previously negotiated the Confederation of Monzón that created an interim government. As an international statesman he intervened in disputes among the nobility on both sides of the Pyrenees, and in 1227, presided over the Tribunal of Alcalá, where he continued to delimit Fernando III of Castile's designs on the Crown of Aragón. For the papacy he investigated the dealings of Archbishop Rodrigo of Toledo. He helped young Jaime I get an annulment of his first marriage, and in contrast to his support for keeping of the internal peace, he promoted the crusade against Valencia.

In line with his papal service but his guarded stance against all external intervention, Espárec hosted the legation of Cardinal Jean of Abbeville but less enthusiastically promoted the post-Lateran reforms advocated by the legate. It was only under pressure that he called the reform Council of Lleida (1230), which only four suffragans attended, and followed it with another council in Tarragona. The legate's demand for the Tarragona chapter's reform and election of more canons for the care of souls was resisted by the chapter and not enforced by their archbishop. More positively, Espárec continued the repopulation of Tarragona; dedicated a parish church to St. Michael for the port district; initiated the use of the cathedral of Tarragona, which continued under construction; and after 1218 sponsored the Carthusians by founding Scala Dei monastery. In a further effort to incorporate into his diocese the Priorat, the mountainous region that had been the Muslim March of Ciurana and that continued to resist assimilation, he introduced the Inquisition from Provence. He died at Tarragona on 3 March 1233.

Lawrence McCrank

Bibliography

Linehan, P. *The Spanish Church and the Papacy in the Thirteenth Century*. Cambridge Studies in Medieval Life and Thought, ser. 3, vol. 4. Cambridge, 1971. 9–53.

Morera Llauradó, E. *Tarragona cristiana. La historia del arzobispado de Tarragona*, Vol. 2. Tarragona. 3–40.

ESPINA, ALONSO (ALFONSO) DE

An Observant Franciscan, Espina preached sermons against the *conversos* (Jews who had converted to Christianity) and Muslims in towns such as Valladolid and Medina del Campo during the 1450s. Attached to the friaries of Valladolid and El Abrojo, he was by 1452 a regent of studies at the University of Salamanca and subsequently became confessor to Enrique IV of Castile (r. 1454–1474). However, given the opposed views of the two men, it is doubtful that his role as confessor had any practical significance.

In 1461 Espina was one of the instigators of a Franciscan plan that demanded the setting up of an inquisition. Shortly afterward he was involved in a scandal in which another Observant Franciscan, Hernando de la Plaza, preached a sermon at the royal court alleging that the Observant Franciscans had in their possession the foreskins of circumcised New Christians, an allegation that Enrique IV quickly demonstrated was without foundation. Between 1458 and 1461 Espina wrote his *Fortalitium fidei contra iudaeos, sarracenos et alios christianae fidei inimicos*, which constitutes his main claim to fame, if only because it provided a "blueprint" for the later Spanish Inquisition. Earlier he had written *Sermones de nomine Iesu*.

The *Fortalitium* consists of five books, four of which are directed against the enemies of the Catholic faith: Jews, heretics (meaning mainly Muslims), and demons. The importance of the treatise does not lie in its originality; indeed, Espina tended to copy from his sources word for word. What was important was that he produced a compendium of fictional stories and allegations from all over Europe, the end result being to emphasize a conspiracy against Christianity and the need for the inquisition. Clearly a fanatic, Espina had the knack of combining the wildest stories (for example, about host desecration, ritual murders, and incubi and succubi) with an apparently logical and theological approach designed to prove the existence of a Hebraic-Crypto-Judaic-Islamic-demonic threat to Christianity.

It has been alleged that Espina was himself a converso, but there is no firm evidence to support this. It has also been asserted that he was made a bishop in "partibus infidelium" about 1491; inquisitorial records, however, indicate that he died in Madrid toward the end of Enrique IV's reign.

Espina had alleged that leading nobles and churchmen at the royal court actively protected the Jews and conversos. Among other things he claimed that Jewish physicians deliberately poisoned Old Christians. When he himself fell ill, witnesses affirmed that the king's minister, Diego Arias Dávila, persuaded Enrique's Jewish physician, Maestre Samaya, to poison Espina. Thus on his deathbed Espina provided yet another example to bolster his conspiracy theory.

ANGUS MACKAY

Bibliography

Beinart, H. *Conversos on Trial: The Inquisition in Ciudad Real*. Jerusalem, 1981.

Carrete Parrondo, C. (ed.) *Proceso inquisitorial contra los Arias Dávila segovianos: Un enfrentamiento entre judíos y conversos*. Salamanca, 1986.

Netanyahu, B. "Alonso de Espina: Was He a New Christian?" *Proceedings of the American Academy of Jewish Research*. 43 (1976), 107–65.

ESTADOS *See* ESTATES

ESTAMENTS *See* ESTATES

ESTATES

In the High and Late Middle Ages, European society was hierarchically organized and composed of three orders or estates (*estados*, *estaments*). This reflected the scholastic concern for categorization as a device for giving meaning and order to the social structure. It was also the result in part of the revival of the Roman legal concept of *status* or juridical condition. Reference to this condition (*estado de los homes*) appeared in Alfonso X's *Siete Partidas* in the sense that human beings were considered as free, slaves, or freed from slavery. In his *Planeta* (1218) the chancellor of Castile, Diego García, mentioned the threefold division of society—*oratores*, *cultores*, *defensores*—but but it remained for the *Siete partidas* to elaborate the theme. The three estates established by God to maintain the world were the clergy (*oradores*), who prayed to God to protect his people; the nobles (*defensores*), whose characteristic function was warfare, theoretically in defense of the community; and the workers (*labradores*), who cultivated the fields or labored in the towns. Each person existed as a member of an estate, carrying out its characteristic duties and enjoying its distinctive juridical condition.

In his *Libro del caballero et del escudero*, Alfonso X's nephew, Infante Juan Manuel (1282–1347), declared that one could save one's soul in any of the three estates, because each one was good. Nevertheless, the highest estate was that of the clergy because of their sacramental function. The most honored estate among the laity was that of the nobles, "because the knights have to defend and do defend the others." While accepting the traditional division into three estates, Juan Manuel, in his *Libro de los estados*, divided society broadly into the two estates of clergy and laity. Just as the pope had the highest rank in the clerical estate, so the emperor ranked highest in the lay estate. The Catalan Francesch Eiximenis (1330/35–1409), in his *Regiment de prínceps*, offered a somewhat different tripartite division of society based on wealth and power. In his view the *maiors* included the aristocracy of birth and wealth, both lay and clerical. The *mitjans* were the middle class of professional people and merchants, and the *menors* were the workers and peasants.

The king constituted an estate of his own (*estado del rey*), in which he was placed by God. It was an estate greater than all others, except that of the emperor. Taken together, the estates constituted the people of the realm, an assembly of all ranks of men. The king was obliged to love, honor, and guard his people, "each one in his estate." Together with "all the men of the realm," the king formed a single body of which "he was the head, the heart, and soul, and they were the members." This belief in the organic structure of society composed of three estates logically led to the notion that when the king assembled the estates in the *cortes*, the entire community of the realm was present before him and capable of acting as one legal person. The consent of the representatives of the estates was tantamount to the consent of all the men of the realm. Thus the meetings of the *cortes* gave the estates the opportunity to came together as one and to participate with the king in the determination of the public business.

JOSEPH F. O'CALLAGHAN

Bibliography

Stefano, L. de. *La sociedad estamental de la Baja Edad Media española a la luz de la literatura de la época*. Caracas, 1964.

ESTORIA DE ESPAÑA *See* ALFONSO X; ILLUMINATION

ESTÚÑIGA, LOPE DE

Born probably between 1406 and 1410, Estúñiga was a member of the powerful Estúñiga clan. The first recorded event of his life has his participation in Suero de Quiñones' *Paso honroso*, one of the great chivalric challenges of the time, at a bridge on the Obrigo River in 1434. Nothing more of him is known until 1439, when, defying Juan II and Don Alvaro de Luna, he aided his brothers and his father, Iñigo Ortiz de Estúñiga, in the takeover of the city of Valladolid. Subsequently jailed by both Don Alvaro and Enrqiue IV, Lope de Estúñiga was known for his impulsiveness and quick temper. His fickle disposition involved him in numerous scandals throughout his life, most notably in 1462 when his wife fled home to seek refuge from him in the convent of Santo Domino el Real in Toledo. Knocking down the doors of the convent, Lope compelled her to return home and promised not to ill treat her. The last years of his life were spent in Toledo, where he died between 1477 and 1480.

Lope de Estúñiga is best known as a poet and for the important collection of *cancionero* verse that bears his name. His poetic personality stands out from among the many cancionero poets of the fifteenth century for its lyrical intensity and subtlety.

E. MICHAEL GERLI

Bibliography

Battesti-Pelegrin, J. *Lope de Stúñiga: Receherches sur la poésie espagnole au XVème siècle*. 3 vols. Aix en Provence, 1982.

Benito Ruano, E. "Lope de Stúñiga: vida y cancionero," *Revista de Filología Española* 51 (1968), 107–19.

Salvador Miguel, N. *La poesía cancioneril: El Cancionero de Estúñiga*. Madrid, 1977. 107–22.

ETYMOLOGIAE *See* ISIDORE OF SEVILLE

EUGENE I, BISHOP OF TOLEDO

The little that is known about Eugene I comes almost exclusively from the paragraph dedicated to him in St. Ildefonso's *De viris illustribus*. Eugene was a monk until drafted by Bishop Helladius (615–633) to assist in running the Toledan see. He served as *collector* under Helladius's successor, Justus (633–636), and succeeded Justus as bishop (636–646), attending the fifth (636) and sixth (638) councils of Toledo. According to Ildefonso, Eugene was an expert in astronomy. In a letter to Braulio of Zaragoza, his successor, Eugene II, referred to an episode in which Eugene I, obliged by the king to promote a man he regarded as an unworthy candidate to the priesthood, sabotaged the ordination by administering a curse rather than a blessing.

KENNETH B. WOLF

Bibliography

Braulio of Zaragoza. *Epistolae*. Trans. C. Barlow. Fathers of the Church, vol. 63. Washington, D.C., 1969. Epistle 35.

Ildephonsus. *De viris illustribus*. Ed. C. Codoñer Merino. Salamanca, 1972. 13.

EUGENE II, BISHOP OF TOLEDO

A native of Toledo, Eugene served as a cleric there prior to entering a monastery in Zaragoza. In 631, when Braulio succeeded his brother John as bishop of Zaragoza, he appointed Eugene archdeacon of the Church of San Vicente. Braulio apparently intended for Eugene to succeed him, but when Bishop Eugene I of Toledo died in 646, King Chindaswinth chose the younger Eugene to succeed him. As the metropolitan of Toledo, Eugene attended the Toledan councils of 646, 653, 655, and 656. He died in 657.

With the exception of letters to Braulio, Chindaswinth, and Bishop Protasio of Tarragona, Eugene's prose works, which included a treatise on the Trinity, have not survived. His efforts in verse have fared better. He revised the first book of the *Laudes Dei*, written by the late fifth-century Carthaginian poet Dracontius, as well as the *Satisfacio* that Dracontius addressed to the Vandal king who had arrested him. Eugene also composed over one hundred short poems that influenced subsequent Spanish poets, including Pablo Álvaro of Córdoba. According to Ildefonso, who succeeded him, Eugene was responsible for composing hymns and revising the Visigothic liturgy.

KENNETH B. WOLF

Bibliography

Braulio of Zaragoza. *Epistolae*. Trans. C. Barlow. Fathers of the Church. Vol. 63. Washington, D.C., 1969. Epistles 31–33, 35.

Collins, R. *Early Medieval Spain: Unity in Diversity, 400–1000*. New York, 1983.

Eugene II. *Monumenta Germaniae Historica, Auctores Antiguissimi*. Vol. 14 (1905): 27–69 (*Laudes Dei*), 115–29 (*Satisfacio*), 231–70 (poems).

Ildephonsus. *De viris illustribus*. Ed. C. Codoñer Merino. Salamanca, 1972. 14.

EULOGIUS OF CÓRDOBA

Priest and apologist for the Martyrs of Córdoba who died in 859 Eulogius was born (c. 800) into a noble Christian family in Córdoba. His parents dedicated him as a child to the Church of St. Zoylus, where he was educated and trained for the priesthood by the abbot Speraindeo. There he met and befriended Paulus Alvarus, later the author of the *Vita Eulogii*, upon which much modern knowledge of Eulogius is based. After his ordination Eulogius seems to have replaced Speraindeo as the *magister* responsible for training future priests. Around 849 or 850 Eulogius traveled north, visiting Navarrese monasteries and acquiring books.

Shortly after Eulogius's return, a monk named Isaac was arrested by the Muslim authorities for blaspheming Islam and was executed on 3 June 851. Within two months ten more Christians followed Isaac's example, launching what has come to be known as the Córdoban Martyrs' Movement. Sometime during that summer Eulogius took it upon himself to begin composing the *Memoriale sanctorum*, a martyrology containing brief accounts of the passions of the executed Christians. Shortly thereafter the Muslim authorities, looking for a way to stem the growing tide of dissent, ordered the arrest of the Córdoban clergy. Among those incarcerated was Eulogius. During his detention he continued to work on the *Memoriale sanctorum*, to which he added a preface designed to convince skeptical members of the Córdoban Christian community that the executed Christians were indeed legitimate martyrs who had suffered as the result of actual persecution. He also wrote the *Documentum martyriale*, a hortative treatise designed to encourage Flora and Maria, who had been arrested for apostasy and blasphemy, respectively, to maintain their resolve to become martyrs.

Eulogius was released in late November 851, but his relations with the local authorities, both Muslim and Christian, became increasingly strained. At one point he contemplated suspending himself from celebrating Mass in order to dramatize his dissatisfaction with the Church authorities who seemed intent on working with the emir to bring the martyrdoms to an end. The unpopularity of Eulogius's position seems to have prevented him from accepting his nomination to succeed Wistremirus as metropolitan of Toledo in early 852. That summer he had to hide to avoid being arrested a second time and was subsequently denounced at an episcopal council that had been convened by the emir to deal with the problem of the martyrs. Little is known about Eulogius's life over the next five years except that he continued to add to the *Memoriale sanctorum* as the executions continued. Sometime after March 857 he wrote another martyrology, the *Liber apologeticus martyrum*, dedicated to Rudericus and Salomon, who were put to death as apostate Muslims at that time. It also is known, from an independent source, that in 858 Eulogius met with the monks Usuard and Odilard, who had come from Paris to Zaragoza in search of relics and had been referred to Córdoba. In the late winter of 859 Eulogius was arrested for harboring a fugitive apostate named Leocritia. He defended himself by claiming that as a priest he was bound to instruct anyone seeking knowledge of the faith. When the judge ordered him whipped, Eulogius responded by denouncing Islam and was executed for blasphemy on 11 March 859.

Most assume that Eulogius's role vis-à-vis the martyrdoms was that of an orchestrator of a martyrs' movement. Yet a close look at the sources reveals that he had personal contact with only a few of the martyrs. His self-appointed function seems instead to have been one of promoting their cult when many of the Córdoban Christians seemed inclined to reject the would-be martyrs as suicides whose actions jeopardized their day-to-day relations with the Muslims. To this end Eulogius struggled in his writings to cast the Muslims as persecutors of the ancient Roman type and to portray Islam as a diabolically inspired false prophecy. Eulogius's apologetic treatises are important, then, not only as evidence of the wide spectrum of Christian responses to life under Muslim rule—from outright rejection to almost complete assimilation—but also as one of the earliest extant sources for Western views of Islam.

KENNETH B. WOLF

Bibliography

Colbert, E. "The Martyrs of Córdoba (850–859): A Study of the Sources." Ph.D. diss., Catholic University of America, 1962.

Gil, J. (ed.) *Corpus scriptorum muzarabicorum*. Vol. 2. Madrid, 1973. 363–503.

Wolf, K. *Christian Martyrs in Muslim Spain*. Cambridge, 1988.

EXEMPLA

The classic view on the genre of exempla continues to be the one described by Welter. This entry considers the importance of the compilations of exempla collected by French and English mendicants in the thirteenth and fourteenth centuries, as well as the various ways of organizing the material. The period coincides with the reformist stimulus of the Fourth Lateran Council (1215), when the new religious orders, especially the Franciscans and Dominicans, made wide use of exempla in preaching. That use is reflected both in the considerable extension of the exempla sources and in the appearance of compilations of doctrinal exempla. Parables, miracles, Eastern short stories, descriptions of tales related to animals, and many more—with some modifications—enlarged the preachers' compendia. Although the effects of the Lateran Council were not immediate, the great compilations that appeared in France and England are widely represented in the Spanish libraries, and a clear reflection of this circulation was the late appearance of the Romance books of examples.

In the same codex the *Libro de los gatos* and the *Libro de los exenplos por a.b.c.* by Clemente Sánchez de Vercial are copied. The first is a version of the *Fabulae* by Odo of Cheriton (1180–1190), written by the middle of the fourteenth century. Between the Latin original and the Romance version there is not an important lapse of time but there are a number of modifications. The first of them, and the only one that has concerned the critics, is the mysterious title, for which there are no explanations in the oriqinal.

The reduction in the number of tales (from seventy-five to fifty-eight) may be due to a mistransmission because, except for some isolated cases, the absences are concentrated at the beginning and at the end. Under every heading there is a story and the moral that can be taken from it. The stories range from those with a minimum narrative to folk tales or tales related to animals. The moral is usually addressed to important churchmen and laymen, criticizing the numerous social problems existing in Castile in the fourteenth century.

The *Libro de los exenplos por a.b.c.*, in two manuscripts, is the only Spanish book of doctrinal exampla considerated to be original. Its author, the archdeacon of Valderas (León), wrote it in the first third of the fifteenth century, following a strict alphabetical order (from *Abbas* to *Ypocritas*), in the same way the Franciscans had done in their collections. It includes 438 headings with up to 547 examples each. Although its disposition may indicate a sermonlike use, the brief preface reveals the desire to teach readers. Study of the text shows several differences from the most representative works in that genre: in the selection of sources there are plenty of examples from Valerius Maximus, and there are hardly any stories whose main characters belong to the mendicant orders; every example is preceded by a Latin *addagio* followed by its versified translation, forming a unit that recalls the scholarly apparatus of the quotation and its gloss. Finally, the examples, thought of being read directly without the oral support of preaching, are more developed in comparison with the Latin records. By the middle of the fifteenth century, the Spanish version of the *Speculum* (from the end of the thirteenth century and produced by an English Franciscan) had been produced. The translation, known as *Espéculo de los legos*, faithfully follows the Latin original and could also have been used, as shown in the manuscript, as pleasant reading in the conventual environment.

Manuscript 5626, in the National Library of Madrid, has an incomplete version of a book of doctrinal examples that, given its close relationship with the work by Vincent of Beauvais, may have come from a Dominican convent.

MARÍA JESÚS LACARRA

Bibliography

Bremmond, C., J. Le Goff, and J.C. Schmitt. *L'exemplum*. Louvain, 1982.

Welter, J.-T. *L'exemplum dans la littérature religieuse et didactique du moyen âge*. Paris, 1927.

EXPLORATIONS, CASTILIAN

The literature of antiquity was filled with references to islands in the western sea, the so-called Blessed or Fortunate Isles. Pliny speaks of them, evoking their climatic diversity. The description he gives of one of them, Nivaria, could well be taken for Tenerife, one of the largest of the Canary Islands, with its snow-capped peak rising out of the ocean. Their mention is repeated in Solinus and Isidore of Seville, both of whom served as key intermediaries for the transmission of classical knowledge to the medieval world. Throughout the Middle Ages, mention of islands in the western ocean continued to surface in vague evocations. It is not until the 1337, however, that a reasonably accurate allusion to them appears in Petrarch, who notes that Genoese ships had been sailing to them within the memory of his parents.

Although the chronology of the mapping and exploration of the archipelago of the eastern Atlantic, known as the Canary Islands during the Middle Ages, cannot be reconstructed with any certainty, it was already well underway before the 1330s, according to reliable information. The name Canary Isles, current from the 1340s, reflect a debt to Pliny, who had named one of the Fortunate Isles Canaria. The first authenticated visit to them, probably prior to 1339, is attributed to Lanzarotto Malocello, a Genoese who likely sailed under Portuguese patronage. By 1341 there is detailed information, apparently in Boccaccio's hand, of an expedition that was the product of cooperation between Portuguese and Italians and included Castilian personnel. News of the expedition quickly spread in Seville and Mallorca, and at least four voyages were licensed from the latter place to the Canaries in 1342. In 1345, Alfonso XI of Castile, invoking his rights to the conquest of "all the kingdoms of Africa" based on remote Visigothic predecents, laid claim to the Islands. Exploration and colonization, however, suffered a setback with the advent of the plague in 1348, although there is record of a voyage by Joan Doria and Jaume Segarra from 1351. Another reference from 1366 preserves instructions from the king of Aragón to patrol the archipelago and exclude interlopers. Many of the early reliable mentions of the Canaries also display a knowledge of the Azores further west. In the 1370s, according to tradition, the Canaries served as a theater of war between Portugal and Castile.

It was not until the 1390s, however, that a move to prosecute Castilian rights to the Canaries had begun in earnest. In 1390 Gonzalo Pérez de Martel sought royal permission in Seville for conquest but, according to later references, Enrique III in that year had already granted a license to Fernán Peraza. Peraza joined his interests in 1393 to those of the Conde de Niebla and mounted an expedition manned by Basque and Andalusian mariners that left destruction in its wake. They seized many natives, the so-called Guanches, including a local chief and his wife, and reported back on how easy their conquest had been. From this time forward, despite efforts by the French (Jean de Béthencourt, who held Lanzarote and Fuerteventura for a time) and the Genoese to make incursions there, the Canaries remained under Castilian authority. By the time of the first surviving records from the islands in the mid-fifteenth century, the institutions and the language of the Canary Islands were thoroughly Castilian, and there was a well-established colony of settlers there. The conquest of the islands had been rationalized by the Conde de Niebla and Enrique III in terms of "converting the natives" to Christianity. However, the rights of the pagans to remain undisturbed became an issue of debate. Until their final subjugation in the 1470s, accounted for by Castile in terms of a crusade, many of the native populations of the islands would continue to mount insurgencies and show resistance. The economy of the islands was largely geared to slaving along the African coast and some agriculture, especially on Gran Canaria. Agricultural products included leather and suet as well as native products like orchil, a mosslike substance gathered from rocks used for medicinal purposes. Pastoralism and gathering were features that survived well into the colonial period.

The final completion of the Castilian conquest and pacification of the all the native inhabitants of the Canary Islands in the 1470s would serve as an important prelude for the Castilian enterprise in the New World. By the late fifteenth century, the Canaries would become crucial stopovers in the exploration of the western Atlantic and America. Columbus knew the Canary Islands well.

In 1485, shortly after the pacification of the Canaries, Columbus went from Portugal to Castile, where he would spend nearly seven years attempting to secure the patronage of the crown. He was received at court, given a small annuity, and quickly gained both friends and enemies. An apparent final refusal in 1492 nearly sent Columbus to France, but a last appeal to Queen Isabel proved successful. An agreement between the crown and Columbus set the terms for an expedition to search for a western route to China and the east.

In the summer of 1492, Columbus outfitted three ships at the port of Palos. He was assisted in his efforts by two men—Martín Alonso Pinzón, and his younger brother Vicente Yáñez Pinzón. They left Palos on 3 August 1492, stopped in the Canaries, and sailed west with favorable winds. A landfall was made on the morning of 12 October 1492, at an island in the Bahamas, which Columbus named San Salvador and claimed for the Crown of Castile. Historians have identified it as present-day Watling Island, although Samana Cay, 105 kilometers to the south, has also been named as a candidate.

The landing was met by a friendly local population that Columbus called *Indianos*, thinking they were the native inhabitants of the East Indies. Some days later the expedition sailed on to present-day Cuba, where delegations were landed to seek the court of the Mongol emperor of China and gold. In December they sailed east to La Española (Hispaniola), where one of the ships was wrecked near Cap-Haitien, though the entire crew was saved. Thirty-nine men were left on the island at the settlement of Navidad while Columbus returned to Spain, sailing due north before heading east again to find favorable winds. He landed at Lisbon in March 1493 and was interviewed by the Portuguese king, João II. He then left for Barcelona, where he was welcomed by the Catholic Monarchs. Columbus claimed to have reached the islands just off the coast of Asia and brought with him artifacts, Indians, and gold. Over the course of the next fourteen years, Columbus mounted four expeditions to the New World under Castilian patronage.

Portuguese claims to the Castilian discoveries in the western ocean led Pope Alexander VI to issue bulls in 1493 that divided the world into areas open to colonization by Castile and Portugal. The two nations moved the line of demarcation to 370 leagues west of the Cape Verde Islands, according to the Treaty of Tordesillas (1494), and began exploration and colonization. By the time of Columbus's final return to Castile from his fourth voyage in November 1504, his efforts had brought large portions of America under the jurisdiction of the Castilian crown, which during the sixteenth century under its Habsburg successors would patronize its exploration and colonization.

E. MICHAEL GERLI

Bibliography

Aznar Vallejo, E. *La integración de las Islas Canarias en la corona de Castilla*. Seville-La Laguna, 1984.

Kadir, D. *Columbus and the Ends of the Earth*. Berkeley, 1992.

Fernández Armesto, F. *Before Columbus: Exploration and Colonisation from the Mediterranean to the Atlantic 1229–1492*. London, 1987.

———. *Columbus*. Oxford, 1991.

EXPLORATIONS, PORTUGUESE

Portuguese explorations rest on an Italian base because from the time of King Dinis (r. 1279–1325) until the reign of João I (1385–1433), it was the Genoese mariners and Mallorcan chartmakers in (or associated with) Portuguese royal service who laid the foundations for what was to come, while on the Portuguese side, the growing interest in maritime reconnaissance arose from Lisbon's position as the "wharf between two seas" added to a growing trade with the north in salt,

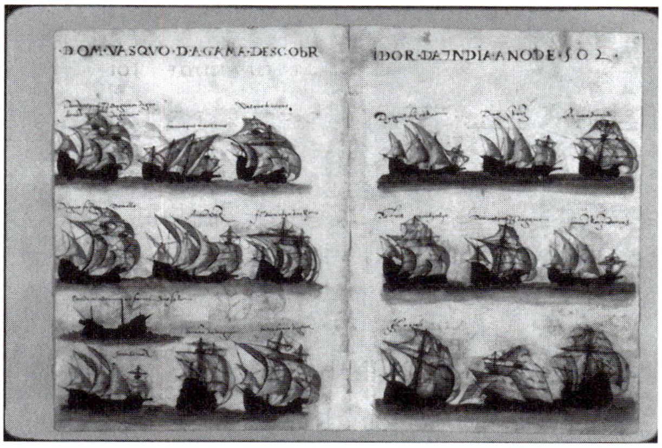

Fleet of Vasco of da Gama. From a manuscript depicting the Lives of the Portuguese Viceroys and Governors in India, by Lizuarte de Abreu, Portugal, ca. 1558. M.525f, 18–19. Copyright © The Pierpont Morgan Library/Art Resource, NY The Pierpont Morgan Library, New York, N.Y., U.S.A.

wine, and local agricultural products. Early Italians in royal service, included Manuel Pessagno and his kinsman Lanzarotto Malocello, both of whom were appointed admirals and became naturalized subjects, they not only created the first Portuguese royal fleets, but also with them visited the Canary Islands and probably discovered the Azores during the course of the fourteenth century. These islands were first represented by Italian portolan makers both in Italy and on the island of Mallorca.

But in the fifteenth century, from the reign of João I, it was the native Portuguese who assumed and continued maritime discovery. Beginning in the 1420s, Infante Henrique, who had become governor of the Algarve, obtained, first from his brother Duarte and, after his death in 1438, from the young king Afonso V, proprietorship of the Madeira Islands, the Canaries (which Portugal later lost to Spain), and the Azores, as well as the exclusive right to license all voyages along the African coast. After Henrique's death in 1460, there followed a six-year period (1469–1475) when the crown granted African voyaging and exploitation rights to the concessionaire Fernão Gomes, but in 1474 Afonso's son, the infante João (later João II), requested and received the rights his uncle had enjoyed. After the Gomes contract expired, pursuit of further discoveries became exclusively a royal prerogative once again.

Although foreigners were frequently enlisted, Portuguese reconnaissance was kept tightly in royal hands: with only Gomes excepted, Infante Henrique and/or the crown sought to license all voyages southward along the coast of Africa and to exclude interlopers;

in this it gained the help of the papacy, for beginning in 1455 Rome added its authority with a series of bulls. The first was the *Romanus Pontifex* of Pope Nicholas V, prohibiting all travel or trade south of Cape Bojador without express Portuguese license.

The pattern of exploration in the fifteenth century began soon after the conquest of Ceuta in 1415; the first islands to be (re)discovered were the Madeiras (1419) and the Azores (from 1427 on). The Canaries areas case apart; they were known from classical times, but Portuguese claims to them were countered by Castilian ones and Portugal finally was forced to abandon them after dismal failure of the military expedition of 1479 intended to counter the accession of Isabel I. The last island group to be discovered was the Cape Verdes (1455), by a Venetian in the service of Henrique, Alvise Ca'da Mosto.

The newly discovered islands (save for the Canaries) were uninhabited, and later were colonized from Europe and Africa; their patterns of settlement were established in contracts between Prince Henrique and the discoverer/proprietors; these, incidentally, became the models after 1500 for the settlement of Brazil. Rather than discovery among the islands, however, it was exploration of the African coast that was most portentous, because it eventually brought the Portuguese flag to the Indian Ocean. Until recently Prince Henrique had been given exclusive credit for the sending of vessels eastward, and even given the posthumous honorific "the Navigator," no doubt due to the panegyric chronicle written by Zurara, one of his retainers, who represented him as a studious visionary overwhelmed by geographical curiosity and the desire to spread the faith. Research has corrected this image: He inaugurated less than half of the coastal voyages and appears to have been far more of a businessman, investing in virtually every contemporary enterprise on land or sea. Nonetheless, at his death in 1460, Portuguese vessels had sailed as far south as Serra Leōa (Sierra Leone). Historians have demonstrated the extreme unlikelihood that Prince Henry could specifically have had the Indian subcontinent in mind when inaugurating his voyages, for in that era its separate existence in the European mind had hardly been established; rather, the expression "Indies" was a catchall for any lands including and east of Turkey and Palestine. Henry was merely looking for the legendary Prester John, whose definite abode had not yet been established within this vague eastern expanse.

It was Henrique's nephew, Infante João II, who succeeded to the throne in 1481, who set Portugal's sights on India; in effect he virtually presented it to his successor as all but a fait accompli. João had petitioned and received the rights of his deceased uncle in 1474, and upon his accession in 1481, he lost no time in resuming Portuguese reconnaissance on a scale hitherto unknown. One of his first steps was to obtain permission to build a fort at Elmina (São Jorge da Mina) on the Guinea coast; cargo ships brought prefabricated stones from Portugal, and a fortress was quickly erected there. It was then used as starting point for further explorations. Among these were the two or three voyages of Diogo Cão resulting in the discovery of the Congo River (1482) and the Cape of Good Hope (1488) by Cão's successor, Bartolomeu Dias. At the same time, in hopes of making contact with Prester John and the source of the spice trade in India (which by then had been identified), João II dispatched overland expeditions from Lisbon and from Elmina; the ones sent across Africa were lost, but one of the two men sent from Lisbon, Pero da Covilha, actually visited India in 1492, whereupon he doubled back to Ethiopia to complete the assignment of his deceased companion, Afonso de Paiva.

The Portuguese medievalist Luis Adão da Fonseca has argued convincingly that after the finding of the Cape of Good Hope, João sent other expeditions into the Atlantic, perhaps seeking a practicable route that square-rigged vessels could follow to round Africa. It is not known when he conceived the idea of reaching the Malabar Coast of India and trading there, but his goal is inherent in all of these activities. So little detail is known, with certainty, however, of João's expeditions after discovery of the Cape of Good Hope that the late Portuguese historian Jaime Cortesão argued that our ignorance is due to a strict policy of *sigilo* (secrecy), pursued by João to keep his discoveries from his Spanish rivals. But this thesis has been attacked by subsequent historians and generally rejected. It is just as likely that either the documents were lost in the great earthquake of 1755 or that the rival factions, the Braganças and their allies, who succeeded to the throne upon João's death in 1495, destroyed them in reprisal for the harsh punishment João had meted out to family members who had plotted against him. At any rate there is fair circumstantial evidence that João's navigators had some idea of lands to the west; otherwise, how would he have known to claim Brazil at Tordesillas, after Columbus's return in 1493? (The context of his actions, however, would point to his lack of interest in uncivilized western lands when India was within reach; it would seem he simply did not wish loss to Castile of any such lands for which his navigators might have established prior claims.)

There is evidence that after Dias's discovery of the Cape of Good Hope, João sent one or more expeditions up the African coast as far as Mozambique and

Socotra, but that these were wrecked—information that the new king, Manuel I, apparently did not wish to make known because it would detract from his own prestige. (It is contained in Damião de Gois's *Chrónica de D. Manuel* and in two Arab sources.) At any rate, in 1498 Vasco da Gama, sent by Manuel, reached Calicut and inaugurated the sea route used to establish a Portuguese presence in India. In 1500, on the second trip to Calicut, the expedition under Pedro Álvares Cabral sailed close to the bulge of Brazil and proclaimed its discovery, though it is possible (because it lay so close to the sailing routes to the Cape of Good Hope) that previous Portuguese reconnaissance had sighted it.

With two possible exceptions, there was no Portuguese discovery thereafter, perhaps because the Asians were expert navigators and their pilots were available to guide the Portuguese wherever they wished to go. In addition the crown, perhaps as a consequence, had ceased to sponsor exploration as it had before. But in or about 1543, three Portuguese freelance traders were blown ashore at Tanegashima, in southern Japan (thereby, one could conceivably argue, discovering it). And, of course, there was a Portuguese captain, one Fernão de Magalhães (also called Magellan) who in 1521 sailed across the Pacific under the Castilian flag because he believed he had been unjustly treated by his own crown in a dispute over spoils from Morocco.

George D. Winius

Bibliography

Albuquerque, L. de. *Navegações e a sua projecção na ciência e na cultura.* Lisbon, 1987.

———. *Náutica e a ciência em Portugal.* Lisbon, 1989.

Diffie, B.W. and G.D. Winius. *Foundations of the Portuguese Empire, 1415–1580.* Minneapolis, 1977.

Winius, G. (ed.) *Portugal, the Pathfinder: Journeys from the Medieval Toward the Modern World, 1300–ca. 1600.* Madison, Wisc. 1995.

EYMERICH, NICOLAU

Nicolau Eymerich, who in 1376 wrote a standard work on heresy and the procedures of the Inquisition, was born at Girona about 1320. Fourteen years later he became a novice in the Dominican convent of his native city. His theological, philosophical, and legal studies quickly led to preaching and writing, and in 1357 he was appointed inquisitor-general for the Crown of Aragón (including Catalonia, Aragón, Valencia, and Mallorca), a post he was to hold, with some interruptions, until his death on 4 January 1399

Eymerich produced a wide range of theological works, including commentaries on the gospels of Mark and John, and a treatise on the divine and human natures of Jesus. His most famous work is his *Directorium inquisitorum*, which not only guided the papal Inquisition in the Aragón of his own day, but also survived as a manual for the refounded Spanish Inquisition of Fernando and Isabel's reign. In the enlarged edition of Francisco Peaña (1578), it became a standard text of the Roman Inquisition during the Counter-Reformation.

During his lifetime Eymerich greatly offended his sovereigns, Pedro IV and Juan I, by upholding the rights of the Inquisition, and by attacking the writings of Ramón Llull and pursuing Llull's, followers both personally and in print. During his two resulting periods of enforced exile from Aragónese domains (1377–1387, 1393–1397), he was attached to the Avignonese popes Gregory XI, Clement VII, and Benedict XIII during the Great Schism of the Catholic Church.

Whatever the violent consequences that were to result from his written and practical work, Eymerich is justly recognized for the knowledge and discrimination shown in his inquisitorial manual. He went beyond the then conventional repetition of laws, previous sentences, and descriptions of heretical views and practices, in an attempt to enter the mind of the "heretic." His fame is thus based on his *Directorium*, rather than his role in the political and ecclesiastical events of his day.

John Edwards

Bibliography

Borromeo A. "A proposito del *Directorium inquisitorum* di Nicolas Eymerich e delle sui edizioni cinquecentesche," *Critica storia* 20 (1983), 499–547.

Eymerich, N. *Manuel des inquisiteurs.* Ed. and trans. L. Sala-Molins. Paris, 1973.

F

FADRIQUE, DUKE OF BENAVENTE

The illegitimate son of Enrique of Trastámara, Fadrique was appointed to the Admiralty of Castile by his father. He married an illegitimate daughter of King Fernando I of Portugal and received the title of Count-Duke of Benavente. He attempted to play an important role in Castilian affairs of the last decades of the fourteenth century, but in the long run his efforts failed. As a result of unsuccessful political machinations, he was deprived of his title in 1394.

As half brother of King Juan I of Castile, Fadrique was sent to Gascony as surety when, in 1388, the Castilians negotiated a settlement with the duke of Lancaster that ended the English claim to the Crown of Castile. Aside from a monetary settlement to be paid the English, the Castilians agreed to the marriage of the heir to the throne, the future Enrique III, to Lancaster's daughter Catherine. Following the wedding, and the payment of the agreed-upon sum, Fadrique was allowed to return to Castile.

Juan I died in 1390, leaving an eleven-year old heir in the care of a regency council sharply divided and unable to govern. Fadrique was one of the most prominent members of the faction within the council that represented the interests of the upper echelons of the aristocracy, at the expense of the crown and the lower aristocracy. The near chaos of this period came to an end when Enrique, though not yet fourteen, was declared old enough to assume the duties of the crown in 1393. He vigorously pursued his opponents, forcing Fadrique, his cause defeated, to capitulate in 1394. He was dispossessed of his titles and some of his properties. A month following the capitulation, Fadrique was taken prisoner and remained thus for the rest of his life. He died in 1404. The resolution of this episode—the apparent victory of the lower aristocracy, and the crown, over the upper aristocracy—constitutes a unique episode in the history of Castile.

CLARA ESTOW

Bibliography

Suárez Fernández, L. *Historia de España antigua y media.* Vol. 2. Madrid, 1976.

FADRIQUE, MASTER OF SANTIAGO

With his twin brother Enrique de Trastámara, Fadrique was the first surviving child of Alfonso XI of Castile and his mistress Leonor de Guzmán. Favored and privileged from his birth in 1332, Fadrique and the rest of his seven surviving siblings, lived close to the king, receiving honors and titles at the expense of the king's legitimate family. While he was still a child, Fadrique was elected master of the Military Order of Santiago at the insistence of his father. Until his violent death on 29 May 1358, Fadrique's political position lacked the single-minded consistency of his brother Enrique.

On a number of occasions Fadrique fought against his half brother Pedro; in 1350 he refused to pay homage to newly crowned Pedro and fled to the lands of the Order of Santiago. In 1354 he joined the growing rebellion in Castile over Pedro's mistreatment of his wife, Blanche of Bourbon. In a complicated series of events that resulted from this episode, he and his brother Enrique fought against Pedro at Toro, Toledo, and Talavera. In spite of early reverses, Pedro was able to prevail; Enrique left the country, and Fadrique sought a pardon and a reconciliation. Two years later he was Pedro's ally in the early stages of Castile's war with Aragón, making available the considerable military resources of the order of Santiago for Pedro's expansionist projects, in spite of efforts by the Aragónese to recruit him to their side.

Enrique, on the other hand, signed a pact with Pere IV of Aragón, Pedro's enemy. Fadrique, savoring a recent military success at the fortress of Jumilla, was summoned to Seville by Pedro in May 1358. When he arrived at the palace, unsuspecting, two mace-wielding guards set upon him and hit him in the head. Pedro was in the next room; finding Fadrique still alive, the king handed a servant a dagger to deliver the coup de grâce.

The fratricide, like several other obscure episodes in the reign of Pedro I, inspired the popular imagination. The *Romancero del rey don Pedro* has preserved two popular versions of the event. In one Pedro ordered Fadrique's death because the Master had had an affair, and a child, with Blanche of Bourbon, Pedro's French wife. In the other the blame falls on Pedro's mistress, María de Padilla, who asked for Fadrique's head as a prize.

CLARA ESTOW

Bibliography

López de Ayala, P. *Crónica del rey don Pedro*. Biblioteca de Autores Españoles. Vol. 66. Madrid, 1953.

FÁFILA, KING OF ASTURIAS

The only known son of Pelayo, the first king of Asturias, Fáfila succeeded his father in 737. He was killed by a bear, probably while hunting, in 739, and the throne in consequence passed to his brother-in-law Alfonso I. During his brief reign Fáfila is reported to have built a church dedicated to the Holy Cross at Cangas de Onís. No traces of it survive other than an inscription, which dates the dedication to Sunday, 27 October 737. This also provides the only evidence for the name of Fáfila's wife, Froiliuba.

ROGER COLLINS

Bibliography

Gil Fernández, J., J.L. Moralejo, and J. I. Ruiz de la Peña (eds.) *Cróanicas asturianas*. Oviedo, 1985. 130–33.

Vives, J. (ed.) *Inscripciones cristianas de la España romana y visigoda*. 2d ed. Barcelona, 1969. No. 315. 107.

FAIRS AND COMMERCE

Fairs, or *nundinae*, trace their origins to Roman times. As distinguished from the regional weekly market day, fairs in the Middle Ages took place once each year over a period of several days. In Iberia, fairs were held regularly at certain places and during certain times of the year, usually on religious feast days. Fairs, more than anything else, were wholesale markets geared to an economy that until the rise of the cities in the Late Middle Ages did not support the existence of daily retail markets. The size of fairs varied from place to place and ranged from a small gathering of merchants and displays to large community efforts guaranteed by royal privileges that offered housing and display spaces for visiting merchants. Revenue in the form of taxes was an important element of all fairs. Displays and shops were taxed, and tolls were often charged on merchants making their way to fairs. Sales taxes, however, could be set aside for the duration of some fairs, which served as an important incentive for attracting local clientele and stimulating consumption of, especially, manufactured goods.

The basic necessities of life were generally available in the villages, estates, and monasteries of medieval Iberia. Luxuries, some raw materials and manufactured goods in particular, however, could only be obtained in the regional *ferias*. From the middle decades of the twelfth century on there was also an increasing commercialization of agricultural products—particularly wool—that were traded at a multiplicity of newly established fairs that became the focal points of increasingly commercial contacts with European industrial centers, particularly those of France, Flanders, Italy, and England, where raw wool was in high demand. In the late Middle Ages fairs became central to advancing widespread trade and commerce and were planned for and anticipated well in advance of their date. The fairs at such places as Medina del Campo and Talavera de la Reina, both close to the geographic center of the Iberian Peninsula, were particularly important because of their strategic location. To ensure their success, the roads leading to them were patrolled to guarantee the safety of all who sought to participate—Christians, Muslims, and Jews. In this way, too, fairs provided secure environments for the commercial interaction of Christians, Jews, and Muslims and offered an open, multicultural climate that incorporated people from as far away as France, Italy, Flanders, and the extreme ends of the Mediterranean. The merchants who gathered at the fairs in medieval Iberia were all of diverse provenance, many of them often of distant foreign origin, like the Genoese at Seville. Still others were Muslims and Jews from all parts of Iberia, especially from across the frontier, and the rest of the Mediterranean world. All of them were multilingual and traveled regularly to North Africa, Egypt, and even had dealings with agents as far away as Persia, India, and on into China.

All manner of items could be purchased or traded at fairs. Everything from agricultural tools (plows, rakes, spades, etc.), weapons, and other iron implements to woolens, rich brocades from Italy, and woven silk from al-Andalus was available and could be bought in small or large quantities. Furs made their way from as far away as Russia, while garments from locally produced leathers and skins were also available—especially items manufactured from sheepskin. Iberian wool from merino sheep was especially prized by foreign merchants and was traded for dried fish, linen, and spun cloth from Flanders and other parts of northern Europe. Spices, salt, pepper, and honey (used for sweetening before the introduction of sugar from the Muslim south), were in great demand and could bring large profits. Cosmetics and perfumes became important commercial items at fairs from the thirteenth century on. Paper, manuscript books, ink, and other writing implements could also be purchased and sold.

In addition to trade and commerce, fairs became important centers in the rise of international banking. They were sites for the exchange, negotiation, and repayment of debt in international commerce, particularly in the cloth trade. They served as clearinghouses for contracts and for other international and commercial business deals.

Fairs filled an important economic need in the Middle Ages, yet they were also common meeting places that served for the communication of ideas, the dissemination of new technologies, and the introduction of new commercial and artesanal techniques of every kind. Physicians, alchemists, and astronomers could be found at fairs, and, as social centers, fairs were also gathering places for musicians, poets, and entertainers of every stripe.

The first fairs in medieval Christian Spain were apparently established in the reign of Alfonso VII of Castile, in Valladolid (1152) and Sahagún (1153). In the latter year, Ramón Berenguer IV appears to have established the first fair in Catalonia, in Moyá. In 1207 Pedro I of Aragón-Catalonia established a fair for the town of Colliure, granting also that all "external Jewish persons" are free to come to it and may travel freely by land or sea. It is peculiar that Jaime I, particularly given his establishment of "king's peace" laws, seems to have shown no interest in establishing fairs. Nevertheless, the *fueros* (municipal charters) of Aragón, compiled during his reign, do refer to the obligation of all citizens to "protect" the fairs and markets. Still, references to specific fairs are virtually lacking for the entire kingdom, including Valencia and Mallorca, throughout the medieval period. This may be due to the frequent wars, and also to the fact that the kingdom tended to develop more along industrial lines (particularly cloth manufacture). Whatever the explanation, the fact remains that merchants had to travel to far-off fairs in Castile, often at great risk of capture and death.

In Castile, early fairs, in addition to those mentioned, were established at Belorado, San Zoilo de Carrión, Sepúlveda, Cuenca and Alcalá de Henares. In the thirteenth century there were added those of Benavente, Brihuega, Cáceres, Badajoz, Mérida, Montiel, Alcázar, Sevilla, Cádiz, Murcia, and Lorca.

Alfonso X was particularly concerned with stimulating the economy through the establishment of fairs such as those of Seville (1254), to be held twice a year—one for a period of fifteen days before and fifteen days after Pentecost (usually in May), and the second for a similar period before and after the feast of St. Michael (September 29). Safe conduct was granted to all—Christians, Muslims and Jews—who came to participate. An almost identical privilege was granted for the establishment of a fair at Baeza in the fuero granted by Alfonso. In 1266, shortly after the restoration of Murcia to Castile, Alfonso established an annual fair of fifteen days after the feast of St. Michael, and in 1270 a similar grant was made to Lorca.

During the reign of Sancho IV the fairs of Brihuega and Alcalá de Henares appear to have been established, since in 1293 Gonzalo, the archbishop of Toledo leased to some Jews his rights and income from these fairs, held twice a year. The fair of Alcalá, seems to have been in existence from much earlier since in 1282 a Christian merchant of Narbonne complained to Pedro III of Aragón that his goods at that fair had been seized by his order on a false pretext. In 1296, as a reward for the loyalty of Palencia, Fernando IV established a fair in that city.

Little is known of fairs in the thirteenth and early fourteenth centuries. One of greatest importance, established by Fernando de Antequera (ca. 1412), was the one at Medina del Campo, because of its central location and its ability to attract Portuguese and Italian merchants.

In 1459 Enrique IV granted a special privilege to Segovia to establish two fairs, and later confirmed the grants to all fairs except those of Segovia and Toledo, and at the *cortes* (parliament) of 1473 he finally reestablished those of Medina del Campo, Valladolid, and others. In 1491 Fernando and Isabel made that of Medina del Campo the general fair for the entire kingdom.

The importance of the fairs, in addition to the obvious stimulation of local economy of the host cities, was that they allowed not only people from the entire peninsula to mingle freely and sell and buy merchandise (with all that implies for cultural exchange and dissemination) but also encouraged foreign merchants and visitors. The guarantee of safety for all encouraged and further promoted the concept of cultural exchange.

While fairs as an economic and social phenomenon persisted well beyond the Middle Ages, their period of maximum influence and energy was from the late fourteenth through the fifteenth centuries in medieval Iberia.

E. MICHAEL GERLI and NORMAN ROTH

Bibliography

Dufourcq, Ch.-E., and J. Gautier-Dalché. *Historia económica y social de la España cristiana en la Edad Media.* Barcelona, 1983.

Torres Fontes, J. "Las ferias de Segovia," *Hispania* III (1943), 133–38.
Verlinden, Charles. "Markets and Fairs." In *Cambridge Economic History of Europe*. Vol. 3. Cambridge, 1952–78.
Vicens Vives, J. *Historia económica y social de España*. Barcelona, 1969.

FALCONRY *See* HUNTING

FAZIENDA DE ULTRAMAR, LA

La Fazienda de Ultramar (MS 1997, Universidad de Salamanca) was first published in 1965, by Moshe Lazar, who believed it might originate as early as the second quarter of the 12th Century. The manuscript, however, appears to date from the first third of the thirteenth century. In any event, this is one of the oldest extant works in Castilian literature.

The work is preceded by two short letters. In the first, Remont, Archbishop of Toledo, asks his old friend Almerich, Archdeacon of Antioch, to send him an account of the Holy Land, including the Latin and Hebrew names of cities and places, the distance between cities, and the miracles that Christ performed in Jerusalem and in all the Holy Land. In the second letter, Almerich promises Remont to learn everything as well as he can by studying the Latin and Hebrew scriptures. The body of the work is a synopsis of the Bible, organized both chronologically and geographically. The account begins in Hebron with Adam and Eve, proceeds through time and space and returns to Hebron, after Samson. The work ends with a number of prophecies about the coming of the Messiah. Although the narrative follows the events of the Old Testament, there are many references to the New Testament. This is done by projecting history over geography, that is to say, by examining the many layers of history that cover each geographical location. For example, when talking about the city of Tyre, a number of Christ's miracles are mentioned, as well as the fact that the city had an archbishop and many martyrs, was attacked by Alexander and Bermudo, and was home to Queen Dido and Yran, Solomon's friend.

According to Lazar, this work is less a pilgrim's itinerary than a Romance Bible, the oldest Romance Bible in all of Europe. However, the second half of the work seems to be more of a pilgrim's itinerary than the first. As the narration progresses, geography becomes more important than history; the narration of events which occurred in a single place becomes more important than that of events occurring in various different locations. The information provided is more specific and seems to be firsthand. In sum, this work appears to be based more on firsthand observation, and less on formulae, than Lazar believes. It is a personal description of places embedded in a literary synopsis of the Bible.

CRISTINA GONZALEZ

Bibliography

Lazar, Moshe (ed.) *La Fazienda de Ultramar*. Salamanca: Acta Salamanticensia, XVIII, 2 (1965).
Rubio Tovar, Joaquin (ed.) *Libros espanoles de viaijes medievales*. Madrid, 1986.

FÉBUS, FRANÇOIS, AND CATHERINE OF NAVARRE

François Fébus (1481–1517) (or Phoebus), count of Foix and Bigorre, and heir of the sovereign principality of Béarn, became king of Navarre at the age of fourteen. His brief reign (1481–1483) suffered all the difficulties arising from a composite state that, straddling the Pyrenees, stretched from Tudela on the Ebro to Tarbes on the Adour, and was constantly threatened with attacks from the kingdom of France and from Spain. His double name reflected both the need to be on good terms with France (the name François pointing to his French ancestry through a sister of Louis XI) and the need to maintain his independence from France (his second name recalled Gaston III Fébus, the prestigious founder of the sovereign principality of Béarn in the fourteenth century).

When François Fébus died, all his estates went to his sister Catherine of Navarre, who had married Jean d'Albret, put forward by the French, rather than the heir of the throne of Castile, whom Navarre had suggested. In 1512 Catherine was ousted by Spain from the part of Navarre south of the Pyrenees. In vain her son Henri II d'Albret (who, caught between Spain and France, saw himself "as a louse between two monkeys") tried to regain Navarre, which was to remain Spanish. However, Henri did retain Navarre north of Ronscesvalles, which he left, together with the title of king to his grandson Henri III of Navarre-Béarn. When this grandson became Henri IV of France in 1589, his lands and his title passed to the Bourbon dynasty, which merged the Foix and Albret families.

PIERRE TUCOO-CHALA

Bibliography

Bordenave, N. *Histoire de Béarn et Navarre*. Paris, 1873.

FELIPE, INFANTE

Infante Felipe (1292–1327) was the son of Sancho IV of Castile (r. 1284–1295) and María de Molina. During the regency of his brother, Fernando IV (r.

1295–1312), Felipe accompanied their mother as she traveled to obtain support for Fernando from cities and regions. While he was still a child, María allocated to him lands in Galicia, where he fought Fernán Rodriguez de Castro. In 1308, after Felipe occupied Ponferrada, a town in Galicia belonging to his uncle, Infante Juan of Castile, the latter tried to foster a quarrel between Felipe and Fernando, but María prevented the development of any lasting animosity between them. After Fernando's death Felipe sided with Constança of Portugal, Fernando's widow, and Infante Juan against María and Felipe's brother Pedro over the regency for Alfonso XI of Castile (r. 1312–1350). Felipe did not recognize Pedro as regent until the Concord of Palazuelos in 1314. The following year Felipe married Margarita, daughter of Alfonso de la Cerda, titular king of Castile and perennial pretender.

When Juan and Pedro both died in battle at the Plains of Granada in June 1319, Felipe became one of the regents for Alfonso XI at the prompting of María de Molina, together with Don Juan Manuel and Juan el Tuerto. As regent with control over Andalucia and part of Castile, Felipe served to counter the ambitions of Juan Manuel by having more towns under his direct control, but he did not otherwise distinguish himself. He disappears from the historical record after Alfonso XI attained his majority in 1325, and Juan Manuel records his death as sometime during April 1327 in Madrid. He left no legitimate issue.

THERESA M. VANN

Bibliography

Benavides, A. *Memorias de D. Fernando IV de Castilla.* Madrid, 1860.

Gaibrois de Ballesteros, M. *María de Molina, tres veces reina.* Madrid, 1967; first published 1936.

FELIX, BISHOP OF URGELL

Felix is best known for his support of the Adoptionist views advanced by Elipandus, Archbishop of Toledo. Because Urgell, located in the Pyrenees, happened to fall under Carolingian jurisdiction, Felix's alignment with Elipandus gave an international dimension to the Adoptionist controversy. In 792 Felix was brought to Ratisbon, where he was forced to abjure the heresy in the presence of Charlemagne and his assembled bishops. He was then sent to Rome, where he made a confession of his faith, but once back in Spain, he resumed his Adoptionist stance. At the Council of Frankfurt in 794, the bishops assembled by Charlemagne condemned the position of Elipandus. In 799 Pope Leo III, at Charlemagne's request, followed suit. Charlemagne sent for Felix and brought him to Aachen, where once again he was forced to abjure. He died, confined in a monastery at Lyons, in 818. Bishop Agobard of Lyons later claimed to have found papers confirming that Felix remained true to his Adoptionist stance to the very end.

KENNETH B. WOLF

Bibliography

Blumenshine, G. (ed.) *Liber Alcuini contra haeresim Felicis.* Vatican City, 1980.

Collins, R. *Early Medieval Spain: Unity in Diversity, 400–1000.* New York, 1983.

FERDINANDO (FERRANTE) OF NAPLES

Ferdinando (Ferrante) was born in 1424, the illegitimate (and only) son of Alfonso V of Aragón, and spent his childhood in Valencia. Summoned to Italy by his father in 1438, he became heir to the newly conquered kingdom of Naples in 1443. In the war between Alfonso and Florence (1452–1454) he led the Aragónese army in Tuscany without notable success. On his father's death (1458) he duly inherited the kingdom but had to overcome a baronial rebellion and an Angevin invasion before his possession was secure. There followed two decades of internal peace buttressed externally by alliance with his uncle Juan II of Aragón and Sforza Milan, and internally by a redistribution of lands and titles in which his numerous progeny (six legitimate and at least eight illegitimate) figured prominently. Traitors were eliminated by stratagems that, though familiar enough in that age, furnished his enemies with material for a "black legend." Ruling without recourse to a parliament from 1459 until 1491, he tightened administrative and fiscal controls in a drive to enhance royal authority and revenues in tandem with an expanding economy. He continued his father's patronage of the arts, especially in music and book collecting, and revived the University of Naples. Ties with Spain were reinforced in 1477 through marriage to his cousin Juana of Aragón.

Foreign adventures, beginning with seemingly victorious participation in a war against Florence (1478–1480), and a Turkish invasion of the kingdom (1480–1481) threatened this achievement. Venice and Rome fell upon a weakened Naples, and no sooner had he extricated himself—with Spanish and Milanese aid—from those dangers than a new baronial revolt exploded in 1485. Thanks to years of reorganization that had left the crown with overwhelming military advantage, it took only one year to crush the rebels, including sympathizers within government ranks. However, peace could not be made with their ally, Pope Innocent VIII, until 1492.

Ferdinando ended his reign unchallenged master within his kingdom, yet threatened from without by the antagonism of a new pope, Alexander VI; Ludovico Sforza in Milan; and the young Charles VIII of France, heir to Angevin claims upon Naples. He died on 25 January 1494, leaving his eldest son, Alfonso, heir to a menaced throne.

ALAN RYDER

Bibliography

Bentley, J. H. *Politics and Culture in Renaissance Naples*. Princeton, N.J., 1987.

Pontieri, E. *Ferrante d'Aragóna, re di Napoli*. 2d ed. Naples, 1969.

FERNÁNDEZ DE CÓRDOBA, GONZALO

Castilian general who served during the reign of the Catholic Monarchs. He distinguished himself in the campaign leading to the fall of Granada in 1492, as well as later in Italy against the French. He belonged to an illustrious Córdoban family of *converso* (Catholic convert) origins and was born in the castle of Montilla on 1 September 1453. His father was Pedro Fernández de Aguilar and his mother Elvira de Herrera, of the powerful Enríquez clan. Like his brother Alonso de Aguilar, count of Cabra, Fernández de Córdoba inherited both wealth and position. When he was thirteen years old, Fernández de Córdoba was sent to serve as a page in the court of Princess Isabel of Castile, whom he would support during the war of succession and continue to serve when she became queen in 1474.

Fernández de Córdoba distinguished himself militarily during the war against Granada, especially in the taking of Loja (1486), in which he led a daring group of 120 lances. In the period leading up to 1492 and the fall of Granada, he was also instrumental diplomatically in dealing with Boabdil, whom he had come to know during the latter's captivity at Porcuna, and al-Zagal. Fernando de Aragón named Fernández de Córdoba to the commission that negotiated the final capitulation of Granada.

The Catholic Monarchs' confidence in Fernández de Córdoba led to their continued patronage. In 1495 Isabel sent him on an expedition against the French in Naples, where he encountered great success. In 1497, at the instance of Pope Alexander VI, Fernández de Córdoba attacked and defeated the French garrison at Ostia near Rome, a feat that won him the acclamation of the Roman people.

Later, in 1500, Fernández de Córdoba returned to Italy at the head of a great army to assist Louis XII of France in the struggle against the Turks. With the help of the Venetian fleet, and after fierce resistance, he vanquished the Turks on the island of Cephalonia, dealing a significant, though only brief, setback to Ottoman expansion in the eastern Mediterranean.

Fernando de Aragón and Louis XII agreed to divide the kingdom of Naples in the Treaty of Granada (1500), but the agreement soon broke down because of border disputes between them; it turned to all-out war in 1502. The Spanish army composed of light cavalry and Swiss pikemen was under the command of Fernández de Córdoba and won decisive victories against the French at Cerignola, Monte Cassino, and Garigliano. Fernández de Córdoba proclaimed the sovereignty of Fernando de Aragón over Sicily and governed it as viceroy under the king's name. Wary of the captain's ambitions, Fernando traveled to Italy to take possession of the kingdom and removed Fernández de Córdoba from power, obliging him to return to the Iberian Peninsula in 1507 as part of the king's retinue. Upon his return to Spain, Fernández de Córdoba retired to Loja. He died in Granada on 2 December 1515.

Fernández de Córdoba is recognized as the great military organizer and creator of the early modern Spanish army. His tactical innovations against the French in the Italian campaigns laid the groundwork for the Spanish military successes of the sixteenth century and won him a reputation throughout Europe as well as the distinction of being called El Gran Capitán.

E. MICHAEL GERLI

Bibliography

De Gaury, G. *The Grand Captain: Gonzalo de Córdoba*. London, 2d 1955.

García Valdecasas, G. *Fernando el Católico y el Gran Capitán*. Granada, 1988.

Montoliu, M. de. *Vida de Gonzalo de Córdoba (el Gran capitán)*. 5th ed. Barcelona, 1933.

Purcell, M. *The Great Captain: Gonzalo Fernández de Córdoba*. Garden City, N.Y., 1962.

Vaca de Osma, J.A. *El Gran Capitán*. Madrid, 1998.

FERNÁNDEZ, LUCAS

As musician, playwright, and cleric, Lucas Fernández was an active participant in the rich intellectual and cultural milieu of late fifteenth-century Salamanca. Born in 1474 and orphaned at the age of fifteen, he came under the tutelage of his uncles, who held important positions in the cathedral and the university. Fernández soon became a member of the cathedral choir and a student at the university, undoubtedly at the same time as Juan del Encina. In 1498 he obtained the position of cathedral cantor—also sought by Encina—and began a steady climb through the city's ecclesiastical and academic ranks, finally being named abbot in 1520 and professor of music in 1522.

Around 1496 Fernández joined the household of the duke of Alba as musician and poet. In that capacity he composed his three secular *comedias* or *farsas*, intended for performance at wedding feasts and other palace celebrations. The influence of Encina, who was also employed by the Alba family at the time, is strongly felt in Fernández's one-act pastoral eclogues, particularly in the character of the shepherd. Fernández's major contribution to the comic role of the *pastor* centers on his speech, the stage jargon known as *sayagués*. By basing it more consistently on a mixture of archaic Castilian and the Leonese dialect spoken around Salamanca, and coarsening its vocabulary considerably, Fernández codified the comic language that was to dominate the Castilian stage throughout the sixteenth century. The simple amorous intrigues dramatized in Fernández's playlets are complicated by the social tensions that arise as the rustics confront soldiers, friars, courtiers, and other upper-class characters. Given Fernández's aristocratic patrons and audience, it is not surprising that the shepherd generally ends up the loser in such encounters. The most vivid example occurs in *Farsa de la doncella* (1497), where the noblewoman whom the shepherd lusts after taunts him for his total ignorance of courtly language and behavior, and an aristocratic rival thrashes him for aspiring to the love of a social superior. Recurring devices in these farces, such as the peasant's proud recitation of his lowly genealogy and his experience of love's pain as a digestive disorder, became comic set pieces among Fernández's successors. Some scholars attribute the satirizing of the peasants' ignorance, social pretension, and, in particular, their identification of honor with bloodline to the dramatist's stigmatized New Christian background, but this aspect of Fernández's biography remains undocumented.

Peasant ignorance and dissension serve a different function in Fernández's two Christmas plays (1500–1502), commissioned by the cathedral council. In *Égloga del nacimiento* the rustics' insolence initially prevents them from attending to the message of Christ's birth, proffered by the learned hermit Macario. This both vividly dramatizes mankind's need for Christ's redemption and serves the playwright's didactic goals, as Macario patiently resolves the shepherds' doubts about the Incarnation and the Virgin's lineage. As in the secular plays, a *villancico* sung in unison brings the action to a harmonious and joyful closure.

Fernández's greatest dramatic accomplishment is the *Auto de la Pasión* (ca. 1500). It is technically noteworthy for its dramatic use of stage directions; the call for the display of a cross, an *Ecce homo*, and a Sacred Host also suggest that it was performed in a church. The fact that the events leading up to the Crucifixion occur entirely offstage heightens the dramatic impact of the play. Its intense emotional effect results from the graphic narration of Christ's suffering by St. Peter, St. Matthew, and the three Marys. The anguished questioning and lamentation of two anachronistic characters, Dionysius of Athens and Jeremiah, direct the audience's response.

In 1514 Fernández published his brief corpus of six plays under the title *Farsas y églogas al modo y estilo pastoril y castellano*, thus ensuring his contribution to the development of early Castilian drama. He died in 1542.

BARBARA F. WEISSBERGER

Bibliography

Fernández, L. *Farsas y églogas*. Ed. M. J. Canellada. Madrid, 1973.

Hermenegildo, A. "Nueva interpretación de un primitivo: Lucas Fernández," *Segismundo* 11 (1966), 1–35.

Lihani, J. *Lucas Fernández*. Boston, 1973.

FERNANDO, II, KING OF ARAGÓN *See* CATHOLIC MONARCHS

FERNANDO DE ANTEQUERA *See* FERNANDO I, KING OF ARAGÓN; ENRIQUE III, KING OF CASTILE; JUAN II, KING OF CASTILE

FERNANDO DE LA CERDA

Fernando de la Cerda, the eldest son and the second child of Alfonso X of Castile and Queen Violante, was born in Valladolid on 23 October 1255 and was baptized on the eve of All Saints Day. Soon after his birth Mencía López de Haro, widow of Sancho II of Portugal, who held extensive estates in Castile, designated the child as her heir, thus laying the foundation for later protests made by other claimants to her property. Entrusted to the tutelage of Jofre de Loaysa, who served as his *ayo*, Fernando was also appointed *mayordomo mayor* (chief steward) in 1255, but others effectively carried out the duties of the office until he reached his majority. His betrothal to Blanche, a daughter of Louis IX of France, was arranged at Saint-Germain-en-Laye on 28 September 1266. When Fernando reached the canonical age of fourteen, the wedding was solemnized on 30 November 1269 in the Cistercian nunnery of Las Huelgas de Burgos. On that occasion Alfonso X knighted his son, who in turn knighted his younger brothers, except Sancho, who refused to receive knighthood from him. Fernando and Blanche had two children, Alfonso, born in 1270, and Fernando, born two years later.

In the course of the rebellion of the nobility in 1272–1273, King Alfonso appointed Fernando and his mother to negotiate with the nobles. In a notable letter to his eldest son, preserved in the royal chronicle, the king condemned the perceived treachery of the rebels. When Alfonso X decided to visit Pope Gregory X at Beaucaire in southern France concerning his imperial claims, he convened the *corte* (parliament) to Burgos in March 1274 and named Fernando as regent. Admonishing him to do justice to all the people of the realm, he entrusted him with the royal seals and authority to appoint all royal officials. Those present promised to accept Fernando as king should his father die during his journey.

As regent Fernando summoned the prelates to a meeting (*vistas*) in April 1275 at Peñafiel, where he attended to their grievances concerning the right of the clergy to be tried only in church courts, the obligation of all to observe ecclesiastical censures, clerical tax exemptions, and the restoration of church lands seized by nobles and others.

Later in the year disaster struck the kingdom. The Marinids of Morocco, taking advantage of the king's absence from the realm, invaded Castile in late spring. At the first news of the invasion, Fernando summoned the host and hastened to the frontier, but fell ill at Villarreal and died suddenly on 25 July 1275. To compound this misfortune, both Núño González de Lara, the *adelantado mayor de la frontera* of the frontier, and Archbishop Sancho II of Toledo were killed in September and October, respectively, while trying to repel the enemy. As Fernando lay dying, he expressed the hope that his son Alfonso, then five years of age, would eventually succeed to the throne, and entrusted him to the care of Juan Núñez de Lara, son of the deceased *adelantado*. Fernando was buried in Las Huelgas de Burgos. His tomb escaped plunder by intruders and was opened in 1943, revealing his remains, princely clothing, jewelry, and arms intact. His death was a grievous blow and created a difficult juridical problem. His older son, Alfonso, could claim recognition as heir to the throne, according to the principle of primogeniture and representation, but Alfonso's uncle Sancho appealed to older custom which indicated that a king's surviving son had a better right. When Alfonso X acknowledged Sancho in the cortes of Burgos in 1276, a struggle over the succession was begun that was not resolved for nearly thirty years.

JOSEPH F. O'CALLAGHAN

Bibliography

Ballesteros y Berreta, A. *Alfonso X*. Barcelona, 1984.

"VII centenario del Infante Don Fernando de la Cerda," *Jornadas de estudio* (April 1975). *Ponencias y Comunicaciones*. Ciudad Real, 1976.

FERNANDO I, KING OF ARAGÓN

Born in 1379, Fernando de Anteguera was the second son of Juan I of Castile and Leonor of Aragón. During his lifetime he enjoyed a golden reputation for chivalrous conduct and honesty, and to a large extent modern historical scholarship has tended to confirm this view. It was a reputation that stemmed in the first instance from the circumstances arising from the problem of the succession to the throne at his elder brother's death.

Enrique III of Castile died at Toledo in 1406, at a time when representatives of the three estates had assembled for a meeting of the *corte*. The presumptive heir to the throne, Juan II, was not yet two years of age, and some believed that Fernando would claim the crown for himself. However, Fernando summoned the representatives of the *corte* to a meeting in the cathedral, persuaded them to accept the young *Infante* Juan as their king, arranged for his public acclamation, and then sent notables to Segovia to perform the ritual kissing of hands (*besamanos*) of the new monarch.

During the regency of the young Juan II, a regency uneasily shared by Fernando and the king's mother, Catherine of Lancaster, his reputation was further enhanced by his military campaigns against the Moors. During these campaigns he captured the stronghold of Antequera in 1410, the difficult and impressive task that earned him his sobriquet.

Shortly before this victory the childless Martín I of Aragón died, and Fernando put forward his claims to the Aragónese succession. The rival claims were considered at Caspe (Compromise of Caspe), and Fernando was proclaimed king in 1412.

As monarch of the Crown of Aragón, Fernando had to deal with several thorny problems. A rival claimant to the throne, Jaime (Jaume), Count of Urgell, initially accepted the decision of Caspe but rebelled in 1413, forcing Fernando to besiege him at Balaguer, confiscate all his possessions, and condemn him to life imprisonment.

In the Mediterranean, Fernando reached an understanding with the Genoese in a truce in 1413, signed treaties of friendship with Muslim powers in Egypt and Fez in 1414; pacified political anarchy in Sicily, eventually appointing his second son, Juan, as viceroy in 1415; and negotiated an end to a rebellion in Sardinia in 1416.

In Castile, Fernando promoted the powers of his sons, the *infantes* of Aragón, two of whom, Juan (later king of Navarre from 1425 and ruler of the Crown of Aragón from 1458 to 1479) and Enrique (master of the Order of Santiago), at various times posed serious threats to the Castilian monarchy.

More strikingly, Fernando resolved the Aragónese problem with respect to the Great Schism by withdrawing his support from Benedict XIII, the pope who, along with Vicente Ferrer, had done so much to promote his candidature to the throne. The Aragónese withdrawal of obedience to Benedict XIII was proclaimed in January 1416. Fernando died in April 1416, and was buried in the monastery of Poblet.

Devoted to the Virgin Mary, Fernando de Antequera fused his religious inclinations with both his political ambitions and his cult of chivalry. On 15 August 1403, for example, he founded the chivalric Order of the Jar and the Griffin in honor of the Virgin at the Annunciation. The white lilies in the jar or pitcher of the order's device are symbolic both of Mary's purity and of the Immaculate Conception, and the griffin represents the defeat of Islam with the Virgin's help. With Fernando's election to the throne of Aragón, the Order of the Jar and the Griffin was transferred to Aragón and became highly prestigious.

Fernando astutely presented himself as the Virgin's candidate at Caspe, thus clearly implying a form of divine intervention—indeed, predestination—and playing down the elective element. Visually this interpretation of his success can be seen in the giant *retablo* in the Prado Museum, *Retablo del Arzobispo Sancho del Rojas*. In it the baby Jesus leans from his mother's lap and personally places a crown on the head of a kneeling Fernando. Not one elector is in sight.

ANGUS MACKAY

Bibliography

Bisson, Thomas N. *The Medieval Crown of Aragón*. Oxford, 1986.

Hillgarth, J.N. *The Spanish Kingdoms, 1250–1516*. 2 vols. Oxford, 1976–1978. II.

Ubieto Arteta, Antonio. *Historia de Aragón: Creación desarrollo de la Corona de Aragón*. Zaragoza, 1987.

FERNANDO I, KING OF LEÓN

The second son of Sancho III Garcés (el Mayor), king of Navarre (r. 1000–1035), and the sister of Count García Sánchez of Castile, Fernando was installed as the count of Castile when García Sánchez was murdered in 1029. Subsequently he was married to Sancha, sister of Vermudo III of León. After his father's death Fernando defeated and killed his father-in-law at Tamarón on 4 September 1037. Vermudo had no direct heirs, so Fernando and Sancha were recognized as the monarchs of León-Castile.

The royal couple seem to have faced no serious internal challenge to their rule. They began the reform of the church of the realm with a council held at Coyanza (modern Valencia de Don Juan) in 1055, although the acts of that meeting show that reform was largely limited to a new policy of enforcing the traditional canon law. However, at some point in the ten years following, Fernando and Sancha entered into a close relationship with the great Burgundian reform monastery of Cluny, which would endure and grow under their heirs and successors. In return for Cluny's prayers for the well-being of their persons and dynasty, the Leonese monarchs began an annual subsidy of 1,000 gold dinars, which would do much to support the construction of a new, third monastic church structure at Cluny.

The royal couple also exerted themselves to enrich and endow the cathedrals and monasteries of their own realm. In 1063 an expedition to the Muslim *ṭāʾifa* (kingdom) of Seville secured the surrender of the relics of St. Isidore of Seville. These were transported to León and installed there in what would later become a major shrine. At the same time other relics were reclaimed from the ruins of Ávila and redistributed among the churches of the north. From what can be determined, Fernando and Sancha were comparatively modest in their patronage of Santiago de Compostela, even though the devotion and pilgrimage to the shrine of St. James was growing substantially during their reign. They were also generous to one of the favorite royal residences, the monastery of Sahagún, which was more central to the kingdom as it was then developing than was Santiago de Compostela. Despite all of this religious activity, relations between the churches of León-Castile and the papacy at Rome were minimal.

In the Christian north of the peninsula, Fernando asserted the hegemony of the new León-Castile that his victory in 1037 had established. During the reign of his father, lands in the Castilian northeast had been detached from that county and added to the kingdom of Navarre. That kingdom had been the portion of his older brother, García IV Sánchez (r. 1035–1054). Following the death of their father, relations between the brothers gradually worsened. On 15 September 1054, the two met in battle at Atapuerca, and García Sánchez was defeated and killed. The district of the Bureba, northeast of Burgos, was reclaimed for León-Castile, and the kingdom of Navarre became a tributary under Fernando's nephew, Sancho García IV (r. 1054–1076).

With the leadership of León-Castille secure in the Christian north, Fernando embarked on an ambitious series of campaigns against the Muslim *ṭāʾifa* kingdoms of the Iberian Peninsula. Perhaps as early as 1055 he launched his offensive against the Portuguese territories of Muslim Badajoz. On 29 November 1057 his forces took the town of Lamego, one hundred kilometers upriver from Christian Oporto. With that victory the valley of the Douro (Duero) River was secured for León. The next objective was the hill city of Viseu, on the Mondego River to the south. It fell to Fernando's troops on 25 July 1058. Nevertheless, clearing the Mondego valley and plain of Muslims proved to be arduous. The key position was occupied by the hilltop fortress city of Coimbra, seventy kilometers southwest of Viseu. Not until 25 July 1064, after a six-month siege, did that city surrender to the Leonese. When it did, the northern two-fifths of modern Portugal had been reclaimed from the Muslims and could be reorganized as a possession of León-Castile.

More directly to the south of Fernando and Sancho's realm lay the *ṭāʾifa* of Toledo. It may have been a tributary as early as 1058, for in that year the last known Mozarabic bishop of Toledo was consecrated in León, presumably because of León's tributary status. Nevertheless, in 1062 Fernando's army invaded that *ṭāʾifa* took Talamanca, north of Madrid; and laid siege to Alcalá. The Muslim king, Al-Ma'mūn, agreed to annual *parias* (tribute payments) to secure Fernando's withdrawal. During the following year Fernando struck deep into Muslim Andalucia, ravaging the lands of the *ṭāʾifas* of Seville and Badajoz. If those two realms had not already pledged the payment of *parias*, they certainly began to do so at this time.

Prior to his southern campaigns Fernando had moved against the great *ṭāʾifa* of Zaragoza on the Middle Ebro River. The chronology is not clear, but probably in about 1060 he seized the territories on the upper Duero with their strongholds at San Esteban de Gormaz, Berlanga, and Vadorrey. He also took control of the rolling country to the south of the river about Santiuste, Huermeces, and Santamara. Most likely Zaragoza paid *parias* from this time, but in 1064 that kingdom broke off payments. The Leonese response involved a victorious campaign that carried all the way to the plains around Valencia on the Mediterranean. That Muslim kingdom had joined with Zaragoza in the attack on the Leonese positions on the upper Duero. It seems to have been turned over to Fernando's ally and tributary, Al-Ma'mūn of Toledo, but Zaragoza itself once again came under Leonese suzerainty.

Fernando now had reached both the apogee of his reign and the end of it. He died on 27 December, 1065, and was buried in the Church of St. Isidore in León. His wife, Sancha, lived until 27 November 1067. On the death of Fernando, the kingdom was divided among his three sons. The oldest, Sancho II (r. 1065–1072), received Castile and the tribute payments of Navarre and Seville.

Bernard F. Reilly

Bibliography

O'Callaghan, J.F. *A History of Medieval Spain.* Ithaca, NY, 1975.

Jackson, G. *The Making of Medieval Spain.* New York, 1972.

Mackay, A. *Spain in the Middle Ages.* New York, 1977.

Reilly, B.F. *The Kingdom of León-Castilla under King Alfonso VI.* Princeton, 1988.

——. *The Kingdom of León-Castilla under Queen Urraca.* Princeton, 1982.

FERNANDO II, KING OF LEÓN

The second surviving son of Alfonso VII of León-Castile and Berengaria, daughter of Count Ramón Berenguer IV of Barcelona, Fernando was born about 1137. He was associated in the government of the realm with his father and brother by 1152 and was knighted in 1155. Following the death of his father, the kingdom was partitioned. Fernando inherited the rule of Asturias de Oviedo, Galicia, a reduced León, and the Leonese Estremadura from Zamora south through Salamanca and Coria. His elder brother, Sancho III (r. 1157–1158), inherited the greater realm, including Asturias de Santillana, the Rioja, New Castile, and an Old Castile swollen to include territories as far west as Sahagún, Medina del Campo, Arévalo, and Ávila.

That division, and the sudden death of his brother, leaving a three-year-old son, the future Alfonso VIII (r. 1158–1214), meant that Fernando could hardly refrain from trying to exercise the regency in Castile. In the latter kingdom the magnate Lara and Castro families vied for control of the child and the government, and Fernando was ordinarily allied with the Castros. Though he never really controlled his young nephew's government, he did long occupy the royal city of Toledo. By 1170 Alfonso VIII had assumed control of his own affairs, and subsequently there was some minor fighting between Fernando and Alfonso over their respective borders.

The contention between Fernando and his cousin Alfonso I Enriques of Portugal (r. 1128–1185) was more serious. Both monarchs continued to claim and contend for control of the valley of the lower Miño, which today forms the border between those countries. In the south an aggressive Portugal made initial gains against the North African Almohads, capturing Alcácer do Sal, Évora, Cáceres, Trujillo, and Badajoz. Alarmed, Fernando intervened in 1169 and, after defeating Alfonso, forced him to surrender Trujillo and Cáceres and to withdraw from Badajoz. The latter recognized the suzerainty of León but retained its own Muslim ruler.

During the first fifteen years of his rule, Fernando II had pursued the Reconquest quite successfully, repopulating Ledesma, Ciudad Rodrigo, and Alcántara in the Leonese Estremadura and adding to these Trujillo and Cáceres, taken from the Portuguese. However, the circumstances changed dramatically in 1172, when the death of Ibn Mardanīsh, the great *tā'ifa* king of Valencia, Murcia, and Upper Andalusia, allowed the Almohads to unite Muslim Iberia. Their caliph, Abū Ya ʿqūb Yūsuf, retook Caćeres and Alcántara in 1174 and pressed north to lay siege to Ciudad Rodrigo, although without success. The Muslims maintained the offensive in the west until their siege of Santarém in 1184. There Fernando came to the aid of Alfonso I Enriques of Portugal; the Almohads were routed and Abū Ya ʿqūb Yūsuf was killed.

The Christian rulers in Iberia at this time came to rely increasingly upon the military orders to carry out the work of reconquest and repopulation. Both the Templars and the Hospitalers were already established in the peninsula, but native orders came to predominate. In the kingdom of León one of these was the Order of Santiago de Compostela, which had its beginnings at Cáceres in 1170 and was formally recognized by Pope Alexander III in 1175. Another was the Order of San Julián de Pereiro, which later changed its name to the Order of Alcántara when Alfonso IX of León conceded that frontier fortress to them in 1213.

Internally the development of the kingdom of León was brisk as agriculture, raising livestock, and the pilgrimage to Santiago de Compostela continued to flourish. In Galicia their growing wealth led the burghers of the towns to become increasingly impatient with the traditional control of secular affairs by their bishops. Fernando had to intervene repeatedly in Lugo to adjust relations between its *concejo* and the bishop, amending the *fueros* (code of laws) of that town. The same sort of problem occurred in Túy, on the sometime border with Portugal. Farther south, Fernando granted a fuero to Benevente, mediated a brief revolt in Zamora, and enlarged the privileges of Salamanca, where discontent had contributed to a short occupation by Alfonso Henriques in 1163.

Fernando II had married Urraca, the daughter of Afonso Henriques, in 1165 as part of a negotiated peace between the two monarchs. However, the royal couple shared a common great-grandfather, in Alfonso VI of León-Castile, and Pope Alexander III finally annulled the marriage in 1175 on grounds of consanguinuity. Subsequently Fernando II had taken the noble Urraca López of Haro as mistress and had married her shortly before his death on 22 January 1188 and she had given birth to a son, Sancho. The king was interred in the cathedral at Santiago de Compostela. His seventeen-year-old son, Alfonso IX (r. 1188–1230), born of the Portuguese marriage, now faced the challenge of the queen mother to his right to succeed.

BERNARD F. REILLY

Bibliography

García de Valdeavellano, L. *Historia de Españá*, 2nd ed. Vol. 1, pt. 2. Madrid, 1955.

González, J. *Regesta de Fernando II*. Madrid, 1943.

FERNANDO III, KING OF CASTILE

Fernando, king of Castile (1217–1252) and León (1230–1252), was the son of Alfonso IX of León and Berenguela, the daughter of Alfonso VIII of Castile. He was born in June or July 1201. After his parents separated in 1204, because of consanguinity, he was reared in his father's court. His mother, summoned him to Castile following the sudden death of her brother, Enrique I (r. 1214–1217). Though she was acknowledged as queen of Castile, she bowed to the wishes of the Castilians assembled at Valladolid and transferred her rights to the throne to her son, and Fernando III was then proclaimed king. When Alfonso IX discovered what had happened, he invaded Castile with the intention of uniting it to the Leonese crown, thereby restoring the unity of the two realms, separated since 1157. Finding little support for his cause, he retreated to León at the end of the summer and recognized Fernando as king of Castile in August 1218. Father and son pledged to live peacefully with one another and to act in concert against the Moors. Following his mother's counsel, Fernando III married Beatrice, daughter of the Holy Roman Emperor, Philip of Swabia and granddaughter of Frederick Barbarossa, at Burgos in 1219. As a consequence, their firstborn child, Alfonso X, was later able to put forward claims to the imperial throne.

As the Almohad empire that dominated Morocco and Muslim Spain began to disintegrate, Fernando directed his energy to the Reconquest. Seizing Quesada in 1224, he also accepted the vassalage of al-Bayasi, the ruler of Baeza, and his brother, Abú Zayd of Valencia, who hoped, with Castilian help, to secure their independence of the Almohads. Al-Bayasi collaborated with Fernando in his campaigns against Jaén and Granada in the summer of 1225, and his fellow Muslims, disgusted by his submissive attitude, murdered him the next year. Soon afterward the Moors of Spain threw off the last vestiges of Almohad authority, but as a result Muslim unity dissolved, thereby giving advantage to the Christian rulers.

While Fernando vainly attempted to besiege Jaén, his father captured Mérida and Badajoz. His death soon afterward, in September 1230, radically altered Fernando's fortunes. Although Alfonso IX had never formally determined the succession to the Leonese throne, Fernando claimed it at once and moved swiftly to take possession. In order to secure an undisputed title, he had to persuade Alfonso IX's two surviving daughters by his first wife, Teresa of Portugal, to renounce their rights. The two former queens of León, Teresa and Berenguela, negotiated the settlement at Benavente on 11 December 1230, which compensated the infantas for their renunciation. Thus the kingdoms of León and Castile, separated since 1157, were reunited under Fernando, who was able to use their combined resources to prosecute the Reconquest.

Meanwhile, rivalry between Ibn Hūd of Murcia and Ibn al-Aḥmar (1232–1273), founder of the Naṣrid dynasty and the kingdom of Granada, benefited Fernando, who launched a major offensive that resulted in the capture of Úbeda in 1232. Elsewhere he laid waste the land around Arjona and Jaén, and threatened Córdoba and Seville. As 1235 drew to a close, a small band of Castilians, after invading the suburbs of Córdoba, quickly summoned Fernando to come to their aid. Receiving their message at Benavente in the middle of January 1236, he rapidly marched south and reached Córdoba on 7 February. In the weeks that followed, the bulk of his army tightened the siege of the city. When it became apparent that they could expect no help from their correligionists, the defenders surrendered on 29 June 1236. Those who wished to do so were permitted to leave, taking whatever they could carry, those who chose to remain were assured of religious liberty. The mosque of Córdoba was consecrated as a cathedral for the newly established Christian bishopric. The bells of Santiago de Compostela, which the Moorish ruler Al-Manṣūr, had carried off in 997 and hung in the mosque, were returned to the Christian shrine in Galicia.

In the years immediately following the conquest of Córdoba, many dependent towns and fortresses in the Guadalquivir valley submitted to Fernando. A few years later Murcia, in the southeast, also acknowledged his sovereignty. The assassination in 1238 of Ibn Hūd, who ruled Murcia, opened the possibility that the area might fall under the domination of Ibn al-Aḥmar, the emir of Tunis. To avert that, Ibn Hūd's family proposed to submit to Fernando as their suzerain and protector. Because he was ill, he sent his oldest son, Alfonso, to receive the homage of the Murcian towns. The Banū Hūd received him at Murcia in April 1243, and Lorca, Cartagena, and other towns, after a show of resistance, also submitted. As vassals of Fernando, the Murcian lords pledged an annual tribute of half their revenues, but otherwise they continued to rule as before. When Alfonso tried to seize Alcira and Játiva, towns reserved for Aragón (according to the Treaty of Cazola, 1179), he encountered opposition from Jaime I of Aragón. After negotiations they concluded the Treaty of Almizra on 26 March 1244, establishing the boundaries between Castilian and Aragónese conquests in that part of the peninsula.

Once he had recovered from his illness, Fernando resumed the offensive, taking Arjona and several neighboring towns in 1244. His next objective was Jaén, a seemingly impregnable fortress. After systematically destroying the crops, the king blockaded the city in August 1245. Ibn al-Aḥmar, now the undisputed master in Granada, Jaén, Málaga, and Almería, was unable to offer any support to the defenders, who faced the real prospect of starvation. Because his hands were tied, Ibn al-Aḥmar authorized them to surrender in March 1246. As the Moors departed, Fernando introduced Christian settlers and converted the mosque into a cathedral. In the hope of preserving himself and his dynasty, Ibn al-Ahmar pledged homage and fealty to Fernando, promising to serve him as a loyal vassal, both in battle and in his court, and to pay a tribute of 150,000 *maravedis* over a term of twenty years.

Seville, the wealthiest city in all of Spain, a port on the lower Guadalquivir River with access to both the Mediterranean and the Atlantic, next attracted Fernando's attention. Preliminary operations disrupted the outer defenses of the city and severed supply lines. Alcalá de Guadaira, Carmona, Constantina, Reina, Lora, Cantillana, Guillena, Gerena, Alcalá del Río, and other adjacent towns capitulated in 1246–1247. A formal siege of Seville was established in July 1247.

The blockade of Seville was completed when Ramón Bonifaz of Burgos, acting on the king's orders, organized a fleet in the ports on the Bay of Cádiz and entered the mouth of the Guadalquivir. Repelling enemy ships, he made his way upriver and broke the bridge of boats connecting Seville and Triana. Their supplies steadily dwindling, the defenders appealed to the Almohads in North Africa for help, but in vain.

Isolated, with no expectation of relief, the defenders of Seville surrendered on 23 November 1248. Fernando III permitted them to leave, carrying their movable property, with safe conduct to Jerez or on Castilian ships to Ceuta, in Morocco. The Moors were given a month to settle their affairs before departure, and a Castilian garrison immediately occupied the *alcázar* fortness Fernando entered the city in triumph on 22 December 1248. An archbishopric was established in Seville, and the king dedicated the remaining years of his reign to the colonization of Seville and the surrounding region, distributing houses and lands to those who had participated in the conquest or who were willing to settle there.

Fernando achieved the greatest success of all the Castilian kings in the Reconquest because the collapse of the Almohad Empire disrupted the unity of Muslim Spain. Taking advantage of the jealousies of rival

Moorish leaders, he gained control of the valley of the Guadalquivir from Úbeda to Seville and reduced the Moors of Murcia and Granada to the tributary status of vassals.

Aside from his efforts to eradicate Muslim rule in Spain, Fernando gave impetus to the development of the institutions and culture of his realm. He tried to reinvigorate the universities of Salamanca and Palencia, and welcomed scholars to his court. In the course of his reign, Castilian supplanted Latin as the official language of government and administration. His son, Alfonso X, eventually brought to fruition Fernando's plan to develop a uniform code of law for the kingdom. The *cortes*, in process of growth for a half-century, appeared as a fully constituted assembly of prelates, magnates, and townsmen representing the estates of the realm at Seville in 1250.

In the expectation of protecting his kingdom against any future Almohad intrusion into the peninsula, Fernando III was planning an invasion of North Africa, but death intervened on 30 May 1252. Buried in the cathedral at Seville, he was declared a saint by Pope Clement X in 1671. By his first wife, Beatrice of Swabia, he had had ten children including Alfonso X who succeed him. Two years after Beatrice's death in 1235, he had married Jeanne de Ponthieu, by whom he had three children.

JOSEPH F. O'CALLAGHAN

Bibliography

González, J. *Reinado y diplomas de Fernando III*. 3 vols. Córdoba, 1980–1986.

Mansilla, D. *Iglesia castellano-leonesa y curia romana en los tiempos del Rey San Fernando*. Madrid, 1945.

FERNANDO IV, KING OF CASTILE

Fernando, the son of Sancho IV and María de Molina, was born on 6 December 1285 at Seville. He was only nine years of age when he succeeded his father on 25 April 1295. For many years his mother, a woman endowed with wisdom, determination, and diplomatic skill, strove to defend him and his throne against numerous enemies. His uncle Juan challenged his right to rule on the grounds that he was illegitimate, because the pope would not validate his parents' marriage. Continuing a quarrel of long standing, Alfonso de la Cerda (a grandson of Alfonso X) denied the rights of both Sancho and Fernando to the throne. Supporting Alfonso's claims, kings Jaime II of Aragón and Dinis of Portugal proposed a partition of Castile for their own advantage, and invaded the kingdom in 1296. The first break in this coalition came the following year, when Dinis agreed to sign the Treaty of Alcañices, whereby Castile ceded certain frontier positions to him.

The new king's future began to take a turn for the better when he came of age in 1301. Pope Boniface VIII legitimated him in that year, thus removing any legal prextext for denying his right to the throne. As an assurance of peaceful relations with Portugal, Fernando married Dinis's daughter Constanza in 1302. Jaime II consented to submit Aragónese claims to Murcia to arbitration. The arbitrators, King Dinis, Infante Juan, and the bishop of Zaragoza, determined in 1304 that Jaime II should retain Alicante, Elche, Orihuela, and the lands north of the Segura River, but that the greater part of Murcia should be restored to Castile, in conformity with earlier treaties between the two kingdoms. Alfonso de la Cerda, in return for the cession of several towns and fortresses, gave up his claims to the Castilian throne.

Although internal peace was restored and the threat of external invasion was now removed, Fernando's relations with the nobility, who perceived him as essentially weak, were difficult. Nevertheless, he decided to resume the war of reconquest, taking advantage of domestic opposition to Muḥammad III, king of Granada. With that in mind, he concluded an alliance with Jaime II in December 1308, allotting to Aragón a sixth of the kingdom of Granada: the port of Almería and its dependencies. Previous treaties between the two kingdoms had reserved the whole of Granada for Castilian conquest. While the Aragónese laid siege to Almería in late July 1309, the Castilians besieged Algeciras and seized Gibraltar in August. Realizing that the the loss of Gibraltar left him in a vulnerable position, Nāṣr, the new king of Granada, who had overthrown his brother, ceded Algeciras to the Marīnids of Morocco, in return for their alliance. Fernando had to abandon the siege of Algeciras in January 1310 because Infante Juan, Juan Manuel, and other discontented nobles withdrew from the royal host. Although the failure of the campaign was attributable in part to poor organization and ineffective coordination between armies and fleets, the primary responsibility rests with the halfhearted efforts of the Castilian nobility. Nevertheless, Fernando did retain possession of Gibraltar, though the Muslims recaptured it in 1333. His ally, Jaime II, had had to withdraw from Almería, returning home empty-handed.

As had happened so often in the past, the king of Granada, recognizing that the Marinids were a threat to his independence, turned away from them and again pledged homage and fealty to Fernando. Renewing the payment of tribute and paying an indemnity, Nasáuár also yielded several castles to Castile. His ambiguous attitude, however, provoked a revolt among his fellow

Muslims, causing him to appeal to Fernando for assistance in suppressing the rebels. The king set out for the frontier and captured Alcaudete, but became ill and died on 7 September 1312. He was only twenty-seven years of age.

By his marriage to Constanza, he had two children: Leonor, who married Alfonso IV of Aragón in 1329, and a son, Alfonso XI, born 13 August 1311, who succeeded him.

JOSEPH F. O'CALLAGHAN

Bibliography

Benavides, A. *Memorias de Fernando IV de Castilla.* 2 vols. Madrid, 1860.

Gónzález Mínguez, C. *Fernando IV (1295–1312): La guerra civil y el predominio de la nobleza.* Valladolid, 1976.

FERNÃO I, KING OF PORTUGAL

Fernão, born in 1345, was the son of Pedro I. Following his ascension to the throne in 1367, he formed alliances with England in hopes of becoming king of Castile. Upon the death of Pedro the Cruel of Castile in 1369, Fernão, citing his descent from Sancho IV and backed by Pedro's supporters and Catalonia-Aragón, claimed the Castilian throne against Enrique of Trastámara (Enrique II). Though Fernão occupied Galicia and blockaded Seville, Enrique defeated him. This and papal intervention in the struggle caused Fernão to make peace in March 1371. Fernão initially had been betrothed to Leonor, daughter of the king of Aragón, but under the provisions of the new Castilian-Portuguese treaty he was betrothed to Enrique II's daughter, also named Leonor. Fernão repudiated this betrothal in order to marry Leonor Teles de Meneses, whose husband, João Lourenço da Cunha, was still alive.

This Castilian-induced rupture with Aragón caused Fernão some personal economic hardship. This, combined with his dislike of the Castilian alliance, caused him to support the pretensions of John of Gaunt, duke of Lancaster, to the Castilian throne in 1372. The English defeats and Enrique's invasion of Portugal in 1373 led Fernão to request military aid from Edward III of England, but he was forced to sign the Treaty of Santarém with Enrique before help arrived. Even though the terms of the treaty stated that Fernão had to break with England and become the ally of Castile and France, he continued diplomatic relations with England. When Enrique died in 1379, Fernão once again openly allied with England, and fighting resumed between Portugal and Castile. Fernão's request for help from Richard II of England brought the earl of Cambridge to Portugal with an army.

Fernão had promised a marriage between his daughter and heir, Beatriz, and Cambridge's heir, but the failure of Cambridge's expedition and possibly the urgings of Queen Leonor caused Fernão to break this treaty and make peace with Castile. In 1383 Fernão married Beatriz to Juan I of Castile, although he later assured the English that he was not in favor of the marriage. Fernão attempted to ensure that Castile would not annex Portugal after he died by fixing the succession upon Beatriz's oldest child and making its grandmother, Queen Leonor, regent. However, when Fernão died on 22 October 1383, Juan claimed the throne on behalf of Beatriz. João, master of the military Order of Avis and Fernão's illegitimate half brother, emerged as King João I from the resulting war over the succession.

Fernão encouraged Portugal's merchant marine and laid the foundations for Portugal's later maritime success. The 1375 *Lei das Sesmarias* was an attempt to recultivate land and to counteract labor shortages caused by wars and plague; however, it was unable to stem the loss of agricultural workers.

THERESA M. VANN

Bibliography

Hillgarth, J. N. *The Spanish Kingdoms 1250–1516.* Vol. 1, *1250–1410, Precarious Balance.* Oxford, 1976.

Oliveira Marquês, A. H. *History of Portugal.* Vol. 1. *From Lusitania to Empire.* New York, 1972.

O'Callaghan, J. F. *A History of Medieval Spain.* Ithaca, N.Y., 1975.

Russell, P. E. *The English Intervention in Spain and Portugal in the Time of Edward III and Richard II.* Oxford, 1955.

FERRANTE, KING OF NAPLES *See* FERDINANDO (FERRANTE) OF NAPLES AND NAPLES, KINGDOM OF

FERRER, VICENTE, ST.

Son of a Girona notary, St. Vicente Ferrer (1350–1419) entered the Order of Preachers, studied theology, philosophy, and logic in Barcelona, Lérida, and Tortosa, having obtained the degree of master of theology by 1389.

After his ordination in 1378 he took up residence in Valencia, where he remained for some years and was known for his preaching and rivalry with his Franciscan contemporary, Francesc Eiximenis.

A lector in theology in the cathedral of Valencia, protected by the royal family and confessor to the heir to the throne Juan and his French wife, Violante, he was a strong supporter of Pope Clement VII in Avignon and later confessor to Benedict XIII. Called upon to form part of the *junta* to settle the question of the papal schism, he was also among those who supported Fernando de Antequera in the Compromise of Caspe in 1412, subsequently enjoying good relations with him and acting as his constant adviser.

Between 1399 and 1412 Vicente traveled extensively throughout the Crown of Aragón, Castile, and even reached Flanders; after this date his missionary endeavors were intensified and his attention seemed to be directed primarily at the conversion of the Jews and Moors who were obliged to listen to his sermons. These occasions, like others from over a century earlier, frequently provoked the people to fervent expressions of faith and violent vituperations against the non-Christians.

Some of the sermons that he preached during the latter years of the fourteenth and beginning of the fifteenth centuries have been preserved, including some forty-three on the subject of Lent, which he preached in Valencia, and others he preached on ceremonial occasions, including one on Palm Sunday 1416 in Toulouse, where he had studied some years earlier. As was his custom he entered the town triumphantly, riding his mule, and preached indefatigably, but bystanders noted his sickly countenance, suggesting that by that date Vicente was no longer in good health. It is for his sermons on a wide variety of topics, many of which have survived in part if not in their entirety, that he is regarded as one of the great Catalan and Latin writers of the late Middle Ages. Studies have been made of his use of the *artes praedicandi*, a use reminiscent of the structure advocated in the treatise of Francesc Eiximenis known as the *Ars praedicandi populo*—a tripartite division consisting of introduction, theme, and exposition of the theme. The text was usually in Catalan and was chosen from the Bible, frequently from the Gospel for the day, but Vicente would frequently append its Latin equivalent. He then proceeded to enunciate the theme and explain its significance in contemporary language, often punctuating his exposé with exclamations and illustrative stories, miracles, lives of the saints, current events, and the occasional personal anecdote, at times dramatizing the stories or adding a touch of humor. His sources were those of any medieval friar—the Bible, patristic literature, lives of the saints, books of *exempla* and other similar compendia of useful material for preachers—but in his hands they took on a new significance, for they became a means of commentary on life around him.

He was a scholar, able to speak to his contemporaries using vocabulary and images they could understand and indicating to them the corruption he saw in all aspects of life. He criticized many of the daily customs and popular beliefs, bewailed the moral depravity seen in the behavior of his contemporaries—lay and clerical alike—regarding the disintegration of society and the confusion that beset the church, characteristic of the late fourteenth and early fifteenth centuries, as signs that the end of the world was near. He is remembered for the sermons he preached in an attempt to make society aware of the problems and redress them before it was too late, and for the active role he played in resolving the questions of the Papal Schism and the royal succession to the Crown of Aragón, but most of all, perhaps, it is his contribution to Catalan language and literature that have ensured him a place in history.

Now regarded as patron of the city of Valencia and revered as a worker of miracles, his canonization process was begun under the Valencian pope, Calixtus III, in 1455, and completed three years later under his successor, Pius II.

Jill R. Webster

Bibliography

Cátdera, Pedro M. *Sermón, sociedad y literatura en la Edad Media: San Vicente Ferrer en Castilla (1411–1414)*. Salamanca, 1994.

Sanchisi Sivera, J. (ed.) *Quaresma de Sant Vicente Ferrer, Predicada a València l'any 1413*. Bercelona 1927.

Schib, G. "Els Sermons de Saut Vicent Ferrer." In *Actes del Tercer Col-loqui Internacional de Llengua i Literatures catalanes celebrat a Cambridge des gal 14 d'abril de 1973*. Oxford, 1976. 325–36.

FEUDALISM

One of greatest changes in western European society to result from the barbarian invasions of the fifth and sixth centuries was the spread of feudal relations. Despite the importance of the system that only in the seventeenth century came to be called feudalism, the real nature of this protective and service-based set of associations between freemen still awaits complete understanding. Recent studies, however, have attempted to show that there is no such thing as "classic" or "bastard" feudalism except in the tidy minds of modern institutional historians. Rather than being a perversion of the "model" of feudalism in northern Europe, then, the feudal relations in medieval Spain can be better understood as an adaptation to the unique conditions of Christian Iberian societies that had been forged in the crucible of war and coexistence with Islam.

The regime of feudal relations entered Spain from two sources, both of which emanated from the flow of barbarian peoples across the western provinces of the Roman Empire. The first source was the Visigothic kingdom that dominated the Iberian Peninsula from the early sixth century until the Muslim invasions (711–718). Though emulating Rome in the issuance of such great law codes as the *Breviary of Alaric* and the *Book of Judges*, Visigothic rulers could scarcely re-create the centralized institutions of the empire. In lieu of a salaried, professional army, they relied on trains of personal retainers who fought in royal campaigns whenever required to. This class of warriors, called either "faithful men" (*fideles*) or "escorts" (*gardingi*), formed an important section of the itinerant royal court, the *aula regia*. Besides serving as the king's army, they formed his bodyguard and routinely garrisoned his fortresses. While seeing to the immediate support of his retainers, the Visigothic monarch was occasionally impelled to reward their loyalty with grants of money or land, both of which came to be called benefices (*beneficia*).

This Visigothic model of retainers maintained by the sovereign whom they served was replicated, with very few changes, in the Visigothic survivor state that came into being in the late eighth century in the mountain fastness of Asturias. Similar societal norms spread to the realms that emerged from the Asturian kingdom: Aragón, Navarre, Castile, and León. As the Reconquest brought much of the Duero and Ebro river basins into Christian hands by the eleventh century, large swaths of land had to be brought under cultivation and held in defense against the ever-present danger of Muslim counterattack. Since the sovereigns of Aragón, Navarre, and León claimed as their own all of the territory they conquered from Islam, they were able to attract settlers into the reconquered lands without losing ultimate control over these valuable additions to their realms. The presence of a hostile frontier with the northern districts of the caliphate of Córdoba made land settlement a crucially important, though dangerous, undertaking that was ultimately fitted into the mosaic of royal government.

The sovereign was supported by a band of retainers, known as "the men of the king's retinue" (*mesnaderos*), knights (*milites*), and the faithful (*fideles*). All of these royal supporters and fellow travelers were rewarded with grants of money or revenue sources (*solidata*) or unconditional gifts of land (*magnificientia, prestamonium, beneficia*). Though the greatest of these retainers, the lords (*seniores*), were given large territories and several castles to administer in the name of the sovereign, their status as warrior/administrators never evolved into that of independent feudal lords whose privileges and immunities effectively walled them off from royal control. The frontier nature of the new lands, coupled with the great influx of freemen into them by the twelfth century made "classical" feudalism effectively impossible in the states that emerged from the Asturian kingdom.

The formal bonds of homage and fealty entered the western realms only in the twelfth century, and even then they seldom implied the same complex of rights and services that formalized in Frankish feudalism. Such oaths were often seen as renewals of a kingdom's allegiance to its king. The existence of such a broad-based feudal bond in Aragón has led Bisson to call it "a land of vassals." In such a situation homage and fealty could imply quite different relationships and tenurial arrangements than in northern Europe. Not all the king's men received fiefs; some were compensated with stipendiary grants instead. Even those holding land from sovereigns and lords did so under many different conditions. Some were given benefices as free gifts; the majority, however, received "tenancies" (*honores*) that in various ways fell under the shadow of royal or seignorial control. In many cases the *honor* remained a temporary grant that the sovereign could reclaim at the end of the tenant's life. Neither were the revenues totally free, since the lord could annually claim at least a portion of them. Such grants were clearly not feudal in the northern European sense, even though the granting of true fiefs did begin, and spasmodically continued, from the thirteenth century. Despite this Catalan and Frankish influence, *honores* largely remained "public lands," and the holders of them attained neither the full range of immunities nor owed the same services as vassals in other European regions. Thus even with such thirteenth-century works as the *Siete Partidas* and the *Fueros of Aragón*, which sought to harmonize western Iberian feudalism with "classical" norms, the "Spanish way" (*mos hispanicus*) of feudal relations was a unique one that owed its special open character to the danger and freedom which emanated from the ever-present frontier with Islam.

In Catalonia the descendant of the Carolingian Spanish March (*Marca Hispanica*), a style of feudal relations much closer to that current in France, came into being. As one branch of the defeated Visigothic realm scattered across the Pyrenees into the land of the Franks in the late eighth century, the "Spaniards" (*Hispani*) rapidly adapted to the tenurial norms of their Frankish benefactors. They gained a land base in southern France through the *aprisio* system, which allowed men to gain full possession of unclaimed land if they cultivated it for a prescribed term. When Charlemagne and Louis the Pious led invasions against the Muslim land between the Pyrenees and Tortosa in the last decades of the eighth century, the Hispani accompanied them and eventually provided the source of the official nobility that would rule the Spanish March. These Frankish agents, who bore the official title of count (*comes*), also referred to themselves as "princes" (*principes*) and "wielders of public authority" (*potes-*

tates). Though the society over which they held jurisdictional sway initially was composed of freemen, it became well experienced in the Frankish regime of fiefs and fealty long before the ninth century had waned. By 877 the Carolingian rulers had given the Hispani the right to receive benefices and pass them on to their heirs. The Spaniards thus increasingly turned to feudal tenure as a means of assuring networks of support and protection in the dark days of the tenth century when the structures of public power in the Spanish March became systemically weakened, though never fully overthrown, by the onslaught of feudalism.

The castle, instead of a distant Carolingian sovereign, became the true core of power in the Spanish March, and the proliferation of such fortresses gave the region the name "land of castellans," which eventually evolved into Catalonia. The castle became a focus of allegiances between great lords, castellans, garrisons, and peasants. The terms of these personal alliances were realized in the ceremony of "homage" (*hominaticum*) and were sealed by oaths of "fealty" (*affidamentum, fidelitas*) made by the vassal (*vassalus, homo*) to his lord. Such proclamations of loyalty and service, generally written down in a pact (*convenientia*), were clearly tied to the lordly grant of a fief (*fevum, terra de feo*) to his vassal. Though originally the fief in Catalonia had been public land that officials used to support themselves, it came to personalize the lord-vassal relationship. Vassalic control of the fief was only provisional, since the lord could claim "control" (*potestas*) of it at any time and theoretically could settle it on anyone he wished when the vassal died. The social and tenurial advantage of feudal relations in Catalonia fueled the proliferation of such bonds between one vassal and several lords. To bring some order to this confusing situation, liege vassalage (*solidancia*) emerged in Catalonia. Declaring one of his many lords to be his liege lord (*melior senior*), the liege vassal swore to honor him above all others. When men began to take more than one liege lord, the complexities of the system became extremely dangerous, especially when two of of a vassal's liege lords waged war on one another and the vassal was caught in the dilemma of rendering military service to them both.

The system of feudal relations in Catalonia was clearly not a perfect one in comparison with the northern European model, yet the two elements that conspired to retard the broader development of Catalan feudalism stood outside it. The first was the continued existence of allodial land, especially in the districts between the Llobregat River and a Tortosa-Lérida line, which came to be called New Catalonia. The second was the persistence of public power in the person of the Catalan counts. From the ranks of the "official" aristocracy, there stepped forward one personage who asserted a fuller sovereignty for his office—the count of Barcelona, Girona, and Ausona. From the reign of Ramón Berenguer I (1035–1076), the rulers of Barcelona began to form a niche in the diffuse and bellicose world that surrounded them. Rather than openly trying to enforce their suzerainty over the other Catalan counts and great lords, Ramón Berenguer I and his immediate successors attempted to rectify the norms of feudal relations and fief-holding while utilizing the public aspect of their comital office to extend their authority. The count of Barcelona as protector of general security—with his espousal of the peace and truce—and "legislator" (*legislator*) cast a much greater shadow than even the greatest of Catalonia's feudal lords. This emergent fusing of public order with the customary law of feudal relations was frozen in legislation in Catalonia's first great code, the *Usatges of Barcelona*. The authors of these laws, the well-trained and well-experienced curials (lawyers) of Ramón Berenguer IV (r. 1131–1162), intimately knew the feudal norms of Catalonia and yet propelled the regalist pretension of their master. As the influence of the count of Barcelona expanded, so did that of the *Usatges*; in the process Catalonia's feudal custom was rectified under the political umbrella of the Barcelona ruler.

The tensions of this hybrid system, which combined feudal law with the structure of comital sovereignty, were all too obvious as the twelfth century waned. In the long and eventful reign of Jaime I (1213–1276), the wedding of crown and feudalism was a stormy one. The great commentator on the *Usatges*, Père Albert, sought to define the cases in which royal prerogative overrode feudal allegiance and vice versa. Despite such attempts to lay out good fences, the crown and the feudal world of Catalonia and Aragón did not often remain good neighbors. Between 1265 and 1348 the differences between feudal and royal law underpinned the intermittent rebellion of the Union of Aragón. Even after this baronial organization was crushed by Pedro IV (r. 1337–1378), the monopoly of Catalan feudalism remained largely intact in the countryside until challenged by a groundswell of peasant revolt (the *remensa* wars) in the late fifteenth century.

DONALD KAGAY

Bibliography

Barbero, A. *La formación del feudalismo en la Península Ibérica*. Barcelona, 1978.

Clemente Ramos, J. *Estructuras señoriales castellanoleonesas: el realengo (siglos XI–XIII)*. Cáceres, 1989.

——. *Sobre los orígenes sociales de la Reconquista.* Esplugues de Llobregat, 1974.

En torno al feudalismo hispánico. I Congreso de Estudios Medievales. Avila, 1987.

García de Cortázar y Ruiz de Aguirre, J. A. *La sociedad rural en la España medieval.* México, D.F. 1988.

García de Valdeavellano, L. *El feudalismo hispánico y otros estudios de historia medieval.* Barcelona, 1981.

García Ormaechea y Mendoza, R. *Supervivencias feudales en España; estudio de legislación y jurisprudencia sobre señoríos.* Madrid, 1932.

Grassotti, H. *Las instituciones feudo-vasalláticas en León y Castilla.* Spoleto, 1969.

Hinojosa y Naveros, E. de. *El régimen señorial y la cuestión agraria en Cataluña, durante la Edad Media.* Madrid, 1905.

Laliena Corbera, C. *Sistema social, estructura agraria y organización del poder en el Bajo Aragón en la Edad Media (siglos XII–XV).* Teruel, 1987.

Moxó, S. de. *Los antiguos señoríos de Toledo.* Toledo, 1973.

Pastor de Togneri, R. *Resistencias y luchas campesinas en la epoca del crecimiento y consolidación de la formación feudal Castilla y León, siglos X–XIII.* Madrid, 1980.

Sánchez-Albornoz, C. *En torno a los orígenes del feudalismo.* 2nd ed. Buenos Aires, 1973.

Sánchez Martínez, M. *Estudios sobre renta, fiscalidad y finanzas en la Cataluña bajomedieval.* Barcelona, 1993.

FINANCE

See ADMINISTRATION, FINANCIAL

FLAGELLANTS, FRANCISCAN ORDER OF THE

See RELIGIOUS ORDERS; FRANCISCANS

FLOR, ROGER DE

Corsair hero of the Sicilian Vespers War and leader of the mercenary Catalan Grand Company that devastated Byzantium, Flor was born about 1268. The memoirist Ramón Muntaner recorded his life, and Catalan letters and art have expanded his myth. In 1268 Roger's father, Richard Blume (Catalan, Flor), knight-falconer to Frederick II of Sicily, lost life and fortune to the Angevins at Tagliacozzo. Roger and his older brother James grew up in the dockside house of his affluent Apulian mother at Brindisi. A Templar sergeant at twenty, and captain of the order's best ship, the *Falcon*, Roger became a renegade when evacuating the Templar treasure from the fallen crusader city of Acre (1291). Hiring out as corsair to Catalan Sicily, with his personal fleet and army he was the scourge of Angevin shipping. Vice admiral and royal counselor by war's end, he leased his force to Byzantium in 1304 (36 ships, 1,500 horse, and 4,000 *almogávers*, Catalan mountaineer irregulars), demanding the title of grand duke (later caesar) and marrying the emperor's niece. Roger was extremely generous and easily made friends; he already spoke Greek "well" and had a nubile daughter "by a lady of Cyprus." The Byzantine scholar Pachymeres describes him as "in the prime of life, with fierce eyes, quick reactions, and hot after adventure." Roger recovered all Anatolia from the Turks in bloody battles, carrying banners of emperor, pope, Sicily, and Aragón. In April 1305 the jealous co-emperor Michael IX Palaeologus invited him to a feast and assassinated him with his entourage, precipitating the "Catalan Vengeance." His son Rogero, born after Roger's death, was still alive in 1325.

ROBERT I. BURNS, S. J.

Bibliography

Burns, R. I. "The Catalan Grand Company and the European Powers, 1305–1311," *Speculum* 29 (1954), 751–71.

Setton, K. *Catalan Domination of Athens 1311–1388.* 2nd.

FLORES, JUAN DE

A courtier, writer, knight, royal administrator, and diplomat, Flores was associated with the court of Garci Álvarez de Toledo, First Duke of Alba and, eventually, with that of the Catholic Monarchs. Extant documentation suggests that he was the nephew of Pedro Álvarez Osorio, third señor of Cabrera y Ribera and the first count of Lemos, and politically allied with the Enríquez, Osorio, Álvarez de Toledo, and Quiñones families. His formative years were probably spent at the ducal palace of Alba (Alba de Tormes), where he enjoyed considerable educational and political advantages, and in Salamanca, where he appears to have been active in local politics. On 20 May 1476 he was appointed official chronicler to Fernando and Isabel, and subsequently joined the royal entourage. During the civil war of the 1470s, he is known to have participated in attacks against the Portuguese and their *juanista* allies; there is evidence that he later joined Fernando in the Granada campaign. Documentation also suggests that he received various judicial assignments in Castile after 1477, and may have held the title of *protonotario de Lucena*. The dates of his birth and death are uncertain, but early genealogical sources suggest a long life, from about 1455 to 1525. He appears to have married Beatriz de Quiñones, a distant relative of Suero de Quiñones, and a son named Gaspar was apparently appointed chaplain to Isabel in 1503.

The extant works bearing Flores's name belong to a large body of courtly prose that examines the tragic nature of human passion, devotion, and intimacy. They include two sentimental romances, *Grisel y Mirabella* and *Grimalte y Gradisa*, and an allegorical vision narrative, *Triunfo de Amor*, recovered in 1976. All probably were written between 1470 and 1477, the period of Flores's affiliation with the first duke of Alba. Of the three works, *Grisel* experienced the greatest commercial success, especially in the sixteenth century, when it was translated into numerous European languages as *(Historia de) Aurelio et Isabel*. It constitutes an ambiguous response to Pere Torroellas's *Coplas de las calidades de las donas* (before 1458), a superficially virulent, but arguably only playful, misogynistic poem. Although *Grisel* implicitly promotes the cause of women by condemning the egocentric nature of male passion and the political abuses of men, there are ironic indications that women lack the virtues they self-righteously claim for themselves. The romance ends with the ritualistic slaughter of Torrellas—a fictional persona of the real-life poet—by the queen of Scotland and her retinue. Flores may have intended to point out the equal contribution of both sexes to illicit love, while underscoring the inherently self-destructive nature of passion.

Owing to its emotional intensity and narrative sophistication, *Grimalte* is now generally recognized as Flores's masterpiece. A continuation and implicit interpretation of the *Elegia di Madonna Fiammetta* of Boccaccio (1313–1375), it seeks to reconcile the contradictory notions of sexual freedom, devotion, and social responsibility as perceived by Fiometa (Fiammetta), her lover Pánfilo, and their counterparts Gradisa and Grimalte. Grimalte's vain attempts to reunite the Italian couple ultimately result in Fiometa's suicide, Pánfilo's self-imposed exile, and the breakup of his own unstable relationship with Gradisa. Philosophically complex and engaging, *Grimalte* explores the selfish motivations for love and the tragedies that ensue from a one-sided passion. *Grimalte* became a favorite source of sentimental material for later chivalric romances, including *Tristán de Leonis* (1501) and the *Quarta parte de don Clarián de Landanís* (1528), which contain substantial plagiarisms.

Though largely addressing the same erotic themes as the romances, *Triunfo* is more lighthearted. A felicitous combination of courtly romance, political allegory, and fictionalized chronicle, it tells the story of Cupid's capture by disgruntled dead lovers seeking redress for their amorous suffering. Following a trial and death sentence, the god of love is rescued, and his supporters receive as a reward the reversal of the customary courting ritual: men replace women as the custodians of virtue and women importune them for sexual favors. In response to the social turmoil of the period, political issues receive prominent attention, but Flores tends to exploit them as a vehicle for exploring the inevitable tension between joyous and tragic love.

Three other texts have been attributed to Flores with reasonable certainty: (1) *La coronación de la señora Gracisla*, (2) a short epistolary exchange between Tristan and Isolde, and (3) a fragmentary royal chronicle, the *Crónica incompleta de los Reyes Católicos*. Once thought to be artistically flawed, *Gracisla* is in fact a subtle *consolatio* written for Leonor de Acuña, the eldest daughter of Juan de Acuña, the second count of Valencia de don Juan, after the failure of her engagement to Pedro Álvarez Osorio, the third marquis of Astorga (April 1475). The work's plot, which relates the experiences of Gracisla, a Castilian maiden, at a beauty contest sponsored by the king of France, closely follows that of *Grisel*, and incorporates a number of allusions to actual events and individuals from the 1470s.

The *Crónica incompleta* represents Flores's official production as chronicler to the Catholic Monarchs. It is the most important source of information on his life and personal attitudes, since it contains circumstantial evidence of his activities in support of Isabel, most of which take place around Salamanca between 1475 and 1476. The extant text of the chronicle is evidently the copy of a working draft and has numerous gaps and inconsistencies. Nonetheless, it contains detailed information found in no other contemporary sources and has attracted the attention of historians. As a literary document it has hardly been studied.

Flores's works are known for their imagination, vividness of expression, and narrative complexity. He is a representative of a class of humanist knights dedicated to the ideals of the chivalric lifestyle, including the pursuit of literature as entertainment for the social elite. He is indisputably one of late medieval Spain's most prolific and versatile writers.

Joseph J. Gwara

Bibliography

Gwara, J.J. "A Study of the Works of Juan de Flores, with a Critical Edition of *La historia de Grisel y Mirabella*." Ph.D. diss., Westfield College, University of London, 1988.

Matulka, B. *The Novels of Juan de Flores and Their European Diffusion: A Study in Comparative Literature*. New York, 1931. Repr. Geneva, 1974.

FOIX, HOUSE OF

The house of Foix had its origins in the family of the counts of Comminges-Couserans. In the eleventh century a partition of the domains of Count Roger the Old of Comminges produced the branch of the counts of

Foix. The counts emerged into prominence during the Albigensian crusades of the early thirteenth century, when Count Raymond-Roger assumed a leading role in resistence to the northern invaders. On the death of Raymond VII of Toulouse in 1249, the counts of Foix became the most important remaining independent lords of lower Languedoc.

During the fourteenth century the counts began to assemble the elements of the trans-Pyrenees principality that came to include the kingdom of Navarre. Through the marriage of Count Roger-Bernard III to Marguérite de Moncada they acquired a claim to the viscounty of Béarn in 1290. This inheritance was disputed by the counts of Armagnac, initiating the struggle between Armagnac and Foix that continued through the reign of the mercurial Count Gaston III Phoebus (1343–1391).

Frequently allied with the English during the Hundred Years' War, the counts of Foix became reconciled to the monarchy of France on the accession of Charles VII. Their domains reached their greatest extent with the marriage of Count Gaston IV (1436–1472) to Eleanor, heiress to the kingdom of Navarre. Following the reign of François Phoebus (1479–1483), Catherine of Foix and her husband, Jean d'Albret, ruled the united principality of Foix, Béarn, and Navarre into the sixteenth century. The inheritance, less the territory of upper Navarre conquered by Fernando II of Aragón in 1512, passed to the future Henri IV of France in 1572.

Alan Friedlander

Bibliography

Courteault, H. *Gaston IV comte de Foix, vicomte souverain de Béarn, prince de Navarre, 1423–1472*. Geneva, 1980.

Tucoo-Chala, P. *Gaston Fébus, un grand prince d'Occident au XIV siècle*. Pau, 1983.

FOLKLORE

Not far beneath every genre of written literature in medieval Spain lay a substratum of oral folk literature that was always available to, and often utilized by, authors who wrote in Latin, Hebrew, Arabic, or the vernacular languages. The poet who composed, probably in the twelfth century, the *Poema de Mio Cid* used popular sources, motifs, beliefs, and superstitions. In the thirteenth century Gil de Zamora in his *Liber Mariae* used folk miracles, and Gonzalo de Berceo in his *Milagros de Nuestra Señora* enlivened and embellished his anthology with folk speech, proverbial expressions and motifs, and, in the twenty-fifth miracle—the only original one in the *Milagros*—he relied upon local lore and legend, and possibly folk law. Even the erudite King Alfonso X el Sabio inserted many folk miracles into his *Cantigas de Santa María*, and his son, Sancho IV, followed in his father's footsteps in *Castigos e documentos*. In the fourteenth century Alfonso's nephew, Juan Manuel, in his *Conde Lucanor*, utilized stories and motifs from oral sources, and his contemporary Juan Ruiz, in his *Libro de buen amor*, used tales, proverbs, and colloquial expressions garnered from oral lore.

Writers of novelesque pieces in the fourteenth and fifteenth centuries included much folkloristic material in their works, for example, in *Libro del cavallero Zifar, Amadís de Gaula*, and *Gran conquista de Ultramar*. In the fifteenth century Clemente Sánchez de Vercial in his *Libro de los exenplos por a.b.c.* and the writer who translated Odo of Cheriton's *Fabulae* into Spanish as the *Libro de los gatos*, included folk material. Alfonso Martínez de Toledo in his *Corbacho* likewise made folklore a vital part of his work, not only in the area of folk speech but also in some of his brief narratives. The vast body of Spanish ballads of the fifteenth and later centuries always made folklore a significant part of their language and subject matter. In that same century *Lazarillo de Tormes*, the *Abencerraje*, and the *Guerras civiles de Granada* depended to a considerable extent upon folk sources. In the Renaissance and the Golden Age authors often dipped into folklore: Juan de Timoneda, Cervantes, Lope de Vega, Guillén de Castro, Calderón de la Barca, and many, many others made use of popular lore for their most important works.

The substratum of folklore—folk language and literature, folk art and folk music—will never be exhausted, not only because it is rich in sempeternal motifs but also because it is self-perpetuating and continually creative. Albert Lord in his *The Singer of Tales* clarified the creative powers of epicry, including the *Poema de Mio Cid*, and Stith Thompson in his *The Folktale* and *Motif-Index of Folk Literature* proved the debt that from its earliest beginnings brief narrative owes to folktales.

In the Iberian Peninsula folklore absorbed a great deal of the *Matière de Rome* and the *Matière de Bretagne*, along with the folklore of the Visigoths and of the Muslim invaders, as well as from the Jews. The folk heritage, while not as important in the formation of medieval thought and religion, was ever present, and to a degree it even made itself felt in erudite and ecclesiastical circles. Whether it came from the age-old "native folk heritage" stemming from the Iberians, Phoenicians, Greeks, and Romans; from the Celtic and Germanic backgrounds and from the literary echoes of these sources; from the literature and/or the folklore of the East; or from other European cultures, Spanish folklore had a powerful impact upon formal literature and upon contemporary popular culture. The fact that so much of folklore and folk literature was first narrated and later written in the vernaculars of Spain may have done much to separate it from the heritage of erudition. But in spite of this or other reasons, vernacular literature in its oral form was from the Middle Ages onward as integral a part of Spanish letters as any or all other literary elements.

JOHN E. KELLER

Bibliography

Keller, J. E. "El cuento folklórico en España y en Hispanoamérica," *Folklore Américas* 14 (1954), 1–14. Repr. in *Collectanea Hispanica: Folklore and and Brief Narrative Studies by John Esten Keller*. Newark, Del., 1987. 1–14.

Thompson, S. *Motif-Index of Folk Literature*. Enl. and rev. ed. 6 vols. Bloomington, Ind., 1955–58.

FORAL

The *foral* (pl., *forais*) was a municipal regulation granted in Portugal by a king or a lord (church or secular nobility) to existing towns or to groups of families settled in new occupied areas. The *forais* rarely created new institutions and were little concerned about municipal organization. Their main goal was to define and specify taxation and the organization of justice. Nonetheless, they mentioned many local features that enable historians to study municipal governement and daily life.

During the twelfth and thirteenth centuries *forais* were granted to most of the towns and large villages. A few were still granted in the fourteenth and fifteenth centuries. Their pattern differed somewhat according to the epoch, the size of the settlement, the purposes of the lord, and the legal training of the royal adviser. Some forms were imported from León and Castile; others were typically Portuguese. It has been possible to determine some six basic types of *forais* and to establish a sort of "family tree" connecting similar ones within each type. The *forais* should not be confused with communal charters. They did not create communes, the principle of which was very far from the Iberian tradition of community government. Self-rule was accepted, true, but only to a limited extent. In many cases all the officers had to be confirmed by the town's lord, generally the king. Self-administration was greatly reduced by a rigid system of taxation and a limited sphere of local justice. The king had the right to interfere frequently. Few attempts were made to secure a greater degree of self-government, which was neither in the Islamic tradition nor in the conditions of life of early Portugal, where a strong central command was required.

Forais were also granted for other purposes, its name being gradually identified with "charter" or "bill of rights." Communities of free Muslims, for instance, had their own *forais*. Customs regulations, where taxation on imported and exported merchandise was established, were also called *forais*.

From 1472 on, a general revision of the *forais* was undertaken, first as a response to several municipal complaints against exaggerated and illegal taxation, then as a royal attempt to standardize the multiple forms and kinds of local revenues. Effective reform started only under King Manuel I, covering approximately the years 1497–1520. The new *forais* were now practically restricted to lists of taxes to be paid to the king or the feudal lords in each municipality. Furthermore, taxes were rendered more or less uniform, which incidentally reduced the historical interest of the charters for the study of common law and local life.

In the overseas dominions of the Portuguese crown, *forais* were granted to most towns throughout the fifteenth and sixteenth centuries. Thus, Funchal in Madeira, Ponta Delgada in the Azores, Goa in India, Macao in China, and Bahia in Brazil each had its *foral*, which was very often copied from a metropolitan charter granted to an important town. In this way patterns of administration and taxation were always similar to those in Portugal.

A. H. OLIVEIRA MARQUES

Bibliography

Boxer, C. R. *Portuguese Society in the Tropics: The Municipal Councils of Goa, Macao, Bahia, and Luanda, 1510–1800.* Madison, Wisc., 1965.

Oliveira Marques, A.H. de. *History of Portugal*. 2d ed. New York, 1976.

FORMULAIC COMPOSITION

One of the principal characteristics of oral traditional poetry is its formulaic diction. According to Parry and Lord's definition, a formula is "a group of words which is regularly employed under the same metrical conditions to express a given essential idea." That is, a formula has both rhythmic and acoustic value together with a narrative function. Formulas are the basic elements of the grammar of oral traditional poetry. They are adaptable in both content and prosodic form to a variety of contexts. The more permissive the verse form, the greater the variability of the formulas. There are fixed formulas, syntactic formulas, and formula patterns. The basic compositional unit is the hemistich, but formulas can be extended to fill a full line or combined into longer series.

Command of basic formula patterns by the bard involves the development of substitution systems in which new phrases are created by analogy to those already in existence. The verse is a complete unit, to which subsequent verses may be linked by rhythmic and acoustic patterns as well as by paratactic devices like parallelism, opposition, and alliteration. This is the practice of a specialized art, characterized by controlled variation, which was learned during a long period of apprenticeship. Instead of restricting the performer, it offered him a wide range of appropriate phrases to draw upon. Variation from one performance to another was probably not great. The poet/singer's skill in the use of formulas determined to a large degree the quality of the product.

The oral-formulaic theory of poetic composition originated in response to the Homeric question. In his study of the noun-epithet formulas in Homer, Parry revealed the systematization of Homeric diction as evidence of its oral character. Since this theory was not generally acceptable to Homeric scholars at the time, he turned to the South Slavic oral epic tradition as a living analogue. This work was extended and completed by Albert Lord. In *The Singer of Tales*, the single most important work in the field, Lord studied the training and performance habits of the Serbo-Croatian bards as well as formulas, themes, and story patterns, and how they were used. His conclusions supported Parry's hypothesis concerning the oral traditional origin of the Homeric epics. Lord then applied his methodology to the medieval epic, reaching similar conclusions.

RUTH H. WEBBER

Bibliography

Foley, J. M. *The Theory of Oral Composition: History and Methodology*. Bloomington, Ind., 1988.

Lord, A. B. *The Singer of Tales*. Harvard Studies in Comparative Literature 24. Cambridge, Mass., 1960. Repr. New York, 1965.

FRANCISCANS

Franciscans first appeared in the Iberian Peninsula shortly after the foundation of the Order of Friars Minor in 1209; in 1213 or 1214 St. Francis himself is said to have gone to Spain on his way to preach to the Muslims in North Africa, a journey that gave rise to numerous claims by towns as far apart as Barcelona and Santiago de Compostela that he either stayed in them or founded a house of his friars nearby. References are also made to the presence of some of his followers who undertook missionary voyages to the peninsula, but the arrival of John Parenti in 1219 as provincial minister for Spain seems to herald the beginning of an organizational structure.

The first houses in the peninsula date from the 1220s, although in most cases their archives have disappeared; Barcelona, Girona, Lisbon, and Vic are among the few that possess records of their medieval houses, but for only Girona and Lisbon are they complete. By the 1230s many houses had been founded from Aragón and Catalonia to Galicia and Portugal, in Valencia and Mallorca, Navarre and Castile, and it was clear that the province must be subdivided into more manageable areas; hence the provinces of Aragón, Castile, Portugal (or Santiago), and Navarre. Each province was further divided into smaller groups of houses (custodies). By 1300 there were Franciscan houses throughout the peninsula, even in the territory held by the Moors in Andalusia.

The Franciscans, like all religious orders, received protection from the pope and from the king; they were exempt from episcopal jurisdiction, a privilege that brought them into conflict with the secular clergy, and in addition to their spiritual duties, they were frequently required to act as nuncios or ambassadors, look after valuables and important documents, dispense charity to the poor, and attend to outcasts such as lepers. In return they received gifts of land and privileges to draw water from royal wells and to transport grain from one area to another. Most significant of all, however, testators included them in their wills, frequently leaving them handsome sums of money that were sometimes beyond the capacity of their estate. They were not required to pay the tax on books demanded of other travelers, and because they traveled to centers of study beyond the peninsula, they often returned to their native area with new ideas.

In Catalonia and Mallorca especially, the Franciscans were influenced by the unorthodox beliefs of Joachim of Fiore and Peter John Olivi, and some were even imprisoned for their heretical beliefs. A few who had studied Arabic for missionary work in Africa embraced Islam; the most famous of them, Anselm Turmeda, died in Tunis, where the custody of Barcelona had a vicariate. Others, usually from privileged backgrounds, like Sancho López de Ayala, archbishop of Tarazona and then of Tarragona, and a relative of the king, reached the peak of the ecclesiastical hierarchy; some, like St. Anthony of Lisbon (or Padua) and Francesc Eiximenis, were renowned for their sermons and literary ability.

In addition to those who took the habit, lay men and women joined the Third Order of St. Francis and sought to follow the rule of poverty and service to others in their daily lives. Some formed confraternities that, although they were not, strictly speaking, part of the Third Order, used the Rule of St. Francis as a basis for their organization and met on a regular basis in the Franciscan church with the superior or guardian of the house as their spiritual adviser.

By the late fourteenth century splendid conventual buildings had been erected, and many of the Gothic churches extant today owe much to Franciscan spirituality. Examples of fine medieval cloisters can be seen in Sangüesa, Mallorca, and Morella; the churches at Montblanc and Teruel show the size and simplicity of Gothic church architecture. Artists like Ferrer Bassa (his mural in the chapel of St. Michael at the convent of the Poor Clares at Pedralbes, Barcelona, still survives) and Lluís Borrasá (his most outstanding Franciscan painting depicts the three Orders of St. Francis gathered round their founder) painted scenes from the lives of St. Francis, St. Louis, and St. Clare, most of which have disappeared. Craftsmen of all kinds were employed in a variety of ways, and the visual impact of the Franciscan churches helped to illustrate their sermons both to Christians and to Jews, to whom they had a special mission.

Success brought prosperity, and prosperity threatened the simplicity of their founder's message; by 1400 the crisis within the order over how to interpret the Rule of St. Francis became more marked, and the houses in the Iberian Peninsula were divided into conventuals and observants, according to the way in which they conceived their spiritual calling and how it related to the rule. The rift contained the seeds of the troubled times of the fifteenth century and led up to the more serious issues of the Reformation.

JILL R. WEBSTER

Bibliography

García Oro, J. *Francisco de Asís en la España medieval.* Santiago de Compostela, 1988.

Moorman, J.R.H. *A History of the Franciscan Order from Its Origins to the Year 1517.* Oxford, 1968.

Webster, J.R. *Els Menorets: The Franciscans in the Realms of Aragón from St. Francis to the Black Death.* Toronto, 1993.

FRIARS

See DOMINICANS; FRANCISCANS; RELIGIOUS ORDERS

FRÓILAZ, PEDRO, COUNT OF TRAVA

Pedro, Fróilaz, Count of Trava (?–ca.1123) was Alfonso VII's guardian during the reign of his mother, Queen Urraca of León. A prominent Galician magnate at the court of Urraca and her first husband, Raimundo de Borgoña, he became the preceptor of their son, Alfonso. When Alfonso VI arranged Urraca's second marriage to Alfonso I in 1109, Fróilaz fomented a rebellion in Galicia, possibly in order to secure his charge's rights in case of offspring from Urraca's new marriage. Fróilaz lacked the support of the archbishop of Santiago, Diego Gelmírez, but his family held the northern lands of the province, and his stand provoked civil war. The crowning of Urraca's son Alfonso in 1111 mitigated the count's demands, but in the interim civil war broke out between Urraca and her spouse. Pedro Fróilaz and Bishop Gelmírez formed an army and recaptured Lugo, held by Alfonso I, and marched into León, where Alfonso I captured Pedro but Alfonso VII and Archbishop Gelmírez escaped. The count was released at some point and joined forces with Gelmírez, remaining at Alfonso VII's side. By 116 Fróilaz and Alfonso VII campaigned against Aragónese forces, possibly at Urraca's request. In 1117 he assisted Urraca in the siege of Compostela, held against the townspeople who had rioted against Urraca and Gelmírez. This unity did not last; in 1120 Urraca campaigned against some of his followers in Galicia. Perhaps because of his activities Urraca considered him an overmighty vassal; his children's alliances with her sister, Teresa of Portugal, did not raise him in the queen's estimation, nor his control over Galicia. Urraca had Pedro Fróilaz imprisoned in 1123; there is no record of him after that.

Fróilaz married twice. The children of his first marriage with Urraca were Vermudo (who married Urraca Enriquez, daughter of Teresa of Portugal); Fernando (lover of Teresa of Portugal), Lupa, and Jimena. The children of his second marriage with Guntroda or Mayor Rodríguez, were Rodrigo, García, Velasco, and seven daughters.

THERESA M. VANN

Bibliography

Reilly, B.F. *The Kingdom of León-Castilla under Queen Urraca (1109–1126).* Princeton, N.J., 1982.

Sánchez Belda, L. "Pedro Fróilaz, Conde de Traba." In *Diccionario de Historia de España.* Madrid, 1979.

FRONTIER

In the Iberian Peninsula the frontier was the strip of territory between Christian and Muslim Spain. From the eighth to the fifteenth century, Spain was divided by a ragged no-man's-land separating the Christian and Muslim realms of the peninsula. This intermediate zone, whether referred to as *frontera*, *marca*, or *limes*, served an extremely important military function as the site for both Muslim and Christian castle networks.

Despite the difficulties in tracing this rather amorphous buffer zone, certain very definite conclusions can be drawn about its configuration at any one time by a study of the military relations of the two Spains. By and large the Muslims, after the initial conquests, were unable to make large gains at the expense of their Christian neighbors. It was the Christians of Castile-León, the Crown of Aragón, and Portugal who, by individual settlement and concerted royal attack, pushed the frontier steadily southward. With the breakup of the caliphate of Córdoba in the early eleventh century, this movement was intensified, and by the end of the thirteenth century, the Christian states, with the conquests of Lérida, Tortosa, Córdoba, and Seville between 1148 and 1248, had driven the frontier to the Guadarramas, the *cordillera* that marked the doorway of the kingdom of Granada. Seemingly poised for the final extension of its borders, Castile, the only late medieval Christian state to share a frontier with Granada, was diverted by a series of disastrous civil wars from its reconquest mission until the accession of the Catholic Monarchs.

The Spanish, and indeed every, frontier stands as "a wild place coming under order." The presence of a hostile boundary could not fail to mold the society of Castile. Initially composed of men drawn to a realm of both danger and freedom that was spoken eloquently of in the *fueros* (charters) of the border settlements, the Castilian frontier society eventually came to be bound more by clan than by legal ties and was a world of quick and violent response to affronts that caused *vergüenza* (shame) to clan honor. On the Muslim side of the frontier, the society was molded by a siege mentality that periodically brought volunteers from all Islam to defend the beleaguered kingdom of Granada against the infidel.

While the Iberian frontier came to symbolize the holy and chivalric war that would be fought and imagined as the Spanish reconquest, it had as much to do with forging connections between the two Spains. Though attempts were made to control it, commerce—much of it in the form of smuggling—flowed across the border. The border was also permeable to a composite Muslim-Christian justice that sent agents (*rastreros*, *alfaqueques*) to settle disputes and punish crimes that involved men of different faiths. This was rendered possible by the linguistic continuum of the Iberian frontier, which routinely provided individuals fluent in both Arabic and Castilian. Such a language bridge facilitated a remarkable cultural interaction that manifested itself in a set of unique hybrid artistic, literary, and musical forms.

Even with these connections, the frontier remained for Castile a symbol of an unending but also neglected war with the Muslim infidel, as many Franciscan preachers reiterated during the later Middle Ages. Added to this call to arms against Muslim neighbors was an overlay of millennarianism that saw the defeat of the Muslims by an Iberian ruler as fulfillment of prophecy that would lead inexorably to the last days. From this brand of fanaticism came a certitude that even the existence of a frontier with Islam was unconscionable. In 1492 the frontier was eradicated with the conquest of Granada. Nevertheless, the lessons it had taught in language, politics, commerce, and stock raising, as well as the cultural norms it had imparted, continued to define a Spanish national character that was transported to the New World, and there was duly transmuted by yet another set of frontiers.

DONALD KAGAY

Bibliography

Burns, Robert I. *The Crusader Kingdom of Valencia, Reconstruction on a Medieval Frontier*. 2 vols. Cambridge, Mass., 1967.

Las tomas: antropología histórica de la ocupación territorial del reino de Granada. Ed. José Antonio González Alcantus and Manuel Barrios Aguilera. Granada, 2000.

MacKay, Angus. *Money, Prices, and Politics in Fifteenth-century Castile*. London, 1981.

——. *Spain in the Middle Ages: From Frontier to Empire, 1000–1500*. London, 1977.

Medieval frontier societies. Ed. Robert Bartlett and Angus MacKay. Oxford; New York, 1989.

FRUCTUOSUS OF BRAGA, ST.

Fructuosus, very likely the most important figure in Visigothic church history after the death of St. Isidore of Seville (636), nevertheless is quite inadequately known because the sources, principally his own *Regula monachorum*, certain *decretals* of the Tenth Council of Toledo (656), and the anonymous *Vita sancti Fructuosi* composed between 670 and 680, cast light on his ascetic spirituality but are notably reticent on the major events of his monastic-episcopal career.

Born in 610/15 to a Visigothic noble family rooted in the Narbonensis, Fructuosus became closely associated with Galicia through his father's rank as duke of that province, which still extended, as in Roman and Suevic times, to the Douro (Duero) River. Attracted to the monastic life under Bishop Conantius of Astorga, he founded in the nearby Bierzo wilderness a cenobium for which, between 635 and 640, he wrote his extremely rigorous *Regula monachorum*. Other foundations followed, generating a widespread monastic movement in religiously backward Galicia in which the nun Benedicta played a significant role. Close to 650, apparently just after Fructuosus traveled to Baetica (Andalusia) and founded two monastic houses there, he prepared to depart Spain for the revered homelands of monasticism in the Byzantine East. Halted in this plan by King Reccesvinth and brought before the monarch at Toledo, Fructuosus evidently persuaded this able ruler to support him in bringing about, along monastic lines, a thorough reform of the decadent Galician church.

The campaign opened in 654 with the deposition of the abbot-bishop Riccimir of Dumio, and in 656 that of the metropolitan bishop Potamius of Braga; in both instances Fructuosus took over the see, holding them simultaneously. This fact alone demonstrates beyond question, despite the complete silence of the sources in this regard, that Fructuosus now regarded himself as the heir and renewer of the project of St. Martin of Braga (d. 579), who, after founding the abbey-bishopric of Dumio and linking it, as *episcous sub regula*, with his subsequent office as metropolitan of Braga, sought to create a sternly monasticized clergy in Galicia. The effort failed, not least through the Visigothic Eingeovigild's annexation of Suevic Galicia. Now, in his termial decade as *sub regula* of the again conjoined sees of Dumio and Braga, Fructuosus undertook to reverse the secularizing and decadent course of the provincial church, an effort of which all too little is known, although it was manifestly the subject of conflict in the final half-century of the Visigothic state. At his death around 665, Fructuosus was buried in a monastery of his own foundation located between Dumio and Braga.

Dimly though they are known, Fructuosus's devoted labors on behalf of monasticism and the church as a whole are impressive and undoubtedly, along with his cult, survived in some degree into the early Reconquest. He must not, however, contrary to much tradition, be assigned authorship of the *Regula communis*, a collection of decrees.

C. Julian Bishko

Bibliography

Díaz y Díaz, M. *La vida de San Fructuoso de Braga*. Braga, 1974.

Linage Conde, A. "Fructueux de Braga." In *Dictionnaire d'histoire et de géographie ecclésiastique*. Paris, 1981. 208–30.

Nock, F. C. *The Vita Sancti Fructuosi*. Washington, D.C., 1946.

FUEROS, ARAGONESE

Aragón was a small and swiftly expanding country, and its early *fueros* (charters) were granted primarily to attract settlers. As a consequence they generally conferred immunities and protection rather than imposing obligations and restrictions. In Aragón, the word *fuero* became synonymous with "privilege." The nature of such privileges depended on the quality of settlers being sought. Three families of Aragónese *fueros* thus emerged, geographically differentiated and corresponding to the three major classes of Aragónese society.

In the Pyrenees region the purpose of settlement was economic development. The *fueros* of Jaca (1077) were intended to attract merchants and artisans, particularly from France. They were characterized by a general equality of classes under the law, strict protection of private property, freedom of the individual from imposts and seigneurial monopolies, restraint of violence, and a due respect for weights and measures. The example of Jaca spread swiftly throughout the Pyrenees region; by the thirteenth century the *fuero* of Jaca applied to virtually all of Aragón north of the Guara Mountains.

South of this area, in the plains and river valleys conquered in the course of the twelfth century, mounted warriors were needed to govern the land and fight the Muslims. Here the monarchs offered *fueros* favoring the noble, or *infanzón*, class. The *fueros* of Barbastro (1100) and Zaragoza (1119) are good examples of this family of privileges, which was characterized by legal discrimination in favor of the nobility, and the enhancement and protection of seigneurial rights. *Infanzones* were required to perform only three days of military service at their own cost, could clear themselves in court by either oath or battle, were free of taxes on flocks throughout the realm, and had the right to farm open land at will. This family of *fueros* became the most widely diffused in Aragón south of the Guaras.

Infantry was needed along the immediate frontier with Castile and the Muslims, and peasant/warriors were sought. The *fuero* of Calatayud typifies this third family. The community was granted judicial autonomy, and authority was vested in a council with an elected judge. Settlers were pardoned of all previous crimes, and status was regarded less as a matter of birth than of personal accomplishments and finances. Kindred were expected to seek vengeance for wrongs, and relatively high levels of civil violence were tolerated. Immunity from numerous restrictions, obligations, and monopolies attracted men and women to dangerous and undeveloped frontier outposts.

In Jaca the local fueros were amplified and extended throughout the course of the twelfth century in a manner that reflected the ascendancy of the aristocracy in both political and economic affairs, as well as a growing acceptance of the concept of the territoriality of the law. This modified fuero of Jaca became regarded as the fuero of Aragón, and by the thirteenth century versions of it guided jurists in Huesca, Borja, and Zaragoza.

In 1247 King Jaime I convened *cortes* (parliament) in Huesca, where he entrusted the compilation of the *fueros* of Aragón to Vidal de Canellas, bishop of Huesca. The result was the Código de Huesca, actually one compilation for the use of the *cortes* and a second, more elaborate work for the guidance of the jurists and administrators of the realm. These compilations clearly promoted the privileged status of the *infanzón* class, and at the same time impeded the growth of royal power by restricting the application of Roman law in Aragón. Later *cortes* and kings added to the Fueros of Aragón, basic elements of which, having survived many vicissitudes, continue in force today.

The *fueros* of Aragón contained many noteworthy and admirable features, not the least of which was the *ley de manifestación*, which in the seventeenth century served the British Parliament as a model in the formulation of the Habeas Corpus Act.

Lynn H. Nelson

Bibliography

Lalinde Abadía, J. *Los fueros de Aragón*. Zaragoza, 1976.

Molho, M. (ed.) *El fuero de Jaca. Edición critica*. Zaragoza, 1964.

Tilander, G. (ed.) *Vidal Mayor*. 3 vols. Lund, 1956.

FUEROS, CASTILIAN

Fuero is a term used in medieval Castile to indicate a body of rights and exemptions from standing obligations, or a contract governing the use of land between agreeing parties. The term derives from the Latin *forum*, and its application in Spain is especially tied to the fact that in Roman towns the forum constituted the place for administrating justice. As a concept, *forum* received its widest territorial application as the title of the great code of law compiled by Hispanic and Visigothic jurists called the *Forum iudicum* (also *Liber iudiciorum*), later translated as the *Fuero juzgo*. The Asturian and Leonese monarchies strove to revive the *Fuero juzgo* in the ninth and tenth centuries with very limited success. This territorial use of the term *fuero* was renewed again in the thirteenth century by the Castilian kings Fernando III (r. 1217–1252) and Alfonso X (r. 1252–1284), when they attempted to apply the *Fuero juzgo* to the newly conquered towns in Estremadura and Andalusia. Meanwhile the term *fuero* had found other uses at the local level, especially in the nascent towns of the High Middle Ages.

By the tenth century *fuero* had come to denote local grants of rights and immunities by local authorities, and occasionally by the king, to communities of persons. Portuguese and Catalan variants (*forais*, *furs*) appeared by the thirteenth century. Much of the inspiration for such grants arose from the need to populate the frontier lands acquired during the Reconquest. *Fueros* for villages and towns often took the form of *cartas pueblas*, documents that established the rights and obligations of the new settlers, along with a description of the municipal boundaries. Until the twelfth century the municipal *fueros* in Castile were comparatively brief. The *fuero* of León, given to that city between 1017 and 1020 by Alfonso V, became the landmark charter of this earlier type, and influenced a number of others in the eleventh century. That foral influences could cross political frontiers becomes clear when Sepálveda (1076) in Castile and Jaca (1077) in Aragón received fueros with similarly worded military service requirements.

Once larger towns like Toledo fell into Castilian hands, the king granted *fueros* to particular groups within the municipality, as Alfonso VI did for the Mozarabs (1101) and Alfonso VII for the French settlers (1136). Such grants consisted of compromises between royal needs and local customs, then were worked into written form by the king's redactors. Periodically the monarchs would reconfirm them, making occasional revisions. During the twelfth century the municipal *fueros* grew steadily fuller and more comprehensive, evolving by century's end into municipal law codes occupying over a hundred folios in the contemporary manuscripts. The redactors of the charters often borrowed single laws and even entire charters from earlier municipal collections. The result was the creation of several models of municipal charters that spread through the various towns of a region, each model with individual aspects highly similar, if not identical, to other charters in that group. Such models with their variations are usually referred to as formularies or families.

The evolution of urban law between 1158 and 1190 has long been dominated by two monumental municipal charters that appear at the end of this period: the *fueros* of Cuenca and Teruel, given by Alfonso VIII of Castile and Alfonso II of Aragón, respectively. Municipal and legal historians have long sought the origins and purposes of the law contained in these codes, but the great complexity of the variables that contributed to their formation has defied easy generalization. Our understanding of regional law is further complicated by the occasional migration of laws and even entire codes from one kingdom to another. In general, Aragónese and Navarrese contributions to the process have tended to be disproportionately undervalued in favor of Castilian law. In fact, each of these regions produced *fueros* whose accumulation of precedents clearly shaped the ultimate content of the Cuenca-Teruel family. From the Castilian side of the Iberian Cordillera, the charter that seems to be a harbinger of the law of Cuenca-Teruel is the *fuero* of Uclés, granted by the master of the Order of Santiago and subsequently confirmed by Alfonso VIII in 1179. The *fuero* of Zorita de los Canes of 1180 also is often singled out as significant. In the non-Castilian lands of the *cordillera*, two Aragónese fueros are noteworthy, the charters of Alfambra (1174–1176) and of Medinaceli (probably given in the 1180s).

In addition to royal initiatives, the regional law of the *cordillera* itself provided a source for the legal materials contained in the charters of Cuenca and Teruel. The *cordillera* proved to be a region of legal creativity embracing the southern frontier of Navarre, the eastern frontier of Castile, and the western frontier of Aragón. The fully elaborated *fueros* of Cuenca and Teruel contain remarkably complete municipal law codes for the late twelfth century. For example, the manner of electing municipal officials and the definition of their offices are treated in connection with the administrative layout of the town. Military topics include the raising of the town militia for offensive and defensive purposes, and the system of vigilance that guarded the territories of the town and assured the garrisoning of its walls. The management of the livestock herds occupies considerable space in these records, suggesting the importance of sheep in the Castilian economy. Social legislation informs us in detail about the role of women in the town, the place of the Muslim and Jewish minorities, and even the operation of the marketplace and the administration of the municipal bathhouses.

During the reign of Fernando III, the Cuenca format was granted initially or renewed at a considerable number of towns. The geographic situation of these municipalities can largely be organized into three groups. One extended along the *cordillera* frontier with Aragón, and another concentration was established in the La Mancha and Calatrava area north of the Sierra Morena Mountains. Finally, as pressure increased on Jaén and upper Andalucía was absorbed, a third group of Cuencan charters was granted in the upper Guadalquivir. As was the case in León and Portugal, the Cuenca pattern was granted by military orders and bishops as well as by the king. If there is any effective explanation for the movement of this cordilleran municipal law across the *meseta* (plateau) into La Mancha (and even Plasencia on the Leonese frontier), as well as its penetration into upper Andalucía, it probably lies with the great body of livestock laws in the pattern that tied the grazing zones of La Mancha and upper Andalusia to the *cordillera* frontier towns established there after their conquest.

While not as full in content as the rich Cuenca-Teruel formularies, other important families of charters can be identified. García Gallo has argued in behalf of such a family in central Castile, based initially on grants given to Toledo at various points in the twelfth century. Of the charters assigned to the latter half of the century, the most interesting are the reconfirmation of the fueros of Toledo by Alfonso VIII (ca. 1166) and the portions of the *fuero* of Escalona that García Gallo dates to the later twelfth century. Fernando III revitalized this family in the first decade of his reign (1217–1227). A number of his early grants appear to have strong ties to the twelfth-century Toledan pattern, especially those to Guadalajara, Palenzuela, Talamanca, Ávila, Uceda, Peñafiel, and Madrid. The capture of Córdoba in 1236 provided the opportunity to enlarge the size and content of the Toledan format. Córdoba was the largest town captured in the Reconquest since the taking of Toledo in 1085, and this justified a reworking of the Toledo charter structure in order to give the new populace of settlers a proper fuero. Córdoba's new charter also marked an effort to provide an effective and updated counterpoise to the more liberal and rapidly spreading pattern of Cuenca-Teruel to the east and southeast. Thus, in 1241 a fuero was granted to Córdoba, a charter subsequently awarded to a number of towns in the remaining years of Fernando's reign, particularly Mula (1245), Cartagena (1246), Jaén (1248), Arjona (ca. 1248), Seville (1251), and Carmona (1252).

A third important area of influence emerged during the twelfth century in the kingdom of León (while it was temporarily separated from Castile) and in Portugal. A family of large-scale charters developed on the frontier of León and Portugal after 1190. Indeed, the symmetrical opposite of the Cuenca-Teruel family seemed to be developing on the Leonese-Portuguese frontier, with four Portuguese and three Leonese variants surviving. However, the law contained therein does not represent the balance of Portuguese and Leonese contributions across the political frontier that can be observed in Cuenca-Teruel. Rather, the law is almost exclusively Leonese, and all of the surviving examples were originally granted by Leonese-Castilian monarchs during the thirteenth century. Although four of the places receiving these charters were subsequently absorbed into Portugal, there is little evidence that they influenced the later law of Portugal or that prior Portuguese law influenced the content of the foral family. Martínez Díez worked out a relationship among the surviving charters and named the group the Coria Cima-Coa family. The Latin original granted to

Ciudad Rodrigo after 1190 does not survive, but a copy made from it for Alfaiates exists, and a copy made for Castelo Rodrigo after 1230 survives in two direct descendants from the thirteenth century at Castelo Rodrigo and Castelo Melhor. By 1227 the town of Coria had been awarded a Latin version of this charter, leading to subsequent versions at Castelo Bom, Cáceres, and Usagre, and a late surviving vernacular version of Coria. The original was granted to Ciudad Rodrigo by Alfonso IX of León almost certainly with the extensive model of Cuenca-Teruel in mind, and was designed to summarize territorial law in the same manner.

The rather considerable number of freedoms granted and the sense of municipal independence connoted by the Cuenca-Teruel fueros posed problems for Fernando III and Alfonso X. Both to seek more uniformity in regional law and to reassert the place of the king as the central authority, Fernando made the aforementioned attempt to apply the *Fuero juzgo* to a number of towns. Alfonso followed by creating a new format, based on the Toledo family of laws, called the *Fuero real* and granted to a number of towns. The revolts of the Muslims, townsmen, and nobles at various points in the last twenty years of Alfonso's reign seems to have thwarted the learned king's effort to make this universal. However, his great Romanized collection, the *Siete Partidas*, would ultimately gain dominance in later centuries by establishing royal law over the regionalized customs represented by the *fueros.*

JAMES POWERS

Bibliography

García Gallo, A. "Los fueros de Toledo," *Anuario de historia del derecho español* 45 (1975), 341–488.

———. *Manual de historia del derecho español.* 2 vols. Madrid, 1984.

García Ulecia, A. *Los factores de diferenciación entre las personas en los fueros de la Extremadura castellano-aragonesa.* Seville, 1975.

Powers, J. F. "The Creative Interaction Between Portuguese and Leonese Municipal Military Law," *Speculum* 62 (1987), 53–80.

———. *A Society Organized for War: The Iberian Municipal Militias in the Central Middle Ages, 1000–1284.* Berkeley, 1988.

FUEROS, VALENCIAN AND CATALAN

A *fuero* was the customary law of a Spanish place (local) or region (territorial), eventually organized in writing and approved by the ruler or regranted elsewhere by him, from then on, it could not be changed unilaterally. Notable collections in Catalan lands include Barcelona's *Usatges*, the *Costums de Catalunya*, and the *Costums* of Girona, Lérida, Mallorca, Roussillon, and Tortosa, as well as the maritime *Costums de mar* (*Libre del Consolat del mar*). *Fueros* (also *furs*) were distinct from the *actes* issued by one or two estates of a *corte* and from a *constitució* issued by the ruler backed by all three estates (as at Barcelona in 1283). The *usatges*, in various compilations from the eleventh century to the definitive redaction in the thirteenth, represented the comital rule and often framed or supplemented other *fueros.* Lérida's and Tortosa's compilations date from the thirteenth century; Girona's and Perpignan's, from the early fourteenth. Below these larger codes were settlement charters (*cartes de població*), collective agrarian contracts issued by public authority either to attract or to establish settlers on new lands as a kind of colonial constitution. Font i Rius has gathered nearly 400 of these for Catalán lands over seven medieval centuries; Miguel Gual Camarena collected 300 for Valencia.

Valencia was unique in the thirteenth century. Antipathetic juridical imports contended in a conquered Islamic kingdom. Before its first *costum* filled this vacuum, at least nineteen places had borrowed the *fuero* of Aragónese Zaragoza and seven, the fueros of Catalan Lérida. Roman law enthusiasm and practitioners were prominent, meanwhile, and a Catalan-dominated capital made possible an advanced, monarchical code against conservative Aragónese influence. King Jaime I promulgated the highly Romanized Latin *Fori* or *Costums de Valencia* around 1240, long before the whole realm was conquered. Conferred for the city of Valencia, a provision assured that it was meant to spread over the kingdom. Indeed, it was the earliest Roman law code of general application in Europe, against the claim of codes like that of Frederick II. The fuller *Furs de Valencia* in 1261 (revised in 1271) was in Catalan, promulgated by king and Valencian *corte.* Technically this *furs* was not a *fuero* but the cooperative new work of *corte* and ruler, like Barcelona's *constitució* growing regularly thereafter by additional *furs* from each Valencian *corte.* The *furs* was printed in its proper chronological form in 1482, by traditional rubrics in 1547–1548, and in a critical edition beginning in 1970, the original Latin *Fori* in 1967.

ROBERT I. BURNS, S. J.

Bibliography

Font i Rius, J. M. *Estudis sobre els drets institucionales locales en la Catalunya medieval.* Barcelona, 1985.

Furs de Valencia. Ed. G. Colón and A. García. Barcelona, 1970.

G

GALAICO-PORTUGUESE LANGUAGE

Galaico-Portuguese developed from the Latin/Romance dialect spoken in the northwest corner of the Iberian Peninsula, in what had been the Roman province of Gallaecia (modern Galicia). It was brought south with the conquest of the Muslim-dominated areas, eventually replacing the southern Romance dialects.

Isolated from the main centers of linguistic innovations of late imperial times, Galaico-Portuguese has a phonetic structure that is, unsurprisingly, characterized by a general conservatism. The tonic vowel system is that of western Late Latin, the isochronic system of seven vowels, with open and closed midvowels in the front and back series: /i/ /ẹ/ /ę/ /a/ /ǫ/ /ọ/ /u/—*lide* "battle" < LĪTE(M), *verde* "green" < VIRIDE(M), *azedo* "acetic" < ACĒTU(M), *dez* "ten" < DECE(M), *cabo* "end" < CAPUT, *forte* "strong" < FORTE(M), *nume* "name" < NŌMEN, *outono* "autumn" < AUTUMNU(M), *escudo* "shield" < SCŪTU(M).

This system remained without further basic change, unaffected by the wave of diphthongization that reached the central Hispano-Romance dialects. The atonic vowels likewise were /i/ /e/ /a/ /o/ /u/. The wave of syncope of posttonic vowels that affected most of early Western Romance evidently did not reach Galaico-Portuguese. Posttonic front vowels in contact with liquids consonants, and between /s/ or a nasal and another consonant, did drop, for the most part: for instance, *galgo* "greyhound" < GALLICU(M), *manga* "sleeve" < *MANICA(M)*. However, many postatonic vowels remained in the medieval period, producing an accentual effect more like that of Italian: for examples, *bebera* "early fig" < BIFERA(M), *covedo* "elbow" < CUBITU(M), *divida* "debt" < DEBITA(M), dúvida "doubt" < *DUBITA, *lídimo* "legitimate" < LĒGITIMUS, *pessego* "peach" < (MALUM) PERSICU(M). Similarly, pretonic vowels not preceded by liquid consonants or nasals survived in medieval Portuguese: *cabedal* "capital" < CAPITĀLE, *saudar* "to greet" < SALŪTĀRE.

The preservation of the Late Latin yod, and other common changes, produced a number of offgliding diphthongs: FRUCTUS "fruit" > *fruito*, NOCTE "night" > *noite*, MAGIS "more" > *mais*. The Late Latin offgliding diphthong /ai/ evolved to /ei/: JĀNUĀRIUS > *janeiro*. The /au/ likewise became /ou/, as in CAUSA "cause" or "thing" > *cousa*.

A notable innovation of Portuguese is the weakening of intervocalic and syllable-final nasal consonants, resulting in a regular series of nasal vowels. Between like vowels, nasalization of the merged vowels was found: *bom* [bõ] < boo < Lat. BONU, *lã* [lã] "wool" < *laa* < LANA, *tens* [tes] "you have, hold" < *tees* < TENĒS. Between unlike vowels, nasalization tended to produce nasal diphthongs: *mão* "hand" < MANU, *irmão* "brother" < GERMĀNU, *pões* "you put, place" < PŌNES, *cães* "dogs" < CANĒS. In some words an initial nasal likewise produced nasalization of a following vowel: *mãe* "mother" < MĀTRE. In a number of words the nasal quality of an earlier vowel was subsequently lost: *areia* "sand" < *arẽa* < ARENA, *boa* "good" (fem.) < *bõa* < BONA.

The metaphonic influence of final vowels on preceding tonic vowels also characterizes Portuguese. In modern standard Portuguese only three vowels are found in word-final position: a central vowel [∂], < Latin /-a/, and two high vowels [i u] that are reflexes of the merger of all Latin front and back vowels into a single front or back vowel. The effect of the high final vowels was to raise preceding tonic vowels: for instance, *isto* "this" (neuter) < ISTUD, *tudo* "all" (neuter) < *TŌTTU (C. L. TŌTUS). It is not certain whether the raising of final vowels goes back to Late Latin or is a medieval development. The evidence of modern Galician, in which the final back vowel is a close mid vowel [ọ], would indicate that the closing of final vowels is a modern phenomenon.

In consonantal development, too, Galaico-Portuguese tends to be fairly conservative, with a few distinctive changes. The initial consonant groups of a voiceless consonant with a lateral—in a way similar to Castilian, Leonese, and Italian—palatalized the /l/. The resulting group then became a voiceless palatal affricate /tʃ/—PLENU "full" > *cheio*, CLAMĀRE "to call" > *chamar*, FLAMMA "flame" > *chama*—and later a hushing fricative [ʃ].

Similar to the loss of single intervocalic nasals was the loss of the single intervocalic lateral /l/, as in *nevoa* "cloud" < NEBULA(M), *sair* "to leave" < SALĪRE "to jump, leap," *povo* "people" < *povoo* < POPULU. The medial Latin /d/ also was dropped in a number of words: LAMPADA "lamp" > *lampaa*, NĪDU "nest" > *nio*. The loss of medial consonants produced a relatively large number of words with vowels in hiatus, including *nevoa*, *area*, *boa*, *saudar*, *nomear* < NŌMINĀRE, *vaidade* < VĀNITĀTE. When the same vowel appears in both syllables, they generally merged fairly soon: *povoo* > *povo* "people," *viinte* > *vinte*, *seelo* > *selo*, *paaço* > *paço*. Other hiatus groups also tended to merge: ANELLUM "ring" > *eelo* > *elo*, VENĪRE "to come" > *viir* > *vir*, MONACHUM "monk" > *moago* > *mogo*, PALUMBUM "dove" > *paombo* > *pombo*. Geminate nasals and laterals simplified to a single nasal: ANNU "year" > *ano*. The loss of single intervocalic laterals and nasals must have been characteristic of the northern source of Galaico-Portuguese, for place names from Mozarabic dialects in southern Portugal reveal preservation: BASILICA > *Baselga*, FONTĀNĀS > *Fontanas*.

The affricates that developed in Late Latin from the combination of an occlusive and a yod, and from velar stops before a front vowel, are found in Galaico-Portuguese: FORTIA "strength" > *força*, RATIŌNE "reason" > *razão*, FACIŌ "I make, do" > *faço*, JŪDĪCIU "judgment" > *juizo*. The Western Romance voicing of simple intervocalic occlusives that one expects between vowels is frequently not found in the case of these affricates: PUTEU "well" > *poço*.

Medieval spelling is often inconsistent, especially in representing sounds not found in earlier Latin. Normally Latin spelling was used wherever possible. The nasal and lateral palatals were represented by digraphs, probably borrowed from Provençal spelling: *ob* as in TENEŌ "I hold, have" > *tenho*, FĪLIU "son" > *filho*. The palatal affricate /tʃ/ also was spelled by a digraph, *ch*, and the apical affricates /dz/ and /ts/ by *z* and *ç* (c before *e i*), respectively. The palatal fricative /ʃ/ was written *x*. The nasal vowels were often represented solely by preservation of Latin spelling, or by a final *m*, as in *bom*. The tilde likewise was used to spell nasal vowels, as in *razon* or *razõ*.

In morphology the loss of intervocalic /n/ and /l/ had important effects of derivation. Nouns and adjectives ending in these consonants formed plurals without them: For instance, *sinal* "sign" and *sinaes*, *leon* "lion" and *leões*, *cao* "dog" and *cães*. The same phonetic change produced definite articles consisting of a single vowel: *o* and *a*. Verbs sometimes preserved older forms of the first-person singular indicative, as in MENTIO(R) "I lie" > *menço*, SENTIŌ "I feel, perceive" > *senço*, ARDEŌ "I burn" > *arço*. "Strong" verbs maintain the atonic *-i* of the first-person singular in the oldest texts—for example, STETĪ "I stood" > *estivi*, PŌTUĪ "I was able" > *pudi*—but by the beginning of the fourteenth century the reduction of atonic final vowels to a mid front vowel produced the standard ending *-e*. The Late Latin third-person singular ending /-u/ was often found as *-o*, alternating with zero (e.g., *fizo* vs. *fez*).

One distinctive feature of the Portuguese verb system was and is the "personal infinitive," or what appears synchronically to be identical with the regular infinitive with certain personal endings added (e.g., *sem o sabermos* "without our knowing it"). One widely accepted theory perceives the origin of this form in the Latin imperfect subjunctive, which for the most part disappeared in Late Latin, replaced by the pluperfect subjunctive. Others have suggested an analogical source.

Galician became separated from Portuguese in the fourteenth century, preserving the apicoalveolar sibilant (known as the *geada*) also found in Castilian and distinct from the sibilant resulting from the simplification of the older affricates /ts, dz/. Standard Portuguese has been based for the most part on the central forms of the language found from Coimbra south, while Galician has undergone a massive influence of Castilian, both in pronunciation and in vocabulary.

PAUL M. LLOYD

Bibliography

Camara, Jr., J. M. *The Portuguese Language*. Trans. A. J. Naro. Chicago, 1972.

Silva Neto, S. da. *História da língua portuguesa*. 2d ed. Rio de Janeiro, 1970.

Teyssier, P. *Histoire de la langue portugaise*. Paris, 1980.

Williams, E. B. *From Latin to Portuguese: Historical Phonology and Morphology of the Portuguese Language*. 2d ed. Philadelphia, 1962.

GALAICO-PORTUGUESE LYRIC POETRY

Whether Portuguese literature today—with its offshoots in Brazil and the five Portuguese-speaking African countries—should be considered the most nearly major of the minor literatures or the most nearly minor of the major ones is a moot point. Old Portuguese poetry, at least from the late eleventh century to the early fourteenth, was unrivaled in an Italy as yet without Petrarch, a France without Villon or Ronsard, an England without Chaucer, and a Spain with not one lyric poet whose name has survived.

The corpus of secular poetry in Old Portuguese (or Galaico-Portuguese, the languages of Portugal and Galicia not having diverged until after the period concerned) consists of some 1,680 songs, preserved in the *Cancioneiro da Ajuda*, in Lisbon; the *Cancioneiro da Vaticana*; and the *Cancionetro da Biblioteca nacional*, Lisbon—the last two compiled in Italy some two hundred years later (available in 1973 and 1982 facsimile editions, respectively). Such was the prestige of these songs that Castilians, Leonese, Aragonese, Catalan, and even Italian poets tried their hand at composing them; among Castilians, Alfonso X complemented the troubadours' secular output by organizing a collection of 420 devotional *Cantigas de Santa María*, many presumably his own.

The secular poetry is conventionally and not altogether satisfactorily grouped under the three main headings of *cantigas de amigo*, *cantigas de amor*, and *cantigas de escarnho e mal dizer*, or flytings. The last are of chiefly psychological interest for their virulent misogyny and the coarsely explicit sexual insults the poets exchange, in contrast to the courtly elegance of their Provençal-inspired love songs and the tenderness and delicacy of the *cantigas de amigo*. If the former are of particular significance for the literary historian, they are by no means so devoid of genuine poetic interest as their relative neglect in favor of the latter might suggest.

The neglect is forgivable: the charm and freshness of the *cantigas de amigo* make them immediately accessible and attractive to modern sensibilities, and many of them are among the most captivating lyrics written anywhere in the Middle Ages. Subgenres include locally acclimatized forms of the general European pastorale, aubade, dance song, and barcarole, plus the indigenous pilgrimage song, all but the first being typically attributed wholly or in part to a female speaker addressing, referring to, or conversing with a lover, and all deriving from a convergence of Provençal influence with a native folk-song tradition of great antiquity and probably ritual origins. While the songs in their present form are the work of sophisticated poets, it is the latter strand that accounts for both the mysterious and hieratic atmosphere and the parallelistic form of the loveliest of them; the potentialities of the immemorial and universal device of parallelism, indeed, were arguably developed with more subtlety and ingenuity by these poets than by any before or since. Even the *cantiga de amor*, though heavily indebted to Provence, retains traces of the indigenous tradition, and its practitioners do not doubt their superiority to their more cerebral mentors in emotional intensity, if not in the intellectual convolutions of *canso* (a type of song) and *trobar clus* (a type of obscure poetry).

What is most notable about the *cantiga de amigo*, however, is not its comparably convoluted parallelism. Dante ascribed the origin of vernacular poetry to one poet's wish to be understood by a lady to whom "era malagevole ad intendere i versi latini" ["Latin verses were difficult to understand"]: the great innovation of the *cantiga de amigo* lies in the engagement of some hundred poets, for almost a century and a half, in the common enterprise of trying to imagine what such a *donna* might say if she herself were writing the verses: perhaps the first example (outside China, where such songs proliferated in the fifth and sixth centuries) of a concerted and persistent effort to break out of the prison of the self, experienced as a gender-specific identity.

Of the 153 poets of the *Cancioneiros* only a few can be named here: the Villonesque Bernal de Bonaval; Garcia de Guilhade, ironic and innovative; Fernández Torneol, author of one of the most magically perfect aubades ever written; the proto-Freudians Portocarreyro and Pero Meogo, singer of phallic stags, symbolic fountains, and dresses torn in the dance, who would surely rank as one of the major poets of the Middle Ages if more than nine of his songs had survived. Others, the number of whose extant works is in inverse proportion to their quality, are the barcarole poets Meendinho, whose one poem some consider the finest *cantiga de amigo* of all, and Martim Códax, the music of six of whose seven "sea chanties," exceptionally, has survived, as has that of King Alfonso's Marian *cantigas*. Gómez Charinho, a Galician admiral in Alfonso's service, depicts his mistress longing to go with him on campaign against the Moors but later rejoicing at his dismissal from his post, since now she no longer need fear for those in peril on the sea. Ayras Núnez, a fine poet and worldly priest "in Galice at Seint-Jame" a century before the Wife of Bath made her pilgrimage there, wrote delicious and ingeniously crafted dance songs and pastorales.

The poet with the largest number (138) of extant songs is Dinis, the sixth king of Portugal. Survival value here was clearly not dictated by hierarchy alone: the poet-king was also famous for a farsighted afforestation scheme whose vestiges may still be seen near Leiria.

STEPHEN RECKERTT

Bibliography

Nunes, J.J. *Cantigas d'amor dos trovadores galego-portugueses*. 2d ed. Lisbon, 1972. 171–92.

———. *Cantigas d'amigo dos trovadores galego-portugueses.* 2d ed. Lisbon, 1973.

Pellegrini, S., and G. Marroni. *Nuovo repertorio bibliografico della prima lirica galego-portoghese.* L'Aquila, 1981.

Rodrigues Lapa, M. *Cantigas d'escarnho e de mal dizer dos cancioneiros medievais galego-portugueses.* 2d ed. Vigo, 1970.

———. *Lições de literatura portuguesa: Época medieval.* 10th ed. Coimbra, 1981.

GALICIA

Today, the word *Galicia* designates the territory, in the northwestern corner of the Iberian Peninsula, that is bounded by the Atlantic Ocean, the Cantabrian Sea, the Galaicodurian Massif and the lower reaches of the River Miño. This territorial and social entity is a creation of the middle centuries of the medieval period. Before this time, according to the *Abledan Chronicle* and the two versions of the *Chronicle* of Alfonso II, Galicia was a much larger territory extending as far south as the Duero River valley. This *provincia* or *urbs Gallecie* remained as the successor-state to the *Gallaecia* established by the late-Roman administrative reform of Diocletian and of the Gallaecia occupied by the Sueves and subsequently incorporated into the Visigothic kingdom. As late as the eleventh century, the realm inherited by García, son of Fernando I, was still the old Gallaecia, expanded by the lands recaptured—or expected to be recaptured—from the Moors. The old territorial notion still persisted when Alfonso VI bestowed the countship of Galicia on Raymond of Burgundy. Five years later, however, the county of Portugal was to be separated from Galicia and, under Count Henriques and Countess Teresa, to begin its path toward independence; and by the beginning of the XIIth century, when the *Historia Compostelana* was written, Galicia was the Galicia of today, the lower reaches of the river Miño having acquired their definitive frontier character: *fluvius enim iste Portugalensem terram disterminat a Gallaetia.*

The earlier, wider conception of Galicia is, as a survival of the era initiated by the Roman conquest, typical of the high medieval period between the eighth and eleventh centuries in areas like Galicia, where the effects of the Islamic invasion did not involve an abrupt break with preceding developments. The most remarkable and renowned event in high medieval Galician history—the discovery of the tomb of St. James the Great—is certainly related to such survivals; specifically, to the tradition that, since the seventh century, had represented St. James as the direct promotor of Christianity in Hispania. It is awareness of this tradition by the clergy of the never-abandoned see of Iria that can explain the attribution immediately made of the early-ninth-century discovery. The medium- and long-term consequences of this—the pilgrimages and the *Camino de Santiago*—were momentous. In the short term, the presence of the Asturian monarch Alfonso II and the protection he afforded to what was to become Compostela served to consolidate the incorporation of Galicia into the northern kingdom. This meant that just as Alfonso was formulating his neo-Visigothic program a territory was incorporated that shared with the lands to the north of the Cantabrian *cordillera* a virtual lack of Islamic influence, but which, unlike the latter region, had experienced relatively intense Roman and Germanic transformations.

Features characteristic of earlier times also manifested themselves in the social patterns of the Galicia of the ninth and tenth centuries, as evidenced by written sources, which at this time began to provide information about the fabric of society. These persistent traits are quite clear, ranging from the spatial distribution of the population—the basic unit is the *villa*, the small hamlet that had replaced the ancient hill forts in a process begun with the Roman conquest—to the pattern of social stratification characterized by the presence of a large serf population, a still significant number of land-holding peasants, and an aristocratic elite devoted to the expansion of the kingdom under the direction of the monarch, to ecclesiastical habits—such as territorial organization in parishes and monasteries inherited from the Germanic period.

This older pattern began to break up in the mid-twelfth century, being replaced by an idiosyncratic form of feudalism. Both internal and external factors were responsible for this change. Ranking high among the latter was the surge in pilgrimages, which made Santiago a center of incessant activity characterized on the one hand by its dynamic civic life and on the other by the growing prestige of the episcopal see eventually raised to metropolitan status thanks to the efforts of Diego Gelmírez.

The rise of the pilgrim route to Compostela, which connected Galicia with the rest of the Castilian-Leonese kingdom and, further afield, with the centers of western Christendom, combined with internal trends—demographic growth, intensification of agricultural activity, the spread of urban nuclei—in driving overall social change; but the specific social forms that arose were also influenced by political factors. After the twelfth century, Galicia lost the relatively central position it had held in the Castilian-Leonese kingdom. Portuguese independence, the reunification of Castile and León in the thirteenth century and finally the rapid advance of the Reconquest led to the centers of power moving away from Galicia and to a reduction in its contribution to the repopulation of the regained territories. The adverse effects of the new situation seem to have been felt most by the lay nobility. The result of it all was the establishment of a feudal society whose chief features were the reduction in the number of small holders and their replacement by a dependent peasantry; the concomitant concentration of property, largely to the benefit of ecclesiastical institutions, Benedictine and Cistercian monasteries especially; and the division of power between the monarchy and other social groups, which favored the clerical sector—the principal recipients of jurisdictional suzerainties, from the Tierra de Santiago to monastic fiefs—at the expense of lay nobility and citizenry, whose power was limited following the abortive anti-episcopal revolts of 1117 and 1137 in Compostela.

The contradictions in the social structure were to be highlighted by the late medieval crisis. The new nobility that emerged from the Trastámaran civil war, lacking a solid financial basis, sustained its social position by the abuse of power. The reaction of the citizenry and peasantry against such abuse came to a head in the Irmandiño Revolt of 1466–1469. Yet neither the revolt nor the short-lived triumph of the nobility (immediately emptied of content by the centralizing policies of the Catholic Monarchs) gave rise to significant changes in the social system established in the preceding centuries. Rather, one is led to the conclusion that the crises of the fourteenth century and the conflicts of the fifteenth were shake-ups that helped to consolidate its basic features for a long time to come.

ERMELINDO PORTELA SILVA

Bibliography

Fletcher, R.A. *Saint James' Catapult: The Life and Times of Die go Gelmírez of Santiago de Compostela*. Oxford, 1984.

Ferreira Priegue, E. *Galicia en el comercio marítimo medieval*. La Coruña, 1988.

Garcia Oro, J. *La nobleza gallega en la Baja Edad Media*. Santiago de Compostela, 1981.

López Ferreiro, A. *Historia de la Santa A.M. Iglesia de Santiago de Compostela*. 7 vols. Santiago de Compostela, 1898–1904.

López Alsina, F. *La ciudad de Santiago de Compostela en la Alta Edad Media*. Santiago de Compostela, 1988.

Pallares Méndez, Ma C. *El monasterio de Sobrado: Un ejemplo del protagonismo monástico en la Galicia medieval*. La Coruña, 1979.

Pallares Méndez, Ma C. y Portela Silva, E. *Galicia en la época medieval*. La Coruña, 1992.

Portela Silva, E. y Pallares Mendez, Ma C. "Historiografía sobre la Edad Media de Galicia en los diez últimos años (1976–1986)," *Studia Historica* 6 (1988), 7–25.

Portela Silva, E. *La colonización cisterciense en Galicia (1142–1250)*. Santiago de Compostela, 1981.

GALÍNDEZ DE CARVAJAL, LORENZO

Royal secretary, historian, and editor, Galíndez was born in Plasencia on 23 December 1472 and died around 1530. The illegitimate son of an archdeacon of Coria (later legitimized), he took his mother's family name first and his father's second. He read law at Salamanca University and later occupied a chair there. He married Beatriz Dávila, daughter of Pedro, *señor de las Navas*. In 1499 Galíndez was named judge on the Valladolid circuit, and three years later was promoted to the Royal Council. He was awarded the degree of Doctor of Laws in 1503, and at the relatively young age of thirty-one had so gained the confidence of Queen Isabel that she asked him to be present when she drew up her will. His first task as a civil servant was to list the laws and ordinances of all previous monarchs, a laborious work that was never published; it was also said that he had begun a collation of the *Partidas*. Galíndez accompanied the Catholic Monarchs through the main events of their reign, and on Fernando's death in 1516 was appointed to go and meet the new king, Carlos I, at Aguilar de Campóo; for Carlos's guidance he prepared an *Informe sobre los miembros del Consejo Real*. We know little of his activities in the last years of his life; it is assumed he retired to his native city about 1525.

Posterity remembers Galíndez not as a civil servant or a legal adviser but as a historian, an editor of historical texts, and an early critic of historiography, acutely aware of the partisanship of his near contemporaries. He compiled two genealogical monographs, but more significant was his *Memorial o registro breve*, an annual itinerary of the Catholic Monarchs from 1468 to 1516. He prefaced this with the first extensive set of observations on the problems and aims of official historians, which, according to some, was a prelude to a history of Spain or at least of the Catholic Monarchs. At Fernando's request he had been collecting and revising manuscripts of major chronicles past and contemporary, at least from Pedro López de Ayala onward. Whatever his intentions, only one was published, that of Juan II of Castile (Logroño, 1517). He also added four biographies to the *Generaciones* of Fernán Pérez de Guzmán, revised a copy of Hernando del Pulgar's *Crónica de los reyes católicos*, which he gave to Antonio de Nebrija to adapt and translate as the *Decades duae*. He also revised Diego Enríquez del Castillo's chronicle of Enrique IV and Diego de Valera's *Memorial de diversas hazañas*, and possibly commissioned the work of Lucio Marineo Sículo.

ROBERT B. TATE

Bibliography

Rodríguez Moñino, A. *Historia literaria de Extremadura: Edad Media y reyes católicos*. Badajoz, 1950. 82–90.

Torres Fontes, J. *Estudio sobre la "Crónica de Enrique IV" del Dr. Galíndez de Carvajal*. Murcia, 1946.

GAMA, VASCO DA

Vasco da Gama was born about 1460 in Sines. He was the son of Estevão da Gama, a minor noble who had fought in North Africa and later became admiral of Portugal and governor of Sines.

The rounding of the Cape of Good Hope by Bartolomeu Dias in 1488 had confirmed the existence of a sea route from western Europe to Asia; consequently King Manuel I of Portugal ordered another, larger expedition and put the young Vasco de Gama in command of it. His fleet consisted of four ships: two *naus*, the *São Gabriel*, captained by Gama himself, and the *São Rafael*, captained by his brother Paulo; the *Bérrio*, a smaller ship, probably a caravel, captained by Nicolau Coelho; and a large supply ship captained by Gonçalo Nunes. The number of sailors and soldiers who took ship on Gama's first voyage was between 150 and 200 men.

Anonymous, 16th century. Portrait of Vasco da Gama. Manuscript illumination, Ms. port. 1 fol. 13. Copyright © Giraudon/Art Resource, NY. Bibliotheque Nationale, Paris, France.

Gama sailed out of the Tagus on 8 July 1497. He reprovisioned in the Cape Verde Islands, leaving there on 3 August and heading southwest to avoid the doldrums. Like Dias he picked up the westerlies and, turning east, made his first South African landfall at Saint Helena Bay on 7 or 8 November. He rounded the Cape of Good Hope on 22 November and anchored in Mossel Bay. Having abandoned his supply ship and redistributed its remaining provisions, he sailed on, reaching the Great Fish River on 16 December. Soon thereafter he was at present-day Natal Point, so named by Gama because it was sighted on Christmas Day. He reached Quelimane on 24 January 1498, Mozambique Island on 2 March, Mombasa on 7 April, and Malindi on 13 April. Favorably received there by the sultan, who liberally resupplied him, Gama set out to cross the Indian Ocean on 24 April. He was able to profit from the southwest summer monsoon wind, which took him to India in under a month. By 20 May he was anchored off the Malabar coast just above Calicut. The *samorin* of Calicut received him coldly, and at one point held Gama and his retinue prisoner. By a judicious mixture of threats and astuteness, Gama extricated his fleet and left India at the end of August 1498.

The return journey was disastrous: he was obliged to burn Paulo's ship for lack of men to sail her, for many had died of scurvy and dysentery; Paulo died on Ilha Terceira in the Azores. Gama arrived in Lisbon at the beginning of September and was rewarded magnificently by Manuel I with three pensions, the admiralty of India, and, much later, the countship of Vidigueira.

In 1502 Gama made his second exploratory expedition with a fleet of twenty ships that bombarded Calicut and left a five-warship guard at the entrance of the Red Sea to thwart Muslim trading competition. He also cemented an alliance with the more friendly Malabar state of Cochin. He returned briefly to India as viceroy of Portuguese India in 1524, dying there at the close of that year.

Vasco da Gama's achievement cannot be overestimated: he circumnavigated the African continent, directly linking the Indian Ocean with Europe, and he effectively sent into economic and political decline the powers of the eastern Mediterranean (Venice, Genoa, Egypt, and Turkey) so that economic power would shift permanently to the Atlantic. The consequent European dominance of western Asiatic waters was to continue until 1941–1942, when the Japanese overthrew British, French, and Dutch power; thus some Indian historians still call the period 1497–1941 "the Vasco de Gama era" of Indian history.

ROBERT OAKLEY

Bibliography

Jayne, K.G. *Vasco da Gama and His Successors: 1460–1580*. London, 1910.

Velho, A., *Roteiro da viagem que em descobrimento da India pelo Cabo da Boa Esperança fez dom Vasco da Gama em 1497–1499*. 2 vols. Oporto, 1945.

GAMES AND GAMBLING

The gloomier moments of medieval life were partially brightened by an array of games and other diversions. Ranging from the silly to the sedate, from the physical to the cerebral, these entertainments had broad appeal to a highly stratified society. Some of these activities parallel modern spectator sports: French-inspired tournaments, for example, played to leisure-class audiences. More plebeian sports included ball games, such as handball and a forerunner of baseball, the latter depicted in the thirteenth-century *Cantigas de Santa María* (*cantiga* 42).

Sedentary players preferred chess and backgammon, both of which formed part of the Oriental culture brought by the Muslims to Christian Europe. The lavishly illustrated *Libro de acedrex, dados e tablas*, commissioned by the polymath Alfonso X the Learned, appeared in 1283 and was the most elaborate medieval treatise on these games. Two centuries later Luis de Lucena coupled the games of love and chess in his *Repetición de amores y arte de ajedrez*. Of all the instruments of play, dice possessed the oldest, if hardly the most illustrious, pedigree. Playing cards, on the other hand, did not arrive at the Iberian Peninsula until about 1375, having first appeared in Italy. The advent of printing a century later ensured that playing cards would enjoy accurate reproduction and widespread distribution.

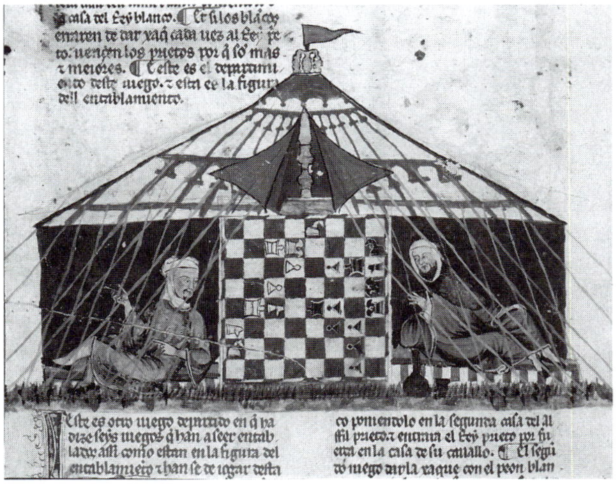

13th century. Two Arabs playing chess in a tent. Alfonso X the Wise, *Libro de ajedrez, dados, y tablas,* Fol. 62v. Spanish, 1282. Copyright © Giraudon/Art Resource, NY. Biblioteca Real, El Escorial, Madrid, Spain.

Gambling, that raffish progeny of innocuous games, likewise played a prominent role in medieval pastimes. Adaptability was gambling's virtue, since any game could be transformed by the addition of a wager, just as any locale could become an informal gambling den. Numerous references to Christian, Muslim, Jewish, women, clerical, and student players testify to the general allure of gambling. Although church and state sought to limit gambling in an effort to preserve social order and prevent moral decay, their injunctions often proved ineffective. Indeed, recognizing the material gain that would accrue to the royal fisc, Alfonso X, the putative author of the *Ordenamiento de las tafurerias*, sought to establish a monopoly on organized gambling.

DWAYNE E. CARPENTER

Bibliography

Carpenter, D. E. "Fickle Fortune: Gambling in Medieval Spain," *Studies in Philology* 85 (1988), 267–78.

Wohlhaupfer, E. "Zur Rechtsgeschichte des Spiels in Spanien." In *Spanische Forschungen der Görresgesellschaft*. 1st series. *Gesammelte Aufsätze zur Kulturgeschichte Spaniens* 3 (1931), 55–128.

GARCÍA DE SALAZAR, LOPE

Lope García de Salazar (1399–1476) was a Basque nobleman best known for a vast compilation, the *Libro de las bienandanzas e fortunas*, written between 1471 and 1476 while he was held prisoner by two of his sons. Earlier, in 1454, he had compiled a shorter work, the *Crónica de Vizcaya*. The *Bienandanzas* consists of twenty-five books, the last six treating northern Spain, particularly Salazar's native Vizcaya. Salazar's stated purpose was to preserve knowledge of the past for future generations. For his history of Spain and other countries and peoples, he favored a genealogical approach, tracing the rise and fall of leading figures, summarizing and often copying verbatim texts from his own library, collected, he informs us, from various parts of Spain and abroad.

Twentieth-century scholars discovered in the *Bienandanzas e fortunas* a wealth of information on historiographical and literary texts, including some now lost, as well as legends that circulated in northern Spain in the fifteenth century. In Salazar's books on the history of Spain, interest has focused principally on his use of epic material (*Roncesvalles*, *Fernán González*, the *Mocedades de Rodrigo*, etc.). Concerning other sections of the work, attention has been given to his use of the *Libro de buen amor* and the pseudo travel book attributed to the Infante Dom Pedro de Portugal (a work otherwise known only in later printings); a now lost Alexander prose romance, the *Poridat de las poridades*, and the Aristotle and Phyllis legend in his history of Greece; Trojan and Arthurian romance in his history of England; the Flores and Blancaflor romance and epic tales concerning Berta and Mainete in his history of France; a version of the Melusine romance and a story of the descent into hell in his history of Flanders; and the *Gran conquista de Ultramar*, including the *Caballero del Cisne*, in his history of the Crusades. Salazar frequently alters his written source with information derived from oral tradition, for example, an account told by English seamen of the passing of King Arthur to the Island of Brasil in his condensation of the post-Vulgate *Roman du Graal*.

Harvey L. Sharrer

Bibliography

Marín Sánchez, A. M. (ed.) *Istoria de las bienandanzas e fortunas de Lope García de Salazar (Ms. 9–10–2/2100 R.A.H.). Licenciate* thesis, University of Zaragoza, 1993.

Sharrer, H. L. (ed.) *The Legendary History of Britain in Lope García de Salazar's "Libro de las bienandanzas e fortunas"*. Philadelphia, 1979.

Rodríguez Herrero, A. (ed.) *Las bienandanzas e fortunas*. 4 vols. Bilbao, 1967.

GARCÍA DE SANTA MARÍA, ALVAR

Royal secretary and historian, García was born in Burgos about 370, into an old Jewish family. His elder brother Solomon converted to Christianity under the name of Pablo de Santa María and led the rest of the family to be baptized around 1390. The family preserved and improved their social standing in the church and royal household as loyal servants of the crown. In 1400 García married Marina Méndez from Toledo; there was no issue, so he legitimized a natural daughter conceived before his marriage. He was introduced early to the court of the regent Fernando de Antequera and in 1408 was appointed to the royal scriptorium. In 1410 he was proclaimed by the regent as "noble ciudadano, regidor, secretario de su cámara, su coronista y consejero, libre de todo pecho" ["noble citizen, rector, secretary of his chamber, chronicler and counselor, free of all taxes"]. When Fernando became king of Aragón in 1412, García briefly followed him there. After Fernando's death in 1416 he returned to Castile to continue in his position as royal chronicler until the 1450s, when, according to Alfonso de Palencia, he fell into disgrace. Following his death on 21 March 1460, he was buried in the main chapel of the monastery of San Juan, Burgos, where, according to Galíndez, manuscripts of his work were deposited.

Alvar is known to posterity as the main author of the *Crónica de don Juan II de Castilla*. According to Fernán Pérez de Guzmán, he was a "notable e discreto onbre que non le falleçería saber para ordenar e conçiençia para guardar la verdad" ["a notable, discreet man whose wisdom and conscience for keeping to the truth would never falter"] who was replaced as historian, with the result that the remainder of the history lacked authority. It is hard to decipher his contribution to the *Crónica*, given the difficulty of assessing authorship of the surviving manuscripts. Galíndez's opinion, as the text's first editor, was that Alvar had started in 1406 (with a gap of some ten years from where López de Ayala left off) and continued to 1420, when he left off. It was continued by another to 1435, and a third from after 1435 to the death of Juan II (1453); after this it was revised by Pérez de Guzmán, whose text Galíndez claimed to respect.

His views have not been totally accepted by modern critics in their examination of the three main manuscripts. But despite the observations of Cantera, Carriazo, Terracini and Donatello Ferro, the balance between original and *refacimenti* has not been totally worked out. The first volume of a "critical" text by Carriazo contains the bare text up to 1411 without any critical apparatus. Overall, the treatment is very traditional; the deliberate anonymity of the author echoes that of previous chronicles. Like Ayala he must have had access to official documents, probably assembled in annual registers before being gathered into a royal itinerary that forms the basis of the narrative. This narrative follows Fernando in the early part, then alternates between Juan II and Álvaro de Luna in the later part. Stylistically there is no great variation (until the last years) in expressive devices. One abiding characteristic is the detailed description of rituals. The chronicle marks the end of a long series.

Robert B. Tate

Bibliography

Carriazo, J. de M. "Notas para una edición de la *Crónica* de Alvar García." In *Estudios dedicados a Menéndez Pidal*. Vol. 3. Madrid, 1952. 489–505.

Crónica de Juan II de Castilla. Ed. J. de M. Carriazo. Vol. 1, 1406–1411. Madrid, 1982.

Ferro, D. *Le parte inedite della "Crónica de Juan II" de Alvar García de Santa María.* Venice, 1972.
Terracini, L. *Intorno alla "Crónica de Juan II."* Rome, 1961.

GARCÍA DE SANTA MARÍA, GONZALO

García (b. 31 May 1447) was a grandson of Tomás García de Santa María of Zaragoza, a first cousin of Pablo de Santa María, *converso* bishop of Burgos, and son of Gonzalo de Santa María, also of *converso* (Christian convert) stock, merchant and moneylender of the same town. By training and profession he was a legal officer, serving as councillor to the chief justice of Aragón, Juan de Lanuza, and also to the governor of Aragón, Archbishop Alfonso de Aragón. He was involved in property and other deals that brought him into conflict with the law (1469). In 1499 he claimed that the servants of the viscount of Evol tried to assassinate him; no reason was given. Like many of his contemporaries, he had brushes with the Holy Office. The *Libro verde de Aragón* claims that the Inquisition had disciplined him and his wife, a Valencian *converso*, Violant de Bellviure.

García's small but choice library gives some measure of his cultural background. Most of the books are in manuscript form and in Latin, equally divided between law and letters. He does not give the titles of those in Greek and Romance, merely listing an important nucleus, including Diogenes Laertius's *Lives of the Philosophers* in an Italian hand, four treatises of Cicero, Trogus Pompeius, Virgil's *Aeneid*, Juvenal, and St. Jerome, plus two volumes of Lorenzo Valla's works. In his own words, he valued these books above all else. Despite his complaint that the new printing presses had lowered the price, he was still enthusiastic about this novelty, and worked for Paulus Hurus and his successors.

The bulk of García's work was translation of moral treatises into the vernacular. Although he regarded this as a laborious task, he had significant things to say about the art of translation and, before Antonio de Nebrija, about the connection between the spread of the mother tongue and political power. He also edited the corpus of Aragonese law (1494), the *Dialogus pro ecclesia contra sinagogam* (1497), and the synodal constitutions of the archbishopric of Zaragoza (1498). He also played some role, according to Fabricio de Vagad, in encouraging the latter to write his *Crónica de Aragón* (1497). We have data on three historical works in Latin related to the Crown of Aragón: a general history of Aragón, of which only fragments remain; a genealogical work whose aim was to secure and confirm the links between the Crown of Aragón and Castile; and an official Latin biography of Juan II of Navarre and Aragón, commissioned by his son Fernando and inspired by Sallust's *Catiline Conspiracy*, which illustrates the triumph of the king over the rebellious Catalan patricians in the 1460s. It can be classified as the first true humanistic product of Iberian historiography. It was utilized, directly or indirectly, in the later works of Lucio Marineo Sículo on Aragonese history.

ROBERT B. TATE

Bibliography

Tate, R. B. *Ensayos sobre la historiografía peninsular del siglo XV.* Madrid, 1970. 212–62.

GAYA CIENCIA

Gaya Ciencia is a late medieval synonym for the art of composing troubadour poetry, probably coined by the Consistòri del Gai Saber, a bourgeois institution with academic pretensions founded at Toulouse in 1323, which aimed to promote a troubadour revival. Arnaut Vidal, the first winner in the May Day competition, was awarded a "doctorate in *gaya sciensia*" in 1324 for a poem ostensibly in praise of the Virgin Mary. This science is defined as "gay" because the joy of love (in Provençal, *joy*; adj. *gai*, fem. *gaia*) was a key concept in both Provençal and Arabic love poetry. Indeed, the word *trobar* itself almost certainly derives from the Arabic *taraba*, "to be moved by joy or grief; to sing, to play music." The Toulouse consistory commissioned a large treatise on Provençal grammar and poetics, *Las Flors del gay saber, estier dichas las leys d'amors* (1328–1337); one of the founders, Raimon de Cornet, wrote a *Doctrinal de trobar* in verse (1324).

This institution was fostered by Pere IV of Aragón after his annexation of Toulouse in 1344. His successor, Joan I, established a poetic academy in Barcelona in 1393, modeled on that of Toulouse. Jaume March (uncle of Ausiàs) and Lluís d'Aversó were appointed as *mantenedors* (overseers); both wrote theoretical works on poetry. There was also a Catalan version of *Las Flors del gay saber*. Learned vernacular culture was further encouraged by Martí I of Aragón: in 1396 he established a faculty of Limousin or Provençal at the University of Huesca, the earliest faculty of the modern humanities in Europe. The almost miraculous civilizing properties ascribed to the gay science by Joan I and Martí I are similar to those mentioned by Ibn Hazm, Guillaume IX, Raimbaut de Vaqueiras, Juan Ruiz, Rodrigo Cota, and others with reference to love: "purissimo, honesto, et curiali nitens eloquio, rudes erudit . . . cor laetificat, excitat mentem, sensum clarificat atque purgat." In 1413 Fernando de Antequera confirmed the concessions "pro gaya sciencia" granted by his royal predesessors. Enrique de Aragón (also known as as de Villena), a *mantenedor* of the Barcelona consistory, then wrote the earliest surviving treatise on poetry in Castilian. This fragmentary *arte de trovar*, addressed to the Marqués de Santillana, contains an eyewitness account of the solemn ritual of electing a poet laureate. Santillana, in turn, summarized his views on poetry in the preface to his collected verse, dedicated to Pedro, Constable of Portugal, in 1449. *Gaya sciencia* is here defined as a divinely inspired craving for perfection to which noble and perspicacious minds are susceptible.

The theory that to be technically proficient a poet requires both nobility and divine inspiration was expressed by Juan Alfonso de Baena in the preface of the *Cancionero*, which he compiled for Juan II of Castile in 1445: "el arte de la poetrya e gaya çiençia es una escryptura e conpusyçion muy sotil e byen graçiosa . . . alcançada por graçia infusa del señor Dios"; the practitioner of this science must be courtly, amorous, and of noble birth: "que sea noble fydalgo e cortes e mesurado . . . que sea amador e que siempre se preçie e se finja de ser enamorado." This antibourgeois definition of *gaya ciencia* was espoused by the impoverished *hidalgo* Alvarez de Villasandino in his hostility to the learned school of Imperial. It was thus that Provençal poetics, in a modified form, influenced the Castilian courtly lyric. One of the last theoretical works in this tradition was a Castilian rhyming dictionary, *La gaya ciencia*, compiled (ca. 1474–1779) for Alfonso Carrillo, Archbishop of Toledo, by Pero Guillén de Segovia.

ROGER BOASE

Bibliography

Boase, R. *The Troubadour Revival: A Study of Social Change and Traditionalism in Late Medieval Spain.* London, 1978.

Chabaneau, C. *Origine et établissement de l'Académie des Jeux Floraux.* Toulouse, 1885.

Las Joyas del gay saber: Recueil de poésies en langue romane couronnées par le Consistoire de la Gaie-Science de Toulouse (1324–1498). Ed. A. Gatien-Arnoult. Toulouse, 1849.

GELMÍREZ, DIEGO, ARCHBISHOP OF COMPOSTELA

This most famous and most powerful ordinary of the shrine of Santiago de Compostela was a native of Galicia, born about 1070 into a family of the minor nobility of that province. He probably was educated in part at the court of Alfonso VI (1065–1109) of León-Castile and in part within the clerical community of the cathedral. In 1090, and again in 1096, Gelmírez was the royal administrator for the possessions of the then vacant see of Compostela. In 1094 he had become the notary of Count Raymond of Galicia (1090–1107), originally from Burgundy, who held the province by virtue of his marriage to Urraca, daughter of King Alfonso. The choice of both king and count, Gelmírez was elected bishop of Compostela perhaps as early as 1098, and certainly by 1100. He was consecrated on 21 April 1101. The see to which he succeeded had been famous since the ninth century as the shrine-church purportedly housing the relics of the apostle St. James the Great. As the only site of apostolic remains in the Western world except Rome, it had long been the destination of pilgrims. In 1095 Pope Urban II had approved the exemption of the see from its traditional metropolitan, Portuguese Braga, and made it directly dependent on Rome.

Gelmírez's major triumph was to secure the transfer of the former metropolitanate of Visigothic Mérida to Compostela by Pope Calixtus II in 1120. As a result Compostela immediately became the metropolitan see for Ávila, Salamanca, and Coimbra, and Gelmírez, an archbishop. The suffragan see of Coimbra finally could not be retained, but in the long rivalry for power that ensued, Compostela ultimately wrested the Galician sees of Túy, Lugo, Mondoñedo, and Orense away from Braga.

In addition Gelmírez had been named papal legate for the ecclesiastical provinces of both Braga and Mérida by Calixtus II, and used his power for the aggrandizement of his own church. He also hoped to have Compostela replace Toledo as the primatial see of Iberia, but fell short of his goal. He was also an energetic reformer of the church and cathedral chapter of Santiago de Compostela, and carried out much of the construction of a major new Romanesque cathedral there, begun a quarter of a century earlier.

Gelmíez was also a major political figure of the realm of León–Castile. He was guardian, along with the Galician magnate Count Pedro of Traba, of the only son of Count Raymond and Alfonso VI's daughter, Urraca. When Urraca succeeded to her father's realm in 1109 and married King Alfonso I of Aragón (r. 1105–1134), Gelmírez and Pedro raised a revolt against the royal couple in the name of the rights of the future Alfonso VII. The Galician prelate was sometimes the soul of the opposition to Queen Urraca and sometimes, particularly after her separation from Alfonso in 1112, her close collaborator. With the death of Urraca in 1126 and the succession of her son as Alfonso VII (r. 1126–1157), Gelmírez initially shared the glory of his former protégé. At the Council of León in 1130 he was able to place canons of his church in the bishoprics of the royal city of León and of Salamanca. Three years later another canon of Compostela became bishop of Orense.

But royal favor was inconstant, and as early as 1127 Gelmírez found himself the subject of extortion at the hands of a needy Alfonso VII. After 1134 the archbishop was increasingly eclipsed by the rising influence of the archbishop of Toledo, who placed his own canons as royal chancellor and then in Compostela's suffragan see of Salamanca in 1135. The following year the king collaborated in an attempt to have Gelmírez removed from his ecclesiastical dignity. At the Council of Burgos in 1136 the Galician prelate was rescued only by the support of the papacy and the ineptitude of the conspirators. Nevertheless, the cost of maintaining his office again came at the price of substantial future subsidies to the king.

The troubles of the archbishop of Santiago de Compostela were, in good part, due to his position as one of the great magnates of Galicia as well as a prelate there. His office made him the administrator of widespread royal lands, and these, combined with the lands of the shrine–church itself, automatically established him as the most powerful figure of central Galica. There he was caught between the ambitions of the Trastámara counts of Traba in the north and of the monarchs Teresa (r. 1112–1128) and Afonso I Enriques (r. 1139–1185) of Portugal in the south.

By royal grant and policy Gelmírez was also the lessee of the royal mint in Compostela and the city's civil administrator. In the latter capacity he resisted the ambitions of a nascent citizen commune to a share in the goverment of the town, although he did grant a measure of participation to it. The communal movement had allies even within the cathedral chapter. When his troubles in the larger political arena became acute, he faced outright revolt in 1117 and again in 1135. Both began with unsuccessful attempts on his life that failed only by the narrowest of margins. In each case the crown had initially encouraged Gelmírez's enemies, and repudiated them only when their attempt at assassination had failed.

After 1136 Gelmírez played only a small part in the life of the realm, and his activities in the church seem to have tapered down as well. From 1138 he was probably intermittently ill, and he died on 31 March 1140.

BERNARD F. REILLY

Bibliography

Briggs, A. G. *Diego Gelmírez, First Archbishop of Compostela*. Washington, D. C., 1949.

Falque Rey, E. (ed.) *Historia compostelana*. Turnhout, 1988.

Fletcher, R. A. *Saint James's Catapult: The Life and Times of Diego Gelmírez of Santiago de Compostela*. Oxford, 1984.

GENERAL ESTORIA *See* ALFONSO X, KING OF CASTILE; ILLUMINATION

GENERALITAT

The Generalitat originally an ad hoc, temporary administrative delegation from the *corts* (parliaments) of Catalonia called the Diputació del General, had evolved by the end of the Middle Ages into an important governing body. The Diputació appeared first in Catalonia in the mid-fourteenth century, and by example it was extended to Aragón and Valencia in the early fifteenth century, and into Navarre roughly fifty years later.

The original function of the Diputació del General was to supervise the implemenation of acts voted on in the *corts*, especially those concerned with fiscal collection and anything connected to the privileges of Catalonia. The mandate of its authority initially was limited to the period between meetings of the *corts*. In 1359 Pedro IV (r. 1336–1387) granted this ad hoc commission a permanent status to the Diputació del General, composed of three representatives, or *diputats del general*, one from each of the three estates of the *corts* and elected by the members of the *corts*. The representative from the ecclesiastical estate presided over the Diputació. Local *diputats*, whose number varied considerably, represented the Diputació in the principal cities. All *diputats* received a salary, and an audit was conducted every three years in an attempt to limit fraud. The Diputació resided permanently in Barcelona.

By 1365 the Diputació's jurisdiction was extended to include the counties of Roselló and Cerdaña. In 1413 Fernando I of Antequera, in recognition of the growing importance of the Diputació, created three additional *diputats*, the *oidors de comptes*, who were directly responsible for finances. All *diputats*, both local as well as the Diputacío del General, were limited to a three-year term, but successors were appointed by the incumbents, thus creating an influential, closely held oligarchy. Within a few years the Diputació had become an administrative body with a status roughly equivalent to that of the royal court.

Although as an institution the Diputació had grown in prestige and influence, during the fifteenth century the membership began to change, reflecting new social and political alignments and weakening its oligarchical nature. In 1454 a bloc of newly influential artisans and merchants in Barcelona protested the selection procedures. Alfonso V (r. 1416–1458) responded with an order that all future elections be a mixture of election and lottery; by 1493 all elections were by lottery only.

The Diputació was immensely valuable to the king in terms of collection of sums approved by the *corts*, and to the Catalans themselves as a guardian of traditional liberties and privileges. By the mid-fifteenth century, however, it no longer was simply on a par with royal governing bodies—it had become a potent counterbalance to royal authority. During the 1440s and 1450s, after decades of increasingly violent unrest in the countryside, Alfonso V decided to liberate the *remenses*, peasants in northeast Catalonia who were bound to their secular and ecclesiastical lords under harsh servile conditions. The *diputats*, landholders whose economic and political interests were seriously threatened by Alfonso's decision, argued that the order was contrary to the traditional liberties of Catalonia and fiercely opposed the action. Led by the archbishop of Tarragona, the *diputats* allied with Barcelona's town council, the Consell de Cent, and forced Alfonso to revoke his order.

The confict continued during the reign of Juan II (1458–1479), and once again royal prerogative was challenged by the Diputació, and not just with respect to the *remenses*. In 1460, when Juan ordered the arrest of his son, the popular Carlos of Viana, on charges of treason, the *cort* immediately denounced it as contrary to the privileges of Catalonia, and before disbanding, granted emergency powers to the Diputació. Joining with other factions from Barcelona in defiance of Juan, and with support from throughout the other crown realms, in 1461 the Diputació forced Juan to sign the Capitulation of Vilafranca, which recognized Carlos as the legitimate heir. It was an unambiguous victory of the Catalans as well as a demonstration of the immense power of the Diputació. In the civil war that followed (1462–1472), the Diputació maintained its defiance of the king until the end, when royalist forces besieged Barcelona and forced a negotiated settlement. Its political power dwindled progressively after the union of Castile and Aragón in 1479, its function limited to administration under the dominance of the government of Madrid.

THERESA EARENFIGHT

Bibliography

Font Rius, J.M. "The Institutions of the Crown of Aragon in the First Half of the Fifteenth Century." *In Spain in the Fifteenth Century*. Ed. J. R. L. Highfield. London, 1972.

———. *Estudis sobre els drets i institucions locals en la Catalunya medieval*. Barcelona, 1985.

Rubio y Cambronero, I. *La deputació del General de Cataluña en los siglos XV y XVI*. 2 vols. Barcelona, 1950.

Rycroft, P. "The Role of the Catalan Corts in the Late Middle Ages," *English Historical Review* 89 (1974), 241–69.

GERMANIC INVASIONS

The origins of the movements of population that often are called the Germanic invasions are not easy to determine, largely because most of the literary evidence relating to them is Roman in origin, and is limited in quantity, especially for what appear to be some of the more crucial periods. In general, Roman authors, whose sense of the cultural superiority of their own civilization in relation to that of the "barbarians" beyond the frontiers was highly developed, were not interested in investigating or providing their readers with details of the social organization and value systems of such alien societies.

However, contrary to old stereotypes, it should not be imagined that the Germanic societies beyond the imperial frontiers, roughly represented by the Rhine and Danube Rivers, were constantly pressing on those barriers, anxious to break into the empire and establish themselves on Roman soil. Their own societies, if more fissile than that of Rome, were normally stable, and they possessed traditional lands of their own. Moreover, a mutually beneficial relationship of trade and employment existed between the empire and its neighbors. Increasingly during the late Roman Empire, groups and individuals were recruited from among the Germanic peoples beyond the frontiers to serve Rome's military needs. In such ways, as well as in trade, elements of the material culture of the Roman Empire came to be established among the Germans.

By the late fourth century, other than in language, there was little to distinguish the Germans from the inhabitants of the frontier provinces of the empire. The causes of the breakdown of this relatively stable set of relationships and the period of upheaval that marked most of the fifth century are not easily determined. Ecological changes in the vast region stretching north from the Danube and around the top of the Black Sea precipitated the disintegration of the dominant Gothic societies in that area, and this in turn seems to have had a slightly delayed effect on the smaller ethnic groups facing the empire along the Rhine.

In the East the first manifestation was the flight of those who were to re-form themselves into the confederacy of the Visigoths toward the imperial frontiers and their crossing into Roman territory in 376. In the West the freezing of the Rhine in the winter of 406 allowed a racially mixed alliance of three smaller confederacies to cross the river on 31 December and enter Gaul. The four groups involved—the Hasding and Siling Vandals, the Alans, and the Suevi—moved across Gaul from a point in the Central Rhine Valley near Mainz, causing the breakdown of local order and ravaging the countryside through which they passed. Being in movement, they could support themselves only from what they could take, and needed security before they could reestablish themselves as economically self-supporting communities.

On the other hand, they were forced to continue moving, in that their needs for food and maintenance could be met only by finding new victims. Thus, in September or October 409 they reached the Pyrenees, and were able to cross into Spain, either through the negligence or with the deliberate assistance of the imperial troops defending the passes. Once in the peninsula, following a further period of movement and depredation, it became possible for them to establish themselves in the role previously played by the Roman army. A treaty made with the regime of the rebel emperor Maximus may have been the cause of this. The Alans and Siling Vandals settled in the southern provinces while the Hasding Vandals and Suevi occupied the former imperial military zone in the northwest. It may be assumed that they established themselves as garrisons in the major towns, and received pay and supplies from the local administrations.

The treaty made with Maximus was not recognized by the legitimate imperial government, which attempted to remove these unwanted peoples and regain its tax revenues. In 416 the Visigoths, led by Wallia, were employed by Emperor Honorius (r. 395–423) to carry out this task. They destroyed the Alan and Siling Vandal confederacies but had to be recalled to Gaul in 418 when it seemed likely that they were planning to move on to the wealthy but poorly defended African provinces. This, however, was achieved in 429 by the Hasding Vandals. Their removal to North Africa left the Suevi as the dominant military force in the Iberian Peninsula, and they established control over most of it, other than the northeast, with a capital at Mérida.

A renewed military alliance in 456 between the Visigoths and the imperial government, now dominated by a soldier of mixed Visigothic and Suevic origin named Flavius Ricimer, involved a further invasion of Spain. The Visigoths under Theoderic II (r. 453–466) crossed the Pyrenees and destroyed the Suevic kingdom in the south of the peninsula. A small version of it was reconstructed in the northwest, and survived until absorbed into the Visigothic kingdom of Leovigild in 584. The year 456, though, may be said to date the establishment of continuous Visigothic rule over the greater part of Spain.

ROGER COLLINS

Bibliography

Collins, R. *Early Medieval Spain: Unity in Diversity, 400–1000*. London, 1983. 1–24.

Goffart, W. *Barbarians and Romans, A.D. 418–584: The Techniques of Accommodation*. Princeton, N. J., 1980. 3–55, 103–26.

Musset, L. *The Germanic Invasions: The Making of Europe A.D. 400–600*. Trans. E. and C. James. London, 1975.

Thompson, E.A. "The Visigoths from Fritigen to Euric," *Historia* 12 (1963). 105–26.

GERONA (GIRONA), CITY OF

Gerona (in Catalan, Girona) is situated on relatively high ground in the valley of the Ter River between the small Onyar, Güell, and Galligants streams. It controlled the main route from Barcelona into the Midi and is at the center of a rich agricultural region, and was beseiged on many occasions.

Gerona was a fortified place on the Roman Via Augusta. Settlement centered around what is now the cathedral, the Gironella tower, and the Church of St. Feliu. In the late fourth century, when the poet Prudentius wrote his *Crowns of Martyrdom*, devotion was already centered on the martyr Felix. A collegiate church built in his honor, along with the cathedral, were the oldest ecclesiastical foundations. Gerona was an episcopal see from at least the fifth century, and this status, as well as the relics of St. Felix and the town's strategic position, assured its survival during the Visigothic era.

The Muslim occupation lasted from about 715 until 785, when the citizens delivered the city to Frankish forces. Gerona was thus the first substantial permanent conquest of Charlemagne's forces (Barcelona would fall sixteen years later). Charlemagne was revered in Gerona and worshiped as a saint in the late Middle Ages.

Gerona was the center of a county and a diocese in the Carolingian Empire. Although controlled at times by the counts of Cerdaña-Besalú, by the eleventh century Gerona was firmly in the hands of the counts of Barcelona and was closely identified with the fortunes of Ermessenda, wife of Ramón Borrell and regent for many years after his death. A Romanesque cathedral was consecrated in 1038 (of which the bell tower remains, visible only from within the cloister). A Gothic structure was erected in the fourteenth century. The cathedral contains the largest single nave among medieval Iberian churches.

The population and prosperity of the town grew in the twelfth and thirteenth century. A municipal government of six (later four) *jurats* and a council of eighty was reformed in the fifteenth century to assure a less oligarchical system of election and political control. A Jewish population of perhaps 500 flourished until the late fourteenth century.

Before the Black Death of 1348, Gerona was the second most populous town in Catalonia. Its population may have approached 10,000 and certainly surpassed 8,000. The mortality figure from the first great epidemic was about 15 percent, but the decline in population continued throughout most of the late fourteenth and fifteenth centuries. In 1497 Gerona had 4,750 inhabitants.

Gerona suffered greatly during the civil war of 1462–1472. It sympathies lay with the Generalitat of Catalonia and the citizens of Barcelona who opposed King Juan II. Nevertheless, at the opening of the war, Queen Juana Enríquez and her son (the future Fernando II of Aragón) withstood a siege of Gerona by an army of the rebels led by the count of Pallars until the invading forces of Louis XI of France came to her aid. Other sieges occurred place in 1463 and 1467, and Gerona changed hands more than once during the war.

PAUL FREEDMAN

Bibliography

Alberech i Figueras, R., and J. Nadal i Farreras. *Bibliografia històrica des les comargues gironines*. Gerona, 1982.

———. *Aproximació a la història de Girona*. Gerona, 1980.

Guilleré, P. *Diner: Poder i societat a la Girona del segle XIV*. Gerona, 1984.

Rahola i Llorens, C. *La ciutat de Girona*. 2 vols. Barcelona, 1929.

GERONA, COUNCIL OF

An important early provincial church council, the Gerona meeting in June 517 promulgated legislation concerning liturgy, baptism, and clerical celibacy. It took place at a time when the Visigothic rulers, who were Arians, tolerated Catholicism and allowed contacts with the papacy.

The Council of Gerona was presided over by Juan, Archbishop of Tarragona. It followed a council in Tarragona that had taken place in 516 and represented an attempt to institute regular provincial gatherings. In attendance were six of the suffragans of the metropolitan: Frontinianus of Gerona, Paul of Ampurias (a see that would not survive the Muslim period), Agrippius of Barcelona, Nibridius of Egara (another later-to-be-abandoned see), Orontius of Lérida, and Cynidius of Ausona (later Vic).

The second and third canons established two series of Rogation Days, periods of fasting and prayer from the Thursday to the Saturday after Pentecost and on the three days beginning on November 1. This followed a practice first attested in the province of Vienne, but antedated acceptance by Rome (which would take place under Gregory I the Great) and the church as a whole.

The power of the archbishop of a province to set a standard liturgy for all suffragen churches was recognized by the first canon. Another step toward liturgical uniformity was to require recitation of the Lord's Prayer after matins and vespers (canon 10). These two liturgical provisions would be cited in the *Decretum* of Gratian in the twelfth century (*De consecratione*, dist. IV, c. 15 and dist. V, c. 14, respectively).

In the early church, baptism was performed only at Easter. A century after the beginning of the Pelagian controversy, the Gerona Council upheld and extended the practice of infant baptism by requiring immediate baptism of sick newborns. This canon (canon 5) went against Pelagian opposition to infant baptism and the notion of original sin. An adult Christian not yet baptized (catechumen), less common by 517 than in earlier centuries, was to be baptized on Easter or Christmas, but here, too, exception was to be made for the sick (canon 4).

The most significant conciliar acts for the later history of the church were those concerning clerical discipline and admission to clerical office. Married men entering holy orders at the level of subdeacon or above were encouraged to live separately from their wives (canon 6). Unmarried clergy were not to entrust their household to women not related to them (canon 7). Men who married widows or divorced women were barred from holy orders (canon 8, cited in *Decretum*, dist. XXXIV, c. 8). Rules on the admission of penitents to orders were defined according to the severity of their offense and the type of penance performed (canons 9 and 9bis).

PAUL H. FREEDMAN

Bibliography

Hefele, C. J., and Leclerq, H. *Histoire des conciles*. Vol. 2, p. 2. Paris, 1908. 1029–30.

Vives, J. ed. *Concilios visigóticos e hispano-romanos*. Madrid, 1963. 39–41.

GERSONIDES *See* LEVI IBN GERSHOM

GESTA COMITUM BARCINONENSIUM

Catalan historiography of the Reconquest began in the twelfth century in such ecclesiastical centers as Cuixá, Ripoll, and La Roda. It took the form of short monastic annals in Latin linked primarily with French rather than universal or Hispanic history. The annals are calendrical, studded with historical events but possessing a meaegr organic structure. The first formally conscious chronicle of Catalan history, the *Gesta comitum* originated in the monastery of Santa María de Ripoll in various versions that eventually included the early kings of Aragón. The earliest Latin version is structured around the legend of Count Wilfred the Hairy (Guifré el Pelós) and the origins of the counties of Barcelona, Urgell, Besalú, and Cerdanya and covers the period up to the death of Ramón Berenguer IV (1162). It was written by the same author in three stages and completed between 1162 and 1184. A first addition containing the kings of Aragón corresponds to the reign of Alfonso I (1103–1134), written probably between 1200 and 1208; a second contains the reigns of Pedro II (1196–1213) and the minority of Jaime I, which can be dated 1214–1218, and a conclusion covering almost all the reign of the latter (1214–1276), ascribed to 1270–1275.

An intermediate version—based on the earliest text, with additions from the *Chronicones Rivipullenses*, the eulogy of the Abbot Oliba of Ripoll, the *Brevis historia monasterii Rivipullensis* and Rodrigo Jiménez de Rada's *Historia gothica*—was finished between 1268 and 1270. This was the basis of a Catalan version, slightly abbreviated, datable to 1268–1283. The definitive version derives from the intermediate, extended up to 1299 by a very detailed narrative and completed between 1304 and 1314. Historians consider that this continuation offers the most striking passages of the totality, both as literature and as history.

ROBERT B. TATE

Bibliography

Gesta comitum Barcinonensium. Ed. L. Barrau Dihigo and J. Massó Torrents. Barcelona, 1925.

Rubió Balaguer, J. "Literatura catalana." In *Historia general de las literaturas hispánicas*. Ed. G. Díaz Plaja. Vol. 1. Barcelona, 1949.

AL-GHĀZALI (ALGAZEL)

See PHILOSOPHY, ISLAMIC

GIBRALTAR

Gibraltar, a strategically important peninsula on the Iberian coast in the Mediterranean Sea, was under Muslim rule from 711 until 1462, with a brief period under Christian domination at the beginning of the fourteenth century. The name Gibraltar does not appear until 1310; in the ninth century it was known as Jabal Ṭāriq, "Mount of Ṭāriq"; in the twelfth century the name was officially changed to Jabal al-Fatḥ, the "Mount of Victory." The official name of Gibraltar for the rock and the surrounding peninsula dates from the 1713 Treaty of Utrecht, which allocated Gibraltar to Great Britain. Gibraltar lacked an indigenous economy, but both the Christians and Muslims recognized Gibraltar's military importance.

There is, however, no documentary evidence of settlement until Fernando IV attempted to populate the peninsula after he captured Gibraltar in 1309; he also built a dockyard and a keep. The Marīnids, at the request of the king of Granada, recaptured Gibraltar in 1333. Alfonso XI, who had arrived too late to relieve the garrison, immediately planned the recapture of Gibraltar. This siege was not successful; it also permitted the possible recapture of Tarifa by the Muslims, which was prevented only by the battle of Salado. Alfonso was again besieging Gibraltar in 1349–1350 when the bubonic plague struck his army and included the king among its victims. After ten sieges Gibraltar surrendered in 1462 to the duke of Medina Sidonia, who later turned it over to the crown.

THERESA M. VANN

Bibliography

Hills, G. *Rock of Contention: A History of Gibraltar*. London, 1974.

GIL DE ZAMORA, JUAN

Juan Gil de Zamora (d. after 1318), a Franciscan friar and historian, was appointed by Alfonso X of Castile as the tutor of his son and eventual successor, Sancho IV. Born perhaps about 1241, Juan entered the Franciscan order and was sent to study at the University of Paris (ca. 1272–1273) and later at Siena. Returning to Castile around 1278 with the title of master, he served as lector (teacher) in various Franciscan houses of study. After holding other administrative positions in the order, he was named provincial minister of the province of Santiago about 1300. In the meantime he served Alfonso X and his son, comparing his own relationship to Sancho with that of Aristotle and his disciple, Alexander the Great.

Juan's principal work, written about 1278 and dedicated to his distinguished pupil, was the *Liber de preconiis Hispaniae*, a book extolling the glories of Spain. A confusing mélange of historical and geographical information, as well as ethical principles, it clearly reveals the author's pedagogical purpose.

Juan's broad acquaintance with the Bible, classical writers, Aristotle's philosophical treatises, John of Salisbury's *Policraticus*, and the principal peninsular historians is displayed on every page. His warning that royal avarice and unaccustomed exactions could result in the impoverishment of the kingdom seems to be a veiled criticism of Alfonso X.

Juan's *Liber de preconiis civitatis Numantine* (finished in 1282) was written in praise of his native Zamora, which he identified with ancient Numantia, famed for its resistance to Roman conquest. Also notable is his *Liber illustrium personarum*, a biographical dictionary with useful data concerning recent and contemporary figures such as Alfonso IX, Fernando III, and Alfonso X. He also contributed to the formation of Alfonso X's *Cantigas de Santa María* by collecting stories of the Virgin Mary's miraculous intervention in the lives of various saints. These were included in his *Liber Mariae*, a book hailing Mary's glories. As part of this work he also composed at the king's request (probably about 1278) Latin hymns for the Office of the Virgin Mary. Other unpublished philosophical and theological works include *Ars dictandi*, *Historia naturalis*, *Liber contra venena et animalia venenosa*, *Liber de arte musicae*, and *Proslogion seu de accentu et de dubilibus biblie*.

JOSEPH F. O'CALLAGHAN

Bibliography

Gil de Zamora, J. *De preconiis Hispaniae*. Ed. M. de Castro y Castro. Madrid, 1955.

GIL DE ZAMORA, JUAN, ON MUSIC

After accompanying the royal court to Seville in 1260, Juan Gil (Aegidius Zamorensis) served no later than 1278 as *scriptor suus* (secretary) to Alfonso X's son and heir Sancho IV. In 1295 Gil became *vicario provincial*, and in 1300 *ministro provincial* for Santiago province of his Franciscan Order. The Franciscan minister general, Giovanni Buralli of Parma (r. 1247–1257) commissioned him to write "a succinct and easily understood introduction to music—omitting already familiar music examples." During Giovanni of Parma's visit to Spain in 1248, he became lost one stormy evening in the mountains, thereafter asking that houses of the Franciscan order sing after compline the first nocturn of Our Lady's Office, which begins with the so-called *Benedicta* antiphon, then singing Psalm 66 and concluding with a prayer for the safety of prelates. Within Giovanni of Parma's musical context his asking the Spaniard Gil to write a music treatise becomes the more understandable.

In compliance with the minister-provincial's request for an elementary music treatise, Gil's seventeen chapters contain constant citations from Scripture. His musical authorities—later constantly invoked Boethius and Isidore—include Rabanus Maurus, Walfridus Strabo, Petrus Comestor and John of Afflighem. Like the latter, Gil distinguished between *musicus* and *cantor*, the mere singer being of a much lower order than the scientific musician. He assigns each of the eight modes a distinctive emotional property, mode 1 being suited to all sentiments (including those in the Song of Songs). Mode 2 expresses sad or melancholy sentiments (the Lamentations of Jeremiah), mode 3 voices severity or harshness, mode 4 caresses, mode 5 comforts the despairing, mode 6 conduces piety and contrition mode 7 expresses adolescent joyousness, and mode 8 varies between the sweet and the morose.

Gil's Spanish upbringing shows itself in his chapter 8 dealing with mutations. His use of the word *regula* to mean line on a staff is also a distinctively Spanish usage. In chapter 17 on instruments he mentions the *canon*, guitar, and *rabé*, instruments known in Spain but not mentioned by Isidore from whom he copies most of his observations on musical instruments. Peculiar to Gil is the oft-quoted warning that only the organ befits divine service, the other instruments having become sullied by their use in secular environs.

Bartholomaeus Anglicus shared a portion of Gil's treatise (*De proprietatibus rerum*, book 19, chapters 132–146), the same portion transmitted in John of Trevisa's 1398 English translation (published in London in 1495).

ROBERT STEVENSON

Bibliography

Atlas, A.W. *Music at the Aragonese Court of Naples*. (Cambridge, 1985). 200–203.

Massenkeil, G. *Mehrstimmige Lamentationum aus der ersten Hälfte des 16. Jahrhunderts*. Mainz, 1965).

Stevenson, R. "Iberian Musical Outreach Before the Encounter with the New World," *Inter-American Music Review*, 8, no. 2 (1987), 70–73.

GIRALDES, AFONSO

Afonso Giraldes is universally considered to be the author of the *Poema da batalha do Salado*, a laudatory poem about Afonso IV of Portugal, who participated, along with his son-in-law, Alfonso XI of Castile and León, in the Battle of Salado (1340). This work is written in octosyllabic quatrains rhyming *abab*, and reveals remarkable similarities with the *Poema de Alfonso XI*, written in 1348 by Rodrigo Yáñez, a poet probably of Leonese descent. The two texts share a similar purpose, employ the same metrical form, and contain identical lines, but still it cannot be affirmed that one author copied from the other. The length of the *Poema da batalha do Salado* is uncertain—only fifty-six lines have survived.

Both poems have been referred to by some critics as "rhymed chronicles," but such a classification seems inappropriate. It appears that both poets rely on their own memories of contemporary events, and that their common expressions belong to a stock of formulas from a powerful oral tradition. Perhaps it would be better to designate the poems as "new epics" that react against the excesses of the heroic epic, especially because both stem from a court tradition yet employ some devices of the traditional epic style.

MERCEDES VAQUERO

Bibliography

Vaquero, M. "The *Poema da batalha do Salado*: Some New Stanzas and the *Poema*'s Relation to Castilian and Latin Texts," *Portuguese Studies* 3 (1987), 56–69.

———. "Relación entre el *Poema de Alfonso XI* y el *Poema da batalha do Salado*." In *Actas del I Congreso de la Asociación hispánica de literatura medieval.* Ed. V. Beltrán. Barcelona, 1988. 581–93.

Vaquero, M. *Tradiciones orales en la historiografía de fines de la Edad Media.* Madison Wisc., 1990.

GIRONA, CERVERÍ DE

A thirteenth-century Catalan troubadour whose professional name was taken from the town where he was born (Cervera, in the province of Lleida), he once used his original name, Guillem de Cervera, when addressing a verse book of proverbs, *Proverbis*, to his sons. His large production, written in the second half of the century (before 1285), makes him the last great troubadour and is closely related to his poetical service to the Aragonese kings and princes, especially Jaime I the Conqueror and his son Pedro III. However, despite acting as an official troubadour, and not as a *joglar*, he was inclined to raise his voice to criticize political events of his time. This relates, rather than to the role of moral adviser he played in many poems dealing with the decline of courtly virtue, to an asserting of proud awareness of his status in the court.

The same can be said as regards his personal remarks on the subtlety of his *trobar ric*, and certainly most of his witty lyrics show off both his metric and his wordplay virtuosity, which was highly appreciated by later courtly poets, such as Andreu Febrer and Jordi de Sant Jordi. Generally his 119 poems (five of them are narratives) cover the widest range of troubadour styles, genres, and topics, and even include unique examples of minor genres, often drawing on traditional lyrics, as in his parallelistic *Viadeyra*, which is virtually a *chanson de malmariée*.

The gaiety of these pieces and of some *pastorelas* contrasts with much of his love poetry, as does the sentimentalism of the latter with his misogynist poems (his *maldit bendit*, for instance, was meaningfully quoted in Eiximenis's *Terç*). Cerverí's verse *Sermó* points to some clerical Latin learning, reinforced by the above-mentioned *Proverbis* or, among other pieces, by his splendid religious *Alba*.

LLUÍS CABRÉ

Bibliography

Riquer, M. de. *Obras completas del trovador Cerverí de Girona*. Barcelona, 1947.

———. "Cerverí de Girona." In *Història de la literatura catalana. Part antiga.* Vol. 10. Barcelona, 1984. 125–61.

GOLD, AFRICAN

The search for precious metals was one of the prime movers of early European expansion, and it goes without saying that only Spain and Portugal were in a position to achieve a supply of it from overseas before the end of the fifteenth century—Portugal from its African discoveries as early as mid-century and Spain from the Antilles, especially Hispaniola, Cuba, and Puerto Rico, in its very closing years. In both cases the gold appears to have been largely alluvial. The Portuguese never extracted theirs from areas under their control, but always traded for it—in contrast, the Spaniards conducted or supervised the panning or sluicing operations on a fairly extensive scale. In neither case are there reliable figures available on the amounts gained.

The African gold trade was far older than the Portuguese participation in it, and in fact is mentioned by Herodotus. It was always accompanied by the slave trade, but it was entirely a trans-Saharan caravan trade, or at least until Fez or one of the North African ports had been reached, especially Tripoli or Ceuta. From there, caravans carrying trading goods or food moved south along any of a number of Saharan routes, usually calling at the mid-desert salt mines of Taghaza, where they exchanged the food for salt. Then they proceeded to Timbuktu, where they traded their salt or other goods for slaves or gold, the gold having been obtained by another set of traders from the Niger basin in exchange for the salt in the famous transactions known as the "silent trade." Then the caravans returned by the same routes.

The Portuguese probably did not make significant inroads into this trade, but they did manage to syphon their gold supplies from much the same regions, though from the coastal regions—first from informal barter along the coasts, but soon after mid-century from a *feitoria* (trading post) on Arguin Island, which remained active until around 1505, and after 1482 at São Jorge da Mina, or, as it came to be called after its loss to the Dutch in 1642, Elmina, on the Gold Coast (modern Ghana). In both cases beads, cloth, mirrors, and manufactured metal objects were traded for the gold, as well as for slaves—in both cases through intermediaries. Exactly how much was traded remains unknown, but to judge from the coining of Portuguese gold *dobras* after mid-century, the amounts obtained must have been considerable. There appears to be little ground, however, for assertions that the trade dealt a significant economic blow to the Muslim "enemy" across the Straits of Gibraltar.

George D. Winiies

Bibliography

Bovill, E.W. *The Golden Trade of the Moors*. London, 1958.

Magalhães Godinho, V. *A economia dos descobrimentos henriquinos*. Lisbon, 1962.

GONÇALVES, NUNO

A Portuguese painter, Gonçalves (ca. 1425–ca. 1491) lived during the reigns of of four kings—João I, Duarte, Afonso V, and João II. These were the most eventful years of Portuguese history, when the country moved from the old feudal order into a precapitalist mercantile society. It was a period of great contrasts, of royal deaths and public festivals, enlivened by the exciting news of the navigations and the discovery of new lands. Gonçalves expressed in his paintings the mood and the spirit of his age. His masterpiece is the polyptych of St. Vincent in the Lisbon cathedral. It consists of six wood panels representing St. Vincent, patron of Lisbon, being worshiped by the king, the court, and various communities. This vast work, comprehending sixty figures, was produced between about 1467 and 1481. Its portraits are remarkable for the accuracy of the physical detail that reveals the characters of the subjects: merchants, knights, princes, kings, bishops, the lower clergy, and ordinary people. The polyptych, as it survives, is incomplete. The entire work probably was presented to the cathedral by Afonso V to commemorate his victories in Morocco. St. Vincent holds a missal open to a passage of the Gospel according to John (14:30–14:31), where the reference to the prince of the world, Satan, has been interpreted as an allusion to Islam.

Gonçalves produced other paintings and probably drew the scenes of the Pastrana tapestry, which shows Afonso V at Arzila. The monumental representation of the human figure, in contrast to his inability to work out the perspective, makes him a foremost painter of the fifteenth century. In recognition of his services, Afonso V knighted him around 1470. Gonçalves' portrait of Henrique "the Navigator" illustrates the entry on Henrique, Prince of Portugal in this encyclopedia.

Luis Rebelo

Bibliography

Belard da Fonseca, A. *O mistério dos painéis*. 5 vols. Lisbon, 1957–67.

Gusmão, A. de. *Nuno Gonçalves*. Lisbon, 1957.

Markl, D. *O essencial sobre Nuno Gonçalves*. Lisbon, 1987.

Santos, R. dos. *Nuno Gonçalves*. London, 1954.

GONZÁLEZ DE CLAVIJO, RUY

Fifteenth-century Castilian traveler born in Madrid (year uncertain). After Sotomayor and Palazuelos, who had been sent by Enrique III as ambassadors to the east, returned to Castile, the king called upon Clavijo to undertake an embassy to Tamburlain (Timur). Clavijo afterward wrote an account of the trip known under the title of *Embajada a Tamorlán*. It is the first known Castilian book of travels and includes both factual and fabulous information. Many of the places it names are difficult to determine with any precision. However, Clavijo departed from Seville in May 1403 in the company of two colleagues, one of whom was a theologian. They were loaded with gifts for Tamburlain. The ambassadors sailed the Mediterranean, reached Constantinople, traveled along the coast of the Black Sea, and landed at Trebizond, from whence they went to Tabriz, Teheran, and Meschud, arriving in Samarchand on 4 September 1404. There they were favorably received by Tamburlain, who, though mortally ill, nevertheless bestowed rich presents upon them. González de Clavijo was married to Mayor Arias, one of the few known women poets of the fifteenth century, who during her husband's absence wrote a lyrical address to the sea pleading for his safe passage and return. Upon returning to the Iberian Peninsula in 1406, Clavijo and his party proceeded directly to Alcalá de Henares, where the king conferred the title of chamberlain upon him in recognition of his exploits. After Enrique III's death Clavijo retired to Madrid, where he died in April 1412.

The account of González de Clavijo's travels, along with a brief biographical sketch, was first published at Seville in 1582 by Argote de Molina. Recent research into the *Embajada a Tamorlán* by López Estrada, however, has placed into question González de Clavijo's sole authorship, proposing that the bulk of the work was composed by Alfonso Páez de Santa María, the theologian who accompanied Clavijo on his embassy, and may even include material from Muhammad Alcagí, one of Tamburlain's envoys to Castile.

E. Michael Gerli

Bibliography

González de Clavijo, R. *Embajada a Tamorlán*. Ed. Francisco López Estrada. Madrid, 1943.

López Estrada, F. "Procedimientos narrativos en la Embajada a Tamorlán," *El Crotalón: Anuario de Filología Española* 1 (1984), 129–46.

Pérez Priego, M.A. "Estudio literario de los libros de viajes medievales." *Epos* 1 (1984), 217–39.

GONZÁLEZ DE MENDOZA, PEDRO

Lawyer, priest, statesman, patron of the arts, and operative head of Spain's most powerful clan, Pedro González de Mendoza (1420/1428–1495) was the fifth son of Catalina Suárez de Figueroa and Íñigo López de Mendoza, Marquis of Santillana. He studied civil and canon law at the University of Salamanca; responded to his father's request to translate into Castilian Virgil's *Aeneid*, celebrating the origins of the Roman empire; then became an architect of the Spanish Empire being referred to as "the Third King" during the reign of Fernando and Isabel.

González de Mendoza showed himself an able proponent of a strong monarchy and Spanish unity under Castilian hegemony while a member of Enrique IV's council, and in coming to support the succession of Isabel and Fernando against the young, single, and seemingly weaker claimant Juana, who may or may not have been Enrique's daughter. In 1476 Isabel legitimated his sons, Rodrigo, Diego, and Juan. Named archbishop of Seville and cardinal of Sancta Maria in Domini in 1473, González de Mendoza became archbishop of Toledo in 1485. Known as the Cardinal of Spain, advising Isabel in particular, he presided over the royal council for twenty years.

González de Mendoza's armies and money, and his role in requisitioning ecclesiastical wealth, were crucial in defeating the Portuguese, and in 1476 he emerged as hero of the decisive Battle of Toro, which assured Castile to Isabel. He prepared the way for reasserting royal authority in Seville, officiated at the baptism of Prince Juan, negotiated the neutrality of Louis XI of France, advised on peace terms with Portugal, enhanced royal revenues by revoking *juros* (bonds) issued during civil war in the reign of Enrique IV, then performed a range of services crucial to winning the war against Muslim Granada. González de Mendoza was nearly always at Isabel's side, and it was his great silver cross, placed atop the Alhambra, that signaled victory in 1492. He commissioned Rodrigo Alemán to carve the fifty-odd scenes of Muslim towns surrendering on the choir stalls in Toledo's cathedral. And he advised Isabel to sponsor the initial voyage of Christopher Columbus, arguing there was little to lose in providing three ships and perhaps much to gain.

González de Mendoza was the principal Spanish mediator with the papacy in the process of instituting the Spanish Inquisition. Earlier he had issued a pastoral letter (now lost) instructing clergy to catechize backsliding converts from Judaism. Hernando del Pulgar characterized him as a moderate opposed to inquisitorial methods. Yet although nondoctrinaire, worldly, and pragmatic, clearly he worked toward an exclusively Christian Spain, sanctioning force when persuasion failed. Powerful in patronage, he suggested that Isabel choose first Hernando de Talavera, and then Francisco Jiménez de Cisneros, as her confessor and adviser, and then that she select Jiménez as his successor both as archbishop of Toledo and as first minister. Ill with kidney disease for a year, he died in January 1495.

González de Mendoza amassed positions for his relatives and titles and fortunes for his sons, and supported religious and charitable foundations—the Church of the Holy Sepulcher in Jerusalem and the Church of the Holy Cross in Rome. He founded and endowed the Hospital de Santa Cruz in Toledo and the Colegio de Santa Cruz in Valladolid, where on the facade he had himself portrayed as donor, with balding head and sensible workaday face. Yet chronicles, other texts, art, and architecture belie that portrait's simplicity.

Peggy Liss

Bibliography

Medina Mendoza, F. de. "Vida del Cardenal D. Pedro González de Mendoza," *Memorial histórico español* 6 (1853): 151–310.

Salazar, P. de. *Cŕonica del gran Cardenal de España, don Pedro Gónzalez de Mendoza*. Toledo, 1625.

GONZÁLEZ, DOMINGO (DOMINICUS GUNDISALVUS)

Domingo González, or Dominicus Gundisalvus (or Gundisalinus, among other variants), Archdeacon of Segovia, was chief assistant to Raimundo I, Archbishop of Toledo, founder and driving force of the twelfth-century Toledo School of Translators. Gundisalvus's contemporaries associated with the school include John of Spain, a converted Jew and Gundisalvus's partner in translation, Hermann of Carinthia, Robert of Chester, Adelard of Bath, Walter of Malvern, Michael Scot, Hugo of Santalla, and other intellectual elites of western Europe. Gundisalvus was active in the second quarter of the twelfth century and is known both for translations and for original works extant in codices housed in the National Library in Paris.

Twelve known translations from Arabic into Latin that are due at least in part to his involvement include

Avicenna's (Ibn Sīnā) *Metaphysica Avicennae . . . sive de prima philosophia*, *Physicorum Avicennae liber primus*, *Liber de anima Avicennae*, *Liber Avicennae, de coelo et mundo*, *Logica Avicennae*, and *Liber Avicennae de ortu scientiarum*; (Al-Ghazālī's) *Physica*, *Logica*, *Metaphysica*, and *Philosphia*; Avicebron's *Fons vitae*; and al-Fārābī's *De scientiis*, the translation of which is also attributed to Gerard of Cremona. The prologue to his translation of Avicenna's *De anima* reveals the collaborative method of translation probably used in the School of Translators.

Given the essentially Aristotelian and (Neo-) Platonic thrust of his sources—Al-Fārābī, Avicenna, Avicebron, and Algazel—it cannot be too surprising that Gundisalvus should manifest the same thrust in his original philosophical writings, of which five are known: *De processione mundi*, *De anima*, *De unitate*, *De divisione philosophiae*, and *De inmortalitate animae*. The influence of his sources is so great that some maintain that these originals are little more than translations with elaborations. Although Gundisalvus distinguishes theology (*scientia divina*) from philosophy (*scientia humana*), Sarton provides the following maxim that makes Gundisalvus's view of philosophy patent: "nulla est scientia quae philosophiae not [*sic*] sit aliqua pars." Furthermore, Sarton presents, Gundisalvus's classification of knowledge as follows: propaedeutics (comprising grammar, poetics, and rhetoric), logic, and the sciences of wisdom (*scientiae sapientiae*). The *scientiae sapientiae* are divided into the theoretical and the practical: "The theoretical branches are (a) Physics (*scientia naturalis*), divided into *medicina*, *indicia*, *nigromantia*, *ymagines*, *agricultura*, *navigatio*, *specula*, *alquimia*; (b) Mathematics, divided into *arithmetica*, *geometria* (and optics), *musica*, *astrologia*, *scientia de aspectibus*, *de ponderibus*, *de ingeniis*; (c) Metaphysics. The practical branches are politics, economics and ethics." Sarton observes that the writings of subsequent philosophers—Michael Scot, Albert the Great, and Robert Kilwardby—reflect Gundisalvus's classification in their own writings.

Gundisalvus's primary contribution can be summarized, then, as his having transmitted, from Arabic culture to Western Christendom, Arabic Aristotelianism combined with (Neo)Platonism, filtered to some extent through Christian theology.

ANTHONY CÁRDENAS

Bibliography

Menéndez y Pelayo, M. "Entrada del panteísmo semítico en las escuelas cristianas: Domingo Gundisalvo, Juan Hispalense, El español Mauricio." In *Historia de los heterodoxos españoles*. Vol. 3, sec. 2, *Ciencias*. Buenos Aires, 1945. 99–151.

Sarton, G. "The Translators (First Half of Twelfth Century). I. From Arabic into Latin." In *Introduction to the History of Science*. Vol. 2, *From Rabbi ben Ezra to Roger Bacon*, 1. Baltimore, 1931. 167–81.

GONZÁLEZ, FERNÁN

Fernán González (ca. 910–970), "first count of Castile," gained Castile's independence from the kingdom of León through military skill, luck, and shrewd political maneuvering. His popularity can be seen in the large number of ballad, poetic, and chronicle sources that describe his exploits and make him the most famous Castilian hero next to El Cid.

During the dynastic dispute that followed the death of Ordoño II of León (924), Fernán González supported Ramiro II over his older brother, Alfonso IV (the Monk) as king of León. The strength of the alliance was recognized by Queen Toda of Navarre when she arranged the marriage of her daughter Sancha to Fernán in 932 and her daughter Urraca to Ramiro II.

While supporting Ramiro II, Fernán distinguished himself in battle against the Moors at Toledo (933), Osma (934), and Simancas (939). As Fernán founded and protected monasteries, and expanded his territory, he began using the title *gratia Dios comes* (count by the grace of God), suggesting a hereditary title and not a temporary grant by the king of León. Ramiro, fearing that Fernán was not acknowledging his feudal bonds, intervened by sending his son, Prince Sancho the Fat, to harass Castile and capture Fernán González. In 944, the count was imprisoned until his wife and vassals finally gained his release. After his release Fernán demonstrated his loyalty to Ramiro by marrying his daughter Urraca to Ramiro's son Ordoño III.

Fernán González was at the peak of his power in the mid-tenth century. By 947 he was again using the title "count by the grace of God," and upon Ramiro II's death in 951, Fernán's daughter became queen of León. However, Ordoño III died without heir in 956, and the count's enemy, Sancho the Fat, claimed the throne. Unwilling to allow the ravager of Castile to sit on the throne, Fernán González married his widowed daughter to the son of Alfonso IV and installed him as Ordoño IV while Sancho was on a weight reduction visit in Pamplona. Ordoño IV ruled for two years until a slimmer Sancho I returned and forced Ordoño to flee in 960. Fernán González was thrown in prison a second time (960–962) and released only through the intervention of his mother-in-law, Queen Toda, who wanted to put down a revolt by Fernán's loyal vassals and, perhaps, to ensure that her grandson would inherit the title Count of Castile. Upon his release the count arranged his daughter's divorce from Ordoño IV and married her to the heir of the Navarrese throne. The now widowed Fernán wed the daughter of King García II Sánchez of Navarre and spent the rest of his life in relative peace.

Though only a handful of documents mention the historical Fernán González, the legendary figure appears in numerous ballad, poetic and narrative sources. The best known of these is the *Poema de Fernán González*, written about 1250 by a monk from the Benedictine monastery of San Pedro de Arlanza. Prosified versions of the *Poema* also appear in the *Primera crónica general* and the *Crónica General de 1344*. Unlike the historical figure, the poetic Count Fernán is a crusader who wins much land from the Moors and gains Castile's independence from the kingdom of León through a shrewd economic deal. He is married only once, to Doña Sancha, who helps him escape from prison twice. Regardless of the activities of the historical count, the presence of the fictional count in poems, ballads, and chronicles suggests a strong and lasting fascination with Fernán González, first count of Castile.

CHAD WIGHT

Bibliography

Márquez-Sterling, M. *Fernán González, First Count of Castile: The Man and the Legend*. Romance Monographs 40. Valencia, 1980.

Menéndez y Pelayo, M. "Tratado de los romances viejos." In Vol. 11. *Antología de poetas líricos castellanos*. Madrid, 1903.

Menéndez Pidal, R. *Reliquias de la poesía épica española*. Madrid, 1951.

O'Callaghan, J. F. *A History of Medieval Spain*. Ithaca, N.Y., 1987.

Pérez de Urbel, J. *El condado de Castilla*. Vol. 2. Madrid, 1970.

Poema de Fernán González, Edición facsimil del manuscrito depositado en el monasterio de el Escorial. Burgos, 1989.

West, B. *Epic, Folk, and Christian Traditions in the Poema de Fernán González*. Potomac, Md., 1983.

Zamora Vicente, A. (ed.) *Poema de Fernán González*. Madrid, 1963.

GOTHS *See* GERMANIC INVASIONS

GOVERNMENT *See* ADMINISTRATION

GRAN CONQUISTA DE ULTRAMAR, LA

The only Castilian chronicle about the Crusades, *La gran conquista de Ultramar* is a long work that survives in four manuscripts (1187, 1920, and 2454, Biblioteca Nacional de Madrid; 1698, Biblioteca Universitaria de Salamanca) and a print version (Salamanca, 1503), yet none of the manuscripts is complete. In fact, together they cover only about 73.5 percent of the text; 26.5 percent of the text is covered exclusively by the Salamanca print, the sole complete version of the work. In addition to a number of partial editions of the work, which transcribe most of the manuscripts, there are two complete editions. The first, by Pascual de Gayangos (Madrid, 1858), follows the Salamanca print and manuscript 1187. The second, by Louis Cooper (Bogotá, 1979), follows the Salamanca print alone. The *Conquista* was included, in a condensed form, in the fifteenth-century Galician *Crónica general de 1404*, an interesting chronicle, yet to be edited, that also includes several Arthurian legends (Hispanic Society of America, B2278).

The most studied issue regarding the *Conquista* is the matter of its author. The Salamanca print attributes the work to Alfonso X, an attribution never questioned until Gayangos, in the prologue to his edition, argued against it and in favor of a much later date of composition, which he placed in the fourteenth century. Although many of his arguments were not accepted by the critics, who settled the question by attributing the work to Sancho IV, its basic line of reasoning prevailed. Gayangos discovered that except for the attribution clause, the text of the prologue was the same as that of the *Bocados de oro*. This caused him to conclude that the editor of the *Conquista* had copied the prologue from that work. However, although the *Bocados de oro* dates from before the *Conquista*, its prologue appears to be a fifteenth-century addition, so it is difficult to know which work borrowed it from the other, or if they both borrowed it from a third source. In any event, even if the prologue had been borrowed at some point, that would not necessarily mean the accompanying attribution clause, present in the *Conquista* but not in the *Bocados de oro*, was false. Gayangos thinks it is, because the oldest manuscript, 1187, attributes the work to Sancho IV. However, this manuscript covers only the end of the work. Therefore, its attribution does not guarantee that Sancho was also the author of the beginning of the work. Indeed, manuscript 1920, which also attributes the work to Sancho IV, says he ordered the scribe to translate this work "from the conquest of Antioch on." This could mean that was the portion of the work done by the scribe, but also mean that it was the portion of the work undertaken by Sancho. Since manuscript 1698 attributes the work to Alfonso X, this attribution cannot be a forgery by the editor of the Salamanca print.

Operating with positivistic presuppositions, Gayangos did not take into account the way medieval chronicles were composed: by different kings and scribes over a long period of time. The attributions to Alfonso X and Sancho IV are not really contradictory, for it is perfectly possible, and in fact most likely, that the project was conceived and started by the father, continued by the son, and finished at a later date. This would make sense, since Alfonso, in addition to having a known passion for writing chronicles, was clearly obsessed with the Holy Land and dreamed about leading a European crusade, following in Louis IX's steps, as he showed in his letters and wills, as well as in the *Cantigas*. His capture, in the first years of his reign, of the North African city of Salé, shows his early interest in the project. This interest seems to have increased in the last years of his life, when, in all probability, he ordered the composition of the *Conquista* out of frustration, nostalgia, and hope.

This chronicle, which is a translation not only of the *Eracles*, but also of several French epics about the Crusades, all combined in Alfonso X's customary style, begins with the uprising of Muḥammad and ends with Louis IX's expeditions to North Africa, the enterprise Alfonso so much wanted to continue. The most famous part of the work is the Swan Knight episode, which has traditionally been considered a chivalric romance (fiction) included in a chronicle (history). However, according both to recent theories of historiography and to medieval views on the matter, chronicles must be read as a whole and cannot be divided into "historical" and "fictional" parts. When approached in this manner, the links between this episode and the rest of the chronicle become obvious. The Swan Knight is a chivalric archetype, and Godfrey of Bouillon's life follows it faithfully. In the *Conquista* the successes and failures of the Christians in the Holy Land are presented as depending on their following or deviating from the chivalric model offered by the Swan Knight and his grandson, Godfrey of Bouillon. This provides an explanation for their rather depressing defeats and a recipe for much-desired victories at the same time. This work is, therefore, a chivalric chronicle. Its structure was reproduced in *Amadís de Gaula* and the chivalric romances of the Golden Age, which are basically long accounts of the ups and downs of knights involved in crusade-like adventures in distant lands. Alfonso X's great love for chivalry is well documented. In his other chronicles he included chivalric episodes, such as the tale of Pirus in the *Estoria de España* and the tale of Bruto in the *General estoria*. In *La gran conquista de Ultramar*, he did the same thing, only on a larger scale, as was called for by the more chivalric framework of this chronicle, the subject of which was the closest to his heart.

CRISTINA GONZÁLEZ

Bibliography

González, C. *La tercera crónica de Alfonso X: "La gran conquista de Ultramar*. London, 1992.

Stresau, C. "*La gran conquista de ultramar*: Its Sources and Composition." Ph.D. diss. University of North Carolina, 1977.

GRANADA, CITY OF

Granada was founded as a walled city in the turbulent period following the collapse of the Islamic caliphate in the eleventh century. ʿAbd Allah ibn Buluggīn, last of the Zīrid line there, tells in his memoirs how his forebear Zāwī ibn Zīri had proposed to the inhabitants of Elvira, capital of that region (*kūra*) in caliphal times, the selection of a suitable nearby hilltop defensive position (*maqil*) to which they, together with him and his Sanhāja Berbers, should move. To these original Andalusi and Berber elements was added a considerable Jewish presence, and Bargebuhr has argued that the oldest parts of the Alhambra incorporate the palace of the Jewish minister Joseph ibn Naghrilla. Under the Zīrids, Granada flourished as capital of their *tā'ifa* state, and this prosperity continued under the Almoravids and Almohads. After the Almohad rule collapsed, and with Christian forces perilously close, dignitaries from the city invited the caudillo of Arjona, Muḥammad ibn Naṣr, to enter, which he did in 1238. The city began to expand as Muslim refugees flocked in from areas falling to the Christians.

Making use of old Zīrid fortifications, Muḥammad soon converted the Alhambra hill into a palace-citadel of great defensive strength (and incomparable beauty) that would serve the Naṣrid dynasty he founded until the end, in 1492. The city proper (*madīna*) lay below, with the principal public buildings: the mosque (the cathedral now occupies the site); the caravanserai (*funduq*) for merchants, in the building now known as the Corral del Carbón; the covered market or *alcaicería* (Arabic, *al-qaysariyya*, the word for officially administered markets in a number of cities, not just in Granada); the hospital (*maristan*); the college (*madrāsa*) founded in 1349. The city's economic prosperity rested in part on the trade in locally produced silk, and on its processing and weaving; the industry was carefully regulated by a powerful trade guild.

Walled suburbs (Arabic, *rabād*; plural, *arbād*) spread over the hills of Granada's magnificent site; one in the south was called Najd (Uplands, perhaps to recall a place-name in the Arabian Peninsula). Some quarters had names indicating the principal occupation of the inhabitants (e.g., *Al-Fakhkharīn*, "of the potters"); others, the place of origin of the original inhabitants (e.g., Antequeruela, settled by refugees from

Antequera after 1410). The existence of strong walls, not only around the whole city but also between one *rabād* and another, was of particular importance in the final period, when factional discord brought internecine strife.

Watered by aqueducts and other channels, broad green zones planted with trees, and interspersed with pleasure palaces and summer residences (of which the Generalife is an outstanding surviving example), surrounded the city. Irrigation reached up to levels abandoned to *secano* (dry lands) in modern times.

Population in Zīrid times has been estimated at 26,000. Under the Naṣrids immigration took the figure much higher. The estimate for 1492 of 40,000, given by Andrés Bernáldez, the curate of Los Palacios, is very low, and presumably refers only to remaining permanent residents. L. Marineus Siculus speaks of 150,000, a high figure presumably reflecting the influx of troops and of refugees. For the German traveler Munzer, in Granada shortly after the surrender, there was no greater city in Europe or in Africa. There is an unresolved controversy both with regard to the exact spatial relationship of Granada to earlier cities thereabouts (Ilibira, Qastiliya, Illiberis) and to the antiquity and etymology of the name Granada. That a place-name Garnata existed before the Zīrid foundation is clear. Pocklington reviews the bibliography on the etymology very fully and argues that Garnata is of Romance origin, from *granata*, not in the primary sense of "pomegranate," but rather in the derived sense of "red" (because of the local soil). It seems unlikely that this debate is closed.

L. PATRICK HARVEY

Bibliography

Bargebuhr, F.P. *The Alhambra: A Cycle of Studies on the Eleventh Century in Moorish Spain*. Berlin, 1968.

Gallego Burín, A. *Granada: Guía artística e histórica de la ciudad*. Granada, 1982.

Gómez-Moreno González, M. "*Guía de Granada*. Granada, 1892; facsimile ed., Granada, 1982.

Grabar, O. *The Alhambra*. London, 1978.

Pocklington, R. "La etimología del topónimo 'Granada'," *Al-Qānṭara* 9 (1988), 375–402.

Torres Balbás, L. "Esquema demográfico de la ciudad de Granada." *Al-Andalus* 21 (1956), 131–46.

———. *Ciudades hispano-musulmanas*. 2d ed. Madrid, 1985.

GRANADA, KINGDOM OF

The Berber *ṭāʾifa* kingdom of Granada was created by Zāwī ibn Zīrī, and, after his return to North Africa in 1020, it continued to be ruled by his family until the Almoravids deposed ʿAbd Allāh (b. Buluggīn) in 1090.

The kingdom of Granada again achieved autonomy in the mid-thirteenth century, but now it was the sole surviving Islamic state (it covered, beside the modern province of Granada, that of Málaga and Ronda, as well as parts of Jaén and other areas). The dynasty that ruled it up to 1492, the Banū'l-Aḥmar or Banū Naṣr, came from Arjona, where, in 1232, they had made a reputation for themselves rallying their fellow Muslims to the *jihād*. In the years immediately following, their campaigns were scattered (in Jaén, Córdoba, Seville, Jerez), and had no lasting effect, but in Granada the activities of Muḥammad Ibn al-Aḥmar found the necessary focus. Orthodox Muslim opinion disapproved of Muslims remaining as subjects of Christian rulers, so large numbers of the pious, especially the well-to-do and the well-educated, emigrated to the kingdom of Granada. The resettlement of so many refugees posed many problems, but the prosperity which this mountain kingdom was to achieve rested on the basis of the presence there of a large skilled population committed to wresting a living from difficult terrain by intensive methods of agriculture.

While elsewhere Romance speech and Arabic coexisted; in Granada, however only Arabic was spoken. And since the inhabitants were those who had opted to live in an Islamic state, this was a pious society where men of religion, the ʿulamāʾ and *fuqahā'*, enjoyed prestige and power. It was a culturally cohesive and monoglot nation state. In some places—Granada itself, Málaga, and, above all, Lucena—there were large Jewish communities, but of the other *dhimmīs*, the Christians, we hear little, and indeed nothing is known of surviving Mozarabic Christians; such Christians as there were came from outside: slaves, resident foreigners, fugitives from justice.

The key to the survival of the kingdom of Granada through the difficult early days lay in the deal struck between Muḥammad I and Fernando III of Castile at Jaén in 1246. All Christian sources agree that Muḥammad became the vassal of the Castilian monarch, and thereafter provided sustained military help to him in his enterprises—at the conquest of Seville, for example. At Fernando's death in 1252, Muḥammad and all his people mourned. In the Castilian view, a permanent bond was established, and the kingdom of Granada acquired an indelible vassal status. For Granada to pursue an independent policy thereafter was treasonable. There is no indication that the Granadans shared this view at all. In Islamic law, a ruler is not able to place himself, still less his Muslim subjects, in permanent subordination to a Christian monarch. To protect its independence Granada needed to find a North African counterbalance to the power of the Christians. The danger was that, as in 1090, protectors would become dominant masters. The principal skill required of the rulers of the Granadan state was the ability to juggle alliances, and at times the rapid switches of alignment which proved necessary are disconcerting.

During the late thirteenth and early fourteenth centuries it was the Marīnids who provided most of the military assistance. Their first large-scale intervention came in 1275, when 5,000 cavalry crossed from Tangier, and from then onward there were North Africans fighting in almost all the campaigns, sometimes in their own formations, occupying territory as their own, sometimes in units incorporated into the Granadan forces, sometimes as individual volunteers motivated by the duty to sustain the *jihād*. Without North African assistance, it is difficult to imagine that Granada would have survived as long as it did.

Muḥammad I died in a riding accident and was succeeded by his son Muḥammad II (1273–1302). Such stability is difficult to match in later reigns. Muḥammad II possessed a strong but warped personality: there is a strong suspicion that he murdered his own father. His short reign was brought to an end by public indignation at insane policies that led Granada into conflict not only with Aragón and Castile, but with the Marīnids as well. The reign of Naṣr (1309–1314) was not without its successes: a determined Aragonese onslaught on Almería was beaten off, but the loss of Gibraltar to the Castilians was much lamented. In 1314, power passed for the first time away from the line of Muḥammad I to a collateral branch. Ismāʿīl (1314–1325) had presented to him a great opportunity when the foolhardy Castilian regents, Pedro and Juan, exposed their forces rashly near to Granada itself and suffered an ignominious defeat. Ismāʿīl's aggressive policies seemed vindicated, but he was to die in an affray inside the Alhambra. It was his youngest son, Muḥammad IV (1325–1333) who was proclaimed ruler by the minister Ibn al-Maḥrūq. Far from bearing this minister gratitude, Muḥammad had him assassinated before three years' time, allegedly because he was in negotiation with the Castilians. Thus did the history of the kingdom of Granada settle into a bloody pattern according to which changes of government were brought about by assassination. That the state was to survive in spite of this for another century and a half is due, in large measure, to the political genius of Yūsuf I (1333–1354). His was a golden age of Granadan culture, and some of the finest of the buildings of the Alhambra stand as his monument. Although Granada experienced some reverses, notably at Salado in 1340, Yūsuf seems not to have been held responsible. His reign ended when a madman stabbed him to death in the mosque.

Muḥammad V came to the throne in 1354 and his reign closed with his death in 1391, but this span of thirty-seven years was interrupted by the reigns of Ismāʿīl II and Muḥammad VI. Such interrupted reigns are a peculiar feature of Granadan political life. A political faction could launch a coup with success, but their creature could not consolidate his grasp on power. Another feature of this coup that was to be repeated was the role played by one of the powerful ladies of the royal family, Maryam, one of the wives of Yūsuf I. Ismāʿīl II (1359) is described as soft and effeminate. Muḥammad VI, who replaced him, is portrayed with equal hostility, as coarse and lacking in refinement, ready to roll up his sleeves and to go about bareheaded. His misfortune was that an even tougher prince, Pedro the Cruel of Castile, held a grudge against him. Most unwisely Muḥammad VI cast himself on Pedro's mercy in Seville: Pedro had none, and chopped off his head. In 1362 Muḥammad V could thus take over the kingdom once more: he was to remain in power for nearly thirty years.

Yūsuf II succeeded his father without violence in 1391, but his short reign proved a bloodbath. He had a faithful minister, Khālid, hacked to pieces before his own eyes, and three of his brothers met their death. His own death is alleged to have come when he put on a poisoned tunic, a gift from the King of Fez.

A policy of negotiating truces with the Castilians in return for tribute had given the Granadans in the late fourteenth century the peace that enabled them to build up their economic strength. Yūsuf II's younger son and successor, Muḥammad VII (1392–1408) refused to pay for truces. Blood now flowed on the frontiers. When he died, in 1408, his elder brother, brought out of prison in Salobreña to reign, tried to negotiate for peace once more, but facing him was Fernando, to be known as *el de Antequera*. Yūsuf pointed to the harm both sides suffered from "pointless loss of life and property inflicted on great knights and good men." If Yūsuf wanted peace, Fernando countered, let him acknowledge himself a vassal of Castile "and pay the tribute which they used to give to Alfonso the son of Fernando who conquered Seville." This in essence was the Castilian position from this point on: vassalage or nothing.

The period following the death of Yūsuf II provides an extreme example of multiple interlocking reigns. Muḥammad IX came to the throne in 1417, but in following years power was to pass between Muḥammad X and XI and Yūsuf IV and V. The initial impression is of extreme political instability, but if we note that over a period of thirty-five years one ruler (Muḥammad IX) ruled for twenty-seven years; another (Muḥammad VIII) for four; and the other three for less than a year apiece, Granada may appear less volatile than many other states. Muḥammad IX stood out against the Castilian demands that their suzereinty be recognized, and so the Castilians sought to replace him by puppets who did not prove acceptable to the Granadan people. It was Muḥammad IX's desire to arrange for the transfer of power after his death to his own nominee, but a rival claimant emerged: Saʿd (Cirizá in Castilian sources). From 1455 Saʿd was to rule without a rival until in 1464 his own son, Abū'l-Ḥasan ʿAlī rose against him. Abū'l-Ḥasan and then his brother al-Zagal were to provide aggressive leadership until very near the end for the people of this beleaguered kingdom. Romantic history seeks to connect the fall of Granada with Abū'l-Ḥasan's turbulent private life: his alleged preference for the beautiful Isabel de Solís over his noble Arab first wife. No doubt harem politics had some impact on the conduct of public affairs, but the kingdom of Granada fell because, on the one hand, the sustained policy of the Castilians of wrecking Granadan agriculture by destructive raids (*talas*) was finally having the desired effect, and, on the other, the Castilian crown had at last found the determination and the means to keep sufficient troops, and sufficient artillery, in the field for long enough to batter down the defenses of the principal Granadan strongholds. At a time when the new artillery was swinging the balance in favor of those who attacked, the defenders of Granada's castles found it difficult to hold out.

The one monarch so far unmentioned is Muḥammad Abū ʿAbd Allāh (Boabdil). It is highly likely that the Castilians intended to use this prince as a malleable puppet in order to outmaneuver the "old king" Abū'l-Ḥasan, and indeed in 1492 it was Boabdil who finally handed over the keys to the Alhambra. But Boabdil's motives were enigmatic, and his actions at times under siege were heroic. The capitulations he negotiated would have provided protection for his people if the Castilians had kept their part of the bargain. The problems that arose came after the kingdom of Granada had ceased to exist, when there were no sanctions that could be invoked against those who broke their word. The existence of a Muslim kingdom of Granada had been the ultimate guarantee of the rights of Muslims throughout the Iberian Peninsula for a quarter of a millennium. The rapidity with which forcible conversion to Christianity followed after 1492 was a clear demonstration of how necessary to the Muslim cause the existence of this kingdom had been.

L. PATRICK HARVEY

Bibliography

ʿAbd Allah (b. Buluggin). *Kitab al-tibyan*. Arabic text under title *Mudhakkirat al-amir ʿAbd Allah*. Ed. Lévi Provençal, E. Dar al-maʿarif, Cairo, 1955; trans. García Gómez, F. *El siglo XI en Iª persona*. Madrid, 1980. Tibi, A., *The Tibyan*. Leiden, 1986.

Arié, R. *L'Espagne musulmane au temps des Nasrides: 1232–1492*. Paris, 1973.

Harvey, L.P. *Islamic Spain, 1250–1500*. Chicago, 1990.

Ladero Quesada, M.A. *Castilla y la conquista del Reino de Granada*. Granada, 1987.

——— *Granada: historia de un país islámico*. 2d ed. Madrid, 1979.

Peinado Santaella, R.G., and J.E. López de Coca Castañer. *Historia de Granada*. Vol. 2, *Lá época medieval: siglos VIII–XV*. Granada, 1987.

Seco de Lucena Paredes, L. *Muhammad IX, sultán de Granada*. Alhambra, 1978.

GRANDE *See* NOBLES AND NOBILITY

GUADALETE, BATTLE OF

Guadalete is the name most commonly glven to the battle between the Visigothic king Roderic and the invading army of Arabs and Berbers led by Tāriq ibn Ziyād. In this encounter, fought almost certainly in 711, the Arabs were victorious, thus opening the way to their rapid conquest of Spain. Arab sources are almost unanimous in locating the battle at a site called Wadilaqqa, but the identification of this with the valley of the Guadalete River, between Medina Sidonia and Jerez de la Frontera, was first made in the *De rebus Hispaniae* of Archbishop Rodrigo Jiménez de Rada and has not always been accepted by modern historians. Some have preferred to locate the battle in the vicinity of the Laguna de Janda, south of Medina Sidonia. However, it is not clear how much weight should be given to any Arab accounts of the battle, which are heavily laden with legendary accretions and none of which dates in present form to before the eleventh century. The near contemporary Christian Latin Chronicle of 754 merely locates the battle in "the Transductine Promontories." This source also makes the battle part of a longer and more complex Arab and Berber campaign in Spain in 711–712 than the simple invasion and decisive victory that the Arab histories imply. In the legendary historical traditions of the Asturian kingdom, contained principally in the two versions of the *Chronicle of Alfonso III*, Roderic's defeat is attributed to the treasonable actions of the two sons of his predecessor, Wittiza. This needs to be regarded with considerable skepticism.

ROGER COLLINS

Bibliography

Collins, R. *The Arab Conquest of Spain, 710–797*. Oxford, 1989.

Sánchez-Albornoz, C. "Guadalete." In his *Orígenes de la nación española*: *El reino de Asturias*. Vol. 1. Oviedo, 1972. 271–317.

GUDIEL, GONZALO PÉREZ

One of thirteenth-century Castile's outstanding churchmen, successively the bishop of Cuenca (1272) and Burgos (1275), the archbishop of Toledo (1280) and the cardinal-bishop of Albano (1298). He was a confidant and counselor to both Alfonso X and Sancho IV, a rare achievement that testifies to the diplomatic skills he had acquired in his years abroad (during which he was active at the papal curia and figured as rector of the University of Padua). He came from a Mozarab family and was the first of that descent since 1085 to achieve the highest office in the Castilian church. As notary for Castile and chancellor during the critical years of Alfonso X's reign, he was well placed, and (if the contents of his remarkable library provide any guide) no less qualified to assist in all departments of that king's intellectual endeavors—legal, historical, and scientific. His domination during Sancho's reign seems to have been even more complete. However, the reaction after the latter's death involved Gudiel's political marginalization: the *corte* (parliament) of Valladolid (1295) marked the low point of his fortunes. But from this he made a triumphant recovery. Summoned to Rome in disgrace, on arriving there he received the red hat. The Maecenas of his generation, he counted among his intellectual intimates both Jofre de Loaisa and Ferrán Martínez, author of the *Libro de caballero Zifar*, the prologue to which records the return of the cardinal's corpse to his native city.

PETER LINEHAN

Bibliography

Hernández, F. J. "Noticias sobre Jofre de Loaisa y Ferrán Martínez," *Revista Canadiense de Estudios Hispánicos* 4 (1980), 281–309.

Linehan, P. *History and the Historians of Medieval Spain* Oxford 1993, chaps. 13–14.

GUESCLIN, BERTRAND DU

Known in fourteenth-century Castilian sources as Bertrán Claquín (because of mythical Muslim ancestry), Guesclin occupies an important place in French history and lore not unlike Castile's Cid Campeador. His exploits on the battlefield in defense of king and honor are celebrated in chronicle and verse; he is portrayed as patriotic and loyal, fierce and courageous, just, eloquent, and wise. This reputation notwithstanding, Guesclin, like Díaz de Vivar, was primarily a highly successful mercenary.

Born around 1314 in Motte-Broon to a family of the lesser nobility of Brittany, he distinguished himself for his courage and military prowess during a period of European history—the Hundred Years' War—that afforded him ample professional opportunities. He excelled as commander of mercenary troops. Left idle by a truce between the English and the French, the main antagonists of the war, Guesclin twice signed on to lead armies into Castile to help Enrique de Trastámara usurp the throne from his half brother, King Pedro I. Financing for these ventures came mostly from the papacy in Avignon and King Charles V; they were eager to rid France of the disruptive and violent presence of large bands of unemployed soldiers and to install a pro-France ruler in Castile.

Guesclin first entered Castile in early 1366 at the head an international force of some ten thousand mercenaries, and by March, Enrique was crowned king of Castile. Guesclin returned to France, only to be recalled by Enrique the following year when Pedro I reentered Castile from forced exile, followed by ten thousand English soldiers.

On 3 April 1367, at the battle of Nájera, Pedro carried the day. Enrique escaped to France; Guesclin was taken prisoner but was soon freed. Pedro's victory proved ephemeral. His English allies left the peninsula, and he was outnumbered when Enrique reappeared in the fall of of 1367 and was later joined by Guesclin. A few miles south of Toledo, the two armies met again. Pedro, routed, sought refuge at the fortress of Montiel, from which he negotiated his escape with Guesclin. Instead, the French commander delivered Pedro to Enrique, who stabbed Pedro to death on 23 March 1369.

Guesclin, rich with Castilian titles and lands, returned to his native land and was appointed constable of France in 1370. He sold his Castilian holdings back to Enrique II and spent the rest of his life in the service of the French until his death from illness, at age sixty-six, during a siege in Languedoc on 13 July 1380. He was buried at St. Denis with great honors.

CLARA ESTOW

Bibliography

Cuvelier, Jean. *Chronique de Bertrand du Guesclin*. Edited by E. Charrière. 2 vols. Paris, 1839.

Delachenal, R. *Histoire de Charles V*. 5 vols. Paris, 1909–31.

GUILDS *See* COFRADÍA

GUZMÁN, DOMINGO DE

Domingo's birth at Calaruega, Castile, about 1170 and his infancy were said to have been attended by marvels forecasting his sanctity and great achievements. From the ages of seven to fourteen he studied under the tutelage of his uncle, the archpriest Gumiel de Izán. In 1184 Domingo entered the University of Palencia, where he remained as a student for ten years. On one occasion he sold his books to help the poor and homeless of Palencia. His biographer, Bartholomew of

Trent, says that he twice tried to sell himself into slavery to raise money to free captives held by the Moors.

The date of Domingo's ordination to the priesthood is unknown. He was a student at Palencia when Martín de Bazán, bishop of Osma, called him to be a member of the cathedral chapter and to assist in its reform. In recognition of his success, Domingo was appointed subprior of the reformed chapter. On the accession of Diego de Azevedo to the bishopric of Osma in 1201, Domingo became prior of the chapter. As a canon of Osma, he spent nine years in contemplation, scarcely ever leaving the chapter house. In 1203 King Alfonso IX of Castile deputized the bishop of Osma to ask for the hand of a Danish princess on behalf of his son, Prince Fernando. The bishop chose Domingo to accompany him. Passing through Toulouse, they witnessed with consternation the effects of the Albigensian heresy. As a result Domingo conceived the idea of founding an order for combating heresy and spreading the Gospel by preaching throughout the world. After completing their mission in 1204, Diego and Domingo went to Rome, and from there they were sent by Pope Innocent III to join forces with the Cistercians, who had been entrusted with the crusade against the Albigensians. The pair quickly saw that the failure of the Cistercians was due to the monks' indulgent habits, and prevailed upon them to adopt a more austere life. The result was a greatly increased number of converts. Theological disputations played a prominent part in the preaching to the heretics, and Domingo and his companion lost no time in engaging in them. Unable to refute his arguments or counteract the influence of his preaching, the heretics often made Domingo the target of insults and threats.

Domingo realized the need for an institution that would protect women from the influence of the heretics. Many of them had already embraced Albigensianism and were among its most active advocates. With the permission of Foulque, bishop of Toulouse, he established a convent for women at Prouille in 1206. To this community he gave the rule and constitution that to the present day guide the nuns of the Second Order of Saint Dominic. On 15 January 1208 Pierre de Castelnau, a Cistercian legate, was assassinated, an event that precipitated the Albigensian Crusade under Simon de Montfort and led to the temporary subjugation of the heretics. During the crusade Domingo followed the Catholic army, seeking to revive religion and reconcile heretics in the cities that capitulated to Montfort. In September 1209 he came into direct contact with Montfort and formed a close friendship that would last until Montfort's death at Toulouse in 1218. Montfort regarded his victory at Muret as a miracle attributable to Domingo's prayers. Domingo's reputation for sanctity, apostolic zeal, and learning made him a much sought-after candidate for various bishoprics, all of which he refused, preferring to preach. The foundation of the Inquisition, and his appointment as the first inquisitor, is ascribed to Domingo during this period, although there is evidence to indicate that the Inquisition was functioning as early as 1198.

By 1214 the influence of Domingo's preaching and his reputation for holiness had drawn a group of disciples around him. The time was right for the realization of his desire to found a religious order to propagate the faith and combat heresy. With the approval of Bishop Foulque of Toulouse, who made him chaplain of Fanjeaux in July 1215, he organized and canonically established a community of followers as a religious congregation whose mission was the propagation of true doctrine and good morals, and the eradication of heresy. Pierre Seilan, a wealthy citizen of Toulouse, placed himself under Domingo's direction and put his large house at Domingo's disposal. There the first convent of the future Order of Preachers (now known as the Dominicans) was established on 25 April 1215.

In November 1215 an ecumenical council convened in Rome to deliberate on the improvement of morals, the extinction of heresy, and the strengthening of the faith, an agenda identical to the mission of Domingo's new order. Along with the bishop of Toulouse, Domingo went to Rome to petition that his new order carry out the mandates of the council. His request, however, was not granted. Returning to Languedoc in December 1215, he informed his followers of the council's mandate that there be no new rules for religious orders. As a result the community adopted the rule of St. Augustine, which, because of its generality, easily lent itself to any form they might wish. In August 1216 Domingo returned to Rome and appeared before Pope Honorius III to solicit confirmation for his order. The bull of confirmation was issued on 22 December 1216.

In 1218, to facilitate the spread of the order, Pope Honorius III addressed a bull to all archbishops, bishops, abbots, and priors, requesting them to show favor toward the Order of Preachers. Later Honorius bestowed the Church of Saint Sixtus in Rome upon the order. In February 1219 Domingo founded the first monastery of the order in Spain at Segovia, followed by a convent for women at Madrid. It is probable that on this journey he also presided over the establishment of a convent in connection with the University of Palencia and, at the invitation of the bishop of Barcelona, a house of the order was founded in that city. Shortly before his death on 6 August 1221, Domingo returned to Rome for the last time and received many new, valuable concessions for his order. He was canonized on 13 July 1234 by Pope Gregory IX, who declared him to be as saintly as Peter and Paul.

E. Michael Gerli

Bibliography

Galmés, L., and V.T. Gómez. (eds.) *Santo Domingo de Guzmán. Fuentes para su conocimiento*. Madrid, 1987.

Vicaire, M.-H. *Saint Dominic and His Times*. Trans. Kathleen Pond. New York, 1964.

GUZMÁN, NUÑO DE

The youngest of the illegitimate children of Luis González de Guzmán, master of the military order of Calatrava (1406–1407 and 1414–1443), by Inés de Torres, a wealthy heiress from Zamora, Nuño de Guzmán was educated by private tutor in the maternal home in Córdoba during a period of estrangement between his parents (1416–1430). Under his mother's guidance he became deeply interested in literature, "so that a day spent without reading seemed to me utterly wasted" (*Apologia Nunnii*), but he did not learn Latin. In 1430 he undertook a pilgrimage to Jerusalem and Sinai, returning via Cairo, the Aegean islands, Venice, Rome, Siena, Bologna, Genoa, Milan, Bohemia, Basle, Cologne, Lyon, and Tours before arriving at the court of Duke Philip the Good of Burgundy in Bruges (autumn 1432), where by his own account he was given an important office (*magistratus*), probably in the household of the duke's wife, Isabel of Portugal. On his return to Spain (ca. 1435) Guzmán found himself in the bad graces of his father, despite the personal intervention of Juan II and the support of his mother; consequently he set out for Burgundy again in 1439, but decided to visit Florence first, where the ecumenical council called by Pope Eugenius IV for reunion with the Eastern Church was just beginning. Guzmán was instantly dazzled by the intellectual ferment he encountered in Florence and, abandoning his Burgundian trip in favor of a vocation as literary patron and book collector, he befriended the celebrated *libralo* Vespasiano da Bisticci, Leonardo Bruni, Pier Candido Decembrio, and other humanists. He had Bruni's apologetic life of Cicero (*Cicero Nouus*) and his humanist version of Aristotle's *Ethics* translated into Tuscan, and received the dedications of Decembrio's Italian translations of Seneca's *Apocolocyntosis diui Claudii* and Quintus Curtius's *Life of Alexander*, while commissioning many superb *lettera antica* manuscripts from Vespasiano's *bottega*. In later years, Vespasiano tells us, Guzmán continued to commission Tuscan translations of classical and humanistic works, among which we know of Quintilian's *Declamationes maiores* (1456), Cicero's *Disputationes Tusculanae* (1456) and *De oratore* (date unknown), and Macrobius's *Sanumalia* (1463 or later). The most important fruit of his Florentine visit, however, was his personal friendship with the humanist Giannozzo Manetti (1396–1459), who dedicated his *De illustribus longaeuis* (1439) to Guzmán's father and his pathfinding Plutarchan parallel lives of Socrates and Seneca to Guzmán himself (1440, with notes on Seneca's Córdoban connections supplied by the addressee). In addition, Manetti cast two works into humanist Latin from notes prepared by Guzmán (1439); *Apologia Nunnii*, an autobiographical selfjustification addressed to his father, and *Laudatio Agnetis Numantinae*, an extended eulogy of his mother supposedly replacing a lost *alabanza* (works of praise) by Enrique de Villena. After returning to Seville in early 1440 Guzmán corresponded on literary matters with Alfonso de Cartagena, Alfonso de Palencia, and the Marquis of Santillana. The only works definitely attributable to Guzmán's own hand are his translation of Manetti's epideictic Tuscan oration on the qualities of the military commander, *Orazione a Gismondo Pandolfo de' Malatesia* (1453), made for the Marquis of Santillana (c. 1455); a revision of the Alfonsine translation of Seneca's *De ira* made (probably) for his mother (1445); and a highly popular vernacular compendium of Aristotle's *Ethics* made for his brother Juan de Guzmán, *señor* of La Algaba, (1467) and subsequently copied and printed a number of times either without attribution, or under false ascriptions to Alfonso de Cartagena and Alfonso de la Torre. It is highly probable, however, that Guzmán was instrumental in the Castilian translations of Bruni's *Vita di Marco Tullio Cicerone* and of Decembrio's versions of the works by Seneca and Quintus Curtius mentioned above, as well as the dissemination of other classical texts. When Guzmán died in Seville at some date between 1467 and 1490, Vespasiano tells us in his curious *Vita di messer Nugno di casa reale di Gusmano* (our fullest contemporary source) that Guzmán's splendid library came to a bad end. Nevertheless, Schiff's judgment that he was one of those to whom early Spanish humanism owed the most is fully justified.

JEREMY LAWRANCE

Bibliography

Bisticci, V. da. *Le vite*. Vol. 1. Ed. A. Greco. Florence, 1970. 435–41.

Lawrance, J. *Un episodio del proto-humanismo español: tres opúsculos de Nuño de Guzmán y Giannozzo Manetti*. Salamanca, 1989.

Morel-Fatio, A. "Notice au trois manuscrits de la bibliothèque d'Osuna," *Romania* 14 (1885), 94–108.

Russell, P.E., and A.R.D. Pagden. "Nueva luz sobre una versión de la *Ética a Nicómaco*: Bodleian Library MS Span. D. 1." In *Homenaje a Guillenno Guastavino*. Madrid, 1974. 125–46.

Schiff M. *La Bibliothèque du Marquis de Santillane*. Paris, 1905. 449–59.

H

ḤAFṢA BINT AL-HAYY AR-RAKUNIYYA

A poet who lived in Granada in the twelfth century, Ḥafṣa belonged to a noble family and received a superior education, which enabled her to become a teacher later in life. Like Wallādah, she was the lover of a poet, Abū Yafar, and many of her poems take the form of a dialogue with him. For example:

> Shall I go to your house, or will you come to mine?
> My heart always goes where you desire.
> You may be sure you will not be thirsty or hot when you meet me.
> A fountain fresh and sweet are my lips, and the branches of my braids cast a thick shadow.
> Answer me quickly, for it would be wrong to make your Butaynah wait, oh, my Yamil.

No less loving than the famous poet Yamil to his beloved Butaynah, Abū Yafar replied to Ḥafṣa:

> If I can find a way, I will go to you.
> You are too important to come to me.
> The garden does not move, but receives the soft puff of the breeze.

Ḥafsa also was being courted by the governor, Abū Saʾīd, whose great passion for her she did not dare reject, and probably enjoyed to some extent. Mutual jealousy caused the relationship between Abū Saʾīd and Abū Yafar, who was his secretary, to deteriorate. Eventually the former had the latter killed. Despite the danger, Ḥafsa did not hide her grief, and wrote the following lines:

> They threaten me for mourning a lover they killed by sword.
> May God be merciful to one generous with her tears
> or to her who cries for one killed by his rivals,
> and may the afternoon clouds so generously drench the land wherever she may go.

After Abū Yafar's death Ḥafṣa went to Marrakech, where she became tutor to the princesses.

All seventeen of Ḥafṣa's known poems were written in the earlier part of her life. Although she produced some satirical and panegyrical poems, most of her works are love poems, at which she excelled. Of the almost forty women poets of al-Andalus, Ḥafṣa is the most representative and the best known.

CRISTINA GONZÁLEZ

Bibliography

Garulo, T. *Diwan de las poetisas de al-Andalus*. Madrid, 1986.

Sobh, M. (comp.) *Poetisas arábigo-andaluzas*. Granada, 1985.

HAGIOGRAPHY

Medieval hagiography differs from the part of modern historiography that consists of scientific research on the lives of saints. If medieval chronicles in general very often included legendary components, the conventional patterns and the appeal to wonder operated especially in the lives of saints.

The oldest data on the custom of reading hagiographic texts in the church have been interpreted as readings during the Mass, and though testimonies of this kind are scarce later than the eighth century, there is a Hispanic particularity: in Mozarabic liturgy such a custom is documented until the eleventh century. Those readings were most frequent in matins, and apart from other offices, they must have occurred in convents during meals and work. Therefore the audience of hagiography consisted fundamentally of the religious living in communities. The rest of the faithful received the hagiographic stories through the examples that preachers took from legendaries, especially from the thirteenth century on.

In terms of a wider diffusion, minstrels may have included lives of saints, as well as *chansons de geste*, in their repertoires. Hence, the hagiographic poems of the *mester de clerecía* could have been recited on pilgrimages. In any case there is no doubt that the new dimension of hagiography in Romance languages which began to develop in the thirteenth century indicates the desire that it be accessible to everyone, not just to those who were fluent in Latin. Provisional data show that the references in Spanish and Catalan account for one-third of the total in the first century of vernacular hagiography, and reach 75 percent of all hagiographic production in the fifteenth century.

Though the first examples of Castilian hagiography were written in verse, by the fourteenth century prose prevailed. The reading aloud or the recitation of the poems seemed inadequate for prose, which tended to be linked with private reading. However, prose did not imply a decline in the popularity of the hagiographic genre, since the legends had become part of common knowledge thanks to the poems. On the other hand, as the Renaissance approached, the custom of private reading increased, facilitated in this genre by the *flores sanctorum*, abbreviated compilations that proliferated in the fourteenth and fifteenth centuries, most of them following Jacopo da Voragine's *Legenda aurea*.

The Castilian hagiography has a generic character that could coincide with that of Latin hagiography or any other field of medieval literature. Since every hagiographic writing is the story of a sanctification process, its internal structure may be put in a sequence of three parts: the wish for sanctity, the improvement process, and the proofs of success (miracles while living, death, and postmortem miracles). The basic type of lives of saints is the one represented by Gonzalo de Berceo's writings devoted to San Millán and Santo Domingo de Silos. Sometimes the structure becomes more complicated when the narration of an earlier, impious life is included. The meaning of the story would be similar to that of other hagiographic writings, with the only difference that, in the *Vida de Santa María Egipciaca*, for example, the starting point is not a positive degree of sanctity, but a very negative one, a violent contrast that would appeal to the reading public.

There is another type of hagiography that, though following the same basic structure, is developed more in the other world than in this one. Perhaps the most famous example of vision literature is the *Poema de Santa Oria*, by Berceo, to which could be joined a story linked with travel literature, the *Vida de San Amaro*. In addition, the *Martirio de San Lorenzo*, by Berceo, and the *Vida de San Vitores*, by Andrés Gutiérrez de Cerezo, are late examples of what was the predominant hagiographic form in Iberia until the tenth century: the literature of martyrs. The passions present a story centered on the execution and its preliminaries, a specific and violent opposition between the sacred and the profane, opposite to the gradual developing of the lives of "confessors."

The hagiographic story of course centers on the saint; the rest of the characters serve to enhance the success of his life and fall into two dichotomous categories: supporters or antagonists of sanctity, and human or supernatural. Type characters that belong to those categories are parents, teachers, members of the religious community, authorities of the ecclesiastical or civil hierarchy, those who benefit from miracles, God, Christ, the Virgin Mary, and the rest of the heavenly court: and invidious clerks, deceivers, Moors, heretics, powerful people, and the devil, the enemy par excellence.

The analysis of the structure, characters, and vision of the world in Castilian hagiography shows that its essential meaning is the subject's life as an example. Nevertheless, the greater glory of the saint also confers benefits on the local centers that were connected with him or sheltered his relics. The ecclesiastical institutions that profited from these stories ranged from dioceses to religious orders to monasteries. The *Vida de San Millán* and *Vida de Santo Domingo de Silos*, by Berceo, are two very good examples because of their explicit mention of the tributes.

FERNANDO BAÑOS VALLEJO

Bibliography

Almeida Lucas, M. C. de. *Hagiografía medieval portuguesa*. Lisbon, 1984.

Baños Vallejo, F. *La hagiografía como género literario en la Edad media: Tipología de doce "vidas" individuales castellanas*. Oviedo, 1989.

Gaiffier, B. de. "Hagiographie hispanique." In *Études critiques d'hagiographie et d'iconologie*. Brussels, 1967. 81–167.

Romero Tobar, L. "La prosa narrativa religiosa." In *Grundriss der Romanischen Literaturen des Mittelalters*. Vol. 9, 1, 4. Heidelberg, 1985. 44–53.

Walsh, J. K., and B.B. Thompson. "Old Spanish Manuscripts of Prose Lives of the Saints and Their Affiliations. I: Compilation A (the *Gran Flos Sanctorum*)," *La Corónica* 15, no. 1 (1986–87), 17–28.

AL-ḤAKAM II, CALIPH OF CÓRDOBA

Al-Ḥakam II b. ʿAbd Al-Raḥmān III ruled as caliph of al-Andalus from 961 to 976 with the throne name of Al-Mustanṣir. His reign is noted for its political continuity and cultural production.

Al-Ḥakam II was designated his father's successor as early as 919 at the age of four. Though ʿAbd al-Raḥmān III lived for forty-two more years, Al-Ḥakam II participated actively in the caliph's administration and gained a breadth of experience in the palace and on military campaigns. By the time he came to power in 961, Al-Ḥakam II had witnessed his father's consolidation of power and understood well how to maintain it. He was particularly adept at delegating administrative duties and was fortunate to have many political advisers and military leaders that he could trust.

Al-Ḥakam II's most significant political achievements involved maintaining the borders in the north, co-opting the majority of the powerful provincial families into the Córdoban aristocracy and military, and subduing the Idrīsīds of Morocco. The only real outside threat he faced was a raid by the Vikings in 971, which was quickly repelled. He continued the practice of obtaining soldiers from outside al-Andalus but turned south, recruiting Berber horsemen from Morocco instead of buying slaves from the north. Either more pious or more recognizant of the vital political role of the Muslim jurists than his father was, Al-Ḥakam II often consulted the leading *faqīhs* of Al-Andalus, and their power increased significantly during his reign. Al-Ḥakam II gained enough esteem among the Christian kings to the north that they regularly solicited his arbitration in their own disputes. The mother of his only son and heir, Hishām II, was a Basque princess. Al-Ḥakam II sent the Jewish doctor Ibrāhīm b. Jacob on a diplomatic mission to Otto I and commissioned the translation of the Talmud into Arabic.

Al-Ḥakam II is better known for his patronage of the arts and culture than he is for his political exploits. His library of over 400,000 volumes and a forty-four-volume catalog was one of the largest Islamic collections of the time. Al-Ḥakam II was himself a fairly good poet, and during his reign Córdoba became one of the leading centers of Islamic culture. He encouraged the study of astronomy and mathematics at the increasingly opulent court of Madīnat al-Zahrā, the palace complex outside Córdoba that his father had built. The Byzantine mosiac workers he continued to import to adorn Madīnat al-Zahrā worked as well on the Great Mosque of Córdoba, which Al-Ḥakam II enlarged yet again.

Al-Ḥakam II suffered a stroke in his latter years, and this might account for his not providing his young heir Hishām II with the political training and confidence that had proved so important in Al-Ḥakam's own reign. Al-Ḥakam II died in 976 leaving the fifteen-year-old Hishām II to the mercy of the increasingly powerful *ḥājib* (chamberlain) Al-Manṣūr. Although al-Manṣūr provided strong leadership from Córdoba until his death in 1002, the weakened Umayyad caliphate only lasted another thirty years.

MARILYN HIGBEE WALKER

Bibliography

Kennedy, H. *Muslim Spain and Portugal: A Political History of al-Andalus*. London, 1996.

Lévi-Provençal, E. *Histoire de l'Espagne Musulmane*. 3 vols. Leiden, 1950–53.

HALEVI, YEHUDA *See* YEHUDA HA-LEVI

HARO FAMILY

Descended from Iñigo López, the *mayordomo* of King Sancho III of Navarre (r. 1000–1035), the Haro family first came to prominence in the region that overlapped the modern Spanish provinces of Vizcaya, Álava, and Rioja. The twelfth century marked the emergence of the Haros as important officials in the courts of both the Navarrese and the Castilian kings. Diego López de Haro had a long official career that centered on his post as count of Nájera. His grandson and namesake, the royal standard-bearer (*alférez real*) for the Alfonso VIII of Castile, played crucial roles as commander of the rear guard at the Battle of Alarcos (1195) and as commander of the vanguard in the Battle of Las Navas de Tolosa (1212).

The thirteenth century saw the extension of Haro power eastward into Aragón as a cadet branch of the clan, the Azagras, became lords of Albarracín and Tragacete, and proved to be extremely rebellious subjects of the monarchs of the Crown of Aragón. The Haro clan's base, however, remained Vizcaya, and their power was derived from the offices they held in the Castilian court and parliament. The most important of these was that of standard-bearer, a post held by a Haro throughout the Middle Ages.

Undoubtedly the most influential of the thirteenth-century Haros was Lope Díaz de Haro, the nephew of the hero of Las Navas, who used his position in the court of Sancho IV of Castile to expand the power of his family at the expenses of its archenemies at court, the Laras. His cruel regime precipitated a wide-ranging revolt of the brotherhoods (*hermandades*) of the Castilian nobility in 1286–1287. Though the royalist forces under Haro were able to put down the Lara-led revolt, the unity of the victors soon began to unravel in 1287. When Haro showed himself to be an unreliable vassal, he was killed by other members of Sancho IV's retinue.

The fortunes of the family were saved with the escape of Lope's brother, Juan López de Haro, who became a leader of the Castilian noble brotherhoods in the early decades of the fourteenth century and, in that position, dominated the activities of the Castilian *cortes* and the royal court of Sancho IV's son, Fernando IV. In the later decades of the Middle Ages and into the early modern period, the Haros remained significant court agents who through marriage became allied to such highly placed officials as the Count-Duke of Olivares.

DONALD KAGAY

Bibliography

Mitre Fernández, E. *Evolución de la nobleza en Castilla bajo Enrique III (1396–1406)*. Valladolid, 1968.

Suárez Fernández, L. *Nobleza y monarquía: puntos de vista sobre la historia castellana del siglo XV*. 2d ed. Valladolid, 1975.

Valdeón Baruque, J. *Los conflictos sociales en el reino de Castilla en los siglos XIV y XV*. 2d ed. Madrid, 1975.

ḤASDAI IBN SHAPRŪT *See* IBN SHAPRŪT

HEBREW LANGUAGE AND LITERATURE

Language

Hebrew as a spoken language fell into desuetude in the Diaspora as early as the biblical period, and in Palestine itself during the Greek and Roman eras. Jews in Visigothic Spain spoke the language of the people, and following the Muslim conquest (711) began using Arabic, already the dominant language of the majority of the Jews in the world. However, in part as a response to the *ʿArabiyya* reaction in the Muslim world, in the tenth century there was a nationalist revival among Jews of al-Andalus that gave rise to the first scientific study of Hebrew grammar and lexicography and resulted in a renaissance of the Hebrew language—not as a spoken language but for literary purposes. Menahem ibn Sarūq and his opponent Dūnash ibn Labrat and their students engaged in heated controversy from which there gradually emerged a correct knowledge of Hebrew grammar.

Judah ben David Hayyūj (11th century), probably a teacher of the famous poet Samuel ibn Naghrilla, and Judah ibn Balsam were two of the important grammarians of the next generation. However, it was Jonah ibn Janāh who dominated that generation, with his works on grammar and his Hebrew dictionary, the first accurate one of its kind. Moses ibn Ezra, renowned poet of Granada, names Ibrahim ibn Saqtar as one of the two greatest grammarians, along with Ibn Janah. Isaac ibn Barūn (twelfth century) was another great grammarian; his *Kitāb al-muwazanah* marks the first scientific effort at comparative linguistics (Hebrew and Arabic), although his predecessors, particularly Ibn Janāh, drew heavily on their knowledge of Arabic in analyzinq Hebrew. Later important contributions were made by Abraham ibn Ezra, David Kimhi, Joseph ibn Caspi, Profiat Duran, and others.

However, the foundation of Hebrew grammar had been firmly established by the end of the twelfth century. All of these works on Hebrew grammar, except for the dictionary of Menahem, were written in Judeo-Arabic and later had to be translated into Hebrew, chiefly for use in Provence and Aragón-Catalonia in the later medieval period when Arabic was no longer known.

Nowhere in Spain, of course, did Hebrew become a commonly spoken language. Spanish was everywhere the language of the Jews, with Arabic prevailing as a strong secondary language in Castile, particularly in Toledo. However, the Hebrew renaissance showed itself in biblical commentary, poetry, and literature; these in turn influenced the style of Hebrew writing not only in scholarly treatises (rabbinic, philosophical, or scientific) but also in the everyday letters of the people.

Some Christians became proficient in Hebrew. "Schools" of Hebrew (actually single teachers at various monasteries) were established by the Dominicans, and to a lesser extent by the Franciscans, in the thirteenth century. Such instruction was usually given by *conversos* (converts to Christianity), but in some cases by Jews (as at Murcia, Barcelona, and Valencia); at Játiva in 1302–1303 a Christian taught Hebrew and a Jew taught Arabic (earlier a Jew had been the instructor in Hebrew there). There also were Christian noblemen who learned Hebrew for its own sake. Juan Fernández de Ixar, author of the *cancionero* that bears his name, was one of these; the important Aragónese Jewish poet Solomon de Piera addressed Hebrew poems to him. The daily contacts between Jews and Christians, and the necessity for the kings to know Jewish law, explain the ever-increasing number of Hebrew words that became part of the standard Spanish vocabulary in the medieval period, some of which survive in modern Spanish. The fifteenth-century *cancioneros*, of course, containing many poems by *conversos*, are full of Hebrew terms, but this may not be evidence of a general knowledge of these words in the way that unquestionably is the case with royal and other documents.

Literature

The first problem is to define precisely what is meant by "literature." Even Hayyim Schirmann, the great authority on Hebrew poetry and literature of medieval Spain, included as "literature" Hebrew works that were essentially philosophical or educational, simply because they were written, in part or in whole, in rhymed prose.

By "literature" we understand a work of fiction, clearly recognizable as such, that, while it may have a secondary aim of moral instruction, is primarily intended to entertain. In the case of the Hebrew literature of medieval Spain, we can be even more specific, since it is invariably of a single genre, borrowed from the

Arabic. This is *maqāma*, a term of unclear origin, perhaps meaning "sitting" or "standing." In any case it appears to refer to the recital of tales to an audience. The style was first used in the ninth century, apparently by Al-Jāhiz, but the Muslim authors with whom the style is most associated are Al-Hamadhānī (967–1008) and Al-Ḥarīrī (1045–1122), whose *maqāmat* was translated into Hebrew by Judah al-Harizi.

The characteristics of this style, whether in Arabic or in Hebrew, are rhymed prose interspersed with actual poetry (metric); obviously fictitious, even mythical or legendary, names of heroes; a protagonist who is often the author himself (particularly in the Hebrew form); and an antagonist who is a trickster and almost always a mythical or "nonreal" person.

The first known Hebrew *maqāma*, which has not survived in its entirety, is that of Solomon ibn Saqbel (mid-twelfth century). A unique feature of the Hebrew form, which was to be imitated by his successors, was the parody of the biblical prophetic "call," where God (or at least a voice) addresses the author in pseudoprophetic language, in an amusing manner, to arouse him to his task. Ibn Saqbel also set the tone of this genre in Spain, where, unlike the relatively few examples of Hebrew literature from other lands, these stories are totally secular, with no religious or moral elements of instruction whatever. Indeed, love and sex play a prominent role in almost all the Hebrew *maqāmat*. The element of deceit is also central. One of the most entertaining stories, for example, finds the hero enticed into a harem where he believes the most beautiful woman is madly in love with him. To his surprise, he finds that this "beauty" is a man disguised to trick him; it is, of course, the mythical antagonist. The skill of the author is manifest in having already planted clues to alert the careful reader and arouse suspicion before the trick is revealed.

Interestingly, the second Hebrew *maqāma* that has survived comes not from al-Andalus but from Barcelona: Joseph ibn Zabara's (twelfth century) *Seferhasha Cashucim* (*Book of Delights*; available in a poor English translation, a very good Catalan translation, and a fairly good Spanish one). While generally lacking the humor, and certainly the outright sexuality, of the Andalusian examples, this work is rightly considered one of the most important of Hebrew literature. (Its supposed influence on the *Libro de buen amor* is, however, highly doubtful.)

Judah ibn Shabbetai (thirteenth century; Toledo and Zaragoza) introduced another important motif that was to have a lasting influence in Hebrew literature and may, indeed, have influenced subsequent Spanish literature: the wiles, or deceitfulness, of women. His totally fictitious work was taken seriously in Provence, where it aroused several responses defending women. We find thereafter many humorous tales of women that demonstrate not so much their deceitfulness as their cleverness and quick wit in turning a potentially dangerous situation (usually sexual) to their advantage.

Judah al-Harizi, known also for his poetry and particularly for his Hebrew translation of Maimonides' *Guide for the Perplexed*, composed the largest example of the genre, *Tahkemoni* (available in a good English and a recent Spanish translation). This work accurately reflects his own travels but is interspersed with many humorous fictitious tales and includes a chapter of great importance on Hebrew poets.

Of major importance also is the work of Isaac ibn Sahulah of Guadalajara (ca. 1281), *Meshal ha-qadmoniy* (*Tale of the Ancient One*), which contains many delightful tales and became one of the most lavishly illustrated Hebrew books.

Jacob ben Elʿazar of Toledo (early thirteenth century), who also composed a Judeo-Arabic grammatical treatise, produced a *maqāma*, unfortunately not complete, which ranks alongside that of Ibn Saqbel for sheer entertainment and brilliance of style. Problematic are some works that, while definitely in the maqāma style, may not entirely fit the definition of "literature" we have suggested. One of these is *Ben ha-melekh ve-ha-nazir* (*The Prince and the Ascete*) of Abraham ibn Hasdai (Barcelona, early thirteenth century). This is, in essence, a translation of an Arabic version of the Barlaam and Josaphat stories, apparently through an intermediary (Persian?) version. However, Abraham has added much of his own material to the work. Nevertheless, in the final analysis it belongs more in the realm of didactic and ethical writing, of which there are many other examples, such as the two Hebrew versions (one by the above Jacob ben Elʿazar) of the *Kalīla wa-Dimna*.

Still problematic is the *Mishley sendebar* (*Tales of Sendebar*; available in English and Spanish translations). While this anonymous composition probably was written in Spain, its style is crude in comparison to other *maqamāt.* The Hebrew version is hardly the "original," as claimed by its editor but derives from a lost Arabic version that has been heavily reworked in a pseudobiblical style.

Some minor examples exist from Provence, where this style of Hebrew literature was extremely popular. In fourteenth- and fifteenth-century Aragón-Catalonia, the *maqāma* had a brief revival (En-Maimon Gallipapa, Vidal Benveniste, Vidal Alrabi, and others), but these works are less satisfying from a literary point of view, however historically important they may be.

Norman Roth

Bibliography

Language

Del Valle Rodríguez, C. *La escuela hebrea de Córdoba.* Madrid, 1981.

Roth, N. "Jewish Reactions to the *Arabiyya* and the Renaissance of Hebrew in Spain," *Journal of Semitic Studies* 28 (1983), 63–84.

Literature

Gonzalo Maeso, D. *Manual de historia de la literatura hebrea.* Madrid, 1960.

Roth, N. "The 'Wiles of Women' Motif in Medieval Hebrew Literature of Spain," *Hebrew Annual Review* 2 (1978), 145–65.

———. "La lengua hebrea entre los cristianos españoles medievales: Voces hebreas en español," *Revista de Filología Española* (1991): 137–43.

HENRY OF BURGUNDY

Count of Portugal from 1093 to 1112, Henry was married to Teresa, natural daughter of Alfonso VI of León-Castile, who was his consort and successor. Together with his cousin, Count Raymond of Burgundy and of Galicia, he was a major court figure until the death of Alfonso VI in 1109. He and his wife then began an attempt to replace Teresa's half sister, Urraca (r. 1109–1126) on the throne of the kingdom. This sometimes involved alliance with Urraca's estranged husband, Alfonso I of Aragón, and at others with the supporters of Alfonso Raimūndez, Urraca's young son by her first husband, Count Raymond of Burgundy. Henry died before 22 May 1112, at Astorga, probably as the result of the fighting near that city. He was the younger brother of Duke Eudes I of Burgundy and probably had come to Iberia in the entourage of that magnate in the late winter or spring of 1087. His career is obscure before his appointment to the county of Portugal, but about 1095 he had conspired with his cousin to partition the kingdom of León-Castile at whatever time Alfonso VI should die.

BERNARD F. REILLY

Bibliography

Defourneaux, M. *Les français en Espagne aux XIē et XIIē siècles.* Paris, 1949.

Sousa Soares, T. de. "O governo de Portugal pelo Conde Henrique de Borgonha: Sus relações com as monarquias Leonesa-Castelhana e Aragónesa," *Revista portuquesa de historia* 14 (1974), 365–97.

HENRIQUE, PRINCE OF PORTUGAL

Conventionally known as "the Navigator," Henrique was born in Oporto (Portuguese: Porto) on 4 March 1394. His father, João I, was a bastard who had fought his way to the throne. The chivalric culture of the court in which Henrique grew up cloaked the imperfections of the new dynasty's credentials.

As the fourth of the king's sons, Henrique had no prospect of the crown. He had, however, the example of his grandfather, John of Gaunt, who maintained an affinity of kingly proportions and sought a crown of his own in Spain through wars, conducted to resemble knightly cavalcades. Though little direct evidence survives of Henrique's life up to 1415, the priorities of an upbringing dominated by knightly exercises are conveyed in the treatise on chivalry attributed to his eldest brother. The chivalric ideal informed his whole career. Though he was later obliged to become involved in commerce and industry in an effort to maintain his estate, he always projected the self-perception of a perfect knight, espousing celibacy, practicing asceticism, and professing religious motives for slave raids and attempted conquests.

After contemplating a tournament of unprecedented magnificence to celebrate the knighting of his

Nuno Goncalves (2d half 15th). Henry the Navigator. Detail from the panel of the Infant of the Saint Vincent polyptych. Ca. 1465. Copyright © Giraudon/Art Resource, NY. Museu Nacional de Arte Antiga, Lisbon, Portugal.

sons, the king decided in 1415 to launch instead a real *chevauchée* (chivalric attack) against a traditional enemy, the Muslims of Ceuta. The princes themselves were said to have urged this change of plan. The chronicle tradition assigns Henrique a prominent part in the conquest and in the next few years he earned offices of honor and profit comparable to those of his brothers. By 1423 he was the duke of Viseu, the governor of Ceuta and the Algarve, and the administrator of the Order of Christ. He remained, however, a cadet prince with an ill-defined role who chose to reside away from court, chiefly in the Algarve, and to surround himself with a retinue of "knights" and "squires" whom he maintained at great cost and no small trouble: documents concerning crimes by members of his household cover murder, rape, and piracy. This entourage was not only evidence of Henrique's pretensions; it also committed him to a quest for patronage with which to reward his followers.

His ambitions are suggested in a memorandum addressed to his father in April 1432: the Count of Arraiolos, who knew Henrique well, observed that he might acquire a kingdom in Morocco, Granada, Castile, or the Canary Islands, "and have the affairs of this kingdom [Portugal] in the palm of his hand." Little survives of any writing of Henriques's own, but the two probably authentic memoranda from his pen recommend crusades against Tangier and Málaga. His attempt to conquer Tangier in 1437, however, was a costly failure, and thereafter he concentrated on alternative fields of endeavor in which he had already dabbled: maritime deeds and, in particular, his effort to acquire a realm in the Canary Islands.

Many chivalric romances of the period had a seaborne setting, and a common denouement placed the hero in an island-kingdom. Portuguese ports had played a part in the exploration of the eastern Atlantic since the 1340s and there is evidence in chronicles and maps that Portuguese navigation intensified in that arena in the 1420s. That Henrique was already involved is an assertion of a chronicle he later commissioned. In the following decade, however, independent documents confirmed his interest. In 1432 his claims to the Canaries led the pope to solicit opinions from jurists on the question of the legitimacy of war against the pagan inhabitants. It is evident from friars' protests that Henrique's career as a slaver, to be continued in the next decade on the African coast, began in the Canaries by 1434. His efforts to secure a base in the archipelago continued with few interruptions almost until his death but were rewarded with no permanent success: some islands remained in the natives' hands, others in those of Castilian adventures or settlers.

After his father's death in 1433, the sense of vocation attributed to him by contemporaries seems to have deepened. He felt destined for great deeds by his horoscope—his chronicler tells us—and endowed, by inheritance from King João, with a "talent" that had to "shine forth." Portuguese ambassadors in 1437 told the pope that Henrique's aim was "expressly to fulfil the image and likeness of King João." Between 1438 and 1449, all his surviving brothers died. The death of the Infante Fernando, in captivity in Fez in 1443, was a heavy charge on his conscience, for Fernando was a victim of the debacle at Tangier and Henrique had opposed the possible surrender of Ceuta in ransom. In adopting a homonymous nephew as his heir, he shouldered a fatherly responsibility. In 1449 he became the senior surviving prince of his line when his elder brother, Pedro, fell in rebellion against the crown.

Meanwhile, he had accumulated resources to invest in his offshore activities. As well as the income from the Order of Christ and the revenues of his many fiefs, he controlled extensive fishing rights, including the monopoly of the tuna-curing industry of the Algarve; the monopoly of soap manufacture throughout the kingdom was his, as was that of coral gathering off Ceuta. His maritime activities were exempt from the royal tax on booty and he had the sole right to license voyages to Madeira, the Azores, and the Atlantic coast of Africa.

These arenas occupied an increasing amount of his attention as his prospects in Morocco and the Canaries waned. He expressed interest in settling a colony on Madeira as early as 1433; in June and July 1439, seed and sheep were shipped to Madeira and at least one of the Azores; thereafter, colonization was farmed out to enterprising intermediate lords, who were normally Henrique's dependents (though his brother and nephew were the superior lords in some cases). Henrique was a partner in the building of the first recorded sugar-mill in Madeira in 1452: this made him a founding patron of an important new industry of the late Middle Ages.

Meanwhile, navigation under Henrique's patronage, or with his license, extended along the African coast. The chronicle he commissioned established the belief, which historians continued to uphold until very recently, that African exploration was the primary focus of the prince's endeavours. The much-vaunted rounding of Cape Bojador in 1434 was a minor byproduct of the effort to sieze the Canaries; to judge from surviving maps and sailing directions, "Cape Bojador" probably signified nothing more remote than the modern Cape Juby. The great series of African voyages began in earnest only in 1441. From the mid-1440s, this enterprise began to yield appreciable amounts of gold and slaves. Around the middle of the next decade, when Henrique employed Genoese technicians to supplement his household personnel, significant progress in navigation was made when the Senegal and Gambia Rivers were investigated and the Cape Verde Islands discovered. The big advances, however, both in the reach of exploration and the yield of exploitable resources, came in the generation after Henrique's death, as Portuguese navigators worked their way around Africa's bulge. Meanwhile, in 1458, Portugal's crusading vocation in the Maghrib was briefly revived and Henrique accompanied the royal expedition that seized Al-Qasr Kebir, near Ceuta.

Henrique died in Sagres on 13 November 1460. The Canaries still eluded him; no crown adorned his head; of the gold of Africa only a few threads had come within his grasp; and he was heavily in debt. He had, however, invested wisely in posthumous fame and has enjoyed an enduring reputation as Portugal's culture hero, credited anachronistically with the foundation of the Portuguese Empire and with the inauguration of a tradition of scientific exploration. Modern scholarship disavows these claims, but as a patron of the colonization of Madeira and the Azores he can genuinely be counted among the creators of Atlantic colonial societies.

FELIPE FERNÁNDEZ–ARMESTO

Bibliography

Dias Dinis, A.J. *Estudos henriquinos*. Coimbra, 1960.
Monumenta Henricina. 15 vols. Coimbra, 1960–75.
Russell, P. E. *Henry the Navigator*. New Haven, Conn. 2001.
———. *Prince Henry the Navigator: The Rise and Fall of a Culture-Hero*. Oxford, 1984.
Zurara, G.E. de. *Cronica dos feitos notáveis que se passaram na conquista da Guiné*. Ed. T. de Sousa Soares. Lisbon, 1978.

HERALDRY

Studies dedicated to heraldic emblems and armorial bearings have almost been reduced to the merely descriptive, focusing overwhelmingly on formal aspects. From a historical point of view, however, the human aspects—the use of these emblems on a societal level, and the reasons they were represented and displayed in such a wide variety of cultural circumstances in different countries and ages—are much more interesting.

Armorial bearings were initially personal distinguishing marks that could be passed on to other people. The channels of this transmission were social structures, and the fact that the emblems were transferred indicates the existence of an essential hierarchy within the structure. Transmission by inheritance within the most immediate social structure, the family, caused these emblems to acquire a double meaning, both personal and familial. The continuous inherited possession of territorial jurisdiction also caused the armorial bearings to be affiliated with specific geographic territories, a third meaning added to the first two. Finally, the hierarchical nature of these social structures meant that the armorial bearings were often passed from superiors to their subordinates. Naturally, the different ways that these transmissions were adopted in each period and in each country reveal how the social structures from which they arise were understood.

The period in which the heraldic emblem began to be widely used is roughly the same in the Iberian Christian kingdoms and in the countries of the English Channel: the south of England and continental territories from the north of France to Rhineland Germany. In Iberia, this occurs during the latter part of the reign of Alfonso VII, between 1135 and 1157, coinciding with the favorable circumstances caused by the political union (under Alfonso's rule) of territories from Galicia and Portugal to Gascony and Languedoc. In short, the phenomenon was yet another manifestation of the progressive movement that became known as the twelfth-century Renaissance. There is evidence showing that Alfonso VII, King of León and Castile, used a lion as a heraldic emblem, and that Ramón Berenguer IV, Count of Barcelona and Prince of Aragón, used a paled shield.

In the first stage of the evolution of heraldry, there was significant diversity, not only in the graphic patterns of the emblems, but also in the material foundations upon which they were represented, as well as in the meanings and purposes for which they were used. In a later stage, these different purposes were fused, forming the thirteenth- and fourteenth-century conception of heraldry familiar to the modern student. This development occured more slowly in Iberia, making it easier to follow the successive phases of the process than it would be in other European regions. The plural nature of heraldic history, combined with the notably rapid diffusion of the heraldic emblem's use outside the military, suggest that there has been an exaggerated importance placed on the emblem's usefulness as a means to recognize soldiers whose faces were hidden. Much more effective is the use of the armorial bearing as an indication of fashion tendencies and as a source of aesthetic value.

The use of heraldry becomes rooted in society with the emblem's increasing presence outside the military sphere. This made the heraldic emblem available to those that had no connection with the world of war, and gave rise to the use of armorial bearings on everyday objects and in everyday occasions. In terms of quantity, this newfound domestic availability was very important: civil heraldic representations were much more numerous than their military counterparts, and were created on much more durable materials. Consequently, their influence in the configuration of the heraldic system was much greater. Previously, these emblems were not conceived as abstractions that preceded their visual, material manifestations; they were merely created and developed in the moment of execution, and not in some preexistent theoretical plane.

The structuralizations of the society and family in different countries had direct repercussions in the way the heraldic emblems were used. In France and England, heraldry took on a strongly personal character: each coat of arms represented one person exclusively, and only the eldest son could inherit the unaltered emblem. In the Hispanic world, on the other hand, the heraldic emblem belonged to all individuals sharing the same lineage, and any of them could use it in its pure, unaltered form. The reason for this discrepancy is that the use of a particular coat of arms in Anglo-French regions was considered to be directly linked to the possession of feudal territory. In Iberia before the fourteenth century, only the coats of arms of certain kings were considered to be connected to the territories they owned.

The heraldic emblems' definitive installation in society seems to depend not only on those that used them, but also on a more general penchant for heraldry that spread throughout Western Europe during the last stretch of the twelfth century and the beginning of the thirteenth. Heraldic manifestations in literature and the plastic arts demonstrate the varied characteristics the emblem had in different countries. In the territories of the English Channel, interest in heraldry was aroused by the admiration of chivalry. The coats of arms of the most famous figures were well known, reproduced, and collected by many people from various social classes. In Hispanic territories this interest was based more on an increasing awareness of the decorative value of the heraldic emblems; this aesthetic regard for heraldry was especially strong during the reigns of Fernando III and Alfonso X in the southern regions of Castile, from Toledo to Seville. During this period, repetitive ornamental patterns inspired by Mudéjar art were formed. These patterns allowed two coats of armor to be assembled in one shield, a useful development since maternal and paternal emblems were habitually incorporated together because of the emblem's familial nature. The quartering of the shield to incorporate two family crests was a Castilian invention that later spread throughout Europe, as was the charged bordure.

The Anglo-French interest in heraldry, founded in a more general passion for chivalry, had two important consequences. The frequent description of the armorial bearings in literature, used to establish a narrative setting, gave rise to the formulation of a specific heraldic vocabulary with its own terminology and expressions. In addition, the tradition of collecting coats of arms led to the birth of the heraldic index or armorial. Because these premises were not in place in the region, the Iberian Romance languages did not have their own original heraldic terminology and did not display an early tradition of heraldic books.

Because heraldry was not associated with a specific economic class in Iberia, the use of the emblem in the peninsula was initially unhampered by social prescription. In the early age of Iberian heraldry, the very concept of the right to use armorial bearings as a prerequisite to actually using them made little sense. Anyone who needed to display heraldic emblems in a given occasion, place, and on a given object could do so. Even the Jewish and Moorish populations residing in Christian territories used coats of arms in their seals.

A new era for peninsular heraldry began in the middle of the fourteenth century, when the formal models and concepts used by the Anglo-French nobility reached the Iberian kingdoms. This influence started in Navarre and Catalonia; Portugal would later be directly influenced by England. The first consequence of this shift was the heraldic emblem's increasingly personal character. The shield containing the family coat of arms would now appear surrounded by ornamental elements like *timbres* (helmets, crowns, crosiers), insignias designating rank, collars of various knightly orders, and so on. In these and other exterior elements, two functions are combined: a signifying function individualizing the coat of arms, and an ornamental function that displayed a fondness for the complicated, the ostentatious, and the surprising. The predominance of the individual character of the emblem is also evident in the use of the *divisa*, a type of emblem that came into use at the same time as the armorial bearings.

The final stage of development occured in the early fifteenth century, assuring that the use of heraldry would survive into the modern era. In this period, emblems acquired a strong noble connotation; ever since, the presence of armorial bearings signified first and foremost that the user belonged to a distinguished social class, with only a secondary personal or familial meaning. With this new characteristic, heraldry also attains a sense of nostalgia for the past that it had not had previously, as well as the popular belief that the symbols and colors on the coat of arms perpetuated the memory of an ancestor's deeds. This way of thinking gave rise to the creation of legends that sought to explain the heraldic emblems as graphic expressions of heroic or portentous acts. Of course, nobody in the twelfth or thirteenth centuries ever adopted a specific emblem for the express purpose of reminding descendants of such deeds. Another important consequence was that once the emblems were considered marks of honor and nobility, their regulation belonged to royal authority, unlike the free use permitted and practiced previously.

FAUSTINO MENÉNDEZ PIDAL DE NAVASCUÉS

Bibliography

Menéndez Pidal, F. *Heráldica Medieval Española*. Vol. 1, *La Casa Real de León y Castilla*. Madrid, 1982.

———. "Panorama heráldico español. Epocas y regiones en el período medieval." In *I Seminario sobre heráldica y genealogía. Ponencias*. Zaragoza, 1988. 5–21.

Riquer, Martín de. *Heráldica castellana en tiempos de los Reyes Católicos*. Barcelona, 1986.

———. *Heráldica catalana des de l'any 1150 a 1550*. 2 vols. Barcelona, 1983.

HERBALS

Herbals are manuals that deal mainly with plants, but also with elements of mineral and animal origin (*simples*—i.e., primitive elements, uncompounded substances; Latin, *simplicia*; Arabic, *adwīya mufrāda*). They provide information on the appearance of these elements, their nomenclature, how to identify them, where they are found, and, primarily, their medical properties and use, often including a strong component of magic and superstition.

The tradition of herbals relevant to the Middle Ages begins in the first century A.D. with Pedanios Dioscorides (*De materia medica*) and Pliny the Elder (*Naturalis historia*, books XII–XXVII). Dioscorides' work survived through various Latin versions, one of which is supposed to have been used by Isidore of Seville. In turn, Isidore's description of plants (*Etymologiae*, book XVII, chaps. 7–11), the first example of herbal literature on the Iberian Peninsula, served as a source for other medieval herbalists.

The Greek text by Dioscorides was translated into Arabic, and became a fundamental text in the Islamic world. In Muslim Iberia the study of Dioscorides became even more important after ʿAbd al-Raḥmān III received an illustrated Greek manuscript of Dioscorides from the Byzantine emperor in 948. Among the many pharmacological authors are Ibn Juljul al-Andalusi, who wrote a commentary on Dioscorides (982), and Ibn al-Wāfiḍ (1007–1074), who composed a book about the simples (*Kitāb fi l-adwīya al-mufrāda*). His work was translated into Latin by Gerard of Cremona (twelfth century) and later into Catalan (*Llibre de les medicines particulars*, fourteenth century). Gerard also translated the works of Galen from Arabic, including *De simplicium medicamentorum facultatibus*. Arabic pharmacological writing reached its apex in Al-Andalus between 1150 and 1250 with the extensive and influential works about the simples of Al-Ghāfīqí and Ibn al-Baytār.

In the Christian world one of the most important herbals was the *Circainstans* by the Salernitan physician Matthaeus Platearius (ca. 1150), of which a fragmentary Catalan version is extant. It seems that the most widely influential work on the peninsula was *De virtutibus herbarum*, composed in verse and partly based on Pliny and Dioscorides. The writer's name, Macer Floridus, is a pseudonym alluding to Aemilius Macer, the author of a lost herbal from the first century B.C. The real author was probably Odo of Meun (twelfth century A.D.). There are interrelated prose versions of it in Castilian and Catalan, and the renown of Macer Floridus can also be seen from the fact that an herbal dating from the early sixteenth century was published as *Libro de medicina llamado Macer* (Granada, 1518). As to original works from the peninsula, there are a few minor anonymous ones in Latin, probably of Spanish origin. Arnald of Villanova (ca. 1235–1311) composed a register of medicinal plants (*De simplicibus medicinis*), and he is also the alleged author of some small treatises on individual plants (*Proprietates roris marini*, *Virtutes herbe tunice*, *De virtute quercus*), partly translated into Romance. However, the attribution to him of the authorship of the *Herbarius latinus*, which first appeared in printed versions in the late fifteenth century, is definitely in error.

After the Middle Ages the tradition of herbals in Spain and Portugal survived mainly in three ways. First, classical and medieval herbals appeared in printed editions. Second, Andrés de Laguna composed an annotated translation of Dioscorides from Greek manuscripts (1555), and João Rodrigues de Castelo Branco (Amatus Lusitanus) wrote an important commentary on Dioscorides (1553). In their works are many references to the medieval tradition. Third, the medieval influence is still in evidence also in the works of such authors as Nicolás de Monardes, Francisco Hernández and García de Orta, who composed herbals describing plants, animals, and minerals that could be found in the New World.

GUIDO MENSCHING

Bibliography

Anderson, F. J. *An Illustrated History of the Herbals*. New York, 1977.

Beaujouan, G. "Manuscrits médicaux du moyen age conservés en Espagne." In *Mélanges de la Casa de Velázquez*. Vol. 8. Paris, 1972. 161–221.

Dubler, C. E. *La "Materia médica" de Dioscórides. Transmisión medieval y renacentista*. 5 vols. Barcelona, 1953–54.

HEREDIA, PABLO DE

Pablo de Heredia (ca. 1420–ca. 1490), a Jewish convert to Christianity, apparently was from Aragón. His Jewish name is unknown. He converted to Christianity in Rome, where he died. Prior to his conversion he wandered through various countries, including North Africa and Sicily, and apparently had lived in or visited several areas of Spain. Although he most certainly was not a rabbi, and in fact had a rather poor knowledge of Hebrew, he was influenced by doctrines of cabala, especially of the *Zohar* and that of Abraham Abulafia. He claimed to have had a revelation from Elijah and to have "discovered" in Sicily certain mystical Hebrew books, prior to his conversion to Christianity in Rome, that were the supposed source for his own writings.

His first work, and the only one published, was *Epistolae de secretis Neumiae fili Haccanae* (published in Rome, ca. 1488; also Florence, perhaps 1482; a copy of the rare Rome edition is in the Biblioteca Nacional, Madrid). The work was dedicated to Íñigo de Mendoza (not López de Mendoza, as some have written), who was ambassador to Rome (1486–1488). The work purports to be a translation from Hebrew of letters between Neumie (Nehemiah? Nehunyah?) and his son Hacanne. The main part of the work, however, claims to be taken from the *Libro gale razaya* (*Galley razaya*) and *Niggherth hazodoth* (*Igeret ha-sodott*) of the exchanges between Judah ha-Nasi (Rabbenu Judah ha-Qodeshll) and the Roman emperor Antonius. In fact, both of these works are spurious, probably the forgery of Pablo himself. To this he adds forged citations of the *Zohar*, all with the intent of proving the truth of the Christian religion. The work contains other citations of Jewish sources, some genuine (if misinterpreted to suit his arguments) and some spurious. Appended to this work is his *Corona regia*, on the virgin birth, original sin, and other topics. It is dedicated to Innocent VIII, and was written in 1488.

Still extant in manuscript, although excerpts have been published, is his *Ensis Pauli*, which he specifically says was written before the *Epistolae de secretis* (this fact has not been noted by scholars), and which deals at greater length with some of the same ideas. It also contains some references to Jewish works and mentions his "revelation" by Elijah. The dedication of this work to Fernando and Isabel contains harsh attacks on the Jews. The interest of the second work, which deserves further study, is primarily in its relation to some of the cabalistic ideas of Abraham Abulafia, Moses de León, and others.

NORMAN ROTH

Bibliography

Roth, N. *Conversos, Inquisition and the Expulsion of the Jews from Spain*. Madison, Wisc. 1995.

Secret, F. "L'*Ensis Pauli* de Paulus de Heredia," *Sefarad* 26 (1966), 79–102, 253–71.

HERESY

Heresy, the "wrong choice" in religion, is a term used in the Catholic Church to refer to those who "choose" to reject the official teaching of that church and follow some other version of belief and practice. In the eyes of the ecclesiastical authorities, any such error leads automatically to hell and damnation, the signs of which may appear in this world and not just in the next. Up to the eleventh century, heresy seems to have been regarded largely in doctrinal terms, rather than as an error to be detected and punished in the mass of believers. In Iberia the Visigothic kings adopted the Arian heresy until Reccared was converted, partly through the intervention of Bishop Leander of Seville in 587, a decision ratified two years later by the Third Council of Toledo. The dispute between Arius and his followers and the Catholic Church was one of many that vexed Christians in late Roman and early medieval times: the proper interpretation of the relationship between the divine and human natures of Jesus Christ. Defense against the growing power of Islam in the Iberian Peninsula seems largely to have suppressed such disputes thereafter, as bishops devoted themselves to keeping the faith alive and protecting their flocks against conversion to Islam.

In much of western Europe the growth of papal authority and the desire for reform were beginning to lead, by 1100, to a greater effort to target not only poor performance by bishops and priests but also the resulting ignorance of the laity. Such developments reached Spain in the 1080s, when the Castilian monarchy became influenced by papal and monastic reformers, especially from Cluny in France. There is little evidence, however, that the preoccupation with heresy that resulted from such developments in France and Italy was transferred to the Iberian Peninsula. Indeed, heretical movements of the kind found north of the Pyrenees in the late Middle Ages seem to have been nonexistent, or else not sought out or discovered. Thus there are no known Spanish or Portuguese equivalents of French and Italian Catharism and Waldensianism, English Lollardy, or Bohemian Hussitism. It is impossible to say whether Christian heresy was unknown in the peninsula, or whether ecclesiastical and secular hierarchies were so preoccupied with their struggle against Islam that they omitted to notice the laity's unorthodox views.

Only in the 1480s, when the newly founded Inquisition of Fernando and Isabel began its systematic investigation of "heretical" views among converts from Judaism to Christianity and their descendants, did such evidence come to light. For the church and the monarchs "heresy" in these people meant adherence to Jewish belief and practice, and if the Inquisition and its witnesses are to be believed (which they are, at least in part), then both these things were widespread among *conversos*. However, as the inquisitorial tribunals in Soria and Burgo de Osma revealed, numerous inhabitants of northeastern Castile in the second half of the fifteenth century were not simply harking back to a Jewish faith and practice formerly adhered to by themselves or by their ancestors, but expressing religious skepticism of a kind to be found in many other parts of Europe where Judaism was not an issue. They had little respect for the clergy, especially those known to them; they found the doctrines of the Catholic Church contradictory and absurd, and its practices abusive; and they doubted the existence of heaven and hell, on the grounds that such stories were invented to keep the laity in order. This should not be forgotten when attention is, quite properly, paid to the continued adherence of so many Spaniards, even after conversion, to Jewish faith and practice. Before the sixteenth century inquisitors paid little attention to such views, because "judaizers" were their main target, but many of the developments after 1500, such as the influence of Protestantism and the more indigenous illuminist (*alumbrado*) movement of the 1520s and later, developed in a climate of dissent as much as one of slavish orthodoxy.

Nevertheless, it does appear that the particular Iberian situation, in which a political as well as a religious confrontation between faiths had primacy for so many centuries, required at least an external adherence to orthodoxy from Christians, Muslims, and Jews alike. There were, of course, doctrinal disputes in the Muslim and Jewish communities, which at times impinged on relations with Christian authority. For example, the protests of some Iberian rabbis, in the early thirteenth century, against the supposedly "rationalist" views of Maimonides led to the burning of his works. Unfortunately, there are no inquisitorial records to indicate whether or not such defenses of orthodoxy by rabbis or imams had any more effect on the Jewish and Muslim faithful than the efforts of the Christian clergy to keep their own flock in order. It is probably not a paradox that medieval Spain apparently was simultaneously a bastion of internal blasphemy and official orthodoxy.

JOHN EDWARDS

Bibliography

Beinart, H. *Conversos on Trial: The Inquisition in Ciudad Real*. Jerusalem, 1981.

Collins, R. *Early Medieval Spain: Unity in Diversity*. London, 1983.

Edwards, J. "Religious Faith and Doubt in Late Medieval Spain: Soria *circa* 1450–1500." *Past and Present* 120 (1988), 3–25. Repr. in *Religion and Society in Spain c. 1492*. Aldershot, U.K., 1996.

Kamen, H. *Inquisition and Society in Sixteenth and Seventeenth Century Spain*. London, 1985.

HERMANDAD

The term *hermandad* (brotherhood) refers to associations of towns that first appeared in Castile and León on a regional basis at the beginning of the thirteenth century. By the end of the century, these associations had spread throughout the realm. Several Andalusian towns, for example, formed an association for mutual defense against the Moors in 1265. When Infante Sancho, following the policies of his father, Alfonso X, summoned the estates of the realm to Valladolid in April 1282, the towns of Castile, León, Galicia, Estremadura, and Andalusia organized to defend their liberties against royal violation of their rights and privileges. Each *hermandad* planned to meet annually, and they seem to have done so until Sancho IV dissolved them all in the *corte* Parliament of Valladolid in 1282.

During the turbulent minority of Fernando IV, the towns once again coalesced in *hermandades* to uphold the king's right to the throne against various claimants and to defend their own liberties. Again they proposed to hold annual assemblies, but when the king came of age in 1302, they seem to have disbanded of their own accord. No more is heard about them until the minority of Alfonso XI. For thirteen chaotic years the *hermandades* tried to preserve municipal rights and the authority of the king. At the *cortes* of 1315 the *hermandades* of Castile and León had an important voice in determining the regency for the child-king, and in 1317 the *hermandad* meeting at Carrión was quite blunt in its dealings with the regents. When Alfonso XI came of age in 1323 the *hermandades* again faded from the scene, and little more was heard of them until the reign of Fernando and Isabel.

As a means of curtailing the crime and disorder that prevailed at the outset of their reign, Fernando and Isabel revived the older institution, establishing the Santa Hermandad in the *corte* of Madrid in 1476.

The Consejo de la Santa Hermandad, whose members were appointed by the crown, was given full authority to direct its activities. In order to guarantee the safety of the highways and to suppress robbery and brigandage, the hermandad had at its disposal about two thousand mounted soldiers. The towns provided funds for the maintenance and support of this force. Local *alcaldes de la hermandad* were assigned to try persons accused of crime by the officers of the *hermandad*. The financial burden of maintaining the *hermandad* eventually prompted the towns to ask that it be suppressed, but it was not until 1498 that the monarchs dissolved the Consejo. The *hermandades* of the late thirteenth and fourteenth centuries were essentially controlled by the municipalities and at times were a threat to the monarchy, so much so that kings were glad to be rid of them, once an emergency situation had passed. Fernando and Isabel utilized this medieval institution as an instrument of royal policy but, like their predecessors, eliminated it once the crisis that brought it into being was over.

JOSEPH F. O'CALLAGHAN

Bibliography

Álvarez de Morales, A. *Las hermandades: Expresión del movimiento comunitario en Espana*. Valladolid, 1974.

Lunenfeld, M. *The Council of the Santa Hermandad. A Study of the Pacification Forces of Fernando and Isabel*. Coral Gables, Fla., 1970.

HERMENEGILD

The eldest son of Leovigild by an unnamed first wife, Hermenegild was made joint ruler with his father, together with his younger brother Reccared, in 573. This may have meant little in practice until, in 579, he was entrusted with authority over the south of the Iberian Peninsula and given a separate seat of government at Seville. This occurred at the same time as his marriage to Ingundis, the daughter of the Austrasian Frankish king Sigebert I and his wife Brunechildis, the latter was a daughter of the former Visigothic king Athanagild. This marriage, which should have cemented ties between the new and the old ruling houses of the Visigothic kingdom, had the opposite effect. In 580 Hermenegild was persuaded to revolt by his wife's grandmother Goisuintha, who, although she had become Leovigild's second wife, appears to have wanted to see an independent kingdom created for the descendants of her former husband, Athanagild. Significantly, this was also the name given to Hermenegild and Ingundls's only son.

From 580 on Hermenegild ruled over Baetica and southern Lusitania, and initially Leovigild made no move against his son. In 582, however, Hermenegild converted from Arianism to Catholicism, as part of a rapprochement with Byzantium. Particularly involved in this was Bishop Leander of Seville, who had undertaken a diplomatic mission to Constantinople for Hermenegild. In 583 Leovigild launched an attack on his son's kingdom, taking Lérida and besieging Seville. In 584 he captured Hermenegild at Córdoba. Hermenegild was sent into exile but was murdered or executed the following year at Tarragona by a certain Sisbert. His wife and son had escaped to the Byzantine enclave in southeast Spain, but Ingundis died at Carthage on the way to Constantinople. There the young Athanagild disappears from view, despite efforts by his Visigothic grandmother Brunechildis to have him returned. Condemned by both John of Biclaro and Isidore of Seville, Hermenegild features as a martyr in the work of Valerius of Bierzo (690s), largely through the influence of the *Dialogues* of Pope Gregory I the Great, who presented him, somewhat erroneously, as a victim of Arian persecution.

ROGER COLLINS

Bibliography

Collins, R. "Mérida and Toledo, 550–585." In *Visigothic Spain: New Approaches*. Ed. E. James. Oxford, 1980. 189–219.

Goffart, W. "Byzantine Policy in the West under Tiberius I I and Maurice: The Pretenders Hermenegild and Gundovald (579–585)," *Traditio* 19 (1957) 75–118.

Hillgarth, J. N. "Coins and Chronicles: Propaganda in Sixth-Century Spain and the Byzantine Background," *Historia* 15 (1966), 483–508.

HIDALGO *See* NOBLES AND NOBILITY

ḤIMYARĪ

About Ibn ʿAbd al-Munʿim al-Ḥimyarī little more is known beyond his immediate North African origins. His *nisba* (kinship name) points ultimately to his forebears' South Arabian descent. We know that Al-Ḥimyarī was a man of religious law (*faqīh*) and a notary (ʿ*adl*). He was the author of an extensive geographical dictionary entitled *Kitāb al-Rawḍ al-miʿtar fī khabar al-aqtār* (*The Fragrant Garden of Information Concerning the Regions of the World*). To the great French Arabist, Lévi-Provençal we owe the discovery and a partial edition of Al-Ḥimyarī's work. There are many manuscripts. The Timbuktu manuscript gives what may be the correct date of compilation: 1461. The *Rawḍ*, which draws on several important antecedents, including Al-Idrīsī's *Nuzhat al-mushtāq fī ikhtirāq al-āfāq* (*The Delight of the One Who Yearns to Traverse* *the Horizons*), is arranged alphabetically (*alif-bā*). The lengthy section devoted to Al-Andalus begins with a substantial account of the Muslim conquest, followed by detailed descriptions of cities and towns, interspersed with poems, and including much historical material: the *tā'ífas* (party kingdoms) the taking, plundering, and recapture of Barbastro, the fall of Valencia to Jaime II, the battles of Zallāqah and Las Navas de Tolosa, among other subjects. There are also entries on Narbonne (the farthest town conquered by Muslims), France, the Atlantic Ocean, Bordeaux, and other extrapeninsular topics. The descriptions of the mosque at Córdoba, of Mérida's ruins, of Almería's famous textiles, and the account of King Solomon's fabulous table at Toledo are all worthy of note. Particularly intriguing is Al-Ḥimyarī's account, taken from Al-Īdrīsī, of the adventurers, eight cousins who set sail from Lisbon, westward and then southward and, after enduring storms and darkness, reached an island populated by tall, blond or red-haired men and beautiful women, where they were imprisoned, interviewed by a lone speaker of Arabic, and finally, after being blindfolded and taken eastward on a three-day boat journey, were released on the coast of Morocco. But, asks Sánchez Albornoz, in a thought-provoking study, if those twelfth-century Muslim adventurers actually had reached America and returned, how might the course of history have changed?

SAMUEL G. ARMISTEAD

Bibliography

Lévi-Provençal, E. *La Péninsule Ibérique au Moyen Age*. Leiden, 1938.

Lewicki, T. "Ibn ʿAbd al-Munʿim al-Ḥimyarī." *Encyclopaedia of Islam*. 2d ed. Vol. 3. Leiden, 1971.

Maestro González, M.P. (trans.). *Al-Himyari: Kitab ar-Rawd al-mi'tar*. Valencia, 1963.

Sánchez Albornoz, C. *De ayer y de hoy*. Madrid, 1958.

HISTORIA ARABUM *See* JIMÉNEZ DE RADA, RODRIGO

HISTORIA COMPOSTELANA

This Latin work is in all probability incomplete, and in the form that survives, postdates 1139. The *Historia* is a composite work of multiple authors. The largest portion of it consists of a history (*gesta*) of the episcopate of Archbishop Diego Gelmírez of Santiago de Compostela (1101–1140) that stops short of relating his death, which occurred on 6 April 1140. This history was the work of a canon of the Church of Santiago de Compostela, Gerald, who was French (probably from Beauvais). An earlier portion of the work is a register of documents that records gifts to the church and short accounts of the circumstances surrounding the donations. This register was composed by Muño Alfonso, then treasurer of the church and later Bishop of Mondoñedo (1113–1136). Still earlier in the manuscript, and probably in time, is a *translatio* recounting the pious theft of some relics from churches in Braga by Bishop Gelmírez in 1102 and their redistribution to churches in Compostela. This piece was the work of Hugh, the canon and archdeacon of Santiago de Compostela and later bishop of Oporto (1113–1136). All of these are preceded by a brief history of Saint James the Great in Spain and the shrine church that had come to bear his name.

Despite some assertions to the contrary, the *Historia* had no effect on the historiography of medieval Iberia. It remained a local and unknown work. Nevertheless, it is important for the no less than 161 documents: royal charters, papal bulls, acts of church councils, and others are incorporated in its text and otherwise largely unknown. Though obviously biased in Gelmírez's favor, the *Historia* is also most important as a contemporary source for some of the events of the reigns of Alfonso VI (1065–1109) of León-Castile, of his daughter Urraca (1109–1126), and of his grandson Alfonso VII (1126–1157), in events of which Gelmírez was often deeply involved.

Today some nineteen manuscripts of the history are known, the oldest of which is a thirteenth-century copy in the library of the University of Salamanca. In most of the manuscipts the much shorter *Chronicon Iriense*, the *Chonicon Compostellam*, a list of the archbishops of Compostela, and a chronicle of the troubled episcopate of the fourteenth-century Archbishop Berenguer of Landoria are appended.

BERNARD F. REILLY

Bibliography

Falque Rey, E. (ed.) *Historia Compostelana*. Corpus Christianorum: Continuatio Medievalis, vol. 70. Turnhout, 1988.

Vones, L. *Die "Historia Compostelana" und die Kirchenpolitik des nordwestspanischen Raumes*. Cologne, 1980.

HISTORIA DE LA DONZELLA TEODOR

The *Historia* is based on a tale in *The Thousand and One Nights*. In it the beautiful and wise slave girl Tawaddud saves her impoverished owner from distress by answering correctly, in the presence of the caliph Harun ar-Rashid, to whom she had been offered for sale, the questions of specialists in very different fields of knowledge.

The tale, composed in Baghdad, probably in the second half of the ninth century, possibly has a Greek origin, was later reshaped in Egypt, and also circulated independently from *The Thousand and One Nights*. The frame is of secondary importance to the examination, consisting of questions and riddles. At some point in the transmission, the name of the heroine was misread as *Tudur*—hence *Teodor* in the Spanish translation or adaptation (thirteenth or, at the latest, fourteenth century).

The oldest Spanish versions of the tale—as an additional chapter of the *Bocados de oro* in four fifteenth-century manuscripts; a fragment of another manuscript of the same period; and an incunabulum without year and place (Toledo, ca. 1498) differ very widely from one another, thus presupposing a rather long and complicated transmission. The number of examiners has been reduced to three (a theologian and jurist, a physician, a grammarian and rhetorician); the scene transferred to Babilonia (i.e., Cairo) or, in the printed versions, in which Teodor is a Christian slave from Spain and her master a Hungarian merchant, to North Africa ("en los reynos de Túnez"), and instead of the caliph there is a king or an emir named Almançor.

The printed text was enriched with materials from various sources, such as the *Repertorio de los tienpos* by Andrés de Li and the Spanish version of the *Altercatio Hadriani cum Epicteto*, and in the course of several elaborations underwent profound changes. As a chapbook (*libro de cordel*) the *Historia de la donzella Teodor* (in some of the later editions *Teodora*) enjoyed extraordinary popularity through the centuries. More than forty Spanish editions before about 1890 are known, and the work was translated three times into Portuguese during the seventeenth and eighteenth centuries, and even into the Mayan language. In the form of ballads it still lives today in northeastern Brazil. Lope de Vega wrote a *comedia* about the wise slave, whose name has become proverbial.

WALTER METTMANN

Bibliography

Mettmann, W. *La Historia de la donzella Teodor*. Wiesbaden, 1962.

Mettmann, W. *La historia de la Donzella Teodor; ein spanisches Volksbuch arabischen Ursprungs; Untersuchung und kritische Ausgabe der altesten*. Mainz, 1962.

Parker, M. *The Story of a Story Across Cultures: The Case of the Doncella Teodor*. Woodbridge, Suffolk, UK; Rochester, N.Y., 1996.

HISTORIA DE LA LINDA MELOSINA

The *Historia de la linda Melosina*, an Old Spanish translation of Jean d'Arras's prose romance *Livre de Mélusine o Noble histoire de Lusignan* (ca. 1387), was first published at Toulouse in 1489 by the German printers Johnnes Paris and Stefan Clebat. The translation was seemingly made from the 1478 Geneva edition of Arras's text printed by Adam Steinschaber, and follows the French closely. There is a second, less slavish Old Spanish version (1526), as well as record of a 1512 Valencia edition, of which there is no known extant exemplar.

The romance, based on written and traditional matter, recounts the establishment of Lusignan, its ruling line, and their conquests. Melusina, Lusignan's founder, is a fairy princess who, as punishment for acts against her father, is to be transformed into a serpent from the waist down every Saturday (although in some legendary accounts she adopts a mermaid's form). She must hide this metamorphosis from her husband in order to remain in the mortal world. In the end, however, her husband, Raimondin, discovers the secret, which forces Melusina to leave her human form forever.

The Spanish translations, like the French original, are rich in chivalric conquest and folkloric motifs. The romance contains many references to Aragónese and Catalan locations, which, as critics have suggested, could have influenced the Count of Cardona to grant asylum to Thomas of Lusignan after the Turks ousted him from Cyprus in the late fifteenth century. As Alan Deyermond has discussed, the date of the first Spanish translation coincides with those political actions, suggesting the importance of *Melosina* in the Iberian Peninsula.

IVY A. CORFIS

Bibliography

Corfis, I.A. (ed.) *Historia de la linda Melosina*. Madison, Wisco, 1986.

Deyermond, A.D. "*La historia de la linda Melosina*: Two Spanish Versions of a French Romance." In *Medieval Studies Presented to Rita Hamilton*. Ed. A.D. Deyermond. London, 1976. pp 57–65.

HISTORIA GOTHORUM *See* JIMÉNEZ DE RADA, RODRIGO

HISTORIA SILENSE

The *Historia* is a Leonese chronicle of unknown authorship composed in the first third of the twelfth century. The author set out, apparently, to compose a history or *aesta* of Alfonso VI of León-Castile (1065–1109), but what he produced is, in large measure, the best surviving narrative account of the reign of Fernando I (1035–1065). All that he accomplished for the reign of Alfonso is a short introduction to the period 1065–1073.

This history of León-Castille in the first two-thirds of the eleventh century is set against a fairly traditional chronicle background that begins with the late-seventh-century Visigothic kings and then relates the history of the kings of Asturias and León up to the time of Fernando and Alfonso. For these earlier reigns he draws upon the seventh-century histories of Isidore of Seville and of Julianus of Toledo, the ninth-century *Chronicle of Alfonso III*, the eleventh-century chronicle of Bishop Sampiro of Astorga (1034–1042), and the reworking of Sampiro's chronicle by Bishop Pelayo of Oviedo (1102–1130). The *Silense* has historiographical importance because the chronicle of Sampiro does not survive independently.

In actuality the title *Historia silense* is a misnomer. The author refers to himself as a monk of a monastery that he calls "domus Seminis" and that modern scholarship early identified with the monastery of Santo Domingo de Silos in Castile. It has recently been demonstrated that the author was a member of the Leonese monastery of Sahagún, which enjoyed the closest of ties with Fernando I, thus giving the account a peculiar authority for that reign.

The problems of composition and authorship of the text have been aggravated by the fact that none of the eight surviving known manuscripts is older than the fifteenth century.

BERNARD F. REILLY

Bibliography

Canal Sánchez Pagín, J.M. "*Crónica silense* o *Cronica Domnis Sanctis*?" *Cuadernos de historia de España* 63–64 (1980), 94–103.

Pérez de Urbel, J., and A. González Ruiz-Zorrilla (eds.) *Historia Silense*. Madrid, 1959.

Santos Coco, F. (ed.) *Historia Silense*. Madrid, 1921.

HISTORIOGRAPHY: *ESTORIA DE ESPAÑA* AND ITS DERIVATIVES

Alfonso X's project for writing a history of Spain, the *Estoria de España*, was begun early in his reign, and a first draft was probably completed by the 1270s. Some four hundred chapters appear to have been completed by about 1272, when Alfonso's attention moved to the more universal *Grande e general estoria*. The more parochial project continued, however, and a number of succeeding attempts were made to finish it, albeit in a less professional manner than in the period of Alfonso's direct interest.

The earlier chapters, dealing with the history of Spain up to the Moorish invasion, exist in a relatively definitive version and have attracted less critical attention; their sources are clear: Orosius and Eusebius of Caesarea figure prominently, and for the Visigothic period much use is made of earlier medieval Spanish chroniclers in Latin, particularly Rodrigo Jiménez de Rada, Archbishop of Toledo (*El toledano*) and Lucas, Bishop of Túy (*El tudense*). It is with the history of the Reconquest, however, that the historiographical tradition becomes more complex in a way which has attracted much critical attention. One of the reasons for this is undoubtedly the compilers' desire to introduce popular poetic material ("epic" poems) into their narrative. This often led to problems of both chronology and verisimilitude, and it is not uncommon for successive chronicle compilers to give substantially different accounts of the same event. Whether these differences are due to the chroniclers' own inventiveness or reflect knowledge of successively differing oral poetic traditions, is a matter of ongoing critical debate.

The title *Estoria de España* (EE), while useful as a name for the original enterprise, cannot properly be used for any one version or manuscript in its entirety. An older critical tradition used the name *Primera crónica general* (PCG), now best reserved for the version published under that title by Ramón Menéndez Pidal (originally in 1906). That version, covering the period from the start of the Reconquest on, is a composite one, belonging to what is called the *versión regia* of the EE. Contrasting with this is the *versión vulgar*, characterized by a more concise, and presumably more primitive, version of the original draft on which the EE was to be based. By contrast, the *versión regia* is marked by a tendency to expansion, sometimes merely rhetorical but on other occasions attempting to explain and justify the actions of characters or to make them more exemplary, and on occasion introducing new legendary material. Sometimes groups of manuscripts within what is recognizably the same version of introduce their own idiosyncrasies: thus a number of manuscripts of the *versión regia*, known as the *Crónica fragmentaria*, show a critical spirit toward their sources that demonstrates how the process of compilation continued, with a new chronicler deliberately introducing his own reservations about the narrative sequence he was relating.

Alongside the *versión vulgar* of the EE one should next place two other chronicle versions that seem to go back to the same early stage of the Alfonsine draft (*borrador*). These are the *Crónica de veinte reyes* (CVR) and the *Crónica general "vulgata"* (CGV). The CVR is relatively the most concise chronicle, of this group, though not consistently so. It is the first to make use of the legendary material dealing with the partition of the kingdoms by Fernando I, and it also offers a substantially revised and reorganized version of the events of the reign of the succeeding king, Sancho II. The most interesting aspect of the CVR, however, is that it tells the story of El Cid in substantially the same terms as the extant *Poema de mío Cid*, while all other chronicles introduce much new material, either from different sources or on their own initiative.

The CGV, while apparently going back to the same *borrador* as the *versión vulgar* and the CVR, has its idiosyncrasies. It sometimes has minor structural peculiarities, adds editorial notes and some details, and on occasion strongly prefers a popular source over the historiographical tradition that is normally followed: this is the case in the novelistic story of the murder of Infante García of Castile, for example. The CGV was one of the first Alfonsine works to be printed, and this version was used for much of the text published in the sixteenth century by the historiographer Florián de Ocampo. In *Las quatro partes enteras de la Crónica de España* (1541), Ocampo used the CGV for the part of the story up to the union of Castile and León under Fernando I in 1037.

A final version of the original Alfonsine draft survives only indirectly, in that it seems to underlie the now lost chronicle possessed by Alfonso's nephew, Infante Juan Manuel, summarized in the latter's *Crónica abreviada*.

Turning to later, expanded versions of the EE, mention has already been made of the *versión regia*, which we know best as the PCG. This formed the basis for a number of later elaborations. The most common of these (in terms of numbers of manuscripts) is the *Crónica de los reyes de Castilla* or *Crónica de Castilla* (CrC). This version begins with the accession of Fernando I to the throne of León in 1037, and may be regarded as a greatly expanded and amplified version of the *versión regia* from this point on. Of all chronicle versions under discussion, the CrC makes the most frequent and uncritical use of legendary material, often in a highly novelesque way. This is seen consistently, but perhaps most strikingly in the account of the later years of El Cid's life and his death. The CrC gave rise to another early printed text, the *Crónica del famoso cauallero Cid Ruy Diez, campeador* (Burgos, 1512), commonly called the *Crónica particular del Cid*, which is an extract from the longer CrC.

Another later derivation from the Alfonsine EE, and probably the best known, is the *Crónica de 1344* (Cr 1344), whose genesis is complex. There a small number of Galician-Portuguese manuscripts that are composite versions, combining the *versión regia* of the EE up to 1037 and the CrC thereafter. These are the ancestors of the Cr 1344. The chronicle was originally composed in Portuguese in 1344, translated into Castilian, revised in an expanded version (ca. 1400) in Portuguese, and then translated into Castilian once more. Of all the chronicle versions discussed, the Cr 1344 represents the most radical and critical rewriting of its sources, whether the *versión regia* or the CrC. Sometimes it involves new sources (the story of the Infantes de Lara is extensively revised, apparently from a poetic source) or other chronicle versions (the story of Fernando I's division of his kingdoms and the ensuing reign of Sancho II is apparently rewritten in the light of the alternative version offered by the CVR). It is always clear in the Cr 1344 that a new and critical spirit is at work, one with a strong tendency to rearrange structural elements and expand the narrative in ways that include the rhetorical but do not stop there.

Another version similar to the CrC and the Cr 1344 is the chronicle with which Ocampo completed his edition of the CGV. Generally referred to as the *Crónica ocampiana*, it takes up the story from the accession of Fernando I (1037) with what is in fact a blend of the *versión regia* and the CrC. It has more features in common with the latter, however, to the point where it might be argued that to talk about the *Ocampiana* as a separate chronicle family is misleading.

Brief reference must be made to two idiosyncratic versions. One is generally known as the *Versión interpolada de la CGV*, and is a one-manuscript derivative of that chronicle that interpolates material which is frequently of a sententious or religious nature and which may, on occasion, reflect the use of new, later versions of epic legends (e.g., the Infantes de Lara). The second is the *Refundición toledana de la Crónica 1344*, a novelesque and rhetorical expansion of the chronicle in question dating from the fifteenth century.

The chronology of the various texts discussed here is difficult to establish, given that few of the manuscripts contain dates of composition, and the majority of them were produced in the fourteenth and fifteenth centuries. One may provisionally divide the chronicle versions into four groups: (1) the first part of the *Estoria de España*, up to the Moorish invasion, completed in Alfonso's lifetime; (2) an early version of the remainder of the narrative, based on the Alfonsine *borrador* and completed at the end of the thirteenth century or the beginning of the fourteenth century: the *versión vulgar* of the *Estoria de España*; the *Crónica de veinte* reyes; the *Crónica general "Vulgata"*; (3) a series of more elaborate fourteenth-century versions comprising, in order, the *versión regia* or *Primera crónica general*, the *Crónica de Castilla*, the *Crónica de 1344*, and the *Crónica ocampiana*; and (4) later derivative versions, probably of the fifteenth century, the *Versión interpolada de la Crónica general "Vulgata"* and the

Refundición toledana de la Crónica de 1344, as well as other novelesque versions not discussed here, such as García de Salazar's *Libro de las bienandanzas* and Rodríguez de Almela's *Compendio historial*.

DAVID PATTISON

Bibliography

Catalán, D., and R. Menéndez Pidal. *De Alfonso X al conde de Barcelos*. Cuatro estudios sobre el nacimiento de la historiografía romance en Castilla y Portugal. Madrid, 1962.

Chalon, L. *L'Histoire et l'épopée castillane du Moyen Âge*. Nouvelle Bibliothèque du Moyen Âge. Vol. 5. Paris, 1976.

Crónica general de España de 1344. Ed. D. Catalán and M. S. de Andrés. Vol. 1. Madrid, 1970.

Menéndez Pidal, R. *Reliquias de la poesía épica española*. 2d ed. Madrid, 1980.

Pattison, D.G. *From Legend to Chronicle: The Treatment of Epic Material in Alphonsine Historiography*. Medium Aevum Monographs, n. s., 13. Oxford, 1983.

Primera crónica general de España. Ed. R. Menéndez Pidal, 2 vols. 2d ed. Madrid, 1955.

HISTORIOGRAPHY, HEBREW

Medieval Jewish chronicles of Spain are few in number and generally poor in quality. Fortunately, however, there are other Hebrew sources of greater value. Medieval Jewish historiography generally followed neither the Bible nor the Talmud, much less such sound historiographical "good sense" as exhibited in 2 Maccabees 2: 24–31. Rather, it was chiefly concerned with lamenting supposed "persecutions" and other disasters, real or imagined. This has aptly been termed the "lachrymose conception" of Jewish history, all too prevalent also in modern writing. Thus, there are such (non-Spanish) chronicles as *The Vale of Tears*. In Spanish Jewish historiography, this is most exemplified in the work of one of the latest writers, Samuel Ibn Verga (fifteenth century), one of the exiles, whose *Shevet Yehudah* (available in Spanish translation) is filled with misleading and false information about the terrible persecutions suffered. Nevertheless, it sometimes contains accurate details of certain events, and like all Spanish Jews, Ibn Verga showed his veneration for the rulers.

Turning from the last to the first, we find an entirely different plan in the work of Abraham Ibn Daud of Toledo (ca. 1110–1180), whose *Sefer ha-qabbalah* (available in both Spanish and English translations) describes the whole of Jewish history from the Bible to his own day. It is highly programmatic, however, as has been shown by its modern editor, with anti-Qaraite polemical intent and possible messianic views. Nevertheless, Ibn Daud, also an important philosopher and scientist, is a generally reliable source for certain maior personalities and events of al-Andalus in his own generation and the immediately preceding years.

The only surviving complete Hebrew chronicles from Spain are from the fifteenth and early sixteenth centuries. Joseph Ibn Saddiq of Arévalo (ca. 1467) left a brief chronicle, which served in turn as the main source for that of Abraham ben Solomon (of "Torrutiel" is impossible; perhaps "Ardutiel," in 1510). Both (also in Spanish translations) are essentially records of the lives and activities of famous Jewish scholars, with only brief details on major "events" in Spanish-Jewish history, often with errors of dates, and other matters. Finally, Abraham Zacut, the noted astronomer of the late fifteenth and early sixteenth centuries (again, one of the exiles) wrote a much more valuable chronicle, *Sefer Yuhasin* (untranslated and virtually unstudied). Like Ibn Daud's work it details the whole of Jewish history, but without any obvious "program" or polemic. His chronicle of personalities and events of Jewish Spain is interspersed indiscriminately with general medieval Jewish history. However, he appears to have used reliable sources, and generally his information is useful and at times uniquely valuable.

Other Jewish writers of Spain, without intentionally setting out to be "chroniclers," have nevertheless left chronicles and other historically valuable material in their writings. Well-known examples include Menahem ben Solomon ha-Meiri of Perpignan (ca. 1300), who provides not only important information on scholars of Provence and Spain but also other historical notices; Menahem Ibn Zerah (originally from Navarre, also lived in Toledo; d. 1385), whose introduction to his *Sedehla-derekh* (untranslated) gives eyewitness accounts of important events, such as the massacre of 1328 in Navarre, and of personalities with whom he was personally acquainted. Less-known writers are Isaac ben Joseph Israeli of Toledo (1310), whose astronomical treatise *Yesod olam* contains a chapter chronicling various scholars and events (the text in the published edition is very poor, and must be read in Zacuto's *Sefer Yuhasin*; Kraków, 1581 only, chap. 18). Much of it is copied verbatim from Ibn Daud. Samuel Zarza of Palencia (1368) has left some important information in his *Megor hayyim* (appendix in Wiener's ed. of Ibn Verga, *Shevet Yehudah*, and in the Spanish translation). Isaac ben Jacob de Lattes (1372; often erroneously identified by Jewish scholars with a later Isaac de Lattes) wrote a chronicle, *Shaʿarey Siyyon*, which is generally a mere catalog of rabbis but does have some important information. Saʿadyah ben Maimon Ibn Danan (Granada, 1468–1485) also left such a chronicle, of limited value.

Of importance for the history of Jews in Spain, though not written by Spanish Jews, are such chronicles as Joseph h. Joshua ha-Kohen's (Provence, fourteenth century), *ʿEmeq ha-baka* (available in English and Spanish translations) and, of a far different quality, the tremendously important work of Elijah Kapsali of Candia *Seder Eliyahu zuta* (1523; now available in a critical edition) on the Jews of the Ottoman Empire, which gives much valuable information on Spanish Jews before and after the exile.

Jewish historiography of medieval Spain is of interest not only for the Jewish historian. Since Spanish Jews were on intimate terms with Muslims and Christians, and often closely involved with the government, it is not surprising that these works reveal some awareness of the general events of the time. Ibn Daud, for example, compiled a Hebrew history of Rome up to the rise of the Muslim Empire, and in his *Sefer ha-qabbalah* there are references to Rome, Persia, and other places, as well as some of the Spanish kings. Yet while the other medieval chroniclers (Ibn Saddiq and his imitator Abraham ben Solomon) show some awareness and even appreciation of medieval kings and certain events of history (though often with erroneous names and dates), it is not until Abraham Zacut that we encounter a genuine awareness and appreciation of non-Jewish—history in a favorable or at least neutral manner; he mentions important church figures, the commentary on Job of Gregory I (which he calls a "great work"), the discovery of the Shroud of Turin, the Council of Basel. (Such relatively objective reporting of Christian personalities and events is generally considered to appear first in the work of Azariah de Rossi in Italy, in the sixteenth century; obviously this is incorrect.) Zacut was not unaware of Muslim history, he reports favorably on certain Muslim scientists and physicians. This work, particularly in its careful edition from manuscript, contains much valuable general historical information, and it is obvious that Zacut drew on Spanish and probably Latin (perhaps also Arabic) sources.

Finally, mention should be made of *Zikaron ha-shmaddof*, a supposed Hebrew chronicle of persecutions (lost, if it ever existed) that Grayzel, Baer, and others insisted was composed by Profiat Duran (fifteenth century). While quotations from such a work do appear, it is at best doubtful that Duran was the author. We also should take note of the specialized "historiography"—really polemics and philosophico-theological schemata—of such authors as Judah ben Barzilai (Barcelona, twelfth century), *Peirush Sefer Yesirah*, and his contemporary Abraham bar Ḥiyya (or Hayya), *Meqillat ha-Megalleh* (an excellent Catalan translation), and in the fifteenth century, of the writer and statesman Isaac Abravanel.

NORMAN ROTH

Bibliography

Baron, S. W. *A Social and Religious History of the Jews*. Philadelphia, 1952–60. Vol. 6. 204 ff.

Roth, N. " 'Seis edades durará el mundo': Temas de la polémica judía española." *Ciudad de Dios* 199 (1986). 45–65.

Steinschneider, M. *Die Geshichstliteratur der Juden*. Frankfurt am Main, 1905.

HISTORIOGRAPHY: ANNALS AND LATIN CHRONICLES UP TO *DE REBUS HISPANIAE*

Christian historiography in the period 500–1250 produced relatively few works. Before the twelfth century in particular, histories that have survived are limited in number and in length, and there is little evidence that many have been lost. In the twelfth century there was some increase in activity that carried on into the thirteenth, when longer and more comprehensive histories finally emerged. In addition to the overall paucity of texts, problems arise because many earlier texts are known only in copies that have been amended, deliberately or accidentally, by their transmitters, while later texts are often reliant on earlier ones for their information.

The principal historical works from the year 500 on are basically annalistic, setting down events in chronological order, in a time frame expressed in relation to major sequences. These are principally the calendar year, expressed as the Spanish Era only or with the addition of *anno domini*, and the year of the reign of the monarch. Besides the latter there can be indicators of the year of the reign of the Roman emperor, the Muslim year, and other markers. For the most part, years are mentioned only when something of note occurs in them, and the length of the entries vary according to the events recorded. In addition to events there are often genealogies, important for ruling houses. Most (if not all) writers were clerics, frequently holders of high office and with close links to the ruling elite. These circumstances had predictable consequences both for the tone of the texts and for the attitudes toward royalty. Texts are in Latin, and the early ones in particular are short. (Those mentioned below are all longer than the annals that have survived from various parts of Iberia.)

Two models were established for later writers in the time of Visigothic domination, by John of Biclaro, bishop of Girona, and Isidore, bishop of Seville. Both described themselves as continuers of earlier historians, such as Eusebius of Caesarea and Jerome, and considered their role to be to add to their writings in order to bring them up to contemporary times. John of Biclaro's model is the universal chronicle, which begins at the Creation, and includes biblical and classical history before reaching Iberia. The other model is provided by Isidore's history of the Goths from legendary origins to their rule of Spain. One task they both performed was to place the Visigoths within an continuum in a way that gave them historical legitimacy as rulers and provided a perspective that would inspire central Spain's view of itself for many centuries. John's chronicle adds to earlier writers the period 567–590, includes the conversion of the Visigoths to Catholicism and compares Reccared to Constantine. Isidore also produced a short history on the universal model, but his *Historia Gothorum*, with short accounts of the Suevi and Vandals, was more influential in the long term. Despite an inconsistent format resulting from its variety of sources, the *Historia* recounts the progress of the Visigoths to 625, portraying them as legitimate conquerors of, and successors to, the Romans. Its opening "Laus Spaniae," in praise of Iberia, became a commonplace. One other work of the pre-Conquest period is the *Historia Wambae* of Julianus of Toledo, which describes the election of Wamba in 672 and the rebellion of Paulus a year later.

After the Muslim entry into Spain, there is a long pause before histories appear in Christian-controlled areas. Elsewhere, in al-Andalus, a cleric aware of Isidore's writings composed the *Crónica mozárabe* (754). It includes Byzantine, Arabic, and Visigothic affairs, and, while bemoaning the Muslim Conquest, recounts events within the church in Muslim Spain without being anti-Muslim. The reign of Alfonso III of Asturias saw the first flowering of historiography in Christian Spain with the *Crónica albeldense* and the *Crónica de Alfonso III*, both probably composed in the 880s, although surviving only in much later texts. While differing over some matters, they focus on the historical context for the Asturian monarchy up to Alfonso III. The *Albeldense* uses the universal model, including Roman history, while the *Alfonso III* is more like Isidore's *Historia Gothorum*. In them, the Asturian nobility emerges as legitimate heirs of the Visigoths with a claim to all their lost kingdom. The *Alfonso III* ends with that king's accession in 866 and shows strong evidence of royal approval of its composition, but it is the *Albeldense* that includes events of Alfonso's reign up to 883.

It may also have been in this period that series of brief annals began to be recorded in religious houses. These laconic lists of events of variable significance, set down in chronological order, were not compiled by one author at one time, but grew up over many years as different contributors added to a sequence sometimes stretching over centuries. Such annals, or evidence of them, have survived from most Christian zones, as in the *annales conimbricenses* in Portugal and the *annales compostellani* in Galicia. Annals of this type were compiled in Castile and in the more eastern areas of the Iberián Peninsula as well. After the emergence of historiography in Asturias in the 880s, another long period followed without major activity beyond the revision of older texts such as the *Crónica de Alfonso III*. For the tenth and eleventh centuries, all we have, apart from annals, is a history by Sampiro of Astorga of the kingdom of Asturias-León, from the end of the *Crónica de Alfonso III* to 984. Although likely to have been composed shortly after that date, it survives only in the twelfth-century compilations mentioned below.

It was not until the twelfth century that more, and more varied, historiographic activity began. In its early decades the disordered but interesting *Historia silense*, composed in León, used the works cited above and added new material to bring events up to the death of Fernando of Castile I in 1065, explicitly as preparation for a life of Alfonso VI that does not survive (and was probably never written). Of the same period, the compilation *Ab exordio mundi usque eram mclxx*, by Bishop Pelayo of Oviedo, adds to previous sources a brief and uninspired history of Alfonso.

But along with continuers of the previous patterns of historiography, the twelfth century also saw innovators. The *Chronica Adefonsi imperatoris* is a consciously literary eulogy of the life of Alfonso VII that becomes a poem on his capture of Almería. A nonroyal lay personage, Rodrigo Díaz, el Cid, is honored with a history of his own, the *Gesta Roderici Campi Doctoris*, which may have used documentary sources. In Galicia, the *Cronicón iriense*, although brief, is idiosyncratic, as is the *Historia compostelana*, which records the history of the see of Santiago. This broader geographical spread of activity is confirmed, in the second half of the century, by the composition farther east of the *Crónica najerense*, best known for its inclusion of more material from popular legends than in previous chronicles, alongside sources such as the *Silense*. In Catalonia, this period saw the creation of the first history beyond annalistic notes with the composition in the monastery of Ripoll of the *Gesta Comitum Barcinonensium*, continued in various versions for more than a century. In Navarre, shortly before 1200, the *Liber regum*, a series of genealogies, was put together, along with a brief text about El Cid. It is worthy of particular mention because it is the first historiographical text in a vernacular Spanish dialect, not Latin.

The first half of the thirteenth century saw the appearance of a *Crónica latina* concentrating on Castilian history up to 1236 and also the two most substantial histories of the period under discussion, both continuations of the semiofficial line of Visigothic-Asturian-Leonese-Castilian histories. The first of these, the *Chronicon mundi* of Lucas of Túy, takes the universal model, beginning with the Creation. The fourth of its four books describes Spanish history in the period 711–1236. Written in Léon in the late 1230s at royal behest, the chronicle combines sources mentioned above more skillfully and comprehensively than previously, and adds others—ecclesiastical, political, and popular—to create a work that enhanced not only royal prestige but also the status of León and its church. The other major work follows the alternative model. The *Historia gothica* or *Historia de rebus Hispaniae* of Rodrigo Jiménez de Rada, archbishop of Toledo, was completed in 1243. Though it relies on Lucas for much of its structure and content, it also exploits a variety of materials gathered and collated by a team employed by Rodrigo, who also composed histories of the Romans, the Moors, and various Germanic tribes. Rodrigo's principal interest was the promotion of Toledo as metropolitan see of Spain against rivalry from León, Santiago, and, potentially, Seville. To this end he was ruthless in amending his sources while making his final text sufficiently convincing to stand alongside the *Chronicon mundi* as a major structural basis for Alfonso X's vernacular history in the second half of the century.

BRIAN POWELL

Bibliography

Díaz y Díaz, M.C. *De Isidoro al siglo X: Ocho estudios sobre la vida literaria peninsular.* Barcelona, 1976.

Jiménez de Rada, R. *Historia de los hechos de España.* Ed. and trans. J. Fernández Valverde. Madrid, 1989.

Linehan, P. *History and the Historians of Medieval Spain.* Oxford, 1993.

Sánchez Albornoz, C. *Investigaciones sobre la historiografía hispana medieval (siglos VIII al XII).* Buenos Aires, 1967.

Sánchez Alonso, B. *Historia de la historiografía española.* Vol. 1. Madrid, 1947.

HISTORIOGRAPHY: ANNALS AND CHRONICLES, FIFTEENTH CENTURY

The historiography of the fifteenth century can be taken to run from the vernacular chronicles of Pero López de Ayala to those of the reign of the Catholic Monarchs. Compared with the previous century, the variety of approach, of form, of spatial and temporal scope, and of language has increased remarkably, as have the frequent observations on the nature and value of history, from Enrique de Villena through Fernán Pérez de Guzmán to Fernando del Pulgar and Lucius Marineus Siculus.

Several factors can be adduced to explain this development. First, there emerged a lay reading public independent of ecclesiastical influences. As libraries of the period show, the average noble drew upon history rather than fiction or collections of exempla for his education; new vernacular translations of Valerius Maximus, Livy, Caesar, Sallust, Quintus Curtius, Suetonius, and Justinus were frequent. Second, unstable political and social situations stimulated a variety of historical judgments. Third, there emerged a growing consciousness of the part to be played by historiography in national and international propaganda, to which may be linked the increasing use of Latin as a means of reaching a wider audience. Fourth, the increase in available texts of Latin and Greek historians allowed the elaboration of the prehistory of the Iberian Peninsula, together with its historical geography and topography. Finally, there was a gradual emergence of the post of royal chronicler, who could be a household scribe with some legal experience, a chaplain or a lay scholar with a university background, a native or immigrant working on commission.

A strong continuity of practice, however, was maintained, as can be seen in the traditional regnal chronicles of the crown in the vernacular, usually the responsibility of the chancellor of the realm. Pedro López de Ayala continues from Fernán Sánchez de Valladolid, covering the usurpation of the royal line by the Trastámaras across the reigns of Pedro I, Enrique II, Juan I, and Enrique III, which were meant to be read as a single block. López de Ayala's procedures are not significantly innovative, but his political insights are sharp. His material is coded according to the principles of chivalry, and exemplified in the deeds and misdeeds of magnates whose families were to dominate in subsequent years. The vision of his successor was politically and culturally less developed. Still maintaining the regnal itinerary as a structural guide, Alvar García took over in the reign of Juan II of Castile, leaving an unexplained ten-year gap. The *Crónica del rey don Juan el segundo* was taken over by others before mid-century, including Fernán Pérez de Guzmán, and revised at the end of the century by Galíndez de Carvajal; no complete, authoritative edition is yet available.

The first clearly documented appointment of an offical historian came in the following reign, that of Enrique IV of Castile, in December 1456, when Alfonso de Palencia was named successor to Juan de

Mena as both chronicler and secretary of Latin letters. Nothing is known of the activity of Mena as historian, although many of his contemporaries refer to him as such. This combination of posts marks a change from the nomination of an *escribano de cámara* to an educated scholar with a knowledge of Latin. Palencia's *Gesta hispaniensis ex annalibus suorum dierum colligentis* (*Décadas* for short) was formally planned in ten books up to the year l48O. The Granada campaign was also to have ten books, but it breaks off in l489, after the siege of Almería. This work has never been published in the original Latin, only in a modern Castilian translation. It contains trenchant and bitter attacks on the moral and political behavior of the nobility by a dedicated supporter of King Fernando V.

By 1460, however, the post of official chronicler proliferated into three further appointments. The only one whose complete work is known is Diego Enríquez del Castillo, the royal chaplain (born 1443). His working copy was captured by rebel troops at Segovia in 1469 and rewritten from memory in the reign of Isabel, who had little sympathy for him. His *Crónica de don Enrique IV* is an effusive eulogy of a king in the grip of circumstances too powerful for him to control, a vision quite contrary to that of Palencia, but infinitely better known at home and abroad.

The reign of Fernando and Isabel is treated extensively and variously by a range of historians, commissioned or otherwise, in both Latin and the vernacular. Juan de Flores, a nobleman from the household of the duke of Alba, author of the sentimental romances *Grimalte y Gradissa* and *Grisel y Mirabella*, has recently been identified as another official chronicler and the author of the *Crónica incompleta de los reyes católicos*. He was appointed in l476, and what survives of the text covers from l469 to l476. Fernando del Pulgar, royal secretary in the previous reign, was appointed chronicler by Isabel in l480 because she disapproved of Palencia's views. She supervised drafts of the *Crónica de los reyes católicos* sent in by Pulgar, who followed the court on active service up to the last years of the Granada campaign. This account became a quarry for subsequent narratives in Latin by Lucius Marineus Siculus and Antonio de Nebrija, all of whom gave wide currency to the concept of the reign of Fernando and Isabel as a dramatic climax to decades of strife and a portent of a glorious future. This was most fulsomely elaborated in the vernacular pulpit oratory of Andrés Bernáldez, chaplain to the archbishop of Seville and under the patronage of Rodrigo Ponce de León, duke of Cádiz. Andalusia is the main scene of this narrative, which includes the Granada campaign, the expulsion of the Jews, and the discovery of the Indies.

Diego de Valera, minor noble, wandering knight, royal councillor and envoy, and compulsive writer of letters and treatises on all manner of topics concerning chivalry and government, planned an extensive account of Castile's past and present history, ending in an detailed narrative of the reigns of Juan II, Enrique IV, and Fernando and Isabel. Its various parts are known as the *Crónica abreviada* (up to Juan II), *Memorial de diversas hazañas* (reign of Enrique IV), and *Crónica de los reyes católicos* (up to the middle of the Granada campaign). The whole is remarkably comprehensive for its time, if not innovative in method. It is dedicated to Isabel, and she and her husband looked upon as saviors of their kingdoms sent by providence to impose law and order. Galíndez de Carvajal's *Anales breves* of this reign are noteworthy not only for their precision and conscious attempt to avoid prejudice and eulogy, but also for the prologue dealing with the value of history, criticisms of previous historians, and the role of the official historian. He also wrote a *Crónica de Enrique IV* that drew in the main upon a vernacular version of Palencia's *Décadas* and Valera's *Memorial*. Galíndez was typical of the new bureaucracy of the Catholic Monarchs, a *letrado* conscious of his duties to the crown and unyielding to the pressures of aristocracy.

In the time of the Crown of Aragón, the most significant event, politically and culturally, was the annexation of the Kingdom of the Two Sicilies by Alfonso V. This king was credited with a voracious appetite for history; his court in Naples attracted many Italian scholars eager for patronage and willing to record, for payment, the lives and deeds of the royal line. Lorenzo Valla's life of Alfonso's father, Fernando de Antequera, *De rebus a Fernandoo Aragóniae rege gestis libri tres* was finished about l445. It is valuable for the discussion in the prologue of the comparative educational merits of literature and philosophy, as well as observations on the nature of historical evidence and textual criticism. The narrative is derived from a version of Alvar García de Santa María's chronicle, and is structured around the moral and military virtues of the protagonist. The *De rebus ab Alphonso Primo Neapolitanorum rege commentariorum libri decem* by Bartolommeo Fazio is also an at tempt to ceate a classical hero figure on the model of Caesar's *Commentaries*, illustrating through his campaigns the virtues of constancy and fortitude. Antonio Beccadelli (*il Panormitano*) has much more to say about Alfonso's cultural pursuits in *De dictis et factis regis Aragónum*, inspired by Xenephon's *Cyropaedia*, which he had previously translated. In the Crown of Aragón proper (with Navarre) there occurred a remarkable lapse in historical writing on contemporary subjects. Carlos de Viana's *Crónica de los reyes de Navarra* goes only as far as Carlos III (died 1425) and was never finished.

In Catalonia the great fourteenth-century tradition of chronicle writing is broken, and resumed only with the advent of Fernando V, who issued commissions Gonzalo García de Santa María and Lucius Marineus Siculus to write biographies of Juan II of Aragón, His illegimate son, Alfonso de Aragón, archbishop of Zaragoza, was a great patron of historical writing, encouraging both Lucius and the Aragónese Gauberte Fabricio de Vagad, who wrote a *Crónica de Aragón* (Zaragoza, 1499) covering the period from the election of Íñigo de Arista to the death of Alfonso V. There is little of consequence in Catalan chronicles until Miquel Carbonell's *Chroniques de Espanya* (finished 1513, printed at Barcelona in 1546). Both these chronicles mark the reign of Alfonso V as a cultural climax in the history of the Crown of Aragón. Carbonell does not take his praise for the kingdom to the exaggerated lengths of Vagad, eager to dismiss Italian claims of superiority.

This sense of cultural competition marks a number of historical works commissioned by Fernando IV. Antonio de Nebrija was asked to revise Pulgar's *Crónica de los reyes católicos* on the basis of a version edited by Galíndez Carvajal, *Rerum a Fernandoo et Elisabe Hispaniarum regibus gestarum Decades Duae* (Granada, 1545). In the same vein, Nebrija reworked Luis Correa's *La conquista del reyno de Navarra* (Salamanca, 1513), which is normally printed with the *Décadas* (Granada, 1545) under the *title De bello Navariensi libri duo*. Both of these Latin works, together with a sequence commissioned from Lucius Marineus, were intended for a wide European circulation and herald in their prologues and conclusions the apotheosis of Hispania restored to its ancient borders in Navarre, Rousillon, and Granada, and about to embark on a new age under the Catholic Monarchs.

The general chronicle of Spain in the Alfonsine tradition also underwent significant changes in the fifteenth century, not so much in the vernacular versions of the *Estoria de España* or Jiménez de Rada's *Historia gothica* as in the new Latin *rifacimenti*. The *Estoria* is reproduced with modifications and additions through the *Crónica general de 1344* and *de 1404*, the *Cuarta crónica general de 1460* and the fanciful *Crónica sarracina* by Pedro del Corral. The heritage is also evident in the *Suma de las crónicas de España* and the *Edades trovadas* of Pablo de Santa María, *converso* (Jewish convert to Christianity) bishop of Burgos. Both are written, in prose and verse, as educational treatises for Juan II of Castile.

Other examples of the general chronicle are the *Atalaya de las crónicas* by Alfonso Martínez de Toledo, the various compilations of Diego Rodríguez de Almela; *Copilación de las batallas campales que son contenidas en las estorias escolásticas y de España* (Murcia, 1487) and *Valerio de las hystorias escolásticas* (finished 1483; Seville, 1542), based formally on Valerius Maximus, but drawing mostly on the *Crónica de 1344*; and the *Crónica abreviada* or *Valeriana* of Diego de Valera, the *Bela Farfana* by Antón Farfán de los Godos, the *Compendio universal* by Alonso de Ávila (?) and Lope García de Salazar's *Bienandanzas e fortunas*. All of these lead back to some version of the Alfonsine heritage, with additions and regional variations, as in the *Bienandanzas*, which concentrates on the feuds in the Basque provinces.

More drastic remodeling rather than reorganization of traditional sources is manifest in the rebirth of Latin historiography in the mid-fifteenth century with the *Anacephaleosis* or *Recapitulation* of Alfonso García de Santa María, *converso* bishop of Burgos (Alfonso de Cartagena). In order to assert the claims of the throne of Castile to offshore islands and the coast of North Africa, Alfonso resurrects the old myth of unbroken royal lineage from the Visigoths and raises Castile to the dominant power in the peninsula. The work goes up to the first years of Enrique IV, and was printed at Granada in 1545. Rodrigo Sánchez de Arévalo's *Compendiosa historia hispánica* (Rome, 1470), the first general history of Spain to be printed, elaborates the same theme and goes further. Challenging Italian humanist accusations of cultural barbarity, Rodrigo draws on the evidence of newly available classical texts to extend the antiquity of Spain to before that of Rome.

This area of prehistory is specifically explored in Alfonso de Palencia's lost *Ten Books on the Antiquities of Spain*, probably in Latin, and in great detail by the Catalan bishop of Girona, Joan Margarit in his *Paralipomenon Hispaniae libri decem* (finished about 1480; printed at Granada, 1545). Margarit has no interest in the Gothic myth; his main intention is to destroy the misconceptions circulated by Jiménez de Rada about the ancient history of Hispania, using Roman texts and Greek texts in recent Latin translation. He also juxtaposes the Augustan unity of Hispania with the union of the crowns of Castile and Aragón. The last stage in this burst of political antiquarianism is marked by Nebrija's *Muestra de la historia de las antigüedades de España* (Burgos, 1499), a foretaste in Castilian of a five-volume Latin work that was never written. One assumes he intended to overshadow all previous efforts to eradicate mistakes, yet he in turn surrenders to the egregious fantasies of the Italian Giovanni Nanni (Annius of Viterbo; Rome, 1498), the first of many sixteenth-century pseudochronicles that push Iberian civilization well before that of the Greek city-states.

ROBERT B. TATE

Bibliography

Cirot, G. *Études sur l'historiographie espagnole: Les Histoires générales d'Espagne entre Alphonse X et Philippe II. 1284–1556.* Bordeaux, 1904.

Linehan, P. *History and the Historians of Medieval Spain.* Oxford, 1993.

Menéndez Pidal, R. *Crónicas generales de España.* 3d ed. Madrid, 1918.

Sánchez Alonso, B. *Historia de la historiografía española.* Madrid, 1941.

Tate, R.B. *Ensayos sobre la historiografía peninsular del siglo XV.* Madrid, 1970.

HITA, ARCHPRIEST OF *See* LIBRO DE BUEN AMOR

HOLY OFFICE *See* INQUISITION

HOMOSEXUALITY

Homosexuality was a key symbolic issue throughout the Middle Ages in Iberia. As was customary everywhere until the nineteenth century, homosexuality was not viewed as a congenital disposition or "identity"; the focus was on nonprocreative sexual practices, of which sodomy was the most controversial. Female homosexual behavior was ignored, and almost nothing is known about it.

In al-Andalus homosexual pleasures were much indulged in by the intellectual and political elite. Evidence includes the behavior of rulers, such as Abd al-Raḥmān III, Al-Ḥakam II, Hishām II, and Al-Muʿtamid, who openly kept male harems; the memoirs of Bādīs, last Zīrid king of Granada, makes references to male prostitutes, who charged higher fees and had a higher class of clientele than did their female counterparts; the repeated criticisms of Christians; and especially the abundant poetry. Both pederasty and love between adult males are found. Although homosexual practices were never officially condoned, prohibitions against them were rarely enforced, and usually there was not even a pretense of doing so.

During the final centuries of Islamic Spain, because of Christian opposition to it and because of immigration and conversion of those who were sympathetic, homosexuality took on a greater ideological role. It had an important place in Islamic mysticism and monasticism; the contemplation of the beardless youth was "an act of worship," the contemplation of God in human form.

Many Christians in northern Iberia and elsewhere in Europe were scandalized by or terrified of Andalusian sexual behavior, which relied heavily on slavery; homosexual indulgence, viewed as an incurable and contagious vice, was seen as a threat to the fighting strength of the army, and thus to the integrity of the state. The boy-martyr San Pelagio, executed for refusing the amorous intentions of Abd al-Raḥmān III, was a hero and the subject of a poem by Hrotswitha. The Christian states worked to rescue captive Christians, prevent slaving raids, set up a bulwark to prevent Islamic expansion northward, and suppress homosexuality within the Christian states themselves. The Castilian emphasis on virginity and marriage, its rejection of lyric poetry, the delayed implantation of clerical celibacy in Castile, and the western European cult of the Virgin Mary all may well have their origin in this confrontation. The possible homosexual elements may be a reason why the theory of the Islamic origin of courtly love and troubadour poetry has had such a poor reception.

Juan II of Castile and his lover Álvaro de Luna were the most famous homosexual couple in medieval Christian Spain. The execution of Álvaro de Luna, arranged by Juan's second wife, Isabel of Portugal, remained into the seventeenth century an event symbolic of the repression of homosexuality. In the Farce of Ávila, Enrique IV was dethroned in effigy as *puto* (faggot); his incapacity as ruler was seen as a result not of illness, as today seems likely, but of moral depravity. Homosexuality was tolerated in the court of Alfonso V of Aragón after its move to Naples.

In the background of the conflict over homosexuality in Iberia are the Jews. Throughout Spanish history Judaism and variant sexuality have been associated by those hostile to either. One reason Jews were excluded from some countries after their expulsion from Spain was because they allegedly took homosexuality with them. Judaism and homosexuality are linked in Golden Age literature (e.g., in Francisco de Quevedo's poetry), and in the early twentieth century homosexuals were referred to as *judíos*, and in the aggregate called a "sect."

The discovery and publication of much poetry thought lost, and the pioneering studies of it by Schirmann and Roth, have given us surprising new perspectives on Sephardic sexuality. There are scores of pederastic poems by the greatest Jewish authors of the period: Ibn Gabirol, Samuel ha-Nagid, Moses ibn Ezra, Judah ha-Levi, and others. From this poetry, "refined, sensual, and unabashedly hedonistic," we know that homosexuality was widespread among the Jewish elite in al-Andalus, apparently more prevalent than among the Muslims. Zīrid Granada, a Jewish state in all but name, was the center of "a courtly aristocratic culture involving romantic individualism [in which there was] intense exploration of all forms of liberating sexuality, heterosexuality, bisexuality, homosexuality." As with the Muslims, homosexuality and religious devotion were combined; Israel's love of God was sometimes expressed as the love of a male. The influence of Sephardic homosexuality has yet to be traced, but it is hard not to see it in the poetry of St. John of the Cross.

DANIEL EISENBERG

Bibliography

García Gómez, E. (ed. and trans.) *Poemas arábigo andaluces.* Madrid, 1930.

Ibn Said al-Maghribi. *The Banners of the Champions.* Trans. J. Bellamy and P. Steiner. Madison, Wisc., 1988.

Roth, N. " 'Deal Gently with the Young Man': Love of Boys in Medieval Hebrew Poetry of Spain," *Speculum* 57 (1982): 20–51.

———. " 'My Beloved Is like a Gazelle': Imagery of the Beloved Boy in Religious Hebrew Poetry," *Hebrew Annual Review* 8 (1984): 143–65.

Schirmann, J. "The Ephebe in Medieval Hebrew Poetry," *Sefarad* 15 (1955), 55–68.

HOSIUS, BISHOP OF CÓRDOBA

Hosius (or Ossius) was said to have been approximately a hundred years old at the time of his death around 357 and to have held the office of bishop of Córdoba for nearly sixty years. This would appear to place his birth in the middle of the third century, and his elevation to the episcopate to around the year 300. He referred in a letter to having suffered during the last imperial persecution of Christianity (303–305). He came into contact with Emperor Constantine I (r. 306–337) soon after the latter's conversion in 312, and became his principal Western ecclesiastical adviser. The African schismatics known as Donatists later claimed that it was Hosius who persuaded Constantine to condemn them in 316, and he was certainly used by the emperor as his envoy to the church in Alexandria in 324, in an attempt to heal the conflict over the teachings of Arius concerning the Persons of the Trinity. After the failure of this mission, Hosius played a prominent part in the ecumenical council held at Nicaea in 325, which sought to settle the growing Arian controversy. For reasons that are not clear, this marked the end of his period of influence at the imperial court, and he spent the next twenty years back in his diocese. In his final years he was again involved in a series of councils and meetings intended to resolve the continuing rift in the church over the doctrine of the Trinity. In 347 he presided at the Council of Serdica, in which the Western bishops made clear their support for Athanasius of Alexandria, the principal opponent of the Arians. But after Constantius II (r. 337–361) united both parts of the empire under his rule, attempts were made to force the westerners to modify their stand. Hosius was summoned to the imperial court at Milan in 355, and detained. He was eventually coerced into signing the acts of the council held at Sirmium in 357, which condemned Athanasius. He died soon after.

ROGER COLLINS

Bibliography

De Clercq, J.C. *Ossius of Cordova: A Contribution to the History of the Constantinian Period.* Washington, D. C., 1954.

Lietzmann, H. *A History of the Early Church.* Vol. 3, *From Constantine to Julian.* Trans. B. L. Woolf. London, 1950.

HOSPITAL, ORDER OF THE

See MILITARY ORDERS

HOSPITALS

Hospitals were houses where pilgrims, the poor, the sick, and outcast could find lodging and, if necessary, medical assistance. In the early Middle Ages they usually were run by religious orders or lay confraternities, or even attached to cathedrals, as at Manresa and Vic. The first such institution in Christian Spain was founded in 580 at Mérida, and from then on, hospitals were to be found in all urban areas, some of them providing shelter for those with diseases like leprosy, smallpox, and the plague.

Few records remain to describe the majority of these institutions, but studies published on the hospitals of Barcelona and Valencia show that by the thirteenth century their number had increased significantly. New institutions had been founded by rich merchants like Bernat dez Clapers in Valencia and Arnau de Cloquer in Vic. Some, like the Hospital del Rey in Burgos and the Hospital de la Reina in Valencia, owed their existence to royal donations. Others, like the Hospital d'En Colom in Barcelona and the Hospital dels Folls in Valencia (1409), looked after the mentally ill; the latter is regarded as the first institution in Europe founded for this purpose.

Initially all hospitals were dependent on private donations, legacies, gifts in kind such as beds and linen, or received assistance from ecclesiastical or lay organizations; gradually the municipalities supplemented or replaced these groups, especially after the Black Death of 1348, when medical resources had been

16th century. Facade 1504–1515. Copyright © SEF/Art
Hospital of Santa Cruz, Resource, NY. Toledo, Spain.

strained to their utmost. By the end of the fourteenth century, throughout the Iberian Peninsula a need for consolidation and specialization became evident, and the separation of the sick from the poor began to take effect. Smaller institutions were incorporated into larger ones: the earliest example of this is the Hospital de la Santa Creu in Barcelona (1401), and in Zaragoza, Nuestra Señora de Gracia was formed in 1425 with the specific purpose of unifying hospital care in the town.

JILL R. WEBSTER

Bibliography

Cabal González, M. *Hospitales antiguos de Oviedo*. Oviedo, 1985.

Durán Gudiol, A. *El Hospital de Somport entre Aragón y Bearn (siglos XII y XIII)*. Zaragoza, 1986.

Gask, G.E. and J.T. "The origins of Hospitals." In *Science, Medicine, and History*. Ed. E. Ashworth Underwood. New York, 1975.

Imbert, Jean. *Les hôpitaux en droit canonique: du décret de Gratien à la sécularisation de l'administration de l'Hôtel-Dieu de Paris en 1505*. Paris, 1947.

La vida hospitalaria en Jaca. Ed. Joaquín Carrasco Almazor, et al. Jaca, 1983.

HOSTIGESIS

Hostigesis was bishop of Málaga in the mid-ninth century. What we know about him comes from the *Apologeticus* (864) of the abbot Samson, which was written largely as a defense against accusations of doctrinal deviance that Hostigesis leveled against Samson. The picture of Hostigesis—whose name Samson altered for polemical reasons to Hostis Ihesu (enemy of Jesus)—is, as a result, rather uncomplimentary and suspect. According to Samson, Hostigesis's father, Auvarnus, was a tax collector who had converted to Islam. His uncle Samuel had done the same after having been deposed as the bishop of Elvira. Through simony Hostigesis rose to the see of Málaga at the uncanonically young age of nineteen. He enriched himself through the corrupt administration of his office and spent most of his time at the emir's court. In conjunction with Count Servandus of Córdoba, he increased the tax burden on the Christian community. He arranged for Samson to be condemned for doctrinal deviance in an episcopal council in 862 and again, a short time later, at another council convened in Córdoba, at which Bishop Valerius of Córdoba was deposed. Samson devoted the second book of his *Apologeticus* (which he wrote at Martos, near Jaén, where he had fled after the second council) to his own defense, accusing Hostigesis of being a heretic for misunderstanding the extent to which God is present in the things he created.

KENNETH B. WOLF

Bibliography

Colbert, E. "The Martyrs of Córdoba (850–859): A Study of the Sources." Ph.D. diss., Catholic University of America, 1962. 357–81.

Gil, J. (ed.) *Corpus scriptorum mozarabicorum*. Madrid, 1973. Vol. 2. 506–658.

HUELGAS CODEX, LAS

Las Huelgas (a musical codex, sigla *Hu*, listed in I. Fernández de la Cuesta under BUH 1) is an early fourteenth-century manuscript preserved at Las Huelgas, the famous Cistercian convent founded about 1180 on the outskirts of Burgos. The convent since its inception has been associated with the Church of Santa María la Real.

Surviving the nineteenth-century plunderings of the French during the Napoleonic Wars, as well as the entails of Juan Álvarez Mendizábal, the manuscript was discovered in 1904 by Dom Luciano Serrano. With the twelfth-century Codex Calixtinus (of Compostela) and the mid-fourteenth-century *Llibre vermell* (of Montserrat), it constitutes the triumvirate of Spanish musical sources that contain examples of medieval polyphony. The music of the Las Huelgas codex, copied in Spain in early mensural pre-Franconian notation, bears a stylistic affinity with coexisting French models. A composer associated with several pieces in the codex was identified as Johan Rodrigues (fl. 1325).

Of its 186 examples, notated on 170 parchment folios, 45 are monophonic (20 sequences, 15 *conducti*, 10 *Benedicamus* tropes) and 141 are polyphonic, written for two, three, and four voices. The latter include the following genres: *conductus* (including a Credo), Latin motet, Sanctus settings, Kyrie, Gloria, Sanctus, Agnus Dei, Benedicamus Domino and Benedicamus tropes, proses (sequences), organa, graduals, alleluias, an offertory trope, an exercise in solfeggio, and a textless monody.

ISRAEL J. KATZ

Bibliography

Anglès, H. (ed.) *El códex musical de las Huelgas*. 3 vols. Barcelona, 1931.

Dittmer, L. "Las Huelgas." In *Musik in Gesschichte und Gegenwart*. Vol. 8. 1960. 242.

Fernández de la Cuesta, I. *Manuscritos y fuentes musicales en España: Edad media*. Madrid, 1980.

Serrano, Dom L. *¿Qué es canto gregoriano?* Barcelona, 1905.

Stevenson, R.M. *Spanish Music in the Age of Columbus*. The Hague, 1964.

Vega Cernuda, D. "El códice de las Huelgas: Estudio de su técnica polifónica," *Revista de musicología*, 1, no. 2 (1978), 9–60.

HUGO OF SANTALLA

Hugo of Santalla (fl. 1145) was a translator of scientific texts from Arabic into Latin. He presumably came from one of the several Leonese villages named Santalla and apparently spent his life in Aragón since the majority of his works are dedicated to Michael, bishop of Tarazona (1119–1151); the remaining works have no dedications. His patron acquired at least one Arabic manuscript for him from Rueda de Jalón. Hugo must be the "magister Hugo" who witnessed two charters at Tarazona on 11 November 1145. His principal interests were astronomy, astrology, and the divinatory sciences. He was apparently the first to translate a text on "sand divination," for which he coined the word "geomancy"; this kind of divination, using figures made up of four rows of single or double dots, became extremely popular. His texts on divination from the shoulder blades of sheep (scapulimancy) had less influence, but are interesting for the insights they give on Spanish-Arabic society and politics. He translated a commentary on a set of astronomical tables and several sets of astrological "judgments." His *Aristotle's Book Based on 255 Indian Volumes of Universal Questions* is a translation of a lost Arabic text that offers precious testimony on the state of astrological knowledge in late eighth-century Baghdad. His translation of the cosmogony and set of questions on nature known in Arabic as the *Sirr al-khal-aga*, of Apollonius of Tyana, the earliest Latin text to include the Emerald Table of Hermes, became a key text for alchemists.

CHARLES BURNETT

Bibliography

Burnett, C. "Divination from Sheep's Shoulder Blades: A Reflection on Andalusian Society." In *Cultures in Contact in Medieval Spain: Historical and Literary Essays Presented to L. P. Harvey*. Ed. D. Hook and B. Taylor. London, 1990. 29–45.

Haskins, C.H. *Studies in the History of Mediaeval Science*. 2d ed. Cambridge, Mass. 1927. 67–81.

HUNTING LITERATURE

Hunting, the principal method of food gathering for pre-agricultural societies, had become a refined courtly pastime in parts of western Europe by the twelfth century. Monarchs and noblemen ordered books dealing with the subject to be written in order to establish a social etiquette, disseminate effective techniques of falconry and venery, and promulgate laws governing the well-being of huntsmen. The same texts usually contain information on the nature and care of falcons and hunting dogs, the accoutrements necessary for the chase, and the best locations for large and small game in all seasons. The earliest hunting literature in Spain is greatly indebted to Arabic scientific treatises, notably the *Kitāb al-yawārih*, composed by Moamin, falconer and astronomer of Baghdad (d. 859 or 860). This text inspired a pan-European tradition, for there exist versions in Latin, Franco-Italian, and Spanish. The first of these was ordered by Frederick II of Sicily about 1240, and may have influenced his famous *De arte venandi cum avibus* (1248); the last, *Libro de las animalias que casan*, appears to have been produced at the command of the future Alfonso X, in 1250, while he was still a prince. (The most complete codices of the work are Biblioteca Nacional, Madrid, MS Res. 270; and Escorial, MS V.II.19, which also contains several brief falconry treatises, such as *Dancus rex* and *Guillelmus falconarius*.)

15th century. Pheasant hunt. Tacunium Sanitatis. Ms.65, f.86v. Paper. Italy, Lombardy, ca. 1475. Astor, Lenox, and Tilden Foundations. Copyright © The New York Public Library/Art Resource, NY. Spencer Collection, The New York Public Library, New York, N.Y., U.S.A.

Three-fifths of the Spanish *Animalias* deal with falconry; the remainder are dedicated to venery, hunting with quadrupeds that kill "with their teeth": dogs, leopards, and other animals. Each of these types would influence later hunting texts on *caza* and *montería* (i.e., falconry and venery, a lexical distinction that was generally maintained until the 1400s). Juan Manuel (1282–1348), nephew of Alfonso X, composed a *Libro de la caça* (ca. 1325–1335) in which he alludes to a *Libro del venar* ordered by his uncle—probably the *Animalias*. He tries to go beyond that work's scope in developing a manual that is more practical, more up-to-date, and less theoretical. The *Caça* expounds on falconry and the nature of falcons in chapters 1–10, provides veterinary information for their care in chapter 11, and in chapter 12 describes the best locations for falconry known to the author. A work of apparently even greater circulation during its day than Juan Manuel's is the *Libro de la caça de las aves* (1386) of Pedro López de Ayala (1332–1407). Possible examples of direct influence of the *Libro de la caça* in López's book are few: he prefers to rely on hunts in which he has participated, conversations with professional falconers from Spain and abroad, and details he has noted. A key written source is the *Livro de falcoaria* by Pero Menino, falconer of Fernão I of Portugal: this text is plagiarized almost in its entirety; López uses it as the basis for chapters 11, 15, 17–32, 34–37, and 39. The *Caça de las aves*, important for its sociological and literary aspects, would influence (among others) the following fifteenth-century writers: Alfonso de Madrigal (El Tostado), *Un libro . . . de curar alcones, azores gavilanes*, and Juan de Sahagún (falconer to Juan II), *Libro de cetrería*; and, from the sixteenth century, Joan Valles, *Libro de la cetreria y montería* (1556). There is also a Portuguese translation.

Books (*tratados*) 4–5 of the Spanish *Animalias*, which deal with *caza mayor*, would have considerable influence on the *Libro de la montería* (ca. 1345–1350), produced at the behest of Alfonso XI, great-grandson of Alfonso X. The *Montería* deals exclusively with the pursuit of deer, wild boar, bear, and *enzebra* (probably wild ass rather than zebra). A possible complement to Juan Manuel's *Libro de la caça*, describes procedures for hunting large game and the nature of hunting dogs in book 1; provides information on veterinary surgery and useful pharmacological compounds in book 2 (in two parts); and in book 3 catalog over 1500 areas in Spain for *caza mayor*, encompassing more than 9000 place-names. Like López de Ayala's falconry treatise, the *Montería* was a popular work: texts apparently modeled on or influenced directly by it include the Portuguese *Livro da montaria* (1415, written at the command of King João I; an anonymous *Tratado de montería del siglo XV*; British Library, MS Add. 28709); Gonzalo Argote de Molina, *Libro de la montería de Alfonso XI* (1582); and Pedro de Pedraza Gaitán's *Libro de montería* (seventeenth century; Biblioteca Nacional, Madrid, MS 8285).

DENNIS P. SENIFF

Bibliography

Alfonso XI. *Libro de la montería*. Ed. D. P. Seniff. Madison, Wisc., 1983.

Fradejas Rueda, J.M. (ed.) *Tratados de cetrería*. 2 vols. Madrid, 1985.

———. "Los manuscritos del *Libro de la caza de las aves*: Intento de un censo y descripción del MS Krahe," *Epos* (Madrid) 5 (1989), 497–504.

Juan Manuel. *Libro de la caza*. In *Cinco tratados*. Ed. R. Ayerbe-Chaux. Madison, Wisc., 1989. 177–251.

López de Ayala, P. *Libro de la caça de las aves*: *El MS 16.392* (British Library, London) Ed. J. G. Cummins. London, 1986.

Muhammad ibn ʿAbd Allāh ibn ʿUmar al-Bayzar (Moamyn). *Libro de los animales que cazan (Kitab al-yawarih)*. Ed. J.M. Fradejas Rueda. Madrid, 1987. Also available as a microfiche transcription of Biblioteca Nacional, Madrid, MS Res. 270, *Libro de las animalias que caçan*. Ed. A.J. Cardenas. Madison, Wisc., 1987.

Seniff, D.P. " 'Munchos libros buenos': The New MSS of Alfonso XI's *Libro de la montería* and Moamyn/Alfonso X's *Libro de las animalias que caçan*" and "Notes," *Studia Neophilologica* 60 (1988): 251–62 and 61 (1989): 249–50.

———. "The Hunt in Medieval Spain and the *Romancero histórico*: Epic Poetry, Lyric Poetry, and Reality," *Anuario Medieval* 2 (1990): 23–40.

HURTADO DE MENDOZA, DIEGO

Eldest son of the magnate of Pedro Gonzálzez de Mendoza, who had allied himself with the new Trastámaran dynasty to become *mayordomo mayor* for King Juan I. Diego held the title of Admiral of Castile and continued his father's advantageous policy of active military and political support of the new royal house, going on to become one of the most powerful men in Castile by the beginning of the fifteenth century. Father and son helped transform the Mendoza family from a provincial military clan into a wealthy, aristocratic house that dominated an entire city and province and held the highest national offices. As such, they were able to extend their family ties to a powerful network of prestigious houses, including the royal family itself.

The admiral's career from early on was a glorious succession of victories, rendering important military services in the wars against Portugal by defeating Portuguese fleets in three separate naval engagements. In the power struggle during the minority of Enrique III (1390–1406), the admiral supported the winning side by allying himself with his uncles, Pedro López de Ayala and Juan Hurtado de Mendoza, thus becoming a counselor to the monarchy and joining that small group of men whose members were entitled to be known as the *consejo del rey* (council of the king). It was during this same period that Pedro López de Ayala served as *canciller mayor* (senior chancellor) of Castile. Immensely proud of his family's heritage and influence, Enrique III was known to have complained about the admiral's social daring and informal ways. Sometime before 1395, the admiral received a royal grant for the patronage of the city offices of Guadalajara. Earlier he had also been granted the right for himself and his descendants to name the city's representatives to the *cortes*, thus ensuring his family's dominance in the city and province of Guadalajara.

Diego inherited a large fortune from his father and added large tracts of land to the Mendoza estates, receiving *mercedes* (grants) from both Juan I and Enrique III that increased his holdings in the provinces of Guadalajara and Madrid. In addition, he extended his interests into Asturias through a second marriage, to Leonor de la Vega in 1387. As the sole heiress of the large Vega fortune, Leonor brought extensive seigneurial lands in Asturias into the Mendoza estate, including sheep-grazing lands, salt mines, and harbors, sources of an important part of the Mendoza clan's income in a period of extensive wool trade between Castile and Flanders. Although the admiral's decision to marry Leonor de la Vega was his own, made after his father died in the Battle of Aljubarrota (1385), it appears that the couple were at odds from the beginning. The admiral was away when their first son was born, and Leonor had the child baptized Garcilaso in honor of her ancestors. In an early will, the admiral stipulated that the boy's name should be changed to Juan Hurtado de Mendoza in honor of his uncle. A poet as well as a man of intellectual interests, Diego was also the father of the greatest humanist and one of the most influential noblemen in Castile during the fifteenth century, Iñigo López de Mendoza, the first marquis of Santillana (1398–1458), whose reputation in Spanish history rests on his great literary achievements.

Before the admiral died, he tried to assure the inheritance of his small children by naming two of his powerful uncles as their tutors, Pedro López de Ayala, and Juan Hurtado de Mendoza, *prestamero mayor* (military governor) of Vizcaya. By the time of his death in 1404, Diego Hurtado de Mendoza was reputed to be the richest man in Castile. His efforts to ensure the inheritance of his children, however, were doomed to failure because of internal family disputes. The recuperation and preservation of the Mendoza fortune was left for Santillana to carry out, who during the next generation was successful in stemming off a series of threats to the family during period of internal and external attacks on the Trastamaran political order.

E. MICHAEL GERLI

Bibliography

Nader, H. *The Mendoza Family in the Spanish Renaissance, 1350–1550*. Rutgers, N.J., 1979.

HYDATIUS

Bishop of Aquae Flaviae (Chaves, northern Portugal) and sole contemporary chronicler of the Suevic kingdom in Roman Gallaecia (now northern Portugal), Hydatius was born about 380 in Civitas Limicorum (now Ginzo). He was educated in the East, ordained in 416, and promoted to bishop in 427; he is presumed to have died shortly after his chronicle terminates in 469. His unusual name is that of the persecutor of Priscillian, and he may have been appointed to resume the orthodox evangelization of Paulus Orosius. His chronicle professes to continue Eusebius's *Ecclesiastical History*, latinized by St. Jerome. Aquae Flaviae was not previously a see, and Hydatius was increasingly occupied in representing Galaeco-Roman interests against the Suevic rulers. This took him to Gaul to confer with Flavius Aetius in and brought about his arrest from August to November forty-five.

Hydatius covers the reigns of the first Suevic ruler, Hermeric; his son Rechila; and his grandson Rechiarius, the first barbarian ruler to be a Catholic, who was soon defeated and killed by Arian Visigoths (461); and a period of internal strife. He does not exult over the succession of a Catholic and, while not questioning the legitimacy of the Suevic kingdom, denounces the Suevi failure to observe the *foedus*. He negotiates with the Visigoths, but finds the imposition of Arianism even more abhorrent. He ends with the Gothic occupation of Mérida and a combined Suevo-Roman appeal to the emperor, the result of which is unrecorded.

Most of Hydatius's 253 entries are short, the longest being of twenty-two lines. His use of portents without interpretation creates problems, as does his adoption of olympiads, confusing to later scribes. Despite these difficulties he remains a unique source to which Isidore's pages on the Suevi add little.

H.V. Livermore

Bibliography

Monumenta Germania Historica, Auctores Antiguissimi. Vols. 9 and 11.

Tranoy, A. *Hydace, Chromigul.* Sources Chrétienne nos. 218–19. Paris, 1974.

HYMNS, CHRISTIAN

Latin hymnody in Iberia is on the whole one of the most original phenomena of medieval religious poetry. Its roots go back to the turn of the fifth century. The *Cathemerinon*, the first hymn collection of the Iberian statesman Aurelius Prudentius Clemens, was geared toward the daily spiritual needs of the christianized provincial gentry with traditional Roman culture. His other hymn collection, the *Peristephanon*, was the first collection of martyr hymns. It was conceived as a programmatic Christian substitute for pagan mythological poetry and included local, Hispanic, Italic, and Roman material. Along with some of the Milanese hymns by Ambrosius, they became models for later medieval hymns on martyrs and saints. The hymns by Prudentius, in their original forms too long for liturgical use, were later adopted in the form of *centos* in Visigothic-Mozarabic and, from the eleventh century on, also in monastic liturgy beyond the Iberian Peninsula. Only a few other hymns can be identified as early Iberian products (such as a Saturninus hymn).

The hymns of the Visigothic and Mozarabic period are preserved chiefly in tenth-century liturgical sources. A precise chronological ordering of these hymns (as undertaken by Pérez de Urbel and Díaz y Díaz) is desirable but remains elusive. Among them are hymns celebrating saints as well as some that were inserted in the Old Iberian daily and seasonal liturgy. The number of hymns to saints of various backgrounds (including some Eastern saints) is remarkably large. In addition to local Iberian hymns there are adaptations of early northern Italian hymns with historical allusions. Ascriptions to Visigothic authors (Maximus and John of Zaragoza, Braulio of Zaragoza, St. Ildefonsus and Julianus of Toledo, Quiricus and Conantius of Barcelona) are based mostly on uncertain assumptions.

A great deal of the poetry of Eugenius III of Toledo is identifiable, but most of the ascriptions of hymns to Isidore of Seville cannot be verified today. The monastic hymns inserted into the daily prayer cycle of the liturgy through Fructuosus of Braga display strong affinities with models elsewhere in Europe. A peculiarity of Visigothic hymnody is the use of "politically accentuated" hymns (designed for state and ecclesiastical events, such as coronations, episcopal consecrations, wars, and departures of the army against the enemy). The Arab Conquest of Iberia promoted the creation of Mozarabic hymns containing allusions to the suppression of the Christian faith by the Arabs and the Muslim rule in Iberia. While the hymns on the saints (now including local martyrs) often reflect the influence of the Hispanic *Passionarium* and are mostly very long, the hymns for "De tempore" are far shorter and more traditional in wording and tone.

In the Carolingian period there are indications of contact with hymnody beyond the peninsula (e.g., a Peter and Paul hymn). An outstanding Iberian poet in the Frankish courtly circle was Theodulf of Orléans, whose production of hymns was limited. Among the Mozarabic hymnodists were the martyr Eulogius of Córdoba and his friend Paulus Alvaro, author of the only St. Jerome hymn existing before the fourteenth century. Another distinctive feature of the age is the use of nuptial hymns. Hymns on St. James of Compostela appear relatively late. The dramatization of the liturgy is signaled by a hymn for the "farewell to the Alleluia," and by a Holy Cross hymn with strong patristic-eschatological elements.

The number of hymns in sources from the tenth century (including some from Silos) is very large. In the eleventh century Ripoll produced some remarkable hymns (on Saints Michael, Peter, and Paul). The long moralistic-religious poem "De vita christiana" was composed during the investiture conflict. The pontificate of Pope Gregory VII (1073–1085) brought the forcible general introduction of the Roman liturgical traditions at the expense of the Mozarabic rite, which survived in Toledo and reemerged at the end of the fifteenth century. At first there was only a limited use of sequences in the Iberian sources.

In hymnody and liturgical music Catalonia gained prominence from the eleventh century on. The sequence, which has a very important role in musical composition, achieved great visibility in Catalan sources, and the *verbeta*, the liturgical hymns (mainly associated with new liturgical feasts and local cults), poetic offices, and paraliturgical songs also were in greater demand. In the twelfth century an important document of the cult of St. James the Great, the *Codex Calixtinus*, stands out as an example of close links between Iberian and southern French culture. In this framework the *conductus* form with its musical implications attained special significance and polyphony took a central position. The spirit of the Reconquest is reflected in some Huesca sequences. There was a further accumulation of Catalan sequences at San Juan de la Peña (Aragón) and San Millán de la Cogolla (Castile), as well as the popularity of the liturgical *verbeta* at San Cugat (Catalonia) and new poetic offices. Some remarkable hymns were composed in the circle of Alfonso X by Juan Gil de Zamora.

The composition of polyphonic poetic offices attained a significant place in the musical and hymnic production of the last centuries of the Middle Ages, especially in the Portuguese realm. The pilgrims' songs of Montserrat, used as "spiritual dance tunes," stand between popular ritual and liturgical hymn compositions. The paraliturgical compositions often display very complex musical and poetic structures. Copied at the beginning of the fourteenth century, the Huelgas manuscript from Burgos was a depository of (mostly polyphonic) products of the *ars antiqua* (some 186 items). Among them are not less than 144 organa, motets, conductus, and sequences, alongwith a number of important secular songs (laments, etc.), some of which were entirely unknown before the edition of Anglès.

A large number of liturgical books, found or written in Tarragona, the Escorial, Tortosa, Alcobaça, Huesca, Vic, and Toledo, offer new or hitherto not recorded hymns. Fourteenth-century hymns celebrate the Christian victory at Río Salado (1340) over the ruler of Morocco and the king of Granada. In the late Middle Ages Portuguese poetic offices preserved Latin hymns (Soeiro in Braga, Coimbra, etc.). A number of Spanish sequences also have survived from the fourteenth century.

Short hymns in the popular "private prayer books" (*horae*, etc.) of the fourteenth and fifteenth centuries present novel features. While a considerable number of handwritten liturgical sources with hymns for old and new feasts, and for cults, survive from the fifteenth century, books printed in German workshops also testify to the hymnological production of the Iberian lands. Some of these "new" hymns may have been taken from older manuscripts, later destroyed, and others are manifestly inspired by humanism. Some poets are known to have contributed to early sixteenth-century Spanish hymnody, which preserved its medieval features well into the middle of that century. The final act of the Reconquest, the victory at Granada (1492), inspired liturgical hymns. At the turn of the sixteenth century the canon Alphonsus Ortiz edited the ancient Mozarabic liturgical books (*Missale mixtum*, *Breviarium*) under the patronage of Cardinal Francisco Jiménez de Cisneros. A definitive history of the rich, and in some respects unique, Iberian Latin hymnody is still to be written.

Joseph Szövérffy

Bibliography

Anglès, H. *El codex musical de Las Huelgas*. Barcelona, 1931.

———. *La música a Catalunya fins al segle XIII*. Barcelona, 1935.

Brou, L. "Études sur le missel et le breviaire mozarabes imprimés," *Hispania Sacra* 11 (1958), 239–387.

Corbin, S. *Essai sur la musique religieuse portugaise au Moyen Âge*. Paris, 1952.

Díaz y Díaz, M.C. *Index scriptorum latinorum medii aevi hispanorum*. Madrid, 1959.

———. "A study of Ancient Texts Bearing on Saint James the Greater," *Classical Folia* 24 (1970), 135–76.

Martins, M. "A nossa poesia religiosa em latim rímico." In *Estudos de literatura medieval*. Braga, 1956.

Messenger, R. E. "Mozarabic Hymns in Relation to Contemporary Culture in Spain." *Traditio* 4 (1946), 149–77.

Pérez de Urbel, J. "Origen de los himnos mozárabes," *Bulletin hispanique* 28 (1926), 113–39.

Szövérffy, J. *Iberian Hymnody*. Albany, N.Y., 1971.

Thorsberg, B. *Études sur l'hymnologie mozarabe*. Stockholm, 1962.

HYMNS, HEBREW

About the middle of the tenth century, Spanish Jews became relatively independent from the East, but for several generations their liturgical poetry continued the tradition established by the Palestinian poets of the Byzantine period. The major genres, such as the *qerobah* and the *yotser*, conserved their fixed structure and the sequence of their minor units in the poetry of the first Spanish liturgical poets, such as Yishaq Ibn Marsaoaʿul from Lucena and Yosef ibn Abitur from Mérida, even if the deep changes that affected Spanish poetry, creating a new model of metrical patterns on secular themes in pure biblical language, left an increasing trace in the poems written for the synagogue. The components of those major genres attained an independent life, and in some cases they enlarged their extension.

Among the hymns cultivated in that period are mention the *ʿofan*, in which the angels sing the glory of God; the *qedushah*, proclaming his holiness; and the *meʿorot*, depicting the wonders of the godly creation of the heavenly bodies. Others, such as the *zulat* and the *mi kamoka*, emphasize the uniqueness and greatness of God. The *ʿalvodah* is specifically for the Day of Atonement. New techniques, such as the Arabic-like meter, appeared in those hymns. Scholars opposed to radical changes elaborated another metrical system based on the number of full syllables. At the middle of the tenth century, a new Andalusian pattern of strophic poetry, called *muwashshaḥ*, appeared in the liturgical hymns, particularly in *meʿorot* and other compositions praising the glory of God, and in the *ʿahabot*. The Jews of Sefarad were particularly found of these *ʿahabot*, which usually alluded to the mutual love of Israel and God, with expressions taken from the Song of Songs, and the *geʿulot*, expressing the desire for redemption and the end of the exile.

At the middle of the eleventh century, during the *tā'ifa* kingdoms, the golden period of Spanish-Hebrew poetry began. Solomon Ibn Gabirol (ca. 1020–ca. 1057), born in Málaga, introduced new forms, techniques, and content into the synagoge poetry, with some psychological, philosophical, and even mystical elements. One of his most famous compositions is "The Kingly Crown," written in rhymed prose, praising God and his attributes, describing the works of the creation, and contrasting the insignificance of the human being with the Lord's greatness.

Yishaq Ibn Gayat (1038–1089), spiritual leader of Lucena, wrote several hundred liturgical poems in pure Sephardic style, with many allusions to the science and philosophy of the epoch. Judah ha-Levi (ca. 1075–1141), a very prolific and delicate author, wrote, among many other well-known poems for the prayer of the communities, a long *qedushah* that has been called "Hymn of the Creation." Abraham Ibn Ezra (1089–1164) wrote more than five hundred religious poems, as well as a long composition, the *Hay ben Meqis*, describing a journey through creation as far as the highest heaven.

When the Almohads entered al-Andalus in the mid-twelfth century and destroyed most of the Andalusian Jewish centers, the legacy of this brilliant epoch passed to the north, to Christian Spain, where many leaders of the comunities continued to write liturgical compositions that remained more or less faithful to the same tradition. But they never attained the same degree of brightness.

ANGEL SÁENZ-BADILLOS

Bibliography

Carmin, T. (ed. and trans.) *The Penguin Book of Hebrew Verse*. New York, 1981.

Fleischer, E. "Piyyut." In *Encyclopaedia Judaica*. Vol. 13.

I

IBN ʿABDŪN, ABŪ MUHAMMAD ʿABD AL-MAJĪD IBN ʿABDŪN AL-FIHRI

Ibn ʿAbdūn, a poet, scholar, and statesman, was born in Évora (Yābura) and died there in 1134. Renowned for his elegant prose style, his prodigious memory, and his keen wit, and credited with being able to recite from memory such literary works as *Kitāb al-aghānī*, he began in 1080 to serve as *khātib* (secretary), and later vizier, to ʿUmar al-Mutawakkil (of the Banū l-Afṭas), ruler of Badajoz (Batalyaws). Al-Mutawakkil's father, Al-Muẓaffar, had loved scholarship and had made his court a haven for scholars and men of letters, a tradition maintained by his son, himself a poet. In 1095 Al-Mutawakkil and his two sons fell into the hands of the Almoravid army of Yūsuf ibn Tāshfīn. An account by Ibn Khāqān has it that Al-Mutawakkil's sons were executed in his presence before he met the same fate.

Immortalizing this tragic event and the memory of these three persons, Ibn ʿAbdūn composed a seventy-five-verse elegy that has come to be regarded as one of the most outstanding elegies composed in Arabic, remarkable for its technique and originality. Vibrant with feeling and rhetorical power, it laments the fall of the Banū ʿl-Afṭas, presenting this tragedy as the culmination of tragedies brought about by the vicissitudes of time. It recounts with emotion the hand of Fate in bringing about the demise of previous rulers, Persian and Greek heroes of antiquity and Arab heroes alike. Then it laments the loss to humanity of Al-Mutawakkil and his sons. The erudite historical references of this innovative ode occasioned the writing of several commentaries, the most complete of which is by Ibn Badrūn of Silves (twelfth/early thirteenth century). After the fall of the Banū ʿl-Afṭas, Ibn ʿAbdūn became a *khātib*, perhaps by necessity, to the Almoravid ruler Ibn Yūsuf ibn Tāshfīn.

DUSTIN COWELL

Bibliography

Monroe, J. T. *Hispano-Arabic Poetry: A Student Anthology*. Berkeley, 1974.

Nykl, A. R. *Hispano-Arabic Poetry*. Baltimore, 1946.

IBN ADRET, SOLOMON

Solomon ibn Adret (ca. 1233–ca. 1310) was the most important rabbinical authority in Spain in his period, and one of the most important of all time. We possess from his pen several volumes of commentaries on most of the tractates of the Talmud and several more volumes of legal responsa numbering in the thousands. All of these are a major source of information on the history of the period, of both Jews and non-Jews. He was the student of two great masters, both of Barcelona—Rabbi Jonah Gerundi and Moses ben Naḥman (Naḥmanides; not a rabbi)—and succeeded them as chief authority of the Aragón-Catalonia Jewish community. He had many famous students, almost all of whom became outstanding legal authorities and rabbis of the next generation in Aragón-Catalonia, Tudela, and Castile. Aside from Moses ben Maimon (Maimonides), who left Muslim Spain in his youth, no other Spanish Jewish scholar had as lasting an influence as Ibn Adret. (Nevertheless, scholars have made incredible errors in naming his students, and Scholem attributed to him the founding of a "school" of *qabbalah* based on his confusion of two sources with similar names, one written by a student of Ibn Adret but having nothing to do with *qabbalah* and the other written centuries later.)

However, Ibn Adret was strongly influenced by *qabbalah* in ways unknown to Scholem. He sometimes borrowed whole sections verbatim from the *qabbalist* ʿAzriel of Girona in his commentaries on the *aggadot* (homilies) of the Talmud; indeed, the order of the commentaries is based on that of ʿAzriel. Additional *qabbalistic* interpretations of Ibn Adret are cited in his student Meir Ibn Sahulah's (attributed) commentary on Naḥmanides on the Torah.

Ibn Adret joined in the controversy against the allegorical interpretation of the Bible and commandments fostered by those who misunderstood Maimonides, and even signed his name to the ban against the study of philosophy. Nevertheless, while he frequently wrote harsh criticisms of philosophy, he was deeply indebted to it, and matter-of-factly accepted certain of Maimonides' most "extreme" interpretations. He was the first anywhere to cite Maimonides' commentary on the Mishnah, and in fact arranged for its translation from Judeo-Arabic into Hebrew. He had, indeed, the greatest respect for Maimonides, whom he frequently cited.

His importance as communal leader and representative of the Catalan Jews cannot be overemphasized. Ibn Adret served as adviser to three rulers: Jaime I, Pedro III, and Jaime II (the last addressed a letter to him as "faithful" servant). He frequently was appointed by the kings as executor of important estates, and also served at various times as tax collector and secretary of the Jewish community of Barcelona.

Late in his life Ibn Adret composed other legal works, such as the *Torat ha-bayit ha-arokh* and a commentary on his own earlier abridged version of that work, which also serve as important source material for certain issues of the time. He left two, or possibly three, sons who were also scholars but never attained to their father's importance.

NORMAN ROTH

Bibliography

Epstein, I. *The "Responsa" of Rabbi Solomon Ben Adreth* [sic] *of Barcelona as a Source of the History of Spain*. New York, 1968. (First published 1925.) (Of limited value.)

R. Salomo b. Abraham b. Adereth [sic]. Breslau, 1863. (In German; of limited value, but better than Epstein.)

Scholem, G. *Kabbalah*. New York, 1974.

IBN BĀJJA (AVEMPACE) *See* PHILOSOPHY

IBN BASSĀM

Abū al-Ḥasan ʿAlī ibn Bassām al-Shantarīnī (d. 1147) was a vastly knowledgeable and widely read Hispano-Arabic poet and anthologist. When his native Santarem fell to the Christians (1092–1093), he took refuge, first in Córdoba and later in Seville, where he began to compile his *Kitāb al-Dhakhīra fī maḥāsin ahl al-Jazīra* (*Treasury of the Good Qualities of the People of the Peninsula*), his only surviving work. Decrying his fellow Andalusians' obsession with the writings of Eastern Muslims—"If a crow croaked [in the East] or a fly buzzed in the far reaches of Syria or Iraq they would kneel in reverence before such a remarkable achievement"—Ibn Bassām decided to collect, in seven volumes, an extensive anthology devoted to the works (both poetry and prose) of the best Andalusian writers. There are four parts, arranged geographically: (1) Córdoba; (2) the west of al-Andalus; (3) the East; (4) foreign writers residing in Muslim Spain. Each entry embodies a biographical section in rhymed prose, followed by laudatory comments and extracts from the author's works. A compendious version of the *Dhakhīra* was redacted by the Egyptian littérateur, Ibn Mammātī (1147–1209), with the title *Laṭā'if al-Dhakhīra wā-ṭarā 'if al-Jazīra* (*The Subtleties of the Treasury and the Exquisiteness of the Peninsula*). The *Dhakhīra* is, of course, an invaluable source for the study of Hispano-Arabic literature, including, among its selections, numerous unique texts preserved nowhere else. (For a survey of the authors covered, see García Gómez's review of the Cairo edition of *Al-Dhakhīra*.) The *Dhakhīra* is also an indispensable document for the history of Al-Andalus, preserving, for example, among other crucially important sources, extensive passages from Ibn Ḥayyān's otherwise lost, multivolume *al-Matīn* (*The Solid [History]*). For Hispanomedievalists, Romanists, and comparativists, perhaps the most interesting feature of Ibn Bassām's anthology is his detailed commentary on the *muwashshaḥat* style of poetry and its origins. Comparing the Arabic original with all previous attempts to translate and interpret this difficult passage, James Monroe proposes a new translation (quoted here only in part): "The first to compose the measures of these *muwashshaḥat* in our country, and to invent their method of composition, as far as I have determined, was Muḥammad ibn Maḥmūd al-Qabrī, the Blind. He used to compose them after the manner of the hemistichs of classical Arabic poetry (except that most of them were [composed] after the manner of the non-existent, hypothetical meters [*muhmala*] that are not used [in classical Arabic poetry]), adopting colloquial Arabic and Romance diction, which he called the *markaz* [= *kharja*], and basing the *muwashshaḥa* upon it. . . ." In agreement with such an appraisal, Ibn Bassām—with his profound knowledge of classical Arabic poetics—excludes the muwashshaḥat from his anthology, as alien to classical Khalīlian metrics: "The measures of these muwashshaḥat lie beyond the scope of this anthology, since the majority of them are not [composed] after the manner of the meters [found] in the classical poems of the Arabs." As Monroe points out, Ibn Bassām has given us a crucially important document in support of the muwashshaḥa's Romance origin and its non-classical, stress-syllabic metrics.

SAMUEL G. ARMISTEAD

Bibliography

García Gómez, E. Review of Ibn Bassām al-Shantarīnī, *Al-Dhakhīra. Al-Andalus* 5 (1940), 11 (1946).

Monroe, J. T. "On Re-Reading Ibn Bassām." *Actas del Congreso Romancero-Cancionero UCLA (1984)*. Ed. E. Rodríguez Cepeda et al. Vol. 2. Madrid, 1990. 409–46.

Pellat, C. "Ibn Bassām." *The Encyclopedia of Islam*. 2d ed. Leiden, 1971.

Vernet, J. *Literatura árabe*. Barcelona, 1968.

Viguera Molins, M. J., et al. *Los reinos de Taifas*. Madrid, 1994.

IBN DARRĀJ AL-QASṬALLĪ

One of the most distinguished Arabic poets of al-Andalus in the Amirid and early *ṭā'ifa* period, Ibn Darrāj (958–1030) first won recognition in 992 for a panegyric to Ibn Abī ʿAmir al-Manṣūr and became court poet to him and his two successors. His panegyrics portraying Al-Manṣūr as the champion of Islam against the Christians recall those addressed by Al-Mutanabbī to Saif al-Daula, and won him acclaim as the Mutanabbī of the West. His poems treat the important political and diplomatic events of the age, including battles, thanks to the practice of bringing court poets along with the troops to record military events. Following the conquest of Santiago de Compostela in 997, he was one of the poets chosen by Al-Manṣūr to write the official communication describing the victory to the caliph. His epistle is not extant, but three of his poems commemorating the event survive, including one containing a description of the shrine.

Ibn Darrāj's position at court weakened under Al-Manṣūr's successors as the stability of the court weakened. His *dīwān* records his shifting alliances during the civil war; in general he supported the Berber party. In 1014 he left Córdoba for Ceuta, to try to win a position as panegyrist for Alī Ibn Daūd, to whom he addressed a celebrated ode. Finding no satisfaction there, he returned to al-Andalus to seek a position in the Slav states headed by former Amirid courtiers: Almería, Valencia, Játiva, Tortosa. One of his most famous poems is a panegyric composed during this period for Khairām of Almería; but Khairā treated him so shabbily that the incident became proverbial.

In 1018 Ibn Darrāj arrived in Zaragoza and became attached to the court of Mundhir ibn Yahyā and his son Yahyā ibn Mundhir. Here he regained the stability that he had sought since leaving Córdoba, though he continued to express nostalgia for the Amirid court. For Mundhir he composed a panegyric imitating one composed by al-Mutanabbi for Saif al-Daula. He may have ended his career in Zaragoza, or perhaps (from 1028) at the court of Mujāmhid of Denia.

Ibn Darrāj was the first Andalusian poet to be appreciated in the Muslim East, thanks to his mastery of the neoclassical style of Arabic courtly poetry that was in vogue there. His poetry is widely quoted in both Andalusian and Eastern works, and a large *dīwān* has survived. His works consist entirely of official *qaṣīda* and completely avoid the aristocratic frivolity of the *muwashshaḥ*. In the "erotic" prelude (*nasīb*) of his panegyrics he avoids the traditional erotic themes; instead he often substitutes for the evocation of the lost beloved his longing for his wife and daughter, a most unusual personal note. He sometimes employs floral themes in the *nasīb*, prefiguring the obsession with flowers of some later Andalusian poets. He inclines to heroic portrayal of the patron, depicting him as the champion of Islam and his wars as just wars. He seems to have invented the practice of ending the poem with an envoi using parallelism, a common feature among later Hispano-Arabic poets.

R. Scheindlin

Bibliography

Blachère, R. "La Vie et l'oeuvre du poēte-pistolier Andalou Ibn Darraj al Qasṭallī." *Hesperis* 16 (1933), 99–121.

Makki, M. A. (ed.) *Ibn Darrāj al-Qasṭallī: Dīwān*. Damascus, 1961.

Monroe, J. T. *Risālat at-tawāmbī' wa z-zawābī': The Treatise of Familiar Spirits and Demons by Abū ʿAmir ibn Shuhaid al-Ashjā'ī al-Andalusī*. Berkeley, 1971.

IBN DAŪD, ABRAHAM

Abraham ibn Daūd, who was born in al-Andalus about 1110 or later and died (supposedly a martyr's death) possibly in 1180 at Toledo, is an important if neglected figure in the cultural history of the Jews of al-Andalus.

He was apparently the first to introduce Aristotelian philosophy to the Jews of Spain; his work is extant only in the medieval Hebrew translation, *ha-Emunah ha-ramah* (edited with German translation, 1853; there is a very poor modern English translation). In particular he utilized the philosophy of Ibn Sīnā (Avicenna), and was the first to argue for the agreement between Judaism and rational philosophical thought. Neither Jewish nor Muslim philosophers, of course, had any "double faith" or "reason versus revelation" conflict, which later plagued the Scholastics, so one should not view Ibn Daūd's effort as an attempt to convince readers that it was unnecessary to choose between religion and philosophy. Rather, somewhat like Maimonides after him, he was concerned with demonstrating the harmony between religion and reason in achieving the same truth. It was left to the far greater capacity of Maimonides to make this demonstration (which explains the lack of influence of Ibn Daūd's work on later thought).

More significantly, Ibn Daūd was first in another area: he was the first (and, in fact, the only) Jewish writer of al-Andalus to compose historical chronicles. He composed two such treatises, one of minor importance, on the history of the Second Temple and the Roman Empire, with an abridged version of the medieval Hebrew *Yossifon*, and the much more interesting and significant *Sefer ha-qabbalah* (*Book of Tradition*). Both of these works, like his philosophical work (in part), were written with a certain degree of polemical propaganda. While it is true that they were produced during the period of Almoravid dominance of al-Andalus, a time of some persecution (it is, however, scarcely true that "thousands" of Christians were "wiped out," or that "thousands" of Jews converted, as has been claimed), these works show no evidence of anti-Muslim hostility.

On the contrary, the latter book in particular seems to have been directed primarily against the Qaraite sectarians of Judaism. It purports to be a history of the Jews from the biblical period to Ibn Daūd's day. Much of the work is of interest only to the specialist in Jewish historiography, therefore, but the relatively small portion on Jews in medieval al-Andalus is obviously of great value, chiefly for biographical information on important scholars and other persons. Some light is also shed on historical events and on the general culture of Jews at the time.

Thus, *Sefer ha-qabbalah* served as a major source for the few later medieval Hebrew chronicles composed in Spain, and entire sections were utilized by Abraham Zacut; for example. Aside from these three or four chronicles, however, neither the author nor his work seems to have left any lasting impression on the Jews of Spain.

There is yet another aspect of Ibn Daūd's career to mention. It has frequently been claimed (even by the editor-translator of *Sefer ha-qabbalah*) that he was the famous "Avendauth" who, with the archdeacon Domingo Gundisalvo, translated numerous Arabic philosophical and scientific treatises into Latin. In fact, this is a confusion with a Jewish philosopher (virtually unknown) by the name of Solomon ibn Daūd, who converted to Christianity and was known as Juan Hispano (*not* Johannes Hispalensis, which has caused further confusion between him and a supposed John of Seville and even a Juan who was archbishop of Toledo in 1166). In Latin this converted Jew was known as Johannes Avendaut or Avendehut. Only Albertus Magnus calls him "archbishop of Toledo," undoubtedly confusing him with the previously mentioned Juan. Who this David Iudaeus, whom Albert says included "dicta" of several Muslim philosophers in his writing, may be is unclear; there is the possibility that this reference is to Abraham ibn Daūd.

Finally, when the fourteenth-century Jewish astronomer of Toledo, Isaac Israeli, stated that Ibn Daūd wrote a treatise on astronomy, otherwise unknown, he may very well have confused it with one of the translations done by Avendaut. More research on all of this is still needed.

NORMAN ROTH

Bibliography

Guttmann, J. *Philosophies of Judaism*. New York, 1964. pp. 143–52.

Ibn Daūd, A. *Sefer ha-Qabbalah*: *The Book of Tradition*. Ed. and Trans. G. Cohen. Philadelphia, 1967.

IBN EZRA, ABRAHAM

Abraham ibn Ezra of Tudela (1089–1164) was a Hispano-Jewish polymath whose career spanned the transition in Jewish society and culture from Muslim al-Andalus to Christian Spain. A Hebrew grammarian, literary critic, and prolific poet of devotional and secular Hebrew verse; a Neoplatonic philosopher, astronomer, and astrologer; and above all a seminal biblical exegete, Ibn Ezra left Spain in 1140 and spent the remainder of his adult life wandering through North Africa, Italy, France, and England.

Ibn Ezra originally produced biblical commentaries on all the books of the Hebrew Bible. Some of these texts are no longer extant, whereas others have survived in more than one recension. Ibn Ezra's witty and frequently acerbic commentaries are written in an unmistakable style. They reflect a synthesis of the diverse hermeneutical trends prevalent in the Spanish school of biblical exegesis and probably represent the way in which the Hebrew Bible was understood by Andalusian Jewish literary intellectuals. On the one hand Ibn Ezra's commentaries focus upon the grammatical, lexical, and stylistic features of the biblical text. In this respect their aim is to clarify the "plain sense" of Scripture. On the other hand they are suffused with highly laconic and frequently enigmatic philosophical and scientific observations, and they contain obscure excursuses often designed to suggest esoteric cosmological and theological doctrines ("the wise will understand"). Although he did not apply them as extremely as some other Spanish exegetes, notably Moses ibn Giqatilla and Isaac ibn Yashush, the methods Ibn Ezra typically employs are rationalistic. For instance, he is thought to be the first to ascribe the second part of the Book of Isaiah to an anonymous prophet of the Babylonian Exile. He also alludes to the likelihood of post-Mosaic interpolations in the Pentateuch.

Ibn Ezra's verse reflects the poet's interest in cultivating strophic forms of composition and his apparent preference for liturgical over secular poetry. From the thematic standpoint Ibn Ezra's lyrics exhibit an openness to treating more realistic and personal motifs than those represented in the conventional matrix established by his predecessors. In terms of its language his poetry upholds the Andalusians' exclusive reliance on biblical Hebrew.

Ibn Ezra's history of the Andalusian philological and linguistic tradition and his Hebrew grammar, as well as his two commentaries on the Book of Psalms, were of great importance for the dissemination of Hispano-Hebrew poetry and poetics. These writings reveal him to be a devotee of Arabic prosody and style, as well as a passionate advocate of the divinely inspired sacred poetry of ancient Israel. Through Ibn Ezra's attempts to promulgate golden age learning and its approach to knowledge, Hispano-Hebrew culture came to exert a powerful influence over the Jews of other Mediterranean lands.

Ross Brann

Bibliography

Díaz Esteban, F. (ed.) *Abraham ibn Ezra y su tiempo*. Madrid, 1990.

Levin, I. *Abraham ibn Ezra: His Life and His Poetry*. Tel Aviv, 1976. (In Hebrew.)

IBN EZRA, MOSES

Moses ibn Ezra (ca. 1055–1138) was the second of four sons in an influential family of Granadan Jewish patricians, and the first important Hebrew poet born during the politically turbulent but culturally productive period of the *muluk at-tawā'if* (*los reyes de taifas*, the party kings). Civil disturbances connected with the 1066 murder of Yehosef ibn Naghrila forced the family to flee to nearby Lucena, where Moses studied with Isaac ibn Ghiyath, the master rabbi associated with the famous Talmudic academy of that town. When the clan returned to Granada, Moses enjoyed the material culture and stimulating intellectual and social life characteristic of the Jewish nobility. During the years prior to 1090 he came into his own as a courtier-rabbi and won acclaim as a poet's poet.

In 1090 the Almoravid invasion broke the sociopolitical stability of Granada, whose Jewish community was devastated for the second time in twenty-five years. For reasons that are unclear, Moses did not join his brothers' exodus to Córdoba and Toledo. He remained alone in Granada, "a resident alien" in his desolate native land. Subsequently, sometime between 1090 and 1095, Ibn Ezra was mysteriously compelled to abandon his wife and children, and leave Granada for exile in Christian Spain. So began the poet's forty-year odyssey though the towns of Castile, Navarre, and, it appears, Aragón. This tragic event proved to be the turning point in Ibn Ezra's personal, intellectual, and artistic life because he was never able to reconcile himself to an environment that he believed was socially, culturally, and intellectually inferior to that of his native Muslim Spain.

Ibn Ezra was, arguably, the most conservative of the Andalusian school of Hebrew poets. He initiated no major genres; his classicizing language and style are manifest in both his secular and his liturgical verse; he revived, in Hebrew form, the traditional structure of the neoclassical Arabic ode (*qaṣida*); and he was the first Hebrew poet to compose an Arabic-style book of manneristic homonym poems. Even Ibn Ezra's most identifiably personal occasional poems, the lyrical complaints in which the poet laments his exile from Granada, are stylized in form and conventional in content. It would be incorrect to conclude, however, that his poetry is lacking in either originality or self-expression. On the contrary, he achieved distinction as a poet through his creative reworking of poetic tradition and his artistic mastery of rhetorical style.

Apart from his literary conservatism, what immediately distinguishes Ibn Ezra from other poets of the school are his Judeo-Arabic prose writings on Hebrew poetry and Andalusian Jewish culture. *The Book of Discussion and Conversation*, the most complete and comprehensive work on Hebrew poetics to come down from the Middle Ages, is a prescriptive and probing treatment of the legitimacy of Arabic-style Hebrew poetry. *The Treatise of the Garden on Metaphorical and Literal Language* is a theoretical study of the nature of poetic diction as manifested in the Hebrew Bible. Along with his substantial corpus of secular and devotional Hebrew poetry, these works serve to identify Ibn Ezra as the embodiment of the traditions and ideals of Andalusian Jewish literary intellectuals of the period.

Ross Brann

Bibliography

Pagis, D. *Secular Poetry and Poetic Theory: Moses Ibn Ezra and His Contemporaries*. Jerusalem, 1970. (In Hebrew.)

Scheindlin, R. P. "Rabbi Moshe ibn Ezra on the Legitimacy of Poetry." In *Medievalia et Humanistica*, new series, Vol. 7. Ed. by Paul M. Clogan. Cambridge, 1976. 101–15.

IBN GABIROL, SOLOMON

Abū Ayyūb Sulaimān (Solomon) ibn Yahyā (Judah?) was born in Málaga, though his father came from Córdoba. His last name is problematic; usually spelled today as Ibn Gabirol, it may more correctly be Ibn Jabirol or Jabirel (referring either to a bone setter, or doctor, or to the angel Gabriel). He was born in 1021 or 1022, but the date of his death is uncertain. According to an Andalusian Muslim author who praised him highly, he died in 1056 or 1057, but in light of what Moses Ibn Ezra wrote, it may have been between 1052 and 1055. He apparently was sickly for several years (possibly suffering from tuberculosis) and did not marry.

Ibn Gabirol, like other Jews of the Muslim period, was an accomplished scholar in many fields. He remains famous primarily as a poet, having written hundreds of secular and "religious" poems, beginning at the age of sixteen. He lived also in Zaragoza, where he continued to write poetry, including a damning attack on the ignorance of the Jews there, and in Valencia. His secular verse is outstanding and uniquely individual, with an easily identifiable style. One of his main themes is the constant struggle between the desire to acquire wisdom and the temptations of worldly pleasures (wine and love, particularly). He wrote many love poems about boys, but an equal number about women. Too much has been made of this, and also of his (possible) illness, which certainly did not last all his life or prevent him from falling in love.

His religious poetry stands out among the finest of this genre, with many poems expressing a mystical longing found also in his other writings (the most famous of these poems is *Keter malkhut*, *Crown of Kingship*, a lengthy mystical poem that combines elements of philosophy and even science).

Tradition has it that Ibn Gabirol composed some twenty-one philosophical treatises, but the accuracy of this statement is perhaps debatable. In any case several important authentic works have survived, foremost among them the Arabic treatise translated into Latin as *Fons vitae* by Johannes Hispalense and Dominigo Gundisalvo, which throughout the Middle Ages was thought to be by a Christian author. Second is the "Improvement of Moral Qualities," composed in Zaragoza in 1045 (Hebrew translation, Arabic original, and English translations are available). Finally, there is the *Mivhar ha-peninim* (*Choice of Pearls*, extant only in a Hebrew translation and an antiquated English one), which is an interesting collection of philosophical and moral maxims.

Ibn Gabirol's mysticism and possible relationship with the later development of *qabbalah* are other factors of importance. The *Fons vitae*, although translated into Hebrew in the medieval period, exerted no demonstrable influence on Jewish thought, although it had a strong impact upon the scholastics. Among modern Spanish scholars Menéndez Pelayo devoted many pages to Ibn Gabirol; interest in him continues today.

NORMAN ROTH

Bibliography

Millás-Vallicrosa, J. M. *Selomó Ibn Gabirol como poeta y filósofo*. Madrid and Barcelona, 1945.

Selected Religious Poems of Solomon Ibn Gabirol. Ed. (in Hebrew) by H. Brody. English translation by I. Zangwill. Philadelphia, 1923.

IBN ḤAFṢŪN, ʿUMAR

Ibn Ḥafṣūn was the most successful of many local Andalusian leaders who, during the late ninth and early tenth centuries, rebelled against the emirate and later against the caliphate of Córdoba. Like many of these rebel chieftains and their followers, he was of New Muslim ancestry (Arabic, *Muwalladūn*; Spanish, *muladí*). His grandfather Jaʿfar had converted to Islam, but all his earlier ancestors had been Christians, and bore Hispanic or Visigothic names. Ibn Ḥafṣūn's father was a prosperous landowner. His son had an impatient, fiery temperament, and after a violent quarrel that led to the death of a neighbor, Ibn Ḥafṣūn escaped into the mountains, then fled to Morocco, and later, fearing he would be discovered, returned to Spain (850) to become leader of a small robber band in the mountain fastness of Málaga (between Ronda and Antequera). His center of operations was Bobastro, an impregnable fortified redoubt high in the Sierra de Ronda. Ibn Ḥafṣūn's banditry, which earned him fame as a daring leader, gradually turned into a full-scale rebellion against Muslim authority. In 883 he briefly made peace with Córdoba and even joined the emir's army, but he soon became impatient with the scorn to which *muladíes* were subjected and returned to the mountains.

From Bobastro, Ibn Ḥafṣūn gradually extended his power over neighboring towns and villages, even seizing or controlling through alliances important and distant centers such as Archidona, Écija, Lucena, Priego, Baeza, and Úbeda. Córdoba, often successful in crushing local rebel leaders, could do nothing against Ibn Ḥafṣūn, who became an independent leader in his own right, even conducting correspondence with Muslim rulers in Tunis and with powerful Moroccans, whose boats from time to time brought him supplies. His activities certainly benefited the territorial aspirations of Alfonso III of Asturias (r. 866–910), though Ibn Ḥafṣūn seems never to have made contact with Christian leaders to the north of the *frontera*.

In 899 Ibn Ḥafṣūn proclaimed his conversion to the religion of his ancestors and started the construction, at Bobastro, of a small stone church whose ruins survive to this day. The conversion was a disastrous tactical blunder; though it was enthusiastically welcomed by *mozárabes*, it lost him the support of many *muladíes*, who were sincere converts to Islam. From the moment of his accession, caliph ʿAbd al-Raḥmān III (r 912–961) vigorously and successfully undertook to suppress rebellious factions throughout his territory, reclaiming most of the fortified towns once controlled by Ibn Ḥafṣūn. But Ibn Ḥafṣūn and his fortress of Bobastro remained unvanquished. He died in September 917. His sons, though divided against one another, held out at Bobastro until 19 January 928. After the fortress surrendered, the tombs of Ibn Ḥafṣūn and his grandfather Jaʿfar were opened, and their bodies were taken to Córdoba and exposed to public desecration. Ibn Ḥafṣūn's daughter, Argentea—who had converted at the same time as her father, her mother, Columba, and her oldest brother, Jaʿfar—entered a convent in Córdoba, but later chose a martyr's death and was beheaded in 937.

SAMUEL G. ARMISTEAD

Bibliography

Acién Almansa, M. *Entre el feudalismo y el Islam: Umar ibn Ḥafṣūn y los historiadores*. Jaén, 1994.

Dozy, R. *Spanish Islam*. Translated by F. G. Stokes. New York, 1913.

Fierro, M. "Cuatro preguntas entorno a Ibn Ḥafṣūn." *Al-Qanṭara* 16 (1995), 221–57.

Hoenerbach, W. *Islamische Geschichte Spaniens*. Zurich-Stuttgart, 1970.

Lévi-Provençal, E. *España musulmana*. Translated by E. García Gómez. 2 vols. Madrid, 1957–65.

IBN ḤAYYĀN

For his contemporaries, Abū Marwān ibn Ḥayyān was "the master of scholarship and of the historians in our land" (shaykh al-'adab wa-l-mu'arrikhīn bi-baladi-nā) and, for modern critics, he is "without doubt the greatest historian of the Middle Ages in all Spain, both Muslim and Christian". (Only centuries later, with the *Muqaddima* of Ibn Khaldūn and the encyclopedic histories of Alfonso X, do we find anything quite comparable to the great historiographic achievements of this Córdoban scholar (ca. 987–1076), concerning whose life, however, despite his distinguished reputation, we know precious little. Ibn Ḥayyān seems to have lived in humble—even impoverished—circumstances until his appointment to the government chancellery. His writings reveal a highly critical, notably acerbic attitude toward many of his contemporaries and, very especially, his deep and bitter resentment of the political instability that wracked al-Andalus during the chaotic epoch of the Ṭā'ifas. Ibn Ḥayyān's writings have reached us only as mutilated, isolated fragments, pitiful vestiges of a vast and brilliantly systematic historiographic enterprise. Several works—possibly seven in all—have been lost in their entirety, but some of these may only have been segments separated from Ibn Hayyān's two major histories: the *Muqtabis* and the *Matīn*. His contemporaries cite and attribute to him the "great history" (*Al-ta'rīkh al-kabīr*), but it remains unclear as to which of these principal works, or their pieces and parts, such references may allude. The *Muqtabis*, in ten volumes, probably written before the *Matīn*, covered the history of Muslim Spain from the Conquest up to the author's time. There are modern Arabic editions of three surviving parts. In the *Muqtabis*, Ibn Hayyān assembled a vast, critical anthology of earlier Muslim historians who wrote about al-Andalus. This work thus cannot properly be said to have been "written" by Ibn Ḥayyān. The title can be roughly translated as "a book copied from other authors." (The verb *qabasa*, "to take, or seek to take, a brand [from someone else's fire]," can also mean "to derive, acquire, borrow, take over." With brilliant control and surprisingly modern editorial criteria—indicating lacunae, adding editorial notes and clarifications—Ibn Ḥayyān assembled and commented on a great number of earlier historians. The *Kitāb al-Matīn* (*The Solid Book*), in an astounding seventy volumes or parts, was something very different. Here Ibn Ḥayyān was writing about, analyzing, and criticizing the chaotic events of his own time, what he himself had witnessed, to reveal—in Dozy's words—"a rare political understanding of events." Thanks to his admiring disciple, Ibn Bassām, substantial portions of the *Matīn* have been preserved for us as part of the *Dhakhīra*. Had the *Muqtabis* and the *Matīn* both survived the ravages of time, they would surely have made up a "great history" indeed.

SAMUEL G. ARMISTEAD

Bibliography

Avila, M. L. "La fecha de redacción del *Muqtabis*." *Al-Qanṭara* 5 (1984).

García Gómez, E. "A propósito de Ibn Ḥayyān." *Al-Andalus* 11 (1946).

——— (trans.). *El Califato de Córdoba en el «Muqtabis» de Ibn Ḥayyān*. Madrid, 1967.

Huici Miranda, A. "Ibn Ḥayyān." *Encyclopaedia of Islam*. 2d ed. Vol. 3. Leiden, 1971.

Viguera Molins, M. J. et al. (trans.) Ibn Ḥayyān de Córdoba. *Crónica del Califa ʿAbdarraḥmān III an-Nāṣir entre los años 912 y 942 (al-Muqtabis V)*. Zaragoza, 1981.

IBN ḤAZM

Abū Muhammad ʿAlī ibn Ḥazm was born in 994 at Munyat al-Mughīra, a suburb of Córdoba, and died on Mont Lishan, near Huelva, in 1063. He enjoyed the luxury and the education of the wealthy during the last years of the last Córdoban caliph, ʿAbd al-Raḥmān IV, at whose court his father was a high-ranking official. His first attempts to follow in his father's steps in political life proved unsuccessful. After the fall of Córdoba, and some years of residence in various places, in 1016 he sought refuge in Játiva, near Valencia. Between 1016 and 1023 he was minister during the short reign of the Ummayyad caliph, and after the latter's assasination Ibn Ḥazm was thrown into prison. Between 1027 and 1031 he seems to have been active again in political life, from which he withdrew to turn to scholarship.

Ibn Ḥazm's education, with the best-known teachers of his time, encompassed the Qur'ān and religious sciences, theology, literature, medicine, history, and logic. He was a prolific author, with some four hundred titles attributed to him, of which only fourteen(?) are extant.

Ibn Ḥazm is especially well known in the West for his book *Tawq al-hamāma* (*The Dove's Necklace*), written during his exile in Játiva and thus a work of his youth. It is in the strictest sense a literary epistle (*risāla*), a mixture of prose and his own poetry. It offers, in thirty chapters, a rather nostalgic contemplation of the nature and experience of love, which he treats with some autobiographical references, a considerable amount of sensuality, and a great deal of sensitivity. A book on love of enduring appeal, it has been incongruently compared to Ovid's and Andreas Capellanus's somewhat similar works.

Of greater importance, yet lesser known, are his other books, works in which the image of the playful and sensitive youth dissipates, replaced by that of the pious, often rigid Muslim scholar that he was. In his *Maratib al-'ulum* (*Categories of Sciences*) he encourages the study of all sciences, but with an objective that is clearly religious, for in his opinion religion should be the aim of all learning. Less important in his view is the study of poetry, especially the lyrical (*ghazal*), which may lead to temptation, and the panegyrical (*madḥ*), which tends toward deceitful exaggerations. His moral concerns are the topic of another book, the *Kitāb al-akhlāq wa'lī-siyar* (*Book of Conduct*) consisting of twelve chapters in the form of admonishments and reflections on virtuous life.

The most important of all Ibn Ḥazm's extant works is his voluminous *Kitāb al-fisal fī'l-milal* (*Decision Among Religions*). Aiming at demonstrating the truth of Islam in comparison with all other religions, Ibn Ḥazm writes what has been considered a treatise on comparative religion. Beginning with the religious and philosophical doctrines farthest removed from the truth of Islam, such as the cynics for their rejection of any truth, and atheists, for their repudiation of the existence of a God, he progresses to discuss the polytheists, as such Zoroastrians and Manichaeans, who recognize God but not his uniqueness. Christianity is included here because of the Trinitarian doctrine, which he understands to be a form of polytheism. Judaism is, in his view, the religion closest to Islam, except for its adulteration of the divine revelation, which he proves with reference to such Jewish sects as the Samaritans, Sadducees, and Talmudites. His analysis of the various religious doctrines is solidly based on textual references that show his vast erudition.

Dealing with Islam, Ibn Ḥazm refers to its various sects, from the Muʿtazilites to the Kharigites, which he sees to have in common their esoteric and allegorical interpretations of the Revelation. To avoid this, the true Muslim must follow the obvious (*ẓahīr*) and the literal meaning of the Qur'ān. In this way he justifies the school of the literalist Thahimites that for a time became popular in al-Andalus.

Points of great importance in Ibn Ḥazm's theology are harmony between faith and reason, divine predetermination, and free will. Possibly the most important is his effort to demonstrate the existence of God and the temporality of the world, and the necessity of divine revelation. Because of them, Ibn Ḥazm is considered a precursor of Christian scholasticism.

Ibn Ḥazm exerted a great influence, and his doctrine of literal interpretation became mainstream among the Zahīrites, and was continued by his followers, known as Hazmites. Of his direct students many are known in their own right. Well known also in the Orient, Ibn Ḥazm was praised by Al-Ghazālī, and his influence extended to the end of the sixteenth century, when it disappeared under bloody persecution. In the Maghrib the favor shown to his doctrines by the Almohad reformer Muhammad ibn Tūmart al-Mahdī helped to enhance the political influence of his followers in North Africa and al-Andalus. Among the most famous scholars that totally or partially followed Ibn Ḥazm's doctrines are the philosopher Averroës and the mystic Ibn al-ʿArabī.

VICENTE CANTARINO

Bibliography

Asín Palacios, M. *Abenházam de Córdoba y su historia crítica de las ideas religiosas*. 5 vols. Madrid, 1927–32.

García Gómez, E. *El collar de la paloma, tratado sobre el amor y los amantes, de Ibn Hazm de Córdoba*. Madrid, 1952.

Ibn Hazm. *A Book Containing the Risāla Known as The Dove's Neckring*. Translated by A. R. Nykl. Paris, 1931.

———. *The Ring of the Dove*. Translated by A. J. Arberry. London, 1953.

IBN HŪD, MUHAMMAD IBN YŪSUF

Ibn Hūd died in 1237, but the date of his birth is unknown. The most important of a group of independent governors and magnates to emerge in al-Andalus after the decline of Almohad power, he was a descendant of the governing Banū Hūd clan of Zaragoza that had been deposed in 1118.

Ibn Hūd filled a power vacuum in Muslim Iberia at the beginning of the thirteenth century. He began his career in the army of Murcia, but deserted and quickly dedicated himself to brigandage, acquiring wealth, followers, and a reputation in a very short time. Defender of the Islamic cause, he fought against the Christians and took Murcia in 1228, subsequently extending his power to Córdoba, Seville, Granada, Almería, Algeciras, and across the Strait of Gibraltar to Ceuta. He recognized the Abbasíd al-Mustanṣir as caliph, took a number of impressive titles for himself like "Prince of the Faithful," and became the most powerful ruler in al-Andalus during the first third of the thirteenth century. Ibn Hūd's authority was soon challenged by individuals like Zayyān ibn Mardanīsh of Valencia and Muhammad ibn Yūsuf ibn Naṣr, who in 1231 declared himself ruler of his native Arjona, and then took Jaén, Guadix, Baeza, and other districts. Ibn Mardanīsh's actions culminated in a clash with Ibn Hūd that greatly weakened the power structures of al-Andalus. At the same time, the king of Castile, Fernando III, took advantage of the instability created by the situation among the warring Muslims and, moving south, forced Ibn Hūd to cede several strongholds to him and become his tributary.

Ibn Hūd's influence lasted but a short time. Even during the height of his power, he was continually menaced by Castile and Aragón. By 1236, Córdoba had fallen into the hands of Fernando III, and by 1238, a year after Ibn Hūd's death, all of al-Andalus had become an easy target of opportunism for the Christian kingdoms of Iberia.

E. Michael Gerli

Bibliography

Arié, R. *España musulmana (siglos VIII–XV)*. Barcelona, 1982.

Chejne, Anwar G. *Muslim Spain: Its History and Culture*. Minneapolis, 1974.

IBN AL-KARDABŪS

Abū Marwān ʿAbd al-Malik ibn al-Kardabūs al-Tawzarī (mid-twelveth century to early thirteenth) was born in the town of Tawzar, in southwestern Tunisia, in a frontier region of Ifrīqiya, which—like its peninsular homonym—came to be known, in late North African Latin, as *Qasṭīliya*, and where, even during our author's time—as Al-Idrīsī assures us—a now extinct northern African variety of Romance (*al-laṭīnī al-afrīqī*) may still have been spoken. As his patronymic would suggest (*Kardabūs = Cordobés?*), the historian's forebears, probably muwallādūn, must have emigrated to North Africa from al-Andalus. We know very little about Ibn al-Kardabūs' life. He seems to have lived for a time in Egypt, where he studied with a famous expert on the *ḥadīth*, Abū Tāhir al-Silafī. Whether he ever traveled to al-Andalus remains in doubt. Nor do we know much of anything about the sources he used to compile his *Kitāb al-iktifā' fī akhbār al-khulafā'* (*The Adequate Book Concerning Information about the Caliphs*). Ibn al-Kardabūs's narrative on occasion offers surprising details: In contrast to most other sources, Tāriq's invasion was not a surprise pushover against unsuspecting Christians. He encountered well-prepared and well-armed defenders, who repulsed his initial attack, forcing him to land with difficulty on a rocky shore, whence he was later able to outflank and defeat the Christians. Like Cortés, Tāriq burned his boats: "*Fight or die!*" he challenged his men. The *Kitūb* includes its own version of the widely known "Locked House of Toledo," of Count Yulyān's treason, and of Tāriq's feigned cannibalism. The defeated Rodrigo drowns in a river. We are told of the Ṭā'ifa kingdoms and of ensuing Christian conquests in which Alfonso VI and Alvar Háñez play their parts: "May God's curse be upon them!" At Zallāqa (Sagrajas), Yūsuf ibn Tāshfīn, on seeing the Christians initially rout the Andalusians, slyly observes, "Let both groups perish, for both are enemies." El Cid besieges and takes Valencia, but dies of sorrow when defeated by the Muslims. Yūsuf ibn Tashfīn comes to Spain accompanied by Sīr ibn Abī Bakr, presumably the "rey Búcar" of the *Cantar de Mio Cid*. Ironically, Alvar Háñez is killed in a battle with Christians. Always interesting, Ibn al-Kardabūs offers us a wealth of unusual or otherwise unedited material.

Samuel G. Armistead

Bibliography

Arié, R. *España musulmana (siglos VIII–XV)*. Barcelona, 1982.

Lewicki, T. "Une langue romane oubliée de l'Afrique du Nord." *Rocznik Orientalistyczny* 17 (1951–52).

Maíllo Salgado, F. (trans.) Ibn al-Kardabūs. *Historia de al-Andalus (Kitāb al-iktifā')*. Madrid, 1986.

IBN KHALDŪN

Born 27 May 1332 and died 16 March 1406, he is regarded as one of the greatest of all historians, but especially of the Muslim world. He developed a theory, method, and philosophy of history he called

ʿumrān al-basharī, or the social study of human civilization. As a result, many credit Ibn Khaldūn with the invention of sociology. Born into a distinguished family of Andalusí origins in Tunisia (they had emigrated from Seville), Ibn Khaldūn received a thorough education at home, in the mosque, and among the many Iberian Muslim intellectuals who were refugees in North Africa. In 1345, his parents died of the plague, and he found employment at the court of the Hafsids. For almost thirty years thereafter, he was deeply involved in the turbulent politics of North Africa and Spain. At one point, he was imprisoned for his political activities. In 1362 he went to Granada, where he was well received by the vizier, Ibn al-Khatīb. There he was enlisted to serve on a diplomatic mission to Seville and the court of Pedro I of Castile. Disillusioned by what he found in Iberia, he returned to Tunisia, where he became *hājib*, or chamberlain to the ruler. Soon embroiled again in political intrigue, he decided on voluntary retirement to the oasis of Baskarah in what today is Algeria. Circumstances, however, compelled him to return to politics, even though he foresaw dangerous consequences. In 1375 he withdrew again from court life to a castle in Oran, where during the course of the next five years he wrote *Al-Muqaddimah*, his greatest work. Drawn back into politics in 1380, his experience proved nearly fatal and, in 1382, he left Tunis never to return. He went to Egypt, where he became a Mālikite *qāḍi*, or judge, and a prominent teacher of Islamic law at Al-Azhar University.

Ibn Khaldūn's *Muqaddimah* serves as an introduction to his *Universal History. Kitāb al-ʿIbar Kitāb al-ʿIbar* is a valuable source for the history of North Africa and Iberia, but the *Muqaddimah* is a brilliant exposition of the methodological and cultural knowledge necessary to produce a scientific understanding of the past. Ibn Khaldūn was interested primarily in the reasons for the rise and fall of human civilizations; he contended that the basic causes of historical evolution are to be sought in the economic and social structure of society. In his work, he emphasizes environment, politics, economics, and religion as the determining factors in the development of societies. He surveys the sciences, refuting some like alchemy and astrology, and reflects on the manner of acquiring and using them. History, like science, involves more than a description of events, it calls for speculation, discrimination, and an attempt to identify the true causes and origins of existing things. The historian needs to possess a clear knowledge of customs, social organization, and beliefs and use critical judgment in dealing always with all the versions of the past. As such, history merits a place in the realm of philosophy. While *Al-Muqaddimah* serves as the introduction to *Kitāb al-ʿIbar*, in the six parts that follow *Al-Muqaddimah* he goes on to apply his ideas to the entire history of humankind. The work is, for the most part, a political history and is arranged around individuals, dynasties, rulers, and important events, but also includes striking reflections on human association as a dynamic interaction of many motives. Ibn Khaldūn's work stands as a monument to the history of history itself and remains an extremely important source of scholarship for the late medieval Maghrib and Iberia in particular.

E. Michael Gerli

Bibliography

Al-Azmeh, Aziz, *Ibn Khaldūn: A Reinterpretation*. London, 1990.

Ibn Khaldūn. *The Muquaddimah*. 2 vols. Trans. Franz Rosenthal. Princeton, N.J., 1967.

Mahdi, Muhsin. *Ibn Khaldūn's Philosophy of History: A Study in the Philosophic Foundation of the Science of Culture*. London, 1957.

IBN AL-KHATĪB

Known as ā Lisān al-Dīn (1313–1374), Ibn al-Khatīb was the greatest Muslim writer of Granada and the last great intellectual, writer, and statesman of Muslim Spain. Son of a Granadine court official, he received an excellent education. He was vizier to Yūsuf I from 1349 to 1354, and continued, with one interruption, under Yūsuf's son Muḥammad V. Among his friends and pupils was Ibn Khaldūn, who was present for a period in the court. Ibn Zamrak, the poet and secretary of Muḥammad V whose verses adorn the walls of the Alhambra, was also a pupil of Ibn al-Khatīb. In 1371 or 1372 Ibn al-Khatīb was accused of heresy, and fled to Morocco. He was imprisoned in 1374, and killed in prison by hired assassins while an investigative commission studied the charges of heresy and disloyalty to Muḥammad V. Ibn Zamrak was accused of complicity.

Ibn al-Khatīb's linguistically and stylistically sophisticated works are numerous. Remembered primarily as a historian, he wrote extensively on the history and geography of the kingdom of Granada. His al-*Ihāta fī ta'rīkn Gharnata*, an encyclopedia of Granadine history, has yet to be completely published or translated. Ibn al-Khatīb was the first Arabic historian to write on Andalusian history in its entirety, and his works are the principal sources for important periods in the history of Naṣrid Granada. He also wrote extensively on Islamic history in general, travel, government, medicine, philosophy, and mysticism, and he is the author of many *muwashsḥahs* and other poems. We lack an adequate understanding of the significance of Ibn al-Khatīb, who was well known and respected, though not always liked, by his contemporaries. The extensive treatment of him by Al-Maqqarī in *Nafh al-Tīb* has not been translated. Much of Ibn al-Khatīb's writing remains unpublished. The Escorial has an important collection of his manuscripts.

DANIEL B. EISENBERG

Bibliography

Arié, R. "Lisān al-Dīn b. al-Khatīb: Quelques aspects de son oeuvre." In *Atti del terzo Congresso di studi arabi e islamici*. Naples, 1967. 69–81.

García Gómez, E. *Foco de antigua luz sobre la Alhambra desde un texto de Ibn al-Jatīb en 1362*. Madrid, 1988.

Santiago Simón, E. de. *El polígrafo granadino Ibn al-jatīb y el sufismo: Aportaciones para su estudio*. Granada, 1983.

IBN MASARRA, MOḤAMMED

Little is known of Moḥammed ibn Masarra's life. His father ʿAbdalla, a merchant, had studied theology in Baṣrah, where he became attracted to the movement of rational theology known as the *muʿtazila*. Some years after his return to al-Andalus, and possibly to avoid persecution by the conservative jurists of the Mālikī school predominant in al-Andalus, he emigrated to Mecca, where he died in 899. Ibn Masarra followed his father's inclination to the Muʿtazilites. While still a youth he began to attract disciples, with whom he moved to a house he had in the mountains near Córdoba. This isolation did not prevent his teachings from spreading nor the Mālikī jurists (*fuqahā*) from becaming suspicious of his orthodoxy. To avoid their persecution, he left for Mecca under pretense of the pilgrimage. About 912, when ʿAbd al-Raḥmān III became caliph, Ibn Masarra returned to his Córdoban isolation, where, in spite of the increasing opposition by conservative jurists and theologians, he continued teaching until his death in 931.

None of the books written by Ibn Masarra has survived. His life and his doctrines are only partially known on the basis of quotations, not all authentic, attributed to him by his followers, both Andalusian (Ibn Ḥazm, Ibn Saʿīd, Ibn al-ʿArabī) and Oriental, (Shahrazuri, al-Shahrastānī, Qifti). From all these sources Miguel Asín Palacios reconstructed the body of his doctrines.

Ibn Masarra is considered the initiator in al-Andalus of the study of philosophy and of its esoteric application, mysticism. It seems that he followed an ecclectic array of doctrines related to the gnostic Neoplatonism then in vogue in Alexandria and wrongly attributed to the Greek philosopher Empedocles. His importance rests on his having introduced into Andalusian thought the concept of a spiritual matter common to all beings, thus opening the way to a doctrine of emanation, which later theologians and mystic writers interpreted in various ways.

VINCENTE CANTARINO

Bibliography

Asín Palacios, M. "Abenmasarra y su escuela." In *Obras escogidas*. Vol. 1, pp. 1–169. Madrid, 1946.

IBN NAGHRĪLLAH, SAMUEL

One of the most important and fascinating Jewish figures of al-Andalus was Samuel (Ismaʿil in Arabic) Ibn Naghrīllah (993–1056). Having fled Córdoba around 1013, after the civil war, he entered the service of the ruler of the Granada *ṭāʾifa* first as a secretary and then rose to the dual positions of prime minister and commander of the army. Whereas other Jews also held such posts for other ṭāʾifa rulers, Granada was the most important of the kingdoms, and the hostility of Muslim fanatics over the appointment of a Jew to such a post led to constant warfare with Granada. For eighteen years Ibn Naghrīllah was continuously in battle with his Muslim troops against these enemies, all of whom he vanquished.

Not only was he thus the first (and only) Jewish general since the time of Cleopatra, but as prime minister he had to oversee the growth and prosperity of the kingdom. In the midst of all this he found time to compose thousands of Hebrew poems, collected by his sons into three massive volumes. To these he assigned significant symbolic titles: *Ben Tehillim* (*Son of Psalms*), *Ben Mishley* (*Son of Proverbs*) and *Ben Qohelet* (*Son of Ecclesiastes*), which reveal his desire to equate himself with the biblical and heroic traditions of David and Solomon. This is expressed also in his poetry, where he more than once compares himself to David, the warrior-king and poet. His skill in poetry was profound, and he was not only the first great Hebrew poet but remains perhaps the shining star in that heaven (to borrow Heine's famous phrase, though unfortunately he did not know Ibn Naghrīllah's poetry to compare with that of ha-Levy and Ibn Gabriol).

His poetry introduced not only many of the Arabic meters into Hebrew (to which he added numerous new ones), but also most of the themes which characterized later Hebrew verse, such as love, wine, nature, and other motifs. *Ben Tehillim* contains numerous poems concerning his battles and victories, of course, as well as touching poems addressed to his beloved young son Yūsuf, who was to succeed his father as prime-minister of Granada. The vitriolic treatment of Yūsuf in the

Arabic source is not confirmed by what we know of his actual life. However, his use of tax money to complete his own palace (very probably the Alhambra), although merely copying what the king himself did, led to a riot in which not only he but most of the Jews of the city lost their lives.

Samuel, who—as he had predicted—died peacefully in bed, was also a renowned authority on Jewish law. Only fragments of his legal work survive, but there are numerous quotations of him in later rabbinical literature. He was also engaged in a polemic with his former friend, from his youth in Córdoba, Ibn Ḥazm, who since had become a zealous Muslim judge. He was not, however, as modern writers continue to err in saying, the author of the well-known introduction to the Talmud.

NORMAN ROTH

Bibliography:

Ashtor, E. *The Jews of Moslem Spain*. Philadelphia, 1979, Vol. 2 (ch. 2). (Unfortunately mostly erroneous.)

Roth, N. *Jews Visigoths & Muslims in Medieval Spain*. Leiden, 1994. (See Index.)

IBN QASĪ *See* BANŪ QASĪM

IBN AL-QŪṬIYYA

Abū Bakr ibn ʿUmar ibn ʿAbd al-ʿAzīz Ibn al-Qūṭiyya (d. 977), a grammarian, lexicographer, poet, and historian, was known by his *laqab* (surname or nickname), as "the son of the Gothic woman," thus being a descendant of Visigothic nobility, since one of his ancestors was Sāra, the granddaughter of Vitiza (r. 700–10), the next-to-last Visigothic king. Ibn al-Qūṭiyya was born in Seville, where he studied under various distinguished teachers, before moving to Córdoba to teach grammar, law, and *ḥadīth* (religious traditions). The idea that he was to become a *qāḍī* (judge) in Córdoba would seem to have been suggested by an erroneous reading of a passage by the tenth- to eleventh-century biographer, Ibn al-Faraḍī, in *Kitāb Ta'rīkh ʿulāma' al-Andalus* (*History of the Learned Men of al-Andalus*) Ibn al-Qūṭiyya was the author of various works, some of which have been lost. Two that survive are his *Kitāb Taṣārif al-afʿāl* (*Conjugation of verbs*) and *Ta'rīkh iftitāh* (or *fatḥ*) *al-Andalus* (*History of the Conquest of Spain*). The *Ta'rīkh* probably was dictated by Ibn al-Qūṭiyya and written down and edited by one of his pupils, though the possible use of additional written sources cannot be ruled out. The narrative, as if reflecting somewhat disconnected classroom notes, may have been known in various different redactions (Ibn ʿAzzūz). Various citations attributed to Ibn al-Qūṭiyya by other tenth-century Hispano-Arabic historians are not to be found in the *Ta'rīkh*, suggesting, among other possibilities, that the surviving text may perhaps be an abbreviation (Fierro, pp. 491–92). Ibn al-Qūṭiyya was one of the earliest historians of Islamic Spain. His *History* is invaluable in preserving for us materials heard from his teachers, anecdotes, personal impressions, and commentaries, found nowhere else, and possibly also family traditions and perhaps even prose summaries from a lost Romance (Mozarabic) epic tradition. Characteristic episodes from the *Ta'rīkh* concern the defeat of King Rodrigo (r. 710–11), the treachery of Vitiza's sons, the "Locked House of Toledo," and the account of a revolt against Al-Ḥakam I (r. 796–822).

SAMUEL G. ARMISTEAD

Bibliography

Arié, R. *España musulmana (siglos VIII–XV)*. Barcelona, 1982.

Bosch Vilá, J. "Ibn al-Ḳūṭiyya." *Encyclopaedia of Islam*. 2d ed. Vol. 3. Leiden, 1971.

Constable, O. R. *Medieval Iberia*. Philadelphia, 1997.

Fierro, M. I. "La obra histórica de Ibn Qūṭiyya," *Al-Qanṭara* 10 (1989).

Ibn ʿAzzūz, M. "Una edición parcial poco conocida de la «Historia» de Ibn al-Qūṭiyya," *Al-Andalus* 17 (1952), 1–75.

Menéndez Pidal, R. *Reliquias de la poesía épica española*. 2d ed. Madrid, 1980.

IBN QUZMĀN

Abū Bakr Muhammad ibn ʿIsā ibn ʿAbd al-Malik ibn Quzmān al-Asghar al-Zajjāl was born in Córdoba, probably just after the battle of Zallāqah (Sagrajas) in 1086, and died in 1160. He called himself *wazīr* (vizir), and his family had produced several such, as well as other minor dignitaries, so the title may have been authentic, though it was a debased coinage by his time. Little else of his biography is certain, even his legendary ugliness, there being much confusion in the minds of later medieval as well as modern literary historians between him and at least one of his eponymous relatives. Much of what is commonly said to be descriptive of him and his life is gained from the internal evidence of his poetry, which by definition is subject to poetic license.

What we do know with certainly is that he had as patrons some of the more important political figures of Córdoba, Seville, and Granada during the turbulent years of his lifetime, which more or less coincided with the first seventy years of Almoravid domination. He was considered to be an important literary figure shortly after his death, and even gained some renown in the Arab East, despite the fact that his poetry was written principally in the dialect of southern al-Andalus and in a form outside the normal canon of Arabic poetry.

Our sources for Ibn Quzmān's work consist primarily of one manuscript of his *Dīwān* (collected poems), copied in Safad (Palestine) a century or so after the poet's death. This is known as the "lesser" *Dīwān* because the existence of a more complete one may be inferred from citations by anthologists and historians, who provide a number of fragmentary, and a few complete, *zajals* as well as Ibn Quzmān's surviving poems in classical Arabic, including one *muwashsahaḥa*.

Ibn Quzmān considered himself to be the master of an Andalusian poetic form he did not invent, but perfected, as he immodestly claims in the prologue to the St. Petersburg manuscript of his *Dīwān*, though he does express admiration for one predecessor (Ibn Numāra, about whom next to nothing is known). The *zajal* is a strophic poem apparently derived from the *muwashshaḥ*: the rhyme scheme is similar (mostly AB-cccAB or AA cccAA or AA cccA, the latter differing slightly from the standard muwashshaḥ scheme AA(orAB) cccAA(or AB), but whereas the muwashshaḥ is not meant to exceed five to seven strophes, the zajal may do so. The muwashshaḥ is in classical Arabic, with only the final refrain (*kharja*) in colloquial Arabic, Romance, or a mixture of both, whereas the zajal is entirely in the Arabic dialect of Córdoba, with an occasional sprinkling of pithy Romance words and phrases. The Arabic shows occasional lapses from the colloquial, probably for metrical reasons, possibly playing on different registers or levels of style.

The meter of the zajal, like that of the muwashshaḥ, has been the subject of virulent controversy. Most scholars who have studied Ibn Quzmān since he came to light in the late nineteenth century have concluded that the materical basis of his songs is closely related to the quantitative rhythmic patterns of classical Arabic prosody. Another group, composed mostly of Spanish scholars, argues that the zajal is governed by syllable count and accent, like old Spanish poetry. Given the uncertainties involved, it is doubtful that the issue will ever be proved one way or the other, certainly not to the satisfaction of all.

The literary quality of Ibn Quzmān's zajals has not been questioned, and if his is not a "voice in the street," it is an original and vivid one. Even the long odes to the talent, good looks, and generosity of his benefactors are not devoid of local color and vividly expressed feeling; the occasional poems can be sublime, especially the love poems such as the famous

> Now do I love you, Laleima, little star (zajal 10, l. 1)
>
> or
>
> Strangeness and solitude and violent passion—
> Such is my lot: I am the lonely stranger! (zajal 124, ll. 1–2)

Ibn Quzmān's emotional palette ranges from pathetic, unrequited love to graphic description of lovemaking with a Berber girl. Wine, food, companionship in revelry, music, and money or (more often) the lack thereof, as of other refinements such as elegant clothes, are favorite themes. His poems, even at their most conventional (the long panegyrics), are well crafted, often playfully evoking the conventional loci of Arabic verse for the dramatic or lyrical purposes of his piece. He paints an irreplaceably vivid picture of twelfth-century Córdoba, a city, a civilization conscious that its glory days were past:

> Where is Ibn . . .'s Lane, with its bustle?
> Where is the Mosque Quarter, and its beauty?
> Laden it is with more spite than it can bear—
> Come close! you'll see a
> Field to plough and seed;
> The rest infested
> Head-high with weed. (zajal 147, strophe 3 and refrain)

T. J. Gorton

Bibliography

An-Nawājī, Shams ad-Dīn Muhammad ibh Hasan. *ʿUqūd al-la'l fi'l-muwashshaḥat wa'l-azjāl*. Ms. Escorial 434.

Colin, G. S. "Ibn Kuzmān." In *Encyclopaedia of Islam*. New ed. Vol. 3. Leiden, 1960. 849–52.

Corriente, F. *Gramática, métrica, y texto del cancionero hispanoárabe de Abén Quzmán*. Madrid, 1980. 69ff.

García Gómez, E. *Todo Ben Guzmān*. Madrid, 1933.

Gorton, T. J. "The Metre of Ibn Quzmān: A 'Classical' Approach." *Journal of Arabic Literature* 6 (1975), 1–29.

———. "Back to Ibn Quzmān." In *Cultures in Contact in Medieval Spain: Historical and Literary Essays Presented to L. P. Harvey*. Eds. D. Hook and B. Taylor. London, 1990. 103–09.

Gunzburg, D. de. *Le Divan d'Ibn Guzman: Texte, traduction, commentaire*. Fasc. 1, *Le Texte d'après le manuscrit unique du Musée impériale de St-Pétersbourg*. Berlin, 1896.

Monroe, J. T. "Romance Prosody in the Poetry of Ibn Quzmān." In *Perspectives on Arabic Linguistics*. Vol. 6, *Papers from the Sixth Annual Symposium on Arabic Linguistics*. Ed. Mushira Eid et al. Amsterdam, 1994, 63–87.

Nykl, A. R. (ed.) *El cancionero de Abén Guzmán*. Madrid, 1933.

Stern, S. M. *Hispano-Arabic Strophic Poetry*. Ed. L. P. Harvey. Oxford, 1974. Ch. 4.

IBN RUSHD *See* AVERROES; PHILOSOPHY

IBN SAʿĪD, ABŪ ʿL-ḤASAN ʿALĪ B. MŪSĀ B. MUḤAMMAD B. ʿABD AL-MALIK B. SAʿĪD

Poet, traveler and adventurer, geographer, literary historian and anthologist, Ibn Saʿī (1208/13–1286) is recognized as a leading exponent of Andalusian culture of the thirteenth century. He was born into a noble family of Yemeni ancestry that, during the period of the Ṭāʾifas, came to govern a fortress at the present site of Alcalá la Real to the northwest of Granada. Ibn Saʿīd's grandfather had served as *wālī* (governor) of both Seville and Granada, and his father apparently left the family fortress definitively in 1224 to become *wālī* of Algeciras. Ibn Saʿīd spent much of his youth at Seville, the leading intellectual center of al-Andalus at the time, where he studied under the tutelage of many of the outstanding scholars of his day. His father, who loved learning and scholarship more than politics, instilled in his son the same zest for learning and inquiry, and the two traveled about al-Andalus and Morocco to seek out rare books for their literary research. Father and son left al-Andalus in 1241 at a time when their political fortunes had been reversed, declaring their intention to perform the pilgrimage, though neither ever returned to his native land. The father fell ill and died in Alexandria in 1242, and Ibn Saʿīd then proceeded to Cairo, where he found an enthusiastic reception and was admired for his scholarship and literary talents. In an age of political uncertainty, Ibn Saʿīd's scholarship coincided with the fervent desire of many scholars to preserve the legacy of Arab civilization. Ibn Saʿīd traveled extensively, and his travels took him to Arabia, Syria, Iraq, Iran, and Armenia.

Much of Ibn Saʿīd's fame rests on a multivolume work entitled *Al-Mughrib fi Ḥulā ʿl-Maghrib*, a work to which he put on the finishing touches, but which in actuality took shape gradually over a period of about eleven decades. In 1135–1136, a man of letters by the name of Al-Ḥidjārī visited the family fortress, and the great-grandfather of Ibn Saʿīd encouraged the visitor to compile an anthology of Andalusian poets. In this anthology the author arranged all the poets according to the town or district to which they belonged. Then, for over a century, the original patron, his son, his grandson, and finally his great-grandson (our Ibn Saʿīd) sought to improve upon the work and to make numerous additions. In its final form it came to deal with the literary history and geography of not only al-Andalus, but of North Africa, Sicily, and Egypt, as well. The section devoted to al-Andalus, conserved in almost its entirety, gives brief geographical descriptions of each area as well as biographical notes of important personages, seasoned with anecdotes and poetical excerpts. Aside from its literary value, this work tells us much about the intellectual and social life of al-Andalus up until the time of the work's completion. Drawing principally on materials from this anthology, Ibn Saʿīd composed short works for patrons on given topics or themes. There have come down to us several volumes of a companion work to *Al-Mughrib* identical in format, dealing with the literary history of the Arab East, and originally conceived of by Ibn Saʿīd's father.

Though Ibn Saʿīd's *dīwān* has been lost, a number of his poems have come down to us. His poetry is conventional in many ways; nevertheless, his verses of nostalgia recalling the days of his youth in al-Andalus speak of a heartfelt yearning to return and are rich in many imaginative images often succeeding one another in an almost dizzying kaleidoscopic fashion.

Even though Ibn Saʿīd's contributions to literary history are remarkable, no less so is the geographical information he either recorded from personal observation or culled from the sources he consulted in libraries throughout the many countries he visited. Among works attributed to him are travel accounts and a number of geographical and historical treatises.

DUSTIN COWELL

Bibliography

Arberry, A. J. *Moorish Poetry: A Translation of the Pennants, an Anthology Compiled in 1243 by the Andalusian Ibn Saʿīd.* Cambridge, 1953.

Arié, R. "Un lettré andalou en Ifriqiya et en Orient au XIIIe siècle: Ibn Saʿīd." In *L'occident musulman au bas Moyen Age.* Ed. R. Arié. Paris, 1992.

IBN SHAPRŪT, ḤASDĀI

Abū Yūsuf Ḥasdai ibn Shaprūṭ was a Jew born in the tenth century at Jaén who rose to great power at the court of ʿAbd al-Raḥmān III at Córdoba. Learned in medicine (though there is no evidence he ever practiced it), he discovered the proper ingredients for synthesizing the long-sought ancient Greek "miracle drug" (*Al-fārūq*). Most important, however, he assisted in the translation of the essential work on drugs of the famous Greek physician Dioscorides, a manuscript of which was sent as a gift to the caliph by the Byzantine emperor. As Ibn Juljul, the famous Muslim physician who was a contemporary of Ibn Shaprūṭ in Córdoba tells us, Ḥasdāi was the one "most interested" in making this translation. The availability of this work, with correct translation of the names of various drugs and their preparation, was of inestimable value for medieval medicine.

On the political level Ḥasdāi served as a sort of "secretary of state" for the caliph, receiving embassies (that included Jewish interpreters) from Otto I of the

Holy Roman Empire, as well as the Byzantine Empire and other lands. He also used his position to gain improved treatment of Jews in these countries, particularly in Italy. Ḥasdāi negotiated the delicate matter of a cure for the obese Sancho I, the new king of Navarre, and persuaded Sancho and his mother, Queen Toda, to come to Córdoba to be attended by physicians. There delicate diplomatic negotiations, in which Ḥasdāi played a role, also took place.

During his international negotiations, rumors reached Ḥasdāi of a Jewish kingdom in the Crimea (the Khazars). He sent a letter in Hebrew to their king, inquiring as to their history and situation, and received a reply. Thus, news of this kingdom converted to Judaism spread among the Jews of Spain and resulted ultimately in Judah ha-Levi's *Sefer ha-Kuzari*.

Ḥasdāi attained a position of leadership of the Jewish community in al-Andalus, and was responsible for the support of developing Jewish educational institutions and the financial encouragement of emerging Hebrew poets. Apparently he also had a knowledge of mathematics and astrology, for Juan Vernet believes that he and Rabīʿ ibn Zaid (Christian bishop of Córdoba, ca. 961) were responsible for the *Mathematica Alhandrei summi astrologi*.

NORMAN ROTH

Bibliography

Ashtor, E. *The Jews of Moslem Spain*. Philadelphia, 1973. Vol. 1, ch. 5. (With numerous errors and unfounded statements.)

Gonzalo Maeso, D. "Un jaenés ilustre ministro de dos califas." *Boletín del Instituto de estudios giennenses* 8 (1956): 63–93.

IBN SŪSAN FAMILY

One of the most powerful Jewish families of Toledo was that of Ibn Sūsan. (The name is sometimes erroneously spelled Ibn Shoshan, and is not to be confused with another important Toledo family, Sason.) Some were local government officials in Toledo in the twelfth century, holding important offices and highly esteemed by the Christians. One of these, Joseph (d. 1205), owned vast amounts of property in and around Toledo, and built a famous synagogue in Toledo. He also was *almoxarife* of Alfonso VIII, who granted him much property, and played an important role in Jewish scholarship. His son Solomon (d. 1221) inherited his position. The Talmudic commentator Meir Abulafia was his son-in-law. Another son-in-law, Abraham ibn al-Fakhkhār, was an important diplomat and accomplished poet. Ziza, the grandson of another of Joseph's sons, was the grandfather of the important astronomer Judah ben Solomon ha-Kohen, who wrote some of the treatises of the Alfonsine astronomical corpus.

Another member of the family, Meir ibn Sūsan, was the *almoxarife mayor* of Alfonso X, and in 1276 was sent on a diplomatic mission to Morocco. He was also a doctor and head of the Jewish community in Toledo, and a close friend of Nahmanides, the famous scholar of Barcelona. Meir's son Abraham was *arrendador* of all the taxes of the kingdom for Alfonso X for two years, and also of the *mesta* taxes. In addition he was an important scholar, cited frequently by prominent Toledo rabbis of the next generation and later. Isaac (Çag) Abenxuxen, probably of this family, was *almoxarife* of Sancho IV (1292). Members of the family continued to play prominent roles, mostly in Toledo, throughout the medieval period. In the fifteenth century Jacob ibn Sūsan was a wealthy landowner and *arrendador* of taxes in Talavera, and in 1470 was the *mayordomo* of Juan de Oviedo, royal secretary and *jurado* of Toledo. Though many Jews served in government positions, no single Jewish family in Castile was as continously involved in government as the Ibn Sūsans.

NORMAN ROTH

Bibliography

Roth, N. "Again Alfonso VI, 'Imbaratur dhu' l-Millatayn,' and Some New Data." *Bulletin of Hispanic Studies* 51 (1984), 165–69.

———. "New Light on the Jews of Mozarabic Toledo." *Association for Jewish Studies Review* 11 (1986), 189–220.

IBN TUFAYL

Little is known about Ibn Tufayl's early life. He was born in Guadix in 1106, may have studied under Ibn Bājjah, and was a physician to the governor of Granada. Ibn Tufayl's medical fame soon spread and he was called to serve ʿAbd al-Mu'min, the Almohad sultan, at Ceuta in the same capacity. Around 1163, he was named court physician and vizier to Abū Yaʿqūb Yūsuf, the second sultan of the Almohads, who encouraged Ibn Tufayl to form a court circle of intellectuals that attracted the best talents of his day. Ibn Tufayl was followed as court physician by Ibn Rushd (Averroes), whom he had attracted to his circle, although he himself kept the post of vizier until his death in 1189. Ibn Tufayl's fame was such that his funeral was attended by Al-Manṣūr Yūsuf Ibn Yaʿqūb, who was then Almohad sultan.

Ibn Tufayl was the author of several medical and astronomical works. However, his universal fame rests on his *Risālat Hayy ibn Yaqzīn* (*Alive, Son of the Awake*), which became a classic of Arabic literature.

In this work, Ibn Tufayl develops the idea of the solitary man, first articulated in the writings of Ibn Bājjah. *Hayy ibn Yaqzīn* tells the story of a man from birth through adulthood, characterizing each of the processes and stages of his development. Hayy Ibn Yaqzīn appears mysteriously on a deserted island. His cry attracts a gazelle who has lost her fawn and who suckles and adopts the boy. Never exposed to language, aided only by his natural reason, the youth learns what is necessary to live and to explain the cosmos and life itself. Observation, experience, and thought lead him to conclude that there is a supreme being, creator and giver of all life, to whom all owe reverence. Knowledge originates from the combined experience of the physical and metaphysical and the human soul, formed in three successive stages (the vegetative, sentient, and rational), is capable of discovering the idea of God as agent and final cause of all things. This story of autodidactic human development permits Ibn Tufayl to expatiate on his scientific theories concerning the processes involved in nature and in the development of life. Later, Hayy encounters Asāl, a man from a neighboring island, who teaches him to speak. They discover that their ideas on Creation and absolute knowledge coincide, and that Asāl's formal religious training is merely a different form of the same eternal truth. When Hayy and Asāl visit another island with the intention of teaching the ways of truth and contemplation, they find that its ignorant inhabitants will not accept the true sense of things. The two become convinced of the defect of living in society and decide to return to uncorrupted isolation and pass the rest of their lives in the contemplation of eternal truth.

Hayy ibn Yaqzīn acknowledges Islam as a valid revealed religion and as a sure path to the truth but at the same time it proposes that philosophy can achieve the same end. Knowledge, perfection, and happiness may be attained by intellectual means and in conformity with human nature. For this reason, the work was central to the revival of philosophy in al-Andalus in the twelfth century under the patronage of the Almohad sultans. Ibn Tufayl's allegory of the harmony of reason and faith must have been known in the West through contact with al-Andalus. Although no early Latin translations are known to exist, it was translated into Hebrew in 1349 by Moses of Narbonne. Moses's text was subsequently translated into Latin and edited by E. Pococke in 1671 under the title *Philosophus Autodidactus*, from where it was rendered into several European languages. Ibn Tufayl's themes are repeated in almost identical fashion by Baltasar Gracián in his *Criticón* during the seventeenth century and were taken up by Daniel Defoe with striking similarity in *Robinson Crusoe*.

E. Michael Gerli

Bibliography

Chejne, A. *Muslim Spain. Its History and Culture*. Minneapolis, 1974

Cruz Hernández, M. "Islamic Thought in the Iberian Peninsula." In *The Legacy of Muslim Spain*. Ed. Salma Khadra Jayussi. Vol. 2. Leiden, 1994. 777–803.

Sharif, M. *A History of Muslim Philosophy*. Wiesbaden, 1969.

IBN WAQĀR FAMILY

One law of the *Siete Partidas* that, like most of those concerning Jews, was never enforced and was never intended to be, prohibited the use of Jewish physicians. Nevertheless, like every king, Alfonso X had as his physician a Jew, named Abraham ibn Waqār, who was also a learned astronomer who wrote part of the Alfonsine astrological corpus. Juan Manuel relates that at the death of Sancho IV, present at the bedside were his physician, Abraham ibn Waqār, and Abraham's older brother don Çag, who later was Juan Manuel's own doctor; he adds that the brothers had also served Alfonso X and Juan Manuel's own father, Infante Manuel. Çag (Isaac) ibn Waqār was often highly praised by Juan Manuel, and appears to have served as a confidant regarding delicate relations with Jaime II of Aragón-Catalonia (1303). In 1303 and again in 1306, Jaime granted lands taken from Muslims in Valencia to Isaac. The service of both Abraham and Isaac to Sancho IV is confirmed by grants of money to them from that ruler. Another member of the family, also in the service of Sancho, was Mosé (Moses), who also was given gifts of clothing by Pedro III of Aragón-Catalonia, while physician to the queen.

Samuel (possibly Ibn Waqār) was supposedly the author of an Arabic work on cures (ca. 1311) for Fernando IV. Perhaps it was this same Samuel who, with a relative named Abraham, was physician to Alfonso XI and owned several houses in Toledo. In 1331 he rented the privilege of minting the new coins from the king and administered the taxes of the frontier, which aroused the jealousy of Yuçaf de Écija and led to a violation of the treaty with Granada, resulting in war.

Çag Aboacar (Ibn Waqār) of Guadalajara, possibly the son of Moses, was physician of the powerful marquis of Santillana (Íñigo López de Mendoza), and was exempted from taxes by Enrique IV in 1465 and by the Catholic Monarchs in 1488. Among the Jews expelled in 1492 who returned to be baptized and live in Spain was this Çag, who became (or already had been) the physician of Cardinal Pedro de Mendoza (1493), and was taken under his protection.

Norman Roth

Bibliography

Baer, F. *Die Juden im christlichen Spanien.* Berlin, 1936, Vol. 2, nos. 317, 391.

Giménez Soler, A. *Don Juan Manuel.* Zaragoza, 1932, p. 297 (doc. XCI), 688.

IBN ZAYDŪN

Abuʾ l-Walid Ahmad ibn ʾAbdullah ibn Ahmad ibn Ghalib al-Makhzumi ibn Zaydūn was born in Córdoba in 1003, and died in Seville in 1071. He became famous as one of the best neoclassical poets in al-Andalus, and more specifically for his love poetry to the Umayyad princess Wallāda. The fact that three editions of his *Dīwān*, two of them also containing his letters, are available attests to his popularity among his contemporaries as well as twentieth-century Arabs who edited them.

Ibn Zaydūn was born into an illustrious family of Arab origin during a period of great cultural splendor in Muslim Spain that was also the beginning of an era of political instability. He was in a position to acquire an extensive education in literary culture, specifically classical Arabic literature, and he started writing his own verse when he was very young. He was first publicly recognized at the age of nineteen for a long elegy upon the death of one of his teachers, Ibn Dhāqwan, whom he admired very much.

After Caliph Al-Mustakfi was killed in 1025, his unconventional daughter Wallāda, herself a poet, became the center of Córdoba's literary circles, in which Ibn Zaydūn played an active part. Poems tracing the stages of his love for Wallāda dominate the greatest part of Ibn Zaydūn's ensuing literary work and also show its most original poetic aspects, though he also drew on his extensive literary training to produce erudite, beautifully crafted poems in a more traditional style, such as one *qaṣīda* against his rival Ibn Abdūs.

In his love poetry Ibn Zaydūn uses many stock themes of courtly love poetry as well as the poetic code of classical Arabic poetry, but he excels in endowing them with new suggestive power and poetic intensity. His first poems give expression to happy union, the elevation of the beloved, and the submission of the lover to the point where a glance is enough and he is even ready to die for her. Their union is threatened only by "the envious" and "slanderers." Soon, however, his poems deal with themes of separation because of her rejection and with his imprisonment, which probably had to do with his political aspirations. He fled from prison and then tried to entice Wallāda to join him.

Ibn Zaydūn's most famous poems spring from this era: the *Nūnīya* and his memories in the garden of Medīnat al-Zahrā. In the *Nūnīya*, he tries to induce his beloved to go with him. With the repeated rhyme *na*, meaning "us," in addition to the frequent use of the sixth verbal form, suggesting mutuality, he endows language forms and the accepted poetic code (monorhyme) with the suggestive power to express his hope. Numerous other acoustic and structural patterns that are derived from the tradition of classical Arabic literature are creatively employed to support the poetic message in subtle ways. In his famous poem from *Al-Zahrā*, he uses the acoustic effects of the rhyme *aqa*, which together with frequent other guttural sounds reflects the melancholy, dark mood of yearning in a way that could not be achieved through rational verbalization alone.

Ibn Zaydūn's use of concepts goes far beyond a beautiful reworking of well-known images. Traditionally parts of nature were often compared to the beloved's beauty. Ibn Zaydūn, however, humanizes and spiritualizes nature by describing it as capable of feelings and their manifestations. For instance, the breeze becomes a friendly spirit sympathizing with the lover's sickness, and the flowers drooping under the morning dew are weeping with him.

Ibn Zaydūn also incorporates many Neoplatonic spiritual ideas into his love poetry, including love as the upsurge of the soul, love having its seat in the soul, and the purity of love, which—in its mixture with sensuality—is quite different from central European courtly love poetry.

After an extended exile Ibn Zaydūn was granted permission to return to Córdoba, where he became court poet at the age of thirty-eight. He left Córdoba again, however, and spent his last years at the court of Seville, as court adviser and poet of panegyrics. In the last year of his life, he was able to return to Córdoba in triumph because his patron, Al-Mutʿamid, took over the city.

Ibn Zaydūn enriched the tradition of classical Arabic poetry with his conceptual innovativeness and his creative use of accepted acoustic and structural elements.

SIEGLINDE LUG

Bibliography

Cour, A. *Un Poète arabe d'Andalousie: Ibn Zaidoun.* Constantine, Algeria, 1920.

Lug, S. *Poetic Techniques and Conceptual Elements in Ibn Zaydūn's Love Poetry.* Washington, D.C., 1982.

IBN ZUHR, ABŪ MARWĀN ʿABD AL-MĀLIK

(1092?–1161?) Called Avenzoar in Latin translations, he was one of the most important physicians in the history of al-Andalus. Born circa 1092 into an important family of physicians: his grandfather, ʿAbd Al-

Mālik ibn Zuhr (d. ca. 1078) studied medicine in Cairo and, when he returned, became personal doctor to al-Mujāhid, king of the *ṭāʾifa* (free kingdom) of Denia (ca. 1010–1045). His father, Abū-l-ʿAlāʾ Zuhr, served as a physician to King al-Muʿtamid of Seville (1069–1091) and, later, to the Almoravids Yūsuf ibn Tashfīn (d. 1106) and ʿAli ibn Yūsuf (d. 1143). Abū Marwān was born and died in Seville but after 1120 spent a good part of his life in Marrākesh, where he inherited his father's post as royal physician to ʿAli ibn Yūsuf. Difficulties with this emir, due to obscure reasons, took him into prison (ca. 1131–ca. 1140). With the arrival of the Almohads he became, once more and until his death, personal physician to Caliph ʿAbd al-Mu'min (1130–1163). His son, Abū Bakr (1113–1199), served in the same way to Caliph Yaʿqūb al-Manṣūr (1184–1199).

Unlike his friend, the famous philosopher and physician Ibn Rushd (Averroë's), and following his family tradition, his attitude toward medicine is essentially practical and his works always contain case records and other observations drawn from his own personal experience or from that of other members of his family. Among his extant works, a few merit special attention. *Kitāb al-iqtiṣād fī iṣlāḥ al-anfus wa-l-ajsād* (On the Adequate Way to Treat Souls and Bodies) is a collection of texts of approximately equal length, written when the author was about thirty years old, to be read to prince Ibrahīm Ibn Yūsuf Ibn Tashf'īn, Almoravid governor of Seville, to whom Abū Marwān was introduced in 1031. It deals with (*zina*) (cosmetics), i.e., the different ways to preserve and embellish the external parts of the human body, including plastic surgery and sexual hygiene, to which Abū Marwān adds a handbook on pathology that deals with the description and treatment of all known diseases classified "from head to toe." *Kitāb al-taysīr fī-l-mudāwā wa-l-tadbīr* (Simplification of Medical Treatment with Drugs and Diet), written after 1147 as an attempt by a cultivated, mature physician to improve the quality of the purely practical therapeutical treatises known as *kunnāsh*, is an excellent handbook of pathology and therapeutics for the daily use of the practicing physician written by a man with both a long medical experience and an excellent knowledge of medical theory. *Kitāb al-jāmiʿ fī-l-ashriba wa-l-maʿfājin* (A Comprehensive List of Syrups and Electuaries), written—like his *Kitāb al-aghdhiya* (On Food)—for Caliph ʿAbd al-Mu'min, it is usually considered a kind of appendix to the *Taysīr*, and both appear together in the edition by *M. Khūri* (Damascus, 1983). It proves the interest Abū Marwān had in practical pharmacology: it consists of a collection of recipes for the preparation of compounded drugs (syrups, electuaries, pills, ointments, and so on). To this list one should, perhaps, add the *Al-Tadhkira fī-l-adwā' al-mushila wa ghayri-hā* (Memento on Laxative and Nonlaxative Drugs), a short treatise ascribed by G. S. Colin to Abū-l-ʿAlāʾ Zuhr, though Khaṭ ṭ ābī has given, recently, arguments in favor of Abū Marwān's authorship. It is a work that shows that its author had a solid knowledge in pharmaceutical theory and a very cautious attitude toward the administration of drugs to patients.

JULIO SAMSÓ

Bibliography

Arnáldez, R. "Ibn Zuhr." In *Encyclopédie de l'Islam*. Vol. 3. Leyden-Paris, 1971, 1001–03.

Colin, G. S., *La Tedhkira d'Aboul 'Alā'*. Paris, 1911.

Khaṭ ṭ ābi, M. A. *al-Ṭibb wa-l-aṭibbā' fī-l-Andalus*, Vol. 1. Beirut, 1988. 277–317.

Ibn Zuhr, A. *Taysīr*, Ed. M. Khūrī. Damascus, 1983

ICART (YCART), BERNARDO

Icart, a Spanish composer and theorist, was born about 1440, perhaps at Tortosa, and died after 1480, perhaps at Naples. Awarded an abbacy yielding an annual fifty gold cameral florins by Pope Sixtus IV on 27 October 1478, Icart was named a *clericus dertutensis diocesis*. In 1479 he was among the chapel singers employed at the Neapolitan court of Ferrante I (son of Alfonso V of Aragón)—his name, "Bernar Hicart," appears immediately before that of the famous Flemish theorist Johannes Tinctoris (ca. 1435–ca. 1511) in the chapel list. On 27 October 1480, Icart received an allowance of approximately three meters of blue cloth for a choir gown. Francesco Florimo asserts that Icart rose from being a mere singer to *maestro di cappella* in the Neapolitan court.

In the *Dialogus Johannis Ottobi Anglici in arte musica* John Hothby, an English Carmelite based at Lucca after 1467, mentioned Ycart (Icart) as a composer fond of verbal canons (directions for singing) superscribed over tenors. For instance, "When he wished to have black notes sung as white notes, he wrote over them *Ethiopians have white teeth.*" Franchino Gaffurio, (1451–1522), who spent 1478–1480 at Naples, called Icart one of the *clarissimi musici* with whom he consorted, and in his first theoretical treatise exemplified a correctly used *punctus transportationis* with a nine-note excerpt from the tenor of a now lost *Missa voltate in qua* by "Bernardus Ycart." Gaffurio also mentioned one other, now lost, Icart Mass, a *Missa de amor tu dormi*.

The *Lamentationum Jeremie prophete Liber primus*, published 8 April 1506 at Venice by Petrucci, contains at folios 7–13 Icart's settings for the last three days of Holy Week: (1) Lamentations 1:1–3 plus the refrain "Jerusalem convertere"; (2) Lamentations 2: 1–2, 9, refrain; (3) Lamentations 5:1–8, refrain. Neither Tinctoris nor Icart, who are among the eight named composers, quote chant, except for Icart in the *Oratio Jeremiae*. Icart's six other extant sacred works are found at the Biblioteca Comunale at Faenza in codex 117 (three movements of a Mass, three even-verse Magnificats). The twenty-six-note tenor in the four-voice Kyrie, *Et in terra pax*, and *Qui tollis* movements duplicates the tenor in Icart's *Magnificat sexti toni*, thus entitling him to be called the composer of the first "parody" Magnificat. The Pixérécourt *chansonnier* (Paris, Bibliothèque nationale, 15123), folios 62v–63, exhibits a picaresque four-voice item titled *Non toches a moi car son trop*, attributed to "b. ycart." The *chapurrado* text mixes a gibberish of French, Italian, and nonsense syllables, with "nichí, nichí, nioch" recurring as a refrain at the close of both the *estribillo* and the *coplas*.

ROBERT STEVENSON

Bibliography

Atlas, A. W. *Music at the Aragónese Court of Naples*. Cambridge, 1985, 200–203.

Caretta, A., et al. *Franchino Gaffurio*. Lodi, 1951, 21–22.

Florimo, Francesco. *La scuola musicale di Napoli*. Vol. 1. Naples, 1881, 67, 74.

Herman, M. M. "Two Volumes of Lamentation Settings (Petrucci, 1506)." M.A. thesis, Yale University, 1952.

Massenkeil, G. *Mehrstimmige Lamentationum aus der ersten Hälfte des 16. Jahrhunderts*. Mainz 1965.

Stevenson, R. "Iberian Musical Outreach before the Encounter with the New World." *Inter-American Music Review* 8, no. 2 (1987), 70–73.

ILLIBERIS *See* CHURCH; WITCHCRAFT

ILDEFONSUS, ST., BISHOP OF TOLEDO

Of Visigothic origin, Ildefonsus (b. ca. 607) was a monk and then abbot of the important monastery of Agali in the vicinity of Toledo, prior to succeeding Eugenius II as metropolitan bishop of the city in 657. During this time he also founded a convent for nuns from his own resources. During his episcopate (657–667), Ildefonsus wrote a continuation of Isidore's *De viris illustribus*, providing brief accounts of the lives and writings of thirteen Spanish ecclesiastics of the mid-seventh century, including Isidore himself. In due course Bishop Julian of Toledo (680–690) added to this collection a short "Eulogy" of Ildefonsus, the principal source for our knowledge of his life. Of

El Greco (1541–1614). St. Ildefonso. Copyright © Scala/Art Resource, NY. Church of Charity, Illescas, Spain.

the writings of Ildefonsus referred to by Julian, only three are now known: two brief books of patristic excerpts on the subject of baptism and the ideal life of the baptized Christian, and his most substantial work, a defense of the perpetual virginity of the Virgin Mary. This was written in the "synonymous style" developed by Isidore, with each statement repeated as many times as there were different synonyms to employ in it. From this work grew the legend of the reward that the Virgin gave to Ildefonsus for his defense of her, which first appears in the mid-eighth-century *Life of Ildefonsus*, almost certainly written by Bishop Cixila of Toledo (744–753). The unspecified "treasure" of the *Life* was transformed into a chasuble in the later artistic depictions of the event. The *De perpetua virginitate* was dedicated to Bishop Quiricus of Barcelona, who may be the Quiricus (667–680) who succeeded Ildefonsus as bishop of Toledo.

ROGER COLLINS

Bibliography

Braegelmann, A. *The Life and Writings of Saint Ildefonsus of Toledo*. Washington D.C., 1942.

Codoñer Merino, C. (ed.) *El "De Viris Illustribus" de Ildefonso de Toledo*. Salamanca, 1972.

IMPERIAL, FRANCISCO

The known historical documents concerning Micer Francisco Imperial reveal only that in 1403 he was vice admiral of Castile and that he may have died sometime before April 1409. In addition, Juan Alfonso de Baena, the first known editor of Imperial's poems, states that Imperial was born in Genoa and lived for some time in Seville. In July 1404 the admiral of Castile, Diego Hurtado de Mendoza, died. If Imperial entertained any hopes of being named admiral at that time, he must have been disappointed when on 4 April 1405, King Enrigue III named Alonso Enríquez to the position. Many of Imperial's poems, including the two long poems for which he is best known, were composed after this disappointment, which probably explains why the theme of Fortune is predominant in them. The theme of Fortune is also crucial to the understanding of Baena's anthology, which features Imperial's poems and is a political document aimed at bringing the king's attention to focus on the plight of Jews and *conversos* in Spain, especially after the bloody pogroms of 1391.

Imperial is best known for two long poems, *Dezir al nacimiento del rey Don Juan* and *Dezir a las syete virtudes*. The first poem was composed shortly after the birth of the Castilian prince who later became King Juan II. It describes a vision a poet had in a *locus amoenus* where the seven planets and *Fortuna* were gathered to bestow their gifts on the infant soon to be born. Fortuna, who has the last word, claims that the gifts of all the other speakers are worthless without hers. After Fortuna's speech the poet is afforded a glimpse of the infant and is then expelled from the setting by the gardener.

In *Dezir a las syete virtudes* the poet, with the help of a guide who carries a copy of Dante's *Commedia*, relates a vision of the Virtues and Vices as they affect Castile. Most of the fifty-eight stanzas of this poem contain references to Dante's *Commedia*. Like Dante, the poet clearly had it in mind to denounce a favorite city of Castile in the manner that Dante condemned Florence. There are also important references to the Bible, especially to Revelation (in which Babylon is condemned). The poem in this way belongs to the apocalyptic tradition of the vision granted to a virtuous individual.

All eighteen of Imperial's poems, as anthologized in the *Cancionero de Baena* (1445), were written in accordance with Provençal literary theory as explained in treatises like the *Leys d'amors*. They therefore respond to true historical events (*vertatz*), veiling them subtly under literary and theological artistic adornments. Spain's most pressing truth, at the time Imperial was writing, was the treatment of Jews and *conversos*.

COLBERT I. NEPAULSINGH

Bibliography

Imperial, Miçer Francisco. *"El dezir a las syete virtudes" y otros poemas*. Ed., introd. y notas de Colbert I. Nepaulsingh. Madrid, 1977.

INFANTE

Besides its meaning of "child," this derivative in Castilian of the Latin *infante(m)* with the same application acquired at least two other meanings of importance during the Middle Ages.

One was "legitimate child of a noble father," and the word was followed by the name of the family seat. The usage ceased to be employed in the thirteenth century, enduring thereafter only in epic and ballad (the *infantes* of Salas, the *infantes* of Carrión). The term was not restricted to unmarried children or youths; it included those who had been knighted and were married until they succeeded to their father's estate. The female equivalent of *infante* was *infantissa*.

The second meaning was "legitimate child of the king." This usage, datable to the ninth century, became the primary one in thirteenth-century Castilian, and from then on is found in Catalan and Portuguese also. In Castile the term is found in the *Especulo* (*Fuero real*; ca. 1252/1255) and in the *Siete Partidas* (1256–1265) with reference to all the king's legitimate children; other royal Castilian documents of the period make it clear that *fijos* included royal daughters as well as sons. (The form *infanta* dates at least to the middle of the twelfth century, but appears not to have become general, at least in this type of document, before the reign of Sancho IV.)

The title *infante* occasionally has been applied to Juan Manuel, nephew of Alfonso X, but the famous politician and prose stylist himself refuted the accuracy of the application. The heir to the throne of Castile became known as the prince of Asturias at the time (1388) the future Enrique III was married to Catherine of Lancaster. Adoption of this title has been attributed to English influence.

ROBERT A. MACDONALD

Bibliography

Cantar de Mío Cid. Ed. R. Menéndez Pidal. 3 vols. 3d ed. Madrid, 1954.

Salazar de Mendoza, P. *Origen de las dignidades seglares de Castilla y León*. Madrid, 1794.

INFANTES OF ARAGÓN

The term "*infantes* of Aragón" is frequently used to refer to the sons of Fernando I, king of Aragón (r. 1412–1416). Before his death in 1406, Enrique III of

Castile had foreseen the problem of a minority, and he left the government of the kingdom to a regency of which his brother Fernando was to be the dominant personality. He used his position to promote the interests of his family, promoting their powers in both Castile and the other Iberian kingdoms.

Two of the *infantes* of Aragón were to dominate the political scene in Castile. In 1409 Fernando obtained the mastership of the military Order of Santiago for Infante Enrique, who was to be involved in political intrigue until his death in 1445. His elder brother, Infante Juan, not only owned vast landed possessions in Castile but also became king of Navarre in 1425 and succeeded the eldest son, Alfonso V (r. 1416–1458), as ruler of the Crown of Aragón (1458–1479). Fernando's daughter, María of Aragón, was married to the young Juan II of Castile in 1418, and Juan's sister was married to Fernando's son, Alfonso. All in all, the infantes of Aragón virtually monopolized political power in Castile.

Nevertheless, Juan II of Castile, ably supported by his favorite Álvaro de Luna, launched a protracted attack on the power of the infantes of Aragón from the early 1420s on, and after a complicated series of successes and reversals, finally broke the powers of the Aragónese party in Castile at the battle of Olmedo in 1445.

At issue were two radically opposed notions about the nature of monarchy and political power in Castile. The infantes of Aragón thought in terms of a series of complicated family relationships that encompassed many of the great nobility: they were the king's natural advisers and councillors. It followed that major problems should be considered by the king in council—that is, by the king in association with the leading aristocrats, who happened to be his relatives as well—and with the help of technical experts, *letrados*, who would see that the details of routine business were implemented once the key decisions had been made. Yet the infantes of Aragón were no great lovers of constitutional restraints on the monarchy. Juan II and Álvaro de Luna were fond of stressing the king's right to decide matters on the basis of his "own will, certain knowledge, and absolute royal power." The infantes of Aragón did not wish to deny the king's right to use his absolute power; what they wanted to do was to ensure that he wielded this power on behalf of their relations and the nobility. Their concept of power was, above all, aristocratic.

ANGUS MACKAY

Bibliography

Suárez Fernández, L. *Nobleza y monarquía*. 2d ed. Valladolid, 1975.

INFANTES DE LA CERDA

The Infantes de la Cerda, Alfonso and Fernando, were the sons of Fernando de la Cerda, the oldest son of Alfonso X of Castile (r. 1252–1284). Fernando de la Cerda died unexpectedly in 1275 while raising an army against the Benimerines, who were invading from Morocco. Since Alfonso X was out of the country, Sancho, the next oldest son, took command of the army and successfully fought the Benimerines. At the urging of the Haro family, Sancho claimed the title of heir to the throne, but Juan Núñez de Lara, to whom Fernando had entrusted his minor children, upheld their rights. Alfonso X initially approved Sancho's claim, as did the *cortes* (parliaments) of Burgos in 1276, but when Sancho revolted against him in 1282, the king chose Alfonso de la Cerda as his heir.

The Infantes thus became the center of a succession crisis that had at its root the interpretation of Castilian law. Alfonso cited the *Siete Partidas*, based on the concepts of primogeniture and representation, to designate Alfonso de la Cerda as his rightful heir, while Sancho claim was based on customary principles of elective monarchy, as exemplified by his ratification by the cortes of Burgos. Queen Violante and Blanche of France, the grandmother and mother of the Infantes, removed them to Aragón in January 1277/1278, to the protection of their great-uncle Pedro III (r. 1276–1285), but Sancho persuaded Pedro to hold them captive. Philip III of France, persuaded by his sister Blanche, insisted on the Infantes' rights, but Sancho convinced Philip IV to abandon the Infantes. Alfonso III (r. 1285–1291) of Aragón recognized the Infantes, released them from custody, and had Alfonso proclaimed king of Castile at Jaca in 1288. The Treaty of Bayonne (1290), between France and Castile, and the death of Alfonso III of Aragón in 1291 marked the end of foreign support for the Infantes until Sancho IV's death in 1295, when Aragón and Portugal launched an unsuccessful invasion of Castile to make Alfonso de la Cerda king. The resulting peace settlement effectively eliminated the Infantes from serious contention for the throne, although Alfonso de la Cerda maintained his claim until 1331, when he pledged homage to Alfonso XI of Castile (r. 1312–1350).

THERESA M. VANN

Bibliography

Benito Ruano, El. "El problema sucesorio de la corona de Castilla a la muerte de Don Fernando de la Cerda." In *VII centenario del Infante Don Fernando de la Cerda. Jornadas de Estudio Ciudad Real, abril 1975*. Madrid, 1976. pp. 217–25.

Díaz-Madroñero, C., and López de Pablos. "El problema sucesorio a la muerte de Don Fernando de la Cerda." In

VII centenario del Infante Don Fernando de la Cerda. Jornadas de Estudio Ciudad Real, abril 1975. Madrid, 1976, pp. 227–34.

INQUISITION, SPAIN AND PORTUGAL

In the Iberian Peninsula the Inquisition had two distinct phases: the medieval and the modern. The medieval Inquisition in Europe was not an institution but a special commission granted by the pope to specific persons (invariably from the Dominican order) in certain areas to investigate heresy by cooperating with the normal machinery of the bishops' courts. The first extensive use of these commissions was in southern France in the early thirteenth century, against the Albigensian movement. Because the heresies of southern France spilled over into Catalan territory, in the 1230s the see of Tarragona was asked to help in vigilance. In 1231 Pope Gregory IX established permanent local inquisitions in various territories. No commissions for inquisition were issued in Iberia except in the Crown of Aragón, where the formative steps were taken under Jaime I the Conqueror; and in 1242, under the guidance of the Catalan Dominican Ramón de Penyafort, the Inquisition in the Crown of Aragón was formally adopted when the provincial council of Tarragona laid down rules for its functioning and accepted the imposition of the death penalty for heresy. At this period the Cathars were the perceived heresy, but they were not active in Catalonia. As a result there was little active persecution, the only notable case being the condemnation of heretics at Castelló.

After the fourteenth century the inquisitorial commissions in the Crown of Aragón were dormant, intervening sporadically in cases such as the suppression of the Templars in 1312. When the Catalan Nicolau Eymerich was appointed inquisitor in 1356, he renewed the severity of earlier days, and also wrote a key guidebook, the *Manual for Inquisitors*. After his death in 1399 very few prosecutions took place. Finally, in 1483, the papal Inquisition of Aragón was replaced by the new Castilian Inquisition, which, like that of Portugal, had a long and eventful history of some three hundred years (and consequently will be outlined here only for the period up to the early sixteenth century).

In Castile there had been no medieval inquisitions and little awareness of "heresy," which was normally dealt with in episcopal courts. Social tensions in the south of Castile between the growing minority of converted Jews (*conversos*) and the majority Old Christian population led in the fifteenth century to growing concern over the orthodoxy of the *conversos*, and hence to demands for the establishment of an inquisition on the French model. In 1478 Pope Sixtus IV granted Fernando and Isabel a bull commissioning two or three inquisitors; the appointments were not made until 1480, when two Dominicans were authorized to start proceedings. Seven more appointments, among them that of Tomás de Torquemada, were made in 1482; and from this time the Spanish Inquisition came into existence as a formal institution, a governing supreme council (or *Suprema*) being set up in 1483.

The early years of the modern Inquisition were highly conflictive. There was bitter opposition in Catalonia and Valencia to the abolition of the old papal commissions and the appointment of new Castilian inquisitors; and in Aragón opposition culminated in the murder (in 1485) of the inquisitor Pedro Arbués. The pope tried to retain authority over the inquisitors, but in 1483 gave way and conceded complete control to Fernando, who that year appointed Torquemada as inquisitor general over the inquisitions in all the Spanish realms. In Castile conflict concentrated in the south, where the arrest and execution of *conversos* (those who converted to Christianity) suspected of heresy took on Holocaust dimensions.

Also in Castile an important controversy took place—in reality the continuation of one that had begun in the 1450s—over the role of conversos in society, and whether force was the appropriate method for dealing with deviation in religion: Queen Isabel's secretary, Fernando dePulgar, felt the use of the death sentence to be both cruel and unhelpful. By the end of the century a network of tribunals was established across Spain devoted primarily to investigating the orthodoxy of the Jews, who, since 1492, and the Muslims of Castile since 1500, had been forced to accept the Catholic faith. Of the sixteen permanent tribunals of peninsular Spain, eleven were founded by 1500, three between 1505 and 1526, and one (Santiago) in 1574; the last, established in 1640, was that of Madrid.

The activity of the tribunal in its first twenty-five years was directed almost exclusively against conversos; a contemporary estimated that in its first ten years it burned two thousand people and punished fifteen thousand others. After this period people of Jewish origin featured far less in trials. The early, savagely anti-Semitic years with their unparalleled death rate, were untypical of the rest of the three centuries of the Inquisition, and historians consequently have taken care to distinguish between the different phases in its evolution. From the early sixteenth century, converted Muslims (Moriscos), and later Protestants, absorbed the attention of the inquisitors.

The Inquisition's procedure, which was laid down by various *Instrucciones* from 1484 on, was based closely on the medieval French model. Those suspected of heresy (which was treated as a capital crime) were interrogated in secret, were occasionally tortured, and had their property seized; public proceedings took the form of an auto da fe, at which Mass was said and punishments were decreed. Judicial penalties ranged from being burned alive at the stake (a sentence never carried out by the Inquisition, which as an ecclesiastical tribunal could not pass sentences of blood, but by the secular authorities, to whom the condemned person was "relaxed"), to the wearing of penitential garments called *sambenitos*. Each tribunal had two or three inquisitors, invariably from the Dominican order and trained either in theology or in law; they were assisted by a small staff including a secretary and a jailer. To help with distribution of orders and arrest of suspects, the tribunal had the aid of laymen ("familiars") who, contrary to popular legend, played no part in the denunciation of people. In addition, members of the local clergy were appointed as *comisarios* to help in collecting information.

Up to the mid-sixteenth century the Inquisition was financed exclusively out of confiscations and received no regular income, which may have stimulated its prosecution of propertied people. Though the medieval Inquisition had been theoretically under the control of the local bishop, the Spanish one, like the later Portuguese Inquisition, was dependent directly on the crown, and consequently was an organ of state, even though its character remained ecclesiastical.

Portugal, like Castile, had no medieval Inquisition, and attempts of the authorities to introduce one on the Castilian model foundered until the 1530s. Long before then socioreligious conflict—signaled, for instance, by the 1506 massacre of New Christians in Lisbon—had surfaced. In 1536 Pope Paul III yielded to crown pressure and sanctioned an inquisition, but reserved control over aspects of it; the new body came into existence in 1539 and held its first auto da fe in September 1540. The strong converso lobby in Portugal backed efforts to suppress it, and in 1544 the pope suspended its operations. As a result it was not until a papal bull of July 1547 (*Meditatio cordis*) that the Inquisition was fully introduced, with the same system as the Spanish. The first years, as in Spain, were harsh; but severity came mainly in the 1580s, when the integration of Portugal into the Spanish monarchy brought a corresponding rise in prosecutions.

The Iberian inquisitions enjoyed a lengthy existence at home and also were exported into the non-European empires. The inquisition of Portugal was introduced into Goa in 1560, and into Brazil later that century; in the metropolis it held its last auto da fe in 1765, and was abolished by decree in 1821. The Spanish Inquisition was established in Peru in 1570 and in Mexico the year after; at home it survived until the early nineteenth century, when it was finally abolished in 1834.

The polemical work of the scholars Américo Castro and Claudio Sánchez-Albornoz has suggested that the modern inquisition drew on medieval Jewish models for its philosophy, but the view is generally considered untenable. It is undeniable that relations between Christians and Jews dictated certain developments, such as the adoption by the Inquisition of *limpieza de sangre* (purity of blood) regulations, which discriminated against people of Jewish blood.

Because the Inquisition always made secrecy its rule, its role was invariably distorted, and no proper account of its activities could be written until the nineteenth century. The traditional picture of a machine of terror is justified only for the early period, when Jewish *conversos* were the victims; the Inquisition also played a key role in Jewish history by bringing about the expulsion of the Jews of Spain in 1492. Subsequently the tribunal extended its interests into a large number of areas affecting faith and morals (blasphemy, bigamy, superstition, witchcraft), and from the mid-sixteenth century began to play a role in cultural censorship through its indexes of prohibited books. It never, however, possessed the power to play the role often attributed to it—of a secret police force that determined the political and religious fate of the country—and its intervention in political matters was infrequent.

From the beginning the Inquisition was primarily an urban institution, reflecting the tensions and problems of life in cities such as Seville, Toledo, and Córdoba. Although attempts were made in later years to take it into the rural areas through the mechanism of "visitations," the Inquisition never succeeded in establishing a convincing presence in the countryside, where most people lived.

The number of its victims in the early years was, as noted above, enormous; but the rough calculation that those two decades over three-fourths of all those who perished under the Inquisition brings home the fact that very few suffered in later periods. It has been estimated that in the sixteenth and seventeenth centuries fewer than three people a year were executed by the Inquisition in the entire Spanish monarchy.

Henry Kamen

Bibliography

Historia de la inquisición en España y América. Madrid, 1984.

Kamen, H. *Inquisition and Society in Spain in the Sixteenth and Seventeenth Centuries*. London, 1985.

Lea, H. C. *A History of the Inquisition of the Middle Ages*. 3 vols. New York, 1887–88.
———. *A History of the Inquisition of Spain*. 4 vols. New York, 1906–08.

IRANZO, MIGUEL LUCAS DE

Miguel Lucas de Iranzo was a courtier of humble *converso* (Christian convert) origins who moved in the circle of Enrique IV of Castile. An astute politician who was rumored to be Enrigue IV's homosexual lover, he rose to the rank of *condestable* (constable) but when faced with opposition from Juan Pacheco, the marqués de Villena and the king's favorite, Iranzo retired to Jaén on the Granadan frontier as the *alcaide* (castellan) of the fortress there. While in Jaén between the years 1458–1471, he organized raids into Muslim territory to capture booty and slaves, greatly increasing his personal fortune. During his years at Jaén he became very influential in the region and established a dazzling provincial court that was the center of great social activity. Iranzo's absence from Fernando del Pulgar's *Claros varones de Castilla* is significant and probably the result of being considered a social climber. Iranzo was murdered by anti-converso sympathizers in the church at Jaén as he was hearing mass in 1471.

Aside from his political activities and his military exploits along the frontier, Miguel Lucas de Iranzo is best known through his association with an anonymous chronicle of his life in Jaén known as the *Hechos del Condestable Miguel Lucas de Iranzo*, attributed by some to Iranzo's secretary, Luis del Castillo, and by others to Pedro de Escavias, the governor of Andújar, and still others to Juan de Olid and Diego de Gámez. The latter work records in striking detail life at the condestable's court in Jaén on the frontier during the third quarter of the fifteenth century. The relation of the astonishingly elaborate and sumptuous feasts and tourneys, the games and pastimes of the nobility, the costly celebrations of Christmas, Carnival, Easter, and other festivals, all complemented by pageants, plays, and other theatrical performances, constitute an invaluable source for envisioning aristocratic life in Castile, and for gaining access to revealing personal anecdotes that betray much about politics in the realm during the waning of the Middle Ages.

E. MICHAEL GERLI

Bibliography

Aubrun, C. V. "La Chronique de Miguel Lucas de Iranzo." *Bulletin Hispanique* 44 (1942), 42–60.
Hechos del condestable don Miguel Lucas de Iranzo (Crónica del siglo XV). Ed. Juan de Mata Carriazo. Madrid, 1940.

ISA OF SEGOVIA (ʿISĀ IBN JĀBIR)

Important Mudéjar scholar from Segovia (fl. ca. 1450) whose precise name is uncertain. On the basis of extant sources we may deduce that he was perhaps called ʿIsāal-Shēdhilq̄. Christian contemporaries in their writings refer to him as Yça Gidelli.

In the middle of the fifteenth century Yça's life evolved around the Mudéjar community (*aljama*) of Segovia; around 1450 he probably was its *alcalde* and *alfaquí*. He was also known as a *mufti*, sometimes called "mufti of the aljama of Segovia," but also "mufti of all the Mudéjars of Castile." Apparently he enjoyed great religious prestige and was asked to give expert religious opinions.

In 1455 to 1456 Yça traveled, at the request of John of Segovia, to Savoy (France), where he did a literal (*de pe a pa*) Spanish translation of the Quʾrān for the theologian. In 1462 he wrote the *Breviario Sunni*, a work on Islamic law, accompanied by a creed comprising thirteen articles, a prayer supplicating forgiveness of sins, and a chapter dealing with the signs heralding the imminent end of time. Yça was involved in a religious polemic with the theologian Juan López de Salamanca. His works continued to influence later Mudéjar and Morisco authors, such as the enigmatic author known as El Mancebo de Arévalo, Muḥammad Rabadán, and others.

G. A. WIEGERS

Bibliography

Cabanelas Rodríguez, D. *Juan de Segovia y el problema islámico*. Madrid, 1952.
Harvey, L. P. *Islamic Spain 1250–1500*. Chicago, 1990.
———. "The Thirteen Articles of the Faith" and "The Twelve Degrees in Which the World Is Governed": Two Passages in a Sixteenth-Century Morisco Manuscript and Their Antecedents." In *Medieval and Renaissance Studies on Spain and Portugal in Honour of P. E. Russell*. Ed. F. W. Hodcroft, et al. Oxford, 1981. 15–29.
Wiegers, G. A. *Islamic Literature in Spanish and Aljamiado: Yça of Segovia, His Antecedents and Successors*. Leiden, 1994.

ISABEL, ST., WIFE OF DINIS OF PORTUGAL

See DINIS, KING OF PORTUGAL

ISABEL I, QUEEN OF CASTILE

See CATHOLIC MONARCHS ISABEL I OF CASTILE AND FERNANDO II OF ARAGÓN

ISIDORE OF SEVILLE, ST.

Isidore, born in the 560s, was the younger brother of Leander, bishop of Seville from 576, who met Pope Gregory I the Great at Constantinople about 580 and subsequently played a central part in the official conversion of the Visigothic state from Arianism to Catholicism (589). The southern fringe of the Iberian Peninsula was under Byzantine influence after 552, and Isidore's family, from Cartagena, may have been of Greek descent. He was probably born in Seville. There was a sister, Florentina, and an intermediate brother, Fulgentius. The Catholic conversion offered a potent prospect of achieving religious and political unity, in which Isidore was the single most influential intellectual figure. He succeeded to the bishopric about 601, and presided over the influential Second Council of Seville (619) and the seminal Fourth Council of Toledo (633), which, among other things, threatened excommunication for opponents of the king, at a time when kings had come to feel the need for episcopal legitimization.

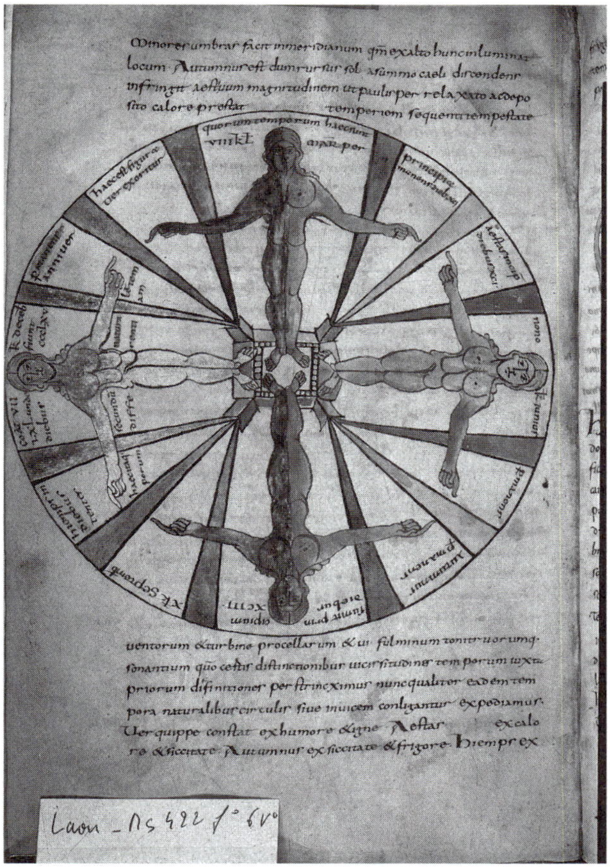

The Wheel of Seasons and Months. Isidore of Seville, De natura rerum. Ms.422, fol.6v. France, ninth century. Copyright © Giraudon/Art Resource, NY. Bibliotheque Municipale, Laon, France.

Isidore died on 4 April 636. His main professional aim had been to consolidate the doctrinal, political, and intellectual triumphs of Catholicism, and he succeeded in inspiring what is sometimes called the "Visigothic Renaissance"; the realm was not as united, educated, and Catholic as subsequent myth came to suggest, but it was the most educated part of western Europe, and Isidore deserves large credit for that. His personality is largely indecipherable, although Díaz y Díaz decided that he was shy, lacking in confidence, eager to please, and obsessively hardworking. Braulio of Zaragoza, his biographer, said that his eloquence would move any kind of hearer.

Isidore's intellectual education was largely in the hands of Leander, who built up the episcopal library (with the works of Augustine, Gregory, African grammarians, etc.). Isidore's 633 council required all bishops to run schools, and he felt a didactic need to raise educational levels; part of his success was that Spanish Christian education and culture remained in his tradition for another five centuries. After his death he slowly metamorphosed from intellectual into saint; his body was translated to León in 1063 as part of Fernando I's affirmation of links with the glorious Gothic past, 4 April was given a special office bearing his name, and, as "Esidre," he was invoked as a national patron (e.g., three times by Alfonso VI in the *Poema de Mío Cid*). He was named doctor of the church in 1722.

Outside the peninsula, Isidore's historical and institutional importance was rarely understood, and he became a mere name appended to influential texts. Surviving early manuscripts are from Irish, English, and Gaulish, rather than Iberian, centers. The works are listed here in tentative chronological order (the precise titles are often later inventions). The *De differentiis verborum*, on semantic distinctions, may precede his episcopacy. The *De differentiis rerum* was prepared independently. The *In libros veteris ac novi testamenti proemia* and the *De ortu et obitu patrum* are biblical and doctrinal; the *De ecclesiasticis officiis* is still a vital source of evidence on the history of the liturgy and the different roles of contemporary clerics. The *Synonyma*, an ascetic confession of and repentance for sins (ca. 610), developed the eventually fashionable style for piling up synonyms. The *De natura rerum*, commissioned by the Visigothic king Sisebut about 613, combines pagan (Lucretian) and Christian views on cosmography (and related allegory).

The *De numeris* considers the symbolism of numbers found in biblical texts. The *Allegoriae quaedam sacrae scripturae* comments on nearly three hundred biblical characters; the *De haeresibus*, on eighty-four sects. The *Sententiae* is Isidore's main spiritual work, combining knowledge and personal experience into a practical guide to Christian life. The *Chronica* is a history of the world from the beginning to A.D. 615. The *De fide catholica contra Judaeos* is polemical. The *De viris illustribus* contains brief summaries of the works (rather than the lives) of thirty-three churchmen, mostly African and Spanish, of the previous two centuries. The *Historia Gothorum, Vandalorum et Sueborum* (625–626) begins with the famous *Laus Hispaniae* and suggests that the Goths, rather than the Byzantines, are the genuine inheritors of Roman culture. The *Quaestiones in vetus testamentum* consists of commentaries.

Various minor works also survive, plus the conciliar and liturgical texts Isidore helped draft, monastic rules, and brief letters (mostly to Braulio); others are forgeries or apocryphally attributed; but his fame came to rest on his main work, still unfinished at his death, which subsumed much previous study and developed from his increasing appreciation of pagan learning: the *Etymologiae*.

The *Etymologiae* is an enormous encyclopedia, of both objectively erudite and pastorally didactic intent, meant to preserve and convey an all-inclusive synthesis of all fields of knowledge available in respectably ancient texts, with added comments from Isidore's own experience to make it relevant to his readers; it is mostly, therefore, written in the present tense, referring to fifty-two classical authors and only twenty Christian ones (plus the Bible). Braulio advised readers to read it through entire, often and carefully, and then they would know everything; thus it is prepared in a simpler style than many Visigothic works. The title is explained by Isidore's persistent attempts to explain why words have the written form they do; in modern terms, this is "popular etymology" (largely accidental word association given unconvincingly mystical explanatory force), not philology.

The *Etymologiae* was probably begun about 615, and a preliminary version of probably ten books (titled *Origines*) was circulating by 621. It is much more than a traditional glossary since, in essence, it presents an accumulation of compartmentalized detail rather than overviews, it is possible to deduce that Isidore worked with a kind of index-card system, preparing lemmas first and adding details as he found them later; this would explain both why several subheadings are left unexplained (particularly in the more technical chapters), and why the latest manuscript versions (from Spain) have additional material at the end of sections not attested in earlier versions. Even though the task covered twenty years, the amount of material is such that Isidore may have had collaborators. If we can overcome the modern scholarly obsession with sources, we can see that the didactic intention (looking to the future) often overrides the scientific (recording the ancient); to this extent the *Etymologiae* was astonishingly successful, being read, studied, and copied in European intellectual centers for another eight hundred years. Modern editions of all Isidore's texts, however, unhelpfully overclassicize the language of the early manuscripts.

ROGER WRIGHT

Bibliography

Díaz y Díaz, M. C. "Introducción." In *San Isidoro de Sevilla. Etimologías (edición bilingüe)*. Ed. J. Oroz Reta. Madrid, 1982. 1–257.

———, ed. *Isidoriana*. León, 1961.

Fontaine, J. *Isidore de Séville et la culture classique dans l'Espagne wisigothique*. 2d ed. 3 vols. Paris, 1983.

J

JACOBO DE LAS LEYES

Jacobo (sometimes found as Jacomo) was the form of the Latin Iacobus used in the Iberian Peninsula at the time only by Italians. On the basis of his son's name and of a sixteenth-century document that records information related to the father's burial, his surname appears to have been Junta, a Hispanizing of the Italian Giunta (-i) or Zonta. Jacobo is thought to have studied at Bologna before arriving in Castile in the period 1250/1252. He is first documented as the principal allocator (*repartidor*) in the land distribution that followed the Christians' reconquest of Murcia (1266), a post that implies his presence in the kingdoms of Alfonso X before then. In a royal document of 1267 he is addressed as "Maestre Jacobo de las leys," and in one of 1268 as "Maestre Jacobo, nuestro juez." His residence in and association with Murcia seems certain by 1274, and he held appointments there as a royal judge and as collector of royal income or auditor of royal accounts. Among his other assignments were those of principal in the second *repartimiento* of Lorca (1268–1272); confirmer, with two others, of the repartimiento of the Campo de Cartagena (1269); and participant in a mission to Aragón to seek aid against the Muslims during the campaign of 1278–1279.

Works undisputably by Jacobo are the *Suma de los noue tienpos de los pleytos*, a brief compendium on phases of litigation; the *Flores de derecho*, a selection of texts of common law taken from Roman and, to a lesser extent, from canon law; and the *Dotrinal que fabla de los juyzios*, a selection of texts on trial law taken from common law. The case has been made persuasively for Jacobo as chief of the team that drew up the *Siete Partidas* (1256–1265). Earlier in the decade he may have participated in the redaction of books 4 and 5 of the *Espéculo* and of parts of the *Fuero real*, but this, and certainly his heading of these projects, remain conjectural in the absence of documentary evidence.

Jacobo's wife's name was Juana, and the couple had at least one son, for whom the judge prepared his *dotrinal*. Jacobo died on 2 May 1294, and his body was interred in the cathedral church of Murcia.

ROBERT A. MACDONALD

Bibliography

Jacobo de Junta. *Oeuvres*. Vol. 1, *Summa de los nueve tiempos de los pleitos*. J. Roudil. Paris, 1986.

Pérez Martín, A. "Murcia y la obra legislativa alfonsina: Pasado y presente." *Anales de Derecho* (University of Murcia) 8 (1985), 93–128.

JACOPO DEL HOSPITAL *See* ARAGÓN, LAW

JAIME (JAUME) I OF ARAGÓN-CATALONIA

Jaime (Jaume) I "the Conqueror," count-king of the realms (*regnes*) of Aragón-Catalonia (1208–1276), was the leading figure of the Reconquest in eastern Spain, founder of his realms' greatness in the western Mediterranean, and an innovative contributor to Europe's administrative, educational, legal, and literary evolution. The only son of Pedro II (Pere I of Catalonia), "the Catholic," he was born in a townsman's home at Montpellier, the principality inherited by his half-Byzantine mother, Marie. His father, hero of the battle of Las Navas (1212), which opened Almohad Islam to Jaime's later conquests, died at Muret. (1213) at battle in the Albigensian crusade in Occitania. Simon de Montfort, leader of the Albigensian crusade, kidnapped Jaime and held him at Carcassonne. Jaime was rescued by Pope Innocent III, who then placed his realms under Templar protection. The orphan Jaime—his mother had died at Rome—was brought up from his sixth to his ninth years at the Templar headquarters castle of Monzón in Aragón. By the time he was almost ten, he had begun his personal rule (1217), and had captained armies in a league for order—the beginning of his intermittent domestic wars with refractory nobles (particularly in 1227 and 1273–1275).

In 1225 Jaime led an abortive crusade against Peñíscola in Islamic Valencia. Four years later he mounted a successful amphibious invasion of Mallorca, adding Minorca in 1232 and Ibiza in 1235 as tributaries. Organizing his Balearic conquests as a separate kingdom of Mallorca, Jaime embarked on a nearly fifteen-year campaign to conquer Almohad Valencia piecemeal (1232–1245). Only three major cities fell to siege (Burriana, Valencia, Biar), with consequent expulsion of Muslims, and Játiva succumbed to a combination of siege, feint, and negotiated arrangements from 1239 to 1248 and on to 1252. One set-piece battle was fought in 1237 at Puig; and Valencia surrendered in 1238. Flanking naval power supplied Jaime's war and fended off Tunisian help. Alfonso X of Castile was conquering northward out of Murcia, and the two kings narrowly averted war over southernmost Valencia by the treaty of Almizra in 1244.

Historians have followed Jaime's own account in ending this crusade (actually a series of papal crusades) in 1245, followed by Mudéjar revolts in the 1250s, 1260s, and 1270s. It now seems clear that he patched up a truce with Al-Azraq, the last leader in the field, to take advantage of his last opportunity to recover Provence. He rushed north, personally led a raid to kidnap the heiress of Provence at Marseilles, was foiled by a counterraid by Charles of Anjou, protested noisily to the pope, and withdrew. Hailed as a hero of Christendom for his conquest of Valencia at this lowest point of Europe's crusading movement, in 1246 Jaime rashly announced a crusade to help Latin Byzantium. However, Al-Azraq plunged Valencia into a decade of countercrusade (1247–1258), put down piecemeal again by Jaime in a new papal crusade. Jaime continually organized his Valencian realm as his original invasion progressed, down to his last years of life. Some of his massive land distribution is recorded in his detailed *Repartiment*. His Mudéjar treaties set up semiautonomous Muslim enclaves throughout Valencia, on a scale unmatched elsewhere in Spain, forming a colonialist society with a thin grid of Christians dominating until the following century. He brought in more Muslims, and also attracted Jewish settlers from Occitania and North Africa, as part of a planned program. He set up Valencia as a separate kingdom with its own law code, money, parliament, and administration.

Meanwhile, Jaime signed away all but his coastal rights in Occitania to Louis IX of France in the treaty of Corbeil (1258). His peninsular politics, notably with Alfonso X of Castile, are only beginning to be explored in depth. Both kings were ambitious to absorb Navarre; they confronted one another as champions, respectively, of the Guelph and Ghibelline movements in the Mediterranean, especially after Jaime married his heir, Pedro, to the Hohenstaufen heiress, Constance of Sicily. In 1265–1266 Jaime helped Alfonso recover the Murcian kingdom from Mudéjar rebellion, an adventure counted as Jaime's third conquest of an Islamic power. From that time on, the confrontational character of their mutual policies turned to friendship.

Jaime also negotiated with the Mongols, who wanted allies against Islam, in 1267. In 1269 he finally mounted his long-awaited crusade to the Holy Land, but abandoned his fleet due to storms (his own excuse) or to reluctance to leave his mistress (the charge by his enemies). After a brief estrangement from his heir, Pedro, and a bitter baronial revolt led by Jaime's bastard son Ferran Sanxis, the conqueror had a moment of triumph again on the world stage. Pope Gregory X summoned him to the Second Ecumenical Council of Lyons in 1274, particularly for his expertise in crusading; Jaime devoted twenty chapters of his autobiography to recounting his reception and activities there. In 1276 the worst of Valencia's Mudéjar revolts erupted, a sustained effort with North African and Granadan help, to recover the land. Jaime fell ill while fighting at Alcira (20 July 1276) and died at Valencia (27 July).

He abdicated on his deathbed, to take the vows and habit of a Cistercian monk, a not uncommon deathbed piety then. The Mudéjar war required his burial at Valencia; only in May 1278 could his successor inter him properly at Poblet monastery near Tarragona. When mobs sacked his tomb during the nineteenth-century Carlist wars, his body was removed to Tarragona cathedral, and only recently has been returned to Poblet. At his death the troubadour Matieu de Carsin hailed him as exalter of the cross "beyond all kings here or overseas," another Arthur of Camelot. His younger contemporary Ramón Muntaner records that people called him "the Good King"; another chronicler records his title as "James the Fortunate," founder of two thousand churches. A myth grew that he had cofounded the Mercedarian ransomer order. A later movement to canonize him did not receive ecclesiastical encouragement.

Jaime had his dark side, however. He could be cruel in warfare after the manner of the times. He cut out the tongue of the bishop of Girona in 1246, for which he suffered papal thunders and public penance. And he was notoriously a womanizer. His guardians had married him in 1221 to an older woman, Leonor, the sister of Fernando III of Castile, for reasons of state. When he was able to consummate the union, Jaime produced his son and first heir, Alfonso (who died in 1260). Rome annulled the marriage in 1229, and in 1235 he married the true love of his life, Violante, the daughter of King Bela IV of Hungary, by whom he had two sons and two daughters. She died in 1251, and in 1255 Jaime married Teresa Gil de Vidaure, by whom he had two sons. Historians often count Teresa as a mistress, but Pope Gregory X regarded the marriage as firm in his thunders against Jaime's efforts to divorce her (1274) after he had relegated her to a nunnery in Valencia. Jaime also had seven formal or contract mistresses and at least five illegitimate children. This led some moderns to dub him "the Henry VIII of Spain."

Jaime promulgated the first Romanized law code of general application, the *furs* of Valencia (1261), as well as the *fueros* of Aragón (1247), the Lérida *Costums* (1258), and the *Costums de la mar* (ca. 1240). Besides founding the papal University of Valencia (1245), he reorganized the statutes of the University of Montpellier to make it the first effective royal university in Europe. He fully supported the mendicant movement and its Arabic/Hebrew language schools, including the Dominicans' 1263 Disputation of Barcelona with the Jews. By his prodigal use of Játiva paper he elaborated the first substantial archives in Europe after the papacy's, leaving a remarkable record of life and administration in his registers. He promoted commerce in many ways, particularly by his trade monopoly at Alexandria, his tributary control of Ḥafṣid Tunis, the North Africa–Valencia–Mallorca–Occitania trade, and his monetary policy. He presided over a literary court (Bernat Desclot and the troubadour Cerverí de Girona stand out) and contributed his *Llibre dels feyts*, the only autobiography by a medieval king except for his great-great-grandson's imitation, to European letters. Done by collaborators at Játiva in 1244 (the first three hundred chapters) and at Barcelona in 1274, it is a lively personal account of himself as a military Roland or Cid. Desclot describes him as taller than most, with athletic frame and reddish-blond hair, a man cordial to everyone and adventurously bold. His skeletal remains confirm the physical details, and a portrait in Alfonso X's *Cantigas de Santa María* shows him at around sixty, majestic, with his short beard gone white.

ROBERT I. BURNS, S. J.

Bibliography

Belenguer Cebrià, E. *Jaume I a través de la història.* 2 vols. Valencia, 1984.

Burns, R. I. *Society and Documentation in Crusader Valencia.* Princeton, N.J., 1985.

———, ed. *The Worlds of Alfonso the Learned and James the Conqueror: Intellect and Force in the Middle Ages.* Princeton, N.J., 1985.

Jaime I y su época: X Congrés d'història de la Corona d'Aragó. 5 vols. in 2. Zaragoza, 1979–82.

Tourtoulon, C. de. *Études sur la maison de Barcelone: Jacme 1er le Conquérant, roi d'Aragón.* 2 vols. Montpellier, 1863–67. Rev. in trans. by Teodoro L'orente. *Don Jaime I el Conquistador.* 2 vols. Valencia, 1874.

JAIME II

Second son of Pedro III (r. 1276–1285) and Constanza de Hohenstaufen, Jaime II (1267–1327) was an amalgam of the stubborn courage of his grandfather Jaime I (1213–1276) and a keen and crafty mind that provided a clear ruling template for his grandson Pedro IV (1336–1387). With his father's acquisition of Sicily in 1283, Jaime as a teenager became a pivotal figure in central Mediterranean affairs, serving as king of Sicily from 1285 to 1291. In this post, he developed a ruling style which combined unbridled force with patient diplomacy. Holding at bay his family's archenemy, Charles of Anjou, by the development of a strong fleet, Jaime established such an efficient Sicilian government that, according to one chronicler, the island population "grew prosperous in a very short time."

With the death of his brother, the ineffectual Alfonso III (1285–1291), Jaime quickly realized that far greater power was open to him on the Iberian mainland than as Sicilian ruler. Shamefully deserting his island vassals, the new Aragónese sovereign began transforming old enemies into new friends. Making peace with Charles of Anjou and sealing the new relationship by marrying his old foe's daughter in 1295, Jaime then rapidly mended fences with Pope Boniface VIII (papacy 1294–1303), becoming the standard bearer and protector of the papacy in exchange for conquest rights to Sardinia and Corsica. The changed reality of this *realpolitik* was especially dramatic in regard to Sicily, which chose Jaime's younger brother, Fadrique, as its sovereign and then supported their new lord in a war of survival with his sibling (1296–1298) that guaranteed at least temporarily Sicilian independence.

The combination of specifically applied force and wide-ranging diplomatic activity marked all of Jaime's subsequent forays into foreign affairs. Maintaining generally peaceful relations with Castile, he used the death of his cousin, Sancho IV of Castile (1284–1296) to block the accession of the young heir, Fernando IV (1296–1312), in favor of another contender for the Castilian crown, hoping to gain the pivotal district of Murcia in the process. Though this conspiracy proved unsuccessful, Jaime persistently pressed his claim to Murcia. By 1304, the Castilians relented partially and granted Jaime the right to conquer Almería and its surroundings. Since the region was still under Muslim control, an Aragónese attack of the city brought overwhelming response from the Granada emir, Muḥammad III (1302–1309) and this effectively ended Aragónese military operations in Andalusia until the era of the Catholic kings.

Despite these aftershocks of the great Reconquest, events soon convinced Jaime that much greater geopolitical prizes awaited him in the Mediterranean than on the Iberian Peninsula. When the Sicilian war ended in 1302, mercenary forces (*almogávares*) who had served Fadrique were out of a job. Accepting an offer for employment from the Byzantine emperor Michael IX (1295–1320), the company was soon thrown out of work again by a premature peace with the Ottoman Turks and then went into business for itself by ravaging much of the central Mediterranean and establishing a loose colonial structure, the Duchy of Athens, which remained in Catalan hands until 1388. Indirectly thrust into Mediterranean affairs by this "Catalan Vengeance," Jaime bided time until 1322 when he attempted to make good his claim to Sardinia with extensive military operations that, however, never brought the island under his control and ultimately consumed the very Barcelona dynasty itself when in 1410 the last heir to the dynasty died putting down yet another Sardinian uprising. Despite this lingering Sardinian debacle, Jaime's reign had ushered in a new economic era in the Mediterranean that made the Catalans, with bases in Athens, Sardinia, the North African litoral, and the Balearics, a strong rival to Pisa and Genoa for market dominance.

Jaime also played a significant role in domestic affairs. Trained in Sicilian politics, which gave much greater power to the sovereign, Jaime brought to eastern Spain not a revolution, but a steady manipulation of legal and constitutional norms. Under his tutelage, royal government became steadily more efficient and productive. Quickly realizing the disparate nature of his realms, the king soon moved to set up structures that firmly tied the ruling center to its many peripheries. His most far-reaching action in this regard was the Privilege of Union (1319), which affirmed "whoever was the king of Aragón would also be the king of Valencia and the count of Barcelona." To further this unity, Jaime completely reformed royal government, dividing it into such departments as the chancellery and the treasury, and staffing these with university educated specialists such as the chancellor, treasurer, and master of accounts. From this pool of curial talent, he chose advisers who, along with trusted nobles and clergy, constituted the royal council.

The wholesale administrative changes that accompanied Jaime's accession enraged his conservative realms of Aragón and Valencia, which had spent the last three decades in stamping out royal "innovations" and in legally subordinating the crown to baronial control. Rather than using military means to confront this insurgency (occasionally bound together as the *Unión*), the king, in August 1301, used the very laws forced on his ancestors to charge his rebellious barons with treason and did so before the unionist functionary, the *Justicia de Aragón*. Despite this temporary triumph, Jaime knew he could not fully defeat the barons and admitted as much in the *Declaration of the General Privilege* (1325), in which he formally accepted many of the legal restrictions the *Unión* had previously imposed on the crown.

Jaime II died on 2 November 1327. He married four times: to Isabel of Castile (1291), Blanche of Anjou (1295), Maria de Lusignan (1317), and Elisenda de Montcada (1322). The most fecund of these unions was the second, which produced ten children, including the princes Jaime, Alfonso (the eventual successor), and Juan (late archbishop of Tarragona). To later historians, Jaime was known as "the Just" or "the Justiciar" because he would allow no one but himself to "render verdicts for disputes." Despite these judicial sobriquets, his greatest accomplishment was the transformation of the Crown of Aragón from a solely Iberian to a strong Mediterranean power.

DONALD J. KAGAY

Bibliography

Abulafia D., *A Mediterranean Emporium: The Catalan Kingdom of Majorca*. Cambridge, 1994.

Archivo de la Corona de Aragón, Cancillería real, Regs. 90–350; Pergaminos, Carp. 128–214.

Kagay D. J. "Rebellion on Trial: The Aragónese *Union* and Its Uneasy Connection to Royal Law, 1265–1301," *Journal of Legal History* 18, no. 3(1997): 30–43.

Martínez Ferrando, J. E. "Jaime II," in *Els Descendents de Pere el Gran*. Barcelona, 1980.

Salavert, V. *Cerdena y la expansion mediterránea de la Corona de Aragón, 1297–1314*. Madrid, 1956.

JAMES THE GREAT, ST.

James was apostle and leader of the Christian church in Jerusalem until beheaded (ca. A.D. 44) at the orders of Herod Agrippa. According to the legend received in Spain during the medieval period, he had preached in Spain, and some of his followers rescued his remains and transported them to Galicia for reburial. During the turmoil following the collapse of the Roman Empire in the West, the Germanic invasions of the Iberian Peninsula, and the Muslim conquest of the early eighth century, they were forgotten until the site was miraculously revealed to Bishop Theodemir of Iria Flavia (ca. 819–847). Beginning with Alfonso II (r. 791–842), the grave became a shrine church and St. James (Santiago) eventually became the patron saint of Spain.

Santiago de Compostela became an object of pilgrimage whose importance during the Middle Ages would be scarcely less than that of Rome in the European West from the eleventh century on. The old Roman see of Iria Flavia was transferred there in 1095 by the action of Pope Urban II in connection with the Council of Clermont. A quarter of a century later, Pope Calixtus II raised Santiago de Compostela to the dignity of an archbishopric in 1120, transferring to it the ecclesiastical province held by Mérida in antiquity, with Salamanca and Coimbra as suffragan sees. Since Iria Flavia had been a suffragan see of Braga in late antiquity, along with all of the other sees of Galicia that surround Santiago de Compostela, the papal action set off claims and counterclaims that were heard at Rome into the thirteenth century. Nevertheless, the church of Santiago became one of the five great archepiscopal sees of the peninsula, ranking with Braga, Toledo, Seville, and Tarragona, even though it lacked their ancient prestige.

At the same time the constantly growing pilgrimage and religious prestige of Santiago made it increasingly important to the kingdom and the kings of León-Castile. While those kings still upheld the rights of the archbishops of Toledo to the primatial dignity, they did bestow the post of royal chancellor on the archbishops of Compostela, and were very generous with royal bequests to that see. As a consequence Santiago de Compostela became a center of artistic and architectural development. Its Romanesque cathedral was begun in 1076 but was still being embellished into the sixteenth century. During the latter period Fernando and Isabel underwrote construction there of a great hospital for pilgrims out of the spoils of their conquest of the Muslim kingdom of Granada in 1492.

Bernard F. Reilly

Bibliography

López Ferreiro, A. *Historia de la santa apostólica metropolitana iglesia de Santiago de Compostela*. 11 vols., Santiago de Compostela, 1898–1911.

Vázquez de Parga, L., J. M. Lacarra, and J. Uría Riu. *Las peregrinaciones a Santiago de Compostela*. 3 vols. Madrid, 1948–49.

JARCHA *See* MUWASHSHAḤA

JAUME II, KING OF MALLORCA

Jaume II of Mallorca, born in 1243, was the second eldest son of Jaime I of Aragón and Queen Violante of Hungary. After his half brother Alfonso died in 1260, the lands of the Crown of Aragón were divided between Jaume's brother Pedro, who was to receive Aragón, Valencia, and Catalonia, and Jaume, who was to receive the kingdom of Mallorca (comprising Mallorca island, Ibiza, and tribute from Islamic Minorca), the counties of Roussillon and Cerdagne, and the lordship of Montpellier. Relations between Pedro and Jaume were never cordial, especially after the death of their father Jaime I of Aragón in 1276, and Jaume II was forced to pay homage for Mallorca to his brother in 1279. Jaume supported the French against Aragón during the political crusade of 1285, and after it failed Pedro announced his intention to retaliate; Pedro's subsequent heir, Alfonso of Aragón (1285–1291), conquered Mallorca in 1286. Jaume II of Mallorca retained, however, possession of his southern French holdings, and ruled for a period of time from Perpignan where he built the formidable Palace of the Kings of Mallorca. As part of the papally-inspired settlement that would eventually bring an end to the War of the Sicilian Vespers, begun in 1282, Jaime II of Aragón (1291–1327) was forced to surrender the kingdom of Mallorca to his uncle, Jaume II of Mallorca, who would nevertheless hold the kingdom as a vassal of Aragón.

It is this second period (1298–1311) of Jaume II's reign in Mallorca that inaugurated the kingdom's acknowledged prosperity during the early fourteenth century. The chronicler Ramon Muntaner, who knew most of the Mediterranean quite well, believed the Mallorcans to be among the most prosperous in the world. Jaume spent more of this second Mallorcan period resident on the island, converting the former fortress of the Almudaina into a suitable palace of ceremony; he also constructed the large, circular castle of Bellver, which dominates the port of Mallorca city and stands on a hill to the west of the city. At the same time that Jaume actively supported the expansion of overseas commerce, he laid the foundation for or reorganization of eleven new inland towns which he hoped would encourage agricultural development and also the production of raw wool for Mallorca's fledgling textile industry. It was during his reign that Mallorca began minting its own coinage; later, at Perpignan, gold coins would be minted in the Mallorcan realms. Jaume championed the usual number of charitable causes, but gave especially strong support to the Franciscans (his eldest son Jaume entered the Franciscans; his successor, Sanç, was his second son). He also gave support to Ramón Llull, especially assisting Llull and the Franciscans in the foundation of a school of Arabic studies at Miramar on the northwest coast of Mallorca; for this he appears in Llull's *Blanquerna* as "a man of noble customs" who "has much devotion as to the manner wherein Jesus Christ may be honoured by preaching among the unbelievers." Jaume is depicted in several detailed, color miniatures in the *Códice de los Privilegios*, preserved in the archives of the kingdom of Mallorca, and is interred in a chapel, unfortunately not open to the public, in Mallorca's magnificent Gothic cathedral.

LARRY J. SIMON

Bibliography

Alomar Esteve, G. *Urbanismo regional en la Edad Media: las "Ordinacions" de Jaime II (1300) en el reino de Mallorca*. Barcelona, 1976.

Cateura Bennàsser, P. *Sociedad, jerarquía y poder en la Mallorca medieval*. Palma de Mallorca, 1984.

Durliat, M. *L'Art dans le Royaume de Majorque*. Toulouse, 1962.

Pons, A. "El Reino Privativo de Mallorca: Jaime II," in *Historia de Mallorca*. Ed. J. Mascaró Pasarius. Vol. 3. Palma de Mallorca, 1978. 52–122.

Riera Melis, A. *La Corona de Aragón y el reino de Mallorca en el primer cuarto del siglo XIV*. vol. 1, *Las repercussiones arancelarias de la autonomía balear (1298–1311)*. Madrid, 1986.

JAUME III, KING OF MALLORCA *See* MALLORCA, KINGDOM OF

JEROME, BISHOP OF VALENCIA

A native of Périgord in France, Jerome was one of the clerical recruits brought to the Iberian Peninsula by Archbishop Bernard of Toledo in 1096. His first post was as a canon of Bernard's church at Toledo, but in 1097/1098 he was appointed to the bishopric of Valencia, where the Cid wanted a Latin replacement for the former Mozarabic bishop. Jerome remained bishop of Valencia until that see and city were lost in the Castilian evacuation and the Almoravid occupation of 1102.

Subsequently Jerome was appointed bishop of Salamanca (1102–1120). That city was then still something of a frontier post, and Jerome seems never to have lived there but to have resided in Zamora, on the north bank of the Duero. From there he cooperated with Count Raymond of Burgundy, son-in-law of Alfonso VI of León-Castile, in the repopulation and organization of both Salamanca and Ávila. He seems also to have been the administrator of Ávila in an ecclesiastical sense, for there is no reliable record of an independent bishop of Ávila before 1121. Jerome must have been the most important figure in the direction of both of these nascent communities, for Count Raymond died in 1107, Alfonso VI died in 1109, and the reign of the latter's daughter, Urraca (1109–1126), was too troubled for that monarch to give much attention to such outlying areas. Neither are there any reliable notices of secular officials in the Ávila-Salamanca region before Jerome's death. At the height of the civil war during Urraca's reign, Jerome seems to have flirted briefly with her rival and half sister, Countess Teresa of Portugal, for he confirmed the latter's charter of 1 August 1112.

After his death (ca. 1120) Jerome's long residence in Zamora encouraged the citizens to seek a bishopric of their own. Queen Urraca acquiesced in their desires, and another Frenchman and protégé of Archbishop Bernard of Toledo, Bernard of Périgord, was installed there. The creation of a new bishopric meant long border disputes with adjacent sees, and the matter had to be adjudicated by the papacy on more than one occasion.

BERNARD F. REILLY

Bibliography

Fernández Conde, F. J. (ed.) *Historia de la iglesia en España*. Vol. 2. Madrid, 1982.

Reilly, B. F. *The Kingdom of Leon-Castilla Under Queen Urraca, 1109–1126*. Princeton, N.J., 1982.

———. *The Kingdom of Leon-Castilla Under King Alfonso VI, 1065–1109*. Princeton, N.J., 1988.

JEROME, ORDER OF ST. *See* RELIGIOUS ORDERS

"JEWESS OF TOLEDO" LEGEND

Many legends and folkloristic tales concerning the Jews existed in medieval Spain and later. One of the most famous of these concerns a beautiful Jewess named Fermosa (a variant of "beauty") with whom Alfonso VIII supposedly fell in love when he arrived at Burgos to marry Eleanor of England. The *General Estoria* of Alfonso X, the first source for the legend, relates that the king, who in fact was particularly well inclined toward Jews, forgot his new wife altogether and lived "inclosed" with Fermosa for seven years, neglecting his realm and everything else. There is also a marginal note to a thirteenth-century manuscript of the *Primera crónica general* (also composed in the reign of Alfonso X, in 1289) that attributes the establishment of the famous monastery of Las Huelgas in Burgos by Alfonso VIII to his love of God, the nobility of his "body and soul," and his having "sinned against God for seven years when he lived in the *judería* of Toledo with a Jewess." (Nothing about Toledo is mentioned in the *General Estoria*, but it became universally believed that Fermosa was from Toledo.) Later, after the disaster of the battle of Alarcos, God is said to have sent an angel to tell the king of God's anger for his "sin" with the Jewess, because of which he lost the battle and his daughter would inherit his throne.

Essentially the same version appears in the *Castigos e documentos* (ca. 1350), attributed to Sancho IV. The totally fictitious nature of all this is evidenced by, among other things, the failure of Rodrigo Jiménez to even mention it.

The legend was significantly elaborated in the *Crónica general de 1344*, but the period the lovers lived together is changed from seven years to a more believable seven months. Certain nobles finally conspired to kill the Jewess. Other later versions generally follow this account. In one of these she is given the name Raquel. The fifteenth-century romantic chronicle *Victorial*, notably anti-Jewish, makes only a brief reference to the king's having done "injustice" to the nobles by the counsel of a Jew (male; possibly *judía* should be read), and thus he lost the battle of Alarcos.

Lope de Vega, a seventeenth-century poet and playwright descended from *conversos* (Jewish converts to Christianity), kept the name Raquel for his version of the legend (*Jerusalén conquistada*; 1609) and also used it in his famous comedy *Las paces de los reyes y judía de Toledo* (1617). Another converso poet, who converted back to Judaism, Miguel (Daniel Lévi) de Barrios of Amsterdam, also referred to the legend. Other authors followed throughout later centuries, so that dozens of plays, poems, operas, and even a ballet and movie version have appeared. The well-known (German) Jewish novelist Lion Feuchtwanger wrote a novel, translated into English as *Raquel, the Jewess of Toledo* (1956).

An unnoticed "source" is the seventeenth-century chronicle of Alfonso Núñez de Castro, of little value other than as a literary curiosity, which tells of the Jewess of Toledo, "a woman of the Hebrew nation, of very dangerous beauty, which the courtiers confirm, and her name was [she was known as] the beautiful Jewess." He is, apparently, the first, and perhaps the only one, to confess that he did not believe the story. This is more than can be said for such important nineteenth-century scholars of the Jews of Spain as Amador de los Ríos and Menéndez y Pelayo, who did believe it. It is not, of course, impossible to imagine a king in medieval Spain (or, for that matter, in other lands where such a thing really did happen) falling in love with a Jewish woman; but that he could have lived openly with her for seven years stretches the imagination. It should be noted that this is one of several legends concerning Jews in Toledo, as well as in Seville, many of which have to do with "beautiful women" who were in love with Christians.

NORMAN ROTH

Bibliography

Aizenberg, E. "Una judía muy fermosa: Jewess as Sex Object in Medieval Spanish Literature." *La Corónica* 12 (1984), 187–94.

González, J. *El reino de Castilla en la época de Alfonso VIII*. Vol. 1 Madrid, 1960. 27–38.

JEWS

Setting aside legends that Jews arrived in Spain as early as the biblical era, the earliest evidence for their presence dates from about A.D. 300. Under the Visigoths (after their conversion to orthodox Catholicism) the Jews suffered severe persecution and various attempts at forced baptism. The notorious anti-Jewish legislation of the Toledo national councils, though it left its mark in canon law and in the early medieval *Fuero Juzgo*, nevertheless had no lasting effect on the status of Jews.

The Muslim invasion (711) brought a complete change, ushering in a long era of cooperation and general harmony in the "caliphal period" of Muslim Spain that ended in the civil war of 1013–1016. This was the period of great Jewish cultural renaissance. When Muslim Spain broke up into the independent *ṭāʾifas*, or kingdom-states, Jews continued to flourish, often rising to positions of great political power. In Granda, Seville, and elsewhere, Jews even became prime ministers.

The successive Almoravid and Almohad invasions from North Africa in the twelfth century actually changed little, although it is true that in the first years of the Almohad conquest, Jewish communities were depleted and Jews were persecuted. Nevertheless, contrary to a widely believed myth, not all Jews were forcefully converted to Islam, nor were all the Jewish communities destroyed, by any means. The Almohad rulers of al-Andalus quickly adopted the ways of the new land, and both Muslim and Jewish secular cultures were once again flourishing. The Christian Mozarabic population in cities such as Toledo and Córdoba was also an important factor, and it was precisely in this period (twelfth and early thirteenth centuries) that the Jewish community, especially in Toledo, reached new heights of economic and political power and influence. There is little evidence of tensions or hostility between the Jewish, Christian, and Muslim communities. The Arabic language was, and continued to be (at least to the end of the fourteenth century), the dominant language of Toledo's Jews, as well as that of many in al-Andalus.

Meanwhile, in Christian Spain (Old Castile, León, and what was to become the united kingdom of Aragón-Catalonia), the already significant indigenous

Jewish population was enlarged by an increasing number of immigrants from al-Andalus, France, and other lands. From the tenth and eleventh centuries, the laws were scrupulously fair in granting absolute equality to Jewish citizens. Indeed, in contrast to other European countries, Jews were recognized as citizens with full rights and protection. Jews were already playing a prominent role in government and as ambassadors and translators, from at least the twelfth century. This role increased rather than decreased in importance throughout the medieval period.

The gradual reconquest of Muslim Spain brought with it this beneficial, and even privileged, treatment of Jews in the reconquered territories. Indeed, whereas Alfonso X (who actually wrote very few, if any, of the works attributed to him) is popularly thought to be the special champion of Jews, in fact his treatment of them fluctuated according to whim and economic and political conditions. It was, rather, such rulers as Alfonso VIII and Fernando III who should be singled out for their particularly positive relations with Jews. In Aragón-Catalonia it was unquestionably Jaime I who filled that role, for during his long reign Jews flourished and reached unparalleled heights of economic development and political influence.

The ill-fated efforts, not of the church but of the Dominican and (to a lesser extent) the Franciscan orders, to impose legislative controls and even censorship had no tangible results. The *Siete Partidas*, largely the work of Ramón de Peñafort, were never enforced, nor did the censorship commission that he headed in Barcelona have a long period of success in convincing the king. The Barcelona disputations also had little impact on Jewish life. Jews settled and prospered in Valencia, Murcia, and Mallorca in this century, adding to the existing Jewish communities there.

Unrest made itself felt, particularly in laws enacted by the *cortes* (parliament) in Castile during the fourteenth century. The unfortunate long succession of minor kings, beginning with Alfonso XI, no doubt contributed to this. Erroneous theories about the supposed anti-Semitism aroused by the Black Death are totally without support, and ignore such obvious and more important factors as the infamous *Ordenamiento* of Alcalá (1348) and the social and political changes. The protracted wars with Aragón and especially the Trastámara civil war (1366) had disastrous consequences for the Jews of Castile (whereas, essentially, there was little change in the condition of Jews in Aragón-Catalonia). The most dramatic events were, however, the pogroms of 1391, when rabble stirred up by the ravings of an anti-Semitic archdeacon of Seville attacked Jewish quarters throughout the peninsula (and Mallorca) in the summer of 1391. The kings acted promptly to punish the perpetrators and restore order, but many of the Jews converted. Far more significant was the preaching of Vicente Ferrer (1410–1411), resulting in the conversion of thousands of Jews throughout Spain. It is important to realize that these were not "forced" conversions but entirely voluntary, a new phenomenon in Jewish history.

The Jewish population was hardly "decimated," but certainly was depleted in a significant manner. Many synagogues were converted into churches, and some communities ceased to exist entirely. Others, like the Jews of Burgos, moved to smaller villages in the area and continued to prosper. The fifteenth century, particularly in Andalusia, witnessed increasing hostility to Jews, especially from the middle classes. Contrary to another popular myth, Fernando and Isabel hardly pursued an "anti-Semitic" policy. On the contrary, they protected the Jews and were scrupulously fair in their dealings with them. Nevertheless, the twin factors of rising anti-Jewish sentiment in the cities and the false accusations of the "Judaizing heresey" of the *conversos*, leading to the establishment of the Inquisition in 1480 in Castile—combined, perhaps, with a desire for a unified "Christian Spain" after the conquest of Muslim Granada—compelled the Catholic Monarchs to expel the Jews in 1492. Most converted rather than leave their homeland.

NORMAN ROTH

Bibliography

Amador de los Ríos, J. *Historia social, política y religiosa de los judíos de España y Portugal*. 3 vols. Madrid, 1875–76.

Baer, Y. *A History of the Jews in Christian Spain*. Philadelphia, 1966. (Abridged translation of this highly unreliable book.)

———. *Historia de los judíos en la España cristiana*. Trans. J. L. Lacave. 2 vols. Madrid, 1981.

Roth, N. *Conversos, Inquisition, and the Expulsion of the Jews from Spain*, Madison, Wisc., 1995.

Roth, N. "Some Aspects of Muslim-Jewish Relations in Spain." In *Estudios en homenaje a don Claudio Sánchez Albornoz en sus 90 años*. Vol. 2. Buenos Aires, 1983. 179–214.

Suárez Fernández, L. *Judíos españoles en la Edad Media*. Madrid, 1980. (Shorter and more reliable than Baer.)

JIMENA, WIFE OF THE CID *See* DÍAZ DE VIVAR, RODRIGO

JIMÉNEZ DE CISNEROS, FRANCISCO

Jiménez, the son of respectable but not affluent noble parents from Cisneros, in the region of Palencia, was born in 1436. He began his studies at Roa, moved on to the Franciscan seminary at Alcalá de Henares, and then graduated in law at the University of Salamanca. After a stay in Rome (1459–1466), he was made archpriest of Uceda by Pope Paul II. The appointment annoyed the archbishop of Toledo, Alfonso Carrillo, who had planned to appoint one of his relatives to the benefice, and as a result Jiménez spent some time in prison. On his release he sought the protection and help of Cardinal Pedro González de Mendoza, and held office in the latter's cathedral church and bishopric of Sigüenza.

In 1484, however, Jiménez made up his mind to join the Observant Franciscans, and spent the following years, withdrawn from the world, in the strict and famous Franciscan houses of El Castañar and La Salceda. His retirement came to an end when Queen Isabel chose him as her confessor in 1492. The appointment was followed by rapid advancement within the Franciscan hierarchy, and then his promotion, backed by Isabel, to the archbishopric of Toledo in 1495. Jiménez now threw himself into the immense task of reforming both the secular and the regular clergy, concentrating particularly on his own archdiocese and on the Franciscan order.

In 1499 Jiménez took over from Archbishop Hernando de Talavera the difficult task of converting the Muslims of Granada, which had fallen in 1492. But whereas Talavera had approached this task in an envangelical spirit of remarkable tolerance, stressing gentle persuasion and religious instruction, Jiménez used threats and force, provoked serious and dangerous uprisings in Granada and the Alpujarras, and finally forced the Muslims to choose starkly between expulsion or conversion in 1502.

On the death of Queen Isabel in 1504, Jiménez supported the political claims of her husband, Fernando, against those of Felipe II the Fair of Castile, and when the latter died in 1506, he set up a regency in Fernando's absence, for which he was rewarded in 1507 with a cardinal's hat and virtual control of the Spanish Church and Inquisition. Inbued with a genuine crusading spirit, he turned his attention to North Africa, personally helped to finance the conquest of Mers-el-Kébir in 1507, and led the successful expedition against Oran in 1509.

Following the death of Fernando, Jiménez once again became regent in 1516 in the problematical absence of Carlos I (later Emperor Charles V), and astutely dealt with episodes of noble and urban unrest, principally in Valladolid, Burgos, and some Andalusian towns; intervened successfully against French intrigues in Navarre; and vainly attempted to deal with the perennial problem of Mediterranean piracy. When Carlos finally returned to Spain in September 1517, Jiménez traveled north to meet him. He died during the journey at Roa on, 8 November.

Though he was a prominent, indeed outstanding, churchman and political personality Jiménez's fame and reputation are also intimately linked to his cultural achievements, particularly the ambitious biblical project that he initiated and that was linked to his foundation and patronage of the Trilingual College and University of Alcalá de Henares. This resulted in the publication of the six volumes of the prestigious Complutensian Polyglot Bible, a task in which Spain's leading humanist scholar, Antonio de Nebrija, was for a time involved. But Jiménez was not really a humanist, and Nebrija soon discovered that the cardinal was not genuinely interested in textual changes or even the correction of mistranslations contained in the Vulgate. Jiménez was interested in scholarship so long as it was placed at the service of God and religion and not Renaissance philology, and his religious spirit was in turn shaped by the ideals of the Devotio Moderna, Franciscan mysticism, and the Observant movements.

Angus MacKay

Bibliography

Bataillon, M. *Erasmo y España.* Mexico City, 1956.

JIMÉNEZ DE RADA, RODRIGO

Jiménez was born about 1170 in Puente la Reina in Navarre, to a family of the minor nobility. His father was Jimeno Pérez de Rada, and his mother, Eva de Finojosa. His uncle, Martín, was abbot of the monastery of Santa María ais de la Huerta. Family connections probably led to a stay at the royal court of Navarre before his departure to secure a higher education at the Universities of Bologna and of Paris. The dates of his stay at those institutions are unknown, although it appears that he was in Paris in 1201. He had returned to Navarre and the court of Sancho VII well before 1207. In that year he participated in the negotiation of a peace between Sancho and Alfonso VIII of Castile. His ambition and talent must have recommended Rodrigo instantly to the latter, to whom he became a major adviser and confidant for the rest of his reign.

Their relationship had become so strong by 1208 that Jiménez, not yet an ordained a priest, was nominated by Alfonso to the see of Osma, although he was never consecrated to it. Instead, further royal favor propelled him in that same year into the primatial see of Toledo. In that capacity he toured western Europe in 1211, soliciting aid for a crusade against Muslim Andalusia. In July 1212 he was present in the army of Alfonso VIII when the great victory over Muslim forces from North Africa was won at Las Navas de Tolosa.

During the next few years the debility of the king and realm prevented any immediate exploitation of that victory, but Jiménez was active in consolidating the resultant territorial gains of the kingdom and of his see in La Mancha. He was a major political figure in the brief reign of Enrique I (1214–1217) and again during the minority of Fernando III. When the latter reached his majority, Jiménez became a royal confidant and one of the chief royal advisers as Fernando ruled Castile (1217–1252) and then León (1230–1252) after the reunion of the two realms. In those capacities he assisted the king in the campaigns that saw the definitive conquest of eastern and central Andalusia—Baeza (1225), Úbeda (1233), and Córdoba (1236)—although he did not live to see the conquest of Seville (1248).

Jiménez's tenure as archbishop also saw the territorial and juridical consolidation of the see of Toledo, whose aggrandizement was one of the great passions of his life. The other peninsular archiepiscopates—Braga, Santiago de Compostela, and Tarragona—were forced to recognize the primacy of Toledo. Bishoprics for the newly conquered cities of Baeza and Córdoba in Andalusia were made suffragans of Toledo. However, claims to Zamora and Plasencia, where sees had been created during the earlier reconquest period, were lost to Santiago de Compostela. Also, despite much acrimony, newly conquered Valencia was assigned by Rome to Tarragona rather than Toledo, and the ancient see of Oviedo in the north continued to be exempt from all metropolitan jurisdiction.

Given the conditions of the age, none of this could be carried through without the cooperation of the papacy, and Jiménez was well known at Rome. He had gone there first in 1211 to secure backing for the campaign of Alfonso VIII against the Almohads in 1212. He returned there to attend the Fourth Lateran Council in 1215. And in 1236 and 1241 he visited the pope. In 1218 he was named papal legate in the peninsula, and from 1224 was entrusted by the papacy with a contemplated creation of a diocese for North Africa in Morocco. Nevertheless, Jiménez had his problems with Rome. Often they flowed from the collection and utilization of ecclesiastical revenues for the reconquest of the south. Jiménez had helped to persuade Rome of their necessity, and was involved in their application to the benefit of the crown. Inevitably he was caught between the necessities of the crown, the reluctance of the Spanish clergy, and the suspicions of Rome.

Some of the moneys from this source certainly contributed, directly or indirectly, to the glorification of the church at Toledo and of its archbishop. Jiménez had hardly been consecrated when he began the construction of a new archiepiscopal palace in Alcalá de Henares (ca. 1209). The present Gothic cathedral at Toledo was begun under his aegis (ca. 1221) to replace the mosque that had served as a cathedral since 1085.

Without question Jiménez was the dominant figure in the Iberian Church during the first half of the thirteenth century, and a major political and court figure as well. Even so, he found time to produce six historical works, and so became the major historian of that period. The most important of these is his *De rebus Hispaniae*, in which he carried on the tradition of the Latin chronicle from Genesis down to the recent conquest of Córdoba. In large measure he continued the work of his older contemporary, Lucas of Túy, and supplied the materials that would underpin the new vernacular history of the *Primera crónica general*, begun in the second half of the century. His *Historia Arabum*, on the other hand, had no known precursor in Christian Iberia, and few in western Europe. Beginning with the biography of Muḥammad, the work deals primarily with the Muslim conquest of Iberia down through the arrival in the peninsula of the North African Murābit (Almoravids). It demonstrates his acquaintance with both the Arabic language and some of the Muslim historians, as well as the breadth of his interests. A *Historia Romanorum* displays his classical interests, and a *Historia Ostrogothorum* and a *Historia Hunnorum, Vandalorum, Suevorum, Alanorum, et Silingorum* demonstrate his debt to the school of Iberian historians of Visigothic times, especially Isidore of Seville.

During the spring of 1247 Jiménez traveled to France to visit Pope Innocent IV at Lyons. On his return journey to Iberia he drowned in the Rhone on 10 June. His body was embalmed and returned to the monastery of Santa María de la Huerta, where it was entombed. His tomb was opened for examination as recently as 1907.

BERNARD F. REILLY

Bibliography

Ballesteros Gaibros, M. *Don Rodrigo Jiménez de Rada.* Madrid, 1943. (A highly laudatory and semipopular introduction.)

Gorosterratzu, J. *Don Rodrigo Jimémez de Rada: Gran estadista, escritor y prelado.* Pamplona, 1925. (The only modern biography; old-fashioned, but thorough.)

Jimémez de Rada, Rodrigo. *Rodericus Ximenius de Rada. Opera.* Ed. María Desamparades Cabanes Pecourt. Valencia, 1968. (Reprint of the 1793 complete edition of his work.)

———. *Historia Arabum*. Ed. J. Lozano Sánchez. Anales de la Universidad Hispalense, serie Filosofía y Letras, Vol. 21. Seville, 1974.

———. *Historia de rebus Hispaniae sive Historia gothica*. Ed. J. Hernández Valverde. Corpus Christianorum, Continuatio Medievalia, Vol. 72. Turnhout, 1987.

JOÃO I, KING OF PORTUGAL

João, the illegitimate son of Pedro I and Teresa Lourenço, was born probably in Lisbon on 14 August 1357 and died there on 14 August 1433. In 1363, when he was still a child, he became the master of the Order of Avis.

In normal circumstances, he would never have acceded to the throne, but the situation created in the latter years of Fernando I's reign (1367–1383) opened a crisis of succession. By his marriage to Leonor Teles in 1372, Fernando had a daughter, Beatriz (1372–ca. 1409), who married Juan I of Castile in 1383. Under Fernando, Portugal had had three wars with Castile, and this marriage was intended to settle the conflict between the two countries. The marriage contract laid down that Portugal would be ruled by the first heir born to Beatriz, and until the child reached fourteen, Queen Leonor would govern the country as regent. This marriage gave Juan I the possibility of one day sitting on the Portuguese throne. However, Queen Leonor, in collusion with her lover, João Fernandes Andeiro, kept an oligarchic rule that excluded the merchants from the privy council. These, fearing the regency by the queen, persuaded João to kill Andeiro in order to force an accommodation with her. But, following the death of Andeiro and the rising of the people against her, the queen appealed to Juan I, who invaded Portugal.

João immediately organized the defense of Lisbon, relying on the military support of Nuno' Alvares Pereira (Nun' Alvares), a knight who proved to be a supreme strategist. The peasants, artisans, and merchants rallied to Dom João's cause, and the younger sons of noble families with no land of their own joined his forces. While João held Lisbon against the Castilian army, Nun' Alvares fought in the south and eventually neared Almada, close to Lisbon, wreaking havoc upon the Castilians. On 3 September 1384, Juan I, fearing the plague that had smitten his camp, lifted the siege of the city, which had lasted four months, and withdrew to Castile. *Cortes* (parliament) were convened at Coimbra to solve the problem of succession. And while João besieged the castles loyal to Beatriz, Nun' Alvares harassed the Castilian loyalists.

João and Nun' Alvares arrived in Coimbra on 3 March 1385. At the *cortes*, the lawyer João Afonso das Regras argued João's case, showing that the other pretenders, the sons of Pedro I and Inês de Castro, were illegitimate in view of the irregular relationship between their parents. As for Juan I, his invasion of Portugal had disqualified him, because it was a breach of the treaty. Having disposed of the argument of rights by birth, João das Regras claimed that since João was the one who had taken up arms to defend the realm from the Castilian invader, he deserved to be king. By acclamation he became João I on 6 April 1385.

Yet the war with Castile was not over. Following Fernando's previous policy of getting military support from England, João I gained some assistance from the duke of Lancaster. An English contingent fought alongside the Portuguese in the battle of Aljubarrota (14 August 1385), which was a decisive victory for the Portuguese. Portugal's ties with England were strengthened by the Treaty of Windsor (9 May 1386), a military alliance between the two countries. This was followed by the marriage of João I to Philippa of Lancaster (1359–1415), daughter of John of Gaunt, duke of Lancaster, on 2 February 1387. From this marriage were born Duarte (1391), Pedro (1392), Henrique (1394, known as Prince Henry the Navigator), João (1400), and Fernando (1402). In 1415, four years after the peace treaty with Castile had been signed, João I, encouraged by his minister of the treasury, complied with the wishes of his sons and led an expedition to Ceuta in Morocco, taking the city. This initiated the period of Portuguese expansion in which all the princes were deeply involved. Between 1418 and 1427, Prince Henrique promoted the discovery of the islands of Madeira and the Azores.

João I was a popular king who listened to his subjects and tried to satisfy their demands. The dynastic crisis of 1383–1385 gave Portugal its independence and enabled the productive classes—traders, merchants, and artisans—to take a leading role in the development of the country. By relieving the people of Lisbon and Oporto from the payment of tithes and seigniorial rights, João I paved the way for a new age. He was a cultivated man and wrote a remarkable treatise on hunting (*Livro da montaria*) that reflects his views on court life and a pre-Renaissance awareness of the value of the human body.

LUIS REBELO

Bibliography

Bernardino, T. *A revolução portuguesa de 1383–1385*. Lisbon, 1984.

Eannes de Zurara, G. *Crónica da tomada de Ceuta por el rei dom João I*. Lisbon, 1915.

Lopes, F. *Crónica de dom Pedro*. Rome, 1966.

———. *Crónica del rei dom Johan I.* 2 vols. Lisbon, 1968–73.

———. *Crónica de dom Fernando.* Lisbon, 1975. Peres, D. *Dom João I.* Oporto, 1983.

Suárez Fernández, L. *Historia del reinado de Juan I de Castilla.* 2 vols. Madrid, 1977.

JOÃO II, KING OF PORTUGAL

João, the legitimate son of Afonso V and Isabel la Poloma, daughter of Pedro, duke of Coimbra, was born in Lisbon on 3 March 1455. In January 1471 he married Leonor, daughter of Fernando, duke of Viseu, who was the son of King Duarte and Beatriz, granddaughter on her mother's side of Afonso, the first duke of Braganza. By Leonor, João had a son, Afonso (1475–1491), who in 1490 married Isabel, the daughter of the Catholic Monarchs of Spain. João had pinned great hopes on Afonso, whom he expected to be the ruler of an Iberian kingdom. But Afonso's untimely death in a riding accident shattered his dream. By Ana de Mendonça, João had an illegitimate son, Jorge de Lencastre (1481–1550). Between 1491 and 1494 he tried unsuccessfully to make him his heir to the throne. But in the face of strong opposition he chose Manuel, his brother-in-law, to succeed him.

João was acquainted with the affairs of state from a very early age. When his father campaigned in Morocco in 1464, he was made regent, in spite of being only nine years old. Later he fought alongside Afonso V in the conquest of Arzila (1471). He also was directly involved with the Spanish policy of Afonso V. In the succession conflict between Juana of Castile, the niece of Afonso V, and Isabel, the sister of Enrique IV, João supported his father and waged war on Castile with him. The battle of Toro (2 March 1476) was inconclusive. João's army was victorious. Convinced that he could defeat Castile only with the aid of France, Afonso V left for Paris in August 1476. He failed to make an alliance with Louis XI and returned to Portugal on 15 November 1477. In his absence João had been the regent and had defended the Portuguese borders against Castilian raids. He continued to rule in the last six years of Afonso's reign, although he was not the monarch.

João ascended the throne on 28 August 1481 and began to pursue his own policy after the *cortes* (parliaments) held at Évora (1481–1482). He realized that with constant wars in Morocco and Castile, his father had given excessive rewards of land and money to the nobility. João's intent was to centralize power in the crown, and he abolished many seigniorial privileges. The third duke of Braganza, Fernando, objected vigorously to these changes. On being informed that the duke was the leader of a plot against him, João acted swiftly. He had the duke arrested on 28 May 1483, and after a summary trial the duke was beheaded on 20 June. The large estates of the Braganzas in northern Portugal then became crown property. In 1484 João aborted another conspiracy against him by stabbing Diogo, duke of Viseu, his cousin and brother-in-law.

Firmly established at home, João pursued the policy of exploration of the West African coast he had started in 1474. In 1482 he had the fortress of São Jorge da Mina built on the Gold Coast to protect the commercial interests of Portugal. From there Diogo Cão explored the Angolan coast, sailed up the Congo River, and brought back news of the Congo.

He was convinced after this voyage (1482–1485), that Cão had been near the Arabian Sea. When the king realized his mistake, he sent Cão on a new voyage. In 1487 João implemented a triple plan, looking south and east. He sent out Bartolomeu Dias, who discovered the Cape of Good Hope; he tried to penetrate the interior of Africa with the expedition of Gonçalo Eanes to Tombuctou; and he attempted to reach the East and Prester John (Ethiopia) by sending Afonso de Paiva and Pero da Covilhão overland as envoys. Politically, he secured the right to lands discovered and to be discovered by signing the Treaty of Tordesillas (7 June 1494) with the Catholic Monarchs. At his demand a line of demarcation was set 370 leagues beyond the Cape Verde Island, which gave Portugal a legal claim to Brazil (yet to be discovered). By this treaty, which was sanctioned by Pope Alexander VI, João introduced the principle of *mare clausum*: the seas belong to those who discover them. At the time of his death in 1495, João knew that the route to the Indian Ocean was open to Portugal.

LUIS REBELO

Bibliography

Diffie, B. W., and G. D. Winius. *Foundations of the Portuguese Empire 1415–1580.* Vol. 1. Minneapolis, 1977.

Góis, D. de. *Chrónica do príncipe dom Joan.* Lisbon, 1567.

Mondonça, M. *D. João II.* Lisbon, 1991.

Pina, R. de. *Crónica de el-rei D. João II.* Coimbra, 1950.

Resenda, G. de. *Crónica de D. João II e miscelânea.* Lisbon, 1973.

Veríssimo Serrão, J. *História de Portugal (1415–1495).* Vol. 2. Lisbon, 1980.

JOGRAL *See* JUGLAR

JOHANNES HISPANUS DE PETESELLA (IOANNES COMPOSTELLANUS)

Originally from Santiago de Compostela, he appears in Bologna on 31 March 1223, taking part in an accord with Tancredo of Bologna and a certain Pedro Hispano. The name Petesella that appears in the document is without doubt a corruption of Compostella. In fact, in the prologue to his *Summa super titulis decretalium* he refers to himself as "ego Ioannes Hispanus Compostellanus natione," which he repeats in one of the codices at the end of his work. From Bologna he went to Padova, where he shows up in a 1229 record. After Padova it appears that he returned to Bologna, where he composed the *Summa super titulis decretalium* (1235–1236), dedicated to Alfonso, *infante* of León. The work is also the first known *summa* of the decrees of Pope Gregory IX promulgated in 1234. Modern research has attributed great value to this work, due to the author's solid knowledge of civil and canon law, and to the frequent historical references the work contains. The *Summa* enjoyed a relatively wide presence in the West, and manuscripts are preserved in Leipzig, Oxford, Seo de Urgel, and the Vatican.

ANTONIO GARCÍA Y GARCÍA

Bibliography

García y García, A. "Canonistas gallegos medievales," *Compostellanum* 16 (1971), 114–15.

Kuttner, S. *Repertorium der Kanonistik. Prodromus Corporis glossarum.* Città del Vaticano, 1937.

JOHN OF BICLARO

John, of Gothic origin, was born about 540 at Santarém in Lusitania. He spent seven years living in Constantinople, probably from about 570 to 577. Soon after his return he fell under the suspicion of King Leovigild (r. 569–586), and was sent into exile in Barcelona (about 580). According to Isidore of Seville he was harassed by the Arians for the next ten years. At some point, possibly following the death of Leovigild, he founded a monastery at Biclar, an unidentified site in Catalonia. For this he wrote a monastic rule, which has not survived. His principal literary work is his *Chronicle*, a continuation for the years 568–589 of the work of the African bishop Victor of Tunnunna, the text of which he brought back to Spain from Constantinople. This chronicle is the most important source for the history of the Visigothic period in the years that it covers, and was used extensively by Isidore. John's work is also of value, despite some disorder in the present state of the text, for the history of the Eastern Roman Empire in the same period. Isidore states in the entry on John in his *De viris illustribus* that other writings by John existed but that he himself had not read them. None of these works has survived. In 590 or 591 John became bishop of Girona, and he died about 620.

ROGER COLLINS

Bibliography

Campos, J. *Juan de Biclaro, obispo de Girona: Su vida y su obra.* Madrid, 1960.

Díaz y Díaz, M. C. "La transmissión textual del Biclarense." *Analecta Sacra Tarraconensia* 35 (1963): 57–76.

JOHN OF GAUNT

John of Gaunt, duke of Lancaster, was born in 1340 at Ghent, the fourth son of Edward III of England. In 1367 he led a large retinue in the army with which his brother Edward, Prince of Wales (the Black Prince), invaded Castile in order to restore Pedro I. Lancaster was commander of the vanguard at Nájera, where the usurper Enrique of Trastámara was defeated. In 1371, in response to Enrique's alliance with the French crown, Lancaster married Pedro's daughter and heir Constanza; in 1372 he was recognized by his father as king of Castile in her right. Lancaster maintained a royal Castilian chancery and retained legitimist refugees. In the 1370s and early 1380s, with the English crown he sought alliances against Enrique II and his son Juan I, principally with Pedro IV of Aragón but also with Fernando I of Portugal and Carlos II of Navarre. The alliances failed principally because of Lancaster's absorbtion in the war with France and in domestic problems.

The revolution of 1384–1385 in Portugal transformed Lancaster's prospects. In 1386, with a small English army, he invaded Galicia; unopposed by Juan I, he was recognized as king in Santiago and other Galician communities. On 11 November, at Ponte do Mouro, he ratified an alliance with João I of Portugal, in accordance with whose terms João married Lancaster's daughter Philippa in the Oporto cathedral (February 1387). Soon after João and Lancaster jointly invaded the kingdom of León. The Anglo-Portuguese campaign, a humiliating failure, led to Castilian negotiations for a settlement with Lancaster at Trancoso (June/July 1387) and his ratification of a peace treaty with Juan I at Bayonne on 8 July 1388. Lancaster and Constanza gave up their regal claims in favor of Juan and his successors, in return for a huge indemnity and annual pension, and the marriage of their sole child, Catalina, to Juan's son and heir (the future Enrique III).

Lancaster's subsequent attempts to persuade Juan to make peace with Richard II and jointly sponsor a conference of Spanish kings to work for the resolution of the Great Schism failed. The grant to him by Richard II of the duchy of Aquitaine in 1390 increased his familial interest in Iberian affairs, but the minority government of Enrique III determinedly excluded his influence and the Aragónese court regarded him with suspicion. His relations with the courts of Navarre and Portugal were cordial, but his earlier policies had reinforced Francophile and Anglophobe inclinations in Spanish governing circles. Lancaster died in 1399.

ANTHONY GOODMAN

Bibliography

Goodman, A. *John of Gaunt*. London, 1992.

Russell, P. E. *The English Intervention in Spain and Portugal in the Time of Edward III and Richard II*. Oxford, 1955.

JOHN OF SEVILLE

John of Seville (fl. 1133–1135) was an astrologer and translator of scientific works from Arabic into Latin. His full name appears to have been Iohannes Hispalensis et Lunensis (or Limiensis). Attempts to identify him with Avendauth, the collaborator of Dominigo Gundisalvo, John David of Toledo, and other Johns are not convincing. He is known only through his translations, which include Abū Maʿshar's *Greater Introduction to Astrology* (1133), Al-Farghānī's *Rudiments of Astronomy* (1135), ʿUmar ibn al-Farrukhān's *Universal Book* (on astrology), Al-Qabīsī's *Introduction to Astrology*, Thābit ibn Qurra's *On Talismans (De imaginibus)* and astrological works by Mšhā'allāh and Sahl ibn Bishr. These were the most important texts on astrology in the Arabic world, and established Latin astrology on a firm scientific footing. To them, John added his own *Epitome of Astrology* or *Liber quadripartitus* (1135), which covered all the main aspects of astrology and, having four books, was clearly meant to be analogous to, and perhaps to replace, the best-known text on astrology from classical antiquity, Ptolemy's *Quadripartitum*.

John appears to have ventured also into the field of medicine, for he is credited with a translation of the medical portion of Pseudo-Aristotle's *Secret of Secrets*, *On the Regimen of Health*, and Qusta ibn Lāqā's *On the Difference between the Spirit and the Soul*. These medical texts are the only works that put their author into a historical context, since the first is dedicated to a queen of Spain with the initial T.—often identified with Tharasia, daughter of Alfonso VI of Castile and León, who married Henry of Burgundy, count of Portugal (1057–1114), and the second is dedicated to Raymond, archbishop of Toledo (1125–1152), and thereby is the earliest text to have some connection with the cathedral.

John's astrological translations are pedantically literal, suggesting that Arabic may have been his first language. The medical translations are more fluent, and the excerpt from the *Secret of Secrets* is preceded by a preface in which the translator justifies departing from the literal sense of the original. Both the astrological and the medical texts remained popular throughout the Middle Ages and several of the astrological texts, including the *Epitome*, were printed in the Renaissance.

CHARLES BURNETT

Bibliography

Lemay, R. *Abū Maʿshar and Latin Aristotelianism in the Twelfth Century*. Beirut, 1962.

Thorndike, L. "John of Seville." *Speculum* 34 (1959): 20–38.

JUAN DE SEGOVIA

Juan de Segovia (1393–1458) was a historian, theologian, and theoretician of dialogue with Islam. Born in Castile, he attended the University of Salamanca from 1407 and taught there until 1433. Juan's earliest ecclesiological opinions were papalist, but his arrival at the Council of Basel in 1433 to represent the university led to a change of mind. Incorporated into the council as a member of the Castilian delegation, Juan played a prominent role in the deliberations of the Faith Deputation. He adopted conciliarist views and defended the doctrine of the Immaculate Conception against the objections of the Thomists. His report on the 1434 debate concerning the presidency of the council reveals a talent for writing history.

Juan emerged as a key figure at the council during the divisive dispute over the site of a council of union with the Greeks. After failing to reconcile the council's factions, he became a spokesman for the majority. Within the assembly he was active in the debates over the definition of conciliar supremacy as a dogma and the deposition of Pope Eugenius IV. Felix V (Amadeus VIII of Savoy), Basel's choice to succeed Eugenius, named Juan a cardinal in 1440. Even before then Juan had become one of the council's chief representatives to diplomatic assemblies in France and Germany.

In 1449, after Felix and Basel gave up their efforts to gain control of the church, Eugenius's successor, Nicholas V, pensioned Juan. In 1453 he retired to Aiton in Savoy, where he continued writing on ecclesiological themes until his death. More important, Juan completed his monumental history of the Council of Basel and began writing to Nicholas of Cusa about dialogue with Islam. Juan even planned a trilingual translation of the Qurʾān, but this project was never realized.

THOMAS M. IZBICKI

Bibliography

Black, A. *Council and Commune: The Conciliar Movement and the Fifteenth-Century Heritage*. London, 1979.

JUAN I, KING OF ARAGÓN

The eldest son of Pedro IV (the Ceremonious), Juan was born in 1350. His secretary, Bernat Metge, described him as in medium stature, grave of countenance, elegantly garbed, and typically surrounded by a pack of hunting dogs. Fits of epilepsy probably bred a touch of hypochondria in his makeup, which was otherwise impulsive and sentimental. While heir apparent he had three wives, all of them French. He married Jeanne de Valois in 1370, but she died before reaching Aragón, (Juan hastened incognito into France to her bedside); the second marriage, to Marthe d'Armagnac (1472), ended with her death in 1378. Then came a love match with Yolande de Bar (1379), contracted against parental wishes; it brought into Aragón a spirited, cultured woman who soon gained such an ascendancy over her easygoing husband that it set him at odds with his father in foreign and domestic affairs.

On becoming king in 1387, Juan swiftly reversed Aragónese policy to a pacific, Francophile stance. This led to friendship with Castile, peace with Granada, and recognition of the Avignon pope. At home, too, he sought a quiet life by dropping Pedro's confrontational attitude toward the nobility. His energies and resources turned instead to hunting (hence his sobriquet "El rey cazador") and, under Yolande's influence, to cultivation of the arts. In an atmosphere of courtly refinement, music and poetry found an authentic Catalan voice. Juan himself ("amador de toda gentileza") wrote verse. Nor were his endeavors restricted to an aristocratic circle, for in 1393 he established a festival of poetry (the *Jochs Florals*) in Barcelona.

For most of his subjects, however, this was a reign of darker hues. It began with a savage attack on his father's widow and counselors. There followed a confrontation with the towns at the *cortes* of Monzón over Juan's demand for larger subsidies to support a household whose composition and behavior were giving offense. Denied aid by his subjects, he turned to Italian bankers, whom he rewarded with privileges that aggravated Catalonia's commercial problems, and in turn provoked more ruthless exploitation of the *remensa* peasantry. In 1391 pogroms exterminated many Jewish communities supposedly living under royal protection.

Abroad, Juan failed to display the vigor he had urged upon his father. An invasion mounted by the count of Armagnac in 1390 penetrated as far as Girona before Juan could muster an army to repel it. The following year revolt in Sardinia threatened the total destruction of the Aragónese position there; to the dismay of his merchant subjects, Juan failed to take effective counteraction. His brother Martín, whose son (also named Martín) had married the heiress of Sicily, received inadequate support when in 1392 he attempted to impose Aragónese authority in that island. Nor was any aid given to the Catalan duchies of Athens and Neopatras to save them from falling to a Florentine and, in 1394, to the Turks. This string of catastrophes was attributed by his subjects, not entirely justly, to regal profligacy in pursuit of pleasure.

Juan died in a hunting accident on 19 May 1395, still engaged in acrimonious dispute with Barcelona and Valencia over money for the rescue of Sardinia.

ALAN RYDER

Bibliography

Bofarull y Mascaró, P. de. "Generación de Juan I de Aragón. Apéndice documentado a los condes de Barcelona vindicados." In *Memorias de la Real Academia de Buenas Letras*. Vol. 6. Barcelona, 1898.

Regla Campistol, J. "La corona de Aragón (1336–1410)." In *Historia de España*. Vol. 14. Ed. R. Menéndez Pidal. Madrid, 1966.

JUAN I, KING OF CASTILE

If by all accounts, contemporary or near-contemporary, Juan I was a depressive, the problems that faced him during his youth and his reign would explain his personality.

Plagued by uncertainties, he heroically triumphed over serious doubts regarding his legitimacy as king and the never-ending intrigues fomented by his adversaries about the succession to Castile.

Much of his reign and his personality can only be understood in terms of Castile's role in the Hundred Years' War, in which the kingdom of Castile, allied to France, had to face the problem of Lancastrian (or English) claims to the Castilian throne. In particular, John of Gaunt, duke of Lancaster, and the son of Edward III of England, by his marriage to Constanza, daughter of Pedro I, the defeated ex-king of Castile, claimed the throne of the kingdom and, using England's links with Portugal as well as internal dissensions in Castile, pushed England and Portugal into conflict with Castile, thus widening the spheres of Anglo-French belligerence and implanting them firmly onto Iberian soil. At issue also was the way in which Castile's formidable naval power was to be deployed, a spectacular example being the attacks launched at various points along the southern coast of England. Juan I, attempting to gain Portugal, suffered a humiliating defeat at the battle of Aljubarrota in 1385. Nevertheless, the real threat was posed by the invasion of the duke of Lancaster in 1386–1389. Juan I astutely countered this by refusing a decisive engagement, extending the enemy's lines of supply and employing a "scorched-earth" policy, thus forcing the exhausted and disease-ridden English forces to withdraw. In the negotiations that followed, a marriage between Gaunt's daughter, Catherine of Lancaster, and Juan I's heir, the future Enique III, was arranged, the Castillians bought off Lancaster's claims to the throne, and the truces of Leulingham and Moncão (1389) brought the Spanish phase of the Hundred Years' War to an end.

Yet Juan I had to pay a price for his success. John of Gaunt only finally surrendered his personal interests in Castile on payment of 100,000 pounds, an annual pension of 6,600 pounds and the marriage of his daughter to Juan I's heir. In addition the crisis had moved this introspective king to ponder on the fact that his position was due to a traditional involvement by others in the tasks of government, tasks in which the great nobility, prelates, doctors of law, and even representatives from the royal towns attending the *cortes* (parliaments) expected to participate. During precisely those years when the crises were most dangerous, the powers of the cortes grew. Juan I did not enjoy unlimited power but was bound by the laws of the kingdom. The making of law and the threats posed to the stability of the kingdom were matters that had to be dealt with by the king and *cortes* together.

Given the long years of alliance with the French, it is not surprising that Juan I's reign witnessed French influence on the development of Castilian institutions, particularly with respect to taxation and finance (the *contadurías*) and the army (the creation of the offices of marshal and constable).

An intensely religious man, Juan I even worked with his opponents to try and heal divisions in the church, particularly with respect to ending the Great Schism. The chronicler Pero López de Ayala, for example, emphasizes the bonds that grew between the king and Gaunt because of their mutual love and devotion to the Virgin Mary, a matter of universal concern at a time when the church was divided by the Great Schism. In this, Juan I was perhaps moved by a sense of family devotion: Enique II had been particularly devoted to the Virgin.

ANGUS MACKAY

Bibliography

Suárez Fernández, L. *Juan I, rey de Castilla (1379–1390)*. 2d ed. Madrid, 1978.

JUAN II, KING OF ARAGÓN

Juan was born in 1398 at Medina del Campo. His father, Fernando of Antequera, having become Fernando I of Aragón (1412), Juan was betrothed to Queen Giovanna II of Naples and appointed viceroy of Sicily (1415). The marriage fell through, however, and Fernando's death (1416) brought Juan back to Spain to assume control of the family's huge Castilian estates. At the court of Castile he immediately became embroiled in power struggles with Álvaro de Luna and his own brother Enrique. These came to a head in 1420 when Enrique, taking advantage of Juan's absence in Navarre (he had gone there to marry Blanche, heiress to that kingdom) staged a palace coup. There ensued years of political chaos that played into Luna's hands, provoked two invasions of Castile (1425 and 1428) by Juan's elder brother Alfonso, king of Aragón, and led to the confiscation of all Juan's Castilian estates.

Meanwhile Juan had become king of Navarre (1425), and in 1432 he gained control of Aragón as Alfonso's *locumtenens*; he used both positions as springboards to restore his Castilian fortunes. In 1434 pursuit of that obsessive design took him to Sicily, bent on securing Alfonso's participation. Instead he found himself caught up in his brother's Neapolitan schemes that led to the naval disaster at Ponza (1435) and Juan's brief captivity, first in Genoa and then in Milan.

Juan returned to Aragón charged with organizing support for Alfonso's conquest of Naples and making peace with Castile. The latter duty he undertook with extreme reluctance, for the treaty (September 1436) promised only to constitute his lost lands into a dowry for his daughter on her marriage to Infante Enrique of Castile. Redemption of honor and fortune seemingly beckoned in 1439 when the king of Castile invited Juan and his brother Enrique to return. Unhesitatingly they seized the opportunity, only to flounder in familiar intrigue until 1443, when, having in desperation laid hands on the king, they found themselves again driven from Castile. Staking everything on battle, they suffered a disastrous defeat at Olmedo (19 May 1445).

War then flared along the Castile/Aragón frontier, and in 1450 spread to Navarre, where Juan had maintained his royal title and authority since the death of his wife (1441), despite the claims of his son Carlos de Viana. Internal Navarrese factions had set father and son at odds, and now drove Carlos into the arms of Castile, thereby kindling a civil war that raged for forty years. Denied aid by Catalonia and Valencia, Juan saw King Alfonso make peace with Castile over his head (1454), a peace that definitively stripped him of the Castilian heritage he had striven so bitterly to preserve. Carlos bore the brunt of his wrath: stigmatized a traitor, he was declared to have forfeited his throne.

In 1450, still hearty though half blinded by cataracts, Juan succeeded Alfonso as king of Aragón. His long career as *locumtenens* had won him little popularity, least of all with the Catalan oligarchy, which resented his championship of the popular cause in Barcelona and the *remensa* peasantry. When he seized Carlos at the *cortes* of Lérida (December 1460) on a charge of renewed plotting, the Catalans joined forces with discontented Navarrese to threaten insurrection in the name of their "liberties." With Castile, too, hostile, Juan had no choice but to free Carlos and capitulate to Catalan demands at Vilafranca del Penedés (21 June 1461). Carlos's sudden death (23 September 1461) might have calmed passions had not the triumphant oligarchs resolved to press their advantage against the cowed royalist elements in Catalonia, thereby igniting a decade of civil war.

Unbowed by age and with sight restored, Juan fought back mightily with the devoted support of Juana Enríquez, his second wife, whom he had married in 1447, and their son Fernando. Yet despite a steady string of military successes, victory constantly receded as one foreign power after another brought aid to the rebels. France he managed to buy off by ceding Roussillon and Cerdagne; Castile he astutely turned from foe to friend by marrying Fernando to the infanta Isabel (1469). But only death removed two other rivals called in by the Catalans—Pedro, constable of Portugal, and Jean of Anjou—and only total exhaustion and demoralization brought the hard-core Catalan resistance to surrender (October 1472) on terms that restored the status quo.

Instead of confronting the social and economic wounds left festering in Catalonia, Juan proceeded to drain his subjects' last resources in a doomed endeavor to regain the lost Pyrenees provinces from France (1473–1475). Comparative tranquillity descended upon the last years of his life, which ended in 1479 with a chill caught while hunting in winter snow.

ALAN RYDER

Bibliography

Suárez Fernández, L. *Los Trastámara y los Reyes Católicos. Historia de España*, Vol. 7 of Madrid, 1985.

Vicens Vives, J. *Juan II de Aragón (1398–1479): Monarquía y revolución en la España del siglo XV*. Barcelona, 1953.

———. *Els Trastámares*. Barcelona, 1956.

JUAN II, KING OF CASTILE AND LEÓN

Juan was born 6 March 1405 and died 21 July 1454. He was the son of Enrique III and Catalina de Lancaster. He acceded to throne on 25 December 1406, before his second birthday, and upon the death of his father. His mother and his uncle, Fernando (later Fernando I of Aragón), were coregents of the realm until the latter left Castile to occupy the throne of the Crown of Aragón in 1412. Their coregency proved remarkably peaceful, with Fernando occupying himself with the Muslims on the Granadan frontier and Catalina with young Juan's education. When Fernando died in 1416, he left titles and vast estates in Castile to two of his three sons, Juan and Enrique; a third son would inherit the Crown of Aragón and reign as Alfonso V. Fernando's sons would remain thorns in the side of the Castilian monarchy for most of Juan II's reign.

Siloé, Gil de. Tomb of Juan II and Isabel of Portugal. Designed in 1486, executed between 1489–1493. Copyright © Scala/Art Resource, NY. Cartuja de Milaflores, Burgos, Spain.

Very early in his life Juan, who would prove weak and disinterested in governing and in affairs of state and much more interested in poetry, music, and the arts, came under the influence of Álvaro de Luna, an adolescent petty noble who had been sent to court to be educated. Their lives would be inextricably intertwined and Álvaro would remain the king's favorite until March 1453, when, at the urging of some of the magnates and his second wife, Isabel of Portugal, the king ordered Luna taken prisoner and executed at Valladolid. From the moment Juan came of age, Don Álvaro became the real governing force of the kingdom.

His influence over the monarch inspired both envy and gossip, at one point leading the nobles to denounce Luna and accuse him of having introduced abominable practices at court, alluding to a rumored homosexual relationship with the king. Led by the two sons of Fernando I, Juan and Enrique, known as the Infantes de Aragón, the nobles saw an opportunity to increase their power and privileges at the expense of Don Álavro and the monarchy. Don Álvaro, however, remained confident of the king's support and relied heavily on the backing of others who associated the crown's interests with their own, namely the lower and middle layers of society. Luna brilliantly exploited the concerns and aspirations of the non-noble sectors of society and successfully increased his own influence and estate as he sought to centralize the power of the monarchy.

Luna's power, however, was sometimes undermined by intrigues and, through the duration of his career, he received inconsistent support from the king. On various occasions, as Juan fell under the influence of the nobles, Luna was exiled from the realm, only to have the king recall him later. Even when Juan II and Luna triumphed militarily against the nobility and the Infantes, as they did at Olmedo in 1445, victory was soon clouded by intrigues. For the entire duration of Juan II's reign the monarchy found itself at odds with the nobles and consistently in crisis.

The House of Trastámara, in order to gain the support of the nobles at the end of the civil wars of the fourteenth century, had been obliged to assign the nobility vastly increased power in the form of *mercedes*, or grants, which greatly reduced the royal treasury. The regents of the realm also paid the price of stability during Juan II's minority in a similar fashion. The burdened royal finances could not give the crown the superiority over the nobility that it needed if it was to maintain an independent policy. Taxes were raised but they never reached the treasury, and by 1442 it had become necessary to pass a law against nobles who seized royal revenues in order to ensure the grants owed them by the crown. The kings' revenues, when not seized by nobles or committed to them in advance, were insufficient for the creation of a permanent armed force to protect them. To make matters worse, the affluent, mostly rural nobility maintained their own armed forces, resulting in pitched battles and sieges against the monarchy and among themselves. The power of the cities declined from 1419–1430 as the Infantes de Aragón and Luna, in the king's name, vied for their support. Even the intellectuals were divided. On the one hand, the marqués de Santillana, one of the great humanists of his age, logically supported the nobles; on the other, Juan de Mena, the king's secretary and one of the most notable scholars of the fifteenth century, staunchly defended the monarchy, calling upon Juan II to recognize his greatness, shake off tyranny, and restore the law to the kingdom.

After years of conflict, and shortly after Luna's execution in June 1453, a letter under the king's signature circulated in the realm. It explained Luna's downfall as the result of a joint demand of both the noble and non-noble classes. Although the letter was probably written by one of Luna's sworn enemies, Diego de Valera, and not the king, the *cortes* duly congratulated the king on seizing the reigns of government for himself. In fact, however, Juan II failed to govern up until his death a year later, turning over affairs of state to two clerics, one of whom had been Luna's ally.

When Juan II died, he left three children: Enrique, by his first wife, María de Aragón, who would succeed him as Enrique IV; and the Infantes Alfonso and Isabel by his second wife, Isabel of Portugal. His daughter Isabel would succeed her half-brother Enrique IV in 1474 and become known as Isabel the Catholic.

Despite his weak character, Juan II was a discerning, intelligent individual and a lover of the arts. During his reign poetry, music, and the arts flourished at court. He had a strong sense of the importance of literature and culture, and was himself an accomplished poet and musician. He is buried at Burgos in the Carthusian monastery of Miraflores next to his second wife, Isabel of Portugal. His magnificent tomb, sculpted by Gil de Siloé, stands as a memorial to an almost forgotten king who was a major patron of the arts.

E. Michael Gerli

Bibliography

Benito Ruano, E. *Los Infantes de Aragón*. Madrid, 1952.

Hillgarth, J. N. *The Spanish Kingdoms 1250–1516*. Vol. 2. Oxford, 1978.

Suárez Fernández, Luis. *Nobleza y monarquía, puntos de vista sobre la historia castellana del siglo XV*. Valladolid, 1959.

JUAN MANUEL

Son of Alfonso X's younger brother, Manuel, and grandson of Fernando III; born in Escalona (Toledo) in 1282. From a very young age, he participated both in war (particularly in the advances on Murcia, which lasted from 1284 to 1339) and in politics, though not without differences with his council.

Along with his hectic political life during the reigns of Fernando IV (1295–1312) and Alfonso XI (1312–1350), which was largely motivated, as he himself says, by questions of *onra* [honor/reputation] and *facienda* [property/wealth], Juan Manuel displayed an encyclopedic knowledge that was indicative of his desire to emulate his uncle, Alfonso X, whom he admired from an exclusively cultural (and not political) perspective. He was also a devout man, influenced by the Dominican tradition, which he followed throughout the various didactic works of his career. After retiring from active political life, Juan Manuel died in 1348; he is buried in the monastery at Peñafiel, which he founded.

In the general prologue to his works, the author expresses the philological/critical anxiety that his texts might be poorly copied, declaring that the authentic, original books, against which any potentially confusing transcripts can be compared, are in the convent at Peñafiel. Although this is essentially nothing more than a repetition of what Nicolás de Lira had already said, this disclaimer serves as a mark of authenticity for Juan Manuel's work. With this notice, the author participates in the medieval concept of an ethics of language opposing the lie, and is thus able to forestall any willful error on his part. For those inevitable involuntary errors, he resorts to the *topos* of modesty—already in use since antiquity—attributing such lapses to his lack of intelligence. Juan Manuel manipulates the vernacular language in a fresh, renewed manner, and with a wider vocabulary and a more purified syntax than Alfonso X. He is partial to concision and clarity, qualities he praises in his uncle's writing, although he does experiment with a more hermetic, obtuse style. The discovery of a skillful use of dialogue is frequently attributed to Juan Manuel, who arguably anticipates certain subtleties of the Renaissance.

A list of Juan Manuel's works appears both in the *Prólogo general* and in the prologue to *El conde Lucanor*, although there are discrepancies between the two prologues with regard to the order and number of works listed. Without the lost Peñafiel codex, what remains of the author's writings is found in various fourteenth-century manuscripts, among them Manuscript 6376 in the Biblioteca Nacional in Madrid. This manuscript lacks the *Crónica abreviada*, which in turn was found by Sánchez Alonso (in MS. F. 81 [now 1356]), also in the Biblioteca Nacional. Both have served as the basis for the edition of Juan Manuel's *Obras completas*.

Of the preserved texts one must first cite the *Libro del cavallero et del escudero*. Written before 1330, the work is one of many encyclopedic treatises of the time. Similar to Ramón Llull's *Llibre de l'ordre de cavalleria*, to which Juan Manuel seems to allude, the plot consists of the encounter between a young squire on his way to the court, and a former knight—now a hermit—who answers the young man's numerous questions. The hermit upholds knighthood as the most honorable estate in this world and indoctrinates the squire through a brief discourse on chivalry; later, the former knight gives the young man, now a novice *caballero*, a treatise on theology, another on astrology, and several expositions on the animal, vegetable, and mineral kingdoms; finally he tells the young man about the sea and the land, ending with an exaltation of creation as "manifestación de la gloria de Dios" (manifestation of God's glory).

Libro de los estados, finished in 1330, consists of two books distributed in three parts: the first book's hundred chapters, which address different religions and the estates of the lay population; the first fifty chapters of the second book, concerning the different laws (among which only the Christian law is true) as well as the mysteries of Christ and the estates of the secular clergy; and the fifty-first chapter of the second book, dedicated to religious orders and their regulations, especially the orders of preaching friars and of lesser friars. The structure is that of a work within a work, all written using dialogue as a technique supported by the main characters: the pagan king Morobán, the *infante* Johas and his tutor/teacher Turín, and a Christian preacher named Julio. The basic framework is similar to that of *Barlaam y Josafat*. Turín, committed to avoid having to address the concept of mortality, ends his phase of the prince's education by explaining the meaning of death in front of a fortuitously discovered cadaver. Chapter 22 introduces the Castilian preacher Julio, "omne muy letrado et muy entendido'' [a very educated and intelligent man] in matters of Christian doctrine. Julio claims to be tutor to Prince Juan, son of the *infante* Don Manuel, and from that moment on he will carry the burden of Prince Johas's education. The work teaches that, in order to be saved, he who did not keep the law of nature should follow Christian law, which fulfilled Old Testament designs. This law is contained in the Holy Scriptures and is preached by the church, whose accepted hierarchy, divided into "legos" [the lay population] and "eclesiásticos" [the clergy], is described in detail.

Crónica abreviada, written during the tutelage of Alfonso XI (around 1320), was thought lost until Sánchez Alonso found it in 1941. It is a summary of Alfonso X's *Estoria de España*, and though Juan Manuel claims to follow his uncle's work step by step, it is actually much more than just a faithful copy.

Libro de la caza, thought by some to be written late in the author's life, is a treatise on the art of falconry, addressing the care, training, and medication of falcons and hawks. Juan Manuel relates not only his knowledge of the hunt, but also his own personal experience, to which he alludes in the text.

Libro infinido, or *Castigos y consejos a su hijo don Fernando* (1337), is inscribed within the tradition of the education of princes, although it also contains a strong dose of personal and autobiographical content. It refers frequently to *Libro de los estados*.

Libro de las armas, or *Libro de las tres razones*, written after 1335, addresses three issues: the meaning of the coat of arms given to Juan Manuel's father; the reason a person may knight others without having been knighted himself; and the content of Juan Manuel's conversation with King Sancho at his deathbed (1295). The author explains the symbolism of the coat of arms (especially the angelic *ala* [wing]) that appeared in his grandfather's prophetic vision while his father, Don Manuel, was in the womb. He relates various anecdotes told both to his father and to himself, among them the legend of Doña Sancha de Aragón, similar to the legend of Saint Alexis. He concludes that both his uncle, Alfonso X, and his father had wanted him to knight others during their lifetime. Finally, the author describes King Sancho's deathbed speech, in which he tells Juan Manuel of the anguish caused by his parents' misfortune, and entrusts the young man to the king's wife María and their son Fernando. This work, which has been praised by Américo Castro as "la primera página, íntima y palpitante de una confesión escrita en castellano" [the first intimate, true life confession written in the Spanish language], has recently been analyzed from a literary perspective.

Tratado de la Asunción de la Virgen María was likely the last work to leave Juan Manuel's pen. A brief theological treatise on the Christian miracle of the Virgin's Assumption, the work gives several reasons why "omne del mundo no deve dubdar que sancta María no sea en cielo" [men in this world should not doubt that Saint Mary is in heaven].

Finally, *Libro del conde Lucanor*, (or *Libro de los Enxiemplos del conde Lucanor et de Patronio*), finished in 1335, has come down to the modern reader in a rather contaminated state. The preservation of five manuscripts, all from the fifteenth century, attest to its wide diffusion. The work is divided into five parts, of which the first is the most extensive, consisting of fifty-one known *exempla*. In the second part the style changes, and in its prologue the author praises the use of subtlety as a way of making the merit of his work known. Books 2, 3, and 4 are essentially one book of proverbs, and the fifth and final book is a general reflection on Christian doctrine. It is difficult to separate the didactic from the narrative; the work's rhetoric manages to overcome the dichotomy of the two elements.

The sources—especially of the *exiemplos*—can be found in stories of Oriental origin that, like the *Disciplina clericalis*, were well known in the Western world through their Latin versions. It is important to remember that in Alfonso X's day *Calila e Dinna* and *Sendebar* had already been translated into Castilian. Other works also circulated in medieval translations, including Aesop's fables, *Barlaan e Josafat*, *Sintipas*, the *Gesta romanorum*, the *Legenda aurea*, which was used by preachers who collected exempla, and contemporary works such as chronicles and bestiaries.

Some of the exempla may come from oral sources later recorded in some textual form selected by the author. Others are indications of Juan Manuel's own originality as a creator, as well as his artistic manner of reelaborating extant texts.

The purpose of the majority of Juan Manuel's writings is to teach through pleasure (*docere delectando*); in several occasions, the author expresses his goal of morally attending to his readers, orienting their conduct—including the increase of *onras* and *faciendas*—according to their estate. Consequently, and especially in *El conde Lucanor*, the author filled his exiemplos with the most useful and entertaining stories he knew, hoping that his readers would benefit from the work's *palabras falagueras et apuestas* (delightful and elegant words), while at the same time taking in the *cosas aprovechosas* (useful things) mixed in.

Starting in the thirteenth century, the exemplum played a didactic role, offering models of behavior for its readers. With Juan Manuel, however, the exemplum becomes something much more: it is an explicitly structural, well-determined genre chosen consciously by the author. Furthermore, it allows Juan Manuel to establish a perfect accord between the duelling narrative and didactic elements, a desire already implicit in the prologue's affirmations.

JESÚS MONTOYA MARTÍNEZ

Bibliography

Caldera, E. "Retórica narrativa e didáttica nel "Conde Lucanor," *Miscellanea di studi ispanici*, 14 (1966–67), 5–120.

Catalán, D. "Don Juan Manuel ante el modelo alfonsí. El testimonio de la *Crónica abreviada*." In *Juan Manuel Studies*. Ed. I. Macpherson. London, 1977, 17–51.

Don Juan Manuel. VII Centenario. Murcia, 1982.

Giménez Soler, A. *Don Juan Manuel. Biografía y estudio crítico*. Zaragoza, 1932.

Juan Manuel, *Obras Completas*. Ed., prologue, and notes by J. M. Blecua. Vols. 1–2. Madrid, 1983.

Rico, F., "Crítica del texto y modelos de cultura en el *Prólogo General* de Don Juan Manuel." In *Studia in honorem prof. M. de Riquer*. Vol. 1. Barcelona, 1990, 409–423.

JUAN, PRINCE, SON OF CATHOLIC MONARCHS SEE CATHOLIC MONARCHS

JUAN, INFANTE AND REGENT OF CASTILE

Juan (1264–1319), Infante of Castile was regent for Alfonso XI (r. 1312–1350) of Castile. Juan was a son of Alfonso X (1252–1284) and Queen Violante. During the conflict between his older brother Sancho (Sancho IV, r. 1284–1296) and Alfonso X, Juan initially sided with Sancho in 1282, but later joined his father. In his will Alfonso rewarded him with the kingdoms of Seville and Badajoz, to be held as vassal to Alfonso de la Cerda, the king's grandson and designated heir to Castile. The will was not executed because Sancho secured the entire inheritance. In 1287 Juan married María Díaz, daughter of Sancho's most powerful noble, Lope Díaz de Haro, and with the latter's support tried to gain the throne. Sancho caused the death of Lope Díaz and briefly imprisoned Juan. Juan took part in the conquest of Tarifa (1292), but after quarreling with Sancho he went to Portugal. In 1293 he joined Juan Núñez de Lara in a scheme to seek the help of Portugal in deposing Sancho, but following Juan Núñez's death the following year nothing more was done. In 1295 Juan offered his services to Abū Ya ʿqūb, king of Morocco, for an attack on Tarifa. Juan led the Moroccan forces at this siege, where he killed the son of Alfonso Pérez de Guzmán, governor of Tarifa, when he refused to surrender the city.

Sancho's death in 1296 left a minor, Fernando IV (r. 1295–1312), whose technical illegitimacy provided a pretext for Juan to claim the throne of León according to Alfonso X's will. Supported by the troops of Jaime II of Aragón and Dinis of Portugal, Juan was proclaimed king in León in 1296. The Portuguese, however, signed the Treaty of Alcañices, recognizing Fernando IV as king. María de Molina, the king's mother, was able to fight off the Aragónese and to obtain papal recognition of her son's legitimacy. Without Aragónese or Portuguese backing, revolt was not feasible, so Juan cultivated Fernando IV instead. He received favorable judgment in the *cortes* of Valladolid (1307) over inheritance of the lordship of Vizcaya, a former possession of his late father-in-law. In 1309 he proposed that the crown raise money by collecting tax arrears, thus preventing the *cortes* from approving new revenues. When Fernando IV died in 1312, leaving as his heir the infant Alfonso XI, Juan was named regent with María de Molina and the Infante Pedro in the Concord of Palazuelos (1314). Juan's troublesome career came to an end on 25 June 1319 when he and his coregent, Pedro, advancing to war against the Muslims, died on the plains of Granada.

Juan's first marriage, to Margarita of Monferrat, daughter of Guillermo VII, took place in 1281 and produced one son, known as Alfonso de Castilla. His second marriage, to María Díaz de Haro, produced two children, Juan de Castilla, ("one-eyed" because of a defective eye) called "el Tuerto" and a daughter (name unknown) who was betrothed to Juan Núñez de Lara.

THERESA M. VANN

Bibliography

Benavides, A. *Memorias de D. Fernando IV de Castilla.* 2 vols. Madrid, 1860.

Hillgarth, J. N. *The Spanish Kingdoms 1250–1516.* 2 vols. Oxford, 1976.

"Juan, Infante de Castilla." *Diccionario de historia de España.* Vol. 2. Madrid, 1952. 118–119.

O'Callaghan, J. F. *A History of Medieval Spain.* Ithaca, N.Y., 1975.

JUANA, DAUGHTER OF FERNANDO AND ISABEL SEE CATHOLIC MONARCHS

JUANA, PRINCESS AND QUEEN OF CASTILE

The exact date of Juana's birth is unknown, but she appears to have been conceived in or around April 1461. Her mother was the wife of Enrique IV, known as Juana of Portugal, queen of Castile. Whether Enrique was her father remains in dispute, hence her also often being called Juana "la Beltraneja," reflecting that her real father may have been Juan Beltrán, a high official at court reputed to have been her mother's lover.

The consequences of Juana's disputed legitimacy are important for monarchical succession in Castile during the last quarter of the fifteenth century. By 9 May 1462 the *cortes* of Castile, attended by leading churchmen and the magnates of the realm, had sworn allegiance to Juana as heir to Enrique IV. Shortly thereafter, the king instructed all jurisdictions in the kingdom to do the same. Soon, however, a campaign began among sectors of the disgruntled nobility to replace Enrique IV as king with his younger half brother, the Infante Alfonso, culminating in the so-called Farce of Avila in June of 1465, where Enrique was deposed in effigy. As part of the campaign to remove the king, especially after the mysterious death of the Infante in 1468, the allegations of Juana's illegitimacy began to circulate publically, placing her at the center of the controversy concerning Enrique's continued reign and his succession. Pressured by the nobles, who now favored the succession of Enrique's half sister, Isabel of Castile, the king disinherited Juana and recognized Isabel as his immediate heir. Some historians have generally been willing to interpret this act of Enrique IV as an implicit acknowledgment that Juana was not his daughter. However, even if she were his daughter, as she was by juridical presumption, he might have yielded to the pressure exerted by the nobles, who sought to give the crown immediately to Isabel. It is therefore possible that Enrique may have compromised with the nobles by making Isabel his heir, as he did at Los Toros de Guisando on 19 September 1468.

On 12 December 1474, the day after the death of Enrique IV at Madrid, Isabel, who was at Segovia, had herself proclaimed queen of Castile. Juana, who had been betrothed to Afonso V of Portugal and had been reinstated as Enrique's heir when he subsequently revoked the Pact of Los Toros de Guisando and again proclaimed her successor to his dominions, sought to press her claims via an alliance with the Portuguese. The archbishop of Toledo, the marqués de Villena, and other nobles who in Enrique's lifetime had denied Juana's legitimacy now defended her claims. The conflict set off a five-year war between Castile and Portugal that ended in 1479, when Juana abandoned her case and retired to the monastery of Santa Clara of Coimbra (1480), from where she was never allowed to leave, thus opening the way for legitimizing Isabel's claim to the throne of Castile. Juana died at Coimbra in 1530.

E. MICHAEL GERLI

Bibliography

Azcona, T. *Juana de Castilla, mal llamada La Beltraneja*. Madrid, 1998.

Edwards, J. *The Spain of the Catholic Monarchs, 1474–1520*. Cambridge, 2000.

JUDAH ḤA-LEVĪ *See* YEHUDAH ḤA-LEVĪ

JUDERÍA

In Castile-León (and to some extent elsewhere)the term *judería* refers to the Jewish quarter of a town or city. In fact, however, there was no restricted quarter where Jews were compelled to live until the fifteenth century, with rare exceptions such as Murcia (1267) and Valladolid (1351), when Pedro I agreed that in those places where priests had an agreement with Jews to live apart from Christians, this should be done. Under the influence of Vicente Ferrer, the Ordinances of Valladolid (1412) supposedly imposed a separate Jewish quarter for each town and city (in fact, this was not always done). A bull from Pope Eugenius IV (1442) also ordered that Jews live only in separate juderías, but again this was not actually enforced. It was not until 1480, when the Catholic Monarchs ordered the establishment of juderías, that some attempt was made actually to enforce this law. Even so, major cities ignored it, and as late as 1492 Toledo, for instance, still had no official judería.

In Aragón-Catalonia (including Valencia and Mallorca) the term *call*, derived from the Hebrew *qahal*, was used at least from 1238 to refer to the Jewish quarter. By 1290 a call was established in Mallorca. The most famous *calls* were those of Barcelona and Girona, but sources attest to the existence of the *call* everywhere in these kingdoms. In many towns in Spain today it is easy to locate these former Jewish quarters.

NORMAN ROTH

Biography

Ashtor, Eliyahu. *The Jews of Muslim Spain*. 3 vols. Philadelphia, 1973–84.

Baer, Yitzak. *Historia de los judíos en la España cristina*. Trans. José Luis Lacave. Madrid, 1981.

Baron, Salo Wittmayer. *A Social and Religious History of the Jews*. New York, 1965. X.

JUGLAR

This term has many meanings and may be understood in various ways according to place, time, and circumstance. It refers principally and broadly, however, to professional medieval entertainers or minstrels. The word *jokulare*, from which *juglar* derives, is first documented in the Iberin Peninsula in Aragónese Latin in the year 1062. Its Romance forms, *joglares* and *joglar*, are subsequently found in Gonzalo de Berceo, *Vida de Santo Domingo de Silos*, 318b y 775b. Its sense when used as an adjective is synonymous with happy (*alegre*) or jesting, jocular (*burlón*): *sermón juglar*, *lengua juglara* as nouns designate a type of speech used by someone to entertain others. Its sense is related to *jocus*, with the acception of joke (*burla*) or fun, jest (*chanza*).

Medieval Spanish legislation relative to the sphere of the court records the tradition of the Roman *mimos* and the barbarian *scopas*, actors and entertainers who provided diversions and entertainments for the nobility. In his *Siete Partidas*, Alfonso X recommends that the king, especially, should take respite from governing by means of leisure pursued publically amid the court, or *a modo palatino*, listening to and watching amusing pastimes. Diversion, especially during meals, consisted in conversation with other members of the court, in listening to stories, and, especially, in verbal games, or *jugar de palabra*. That is, cultivating double entendre, jokes, and verbal play whose object is laughter, because, as was noted "there would be no fun where no one laughs" ("non serie juego onde omne non rrye"). Play is thus associated with laughter and joy in a courtly setting. It is often produced by *juglares*, or entertainers. Playful diversions were referred to as *alegrías*, or joys provoked by juglares, or professional performers, who by playing instruments and singing their own as well as songs composed by others provided amusement for the king, as recorded in the *Partida Segunda*.

The term *trobador*, often associated with *juglar*, is also first documented in the eleventh century, but with the sense of someone who verbally invents or creates song or poetry. The term *juglar* seems to have been applied to all performers who played instruments and sang. These entertainers were generally also distinguished by the type of instruments they played.

Other related terms are *remedador* and *cazurro*, who were also designated juglares. Guiraut Riquier laments that he, a juglar, was often confused with them. In 1275 Guiraut composed a *Supplica*, or petition, addressed to Alfonso X where he begs the king to define the function of remedadores and cazurros so that he will not be mistaken for one of them. Opinion is divided on whether Riquier's request was motivated by economics or by a concern for his social status. The remedadores and cazurros were juglares who were mimes and jesters. They imitated their social superiors and recited nonsense verses often in the streets and public places, usually in the company of puppeteers, cardsharps, saltimbanques, or animal trainers, all of whom also often went under the name of *juglar*.

Segreles, or professional entertainers of a higher class were also referred to as *juglares*. Segreles traveled from court to court offering their brand of more exclusive diversion for compensation in the form of gifts, shelter, or other emoluments. To be sure, some juglares were known to be permanently retained at certain courts, where their presence is documented in account books and lists of payments by the lord. In Alfonso X's *Partida Segunda*, as well as in the *Llibre de cavalleria* of Pedro III of Aragón, there are references to the requirement that juglares should not sing anything but songs of military deeds (*fechos de armas*) before an audience of knights, which indicates that, in addition to courtly entertainments, part of the repertoire of certain juglarles consisted of epic songs, or *cantares de gesta*. These were known as *juglares de voz*. In a thirteenth-century *ensenhamen* (instruction poem of praise or blame that Guerau de Cabrera directed at a juglar known as Cabra, Guerau provides a list of activities he describes as Cabra's repertoire. The latter includes a broad range of lyric and narrative compositions that every juglar should master and perform in exercising their profesional duties. Finally, there were *juglares de péñola*, or those who composed in writing for themselves.

Itinerant juglares, especially those who sold their services, were generally looked down upon, designated as *viles e infames*. The ones who played or amused others for their own entertainment, however, were considered socially acceptable. During the Fourth Lateran Council (1215) the church pronounced excommunication against all juglares identified as viles and infames and strictly prohibited the clergy from associating with them. This legislation was subsequently incorporated by Alfonso X in the *Partida Séptima*.

Jesús Montoya Martínez

Bibliography

Bertolucci Pizzorusso, V. "La *Supplica* de Guiraut Riquier." *Studi Mediolatini e Volgari* 14 (1966), 11–135.

Menéndez Pidal, R. *Poesía juglaresca y orígenes de las literaturas románicas*. 6th ed. Madrid, 1957.

JULIAN, COUNT

The reality of Count Julian's existence is open to serious doubt, and it is probable that he is no more than a literary figure created to help give a human dimension to the explanations for the rapid and triumphant Arab conquest of Spain in 711. He features in a number of Arab accounts of the invasion as the Visigothic governor of Ceuta, whose assistance to Ṭāriq ibn Ziyād was motivated by his desire for revenge against King Roderic. According to these stories, the Visigothic ruler is said to have raped or seduced the count's daughter while she was entrusted to his court in Toledo for her education. In consequence the enraged Julian provided the Arabs with the five (or seven) ships that they needed to cross the Strait of Gibraltar.

Julian does not feature in the Christian historical tradition at all, and, most significantly, there is no mention of him in the Latin *Chronicle of 754*, the only eighth-century account of the Arab conquest in any language. The story of Julian and his daughter belongs with similar tales, such as those of Roderic and the locked tower in Toledo or of Ṭāriq and the Table of Solomon. These are all part of an essentially literary elaboration of the events of the conquest by Arab authors of the tenth and eleventh centuries, and lack historical foundations. A ruined building on the banks of the Tagus in Toledo was long claimed to be the Baños de la Cava where Roderic was said first to have caught sight of Julian's daughter, but in reality this structure is the remains of a ninth-century Arab bridge.

Roger Collins

Bibliography

Basset, R. *La Maison fermée de Tolède*. Oran, 1898.

Collins, R. *The Arab Conquest of Spain: 710–797*. Oxford, 1989.

JULIAN OF TOLEDO

Born around 640, Julian was of partly Jewish descent. Knowledge of his career comes primarily from the brief "Eulogy" of him written by Bishop Felix of Toledo (693–ca. 700). He was a pupil of Bishop Eugenius ll (647–657), and subsequently became a member of the clergy of the church in Toledo while following a rigorous ascetic regime. Following the death of Bishop Quiricus (667–680) he was chosen by King Wamba to take over the see. The choice may have been influenced by Julian's eulogistic *Historia Wambae*, an account of the opening events of that king's reign. However, before the end of 680 Julian had been caught up in, or even had initiated, the chain of events leading to Wamba's enforced abdication and retirement to a monastery. With the new king, Ervig (680–687), to whom he had previously dedicated a now lost work on divine judgment, Julian seems to have cooperated closely. In 686 he dedicated to the king his most significant surviving book, *On the Proof of the Sixth Age*, a polemical reply to Jewish denials of Christ's messiahship. This work redefined the chronological framework of human history within an apocalyptic context, and was to be highly influential in Spain and western Europe throughout the Middle Ages. He died in Gao.

Other extant writings by Julian include the *Antikeimenon* and *the Prognosticum futuri saeculi*. In these, as in lost collections referred to in the "Eulogy," Julian is revealed as an assiduous reader of the works of Augustine. Like Ildefonsus, Julian is credited by Felix with the composition of verse and also of a substantial body of liturgy. The latter cannot be disentangled from the vast corpus of Mozarabic liturgical texts.

During his episcopate Julianus presided over four Councils of Toledo: the twelfth (680–681), thirteenth (683), fourteenth (684), and fifteenth (688). The first of these formalized the primacy of Toledo over all the other churches of the Visigothic kingdom. Julian himself contributed to this by his emphasis on the role of the anointing of the king in the "royal city" as a precondition for a new ruler's legitimacy.

ROGER COLLINS

Bibliography

Collins, R. "Julian of Toledo and the Royal Succession in Late Seventh-Century Spain." In *Early Medieval Kingship*. Eds. P. Sawyer and I. Wood. Leeds, 1977. 30–49.

Hillgarth, J. N. "St. Julian of Toledo in the Middle Ages." *Journal of the Warburg and Courtauld Institutes* 21 (1958), 7–26.

Murphy, F. X. "Julian of Toledo and the Fall of the Visigothic Kingdom in Spain." *Speculum* 27 (1952), 1–21.

JURA DE SANTA GADEA

Jura de Santa Gadea is an epic story preserved in traditional ballads and prosified in chronicles. Its hero, El Cid, compels his new lord, Alfonso VI, to swear three times in the church of Santa Gadea that he is innocent of the murder of his brother Sancho II. The murder is narrated in the lost *Cantar de Sancho II y cerco de Zamora*. Critics disagree as to whether the *Jura* was the final episode of this *Cantar*, or was composed later (ca. 1200) and separately for the purpose of linking the *Sancho II* epic and the *Cantar de Mío Cid* into a cyclical poetic life of the Cid, or was simply a ballad.

There are common features in all of the versions of the *Jura*: anti-Alfonsine sentiment and the presentation of the Cid as a rebellious vassal. Consequently the possibility that it was the epilogue of an anti-Leonese *Sancho II* cannot be excluded. It also may have been the beginning of a lost *Cantar del destierro del Cid*, in which the hero is presented as rebellious against his monarch. This can be observed better in the *Crónica de Castilla* (late thirteenth or early fourteenth century). It has also been suggested that the epic tradition of the Cid as a rebellious vassal (the best example being the *Mocedades de Rodrigo*, probably from the 1360s) may well have derived from the *Jura* tradition.

MERCEDES VAQUERO

Bibliography

Vaquero, M. "El cantar de la *Jura de Santa Gadea* y la tradición del Cid como vasallo rebelde." *Olifant* 15, no. 1 (1990), 47–84.

Horrent, J. "La *Jura de Santa Gadea*: Historia y poesía." In *Studia philologica*: *Homenaje ofrecido a Dámaso Alonso*. Vol. 2. Madrid, 1961: 241–65.

JUSTICE, CHRISTIAN, ISLAMIC *See* ADMINISTRATION, JUDICIAL

JUSTICIA OF ARAGÓN

The *justicia* of Aragón was a judicial intermediary between the Crown of Aragón and the people. Though long thought to have roots in the judiciary of Muslim Spain or in the *fueros* (civil codes) of Sobrarbe, the justicia has been shown to have originated from a class of officials of twelfth-century Zaragoza, most especially the *zalmedina*. His road from minor judge to true national voice was begun during the unionist revolt of 1265–1266. At the *cortes* (parliament) of Exea in 1265, the justicia was made judge of record in suits between the king and the Aragónese nobles. To prevent his being suborned by either side, the office was to be held only by a knight. During the revolt of the *Unioń* (1283–1287), the justicia, in conjunction with the Aragónese cortes, became a countervailing force to the crown. The power of the office escalated to such an extent that for the next century, even after the final defeat of the Union in 1348–1349, Pedro IV and his successors still retained the justicia as one of the greatest judges of Aragón who performed many of his earlier functions as advocate of the Aragónese people. As the supreme interpreter of Aragón's foral law, the justicia also stood as the protector of individual litigants who could intervene in any suit in which Aragónese fueros (civil codes) were being violated by other royal judges. These functions of foral protection (*manifestación*) and litigant advocacy (*firma de derecho*) continued as long as the office of *justicia* persisted. In all, fifty-nine justicias served in Aragón between 1123 and 1707, when the office was abrogated by Philip V's *Decreto de Nueva Planta*.

DONALD KAGAY

Bibliography

Bisson, Thomas N. *The Medieval Crown of Aragón*. Oxford, 1986.

Bonet y Navarro, Angel. *El justicia de Aragón: historia y derecho*. Estudio introductorio Angel Bonet Navarro, Esteban Sarasa Sánchez, Guillermo Redondo Veintemillas. Zaragoza: Cortes de Aragón, 1985.

Ubieto Arteta, Antonio. *Historia de Aragón: Creación y desarrollo de la Corona de Aragón*. Zaragoza, 1987.

K

KHABALLA *See* LEÓN, MÓSES DE

KHARJA *See* MUWASHSHAḤA

KINGSHIP

The authority of the first Visigothic kings rested on their military success. Once settled in Spain, under the influence of Roman tradition they assumed much of the authority of the emperor. Leovigild (r. 568–586) adopted royal vestments and other trappings of kingship. The monarchy was elective, but by associating their sons on the throne, kings tried to transform it into a hereditary institution. The Visigoths unfortunately tended to assassinate their kings. To safeguard the monarchy the Fourth Council of Toledo in 633 established a procedure for a royal election. The newly elected king probably was raised on a shield and acclaimed by the assembly, who swore allegiance to him. Another protective device was anointing, a practice first used in Wamba's (r. 672–680) time and then copied elsewhere in Europe. Toledo was the favorite residence of the Visigothic kings. Isidore of Seville (d. 636) stressed the king's responsibility to rule justly; otherwise he would not be entitled to be called king.

The kings of Asturias-León, inspired by Visigothic tradition, claimed to continue the Visigothic monarchy. The principle of hereditary succession gradually came into operation as rulers were descended from Pelayo (r. 718–737) and his son-in-law Alfonso I (r. 739–757). There were three minorities in 966, and others in 999 and 1028. Royal anointing was employed sporadically, as in the case of Alfonso II in 791. After the acclamation of Ordoño II in 914, a diadem was placed on his head and he was anointed. The *Antiphonary of León* contains an *ordo* (procedure) for making a king. The king's authority was rather rudimentary. He was primarily a military leader responsible for defense, but by the end of the ninth century his obligation to expel the Muslims from Spain was clearly stated. In addition he maintained the peace and dispensed justice.

In response to the revival of Roman law, the recovery of Aristotle's *Politics*, and changing economic and social circumstances, the nature of kingship changed substantially from the twelfth century onward. The kingdoms of Castile, León, Portugal, Aragón-Catalonia, and Navarre were now well defined. The principle of hereditary succession and primogeniture was also established. Fathers often designated their sons as heirs to the throne. On several occasions between 1065 and 1230 Castile and León were separated to provide for more than one son. The right of minors to inherit the throne was acknowledged—for example, in the cases of Jaime I of Aragón (1213); Afonso V of Portugal (1438); and the Castilian kings Alfonso VIII (1158), Enrique I (1214), Fernando IV (1295), Alfonso XI (1312), Enrique III (1390), and Juan II (1406). The right of females to inherit was also accepted in Castile in the case of Urraca (r. 1109–1126); Berenguela, who ceded her right to her son, Fernando III (r. 1217–1252), and Isabel I the Catholic (r. 1474–1504). In Aragón the rights of Petronilla (r. 1137–1174) were recognized, as were those of Constanza, daughter of Pedro IV, in 1347, although she did not succeed him. In Castile a difficult situation arose when Alfonso X's oldest son and heir, Fernando de la Cerda, predeceased him in 1275. The king recognized his second son, Sancho, but opponents favoring the claims of Fernando's heirs, the Infantes de la Cerda, initiated a struggle that lasted until 1304. Although illegitimate children were barred from succession, Enrique II of Castile (r. 1369–1379) and João I of Portugal (r. 1385–1433) both gained power in revolutionary circumstances. In each case it was claimed that the people had the right to choose their king.

Although texts commonly speak of the king being raised to the kingship, that should be taken figuratively. There is no reason to believe that the Germanic custom of raising him on a shield persisted in medieval Spain. The new monarch was acclaimed and received a pledge of homage and allegiance from his people.

The custom of anointing and coronation seems to have fallen into desuetude except in Aragón, and was used elsewhere only when a king needed to stress his right to rule. Alfonso X may have crowned himself at Toledo in 1254; Sancho IV crowned himself there in 1284, primarily to strengthen his claims against Alfonso de la Cerda. Fernando IV apparently also was crowned there in 1295. Alfonso XI crowned himself at Las Huelgas de Burgos after being knighted by a mechanical statue of St. James. Of the succeeding kings only Juan I was crowned. Pedro II of Aragón was crowned in Rome by the pope in 1204, but later kings were crowned in Zaragoza by the archbishop of Tarragona. Pedro IV, however, crowned himself.

The concept of royal power was greatly enlarged during this time. The king was expected to do justice, but this was taken in a much more active sense. The king assumed the responsibility of amending old laws, and also of making new ones. His duty was to obey the law and to do justice to every person. In addition he claimed the right to levy extraordinary taxes to carry on his activities for the benefit of the kingdom, but he had to ask the consent of the people, which was usually given in the *cortes* (parliament). He was responsible for defense and for the prosecution of the reconquest.

From time to time kings were charged with incompetence or tyranny. Charged by the papacy in 1245 with tolerating anarchy, Sancho II of Portugal was effectively deprived of royal power as custody of the realm was entrusted to his brother Afonso III (r. 1248–1279). The accumulated grievances of the Castilians concerning Alfonso X's innovations in law and taxation, and a dispute over the succession, resulted in his being stripped of royal authority in 1282. Though he retained the royal title, his powers were transferred to his son Sancho IV. Years later Pedro I was challenged by his half brother Enrique of Trastámara, who finally murdered him in 1369. Juan II of Aragón had to contend with the revolt of the Catalans, who denounced him as an enemy of Catalonia in 1462. The Castilian nobility formally declared the deposition of Enrique IV in 1465 and vainly attempted to transfer the crown to his younger brother Alfonso of Ávila. The task of restoring the prestige and authority of monarchy fell to Fernando and Isabel at the close of the medieval era.

JOSEPH F. O'CALLAGHAN

Bibliography

Nieto Soria, J. M. *Fundamentos ideológicos del poder real en Castilla (siglos XIII–XVI)*. Madrid, 1988.

O'Callaghan, J. F. *A History of Medieval Spain*. Ithaca, N.Y., 1975.

KIṬĀB SEGOBIANO *See* YÇA IBN JABIR

KNIGHTS HOSPITALERS *See* MILITARY ORDERS

KORAN *See* QUR'AN

KUZARI

Judah ha-Levi (ca. 1075–1141) was an important Hebrew poet. Sometime prior to his ill-fated voyage to live in Palestine (he died on the way in a storm), he composed what he himself refers to as an "insignificant" little work in Arabic, known by its Hebrew translation as the *Kuzari*. It is not, as often erroneously claimed, a "philosophical" work, but rather a theological one, modeled fictitiously on a debate between the king of the Kuzars (who actually had converted to Judaism) and a Muslim, Christian, and Jewish spokesman, each setting forth the validity of his religion. Its aims were three: to assert the superiority of Judaism over Christianity and Islam, to assert the superiority of revealed religion over Aristotelian philosophy, and primarily to attack the Qaraite heresy. Most interesting are his "Zionist" ideals: the interdependence of God, the Land, and the Jewish people. Nevertheless, the work had little or no impact upon the Jews of Spain. It did, however, on Spanish literature, for it certainly influenced Juan Manuel (*Libro de los estados*) and Ramón Llull (*De el Gentil y de los tres sabios*). A medieval Spanish translation is extant (being edited) and a seventeenth-century one by a Jew of Amsterdam has been frequently published. English translations and others exist.

NORMAN ROTH

Bibliography

Buber, M. "The Voice of the Exile." In his *Israel and Palestine*. New York, 1952. 61–72.

Menéndez y Pelayo, M. *Historia de las ideas estéticas en España*. 4th ed. Vol. 1. Madrid, 1974.

———. *Orígenes de la novela*. Vol. 1. Buenos Aires, 1946.

L

LANGUAGES *See*, ARABIC LANGUAGE, ARAGÓNESE LANGUAGE, BASQUE LANGUAGE, CASTILIAN LANGUAGE, CATALAN LANGUAGE, GALAICO-PORTUGUESE LANGUAGE, HEBREW AND JUDEO-SPANISH LANGUAGE, LATIN LANGUAGE AND LITERATURE, MOZARABIC LANGUAGE

LAPIDARIES

Lapidaries are books that describe stones and their therapeutic virtues. Three types can be distinguished: medical-descriptive, magical, and symbolic interpretations of the twelve biblical stones.

The lapidary inserted in St. Isidore of Seville's (c. 560–636) *Etymologiae* follows Pliny the Elder's and Solinus's lapidaries. It shows Pliny's subdivision of stones, gems, and metals. Among stones, Isidore distinguishes ordinary, luxurious, and marble; his classification and terminology rely on external forms, so that variations of color gives rise to different names. Although he rejects superstitious practices, Isidore recognizes the existence of magical powers in Nature due to the relation between macrocosmos and microcosmos that the physician will use only for therapeutic purposes. The main interest of the work, which had an extraordinarily wide diffusion, is the etymological aspect.

Among Arabic lapidaries it is important to highlight the geological and chemical part of Avicenna's (980–1037) *Kītāb al-Shifā'*, which follows the classification of stones, sulfides, metals, and salts, and the mineralogical part of Ibn al-Baitar's (1197–1248) *Simple Treatise*. The latter contains alphabetically ordered descriptions of precious stones to be used in the Muslim pharmacopoeia.

Alfonso X (r. 1252–1284) ordered the *Lapidario*, considered to be the main work of astrological learning; derived from a Greek original transmitted in an Arabic version, it belonged to a vast body of research on the microcosmos as a whole. This work (the only one remaining in the Western world with miniatures) reflects diverse graphic sources, among them Muslim adaptations of the Gothic style. It consists of four lapidaries. The first one is divided into twelve sections corresponding to the constellations of the zodiac; each section has thirty chapters, corresponding to thirty degrees of every sign; each chapter covers one stone and the star(s) to which it is astrologically linked. The text names it in three languages and describes its features, the lands where it can be found, and its qualities. This work has illustrations of two types: capital letters depicting the finding or obtaining of the stones by a savant and his helper, and round medallions enclosing one of the forty-eight constellations from the *Ochava esfera*, which illustrate each stone's qualities and virtues. In all there are 360 stones, corresponding to the zodiac's 360 degrees. Each section is illustrated by a big wheel whose center features the corresponding sign of the zodiac. From each wheel thirty arms radiate, each of them bearing the constellation that influences the corresponding stone.

Juan Gil de Zamora (ca.1241–ca.1318) included a lapidary in his *Historia naturalis* (ca.1282), which reveals the influence of Pliny the Elder.

In the fifteenth century three anonymous Catalonian lapidaries of an astrological-popular character were derived from one of the compilations of the *De mineral ibus* of Albertus Magnus (1193–1280).

CARLOS MIRANDA-GARCÍA

Bibliography

Alfonso X. *Lapidario*. Complete text. Ed. Marĭa Brey Mariño. Madrid, 1983.

Amasuno, M. V. *La materia médica de Dioscórides en el Lapidario de Alfonso X el Sabio. Literatura y ciencia en la Castilla del siglo XIII*. Madrid, 1987.

Domínguez Rodríguez, A. *Astrología y arte en el Lapidario de Alfonso X el Sabio*. Madrid, 1984.

Fontaine, J. *Isidore de Séville et la culture classique dans l'Espagne Visigothíque*. 2 vols. Paris, 1959.

García Aviles, A. "*La miniatura astrológica en los reinos medievales hispánicos (sigios XI–XIII): Iconografía y contexto cultural*." 2 vols. Ph.D. diss., University of Murcia, 1994.

Isidore of Seville. *Etimologías*. 2 vols. Ed. by J. Oroz Reta and M. A. Marcos Casquero. Madrid, 1982–83.

Lapidari. Tractad de pedres precioses. Manuscrit del segle XV. Text, intro., and glossary by Joan Gili. Oxford, 1977.

Nunemaker, J. H. "An Additional Chapter on Magic in Mediaeval Spanish Literature." *Speculum* 7 (1932), 556–64.

Sarton, G. *Introduction of the History of Science*. 3 vols. in 5. Baltimore, 1927–47.

Zamora, J. G. De. *Historia naturalis*. Critical ed. and Spanish trans. A. Domínguez García and L. García Ballester. 3 vols. N.p., 1994.

LARA FAMILY

One of Castile's great noble families, the Laras initially based their power at the village of Lara in the present-day Spanish province of Burgos. They emerged in the eleventh century as minor retainers of the first Castilian Count Fernán González. The era of clan violence and court intrigue in which the Laras began their climb to prominence can be gleaned from the Castilian epic *Infantes de Lara*. In such an atmosphere of social flux, the Laras rapidly moved to the forefront of the Castilian nobility by the twelfth century. Vying with their major early rivals in the baronage, the Castros, for control of such centers as Toledo, the Laras by the thirteenth century had become power brokers for the Castilian crown and the realm's parliament, or *cortes*. One of the greatest scions of the family, Álvaro Núñez de Lara, served as procurator for Castile after the death of Alfonso VIII in 1214. When Crown Prince Enrique I, died in 1217, as the result of an accident, Álvaro tried desperately to retain his position of power, but was finally forced to acknowledge the rule of Enrique's brother, Fernando III.

With the union of Castile and León in 1230, the Laras occupied a number of official posts, including those of *mayordomo mayor* and *adelantado mayor*. The most notable Lara in the late thirteenth century was Nuño González de Lara, who, as *adelantado* of the frontier, commanded a great Castilian army that was disastrously defeated—and he himself was killed—in July 1275 at Écija. Despite such sacrifices the Laras saw the Castilian monarchy slip under the influence of their archenemies, the Haro clan. Due to Sancho IV's weakness, a widening power base was carved out in the Castilian court by Lope Díaz de Haro. Rousing the majority of the Castilian nobility against Haro's dictatorial regime, Álvar Núñez de Lara fomented rebellion against Haro as far afield as Portugal.

When Lara was deserted in 1287 by his Portuguese backers, notably King Dinis I, his rebellion collapsed and he died shortly afterward. Despite this setback the Laras retained much of their local power and gained increased influence at the Castilian court with Juan Núñez de Lara, who served as adviser to Sancho IV's son, Fernando IV. The traditional position of the Laras at the forefront of the Castilian nobility was recognized, even after the family had lost influence in the later medieval period to new noble clans through the practice of having one of its members serve as spokesman for the nobility in Castile's cortes.

DONALD KAGAY

Bibliography

Doubleday, Simon R. *The Lara Family: Crown and Nobility in Medieval Spain*. Cambridge, MA, 2001.

LATERAN REFORMS

The movement of religious reform of the medieval church began under Pope Gregory VII in the eleventh century, with the intent to accomplish three things: a recovery of papal influence and power in the church, a reconquest of territory possessed by the Moslems since 640, and, most important, a rededication to the moral rectitude of the clergy. The first two aims of the movement, and to a certain extent the third, were generally quite successful in the twelfth century. By 1200, though, the process had slowed down and lost its effect: Moslems won important battles at Hattin and Alarcos, the monarchy still controlled the English and Spanish clergy, and the church faced anticlericalism, materialism, Catharist and apocalyptic propaganda, and a clergy that was still often corrupt and ignorant.

A revival of the reform movement took place in the early thirteenth century: St. Francis of Assisi emphasized preaching, missions, and charity work; Dominic organized his friars for similar purposes; schools and universities were established to train a more educated and dedicated clergy; canon law became more effectively codified. In an attempt to systematize this multifaceted movement, Pope Innocent III called a churchwide council in 1215, convening in the basilica of Saint John Lateran. Because of the location of the meeting, this council was known as the fourth Lateran Council, and the whole reforming phenomenon as the Lateran Reforms, even though many of the elements associated with ecclesiastical reform of the period were not a direct result of the Lateran councils.

The effect of the Lateran Reforms on Christian culture and literature in some regions (England, for example) has been well documented. Until Derek Lomax's important study in 1969, however, there was virtually no attention paid to their effects on Iberian society and civilization. As Lomax points out, the Spanish church leadership, headed by Rodrigo Jiménez de Rada, archbishop of Toledo, was well represented at the Fourth Council. In other regions, the clergy held synods and issued decrees to pass on the legislation of the Fourth Lateran Council to the diocese. In Castile, the effect of the reforms is much more indirect and diffuse: bishops surely knew about the decrees, but were distracted by the reconquest of southern Spain and the overwhelming task of establishing a completely new Christian Church in those regions, and as a result they only rarely summoned diocesan councils and synods. They may, however, have put the Lateran decrees into practice without officially promulgating them, and many of the reform movement's effects—establishment of schools and universities, foundation of new religious orders, administration of the sacraments, etc.—were as evident in Castile as they were elsewhere.

The cultural fruits of the so-called Lateran Reforms can perhaps best be seen throughout the two centuries following the Fourth Lateran Council, when religious literature experiences a significant boom and a change in focus. This can be seen in the production of vernacular hagiography, the increased emphasis placed on confession (which was prescribed as an annual duty by the Fourth Lateran Council), and the valorization of moralizing literature, especially of the sermon and its source material. These didactic tools of the clergy slowly made their way into the lay population. Books of exempla, first compiled by clerics for other clerics (as in the case of *Disciplina clericalis*), were soon revised for the layman's use or produced as devotional reading (see the *Libro de los examplos*). At the same time, authors began to use the exempla model for both didactic and entertainment purposes (the latter increasingly overshadowing the former), sometimes calling attention to the problematics of reading such works (see the *Libro de buen amor*). Finally, as the example of Juan Manuel shows, other lay authors began to employ the didacticism of the exemplum to communicate moral lessons that were sometimes nearly devoid of uniquely Christian teachings.

The presence and relevance of canon law in the literature of this period has only recently been articulated. It is clear, however, that church legislation on such matters as confession and marriage provided source material for the *Arcipreste de Talavera*, the *Libro de buen amor*, and in a more indirect manner, for vernacular short narratives, which seem to use as points of departure the cases that canon law lecturers like Bernardo de Compostela addressed in their *quaestiones*.

The reform movement of the thirteenth century clearly achieved a significant degree of success, resulting in a greater knowledge of theology and canon law among its clergy, as well as a greater appreciation of works that satirized and parodied these subjects.

MATTHEW T. BENTLEY

Bibliography

Lomax, Derek W. "The Lateran Reforms and Spanish Literature." *Iberoromania* 1 (1969): 299–313.

LATIN LANGUAGE AND LITERATURE

Latin literature of the Hispanic Middle Ages is brought about by the successive introduction of three factors: the Arabic invasion (early eighth century), the establishment of the Mozarabic population (tenth century, with a subsequent dispersion in the eleventh century), and the entrance of the Cluniac mission into the peninsula (eleventh century), which would put an end to the Spanish Mozarabic liturgy, but would also promote the diffusion of European culture.

From this perspective, the eighth century can be characterized on the one hand by the fact that communication and cultural activity between the Arabic and Christian parts of the Iberian Peninsula had not yet been broken; and on the other, by the influence of the Carolingian reforms of the last quarter of the century.

Within the Visigothic tradition, two famous epistolographers stand out: Ascárico (author of a cento based on the writings of Prudentius and Sedulius, and a theological epistle) and Tuseredo, an unknown individual who was the author of an surprisingly insightful epistle to Ascárico that addresses the problem of the Resurrection and the Glory. The abbot Pirminio, the founder of Reichenau and Murbach and a good example of a cleric who successfully fled the Arabic invasion, was the author of *De cunctis libris Scripturarum scarapsus*, which is a very useful example of Visigothic preaching.

Of greater interest and merit are the doctrinal and polemical works by the Adoptionist, Elipando de Toledo, an adversary of Alcuin who led the Hispanic resistance to the interests of Charlemagne. Besides several epistles, he is also the author of a *Symbolum* and an *Adversus Alcuinum*. The Adoptionism of Elipando (who never ceased to be closely observed because of the political problems posed by his opposition to French influence) was more a result of his heated debates with Alcuin and Beato de Liébana than of a sincere belief.

Beato, a northerner and a supporter of Charlemagne's expansionist campaign, was Elipando's first Spanish adversary, and won the approval of Alcuin. His work is fairly unoriginal, especially the *In Apocalipsim libri duodecim* which, nevertheless, is fundamental for the study of medieval art. The *Adversus Elipan-*

dum, of a narrower diffusion, is more prophetic than theological; in this work Beato attacks the possible reconciliation with the Arabs living in traditionally Hispanic sectors. The growing hostility toward the Moors explains the appearance in the south of the *Historia de Mammeth pseudopropheta*, a compilation of the major ideas of anti-Islamic European literature.

Eighth-century historiography includes two Mozarabic chronicles written as supposed continuations of Isidore of Seville: the *Crónica de 741*, which treats foreign, Byzantine, and Arabic topics along the lines of John of Biclaro; and the *Crónica de 754* or *Chronica Mozarabica* which, with its very precise structure, deals with Hispanic, Arabic, and "Roman" matters successively.

The ninth century produced little original work, and is distinguished by the proliferation of *scriptoria*. In the Christian zone to the north, Latin literary production was limited to politically charged historiography. The first book of the *Annales Portugalenses Ueteres*, for example, deals with the historical legitimacy of the Asturian monarchy as heirs of the Visigothic monarchy. The *Crónica de Alfonso III* had a similar intention, though it is hidden among the jumble of contributing materials. In the last quarter of the century the third of the great political chronicles, the *Chronicon Albeldense*, was composed. It is a *historia mundi* in which news of the peninsula is interwoven with a clear pro-Asturian agenda.

The particular situation of the Mozarabic communities explains, in part, the successful preservation and persistence of Hispanic-Visigothic traditions. Around midcentury, a strong sentiment of religious and cultural opposition to Islamic power was unleashed in Córdoba, spawning a wave of persecutions. The first name among the Mozarabic ranks worthy of citation is that of the abbot Speraindeo, teacher and spiritual director of Eulogio and Paulo Alvarus, who were the most important figures of the time. Around 845, Eulogio, who belonged to a wealthy family, felt the need to travel to the Pyrenees, where he would have the opportunity to become acquainted with Christian Hispania and with the monastic libraries of Leire and San Zacarías; his journey provided him with a notable collection of books to take back to Córdoba. Eulogio allied himself with those that venerated the martyrs of the Islamic persecution, and as result was incarcerated; during his confinement he wrote the *Documentum martyriale*, the *Memoriale martyrum*, and the *Liber apologeticus martyrum*, and prepared a Latin prosody. He was martyred by decapitation in 859.

Paulo Alvarus, a friend, companion, and biographer of Eulogio, was a highly cultured layman who had read Vergil and Horace. His *Indiculus luminosus* is a polemical anti-Islamic work complemented by the judgments expressed in the *Vita Eulogii*. Alvarus the theologian is revealed above all in his *Epistulae*; his fame, however, is mostly due to his poetic talents. He was the most accurate of the Mozarabic poets: he tried to reach the artistic heights of Eugenio de Toledo (his subject matter is very similar), but was not successful.

The tension provoked by the persecutions in al-Andalus gave rise to differences between the most strict Christians and those that, with their dominators, opted for compromise; the fiercest example among these conflicts was that of the steadfast Sansón of Córdoba and the inconstant Hostigesis of Málaga. Because the first is the only source of the second, the root of the conflict is not clear: needless to say, the *Apologeticus* demonstrates a vehemence not found even in the anti-Islamic literature.

The tenth century is dominated by the Mozarabic diaspora, which would bring with it a multitude of books only preserved by the Mozarabs. Apart from these, a biography of the child Pelayo by a priest named Raguel, along with the *Libellus a regula Sancti Benedicti subtractus* by Salvo de Albelda, are the only works of much importance that have reached our times. Introducing what would be a major cultural focus in the next century, Lupito de Barcelona composed a *Tractatus de astrolabio* that attained significant exposure throughout Europe.

With respect to poetry, one notable work is the *Epithalamium Leodegundiae*, probably of Navarrese origin. In the Ripoll monastery, a few compositions of certain quality were written in the Latin European style, "a la europea."

The eleventh century is the period of the great dispute between the supporters of European integration under the rule of the papacy and the supporters of the old Hispanic traditions. It is the century of the Cluniac mission in Spain, the introduction of the Roman liturgy, and the conquest of Toledo. The most original literary works come from Catalonia, and more specifically from the Ripoll region, where the production that began in the previous century continued. Among literary figures, both Olibas stand out: the first, from Vic, was abbot of Cuixá, bishop of Vic, and the son of the count of Besalú, and was an accomplished letter writer and a scholastic poet. The second, from Ripoll, was a scientific writer of mathematics, astronomy, and musicology. Homobono de Barcelona also flourished in the Catalan area—he was a cleric who summarized and updated the compilation of Visigothic law in a work named *Liber iudicum popularis*.

The question of the Roman liturgy imposed by the Cluniacs provoked a whole series of lively works both in favor and in opposition to the reform—the majority of the works against the phenomenon have been lost. In part because of the influence of European satire in the work, and in part because of its decidedly anti-Roman atmosphere, it is probable that the composition of the *Garsuinis* or *Tractatus de reliquiis preciosorum martyrum Albini et Rufini* was connected to the antireform faction. This Hispanic work is a cruel and agile satire of simony (we are in the age of investiture) and the reprehensible life of the Roman Curia. Of a different vein, and with epic characteristics, is the *Carmen Campidoctoris* on the subject of El Cid (likely composed in Ripoll at the end of the century), written in Sapphic meter by someone that may have known the protagonist.

The overall importance of the twelfth century should be emphasized, as should the fact that this period in Spain does not exactly correspond to twelfth-century Europe; among the works of literary production, the *Gesta Roderici* stands out as a narrative without plot in which very reliable anecdotes of the Cid and his world are juxtaposed. In Iberian historiography, this work is complemented by the famous *Historia Silense*, a very polemical work by a very erudite author that never quite reached its intended chronological scope (the final years of the eleventh century), but that radiates Leonese patriotism.

The *Chronica Adefonsi Imperatoris*, written around 1148, is of interest as much for its subject matter—the reign of Alfonso VII—as for the addition at the end of an epic composition in hexameter that has been designated *Poema de Almería*, and includes an imitation of the time-honored "catalogs" of the *Iliad* or the *Aeneid*. The *Crónica Najerense* is a history *ab origine mundi* covering up to the reign of Alfonso VI that, apropos of the siege of Zamora, glosses what Entwistle considers a *Carmen de morte Sanctii regis*. Both histories pose the problem of the questionable existence of a medieval Hispanic Latin epic. The *Historia Compostellana* (ending abruptly with the year 1139) is not so much a history of that diocese as a *gesta* (chronicle of deeds) about Diego Gelmírez, its first archbishop. It displays both the verisimilitude of its contemporary setting and the drawbacks inherent in an imagined history; nevertheless, from a literary point of view these qualities make the history a key work of peninsular Latin literature.

The best known figure of the twelfth century is the Aragónese *converso* (Christian convert) Pedro Alfonso, who was the physician of Alfonso el Batallador and a prolific author. His works include a treatise, *De Astronomia*, a *Dialogus contra judaeos*, and the first European example of an apology of Oriental extraction, the *Disciplina clericalis*. The work is a series of exempla that the author, with a certain degree of impudence, presents as a *via ad caelum* (path to heaven) for enlighted readers.

In terms of poetry, aside from the Latin compositions of epic style, almost all religious and secular literary production takes place in Ripoll or the surrounding regions, and are by anonymous authors. Among these works are the *Carmina Rivipulliensia*, twenty compositions—probably of Hispanic origin—of Goliardic nature with amorous subject matter.

With the exception of certain liturgical compositions (above all of the Ripoll and Montserrat schools) and the poem *Rithmi de Iulia Romula seu Ispalensi Urbe* by Guillermo Pérez de la Calzada (1250), all of the notable works of the thirteenth century are in prose, and most are histories. Lucas de Túy, who studied in Italy and joined the crusade against the Albigensians in France, became bishop of Túy and composed a *Chronicon mundi* inspired by Isidore of Seville and a curious hagiographic work, *De miraculis sancti Isidori liber*. More important was Rodrigo Ximénez de Rada, the archbishop of Toledo and author of the *Historia Gothica* (1243), a work that served as a basis for Alfonsine historiography and for less important histories of considerable quality and interest: *Historia Arabum*, *Historia Romanorum*, *Ostrogothorum Historia*, etc.

Juan Gil de Zamora, a collaborator of Alfonso X, wrote a *Tractatus Historiae Canonicae et Civilis*, a biographical collection with moral aims: his *De preconiis civitatis Numantinae* and *De preconiis Hispaniae* are representative of the patriotic current of the period.

Diego García "de Campos," chancellor of Enrique I, was the author of a surprising work of scholastic content and deep erudition entitled *Planeta*, in which he shows off a unique yet overwrought style. Of a very different nature is the work by the Galician, Alvaro Pelayo, who studied in Italy and wrote an allegation in favor of papal supremacy, *De planctu ecclesiae*; a treatise of political theory for the instruction of princes, *Speculum regum*; and an exegetical work.

Rámon Llull (ca. 1235–1316), a Mallorcan of encyclopedic intellect, is a special case. He composed more than five hundred works of an essentially Platonic/Augustinian character. Despite his beatific status, the church always considered him with suspicion. His *Ars Magna*, about the organization of the universe, stands out amid his prolific production. Among his writings there are works of theology, astronomy, mathematics, medicine, and even enlightened spiritual meditation. The first formalization of the Catalan language owes itself to Llull.

José Manuel Díaz de Bustamante

Bibliography:

Díaz y Díaz, M. C. *Index Scriptorum Latinorum Medii Aevi Hispanorum*, Madrid, 1959.

Moralejo Alvarez, J. L. "Literatura hispano-latina (siglos V–XVI)." In *Historia de las literaturas hispánicas no castellanas*. Ed. J. M. Díez Borque. Madrid, 1980. 14–137.

Rico Manrique F. "Las letras latinas del siglo XII en Galicia, León y Castilla," *Abaco* 2 (1962), 1–120.

LAURENTIUS HISPANUS

Laurentius Hispanus's birthplace and date are unknown; he died in 1248. He studied law at the University of Bologna, where he was a disciple of, among others, the Romanist Azzo; he also taught canon law there between 1210 and 1215. Among his likely disciples were Tancredo de Bolonia and Bartolomé de Brescia. Documentation of the Cathedral of Orense shows Laurentius as *maestrescuela* (schoolmaster) in 1214, 1215, and 1218. He was the bishop of Orense from 1218 or 1219 until 1248. Besides his activities in the Orense diocese, he was entrusted with various assignments in other dioceses by the popes Honorius III, Gregory IX, and Innocent IV in letters directed to him or mentioning him. His works, produced in Bologna before 1215, set him apart as one of the best canonists of his time. They include: (1) *Apparatus* to the *Decretum* of Gratian, preserved in a fairly inconsistent manuscript; (2) *Glossa Palatina*, which seems to represent the last phase of his *Apparatus* to the *Decretum* (many of Laurentius's glosses on the *Decretum* made their way into the celebrated *Glossa Ordinaria*; in fact, a considerable group of fourteenth-century manuscripts, known as *Laurentiustyp* (Laurentian type) explicitly attribute many glosses to Laurentius); (3) *Apparatus* to the *Tractatus de poenitentia* from the *Decretum* of Gratian; (4–5) isolated glosses on the *Compilatio prima antiqua* and the *Compilatio secunda antiqua*, written before 1210; (6) *Apparatus* to the *Compilatio tertia antiqua*; and (7) possible commentaries on the constitutions of the Fourth Lateran Council of 1215, but none of these has been found.

ANTONIO GARCÍA Y GARCÍA

Bibliography

García y García, A. *Laurentius Hispanus. Datos biográficos y estudio crítico de sus obras*. Rome, 1956.

Stickler, M. "Il decretista Laurentius Hispanus," *Studia Gratiana* 9. (1966), 461–549.

LAW, CANON

Each section that follows discusses the period's important texts and figures associated with canon law.

1. Roman/Visigothic Period (Fourth through Seventh Centuries)

Canon law texts of the Roman period (fourth and fifth centuries) were established by councils and various papal letters. The earliest Hispanic council was that of Elvira (ca. 295–314), followed by the first Council of Zaragoza (380), and the first Council of Toledo (400). Among the pontifical documents addressing disciplinary matters (decretals), the letter from Pope Siricius to Himerius, archbishop of Tarragona (385), stands out.

With the creation of the Visigothic kingdom in the Iberian Peninsula and the south of France, conciliar activity was reactivated, and flourished particularly during the Visigothic era (sixth and seventh centuries), with the Councils of Toledo (I–XVII), Tarragona, Girona, Barcelona (I–II), Lérida, Valencia, Braga (I–III), Narbona, Seville (I–II), Zaragoza (II–III), Huesca, and Mérida. Pontifical letters in this period were also more abundant than they were in the Roman period. The Visigothic era is divided into two clearly distinct periods: the Arian era and the Catholic era, which began with the conversion of Recared, made official in the Third Council of Toledo (589).

Several different canonical collections were formed based on the councils and the papal decretals, including the *Capitula Martini*, the Spanish *Epitome*, the collection of Novara, and other lost compilations. These canonical anthologies culminated in the *Hispana* (ca. 634), a collection that not only reveals much about the life of the Visigothic monarchy and church, but also about the Mozarabic world and the Christian culture of the Reconquest up until the mid-twelfth century.

2. Early Middle Ages (Eighth through Twelfth Centuries)

With the fall of the Iberian Peninsula to the Muslims, the Visigothic political apparatus broke down, with only faint traces apparent in the Christian kingdoms of the Reconquest. Visigothic canon law, on the other hand, which was more universal in nature, managed to survive not only in medieval Iberia, but also beyond the Pyrenees. The codices of the *Hispana* traveled with some of their owners to Merovingian and Carolingian territories, where some can still be found. In Charlemagne's time, the *Hispana* was included in the *Dacheriana*, which was the most important collection of canon texts in the Carolingian empire in the first half of the eleventh century, and continued to be influential until the end of the century. In the middle of the ninth century in the same kingdom, a series of falsified canonical texts were produced; these writings were known as pseudo-Isidorean decretals because of the pseudonym used by the compiler. The "Hispana" appeared in a number of these spurious collections, although as a distorted and manipulated version. These false decretals exerted enormous influence in the Latin church until the mid-twelfth century.

During this period, two canon law movements from beyond the Pyrenees can be observed, both of which influence Iberian culture to a certain extent; this influence is, however, quite small, due to the consistency of Visigothic ecclesiastical law already contained in the *Hispana*. The first of these trends, which was especially strong in the Celtic and Anglo-Saxon churches, was the increasing presence of the penitential books that were well known in continental Europe. In the Iberian Peninsula, only a few *Libri Poenitentiales* are known: the *Albeldense* (976), the *Silense* (late tenth century), and the *Pseudojeronimiano* (eighth and ninth centuries). The other movement was the ecclesiastical reformation of the eleventh century that became known as the Gregorian reformation because one of its greatest proponents was Pope Gregory VII (1073–1085). In terms of its effect on legatine councils (directed by papel legates) and papal documents, this reform had a noticeable influence in the Hispanic world. On the level of canonical collections, however, its impact only reaches Catalonia, where two compilations of Gregorian tendency were created, presently known as the *Liber Tarraconensis* and the *Collectio Caesaraugustana*.

Visigothic canon law, therefore, informed the way of life of the Iberian church and society until the middle of the twelfth century, when it was replaced by medieval Roman canon law.

3. Late Middle Ages (Twelfth through Fifteenth Centuries)

Until the mid-twelfth century, canonical texts were collected successively and superimposed in countless canonical compilations. But around 1140–1150, Johannes Gratian, a Camaldolese monk, published his *Concordia discordantium canonum* (known historically as *Decretum*) at the University of Bologna. As the original title indicates, Gratian chose not to simply place the texts together in a random or chronological order, but rather to set them in opposition and compare them, thereby introducing Aristotelian logic and dialectic to the canonical text, and giving rise to a science and systematization of canon law. As mentioned, there were roughly eight hundred Visigothic canonical texts; Gratian's new approach essentially wiped out all previously circulating canonical collections, among them the *Hispana*, whose texts, save those that had the fortune to be incorporated into Gratian's *Decretum*, became objects of historification.

For the duration of the Middle Ages, the *Decretum* was the canon law text used in schools and in forums throughout the Christian Latin world. Medieval church fathers would supplement these legal texts with collections of their own decretals, giving rise to those collections making up the *Corpus iuris canonici*: the *Liber Extra* or decretals of Gregory IX (1234), the *Liber Sextus* of Boniface VIII (1298), decretals of Clement (1317), *Extravagantes* of John XXII (1325), and *Extravagantes Comunes* (1500, 1503). These compilations were in use in the Roman church, including that of the Iberian Peninsula, for the rest of the Middle Ages.

Apart from these general collections of ecclesiastical law, there were various unofficial private collections of pontifical letters or decretals produced in Iberia, including the *Collectio Seguntina*, *Collectiones Dertusenses I–III*, *Collectiones Alcobacenses I–III*, and the *Collectio Romana*, compiled by Bernardus Compostelanus Antiquo in Bologna. The first three date from the late twelfth century, and the other two from the early thirteenth century. (The decretals of Gregory IX were compiled by another Iberian, San Raimundo de Peñafort.)

Among Hispanic canon law experts of this period, the group associated with the University of Bologna in the late twelfth and early thirteenth centuries is especially notable: Melendus Hispanus, Petrus Hispanus, Laurentius Hispanus, Vincentius Hispanus, Bernardus Compostelanus Antiquo, San Raimundo de Peñafort, Ioannes Hispanus de Petesella (de Compostela), João de Deus, and others. In the fourteenth century, authors such as Alvaro Pelagio and Juan de Torquemada stand out. In the fourteenth and fifteenth centuries there was a group of notable *canonistas* at the University of Salamanca, including Juan Alfonso de Benavente, Juan González, Juan de Castilla, and Gonzalo García de Villadiego.

In order to apply canon law on a local level, annual councils and synods were organized. A study and edition of these texts in medieval Iberia can be consulted in the *Synodicon hispanum*.

ANTONIO GARCÍA Y GARCÍA

Bibliography

García y García, A. "La canonística ibérica medieval posterior al *Decreto* de Graciano." *Repertorio de Historia de las Ciencias Eclesiásticas en España* 1 (1967), 397–434; 2 (1971), 183–214; and 5 (1976), 351–402.

———. *Iglesia, Sociedad y Derecho* 1 (1985), 164–96 and 2 (1987), 75–91.

García y García, A. (ed.) *Synodicon hispanum*. Vols. 1–4. Madrid, 1981–87.

Martínez Díez, G., and F. Rodríguez. *La Colección Canónica Hispana*. Vols. 1–4. Madrid, 1966–84.
Orlandis, J., and D. Ramos Lisón. *Historia de los concilios de la España romana y visigoda*. Pamplona, 1986.

LAW, CIVIL

Civil law as treated here consists of certain legal traditions and of the law they informed that was made by secular authorities in the Asturian-Leonese-Castilian kingdom. This same law influenced that of other peninsular kingdoms and in time came to dominate even as regional differences continued to be valid in the postmedieval world.

The private law of the Hispano-Romans had its sources in the writings by certain lawyers of the imperial era; in collections, codices, and *novellae* published by the emperors; and in elements from indigenous customary law. The sources of public law were the dispositions known as *datae* and *dictae*, magisterial edicts, imperial constitutions, and other imperial ordinances pertaining to Hispania. Justinian's law may be presumed to have been introduced during Byzantine occupation of southern parts of the Iberian Peninsula for at least seventy-five years, beginning in the middle of the sixth century.

In the Visigothic kingdom of Toledo, which flourished in the sixth and seventh centuries, religious and cultural attitudes are cited as causes of the failure of legal compilations made during the two preceding centuries to prosper. More enduring was the seventh-century *Liber iudiciorum*, or *Lex Visigothorum*, a code of twelve books, in the revision of 681, that represented a combination of existing Visigothic law and pre-Justinian Roman law applicable territorially (that is, to all the inhabitants). Amendments, including a preliminary title on public law appended during this period, were added during the early years of the Reconquest; the result is called the *Lex Visigothorum vulgata*. The *Liber iudiciorum* has been said to have enjoyed, next to Justinian's legislation, a wider authority for a longer time than any other code of law. Apart from the royal law mentioned, popular customary legal elements sometimes entered the law, and they prevailed in areas where non-Visigothic traditions had a long history.

The period from 711 to 1248 covers the apogee of Muslim power in the peninsula and the uneven progress by the Christians that eventuated in the latter's victory. In law the period may be described as one of diversity and complexity that corresponded to the territorial fragmentation of Hispania into kingdoms whose boundaries changed frequently and whose independence at times was ephemeral. The numerous local laws that appeared were influenced to varying degrees by pre-Roman law, vulgar Roman law, Germanic customary law (Castile), and Frankish law (Catalonia). The Roman distinction between private and public law fell into disuse. Newly created law derived from custom, royal legislation consisting of dispositions announced in the presence of the royal council for territorial application, seigneurial and conciliar (municipal) administrative standards, and sentences. The last originated in the decisions made in Germanic popular assemblies; in time they evolved into decisions made by judges acting for the whole, later into the decisions (*juicios de albedrío*) made by judges acting according to the legal merits of the case, and finally into the binding precedents known as *fazañas*.

The various sources of law may be described as general, territorial, and privilege. With both a general norm and territorial application, the *Liber iudiciorum vulgata* continued to undergo change as it became known as the *Forum iudicum*. It took root in León and Aragón but was rejected by Castilians when they established their independence from the Leonese in the middle of the tenth century. (The story of their burning all copies of the code merely symbolized local sentiment.)

Territorial law grew more slowly, contributing royal legislation, private written collections of juridical norms (unsystematic in their earliest redactions), and municipal law (notably the *fueros extensos*). In León such law included the Laws of 1017 and the Decrees of Coyanza (c. 1055) and León (1188); in Castile the *cortes* (parliament) of Nájera (1217–1218), the *Libro de los fueros de Castilla* (c. 1248), the *Fuero víejo de Castilla* (*c*. 1248), and the statements of enactments resulting from particular cortes (*ordenamientos de cortes*) as well as other works; in Navarre and Aragón the Fueros de Aragón, or *Código de Huesca* (1247) that derived from the *Fuero general de Navarra*, the fueros of Jaca and Tudela, and private territorial compilations; and in Catalonia the *capitulares* of Frankish kings and the collection known as the *Usatici* (*Usatges*, redactions from 1086 to 1251).

Laws of privilege may be classified according to their local application (municipal fueros such as those of León, Benavente, Toledo, Cuenca-Teruel, and many others, whether individual or in a series or family; *costums* in Catalonia) or to their application to a person (foundation charters for towns, privileges of one kind or another to an individual), or to a class (nobles, ecclesiastics, merchants, religious groups, foreigners). The complexity of the situation, only hinted here, is underlined by the use of different laws in appellate courts. Where laws were in conflict, the tendency was for the law of the judge's seat to prevail. When possible, local law was preferred to the law of higher or larger units.

The extensive conquests realized by the Christians at the expense of the Muslims in the first half of the thirteenth century made apparent the need for new territorial legislation. The resulting realization of plans was facilitated by contact with scholars involved in the revival of knowledge of Roman law by way of Justinian's legislation, by the preparation of a canon law for the ecclesiastical world and of a *ius commune* (made up of a mixture of Roman, canon, and feudal law) for the secular world, and by the examples provided by compilations of both canon law (*Decretals*, 1234) and secular territorial law (Valencia, 1238; Aragón, 1247).

A reversal of the previous trend toward fragmentation in the peninsula now led in the direction of integration, helped in the case of Castile and León by the final union (1230) of the two crowns and rationalized in citing the memory of legislative unity associated with the Visigothic kingdom, a situation in contrast to the confusion generated when a multiplicity of laws appeared in the same area. Early examples of the royal policy in favor of unification or standardization were the spread of the *Forum iudicum* in its Romance translation, the *Fuero juzgo* (1241), and certain municipal fueros (Toledo, Seville) that incorporated all or parts of the *Fuero juzgo* during the reigns of Fernando III and Alfonso X. Alfonso sought to strengthen the policy by using a similar system for disseminating the *Espéculo* and the *Fuero real*, but economic and political circumstances combined to thwart his efforts.

A contest arose between traditionalist elements who benefited from customary law and the royal patrons of territorialized legislation. A second contest originated when the official prohibition of legal sources from outside the realm began in the middle of the thirteenth century. The prohibition represented royal reaction against common law, but the reaction quickly weakened as both common and commercial law infiltrated the judiciary and the university-trained personnel who then propagated it. From the middle of the thirteenth century to the end of the fifteenth, the sources of created law in Castile consisted mainly of royal legislation (*Ordenamientos de Cortes*), charters of privilege, letters of various types and other documents used in government and administration, legal codes, judicial decisions, *Leyes nuevas* (a private written collection of the clarifications and interpretations of codified law, mainly Alfonsine), the *Leyes del estilo* (interpretations made in the royal tribunal), and custom (already losing importance unless it applied to the whole kingdom).

The territorial law created in the court of Alfonso X languished officially from 1272 until 1348, when Alfonso XI, in the *Ordenamiento de Alcalá*, established the order of precedence of codes used in resolving a legal question: the *Ordenamiento* itself, active and valid municipal fueros (hence including the *Fuero real*), the *Siete Partidas*, and royal sentences. From 1433 to 1504 efforts to prepare a royally approved compilation culminated in the *Copilaçión de leyes* (1484) of Alonso Díaz de Montalvo.

ROBERT A. MACDONALD

Bibliography

Gacto Fernández, E., J. A. Alejandre García, and J. M. García Marín. *El derecho histórico de los pueblos de España*. 5th ed. Madrid, 1988.

Pérez-Prendes y Muñoz de Arracó, J. M. *Curso de historia del derecho español*. 4th ed. Madrid, 1984.

LAW, ISLAMIC

The history of Islamic law in al-Andalus begins with the introduction of the legal school of the Syrian jurist Al-Awzāʿī (d. 774) during the reign of ʿAbd al-Raḥmān I (r. 756–788). Al-Awzāʿī's system was rudimentary and relied primarily on the "living tradition," that is, the uninterrupted practice of the Muslims, as verified by the scholars, extending from the time of the Prophet through much of the Umayyad period in the East. For geopolitical reasons this Syrian legal tradition appealed to the Umayyad regime in Spain, which opposed the ʿAbbāsid caliphate in Baghdad, and its simplicity and the attention it devoted to military problems were well suited to a country only recently conquered and minimally Islamized.

During the reigns of Hishām I (788–796) and Al-Ḥakam I (796–822) the school (*madhhab*) of the Medinese jurist Mālik ibn Anas (d. 796) began to supersede that of Al-Awzāʿī. It became the "official" school of law under ʿAbd al-Raḥmān II (r. 822–852) and maintained its preeminence in al-Andalus until the fall of Naṣrid Granada in 1492. The promoters of this change were Andalusian jurists (*fuqahā'*) who had studied in Medina with Mālik himself or with his disciples, and who brought to Spain Mālik's great legal work *Al-Muwaṭṭa'* (The Smoothed Path). The most important among them, especially Yaḥyā ibn Yaḥyā al-Laythī (d. 848), gradually formed a school and propagated Mālikī doctrine with the support of the Umayyad emirs.

Mālikī law, like that of the other schools of Sunnī Islam, is based on the Qur'ān and the Sunna (the sayings and actions of the prophet Muḥammad and his companions conveyed in traditions, or *ḥadīth*s, and established as legally binding precedents). The *Muwaṭṭa'* studied by the Andalusian jurists of the eighth and ninth centuries constituted the foundation for the further development of Mālikī jurisprudence and was, in essence, Mālik's codification and systematization of the law in accordance with the consensus of scholarly opinion in Medina, his supreme criterion. Mālik considered and interpreted *ḥadīth*s in the light of his own reasoning and the local legal tradition.

Mālikism triumphed because it responded to the needs of a rapidly changing and increasingly complex Hispano-Muslim society. Islamic law, which treats both religious and secular concerns, acted as an integrative and stabilizing force in al-Andalus by providing a common Islamic framework to an ethnically diverse Muslim population composed of Arabs, Berbers, and a growing body of New Muslims. The general adherence of Andalusian Muslims to one school of law, Mālikism, enhanced orthodoxy, particularly when that school privileged the tradition of Medina, the cradle of Islam, where the Prophet had enunciated Qur'ānic and non-Qur'anic (contained in *ḥadīths*) legislation. Moreover, the Umayyad emirs and caliphs promoted Mālikism, and allowed the jurists influence in the government. They did so because they needed the support of the jurists, who, by virtue of their knowledge and piety, enjoyed great prestige among the urban populace, and because a rigid Mālikī orthodoxy shielded al-Andalus from external religiopolitical threats.

During the Umayyad period the Mālikī jurists largely devoted themselves to the study of the manuals of jurisprudence of Mālik and his most important disciples, the Egyptian Ibn al-Qāsim (d. 806) and Saḥnūn (d. 854) of Kairouan. In focusing exclusively on works of positive law (*furū'*)—that is, the law as practically applied in the form of the master's and his disciples' responses (*masā'il*) to specific problems—they neglected the study of the sources of the law (*uṣūl*), such as *ḥadīth*s, which formed the base of Mālik's system. Typical of this mode of scholarship were the *Wāḍiḥa* of Ibn Ḥabīb (d. 845), a commentary on Mālik's *Muwaṭṭa'*, and the *'Utbīya* of Al-'Utbī (d. 869), a collection of the responses of the great Mālikī jurists. Hence, Andalusian Mālikism was reduced to a strict adherence to and servile imitation of the teaching of the master (*taqlīd*). While Mālikī jurists had, to a certain degree, to take local realities into account when making legal decisions, independent interpretation (*ijtihād*) of the sources of the law was proscribed and the development of a jurisprudential method was impeded.

Still, even with the dominance of a rigid and conservative Mālikī school, Andalusian jurists were influenced by important developments in the field of law occurring in the East. Most influential were the ideas of Muḥammad ibn Idris al-Shāfi'ī (767–820), who was primarily responsible for formulating what would become the classical doctrine of Islamic jurisprudence. According to Al-Shāfi'ī, legal reasoning was to be based on the four sources (*uṣūl*) of the law: the Qur'ān; the Sunna, now identified solely with the divinely inspired practice of the Prophet, which had to be verified through the criticism of *ḥadīths*; the consensus (*ijmā'*) of the entire Muslim community, as opposed to the more limited consensus of the scholars of Medina; and strict analogical reasoning (*qiyās*), which must have as its starting point the revealed sources (Qur'ān and Sunna).

In al-Andalus the practical result of the infiltration of Shāfi'ī ideas, which took place with the tacit approval of Emir Muḥammad I (r. 852–866), was the development of a school of *ḥadīth*. The forerunner of this school was Muḥammad ibn Waḍḍāh (d. 900); he had studied with the great traditionists in the East and he adopted al-Shāfi'ī's method of *ḥadīth* criticism. But it was Baqī ibn Makhlad (d. 901) who was the real protagonist of jurisprudential reform in al-Andalus. He, too, studied in the East, and was the first to bring works of al-Shāfi'ī into Spain. Baqī was not attached to a particular legal school, and because so many students in Córdoba were attracted to his teaching, he came into conflict with the Mālikī jurists. However, the emir protected Baqī, and as a result the solid foundations of a school of *ḥadīth* were laid. The fact that many of the followers of Ibn Waḍḍāh and Baqī ibn Makhlad were adherents of the Mālikī school allowed for some reconciliation between the students of *ḥadīth* and the conservative Mālikī jurists.

Simultaneous with the infiltration of Shāfi'ism, the Ẓāhirī school entered Al-Andalus. Founded in Iraq by Dāwūd ibn 'Alī (d. 883), this school expounded the principle that law should be based only on the literal and evident (*ẓāhir*) meaning of the texts of the Qur'ān and the *ḥadīth*s. An Andulusian disciple of Dāwūd, 'Abd Allāh ibn Qasim, introduced Zāhirism at Córdoba during the reign of Muḥammad I. In the tenth century the most notable Ẓāhirī was Mundhir ibn Sa'īd al-Ballūṭī (d. 966), a jurist, theologian, and judge of Córdoba. Ultimately neither Shāfi'ism nor Ẓāhirism presented an effective challenge to the government supported Mālikī orthodoxy prevalent in al-Andalus. In fact, the followers of the Shāfi'ī and Ẓāhirī schools, when they functioned as magistrates and jurisconsults, felt compelled to conform to Mālikī doctrine in practice, as did Al-Ballūṭī. Furthermore, the study of *ḥadīth*s, which had emerged with such promise in the ninth century, slowed considerably in the tenth century as the powerful caliph 'Abd al-Raḥmān III (r. 912–961) reduced the jurists to the role of government functionaries, which diverted them from more scholarly pursuits. Consequently, if the ideas of Al-Shāfi'ī and the return to the sources of the law contributed to some invigoration of a Mālikism excessively confined by *taqlīd*, the tangible results were, by the end of the caliphal period, limited.

The political and cultural decentralization of the era of the party kings (1009–1091) provided somewhat more freedom to the adherents of the Ẓāhirī and Shāfiʿī schools, and at the same time were conducive to an internal renewal of Andalusian Mālikism. The great Ibn Ḥazm of Córdoba (d. 1064) abandoned the Mālikī doctrine in which he was first educated for the Shāfiʿī school and undertook a study of *ḥadīth* in Shāfiʿī fashion; his subsequent rejection of analogical reasoning, one of the foundations of Shāfiʿism, led him, finally, to become a zealous proponent of Ẓāhirism. Wishing to challenge the dominance of the Mālikī school, he attacked it for its *taqlīd* and its privileging of the practice and consensus of Medina. However, Ibn Ḥazm, who tried to reconstruct Islamic law as it was in the time of the Prophet and his companions by eliminating those elements he believed had been added by later jurists, has been criticized for ignoring the social and political context within which the law developed and for being, therefore, more impractical than the Mālikī jurists he criticized.

The internal renewal of Mālikism involved the study of other legal schools and their methods, at times for polemical purposes, and a far greater interest in the sources of the law and in jurisprudential methodology. Its most representative figures were Ibn ʿAbd al-Barr (d. 1070) and Al-Bājī (d. 1081). The career of Ibn ʿAbd al-Barr followed a course opposite to that of his friend Ibn Ḥazm: he first inclined toward Ẓāhirism, then left it for Shāfiʿism, and finally became a Mālikī judge in Lisbon, though maintaining certain Shāfiʿī tendencies. He rejected the *taqlīd* characteristic of tenth-century Mālikism and gained a reputation as the best traditionist of his day. Al-Bājī was the great defender of Andalusian Mālikism. He debated with Ibn Ḥazm on Mallorca in 1047, and among his various works on Mālikī law were some devoted to polemics with other schools on the principles of jurisprudential method. In his acceptance of analogical reasoning, though in a manner more restricted than Al-Shāfiʿī, Al-Bājī evidences the change that Andulusian Mālikism was undergoing, for the early Mālikīs had not acknowledged this mode of legal reasoning.

Under the Almoravid regime (1090–1145), Mālikism regained an uncontested supremacy in al-Andalus. The legalism and moral austerity of the Almoravids, while resulting in a resurgence of the literature on positive law, did not mean an abandonment of the study of jurisprudential method, for the science of *uṣūl* had become well integrated into Andalusian Mālikism.

Almohad rule (1147–1232) was, from an ideological perspective, uncongenial to the Mālikī jurists, who had been supporters of the Almoravids. The Almohads, for instance, criticized the Mālikīs for their excessive reliance on the established authorities of their school, instead of focusing more rigorously on the sources of the law. However, in practice, even though they showed favor to some Ẓāhirī jurists, the Almohads ultimately were forced to conciliate with the popular Mālikī jurists and to leave the existing judicial system in place. The most illustrious legal thinker of the Almohad era was Averroës (Ibn Rushd, 1126–1198). A Mālikī from a family of jurists, he served as judge of Seville and then of Córdoba. His great work of jurisprudence, the *Bidāya* (Beginning [for those attempting individual interpretation]), analyzes the differences between the diverse schools of law, especially with respect to their modes of deducing decisions from the law's sources. Yet the work is not a polemical defense of Mālikism; rather, it is marked by a spirit of objective criticism and an exacting rationality.

In the Naṣrid sultanate of Granada (1232–1492) the Mālikī jurists continued to play a preeminent role by virtue of their social prestige, influence with the sultan, and teaching in the *madrasa* (school) of Granada founded by Yūsuf I in 1349. The legal opinions (*fatwā*) of leading jurists, such as Al-Shātibī and Ibn Sirāj, show that in its final centuries Andalusian Mālikism continued to adapt to changing social and political conditions.

MARK D. MEYERSON

Bibliography

Brunschvig, R. "Averroès juriste." In *Études d'orientalisme dédiées à la mémoire de Lévi-Provençal*. Vol. 1. Paris, 1962, 35–68.

Lévi-Provençal, E. *Histoire de l'Espagne musulmane*. 3 vols. Paris, 1950–53.

Makkī, M. A. *Ensayo sobre las aportaciones orientales en la España musulmana y su influencia en la formación de la cultura hispano-árabe*. Madrid, 1968.

Monés, H. "Le rôle des hommes de religion dans l'histoire de l'Espagne musulmane jusqu'a la fin du califat." *Studia Islamica* 20 (1964), 47–88.

Urvoy, D. *Le monde des ulemas andalous du V/XIe au VII/XIIIe siècle: Étude sociologique*. Geneva, 1978.

LAW, JEWISH

The Bible (particularly the Torah, or Pentateuch) is, of course, the foundation of Jewish law. Of primary importance, however, is the Talmud, which constitutes the rabbinical exegesis and development of that law over a period of nearly five hundred years. In Spain, from at least the tenth century, the rabbis studied and interpreted this law and added significantly to it. It was Moses b. Maimon (Maimonides) whose work laid the most important foundation for the medieval development of Jewish law, not only in Spain but throughout the world.

Developments in Jewish law in Spain (paralleled, though in a less significant way, in other lands) consisted of commentaries on the Talmud, rabbinical responsa, and independent books of customs and laws. Jewish law covered all of life, since there is no separate concept of "religion." Indeed, what we would call "civil law" played a far more prominent role than ceremonial or cult observances. The autonomy of Jewish community control was scrupulously observed by the kings in Spain, and local Jewish courts (the *bet din*) adjudicated disputes over contracts, property rights, partnerships, marriage and divorce, and all other aspects of life. Matters that were either too complex for the local court to decide, or were only of a theoretical nature, were referred to leading rabbinical scholars for their decision (the responsa). Other important interpretations, which often became legal precedent, were set down by these same scholars in their numerous Talmudic commentaries. Many of these were cited by subsequent rabbis in their responsa, or were codified in such major legal compendia as the *Ṭur* (technically, *Arbaʿah ṭurim* (four rows), referring to the four divisions of laws) of Jacob ben Asher (fourteenth century). Another major independent legal codification composed in Spain was that of Isaac al-Fāsī (twelfth century), which to an extent served as a model for Maimonides.

Independent treatises on laws and customs are almost too numerous to detail. Examples include works by Judah ben Barzilai (eleventh–twelfth centuries), Moses ben Naḥman (Nahmanides), Jonah Gerundi, and perhaps especially Abraham ben Natan's *Sēfer ha-manhig* (Book of Custom, or Practice), which, along with similar works of Menaḥem ha-Meiri of Provence, was the most important of that genre.

Spanish Jews nevertheless routinely utilized Gentile courts (Muslim and Christian), even when this clearly was against Jewish law. The kings were personally the court of last appeal (sometimes even of first resort) and were required to know Jewish law. Spanish rabbis had the greatest respect for their kings, and often referred to Spanish law in their own responsa or commentaries. A unique feature of Jewish law in Spain was the right of capital punishment, particularly for the *malshin* (informer).

Norman Roth

Bibliography

Peres-Prendes, J. M. "Sobre la pervivencia del derecho privado de los comunidades sefardíes" and "Apuntes para la bibliografía histórica del derecho hebreo." In *Actas del primero simposio de estudios sefardiés*. Madrid, 1970.

Roth, N. "Dar 'una voz' a los judíos: Representación en la España medieval." *Anuario de Historia del Derecho Español* (1986), 943–52.

LAWYERS

Despite a number of fine studies of law and judicial institutions in medieval Iberian kingdoms, no systematic research has been done on lawyers as a group in any of them. Traditional styles of scholarship on law and institutions have not provided a fertile ground for a social history of legists. Nevertheless, given the importance of jurists in the late Middle Ages, the lack of a prosopographical study of the group in any community or period is shocking, since the political and intellectual developments in the area of law were to some extent an expression of lawyers' interests and aspirations. Without this context it is hard to grasp the significance for contemporaries of the work of men of the law who served as codifiers, judges, prelates, and bureaucrats with increasing prominence.

Who were these men? Any study of lawyers will have to discover their career paths, their social and regional origins, their marriage patterns, their business activities, their opportunities for political action, their lifestyles, and their characteristic religious and social attitudes. Especially in the early period, from the late twelfth century, the legal experts were itinerant. (Their mobility will be a major hurdle for scholars, who may find it wise to work as a group using a computer-linked data bank for nominal record linkage.)

How and where were they educated? Until the late thirteenth century Bologna was the mother of jurists in the Iberian Peninsula, sending its graduates west and receiving, initially from Catalonia, Iberians among its students and teachers. In the fourteenth century the *studia* of Montpellier and Toulouse became important centers of legal training, although Bologna reasserted its role, at least for Castilians, with the establishment of the Spanish College through a bequest by Cardinal Gil Albornoz. However, as law graduates became more important to their ecclesiastical, royal, and seignorial employers, domestic institutions at Coimbra and Salamanca (among others) began to undermine the traditional internationalism of universities. Indeed, the transition from a group of itinerant, cosmopolitan internationalists and the political impact of this change would be an important part of any study of medieval Iberian lawyers.

Of course, to deal with questions like these, it will be necessary to define carefully who should be included in the study. Here it would be best to use the broad category "men of the law" so that notaries and procurators can be included with attorneys, since all of these professionals played a role in the emergence of family dynasties of jurists. Moreover, ecclesiastical legists, especially those who belonged to the vast, unstudied group of clergy who had taken minor orders, must receive attention; they have been almost forgotten in the few references to lawyers that exist.

As the basis for research on lawyers, scholars can take advantage of ongoing work on particular jurists, such as that of Jean Roudil on Jacobo de Junta. And there are numerous fine histories of law as well as often massive studies, like that of Henrique da Gama Barros on Portugal, of the legal environment in which lawyers developed as a group.

The emergence of the lawyer's office as a public one has been best studied for Castile, where the role was defined as part of the codification work of the thirteenth century, particularly in the *Siete Partidas* (especially *Partida* 3, title 6). The Alfonsine legislation had an impact on Portugal through the circulation of translations, and the various law codes of the eastern kingdoms provided increasingly precise definitions of the lawyer and related officials. However, in the absence of a study of men of the law, it is difficult to know to what degree jurists' activities corresponded to the legislation.

While the final three medieval centuries saw a progressive increase in the prominence of lawyers, the establishment of the new Trastámara and Avis dynasties in Castile and Portugal, respectively, in the fourteenth century appears to have stimulated a dramatic increase in the reliance on legists by the crown, as well as by municipalities and magnates. The chronology is not as sharply delineated in the eastern kingdoms, but the increasing professionalism of the courts of the *justicias* of Aragón and Valencia had something of the same effect there. The role of trained jurists was already pronounced in Catalonia in the early thirteenth century as a result of the principality's closer connection to international commerce, the legal predominance of the judges of Barcelona, and the codification efforts of Ramón Berenguer IV. Everywhere the advancement of the university-trained lawyer was tied to the triumph of territorial over local law and the substitution of legal principles and procedures from Roman and canon sources for customs and *fueros*.

John B. Owens

Bibliography

Fernández Serrano, A. *La abogacía en España y en el mundo*. 3 vols. 2d ed. Madrid, 1955.

Jacobo de Junta. *Oeuvres*, 3 vols. Ed. J. Roudil. Paris, 1986.

Gama Barros, Henrique da. *História da administraçäo Publica em Portugal nos seculos xii–xv*, 2d ed. 2 vols. Lisbon, 1945–1954.

Valls-Taberner, F. "Los abogados en Cataluña durante la Edad Media." In *Obras selectas de Fernando Valls-Taberner*. Vol. 2, *Estudios histórico-jurídicos*. Madrid, 1954. 281–318.

LEANDER OF SEVILLE

The family of Leander of Seville moved to that city from Cartagena after the Byzantine occupation of the southeastern seaboard of the Iberian Peninsula in 551. Little is known of Leander's early life beyond the statement in his brother Isidore's *De viris illustribus* that he had been a monk. The flight of monks from Africa into Spain as a result of conflict with Emperor Justinian I over his theological policies (the "Three Chapters Controversy") probably provides the context for the emergence at this time of monastic institutions in southern Spain, where there is no evidence for their previous existence.

At some point in the 570s, Leander was made bishop of Seville, which in 579 became the royal residence of Hermenegild. When the latter rebelled against his father, Leovigild, in 580, Leander was one of his partisans, and early in the 580s undertook a mission for him to Constantinople. In Constantinople, Leander became a friend of the papal envoy and future pope, Gregory I the Great (590–604). There, at Leander's request, Gregory undertook his series of homilies on Job, the *Moralia*. Hermenegild's conversion from Arianism to Catholicism, probably in 582, was attributed by Gregory in his *Dialogues* to Leander's influence, and this must have occurred after the bishop had returned from Constantinople.

The fall of Seville to Leovigild and the crushing of Hermenegild's revolt in 584 led to a period of exile for Leander, but with the accession of Reccared in 586 and the new king's determination to resolve the religious division within the kingdom, he regained a position of influence. Isidore attributes Reccared's personal decision to convert to Catholicism in 587 to the work of Leander. He was also, although not the most senior of the hierarchy by date of consecration, the most influential of the bishops at the Third Council of Toledo (589), and the text of the sermon he delivered to it has been preserved. Leander's other works have not fared so well. Of the writings against the Arians that Isidore refers to, none have survived. Leander's only extant treatise is a short work on the monastic life for women, *De institutione virginum*, which he dedicated to his sister, the nun Florentina.

After the conclusion of the First Council of Seville in 590, which was held under his direction to implement some of the decisions of the Third Council of Toledo, little is known of Leander's activities. It has been deduced that he died around 599, and was succeeded as bishop of Seville by his younger brother Isidore. Another brother, Fulgentius, became bishop of Écija by 619.

Roger Collins

Bibliography

Domínguez del Val, U. *Leandro de Sevilla y la lucha contra el Arrianismo.* Madrid, 1981.

Fontaine, J. "Qui a chassé de Carthaginoise Severianus et les siens? Observations sur l'histoire familiale d'Isidore de Séville." In *Estudios en homenaje a Don Claudio Sánchez Albornoz.* Vol. 1. Buenos Aires, 1983. 349–400.

Velázquez, J., ed. *De la instrucción de las vírgenes y desprecio del mundo.* Madrid, 1979.

LEGISLATION, PORTUGAL

See LAW; CHARTERS, FUEROS

LEODEGUNDIA

In addition to Egeria, other Iberian women were involved in literary activities in the early Middle Ages. Some wrote letters of a more or less artistic nature. Some participated, in various ways, in producing texts. Such is the case with Leodegundia of Bobadilla, a Galician nun who wrote a *Codex regularum*, a Visigothic compendium that was widely read for centuries. Her manuscript is one of the oldest versions of this work, which typically contains the teachings and lives of the holy fathers of the church.

The manuscript, which was moved from Oviedo to the Escorial (a.I.13) in the sixteenth century, includes the following colophon: "O vos omnes qui legeritis hunc codicem mementote/clientula et exigua Leodigundia qui hunc scripsi in monasterio Bobatelle regnante Adefonso principe in era 950 quisquis pro alium oraver it semetipsum deum commendat." The manuscript appears to refer to King Alfonso II and presumably was written in 850 rather than 950.

Leodegundia's calligraphy has been highly praised. However, it is logical to assume she did more than copy the manuscript. In addition to the usual teachings and lives of the holy fathers, her version of the *Codex regularum* contains St. Jerome's letters to women friends, St. Augustine's letter to his sister Marceline, St. Leander's letters to his sister Florentina, and the lives of a number of women saints. That the additions have to do with women would seem not to be a coincidence. Neither would the fact that some of the women saints are of Spanish origin, and one, St. Melanie, is believed to have made her living by writing. Rather, this collection appears to be a mirror in which its author and her audience, the nuns of her convent, recognize themselves, a feminine adaptation of a masculine work.

Cristina González

Bibliography

Antolín, G. "Historia y descripción de un *Codex regularum* del siglo IX (Biblioteca del Escorial: a.I.13)." *Ciudad de Dios* 75 (1908), 23–33, 304–16, 460–71, 637–49.

Benedictines of Bouvert. *Colophons de manuscrits occidentaux des origines au XVI*[e] *siècle.* Fribourg, 1976, 36.

Pérez de Urbel, J. *Los monjes españoles en la Edad Media.* 2 vols. Madrid, 1934.

LEÓN, COUNCIL OF (1090)

A council of the church and realm of León-Castile held in the royal city of León in late March. Though the *acta* of the council do not survive, the meeting is known from a variety of literary sources of the early twelfth century. The Roman Cardinal Rainerius, later Pope Paschal II (1099–1118), presided.

In one piece of business, Bishop Pedro of Santiago de Compostela was deposed and the tangled succession to that great shrine-church was deferred while the earlier bishop, Diego Peláez, deposed at the Council of Husillos in 1088, appealed his case to Rome. Pedro, bishop of Braga, unsuccessfully sought the restoration of the ancient metropolitan dignity of his see.

In affairs at once secular and ecclesiastical, Alfonso VI seized on the occasion to formally inter the body of his newly deceased younger brother, García, there. García, independent king of Galicia-Portugal, had been overthrown, seized, and imprisoned by Alfonso in 1073. The king also probably asked the council to confirm his decision to double the annual payment of 1,000 gold *dinars* made to the Burgundian abbey of Cluny since the time of his father, Fernando I. He certainly had council members confirm a great grant to the episcopal church of Palencia.

Bernard F. Reilly

Bibliography

Diccionario de historia eclesiástica de España. 4 vols. Ed. Quintín Aldea Vaquero et al. Madrid, 1972. I

Historia de la iglesia en España. 7 vols. Ed. Javier Fernández Conde. Madrid, 1979–1983. II.

Historia del obispado de Burgos. 3 vols. Madrid, 1935. I.

LEÓN, KINGDOM OF

The kingdom of León was the successor to the kingdom of Asturias, which it subsequently always included. The former may be said to have originated when Ordoño II (r. 910–925) moved the royal city from Oviedo to León in 914, and raised a cathedral and a royal palace there. It was united to the kingdom of Castile under Fernando III (r. 1217–1252) following the death of Alfonso IX of León, Fernando's father, in 1230. Thereafter the history of the two kingdoms was permanently linked.

The history of the kingdom falls naturally into three major periods. During the first, between the reign of Ordoño II and through that of Vermudo III (1028–1037), it generally existed in the shadow of the great caliphate of Córdoba and was subject to periodic raids from the Muslim south, though never seriously in danger of outright conquest from that quarter. The second period extends from the reign of Fernando I (1037–1065) through that of Alfonso VII (1126–1157) and is the period of its greatest splendor. The kingdom

Kings of León and Castile, 1214–1504

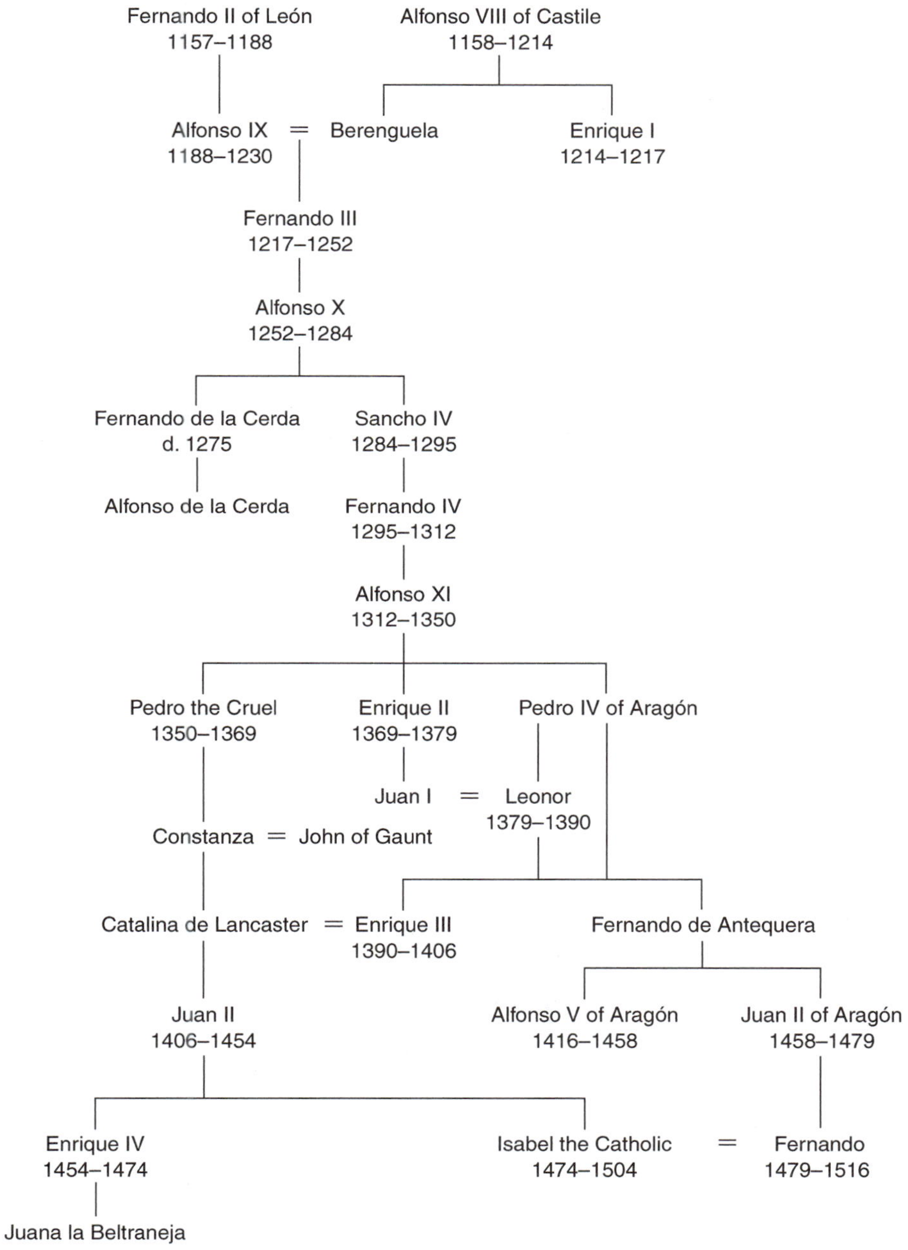

then was ordinarily the most powerful realm in the peninsula, either Christian or Muslim, and most of these paid the king of León either homage or outright tribute. The third period begins with the separation of León and Castile following the death of Alfonso VII, Castile going to Sancho III (r. 1157–1158) and León to Fernando II (r. 1157–1188). In general the terms of that division favored Castile, which heretofore had been subordinated to León, and Castilian ascendancy is marked through most of this era.

The most remarkable and important feature of the early period was the appropriation and repopulation of the *meseta* (plateau) north of the Duero River from the mountain lands north of the Cantabrians in Asturias, from northwest of the mountains of León in Galicia and the Bierzo, and from the Basque country and the Rioja in the northeast. The movement south was not absolutely new, but in contrast to the halting progress of the Asturian period, the long episodes of weakness in the history of the caliphate at Córdoba now allowed the steady seizure of the meseta from its heights in the country east of Burgos to the territories between the Miño and the Duero, where the latter debouches into the Atlantic at Oporto. This movement of Christians from the north onto the meseta was equaled in importance by a corresponding movement of Christian Mozarabs north from Islamic al-Andalus into the territories of León. The Mozarabs brought with them the superior agricultural techniques of Islam and a religious and cultural baggage that cemented the identity of the emerging north with its Visigothic and classical past.

Various attempts were made to push repopulation south of the line of the Duero, into the lands between it and the Guadarrama Mountains at points such as Sepúlveda and Salamanca, but raids from the Muslim south made life there too hazardous. Near the end of its first period, the Muslim dictator Al-Manṣūr (976–1002) and his son ʿAbd al-Mālik (1002–1008) launched a series of almost annual great raids that penetrated the Leonese kingdom and sacked such towns as Burgos, Santiago de Compostela, and León itself. Still, the Leonese appropriation of the lands north of the Duero could not be reversed.

During this era the kingdom was virtually synonomous with the dynasty that ruled it. The royal charters fail to indicate any regular administrative subdivisions, and in those documents the kings never refer to themselves as territorial rulers, but only by those patronymics on which their right to rule was based. The essential resource of the dynasty was the land of the royal fisc, and its chief agent was the *merino*, at once estate supervisor, local peace officer, dispenser of justice on crown lands, and leader of the local contingent to the royal host. The crown ruled in concert with the bishops and abbots of the church, whom it ordinarily had appointed and who were its most valuable subordinates (and the only formally educated ones). Bishoprics were inherited from the Visigothic Church at Lugo, Santiago de Compostela, Túy, Orense, Braga, and Astorga, and the Asturian monarchy had established new ones at Oviedo and León. A powerful magnate class flourished both as castellans in royal territories and as virtual miniature monarchs within their hereditary lands. The most potent of these existed at the far extremities of the realm, in Galicia in the west and Castile in the east. Count Fernán González of Castile (923–970) achieved near independence.

The reign of Fernando I (1037–1065) marked the beginning of a new epoch in the history of the kingdom. He carried the Leonese frontier southward to Viseu, Lamego, and finally Coimbra in the Portuguese west, and expanded his Castilian kingdom to Burgo de Osma and San Esteban de Gormaz in the Sorian highlands to the east. Moreover, he forced the major *ṭāʾifas*, successor kingdoms to the caliphate, of Zaragoza, Toledo, and Badajoz into the position of tributaries, paying *parias* (annual subsidies) to León. His son, Alfonso VI (1065–1109), carried out the conquest of Toledo in 1085, projecting the frontier south of the Guadarrama and the Tajo (Tagus) rivers, deep into La Mancha and the southern meseta. The appeal of the remining ṭāʾifas to the Muslim fundamentalist and Moroccan dynasty of the Almoravids led to the invasion of Iberia by Emir Yūsuf ibn Tāshfin, who defeated Alfonso VI at Zallāqah near Badajoz, on 23 October 1086. Subsequently the Almoravids absorbed the ṭāʾifas and al-Andalus became a province of that Moroccan empire. Gradually the Christians were pushed back in La Mancha until the frontier became Toledo, and during the reign of Alfonso's daughter and successor, Urraca (1109–1126), it moved to the Tagus River basin.

During the rule of Urraca's son, Alfonso VII (1126–1157), a new period of advance began. Coria in the Leonese Estremadura was taken in 1142 and the south bank of the Tagus, north of the Mountains of Toledo, was consolidated. In 1146, taking advantage of the collapse of the Almoravid empire in North Africa, Alfonso swept south into Upper Andalusia, taking Baeza, Úbeda, and finally the port of Almería on the Mediterranean in 1147. In the latter he had the assistance of the Genoese, Navarrese, and Catalans. However, Upper Andalusia and Almería proved impossible to hold against the rise of the new North African empire of the Almohads, and were lost to the latter in 1157, the year of Alfonso's death.

Among the Christian kingdoms of northern Iberia, León held the preeminence, symbolized by Alfonso's coronation as "emperor" at León on Pentecost, 26 May 1135. After his succession in 1126, the Leonese had forced his stepfather, Alfonso I of Aragón, out of Castile, and on the latter's death in 1134 had reclaimed the Rioja, which had first been annexed by Alfonso VI of León in 1076. Yet in the three-cornered struggle that ensued, the Leonese was unable to prevent Count Ramón Berenguer IV of Barcelona from absorbing most of Aragón, including Zaragoza, for which the count did homage to him. Nor was Alfonso able to forestall the reemergence of Navarre under García V Ramírez (r. 1134–1150), although that king, too, did homage to him. Count Alphonse Jourdain of Toulouse, his cousin, also became his vassal. The situation was similar in the west, where an independent Portugal had grown under his aunt, Queen Teresa (1096–1128). After a series of struggles with his cousin Afonso Henriques (r. 1128–1185), the Leonese monarch was forced to recognize that monarchy as well, although it was subject to his suzerainty.

Internally, the paramount development in the Leonese realm was the expansion of its agricultural society with the widespread application of irrigation techniques, the increasing use of water mills, and the wider utilization of plow culture and transhumance stock raising in Asturias and Galicia. The ensuing growth of farm size, production, and population allowed the appropriation of the southern half of the Duero basin after 1076, and then of the Tagus basin and the Leonese Estremadura south and west of Salamanca after 1130. Foundations of restored bishoprics at Salamanca (1102), Burgo de Osma (ca. 1102), Segovia (1120), Ávila (1121), Zamora (1122), Sigüenza (1123), and Coria (1142), and the restoration of the archiepiscopal see at Toledo in 1086, gave a stiffening administrative structure to much of these new territories.

The structure and ideology of the monarchy also developed apace. With Alfonso VI the Leonese kings begin to style themselves "imperator totius ispaniae" in their documents, and the dating formula lists the constituent parts of the kingdom. The action of the royal chancery becomes sufficiently regular to be studied, and the title of chancellor is usual from the reign of Alfonso VII. The major court officials, *mayordomo* and *alférez*, become traceable, and it is evident that they are held by an emerging nobility that is also a court nobility in its training. Education at court and service in its offices prepared the holder for subsequent elevation to what was, ordinarily, a family countship. Regular counties are detectable in the various provinces, and fisc lands (*comitatae*) are assigned at least to their partial support. Other fisc lands (*infantaticum*) are allocated to the maintenance of junior members of the dynasty and are administered by them. Experiments were sometimes made, as well, in providing territorial administration by such dynasts, as in Galicia (1090–1107), which was governed by Infanta Urraca and her husband, Count Raymond of Burgundy. A similar provision in the county of Portugal between 1096 and 1109 under Infanta Teresa and her husband, Count Henri of Burgundy, was to lead instead to the independence of that territory after the death of Alfonso VI.

Although the pilgrimage had some earlier history, this period saw the great flowering of the cult of Santiago. The route across the north to Santiago de Compostela became the artery of León and the avenue of European influence. The towns along it, although still diminutive, doubled their size as a result, and churches in the new Romanesque style rose in them while many developed a French "barrio" as well. Fernando I initiated a personal relationship between the dynasty and the French abbey of Cluny, while Alfonso VI and Urraca began a patronage that would establish a Cluniac Leonese province of formerly independent Iberian monasteries. Alfonso VII would do the same for the newer order of Cîteaux. Simultaneously Alfonso VI's reign saw the initiation of regular relationships between the Iberian Church and Rome. The old Mozarabic ritual was abolished in favor of the Roman one, papal legates held councils in the peninsula, new episcopal sees were established, and bishops were installed with papal approbation. The appointment of a former Cluniac, Archbishop Bernard, at Toledo (1086–1125) opened an era in which Osma, Palencia, Sigüenza, Segovia, and Salamanca were ordinarily held by bishops with a French monastic background.

All of these developments were constrained to some degree by the division of the old kingdom after 1157. That partition was much more favorable to Castile than to León. The line ran just west of Sahagún, Medina del Campo, and Ávila, territories historically more associated with León than with Castile, and included all of the Toledan lands to the south of the Guadarrama as well. Consequently, most of the next three-quarters of a century was spent in sterile border disputes between the sister realms. This was especially true of the reign of Fernando II (1157–1188) because he was tempted additionally by the quick demise of his brother, Sancho III (1157–1158), and the ensuing minority of the latter's son, Alfonso VIII (1158–1214). Fernando made common cause with the Castilian noble house of Castro against that of Lara in an attempt to control the regency of the three-year-old monarch. He had no more success than would his son and successor, Alfonso IX (r. 1188–1230), who continued the disputes with his now grown cousin of Castile. One abortive effort at a solution was the marriage in 1197 of Alfonso IX and Berenguela, daughter of Alfonso VIII. The papacy forced a dissolution on the grounds of consanguinity in 1204 but the marriage had by then produced that child who would become king of Castile as Fernando III in 1217 and king of León as well on the death of his father in 1230, reuniting the two permanently.

Under these circumstances, and given the contemporary strength of the Almohads in Andalusia, the Reconquest progressed slowly, although Fernando II did manage to repopulate Ledesma and Ciudad Rodrigo. Such other gains as he was able to effect were lost again, but his son was able to take advantage of the virtual collapse of the Almohads after 1212. Alfonso IX took Alcántara on the line of the Tagus in 1213; Cáceres, which controlled the advance into the valley of the Guadiana, in 1227; and Mérida and Badajoz, in the middle reaches of that river, in 1230. During this process the Leonese kings founded the military orders of Santiago (1175/1175) and Alcántara (1213/1218).

The advance to the south was accompanied by continuous border disputes with the new Portuguese monarchy. Fernando struggled to maintain control in the valley of the Miño River and had to intervene to forestall a Portuguese advance into the valley of the Guadiana in 1169. Nevertheless, he helped to defeat the Almohad attack on Santarém in 1184.

Internally the major development of the period was the appearance of the *cortes* (parliament) in 1188. Threatened at his accession by the claims of a stepbrother who was supported by the queen mother, and the pretensions of his uncle, Alfonso VIII of Castile, the young Alfonso IX convened a *curia* at León to which the good men of the towns of the realm were also summoned. To secure the support of that first cortes of the realm, Alfonso IX pledged himself to obey the laws of the kingdom and not to make war or conclude peace without consulting it. In a subsequent *corte* at Benevente in 1202, the king promised that he would not issue a new coinage for seven years if the assembly would grant him an aid.

The growing importance of the towns had already become evident in the increased activity of his father, Fernando II, in the granting of municipal *fueros* (charters). Salamanca, Zamora, Benevente, Túy, and Lugo all experienced royal intervention to enlarge or modify preexisting fueros or to grant new ones. Alfonso IX himself saw the trade of ports such as La Coruña and Gijón grow remarkably, and was active in the granting of municipal charters to Oviedo, Toro, and Mansilla in the north of his realm, and to Cáceres and Alcántara in the south.

Bernard F. Reilly

Bibliography

González, J. *Regesta de Fernando II*. Madrid, 1943.
———. *Alfonso IX*. 2 vols. Madrid, 1944.
Procter, E. S. *Curia and Cortes in León and Castile, 1072–1295*. Cambridge, 1980.
Reilly, B. F. *The Kingdom of León-Castilla under King Alfonso VI, 1065–1109*. Princeton, N.J., 1988.
———. *The Kingdom of León-Castilla under Queen Urraca, 1109–1126*. Princeton, N.J., 1982.
Recuero Astray, M. *Alfonso VII, emperador*. León, 1979.
Sánchez Candeira, A. *El "Regnum-Imperium" leonés hasta 1037*. Madrid, 1951.

LEÓN, MOSÉS DE

Spanish cabalist. (1250–1305). *Cabala* means "receiving," referring to that which has been handed down by tradition. By the time of Mosés de León, the term was used to denote the mystic and esoteric teachings and practices of a growing body of mystical literature.

Little is known about his life; he settled in Guadalajara sometime between 1275 and 1280 and relocated to Avila sometime after 1291. Best known for his revelation of the *Zohar* (*The Book of Splendor or Enlightenment*) to fellow cabalists, he also composed twenty cabalistic works, only two of which have been printed: *Ha-Nephesh ha Hakhamah* (*The Wise Soul*) and *Shekel ha-Kodesh*. (*The Holy Shekel, or Weight*). By 1264 he undertook the study of Maimonides' Neoplatonic philosophy, a belief system that rejected a literal interpretation of Torah and sought to spiritualize its teachings.

While in Guadalajara, Mosés de León composed a mystical midrash, which he titled *Midrash ha-Ne'elam* (*Concealed, Esoteric Midrash*). A midrash is an analytical text that seeks to uncover the meaning of biblical passages, words and phrases and often employs philology, etymology, hermeneutics, homiletics, and imagination. This work represents the earliest stratum of the *Zohar* and contains commentary on parts of the Torah and the Book of Ruth. Between 1280 and 1286, he produced the main body of the *Zohar*, a mystical commentary on the Torah written in Aramaic, which is spoken by Rabbi Shim'on ben Yohai and his disciples as they ruminate over distinct passages of the Torah.

The text upon which the *Zohar* was purportedly based was said to have been sent from Israel to Catalonia, where it fell into the hands of Mosés de León of Guadalajara, who assumed the task of copying and disseminating different portions of it from the original manuscript. After the Mamluk conquest of the city of Acre (Israel) in 1291, Isaac, son of Samuel, was one of the few to escape to Spain. When he arrived in Toledo in 1305, he heard reports about the existence of a newly discovered midrash of Rabbi Shim'on ben Yohai. Ostensibly written in Israel, the manuscript was unfamiliar to Isaac. He sought out Mosés de León, who assured him that he owned the original ancient manuscript upon which the *Zohar* was based and offered to show it to him if he came to his residence in Avila. After their separation, Moses became ill and died in Arévalo on his way home. When Isaac learned of the news, he traveled to Avila, where he was told that the wife of provincial tax-collector Joseph of Avila was living. After Mosés de León's death, Joseph de Avila's wife had made a deal in which she would offer her son's hand in marriage to the daughter of Mosés de León's widow in exchange for the ancient manuscript. During Isaac's visit, Joseph de Avila's wife denied that her late husband had ever possessed such a book, insisting instead that Mosés de León had composed it himself.

Mosés de León attributed the work to Shim'on ben Yohai, a famous teacher of the second century A.D. known for his piety and mysticism. Ben Yohai lived in Israel, where he reportedly spent twelve years in seclusion in a cave. After his death, his book was either hidden away or secretly transmitted from master to disciple. When Mosés de León began circulating booklets among his friends containing previously unknown teachings and tales, he claimed to be a mere scribe copying from an ancient book of wisdom. In addition, he distributed portions of the book rather than entire copies. No complete manuscript of the work has ever been found. When the *Zohar* was first printed in Italy in the fifteenth century, the editors combined several manuscripts to produce a complete text. Other manuscripts located later were added to an additional volume which was printed later. Today, most standard editions comprise some 1,100 leaves consisting of at least two dozen separate compositions.

The *Zohar* consists of a mystical commentary on the Pentateuch, describing how God—referred to by the cabalists as *Ein Sof* (the infinite, endless)—rules the universe through the Ten *Sefirot* (Ten Spheres). In other cabalistic texts, the sefirot are often organized in the form of a hierarchy of divine emanations from the apex of the Godhead with *Keter* or *Da'at* (the highest aspect of God) being followed by *Hokhmah* and *Binah* (divine wisdom and understanding respectively). Ein Sof is rarely emphasized in the *Zohar*. Instead, the work focuses on the sefirot as the manifestations of Ein Sof, its mystical attributes in which God thinks, feels, and responds to the human realm. The characters include Rabbi Shim'on and his comrades, biblical figures and the sefirot. At times the distinction between the latter two is ambiguous. Throughout the work, the *Zohar* never loses sight of its goal: to create a mystical commentary on the Torah in which God is simultaneously revealed and concealed. To study Torah is to meditate on the name of God. As Daniel C. Matt explains, "*Zohar* is an adventure, a challenge to the normal workings of consciousness. It dares you to examine your usual ways of making sense, your assumptions about tradition, God, and self. Textual analysis is essential, but you must engage *Zohar* and cultivate a taste for its multiple layers of meaning. It is tempting and safe to reduce the symbols to a familiar scheme: psychological, historical, literary, or religious. But do not forfeit wonder."

The authorship of the text, its method of composition and its use of sources (contemporary or ancient) have remained polemical among scholars. Among the most representative opinions in this controversy are Jellinek, Graetz, Scholem, and Giller. Jellinek concluded that many of the passages in the *Zohar* were derived from ancient sources and that Mosés de León was at least one of the authors of the work. Graetz concurred with Jellinek on the nature of its sources, but believed that the text represented a forgery executed entirely by Mosés de León. Scholem argued that the text was purely a product of the thirteenth century and was based on medieval Jewish Neoplatonism and Gnosticism. For him, the author and the translator were one and the same. More recent scholarship in the tradition of Giller and Liebes tends to view the *Zohar* as the product of a group collaboration among thinkers who grappled with cabalistic doctrine. Mosés de León was a main figure in this group but is not the sole author.

Regarding the overall structure of the *Zohar*, there is some consensus among scholars. The work is divided into distinct sections or strata, each of which has its own literary nature and mystical doctrines which are unique to it. The *Midrash ha-Ne'elam* is the earliest and is followed by the long midrash on the Torah and another group of compositions resembling it; the *Tiqqunei ha-Zohar* (*Embellishments on the Zohar*) and the *Ra'aya Meheimna* (*The Faithful Shepherd*) constitute another stratum. The *Midrash ha-Ne'elam* establishes an organizing fulcrum for the entire work in creating a protagonist Shim'on bar Yohai who does not appear until later. Until his subsequent appearance in the text, the teachings are conveyed by other rabbis from the second century with no single dominant figure. Further, there is a pattern of development in which certain ideas and themes are developed and reach their culmination over the course of the work's composition.

The *Zohar* was not accepted immediately as an ancient work. Students of Rabbi Solomon ibn Adret of Barcelona treated it with restraint. In 1340, the philosopher and cabalist Joseph ibn Waqqar warned about the preponderance of errors in the book. Slowly, its antiquity became accepted by cabalists, but as late as the mid-fifteenth century was not read or circulated except in small circles. It did not become the Bible of the Cabalah movement until after the Jewish expulsion from Spain in 1492. After 1530, Safed (Israel) gained importance as a meeting place for cabalists. Among them was Mosés Cordovero who wrote two systematic books based on the *Zohar*, along with an extensive commentary. Isaac Luria developed a new system based on Cabalah that relied heavily on portions of the *Zohar*. The trend of mystical-ethical literature emerging from this circle helped popularize the *Zohar*'s teachings as did the messianic fervor that encouraged the dissemination of its enigmas. If early qabbalists had drawn an analogy between spread of Cabalah and the redemption of Israel, in the sixteenth century, studying the *Zohar* became elevated to the level of a divine command, equal in importance to studying the Bible and the Talmud. Today, the *Zohar* retains its distinction as the fundamental text of cabalistic thought.

MATTHEW B. RADEN

Bibliography

Fine, L. *Essential Papers on Kabbalah*. New York, 1995.

Giller, P. *Reading the Zohar: The Sacred Text of the Kabbalah*. Oxford, 2001.

Holtz, B. (ed.) *Back to the Sources: Reading the Classic Jewish Texts*. New York, 1984.

Liebes, Y. *Studies in the Zohar*. Trans. A. Schwartz, St. Nakache, and P. Peli. Albany, N.Y., 1993.

Matt, D. C. (ed.) *Zohar: Book of Enlightenment*. New York, 1983. 38.

LEONOR DE GUZMÁN *See* ALFONSO XI

LEOVIGILD

The brother of Liuva I (r. 568–72/3), who made him coruler in 569, with responsibility for the south and center of the Iberian Peninsula, Leovigild proved to be perhaps the greatest of the kings of Visigothic Spain. Even those who opposed his religious policies, such as Isidore of Seville and John of Biclaro, admired his military capacity and achievements. At the time of his accession the kingdom was threatened by Frankish aggression from the north and Byzantine aggression in the southeast. Much of the north of the peninsula and various areas in the south, including the city of Córdoba, had broken free of royal control. An independent Suevic kingdom survived in the northwest. Leovigild's initial campaigns were directed against the Byzantine enclave, and he regained Sidonia and Málaga. In 572, he reimposed Visigothic rule on Córdoba. Following the death of his brother Liuva I, Leovigild turned his attention northward, and in a series of campaigns between 573 and 577 made himself master of most of the north of the peninsula, from the Rioja to the frontiers of the Suevic kingdom, whose ruler Miro became tributary to him. In the peaceful years of 578 and 579, the king established the new town of Reccopolis, named after his younger son, and also set up his elder son Hermenegild in Seville as coruler with responsibility for the south. This failed when Hermenegild rebelled, at the instigation of Leovigild's second wife, Goisuintha, widow of the former Visigothic king Athanagild (r. 554–568). Initially Leovigild made no move to curtail his son's independence, and in 581 launched a campaign northward to contain the Basques. There he founded another new town, called Victoriacum (probably Olite in Navarre). Only when an alliance between Hermenegild and the Byzantines developed, symbolized by the former's conversion to Catholicism, did Leovigild act. In 583 he took Mérida and Seville, and in 584 Córdoba, where Hermenegild was captured. After the suppression of the revolt in the south, Leovigild overran the Suevic kingdom in the northwest, where the son of his former ally Miro had recently been overthrown by a usurper. With this achieved, the Basques temporarily pacified, and a Frankish invasion of the province of Narbonensis repelled in 585, Leovigild had achieved a military reunification of the Visigothic kingdom in the peninsula and Septimania. To turn this into a genuine political and cultural unification required the solution of the theological division between Arians and Catholics, which had provided a context for factionalism and local power struggles. This problem Leovigild hoped to tackle by holding a council in Toledo in 580 with the aim of modifying the theological tenets of Arianism, to make this view of the Trinity more acceptable. In the outcome, the polarization of religious and political opinion following the conversion of Hermenegild in 582 made such a compromise unworkable. The only solution was the acceptance by all of the uncompromising doctrinal stand of the Catholics. It is reported in Gregory of Tours's *histories* that Leovigild himself secretly converted prior to his death in 586, but the public resolution of the issue was left to his heir Reccared.

ROGER COLLINS

Bibliography

Collins, R. "Mérida and Toledo, 550–585." In Visigothic Spain: New Approaches. Ed. E. James: Oxford, 1980. 189–219.

Stroheker, K. F. "Leowigild. Aus einer Wendezeit westgotischer Geschichte," Die Welt als Geschichte 5 (1939), 446–485.

Thompson, E. A. The Goths in Spain. Oxford, 1969, 57–91.

LETRADOS

Widely used in the scholarly literature on the late medieval and early modern periods, the term *letrados* has been a source of confusion. Its core meaning emerges from the much-cited passage, probably written in the early 1570s, of Diego Hurtado de Mendoza's *Guerra de Granada*, in which the author ties the Catholic Monarchs' political program of the recruitment of *letrados* for judicial and public administration. *Letrados* were those with university law degrees, their prominence dating from the Castilian Trastámara and Portuguese Avís dynasties, who increasingly dominated royal bureaucratic institutions and developed a group consciousness. Whether educated in canon or civil law, *letrados* had mastered a type of reasoning useful for clarifying and debating opposing viewpoints, and this training recommended them as judges and advisory officials. Self-interest and exposure to Romanist political theory made *letrados* active proponents of monarchical authority, and their influence in crown affairs opened numerous opportunities for them in urban, aristocratic, and ecclesiastical administration.

Confusion has resulted from the multiple meanings of *letrado* in the sources; the word could refer to a literate person, to someone with considerable formal education, to an individual both learned and wise, or to a university graduate (sometimes without reference to his actual degree). Historians often appear unsure whether to restrict the term to its fifteenth- or sixteenth-century usage or to add it to our modern technical jargon. When it is used in the latter manner, writers have discussed *letrados* prior to the fourteenth century or in the eastern Iberian kingdoms; they have debated whether clergymen were *letrados*; and they have included groups like notaries and fiscal agents. Some influential historians, such as S. de Moxó and A. Rucquoi, have expanded the word *letrados* to cover so many people that the individuals involved surely lacked the sense of group consciousness that J. Maravall and Pelorson have felt made the term worth including in contemporary historical discourse.

Due to such extensions to heterogeneous sets of people and to the general lack of precision in the term's use, important hypotheses about the role of *letrados* as a sociological class in cultural, commercial, and administrative developments have often been hard to evaluate. For example, this problem has troubled discussions of Nader's argument that *letrados* did not play a significant role in the development of Castilian Renaissance humanism, of Carande's contention that *letrado* public administrators had an antimerchant mentality that damaged Spanish commercial growth, and of the assertion of J. Vicens Vives that *letrado* emphasis on legal studies retarded the elaboration of administrative theory. The word is probably best avoided in English-language studies of Iberian medieval history in favor of more precise references to more clearly definable groups like law graduates, lawyers, jurists, legists, or bureaucrats.

JOHN B. OWENS

Bibliography

Maravall, J. A. "Los 'hombres de saber' o letrados y la formación de su conciencia estamental." In *Estudios de historia del pensamiento español*. Madrid, 1967. 357–89. (First published 1953.)

Moxó, S. de. "La elevación de los 'letrados' en la sociedad estamental del siglo XIV." In *XII Semana de estudios medievales*. Ed. V. Galbete Guerendiáin. Pamplona, 1976. 183–215.

Nader, H. *The Mendoza Family in the Spanish Renaissance*. Rutgers, N.J., 1978

LETTERS AND LETTER WRITING

In medieval Spain, long-distance communication by means of letters generally involved four people: the sender, the scribe, the messenger, and the recipient. A broad look at these four parties gives a good sense of the process and style of medieval letter writing.

The senders and recipients of letters were usually from the nobility and/or the church. The topics of these letters ranged widely, from mundane themes to legal documents to travel commentaries to protest petitions. Of the letters and letter collections in Spanish, some of the better known are those of Juan Manuel, Fernando and Isabel, Alfonso de Palencia, Juan Álvarez Gato, Alonso Carillo, Christopher Columbus, Enrique IV, Juan II, Francisco Jiménez de Cisneros, Pedro López de Ayala, Diego Rodríguez de Almela, and Hernando de Talavera. These are found published singly or as part of literary and historical document collections.

Senders generally dictated their correspondence, and with some exceptions the style of a letter can be attributed to the scribe and the medieval art of letter writing. A letter's style as presented by most scribes was firmly grounded in the medieval art of letter writing, the *ars dictaminis*. A letter consisted of five parts that could be elaborated or omitted at a writer's discretion: the *salutatio*, or formulaic greeting; the *captatio benevolentiae* or *exordium*, which captured the goodwill or, at least, the attention of the recipient; the *narratio*, or narration of facts; the *petitio*, which argued, pled, or simply stated the opinions, needs, and facts as they stood at the moment; and the *conclusio*, a closing phrase of a general nature or a recapitulation of essential arguments and points.

Scribes learned their craft through the Latin *artes dictandi*, rhetorical treatises on the art of letter writing, or from collections of model letters and model letter parts. Whether or not a letter was dictated to a scribe or penned by the sender, the general format of ars dictaminis was followed. It was in fact pervasive, and use of proper format should not be seen as a direct link to knowledge of the artes dictandi.

Letters in medieval Spain were written in a variety of languages. The majority of letters from the early Middle Ages were in Latin, and Latin continued to be used for most international correspondence, particularly from the church. Both Hebrew and Arabic letters from the Middle Ages survive. Catalan was the language chosen for many challenge letters, and French was occasionally used in nobles' letters to parties outside of Spanish-speaking areas.

Delivery of the correspondence fell to the messenger. The type of messenger used depended on the sender's social rank, the nature of the message, and the distance the letter was sent. The messenger could be a trusted servant, an official envoy, a good friend, or merely a person going to the same destination as the letter. Royalty had at its disposal many trusted messengers who were used regularly and to whom additional, verbal messages were often entrusted.

In ancient civilizations the majority of long-distance communication was oral, although the evolution of the written message occurred very early as a method of jogging the messengers' memories. All through the Middle Ages and beyond, both oral and written communications continued to be employed. Certain types of letters, most notably letters of challenge, long remained fossilized in an oral tradition that had passed out of use in more everyday correspondence. The fluctuation between oral and written presentation of messages allowed letters to take on the quality of "half a conversation" as described by the *dictatores*.

The conversational and intimate aspect of letters, combined with their earlier role as legal, and therefore true, documents made letters a very appealing device to authors, who used them for short treatises, demonstrations of stylistic expertise, and literary devices within their texts. Differentiating literary letters from everyday letters is not a simple task. Their subject matter varies widely and encompasses many of the subjects treated in everyday correspondence. Certainly the authors of literary letters lavished careful attention on style and composition, but scribes, trained in the art of letter writing, employed similar standards for the letters they composed. Perhaps the best, albeit by no means conclusive, indication is that although commonly addressed to a single recipient, literary letters were written with an eye to public circulation. Composed in both prose and verse, literary letters circulated in single copies, in collections, and as parts of other works. Public circulation and extensive copying, as well as their collection, indicate that the value of these letters extended beyond their news-bearing ability, to include interest in the artistry of their composition and the facts and opinions presented by the author. Authors of literary letters include Diego de Valera, Hernando del Pulgar, Francisco de la Torre, Íñigo de Mendoza, Alfonso de Madrigal, Gómez Manrique, Juan de Lucena, Enrique de Villena, Juan Rodríguez del Padrón, and the many authors of challenge letters.

CAROL A. COPENHAGEN

Bibliography

Copenhagen, Carol. "Las *Cartas mensajeras* de Alfonso Ortiz: ejemplo epistolar de la Edad Media." *El Crotalón: Anuario de Filología Española* 1 (1984), 467–483.

———. "Salutations in Fifteenth-century Spanish Letters." *La Corónica* 13 (1984–1985), 196–205.

———. "*Narratio* and *Petitio* in Fifteenth-century Spanish Letters." *La Corónica* 14 (1985–1986), 6–14.

———. "The *Conclusio* in Fifteenth-century Spanish Letters." *La Corónica* 14 (1985–1986), 213–219.

LEVI BEN GERSHOM (GERSONIDES)

Although he was born and lived his entire life in then French Provence, Gersonides (1288–1344) was the heir of the Spanish Hebrew-Arabic medieval culture. Deeply influenced by Averroës and Maimonides in philosophy and by Abraham ibn Ezra in biblical exegesis, Gersonides not only excelled in both these areas but also made important contributions to astronomy and mathematics. Besides inventing or improving upon several astronomical observational instruments, he compiled his own astronomical tables, made many of his own observations, and engaged in a critical analysis of several of Ptolemy's hypotheses. In mathematics he wrote a commentary on parts of Euclid's *Elements* and a treatise on trigonometry.

But it was in philosophy and biblical exegesis that Gersonides was most influential. Continuing the tradition of the Córdoban philosopher Averroës, Gersonides wrote many supercommentaries on Averroës's commentaries on Aristotle, in which he exhibited a critical and independent approach to both his predecessors. But it is *The Wars of the Lord* that is his most important philosophical work. In this long treatise most of the topics of medieval philosophy and science are discussed in detail and with acuity. Some of his more novel or radical conclusions were (1) the individual human intellect is immortal (contrary to Averroës); (2) God does not have knowledge of particular future contingent events (contrary to Maimonides); (3) yet there is divine providence over deserving individuals;

(4) the universe was divinely created out of an eternal shapeless body (contrary to Averroës and Maimonides); (5) although it has a beginning, the universe is indestructible (contrary to Aristotle).

Whereas *The Wars of the Lord* elicited considerable criticism from his coreligionists, Gersonides' commentaries upon the Bible were widely studied, even among nonphilosophical Jews; his *Commentary on Job* was particularly popular. This is remarkable because in these commentaries Gersonides pulls no punches: the ideas of *The Wars of the Lord* are repeated or assumed, and there is no effort to mute their impact. He did not obey Averroës's and Maimonides' rule that the teaching of philosophy ought to be reserved for the philosophers alone. In his *Commentary on Job*, for example, he has each character represent a distinct philosophical position on the question of divine providence. These various positions are philosophically analyzed, and eventually one emerges as the true solution to Job's predicament. Thus, the Book of Job is transformed into a Platonic dialogue.

SEYMOUR FELDMAN

Bibliography

Levi ben Gershom. *The Wars of the Lord*. 2 vols. Trans. Seymour Feldman. Phildelphia, 1984–87.

Touati, C. *La Pensée philosophique et théologique de Gersonide*. Paris, 1974.

LEYES DE MOROS

Leyes de moros, the laws concerning the Muslims (Mudéjars) living in the Christian kingdoms, are found in royal and municipal law codes and in the legislation of regional *cortes* (parliaments). They constitute an elaboration upon the surrender treaties reached between the Christian kings and the conquered Muslim populations—which granted the Muslims the basic privileges of religious freedom and communal autonomy—and define the Muslims' status in a Christian society and regulate their relations with the Christian populace. Many laws intended the segregation of the Muslims in order to shield the faith and morals of Christians. For instance, Muslims were to reside in separate quarters and to wear distinctive clothing and haircuts; sexual relations between Muslims and Christians were prohibited and harshly penalized. Other laws affirmed Christianity's present domination of Islam by requiring Muslims to kneel in the presence of Christian religious processions or increasingly restricting the Islamic call to prayer.

Concomitant to such laws were those banning Christian conversion to Islam and encouraging the proper treatment of baptized Muslims. Laws also reinforced Christian sociopolitical power in their proscription of Muslims holding public office over Christians, employing Christian servants, or owning Christian slaves. Christians could own Muslim slaves, either Mudéjar or foreign, and laws regulated their treatment and manumission. Beyond granting Muslim judges jurisdiction over civil suits between Muslims, laws established guidelines for judicial procedure in litigations involving Muslims and Christians, which normally were adjudicated in Christian courts. The royal and seigneurial lords of Muslims, in order to protect their own economic interests, enacted laws that restricted Mudéjar emigration to Islamic lands and controlled Mudéjar movement from one lord to another. The crown, however, did not consistently enforce many of the harsher segregative provisions. Most royal measures to protect Muslim interests were of an ad hoc nature and do not appear in the law codes.

MARK D. MEYERSON

Bibliography

Boswell, J. *The Royal Treasure: Muslim Communities under the Crown of Aragón in the Fourteenth Century*. New Haven, Conn., 1977.

Fernández y González, F. *Estado social y político de los mudéjares de Castilla*. Madrid, 1985. (Reprint of 1866 ed.)

LEYES DE MOROS (II)

Leyes de moros is the title under which Pascual de Gayangos published in 1853 a Latin-character (not *aljamiado*) text of which the original had already been lost, so that exact dating is now impossible. The original may have been from as early as the thirteenth century, and is certainly earlier than the fifteenth-century *Breviario sunnī*. The *Leyes de moros*, like the not-dissimilar Catalan *Llibre de la Cuna* recently discovered and published by Barceló, provide a short Romance manual of some aspects of Islamic law (*fiqh*). The text appears to be primarily intended for the use of Christian administrators and functionaries rather than for Muslims. Although their Mudéjar status guaranteed to subject Muslims that they would be judged according to their own laws, administered by their own *qāḍī*, inevitably there were conflicts of jurisdiction, and sometimes Muslims, anxious to escape the rigors of the *ḥadd* obligatory capital punishment, sought to have their offense tried before a royal court. (In any case, the crown provided the ultimate court of appeal.) Christian lawyers and others needed a statement of Islamic law they were asked to apply. The *Leyes de moros* certainly did not cover the whole range of *fiqh*, but although Gayangos' description of them as a "civil code" goes too far (no Islamic code is devoid of theological content), it is true that they avoid purely ritual issues. They are based on entirely orthodox Mālikī juridical writings in Arabic, and indeed some of the cases discussed arise from the needs of a camel-herding society, and so will have been quite irrelevant to the circumstances of the Mudéjars of the Iberian Peninsula.

L. PATRICK HARVEY

Bibliography

Barceló, C. (ed.) *Un tratado calalán medieval de derecho islámico: el Llibre de la Cuna*. Córdoba, 1989.

Gayangos, Pascual de (ed.) *Tratados de legislación musulmana. Memorial histórico español* V. Madrid, 1853.

Harvey, L. P. *Islamic Spain, 1250–1500*. Chicago, 1990. 74–97.

LEYES DEL ESTILO

Leyes del estilo o declaración de las leyes is the title of the first printed edition (Salamanca, 1497) of a private compilation created by unknown author(s), probably during the reign of Fernando IV of Castile (1295–1312), according to some easily datable references from the period 1290–1309. The known half-dozen manuscripts, showing some variation in title, date mainly from the fourteenth century. The editions include four other confirmed incunabula of different dates, nine editions from the sixteenth century, and one edition by the Royal Academy of History published in 1836. The latter contains 252 *leyes*, units more appropriately called *chapters* because the collection was not promulgated. Like the *Leyes nuevas*, the *Leyes del estilo* were intended to fill gaps perceived in existing law, mainly in the *Fuero real*, although numerous sources in Roman, canon, customary, and Alfonsine juridical literature are cited as well.

The *Leyes* may be described generally as comprising a systematic compilation of interpretations, clarifications, explanations, and examples of carrying out the law emanating from decisions of the royal tribunal. The compilation was much cited by jurists into the sixteenth century. Eventually some of the chapters acquired legal status on being incorporated into the *Novísima recopilación* (1805). The *Libro de los juyzios*, contained in a manuscript written mainly in an early fifteenth-century hand, is related to the *Leyes del estilo* and has been called a version of it. It has been said to show even more receptiveness to the *Fuero real* than that appearing in the *Leyes*; both works are cited as showing evidence of the differences between the new law represented by the *Fuero real* and traditional law as represented by municipal *fueros* generally and by customary law.

ROBERT A. MACDONALD

Bibliography

"Leyes del Estilo." In *Nueva enciclopedia jurídica* Ed C. E. Mascareño, Barcelona, 1970. Vol. 9, 211–13.

Prieto Bances, R. "Caridad y justicia en las *Leyes del estilo*." In *Homenaje a D. Nicolás Pérez Serrano*. Vol. 1 Madrid, 1959. 161–91.

LEYES NUEVAS

The thirteenth century was the most important throughout Spain for the codification and promulgation of laws. In the kingdom of Castile, Alfonso X especially is noted for his sponsorship (hardly "authorship") of various legal codes. Whereas the *Siete Partidas* was intended as a theoretical codification, a kind of "encyclopedia" of civil and canon law, for use in the royal court, the king was very serious about his effort to impose the *Fuero real* as a universal code upon the municipalities of Castile and Extre madura. He reserved to himself (i.e., the royal judges) the right of appeal, as well as of the interpretation and emendation of the law.

The *Leyes nuevas* (ca. 1263) represent, in effect, a collection of such interpretation, in response to queries from judges of Burgos. These laws played an important role in later legislative developments and *fueros*.

In addition they are of particular importance for Jewish history and the issue of usury, inasmuch as the majority deal with these questions. Lengthy formulas of oaths for Christians, Muslims, and Jews in matters of debts are also prescribed. Other laws attempt to redress earlier injustices against Jews, such as the matter of "seizure" (hostage) for debt.

NORMAN ROTH

Bibliography

Los códigos españoles. Vol. 6. Madrid, 1872. 225–37.

López Ortiz, J. "La colección conocida con el titulo 'Leyes nuevas' y atribuida a Alfonso el Sabio." *Anuario de Historia del Derecho Español* 16 (1945), 5–70. (Also offprint, Madrid, 1945.)

LIBER JUDICIORUM *See* FUEROS

LIBER REGUM *See* HISTORIOGRAPHY

LIBRARIES

The earliest reference to a Spanish library is found in the verses inscribed on the walls of the library of St. Isidore of Seville (ca. 560–636), but the first one documented is that of Villeña (Santander), which received a donation of five liturgical works in 796. Those known during the early years of the Reconquest (ninth–eleventh centuries) are primarily of the same type: small collections of liturgical works with, occasionally, some patristic texts. Larger collections, especially with secular works, are rare, although St. Eulogius of Córdoba visited the monastery of San Zacarías of Navarre in 848 and brought back to Córdoba texts of Virgil, Juvenal, and Horace. (More commonly books were brought from al-Andalus to the north as Mozarabic Christians fled increasingly severe religious persecution.) Thus a library inventory from 882 (Escorial, Ms. R.II.18, variously ascribed to Córdoba, Toledo, Oviedo, or Zaragoza) stands out for its size (forty-two books) and variety (Virgil and Juvenal; the histories of Eusebius, Paulus Orosius, and St. Isidore; Christian Latin poets like Prudentius and Sedulius Scottus; and the more common works of the church fathers).

Evidence for contemporary Islamic libraries is entirely anecdotal, since there are no extant inventories. The commonly cited figure of 400,000 volumes for the library of Al-Ḥakam II, caliph of Córdoba (961–976), is suspicious, since in Arabic 400,000 frequently means only "innumerable, beyond count." Nevertheless, it is generally accepted that there were large collections not only in Córdoba but also in the sucessor *ṭā'ifa* kingdoms of the eleventh century (e.g., Seville, Almería, Granada, Zaragoza, Valencia).

Documentation for the major monastic centers in Castile and León (e.g., Santo Domingo de Silos and San Pedro de Cardeña [Burgos], San Millán de la Cogolla and San Martín de Albelda [Logroño]) has not survived, but extant codices indicate that their libraries were almost exclusively religious and relatively small. By far the richest and most impressive library in Christian Spain was that of Santa María de Ripoll (Girona) in the Catalan Pyrenees. In 979 it had sixty-five books; by the time of the death of Abbot Oliba (1047), its collection of 246 books included Juvenal, Caesar, Horace, Terence, Cicero, Virgil (with the commentaries of Servius), the grammars of Donatus and Priscian, and the logical texts of Porphyry and Boethius as well as arithmetical and musical works. In contrast, more than a century and a half later, San Salvador de Oña (Burgos) had only 117 books, and somewhat later in the thirteenth century Silos had 146, almost all of them liturgical or patristic.

By the thirteenth century the cathedrals, called upon to create schools by the Third (1179) and Fourth (1215) Lateran Councils, began to build increasingly substantial libraries through purchase or legacies from canons and bishops. The collections at Toledo, Burgo de Osma, Burgos, Sigüenza, Barcelona, Valencia, Pamplona, Tortosa, and Vich can be traced to this period, and are essentially intact today. Burgo de Osma had 149 books at the end of the thirteenth century, and Sigüenza's collection grew from twenty in 1242 to 280 in 1339. In contrast, at the end of the fourteenth century the cathedral of Oviedo had only seventy-six books; at roughly the same time there were eighty-six in Burgos. The collections themselves served as texts for the cathedral schools and as a source of income to the cathedral, since they were frequently rented out.

We may surmise the existence of royal or noble libraries during the high Middle Ages, but it is only toward the end of the thirteenth century that they are documented. Attempts to reconstruct the library of Alfonso X of Castile and León (r.1252–1284) are based on the sources used in his works as well as on documents listing books borrowed from Riojan monasteries around 1270. For the Crown of Aragón we have concrete information only from the reign of Jaume II (1291–1327) onward. In 1323 the *cámara real* contained a collection of eighty-eight books, mostly confiscated from the Knights Templars. This library did not form part of the royal patrimony, and many of its manuscripts were donated to other members of the royal family or to royal favorites.

The bibliophilia of the last kings of the Aragónese dynasty (Pedro IV [r.1336–1387] and his sons Juan I [r.1387–1395] and Martín I [r.1395–1410]) is well documented; and the inventory of the latter's collection of 349 books provides in some respects the final record of that passion. It contained texts in Latin (56 percent), Catalan (19 percent), French (14 percent), Castilian (4.6 percent), and Aragónese (3.4 percent), as well as scattered items in Provençal, Sicilian, Hebrew, and Arabic. Resolutely medieval in its outlook, it held fifty-five legal works (15 percent), fifty-five astronomical and astrological ones, and thirty-nine historical texts (11 percent), but almost no classical or humanistic materials and very little vernacular imaginative literature.

Carlos of Aragón (1421–1461), prince of Viana and son of Juan II, had a library of one hundred volumes that reflected the intellectual interests of his uncle Alfonso V the Magnanimous, whose library at Naples, with its magnificent classical and humanistic manuscripts, was one of the glories of the Italian Renaissance. We find no record of the Castilian royal library until Isabel I's was cataloged in 1503. However, from its contents and composition (199 manuscripts and only five printed books), it is plain that its nucleus dates from the reign of her father, Juan II of Castile and León (1406–1454). Almost half of its texts are in Castilian and the rest in Latin, with but a scattering in French, Catalan, and Italian. Law and religion are the most numerous subjects, and there is a good collection of vernacular Castilian literature, including such canonical texts as the *Libro de buen amor* and Juan Manuel's *Conde Lucanor*, but very little humanistic or classical literature. From this time on, the royal library was a possession of the crown, which explains why many of the books mentioned in the 1503 inventory eventually found their way into the Escorial, the Biblioteca Nacional, and the royal library (Biblioteca de Palacio).

During the reign of Juan II both the upper and the lower nobility began to collect books seriously. The largest noble library was probably that of Íñigo López de Mendoza (1398–1458), first marquis of Santillana; but its reconstruction is problematic, since it is based on a study of extant manuscripts. More useful as touchstones of the intellectual interests of the nobility are the libraries of Alfonso Pimentel, the third count of Benavente (1440–1461), who about 1447 owned 126 books, and of Pedro Fernández de Velasco (1400–1470), first count of Haro, who had seventy-nine in 1455. There is little imaginative literature in these libraries; legal and religious texts, histories, and didactic and exemplary works of various kinds predominate. Inventories of the libraries of a few well-known writers are still extant, such as those of Ausiàs March and Joanot Martorell in Valencia; of Alvar García de Santa María, *cronista* of Juan II of Castile; and of the poet Fernán Pérez de Guzmán. They tend to reflect the same interests as the libraries of the nobility.

University and school libraries were generally limited to textbooks: grammatical and logical texts at the lower levels, theological and legal works at the higher. In the earlier period provision of texts was in the hands of the *stationarius*, who rented out manuscripts for students to copy. In Salamanca, for example, the university library is not even documented until well into the fifteenth century, and appears not to have grown substantially until the second half of the century.

Through the end of the fourteenth century, private libraries remained small and tended to focus on their owners' professional concerns: lawyers owned legal texts; doctors, medical treatises. During the fifteenth century they became increasingly common, even before the advent of the printed book in the last quarter of the century. While the inventories of such libraries—generally compiled for testamentary purposes—are far more numerous in the Crown of Aragón than in the Crown of Castile, it is not clear whether this in fact corresponds to a real difference between the two regions or is merely a reflection of the earlier establishment of notarial archives in the eastern kingdoms, which preserved such inventories in far greater numbers than did Castile. Private libraries of all classes become more common in the fifteenth century, due to an increase in demand—a higher literacy rate with the spread of grammar schools—as well as in supply—the increasing substitution of paper for parchment as a writing material; they increased dramatically in numbers, size, and content after the introduction of the printing press. Luis de Acuña, bishop of Burgos, possessed 363 books in 1496, and an obscure Mallorcan notary, Miquel Abeyar, owned 471 in 1493. Berger shows that in Valencia even some 10–15 percent of the manual laborers owned books, as opposed to 30 percent of the merchants and fully 75 percent of the professional classes. Library size ranged from one to two books for the first group to some thirty or forty for the last. Fewer women had libraries, and those who did generally owned no more than three or four books, regardless of social class.

CHARLES B. FAULHABER

Bibliography

Beceiro Pita, I., and A. Franco Silva. "Cultura nobiliar y bibliotecas: Cinco ejemplos de las postrimerías del siglo XIV a mediados del XVI." *Historia. Instituciones. Documentos* 12 (1985), 277–350.

Beer, R. *Handschriftenschätze Spaniens*. Vienna, 1894.

Berger, P. "La Lecture à Valence de 1474 à 1504 (quelques données numériques)." *Mélanges de la Casa de Velázquez* 11 (1975), 99–118.

Faulhaber, C. B. *Libros y bibliotecas en la España medieval*. Research Bibliographies and Checklists, 47. London, 1987.

Marín, T. "Bibliotecas eclesiásticas." In *Diccionario de historia eclesiástica de España,* Vol. 1. Ed. Quintín Aldea Vaquero et al. Madrid, 1972. 250–62.

LIBRO DE ALEXANDRE

The anonymous early thirteenth-century *Libro de Alexandre* narrates in verse the life of Alexander the Great, and thus represents the Spanish contribution to the widespread medieval Alexander tradition, which produced numerous retellings of the Macedonian hero's life in Latin, in Arabic, and in various European vernacular languages. To medieval Europeans, Alexander represented a classical figure worthy of imitation due to his sagacity, determination, and prowess as a warrior, yet he also came to signify the dangers of excessive ambition and unrestrained quest for fame. The Spanish poem clearly reflects this ambiguity by means of a detailed medievalization and Christianization of the story.

The 2,675 quatrains begin with the hero's birth, infancy, and tutelage by Aristotle. Alexander then takes arms in a scene that anachronistically reflects the rituals of medieval knighthood. After several preliminary military victories, Alexander's father, King Philip, dies, and the son ascends to the thrown. The new king invades Asia in the hope of conquering the

Persian king Darius and liberating Greece from Persian domination. At Troy, 472 stanzas relate the story of the Trojan War, which instructs and inspires Alexander's troops. Alexander goes on to defeat Darius and to advance through Asia conquering and occupying territory. As the poem draws to a close, Alexander, "emperador del mundo," enters Babylon victorious, erects his magnificent tent, and contemplates his vast gains. Here at the pinnacle of his power, Alexander's nemesis Antipater poisons the great man's wine glass and when Alexander drinks, the poison kills him. The final stanzas of the poem meditate on the unreliability of earthly riches and glory and the need to serve and have faith in God's eternal kingdom in the afterlife.

Differences between the two extant manuscripts raise various questions regarding the original poem's composition. The language of Manuscript O (Biblioteca del Duque de Osuna) contains Leonese dialectal characteristics, and the last stanza attributes composition to Juan Lorenzo de Astorga. The language of Manuscript P (Bibliothèque Nationale, Paris) is more typical of the Aragónese dialect, and ends with an attribution to Gonzalo de Berceo. However, stanza 1548 in Manuscript O refers to a "Gonçalo," and in P the same *copla* cites "Lorente." For over one hundred years, scholars have attempted to explain these differences and contradictions, often arguing for either an Aragónese original by Gonzalo de Berceo or for Leonese composition by Juan Lorenzo. In 1979, Dana Nelson took the daring step of publishing an edition, or "reconstrucción crítica," of the *Libro de Alexandre* bearing Gonzalo de Berceo's name as author. Today the general consensus leans toward accepting the *Libro de Alexandre*'s anonymity yet recognizing the close connection between that work and the writings of Gonzalo de Berceo, perhaps due to a shared association with the University of Palencia.

The question of the *Libro de Alexandre*'s sources has been far less difficult for scholars to resolve. Two twelfth-century Alexander narratives, the Latin *Alexandreis* of Gautier de Chatillon and the French *Roman d'Alixandre*, in addition to the tenth-century Latin *Historia Proeliis* served as sources for the principal story line. Much of the Troy material comes from a first-century Latin Homeric summary, the *Ilias*. Scholars have not only identified the principal sources for both the primary narrative and the digressions, but have also studied in some detail the relationship between the Spanish poem and its roots.

Scholars consider the *Libro de Alexandre* prototypical of the thirteenth-century Spanish school of poetry known as *mester de clerecía*. In fact, nineteenth-century readers coined the term from the *Libro de Alexandre*'s second stanza, where "mester de clerecía" refers to the poem's regular versification (rhymed quatrains of fourteen-syllable lines) in contrast to *joglaría*, or poetry tied more closely to the oral tradition with much looser metrics and rhyme. More recently, mester de clerecía has come to encompass a broader range of characteristics including content (learned material reflecting the thirteenth-century intellectual tradition of the nascent Spanish universities, such as Palencia) and purpose (the sharing of information for instruction and moral edification).

This didactic intent is most obvious in the many digressions, which include a lesson on how to hunt elephants, a catalog of the wonders of the Orient, a map of the world, and an allegory on the four seasons of the year. The moralistic orientation of many digressions is clear in, for example, the diatribe against social corruption, and a description of hell that enumerates the Seven Deadly Sins. Scholars agree that such "digressions" play an important structural role in that they reinforce the didactic and moralizing intent of the principal story line.

MARY JANE KELLEY

Bibliography

Cary, G. *The Medieval Alexander*. Cambridge, 1956.

Michael, I. *The Treatment of Classical Material in the* Libro de Alexandre. Manchester, 1970.

Rico, F. "La clerecía del mester." *Hispanic Review* 53 (1985), 1–23; 127–50.

LIBRO DE APOLONIO

An anonymous work composed of some 650 monorhymed cuartets in the style of the so-called *Mester de clerecía* that dates from circa 1250 and comprises an imaginative portrayal of late classical antiquity. It is uniquely preserved in Escorial manuscript III-K-4. The *Libro* tells the story of Apollonius, king of Tyre, who, after many complicated trials and adventures in the eastern Mediterranean, is reunited with his lost wife, Luciana, and his daughter, Tarciana, who had nearly fallen into prostitution and become a *jongleur*. Apollonius, urbane and expert at solving riddles, is also a master of music and court entertainments who uses his skills to overcome adversity. A tale essentially of exile and return, the peripatetic adventures of the *Libro de Apolonio* follow the structure of the late Byzantine romances, with chance encounters, mistaken identities, and surprise endings. Although probably inspired by a French or Provençal model of the story, the poet was most likely also familiar with Latin versions of the tale, among them the *Historia Apolloni regis Tyri*, attributed to Symposius, the *Phanteon* of Godfrey of Viterbo, the tenth-century *Gesta Apolloni*, and the shorter version of it in the *Gesta Romanorum*.

More than entertainment, the *Libro de Apolonio* is noteworthy for its conflation of courtly attitudes, hagiographic discourse, folklore, and secular knowledge, demonstrating the desire to forge a new intellectual and social alliance between the laity, especially the aristocracy, and the world of clerical learning. Its vision of the world of prostitution and an almost primeval monarchy corrupted by incest that is revealed, and eventually overcome, by the virtuous and learned Apolonio exhibits a care for the interaction and involvement of Christian and human values in a fallen secular universe. Its exaltation of liberal learning in both the active and the contemplative life seeks to show the wisdom and efficacy of an education in coming to terms with the problems of the world.

E. Michael Gerli

Bibliography

Alvar, M. "Apolonio, clérigo entendido." In *Symposium in honorem profesor Martín de Riquer*. Ed. A. Vilanova Barcelona, 1986.

Brownlee, M. S. "Writing and Scripture in the *Libro de Apolonio*: The Conflation of Hagiography and Romance," *Hispanic Review* 51 (1983), 159–74.

Rico, F. "La clerecía del mester," *Hispanic Review* 53 (1985), 1–23, 127–50.

LIBRO DE BUEN AMOR

The *Libro de buen amor* is by far the most enigmatic work in medieval Spanish literature, and probably in the literature of all medieval Europe. It is intentionally ambiguous, it is pervasively parodic, the relationship between the first-person narrator and the implied author is unusually complex, there is a kaleidoscopic interplay between the didactic message(s) and the subversive (sometimes obscene) humor, and even the genre of the book is hard to pin down.

The authorial title is given in a characteristically elusive way, and it passed unnoticed for over five hundred years (early readers knew it as *El libro del Arcipreste*, *El Arcipreste de Fita en su tractado*, *Las coplas del Arcipreste de Hita*, or *Cancionero del Arcipreste*). Yet there should be no doubt about the title: the narrator-protagonist tells us that as a tribute to one of the characters, "buen amor dixe al libro." The character in question is his go-between, the old bawd Trotaconventos, who had commanded "llamatme Buen Amor"; nevertheless, the prose prologue insists that "buen amor" means the love of God.

The *Libro de buen amor* as it has come down to us is not a unitary work: it has an extensive narrative core, into which some lyrics are firmly integrated (others, announced in the text, are missing), and around which other lyrics and one episode have been gathered. The core is a fictional autobiography, treated in a parodic manner and centered on the protagonist's comically unsuccessful pursuit of women. The only episode in which he is unquestionably successful is that of Doña Endrina, whose seduction (with the help of Trotaconventos) follows advice from the allegorical figure of Don Amor and then from Venus; but in this sequence (which occupies 42 percent of the *Libro*) the protagonist's name changes, and there are so many anomalous features that only if we regard the whole sequence as a dream does everything fall into place. If we add associated episodes that follow soon after (the allegorical battle between Carnival and Lent, the triumphal entry of Don Amor), dream narrative rises to 56 percent of the *Libro* and an even higher percentage of the narrative core.

Sources or close analogues have been found for all the major elements of the *Libro*: for instance, the Endrina episode is a reworking of the medieval Latin comedy *Pamphilus*, Don Amor's advice adapts Ovid's *Ars amatoria*, many of the tales used by the characters as *exempla* to support their arguments come from medieval Aesopic collections, and the battle between Carnival and Lent derives from a European tradition, perhaps in its French form. The four *serrana* episodes, in which the protagonist encounters mountain women, parody the *pastorelas* of the troubadours (these episodes, like the allegorical battle that follows them, are now widely seen as evidence of a carnivalesque spirit in the *Libro*). All of the episodes and the inset tales and lyrics are firmly within the Western, Christian tradition (even the one tale that has a Moorish setting seems to derive from Arthurian literature). It is at first sight surprising, therefore, that several eminent scholars have detected an Islamic or Hebrew inspiration for the autobiographical, episodic structure and for the work's pervasive ambiguity. Recent research has, however, found, at several points in the *Libro*, convincing evidence of contact between the poet and Islamic culture. It is here that the question of literary influences connects with research on the poet's life.

The narrator-protagonist tells us that his name is Juan Ruiz and that he is archpriest of Hita; some other snippets of information are added (e.g., that he is "de Alcalá"). Until the early 1970s there was only speculation, but since then three serious hypotheses have been built on firm documentary evidence. First, that the poet is Juan Ruiz de Cisneros, born in Muslim Spain (Alcalá la Real?) to Christian parents who never married; in his early teens he went with his father to Castile, and eventually rose to prominence in the church. Secondly, that he is the Juan Ruiz mentioned in documents in the Toledo cathedral archives. Thirdly, that he is the composer named as Johannes Roderici in a Latin musical manuscript. There are dangerous gaps in the evidence for each hypothesis, but there are attractive features in each. Moreover, they are not incompatible: any two, or even all three, could be correct. And if our poet Juan Ruiz is Johannes Roderici, the interest in music shown in the *Libro* is explained; if he is Juan Ruiz de Cisneros, he has a personal history that would generate elements of Islamic culture within a generally Western, Christian pattern of sources.

The textual history of the *Libro* is as problematic as the poet's biography. Scholars agree that some parts had an independent existence (and were probably written for public performance) before the work as a whole took shape, and that other parts were probably composed after the narrative core was constructed. Throughout most of the twentieth century the majority view was that there were two versions of the *Libro*, one completed in 1330 and represented by two of the three manuscripts (Gayoso and Toledo), the other, represented by the longer Salamanca manuscript, being an expansion dating from 1343. Majority opinion has now swung against the two-versions hypothesis, concluding that there was a single version (completed in 1343?) and that the differences between the two states of the text are the result of manuscript transmission and reception, not of authorial expansion. It may, however, be too early to dismiss the two-versions hypothesis out of hand, and in any case there is still controversy about the date: one scholar has suggested much later composition, in the 1380s. If this were true all the biographical hypotheses would collapse, and the *Libro* would no longer be innovatory in its abundant lyrics in Castilian (but the weight of the evidence is against this redating).

The poet's metrical virtuosity is impressive. Most of the *Libro* is in the *cuaderna vía* (monorhymed Alexandrine quatrains) that dominated learned poetry throughout the thirteenth century and most of the fourteenth, but the lyrics exhibit a variety of metrical forms, and the poet announces that one of his aims was "dar [a] algunos lecíón e muestra de metrificar e rimar e de trobar" (to provide a lesson and example for some of prosody, rhyming, and making poetry)." There is a period of influence on Castilian court poems from about 1380 to the beginning of the fifteenth century, but if the *Libro* was completed around 1343, the emergence of Castilian as the dominant vehicle for court lyric, a few decades later, may show that Juan Ruiz's example had been rapidly effective.

The Salamanca manuscript was copied in about 1415, and within twenty-five years was in the library of one of the university's colleges. It is unlikely to be mere coincidence that, after the short period of poetic influence, the *Libro*'s presence in the fifteenth century was primarily learned (influence on *Celestina*, another product of the University of Salamanca, no longer seems improbable). The *Libro* seems to have been read in the light radical Aristotelianism, which saw love in the context of the natural impulse to reproduction, and that current of thought may well be present in the *Libro* itself (where it blends with the Ovidian attitude to love), not just in its fifteenth-century reception. That, however, is by no means the only intellectual current relevant to the work: St Augustine, especially in *De doctrina christiana* and *De magistro*, is now seen as a major influence on Juan Ruiz's ambivalent attitude to the interpretation of his work; in addition, the *Confessiones* may be a subtext of the autobiographical narrative, though this by no means excludes the formative role of the late-medieval European genre of the erotic pseudoautobiography.

Juan Ruiz insists that he aims to "dar solaz a todos" (give pleasure to all), and that his book provides "la santidat mucha" (much sanctity) but also "de juego e de burla" (jest and fun). It is generally assumed that much of the *Libro* was intended for public performance, but we have no evidence of such a performance (it would have been surprising if any record had been kept). If we knew how it had been performed, we should learn a great deal, and many of the ambiguities might be resolved (though, in this supremely ambiguous book, many would remain). It is likely that the *Libro*'s reception in the fourteenth century differed markedly from its mainly learned reception in the fifteenth. And its influence may have spread beyond Spain. Similarities between the *Libro* and *The Canterbury Tales* have often been noticed. Now it seems highly probable that Chaucer visited Spain in 1366, halfway between the completion of the *Libro* and the beginning of the *Tales*. The possibility that Juan Ruiz's work may have inspired Chaucer needs more thorough investigation. For the present, the question remains tantalizingly open, like so much in *Libro de buen amor* studies.

ALAN DEYERMOND

Bibliography

Arcipreste de Hita, *Libro de buen amor*, Clásicos Castellanos Vols. 14 and 17. Ed. J. Joset, Madrid, 1974.

Dagenais, J. *The Ethics of Reading in Manuscript Culture: Glossing the "Libro de Buen Amor."* Princeton, N.J., 1994.

Gybbon-Monypenny, G. B. (ed.,) *"Libro de buen amor" Studies*. Colección Támesis, A12. London, 1970.

———, (ed.,) Arcipreste de Hita, *Libro de buen amor*. Clásicos Castalia, Vol. 161. Madrid, 1988.

Lecoy, F. *Recherches sur le "Libro de Buen Amor" de Juan Ruiz, Archiprêtre de Hita*. 2d ed. Ed. A. D. Deyermond. Farnborough, England, 1974.

Juan Ruiz, *Libro de Buen Amor*. Ed. and trans. R. S. Willis. Princeton, N.J., 1972.

Juan Ruiz, Arcipreste de Hita, *Libro de buen amor*. Letras Hispánicas, Vol. 70. Ed. A. Blecua. Madrid, 1990.

LIBRO DE LOS ENGAÑOS

Libro de los Engaños (Book of the Wiles of Women) is the title of the first Spanish translation of *Sendebar*, a collection of short stories. It is supposed that, following a process similar to *Calila e Digna*, its origin goes back to India and that, via Persia, it reached the Arab world, though the lack of evidence makes this journey purely hypothetical. It was pointed out that the book was written in Persian in the sixth century, and, later, part of its narrative material migrated toward the East; on the other hand the importance of the Hebrew version, which served as a link between the Eastern and the Western version has also been shown. The Spanish translation was requested by Fadrique, brother of Alfonso X, in 1253, and was done from an Arabic original. The lack of a proper team, like the one gathered around Alfonso X, may explain its faults, with some passages not decipherable. There remains one manuscript written by the beginning of the fifteenth-century, corrected quite a few times at the end of that century or the beginning of the sixteenth. The corrections are very interesting for a linguistic study.

The work is one of the most perfect and simple narrative models. A prince is sentenced to death as a result of a false charge made by of one of the king's wives. But the execution is postponed—as is the main narrative—because the royal advisers and the wife try, with their stories, to change the king's decision. Altogether there are twenty-three stories: five from the wicked wife, who tries to validate the accusation with them and save her life; thirteen from the seven advisers (there is one story missing), who ask the king to spare the prince and present misogynist arguments; and five stories in which the prince defends himself and shows the wisdom he has achieved. The main story, very similar in most of the Eastern versions, is a strange mix of traces of old initiation rites, folk motifs, and diverse literary traditions. Within the inserted stories there is a wide variety: some of them (such as 6 and 8) are hardly found in medieval literature; others are very close to classic tales (such as 12) or to *fabliaux* (such as 5, 10, and 13). Some were already known in the Iberian Peninsula, having appeared in the *Disciplina clericalis* of Petrus Alfonsi, and, due to their remarkable misogynist character, were widely disseminated. The work was well known in Spain, but in a much more Western version, *Siete sabios de Roma*, which derives from the *Liber de septem sapientibus* (twelfth century).

María Jesús Lacarra

Bibliography

Kantor, S. *El libro de Sindibād: Variacions en torno al eje temático "engaño-error."* Madrid, 1988.

Sendebar. Ed M. J. Lacarra. Madrid, 1989.

LIBRO DE MISERIA D'OMNE

The *Libro de miseria d'omne*, a poetic adaptation of the *De miseria condicionis humanae* by Pope Innocent III, is a *cuaderna vía* piece copied in prose form and consisting of 502 strophes cast in sixteen-syllable verse. In his paleographic edition of the poem, Miguel Artigas, pointing to the eight-510 syllable hemistiches, imperfect rhyme, and poetic ineptness, classified it as a representation of the decline of the Alexandrine and dated its composition at the end of the fourteenth century. Agreeing with this assessment, subsequent scholars held the poem in low esteem, categorizing it as an uninspired translation and an example of the degeneration of *cuaderna vía* (quatrains). Recent studies have, however, shown the need to reevaluate the position and importance of the poem.

In her study of the *Miseria* Jane E. Connolly rejects the classification of the poem as a translation, arguing that the Spanish poet transforms rather than translates his source: he amplifies, abbreviates, or reorders the Latin material in order to emphasize clarity and coherence; he replaces the elevated rhetoric of Innocent with imaginative and descriptive language; he eliminates unsuitable topics while adding sections containing sharp social criticism and fundamental church doctrine; and he recasts the treatise in the more popular cuaderna vía. In adapting and re-creating the Latin treatise to meet his own artistic and personal designs, the attitude of the Spanish poet toward his source resembles that of Gonzalo de Berceo or the authors of the *Roman d'Alexandre* and *Libro de Apolonio*.

John K. Walsh and Connolly suggest an early date of composition for the poem: in their view the poet clearly expected his work to be understood within the context of the thirteenth-century *clerecía* texts, an intention reinforced by the inclusion of strophe 4, which is a deliberate echo of the prologue of the *Libro de Alexandre*. Connolly attributes many of the imperfections in the only extant version of the poem to errors of the prosifying copyist, and she reconstructs the poem, showing that the meter, rhyme, and formulas tie it to the practices of the thirteenth-century cuaderna vía poets. Walsh and Connolly situate the *Miseria* in the homiletic literature of the late thirteenth century, pointing to the numerous thematic similarities with the *Castigos de Catón* and especially the *Proverbios de Salamón*. Connolly supports this claim by citing historical documents of the period, which reveal that the social criticism in the *Miseria* reflects the general sense of malaise at the turn of the century.

The *Miseria* belongs to the cycle of late thirteenth-century didactic poetry and may have influenced later cuaderna vía works. Indeed, Walsh argues that Juan Ruíz parodied the *Miseria* in his *Libro de buen amor*, and Connolly suggests that the author of the *Alhotba arrimada* was familiar with it.

JANE E. CONNOLLY

Bibliography

Connolly, J. E. *Translation and Poetization in the "Quaderna Vía": Study and Edition of the "Libro de miseria d'omne."* Madison, Wisc., 1987.

Walsh, J. K. "Juan Ruiz and the *mester de clerezía*: Lost Context and Lost Parody in the *Libro de buen amor*." *Romance Philology* 33 (1979–80), 62–87.

LIBRO DEL CAVALLERO ZIFAR

The *Libro del cavallero Zifar* (also written Cifar and Çifar) is an anonymous fourteenth-century prose romance that is divided into three main parts, two sets of adventures and a long moralizing discourse. The first section contains the life history of the knight Zifar, who rises from poverty to wealth; the second presents a series of lectures that Zifar delivers to his two sons on how to rule; and the third narrates the adventures of Zifar's son Roboán, who begins his quest as an obscure figure and ends it with fame and fortune. The journeys of both men are filled with numerous digressions, including two in fantasy worlds that provide variety and humor to the basic narrative.

The extensive and complex adventures of Zifar are best understood if they are separated into three phases: the first, in which the family is together; the second, dealing with the life of Zifar after the separation of the family; and the third, depicting circumstances in Mentón, where the family is reunited. The romance begins in a land of uncertain location called "las Yndias," where Zifar, the son of a noble, wealthy, and distinguished family, is living with his wife, Grima, and two young sons, Garfín and Roboán. Despite his noble birth and talent as a knight, Zifar's life is plagued with obstacles caused by a curse placed on him by an evil ancestor.

Because of the malediction Zifar's horses die every ten days, a phenomenon that has far-reaching consequences. Although the details are not totally clear, the main impact of the curse is economic, because the high cost of replacing the animals has made it impossible for the family to live with the comforts normally available to aristocrats. It is also evident that the curse undermines Zifar's authority and effectiveness as a knight, for when his horses collapse and expire in the middle of a major conflict, his role as a leader is inhibited until the animal has been replaced.

Tired of living in poverty and unable to overcome its cause, Zifar and his wife decide to leave the area, hoping that a change in location will enable them to regain wealth and prestige. After packing their belongings, the family departs and eventually reaches the kingdom of Galapia, where Zifar is instrumental in settling a dispute between the woman ruler of Galapia and a king who controls the adjacent land. The two figures end their conflict by marrying; after the wedding Zifar and his family continue their journey and almost immediately become separated due to circumstances beyond their control: Garfín is kidnapped by a lioness, Grima is abducted by some sailors and carried on a magic ship to a distant land, and Roboán becomes lost while searching for his mother.

With the separation of the family, Zifar enters a new phase of his life. He travels alone until he unexpectedly comes upon a hermit. After the two men share a meal, the hermit has a vision in which he miraculously foresees Zifar's future life. Later the hermit introduces Zifar to a squire; Zifar and the squire leave the area and embark on a series of adventures that end in the land of Mentón.

In this final phase of his journey, Zifar's economic and political status begins to change dramatically, for he meets and marries the king's daughter, thereby placing himself in a position to inherit the throne. When in the course of time his father-in-law does die, Zifar automatically succeeds him as king. Now that he holds the highest position in the kingdom, he has attained the wealth and prestige that he had previously been denied.

Until Zifar reaches Mentón, the fate of his first wife and sons is a mystery. After he becomes king, however, their whereabouts is unexpectedly clarified, for one day Grima, Garfín, and Roboán all appear. This pleasant surprise creates a major problem for Zifar, who is now married to another woman. The dilemma is miraculously settled, however, when his second wife suddenly becomes ill and dies, thereby leaving him free to reunite with Grima.

Zifar's central portion is devoted to a series of lectures on how to rule wisely that Zifar delivers to his sons. Most of the discussion is an elaboration of the meaning and importance of concepts considered significant in the medieval period: humility, meekness, chastity, charity, temperance, and diligence. In one part, however, Zifar abandons this highly idealistic view and discloses unexpected prejudices: he issues a very stern warning about the disastrous consequences of accepting advice from Jews.

The final section of the romance is dedicated to Roboán, who leaves Mentón in search of his own set of adventures. Shortly after beginning the journey he meets Seringa, the woman who will eventually become his wife. At this stage of his career, however, he decides to postpone marriage and to continue his journey. During his expedition he slowly acquires prominence and eventually becomes emperor. Now, as principal ruler of the land, he needs an heir to the throne, a problem that his advisers resolve by recommending matrimony. He returns to visit Seringa, whom he marries, and after the birth of their first child, Roboán and his wife return to Mentón for a reunion with his family.

For many years scholars believed that the three major parts of the romance were almost totally unrelated. The adventures of Roboán were considered to be dissociated from those of his father, and the series of lectures comprising the central, moral section were normally disregarded as insignificant and unrelated to the activities of Zifar and Roboán. In recent years, however, scholars have reversed their position, since strong similarities have been found between the lives of father and son. Furthermore, the topics stressed in Zifar's lectures have been identified as those most elaborated in the two sets of adventures.

One of the most complex and inconclusive topics concerning the *Zifar* is its sources. Investigation has concentrated primarily on three main areas of the romance: the two otherworld episodes, the adventures of Zifar, and the advice Zifar gives to his sons. Studies analyzing the two otherworld adventures have produced the least conclusive results, since sources from both Arabic and Celtic material have been found. In one of these episodes a passing reference to King Arthur led some scholars to suspect that the entire work may have derived from the Arthurian material, but a closer examination revealed few similarities with either the Vulgate or the post-Vulgate cycle.

The adventures of Zifar have revealed similarities with three sources: the eastern and western branches of the legend of St. Eustachius, formerly a Roman general named Placidus; "The Tale of the King Who Lost Kingdom and Wife and Wealth and Allah Restored Them to Him" in the *Thousand and One Nights*; and the French epic *Chanson de Floovant*, which is directly related to the legend of Octavian. Despite the strong parallels that may be drawn between the *Zifar* and all of these works, however, major differences also exist.

The main source of the second section of the romance is far easier to document, although care needs to be taken not to oversimplify an intricate situation. The point of departure for these lectures is almost certainly the Arabic treatise *Flores de filosofía*, but since the *Zifar* author has greatly expanded and rearranged the original, he may also have taken material from other sources. It is also important to point out that the *Flores* is closely related to such other thirteenth- and fourteenth-century didactic works as *Bocados de oro, Poridat de las poridades, Castigos e documentos del rey don Sancho*, and the *Siete Partidas* of Alfonso X, all of which draw on Semitic originals.

The question of sources is complicated even further when one takes into consideration a statement in the prologue indicating that the work is a translation. This comment is frequently disregarded because authors have been known to make similar assertions even though their work may not have been translated. However, since other Hispanic books produced in the fourteenth century state that they are translated, and historical evidence proves this to be true, many scholars suspect that the *Zifar* may also have been a translation.

If one does accept the possibility that the *Zifar* was translated, the second question to be addressed concerns the meaning of "Chaldean," the original language from which it reportedly was translated. The term normally designates Syriac, a dialect of Aramaic, but some Hispanists have found evidence that leads them to believe that *caldeo* may also have referred to Arabic.

Little is known about the date of the *Zifar*, although most scholars agree that the romance was composed during the first half of the fourteenth century. Since the Jubilee of 1300 is mentioned in the prologue, this year is considered the earliest possible date of composition, although it should be taken into consideration that prologues were normally written after a work had been finished. We also may confirm that the work was terminated by 27 October 1361, for on this day Pedro IV of Aragón wrote a letter in which he requests a copy of the *Siffar*. Within these broad limits, however, opinion varies, and definitive conclusions have yet to be reached.

The question of authorship is also complex, especially if the work is a translation, for we do not know the role of the person or the people who had a part in translating, copying, expanding, or editing the material. Whatever the process might have been, however, we may affirm that the author of the first Spanish version is unknown, although some attempts have been made to attribute the romance to Archdeacon Ferrand Martínes. This idea was first suggested by Menéndez y Pelayo, and it has been supported primarily on the basis that the archdeacon is mentioned in the prologue, that he lived during the first years of the fourteenth century, and that he had the preparation and knowledge necessary to compose the work. Although some Hispanists continue to favor this theory, most now agree that the evidence available at this time is still inconclusive.

MARILYN A. OLSEN

Bibliography

Burke, J. F. *History and Vision: The Figural Structure of the "Libro del cavallero Zifar."* London, 1972.

González, Cristina. *El* Cavallero Zifar *y el reino lejano* Madrid, 1984.

Olsen, M. A. (ed.) *Libro del cauallero Cifar.* Madison, Wisc., 1975.

Ruíz de Conde, J. *El amor y el matrimonio secreto en los libros de caballerías.* Madrid, 1948.

Wagner, C. P. (ed.) *El Libro del cauallero Zifar (El Libro del cauallero de Dios).* Part I, *Text.* Ann Arbor, Mich., 1929. Repr., Millwood, N.Y., 1971.

Walker, R. M. *Tradition and Technique in "El libro del cavallero Zifar."* London, 1974.

LIBRO DEL PASSO HONROSO

In the summer of 1434, the Castilian knight Suero de Quiñones, together with nine other friends, celebrated a pass of arms on the Órbigo River bridge near Astorga (León), on the pilgrimage road to Santiago de Compostela.

From 12 July until 9 August the ten defenders and the sixty-three challengers broke a total of 180 lances, considerably less than the 300 that had been agreed in the chapters publicized in the various courts of the Iberian Peninsula and elsewhere in Europe.

A detailed account of the events at the bridge by Pero Rodríguez de Lena is preserved in the El Escorial Library (Ms. f.II.19); two partial manuscripts are in the Biblioteca Menéndez Pelayo, (Ms. 75) and the Real Academia de la Historia, Madrid (Ms. B-104); and there is an abbreviated version by Juan de Pineda (Salamanca, 1558), that contains material not found in the Escorial manuscript or either of the two partial manuscripts.

The events of July and August 1434 had implications beyond the purely anecdotal: a knight who wants to free himself of a vow, or a number of knights engaged in re-creating literary interpretations of a bygone chivalric age. Riquer has proven convincingly that the *Passo honroso* was the answer of Álvaro de Luna and members of his house to the *Passo de la fuerte ventura*, organized by Enrique of Aragón, which had surpassed a previous pass of arms organized by Álvaro de Luna. The clear interest of some Aragónese challengers in tarnishing Suero's pass—the letters exchanged between them and the Castilians, and the fact that there were several scribes present, one of them Juan de Mena, with the explicit purpose of keeping King Juan II informed of the daily events—clearly indicates that the *Passo honroso* was part, albeit a small one, of the political intrigues of the fifteenth century.

JUAN ESPADAS

Bibliography

Espadas, J. "Pedro Rodríguez de Lena y su papel en el *Libro del Passo Honroso.*" *La Corónica* 10, no. 2 (1980): 179–85.

Ferrer: Gironès, F. *Lletres de batalla.* Barcelona, 1963.

Riquer, M. de. *Caballeros andantes españoles.* Madrid, 1967.

LINGUISTIC STANDARDIZATION

Linguistic standardization is an artificial phenomenon; languages only acquire "standards" if there has been a conscious decision as to which forms belong to the canon. In their natural state languages have stylistic, sociolinguistic, and geographical variation. Standardization is usually part of a wider process of the establishment of literacy. Standard written Latin in the early Middle Ages, in the Iberian Peninsula as elsewhere, was based on the *Ars Minor* (fourth century A.D.) of Aelius Donatus and his commentators. All grammars of the age focused on writing, and took the form of a limitation of the linguistic options found in speech. These *artes* concentrated especially on correct written morphology, which apparently came to be thought of as a branch of orthography as much as of syntax; Romance speakers were taught and expected to write their own language by following standard spellings plus the rules of Donatus concerning word endings.

In Muslim Spain this system never changed, although from the late ninth century the many Arabic-Romance bilinguals seem to have confined their literacy to Arabic, already essentially standardized. In the north, however, polishing texts to conform to Donatus became increasingly arduous; in the *Chronica* said to be by Alfonso III, for example, surviving versions attest to differing stages of the polishing process, but the lawyers who drew up bills of sale and other practical documents had less leisure. Yet their nonstandard morphosyntax and orthography is not merely whimsical; we see occasional glimpses of pragmatic accommodations according to less rigid standards (in the tenth and early eleventh centuries), wherein vernacular noun and verb morphology is accepted in writing, and several orthographic approximations, both logographically for whole words and morphemes and phonographically for sounds, seem to have been taught and learned. These documents are not easy to study; Menéndez Pidal's pioneering analysis implied in many cases that the scribes operated a phonetic script, but the existence of partial alternative localized unofficial standards seems more plausible.

The problems came to a head in ninth-century France, where scholars established for the first time a standard spoken form in church contexts, based not only on the ancient morphosyntax prescribed by Donatus but also on the artificial spelling-pronunciation techniques already used as standard by Germanic speakers, where every written letter had a specified sound (as we still read Latin today). Thus for the first time written texts became generally unintelligible when read aloud. This system, reinforced by newly fashionable respect for Priscian's *Institutionis grammaticae*, led to an otherwise unnecessary conceptual break between Latin and Romance, eventually seen (in educated circles) as being two different languages. This gave rise to a need for a separate written standard for any text desired to be read aloud intelligibly to a nonclerical audience; in this, spoken morphosyntax could be allied to an orthography that used the letter-sound correspondences of the new Latin pronunciation in reverse to produce new standard spellings different from the Latin forms of the same words. Even in orthography, however, this "Old French" standardization was never as rigid as that of Latin. The new medieval Latin standard came to Catalonia in the late ninth century, but to the rest of the Iberian Peninsula only in the Twelfth-century Renaissance, when many French and French-trained scholars worked there. There then arose similar consequential needs for vernacular standards.

Techniques using roughly the same principles as in France were elaborated experimentally (as we see first now in the famous eleventh-century Riojan glosses). Different scribal centers experimented along different lines; Vairão, in Portugal, for example, seems to have had its own enterprising ideas. In due course, different political units tended to want different new standards as symbols of their own separately affirmed identities (as in the modern Spanish *autonomías*). Thus the Catalans chose to standardize a separate written system only after, and perhaps as an indirect consequence of, the battle of Muret (1213), whereas Catalan speakers had previously followed the Provençal standard. In both León and Castile the first important document written in Romance is the Treaty of Cabreros (1206). Some details suggest that already the chanceries had standardized the written forms of several words and morphemes, often differently in the two kingdoms, but the scribes had difficulty in abandoning entirely their old ''correct'' instincts. The conceptual splitting of Romance into separate standard languages was thus a direct consequence of the Latin-Romance split, both processes unnecessary in the previous increasingly logographic culture but precipitated (in Romance Europe) by the heightened consciousness of the grapheme-phoneme anisomorphism and a perceived need for new local standardizations.

Later in the thirteenth century, the Castilian court worked out a kingdom-wide norm for many features of written Castilian, as used in the later Alfonsine chronicles, probably based on a selection of features from different areas (as in modern standard written Galego) rather than choosing one complete local linguistic system to be the general standard (as in modern standard written Basque). There seems to have been no general medieval Aragónese standard at all; Basque, being still unwritten, did not need one. The creators of standard written Portuguese deliberately accentuated its individuality by choosing some southern French rather than Castilian and Galician sound-letter correspondences (*nh* and *ñ* represent the same sound, for example), with the same *''diferencialismo''* that characterizes those modern *autonomias* that spell [k] with *k*. The Romance standardizations are thus both symptoms and catalysts of nationalism, of a decrease in international cultural relations, and an increase in internal social divisions, so it was as well that there was no rigid or dogmatic standardization of Castilian language (or even texts) before the founding of the Real Academia (1713). Even then it hardly affected speech at all; medieval standardization only really affected Latin (and Arabic), a fact that largely caused the general but erroneous view that vernaculars had no grammar.

ROGER WRIGHT

Bibliography

Joseph, J. *Eloquence and Power: The Rise of Language Standards and Standard Languages*. London, 1987.

Lapesa, R. "Contienda de normas lingüísticas en el castellano alfonsí." In *Actas del coloquio hispano-alemán Menéndez Pidal*. Ed. W. Hempel and D. Briesemeister. Tübingen, 1982. 172–90.

Menéndez Pidal, R. *Orígenes del Español*. Madrid, 1926.

Wright, R. *Early Iberoromance*. Newark, Del., 1995.

LISBON, CITY

Capital of Portugal. Lisbon was already an important trading center for Africa and a large part of Europe before Afonso Henriques, king of the Portuguese, captured it from the Moors in 1147. He did not have the resources or the men to assault it, but when a fleet carrying an expeditionary force of the Second Crusade put in at Oporto, the bishop of the city negotiated with the crusaders for their participation in the king's plan to take Lisbon. They agreed and sailed up the Tagus River on 28 June 1147. The siege, a joint operation that involved Portuguese, Flemings, Germans, Normans, and English lasted seventeen weeks. Weakened by war, hunger, and pestilence, the Moors surrendered after putting up a ferocious resistance.

In Christian hands, Lisbon became no less a coveted prey for marauders and invaders in view of its wealth and geographical position. Portuguese kings were eager to develop Lisbon as a maritime and commercial center. Afonso III (r. 1248–1279) made Lisbon the capital of the kingdom. He promoted a large market of stall-holders, renting booths that rendered good profits to the crown. Lisbon grew in prosperity and soon its merchants were trading with the main ports of Europe. King Fernando (1367–1383), after successive and unsuccessful sieges of the city by the Castilians, had its walls rebuilt between 1373 and 1376. It was behind these walls that the people of Lisbon fought off a nine-month Castilian siege in 1384. With the voyages of discovery, Lisbon became an international emporium, being one of the most beautiful cities in Europe.

LUIS REBELO

Bibliography

Caetano, M. *A Administração Municipal de Lisboa durante a Primeira Dinastia (1179–1383)*. Lisbon, 1951.

Castilho, J. de. *Lisboa Antiga*. Coimbra, 1884.

David, C. W. *De Expugnatione Lyxbonensi: The Conquest of Lisbon*. New York, 1936.

Góis, D. de. *Vrbis Olisiponis Descriptio*. Evora, 1554.

Livermore, H. "The Conquest of Lisbon and Its Author." *Portuguese Studies* 6 (1990), 1–6.

LISBON, CONQUEST OF

Afonso Henriques, king of Portugal, accompanied by a large force of crusaders recruited by St. Bernard for the Second Crusade, took the city after a lengthy siege on 24 October 1147. The feat is described by a crusader known only as R. in a letter to Osbert of Bawdsey, *De Expugnatione Lyxbonensi*.

Lisbon had formed part of the Berber state of Badajoz, whose ruler had offered it to Alfonso VI of León in return for protection from the Almoravids, who, however, seized Badajoz. Alfonso could not hold Lisbon: Santarém and the Tagus River valley were also lost to the Christians in 1111. On becoming king, Alfonso Henriques made a first unsuccessful attempt to conquer Lisbon in 1142–1143. In March 1147 he took Santarém by a surprise attack. St. Bernard had launched the Second Crusade, for which men from England, the Low Countries, and southern Germany gathered at Dartmouth in 164 ships. On their putting in at Oporto, Bishop John Peculiar persuaded them to join Afonso before Lisbon, which held out unrelieved for nearly four months. The crusaders went on to Palestine in the spring, but some remained to settle, and an English priest, Gilbert of Hastings, became bishop of the new see. R.'s letter shows the part played by Hervey de Glanvill, constable for the East Anglian contingent, in this.

The feat assured the continuity of the Portuguese monarchy, greatly increased the authority of Afonso Henriques, and almost doubled the territory of Portugal, which until then consisted of the old county and that of Coimbra, annexed in 1064. It provided Portugal with the physical base for the fourteenth-century enterprise of the voyages of discovery. The taking of Lisbon was followed at once by the annexation of Sintra and Palmela. R. s letter survives in the unique copy at Corpus Christi College, Cambridge, and was first edited by Herculano in *Portugaliae Monumenta Historica* (1861).

H. V. LIVERMORE

Bibliography

The Conquest of Lisbon. Ed. C. W. David, New York, 1936.

Livermore, H. "The Conquest of Lisbon and Its Author." *Portuguese Studies* 6 (1990), 1–6.

LITERACY

Western Christendom has been literate, in the sense of depending upon written records for the essential transactions of its civil and religious life, without interruption since Roman times. But in the Middle Ages the dissemination of literacy rested on radically different postulates from those that obtained in antiquity, or in early modern Europe: training and skill in letters (*grammatica*) was the highly specialized professional preserve of a unique social group known as the clergy, whose distinctive function was "scripture"—the guardianship of the written religious law and liturgy. This intimate connection between literacy and scripture was also fundamental to the culture and education of the Jewish and (after 711) Muslim communities of Iberia; what made the Christian case unique was its restriction (probably deriving from primitive Germanic notions of the sacral power of runes and spells, and from a caste system that separated bards from warriors) to a closed community of celibate males who, from early puberty, wore distinctive haircuts and vestments and used a special hieratic language, Latin. Consequently the word *litteratus* itself, and its Romance derivatives *letrado* and *lletrat*, meant not "literate" but "Latinate." Reading was taught exclusively through the medium of Latin, using as a primer (*cartilla*) the *common prayers*, Ten Commandments, and catechism, and the aim was to train clerics to recite aloud the Latin liturgy (*psalterium discere*). At seven, the canonical age of discretion, boys memorized the alphabet with simple phonic exercises and then proceeded directly to reading aloud from the primer (which need not be understood, only accurately recited). Explicit Spanish testimony of this process is given by a vernacular annotation in a fifteenth-century grammar book and glossary (Madrid, BPal MS 1344, fol. 116^v): "*Item* nota el orden que has de tener en enseñar a ler; lo primero enséñale la señal de la crux e los X mandamientos en romançe . . .; lo segundo IV oraçiones dominicales *Aue Maria, Patemoster, Credo, Salue Regina* vulgarmente [in the vernacular], porque todo fiel christiano siete años pasados es obligado . . .; lo terçero el ABC, conosçer las letras ansí vocales como consonantes e juntar e por síllabas deletrear, scilicet *ba be bi bo bu*, e las IV oraçiones sobredichas *en Latino sermone*" (*Item*: Note the order in which you should teach reading; first teach the sign of the cross and the Ten Commandments in Romance; second, the four Sunday prayers, *Ave Maria*, *Paternoster*, *Credo*, *Salve Regina* in the vernacular because every faithful Christian above the age of seven is obliged to know them; third, the ABC, to know the letters and the vowels and consonants and to join and spell by syllables, namely *ba be bi bo bu*.) Training in the skill of writing was a separate process, undertaken later by professional scribes who had to learn not only the Gothic scripts and their complex systems of abbreviation but also the various technicalities of penmanship, ink manufacture, and preparation of manuscript codices. More competent students might proceed to study ecclesiastical Latin grammar and composition, but this remained a subsidiary requirement; throughout the Middle Ages the proof of literacy that conferred benefit of clergy (exemption from secular legal jurisdiction) remained, not the ability to construe the Sacred Page, but the ability to read out a Latin passage (in England the "neck-versel," Ps. 51:1; in Spain more often the Creed or Paternoster). The history of medieval literacy therefore concerns the processes that loosened the clergy's stranglehold on literate skills, and then opened reading and writing to lay society in general. Among these processes two stand out: the rise of vernacular literature, and the growing prestige and professionalism of lawyers and bureaucrats.

Early Middle Ages (to 1080)

Visigothic Spain in the age of Isidore (bishop of Seville, 602–636) had the most sophisticated literary culture in the Latin West. Clerical monopolization of literacy, however, had taken place; the teaching of reading was entirely in the hands of the church and the aristocracy were, in our modern sense, illiterate. It is clear from the abundant liturgical texts of this period, and from Isidore's own voluminous lexicographical works, that the vulgar Latin spoken by the Goths (who were Romanized before they conquered the Iberian Peninsula in 589) had evolved many Romance features not reflected in orthography; writing and reading were moving inexorably away from the spoken language, although it is doubtful whether even Isidore was yet aware of the conceptual distinction. After the Muslim conquest in 711, this separation advanced further: the daily languages of Christians were Arabic and Mozarabic Romance, while formal Latin remained as a liturgical *Schriftsprache*, preserved (along with the Visigothic rite and script) with fervid but inefficacious zeal by the clergy. Even in the most accomplished literary circle of this period, which the caliphs tolerated to gather round Eulogius in ninth-century Córdoba, Paulus Alvarus complained that his Christian flock were better versed in Arabic poetry and rhetoric than in Latin letters (*Indiculus luminosus*, c. 850). In the Christian petty kingdoms of Asturias, León, Navarre, and the Frankish March, literacy was confined to the monasteries, where the influence of French Benedictinism produced flourishing schools, first in Catalonia (at Ripoll, ninth–tenth centuries), and then in La Rioja (in the abbeys of Albelda and San Millán de la Cogolla, late tenth century). An important development occurred when monastic manuscripts began to be furnished with interlinear Romance glosses, marking a recognition of the distinction between "literate" and spoken forms; the most celebrated example, a ninth-century sermonary from San Millán de la Cogolla, includes among its glosses (inserted around 1020–1045) a transcription of the doxology commonly cited as the first extant example of Spanish prose: "Cono ajutorio de nuestro dueno, dueno Christo, dueno Salbatore, qual dueno get ena honore e qual duenno tienet ela mandatjone cono Patre cono Spiritu Sancto enos sieculos delosieculos, facanos Deus omnipotes tal serbitio fere ke denante ela sua face guadioso segamus, Amen" (With help from our lord, lord Christ, lord Savior, Who is honored and shares dominion with the Father and the Holy Ghost for ever and ever, give us omnipotent God the gift that we may be before your face and share joy among us.) (Madrid, RAH Ms. 60, fol. 72). Glosses such as *ibi: obe* or *sicitates: seketates, saltare: sotare* (the latter from an eleventh-century manuscript from Santo Domingo de Silos, London BL Add. 25,600) show that their purpose was not to help monkish readers construe the text, but to facilitate oral delivery for the benefit of the laity. The other significant development in these northern kingdoms occurred, however, not in the monastic *scholae* but in the field of civil law, where the remarkable preservation of the Visigothic *Forum iudicum* (the basis of judicial process down to the thirteenth century), brought literacy into everyday life; for although lawsuits were still conducted by the Germanic procedures of oral testimony, oath-helping, and ordeal, the *Forum* attached fundamental importance to written title, records, and codified enactments. Everyday disputes thus generated a copious documentation of charters, formally subscribed to by witnesses; the instruments themselves were redacted by professional notaries, and although we have no evidence of how these men were taught, their orthography and language, heavily Romance in phonology, phrasing, and vocabulary, was clearly designed, despite its Latin formulae, to be intelligible when read aloud to the litigants—evidence of a training in functional literacy quite distinct from the clerical literacy of the monasteries.

Central Middle Ages (1080–1300)

At the Council of Burgos (1080), King Alfonso VI of Castile abolished the Visigothic liturgy in favor of the Roman (similar measures had been taken in Aragón in 1474 and Navarre in 1076). According to the chronicles the king also banned Visigothic script (*Toletana littera*, supposedly invented by Ulfilas) and enjoined the use of Carolingian minuscule (*Gallica littera*, from which modern roman scripts are derived). Although the definitive abandonment of the Visigothic heritage took time (so that a Leonese charter as late as 1155 might be written in Visigothic script with a conversion table of Carolingian letter-forms at the foot, and the recopying of San Millán de la Cogolla's Visigothic manuscripts into the new script did not take place until around 1200), 1080 marked a watershed in the history of Iberian literacy. The direct effect was to provoke a reform of Latinity in favor of more classical orthography and accidence; the indirect consequence was to clarify the conceptual distinction between this reformed ecclesiastical Latin and the Romance of everyday speech. Before long, therefore, we find texts consciously transcribed in the vernacular. In Catalonia *Homilies d'Organyà* and a version of *Forum iudicum* (both twelfth century) and in Navarre *Fueros of Novenera* (c. 1170) and *Corónicas navarras* (co. 1206), show that scribes turned to Provençal for inspiration in adapting orthography and script to the vernacular; the first datable documents in undisguised Portuguese are the charters of Vairão (1192) and Galician-Portuguese *cancioneiro* lyrics were perhaps written down as early as the reign of Sancho I (1185–1211). In Castile the decade around 1200 marks the full recognition of the written vernacular not only by the crown (Treaty of Cabreros, 1206), but also in literature (*Auto de los reyes magos, Cantar de Mio Cid, Libro de Alexandre*, followed in 1220–1245 by the works of Gonzalo de Berceo). The chief motor for the spread of vernacular writing was the official adoption of the national languages by royal chanceries, a process that reached its culmination in the reigns of Alfonso X of Castile and Jaime I of Aragón; the Castilian and Catalan orthographies designed at this period have lasted, with only superficial changes, to modern times. By 1300, therefore, while the clergy still retained their monopoly on Latin literacy (now highly technical, and taught not in monastic or episcopal schools but in the new universities), there had grown up a parallel group of court bureaucrats who were no less skilled, trained in Roman as well as foral law, but whose literacy was firmly vernacular.

The Late Middle Ages, 1300–1450

The inevitable next stage was the spread of literacy skills among the amateur laity. Non–professional literacy, however, could mean anything from the mere ability to spell one's name to deep book-learning, with wide discrepancies in distribution between regions, classes, town, and country. In the fourteenth century the normal method of diffusion remained oral, by social reading: The *Libro de buen amor*, for example, contains frequent addresses to an audience that included *dueñas*, and there are abundant testimonies reaching the fifteenth century of texts being read aloud to groups of nobles (as Cervantes was later to portray the romances of chivalry being read to harvesters in the *posadas* of La Mancha). Likewise, when a nonprofessional engaged in literary composition he dictated the text to professional amanuenses, as the Infante Juan Manuel, for example, states at the end of each *exemplum* in his *Libro del conde Lucanor*—although autograph documents show that he himself could write. But as increasing prosperity, leisure, and new forms of privacy in the architecture of private houses provided the conditions for lay study, these oral substitutes for reading and writing began slowly to coexist, for the first time since antiquity, with the novel practice of private (silent) reading. By 1440 inventories of private libraries, evidence of lay patronage and authorship, and a large increase in the range of works available in the vernacular, as well the growing number of manuscript copies, indicate the rise of what we may properly call a lay reading public. Literacy, even in theory, was no longer thought of as the preserve of the *clerici*; a Jewish writer, R. Moshe Arragel of Guadalajara, noted in the 1430s that "la sçiençia e lengua latina" was so widespread that even "cavalleros e escuderos e çibdadanos han dexado el puro castellano e con ello han mixto mucho latino" (*Biblia de Alba*, Prólogo, V), while the Salamanca-trained canonist and bishop of Burgos Alfonso de Cartagena, in a Latin epistle to the count of Haro around 1441, enthusiastically argued for the desirability of noblemen learning "the language of literacy which we call grammatical [that is, Latin] speech" (*idioma litterale quod grammatice locutionem uocamus*—Haro himself, he informs us, learned Latin in a school at the court of John II). Cartagena mentioned as a matter of course that most knights possessed "an abundant store of books"; his only concern was that their "unbridled passion for reading [made them] rush to read and hear any book, without discrimination of subject-matter." Cartagena's solution was to propose a discreet form of censorship; growing ecclesiastical opposition to lay literacy was to become a feature of the age, beginning in 1434 with the cause célèbre of the burning of the *libros vedados* (chiefly of Arabic science and supposed "black arts") in the private library of the most learned man in Castile, the nobleman Enrique de Villena, and culminating in attempts to suppress the vernacular versions of the Scriptures that had hitherto flourished in Iberia (despite the ban on Bibles *in Romancio* imposed by the the Fourth Lateran Council, 1215). But this belated clerical backlash in defense of their monopoly of literacy was swept away by the last development in medieval literacy, the invention of the serially printed book. The first native Iberian presses date from the early 1470s, and they issued nearly a thousand incunable editions, almost all in the vernaculars and frequently in runs of four hundred or more copies. By 1500 the archival evidence from wills of book ownership and the statistics of the book trade show that literacy (defined simply as the ability to read and write) was general among the upper aristocracy and urban patriciate (men and women), common in the merchant classes of large cities, by no means unknown among humble artisans, and even occasionally found among rural hidalgos and parish priests. This gradual permeation of society by book-culture through printing meant the end of the medieval clerical monopoly. Iberia, like the rest of preindustrial Europe, reached by 1520 the overall rate of literacy (perhaps 30 to 40 percent) that was to obtain, more or less unchanged, until the educational revolution of the industrial nineteenth century.

JEREMY N.H. LAWRANCE

Bibliography

Berger, P. "La Lecture à Valence de 1474 à 1504. quelques données numériques." *Mélanges de la Casa de Velázquez* 11 (1975), 99–118.

Díaz y Díaz, M. C. et al. *Libros y librerías en la Rioja altomedieval*. Logroño, 1979.

———. *Livre et lecture en Espagne et en France sous l'Ancien Régime: Colloque de la Casa de Velázauez*. Paris, 1981.

Lawrance, J. "The Spread of Lay Literacy in Late Medieval Castile," *Bulletin of Hispanic Studies* 62 (1985), 79–94.

Sánchez Albornoz, C. "Nota sobre los libros leídos en el reino de León hace mil años." *Cuadernos de Historia de España* 1–2 (1944), 222–38.

LITERARY THEORY AND POETICS

In the romance vernaculars of Iberia, the composition of poetic treatises began around 1200 with the desire to codify and transmit the literary practices of the earlier Occitan troubadours for the benefit of courtiers in the kingdom of Aragón. Of the first group of six treatises, the three most significant are Raimon Vidal's *Razos de trobar* (c. 1200) Jofre de Foixà's *Regles de trobar* (c. 1286–1291), and Berenguer d'Anoya's *Mirall de trobar* (early fourteenth century). Though they differed in scope and emphasis, taken together these treatises offered grammatical instruction in Occitan (which was the poetic language of Aragón until the later Middle Ages), and explained the form and function of the most authoritative fixed verse forms, illustrated by examples from classical troubadours. There are also scattered remarks on the nature of poetry itself; for example, both Vidal and Foixà claim the universality of poetry as a defining human activity (an idea that would resurface in Santillana's writings, see below). However, the primary theoretical underpinning of these treatises is that poetry is a rhetorical display of courtliness.

Similar concerns are a feature of the fourteenth-century treatises, associated with the "Poetic consistories" of Toulouse (1323 onward), Lérida ([Lleida], 1338) and Barcelona (1394 onward). These consistories were competitive assemblies designed to conserve and regulate the traditions of Occitan troubadour verse within an orthodox moral and religious framework. The need to award prizes objectively generated poetic treatises that defined linguistic and metrical standards. The largest, and most popular, of these was Guilhem Molinier's vast grammatical *Leys d'amors*, which exists in three redactions (1328–1355), and among texts were a rhyming dictionary by Jacme March (1371), and the *Torcimany* (*The Interpreter*) by Lluis d'Averçó (c. 1400), which, drawing on Molinier's *Leys* and Johan de Castelnou's *Compendi*, combines grammatical and metrical instruction with a rhyme dictionary.

Sponsored by the Aragónese monarchs Pedro the Ceremonious, Juan I, and Martín the Humane, the Catalan consistories enabled the urban oligarchies to acquire the pedigree of courtliness offered by what was called "la gaya sciència de trobar" (the delightful science of poetry).

The social premises of this "gay science" were definitely passed down to fifteenth-century Castile through the ideas of Enrique de Villena and Juan Alfonso de Baena (see below), but it is possible that the ideals of the Catalan-Occitan school may have been popularized earlier in the fourteenth by the Castilian magnate Juan Manuel, who had close contacts with the kingdom of Aragón. Among his numerous treatises on the education, pastimes, and social duties of the nobility, is a lost *ars poetica*, the *Libro de las reglas de cómo se debe trobar*. However, in the early fourteenth century Castilians were also familiar with lyric written in Galician-Portuguese. And for this school, we possess a two-hundred-line fragment of an *Arte de trovar* (ca. 1340) copied out at the start of the *Cancioneiro da Biblioteca Nacional*. Its six sections are irregularly subdivided, and the extant fragment deals primarily with poetic forms, versification, rhyme and the consistent use of tenses (an instance of the author's interest in the proper harmony between the parts of a poem). As far as one can tell, this treatise, like Raimon Vidal's *Razos de trobar*, was conceived as a practical guide in poetic taste and composition, although no poetic examples are cited. Its survey of accepted aesthetic practice generally refrains from the technical grammatical explanations of the contemporary *Leys d'amors*, except for the two most common errors, hiatus and *caçafaton* (lexical vulgarity).

In Castilian, the first significant work is the *Cancionero* compiled around 1430 by Juan Alfonso de Baena. This anthology contains numerous debates over the nature of *la gaya ciencia* (the term betrays a debt to the Catalan tradition), in particular over divine inspiration, the relationship between natural talent and craftsmanship, wit and decorum. These debates, between such poets as Alfonso Álvarez de Villasandino and Ferrán Manuel de Lando, are symptoms of the changing status and intellectual range of poetry within an expanding and increasingly literate courtier caste. Their social and esthetic ideals also figure in Baena's critical rubrics, as well as in his two prose prefaces, which are not only the first of several literary-theoretical prologues in fifteenth-century Castile, but also the first critical introduction to any European verse anthology. Acting as arbiter of literary taste for the court of Juan II, Baena offers a defense of letters (mostly cribbed from Alfonso X), and consolidates the status of poetry as a noble court pastime, of intellectual and therapeutic significance. The prologue ends with a sketch of the ideal poet, who, among other virtues, is divinely inspired, widely read and travelled, eloquent and witty, and, above all, a lover, because love is the source of all worthy doctrine.

More ambitious are the claims made in Enrique de Villena's *Arte de trovar* (1433), which survives only in excerpts made by the sixteenth-century humanist Alvar Gómez de Castro. Most of the extant text was probably extracted from the original work's prologue, which describes Villena's role in the Barcelona Poetic Consistory and surveys earlier poetic treatises such as those by Raimon Vidal, Jofre de Foixà, Berenguer de Noya, and Guilhem Molinier. Although what survives of the treatise itself deals with orthography, punctuation, and euphony, overall the work is infused with the civic concerns of the Catalan school, though perhaps also modulated by Italian civic humanism: as the effective communication of thought, poetry benefits "la vida civil," and enables the intellectual elite to stand out from the ranks of the "ediothas" and to take a leading role in society. Villena argues that poetry should possess the dignity of a *scientia*, a fully fledged branch of knowledge, with its immutable and divinely ordained laws, and that by the process of *translatio studii*, this poetic knowledge has now passed to the new poetic language of Castilian. This concern to ennoble poetry, and to set it within a historical framework, was inherited by the dedicatee of the treatise, the marqués de Santillana, Iñigo López de Mendoza.

Santillana epitomized the union of arms and letters, which was a central ideal of early modern vernacular humanism. Although several prologues and epistles bear witness to his interest in literary theory and history, the most significant is his *Proemio e carta al condestable don Pedro de Portugal* (1445–1449). On a theoretical level, this treatise is notable less for the originality of its ideas than for its impressive cultural framework, conceptual scope, and rhetorical elegance. Many issues—formal, philosophical, and historical—are addressed in the course of the prologue: in essence, however, Santillana claims that poetry combines allegory, metrical and rhetorical perfection, and music in a creative act that is characteristically human, and is mankind's mark of divine favor. Santillana's sources include Boccaccio, Isidore, Dante commentaries, and, indirectly Horace and Cicero: but by and large his ideas stem from the common stock of medieval and early renaissance poetic and rhetorical theory. It is Santillana's historical survey of poetry, however, that sets this prologue apart from its European counterparts. Drawing on the ample resources of his own library, Santillana traces the history of poetry from its biblical origins, through classical antiquity, Italy,

France, and the various schools of the Iberian Peninsula. This eulogy of poetry, with its striking historical emphasis, is part of a large and complex cultural shift: as modern Castilian poets strove to emulate the classical *auctores*, to confer dignity upon vernacular letters, and to justify them as an essential ingredient of true nobility, they laid the basis for modern notions of "literature."

This trend is also apparent in the widespread application to vernacular texts of the academic terminology of the *accessus ad auctores* (a formalized scholastic prologue used in grammatical study), and in the popularity of commentaries and glosses attached to translations of the classics, Dante, and to contemporary Castilian texts. Villena's commentary to his translation of the *Aeneid* (which contains a fervent defense of allegorical poetry as a central component in the education of an aristocratic elite), Juan de Mena's self-exegesis of his *Coronación*, Santillana's own historical glosses to his *Proverbios*, and Alfonso de Madrigal's commentary on Eusebius are among the major examples before the close of the fifteenth century.

Although there are other instances of literary theorizing and poetics (e.g., a rhyming dictionary in the Occitan-Catalan tradition, *La gaya sciencia*, by Pero Guillén de Segovia [1475], a lost poetics attributed to Juan de Mena, and a treatise on the reading matter appropriate for the noble layman, Alonso de Cartagena's Latin epistle to the count of Haro, ca. 1440), the remaining works of significance were the product of the humanist movement of the final decade of the century.

Antonio de Nebrija not only wrote commentaries on the Christian poets Sedulius, Prudentius, and Persius, but also included a brief metrical treatise within his famous *Gramática de la lengua castellana* (1492). Nebrija examines the principles of Castilian meter, surveys the most authoritative rhyme forms, defines the function of the stanza, and illustrates his points with examples drawn from modern authorities, principally Juan de Mena (for whose "vulgar latinity" he reserves some withering criticism). Although Nebrija expresses reservations about the *mendacia poetarum*, compares Castilian practice negatively with the classical quantitative system, and castigates his contemporaries for being overly fond of rhyme (in this he anticipates the esthetic prejudices of the Renaissance poets Garcilaso and Boscán), his treatment nonetheless acknowledges the elevated cultural status that vernacular poetry had acquired over the previous half century.

Prefixed as a prologue to the first printed edition of his work (1496), Juan del Encina's *Arte de poesía castellana* is made up of nine chapters, divided more or less equally between a eulogy of poetry (especially Castilian verse), and a prescriptive treatment of various aspects of composition. Although many of Encina's ideas (e.g., about the biblical origins of verse, or the philosophical poet) had been anticipated by Santillana, he draws directly upon the newly accessible Renaissance authorities Horace and Cicero. Like his mentor Nebrija, Encina was motivated by an incipient Castilian cultural nationalism as well as by the desire for self-publicity (as examples of fine verse, he quotes not only Mena but also himself). Unlike Nebrija, Encina—who was after all a musician as well as a poet—displays a keen sense of the semantic possibilities and the musicality of Castilian meter and rhyme.

The gradual elevation in cultural status of vernacular poetry culminated in the publication, in 1499, of the first critical edition of Juan de Mena's *Laberinto de Fortuna*, compiled by the classical scholar Hernán Núñez de Toledo. Núñez endowed the poem with a long and erudite commentary, which he revised in a second edition (1505) that was to become a sixteenth-century "best-seller," and which consolidated Mena as a modern Spanish classic. The edition and commentary is a prime example of early modern textual criticism in its attempt to "purge" the text (sometimes rather arbitrarily by modern standards) of the errors of scribes and compositors. Although there is little evaluative commentary upon the poem, Núñez consistently praises the work's eloquence, all-embracing wisdom, abundant aphorisms, and wealth of myths and legends, all of which demonstrated the educational value of poetry (which elsewhere he claims on the authority of the Greek geographer Strabo). Apart from his handling of a complex structure, Mena is also praised for the power of his similes and his ability to represent a scene with poetic force (what classical and renaissance theorists called *energeia*). Núñez also undertakes an exhaustive study of Mena's sources (Lucan, Ovid, Virgil), historical references, and vocabulary; and his glosses have been mercilessly plundered by modern scholars. He cannot display unqualified admiration for Mena, however; as a professional humanist, he scorns Mena's reliance on corrupt manuscripts and discredited authorities (e.g., pseudo-Anselm), which led to the poem's various factual blunders in cosmological and other matters. In short, the edition and commentary are a celebration not only of a national classic, but also of a new philological approach to the vernacular that, albeit in different modes, survives to this day.

Julian M. Weiss

Bibliography

Johnston, M. D. "Literary Tradition and the Idea of Language in the *Artes de trobar*," *Dispositio* 2 (1977), 208–18.

———. "The translation of the troubadour tradition in the *Torcimany* of Lluis d'Averçó," *Studies in Philology* 78 (1981), 151–67.
———. "Poetry and courtliness in Baena's Prologue," *La Corónica*, 25 (1996), 93–105.
Kohut, K. *Las teorías literarias en España y Portugal durante los siglos XV y XVI: estado de la investigación y problemática*. Madrid, 1973.
Weiss, J. M. *The Poet's Art: Literary Theory in Castile c. 1400–60*. Oxford, 1990.
———. "Medieval Poetics and the Social Meaning of Form," *Atalaya: Revue Française d'Études Médiévales Hispaniques* 8 (1997–98), 171–86
———. "Tiempo y materia en la poética de Juan del Encina." *Humanismo y literatura en tiempos de Juan del Encina*. Ed. J. G. Ceballos. Salamanca, 1999. 241–57.

LITERATURE, ARABIC

Even before Islam was born in the sixth century of our era, the Arabs had a deeply rooted, well-developed, and powerful poetic tradition that had produced masterpieces in the form of monorhyme odes with a limited number of quantitative meters, embodying mainly the ethos of desert life. The Islamic dogma that then made Arabic the only true language of revelation and deemed the eloquence of the Qur'ān to be the prophet Muḥammad's sole authenticating miracle further strengthened the hold of the inherited corpus of poetry, pagan though it was, as an embodiment of the purest form of the language.

The creation of a vast empire incorporating diverse lands, inhabited by races that were heirs to different cultures, soon generated ways of life far removed from that of the desert. Inevitably, modes of expression changed, but not as radically as they might have done with a different tradition. The old poetry remained normative for many centuries, conventional forms and motifs holding pride of place. The most obvious modification was a growing taste for verbal ornaments, chief among which were the paronomasia and the double entendre, but with the addition of ever more ingenious devices to which the phonemes of Arabic and even its script can lend themselves.

Local and everyday concerns, however, appear to have found an outlet in regional folk literatures; but if only because these were couched in colloquial forms of the language regarded as corruptions, they have been largely ignored if not despised by the scholars. They are, therefore, almost entirely undocumented, their early existence attested only by casual, and often derogatory, references. Only exceptionally have some features of them passed into the canon, usually when a learned writer deigned to recast them in the idiom of the "high" literature.

Al-Andalus—as Arabs and Arabists call those parts of Iberia that came under Muslim sway—is of absorbing interest in this context. It was geographically remote from the Islamic heartlands, and politically separate. Among the so-called Moors of Spain, only a small minority was of Arab stock. Far more significantly—for many of the giants of Arabic culture were not ethnically Arab—the region was never thoroughly Islamized or Arabized. For nearly eight centuries, Muslims, Christians, and Jews, speakers of Arabic and of Romance, lived side by side. Converts were not totally estranged from kinsmen who remained attached to the older faith—indeed, calendars were adjusted to enable some Muslim and Christian festivals to coincide. Soldiers of fortune such as El Cid served masters with different religious labels. There were mixed marriages between princely families and between itinerant singers alike. Al-Andalus was thus a supreme testing ground both for the homogeneity of the "high" Arabic literature and for the vitality of its folk arts.

That the initial impulse was imported is self-evident. The attachment of the newcomers to their roots is well exemplified by the founder of the first independent dynasty in Córdoba, a scion of the dispossessed Umayyads of Damascus, who retained a lifelong nostalgia for his Syrian home. Andalusians took to heart the Prophet's injunction to travel far and wide in search of knowledge, and willingly sat at the feet of masters in the heartlands. Conversely, scholarly émigrés from the east were welcome in al-Andalus. Such was the musician Ziryāb (d. 852) who not only trained singing girls but seems also to have been accepted as an arbiter of good manners. Such also was Abū Alī al-Kālī (d. 867), whose comments—mainly philological, but often implying literary judgments—were collected under the appropriate title of *Amālī* (*Dictations*).

Eventually—and not least after the breakdown of central authority had resulted in a multiplicity of city-states whose courts vied with one another in the patronage of men of letters—al-Andalus produced its own masters of the monorhyme ode, ranging from Ibn Hānī (d. 973) with his grandiloquent panegyrics and celebrations of the great events of his day, to Ibn Zamrak (1333–1393), whose verses in praise of his princely patrons are inscribed on the walls of the Alhambra much as royal portraits are hung in European palaces.

Understandably, specialists in this field have dwelled on what is distinctive of Andalusian poetry, and especially on features of Arabic literature that bring it close to European practice and taste. Much has been made of the Andalusians' delight in the beauties of a bountiful and sympathetic nature. And indeed, descriptions of flowers and of gardens abound, notably in the poetry of Ibn Khafāja (1050–1139), and the compiler of one of our main sources for the study of this literature, the North African Al-Maqqarī (1591/2 –1632), observed that in their love poems the Andalusians "fashioned cheeks out of roses, eyes out of narcissi, ears out of lilies, breasts out of quinces, waists out of sugar cane, lips out of almond kernels or apple dimples, and saliva out of the daughter of the vine."[1] Some have also stressed the tenderness of an Ibn Zaydūn (1003–1070), a midness of disposition and an attitude to women that Pérès[2] is tempted to characterize as Christian, perhaps even a greater consistency in imagery than is found in the East. Yet these are, at most, differences of degree. The poetry of the heartlands, not least that of the immensely talented al-Mutanabbī never ceased to be admired and imitated in al-Andalus, the eminence of several of its poets being marked by dubbing each of them "the Mutanabbī of the West."

It is in the creation of two radically new verse forms that Andalusian originality is unquestionable. These are the *muwashsḥaha* and the *zaḥjal.*

A *muwashsḥaha* consists of a number of strophes, usually five, with an intricate pattern of rhymes maintained in each, but also with a binding rhyme that may be established in an opening Arabic literature couplet and may then be used as a refrain, but will also be echoed at the close of each strophe, so that a common arrangement (capable of further elaboration) may be schematized as:

AA bcbcbcAA(AA) dedede AA(AA)

Of particular importance is the final couplet known as the *Kharja*[3] which may be borrowed from another composition and may be in a mixture of the local vernacular and of Romance, in which case it usually takes the form of a provocative statement made by a woman.[4]

Most of the muwashshaḥs that have come down to us conform with classical Arabic meters, but the testimony of Ibn Sanā' al-Mulk (ca.1155–1211), who wrote the first treatise on the subject is that by far the larger number known to him did not. This indicates that the scholarly compilers filtered out compositions that they found difficult to reconcile with the norms they had inherited, yet the multiplicity of rhymes was not only in itself a striking departure from poetic tradition; it also made the strophe rather than the line the basic unit of the poem, and lent itself to a lyricism exploited with skill and often with great charm by Andalusians, mainly in love poems, though they also used the new metrical form in panegyrics and in expressions of asceticism. Other subtleties can be detected in the muwashsḥaha. Some at least have a "ring structure" with the pith of the poet's concern in the central strophe. And a case can be made for considering the bilingual muwashsḥah as a separate subgenre with a stronger feminine element and a somewhat different range of images and characters from those found in the monolingual ones.

The *zaḥjal* is clearly a related genre, for it has a similar strophic structure, though usually with a simpler rhyme scheme. It differs from the muwashsḥah principally in that it is entirely in the colloquial Arabic of the region. It gained distinction at the hands of Ibn Quzmān, known in Spanish as Abenguzmán (d. 1160/1169). Although he himself names a long list of predecessors, to the zaḥjal, its late appearance has led to the assumption, especially among Arab writers, that it was an offshoot of the muwashshaḥ. Yet there are musical and prosodic indications—mainly that the trend in parallel developments has been toward the elaboration of rhyme schemes, not their simplification—either that the reverse is true or that both branched out of a common stem.[5] Incomplete though the documentation is, to al-Andalus and its mixed population belongs the distinction of first giving a measure of recognition to an Arabic folk art.

Unlike poetry, fine prose flourished in early Arabia only in the form of oratory. Its tradition grew later, mainly out of the activities of court secretaries, who took pride in the elegance of their correspondence, and who readily adopted the poets' taste for linguistic purity and rhetorical artifice. Belles-lettres therefore took the form of epistles, of a kind of essay that grew out of such epistles in which, for example, spring and summer flowers were compared, of analecta and literary curiosities, the enormous *adab* books that eventually appeared being essentially collections of such short pieces.

Mere storytelling was considered unworthy of serious men of letters, and was left to folk literature. Anonymous tales and legends, some originating as far away as in India, gained currency in al-Andalus; their status and their public may be inferred from the fact that they have sometimes been preserved only in Romance translations. The only narrative genre to secure a foothold within the canon was the *maqāma*, the story of a petty fraud perpetrated by an amiable rogue, with no greater prize in view than a free meal or some meager booty. The folk origin of such anecdotes is patent, but they gained acceptance in the East when Badī' al-Zamān al-Hamadhānī (969–1009) clothed them in the high style of which he was a celebrated master. Within a century, the genre had been brought to a peak of stylistic virtuosity by Al-Harīrī of Basra (1051–1122), who reduced the narrative element to a mere framework within which his antihero reached his ends almost invariably by a dazzling display of verbal acrobatics.

The Andalusians did not lag behind their Eastern models in producing an elegant prose in which rhyme was only one of many rhetorical embellishments, and which almost always was studded with gemlike verses. Several of them are known to have heard the maqāmas of Al-Harīrī expounded by the author himself, and the standard commentary on them was written by Al-Sharīshī of Xeres (d. 1222). Of his imitators, the most celebrated was the versatile Lisān al-Dīn ibn al-Khatīb (1313–1374). Yet it seems that it was the style that impressed itself on Andalusians as the supreme feature, for among them many a piece of finely wrought prose was labeled a maqāma, even if it contained no narrative element at all.

It follows from the primacy given to such genres that, until modern times, Arabic literature produced only a handful of books of unified conception and sustained invention, and these were due to the creativity of individuals who left no direct line of succession. It is noteworthy that three of the most original of these works saw the light of day in al-Andalus.

The first is the *Risālat al-Tawābiʾ wa al-Zawabiʾ*[6] by the poet Ibn Shuhaid (992–1035). In this—possibly following a lead from one of the maqāmas of Al-Hamadhāni—he seized upon the pre-Islamic belief that each poet had a familiar spirit and imagined a series of encounters with such spirits as well as with other genii and even some articulate animals in their realm, more often than not to compare the styles of his predecessors with his own or to discuss issues of literary interest. Although sparked off by a desire to answer some detractors, it works well as a fanciful way of presenting literary criticism.

Even more substantial is a treatise on love by the jurist Ibn Ḥazm (994–1064).[7] Rooted in Platonic thought and kept in strict conformity with Islamic law, it is also informed by his own experiences and those of individuals well known to him, and it is abundantly illustrated with verses, mostly by himself. It treats the attraction between individuals of opposite sexes or of the same sex with equal delicacy, always extolling spiritual rather than physical union. It also has revealing sidelights on the refinement of high Córdoban society in his day.

Finally, drawing on a folktale and borrowing the names of his characters from some of the writings of Avicenna, Ibn Tufayl (d. 1185) elaborated on both in the remarkably cogent philosophical romance of *Hayy ibn Yaqzan*. In it the hero, whose name means "Alive, son of the Awake," drifts while yet a child on to an uninhabited island where he is nurtured by a gazelle. There, by the exercise of his human faculties alone, he masters not only the means of survival, but also the principles of natural philosophy, and eventually, by dint of mystic contemplation not divorced from reason, he comes to a knowledge of God. When he makes contact with the inhabitants of another island who have had the benefit of revelation, he finds himself at one with the thoughtful and subtle Asāl, but less so with the literal-minded Salamān, and not at all with the masses, who are ruled by gross appetites.

The place of Islamic thought, including Ibn Tufayl's, in world culture has been much studied; but the literary crosscurrents generated by the meeting of cultures in al-Andalus are more problematic. On the whole, the "high" literature of Islamic Spain bears witness above all to the homogeneity and persistence of the Arab literary tradition; but that the nonclassical forms grew out of an intimate blending of local and imported elements is both likely and supported by at least fragmentary evidence.

Conversely, classical Arabic was embraced by the Jews of Spain with such enthusiasm and thoroughness that some, like the great Maimonides, wrote their own works in the borrowed language, and translations and imitations of Arabic poems and *maqāmas* loomed large in the Hebrew literature of the thirteenth and fourteenth centuries.

Few Christians, however, were inclined to emulate the Jews, so that once again it is at the popular level that fruitful contacts were made. If Dante needed the stimulation of an Arabic extraterrestrial adventure to inspire his *Divine Comedy*, it came more probably from a popular account of the prophet Muḥammad's ascent to the heavens than from either Al-Maʿarrî in the east or Ibn Shuhaid in al-Andalus.[9] Similarities in strophic structure and in the stock characters of love poetry suggest at least short-lived Arabic influences on the Provençal troubadours, but the subject requires a mastery of two specialized fields, at which A.R. Nykl made a brave but not altogether convincing attempt.[10] As for the possibility of a direct line of descent from the Andalusian *maqāma* to the Spanish picaresque novel of the sixteenth and seventeeth centuries, it must be deemed less than likely when one considers the lapse of time and the fact that the Muslims of Spain downplayed the narrative character of the genre.

Unfortunately, these issues have too often been approached in a contentious and immoderate spirit,[11] as if the acceptance of a literary model were demeaning, whereas cross-fertilization is a process in which admiration passes imperceptibly into imitation, emulation, adaptation, and a new creativity. Of this there is no clearer example than that the very Hebrew poets who closely imitated individual Arabic muwashshaḥs also adapted the form to liturgical uses, which it never had in an Islamic environment. Reaching out for the best that is known, thought, or practiced anywhere is less a debt than an enrichment.

PIERRE CACHIA

Notes

1. See al-Rikābī, D. *Al-Tabī'a fī al-Shi'r al-Andalusī*. Damascus, 1959. 43–49.
2. Pérès, H. *La Poésie Andalouse en Arabe Classique au XIe Siècle*. 2d ed. Paris, 1953. 473–75.
3. Monroe, J. T. "The Structure of an Arabic *Muwashshah* with a Bilingual *Kharja*," *Edebiyyat* 1 (1976), 113–23, and "Prolegomena to the Study of Ibn Quzmān: The Poet as Jongleur," in *El Romancero Hoy: Historia, Comparatismo, Bibliografiá, Crítica* 4 (1979), 77–129.
4. Compton, L. F. *Andalusian Lyrical Poetry and Old Spanish Love Songs*. New York, 1976.
5. See Cachia, P. *Popular Narrative Ballads of Modern Egypt*. Oxford, 1989. 11–12.
6. Trans. with the subtitle *The Treatise of Familiar Spirits and Demons*, by J. T. Monroe. Berkeley, 1971.
7. *The Ring of the Dove*. Trans. A. J. Arberry. London, 1953.
8. The most recent translation is by L. E. Goodman. 2nd ed. Los Angeles, 1983.
9. Asín Palacios, M. *La Escatología musulmana en la Diyina Comedia*. Madrid, 1919.
10. Nykl, A. R. *Hispano-Arabic Poetry and Its Relations with the Old Provençal Troubadours*. Baltimore, 1946.
11. See, e.g., Gorton, T. J. "Zajal and Muwassah: The Continuing Metrical Debate," *Journal of Arabic Literature* 9 (1978), 32–40.

Bibliography

García Gómez, E. *Poesía Arábigoandaluza*. Madrid, 1952.

Monroe, J. T. *Hispano-Arabic Poetry: A Student Anthology*. Berkeley, 1974.

Pérès, H. *La Poésie Andalouse en Arabe Classique, au XIe Siècle: Ses Aspects Généraux et sa Valeur Documentaire*. 2d ed. Paris, 1953.

Stern, S. M. *Hispano-Arabic Strophic Poetry—Studies*. Sel. and ed. L. P. Harvey. Oxford, 1974.

LITERATURE, BASQUE

Basque literature possesses a series of specific characteristics that complicate any comparison. In the first place, the great periods that make up the history of the major Western literatures do not apply to their Basque counterparts. Secondly, Basque literature has been basically a servant of linguistic necessities. The primary protagonist of this literature has been *Euskara*, or the Basque language. It has been accepted as an axiom that the Basques have no literature, but Basque popular and oral literature is very rich, especially in its poetry.

Although the Basque language was not used for literary purposes in the Middle Ages, it exists in inscriptions, sentences, and short texts. The oldest sentences that we know about are called "Glosas Emilianenses" of the tenth century, which are in San Millán de la Cogolla. The most ancient testimonies of popular Basque literature date from the fourteenth century and are evidence of the medieval Basque language.

Poetical texts were kept by the oral tradition and were recorded in writing by some Basque historians (like Garibay, Zaldibia, in the sixteenth and seventeenth centuries). These texts of medieval poetry are fragmentary except for some ballads, including "Song of Berreterretxe," "Ballad of Urtsua," and "Lady of Urruty."

The themes of this epical and familial poetry are of two types and are constantly repeated. On one side are the family wars, bloody fights that destroyed all the Basque country, as much in the north (Agramonteses and Beamonteses) as in the south (Oacinos and Gamboinos), especially in the fifteenth century. Specifically, these poetical themes were related to the death of the chief and the defeat of the enemies. On the other hand there exists the theme of love and familial problems, as typified by the "Song of Berreterretxe." This fifteenth-century song, a poem by an anonymous writer, deals with a murder that shocked and angered the Basque people of Zuberoa. The facts narrated in its fifteen stanzas can be presented in four sections: (1 the indignation and pain of the poet; (2) the arrest of Berreterretxe; (3) the anxious search of Marisantz, his mother; and (4) and the horror of the young Berreterretxe's murder at the hands of the soldiers of the count of Lerín.

The rich oral Basque literature—including its *bertsolariak*, or troubadors; the pastorales; the *chiarivariak*, or carnivals; ballads, proverbs; and masquerades—is a very unique patrimony of this small nation whose origins still remain unknown.

GORKA AULESTIA

Bibliography

Villasante, L. *Historia de la literatura Vasca*. 2d ed. Oñate, Guipúzcoa, Spain, 1979.

Vinson, J. *Literatura popular del Paīs Vasco*, Trans. I. Urdanibia. San Sebastián, 1988.

LITERATURE, CATALAN

The Late Middle Ages produced the best of Catalan literature, which, after a period of decline, underwent a strong renewal during the nineteenth century and flourished again in the twentieth. Medieval Catalan writers were subjects of the Crown of Aragón (Aragón, Catalonia, the Balearic Islands, Valencia), a Spanish kingdom that reached its period of greatest power in the second half of the thirteenth century. The Crown of Aragón actually existed until 1714, although after the beginning of the sixteenth century it was absorbed by the new kingdom of Spain. Throughout the thirteenth and fourteenth centuries the Aragónese monarchs, although ruling a plurilingual country, showed a clear preference for the Catalan sector of their possessions; Catalan medieval literature is consistently linked to the royal house. Thus, the first significant Catalan literary texts are four chronicles of contemporary events endowed with epic inspiration. Two of them are written in the form of a royal autobiography: the *Llibre dels feits*, narrating the life of King Jaime I the Conqueror (1208–1276), the true founder of Aragón; and the *Crònica* of Pedro III (1336–1386). The latter work is a political tract written by officers of the chancellery and supervised personally by the king; we presume that Jaime I used a similar method. The other two Catalan chronicles were the work of Bernat Desclot and Ramon Muntaner. The first mainly narrated the life of Pedro II the Great (1276–1285), who conquered Sicily and turned back a French invasion. Muntaner compiled a very colorful narrative of events from the reigns of all the monarchs he had personally known (Jaime I, Pedro II, Alfonso II, and Jaime II). The most powerfully original writer of the Catalan Middle Ages was Ramon Llull (1232–1316), who left the king's court in Mallorca to become a Christian apologist and missionary. He wrote more than 260 works in every discipline and literary genre, and he was the first in Europe to use a vernacular language for philosophical subjects. His *Art* is a complex system designed as a weapon of controversy against unbelievers, one that attempts to explain logically the truths of Christian dogma. Llull also wrote didactic novels that describe the contemporary world (*Blaquerna*, *Fèlix o Llibre de Meravelles*), poetry (*Desconhort*, *Plany de la Verge*, *Cant de Ramon*), and other mystical, apologetic, and didactic works (*Llibre de contemplació en Déu*, *Llibre del Gentil e dels tres savis*, *Llibre d'amic e Amat*, *Llibre de santa Maria*, *Arbre de Ciència*). Moreover, Llull wrote Catalan verse for moral purposes at a time when nobody was doing so in the Catalan-speaking regions. Catalan poetry, in fact, was born as a local branch of the troubadour lyric. Guillem de Berguedà and Guillem de Cabestány in the twelfth century and Cerverí de Girona in the thirteenth had strong personalities and produced very good poems, but wrote them in Occitanian. The Occitanian of the troubadours, with a gradual admixing of Catalan, remained the linguistic vehicle of Catalan poets until the emergence of the Valencian Ausiàs March (ca. 1425). The annual poetry competition of Toulouse, the Jocs Florals (begun in 1324), and the poetical treatise *Las leis d'amors*, conceived as a tool for writing verse, had a long success in the Crown of Aragón to the extent that in 1393 King Juan I instituted Jocs Florals in Barcelona. Thus Andreu Febrer, Gilabert de Pròixita, Pere March, Jaume March, Jordi de Sant Jordi, and other minor poets, whose poems are collected in the Catalan *Cançoners*, attempted to follow the troubadours' path. The Occitanian-Catalan hybrid language they used was also the vehicle for anonymous religious poetry (the oldest metrical Catalan text is the vernacular *Planctus Mariae*, in the early thirteenth century), as well as of narrative verse. Borrowing from Occitanian and French literature the idea of the *roman courtois*, Catalan writers produced a certain number of minor fourteenth-century novels in verse, dealing with courtly and allegorical subjects; the best are the anonymous *Fraire de Joi* and *Sor de Plaser* (a literary version of the "Sleeping Beauty" folktale), the *Faula* of Guillem de Torroella (in which King Arthur is located in a sort of earthly paradise) and the also anonymous *Salut d'amor*. In 1460 the Valencian doctor Jaume Roig produced a long misogynous treatise written in quadrisyllabic verse, containing an interesting pseudo-autobiography of the author, *l'Espill* or *El llibre de les dones*, the last narrative poem of the Catalan Middle Ages. The greatest medieval Catalan poet, Ausiàs March, possessed an enormously tortured lyric temperament. He not only wrote in a pure Catalan of Valencia, but also fashioned his own new poetry, both metrically and rhetorically, from the troubadour tradition even though he was in a continuous ideological struggle against it. Ausiàs March died in 1459 and most of the minor poets of the second half of the century modeled their verse on his.

Around 1380, Italian cultural developments began to change the Catalan literary scene. Dante, Petrarch, and Boccaccio were read and admired, and a local tradition of intellectuals at the service of the royal chancellery (scribes, notaries, secretaries, lawyers) learned a new elegant and refined prose style. Bernat Metge (1324–1413) was a very talented, if not very honest, servant of the crown who produced a masterpiece of artistic prose, *Lo Somni* (1398). In it, Metge compiled a brilliant self-apology, borrowing from Cicero, Ovid, Boccaccio, Petrarch, and the Church Fathers. This work, a fictitious dialogue between the author and three dead men who come to him while he is asleep in prison, contains solemn and elegant pages mixed with others that are coarse and very funny. Translation from Latin and Italian was the actual source of the new Catalan artistic prose: Antoni Canals, a severe Dominican inquisitor, produced some versions of Seneca, Valerius Maximus, and Petrarch for moral purposes. Other translators were interested in history (the

Decades of Livy, the *Historia Troiana* of Guido delle Colonne), or in literature (the *Divina Commedia* of Dante, the *Decameron* of Boccaccio). The two long chivalric novels of the fifteenth century, the *Tirant lo Blanch* of Joanot Martorell (1460, printed 1490) and the anonymous *Curial and Güelfa*, benefited from this artistic prose writing. Although the authors of both books borrowed from the romance narrative tradition (the French prose *roman*, the troubadours, Dante), as well from that of Catalonia itself (Ramon Llull, the chroniclers Desclot and Muntaner, verse narrative novels), they created quite a new narrative pattern, with no exact parallels in their age.

Some outstanding Catalan writers of the late Middle Ages, however, ignored and even opposed this learned fashion. They were intellectuals of the Mendicant orders, devoted to their pastoral concerns. Thus Francesc Eiximenis, a Franciscan vernacular encyclopedist, and Vicent, Ferrer, a Dominican popular preacher, found their literary way through scholasticism and the mendicant homiletic tradition. The same is true of the only woman writer of the Catalan Middle Ages, the abbess Isabel de Villena, who wrote a *Life of Christ* in a beautiful colloquial Catalan. Anselm Turmeda, a Franciscan friar converted to Islam, wrote very successful moral poetry and prose; the knight Ramon de Perellós narrated in colloquial prose his travel to the Purgatory of Saint Patrick in Ireland. The last great Catalan writer was a Valencian theologian and preacher, Joan Roís de Corella. He translated devotional works into Catalan and used printing to disseminate some of his writings. He was also a lyric poet, and in a rhetorical narrative tradition deeply indebted to Boccaccio, he produced some retellings of Ovid's tragic stories.

The extant texts of medieval Catalan theater belong to the Easter and Christmas cycles, or develop themes from the Old Testament. A liturgical drama on the Assumption of Mary (the *Misteri d'Elx*), which originated in the fifteenth century, is still performed each year in the city of that name.

LOLA BADÍA

Bibliography

Molas, J. and J. Massot (eds.) *Diccionari de la literatura catalana*. Barcelona, 1979.

Riquer, M. de, A. Comas, and J. Molas. *Història de la literatura catalana*. 11 vols. Barcelona, 1964–1988.

Roca Pons, J. *Introduction to Catalan Literature*. Bloomington, Ind., 1977.

Rubió Balaguer, J. *Història de la literatura catalana*. 3 vols. In *Obres Completes de J. Rubió Balaguer I, III, IV*. Barcelona, 1984–1986.

Terry, A. *Catalan Literature*. In *A Literary History of Spain* 8. Ed. R. O. Jones. London, 1972.

LITERATURE, HEBREW

See HEBREW LANGUAGE AND LITERATURE

LITERATURE, LATIN

See LATIN LANGUAGE AND LITERATURE

LITERATURE, LOST

The farther we go back in time, the greater the proportion of written literature that is lost (oral literature—works composed and transmitted orally—has always had a very high rate of loss, regardless of its age). Yet lost works often leave traces, and it is important for us to know as much as we can about what has been lost. If we do not—if we attend only to the texts that have survived—our picture of the literature of the past will not only be incomplete, it may be seriously misleading. This is especially true of genres where the rate of loss is above average: the medieval epic, for example.

Tomás Antonio Sánchez, in the preface to his great collection of medieval Spanish texts, wrote, "Siempre he creído que un gran caudal de nuestra lengua, de nuestra historia, de nuestras costumbres y literatura antigua, yacía como mudo entre las tinieblas del más profundo olvido y abandono." (I have always believed that a great wealth of our language our history, our customs and ancient literature lay silent, Forgotten, and abandoned amid the darkness). That was in 1779, and it remains true today. The fact that so many works survive today in a single, and sometimes incomplete, manuscript or copy of an incunable (the *Cantar de Mio Cid*, the *Libro de Apolonio*, the *Vida de Santa María Egipciaca*, for instance) shows how easily a work could disappear from view. Sánchez mentioned "el tiempo, los incendios, la polilla" (time, fire, and vermin) as the main causes of loss; the causes are numerous, and may be classified as follows:

1. Fires in libraries and archives: more than four-thousand manuscripts were destroyed in the fire in the Escorial Library (1671), a loss perhaps even greater than that of the most disastrous English equivalent, the Cotton Library fire of 1731.
2. War and revolution: the library of one of Spain's greatest scholar-bibliophiles, Bartolomé Gallardo, was sacked in the Seville riots of 1823.
3. The dissolution of the monasteries in 1835–1836.
4. Theft of manuscripts and incunables by readers—and also by underpaid librarians. The Biblioteca Colombina in Seville, founded by Hernando

Colón in the early sixteenth century, now has only a fraction of its former holdings.

5. Bad conditions in libraries: damp, rodents, worms. These, however, usually damage books rather than destroying them totally.
6. Loss of leaves or of whole gatherings from intensively used books (the first and last leaves are especially vulnerable).
7. Political, religious, or moral censorship. When Enrique de Trastámara murdered his half-brother and seized the throne in 1369, the new dynasty was eager to suppress any evidence that cast doubt on its claim to legitimacy. It was dangerous to be caught in possession of ballads attacking Enrique and his followers, or of chronicles that gave a different version of the events.
8. Those who inherited great private libraries and archives might lack interest in them and sell them off cheaply—even to a wastepaper merchant (the Duque de Sessa, 1869). In extreme cases, manuscripts might be used as toilet paper, or to light the fire.
9. Manuscripts and incunables might be broken up to serve as pastedowns in the binding of other, newer books. This was the fate of the unique manuscript of the *Roncesvalles* epic.
10. A manuscript or incunable misplaced in a library, or sold to a secretive collector, may disappear from view for decades—sometimes, one assumes, for centuries.
11. Responsible for far more losses than any of these is that many medieval works lived only in oral tradition, and very soon changed drastically or died out altogether.

How can we learn something of what has been lost? The difficulty is greatest in the case of oral works, though even here something may be retrieved: some were written down, some survived in the oral tradition for centuries (notably, the ballads preserved in the Sephardic communities), and even though both kinds of preservation imply major changes, we can glimpse something, especially if the same work was written down by a literate poet and also preserved by singers. If a fragment survives (the single leaf of *Roncesvalles*, the fragment of the first version of *Amadís de Gaula*), we not only have incontrovertible evidence that the work once existed, but can form an idea of its characteristics. An author will sometimes refer, in an extant work, to one that is now lost. Juan Manuel is the most prolific source of such information: he carefully listed his works, five of which do not correspond to any that we have (the titles usually give a fairly clear indication of the content). Three titles of lost works emerge from a shorter list by Alfonso de Palencia (though in his case it is less certain that the books were completed). And the preface to the second version of Diego Enríquez del Castillo's *Crónica de Enrique IV* gives a graphic account of the way in which the unfinished first version and its documentary sources were lost. References by other authors may also give us the title of a lost work, and occasionally may give us much more. The extreme case is Hernando de Talavera's *Católica impugnación*, which goes into such detail about a pamphlet, called by him the *Herético libelo*, that we are able to reconstruct its structure and much of its content; had he stayed his hand, the pamphlet to which he objects so strongly would be unknown to us. Some *cancionero* poems are largely composed of quotations from others; some of these other poems are extant, but some are known only through the quotations. A translation may survive when the original is lost: we have a Latin translation of one lost work from the circle of Alfonso X, and a French translation of another. A great deal of information comes from library catalogues, inventories attached to wills, and inventories of donations, though the information is of uneven quality: sometimes we have an identifiable title, sometimes not. A more precise, though much less frequent, source of information is the table of contents of a manuscript containing a number of works, from which leaves are missing; in this way, we can be sure that a Salamanca University Library manuscript once included the *Libro del arra del ánima*. An unlikely, but occasionally fruitful, source is an account book: one from Toledo cathedral gives us the titles of fourteen otherwise unknown plays from the end of the fifteenth century and the beginning of the sixteenth. The writings of bibliophiles, from the sixteenth century onward, can supplement the other sources, and may even put us on the track of a lost work recorded nowhere else. Finally, the content of lost oral epics is sometimes preserved in chronicle prosifications. This information needs to be assessed with greater care than has sometimes been used, but it is thanks to such prosifications that we know about the *Siete infantes de Lara*, the *Cantar de Sancho II*, and the *Romanz del Infant García*; whether the differences between chronicles reflect the existence of more than one version of the epic, or whether they are due to the initiative of the chroniclers, is a question now being vigorously debated.

Not every loss is irretrievable. In the past half-century, several lost *cancioneros* have been located (usually thanks to the extraordinary efforts of Brian Dutton). The *Triunfo de Amor* of Juan de Flores, dismissed for over a hundred years as a bibliographical ghost, is now known in two manuscripts. Perhaps more surprisingly, some works that had left no trace at all have been discovered: *Ay Jherusalem!* in the 1950s, the *Fazienda de Ultra Mar* in the 1960s, the *Auto de la Pasión* and the *Coronación de la señora Gracisla* in the 1970s, and the *Devocionario* of doña Constanza in the 1980s. The likelihood of further discoveries and rediscoveries must diminish as the search goes on, but it would be rash to assert than we have reached the end of the process. And each discovery of a hitherto lost work, each reassessment of the evidence for works that are still lost, redraws to a greater or lesser extent the map of medieval Spanish literature.

ALAN DEYERMOND

Bibliography

Deyermond, A. "Evidence for Lost Literature by Jews and *Conversos* in Medieval Castile and Aragón," *Donaire* 6 (1996), 19–30.

———. *La literatura perdida de la Edad Media castellana: catálogo y estudio, I: Épica y romances*. Obras de Referencia, Vol. 7 Salamanca, 1995.

Lobera Serrano, F. J. "Los conversos sevillanos y la Inquisición: el *Libello* perdido de 1480," *Cultura Neolatina*, 49, (1989), 7–53.

López-Baralt, L. "Crónica de la destrucción de un mundo: la literatura aljamiado-morisca," *Bulletin Hispanique* 82 (1980), 16–58.

Menéndez Pidal, R., et al., *Reliquias de la poesía épica española*. Madrid, 1951.

Smith, C. "On the 'Lost Literature' of Medieval Spain," in *'Guillaume d'Orange" and the "Chanson de geste": Essays Presented to Duncan McMillan in Celebration of His Seventieth Birthday*. Reading, 1984, 137–50.

LITERATURE, ORAL AND WRITTEN

As with other literatures of medieval Europe, that of Spain composed between the twelfth and fifteenth centuries reflects the transition of a culture from a predominantly oral state to an increasingly literate one, with the result that a determined literary work (e.g., the *Poema de Mio Cid*), may contain traces of primary orality (repetition and formulaic phrases; see the classic 1960 study by Lord) as well as certain learned features (diplomatic and accounting references). This convergence of oral and written elements can be studied in genres as diverse as lyric and epic poetry, the *romancero*, and even prose works (notably the folktale and the proverb) with respect to their sources, composition, and diffusion.

One of the goals of the medieval narrator was to captivate his audience and to convince it of the importance and veracity of his work: the author/poet's personal word was his "bond" with that group. Written documents were often suspect, having a connotation in the epic, for example, of privilege and secrecy, the insidious commands that they contain often backfiring or ridiculing the executors of the documents (Montgomery studies the issue for the *Poema de Mio Cid*, the *Siete infantes de Lara*, the *Mocedades de Rodrigo*, and other works). Thus it behooved the narrator to personalize his text in an ingratiating, often "chatty" manner (although chroniclers citing time-honored written *auctoritates* as an integral part of their own narratives usually dispensed with this nicety). A poet would write down his lines, imagining himself declaiming them to an audience (real or fictional; see the 1965 study by Gybbon-Monypenny on the works of Gonzalo de Berceo and the *Libro de Alexandre*); and prose texts as diverse as *Calila e Dimna* (ca. 1250) and some *exempla* of Juan Manuel's *Conde Lucanor* (1335), would present narratives in a scholastic objection-and-response form so that the reader can imagine himself involved in an oral disputation, that is, in the form of a "frame story" that allows him the fiction of becoming part of the listening company. In offering several theorems of literary history, Ong comments on the "intriguing" nature of medieval literature, given the influence on it of a "strange new mixture of orality (disputations) and textuality (commentaries on written works) in medieval academia," observing too that "probably most medieval writers across Europe continued the classical practice of writing their literary works to be read aloud. . . . This helped determine the always rhetorical style as well as the nature of plot and characterization." This oral delivery is most evident, according to Crosby in "the use of direct address not to the reader, but to those listeners who are present at the recitation," and results in the presence of epideictic 'demonstrative' locutions ("afevos aqui," "ya oyestes") in works as diverse as poetic hagiographic texts (e.g., the thirteenth-century *Vida de Santa María Egipçiaca*; early chivalresque prose romances (e.g., the *Libro del cavallero Zifar*, ca. 1300) and prose histories (e.g., the fifteenth-century *Crónica de Juan II*) and scientific treatises (e.g., Bernardo Gordonio's *Lilio de medicina*, 1495. Formulaic phrases typical of minstrel epic poetry may also be found in prose chronicles and chivalresque romances (see the studies by Gómez Redondo and Walker. As well, many belletristic texts like the *Libro de buen amor* (1330, 1343) and the *Arcipreste de Talavera o Corbacho* (1438) were probably first diffused orally for their sermonic value or for clerical instruction, being read silently only thereafter.

A useful evaluation of medieval Spanish literature in terms of *diglossia*, or coexistence of two oral and written linguistic systems (e.g., Latin and Spanish)—now popular, now learned—in a specific environment was made in 1989 by Seniff; the same work offers a series of tests under the categories "Aspectos orales" and "Aspectos textuales [= escritos]" for examining the literary production of Alfonso X, Juan Manuel, Alfonso Martínez de Toledo, Diego de San Pedro, and Fernando de Rojas. The work of each author is shown to describe some degree of convergence of orality (now spontaneous, now elaborately rhetorical) and writing with respect to their sources, composition, and—perhaps most commonly—diffusion. A cultural milestone is attained in the case of the last two authors: the popularity of San Pedro's *Cárcel de Amor* (1492) and Rojas' *Celestina* (ca. 1499, 1502), which appeared shortly after the advent of the printing press and were doubtless read aloud to small groups as well as in silence by individuals, may qualify them as the first "best-sellers" in Spanish literature. Yet of all genres described above, the ballad remains as Spain's great living contribution to international oral literature, and is currently the object of intense fieldwork by researchers throughout the Hispanic world.

DENNIS P. SENIFF

Bibliography

Crosby, R. "Oral Delivery in the Middle Ages," *Speculum* 11 (1936), 88–110.

Ferguson, C. A. "Diglossia," *Word* 15 (1959), 325–40.

Foley, J. M. (ed.) *Oral-Formulaic Theory and Research: An Introduction and Annotated Bibliography*. New York, 1985.

Gómez Redondo, F. "Fórmulas juglarescas en la historiografía romance de los siglos XIII y XIV," *La Corónica* 15 (1986–87), 225–39.

Gybbon-Monypenny, G. B. "The Spanish *mester de clerecía* and Its Intended Audience." In *Medieval Miscellany Presented to Eugène Vinaver*. Ed. F. Whitehead. Manchester, 1965. 230–44.

Joset, J. *Nuevas investigaciones sobre el "Libro de buen amor."* Madrid, 1988.

Lawrance, J. N. H. "The Spread of Lay Literacy in Late Medieval Castile," *Bulletin of Hispanic Studies* 62 (1985), 79–94.

Lord, A. B. *The Singer of Tales*. Cambridge, Mass., 1960.

Montgomery, T. "The Uses of Writing in the Spanish Epic," *La Corónica* 15 (1986–87), 179–85.

Ong, W. J., S. J. *Orality and Literacy: The Technologizing of the Word*. London, 1982.

Seniff, D. P. "Aproximación a la oralidad y textualidad en la prosa castellana medieval." In *Actas del IX Congreso de la Asociación Internacional de Hispanistas: 18–23 agosto 1986 Berlin*. Vol. 1. Ed. S. Neumeister. Frankfurt-am-Main, 1989. 263–77.

Stock, B. *The Implications of Literacy: Written Language and Models of Interpretation in the Eleventh and Twelfth Centuries*. Princeton, N. J., 1983.

Walker, R. M. "Oral Delivery or Private Reading?: A Contribution to the Debate on the Dissemination of Medieval Literature," *Forum for Modern Language Studies* 7 (1971), 36–42.

Webber, R. H. "Hispanic Oral Literature: Accomplishments and Perspectives," *Oral Tradition* 1 (1986), 344–80.

———. (ed.) *Hispanic Balladry Today*. Monographic edition of *Oral Tradition* 2 (1987), 395–690.

LIVESTOCK

Given the pervasive impact of pastoralism and of livestock upon the formative medieval centuries of the Iberian economic, social, and military structures, it is unfortunate that so little scholarly work has been done on the subject, despite abundant data in royal law codes and charters, the municipal *fueros* or *forais*, and in private documentation such as deeds of purchase and wills. Spanish and Portuguese linguistic usage subdivides livestock and its raising (*ganadería*; Portuguese *pastoreio*) into two principal categories: *ganado mayor* (Portuguese *gado grosso*), including such larger animals as horses, camels, cattle, mules, and donkeys; and *ganado menor* (*gado miudo*), chiefly sheep, goats, and pigs. Other articles here deal with sheep and cattle; this one will devote itself largely to horses, with briefer comment on other domesticated species.

So far as the horse is concerned, major attention has customarily been paid to the effects of the centuries-long importation of peerless Arabian and Barb (that is, Berber) stock all through the Hispano-Islamic Middle Ages. A hardly less pressing, if neglected, question has to do with the indigenous breeds carried over from the Roman and Visigothic epochs into the life and warfare of the Asturo-Leonese and Navarrese monarchies and the Arago-Catalan counties of the early Reconquest. That such native strains bore any marked resemblance to the still surviving Sorrais breed of primitive Tarpon-like ponies seems unlikely; but how far the handsome Andalusian equine of the south, often styled the "Spanish horse" par excellence, depends upon its classification as either a purely Iberian Barb or a cross of indigenous and African Barb strains. Centers of horse breeding tended to lie off the *meseta* (plateau) in the Middle Ages: in Andalusia, for both Muslims and Christians; in Catalonia all the way from around Vic and Girona to the lower Ebro River; in Portugal, near the coast and perhaps in Ribatejo.

In medieval Iberia the dominant function of the horse was military; travel and carriage uses were distinctly secondary and employment for plowing, as in ultra-Pyrenean manorial Europe, completely undocumented. The physiography of the meseta, the extensive tracts of *despoblado* (wasteland), and the Arabo-Bebber fondness for mobile warfare combined to stress mounted combat for both sides during the Reconquest and this directly affected the need for, and breeding of, horses. The armored knight astride a sturdy charger was, of course, a familiar figure below the Pyrenees among aristocratic *afrancesados* (Frenchified people); but far more typical, and constituting a much larger market for horses, were the urban militias of the towns and comparable bodies of lightly armed troopers that required swift steeds of spirit and endurance for long raids or intricate battle tactics. It was upon such horses, as upon donkeys and mules, that the local and regional livestock fairs depended so heavily, supporting an as yet poorly known class of professional livestock traders.

Occupation of the southern meseta by the Christian kingdoms from around 1200 on led to increasing adoption of the donkey or burro, and the mule, widespread in al-Andalus, whether for travel, carriage, or farming. This was, in effect, the taking over of Mediterranean livestock patterns. The mule, however, stronger than the donkey and faster than the ox (although because it required grain supplement to its feeding, more expensive), gained popularity all over the later medieval peninsula for riding, draft, and agricultural purposes. In view of its importance before and after 1500 in Iberia and the Americas, the mule merits investigation of the foral and charter references.

Goats readily adapted to dry regions and were valued for their milk and mohair. They appear in the sources but were apparently less numerous throughout the Middle Ages than afterward. Rather more is known of pigs, found everywhere in Christian Iberia, but raised in the largest numbers in Galicia, in southern León—where the transhumant porkers of Salamanca are driven south each fall to gorge on the acorn mast of the Extremaduran oak forests was regulated in that town's *fuero*—and in Extremadura itself, already famous for its succulent hams. Much further research on these animals, their economic and human connections, as well as on medieval Iberian livestock in general is imperative.

C. Julian Bishko

Bibliography

Mason, L. *A World Dictionary of Breeds, Types and Varieties of Livestock*. Slough, U.K., 1960.

Togneri, R. de. "Ganadería y precios." *Cuadernos de Hiztoria de España* 35–36 (1962), 37–55.

Vicens Vives, J. *An Economic History of Spain*. Princeton, N.J., 1969.

LLIBRE DEL CONSOLAT DE MAR

The *Llibre del consolat de mar* (LCM) was the most systematic and widely used compilation of maritime law in the medieval Mediterranean. The code served to expedite disputes heard in various "consulates of the sea" (*consolats de mar*), the maritime guild courts. First established in Italy, maritime consulates spread to eastern Iberia in the thirteenth century. In 1258, King Jaime I authorized the "notables of the shore district" (*prohoms de la ribera*) of Barcelona to supervise the port area, shipping, and naval defense. This first attempt to establish an independent maritime institution proved ephemeral and was superseded by a consulate of the sea. Similar institutions were later established in Valencia (1283–1284), Mallorca (1326), and other important ports in the Crown of Aragón.

The compilation known as the LCM grew in stages corresponding to the development of the principal maritime consulates. Its primitive nucleus, probably redacted in Latin at Barcelona between 1266 and 1271, drew upon two different sources: One, possibly oral, dealt with questions of commercial navigation, including obligations among captains, shipowners, sailors, passengers, and merchants; the other, an older set of regulations, was devoted to armament, seizures, and raids. The growth of maritime trade led to the inclusion of new chapters both practical and moral in nature, first at Valencia, where a Catalan version existed, after the establishment of its consulate and then at Mallorca. With the inclusion of new ordinances promulgated by Pedro IV the Ceremonious, by 1353 the LCM attained its final form at Barcelona. This version came into general use in the consulates of the Crown of Aragón and throughout the Mediterranean. Although influenced by Roman law, the LCM draws most heavily on the practical experience of Catalan merchants and sailors. Gradually formed in the three major ports of the crown, the LCM stands as a monument to the cohesiveness and sophistication of Catalan maritime civilization.

Stephen P. Bensch

Bibliography

Colón, G., and García, A. (eds.) *Llibre del consolat de mar*. 4 vols. Barcelona, 1981–87.

The Consulate of the Sea and Related Documents. Trans. S. J. Jados. Tuscaloosa, Ala., 1975.

LLIBRE DELS FEYTS *See* JAIME I, KING OF ARAGÓN; AUTOBIOGRAPHY

LLIBRE VERMELL

Known as the "Red Book" (Bibliot. Mont. ms. 1), this most revered manuscript, containing ascetic treatises, together with the music and texts of twelve pilgrim songs, belongs to the Benedictine Monastery at Montserrat. It was completed in 1399 and had for long remained obscure until it was discovered by the Dominican monk Jaime Villanueva, who mentioned it in the seventh volume of his *Viage literario a las iglesias de España* (Valencia, 1821). Fortunately the manuscript was among the few items that survived a fire in the monastery's scriptorium in 1811 during the Napoleonic War. It takes its name from the red velvet binding in which 137 of its original 172 folios are preserved.

The monastery, situated about fifty kilometers northwest of Barcelona, was founded in 1027 by the abbot Oliba of Ripoll and is considered to be Catalonia's most famous religious shrine, honoring the Virgin of Montserrat. According to legend, the black image of the Virgin that was carved by St. Luke, who brought it there from the Galilee, "was hidden on the mountain at the time of the Moorish invasion and miraculously revealed to the shepherds in the 10th century." Montserrat was also purported to be the site of the Holy Grail, which inspired Richard Wagner's *Parsifal*.

The pilgrim songs (*Els cants dels romeus*), listed according to their order in the *Llibre*, are: (1) *O virgo splendens* (fol. 21^{v}–22); (2) *Stella splendens in monte* (fol. 22^{v}); (3a) *Laudemus virginem* (fol. 23); (3b) *Plangamus scelera*; (4a) *Splendens ceptigera*; (4b) *Tundentes pectora*; (5) *Los set goyts recomptarem*, with the Latin refrain, *Ave Maria, gratia plena* (fol. 23^{v}); (6) *Cuncti simus concanentes* (fol. 24^{r}); (7) *Polorum regina* (fol. 24^{v}); (8) *Mariam matrem virginem/Mariam/Mariam* (fol. 25); (9) *Imperayritz de la ciutat ioyosa/Verges ses par misericordiosa* (fol. 25^{v}); and (10) *Ad mortem festinamus* (fol. 26^{v}). It should be pointed out that the respective texts of the pairs 3a–b and 4a–b share the same music.

As for language, all the songs are in Latin, except numbers 5 and 9, which are in Catalan. Regarding the settings, five (numbers 1, 3a–b, 4a–b, and 8) were written for three voices, the latter for voice and instruments; two were written for two voices (numbers 2 and 9); and the remaining are monophonic. As for notation, all but the first (in square notation) were notated in the mensural notation of the French Ars Nova. Noting the forms, an antiphon (number 1, with its corresponding *versillo* and *oración*), may be considered the earliest canon discovered on the Iberian Peninsula; there exist also examples of the *virelai* (numbers 2, 6, 7, 8, and 10), a precursor of the Spanish *villancico* (the melody and text of an additional *virelai*, *Rosa plasent*, was lost among the missing folios); the canon or round (*caça* in Catalan) for two or three voices (numbers 1, 3a–b, 4a–b); the *canción a dos voces vocales* (number 5), whose two distinct texts, according to Anglés, were not sung simultaneously (that is, the former text was sung before the latter, or each of their respective six strophes were sung one after the other); and the motet, in the French style (number 9), alternating between two and three voices. Numbers 2, 5, 6, 7, and 10 are also responsorial dance songs, of the circle type (*a ball rendon*), which were unique among medieval dances. Authorized by the clergy to be danced during vigils or during the daytime hours in the open squares adjoining the shrine, this Catalan creation, whose purpose was both recreational and devotional, may be considered a precursor of the *sardana*. In noting meter, number 1, predating the other examples by its square notation, comprises the only nonmeasured example. Seven are in the predominating duple meter (numbers 2, 3a–b, 4a–b, 5, and 9, the latter in compound duple 6/4), while the remaining three are in triple (numbers 6, 7, and 10).

Ad mortem festinamus appears to have been the oldest surviving music for a "dance of death." Three of its nine stanzas were found in an earlier *Contemptus mundi* of 1267. Moreover, both its text and that of *Plangamus scelera* are penitential. It should also be noted that the tune for *Polorum regina* reappeared two centuries later in Francisco de Salinas's *Libri septem de musiċa* (Salamanca, 1577).

ISRAEL J. KATZ

Bibliography

Anglés, H. "El 'Llibre Vermell' de Montserrat y los cantos y la danza sacra de los peregrinos durante el siglo XIV." *Anuario Musical* 10 (1955), 45–78.

Gómez i Muntané, M. C. *El Llibre Vermell de Montserrat: Cantos y danzas, s. XIV.* San Cugat de Valles, 1990.

Suñol, G. M. "Estudio crítico y transcripción de las canciones en este manuscrito *Els cants dels Romeus* (segle XIV)." *Analecta Montserrantensia* 1 (1918), 100–192.

Whyte, F. *The Dance of Death in Spain and Catalonia.* Baltimore, 1931.

LLULL, RAMÓN

Catalan lay missionary, philosopher, mystic, poet, and novelist, Ramón Llull (1232/3–1316) was one of the creators of literary Catalan; the first European to write philosophy and theology in a vernacular tongue; the first to write prose novels on contemporary themes; and the founder of a combinatory "art" that was a distant forerunner of computer science. He wrote some 265 works in Catalan, Latin, Arabic (none of these last have been preserved), and perhaps Provençal. In addition we have medieval translations of his works into Spanish, French, and Italian.

Life

Born on the island of Mallorca (modern-day Majorca), which had only recently been reconquered (at the end of 1229), and brought up in a wealthy family in a colonial situation, amid a still considerable Muslim population (perhaps a third of the entire population of the island), Llull's youth was that of a courtier who dabbled in troubadour verse. He married, had two children, and was appointed seneschal to the future Jaume II of Mallorca. Then, in 1263, repeated visions of the Crucifixion made him decide to dedicate his life to the service of Christ, and specifically to carrying out three aims: to try to convert Muslims even if it meant risking his life; to "write a book, the best in the world, against the errors of unbelievers"; and to found monasteries for the teaching of languages to missionaries. Llull bought a Muslim slave in order to learn Arabic and began nine years of study not only of that language, but also of Latin, philosophy, theology, and logic, as well as a certain amount of law, medicine (surely in Montpellier), and astronomy. At the end of this period he wrote a compendium of Al-Ghazālī's logic and the *Llibre de contemplació en Déu* (Book of Contemplation), a vast work combining semi-mystic effusions with the germs of most of his later thought. The changing methodological tactics of the work, however, were finally resolved on Mount Randa in Mallorca, where, after a week's meditation, "The Lord suddenly illuminated his mind, giving him the form and method for writing the aforementioned book against the errors of the unbelievers." (See below for *Contemporary Life* from which this and other passages are quoted.) This "form and method" was the art, of which he now wrote the first work (*Ars compendiosa inveniendi veritatem*, c. 1274), thereby fulfilling the second of his three aims. The third was soon (1276) to be fulfilled with the founding of the monastery of Miramar on the northwest coast of Mallorca for the teaching of Arabic to thirteen Franciscan missionaries.

From this point on, apart from his feverish literary activity, Llull's life became one of ceaseless travel in an attempt to interest the world in his missionary projects. Using Montpellier as a base (it then formed part of the kingdom of Mallorca), he visited Paris four times, where he lectured at the university and had audiences with the king (Philippe IV the Fair, nephew of his patron, Jaume II of Mallorca); he traveled to Italy some six times (to Genoa, where he was in contact with rich merchants, to Pisa, to Rome, where he had audiences with at least three popes, to Naples, and near the end of his life to Sicily); he went three times to North Africa (Tunis and Bougie [modern-day Bejaïa]), thereby fulfilling the first of his three proseltyzing aims; and once to Cyprus (from where he visited the Turkish port of Ayas, and perhaps Jerusalem). Llull's lack of success was typical for an idealist approaching practical politicians with schemes for the betterment of mankind. As he himself admitted in a work of the same title, he was everywhere treated as a *phantasticus*, or as he put it in earlier works, "Ramon lo Foll." And in a touching passage from the poem *Desconhort* (1295), he complained that people read his art "like a cat passing rapidly over hot coals." But these epithets and complaints must not make us forget that he did manage to have the ear of kings and popes, that he presented them with political tracts that recent research has shown to have been far more realistic than was formerly believed. Nor must we forget that on his last trip to Paris, overcoming at last the incomprehensions attendant on his former attempts to teach his peculiar system there, Llull received (1310–1311) letters of commendation from Philippe IV and the chancellor of the university, as well as a document in which forty masters and bachelors in arts and medicine approved of Llull's lectures in *Ars brevis*. The Council of Vienne (1311–1312) subsequently endorsed his proposal for the founding of schools of Oriental languages.

After Llull's discovery of the methodology of the art, his literary and philosophical production can be divided into three periods.

The Quaternary Phase (ca. 1274–1289). This was so called because the basic components of the art (divine attributes, relative principles, and elements) appear in multiples of four. The first work of the art, *Ars compendiosa inveniendi veritatem*, was rapidly accompanied by a series of satellite works explaining it and showing the other fields to which it could be applied. Among these, the most important was *Llibre del gentil e dels tres savis* (Book of the Gentile and the Three Wise Men), Llull's principal apologetic work. It was also around this same time that Llull wrote a pedagogical tract for his son, *Doctrina pueril*, and a manual of knighthood, the *Llibre de l'orde de cavalleria* (*Book of the Order of Chivalry*), destined to become popular in its French translation, and later translated into English by William Caxton. It was also during this time (1283) that he wrote his first didactic novel, *Blaquerna* (this seems to have been the original form of the name, and not the later *Blanquerna*), which included his most famous mystic work, the *Llibre d'amic e amat* (*Book of the Lover and the Beloved*).

In the same year of 1283, Llull decided to refashion many minor aspects of his system in a new version called *Ars demonstrativa*, around which he wrote a new cycle of explicative and satellite works. It was during this period that he wrote his second didactic novel, *Félix o El libre de meravelles* (Felix, or the Book of Wonders), which includes the political animal fable, *Llibre de les bèsties* (*Book of the Beasts*).

The Ternary Phase (1290–1308). In this phase the principles of the art appear in multiples of three (and the four elements disappear as one of its foundations). Because of "the weakness of human intellect" that Llull encountered on his first trip to Paris, he reduced the number of figures with which his system invariably began from twelve (or sixteen) to four, and he removed all algebraic notation from the actual discourse of the art. This phase begins not with a single work surrounded by satellites, but with twin works: *Ars inventiva veritatis* which, as Llull says, treats *ciència* or knowledge, and *Ars amativa* which treats *amància* or love of God; it ends with the final formulation of his system in *Ars generalis ultima* (1305–1308), and in shorter form in *Ars brevis* (1308). This period is rich in important works, among which one might mention the immense encyclopedia, *Arbre de ciència* (Tree of Science, 1295–1296), as well as his principal work on logic, epistemology, and politics, *Logica nova* (1303), *Liber de ascensu et descensu intellectus* (1305), and *Liber de fine* (also 1305).

The Postart Phase (1308–1315). With the definitive formulation of his system now out of the way, Llull is free to concentrate on specific logical and epistemological topics, many directed toward his campaign against the Parisian "Averröists" while on his last trip there (1309–1311). It was at the end of this stay that he dictated what has come to be known in its English translation as *Contemporary Life*. He also became more and more involved in the art of preaching, writing a vast *Summa sermonum* in Mallorca (1312–1313).

Llull's last works are dated from Tunis, December 1315, after which he disappears from history. He probably died early the following year, either there on the ship returning to his native Mallorca, or on the island itself, where he is buried. The story of his martyrdom (he was stoned to death) is a legend bolstered by pious falsifications in the early seventeenth century, in which an earlier (1307) stoning in Bejaïa was transposed and made into the cause of his death.

Thought and Influence

The unusual nature of Llull's system and of his thought in general is due to his insistence that any apologetic system that hoped to persuade Muslims and Jews would have to abandon the use of Scripture, which only caused endless discussions over validity and interpretation, and try to prove the articles of the Christian faith, above all those of the Trinity and Incarnation that Muslims and Jews found most difficult to accept. The first consideration forced Llull to forge an abstract system that could stand completely by itself. This was the art, each work of which begins with a series of of concepts distributed amid geometric figures, and then proceeds to describe the correct method of combining these concepts. The point was to display the basic structure of reality, which, noted Llull, begins with the attributes of God, goodness, greatness, eternity, and so forth, which are not static but unfold into three correlatives of action. Thus *bonitas* (goodness) unfolds into an agent (*bonificativum*) and a patient (*bonificabile*), and the act joining them (*bonificare*). Their necessary activity *ad intra* produces the Trinity, and their contingent activity *ad extra* the act of creation. Moreover, this triad of action is then reproduced at every level of creation, so that, for instance, man's intellect is composed of *intellectivum*, *intelligibile*, and *intelligere*, and fire of *ignificativum*, *ignificabile*, and *ignificare*.

This metaphysics of action exerted a strong influence on Nicholas of Cusa, as did the combinatorial art on Giordano Bruno and Gottfried Wilhelm Leibniz. But at the same time, Llull's system was taken over by alchemists, and eventually over one hundred such works were falsely attributed to him. This, plus his self-image as a *phantasticus*, the unusual nature of his system, and the fact that his attempts to prove the articles of the faith made him suspect to the Inquisition, helped propagate the image of a peculiar, countercultural figure.

Llull's influence in the Iberian Peninsula was less hetorodox and countercultural than in the rest of Europe. Aside from the fifteenth-century Llullist schools of Mallorca and Barcelona, there were a certain number of Castilian translations of his works done in the later Middle Ages, although interest in him seems to have been of a dispersed, sporadic nature, at least until the beginning of the sixteenth century. Then we find a Lullist school at Valencia (where some of his works were published), the chief figure of which was the humanist Alonso de Proaza. He in turn was in contact with Cardinal Francisco Jiménez de Cisneros, who in his foundation in 1508 of the University of Alcalá de Henares, instuted a chair of Lullian philosophy and theology. Later in the century, Felipe II was an admirer of Llull, as was his chief architect, Juan de Herrera, who not only wrote a *Tratado del cuerpo cúbico* based on Llull's art, but in 1582 founded a mathematical-philosophical academy in Madrid in whose program the art was to have a prominent place.

Literary Works

Llull's most unusual literary feature is that he dared to modify the conventional genres of contemporary romance tradition to fit his own didactic needs. Llull first attempted the novel, in the *Libre de Evast e Blaquerna* (Book of Evast and Blaquerna, 1283), and *Félix o El libre de meravelles* (Felix, or the Book of Wonders, 1288) he recounted stories morally useful to his readers. He similarly adjusted the narrative wrapping of an early apologetical work, the *Llibre del gentil e dels tres savis* (Book of the Gentile and the Three Wise Men), in which an unbeliever struggles to find the truth and finally embraces the faith.

The plot of *Blaquerna* follows the outline of a hero's biography; the main character is endowed with the mental strength permitting him to overcome the obstacles in the way of his becoming a contemplative hermit. These "obstacles" are the ties that link a man to society: a family, a religious order, a diocese, and the whole of Christianity ruled by the pope. Blaquerna abandons his parents, Evast and Aloma, and convinces his bride, Natana, to become an exemplary nun, whereupon he enters a monastery and becomes a reforming abbot who is then elected bishop. Blaquerna improves the spiritual life of his diocese and as a result is elected pope; from Rome Blaquerna manages to reorganize the world and to change the moral attitudes of people. Finally he renounces the papacy and becomes the perfect hermit, which permits him to write *Llibre d'amic e amat* (*Book of the Lover and the Beloved*), a collection of short mystical proverbs lyrically embellished and artistically constructed.

The *Book of Wonders* follows the spiritual journey of Felix through events that cause him "wonder" because they seem to be contrary to God's will, and that allow various hermits and philosophers to explain the fundamental points of Christian knowledge about God, angels, the heavens, the elements, plants, minerals, animals, man, paradise, and hell. Like *Blaquerna*, this novel offers plenty of morally meaningful exempla, but unlike the earlier work, it betrays considerable pessimism about the capacity of mankind to better its moral behavior. One chapter of *Félix* has become particularly famous: *Llibre de les baèsties* (*Book of the Beasts*), a Llullian adaptation of the old Iranian *Book of Kalila and Dimna* with some references to the French *Roman de Renard*.

In search of a literary vehicle for his message, Llull attempted autobiography, so *Desconhort* (1295) and *Cant de Ramon* (1300), two splendid lyric poems, explain from a personal point of view the disappointments and failures of his career. In the process Llull himself becomes a new literary character: a poor, old, and despised man who has devoted his life to revealing a treasury of knowledge, an art given to him by God. A short late prose work, *Phantasticus* (1311), offers the most complete picture of this personage, whom, as was noted above, he sometimes called "Ramon lo Foll."

Plant de la Verge and *Llibre de Santa Maria*, both probably written between 1290 and 1293, are two pieces of devotional literature: the former, in verse, is a moving description of Christ's Passion, the latter, in prose, an unusual application of the Llullian art to a prayer to the Virgin Mary. Another treatise with rich literary contents is the *Arbre de filosofia d'amor* (*Tree of Philosophy of Love*, 1289), which encloses a short, touching mystical novel.

In his immense encyclopedia of 1295–1296, the (*Arbre de ciència*) (Tree of Science) Llull included a little *Arbre exemplifical* (Tree of Examples), in which a preacher could find the way to "translate science into exemplary literature." This work is the first of Llull's contributions to homiletics, a trend that later developed both into theoretical treatises—*Rhetorica nova* (1302), *Liber de praedicatione* (1304), *Ars brevis pradicationis* (1313)—and sermon writing. Llull in later years, in fact, put aside romance literary genres and devoted himself to sermon collections; the most important being *Summa sermonum* of 1312–1313, which offers an unusual model for preaching, since Llull wanted to persuade lay audiences intellectually rather than to touch their hearts with moving anecdotes.

ANTHONY BONNER AND LOLA BADÍA

Bibliography

Bonner, A., and Badia, L. *Ramon Llull: Vida, pensament i obra literària*. Barcelona, 1988.

Carreras y Artau, T., and J. *Historia de la filosofía española: Filosofía cristiana de los siglos XIII al XV*. 2 vols. Madrid, 1939–43.

Hillgarth, J. N. *Ramon Lull and Lullism in Fourteenth-Century France*. Oxford, 1971.

Llull, R. *Obres essencials*. 2 vols. Barcelona, 1957–60.

———. *Selected Works of Ramon Llull (1232–1316)*. 2 vols. Ed. A. Bonner. Princeton, N.J., 1985. Catalan version in *Obres selectes de Ramon Llull (1232–1316)*. 2 vols. Majorca, 1989.

LOPES, FERNÃO

The date of Lopes' birth is unknown but he was said to be quite old when he died in 1459. He was the most significant Portuguese chronicler of the Middle Ages, and flourished during the reign of Duarte and the regency of the Infante Pedro. Lopes seems to have fallen from favor after the accession of Afonso V (1448), when Gomes Eanes de Zurara began to be active. By

1454 Lopes had been replaced as custodian of the Torre do Tombo, the royal archive he directed from 1418 on. Lopes's historical accounts cover the period from 1357–1433. They are based on documentary investigations carried out by him in the Torre do Tombo and on earlier, now lost, narratives. Lopes's historical writing was probably initiated at the instance of the Infante Dom Duarte, who by 1419 was responsible for overseeing the reaction of chronicles dealing with the first Portuguese kings. Dom Duarte's interest in history continued after he became king in 1434. Duarte officially commissioned Lopes to continue chronicling Portuguese history from the reign of Dom João I forward. Lopes's historical accounts are often compared favorably with those of Jean Froissart and Pero López de Ayala, both of whom chronicled many of the same events of the effects of the Hundred Years' War in the Iberian Peninsula.

Fernão Lopes's chronicles are distinguished for their realistic portraits of individuals and for their portrayal and basic analysis of motivational factors in historical events. Lopes's *Crónica de D. João I* is perhaps his best known work for its heroic portrait and close scrutiny of Nuno Alvares Pereira, *condestavel* (Constable) of the realm during the reign of João I.

E. Michael Gerli

Bibliography

Lozoya, Marqués de. *El cronista don Pedro López de Ayala y la historiografía portuguesa.* Madrid, 1931.

Rodrigues Lapa, M. *Froissart e Fernão Lopes.* Lisboa, 1930.

Russell, P. E. *The English Intervention in Spain and Portugal in the Time of Edward III and Richard II.* Oxford, 1955.

Saraiva, A. J. *Fernão Lopes.* 2nd ed. Lisboa, 1965.

LÓPEZ DE AYALA, PERO

Pero López de Ayala (1332–1407) was a chronicler, poet, and statesman who lived in a period that spanned the reigns of five Castilian kings. He was born into a wealthy, noble family in the northern province of Álava. Although not a great deal is known of his youth, Ayala's knowledge of Latin and French, plus his interest in the Bible and other religious writings may have come from early ecclesiastical training by his uncle, Cardinal Pedro Gómez Barroso, who raised and educated him. Much of what is known of Ayala's activities is derived from the chronicles he wrote describing the reigns of Pedro I (1350–1369), Enrique II (1369–1379), Juan I (1379–1390), and Enrique III (1390–1406). Beginning with his first appearance in the *Crónicas des los reyes de Castilla: don Pedro* (Chronicle of the Kings of Castile: Peter I) in 1353 as a page selected to carry the king's banner, Ayala served Pedro in various capacities for over a dozen years. By 1367, however, he had joined Enrique of Trastámara, Pedro's illegitimate half-brother and rival for the throne. Shortly afterward, Ayala was taken prisoner by the English at the battle of Nájera.

During the reign of Enrique II, Ayala received many royal favors, including territorial possessions and political posts. His political activity greatly increased during the reign of Juan I, when he served as royal counselor and as ambassador to France. Although he opposed the plan of Juan I to assume the Portuguese throne and thereby unite the two kingdoms, Ayala participated in the disastrous battle of Aljubarrota, where he was captured by the Portuguese and imprisoned for two years. It is probable that some of his writings were done during this period, especially the *Libro de la caza de las aves* and some poetic works. Ayala's importance and influence continued to grow during the reign of Enrique III. He was a member of the Council of Regents during the king's minority and served as a negotiator in the peace talks with Portugal. In the mid-1390s, Ayala spent several years in semiretirement at his estate in Álava and at the adjacent Hieronymite monastery. It is believed that he wrote his chronicles and *Libro del linaje de Ayala* during this time. In 1399, he was appointed grand chancellor of Castile.

In addition to being an impressive political and military leader who was personally acquainted with popes and kings, Ayala must also be acknowledged as one of the three major literary figures of his century. Juan Ruiz, Juan Manuel, and Pero López de Ayala all in their own way reflect the social, economic, and political milieu in which they lived as well as their own personal reactions to their circumstances. Although a self-consciousness as literary creators is apparent in the work of each of these authors, their primary purpose remains didactic—ranging from the jocular tongue-in-cheek admonitions of Ruiz to the chivalric preoccupations and moralizing of Manuel to the almost ascetic severity of Ayala. As the most important writer of the last half of the fourteenth century, Ayala's prose and poetic works are significant for a number of reasons. Linguistically, they comprise an extensive and reliable source of late-fourteenth- and early-fifteenth-century Spanish. His chronicles are of great historical value as they are a major source of information concerning events in Spain from 1350 to 1396. The epoch that Ayala chronicles is a period of crisis and of such peninsular and international conflicts as civil and religious wars in Spain, the Hundred Years' War, the Black Death, and the schism in the Catholic Church. An eyewitness to many of these events, Ayala identifies himself with the purpose and norms of ancient chroniclers, explaining in his preface that the purpose of knowing about events in the past is to serve as a guide for present actions. He further comments that his sole intention is to tell the truth based on what he himself observed and from testimony of trustworthy persons. Nevertheless, the chronicler's impartiality, and at times even his veracity, has been questioned because he reports so many barbarous acts, and because he views Pedro I primarily as a negative example. Ayala's support of the Trastámaran pretender and his later involvement in the royal court further clouds the picture. The two manuscript traditions *abreviada* and *vulgar* suggest a process of revision that served to soften the condemnation of Pedro I after the reconciliation of the two dynastic lines, with the marriage of the grandchildren of the two contenders.

The literary nature of these narratives and the chronicler's acute awareness of literary style must also be taken into account. Among the variety of literary devices used in the chronicles, Ayala includes the skillful arrangement of all the contributing elements to form an organic unity: tense choice, paired words or doublets, alternation, contrast, parallelism, repetition, and portraiture. The author's skill in the use of direct address such as dialogues, one-liners, discourses, letters, and sayings enliven narrative passages and reveal the dramatic nature of the events. The dramatic structure of the death scenes is also evident in other episodes; for example, the farewell scene between Leonor de Guzmán and her son Fadrique, the confrontation with the Queen Mother at Toro, the departure of Pedro I from Burgos, and the papal election that began the schism. Ayala must be recognized as a talented prose stylist as he relates events more varied and fascinating than many fictional sagas, consisting of wars, fratricides, marriages, mistresses, international intrigues, and power struggles at the highest levels of government.

Ayala's long poetic work *Rimado de Palacio*, completed in 1404, is a highly personal and creative expression of the author's moral and philosophical preoccupations. Most of its 2,168 stanzas (totalling more than 8,000 lines) are written in the verse form *cuaderna vía*, characterized by four-line stanzas, each fourteen-syllable line divided by a caesura after the seventh syllable and ending in uniform consonantal rhyme. In spite of being the last of the *cuaderna vía* poets, Ayala demonstrates poetic innovations that include increased use of the eight-syllable line and the introduction of *arte mayor*, both most apparent in the *Cancionero* portion, stanzas 732–919. At the center of *Cancionero*, the poet again reveals his concern for the Church in a long allegory in which the ship of St. Peter is being torn apart by the destructive storm of the Great Schism.

The *Rimado* consists of a large number of poems of varied content and structure whose composition undoubtedly spans decades and whose impetus springs from the experiences of a long, adventurous life as well as from periods of reading and meditation. To say that it is a didactic-moral work or a long confessional poem is true. Nonetheless, this would slight the literary value and variety of Ayala's forcefully sober verse. Ayala's fine, satirically traced pictures of medieval society have, above all else, attracted readers to *Rimado*. These vigorous scenes of contemporary society and court life are found in the first part of the book, along with other poems that arise from the chancellor's personal experiences and his reflections. The poet's description of personages in the royal courts, the almost caricaturelike presentation of merchants and lawyers, prefigure later satirical works that culminate in the mordant sarcasm and ridicule of Francisco Quevedo, as well as in subsequent vignettes of manners and customs.

The more extensive final part of the work provides a focus on doctrine rather than experience. Ayala demonstrates originality in combining confessional and doctrinal themes and materials based on the Bible and the *Morals* of St. Gregory in order to produce a didactic exposition in verse. Many of the themes of the fifteenth-century rhymmed confessions undoubtedly received some impetus from the meditations on life, death, original sin, and the brief duration of worldly gains portrayed in *Rimado*. In addition to influencing the verse forms, topics, and themes of later poets, Ayala's devout and moving poems dedicated to the Virgin had an impact on religious lyrical poetry of the fifteenth century. Ayala also made an important contribution to Castilian intellectual life through his translations of works of Livy, Gregory, Isidore, and Boethius.

CONSTANCE L. WILKINS

Bibliography

García, M. *Obra y personalidad del Canciller Ayala*. Madrid, 1983.

López de Ayala, P. *Libro Rimado de Palacio*. 2 vols. Ed. J. Joset. Madrid, 1978.

Strong, E. B. "The *Rimado de Palacio*: López de Ayala's Rimed Confession." *Hispanic Review* 37 (1969), 439–51.

Tate, R. B. "López de Ayala, Humanist Historian?" *Hispanic Review* 25 (1957), 157–74.

Wilkins, C. *Pero López de Ayala*. Boston, 1989.

LÓPEZ DE CÓRDOBA, LEONOR

Born in 1362, Leonor López de Córdoba composed one of the most singular chronicles of the late Middle Ages in Castile. Her *Memorias*, which were dictated to a scribe around the beginning of the fifteenth century, are a personal testimony of a society ravaged by civil war, pestilence, and class upheaval.

Due to the dramatic circumstances of the narrator's life, the *Memorias* present a point of view that is rare in the historiography of this period. Leonor López was the sole survivor of a family destroyed because of its allegiance to Pedro I, the legitimate king of Castile, during the dynastic struggle he waged against his half-brother, Enrique de Trastámara. The social climate of the decades following this civil war was dominated by the usurper's followers, who spread propaganda alluding to the brutality of Pedro "the Cruel," and the low social class of his supporters, as a means of justifying their overthrow of the rightful monarch. In an effort to repudiate such rumors in her *Memorias*, Leonor López described in detail the nobility of her lineage, the bravery of her father in defense of the loyalist cause, and the atrocities that Enrique de Trastámara himself inflicted upon her family. Her work is a historical curiosity, both as a document of a dispossessed class, and as a feat of honor performed verbally by a woman.

Memorias also merits attention for its literary significance as one of the earliest examples of autobiographical expression produced in medieval Spain. In order to exonerate herself, Leonor López elaborated a self-portrait that exemplified the conduct deemed appropriate for a noble lady. Her persuasive manipulation of language is particularly evident in her use of motifs derived from pious literature to associate herself with a popular ideal of Christian virtue.

Despite their limitations as a historical record and artistic work, the *Memorias* of Leonor López are notable as a re-creation of the past that preserves a uniquely feminine interpretation of the values of medieval Castilian society.

AMANDA CURRY

Bibliography

Ayerbe-Chaux, R. "Las memorias de Leonor López de Córdoba." *Journal of Hispanic Philology* 2 (1977–78), 11–33.

Deyermond, A. "Spain's First Women Writers." In *Women in Hispanic Literature: Icons and Fallen Idols*. Ed. B. Miller, Berkeley, Calif., 1983. 26–52.

LÓPEZ DE CÓRDOBA, MARTÍN

The Castilian official most identified with the last stages of Pedro I's reign, Martín López (ca. 1315–1371) remained loyal to the king's cause even after Pedro's death in 1369. A knight of relatively humble origins, he first came to Pedro's attention as a subaltern of his *canciller mayor* (senior chancellor) Juan Fernández de Henestrosa. His first known important function was as *comendador* (commander) of the houses of Seville of the Military Order of Calatrava. López de Córdoba rose rapidly in the royal service, entrenched himself at court, and occupied a series of increasingly important posts from *camarero mayor* (senior steward) in 1359 to *repostero mayor* (senior butler) the following year. In 1365 he was elected master of the Order of Alcántara and appointed *adelantado mayor* (senior governor) of Murcia. Before 1367 he was elected master of the Order of Calatrava, and was sent by Pedro as his ambassador to the English court. Pedro López de Ayala, the chronicler of Pedro's reign, asserts that Pedro entrusted Martín López with the delicate task of eliminating some of his enemies, and that the master's success in carrying out the task accounted for his rapid ascent.

Martín López did not accompany Pedro on his fateful march northward from Seville to meet the armies of his challenger Enrique de Trastámara in the early spring of 1369. When Enrique's superior army and clever strategy forced Pedro to seek refuge at a nearby fortress following the battle of Montiel on 14 March 1369, López de Córdoba attempted to reach the fortress to relieve the king. But before he arrived, Pedro had been killed by Enrique. López de Córdoba then turned around and returned to Andalusia where he tried unsuccessfully to raise a large army to march against Enrique. As not much support materialized, he took his own family, some of Pedro's illegitimate children, an armed contingent of eight hundred knights, and what remained of the king's treasury and set up residence behind the walls of the fortress of Carmona, outside Seville, a splendidly located strategic site that had been provisioned to withstand a long siege.

After holding out for two years, and giving up hope of reinforcements from the outside, Martín López entered into negotiations with Enrique, who appeared disposed to offer the rebels reasonable terms, promising a safe-conduct abroad in exchange for their surrender and the return of what was left of Pedro's treasury. On 10 May 1371, when the gates of Carmona opened, Enrique reneged. He had many of the notables, including Pedro's children, bound in chains and carted off to prison in Seville.

López de Córdoba and the other principal defender of Carmona, Mateo Fernández, were paraded through the streets of the town, taken to a public square, and mutilated and burned to death. Before his execution, Martín López is reported to have said to Bertrand du Guesclin, the French mercenary in Enrique's employ whose betrayal of Pedro had led to the king's death: "It is better to die a loyalist, as I do, than to live as a traitor, as you do."

It was Martín López de Córdoba's loyalty to Pedro, more than any other quality, that defined his relationship to the king during the last years of the reign. This was a period plagued by political instability, the defection from the royal cause of important individuals, and the violent response of the king to adverse circumstances. Martín López defied the trend and was rewarded for it with Pedro's trust and the prestige and rents of high office.

Martín López's death effectively marked the end of internal opposition to the Trastámaran usurpation. Martín López's daughter, Leonor López de Córdoba, a prisoner in Seville following the surrender of Carmona, left a set of memoirs recollecting the fate of the prisoners after the death of her father. She eventually became an important figure in the Castilian court of Catherine of Lancaster, wife of Enrique III and granddaughter of Pedro I.

Clara Estow

Bibliography

Estow, C. "Leonor López de Córdoba: Portrait of a Medieval Courtier." *Fifteenth Century Studies* 5 (1982), 23–46.

O'Callaghan, J. "The Masters of Calatrava and the Castilian Civil War 1350–1369." In *Die geistlichen Ritterodern Europas*. Sigmaringen, Germany, 1980. 353–74.

LÓPEZ DE MENDOZA, IÑIGO

Born in 1398, Iñigo López de Mendoza (first marqués de Santillana, and señor de Hita and Buitrago) was the son of Diego Hurtado de Mendoza, the influential admiral of Castile. His uncle was Pero López de Ayala, poet, statesman, military figure, and the commanding chancellor of Castile during the last quarter of the fourteenth century. During the reign of Juan II of Castile, López de Mendoza was head of the powerful Mendoza clan, which was connected through marriage to many of the most influential families of the kingdom.

López de Mendoza is one of the major cultural and political figures of the fifteenth century. He spent a part of his youth in Aragón, where he became friends and shared intellectual pursuits with Enrique de Villena, one of the great learned men of his time. López de Mendoza distinguished himself both militarily and literarily on the Granadan frontier, at Ágreda in 1429 and again at Jaén in 1438. Although he fought alongside Juan II and his confidant Álvaro de Luna, Constable of Castile, at the battle of Olmedo in 1445 defending the interests of the monarchy against the challenges of the Infantes de Aragón, López de Mendoza quickly became don Álvaro's sworn enemy. Along with other powerful nobles, López de Mendoza then conspired to topple Luna from power and went on to write admonitory poetry about the example of Luna's life and execution in 1453.

The Marqués, as López de Mendoza was referred to simply in his time, surrounded himself in Guadalajara with artists, writers, and thinkers like Nuño de Guzmán, Pero Díaz de Toledo, and Martín González de Lucena, and was perhaps the greatest single cultural and artistic force of his time. As both intellectual and patron, López de Mendoza was the single most important figure in the propagation of humanistic knowledge in Castile during the first half of the fifteenth century. In addition to having gathered in Guadalajara the most significant library of humanistic works in lay hands and patronized the translation of Homer's *Iliad*, Plato, Ovid, Cicero, Seneca, Dante, and Boccaccio into Castilian, López de Mendoza was in his own right a celebrated poet, literary critic, and theoretician. Although he collected Latin manuscripts, he could not read Latin, but he read several vernaculars fluently and was aware of contemporary developments in European poetry, especially in France and Italy. His *Carta e prohemio al Condestable de Portugal*, which draws heavily on classical and patristic writers as well as Boccaccio's *De genealogia deorum*, is considered the first concerted work of literary theory and criticism in Castilian. Its novelty lies in its historical descriptions of different genres and the catalogue of works that it contains, just as it offers an evaluation of the qualities and defects of the poets he mentions. In addition, his *Sonetos fechos al itálico modo* (1438), which follow the example of Dante and Petrarch, mark the first coherent attempt to cultivate the sonnet form in Castilian. Besides these two works and his patronage, López de Mendoza was a prolific writer responsible for a vast body of work in both prose and verse that deals with moral, religious, political, and sentimental themes, all of which contributed to his vast fame during his lifetime. Among the best known of his lyrical works are his *serranillas*, or pastourelles, that tell of rural love encounters between knights and rustic shepherdesses. His ambitious narrative and allegorical poems, known as *decires* (*Bías contra Fortuna, Doctrinal de Privados, Comedieta de Ponza*), are replete with mythological, biblical, and other learned themes that attest to his humanistic knowledge and intellectual aspirations. The *Comedieta* (1436), a patriotic composition that exalts the Aragónese in their Italian campaign at the naval battle of Ponza, represents the culmination of López de Mendoza's allegorical works. It is built upon a complicated image pattern developed through the use of highly learned language and allusion. *Bías contra*

Fortuna, written in 1448 as a consolation to mark the political imprisonment of a cousin by don Álvaro de Luna, marks the climax of the theme of Fortune in his work. In contradistinction to the difficult allegory of the *Comedieta*, Bías, the Greek philosopher who is the spokesperson for Santillana, makes his views on Fortune and the world clearly known. The *Doctrinal* reveals a final vindictive side of López de Mendoza's character, in which he employs Fortune and confession to make Álvaro de Luna, his dead enemy, denounce his own transgressions.

When López de Mendoza died in 1458, the event inspired his contemporaries to write a number of elegies and other literary compositions to mourn his passing.

E. Michael Gerli

Bibliography

Lapesa, R. *La obra literaria del Marqués de Santillana*. Madrid, 1959.

Nader, H. *The Mendoza Family in the Spanish Renaissance, 1350–1550*. Rutgers, N.J., 1979.

Schiff, M. *La bibliothèque du marquis de Santillane*. Paris, 1905.

LUCAS OF TÚY

Lucas of Túy (fl. thirteenth century) was the bishop of the small see of Túy in Galicia on the Portuguese frontier between 1239 and 1249 where he had also been *magister scolarum* and canon just previously. His episcopate was not particularly significant and he is known to us chiefly as an author. Lucas was likely a native rather of the city of León or its environs and, before he came to Túy, had been a canon and deacon of the cathedral of León. While in that position, he had written a *translatio* detailing the movement in the eleventh-century of the relics of St. Isidore of Seville from that city to the great shrine church built for them in León. There as well he also wrote an apologetic tract against the Albigensian heresy.

These works may have brought him to the attention of the Queen Mother Berenguela, former wife of Alfonso IX of León, who asked him to compile a history of the realm. The result was his most famous work, *Chronicon Mundi*, composed before 1238. A world chronicle in form, the work largely follows Isidore of Seville for the earlier period and only with the fourth book, which covers the time from the Muslim invasion of 711 down to the recapture of Córdoba by Fernando III in 1236, is it of independent interest. Lucas excerpted freely from the chronicles of the Alfonso III cycle, from *Historia Silense*, and from *Crónica del obispo Don Pelayo*. It is possible, as well, that he used *Crónica Nájerense* and *Crónica latina de los reyes de Castilla*. However, for his twelfth and thirteen-century narrative he employed sources now apparently lost. He does not utilize *Historia Compostelana* or *Chronica Adefonsi Imperatoris*.

In addition to earlier but lost chronicles as such, he also freely employed epic materials. That of Bernardo del Carpio first appears in Lucas's text. He also incorporates epic materials dealing with the reigns of Sancho II of Castile (r. 1065–1072) and Alfonso VI of León and Castile (r. 1065–1109). There are also minor tales, including that of the pilgrimage of Louis VII of France to Santiago de Compostela in 1154. Writing slightly later, Rodrigo Jiménez de Rada incorporated these materials almost verbatim into his *De rebus Hispaniae* and from there they became the common property of subsequent historians.

Bernard F. Reilly

Bibliography

Reilly, B. F. "Sources of the Fourth Book of Lucas of Túy's *Chronicon Mundi*." *Classical Folia* 30 (1976), 127–37.

Túy, L. de "Chronicon Mundi ab Origine Mundi usque ad Eram MCCLXXIV." In *Hispaniae Illustratae*. Ed. Andreas Schottus. Frankfurt, 1608, 1–116.

LUCIDARIO

The Latin *Elucidarium*, composed around 1095 by Anselm of Canterbury's disciple Honorius Augustodunensis (c. 1075–c. 1156), was a highly popular work translated soon after its creation into every major European language. The Castilian version, the *Lucidario*, was commissioned by Sancho IV (r. 1284–1295) around 1293 and forms a complement to the other minor encyclopedic works from the reign of the second son of Alfonso el Sabio: the *Castigos e documentos* and a translation of Brunetto Latini's *Li Livres dou trésor*. *Lucidario* is extant in five manuscript copies ranging from the late fourteenth or early fifteenth to the early sixteenth centuries. Like the original *Elucidarium* and its vernacular congeners, the Castilian rendition is couched in the form of a dialogue between a master and his pupil wherein the student poses a question to which the master duly responds with a conventional answer based on the interplay between the fundamental medieval doctrines of *lex naturalis* or laws of nature and *lex theologiae* or laws of God. In this respect, the work was a highly successful attempt to reconcile the pagan Aristotelian scientific corpus with the essential canons of Christian dogma. As such, the Castilian *Lucidario* became a standard text of Christian orthodoxy at the level of the cathedral schools where it was utilized as a most effective if rather limited and rudimentary mode of instructing Christian cosmogony and cosmography. In the process of reproducing and translating the primitive text of the *Elucidarium*, scribes frequently incorporated additional questions and answers which were then suitably accommodated and passed on as if they had been part of the original work, thus accounting for the variety of contents found in the extant Castilian codices of the *Lucidario*, which range from 59 to 113 chapters. The title *Lucidario* eventually came to be used as a generic term for a variety of encyclopedic works cast in the master-disciple format of question and answer. Today its value resides precisely in that aspect of the text that made it so popular during the Middle Ages: the certainty that it accurately reflects the orthodox Christian views of the average Spaniard between the thirteenth century and the demise of Aristotelianism some four hundred years later when, in testament to the esteem it continued to enjoy, an abbreviated Latin translation based on the Castilian version was made by Padre Juan Eusebio Nieremberg (1595–1658).

RICHARD P. KINKADE

Bibliography

Kinkade, R. (ed.) *Los "Lucidarios" españoles*. Madrid, 1968.

"Sancho IV: Puente literario entre Alfonso el Sabio y Juan Manuel." *Publications of the Modern Language Association* 87 (1972), 1039–51.

LUNA, ÁLVARO DE

Don Álvaro, as he is commonly referred to, was the illegitimate son of a minor noble of Aragónese origin by the same name. He was born in Castile at Cañete in 1388, and his mother was from that village. When his father died in 1395, Álvaro was taken in by his uncle, Juan Martínez de Luna. In 1408 Álvaro de Luna was sent to court to further his education. There he was known for his elegance and wit, and quickly became the friend, companion, and favorite of Prince Juan, the considerably younger boy who had inherited the throne during infancy and would become Juan II, king of Castile. From their earliest days together, Luna and the king were constant companions and confidantes. Fearing the worst of the association, the young prince's mother, the Queen Regent Catalina de Lancaster, arranged to have Luna removed from court in 1415. Juan was miserable without his friend's company, and Luna was quickly recalled. By 1418, when Catalina had died, Luna and the king's relationship had grown to the point that it inspired both public gossip and private envy among many of the nobles, who sought influence to augment their power at the expense of the crown. (In later years the king would be confronted by the nobles with rumors of their homosexual relationship). Luna, however, remained confident of the king's support and relied heavily on the backing of others who associated the crown's interests with their own, namely the lower and middle layers of society. Luna brilliantly exploited the concerns and aspirations of the non-noble sectors of society and, at the same time, sought to increase his own influence as well as centralize the power of the monarchy. As a result, he undermined the power of the *cortes* (parliament) and the local municipalities, as he gathered more and more power for the crown and for himself. The king, who remained largely disinterested in affairs of state, became a virtual pawn of the ambitious Luna.

In 1420 Luna, who had been elevated to count and been given large estates, rescued the king from the Infantes de Aragón, who had seized the monarch and taken him to Talavera de la Reina. The Infantes, brothers of Alfonso V of Aragón, were closely allied with the Castilian nobles who sought to curb the power of the monarchy in the kingdom. Both had regal ambitions themselves and looked to protect their family's enormous interests in Castile. Luna was made the constable of Castile in 1423, a step which greatly increased his power and influence by making them official. The move provoked the nobles and the Infantes to multiply their efforts against him, which met with success in 1427, when they and the other nobles forced the king to exile Luna. Neither the king nor the nobles, however, were capable of governing Castile without Luna, whose talents had ensured his indispensability. As a result, he was quickly recalled and fully reinstated. The Castilian victory in the war against Aragón (1429) not only restored but amplified Luna's power and influence.

Luna seemed unstoppable. At one point, the mastery of the military Order of Santiago was conferred upon him after it had been stripped from the Infante Enrique, heir to the throne. With this new power in hand, Luna began to campaign against the Muslim south and led the Castilians to an important victory at the battle of La Higueruela in 1431. The nobles, presided over by the Manrique and Enríquez clans, continued to resist Luna and plot against him at court. Although their efforts led to a second exile in 1438, by 1445 Luna had been restored to favor and had handed the nobles a resounding defeat at the battle of Olmedo. Only King Juan's second wife, Isabel of Portugal, managed to rid the kingdom of Luna. With the collaboration of the nobles, especially the conde de Haro and the marqués de Santillana, she persuaded the king to arrest Luna and condemn him to death. He was taken prisoner at Easter, 1453, and publically beheaded at Valladolid on 22 June of that year.

As he went to his death, Luna, whose bravery was legendary, calmly requested that his executioner not tie his hands with the customary rope but with the silk cord he had brought for that purpose. Luna's spectacular rise and dramatic fall would continue to haunt the Castilian imagination for the next several centuries as an example of the whims of Fortune, inspiring many literary works that commemorated it. He is buried in the cathedral at Toledo. Juan II died the year after Luna's execution, overcome by personal grief and remorse.

Álvaro de Luna's diplomatic and military skills rank him among the most influential Iberian political leaders of the fifteenth century. Committed to a powerful monarchy and centralized authority based on broad popular support, his vision was only betrayed by an indecisive king and his own venality.

E. Michael Gerli

Bibliography

Round, N. G. *The Greatest Man Uncrowned: A Study of the Fall of Don Alvaro de Luna*. London, 1986.

LUNA, MARÍA DE

The first wife of Martín I, "the Humane," king of Sicily (1409–1410) and king of the Crown of Aragón (1395–1410), María de Luna was born in 1357. The daugher of the powerful Lope, count of Luna, María was betrothed to Martín at the age of four. The couple married in 1372 and had four children, although only one, Martín the younger, born in 1376, survived to adulthood.

In 1395 King Juan I, Martín's brother, died without a male heir. Martín was proclaimed king but because he was in Sicily, María stepped in as regent until her husband's return in 1397. The new queen demonstrated prudence and strength during this difficult regency. She first had to contend with a threat to the legitimacy of her husband's royal inheritance from Juan's widow, Yolanda, who claimed to be pregnant. Then, in October 1396, she successfully warded off an invasion by the count of Foix who sought to recover lands in Aragón for his wife, Juana, daughter of King Juan.

María remained active in government even after Martín's return. She worked toward the pacification of feuding factions in Valencia and Aragón, but the peace accords were not effective until 1407. One of her most enduring accomplishments was her intervention in 1402 on behalf of the *remensa* peasants of Catalonia. María appealed to her kinsman, the antipope Benedict XIII, for a formal admonition of the harsh treatment of the peasants by the ecclesiastical lords. María's actions served as precedent for later settlements in the 1460s and 1480s. Deeply religious and an active proponent of arts and culture, María died in 1406 in Villareal (Castellón).

Theresa Earenfight

Bibliography

Bisson, T. N. *The Medieval Crown of Aragón*. Oxford, 1986.
Fita, F. "Lo Papa Benet XIII y los Pagesos de Remensa." *Renaixensa* 11 (1895), 11–16, 81–85, 122–30.
Javierre Mur, A. L. *María de Luna, reina de Aragón*. Madrid, 1942.

LUNA, PEDRO DE

Antipope under the name of Benedict XIII, born Illueca, Aragón, 1328; died at Peñíscola, Spain, either 29 November 1422 or 23 May 1423. He was elected pope 28 September 1394 and deposed at the Council of Constance 26 July 1417. He belonged to the de Luna family and was distantly related to Álvaro de Luna, constable of Castile. He studied law at Montpellier, where he obtained a doctor's degree and later taught canon law. On 30 December 1375, Gregory XI made him cardinal deacon of S. Maria in Cosmedin. As cardinal he returned to Rome with Gregory XI, after whose death in 1378 he took part in the conclave that elected Urban VI, for whom he voted. The conclave was attacked by the citizens of Rome. Later, he joined the other non-Italian cardinals at Anagni, where he became convinced of the invalidity of the vote for Urban VI. Pedro de Luna took part in the election of Robert of Geneva (Clement VII) at Fondi on 20 September 1378, and became one of his adherents, energetically defending his legality. When Clement VII died, Pedro de Luna was unanimously chosen on 28 September 1394 to succeed him. The choice of Cardinal de Luna was welcomed by the French court. His desire to put an end to the schism in the church, even if he had to renounce the papacy, was a strong inducement for the cardinals obedient to Avignon to vote in his favor. As he was only a deacon at the time of his election, he was made a priest, consecrated bishop, and enthroned as pope under the name Benedict XIII. Benedict XIII was highly esteemed because of his austere lifestyle and personal ability.

In 1396 an embassy, headed by three of the most powerful French princes, brought a resolution to Benedict that both he and Boniface IX, the Roman pope, abdicate. Benedict obstinately opposed the proposal, despite the fact that the cardinals at Avignon sided with the embassy. He insisted that personal negotiations between both popes was the only course to pursue and clung tenaciously to his opinion. Like Benedict, Boniface IX, refused to hear of resigning, remaining as firmly convinced as Benedict that he was the legitimate pope. The schism in the church remained, while general discontent reigned in all Christian countries.

In 1398 Geoffroy Boucicout occupied Avignon and besieged the pope in his palace, but failed to take the papal fortress. Benedict was, however, obliged to deal with his enemies; in an understanding with his cardinals he pledged to renounce the papacy if the Roman pope would do the same. Nevertheless, on 9 May 1399, the pope protested that these stipulations were obtained by force. Benedict ensured that long negotiations ensued as to who would be the custodian of the pope in the palace at Avignon. On 12 March 1403, Benedict took flight from Avignon and reached safe territory. Avignon immediately submitted again to him and the cardinals likewise recognized him. His obedience was reestablished in all of France.

Benedict XIII pursued negotiations with the Roman pope, and in 1404 suggested to Boniface IX that they and both colleges of cardinals should meet at a mutually agreeable place to put an end to the schism. Boniface would have nothing of it. After the latter's death (1 October 1404), Benedict's envoys continued to negotiate with the Roman cardinals. These however elected Innocent VII on 17 October, who also refused all negotiations. When Innocent VII died in Rome on 6 November 1406, Gregory XII was chosen on 30 November as his successor. The latter wrote immediately to Benedict and announced that he was ready to abdicate on condition that Benedict would do likewise, and that afterward the cardinals of Avignon would unite with those of Rome for a unanimous papal election. Benedict replied 31 January 1407, accepting the proposition.

A meeting at Savona was planned for this purpose but never took place. Benedict went to Savona. Gregory failed to appear. Benedict's position worsened; on 23 November 1407, his principal protector in France, Louis of Orléans, was murdered. Benedict no longer received revenues from French benefices, and when he wrote a threatening letter to King Charles VI, the latter tore it up. On 25 May 1408, the king declared France's neutrality toward both papal pretenders.

A number of cardinals belonging to both sides met at Pisa for the purpose of convening a universal council. Benedict XIII fled to Roussillon and called a council at Perpignan, which opened on 21 November 1408. Both popes were deposed at the Council of Pisa. The delegation that Benedict sent there arrived too late. In spite of this, the Avignon pope was still recognized by Scotland, Aragón, Castile, and the island of Sicily. Avignon was seized in 1411 for the Pisan pope (Alexander V).

Emperor Sigismund went to Perpignan on 19 September 1415, as a delegate of the Council of Constance, to urge Benedict to abdicate, but to no avail. A conference was held at Narbonne in December 1415, between the representatives of those countries who acknowledged Benedict. The conferees withdrew their obedience to Benedict on account of his obstinacy. Benedict retired to his family's castle at Peñíscola, near Valencia. An embassy from the Council of Constance failed to convince him to abdicate, and he was deposed by the council 27 July 1417. He never submitted, continuing to consider himself the only legitimate pope. He died at Peñíscola either 29 November 1422 or 23 May 1423. His remaining adherents elected a successor, Muñoz, who for a time continued the schism.

E. Michael Gerli

Bibliography

Benedicti XIII. Ed. Franz Ehrle. Paderborn, 1906.

Ehrle, Franz. "Neue Materialen zur Geschichte Peters von Luna." *Archiv für Literatur-und Kïrchengeschichte des Mittelalters*, VI, 139–308.

Glasfurd, Alexander Lamont. *The Antipope: Peter de Luna, 1342–1423: A Study in Obstinacy*. London, (1965).

LYRIC *See* POETRY, LYRIC

M

MACIAS

Macías is one of the earliest known *cancionero* poets of the late Middle Ages. As such, he wrote still very much in the vein of the Galaico-Portuguese lyric of the middle of the fourteenth century. Little of any certainty is known about him, although he appears to have been from Galicia in the northwest of the Iberian Peninsula and to have flourished between 1340–1370. His poetry, which received wide circulation through *cancioneros* especially in Castile during the fifteenth century, is dominated by themes of catastrophic love and sacrificial desire. As in the case of many of the earlier Provençal troubadours, the tragic incidents to which his poems refer led to the creation of a legend around Macías as a martyr to love. Don Pedro, Condestable de Portugal, Juan Rodríguez del Padrón, Hernán Núñez, and much later Argote de Molina, all recall dramatic anecdotes about him. These tell how Macías was slain by a jealous husband, who discovered the poet's love for his wife. Macías's fame as a martyr of romantic love extended itself into literature well beyond the fifteenth century. In both the early modern theater and nineteenth-century literature the legendary figure of Macías became synonymous with paradigmatic tragic lover. Lope de Vega made Macías the protagonist of his drama *Porfiar hasta morir*, and Mariano José de Larra was inspired to write a play titled *Macías* and a novel called *El doncel de don Enrique el Doliente* based on his celebrated exploits.

E. Michael Gerli

Bibliography

Avalle-Arce, J. B. "Macías: Trovas, Amor y Muerte." In *Estudios Galegos Medievais*. Ed. Antonio Cortijo Ocaña, et al. Santa Barbara, Calif., 2001. 177–88.

Lapesa, R. "La lengua de la poesía lírica desde Macías hasta Villasandino." *Romance Philology* 7 (1953–1954), 51–59.

Martínez Barbeito, C. *Macías el enamorado y Juan Rodríguez del Padrón*. Santiago de Compostela, 1951.

Rennert, H. A. *Macías "No Namorado": A Galician Troubador*. Philadelphia, 1900.

Vanderford, K. H. "Macías in Legend and Literature." *Modern Philology* 31 (1933), 35–64.

MADEIRA *See* EXPLORATIONS, PORTUGAL

MADĪNAT AL-ZAHRĀ

Madīnat al-Zahrā was founded in 936 by the Umayyad caliph ʿAbd al-Raḥmān III al-Naṣir (r. 912–961) approximately five kilometers east of Córdoba. It became the caliph's personal residence where he entertained a brilliant court of scholars and artists from al-Andalus and abroad. Built after he declared himself caliph in 929, the palace-city was larger and more magnificent than any of the earlier palaces in the environs of Córdoba. It was a huge complex with double-enclosure walls and extended across three stepped terraces carved from the foot of a gently sloping hill.

Of the four gates described by historians, the only one extant is the Bāb al-Sudda (reconstructed), located at the entrance to the Dār al-Jund (reconstructed), the military headquarters. With stabling for horses and a hall giving onto the corral, this quarter was a protective intermediary between the lower levels of the city and the upper level of reception halls and elite residences. Among the latter, a residence with rich stucco wall decoration has been identified as the Dar al-Mulk, or caliphal quarters; another elegant residence was distinguished by columned porticos facing a small garden with a pool and water channels.

The Salón Rico (reconstructed) was a handsomely decorated reception hall of three naves that looked out through a screen of marble columns to a large quadripartite garden (the first in western Islam) with paved walkways, pools, and a small pavilion. To one side were baths; on the other were service rooms and a ramp leading down to a second quadripartite garden on the lower level. Excavations and inscriptions indicate that the Salón Rico was built in 953–957 and replaced older buildings. Near it was the congregational mosque (finished 940–941), distinguished by its square minaret placed to one side of the axis leading to the *mihrab*, its double *qibla* wall, and its prayer hall of five aisles separated by marble columns bearing arches. A second mosque in the southwest corner of the city (unexcavated but evident in aerial photographs) probably served the soldiers of the barracks there. A mint, zoo, aviary, fish ponds, prison, and factories are mentioned in medieval histories. The histories' detailed accounts of the materials used, numbers of workers and occupations, and their salaries provide an extraordinary glimpse into the organization of a medieval Islamic construction site.

The palace-city was continually built during the reign of ʿAbd al-Raḥmān III and the reign of his son and successor, Al-Ḥakam II (961–976). Subsequent revisions during the reign of Hishām II (976–1009 and 1010–1013) were, it seems, not for expansion but to confine the young ruler when his regent, Al-Manṣūr (Muḥammad ibn Abī ʿAmir, also known as Al-Manṣūr) seized control. When Al-Manṣūr built his own palace-city, Madīnat al-Zāhira, west of Córdoba, the political importance of Madīnat al-Zahrā waned. During the civil war of 1010–1011, both palaces were sacked and destroyed, and ultimately their whereabouts forgotten. Nonetheless, Madinat al-Zahrā retained its reputation as an splendid architectural ideal and, despite its short life, was the progenitor of subsequent palaces such as the Alhambra.

Madīnat al-Zahrā was rediscovered in the mid–nineteenth century; excavations began in 1910; today about 10 percent of the buildings have been unearthed.

D. FAIRCHILD RUGGLES

Bibliography

Ruggles, D. F. "Historiography and the Rediscovery of Madinat al-Zahra'." *Islamic Studies* 30 (1991), 129–40.

Vallejo Triano, A. "Madinat al-Zahra': the Triumph of the Islamic State." In *Al-Andalus: The Arts of Islamic Spain*. Ed. J. Dodds. New York, 1992. 27–39.

MADRID

The name Madrid derives from the Celtiberian word Mageterito-Vadoluengo meaning long ford. In heraldry from the twelfth to the end of the fifteenth century, it was represented as a she-bear on all fours, and from the end of the fifteenth to the beginning of the sixteenth century as a standing she-bear leaning against the right side of a tree.

Initially a modest village in New Castile, Madrid is centrally located and well situated on a steep slope of the Manzanares River with a healthy climate. In medieval times there was abundant water, forests for hunting major game, olive groves, and vineyards. The economy was rural and artisan; it obtained in 1447 two annual fairs, and in 1463, a free market and three regular ones. The population in the fifteenth century was approximately 2,500. Moors had fewer rights than Christians but they coexisted peacefully. The same was true for the Jews, except in 1392, when serious confrontations took place with Christians. The Jews were eventually expelled in 1492.

Madrid has many paleolithic remains, but there is little evidence of the Romans and Visigoths. It gained strategic importance (defending Toledo) with the coming of the Arabs; but was reconquered by Alfonso VI in 1085–1095. Madrid grew out from around its castle, which was destroyed in 1724, into two areas with walls in the ninth and eleventh centuries (there are some remains): the citadel proper (eight hectares) and the town (twenty-six hectares). In the fifteenth century, areas outside the walls were incorporated, and this doubled the expansion. Madrid has several gates: Santa María, Albega, De Moros, Cerrada, De Guadalajara, and De Balnadú, as well as narrow and winding streets. In medieval times the housing was generally poorly constructed. The principal monasteries were San Francisco, Santo Domingo, San Martín, and San Jerónimo. There are remains of Mudéjar culture in the towers of San Nicolás (twelfth century) and San Pedro (fourteenth century), as well as late Gothic remains in San Jerónimo, the front of the Hospital of La Latina, and buildings in La Plaza de la Villa.

The town's grammar school was founded by Alfonso XI in 13–16. The works of the writers Alvarez Gato and Ruy González de Clavijo (fifteenth century) were well known. There was a special devotion to Santa María of Atocha and to Isidro Labrador (canonized in 1622). During the civil wars, Madrid supported Pedro I and Enrique IV; it delayed in recognizing Isabel I the Catholic as queen; and it was the meeting place of the *cortes* (parliaments) in 1309, 1339, 1391, 1393, and 1433. It continued to litigate with the municipality of Segovia and with the church hierarchy in Toledo.

Administratively, Madrid was organized as "la Villa" and its "tierra" (outlying territory). The villa was divided into ten districts: Santa María, San Andrés, San Pedro, San Miguel de los Octoes, San Justo, San Salvador, San Nicolás, San Juan, San Jacobo, and San Miguel de la Sagra. The outlying territory (almost the size of the current province) was organized into three large districts called *sexmos*: Vallecas, Villaverde, and Aravaca. They belonged to the crown except for a short period (1383–1393) when they were under the feudal authority of Leon V of Armenia, who was living in exile in Castile. It was governed by a *fuero* (municipal code, established in 1202) and its corresponding *Carta de Otorgamento* (1219). In total, there were 110 precepts on criminal law, legal procedure, and municipal law (the codex still exists, in thirty-two folios). Alfonso X gave Madrid (1262) a *fuero real*. In 1346 Alfonso XI named a fixed number (twelve) of town council members. In 1480 Madrid was influenced by legislation approved by the Cortes of Toledo, whose intention was to strengthen municipalities.

José María Bernáldez Montalvo

Bibliography

Documentos del Archivo General del Ayuntamiento de Madrid. Madrid, 1888–1909.

Gibert y Sánchez de la Vega, R. *El Concejo de Madrid*. Madrid, 1949.

Libros de Acuerdos del Concejo madrileño. 4 vols. Madrid, 1932–82.

MADRIGAL, ALFONSO FERNÁNDEZ DE

Eminent theologian, canonist, and philosopher known also as *El Tostado*. He was born in Madrigal de las Altas Torres around 1410 and died at Bonilla de la Sierra, Avila, on 3 September 1455. Madrigal was educated at the Colegio de San Bartolomé of the University of Salamanca, of which he later became rector. He studied Greek, Latin, and Hebrew from an early age. Madrigal received the title of *maestro* in 1432 and then studied theology from 1432–1441, when he was conferred the title of master of theology. Madrigal occupied the chair in poetry in the faculty of arts at Salamanca and, most probably, the one in moral philosophy as well. In addition, he held the chair in biblical studies in the faculty of theology. During his career, he was also canon of the cathedral and finally chancellor of the university.

By the time Madrigal was twenty-five he had acquired the reputation of a polymath and sage. He wrote commentaries on Aristotle and Thomas Aquinas and, at one point, fell under the influence of Scotus in theology later to return almost entirely to Aquinas. On the whole, his work was notable for its originality and independence of thought. He was invited to participate in the Council of Basel but failed to do so. Rather, he went to Siena and presented twenty-one propositions to Pope Eugene IV, three of which displeased the pontiff greatly. The latter dealt with absolution of sin and the date of Jesus' death and were censured by the bishops of Reggio and Ancona. Eugene IV ordered Cardinal Juan de Torquemada, an eminent Castilian theologian, to challenge Madrigal on these points. Madrigal responded to Torquemada with his *Defensorium trium propositionum*, made public after Madrigal's death.

Disillusioned by his experience at the curia, Madrigal returned to the Carthusian monastery of Scala-Dei in Catalonia with the desire to become a monk. He became a novitiate there on 16 January 1444 and stayed only until 11 April of that year, when Juan II called him to Castile to serve as a counselor at court. After his return to Castile, Madrigal, who was the author of numerous vernacular works, wrote several opuscules like the *Tratado por el qual prueva como al home es necesario amar*, which became influential in the debates centering on Aristotelian naturalism and love carried out among the intellectual circles associated with the University of Salamanca during the second half of the fifteenth century. These debates had a profound influence on the evolution of vernacular imaginative literature during that period.

When Madrigal returned to Castile and established himself at court, Juan II appealed to the pope that he name Madrigal bishop of Avila, which he did on 11 February 1445. Madrigal's elaborately sculpted tomb, with its inscription referring to him as *stupor mundi* (marvel of the world), is in the cathedral of Avila.

E. Michael Gerli

Bibliography

Blázquez Hernández, J. M. *El Tostado, alumno graduado y profesor de la Universidad de Salamanca*. Madrid, 1956.

Cátedra, P. M. *Amor y pedagogía en la Edad Media*. Salamanca, 1989.

Fernández Vallina, E. "Introducción al Tostado. De su vida y obra." *Cuadernos Salmatinos de Filosofía*, 1988.

MAHOMAT EL XARTOSSE

The heading to the only poem by Mahomat el Xartosse to have survived (*Cancionero de Baena* no. 522, "Preguntador de cara pregunta") describes him as a Moor (that is, Muslim), formerly physician to Diego Hurtado de Mendoza, the admiral of Castile (d. 1405), and as being from Guadalajara (one of the few places in Castilian territory at that time where Arabic medical science continued to be transmitted in Arabic). His 168-line *respuesta*, one of seven to a *pregunta* by Ferrán Sánchez Calavera (or Talavera) was criticized by Juan Alfonso de Baena for its failure to respect the rhyme scheme of the pregunta. (It is only fair to add that of the six others to participate in this literary debate, only three poets did manage to adhere to the rules, among them the great Pero López de Ayala; three did not, among them Francisco Imperial.) Mahomat's handling of the subject, free will versus determinism, is praised by Baena as "very subtle." In such distinguished literary company, Mahomat acquits himself well, but the poem is an isolated curiosity from which it would be unwise to draw general conclusions.

PATRICK I. HARVEY

Bibliography

Cancionero de Juan Alfonso de Baena. Critical ed. by J. M. Azáceta. Vol. 3. Madrid, 1966, 1038–44.

Fraker, C. F. Jr. *Studies on the Cancionero de Baena*. Chapel Hill, N.C., 1966.

———. "The Theme of Predestination in the Cancionero de Baena," *Bulletin of Hispanic Studies* 51 (1974), 228–43.

MAGIC *See* WITCHCRAFT

MAIMONIDES

Likened by more than one medieval Jewish writer to the prophet Moses ("From Moses to Moses there was none like Moses"), Moses ben Maimon (correctly, Maimūn) was born in Córdoba not in 1135, as is usually assumed (and so the 850th anniversary was universally celebrated in 1985) but in 1138, where he was educated and began writing his first works.

His father, Maimūn, was a *dayan* (religious judge) of the Jewish community of Córdoba, and a student of the great Joseph ibn Megash, and himself author of some responsa and "Letters of Consolation" meant to strengthen the Jews in the face of the Almohad persecution. It was due to this that the family left Spain around 1160, settling first in Fez, Morocco, and then briefly in Palestine. From there they went to Egypt and settled at Fustat, a suburb of Cairo, where Jews were allowed to live. The twin tragedies of the death of his father and then his brother David devasted the young scholar, who had to support himself and his family by becoming a doctor and court physician to the *wazīr* (prime minister) and his son. Never did he convert, or even appear outwardly to do so, to Islam, as a long-discredited legend maintains.

Within a few years he had become by reputation the most famous physician of the Muslim world. At the same time, his reputation in Jewish learning, established already by his brilliant commentary on the Mishnah, was growing. Questions poured in from all parts of the world. Working almost entirely from memory, and under the most difficult conditions imposed upon him by the demands of his medical practice, he composed in clear and simple Hebrew the *Mishneh Torah*, a work in fourteen volumes that encompasses the whole of Jewish law. This work quickly became the accepted authority for Jewish law, the only such composition ever written by someone who was not a rabbi.

Nevertheless, there were critics. First, he had not cited his sources, and although sources have been found for virtually every statement, lesser scholars had difficulty in accepting some of his rulings. Second, there were disagreements in some cases as to the rulings themselves. Finally, certain religious zealots who lacked training in philosophy objected strenuously to his philosophical notions, contained both in his commentary on the Mishnah and in the legal code. The situation worsened when he wrote his great philosophical work, *Dalālat al-bā'irīn* (*Guide for the Perplexed*). Clearly intended only for those with the necessary preliminary background of rigorous study, the book was translated twice from Judeo-Arabic into Hebrew and thus soon fell into the hands of those without such background. Its clear denial of such fundamental popular beliefs as miracles, creation in time, resurrection, and so forth combined with allegorizing of many biblical and rabbinic statements, gave rise to charges of heresy. The result was a controversy that lasted in Spain and Provence for hundreds of years, and actually led to Jewish-inspired condemnation and burning of the book at Montpellier around 1232.

In spite of the philosophical controversy, Maimonides continued to be revered as a legal authority throughout the Middle Ages in Spain and elsewhere. Even those who disagreed with him, such as Naḥmanides and Ibn Adret, cite him constantly and respectfully. Communities, such as Tudela, enacted decrees according to which only his rulings were to be followed; similar decisions were made throughout North Africa and Yemen.

No less important was his impact on Christians in Spain. In Aragón-Catalonia, various kings ordered translations of the *Guide* and even of the *Mishneh Torah*. Philosophers in Spain (and, of course, the scholastics in general) who were influenced by him include Poncio Carbonell (fourteenth century) and, more important, Alfonso de la Torre (fifteenth century). Sancho, son of Jaime I, archbishop of Toledo (1266–1275), and Archbishop Gonzalo García Gudiel (1280–1299) both possessed copies of his work. In the fifteenth century, Pedro Díaz de Toledo, possibly a *converso* (Jewish convert to Christianity), made a Spanish translation of the *Guide*.

Maimonides died in 1204, and tradition maintains that his grave is near Tiberias.

NORMAN ROTH

Bibliography

Maimonides. *Guide for the Perplexed*. Trans. P. Díaz de Toledo. Ed. Moshé Lazar. Madison, Wisc., 1989.

Ormsby, E. (ed.) *Moses Maimonides and His Time*. Washington, D. C., 1989.
Roth, N. *Maimonides: Essays and Texts*. Madison, Wisc., 1985 (also with bibliographies, including Spanish).

MĀLIKITES

The administration of justice in Muslim society was originally in the hands of the rulers and was often delegated to warriors and politicians. As the new Muslim society acquired a more permanent amd more complex status, and as new laws (and reinterpretation of old ones) became necessary, the duties were increasingly delegated to others, who in this way became a special class—the jurists (*fuqahā'*) of Islamic law.

Already under the Umayyads there was a preoccupation with maintaining the revealed law. Under the ʿAbbasids, and coinciding with the study of its theological and philosophical aspects, the study of revealed law also began to shape its technical interpretation. The result was four main schools of legal thought: Hanīfite, Mālikite, Shafīʿite, and Hanbalite, thus named by their founders. Each became predominant in various parts of the Islamic empire for social as well as political reasons. In their scope, the schools extended beyond the legal interpretation of Muslim law to encompass liturgical and even social behavior. The interpretations of law could also had political implications, so the *fuqahā'* achieved at times extrordinary power.

Although other schools had their followers, in al-Andalus, Mālikism achieved such an importance, and often even official endorsement by the rulers, that it is generally identified with Andalusian Islam, and more concretely as a sign of Andalusian traditional conservatism. A major factor in this acceptance, however, was also political, most specifically the victory of the ʿAbbasids in the east over the Umayyads in Syria, and the enduring animosity that Andalusian Umayyads felt toward the ʿAbbasids.

Against the philosophical principles—analogy (*qiyās*) and preference (*ijtihad*)—introduced in the interpretation of law by the school of Abū Hanīfa, which was favored in the east, Al-Awzāʿi (d. 795), a Syrian, defended more traditional interpretations. From this conflict a new school grew formed by Mālik ibn Anas (ca. 715–795), who insisted on a strict adherence to the Qurʾān and the traditions (*ḥadīth, sunna*), with the help of the principles, general consensus (*ijmāʿ*) and communal interest (*istislah*).

Andalusian Umayyads, suspicious of the the ʿAbbasids, preferred the more conservative Syrian interpretation. The introduction of Mālik's doctrine in al-Andalus is attributed by some Arab historians to the time of Emir ʿAbd al-Raḥmān I (756–788). It became predominant during the reign of Hishām I (788–796) because of the favored position he granted to Yaḥyā ibn Yaḥyā al-Laiythi, one of Mālik's students.

During the Almoravid period, Mālikism tended to include more than just legal scholarship. The school's most eminent scholars were Ibn Ḥazm and Abū al-Walīd Muḥammad ibn Rushd, grandfather of the philosopher Averroës.

As the threat from the Almohads began to appear in Africa from about 1125 onward, the Mālikites supporting the Almoravids felt compelled to attack their leader, Ibn Tūmart. The Almohads tried at first to do without the Mālikites, who, for a time, lost most of the political favor they had previously enjoyed. However, the new lords soon recognized that they needed the Mālikite jurists and the population they represented.

Andalusian Mālikism did not help the formation of a real school of legal thought in al-Andalus. Rather, Andalusian jurists preferred to follow the solutions already provided by noted Mālikite scholars in their manuals, to the point of a narrow-minded exclusivism. With them, an excessive reliance on the school tradition was established by the great jurists that took precedent over the study the Qurʾān and the *sunna*, *ḥadīth* tradition as Mālik had established it. As a consequence, this school became repetitive and ritualistic even to the point of neglect of direct study of the texts.

VICENTE CANTARINO

Bibliography

Ortíz, J. L. "La recepción de la Escuela Malequí en España." In *Anuario de Historia de Derecho Español*. Vol. 7. Madrid, 1930.
Shacht, J. *The Origins of Mohammedan Jurisprudence*. Oxford, 1950.

MALLORCA, CONSTANZA DE

An early fifteenth-century manuscript (Biblioteca de Catalunya, *Cançoner Vega-Aguiló*, 7) includes a poem attributed to the queen of Mallorca (modern-day Majorca). The poet is believed to be Jaime III's first wife, Constanza, daughter of Alfonso IV of Aragón. Her family was very literary: her great-grandfather, Pedro III of Aragón, her grandfather, Jaime II of Aragón, and her brother, Pedro IV of Aragón, wrote poems in Provençal, as did Constanza herself. Constanza was born in 1313, married in 1325, and died in 1346, two years after her husband lost his kingdom to her brother.

Her poem begins with a declaration of her lover's perfection and her total devotion for him. She then expresses her desperation at his being away in France: "I fear the yearning and great desire I have for you will kill me, my sweet dear lord, and I may soon die for you, whom I love and want so much, if I do not see you return to me soon, for I miss the embraces, the talk and all." She sounds like a woman addressing her lover, but at the end says: "Grace, my husband, that I spend my time enduring the suffering you have given me, you should return, for no treasure is worth a heart dying for you in loving thought."

It has been considered surprising that Constança does not seem to follow the conventions of courtly love. However, most women writers knew better than to imagine they were the dominant parties in their love relationships with men and did not show themselves in that light, particularly if they were married. In addition, an entire genre, the earlier Galician *cantigas de amigo*, concerns women who lament the absence of their lovers. In a limited way, Galician poetry became known in fourteenth-century Aragón, and this poem is a *cantiga de amigo* of sorts. Thus, a woman at the crossroads of regional traditions, the queen of Mallorca composed a poem in Provençal with a Galician topic, appropriate to the circumstances of a lonely wife. Her rather original work must have become known to some extent, since the first part of it was reproduced with modifications in a 1429 Catalan translation of the *Decamerone*.

CRISTINA GONZÁLEZ

Bibliography

Cluzel, I. "Princes et troubadours de la maison royale de Barcelone-Aragón." *Boletín de la Real Academia de Buenas Letras de Barcelona* 27 (1957–58), 321–73.

Jeanroy, A. "La poésie provençale en Catalogne." *Histoire Littéraire de la France*. 38, no. 1 (1941), 191–201.

MALLORCA, KINGDOM OF

The Balearic and Pitusian Islands in the western Mediterranean include Mallorca (3,640 square kilometers), Minorca (702 sq. kms.), Ibiza (541 sq. kms.), Formentera (82 sq. kms.), and assorted other islets. In the Middle Ages these islands were the commercial and to some degree cultural crossroads of the western Mediterranean, and, whether under Muslim or Christian domination, were coveted by the Catalans, French and southern French, Italians, and various North Africans. Conquered by the Muslims in the year 902—the same year Sicily was conquered by Muslims from Tunis—when troops of the emir (later caliph) of Córdoba invaded the islands, Mallorca was, after the collapse of the caliphate, joined to a peninsular landmass which included Denia, Alicante, Cartagena, and Murcia. For a brief period (1075–1115) Mallorca constituted an independent Islamic state, but this independence fell to a combined Pisan and Catalan crusade led by Ramón

Moorish art, 1229 A.D., from the Palacio Berenguer de Aguilar, Spain. Fresco: The Conquest of Mallorca—detail showing city fortifications. Copyright © Werner Forman/ Art Resource, NY. Museu d'Art de Cataluna, Barcelona, Spain.

Berenguer III. Unable to sustain a serious effort at colonization, the Pisans and Catalans departed, and the island was peaceably reconstituted in 1116 under the Muslim control of the Banu Ghaniyah who ruled in the name of the Almoravids. The Ghaniyah resisted the Almohads, even attacking and capturing Bougie and Algiers in 1185, but the Almohads nevertheless prevailed and conquered Mallorca in 1203. The final years of Muslim domination of the island were under a *wālī* (governor) appointed from Marrakesh.

The kingdom of Mallorca was founded by Jaime I, king of Aragón, who led a fleet of 150 ships and 1,300 knights on an official crusade, accompanied by the papal legate Cardinal Jean d'Abbéville, to the island in 1229. Victories were won by the Christians on 12 and 13 September, and by 15 September the city of Mallorca (Present day Palma) was under siege by land and sea. On 31 December, as retold in the king's own autobiography, the crusaders successfully stormed the walls in a bloody assault that led to widespread slaughter and enslavement of Muslims. By the spring of 1230 the eastern sections of the island had been overrun, and in 1231 and 1232 Jaime returned to the island for final operations in the more mountainous northern and western sections of the island. In 1231 Jaime successfully negotiated tribute and homage from the Muslims of neighboring Minorca. Jaime sold the right to conquer Ibiza to Nunyo Sanç, lord of Roussillon and Cerdagne, and to a Prince Pedro of Portugal; he later reallocated this right to Guillem de Montgrí, sacristan of Girona cathedral and archbishop-elect of Tarragona; the three completed the conquest in the summer of 1235.

Jaime's first and most lasting act as king of Mallorca was to oversee the land division. By right of conquest the king received half of the land of the island, principally Montuïri in the southeast, Sineu-Petra in the center, Artà in the northeast, and Inca, Muntanyes and Pollença in the north, and half of the houses, workshops, ovens, and baths in Mallorca City. The *repartiment* or land division that survives describes the subdivision and distribution of this royal half. The major beneficiaries of royal largesse were nobles such as Ramon Alemany, Ramon de Plegaman, Guillem de Claramunt, and members of the Montcada family; various religious orders, especially the Knights Templar, who were endowed with land in Mallorca City and in Inca and Pollença; and a very large number of small proprietors from Barcelona, Marseilles, Tarragona, Lérida, and Montpellier. Little is yet known about the subdivision of the seigneurial lands that comprised the other half of the island, but Nunyo Sanç controlled Bunyola and Valldemossa, the count of Ampurias controlled Muro and Sóller, the bishop of Barcelona Andratx, and the viscount of Béarn controlled Canarossa in the center of the island, including the key castle of Alaró. Jaime specifically constituted Mallorca as its own kingdom; despite his enormous pride in the conquest and his new kingdom, he subsequently returned there only once, briefly in 1269 while planning a crusade to the Holy Land, before his death in 1276.

When Jaime's only heir from his first marriage died in 1260, the royal patrimony was divided in two: his eldest surviving son Pere was to receive Valencia, Aragón, and Catalonia, while his son Jaume was to receive the Balearics, Roussillon, Cerdagne, and Montpellier. Jaume II of Mallorca ascended the throne in 1276, though he was forced to pay homage to his brother in 1279. The kingdom of Mallorca (or, occasionally the "Mallorcas," or the Balearics) refers only to the Mediterranean islands and not to mainland holdings; Jaume II was king of Mallorca, count of Roussillon and Cerdagne, and lord of Montpellier, and the three disparate entities, correctly identified as the Crown of Mallorca or the lands of the Crown of Mallorca, were only linked via the monarchy. After Jaume sided with the invading French against his brother in the political crusade of 1285, Pere vowed to conquer the Balearics in retaliation, but fell ill and died shortly after setting out from Barcelona in November 1285. His heir Alfonso III of Aragón continued the expedition, recapturing Mallorca and Ibiza for the Aragónese crown; in January of 1287 Alfonso conquered Minorca, whose Muslims had supposedly advised coreligionists in North Africa of Aragónese troop movements on the eve of the War of the Sicilian Vespers. In 1298 Jaime II of Aragón, successor to Alfonso III after 1291, returned at papal insistence the Balearics to his uncle Jaume II of Mallorca, who had held on to his southern French lands and ruled from the royal palace of the kings of Mallorca at Perpignan, as a part of the agreement that would eventually bring the War of the Sicilian Vespers to a close.

Mallorca's greatest period of prosperity dates from this second and final period of its independence: the years when the kingdom was ruled by Jaume II for a second time (1298–1311), by Sanç of Mallorca (1311–1324), and by Jaume III of Mallorca (1324–1343). In 1343 Pedro IV of Aragón permanently reincorporated the Balearics into his crown, and Jaume III died in 1349 on the battlefield at Llucmajor in an attempt to reclaim his patrimony. Jaume III's son Jaume IV married Joana of Naples, invaded Roussillon in 1374, and died in 1375. If the royal house of Mallorca reached a sad and dismal ending with the deaths of Jaume III and Jaume IV, and the subsequent pretensions of Jaume IV's sister Isabel, the separately constituted kingdom of Mallorca, with its own laws and customs, and even its own coinage, would endure well beyond the end of the Middle Ages. The elaborately illuminated codex of *Palatine Laws*, now housed in the Royal Library of Brussels, gives a detailed glimpse of the Mallorcan royal household and administration during the reign of Jaume III; the *Ordenacions* of Pedro IV of Aragón are a Catalan collection closely modeled on this earlier Mallorcan antecedent.

Mallorca's strategic position in the Mediterranean made it of great significance in the commercial networks of Catalan and Italian merchants. The Balearics are almost equidistant between Barcelona and Algeria, and Catalan trade with Bougie and Tunis blossomed after the conquest. The Genoese had signed treaties with Islamic Mallorca in 1181 and 1188, and they were quick to work out agreements with the new Christian rulers of Mallorca after the conquest. Pisans and later the Florentines maintained active interests in Mallorca, and like the Genoese occasionally became permanent residents; Francesco Datini, the celebrated merchant of Prato, had notable ties with Mallorca in the years around 1400. Mallorcan port registers show 617 foreign ships visiting the island in 1340, and Mallorcan merchants themselves were as active and acquisitive as the foreign merchants who visited the kingdom. Some 261 Mallorcan merchants are documented as trading with North Africa in the years 1308 to 1331; in addition to Mallorcan consulates being located in ten North African ports, they are found in the early fourteenth century in Seville, Málaga, Granada, Naples, Pisa, Genoa, Constantinople, and Bruges. Figs, raisins, honey, almonds, and olive oil were exported from Mallorca, as was cheese from Minorca and salt from Ibiza. Slaves were both imported and exported from the Balearics in large numbers throughout the Middle Ages.

Mallorca's main cultural contributions are intimately linked to its Jewish and Muslim minorities. The city of Mallorca, and later Inca, in the center of the island, possessed sizable Jewish populations; these included Arabic-speaking Jews who the Christian conquerors found upon their arrival, and both Arabic-speaking Jews fleeing Almohad persecution and Romance-speaking Jews from French and Catalan lands who were actively encouraged to settle on the island. Numerous royal charters to Mallorca's Jews have survived; they confirmed their right to buy and sell land, property, and slaves, to engage in a wide variety of trades, to establish separate court systems and a communal system of tax collection, and to freely practice their religion. The fate of the Muslim population of Mallorca island after the conquest is unknown; it seems likely, however, that many were enslaved, the wealthy perhaps purchasing their freedom and right of emigration to North Africa. Many Muslims remained as semifree tenant farmers, but records indicate that many of these accepted baptism and became Christians. Although there was not only a sizable Muslim slave population but also a population of free and foreign Muslims on the island, there is no record of Muslim communal organization or judicial or religious officials.

The post-mystic and missionary-philosopher Ramon Llull was born on Mallorca around 1232, learned Arabic from one of his Muslim slaves, and, despite a peripatetic existence, wrote many of his several hundred Catalan works while resident on the island. Llull assisted, with the support of Jaume II of Mallorca, the Franciscans in founding at Miramar on the northwest coast of Mallorca a school of Arabic studies—similar to Dominican establishments at Játiva, Tunis, and elsewhere—for the training of missionaries. The school did not, however, survive into the fourteenth century. Mallorca city was also the site in 1286 of a disputation between Mallorcan Jews and a Genoese merchant by the name of Inghetto Contardo. The Latin transcript of this disputation survives in two editions printed in Venice in 1524 and 1627 and at least seventeen manuscript copies, but only recently has it received a critical edition and scholarly attention. One of the more enigmatic Catalan writers of the late fourteenth and early fifteenth centuries is Anselm of Turmeda, a Franciscan on Mallorca, who as a result of a spiritual crisis moved to Tunis and converted to Islam. Mallorcan cartographers in the fourteenth century were among the best in Europe, and some of these were Mallorcan Jews, such as Abraham Crescas, whose celebrated Catalan Atlas of the World (1375) is in Paris, or *conversos*, converts to Christianity, such as Abraham's son Jahuda or Jafuda Crescas, later known as Master Jaume of Mallorca.

There is a tendency in Mallorcan historiography to attribute its comparative decline in the late fourteenth century and throughout the fifteenth centuries to its return to the Crown of Aragón. The case may be overstated in some of the historiography, especially of a local variety, and the causality certainly unproven, but the correlation between Aragónese governance and decline would appear to be empirical. Mallorca was hit hard by the Black Death of 1348–1351, suffered recurring demographic setbacks, including a further visit from the plague in 1440, and did not recover its 1329 population until 1573. Although the city of Mallorca built a beautiful new *lonja*, or trading exchange, between the years 1426 and 1456, Mallorcan shipbuilding and merchant enterprise were becoming eclipsed by activity in Barcelona and Valencia. The endless Catalan and Genoese naval war of the fourteenth century exacted a toll, and Muslim piracy and its threat would plague the Balearics well into the early modern era. Some wounds were self-inflicted. Mallorca city was one of several Iberian cities that witnessed violent pogroms against Jews in 1391, yet Mallorca's Jews played a far greater role in trade and the Mallorcan economy than Jews did in many of the other cities. Although several hundred Portuguese Jews settled on the island in the 1390s and some Mallorcan Jews returned from North Africa following 1391, the entire Jewish community was converted en masse in 1435. Soon after the creation of the Spanish Inquisition a tribunal was established in Mallorca. Civic conflicts between the elite who controlled Mallorca city and the smaller towns of the island were constant throughout the fifteenth century and erupted into a civil war in the years 1450–1453.

LARRY J. SIMON

Bibliography

Abulafia, D. *A Mediterranean Emporium: The Catalan Kingdom of Majorca*. Cambridge, 1994.

Barceló Crespí, M. *Ciutat de Mallorca en el Trànsit a la Modernitat*. Palma de Mallorca, 1988.

Braunstein, B. *The Chuetas of Majorca: Conversos and the Inquistion of Majorca*. New York, 1936.

Cateura Bennàsser, P. *Politica y finanzas del reino de Mallorca bajo Pedro IV de Aragón*. Palma de Mallorca, 1982.

Dufourcq, C.-E. *L'Espagne Catalane et le Maghrib aux XIIIe et XIVe siècles*. Paris, 1966.

Historia de Mallorca. 5 vols. Ed. J. Mascaró Pasarius. Palma, 1971–74; repr. 1978 in 10 vols.

Martínez Ferrando, J. E. *La Tràgica Història dels Reis de Mallorca*. 2d ed. Barcelona, 1979.
Santamaría Arández, Alvaro. *Ejecutoria del Reino de Mallorca*. Palma de Mallorca, 1990.
———. *El reino de Mallorca en la primera mitad del siglo XV*. Palma de Mallorca, 1955.

MANRIQUE, GÓMEZ

The fifth child of the *adelantado* (governor) of León, Pedro Manrique, and Leonor of Castile, Gómez Manrique was born in Amusco (Palencia) around 1412. (He was probably named to honor the memory of his uncle who died late in 1411.) He tells us in his *cancionero* that his formative years were spent in the household of his older brother Rodrigo for whom he had deep affection and respect and with whom he engaged in several military campaigns. Caught up politically in the tumultuous years of the reigns of Juan II (1406–1454) and Enrique IV (1425–1474), Manrique sided with his brothers and their extended families, ultimately supporting Enrique's brother Alfonso, and then his sister Isabel, as legitimate heirs to the throne. His active support of the marriage of Fernando and Isabel, and thus of the alliance of Castile and Aragón, was clearly instrumental in his being appointed *corregidor* (magistrate) of Toledo, a post he held for some fourteen years until his death in November 1490.

Gómez Manrique's fame is usually based more on his reputation as a man of letters than as a politician. After the deaths of Juan de Mena (1411–1456) and of Manrique's uncle, Iñigo López de Mendoza, the Marqués de Santillana (1398–1458), Manrique gained a lasting reputation as one of Castile's most respected poets by completing Mena's already lengthy but unfinished *Contra los pecados mortales*. And in Manrique's elegy on the death of Santillana—the man in his words who first "congregó la ciencia con la caualleria, e la loriga con la toga" (joined science with chivalry, and the lorica with the toga.) (*El planto de las virtudes*)—he sets himself up as the messenger through whom poetry will lament the loss of his friend and relative whose poetic talent excels even that of Dante. Although Manrique's efforts to assume the mantle passed on by Mena and Santillana is articulated through his references to his own unworthiness, his goal is unequivocal even as he tries to pass off this grave responsibility to the oldest and most famous writer of the time, Fernán Pérez de Guzmán.

Manrique's poetry can be roughly divided into work composed before and after the deaths of Mena and Santillana. His early poems are almost indistinguishable from those of his contemporaries: *canciones*, *cartas de amores*, *apartamientos*, *preguntas y respuestas*, *estrenas, quejas y comparaciones*, and *glosas*. Often larded with courtly love imagery and themes, riddles and allegories, he characterized them late in life simply as *trobas*: "solía hazer en un día quinze o veynte trobas sin perder sueño." (I used to compose fifteen or twenty poems in a day without losing sleep.) He came to realize that his emphasis on the technical aspects of poetry (verse form, rhyme scheme) did not make him a *poeta* as defined by Mena and Santillana; serious poetry demands transcendental themes. His production of didactic and moral works rose sharply when he began to concentrate on Christian life and death. His elegy on the death of Garci Laso de la Vega (around 1455) consoles the living by finding solutions in the afterlife: Garci Laso gains immortality because he was killed by fighting the Muslims in the service of king and God. Manrique reminded Ferdando and Isabel, in his *Regimiento de príncipes* (around 1469), that political turmoil and bad government are the result of misguided kings and their counselors. Most *consejeros* "corren tras sus apetitos/con consejos lisonjeros/ no buenos, mas voluntarios." (Run after their appetites/ with flattering advice/not good, but voluntary.) Only by fearing God and following Christian virtues (justice, prudence, charity, temperance, and fortitude) can kings sustain their earthly powers: "es a saber, que temáis/príncipes esclarescidos/aquel Dios por quien regnáis,/amándole, si deseáis/ser amados y temidos." (Take note, you should fear,/enlightened princes,/that God for whom you reign,/loving Him, if you wish/to be loved and feared.) Manrique's poems about consolation and civic behavior are built on examples from the past. Pagan examples are mentioned only to be discarded in favor of biblical precepts, and a poet's true reputation is based not on knowledge and book learning but rather on Christian wisdom and faith.

Manrique's moral and didactic motives reappear in his *Representación del nacimiento de nuestro señor* (1468), a liturgical play written at the request of his sister, the abbess of the convent of Calabazanos. The play opens with Joseph's suspicion and disbelief at his wife's unexpected pregnancy. His moral blindness can be healed only by divine intervention and by witnessing the faith of uneducated shepherds who come to worship the new king. The tortures through which the child will later pass as a man to death and resurrection constitute a visible portrait of the world's temporal and deceptive nature, and emphasize the certainty of life after death. Manrique's humanism, based principally on the reading of a Christianized Seneca and of biblically inspired treatises, is reflected in that poetry that constitutes his lasting reputation.

HARRY SIEBER

Bibliography

Editions

Foulché Delbosc, R. (ed.) *Cancionero castellano del siglo XV*. Nueva Biblioteca de Autores Españoles, Vol. 2. Madrid, 1915. 1–154.

Paz y Melia, A. (ed.) *Cancionero*. 2 vols. Madrid, 1885. Reprt., facsimile ed. Palencia, 1991.

Criticism

Battesti-Pelegrin, J. "Les Poètes convers et le Pouvoir: Le Débat poétique entre Gómez Manrique et Juan de Valladolid." In *Ecrire à la fin du Moyen-Age: Le Pouvoir et l'écriture en Espagne et en Italie (1450–1530)*. Ed. J. Battesti-Pelegrin and G. Ulysse. Aix-en Provence, 1990. 241–52.

Caunedo del Potro, B. "Un inventario de bienes de Gómez Manrique." In *Estudios de historia medieval: homenaje a Luis Suarez*. Valladolid, 1991. 95–114.

Lapesa, R. "Poesía docta y afectividad en las 'consolatorias' de Gómez Manrique." In *Estudios sobre literatura y arte dedicados al profesor Emilio Orozco Díaz*. Vol. 2. Granada, 1974. 231–39.

Leal de Martínez, M. *Gómez Manrique, su tiempo y su obra*. Recife, 1959.

Scholberg, K. *Introducción a la poesía de Gómez Manrique*. Madison, Wisc., 1984.

Sieber, H. "Dramatic Symmetry in Gómez Manrique's *La Representación del Nacimiento de Nuestro Señor*." *Hispanic Review* 33 (1965), 118–35.

———. "Gómez Manrique's Last Poem: *Consolatoria para Doña Juan de Mendoça*." In *Letters and Society in Fifteenth-Century Spain: Studies Presented to P. E. Russell on His Eightieth Birthday*. Eds. A. Deyermond and J. Lawrence. Llangrannog, Wales, 1993. 153–63.

———. "Narrative and Elegiac Structure in Gómez Manrique's *Defunzión del noble cavallero Garci Laso de la Vega*." In *Studies in Honor of Bruce W. Wardropper*. Eds. D. Fox, H. Sieber, and R. ter Horst. Newark, Del., 1989. 279–90.

———. "Sobre la fecha de la muerte de Gómez Manrique." *Boletín de la Biblioteca Menéndez y Pelaye* 59 (1983), 5–10.

Zimic, S. "El teatro religioso de Gómez Manrique (1412–1491)." *Boletín de la Real Academia Española* 57 (1977), 353–400.

MANRIQUE, JORGE

The reputation of Jorge Manrique (ca. 1440–1479) has long rested principally upon his *Coplas por la muerte de su padre*, most familiar to English-speaking readers through Longfellow's translation. His poetic range extends, however, beyond the serious mood of the *Coplas* to a wide variety of compositions found in the late medieval and fifteenth-century *cancioneros*, in which Manrique demonstrates a fluent handling of the current verbal and conceptual conventions of the genres and categories involved. These include personal satire and various approaches to conventional amorous themes, among them verses in which a lady's name is conveyed acrostically, and renderings of the traditional motif of love as a siege (*Escala de amor*), a castle (*Castillo de amor*), or membership of a religious order (*Profesion que hizo en la orden de amor*). Critical evaluation of Manrique's verse has concentrated primarily upon the *Coplas*, but the importance of his other writings is now generally recognized.

Jorge Manrique's life was marked by active involvement in the politics of his day and their military extension. His family was prominent in the turbulent events of the reign of Enrique IV; his father Rodrigo (1406–1476), count of Paredes and a master of the Order of Santiago, was involved in the abortive elevation of the puppet-king Alfonso against Enrique (an event alluded to in the *Coplas*). To Jorge fell the role of maintaining this involvement in the next phase of the succession dispute, and, having actively espoused the cause of Fernando and Isabel he was fatally wounded in a minor action.

The military aspect of Manrique's career fundamentally marked his poetry; his work stands comparison with that of any war poet of any period. Imagery drawn from the experience and equipment of medieval warfare abounds even in the amorous poems (it is, indeed, the very foundation of *Escala* and *Castillo*, while isolated images occur in other poems), and permeates the *Coplas*, where death is expressed in terms of an ambush and an arrow, against whose force the strongest fortifications and armies are powerless and ineffective. The tournament panoply of the warrior caste (among other dimensions of its courtly existence such as music and dancing) is richly evoked in the poet's examination of the meaning of life. For Manrique, war is a necessary element in existence: the noble's duty is to fight for his faith against its enemies (just as that of the priest is to pray), and by doing so he merits salvation. His father, Rodrigo, is praised for his effectiveness in this sphere, and his entry to paradise is, as a result, taken for granted in the idealized deathbed scene that closes the poem. But Rodrigo is also commended by the poet for his part in the civil wars in support of the legitimate candidate for the throne, and also for fighting fellow-Christians in the maintenance of his own status and domains. The political aspect of his career is thus an essential element in the poet's eulogy of his father Rodrigo's greatness. In this Jorge Manrique is merely reflecting the importance attached to *estado* (state) and to the behavior appropriate to one's rank, in contemporary thinking; beyond mere physical existence lies a further dimension of *fama*, the existence implied in one's reputation, which survives after death; this itself is, of course, a poor second to eternal life, though an essential prerequisite for it in so far as it indicates a worthy life. In addition to the doctrinal statements made and political points scored in the poem, various conscious statements of literary attitude are explicit, as in the rejection of traditional poetic invocations and classical examples in the *Ubi sunt?*, while others remain implicit. Although the *Coplas* have been widely praised, and is indubitably in many respects a masterpiece, problems have been noted in various aspects of the poem from the earliest commentators to the present. The *Coplas* make use of a wide range of traditional imagery drawn from the Bible and other sources in addition to the author's military experience, with the transience of earthly life and the inevitability of death being conveyed in a densely textured series of metaphors. The skillful updating of the topos of the *Ubi sunt?* by reference to politically prominent persons of recent memory is but one dimension of Manrique's artistry in handling traditional concepts and poetic commonplaces. The eulogy of his father (apparently controversial among early commentators, and ignored by most glossators) draws upon classical archetypes and established medieval concepts of hierarchy and makes effective use of the personification of death.

Despite the prominence traditionally assigned to the *Coplas* in Spanish literary studies, the first truly critical edition (which is likely to become the standard text) was not published until 1991; the many previous editions vary, because of problems in the complex transmission of the text, both in the number of stanzas (forty or forty-two) and in their order. The stanza that begins "Si fuesse en nuestro poder," in particular, has been variously placed as number seven or thirteen; the earlier location is undoubtedly the original. The additional two stanzas found in many early editions (and in Longfellow's translation) are problematic; they do not form a natural part of the poem. Their attribution to Manrique remains questionable; even if ultimately proven to be by his hand, they are best viewed as originally independent stanzas that later became an accretion to the *Coplas*. During the sixteenth century, the *Coplas* were frequently printed, and private manuscript copies further attest their popularity. It is clear that the poem circulated in a wide variety of forms and contexts. Important among these are the early printed editions in which the text is accompanied by a poetic gloss; the *Coplas* soon attracted the attention of glossators, the earliest of whom was Alonso de Cervantes (first printed in 1501).

DAVID HOOK

Bibliography

Editions

Beltrán, V. *Coplas que hizo Jorge Manrique a la muerte de su padre*. Barcelona, 1991.

Serrano de Haro, A. *Jorge Manrique; Obras*. Madrid, 1986.

Studies

Domínguez, F. A. *Love and Remembrance: The Poetry of Jorge Manrique*. Lexington, Ky., 1988.

Serrano de Haro, A. *Personalidad y destino de Jorge Manrique*. 2d ed. Madrid, 1975.

MANṢŪR, AL-

Ibn ʿAbī Āmir, later known as Al-Manṣūr, was the last of the great rulers during the caliphate period in al-Andalus. Initially he served as vizir, virtually assuming effective control of the caliphate after the death of Al-Ḥakam II, who appointed his young son Hishām to succeed him in 976. Allegedly acting on Hishām's behalf, Al-Manṣūr eliminated all who wished to compete for power, including his father-in-law Al-Ghālib, securing it all for himself. Al-Manṣūr remained in power from 976 to 1002 and was feared and noted for his decisive action, vigilance, and ruthlessness; it was in 981 that he assumed the sobriquet (*laqab*) Al-Manṣūr, "The Victorious."

The caliph Hishām, who was a virtual captive of Al-Manṣūr, was a weak individual who allowed his weaknesses to be exploited. A brilliant politician, Al-Manṣūr filled the political vacuum created by the death of Hishām's father, Al-Ḥakam II. He ruled with an iron hand, galvanizing the army and leading daring incursions into Christian territory that struck terror into the hearts of the northern populations. His name alone was enough to make them shudder with fear. As a response to the Christians who, sensing disunity among the Muslims in al-Andalus, had begun to make their first incursions into Muslim territories, Al-Manṣūr led some fifty expeditions against the Christians. In 997 he struck at their very heart, taking Santiago de Compostela, the alleged burial place of the apostle James. When he entered Santiago the town was all but deserted, except for a Christian monk whom Al-Manṣūr allowed to go free. Although Al-Manṣūr rode his horse into the cathedral to show his contempt for Christianity, the tomb of the apostle was not disturbed. He destroyed all the surrounding buildings and took the bells of the cathedral back to Córdoba both as booty and as a sign of humiliation. He converted the bells into lamps for the mosque, where they remained until the thirteenth century. Besides warrior and statesman, Al-Manṣūr was a poet and a builder, and he expanded the Great Mosque of Córdoba. A devout religious man, he publically abjured philosophy and science by burning the books in Al-Ḥakam II's library that dealt with these subjects, and always carried with him a Qu'rān that was copied out in his own hand. Whenever the name of Allah was uttered in his presence, he never failed to repeat it. If tempted to act in an impious way, he was reputed always to have resisted temptation. Nevertheless, he was known to have enjoyed all pleasures—even wine, which he failed to renounce until two years before his death.

In 991, virtually ignoring Hishām, he made his eighteen-year-old son ʿAbd al- Mālik chamberlain, and later designated ʿAbd al- Mālik as his successor. Al-Manṣūr died in 1002 while on an expedition against the Christians. His other son, Al-Muzaffar, succeeded him, but died six years later. Al-Muzaffar was briefly succeeded by his brother, ʿAbd al-Rahmān, known as Sanchuelo, who conspired to grasp the title of caliph for himself. The death of Al-Manṣūr was followed by a crisis of authority and struggles among his family; Hishām II, the grandson of ʿAbd al-Raḥmān III, who was incapable of ruling; and several other contenders, including Al-Mahdi, who eventually seized power. Al-Manṣūr's biography, *al-Ma'āthir al-ʿĀmiriyyah* was written by Husayn Ibn ʿĀsim at the end of the eleventh century.

E. Michael Gerli

Bibliography

Chejne, A. G. *Muslim Spain: Its History and Culture*. Minneapolis, 1974.

MANUEL I, KING OF PORTUGAL

Born at Alcochete on 31 May 1469, died in Lisbon on December 13, 1521. Manuel was the ninth child of Fernando (1433–1470), the second duke of Viseu and first duke of Beja, and Beatriz (1430–1506), the daughter of João (1400–1442), son of King João I. Manuel was the grandson of King Duarte, great-grandson of João I and the brother of Leonor (1458–1525), wife of João II. His ascent to the throne was the result of accidental circumstances. The unexpected death of Afonso, the heir of João II, created a problem of succession. João II tried hard to have Jorge de Lancastre, his illegitimate son by Dona Ana de Mendonça, accepted as his successor, but he faced vigorous opposition from the queen. In his will he left the throne to his cousin and brother-in-law. Manuel had shown total loyalty to João II and never rebuked him for the death of his brother Diogo, involved in a plot against the king.

In 1497 Manuel married Isabel, daughter of Fernando and Isabel of Spain and widow of Prince Afonso; she died in childbirth the following year. In 1500, Manuel married her sister, Maria, who gave him eight children, including the heir to the throne, João III. Widowed in 1517, he married Leonor, sister of Charles V, who had been previously promised to his son João.

When Manuel I came to power he found a centralized state that was the work of his predecessor, he had only to consolidate what had been done to achieve royal absolutism. The measures agreed to at the *cortes* (parliament) of Montemor-o-Novo, in November 1495, put public administration under the direct control of the crown. On the other hand, he invited the nobility that had sought political asylum in Spain at the time of João II to return, and changed the conditions that had kept the Jews in a state of slavery. In 1496, however, to satisfy Isabel and the Catholic Monarchs, he decreed that all Jews who refused baptism had to leave the country or lose their property and lives. Yet, before the time for their departure expired, he had them all converted by a royal decree. By the law of 4 May 1497, he forbade all enquiries into the beliefs of the converted and by the royal order of 1499 prohibited them from leaving the kingdom. Manuel I was not interested in losing the Jews but wanted them to lose their juridical identity. This identity was ignored in the *Ordenações Manuelinas*, the royal civil law code.

Manuel inherited from his predecessor all plans and preparations for overseas voyages; he had only to implement them. In 1497 he sent Vasco da Gama on a voyage to India, which he completed successfully when his ships put in at Calicut on 20 May 1498; the sea route to India had been discovered. In 1500, Manuel ordered a larger fleet, under the command of Pedro Álvares Cabral, to establish commercial relations with the East and show off the power of Portugal in view of the difficulties Vasco da Gama had encountered. Cabral followed a longer route to the southwest and discovered Brazil on 22 April 1500. He proceeded then to Calicut, but Muslim hostility made him move to Cochin, where he was allowed to establish a factory. Yet his bombardment of Calicut had stiffened Muslim resistance to the Portuguese presence in the area. The armadas of Vasco da Gama and Dom Francisco de Almeida, sent out respectively in 1502 and 1503, had the purpose of imposing Portuguese control over the Indian Ocean. But these expeditions proved costly. The problem was temporarily solved when Afonso de Albuquerque occupied key positions in the Indian subcontinent by conquering Ormuz (1507), Goa (1510), and Malacca (1511). He promoted intermarriage between the Indians and the Portuguese, laying the foundations for a durable empire. During the reign of Manuel I Portuguese expansion reached its peak and arts and letters flourished with the spirit of the New Age. The Manueline style in architecture, characterized by exhuberant maritime motifs, produced masterpieces such as the monastery of Jerónimos in Lisbon.

LUIS REBELO

Bibliography

Góis, D. de. *Crónica do Felicíssimo Rei D. Manuel.* 2 vols. Coimbra, 1949–55.

Osório, J. *Da Vida e Feitos del Rel D. Manuel.* Porto, 1945.

Serrão, J. V. *História de Portugal 1495–1580.* Vol. 3. Lisbon, 1980.

MANUSCRIPT ILLUMINATION

The terms *illumination* and *miniature* are equivalent in the modern terminology of the art historian, and both refer to paintings in manuscript texts. Strictly speaking, *illumination* alludes to the use of gold leaf in the painting, and this technique is quite uncommon in the Iberian Peninsula, or at least in Castile.

The first great age of the Spanish miniature is the Mozarabic age, principally during the tenth century and the beginning of the eleventh century, and which reached a splendor with no known equivalent in the Visigothic era notwithstanding the Asturian and Isidorean cultural achievements of the period. Beginning with Gómez Moreno, the term *Mozárabe* has been applied to the manuscripts in Castile and León supposedly written and illuminated by Christians under Muslim rule. Starting with Camón Aznar, this style has also been called the "art of repopulation," implying that its characteristics are similar not just to Muslim artistic contributions, but also to Christian art of the same period. Compared to Carolingian art, which was implicated in an extensive renovation of ancient classicism, Mozarabic art (with some exceptions) seems to be situated in the margins of older artistic legacies. There are certain undeniable Islamic traits, including the frequent use of the horseshoe arch and the existence of Abbasid imagery such as the image of the woman on horseback (with the cup of the world in her hand). Its profound originality is its most notable characteristic, and it is rooted in an aesthetic radically different from classical art, with very linear form and stylized, abstract drawings. The works display a radical bidimensionality that makes few concessions to illusionism and applies strongly contrasting and deeply expressive coloring.

The *Biblia Hispalense* (Madrid, Biblioteca Nacional, MS. Vit. 13–1.), written in Seville around 900, is the earliest Mozarabic codex. In its miniatures two styles contrast, resulting perhaps from two distinct stages. The date cited above would apply to the atypically illusionistic paintings that accompany the canons of Luke and John (f. 278), portraying the animal heads of the two evangelists in a classic style. The images of the prophets Micah (f. 161) and Nahum (f. 162v.) were painted around 988, displaying an abstract, distorted two-dimensionality typical of the Mozarabic style.

The *Biblia del año 920* (MS. 6, now in the Cathedral of León) was prepared in a Leonese monastery under the direction of a monk named Vimara, but was written and illustrated by Iohannes. Along with smaller decorations, the work's illustrations include full page miniatures of a fully developed Mozarabic style. In the St. Luke miniature (f. 211), for example, the evangelist appears encircled by five colored discs that frame his distorted face, which in a daring metamorphosis gradually changes into the body of a bull, St. Luke's symbol.

The most characteristic Mozarabic miniatures are the illuminations of the *Beatos*, the name given to the manuscripts copying the "Comentarios al Apocalípsis" of Beato of Liébana. Given their importance for Spanish art throughout time and their international renown, the *Beatos* are studied separately in this encyclopedia.

Continuing in chronological order, another important manuscript is the *Moralia in Job* (Madrid, Biblioteca Nacional, MS. 80), a work of great artistic importance that sets it apart from the numerous manuscript versions of this famous text: the commentaries on the Book of Job written by Pope Gregory the Great at the request of San Leandro of Seville. The illuminator, Florentius, signs his name on a beautiful page accompanying an abstract miniature in the style of a tapestry. The "Majestas Domini" (f. 2) portrays a Christ amidst angels holding the book of life, and uses intense yellow hues that stand out from the vivid red background.

The *Biblia del año 960* (León, Colegiata de San Isidoro, MS. 2) is a magnificent work signed by two monks, Florentius and Sanctius, who appear in the miniature on the last page of the book (f. 514, marked with the Greek letter *omega*), toasting each other for having finished the work. The numerous miniatures that illustrate this work are inserted into the text in two ways. Some are displayed without a frame to separate the figures from the texts. Others, more developed, are situated within a frame that accentuates the illustration's beauty and pictoric value.

Aside from Bibles and the *Beatos*, the most numerous and representative manuscripts, other works deserve mentioning. The *Códice Albeldense* (Escorial, MS. d.I.2.), a collection of canon law texts, was finished in 976 in the Navarrese monastery of San Martín de Albelda by a scribe named Vigila. One of its miniatures (f. 142) contains an image that alludes to the

Toledan councils: Toledo, the regal city, appears up high, and although it culminates in typical medieval battlements, the miniature lacks the horseshoe arches and the vivid color schemes associated with Mozarabic illumination. In folio 428 a miniature with nine panels displays the portraits of six important figures: three Visigothic monarchs in the top level, starting with Chindasvintoh; three contemporary Navarrese kings in the middle; and the three authors of the manuscript—the scribe Vigila, his partner Sarracinus, and his disciple Garsia—at the bottom. The *Códice Emilianense* (Escorial, MS. d.I.2.) is a similar work, finished in 994.

The *Antifonario Mozárabe* (Cathedral of León, MS. 8) was written for the abbot Ikila by the copyist, abbot Totmundo—the date of the work has long been disputed, but is now considered to date from the tenth century. Its renown stems mostly from its musical notation, which has not yet been possible to transcribe, and from its extremely valuable text, containing all of the pieces of the Visigothic-Mozarabic liturgy that were sung. Its miniatures are excellent works produced by the school of the painter Magio (also the author of the *Morgan Beatus*), although they are more worthy because of their imagery and their appearance in an *antifonario* (antiphonary) than because of their pictorial quality.

A *De Virginitate Mariae* of San Ildefonso (Florence, Biblia Laurenciana, MS. Ashb.17.), written in Toledo in 1067, contains only one miniature—it depicts the Annunciation and employs a style notably archaic for the late eleventh century.

In the Romanesque period, manuscripts can be divided into three chronological subdivisions. Among representative works of the early Romanesque period are two Catalan Bibles written and illuminated in Ripoll. Through a series of misadventures, these works passed through the possession of various monasteries, with one (*Biblia de Roda*, Bibl. Nationale, MS. lat. 6) eventually landing in Paris and the other (Bibl. Vaticana, MS. lat. 5728) in Rome. These works are of exceptional importance for the history of the Catalan and European miniature, despite the fact that neither has been completely preserved. There is significant iconographic similarity between the two works, implying that they both descend from a common antecedent. In terms of both imagery and stylistics, the works display traits similar to previous Carolingian manuscripts, and are quite different from other Castilian or Leonese works.

In the kingdom of León, a royal scriptorium established to serve the imperial ambitions of Fernando I and doña Sancha produced a *Diurnal* o *Libro de Oraciones* for the royal couple (Biblioteca de la Universidad de Santiago de Compostela, MS. Res.1), as well as a *Beatos* (discussed in a separate article). Written in 1055, the *Diurnal* seems to reflect the economic glory of the kingdom after the progress of the reconquest in the south, as well as the new ties with trans-Pyreneen Europe. Folio 3 depicts the two monarchs standing beneath solemn curtainry; between them is a figure holding a book. This person has been variously interpreted as the scribe Fructuosus and as King David, the author of the Psalms that appear in the text.

In the high Romanesque period (1075–1150), the most important works are the Castilian-Leonese *Beatos*, studied in a separate article. Among other significant works is the *Biblia de 1162* at the Colegiata de San Isidoro de León (MS. 3), which is a copy of the Mozarabic Bible of 960 that is preserved in the same collegiate church. This text is one of a long series of Castilian Bibles written in Latin that reach the thirteenth century preserving Visigothic and Mozarabic traditions. Its numerous miniatures, though copied from the previous text, are adapted to the Romanesque style and display other novel qualities. In Santiago de Compostela two exceptional works were illuminated in the same period. The first is the *Tumbo A* of the cathedral of Santiago, a *cartulario* (cartulary) containing privileges granted to the cathedral between 1125 and 1255. In an early stage, the illuminator produced twenty-four images of monarchs and other royal figures. The king appears as a donor, seated on a throne with a majestic attitude, and is surely influenced by Carolingian or Ottonian models. The portrait of Fruela II (f. 11) is notable for its pliant, flexible style; Fernando II's image (f. 44v.) gives rise to a new iconographic type, with the king mounted on horseback. This miniature also occupies the whole page, the bottom of which displays a heraldic lion with the royal shield. The portrait of Fernando II belongs to the late Romanesque period (or the Romanesque in transition) and in its style a new Byzantine naturalism is apparent. The *Codex Calixtinus* is another important work produced in Santiago during the high Romanesque period. It contains beautifully decorated capital letters that are representative of one of the most creative aspects of the Romanesque. It also contains several miniatures. Its style recalls English works connected to the *Psalter of Saint Albans*.

The late Romanesque or Proto-Gothic period occurs around the year 1200, when a wave of Byzantine influence explodes in Europe, with varying intensity according to the place. In Castile and León the *Beatos* enjoy a final moment of glory, and two Bibles also stand out.

The *Biblia de Burgos* (Burgos, Biblioteca Pública del Estado), produced in the scriptorium of San Pedro de Cardeña between 1190 and 1200, is one of the most remarkable examples of the Romanesque miniature in Spain, despite the fact that it only contains two miniatures, both of considerable size. Both the Epiphany (f.8 v.) and the Genesis cycle (f.12v.) are of great iconographic originality. The *Biblia de Avila* (Madrid, Bibl. Nac. MS. Vit.15–1) contains an initial Italian section to which was added a Spanish part. The Spanish section's miniatures are of a strong expressionism recalling the paintings of San Justo of Segovia.

The *cartularios* (cartularies) of this same period are of great aesthetic significance. The *Libro de los Testamentos* (Archivo de la Catedral de Oviedo) was commissioned by Pelayo, the bishop of Oviedo, to try to save the Oviedan diocese from considerable decadence. Its eight large paintings have been considered some of the most beautiful miniatures of the Spanish Romanesque. They were created by a visionary artist with a very personal style who used beautiful and diverse colors, creating a few figures that are completely expressionistic.

The *Libro de las Estampas* (Catedral de León, MS. 25) contains seven preserved miniatures that portray the kings who bequeathed their legacies to the cathedral. The enthroned figures are represented in a Byzantine, classicist style. The *Obras de Santo Martino* (San Isidoro de León, cod. 11) are of a similar style, with beautifully illuminated capital letters and a sizeable portrait of the author.

The *Biblia de Lérida* is a remarkable Aragónese work (Archivo de la Catedral), with handsome ornamental initials depicting battles between men, animals, and fantastic beings. The work was likely produced in a scriptorium in Calahorra. In Catalonia, two cartularios stand out: the *Liber feudorum maior* (Archivo de la Corona de Aragón, ms. 1) and the *Liber feudorum ceritaniae* (Archivo de la Corona de Aragón, MS. 2). The first is the masterpiece of Catalan illumination of the period, with two particularly notable miniatures: one (f.1) portrays the compiler of the documents, Raimundo de Caldes, before king Alfonso I.

In the Gothic period (1225–1500), as in the Romanesque, the miniature employs various styles.

In this encyclopedia a separate entry is dedicated to the Alfonsine miniature, given its fundamental role in Hispanic illustration in the late Middle Ages.

The kingdom of Castile achieved artistic preeminence in the thirteenth century through the works of Alfonso X, which are characterized by an authentic aesthetic experimentalism and by other exceptional qualities. In Aragón, the existent miniatures show a clear French Gothic style, especially in the backgrounds, which are dominated by golds, reds, and blues and decorated with white dots. The figures are cast in curved lines characteristic of the period. The *Vidal Mayor* (J. Paul Getty Foundation, Malibu, California, Getty Museum, Ludwig XIV 4) seems to have been illuminated by a talented Catalan, Aragónese, or French artist at the service of King Jaime I, who appears in the first miniature of the book (f. 1), accompanied by members of his court, in the act of commissioning the compilation of the *fueros* of Aragón to Vidal de Canellas, bishop of Huesca. The most opulent miniature (f.72v.) portrays the enthroned king, with the sword of justice in hand, presiding over a group of common people and public officials. The marginalia or *drôleries* of the work are particularly remarkable, shooting off from the capitals to form sketches with elements of humor and of plant life. In Castile, marginal decorations only appear in the Alphonsine *Lapidario*, though in the same period the phenomenon is evident in the Bolognese schools and on both sides of the English Channel.

In the fourteenth century the Castilian miniature cultivated a linear Gothic style influenced by the French, except for a very few number of works that expand on the Alphonsine style. One group of texts attributed to King Alfonso XI contains two juridical manuscripts that are different versions of the same document, the *Ordenamiento de Alcalá*. Both manuscripts are decorated with elaborate miniatures: the version in the Escorial (MS. Z.III.9.) contains two full-page miniatures with marginal decoration; the other, in the Biblioteca Nacional of Madrid (MS. Res 9) is more modest, but does contain a portrait of the enthroned Alfonso XI with a scepter and a globe in each hand, both symbols of power linked together, in my opinion, in the king's concept of monarchy as a contract supported by the court. Both manuscripts were written by Nicolás González, who also produced the masterpiece of Castilian illumination of this period, the *Crónica Troyana* (Escorial, MS. h.I.6.). With more than one hundred miniatures, many of them occupying the whole page, this codex echoes the French and Italian traditions of illuminating literary texts about the Trojan War. Compared with the uniquely Castilian character of the Alphonsine miniature, both in textual and stylistic terms, the *Crónica Troyana* is a rich, sumptuous work derived from European sources. There are no allusions in its miniatures to Islamic imagery, unlike the *Cantigas* and other manuscripts of Alfonso X, and the style is linear Gothic. The history of the ancient Greeks and Trojans is interpreted by Gothic heroes in a Gothic setting, while in the Alphonsine works there was a conscientious effort to revive ancient astrological and mythological themes. The land and sea battle scenes are very decorative, as are the visions of the besieged city of Troy, depicted with brightly colored walls.

The Italo-Gothic style, influenced by *Trecento* Italian painting, is fully expressed in Catalonia, both in the miniature and in panel painting. The Maestro de los Privilegios, who worked for the monarchy in Mallorca during its brief period as an independent kingdom, was one of the most talented illustrators. His most important work is the *Llibre del Privilegis* (Archivo Histórico de Palma de Mallorca), containing a miniature in which Jaime I appears in a majestic vision surrounded by his court, receiving the crown from two angels while another two play music. The same painter illustrated the *Leyes Palatinas de Mallorca* (Brussels, Bibliothèque Royale, ms. 9169) as well as a series of works on panels. Ferrer Bassa introduced the Italian style to Catalonia; he was famous for his murals in Poblet, and recently the *Horas de María de Navarra* (Venice, Biblioteca Marciana, MS. lat.1.104/12.640) have been attributed to him, though others have suggested that they are the work of the Maestro de San Marcos (creator of a famous altarpiece) or of Arnau Bassa, Ferrer's son. The most famous work of this artistic group is the *Salterio Anglocatalán* (Paris, Bibliothèque Nationale, MS. lat.8846). Illumination of the work began in Canterbury around 1200, but it was finished in Catalonia in the fourteenth century; these two stages are evident in both the style and the iconography of the work.

In Castile the Italo-Gothic style is introduced through Gerardo Starnina, a Florentine painter who came to Toledo at the end of the fourteenth century. We know very little about the extent of this style's influence in Castile, because the contemporary manuscripts of the cathedral of Toledo remain incomplete. In the *Siete Partidas* (Bibl. Nacional, MS. 12.793), an extraordinary Last Judgment (folio 7) demonstrates a style clearly derived from the Italian *Trecento*.

Illuminated manuscripts intended for Spanish Jews, such as certain Bibles and the *Haggadot*, are studied separately in this encyclopedia along with other Jewish art.

The international Gothic style of the early fifteenth century was most successful in Aragón. In Catalonia the most eminent work is the *Breviario* of King Martín I the Humane (Paris, Bibl. Nat., MS. Rothschild 2529); the setbacks associated with the process of the work's production are well documented, and the work was completed by Martín's heir, Alfonso V the Magnanimous. The illustrations from Martín's period resemble the Parisian manuscripts of the Valois in their use of calendar iconography, but in terms of style, the work alternates between Parisian and Catalan influences. The most famous work of the international Gothic in Catalonia is the *Misal de Santa Eulalia* (Archivo de la catedral de Barcelona, cod.116), the masterpiece of the painter and illuminator, Rafael Destorrents. Its Last Judgment (folio 7) expresses incredible refinement. With a rather original format, the illustration occupies every bit of the four margins, leaving the text in the center. The Glory of the upper margin is painted in luminous tones that gradually get darker and darker toward the bottom of the page, where the depths of Hell are represented. The codex also has eighteen exquisitely illuminated initials—the Annunciation stands out especially.

In Mallorca, the illuminated atlases and *portolanos* are of note, particularly the *Catalán Atlas* (Paris, Bibl. Nat., MS. Espagnol 30), produced around 1375.

The Crespí family dominated the scene in Valencia. Domingo Crespí was the author of a *Llibre del Consolat del Mar* (Archivo Municipal de Valencia). His son Leonardo produced the Valencian masterwork of the period, the *Salterio-Libro de Horas de Alfonso V el Magnánimo* (London, British Museum, MS. add.28962). This rich work contains several types of illustrations and employs original imagery, especially in the "Oficio de Difuntos" (Office of the Dead), whose central figure is Death riding an ox and shooting his arrows at the living, a fairly uncommon variation on the Dance of Death.

In Castile, the International Gothic is concentrated in two cities, Toledo and Seville. Around 1430, a Maestro de los Cipreses illuminated numerous choirbooks for the cathedral of Seville; he might be identified as a Pedro de Toledo who worked in the cathedral during those years. The beautiful miniatures of this work are characterized by their winding drawings with background landscapes of cypresses: two of the especially remarkable miniatures are the images of King David (Libro 44, f.21) and the Virgin with Child (Libro 4, f.20v.). The same artist collaborated in the illustration of a *Biblia romanceada* (Escorial, MS. I.1.3.) along with another master of inferior quality. The Maestro de los Cipreses is attributed with the representations of the death of Absalom (f.184v.) and the story of Samson (f.149v.); the other artist, who is in my opinion comparable to the master of the altarpiece of D. Sancho de Rojas (Museo del Prado), is attributed with, among other miniatures, the stories of Noah's Ark and the Sacrifice of Isaac.

The most famous Castilian work of the fifteenth century Gothic is the *Biblia de Alba* (Palacio de Liria, Madrid, MS. 399), whose fame is rooted above all in its text, translated from the Hebrew to Romance by a rabbi in Guadalajara at the request of Don Luis de Guzmán, a great *maestre* of the Order of Calatrava. It contains 334 miniatures of variable quality and of a clear Toledan style: the prologue indicates that once the text was written, the codex was brought to Toledo to be illuminated. Gutmann believes that the Christian tradition is very strong in the miniatures, and that the work found more inspiration in Christian works than in Jewish ones, a theory opposing the thesis defended by Nordström in his monograph.

Two other works exist from the Toledo school, both written on paper instead of parchment. Despite their inferior quality, these texts contain highly original illustrations. The *Castigos del Rey Don Sancho* (Madrid, Bibl. Naci., MS. 3995) is a moralizing work whose first miniature depicts the enthroned Salomon before the kneeling King Sancho, all in a high quality chiaroscuro. The *Décadas de Tito Livio* (Madrid, Bibl. Nac., MS. Res.204) were illustrated by a naive but expressive artist who was especially adept at portraying scenes of cruelty, like that of Tulia driving her carriage over her father's body (f.16v.). Its thirteen full-page miniatures are, in my opinion, of great interest for modern aesthetics.

The Hispano-Flemish miniature (1450–1500) is still insufficiently known, but it seems that it reached considerable development in Castile. The two best-known works are of a literary nature and were produced for Enrique IV: the *Libro del caballero Zifar* and the *Libro de la montería*. The *Genealogía de los reyes de España* was likely written and illuminated for the same king. The most significant development of the period is the boom in liturgical works that were fashionable in Europe since the thirteenth century but only recently in Castile: breviaries, psalters, books of hours, missals, and choirbooks were also popular.

The *Libro del caballero Zifar* (Paris, Bibl. Nat. MS. Espagnol 36) contains 242 beautiful miniatures that are of particular interest because of the civil and military documentation they offer. The principal illuminator has been identified as Juan de Carrión, a prolific artist who signed the choirbooks of Avila and who merits more study.

The *Libro de la montería* (Madrid, Biblioteca de Palacio, MS.2105) is one of the existing copies of the famous hunting treatise by Alfonso XI, and was written and illustrated for Enrique IV, with Juan de Carrión creating the miniatures.

The *Genealogía de los reyes de España* (Madrid, Bibl. de Palacio, MS. Z-LI-2) is an elaborate work with eighty-two ink drawings that depict Spanish kings and princes from Atanárico to Enrique IV. Its precious and highly detailed style is unmatched in the field of the miniature and of painting in general.

The Catholic Monarchs promoted the production of various manuscripts that have yet to be studied sufficiently. The *Libro de Horas del Infante D. Alfonso* (New York, Pierpont Morgan, Library MS. 854) was clearly commissioned by Isabel at the death of her brother, and though the work is not very elaborate, it applies original imagery, especially in the "Oficio de Difuntos" (f.161v.). Here, Death rides with the horseman of the Apocalypse, wounding with his arrows a cardinal, a bishop, a pope, a monk, and the already dead prince. Behind is a queen, possibly Isabel, dressed in white. The *Misal Vitrina 8* of the Escorial has not yet been studied, and there is doubt as to whether the work is Spanish (which is Durrieu's opinion) or Flemish. Another *Misal de Isabel la Católica*, in the Capilla Real of Granada, was written in 1496 by Francisco Flórez for the queen, who appears in two portraits of the manuscript. Two breviaries are of interest: the *Breviario de Isabel la Católica* (Madrid, Bibl. Nacional, Vit.18–8), with several decorated letters; and the *Breviario del Escorial* (b.II.15), which displays the shields and emblems of the Catholic Monarchs and contains 115 miniatures. The choirbooks of the Capilla Real of Granada and of the cathedral of Badajoz also contain the shields of the Catholic monarchs. There are few illuminated works belonging to the Castilian nobility. Iñigo López de Mendoza, the Marqués de Santillana, used the painter Jorge Inglés as a miniaturist; Inglés participated in the *Conocimiento de todas las Cosas* (Madrid, Bibl. Nac., MS. 1197) and the *Fedón* (Madrid, Bibl. Nac., ms. Vit.17–4). The Zúñiga family commissioned numerous works, including Antonio de Nebrija's *Gramática latina* (Madrid, Bibl. Nac. MS. Vit.17–1).

Toledo played a significant role in the production of liturgical manuscripts—recently studied by Lynette M. F. Bosch—although the phenomenon was very closely connected to production in Avila and even Burgos. Especially notable among the monastic *scriptoria* was the monastery of Guadalupe, which specialized in the illumination of choirbooks. The majority of their fifteenth century choirbooks were sold in the sixteenth century and substituted with more modern versions.

Ana Domínguez Rodríguez

Bibliography

Alcoy, R. "Los maestros del *Libro de Horas de la reina María de Navarra*: avance sobre un problema complejo," *Boletín del Museo e Instituto Camón Aznar* 34 (1988), 105–34.

Angulo Iñiguez, D. "La miniatura en Sevilla. El maestro de los Cipreses," *Archivo Español de Arte y Arqueología* 2 (1928), 65–96.

———. "Libros corales de la catedral de Sevilla. Siglos XV y XVI," in *La catedral de Sevilla*. Seville, 1984. 513 ff.

Avril, F. et al. *Manuscrits enluminés de la Bibliothèque Nationale. Manuscrits de la Peninsule Ibérique*. Paris, 1983.

Bohigas, P. *La ilustración y la decoración del libro manuscrito en Cataluña*. Barcelona, 1960.

Büchtal, H. *Historia Troiana. Studies in the History of Mediaeval Secular Illustration*. London, 1971.

———. *Pintura medieval española*. Madrid, 1966.

Domínguez Bordona, J. "La ilustración de manuscritos en Castilla (siglos XIV al XV)," *Arte Español* 7 (1924–25), 133–39.

———. *La miniatura española*. 2 vols. Barcelona, 1930.

———. *Manuscritos con pinturas*. 2 vols. Madrid, 1933.

———. *Miniatura*. Vol. 18 of *Ars Hispaniae*. Madrid, 1962.

Domínguez Rodríguez, A. "El libro ilustrado medieval," in *Historia ilustrada del libro español*. Ed. H. Escolar. Madrid, 1994.

Fernández González, E. *Abecedario-Bestiario de los códices de Santo Martino*. León, 1985.

Gudiol i Cunill, J. *La miniatura catalana*. Barcelona, 1954.

Kauffmann, C. M. "Vidal Mayor, Ein spanisches Gesetzbuch aus dem 13 Jahrhundert in Aachener Privatbesitz," *Aachener Kunstblätter* 29 (1964), 109–38.

Keller, J. E. and Kinkade, R. P. *Iconography in Medieval Spanish Literature*. Lexington, KY, 1984.

Lacarra Ducay, M. C. *Vidal Mayor. Estudis*. Facsimile ed. Huesca, 1989. 119 ff.

Meiss, M. "Italian Style in Catalonia and a Fourteenth-century Catalan Workshop," *Journal of the Walters Art Gallery* 4 (1941), 45–87.

Mentré, M. *Contribución al estudio de la miniatura en León y Castilla en la Alta Edad Media*. León, 1976.

Moralejo Alvarez, S. "La miniatura en los Tumbos A y B." In *Los Tumbos de Compostela*. Madrid, 1985. 45–62.

Mundó, A. M. "Las Biblias románicas de Ripoll," *Actas del 23⁰ Congreso Internacional de Historia del Arte*. Vol. 1. Granada. 1976. 435–36.

Neuss, W. *Die Katalanische Bibelillustration um die wende des ersten Jahrtausends und die altspanische Buchmalerei*, Leipzig, 1922.

Nordström, C. O. *The Duke of Alba's Castilian Bible (A Study of the Rabbinicial Features of the Miniatures)*, Uppsala, 1967.

Pazy Meliá, A. "Código de las Siete Partidas. Breviario romano y códices que pertenecieron a Isabel la Católica" and "Códices más notables," *Revista de Archivos Bibliotecas y Museos* 11, no. 2 (1904), 437–440.

Planas, J. "El Misal de Santa Eulalia," *Boletín del Museo e Instituto "Camón Aznar"* 16 (1984), 32–62.

Raizman, D. "A Rediscovered Illuminated Manuscript of St. Ildefonsus's *De Virginitate Beatae Mariae* in the Biblioteca Nacional in Madrid," *Gesta* 26 (1987), 37–46.

Sánchez Mariana, J. "Biblia de Avila." In *Las Edades del Hombre. Libros y Documentos en la Iglesia de Castilla y León*. Burgos, 1990, p. 19.

Schapiro, M. *The Parma Ildefonsus. A Romanesque Illuminated Manuscript from Cluny and Related Works*. New York, 1964.

Sicart, A. *Pintura medieval: la miniatura, "Arte Galega Sánchez Cantón."* Santiago de Compostela, 1981.

Silva y Verástegui, S. *Iconografía del siglo X en el Reino de Pamplona-Nájera*. Pamplona, 1984.

Villalba Dávalos, A. *La miniatura valenciana en los siglos XIV y XV*, Valencia, 1964.

Viñayo González, A. "El abad Totmundo" y el "Libro de las Estampas," *Las Edades del Hombre. Libros y Documentos en la Iglesia de Castilla y León*. Valladolid, 1990, p. 14 and p. 43.

Werckmeister, O. K. "Die Bilder der drei Propheten in der Biblia Hispalense," in *Mitteilungen des Deutsches Archäelogisches Institut* [Madrid] 4 (1963), 141–88.

———. "Islamische Formen in spanischen Miniaturen des 10 Jahrhunderts und das Problem der mozarabischen Buchmalerei." In *Settimane di Studio del Centro italiano di Studi sull' alto medioevo*. Spoleto, 1965. 933–67.

———. "Das Bild zur liste der Bistümer spaniens im Codex Aemilianensis," *Mitteilungen des Deutsches Archäelogisches Institut* [Madrid] 9 (1968), 399–423.

Williams, J. "A Castilian Tradition of Bible Illustration: The Romanesque Bible from San Millán," *Journal of the Warburg and Courtauld Institutes* 28 (1965), 66–85.

———. *Early Spanish Manuscript Illumination*. New York, 1977.

Yarza Luaces, J. "Las miniaturas del *Antifonario de León*," *Boletín del Seminario de Estudios de Arte y Arqueología de la Universidad de Valladolid* 35 (1976), 181–205.

———. *Arte y Arquitectura en España, 500/1250*. Madrid, 1979.

———. *La Edad Media*. Vol. 2 of *Historia del Arte Hispánico*. Madrid, 1980.

———. "Notas sobre la relación texto-imagen, principalmente en el libro hispano medieval," in *Actas del V Congrés Espanyol d'Historia de l'Art*. Barcelona, 1986.

———. "Reflexiones sobre la iconografía medieval hispana," *Actas del Primer Coloquio de Iconografía, Cuadernos de Arte e Iconografía* 2, no. 3 (1989), 27–46.

———. "La miniatura románica. Estado de la cuestión," *Anuario del Departamento de Historia y Teoría del Arte* 2 (1990), 9–25.

———. "Funzione e uso della miniatura ispana nel X⁰ secolo." In *Settimane di Studio del Centro Italiano di Studi sull'Alto Medioevo*. Spoleto, 1990.

MAQĀMA

The *maqāma* (pl. *maqāmāt*) is a classic Arabic narrative genre. The term is usually translated as "session" or "assembly." The genre's invention is credited to the Arabic-Persian author, Aḥmad Badīʿ al-Zamān al-Hamadhānī (968–1008). His greatest successor, Abū Muḥammad al-Qāsim al-Ḥarīrī al-Baṣrī (1054–1122) established the generic norm, followed—though often with radical modifications—by subsequent generations up through the nineteenth century. The maqāma came to be cultivated throughout the medieval Arabic world and beyond, as a vehicle for Muslim and Christian writers alike, spreading all across North Africa, to the Maghrib and to Spain; it was also cultivated in Persian and Syriac, as well as in Hebrew by Hispano-Jewish authors. Taking Al-Hamadhānī's pathbreaking work as a model, the genre can be characterized as follows: The maqāmāt are written in rhymed and rhythmic prose, occasionally interspersed with verse. Each maqāma represents a separate episode or adventure; there is no temporal or spatial link between the different episodes; chronological sequence is unimportant; the narrative is essentially synchronic, rather than diachronic, and covers a wide variety of geographic milieus. The various maqāmāt achieve a certain unity in the usual—though not totally consistent—presence of a principal protagonist, a roguish, morally ambivalent character (Abū'l Fatḥ al-Iskandarī), capable of unexpected and bizarre disguises and transformations, who, in one episode, may appear as aged, but subsequently be represented as youthful. The encounters with this protagonist are told by a narrator (ʿĪsā ibn Hishām). The maqāmāt are characterized by a concern with eloquence and word play, and with rare, recondite, multivalent, deceptive vocabulary; language is seen as essentially "misrepresentational." Central to Al-Hamadhānī's narrative is the problem of deceptive appearances, the contrast between image and essence, the external and the internal; social corruption and preaching vs. practice; the problem of meaning; the world and the characters of the maqāmāt are essentially unstable. Free will vs. predestination is another basic concern (a Shī ʿite vs. Sunnī polemic). Irony and parody, including parody of sermons and heroic narrative, are also crucial features. Reality in the maqāmāt is conceived as cyclical and ring composition is essential to the organization of individual episodes. Authorial intent suggests both entertainment and instruction, by combining serious and comic perspectives.

As the genre was taken up by later authors, the maqāmāt came to vary greatly in form, content, and artistic intent. The opposition between protagonist and narrator was often eliminated, the first becoming identified with the second. The maqāma sometimes came to be confused with other genres, such as the *riṣāla* (epistolary treatise) and the *ḥadīth* (multigenerational tradition of consecutive narrators). In Spain, the maqāmāt were much cultivated in both Arabic and Hebrew. The outstanding Arabic practitioner was Abū Tāhir al-Ashtarkūwī al-Saraqusṭī (d. 1143), whose *Maqāmāt al-luzumiyya* (*Double-Rhymed* Maqāmāt) is the only Hispano-Arabic example to embody the classic fifty episodes (on the model of Al-Ḥarīrī). Among important Hispano-Jewish authors are Yĕhûdāh bēn Shĕlōmōh al-Ḥarīzī (1170–1235), who translated Al-Ḥarīrī and also wrote his own *Sēfer Ṭaḥkĕmônî*(Book of the Wise Counselor)—consisting of the traditional fifty maqa-ímāt—and Yôsēf bēn Mē'îr ibn Zabāra (ca. 1140) whose *Sēfer Shaʿăshû ʿîm* (*Book of Entertainments*) is considered a masterpiece of the genre.

The putative influence of maqāmāt on Hispano-Romance literature is highly controversial. A number of parallels with Juan Ruiz's *Libro de buen amor*, perceptively pointed out by M. R. Lida de Malkiel, have, in general, not been favorably looked upon by contemporary criticism. Abundant analogies with Spanish picaresque novels may or may not reflect some genetic connection. No medieval translations of maqāmāt into Latin or Romance are known, though a thirteenth-century Arabic religious debate reveals a Christian monk well versed in the complexities of Al-Ḥarīrī's masterpiece.

Samuel G. Armistead

Bibliography

Fanjul, S. (trans.) Al-Hamadhānī. *Venturas y desventuras del pícaro Abū l-Fatḥ de Alejandría*. Madrid, 1988.

Granja, F. de la. *Maqāmas y risālas andaluzas*. Madrid, 1976.

Lida de Malkiel, M. R. *Two Spanish Masterpieces*. Urbana, Ill., 1961.

Márquez, F. *Orígenes y sociología del tema celestinesco*. Barcelona, 1993.

Monroe, J. T. *The Art of Badīʿ az-Zamān al-Hamadhānī* . Beirut, 1983.

———, trans. Al-Saraqusṭī. *Al-maqāmāt al-luzūmīyah*. Leiden, 2002.

Prendergast, W. J. (trans.) *The Maqāmāt of Badīʿ al-Zamān al-Hamadhānī*. London, 1973.

Segal, D. S. (trans.) Judah Alḥarizi. *Taḥkemoni*. London, 2001.

Zabara, Joseph ben Meir. *The Book of Delight*. Trans. Moses Hadas. New York, 1960.

MARCH, AUSIÀS

Valencian knight and poet (1397–1459). His uncle Jaume and his father Pere were both courtly poets and the latter bequeathed to Ausiàs the lordship of Beniarjó, a village next to Gandía. He attended Alfonso V the Magnanimous's court and took part in the royal expeditions to Italy as Jordi de Sant Jordi did. However, this link became gradually weaker after 1424, when he retired to manage his property. At this stage, he started writing a kind of personal poetry; Ausiàs's work consists of 128 poems (one, at least, of dubious attribution) that mostly follow the traditional verse pattern of Catalan post-troubadour lyric (stanzas of eight decasyllables), though he was the first to use a Catalan deprived of Occitan features as a poetic vehicle. This outward ambivalence can be extended to many other aspects of Ausiàs's poetry. On one hand, there is a courtly love framework that would group a majority of his poems in cycles according to the *senhal* (*Plena de seny* and the biblical *Llir entre cards* are the earliest), although any hypothetical order is still controversial. Ausiàs, however, carries the tradition to extremes, mainly through self-awareness, and even argues against it to emphasize his ideas about honorable love. This struggle results in a range of limited situations, often expressed by means of broad analogies that draw on a variety of sources (moral literature and preaching, classical authors, Dante, and so on), so much so that, in fact, courtly commonplace turns into moral judgment of human nature and love, nearly always focusing rhetorically on the poet's unique condition. From this viewpoint the lady can either represent an ideal of wisdom or be blamed for her inability to love, and the poet, in turn, can temporarily dream of a heavenly human happiness, regret the weakness of the flesh or even reject openly any deceitful illusion (especially in the later cycle *Oh folla Amor*). Furthermore, on some occasions March explained his conceptions of love, virtue, and double human nature theoretically, via some elemental philosophical ideas of his time onto which he gradually imposed his own thoughts. In some measure, this aspect grew as he became older, and it eventually led to longer didactic verse compositions (*Cants morals*) in his last years. His splendid *Cant espiritual* and his *Cants de mort* give a complementary view of Ausiàs's tortuous thought. In the former he enacts a dramatic monologue with God to express both faith and doubt while reflecting that an interest in such theological points as predestination had arisen among learned laymen. The latter stress Ausiàs's spiritual concerns, as when he felt guilty after the death of his second wife Joana Scorna (1454). Thirteen manuscripts, five editions, and some translations into Spanish and Latin account for March's posterity. His ability to refurbish an ancient tradition and his claim for truth in poetry, both in a sentimental and moral sense, impressed his followers. Thus one should consider an early fifteenth-century Catalan Ausias Marchism different from the deeper influence he had on Castilian Golden Age poetry.

Lluis Cabré

Bibliography

Archer, R. *The Pervasive Image: The Role of Analogy in the Poetry of Ausiàs March.* Amsterdam, 1985.

March, A. *Poesies.* 5 vols. Ed. P. Bohigas. Barcelona, 1952–59.

MARCH, PERE

Pere March (1336/7–1413) was a Valencian knight and poet who spent most of his life serving Pedro of Aragón, count of Empúries, and the latter's son, Alfonso, the marquis of Villena (and later the duke of Gandía). The influence of March's lineage as well as his merits as a warrior eventually brought him promotion to the post of Alfonso's general deputy (ca. 1370–1412), from which he mainly took benefit when given the lordship of Beniarjó, later inherited by his son, the great poet Ausiàs March. Much of Pere's poetry was written from 1372 on and reflects to a large extent both his responsibilities and Alfonso's interest in moral culture. In *Lo compte final*, after asking ironically for the reward he deserved, Pere reminds his lord of his father's exemplary ruling and ends by quoting a proverb of Cerverí de Girona. Like these precursors, March cast himself in the role of moral adviser and offered yet another poem in *noves rimades* to Alfonso (*L'arnès del cavaller*). This is a long didactic exegesis of the Christ-knight's *similitudo*, sometimes echoing preaching modes. Vices and virtues as well as precepts for ruling are also the subject of five of March's poems in *cobles*, in which he managed to turn moral commonplace into highly convincing verse (*Al punt c'om naix comensa de morir*). Apart from other minor poems, a second, perhaps earlier, aspect of March's work is provided by his *Plazer* and his narrative *Lo mal d'amor*. The former gives a lively outline of a range of activities in courtly life. The latter seems to be just a courtly epistle to advise a certain real lady who suffers from love, though, in fact, the framework and the poet's pretense to be an expert doctor hardly cover an adulterous act of seduction. This aspect, however, did not survive Pere as well as did the moral side, as we can see in his son Ausiàs's poetry.

Lluis Cabré

Bibliography

Pagès, A. *Les "coblas" ou les poésies lyriques provençocatalanes de Jacme, Pere et Arnau March.* Toulouse, 1949.

Romeu i Figueras, J. "Pere March, *Al punt co.m naix comença de morir.*" In *Miscel·lània Pere Bohigas.* Barcelona, 1983. Vol. 3, 85–119.

MARGARIT I PAU, JOAN

Humanist historian and churchman, Margarit was born in Girona in 1422 and died in Rome in 1484. His father's family belonged to the minor nobility of the Ampurdán; his mother's family came from Roussillon, which contributed to his frontier mentality. Destined from an early age for the priesthood, he went to Bologne to study law; in 1443 he got his doctorate. After five years as vicar general to his uncle Bernat de Pau, bishop of Girona, he returned to Italy and served as emissary between Alfonso V and the Vatican during the strife between Naples and Anjou. In 1453 he was nominated bishop of Elna, which he administered mainly as an absentee. From this moment his career as a politician began. On 16 October 1454, as a member of the *cortes* (parliament), he delivered his famous welcome address in Catalan to Juan II of Naverre, who was being sworn in as lieutenant general of Catalonia. Eventually he returned to the Vatican as the royal representative when Juan became king of Aragón in 1458. He delivered a public address on the arrival of the Aragónese embassy on 12 August 1459 at the Congress of Mantua to discuss the crusade against the Turks. There were few positive results for the pope, but Margarit may have met major Italian and Spanish scholars there. He returned to Catalonia to collect the tithes for Pius II's ill-fated plan of crusade and became involved in the preliminaries to the Catalan civil war. Rewarded for his services to the crown with the bishopric of Girona, he found himself defending the inner redoubt of that city, to which Queen Juana and her young son, the future Fernando the Catholic, had fled against the army of the Generalitat. They escaped, but in June 1469 the city eventually capitulated to French forces, allies of the rebel Catalans. Two years later, Margarit declared his support for the crown as Juan was advancing from the south. The king rewarded Margarit by making him chancellor, and the bishop served the king loyally until his death in 1479. Fernando reappointed him chancellor and sent him back to Italy as a roving ambassador to the Italian states, traveling between Ferrara, Venice, Naples, and Rome. During these negotiations he received his cardinal's hat at Sixtus IV's last creation; he died shortly after on 20 November 1484. Margarit was a typical product of cultural relations between Italy and Catalonia during the humanist period; he wrote normally in Latin. *Templum Domini* was a pamphlet on the relations between the church and the state, provoked by events during the civil war. He also dedicated to Fernando an educational treatise, the *Corona Regum*, structured around the names of precious stones. His best-known works are on early history, *De origine regum Hispaniae et Gothorum* and *Paralipomenon Hispaniae libri decem*. The latter was first published by Elio Antonio de Nebrija's son Sancho (Granada, 1545) and represents a significant advance in the treatment of pre-Gothic Iberian Peninsular history through an intelligent use of recently translated Greek texts. The copy of Ptolemy's *Geography* bearing his arms is preserved in the Salamanca University library. His own library was dispersed after his death.

ROBERT B. TATE

Bibliography

Vicens Vives, J. *Juan II de Aragón. Monarquía y revolución en la España del siglo xv*. Barcelona, 1953.

Tate, R. B. *Joan Margarit i Pau, cardenal i bisbe de Girona*. Barcelona, 1976.

MARINEO SÍCULO LUCIO

Humanist, letter-writer, historian, and grammarian, Marineo (Luca de Marinis, Lucius Marineus Sículus; ca. 1444–1533) was born near Catania, Sicily, a subject of the Crown of Aragón. He studied in Rome and Palermo, and taught in Palermo from 1479 to 1484, when Fadrique Enríquez de Cabrera, son of Almirante Alfonso Enríquez, brought him to Spain. Appointed to one of the new chairs of humanities in Salamanca in 1484, overlapping with Pedro Mártir and Elio Antonio de Nebrija, he taught poetry and oratory and attempted to revive the use of Latin. He never met Nebrija, who disliked all immigrant scholars, and eventually moved to the royal household at Toledo where he acted as tutor to young nobles, one of whom was Juan Boscán. To further his career he took holy orders and was given a benefice by Fernando V; upon the king's death he became chaplain to Carlos V. His published collection of letters (Valladolid, 1514) contains 250 of his own and 150 from his friends. It was the first of its kind in Spain and aimed at promoting a high standard of informal epistolography in Latin. These letters may have reached figures of importance, but his closest friends do not seem to have risen above the secretarial level. It is not surprising that he was sensitive about his learning, sycophantic to his superiors, and dismissive of those that did not care for his view of culture. His *De laudibus Hispaniae* (1491) was a characteristic eulogy of Spain and its most famous inhabitants, with particular reference to Salamanca. As a result he received a commission from King Fernando to write a biography of his father Juan II of Aragón at the same time that Gonzalo García de Santa María received his. The patronage of Alfonso de Aragón, archbishop of Zaragoza, and others led to a series of historical works, like *De geneælogia regum* (Zaragoza, 1509) on the kings of Aragón, and an account of the reign of the Catholic Monarchs that was never published separately, but subsumed with other items in his major work, *De rebus Hispaniae memorabilibus opus libris XXII comprehensum* (Alcalá de Henares, 1530), dedicated to Carlos V. The geographical introduction was the most extensive yet for any Iberian Peninsular history, and it branched out into new topics, like the Spanish language of past and present. Marineo is not, on the whole, an impressive figue, but he is typical of the period, the expatriate scholar, living by commissions, and a contributor to the propaganda campaign supporting the achievements of the Catholic Monarchs.

ROBERT B. TATE

Bibliography

Lynn, C. *A College Professor of the Renaissance: Lucius Marineus Sículus among the Spanish Humanists*. Chicago, 1937.

Lawrance, J. N. H. "The Impact of Humanism in the Iberian Peninsula." In *The Impact of Humanism in Western Europe during the Renaissance*. Eds. A. E. Goodman and A. I. MacKay. London, 1990.

MARRANOS *See* CONVERSOS

MARRIAGE AND DIVORCE

Marriage in the Middle Ages was a contract negotiated between two families, an institution rather than a companionship. On the average, women married at sixteen and men at nineteen years of age, though much earlier ages were legally acceptable. Many young people were bound to each other by means of a formal betrothal if they were over the age of seven. The church's sanction was not necessary at the time of the betrothal, thereby revealing the contractual nature of this step. Children could not commit themselves to matrimony without parental approval. Although free to refuse their parents' choice, they had to choose between marrying a mate chosen against their will or living life disinherited. The *Siete Partidas* recognized that a parent might be mistaken or might have delayed marriage beyond reasonable expectations and ruled that children were not deserving of such harsh treatment.

Having chosen a spouse for one's child, the father arranged the exchanges of dowry, or *arras*, which served as a guarantee that the marriage would take place. With this exchange, the bridegroom and his family assigned a part of his belongings or future inheritance to his prospective bride. In some cases, especially in the late Middle Ages, the girl would also bring her marriage portion, or *dote*, to the marriage. These possessions would be administered by the husband, but they would always legally belong to her and would be hers to use as she wished if widowed. Her widow's settlement would also include any future inheritances as well as her share of future gains made by the couple, including movable and immovable goods. The amount given as dowry varied greatly, not just between classes but also depending on where the couple lived. Already in the *Fuero Juzgo*, just the giving of *arras* was well controlled by law: in this code, one-tenth of a man's belongings were to be exchanged. These would revert to the man or his relatives should she not produce children. Customary law dictated that in Castile, one-third of his possessions be granted to her whereas, in León, one-half was given. The legal literature is explicit, requiring different payments depending on the bride's social origins and previous marital status.

Marriage, second only to feudal loyalties, formed the cornerstone of medieval society. Great care, therefore, was dictated in the choice of a spouse. In the case of royal daughters, for example, the *Siete Partidas* emphasized four principal characteristics: lineage, beauty, comportment, and wealth. These were no doubt sought by all fathers of marriageable children. Kings could well afford to list wealth as fourth and last; other fathers probably put higher value on that attribute.

Fathers usually arranged the marriages of their children, but the decision was to be mutually pleasing to both parents. If the father had died, the mother assumed this duty. Brothers or uncles took charge of orphans. In the case of other nobility, the king or other high-ranking nobles often arranged the marriages of the children of their vassals. The church at the time was flexible regarding the marriage ceremony, which was still not solidly established as a sacrament. Clandestine marriages, to which there were no witnesses, were considered valid. As a legal obligation, established practices later were given sacramental connotations. Just as the king was consecrated and the knight initiated in a religious ceremony, so too was marriage sanctified and given spiritual value.

Most impediments to marriage grew out of established local customs. The more obvious impediments concerned the mistaken identity of people, lineage, social class, religion, and—in the case of a supposed virgin bride—previous sexual activity. Weddings performed under duress were not considered valid, nor were marriages to impotent men or to the insane. Incest was strictly forbidden as were marriages in which there existed a kinship closer than the seventh degree and, after the Fourth Lateran Council in 1215, from the fourth degree. This included relatives by marriage, as well as godparents and their chidlren. Age, as an important consideration for procreation, could be cited as an impediment to marriage as were marriages between the infirm. Because the church approved of matrimony strictly for the purpose of procreation, these customs were incorporated into medieval Spanish law.

To love, honor, and maintain his wife were the husband's responsibilities because she reflected his honor and was the mother of his children. By doing so, he could expect in turn to be loved, honored, and cared for by her. The wife's obligations were less self-centered, spanning both peace and wartime. Despite rulings that forbade women and children to intervene in military matters, women were not shielded from warfare. Just as in war, the law emphasized the solidarity of the family. A wife and children could be held responsible for debts incurred or crimes committed by the husband and father; even common-law wives were so bound.

Through marriage, women were given and taken by father and husband. One aim of political marriages was to enlarge boundaries and extend power. They were also used as gifts to reward deserving vassals and formed one way in which a man could improve his status. The reverse was also applicable in that one way to dishonor a rival was to kidnap his wife or daughter. Repudiation was the most favored method by which a woman could be used to shame an enemy.

Women bore many children in order to keep a few. Because of the high rate of infant mortality and the physical burden of repeated childbearing, early marriage was advised. A high rate of fertility has been documented, with an average of two years between births, yet royal couples produced only an average of 3.6 children, nobles 3.5, and other families only 2.3 who survived to adulthood. Motherhood in the Middle Ages did not greatly differ from other times. One way in which a mother did serve her offspring was to ensure their inheritance and to maintain the economic level of the family. Her children's later well-being could depend on her ability and chastity. The family was not necessarily tied to each other by emotions; it was a moral and social entity. It was a woman's duty to assure its survival from generation to generation.

Regulations regarding inheritance came into effect as soon as a couple was wed. According to the *Fuero Juzgo*, the moment a marriage was finalized, the wife could inherit half her husband's belongings. Later law codes insisted that the marriage be consummated before the wife could inherit. Daughters could inherit equally with their brothers. Recognized illegitimate children could also inherit a part of their parent's estates.

Mothers had very little decision-making power over the choice of a legal guardian for their children, should they be orphaned by their father. A woman could appoint a guardian only if she left her child an inheritance. A father's wishes were to be obeyed and only if he died intestate could the mother or grandmother automatically become the child's guardian. Women who were not mothers could not be guardians. Upon remarriage, parents were not obliged to care for the children of a previous marriage. A widower could choose between keeping the children with him or putting them into the care of a guardian chosen from among his late wife's relatives. Widows did not have this choice. A woman wishing to remarry was forced to relinquish her children.

The indissolubility of the conjugal tie was proclaimed by the church and divorce was technically forbidden by the eighth century. Nevertheless, at least among the upper classes, repudiations, annulments, and separations were frequent. It was not unlikely in medieval Spain to find women who had been married and repudiated various times. Annulments could be obtained from the church for the lightest motives: consanguinity of a close or imagined degree, the minutest of physical defects, or a simple illness were given and accepted as excuses. The church accepted cruelty, adultery, and forced marriages as grounds for annulments. Other grounds were when one partner was unwilling to have children or when one partner forced the other into prostitution. Still another was religious conversion.

Wars, crusades, and pilgrimages of the Middle Ages produced many widows. Because proof of death was hard to obtain, care had to be taken to avoid bigamy. The *Fuero Juzgo* ruled that a woman who remarried could be severely punished if it later became known that her first husband was alive. Both she and her new spouse could be sold as serfs. The more liberal *Siete Partidas* absolved women from prosecution, allowing them to claim ignorance. This law code did, however, establish stringent minimum waiting periods of from five to ten years depending on where the husband was said to have died.

Certain segments of medieval Spanish society were exempted from their feudal duties and widows were included in this group. Widows were also granted extra physical and emotional protection. Most widows lived off their marrige settlements and their portion of their husband's estates. If a man died in battle, his widow was to receive compensation, the amount depending on his social class. Nevertheless, a careful reading of epic poetry shows that no mention of these pensions is made when spoils are divided. Given the state of the royal treasury through the Middle Ages in Spain, one wonders how often, if ever, these benefits were paid to deserving widows and orphans. Not a few widows entered convents.

In medieval Spain the physical security of women was assured; they could refuse to marry anyone; their dowries were safeguarded from husbands' abuse; their children's inheritances were guaranteed. As symbols of the weak and custodians of family honor, medieval Spanish women were well protected.

Marjorie Ratcliffe

Bibliography

Alfonso X, *El Libro de las Siete Partidas*. 3 vols. Madrid, 1807.

El Fuero Juzgo. Madrid, 1815.

Kofman de Guarrochena, L. C., and M. K. Carzolio de Rossi. "Acerca de la demografía astur-leonesa y castellana en la Alta Edad Media." *Cuadernos de Historia de España* 47–48(1968), 136–65.

Pastor de Togneri, R. "Historia de las familias en Castilla y en León (siglos X–XIV) y su relación con la formación de los grandes dominios eclesiásticos," *Cuadernos de Historia de España* 43–44 (1967), 88–118.

Roudil, J. (ed.) *El Fuero de Baeza*. The Hague, 1962.

MARTÍ, RAMÓN

The most erudite and accomplished Arabist and Hebraist of his day, missionary to Muslims and fierce polemicist against Jews, Ramón Martí was born at Subirats near Barcelona (ca. 1210/15). He joined the Dominican mendicants at Barcelona's Santa Caterina priory by 1240, and studied at Saint-Jacques College of the University of Paris alongside Thomas Aquinas under Albert the Great (Albertus Magnus). The order sent him in 1250 to help found a missionary school of Arabic at Tunis. In 1264 King Jaime I commissioned him to censor rabbinic texts at Barcelona (but probably he had no role or presence at the Barcelona Disputations of 1263). Martí perhaps worked at the Murcia Arabicum in 1266; in 1268 he was again at Tunis. In 1269 he successfully visited Louis IX of France to urge a North African crusade; while there he probably commissioned Thomas Aquinas, for the order's master general, to write his masterwork the *Contra gentiles*. Martí spent the 1270s and 1280s at Barcelona, where he held the chair of Hebrew in 1281. His contemporary Marsili titled him "Philosophus in arabico," and "beloved intimate" not only of Jaime I and Louis IX but of "the good king of Tunis." Martí's friend Ramon Llull has an anecdote about his nearly converting that Muslim ruler. King Jaime mentions him as a friend in his own autobiography, noting his trip from Tunis to Montpellier. Arnau de Villanova was one of his students.

Martí's prolific writings are a key to the contemporary anti-Talmudism and growing animosity toward Jews. Until 1260 his main focus had been the conversion of Muslims, beginning with his *Explanatio symboli apostolorum* at Tunis in 1257. He is most probably the author of the *Vocabulista in arabico*, an Arabic word list of some 650 printed pages in Celestino Schiaparelli's edition, a missionarys' dictionary of unrivaled importance today for studying the Arabic of eastern Spain. His Islamic phase ended in 1260 with the now lost *Summa* against the Quʿrān. In 1267 came his *Capistrum iudeorum*, which Aquinas seems to have used for his own *Contra gentiles*. Martí's masterwork was *Pugio fidei contra Mauros et iudeos* (*Dagger of Faith*), finished in 1281, filling over a thousand pages in its printed version, of wide influence over the next three centuries. Recent redating of Aquinas's *Contra gentiles* suggests that the hundreds of parallels between these two works show a strong dependence on Martí. With a wealth of rabbinic materials from and in Hebrew, *Pugio* is the most thorough of all the medieval anti-Judaic polemical works. Martí's writings are currently being studied intensively.

ROBERT I. BURNS, S. J.

Bibliography

Cohen, J. *The Friars and the Jews*. Ithaca, N.Y., 1982. Chap. 6.

Robles, L. *Escritores dominicos de la corona de Aragón, siglos XIII–XV*. Salamanca, 1972.

MARTIN OF BRAGA, ST.

Martin (A.D. ca. (520–ca. 579), stands forth as one of the most illustrious figures of the early Middle Ages in the Iberian Peninsula. Born in Pannonia, present-day Hungary, he ventured east to the Holy Land where he lived a monastic life. From the East he sailed westward to Galicia in the northwestern corner of the Iberian Peninsula. Martin is credited by the contemporary chroniclers, notably Gregory of Tours and Isidore of Seville, for the conversion of the Sueves to Catholicism. In Galicia, he founded churches and monasteries and successfully converted the Sueves to Catholicism. An important factor that facilitated his ministry among the Sueves was the friendly relations he maintained with the Suevic rulers. From about 550 to 579, Martin had succeeded in working with four distinct Suevic leaders: Chararic, Ariamir, Theodomir, and Miro. All came under his heavy influence. He played a pivotal role in the Galician Church to extirpate the Arian and Priscillianist heresies, including attempts to suppress paganism. Of the highlights of his ministry were the meeting of two councils at Braga held in 561 and 572. In the First Council of Braga, Martin was one of many signatories gathered; by 572 he had become the metropolitan bishop, which allowed him to preside over the Second Council. At that council Martin promulgated a collection of canons of the eastern councils called the *Capitula Martini*, which is one of the oldest canonical collections of the Iberian Church. The bishops also made the bold claim that unity of faith and orthodoxy had been firmly established in Galicia, thus contributing to the claim that Martin was the "Apostle of the Sueves." His labors in Galicia resulted in the establishment of a permanent church among a people that had displayed a great deal of ambivalence in matters of religion.

Martin of Braga is also well known for his literary works, which are not abundant in number but had remarkable circulation and popularity in the Middle Ages. The most significant is *Formula vitae honestae*, based loosely on a lost work of Seneca, one that emphasized the four cardinal virtues. Of equal importance is *De correctione rusticorum*, a work intended to refute pagan practices, and one that offers us enormous insight into rural popular religion in early medieval Galicia. Other works by Martin of Braga include translations, from Greek into Latin, of *Sayings of the Egyptian Fathers* and *Questions and Answers of the Greek Fathers*, both of which made contributions to monastic life in Galicia.

ALBERTO FERREIRO

Bibliography

Barlow C. W. (ed.) *Martini Episcopi Bracarensis Opera Omnia*. New Haven, Conn., 1950.

Ferreiro, A. "The Missionary Labors of St. Martin of Braga in Sixth-Century Galicia," *Studia Monastica* 23, no. 1 (1981), 11–26.

MARTÍN THE HUMANE, KING OF ARAGÓN

Born in 1356, Martín was the second son of Pedro IV (1336–1387) King of Aragón and Sicily. In 1372 he married María de Luna; they had four children, although only one, Martín the Younger, survived to adulthood. Martín the Humane served his father ably as lieutenant in Valencia between 1378 and 1384 and as leader of expeditions to Sicily to secure the crown's succession there.

In 1395 his brother, King Juan I, died without a male heir. Martín was proclaimed king although the legitimacy of his right to rule was challenged by Juan's widow, Yolanda, who believed herself, erroneously, to be pregnant. Because Martín was on a military campaign in Sicily, María served as regent of the peninsular realms until her husband's return two years later; he was crowned in 1399 at Zaragoza.

On his return from Sicily in 1397, Martín stopped at Avignon to meet with the antipope Benedict XIII, his wife's kinsman. His unfaltering support for Benedict in the face of a rival pope in Rome and the powerful enemies that engendered, intensified the contentious dilemma provoked by the schism of the Western church. Their alliance, however, provided both parties with important benefits. In 1397 Martin's attacks against Berber piracy on the Valencian coast were designated a crusade by Benedict; in return Martín physically saved Benedict in 1403 from a French army that had captured Avignon.

His involvement in papal affairs marks Martín's principal foray into external politics; in fact, most of his reign was concerned with domestic matters that often brought him into conflict with powerful nobles and townspeople. In order to strengthen crown finances he struggled vigorously to recover former royal territories that had been sold off to local lords by his father and brother. His attempts to quell chronic violent factional unrest in Valencia and Aragón infuriated both the local lords and the urban oligarchies, which viewed royal intervention as a threat to traditional liberties and privileges.

Outside the Iberian Peninsula, his Mediterranean possessions remained persistent concerns. He sent troops to Sicily between 1392 and 1398 to suppress partisan opposition to Aragónese rule. Genoa continued to pose a threat to the crown territories in Sardinia and Corsica, but it was local rebellion in Sardinia that was a more intractable problem. In 1409 an exasperated king sent his son to Sardinia at the head of a large army. Although his son Martín won an important battle at Sanduri, he died of malaria a month later, leaving his father with a serious crisis of succession.

Martín's first wife, María de Luna, had died in 1406; his advisers had urged him to remarry but he resisted because he favored Federico, his illegitimate grandson. Even though Federico had been legitimatized by Martín the Younger in order to grant him the lordship of Luna and the Segorbe, in the end, Martín the Humane gave in to his advisers. In 1409 he married Margarita de Prades, daughter of Pedro, the constable of Aragón, but they had no children. As he was gravely ill by this time, Martín's advisers tried in vain to get him to designate an heir.

The question of the succession was not resolved before his death on 31 May 1410; the kingdom remained in disarry for two years while four candidates claimed the throne. The contest was settled by the Compromise of Caspe, which brought a Castilian family, the Trastámaras, to rule the Crown of Aragón.

THERESA EARENFIGHT

Bibliography

Bisson, T. N. *The Medieval Crown of Aragón*. Oxford, 1986.

Ferrer i Mallol, M. T. "L'infant Martí i un projecte d'intervenció en la guerra de Portugal (1381)." In *La Corona de Aragón en el siglo XIV*. VIII Congreso de Historia de la Corona de Aragón, 1967. Valencia, 1973, 205–33.

———. "El patrimoni reial i la recuperació dels senyorius jurisdiccionals en les estats catalano-aragonesos a la fi del segle XIV." *Anuario de Estudios Medievales* 7 (1970–71), 351–491.

MARTÍN THE YOUNGER, KING OF SICILY

The son of the Aragónese king Martín the Humane (1376–1410) and María de Luna, Martín the Younger is noted less for his accomplishments as king of Sicily than for the serious crisis of succession provoked by his death at age thirty-four. At the head of a large army gathered in Sardinia to suppress chronic local unrest, Martín defeated a joint army of Sards, Genoese, and French at Sanduri on 25 July 1409, only to die of malaria one month later. With him died the last hope for a peaceful succession for the family that had since 1137 possessed the extraordinary good fortune of an unbroken string of male heirs to rule the Crown of Aragón. Less than a year later his father died and the kingdom suffered a contentious two-year interregnum that was settled by the Compromise of Caspe in favor of the powerful Castilian family, the Trastámaras.

The only one of the four children of Martín the Humane to survive to adulthood, Martín the Younger was born in 1376–1410. He married María of Sicily in 1390, thus securing Aragónese control of that Mediterranean kingdom. Their one son, Pedro, died in 1400.

Martín was designated heir to the Crown of Aragón in 1398 and began the traditional education of Aragónese princes as his father's lieutenant in various royal realms. Prudent, athletic, and cultivated in the arts and sciences, Martín was also a fine soldier. He was concerned mainly with the governance of the crown's Mediterranean possessions—Sardinia, Corsica, and above all, Sicily. Sardinia, with its combination of external threats from the Genoese that harassed Catalan shipping and internal rebellion against Aragónese rule, proved to be the most vexing problem. The tense situation there necessitated continued military intervention. By contrast, a more peaceful atmosphere prevailed in Sicily after the campaigns of the early 1490s. In fact, Martín the Younger's claim to rule Sicily was not challenged when his wife died in 1401. He remained in charge as his father's heir and viceroy, and on his death he left Sicily to his father.

In 1402 he married Blanche of Navarre; they had one son, Martín, who died in 1407. He had an illegitimate son, Federico, whom he later legitimized to permit him to inherit the counties of Luna and the Segorbe. On the death of Martín the Humane in 1410, Federico was a principal claimant in the four-way succession dispute that he lost in the end to the Trastámara candidate, Fernando of Antequera (r.1412–1416).

THERESA EARENFIGHT

Bibliography

Bisson, T. N. *The Medieval Crown of Aragón*. Oxford, 1886.

Girona i Llagostera, D. *Martí, rey de Sicilia, primogénito Aragó. Barcelona, 1919.*

MARTÍNEZ DE TOLEDO, ALFONSO

Fifteenth-century writer and cleric from Toledo (1398–1460). He held the title of bachiller en decretos (bachelor in decretals) and was probably educated at the University of Salamanca. Martínez de Toledo was archpriest of Talavera de la Reina, prebend of Santa María de Nieva in Segovia, and chaplain of the Capilla de don Sancho, or Reyes Viejos, in Toledo cathedral, where he was responsible for organizing short plays for the celebration of Corpus Christi. He is buried in Toledo cathedral. Martínez de Toledo traveled widely in the Iberian Peninsula during his youth, especially in the Crown of Aragón, and visited Rome. Sometime between 1438 and 1444 he received the title of royal chronicler.

Martínez de Toledo is best known for the book he named after one of his ecclesiastical benefices, *Arcipreste de Talavera* (also called *Corbacho*), composed in 1438, which survives in one manuscript, two incunabula, and several later editions. The latter is a tract directed against misguided love that takes up the tradition of the complaint against women (*demanda de las mugeres*). Derived from diverse sources (principally book 3 of Andreas Capellanus' *De Amore*, the *Secreta secretorum pseudo-Aristotelis*, and Boccaccio's *De casibus virorum illustrium*) it is central to the understanding of the pro- and antifeminist debate in Castile and Aragón during the fifteenth century. Although much of this work derives from bookish sources, Martínez de Toledo's elaboration of them points to contemporary cultural tensions produced by evolving sentimental attitudes at court and society at large. Part sermon, part essay, and part fiction, the tract, which is divided into four parts and composed in both high and low styles, is often punctuated by amusing or shocking illustrative exempla that reveal this author's ability to capture colloquial language and create impressive scenes of imaginative prose.

Martínez de Toledo was also author of the *Atalaya de las crónicas* (begun in 1443), an important digest of medieval Castilian chronicles critical for the understanding of the evolution of historiography in fifteenth-century Castile, and two hagiographies from 1444, the *Vida de Sant Ildefonso*, archbishop of Toledo (657–667) and the *Vida de San Isidoro*, or Saint Isidore of Seville.

E. MICHAEL GERLI

Bibliography

Gerli, E. M. *Alfonso Martínez de Toledo*. Boston, 1976.

Mañero, S. El Arcipreste de Talavera *de Alfonso Martínez de Toledo*. Toledo, 1997.

MARTÍNEZ, FERNANDO (ALSO FERNÁN, FERRANT)

Martínez's, whose only claim to historical fame lies in his responsibility for sparking off the series of massacres of Jews that took place in Spain in 1391. He was archdeacon of Ecija, in the archdiocese of Seville, and hence a canon in the cathedral of Seville. Evidently he started trouble in the middle of the 1370s, preaching rabble-rousing sermons against the Jews, threatening town councils that allowed them to live in their midst, and subsequently ordering the destruction of synagogues. On 25 August 1378, King Enrique II of Castile ordered him to desist from his anti-Jewish campaign, orders that were subsequently repeated by his son and heir, Juan I (1379–1390) in 1383. These royal actions calmed matters for a time, but Martínez soon ignored them, and even began to claim that the king and queen secretly supported any attempt to kill Jews.

Martínez' opportunity came in 1390 when both Juan I of Castile and the archbishop of Seville died, and, the archbishopric, being *sede vacante*, Martínez became its administrator. As a result of the power vacuum and his demagoguery, the massacres began on 6 June 1391 in Seville and quickly spread to the other cities of Andalcía, and then to all the cities of the kingdom of Castile and the Crown of Aragón. Hardly a town escaped.

The size and wealth of the Jewish communities suffered drastically as a result of the massacres, the Jews either forsaking the towns and cities for smaller rural communities or accepting forced conversion. The pogrom of 1391 should have brought an end to the history of the Jews in Spain, but it did not. Thousands survived as New Christians or *conversos*.

ANGUS MACKAY

Bibliography

Wolff, P. "The 1391 Pogrom in Spain: Social Crisis or Not?" *Past and Present* 50 (1971), 4–18.

MARY OF EGYPT, ST.

Fifth-century penitent who has been depicted in literature from the seventh century to the present, and in iconography from the eighth century to the present. The unique Spanish poetic text of her life exists in manuscript III-K-4 of the Biblioteca del Escorial and is of the early thirteenth century; a unique prose version is in manuscript h-I-13 of the Biblioteca del Escorial and dates from the late fourteenth century. Both prose and poetic texts are believed to have been redacted from texts in Old French and Latin. To date there exist five translations of Jacobus de Voragine's life of Mary the Egyptian in Spanish versions of his *Legenda aurea Golden* (*Legend*), which probably derives from the *Speculum Historiale* of Vincent de Beauvais. There is also a fourteenth-century Spanish translation of Paul the Deacon's *Vita Sanctae Mariae Aegyptiacae* (MS. h-III-22 Escorial, and Biblioteca Nacional 780), which is based on the *Golden Legend.* A third prose Latin treatment, represented in a Portuguese translation, *Vida de Sancta María Egipcia*, survives in two manuscripts, Alcobaça CCLXVI and CCLXX.

The original legend derives from numerous Greek sources and may be summarized as follows: The daughter of a wealthy Egyptian family engages in prostitution for personal satisfaction. After seventeen years of sinful behavior she begins her repentence when she is miraculously forbidden entry on Ascension Day to the Church of the Holy Sepulchre and hears a voice directing her to the monastery of Saint John on the banks of the Jordan. For forty-seven years she roams the desert living on seeds, nuts, water, and three loaves of bread. Her hair replaces her decayed clothing, and her physical beauty disappears as her body blackens and shrivels, while the blackness of her soul becomes purified. When she meets Zosimas, a vainglorious ascetic, she causes him to repent of his sin, and he witnesses her miracles of levitation, walking over the Jordan, and finding her deceased body intact in the desert after one year with her identity written in the sand. A tame lion assists him with her burial.

The legend of Saint Mary of Egypt clearly enjoyed great popularity in the Iberian Peninsula. In Granada there was a convent dedicated to her, and iconography depicting her miracles can be found in the Church of San Juan Bautista in that city, as well as in the Museo del Prado.

MICHÈLE S. DE CRUZ-SÁENZ

Bibliography

Cruz-Sáenz, M. S. de. *The Life of Saint Mary of Egypt: An Edition and Study of the Medieval French and Spanish Verse Redactions*. Barcelona, 1979.

Walker, R. M. *Estoria de Santa Maria Egipciaca*, 2d ed. Exeter, 1977.

MASLAMA DE MADRID

Abū-l-Qāsim Maslama ibn Aḥmad al-Majrīṭī, (d. 1007), Andalusian astronomer and mathematician, was born in Majrīṭ (Madrid). He studied in Córdoba and practiced astrology: interested by the Saturn-Jupiter conjunction that took place in 1007, he predicted a series of catastrophes usually associated with the fall of the caliphate and the period of civil wars (*fitna*, 1009–1031). He is the author of the first documented astronomical observation in al-Andalus (the longitude of *Qalb al-Asad*, Regulus, 135° 40′ in 977 or 979). He wrote a set of notes on the only trigonometrical tool used in antiquity, Menelaos' theorem (*al-shakl al-qaṭṭāʿ*), as well as a commentary, with frequent original digressions, on Ptolemy's *Planisphaerium*, which is the first of the studies dedicated by Andalusian astronomers to the astrolabe: its influence is clear in the thirteen-century Latin compilation on the instrument ascribed to Messahalla (Māshā'allāh, fl. Baṣra, 762–809) the echoes of which reach the treatises on the astrolabe written by the collaborators of Alfonso X and by Geoffrey Chaucer (ca. 1340–1400). He is the creator of an important school of mathematicians and astronomers, and two of his disciples (Aḥmad ibn al-Ṣaffār and Abū-l-Qāsim Aṣbag ibn al-Samḥ) collaborated with him in his revision of the *Sindhind zīj* (astronomical handbook with tables) of Al-Khwārizmī (fl. 800–847), a work having an Indian pre-Ptolemaic origin, probably known in Al-Andalus since ca. 850. This revision, extant in a Latin translation by Adelard of Bath (fl. 1116–1142), adapted certain tables to the geographical coordinates of Córdoba, changed the Persian calendar used in the original for the Hijra calendar, introduced Hispanic and, possibly, Ptolemaic materials and added a considerable amount of new astrological tables (about one-fifth of the extant set of numerical tables), which improve considerably the techniques used by Al-Khwārizmī himself. He also introduced Ptolemaic astronomy in al-Andalus: he studied the *Almagest* and wrote astrological additions for the Ptolemaic *zīj* of Al-Battānī (d. 929).

JULIO SAMSÓ

Bibliography

Burnett, C. (ed.) *Adelard of Bath: An English Scientist of the Early Twelfth Century*. London, 1987. 87–118.

Mercier, R. *Astronomical Tables in the Twelfth Century*. London, 1988.

Neugebauer, O. *The Astronomical Tables of Al-Khwārizmī*. Trans. with commentary by H. Suter. Copenhagen, 1962.

Samsó, J. *Las Ciencias de los Antiguos en al-Andalus*. Madrid, 1992. 84–98.

Suter, H. *Die Astonomischen Tafeln des Muḥammed ibn Mūsā al-Khwārizmī in der Bearbeitung des malama ibn Ahmed al-Madjrīṭī und der latein. Uebersetzung des Athelhard von Bath*. Copenhagen, 1914.

Vernet, J., and M. A. Catalá. "Las obras matemáticas de Maslama de Madrid." In *Estudios sobre Historia de la Ciencia Medieval*. Ed. J. Vernet. Barcelona, 1979. 241–71.

MASS *See* MOZARABIC RITE

MATHEMATICS, MUSLIM

Andalusian mathematics did not have the same importance as did astronomy. Very little is known about its origins apart from the existence, in the tenth century, of a practical handbook on land surveying (*taksīr*) by Ibn ʿAbdūn al-Jabalī as well as treatises on commercial arithmetic (*muʿāmalāt*) written by members of the school of Maslama ibn Aḥmad al-Majrīṭī (d. 1007). An idea of their contents can be obtained through the *Liber mahameleth*, a Latin translation ascribed to John of Seville of an Andalusian treatise on the same subject. Arithmetic and geometry were cultivated by Abū-l-Qāsim Aḥmad ibn al-Samḥ (d. 1035) but his works on these subjects seem to be lost. Nothing is known, on the other hand, on the development of algebra in Al-Andalus until the Naṣrid period (1232–1492) toward the end of which flourished Abū-l-Ḥasan ʿAlī ibn Muḥammad al-Basṭī al-Qalaṣādī (ca. 1412–1486 or 1506), who wrote extensively on it as well as on arithmetic, algebra and *parā'iḍ* (the partition of inheritances). Strongly influenced by the Moroccan mathematician Ibn al-Bannā' al-Marrākushī (1256–1321), his originality has been exagerated by modern scholarship. Thus, in spite of the fact that he made interesting improvements to the method of successive approximations of imperfect square roots, the way he dealt with summations of series of squares and cubes and used algebraical symbolism merely followed the lead of many predecessors both in eastern and western Islam.

Geometry and spherical trigonometry had, however, important developments in the eleventh century. Abū ʿAmir Yūsuf ibn Aḥmad al-Mu'taman, king of the *ṭā'ifa* of Zaragoza (1081–1085) wrote an important geometrical treatise called *Al-Istikmāl* (*Perfection*) of which four incomplete manuscripts have been recently discovered. They deal with number theory, plane geometry, the study of the concepts of ratio and proportion (following Books 5 and 6 of Euclid's *Elements*), geometry of the sphere and of other solid bodies and conic sections, and they prove that the royal library in Zaragoza contained the best books—both Greek, in Arabic translation, and Arabic—available at the time for the study of higher mathematics. Al-Mu'taman did not limit himself to a reproduction of his sources but offered often original solutions that prove that he was an excellent geometer. Geometrical research was also developed by Abū Zayd ʿAbd al-Raḥmān ibn Sayyid (fl. Valencia 1063–1096) the master of Ibn Bājja (Avempace, 1070?–1138), who wrote on arithmetical series and conic sections, and by the *qāḍī* of Jaén Abū ʿAbd Allāh Muḥammad ibn Muʿādh al-Jayyānī (d. 1093), whose *Maqāla fī sharḥ al-nisba* (*Commentary on the Concept of Ratio*) seems to be the first known instance of an adequate comprehension of the Euclidean conception of ratio (*Elements* V, def. 5) before the seventeenth century. On the other hand, his *Kitāb majhūlāt qisī al-kura* (*Unknown Arcs of the Sphere*) is the first treatise on spherical trigonometry compiled in western Islam as well as the first known instance in which this mathematical discipline becomes independent from astronomy. It introduces six new trigonometrical theorems discovered in eastern Islam toward the end of the tenth and beginning of the eleventh centuries that allow the solution of spherical triangles in a way that is far more simple than that used in classical antiquity, in which the only known trigonometrical tool was the so-called Menelaos' theorem (*shakl al-qaṭṭā*ʿ in Arabic). He was the first, in the West, to use a method of quadratic interpolation and to compute a tangent table for $r = 1$. It is difficult to establish up to what extent there is some originality in this work but it seems, for example, that his use of a polar triangle is independent from that of his Eastern predecessor Abū Naṣr Manṣūr ibn ʿIrāq (d. e. (–ca. 1036). Ibn Muʿādh's book was not translated into Latin and its influence in medieval Europe was exerted indirectly, through the *Iṣlāḥ al-Majisṭī* written by Abū Muḥammad Jābir ibn Aflaḥ toward the middle of the twelfth century, a work translated both into Latin and into Hebrew, in which four of Ibn Muʿādh's trigonometrical theorems appear.

JULIO SAMSÓ

Bibliography

Djebbar, A. "Las matemáticas en al-Andalus a través de las actividades de tres sabios del siglo XI." In *El legado científico andalusí*. Eds. J. Vernet and J. Samsó. Madrid, 1992. 23–35.

Plooij, E. B. *Euclid's Conception of Ratio and His Definition of Proportional Magnitudes as Criticized by Arabian Commentators*. Rotterdam, 1950.

Saidan, A. S. al-Qalaṣādī. *Dictionary of Scientific Biography*. Vol. 11. New York, 1975. 229–30.

Samsó J. *Las Ciencias de los Antiguos en al-Andalus*. Madrid, 1992. 81–83, 132–144, 402–9. English summary: Samso, J. "The Exact Sciences in al-Andalus," In *The Legacy of Muslim Spain*. Ed. S. K. Jayyusi. Leiden, 1992. 952–57.

Sesiano, J. "*Le Liber mahameleth*, un traité mathématique latin composé au XIIᵉ siècle en Espagne." In *Actes du Premier Colloque International d'Alger sur l'Histoire des Mathématiques Arabes*." Alger, 1988. 69–98.

Villuendas, M. V. *La trigonometría europea en el siglo XI. Estudio de la obra de Ibn Muʿād. El Kitāb maŷhūlāt*. Barcelona, 1979

MAURICIO, BISHOP OF BURGOS

Mauricio's origins have been a topic of discussion among those researchers who believe that he was born in Medina de Pomar (Burgos) at the end of the twelfth century, but to an English or Gascon family stationed in Castile. He appears to have studied law in Paris, and in 1209 he was the archdeacon of Toledo, where he displayed his juridical instincts, intervening as ecclesiastical judge in several matters of the archbishopric of Toledo and the bishopric of Burgos because of his reputation as a jurist before the Holy See. In August of 1213, he was elected the bishop of Burgos, backed by the archbishop of Toledo, Rodrigo Jiménez de Rada. He was consecrated in 1215, and in September of the same year traveled to Rome to attend the Fourth Lateran Council, whose regulations he tried to put into practice in Burgos. His good relationships with royalty, especially with Doña Berenguela, led him to participate actively in national politics. He helped put Fernando III on the throne, and in 1219, under the guidance of the queen, traveled to Germany to meet Beatriz de Swabia, Fernando's future wife, and accompany her back to Castile: Mauricio performed their marriage on 30 November 1219 in the Romanesque cathedral, having knighted the king earlier in the monastery de Las Huelgas.

Mauricio filled an important spiritual role in the diocese. He promoted its statutes in an effort to reform his chapter, establishing the so-called *Concordia mauriciana*. He attended the Valladolid Councils in 1228 and the Tarazona Council in 1229. During his term as bishop he authorized the foundation of several different religious orders: the Franciscans in 1214, the Trinitarians in 1221, and the Dominicans in 1227, as well as the orders of Saint Clare and of Calatrava. He also approved the establishment of the Cistercian nuns in Vileña and in Villamayor de los Montes. Mauricio died on 12 October 1238 and was buried in the presbytery of the same Gothic cathedral for which he and the monarchy had earlier laid the first stone on 20 July 1221.

Mauricio dedicated himself passionately to gathering sufficient resources to build the magnificent cathedral. In 1230 worship services were first held in the new building, which was definitively consecrated in 1260. Its stylistic elements, both architectural and sculptural, reveal its dependence on French Gothic art, and several artists from France worked on the cathedral. The bishop left an extraordinary mark on all of the arts, including funerary monuments: the recumbent statue portraying the bishop is considered by specialists to be an exceptional work in terms of the material and techniques applied. It is made of wood coated with gold-plated copper and decorated with *champlevée* enamel, a technique frequently employed in the Limoges workshops. This has led specialists to conclude that this interesting work of the mid-thirteenth century was a French product.

MARÍA JESÚS GÓMEZ BÁRCENA

Bibliography

Serrano, L. *Don Mauricio. Obispo de Burgos y fundador de su catedral.* Madrid, 1922.

MAYORAZGO (PRIMOGENITURE/INHERITANCE)

In Castile and León, more so than in other medieval kingdoms, laws protected the hereditary transferral of property within the family, and permitted a sole heir to inherit a large part of the estate, thereby favoring aristocratic practices that tended to keep most of the wealth together instead of splitting it up. The *Liber iudiciorum* (ca. 654) combined the freedom of the testator with the concept of the obligatory heir (*herederos forzosos*). Four-fifths of the estate (*reserva*) was set apart for these compulsory beneficiaries, who were primarily legitimate children of the testator, though in some cases they were more distant relatives, sometimes up to the seventh degree. Only the other fifth of the estate (*quinto*) was allowed to be freely distributed by the testator. The reserva could be divided equally among all of the obligatory heirs; alternatively, a third of the reserva (*mejora del tercio*) could instead be set apart for one specific heir, with the rest distributed equally among remaining heirs. Despite negative reactions, these regulations were ratified in medieval Castilian law and included in the *Fuero Juzgo*, *Fuero Real*, *Leyes del Estilo*, and *Leyes de Toro*.

Added to this system, which was the most common, was the establishment of primogeniture (*mayorazgo*), which was the transferral of a mass of wealth following habitual lines of succession and favoring one sole heir. The first examples date from the latter part of the twelfth century, but the practice didn't become common among the high nobility until 1369, when royal gifts of seigneurial lands and property increased and when the monarchy permitted inheritance through illegitimate children when there were no legitimate heirs. To establish or increase a mayorazgo required royal authorization, as did the severance or disassociation of the wealth entailed in primogeniture. However, the *Leyes de Toro* (1505) allowed the formation of *mayorazgos cortos*, dictating the bestowal of the mejora de tercio or the quinto, without previous authorization. The lower nobility, as well as those of non-noble rank, established many of these smaller mayorazgos beginning in the sixteenth century.

The mayorazgo was formulated through public documents that detailed the property linked to the inheritance. Even if it did not bestow any property, this system complied with the principle of primogeniture and of succession to the throne described in the *Siate Partidas*, and included the so-called *derecho de representación* (right to representation).

In summary, mayorazgo and the stable transmission of estate and of aristocratic power in the noble family were inseparable realities: the system of primogeniture consolidated and stabilized the nobiliary structure of Castilian society between the fourteenth and eighteenth centuries.

Miguel Ángel Ladero Quesasa

Bibliography

Clavero Salvador, B *Mayorazgo. Propiedad fuedal en Castilla, 1369–1836.* Madrid, 1974.

Gerbet, M. C. *La noblesse dans le royaume de Castille. Étude sur ses structures sociales en Estremadure de 1454 à 1516.* Paris, 1979.

MEDICAL TREATISES

During the Visigothic period (sixth century) St. Isidore of Seville dedicated the whole of book 4 of his *Etymologies* to medicine.

Apart from St. Isidore, the most important treatises may be divided into four groups: those written in Arabic by Spanish doctors; translations from Arabic into Latin; translations from Latin and Arabic into Castilian; and finally, works composed in Latin or Castilian by Spanish authors.

Group 1 includes: *The Book of Generations of Doctors* by Ibn Juljul of Córdoba, (tenth century), which discusses Dioscorides, *Materia medica* and tells how to identify and locate the simples described there. The *Kitāb al-Tasrif* or *Book of Surgery* by Abūal-Qāsim Khalaf al-Zahrāwi, known as Albucasis (ninth century), was still being printed in Latin in the sixteenth-century. The *Kitāb al-kulliyāt fi-l-tibb* by the Córdoan Abūal-Walīd Muḥammad ibn Aḥmad ibn Rushd or Averroës (1126–1198), was translated into Latin as *Colliget*. The *Amal mān tābba li-man habbā* or *Treatise on General and Special Pathology* by Muḥammad ibn ʿAbd Allāh ibn al-Khatīb (1313–1374) from Granada.

Group 2 includes translations into Latin by Gerard of Cremona of the *Kitāb al-hawi fi-l-tībb*, known as *Continens*, by the Persian Abū Bakr Muḥammad ibn Zakarīyā al-Rāzī, known as Rhazes (865–925), an extensive work that includes all Greek and Eastern medicine, plus the latest developments. A more compact and hence more widely used work is the *Kitāb al-Manṣūri fi-l-tībb* or *Liber Medicinae ad almansorem*, studied and imitated for centuries by Western doctors.

Special mention must be made of *Qanun fi-l-tībb* by Abū ʿAlī al-Husayn ibn Sīnā, known as Avicenna (980–1037), known in Latin as his *Canon*. The work covers the entire field of medicine as then known in five books. A shorter version of this work was widely known in the West as the *Canticas*, being a summary in verse of the pathology contained in the *Canon*. The aim of this work was to impart the most essential knowledge, and the verse was meant as a memory aid.

Group 3 includes translations into Castilian of Latin works by medical professors from northern Italian and French universities. The *Lilium medicinae* or *Lilio de medicina* (1305) by Bernard of Gordon is a general pathology that follows closely Arabized Galenism, but one colored by the personal experiences of the author. The *Compendio de la salud humana* by John of Ketham is a schematic but poorly systematized summary in six chapters of the commonest pathology of the period.

Kitāb al-hummayāt or *Treatise on Fevers* by Isaac ben Solomon Israelī, translated into Latin by Constantine the African, from Latin into Hebrew in the twelfth century and into Castilian in the fifteenth, is a monograph on the diagnosis and treatment of fevers, based in the traditional authorities. Three books on surgery exist by Theodoric of Lucca (1206–1298), Guy Lanfranchi of Milan (d. 1305), and Guy de Chauliac, originally from Bologna (ca.1300–1368). All three were internationally famous university professors and their works were translated into several European languages.

Group 4 has original works including an anonymous treatise on pathology in an acephalous and defective manuscript of the late fourteenth century. It is not very original since it follows very closely an Arabic manual, to the point that many technical terms are mere transliterations of the Arabic. *El menor daño de la medicina* by Alonso de Chirino (1428) contains two basic treatises, one on hygiene and one on pathology, that are more concerned with prevention than cures. The *Tratado de apostemas* by Diego del Covo contains a part of his lost *Cirurgía rimada*, composed in 1412. The surviving fragment was copied in 1493. *Sevillana medicina* by Jean de Avignon, composed in the early years of the fifteenth century, survives in an edition by Monardes of the year 1545. It is one of the first European medical topographies, but from the indications in the prologue, the edition appears to be incomplete. The *Sumario de la medicina con un tratado sobre las pestíferas bubas* (1498) was written in verse by Francisco López de Villalobos, then a student in Salamanca, following Avicenna's *Cantica* very closely. The rhymes were meant to help the reader memorize, and while the aim was divulgation, it retains technical medical terminology and Arabisms. The *Suma de de la flor de cirugía* by Alonso de Córdoba survives only in a very incomplete and corrupt copy.

María Teresa Herrera

Bibliography

Beaujouan, G. *Manuscrits scientifiques médiévaux de l'Université de Salamanque et de ses "colegios mayores."* Bordeaux, 1962.

———. *Médecine humaine et vétérinaire á la fin du Moyen Āge*. Genéve, Paris, 1966.

García Ballester, L. et al. *Medical Licensing and Learning in Fourteenth-century* Valencia. Philadelphia, 1989.

McVaugh, M. R. *Medicine before the Plague: Practitioners and Their Patients in the Crown of Aragón, 1285–1345.* New York, 1993.

MEDICINE

Roman domination of the Iberian Peninsula and the Romanized Christianity that later flourished there led to the widespread practice of medical doctrines inherited from Greece by the empire. The outstanding Greek authority was Galen of Pergamum (ca.130–ca.200), who strove to systematize Hypocratic medical teaching and theory to link them with practical medicine, thus becoming the creator of rational scientific approaches through the study of animal anatomy and experimental vivisection. His basic concept of man as the creation of a Supreme Being, the body being merely the vessel of the soul, won ecclesiastical approval and resulted in the universal acceptance of Galenic medicine in the West until the seventeenth century. Galen took up residence in Rome when he was thirty-three and began to practice, treating the ailments of emperors and aristocrats, but also teaching medicine and writing manuals that covered all aspects of the science: anatomy, pathology, hygiene, pharmacology, and so on. Galenic medicine, as part of Greek science transmitted to the Latins, was based on a rational knowledge of the human body, of diseases, and of methods of treatment, reached the Iberian Peninsula, but did not supplant popular empirical or magical medicine, which had a fundamentally different view of illness. If the harm to an organism was due to external causes such as wounds, bites, fractures, and so forth, time-proven remedies were applied. On the other hand, if the cause was some moral transgression that provoked divine punishment, then the gods had to be appeased with religious or magic rites and formulas capable of restoring the broken bond.

From the fifth century onward, barbarian invasions fragmented the western Roman Empire, impeding communications between the various imperial provinces, whose isolation led to cultural decline. The resultant economic collapse and general insecurity produced a flight from the cities to the countryside, which was under stress from the large numbers seeking refuge there. The outcome was a severe decline in those cultural contacts that had been natural to city life. Medicine continued to be practiced, but there was a lack of development and advances, and a reliance solely on what had survived of the Graeco-Roman science transmitted by personal instruction, usually through direct experience in medical practice from those who continued the profession.

In general terms, culture took refuge in the episcopal schools, and only the aristocracy and the clergy could take advantage of it. Hence we find the lay doctor alongside the priest doctor from the secular clergy or, with the rise of the monasteries, among the monks. The most outstanding figure of the period is St. Isidore of Seville (560?–636). Book 7 of his *Etymologiae* deals with the scientific medical terminology most commonly in use in his time. Chapter 13 explains that medicine cannot be included among the other liberal arts because they deal with individual areas of study under the general heading of philosophy, whereas medicine too must cover them all. For this reason, he states that it must be considered a "second philosophy," since it claims for itself the entire man, and "if the first heals the soul, then this second philosophy cures the body." St. Isidore's encyclopedia was known and used far beyond the confines of the Visigothic kingdom in Spain, influencing European culture generally. In the court of Charlemagne (742–814), the erudite philosopher Alcuin knew and admired this Spanish author, but Charlemagne's general prohibition of the use of superstitious practices, favoring a more technical approach to medicine, itself indicates that in spite of his prohibition, magical arts continued to hold sway in his kingdom, not only in the Spanish Marches, but well beyond them.

The Arab invasion of 711 and their conquest of Iberia produced a radical change in science in general and medicine in particular. The recovery of many of the lost Greek medical manuals came about as a result of Arabic translations, refined and expanded in the Muslim East, that reached the peninsula after the establishment of the caliphate of Córdoba. However, the first century of the Arab conquest is culturally quite poor, owing to the massive time and effort needed to establish the understructures for security and political government. Hence Visigothic culture survived and continued, and St. Isidore remained the supreme authority.

During the tenth century a cultural awakening is perceptible. In various regions groups of scholars undertook translations from Arabic into Latin of the most important scientific works that had come from the East. The monastery of Ripoll in Catalonia is one of these centers, where the translation of medical texts in summary or abstracts strove to disseminate this knowledge, without showing any concern for the original authorship or the name of the translator in almost all cases. This activity, combined with the large numbers of Mozarabs who fled from Muslim domination to find refuge there, made Ripoll an extremely important cultural center.

In the eleventh century, as political factors brought about a cultural decline in the Middle East, Arab culture flourished in the conquered territories of the West that were now independent. In Spain, the sovereign caliphate favored this cultural growth. Ibn Wāfīd (1007–1074) wrote *On Simple Medicines* and *The Bedside Book* in Toledo, his treatises *On Agriculture* and *On Bath Treatments* were translated into Latin. In the early years of the twelfth century Ibn Rushd (Averroës; 1126–1198) composed in Córdoba his medical encyclopedia *Coliget*. In the middle of the twelfth century Archbishop Raymond de Sauvetot (1125–1151) formed a school of translators in Toledo who made available in Latin numerous Arabic treatises on a wide variety of subjects. Among the most outstanding translators was Gerard of Cremona (1114–1187), who practically headed a team of Arabs, Jews, and Spaniards that was to put the latest medical science of the Arab world within the reach of Western scholars. Among the most important authors translated into Latin was Ḥunayn ibn Isḥāq al-Ibādī (809–873), known in the West as Johannitius, who during his lifetime had translated from Greek into Arabic 129 treatises by Galen, as well as the *Alexandrian Summaries*, while his own compilation *Kitābal-mudjal* or *Isagoge ad tegni Galeni* is a faithful reflection of Galenic medicine that does not lose sight of the contributions of the Alexandrian school. His work, while not original, was concise and orderly. It became widely known in medieval universities, thus renewing and invigorating European knowledge of Galen. Editions of Johannitius's works were in print constantly from the fifteenth to the seventeenth centuries.

Also of extraordinary importance for medieval medicine were the translations of works by Abū Bakr Muḥammad ibn Zakarīyā al-Rāzī (865–925), known as Rhazes. His *Continens* is an treatise that incorporates into an organic whole Greek and Indian medicine, and the new Arab discoveries. A shorter work was his ten-volume *Kitāb al-Manṣūri fi-l-tībb*, known as the *Liber medicinae ad almansorem*, equally divided between theory and practice. Being less extensive than *Continens*, and hence more manageable, it became indispensable for medical practitioners. Equally important for its effects on later development was the *Canon* by Avicenna (980–1037), which gives complete coverage of the medical science of the age; it was translated several times into Latin and in use in numerous editions for centuries. We know that even in the seventeenth century it was still a required text for medical students at the University of Salamanca.

As for surgery, mention must be made of the translation done by Gerard of Cremona of the *Book of Surgery* by the Córdoan Abual-Qāsim Khālaf al-Zahrāwi (ninth century), known as Abulcasis, in which we have the first known descriptions of hemophilia and leprosy. Abulcasis not only covered in detail previous surgical knowledge, but also introduced several advances and new methods, such as sutures and cauteries. Thanks to the Latin translation, this work could be studied by the top surgeons of the fourteenth and fifteenth centuries, who, using this firm basis, vigorously developed the new science.

During the following centuries radical changes came about in the structure of society that gradually left behind the feudal world and opened out into a more burgeois social system in the cities and towns, offering greater freedom and requiring different modes of social behavior. Concommitant changes in medical practice were soon felt. Ecclesiatical medicine gradually disappeared (except in rural areas, where the monasteries continued to function as clinics until the nineteenth century) and medicine was quite definitely separated from the church, becoming progressively more rationalized and demanding its proper place, like any other human endeavor. In this new social order, the transmission of knowledge also underwent important changes. The cathedral schools were replaced by or developed into the new *studium generale* or university, but as these studies began to set themselves within the framework of the universities, medicine tended to be left behind, and we know that it was only through the agency of Alfonso X the Wise (1252–1284) that the *studium generale* of Castile created chairs of medicine. This coincides with attempts to regulate the practice of medicine. Medical professionals would have to complete special studies and obtain an official license to practice. We know that, following Eastern custom, Muslim Spain did not have such a general system until the thirteenth century, which was gradually consolidated in the fourteenth. For a very long period doctors with a degree coexisted with those who simply practiced medicine after having learned it by working with an experienced physician.

The new medical studies in the universities went no further than teaching the Arabized Galenism contained in the Latin translations of Arab authorities, to which Scholastic methods were applied to a greater or lesser degree, as the all-embracing source of all knowledge: philosophy. Medical education was based on a theoretical view, based solidly on the authorities, without any experimental approach that might have led to systematic constructive criticism, and hence effective advances. However, the authorities as a basic foundation did not prevent practical nonacademic criticism that gradually modified criteria as a result of daily contact with patients whose individual clinical record in terms of climate and social and physical factors differed from what the books indicated and made the doctor depart from the authorities and change his approach, leading to different and new treatments.

As it had for centuries, Latin continued to be the language used in this science and also in the new medical education programs, although Castilian in the Alfonsine schools has already managed to achieve the level of a scientific language quite capable of expressing Graeco-Roman knowledge as transmitted in Arabic. However, although Alfonso the Wise ordered that the scientific writings created by his school be written in the vernacular, no purely medical works were produced, although several medical topics appear in others.

Medical treatises written in Castilian in the fourteenth and fifteenth centuries may be divided into two quite distinct groups. There are a large number of translations of the most important Western medical books written by doctors, usually university professors who, for teaching purposes, composed manuals, summaries, and monographs that are little more than compilations of existing knowledge, to which they added those advances acquired through their medical practice. On the other hand, we have works or fragments of works in Castilian, often anonymous through the loss of initial folios or because the copy derives from such a fragment. These are sometimes partial translations from Latin or Arabic, summaries compiled as a handbook for personal reference. These two groups have distinct characteristics. The first shows us the state of the art in the late Middle Ages as an outcome of the systematization of the *materia medica*. The second group introduces us to a more popular type of medicine, quite alien to Latin and often not deriving from theoretical studies. The texts preserved are not treatises but compendia or monographs whose aim is to teach in the shortest possible time all that the professional would need to know. However, in both groups the contents derive from Arabic sources, to differing degrees reworked, adapted, and modified by practical knowledge acquired in general practice.

During this period we have Castilian translations of important and extensive medical works in Latin, as well as compendia and monographs written in the general area of northern Italian and southern French universities. One such work is *Lilium medicinae* or *Lily of Medicine*, 1305 by Bernard of Gordon. Three treatises on surgery were also translated, those by Theodoric of Lucca (1206–1298), Guy Lanfranchi of

Milan (d. 1305) and Guy de Chauliac from Bologna (1300–1368). All three were designed to aid in the study of medicine in their respective universities, but their fame and prestige carried them far and wide and they were quickly translated into many languages. The surgery inherited from the ancients as transmitted by the works of Abulcasis did not cease to advance, thanks in great part to the dissection of cadavers, which increased anatomical knowledge considerably, and also to the fine education and great ingenuity of these three great surgeons.

Within the second group, works written in Castilian, we have compendia and monographs, always with didactic aims in mind, or as in the case of *El menor daño de la medicina* or Lesser Harm of Medicine (1428) by Alonso de Chirino, a warning to healers or those who might suffer the consequences of treatment by poorly trained doctors. In this group we have only one extensive work, a treatise on pathology in an anonymous manuscript, whose beginning is lost, that is also defective and mutilated. Its formal structure and content are not original. It must have been put together following very closely some Arabic treatise, since its terminology often derives from a mere transliteration of the Arabic terms.

Medical theory and practice in the Middle Ages were, in general terms, the continuation of Arabized Galenism, transmitted in Arabic versions and commentaries, translated into Latin, reworked and adapted to the methodology of Scholasticism. However, direct contact with reality and with patients gradually altered medical practice, which bit by bit changed theory as a result of experimental proof of hypotheses, modifying practice (albeit slowly), rationalizing it, and making it more technical, marking a slow but steady progress in this incipient new science. There always existed alongside, however, a more or less magico-religious medicine that at times affects the more rational arts of healing.

To sum up, the content of this new science is as follows: In anatomy it distinguished two main constituents of the human body, the extremities and the main cavities, cephalic, thoracic, and abdominal. These cavities are occupied by the organs, which are nurtured by the veins, a term that also includes what we now know as nerves, tendons, and so on—in general the vessels through which the humors and spirits that sustain the organism circulate. Physiology is governed by four humors: blood, phlegm, bile, and melancholy (black bile), the predominance of any of which gives rise to four human biological types: sanguine, phlegmatic, choleric, and melancholic. The balance among these humors favors health and well-being. The movers that drive life are the spirits that set in motion the powers needed to maintain the vital functions. The body is healthy if the humors are in balance, that is, if they are mixed in due proportion and circulate freely through the vessels. Good health is lost if this balance is altered or the circulation of the humors is hampered by obstruction of the vessels or excessive density or fluidity of the liquids and gasses necessary for life. The causes of the anomalies may be internal, such as an excess or lack of some humor that upsets the conditions for the sound functioning of the organism, or external, such as disorders caused by poisons, wounds, or a bad lifestyle. Health is reestablished by restoring the humoral or organic balance, if the cause is internal; if it is external, by correcting the agencies that cause harm, for example by purifying corrupted air in plagues or using surgical methods for wounds, factures, or abscesses. To this end, medicaments are applied, either simple or compound. Any substance capable of modifying the functions of the organism can constitute a remedy—that is, a means of healing. The vegetable, animal, and mineral worlds, above all the first, are the basis for the pharmaceuticals used directly as simple medicaments or combined with other elements to form the composites.

The philosophy underlying all healing relied on the use of opposites. If the cause of the illness is cold, then remedies of a warm type are applied, and vice versa. The degree of effectiveness of each pharmaceutical also needs to be known—whence came the development achieved by pharmacology. The general manuals in Arabic devoted a great deal of space to the discussion of medicines, and they were followed by the doctors. Galen had already indicated the possibility of determining the degrees in the qualities of medicines, that is, warm, cold, dry, and humid, and basing themselves on this, Arab and Western doctors developed a scale of degrees in all natural elements of which medicines are composed, and thus devised a suitable therapy in each case. The starting point for this pharmalogical system was the *Materia medica* of Dioscorides (first century), which the Arabs modified and expanded with a large number of new simples and composites, many of which were widely used in the Middle Ages and even in later centuries. Dioscorides' work was still used in the sixteenth century when Laguna translated it into Castilian, adding learned commentaries, thanks to which we can know the previous fundamentals of pharmacology and the continued use of the old medicaments in later centuries. The evolution of medicine was to rely on a praxis that would gradually modify the old conception, interpreting and rationalizing the new discoveries, but still, in the sixteenth century and the beginning of the seventeenth, we see theories and fundamental concepts completely rooted in medieval ideas.

Veterinary Medicine

The Greeks tell us that the origin of veterinary medicine is to be found in the centaur Chiron. Virgil mentions him, and St. Isidore, in book 9 of his *Etymologiae* stated, "Animal medicine was created by a Greek named Chiron, who is portrayed as half man and half horse." However, in the Iberian Peninsula veterinary medicine originated with shepherds tending their flocks, who followed a lore acquired from direct experience and family traditions, but we have no systemized doctrine for this knowledge. Generally, animal pathology followed human pathology, growing out of the shepherds' folk medicine into the clinical veterinary. The care of stock, and above all horses as a necessary factor in warfare and the rise of knighthood as a social class in the Middle Ages, led to a special concern for its welfare and to great advances in the knowledge of its anatomy, hygiene, and pathology. Several surviving manuscripts reveal this interest, among them an anonymous thirteenth-century *Book of the Horse* and *Book of Hunting*, or the treatise composed by Theodoric of Lucca on equine pathology. Falconry produced similar results in avian medicine. This new science, however, may be viewed as really beginning its true development with the creation at the close of the fourteenth century of the Royal Tribunal for Animal Medicine, charged with the examination and certification of future veterinaries.

MARÍA TERESA HERRERA

Bibliography

Beaujouan, G. "Visión sinóptica de la ciencia medieval en Occidente." In *Historia universal de la medicina*. 7 vols. Ed. P. Laín Entralgo. Barcelona, 1972–75.

Crombie, A. C. *Historia de la ciencia*. Trans. J. Bernia. 2 vols. Madrid, 1987.

García Ballester, L. *Los moriscos y la medicina*. Barcelona, 1984.

García Guillén, D., and J. L. Peset. "La medicina en la Baja Edad Media latina." In *Historia universal de la Medicina*. 7 vols. Ed. P. Laín Entralgo. Barcelona, 1972–75.

Isidore of Seville. *Etimologías*. Bilingual ed. by J. Oroz Reta and M. Marcos Casquero. 2 vols. Madrid, 1982.

Laín Entralgo, P. *Historia universal de la medicína* 3d ed. Barcelona, 1979.

——— "La sciencie dans l'Occidente médieval chrétien." In *Histoire général des sciences*. 4 vols. Paris, 1957–64.

Sanz Egana, C. *Historia de la veterinaria española*. Madrid, 1941.

Schipperges, H. "La medicina árabe y la medicina en la Edad Media latina." In *Historia universal de la medicina*. Ed. P. Laín Entralgo. 7 vols. Barcelona, 1972–75.

MEDINA SIDONIA, HOUSE OF

In the late thirteenth century, under Sancho IV and Fernando IV, Alfonso Pérez de Guzmán the Good married María Alonso Coronel in Seville, and thus acquired significant property in the area to begin his family's progression toward Castilian upper nobility. Between 1282 and 1303, Alfonso gained control of lands that appeared to be of little importance at the time, but were to form the basis of a huge territorial empire in southwestern Spain. As with so many other grandee noble houses in the later Middle Ages, the big opportunity for Guzmán came with the Trastámaran victory in the Castilian civil war of 1366–1369. Juan Alfonso de Guzmán fought for the victorious Enrique II, and was awarded not only the hand of the new king's niece, Juana de Castilla, but also the extremely valuable county of Niebla. Juan and his successors steadily accumulated lordships and other properties in western Andalusia until, in 1445, a later count, Juan Alfonso, was granted the duchy of Medina Sidonia. Both the new duke and his tardily legitimized heir Enrique took full advantage of the political difficulties of Juan II and Enrique IV. Not only did they succeed in greatly expanding their seigneurial possessions, mainly in the modern provinces of Huelva, Seville, and Cádiz, but they also intervened increasingly in the government of the growing port of Seville itself. This was despite the fact that the city's council was supposedly directly subject to the crown.

The influence and wealth thus gained by Duke Juan Alfonso was greatly added to by his son, in the last years of Enrique IV's reign, between 1468 and 1474. In this period, Duke Enrique gained virtually complete control of Seville, in the process driving out the rival Ponce de León family, lords of Arcos and Marchena, and their supporters. The height of the political power of the house of Medina was in the 1470s, when Duke Enrique was chief magistrate (*alcalde mayor*) of Seville and also held various other significant and lucrative offices. Although Fernando and Isabel came to the region in 1477–1478 to curb the power of magnates such as these, their success was limited. Duke Enrique was suspended from his Seville magistracy, but the Granada war assisted his rehabilitation, and in 1488, Isabel made him marquis of Gibraltar. Only in 1502 did she succeed in regaining this jurisdiction, but even so, when the Guzmán entail (*mayorazgo*) was put together in 1503, it was still possible to travel across western Andalusia without ever leaving Medina Sidonia land. The ducal accounts of 1509 indicate the vast range of the family's interests, equivalent to those of a holding company of the present day. In that year, apart from the rents and dues from their numerous urban houses and rural estates, they also gained income from taxes and duties on trade through their various seaports, and from the proceeds of fisheries, salt pans, butcheries, tanneries, banks, and brothels, as well as royal taxation revenue of various kinds that had been diverted legally into the ducal coffers. It was not surprising that Charles V declared the dukes of Medina Sidonia grandees of Spain.

JOHN EDWARDS

Bibliography

Ladero Quesada, M. A. *Andalucía en el siglo XV: Estudios de historia política*. Madrid, 1973.

Solano Ruiz, E. "La hacienda de las casas de Medina Sidonia y Arcos en la Andalucía del siglo XV," *Archivo Hispalense* 168 (1972), 85–176.

MEDINACELI, HOUSE OF

The De la Cerda family, counts of Medinaceli and marquises of Cogolludo (Guadalajara) were descended from an illegitimate branch of the house of Béarn, in the Pyrenees. Bernard de Foix, known as the Bastard of Béarn, married into the De la Cerda branch of the family of Alfonso X. They became naturalized Castilians in the early fourteenth century, with seignorial jurisdiction over Medinaceli (Soria) and Arcos, near the Aragónese border. Their rise predated the development of a new upper nobility in the late fourteenth and early fifteenth centuries, as the victorious Trastámaran kings granted increased resources to their noble supporters in the Castilian civil war of 1366–1369. Thus it was not until the reigns of Ferdando and Isabel that the De la Cerda made further advances, but by then Fernando del Pulgar, in his *Libro de los claros varones de Castilla*, had left a vivid description of Count Gastón de la Cerda, whom he portrays as having been loyal to Enrique IV, in contrast to his father Count Luis, though he was also said to have been "ome vencido del amor de las mugeres, e él fue amado dellas!" (a man conquered by the love of women, and beloved by them)

Whatever the truth of this, it is undeniable that the De la Cerda family gained greatly from having supported Isabel and Fernando in their conflict with Juana la Beltraneja and Afonso V of Portugal. In 1476, they received from the crown a massive grant of 406,000 *maravedís* a year, while in 1479, the county of Medinaceli was upgraded to a duchy. Thus they became part of the elite nobility of the Catholic kings, and grandees under Carlos V. More significantly in some respects, the De la Cerda family also received in 1479 the county of Puerto de Santa María. This was a small seaport south of Cádiz that had scarcely been developed at the time. In the climate of economic optimism that had been created in Spain and Portugal by growing trade and discoveries in the Atlantic and Africa, El Gran Puerto might have become a major center to rival not only Cádiz and the duke of Medina Sidonia's port of San Lúcar de Barrameda, but even Seville itself. In the event this did not occur, though, by his own account, the duke was asked for sponsorship by Christopher Columbus, a request that entirely accorded with his ambitions for Puerto de Santa María. He appears to have refused so as not to offend his royal mistress and master, from whom he had so recently received rewards and preferment and who were intent on clipping the wings of the main magnates of the region and developing both Cádiz and Seville under crown control.

Nevertheless, the house of Medinaceli continued to add to its Andalusian interests as the sixteenth century began, eventually acquiring by intermarriage with the Ribera family that great monument to seignorial pride and classical and Islamic culture the Casa de Pilatos in Seville.

JOHN EDWARDS

Bibliography

Highfield, J. R. L. "The Catholic Kings and the Titled Nobility of Castile." In *Europe in the Late Middle Ages*. Eds. J. Hale, R. Highfield, and B. Smalley, London, 1965. 358–85.

———. "The De la Cerda, the Pimentel and the So-called 'Price Revolution.' " *English Historical Review* 87 (1952), 495–512.

Pulgar, F. del. *Claros varones de Castilla: A Critical Edition*. Ed. R. B. Tate. Oxford, 1971. 47–48.

MENA, JUAN DE

Secretary and chronicler of Juan II of Castile and one of the outstanding poets of his time. Author of two long narrative poems, *La coronación del marqués de Santillana* (c.1438), and his masterpiece, *El laberinto de Fortuna* (1444); an allegorical debate, *Coplas de los pecados mortales* (also known as *Debate de la Razón contra la Voluntad*), left incomplete at his death; and some fifty shorter compositions typical of the courtly verse of his day: queries and responses to other poets, occasional pieces, riddles, love poems, and satiric verse. His prose works include a prologue and commentary to his *Coronación*; *La Ilíada en romance*, a translation of the *Ilias latina*, with prologue (c.1442); *Tratado de amor* (c.1444); *Tratado del título de duque* (1445); a prologue to Alvaro de Luna's *Libro de las virtuosas e claras mugeres* (c.1446); and the fragmentary *Memorias de algunos linajes antiquas é nobles de Castilla* (1448).

Reliable data on Mena's life is sparse. He was born in late December 1411 in Córdoba, and was named alderman (*veinticuatro*) there possibly as early as 1435. In his *Memorias* he traces the Mena lineage to the valley of Mena in La Montaña. Vatican archival documents place him in Florence in 1442–1443 at the court of Pope Eugene IV, from whom he unsuccessfully sought ecclesiastical benefices in Córdoba. He was appointed secretary for Latin and royal chronicler by King Juan II of Castile probably in the mid-1440s, although the earliest extant document which refers to him with either of these titles is his own *Memorias* (1448). He married Marina Méndez, some twenty years his junior, around 1450. Upon the death of King Juan II in 1454 he remained in the service of King Enrique IV; he died in Torrelaguna in 1456, leaving no descendants.

The poet's first editor, Hernán Núñez, supplies additional biographical data that cannot be corroborated: that he was the son of Pedrarias and of a sister of Ruy Fernández de Peñalosa, lord of Almenara and *veinticuatro* of Córdoba; that both parents died when he was very young; that he began his studies in Córdoba and continued them in Salamanca; and that he was married in Córdoba to a sister of García de Vaca and Lope de Vaca. Other early biographical accounts derive from Núñez, although they differ in some particulars.

Throughout his adult life Mena divided his time between Córdoba and the royal court. He was a loyal supporter of King Juan II and an unabashed admirer of Alvaro de Luna; at the same time, his friendship with the Marquis of Santillana transcended the political turmoil of the time and survived the Marquis's disaffection with the crown and the *condestable*.

El laberinto de Fortuna (popularly called *Las trescientas*), a narrative poem of 297 *arte mayor* stanzas, was presented to King Juan II in February 1444. The poet inveighs against capricious Fortune, and is forthwith transported in a visionary journey to her palace. There he is met by Providence, who will serve as his guide. Providence shows him the three wheels of Fortune corresponding to the past, present, and future, each with seven circles governed by the seven planets. The wheel of the unknowable future remains veiled, but the poet will be permitted to see those of the past and the present.

The main body of the poem (stanzas 61–238) recounts the histories of exemplary figures (exalted and condemned) in each of the seven circles. The first four circles (Diana, Mercury, Venus, and Phoebus) stress figures from the past and ethical concerns, while the last three (Mars, Jupiter, and Saturn) emphasize the present (and, by extension, the recent past). Here Fortune holds sway; only Alvaro de Luna has been able to conquer her, and the king must emulate his example if he is to attain the greatness foretold for him.

The work concludes with Providence's prophecy of future glory for the king, whose fame will eclipse that of his ancestors; the vision fades, however, before the poet can inquire of his guide as to the particulars of the king's future accomplishments. His task is clear: he must put an end to civil strife ("las guerras que vimos de nuestra Castilla," 141b) and unite the warring factions in a final push to victory over the Muslims (the "virtuosa, magnífica guerra" of 152a).

Mena drew selectively and deftly from a wide variety of sources. His allegorical construct owes much to such works as *Anticlaudianus*, *Roman de la rose*, and Dante's *Divine Comedy*, though he appears to have made his own contribution to the symbology of Fortune in the concept of the three wheels. He knew and utilized Latin epic poets (Virgil, Lucan, Statius) and relied heavily on Ovid's *Metamorphoses* for Greco-Roman mythology.

The language of the *Laberinto* is a language of poetic innovation. It is characterized by an abundance of neologisms coined from Latin roots, a tendency toward Latinate morphology and syntax, and the extensive use of a wide variety of rhetorical devices. Yet the poet does not hesitate to juxtapose a vulgar, archaic vernacular word and an elegant Latinism: "*fondón* del *çilénico* çerco segundo" (at the deepest bottom of the second celaenic [i.e., Meraniel] circle) (92b) or "con *túrbido* velo su *mote* cubría" (with turbid veil covered their riddle 57d). The result is a compendium of tragic, satiric, and comedic styles consistent with principles enunciated earlier by the poet (*Coronación*, prologue).

La coronación del marqués de Santillana was composed to celebrate Santillana's victory over the Moors in the Battle of Huelma in 1438. It consists of fifty-one octosyllabic *coplas reales*, accompanied by the author's extensive prose commentary in which he explicates each stanza, clarifying classical allusions and glossing his neologisms. Mena coined the term *calamicleos* (from the Latin *calamitas* and Greek *cleos*) to describe the work, "a treatise on the misery of evildoers and the glory of the good." The poet describes his allegorical journey through the valleys of Thessaly, where he contemplates the fate of figures from antiquity such as Ninus of Babylon (armless in punishment for his failure to raise his arms in defense of his city) and Jason (afire in punishment for his lust). He then makes his way through a forest of knowledge and ascends Mt Parnassus, reaching a place reserved for those who have attained fame through their works: Solomon, David, Homer, Lucan, Virgil, Seneca, and others. Under a canopy, attended by the immortal authors and the Muses, is the Marquis of Santillana; the poet watches as he receives the laurel crown from four maidens who represent the cardinal virtues, and exhorts the goddess Fame to spread the news of the event worldwide.

Stanza 42 and its commentary reveal that Santillana is being recognized for his diligence, loyalty, and valor in the service of the king against the Muslims rather than for his accomplishments as a writer. By implication, the poet's condemnation of those being punished for cowardice or irresponsibility could be extended to some of his contemporaries; the example of Santillana (like that of Alvaro de Luna in *Laberinto*) is worthy of emulation.

In *Coplas de los pecados mortales*, the poet invokes the Christian muse, disavowing the "dulçura enponzoñada" of his earlier works and ruing time misspent in the study of pagan antiquity. Written in octosyllabic *arte menor* stanzas and structured as an allegorical debate between Reason and the Seven Deadly Sins, represented as seven faces of Will, the work leaves off at Stanza 106, during the debate between Reason and Anger. An indication of the work's reception in its own time are the continuations of it written by Gómez Manrique, Pero Guillén de Segovia, and Fray Jerónimo de Olivares.

Mena's earliest prose work is probably his commentary to the *Coronación*. There he cultivates several styles, ranging from elaborate Latinate through simpler narrative to direct didactic. The *Ilias latina* is his translation of an abridged version of the Homeric epic in 1,070 Latin hexameters. *Tratado de amor*, in relatively straightforward didactic style, reveals some of the author's subtle humor as he concentrates on "el amor no líçito e insano" and devotes almost equal attention to that which engenders it as to that which repels it. *Tratado sobre el título de duque* purports to trace the origins, rights, privileges, insignia, and prerogatives of dukes but serves as a vehicle for the poet's praise of the duke of Medina Sidonia and count of Niebla, Juan de Guzmán, to whom it is dedicated. In his brief prologue to Alvaro de Luna's *Libro de las virtuosas e claras mugeres*, Mena renders thanks at the behest, he says, of many well-born ladies to Alvaro for his defense of their honor; finally, the fragmentary *Memorias de algunos linages antiguos é nobles de Castilla* are brief sketches of the historical and geographical origins of fourteen lineages, including his own.

Mena's works—particularly the *Laberinto*—were well known to his contemporaries and to posterity. He was cited extensively by Elio Antonio de Nebrija and Juan del Encina, annotated by Hernán Núñez and Francisco Sánchez de las Brozas, and his influence can be found throughout the sixteenth century (in Cristóbal de Castillejo and Fernando de Herrera, for example), and into the seventeenth (Luis de Góngora). The point of departure for modern Mena scholarship is Lida de Malkiel's monumental study (1950).

Philip O. Gericke
Colbert I. Nepaulsingh

Bibliography

Deyermond, A. D. "Structure and Style as Instruments of Propaganda in Juan de Mena's *Laberinto de Fortuna*." *Proceedings of the Patristic, Medieval, and Renaissance Conference* 5 (1980), 159–67.

Gericke, P. O. "The Narrative Structure of the *Laberinto de Fortuna*." *Romance Philology* 21 (1968), 512–22.

Lida de Malkiel, M. R. *Juan de Mena, poeta del prerrenacimiento español*. 2d ed. Mexico City, 1984.

Mena, J. de. *Obras completas*. Ed. M. A. Pérez Priego. Barcelona, 1989.

———. *Tratado sobre el título de duque*. Ed. L. Vasvari Fainberg. London, 1976.

MENDOZA, FRAY IÑIGO DE

Franciscan friar (c. 1424–c.1507) related to the aristocratic Mendoza family and to the Jewish convert Santa María family. He appears in Enrique IV's court and later in the court of the Catholic Monarchs, of whom he was an ardent supporter as well as Isabel's personal preacher. The first version of his major work, the *Coplas de vita Christi*, dates from 1467 to 1468, and interspersed in it are numerous extensive passages of criticism against King Enrique, his protegés, and other personalities (Pedro Girón, Juan Pacheco, Beltrán de la Cueva, Alonso Carrillo, for example), as well as Alvaro de Luna, the high constable to Juan II. Mendoza was obligated to rewrite a second version of this work excluding the personal references but he managed to maintain the same critical tone. The first edition (actually a third version of the poem) appeared in Zamora in 1482, with almost four hundred double five-line octosyllabic stanzas and one ballad (perhaps the first ever printed) with its *desfecha* (gloss). The text includes a pastoral Christmas episode with clearly theatrical connotations. Imbued with both cultured and popular styles, *Vita Christi* also conveys the typical Franciscan spirit of the time with a didactic, moralizing tone. The influence of this poem is notable in Comendador Román, Juan de Padilla, and Ambrosio Montesino, among others; important traces of the pastoral episode appear in Juan del Encina, Torres Naharro, and in other authors prior to Lope de Vega. Shortly before *Vita Christi* appeared, another poem by Mendoza was published, the popular *Coplas de Mingo Revulgo*, also directed against Enrique IV and his protegés.

Mendoza was, in addition, the author of strictly religious poems, among which *Los gozos de Nuestra Señora* and *Coplas a la Verónica* are particularly noteworthy. Two works of moral intention were reprinted frequently during the period up to 1509: *Coplas en vituperio de las malas hembras* and *Historia de la cuestión y diferencia que ay entre la Razón y la Sensualidad*; the latter follows very closely the *Debate de la Razón y la Voluntad* by Juan de Mena. During the same period a series of political works by Mendoza in defense of the Catholic monarchs enjoyed considerable fame and in them the political and military instability inherited from the previous reign was reflected. In the *Dechado* (1475–1476) addressed to Isabel, he encouraged the queen in her struggle against Juana la Beltraneja's supporters and foreign allies, and predicted her coming victory. In his *Coplas en que declara como por el aduenimiento destos muy altos señores es reparada nuestra Castilla* (composed around 1479), he prophesies an extraordinary, messianic future for Castile and its monarchs Fernando and Isabel, and recommends the relentless application of justice in dealing with rebels who challenge royal authority. It is therefore evident that Mendoza is not simply a religious poet, but rather his works, of great variety and complexity, encompass other important topics that make this author one of the most interesting writers of late-fifteenth-century Castile.

JULIO RODRÍGUEZ PUÉRTOLAS

Bibliography

Mendoza, Iñigo de. *Cancionero de fray Iñigo de Mendoza.* Ed. J. Rodríguez-Puértolas, Madrid, 1968.

Rodríguez Puértolas, J. *Fray Iñigo de Mendoza y sus "Coplas de Vita Christi."* Madrid, 1968.

MERCEDARIANS, ORDER OF OUR LADY OF MERCY *See* CHURCH, RELIGIOUS ORDERS

MERINIDS

The Merinids, often referred to as the Benimerines, were a North African dynasty probably of Berber origin, although they claimed Arab ancestry. Essentially nomadic, they struggled with the Almohads in Morocco, and in 1145 were driven into the Sahara. In subsequent clashes with the Almohads they emerged victorious and by 1246 had taken the Almohad capital of Marrakesh, Tangiers by 1273, and Ceuta by 1275. They first appeared in Al-Andalus at the time of the Mudéjar revolts of 1264–1266, when they were welcomed by Ibn al-Aḥmar and seen as the instruments for frustrating Christian gains in the south. On several occasions, they came to the aid of Granada against the encroachments of Alfonso X and Sancho IV. After the disintegration of Almohad power in Al-Andalus, the Merinids by the fourteenth century had hoped to build an empire that could counter the influence of Castile and Aragón in Iberia. Their attempts, however, failed and they were compelled to return to Morocco after a resounding defeat at the battle of the Río Salado in 1340.

Contrary to the Almoravids and the Almohads, the Merinids had no sectarian or ideological foundation for their authority. Their power had been won by means of tribal conquest and established by force rather than through religious reform. Despite the secular origins of their dominance, they perceived themselves as the heirs and successors of the Almohads and sought to intervene in Al-Andalus on the basis of protecting the Muslim faith and their coreligionists there. Their leadership in campaigns against Iberian Christians not only signaled their political initiative but their sponsorship of *jihād* and, therefore, their right to ascendancy. The Merinid armies were highly mobile, composed of light cavalry, reflecting their desert origins and ties to the Zanāta Berbers. With this type of force they were successful in raiding and claiming booty, but not in retaining territory or carrying out successful sieges of cities and fortresses.

The Merinid interest in Al-Andalus led to Merinid involvement in the internal affairs of the Iberian Muslims, especially in Granada. Their presence contributed greatly to the deterioration of relations between Iberian Muslims and Christians and led the latter to introduce oppressive measures against Muslims living in their territories. Merinid intercession in Al-Andalus proved almost as dangerous for the Muslims of Iberia as had the intervention of the Almoravids and the Almohads, plus any alliance that had been wrought with the Christians.

E. MICHAEL GERLI

Bibliography

Arié, R. *L'Espagne musulmane au temps des Nasvids (1232–1492).* 2d ed. Paris, 1990.

Harvey, L. P. *Islamic Spain 1250–1500.* Chicago, 1990.

Manzano Rodríguez, M. A. *La intervención de los benimerines en la península ibérica.* Madrid, 1992.

MERINO

The *maiorinus* in the Astur-Leonese kingdom was the administrative official named by a count or *tenente* to collect payments, especially those judicial in origin, in a given district. In the tenth century the term generally replaced the earlier *vílico* as the king appointed a nobleman to function at court as an assistant *mayordomo* or to take charge of a jurisdiction. Analogously, lay and ecclesíastical lords began to appoint *merinos* in lands under their authority. In the eleventh century public administration acquired a more civil character as the king gradually replaced counts and tenentes with merinos (whose names were listed in royal documents) and the former counties with *merindades* that might or might not have the same boundaries as their predecessors. The merino also came to be entrusted with the tenancy of castles and towers, thus gaining responsibility for keeping local peace and order. At the same time, the rise of towns as corporate authorities with their own *fueros* (municipal charters) resulted in the appearance of *merinos concejiles* who eventually functioned under the authority of the municipal judges (*alcaldes, jueces*). Concomitant with the legal organization of municipal corporations was the limit thus placed on the authority of seigneurial or ecclesiastical merinos, although not on that of royal judges or judges from the same town. As early as the end of the twelfth century some *concejos* began to participate in choosing their merino, hitherto appointed by the king or lord. By the thirteenth century the merino in Castile and León—whether royal, seigneurial (either lay or ecclesiastical), or municipal, and whether located at the seat of highest authority or in an inferior jurisdiction—can be described generally as fulfilling fiscal responsibilities, exercising judicial power as the logical extension of delegated authority, carrying out judicial decisions, and recruiting and leading soldiers in maintaining public order.

At the beginning of the reign of Alfonso X (1252) there were four *merindades mayores*: Galicia, León, Castile, and Murcia. The Alfonsine *Espéculo* describes the *merino mayor* only in terms of his executive authority; he was the superior officer in charge of meting out justice and carrying out the law, and he oversaw the merinos *menores* of the lesser territorial jurisdictions within his region. (In the *Segunda Partida* the merinos menores could also be appointed by an *adelantado* [governor] and the merino's powers were specified.) In 1258 Alfonso suppressed the *merindades mayores* in Castile and Murcia, replacing them with *adelantamientos* (governorships). Later he also suppressed the adelantamientos without appointing new merinos, the latter action no doubt in response to the specific demand made by the nobles in the *cortes* (parliament) of Burgos (1272). The merinos mayores in Galicia, León, and Castile reappeared early in the reign of Sancho IV, but by the end of the reign were replaced by adelantados mayores. In the *Ordenamiento de Alcalá* (1348) Alfonso XI referred to merinos mayores for Castile, León, and Galicia, adelantados mayores for Andalusia and Murcia, and merinos for Guipúzcoa, Alava, and Asturias. Enrique II created (1371) the *audiencia* to serve under the chancery and over the merinos mayores, but from the middle of the century the merino already had begun to lose ordinary judicial authority to a new official, the *corregidor*. By 1500 Castilian territory had been divided into sixty-five *corregimientos*.

Robert A. MacDonald

Bibliography

Pérez-Bustamante, R. *El gobierno y la administración de los reinos de la Corona de Castilla (1230–1474)*. 2 vols. Madrid, 1976.

Sinués Ruiz, A. *El merino*. Zaragoza, 1954.

MESTA

A specifically Castilian term, derived from the Berber *meshtā*, meaning the annual winter encampment of migratory shepherds, denotes in common usage the great royal-chartered corporation of sheepmen in medieval and modern Castile alternatively known as the *Mesta Real* or *Honrado Concejo de la Mesta de los Pastores del Reino*. But it can also apply to a comparable body based on a single municipality or district, and, in its original sense as a seasonal meeting of sheepowners and herdsmen to redistribute stray animals (*mesteñas*), settle disputes, and enforce pastoral law.

The two and one-half centuries of medieval mesta history from around 1260 to 1500 have tended to be overshadowed by a traditional focus on the modern period, and by the hostile polemical literature of Spanish agrarian reformers from the eighteenth century on, charging the Mesta with having ruined the nation's agriculture and peasantry. In consequence, much remains to be learned regarding the Mesta's genesis, structure, membership, and operation in the Middle Ages when it almost certainly played a beneficent role in society and agropecuarial economy.

The Mesta's obscure origins in the second half of the thirteenth century are irrefutably linked to that dynamic extension of long-distance transhumance across the Iberian *meseta* (plateau) made possible by the major Reconquest advances of Alfonso VI and his successors. These opened up to entrepreneurial sheepraisers—nobles, monasteries, churches, military orders, and, above all, townsmen—vast new areas ideal for winter grazing grounds (*invernaderos*) in Extremadura, New Castile, Murcia, and Andalusia. Out of the network of sheepwalks linking these southern regions with the older summer pastures (*agostaderos*) in Galicia, León, Old Castile, the Rioja, the central Sierras, and Serranía de Cuenca, emerge the four great north-south sheep highways (*cañadas*)—the Leonesa, Segoviana, Soriana, and Cuenca—upon which the Mesta will center its activities. It is probably from associations (*cuadrillas* of herdsmen banding together on each *cañada* to elect their own *alcaldes* [judges] and handle mutual problems) that arose, no doubt under royal pressure, and not from the often alleged merger of mythical local mestas. Contrary also to the frequent affirmation of 1273 as its date of establishment, the Mesta's existence can unquestionably be carried back to Alfonso X's first set of Mesta charters, around 1260. These charters, four in number, recognized the Mesta as a legal corporation, conceded it pasturage privileges in the royal domain (*realengo*), and defined various protective rights. At the same time, the king moved to ensure crown control by assigning the Mesta on each *cañada* itinerant royal justices (*alcaldes entregadores*) for adjudicating the Mesta's claims to its stray sheep, its rights of pasturage access, and protection against excessive tolls and rents imposed by *concejos* or military orders; and by imposing upon it royal taxes of passage and pasturage (the *servicio y montazgo*) to be collected at toll stations strategically located along the *cañadas*.

It should be kept in mind that the Mesta of the Middle Ages was not, as it later became, an oligarchical body of high nobles and large ecceslastical corporations, but an organization whose membership was largely of the urban and rural middle classes. Whether these holders of relatively modest flocks actually controlled elections of *alcaldes de cuadrilla* who made up the governing board that presided at the supreme annual juntas held at Montemolín in Extremadura and elsewhere, and whether in consequence Mesta government was democratic, continues to be a subject of debate. There is the problem also of when and how speedily the Mesta came to convert its flocks to the high-quality, fine-wooled sheep of the celebrated Merino breed. Vicens Vives has argued that the Merino's introduction into the Iberian Peninsula before 1200 resulted in a "wool revolution" that in turn led to the creation of the Mesta; but all our documentary evidence indicates that the advent of the new breed from North Africa did not much predate 1350, a century after the Mesta's foundation.

Other questions revolve, on the internal side, around the little known prosopography of the actual Mesta membership and their alignments during the political disturbances of late medieval Castile; around the power and familial appropriation of the top royal judicial office, that of the *alcalde entregador mayor*; and how far the Mesta's difficulties with agararian and other opponents of its sweeping privileges actually constituted, as has been often supposed, a struggle between farmer and pastoralist.

What is certain is that whatever the magnitude of the profits and losses, the members of the Mesta experienced in the fourteenth and fifteenth centuries due to wool price fluctuations or the semianarchy of the Castilian kingdom, the *honrado concejo* (hononable council) comes over basically unscathed into the reign of the Catholic Monarchs (1474–1516) as a major producer of national wealth, fielding some two million animals for its annual clip; receiving now from the centralizing monarchy a president, henceforth taken from the senior members of the royal council; and embarking upon its greatest age of importance in the sixteenth century as an ever greater supplier of prime Merino wools to the bustling clothmaking centers of western Europe from the Low Countries to Italy.

C. Julian Bishko

Bibliography

Díez Navarro, A. (ed.) *Quaderno de leyes y privilegios del Honrado Concejo de la Mesta*. Madrid, 1731.

García Martín, P. *The Mesta*. Madrid, 1990.

García Martín, P., and J. M. Sánchez Benito. *Contribución a la historia de la trashumancia en España*. Madrid, 1986.

Klein, J. *The Mesta*. Cambridge, Mass., 1920.

MESTER DE CLERECÍA

In accord with the derivation of *mester* from the Latin *ministerium* ("profession"), in its broader sense *mester de clerecía* refers to the profession of the clerk, but its connection with the verse form known as *cuaderna vía* was established in the second stanza of the *Libro de Alexandre*, so that *mester de clerecía* now refers to a monorhyme tetrastrope of Alexandrine lines (fourteen syllables per line, divided into two equal hemistichs).

The form first appeared toward the middle of the thirteenth century: the most important examples are the *Libro de Alexandre*, the works of Gonzalo de Berceo, and the *Libro de Apolonio*; near the end of its popularity in the middle of the fourteenth century, the cuaderna vía still predominates in the *Libro de buen amor* and the *Rimado de palacio*.

It has long been held that the works were composed in regular fourteen-syllable lines; however, the manuscript witness reveals many irregular lines, and in the case of the *Libro de Alexandre* the fourteen-syllable line represents only 70 to 75 percent of the total. A majority of scholars also concur in the uniform observance of hiatus between contiguous vowels in adjacent words; some proponents even attribute to obligatory hiatus a certain esthetic status, in that the poet dignifies the language by preserving the integrity of the vowel locutions, in imitation of the vowel autonomy of Latin poetry. On the other hand, complete elimination of vowels through the widespread apheresis, syncope, and elision is a salient characteristic of the Castilian language in the thirteenth century, and is reflected in the manuscripts themselves, especially those of the *Libro de Alexandre*.

SPURGEON BALDWIN

Bibliography

Fitzgerald, J. D. *Versification of the Cuaderna Via*. New York, 1905.

Rico, F. "La clerecía del mester." *Hispanic Review* 53 (1985), 1–23, 127–150.

METALINGUISTICS

The language spoken by non-Basque inhabitants of the Iberian Peninsula continued to be called *lingua latina* after the end of the Western Roman Empire. St Isidore referred to the Latin of his own time (seventh century) as being *mixta*, translating the Greek κοινη: "id est mixta, sive communis quam omnes utuntur." (It is mixed in the common way men are). Isidore had a concern for careful usage, but saw his society as essentially monolingual. This perspective probably survived for another four hundred years. Our own data for the language of the period preceding the general use of reformed written Romance comes from two sources: reconstruction on the basis of later Romance evidence, and the texts of the time. Their evidence appears to conflict, so some modern scholars have visualized those centuries as being bilingual (or diglossic), Latin and Romance; Menéndez Pidal postulated a third intermediate language (Leonese Vulgar Latin). The speakers of the time seems to have made no such metalinguistic distinctions, not even the erudite stylists in Muslim Spain; they distinguished Arabic, Hebrew, and undifferentiated Latin/Romance. Their own speech, now called *Mozárabe* (Mozarabic), was neither distinguished nor probably distinguishable from that farther north. Historians suggest now that in these centuries the majority of the population were not, as used to be thought, cut off from literate culture and a society whose functioning was still based on documentation; a few could write, many more could read, and virtually everybody (then as now) could usually understand written texts read aloud to them (orders, letters, sermons, the details of legal documents, saints lives, even histories). This fits a metalinguistic perspective of sociolinguistically complex monolingualism, with wide social and stylistic variation (as is normal everywhere) and a gap between most people's active and passive competence, but not the postulated rigid divide between the language of the literate (supposedly attested by texts) and the illiterate (attested through reconstruction); older and newer grammatical and morphological features coexisted, and everyone's pronunciation was evolved. Learning to write was thus as complicated then as it is in the modern English-speaking world. Nor do we have in these early centuries any sign of geographically based metalinguistic distinctions; such words as *Galleco* seem to have merely geographical reference. Spatial variations existed, naturally, but were still perceived as language-internal.

The metalinguistic situation changed drastically between 1080 and 1300. Catalonia, being Frankish, may have seen a conscious Latin-Romance conceptual distinction in some church centers from the ninth century (when the distinction was invented by Carolingian scholars); elsewhere, such a metalinguistic distinction seems not to have occurred to Spaniards until after the French liturgy replaced the Toledan liturgy (1080), needing to be pronounced in the standard European way (producing a specified sound for every written letter) that we now call "Medieval Latin." Outside progressive church circles the distinction was probably not generally felt until the thirteenth century, and even Alfonso X el Sabio still occasionally treated them as two modes of one language. Subsequently, the distinction was clear, and people could become literate in the vernacular without necessarily first becoming literate in Latin.

This metalinguistic development probably arose parallel with new geographically based ones. Alfonso X referred to *romance*, but regularly also to *romance castellano*, distinguished in his own mind from the *romance gallego* in which he composed poetry; clear distinctions from Leonese and Aragónese were probably also invented in that century (for political reasons), even though these had no internal standardization process. Catalan, also for political reasons, acquired a separate standardized written form then to distinguish it conceptually from the written form they had used before (Provenzal). The fourteenth-century conceptual erection of a Portuguese-Galician divide was similarly only thought worthwhile because of their political separation. For such diatopic distinctions are never based on a list of sufficient and necessary conditions for regarding related languages as separate; they are always political decisions, usually accompanying, or even following, the elaboration of new separate written forms. Thus before 1080 the peninsula was metalinguistically comparable to the modern English-speaking world (one language with wide variation), but by 1300 it was comparable to Spain in the late 1990s (where several newly identified geographically based separately written languages are claimed to exist). Meanwhile, actual linguistic changes continued largely unconnected with such metalinguistic revolutions.

ROGER WRIGHT

Bibliography

Niederehe, J. *Alfonso X el Sabio y la Lingüística de su tiempo*. Madrid, 1987.

Wright, R. (ed.) *Latin and the Romance Languages in the Early Middle Ages*. London, 1991.

METGE, BERNAT (505)

Bernat Metge (1340/6–1413) was a learned Catalan writer. His stepfather, Ferrer Sayol, the principal notary of Queen Leonor of Sicily, translated into Catalan the *De re rustica* (1380–1385) of the Latin writer Palladius Rutilius, so we presume that he initiated Metge both into the field of classical letters and into the royal court. In 1371 Metge entered the service of the queen and in 1375 he was appointed scribe to her son, Metge's protector, who began to reign in 1387 as Juan I of Aragón. In 1390 Metge was promoted to the position of secretary to the king and his wife, Queen Violant, even though his honesty as a royal servant had been questioned; he was, in fact, involved in at least three lawsuits. As the records of the last of these trials (1397) have been preserved, we know exactly how serious the charges were against him. Such legal problems became the subject of very interesting literary writings that illustrate the discovery of the value of learned prose by Catalan intellectuals toward the end of the fourteenth century. In 1381, in fact, Metge wrote his first self-defense in traditional Occitanian-Catalan verse, the *Llibre de fortuna e prudència*, in which he wittily borrowed from Dante and Jean de Meun as well as from Latin writers such as Alain de Lille and Arrigo da Settimello. Metge also parodied preaching in the verses of his *Sermó*, and adapted to Catalan prose the second book of the medieval pseudo-Ovidian poem *De vetula*, which is known as *Ovidi enamorat*. From 1388 on, he began a new literary fashion with his translation of the last novella of Boccaccio's *Decameron*, the story of Walter and the patient Griselidis. Metge, who felt himself to be the first Petrarchist in Catalan vernacular literature, used the Latin version of Boccaccio's text included by Petrarch in one of his *Seniles*. His Italian masters acquainted Metge with classical Latin literature, as we can see in his unfinished *Apologia* (1395? 1408?), and in his masterpiece, *Lo somni* (1399). This work was conceived as a dialogue between the author and three dead men that come to him when he is asleep in prison. Metge tries to prove that he is innocent of the charges of treachery and immorality that have put him in jail after the unexpected death of King Juan I in 1396, so he agrees to be converted to the "true faith" from cynic skepticism—which he calls Epicurism—and also promises that in the future he will restrain his excessive devotion to women. This part of *Lo somni*, which Metge borrowed from Cicero, Ovid, and the church Fathers and Doctors, shines with Platonic solemnity and elegance, but there is also a coarser and extremely funny part that comes straight from Boccaccio's *Corbaccio*. *Lo somni* is such a unique achievement that it does not fit into any scheme of medieval literary history. There is a scholarly tradition in modern Catalonia that makes Metge a humanist *ante litteram*, even though he is at least as medieval as his main source, Boccaccio.

LOLA BADÍA

Bibliography

Badia, L. *De Bernat Metge a Joan Roís de Corella*. Barcelona, 1988.

Metge, B. *Obras. de Bernat Metge*. Ed. M. Riguer. Barcelona, 1959.

MIERES, TOMÁS

Catalan jurist and counselor to King Alfonso IV, Tomás Mieres is best known for his glosses and recompilations of the constitutions of Catalonia, the acts of the Catalan courts, and the local and provincial customary law known as the *Usatges* of Barcelona. A native of Girona, born in the late fourteenth century, Mieres studied law in Italy. He worked as a lawyer and judge of the curia in Girona; later Mieres was named legal council to the Real Patrimonio by Alfonso IV and made a member of the the royal *curia* (court).

In 1430 Mieres began a new compilation of the customary law codes of Girona that were concerned with feudal and seignorial landholding. Due to the contradictory nature of the texts, Mieres had to reorganize thoroughly the older codes into a new compilation and concordance. This work, the *Consuetudines diocesis gerundensis*, published in 1439, provided a solid base for feudal institutions in Girona and thus became a key argument used by secular and legal lords in defense of their landholding practices in the face of demands for liberation by the *remensa* peasants.

In the same year as the publication of the *Consuetudines*, Mieres began work on a gloss on the constitutions of Catalonia and the promulgations of the *corts* of Catalonia up to 1432. Completed in 1446, the *Apparatus super constitutionum curiarum generalium Cathalonie* attempts to harmonize older native customary laws that emphasized monarchical aspirations of control with demands by the new class of bourgeoisie for greater liberty and political control.

THERESA EARENFIGHT

Bibliography

Freedman, P. *The Origins of Peasant Servitude in Medieval Catalunya*. Cambridge, 1991.

Hinojosa y Naveros, E. de. *El régimen señorial y la cuestión agraria en Cataluña durante la Edad Media*. Madrid, 1905.

MILLÁN DE LA COGOLLA, SAN

Millán of the Cogolla was born in 473 in Berceo, a village in the Rioja Alta, near the place today known as San Millán de la Cogolla, a name taken from the saint and from a high peak that was called, in ancient times, Cogolla (*cuculla*), according to a Latin document from 1016.

The main source of information about Millán of the Cogolla is the *Vita Beati Aemiliani* by St. Braulius, bishop of Zaragoza (631–651), who was one of the most outstanding figures of the Visigothic culture. Millán was a young shepherd in the Distercian Mountains; he then lived for a while in Bilibio (Haro?) as a disciple of the holy anchorite Felices, who taught him holy science and wisdom. After this period of learning he went back to his native land and to his family. However, he soon decided to abandon life among men and to retire into the wilderness of the Distercian Mountains, where he lived as a hermit for some forty years. Word of his virtues came to Didimus, bishop of Taragona, who ordained him a priest and entrusted him the church at Berceo. When he was an old man, he retired again to a cave in the folds of the Distercian Mountains, where he led a community of monks and another of women who had been consecrated to God. In such a way began the cenobite cell of San Millán de Suso.

Millán died in 574, and was buried in the same cave where he had lived. In 1030 his relics were transferred to the church of San Millán de Suso and in 1067 they were transferred again to the new church, San Millán de Yuso, where they were placed in a rich casket covered with ivory panels that is still kept in an oratory.

ISABEL URÍA-MAQUA

Bibliography

Dutton, Brian (ed.) *La Vida de San Millán de la Cogolla: Estudio y edición crítica*. 2d ed. London, 1984.

MILITARY ORDERS

Military orders had their origin in the Crusades and were founded in Jerusalem in the twelfth century to fight against infidels. Their members had a double condition: they were both monks and soldiers. In Spain, military orders were also founded to fight against the Muslims and to help the kings during the Reconquest; their organization was very similar to the international orders. When the Moors were expelled from the Iberian Peninsula, Catholic Monarchs Fernando and Isabel incorporated the Hispanic military orders into the crown in 1493.

Internationals Orders

The order of Saint John of Jerusalem (or the Hospital, known as the Hospitalers) was founded in Jerusalem in 1104 by St. Gerard of Provence to take care of the sick pilgrims and to offer help to the crusaders. Their members took the standard vows of poverty, chastity, and obedience and another vow of arms. Their habit was a black mantle with the white Hospitaler cross. This order expanded through the Western Christianity, including the Hispanic kingdoms. Hospitalers in Spain were endowed to fight against the Muslims and to encourage Christian resettlement within the peninsula. They enjoyed an exceptionally prominent position in Roussillon, Catalonia, Aragón, and Valencia. Hospitaler properties were divided in two *lenguas* or languages: Castile and Aragón. That of Aragón embraced the *Castellanía de Amposta* and the priories of Catalonia and Navarra. In Aragón there were also two convents of Hospitaler sisters: Grisén, founded in 1177, and the important monastery of Sijena, founded in 1188 by Queen Sancha, where many king's daugthers and women of noble extraction professed. Hospitalers reached their highest power in the fourteenth century with such important personalities as Master Juan Fernández de Heredia and the prior of Catalonia, Guillem de Guimerà. Afterward, Hospitalers began to decline, especially as a result of the incomes produced by the sustenance of Rodas, where the master had his court.

The Order of Knights of the Temple of Solomon (known as Knights Templars) was founded in 1118 by Hugues de Payens and other French knights to defend the pilgrims who visited the Holy Land. Its expansion through Europe was rapid, and in the mid-twelfth century there were twelve provinces in the West and five in the East. The exact date of the entrance of the Templars into Spain is unknown, but it seems probable that before 1128 they were in Aragón and a bit later they arrived in Castile. There the Templars served in the fight against the Moors during the twelfth and thirteenth centuries. After the conquest of Seville, King Fernando III gave them the town of Fregenal. Like other military orders, the Templars had their properties grouped in *encomiendas* and commanded by a preceptor or *comendador*. The most important *encomiendas* in the Crown of Aragón were Monzón, Tortosa, Gardeny, Barberà, Horta, Peñíscola, Ares, Borriana, and Miravet. Both Templars and Hospitalers gave much military service to the kings during the Reconquest and they received so many rewards that the Order of Temple acquired great financial power. This economic power worked against them and they were dissolved in 1312 by Pope Clement V. Their possessions in Catalonia, Aragón, and Mallorca passed to the Hospitalers, while the Valencian properties would endow the new national Order of Montesa founded in 1317.

Hispanic Orders

The Order of Calatrava is the oldest military order in Spain. It was founded by King Sancho III of Castile, who in 1158 commited the defense of Calatrava castle to Raimond Serrat, abbot of the Cistercian monastery of Fitero. Afterward, he clustered the defenders of Calatrava in a military order that adopted the Cistercian rule and was recognized by Pope Alexander III in 1164. This order was composed of knights and clerks. They were committed to vows of poverty, chastity, and obedience, but in 1540 Pope Paul III freed them from the vow of celibacy. The order's purpose was to defend the roads between Andalusia and Toledo against the Almohads. As a reward, Fernando III and Alfonso X gave the dominion of Jaén to the knights. There the order had got nine preceptories in the fourteenth century. Other important preceptories in Andalusia were Fuenteovejuna and Osuna. In Aragón the Calatrava Order was introduced by King Alfonso II, who gave it lands and the town of Alcáñiz, where a big preceptory was established. Calatravas helped in the reconquest of the Balearics and the Valencia kingdom. Calanda, Alcorisa, Maella, and Monroyo were important preceptories in Aragón. The master lived in Almagro.

The Order of Alcántara was at the beginning only a fraternity of knights placed in the San Julián de Pereiro Convent. It was founded in 1156 by Suero Fernández Barrientos and approved by Pope Alexander III in 1177. It followed the Cistercian rule and after 1212 the order was subjected to that of Calatrava. In 1218 King Alfonso IX of León gave the town of Alcántara to the order. Its aim was to fight against the Muslims and to defend Estremadura against the Portuguese. The Alcántara knights received as a reward the towns of La Serena, Benquerencia, Zalamea, Villanueva de la Serena, and Magacela in Extremadura, and Morón and Cote in Andalusia. Their contribution to the repopulation of much of the land was very important. Their habit was white, with a gold and green cross in the left side.

The Order of Santiago was a Christian military-religious order founded in 1171 to fight against the Muslims of the peninsula and to protect European pilgrims who were going to visit the Sepulcher at Santiago de Compostela. In 1174 King Alfonso VII of Castile gave it the town of Uclés, which became the main center of the order, where the master lived. This order grew very quickly especially in the territories of Ciudad Real, Cuenca, and Toledo, and in the fourteenth century there were five big preceptories: Portugal, León, Castile, Aragón, and Gascuña, and two priories, Uclés and San Marcos of León. The first members of the order in Aragón had been there since the beginning of thirteenth century and they received the Montalbán town that became the main preceptory of Aragón. The *freires* took vows of poverty and obedience, and the clerks also took vows of chastity, because the Santiago order was the only one that alowed the knights to get married. The Santiago order also had some hospitals for the care of pilgrims (San Marcos of León), for the care of lepers (Carrión) and, especially, to redeem those Christians captured by infidels (Toledo, Cuenca, Alarcón, and Talavera).

The Order of Montesa was born as a consequence of the dissolution of the Templars, whose properties and those of the Hospitalers in Valencia—except the town of Torrente and the House of Valencia—were ascribed to the Montesa order. It was founded in 1317 by Pope John XXII, under the Cistercian rule and as filial to the Calatrava order. Its purpose was to fight against the Muslims on the Valencian frontier. King Jaime II gave them Montesa castle, where the main convent was set up. Montesa properties were subject to a master and were clustered in two *bailías*, Cervera and Montcada, and in *encomiendas*, the most important of which were Peñíscola, Culla, Benassal, Onda, Borriana, and Ademús. In 1400, the Order of San Jorge de Alfama was joined with Montesa, after which it was called the Order of Montesa and San Jorge de Alfama.

The Order of San Jorge de Alfama was a Catalan order founded in 1201 by King Pedro II to defend and repopulate the Mediterraneen coast between Ampolla and Balaguer, whose wilderness provoked frequent attacks by Muslim ships. Their members had also to help the pilgrims who arrived at the Alfama castle, where their convent was. The order had properties in Catalonia; Valencia, where a priory was created; the Balearics, and Sardinia. Their members, both clerics and lay men, lived under the St. Augustine rule and wore a white habit with a red cross. The order was not approved by the pope until 1371. Poverty and a scarcity of members ended in 1400, when it was incorporated into the Order of Montesa and thereafter known as the Order of Montesa and San Jorge de Alfama.

During the Middle Ages other military groups were formed, such as the Order of Santa María de Montegaudio, with a more severe rule, founded by one of the founders of the Order of Santiago. It was then known as the Order of Monsfragüe until 1221, when it was joined with the Order of Calatrava. The Milicia de Cristo appeared in Trujillo during the reign of Alfonso IX of León, and was later joined with the Order of Calatrava by the king. In Portugal, the Order of Avis was founded in 1147 in the town of Aviz, under the rule of the Cistercians, to fight against the Muslims. In the mid-thirteenth century, King Alfonso X founded the Order of Santa María de España to defend his conquests in Andalusia. Its history was very short, because in 1280 the knights were incorporated into the Santiago order.

REGINA SÁINZ DE LA MAZA LASOLI

Bibliography

Forey, A. J. *The Templars in the Crown of de Aragón*. London 1973.
———. *The Fall of the Templars in the Crown of Aragón*. U.K., 2001.
García Larragueta, S. *El gran priorato de Navarra de la Orden de San Juan de Jerusalén*. Pamplona, 1957.
Gutton, F. *L'Ordre de Calatrava*. Paris, 1955.
———. *L'Orde de Montesa, Achel, abbaye Cistercienne*, Paris 1975.
——— Ledesma Rubio, M. L. *Templarios y hospitalarios en el reino de Aragón*, Zaragoza 1982.
Lomax, D. W. *La Orden de Santiago (1170–1275)*, Madrid, 1965.
Miret i Sans, J. *Les Cases de Templers i Hospitalers de Catalunya*. Barcelona, 1910.
Rades y Andrada, F. *Chronica de las tres Ordenes y cavallerias de Sanctiago, Calatrava y Alcantara*. Toledo, 1572.
Sáinz de la Maza Lasoli, R. *La Orden de San Jorge de Alfama: Approximación a su historia*. Barcelona, 1990.
———. *La orden de Santiago en la corona de Aragón*. Vol. 1, *La encomienda de Montalbán (1210–1327)*. Zaragoza, 1980.
———. *La Orden de Santiago en la Corona de Aragón*. Vol. 2, *La Encomienda de Montalbán (1327–1357)*, Zaragoza, 1988.

MINIATURES *See* ALFONSO X, EL SABIO, ARTISTIC PATRONAGE; ALSO ILLUMINATION

MINSTRELS *See* JUGLARES

MIRROR OF PRINCES, THE

An ethical treatise adapted to the particular interests of rulers. Although princely concerns are discernible in the wisdom corpus, *Calila, Zifar* and the works of Juan Manuel, the earliest vernacular example of the pure form of the genre in the Iberian Peninsular is the *Libro de los doze sabios*, probably produced at the court of Fernando III (c. 1237). A number of works emanated from the Castilian court: the Alfonsine *Setenario* (c. 1250), the *Castigos e documentos* (1293) commissioned by Sancho IV, the *Speculum regum* of the Galician Franciscan Alvarus Pelagius (Alvaro Pais, c. 1280–1349), dedicated to Alfonso XI, and the Isabelline *Repertorio de principes*. The *De regimine principum* (1287) of Giles of Rome was translated and glossed with numerous exempla (c. 1345) by the Franciscan Juan García de Castrogeriz for Bernabé, bishop of Osma (c. 1290–1351), tutor to Pedro I when prince. In the extensive gloss the focus on statecraft is blurred, perhaps reflecting its origins on the periphery of the court rather than at its center. The gloss, which circulated separately from and in considerably more witnesses than the simple translation, is the source for the additional matter in the longer redaction of the *Castigos e documentos*. There were also Portuguese and Catalan translations of Giles, and a Castilian translation of the Dominican Thomas Aquinas's *De regimine principum ad Regem Cypri*.

In Catalonia, the theme of princely instruction is present in the works of Arnau de Vilanova, Francesc Eiximenis, and Ramón Llull (whose book of proverbs of statecraft dedicated to Jaime II is lost), and in chronicles. One monograph on the subject is the scripturally centered *Tractatus de vita moribus et regimine principum* written by infante Pere, count of Ribagorça, after entering the Franciscan Order in 1358. The presence of the preaching orders is thus striking.

The Portuguese representative of the genre, the *Leal conselheiro* of King Duarte (r. 1433–1438) is unusual in that it is a work on kingship written by a king.

The dedication of *Castigos e documentos* shows the dual nature of the genre: "ordené fazer este libro para mi fijo, e dende para todos aquellos que del algund bien quiseren tomar . . ." (I ordered this book made for my son and for all who wish to take some good from it). The mirror tends to address both the prince and the broader community. Pragmatism and piety coexist throughout the history of the genre, but the latter seems to predominate toward the end of the medieval period.

The Secret of Secrets

Straddling the wisdom genre and the mirror of princes is the *Secret of Secrets*, ostensibly a letter from Aristotle to Alexander the Great on the government of self, household, and state, including advice on diet, hygiene, and divination (this last topic is censored in some versions). A hermetic element is present. Its ethos is generally more Machiavellian than that of the mirror.

The peninsula knew this text in translations from two redactions. The Western version, in the form of the Arabic *Sirr al-asrar*, supplied the first Hispanic translation, the Castilian *Poridat de las poridades*, known to Alfonso X. *Poridat* is to a degree implicated in the textual transmission of *Buenos proverbios*: both have material on Alexander the Great; of the six *Poridat* manuscripts, four include *Buenos proverbios*; in Catalonia, they are probably the twin sources of the *Llibre de saviesa*. The Eastern version is represented in the peninsula by the Aragónese, Castilian, Catalan, and Portuguese translations from the Latin abbreviated version of the translation of Philip of Tripoli (first half of the thirteenth century). This version seems to have been the more popular: unlike *Poridat*, it survived into the printing age.

BARRY TAYLOR

Bibliography

Jones, P. B. "Three Iberian Manuscripts of the *Secret of Secrets*." In *Josep Maria Solà-Solé: homage, homenaje, homenatge (Miscelánea de estûdios de amigos y discipulos)*. Vol. 1. Ed. A. Torres-Alcalá, et al. Barcelona, 1984, 297–309.

Wittlin, C. J. "Consells per a prínceps catalans de Jaume I a Francesc Eiximenis." In *Josep Maria Solà-Solé: homage, homenaje, homenatge (Miscelánea de estûdios de amigos y discípulos)*. Vol. 1. Ed. A. Torres-Alcalá, et al. Barcelona, 1984. 151–58.

MISA DE AMORES

Two major surviving compositions are generally given the title *Misa de amor* (or *amores*). One is attributed to Juan de Dueñas, "Beati de amores adsit" (Dutton 0369), and the other to Suero de Ribera, "Amor en nuestros trabajos" (Dutton 0034). A further fragment of a "love mass" is found in a four-line *Sanctus* to love by Juan de Tapia in the *Cancionero de Estúñiga* (Dutton 0559). The poets make use of the form of the Christian liturgy of the Mass (confession, creed, and the like) to write about love, or to address love as a god. To dismiss this as irreverent blasphemy, as some have done, is to make an inadequate critical response to the works themselves and also to late medieval religious sensibility. Evidence of censorship of such works does exist, but it looks to be the product of a later hand. The court anthologies of the fifteenth and early sixteenth centuries appear to allow for a creative juxtaposition of the sacred and the secular. At some times there is a clear parodic intent; at others the effect is less easy to categorize. This is true in the case of a third intact *Misa de amor*, which is less well known than those mentioned above. It comes in a composition by Nicolás Núñez in the *Cancionero general* of 1511, "Estas oras rezaréys" (Dutton 6621). The poet is ostensibly directing his lady in the devotional use of her Book of Hours. Each of the liturgical hours is accorded just one stanza, except the office of Terce, where some sixteen stanzas are devoted to the lady's attendance at the mass accompanying this service. Here the poet not only employs the structural form of his source but he also appeals to its spiritual and moral content.

JANE YVONNE TILLIER

Bibliography

Dutton, B., et al. *Catálogo-índice de la poesía cancioneril del siglo XV*. Madison, Wisc. 1982.

Piccus, J. "La *Misa de amores* de Juan de Dueñas." *Nueva Revista de Filología Hispánica* 14 (1960), 322–25.

MISSIONARIES *See* CHURCH; DOMINICAN ORDER; FRANCISCANS; RELIGIOUS ORDER

MOCEDADES DE RODRIGO

As one of only three epic narratives surviving in rhymed form, the *Mocedades de Rodrigo* is a document of major importance. The poem's unique, lacunous, poorly copied codex (Bib. Nat. Paris, MS. Espagnol 12), discovered in 1844, was studied and edited by A. D. Deyermond. Neotraditionalist criticism saw in the *Mocedades* only a late, aberrant, decadent epic. Deyermond has determined the poem's date (*c.* 1365) and has demonstrated that, in its present form, it embodies ecclesiastical propaganda in favor of the bishopric of Palencia, thus providing evidence of learned intervention in the diffusion of this late Spanish epic. However, the poem is not the only extant *Mocedades* narrative. Evidence of a *Mocedades* tradition dates from the late thirteenth century. An extensive prose rendering of similar structure and narrative content, thought to reflect an oral verse version (a lost *Gesta de las Mocedades*), was absorbed in the *Crónica de Castilla* (1300); the Portuguese *Crónica de 1344* attests to further possible evidence of the oral tradition. Vestiges of still other variants appear, after the extant *Mocedades*, in the *Bienandanzas e fortunas* (1471–1476) of Lope García Salazar, in a revision of Diego Rodríguez de Almela's *Compendio historial* (1504–1516), and in ballads from the late sixteenth century as well as in the modern oral tradition. From a neotraditionalist perspective, such texts document an epic tradition concerning El Cid's youthful deeds beginning in the late 1200s and lasting until the end of the Middle Ages and, in ballad form, until even later.

The *Mocedades de Rodrigo* will continue to be a crucial witness in the ongoing dialogue between neotraditionalist and neoindividualist critics concerning the origins and nature of the epic on the Iberian Peninsula.

SAMUEL G. ARMISTEAD

Bibliography

Armistead, S. G. "The *Mocedades de Rodrigo* and Neo-Individualist Theory." *Hispanic Review* 46 (1978), 313–27.

———. *La tradición épica de las Mocedades* de Rodrigo. Salamanca, 2000.

Deyermond, A. D. *Epic Poetry and the Clergy*. London, 1969.

MOLINA, MARÍA DE

Queen of Castile María (c. 1270–1321) was the wife of Sancho IV (r.1284–1295) and the mother of Fernando IV (c.1295–1312). As the daughter of Alfonso de Molina and Mayor Téllez de Meneses, she was a niece of Fernando III and a first cousin of Alfonso X. In June 1282 at Toledo she married Infante Sancho, the son and heir of Alfonso X, even though they were related within the prohibited degrees of kindred. Threatening them with excommunication and interdict, Pope Martin IV ordered them to separate in 1283, but they would not do so. Inasmuch as they lacked a papal dispensation, their enemies regarded the marriage as invalid and their children as illegitimate. María was crowned with Sancho IV at Toledo in April 1284. She seems to have been an active counselor to her husband, but her powerful presence in Castilian politics was particularly felt after his death in 1295.

As guardian of their firstborn, Fernando IV, her responsibility was to protect his person and to repel those who challenged his right to the throne. Her brother-in-law, Infante Juan, denied Fernando IV's claims on the grounds that he was illegitimate. Alfonso de la Cerda, as the son of Fernando de la Cerda, Alfonso X's eldest son, alleged that he had a better right to rule. She also had to contend with Sancho IV's uncle, Infante Enrique, who, after long years in exile in Italy, returned home and now demanded the right to act as regent for the boy king. María skillfully won over the towns of the realm, who formed their *hermandades* (military and religions fraternities) in defense of their liberties and the rights of Fernando IV. Through her impassioned appeal the *cortes* (parliament) of Valladolid in 1295 recognized him as king, giving María custody of his person and naming Enrique as guardian of the realm. In the turmoil of the next few years she succeeded in keeping her son's domestic enemies at bay and eventually made peace with his external enemies, Portugal and Aragón. She then arranged his betrothal to Constanza, daughter of King Dinis of Portugal. When Fernando came of age in 1302 he wished to be free of his mother's control and so there followed a period of estrangement. Though forced to withdraw into the background, she later endeavored to induce the nobles to abandon their hostility toward her son.

After the sudden death of Fernando IV in 1312 and of Queen Constanza in 1313, María de Molina emerged once more as a central figure in Castilian politics, championing the cause of her grandson, Alfonso XI (r. 1312–1350), then an infant. Summoned to determine who should be regent, the cortes of Palencia in 1313 were unfortunately divided, some acknowledging her brother-in-law, Infante Juan, while others accepted María and her son, Infante Pedro. After a year of diplomatic, political, and military maneuvering, María took the lead in persuading the infantes to collaborate. The cortes of Burgos in 1315 acknowledged the unified regency, entrusting María with custody of the king. She successfully maintained the unity of the regency, despite the tensions between Juan and Pedro, but after both men died on the plains of Granada in 1319, her skill was tried to the utmost. Her son Felipe, Juan's son Juan, and Infante Juan Manuel, the distinguished writer, now all demanded a share in the regency. Insisting that nothing could be done without the consent of the cortes, she summoned them to Valladolid in 1321, but she fell gravely ill. After making her will on 29 June, she died the next day and was buried in the Cistercian nunnery in Valladolid. By her marriage to Sancho IV she had several children: Fernando IV, Alfonso, Enrique, Pedro, Felipe, and Beatriz. A truly remarkable woman, she deserves to be ranked among those who most effectively governed medieval Castile. In many respects both Fernando IV and Alfonso XI owed their thrones to her.

JOSEPH F. O'CALLAGHAN

Bibliography

Gaibrois de Ballesteros, M. *Doña María de Molina*. Madrid, 1936.

MONARCHY, PORTUGAL

See KINGSHIP; QUEENSHIP

MONARCHY, SPAIN

See KINGSHIP; QUEENSHIP

MONASTERIES, CROWN OF ARAGÓN

Pre-Benedictine monasticism spread from Gaul to northeastern Romano-Visigothic Spain (the Tarraconensis) before the time of King Leovigild (r. 569–586), when it became more common throughout the Iberian Peninsula. Both Antonian eremitic or anchoritic, and cenobitic or communal forms existed, including double monasteries, using the guidelines from John Cassian or Caesarius of Arles, with indirect Basilian influence from the East and later that of St. Fructuosus from the West, and the old Isidorian or Mozarabic rites. The extent of continuity in monastic life at the oldest sites through the severe interruptions of the Arian controversy and Germanic invasions, is, however, debatable; and the Muslim conquest (711–718) was an even more severe interregnum. Monks who fled to mountain refuges do not seem to have retained their communities intact. Even when houses in the Hispanic March of northeastern Spain and farther west, in what would become Aragón and Navarre, trace their origins to late antique foundations either by oral tradition or because of archaeological remains, their recorded history usually begins anew in Carolingian times.

Normalized communal monastic discipline under the Rule of St. Benedict (480–543) usually dates after the promulgation in 817 of the *capitula* of Aachen and the ninth-century reforms of St. Benedict of Aniane. The general pattern was that a few houses in the Pyrenees spread their influence into mountain valleys, received patronage from local nobility, and enlarged their domains, then joined into some form of congregation for mutual support partially to ward off their patrons intervention and exploitation. These federated communities would found daughter houses in the lower piedmont country of northeastern Spain and spread monasticism farther south behind the lines of frontier action by the Catalan counts and upstart kings in Aragón who were able to encroach on Muslim territory. There is no evidence of the survival of Mozarabic monasticism in Muslim territory or the Hispanic March, which was embroiled in more than three centuries of intermittent warfare. However, the ideal of Romano-Visigothic monastic culture exemplified by the chronicler John Biclaro (d. 589), the monk-bishop of Girona, was later revived. As a learned Visigoth from Lusitania and traveler to Constantinople, he could have brought Fructuosan and Basilian monasticism to Catalonia, but the site (Vallclara?) of the monastery of Biclaro cannot even be located for certain. Medieval monasticism must be seen as a re-creation and renewal—largely spreading in a north-to-south movement with the Reconquest—that resurrected oral traditions, fostered a nostalgia for an often romanticized past, and revered places hallowed by events in pre-Muslim history.

Stronger evidence for continual monastic life after the Carolingian intervention pertains to key Pyrenean foundations such as Sant Miquel de Cuixà in the conflent where some Mozarabic influence can be detected. Founded in 879 by the archpriest Protasius and monks from Sant Andreu d'Eixlada, it would last until 1790. Santa Maria de Ripoll, whose church was dedicated in 888, was founded about the same time by Count Guifré and his protégé, the priest Dagui (880–902); it would continue until the exclaustration of its last eighteen monks in 1835. Ripoll had a dual house for women, Sant Joan de les Abadesses, which the count erected in 885 for his second daughter, Abbess Emma (898–942). Later (1001–1007) Sant Martí del Canigó, organized by the monk Solua (c.1004) from Ripoll, was patronized by Count Guifré II of Cerdanya (c.–1049) who would retire there. It would hold the relics of St. Goldrio, the patron of Catalan peasants. Other centers included Banyolas, Besalú, Camprodón, and revival of the old eighth-century foundation at Labaix.

Organizational reforms were directed by the famous abbot Oliba of Ripoll and Cuixà (1008–1048) who became bishop of Ausona (Vic). Oliba owed his education and inspiration to his predecessor at Cuixà, Abbot Garí (956–998), who continued the building program started by Abbot Ponç in 956, and who introduced the Cluniac (910) reform to the Pyrenean monasteries. Bishop Oliba continued building Cuixà, which is still known for its fine Romanesque architecture, and made it a center of learning with an active scriptorium that began producing chronicles in 985 and continued this tradition through the twelfth century. Ripoll likewise flourished as the pantheon of the comital house of Barcelona in its new church of Sant Pere (890) and monastic school that would later attract scholars like Gerbert (Gerbert d'Orlhac who became Pope Sylvester II) from the north to use its 121 manuscripts (catalog of 1008; 246 codices by 1046). Comital patronage of Ripoll's scriptorium, especially by counts Ramón Berenguer III and IV, resulted in numerous productions, some still extant: Bibles, the *Carmen Campidoctoris* (1098–1099) memorializing El Cid, the *Brevis historia* of Ripoll (1147), and an important version of the *Gesta comitum barcinonensium et regum Bragonum.*

In addition to Canigó, Ripoll (which numbered seventy-five monks in 1169) founded houses dedicated to St. Peter at La Portella and Casseres, and Sant Sadurní de Tavérnoles. After a feudal intervention by the counts of Besalú, the monks influenced by the Gregorian Reform sought union in 1070 with the congregation of St. Victor of Marseilles. Previous federation attempts were spread through the congregations of St. Ponce de Thomières and from La Grasse to incorporate Catalan Benedictine houses. In the 1070s many of these Benedictine monasteries became Cluniac. This pan-Pyrenean congregationalism encouraged cultural exchange between Catalonia, Provence, and Languedoc, which in turn supported Barcelonan dynastic interests in southern France. Filial priories were established by Ripoll at Cervera, Meía, Banyeres in the upper Penedés, Mediona, and Urgellet. Other important houses included Santa Maria de Amer and Santa Maria de O. The most important of these sub-Pyrenean monasteries, however, was Sant Cugat del Vallés, founded around 870 on first-century Roman ruins to commemorate this saint's martyrdom. Its early foundation so far south in a fertile but open valley left the monastery vulnerable to Muslim raids, as when Al-Manṣūr in 985 laid siege to Barcelona or as late as 1112–1118 when the Almoradvids penetrated Catalonia and threatened to cross the Llobregat River, also placed it in position to dominate the eleventh-century affairs of Barcelona's church and county.

Further west the Riojan borderland between Narvarre-Aragón and Castile had eight monasteries, of which all but two were tenth-century foundations. Of these, San Martín of Albelda (924) proved to be one of the most influential by spreading the Cluniac reform; and San Millán de la Cogolla, actually a Castilian foundation on an old hermitage site, was to become another major cultural center. The most important Benedictine houses in Aragón proper were San Victorio and Alaón, and San Juan de la Peña which was to become the pantheon for the kings of Aragón. Leyre and Irache were the dominant houses in Navarre. These were reestablished from southern France and reformed as Cluniac houses that played a significant role in the abolition in 1071 of the Mozarabic rite and its replacement by the Roman rite, and that supplied monks and bishops for restored churches and frontier monasteries both in Reconquest Castile-León and Aragón. The post-tenth-century migration of monks into peninsular houses has been called an "ultra-Pyrenean monastic invasion"; their pervasive influence on both Castile-León and Arago-Catalonia was much critized by anti-French Spanish historians writing after the Napoleonic occupation. The attribution to Cluniac Benedictines of the conversion of the Reconquest into something more militant than it had been, is not tenable; the papacy deserves this credit.

The most famous Catalan Benedictine monastery today is Montserrat, a monument of Catalan nationalism, culture, and regional pride, built on a "holy mountain"—a unique geological formation that is genuinely spectacular. Its foundation in 888 by Ripoll, also owed to the largess of Count Guifré, was confirmed by the Emperor Lothar in 982 and Pope Sergius in 1011, but it was not as important as Sant Benet de Bagés and other houses in the counties of Ausona and Barcelona until much later. Montserrat began humbly as four hermitages, two at the base of the mountain and two perched on ledges in a large crevice on the northeastern side. It became somewhat infamous in the late tenth century when in 971 one of its monks, Ceasarius of Santa Cecília de Montserrat, pretended to be the archbishop of Tarragona in exile. Around 1025 the hermits and various unorganized cenobitic communities around Montserrat were gathered together to form a monastery that embraced the Cluniac reform. Like its motherhouse, it later joined the congregation of St. Victor and during the twelfth century developed its famous cult of the Black Virgin. Its status, however, was only that of priory from 1082 until 1409 when Montserrat became an abbey. Its early years were upstaged by the abbey of Sant Llorenç del Munt, a castle (882) turned into a monastery by the monks of Sant Marçal de Montseny in 1067. A century later in 1161, Sant Llorenç faced a reform challenge that transformed several Benedictine monasteries: its monks converted themselves into a community of Augustinian canons.

Although the Benedictines were influenced by waves of reform in succession after the Cluniac (Camaldulesian, Vallumbrosan, Gramuntese), they were split permanently between the Black Monks and the new White Monks or Cistercians after the latter reform movement began in 1098 at Cîteaux and gained renown from the reputation of St. Bernard of Clairvaux (c.1090–1153). The Cistercians, reputed for their land reclamation elsewhere, appeared south of the Pyrenees as vanguard colonists in the late 1140s, contemporary with the most rigorous conversion of the Reconquest into a crusade. This conversion came in reaction to the Almoradvid invasion from Africa and to a revival of Islamic militantism in the 1130s, with consequent Christian drives to secure Tarragona (1118–1129), and take Tortosa and Lleida (1148–1149). Invited south by Count Ramón Berenguer IV and the seneschal Guillem de Moncada, the first White Monks from Grandselve (founded only a few years earlier, in 1145) settled temporarily in Valldaura by 1150 and moved on to the Tarragona frontier two years later. This monastery, Santa Maria de Santes Creus, which had an abbot by 1152, was followed shortly by a second colony from Fontfroide (1146) to occupy land donated after 1150 at the very base of the highland Muslim march of Ciurana, which was being subdued while the monks took position at Poblet. Its first abbot, Guerau, took office in 1153, the year Ciurana castle fell to the Christian allies. Their Cistercian cartularies document thereafter the assimilation of this Muslim territory, New Catalonia, into the Crown of Aragón. These two royal monasteries constituted the epitome of monastic institutionalization in northeastern Spain.

Santes Creus by 1158 consolidated its domain on the upper Campo de Tarragona (documented in its cartulary, *Llibre blanch*, compiled between 1194 and 1197), began construction of its exemplary Gothic-styled church in 1174 along with a major building program consisting of a chapter hall, dormitories, cloisters, courtyards, and outbuildings, followed after 1313 by a refectory and major cloister. Its scribes served the royal and archiepiscopal chanceries and by 1213 developed a reference library of more than sixty codices (which was to grow to 262 manuscripts and 150 incunabula by 1500). The monks built a hospital in 1129 and attracted the special patronage of King Pedro II who in 1285 was entombed there. During its apogee Santes Creus founded daughter houses at Valldigna (1298) in Valencia and Altofonte in Sicily (1308), and assisted in creating the military Order of Montesa (1319).

Poblet's domain grew more rapidly because of conversion of Muslim lands into its seignorial domain and King Alfonso II's patronage of his father's foundation; but its monastic complex developed somewhat differently from Santes Creus. It took over an old hermitage with a small chapel, the buildings turned into a refectory and hospital, and outlying Muslim castles that were converted into granges. These monks also began a magnificent Gothic church and cloister; and they inaugurated such a building program, including chapter hall and new refectory, sacristy, two dormitories for monks and conversos, a hospital, cellars, and forecourt, that by the end of the thirteenth century the abbots faced a financial crisis. When Alfonso II elected to be buried there, Poblet became the royal pantheon for the Crown of Aragón; the stunning royal tombs elevated on majestic arches on both sides of the main nave before the high altar were dedicated in 1340 by King Pedro III. The official character of Poblet's massive complex underscores the extent of its domain, the power of its abbots who became bishops of neighboring sees and served the crown as its treasures, and the influence of its scriptorium. The scriptorium saw much charter production and cartulary compilation, as well as the deeds of King Jaime I in his official *Chronica*, and records of the frequent stops by the royal court as it journeyed back and forth between Catalonia and Aragón along the old Roman road from Lleida to Tarragona. After 1369 the monastery was enclosed by massive walls and towers, and King Martín built his own residence there (1397–1406). Poblet's monks founded daughterhouses at Piedra (1194) on the other side of Zaragoza, at Benifassá (1233) in the kingdom of Valencia, and La Real (1239) in Mallorca; in 1287 they took over Valencia city's major shrine to St. Vincent.

The Cistercian impact on the settlement and evolution of the Crown of Aragón was profound. Cistercian sheep grazed from the foothills of the Pyrenees at the headwaters of the Tet, Segre, and Llobregat Rivers, to the south past Muslim boundaries by special privilege of the Almohads (1217) long before the Christian Reconquest. New Catalonia was resettled both by subcontracts to laymen and by the grange system that encompassed the entire drainage basin of the Segre River below Urgel and the Plains of Tarragona. Their trade goods were exchanged at permanent factories in Lleida, Tortosa, Tarragona, and latter Barcelona. White Monks took over the Benedictine sites of Clariana (1162), in the conflent and Labaix (1235), in Alta Ribagorça; and they founded abbeys at Escarp (1214) at the confluence of the Segre and Ebro Rivers, Vallbona (1242) in the Vallespir, Valldigna (1279) in Valencia, and Sant Bernat de Rascanya (1372), with priories of Roqueta (1287) at a Valencian shrine and Nazaret (1311) in Barcelona, with continued expansion at Les Franqueses (1452) in Noguera, Sant Pau (1472) at Manresa, and Tallat (1509) in Urgell. Of non-Catalan Cistercian houses, Fitero in Navarra (1140) was the most famous.

The convents of Cistercian nuns were far more numerous than older Benedictine convents. After the initial foundation at Valldemaria (1158) at Selva, they established houses at Cadins (1169) in old Empurias, Vallverd (1172) in Noguera; Vallbona de les Monges (1175) in the march of Urgell above Poblet; Les Franqueses (1186) long before its latter conversion to a male priory; La Bouera in Urgell (1195, translated to Vallsanta, 1249); Sant Hilari (1204) near Lleida, which moved to Tamarit; Bonrepòs (1210) in the former Muslim march of Ciurana that became known as the Priorat; Valldonzella (1237) in Barcelona; Valldaura (1237) in Berguedea; l'Eula (1247) in Perpgnan; Vallsantos (1249); and in Valencia at La Saïda (1268). By 1492, when many convents or women's houses were consolidated or abandoned, fourteen men's and eighteen women's monasteries had been founded in Catalonia and more in Aragón. Nearly all were destroyed in the uprisings of 1835.

Although monasticism thrived in the Crown of Aragón throughout the Middle Ages, after the thirteenth century cloistered living came under severe competition from the semimonastic but more socially active mendicant orders. The Benedictines and Cistercians were affected by the reform canons of the Fourth Lateran Council (1215). The Cistercians had always congregated into some kind of suprastructure; the Black Monks were reorganized into the Congregación Claustral Tarraconensis, but later the Benedictines of Navarre separated from the Aragónese and Catalan houses. In 1336, Pope Benedict XII divided the Tarraconensian congregation into those centered at Zaragoza for the Aragónese and those at Tarragona for the Catalans. The latter congregation subsequently split again when in the fifteenth century Montserrat, Cuixols, and Bagés were influenced by the reform from Valladollid.

LAWRENCE J. MCCRANK

Bibliography

Abadal i de Vinyals, R. d. *Dels Visigots als Catalans*. In *Collecció estudis i documents*, 2 vols. Barcelona, 1969–1970, 13–14. This also includes his *L'Abat Oliba, bisbe de Vic i la seva època*. Barcelona, 1948; 3d ed., Barcelona, 1962.

Altisent, A. *Història de Poblet*. Poblet, 1974.

Bishko, C. J. *Studies in Medieval Spanish Frontier History*. London, 1980.

Fort i Cogul, E. "La Congregación Cisterciense de la Corona de Aragón y Navarra: Aspectos de su gestación a través de documentos de Santes Creus." *Yermo* 8 (1970), 3–98.

Lewis, A. R. *The Development of Southern French and Catalan Society, 718–1050*. Austin, Tex., 1965.

Linaje Conde, A. *Los orígenes del monacato benedictino en la Península Ibérica*. 2 vols. León, 1973.

McCrank, L. J. "Monastic Inland Empires and the Meditteranean Coastal Reconquest in New Catalonia, 1050–1276." In *Spain and the Mediterranean*. Eds. B. Taggie, R. Clement, and J. Caraway. Kirksville, MO, 1992. 21–34.

Mundó, A. M. "Regles i observances monàstiques a Catalunya." II Colloqui d'Història del Monaquisme Català, 1970. *Scriptorium Populeti* 9 (1974), 7–24.

MONASTERIES, LEÓN AND CASTILE

The main characteristics of monasticism and its development in León and Castile may be reasonably divided into three broad chronological periods. The first of these, from the foundation of the Asturian kingdom in the early eighth century to roughly 1075, was marked by the predominance of Iberian peninsular forms and rules derived from the Visigothic era and a fundamental independence of houses, one from the other. The second period began about 1075 with the advent of Cluniac organization and flourished down until about 1220. It was notable both for the spread in the peninsula of orders founded elsewhere in Europe, notably the Benedictines of Cluny, the Cistercians, and the Carthusians, and for the marshaling of formerly independent houses into orders and provinces of orders. The final medieval period may be said to begin with the foundation of their Madrid house in 1218 by the Dominicans and was the great age of the friars, which continued until the time of the Catholic monarchs and St. Ignatius Loyola.

In the oldest period the indigenous rules of Bishop Isidore of Seville (600–630) and St. Fructuosus of Braga (c.600–665) largely governed monastic life and, in fact, most of the monasteries of the Christian north in Galicia, northern Portugal, and Old Castile either corporately survived from that period or were founded from the south by Mozarab refugees. During the Visigothic period, monasticism, like other formal Christian institutions, had been largely unknown in Asturias proper and in northern León and Galicia. The monastery at Liébana, flourishing in the late eighth century, is one of the earliest known. Nevertheless, there must have been dozens of others, for when the documentary record becomes substantial, the tiny monastery was typical. Founded very often by a family, some of whose members formed its first congregation, its lifetime might most often be limited to that of the family itself. Others, gathered about an influential anchorite, might also not outlive the founder who had given it impulse. Such small foundations not infrequently were double monasteries composed of houses of both men and women, both presided over by an abbess or an abbot. While many of them seem to have adhered to the rule of St. Isidore or St. Fructuosus, others were marked by a "pactual" form in which the authority and discipline were determined by an initial agreement between the monks and their abbot-to-be. This peculiar practice originated in the northwest of the peninsula in Visigothic times and subsequently spread west as far as the borders of the Rioja.

But if the typical monastery was a spontaneous and very local phenomenon, those that survived to have a wider, more enduring influence were likely to have been of episcopal or even royal foundation. Such were Valpuesta in the Rioja, founded by Bishop Juan in 804, or San Pedro de Montes in the Bierzo by Ramiro II in collaboration with San Genadio, bishop of Astorga, in 935, or again, Celanova south of Orense in 942, the work of Bishop San Rosendo of Mondoñedo, cousin of the same monarch. Such foundations had the prestige and the endowment that allowed them a chance at continuous existence. So too, more often, had the monasteries founded not in the countryside but in the towns, which at this time were little more than cult centers. The most favored houses of this type were, in fact, dedicated to the service of an episcopal cathedral or an important local saint's shrine. The monasteries of San Payo de Antealtares and San Martín de Pinario at Santiago de Compostela and the earliest history of San Isidoro of León are the most famous instances of this type of house.

These greater monasteries were the centers of such high culture as existed in the north during the early Middle Ages. This was a religious culture, of course, concerned with the teaching of Latin grammar so that the Scriptures could be read and appreciated. Beyond that, the *scriptoria* of these houses must see to the recopying of the various ordinals and antiphonals, service books central to the proper celebration of the liturgical life of the house. Some recopying of the patristic commentaries was also obligatory for such a house. But the greatest of them went beyond these merest necessities. At Liébana in the late eighth century a literature of controversy, centering on the adoptionist heresy championed by the metropolitan Elipandus of Toledo, was produced but one of the protagonists also wrote a *Commentary on the Apocalypse*. Ironically, the work has become world famous not for its theology but for the extraordinary illuminations of its manuscripts.

From the scriptorium of the monastery of Berlanga in the Sorian highlands we have not simply two manuscripts of the Bible, but also copies of some of the works of Cassiodorus and one of the homilies of the Carolingian author Smaragdus. The chronicle cycle of Alfonso III (866–910) found one of its major expressions in a version produced in the Riojan house at Albelda. From the nearby San Millán de La Cogalla a late tenth-century copy exists of the great, late Visigothic collection of church canons, the *Hispana*. The continued availability to at least that critical, literate portion of northern society of the latter work, which displayed the Visigothic Christian church at its most grand, and the associated collection of Roman and Visigothic law, the *Liber Judiciorum* or *Fuero Juzgo*, which did the same for the Visigothic monarchy, supplied a fundamental intellectual identity to the emerging Christian society.

The initiation of a new era in Iberian monasticism was signaled by the formation of a close liturgical bond between the Burgundian monastery of Cluny under abbot Hugh the Great (1079–1109) and Fernando I (1037–1065). That arrangement provided for the payment of an annual *census* to Cluny by the Leonese in return for Cluniac intercession for the king and dynasty. But while these, and other initiatives were important, the growth of an actual Cluniac province made up of formerly independent Leonese houses is datable to the period 1073–1077 when Alfonso VI bestowed four monasteries on the French house. His daughter Urraca (1109–1126) was to be quite as generous and the nobility of the realm tended to follow the lead of the crown. By the mid-twelfth century the Burgundian dependencies in León-Castile numbered no less than fourteen houses. That represented, however, the high point of Cluniac expansion.

Urraca's son, Alfonso VII (1126–1157) rather favored the new order of Cîteaux in his benefactions. The Cistercians secured their first house, in Fitero, at his hands in 1140 and his successors followed his lead. By the end of the century the order boasted no fewer than twenty-nine houses in the realm, although most of these were affiliated with Clairvaux and Morimond rather than Cîteaux itself. At the same time, no fewer than four Cistercian monasteries in León-Castile were houses for nuns.

The spread of houses of women was, strictly speaking, not new but the reforming conceptions of the late eleventh and early twelfth centuries had been hostile to the older houses. The Cistercians were, on the other hand, eminently respectable. So too was the French order of Fontevrault. Its first house in León-Castile, Nuestra Señora de las Nieves near Mayorga, was secured in 1125. Three others are known before the century's end.

Of course, these orders all grew, to large extent, by the appropriation of existing monasteries. The contemporary ideas of reform encouraged that process as they also favored the consolidation of the monastic world. Many small monasteries, under family or even royal patronage, were donated to these new and larger monasteries affiliated with a prestigious order. In short, monastic houses became radically fewer but larger in both community and endowment. A perhaps much older impulse toward a strictly contemplative and liturgical monasticism, even if embodied in a new and wider incarnation, such as the Carthusian ideal, grew most slowly in these centuries and the hermits of La Grand Chartreuse did not establish a presence in Castile until almost the end of the fourteenth century.

Yet other orders that saw some development in León and Castile in this period were those corporations of military monks founded in the Holy Land in the aftermath of the First Crusade. As early as the reign of Urraca there is some evidence for the royal patronage of Templars and Hospitalers but neither of them saw the sort of solid expansion in the west of the peninsula that they did in Aragón or Catalonia. In 1146 Alfonso VII surrendered the newly taken fortress of Calatrava to the Templars but the order proved unequal to the demands of the defense of that exposed position. In 1158, Sancho III of Castile redonated it to a group of individuals who subsequently organized themselves as the Order of Calatrava, which received papal sanction in 1164 and affiliated with Cîteaux in 1187.

At much the same time, in the kingdom of León, another military order was taking shape—that of San Julián del Pereiro, which was later to take the name of the Order of Alcántara after Alfonso IX of León (r.1188–1230) established them in that city in 1218.

Also contemporary in foundation was the Order of Santiago, which was organized first in Cáceres in 1170 and had received papal approval by 1175. It had the blessing from the first of Fernando II of León (r.1157–1188) who was much interested in the acquisition of that city. But during the reign of Alfonso VIII of Castile (1158–1213) it gained favor in that kingdom as well and expanded southward from its new headquarters at Uclés.

At this same time, those monastic houses associated with a cathedral were either becoming distinct from it or were themselves being converted into chapters of canons regular. The process has not thus far been much studied because it has not been recognized for what it was. At Santiago de Compostela, for example, the separation of San Payo de Antealtares from the official worship of the cathedral may have occurred simultaneously with the initiation of work on the new Romanesque cathedral there in 1076. The organization of cathedral chapters is also difficult to study for such documents as do exist have ordinarily been altered subsequently in the course of disputes between bishops and their chapters. This is the case with the cathedral chapter of Palencia, ordinarily said to have been formed in 1090 but the crucial document is not entirely reliable. In any event, from roughly 1080 to 1130 the transition to cathedral chapters was taking place.

The resultant corporations of canons regular were often reputed to have taken the Rule of St. Augustine but, in fact, their customs and constitutions were shaped by their local history combined with a certain borrowing from the monastic world proper. On a wider stage, something of the same sort was to create the Order of Premontré, or Norbertines, during the twelfth century. The history of that latter begins in León-Castile with the foundation of La Vid near Aranda de Duero sometime in the 1140s. During the twelfth and thirteenth centuries in Iberia, higher learning was, by and large, most conspicuous in the new cathedral schools that grew to provide for the professional training of chapter members and potential members. That scholarship continued to be marked by a concentration on Latin grammar and style, biblical studies, and scriptural commentary, and the most typical products of the chapter *scriptoria* continued to be mass books. The author of the *Chronicon Mundi*, Lucas of Túy, had been a canon of Léon and Rodrigo Jiménez de Rada, archbishop of Toledo (1208–1247) and author of the *De rebus Hispaniae* among other works, was closely associated with the cathedral school. In fact, by far the most famous of all of these schools in the peninsula was that of Toledo. Especially under Archbishop Raymond (1126–1151), Toledo became the center for a variety of scholars, both native and from beyond the Pyrenees, who worked to translate the works of Greek science, of Aristotle's philosophy, and of Jewish and Muslim philosophy, theology, mathematics, and medicine, into Latin and so made them available to the remainder of the West. However, when the further development of the cathedral schools and their learning into universities took place, it was first of all at Palencia but most importantly at Salamanca, where some ten masters attached to the chapter may be identified in the last half of the twelfth century, that it took root, rather than at Toledo.

From the beginning of the thirteenth century, the monastic world in León-Castile displayed much of the same features prominent elsewhere in the medieval West. That is, the new orders of friars, above all the Dominicans and Franciscans, tended to eclipse the older ones. Organizationally, the new friars were more truly international in character with a membership that attached the individual friar to the order rather than to a particular house and in subjection to a "general" at Rome rather than to a local abbot or prior. Moreover, the primary liturgical focus of the corporate life of earlier monasticism gave way, in some degree, to an increasing role of some mission in Christian society, such as preaching or evangelization. The former was of rather more importance in Iberia for it drew peninsulars more fully into the life of western Europe and contributed to the further integration of Spain into that society.

Indeed, St. Domingo de Guzmán (c.1170–1221) may be said to be the first great Castilian churchman whose life and work had a general European resonance since the end of antiquity. Fittingly, the spread of the Order of Preachers in León-Castile was swift. Already in 1221 a Spanish province was created by the second general chapter and by 1301 it had become desirable to divide that province into a Castilian and an Aragónese one.

St. Francis of Assisi (1182–1226) had made the pilgrimage to Santiago de Compostela in 1213–1214 and a fair number of the houses of the Friars Minor in the peninsula subsequently would trace their foundation to the saint himself, while being unable to document that circumstance. Nevertheless, the Franciscan general chapter of 1219 would name Juan Parente provincial for a Spanish province and in 1227, Parente would become general of the order. Already by 1232 the popularity of the order in Iberia was such that it was regarded as necessary to subdivide the province into three—Santiago de Compostela, Castile, and Aragón.

Both orders of friars would boast women's houses from the earliest days, of course, and the latter would contribute to the increasing popularity of women's convents in the peninsula. The Poor Clares, as the Franciscans were called, numbered no less than forty-nine houses in Spain by the end of their first century. The Dominican women's houses spread much more slowly even though that of Madrid dated to the lifetime of St. Domingo himself. There were but seven in the entire peninsula by 1300. Moreover, unlike the male friars, the nuns of those orders tended to be contemplatives rather than developing a social apostolate.

The later orders of friars also found their way into the peninsula, if more slowly and in fewer numbers. The Carmelites decreed a Spanish province in their general chapter of 1256 but the first known house in León-Castile only appears near Medina del Campo in 1315 and separate Aragónese and Castilian provinces were not created until 1416. The Augustinian mendicants, as distinct from canons regular who followed some variant of the Rule of St. Augustine, grew out of the "Grand Union" of 1256 and the creation of a Spanish province followed hard on that event. A Toledan convent existed by 1260. Further houses at Murcia, Seville, Córdoba, Casarrubias, and Badajoz had swelled the new congregation during the thirteenth century.

Two other new orders found particular occupation in the peninsula by reason of their primary mission. The first was the Trinitarian, founded in France in the latter twelfth century. Its purpose was the ransom of Christian captives in Muslim hands. Houses were established by the founder, Juan de Mata, in Toledo in 1206 and in Burgos in 1207. By 1221 two distinct provinces had been formed for Castile and for Aragón. In 1312 the former was divided into into a Castilian and a Portuguese province. The peninsula constituted a unique field for such work and the Mercedarian Order was itself founded in Catalonia. It had a house in Seville already in 1248 as a result of the Reconquest there. By 1311 its possessions were divided between the two provinces of Catalonia and Castile.

All these orders of friars soon produced associations of lay tertiaries that contributed to the former's material support and that enjoyed some benefits from the liturgical intercession of the full members. The latter of such practices tended, insensibly, to conform the newer orders somewhat to the older monastic tradition and practice. On the other hand, the friars' preaching, the saying of Mass, and the hearing of confession brought them into competition and conflict with the secular clergy and, above all, the bishops. At the same time, the superior educational opportunities of the order clergy would prove to give them an advantage in the competition for promotion to the episcopacy itself, which frequently overcame the general reluctance to permit the consecration of members of religious orders to that office and further confused lines of authority in the church.

Nevertheless, the organizational model of the new orders recommended itself for the modification of the older monasticism as well. As early as the Fourth Lateran Council (1215) the practice of triennial abbatial chapters were enjoined for the otherwise unassociated monasteries in each ecclesiastical province. By 1336 Pope Benedict XII, a Cistercian himself, would work out a universal plan of such that provided for congregations of Santiago de Compostela in Seville and of Toledo in León-Castile. None of these plans prospered, though they clearly foreshadowed the future congregation of Valladolid.

That same pope also addressed himself to the stimulation of education among the more traditional monasteries and, for a time in the fourteenth century, the great Benedictine abbey of Sahagún responded with an attempt to broaden and revivify its school. Such attempts were destined to fail in the new age emerging, however, unless they could be assimilated to the newer university structures. The new orders, on the other hand, more routinely sent their members to study in Paris, Bologna, or Rome. There and in the peninsula they established houses of study in conjunction with the universities, such as the Dominican San Esteban in Salamanca, functioning already by 1265. Indeed, when a faculty of theology was at last instituted at Salamanca at the end of the fourteenth century, Dominicans and Franciscans made up the bulk of its members.

Under these circumstances, most of the identifiable scholars of León-Castile in the later Middle Ages are members of the regular clergy. Juan Gil de Zamora (c.1250–c.1319), author of the *Liber de Preconiis Hispaniae* and the *Liber Illustrium Personarum* was a Franciscan. Juan Puigventos was a Dominican educated in Murcia who later taught Arabic in Valencia. Also a Dominican was the Marian theologian Pedro of Compostela. The Augustinian and scholastic philosopher Alonso Fernández de Toledo y Vargas (1300–1366) taught at Paris and subsequently became bishop, in turn, of Badajoz, Osma, and then Seville. Curiously, however, the circle of scholars other than Gil de Zamora who collaborated with Alfonso X (c.1252–1284) and produced such a brilliant array of works, seem not to have been friars or even clerics.

BERNARD F. REILLY

Bibliography

Ajo González y Sáinz de Zúñiga, C.M. *Historia de las universidades hispánicas: Orígenes y desarrollo desde su aparición hasta nuestros días*. Vol. 1, *Medievo y Renacimiento universitario*. Madrid, 1957.

Bishko, C.J. "Fernando I and the Origins of the Leonese-Castilian Alliance with Cluny." In *Studies in Medieval Spanish Frontier History*. London, 1980, 1–136.

Brodman, J.W. *Ransoming Captives in Crusader Spain: The Order of Merced on the Christian-Islamic Frontier*. Philadelphia, 1986.

Cocheril, M. *Études sur le monachisme en Espagne et au Portugal*. Lisbon, 1966.

Fernández Conde, J. (ed.) *Historia de la Iglesia en España*. Vol. 2, parts 1–2. Madrid, 1982.

Hinnebusch, W.A. *The History of the Dominican Order*. Vol. 1. New York, 1965.

Linage Conde, A. *Los orígenes del monacato benedictino en la península ibérica*. 3 vols. Leon, 1973.

Lomax, D.W. *Las órdenes militares en la peninsula ibérica durante la Edad Media*. Salamanca, 1976.

López, A. *La Provincia de España de los frailes menores: Apuntes histórico-críticos sobre los orígenes de la orden franciscana en Espãna*. Santiago de Compostela, 1915.

Moral, T. "Hacia una historia de la Orden praemonstratense en España y Portugal." *Boletín de la Real Academia de la Historia* 165 (1969), 219–53.

Sanz Pascual, A. *Historia de los augustinos españoles*. Madrid, 1947.

MONASTERIES, PORTUGAL

The Portuguese territory as it is today had in the past a great quantity of monasteries unevenly distributed, side by side with the also uneven distribution of the population. The monasteries were extremely numerous in the north, but practically absent in the center and south. These latter regions, definitively conquered from the Muslims between 1227 and 1249, were much less inhabited. The distribution of monastic observances was also always unequal due to the correlation between the political and ecclesiastical phases of establishment in the territories conquered by Islam and the evolution of religious orders. Thus, there were mainly Benedictines and regular canons in Entre-Douro-e-Minho; Cistercians in Trás-os-Montes, Alto Minho, and Alto Douro; canons regular, Cistercians, and Jerónimos in Beira Litoral and Estremadura; Paulines in Alentejo.

Pre-Benedictine Observances

The monastic tradition in the north of Portugal has its origins in an era prior to St. Martinho of Dume but it was he who greatly influenced the region with his monastery of Dume (Braga). We do not know of other monasteries previous to the one founded the next century by St. Fructuosus (c.600–665) in Montélios, very close to Dume. Nevertheless, the existence of numerous monasteries at that time is clear. Several were associated in congregations and adopted the practices contained in *Regula communis* due to the influence of Fructuosus. Some had double communities (monks and nuns), reserved the admission of their members to the relatives of the founding families (familiar monasteries) and practiced the monastic pact that restrained the abbot's power. Some of these practices were contested by St. Fructuosus but they endured and even took root because of the ecclesiastical and political disorganization resulting from the Muslim invasions (711). Such disorganization did not prevent the foundation of numerous monastic communities in the north of Portugal, mainly between the Douro and Lima Rivers before the reorganization started in 868. By that time, the counts who took power as the Asturian king's delegates also protected monastic life but preferred rich and large communities, true observant ones, as opposed to the surviving small monasteries, which were poor and unstable. The prototype for the new abbeys was the monastery of Guimarães, founded around 950 by Mumadona Dias, a relative of the monastic reformer St. Rosendo (d.966). The monastery of Lorvão may also be included in this type. It was probably founded before the Christian occupation of Coimbra (878) but protected by the count of Coimbra, who was also related to St. Rosendo. In this way, we have documentary evidence of about thirty monasteries in Entre-Douro-e-Minho founded before 1000, and of seventy-six founded between 1000 and 1100. From the Council of Coyanza (1055) on, the divisions between the monasteries considered observant and the ones considered relaxed became deeper. Some foundations were inspired by an ideal of austerity and tried to restore the ancient Fructuosan observances, as in Pendorada in 1054 or Vacariça, founded earlier.

Benedictines

Although the Council of Coyanza agreed that the observant monasteries might follow the Rule of St. Benedict, no Portuguese monastery is known to have adopted it before 1084. Probably the change occurred when the Hispanic liturgical rite was replaced by the Roman rite, decreed in the Council of Burgos (1080). There is surely a relation between this change and the introduction of French culture and the establishment of French institutions supported by Alfonso VI. The French influence achieved great success among the Portuguese nobles who had recently obtained feudal powers. Until then several monasteries under their protection that had followed the peninsular rules adopted the Rule of St. Benedict and Cluniac practices. They did not, however, affiliate with Cluny. Pendorada, Santo Tirso, Pombeiro, Tibães, and Arouca, protected by the most powerful noble families, are some examples. The movement spread rapidly, mainly after the impulse given by the bishops of Coimbra, Crescónio (1092–1098), Maurício Burdino (1099–1109), and Bernardo (1128–1146), and the bishops of Braga, Geraldo (1099–1108) and Maurício Burdino (1109–1118). The renewal of monastic practice led to a time of great prosperity and the Benedictines could become the owners of many small monasteries that were transformed into dependent churches. The rare new monasteries were founded by Cluny between 1100 and 1127, Rates, Vimieiro, and St. Justa of Coimbra, but they fell into decay, especially from the thirteenth century on. The other Benedictine monasteries were dependent on the bishop of their dioceses and did not constitute a congregation until 1567. They also started falling into decay mainly from the beginning of the fourteenth century. Some disappeared in the fourteenth or fifteenth centuries. The richest ones started to be ruled by commendatory abbots who had not taken vows as monks and contributed to the complete corruption of monastic life. The first reform movements took place in the fifteenth century in Paço de Sousa and Pendorada, under the influence of monks who had been in Flanders or Italy, and later in Santo Tirso, Tibães, and Rendufe, under the influence of the Valladolid Congregation and the Jerónimos monks.

Cistercians

The Order of Cister was established in Portugal in 1143 or 1144 in the monastery of Tarouca, where a hermitic community following St. Benedict's Rule already existed. Soon later, other hermitic groups in Lafões and Salzedas followed suit. The adhesion of hermits and other communities to Cister continued until the end of the twelfth century, involving monasteries such as Fiães, Bouro, and Aguiar. The only new foundation was Alcobaça, which was given immunity in 1153 by Afonso Henriques, the first Portuguese king. Although the Alcobaça community had had a modest origin, the abbey developed within in a short period of time, thanks to its agricultural production and its rapid commercialization, having become a supplier of the city of Lisbon. Its prosperity is evident in the large abbatial church, built in the beginning of the thirteenth century, and in the library with its codex collection, accumulated between the twelfth and fifteenth centuries. Some kings, such as Alfonso II, Alfonso III, and Pedro I, wished to be buried in the abbey. From 1210 on, some ancient Benedictine monasteries became feminine Cistercian communities such as Lorvão and Arouca (1223); others were new foundations such as Celas in Coimbra (1214), Almoster (1287), and Odivelas (1295). Opposite to what happened to the Benedictines, and despite the general decadence, the Cistercians experienced less corruption in part due to the action of visitors from Clairvaux. They started as an independent congregation in 1567.

Canons Regular

Apparently some pre-Benedictine monasteries in the north resisted the adoption of the Rule of St. Benedict. Later, many of them became canons regular of St. Augustine, following the practices of Santa Cruz of Coimbra, probably because they were influenced by some Augustine bishops who had occupied the sees of Braga and Oporto since 1136. Santa Cruz had been founded in 1131 by Tello and St. Teotónio and adopted the rules of St. Ruf of Avignon shortly after. It was protected by kings Afonso Henriques and Sancho I, who are buried there. It came into possession of large estates in central Portugal and founded the monastery of St. Vincent in Lisbon immediately after the city was conquered from the Moors in 1147. It played an important cultural role by preserving some Mozarabic traditions and establishing an important manuscript library. Among the northern monasteries that adhered to its rules are Moreira da Maia, Grijó, Refojos de Lima, and Cárquere. Like other monastic orders, they were also afflicted by religious decadence in the fourteenth century and subjected to commendatory abbots during the fifteenth and sixteenth centuries. However, one can mention an important effort of religious reformation led by Prior Gomez, appointed as commendatory abbot (1441–1459). He had already actively participated in the reform of the Benedictine monks of St. Justina of Padova at the monastery of Florence and in the reform of the Italian Camaldoli monks. But the definitive process of reform came later, in 1556, with the congregation of Santa Cruz of Coimbra.

Other Monastic Orders

The other monastic orders were not so significant in Portugal. One can mention the Premonstratensians, who owned two small monasteries in Ermida de Paiva and Vandoma during the twelfth and thirteenth centuries, and the Paulines or Hermits of St. Paulo da Serra de Ossa. The Paulines founded several small hermitages in Alentejo that had been independent up to then. These hermitages formed a confederation in 1465 and a congregation approved by the Holy See in 1536. The Jerónimos, founded in Spain in 1374, were more important than the other two orders. They founded in Portugal the monastery of Penhalonga in 1390, and later, protected by several kings, especially Manuel I, founded other monasteries. The most important one is the monastery of Jerónimos in Lisbon (1498).

José Mattoso

Bibliography

Caetano Damásio, M. de S. *Thebaida portuguesa*. Lisbon, 1793.

Cocheril, M. *Routier des abbayes cisterciennes du Portugal*. Paris, 1986.

Mattoso, J. *Le monachisme ibérique et Cluny*. Louvain, 1968.

O'Malley, A. *Tello and Theotonio, the Twelfth-Century Founders of Santa Cruz of Coimbra*. Washington, D.C., 1954.

Santos, C. dos. *Os Jerónimos em Portugal*. Lisbon, 1980.

MONASTICISM

The multifaceted story of monachism in medieval Spain and Portugal commences obscurely in late Roman Hispania, when powerful currents of ascetic-encratitic spirituality reached the Iberian Peninsula directly from the Christian east or by way of surrounding North Africa, Italy, and Gaul. By about 300–306, the Council of Elvira (Granada) was regulating the life of consecrated women (*velandae*, *devotae*), and later in the fourth century there are references to *monachi* (anchorites), who are carefully distinguished from comparable adherents of the widely popular dissident rigoristic movement of Priscillianism, by the Council of Zaragoza (380) and the First Council of Toledo (400), and in the correspondence of Metropolitan Himerius of Tarragona with Pope Siricius (384–385).

The turbulent fifth century of Germanic invasions is painfully lacking in monastic data; but the sixth century provides more than sufficient evidence that in both the Visigothic monarchy of Toledo and that of the Suevi at Braga in Galicia, not only anchorites and semi-anchorites, like St. Aemilian (San Millán; d. 574), but also organized communities of monks (*monasteria*, *coenobia*) are well documented. For the latter the pattern is a visibly regionalistic one: numerous houses in the Tarraconensian northeast under strong south Gallic influences; in the east and south, prototypical foundations established by refugee monks from North Africa; and in remote Galicia, the remarkable abbey-bishopric of Dumio (Dume), which its founder, St. Martin of Braga (fl. 550–580), made the protomonastery of the Suevi and conjoined it to his metropolitan church of Braga.

The conversion of the Visigoths to Catholicism (589) was followed by a widespread series of monastic foundations by kings, nobles, and bishops, with abundant legislation by the Fourth Council of Toledo (633) and later councils, and in the royal *Leges Visigothorum*, aimed at enforcing uniformity of observance, liturgy, and relations with crown and episcopate throughout the monasteries of the kingdom. In this seventh-century golden age of Visiogthic monachism, the traditional cenobitic sources associated with Pachomius, Basil, St. John Cassian, Augustine, and others were richly supplemented by new, distinctly Hispanic rules: Leander of Seville's *De institutione virginum* (590–595?), Isidore of Seville's *Regula monachorum* (c. 620–625?), and the austere, similarly titled code of Fructuosus of Braga (ca. 635–640). Circulation in the peninsula of the Rule of St. Benedict, often defended, has yet to be proved; unquestionably no true Benedictine abbey can be found there before 711.

At the same time it is essential to allow, alongside the main Visigothic tradition, for a second, constitutionally distinct, cenobitism found in late seventh-century Galicia. This is the so-called pactual monasticism, in which the orthodox individual act of profession, pledging obedience to a monarchical abbot, is replaced by a synallagmatic covenant (*pactum*)—in effect a contract between abbot and monks defining the rights and duties of each and reserving to the monks the right of rebellion against abbatial misrule. This particular cenobitism—often mistakenly ascribed to St. Fructuosus of Braga—can be traced through such texts as the *Consensoria monachum*, the *De* [*septimo*] *genere monachorum* of Valerius of Bierzo, and—above all—the *Regula communis* and its terminal *pactum*, a collection of decrees by Gallegan abbatial synods of about 675–690. The phenomenon is of great historical interest in itself and for the transmission of pactualism as the basis of early Reconquest cenobitism in comital Castile and the Rioja.

For Iberian monasticism in general, the consequences of the catastrophic Arab-Berber overthrow of the Visigothic state in 711–714 may be classified under three heads. First, many houses, with their libraries and temporalities, simply disappeared. Second, a limited number of communities, chiefly around Toledo and Córdoba, survived into the earlier Islamic centuries; these constitute the so-called Mozarabic monasticism, best known from the *Memoriale sanctorum* of Eulogius of Córdoba, and sporadically sent monks and manuscripts to new centers on Christian soil. Third, scores of houses, founded by refugee monks from the south and by their soon far more numerous successors in the Cantabrian-Pyrenees zone and its extensions, sprang up in proto-Christian Spain. From there they spread monasticism in the wake of the Reconquest, creating new centers of ascetic spirituality and agrarian development while attracting lay settlers into desolate *despoblados*.

These monasteries of the early Reconquest clung tenaciously to monastic, literary, and artistic continuities with the Visigothic past, a notable example being the composition by the monk Beatus of Liébana of his famous, richly illustrated, and much copied *Commentary on the Apocalypse* (c. 786). As regards observance, these monasteries of the early Reconquest in Asturias, León, Navarre, Aragón, and the northeast followed no single rule (*regula unica*) but selectively used traditional codes collected in *codices regularum* (*regula mixta*). At two key points Europeanizing Benedictinism entered the pensinsula for the first time: early, in the Catalan northeast close to Aquitaine; later, in the late ninth and tenth centuries, in the pactualized zones of comital Castile and the Rioja, where the *Regula s. Benedicti* came to circulate embedded in the massive by-product of Carolingian reform Benedictinism, the *Expositio* of Smaragdus of St. Mihiel. Here there occurred a remarkable if ultimately frustrated effort to combine the pactual and Benedictine traditions, a synthesis clearly visible in the nuns' rule composed between 951 and 962 by the abbot Salvus of Albelda, and in the monastic sections of the *Liber ordinum* of the eleventh century.

By the early eleventh century, documentary evidence all across the Christian north showed clear signs of spiritual and disciplinary decline in this conservative, relatively isolated cenobitism. This in turn led to energetic royal, episcopal, and aristocratic efforts to reinforce policies of internal development and territorial expansion through programs of monastic revitalization along "Benedictinizing" (i.e., "Europeanizing") lines. These circumstances underlie the powerful attraction to peninsular rulers and churchmen of the Burgundian abbey of Cluny. King Sancho III Garcés of Navarre (r. 1000–1035) initiated formal Hispano-Cluniac ties west of Catalonia, but his aims were intercessional, not reformist. It was his son, Fernando I of León-Castile (r. 1037–1065), who enlisted the Cluniacs in support of his program of complete Benedictinization as well as of his claims to imperial rule over all Iberia. In 1063 he established a veritable dynastic alliance (*coniunctio*) with the abbey and endowed it with a rich annual subsidy of 1000 gold dinars (*metcales*) out of the tributary *parias* of his *ṭā'ifa* vassals. In turn Fernando's son, Alfonso VI (r. 1065–1109), doubled this stipend in 1077; and in 1073 he had already given the Cluniacs their first peninsular dependency, San Isidro de Dueñas. Other such transfers of established houses followed from Leonese-Castilian rulers and nobles, creating a string of what the Cluniacs organized as priories under the Burgundian abbot. Others were added: three in Portugal, another three in Catalonia. Hispano-Cluny, however, always remained a basically Leonese-Castilian phenomenon, the priories radiating reformist influences and contributing to the advance of Europeanization below the Pyrenees; never a widespread or popular movement, its impact was confined to monarchs and the upper layers of Luso-Hispanic society.

By the mid-twelfth century, with Cluniac energies and prestige visibly waning, a new chapter in Iberian monastic history opened with the advent of the Cistercians, who represented a new fervent, mystical spirituality and crusading ardor and, in terms of geograpical expansion and recruitment of large numbers of peasant *conversi*, constituted a more widely established, socially much more inclusive, movement of far broader appeal than the Cluniacs. Warmly welcomed from the 1140s and 1150s by such rulers as Alfonso VII of León-Castile, Afonso Henriques of Portugal, and Ramón Berenguer IV of Barcelona, the White Monks took over and organized as relatively independent abbeys numerous male and female houses throughout northern Spain and Portugal, as far south as the Tagus and Júcar Rivers, leaving the dangerous zones of Reconquest warfare beyond to the rising military orders. The siting of many of their abbeys, such as Alcobaça in Portuguese Estremadura and Santes Creus and Poblet in New Catalonia, and others in the two Castiles, clearly reflects the Cistercian predilection for isolation and the reduction of wilderness and frontier districts to human settlement.

From about 1250 the picture changed once again. Both Black and White Monks—with important exceptions of still vigorous communities—passed into a twilight zone of fading energies, sharp reduction in postulants, and a lamentable debasement of disciplinary, spiritual, liturgical, and intellectual standards, a decline intensified by the attacks upon them and their temporalities by kings, nobles, bishops, peasants, and townsmen. The condition was made worse by the emphatic swing of royal and popular enthusiasm to the new mendicant orders, with their greater attraction to an increasingly urban-oriented medieval society. Nevertheless, it would be erroneous to dismiss the Luso-Hispanic monastic tradition of the later Middle Ages as moribund, for countercurrents of renewed monastic faith and creativity also appeared, encouraged in part by the pervasive effects of the Observant reformism among the Franciscans and other mendicants, and in part by the new ascetico-mystico-interiorist piety flowing into the peninsula from Italy and the Low Countries.

Thus, the fourteenth century brought the rise of a major new semi-anchoritic order of marked austerity, that of St. Jerome, of Italian origin but very quickly transformed into a distinctly Iberian movement. Approved by Pope Gregory XI in 1373, and spreading rapidly from San Bartolomé de Lupiana (Guadalajara) in Castile, Portugal, and the Crown of Aragón, the

Jeronymites (Hieronymites) attracted rich benefactions from Juan I of Castile, other monarchs, and the aristocracy, drawing into their houses numbers of nobles and upper-class *conversos* (converts to Chastianity). In 1389 they acquired their chief Spanish base, the celebrated Estremaduran monastery and Marian pilgrimage center of Nuestra Señora de Guadalupe; and in the fifteenth century, under such able generals of the order as Pedro de Alarcón and Lope de Olmedo, the Jeronymite Order enjoyed high prestige, great wealth, and a fruitful influence upon the church in Spain and Portugal. Also from the late fourteenth century on, the comparably rigoristic, semi-anchoritic Carthusian Order became established in the peninsula, with leading centers at Miraflores (near Burgos), EI Paular (Segovia), and elsewhere.

In addition a revived, robust Benedictinism appeared with the foundation by Juan I of Castile, in 1390, of a deliberately organized monastic reform house that quickly became the head of an alliance of Black Monk monasteries joined in the strongly reform-oriented Congregation of Valladolid. Among these was the celebrated abbey of Nuestra Señora de Montserrat in Catalonia, the gifted abbot of which, García de Cisneros (1455–1510), wrote one of the leading manuals of fifteenth-century Iberian spirituality, the *Exercitorio de la vida spiritual*, later a principal guide for Ignatius Loyola. Nor were the Cistercians remote from these strong new religious forces: from the early fifteenth century on, under the inspiration of such abbeys as Alcobaça and Poblet, much reformist legislation by their chapters-general, and the activities of talented generals of the order, gave the White Monks a significant role in the monastic revival.

All this dynamic reformism leavening the monastic life of the Iberian later Middle Ages constructed the foundations upon which, after 1574, Cardinal Cisneros and the Catholic Monarchs, and comparable royal and ecclesiastical leadership in Portugal, built. The long Luso-Hispanic monastic tradition thus continued unbroken into the age of comprehensive, innovative modernization, deeper spiritual exploration, and expansionist impetus that characterized the monastic, and in general the religious, life of early modern Iberia.

C.J. Bishko

Bibliography

Bishko, C. J. *Spanish and Portuguese Monastic History, 600–1300*. London, 1984.

Cocheril, M. *Études sur le monachisme en Espagne et au Portugal*. Paris, 1966.

García Oro, J. "La reforma de las órdenes religiosas en los siglos XV y XVI." In *Historia de la iglesia en España*, Vol. 3, pt.1. Ed. R. García Villoslada. Madrid, 1980. 211–90.

Linage Conde, A. *Los orígenes del monacato benedictino en la Península Ibérica*. 3 vols. León, 1973.

MONTCADA, HOUSE OF

Guillem de Montcada (d. 1040) took his name from the castle of Moncada (Catalan, Montcada), that dominates the gap through which the Besòs River flows into the plain of Barcelona. Through association with the count-kings of Catalonia-Aragón, his descendants grew in stature and importance. The family also established branches outside the kingdom of Aragón in Béarn and Sicily.

The Montcada name was long associated with the hereditary office of seneschal in Catalonia. This resulted from the marriage of Guillem Ramón II (c. 1090–1173), "The Great Seneschal" (whose ancestors were not related to the Montcadas), to Beatriu de Montcada in 1117.

Prominent early Montcadas included Guillem de Montcada II (c. 1120–1172), who acquired the viscounty of Béarn for his lineage (by marriage to Maria of Béarn); Guillem Ramón de Montcada I (c. 1165–1224), second Montcada viscount of Béarn, noted for his assassination of Archbishop Berenguer de Vilademuls in 1194; and Guillem de Montcada III (c. 1185–1229), an influential royal counselor during the minority of Jaume I.

Later generations of Montcadas included Pere de Montcada (d. 1282), master of the Knights Templar in Catalonia-Aragón; Guillem de Montcada i d'Aragó (d. 1283), bishop of Lleida; Guillem de Montcada (d. 1308), bishop of Urgell; Elisenda de Montcada (d. 1364), wife of King Jaime II of Aragón; and Ot de Moncada i de Luna (d. 1473), bishop of Tortosa and cardinal during the final years of the Great Schism.

Advantageous marriages contributed to the influence of the Montcada lineage, and many Montcada women were prominent as baronesses. Some Montcada women entered the church; two became abbesses.

John C. Shideler

Bibliography

Fluvià, A. de, and M. M. Costa. "Montcada." In *Gran enciclopedia catalana*. Vol. 1. Ed. J. Carreras i Martí. Barcelona, 1977. 222–30.

Shideler, J. C. *A Medieval Catalan Noble Family: The Montcadas, 1000–1230*. Berkeley, 1984. Catalan translation by G. Lletjós i Llambias and J. M. Masferrer. *Els Montcada: Una família de nobles catalans a l'edad mitjana (1000–1230)*. Barcelona, 1987.

MONTESA, ORDER OF *See* MILITARY ORDERS

MONTESINO, FRA AMBROSIO

Montesino (ca. 1440/1450–1514), a Franciscan friar who attained a high rank in the ecclesiastical bureaucracy (bishop of Sarda, in Albania), was a protégé of Cardinal Francisco Jiménez de Cisneros and of Queen Isabel, for whom he was both personal confessor and preacher. He was the author of prose religious texts, among which his collection *Epístolas y euangelios por todo el año* (Toledo, 1512), with numerous later editions, is especially worthy of mention. A work of major importance was his Castilian translation of Ludolph of Saxony's renowned text *Vita Christi, cartuxano romançado*, in four volumes (1502–1503), the first book published by the Renaissance presses of Alcalá de Henares. It had great influence on religious literature and thought.

In addition Montesino wrote religious poems. These appeared in two collections: *Coplas sobre diuersas deuoçiones y misterios de nuestra sancta fe catholica* (Toledo, ca. 1485) and *Cancionero de diuersas obras de nueuo trobadas* (Toledo, 1508). The *Coplas* consists of fourteen compositions later revised in part and included in the *Cancionero* along with other texts for a total of thirty-four in verse and three in prose. This work presents a series of meditations on the Virgin Mary, Christ, and the lives of certain saints, and includes apocryphal themes.

Besides the customary double five-line octosyllabic stanzas of this period, the presence of nine ballads—one nonreligious—should be mentioned, and of special note is the use of religious *contrafacta*. Occasional criticism of customs adorns the poems, and many cultured forms and, on the whole, an elegant, sophisticated style are found throughout. A preacher-turned-poet, Montesino was clearly influenced by another Franciscan, Íñigo de Mendoza, an influence that in certain instances lends itself to plagiarism.

JULIO RODRÍGUEZ-PUÉRTOLAS

Bibliography

Álvarez Pellitero, A. M. *La obra lingüística y literaria de fray Ambrosio Montesino*. Valladolid, 1976.

Rodríguez Puértolas, J. *Cancionero de fray Ambrosio Montesino*. Cuenca, 1987.

MONTIEL, BATTLE OF

The battle of Monteil, which took place on 14 March 1369, represents the last stage of the civil war fought between Pedro I of Castile and his illegitimate half-brother Enrique de Trastámara from 1366 to 1369.

The two sides in this contest represented different interests, and both sides relied on military support from abroad. Unfortunately for Pedro, the English, who had backed him during the earlier stages of the war but had not received the expected compensation, refused to commit additional troops after 1367. The only foreign soldiers supporting Pedro after that date were from the Muslim kingdom of Granada. Enrique's allies, the French, were more consistent in their commitment; the French king, Charles V, paid, a second time, for the military services of the mercenary captains Bertrand du Guesclin and Arnoul d'Audrehem, who arrived in Castile in January 1369.

In the early months of 1369 Enrique and his allies assembled their thirty-six hundred lancers at Orgaz, south of Toledo. Pedro had decided to travel north from his headquarters in Seville to meet his opponent. His force consisted of fifteen hundred Moorish cavalry and three thousand lancers. After a long and meandering march, he stationed part of his army in Montiel while the rest foraged in the surrounding countryside. On the evening of 13 March the garrison commander at Montiel, upon seeing torchlights, alerted Pedro to the possible approach of the enemy. Pedro dismissed this report, and the next morning, to his dismay, found himself surrounded by Enrique's soldiers, who had marched during the night. Because Pedro's troops were scattered, Enrique was able to win a quick victory.

Pedro sought refuge at the fortress of Montiel, and because it was a position ill suited to sustain a long siege, he began negotiations with Guesclin to buy his release. The French commander, after an initial refusal, agreed to help Pedro escape in return for highly generous promises of rents, titles, and lands, among them the towns of Soria and Atienza. On the evening of 23 March, however, Guesclin delivered Pedro to Enrique instead, whereupon Enrique stabbed the king to death. Guesclin, combining his best mercenary instincts and his loyalty to his employer, had been persuaded by his comrades in arms to place the offer before Enrique rather than refuse it outright. Since Enrique agreed to the terms, Pedro's fate was sealed.

The death of the king secured Enrique's claim to the throne, although several individuals and localities loyal to Pedro continued to resist the usurpation some two years after his death. The battle of Montiel, however, made possible the final Trastámaran victory and the establishment of that bastard dynasty on the throne of Castile.

CLARA ESTOW

Bibliography

López de Ayala, P. *Corónica del rey don Pedro*. Eds. C. Wilkins and H. M. Wilkins. Madison, Wisc., 1986.

MONTORO, ANTÓN DE

A *converso* (Christian convert) and a poet, he was probably born around 1404 in the town of Montoro near Córdoba. The area around Córdoba was known for its large Arabic-speaking Jewish population in the late Middle Ages. The Jewish community there specialized in the making and marketing of textiles, especially silk, brocades, and other fine cloth. A great many Córdoban Jews were massacred in the anti-Semitic riots of 1391 while the remaining part converted to Christianity. Montoro seems to have been born to parents who converted to Christianity in 1391 or shortly thereafter, or to have converted himself at a very young age. The greater part of his life was spent in Córdoba, where he was a tailor and vendor of textiles, whence the sobriquet El Ropero de Córdoba. Montoro must have died in late 1477 or early 1478, since he professed to being mortally ill when he dictated his last will and testament in September 1477.

Throughout his life, Montoro was the target of the satire of other converso poets like Juan de Valladolid (also known as Juan Poeta), Rodrigo Cota, and Juan Agraz, who attacked him for being a tailor, ridiculed his low birth and infamous family origins, plus mocked his status as a "new Christian." Montoro responded in kind with brilliant satirical verse that shows great imagination, linguistic acumen, and merciless wit.

Although Montoro often denigrated himself in his own poetry, highlighting his status as an outsider and a newcomer (at one point he refers to himself as an "old Jewish faggot" *viejo puto, judío*), he quite consciously cultivated a subaltern identity and lower class status to gain access to influence and power at court by means of laughter. Although Montoro was indeed a tailor, it was to the fashion-conscious members of the Castilian aristocracy that he ministered his services. Using his sartorial talents and his poetic wit, Montoro became a well-connected individual at court, who during the course of his life corresponded poetically with, and even had the audacity to lecture, the marqués de Santillana, Juan de Mena, Gómez Manrique, Miguel Lucas de Iranzo, the conde de Cabra, Pedro de Escavias, Queen Isabel of Castile, and other distinguished members of the high nobility, with whom he maintained cordial relations. During Easter week of 1473, Montoro witnessed the anti-Semitic riots in Córdoba, which he evokes in a poem addressed to Alonso de Aguilar, himself a converso and a member of one of the leading families of the city.

Montoro's verse displays an astonishing range of registers: amorous, burlesque, angry, religious, satirical, even grossly obscene. He is one of the most complicated and subtle personalities to be found among the vast number of *cancionero* poets in fifteenth-century Castile.

E. Michael Gerli

Bibliography

Aubrun, C. V. "Conversos del siglo XV: a propósito de Antón de Montoro," *Filología* 13 (1968–69): 59–63.

Gerli, E. M. "Antón de Montoro and the Wages of Eloquence: Poverty, Patronage, and Poetry in Fifteenth-Century Castile," *Romance Philology* 48 (1994–95), 265–77.

Mai, R. *Die Dichtung Anton de Montoros, eines Cancionerodichters des 15 Jahrhunderts*. Frankfurt, 1983.

Mitrani-Samarian, S. "Le sac de Cordue el le testament de Antón de Montoro," *Révue de Etudes Juifs* 54 (1907), 36–40.

Montoro, A. de. *Cancionero de Antón de Montoro*. Ed. J. Rodríguez Puértolas y Marcella Ciceri. Salamanca, 1991.

———. *Poesía completa*. Ed. and with notes by M. Costa. Cleveland, 1990.

Scholberg, K. R. *Sátira e invectiva en la España medieval*. Madrid, 1971.

MORISCOS

Moriscos is a term often applied in modern historical literature to Muslims who, after the Reconquest, were baptized and remained in Spain. The word "*Morisco*" in this sense (rather than in the older one, *Moorish*) does not occur in the historical source material until the mid-sixteenth century: before that, such general expressions as "new converts" and "the newly baptized" were in use. Forcible conversion of individuals had occurred in the last decade of the fifteenth century, especially in Granada (by 1525 Muslims in all parts of the Iberian Peninsula had been forced to accept Christianity). The Granadan Muslims should have been amply protected by the terms on which the city was surrendered (negotiated in December 1491). In accordance with the well-established medieval pattern, they had the right to continue to practice their own religion guaranteed; the capitulations also forbade any molestation of former Christians who had converted to Islam (the *elches*).

In the years immediately following the occupation of Granada, these terms were by and large respected. There were some individual conversions, notably that of Yaḥyā al-Najjār, who after baptism became Pedro de Granada Venegas, *alguacil mayor* of the city. (Significantly, such powerful and successful converts are never stigmatized as Moriscos.) The majority of the Granadan Muslims, however, held fast to the old faith. Francisco Jimérez de Cisneros, impatient at the slow progress being made by Archbishop Hernando de Talavera and other missionaries, launched a new and more vigorous drive to secure converts by all available means, including duress. A leading figure who succumbed after a period of rigorous confinement was El-

Zegrí Azaator, baptized as Gonzalo Hernández. At the same time the harassment of the elches led to widespread realization that the promises made in 1492 would not be kept.

A large section of the Muslim population of Granada and other parts of the kingdom took up arms in 1500 against the Castilian occupiers. The immediate consequence was that Cisneros fell from favor: "His rashness has lost us in a few hours what we have been years in acquiring," noted Fernando. In the longer term, however, it was the policy of Cisneros that prevailed. By driving exasperated Muslims into open rebellion, he effectively brought the Mudéjar period to an end in the lands of Castile. Forcible converts were rarely sincere converts, but Muslims who wished to continue to live in their homeland had to pretend outwardly to be Christians. Islam did not cease to exist, but it was driven underground. At the very end of the medieval period the intractable Morisco problem had been created. It was to continue to preoccupy Spain's rulers until a plan of expulsion was adopted in 1609–1611.

L. PATRICK HARVEY

Bibliography

Boronat y Barrachina, P. *Los moriscos españoles y su expulsión: Estudio histórico-crítico*. Valencia, 1901. Vol. 1, pp. 103–16.

Caro Baroja, J. *Los moriscos del reino de Granada*. Madrid, 1957.

Harvey, L. P. "Yuse Banegas: Un moro noble en Granada bajo los Reyes Católicos." *Al-Andalus* 21 (1956), 297–302.

Ladero Quesada, M. A. *Los mudéjares de Castilla en tiempo de Isabel I*. Valladolid, 1969.

———. *Granada después de la conquista. Repobladores y mudéjares*. Granada, 1988.

Paz Fernández, F. *Moriscos, repertorio bibliográfico Cuadernos de la Biblioteca slámica, "Félix María Pareja,"* no. 19, 1989. (The previous number, 18, on Mudéjares, also contains much relevant material.)

Peinado Santaella, R. G., and J. E. López de Coca Castañer. *Historia de Granada: La época medieval, siglos VIII–XV*. Granada, 1987. Vol. 2, pp. 358–68.

MOSES BEN NAHMAN

Moses ben Naḥman (Naḥmanides), rabbi of the Jewish community of Girona during the middle decades of the thirteenth century, was a leader of Iberian Jewry during his lifetime, and one of the most distinguished intellectual and spiritual figures in all of medieval Jewry. Like so many Iberian Jewish luminaries, Naḥmanides is striking for the remarkable range of his intellectual abilities and achievements. He was a master of Jewish law, mentoring important students and composing important *novellae* to major Talmudic tractates. He was, at the same time, a keen student of the Bible, composing an extensive commmentary on the Pentateuch that is rich in exegetical insight and is still widely studied. He was one of the leaders in the rapidly developing school of Spanish Jewish mysticism, rather conservative in his approach to the explosive issues associated with the new mystical speculation but extremely important for the more traditional prestige and acumen that he brought to bear on the development of mystical teachings. His remarkable command of the Hebrew language in all its styles linked him to earlier tendencies in Iberian Jewry. The account that he composed of his public disputation with a former Jew, Pablo Christiani, who had become a Dominican friar, is a masterpiece of narrative art and one of the most effective Jewish polemical treatises of the Middle Ages.

That famous disputation highlights the public career of Naḥmanides. Prior to this engagement the rabbi was already known to King Jaime I of Aragón. In the face of the missionizing assault of the Dominicans, Rabbi Moses ben Naḥman was chosen as the Jewish spokesman for the encounter. Essentially the carefully contrived disputation involved an effort by the Dominican spokesman to prove to the Jews, from materials including both commentary on the Bible and rabbinic dicta, the truth of key Christian doctrines, most importantly the Christian claim that the promised Messiah had already appeared.

The role of the Jewish spokesman was to be limited to rebuttal of the Christian use of rabbinic texts only, with no allowance for Jewish negation of Christian teachings. Whether or not the limited parameters of Jewish rebuttal were in fact rigidly maintained is not altogether certain. In his brilliant narrative account of the disputation, Naḥmanides portrays himself as ranging far and wide in direct attack on central tenets of Christianity and on fundamental characteristics of Christian society. While modern researchers have questioned the reliability of these aspects of Naḥmanides' narrative, it is clear that the rabbi of Girona composed a captivating account of his public encounter and, in the process, provided his Jewish readers with appealing argumentation for the superiority of the Jewish faith.

The publication of Naḥmanides' narrative aroused the ire of ecclesiastical leadership and produced calls for punishment of the aged rabbi of Girona. The king of Aragón, who is portrayed most sympathetically in Naḥmanides' narrative, proved an effective supporter, although by 1267 Naḥmanides had made his way to the Holy Land. It is by no means clear whether this move reflects the pressures brought to bear against him or whether it resulted from his personal religiosity. He exercised leadership briefly within the Jewish community of Jerusalem, and died shortly thereafter.

Bibliography

Baer, Y. *A History of the Jews in Christian Spain*. 2 vols. Trans. by L. Schoffman et al. Philadelphia, 1961–66.

Chazan, R. *Barcelona and Beyond: The Disputation of 1263 and Its Aftermath*. Berkeley, 1992.

Twersky, I. (ed.) *Rabbi Moses ben Naḥman (Ramban): Explorations in His Religious and Literary Virtuosity*. Cambridge, Mass., 1983.

Wolfson, E. R. " 'By Way of Truth': Aspects of Naḥmanides' Kabbalistic Hermeneutic." *Association for Jewish Studies Review* 14 (1989), 103–78.

———. "The Secret of the Garment in Naḥmanides." *Daat* 24 (1990), Eng. sec., xxv–xlix.

MOSQUE OF CÓRDOBA

Córdoba's congregational mosque, the first in Spain, was built in stages over two hundred years. The first structure, by Emir ʿAbd al-Raḥmān I in 786–787, occupied a site purported to be that of an older Visigothic church, San Vicente, and an even earlier Roman temple. The mosque's orientation is incorrect, which is only partly explained by the orientation of the former church. Instead of facing Mecca (east), as would be expected, it faces south, adopting the orientation of the Umayyad mosque of Damascus; politicoideological allegiances with the Umayyad and Syrian past, expressed in this manner, proved more important than correct direction of prayer.

Interior of the mosque. Umayyad caliphate tenth century. Copyright © Scala/Art Resource, NY. Mosque, Córdoba, Spain.

The first mosque was a rectangular enclosure consisting of an open courtyard and a roofed hypostyle prayer hall with eleven aisles perpendicular to the *qiblah* wall, similar to the plan of eastern mosques, such as Al-Aqsā in Jerusalem. Its simple layout may be due to the transmission of architectural information by numbers and geometrical proportions rather than a written plan. In contrast, its elevation was extraordinary and unique. Architectural spolia were used in part because Roman and Visigothic materials were available and inexpensive, and in part to suggest the triumph of Islam over previous civilizations. Marble columns and capitals supported rhythmic arcades of colorful horseshoes arches (a Visigothic form) of white stone and red brick. The lower arcade bore a second tier, piggyback-style, that supported a flat pine ceiling bearing a roof of parallel gables. These techniques for heightening the interior and adding color appear to have been learned from the Roman aqueducts of Mérida. The shape, doubling, and polychromy of the arches demonstrate Muslim architects' willingness to adapt pre-Islamic building techniques and decoration to new ends.

The second emir, Hishām I (r. 788–796), added a staircase minaret that reached only to the height of the courtyard walls. In 836 ʿAbd al-Raḥmān II expanded the prayer hall eight bays to the south, replacing the *qiblah* wall and commissioning new columns and capitals. Muḥammad I restored the Portal of San Esteban in 855. A blind horseshoe arch with alternating voussoirs of red brick and white stucco with vegetal designs, it is the earliest known monumental exterior portal in a mosque.

In 951 Caliph ʿAbd al-Raḥmān III al-Nāṣir extended the courtyard to the north and built a new minaret next to the *miḥrāb* axis. This tall minaret survives today with seventeenth-century facing. Al-Naṣir also added arcades (*riwaq*s) in the courtyard and planned other improvements to the mosque that were finished by his son, Al-Ḥakam II. In 962 the latter added twelve bays to the *qiblah* end of the prayer hall, doubled the *qiblah*-wall, and added ribbed vaults in three spectacularly decorated bays that defined a reserved place (*maqsūrah*) in front of the new *miḥrāb*. The miḥrāb is a small octagonal chamber decorated inside with stucco and faced on the outside with glittering gold, red, and blue mosaics, the work of visiting Byzantine artists. The inscriptions inside and framing the miḥrāb and flanking chambers are from the Qur'ān and offer lengthy foundation texts giving the date of completion and the patron's name. The *maqsūrah* is articulated by three domes on squinches, the centermost encrusted with mosaics; at midlevel, interlaced polylobed arches form a visual screen that vigorously intensifies the already highly ornamental pattern of arches and alternating voussoirs elsewhere in the prayer hall. This screen, together with a corresponding fence at ground level, demarcated a ceremonial space for the caliph that was reached directly from the palace next door by a private entrance and raised passage (*sabat*). In the mosaics, the lofty interior of the prayer hall, and the alternating columns and piers of the courtyard, the Umayyad mosque of Damascus was evoked in conscious reference to the Hispano-Umayyads' lineage and source of authority.

In 987–988 the entire mosque was extended eastward by eight aisles. The river may have been a limiting factor, but the sideways direction of growth was probably due as much to political and aesthetic considerations as to lack of space. The addition to the great Umayyad mosque was ordered not by one of the Umayyad rulers but by Muḥammad Ibn Abū ʿĀmir, called Al-Manṣūr (Almanzor), who, as regent for young Hishām II, had seized power in 981. Al-Manṣūr astutely realized that his extension must conform to the existing fabric of the legitimate rulers and saw that destruction of Al-Ḥakam II's spectacular miḥrāb, the most highly charged place in the mosque, would be unacceptable to the Córdoban populace. Hence the remarkable conservatism of the extension; he did not try to surpass, but to conform to, previous stages of the mosque.

The mosque was converted to a church in 1236 when Córdoba was conquered by Castile; later alterations were made beginning in 1523, when the architects of Holy Roman Emperor Charles V (Carlos I of Spain) inserted a Gothic cathedral into the center of the prayer hall and added chapels along its side walls. Today the building continues to serve as a church.

D. FAIRCHILD RUGGLES

Bibliography

Creswell, K. A. C. *Early Muslim Architecture*. Vol. 2. Oxford, 1940. 138–61.

Dodds, J. "The Great Mosque of Córdoba." In *Al-Andalus: The Art of Islamic Spain*. Ed. J. Dodds. New York, 1992. 11–25.

Ewert, C. *Spanisch-islamische Systeme sich kreuzender Bögen*. Berlin, 1968.

Hillenbrand, R. "Medieval Córdoba as a Cultural Centre. Appendix: The Great Mosque of Córdoba." In *The Legacy of Muslim Spain*. Ed. S. K. Jayyusi. Leiden, 1992. 129–35.

Stern, H. *Les Mosaïques de la grande mosquée de Cordoue*. Berlin, 1976.

MOZARABIC CHANT *See* MOZARABIC RITE

MOZARABIC CHRONICLE OF 754

The *Mozarabic Chronicle of 754* is one of two anonymous chronicles written by Iberian Christians living under Muslim rule in the generation after the invasion of 711, the other being the *Arabic-Byzantine Chronicle of 741*. Unlike the earlier chronicle, the *Mozarabic Chronicle* focuses on events in Spain. In fact, it is the only contemporary source for Iberian events from the invasion through the period of the Muslim governors, which ended shortly after the chronicler did, with the establishment of the Umayyad emirate of Spain in 756.

The *Mozarabic Chronicle* was designed as an installment of the universal chronicle begun by Eusebius of Caesarea and continued in succession by St. Jerome, Prosper of Aquitaine, Victor of Tunnuna, and John of Biclaro, all of which Isidore summarized and extended to the year 615 in his *Chronica*. The chronicler of 754 began where Isidore left off—with the reigns of Emperor Heraclius and King Sisebut of Spain—recounting the events leading up to the Islamic conquest of imperial territory in the east and then backtracking to cover, albeit in a cursory way, contemporaneous events in Spain. When, shortly before the midpoint of the chronicle, the Visigoths are defeated by the Muslims, the chronicler simply replaces the Visigothic kings with the Muslim governors, and continues moving back and forth between Damascus and Constantinople in the east and Córdoba in the west. Fortunately the chronicler knew a great deal more about Spanish history after the invasion than before, his account of peninsular events becoming more detailed as he approaches his own day. He refers in three places to another, more detailed history that he wrote on the civil wars within Muslim Spain in the early 740s, but that work has not been recovered.

All that can be determined with any certainty about the author is that he was a Christian living within Muslim Spain. It is very likely, given his attention to Toledan councils and distinguished Iberian churchmen, that he was an ecclesiastic. Where he lived within

Spain is a point of contention. Córdoba and Toledo have been the traditional choices, although recently a case has been made for the Murcia region. He seems to have had access to the same source for Arab events in the east as the chronicler of 741, as evidenced by the similarity in treatment by the two chronicles. It seems likely, given his use of the Arabic calendar and the regnal years of the caliphs alongside the more Isidorean years of the emperor and the "era," and his occasional use of some very Arabic-sounding similes, that he had access to Arabic sources, either written or oral.

Though he depicts the Arab victory over the forces of Heraclius as a scourge, he does not attempt to moralize the defeat of the Visigoths. He laments the fall of Spain with rhetorical flourish, but does not seem to hold it against the new rulers. He evaluates them according to their success in promoting peace and justice in Spain rather than according to their religious affiliation. There is virtually no information in the chronicle about Islam as a religion; only once is Muḥammad even identified as a prophet, and then only in passing, without further elaboration. Though the chronicler does not go so far as to applaud the Muslims for conquering Spain—as Isidore had done for the Visigoths in his *History of the Goths*—his willingness to ignore the religious identity of the invaders and evaluate them on political grounds served, as Isidore's work had for the Gothic monarchy, to lend some legitimacy to the Muslim regime by giving it a place in Latin history.

KENNETH B. WOLF

Bibliography

Collins, R. *The Arab Conquest of Spain, 710–797*. Oxford, 1989.

Wolf, K. *Conquerors and Chroniclers of Early Medieval Spain*. Liverpool, 1990.

MOZARABIC LANGUAGE

Mozarabic (< Arabic *mustʿarab*, "quasi-Arab") designates the Romance dialect, or group of dialects, spoken in Muslim Spain. Since there are exceedingly few direct attestations of Mozarabic, scholars have been obliged, in their attempts to determine its basic characteristics, to rely on the testimony of Hispano-Arabic authors, on the evidence provided by documents, and on the analysis of numerous putative Mozarabic loanwords in the other Romance vernaculars of the peninsula and in Arabic. As a literary dialect Mozarabic's only claim to fame is its use in the *kharjas*, but the reconstructions of those elusive texts that have so far been attempted remain linguistically so problematic as to be of limited value in describing the dialect's most salient features.

There is a broad consensus among scholars of Mozarabic on the following points: the preservation of the diphthongs /aj/ and /aw/, though the former may have evolved to /ej/ as in Galician-Portuguese; the diphthongization of the mid-open vowels /ĕ/ and /ŏ/; the appearance of the alveolo-palatal affricate /č/ as the regular solution for the Latin /k/ before front vowels vs. the alveolar affricate /ts/ that became the norm in the other Romance languages of the peninsula; the maintenance of the palatal fricative /y/ before front vowels; and the shift to /-es/ of the feminine plural ending / − as/. The occurrence of other fundamental changes (i.e., lenition of the voiceless obstruents /p/, /t/, /k/, /f/, and /s/, and the palatalization of the geminate lateral /ll/ and nasal /nn/) remains a matter of controversy, largely because the Arabic script in which most Mozarabic material is preserved, though in principle perfectly capable of providing an accurate reflection of such shifts, in fact turns out to be opaque or ambiguous with regard to these and many other crucial linguistic issues.

The chief Arabic sources for Mozarabic are the *Glossarium latino-arabicum* (Leiden University Library Codex or. 231), the *Vocabulista in arábico* (Bibliotèca Riccardiana, Florence, MS 217), the botanical treatise of the Anónimo sevillano (Academia de la Historia, Madrid, Col. Gayangos, ms XL), the vast collection of Toledan documents published by González Palencia, the *Vocabulista arauigo* of Pedro de Alcalá, the twelfth-century Córdoban poet Ibn Quzmān, and the *kharjas*. The single most important source for Mozarabic in Romance documents is the resettlement rolls drawn up by the Christian authorities shortly after their conquest of Seville, Murcia, Mallorca, and Valencia, though the rolls tend to be more relevant for onomastics (anthroponomy and toponymy) than for other aspects of the language. For the rest one must consult the major etymological dictionaries of the peninsular languages, as well as the specialized literature in the field.

JERRY R. CRADDOCK

Bibliography

Galmés de Fuentes, A. *Dialectología mozárabe*. Biblioteca Románica Hispánica, 3, Manuales, 58. Madrid, 1983.

Sanchis Guarner, M. "El mozárabe peninsular." In *Enciclopedia lingüística hispánica*. Vol. 1, *Antecedentes y onomástica*. Madrid, 1960. 293–342.

MOZARABIC MARTYRS *See* CÓRDOBA, MARTYRS OF

MOZARABIC RITE

Although *Mozarabic* refers to the period under Muslim domination, the liturgy was established earlier, during the Visigothic period. Hence it might properly be called the Visigothic rite or the rite of Toledo. This rite shares basic elements with Western liturgies, but issues of this earlier period are reflected in the prayers and are invoked as the motive for papal intervention in the eleventh century.

From 507 the Visigoths, who were Arian Christians, maintained their kingdom at Toledo. Though reasonably tolerant, they controlled episcopal appointments. These factors may have provoked the first extant expression of papal concern in Pope Vigilius's letter to the bishop of Braga in 538, dealing with baptism, penance, and reconsecration of churches. Among bishops sympathetic to Rome was Leander, archbishop of Seville (584–601), who had formed a friendship with Gregory I the Great while on embassies in Constantinople. Leander presided over the Third Council of Toledo in 589, during which the Visigothic king Reccared formally brought the Visigoths into Catholicism. The same council also formally introduced the *Filioque* clause into the Nicene Creed, later a provocation for the schism of 1054. Isidore, Leander's brother and successor as archbishop of Seville (601–636), presided over the Fourth Council of Toledo (633), which established uniform chants for the divine office and rites of the Eucharist. Concerns over ritual practices were reflected in his *De ecclesiasticis officiis*.

Among bishops with Visigothic roots was Eugenius II, archbishop of Toledo (647–657), who presided over four councils and took an interest in liturgical chants and the religious calendar. He continued Iberian interest in trinitarian theology with his *De Trinitate*, now lost. Ildefonso, his nephew and successor at Toledo (657–667), wrote *De cognitione baptismi*, possibly reflecting an anti-Arian position with the provision for a single dipping. Julian, from a family of *conversos*, presided as archbishop of Toledo (680–690) over four councils and was responsible for revisions to the *Hispana*, the Spanish collection of canon law, and to the liturgical rites. This concluded the creative development of this rite before the Moorish conquest of 711.

No definitive study has sought to explore possible Moorish influences on Christian liturgy. Rather than a response to the monotheism of Islam, the distinctive emphasis on "Trinity" as a title of address in many of the prayers of this liturgy has long been interpreted as a reaction to the Arianism of Visigothic origins. The *Filioque*, affirming the procession of the Holy Spirit from both Father and Son, reflects preoccupations with consubstantiality against a form of Arianism.

The five elements of the Eucharistic liturgy can be reconstructed from canonical legislation, treatises, manuscripts, and early editions.

The preparation includes the double washing of the celebrant's hands, prayers for each vestment, approaching the altar with psalms, a sign of the cross, a kiss, and possibly the preparing of the chalice.

The liturgy of the Word begins with the Gloria, except on Sundays in Advent and Lent, and a lengthy prayer often related to the Gloria. There follow readings from Scripture, with chants after the first reading and the Gospel. Normally there is one reading each from the Old Testament, the Epistles, and the Gospels. By the time of Isidore, deacons do the readings. There is a Gospel procession attended by incense and candles.

The offertory includes presentation of bread and wine by the people and preparation of the host by a deacon. Then come several prayers, including a call to prayer, commemoration of names, intercessions, and prayers for peace and for reconciliation. The kiss of peace follows in the Byzantine Order.

The canon opens with an invocation to the Father and Son in a preface, then continues with the consecration, the epiclesis, and a second elevation with the words "The faith which we believe in our hearts let us proclaim with our lips." Then comes the Nicene Creed following the Byzantine order. This was the first Western rite to include the recitation of the creed, probably in reaction to Visigothic Arian roots.

The service continues with the Lord's Prayer, the people responding "Amen" after each phrase, and after the "daily bread" with "Because you are God." Then the host is fractured into nine pieces, seven of them representing a mystery of Christ from his incarnation to his resurrection. There follow the Communion, a thanksgiving prayer, a dismissal, and a prayer in honor of Mary.

As Muslim power declined, Rome took an active interest in Spain. Pope Gregory VII (1073–1085) was a strong proponent of the Cluniac reform, and encouraged these monks to exert influence in Spain. To advance his centralizing interests, he wrote to the kings of León and Castile on 19 March 1074 that the rite of Toledo was contaminated by the heresies of Arianism and Priscillianism, and urged them to follow Roman practice. Catalonia in the north, under Cluniac influence, had made the change; Aragón had accepted it in 1071. El Cid is reported to have established a Cluniac as bishop of Valencia. Alfonso VI of León wanted outside, including papal, support. To offset enthusiasm for the Mozarabic tradition, he reputedly submitted texts of the Mozarabic and Roman rites to trial by ordeal. The Council of Burgos in 1080 officially sanctioned the Roman rite. To placate popular resistance, six parishes in Toledo were allowed to continue the Mozarabic rite. The Roman rite being imposed was the creative Gallic rite that Cluniac monks had taken to Rome. It was distinguished by dramatic ceremonials such as the procession of psalms, the washing of feet, the veneration of the Cross with reproaches, the blessing of the new fire, the Paschal candle, and the Exultet. The papal policy was completed at the Council of León in 1090 by eliminating Visigothic script from ecclesiastical books.

The last phase of the Mozarabic rite began after the defeat of the Muslims at Granada in 1492. Francisco Jiménez de Cisneros, archbishop of Toledo (1495–1517), had Mozarabic texts prepared, and in 1504 designated a cathedral chapel at Toledo for this rite. So there, and occasionally in the Talavera Chapel in Salamanca, the Mozarabic rite of the Eucharist is still celebrated.

PAUL C. BURNS

Bibliography

Emerton, E. *The Correspondence of Pope Gregory VII: Selections of Letters from the Registrum.* New York, 1932. 29, 144–46, 160–61, 176–78.

Férotin, M. *Le Liber ordinum enusage dans l'eglise wisigothique et mozarabe d'Espagne du Ve au XIe siecle.* Paris, 1904.

———. *Le Liber mozarabicus sacramentorum et les manuscrits mozarabes.* Paris, 1912.

Hope, D. M., and G. Woolfenden. "The Medieval Western Rites." In *The Study of Liturgy.* Ed. C. Jones et al. Oxford, 1992. 264–85.

MOZARABS

The term *Mozarabs* is used by modern historians to refer to Christians in Spain who lived under Muslim rule. They are distinguished from the *Muwallads*, who were originally Christians but had converted to Islam. The generally accepted etymology of Mozarab is "musta'rib," Arabic for "Arabized." Although this is probably accurate, it is misleading in two ways. First of all, though Arabic in derivation, Mozarab was not used by the Muslims in Spain to describe subject Christians. As elsewhere they tended to refer to them as "unbelievers" or "Nazarenes." Secondly, "Arabized" implies a level of acculturation that was certainly not typical of every Christian living under Muslim rule. Some historians have avoided Mozarab altogether, preferring more neutral terms such as "Andalusian Christian." But the adjectival form of the word, used, for instance, by art historians to describe a distinctive architectural style, is more firmly entrenched.

From a Muslim point of view, the Mozarabs were a "People of the Book" and therefore, in accordance with Islamic law were allowed to maintain their separate religious identity and keep their property in exchange for their recognition of Muslim rule and their payment of a special tax (*jizya*). The Christians (or Jews) subject to such an agreement (*dhimma*, "pact") were referred to collectively by the Muslims as *dhimmis*. The most famous *dhimma* was the so-called Pact of Umar', which came to be considered normative by Islamic legal schools as early as the eighth century, included many restrictions aimed at limiting those aspects of the Christian cult that seemed to compromise Islam: the construction of new churches, bell ringing, processions, public funerals, and especially blaspheming Islam or its prophet. Others were designed to keep dhimmis from melting into Islamic society by prohibiting their adoption of Arab styles of clothing or the use of arms or saddles. Dhimmis were not allowed to assume government positions that would give them any kind of power over Muslims nor were they permitted to own Muslim slaves or even to marry Muslim women, although Muslim males could and frequently did marry dhimmi women.

The fact that the Mozarabs of Spain, as dhimmis, were subject to these restrictions de jure did not mean that they were de facto obliged to live in accordance with them. The Latin literature that survives from the ninth century—in particular that pertaining to the martyrs of Córdoba—reveals that Christians were paying the *jizya* and they were being executed for publicly disparaging Islam. But it also shows that bells were ringing in the streets of Córdoba, Christian processions were passing through Muslim neighborhoods, new monasteries were being founded all around the city, and at least some Christian youths were dressing as Muslims and studying Arabic. There is also evidence of Christians in the ninth century serving as soldiers, bodyguards, translators, and tax collectors in addition to the many who held positions within the Córdoban government that were designed to manage the affairs of the Christian population that, at that time, probably still outnumbered that of the Muslims.

The spectrum of Mozarab responses to Islamic society was wide, ranging from complete rejection to almost total assimilation. Mozarabs who lived outside of the cities, whether as farmers or as monks, had very little contact with Muslims, and as a result tended to maintain their pre-conquest cultural identity much longer than their urban coreligionists. The famous lament of Paulus Alvarus (864) about Christian youths in Córdoba who had forsaken Christian literature and the Latin language for Arabic studies, reveals the other extreme. It is interesting, in light of Alvarus's complaint, that there is so little in the way of extant Christian Arabic literature from Spain. Bishop Recemund's calendar (962), written in Arabic and dedicated to the new caliph, is apparently the closest that the bilingual

Christians of Spain came to producing anything in their adopted tongue. This is all the more remarkable when we consider the efflorescence of Jewish-Arabic literature in Muslim Spain beginning in the mid-tenth century with the groundbreaking efforts of Dunash ben Labrat and blossoming in the eleventh and twelfth centuries into a veritable Jewish renaissance.

The Mozarabs left a more enduring mark on Christian Spain. The *Chronicle of Alfonso III* (late ninth century) reports that King Ordoño I (850–866) populated a number of deserted cities in the north in part with people coming up out of Muslim Spain, one of the earliest references to the late-ninth and tenth-century northern migration of Mozarabs. Foundation inscriptions on churches, monastic charters, and the names of new settlements, especially in the Duero River Valley, confirm this. The reasons for the migration are not clear. Though many have pointed to increased persecution, the civil wars within Muslim Spain are perhaps a more likely cause of Mozarab dislocation. The influx of immigrants not only provided the northern kingdoms with much-needed frontier settlers, but led to an infusion of distinctive cultural elements. The Duero Valley contains some of the best examples of Mozarabic architecture, for instance, the church of San Miguel de la Escalada near Léon, with its distinctive horseshoe or keyhole arches. The famous illuminations in the manuscripts of Beatus's commentary on the Apocalypse (tenth through twelfth centuries) are the most famous example of Mozarabic art. The newly arrived Christians may also have left their mark in historiography, if they were indeed the ones who suggested to the Asturian monarchy that they could consider themselves the heirs of the Visigothic kings of Toledo. The Mozarabs may also have been the first to introduce Arabic urban institutions and agricultural products to the north. But they were also the cause of a liturgical dispute, when they insisted on performing the rite that they had inherited from the Visigothic church despite the Roman-sponsored changes that had taken place in the north. The crisis came to a head in 1080, when Pope Gregory VII decreed that Spain uniformly adopt the Roman rite. Local resistance led to something of a compromise which allowed a handful of Toledan churches to continue following the Mozarabic rite.

When the active phase of the Reconquista began with the takeover of Toledo in 1085 and Zaragoza in 1118, whole communities of Mozarabs found themselves within Christian territory without ever having moved. The Mozarabs in Toledo had become entirely Arabic speaking by that time and there is evidence that their descendants were still using Arabic to some degree two centuries later.

KENNETH B. WOLF

Bibliography

Epalza, Mikel. "Mozarabs: An Emblematic Christian–Minority in Islamic Al-Andalus." In *The Legacy of Muslim Spain*. Vol. 1. Ed. S. K. Jayyusi. New York, 1992. 149–70.

Gil, J. (ed.) *Corpus scriptorum muzarabicorum*. 2 vols. Madrid, 1973.

———. "Judíos y cristianos en hispania" (s. VII–IX). *Hispania Sacra* 31 (1978–79), 9–88.

Glick, T. *Islamic and Christian Spain in the Early Middle Ages*. Princeton, N.J., 1979.

Millet-Gérard, D. *Chrétiens mozarabes et culture islamique dan l'Espagne des VIIIe-IXe siècles*. Paris, 1984.

Wolf, K. *Christian Martyrs in Muslim Spain*. Cambridge, 1988.

MUDÉJARS

As the eleventh-century Reconquest advanced, Muslims lived in greater number under Christians not only as slaves, freedmen, scattered individuals, and alien merchants, but also as integral surrendered communities. Still called Saracens and Moors, they received from Castilians the more specific name Mudéjars, probably from the Arabic *mudajjan*, "allowed to remain," as in the tributary Muslim groups under treaty in Islamic chronicles (*ahl al-dajjan*). Their surrender compacts, whether written or understood or applied as routine custom, established a parallel society with its own religious, legal, administrative, and fiscal autonomy and institutions, with adaptive mechanisms for subordination to Christian public authority, both royal and seigneurial. Probably borrowed from the analogous Qurʾānic *dhimma* for Jews and Christians, the status was prepared for and reinforced by general structures of Mediterranean and Christian society. In the sixteenth century, as forced or assumed converts, these Muslims continued an underground Islamic life as Moriscos until their expulsion.

Long debate about Islamic "continuity" or "discontinuity" in the Mudéjar enclaves is beside the point: they were survival cultures, a unique form of Islam whose continuities were discontinuous due to reactive acculturation. Modern Enlightenment "tolerance" is also irrelevant: Muslim and Christian societies then, religious in root and branch, recoiled from one another in mutual contempt, demanded civic expression of their respective revelations, and feared any assimilation or taint from the infidel. If overt interaction was discouraged by segregation and discrimination, however, constant colonialist interchange at many levels was inevitable.

The Mudéjar *aljama* was a jurisdictional unit that might include one or more Moorish quarters (*morerías*). The morería was at first a privileged sanctuary, usually suburban, but in the fifteenth century became a compulsory ghetto. The basic structure of an *aljama* involved a governing *qāḍī* and/or *qā'id*, a Qurʾānically learned *faqīh* stratum, sheiks or notables in council (also called *aljama*), one or more *amīn* functionaries as fiscal liaison with the Christian ruler, and officials including the consumer advocate (*muḥtasib*), muezzin, prayer leader (*ṣaḥib al-ṣalāt*), secretary (*kātib*), and tax collector (*mushrif*). This public structure and the quality of Mudéjar life depended on the defining contexts of place and time; and actual life, both public and private, could differ radically according to those circumstances. An early or a rural Mudéjar, for example, might inhabit an entirely Islamic ambience; seigneurial *aljamas* on the Ebro River might live as valued and affluent tenants, while town *morerías* suffered pogroms.

Castile soon drove out most of its Mudéjars, whereas Valencia kept and even imported them as economically essential. Mallorca had no *aljamas*, only numerous acephalous individuals; Catalonia's population was less than 3 percent Mudéjars, and those only on its borders; Aragón's population in the late fourteenth century was one-third, but its sister kingdom Valencia was two-thirds, Mudéjar. Sustained general scholarship on Mudéjars dates only from the 1980s, with most of it from the 1990s. Regular international congresses on Mudéjarism, Míkel de Epalza's annual bibliographies, surveys of Navarrese Mudéjars by Akio Ozaki and Mercedes García Arenal, of Murcia's by Juan Torres Fontes, of Aragón's by José Lacarra, of Castile's by M. A. Ladero Quesada and Joseph O'Callaghan, of Catalonia's by Rodrigo Pita Mercé, of Mallorca's by Elena Lourie and Ricardo Soto Company, and of Valencia's by M. C. Barceló Torres, John Boswell, Robert Burns, M. T. Ferrer i Mallol, Pierre Guichard, and Mark Meyerson are the beginning of those regional, and eventually local, studies essential before generalizations can be attempted about Mudéjars a a whole. Meyerson has already shaken the universal assumption that the Mudéjar condition worsened linearly with each generation, culminating logically in the expulsion of the Muslims. He finds Valencian history cyclical, with relatively acceptable circumstances in the thirteenth and fifteenth centuries and catastrophic circumstances in the fourteenth and sixteenth. He also notes the wholly opposing policies of Fernando the Catholic toward Castilian and Valencian Mudéjarism. Another assumption, that Muslim elites entirely fled at any conquest, leaving only rural peasants and a few artisans, needs to be carefully adjusted for each area and time span.

Mudéjar art has attracted research for a longer time and on a wider scale than other aspects of Mudéjar culture. From the twelfth to the sixteenth centuries this brickwork Islamo-Christian hybrid flourished, especially in the fourteenth and fifteenth centuries in Aragón and Andalusia. Controversy has continued as to its nature: a form of decoration or stylistic language, or the only architecture besides Gothic truly native to Europe, or essentially Arabic construction borrowed for economic reasons by a Spain fallen on hard times? Though Valencian Mudéjars kept Arabic as their language to the end, with little Romance, Castilian Mudéjars were heavily acculturated to Romance, leaving, for example, the fourteenth-century *Suma* and *Leyes de moros* and (especially in the fifteenth century) the *aljamiado* Romance literature in the Arabic alphabet.

Eleventh-century Christian advance in Castile, followed by mistreatment of Toledo's Mudéjars, had led to Muslim emigration from the center toward the south, the southeast, or even the north. The main Islamic towns, and therefore the Mudéjar communities, came to center on Andalusia (Córdoba, Jaén, Seville) and Murcia. The 1264 Mudéjar revolt there occasioned expulsion and massive flight, until by 1300 only enclaves survived, often on large seigneurial estates.

Valencia always held the largest numbers of Spain's Mudéjars, first under a colonialist minority of Christians, and in 1450 constituted some 30 percent of the population. Though all but two main Valencian towns had surrendered on Mudéjar terms, regular thirteenth-century revolts, as well as paranoid obsession in the fourteenth century with invasion from the Maghrib, increased the townsmen's hostility, though the rural lords protected Mudéjars as tenants and allies. Around 1300 the bishop over the most settled half of the kingdom of Valencia complained that mosques outnumbered churches and that over half his people were Mudéjars. Ferrer i Mallol has surveyed the demographic diminution and ever harsher laws throughout the fourteenth century there; wars, plagues, anti-Moor riots, and (in Granadan invasions of 1304, 1331, and 1332) episodes of flight. Though the Mudéjars individually did help invaders, and as a group exhibited both unity as "the nation" of Valencian Mudéjars and pan-Islamic sentiment, they did not revolt after 1300, and they did fight frequently in the king's armies. In 1456 mobs sacked the capital's *morería*. Despite all blows they remained a proudly functioning Islamic society, prized by king and lords if not by townsmen, down to the 1522 forced conversion.

Robert I. Burns, S. J.

Bibliography

Boswell, J. *The Royal Treasure: Muslim Communities under the Crown of Aragón in the Fourteenth-Century*. New Haven, Conn., 1977.

Burns, R. I. *Islam under the Crusaders: Colonial Survival in the Thirteenth-Century Kingdom of Valencia*. Princeton, N.J., 1974.

———. *Muslims, Christians, and Jews in the Crusader Kingdom of Valencia: Societies in Symbiosis*. Cambridge, 1984.

Ferrer i Mallol, M. T. *Els sarraïns de la corona catalano-aragonesa en el segle XIV: Segregació i discriminació*. Barcelona, 1987.

Powell, J. (ed.) *Muslims under Latin Rule: A Comparative Perspective*. Princeton, N.J., 1989.

MULADÍ *See* MUWALLADŪN

MUNICIPALITIES *See* TOWNS

MUNIO OF ZAMORA *See* DOMINICANS

MUNTANER, RAMÓN

Ramón Muntaner (1265–1336), military man extraordinaire in thirty-two battles on land and sea, crown official and municipal administrator, and cloth merchant, composed a brilliant, novelistic autobiography, the most popular and extensive of Catalonia's four great vernacular chronicles. He was born at Perelada to a high bourgeois family, who were hosts to Jaime I and Alfonso X in 1274. In the entourage of the future Pedro III, Muntaner met Philip III the Bold of France in Paris. He seems to have served for a while in Roger de Lloria's fleet off North Africa. In 1286–1287 he had a major role in the conquest of Menorca, thereafter becoming "a citizen of Mallorca," and in 1300 he defended a section of Messina, Sicily, against the Angevins' siege.

Joining the corsair Roger de Flor, Muntaner served as chancellor and quartermaster of the Catalan Company in Byzantium from 1302 to 1307, distinguishing himself in the siege of Gallipoli (1306) and being taken prisoner at Negropont by the Venetians. Frederick III of Sicily invested him as governor of Djerba island, off North Africa (1309–1315), which he pacified. In 1311 Muntaner transported the future Jaume III of Mallorca, an orphaned infant, from Catania to the Perpignan court. After a term as procurator to the magnate Bernat de Sarrià (1316–1320), he helped organize the conquest of Sardinia (1324).

At his home at Xirivella in the Valencian *huerta*, Muntaner composed his memoirs (1325–1326) and engaged in the cloth trade. As a jurate of Valencia city he attended the coronation of Alfonso IV the Benign in 1328. On Mallorca in 1332 Jaume III made him knight and the bailiff of Ibiza, where he lived with his wife, Valençona, his daughter, Caterina, and his sons Martí and Mascarí until his death there in 1336.

Like Jaime I, Muntaner called his memoirs *Llibre* rather than *Crònica*; both must be assessed under the genre of autobiography, not history. They unabashedly propagandize for the Catalan dynasties at home and abroad, and adopt a lively novelistic style: personal, colloquial, and anecdotal, suitable for reading aloud to an audience. Over fifty chapters on the Catalan Company recount their high point, and provide our main information for that adventure, and the model for *Tirant lo Blanc*. Muntaner's unforgettable scenes of pageantry and war may be our best panorama of fourteenth-century life.

ROBERT I. BURNS, S. J.

Bibliography

Muntaner, Ramon. *Crònica*. In *Les quatre grans cròniques*. Ed. F. Soldevila. Barcelona, 1971. Trans. Lady H. M. Goodenough as *Chronicle*. 2 vols. London, 1920–21.

Riquer, M. de. *Historia de la literatura catalana*. 4 vols. Barcelona, 1964.

MURCIA

In the twelfth century, the Moorish kingdom of Murcia reached great political and economic ascendancy, as well as a cultural brilliance so extraordinary that its capital became the center of the entire eastern region of Al-Andalus. After the disappearance of the Almohads and Ibn Hūd's brief attempt at independence, Castilian rule began in 1243 with the imposition of a military protectorate. According to Ibn ʿIdhāri, "La gente de Levante de al-Andalus pactó con los cristianos por una cantidad fija que les pagasen y los murcianos dieron su alcazaba a los cristianos, quienes la convirtieron en su alcázar" (the people of Eastern Al-Andalus made a pact with the Christians for a set quantity of money, and the Murcians gave their fortress to the Christians, who converted it into their own *alcázar*). The gradual Castilian intervention in Muslim life and the breaking of the Pact of Alcaraz, in which the terms of surrender were set, led to the 1264 uprising of the Mudéjares, whose decisive defeat in 1266 marked the introduction of Castile's complete sovereignty.

Until the end of the Middle Ages, the region's chief characteristic was its role as a frontier kingdom or *marca*, bordering Granada, Aragón, and the Mediterranean. This situation, given the limited number of settlers that came to the region during the *Repartimiento*, led the Castilian monarchs to distribute land to the military orders of the Temple Santiago, San Juan, and Calatrava, whose commanders faithfully protected the Granadan border with the aid of the city of Lorca. If the Christians were indeed able to score significant victories on the frontier, they could not prevent the frequent pillagings by the Granadan raiders, nor the three bloody expeditions of the Nasrid kings in the fifteenth century, which resulted in a great number of casualties and captives.

The repopulation of the cities and rural regions of Murcia, Lorca, and Orihuela led to the settlement of more than four thousand Christians who received territories either through royal donation or inheritance. By royal decision, most of these allotments were small properties, and recipients were required without exception to participate in the defense of the kingdom. The monarchy's concession of exemptions and privileges allowed for the establishment of councils (*concejos*) in all of the crown's populations, although only *hidalgos* and *caballeros* took part in their administration. The Murcian capital, where the *adelantados* (frontier governors) and bishops resided, achieved considerable domination because of its greater economic and human power, and was able to provide military aid to the whole kingdom when necessary.

A decade after the initial repopulation phase, an opposite phenomenon ocurred: a gradual Christian and Mudéjar abandonment of the territory caused by the insecurity that the Granadan raids produced. This decrease in population led to military, economic, and demographic weakness; Jaime II of Aragón took advantage of the situation during Fernando IV's *minority*, annexing the northern part of kingdom. This action was later given official recognition in the judgment of Torrellas (1304), although Castile was able to recuperate part of this territory over the course of the fifteenth century.

The government of the frontier territory (*adelantamiento mayor*) and its territories in Villena and Elche was in the hands of the *infante* Manuel, and his delegates maintained intrusive political participation throughout the kingdom, especially in the resolutions of the concejo in the capital. His son Juan Manuel had interfered even more in the affairs of the kingdom through a period of forty years, although there were moments in which the Murcian citizens were able to assert their independence. Before Juan Manuel's death, small dominions (*señoríos*) within the territory began to be established. Their leaders—Ayala, Calvillo, and Fajardo—worked toward various purposes, but above all aimed to gain the favor of the monarchy, become successors to the throne, and impose their hegemony in the kingdom. At the same time the church in Cartagena acquired the only two territories it ever possessed during the Middle Ages, Alguazas and Alcantarilla; both were inhabited exlusively by Mudéjars who, under the protection of the church, were successful not only in revitalizing the economic development of both areas, but also in putting themselves in prominent positions compared to the rest of the Mudéjar population.

The civil war in Castile paved the way for a conflict between the Murcian señoríos, with the gradual imposition of the Fajardo family in the fourteenth century. The conflict, however, would continue for more than seventy years in the following century, this time among the Fajardos themselves, with Pedro Fajardo ultimately triumphant. The presence of the señoríos led to such an extreme that in 1480 only Murcia and Lorca remained under royal power, although Pedro was still involved in the administration of even these regions, as *alcaide* (mayor, leader) of their fortresses and as *adelantado mayor*. This situation is reflected in the letter written by Hernando del Pulgar in 1473 to the bishop of Coria: "Del Reino de Murcia os puedo bien jurar, señor, que tan ajeno lo reputamos ya de nuestra naturaleza, como el reino de Navarra, porque carta, mensajero, procurador ni cuestor, ni vienen de allá ni van de acá más ha de cinco años" (I swear to you, sir, that we deem the kingdom of Murcia to be as detached from our own character as the kingdom of Navarre, because not a letter, messenger, procurator, nor collector has arrived nor departed for more than five years).

The social and ethnic stratification peculiar to the late Middle Ages was maintained in Murcia without any significant difference: hidalgos, caballeros, plebeians (*pecheros*), Jews, Mudéjars, slaves, and foreigners made up its population, which brought with them juridical, ethnic, and economic differences. All were subject to the exceptional circumstances of the geographical location of the *adelantamiento*, which conditioned much of the area's decisions and activities.

The hidalgos, who enjoyed a privileged position because of their exemptions from royal and regional tributes, struggled successfully to maintain their status, although not all had enough possessions to dispose of the income necessary to maintain the quality of life they believed they deserved. An accord of 1418 recognized them officially, listing 372 men and 84 women, a qualified minority that only partially participated in the city's government. Those *pecheros* with relatively high quantities of money were required to keep a horse and weapons in exchange for tax exemptions, making them essentially equal to the hidalgos. At its highest, this population consisted of 256 people in 1475: this number decreased in the following years, with only 104 in 1489. Their economic benefits were attractive at first, but were later avoided because of the costly requirement of owning a horse dedicated exclusively for military action. Both groups held governing positions on the concejo and maintained their social distinction at all times. The pecheros, permanently in military service like all citizens, practiced all kinds of careers and services both in the city and in the rural areas. They were, however, always subject to the instructions and guidelines set forth by the wealthy urban sector. They made up as much as 70 percent of the kingdom's population.

In 1266, after the Castilian occupation of the capital, Alfonso X established a Jewish neighborhood within the city walls, next to the gate of Orihuela, with the double purpose of offering them the protection mandated in the *Partidas*, and maintaining their separation from the Christian sector. This separation turned out to be beneficial for the Jews, since it guaranteed their security by setting them apart within the city walls, safe from the abuse and theft they would have suffered had they lived among the Christians. At the same time, their situation allowed for the continuity of Jewish customs and ways of life and permitted them to maintain their peculiar traditions. They were also free to leave their precinct during the day and participate in city activities, attending to everyday chores in their small stores, offices, and workshops until they returned to the *judería* before sundown.

The royal protection of the Jews was assumed by the concejo, which lended them strong support in the defense of their people, possessions, and rights. This protection saved the Jewish population from critical situations such as the persecutions of 1391: the city government not only prevented an assault on the judería, but also demanded that the leaders of Orihuela return the possessions left there by the Jews when they were forced to flee the area to avoid being robbed or killed. This was an oasis of peace, but it should be pointed out that the events of 1391 led some of the Jewish population to convert to Christianity through fear of losing all they had. Even more conversions were produced as a result of the long month that San Vicente Ferrer spent preaching in 1411. The Murcian chronicler, Diego Rodríguez de Almela, observed this process with clarity just before 1390: "Fueron tornados muchos judíos christianos por miedo, e asi muchos dellos nunca fueron buenos christianos nin los que dellos vinieron, segund lo que agora poco tiempo ha parecido, e los que fueron convertidos por su grado en la predicacion que fizo Fray Vicente, salieron buenos christianos, mejor que non los que fueron convertidos por fuerça e miedo" (Many Jews turned Christian by fear, and many of them were never good Christians, nor were those that descended from them, as has been shown recently, and those that were converted through Friar Vicente's preaching turned out to be good Christians, better than those that were converted by force and fear).

There are no Jews mentioned among those that worked the land, since they all sought jobs in the city. They were landlords; collectors (or assistants to collectors) of taxes on food products (meat, bread, and wine), textiles, carpentry, shoemaking, and on the Jewish and Moorish populations; inspectors in the three custom houses (*aduanas*); and commercial brokers of clothing, animals, etc. Above all, however, they worked in the clothing industry: in 1409 there were a total of seventy-nine Jewish tailors and dressmakers listed. Fewer in number, though still significant, were those who worked as jewelers, binders, spice merchants, and apothecaries; some also worked as usurers, an occupation that caused great dislike among the humble sectors of the city. The total Jewish population in the last decade of the fifteenth century numbered more than 1,500 people, almost all of which lived in the judería of the capital. This number however, did vary throughout time, due to plague epidemics like that of 1396, in which 450 citizens died; emigration to the neighboring kingdom of Aragón during periods of economic depression; and conversion or escape in times of anti-Jewish crisis.

The treaty of Alcaraz initially promised the Islamic population peace, stability, and continuity of lifestyle, although their fortresses and half of their royal income were transferred to Castile, as well as a few occupied territories not addressed in the treaty. The pact was respected for the first few years, but the influx of the Castilians, their interferences and excesses, the creation of local concejos, and the occupation of Muslim houses and lands caused unrest and silent protest among the Mudéjars. This led first to emigration, then to uprisings of those that remained, who were supported by the king of Granada. After squelching the rebellion, the Castilian sovereignty would not encounter further obstacles.

There were many Mudéjars that died in the war or as captives, and others who were sent as captives away from the Iberian Peninsula. Also contributing to a loss in numbers was the Aragónese occupation of the territory at the end of the thirteenth, which led to the transfer of the most qualified men to Aragón. After the judgment of Torrellas in 1304, Fernando IV made a pathetic (and unheeded) plea to the Mudéjars, soliciting their return with promises of various privileges. Since then, the reduced Mudéjar contingent would be characterized by its economic weakness, and by social/racial discrimination. If the Mudéjars could count on the protection of the concejos, their commanders, and their lords, they did not enjoy such treatment from others, who dealt with them abusively. Lacking coordination and authority, their disunity was their worst destiny; continuous degradation and compliance with their fate were two ills that affected everyone.

Starting in the late fourteenth century, the increased security of the border allowed for the creation of small señoríos in the country and the cultivation of new lands, which improved the living conditions for those Mudéjars that settled in those territories out of economic necessity. There was at the same time greater attention paid to fiscal exemptions for those still living in the urban sectors. Three negative factors, however, continued to dominate: low population, low quality of work, and poverty. The Mudéjar population's relationship with Granada did not benefit them, and emigration did not guarantee them better living conditions. Apart from their work in the fields and farms, the Mudéjars worked as fishermen, sheepherders, smiths, potters, and cutlers. They also worked as laborers in the most menial jobs of daily life. At the end of the fifteenth century there were a score of Mudéjar families in the Arrixaca slums of the capital, and the total population in the kingdom would not have exceeded five thousand. An exception to the misery suffered by the Mudéjar was the advantageous situation of the vassals of the church, both in Alguazas and in Alcantarilla. They benefited not only from the committed protection of their masters, but also from their superior economic possibilities.

The number of Moslem slaves was not great, because very few Mudéjars lost their liberty through crime or frustrated attempts of emigration. Proximity to the border with Granada facilitated escape, especially when the fugitive could count on the assistance of Mudéjar vassals of the military orders near the border; but the welcome that waited them was not always pleasant, as is shown in the return of those that went to the Ricote valley only to be forcibly transferred by Abūl-Ḥasan in 1477. The scarcity of Muslim slaves required masters to turn to the acquisition of African subjects, but their high cost limited their numbers, and therefore they were largely assigned to domestic work.

Since the thirteenth century, even before the Castilian occupation of the kingdom, documents show the presence of merchants from Genoa in Murcian territory. This activity diminished during a long period of economic depression, but is renewed with greater intensity in 1370. These merchants formed businesses connected to members of the oligarchy in the capital, with whom they also established family ties. They were active in many aspects of social and political life: they acquired urban and territorial property; filled whichever municipal and economic positions benefited them (like those associated with the *aduana* [customs house], which provided them a way of controlling the traffic of merchandise); established money-changing stores; loaned high quantities of money to the city treasury, which was always in debt; created industries; and imposed their economic dominion through their monopoly of the dye industry, and especially through Merino wool, which they exported as early as 1372. The Genovese merchants also traded products that the Mediterranean market demanded, including dyes, textiles, grains, weapons, and whatever else would provide them rich economic benefits—always, of course, counting on the support of the city oligarchy.

Agriculture was often burdened with debts caused by many factors: first, a permanent insecurity extended to every corner of the adelantamiento, caused by the Granadan invasions and the presence of a system of bandits; second, there was frequent flooding and prolonged periods of drought; finally, deadly plague epidemics persisted—in 1396 there were 6,080 killed in Murcia—and not only brought about a great number of casualties, but also weakened bodies and efforts, and threatened the Murcian territory unceasingly. Related to all of this is the shortage of population and the necessity to attend to the alimentary needs of those that resided in the urban world and did not work the land. These consequences led to a drastic reduction of land cultivation, which was forced to concentrate on the most essential products (grains and wine) at the expense of other traditional foods like olives, vegetables, almonds, figs, and other fruits. This produced a notable change in the rural landscape compared with the Muslim era and the first years of Castilian occupation. It also resulted in a gradual abandonment of the fields of Lorca and Cartagena, which were subsequently only used by transhumant livestock. As a result, the northern part of the countryside, lacking the necessary drainage, was converted into marshy lands that were only fit for cattle.

The end of the rivalries of the noble factions and the external and internal peace of the first part of the fifteenth century led to a magnificent urban and rural resurgence. The city grew and was beautified, and the increase of the Christian and Mudéjar populations promoted the creation of small señoríos in the countryside. The opening of the irrigation ditches of Monteagudo allowed for the drainage of swampy zones and a gradual increase in cultivation. In 1450, a rapid repopulation of the Murcian countryside of Cartagena began: the council regulated this process by granting the lands for indefinite periods of time or through estate pensions. New cultivations also contributed to the favorable situation: the orange tree ceased to be purely ornamental, and its fruit soon flooded the market, while the varieties of vegetable products multiplied. Finally, the replacement of the black mulberry tree with the white variety made way for the immediate fabrication of silk, which was an enormous economic staple for centuries in Murcia and its rural regions.

Agriculture's decadence was compensated by the livestock industry. Meat and wheat were essential staples in medieval alimentation, and were supported by the concejo, who made sure there was enough in supply. The mobility of sheep gave them the flexibility to use the extensive pastures in the countryside. In 1267, Alfonso X passed legislation regarding Castilian and Aragónese livestock that came to Murcian fields in the winter. Leather, wool, milk, cheese, meat, and manure were fundamental in the medieval Murcian economy, which also benefited from the taxes that were collected from the passage and stay of foreign livestock. A strong textile industry also begins during this period. The industry was already important as early as 1339, when Alfonso XI nurtured the industry through various provisions that kept products in supply. The exportation by the Genovese merchants of large quantities of Merino wool starting in 1372 also attests to this industry's importance. Two significant statistics: first, in 1488, 127,500 heads of transhumant sheep were counted in Murcia, originating from La Mancha, Guadalajara, Cuenca, and the kingdom of Valencia. This figure drops to 102,483 in 1499, when the end of the Granadan war allowed the herds to find other places to winter. Second, we know that in 1452 the Granadans robbed 40,000 head of livestock in one of their invasions. Uncertainty and vulnerability were always inherent characteristics of the Murcian kingdom.

The depopulation of a substantial part of the kingdom led to the growth of the forest and to the prosperity of the hunt. Alfonso XI's *Libro de la montería* and don Juan Manuel's *Libro de la caza* are faithful testimonies to the number and variety of animals in the area: bears, wild boar, deer, partridges, rabbits, hares, wolves, doves, herons, cranes, ducks, etc. Fishing, on the other hand, was less common, until the practice increased considerably in the early fifteenth century due to the concern of the concejos of Murcia and Cartagena, which responded to the increasing demands for fish. The muleteers' reports of the more than twenty types of fish, and the many misadventures described about fishing attest to the demand for and consumption of the product.

An extraordinary cultural era—in part a continuation of a similar period of glory achieved by the Muslims in the twelfth century—was promoted by Alfonso X in Murcia with the creation of an *estudio* (school or university) where works of classical antiquity were translated, and where the writing of the various *Partidas* and the *Cantigas* proceeded. Economic problems would prevent the university's longevity.

JUAN TORRES FONTES

Bibliography

Martínez Carrillo, M. L. *Revolución urbana y autoridad monárquica en Murcia durante la baja Edad Media (1395–1420)*. Murcia, 1980.

Rodríguez Llopis, M. *Los señoríos de la Orden de Santiago en el reino de Murcia (1440–1515)*. Murcia, 1986.

Torres Fontes, J. "La cultura murciana en el reinado de Alfonso X." *Murgetana*, 14 (1960), 57–90.

———. *Don Pedro Fajardo, adelantado mayor del reino de Murcia*, Madrid, 1953.

———. *Estampas medievales*. 3d ed. Murcia, 1988.

———. "Evolución del municipio murciano en la Edad Media." *Murgetana* 71 (1988), 5–47.

———. "Genoveses en Murcia (siglo XV)," *Miscelánea Medieval Murciana* 7 (1976), 69–168.

———. "Los judíos murcianos a fines del siglo XIV y comienzos del XV." *Miscelánea Medieval Murciana* 8 (1981), 55–117.

———. "Los mudéjares murcianos en la Edad Media." In *Actas del III Simposio internacional de mudejarismo*. Murcia 1986, 55–66.

———. *Repartimiento y repoblación de Murcia en el siglo XIII*. 2d ed. Murcia, 1990.

MURET, BATTLE OF

In 1209 the crusade of Legat brought Simon of Montfort and his warriors to the Occitan theater of operations. They were fighting Raymond VI of Toulouse and the counties of the Languedoc territorial principalities, which were suspected of conniving with the Cathars. Raymond called on Pedro II of Aragón, his brother-in-law, who, encouraged by Pope Innocent III, tried at first to avoid the conflict by diplomatic means; the failure of negotiations led to an armed struggle. In January 1213 the king of Aragón received the homage of the counties of Toulouse, Foix, and Comminges; he thus became the lord of Occitania. He directed his troops to the south of Toulouse, to the city of Muret. On 12 September 1213, after having refused to negotiate, he ordered his foot soldiers to attack one of the gates of the town, but they failed to take it. Simon of Montfort's counteroffensive was not long in coming. Although Raymond's forces were more numerous, they were disorganized; Montfort's army, divided into three groups, made three successive charges and approached the enemy lines.

Pedro II, having allowed himself to be seen at the head of his troops, was killed, which caused his men to flee. Many of them perished while trying to cross the Garonne. The French, who had trained in tournaments in the north of the kingdom, and who were encouraged by their religious zeal, demonstrated their military superiority. The disarray of Pedro's army, as much as his death, was a sign of the end of the Catalán-Aragónese hegemony in the south. The confederation, crippled with the debts caused by the expansionist adventures of Raymond, was caught up in internal wars until Jaime I came of age. Later, Jaime gave up the Occitan dream forever, choosing instead an unambiguous Spanish policy against the Muslim kingdoms of Valencia and Mallorca.

MARTÍ AURELL I CARDONA

Bibliography

Roquebert, M. *L'Épopée cathare*. Toulouse, 1970.

Soldevila, F. *Història de Catalunya*. 2d ed. Barcelona, 1963.

MŪSĀ IBN NUSAYR

Mūsā ibn Nusayr, a general of Persian origin who converted to Islam and helped spread Islamic religion and culture to the far ends of the known earth, managed to pacify the Berbers in Africa and delegated two of his sons to put down their rebelion in Al-Maghrib, or Morocco. By 707 his efforts helped him become the governor of all North Africa. Strategically brilliant and tranquilly ruthless, Mūsā ensured Arab dominance for the caliphate all the way to the shores of the Atlantic. By 708 he had marched into Tangier and secured Arab domination over the southern Mediterranean. When he entered Tangier, he appointed Ṭāriq ibn Ziyād as governor there. A master strategist and politician, from his North African redoubt Mūsā immediately recognized the political weakness and disarray of the Visigoths in Iberia. In 710 he encouraged Ṭāriq to cross the Strait of Gibraltar and explore the possibility of conquering the Iberian Peninsula for Islam. At Mūsā's command, Ṭāriq crossed to Iberia a second time, in the late spring of 711, with an army of nine thousand men. Mūsā's military exploits and his reputation as a strategist, as well as the prospects of encircling the Mediterranean, sent terror through the heart of the Byzantine Empire and the rest of the Christian West.

When Ṭāriq encountered relatively minor resistance in Iberia, Mūsā was moved to jealousy. He crossed into Iberia in 712 with his own band of eight thousand men and moved from Algeciras against Seville, then on to Sidonia, Huelva, and Beja. Finally, following the Guadiana River north, he reached Toledo, where, in an effort to humiliate Ṭāriq for his overzealousness and insubordination, he caught up with him and whipped him in public. After the winter of 713, the pair moved east to Zaragoza, Lérida, Barcelona, Narbonne, Avignon, and Lyon. Although his forces were stretched thin, Mūsā, wrote to the caliph in Damascus of his intent to encircle the entire Mediterranean. Wary of his success, al-Walid, the caliph, stopped Mūsā short and ordered him back to the peninsula, where he proceeded to take Galicia and push the opponents of Islam into the mountains of Asturias. In 714, at the behest of the caliph, Mūsā returned to Damascus with booty and captives and too much success. By 716 he had been humiliated, and his meteoric career advanced no further.

E. MICHAEL GERLI

Bibliography

Chejne, A. G. *Muslim Spain: Its History and Culture*. Minneapolis, 1974.

Vernet, J. *La cultura hispanoárabe en oriente y occidente*. Barcelona, 1978.

MŪSĀ IBN QASĪ, *See* BANŪ QASĪM

MUSIC AND MUSIC THEORY, ARABIC

Our knowledge of Arabic music in medieval Spain is confined to three main sources of information: Arabic theorists of the time; supposed influence in the Alfonsine *Cantigas* and elsewhere; and what appear to be survivals of the Iberian tradition in the Maghrib. Unfortunately, these sources are not what they seem. Theorists, then as now, can delude themselves and their readers; the relationships between the apparently *zajal*-esque *virelai* forms of the *Cantigas* and the parallel of the Hebrew or of the Arabic forms *muwashshaḥ* and *zajal* is not as straightforward as is sometimes assumed; and the belief that North African singers have preserved intact the medieval Iberian singing techniques is simplistic, to say the least. Indeed, the interrelationships of the Mediterranean cultures were clearly complex.

Theoretically, Arabic (and parallel Hebrew) song-poetry was dependent on *arūd*. Yet, as with Greek metric, the pleasing patterns of theory were traduced by music. We are fortunate in having the opening of a *qasīda* preserved in a treatise of the thirteenth century. Al Jāhīz gives the impression that this kind of song was typical of the *qaynāt* (singing girls), who in Spain were often Christians. The tablature notation conveys exactly the (relative) pitch of the notes, together with the note values and drumbeat accompaniment. Metric and rhyme schemes are appended.

As can readily be seen, the pattern of longs and shorts demanded by *ʿarūḍ* (*ta'awīl* meter) is only loosely connected with the actual rhythm. Note also the "paragogic" use of the unelided *-I-*.

Such a song may have been the germ of the type of vulgar Arabic zajal made famous by Ibn Quzmān in the twelfth century. It also may have furnished one type of *Kharja* for the muwashshaḥ, mostly written in classical Arabic (e.g., the thirteenth-century Ibn Sahl, one of whose muwashshaḥāt survives today in the Maghribine singing tradition) or the equivalent in Hebrew (e.g., by his contemporary Todros Abulafia;

ḍarb
(drum: rhythm ramal)
etc.
mode: guwāsht
rhythm of tablature
pitch
1. ʿa-la-l-hadjri lā wallāhi ma a-nā ṣā-bi-rū
2. katam-tu-ha wā-- kumkhifa-tan min a-wā-dhi-ī
metre: ṭawīl
rhyme: 1. a a 2. x a
* error
1. wa-ghay-ri ʿa-lā fakdi l-aḥibba-ti kadi-rū
2. wa-ī wa--la- kum ʿinda l-likāʾi sarāʾi-rū

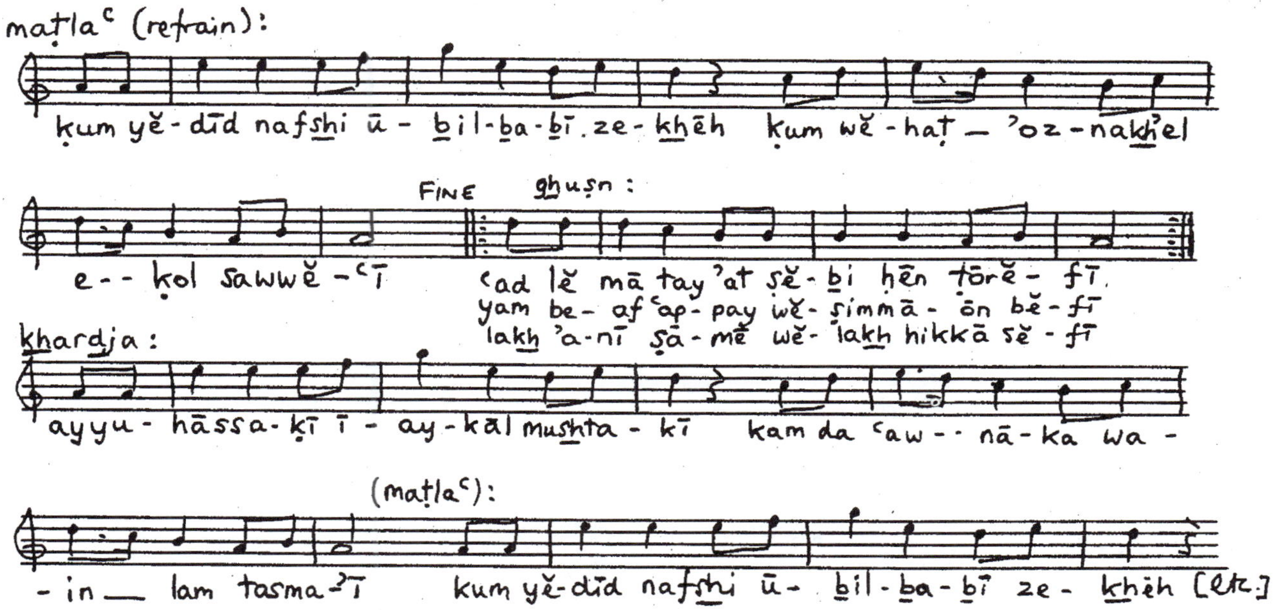
maṭlaʿ (refrain):
kum yĕ-dīd nafshi ū-bil-ba-bī ze-khēh kum wĕ-haṭ—ʾoz-nakhel
e--kol sawwĕ-ʿī
FINE
ghuṣn:
ʿad lĕ mā tayʾat sĕ-bi hēn ṭōrĕ-fī
yam be-afʿap-pay wĕ-simmā-ōn bĕ-fī
lakh ʾa-nī ṣā-mĕ wĕ-lakh hikkā sĕ-fī
khardja:
ayyu-hāssa-kī ī-ay-kāl mushta-kī kam da ʿaw--nā-ka wa-
-in— lam tasmaʾī
(maṭlaʿ):
kum yĕ-dīd nafshi ū-bil-ba-bī ze-khēh [etc.]

again, one of his songs can be reconstructed from tradition—see Example 2). These writers, however, instead include scraps of Romance in the kharja (final section) of some of these lyrics, the significance of which is the subject of dispute, as is the relationship between Romance and Arabic metric and forms. Nonetheless, as Example 1 shows, Arabic rhythm was neither necessarily exotic nor irreconcilable with its Romance counterpart; and, granted the known importation of Arab and Persian musical instruments into Spain (and thence elsewhere), it is hard to believe that the CD player came without any discs, so to speak. Galician and Spanish lyrics mention the *alaude* (*al-ʿūd*, lute), *adufe* (*al-duff*, drum) and many other instruments. The lute, rebec (*al-rabāb*), and *nakers* (small kettle drums, *naqqārāt*) are among the host of instruments that were naturalized into Europe, often tenaciously retaining their Arabic names.

Arabic theorists such as Al-Fārābī (tenth century), were translated into Latin at Toledo, and became known by Vincent of Beauvais, Roger Bacon, Jerome of Moravia, and many other later writers. Although the Western writers tended to adapt the theory to their own ends, the transfer of musical lore was not entirely superficial. For example, "tablature" for the lute and other instruments is found in Europe from the fourteenth century on, but it had been used in Arabic notation for many centuries previously. That the Arabic word for love song (*ghazal*) appears in an Aquitainian song of the twelfth century (as *gazel*) is hardly coincidental; and the word "toccata" is arguably Arabic. Despite a widespread belief in its etymological connection with Italian *toccare* (to touch), the word first seems to mean a fanfare-like piece. A more likely derivation is from *takk* (onomatopoeic, meaning a burst of sound), having to do with the tonguing technique of the "Saracen trumpet."

The musical influence did not necessarily run in one direction only. The muwashshaḥ and zajal emanating from Spain may, like many of the singing girls, have been the product of mixed Romance and Arab parentage. The receptivity of the conquerors to the native culture may well have been heightened by the collapse of the Umayyads in the middle of the eighth century, and the arrival from Baghdad of the famous Persian tenor Ziryāb in 822. The resulting innovations may have found fertile ground in Spain, since neither the Berbers nor the Mozarabs were particularly interested in classical Arabic verse. Be that as it may, it is from this time that the muwashshaḥ seems to have blossomed in Spain. In turn, elements of Spanish Arabic lyric forms (especially their virtuoso rhyme schemes) and their associated music might easily have been transplanted north and east into the rest of Europe, since they were already vigorous hybrids.

As an illustration of this last point, the last stanza of a Hebrew muwashshaḥ by Todros Abulafia is appended. Its tune survives in a Palestinian tradition, to the words of its model, a muwashshaḥ by Ibn Zuhr, of the preceding century. Todros's lyric is thus a *muʿārada*, a contrafaction, borrowing the music and other features of its model. In particular it takes Ibn Zuhr's Arabic refrain (*maṭlaʿ*) and uses it as the kharja, or parting shot, of the Hebrew imitation. But because of the way the music of the latter is heard all through the lyric, the audience anticipates the punch line, a device that seems to have been at the heart of the technique, whether the kharja was borrowed from Arabic or Romance. An additional and striking feature is the rhythm. The Greeks called it Ionic, and associated it with orgiastic cults, such as those of the Celts. The same rhythm occurs in the Alphonsine *Cantigas*, written in *gallego* (Galicia being the Celtic fringe of Iberia). This congruence should not be overemphasized, but it serves to demonstrate the complexity of the problems of the relationship between Arab and European music. It also underlines the disparity between theory and practice, for once again the supposed *ʿarūd* is ridden over roughshod, and the Arabic treatises are silent on this particular rhythm.

DAVID WULSTAN

Bibliography

Wright, O. *The Modal System of Arab and Persian Music, A.D. 1250–1300*. Oxford, 1978.

Wulstan, David. *Boys, Women and Drunkards: Hispano-Mauresque Influences on European Song*. Exeter, U.K., Malta, 1992.

Example 1 (London, British Library, Ms. Or. 2361, collated; see Wright, p. 226, for references and for a slightly different transcription. Wright presents Arabic modal and rhythmic theory in detail, but note his strictures on p. 254).

AL-MUʿTADID, KING OF SEVILLE

See BANŪ ABBĀD

AL-MUʿTAMID, KING OF SEVILLE

See BANŪ ABBĀD

MUWALLADŪN

Muwalladūn means "adopted" and is the past participle of the root *wlld* "to bring up." It is applied to Andalusian native people who adopted the belief of the religious and political dominant class, Islam, and who constituted the great majority of the Hispanic-Islamic population. *Musālima*, a term closely connected, is infrequent in texts and has no precise meaning. The difference generally can be decided by the moment of religious conversion: *musālima* refers to people just converted, and *muwalladūn* refers to a second generation of converts.

The new Muslims generally hid their origin with Arab names or by the *walā'* system, which showed them as clients of the Umayyad emirs.

The *muwalladūn* make a showing in chronical sources that relate to events of the second half of ninth century and the beginning of the tenth. They are shown there as a new group claiming its place in Andalusian society and causing great disturbances to Umayyad government. Their actions during this period, secondarily supported by the Christian element, show that the process of Arabization and/or Islamization of native people had reached an important and significant degree in the middle of the ninth century.

From the tension caused both by the assimilation of new Muslims to Arab-Islamic culture and the situation of "Muslims of second class" emerge the trend of the *šuʿūbiyya*, highly developed among the Persians. According to it, non-Arab Muslims living in the Arab Muslim world praised and claimed their own values.

Ibn García, a Muslim slave of foreign origin in Al-Andalus (a *saqāliba*), showed in his famous epistle the problems of non-Arab Muslims.

With regard to the language spoken by *muladíes*, a complex subjet that has not been much studied, one could assume bilinguism. It is not probable that they spoke Romance after their conversion (at least not immediately); nor did the Mozarabs speak only this language.

Míkel de Epalza

Bibliography

Ibn al-Qūtiyya, *Ta'rīj iftitāh Al-Andalus*. Ed. and tras. J. Ribera y Tarragó. Madrid, 1926. 90–91.

Ibn Hayyān. *Al-Muqtabis fī-ta'rīj riŷāl Al-Andalus*. Ed. M. Martínez Antuña. Paris, 1937.

Dozy, R.P. *Supplément aux dictionnaires arabes*. Vol. 1. Leiden, 1881; reprt. Beirut, 1981, p. 679.

Levi-Provençal, E. *España musulmana hasta la caída del califato de Córdoba (711–1037), Instituciones y vida social e intelectual*. In *Historia de España*. Ed. R. Menéndez Pidal. Vol. 5. 1st ed., Madrid, 1957; 4th ed, Madrid, 1982, 101–105.

Arié, R. "España musulmana (siglos VIII–XV)." In *Historia de España* Ed. M. Tuñón de Lara. Vol. 3. 1st ed., 4th reprt., Barcelona, 1999, 171–72.

Peres, H. *Esplendor de Al-Andalus*. 1st ed. Paris, 1937. Spanish trans., Madrid, 1983. 260–61.

Epalza, M. de. "Mozarabs, a Christian Emblematic Minority in Islamic Al-Andalus." In *The Legacy of Muslim Spain*. Ed. S. K. Jayyusi. Leiden, 1992. 149–70.

Glick, T. F. *Islamic and Christian Spain in the Early Middle Ages*. Princeton, N.J., 1979.

MUWASHSHAḤA

Two highly distinctive poetic genres, the *zajal* and the *muwashshaḥa* originated in Islamic Spain during the Middle Ages. Classical Arabic poetry is monorhymed and quantitative (that is, the verse embodies a combination of long and short vowels), but these two innovative Hispano-Arabic genres exhibit a very different prosody: they are strophic, have variable rhyme schemes, and their meter is stress-syllabic (that is, the verse exhibits various accentuation patterns together with a certain number of syllables per verse). The two genres differ as to language: the zajal is composed in colloquial Hispano-Arabic and sometimes includes words or phrases in Mozarabic (the Hispano-Romance dialect of medieval al-Andalus), the muwashshaḥa, by contrast, is written in classical Arabic (or, in the case of Hispano-Jewish poets, in Hebrew), except for the final refrain (or *kharja* "exit"), which is usually in either Vulgar Hispano-Arabic or in Mozarabic, often in a combination of these two colloquial languages. Both the zajal and the muwashshaḥa embody variations of the following strophic pattern: An initial refrain in (Arabic, *maṭlaʿ*, Spanish, *cabeza*), which establishes the metrical model to which subsequent segments will conform, is followed by verses in which both meter and rhyme change (Ar. *ghuṣn*; Sp. *mudanza*); a third segment is the "return" (Ar. *qufl*, *simṭ*, or *markaz*; Sp. *vuelta*), in which the poem returns to the meter and rhyme of the initial maṭlaʿ. Lastly, after the quft, the maṭlaʿ is repeated—chorally—to complete the cycle. This arrangement is repeated throughout the poem, usually in five successive strophes. The kharja, which usually occurs only in the muwashshaḥa (and not in the zajal), is the poem's final return strophe (qufl), in which the muwashshaḥa once again returns to the meter and rhyme established in the beginning *maṭlaʿ*. The kharja embodies a radical change in language and in tone, by which, from the exquisite, erudite, classical language (Arabic or Hebrew) of the preceding strophes, we are suddenly and shockingly transported into a very different world, a world of everyday, vulgar—indeed sometimes even obscene—colloquial language. According to the twelfth-century Egyptian theorist, Ibn Sanā'al-Mulk, the kharja should be in "the vernacular, hot and burning, close to the language of the common people and the phraseology of thieves . . . the kharja is sometimes composed in the Romance dialect (*ʿajamiyya*) . . . It is the spice of the muwashshaḥ, its salt and sugar, its musk and amber." The kharja's effect on contemporary Hispano-Arabic (or Hispano-Hebraic) listeners must have been electrifying and probably also highly amusing. It is important to bear in mind that both the zajals and the muwashshaḥāt were composed to be sung (not recited). They represent a highly learned complex poetry that was orally performed and orally transmitted. The zajal, composed in colloquial Arabic, in most cases—there are exceptions—does not end with a kharja, whose effect, dependent on a sudden, radical change in language, would in any event have been dissipated by the seemingly popular character of the preceding strophes. Some muwashshaḥāt, for their part, omit the initial, paradigmatic maṭlaʿ and simply start with the first *ghuṣn*; such poems are characterized as *aqraʿ* ("bald"). There are also other differences between the strophic components of zajals and muwashshaḥāt: The zajal generally replicates, in its qufls, only half the rhymes of its beginning maṭlaʿ; the muwashshaḥa, on the other hand, will reproduce the entire rhyme scheme of its maṭla in each of its successive qufls. The typical rhyme scheme of a zajal will, then, exhibit the pattern: AA bbba (AA), ccca (AA), ddda (AA), and so on, while a muwashshaḥa—provided it has a matlaʿ (that is, is not aqraʿ)—will embody the following pattern: [AA] bbbaa (AA), cccaa (AA), dddaa (AA), and so on. The zajal and the muwashshaḥa may combine disparate and, from the perspective of Western readers, seemingly irreconcilable elements in one and the same poem, beginning, for example, with the poet's own erotic complaint about a scornful or unattainable beloved, continuing with panegyric verses in praise of some important patron, and ending with an amorous lamentation, voiced (often said to be sung) by a beautiful (Christian) girl, seeking her mother's advice concerning her unfaithful or absent lover. Yet an attentive reading can reveal the coherence of these elements and the songs sometimes achieve a very tight structure characterized by complex ring composition.

According to Ibn Bassām al-Shantarīnī (d. 1147), the muwashshaḥa was invented, at the end of the nineth or the beginning of the tenth century, by the Andalusian poet Muḥammad ibn Maḥmūd al-Qabrī, the Blind, who adopted, in his poems, "colloquial Arabic and Romance diction" (*al-lafẓa l-ʿāmīya wa-l-ʿajamīya*), while Ibn Saʿid al-Maghribī (d. 1274), in a probably erroneous reference, names Muqaddam ibn Muʿāfā al-Qabrī in an identical role. Among the Muslim and Jewish authors of muwashshaḥāt with Romance (or partially Romance) kharjas, the earliest is the little-known Jewish poet, Yōsēf al-Kātib the Scribe (d. 1042), and the latest is Ṭodrôs ben Yehûdāh Abū-l-ʿĀfia (d. 1306–?), author of three Hebrew muwashshaḥāt. Arabic and Hebrew poets, who composed muwashshaḥāt with colloquial Arabic kharjas, flourished during the same period and, in a number of cases, the same authors, in other poems, also used Romance kharjas. The great author of zajals in colloquial Hispano-Arabic was the unrivaled Córdoban poet, Abū Bakr ʿAbd al-Malik ibn Quzmān (d. 1160), who could boast that his famous zajals were heard even in Iraq. The zajal was, of course, of ancient origin and was cultivated long before Ibn Quzmān, some of whose predecessors (Ibn Numāra; Ibn Rāshid) are known to us, though, at best, their works have been preserved only fragmentarily. After Ibn Quzmān, many other Hispano-Arabic poets cultivated the zajal, though relatively few texts have come down to us. An outstanding exception is the Granadan mystic, Abū-l-Ḥasan ʿAlī ibn ʿAbdallāh al- Shushtarī (d. 1269). The zajal (Sp. *zéjel*) can also be documented in poems composed in Hebrew, Galician-Portuguese, and Castilian. Solomon ben Yehuda, ibn Gabirol, Alfonso X, Juan Ruiz, and Alfonso Alvarez de Villasandino all used the zajal form. Needless to say, the zajal's close relationship to a panoply of similar forms in medieval French, Provençal, and Italian poetry (*virelais*, *baladas*, and *laude*, among others) must be taken into account.

The zajal, the muwashshaḥāt, and the kharja have been the subject of intense and sometimes acrimonious debate. Without attempting to review in detail or resolve such problems here, some of the questions raised are: Which came first, the zajal or the muwashshaḥa? Was the earliest model for Hispano-Arabic strophic poetry a proto-zajal in Hispano-Romance? Was the muwashshaḥa a late, cultured elaboration of an earlier zajal tradition or was the muwashshaḥa the earlier form and the *zajal* merely a secondary derivative? Do zajal and muwashshaḥāt replicate Romance stress-syllabic metrical patterns or did they originate in some modification of classical Arabic quantitative meters? Do the kharjas reproduce—or at least imitate—traditional songs (or parts of traditional songs) in the Mozarabic Romance dialect or are they merely Romance verses arbitrarily invented by learned Arabic and Hebrew poets who composed the muwashshaḥāt? Recently Liu and Monroe, working with medieval Hispano-Arabic muwashshaḥāt surviving in the repertoires of a modern North African singers, have brought forward new evidence in favor of the precedence of the zajal and the Romance origins of Andalusian strophic poetry and its metrics. In regard to the kharja, numerous thematic, metrical, and formulaic parallels between the kharjas and Spanish *villancicos*, Galician-Portuguese *cantigas*, and Old French *refrains* suggest a genetic connection among all these genres, as manifestations of a pan-Romance oral lyric, going back to colloquial Latin origins and ultimately linked to Greek and Near Eastern lyric traditions. In a few cases, it is even possible to identify whole-text parallels between Mozarabic kharjas and Castilian villancicos, as for example, in the following kharja, from a muwashshaḥa by the Jewish poet, Yōsēf ibn Ṣaddīq (d. 1149): "¿Ké faré, mamma? / Meu l-ḥabīb ešt'ad yanna" (What shall I do, mother? / My beloved is at the door). Compare the sixteenth-century villancico: "Xil González llama: / No sé, mi madre, si me le abra" (Gil González is knocking: / I don't known, mother, if I should open for him"). Both poems represent an identical situation, both involve maiden, mother, and lover, and both exhibit the same *ā-a* assonance. In closing, it is, however, important to stress once again the wide differences of critical opinion concerning zajals, muwashshaḥāt, and kharjas, their origins, their relationships, and their interpretation.

SAMUEL G. ARMISTEAD

Bibliography

Armistead, S. G. "A Brief History of *Kharja* Studies." *Hispania* 70 (1987).

Corriente, F. *Ibn Quzmān: El cancionero hispanoárabe*. Madrid, 1984.

———. *Poesía dialectal árabe y romance*. Madrid, 1998.

García Gómez, E. *Las jarchas romances de la serie árabe en su marco*. 2d ed. Barcelona, 1975.

Hitchcock, R. *The Kharjas*. London, 1977.

Jones, A. *Romance Kharjas in Andalusian Arabic Muwashshaḥ Poetry*. London, 1988.

Liu, B. M., and J. T. Monroe. *Ten Hispano-Arabic Strophic Songs in the Modern Oral Tradition*. Berkeley, 1989.

Monroe, J. T. "On Re-Reading Ibn Bassām." In *Actas del Congreso Romancero-Cancionero*. Ed. E. Rodríguez Cepeda. Madrid, 1990.

Sola-Solé, J. M. *Corpus de poesía mozárabe*. Barcelona, 1973.

Stern, S. M. *Hispano-Arabic Strophic Poetry*. Ed. L. P. Harvey. Oxford, 1974.

N

NÁJERA, BATTLE OF

This military encounter on the border of Castile and Navarre on 13 April 1367 is the first of two important battles of the Castilian civil war of 1366–1369. The second and decisive one took place in Montiel two years later. The principal antagonists in this conflict were King Pedro I of Castile and his bastard half-brother Enrique de Trastámara.

Enrique's opposition to Pedro and his ambition to be king had become apparent less that five years after Pedro's ascent to the Castilian throne in 1350. Enrique found refuge and financial and military support for his ambitions in the French court of King Jean II and his heir Charles V.

With a force assembled in France, he marched into Castile against Pedro in 1366 at the head of an impressive army made up of many of Western Europe's most renowned mercenary captains. Given their number, Pedro chose to retreat and look for outside help, traveling first to Portugal, where he was rebuffed, and then to Bordeaux where he found a more sympathetic audience among the English occupying that region of France. In the Treaty of Libourne, signed 23 September 1366, the English, represented by Edward of Wales, the Black Prince and heir to the English throne, and the Navarrese, through whose kingdom any invading force would have to pass, agreed to help Pedro regain the crown in return for substantial financial and territorial concessions.

The Anglo-Castilian expedition arranged for at Libourne entered Castile through Navarre in early March 1367. The Black Prince chose to make his approach in the province of Álava, intending to cross the Ebro River at Miranda rather than the easier crossing at Logroño, the expected route and the scene of Enrique's and the mercenary companies' earlier road into Castile.

Enrique and his French allies were advised by all who knew the impressive military accomplishments of the Black Prince to avoid a pitched battle with him, urging him to wait until the inevitable falling out between the English and the Castilians, given the onerous terms of their alliance and Pedro's inability to pay.

In what proved to be another triumph for the Black Prince on 3 April 1367, he bypassed the area through which he was expected to meet Enrique's armies head-on, outside the town of Nájera on the main road to Burgos, and chose instead to take a detour away from the highway and surprise Enrique the next morning as the sun was rising. In the chaos that ensued, Enrique's soldiers abandoned their positions and fled in the direction of the town of Nájera. Many were killed, including four hundred knights, and a complete slaughter was prevented only because of the financial interest of the English in their prisoners. Among the concessions they had negotiated with Pedro was the right to ransom their captives, which in this case included an impressive number of notables such as the French mercenary soldier Bertrand du Guesclin, Enrique's brother Sancho, and Pedro López de Ayala, the chronicler of Pedro's reign. Enrique, however, managed to escape, first to Aragón and then to France.

The events at Nájera were a temporary success for Pedro, whose alliance with the English, as predicted, soon fell apart, leaving him at the mercy of Enrique and a second contingent of French mercenaries that eventually defeated him at the battle of Montiel in 1369.

Clara Estow

Bibliography

Pope M. K. and E. C. Lodge (eds.) *Life of the Black Prince by the Herald of Sir John Chandos*. Oxford, 1910.

Russell, P. E. *The English Intervention in Spain and Portugal in the Time of Edward III and Richard II*. Oxford, 1955.

NAPLES, KINGDOM OF

It took bands of Norman adventurers led by Robert Guiscard only three decades in the mid-eleventh century to overthrow the Lombard, Greek, and Saracen principalities of mainland Italy and Sicily. The coronation of Roger II in Palermo (1130) united all these territories in the kingdom of Sicily, an association that lasted de jure and de facto for much of the succeeding seven centuries. An eclectic blend of Norman, Byzantine, and Saracen institutions gave the new state, with its capital in Palermo, a vitality unsurpassed in Europe. Papal overlordship sat lightly on its monarchs. It survived the failure of the male line to emerge seemingly more splendid still in the reign of Frederick II of Hohenstaufen. Under his dynamic autocracy the center shifted to the mainland provinces that, through regular parliaments and a uniform administrative system, developed a certain political unity centered upon Naples. In 1224 that city became the seat of a university founded by Frederick to train servants of the state.

Norman, and still more Hohenstaufen, ambitions inevitably clashed with papal pretensions within the kingdom and in Italy at large until the whole peninsula aligned itself in the factions of papal Guelf and imperial Ghibelline. In 1266 their enmity brought Charles of Anjou into Italy as Guelf champion with a French army that overthrew first Frederick's son Manfred, then his grandson Conradin (1268).

Charles made Naples his capital, settled large numbers of French followers and, contrary to expectation, did not lessen the pressures of government and taxation, all of which proved too much for his Sicilian subjects. They rose in revolt (Sicilian Vespers 1282) aided by Pedro III of Aragón, with the result that for the next 150 years an Aragónese dynasty in Sicily confronted an Angevin rival on the mainland with dire consequences for the social and economic health of both regions. During that schism the mainland state became known conventionally as the kingdom of Naples.

Until the death of King Roberto (1343), Naples remained an important cultural center; thereafter it sank to insignificance while the remainder of the kingdom fell prey to feudal mismanagement. Only a brief military revival under King Ladislas (r. 1386–1414) illuminated the subsequent fortunes of the Neapolitan Angevins. They were finally extinguished under the childless Giovanna II, whose reign witnessed a long struggle for the succession between French Angevins and Alfonso V, king of Aragón and Sicily. Alfonso, having emerged victorious in 1442, consolidated his conquest by establishing his seat of government in Naples and making his illegitimate son Fernandoo heir to its throne. His death in 1458 thus brought another division as Sicily passed with Aragón to his brother Juan.

Alfonso and Fernandoo succeeded, despite baronial opposition, in restoring the fabric of royal authority, reviving cultural life, and stimulating economic activity. Fernandoo's death, however, saw French endeavors to reverse the verdict of 1442 come to fruition with Charles VIII's invasion (1494) followed by that of Louis XII (1500). Only the intervention of Fernando the Catholic, heir in the legitimate Aragónese line, sufficed to defeat the French. In the aftermath of his triumph the kingdom settled down to two centuries of existence as a Spanish vice-royalty where, in return for large subsidies in men and money toward imperial ambitions, the rulers of Spain allowed the landowning nobility virtually unfettered sway over economy and society to the detriment of both.

ALAN RYDER

Bibliography

Croce, B. *History of the Kingdom of Naples*. Trans. F. Frenaye. Chicago, 1970.

Storia di Napoli. 10 vols. Naples, 1975–81.

NAṢRID DYNASTY

The Naṣrid dynasty reigned from1231–1492 and arose as a consequence of the decline of Almohad power in Al-Andalus after 1228. By 1238 the dynasty had expanded its influence and come to rule the only Muslim state to survive the twelfth-century Christian territorial expansion into the south of the Iberian Peninsula. The House of Naṣr traces its origins not to Granada but to Arjona, a small town in the present-day province of Jaén. It was there that Muḥammad Ibn Yūsuf Ibn Aḥmad Ibn Naṣr Ibn al-Aḥmar first came to prominence and laid the groundwork for a kingdom his descendants would govern for over two hundred years that stretched along the Mediterranean coast from Tarifa in the west to Almería in the east, and from the Mediterranean coast north to the city of Granada at the foot of the Sierra Nevada.

Muḥammad Ibn al-Aḥmar, later Muḥammad I of Granada, belonged to the Banū Naṣr or Banū al-Aḥmar clan, associated with the Banū Asquilūla, or Banū Escayola clan of Málaga, with family connections in Arjona. Taking advantage of the political turmoil after the breakdown of the Almohad hold on Al-Andalus, and his own reputation as an austere proponent of Islam, by 1234 he had risen to distinction in the region and extended his dealings on into Córdoba, whose leader Ibn Hūd he promptly betrayed in order to assist Fernando III of Castile in the conquest of that city in 1236. In exchange, it is believed that Ibn al-Aḥmar was permitted to take the city of Granada two years later, and establish himself there as its king. From the outset, Ibn al-Aḥmar was thus obliged to recognize Christian sovereignty in the south and cooperate with the Castilians by becoming their tributary, often turning a blind eye in the name of expediency and survival.

Naṣrid Dynasty

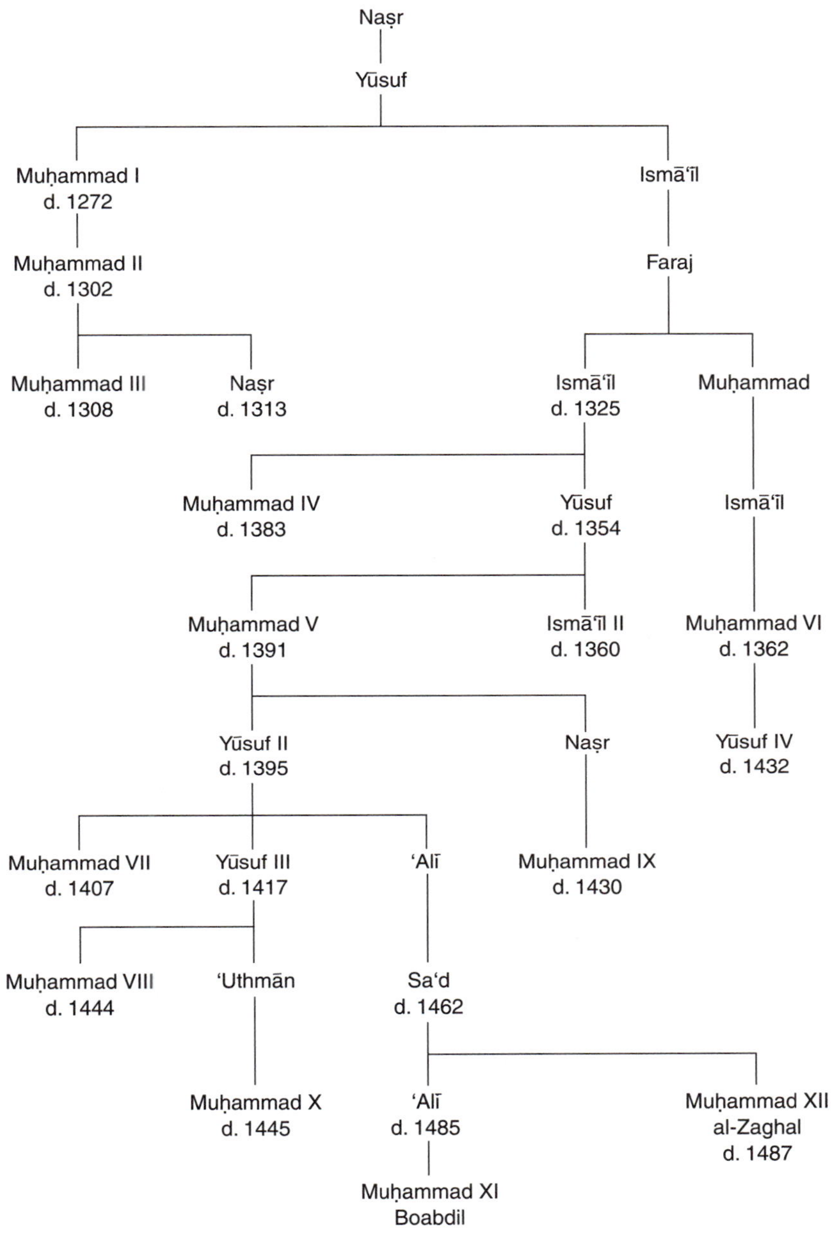

From its start, the Naṣrid hold on Granada was precarious, wedged as it was between the Christians to the north and the North Africans to the south, both of whom laid covetous eyes on the territory ruled by the dynasty. As a result, the Naṣrids throughout their history would rely on diplomacy, cunning, and duplicity to ensure their continued survival.

Ibn al-Aḥmar died in 1273 and was succeeded by his son Muḥammad II (1273–1302), a learned jurist (*faqīh*), who sought to free the kingdom from pressure exerted upon it by the successors of Fernando III, Alfonso X, and Sancho IV of Castile, by entering into an alliance with Merīnids in North Africa, a move that only worsened relations with the Christians and produced greater repression. By the time of his death in 1302, Granada enjoyed an uneasy peace with Aragón and their Merīnid protectors in Africa. His successor, Muḥammad III (1302–1308), known as the Deposed (*Majilū*), was a poet and builder responsible for the Great Mosque of the Alhambra. When he turned over power to his vizier, who attempted to forge a peace with the Castilians, internal and regional dissension proved too much. Supported by prominent members of the Naṣrid clan, Muḥammad's brother Naṣr arranged for the assassination of the vizier and forced Muḥammad to abdicate. Naṣr (1308–1313) was an astronomer and mathematician who was unable to quell dissatisfaction at home. When the Castilians moved to take Gibraltar and Algeciras in 1310, Naṣr was forced to face the situation and counter the immediate threat on his kingdom by paying tribute to Fernando IV, circumstances that aggravated the internal political balance of the clan. Naṣr was himself deposed by his nephew, Ismāʿil (1313–1325). Over the course of the ensuing century and a half, clan rivalries and quarrels would prove the decisive factor in determining the fate and decline of the Naṣrid dynasty.

Ismāʿil was succeeded by his nine-year-old son, Muḥammad IV (1325–1333), who became a virtual captive of his tutor, Ibn Aḥmad al-Mahrūq, During Muḥammad IV's reign the Granadans took back Gibraltar and other Christian strongholds and were successful in holding the North Africans at bay. Muḥammad died at the hands of a Christian assassin in 1233. His brother, Muḥammad Yūsuf I (1333–1354), a reserved and timid individual, was placed on the throne by Ridwān, a powerful minister of the realm. Muḥammad Yūsuf's timidity was exploited by the North Africans, who sent an army to Algeciras and Gibraltar with the intent of taking the entire Iberian Peninsula for themselves. They were met by the combined forces of Castile, Portugal, and Aragón, which in 1340 at the Salado River inflicted a defeat upon the Islamic cause in Iberia second only to Las Navas de Tolosa in 1212. The Kingdom of Granada, alone and virtually unprotected, for the rest of its history would become a client state of the Christians, obliged continually to transact and bargain with them until the end of its days at their hands in 1492.

Yūsuf's successors, Muḥammad V (1354–1359), Muḥammad Ibn Ismāʿil (1360–1362), Muḥammad VI (1362–1391), Yūsuf II (1391–1392), Muḥammad VII (1392–1407), Yūsuf III (1407–1417), Muḥammad VIII (1417–1428, restored to the throne 1430–1432, and again in 1433–1444), Muḥammad IX (1427–1429), and Yūsuf IV (1432), were all deeply affected by clan rivalries, internal civic turmoil, and civil unrest that often led to war and tore at the economic, social, and political stability of the kingdom. By the mid-fifteenth century, whatever little protection the Merīnids of North African could offer had disappeared, forcing the Granadans to turn to Egypt and the Ottoman Empire for moral and diplomatic support. However, by the final fall of Gibraltar into Christian hands in 1462, the Kingdom of Granada found itself completely isolated and could now only depend on its wealth, stealth, legerdemain, and diplomatic acumen to guarantee its continued survival.

Throughout their reigns, Saʿd Ibn ʿAlī (1445–1446) and his son ʿAlī (1462–1482) were alternatively obliged to confront Christian suits for peace followed by demands for tribute, as well as incessant Christian incursions into Granadan territory all along the frontier. Although the Christians were divided in terms of a grand strategy against Granada, the Naṣrids continued to quarrel among themselves and failed to marshal sufficient force to counter their continuous harassment. In 1481 ʿAlī did manage to take back some strongholds along the western frontier and sought to forge a separate peace with Castile. His appeal, however, was met by a series of impossible stipulations imposed on him by Fernando V of Aragón. At the same time, a quarrel between ʿAlī's wife and his Christian concubine for the rights of succession of their respective sons broke out, and this, combined with heightened social unrest in the kingdom, led to a revolt that brought Abū ʿAbdallāh Muḥammad, his wife's son, known as Boabdil, to the throne. ʿAlī fled to Málaga seeking the protection of his brother who governed there until Abū ʿAbdallāh Muḥammad (Boabdil) was taken prisoner by the Christians during an expedition against them. ʿAlī returned to Granada and, when taken ill with epilepsy, handed power over to his brother Abu ʿAbd Allāh (known as Al-Zaghal), who had provided sanctuary for him in Málaga. Boabdil's freedom was obtained by his uncle, with whom he had good relations, in exchange for 400 Christian captives, 12,000 pieces of gold, and the recognition of Fernando of Aragón's sovereignty over the kingdom when Boabdil returned to the throne. Upon his return to Granada in 1487 to reoccupy the throne, Boabdil sent Al-Zaghal to govern the southern part of the kingdom. His actions were to no avail: Málaga fell to the Christians. In the process of his imprisonment and restoration, Boabdil had cooperated with Fernando of Aragón in handing over a number of key strongholds in the kingdom and had been turned into the Christian king's pawn. Despite Granada's attempt to steel itself against the territorial ambitions of Fernando and Isabel, after 1487 the damage was beyond repair. By 1492 Granada and the Naṣrids would fall permanently into the hands of the Christians and the last Muslim stronghold in Europe would cease to exist, bringing to a close a chapter of Iberian history that had lasted over seven centuries.

E. Michael Gerli

Bibliography

Chejne, Anwar G. *Muslim Spain: Its History and Culture.* Minneapolis, 1974.

Edwards, John. *The Spain of the Catholic Monarchs, 1474–1520.* Cambridge, 2000.

Harvey, L. P. *Islamic Spain, 1250–1500.* Chicago, 1992.

Kennedy, H. *Muslim Spain and Portugal.* New York, 1996.

Jayyusi, S. K. (ed.) *The Legacy of Muslim Spain.* 2 vols. Boston, 1994.

NAVARRE, KINGDOM OF

Today, Navarre is only a province located in the north of Spain, as well as Lower Navarre which, to the north of the Pyrenees, is one of the Basque provinces of southern France. During the medieval epoch, these two territories made up a kingdom that was largely spread out around the eleventh century; it then became less extensive, from the Adour to the Ebro rivers, and was hemmed in by the regions of Castile, Aragón, Béarn, and Aquitaine during the thirteenth to fifteenth centuries.

Like the whole of Spain and Aquitaine, the future Navarre was part and parcel of the Holy Roman Empire (Pamplona, its capital, was founded by Pompey) when in the fifth century the Visigothic barbarians crossed the Pyrenees and annexed it, in 476, to their independent kingdom. Navarre was then converted to Christianity, and the bishops of Pamplona took part in the seventh-century councils of Toledo. But this Visigothic kingdom collapsed at the time of the 711 Arab conquest; a governor came under the emirate of Córdoba and sat in Pamplona; Tudela was founded by the Muslim monarchs around 800. Charlemagne crossed the Pyrenees in 778, thinking he could take Zaragoza from the emirs; at the same time he succeeded in settling in the future province of Catalonia, to the east. But his troops sacked Pamplona on their way there; the inhabitants, the native Basco-Navarese, took revenge on his rear guard when he came back, in a high valley of the mountains, at a place called Roncevaux from the twelfth century on, when the *Chanson de Roland* transformed history for the geste, an era when the whole West used this pass to reach Santiago de Compostela.

In 830, the natives chose one of their leaders, Iñigo Arista, as king. Thus the kingdom of Navarre was born, claimed first by the Carolingians of Aquitaine, which was independent. Continually threatened by Muslim forays, Navarre was only a very small state but one that lasted with its dynasty, the Sánchez, who in the tenth century took the place of their relatives the Iñiguez.

Navarre succeeded in largely expanding its territory under King Sancho the Great (1005–1035), who ruled the northern peninsula from Castile to the Val of Aran. A close relative of the princes of Gascony, he received the Lower Navarre from Saint-Jean-Pied-de-Port to the Adour River. This king is mostly known as one of the "God's peace" monarchs, a protector of monasteries and organizer of councils in Leyre, one of those who started the pilgrimages to Santiago by using the Navarrese roads, rapidly giving it its originality and culture. But when Sancho died in 1035, his sons divided his states among themselves, giving rise to the kingdoms of Castile and Aragón on either side of Navarre. Navarre was several times included in the Aragónese sovereignty, and only recovered its permanent independence in 1134. The Navarro-Aragónese then reconquered the Ebro River valley (Tudela in 1119, after reconquering Zaragoza in 1118), Castile and Aragón becoming large states, thanks to the Reconquest; however, Navarre was very much reduced and, in 1200, lost the Basque provinces to Castile. The kingdom of Navarre no longer had a maritime outlet and had to negotiate with Castile for the use of Fuenterrabía, and with Aquitaine for the use of Bayonne.

In 1234, Sancho VII the Strong died without leaving any legitimate heir. (In 1212, he was one of the heroes of the victory of Las Navas de Tolosa, fought between a united Christian army and the last Almohads.) His successor was his sister's son, the Comte Thibaut IV de Champagne. Henceforth, until the fifteenth century, the kings of Navarre came from French dynasties (successively by inheritances and marriage), counts of Champagne (Thibaut I, Thibaut II, Henri the Fat, from 1234 to 1274); kings of France (Philippe the Fair, through his wife Jeanne de Champagne-Navarre, Louis the Hutin, Philippe the Long, Charles the Fair, from 1274 to 1328); and the counts of Evreux (Philippe d'Evreux through, his wife Jeanne de France-Navarre, Charles II, and Charles III, from 1328 to 1425). It was not until the fourteenth and fifteenth centuries that the kings of Navarre–counts of Evreux—actually resided in Pamplona, Tudela, Olite, or Estella, their predecessors having only made brief appearances or none at all in their kingdom, which was administered by a governor. It was a long time, as with French politics, before the kingdom regained an initial independence, with the Evreux dynasty. Charles II, the Bad (r. 1349–1387), is particularly famous for his activities hostile to the Valois kings and for his concern to make people speak of Navarre and himself in all the events that occurred in the Iberian Peninsula as well as in France. His son Charles III the Noble had similar international influence. The princes and princesses of this family married into all the reigning houses of the neighboring kingdoms, and a Navarrese alliance was much sought after during the Hundred Years' War by the English as well as by the French.

Charles III had no heir to succeed him when he died in 1425. His daughter Blanche as heiress brought the rights to Navarre to her husband Juan of Aragón (Juan II in 1458) and to their son Carlos, prince of Viana. But from 1450 to 1460, a civil war broke out in Navarre, a struggle between the nobles and supporters of the prince of Viana and the king of Aragón (who did not want to leave Navarre to his son). The prince's sister, Eleonor, married Gaston IV of Foix-Béarn. Henceforth their heirs bore the titles of King of Navarre, Count of Foix, and Viscount of Béarn. At the end of the fifteenth century, the young queen Catherine (heiress of her brother King François-Fébus) was Jean d'Albret's wife. But then, in 1512, the Castilian troops conquered the Iberian part of Navarre, leaving just Lower Navarre, but still the title king of Navarre, to the sovereigns in the north, and to their descendants: Henri d'Albret-Navarre-Foix-Béarn, his daughter Jeanne, and lastly Henri, the son of Jeanne and Antoine de Bourbon, who in 1589 became King Henri IV of France and of Navarre.

In spite of its size, the small kingdom of Navarre during the thirteenth to the fifteenth centuries had a wide range of landscapes and economic possibilities, from the hills of Lower Navarre to the agropastoral life of the mid-altitude Pyrenees in the mountains, the broad cereal plateaus and the viticulture of the Ribera, and even the *huerta* (farmland) and irrigation of the Ebro River valley around Tudela, where the right to use water was very expensive and could be bequeathed. The Basco-Navarrese were first of all mountain peasants; the Navarrese from the Ebro viticulturists and olive-oil merchants. The country had enough wheat, wine, and meat, but had to buy fish and salt in Bayonne: such trade was a source of wealth for the merchants of Bayonne, who also counted on the king of Navarre's right to pass through their port to reach his Norman possessions. Navarre, which held the Roncevaux Pass, one of the Somport passes, and controled a part of the Ebro, relied even more on trade. The merchants from all Western countries who wanted to go from the French regions to the Spanish lands had to go through Navarre. Moreover, the presence of a royal court in Pamplona, Olite, Tudela, or Estella; an aristocracy; and a bishop and canons in Pamplona represented a continual demand for much sought-after products. The Cruzats and Itoizs from Pamplona, Pons from Estella, and Caritats from Tudela were great bourgeois families that traded horses, spices, and cloth for upper-class Navarrese customers or for the numerous buyers from the border countries. Jews from the main towns took part in this trade and handled the capital for all the customers (as did the bourgeois).

The Navarrese nobility (the *hidalgo*) was made up of about a dozen big families: the Gramonts, Luxes, and Echaux (viscounts of Baïgorry) in the north, and the Montaguts, Aibars, Medranos, and Leets in Iberian Navarre. The knights played a major part as well, but a great proportion of *infanzones* (the lowest order of the nobility) laid claim to hidalgo status, without having the important means of socially asserting themselves and dissociating themselves from the peasantry. However, hidalgo status amounted to a fiscal exemption, and the king, with a charter, could grant it to any deserving individual.

At the time of the armed expeditions of the fourteenth and fifteenth centuries, the sovereigns granted hidalguía and a small income (the *mesnada*) to numerous subjects, who were then forced to serve as an army (cavalry and infantry). Next to this nobility that had representatives in the *cortes* (the assemblies that granted the monies asked for by the sovereigns and that also played a political role) were the prelates of Navarre. Of these, the bishop of Pamplona and the prior of Roncevaux were key; beside them, the abbots of the Benedictine and Cistercian monasteries were much revered. At the end of the Middle Ages, the townspeople gave all their devotions to the mendicant orders. Among these towns people (as a third "arm" of the cortes), an aristocracy made up of tradesmen and head craftsmen was formed by the "Francos," who had came with the pilgrimages to Santiago and with the Reconquest. These were often originally French, but also Navarese and "free bourgeois," keeping the urban councils as much as the origins of their fortunes. A *fuero general* (book of laws and customs) detailed in writing the rights and duties of everybody in the twelfth to thirteenth centuries.

The socioethnic non-native communities were much represented in Navarre. Tudela and the surrounding villages had Moors, witnesses of the Andalusian era, until the sixteenth century, when they were expelled. The Muslims from Navarre, in the thirteenth to fifteenth centuries, were both farmers and craftsmen, specializing in building work and ironwork. A particular *fuero* protects their rights, which they bought with a special yearly contribution: the *pecha* (different from the kingdom's commoners' *pecha* and that of the Jews). The Alpelmi family from Tudela was the most important. Many these Muslims took part in the armed expeditions of Charles II, even in Normandy. The Jews were equally protected by a *fuero*, for a *pecha*. Free in their choice of religious and intellectual life, they had access to landed property, and could also farm that land, and could live by lending money as much as on trade. Some of them were purveyors by appointment to the court, which also entrusted them with embassies and offices in the kingdom's fiscal administration. The Ben Abbas, Menirs, Ben Shuaibs, Falaqueras, and Benvenistes are among the most important of those Jewish families, mostly present in Tudela (where there were three synagogues and two mosques), and in all the Navarrese towns.

Such was this kingdom that had its court officers, provinces, treasury, justice, assembly representatives, state life, and urban and social life. It was located in a remarkably strategic position and represented a tempting prey. The fifteenth-century civil wars weakened it, but it lived on until 1512, when it was no longer able to defeat Fernando the Catholic's armies.

BÉATRICE LEROY

Bibliography

Carrasco Perex, J. *La Población de Navarra en el Siglo XIV.* Pamplona, 1973.

Lacarra, J.M. *Historia política del reino de Navarra: Desde sus orígenes hasta su incorporación a Castilla.* 3 vols. Pamplona, 1973.

Leroy, B. *The Jews in Navarre in the Late Middle Ages, Hispania Judaica,* Vol. 4. Jerusalem, 1985.

———. *La Navarre au Moyen Age.* Paris, 1984.

NAVAS DE TOLOSA, BATTLE OF LAS

The battle of Las Navas de Tolosa (16 July 1212), a victory for the combined Christian armies led by Alfonso VIII of Castile, was the last great battle fought by the Almohads in Spain.

After his defeat at Alarcos in 1195, Alfonso VIII had made a truce with Abū Yūsuf Yaʿqūb al-Manṣūr. But beginning in 1209, Innocent III and the prelates of Spain encouraged the Christian kings of the Iberian Peninsula to continue the Reconquest. Yaʿqūb al-Manṣūr had died in 1199, and the Almohad empire was waning under his son, Muḥammad al-Nāṣir. Alfonso VIII contravened the truce with the Almohads, raiding the provinces of Jaen and Murcia in 1209 and settling the town of Moya in 1210. Pedro II of Aragón also raided in Muslim territory, capturing Adamuz, Castellfabib, and Sertella in the kingdom of Valencia.

In response to these raids, Muḥammad al-Nâṣir landed in the peninsula in 1211 and headed toward the city of Toledo. He besieged and captured the castle of Salvatierra. Alfonso VIII's heir, Fernando, died during the siege. The siege delayed Al-Nāṣir, who decided to return to Córdoba and resume the campaign against Toledo the following spring.

Alfonso VIII, who had been criticized for not waiting for his allies at Alarcos, organized the Christian defense during the winter of 1211–1212. Innocent III proclaimed a crusade, which attracted troops from Aragón, Navarre, León, and north of the Pyrenees. Pedro II of Aragón and Sancho VII of Navarre also joined the campaign. In June 1212, the Christian forces recaptured Calatrava, but most of the French knights left soon after. The Christian army then retook Alarcos, Piedrabuena, Benavente, and Caracuel, arriving at Las Navas de Tolosa on 13 July.

The Muslims, led by the caliph, encamped on the eastern wing of the Sierra Morena. The Christians attacked the morning of 16 July. Al-Nāṣir was unable to hold his troops, and his Andalusian contingent fled, possibly because Al-Nāṣir had executed their general for losing Calatrava. The Christians penetrated the Almohad forces and reached the caliph's tent. Al-Nāṣir escaped, but the Christians captured enormous amounts of booty, which was distributed throughout Christian Spain. Alfonso VIII sent a report of the battle to Innocent; his oldest daughter, Berenguela, wrote an account to her sister, Blanche of Castile.

Both Al-Nāṣir and Alfonso VIII died shortly after the battle. But the battle of Las Navas de Tolosa altered the balance of power in the peninsula. The kingdoms of Castile-León and Aragón were able to capture the great cities of al-Andalus, leaving only Granada under Muslim rule by 1252.

THERESA M. VANN

Bibliography

Huici Miranda, A. *Estudio sobre la campaña de las Navas de Tolosa.* Valencia, 1916.

———. *Las grandes batallas de la reconquista durante las invasiones africanas.* Madrid, 1956.

Monés, H. "Al-ʿIkāb" In *The Encyclopedia of Islam,* New ed. Leiden, 1971.

NAVY AND SEA POWER, PORTUGAL

The growth of naval and sea power in the kingdom of Portugal has a long history. The first important occasion when naval power was utilized by the king of Portugal to achieve a military objectives was in 1147 when Alfonso I contracted with a crusading fleet from England, France, Flanders, and Germany on the way to the Holy Land to assist him in the siege of Lisbon. By blockading the city by sea and by land, the king was able to force its surrender. One of the ships served the king and was commanded by a *rector de galatea regis.* In 1189 Sancho I similarly benefited from the naval power provided by another northern crusading fleet when he besieged and captured Silves in the Algarve. Apparently Portuguese ships (thirty-seven *gales e naves de alto bordo*, and *setias*) also participated. Again in 1217 a northern crusading fleet aided Alfonso II in the capture of Alcácer do Sal. These were ad hoc usages of foreign naval power.

The kings of Portugal evidently recognized the importance of maritime enterprise and granted privileges to mariners in royal service. In 1179 Alfonso I granted the juridical status of knights to the men serving on his ships, including an *alcaide* or ship commander, two *espadeleiros* or helmsmen, two *proeiros*, and a *petintal*; the meaning of the last two words is uncertain. Letters of Sancho I in 1204 and 1210 mention Fernandus Martini, *pretor navigorum* or *pretor navigii*, a ship commander acting in the king's name. During the reign of Sancho II the *palacium navigorum regis* in the parish of Santa Maria Magdalena was cited in 1237; evidently this was the royal shipyard, where ships were built, and also where naval provisions and equipment were stored. According to custom the Jewish community had to supply an anchor and a cable for each new royal ship.

In the late thirteenth century King Dinis extended the rights and privileges of his mariners. The ninety-six *marineiros do conto* or seamen recruited for royal service from maritime towns, and the caulkers (*calafates*) and carpenters of the Ribera de Vila Franca de Xira were granted the status of knights. He confirmed the *foros* and customs of the *alcaides*, *arraizes*, and *pitintaes das galees*, that is, the commanders and crews of royal ships, exempting them from tributes; in 1298 he conferred the rank of *infançâo*, a step above an ordinary knight, on the *alcaides das galés* or ship commanders in 1298.

Most important for the future development of the Portuguese navy, Dinis contracted with the Genoese Emmanuele Pessagno (Manoel Pessanha) in 1317 to build up the royal fleet by recruiting twenty Genoese sea captains, whom he would maintain at his own expense whenever they were not serving the king; Pessagno would receive three thousand *libras* annually in recompense. The king also appointed him as *almirante mor* with the right to transmit that title to his heirs. With an eye to providing material for shipbuilding, the king undertook to plant a pine forest in the region of Leiria.

The most common types of ships were the *galé, galera*, or galley manned by a crew of oarsmen and utilizing a single sail. Much heavier were *naus*, which could carry many men-at-arms and could wreck a smaller ship simply by ramming it. The *barcha, barinel*, and *setia* were ships of about twenty-five to thirty tons, but swift and maneuverable. The *caravela*, which played such an important role in Portuguese overseas expansion, came into use after 1441.

In the fourteenth century both Pedro I and Fernando affirmed the privileges of mariners in royal service and continued to encourage shipbuilding. During his wars with Castile, Fernando had need of fleets and assembled a fleet of thirty-two *galés* and thirty *naus* for an attack on Seville in 1369. He also sent ships to assist England against France in 1374. More than likely, the office of *capitão mor da frota* with authority much like that of an admiral dates from Fernando's reign. In 1377 and again in 1380, he granted additional benefits to shipbuilders, caulkers, and carpenters, exempting them from tolls and other duties. New shipyards (*taraçanas*) were erected near the Ribera Velha. From about this time bread and biscuit for the mariners was baked in ovens on the right bank of the Coina River. Nearby was the arsenal of Telha where arms were kept. The placement of artillery on ships in the fifteenth century demanded much larger crews capable of using these weapons. Many mariners called *vintaneiros* were recruited from maritime towns and were obliged to provide one oarsman from every twenty men (*vintenas do mar*). Captive Moors and criminals were also often set to man the oars.

The most rapid development of Portuguese naval power came in the fifteenth century when João I, prompted by his sons, undertook the capture of Ceuta on the Moroccan coast in 1415. As is well known, the king's son Henrique, better known as Henry the Navigator, sponsored numerous expeditions to explore and colonize the west coast of Africa and the islands of Madeira, the Azores, and the Canaries. Nevertheless, Henry's activities were not necessarily identical with those of the crown. Afonso V was also active in naval affairs, building warships, manufacturing arms, ammunition, and artillery for his attempts to conquer Alcácer Seguir, Arzila, and Tangier.

In general one can say that from the thirteenth century onward Portuguese maritime trade increased steadily along the Atlantic coast, the Bay of Biscay, and the English Channel. The number of merchant ships and seamen obviously grew to meet this challenge, and it is likely that the king, when in need of ships and men for naval warfare was able to draw on the merchant marine. The need to maintain a royal fleet on a permanent footing was not of the greatest importance except during the wars with Castile in the late fourteenth century, and then in the exploratory activities of the late fifteenth century.

JOSEPH F. O'CALLAGHAN

Bibliography

Alburquerque, L. de. *Introdução a história dos descobrimentos*. Coimbra, 1962.

Diffie, B.W., and G.D. Winius. *Foundations of the Portuguese Empire, 1415–1580*. Minneapolis, 1977.

NAVY AND SEA POWER, SPAIN

The development of naval and sea power in the Iberian Peninsula proceeded by fits and starts as needs required. For example, in the seventh century the Visigothic kings organized fleets to expel the Byzantines and to protect the coast against initial Muslim assaults. In like manner ʿAbd al-Raḥmān I (756–788) erected shipyards in Seville, Cartagena, and Tortosa to build ships to protect his realm from attacks by the caliphs of Baghdad. ʿAbd al-Raḥmān III (912–961) constructed new shipyards and sent his ships to guard the coast against pirates.

The first important evidence of the use of fleets in Christian Spain dates from the early twelfth century. The Christian rulers were dependent on the Italian maritime republics of Genoa and Pisa for both mercantile and naval shipping. The Catalan assault on Mallorca in 1114, for example, was carried out with the essential collaboration of a Pisan fleet and the Genoese provided the ships that made possible the capture of Almería in 1147 and Tortosa in 1148. On the Atlantic coast Archbishop Diego Gelmírez of Santiago de Compostela assembled a fleet in 1112 to repel pirate attacks; he also built a shipyard at Padrón and hired a Genoese to supervise construction of two galleys. Similarly crusading fleets from northern Europe enabled the kings of Portugal to capture Lisbon in 1147, Silves in 1189, and Alcácer do Sal in 1217.

Not until the thirteenth century did the Christian rulers develop a naval arm of their own as the port towns of Cantabria along the Bay of Biscay and of Catalonia on the Mediterranean shore began to engage in regular maritime trade. The Cantabrian towns organized an *hermandad de las marismas* to protect their maritime interests. For the first time Christian rulers were able to call on their own people to provide ships for naval operations. Thus when Jaime I of Aragón decided to attack Mallorca in 1227 he was able to utilize Catalan ships. That prompted him to build shipyards at Barcelona, which were reconstructed in the late fourteenth century. His contemporary Fernando III of Castile in 1248 entrusted Ramón Bonifaz with the task of securing Cantabrian ships to assist in the siege of Seville.

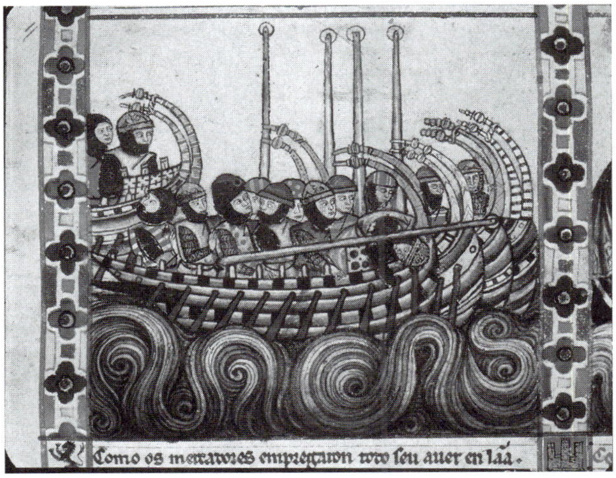

Thirteenth century CE battleships. Alfonso X, the Wise, Cantigas de Santa Maria Spain, 13th c. Copyright © Giraudon/Art Resource, NY. Biblioteca Real, El Escorial, Madrid, Spain.

The beginning of a Castilian royal navy dates from the reign of Alfonso X, who constructed shipyards in Seville, Castrourdiales, and Santander, and hired twenty-one *comitrés* from Cantabria, Catalonia, France, and Italy, each to captain and maintain a galley with a crew of one hundred. He also appointed Ruy López de Mendoza as the first *almirante de la mar* or admiral of the fleet. The position of admiral became hereditary in the Enríquez family, illegitimate descendants of Alfonso XI, who often had little or no naval experience. The admirals' functions in the later medieval centuries tended to be judicial and financial, that is, they adjudicated maritime litigation and were entitled to certain levies on trade.

In the *Siete Partidas* Alfonso X devoted an entire section to the theme of naval warfare, the responsibilities of the admiral, the ship captains (*comitrés*), navigators or pilots (*naucheros*), ordinary seamen, and the marines or armed men. These included *proeres*, stationed in the prow of the ship ready to be the first to go into battle; the *alieres*, who followed next; the *sobresalientes*, whose task was to defend the ship; and archers (*ballesteros*). The *Partidas* also spoke of the need to supply each ship with weapons, armor, biscuit, salt meat, vegetables, cheese, vinegar, and fresh water.

The principal type of warship was the *galea, galera*, or galley, a long ship propelled by oars but carrying an auxiliary sail. Others included the *nao* or *nave*, a large round ship carrying lateen or triangular sails on one or two masts; the *saetía*, a small, swift vessel, and the *ballener*, used to transport troops. In the fifteenth century the *coca* and *carraca*, adaptations of the heavy square-rigged northern cog came into use. The *carabela* or caravel, a small light ship with two or three masts utilizing lateen sails was especially favored during the era of exploration and colonization.

Pedro IV of Aragón also drew up the *Ordinacions Sobre lo Feyt de la Mar*, a code concerning naval armaments and discipline. He gave his admiral charge over the royal shipyards and authority to hear and punish crimes committed both at sea and in the ports. All ships were required to have a seneschal in charge of supplies, a *comiral* or boatswain to direct the sailors, a pilot, and a *comitré* or captain, and a requisite number of seamen who were often recruited in public places. The office of admiral became hereditary in the Catalan family of Cardona.

In the late thirteenth and early fourteenth centuries Castilian fleets were exceedingly busy defending the peninsula from invasion by Moroccan forces. With that end in view the kings besieged by land and sea the ports of Tarifa (taken in 1292), Algeciras (taken in 1344), and Gibraltar (taken in 1309, lost in 1333). In the struggle for control of the straits, Castile continued to utilize the services of Genoese mariners such as Benedetto Zaccaria. In the latter half of the fourteenth century Enrique II supplied France with Castilian ships commanded by the Genoese Ambrosio Bocanegra for service against England. These ships raided the English coast and even sailed up the Thames River. Enrique III also maintained a fleet to pursue pirates. Meantime Catalan fleets had facilitated the conquest not only of the Balearic Islands, but also of Sicily (1282) and Sardinia (1323–1325). Throughout the fourteenth century the kings of Aragón were involved in war with Genoa for control of Sardinia and mastery in the western Mediterranean. In the fifteenth century the Aragónese royal navy declined significantly in the time of Alfonso V and Juan II, while their contemporaries Juan II and Enrique IV of Castile similarly neglected the Castilian navy. Fernando and Isabel revived the royal fleet for use against Portugal during the war of succession and then for the reconquest of Granada.

The maintenance of a permanent fleet by the crown was financially difficult and for the most part the navy was neglected until there was a crisis. Then the monarchy was often dependent on leasing private ships for naval use.

JOSEPH F. O'CALLAGHAN

Bibliography

Fernández Duro, C. *La marina militar de Castilla desde su origen y pugna con la de Inglaterra hasta la refundición en la Armada española.* 2 vols. Madrid, 1890–94.

O'Callaghan, J. F. *A History of Medieval Spain.* Ithaca, N.Y., 1975.

NEBRIJA, ELIO ANTONIO DE

(c. 1441–1522), Spain's leading pre-Renaissance humanist was born Antonio Martínez de Cala e Hinojosa in the Andalusian town of Lebrija. Opinion is divided concerning the year of his birth. In the prologue to his undated Latin-Spanish dictionary he gives his age as fifty-one and states that he was born in the year prior to the battle of Olmedo (1444). However, other observations in the same prologue concerning the age at which he went to Italy, the length of his stay there and of his subsequent service to Alonso de Fonseca, archbishop of Seville, have led some specialists to place Nebrija's date of birth in 1441.

At the age of nineteen Nebrija left for Italy to study in the Spanish College of San Clemente in the University of Bologna, where he was exposed to the writings of Lorenzo Valla and to his critiques of the medieval system of teaching Latin grammar. Nebrija was appalled at the state of Latin instruction in the University of Salamanca, by the teaching manuals employed (typified by the highly popular verse *Doctrinale* of Alexander de Villadei), which stressed rote memorization of paradigms, and by the lack of attention paid to classical authors. Nebrija returned to Spain determined to introduce the reforms advocated by Valla. In 1476 he took posession of the chair of Latin grammar at Salamanca, where he remained until 1487, when he entered the service of his former student Juan de Zúñiga, master of the Order of Alcántara and future cardinal archbishop of Seville. The years spent with Zúñiga were among Nebrija's most productive. At the beginning of the sixteenth century, Nebrija joined the group headed by Cardinal Cisneros, that was preparing the edition of the *Biblia Poliglota* at the newly created University of Alcalá. Nebrija's insistence on applying strict philological criteria to the text of the Latin Bible brought him into conflict with the group's theologians. After Cisneros lent them his support, Nebrija chose to withdraw from the project and returned to the University of Salamanca where he held various chairs. In 1513 Nebrija failed in his bid to win the chair of prima de gramática. Embittered, he left Salamanca. In 1514 Cisneros granted the ageing Nebrija the chair of rhetoric at Alcalá de Henares, which he occupied until his death on 2 July 1522.

Nebrija can be described as Spain's first linguist, perhaps best known today for his studies of Latin, Greek, Hebrew, and the Castilian vernacular. Despite his pioneering work on Castilian, Latin seems to have been Nebrija's primary concern as a linguist. His first major book was *Introductiones Latinae* (1481), a direct result of Nebrija's concern with the quality of Latin teaching at Salamanca and his belief that *grammatica*, the acquisition of Latin, was the key to all other scholarly disciplines. *Introductiones* was designed as a clear and systematic pedagogical manual for university students, with which Nebrija sought to reintroduce into Spain classical models and the premedieval grammatical theory of Donatus and Priscian. This work was an instant success. It was revised and reedited several times during Nebrija's life and frequently reprinted (often under different titles) throughout the sixteenth century in Spain and elsewhere. At the insistence of Queen Isabel, Nebrija published around 1488 (apparently reluctantly) a bilingual Latin and Spanish version of this manual. *Introductiones* became the basic manual for university teaching of Latin in Spain and was one of the books most often exported to the New World during the colonial period. Throughout his career Nebrija published a series of *Repetitiones*, formal university lectures dealing with the pronunciation of Latin, Greek, and Hebrew.

Within the intellectual framework of late-fifteenth-century Spain, Nebrija's Latin-Spanish (1492) and Spanish-Latin dictionaries (c. 1495) as well as his *Gramática de la lengua castellana* (1492) represent major innovations. In all likelihood the two dictionaries were designed to provide access to Latin rather than to constitute repositories of contemporary Spanish. They may well represent the fruits of an announced larger "*obra de vocablos*," which was to include lexicons of civil law, medicine, and the Scriptures (his *Ius Civilis Lexicon* of 1506 and his *Lexicon illarum vocum quae ad medicamentariam artem pertinent* appended to a 1518 edition of a Latin translation of Dioscorides). The Spanish-Latin dictionary was the first systematic and comprehensive work in which Spanish was the source language. Both dictionaries, in many respects quite modern in their lexicographic principles, were revised by Nebrija and underwent several editions. The Latin materials served other early sixteenth-century lexicographers in the preparation of bilingual dictionaries involving Catalan, French, and Sicilian.

According to its prologue, Nebrija published his *Gramática de la lengua castellana* to fix and stabilize the Spanish language in order to prevent its further decay, to facilitate the acquisition of Latin grammar, and to provide a means of learning Spanish for those peoples over whom Spain would one day rule. Within a framework of Latin grammatical theory, Nebrija examines the linguistic facts of Spanish, with emphasis on form rather than on function. The *Gramática* treats orthography and pronunciation, prosody, etymology (that is, morphology), the syntax of the ten parts of speech, and closes with an overview of Spanish for the second-language learner. Motivated by the belief that standardized spelling would contribute to language stability, Nebrija published a second spelling treatise in 1517 under the title *Reglas de orthographía en la lengua castellana*, essentially a resume of book 1 of the *Gramática castellana*. Nebrija's *Gramática* was not reprinted until the eighteenth century and did not seem to have much impact on the work of other sixteenth- and seventeenth-century Spanish grammarians, many of whom may not even have known this work.

In addition to his activities in the realm of language studies, Nebrija composed Latin verse and prepared in that language commentaries on Scripture, rhetorical treatises, works of historiography, geography, and cosmography, as well as editions of and commentaries on the writings of other humanists. Unfortunately, hardly any of these works is available in a modern edition (for titles, see Odriozola).

STEVEN N. DWORKIN

Bibliography

Braselmann, P. *Humanistische Grammatik und Volkssprache. Zur "Gramática de la lengua castellana" von Antonio de Nebrija*. Düsseldorf, 1991.

García de la Concha, V., ed. *Nebrija y la introducción del Renacimiento en España*. Salamanca, 1983.

Nebrija, A. de A. *Gramática de la lengua castellana*. A. Quilis, 3d ed. Madrid, 1989.

Odriozola, Antonio. "La caracola del bibliófilo nebrisense," *Revista de bibliografía nacional* 7 (1946) 3–114.

Rico, F. *Nebrija frente a los bárbaros*. Salamanca, 1978.

NEOTRADITIONALISM

Two opposing theories have dominated discussions about the origins of the medieval epic. The individualists claim that every epic is the product of a single poet who composed his work in writing based on learned sources. The traditionalists consider the medieval epic to be the product of a long oral tradition, the earliest written forms of which were chance survivals. *Neotraditionalism* is the term adopted by Ramón Menéndez Pidal to distinguish his views concerning the origin of the Romance epic from those of his traditionalist predecessors and contemporaries. In opposition to the lyric song (*cantilènes*) theory of Gaston Paris and that of legendary origins espoused by Pio Rajna, among others, Menéndez Pidal argues that the epic came into being as a contemporary account of a historical event, which was then continually revised as it was sung over and over again. It was the need to remember notable happenings and to pass on this knowledge from one generation to another that gave rise to the traditional epic and was responsible for its long and fruitful life.

According to the neotraditionalist view, the poets of the successive versions of an epic remained anonymous, representing the collective voice of the society of which they were a part. It was a collaborative effort in which many individual bards and their audiences participated. During the silence of the early centuries, disturbing to many scholars because of the lack of written testimony, the epic flourished in oral circulation just as the Spanish ballad (*romance*) had during the seventeenth and eighteenth centuries when critics believed that ballad-singing had ceased. Any texts that might have been written down were lost.

Concrete evidence of an epic tradition and lost epics in Spain does not appear until the early twelfth century, the source of which are the chronicles. In France it is not early historiography but rather ecclesiastical documents, monasterial chronicles, and saints' lives that produce proof of an epic tradition a century earlier. A scrutiny of the Spanish chronicles from the early Latin to the great Castilian ones brought to light references to and prosifications of many epics, some unknown from any other source. Furthermore, different chronicles sometimes prosified variant versions of the same *cantar de gesta*, attesting to the fact that these epics had undergone changes as they were being sung.

The most succinct presentation of Menéndez Pidal's ideas is to be found in the introduction to his *Reliquias de la poesía épica española*. A more detailed exposition appears in *La Chanson de Roland y el neotradicionalismo*, where he applies the same theory, now called neotraditionalism, to the French epic in particular and, by extension, to the Romance epic as a whole.

RUTH H. WEBBER

Bibliography

Menéndez Pidal, R. *La Chanson de Roland y el neotradicionalismo (Origenes de la épica románica)*. Madrid, 1959. Revised ed. *La Chanson de Roland et la tradition épique des Francs*. Trans. Paris, 1960.

———, *Reliquias de la poesía épica española*. 2d ed. Madrid, 1980, 7–78.

NIÑO DE LA GUARDIA

One of the most infamous, and earliest, cases of the Inquisition in Castile was the prolonged trial (1490–1491) of some Jews and *conversos* (Christian converts) as well as "Old Christians" accused of having murdered a Christian boy (whose body, as usual in such cases, was never found). The accused were from Toledo, but Torquemada ordered the trial to be under jurisdiction of the Inquisition, in Avila where that court met.

Every effort was made to establish the authority and jurisdiction of the Inquisition by this sensational trial, complete with obviously false testimony and a growing series of charges against the Jew, Yucé Franco, that he and the others had "crucified" the supposed child, and that he had conversed with Christians, attempting to convert them to Judaism! For good measure, it was charged that Franco had also stolen a consecrated host (another common charge in Europe against the Jews). The notorious anti-Semite Alonso de Espina had already fabricated such charges against Jews a few years earlier.

After severe torture, and also the torture of his father, Franco "confessed," and he and several of the others were condemned to death at an auto-da-fé in Avila in November of 1491.

Lope de Vega and other lesser dramatists composed plays on the legendary "holy child" of la Guardia.

NORMAN ROTH

Bibliography

Baer, Y. *A History of the Jews in Christian Spain* Vol. 2. Philadelphia, 1966, 399–423 (with some errors).

Fita, F. "La Inquisición y el santo niño de la Guardia," *Boletín de la Real Academia de la Historia* 11 (1887), 7–160.

NOBLES AND NOBILITY

In the high Middle Ages, nobles in the Christian kingdoms were those who fulfilled administrative and judicial functions in territorial circumscriptions or gave counsel at the king's court: they were the *comites*. During the tenth century, some of them made themselves independent and negotiated as equals with the kings, such as the counts of Castile and those of Barcelona. A lower class of owners of great domains, who had legal powers and who brought to or imposed upon the countrymen their protection, joined them; they were known according to their duties to the public authority as *seniores* and *domini* in the west, as *vicarii* and *castellani* in the east.

Al-Manṣūr's campaigns in the years 980–1002 disorganized Christian society. In the eleventh century, the ancient *vicarii* or *veguers* of the eastern regions became independent from the count's authority and, through vassalic links, submitted to their power a great numbers of *fideles, milites*, and *homines*; they thus contributed to the feudalization of the future Catalonia. In the western kingdoms of the Iberian Peninsula the successful Reconquest and gifts by the king allowed the rising of an aristocracy that often chose to live at the court and was entrusted with the government of lands and cities in the king's name. The *infanzones*, the lowest scale of nobility, disappeared during the twelfth century, being replaced by the *fijosdalgo* or *hidalgos*; as the *ricos hombres* or "rich men" from the royal court. These fijosdalgo or "sons of something" were defined by their wealth and had fiscal and legal privileges. The war of reconquest witnessed the development of urban militias, with horsemen and others who served on foot. The first, called *milites* or *caballeros*, soon took over the government of the cities and, thanks to the profits of warfare and the possession of lands and flocks, succeeded in being considered to have the rank of *hidalgos*.

In the middle of the thirteenth century King Alfonso X in his *Partidas* defined nobility according to its functions within the kingdom. Members of the court and aids in government, from the officials of the court and the central administration to those who exercised power in the king's name in his territories, constituted the first nobility. To this nobility "of function," a heritage from ancient Rome, the king added those who served the common good fighting his battles, the *defensores* or *caballeros*. Eventually, under the influence of Italian lawyers, the *Segunda Partida* gave the same privileges and exemptions of the nobility to the masters and doctors in law.

But the end of the military operations at the time of the Reconquest of Córdoba (1236) and Seville (1248) created a grave crisis. The king could no longer pay his nobles for their services and had to reduce the value of the money. In order to alleviate the loss of income, the nobles tried to increase their landholdings and the fiscal pressure on their dependents, while staying at the court to benefit from rents and gifts; in Castile, the nobles stood up for the future Sancho IV in 1282, and struggled to control the regency during the minorities of kings Fernando IV and Alfonso XI. In Aragón, the nobles had, in 1247, obtained from the king the *ius maletractandi*, or right to ill-treat their dependents; Catalan nobles, in 1283 by the article *En les terres o llocs*, imposed the institutionalization of serfdom. From the years 1340 to 1350, a strong royal policy and new military campaigns against the Moors put an end to the troubles; the civil wars, military operations, and eventually the plague resulted in the extinction of many noble families in Castile and Portugal.

Under cover of the internal struggles between Pedro I of Castile (1350–1369) and his half-brother Enrique II (1369–1379), between Beatriz of Portugal (1383–1385), and Master of Avis João I (1385–1433), new families became important and dominated the political, social, and economic life of the fifteenth-century peninsula. As owners of huge *estados* in which they had jurisdiction and enjoyed some royal rights, the nobles lived in the cities; earned from the king's favor rents, privileges, and titles; acted as *mecenas*; sent their sons to study abroad, and introduced Italian humanism and Flemish art. In the kingdom of Aragón the nobles, divided as high and middle nobility, composed two of the four *brazos* at the *cortes* (parliament), opponents to the royal policy of expansion in Italy, they ended in struggling in each of the crown's kingdoms—Aragón, Catalonia, Valencia, and the Balearic Islands—for their privileges.

The accession to nobility was still easy and the three "ways" mentioned in the *Partidas*—government, military service, and university—allowed a great number of the king's subjects to become hidalgos and caballeros. The trials for *hidalguía* kept at the chancery of Valladolid attest, as do the treatises on nobility, that wealth, real military service, and public offices were considered to be noble characteristics.

Cities often complained about their decreasing incomes due to the increase of *hidalgos* who enjoyed tax exemptions. On the other side, within the nobility, some mechanisms operated to forbid new nobles from enjoying the same privileges and prestige as those of ancient nobility. Lineage, which had always been important, became essential. It was no longer considered just an accumulation of virtues, and so a guarantee that the descendants of such illustrious ancestors would not display fewer virtues; henceforth the antiquity of the line would bestow a guarantee of purity, of the elimination of any lack of virtue and vileness in the ancestors, or of the deep stain of Judaism. The true nobles, at the end of the fifteenth century, were those who had the purest, cleanest blood.

The appearance of the concept of "pure blood" permitted the nobility to establish levels of ranks among themselves, but did not impede the creation of new nobles according to Spanish tradition, and both concepts—based on law and on purity of blood—were operational in modern times.

Adeline Rucquoi

Bibliography

Alfonso X el Sabio. *Las Siete Partidas*, Salamanca, 1555; facsimile ed. Madrid, 1985.

Collins, R. *Early Medieval Spain: Unity in Diversity, 400–1000*, London, 1983.

Fletcher, R. *The Quest for El Cid*. London, 1989.

Freedman, P. *The Origins of Peasant Servitude in Medieval Catalonia*. Cambridge, 1991.

Gerbet, M. C. *La noblesse dans le royaume de Castille: Etude sur ses structures sociales en Estrémadure de 1454 à 1516*. Paris, 1979.

Hernández, F.J. *Las rentas del rey: Sociedad y fisco en el reino castellano del siglo XIII*. 2 vols. Madrid, 1993.

Hidalgos & Hidalguía dans l'Espagne des XVIe–XVIIIe siècles. Paris, 1989.

Lawrance, J. N. H. "The Spread of Lay Literacy in Late Medieval Castile." *Bulletin of Hispanic Studies* 62 (1985), 79–94.

Mexía, F. de. *Nobiliario Vero*. Seville, 1492.

Moreta, S. *Malhechores-Feudales: Violencia, antagonismos y alianzas de clases en Castilla, siglos XIII-XIV*. Madrid, 1978.

Nader, H. *The Mendoza Family in the Spanish Renaissance, 1350–1550*. New Brunswick, N.J., 1979.

Powers, J.F. *A Society Organized for War: The Iberian Municipal Militias in the Central Middle Ages, 1000–1284*. Berkeley, California, 1988.

Rucquoi, A. *Histoire médiévale de la Péninsule ibérique*. Paris, 1993.

Thompson, I. A. A. "Neo-noble Nobility: Concepts of *hidalguía* in Early Modern Castile." *European History Quarterly* 15 (1985), 379–406.

Valera, D. de. *Espejo de verdadera nobleza*. Madrid, 1959, 89–116.

NOTA EMILIANENSE

The earliest witness to a Hispanic *Song of Roland* tradition, the hundred-word Latin *Nota Emilanense* (c. 1065–1075) embodies a highly distinctive narrative: In 778, King Carlus comes to Zaragoza, accompanied by his twelve nephews, including Rodlane, Bertlane, Oggero of the short sword, Ghigelmo of the curved nose, Olibero, and Bishop Torpini, each with three-thousand armored knights. The besieging army endures hunger, until the king's followers persuade him to accept gifts and return home. Rodlane, in the rear guard as the army goes through Sicera Pass, is killed by the Saracens at Rozaballes. The following features are particularly significant: The twelve peers are all Carlus nephews and they include extraneous heroes, by French epic standards: Bertrand, Ogier le Danois, Guillaume d'Orange. The Spanish tradition has apparently sought to reshape the Roncevaux narrative by adding the most famous French heroes of other cycles to Charlemagne's forces. Notable too is the absence of Ganelon: There is no treason; Carlus simply withdraws at the behest of his followers. The *Nota* may thus exemplify a primitive form of the Roland story in which the traitor as yet played no part. The vernacular names *Rodlane* and *Bertlane* are crucial in exemplifying the archaic "paragogic" *-e*, a prosodic feature attested in Spanish epics and in later ballad tradition (and even in the same heroic names, *Roldane* and *Beltrane*). Such features—among others—qualify the *Nota* as a witness to a distinctively Spanish vernacular epic tradition antedating the Oxford *Roland* by a full quarter-century. Traditionalist criticism sees the *Nota* as the first in a series of testimonies documenting the Roland epic on the Iberian Peninsula, either approvingly, as in the *Poema de Almería* (1148), *Roncesvalles* fragment (c.1230), *Vida de San Ginés de la Xara* (c. 1400), and various sixteenth-century and modern ballads, or in a hostile Hispanic reaction to French boasts of conquest, as in the *Chronica Silense* (1110), *Coplas de Zorraquín Sancho* (1158), and *Bernardo del Carpio* (early thirteenth century).

SAMUEL G. ARMISTEAD

Bibliography

Alonso, D. *La primitiva épica francesa a la luz de una Nota Emilianense*. Madrid, 1954.

Menéndez Pidal, R. *La chanson de Roland et la tradition épique des Francs*. Paris, 1960.

NUNEZ, AIRAS

A Galician-Portuguese court poet close to the political center during the reign of Sancho IV. Nunez's career flourished in the 1280s and fifteen songs of an unusual thematic and formal variety comprise his poetic corpus. He shared a reverence for Occitan troubadour art with Alfonso X, king of León and Castile (1252–1284), to whose *Cantigas de Santa María* he may possibly have contributed. In an era when his fellow poets (Johan Zorro, Nuno Fernandez Torneol, and the young Dinis, future king of Portugal, among them) were, in their *cantigas d'amor*, fixated on—and exalting—the theme of the pains and sorrows (*coita*) that love brings, Airas Nunez, more closely identified with his Occitan forebears, was celebrating in his songs the delights and happiness (*ledicia*) to be found as a thrall of love. The poet-lover, devoted and respectful, attains a state of grace and joy in the simple act of loving, celebrated in "Amor faz a mim amar tal senhor" (number 4), "Nostro Señor, ¿e porque foi veer" (number 10), and "Falei n'outro dia con mia senhor" (number 12). Admiration keeps the male persona of his *pastorela*, "Oí og'eu a pastor cantar" (number 1), from approaching the lovely shepherdess, a departure from precedents set in the traditional pastorela. There is a difference, too, in his satirical poems which, instead of the bountiful private satire to be found in many *cantigas d'escarnho y mal dizer*, instead focus on moral and political themes, harking back to the classical Occitan *sirventés* in "Porque no mundo mengou a verdade" (number 2) and "O meu señor, o bispo, na Redondela u dia" (number 13). Airas Nunez expands his repertoire with a spring song, "Que muito m'eu pago d'este verão" (number 3), and two *cantigas d'amigo*, "A Santiagu'en romaria ven" (number 5) and the beautiful and much-anthologized "Bailemos nós ja todas tres, ai amigas" (number 7), a song modeled on Johan Zorro's "Baylemos agora, por Deus, ay velidas." This technique of recycling themes and forms, but giving them new energy and elegance, is characteristic of Airas Nunez's art. This latter song, although by theme and style a *cantiga d'amigo*, does not so much reflect a popular vein in poetic composition as it does a cultivated Occitan strain, one evident in his love songs and his didactic verse as well. His preference for the decasyllable line seems to evince an artistic preference for Occitan metrical forms, as does the frequent use of a seven-line stanza. The mix of lines of differing metrical measures in his refrains, as well as the varying length of refrains even within a single composition, endows his songs with a liveliness that does much to underscore the motif of happily-being-in-love that he so often celebrates.

JOSEPH T. SNOW

Bibliography

Nunez, A. *Le poesie di Ayras Nunez*. Ed. Giuseppe Tavani. Milan, 1964. A Galician translation of this edition is *A Poesía de Airas Nunez*, Vigo, 1992.

NÚÑEZ DE TOLEDO, ALFONSO

Alfonso Núñez de Toledo was born in the early fifteenth century and died after 1481. He is known only through his *Vençimjento del mundo*, an ascetic treatise composed at the behest of Doña Leonor de Ayala and sent to her from Elche on the last day of the year 1481, according to the *explicit* of the work's sole surviving manuscript (Bib. del Escorial, MS h.III.24, folios 67r–79r).

In the *Vençimjento*'s exordium, Núñez de Toledo acknowledges his correspondent's request that he write on the comportment of those who have achieved the state of grace through penance. Choosing to stress the consequences of a fall from grace rather than attempting to inspire a state of greater perfection, he underscores the lasting nature of God's rewards as an incentive for rejecting the world, which offers only "cobdicia de la carne e cobdiçia de los ojos e soberuja de la vida" (I John 2:16). Expostulating against these three evils, he cites three examples of the pernicious effects of each: the deluge, the destruction of Troy, and the fall of Spain to the Moors resulted from sins of the flesh; the Egyptian captivity, the punishment of Giezi, and Judas's death by his own hand stemmed from greed; and pride led to the fall of Lucifer, the expulsion of Adam from Paradise, and the defeat of King Juan I of Castile at Aljubarrota. The author exhorts his reader to combat these worldly enemies with the appropriate weapon (humility against pride, alms against greed, and fasting against carnal desires), to place her trust in divine mercy as illustrated in three New Testament examples (the adulteress, Mary Magdalene, and the good thief), and to join him in wishing for death, "la puerta por donde avemos de entrar a la vida ynfinjta." (the door through which we enter eternal life).

Ostensibly destined for the private edification of Leonor de Ayala, the *Vençimjento* resembles a popular sermon (*divisio extra*) in its structure, rhetorical devices, and use of *exempla*. Sources include the Old and New Testaments, patristic writings (those of saints Augustine, Jerome, Gregory the Great, and Bernard of Clairvaux), Innocent III's *De Contemptu Mundi*, and such "jentiles filósofos" as Socrates, Cicero, Seneca, and Boethius.

PHILIP O. GERICKE

Bibliography

Piero, R.A. del. "El *Vençimjento del mundo*: autor, fecha, estructura." *Nueva Revista de Filología Hispánica* 15 (1961), 377–92.

Piero, R.A. del, and P. O. Gericke. "El *Vençimjento del mundo*, tratado ascético del siglo XV: edición." *Hispanófila* 21 (1964), 1–29.

O

OLIBA

A member of the Cerdanya-Besalú branch of the House of Barcelona, Oliba was born around 971, the son of Count Oliba Cabreta. Oliba shared with his brothers the title of count, but appears to have renounced it shortly after entering the monastery of Ripoll in 1002 or 1003. Oliba became the abbot of Ripoll in 1008 and, at the same time, abbot of Cuixà. He became the bishop of Vic in 1017 while retaining his monastic offices. Oliba was an ally of Ermessenda, widow of Count Borrell of Barcelona. She acted as regent for her son, Berenguer Ramón I, and grandson, Ramon Berenguer I. Oliba cooperated closely with the embattled comital family during a period of aristocratic violence. The Truce of God, proclaimed shortly after 1020, is credited to Oliba and represented an attempt to regulate the times when war could be fought. It extended the earlier Peace of God, which exempted noncombatants and sacred places.

Oliba was also responsible for an artistic efflorescence, sponsoring construction of a new cathedral at Vic, renovating Ripoll, and supporting *scriptoria* at Vic and Ripoll. He died in 1046.

PAUL H. FREEDMAN

Bibliography

Abadal i de Vinyals, R. *L'abat Oliba, bisbe de Vic, i la seva època.* 3d ed. Barcelona, 1962.

OLIVER, BERNARDO

One of the most important church figures in the fourteenth-century kingdom of Aragón-Catalonia was the Augustinian, Bernardo Oliver. Born in Valencia, he studied theology at Paris and became master of theology at the cathedral school of his native city (1320), also becoming prior of the Augustinian convent there and, in 1329, head of the provincial order. Shortly afterward he also came to the attention both of the king (Alfonso IV) and the Avignon pope (Juan XXII). He preached sermons both at the royal court and before the pope. In 1337 he was named bishop of the important see of Huesca and was preacher and a counselor to Pedro IV. When Pope Clement VI decided to intervene against Pedro's campaigns in Mallorca, Oliver was part of the official delegation sent to present the papal bull to the king (1344). In the same year, with the king's approval, Oliver was named to the vacant see of Barcelona, and in 1346 the vacant see of Tortosa was also transferred to the jurisdiction of Barcelona, so that Oliver was from that date bishop both of Barcelona and Tortosa. In 1348 he was sent on a certain diplomatic mission by the king, and upon his return he died as a consequence of the plague.

Of the several works attributed to him or known to be his, mostly in manuscript, mention may be made of a commentary on the "Sentences" of Peter Lombard, the moralistic work *Excitatori de la pensa á Deu* (published 1929, a Valencian version of a Latin original), a concordance of the *Decretum* with biblical passages, and the *Tractatus contra Antichristum.*

Of most importance, however, is his small polemic against the Jews, *Contra caecitatem iudaeorum* (written c. 1317, and thus, apparently, while still at school in Paris). The work shows influences of St. Augustine and Isidore of Seville. A dispassionate work, its main purpose is to show the abrogation of the "old" law (Torah) and the imperfect nature of that law and of those (Jews) who observe it; it utilizes the falacious argument that Jews believe in the "perfection" of the Torah due to miracles, and that the miracles of Jesus are "superior" to those of the Old Testament.

There is nothing either original or persuasive in the argumentation, and the book appears to have had no impact on subsequent polemical literature in Spain (a possible exception might be a minor polemic by another Augustinian, Alonso [Fernando] Vargas of Toledo, the bishop of Badajoz and archbishop of Seville, d. 1366). Nevertheless, Benedict XIII, a notoriously anti-Jewish pope, had not one but *two* copies of Oliver's book, and the possible impact of this on the Tortosa Disputation may be considered.

NORMAN ROTH

Bibliography

Oliver, B. *El tratado "Contra caecitatem iudaeorum" de fray Bernardo Oliver*. Ed. F. Cantera Burgos. Madrid-Barcelona, 1965.

Vendrell de Millás, F., "La obra de polémica antijudáica de fray Bernardo Oliver," *Sefarad* 5 (1945), 303–36.

OPPA

Bishop of Seville (?), early eighth century. The little that we know about Oppa comes from conflicting chronicles. According to the *Mozarabic Chronicle of 754*, he was a son of the Visigothic king Egica (687–702), and therefore a brother to King Witiza (698–710). The same source reports that Oppa assisted Mūṣā ibn Nusayr in rounding up and executing Visigothic nobles who were attempting to flee Toledo during the Muslim conquest of Spain. The late-ninth-century *Chronicle of Alfonso III* also depicts Oppa as a collaborator with the Muslims, but identifies him as a *son* of Witiza and a bishop, either of Seville (according to the Oviedo version of the chronicle) or Toledo (according to the Roda version). There is, in fact, an Oppa listed among the early eighth-century bishops of Seville. The *Chronicle of Alfonso III* describes a legendary encounter between Oppa and Pelayo in which the former, in cooperation with the Muslim army, tried in vain to convince the latter to surrender. Pelayo refused and subsequently defeated the Muslims at the battle of Covadonga (c. 718).

KENNETH B. WOLF

Bibliography

Collins, R. *The Arab Conquest of Spain*. Oxford, 1989.

Wolf, K. *Conquerors and Chroniclers of Early Medieval Spain*. Liverpool, 1990.

ORAL-FORMULAIC COMPOSITION *See* NEO-TRADITIONALISM

ORDENAMIENTO DE ALCALÁ *See* LAW

ORDENAMIENTO DE MENESTRALES

One of the principal outcomes of the Castilian *cortes* (parliament) held at Valladolid in 1351, this piece of legislation attempted to set limits on the wages and prices that laborers and artisans could respectively demand. These measures, applicable to men and women, were deemed necessary to counteract labor shortages and the high cost of staples caused by the first wave of the Black Death that hit Castile from 1348 to 1350. The *Ordenamiento* is important as one of only a handful of such price- and salary-setting documents in the history of medieval Castile. It is also part of the only extant set of cortes proceedings for the reign of Pedro I (1350–1369).

Five regions of Castile received their own *Ordenamiento*, each reflecting local realities: Toledo and Cuenca; Seville, Córdoba, and Cádiz; León, Oviedo, and Astorga; Burgos, Castrojeriz, Valladolid, and Tordesillas; and Murcia. Regulated were farm laborers, planters, pruners, reapers, flax gatherers, grape pickers, harvesters, carpenters, shepherds, masons, roofers, smiths, tailors, shoemakers, furriers, oxdrivers, weavers, jewelers, house servants, nursemaids, saddlemakers, and armorers.

According to the *ordenamiento*, an average agricultural laborer received sufficient monthly income to purchase five quarts of wine, two chickens, one and a half bushels of barley, one lamb, two pairs of inexpensive shoes, and an unlined coat. It would have taken him two months to earn enough for a cow and a full year to buy a saddle. No matter how hard he worked, he would never have been able to afford a charger and a suit of armor.

Although the economy of Castile recovered by the middle of the decade following the meeting of the Cortes, it is not clear, for lack of direct evidence, how these measures contributed to the recovery. It also remains unclear whether the crown had at its disposal the means to enforce the terms of the *ordenamiento*.

CLARA ESTOW

Bibliography

Cortes de los antiguos reinos de León y Castilla. Vol. 2. Madrid, 1861–1863.

Valdeón Baruque, J. "Las cortes castellanas en el siglo XIV." *Anuario de Estudios Medievales* 7(1970–71), 615–21.

ORDER OF CHRIST *See* MILITARY ORDERS

OROPESA, ALONSO DE

General of the Order of San Jerónimo, Alfonso de Oropesa played an important role in the history of Jewish-Christian relations in Castile. He headed the council of nobles that in 1465 settled a peace with Enrique IV and imposed certain demands on the king, among which were a series of anti-Jewish restrictions, the work of Alfonso. He was one of three named by that council to oversee the "welfare of the kingdom"—that is, that the demands were complied with. Alfonso particularly objected to Jews holding public office over Christians and the general influence Jews had at court and with the nobles. Although there is little evidence that these anti-Jewish measures were in fact carried out, the attempt contributed to the growing anti-Jewish sentiment.

Alfonso (who certainly was not a *converso*, a Jew who had converted, as has been claimed) wrote an important treatise defending the *conversos* against the attacks of "Old Christians." In it, he fluctuates between admiration for "Old Testament" Jews and Judaism and contempt and vilification of the "perfidious Jews" of his own time. Arguing at one point that the ancient Jews were the only true people, since only they had a (divine) law and concept of justice, he then attacks the imperfection of the law since the people itself was imperfect. Not only was the Jewish law imperfect—so also was its faith, which did not "reveal" to them the truth of the Trinity; as was the sacrificial cult and the teachings as to the ultimate perfection of man, based on "temporal rewards" not leading to salvation (an old argument, derived from Thomas Aquinas).

Alonso reveals that he was not entirely unfamiliar with rabbinical traditions, and at one point seems to allude to a statement found, in fact, in the *Mekhilta*. Yet if so, he ignored, deliberately or otherwise, the explanations given by Spanish Jewish authorities, Maimonides, and others.

He complains again of Jews holding office, of having Christian servants who live with them and keep the Sabbath, farming the taxes of the kingdom and the churches, and even the old anti-Semitic barb that Jews rape Christian women and are generally suspect of "lewdness."

Nevertheless, he could write that Israel was the "people of God," to whom Christ belonged according to the flesh, and by whom salvation is promised. This, of course, he did in the context of defending conversos. Very important is the correct observation of his editor that his whole book gives the impression that, while there were no doubt some "bad" conversos, these were few in number.

Ironically, after his death, his own powerful Order of the Jeronymites was to be condemned as a hotbed of (supposedly) such "bad" conversos.

NORMAN ROTH

Bibliography

Enríquez de Castillo. *Crónica de don Enrique IV*. Biblioteca de Autores Españoles 70, 140.

Oropesa, A. de. *Luz para conocimiento de los gentiles*. Trans. L. Díaz y Díaz. Madrid, 1979.

Roth, N. *Conversos, Inquisition and the Expulsion of the Jews from Spain*. Madison, Wisc., 1995.

OROSIUS, PAULUS

Orosius was a Spanish priest, probably of the diocese of Braga, who left Spain around the year 413 for reasons that may be related to disturbances in the Iberian Peninsula following the Germanic invasions. Little is known of his earlier life, but he appears to have been involved in opposing the spread of Priscillianism in Spain. He made his way to Hippo in North Africa, to seek the advice of St. Augustine, for whom he wrote his *Liber apologeticus Contra Pelagianos* (Warning concerning the Error of the Pelagianists and Origenists, 414). Augustine replied with the treatise *To Orosius against the Pelagianists and Origenists*. In 415 to 416 he served as an intermediary between Augustine and Jerome in Palestine in their efforts to coordinate Western and Eastern condemnation of the teaching of Pelagius. He returned from Palestine in 416 with relics of St. Stephen the Protomartyr, which were intended for the Church of Braga, but the conflicts in the peninsula between the Visigoths and the Vandals and Sueves prevented him reaching the mainland. He therefore deposited the relics in a church in Minorca. At this time he began his best known work, *Historiarum adversus paganos libri VII* (Seven Books of History against the Pagans), a synoptic history of Rome from the foundation of the city up to 416, which he dedicated to Augustine. This attempted to rebut pagan claims that recent military disasters had befallen the Roman Empire in consequence of it having become Christian. This Orosius sought to deny by arguing, rather unconvincingly, that worse things had occurred before the conversion of Constantine. Nothing more is known of Orosius after he completed this work in 418.

ROGER COLLINS

Bibliography

Mommsen, E. T. "Orosius and Augustine." In his *Medieval and Renaissance Studies*. New York, 1959, 325–48.

Zangemeister, C. (ed.) *Pauli Orosii historiarum adversum paganos libri VII*. Vienna, 1882, reprt. Hildesheim, 1967.

OVID

The works of Publius Ovidius Naso exerted a broad influence on medieval Iberian letters. Whatever the ultimate source of the European love lyric, it is clear that the vast body of amorous poetry written in Galician-Portuguese, Castilian, Catalan, and Provençal throughout the Middle Ages owes many of its themes, classical references, and much of its stylistic expression to the works of the Roman poet Ovid (43 B.C.E.–17 C.E.) Already in the early Middle Ages, Ovid's works were known to writers such as Isidore of Seville (c.560–636), perhaps through florilegia. The earliest known translation of Ovid into a peninsular language is found in the thirteenth-century Alfonso the Wise's *General estoria*, in which passages from the *Metamorphoses* and *Heroides*, together with selections from medieval commentaries on these works, are translated into Castilian.

In fourteenth-century Castile, the *Libro de buen amor* by the archpriest of Hita, possibly influenced by the pseudo-Ovidian *De vetula*, also includes an art of love with clear debts to Ovid's *Ars amatoria*. It is, however, still a matter of debate as to whether the archpriest knew the work directly or in some florilegium or student anthology. Ovid's works were probably taught in centers of higher learning in Spain in the fourteenth and fifteenth centuries. Although little concrete evidence survives this chaotic period of Spanish history, we do have one interesting manuscript of Ovid's *Metamorphoses*, which bears a Latin marginal commentary and a Castilian inscription stating, "This is the Ovid from which the teacher lectured" (Soria, Bibl. Pública, MS 4-H).

The fifteenth century was a veritable *aetas ovidiana* in Castile. The language of the *Ars amatoria*, together with the *Heroides* and *Metamorphoses* enjoyed strong favor with courtly poets. At the same time there arose the "sentimental romance," a genre that draws upon Ovidian themes, situations, and characters, as already received by Giovanni Boccaccio in Italy, for much of its inspiration. Juan Rodríguez del Padrón, the author of the earliest of these romances (*Siervo libre de amor*), also made a new translation of the *Heroides* into Castilian, including in it a medieval Latin commentary on the work.

In eastern Iberia, the influence of Ovid is still more firmly documented. Already in the twelfth century, Guerau de Cabrera recommends a knowledge of several myths from the *Metamorphoses* to would-be troubadours in his Provençal *ensenhamen*. There were at least two medieval translations of Ovid's works into Catalan, one a late-fourteenth-century translation of the *Heroides* attributed to Guillem de Nicolau and another of the *Metamorphoses* by Francesc Alegre, printed in Barcelona in 1494. In the fourteenth century, the influence of Ovid is most strongly seen in the works of Bernat Metge, especially in his *Somni* and in a fragmentary translation of the pseudo-Ovidian *De vetula*.

Ovid flourished in fifteenth-century Catalonia and Valencia. At the turn of the century, Jordi de Sant Jordi composed a *Passio amoris secundum Ovidium* and both Pere Torroella (c. 1436–1486) and, especially, Joan Roís de Corella (d. 1497) show a thorough familiarity with his works. Ovid's influence can also be seen in the moral-theological works of Francesc Eiximenis and in the chivalric romance *Tirant lo Blanch*.

JOHN DAGENAIS

Bibliography

Badia, L. "Per la presència d'Ovidi a l'edat mitjana catalana amb notes sobre les traduccions de les *Heroides* i de les *Metamorfosis* al vulgar." In *Studia in honorem prof. M. de Riquer, pars prima*. Barcelona, 1986, 79–109.

Burkard, R. *The Archpriest of Hita and the Imitators of Ovid*. Newark, Del., 1999.

Schevill, R. *Ovid and the Renascence in Spain*. Berkeley, 1913.

OVIEDO, CITY OF

For the Spanish imagination, the city of Oviedo continues to carry a special significance for monarchy and the idea of a sustained Christian reconquest of Muslim lands during the Middle Ages. Sometime during the

Sta. Maria de Naranco, Oviedo, Spain. Facade, built ca. 842–850, converted to a church after 905. Copyright © Scala/Art Resource, NY.

first part of the ninth century, the royal residence of the kings of Asturias was moved by Alfonso II (791–842) from Cangas de Onís in the mountains to Oviedo, a location with easy access over the Cantabrian range to the Duero River valley. Since that time, the city has been closely identified with the restoration of medieval Christian monarchy in the north of the Iberian Peninsula after the Muslim conquest of 711 and is cited always as the seat of the ancient kings of Asturias, progenitors of the all the great medieval kings of Spain. In Oviedo, Alfonso II not only built a splendid palace and ceremonial space for himself on the mountainside (the present-day Church of Santa María del Naranco), but several other buildings destined for civic and religious use as well. When Alfonso moved the royal residence to Oviedo, he saw to the creation of churches, a bishopric, and a see for the new municipality, a circumstance without precedent in antiquity. At the same time, the king made sure that the name used to designate this new political space and structure centered at Oviedo was "regnum christianorum."

For nearly one hundred years Oviedo served as the seat of the kings of Asturias, until Ordoño II (910–925) moved the royal residence to León, closer still to the Duero River, which served as the frontier between Christian and Muslim lands after the beginning of the tenth century.

E. Michael Gerli

Bibliography

Floriano Cumbreño, A. C. *Estudios de historia de Asturias*. Oviedo, 1962.

P

PABLO CHRISTIANI

While conversion from Judaism to Christianity is documented all through the Middle Ages, beginning in the middle of the thirteenth century the phenomenon of conversion on the part of learned Jews and their subsequent involvement in either attacks on Jewish life or missionizing efforts aimed at their former coreligionists became increasingly prominent. One of the earliest of these new style converts was a southern French Jew probably named Saul, who subsequently took the Christian name Paul and eventually became a member of the Dominican Order. The conversion of this Jew obviously took place during his later years, since he left behind in the Jewish community a wife and children.

As a Christian, Friar Paul, generally known in recent historiography as Pablo Christiani, became heavily involved in activities related to his former coreligionists. Concerned with a wide range of Jewish issues, he is best known for his proselytizing preaching and disputing and is particularly noteworthy for his pioneering efforts to utilize rabbinic materials as the basis for arguing to Jews the truth of Christianity. His most famous missionizing endeavor took place in Barcelona in 1263, when he engaged the distinguished Girona rabbi, Moses ben Naḥman, in a disputation sponsored by King Jaime I of Aragón, one of the most striking proselytizing encounters of the Middle Ages.

Toward the end of his life, during the late 1260s, Pablo Christiani moved northward to the court of the pious King Louis IX of France. He was supported by the monarch in his effort to introduce a special Jewish badge in royal France, as well as in his ongoing missionizing preaching. Once again, he was successful in winning royal backing for a proselytizing disputation with a leading rabbi, this time in Paris in the last year of the 1260s or in the early 1270s. While he does not seem to have been particularly successful in bringing Jews to baptism, the new argumentation that he set in motion eventually does seem to have played some role in the massive conversions on the Iberian Peninsula during the late fourteenth and fifteenth centuries.

ROBERT CHAZAN

Bibliography

Baer, Y. *A History of the Jews in Christian Spain*. Trans. L. Schoffman et al. 2 vols. Philadelphia, 1961–66).

Chazan, R. *Barcelona and Beyond: The Disputation of 1263 and Its Aftermath*. Berkeley, Calif., 1992.

———. R. *Medieval Jewry in Northern France: A Political and Social History*. Baltimore, 1973.

Shatzmiller, I. *La deuxieme controverse de Paris*. Paris, 1994.

PABLO DE SANTA MARÍA

Pablo de Santa María was *converso* bishop of Cartagena (1403–1415) and then archbishop of Burgos (hence sometimes referred to as Pablo de Burgos) until his death. As Bishop of Cartagena, a major diocese that included the kingdom of Murcia, he instituted various reforms, resistance to the "schism," and support for Benedict XIII as pope. Prior to his conversion, he was Solomon ha-Levy, a rabbi of Burgos. He did not convert because of the pogroms of 1391, but rather prior to that date. A hitherto ignored document shows that in 1396 he was already in the service of Benedict XIII. As Bishop of Burgos he became counselor to Enrique III, was appointed Apostolic Nuncio by Benedict, and chancellor of the infante (later king) Juan II. Before his conversion he was a member of a large family (seven brothers and sisters), all of whom eventually converted. The most famous of these was Alvar García de Santa María. Pablo's son, who apparently converted with him, took the name Alonso de Cartagena and succeeded his father as Bishop of Burgos, and another son, Gonzalo García de Santa María, became Bishop of Astorga and Plasencia. Alonso de Burgos, a nephew of Alonso de Cartagena, was bishop of Córdoba, Cuenca, and Palencia, and confessor of Queen Isabel.

Virtually all members of the Santa María–Cartagena family were, for centuries, famous writers, theologians, and churchmen. Yet another of Pablo's sons, Alfonso Díaz, was the father of Juan Díaz de Coca (1389–1477), Bishop of Calahorra.

Pablo himself wrote several works although he was by no means as prolific a writer as other members of the family. Prior to his conversion he wrote a Hebrew satirical "Purim letter" (the historical background of which still needs clarification), and shortly after his conversion he received a letter from his friend Joshua al-Lorqi inquiring as to the reasons for his conversion, to which he replied (in Hebrew). Joshua himself later converted and took the name Jerónimo de Santa Fe. Later in his life, Pablo, who had a thorough theological training, wrote *Scrutinium scriptuarum*, a biblical commentary not without some anti-Jewish polemic (numerous editions from 1469 on) and *Additiones* to the *Postillam* (glosses) of Nicholas de Lyra (also numerous editions, from 1481 to 1498), and a poem, "Las siete edades del mundo" or "Edades trovadas," dedicated to Juan II. In spite of his natural preference for Christianity and orthodox Christian interpretation of the Bible, he never "persecuted" the Jews, as has been falsely suggested. In 1604, Felipe III granted—only to the descendants of Pablo, and not the entire family—the privilege of *limpieza de sangre* ("purity of blood," removing the *converso* (conversion) "taint" from them).

NORMAN ROTH

Bibliography

Cantera Burgos, F. *Alvar García de Santa María*. Madrid, 1952. This adds to and corrects his earlier book on the conversion of Pablo.

Baer, Y. *A History of the Jews in Christian Spain*. Philadelphia, 1961, 140–50. With errors but with valuable information on 473, n. 38.

PACHECO, JUAN MARQUIS OF VILLENA

See ENRIQUE IV, KING OF CASTILE

PADILLA, JUAN DE

A Carthusian friar (c. 1467–1520) of obscure, illegitimate birth—a matter that caused him certain difficulties—Padilla was very active in his religious order, where he reached a high rank. He was the author of two extensive religious poems in *arte mayor* (Stanzas with dodecasyllabic scansion). Fundamental to both are numerical and symbolic organization, based on ancient biblical and medieval roots. The first of these two works is *Retablo de la vida de Christo* (1505), in which he consciously imitates the pictorial art of the times; at the end of the poem, Padilla writes, "Asy como hazen algunos pintores / que tiran el velo delante su obra / quando ni mengua ni falta ni sobra / a las figuras bious colores, / assi los poetas et los oradores / quitan delante sus obras el velo / [. . .] / Assi pues hagamos en esta pintura, / tirando su velo que tiene delante" (Just as some painters do, / who remove the veil over their work. / When their figures and Vivid colors / neither exceed or are lacking, / thus poets and clerics / remove the veil). This piece constitutes an authentic Christology divided in four *tablas* corresponding to the four canonical Gospel books. *Retablo*, which was reprinted in numerous editions, consists of 1,289 eight-line stanzas in arte mayor, plus a series of octosyllabic prayers and lamentations in prose. Despite the obvious influence of Juan de Mena, Padilla explicitly rejected pagan and literary invocations. Both in this poem as well as in *Los doze triumphos de loz doze apóstoles*, numerous details relate the text to Iñigo de Mendoza's *Vita Christi*, including some hidden references to the Franciscan's work.

Of greater complexity is *Los doze triumphos*, a work published posthumously (1521) of 1,144 strophes in arte mayor, with a pompous tone and a decidedly allegorical and cultured form. Padilla shows here the clear influence of Dante, Mena, and, to a lesser degree, Petrarch. Divided into twelve parts corresponding to the twelve apostles, the twelve months, and the twelve Zodiac signs (at the center of which is the sun, that is, Christ), this poem's astrological and, above all, numerical symbolism make it difficult to read. If, on the one hand, the cultured construction and use of latinisms are abundant (*nitente*, *manante*, *rubente*, *clarífico*, *dulcisona*, and *serénico*), on the other it can be considered, also in the fashion of Mena's *Las trescientas*, as a "national" poem, with reference to Castilian topics of the past and of the fifteenth century, as well as an "Isabelline" poem (Granada, the expulsion of the Jews, and so on). Padilla demonstrates a more personal approach in his allusions and comparisons with actual reality (the Medina del Campo fairs, the witches of Durango, and Seville, and the *Torre del Oro*). An important question to consider that has yet to be addressed by scholars is the identity of Padillas readers.

JULIO RODRÍGUEZ-PUÉRTOLAS

Bibliography

Norti Gualdani, E. *Los doce triunfos de los doce apóstoles*. 2 vols. Messina and Florence, 1975–78.

Vries, H. de *Materia Mirable: Estudio de la composición numérico-simbólica en las dos obras contemplativas de Juan de Padilla*. Groningen, 1972.

PADILLA, MARÍA DE

The daughter of a Castilian family of the lesser aristocracy, María de Padilla became Pedro I's favorite in 1352, shortly after meeting through the Pedro's chief minister Juan Alfonso de Alburquerque. María was a member of the household staff of Alburquerque's wife, Isabel de Meneses. In spite of two subsequent marriages, Pedro's attachment to María was the most enduring relationship of his life. It lasted, with brief interruptions, until her death in 1361.

María's reputation has remained largely unscathed, in spite of Pedro's many excesses. Contemporary sources generally praise her for her beauty and charm, and for attempting to soften Pedro's harshness. A notable exception is the collection of anti-Pedro ballads, *Romancero del rey don Pedro*, in which she is portrayed as cruel and vengeful. In Romance 9, for example, she is held responsible for breaking up Pedro's marriage to Blanche de Bourbon in 1353. Jealousy leads María to hire a Jewish necromancer to put a spell on a gem-encrusted belt that Blanche gave the king to wear on their wedding night. As Pedro puts it on, the belt turns into a snake; the king, horrified, flees from his bride.

Pedro's refusal to live with his French wife, and his attachment to María, served as a political excuse for his enemies and resulted in the alienation of Alburquerque. At the same time, María's relatives gained ascendency at court and replaced Alburquerque and his circle. Juan Fernández de Henestrosa, an uncle, became *camarero mayor mayordomo mayor*, and *canciller mayor*. María's brother Diego García de Padilla owed his election as Master of the Order of Calatrava to Pedro's influence. He later became the king's *mayordomo mayor*. A half-brother of María received the *encomienda mayor* of the Order of Santiago, while another relative, Juan Tenorio, became *repostero mayor*.

María, with Pedro's financial support, founded the monastery of Santa Clara at Astudillo in 1354 which, together with an earlier cession of Huelva, constituted the only significant settlement the king made on her.

María died in July 1361. She bore Pedro four children: three daughters and a son. Immediately after her death Pedro proclaimed María queen of Castile and ordered a royal burial at the monastery at Astudillo. The following year, Pedro hastily assembled a meeting of the *cortes* at Seville to declare their son Alfonso, then two years old, heir to the Castilian throne. Upon the child's death the following year, Pedro designated his first daughter Beatriz his heir. He also insisted that he and María had been legally wed and had her remains transferred and buried in the royal chapel at Seville. The Trastámaran usurpation of the Castilian throne in 1369 made Pedro's succession arrangements moot. However, Pedro's line eventually returned to the throne when his granddaughter Catherine of Lancaster, daughter of his and María's second child Constanza and John of Gaunt, duke of Lancaster, wed Enrique III of Castile.

CLARA ESTOW

Bibliography

Romancero del rey don Pedro, 1368–1800. Ed. Antonio Pérez de Gómez. Valencia, 1954.

PAGANISM

Residual traces of pre-Christian beliefs and practices survived in various forms in medieval Spain and Portugal. The purely literary awareness of pre-Christian myth and belief through written sources must here be distinguished from the survival of such practices and beliefs at the level of folk tradition and popular observance. The survival of various manifestations of classical paganism under the Visigothic kingdom is well documented. Some beliefs persisted longer; examples are elements of astrology, and the use of bird-flight as an augury. An *auguriator* appears in a document of 1204; accusation of belief in such auguries was leveled at el Cid in the the late eleventh century and at Alfonso el Batallador of Aragón in the early twelfth. Literary reflections of this mantic practice are found in epic poems (*Poema de Mio Cid, Siete infantes de Lara*). Numerous texts attest a continued vogue for divination by this technique up to the fifteenth century; it appears to have been particularly associated with the office of *adalid*, in connection with which it is still mentioned in a source of 1430. Some popular superstitions, in particular those associated with agricultural magic and personal malefice, have evident pagan roots. Other possible survivals are more obscure and controversial; dancing in the guise of stags (*cervulum facere*) is condemned as a pagan abuse in early church authorities (fourth to seventh centuries), and some such tradition may form part of the background to the image of the lover as stag in the *cantigas* of Pero Meogo in the thirteenth century. The beating of el Cid's daughters in *Poema de Mio Cid* finds parallels in folk customs from cultures as distant chronologically as classical Rome and Victorian Wales; it also, however, has obvious parallels with elements found in Christian martyrology. The reference in *Poema de Mio Cid*, lines 2694–95, to an "Elpha" shut in a cave has been seen as arising from a local tradition concerning otherworld beings, but has also been explained by reference to a contemporary feminine personal name. Further episodes may well have unsuspected pagan substrata. In

Poema de Fernán González, for instance, the adoption of a stone image by the Castilians as their leader during the imprisonment of the Count in Navarre has striking similarities to practices associated with the worship of Cybele in the Mediterranean world and to ancient Germanic and Nordic rituals reported by Tacitus and other sources. That Christian elements may also have contributed to the formation of this incident in a thirteenth-century clerical poem should not surprise us, for, as with much material of this nature, the situation is complicated by the well-documented practice of adapting pre-Christian elements into popular Christian observances. Where, then, parallels exist for a particular literary motif or episode in both Christian and pagan culture, the presumption must generally be in favor of a Christian origin unless specific factors indicate otherwise, always allowing for the possibility of an intermediate Christian source for ultimately pagan material. For popular observance and belief, sources including chronicles and legislation provide information on pagan elements.

David Hook

Bibliography

Garrosa Resina, A. *Magia y superstición en la literatura castellana medieval.* Valladolid, 1987.

Homet, R. "Cultores de prácticas mágicas en Castilla medieval." *Cuadernos de Historia de España.* 63–64 (1980), 178–217.

PALENCIA, ALFONSO DE

Royal secretary, historian, and humanist, Alfonso was born in Palencia, the son of a secretary, in 1423. At seventeen he was in the household of Alfonso García de Santa María (de Cartagena), Bishop of Burgos, and later in 1441 took part in a mission to Álvaro de Luna on behalf of Juan II of Castile. Some years later he appeared in Florence and Rome in the household of Cardinal Bessarion; in later years he recalled the tutoring he received from George of Trebizond ("que didici, tu docuisti"). After the fall of Constantinople he returned to Spain to join the household of Alfonso de Fonseca the elder, Archbishop of Seville. On 6 December 1456 he was named royal chronicler and secretary of Latin letters to Enrique IV. By the 1460s he seems to have taken up residence in Seville and to have openly sided with the nobles in opposition to the king. Several nobles sent him to Paul II in Rome to complain about Enrique's actions. When young Alfonso, Isabel's brother, was proclaimed king at the famous Farce of Avila (June 1465), Palencia claimed he was close to the pretender. At his death in 1468, Palencia shifted his allegiance to Isabel and Fernando, and played a major role in smuggling Fernando into Castile to marry Isabel in Valladolid in October 1469. From then on Palencia became a devoted supporter of Fernando, thick with the conspirators in the conflict with Enrique IV, but with growing suspicions of some of Isabel's advisers, particularly Pedro González de Mendoza, later *el gran Cardenal*, who preferred Isabel to dominate in Castile. Eventually in the 1480s it was clear that Palencia had lost Isabel's support as chronicler; she then appointed Fernando del Pulgar as her own historian. Although it appears that Palencia was still classified as secretary and chronicler up to his death, he did not appear as an active figure in politics. A place was granted to him for his tomb and books in the Seville cathedral, but no trace survives. Palencia was not a cleric but a professional man of letters, like Elio Antonio de Nebrija, whose normal written language was Latin. He collected books for Fonseca and himself; he copied Latin manuscripts translated from the Greek, and maintained correspondence with Italian and Spanish scholars. He wrote political treatises, grammatical and lexicographical compilations, a treatise on ancient Iberian geography, and translations of Plutarch's *Lives* and Josephus's *De Bello Judaico*. Many others have disappeared, like ten books on the antiquities of Spain. His major work, *Gesta Hispaniensis ex annalibus suorum dierum collinentis*, or *Decades* for short, covers the years from 1453 to the end of the Granada campaign. It is a savage political and moral criticism not only of Enrique IV and his main advisers, like Juan Pacheco, Marqués de Villena, for their self-serving behavior, but also in later years, of the counselors of Fernando and Isabel, as well as Isabel herself, whom he did not think as capable as Fernando. No wonder it was never printed. Despite the declared prejudices, it cannot be discarded, since Palencia was well acquainted with most of the protagonists and witnessed many of the events he records. Like Joan Margarit, whose work he knew, Palencia has many affinities with the Italian humanist scholars of his day. He possessed an idiosyncratic Latin style, classical in its inspiration, with a pronounced Terentian flavor in some of his more caustic moods. The history itself started off in traditional fashion as a movement from turbulent darkness into the light of justice, but this crescendo weakens as Palencia seems to lose faith in those he had once trusted.

Robert B. Tate

Bibliography

Palencia, A. de. *Gesta Hispaniensia exannalibus suorum dierem Collecta.* Ed. and trans. Brian Tate and Jeremy Lawrance, 2 Vols. Madrid, 1998

López de Toro, J. *Cuarta Década de Alonso de Palencia.* Madrid, 1970; trans. L. de Toro, Madrid, 1974.

Tate, R. B. "Las Décadas, de Alfonso de Palencia: un análisis historiográfico." In *Estudios dedicados a J. L. Brooks*. Ed. J. M. Ruiz Veintemilla. Barcelona 1984. 223–241.

PAMPLONA

City in present-day Navarre that dates back to Roman times. Possibly founded by Pompei in 75 B.C. it was an episcopal see from the fifth century on and, due to its strategic position, housed both Visigothic and Muslim garrisons during the Middle Ages. During the ninth century, it became the focal point for major political activity, laying the foundation for the emergence of the Kingdom of Pamplona there in the tenth century. The development of pilgrimage along the Road to Santiago de Compostela led to the appearance of new townships and suburbs close to the episcopal seat, the area now called Navarrería. Places like San Cernín and San Nicolás had appeared by the end of the eleventh and the middle of the twelfth centuries respectively. The three townships, each with its own municipal government and fortifications, vied for economic supremacy and control of the urban areas well into the fifteenth century. During this period, the monarch and the episcopate also competed for control of temporal jurisdiction in the city. Tensions between church and monarchy culminated in 1276 in the so-called Guerra de la Navarreria (War of Navarrería), made famous by a Provençal poem of the same name composed by Anelier de Toulouse. With some fifteen hundred households, by the twelfth century Pamplona was the recognized capital of the kingdom of Navarre. It did not become the permanent seat of the royal court, however, until the fifteenth century, after the monarchy had united the three competing townships of Navarrería.

Pamplona is distinguished for its religious architecture. A Romanesque church was erected over a primitive religious structure in 1127, marking the origins of the present cathedral. A Gothic cloister was added between 1286 and 1374, replacing the original Romanesque cloister. After the collapse of the Romanesque church, between the years 1394 and 1501, a Gothic edifice was constructed in its place. The original Romanesque facade, which survived the collapse of the Romanesque church, was replaced with a neoclassical one in 1783. The Church of San Cernín was built in the twelfth century and was reconstructed in 1297. In 1758 the church's Gothic cloister was torn down and replaced with a baroque chapel. The Church of San Nicolás dates from the twelfth century and was restored in the Cistercian style in 1231; a Gothic headwall was added at the end of the thirteenth century. Both San Cernín and San Nicolás have fortified towers. Only two examples of medieval civil architecture remain, each partially preserved, and both in the Gothic style and of uncertain date. These are the Royal Palace and the Palacio del Señor de Otazu, since the sixteenth century referred to as the Cámara de Comptos as the treasury was housed there.

M. Raquel García Arancón

Bibliography

Irurita Lusarreta, M. A. *El municipio de Pamplona en la Edad Media*. Pamplona, 1959.

Martínez Ruiz, J. J. *La Pamplona de los burgos y su evolucion urbana, siglos xii–xvi*. Pamplona, 1975.

PAPER

Paper, used in China by 105, came to the Islamic World in 751, and was manufactured at Baghdad and Damascus before 800. By the early 900s papermaking became a general craft in Islamic Spain; by 1150 Játiva's paper was internationally famed. Exported to Christian Spain, paper became common there only in the thirteenth century, though severely restricted to governmental use. Christian Spain's manufacture dates from Játiva's conquest, especially its full absorption after 1250.

César Dubler's fantasy of how fugitives from the Almoradvids/Almohads multiplied paper mills is now compounded by Oriol Valls's fantasy of twelfth-century Catalan paper mills from the Pyrenees to Tarragona, erroneously argued from the standpoint of the history of cloth mills (especially the 1193 Copons mill). Authorities also unwarrantedly assume Maghribian and therefore Christian production by hydraulic mills; domestic hand processing instead prevailed. Aragón's crown did introduce Játivan mills in the 1280s (the Italian Fabriano's 1268 claim as Europe's pioneer mill cannot be sustained). Hydraulic technology plus proliferating material codices, private use, and royal registers constitute the "paper revolution."

The crown controlled manufacture, quality, marketing, and export. Linen rags, not flax or cotton, were the usual materials. Centers also sprang up in Murcia (1266), Mallorca (1280s), and perhaps Castile. New techniques and marketing sharpened rivalry with Italy in the fourteenth century; identifying watermarks multiplied then. By 1456 Barcelona had a mill, but no notice survives for Castilian mills. Printing definitively expanded both manufacture and use.

Robert I. Burns, S. J.

Bibliography

Burns, R. I. *Society and Documentation in Crusader Valencia*. Princeton, N. J., 1985, chaps. 23–28 and bibliography (esp. O. Valls, J. M. Madurell).

PARTY KINGDOMS *See* ṬĀʾIFA KINGDOMS

PEASANTS AND PEASANTRY

The lives of peasants, the economic and social bonds that linked them to their lords and to the soil, the structure of the village community, and the tenor of their very lives was determined in Castile by where and when the peasants lived. The history of the Castilian peasantry is a complex one indeed, and any attempts to generalize about their status ignores the heterogeneous character of their lives. Most of the standard interpretations and accounts of medieval rural life, the classical formulations of Marc Bloch and others do not fully apply to the Castilian setting; thus, comparisons with the peasantry in better-known regions are not always useful.

In Castile, few peasants were exempted from seignorial dues. Whether these dues were paid to the king (in lands of *realengo*), to the church (*abadengo*) or to lay lords (señorío), the result was much the same. Peasants paid rent for their land, annual contributions to the crown, and to their lords. In some cases, they had to perform labor duties during the high points of the agricultural cycle (the *sernas*) and pay the equivalent of *mainmorte*, entry fees, and a host of other dues for which one finds rough equivalents in the north. Yet peasants in Castile were seldom tied to the soil. In short, servile labor was not the predominant mode of production in Christian Castile. Instead, peasants and their lords were bound by intricate bonds of reciprocity, often oppresive to the peasantry, but also allowing for forms of resistance, denial, and escape.

The dynamic character of Castilian society, dominated by the military tide of the Reconquest and the repopulation of new lands, provided a setting that favored the peasantry. Villages in the northern mountains were, on the whole, small, and the peasants worked under heavier seignorial dues and obligations. Villages south of the area of Burgos and into the Duero River basin were often large, with most of the work duties commuted into money payments. But even in the mountains, the obligations of individual peasants in the same village differed according to status and the nature of their ties to the lords. Everywhere in Castile, as one moves into the later Middle Ages, we find well-to-do peasants building sizable holdings, and fairly independent from seignorial excesses.

The village was the communal focus of peasant life. As such, the community of village "citizens" exercised their collective rights. In times of trouble or litigation with their ecclesiastical and secular lords (and there were an endless number of litigations in the late Middle Ages), one can witness the inhabitants of villages standing as one. At the ringing of the church bells, the petty noblemen, the curate, and those peasants who "owned" a household and property came to the village church or to the opening in front of the church door to voice their opinions and to vote on the pressing issues of the day. In litigation after litigation, it is the rural council that speaks with one voice in its attempt to protect itself and its members from excessive demands or abuses. In the communal world of the Castilian peasantry some were more equal than others, and women, newcomers, and those who lived by hiring themselves to others were not called by the ringing of the bells to make decisions for all. The apparent leveling structure of rural communities was indeed a mirage, and rigid social hierarchies were already in the making in the Castilian countryside by the thirteenth century.

Within villages social gradations and social distinctions based essentially on property or on the enjoying of a beneficial landlease led to the hierarchization of political and economic power at the village level. These distinctions, sharpening with the economic downturn of the thirteenth and fourteenth centuries, were made more onerous by the authority of the village council to sell property or to assign work. Moreover, as urban oligarchs began to purchase houses and land in the countryside around the cities, they acquired not only property but also rights to the village commons.

Along the lines stated above, we can make a very rough typology of the different kinds of peasants living in medieval Castile. First were the peasants in royal lands. They were, for all practical purposes, the proprietors of their holdings, with the right to sell, buy, bequeath, or dispose of their lands or, more accurately, of their *dominium* over the land. Some restrictions on their rights can be found in the extant documentation, limiting their ability to sell land to magnates or monasteries, but these provisions were often disregarded. Peasants working royal lands paid dues to the crown, and their burden was often lighter than that of other peasants. Their obligations were met in kind (mostly in the mountains of the north), in issue (mostly in the plains), or in both. Next were men and women working ecclesiastical and/or seignorial lands who paid dues to the king and to their lords. In older settlements, this also included work duties and other more oppressive obligations. Third were men and women of *behetrías* (free cities), those peasants with the right to choose their own lords and to abandon their service if not satisfied. Fourth, as we move into the late Middle Ages, we find an increasing number of peasants who worked for a wage. There are strong indications that these men and women owned or held small farms of their own, but that these holdings were not sufficient to support them and their families. The tendency to the fragmentation of rural property led to the emergence of a salaried rural underclass. Most of the domains of northern Castilian monasteries were plowed, tended, and their crops harvested by day laborers. Moreover, there is also a clear move to the leasing of land either for life or for a set number of years, with monasteries and lords collecting a share of the crops.

By the mid-fourteenth century, there was a concerted effort by the crown and the nobility, as seen in the ordinances of the *cortes* (parliament) of 1351, to bind the peasantry under more harsh and economically exacting obligations. How successful were these attempts is hard to assess. What it is clear, however, is that by the fifteenth century the overall conditions of the peasantry had deteriorated considerably. Reports of rural poverty and upheaval marked a radical change from the stable conditions of the central Middle Ages.

TEÓFILO F. RUIZ

Bibliography

García de Cortazar, J. A. *La sociedad rural en la España medieval*. Madrid, 1988.

PEDRO ALFONSO, OR PETRUS ALFONSI

Moisés Sefardí, a noted Jew from Huesca, adopted the name Pedro Alfonso when he was baptized on 29 June 1106, with King Alfonso I el Batallador serving as godfather. Pedro Alfonso probably left the Iberian Peninsula soon after his baptism; a few years later he was located in England as a *magister* of liberal arts, where he likely contributed to the diffusion of Arabic science, especially astronomy and calculus, around the monastery of Malvern. Whether he was the physician to both Alfonso I and Henry I of England, as is often claimed, is not certain.

The preserved literary production of Pedro Alfonso is in Latin, and can be separated into three fields of interest: apologetic, scientific, and didactic literature. As a response to the scandal caused by his conversion, he wrote *Diálogos contra los judíos*, in which two characters, Pedro and Moisés, represent the author before and after his baptism. Throughout the work's twelve chapters, Pedro turns to a wide variety of medical, cabbalistic, and theological arguments to show Moisés the error of his ways. At the latter's insistence, in the fifth chapter Pedro traces a broad critical panorama of Islam. If the *Diálogos* enjoyed especially wide distribution, as the more than seventy preserved manuscripts dispersed throughout European libraries prove, the repercussions of this chapter were even greater.

Very few of Pedro Alfonso's scientific works are preserved, and only some incomplete *Tablas astronómicas* can be attributed to him with surety. These tablas are preceded by a curious preliminary text titled "Carta a los estudiosos franceses", which seems to have been motivated by a stay in France, and which becomes an important document with regard to the author's position on the cultural renaissance of the twelfth century. In the letter, Pedro Alfonso criticizes European intellectuals for their bookish culture, far removed from the world of scientific practice. He also addresses the traditional division of the liberal arts, positioning himself among those partial to the quadrivium, which includes the study of medicine; in the trivium only the study of dialectics is saved from the author's condemnation, but is still only regarded as a supplementary subject.

Pedro Alfonso's name has become unquestionably most associated with the *Disciplina clericalis*, a combination of exempla (thirty-four total), comparisons, proverbs, and so on—all focusing on the indoctrination of students as the title indicates. For the subject's organization, the author likely found inspiration in the books of the Bible, Hebrew religious texts, and mixed genres of oriental origin. The dialogue between anonymous characters (father-son, teacher-disciple) creates a frame that reaches its maximum development between examples 9 and 17. The subject matter—knowledge of self and of neighbor, but always remembering the fear of God—corresponds to other similar works of oriental literature. The most popular stories, though, deal with misogynistic themes, and are closer to the *fabliaux* in their narrative scheme. Medieval preachers turned to the *Discliplina clericalis* frequently, explaining its wide diffusion and its importance in the origins of the novel. Because it was written in Latin, the *Disciplina clericalis* became the first pathway through which oriental narrative began to circulate in the West.

MARÍA JESÚS LACARRA

Bibliography

Alfonso, Pedro. *Disciplina clericalis*. Intr. M. J. Lacarra, tran. E. Ducay. Zaragoza, 1980.

Reinhardt, K., and H. Santiago-Otero, *Biblioteca bíblica ibérica medieval*. Madrid, 1986, 250–58.

PEDRO I THE CRUEL, KING OF CASTILE

Born 30 August 1334 in Burgos, Pedro was the only legitimate child and heir of Alfonso XI of Castile (1312–1350). His mother was María daughter of King Afonso IV of Portugal. One of the most controversial kings of the Castilian Middle Ages, he is the only one who came to be known by the sobriquet of "the Cruel" for the many acts of violence associated with the last stages of his rule. Aside from the personal excesses that inspired this reputation, Pedro's reign (1350–1369) is distinctive for a number of other reasons.

His subjects experienced the full economic and demographic effects of the first wave of the Black Death that hit Castile from 1348 to 1350. He led an aggressive war of expansion against Aragón that lasted, intermittently, from 1357 until the end of the reign. His policies and alliances contributed to the involvement of international troops in the peninsular conflict, making Spain, from 1366 to 1369, the main theater for the larger military conflict known as the Hundred Years' War. His treatment of the aristocracy and his poor relations with the Castilian Church and the Avignon papacy alienated a substantial portion of his most important subjects, causing many to side with his chief rival, his half-brother Enrique de Trastámara, during the Castilian civil war of 1366–1369. The reign ended violently with Pedro's death and the usurpation of the throne by Enrique.

Coming to the throne 28 March 1350 shortly before his sixteenth birthday, Pedro spent the first two years under the influence of Juan Alfonso de Alburquerque, a Portuguese nobleman who had been in the service of Queen María, and had become Pedro's first minister. Under the auspices of Alburquerque, Pedro convened the Cortes of Valladolid in 1351, the only such meeting for which we have any detailed records for the entire reign. Through a series of measures redacted during these proceedings, Pedro attempted to remedy some of the economic consequences of the plague such as the abandonment of arable lands, and the steep rise in the cost of living. At the same time, the *cuadernos de cortes* (records of the courts) reveal Pedro's interest in a healthy royal treasury and an effective system of tax-collection. This concern with sound finances remained a constant feature of his reign, and resulted in the unpopular appointment of Samuel Halevi, a Jew, as his chief treasurer and the extensive use of Jews as tax-farmers. These measures, for which Pedro was severely criticized, served as evidence to his detractors of the king's presumed philojudaism, a quality almost as objectionable as his cruelty.

From the early days of his reign, Pedro also had to contend with an endemic feature of Castilian medieval politics, a restless and rebellious aristocracy. In his particular case, the situation was aggravated by the existence of a rival group of wealthy and influential individuals composed of the bastard children of Alfonso XI and his mistress Leonor de Guzmán, their allies, and retainers who challenged Pedro's authority almost from the beginning of the reign. Pedro reacted to these challenges in an increasingly suspicious and retaliatory manner.

In 1353 Pedro married the French princess Blanche de Bourbon and abandoned her two days after the wedding. It is likely that Blanche's sponsor, the French crown, was not able to fulfill the financial obligations of the marriage contract, and that Pedro left her for that reason. The more popular yet unverifiable reason given to explain the king's actions states that he abandoned Blanche because he could not bear to be away from the woman he loved, María de Padilla, whom he had met in 1352.

Whatever his motives, Pedro's refusal to cohabit with Blanche served to alienate his mother and Alburquerque, the principal architects of the marriage contract with the French, and gave his half-brothers a pretext for rebellion. As the minister and the bastards became allies, they were joined by other prominent Castilians displeased with the king's behavior. Outnumbered, Pedro gave himself up to the rebels at Toro only to escape after a month to begin a slow but successful campaign against them. With the capitulation of Toledo in 1355 and Toro in 1356, the main centers of antiroyal activity, Pedro succeeded in defeating the first serious challenge to his authority.

Shortly after this victory, Pedro went to war against Aragón, seeking redress over several territorial and dynastic grievances. Pedro IV was soon joined by Enrique de Trastámara, who had escaped from Castile before Pedro's victory at Toro, and other Castilians who had fled fearing the king's justice while Pedro counted on the support of Pedro's hated half-brother Ferrán. Pedro experienced several successes at Tarazona (1357); Guardamar (1359); Calatayud (1362); Teruel; Segorbe and Murviedo (1363); Alicante, Elche, Denia (1363), and Orihuela (1365); but he was never able to win a decisive victory. Several truces and peace efforts mediated by papal legates did not succeed in bringing a lasting peace between the two kingdoms.

Meanwhile, from the conspiracy at Toro onward Pedro had turned increasingly against those he suspected of treason. He eliminated many of his former allies; several of his half-brothers, among them Fadrique; and his aunt Leonor and her son Juan, and he was believed responsible for the death of his wife Blanche in 1361.

Pedro's policies, Enrique de Trastámara's ambitions, Pedro's predicament, and even the politics of Navarre all contributed to the participation of the French in peninsular affairs, beginning in 1360. The French crown agreed to sponsor Enrique's ambitions by commissioning Bertrand du Guesclin and an army of mercenaries to fight in Castile. When they entered the kingdom in 1366, Pedro was forced to flee in search of outside help, which he finally secured from Edward the Black Prince in Bordeaux. The ensuing battle at Nájera on 13 April 1367 was a resounding, albeit short-lived, victory for Pedro. His alliance with the English collapsed when the Castilian would not meet the terms of their agreement and, as the Black Prince's troops withdrew from the peninsula, Enrique and Guesclin returned in 1368 and received the support of several important regions.

Pedro determined to meet his enemy in the vicinity of Toledo. At the Battle of Montiel on 14 March 1369 Enrique and the French soundly defeated Pedro's scattered army. Pedro, who had fled to a nearby fortress, tried to buy his freedom from Guesclin. Some days later, believing that the French captain had accepted his terms, Pedro went to Guesclin's tent where, within a few minutes, Enrique arrived. He killed Pedro with a dagger, after a short struggle on 23 March 1369. Through this fratricide Enrique became uncontested king of Castile, a title he began to use when he first entered the kingdom alongside the French in 1366.

In addition to his marriage to Blanche de Bourbon, Pedro is said to have married María de Padilla—at least he claimed this following her death in 1361 in order to declare their four children (three daughters and a son, the youngest) legitimate heirs to the throne. Shortly after his marriage to Blanche, he had also wed Juana de Castro, but this marriage was just as ephemeral as his first and left no children. Eventually Pedro's line returned to the Castilian throne when his granddaughter, Catherine of Lancaster, daughter of John of Gaunt and Pedro and María's second daughter Constanza, married the future Enrique III of Castile.

CLARA ESTOW

Bibliography

Díaz Martín, L. V. *Itinerario de Pedro I de Castilla*. Valladolid, 1975.

López de Ayala, P. *Crónica del rey don Pedro*. Biblioteca de Autores Españoles, vol. 66. Madrid, 1953.

Sitges, J. B. *Las mujeres del rey Don Pedro I de Castilla*. Madrid, 1910.

PEDRO III, KING OF ARAGÓN

Pedro III the Great, Pere III of Aragón, Pere II of Catalonia, Pere I of Valencia, and Pere I of Sicily (1240–1285), "was the troubadour-warrior ruler of the realms of Aragón (1276–1285) and liberator-conqueror of Sicily. He was born at Valencia, two years after that Islamic city fell to his father Jaime the Conqueror, of Jaime's second wife Violante of Hungary. Jaime named him heir to Catalonia in 1253, procurator or vice-regent there at seventeen in 1257, and—at the death of Jaime's son Alfonso by his first wife in 1260—procurator of the Catalonia, Aragón, and Valencia realms. (Pedro's brother Jaime became procurator of the Balearics, Roussillon, and Cerdanya.) In 1262 Pedro married Constance, the daughter and heiress of Manfred, the Hohenstaufen ruler of Sicily-Naples. Besides four sons and two daughters by his mistresses María and Agnés Zapata, he had four sons (including his successors Alfonso II and Jaime II, and Frederico III of Sicily), and two daughters (Queen Violante of Naples and Isabel Queen of Portugal).

Although his formal reign lasted only nine years versus his famous father's sixty-three, the Infante Pedro enjoyed a fifteen-year public career as procuratorial co-ruler and soldier before his coronation. He restored feudal order as a teenager, plunged into Mediterranean Ghibelline politics during negotiations for his marriage, championed Occitan refugees after such troubles as the 1263 Marseilles revolt, captained the first phase of the Murcian Crusade in 1265–1266, replaced his father at home during Jaime's abortive Holy Land Crusade in 1269 (and intervened in the Urgell wars of 1268), and prepared an invasion army to seize Toulouse in 1271. Relations with his father deteriorated in 1272, with Pedro stripped of all offices and revenues; reconciliation came the following year. When the northern Catalan nobles revolted, Pedro captured and drowned their leader, his bastard brother Ferran Sanxis. During a diplomatic visit to Paris, he met Philippe the Bold. His greatest test came in 1275–1277, when the Mudéjars of Valencia with Maghribian support revolted and nearly recovered their land. Pedro had one thousand horsemen and five thousand foot soldiers at first, but soon had to assume the entire responsibility when his father died on the field (27 July 1276). Burying Jaime provisionally at Valencia and deferring his coronation at Zaragoza to 17 November, Pedro grimly set about conquering much of Valencia "a second time," as the contemporary memoirist Ramón Muntaner puts it. Meanwhile his brother Jaume II of Mallorca received the Balearics, Cerdanya, Montpellier, and Roussillon.

With the Mudéjar headquarters at Montesa castle fallen (September 1277), Pedro began a vigorous domestic and international program. He demanded tribute from Tunis, harrying it through his admiral Conrad Llança, pressured Jaime II of Mallorca into accepting vassalage, and moved strongly against the still-rebellious northern barons, ending their six-year war by his siege of Balaguer (1281) and winning their support by his clemency. By holding as "guest hostages" the Infantes de la Cerda, he dominated the Castilian succession crisis. His negotiations with Philippe the Bold at Toulouse in 1281, and his treaties of Campillo and Ágreda with Alfonso X and the Infante Sancho of Castile that year, stabilized his peninsular situation. He established understandings with Byzantium, England, Genoa, Granada, Portugal, and the papacy, and was finally ready for his life's coup: to foil the Angevin power that had absorbed Occitania and taken over Sicily-Naples, and to assume the Hohenstaufens' Sicilian kingdom and Ghibelline leadership in the western Mediterranean.

Massing his naval and military strength, he simulated a crusade against Tunis, actually taking Collo there; the pope refused crusade title or aid. Previously in contact with the Sicilians, Pedro now supported the Sicilian Vespers revolt of 30 March 1282. He moved eight hundred knights and fifteen thousand foot soldiers by sea to Trapani, receiving the crown of Sicily-Naples at Palermo and starting a twenty-year war. A succession of naval victories by his admirals, especially Roger de Llúria, established the Catalans as the dominant maritime power of the western Mediterranean after Genoa. Besides Sicily and much of the Italian mainland, Pedro also took Malta and Tunisian Djerba island.

Meanwhile Pope Martin IV, feudal lord of Sicily and proponent of its Angevin king Charles of Anjou, excommunicated Pedro in November 1282, deposed him in March 1283, and transferred all his realms to the son of Philippe the Bold of France, Charles of Valois, in February 1284. The Catalans supported their king, but the Aragónese had been ill-disposed toward the Sicilian adventure from the start. In that long and bloody war, one episode stands out—the Challenge (*desafiament*) of Bordeaux. Anjou offered to settle the war by personal combat with Pedro, but instead arranged a trap for his arrival at English Bordeaux; Pedro still appeared, met the challenge, and escaped, to the edification of Europe's chivalric classes (1283). More formidably, a papal crusade to set Valois during Pedro's reign saw an army of 118,000 foot and 7,000 horse under Philippe the Bold sweep into Catalonia. Pedro delayed this greatest army since ancient Rome at Girona until Llúria's fleet from Sicily could arrive to destroy the French naval flank and logistics, ending the invasion (September 1285). Pedro suppressed a plebeian revolt in Barcelona under Berenguer Oller that same year, negotiated a major commercial treaty with Tunis, and mounted a punitive amphibious expedition against his traitorous brother on Mallorca, but died on the road to join the fleet.

The contemporary memoirist Bernat Desclot calls Pedro "a second Alexander" for his generalship. Dante lauds him as "the heavy-sinewed one [who] bore in his life the seal of every merit"; and he appears both in Boccaccio's *Decameron* and Shakespeare's *Much Ado about Nothing*. Pedro was a troubadour (two of his poems survive) and their patron. He presided over a constitutional revolution (Aragón's Privilege of Union, Catalonia's *Recognoverunt proceres* annual parliament) in 1283–1284. He stabilized coinage with his silver croat, and maritime law with his restructured *Llibre del Consolat* (1283). He protected Jews and gave them important posts in his administration. As a politician and diplomat he is thought superior to his great father, and he presided over a commercial, literary, and architectural flowering in Catalonia.

ROBERT I. BURNS, S. J.

Bibliography

Soldevila, F. *Pere el Gran*. 2 parts in 4 vols. Institut d'Estudis Catalans, Memòries de la Secció Històrico-arqueològica. Vols. 11, 13, 16, 22. Barcelona, 1950–1962.

———. *Vida de Pere el Gran i d'Alfons el Liberal*. Barcelona, 1963. XI Congres de Història de la Corona d'Agó. 3 vols. Palermo, 1983–84.

PEDRO IV

As a product of the new court system ushered in with the Crown of Aragón by Jaime II (1291–1327), Pedro IV was a strange mixture of intellectual brilliance, emotional aloofness, and cruelty. Born in 1319 to a weak father, Alfonso IV (1327–1336) and a strong-willed mother, Teresa Entenza, the prince, feeble and rickety at birth, spent most of his early life in the care of wet nurses. When his mother died in 1329 to be replaced by his father's second wife, Leonor of Castile, the isolation of the young prince seemed to deepen. Despite this emotional upheaval, Pedro attained an excellent education. This conflicting background made Pedro into a man of keen intellect, but with an absolute lack of scruples. A nagging sense of inferiority to such figures of the great reconquest as Jaime I (1213–1276) drove Pedro to accomplish great deeds. The psychological labyrinth of his adolescence informs the long series of foreign and domestic struggles he engaged in, as well as the tragic atmosphere that hung over his personal life.

Pedro's foreign policy was openly motivated by a desire to consolidate his loosely connected realms. Inheriting a number of Mediterranean outposts, he methodically moved to gain clear titles to the Duchy of Athens (1354) and Sicily (1373). Sardinia, however, remained a battle zone that he would never subordinate, despite immense military expenditures and operations. As is evident from the lingering wars in the 1360s and 1370s, Genoa, Catalonia's principal rival in the region, was not prepared to easily accede to this phase of Pedro's aggrandizement.

The most violent response to this Mediterranean policy came not from foreigners but from Pedro's relative, Jaume III of Mallorca (1324–1343). With the death of Jaime I in 1276, the Balearic Islands and certain Pyrenean and southern French holdings were separated from the Crown of Aragón and made into the Kingdom of Mallorca. Though ruled by brothers and then cousins, the two realms became economic rivals and dealt very difficultly with the French: the Mallorcans seeking accommodation with the French monarchy, and the Aragónese harboring undisguised antipathy for it. Even when they became in-laws, the hatred between Jaume III and Pedro was palpable and came to the fore in 1341 when the Mallorcan dynasty was locked in a dispute with France over the rights to Montpellier and Jaume neglected to go through the formality of accepting Pedro (his junior) as his overlord. Pedro quickly moved to declare Jaume a traitor and in 1343–1344 conquered the Balearics and the Pyrenean counties, largely leaving the rest to the French. Though pressing their claims for decades to come, Jaume and his successors would remain ever afterward kings without a kingdom.

Even while the memory of his victory against his cousin lingered, Pedro quickly became entangled in a disastrous war with Castile, the War of the Two Pedros (1356–1367). Though Aragónese relations with Castile had generally been unfriendly for decades past, the war began in the fall of 1356 with the Catalan capture of two Genoese vessels. Allied to Genoa, the Castilian king, Pedro I (1350–1369), declared war on the Crown of Aragón. For the next two years, the Castilian king, principal enemy to Pedro IV, ravaged Valencia and Catalonia, even threatening Barcelona in 1359. When this spurred an Aragónese counterattack on Castile in 1360, the Castilian king agreed to peace at Terrer in May, 1361. Arranging an alliance with Granada, Pedro I started hostilities once more some two months later and by September had captured the Aragónese border town of Calatayud. Pedro IV's new alliances with King Charles the Bad of Navarre and Pedro I's half-brother, Enrique de Trastámara, allowed him to consistently outman his rival, who would soon be occupied with a much more pressing matter—an escalating civil war with his half-brother (1367–1369) which ultimately cost his life.

The unstable record of Pedro IV's foreign wars was reflected in his intrigue-ridden court and the growing opposition his government engendered within his own realms. The royal household was a hotbed of factionalism and favorites. In the first half of Pedro's life, it was dominated by Bernat de Cabrera. Scion of an important Pyreanean clan, Cabrera's advancement in the late 1340s marked the emergence of a strong group of middling nobles, the Roussillon faction. Though surely the most talented of Pedro's advisers, Cabrera quickly gained powerful enemies, such as Queen Leonor of Sicily and the royal uncles Pedro and Ramón Berenguer, who conspired to undermine his position. Sacrificed to Pedro's insatiable distrust, Cabrera was executed for treason in 1364. The dominant figure in Pedro's last years was his fourth wife, Sibilia de Forcia who used bribery and intimidation to establish a stranglehold over the court. The principal victim of Sibilia's regime was the crown prince, Juan, and his young wife, Violante de Bar, who endured one indignity after another until his accession in 1387.

Pedro's policies and the expense they caused had violent repercussions through eastern Spain. The scale of change to royal government and succession infuriated the Aragónese and Valencian barons who gathered at Zaragoza in the summer of 1347 to register their disfavor with the establishment of yet another union. When the king was slow in acceding to unionist demands, war loomed. Though delayed for some months by the intrusion of the Black Death into the Iberian litoral in early 1348, the struggle reached a critical point at Epila (21 June 1348) where the royalist forces emerged victorious. Pedro symbolically ended the historical importance of the *Unión* by burning all its privileges and smashing the seals which had given them legal validity. While Epila was a victory for royal sovereignty, Pedro's profligate spending in the second half of his life ironically undermined his power and endowed great autonomy on his parliaments (*cortes*) which largely took over the logistical and fiscal aspects of his later wars. Because of this, the parliament in all his realms became full-fledged institutions, whose executive committees (Diplutació del General, Generalitat) attained a permanent existence.

Pedro IV died at Barcelona on 30 December 1387. He had been married four times: to María of Navarre (1334), Constanza of Sicily (1347), Leonor of Sicily (1349), and Sibilia de Forcia (1377). The third union produced the princes Juan and Martín, the last sovereigns in the Barcelona line. Known by historians as Pedro the Ceremonious for his wholesale changes to court protocol and de la Punyalet (of the dagger) for the dagger he used to hack apart unionist documents after Epila, Pedro IV was a pillar of the Barcelona dynasty whose life extended its greatness, but also clearly presaged its demise.

DONALD J. KAGAY

Bibliography

Archivo de la Corona de Aragón, Cancillería real, Regs. 585–1561; Cartas reales, nos. 1–7476.

Kagay, Donald J. "*Princeps namque*: Defense of the Crown and the Birth of the Catalan State," *Mediterranean Studies* 8 (1999), 55–88.

Matrinez Ferrando, J. E. *La tràgica història dels reis de Mallorca*. Barcelona, 1979.

Pere III of Catalonia [Pedro IV of Aragón], *Chronicle*. 2 vols. Trans. Mary Hillgarth, ed. J. N. Hillgarth. Toronto, 1980.

Tasis i Marca, Rafael. *La vida del rei En Pere III*. Barcelona, 1961.

PEDRO MÁRTIR

Pedro Mártir (Pietro Martire d'Anghiera, Petrus Martyr; 1457–1526) was a humanist, letter writer, historian, and one of the most important classical scholars to be invited to Spain from Italy during the early Renaissance period. Born in Arona near Anghiera on the shores of Lake Maggiore, he completed his education in Rome. Iñigo López de Mendoza, the second count of Tendilla (and Santillana's grandson), persuaded him to come to Spain in 1487. He visited Zaragoza, Salamanca, and Granada as a tutor to the highest nobility and became acquainted with Arias Barbosa, Elio Antonio de Nebrija, and Marineus Siculus. He entered Queen Isabel's service in 1501 as chaplain and in the same year was sent as royal envoy to Egypt to discuss the spice trade and other mercantile interests. The rest of his life was spent in court as tutor, member of the Council of Indies (1518), and chronicler of the Indies (1520), which gave him access to material brought back by explorers. He became friendly with Carlos V, and this brought him many patrons, like Adrian of Utrecht, later Pope Adrian VI. Like Marineus, he used his acquaintances to further his career, and entered the Church for the same purpose. He was buried in the cathedral of Granada. He was a more prolific letter writer than Marineus. His *Opus epistolarum* was published posthumously (1530). It contains over eight hundred letters covering the years 1488–1525, and addresses major noblemen and churchmen in Spain and Italy. In the letters describing Columbus's arrival in the Caribbean, he is supposed to have used for the first time the expressions "New World" and "Western Hemisphere."

Pedro Mártir is best known for his historical works. *Legatio Babylonica* is the fruit of three reports of his visit to Cairo, which he dedicated to Francisco Jiménez de Cisneros (1511). The first decade of the famous *De orbe novo* was probably completed around 1501; a revised edition was supervised by Nebrija and published in Alcalá de Henares in 1516. The complete ten decades was issued in Alcalá in 1530. Its importance can be calculated from the fact that an unauthorized Italian version of the early part was published in Venice in 1504. Mártir's classical training transforms the New World into the land of the Golden Age, idealizing the Indians and recognizing the legitimacy of their society; he omitted all accounts of atrocities. Modern scholarship has recognized the value of Mártir's work, dismissed by nineteenth and early twentieth-century writers as fantasy or facile journalism.

ROBERT B. TATE

Bibliography

Olmedillas de Pereiras, M. de las. *Pedro Mártir de Anglería y y la mentalidad exoticista*. Madrid, 1974.

Riber, L. *El humanista Pedro Mártir de Anglería*. Barcelona, 1964.

PEDRO AFONSO, CONDE DE BARCELOS

Great-grandson of Alfonso el Sabio and son of the poet-king Dinis of Portugal, Pedro, Conde de Barcelos (c. 1280–1354), is remembered as the man who established a distinctive historiographic tradition in Portugal. One of several illegitimate sons of Dinis, Pedro enjoyed favorable treatment by his father until a rift in the royal family caused his exile in 1317, when he went to Castile. His return to Portugal in 1322 was to help Dinis's son Afonso in rebellion against his father, a dispute that continued sporadically, facing Pedro with conflicts of loyalty until the king's death in 1325. Afterward, under Afonso IV, Pedro lived on his own estates, becoming involved outside only in major events like the defense of Portugal against Castile in 1336, and the joint struggle against the Marinids in 1340.

Like many contemporaries, Pedro wrote *cancionero* poetry. Five love poems and six *cantigas d'escarnio* survive. His will of 1350 confirms this interest, as he bequeathed to Alfonso XI of Castile "o meu livro das cantigas," probably a compilation of poems by contemporaries. A taste for compilation is shown in Pedro's best known and more innovative projects, composed in his later years. *Livro das linhagens* is a genealogical work, using a number of sources to create a history of Portuguese royalty and nobility that gives them an honorable and legitimate place in an Iberian, and partly wider, continuum. Similarly, *Crónica geral de 1344* places the history of Portugal in context. For it, Pedro used various sources such as genealogical material, including *Livro das linhagens*, an Arabic text translated into Portuguese, and a chronicle based on the Alphonsine tradition, to construct his own history to the battle of El Salado. The *Crónica* is inconsistent in form, but it is a landmark in Portuguese historiography and Pedro's finest monument.

BRIAN POWELL

Bibliography

Lindley Cintra, L. F. *Crónica geral de Espanha de 1344*. 3 vols. Lisbon, 1951–61.

Pedro, Conde de Barcelos, *Livro de linhagens*. Ed. J. Mattoso. 2 vols. Lisbon, 1980.

PEDRO, CONSTABLE OF PORTUGAL

Pedro of Portugal (1429–1466), as Constable of Portugal and Master of Avís (1443–1446) and "intruder" king of Aragón and Catalonia (1463–1466) embodies a cultural unification of three Christian Iberian kingdoms. Son of Dom Pedro de Avís, Regent of Portugal, he received an excellent education grounded in Italian humanist ideals via the *Prohemio e carta* from the Marqués de Santillana, considered the first literary history in Castile.

After the death of his father (1449), Pedro fled to Castile where he was welcomed at the court of Juan II and where he completed three works in Castilian representative of then current literary genres and themes. *La sátira de infelice e felice vida* (1450–1453), written in an alternation of prose and verse, is a "sentimental novel" that incorporates elements from Latin rhetoric and allegory, and biography, and includes reflections on the character of women and the subtleties of courtly love. *Las coplas del menosprecio e contempto de las cosas fermosas del mundo* (1453), written as a reaction to the untimely deaths of Don Álvaro de Luna and members of Pedro's own family, is a reflection on the mutability of life and fortune, and the need for Stoic morality in the face of misfortune. *La tragedia de la Insigne Reyna Doña Ysabel* (1457), written in response to the death of his sister, Queen Isabel of Portugal, is the first tragedy so entitled in Castilian and is informed by the medieval concept of tragedy as basically the fall of princes. An innovative composite for Castile of several genres, including tragedy, consolation, elegy, and dream vision, the *Tragedia* focuses on the author's personal lament, situating the queen's death within the context of the family's other famous figures and emphasizing the political influence and fame of Pedro's relations. Influences from Seneca, Boethius, Dante, Petrarch, Boccaccio, and the Marqués de Santillana are discernable throughout the text.

Upon his return to Porgual in 1457, Pedro's titles and privileges were restored. As the only grandson of the last Count of Urgell, he was offered the kingdoms of Aragón and Catalonia in 1463 by the Generalitat of Barcelona as part of its revolt against the legitimate heir Juan II of Navarre and Aragón—thus his title of "intruder king" in Catalan history. It has been argued that Pedro's fame as an intellectual figure was instrumental in his selection as king, thus demonstrating the growing significance of arts and letters in the political arena. He remained in power for almost three years. After several military defeats he died—most likely poisoned—in 1466 at the age of thirty-five.

Elena Gascón Vera

Bibliography

Adão da Fonseca, L. *O condestavel D. Pedro de Portugal* Porto, 1982.

Gascón-Vera, E. *Don Pedro, Condestable de Portugal*. Madrid, 1979.

Gerli, E. M. "Toward a Reevaluation of the Condestable of Portugal's *Sátira de infelice e felice vida*." In *Hispanic Studies in Honor of Alan D. Deyermond: A North American Tribute*. Ed. J. S. Miletich Madison, Wisc., 1986, 107–18.

PEDRO, DUKE OF COIMBRA

Son of João I and Philippa of Lancaster, Pedro (1392–1449) was the second in succession to the throne of Portugal. In 1429 he married Isabel, daughter of Jaime II of Aragón, and had six children by her. He fought alongside his brothers and his father in the assault on Ceuta (1415) and, on his return to Portugal, was made a duke by João I. He was a well-educated man with strong humanistic leanings. At his request, the humanist Vasco Fernandes de Lucena translated into Portuguese the panegyric of Trajan by Pliny the Younger. Between 1433 and 1438, Pedro translated into Portuguese *De Officiis* by Cicero. With the assistance of his confessor, he also produced a version of Seneca's *De Beneficiis*, a work composed intermittently between 1418 and 1433, and enlarged it with his own comments and reflexions. The book closes with a beautiful allegory about the order of the universe and its relations with a hierarchical society.

King Duarte died 19 September 1438, leaving his six-year-old son Afonso V as successor. As he was underage, Pedro was chosen by the *cortes* (Parliament) of Lisbon (1439) as regent and protector of the realm. The regency (1440–1446) was a brilliant period for Portugal. Pedro favored the plans of maritime expansion promoted by his brother Henrique, and in six years, 198 leagues of the West African coast were explored. He strengthened the power of the crown and promoted the publication of the *Ordenações Afonsinas* (1446), the first Portuguese civil code, which broke the medieval mold of the country. Pedro developed a policy that furthered the interests of the merchants. Fearing for its privileges, the old nobility pushed Afonso V into a military confrontation with Pedro, who was killed in the battle of Alfarrobeira (May 1449).

Luis Rebelo

Bibliography

Baquero Moreno, H. *A Batalha de Alfarrobeira*. 2 vols. Coimbra, 1979.

Dias de Landim, G. *O Infante D. Pedro*. Lisbon, 1829–94.

O Livro de Virtuosa Bemfeitoria do Infante D. Pedro. Oporto, 1947.

Pedro, Duke of Coimbra. *Livro dos Oficios de Marco Tullio Ciceram*. Coimbra, 1948.

Rui de Pina, *Crónicas*. Oporto, 1977.

PEDRO, INFANTE OF CASTILE

Pedro, Infante of Castile, (1290–1319), son of Sancho IV of Castile (1284–1295) and María de Molina, was regent to Alfonso XI (1312–1350). During the minority of his brother, Fernando IV (1295–1312), María de Molina left Pedro nominally in command of Valladolid to guard it against the attempt by Jaime II of Aragón and Infante Juan to dispossess Fernando in 1296. Pedro later acted as *mayordomo* to Fernando, but as an adult he was primarily a warrior. His mother arranged a diplomatic marriage for him with María de Aragón, daughter of Jaime II, in 1311. They had no surviving children. Upon the death of Fernando in 1312 Pedro proclaimed Alfonso XI as king, and at first supported Fernando's widow, Constanza, as regent, but soon switched alliances to favor María de Molina. The faction surrounding Constanza, which included the infantes Juan and Felipe, refused to recognize Pedro as regent. After Constanza died in 1313 Pedro, Juan, and María de Molina were designated regents by the Concord of Palazuelos (1 August 1314), confirmed by the *cortes* (parliament) of Burgos in 1315. Most of Pedro's activities as regent focused on military affairs to continue the Reconquest and to subdue noble dissension. Immediately after Fernando's death Pedro had tried to continue his brother's campaigns against Algeciras. He later became involved in the war with Granada, and by 1316 he and his forces advanced almost to the city of Granada and later occupied Tiscar. In 1319 he and his coregent, Infante Juan, made plans for a great campaign on the plains of Granada where the two died in battle on 25 June 1319. Their deaths caused major disruptions in the kingdom—disruptions that lasted until Alfonso XI came of age.

THERESA M. VANN

Bibliography

Benavides, A. *Memorias de D. Fernando IV de Castilla*. Madrid, 1860.

Hillgarth, J. N. *The Spanish Kingdoms 1250–1516*. 2 vols. Oxford, 1976.

PELAYO, BISHOP OF OVIEDO

Appointed bishop in 1101 or 1102, Pelayo continued in that see until deposed by the Council of Carrión of February 1130, apparently at the behest of Alfonso VII of León-Castile. Pelayo appealed his deposition and Pope Innocent II suspended his successor in that office, one Bishop Alfonso. After the death of the latter in 1141, Bishop Pelayo was again named as bishop of Oviedo in private documents of the years 1142–1143 but not in any royal ones. The royal actions were doubtless related to the continuing revolt and civil war in the province of Asturias, although the extent of the involvement of Pelayo in the resistance to royal authority there cannot be determined at present. At the Council of Valladolid in September 1143 the see of Oviedo was newly filled by a Bishop Martín. Nevertheless, according to the calendar of the cathedral of Oviedo, Bishop Pelayo lived until 28 January 1153.

Pelayo had been a court figure during the latter part of the reign of Alfonso VI of León-Castile (1065–1109) and was the chief biographer of that monarch. The (brief) biography appears as the final portion of his continuation of a series of earlier chronicles. The bishop was also an enthusiastic promoter of the dignity and prerogatives of the episcopal see of Oviedo at a time when the spectacular growth of the pilgrimage to Santiago de Compostela was threatening the established position of other episcopal seats and also when the general reorganization of the Church of León-Castile was resulting from the very success of the Reconquest. To further the cause of his church, the bishop is credited with an elaborate series of forgeries of documents, both royal and private.

There are indications that Pelayo was himself of Leonese rather than Asturian origin. While his career before his appointment to Oviedo cannot be presently traced, he was certainly at least a minor court figure in the time of Alfonso VI and continued to be important during the reigns of Urraca (1109–1126) and that of Alfonso VII (1126–1130) before his deposition at Carrión.

BERNARD F. REILLY

Bibliography

Fernández Conde, F. J. *El Libro de Testamentos de la catedral de Oviedo*. Rome, 1971.

Reilly, B. F. "On Getting to be a Bishop in León-Castile: The "Emperor" Alfonso VII and the Post-Gregorian Church." *Studies in Medieval and Renaissance History* 1 (1978), 37–68.

Sánchez Alonso, B. ed. *Crónica del obispo Don Pelayo*. Madrid, 1924.

PELAYO, KING OF ASTURIAS

Pelayo (r. 718/9–737) was was the first ruler of an independent Christian realm in Asturias after the Arab conquest in 711. According to the earliest records, Pelayo was of Visigothic origin—by some accounts of royal stock, by others the royal swordbearer or *alférez*. Fleeing into the mountains of Cantabria sometime during the collapse of the Visigothic kingdom, he organized local resistance there. When this achieved such substance as to attract the attention of the Muslims, Pelayo defeated an Islamic force led by a general named Alkama, accompanied by a Christian bishop of Seville named Oppa, at Covadonga in 718–719. This mountain cave is near Cangas de Onís, about sixty-five kilometers east of Oviedo, and on the edge of the Picos de Europa, the highest portion of the Cantabrian chain of mountains. The battle is generally celebrated as the first victory in the struggle to reclaim the Iberian Peninsula for Christianity and the founding of the Spanish kingdom. The cave at Covadonga is now a national shrine.

BERNARD F. REILLY

Bibliography

Collins, R. *The Arab Conquest of Spain: 710–797*. Oxford, 1989.

Gil, J. F. (ed.) *Crónicas Asturianas*. Oviedo, 1986.

PEÑAFORT, RAMÓN DE

Ramón de Peñafort (c.1180–1275) was the greatest canon lawyer of his century, third master general of the Dominicans, and architect of the century's novel program for proselytizing Muslims and Jews. Born at his father's castle or seignorial residence of Peñafort at Santa Margarida del Penedès, Ramón presumably received his arts education at the cathedral of Barcelona, where he became a cleric and *scriptor* in 1204. A decade later he undertook legal studies at the University of Bologna and subsequently taught there. By 1223 he was back at Barcelona Cathedral as provost canon of its chapter. He soon left all to become a Dominican mendicant, presumably at Barcelona's Santa Caterina priory. He is thought to have assisted Cardinal Jean d'Abbeville, the papal legate, in his travels across Spain beginning in 1228 to reinforce the reforms of the Fourth Lateran Council; he was certainly at Zaragoza in 1229 to decide the annulment of the marriage between Jaime I and Leonor of Castile. In 1230 he was called to Rome as papal chaplain and confessor. Pope Gregory IX commissioned him there to construct the *Decretals*, promulgated in 1234; with Gratian's *Decretum*, this systematization of a century's laws in some two thousand sections remained the code of the church until the twentieth century. Ramón then refused the metropolitanate of Tarragona, and in 1236 returned to the Barcelona priory. Continuously involved in important canonical cases there, he was active at the parliament (*corts*) of Monzón in 1236, was delegated to lift the papal excommunication from Jaime I (whose friend and counselor he was), and became involved in the dismissal of Tortosa's bishop and the provision of Huesca's and Mallorca's bishops. The Dominican chapter general elected him head of the order in 1238. He left a lasting mark especially by his revision of their constitutions and his integration of the order's nuns before suddenly resigning in 1240.

Returning to Santa Caterina priory, he spent the next thirty-five years there on massive missionary projects and in most of the Crown of Aragón's religious crises. He was active against heresy, persuading King Jaime to allow the Inquisition; he was regularly counselor to the king; and he adjudicated important public quarrels. Ramón's main preoccupation was with the founding of language schools for intrusive missionary disputation with Muslims and Jews, and with devising a program of persuasive confrontation and handbooks of polemical argumentation. He opened an Arabic language and disputation center at Tunis in 1245 and at Murcia in 1266. He persuaded Thomas Aquinas to construct his masterwork, *Contra gentiles*, for these missions.

Through the school centers, compulsory sermons in mosques and synagogues, the public disputation of 1263 in Barcelona, censorship of rabbinic books, and the aggressive labors of Dominicans like Pau Cristià and Ramon Martí, Ramón helped turn Mediterranean Spain into a stormy laboratory for the new rationalist-confrontational missionary methods. This was part of the wider mendicant effort to convert India, China, and Islamic countries by polemical dialogue. Jeremy Cohen argues for an even more revolutionary orientation in Ramón's vision: a conviction that Talmudic Judaism was antibiblical, depriving Jews of their right by Christian teaching to practice their faith in Christian lands. Contemporary hagiographers stress instead Ramón's mission to the Muslims of Spain, and he himself reported euphorically on the successful conversion of many. The roots of these movements, and the inevitability of their ultimate failure, have been more recently discussed by authors such as Robert Burns, Jeremy Cohen, and Dominique Urvoy.

Throughout all his activity in public life, missionary disputation, or Dominican administration, Ramón remained a scholar on the cutting edge of Roman and canon law. His legal publications multiplied from the start of his career at Bologna to his last year of life in Barcelona. The writings circulated throughout Europe and had immense influence. The most important were his *Summa iuris canonici*, written at Bologna; his *Summa de casibus poenitentiae* (or *Summa de confessoribus*), written in 1222–1225 but redone in

1234–1236; his *Decretales*, written between 1230 and 1234; and the Dominican constitutions. Some sermons and letters, as well as legal responses (*dubitalia*) survive. The *Decretales* had as great an influence on national codes, like Alfonso el Sabio's *Siete Partidas*, as his confessors' handbook had on the ethical and behavioral life of Christendom. Though a Tarragona Council presented a special report and petition for his canonization in 1279, that honor came only in 1601.

ROBERT I. BURNS, S. J.

Bibliography

Burns, R. I. "Christian-Islamic Confrontation in the West: The Thirteenth-Century Dream of Conversion." *American Historical Review* 76 (1971), 1386–1434.

Rius Serra, J. *San Raimundo de Peñafort: diplomatario*. Barcelona, 1954.

PEÑALOSA, FRANCISCO DE

Classed by Cristóbal de Villalón as a musician who exceeded even the "inventor of music," Apollo, Peñalosa (c.1470–1528) outdistanced every Spanish composer of his generation in gaining court and papal favors. On 11 May 1498 Fernando V appointed him a singer in his chapel choir. Thanks to royal request, Peñalosa was named on 15 December 1505 to a vacant canonry in Seville Cathedral. Only a month later papal bulls arrived at Seville naming an Italian Cardinal, Raffaele Riario, to the canonry, but on 28 September 1506 Peñalosa's father, Pedro Díaz de Segovia, successfully interceded before the Seville chapter on his behalf.

In 1511 he became the teacher and maestro de capilla to Fernando V's like-named grandson. The next year while residing at the royal monastery of San Pedro de Cardeña (near Burgos) he corresponded in elegant Latin with the humanist Lucio Marineo, who saluted him as "prince of musicians" ("musicorum princeps"). Despite occasionally attending Seville Cathedral chapter meetings, Peñalosa continued uninterruptedly in royal service until 1516, the year of Fernando V's death on 23 January.

Following several months residence at Seville, Peñalosa in 1517 responded to Pope Leo X's summons to Rome, where he enjoyed the highest marks of favor until Leo's death on 1 December 1521. Thereafter he resided continually at Seville, where on 24 March 1525 he rose to the position of cathedral treasurer and on 2 April 1527 saw his nephew Luis de Peñalosa appointed a canon.

Peñalosa's complete works include six masses and part of a seventh (written cooperatively with Pedro Fernández, Pedro de Escobar, and Alonso de Alva, all Seville cathedral maestros), one odd-verse and five even-verse magnificats, some thirty motets (one of which, *Sancta mater istud agas*, for four voices, wrongly attributed to Josquin Desprez, was published in Amsterdam in 1969), four hymns, a Maunday Thursday lamentation, and ten secular part-songs (the latter in the *Cancionero musical de palacio*). Peñalosa's compositions—all sacred for four voices—are the most virtuosic before Cristóbal de Morales. They survive in five locations: Barcelona, Coimbra, Madrid, Seville, Tarazona, and Toledo. All of his masses except the Marian, are based on secular tunes (*Adieu mes amours, El ojo, L'homme armé, Nunca fue pena maior, Por la mar*). In the last Agnus of the *Ave Maria Peregrina* he combines the reversed tenor of Hayne van Ghizighem's chanson, *De tous biens plain*, with the Salve Regina plainsong.

ROBERT STEVENSON

Bibliography

Stevenson, R. *La música en la Catedral de Sevilla, 1478–1606, documentos para su estudio*. Madrid, 1985.

———. *Renaissance and Baroque Musical Sources in the Americas*. Washington, D. C., 1970, 56, 29.

———. *Spanish Music in the Age of Columbus*. The Hague 1960, 145–63. With list of works and three musical examples.

———. "The Toledo Manuscript Polyphonic Choirbooks." *Fontes Artis Musicae* 20 (1973), 100, 102.

PER ABBAT *See* CANTAR DE MIO CID

PÉREZ DE GUZMÁN, FERNÁN

Minor noble, poet, translator, and biographer, Fernán Pérez de Guzmán (c.1377–c.1460) was descended from families that had changed sides in the civil war of Castile that led to the Trastámaran succession and prospered under the Trastámaras, like the Ayalas and the Alvarez de Toledo. His grandfather was Pedro Suárez de Toledo, chamberlain to Pedro I, and his father was Pedro Suárez de Guzmán. Fernán was nephew to the chancellor Pedro López de Ayala and uncle to Íñigo de Mendoza, Marqués of Santillana. Never politically very active, he figured first among the followers of the Infante Enrique and then in 1429 as an emissary of the young King Juan II of Castile. A few years later he joined the opposition to Álvaro de Luna, and was probably imprisoned for a short time. There is no further data on his life beyond what Alfonso García de Santa María says in his *Duodenario*, that political disturbances at court left him little time for study. He retired early to his estates in Batres, south of Madrid, and died at an advanced age in this rural retreat.

Pérez de Guzmán was in touch with the major cultural figures of his time, to whom he dedicated his compositions, most of which would have belonged to the later period of his life. The surviving library list at Batres must contain some of his books. His poetic works are in the main devotional, didactic, and allegorical with some light satire; he showed little sympathy for amorous poetry. Best known are long compositions on moral, historical, and patriotic themes, like *Loores de los claros varones de España*. He ordered translations of Seneca's epistles and Sallust's two works; one translation of importance to his biographical work is *Mar de historias*, a version of Giovanni (not Guido, as he claims) della Colonna's *Mare historiarum*, a collection of sketches of classical and biblical kings and heroes and fictional figures. Echoes of this can be found in Fernán's main work, like the choice of certain physical characteristics, reference to family links and lineage, the mixture of vice and virtue in the same person, and glosses on topics like fame, science, and letters. *Generaciones, semblanças e obras de los eçelentes reyes de España, don Enrique el terçeroe e don Juan el segundo e de los venerables perlados e notables cavalleros que en los tienpos destos reyes fueron* is a key text, the prologue of which illustrates an awakening critical sense in the writing of history. Like Enrique de Villena, he deplored the quality of contemporary historians of Castile who had either failed to record what was worthy in the past, or who had agreed to write flattering accounts of their princely employers. And like Villena, he demanded that a historian be a rhetorician, capable of expressing what he had witnessed, or if he had not, to use reliable sources, and that no history of a prince should be published in his lifetime, so that the author is free to express opinions. His preferred model is the history of Rome and its faithful subjects. *Generaciones* reveals traces of the Sallustian and Suetonian approach in thirty-four succinct portraits of three kings, a queen, twenty-two nobles, seven prelates, and one clerk, ordered more or less chronologically from Enrique III to Juan II. The majority are chosen because of their political importance or exemplary behavior, but the criteria of choice for minor figures are not too clear. It is possible that the author knew most of his subjects directly; he acknowledges evidence from others but makes it clear this does not imply acceptance, and he has consulted standard vernacular histories. Presentation of subjects varies in length; some are extensive, others merit only a few lines. A formal schema is evident, consisting of reference to lineage, physical characteristics (which infer a belief in the pseudoscience of physiognomy), temperament, and moral qualities. In general individuals are not seen as exemplars of particular virtues or vices, but as an indefinite composite of both. At times personal glosses break the laconic narrative in passionate indignation at displays of princely or aristocratic self-regard, rivalry for political power, but without revealing any precise political doctrine beyond that of noblesse oblige, a well-defined dedication to the common good, and a balanced exercise of arms and letters. It is difficult to argue in favor of any humanistic impact on Fernán's cultural education. However, he is an example of many of the noble class whose reading does not include the romances of chivalry, nor does he live in the same literary world as the author of the *Crónica de don Pero Niño*. Disabused about the human condition, he affects a Senecan stoicism that counsels fortitude in the face of present adversity.

Robert B. Tate

Bibiography

Pérez de Guzmán, F. *Generaciones y semblanzas*. Ed. R. B. Tate. London, 1965.

Clavería, C. "Notas sobre la caracterización de la personalidad en las *Generaciones*." *Anales de la Universidad de Murcia* 10 (1951–52), 481–526.

PETRONELLA OF ARAGÓN

Born 11 August 1136, Petronella was the only child of Ramiro II el Monje, king of Aragón, and Inés of Poitou, daughter of William IX, duke of Aquitaine. Although a son might better have served his need to resolve the succession crisis in Aragón, Ramiro moved swiftly to secure an advantageous marriage alliance for his daughter. Petronella was betrothed at Barbastro on 11 August 1137 to Ramón Berenguer IV (1113–1162), the count of Barcelona since 1131. According to the marriage agreement, Ramón was to govern Aragón, and the royal title was to pass to his and Petronella's children. Their marriage was celebrated at Lérida in August 1150 when Petronella had reached the minimum marriageable age of thirteen.

Her first child, Pedro, was born in April 1152 in Barcelona, but died sometime before 1158 in Huesca. Her second, the future Alfonso II the Chaste, was born in March 1157, probably in Barcelona. Other children included a second Pedro, Sancho, and Dulce. Ramón Berenguer died at Turin 7 August 1162, leaving Aragón and Barcelona to Alfonso, and placing him under the protection of Henry II of England. The lands of Besalú and Ripas were left to Petronella for her lifetime. On 18 June 1164, Petronella renounced her royal rights to Aragón in favor of her son, an act that made possible the foundation of the Crown of Aragón. She spent much of the remainder of her life in Catalonia, dying in Barcelona, 24 October 1173, at the age of thirty-seven. She requested interment in the cathedral of Barcelona, but no remains of her tomb have survived.

LYNN H. NELSON

Bibiography

Ubieto Arteta, A. *Los esponsales de la reina Petronila y la creación de la Corona de Aragón.* Zaragoza, le 1987.

———. *Historia de Aragón: Creación y desarrollo de la Corona de Aragón.* Zaragoza, 1987. 135–211.

Ventura, J. *Alfons el Cast: El primer comte-rei.* Barcelona, 1961.

PETRUS HISPANUS BONIENSIS

Known also as Petrus Hispanus the Elder to distinguish him from another Petrus Hispanus known as the Younger, he was a decretist and glossator of Gratian's *Decretum* whom William Durandus cites with admiration in his *Speculum iudiciale* (c. 1275). Between 1193 and 1198, Petrus wrote an extensive set of glosses to Bernard of Pavia's *Compilatio prima*, the earliest of the *Quinque compilationes antiquae*. Although no complete text of these glosses survives, their detail and complexity can be perceived through many decretalist commentaries that rely on them. They consist largely of clarifications of Roman law procedure. Petrus had studied with Azzo, one of the great glossators of Roman law.

Documents from the 1220s refer to Petrus Hispanus, the Younger. He was the author of *Notabilia ad Compilationem quartum* (after 1215) and two small expositions on Roman law known as *De ordine iudiciorum*. Many of his contributions were incorporated into the works of Bartolo de Sassoferrato, one of the great legal authorities of the Middle Ages.

E. MICHAEL GERLI

Bibliography

Gillman, F. "Des Petrus Hispanus Glosse zur *Compilatio prima* auf der Würzburger Universitätsbibliothek," *Archiv für katholischen Kirkenrecht* 102 (1922), 119–42.

Kuttner, S. *Repertorium der Kanonistik (1140–1234) Prodromus corporis glossarum.* Rome, 1937.

Stickler, A. "Decretisti bolognesi dimenticati," *Studia Gratiana* 3 (1955), 75–91.

PETRUS HISPANUS PORTUGALENSIS (PEDRO JULIANO REBOLO OR REBELLO)

He was born at Lisbon before 1205 and was the son of one Julianus. Petrus died at Viterbo, Italy, on 20 May 1277. He is the Petrus Hispanus quoted by Ugolino of Orvieto in his *Declaratio musicae discipline* (c. 1430). From 1220 to 1229 he studied at the University of Paris. He visited the north of Spain c. 1231. After stays in Toulouse and Montpellier, he taught medicine at Siena, Italy, between 1245 and 1250. In 1250 he was elected the archbishop of Braga. From 1272 to 1276 he was court physician to Pope Gregory X at Viterbo; he attended the General Council at Lyons in 1273–1274. Elected pope on 15 September 1276, Petrus took the name John XXI and died at Viterbo 20 May 1277.

Ugolino quoted tractatus 1 of Petrus Hispanus's *Summule logicales* concerning the property of sound (*Sonus igitur est quicquid auditu proprie percipitur*). According to Claude Palisca, Ugolino drew many new insights from the works of Petrus Hispanus. The popular medieval handbook *Thesaurus pauperum* has traditionally been regarded as his work, although modern editors have recently questioned his authorship.

ROBERT STEVENSON

Bibliography

Palisca, C. "Ugolino della Gherardesca." *New Grove Dictionary of Music.* N.Y. 1980. vol. 13, 572a.

Peter of Spain (Petrus Hispanus Portugalensis). *Tractatus*, called afterwards *Summule logicales.* 1st critical ed. by L. M. de Rijk. Assen, 1972.

Stevenson R. "Petrus Hispanus," *Inter-American Music Review* 8, no. 2 (1987), 26.

PHILOSOPHY, CHRISTIAN

Iberia's paradoxical location in the intellectual milieu of medieval Europe substantially influenced the development of its Christian philosophy. On the one hand Iberia was a provincial area far from Paris, the cultural capital of Latin Christendom. As such it is not surprising that a great deal of Iberian philosophyzing was derivative and textbookish. On the other hand, the Iberian Peninsula was the arena in which Latin Christendom and the Islamic world overlapped most thoroughly and enduringly; in consequence the great minds of Iberia tended to devote their attention primarily to the important if subsidiary philosophical work of selecting, translating, and adapting great works of Arab philosophy, or to applying philosophy to religious polemic and apologetic.

Islam had not, of course, arisen during the Visigothic period, but what little philosophical thought there was between the fifth and eighth centuries in Iberia was wholly devoted, as in the rest of western Europe, to preserving those aspects of Greco-Roman thought that the great patristic writers had baptized for Christian use. Isidore of Seville (560–636) was by far the most important figure. Although he was not primarily a philosopher, but a bishop and encyclopedist, his works carefully preserve a broad, but eclectic range of philosophical ideas: Stoic ethics, Neoplatonic anthropology, late-Roman dialectic. What Isidore preserved, moreover, became the common repository of philosophical ideas for all of Europe for several centuries to come: his *Etymologiae* was one of the most widely read books in Latin Christendom.

The whole of the peninsula was conquered by Arab Muslims in the second decade of the eighth century, as the eastern and southern Mediterranean coastal lands had been previously. But the response of Iberian Christians to Arab rule was in some ways quite different from that of Christians in other areas of the Islamic world. Where eastern Christians often assimilated to the Arab intellectual milieu at a fairly early date, embracing in the process the fruitful Arab philosophical tradition, the Christians of Iberia tended not to do so. Rather Iberian Christians during the first two centuries of Islamic rule rejected the Arab philosophical tradition entirely, but had little interest in Latin philosophy either, choosing instead to perpetuate in Latin the legacy of Isidore, shorn largely of its philsophical concerns. It is only in the mid-tenth century that we hear of two Arabic-speaking bishops, Reccemund and Abū al-Ḥārith, who were said to have an active interest in Arabic philosophy, but no philosophical works by either of these churchmen, if such works ever existed, survive. The only persuasive evidence we have of Arabic-speaking Iberian Christians actively engaged in the Arab philosophical tradition comes from fully two centuries later in the form of two twelfth-century fragmentary Arabic apologetic works which use, in rather simplistic ways, Arab philosophy to defend the doctrine of the Trinity. And it is notable that these two works were almost certainly written in Christian-controlled northern Spain and under the influence of contemporary Latin thought.

The incremental conquest of al-Andalus by Iberian Christian kings in the High Middle Ages resulted in the incorporation into their kingdoms of enormous numbers of non-Christians. But at the same time, the cultural and spiritual energies of Latin-Christian civilization were flowing into all Christian-controlled Iberia in ever more intensive ways. The effects of these two circumstances on Iberian Christian philosophy in the High Middle Ages were manifold. The twelfth-century Latin fascination with the philosophy and science of the Arabs brought northern European intellectuals such as Gerard of Cremona to the Christian-Muslim frontier in Iberia where they translated important Arabic works into Latin. These immigrant masters were joined by native translators, such as Domingo González or Gundisalvo (d. after 1181), who likewise contributed heavily to this translation project. As a result, scores of Arabic philosophical works found their way into Latin versions, and the story of the enormous influence of these Latin translations on the great scholastic thinkers requires no retelling here. However, some of these twelfth-century translators, most notably Gundisalvo, were creative philosophers in their own right. As Etienne Gilson has pointed out, Gundisalvo was the first philosopher of Latin Christendom to integrate aspects of the Neoplatonized Aristotelian philosophy of the Arabs into his Latin writings. In his *De divisione philosophiae* Gundisalvo anticipates the practice of the great thirteenth-century European universities by recommending the inclusion of Arab-Aristotelian physics, psychology, and metaphysics among the traditional studies of the quadrivium. His *De processione mundi* is a distinctly Avicennan inquiry into the doctrine of creation.

Gundisalvo, therefore, had been both truly philosophical in his interests and notably innovative as well. No thinker of this stripe could be found in Iberia in the thirteenth century. Rather, Iberian philosophers of that century tended to depend on northern-European thought, while the more innovative souls were not primarily philosophers or, at least, did not make their greatest contributions in the area of philosophy. Both the Dominican Bernardo de Trilla (d. 1294) and the Franciscan Gonzalo de Balboa (d. 1313) exemplify the former tendency in closely recapitulating the thought of Thomas Aquinas and Duns Scotus, respectively, and most of the other Iberian philosophers of the thirteenth century did likewise. The greatest Iberian scholastic philosopher of this age was surely Pedro Hispano (1226–1277) whose *Tractatus* eventually became the standard logical manual in the universities. Although it is a textbook that he is most remembered for, however, this handbook is itself a work of brilliant concision and clarity. Moreover, he had wider philosophical interests as well, though these are little understood since his other works have been insufficiently studied.

On the other hand, in the towering thinkers of this age, philosophy was the handmaid that served other, more deeply felt purposes. Ramón Martí's (c. 1230–1286) well-schooled Thomism was but an ancillary tool in religious polemical works such as the *Pugio fidei*, his preferred instruments being scriptural, exegetical, and historical arguments arising from his intimate familiarity with the Hebrew-Aramaic *Talmud*, and the Arabic *Qu'rān* and *Ḥadīth*. Arnau de Villanova (c. 1235–1312), physician, Hebraist, Arabist, and translator, made his greatest contributions in medicine and religious reform. But in his advocacy of medical empiricism he does stand with Roger Bacon as a great, early advocate of the experimental method. Philosophical currents run far deeper in the life and work of the Mallorcan mystic, missionary, and Arabist Ramón Llull (1232–1316). Nevertheless, as many interpreters have pointed out, "when Llull wrote on philosophy, it was not as a philosopher." Combining, in effect, the goals of Marti and Villanova, Llull's dominant desires were conversion of unbelievers and Christian reform. Toward this end, he fashioned a method of persuasion that he called in Catalan his *art* (in Latin *ars*, both words meaning "techique" or "method"), this persuasive art being founded upon a series of Neoplatonic philosophical ideas and nonsectarian monotheistic axioms assented to by nearly all contemporary Jews, Christians, and Muslims. In particular Llull believed, and attempted to demonstrate in more than two hundred Latin and Catalan works, that one could "find truth"—indeed that one could demonstrate such doctrines as the Trinity and Incarnation—by properly extrapolating from the widely recognized attributes of God (goodness, omnipotence, wisdom, will, truth, and so forth) that he called "dignities." In devising his art, Llull made at least two important contributions to Western thought. First he insisted that the "dignities" be seen not only as principles of being, but also as principles of action, thereby introducing "a new category in the history of metaphysics.

His second innovation was the combinatory mechanism at the heart of his persuasive system. To derive new truths from the "dignities" one had to combine them systematically and draw conclusions. The wheels, tables, and procedural rules that Llull devised to achieve this end represented a considerable advance in the "mechanization of thought," one that decisively influenced Gottfried Wilhelm Leibniz in the formation of his justly famous—and similarly named—*Ars combinatoria*.

There is rather little that is notable in fourteenth- and fifteenth-century thought in the peninsula. There were a number of Iberian scholastic thinkers in this age, but their works, though they have been insufficiently studied, appear rather unremarkable. The great preacher Vicente Ferrer (1350–1419) was a thoroughgoing Thomist in his philosophical works, for example, while Antonio Andrés (1280–1320), who studied under Duns Scotus in Paris and commented on the old logic, was a stout defender of Scotist realism against William of Ockham's terminism. Though from the latter fourteenth-century on there were a number of intellectuals, such as the *converso* bishop Alfonso de Cartagena (c. 1385–1456), who had humanist interests, very little in the way of properly Renaissance philosophy was produced. Nevertheless, the most important philosopher in the peninsula in this period, the Catalan Ramon Sibiuda (d. 1436), though he was in many ways a realist follower of Llull, anticipated certain aspects of Renaissance Neoplatonism, especially in his emphasis on man as the focal point of creation.

THOMAS E. BURMAN

Bibliography

Abellán, J. L. *Historia crítica del pensamiento español.* Vol. 1, *Metodología e introducción histórica.* Madrid, 1979.

Bonner, A. (ed. and trans.) *Selected Works of Ramon Llull (1232–1316).* Princeton, N.J., 1985.

Burman, T. *Religious Polemic and the Intellectual History of the Mozarabs, c. 1050–1200.* Leiden, 1994.

Carreras y Artau, T., and J. *Historia de la filosofía española: Filosofía cristiana de los siglos XIII al XV.* 2 vols. Madrid, 1939–43.

Fontaine, J. *Isidore de Seville et la culture classique dans l'Espagne Wisigothique.* 2 vols. Paris, 1959.

PHILOSOPHY, JEWISH

There exists a particularly rich history of Jewish philosophy in Iberia that extends from the eleventh century right up to the expulsion of the Jews in 1492, after which its enforced move produced a significant afterlife through its influence on European philosophy as a whole. The first significant thinker was Solomon ben Yahuda ibn Gabirol (1021/2–1054/8) who produced a number of poetic and philosophical works heavily influenced by Neoplatonism. Despite the brilliance of his writing, his thought failed to win many adherents, largely due to his concentration upon Plato and his failure to address the issue that was to remain the leitmotiv of Jewish philosophy in Iberia that is, the relationship between faith and reason. Judah Halevi (c.1075–1140) also wrote a mixture of poetry and philosophy, but his theoretical works do embody an original defense of Judaism against the objections of a variety of competing ideologies, including philosophy. This came to be much discussed among Jewish philosophers, especially given the interest in Christian areas for public disputations between members of different religions. But even more important was the feeling that there is a difficulty in reconciling religion with philosophy, in particular the tradition of peripatetic philosophy, which had become so elaborately developed in the Islamic world. This philosophy came to have the status of science and modernity, and was in danger of replacing religion in the minds of those intellectuals given to theoretical inquiry.

Hence the great interest in reconciling religion with philosophy, which Aristotelians like Abraham ibn Daūd pursued, but which reached their climax in the thought of Maimonides (1135–1204). It is difficult to exaggerate the importance of Maimonides with respect to Jewish thought right up the present time, and although political instability forced him and his family to leave Córdoba for North Africa and Egypt, he embodied the very finest elements of Iberian culture in his writings. His enduring reputation rests not only on his legal works, but also on his philosophical writings, in particular the enigmatic *Dālālat al-ḥāirīn* (*Guide of the Perplexed*). The real intentions that Maimonides had in writing this work have remained a controversy over the centuries, with most commentators arguing that he sought to hide his genuine heterodox views by the use of deliberately misleading and ambiguous language. The apparent aim of the book is to show how one can reconcile religion with philosophy, with the proviso that one must be careful not to challenge the faith of ordinary believers at the same time as one stimulates the intellectual interests of those capable of a deep philosophical understanding of the real meaning of scriptural passages.

This was very much a theme in the philosophy of Maimonides's Muslim countryman, Averroës, and formed a part of much Jewish philosophy. Certainly if we examine some of the ideas in the *Guide* that Maimonides mentions with apparent approval we are confronted with grave difficulties if at the same time one wishes to adhere to orthodox Judaism. Maimonides provides very radical interpretations of scriptural passages, which seem to have to be understood as in accordance with the sort of philosophy (*falāsifā*) produced by Al-Fārābī and Aristotle. Perhaps most radical is Maimonides's theory of language, according to which there is no relationship whatsoever between ordinary language and our language about God except insofar as the terms themselves are the same. That is, when we say that a person is wise, and when we say that God is wise, we have used the same word but should not be fooled into thinking that they describe the same, or even a similar, property. We can form no positive notion of the deity; we can only describe him using negative expressions, saying what he is not rather than what he is. There is no point in praying to God, since God does not listen to our prayers. Praying is only a custom appropriate to certain times, as sacrifices were appropriate forms of religion in earlier times. God cannot even really be said to know what goes on in our world, since this is to identify him with human-knowing subjects. Maimonides claims that these and other equally challenging doctrines are reconcilable with Judaism, but if Maimonides is to be taken at his word, an immense gap exists in his metaphysical system between the deity and his creation, a gap which his philosophical successors have tried to explain.

The writings of Maimonides caused huge controversy in the Jewish world, perhaps rather more outside the Islamic countries than within them. Philosophy in Iberia turned in a very contrary direction through a renewed interest in mysticism based upon the Cabala, a movement influenced by the writings of Judah ha-Cohen (early thirteenth century), Isaac ibn Latif (c.1210–c.1280), and Abraham Abulafia (1240–c.1291). These philosophers often took the Maimonidean text and emphasized the hidden nature of much of it, interpreting the deity as unknowable and infinite, but also reflected partially in his creation.

The fourteenth century saw the celebrated debate on the comparative merits of Christianity and Judaism put forward by Abner of Burgos and Isaac Pulgar, the former arguing with all the vigor of the apostate for the superiority of Christianity over Judaism. This debate was pursued with considerable philosophical rigor, based upon the ways in which Al-Fārābī and other *falāsifā* had sought to compare religions in terms of their differing qualities and the relationship between these qualities and rationality. This sort of confrontation between a convert and a continuing adherent of Judaism took place quite often in this and the next century, and these arguments are interesting for the ways in which they employ an eclectic approach to the understanding of Jewish philosophy, theology, cabala, and law by disputants of equal intellectual standing and similar cultural background.

There are three major thinkers in fifteenth-century Jewish philosophy. Hasdai ben Abraham Crescas (1340–1412) presents a thorough critique of Maimonides's approach, putting emphasis upon action rather than on thought, but more important, perhaps, seeking to replace Aristotelianism with a metaphysics more amenable to religion. His defense of theology against philosophy has the flavor of the much earlier attack by al-Ghazālī upon peripatetic philosophy in Islam, in seeking to disclose the damaging philosophical attack on religion by using philosophy itself to support and strengthen the rational basis of faith. His disciple, Joseph Albo (ca.1380–ca.1444) directed his attention to a detailed discussion on the nature of divine law, and an argument for the superiority of Jewish law against its alternatives, again within the context of the public disputations in Spain that sought to demonstrate the errors of the Jewish religion. Isaac Abravarel (1437–1509) tried to steer a philosophical course between Maimonides and Crescas, but the greatest originality in his thought is to be found in his discussion of history. He distinguishes between natural and artificial situations, where the latter refers to civilized forms of life and the former to those states like that of Adam before the expulsion from the garden. The arrival of the Messiah will result in the rejection of the false lives implicit in urban civilization and the return to a natural and specifically human form of existence.

Jewish philosophy achieved great things in the Iberian Peninsula. It was very much part of the cultures that surrounded the Jewish community, so much of it was written in Arabic (often in Hebrew characters) and even in Catalan as well as in Hebrew. It was influenced very much by *falāsafā*, Islamic philosophy, and later also by scholastic philosophy from Christian Europe and local antagonistic theologians. The thinkers mentioned here are just a part of what was a very considerable philosophical project, pursued by a large number of Jewish thinkers. One can only admire their productivity, especially when one considers the perilous political and economic circumstances of much of this period, together with the heavy involvement of the leading characters in the lives of their political and religious communities. This philosophical movement entered Western philosophy through its impact on Baruch Spinoza and Gottfried Wilhelm Leibniz, and remains important to this day in the realm of Jewish thought.

OLIVER LEAMAN

Bibliography

Leaman, O. *Moses Maimonides*. London, 1990.

Loewe, R. *Ibn Gabirol*. London, 1989.

Sirat, C. *A History of Jewish Philosophy in the Middle Ages*. Cambridge, 1985.

Wolfson, H. *Crescas' Critique of Aristotle*. Cambridge, Mass., 1929.

———. *Studies in the History of Philosophy and Religion*. Vols. 1 and 2. Cambridge, Mass., 1973, 1977.

PHILOSOPHY, MUSLIM

Muslim Spain (al-Andalus) was a difficult area for philosophy to get a firm grip. The area was often far from stable both politically and militarily, and was in constant contact with anti-Islamic forces. In addition, there were frequent incursions from North Africa (Maghrib) by Berber groups intent on usurping power, and much internal conflict between the divergent Islamic regimes. Even jurisprudence was limited broadly to the school of Mālik ibn Anas, which discouraged speculation concerning the rules of law apart from those aspects of law that can be perspicuously answered. This tended to be accompanied by an unadventurous theology, supported by the Almoravid dynasty and the politically important network of legal figures, the *fuqahā'*, who stoutly defended a rather simplistic view of the limits of Islam.

Despite these apparently unfavorable conditions, philosophy in Al-Andalus reached extraordinary heights. There are four major figures. Ibn Bājjah (Avempace) died in 1139 and lived in Zaragoza, combining a political career as vizier of the Almoravid ruler's brother-in-law with philosophical and political works, many of which are no longer extant. Ibn Bājjah established the philosophical tradition in Al-Andalus as firmly based upon the works of Plato, Aristotle, Alexander of Aphrodisias, and Galen, thus linking Spanish philosophy with that practiced in the eastern regions of the Islamic world and typified by al-Fārābī and Ibn Sīnā (Avicenna). Although Ibn Bājjah is clearly writing within the Neoplatonic tradition of Islamic philosophy as a whole, he produced some very interesting and original texts on a whole variety of topics, ranging from a most unusual interpretation of the notion of the active intellect (that which makes thought possible) to a protracted discussion of the responsibility of the philosopher to a society that rejects him. This latter discussion is surely in some ways a heartfelt response to the rather grim intellectual climate in which philosophy in Al-Andalus initially had to survive.

The overthrow of the Almoravids by the Almohads around the middle of the twelfth century introduced rulers who were interested in discussing philosophy at court, while at the same time preserving the appearance of rigid orthodoxy to the community at large. The ruler Abū Yaʿqūb Yūsuf is said to have attracted scholars to his court to discuss with them the views of the Greek philosophers and their Muslim critics. Both Ibn Ṭufayl and Ibn Rushd attended this court, the latter being introduced by the former. Ibn Ṭufayl (1106–1185) is best known for his philosophical novel, *Risālat Ḥayy ibn Yaqẓān*, in which he explores the notion of attaining scientific, philosophical, and religious knowledge through the application of reason alone. This highly original text, sometimes called a philosophical *Robinson Crusoe*, succeeds in summarizing the views of many of his philosophical sources while at the same time striking out in new directions. A particularly unusual aspect of the book is its conclusion that the highest level of happiness is attainable not through union with the active intellect but with God himself, and without having to go through any intermediaries. In addition, this state of union is available through the application of reason alone, and in such a way as not to contradict any of the teachings of Islam. The text itself embodies a variety of literary techniques, some more accessible to the unsophisticated reader and some only to a reader with philosophical and mystical knowledge.

The outstanding philosopher in Al-Andalus was undoubtedly Ibn Rushd (Averroës, 1126–1298). He spent forty years producing commentaries of the Aristotelian texts that were then available in Arabic, together with other Greek texts surviving in Arabic. These commentaries were produced in a variety of forms, very detailed long commentaries together with middle commentaries and summaries, and this work was very much an official project commissioned by the Almohad authorities. Ibn Rushd's commentaries are far from slavish comments upon the Arabic text.

They are often informed by arguments and discussions from his own philosophy. In addition to the commentaries he produced a large number of philosophical works which take to task the opponents of philosophy in the Islamic world, and argue for the compatibility of *falsafā*, philosophy in the Greek tradition, and Islam. This is despite the very radical conclusions which his arguments have, for example, that there is no such thing as spiritual, let alone corporeal, personal immortality, that the universe is eternal and so not created by God out of nothing, and that philosophy represents the most privileged route to the nature of reality that is available to human beings.

Ibn Rushd tried to free philosophy not only of the assaults on it by the Muslim traditionalists but also of the accretions to Aristotelianism represented by the Neoplatonists among his predecessors. He had very little time for those thinkers who had a deep respect for mysticism as a way of finding out what really exists. He argued that revelation and reason must be different routes to the same reality, the truth, and that different kinds of language are appropriate to different sorts of audience. Ordinary people will require Islam to lead them to the truth, since they are dependent upon figurative and anthropomorphic language, while those more sophisticated can employ philosophical methods to understand the world and the role of human beings within it. He does suggest that philosophy is in many ways the superior means of attaining understanding, and poured scorn on the ways in which theologians (*mutakallimūn*) tried to reserve their interpretative techniques as the most decisive in making sense of scripture. Many commentators suggest that even when he writes that the opinions of ordinary people and non-philosophers have to be respected, since they are just less sophisticated versions of the truth more clearly grasped by philosophers, he is really concealing his own views in order to keep with the religious authorities of the time. Others argue that he should be taken at his word, since the notion of the existence of different routes to the same truth is a logical aspect of his entire approach to the role of language in philosophy.

If there is anything characteristic about philosophy in Al-Andalus, it is this concentration upon the notion and significance of language. Ibn Rushd argues that those who insist upon a literal understanding of Islam are guilty of using language in incoherent ways. They argue that God must really be able to know what goes on in the world, that he has total power over everything that happens, that there is nothing logically possible that he cannot do, and yet if we follow through the implications of these statements we can see that they involve serious damage to the way in which we use language. They imply that things in the world exist only because God maintains them in existence as a direct effect of his will, and yet this is to contradict the possibility of the process of naming things in the world and understanding the course of natural events. The theologians represent the deity as some sort of superman, while the philosophers interpret his qualities as very different from those perceived in his creation, so that when God is said to know what is meant is a very different type of knowledge than that which we human beings experience. Given the radical nature of Ibn Rushd's philosophy, it is hardly surprising that he was tried for heresy in Córdoba in 1195 and spent some time in disgrace in North Africa before he was allowed to return to Al-Andalus.

The philosophy of Averroës came to have enormous influence in Christian Europe, yet disappeared almost without trace in the Islamic world. The thought of Ibn al-ʿArabī of Murcia (1165–1240) has remained popular wherever people have been interested in mysticism. His enormous output of both prose and poetry is replete with metaphysical symbolism designed to move its audience both rationally and imaginatively. He represents a very powerful strain in philosophy in Al-Andalus—namely, the desire to combine personal mystical experience with intellectual argument. He presents a unified view of the world through the person of God, where the world is the manifestation of God together with his reflection. Human beings are images of the divine, and gain some understanding of the deity by apprehending the aesthetic qualities of the world. All religions are to a degree valid, since they all embody the same truths, albeit in different forms. It is a particular feature of Ibn al-ʿArabī's style that he manages to transform the rather technical languages of theology, law, and philosophy into a mystical synthesis of quite remarkable fluency. Most of his extensive output was produced after he left Al-Andalus, where it is likely that his adherence to Sufism did not please the religious authorities, yet his thought is heavily marked by his upbringing in that politically unsettled but culturally rich area of the Islamic world.

Oliver Leaman

Bibliography

Averroës (Ibn Rushd). *Averroes on the Harmony of Religion and Philosophy*. Trans, G. Hourani. London, 1961; repr. 1976.

Hérnandez, M. *Filosofía hispano-musulmana*. Madrid, 1957.

Ibn Ṭufayl *Ḥayy ibn Yaqẓān: A Philosophical Tale*. Trans. L. E. Goodman. New York, 1972.

Leaman, O. *Averroës and his Philosophy*. Oxford, 1988.

———. *An Introduction to Medieval Islamic Philosophy*. Cambridge, 1985.

PICATRIX

The supposed author and the title of the Latin version of the Arabic *Ghāya al-hakīm* (*The Aim of the Wise Man*). The Arabic text was written in Spain in the eleventh century and was ascribed to the well-known mathematician and astronomer from Madrid, Maslama al-Majrīṭī. The Latin text is a translation of the Spanish version of the Arabic text; both Spanish and Latin versions were made in the 1250s under the aegis of Alfonso X, king of Castile and Leon. *Picatrix* is a hodgepodge of prayers to the planets, astrological theory, and recipes for fumigations and talismans, thrown together from Indian, Persian, Egyptian, and Greek sources. Under the veneer of a spurious Neoplatonic cosmology, it gives practical details for performing magical liturgies, which allow the reader to harnass the spiritual powers of the planets and perform wonders, such as changing into the shape of an animal and becoming invisible. The *Picatrix* suddenly acquired popularity as a handbook on magic in the Renaissance, when it was frequently copied and excerpted, and was translated several times into European vernaculars.

CHARLES BURNETT

Bibliography

Pingree, D. "Some of the Sources of the *Ghāya al-hakīm*," *Journal of the Warburg and Courtauld Institutes* 44 (1980), 1–15.

Pingree, D. (ed.) *Picatrix: The Latin Version of the Ghāya al-hakīm*. London, 1986.

PILGRIMAGES

The phenomenon of pilgrimage to a place or thing holy for one reason or another was the commonest of occurences in the medieval Christian West, though far from exclusive to it or to Christianty. The pilgrimages to the Holy Land or to Rome are the best known but any church that possessed or came into the possession of well-known relics of any sort could become an object of pilgrimage from its surrounding countryside or even from much more distant parts if they became very famous.

Iberia was no exception to this. The most famous of all Iberian pilgrimages was that to Santiago de Compostela, where the relics of the apostle, St. James the Great, were believed to have been discovered in the early ninth century. But by the eleventh century that pilgrimage route had become so traveled that it spawned side devotions, so to speak. At León, King Fernando I (1037–1065) had recovered the bones of St. Isidore of Seville and the church of the same name there became not only a mausoleum of the dynasty but also a center of veneration of the saint. At Oviedo, Bishop Pelayo (1100–1130) published a list of all sorts of precious religious marvels supposedly contained in the arca sancta of his cathedral in a successful effort to make his church attractive to pilgrims. The latter could also stop not far outside León at the great royal monastery of Sahagún where the relics of the early Iberian Christian martyrs San Facundo and San Primitivo were housed.

León-Castile was not singular in this respect, however. In Catalonia, from the port of Barcelona, with its cult of Santa Eulalia the early Iberian feminine martyr, the pilgrims could fan out in turn to the miracle-working shrine of the Virgin at the nearby monastery of Montserrat or trudge south to the port of Tarragona to pay their respects to its patron, San Narciso. Should they have come south by land there was the great Cistercian monastery of Santa María de Ripoll to be visited even before they reached Barcelona.

As with León-Castile and Catalonia, the kingdom of Aragón proper also had its pilgrimage shrines. Chief among these was the church of the Virgen of the Pillar in Zaragoza. It was believed to mark the spot where the Virgen appeared to St. James the Great when he preached in the peninsula in apostolic times; particularly after the recapture of the city from the Muslims in 1118 pilgrimage grew in popularity.

BERNARD F. REILLY

Bibliography

Dunn-Wood, Maryjane, and Linda Kay Davidson. *The Pilgrimage to Santiago de Compostela: A Comprehensive, Annotated Bibliography*. New York, 1994.

PINAR, FLORENCIA

A presence at the court of Isabel and Fernando, Florencia Pinar is the sole female poet from the *cancionero* period represented by complete poems, yet almost nothing is known of her life. A few compositions are attributed to her, and may be by her brother, but only three are surely hers: "¡Ay! que ay quien más no vive," "Canción a unas perdizes que le embiaron bivas," and "El amor ha tales mañas." These poems place Florencia as a poetic force at odds with male-centered views of women. In her poems, the dominant attitude toward love is an ambiguous one. The lover is not praised and love, far from being exalted, is portrayed as deceiving and hurtful. Passion overwhelms common sense, it overbalances prudence. In "Canción a unas perdizes," the poetic persona reveals her feeling as parallel to that of the caged partridges at the core of the composition, free spirits now entrapped by the snares of an unavoidable but fatal attraction. Here, as in "El amor ha tales mañas," bestiary imagery is richly explored to the detriment of love perceived as ennobling. The burrowing, cancerous worm of the latter poem makes for a richly allusive attack on love, which wears a sweet mask in the world but, when stripped of it, is revealed as devious, enslaving. The undeniable pleasures that love can bring are exposed as dangerous, even signs of sickness. Images of love, passion, and illness are tools of a poetic craft in which Florencia Pinar is singular for her depictions of its malignant effects on the woman; her male brethren speak only of its deleterious effects on men.

JOSEPH T. SNOW

Bibliography

Deyermond, A. "Spain's First Women Writers." In *Women in Hispanic Literature*. Ed B. Miller. Berkeley, 1983. 27–52, esp. 44–51.

Fulks, B. "The Poet Named Florencia Pinar." *La Corónica* 18 (1989–90), 33–44.

Snow, J. T. "The Spanish Love Poet, Florencia Pinar." In *Medieval Women Writers*. Ed. K. Wilson. Athens, Ga., 1984, 320–32.

Weissberger, B. "The Critics and Florencia Pirar." In *Recovering Spain's Feminist Tradition*. Ed. L. Vollendorf, New York, 2001, 31–47.

PINHEIRA, MARGARIDA

An early-sixteenth-century manuscript contains the history of the convent of Jesus in Aveiro. This manuscript, edited by António Gomes da Rocha Madahil appears to have been written either by Catherina Pinheira or, more likely, her older sister Margarida, both nuns of the convent. The manuscript seems to date from 1525; it could, however, be a copy of, or based on, an earlier work. The work recounts the history of the founding of the convent by Brityz Leytoa, who started her religious career in 1458 and died in 1480. This is followed by the life of the princess (and later saint) Joana of Portugal, who entered the convent in 1472 and died there in 1490. There also are lists of dates relating to the lives of the other nuns of the convent. The work's main theme is that the convent is more attractive than marriage. Brityz Leytoa and her friend Micya Pereyra, both widows, resisted much family pressure to remarry and founded the convent together. Joana of Portugal and her friend Leonor de Meneses resisted the same kind of pressure and entered the convent after corresponding with each other secretly for a very long time.

Other women had an easier time. This was true of Brityz Leytoa's daughters, Catherina and Maria Datayde; Micya Pereyra's niece of the same name, and Ynes Eanes and Margarida and Catherina Pinheira, the three nieces of Johan de Guimarães, a priest who was instrumental in founding the convent. These women entered the convent very young and played an important role in its history, a role that the text stresses repeatedly. Maria Datayde was the convent's third prioress, after Brityz Leytoa and Leonor de Meneses. She died in November 1525, one month after the completion of this manuscript. Only Margarida Pinheira and her sister Catherina, who was the associate prioress and, thus, a natural candidate for the position of prioress, remained at the convent. Catherina Datayde had died in 1466. Ynes Eanes had moved to Leyrea in 1498, and Micya Pereyra had moved to Santarem in 1513.

The author declares her intention to praise God and invoke his help in such evil times. It is possible that there was a political struggle between the old guard and the younger generation. In such circumstances, it would make sense to write or rewrite a book glorifying the convent's founders and emphasizing that Catherina Pinheira had received Brityz Leytoa's special blessing and that Margarida Pinheira had been particularly close to Joana of Portugal. The battle, if there ever was one, was lost. Isabel de Castro, a younger nun, became prioress, Catherina Pinheira continued to be associate prioress until her death in 1528, and Margarida Pinheira left for Setubal in 1529.

CRISTINA GONZÁLEZ

Bibliography

Leitão de Barros, T. *Escritoras de Portugal: Génio feminino revelado na Literatura Portuguesa*. 2 vols. Lisbon, 1924.

Lopes de Oliveira, A. *Escritoras Brasileiras, Galegas e Portuguesas*. Braga, n.d.

POEMA DE ALFONSO XI

The *Poema de Alfonso XI* was probably written by a poet of Leonese descent, Ruy Yáñez, in 1348. It consists of nearly ten thousand octosyllabic lines, in quatrains rhyming *abab*. Some 6,530 lines concern Alfonso's military campaigns, of which the battle of Salado (1340) stands out. It contains remarkable similarities to the Portuguese *Poema da batalha do Salado* by Afonso Giraldes.

There are several hypotheses about the original language of the *Poema de Alfonso XI*. Some critics have argued that the poem was written in Portuguese or Galician, and translated into Castilian. Others believe that it was written in a western Leonese dialect which included some Galician features. A final conclusion has not been reached because some of its linguistic configurations resist classification. The poem has been referred to by some critics as a "rhymed chronicle" because it was wrongly believed to be based on the *Gran crónica de Alfonso XI*. However, in light of new evidence it has been demonstrated that it was the author of the *Gran crónica* who drew on the firsthand information of Ruy Yáñez. Furthermore, the poet does not adopt a given text or use a specific source for his poem, which is also completely independent of Fernán Sánchez de Valladolid's *Crónica de Alfonso XI* (1344). The poem has also been described as a "gesta erudita" or a learned text because it drew some features from the *Libro de Alexandre* and the *Poema de Fernán González*. The *Poema de Alfonso XI* stems from a court tradition but its author—in contrast to those who wrote in *cuaderna via* (monorhymed alexandrine quatrains)—does not boast about his erudition. The *Poema de Alfonso XI* was originally composed in writing and not on the oral tradition. However, its relatively high percentage of oral formulae (18 percent), indicating residues of oral composition, and its many popular epic characteristics clearly prove that it was directed to a popular audience, and was most probably meant to be transmitted by singing. The poet's sympathy for the sufferings of the common people at the hands of the nobles seems to confirm this. Perhaps it would be better to designate it as a "new epic" because it was composed most probably in reaction to the excesses of the heroic epic.

MERCEDES VAQUERO

Bibliography

Catalán Menéndez Pidal, D. (ed.) *Gran crónica de Alfonso XI*, vol. 1. Madrid, 1975, 15–251, esp. 141–42, 162.

———. *Poema de Alfonso XI. fuentes, dialecto, estilo.* Madrid, 1953.

Deyermond, A. *El ''Cantar de Mio Cid'' y la épica medieval española.* Barcelona, 1987, 91–93.

POEMA DE ALMERÍA

The Latin *Chronica Adefonsi Imperatoris* is a prose narrative that covers the internal political events as well as the external battles and victories of King Alfonso VII of León-Castile (1126–1157) against the Moors, who had been occupying Spain since the early years of the eighth century. The *Chronica* ends with 386 Leonine hexameters, known as the *Poema de Almería*. The *Poema* was inspired by the enthusiastic desire of the chronicler to alleviate the boredom of the prose and to sing in a heroic mood the historical siege of the Muslim stronghold of Almería, an event that took place in August 1147. The theme and structure of the *Poema* are very simple and straightforward: to review the preparation for the siege and to describe the Christian contingents that, under the leadership of King Alfonso VII, took part in it. Because the text ends abruptly in the middle of line 386, we do not know if the poet-chronicler ever completed the actual battle scenes and final elegy of the Christian heroes and their victory, that we know did occur historically. On the other hand, perhaps he died before completing his opus. In any case, what remains of the *Poema* was certainly written soon after the siege and most likely during the year 1148. As a literary composition, it is a clear imitation of a classic topos: the "catalogs" of participants in a battle of the classical epic, or a "desfile," or "dénombrement épique," as it is called in Romance epic.

The author of the *Poema* is unknown, but there is strong evidence that it was Arnaldo, bishop of Astorga and active participant at the siege. The name Arnaldo, rare in Castile in the twelfth century, would indicate that he probably was from eastern Iberia; attempts have been made to identify him with Arnaldo of Ripoll, but we should not exclude the possibility that he might have come from France. This hypothesis would explain his familiarity with French epics, although his epic knowledge could have also come from his residence in Astorga, a very important town along the Camino de Santiago, the route frequently traveled by French jongleurs.

The *Poema de Almería* as a literary genre lies on the borderline between chronicle and epic. Contemporary scholars on close examination, consider it the best epic work in Latin of the Spanish Middle Ages, and for its aesthetic values certainly it is much more than a rhymed chronicle. The widest audience, and by far the most admiring one, has been drawn from scholars working in the field of Romance epic, and for good reason. During the late twentieth century this group of researchers subjected the text to a very intense scrutiny in order to unveil the contents of its allusions to the epic legend of Roncesvalles to find out how the poet came to know about it and, more importantly, how was the poet able to connect it with the Cidian epic theme which so preeminently dominates some parts of the text.

The significance of the *Poema de Almería* stands up mostly on two fronts. First, it is an invaluable source for the study of the origins of Romance epic and a witness to its early manifestations. In this respect it has been extremely useful for the purpose of dating it, clarifying its contents, and illuminating other literary and cultural implications. But perhaps its major significance lies in the value of the *Poema* itself. Being at the crossroads of the epic literary history of the Middle Ages, the *Poema* represents a rare and extraordinary example of a popular Latin epic tradition that coexisted with that of the Romance epic. It is this extraordinary concept of epic poetry that has made the *Poema de Almería* a unique and in many ways a special instance of the genre.

H. SALVADOR MARTÍNEZ

Bibliography

Gil, J. (ed.) "*Carmen de expugnatione Almariae vrbis.*" *Habis* 5 (1974), 45–64.

S. Martínez, H. *El "Poema de Almería" y la épica románica*. Madrid, 1975

POEMA DE FERNÁN GONZÁLEZ

A rhymed chronicle about the life and exploits of the emancipator of Castile, Count Fernán González (c.915–970), the *Poema de Fernán González* is thought to have been composed around 1250 by an anonymous monk affiliated with the monastery of San Pedro de Arlanza in Old Castile. The original manuscript has not survived, although an incomplete copy from the fifteenth century, preserved in a codex with four other manuscripts, is housed in the library of the Monastery of San Lorenzo del Escorial (iv. b.21).

Together with Rodrigo Díaz de Vivar, popularly known as el Cid, Fernán González is one of the most revered epic heroes of medieval Spain. His military prowess and piety earned him a reputation that inspired numerous ballads, Golden Age plays, and even a nineteenth-century Spanish novel. The anonymous Arlantine poet sought to portray the first Count of Castile as a self-proclaimed vassal of God whose constant aid and intervention the Judeo-Christian warrior sought in order to guarantee Castilian supremacy over the infidels and other Christian rivals.

In weaving his tale, the poet borrowed from learned sources, including the Scriptures, the *Chronicon mundi* by Lucas of Túy, and St. Isidore's *Historia gothorum*, but he also relied to a considerable degree on legendary materials. He molds the various epic, folkloric, and monastic influences that inform his literary creation into a tripartite structure, the first of which treats the history of Spain prior to the appearance of Fernán González. The second section, most probably based on popular sources, deals with two important battles waged against the Moors as well as the rivalry between the kingdoms of Castile and Navarre. In the last section the Count is imprisoned in Navarre but manages to escape with the help of Princess Sancha who later becomes his wife. Finally, the hero wins the autonomy of the County of Castile in exchange for a horse and hawk, an act which may have some basis in history or may simply be a traditional folk theme.

JOHN S. GEARY

Bibliography

Bailey, Matthew. *The Poema del Cid and the Poema de Fernán González: The Transformation of an Epic Tradition*. Madison, Wisc., 1993.

Hernández, C. (ed.) *Poema de Fernán González*. Vitoria, 1989.

West, B. *Epic, Folk, and Christian Traditions in the "Poema de Fernán González"*. Madrid, 1983.

POEMA DE MIO CID *See CANTAR DE MIO CID*

POEMA DE YÚÇUF

The *Poema de Yúçuf* or *Poema de José*, a narrative poem in Aljamiado consisting of ninety-five stanzas in *cuaderna vía* (monorhymed alexandrine quatrains) and based on the Islamic version of the Joseph legend (Qurʾān, chapter 12). It is one of the principal monuments of *aljamiado* literature. Two manuscripts exist: one, the more complete, was published by Heinrich Morf in Leipzig in 1883; the other, an older version, was published by Ramón Menéndez Pidal. Pascual de Gayangos originally dated the text to the sixteenth century, believing that no *aljamiado* was produced before that time. In fact, the poem should be considered the work of Mudéjares and not Moriscos, and was probably composed in the late thirteenth to early fourteenth centuries (a period closer to the heyday of *cuaderna vía*); the Menéndez Pidal manuscript appears to be of the late fourteenth or first half of the fifteenth.

The poem's version of the Joseph legend departs in several respects from both the Old Testament and the Qurʾānic versions. The wolf that Joseph's brothers accuse of having eaten Joseph miraculously speaks to protest his innocence; on his way to captivity in Egypt Joseph weeps at his mother's tomb; and a harsh storm subsides when the boy forgives the blows of his African guard. In Egypt, Joseph's intercession with God helps the merchant's twelve wives all to conceive and bear twins. Pharaoh's wife, to tempt Joseph from his chastity, has the walls of her chamber painted with lascivious scenes. The poem breaks off with an event that is included in the Qurʾān: the women of Egypt, who are peeling grapefruit when they first see the young man, are so distracted by his beauty that they cut their hands.

The language of *Poema de Yúçuf* shows many Aragónese features, especially in the older manuscript A.

CONSUELO LÓPEZ-MORILLAS

Bibliography

Menéndez Pidal, R. *Poema de Yúçuf: Materiales para su estudio*. Granada, 1952.

POETRY, ARABIC

Provincial Beginnings

Little poetry has come down to us from the century following the Arab conquest of Visigothic Spain in A.D. 711, with the possible exception of the famous poem attributed to the first Umayyad emir, ʿAbd al-Raḥmān I (r. 756–788), in which he likens himself to a palm tree, exiled like him far from his native Syria. This dearth of poetry is hardly surprising in view of the enormous practical task that faced the new masters of the Iberian peninsula, both before and after the establishment of the emirate: settling the various tribes in their respective new homes, consolidating something like political unity, and generally getting used to the place.

With the reign of ʿAbd al-Raḥmān II (822–852), al-Andalus began to acquire the cultural trappings of a province, with the eastern metropolis of Baghdad providing cultural but not political leadership. The most famous case in point is the arrival in 832 of the Persian singer Ziryāb, who brought the newest Baghdad fashions in verse and song to the furthest outpost of Arab society; other easterners followed, bringing the latest in philology or jurisprudence as well as poetry, and many Andalusians visited and studied in the Arab East during the formative ninth and tenth centuries. Soon court poets such as ʿAbbās ibn Nāṣiḥ (d. 844) were imitating the poetry of Abū Nuwās (d. 813), while others such as Mu'min ibn Saʿid (d. 844) emulated Abū Tammām's neoclassical verse. None of the poets of this period was more than proficient at following Eastern themes in Eastern forms, and no poet of greatness or even individuality had yet appeared in al-Andalus.

Maturity

By the reign of ʿAbd al-Raḥmān III (912–961), Córdoba had become a haven for artists, scholars, and poets. The first of the latter to leave us a substantial body of verse that may be said to have more of an Andalusian than a derivative theme (as opposed to form, which is still resolutely Eastern) is Ibn ʿAbd Rabbihi (d. 939 or 940). He is best known for an ingenious reasoned anthology called *al-ʿIqd al-farīd* (*The Unique Necklace*); his own *qaṣīda*s in the Eastern manner, in which he makes a cold and somewhat tentative use of the rhetorically ornamented *badiʿ*style; and a long poem in the "lower"-register *rajaz* meter. This 445-line composition recounts the newly proclaimed Caliph's martial exploits against the Christians in a manner which has been likened to that of the *chansons de geste* and other medieval Romance epics.

Later Andalusian poets of the caliphate, such as Ibn Darrāj al-Qasṭalli (d. 1030) and the Umayyad prince ash-Sharif aṭ-Ṭalīq (d. 1009), also followed the Eastern neoclassical school, widening their palette to cover all the traditional genres of Arabic poetry: *ghazal* (*nasīb*) or love poetry, *nauriyyāt* or floral poetry, *khamriyyāt* or bacchic themes, and *fakhr* or boasting. Prose masterworks of deep relevance to poetry were composed: *Risālat-at-tawābiʿwa-z-zawābiʿ* (*Book of Familiar Spirits and Demons*) by Ibn Shuhaid (d. 1035), a first-rate poet who applied Neoplatonist ideas to form an almost romantic theory of the "poetic soul"; and *Tawq al-hamāma* by Ibn Ḥazm (c.990, 1063). This is a treatise on love and poetry which is one of the extremely rare medieval Arabic prose works of intense human and artistic interest.

Poetry in the Time of Troubles and in the Era of the Party Kings

As the political unity of Al-Andalus unraveled, leading first to chaos (the Time of Troubles from 1009 to 1031), and then to a fragmented mosaic of city-states (the party kings era, from 1031 to 1092), each local court in such places as Zaragoza, Badajoz, Silves, Denia, and Elvira as well as Toledo, Córdoba, Seville, and Granada began to vie with the others for preeminence in poetry, and for the allegiance of the best poets. One poet of this period stands out, perhaps the one name in Andalusian letters that is held in the very highest regard among Arabic poets of all ages and places: Ibn Zaydūn. His briefly requited love affair with the liberated Umayyad princess and poetess Wallāda is as famous in Arabic literature as *Romeo and Juliet* is in the West, but in this case the story is true. His masterpiece, rhymed on the letter *nūn*, deserves to be quoted in full, but two lines (much appreciated by contemporary and later Arab critics for its double *tibāq* or antithesis) conveys something of its taut emotion and brilliant imagery:

> Having lost you, my days have gone all dark
> While with you, even my nights were white.

Whether or not this period was a "golden age," it was a remarkably fertile time for good poets sounding vibrant and creative chords. Thus, Ibn ʿAmmār of Silves (c.1040–1086), famous for his poem beginning:

> pass round the glass for the breeze has arisen
> and the stars have slackened the reins of night-travel.

Even the kings of the various city-states put their hands to poetry, in at least one case with memorable felicity: Al-Muʿtamid of Seville (c.1040–1095). His fateful decision to call in the Almoravids led first to the victory of Zallāqah (Sagrajas) in 1086, and then to the exile and dispossession of his and other ruling familes of the previous era. He left bitter poems of exile and loss, an increasingly recurrent theme in Andalusian poetry, which contrast the verdant gardens of Spain with the drier climes of refuge:

> Would that I knew whether I shall ever again spend a night
> With a garden before me and a pool of water behind me.

Al-Muʿtamid's friend and court poet Ibn al-Labbāna (d. 1113) became famous for his fidelity after his patron's exile and ruin, as well as for his fine poems.

Decadence and Decline

If the later party kings period marks a high point of culture in Al-Andalus, its political fragmentation favored the Reconquest and this in turn led directly to intervention by warlike zealots from North Africa: the Almoravids at the end of the eleventh century, and the Almohads who invaded in 1145. Those invasions also marked the beginning of a decadence and then decline of letters. Good poetry continued to be written, but with increasingly common themes of nostalgia and regret, carpe diem contrasted with premonitions of impending doom, escapist nature poetry in a miniaturist rather than the earlier impressionistic style. This is visible in the work of poets of this period such as Ibn ʿAbdūn, author of a famous elegy and court poet to the Bani Afṭas in Badajoz (d. 1134); or Ibn Khafāja (d. 1138), whose name became synonymous with nature poetry, while his nephew Ibn az-Zaqqāq (d. 1133) wrote satire and sensuous wine and love poetry.

Ar-Ruṣāfī of Valencia (d. 1177), among the better poets of the post–party kings period, was a nature poet of the Ibn Khafāja school. One Andalusian who fled abroad as the Reconquest engulfed Al-Andalus is Ibn al-ʿArabī (d. 1240), a great mystical poet whose wistful odes and *muwashshaḥāt* (rhymed odes) on Sufi themes have stood the test of time. Ḥāzim al-Qarṭājannī (d. 1285) wrote, besides poetry, a prose work entitled *Kitāb sirāj al-bulaghā' wa minhāj al-udabā'* (*Book of the Lamp unto the Eloquent and Pathway for the Lettered*). In it he discusses Aristotle's *Poetics*, holding that imitation—*mimesis*—is a form of embellishment of nature, not slavish copying. Finally, Ibn Zamrak, a court poet and sometime Vizier of Granada, wrote finely crafted *qaṣīda*s (odes) and muwashshaḥāt, some of which decorate the walls of the Alhambra; murdered along with his children in 1393, he was the last great Arabic poet of Muslim Spain, indeed perhaps the last one of real merit.

Innovation: Muwashshaḥ and Zajal

While the Andalusian poets never completely broke with the thematic context of Eastern Arabic poetry, the one truly Andalusian innovation is a formal one: the use of strophic forms, odes broken up into symmetrical strophes and refrains. These have a common rhyme in the opening couplet and the refrain, and differing ones in each stanza: AA bbb AA or, with different internal rhyme in the refrain, AB ccc AB. The most complex structure has multiple internal rhymes: ABCDEC fghfghfgh ABCDEC (the opening couplet rhymed like the refrains is occasionally lacking; without it, the poem is said to be "bald.") Called *muwashshaḥ* or "girdled," these poems are written in quantitative meters identical to or closely derived from those of the classical Arabic; their themes are also similar to those of other Hispano-Arabic poetry, with the notable exception of the finale or *kharja* in Romance or in colloquial Arabic. There was some precedent for strophic forms even in the Abbasid East, but their intricate development (which later spread to Egypt and the East) was new, and the use of nonclassical language—possibly a snippet from a popular song of the day—as "spice" could only have arisen in a bilingual culture such as al-Andalus. Some of the best Hispano-Arabic poets of the party kings era composed muwashshaḥāt: Ibn Bājjah (d. 1138, the "physician-poet" known as Avempace), or the blind poet al-Aʿmā at-Tuṭīlī (d. 1126). The latter's strophic compositions were not originally included in his Dīwān, being considered insufficiently dignified.

The strophic form itself, the origins of which are shrouded in obscurity and clouded by decades of heated scholarly controversy, gave rise to a further innovation. Beginning sometime in the late eleventh or early twelveth century, we find strophic compositions entirely in colloquial Andalusian Arabic. Sometimes these contain Romance words or phrases, providing a uniquely preserved, lively vignette of street dialogue from twelveth-century Córdoba. The most famous practitioner of this colloquial form, known as the *zajal*, was Ibn Quzmān of Córdoba (d. 1160). His choice of the colloquial language effectively excluded his poetry from the mainstream of Arabic letters, but his poems are not only linguistic and societal anecdotes of substantial interest (which they undoubtedly are), but great poetry in their own right, against any standard.

Arab Origins Debate

No account of Hispano-Arabic poetry would be complete without a mention of the various arguments adduced by Romanists (especially) or Arabists to the general premise that the flowering of Romance lyric in the eleventh century was caused or at least influenced by Andalusian poetry in Arabic, and the converse belief that the Hispano-Arabic lyric was influenced in its form and/or content by early Romance poetry or song. The internal evidence for such contamination adduced by proponents of a decisive influence in one direction or the other includes formal similarity between the strophic poetry described above and Hispanic forms like the *villancico*, as well as painstakingly compiled thematic parallels and the possible occurrence of Arabic words in obscure or misunderstood Romance texts. External evidence such as slave girls who might have been captured and brought north of the Pyrenees is no more convincing than the internal evidence adduced so far, and one is thus led to conclude that (1) we will never know; (2) that there is in any case no real anomaly that requires explanation; and therefore (3) we should not waste time on this question.

The Legacy

Besides enriching as it did the corpus of Arabic poetry, at a time—the eleventh, twelfth, and thirteenth centuries—when Arabic literature in the East was going through a period of relative sterility followed by catastrophic decline, the lyric poetry that flourished in al-Andalus for over three centuries has considerable documentary value, as demonstrated in Pérès's invaluable survey. It offers eyewitness accounts of the unique tribal, ethnic, and religious mosaic of Al-Andalus, of popular festivals (including some of Persian origin such as *nawrūz* and *mihrijān*), the life of the palace, street, and bazaar, industry (the poet ar-Ruṣāfī was a weaver of silk), and more of the seamy side of life than in any Eastern poetry (Ibn Quzmān stands out there). New strophic genres were added to the narrow *qaṣīda* form, and Andalusia also produced poet-anthologists to whose labors we owe much of what we know about literary society, the biographies of poets, and a good deal of poetry. Thus Ibn Bassām (d. 1147), whose *al-Dhakhīra fī mahāsin ahl al-jazīra* is (as its name tells us) a treasure-trove of information and poetry; the *Qalā'id al-iqyān*, an anthology by the tendentious Ibn Khāqān (d. 1134 or 1140); or Ibn al-Khatīb (d. 1374), who was a first-rate poet as well and whose anthology *al-Ihāta fī akhbār ahl Gharnata* contains a mine of details about life and poetry in Granada and elsewhere.

T. J. GORTON

Bibliography

Arberry, A. *Moorish Poetry: A Translation of the Pennants: An Anthology Compiled in 1243 by the Andalusian Ibn Sa'id.* Cambridge, 1953.

García Gómez, *Poemas arábigoandaluces.* Madrid, 1940.

Monroe, J. T. *Hispano-Arabic Poetry, a Student Anthology.* Berkeley, 1974.

Nykl, A. R. *Hispano-Arabic Poetry and its Relations with the Old Provençal Troubadours.* Baltimore, 1946; reprt., 1970.

Pérès, H. *La poésie andalouse en arabe classique au 11e siècle.* Paris, 1937.

Stern, S. M. *Hispano-Arabic Strophic Poetry.* Ed. L. P. Harvey. Oxford, 1974.

POETRY, DIDACTIC

A large number of medieval poems have at their foundation a didactic intent; that is, they aim to impart some form of moral or practical instruction. Lessons conveyed by didactic poetry may be of a practical, secular character (for example, advice regarding acceptable modes of social or political conduct) or of a religious nature (for example, instruction relating to questions of devotion and salvation). It should not be surprising, therefore, that much of this poetry was cast by clerkly hands in Alexandrine verse. Indeed, as Alvar and Gómez Moreno indicate, the mere presence of the *Cuaderna vía* (monophymed alexandrine quatrains) was a clear announcement that the poetry at hand was of a didactic, moral type.

Gonzalo de Berceo (c. 1196–c. 1264) wrote three types of poetry—that of the saints' lives, Marian works, and liturgical-doctrinal poems, all of which aspire at some level to instruct the audience. The hagiographic texts (*Vida de San Millán, Vida de Santo Domingo de Silos, Vida de Santa Oria, Martirio de San Lorenzo*) are clearly intended both to offer the positive example of the saint for the audience to emulate and to teach the public devotion to the particular saint, which often includes paying tributes to him; *San Millán*, for example, begins with the claim that the public will gladly render the tributes owed to his monastery upon hearing the poem, and concludes that they will be richly rewarded if they resume payment of the tributes. Like the hagiographic texts, the Marian works (*Duelo que fizo la Virgen*, *Loores de Nuestra Señora*, *Milagros de Nuestra Señora*) have at their center the purpose of instructing the public in devotion to the Virgin, who, Dutton argues, is Our Lady of March at San Millán de Yuso. *Milagros de Nuestra Señora*, the best known and studied of these poems, offers twenty-five miracles relating the fall and the salvation of individuals and illustrating the redemptive role of the Virgin, a role that Berceo invariably highlights at the conclusion of each miracle. The liturgical-doctrinal poems (*Sacrificio de la Misa*, *Himnos*, *Signos del Juicio Final*) are varied in content, but again contain some didactic message. *Signos*, for instance, treats the fifteen signs of the Apocalypse and admonishes "good Christians" in the conclusion that these horrific visions may be avoided by leading better lives, doing penance, and praying.

Three thirteenth-century cuaderna vía poems deal not with the lives of saints but of heroes. *Libro de Alexandre*, a long and complex poem, narrates the life of Alexander the Great, who is unable to dominate his own nature (that is, his arrogance, pride, and lack of restraint), and consequently dies at the hands of a traitor. At the conclusion of the poem, the narrator echoes the *de contemptu mundi* and draws for the audience the lesson to be learned from Alexander's life, instructing them that they should put their faith in God and not in things of this world. In *Libro de Apolonio*, the protagonist represents the opposite of Alexander: a hero who suffers not because of his own sinful nature but because of the persecution of an incestuous and avaricious king; the sinner and his daughter are punished with death and, in the end, the hero is amply rewarded for his constant virtue and faith in God. In the final strophes of the poem the poet makes clear that the audience may find in Apollonius a moral example to be followed. *Poema de Fernán González* is an epic poem that offers in the figure of its hero a model of exemplary Castilian leadership. The extraordinarily devout Fernán González receives divine endorsement for his mission in the form of prophecy (Pelagius promises him victory over the Moors), visions (St. Emilianus and St. Pelagius appear in dreams), and direct intervention (St. James participates in battle).

At the end of the thirteenth and into the early fourteenth centuries, there is a cycle of didactic poetry written in *cuaderna vía* that, Walsh argues, served as a bridge between the earlier *clerezía* (clerical) texts and the *Libro de buen amor*. Many of these poems are homiletic in nature. In *Castigos y ejemplos de Catón*, based on the popular Latin *Disticha Catonis*, Cato offers his son practical and ethical advice against follies such as gambling, money, court proceedings, and astrology. *Proverbios de Salamón*, whose dating is problematic (some argue for composition in the thirteenth century, while others place it in the mid- to late-fourteenth century), derives from Ecclesiastes, which explains its aphoristic character. The poem reflects in many ways the sociopolitical turbulence of the period, focusing on such topics as the relations between the wealthy and the poor and death as the great equalizer. A similar tone is found in *Libro de miseria d'omne*, a poetic adaptation of *De miseria conditionis Humanae* by Innocent III. Perhaps intended for reading at Lent, the *Miseria* encourages its audience through its negative presentation of life, death, and judgment day to abstain from vices and to repent; the poet is especially harsh with regard to social practices such as the abuse of vassals by their lords, the evils of money, the selling of justice, and the abuses of the clergy.

Dating from the first years of the fourteenth century, *Vida de San Alifonso por metros* serves multiple functions. The first of these is common to all hagiographic texts: to inspire veneration of the protagonist, in whom the audience may also find a model to imitate. Ildefonso stands out for his chastity, humility, and most especially his dedication to the Virgin. In addition to instructing the audience to revere Ildefonso, it is clear that the poet intended to illustrate for his audience the importance of Marian devotion as well. The Virgin occupies the position of co-protagonist, appearing to Ildephonsus's mother twice (during her pregnancy and before her death) and to the saint (upon his mother's death), causing him to establish a convent in her honor; Ildefonso later writes a treatise defending her virginity against attacks by nonbelievers, which results in yet another visit by the Virgin. The most clearly didactic function of the poem is its goal of encouraging familial support for a child's decision to enter religious orders. The saint's father initially opposes his son's resolution, while his mother gleefully embraces it, a position which the poet admonishes his audience to follow.

Three poems cast in *cuaderna vía* (*Alhotba arrimada*, *Poema en alabanza de Mahoma,* and *Poema de Yúçuf*) pertain to *aljamiado* literature and may date, as Thompson suggests, to the thirteenth or fourteenth centuries. Of these the most patently didactic is *Alhotba*, a sermon destined for Ramadān. The *Alhotba* derives from the *Sunna* (the Islamic ethical-religious laws and customs), and treats in similar fashion many of the themes found in other didactic poems—notably *Miseria* (see Connolly); and *Castigos* and *Libro de buen amor* (see Thompson).

As Walsh notes, many of the themes (and, indeed, direct passages) of the thirteenth-century *cuaderna vía* are parodied in *Libro de buen amor*, whose inclusion under the heading of didactic poetry is tentative at best. At the beginning of the *Libro* the author instructs the audience to interpret his poem correctly and repeatedly urges the audience to extract the appropriate moral lesson, but he does not aid in this enterprise. He merely states that we must interpret his work according to our understanding, which he repeatedly shows to be variable (for example, the debate of the Greeks and the Romans). The *Libro* includes many of the commonplaces one would expect to find in didactic literature (a treatise on the Seven Deadly Sins, and the evils of money), but these are undercut by the context in which they are found (the Seven Deadly Sins being included in the unsuccessful lover's tirade against Sir Love, and the exposition on money used by Sir Love to illustrate the power of money in amorous pursuits).

Even one of the traditional tools of didactic literature, the *exempla*, is undermined in the *Libro* (for example, the go-between uses *exempla* to lead Doña Endrina into sin rather than away from it). Many scholars have argued that the *Libro* teaches the futility of love through negative example; that is, that the first-person narrator/lover has but fleeting success in his affairs of the heart (as Don Melón, a "fictional" character, and with Doña Garoça, who dies shortly after the affair begins). Whatever the case, it is clear that if the *Libro* has a prescriptive function, it is unlike that of other didactic works.

The end of the fourteenth-century brings with it what may have been the last work written in *cuaderna vía*, *Rimado de Palacio* by Pero López de Ayala. Referred to by its author as a sermon and written in a most somber tone, *Rimado* is a highly didactic work. It includes a confession in which the poet enumerates his sins, social and political criticism that reflects a negative view of contemporary society, a contemplation of the art of governing based on *De regimine principum*, and a long treatise on Job derived from Gregory's *Moralia*.

While a large number of didactic poems were written in *cuaderna vía*, many poets did not avail themselves of this form. Dating from the first half of the thirteenth century, *Vida de Santa María Egipciaca*, cast in *pareados* (paired verses), narrates the life of a prostitute-penitent. The poet's didactic aim is clear from the outset. In the introductory verses he orders the audience to listen attentively, for the story contains a moral lesson: like the sinner-saint, we may save ourselves through repentance.

The most clearly didactic of the debate poems are those that deal with the struggle between the soul and the body, in which the latter is portrayed as a vile prison for the former. The earliest of these, *Disputa del alma y el cuerpo*, written in pareados probably in the late twelfth century, survives only as a fragment. In the fourteenth century there are two versions (*Disputa del cuerpo e del ánimo* and *Revelación de un hermitaño*) of a debate poem in *arte mayor* (dodecasyllabic scansion), which derives not from the earlier Spanish poem but from *Visio Philiberti*. *Tractado del cuerpo e de la ánima* appears at the end of the fifteenth century, and contains a conclusion in which an angel delivers a written condemnation of the two opponents.

The very title of the sole work written in Castilian by the rabbi Santob de Carrión, *Proverbios morales*, indicates the didactic intent of the poem. A contemporary of another moralist, Juan Manuel, Santob describes a world in which man must guide himself through the exercise of caution and moral conduct. The poem aims to speak to two audiences: Pedro I (to whom the poem is dedicated) and his subjects, and, as Perry indicates, the Jewish community (through coded messages).

Much of later didactic poetry treats the topic of death, a common subject throughout Europe in the late Middle Ages owing to the economic, demographic, and emotional devastation produced by the Black Death. *Dança general de la Muerte* dates from the late fourteenth or early fifteenth century, and was later expanded and printed in 1520. The poem pertains to the popular European tradition of the dance of death, and probably derives, directly or indirectly, from the French *danse macabre*. The didactic nature of the poem is evident: it begins with a friar's sermon and ends with promises of repentance by those who have witnessed the horrific dance of the powerful (clergy and lay alike) before death.

Among the best known poems in Spanish is *Coplas que fizo a la muerte de su padre* by Jorge Manrique. The didactic intent of the poet is clear, not only by the choice of subject but by the exhortative tone employed throughout the poem. Like a preacher delivering a sermon, Manrique begins his contemplation of death with an admonition, entreating the soul and the mind to awaken to the fleeting nature of this life and of pleasure and to the certainty of death. He then proceeds with a general consideration of life and death, a review of the fate of the illustrious dead from the recent past, and his father's own encounter with death who, unlike the figure portrayed in the *dança general*, treats him with utmost respect.

As Rico has shown, *Doctrina de la discreçión* (also called *Tractado de la doctrina*) by Pedro de Veragüe dates from the fifteenth century and was inspired by the Catalan *Libre de bons amonestaments* by Anselm Turmeda. Drawing on aphorisms, the *Doctrina* is a work of religious instruction which also offers general moral advice and especially counsels prudence.

As this sampling has shown, the category of didactic poetry is an immense and diverse one encompassing a range of genres—saints' lives, epics, doctrinal works, gnomic literature, debates, elegies, and the *danse macabre*. While the use of the *cuaderna vía* predominates, it is by no means the exclusive metrical form. The poems do, however, share certain characteristics. They teach, for example, by offering positive models for the audience to admire and follow (Apollonius, Fernán González, and saints) or negative ones for them to avoid (Alexander, the incestuous king). They employ many of the same tools (proverbs, exempla), and echoes of the same *topoi* and themes permeate the works (most notably, the *de contemptu mundi*, and *Ubi sunt?*). What ties these poems together is their intent. The poets strive to instruct their audiences on some matter, (practical advice for survival in this world, religious instruction for the soul's redemption in the next), and to this end they avail themselves of many of the same recourses.

JANE E. CONNOLLY

Alvar, C., and A. G. Moreno. *La poesía épica y de clerecía medievales*. Madrid, 1988.

Connolly, J. E. *Transaltion and Poetization in the "Quaderna Vía": Study and Edition of the "Libro de miseria d'omne."* Madison, Wisc., 1986.

Dutton, B. (ed.) *Gonzalo de Berceo: Obras completas I–V*. London, 1967–81.

Perry, T. A. (ed.) *Santob de Carrión: Proverbios morales*. Madison, Wisc., 1986.

Rico, F. "Pedro de Veragüe y fra Anselm Turmeda." *Bulletin of Hispanic Studies 50* (1973), 224–36.

Thompson, B. B. "La *Alhotba arrimada* (o el *Sermón de Rabadán*) y el mester de clerecía." In *Hispanic Studies in Honor of Alan D. Deyermond: A North American Tribute*. Ed. John S. Miletich. Madison Wisc., 1986. 279–89.

Walsh, J. K. "Juan Ruiz and the *mester de clerezía*: Lost Context and Lost Parody in the *Libro de buen amor*," *Romance Philology* 33 (1979–80), 62–87.

POETRY, HEBREW AND JEWISH ROMANCE

Hebrew Poetry

Medieval Hebrew poetry may be classified as either "secular" or "religious," with the latter further subdivided as liturgical (intended for recitation in services) or personal religious expression of the poet. "Religious" poetry (*piyyuṭ*) dates at least to the Talmudic era (fourth century or earlier), as a separate literary genre; of course, such poetry is found already in the Bible. "Secular" Hebrew poetry, on the other hand, originated in al-Andalus directly under Arabic influence not earlier than the middle of the tenth century. The first generation of poets introduced both Arabic meter and themes into their innovation of Hebrew poetry. As early as the eleventh century, Samuel ibn Naghrīllah created many additional meters not found in Arabic poetry and greatly expanded the themes used. Subsequent generations of poets expanded somewhat on these, but generally followed the "classical" forms already set by the Hebrew poets of Muslim Spain.

Hebrew meter, like Arabic, is "quantitative" (based on long and short phoneme elements), with the line divided into two hemistichs (not, however, a cesura, since the division is not of meaning but rather of elements, and can even come in the middle of a word). Rhyme is dictated, to a degree, by the nature of Semitic words. It is untrue that early classical Hebrew poetry was entirely monorhyme; *some* of that poetry was, but a great deal of it (including most of Ibn Naghrīllah) already shows considerable variation.

Themes employed by the Hebrew poets include friendship poems, praise of patrons or famous men, wine (praise of wine-drinking parties), love (of men or women), war (only Ibn Naghrīllah), nature, the vicissitudes of fate, longing for Zion, and so on. There are many uniquely individual themes found in the poetry of the most outstanding poets.

Great care was used in composing poems, with at least equal attention given to form and content. The beautiful opening line was particularly praised—a line that expressed a complete thought and set the tone to follow. Biblical style was used but not slavishly imitated (again, contrary to the belief of some experts, classical Hebrew poetry was extremely innovative in vocabulary and did not merely copy biblical terms). Allusions to lines of other poets, perhaps even citation, was allowed, but actual plagiarism was severely criticized.

In addition to biblical phrases or images, Talmudic and Midrashic literature served as sources, and particularly Arabic poetry and literary ideals. New Hebrew words were coined based on adaptation from Arabic, or were given new meanings in light of Arabic cognates. In many Hebrew poems of the classical period (Muslim Al-Andalus), it is possible to discover actual Arabic sources or similar expressions. Judah ha Levy is known to have translated, sometimes modifying and improving, some Arabic poems.

The names of well over one hundred Hebrew poets of Spain are known, but poetry has not survived for the majority of them. Some of the most important Hebrew poets whose work has survived include: Dunash Ibn Labraṭ, Isaac ibn Khalfun, Joseph ibn Abitur, Samuel ibn Naghrīllah (all of the tenth and eleventh centuries); Solomon ibn Gabirol, Isaac ibn Ghiyāth, Levy ibn al-Tabban, Moses Ibn ʿEzra, Judah Halevi, Abraham ibn ʿEzra (eleventh and twelveth centuries); Judah al-Ḥarizi, Meshullam de Piera, Ṭodros Abulafia (thirteenth and fourteenth centuries). After the fourteenth century, poetry shifted primarily to Aragón-Catalonia, although there certainly was no "school" of Hebrew poets in Girona, as has been erroneously suggested. Important fourteenth- and fifteenth-century poets included Solomon de Piera (who also exchanged Hebrew poetry with Christians), Vidal Benveniste (de la Caballería), and Solomon Bonafed.

The audience for Hebrew poetry was simply the Jewish people in its entirety, chiefly in Spain, but also in Provence and as far away as Yemen. There is no evidence that these poems were "sung," as sometimes claimed, but they may have been recited orally. Certainly, and primarily, they were read and copied, and manuscripts circulated widely. Again, contrary to a common myth, the Hebrew poets were not "court poets"; they belonged to no aristocratic class and only rarely composed panegyrics for a patron. Few, if any, were professional poets who made a living from their poetry. Knowledge of, and ability to compose, poetry spread quickly among all levels of Jewish society. Common letters and numerous writings of Spanish Jews attest to this. Even children became proficient in poetry, and of course the love poems addressed to boys shows that they understood the often sophisticated language. The rabbi Solomon ibn Adret writes that he knew a boy in Lérida who, although he could not read, could compose poetry.

Jewish Romance Poetry

The earliest example of the use of Romance in poetry is to be found in the *muwashshaḥāt*, a special kind of strophic poem of definite meter and length with the final couple (*kharja*) either in Romance or Arabic, or a combination of the two. This form of poetry began among the Muslims of Al-Andalus in the tenth century and was quickly imitated by Hebrew poets. There are many erroneous and unfounded theories about this type of poetry.

Probably the first Jewish poet to write in actual Romance (that is, Spanish), however, was Shem Ṭov de Carrión, whose *Proverbios Morales* has been called the first "absolute poetry" (non-epic) in Spanish. (Prior to this, some Jews, and also women, had written in Arabic.) Moses ibn Zarzal, physician to Enrique III, wrote a Spanish poem on the birth of Juan II. Astruch Rimokh (early fifteenth century) sent a Catalan verse composition to Solomon de Piera (who satirized him, nevertheless, for not writing in Hebrew). Piera also refers to Catalan poems by Moses Abbas. There are also some anonymous Judeo-Catalan (or Provençal) secular and wedding poems of the fourteenth and fifteenth centuries. Mention should also be made of the apparently fifteenth-century (if not, in fact, later) Judeo-Spanish *Coplas de Yoçef.*

Hebrew Poetics

An important contribution of medieval Hebrew poets lies in the various works on poetics they composed. Unlike similar Arabic works, which were written entirely by non-poets and thus are of limited value, these works give real insight into both the historical development and aesthetic standards of Hebrew poetry. The most important such work, now available in an excellent Arabic edition and Spanish translation, is Moses ibn ʿEzra's *Kitāb al-muḥādara*. Other important sources include various works of Abraham ibn ʿEzra, Abraham and Yedaya Bedersi, and Shem Ṭov ibn Falquerah, the *Takhemoni* of Judah al-Ḥarizi, and many others. (Abraham Bedersi, a Provençal Hebrew poet, is particularly interesting because of his unique knowledge of contemporary Christian poets.)

Spanish Hebrew poetry already influenced similar developments in Egypt, North Africa, Yemen, and elsewhere prior to the Expulsion, and afterward this tradition continued to some extent, but Hebrew poetry has never again achieved the heights reached in medieval Spain.

NORMAN ROTH

Bibliography

Carmi, T. (ed. and tr.) *The Penguin Book of Hebrew Verse*. New York, 1981. The best anthology; unfortunately incomplete versions.

Roth, N. "'Deal Gently with the Young Man'—Love of Boys in Medieval Hebrew Poetry of Spain." *Speculum* 57 (1982), 20–51.

———. "The Lyric Tradition in Hebrew Secular Poetry of Medieval Spain." *Hispanic Journal* 2 (1981), 7–26.

———"Panegyric Poetry of Ibn Gabirol: Translations and Analysis." *Hebrew Studies* 25 (1984), 62–81.

Valle Rodríguez, C. del. (tr.) *El Divan poético de Dunash ben Labrat*. Madrid, 1988. The most complete study of Hebrew meter.

POETRY, IMPROVISED

There is no direct evidence for orally improvised poetry in Hispano-Romance during the Middle Ages and there is only one witness in Hispano-Arabic. Monroe has studied a brief improvised poetic duel dating from the eleventh century, at the latest, and very possibly from the tenth. The insulting verses, recorded in Ibn Ḥayyān's *Kitāb al-Muqtabis*, were purportedly shouted from a fortress wall by a supporter of the Hispano-Christian rebel, Ibn Ḥafṣūn, and were immediately answered in verse by a mule driver in the besieging army of the future caliph, ʿAbd al-Raḥmān III. They are the earliest known verses in Colloquial Hispano-Arabic. Such aggressive versified exchanges represent the Arabic *ḥijā'* genre of improvised poetic invective. The custom of a competitive exchange of improvised rhymed insults (*echarse pullas*) is known in Castilian from the early sixteenth century and the related forms *repullar* and *repullón* already figure in the mid-fifteenth-century *Cancionero de Baena*. The custom of improvised poetic competition is known today throughout the Hispanic world, in Basque, Spanish, Portuguese, and Catalán, and on both sides of the Atlantic, while analogous competitions have also been recorded from France and Italy. The thirteenth-century

Sicilian *Contrasto*, written by Cielo d'Alcamo, may represent a literary re-creation of just such an improvised exchange. Similar practices in Latin are commented upon by classical authors (Horace, among them) and there is evidence for the same custom among various ancient peoples. Given such early parallels, as well as the widespread survival of poetic improvisation among modern Hispanic peoples, we would be ill-advised to disclaim its probable existence among Hispano-Romance speakers during the Middle Ages.

SAMUEL G. ARMISTEAD

Bibliography

Armistead, S. G. "La poesía oral improvisada en la tradición hispánica." In *La décima popular*. Ed. M. Trapero. Las Palmas, Grand Canary Island, 1994.

Crawford, J. P. W. "*Echarse pullas*: A popular form of *Tenzone*," *Romanic Review* 6 (1915), 141–55.

Monroe, J. T. "Which Came First, the *Zajal* or the *Muwashshaḥa*?" *Oral Tradition* 4 (1989), 75–90.

POETRY, SPANISH LYRIC

Lyric poetry, as its name suggests, involves elements of music, and so contains rhythm, expressive sounds, and emotional appeal. It may take the form of an independent composition, be a passage in a long poem (for example, the epic), or merely constitute part of a Spanish *kharja* (early woman's song) thus serving in a refrain to an Arabic or Hebrew poem.

Few traces of pre-thirteenth-century Spanish lyric poetry remain. Although Jimena's prayer on behalf of her husband, el Cid (in the *Cantar de Mio Cid*, ca.1200) is not entirely lyric, it may serve as an early example of an emotion portrayed in verse form. This semilyric was preserved because it was shielded by the epic in which it appears. Another instance of the "shielded" lyric is the May song, "El mes era de mayo," buried in the *Libro de Alexandre* (c.1250).

Religious poetry and song—such as Gonzalo de Berceo's early-thirteenth-century *Milagros de Nuestra Señora* or his *Duelo de la Virgen*—have been better preserved than popular lyrics, though profane works in prose were often relieved of monotony by the insertion of such poems as the doleful "Profeçía de Casandra," or the love laments of Troilo and his lady Briseida and their grief at the prospect of parting in *Historia troyana* (c.1270) thus preserving these lyric poems in a prose context.

Lyric narrative is well exemplified in the anonymous early thirteenth-century *Razón feita d'amor*: love is the theme, springtime the setting. Wine and cool water blend with the fragrance of flowers. Lines vary in length, and they all rhyme, but without a set pattern.

The principal reason, apparently, for the paucity of learned lyric poetry in the early period is that poets preferred to employ the Galician Portuguese language, in vogue during the twelfth to the early fourteenth centuries.

The *Libro de buen amor*, attributed to Juan Ruiz, Archpriest of Hita (c.1283–c.1350), begins with a verse prayer followed by lyrical *gozos*, poems in praise of St. Mary, which together indicate that in Spanish lyric verse measure, both octosyllabic and heptasyllabic, as well as varying line-length strophe forms including the *copla de pie quebrado* (stanzas containing half-lines), were fully developed. The prayers and religious songs that relieve the monotony of heavy topics in *Rimado de palacio* by the melancholy Pero López de Ayala (1332–1407), contain strophes in octosyllabic verse and some *coplas de arte mayor* (eight-line stanzas of six-plux-six-syllable verse patterned (Ú) $\acute{-}$ UU $\acute{-}$ (U)/(U) $\acute{-}$ UU $\acute{-}$ (U), with the restriction that syllables five and six may not both be omitted, thus relieving the monotony of the *cuaderna vía* (seven-plus-seven-syllable monorhymed quatrains) and foreshadowing their fifteenth-century predominance in Spanish poetry. (Verse lengths here are given according to Spanish measure, which involves, as appropriate, synalepha, hiatus, syneresis, and dieresis.)

Juan Ruiz's young contemporary, Alfonso XI (1314?–1350), offers further evidence of Spanish employed as a lyric medium: his *cantiga* (song) beginning "Em hum tiempo cogi flores" appears in the Galician Portuguese *Cancioneiro da Vaticana*.

Popular verse is found in the *cossaute* (dance song) by Diego Hurtado de Mendoza (c.1340–1404); monorhymed couplets in oxytonic verse vary in length from nine to twelve syllables. Each couplet is followed by the heptasyllabic refrain.

The major impetus to the development of Spanish lyric verse occurred during the reign of Juan II (1405–1454), at whose court poetry recitation and singing apparently constituted principal forms of entertainment. Much of this verse composition has been preserved in the *Cancionero de Baena* (c.1440), compiled by Juan Alfonso de Baena, which contains works of at least sixty poets. A few selections are in Galician Portuguese. Topics vary from those of love for one's lady to devotion to St. Mary to those of local and general interest. The poet-for-hire Alfonso Álvarez de Villasandino (c.1350–1424) is the most prolific, and one of the earliest poets featured in the collection; his topics range from the pious to the obscene. Other lyric poets include Baena himself, Ferrán Manuel de Lando, Francisco Imperial, and the lovelorn Macías, who is less worthy of note for his poetry than for the romantic love legend his life engendered.

Independent of court activity, Ĭñigo López de Mendoza, Marqués de Santillana (1398–1458) introduced the Italianate sonnet with his *Sonetos fechos at itálico modo*, closely related to a certain *arte mayor* form in the *Cancionero de Baena*—that is, a poem consisting of an octave rhyming ABBAACCA, plus a quatrain rhyming ACCA. Santillana's highly learned style gave direction to a trend in poetic composition that gradually led to the stylized, mannered verse known as Gongorism.

Santillana's contemporaries Juan de Mena (1411–1456), author of the allegorical *Laberinto de la Fortuna*, and Jorge Manrique (1440–1479), whose unforgettable *Coplas por la muerte de su padre*, on the equalizing power of death, are the major mid-century lyric poets.

The medieval period ends with the appearance of the earliest known treatise on Spanish metrics: *Arte de poesía castellana*, included in Juan del Encina's *Cancionero* (1496).

DOROTHY CLOTELLE CLARKE

Bibliography

Clarke, D. C. *Early Spanish Lyric Poetry: Essays and Selections*. New York, n.d.

López Estrada, F. *Introducción a la literatura medieval española*. 5th ed. Madrid, 1990.

POETRY, SPANISH, LYRIC, TRADITIONAL

In a conference in 1919, Menéndez Pidal encouraged literary historians to investigate the popular lyric of the Middle Ages, whose influence he had glimpsed through the *cantigas de amigo*, a few citations from fifteenth-century *cancioneros* (Song books), Renaissance and Baroque adaptations, and imitations from Gil Vicente to Lope de Vega. From this spark of interest were born anthologies that have progressively enriched our knowledge of this field, including collections by J. M. Blecua and Dámaso Alonso (1956), J. M. Alín (1968), and M. Frenk (1987).

Since then, our perspective on popular poetry has changed a great deal. For one, the *Kharjas* (vestiges of women's songs preserved in Hispano-Arabic poetry), the first link in the traditional lyric's development, have been discovered. Scholars have systematically explored Galician-Portuguese, Castilian, and Catalan texts and have studied their content, form, and themes, while in other European literatures such interest has disappeared with the progressive abandonment of traditionalist theories of the origins of the lyric. After these developments, several facts worth taking into account were clarified: like other Romance literature, lyric poetry has very old roots, and is divided into different schools that share some essential characteristics but also differ in more than just a few aspects. It undergoes a marked chronological evolution that doesn't cease until between the fifteenth and eighteenth centuries with the origin of modern folklore, which itself displays traces of the popular lyric. But above all, we must emphasize the fact that there are very few medieval Spanish texts preserved, and the majority date from the fifteenth century.

Essentially, the popular lyric is a poetic mode first recorded around 1500 by the polyphonists (*Cancionero musical de Palacio, Cancionero de Upsala*, and later Juan Vásquez), and continuing with the sixteenth-century *vihuelistas* (Luis Milán, Alonso Mudarra, Luis de Narváez, and Enríquez de Valderrábano). But if these musicians were interested above all in the melody of the lyric, which they adapted to string accompaniment or to polyphonic modes that were then in vogue, there were at the same time poets who were attracted to the lyric's enchantment, and who then attempted to imitate or re-create its allure. The earliest of these was apparently Gil Vicente, but the best poets of the sixteenth and seventeenth centuries also glossed and imitated popular verses: some were interpreted *a lo divino* (given a religious interpretation) by mystical and religious poets, while others served as points of departure for more than a few theatrical works, like Lope de Vega's *El caballero de Olmedo* and *El galán de la Membrilla*, or Tirso de Molina's *La dama del olivar*. It is, therefore, a poetic trend of the Golden Age whose medieval precedents can be reconstructed to a certain point, but only following French and Galician-Portuguese texts.

In terms of form, the popular lyric consists of two- or three-verse *estribillos* (refrains; also called *villancicos*) accompanied at times by glosses of a learned nature, and less often by more popular glosses. The gloss tended to follow the *zéjel* model (a two-verse stanza with estribillo typical of the Galician-Portuguese school and found only—and rarely—in the fifteenth century). Its style is dominated by what we now consider basic vocabulary of the language, with approaches both affectionate (dimunitives, terms like *amigo*, *amor*, *vida*, *madre*, *corazón*, etc.), and intuitive rhetorical questions, exclamations, simple phrases, use of juxtaposition. The limited descriptive elements usually portray the physical landscape, but in a symbolic manner.

In terms of content, the texts are usually put in the voices of women discussing love. Most important, the subject matter selected generally appears to be truncated, without antecedents, without consequences, and without a logical solution for the situation presented in the poem, whose interpretation depends on the cultural background of the reader: "¿Qué me queréis, caballero? / Casada soy, marido tengo. ["What do you wish, Sir? I am married and have a husband."] For those readers familiar with earlier poetry and its subtle conception of emotions and passions (courtly love, Petrarchism), the popular lyric's direct expressions of love, with little repression or shame, prove quite surprising, as do its aspirations for sexual satisfaction. The obstacles to this fulfillment, which generally make up the thematic content of the poem, come from the amigo (the often unfaithful, absent, or deceiving man with whom the woman has fallen in love) or from society (family, war). The young woman voices the pain caused by her situation ("La media noche es pasada / e no viene; / sabedme si hay otra amada / que lo detiene." ["Midnight has passed / and he does not come; / would that I knew if he has another lover / who detains him."]) or dreams of regaining her freedom ("Agora que soy niña / quiero alegría, / que no se sirve Dios / de mi monjía". ["Now that I am still a young girl / I want joy, / God will not gain / if I become a nun."]).

Unlike the tradition of erudite, refined love poetry, the popular lyric frequently expresses happiness, exaltation, the yearning for satisfaction, and the memory of pleasure. Its authors seem to be envisioning a society without repression, where no desire remains unfulfilled; they do so, however, through symbols that shroud the meaning, even for the attentive reader. The spring, river, and stream, settings for the romantic encounter, are enough to evoke this poetic reality ("en la fuente del rosel, / lavan la niña y el doncel." ["In the fountain of the rosebush / the young girl and the young man wash."]); flowers tend to express the fulfillment of love ("Ya florecen los árboles, Juan; / mala seré de guardar." ["Juan, the trees are in bloom; I'll be difficult to keep."]) and, like strands of hair carried away by the breeze, the loss of virginity ("Estos mis cabellos, madre / dos a dos me los lleva el aire." ["These my tresses, mother / the wind blows two by two."] The most omnipresent element, though, is vegetation as a force of nature ("Dentro en el vergel / moriré; / dentro en el rosal / matarm'han," ["Down in the glade / I will die; / down among the rosebushes / they will kill me."] or the well-known "De los álamos vengo, madre / de ver cómo los menea el aire." ["I come from among the poplars, / from seeing how the wind rustles them."])

These elements also frequently represent failed attempts at love, suggesting love's difficulties ("Aquellas sierras, madre, / altas son de subir; / corrían los caños / daban en el torongil." ["Those mountains, mother, / are tall to climb; / the streams ran down, ran down to the lemon garden."]), the sorrows of the present ("Miraba la mar, / la malcasada, / que miraba la mar / cómo es ancha y larga." ["She looked at the sea, / the unhappily married one, / she look at the sea, / how it is wide and / long"]), despair ("Vi los barcos, madre, / vilos y no me vale, ["I saw the ships, mother, I saw them to no avail"), pleas for help ("Aires de mi tierra, / vení y llevadme, / qu'estoy en tierra axena, 'no tengo a nadiel." ["Breezes from home / come and take me / I am in an alien land and have no one"]), or profound hopelessness ("Van y vienen las olas, madre, / a las orillas del mar: / mi pena con las que vienen, / mi bien con las que se van." ["The waves come and go, mother / on the shores of the sea; my grief with those that come, / my happiness with those that go."]).

Some images deserve separate mention, such as the metaphoric use of falconry ("Mal ferida va la garça. / Sola va y gritos daba." ["The heron takes wing badly wounded. / She flies off crying out"]), revisited later by San Juan de la Cruz ("Tras de un amoroso lance, / y no de esperanza falto / volé tan alto, tan alto, / que le di a la caza alcance." ["After an amorous affair, / and not without hope / I flew so high, so high, / that I reached my prey"]). The night, however, stands out as the most important symbol of the popular lyric, expressing the solitude and insomnia caused by love ("Estas noches atan largas / para mí / no solían ser ansi." ["These nights so long / for me / used never to be like that"]); the hope brought by dawn ("¡Quándo salireis, alba galana! / ¡Quándo saliréis, el alba!" ["When you rise, oh beautiful down / when you rise, oh dawn"]); the eagerness with which the lovers await their encounter ("Salga la luna, el caballero, / salga la luna y vámonos luego. ["Let the moon come out, the gentleman, / let the moon come out and we depart"]); desire ("Besáme y abraçáme, / marido mío . . ." ["Kiss me, embrace me, / oh husband of mine"]); or ambiguous dreams ("En la peña, sobre la peña, / duerme la niñá y sueña." ["On the cliff, over the cliff, / the young girl sleeps and dreams"]). Expressions of pleasure and of elegiac nostalgia usually dominate this genre.

At the same time, however, less serious compositions treating the love lyric's components as a joke are not lacking. Sometimes these verses make fun of the general situation ("Por qué me besó Perico, / por qué me besó el traidor?" ["why did Perico kiss me, / why did the traitor kiss me?"]); in other cases, they ridicule the poem's dearest symbols, including water ("Al pasar el arroyo / le vi las piernas, / ¡Ay la puta bellaca, / y qué blancas que eran." ["On crossing the stream / I saw her legs / Ah, the cunning old whore, / and oh they were so white"]) and the wind ("Levantóse un viento / que de la mar salía / y alçome las faldas / de la mi camisa." ["A wind rose up / that came from the sea / and lifted up the flaps of my shirt"]). Occasionally the popular lyric presents the reader with a direct exaltation of the beauty of the body that is rare in Spanish literature ("No me las enseñes más / que me matarás. / Estávase la monja / en el monesterio, / sus tetitas blancas / de so el velo negro . . ." ["Don't show them to me again, / you will kill me. // The nun was in her monastery, her little white breasts / under the black veil"]).

Because of its expressive qualities and its thematic focus, the popular lyric interested more than just philologists. Francisco Asenjo Barbieri's 1890 publication of the *Cancionero musical de Palacio* resulted in that collection's availability among the poets of the so-called Generation of 27 (Lorca Alberti and others), and helped them become acquainted with traditional poetry's merits. The rhythm and dramatism of one of the collection's poems ("En Avila, mis ojos, / dentro en Avila. // En Avila del Rio / mataron a mi amigo, / dentro en Avila." ["In Avila, my eyes, / inside Avila. // In Avila of the River / they killed my lover"]) likely inspired one of the compositions from Rafael Alberti's *Marinero en tierra* ("Mi corza, buen amigo, / mi corza blanca. // Los lobos la mataron / al pie del agua." ["My roe, good friend, my white roe. // The wolves killed her at the edge of the water"]).

Vicenç Beltrán

Bibliography

Alonso, D., and Blecua, J. M. *Antología de la poesía española. Lírica de tipo tradicional.* 2d. rev. ed. Madrid, 1964.

Beltrán, V. *La canción tradicional de la Edad de Oro.* Barcelona, 1990.

———. "*O vento lh'as levava*: Don Denis y la tradición lírica peninsular," *Bulletin Hispanique*, 86 (1984) 5–25.

Frenk, M. *Corpus de la antigua lírica popular hispánica (siglos XV a XVII).* Madrid, 1987.

Morales Blouin, E. *El ciervo y la fuente. Mito y folklore del agua en la lírica tradicional.* Madrid, 1981.

Rogers, E. R. *The Perilous Hunt.* Lexington, Ky., 1980.

Reckert, S. *Lyra minima: Structure and Symbol in Iberian Traditional Verse.* London, 1970.

Sánchez Romeralo, A. *El villancico. Estudios sobre la lírica popular en los siglos XV y XVI.* Madrid, 1969.

POETRY, VERNACULAR, POPULAR, AND LEARNED, ARABIC EPIC

The fundamental role played by oral narrators and *juglares* (minstrels) in the transmission of epic poetry as an outwardly projected expression of the world is well known. In this context, it is important to remember that the historical Cid, in his half-Moorish Valencian court, listened not only to jugalres in Romance but also in Arabic. We also know through Ibn Bassām's testimony that the Cid listened with great admiration and passion to epics about the valiant Moors.

In el Cid's Valencian court, a hybrid of Christian and Moorish *juglaría*, Romance juglares would also have learned Arabic epic poems. In fact, a comparative analysis of Arabic narrative and Castilian epic reveals, firstly, a series of thematic motifs common to both traditions. This is not so much a question of looking for literary models that may have influenced Castilian epic, but rather for shared myths, beliefs, social behavior, ideas, and manifestations (internal and external) of chivalry: in short, the unique poetic code which the Castilian juglares have been able to echo.

The first shared characteristic associated with the chivalric spirit that stands out is the tradition of giving a proper name to the knight's weapon. This practice responds to a concrete historical reality in the Arabic world, while in the Romance epic it is a mere literary device. This nominalization is without doubt related to the Arabic belief that words possessed magical strength. This leads to the Muslim warrior's practice of reciting before combat a few *coplas* (verses) that exalted his own strengths, thereby fulfilling the ritual of *faqhr*, or boasting, that was inherent in the Arabic knight's character. The thematic coincidence here highlights the existential approach to Arabic life that is later transferred to the Castilian epic.

The Muslim influence also sheds light on the very concept of the war against the infidel, which was conceived according to the doctrine of *jihād*, or holy war, as Américo Castro has emphasized. Another crucial element in this type of war is the presence of the angel Gabriel—Jibril, among the Arabs—who appears to the warrior in critical moments, warning him of danger and giving counsel necessary to achieve victory. Also important are the war strategies and schemes that are inherent talents of the Muslim paladin.

Many other characteristics of Arabic origin can also be recognized in the epic, such as: the presence of the woman in war, or the motif of the woman of noble lineage who comforts the captive, both evident in Arabic life and literature; falling in love by hearsay, which follows doctrines of love collected by the poet Ibn Ḥazm de Córdoba; birds as good omens, related to Arabic rules of divination; and treacherous letters commanding the recipient to kill the carrier, a frequent theme in Arabic tradition. Moreover, the disconcerting realism and historicity of the Castilian epic, concentrating on the human condition of the hero instead of his mythic qualities, are made to fit the Arabic models, as are the hero's burden of tolerance and his democratic aspirations; all is made to fit the framework of an irregular meter similar to the Arabic *rajaz* (rhymed prose), which differs from the *qaṣīda* (ode) in the same way as the Castilian *mester de juglaría* and *mester de clerecía*.

To summarize, the Castilian epic could very well have originated from echoes of the Germanic epic. Without doubt, however, it could not have come into existence without the strong decisive mark made by the Arabic chivalric epic. The resulting product, then, is a Mudéjar epic—the equivalent of an embroidered cloth interwoven with Western and Moorish threads.

ALVARO GALMÉS DE FUENTES

Bibliography

Castro, A. *La realidad & histórica de España*. Mexico City, 1966. 419.

Galmés de Fuentes, A. *Épica aŕabe y épica castellana*. Barcelona, 1978.

POETRY, VERNACULAR, POPULAR, AND LEARNED: CANCIONEIROS OF PORTUGAL

The amorous and satirical lyrics composed by Portuguese and Galician poets during a period extending from roughly the end of the twelfth to the middle of the fourteenth centuries are preserved in three major collections, known as *cancioneiros*: *Cancioneiro da Biblioteca Nacional*, *Cancioneiro da Vaticana*, and *Cancioneiro da Ajuda*, which were all brought to light in the nineteenth century. The term derives from Old French *cançoner*, forerunner of Modern French *chansonnier*. The initials that best respect the shelf markings of these collections are *CBN*, *CV*, and *CA*, although some scholars, considering C a superfluous reference to *cancioneiro*, find these abbreviations cumbersome. The proliferation of manuscripts, characteristic of the poetic tradition in medieval France and Italy, is unknown on the Iberian Peninsula, where there normally is only one manuscript, kept in a royal or monastic library.

The *CBN* contains the largest collection by far. Copied down in Italy around 1500 under the direction of the Italian humanist Angelo Colocci, it was discovered by Costantino Corvisieri and Enrico Molteni in the library of the Counts of Brancuti in Cagli. The diplomatic edition, prepared by Molteni, bears the names of the former owners of the manuscript, *Il canzoniere Portoghese Colocci Brancuti*. Published in 1880, it covers only those poems that are not included in the *CV*. The manuscript was later owned by Ernesto Monaci, whose heirs donated it to the Portuguese government in 1924. It is now kept in the National Library of Lisbon. The *CBN* contains a total of 1,567 poems along with a fragmentary *Poética*, which establishes the traditional division of the lyrics into *cantigas* (songs) *de amor*, *cantigas de amigo*, and *cantigas de escarnho* or *maldizer*. The eight-volume Machado edition of the *CBN*, published from 1949 to 1964, is of limited usefulness.

The *CV* manuscript, (Codex Vat. Lat. 4803) was discovered in the Vatican Library by a Portuguese clergyman, Padre J. I. Roquete. It is not known whether Angelo Colocci played a supervisory role in the preparation of this manuscript, copied down in Italy during the late fifteenth or early sixteenth century. The attributions and some of the marginal notes have been traced to Colocci's handwriting, but not the texts themselves. The *CV* manuscript has reached us in a less than perfect state; the initial 390 poems are missing, and there are additional *lacunae*. Partial editions were put together by Varnhagen and Monaci, and a diplomatic edition: *Il canzoniere Portoghese della Biblioteca Vaticana*, was published by Monaci in 1875. Teófilo Braga's 1878 critical edition: *Cancioneiro portuguez da Vaticana*, is unsatisfactory; the accompanying glossary is particularly poor.

The *CA* is the oldest and most reliable of the three major codices and the only one that was copied down in Portugal. Published together with the *Nobiliario do Conde de Barcelos*, the *CA* is incomplete, containing only 310 cantigas without indication of authorship. Colocci's inventory, the *Tavola Colocciana*, permits the attribution of 288 compositions to thirty-two known poets, and Carolina Michaëlis attributes the remaining twenty-two poems to six unidentified authors. Spaces left blank may have been intended for musical notations. The numerical arrangement of the *CA* material corresponds to that of the *CBN* up until numbers 242–45, though with lacunae. The *CA* shares fifty-six poems with the *CV*, 189 with the *CBN*, and is the repository of sixty-four cantigas not transmitted elsewhere. Only the *cantiga de amor* genre is represented. From the place of its discovery, the manuscript was initially labeled *Cancioneiro do Colégio dos Nobres*. It was later transferred to the Biblioteca Real in the vicinity of the Ajuda palace, hence its definitive designation. The early history of the codex is unknown, but it is generally assumed that the manuscript never left Portugal. Partial editions of the *CA* material were put together by Lord Stuart, C. F. Bellermann, and F. A. de Varnhagen. The subtitle to Varnhagen's 1849 edition, *O livro das cantigas do Conde de Barcellos*, is noteworthy in that it bears witness to the editor's belief in single authorship, but the Count of Barcelo's role as a mere compiler of cantigas has since been definitively established. The fate of his collection, bequeathed to the king of Castile, is unknown. These early works are superseded by Carolina Michaëlis's monumental 1904 edition: *Cancioneiro da Ajuda: Edicão crítica e commentada*. Henry H. Carter provided a diplomatic edition in 1941.

The *Tavola Colocciana*, containing an inventory of authors, put together by Colocci, is preserved in

Codex Vat. 3217. The names are preceded by numbers ranging from 1 to 1675 and coinciding with the numbers and attributions proposed by the *CBN*.

The discovery of the *Pergaminho Vindel* lends support to Gustav Gröber's *Liederblätter* (broadside theory), in terms of which medieval poetry was transmitted through *rotuli* or fly leaves, containing all the poems written by each individual author and executed or ordered executed by him for propaganda purposes. Serving as cover for a codex of Cicero's *De Officiis*, this manuscript, containing all seven cantigas by Martin Codax, was discovered in 1914 by the Madrid librarian Pedro Vindel, who published a photographic reproduction in 1915, but the manuscript itself has since been lost. Related to the *CA* in graphical representation, the manuscript may date back to 1300, but is not necessarily the original. Not only does the *Pergamintro Vindel* offer concrete proof of Gröber's Liederblätter theory, but it also holds great importance as the only manuscript to provide musical notations.

The existence of Liederblätter, the uniformity of the manuscripts, and the formal perfection of the poems point to written transmission of the poetry. We may conclude that the cantigas were copied down in carefully executed rotuli for each individual poet, then inserted into cancioneiros.

FREDE JENSEN

Bibliography

Jensen, F. *The Earliest Portuguese Lyrics*. Odense, 1978.

Michaëlis de Vasconcelos, C. *Cancioneiro da Ajuda*. Halle, 1904.

Pellegrini, S. *Repertorio bibliografico della prima lirica portoghese*, Modena, 1939.

Tavani, G. "La tradizione manoscritta della lirica galego-portoghese," *Cultura Neolatina* 27 (1967), 41–94.

———. *Poesia del duecento nella penisola iberica*. Rome, 1969.

POETRY, VERNACULAR, POPULAR, AND LEARNED: CANCIONEROS OF SPAIN

Spanish court poetry of the late Middle Ages is preserved in often substantial manuscript anthologies which were compiled from about 1430 onward. These books, of which some sixty contemporary examples survive, are known as *cancioneros*, (literally, "songbooks," "collections of *canciones*") though none of the early manuscripts contains musical notation, and few give precedence to the *canción*, a short lyric with initial *estribillo*. In the 1480s the first printed cancioneros began to appear, culminating in the enormous *Cancionero general* of 1511. The term "*poesía de cancionero*" or "*cancioneril*," therefore, refers to all the extant court poetry of a 150-year period, from the end of the fourteenth to the beginning of the fifteenth century, a corpus of several thousand poems, written by over five hundred named poets. Almost all of this verse was written in castilian, even by poets of a different linguistic background, like the Catalan Pedro Torrellas, and the Portuguese Juan Manuel. Catalan poetry was collected separately, but no contemporary manuscripts of Portuguese verse survive.

The extraordinary proliferation of poetic collections, on a scale unprecedented in the Iberian Peninsula, has been taken to mark the sudden flowering of Castilian court lyric after two centuries of dominance by the Galician-Portuguese. It would perhaps be safer to say that the survival of so much verse is more an index of consumer interest, or increased literacy, than of heightened productivity. Nonetheless, poetry obviously enjoyed a renewed vogue in the fifteenth century, playing a significant part in the cultural life of the courts and the courtship practices of the individual.

The Poetry

The term "*cancionero* poetry" is often generally used to refer to all forms of love poetry characteristic of the period. This includes various types of lyriconarrative poems (love allegories, dream-visions, *serranillas*), as well as the short lyric canción and the long amorous *dezir* or *coplas*. In fact, the heterogeneity of fifteenth-century verse cannot be overemphasized. It embraces a wide variety of subjects and treatments, including debate poems, disquisitions on moral or doctrinal themes, personal invective, political satire, and misogynist diatribe. The categories of religious verse alone range from Marian hymns to long narrative meditations on the life and Passion of Christ, shading over, rather disturbingly, into amorous parodies of the mass and other liturgical devotions. The poetry of burlesque and bawdy, little known from manuscripts, is elevated to prominence by a special section of *obras de burlas* (works in jest) at the end of the *Cancionero general*, and in its offshoot, the *Cancionero de obras de burlas provocantes a risa* (Valencia, 1519).

Much of this verse was occasional, commemorating events of national importance or trivial incidents at court. And most of it may have been performed, in improvised games, competitions, or semitheatrical entertainments. It is difficult to be sure that even the more intimate poems were intended for private reading rather than public display. Some of the shorter love lyrics must have been sung, but only with the appearance of songbooks in the closing decades of the century do we have a secure indication of poems that were songs.

The Poets

The authors of this verse come from a wide spectrum of backgrounds, ranging from monarchs, high-ranking nobles, statesmen, diplomats, and knights to bureaucrats, clerics, and latter-day *juglares* (minstrels). These differences may be reflected in the output of the dilettante for whom verse writing was a desirable social accomplishment (Juan II, Alvaro de Luna), the professional dependent on it for a living or preferment (Alfonso Alvarez de Villasandino, Montoro), and the dedicated man of letters who made poetry the focus of serious literary endeavor. In this last group we can include all the major poets of the fifteenth century: Francisco Imperial, Marqués de Santillana; Fernán Pérez de Guzmán; Juan de Mena; the two Manriques, Jorge and Gómez; Fray Íñigo de Mendoza; and Garci Sánchez de Badajoz; as well as a number of authors better known for their prose works: Juan Rodríguez del Padrón, Diego de Valera, the Bachiller Alfonso de la Torre, and Diego de San Pedro.

However, archival research has still to unearth biographical data for the great majority of names. All but a handful were men. Florencia Pinar is the only woman credited with more than one complete poem.

The Manuscripts

The latest register of this poetry (Dutton 1990–1992) records over two hundred manuscripts (hereinafter identified by Dutton's *sigla*). By no means are all of these strictly *cancioneros*; some are only fragments of lost collections (BM2, MN29) or prose miscellanies containing a few poems (MN31, PN2). Castilian court lyric also occurs in Catalan poetic manuscripts (BA1, BU1), in French and Italian songbooks (MA1, PN15); and as lyric insertions in sentimental romances (MN5, MN20). But the manuscripts that conserve the bulk of the poems were exclusively dedicated to verse, and such prose pieces as are included are either prefatory matter (Santillana's *Prohemio*, MN8, SA8), learned glosses (for example, of Mena's *Laberinto de Fortuna* in PN7), or related courtly works, such as pseudo-Ovidian epistles (PN4, PN8, PN12, PM1) or correspondence between poets (CO1, MN44), or, in the case of cancioneros devoted primarily to didactic or satirical genres (LB3, SV1), some wisdom literature.

We have in the region of sixty contemporary cancioneros, and another dozen sixteenth-century or later copies of lost collections. Few, if any, of the extant manuscripts are original compilations, but are through copied replicas of lost archetypes, some with local and/or personal additions by the compiler. Others, like EM9, SA9, SA10, and MN6 (the *Cancionero de Ixar*), are factitious, comprising two or more fragments of different date and provenance that have been bound together.

Family relationships between a number of manuscripts reveal a complex network of transmission, suggesting the loss on a massive scale, not only of whole cancioneros, but of the more modest units that may lie behind their composition. Since many collections give prominence to the work of one individual, it is possible that a personal cancionero formed the basis of the extant copy. We have individual manuscripts for Fernán Pérez de Guzmán (MM2, NH4), Santillana (MN8, SA8, TP1), Gómez Manrique (MN24, MP3), Fernando de la Torre (MN44), and Juan Alvarez Gato (MH2), but none for equally or more eminent figures such as Juan de Mena and Jorge Manrique.

The manuscripts vary considerably in quality and condition. Generally they are undistinguished folio or quarto volumes, on paper, with minimal decoration, copied in clear book hands by professional scribes, rather than private aficionados. A small minority were clearly intended as presentation copies, notably three of the manuscripts produced in Italy, *Estúñiga* (MN54), *Marciana* (VM1), and *Roma* (RC1), and one of the personal cancioneros of Gómez Manrique (MP3). These are sumptuously executed on vellum with an illuminated frontispiece and decorated initials. The *Cancionero de Palacio* (SA7), uniquely, is adorned with polychrome sketches in the margins. The sexually explicit nature of some of these drawings led Whinnom to postulate a covertly erotic subtext for its (largely) chaste lyrics.

Codicological and typological studies are still in their infancy. Much remains to be clarified as to provenance, ownership, criteria, and methods of compilation, production, circulation, and readership. The following notes are intended as a rough chronological guide to some of the more important and/or accessible collections.

Cancionero de Juan Alfonso de Baena (PN1). The original *Cancionero de Baena* was completed around 1430; the Paris codex is only a copy, a plain folio volume that incorporates later additions made to its exemplar. It is nonetheless the oldest known manuscript collection, and the only one with a known compiler. Although Juan Alfonso de Baena's dedication and prologue, addressed to Juan II of Castile, suggest he was conscious of setting a precedent, its sheer scope and size (over 550 items covering four reigns from Pedro the Cruel to Juan II) indicate almost certain reliance on written sources. Organized in principle by author with generic subdivisions (*cantigas*, *preguntas*, *dezires*), it gives pride of place to 217 works by Villasandino (ca.1345–1425) and privileges the genres of poetry favored by his contemporaries, commemorative poems and learned debates. Fewer than one-sixth of its compositions are love poems. The compiler and several other contributors were natives of Andalusia, or, like Francisco Imperial, resident there. *Baena* has been published several times, but see especially the edition by B. Dutton and J. González Cuenca, which gives an up-to-date account of its codicological history and a critique of previous editions, including the facsimile by H. R. Lang.

Cancionero de Palacio (Now in Salamanca; SA7). *Cancionero de Palacio* was compiled in the following decade (ca.1437–1440). It has a small overlap with *Baena* (Macías and Villasandino), but is quite different in character. It is devoted almost entirely to love poetry, with a predominance of actual canciones, short lyrics of varying metrical type with an initial *estribillo*. They are not arranged in any discernible order. It contains the earliest extant texts of Santillana, Suero de Ribera, and Pedro de Santa Fe, and a host of minor figures, most of whom do not reappear in any subsequent collection. The presence of a few Catalan poems and some scribal aragonesisms indicate an eastern provenance. The pioneering edition by Vendrell de Millás, still valuable for its introductory study, has been superseded textually by that of A. M. Alvarez Pellitero.

Paris A, E, and H (PN4, PN8, PN12). Of slightly later date (ca.1442) is the lost Castilian archetype (Vàrvaro's *a*) for three manuscripts, now in Paris, which Dutton believes were copied in a Naples scriptorium in the 1460s or 1470s. This archetype, which all follow more or less faithfully, contained a core collection of love poems by Mena, Lope de Stúñiga, the Bachiller de la Torre, Juan Rodríguez del Padrón, and Santillana, some of which were to enjoy wide and continuing, circulation in later collections, up to and including *Cancionero general.*

Cancionero de Gallardo or *de San Román* (MH1). The next most substantial manuscript safely associated with Castile is *Cancionero de Gallardo* or *de San Román*, which dates from about 1454. It was clearly planned as an official register, with spaces left blank for additions to the work of individual poets. It contains most of the known verse of Juan de Dueñas, a key figure of Santillana's generation, as well as unique items by Diego de Valera, Pedro de Escavias, and Santillana himself. It was published in full for the first time by Dutton's volume 1, 1990.

Cancionero de Herberay (LB2). *Herberay*'s claim to uniqueness are the compositions that link it to the Navarrese court of Leonor de Foix in the early 1460s, and a series of anonymous love poems which have been attributed to the diplomat poet Hugo de Urríes. These are incorporated around another core of earlier favorites (Vàrvaro's *v*) by Macias, Mena, Pedro Torrellas, Lope de Stúñiga, Pedro de Santa Fe, and Juan Rodríguez de la Cámara (= del Padrón). The *Cancionero de Modena* (ME1), copied in northern Italy, was based on the same archetype. *Herberay* has been edited by Aubrun.

The Neapolitan "Cancioneros" (MN54, RC1, VM1). The Aragónese court at Naples was the provenance of the last significant family of cancioneros (1465–1475), which graft on to a common base selected from the core represented by Paris A, E, and H (see above) the work of a group of expatriate Spaniards writing in the last years of the reign of Alfonso the Magnanimous. Carvajales is the most interesting poet of this group. The *Cancionero de Estúñiga* (MN54) is the fullest collection; *Roma* (RC1) adds a second section deriving from a complementary core of moral, political, and satirical poems (Vàrvaro's *g*) of peninsular origin; and *Marciana* (VM1) includes Italian verse translations of a portion of its contents. All three manuscripts have been published in modern editions. See especially Salvador Miguel's study and edition of the *Cancionero de Estúñiga.*

The Era of Printing

From the mid-1470s on, the early Spanish presses produced numerous small books and *pliegos sueltos* (short folios) of devotional or moralizing verse, usually by a single author—some new, some already disseminated in manuscript. The first printed anthology, by Ramón de Llavía (c.1486), continues this trend with twenty-two compositions by thirteen poets. Another landmark is the first edition of the cancionero of the prolific and versatile Juan del Encina (1496).

The paucity of new manuscript compilations after about 1470 suggests perhaps a change in market forces as poetry became available to a more bourgeois readership. However, manuscript copies of fifteenth-century verse continued to be made in the sixteenth century and the *Cancionero del British Museum* or *de Rennert* (LB1) is important as one of the few collections to contain court lyric of the Isabelline period.

The Songbooks. Known somewhat tautologically as *cancioneros musicales*, three Spanish songbooks (MP4, SG1, SV1) are preserved from the end of the fifteenth century. The *Cancionero musical de Palacio* (MP4) is the most substantial (458 items), containing works added in stages between about 1505 and 1520. Its contents represent the polyphonic repertoire of Fernando's royal chapel, including predominantly secular songs in Castilian, but also in Catalan, Portuguese, French, and Italian. The textual overlap with poetic collections is negligible. From the literary point of view it is valuable chiefly for the first solid evidence it provides of a court interest in folksong, as it includes settings for numerous traditional *villancicos* and thirty-eight ballads. It has been edited by Romeu Figueras.

Cancionero General de Hernando del Castillo (Valencia, 1511). As he states in his prologue, Castillo spent twenty years (1489–1509) assembling works of the most prominent poets, from Juan de Mena to those of his own time. The result is over one thousand items, more than half of which are unattested elsewhere, arranged partly by author and partly in generic sections. Recent scholarly interest has focused on the section of 156 canciones. It preserves most of the extant love poems of Jorge Manrique, and of other more enigmatic figures such as Cartagena, Guevara, Soria, and Tapia.

The first edition of one thousand copies, only one of which survives, was succeeded by a second edition in 1514 and seven further editions up to 1573. Evidently a publishing coup, it was the source or stimulus for many imitations, the most important being Garcia de Resende's equally vast compilation of Portuguese court poetry, the *Cancioneiro geral* (Lisbon, 1516). The success of Castillo's selection had the incidental effect of fixing the canon of fifteenth-century verse for Golden Age readers such as Juan de Valdés and Gracián. See the 1958 facsimile edition, with an introduction by Rodríguez-Moñino.

JANE WHETNALL

Bibliography

Baena, J. A. *Cancionero de Juan Alfonso de Baena*. Fac. ed. J. R. Lang. New York, 1926; rprt. 1971.

—.*Cancionero de Baena*. Ed. B. Dutton, J. González Cuenca. Madrid. 1993.

Cancioneiro geral de Garcia de Resende. Fac. ed. A. Rodríguez-Moñino. Madrid, 1958.

Cancionero de Estúñiga. Ed. N. Salvador Miguel. Madrid, 1977.

Cancionero de Palacio. Ed. F. Vendrell de Millás. Barcelona, 1945.

Cancionero de Palacio. Ed. A. M. Alvarez Pellitero. Salamanca 1993.

Le Chansonnier espagnol d'Herberay des Essarts. Ed. C. V. Aubrun. Bordeaux, 1951.

Dutton, B. (ed.) *El cancionero del siglo XV, c.1360–1520*. 7 vols. Salamanca, 1990–92.

———. "Spanish Fifteenth-Century *Cancioneros*: A General Survey to 1465." *Kentucky Romance Quarterly*, 26 (1979), 445–60.

Gerli, E. M., and J. Weiss. (eds). *Poetry at Court in Trastamaran Spain*. Tempe, Ariz, 1998.

Romeu Figuera, J. *La música en la corte de los Reyes Catól-icos*. Barcelona, 1947.

Vàrvaro, A. *Premesse ad un' edizione critica delle poesie minori di Juan de Mena*. Naples, 1964.

Whetnall, J. "El *Cancionero general* de 1511: Textos únicos y textos omitidos." In *Actas del V Congreso de la Asociación Hispánica de Literatura Medieval (Granada, 1993)*. Granada, 1995.

Whinnom, K. *Spanish Literary Historiography: Three Forms of Distortion*. Exeter, 1967.

POETRY, VERNACULAR, POPULAR, AND LEARNED: EPIC

Like certain other areas of the Romance world (notably northern France and, to a lesser extent, Provence and northern Italy), Spain, and particularly Castile, developed an autocthonous local tradition of heroic narrative poetry during the Middle Ages. The origins of the Spanish epic—as well as the extent to which lost epic narratives may or may not be reflected in chronistic prosifications and balladic stories—have both been the subject of controversy. It has been argued that the Spanish epic is merely a secondary derivative of the French epic; that it is of ancient Germanic origin, inspired in the heroic poetry of the Visigoths; that it is basically an independent Spanish development; that it is essentially learned, or, again, that it is essentially oral and traditional in character. Each of these arguments merits serious consideration. Medieval minstrels were a multilingual, far-traveled, and cosmopolitan lot. French jongleurs went to Spain and their Spanish counterparts, *juglares*, also went to France. Both significantly influenced the other's epic repertoires. The French epics' influence in Spain was enormously important, not only in numerous Spanish adaptations of French epics and in some narrative components taken over by the Spanish national epics, but also in the innumerable formulaic elements shared by the poetic diction of both traditions. There are indeed some Spanish epic narratives (*Gaiferos*, for instance) and certain narrative themes that are (or, at least, may be) ultimately of Germanic origin, but whether these go back to the traditions of ancient Visigothic invaders or were, rather, taken over from French intermediaries is a debated question. Certainly the epic poetry that developed in Spain, whatever its origins, emerged as eminently and distinctively Spanish in character. Surely there are learned—even ecclesiastic—elements in the few poetic texts that have come down to us and, in some cases, chroniclers undoubtedly intervened to modify—sometimes profoundly—the fragments of epic texts they prosified. An extreme individualist perspective would hold that none of the ancillary chronicle or balladic evidence can be used to reconstruct lost epics and that the only viable texts are the three epics that have been preserved in their "original" poetic form. All the same, the combined evidence of chronicles and ballads has been strengthened by recent traditionalist findings. At the same time, individualist critics have made enormously important contributions in demanding greater rigor in interpreting narrative and poetic elements preserved in secondary sources.

In terms of primary documentation, conditions in Spain contrast radically with those of northern France. There are well over one hundred different epic narratives (*chansons de geste*) in Old French (taking into account the problem of versions versus "different" poems and the flexibility of boundaries between one work and another) represented by an extremely rich manuscript tradition; in Spain, by contrast, only three epics (*cantares de gesta*) have been preserved in their original poetic form and only one, the *Cantar de mio Cid*, has survived essentially intact. The other two epics are *Mocedades de Rodrigo* (Youthful Adventures of the Cid), which is prosified at the beginning and breaks off after some 1,164 verses, and *Roncesvalles* (a Spanish avatar of the French *Chanson de Roland*), of which only two parchment folios—a mere hundred lines—have survived. Such a paucity of primary documents is deceptive. Medieval Spanish chroniclers treated heroic poems as authentic records of the past and consequently they have preserved for us lengthy prosifications of certain *cantares de gesta*, while fragments of various epics also survived in the form of ballads. Based on such secondary evidence, a substantial repertoire of Old Spanish heroic poetry can be partially reconstructed, to the extent that we can be reasonably certain of the poems' narrative content and, in some cases, we can even sample some of their poetry in vestiges of assonant rhyme and traditional formulaic diction imbedded in chronicle prosifications.

The Spanish epic was concerned with two major topics: national narratives, pertaining both to Christian conflicts and to wars against the Muslims and Carolingian narratives brought in from France. Spanish national epics reflect two consecutive historical moments: the cycle of the Counts of Castile: the *Poema de Fernán González, Infantes de Lara* (Lords of Lara), *Romanz del infant don García* (Epic of Prince García), and perhaps also *La condesa traidora* (The Treacherous Countess), and the cycle of the Cid: *Mocedades de Rodrigo, Partición de los reinos* (Division of the Kingdom), *Cerco de Zamora* (Siege of Zamora), *Jura de Santa Gadea* (Oath at Santa Gadea), and *Cantar de mio Cid*. The historical origins of these national narratives go back, respectively, to around 950–1030 and to el Cid's lifetime (c. 1043–1099), though the texts of poems or prosifications that have actually been preserved invariably date from much later times (thirteenth and fourteenth centuries). Carolingian narratives, which generally were not prosified, or even summarized, in the chronicles, are much more difficult, though certainly not impossible to reconstruct. With the help of the *Nota Emilianense*, the *Roncesvalles* fragment, various sixteenth-century ballads, and other evidence, we can form a general idea of what the *Song of Roland*'s Spanish avatars may have been like. Exceptionally, chronistic prose accounts of *Mainete* (*Youthful Adventures of Charlemagne*) have survived and partial outlines of other lost Hispano-Carolingian epics, corresponding to the Old French *Chanson des Saisnes* (*Epic of the Saxons*), *Floovant*, and *Beuve de Hantone* (*Bevis of Hampton*), can be convincingly reconstructed in considerable detail, on the evidence of sixteenth-century and modern traditional ballads (*Belardo y Valdovinos*, *Floresvento*, *Celinos*). Another indirect echo of lost Spanish epics on Carolingian themes is reflected in certain poems that adopt a hostile attitude toward epic accounts of French heroism: *Historia Silense* (c. 1110) bitterly contests minstrel accounts of mythical French victories against the Muslims (for example, *Chanson de Roland*, vv. 1–6). So also, in the lost *gesta* of *Bernardo del Carpio*, the hero organizes a Spanish army, composed of both Christians and Muslims, to defeat Charlemagne's forces at Roncevaux. *La peregrinación del rey Luis de Francia* (*The Pilgrimage of King Louis of France*), known only in a chronistic summary, adapts the Old French epic, *Pélegrinage de Charlemagne* (*The Pilgrimage of Charlemagne*) to a peninsular venue, stressing the superiority of Spain and the nobility of Spaniards. Likewise, in *Mocedades de Rodrigo*, King Fernando I invades France and defeats the French, while the young Cid—anachronistically—beats with his fist on the gates of Paris, challenging to battle the Twelve Peers of France. The legend of *La condesa traidora* also reflects a bitterly Gallophobic perspective.

The meter of Old Spanish epic poetry involved an anisosyllabic verse, divided into two hemistichs of between six and nine syllables, with assonant rhyme in the second hemistich. The percentage of octosyllables seems to have increased somewhat in the fourteenth century (over the twelth and thirteenth), suggesting a gradual drift toward the regular octosyllabism of the ballads, while the earliest ballads are still slightly irregular, having a higher percentage of heptasyllables than most sixteenth-century ballads or those in the modern oral tradition. A significant feature of epic prosody is the "paragogic *-e*," occurring in oxytonic (acute) rhyme words, where the stress falls on the final syllable. In some cases, the paragoge is non-etymological (*acáe* "here"; *avíae* "had"; *sone* "are"), but in others the *-e* is etymological (*ciudade* "city"; *fablare* "speak"), reflecting an archaic phonological stage in the development of Spanish that has not been part of everyday Castilian speech since the tenth century and thus suggesting that epic poetry was already in existence at a time well before the historical events reflected in most of the *gestas* known to us today. The importance of the paragogic *-e* is confirmed by the equally archaic paragogic *-d-*, corresponding to the Latin *-t* of third-person singular verb endings (*diráde, faráde* "will say, will do").

Certain lost epic narratives remain outside the major Castilian cycles. Hotly debated is the possibility of an early Mozarabic epic on *El rey don Rodrigo y la pérdida de España* (*King Rodrigo and the Destruction of Spain*). Traditional accounts absorbed by both Muslim and Christian chronicles are full of novelesque motifs. Whatever the narrative's original form, the story is also reflected in the French epic *Anseïs de Cartage* (c. 1200). Vestiges of assonant verse and epic formulas are present in the prose accounts *El abad don Juan de Montemayor* (*Abbot John of Montemayor*), suggesting a pseudo-hagiographic legend in epic verse, centered on the Portuguese fortress of Montemor o Velho. Though the *Chanson de Roland* is parodied in a thirteenth-century *cantiga d'escarnho* (defamatory song) by Alfonso López de Baian, "Sedia-xi Don Belpelho en ũa sa maison" ("Mr. Fox was sitting in his house"), the epic genre seems to have been little cultivated in medieval Portugal. Chronistic accounts of *La campana de Huesca* (*The Bell of Huesca*), concerning a massacre of rebellious Aragónese nobles by King Ramiro II (d. 1157), are replete with assonant rhymes, suggesting the development of an epic tradition in Aragón, as well as in Castile. Onomastic data attest to the presence of the Old French epic (or more probably Provençal or Catalan adaptations) in Catalonia by the mid-eleventh century and there are ample testimonies in medieval Catalan chronicles to prosifications of Catalan epic poems about battles of the Reconquest. Convincing evidence exists for contacts between Romance epic poetry and heroic narratives in Arabic, both on the Iberian peninsula and elsewhere.

SAMUEL G. ARMISTEAD

Bibliography

Armistead, S. G. "The Paragogic *-d-*. . . ." In *Hispanic Studies in Honor of J. H. Silverman*. Newark, Del. 1988.

Catalán, D. *La épica española*. Madrid, 2000.

Deyermond, A. *Literatura perdida de la Edad Media. . . .* Salamanca, 1995.

Duggan, J. J. "The Manuscript Corpus of the Medieval Romance Epic." *Essays in Honor of D. J. A. Ross*. Millwood, N.Y. 1982.

Jensen, F. *The Earliest Portuguese Lyrics*. Odense, 1978.

Galmés, A. *Epica árabe y épica castellana*. Barcelona, 1978.

Menéndez Pidal, R. *La épica medieval española*, Madrid, 1992.

———. *Los godos y la epopeya española*. Madrid, 1956.

———. *Reliquias de la poesía épica española*. 2d ed. Madrid, 1980.

Riquer, M. de. *Història de la literatura catalana*. Vol. I. Barcelona, 1980.

Vaquero, M. *Tradiciones orales en la historiografía de de la Edad Media*. Madison, Wisc., 1990.

POLEMICS, POLITICAL

All polemics of the later medieval period, including those primarily concerned with religious or social issues, tended to have political overtones, and contemporary chroniclers certainly had political axes to grind, Pero López de Ayala and Alfonso de Palencia perhaps being outstanding in this respect. But some polemics were more overtly political in nature than others.

At an international and sophisticated level, Spaniards made outstanding contributions to the polemics on political power by their interventions in the debates at the General Council of Basel (1431–1449). At the council, the leading champion of what may be termed constitutionalism was Juan de Segovia who, by arguing that power resided with the community (in this case the council) and not an individual (in this case the papal monarch), was advancing theories about constitutional monarchy that anticipated the much later views of John Locke and Jean-Jacques Rousseau. His views were opposed by the *converso* Juan de Torquemada who, in supporting the absolutism of papal and monarchical power, anticipated the political thought of Jean Bodin. Clearly Spanish political thought had much to offer the rest of Europe in terms of sophistication and diversity.

Such diametrically opposed views reflected similar polemics within Spain. In the Crown of Aragón influential theories were developed with respect to *pactismo*: that is, the view that political power, and hence royal power, was ultimately based on contractual arrangements involving election and consent. The nature of such pacts meant that political domination had to be exercised in the interests of the community, it being understood that political power was ultimately vested in the *communitas*. Such views were most clearly expressed by the Franciscan Francesc Eiximenis (1340–1408), but they were also enshrined in the way in which the balance of power between the kings and the various *cortes* of the Crown of Aragón was regulated.

In Castile extreme notions of royal absolutism developed and tended to predominate, especially during the reign of Juan II (1406–1454). The king derived his power from God, not the community, and claimed to make or revoke laws on the basis of his "certain knowledge, own will and absolute royal power." These assertions ran directly counter to conventions that had grown up during the fourteenth century, most notably during the reign of Juan I (1379–1390), whereby the making or revoking of laws was envisaged as a matter of the king and the *cortes* acting together.

Nevertheless, both the prevailing tendencies, constitutionalism in the Crown of Aragón and absolutism in Castile, encountered opposition and gave rise to polemics. In Castile, for example, the nobles used the *cortes* (courts) at one stage to advance notions of pactism, and during the reign of Enrigue IV (1454–1474), particularly during the crisis that culminated in the curious ritual deposition of the king's effigy at the Farce of Avila of 1465, they based their actions on the claim that royal power depended on "election" and "acclamation." But they also resorted to accusing the king of tyranny, justifying their actions by appealing to precedents in Castile (especially Perdo I, the Cruel) and, more vaguely, elsewhere in western Europe, coupling this accusation with that of a *rex inutilis*. The king, therefore, was both a tyrant and useless. The crisis gave rise to an important polemic, although some of the contributions to it have been lost. For example, Francisco de Toledo, a professor of theology, at first railed violently against Enrique IV but changed sides and wrote at length about the illegality of the deposition, the chronicler Fernando del Pulgar referring to this lost work written "against those who cause divisions in kingdoms and presume by their own authority to remove a king and replace him with another." Others who joined in the polemic were the Franciscan Antonio de Alcalá, the Dominican Juan López, and above all the bishop of Calahorra, Pedro González de Mendoza, who delivered a powerful speech in support of the king at a crucial stage. In it he accepted that the king, as head of the *corpus reispublicae mysticum*, suffered from an *ynabilidad* (inability), was unskilled in the art of kingship (*yndoto*), and was *inutilis* (useless). But—crucially—he did not even hint at tyranny, and he argued that the community or *respublica* had absolutely no say in the removal or bestowal of a title that was exclusively God's gift.

During the crisis there were clear echoes of the political polemic that had occurred at the Council of Basel. Indeed one of the leading protagonists at the Farce was Archbishop Carrillo of Toledo who had been the president of the Castilian embassy at Basel. Sophisticated arguments that had been used to justify the deposition of a pope could be used to justify the deposition of a king. Not surprisingly, therefore, the papacy became involved in the Castilian polemic on the royal side and also became the object of acrimonious attack by Alfonso de Palencia.

The sophisticated political polemics that have been briefly reviewed were usually paralleled by a more popular form of polemical literature. An important cycle of ballads, for example, vilified Pedro the Cruel by narrating the gory assassinations of his half-brother, Fadrique, and of his queen, Blanca, as well as by introducing prophetic shepherds and clerics who ostensibly warned the king that he would be suitably punished for his misdeeds. Ayala used some of these popular polemics, incorporating the essence of their contents in his chronicles. The crisis of Enrique IV's reign gave rise to the sophisticated pastoral allegory, couched in popular terms, known as *Coplas de Mingo Revulgo*, which clearly reflects the debate about the relationship between the king (a shepherd), his subjects (the sheep), and rapacious wolves (the nobility). But it also witnessed the circulation of the highly obscene *Coplas del Provincial*, which contain infamous allegations against a long series of individuals at court, both male and female, many of whom are difficult to identify. In addition, the chronicles refer to other examples of popular polemical poems that have not survived.

Most political polemics were concerned with the nature of royal power or the relationship between the king and the nobility. There is evidence, however, of the existence of political polemics at a different level. In particular it is possible to detect a belief in, and support of, notions relating to such concepts as *el común*, *la comunidad*, and even *repúblicas*, all these being expressions of a not unimportant undercurrent of political ideology that surfaced in the revolt of the *comuneros* in 1520. There was, for example, the attempt by the Count of Luna to establish a kind of Italian commune in Seville in 1433; the resistance proferred by the citizens of Seville when threatened by the Infante Enrique in 1444, a resistance apparently eulogized in a chronicle (now lost) by a certain Juan Guillén; an uprising in Fuenteovejuna in 1453 that was followed by the famous rebellion of its comunidad in 1476; and numerous attempts to establish comunidades in Andalusian towns, in some cases expressly aping Italian models, most notably the conspiracy in Seville in 1463, fomented by Archbishop Fonseca, which aimed to free the city completely from royal control and turn it into a comunidad.

It is possible to find echoes of the political polemics to which such episodes gave rise in the chronicles of Palencia and Hernando del Castillo, but their accounts tend to be brief and hostile. Palencia, for example, portrays Fernán Gómez de Guzmán, the *comendador mayor* of Fuenteovejuna fame, as a kind and generous lord who even visited the sick of the town. When Lope de Vega wrote his play about the heroic uprising against the tyrannous *comendador mayor* he drew on a different and later source, the *Crónica* about the military orders of Santiago, Calatrava, and Alcántara written by Rades y Andrada.

ANGUS MACKAY

Bibliography

Burns, J. H. *Lordship, Kingship and Empire: The Idea of Monarchy. 1400–1525.* Oxford, 1992.

MacKay, A. "Ritual and Propaganda in Fifteenth-Century Castile." *Past and Present* 107 (1985), 3–43.

MacKay, A., and G. McKendrick. "The Crowd in Theater and the Crowd in History: Fuenteovejuna." *Renaissance Drama* new se. 17 (1986), 125–47.

Rodríguez-Puértolas, J. *Poesía de protesta en la Edad Media castellana.* Madrid, 1968.

Tate, R. B. *Ensayos sobre la historiografía peninsular del siglo XV.* Madrid, 1970.

POLITICAL THEORY

Medieval Hispanic political theory was founded principally upon the writings of St. Isidore of Seville (c.560–636), who brought together many of the essential ideas of the ancient world concerning kingship, law, and government. Although there are traces of Isidorian political ideas in early medieval Hispanic writings, it was not until the thirteenth century that Spanish authors, influenced by the revival of Roman law and the Aristotelian conception of political society, began to develop a conscious political theory.

The principal repository of these new ideas were the law codes compiled during the reign of Alfonso X of Castile (1252–1284), namely the *Espéculo* and *Siete Partidas*. Both codes accepted the notion of the state as a corporation comparable to the human body. Both also stated the principle that the king had no superior in temporal matters and within his own realm enjoyed the same powers as the emperor.

The genre of "Mirrors of Princes" also began to appear, as for example, *Llibre de la saviesa* attributed to Jaime I of Aragón (1213–1276) and *Libro de la nobleza y lealtad* dating from the reign of Fernando III of Castile (1217–1252). Alfonso X's *Setenario* was intended as a work of counsel for his successors, while Juan Gil de Zamora (d. 1318) composed *De preconiis Hispaniae*, a melange of historical and geographical data, for the instruction of the future Sancho IV (1284–1295). The latter, in 1293, completed his *Castigos e documentos*, a book of advice on the art of kingship addressed to his son, Fernando IV.

Around the beginning of the fourteenth century a certain Master Pedro penned *Libro del consejo y de los consejeros*. For the advice of the future Pedro I, Juan García de Castrogeriz in 1344 completed his adaptation and translation of Giles of Rome's *De regimine principum*. Álvaro Pelayo (d. 1353), in his *Speculum regum* dedicated to Alfonso XI, denounced the sins and failings of kings. His contemporary, Infante Juan Manuel (1282–1348) discussed the three estates constituting human society and the relation between kings and their subjects in his *Libro de los estados*. Later in the century Pero López de Ayala (1332–1407) lamented the failure of kingship in a lengthy poem, *Rimado de Palacio*. The Catalan Franciscan Francesc Eiximenis (c.1340–1408), in his *Regiment de la cosa publica* and the later *Regiment de princeps* or *El Dotze*, expounded the theory of contractual monarchy in which the several estates would have the opportunity to participate.

Many fifteenth-century authors chose to express their views on political society in poetic form. Fernán Pérez de Guzmán (c.1378–c.1460) in his long poem *Loores de los claros varones de España*, drew parallels between contemporary circumstances and the deeds and follies of the great men of earlier times. Juan de Mena's (1411–1456) *Laberinto de Fortuna*, an allegorical commentary on contemporary government marked by a strong sense of patriotism, offered counsel to Juan II, "the great king of Spain, the new Caesar." Iñigo López de Mendoza, Marqués of Santillana (1398–1458), an active politician and humanist, in his *La comedieta de Ponza* reflected on the misfortunes of princes. In his *Doctrinal de privados*, the marquess admonished those who might be tempted to imitate Juan II's erstwhile favorite, Álvaro de Luna, in his quest for power and riches.

In his letters to Juan II and Enrique IV, Diego de Valera (1398–1488) pointed out that unless they corrected their failings the monarchy might be destroyed. Comparing the state to the human body in his *Doctrinal de príncipes*, he stressed that all the members were interdependent and that the king, as head of the body, could not function without the members.

Among the ecclesiastical authors writing in Latin, mention should be made of Alfonso de Madrigal, el Tostado (c.1410–1455), who argued in his *De optima politia* that democracy was the preferable form of government. Juan de Torquemada (1388–1468), in his

Summa de ecclesia, emphasized the pope's right to depose kings or emperors. In his *Opusculum ad honorem romani imperii*, he upheld the claims of the Holy Roman Empire to universal dominion over all other rulers. On the contrary, Rodrigo Sánchez de Arévalo (c.1405–1470), in his *De monarchia orbis*, denied the emperor's sovereignty over the kingdoms of France and Spain. His *Suma de la política*, a vernacular treatise, stressed the need for unity in the body politic, while his *Vergel de príncipes* was a typical mirror of princes.

JOSEPH F. O'CALLAGHAN

Bibliography

Bermejo, J. L. "Principios y apotegmas sobre la ley y el rey en la Baja Edad Media castellana." *Hispania* 35 (1975), 31–48.

Maravall, J. A. "El pensamiento político en España desde el año 400 a 1300." *Journal of World History* 4 (1957), 818–32.

Pérez, J. B. *Historia de las doctrinas políticas*. Madrid, 1950.

PÓRTICO DE LA GLORIA

The Pórtico de la Gloria, located within the western facade of the basilica at Santiago de Compostela, was sculpted by Maestro Mateo, a Frenchman, some time between 1168 and 1188. Its design, inspired by St. John the Divine's apocalyptic vision of the throne (Rev. 5), depicts St. James seated with his pilgrim's staff on the mullion of the central column, representing the tree of Jesse, and flanked, on the outer columns, by the Apostles Peter, Paul, James, and John to his left, and Moses, Isaiah, Daniel, and Jeremiah to his right. Upon these figures rests the magnificent tympanum, whose centerpiece is a twice life-size figure of Christ, ruler of the universe, seated with the palms of his hands facing forward. He is skirted on each side by a pair of angels, three of whom take charge of one of three beasts (eagle, lamb, and one with a human face). The fourth beast, a lion, is represented by two, which support St. James's seat. Christ is also surrounded by a huge chorus of angels. The entire scene is encased by an archivolt bearing the twenty-four elders of the Apocalypse, whom Mateo grouped in pairs, portraying them conversing with one another while tuning stringed instruments. Three types can be distinguished: lute (fiddles or *vielles* of various sizes and shapes, rebecs, and an organistrum); zither (psaltery); and harp.

The bold ciphers enclosed in parentheses designate the position (running clockwise) of each of the elders according to their respective instruments: three-stringed fiddles (1, 7, 11, 14–16, and 24); three-stringed rebecs (9 and 20); four-stringed fiddle (2); five-stringed short-necked fiddle (6 and 23); undefinable fiddles (3 and 22); an organistrum or hurdy-gurdy, whose prototype can be found in the popular Galician *zanfoña* (here, however, its size necessitates two elders; 12–13); nine-stringed vertical psaltery (5 and 18); twelve-stringed horizontal psaltery (10 and 17); and a sixteen-stringed frame harp (8 and 19). Two elders (4 and 21) are depicted without instruments.

Portal of the Portico de la Gloria. Copyright © Scala/Art Resource, NY. Cathedral, Santiago de Compostela, Spain.

Earlier and distinct versions of this scene can be found on tympana of many churches and cathedrals in France and northern Spain whose inspiration may have derived from the miniatures in *In Apocalipsim (Commentary on the Apocalypse*, (c.775) by the Asturian monk Beatus of Liébana. However, their sculptors, like Mateo, avoided a literal interpretation of John's vision (Rev. 5:8), wherein each of the elders held harps, together with golden flasks containing incense. Mateo assigned instruments to twenty-two of them and the flasks to only nine (3, 4, 8, 15–18, 21, and 24).

From a musicological standpoint, certain aspects of Mateo's pórtico are enigmatic. A basic problem is the absence of bows, begging an assumption that the instruments of the lute type were plucked or, in some cases, strummed. Apart from the four- or five-stringed instruments that may have been performed in this manner, it appears more likely that the three-stringed instruments were bowed, with perhaps one of the strings functioning as a drone. Such is the case of the sculpture bearing King David on the south door of the cathedral—that is, the Puerta de las Platerías, where he is shown playing a three-stringed fiddle with a bow in the then customary fashion. Here, indeed, Mateo added a subtle touch, implying their being kept out of view, but not unutilized.

The question of the flasks (*redomas*) has also led to several speculations. They were either used as drinking vessels (carrying water or wine), inferred from the varied shapes sculpted by Mateo, which have the appearance of calabash gourds that are quite plentiful in the region surrounding Compostela, and which the pilgrims used to carry water. They may have also served as rhythmic instruments, as rattles with the insertion of pebbles or beads, or even as gourds emitting a tone when struck with the finger or another object, perhaps pitched to produce a natural drone.

Mateo may have indeed studied other sculptural programs in France, but this has not be substantiated. Inasmuch as Santiago was one of the most progressive music centers during the latter half of the twelveth century, Mateo was indeed exposed to the musical currents of his day. A detailed examination of his sculpted instruments indicates that he modeled them upon existing specimens.

Before the completion of the pórtico, the principal entrance for the pilgrims was the north door, the Puerta Francesa facing the Plaza Fuente San Juan, formerly known as Azabachería.

Israel J. Katz

Bibliography

Beatus of Liebana. *In Apocalipsim*. Ed. Henry A. Sanders. Rome, 1930.

Iglesias Villarelle, A. "Los músicos del Pórtico de la Gloria." *El Museo de Pontevedra* 7 (1952), 35–68.

López-Calo, J. *La música medieval en Galicia*. La Coruña, 1982. 87–102.

López Ferreiro, A. *El Pórtico de la Gloria, platerías y el primitivo altar mayor*. Santiago de Compostela, 1975.

Pita Andrade, J. M. "Las redomas que sostienen los Ancianos del Pórtico de la Gloria." *Cuadernos de Estudios Gallegos* 3 (1948), 213–21.

Rahlres, F. "El Pórtico de la Gloria, del maestro Mateo." In *Catedrales y Monasterios de España*. Barcelona, 1969. 129–39.

Schünemann, G. "Die Muskinstrumente der 24 Alten." *Archiv für Musikforschung* 1 (1936), 42–58.

Silva, J., and J. R. Barreiro. *El Pórtico de la Gloria: Autor e interpretación*. Santiago de Compostela, 1965.

Yarza Luaces, J. *El Pórtico de la Gloria*. Madrid, 1984.

PORTUGAL, KINGDOM OF, EARLIER COUNTY OF

In the aftermath of the Muslim invasion of the Iberian Peninsula in 711, Christians from Asturias slowly pushed southward. During the tenth century, as the various monarchs of Asturias-León partitioned their realm among their children, Galicia, north of present-day Portugal, was given the status of a kingdom. A crucial ingredient in the development of an autonomous sentiment in that part of the northwest which was to become Portugal were the officials whom the monarchs appointed to oversee the affairs of lands recaptured from the Muslims. These officials provided for their regions' defense and helped consolidate the new territories by promoting settlement. They held a variety of titles, the most important being "count."

In 1072 Alfonso VI, king of León and Asturias took over the kingdom of Castile and annexed parts of Galicia and Terra Portucalense to his kingdom of León. He also captured Toledo in 1085. In the late eleventh century, in response to Alfonso VI's pleas for help against continuing Almoravid invasions, several contingents of French knights arrived in the Iberian Peninsula. Two of the most important of these adventurers were Raymond and Henri, countrymen of Alfonso's Burgundian wife, Queen Constance. Raymond married Urraca, Alfonso's daughter and heiress. Alfonso entrusted his son-in-law with the administration of the county of Galicia as well as that of Terra Portucalense and Coimbra as far south as the Muslim frontier along the Tagus River. But Raymond's authority over the region to the south of Galicia was short-lived, as Muslim forces soon overran the Christians southernmost boundaries.

In the meantime, Henri, another Burgundian, had arrived in Iberia and had distinguished himself in battle against the Almoravids. In 1095 he married the young Teresa, Alfonso VI's favorite, albeit illegitimate, daughter. Alfonso VI now awarded this son-in-law the governance of Terra Portucalense. By the end of the year Henry was being addressed as Lord of Coimbra, and by 1197 he was referred to as Count of Portucale. Henry established his capital at Guimarães and stimulated settlement in the territory under his administration. Although he continued to take part in Alfonso VI's campaigns against the Muslims and to advise Alfonso at court, he also sought opportunities to exert greater independence from the monarch. In this endeavor he was aided by the isolation of Terra Portucalense from the other Christian territories in the Iberian

Peninsula. Mountains formed barriers and there was scant communication by water. With the exception of the Douro, none of the rivers that flowed through northern Portugal originate to the east, in what is now Spain. Political factors, such as internal problems in the kingdom of León and Muslim threats to the Spanish kingdoms, strengthened this isolation. Thus local identify and self-reliance were encouraged. The attention of Terra Portucalense was directed to the southwest and to the Atlantic Ocean.

Succession problems in León enabled Henry, and later his widow, Teresa, to gain greater independence for the county of Portucale. Teresa, like her husband before her, encouraged the establishment of new settlements. She also tried to expand her authority beyond the Minho River by allying herself with a faction of Galician nobles headed by Fernando Peres. Some of the wealthiest and most powerful Portuguese nobles opposed Teresa's Galician adventures and rallied around Afonso Henriques, the son of Teresa and Henry, a youth who had been only three years old at the time of his father's death. At the Battle of São Mamede in 1128, Afonso Henriques' forces defeated those of his mother and her supporters. Afonso Henriques exiled Teresa and took over the rule of the county of Portucale. During his long reign Afonso Henriques firmly established his line on the Portuguese throne. Portugal's first ruling house came to be known as the Burgundian dynasty.

Afonso Henriques (also known as Afonso I of Portugal) and his successors had four chief aims: (1) to assert Portugal's independence from León and Castile by establishing a separate kingdom; (2) to drive out the Muslims to the south and carve out the boundaries of what would become the Portuguese nation; (3) to firmly establish the position of monarch with its accompanying sovereign power; and (4) to organize a church independent of León and Castile and then keep this increasingly powerful church in line by subordinating it to the monarchy.

By 1383, when the death of Fernando I of Portugal marked the end of the Burgundian dynasty, the first two goals had been achieved and the latter two were close to fulfillment.

Afonso Henriques made gains steadily in his move toward independence from León and Castile. In 1126 Afonso Henriques's first cousin, Alfonso Raimúndez, assumed power as Alfonso VII, King of León. In 1135, Alfonso VII was crowned by the *cortes* (courts) of León as emperor of the "whole Spain." Afonso Henriques refused to recognize the sovereignty that his cousin claimed over Portugal and was in almost constant revolt. Finally, in 1143, in the Treaty of Zamora, Afonso Henriques promised to stay out of Galician territory and affairs and, in return, Alfonso VIII recognized him as king of Portugal. Afonso Henriques had already taken the title for himself in 1140 and had commended his kingdom to the holy see, declaring himself a vassal of the pope. The papacy of Lucius II accepted this offer in 1144 following the pact between Afonso Henriques and Alfonso VII. However, it was not until 1179 that a pope would address Afonso Henriques as "king."

The threat to Portuguese independence greatly diminished with the death of Alfonso VII in 1157. By 1185, the year when Afonso Henriques died, the task of asserting Portugal's independence from León and Castile was virtually complete. Although the successors of Afonso Henriques came into intermittent conflict with Portugal's Christian neighbors to the east and the north, it was not until the reign of Fernando I of Portugal (1367–1383), when Castilian forces invaded Portugal three times, that Spanish power seriously threatened Portugal's autonomy.

The second major goal of the Burgundian dynasty—to drive the Muslims farther and farther south—was not achieved as readily as the assertion of Portuguese independence. But Afonso Henriques did take some important steps in that direction by making significant inroads into Muslim territory. Early in his reign, he secured the region around Coimbra and transferred his capital there. In 1135 he gave further attention to his southern borders by fortifying Leiria. In 1139 he won an important skirmish at Ourique during one of his raids into Muslim regions. Afonso Henriques was aided by the chaos in Islamic Spain, which resulted from the breakdown of Almoravid rule and the corresponding Almohad revolt in North Africa that was spreading to Muslim Iberia.

Soon, Afonso Henriques began a big push against the Muslim forces along his Tagus River frontier. In the next two decades major territorial gains were achieved. In 1147 Afonso Henriques captured the important city of Santarém. This conquest opened the way to Lisbon, which was taken later the same year after a seventeenth-week siege, carried out with the aid of several thousand northern European knights, participants in the Second Crusade. This was the first of six times that crusaders on their way to the Holy Land would be asked to assist the Portuguese in driving out the Muslims.

With the aid of the Knights Templar and the orders of Santiago and Avis and adventurers like Geraldo "sem Pavor" ("the Fearless"), Afonso Henriques advanced further into Muslim territory. Such Muslim strongholds as Alcácer do Sal on the Sado River south of Lisbon were captured (at last temporarily) along with a number of important towns in the Alentejo and across the Guadiana River in what is now Spanish Estremadura. But after the Almohads gained ascendancy in the southern part of the Iberian Peninsula, the Muslims recaptured many of the strongholds they had lost to Afonso Henriques during the 1160s. Eventually the Portuguese were pushed back to the Tagus. It would not be until 1249 that the last Muslim stronghold in Portugal would be captured.

Afonso Henriques initiated a strong royalist tradition in Portugal. In doing so, he was imitating León. He was aided in his endeavor by the territorial compactness of his kingdom. The great length of Afonso Henriques' reign (1128–1185) was an important factor in the development of royal ascendancy. Also, Afonso Henriques's decision to have his son and heir, Sancho I, rule jointly with him during the last fifteen years of his reign eliminated succession disputes that could have weakened the crown's position. Thus the sovereignty of the crown over the three estates of nobility, clergy, and commoners was established early in Portugal, though it was not unchallenged.

As part of the effort to create an independent Portugal, Afonso Henriques was anxious to establish a church in his kingdom separate from that in Santiago de Compostela and separate also from the church in Toledo, which had been awarded the status of primatial see during the Visigothic domination of Iberia. Afonso Henriques's father, Henri of Burgundy, had backed the archbishop of Braga in his assertion of independence from Toledo. In 1103 the papacy gave Braga control not only over dioceses in Galicia, but also over those of Coimbra, Viseu, and Lamego in Portugal. A decade and a half later, however, Braga was stripped of its control over dioceses south of the Douro River. When Afonso Henriques came to power, he managed to recover the lost dioceses for Braga. However, the conquest of Lisbon and other cities in southern Portugal caused new problems because dioceses in this region had never been subordinate to Braga. Ironically, when the efforts to establish a Portuguese church succeeded, it was the church that offered the crown the fiercest rivalry. Of all the internal struggles for power in Portugal during the Middle Ages, those between crown and church were the most bitter.

The devastation and suffering that resulted from the three wars with Castile during the reign of Fernando I (1367–1383) paved the way for a new Portuguese dynasty. In 1369 Pedro I of Castile was assassinated by his illegitimate half-brother, Enrique of Trastámara, who then became the new king of Castile, Enrique II (1369–1379). Fernando I of Portugal, the nearest legitimate male heir of Pedro I of Castile, also claimed the Castilian throne and entered Galicia and the first of the three wars began. In 1372 Fernando entered into an English-Portuguese alliance against the Trastámaras. By the Treaty of Tagilde, the Portuguese monarch allied himself with John of Gaunt, the duke of Lancaster, who had married an illegitimate daughter of Pedro I of Castile. This pact was followed in 1373 by the Treaty of Wesminister, in which Fernando promised to defend the duke of Lancaster's claim to the Castilian throne. The above-mentioned events were also part of the Iberian Peninsula's role as a side theatre of the Hundred Years War. The same period witnessed the beginning of the Great Western Schism. Portugal initially backed Clement VII in Avignon and received many benefits from the Avignon papacy. But because England backed Pope Urban VI in Rome, the Portuguese switched their allegiance to the popes of Rome.

Shortly before his death in the latter part of 1383, Fernando married his young daughter Beatriz to the recently widowed Juan I of Castile. But hostility toward Castile led to revolution and a new Portuguese dynasty.

The House of Avis was founded by João, the master of Avis and illegitimate son of the Portuguese monarch, Pedro I (r. 1357–1367) and half-brother of King Fernando. On 14 August 1385 outnumbered Portuguese forces managed to route the Castilians under Juan I at the famous battle of Aljubarrota. On 9 May 1386 the Portuguese and the English signed the Treaty of Windsor, "a treaty of perpetual peace and friendship." The following year João married Philippa of Lancaster, daughter of John of Gaunt.

Much of Portugal's history in the fifteenth century revolves around the legitimate and illegitimate children of João I of Avis and their heirs. Duarte, João's eldest legitimate son, succeeded his father on the throne in 1433. Pedro, the second son, famous for his travels thoughout Europe between 1425 and 1428, served as regent from 1439 to 1448 for Duarte's young son, Afonso V (r. 1438–1481), before being killed as a rebel at the battle of Alfarrobeira in 1449. Henrique (Henry the Navigator), the third son, was duke of Viseu and the master of the Order of Christ. He devoted his life to crusading in North Africa, hoping to gain control of the Canary Islands, settling the archipelagos of Madeira and the Azores, and presiding over exploration and commerce down the western coast of Africa. The fourth legitimate son, João, was named master of Santiago and constable of Portugal. One of his daughters, Isabel, married Juan II of Castile and was the mother of Isabel "La Católica." Fernando, the youngest of João I's sons, was named master of Avis and was captured during Portugal's disastrous effort to seize Tangier in 1437 and died in Muslim hands in 1443. João I's legitimate daughter, Isabel, married Philip, Duke of Burgundy, in 1429, thereby helping to strengthen Portugal's commercial ties with Flanders. She was the mother of Philip "the Bold" of Burgundy. Afonso, illegitimate, but the oldest son of João I, became count of Barcelos and later first duke of Bragança. Afonso's two sons played important roles during the fifteenth century in the struggle between the powerful landed aristocracy and those who worked to promote greater centralization and royal power.

Afonso V (r. 1438–1481) was very active in crusading against the Muslims in northern Africa. Because of this, he is sometimes called "the African." During his reign the Portuguese captured Alcácer Seguer (El-Qsar es Sghir), Arzila, and Tangier in Morocco. Afonso V's sister Joana (Juana) married Enrique IV of Castile and was the mother of Juana. Enrique's death in 1474 left Juana heiress to the Castilian throne, although her claim was challenged by Enrique's half-sister Isabel, the latter having married Fernando of Aragón in 1469. In the latter years of his reign Afonso V tried to marry his thirteen-year-old niece, Juana, and invaded Castile on her behalf. But the opposition of the Trastámaras Isabel and Fernando were too strong and after a number of years of warfare the Treaty of Alcáçovas was signed in 1479. It recognized Isabel as queen of Castile and ceded the Canary Islands to her kingdom.

Afonso V was almost profligate in giving lands and privileges to the landed nobility, especially, but not exclusively, to the count of Barcelos and first duke of Bragança and his family, at the expense of the royal patrimony. Afonso V's younger brother Fernando married Beatriz, another daughter of his uncle Prince João, and eventually became master of Santiago and Christ, and succeeded his uncle Henrique as duke of Viseu. When he died in 1470, Fernando was one of the wealthiest men in Portugal. His youngest son, Manuel, became king of Portugal (1495–1521). Manuel's sister, Leonor, married Crown Prince João, Afonso V's heir.

With João II, the Renaissance monarchy began in Portugal. Considered among the ablest European monarchs in the fifteenth century, João was determined to subordinate the landed nobility to the Crown. João II was opposed by Fernando, third duke of Bragança, one of the wealthiest and most powerful men in the entire Iberian Peninsula. Evidence of treason was discovered and the third duke was brought to trial, found guilty as charged, and publicly beheaded in Évora in 1483. The following year, Joao II's first cousin (and brother-in-law), Diogo, fourth duke of Viseu, who had continued to plot against the monarch, was stabbed to death by João II's own hand. Others involved in the conspiracies were executed or imprisoned, or sought refuge in Castile. With the support of the cortes, the extension of royal law and administration was greatly increased. Although the high social and economic status of the nobility remained, any threat the nobility posed to the crown was extinguished.

João II was active in promoting expansion down the coast of Africa. São Jorge da Mina was established in 1482. Later that same year, the Portuguese monarch sent Diogo Cão on the first of two voyages to explore south of the equator. Cão became the first known European to see the Congo River. During his expedition of 1487–1488, Bartolomeu Dias discovered the Cape of Good Hope, thus paving the way for Vasco da Gama's epic voyage to India of 1497–1499.

FRANCIS A. DUTRA

Bibliography

De Oliveira Marques, A. H. *Daily Life in Portugal in the Late Middle Ages*. Madison, Wisc., 1971.

———. *A History of Portugal*. New York, 1972.

Diffie, B. W. *Prelude to Empire: Portugal Overseas before Henry the Navigator*. Lincoln, Neb., 1960.

Livermore, H. V. *A History of Portugal*. Cambridge, U.K., 1947.

Mattoso, J. (ed.) *História de Portugal* Vol. 2. Lisbon, 1993.

Serrão, J. V. (ed.) *História de Portugal*. Vol. 1. Lisbon, 1977.

PORTUGUESE LANGUAGE *See* GALAICO-PORTUGUESE LANGUAGE

PRESTER JOHN

The legend of Prester John was unique in medieval history not because it was taken seriously, but because it became identified with an actual person or persons—the negus, or emperor, of Ethopia. Other legends, such as that of el Dorado, may have been more firmly rooted in fact, but the Iberians (and Germans) who searched for them never imagined or claimed to have realized them; the Portuguese actually awarded the office and title to a living ruler.

The origin of the legend had nothing to do with Portugal, but rather with the German chronicler, Otto von Freising, who claimed that in 1145 he had met a Syrian bishop in Italy who told him of a Christian priest-emperor named John, ruler of a vast realm to the east of Persia, who combined vast wealth with great piety, and who desired to march westward and liberate Jerusalem. Then, twenty-five years later, a hoax in the form of a letter was circulated that purported to be from this personage addressed variously to the pope or the Holy Roman or Byzantine emperors. In it, he proclaimed himself to to be a descendant of the Magi, richer and more powerful than all worldly monarchs combined, and there followed a fanciful tale of seven streams, bottomed with precious stones, flowing from his mountaintop palace and dividing his empire, which included the "three Indias," into seven kingdoms. To Europeans, whose knowledge of extra-European geography was vague and fanciful and who thought of anything beyond Egypt as Asian, the whereabouts of this Christian Shangri-la was subject to continuous readjustment from lands recently known to lands still unexplored.

When reports of a great Christian monarch in Abyssinia began to filter into Christian Europe, curiosity was presently translated into action, in this case by the Portuguese, who were in a unique position to investigate them. From the time of Infante Henrique onward (as demonstrated in the chronicle of Azurara), the quest for Prester John became a major objective of Portuguese expansion, while in the reign of João II (1480–1495) expeditions and individuals were sent in search of his realm, most notably in the persons of Afonso da Paiva and Pero da Covilhã; Covilhã actually found the negus before the end of the fifteenth century, but was not allowed to return to Portugal; instead, the Ethiopian did send an Armenian named Matthew to Portugal as his ambassador, who reached Lisbon in 1514. Then it was not until 1520 that an embassy was returned under Rodrigo da Lima, who was accredited as ambassador to the court of Prester John. It actually made contact with the negus, then Lebna Dengel Dawit, on the Ethiopian plateau in 1520. A priest on the mission, Francisco Álvares, wrote an account of the mission called *Ho Preste Joam das Indias*, published in 1540. While the Portuguese continued to refer to the negus as "Preste João," it is clear that thereafter the title became a mere convention and bore little relationship to belief in the original legend.

George D. Winius

Bibliography

Beckingham, C. F., and G. W. B. Huntingford (eds.) *The Prester John of the Indies*. 2 vols, Cambridge, 1961.

"Preste Joao." In *Dicionário de História de Portugal*. Ed. J. Serrão. Lisbon. n.d.

PRINTING

By the earlier fifteenth century, woodblock books (and perhaps also metal plates) circulated in Spain. As yet, however, no examples known to have been produced in Spain itself before 1473 have been discovered. This primitive form of printing has left short examples produced in the last quarter of the century. Likewise, no examples are known from the single letter, movable wood type (probably the invention of Lorenzo Jansoon Coster of Haarlam), modified by Coster's apprentice, Johannes Gutenberg, at Strasbourg soon after 1450 to arrive at movable, metal type. The primary candidates for the first book thus printed in Spain are *Les obres o trobes de labors dela verge Maria* (Valencia, c.1470), the *Catena aurea* of St. Thomas (Barcelona, c.1471), and a *Sinodal* (Segovia, c.1472). The first printer we can identify is Johann Parix from Heidelberg. The oldest example in the United States (in the collection of the Hispanic Society) of Spanish printing is the commentary on the Athanasian Creed by Pedro Martínez de Osma, printed by Parix at Segovia (c.1472).

The first printers in Spain were immigrants from northern Europe; they were primarily from Germany, but several came from France and elsewhere. Among them were Heinrich Botel, Pedro Hagembach, Johann Luschner, Nicolás Spindeler, Lambert Palmart, and Arnaldo Guillén de Brócar. Over thirty different Germanic printers worked in Spain before 1500 and many were peripatetic in the earlier years. The first known native Spanish printer is Alfonso Fernández de Córdoba (fl. 1477–1495), who first learned his trade at Naples. By the end of the fifteenth century, an almost equal number of native Spaniards had acquired the skill, usually as apprentices to the Germanic printers, and became independent. Some of the most active were Pedro Posa (Barcelona), Antonio Centenera (Zamora), and Juan de Burgos. The earliest books in Spain are printed with Roman type, suggesting that the earliest German printers arrived in Spain without their typefaces in hand and quickly cast less-complicated fonts. The first Gothic type seems to be that of Matthew of Flanders at Zaragoza in late 1475. Soon after, Gothic fonts dominated the publishing industry in Spain and thrived for most of the sixteenth century.

Incunabula, books printed before 1501, followed manuscript traditions with floriated or historiated initials printed with wooden blocks, as were illustrations. Printed on handmade paper with watermarks, the standard Spanish incunabulum tended to be folio page size (34 by 24 centimeters with full watermark in the center of every other page) or quarto (17.5 by 12 centimeters with half of the watermark at the center edge of two pages in every four). The earliest title pages were brief, but the last page, the colophon, gave precise and complete information, usually including day and month as well as year of publication. The art of book illustration developed quickly in the hands of Spain's skilled but anonymous woodcarvers. Notable series include the blocks for Aesop, *Historia de Vaspasiano*, and *Celestina* usually imitated or even recut from tracings for subsequent publishers. Full-page title pages, often portraits with ornate borders, began to emerge, and most printers designed sometimes complicated logos for the colophon, still retained for printing information. Bindings were often of crude parchment with a handlettered spine title. Luxury books were printed with a second color, red, and sometimes bound in tooled leather especially for presentation. Editions were small and all books were extremely costly. They were often subsidized by prominent or wealthy patrons thus meriting a dedicatory preface as well as their portrait.

By the end of the fifteenth century some nine hundred editions had been produced at twenty-five known sites, over 75 percent at only six cities: Seville, Salamanca, Barcelona, Zaragoza, Burgos, and Valencia. The major printers at each site, respectively, were Meinhardus Ungut, Stanislao Polono, the second Gothic group, Johann Rosembach, Paul and Johann Hurus, Fadrique (Biel) de Basilea, and Lope de la Roca. Almost half the texts published in all of Spain were in Latin, 40 percent were in Castilian, and over 10 percent in Catalan. Nine books were printed in Hebrew and one in Portuguese. Immigrant printers from Germany produced 62 percent of the total.

The Latin texts issued are primarily associated with the church, from theology to breviaries, missals, catechisms, and indulgences. Notable items from this group are the Catalan Bible (1478) and the Book of Solomon (1500) as well as a Torah (1490). Another large category, both in Latin and the vernacular, are legal and governmental texts as well as histories and chronicles. Texts in the vernacular reveal the emergence and popularity of secular literature. The most popular of these were the *Claros varones* of Fernando del Pulgar; the *Laberinto de fortuna* of Juan de Mena, as well as his *Coronación*; and *Celestina, Coplas de Mingo Revulgo*, and *Cárcel de Amor* by Diego de San Pedro. Catalan readers favored the novels of Juan de Flores and the chivalresque novel *Tirant lo Blanc*. Roman and Greek classics are well represented in Spanish translation by twenty-three printings with Aesop, Seneca, Aristotle, and Cato predominating. Other notable European authors in Spanish versions include Giovanni Boccaccio, Merlin, Alessandro Piccolomini, and Girolamo Savonarola. Lively interest in languages is indicated by some twenty-five printings of various works of Elio Antonio de Nebrija including his Spanish-Latin dictionaries and his grammar of the Spanish language. A Latin-Spanish dictionary (1490) by Alfonso de Palencia was also published, as were other linguistic treatises. Noteworthy clusters of works appeared in the categories of medicine (including surgery), astronomy, and cosmography, and science and technology including magnetics.

An unknown number of Spanish incunabula have been lost to posterity, but a substantial quantity remain carefully preserved and cataloged by libraries throughout the world. The major collections in Spain include those of the Biblioteca Nacional and the Royal Library and Academies in Madrid as well as those of the Universities of Barcelona and Seville. Important groups and unique copies of Spanish incunabula are to be found throughout Europe and in the Americas, prominent among which are the National Library in Paris, the British Museum, the Herzog August Library (Wolfenbüttel, Germany), the Hispanic Society (New York), Newberry Library (Chicago), and various universities and other libraries in North and South America.

THEODORE S. BEARDSLEY Jr.

Bibliography

Catálogo colectivo provisional de incunables existentes en las bibliotecas Españolas. 2 vols. Madrid, 1970?

Goff, F. R. *Incunabula in American Libraries: A Third Census*. New York, 1964.

Haebler, C. *Bibliografía ibérica del siglo XV*. 2 vols. New York, 1962.

Penney, C. L. "Incunabula." In *A History of the Hispanic Society of America*. New York, 1954. 408–87.

Ramer, J. D. "Fifteenth-Century Spanish Printing." Ph.D. diss., Columbia University, 1969.

PRISCILLIAN AND PRISCILLIANISM

See CHURCH; HERESY; THEOLOGY

PROAZA, ALONSO DE

Asturian-born humanist, poet, editor, translator, and rhetorician, active in the final decades of the fifteenth and the first two decades of the sixteenth. Like others of his day, he was trained, apparently in rhetoric, at Salamanca, and helped promote the new university at Alcalá de Henares, a pet project of a group of humanists led by the powerful Cardenal Cisneros. Proaza's many interests embraced the works of Ramón Llull, some of which he edited and/or translated between 1510 and 1519, and later published with the patronage of Cisneros. No prose of Proaza's survives. As a poet he wrote in both Latin and the Castilian vernacular: a hymn to St. Catherine of Siena, as well as a few playful "*respuestas*"—courtly poems in the *tenso* style—survive in the *Cancionero general* editions of 1511 and 1514. His career ended in and around Valencia where, under the protection of the Duke of Gandía, he held chairs of rhetoric, first at the University of Valencia (1504–1506) and then at Tarazona (1505–1517). In 1505, he published a paean to Valencia, a unique heroic ballad, in his *Oratio luculenta*.

The enduring fame of Proaza, however, largely rests on poems he created corrector, for two acclaimed works of the period, *Sergas de Esplandián* (Seville, 1510, fifth book of the *Amadís de Gaula* cycle), and *Tragicomedia de Calisto y Melibea* or (*Celestina*). To both works he appends original poems (the first to do so in the vernacular, and the first to style them—in the instance of *Celestina*—in his role as corrector of preprinting proofs) that are destined as parting commentaries to readers. The *octavas reales* (verses composed of eight hendecasyllabic lines rhyming abababcc) he provides for *Esplandián* spare little hyperbole in extolling the union of classical epic style with the skills of the author, Garci Rodríguez de Montalvo, and recommends it specifically to men and women of taste and learning.

His intervention in the 1501 Seville printing of the sixteenth-act *Comedia* have had wider repercussions. Proaza's poem at the conclusion of the work opens with references to the attraction of Orphic music and suggests that the reader would do well to speak the text, compares the work favorably to those of earlier playwrights, indicates how the work can be read aloud in small groups in the manner of *lesedrama*, reveals what secrets are to be found in the acrostic verses that form a prologue to the text, and ends by giving the date (Salamanca, 1500; a lost version of another sixteen-act *Comedia*?). Proaza adds to these another stanza, which appears first in the Valencia 1514 *Tragicomedia*, and which argues that the work merits being called a tragicomedy owing to the excesses that are ruefully punished in its pages. Proaza's placing the *Celestina* firmly among dramatic works meant for oral delivery has come to play a crucial role in the ongoing debate over its genre.

JOSEPH T. SNOW

Bibliography

McPheeters, D. W. *El humanista español Alonso de Proaza*. Valencia, 1961.

PROPHETIC CHRONICLE

A curious collection of materials closely related to the *Crónica Albeldense*, although previously thought to be independent. The chronicle contains its own internal dating to April 883, that is, during the reign of King Alfonso III of Asturias. It is chiefly remarkable because it predicts that expulsion of the Muslims from the Iberian Peninsula will take place in November 884 on the basis of a biblical prophecy from Ezekiel that actually does not exist in any known text of Scripture. That strange prediction was included in a potpourri of other materials including lists of the earlier kings of Asturias, of Iberian bishops, and of the Roman provinces of the peninsula. Throughout, the chronicle treats the kings of Asturias as the rightful successors to the Visigothic rulers of the sixth and seventh centuries who are said to have lost their kingdom to the Muslims by reason of their sins and those of their subjects. It is believed to have been inspired by the contemporary successes of Alfonso III against the Muslims.

BERNARD F. REILLY

Bibliography

Gil Fernández, J., J. L. Moralejo, and J. I. Ruiz de la Peña (eds.) *Crónicas asturianas*. Oviedo, 1985.

PROSE, BEGINNINGS OF

The initial period of Castilian prose encompasses the writings of Alfonso X (1221–1284), and this prose becomes the tool for scholarship and literary creation at the royal court. The study of this early period is difficult because of the scarcity of documents and the fact that they are of uncertain dates. Moreover, their literary value is scarce or nonexistent.

Religious Prose

The Church used vernacular language in its preaching, for the purpose of imparting Christian doctrine to the common people. These early sermons and homilies have been lost. They represented the first stage of oral prose used to address public audiences, both courtly and popular. According to Lomax, this practice was increased after the Lateran Council (1215). The incomplete copy of a *Disputa entre un cristiano y un judío* of the first third of the thirteenth century, which was perhaps written by a renegade Jew, is the earliest testimony of an encounter between different religions.

Legal Prose

The law promoted writing in Romance. Under Fernando III the Visigothic *Forum judicum* or *Fuero Juzgo* was translated into the vernacular. Some *fueros* were directly written in this common language. R. Menéndez Pidal proved that notarial practice, especially in documents relating to minor matters, was an important factor in the process of adopting the vernacular in writing. According to Rubio García, the use of the vernacular language in the royal chancellery dates back to the end of the thirteenth century.

Early History

The *Anales*, a simple form of historical narrative, were either written in Castilian or translated into this language at an early date. Such was the case of the *Anales Toledanos*. Royal history was written in Latin.

In the kingdom of Castile, the two main works in the Latin group are the *Chronicon mundi* (1236) by Lucas, bishop of Túy, and the *Historia Gothi* by Rodrigo Jiménez de Rada (1180?–1247).

The first known travel book is *La Fazienda de Ultramar*, whose author is known as Almerich, archdeacon of Antioquia. It describes, using biblical references, an itinerary to the Holy Land. The editor of this work, Lazar, considered the extant text as original, but Lapesa believes it is the Castilian version of a Latin, Provençal, or Gascon original, written in the first third of the thirteenth century. A Castilian cosmography compiled around 1223 by Isidoro and Honorio, the *Semeiança del mundo*, should also be mentioned.

The Vernacular Language: A Bridge between Arabic, Hebrew, and Latin

From the time of Archbishop of Toledo Don Raimundo (1126–1152) on, an oral romance version was used as an intermediate step between the original Arabic or Hebrew text and its Latin translation. The "Escuela de Traductores de Toledo" (School of Translators of Toledo) used this method to translate ibn Sīnā, al-Ghazālī, ibn Gabirol, and ibn Rushd. Such practice may have been a great incentive for the early development of prose.

Translations of Arabic Tales

Together with the great works produced under the sponsorship of Alfonso X, collections of Arabic tales were translated in this period. They represent the first stage in the development of prose-fiction. *Calila e Dimna*, stemming from the Arabic version by ibn al-Mukaffa, is a collection of tales intended to be a "mirror of princes." *Sendebar*, of Sanskrit origin, is another educational tale collection, with a misogynous bias. In both books the stories appear within a frame structure, and they are intended to instruct. Later on, Juan Manuel produced *El Conde Lucanor*, the Castilian masterpiece of the genre.

Counsel Books

Some of the first samples of vernacular didactic writing are books in which learning is imparted by means of proverbs. Such is the case of *Poridat de poridades*, a collection of Arabic sentences presented as advice given by Aristotle to Alexander the Great. In the *Libro de los doze sabios*, twelve wise men counsel a young king. The *Libro de los buenos proverbios* presents a series of diverse advice, some in dialogue form, which are attributed to wise men of the Orient and the Occident. The *Flores de filosofía* and the *Libro de los cien capítulos*, both of uncertain dating, may have been written during the thirteenth century.

In sum, prose becomes established later than verse in literary practice. The process takes place within chronological limits difficult to specify. Vernacular language is subject to the strong influence of the learned languages: Latin, Arabic, and Hebrew. Vernacular prose was adopted by the church, and used for the formulation of laws, as well as for the purpose of teaching.

Francisco López Estrada

Bibliography

Anales Toledanos. Ed M. Gómez Moreno. Madrid, 1917.

Calila e Dimna, Ed. J. M. Cacho Biecua, M. J. Lacarra, Madrid, 1984.

Deyermond, A. "The Sermon and its Uses in Medieval Castilian Literature." *La Corónica* 2 (1980), 126–45.

Disputa entre un cristiana y un judío, ed. A. Castro, *Revista de Filología Española* 1 (1914), 173–80.

Fazienda de ultramar. Ed. Moshé Lazar. Salamanca, 1965.

Flores de filosofía. Ed. H. Knust. Madrid, 1878.

Fuero Juzgo en latín y castellano. Madrid, 1815; facsimile ed. Madrid. 1980.

Lacarra, M. J. *Cuentística medieval en España: Los orígenes*. Zaragoza, 1979.

Lapesa, R. *Historia de la lengua española*. 8th ed. Madrid, 1980. 233.

Libro de los buenos proverbios. Ed. H. Sturm. Lexington, Ken., 1971.

Libro de los cien capítulos. Ed. A. Rey. Bloomington, Ind., 1960.

Libro de los doze sabios. Ed. J. K. Walsh. Madrid, 1975.

Lomax, D. W. "The Lateran Reforms and Spanish Literature," *Iberorromania* 1 (1969), 299–313.

López Estrada, F. *La prosa literaria medieval (Orígenes-Siglo XIV)*. Madrid, 1973.

Menéndez Pidal, R. *Documentos lingüísticos de España*. Madrid, 1966.

———. "España y la introducción de la ciencia árabe en Occidente." In *España, eslabón entre la Cristiandad y el Islam*. Madrid, 1956, 33–60.

———. *Orígenes del español*. 4th ed. Madrid, 1968–69.

Menéndez Pidal, R., et al. (eds.) *Crestomatía del español medieval*. Madrid, 1965.

Pordiat de poridades. Ed. L. Kasten. Madrid, 1957.

Rubio García, L. *Del latín al castellano en las escrituras reales*. Murcia, 1981.

Sánchez Alonso, B. *Historia de la historiografía española*. Vol. 1 2d ed. Madrid, 1947. 87–162.

Sendébar, Ed. M. J. Lacarra. Madrid, 1989.

PROSTITUTION

In the Middle Ages, prostitution was not considered a crime, but rather a necessary evil. Consequently, in order to make sure that they were not confused with respectable women, society isolated prostitutes by making them live in designated places such as brothels (*mancebías*), and by requiring them to wear certain types or colors of clothing. Nevertheless, society accepted the prostitute for the necessary function she filled, as the extensive medieval legislation on prostitution shows.

Although prostitution has always existed, it only acquired a regulated urban presence with the rise of the cities and the middle classes. Prostitutes were generally women of lower social class status who turned to the profession after being left without family and without money. Prostitution was considered necessary because it provided a sexual outlet for men, who outnumbered women and in many cases lacked access to marriage because of a shortage of females.

Cities generally had one or several brothels where prostitutes lived and worked. Laws in the *fueros* (municipal codes) and especially in city ordinances, regulated the prostitutes' activities to assure that the practice did not disturb public order. The brothel had a manager who was responsible for making sure that the operation ran smoothly and that money was handled appropriately. The mancebías belonged to various institutions, including the crown, the Church (as was the case in Córdoba), and most frequently, the city. The crown could also transfer the earnings of its brothels to a particular noble as a reward for his services, as was the case in Málaga and later in Granada. The majority of the problems caused by prostitution occurred when prostitutes left the brothel to work on their own, an offense that was punished with fines.

Prostitution was the greatest form of the economic exploitation of women in the Middle Ages.

CRISTINA SEGURA GRAIÑO
A. C. AL-MUDAYNA

Bibliography

Brundage, J. A. *Law, Sex, and Chrsitian Society in Medieval Europe*. Chicago, 1987.

Bullough, V. and B. Bullough. *Women and Prostitution. A Social History*. Buffalo, N.Y., 1987.

La Prostitution en Espagne: de l'époque des rois catholiques à la IIe République. Études réunies et présentées par Raphaël Carrasco. Paris, 1994.

Las mujeres en las ciudades medievales. Actas de las Terceras Jornadas de Investigación Interdisciplinaria. ed. C. Segura Garíño. Madrid, 1984.

Otis, Leah Lydia. *Prostitution in Medieval Society: The History of an Urban Institution in Languedoc*. Chicago, 1985.

Rossiaud, J. *Medieval Prostitution*. Trans. Lydia G. Cochrane. New York, 1988.

Vázquez García, F. *Poder y prostitución en Sevilla (siglos XIV al XX)*. 2 vols. Sevilla, 1995.

PROVERBS

Eleanor O'Kane, in her seminal work, distinguished among erudite sayings (*proverbios*), popular sayings (*refranes*), and proverbial phrases—grammatically incomplete proverbs.

Erudite sayings in medieval Iberian sentential works introduce a topic and provoke further thought. For this reason they sometimes take the form of enigmas or riddles whose referents need not be guessed: "El saber es nave de los obedientes" ["Knowledge is the ship of the obedient"] (*Libro de los buenos proverbios*). The hearer first conjures up the image and then draws up a mental list of correspondences in order to benefit from the lesson. Patronio, aware of how taxing sentential sayings could be, warns the Conde Lucanor that the *proverbios* listed as a supplement to his exemplary tales are enigmatic: "vos converná de aguzar el entendimiento para las entender" ["You had better sharpen your undestanding to understand them"] (*Cuarta Parte*).

Erudite proverbs occur in dialogues between a sage and a pupil (*Poridat de las poridades, Conde Lucanor*) a father and son in the manner of Proverbs and Ecclesiasticus (*Zifar*, *Vida de Ysopo*), as a transcription of an ancient work (*Libro de los proverbios*), as the proceedings of a meeting of sages (*Libro de los doze sabios*), or in riddle form as the contents of a battle of wits (*La donçella Teodor*).

On the other hand, *refranes* occur in discourse and illustrate, amplify, or reinforce meaning. Their principal function in discourse is to sum up a situation. The defeated Poro in the *Libro de Alexandre* warns Alexandre that fortune is undependable: "Ca son fado e viento malos de retener" ["It is destiny and wind and impossible to keep"]. *Refranes* also recommend a course of action; Trotaconventos in the *Libro de buen amor* tells her customer that her services are valuable: "El que al lobo enbía . . . carne espera" ["He who sends the wolf expects meat"].

The reader envisions the image adduced by the proverb, and selects the meaning that applies to the immediate situation. Unlike sentential sayings, *refranes* become intelligible only through the shared cultural experience of speaker and listener.

At times a proverb alludes to a familiar folktale even though the tale itself is no longer current; for example, "Ay molino te veas casado" ["Oh mill, would that you were married"] in the *Libro de buen amor*. Familiar sayings can appear in truncated form as proverbial phrases—for example, "com al carnero que fue buscar la lana" ["Like the ram that went looking for wool"] (*Poema de Fernán González*)—or they can be transformed comically—for example, "Moço malo, moço malo más val' enfermo que sano" ["A bad helper, a bad helper is worth more sick than well"] (*Libro de buen amor*). Occasionally a speaker will create a chain of *refranes*: "Perezoso nin tardinero non seas en tomar; muchas cosas prometidas se pierden por vagar; Quando te dieren la cabrilla, acorre con la soguilla; Quien te algo prometiere, luego tomando fiere" ["Don't be lazy or late when taking; many promised things are lost because of delay; when they give you the goat, run with the rope; whosoever promises something later wounds by taking"] (*Corbacho*).

Recognizing *refranes* in literary texts from the past, and distinguishing them from sentential sayings or from individual flashes of wit that are preproverbial, is a difficult task in the absence of shared cultural resonance between reader and author. Abrahams defines proverbs as "among the shortest forms of traditional expression that call attention to themselves as formal artistic entities." Frequently, their acontextuality, or strangely inappropriate subject matter, alerts the reader to possible proverbiality, particularly when, as Barley notes, an "underlying logical structure" is discernible: "Oro majado luçe" ["Beaten gold shines"] (Berceo, *Santo Domingo de Silos*).

In some cases the author identifies proverbs explicitly as *parlilla*, *fabla*, *fablilla*, *palavra*, *pastraña*, *derecho*, *prouerbio antiguo*, or *retraer*, or prefaces the saying with such comments as "por ende dizen," ["therefore they say"] or "dizen las viejas" ["old women say"]. Lacking this identification these popular sayings are identifiable by the acontextuality of their image ("ca de pequeña çentella se leuanta gran fuego" ["from a small spark a great fire arises"] or by their structure: *Quien* (He who)—"Quien bien see non se lieue," ["He who sits well should not get up"]. *El que*—"El que suel ser vençido será el vençedor," ["He who is usually conquered will conquer"]; *Mejor es* (It is better to)—"Mejor es tardar e recabdar que non auerse ome a repentir por se rebatar." ["It is better to be late and get what you want than to withdraw"]; *Más vale* (more valuable than)—"Más vale saber que auer," ["Knowledge is more valuable than wealth"]; *No hay . . . sin* (There is no without)—"Non ay paño sin raça," ["There is no cloth without tearing"]; *Tal . . . tal* (He who, gets . . .)—"Qui tal faze, tal prenda," ["What goes around, comes around"] (Berceo, *Milagros*); or *Qual . . . tal*—"Qual aqui fiziere tal avrá de padir," ["He who does gets it back in return"] (*Apolonio*).

Proverbial phrases are even more difficult to validate because they can be confused easily with possibly preproverbial similes or metaphors. In the absence of authorial identification, these colorful fragments can be called proverbial if they appear in complete form elsewhere. Proverbial phrases are often sayings that derive from anecdotes about historical events or from folktales. Consider the saying: "Tijeretas han de ser" ["They must be scissors"] an echo of the tale of the drowning woman who died insisting that she had been right (*Corbacho*). The fragmentary "Amidos faze el perro barvecho" ["The wild dog gets little attention"] is understandable through its equivalent listed in the seventeenth century by Correas: "Perro de barbecho, ladra sin provecho," ["The wild dog's howl is without profit"]. A modern compilation lists it as "Amidos hace el can barbecho."

HARRIET GOLDBERG

Bibliography

Abrahams, Roger. *Talking Black.* Rowley, Mass., 1991.

Barley, Nigel. *The Innocent Anthropologist: Notes from a Mud Hut.* New York, 1992.

Campos, J., and A. Barella. *Diccionario de refranes.* Madrid, 1975.

Correas, Gonzalo. *Vocabulario de refranes y frases proverbiales.* Madrid, 1627; Ed. Louis Combet et. al. Madrid, 2000.

Goldberg, H. "The Proverb in *cuaderna vía* Poetry: A Procedure for Identification." In *Hispanic Studies in Honor of Alan D. Deyermond.* Ed. J. S. Miletich. Madison, Wisc., 1986, 119–33.

O'Kane, E. *Refranes y frases proverbiales españoles de la Edad Media.* Madrid, 1959.

PULGAR, FERNANDO DEL

No complete study exists of the life and works of this royal secretary and official historian. We know little of his personal life, family, and friends. He was married, had a daughter who became a nun, and a brother Rodrigo, murdered in 1474 in obscure circumstances. A document, not fully authenticated, says his father was a court scribe, Diego Rodríguez de Toledo. Indirectly we know he came from the Toledo area (c.1420) and died of old age in Villaverde, a village near Madrid (c. 1490). He may have been educated in the household of the "relator" Fernán Díaz de Toledo and in the chanceries of Juan II and Enrique IV of Castile; the only acquaintance he names with special warmth is Fernán Pérez de Guzmán. From 1457 on his name appears in documents as secretary in the chancery of Enrique IV where no doubt he became acquainted with the official chronicler Alfonso de Palencia.

In the crisis over the succession in Castile, Enrique IV intended to send Pulgar to Rome in early 1473 to get dispensation for the marriage of his daughter Juana to the Infante Enrique Fortuna; the arrangement never came about. On the accession of Queen Isabel, Pulgar was entrusted with the first important mission to France to arrange the terms under which an alliance could be reestablished. It has been suggested that a letter sent to Pedro González de Mendoza, el "Gran Cardenal," accused Pulgar of being a judaizer and of speaking ill of Queen Isabel, and that this forced him out of her favor, but no documentary proof has yet appeared.

In 1480, if Palencia's statements are to be believed, Isabel appointed Pulgar as official chronicler because she did not trust Palencia. From this point on we have two distinct regnal narratives, one favorable to Isabel and Pedro González de Mendoza, and the other more inclined to Fernando. Henceforward, Pulgar devoted his time to the preparation of historical works, and left evidence of his methods in his correspondence; These *Letras* were probably printed posthumously (Zaragoza, 1493). In late 1486 the *Claros varones de Castilla* were printed in Toledo, after his experiences in the Granada campaign. His official chronicle in its original version ended in late 1490, but was not printed until 1565 in Valladolid, falsely attributed to Elio Antonio de Nebrija. This was because Galíndez de Carvajal, as part of his plan to edit and print Castilian chronicles, had given a copy to Nebrija to be translated into Latin; this was completed in 1509 and printed in Granada, 1545. (The 1565 edition was an abbreviated version of the original, which was not itself edited until 1943). Galíndez had mixed feelings about Pulgar's methodology. He approved of his industry but not his selection of events, which gave too much prominence to "el gran Cardenal," nor did he care for the intercalation of harangues and moral commentaries that Pulgar put in the mouth of his protagonists. However, he did sanction the main thrust of the narrative, which traced the dramatic change in the political fortunes of Castile from the marriage of Isabel to Fernando to the last phase of the Granada campaign. Pulgar himself stated he was imitating classical precedent in allowing protagonists to speak, as he says, in their own voices, sometimes using real documents as his inspiration. He identified himself totally with royal policies and gave the Queen his rough drafts to correct. His gloss to the *Coplas de Mingo Revulgo* (Logroño, 1502–1505) is another example of using poetic material for the purpose of educating those in authority in matters of government.

Pulgar is best known for *Claros varones de Castilla*, which, while acknowledging a debt to Fernán Pérez de Guzmán, is much more varied and subtle and drives toward a different goal. He would agree that unregenerate humanity was avaricious, power-hungry, and self-regarding, but he offers as examples to his readers certain lives of Castilian nobles who could outshine the Romans in their *amor patriae*. Where Guzmán admonishes, Pulgar encourages and creates a pantheon of heroes to inspire his aristocratic audience to greater deeds of virtues, to act in unison and bring about the completion of the Granada campaign. Included are one king (Enrique IV), fifteen nobles, eight prelates, and two intercalated addresses to Isabel. A *Tratado de los reyes de Granada* is also attributed to Pulgar.

ROBERT B. TATE

Bibliography

Pulgar, F. del. *Claros varones de Castilla*. Ed. R. B. Tate. Madrid, 1985.

———. *Crónica de los Reyes Catálicos*. Ed. J. de Mata Carriazo. 2 vols. Madrid, 1943.

Q

QABALLAH *See* DE LEÓN, MOSES

QĀḌĪ

Qāḍīs are judges or jurists (*fuqahā'*) appointed by the state who administer Islamic law. *Qāḍīs* are selected from the '*Ulamā*' or the corpus of pious religious scholars in the community. Since qāḍīs were appointed by the state, their judgments could often reflect more local political interests. As a result, they were sometimes the object of censure by the 'Ulamā' and there are repeated expressions of disapproval of them from earliest Umayyad times.

The task of the specific interpretation of the law and its application in individual cases was vested in the *muftīs*, who could either be private individuals or public servants. A verdict on a particular point of law is called a *fatwā*. Over time a large body of fatwās was collected by the Ulamā that was employed by the qāḍīs in applying the law in cases that came before the courts. A muftī is thus an eminent judge or jurisconsultant, a qāḍī simply a judge. The collections of fatwās from the Middle Ages are an important source of knowledge about the nature, application, and integration of customary and Islamic law in Al-Andalus.

E. MICHAEL GERLI

Bibliography

Harvey, L. P. *Islamic Spain, 1250–1500*. Chicago, 1990. 74–97.

Rahman, Fazlur. *Islam*. 2d ed. Chicago. 1979.

Urvoy, Dominique. "The '*Ulamā*' of al-Andalus." In *The Legacy of Muslim Spain*. Ed. S. K. Jayussi. Vol. 2. New York, 1994. 141–55.

QASMŪNA BINT ISMĀ'ĪL

Qasmūna was the first known Jewish woman writer on the Iberian Peninsula. She is believed to have been the daughter of the famous eleventh-century poet, Samuel Ha-Nagid (Ibn Nagrīllah), the vizier of the king of Granada and the leader of the Jewish community. He apparently had four children, three sons and one daughter, Qasmūna, whom he instructed in the art of poetry. He reportedly often began a strophe and called on Qasmūna to finish it, a form of recreation common among medieval Arabic peoples. Indeed the first of the three extant poems by Quasmūna is a reply to a short poem by her father concerning someone who harms his benefactor. Qasmūna's clever response compares that person with the moon, which receives its light from the sun and yet sometimes eclipses it. Tradition has it that, upon hearing this, her father said she was a greater poet than he was.

However, Samuel Ha-Nagid wrote his poems in Hebrew, while Qasmūna wrote hers in Arabic. As a Jewish woman, she had no access to Hebrew poetry and certainly no audience for it, even if she had written it. On the other hand, as a member of the court in Granada, she did have access to Arabic poetry, as well as an audience of like-minded women poets. Indeed, although Jewish, she is considered one of the foremost Arabic women poets of Al-Andalus.

Critics have pointed out some Biblical resonances in Qasmūna's poems. They also have underscored the fact that her poems seem to alude to the importance of marriage for women, a very Jewish concept. In effect, her two other poems are laments about her loneliness. The first is about a garden which is going to waste without a gardener. Youth is passing by and the only thing that remains is something the poet does not dare name. In the second poem, she compares herself with a deer in a garden. Critics have commented that her father seems to have been too busy to select a son-in-law. However, one wonders if this is what Qasmūna was complaining about. Obviously, she felt alienated, but her alienation might have been of a more profound nature. Being the daughter of a powerful Jewish official in an Arab court must not have been easy. Being a talented woman with no outlet for her talent must have been even more difficult. Qasmūna could be talking about her spiritual isolation and the waste of her talent. The deer is a restless animal meant to be free, not confined in a garden, however pleasant. What Qasmūna does not dare name could be her frustration.

CRISTINA GONZÁLEZ

Bibliography

Garulo, T., *Diwan de las poetisas de al-Andalus*. Madrid, 1986.

Sobh, M., *Poetisas arábigo-andaluzas*. Granada, n.d.

QUEENSHIP

Queenship in medieval Aragón, Castile, León, Navarre, and Portugal reflects a distinctive political culture that was both similar to and substantially different from England, France, or the German Empire. All queens faced the imperative to produce an heir and to raise and educate the children; they participated in public ceremonial functions, performed charitable work, and were important patrons of religion and art. Unlike their northern counterparts, however, Spanish and Portuguese queens were more likely to be active in the governance of the realm. The circumstances surrounding the Muslim conquest of 711 and the Christian Reconquest led to a pragmatic, less theocratic monarchy that, for the most part, did not explicitly prohibit women from inheriting or ruling. The resultant dynamic political partnership, sensitive to the prevailing legal customs and local culture, involved both king and queen and took into account individual abilities and temperament.

Birth determined a queen's inheritance rights and her suitability as bride for a foreign prince, but it was marriage that ultimately constituted a queen's political rights and responsibilities. Royal marriages forged alliances of great consequence to the consolidation of power among the Christian kingdoms. The dowry that Sancha, daughter of Alfonso V of Asturias-León (999–1028), brought to her marriage to Fernando I of Castile (1035–1065), enabled them to reunite briefly the two realms and initiate the reconquest. Philippa and Catalina of Lancaster, daughters of John of Gaunt, married João I of Portugal (1385–1433) and Enrique III of Castile (1390–1406), respectively, in a move that effectively ended Castilian and Portuguese intervention in the Hundred Years' War. Marie of Montpellier's marriage to Pedro II of Aragón (1196–1213) opened the door to Aragónese influence north of Pyrenees and set the stage for the conquests of their son, Jaime I (1213–1276). Teresa of Portugal, illegitimate daughter of Alfonso VI of León (1065–1109), married Henry of Burgundy, and together they governed the nascent kingdom of Portugal from 1109 to 1128.

In Castile and León, princesses could legitimately inherit in the absence of a legitimate male heir. Alfonso VI of León (1065–1109) designated his daughter Urraca as his successor and she ruled in her own right from 1109 until 1126. Married twice to powerful men, including Alfonso I of Aragón (1104–1134), Urraca defied the notion that a man who married a ruling queen should automatically share in the governance of his wife's realms. Isabel I, "la Católica" (1474–1504), arguably the most famous Castilian queen, held her realms separate from those of her husband, Fernando II of Aragón (1479–1516), who ruled Aragón in his own right but did not have sovereign power over Isabel; not even after her death could he rule as king of Castile.

It is one thing to inherit, but another to rule. Berenguela, daughter of Alfonso VIII of Castile (1158–1214), was legal heir but renounced her rights in favor of her brother, Enrique I (1214–1217); she was regent throughout his minority, and upon his death ceded her throne rights to Fernando III (1217–1252), her son by her former husband, Alfonso IX of León (1188–1230). Alfonso IX may have named his daughters Sancha and Dulce as his successors, but they renounced their claims in favor of their half-brother Fernando, resulting in the union of the Leonese and Castilian realms. In Aragón, Petronilla, (1137–1162), infant daughter of King Ramiro II (1134–1137), inherited the kingdom in 1137 and married the older (by perhaps twenty-five years) and politically experienced Ramón Berenguer IV, count of Barcelona. After Ramiro retired to a monastery, Ramón Berenguer acknowledged his status in Aragón not as king but as prince-consort, but Petronilla ruled more in name than in fact. When Ramón Berenguer died in 1162, she ceded her throne rights to the united realms of Aragón and Catalunya to their son, Ramón. Petronilla remained regent for her son, now called Alfonso (he ruled as Alfonso II, 1162–1196), until 1164. After 1164, three succession crises loomed, but none were resolved in favor of a female claimant.

The regency was the most common means by which a queen could participate in government. The queen-regent's political authority was accepted, at least in theory, as an extension of her maternal rights as the guardian of her children. In Castile, María de Molina, widow of Sancho IV was regent for both her son, Fernando IV (1295–1312), and grandson, Alfonso XI (1312–1350). Berenguela, regent for Fernando III (1217–1252), maintained order in Castile in the face of threat of invasion by her ex-husband and civil war. In Navarre, Toda Ansúrez, was regent for her son García I Sánchez (926–970); Urraca Fernández and Jimena González, grandmother and mother, respectively, were regents for Sancho III Garcés, el Mayor (1000–1035). There are few regents in Aragón, which had instead the office of the queen-lieutenant. The lieutenancy, devised in the thirteenth century, was a means for both princes and queens to rule the Crown's extensive territorial possessions. It became a route to political power for seven queen-lieutenants: Blanca of Naples, wife of Jaime II, in 1310; Teresa d'Entença, wife of Alfonso IV (1324–1327); Violante of Bar, third wife of Juan I (1388–1430); María de Luna, first wife of Martín (1396–1406); Margarida of Prades, second wife of Martín (1412–1421); María of Castile, wife of Alfonso V (1420–1453); and Juana Enríquez, second wife of Juan II (1461–1477).

Little is known at present of Visigothic queens and many Portuguese and Navarrese queens, especially in the politically unsettled centuries before the reconquest, but a few queens stand out. Isabel, wife of Dinis of Portugal (1279–1325), was noted for her religious devotion. Blanca, daughter of Sancho VI of Navarre (1150–1194), married Thibault of Champagne; his rule, from 1234 to 1253, signaled the linkage of Navarrese and French interests. Another Blanca, daughter of Carlos III (1387–1425), inherited Navarre from her father and, in theory, ruled it jointly with her husband Juan II of Aragón (1458–1479).

THERESA EARENFIGHT

Bibliography

Bisson, T. *The Medieval Crown of Aragón: A Short History*. Oxford, 1986.

Collins, R. "Queens-Dowager and Queens-Regent in Tenth-Century León and Navarre." In *Medieval Queenship*. Ed. J. C. Parsons. New York, 1993. 79–92.

Coll Juliá, N. *Doña Juana Enríquez, lugarteniente real en Cataluña, 1461–68*. 2 vols. Madrid, 1953.

Earenfight, T. "María of Castile, Ruler or Figurehead? A Preliminary Study in Aragónese Queenship." *Mediterranean Studies* 4 (1994), 45–61.

Hernández-León de Sánchez. *Doña María de Castilla, Esposa de Alfonso el Magnánimo*. Valencia, 1959.

Javierre Mur, A. L. *María de Luna, reina de Aragón*. Madrid, 1942.

Kagay, D. "Countess Almodis of Barcelona: 'Illustrious and Distinguished Queen' or 'Woman of Sad, Unbridled Lewdness.' " In *Queens, Regents, and Potentates*. Ed. T. M. Vann. Denton, Tex. 1993. 37–47.

Liss, P. *Isabel the Queen*. New York, 1992.

O'Callaghan, J. F. *A History of Medieval Spain*. Ithaca, N.Y., 1975.

Reilly, B. *The Kingdom of León-Castilla under Queen Urraca, 1109–1126*. Princeton, N.J., 1982.

Segura Graíño, C. "Participación de las Mujeres en el Poder Político." *Anuario de Estudios Medievales* 25, no. 2 (1995), 449–62.

Shadis, M. T. "Berenguela of Castile's Political Motherhood: The Management of Sexuality, Marriage, and Succession." In *Medieval Mothering*. Ed. J. C. Parsons and B. Wheeler. New York, 1996. 335–58.

Stalls, W. C. "Queenship and the Royal Patrimony in Twelfth-Century Iberia: The example of Petronila of Aragón." In *Queens, Regents, and Potentates*. Ed. T. M. Vann. Denton, Tex., 1993. 49–61.

Vann, T. M. "The Theory and Practice of Medieval Castilian Queenship." In *Queens, Regents, and Potentates*. Ed. T. M. Vann. Denton, Tex. 1993. 125–47.

Walker, R. "Images of Royal and Aristocratic Burial in Northern Spain, c. 950–c. 1250." In *Medieval Memories: Men, Women, and the Past, 700–1300*. Ed. E. van Houts, London, 2001. 150–72.

———. "Sancha, Urraca, and Elvira: The Virtues and Vices of Spanish Royal Women 'Dedicated to God.' " *Reading Medieval Studies* 24 (1998), 113–38.

QURʾĀN

Qurʾān, the Holy Scripture of Islam, was revered in Spain from the Arab conquest until the expulsion of the Moriscos in 1609, a span of nine centuries. Considered by Muslims to be the direct word of God as revealed, in Arabic, to his prophet Muḥammad, it holds a unique place in Islamic culture. In the Middle Ages the precepts of the Qurʾān formed the basis for all law, and its memorization was the starting point of all education. Interpretation of, and commentary on, the Qurʾān constitute an important genre of Arabic letters. The Muslims' reverence for the book extends to its physical makeup, a fact that accounts for the luxurious ornamentation of many specimens (as well as for the place occupied by calligraphy in Islamic decorative art). In Spain in Caliphal times, many of the finest Qurʾān calligraphers were said to be women.

In the strictest Islamic view, translation of the Qurʾān is not permitted because God chose to reveal his word in Arabic. The first translations of the Qurʾān known to have existed in Spain were therefore made by and for Christians. In 1141 Peter the Venerable, abbot of Cluny, commissioned an Arabic-to-Latin translation that was carried out in Spain by Robert of Ketton and Hermann of Carinthia, with the assistance of a Muslim known only as Muḥammad. In the same century a Mozarabic Christian, Mark of Toledo, also produced a Latin text. Both of these versions are extant, and both were motivated by a wish to understand Islamic doctrine, the better to preach Christianity to its adherents.

The same purpose inspired, three centuries later, the first known translation of the Qurʾān into Spanish. This version was prepared by ʿIsā ibn Jābir of Segovia, at the behest of Juan de Segovia, in 1456. We know from a statement of ʿIsā's elsewhere that he fleshed out his translation with a running commentary taken from a *tafsir* or interpretation of the Qur'ān that he had in his possession. It is not known whether this work was in Arabic or in Spanish. Since Juan in his turn rendered ʿIsā's Spanish text into Latin (thus producing the first trilingual Qur'àn in Europe), the Spanish version may have been intended only as a transitional text, made necessary by the fact that ʿIsā knew Arabic and Castilian but no Latin.

All of this work except Juan's Latin prologue has been lost. Yet in the sixteenth century we find in circulation in Spain a large number of Aljamiado manuscripts containing the very type of Qur'ānic translation-cum-commentary that ʿIsā claims to have made, though most often they contain only part of the text. For example, where the Qur'ān 79:34 reads *fa'id-haǰa'at al-tamatu l-kubra* ["Then, when the Great Catastrophe comes"], one Aljamiado version renders the phrase by the amplification "I cuando venrrá la fortuna mayor, que será el soflo del cuerno la çaguera vegada, cuando traerán los del aljanna al aljanna y los del fuego al fuego" ["And when the great destiny comes, and when the horn blows the last time, and when the judged come to judgment and those of the fire to the fire"]. One is tempted to relate at least some of these versions to ʿIsā's, although the specific connections are not clear. It is possible that where several Aljamiado Qur'ān translations follow each other closely they descend from a single original; this being the case, that original might have been ʿIsā's. Alternatively, they may go back to the *tafsir* that ʿIsā himself consulted. But some of the extant versions differ so sharply from these that they must represent independent versions (for example, a Latin-letter Morisco Qur'ān of 1606 that translates the verse quoted above without commentary, "Pues cuando vendrá la fortuna mayor").

About seventy Aljamiado Qur'āns are extant. By the early seventeenth century copies must have been rare, for one scribe speaks of having borrowed his model for only a limited time. Most of those surviving texts exist in an abridged form in which the opening chapter or *Fātiha* is followed by only selected verses from the chapters up to 38; from that point on the text is usually complete (there are 114 chapters in all). This means that the Moriscos preferred the Meccan chapters, with their more inspired and hortatory tone, to the Medinan, or law-giving, chapters.

CONSUELO LÓPEZ-MORILLAS

Bibliography

D'Alverny, M. T. "Deux traductions latines du Coran au Moyen-Age." *Archives d'Histoire Doctrinale et Littéraire du Moyen Age* 22–23 (1947–48), 69–131.

López-Morillas, C. *The Qur'ān in Sixteenth-Century Spain: Six Morisco Versions of Sūra 79*. London, 1982.

R

RABBIS

The term *rabbi* in medieval usage was actually an honorary title and denoted generally a scholar proficient in Jewish law, and not necessarily a community functionary. However, virtually every community in medieval Iberia of any size had at least one official rabbi, whose duties were to oversee the conformity to Jewish law, both "religious" and civil, and usually to head the court (*bet din*) of three to adjudicate cases. Some Jewish scholars attained such high level of proficiency in the Talmud and Jewish law that they became national and even international authorities, to whom other rabbis and communities turned to render decisions or explain problems too complex for them to resolve. The decisions (responsa; *she'elot u-teshuvot*) of these scholars serve as an important historical source. Outstanding rabbis, particularly in the earlier periods (tenth and eleventh centuries) even took upon themselves the authority to enact new decrees or set aside earlier ones. (Maimonides, who was not a rabbi but a universally recognized legal authority, sometimes acted in bold and audacious ways in this regard; as did Joseph ibn Megash and others.)

However, not all rabbis were as well trained or knowledgeable as they ought to have been. From the tenth century on we encounter severe criticism and ridicule of such rabbis in our sources, and this continued to be the case down to the fifteenth century. Rabbis in earlier generations were never salaried, and Maimonides particularly disapproved of any who dared receive money for his learning. Yet by the end of the thirteenth century, particularly in Zaragoza and elsewhere in Aragón-Catalonia, rabbis were customarily salaried. Nevertheless, while such rabbis may have taught in the community, they rarely preached sermons and never officiated at services. Only once do we hear of a *cofradía* (guild) that hired a sage to preach sermons in their synagogue every Sabbath. Usually, if sermons were preached at all, this was done by itinerant "preachers." However, before major holidays and on other special occasions, great scholars did preach sermons, many of which have survived.

Court rabbis, sometimes called "chief rabbis" (*rabí mayor*) were often appointed by the king. This position may have originated as early as the reign of Alfonso X, but became fairly widespread in the fourteenth century, when in the reign of Enrique II in Castile we find references to such royally appointed *rabí* or *viejo* (elder—a biblical term). In 1388, Pedro Tenorio, the archbishop of Toledo and *cancillor mayor* (head chancellor), appointed his physician, Rabbi Hayyim ha-Levi, chief rabbi of all the Jewish *aljamas* (communities) in the province, to replace a previously named judge who did not fulfill his duties. In 1395, the archbishop appointed his physician "maestro Pedro" (who may have been the same Rabbi Hayyim, now converted?) to the same post. Sometime in 1383–1384, Juan I appointed David Negro from Portugal as chief rabbi of all Castile. He had joined the king when Juan invaded Portugal following the death of Fernando IV, whose chief rabbi Juda Aben Menir also joined the Castilian king. Maestre Samaya Lubel of Segovia, physician of Enrique IV, was *juez mayor* (head judge) of all the Jewish aljamas (c.1465–1469). Juan II apparently appointed Abraham Benveniste (c.1432) to a similar post.

In Aragón-Catalonia, such court-appointed rabbis were rarer. However, already in 1270 Jaime I appointed a rabbi and judge for Lérida, and the following year appointed Solomon Alfaquim as judge for all cases between the Jews of Zaragoza and the crown. In 1284, Solomon Avenbruch, who had been appointed judge of the Jews of Zaragoza by Pedro IV, was murdered by some Jews. When, in 1294, Solomon Constantin sought the intervention of Queen María de Molina of Castile to be appointed chief rabbi of Aragón, Jaime II refused, noting that he had not exercised that post, to which he had been appointed, in the reigns of Pedro III or Alfonso III.

Some of the many outstanding rabbis of Spain were Joseph ibn Abitur, Isaac ibn Ghiyāth, Joseph ibn

Megash, Isaac al-Fāsī, Jonah Gerundi, Solomon ibn Adret, Moses ben Naḥman, Yom Ṭov Ishbīlī, Nissim Gerundi, Ḥasdai Crescas, Isaac ben Sheset, and Asher ben Yeḥiel and his sons Judah and Jacob. Many volumes of commentaries, responsa, and other material have survived from these authors.

NORMAN ROTH

Bibliography

Neuman, A. *The Jews in Spain*. Philadelphia, 1942. Ch. 7 (with caution).

Pimenta Ferro, M. J. *Os judeus em Portugal no século XIV*. Lisbon, 1979. 25–33. Applicable also to "court rabbis" of Spain.

Roth, N. "Dar 'una voz' a los judíos: Representación en la España medieval." *Anuario de Historia del Derecho Español*, (1986), 943–52.

RAIMUNDO, ARCHBISHOP OF TOLEDO

The second archbishop of Toledo after its reconquest in 1085 by Alfonso VI of León-Castile, Raimundo succeeded Bernard of Sauvetot in 1125 and held the post until his death on 20 August 1152. During his long career he was the chief confidant of Alfonso VII of León-Castile (1126–1157). Like his predecessor, he was an ardent defender of the primatial and archepiscopal prerogatives of Toledo and therefore was frequently in conflict with the archbishops of Braga and Santiago de Compostela over their respective jurisdictions. He managed to install canons of his own church as bishops of Salamanca and Santiago de Compostela. Raimundo is most famous, perhaps, as the patron of a group of Christian, Jewish, and Muslim translators at Toledo who were rendering many of the works of ancient Greek science and Aristotelian philosophy from Arabic into Latin during his episcopate. This process made Greek, as well as much Islamic and Jewish, lore available to the developing universities of western Europe.

Raimundo had been one of the French Cluniac monks recruited for the cathedral chapter of Toledo in 1096 by Bernard of Sauvetot. Before his elevation to Toledo he had been bishop of Burgo de Osma from late 1109 until the middle of 1125, when he was transferred to the former see. In that frontier position, Raimundo had been a leading supporter of Queen Urraca of León-Castile in her struggles with Alfonso I of Aragón (1104–1134).

BERNARD F. REILLY

Bibliography

González Palencia, A. *El arzobispo Don Raimundo de Toledo*. Barcelona, 1942.

Rivera Recio, J. F. *La iglesia de Toledo en el siglo XII*. Rome, 1966.

RAMÓN BERENGUER IV, COUNT OF BARCELONA

On the death of his father in 1131, the young Ramón Berenguer IV (c.1114–1162) became the count of Barcelona at the age of seventeen. The first major event of his reign was the union of the Catalan principalities with the neighboring Kingdom of Aragón. In 1134 Alfonso I the Batallador died childless, and this raised the problem of who was to succeed him. His will, leaving his goods to the military orders, could not be applied; and this, together with the marriage of Ramiro, the brother of Alfonso I, made Alfonso VII of Castile give up all hope of succeeding to the throne. In August 1137 Petronella, born of Ramiro's recent marriage, was immediately promised to Ramón Berenguer, who became prince of Aragón; the marriage took place in 1150. In 1140 the holy see and the military orders gave up their rights over Aragón. It was by diplomatic means that Ramón Berenguer IV ended his disagreement with the king of Castile, whom he met in 1137 and 1140; at these meetings, he swore allegiance to the city of Zaragoza, and prepared a joint expedition against Navarre. Thanks to the diplomatic activities of Oleguer, archbishop of Tarragona, and the seneschal Guillem Ramón de Montcada, the count of Barcelona symbolized the union of the counties inherited from his father with the kingdom of Alfonso I. The Catalano-Aragónese confederation depended on a reciprocal respect for the institutions belonging to each territory.

Ramón Berenguer IV concentrated henceforward on the struggle against Islam. With Alfonso VII he participated in the expeditions to Murcia (1144) and Almería (1147). He later directed campaigns intended to extend his principalities. In 1148 he took Tortosa where the help of Guillem Ramón de Montcada, of the Genoese fleet, and of contingents from Languedoc was decisive for the success of this expedition, recognized by Pope Eugene III as a true crusade. Franchises accorded to the city attracted new inhabitants, while an arrangement with the qādī and the fuqahā' ensured the respect of the Muslim population. On 24 October 1149, the cities of Fraga and Lleida also fell before the troops of Ramón Berenguer IV and Ermengol VII of Urgell. Between 1152 and 1153 Miravet was conquered, and the surviving pockets of Islamic resistance destroyed. Ibn Mardānish, king of Valencia, then swore allegiance to the count of Barcelona, to whom he payed a large tribute. The Ebro River was reached; Ramón Berenguer IV considerably extended the territory of New Catalonia beyond Tarragona. The same thing happened in Aragón, where he annexed Huesca (1154) and Alcáñiz (1157).

His political activities were continued beyond the Pyrenees; the families of Béziers-Carcassonne, of Narbonne and of Montpellier paid homage to him. In 1154 he became the tutor of Gaston V of Béarn; he fought successfully at Toulouse, to which he laid siege with Henri Plantagenet II in 1156. But most of his activities took place in Provence. In 1144, his brother Berenguer Ramón, count of Provence was killed in his wars against the count of Toulouse and the family of Baux, as well as Genoa and Pisa. His son, Ramón Berenguer of Provence, was still a minor and was powerless against so many enemies. In February 1147 Ramón Berenguer IV came to his aid; the leading nobles swore that they would be faithful to him. He wiped out Ramon of Baux, and brought him back in captivity to Catalonia. Three more wars were necessary to put an end to the seditious revolt of Ramon's wife, Stephania of Baux, their children, and their associates. During the summer of 1155 he took their castle at Trinquetaille; at the beginning of 1162, he laid siege to the fortress of Baux and conquered it. He then ensured that Frederick Barbarossa recognized Catalan dominion in Provence, ordering the marriage of his niece Riquilda and his nephew Ramón Berenguer of Provence. It was during the journey to Turin, where he was to meet the emperor, that Ramón Berenguer IV met his death in Borgo San Dalmazzo, on 6 August 1162.

The work of Ramón Berenguer IV was fundamental on institutional and administrative levels. During his youth, in order to oppose the revolt of the Catalan aristocracy, he convened the Assemblies of Peace and Truce. He organized the management of his domain in such a way as to increase his financial resources, which he needed for his expansionary policy. An inspection carried out by Bertran of Castellet in Old Catalonia in 1151 furnished him with a precise inventory of the revenues of his domains; these were administered by bailiffs (*batlles*) or by creditors who accepted them as payment. His vicars (*vicaris*) mainly brought him the fines imposed by tribunals, the tolls levied, and the *parias* (tributes) of the Muslim chiefs. Justice was henceforth carried out by specialists in law, who applied the *Usatges de Barcelona*, a Roman legal code that he had just promulgated. The *Usatges* established the monopoly of the count as regards certain royal rights; castles, mint, and organization of the peace were under his control. The ecclesiastical map was redrawn; the bishoprics of Tortosa and of Lérida (Lleida) were reestablished instead of Roda-Barbastro. In 1154, the metropolitan province of Tarragona, including all the Catalan and Aragónese bishoprics, was also reestablished. Cistercian monks from Grandselve and from Fontfroide founded Santes Creus and Poblet in New Catalonia; the Templars and Hospitalers, who had received indemnities for their renunciation of Alfonso I's will, were also given domains on the frontier. The count welcomed to his court the first Catalan troubadours, Berenguer of Palol and Guerau of Cabrera. In 1162 he was praised in the first version of the *Gesta comitum barchinonensium*, drawn up at Ripoll. In 1157, on the death of Alfonso VII of Castilla-León, Ramón Berenguer IV had become the most important of the Iberian kings, and the arbiter of their struggles; he had a preponderant role in Occitania. His reign laid the basis for the great Mediterranean expansion of the Catalano-Aragónese confederation.

MARTÍ AURELL I CARDONA

Bibliography

Aurell, M. "L'expansion catalane en Provence au XIIe siècle." In *La formació i expansió del feudalisme català*. Ed. J. Portella. Girona, 1985. 175–197.

Bisson, T. N. *Fiscal Accounts of Catalonia under the Early Count-Kings (1151–1213)*. Berkeley, 1984.

———. *The Medieval Crown of Aragón: A Short History*. Oxford, 1986.

Schramm, P. E., J. F. Cabestany, and E. Bagué. *Els primers comtesreis; Ramon Berenguer IV. Alfons el Cast, Pere el Catòlic*. Barcelona, 1963.

Soldevila, F. *Història de Catalunya*. 2d ed. Barcelona, 1963.

RAMÓN BERENGUER V, COUNT OF PROVENCE

The son of Alfons II of Provence and of Garsenda of Forcalquier, Ramón Berenguer V found himself after the death of his father in Aragón under the control of Pedro II (1209). In November 1216 he left the Templar Castle of Monzón for Provence. In 1219 his mother gave him the counties of Provence and Forcalquier. In 1226 he took advantage of the arrival of Louis VIII's troups to oppose the autonomy of the cities of the Rhône; in the aftermath of the fall of Avignon, he abolished the Consulate of Tarascon. He then conquered Grasse (1227) and Nice (1229), but failed to take Marseilles, which offered its government to Raimon VII, the ousted count of Toulouse (1230). From 1240, Raimon VII and the independent communes allied themselves with Frederick II, while Ramón Berenguer V persevered in his pro-French and pontifical policy (in May 1234, he had given his eldest daughter Marguerite to Louis IX in marriage). Success was not long in coming. The episcopal party triumphed at Avignon and Tarascon in 1242; Marseilles fell on 22 June 1243.

Ramón Berenguer V died in August 1245. It was natural, bearing in mind the alliances that he had defended throughout his life, for Romée of Villeneuve, who had been his right-hand man, to arrange for Beatrice, his heir, to marry Charles of Anjou. Provence ceased to be Catalan and became French. During his reign, there was considerable centralization; the development of a central administration, the refining of the judicial system, and the creation of *vigueries* and *baillages* had allowed him to govern his country with efficiency.

MARTÍ AURELL I CARDONA

Bibliography

Aurell, M. *La vielle et l'épée: Troubadours et politique en Provence au XIIIe siècle*. Paris, 1989.

Bourrilly, V. L., and R. Busquet. *La Provence au Moyen Age: Histoire politique; L'eglise, les institutions*. Paris, 1924.

RAMÓN OF FITERO

Ramón (1100?–1161?), abbot (1141–1161) of the Cistercian monastery of Santa María in Fitero, Navarre, was founder of the Order of Calatrava. In the years 1144–1157 Ramón substantially increased the monastery's holdings and received both royal and papal privileges. In 1157, amid rumors of a pending Almohad attack against the strategically important fortress at Calatrava, the Knights Templar, who had garrisoned Calatrava since 1147, asked Sancho III (1157–1158) for permission to withdraw. Ramón was the only person willing to assume the defense of Calatrava. Out of desperation Sancho agreed, and granted Calatrava to the monastery of Fitero and the Cistercian order in January 1158. Ramón then transferred the monastery of Fitero to Calatrava, leaving behind only the aged and sick. His efforts had the support of Juan, archbishop of Toledo, who promised absolution to anyone who joined Ramón in Calatrava. This and Ramón's example inspired volunteers to come or send provisions and supplies. The garrisoning of Calatrava averted the expected attack and created the Military Order of Calatrava. The origins of the order are obscure. It is by no means certain that Ramón intended to establish a religious military order, but the lay defenders of the fortress adopted the monastic habit and Ramón gave them the Rule of St. Benedict. During Ramón's lifetime the knights lived as Cistercians, but after his death differences between knights and monks were recognized. The abbey of Fitero apparently played no further role in the order's development. The order was recognized after Ramón's death by Pope Alexander III in 1164, and it was officially affiliated with the order of Cîteaux in 1187.

THERESA M. VANN

References

Albiac, C. M. *Colección diplomática del monasterio de Fitero (1140–1210)*. Zaragoza, 1978.

O'Callaghan, J. F. "The Affiliation of the Order of Calatrava with the Order of Cîteaux." In *The Spanish Military Order of Calatrava and its Affiliates*. London, 1975.

RAMOS DE PAREJA, BARTOLOMÉ

Spanish theorist (c.1435–c.1491). Initiated into music by the papal singer Juan de Monte, whom he considered the equal of Ockeghem, Busnois, and Dufay, Ramos lectured at Salamanca where he disputed with Pedro Martínez de Osma on the meaning of the diatonic, chromatic, and enharmonic genera. Among his friends he counted such royal maestros as Tristano de Silva and Johannes Urrede.

Before 1482 he lived in Italy, first perhaps at Florence but also at Bologna, where, however, the jealousy of the mathematical faculty prevented his obtaining the chair that Nicolas V had sought to create. After publishing at Bologna in 1482 *Musica practica*, the most important treatise in Latin by a Spaniard before Salinas (1577), he settled in Rome.

In the tuning system advocated by Ramos, he opted for vibration ratios permitting three 5:4 major tri'ads and three 6:5 minor triads. Two major triads, C-E-G and F-A-C reached mathematical perfection denied them in the older Pythagorean tuning system. He also advocated solmization through the octave (equivalent to the modern fixed-*do* system). He permitted certain licenses, such as an occasional tritone and swiftly moving fifths, one perfect, the other imperfect. He was the first writer to mention the "short" octave at the bottom of keyboard instruments. However, his novel doctrines anticipating future musical developments went hand in hand with traditional contrapuntal rules and long venerated modal ethos doctrines.

All his original compositions except a perpetual four-voice canon are lost. This included a magnificat, requiem, and mass composed in Spain, and a motet *Tu lumen* in Bologna.

ROBERT STEVENSON

Bibliography

Stevenson, R. "Iberian Musical Outreach before the Encounter with the New World," *Inter-American Music Review* 8, no. 2 (1987), 26–36.

———. *Spanish Music in the Age of Columbus*. Westport, Conn., 1979. 55–63.

RAVAYA FAMILY

Many Jews rose to prominence in government service in Aragón-Catalonia as well as Castile. Among those in the former kingdom were the Ravayas. In the reign of Jaime II, Jucef Ravaya was banker to the *infante* Pedro el Grande, eventually becoming treasurer and counselor to the future king. His brother Mossé (Moses) held a similar post in Catalonia as inspector of accounts. Jucef was also involved in the negotiations of the marriage of Jaime II, and took part in the Sicily expedition (1282). When Pedro, as king, was out of the country for a year (1283), Mossé was named as *procurador* to administer the kingdoms of Aragón, Catalonia, and Valencia (however, his authority was reduced to Catalonia alone). He was, however, briefly the *baile* (bailiff) of Valencia.

Astrug, another member of the family, was baile of Girona from 1276 to 1281, and as such issued laws and exemptions of taxes to the town of Palamós. These, and various economic regulations, were issued entirely in his own name and countersigned by various local Christians. Pedro III granted him similar privileges for the town of Borrassá, noting that Astrug's son Yucef had undertaken the repopulation of that town (1280). Astrug and his son also were granted the revenues of Girona and Besalú in payment of loans made to the king and Astrug was exempted from paying taxes to his cousin, Solomon ibn Ṣaddoq, *almoxarife* of Castile, after Astrug had moved from Toledo to Girona.

NORMAN ROTH

Bibliography

Romano, D. *Judíos al servicio de Pedro el Grande de Aragón*. Barcelona, 1983.

Font Rius, J. M. (ed.) *Cartas de población y franquicia de Cataluña*. Vol. 1. Madrid, 1969, Vol. 495–98, 502.

RAZÓN DE AMOR

The thirteenth-century lyric poem *Razón de amor*, along with *Denuestos del agua y del vino*, published first by Morel-Fatio in 1887, was edited by Menéndez Pidal; the text was further analyzed in Gardiner London's paleographic edition. Examined as a Christian allegory, it has even been viewed as an allusion to the Cathar heresy. Ley studied its debt to Provenzal literature; Ferraresi dealt with its relationship to courtly love, and Antwerp showed its dependence on popular lyric. Whether the *Razón* and the *Denuestos* were ever intended to be a single poem is subject to debate. For Spitzer, the connective thread is thirst: for relief from the heat, for love, and finally for the soul's ease. A possible compromise is a proposal that an anonymous poet created a new seamless poem out of two distinct dream poems: a midday apparition and a debate vision. Thus the *Denuestos* is a final sequence in a dream narrative in which the wine and water of the first poem are the protagonists of a raucous debate that breaks the amorous mood in a manner characteristic of dreams.

The poem begins with a *juglaresque* (minstrelesque) invitation to the public to listen and to take solace from his performance. The cosmopolitan well-educated poet tells of the time when, hot and tired, he found himself in an orchard at midday. A *dueña* (lady) had placed a cup of wine, covered to protect it from the heat, high in a tree to refresh her lover. Above the wine he saw another cup filled with water drawn from a magical spring. Afraid to drink the water, the poet fell asleep in the shade. Up to this point, there is a certain correspondence with the explicit Christian allegory in Gonzalo de Berceo's *Milagros de Nuestra Señora* where the poet's thoughts turn to the Virgin, but in the *Razón* events susceptible of allegorical interpretation are, at least superficially, erotic.

The poet falls asleep and in a dream arrives at a *locus amoenus* with a spring that cools its surroundings magically, encircled by flowers whose fragrance will resuscitate the dead. His dream beloved, fused with the dueña of the orchard, interrupts his poetic musing, and they spend an amorous interlude, at the end of which she hurries away. The drowsy postcoital poet, still dreaming, sees a white dove that, afraid of the *fuente perenal*, seeks relief from the heat in the cup of water in the tree and spills some water into the wine beneath it. This accidental spillage motivated by fear of the spring recalls the predream uneasiness about the water in the cup. Thus this second interruption becomes a creative bridge between the erotic content of the *Razón* and the traditional water/wine debate.

HARRIET GOLDBERG

Bibliography

Antwerp, M. van, "*Razón de amor* and the Popular Tradition." *Romance Philology*, 32 (1978–1979), 1–17.

Azuela, M. C. "La *Razón de amor* a la luz de la presencia musulmana en España," *Corónica* 20 (1991–92) 16–31.

De Ley, M. "Provençal Biographical Tradition an the *Razón de amor*." *Journal of Hispanic Philology*, 1 (1976–1977), 1–17.

Ferraresi, A. *De amor y poesía en la España medieval*, Mexico City, 1976.

Franchini, E. *El manuscrito, la lengua y el ser literario de la Razón de amor*. Madrid, 1993.

London, G. "The *Razón de amor* and the *Denuestos* del agua y el vino," *Romance Philology* 19 (1965–1966), 28–47.

Menéndez Pidal, R. "*Razón de Amor* con los Denuestos del Agua y Del Vino," *Revue Hispanigue* 13 (1905), 602–18.

Spitzer, L. "*Razón de amor*." In his *Sobre antigua poesía española*. Buenos Aires, 1962, 41–58.

RECCARED

The younger son of Leovigild, Reccared (569–586) was made a nominal co-ruler with his father and elder brother, Hermenegild, in 573, but did not receive a separate area of authority. The city of Reccopolis (probably Zorita de los Canes near Alcalá de Henares), which Leovigild founded in 578, was named after him. A proposed marriage to the Frankish princess Rigunth, daughter of the Neustrian king Chilperic (561–584), was canceled when the bride's father died while she was still on the way to Spain. In 585, following the suppression of his brother's revolt, Reccared was sent successfully to repel a Frankish invasion of the province of Narbonensis. He succeeded his father without opposition in 586, and early in 587 at a meeting with the Arian episcopate he ordered them to reach a definitive solution of the theological disagreements between themselves and Catholics. His own conversion to Catholicism, in which Bishop Leander of Seville was said to have been influential, occurred that year, and those of most of the Visigothic clergy and nobility followed in the course of the next two years. The process of conversion was formalized by the holding of the great Third Council of Toledo in May 589, which was attended by Reccared and his queen, Baddo. He faced revolts in 588 and 589 in Mérida, Toledo, and Narbonne on the part of three Arian metropolitan bishops and a number of disaffected Gothic counts. All of these were quickly suppressed. For the last decade of Reccared's reign very little evidence survives. He died in 601, leaving the throne to a young son Liuva II (601–603), who was subsequently deposed and then murdered in an aristocratic coup, bringing the rule of this dynasty to an end.

ROGER COLLINS

Bibliography

García Moreno, L. A. *Historia de España visigoda*. Madrid, 1989. 113–143.

Thompson, E. A. "The Conversion of the Visigoths to Catholicism," *Nottingham Medieval Studies* 4 (1960), 4–35.

Visigothic, 7th cent, Crown of Recessvinth, Visigoth king, from the treasure of Guarrazar, near Toledo. Copyright © Giraudon/Art Resource, NY. Museo Arqueologico Nacional, Madrid, Spain.

RECCESVINTH

The son of Chindaswinth (642–653), Reccesvinth was associated with his father as joint king in 649. A letter advocating this decision survives in the epistolary collection of Bishop Braulio of Zaragoza. During the period of joint rule a new coinage in both kings' names was issued. After his father's death Reccesvinth ruled alone, and died without known heirs on 1 September 672. His wife's name appears to have been Recciberga. His reign is particularly notable for the promulgation in 654 of the first version of the law code known as the *Forum Iudicum* or *Lex Visigothorum*. Although this may not be the first Visigothic code that was territorial in its application, that is to say provided the exclusive rule of law for all subjects of the king, its size and the attempted comprehensiveness of its contents make it the most substantial piece of legal codification in the West since the promulgation of the Theodosian Code in 438. The early years of Reccesvinth are also notable as a period of considerable conciliar activity, with the Eighth, Ninth, and Tenth Councils of Toledo (held in 653, 655, and 656, respectively). After these no further plenary or national assemblies were convened during the reign. This may in part be due to the very critical tone adopted by the bishops in their demands for reform of abuses and malpractices that had occurred under the apparently despotic regime of Chindaswinth. A tangible record of the reign of Reccesvinth comes in the form of the church of San Juan de Baños, south of Palencia, which, according to its extant dedicatory inscription, was built in 661 by the king in honor of St. John the Baptist. This probably relates to the presence close to the church of a spring enclosed by masonry of the same period. It is likely that the site was part of a royal estate.

ROGER COLLINS

Bibliography

Collins, R., *Early Medieval Spain: Unity in Diversity, 400–1000*. London, 1983, 108–45.

Navascués, J. M. de. *La dedicación de San Juan de Baños*. Palencia, 1961.

Thompson, E. A. *The Goths in Spain*. Oxford, 1969, 199–210.

RECEMUND

Bishop of Elvira and caliphal secretary (mid-tenth century). Known to the Arabs as Rabi ibn Sid al-Usquf, the Christian Recemund served as a secretary under the caliph ʿAbd al-Raḥmān III (929–961). In 953 he was sent by the caliph as an ambassador to Otto I of Germany (936–973), where he managed to defuse a potentially volatile situation caused by a previous exchange of letters that were apparently less than sensitive to the religious inclinations of their recipients. The caliph rewarded Recemund for his services with the recently vacated see of Elvira. While in Germany, Recemund met Liutprand of Cremona, who subsequently dedicated his *Antapodosis* to him. Even as bishop, Recemund continued to serve as an ambassador for the caliph, traveling to Constantinople and Jerusalem. With the accession of Al-Ḥakam II in 961, Recemund dedicated to him a calendar written in Arabic which, interestingly enough, included references to Christian holy days, even some that commemorated a few of the martyrs of Córdoba. Recemund was a contemporary of Hasdai ibn Shaprut, the Jewish physician and intellectual who also served ʿAbd al-Raḥmān III as ambassador.

KENNETH B. WOLF

Bibliography

Colbert, E. "The Martyrs of Córdoba (850–859): A Study of the Sources." Ph.D. Diss., Catholic University of America, 1962, 382–86.

Dozy, R., ed. *Le Calendrier de Cordoue*. Trans. C. Pellat. 2d ed. Leiden, 1961.

RECONQUEST AND REPOPULATION

The Reconquest and the concomitant task of repopulation are the essential threads running through the history of medieval Spain. Spaniards have long believed that their forebears waged nearly continous warfare over seven hundred years to expel the Muslim invaders from North Africa who overthrew the Visigothic kingdom in 711. Modern historians have questioned the validity of this traditional concept, but Derek Lomax pointed out that the Reconquest was "an ideal invented by Spanish Christians soon after 711" and developed in the ninth-century kingdom of Asturias.

Given the failure of the Muslims to occupy the entire Iberian Peninsula, several tiny, independent kingdoms and counties emerged in the foothills of the Cantabrian and Pyrenees mountains, namely, Asturias, León, Castile, Navarre, Aragón, and Catalonia. The idea of reconquest originated in Asturias, where King Pelayo (718–737), the leader of a hardy band of mountaineers, proclaimed his intention to achieve the *salus Spanie*—the "salvation of Spain"—and the restoration of the Gothic people. His victory over the Muslims at Covadonga in 722 is traditionally taken as the beginning of the Reconquest. A ninth-century chronicler affirmed that the Christians would wage war against the Muslims by day and night "until divine predestination commands that they be driven cruelly thence. Amen!" Two ideas were linked here. First there was the determination to expel the Muslims considered as unlawful intruders who had seized land belonging by right to the Christians. Secondly, the task of restoring the Visigothic monarchy to its fullest extent was attributed to the kings of Asturias and their later successors in León and Castile who were hailed as heirs of the Visigoths. The reconquest was a war to recover territory, but it also had a religious character because of the fundamental opposition between between two mutually exclusive societies.

Despite the bravado of the chroniclers, the Christian rulers were in no position to offer serious opposition to Muslim ascendancy during the three hundred years following the initial invasion. Almost every year the emirs and caliphs of Córdoba sent their armies to ravage Christian lands, though never to conquer them. A no-man's-land extending along the Duero river from the Atlantic Ocean to the borders of Aragón separated Christian and Muslim territory, but many years elapsed before the Christians were emboldened to settle that region. Until the late eleventh century, Islamic rule in the northeast reached as far north as the foothills of the Pyrenees. In these circumstances one could hardly speak of reconquest.

Nevertheless, the breakup of the Caliphate of Córdoba early in the eleventh century and the emergence of the petty Muslim kingdoms known as *tā'ifas* enabled the Christian princes to make significant progress in the Reconquest. Alfonso VI of León-Castile (1065–1109) captured Toledo in 1085 and won control of a long stretch of the Tagus River. However, the Almoravids, a Muslim sect from Morocco, defeated

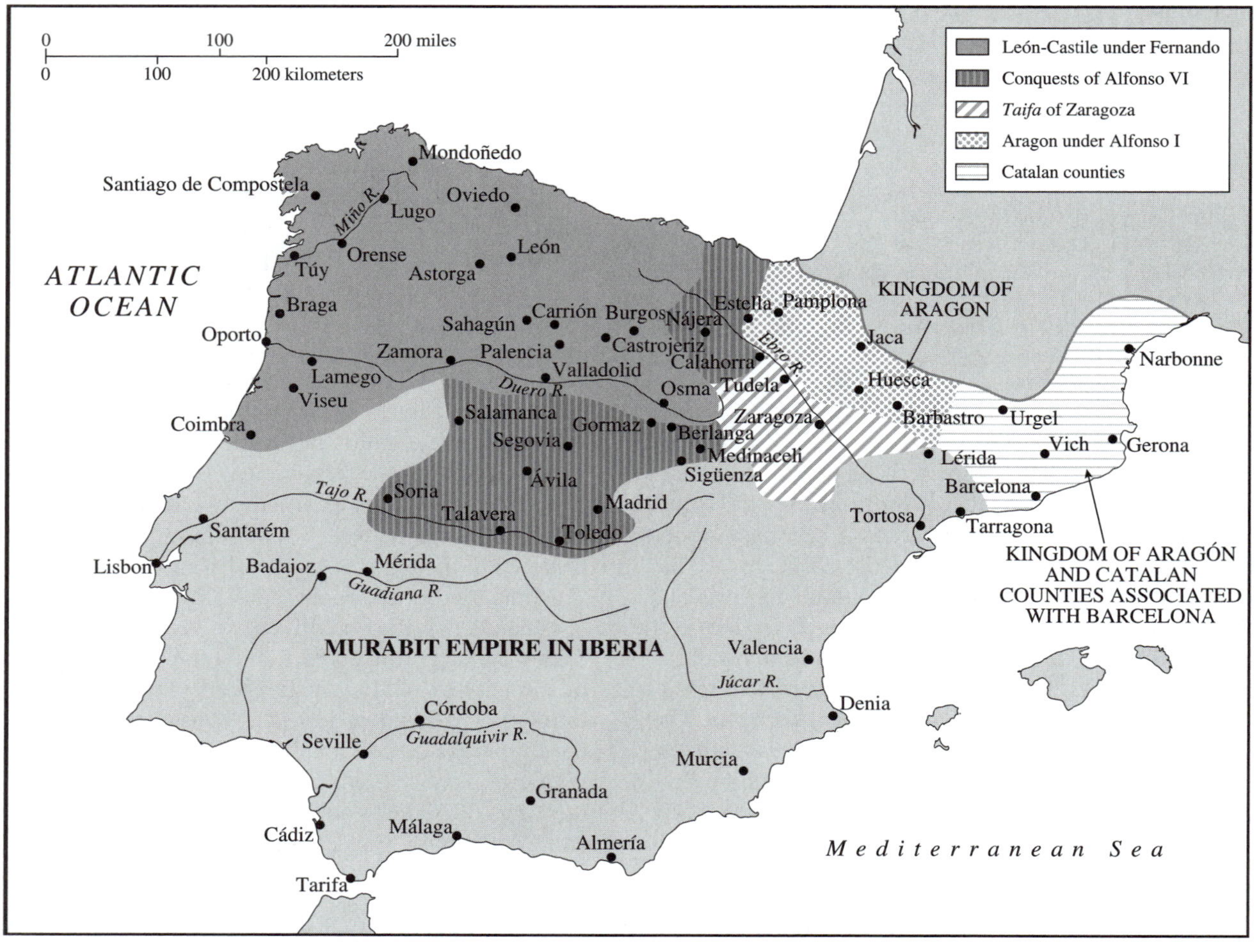

Reconquest and Repopulation. End of eleventh century Iberia.

him at the battle of Sagrajas in 1086 and unified Islamic Spain by swallowing the tā'ifas. Christians once again found themselves on the defensive. As Almoravid power waned the Christians again achieved important gains when Alfonso I of Aragón (1104–1134) conquered Zaragoza on the Ebro River in 1118 and Afonso I of Portugal (1128–1185), with the aid of a fleet of northern crusaders on their way to the Holy Land, seized Lisbon at the mouth of the Tagus River in 1147.

From this point onward the Reconquest assumed the character of a crusade as numerous papal bulls equated the struggle against Islam in Spain with the wars in the Holy Land. The conflict intensified in the second half of the twelfth century when the Almohads, another Muslim sect from Morocco, halted the Christian advance and ravaged Christian territory. In 1195 the Almohads gained an extraordinary triumph at Alarcos over Alfonso VIII of Castile (1158–1214), but in 1212, with the help of a papal bull of crusade, he redeemed himself and routed the Muslims at Las Navas de Tolosa. As a consequence the southern frontier of the kingdom of Toledo was secure and the road to Andalusia was opened. Moreover, the balance of power had now been tipped once and for all in favor of the Christians.

Pressing forward from the Guadiana to the Guadalquivir Rivers, Fernando III of Castile-León (1217–1252) captured Córdoba (1236), Jaén (1246), and Seville (1248) and also received the submission of the Muslim kingdom of Murcia. At the same time the Portuguese occupied the Alentejo and the Algarve thereby completing the territorial expansion of their kingdom. In the east Jaime I of Aragón (1213–1276) subjugated the Balearic Islands and conquered the kingdom of Valencia (1238). In that way the Crown of Aragón consisting of Aragón proper, Catalonia, and

Reconquest and Repopulation. End of thirteenth century Iberia.

Valencia reached its fullest extent within the peninsula. Thus by the middle of the thirteenth century all of Islamic Spain, with the exception of the kingdom of Granada, was ruled by the Christians. The kings of Granada were forced to pay tribute as vassals of the kings of Castile-León.

Only Castile-León had a frontier contiguous to the kingdom of Granada and so had a realistic chance for further peninsular acquisitions. In the late thirteenth and fourteenth centuries the principal concern of the Castilian kings was to seize control of the ports on the Strait of Gibraltar in order to prevent further incursions from Morocco. In preparation for an African crusade, Alfonso X (1252–1284) developed the ports of Cádiz and El Puerto de Santa María, but his plans were thwarted by the revolt of the Muslims subject to his rule in 1264. Another wave of Moroccan invaders, the Banū Marin or Benimerines, put the Christians on the defensive once again. Sancho IV (1284–1295) captured the port of Tarifa in 1292 and his son Fernando IV (1295–1312) seized Gibraltar in 1309, though it was lost in 1333. Alfonso XI (1312–1340) stemmed the final Moroccan invasion at Salado in 1340 and gained Algeciras in 1344, but died during the siege of Gibraltar. For the next century and a half the reconquest was left in abeyance as the kingdom of Granada was not considered a serious threat and no further intrusions from Morocco took place.

As the Muslims withdrew before the Christian advance, reconquered territory had to be repopulated or colonized. The earliest stage in the process occurred when pioneers willing to take the risk of livng on an exposed frontier began to settle in the unoccupied lands of the Duero River valley. In the eleventh and twelfth centuries while the Leonese, Castilians, and Portuguese crossed into Extremadura and then into the Tagus Valley, the Aragónese and Catalans moved south of the Ebro River. Fortified urban settlements

13th century C.E. The Moors regain their castle. Alfonso X the Wise, Cartigas de Santa Maria Spain, 13th c. Copyright © Giraudon/Art Resource, NY. Biblioteca Real, El Escorial, Madrid, Spain.

were established directly dependent upon the king and royal charters assuring personal freedom and other liberties were issued to attract settlers. The military orders founded in the twelfth century received lordships in the frontier region stretching from below the Tagus to the borders of Andalusia. When Andalusia, Valencia, Murcia, and the Algarve were occupied in the thirteenth century, the Muslims were usually evacuated from the principal cities and towns. Books of distribution or *Libros de repartimiento* drawn up on the king's orders distributed houses and lands among the victors. The repartimientos for Valencia and Seville are among the most comprehensive of these documents. A substantial Muslim population, known as Mudéjars, remained in the rural areas and were not fully incorporated into Christian society until the seventeenth century.

Fernando of Aragón (1479–1516) and Isabel of Castile (1474–1504) conquered Granada and brought the Reconquest to an end. Stating their expectation that "these infidels . . . will be ejected and expelled from Spain," they asked the pope in 1485 for crusading indulgences. Then in 1492, they announced that "this kingdom of Granada, which was occupied for over seven hundred and eight years by the infidels . . . has been conquered."

Medieval Spanish Christians, a people always living on a frontier, developed a pioneer psychology through the Reconquest and seemed prepared at any time to move from the more peaceful and settled areas of the north in the expectation of finding a better life in the south. After the conquest of Granada some tried to press Spanish interests in Morocco in accordance with the notion that the Visigoths had once ruled there, but the opening of the New World diverted Spanish energy from that enterprise. Overseas exploration and colonization in the sixteenth and seventeenth centuries in some measure continued the process of reconquest and repopulation within the peninsula.

Although the Christians now dominated all of Spain and Portugal, the continued presence of large numbers of Muslims and Jews, who hitherto had enjoyed religious freedom and juridical autonomy, was seen by many as an impediment to national unity. On that account, the Jews in 1492 and the Muslims of Granada in 1502 were compelled to accept Christianity or to go into exile. In that way a façade of political, juridical, and religious unity was imposed.

In conclusion, though the ideal of reconquest found expression in the ninth-century chroniclers, the Reconquest itself did not really begin until the late eleventh century. Thereafter it was frequently interrupted by truces and sometimes neglected entirely, but it remained the ultimate goal of the Christian rulers of Spain.

JOSEPH F. O'CALLAGHAN

Bibliography

Collins, R. *Early Medieval Spain. Unity in Diversity, 400–1000.* New York, 1983.

Lomax, D. W. *The Reconquest of Spain.* New York, 1978.

MacKay, A. *Spain in the Middle Ages. From Frontier to Empire, 1000–1500.* New York, 1977.

O'Callaghan, J. F. *A History of Medieval Spain.* Ithaca, N.Y., 1975.

REGIDOR *See* TOWNS

RELIGIOUS ORDERS

A religious order is a community of individuals, either male or female, who make a public vow and a religious consecration. It is an institute of perfection whose members subject themselves to the discipline of a rule recognized and approved by ecclesiastical authorities. Through their corporate life and service to the larger community of the church, these individuals seek spiritual growth and ultimately the attainment of salvation. The religious orders of medieval Europe, first appearing during the twelfth century, were an outgrowth of the Gregorian Reform Movement. They were less rural and contemplative than the older monastic communities and generally subscribed to some version of the Augustinian Rule. Their works tended to be evangelistic or caritative, well suited to the needs of emerging urban communities, from which they drew their recruits and material support and which also served as the arena for their various apostolates. These orders fall roughly into three categories: military, evangelistic/mendicant, the hospitaler/caritative.

Medieval Iberia, for the most part, was not the originator of those forces that led to the creation of the new orders. Yet Spain, with its own crusade, developing urban centers, and proximity to France and the Mediterranean, was an early and logical arena of expansion for externally created orders. Hispanic society quickly responded to these examples by developing native variants.

The military orders were among the first to appear in Spain. The Knights of St. John and the Knights Templars had both arrived by 1131, but their reluctance to commit themselves fully to the Spanish reconquest led to the subsequent establishment of indigenous versions. Among these were the Spanish orders of Santiago, Alcántara, Calatrava, Montesa, and Alfama, and the Portuguese orders of Avis and Christ.

The principal mendicant orders active in medieval Iberia were the Franciscans, Dominicans, Carmelites, Sack Friars, Poor Catholics, and Augustinians. Of these, the Franciscans were the most numerous. Tradition has it that Francis of Assisi founded several houses in Castile and Aragón in 1213 and 1214. Spain became a province in 1217, and in 1232 this was subdivided into three. By 1400, these provinces contained twenty-three custodies (or districts) with 123 houses. The Second Order of St. Francis, or the Poor Clares, held some forty-nine convents in Spain at the end of the thirteenth century.

The Order of Preachers, or Black Friars, was established by the Castilian Domingo de Guzmán at Toulouse in 1215. In 1217 and 1218 Domingo and several Spanish friars established the order in Madrid, Segovia, Palencia, Burgos, Zaragoza, Zamora, Barcelona, and Compostela. These houses were organized into the province of the Spains in 1221; Aragón became a separate province in 1301, and Portugal in 1418. There were some twenty houses in the peninsula in 1250, thirty-five in 1275, and forty-two in 1298. While there was a community of Dominican nuns in Madrid as early as 1218, only six other convents were established within the peninsula by 1303, in contrast to the seventy-four in Germany and forty-one in Italy.

The Order of the Virgin Mary of Mount Carmel, better known as the Carmelites or White Friars, grew out of a community of hermits established in Palestine before 1206. Attacked by Muslims in 1238, members migrated to Europe and established themselves in England, France, Spain, and Italy. The loss of Mount Carmel in 1291 cut the order's last ties with Palestine. In 1254 the Englishman Simon Stock was elected general and, with the approval of Pope Innocent IV, reorganized the community as a mendicant order, a status confirmed at the Council of Lyons in 1274. With a rule stricter than those of the Dominicans and Franciscans, the Carmelites established houses in towns and their suburbs; earlier disciplines were relaxed and the original habit with its vertically striped black and white mantle was replaced in 1287 by a white one. In 1291 lay brothers lost the right to vote at meetings of the chapter.

The Carmelite province of Spain was one of the last to be established, probably because few Spaniards had belonged to the original Palestinian community. The first residences were located in the Crown of Aragón, where houses at Lérida and Huesca existed by 1272. Others followed in Sangüesa, Valencia, Zaragoza, Barcelona, Perelada, Girona, and Mallorca. There were none in Castile until 1315 and these, with the exception of foundations in Toledo and Avila, had rural locales. In Andalusia there was a friary in Seville by 1358. The diocesan clergy resisted the Carmelite settlement in Barcelona, Girona, and Mallorca but this was negated in part by royal patronage and, in 1317, by a papal grant of episcopal exemption. Catalonia and the Balearics became a separate province in 1354 and in 1416 Castile and Aragón were divided administratively.

The Carmelites fostered devotion to the Virgin and to the Holy Scapular; its distinct Marian spirituality was developed in the writings of the Catalan friars Felip Ribot and Pere Riu. Houses of study were established at Barcelona (1333) and Valencia (1379); and Guy Terrena, a Perpignanais elected as Carmelite general in 1318, became bishop of Mallorca in 1321 and of Elne in 1332. Another Catalan, Bernat Oller, was elected general in 1375. To judge by the size of the Mallorcan house, Carmelite communities in the fourteenth century contained as many as forty friars. The order was divided by the Great Schism and experienced a much relaxed discipline in the fifteenth century. The observant reform was not introduced into Spain until the sixteenth century. In Portugal, however, the Carmelites prospered during the fifteenth century under the reform of Baltasar Limpo, who became archbishop of Braga in 1479. The first notice of Carmelite nuns dates from a royal act of 1346 granting them permission to seek alms in Barcelona, but their effort at a permanent establishment there seems to have failed.

Like the Carmelites, the Order of Hermits of St. Augustine (or Augustinians) abandoned the contemplative life for the active ministry of the mendicants. The order itself originated through the "Grand Union" of various preexisting Augustinian eremite foundations that was approved by Pope Alexander IV in 1256.

The Province of Spain emerged as one of its twelve regional groupings. These Spanish houses had already attempted confederation on a regional basis; those in Aragón, for example, may have had their own provincial as early as 1216. Much thirteenth-century Augustinian expansion followed the progress of the Reconquest. In Valencia, five houses were established between 1260 and 1300; Murcia's monastery of St. Ginés dates to 1247; and in Andalusia there were foundations in Córdoba (as early as 1236) and Seville (1248). Jaime I of Aragón established a house for them on Formentera in 1257 that endured until piracy forced its abandonment in 1350. Other centers appeared at Toledo (1260), Zaragoza (1286), Badajoz (1298), and Barcelona (1309). Augustinian recruits included former Sack friars and Poor Catholic Brothers. In the fourteenth century, there were Augustinian nuns in Toledo and Seville. Catalonia and Aragón became separate provinces at the end of the thirteenth century and Portugal, with almost twenty establishments, by the mid-fifteenth century. The Augustinian observant movement was inaugurated by Friar Juan de Alarcón near Valladolid in 1438 and by the end of the century most houses had accepted reform.

Least known of the major mendicant groups are the Brothers of the Penitence of Jesus Christ, or the Sack Friars, so called for the pilgrim's tunic worn by each friar. They were established around 1248 by a knight of Hyères in Provence. Despite their distinctly Franciscan spirituality, members adopted the Rule of St. Augustine in 1251. In the quarter century until its formal dissolution at the Council of Lyons (1274), the Order established seven provinces and some eighty houses from Scotland to Palestine. The brothers preached, heard confessions, distributed alms, and helped the poor. Their Spanish foundations were concentrated in the Crown of Aragón where King Jaime I was an important benefactor. After 1274, as the brothers died, their property was turned over to other orders, including the Dominicans, Carmelites, and Mercedarians.

Another little-known mendicant group is that of the Poor Catholics, established at Toulouse in 1207 by Durand of Huesca, a Waldensian reconciled to the church. Pope Innocent III approved this community of preaching clerics and laymen but evidently did not assign them a rule. In 1237, members in Occitania and Catalonia were placed under the spiritual supervision of Dominicans from Tarragona, but the evidence is contradictory as to whether they ever accepted the Augustinian Rule. Members appear to have been absorbed by the other mendicant orders. In Catalonia, many became Dominicans because in 1256 the latter sold to the Mercedarians the Brothers' former house in Castellón de Ampurias.

While mendicants certainly performed works of charity, the care of lepers, foundlings, the aged, the sick and diseased, travelers, pilgrims, captives and prostitutes was the primary focus of a number of hospitaler and caritative orders. While various almshouses and hospices for the needy had already been established by bishops and cathedral chapters in Spain, demographic changes in the twelfth century led to increasing specialization.

New and more narrowly focused hospitals were founded by, among others, religious orders. Several were quite small. The Order of Roncesvalles, for example, was established around 1132 by the bishop of Pamplona and Alfonso I of Aragón to guard the famous pass and to provide shelter for travelers and pilgrims. In the thirteenth century, the order constructed a number of pilgrim hospices along the route to and from Roncesvalles, and another in the city of Valencia. The latter may have served the entirely different purpose of tending to wounded casualties of the Reconquest. Another Pyreneean hospital associated with a religious order was that of Somport, located in the pass of Somport north of Jaca. The hospital there, founded between 1100 and 1108, appears to have been entrusted to the Military Order of the Holy Sepulcher for the purpose of protecting the route from Béarn to Aragón. The latter was established in the early twelfth century as one of two orders, one of canons regular and the other of knights, under the direction of the Latin patriarch of Jerusalem. In 1134 it was one of the three military orders to whom Alfonso I of Aragón bequeathed his realm. Between 1190 and 1210, the ties between Somport and the Knights of the Holy Sepulcher were apparently severed, because the former then called itself the Order of Santa Cristina. This order possessed some thirteen hospitals located around Béarn as well as in Aragón, Navarre, and Castile in the thirteenth century. The other Order of the Holy Sepulcher, that of canons regular, served within the Crown of Aragón as administrators of property that had been willed to the Church of the Holy Sepulcher in Jerusalem. Its chief centers were located at Calatayud and Barcelona, where it administered the Church of St. Anne. Jaime I entrusted to it care of the parish of St. Bartholomew in Valencia. Another branch was established at Logroño. With the fall of Acre and the chapter's transferral to Perugia in the late thirteenth century, most of the order's regional districts, like that in Spain, separated themselves from the chapter's authority and, like the hospitalers of Somport, became independent.

There is a great deal of legend surrounding the establishment of the Order of St. Anthony, or the Antonines. Tradition relates its establishment around 1095 by Gaston of Dauphiné at La-Motte-Saint-Didier for the treatment of ergotism, an epidemic disease also known as "St. Anthony's Fire." The first members were laymen, although the grand master was a priest. In 1218 members took monastic vows and in 1297 became canons regular of St. Augustine. Their almshouse at La-Motte-Saint-Didier is documented from 1150 and the thirteenth-century order had four commanderies: France, Italy, Germany, and Spain. The first Spanish hospital was located at Cervera. Its commander founded another at Barcelona in 1157. There were also hospitals on Mallorca and at Lérida; in Valencia, Antonines were established at Fortaleny in 1276 and after 1333 at Oriols near the capital. In Castile, the Antonines had hospitals at Castrojeriz, possibly dating from the late twelfth century, and at Salamanca from around 1230; in Navarre, there was a hospital in Olite.

The Order of the Holy Spirit was established at Montpellier between 1160 and 1170 by Guy of Montpellier and approved in 1198 by Innocent III. The order, whose rule derived from that of the Hospitalers of St. John, established itself in France, Italy, Germany, Scandinavia, and Spain. Guy himself may have brought the Order to Lérida, where a hospital for foundlings, the sick, the insane, and former prostitutes was functioning after 1214. Two other Spanish hospitals were in existence in 1256 and by the century's end, there were seven. Some estimates, up to thirty in the fifteenth century, are considerably higher, the discrepancy arising out of the difficulty of distinguishing the order's hospitals from others of the same name operated by purely local chapters or confraternities.

It is equally difficult to identify which leper hospitals belonged to the Order of St. Lazarus. The latter was established in Jerusalem around 1142 as a military order of lepers. Until 1253 its grand master had to be a leper. The order, which followed the Rule of St. Augustine, was brought to France by Louis VII after the Second Crusade to run hospices for lepers. From there it spread to central Europe, Italy, Scotland, and Spain. It possessed lazarets in Lérida and Valencia by the mid-thirteenth century, but other hospices also under the invocation of St. Lazarus (for example, at Barcelona and throughout the Asturias) had no connection to the order. The affiliation of others (such as those at Girona and Zamora) remains uncertain.

Ransoming orders were established to purchase the freedom of Christians who had become captives in Muslim lands. The first of these to appear in Spain was that of the Holy Trinity, whose members were also known as Maturins and Donkey Brothers. The order was founded by Jean de Matha and, according to legend, Felix of Valois late in the twelfth century. Its rule, which emulated the customs of St. Victor of Paris, was approved by Innocent III in 1198. While Matha himself was probably a native of Provence, the order's motherhouse was located at Cerfroid, a rural site northeast of Paris. Trinitarian leadership was clerical, but lay brothers were also admitted. Because revenues were divided equally among the poor, captives and the brothers' expenses, the order had two distinct apostolates: assistance to the poor, and the ransoming of Christians. While northern France was the primary sphere of its operation in the thirteenth century, the Islamic wars brought Trinitarians to Palestine and Spain.

Tradition credits Matha himself with the foundation of the first Trinitarian houses in Castile: hospices for captives in Toledo (1206) and Segovia (1208) and another for paupers in Burgos (c. 1207). There were two Portuguese houses in the thirteenth century: at Santarem (1208) and Lisbon (c.1286). In the Crown of Aragón, there was a hospital in Lérida by 1218 and another at nearby Anglesola as early as 1201. Trinitarians followed the Reconquest to Córdoba, Seville, and Valencia, where they were given a medical hospital by the justiciar of the new kingdom. The order's ransoming work, apart from that conducted by the early ransoming hospices, can only be inferred from privileges allowing the brothers to collect alms. Its hospital work is better known; indeed its activities at Valencia and on Mallorca, where it assumed control of an orphanage in 1270, were more demonstrably Hospitaler in nature than redemptionist. Other thirteenth-century houses were located in Valladolid (1256), Murcia (1272), and, less certainly, in Andújar, Tarifa, and Badajoz in the Crown of Castile; and in Avingaña, Tortosa, Monzón, Daroca, and Murviedro in the Crown of Aragón. Houses at Barcelona and Játiva followed in the fourteenth century. After 1221 these were constituted into the separate provinces of Castile and Aragón; Portugal received provincial status in 1312. A single community of Trinitarian nuns, at Avignaña, dates from 1236.

The Order of Our Lady of Mercy for the Ransoming of Captives (the Mercedarians) was established in Catalonia shortly before 1230 when its lay founder, Pere Nolasc, began collecting alms for Christian captives at Barcelona and on Mallorca. Nolasc's order received approval in 1235 from Gregory IX, who assigned it the Rule of St. Augustine. The first Mercedarians were mostly laymen and, until 1317, had a laic master general. Unlike the Trinitarians, the Mercedarians' only charitable work was ransoming. Members followed the advancing Christian armies of the thirteenth-century Reconquest and established themselves as ransomers in the Balearics, Valencia, Murcia, and Andalusia. While returning crusaders and the order's own initiative led to the establishment of houses in Aragón, Catalonia, Roussillon, Navarre, and Occitania, Mercedarians had no significant presence in Castile, apart from Andalusia and Murcia. The order maintained close ties with the House of Barcelona and had a strong Catalan identity: Barcelona was the seat of its motherhouse. The Mercedarians possessed some fifteen houses in 1245, thirty in 1263, and forty-one in 1291. In the early fourteenth century, there were approximately two hundred active Mercedarians.

Because Mercedarians ransomed those unable to pay their own ransoms, much of the order's work was devoted to fund-raising. Brothers would seek alms, frequently accompanied by recently freed Christians who owed six months of such service as repayment for their ransoming. In places like Valencia or Perpignan, the order assembled rural patrimonies as endowments for captives. The funds so collected were customarily entrusted to two ransomers who would bargain for captives in Granada or North Africa late each spring. The Mercedarian fourth vow, which required brothers to offer themselves as ransom for captured Christians, seems to be of post-medieval origin. Estimates for the numbers actually freed vary greatly; it is likely that the annual average was closer to a few dozen than to the hundreds claimed in Mercedarian tradition.

JAMES W. BRODMAN

Bibliography

Aldea Vaquero, Q., T. Marín Martínez, and J. Vives Gatell. (eds.) *Diccionario de historia eclesiástica de España*. 4 vols. Madrid, 1972–75.

Batlle i Gallart, C., and M. Casas i Nadal. "La caritat privada i les institucions benèfiques de Barcelona (segle XIII)." In *La pobreza y la asistencia a los pobres en la Cataluña medieval*. Vol. 1 Ed. M. Riu. Barcelona, 1980–82. 117–90.

Brodman, J. W. *Ransoming Captives in Crusader Spain: The Order of Merced on the Christian-Islamic Frontier*. Philadelphia, 1986.

Burns, R. I., S. J. *The Crusader Kingdom of Valencia: Reconstruction on a Thirteenth-Century Frontier*. 2 vols. Cambridge, Mass., 1967.

Durán Gudiol, A. *El hospital de Somport entre Aragón y Béarn (siglos XII y XIII)*. Zaragoza, 1986.

García-Villoslada, R., (ed.) *Historia de la Iglesia en España*. 6 vols. Madrid, 1979–82.

Pelliccia, G., and G. Roca, (eds.) *Dizionario degli istituti di perfezione*. 8 vols. to date. Rome, 1974–.

Tarragó Valentines, J. *Hospitales en Lérida durante los siglos XII al XVI*. Lérida, 1975.

Vicaire, M. H. (ed.) *Assistance et charité*. Toulouse, 1978.

Webster, J. R. "The Carmelites in Majorca," *Carmelus* 34 (1987), 94–112.

RELIGIOUS PREJUDICE

If only because of the activities of the Inquisition at the end of the Middle Ages, intolerance or prejudice in religious matters is commonly regarded as the predominant feature of the religious life of Spain in earlier as well as later periods. The term *religious prejudice* presumably means a prejudged hostility to other people on the basis of a religious belief, held by the displayer of prejudice, which supposedly justifies such hostility. In the Spanish case, the history of the Middle Ages may be seen as a religious conflict between Christianity and Islam, together with spasmodic and increasing persecution of the Iberian Peninsula's Jews. The Christian Reconquest, as well as attacks on Jews and Jewish Christians between 1391 and 1500, might be adduced as evidence to support such a view. It should always be remembered, however, that religious prejudice, in the modern form of a refusal to tolerate the religious views of others, is quite a recent concept. Toleration, in the sense of official or individual permission to others to believe in and practice a contrary religion, cannot be said to have arisen in Europe before the seventeenth century, so what was the situation in medieval Spain?

Although the notion that there was a conscious and continuous plan among the Christian states that developed after 711 to oppose al-Andalus, and "reconquer" Iberia for Christendom, is hardly justified, conflict between the two faiths undoubtedly existed throughout the later Middle Ages. As far as the Spanish Christian Church was concerned, the presence, and in many cases the dominance, of Islam in the peninsula forced the institutional hierarchy to defend itself and its faithful against the attacks and restrictions of Muslim rulers. The Córdoba Martyrs episode under the emirate in the 850s well illustrates the tensions, which must have existed less spectacularly in many other centuries and circumstances, between the desire to keep and witness the faith on the one hand, and the need to cooperate with Islam and its structures on the other.

The basis on which Iberian Muslim and Christian majorities treated minorities from the "opposing" faith—as well as Jews, who were subject to one or other of the rival "faiths of Abraham" throughout this period—was fairly equivalent. The Christian Church regarded Judaism as an outmoded religion, whose adherents were not only in error but also potentially dangerous to the rest of society, such a perception being of the very essence of religious prejudice. Nevertheless, Jews were, up to the very eve of the 1492 expulsion (1497 in Portugal and 1498 in Navarre), allowed freedom of worship and a certain degree of community autonomy, even though their opportunities in general economic, social, and political life were quite narrowly circumscribed. Muslims under Christian rule were subject to a similar dispensation. Islamic treatment of subject Christians and Jews in Spain was governed by the seventh-century agreement (*dhimma*) credited to the Middle Eastern caliph ʿUmar and laid down similar conditions for their treatment. In practice, though, the lives of religious minorities were governed as much by social and political conditions as by anything done by religious hierarchies. Institutional intolerance might be expressed by leaders of all three faiths from the pulpit and in written polemic, as well as in the laws passed by Muslim or Christian governments. But the stereotypes of other faiths that were included in written texts might be more directly and violently expressed in physical attacks on religious minorities—for example, the violence that drove the family of Moses Maimonides from Córdoba in the mid-twelfth century, and the pogroms against Jews and *conversos* in the fourteenth and fifteenth centuries.

What is more difficult to assess is the extent to which these official prejudices translated themselves to ordinary Iberians in this period. While soldiers clearly fought each other on religious grounds, Christian guilds deliberately excluded Jews, Muslims, and even *conversos*; and rioters and looters seem to have come from all social classes. It was the Spanish Inquisition that lifted the lid on the prejudices of ordinary Christians, if not on those of Jews or Muslims. The conclusion seems to be that official prejudice had indeed been transmitted to the general public, though not always in a form that corresponded to the more recently elaborated notions of religious elites.

John Edwards

Bibliography

Edwards, J. *The Jews in Christian Europe, 1400–1700*. Rev. ed. London, 1991.

———. "Religious Faith and Doubt in Late Medieval Spain: Soria *circa* 1450–1500." *Past and Present* 120 (1988), 3–25.

Kamen, H. *The Rise of Toleration*. London, 1967.

Lomax, D. W. *The Reconquest of Spain*. London, 1978.

REMENSA

The *remenses*, peasants of northeast Catalonia tied to the land in onerous serflike conditions, were the last vestiges of a quasi-feudal landholding system that was antiquated long before its institutional demise in the late fifteenth century. Their name refers to the Catalan term *remensa* (redemption), the monetary payment required to purchase their freedom from a secular or ecclesiastical lord.

The *cort's* (Parliament) of Barcelona in 1283 codified existing practices by defining the legal status of the remenses in terms of the *mals usos*, or bad customs. Some customs were strictly financial—payments of inheritance taxes and levies against a peasant's land whose wife had deserted him—but the most universally despised were those that not only restricted a peasant's freedom but were humiliating as well. For example, a lord could arbitrarily demand labor services, force a nursing woman to serve as a wetnurse, and subject a peasant to unwarranted physical abuse.

Such legally sanctioned routine mistreatment of roughly one-fifth of the population led to widespread peasant unrest that was further intensified in the wake of social and economic chaos caused by the devastations of the plague in the fourteenth century. Despite persistent noble opposition, Juan I made a tentative attempt in 1388 to abolish servile levies. In 1402 Martín I and Queen María de Luna appealed to the antipope Benedict XIII to issue an order to abolish servitude on ecclesiastical lands. Both attempts were temporarily thwarted, but the volatile combination of infuriated nobles and frustrated peasants was fueled by the vacillating policies of Alfonso V during the 1440s and 1450s. In the end, a devastating civil war tore Catalonia apart from 1462 to 1472. The solution to the problem of the *remenses* was eventually resolved by Fernando II in the 1486 Sentencia de Guadalupe. Although the Sentencia improved the peasant's legal status, it left more or less intact the skeleton of an archaic landholding system that would persist into the twentieth century.

Theresa Earenfight

Bibliography

Freedman, P. *The Origins of Peasant Servitude in Medieval Catalunya*. Cambridge, 1991.

Hinojosa y Naveros, E. de. *El régimen señorial y la cuestión agraria en Cataluña durante la Edad Media*. Madrid, 1905.

Serra, E. *Pagesos i senyors a la Catalunya del segle XVII. Baronia de Sentmenat 1590–1729*. Barcelona, 1988.

Vicens Vives, J. *Historia de las remensas en el siglo XV*. Barcelona, 1945.

RHETORIC

Although rhetoric in antiquity focused primarily on developing techniques for effective speaking in the courts, during the Middle Ages—with the notable exception of preaching—it focused primarily on written documents. Nevertheless, the classical tradition, usually in the form of Cicero's *De inventione* and the pseudo-Ciceronian *Rhetorica ad C. Herennium*, was dominant throughout the period, particularly in the schoolroom. The presence of these two texts, frequently called the *Rhetorica prima* or *vetus* and *Rheto-*

rica secunda or *nova*, is first documented in the Iberian Peninsula in Barcelona in 1183 and in Santiago de Compostela around 1225. The more elaborate Ciceronian texts (*De oratore, Orator, Brutus*), Quintilian, and Aristotle do not exercise any influence until well into the fifteenth century, with the advent of Italian humanism.

While the general lines of the development of medieval rhetoric are well known, much work is still needed on regional variations, particularly for Spain, where most of the treatises have been neither edited nor studied and our knowledge of school and university curricula, especially prior to the fifteenth century, is sketchy at best. The earliest of the specifically medieval arts of discourse to arise was the *ars dictandi*, the art of letter writing, which originated in Italy in the late eleventh century in response to the increasing volume of correspondence emanating both from church and secular chanceries. It was apparently taught at the nascent university (*studium generale*) of Palencia around 1220 on the basis of the *Ars dictandi palentina*, a brief theoretical treatise followed by form letters (a standard configuration) probably written by a master trained at the University of Paris. The intellectual filiation of this text is of great interest because of the possible connection between the University of Palencia and the early authors of the *mester de clerecía*. This early French influence was swept away in the late thirteenth century by the flood of Italian dictaminal treatises, particularly those of Guido Faba (c.1196–c.1240) and Boncompagno da Signa (1165–1240). These exercised a major influence on two texts written during the reign of Alfonso X of Castile and León, the *Dictaminis epithalamium* (1277–1282) of Juan Gil de Zamora and the *Ars epistolaris ornatus* (c.1270) of Gaufridus de Everseley, an Englishman in Alfonso's service. Later texts probably follow the same tradition until well into the fifteenth century, although in the absence of editions confirmatory evidence is lacking. The works of the Valencian Joan Serra (mid-fifteenth century) and, especially, the *Flores rethoricae* (printed in Salamanca, c.1488) of Fernando Manzanares, a student of Elio Antonio de Nebrija, represent the triumph of Italian Humanism and a return to the classical Ciceronian tradition.

The *ars poetriae*, the application of rhetoric to the composition of literary texts, arose at the end of the twelveth century in the context of the medieval schoolroom, where one of the most widespread methods of teaching correct Latinity was for students to write pastiches imitating the classical and medieval *auctores* (the canon of texts accepted as models). The various *artes poetriae* were intended primarily to provide rules for such exercises, although they also influenced literary practice outside the schoolroom. The only one that appears to have been known in Spain was the *Poetria nova* (c.1208–1213) of the Englishman Geoffrey of Vinsauf. It is mentioned in library inventories in Catalonia as early as 1329 and as late as 1506, and in Salamanca from the early fifteenth century. There is one Spanish contribution to the genre, the *Breve compendium artis rethorice* attributed to a Martín of Córdoba (Martinus Cordubensis) (first half of the fourteenth century). Extant in two manuscripts, it attempts to mate the structural divisions of Ciceronian rhetoric (invention, disposition, style, delivery, memory) with precepts taken from the *Poetria nova* (natural versus artificial order, techniques for amplification and abbreviation, stylistic variety) in a structure that presages the return to classical principles characteristic of humanism.

The *artes praedicandi*, treatises for the organization of the thematic (because it takes as its theme a passage from Scripture) or university (because the first examples appeared in the University of Paris around 1230) sermon, developed in England and northern France in the first decades of the thirteenth century, rapidly gained currency, especially with the Franciscans, and remained enormously popular until the end of the Middle Ages. Despite this popularity there are no Spanish examples until the *Ars praedicandi populo* of the influential Catalan Franciscan Francesc Eiximenis (c.1340–1409); in its avoidance of overly technical methods in sermon construction and insistence on the moral character of the preacher as much as his rhetorical skills, it may well reflect not only Eiximenis's own experiences but also those of the foremost preacher of the age, St. Vincent Ferrer (1350–1419). An anonymous *Ars praedicandi aragonensis* (c. second quarter of the fifteenth century), probably written by a Spaniard at the University of Toulouse, is more representative of the preceptive tradition of the thematic sermon, although it ends with an atypical section on versification (used as a means of fixing the congregation's attention) of great interest for the study of fifteenth-century Spanish metrical terminology. The only text to originate in Castile is the *Ars praedicandi* of Martín Alfonso de Córdoba, also trained in Toulouse, who died in 1476 and is better known as the author of *Jardín de nobles doncellas*, dedicated to Isabel I the Catholic. The treatise is entirely traditional in its exposition of the basic doctrines of the thematic sermon.

The Catalan mystic Ramón Llull (Raimundo Lulio, c.1232–1316) stands completely outside the currents sketched above. Although his three rhetorical works deal with homiletics, they are based not on the *ars praedicandi* but rather on the application of his great *ars* (the explanation of the created world and all human knowledge as reflections of the nine divine attributes) to the problems of preaching. The *Rhetorica nova* is a theoretical statement, which is then applied, in detail in the *Liber de praedicatione* and more summarily in the *Ars brevis praedicationis*, to the problem of finding materials for the sermon and organizing it.

Treatises on poetics in the vernacular languages (for example, Raimon Vidal de Besalú, *Razos de trobar*; Berenguer de Noya, *Mirall de trobar*; Enrique de Villena, *Arte de trobar*; Pero Guillén de Segovia, *Gaya ciencia*) are largely concerned with technical questions of metrics rather than with composition in the broader sense and must be studied within the context of vernacular versification.

We do not know whether the classical rhetorics or any of the medieval arts formed part of the grammar school or university curriculum in Spain. We may surmise that the *ars dictandi* was taught in the faculty of law, as in Italian universities, but there is no evidence for such teaching. The first documentary reference is found in Salamanca in 1403, in the form of an Italian *magister rhetoricae*, Bartolomeo Sanzio; from that time forward Salamanca had a chair of rhetoric, but we still do not know what was taught; we find similar references to Italian masters in Catalonia from the 1420s onward.

Nor do we know the extent to which rhetorical texts may have influenced contemporary writers. It seems clear that the early writers of the *mester de clerecía* (Gonzalo de Berceo, and the *Alexandre* poet), attuned to European intellectual trends, were familiar with contemporary rhetorical teaching in the first half of the thirteenth century. The prose introduction to the Archpriest of Hita's *Libro de buen amor* is quite evidently a parody of the thematic sermon, and it has also been suggested that sermon techniques underlie Alfonso Martínez de Toledo's *Arcipreste de Talavera* (*Corbacho*). Nevertheless, in the absence of reliable texts, comparisons are difficult to draw.

CHARLES B. FAULHABER

Bibliography

Camargo, M. *Ars dictaminis, ars dictandi*. Typologie des Sources du Moyen Age Occidental, fasc. 59. Turnhout, 1991.

Faulhaber, C. B. *Latin Rhetorical Theory in Thirteenth and Fourteenth Century Castile*. Berkeley, 1972.

———. "Las retóricas hispanolatinas medievales, siglos XIII–XV." *Repertorio de Historia de las Ciencias Eclesiásticas en España* 7 (1979), 11–64.

———. "Rhetoric in Medieval Catalonia: The Evidence of the Library Catalogs." In *Studies in Honor of Gustavo Correa*. Ed. C. B. Faulhaber, et al. Potomac, Md., 1986, 92–126.

Kelly, D. *The Arts of Poetry and Prose*. Typologie des Sources du Moyen Age Occidental, fasc. 59. Turnhout, 1991.

Murphy, J. J. *Rhetoric in the Middle Ages*. Berkeley, 1974.

RHETORIC, ARABIC

In dealing with Arabic rhetoric (*balāgha*) it is necessary to keep in mind that we are dealing with literary theory and criticism; the art of oratory received little attention; that Arabic literary rhetoric was more interested in poetry than in prose (mostly epistolography); and that, as far as we know, there is little that can be qualified as representing an Iberian school of rhetoric and that there is good reason to consider scholars from the western part of North Africa and from Spain as belonging to one and the same group. It also appears reasonable to follow Soudan in distinguishing an eastern Arabic school and a Persian school, to which one could consider adding a somewhat isolated Aristotelian school based on translations and commentaries of Aristotle's *Poetics* and *Rhetoric*. Considerable oversimplification cannot be avoided in an article this size. Moreover it should be kept in mind that some texts are not yet available in print, have not been thoroughly studied, or are not even known to have survived in manuscript.

The origin of Arabic literary rhetoric can be traced to the Fertile Crescent. Numerous collections of poetry quote traditions relating debates on the merits of one poet weighed against the merits of another, plagiarism (a legitimate, even praiseworthy, form of plagiarism was recognized). Characteristic was the discussion of single lines of poetry to which the structure of Arabic poetry lends itself easily. These tendencies can be noticed even in later handbooks and monographs. Leaving aside one early treatise that was apparently completely forgotten, it was the *Kitāb al-Badi* (*Book of the Novel [in Style*) of Ibn al-Muʿtazz and, somewhat later, the *Naqd al-Shiʿr* (*Criticism of Poetry*) of Ḳudāma ibn Djaʿfar that laid the foundation for Arabic rhetoric. Though written, as the title indicates, to discuss a new style sometimes characterized by an excessive use of figures of speech, it was the terminology and exemplification of Ibn al-Muʿtazz's figures of speech that survived through the ages. The result was that *badi* (novel) came to be used as a collective for *figures of speech*. But this did not happen without significant and often confusing changes in the terminology of Ibn al-Muʿtazz, various systems of categorizing figures of speech, and so forth. The same happened to the terminology of Ḳudāma, whose curious arrangement of his material (based on what he knew of Greek philosophy and logic) was soon forgotten.

A new approach was introduced by ʿAbd al-Ḳāhir al-Djurdjāni in two books that are unique in the history of Islamic scholarship: his *Proofs of the Inimitability of the Koran*, according to Ritter a "very subtle theory of syntactic stylistics" and his *Secrets of Eloquence*, essentially his "teaching on simile, metaphor, and analogy" as well as "phantastic aetiology." These two books gave rise to the Persian school that henceforth divided literary theory into *ʿilm al-maʿāni* (the theory of stylistics—that is, style in its relation to syntax), the *ʿilm al-bayān* (the theory of imagery), and the *ʿilm al-badiʿ* (the theory of the figures of speech—a choice from among the figures of speech not discussed under *maʿānī*). This school found, according to Ibn Khaldūn not much favor in the western half of the Islamic world, which instead, preferred to concentrate on the *badiʿ* following the old tradition of Ibn al-Muʿ-tazz and Ḳudāma and their many followers. It should be noted that the Western school showed a degree of interest in adaptations of Aristotle. Initially, however, they derived their interest mostly from an outstanding Tunisian representative of the Eastern school, Ibn Rashīḳ. Incidentally, Ibn Rashīḳ did not limit himself to an analysis of the figures of speech, but also gave attention to such matters as the history of poetry and its position in society, as well as to the technicalities of metre and rhyme. At least two authors show Aristotelian influence very clearly. Averroës (Ibn Rushd) tried, basing himself on a faulty translations and therefore with very little success, to discuss Arabic poetry and oratory in Aristotelian terms. Ḥāzim al-Qartādjanni (d.), parts of whose *Minhādj* (*Plain Road*) have been translated and very carefully analyzed by Heinrichs and Schoeler, reflects Aristotle using earlier and more careful interpretations by dl-Fārābi and Avicenna (Ibn Sīnā) in dealing with such matters as technical terms, the difference between rhetoric and poetry, poetry that is useful and also pleasing, poetry's moral character, the typology of poets, as well as other matters that cannot be dealt with in the context of a brief survey. To the same school belongs the Moroccan al-Sidjilmāsī, whose *al-Manzaʿ al-Badiʿ* has not yet been studied in detail. There is a probably unique work on prose, including oratory, by Ibn ʿAbd al-Ghafūr al-Kalāʿi that mainly follows the Eastern tradition. Tanasi lived in North Africa; his treatise, like that of Ḥāzim, shows a very detailed and careful arrangement, thereby disproving the often heard claim that many Arabic scholarly texts are incoherent. According to Soudan he belonged to the eastern Arabic as well as the Persian Schools, mainly through Ibn Jābir and al-Ruʿayni. Both Ibn Jābir and al-Ruʿayni hailed from Spain, but lived some forty years in the East and died there; consequently it is not easy to determine whether they have to be considered as belonging to the Western school, the more so since a complete edition of their work is not available. Finally it should be mentioned that the Egyptian Ibn Abi ʿl-Iṣbaʿ lists among the texts he used some apparently of Spanish or North African origin.

SEEGER A. BONEBAKKER

Bibliography

Heinrichs, A. *Arabische Dichtung und griechische Poetik.* Beirut, 1969.

——— "Poetik, Rhetorik, Literaturkritik." In *Grundriss der arabischen Philologie*. Vol. 2. Ed. H. Gätje. Wiesbaden, 1987. 177–190.

Al-Jurjāni Abdalqāhir. *Asrār al-balāgha: The Mysteries of Eloquence*. Ed. H. Ritter. Introduction, 1–24.

Ibn Khaldūn. *The Muqaddimah: An Introduction to History*. Vol. 3. 2d ed. Trans. F. Rosenthal: Princeton, N. J., 1967. 286, 335–39, 398–409.

Schoeler, C. *Einige Grundprobleme der autochtonen und der arabischen Literaturtheorie: Hāzim al-Qartāganni's Kapitel über die Zielsetzung der Dichtung und die Vorgeschichte der in ihm dargelegten Gedanken.* Abhandlungen für die Kunde des Morgenlandes. Vol. 41, 4.

Soudan, N. (ed.) *Westarabische Tropik: Nazm IV des Tanasi*. Bibliotheca Islamica 29. Wiesbaden, 1980, Introduction, 3–117.

RICOHOMBRE *See* NOBLES AND NOBILITY

RIDDLES

According to Dundes and Georges, "A riddle is a traditional verbal expression which contains one or more descriptive elements; the referent of the elements is to be guessed." Taylor argues that true riddles compare an object with an entirely different object; all other play questions are enigmas. Riddles and enigmas occur in interpersonal transactions in which power is transferred from poser to successful responder. The poser may even reject one correct answer and insist upon another, as in the tale of Saladin.

Often a relatively powerless person's survival depends on success in a riddle contest whose content is usually doctrinal, cosmological, or theological, for example, in *Donzella Teodor*, St. Catherine and the Infante Epitus confront and defeat officially appointed inquisitors. A clever bishop saves San Andrés from a devil in the guise of a seductive woman who posed cosmological riddles.

The *Libro de Apolonio* begins with a folkloric contest in which the referent is a shameful royal secret.

The reward for a correct response is the hand of the princess, and failure means death. In folktales, a suitor, imitating Samson (Judg. 14:12–19), brings a hermetic, unanswerable riddle to confound a princess famous for riddling skills. Another princess, Tarsiana, Apolonio's daughter, is an entertainer who engages in a playful riddle contest with a mock penalty and reward using popularizations of classical riddles.

HARRIET GOLDBERG

Bibliography

Dundes, A., and R. A. Georges. "Toward a Structural Definition of the Riddle." *Journal of American Folklore* 76 (1963), 111–18.

Goldberg, H. "Riddles and Engimas in Medieval Castilian Literature." *Romance Philology* 36 (1982), 209–21.

Taylor, B. "Juan Manuel's Cipher in the Libro de los estados," *Corónica*, 12 (1983–1984), 32–44.

RIPOLL SONGS

Since Lluis Nicolau d'Olwer's study in 1923, "Ripoll Songs" (*Carmina Rivipullensia*) has been used to refer to eighty-one Latin poems transmitted in seventeen manuscripts from the monastery of Ripoll (Catalonia, Girona), a ninth-century foundation, which from time to time had connections with Fleury and Marseilles. Among the poems that are panegyrical, didactic, and liturgical, those written by Abbot Oliba (1008–1048), are of particular importance. Analysis of the many figures that adorn the facade of the church that Oliba built in Ripoll reveals numerous clues as to the meaning of the Ripoll collection. Many-sided in theme and form—with metrical and accentual—rhythmic verses, final rhyme, alphabetical and acrostic poems—this collection, taken as a whole, is testimony to the monastery's flourishing scholarship up to the thirteenth century. While most of the poems were produced in Ripoll itself, others were only copied there.

By the Ripoll Songs in the narrower sense we mean a collection comprising nineteen items of love poetry, entered onto folios 97v, 98r, and 102r of a tenth-century miscellany by a twelfth-century hand because those folios had remained unfilled due to their defective quality. (The miscellany is in Barcelona, Archivo de la Corona de Aragón, Ripoll 74). The unknown author of these love poems is described by Nicolau as an "anònim enamorat." Opinions differ as to whether the author of these poems is identical with their copyist; Dronke argues persuasively for the identification. Paleographical, formal, and internal grounds make a dating of the collection to the 1170s probable. The poet is plainly familiar with Ovid's works, and imitates them. He appears to have known the works of the poets of the Loire circle—Marbod of Rennes, Hildebert of Lavardin, Baudri of Bourgueil. Echoes of the poem *Foebus abierat*, which was produced in northern Italy, and of *Surgens manerius*, which is dependent on it, are attested in both form and content; equally evident is an acquaintance with *Carmen Buranum* 117.

Evidence of links with France is provided by the inscription of poem 11, "Ad comitissam Frantie" and by the mention of the nunnery of Remiremont, which was known for its "Council of Love."

As general themes and topoi there are attested the "beginning with nature," the *locus amoenus*, hunting metaphors, descriptions of beauty, and the five stages of love; Venus, Amor/Cupido, Diana, Phoebus, nymphs and muses make their appearance from ancient mythology. There is a well-balanced mixture of different line forms, accentual-rhythmical and gathered into strophes, almost all of them rhyming, together with stichistic hexameters and elegiac distichs. Since one is to assume that the author has himself organized the poems in the sequence that has come down to us, variation should be regarded as a ludic motif; Dronke points to musical elements. The fancy of writing poems' inscriptions partly backward (for example, Macimada Ad amicam) is another indicator of this ludic aspect. When one considers the content of the collection, the poems are not juxtaposed as individual texts. Although they do not form a novella, there is a clear beginning and development of a love affair, followed by separation and abandonment. The beginning is signaled by the months of April (c.1) and May (c.2). Dreams and visions alternate with more realistic phases. Poems 1–11 center on a mistress called "Judit" (c.2); 12–17 on one named "Guilibergis." Both cycles are rounded off with an elsewhere attested misogynistic poem attributed to Marbod. On the third folio, which remained free from the gathering (102r), two more substantial poems are entered. They refer back to the mistress Judit. In assessing the poems pride of place should be given to 9 and 19 because of their unconventional, subtle style of argument. All in all, there is a division of opinion as to whether they are stereotypical school exercises or, in the high estimation of Dronke "one of the most original poets of his age."

EWALD KÖNSGEN

Bibliography

Dronke, P. "The Interpretation of the Ripoll Love-Songs," *Romance Philology* 33 (1979), 14–42.

Moralejo, J. L. (ed.) *Cancionero de Ripoll (Anónimo)*. Barcelona, 1986.

Nicolau d'Olwer, L. *L'escola poètica de Ripoll en els segles X–XIII*. Anuari de l'Institut d'Estudis Catalans 6. 1915–19.

RODERIC

The succession of the Visigothic king Roderic (Rodrigo) in 710 appears to have been contentious. He may have been the son of a Visigothic noble called Theodefred, and later sources associate his family with both Córdoba and Mérida. He was certainly no relation to his predecessor Wittiza (692/4–710), and the *Crónica mozárabe del año 754* (*Chronicle of 754*) states that he was chosen as king by the "senate," probably referring to the Visigothic palace nobility. The same chronicle makes it clear that his succession was opposed and some form of civil war was taking place in Spain when the Arabs invaded in 711. A further indication of this may be the lack of coins of Roderic issued by the mints of the towns of the Ebro Valley and Catalonia. Here power was in the hands of a king Achila (c.710–c.713). Regnal lists containing the name of Achila do not mention Roderic. According to some of the Arab sources, Roderic was in the north of the Iberian Peninsula fighting the Basques when the invasion took place. He was defeated by the Arab and Berber armies in the ensuing battle of Guadalete, and, although his death in that conflict is not certain, nothing more is known of him. His widow Egilona subsequently married the Arab governor ʿAbd al-Azīz ibn Mūsā (712–715). The reference to his funerary inscription being seen at Viseu, contained in both versions of the *Crónica de Alfonso III* is to be treated with caution. In the historiographical tradition of the Asturian kingdom, Roderic was made to be a heroic figure, in distinction to his predecessor. Southern traditions, as represented by the *Chronicle of 754*, reverse this verdict on the two kings.

ROGER COLLINS

Bibliography

Collins, R. *The Arab Conquest of Spain, 710–797*. Oxford, 1989.

Menéndez Pidal, R. (ed.), *Floresta de leyendas heróicas españolas*. Vol. 1, *Rodrigo, el último godo*. Madrid, 1925.

RODRIGO DE LA GUITARRA

According to widowed Aragónese Queen Margarita de Prades's letter to Archimbaud of Foix, Rodrigo de la Guitarra (c. 1380–c.1422) had served Fernando I. Dated 30 December 1415, the letter contains this recommendation: "Out of regard and concern for me, I beg you to treat him with singular respect, for by so doing you will please me greatly." In Alfonso the Magnanimous's letter to Juan II of Castile dated 30 July 1417 (Archivo de la Corona de Aragón, Registro 2562, fols. 110ᵛ–111), *el Magnánimo* states that he is sending "his faithful household string player, Rodrigo de la Guitarra, accompanied by Rodrigo's helper Diego, to Juan's court to do him reverence as Juan's vassal, and to serve him and entertain him with his art (el fiel ministrer de cuerda de nuestra camara Rodrigo de la Guitarra, con su criado Dieguiello, de nuestra licencia va asci a vuestra cort por fazer a vos servicio a plazer de au oficio)." When, after a delay, Rodrigo did make the trip in August 1418, he and his entourage went with Alfonso's safe conduct (*salvoconducto*) protecting them and their baggage train laden with gold, silver, money, and clothing. Upon returning to Alfonso's Neapolitan court, Rodrigo was rewarded, on 26 August 1421, with the lucrative post of Castilian consul at Palermo.

The Chantilly manuscript, Musée Condé 564 (olim 1047) contains a Latin ballade, *Angelorum psalat tripudium*, copied at folio 48ᵛ, which according to Gilbert Reaney is "one of the most recent and most complex works in the manuscript." The variety of note forms employed in the Cantus reaches extremes unparalleled even in the Chantilly Codex, and syncopation produces results which can hardly be transcribed in modern notation. Coloration [notes in red] is excessive, but particularly noteworthy is the modal transcription. A two-flat signature (E flat and A flat, B flat being understood) moves the mode Ionian from C to E flat, a unique case in this period.

In Gordon Kay Greene's Indiana University Ph.D. dissertation (1971) he took the inscription below the tenor, *Retro mordens ut fera pessima ante blandis ut faris in vocibus*, to indicate retrograde reading at some section or sections. Such backward reading would conform with the backward inscription of the composer's name above the cantus part: "S. Uciredor" = Rodericus.

To Nors Sigurd Josephson belongs the credit for having solved what to others before him seemed an insoluble riddle, transcription of Rodrigo's cryptic ballade—Rodrigo's sole extant work.

ROBERT STEVENSON

Bibliography

Reaney, G. "The Manuscript Chantilly, Musée Condé 1047," *Musica Disciplina* 8 (1954), 78–79.

Greene, G. K. The Secular Music of Chantilly Manuscript, Musée Condé 564 (olim 1047)," Ph.D. diss. Indiana University, 1971. 285.

Josephson N.S. "Rodericus, *Angelorum Psalat*." *Musica Disciplina* 25 (1971), 113–26.

Stevenson, R. "Therian Musical Outreach before the Encounter with the New World," *Inter-American Music Review* 8, no. 2 (1987), 20, 43–51 (with music facsimile and transcription).

RODRIGO, LEGEND OF THE LAST VISIGOTHIC KING

Following the Arabic invasion of Spain in 711 and the subsequent collapse of the Visigothic monarchy, three principal myths with minor variants arose to explain the destruction of Christian Spain, each reflecting an interpretation of the events by a particular political faction anxious to propagate its own point of view. The original legend, first encountered in the contemporary *Crónica mozárabe del año 754* and later repeated by the *Chronica gothorum* (c.1050), is an expression of the convictions held by the conquered Mozarabic Christians and ascribes the loss of Spain to the indiscretions of the lecherous King Wittiza whose seduction of Count Olián's daughter led the disaffected vassal to seek vengeance by allying himself with an Arabic invasion to overthrow the Visigothic kingdom. Following the reconquest of Toledo in 1085, we find a second version of the legend by yet another Mozarabic Christian, author of the anonymous *Crónica silense* (c.1115), reflecting the perspective of the Arabs and their allies, the defeated Wittiza faction, with an interpretation calculated to cast blame upon the last Visigothic king, Rodrigo, who had overthrown Wittiza and his government. In this account, Rodrigo had promised to marry Count Julian's daughter but instead took her as his concubine. The count then sought revenge by abetting the Arabs in their invasion of Spain. The third version represents the position of the thirteenth-century Castilian-Leonese monarchy which was anxious to disassociate itself from the imagined depravity of the last Visigothic kings from which it was supposedly descended by portraying both Wittiza and Rodrigo as corrupt and lascivious rulers whose unscrupulous and immoral reigns, like Sodom and Gomorrah, were destroyed by divine wrath in the person of the Arabs, *flagellum dei*. This interpretation was promoted by Lucas de Túy in *Chronicon mundi* (1236), substantially embellished by the archbishop of Toledo, Rodrigo Jiménez de Rada in *De rebus Hispaniae* (1243), and repeated by Alfonso X el Sabio in the *Primera crónica general* (c.1275). The legend of Rodrigo as seducer of Count Julian's daughter then took its definitive novelistic shape in the *Crónica de 1344*, which drew substantially upon the so-called *Crónica del moro Rasis* by the Córdoban historian Ahmad al-Rāzī (888–955), who incorporated a number of fictitious episodes. The legend was extensively enlarged by Pedro del Corral in the *Crónica sarracina* (c.1430) and later assimilated as a historical source by the archpriest of Talavera in *Atalaya de las crónicas* (c.1453) and Diego Rodrigo de Almella in *Compilación de las crónicas et estorias de España* (1491), reaching its most factitious extreme in the fantastic reworking by Miguel de Luna, *La verdadera historia del rey don Rodrigo compuesta por Abulcácim Tárif Abentarique* (1592).

RICHARD P. KINKADE

Bibliography

Deyermond, A. "The Death and Rebirth of Visigothic Spain in *Estoria de España*," *Revista Canadiense de Estudios Hispánicos* 9 (1985), 345–67.

Floresta de leyendas heróicas españolas: Rodrigo el último godo, Clásicos castellanos, vols. 62, 71, 84–.

Menéndez Pidal, R. "El rey Rodrigo en la literatura," *Boletín de la Real Academia Española* 11 (1924), 157–97 251–86, 349–87, 519–85; and 12 (1925), 5–38 192–216.

RODRíGUEZ DE LA CÁMARA *See* RODRÍGUEZ DEL PADRÓN, JUAN

RODRÍGUEZ DEL PADRÓN, JUAN (JUAN RODRÍGUEZ DE LA CÁMARA)

Poet and prose writer of Galician origin who flourished around the mid-fifteenth century. Few details are available on the life of Juan Rodríguez del Padrón. From the scant information available, we know that he served in the household of Juan Cervantes, Cardinal of San Pedro and Provincial General of the Francicans, along with Aeneas Silvius Piccolomini and Alfonso de Madrigal. In 1430 he most likely accompanied the cardinal to Assisi and was with him at the Council of Basle in 1438. By 1441, Rodríguez del Padrón had taken Franciscan orders in Jerusalem. He probably belonged to that group of civil, ecclesiastical, and court officials known as *letrados* and, from the range of his writings, was quite cultivated.

Rodríguez del Padrón's surviving works center on three themes, love, worthy women, and nobility. His *Triunfo de las donas* is his response to the complaint against women (*demanda de las mugeres*) touched off by Boccaccio's antifeminist *Corbaccio* and Alfonso Martínez de Toledo's *Arcipreste de Talavera*. The work is comprised of a prologue followed by a series of exemplary portraits of praiseworthy women. Rodríguez del Padrón's *Cadira de Honor* is an extended treatise of nobility that ties into the debate on this subject in the works of Alfonso de Cartagena, Diego de Valera, and others. His *Bursario* is in part a translation and amplification of Ovid's *Heroides*. Rodríguez del Padrón's poetry circulated widely throughout the fifteenth century and is collected in many *cancioneros* (song books).

Rodríguez del Padrón's best known and most important work is *Siervo libre de amor*, which is preserved in a unique manuscript that is possibly incomplete. Couched as an autobiographical epistle, it relates the narrator's unhappy love affair and dream vision of his journey to the other world, a journey based on Guillaume de Deguilleville's *Romant des Trois Pèlerinages*. Composed in both prose and verse, in its midst, the autobiographical narrative is punctuated by the introduction of the *Estoria de dos amadores*, a chivalric-sentimental tale of love and death that the narrator invokes and serves as a dire reminder of love's cruelty. The work is important for the deliberate introduction of shifting points of view and its portrayal, discussion, and analysis of emotions and close experience. It is generally considered to be the first Spanish sentimental romance, a type of fiction that played an important role in laying the groundwork for modern novelistic discourse.

E. Michael Gerli

Bibliography

Gilderman, M. *Juan Rodríguez de la Cámara*. Boston, 1977.

Rodríguez del Padrón, J. *Obras completas*. Ed. César Hernández Alonso. Madrid, 1982.

Rohland de Langbehn, R. *La unidad genérica de la novela sentimental española de los siglos XV y XVI*. London, 1999.

ROÍS DE CORELLA, JOAN

Poet and learned Catalan prose writer (1433/43–1497). Although as heir of a noble family he was expected to become a knight, in 1471 Corella obtained the degree of master of theology. Corella, the last Catalan poet of the Middle Ages, both complains about the treason of a certain Caldesa and longs for the impossible love of other honest ladies, like in his *Balada de la garsa i l'esmerla*. He also wrote some poems to the Mother of God, like the powerful *Oració de la Verge*, as well as some lives of saints, such as *Vida de Santa Anna*, *Història de la Magdalena*, and *Història de Josep*. Some of these, along with his translations into Catalan of Ludolf of Saxony's *Vita Christi* and the *Psalter*, are the religious works that Corella himself wanted to have printed. The minor works of Corella (*Triunfo de les dones* or the letters he interchanged with Prince Carlos de Viana) are written in the same strongly rhetorical fashion as his most famous profane work, the *Tragèdia de Caldesa*. Here, the first-person narrator, clearly meant to be identified with the author himself, briefly recounts in prose and verse how a lady of Valencia deceived her ingenuous and sincere lover by behaving like a courtesan. Corella's disillusionment with human love is also the main subject of his splendid versions of Ovid's tragic love stories: *Història de Jason e Medea, Història de Leànder y Hero, Parlament en casa de Berenguer Mercader*. The Trojan War provides the setting for his retelling of the *Lo joi de Paris*, which shows how a man is misled by passionate love, of the *Raonament de Telamó e de Ulixes*, and of Corella's finest Senecan achievement, *Plant dolorós de la reina Hècuba*, in which decasyllabic verses are skillfully meshed with a rich prose embellished by rhythmic clausulae.

Lola Badía

Bibliography

Badia, L. *De Bernat Metge a Joan Roís de Corella*. Barcelona, 1988.

Miquel i Planas, R. (ed.) *Obres de Joan Roiç de Corella*. Barcelona, 1913.

ROIG, JAUME

Catalan moral writer (1400/10–1478). Starting in 1434 we find Roig documented as a master of medicine in Valencia, in 1456 as doctor to the queen of Aragón, María of Castile, and between 1450 and 1462 as administrator of the Valencian Hospital d'En Clapers. In 1474, a poem of his in honor of the Virgin was published in the first Catalan incunabulum, *Les trobes en laors de la Verge Maria*. Roig produced a long misogynous treatise written in quadrisyllabic verse that contains a pseudo-autobiography: *L'espill*, or, *El llibre de les dones*. If written in prose, *L'espill* would probably have become a great novel since its plot is exciting and it presents a wide range of characters. The misfortunes of a young boy, who is expelled from home after his father's death by a wicked mother, provide, in fact, a shockingly realistic picture of everyday life. Despite the continuous aggressions of perverse women, the hero becomes quite well off by joining a mercenary army in France. Upon his return to Valencia four consecutive attempts at marriage come to disastrous ends because of the unbearably evil nature of women. He tries to marry a young girl, a beguine, a widow, and finally a novice with increasingly bad results. Finally King Solomon advises the hero in dreams. Solomon's long theological lesson is a vindication of the ideals of monastic asceticism. By accepting this advice, Roig manages to end his life peacefully, far from worldly wickedness and chiefly far from women. In the meanwhile we have been given glimpses into hospitals, nunneries, pilgrimages, the private rooms of bourgeois women, public bathhouses, and picturesque marketplaces, among others. Roig was a very gifted social observer and his profession as a doctor certainly helped him. He also created a very personal literary style full of rhymes and with a strange elliptical syntax.

LOLA BADÍA

Bibliography

Miquel i Planas, R. (ed.). *Spill o Libre de Consells*. 2 vols. Barcelona, 1929–50.

Roig, J. *Espejo*. Trans. R. Miquel i Planas, ed. J. Vidal Alcover. Barcelona, 1987.

ROJAS, FERNANDO DE *See* CELESTINA

ROMAN LAW *See* LAW

ROMANCERO *See* BALLAD

ROMANCES, ARTHURIAN

While there exists no evidence that the romances of Thomas, Béroul, or Chrétien de Troyes were translated into any Iberian language, the Arthurian legend nevertheless made its way into the Iberian Peninsula via France and exercised a significant cultural influence during the late Middle Ages. Throughout the Middle Ages allusions to the legend appear in all parts of Iberia and there is strong evidence to believe that it even served as a model for aristocratic conduct. The earliest mention of the legend dates from 1170, while material from Wace's *Roman de Brut* is known to have formed part of a now lost early thirteenth-century Navarese redaction of the *Liber Regum*. At the other end of the chronological spectrum there is a late fifteenth-century sermon composed in Castilian that uses material from Geoffrey of Monmouth's *Historia regum Britanniae* in order to explain and elaborate upon the doctrine of transubstantiation. These witnesses attest to general public knowledge about Arthurian material over a very broad period of time. The Vulgate Cycle, the prose *Tristan*, and the Post-Vulgate *Roman du Graal* appear to be the major sources for the transmission of the Arthurian legend in medieval Iberia. Translations and transformations of the latter texts exist in some twenty-six extant manuscripts and printed books (some of them fragmentary) ranging chronologically from the first part of the fourteenth to the middle of the sixteenth centuries. The derring-do adventure depicted in this last group of romances appears to have held special appeal in the Iberian Peninsula.

Evidence of the circulation of Arthurian legends can be found in the western part of the peninsula as early as 1190, where the name Merlinus is attested to in Portugal, followed by Galván in 1208. In 1200 the name Arturus was used by someone in Salamanca, and throughout the thirteenth and fourteenth centuries the Galaico-Portuguese troubadours frequently alluded to Arthurian subjects, drawing principally from the cyclical prose romances. The cleric João Bivas translated the Post-Vulgate *Roman du Graal* around the year 1313 and testimonials of all three branches of the cycle survive in Galician and Portuguese as well as Castilian. The Conde de Barcelos' fourteenth-century *Livro de Linhagens* adapts material from Wace via the lost Navarese *Liber Regum* mentioned above, and information of a similar type can be found in the *Crónica de 1404* and a fifteenth-century copy of the *Libro de las generaciones* of Martín de Larraya. Fernão Lopes' *Cronica de d. João I*, the Portuguese king who reigned from 1385–1433, demonstrates that the romances were both well known and well read at court. Attestations to knowledge of the Matter of Britain continue to be found in the western part of the Iberian Peninsula well into the sixteenth century, notably in the courtly lyric collected by Garcia de Resende in his *Cancioneiro geral* in 1516.

In the northern and central parts of the peninsula, in a document attached to a manuscript of the Navarro-Aragónese *Fuero general de Navarra* (1196–1212), and in the *Anales Toledanos* (1217), mention is made of Arthur's deadly battle with Mordred. Further references to Arthurian material can be found in the *Libro del cavallero Zifar*, the first known Spanish romance of chivalry (ca. 1300). Later, there are mentions of Arthur and members of his court in Castilian court poetry, and a long version of the *Lancelot* was translated into Castilian around 1414. The latter is extant in a mid-sixteenth-century copy with an addition that connects it with the story of Tristan. In the late fifteenth century the *Libro de las bienandanzas y fortunas* of Lope García de Salazar, a chronicler from Vizcaya, condenses material from several branches of the *Roman du Graal* and is a mine of Arthurian matter, while the *Baladro del sabio Merlín* (Burgs, 1498) and the *Demanda del sancto Grial* (Toledo, 1515) also incorporate a significant amount of material from the last two branches of that romance. A great many other Arthurian allusions are recorded in Castile and the northern center of the Iberian Peninsula, incorporated directly or indirectly into texts from the end of the fourteenth century forward. By their prevalence there and in the ballad tradition they reflect the continuing presence and interest in Arthurian material in Castile well into, and beyond, the sixteenth century.

Finally, in Catalonia, the legend was adapted with appreciable originality during the Middle Ages in works like *Jaufré* and *Baldín de Cornualha*, which evoke Cornish settings and emphasize action over sentimental themes. Cervantes at the beginning of the seventeenth century in his *Don Quijote* mentions an adaptation of the *Jaufré* composed in Castilian under the title *Tablante de Ricamonte* (first printed in 1513). Allusions to Arthurian names and themes in Catalan literature can be found starting in the twelfth century with the lyrics of Guillem de Berguedà and other troubadours. They continue to be appear in Catalan and Valencian poetry and prose throughout the rest of the Middle Ages, while some parish records even indicate that Arthurian names were often given to actual people. The circulation of *Cuiron le Courtois*, *Palamedes*, *Meliadus*, and the *Prophécies de Merlín*, as well as the cyclical romances, is confirmed by allusions to them in Catalan and Aragónese documents. The existence of tapestries and paintings in the medieval Crown of Aragón at the end of the Middle Ages can also be corroborated.

The enormous popularity and intimate knowledge of Arthurian material in the peninsula during the late Middle Ages is confirmed by its pervasive mention in aristocratic milieux, especially in courtly circles, and by the widely used practice of giving Arthurian names to children and even pets in society at large. With the spread of lay literacy throughout the fourteenth and fifteenth centuries, the Matter of Britain gradually became accessible to all strata of society, capturing a broad range of imaginations and leading to the revival, creation, and commercial success of autochthonous Iberian chivalric romances like *Amadís de Gaula*, first printed in 1510 after being amplified by Garci Rodríguez de Montalvo.

E. Michael Gerli

Bibliography

Entwistle, W. J. *The Arthurian Legend in the Literature of the Spanish Peninsula*. London, 1925.

Lida de Malkiel, M. R. "Arthurian Literature in Spain and Portugal." In *Arthurian Literature in the Middle Ages*. Ed. R. S. Loomis. Oxford, 1959.

Sharrer, Harvey L. *A Critical Bibliography of Hispanic Arthurian Material*. London, 1977.

ROMANCE, CAROLINGIAN

Carolingian romances are related to that cycle of stories that were given the name *matière de France* by Jean Bodel in the famous couplet

> Ne sont que trois matières à nul homme attendant,
> De France et de Bretaigne et de Rome le grant.
> (There are only three matters for one to know, / that of France and of Britain and great Rome.)

The plots of these romances take Charlemagne and his relatives as their primary characters. For instance, the romance of *Flores and Blancaflor* is considered to be Carolingian since these two characters are the parents of Berta, who is the wife of Pepin and the mother of Charlemagne. In fact, the connection with Charlemagne and France is often tenuous, thus vitiating to some extent the usefulness of Bodel's classification and the category of Carolingian romance in general. Nevertheless, it is traditional in scholarship to speak of such a category.

All these romances in their Spanish versions are translations from originals in other languages, mostly French, and most have their origin in French epic cycles dealing with the same material. Charlemagne has always been of special interest to Spaniards since he is the legendary founder of the pilgrimage to Santiago de Compostela and because of his heroic struggle against the Moors. In addition to the romance cycle there is a very productive ballad cycle, including such works as *El conde Dirlos*. Some hagiographic traditions are also associated with this material. Indeed, given the popularity of the theme, one wonders at the relative paucity of romance texts.

The following legends have been mentioned as Carolingian:

1. *Flores y Blancaflor* (The story of a couple sometimes identified as the monarchs of Almería, parents of Berta, the mother of Charlemagne.)
2. *Berta* (The story of Berta's betrayal by a chambermaid and of Berta's eventual reinstatement as queen.)
3. *Mainete* (The story of the early adventures of Charlemagne in Spain.)
4. *Historia de los amores de París y Viana* (The amorous adventures of two socially unequal lovers.)
5. *Historia de Enrique Fi de Oliva* (The story of a false accusation of adultery and military expeditions to the Levant.)
6. *Noble cuento del enperador Carlos Maynes e de la buena enperatris, Sevilla, su mugier* (*Hystoria de la reyna Sevilla* in later printings; the story of the falsely accused Sevilla, wife of Charlemagne, and of her eventual reconciliation with the emperor.)

It must be stressed that some of these tales are classified as "oriental" by various scholars, whereas other critics prefer to classify them by themes. Often there exist in these texts little more than references and allusions to the Carolingian legends. Some of the texts are embedded in other works, principally the *Gran conquista de Ultramar* and *Primera crónica general (Estoria de España)* of Alfonso X el Sabio. Others, such as the *Noble cuento*, the last tale in a collection of saints' lives and romances, became quite popular and circulated in various versions and printings as an independent text.

The stories deal with amorous adventures, mistaken identities, false accusations of adultery, soap opera cunning, deception, Byzantine-type travels and family separations, treachery, and so forth. Folkloric elements, such as dogs and asses far wiser than the human characters, are plentiful in these tales. There is also quite a bit of interest in matters of lineage and family origin, which probably explains why several of the legends appear in the *Gran conquista de Ultramar*, a work that deals with the exploits of famous crusaders and their (often fantastic) family origins. The importance given to female characters in these texts is worthy of note as is the relatively negative presentation of a gullible, easily deceived Charlemagne (when he appears as a character at all). Many critics have scant patience for this kind of imaginative fiction and have judged the stories to be absurd works of a degenerate genre. Still other scholars consider them to be works that function on a symbolic or archetypal level and suggest that they are more akin to dreams than to wakeful consciousness, real life, or realistic fiction. Scholars and literary critics in Spain have been slow to recognize these romances as forming a separate genre, and strong biases in favor of realism and so-called historical accuracy have kept these texts from forming part of the canon of medieval Spanish literature.

THOMAS D. SPACCARELLI

Bibliography

Bohigas Balaguer, P. "Orígenes de los libros de caballerías" and "La novela caballeresca, sentimental y de aventuras." In *Historia general de las literaturas hispánicas*. Ed. G. Díaz-Plaja. Barcelona, 1949–51, Vols. 1–2. 522–26; 196–99.

Deyermond, A. D. "The Lost Genre of Medieval Spanish Literature," *Hispanic Review* 43 (1975), 231–59.

Gómez Pérez, J. "Leyendas medievales españolas del ciclo carolingio." *Anuario de Filología* 1–2 (1963–64), 7–136.

Pedraza Jiménez, F. B., and M. Rodríguez Cáceres, *Manual de literatura española*. Vol. 1, *Edad Media*. Tafalla, 1981, 485–90, 800–802.

Rey, A. "Las leyendas del ciclo carolingio en la *Gran Conquista de Ultramar*." *Romance Philology* 3 (1949–50), 172–81.

ROMANCES, CHIVALRIC

Just what might determine the specific criteria for material to be covered in an entry on Chivalric Romance in medieval Iberia is difficult to define, but perhaps this difficulty reflects the complexity of the problem posed by the subject. The evidence for the production of autocthonous chivalric romances in the Iberian Peninsula prior to 1508 is slim. Much of what has come down to us is incomplete when not ephemeral, but precisely because of its fragmentary, elusive nature it is of great interest. In some aspects, a part of what remains represents adaptations or rewritings—as opposed to direct translations—of stories that have English, French, Anglo-Norman, or Franco-Italian origins.

Certainly when dealing with chivalric romance in medieval Iberia one must begin with the *Libro de Alexandre*, a reworking and acclimation of the French *Roman d'Alexandre*, which accommodates themes taken from classical antiquity to a thirteenth-century Hispanic chivalric context. If an important dimension of chivalric fiction is the affirmation of a politics that advocates the combination of chivalry with monarchy, then one must of necessity take special note of the *Alexandre* both for its contribution to the evolution of the theme as well as for having been composed just at the time that these ideas were beginning to come into close contact in Castilian civic life, i.e., during the reign of Alfonso VIII, as recently demonstrated by Amaia Arizaleta.

The *Libro de Alexandre* is not the only work to incorporate heroic chivalric values and motifs. At about the middle of the thirteenth century, many chivalric themes and ideas begin to surface in historiography, which attests to the political significance of chivalry and of chivalric fiction in general, although it draws us away from a strictly fictional European novelistic universe per se, especially that of works composed in French and Middle High German. By the end of the thirteenth century in Spain, classical, and most especially Carolingian, chivalric material was often incorporated in its entirety into historical narratives, above all in the *Gran Conquista de Ultramar* and the various versions of the *Estoria de España* composed during the reigns of Alfonso X and Sancho IV.

That said, however, what is generally recognized as genuinely chivalric material—fabulous tales populated with virtuous damsels, sorcerers, and monsters and comprised of the derring-do adventures of storied medieval knights—only begins to appear in Castile during the reign of Alfonso XI. The composition of two of the great Castilian chivalric romances belong to this period, the *Libro del caballero Zifar* and *Amadís de Gaula*. The *Zifar* is a complicated work composed from a perspective that fails to fit neatly into any European cultural paradigm. In it many literary and generic traditions of different, even Eastern, origins merge, but the work's central core remains the tale of gallant adventure that leads to an affirmation of monarchy and the display of the advantages of a knightly education, themes central to all chivalric fiction. The *Amadís* that was in circulation at this time, known only through fragments, was doubtless a work comprised of three books, as opposed to its later sixteenth-century incarnation in four. Its structure closely reflected that of the *Lancelot* of the French Vulgate Cycle. In addition, the short narratives known as *Otas de Roma*, *El Caballero Plácidas*, *La Emperatriz de Roma*, *Carlos Maynes*, *El Rey Guillermo*, plus various saints' lives contained in an important manuscript commonly referred to as the *Flos Sanctorum* (Escorial H-I-13), are also from this same period. As Francisco Rico has demonstrated, both the *Zifar* and the manuscript of the *Flos Sanctorum* share qualities that are essential to chivalric narrative fiction: Despite the hetereogeneity of their action and composition, they are both tightly unified by themes closely allied to questions of religious, political, and moral education. Something very similar can be discerned in another manuscript miscellany from the fifteenth century (MS 1837 of the Biblioteca Universitaria de Salamanca), which contains adaptations from the Arthurian Post-Vulgate Cycle, in particular a version of *Merlin* and *Lancelot*, along with an account of *Barlaam e Josafat*, plus several lesser texts of a pious nature. The *Amadís* and the works collected in the two manuscripts mentioned above all reflect the configuration of a cultural politics based on the advocacy of chivalry that began to be promulgated during the reign of Alfonso XI, a period that runs roughly between 1330 and 1350.

Around this same time or shortly thereafter, Catalan, Castilian, and Portuguese versions of the post-Vulgate cycle began to appear. These may be characterized as interpretive rewritings that tend toward a more pious and religiously orthodox interpretation of the French Arthurian material they draw on. The majority of the latter texts can be sorted into three main categories distinguished by the *Baladro del sabio Merlín*, *Lanzarote*, and the *Demanda del Santo Grial*. Both the *Baladro* and the *Demanda* appeared in incunable editions. Only mansucript fragments of the *Lanzarote*, however, remain.

The most original contributions to chivalric romance in the fifteenth century, the golden age of medieval Iberian chivalry, are of divers types. On the one hand, one model constituted principally as a political allegory, and one that deserves much further study, is represented by the Catalan *Curial e Güelfa*. In it Italian intellectual interests are artfully combined with courtly themes of French origin to embody a sensibility that could best be categorized as chivalric humanism. On the other, there is the unique work called *Tirant lo Blanc* that represents a union of everything chivalric from the theoretical treatise on chivalry to observations against it, to specific echoes and recollections of the *Matiére de Bretagne*, to gallant poetry and courtly spectacle, that circulated under the authorship of Joanot Martorell and was published at the instance of the printer Martí Joan de Galba, who was to Martorell what William Caxton was to Thomas Malory.

Other fifteenth-century Castilian narrative traditions that embrace chivalric material are also notable for their originality. The earlier synthesis of chivalric fiction and historical narrative that has already been noted persisted in Castile and León but now on a much more individual level, in the biographies of notable personages. Many of the heroic life narratives of the period, like Gonzalo de Chacón's chronicle of the deeds of don Álvaro de Luna and another work on Alonso de Monroy, or even the *Hechos de Alonso Carrillo* composed by Pero Guillén de Segovia (preserved now only in fragments), make ample use of classic chivalric paradigms to relate the lives of their protagonists. Predominant among these biographies is *El Victorial*, or the celebrated *Crónica de don Pero Niño, Conde de Buelna*, by Gutierre Díaz de Games, which gives free rein to chivalric motifs and exploits them in order to draw the portrait of the man who is the subject of the narrative. In consonance with the didactic tendency of many chivalric narratives, *El Victorial* also confers a great deal of space to the discursive development of ideas and to specific teaching, usually in the form of a debate centering on a significant topic. Like the vast majority of chivalric romances, *El Victorial* rests on a thematic core that underscores the importance of the education of the hero, the recuperation of lost honor or diminished family name, and the attainment of social recognition and success based on the hero's personal virtue and loyalty to the institution of monarchy.

The very last examples of medieval Iberian chivalric fiction materialized during the advent of printing in the peninsula. In the last last decade of the fifteenth century in particular, various brief chivalric romances appeared in print, although the majority of them did not see widespread circulation and broad acceptance until later in the sixteenth century. The first known edition of *Amadís de Gaula* in four books by Garci Rodríguez de Montalvo (now lost and probably from 1496) marks the transition from medieval chivalric romance to the great torrent of works that would emulate it and be published in the sixteenth century.

J. Rodríguez Velasco

Bibliography

Arizaleta, A. *La translation d'Alexandre: Recherches sur les structures et les significations du "Libro de Alexandre."* Paris, 1999.

Cátedra, P., and J. D. Rodríguez Velasco. *Creación y difusión de "El Baladro del Sabio Merlín."* Salamanca, 2000.

"Número monográfico sobre la narrativa caballeresca medieval." *Voz y Letra*, 7, no. 2 (1996).

Rico, Francisco. "Entre el códice y el libro (Notas sobre los paradigmas misceláneos y la literatura del siglo XIV." *Romance Philology* 51 (1997–98), 151–69.

Arthur Terry, A. (ed.) *Tirant lo Blanc: New Approaches.* London, 1999.

ROMANCES, SENTIMENTAL

The literary genre in the Iberian Peninsula called "sentimental romance" or "sentimental fiction" is composed of some thirty works written between about 1400 and about 1550. The canonical list of sentimental romances as first established by Whinnom includes the following titles:

1) *Siervo libre de amor* by Juan Rodríguez del Padrón
2) *Tratado e despido a una dama de religión* by Fernando de la Torre;
3) *Sátira de infelice e felice vida* by Dom Pedro de Portugal
4) *Triste deleytaçión*, anonymous (although written by a Catalan author)
5) *Arnalte y Lucenda* by Diego de San Pedro
6) *Cárcel de Amor* by Diego de San Pedro
7) *Triunfo de Amor* by Juan de Flores
8) *Grisel y Mirabella* by Juan de Flores
9) *Grimalte y Gradissa* by Juan de Flores
10) *Repetición de amores* by Luis de Lucena
11) *Cárcel de Amor* by Nicolás Núñez
12) *Tratado de amores*, anonymous
13) *La coronación de la señora Gracisla*, anonymous
14) *Qüestión de Amor*, anonymous
15) *Penitencia de amor* by Pedro Manuel Jiménez de Urrea
16) *Quexa ante el dios de amor* by the Comendador Escrivá
17) *Cartas y coplas para requerir nuevos amores*, anonymous
18) *Veneris tribunal* by Ludovico Scrivà
19) *Tratado llamado notable de amor* by Juan de Cardona
20) *Proceso de cartas de amores* by Juan de Segura
21) *Quexa y aviso contra amor* by Juan de Segura

Although scholars have long considered this genre as exclusively Castilian, recent criticism suggests that some Catalan and Portuguese works should be considered sentimental fictions as well. Thus, while the first canonical sentimental romance written in Castilian dates from about 1440 (*Siervo libre de amor* by Juan Rodríguez del Padrón), several critics have defended that *Frondino i Brisona* (a bilingual work written in Catalan and French about 1400) is already a developed sentimental fiction. As well, the Portuguese *Confissão do Amante* (c. 1430), *Menina e Moça*, and *Naceo e Amperidónia*, among others, and the fifteenth-century Catalan novel, *Les amoroses i sentimentals*, should be included as part of the genre. Among the main literary sources of sentimental fiction, we could mention the Arthurian romance, the French *voir-dit*, Boccaccio's *novelle*, medieval literature of *de regimine principum*, Biblical texts, *cancionero* literature, university *tractatus*, homiletic literature, *relaciones* (descriptions of courtly events), theatrical texts (eclogue, humanistic comedy), and so on.

Critics have long debated the main characteristics of sentimental fiction. Although there is no complete agreement (recent scholars have established that there is *unity* within this genre), some of the most accepted features of the genre include:

- A love story between lovers whose love affair is seldom consummated. In most cases the result of their love affair is tragic, including the death (mostly by suicide) of the male lover. Love is analyzed as a frustrating and frustrated passion and is usually envisioned within both a personal and social framework.
- (Pseudo) Autobiography. Many sentimental stories adopt the first person as the favorite narratological voice to explore the anguish of a tragic love journey. Nevertheless, this first person is usually accompanied by other rhetorical *genera dicendi* which present the love-problem as having a dialectical nature.
- Epistolary technique. Many sentimental fictions include a lengthy exchange of letters between lovers. The use of letters has been linked to the development of the *ars dictandi* both at the university and the nobility and royal *milieux* during the fifteenth century. The *Proceso de cartas de amores* by Juan de Segura is written entirely in this epistolary fashion.
- Critique of courtly love. Most sentimental fictions include a lengthy and developed criticism of the behavioral code of courtly love. Courtly love is usually seen as frustrating, unproductive, and useless in granting lovers a complete satisfaction of their social and physical needs and desires.
- Female voice. Women attain an extremely important role as characters and readers in sentimental fictions. First, it should be noted that women have in this genre—for the first time in literary history—as much importance if not more as male characters. In addition, women are in charge of pointing out the

incoherence and inconsistency of the discourse of courtly love. As a result, they frequently appear as mocking and criticizing their male counterparts as love fools.

- Love debate. Together with the adoption of a female point of view, there is an increasing number of voices that can be heard in sentimental fictions. As well, characters usually debate about the essence of love, thus offering a multiplicity of voices and points of view regarding love (personal and social relations) as a personal and social phenomenon. In addition, there are within these works numerous chapters which belong to the genre of *pro femina/adversus mulieres* literature. There is also a presence of literary subgenres such as *consejos/consells/conselhos* and *de regimine principum*.
- Equality. Strikingly, the debate on love, together with the adoption of a multifaceted range of opinions on love, promotes the idea of love as a somewhat egalitarian force. That is to say, participants in the love-game have a right to express their opinions inasmuch as they are equally subjects of the love-game.
- Sentimental fiction and *Celestina*. Critics have increasingly related sentimental fictions to *Celestina* and many *Celestina*-like works written about 1490–1530. To this extent *Celestina* has been considered a sentimental fiction. Some critics have suggested that *Celestina* is a literary response to *Cárcel de Amor* by Diego de San Pedro.
- Dialogical nature of love plots. The increasing presence of dialogue, letters (*dialogus in absentia*) and debates on love tends to overshadow the role of simple narrative in third person. Love is seen as a topic to be discussed in dialogical fashion, thus prompting an ego-tu dialectics which is at the core of the modern novel.
- Fiction-Realism. As the genre evolves, there is a tendency towards more realistic plots. Thus, some of the Arthurian-like features of the early works give way to a more realistic portrayal of late-fifteenth- and early-sixteenth-century society.
- Sentimental fiction and the eclogue. Critics have linked the genre of sentimental fiction to the development of eclogue as a theatrical genre. From Juan del Enzina to Garcilaso and Bernardim Ribeiro, many eclogues build their plots upon debates on love, tragic love stories, and so on, in a similar fashion to the sentimental romance. Even some sentimental novels include eclogues as part of their plots (*Égloga de Torino*).
- Matrimony. Many female characters of sentimental fictions tend to view matrimony as a valid social solution for the ethical problem of courtly love. "Marry me", they seem to say, "and we will be able to live our love affair to the fullest", thus setting the love-problem within a clear social context.
- Lyric and narrative. Many critics view sentimental fiction as the result of the prosification or narrativization of love lyric poetry (*cancionero* lyric). In fact, many sentimental fictions could be seen as prose developments of lyric *cancionero* poems. In addition, numerous sentimental romances insert lyric compositions in their narrative (*prosimetra*).
- Portrayal of a crisis. Sentimental fiction is neither a medieval nor a Renaissance genre. At the threshold of the Renaissance, sentimental romance is representative of the notion of crisis that defines this period. When talking about love affairs (at first in a very similar fashion to that of the Arthurian novel and *cancionero* poetry), sentimental fictions tend to *narrate* love within a more developed (and realistic) social frame. In doing so, they usually commence where *cancionero* poetry ends. As well, they show a tendency less toward deeds and action (as in the Arthurian novel) and more toward analyzing the essence of the love crisis, both in individual and social terms.

Sentimental fiction, an enormously successful genre, seems to have faded around 1550. New literary genres, such as the pastoral romance, the Byzantine novel and the chivalric romance became the new fashionable genres of the Renaissance. Traces of the influence of sentimental fiction can be perceived in all of them. From Arthurian literature and *chançonnier* poetry to *Don Quijote*, sentimental fiction stands in the frontier of the creation of modern romance. By focusing on love both as a personal and social feeling and by mixing several narratological techniques (*narratio*, dialogue, debate, letters, etc.) which further complicated the status of the narrator and his/her position in the narrative, sentimental fictions gave birth to a new dialogical interest in the individual in communication (debate) with the society that fostered him/her. The social and personal desiderata of the new society (Renaissance) were later explored in novels that focused on the exoticism of travel, the material deeds of adventure and/or the escape toward social utopias.

As for the social milieu that fostered sentimental fiction, it seems to have originated in the literary courts of the fifteenth-century nobility. Nevertheless, the presence of numerous voices interspersed in the narratives (female voices, scholarly and university elements, bourgeois characters, etc.) as well as the portrayal of a crisis (both personal and social) point toward a milieu more complicated than that of the simple upper nobility. In this sense, some critics have even observed the presence of *converso* (Christian convert) voices and structures as well as the presence of incipient bourgeois elements within the genre.

ANTONIO CORTIJO OCAÑA

Bibliography

Cortijo Ocaña, A. *La evolución genérica de la ficción sentimental de los siglos XV y XVI. Género literario y contexto social*. Colección Támesis. Serie A: Monografías, 184. London, 2001.

———, ed. Critical Cluster (Sentimental Romance). *La Corónica* 29, no. 1 (2000).

Deyermond, A. *Tradiciones y puntos de vista en la ficción sentimental*. Mexico, 1993.

Gwara, J. J., and E. M. Gerli. (eds.) *Studies on the Spanish Sentimental Romance (1440–1550): Redefining a Genre*. Colección Támesis. Serie A: Monografías, 168. London, 1997.

Rohland de Langbehn, R. *La unidad genérica de la novela sentimental española de los siglos XV y XVI*. Papers of the Medieval Hispanic Research Seminar, 17. London, 1999.

Whinnom, K. *The Spanish Sentimental Romance 1440–1550: A Critical Bibliography*. Research Bibliographies and Checklists, 41. London, 1983.

ROMANCES, TROY AND ADVENTURE

The tales of the siege and destruction of Troy, with their evocation of the loss of grandeur amidst tragic love, played a special role in stimulating the medieval European imagination. The doomed love of Paris and Helen, plus the courtship of Troilus and Cressida, which emerged from an anecdote in the original story, were turned into paradigmatic legends of love's suffering, chivalry, and sentimentality. The story of Troy circulated widely via several Latin versions: The *Ilias latina*, an inferior Latin summary of Homer's original, and the more influential *Excidium Troiae*. Two spurious eyewitness accounts, the *De excidio Troiae historia*, said to have been written by Dares the Phrygian, a soldier who fought with the Trojans, and the *Ephemerides belli Troiani*, attributed to a combatant in the Greek army called Dictys of Crete, were also well known. The *Roman de Troie* by Benoît de Sainte-Maure, the most widely circulated vernacular version of the story in medieval Europe, is derived from the latter two works. Benoît is, in turn, the source of the thirteenth-century *Historia destructionis Troiae* by Guido delle Colonne, which saw widespread circulation.

Numerous vernacular romances of the story of Troy circulated in the Iberian Peninsula during the late Middle Ages yet little scholarly attention has been given them. A Castilian text written in both prose and poetry from between 1275 and 1300, the *Historia troyana polimétrica*, is probably derived from the French *Roman de Troie en prose* and greatly elaborates the story in the verse passages, inspired in the most emotionally stirring parts of the *Roman*. The poetry in the *Historia troyana* merits special attention: it exhibits great metrical variety, shows a close interest in the love of Troilus and Cressida, and presents a detailed, anachronistic elaboration of the armed conflict between Greeks and Trojans in terms of medieval warfare. However, the story of Troy first appeared in Iberia redacted solely in prose, in Alfonso X's *General estoria* (begun in 1272), which combines material from Benoît, the *Ephemerides* and the *De excidio Troiae historia* attributed to Dares. There are two other known prose versions, both from the fourteenth century. These are a translation of the *Roman de Troie* commissioned in 1350 by Alfonso XI of Castile, and a Galaico-Portuguese version, also based on Benoît, composed before 1373. Also from the fourteenth century is a work by Leomarte, of whom virtually nothing is known. This is the *Sumas de historia de Troya*, based on Alfonso's *General estoria*, Guido delle Colonne's *Historia destructionis Troiae*, and other sources. The *Sumas* appears to be a highly original conflation of Trojan and historiographical materials. Despite his near anonymity, Leomarte was well known and influential in establishing a "Trojan palimpsest" that would emerge allusively in Castilian poetry and prose, particularly in courtly circles during the next century.

Finally, there is an incomplete *Corónica troyana* that derives from the *Historia destructionis Troiae*, as well as complete versions of the story also based on Guido delle Collone in Aragónese and Castillian. During the last quarter of the fifteenth century, Pedro González de Mendoza, el Gran Cardenal, translated the *Iliad* itself from a Latin version by Pier Candido Decembrio.

Numerous romances of adventure, chivalry, and love that did not derive from the story of Troy also circulated in Iberia during the late Middle Ages. Aside from two autochthonous romances of chivalry, *Amadís de Gaula* and the *Libro del caballero Zifar*, the latter were largely adaptations or translations of texts with a foreign provenance and are drawn from various sources: the *Cuento del emperador Carlos Maynes*, a story with a Carolingian theme; the *Historia de Enrique fi de Oliva*, and the *Cuento del enperador Otas*, are all of French epic origin. Several other romances, like the *Fermoso cuento de una santa enperatiz* and *De un cavallero Plácidas*, the *Chronica del rey don Guillermo de Ynglaterra* and the *Estoria del rey Guillelme* all trace their origins to hagiography and saints' legends, especially the legend of St. Eustace.

The *Historia de la linda Melusina*, a tragic tale about a woman who is transformed into a serpent from below the waist once per week, and tries to keep her secret from her husband is a free translation of the French *Mélusine* by Jean d'Arras. *Flores y Blancaflor*, the *Historia del muy valiente Clamades y de la linda Clarmonda*, and the *Libro del esforçado cavallero Partinuplés*, all also trace their origins to beyond the Pyrenees.

E. MICHAEL GERLI

Bibliography

Brownlee, M. "Towards a reappraisal of the *Historia troyana polimétrica*." *La Corónica* 7 (1978–79), 13–17.

———. "The Trojan Palimpsest and Leomarte's Metacritical Forgery." *Modern Language Notes* 100 (1985), 397–405.

Casas Rigall, J. *La materia de Troya en las letras romances del siglo XIII hispano*. Santiago de Compostela, 1999.

Grieve, P. *Floire and Blancheflor and the European Romance*. New York, 1997.

Leomarte. *Sumas de historia troyana*. ed. Agapito Rey. Madrid, 1932.

Solalinde, A. G. "Las versiones españolas del *Roman de Troie*." *Revista de Filología Española* 3 (1916), 121–65.

RONCESVALLES, CANTAR DE

The *Cantar de Roncesvalles* is a one-hundred-verse fragment of a lost Spanish epic about the defeat of the rear guard of the French army under Roland by the Saracens at the pass of Roncesvalles in the Pyrenees. The two badly worn folios were discovered inside a fourteenth-century census register from Navarre. The writing on the folios has been identified as Navarrese from the first years of that century. The text itself, according to Menéndez Pidal, was composed in Castile in the early thirteenth century; Horrent dates it somewhat later.

The fragment tells of Charlemagne's search for Roland's body on the battlefield, where he comes upon the corpses of Bishop Turpin and of Oliver before finally encountering his nephew. Thereupon he utters a long lament and falls unconscious. At the same time Aymón seeks, finds, and mourns over his dead son, Reinaldos de Montalbán. The account is in essence similar to that of the *Chanson de Roland* but with many different details that reveal a peninsular version of the Charlemagne/Roland story founded on an earlier epic tradition (the *Nota Emilianense*) and subsequently carried over into the ballads (*romances*).

The verse form and the diction of *Roncesvalles* are the same as those of *Cantar de Mio Cid* except for the consistent use of the paragogic *e* at line end. The two-hemistich verse with end assonance is irregular in length. Seven-syllable hemistichs dominate, followed by those of eight, six, and nine. The verses are grouped into series of like assonance, *á–e* being favored.

Roncesvalles is of great value for the history of the Spanish epic in that it offers concrete evidence of a long-standing epic tradition in the peninsula and supports the theory of the loss of many texts. It also attests to the independence of the Spanish epic tradition from the French despite considerable borrowing from it.

RUTH H. WEBBER

Bibliography

Horrent, J. *Roncesvalles: Etude sur le fragment de cantar de gesta conservé à l'Archivo de Navarra (Pampelune)*. Bibliotèque de la Faculté de Philosophie et Lettres de l'Université de Liège, 122. Paris, 1951.

Menéndez Pidal, R. "*Roncesvalles*: Un nuevo cantar de gesta español del siglo XIII." *Revista de Filología Española* 4 (1917), 105–204, Reprinted in *Textos medievales españoles: Ediciones críticas y estudios*. Obras Completas de Ramón Menéndez Pidal, 12. Madrid, 1976, 7–102.

S

SAGRAJAS, BATTLE OF *See* ZALLĀQAH, BATTLE OF

SAGRES *See* HENRY THE NAVIGATOR

SAINTS

In Iberia, as in all western Europe during the Middle Ages, the cult of saints and of the Virgin reached its high point, so that they became the main means of expression of popular religiosity. Learned and popular elements were involved in the origin of the devotion to saints; although the concept of sanctity was defined by the church, in a parallel way, but not always hand in hand, people worshipped some saints they believed able to work miracles. The strength of the devotion was so great that it appeared in every aspect of medieval culture, either in theologians' abstractions or in legends, graphically on images or materially in the accumulation of alleged relics. Nevertheless, the main source for the study of the saints worshipped in the Middle Ages, individually and as a general phenomenon, are hagiographic texts. Using this material, it is possible to appreciate the evolution of the cult of saints during the Middle Ages in Iberia.

The Eighth to Eleventh Centuries

As in the rest of the Romance language areas, the stories of martyrs prevail in the writings of this period, with the Hispanic peculiarity of belonging to the Mozarabic rite. The Muslim invasion did not interrupt either the worship of saints or hagiographic production that had reached an important level in the seventh century. In the ninth century the hagiographic literature did not decrease, thanks to the Mozarabic community of Córdoba, and above all to Speraindeo and his disciples Eulogio and Alvaro, but perhaps more texts would have appeared after the large number of martyrs in the persecution of ʿAbd al-Rḥamān II in 850–852. In the tenth and eleventh centuries a remarkable increase of hagiographic production occurred, even when the persecutions suffocated the Mozarabic tradition, because the renewal seems to start in certain northern centers, such as Ripoll, Cardeña, and Silos. For the first time, the stories devoted to martyrs (*passiones*) are not greater in number than those devoted to confessors (*vitae*).

The Twelfth to Thirteenth Centuries

A vigorous cultural activity developed in Santiago, Toledo, and Catalonia. The *Liber Sancti Iacobi* or *Codex Calixtinus* is perhaps the best proof of the role that hagiographic literature had in that activity, as it is the expression of the beginning of a specialized worship of saints. As patrons of the pilgrims to Santiago, for instance, the devotion to Sto. Domingo of the Calzada, St. John of Ortega, St. Marina, and St. Julian the Hospitaler, was extended to St. Christopher. Also a decline of the martyrial subject can be appreciated, since the *passiones* represent only a quarter of the hagiographic texts, giving way to "lives and miracles." As the hagiographic literature reveals, in the thirteenth century an important qualitative change occurred in the cult of saints, one that could be linked with the religious reforms, one of whose manifestations was the founding of mendicant and ransoming orders, and their struggle against the heretics. Parallel to the increase in Latin literature, this new atmosphere, with a clear will of divulgation, favored the flowering of Romance languages. Thus we find stories in Castilian and in Catalan that extol the founders of the new orders and warn against heretics. Although the thirteenth century was an actual "century of saints," above all Dominicans and Mercedarians (Franciscans did not partake of this profusion, probably because of their critical attitude), a new restrictive factor must be taken into account: since 1170, when Pope Alexander III reserved for the Holy See the faculty of recognizing the sanctity of the faithful, the number of canonizations decreased. However, this arrangement was not able to control the dimensions and diversification that the cult of saints had already acquired.

The Fourteenth to Fifteenth Centuries

In the fourteenth century sanctoral, Hispanic saints scarcely can be found, which could be connected with the decline of the church in that period. In hagiographic production, the Dominicans were the only ones to increase it, and that could be explained by the rise of Scholasticism and their rise in the inquisitorial ranks. The martyrial writings at that time were real exceptions, and that was so because the evangelic pattern of sanctity (martyrdom, asceticism, poverty) was in the late Middle Ages giving way to concepts like culture and mysticism. The fifteenth-century individual texts were usually devoted to Hispanic saints, while the compilations followed after Jacobus de Voragine's collection, the *Legenda Aurea*.

The Figure of the Saint

Because of the period in which it developed, medieval Castilian hagiography already integrated the different types of saints that appeared in the history of Christianity, whether they were models deriving from the Bible or from Latin religious literature. All of them in the end refer to Christ, or to the Virgin Mary, in the case of feminine hagiography. Basically the concept of sanctity implies the attribution of theological and cardinal virtues, but medieval texts especially insist on humility: perhaps because at that time pride was considered one of the worst sins. An essential aspect of the medieval archetype of saint, common in every model, is thaumaturgy. Even the martyrs, whose sanctity needed no verification by prodigies as it was evident by their voluntary sacrifice, are finally empowered to propitiate miracles. The most usual prodigies are prophecies, visions, and miraculous cures of every kind of illness, and even exorcisms. More peculiar to Hispanic saints are their apparitions against the Moors (St. James or St. Millán) or the freeing of captives (Sto. Domingo of Silos).

The conventions of the genre already appear in the circumstances of a saint's birth: the parents, usually members of a distinguished family, pray to God for a child (St. Ildefonso, Sta. Oria, S. Juan of Sahagún). In the case of masculine hagiography the wish for sanctity is manifested early in the application to study, so that, following the *puer senex* topic, children show more wisdom than their own teachers, and look down on jokes and laughter. Then Hispanic medieval hagiography presents the saint in several scenes that are sometimes superimposed, combined with some other strange ones, or even contrary to the very concept of sanctity:

Ploughman or Worker-saint. In the *Vida de San Millán* by Gonzalo de Berceo, we can find frequent mentions of the toil of the protagonist in order to gain Paradise, comparing it with the remuneration of workers. Another good example is St. Dominic of Silos.

Penitent. Already the Bible included models of this type, masculine (St. Paul) as well as feminine (Mary Magdalen). The legend most extended by peninsular hagiography, although of foreign origin, is perhaps that of St. Mary of Egypt.

Hero-saint. St. Millán is often presented as a warrior who shines especially in the famous episode of Fernán González's votive offerings, when he and St. James terrify the Saracens. One real warrior was Fernando III, a curious case of saint and king, as was also St. Elizabeth, queen of Portugal.

Martyr. Although in the late Middle Ages saints usually died peacefully, and were not executed, the cult of ancient and early medieval martyrs was still strong. Probably that was because of the analogy with the supreme model of Christ's Passion, that presents the martyr as the sacred-form hero par excellence. St. Lawrence is one of the most celebrated ones, but even confessors are considered "martyrs in will."

Ascetic. According to the previous discussion, when saints are no longer martyred by the enemies of Christianity, they have to mortify themselves by means of every kind of sacrifice. Besides the anchorite life of St. Mary of Egypt, many Hispanic saints lived for a time as hermits (St. Millán, Sto. Domingo of Silos, Sto. Vitores), or severely cloistered (Sta. Oria, for example).

Good Shepherd. In the case of masculine saints, pastoral labor is an important part of their merits, either as monks (Sto. Domingo of Silos, Sto. Domingo of Guzmán, St. Juan of Sahagún) or as secular clerks (St. Millán, St. Lawrence, St. Ildefonso, St. Isidore).

Founder. St. Millán, but more clearly Sto. Domingo of Silos, Sto. Domingo of Guzmán, or St. Peter Nolasco have the image of a saint able to raise or restore ecclesiastical institutions.

Learned Saint. During the late Middle Ages, in the Iberian Peninsula, as in the rest of western Europe, we can appreciate the importance that culture acquired in the pattern of sanctity. Vital for the defense of doctrinal orthodoxy, especially against the danger of the heretics, the church and the people extolled their ancient (St. Isidore, St. Ildefonso) or contemporary doctors (Sto. Domingo of Guzmán, St. Vicente Ferrer).

FERNANDO BAÑOS VALLEJO

Bibliography

Aldea, Q., T. Marín, and J. Vives. "Hagiografía." In *Diccionario de historia eclesiástica de España*. Vol. 2. Madrid, 1972, 1073–78.

Baños Vallejo, F. *La hagiografía como género literario en la Edad Media (Tipología de doce "vidas" individuales castellanas)*. Oviedo, 1989.

Fábrega Grau, A. *Pasionario hispánico (siglos VII–XI)*. 2 vols. Madrid, 1952–55.

Fernández Conde, F. J. "El siglo de los santos," and "El culto y la devoción a los santos." In *Historia de la Iglesia en España*. Vol. 2, *La Iglesia en la España de los siglos VIII–XIV*. Ed. R. García-Villoslada. Madrid, 1982, 248–53, 301–18.

Vauchez, A. *La sainteté en Occident aux derniers siècles du Moyen Age*. Rome, 1988.

SALADO, BATTLE OF

The Battle of Salado (30 October 1340) lifted the siege of Tarifa and was the last great battle of the Reconquest. On one side was Abū al-Ḥasan (sultan of the Benimerines, 1331–1351) of Morocco and Yūsuf I of Granada (1333–1354); on the other were the combined forces of Castile-León, Portugal, Aragón, and France, led by Alfonso XI of Castile-León (1312–1350) and Afonso IV of Portugal (1325–1357). The Benimerines had mounted a series of campaigns in the southern part of the Iberian Peninsula since 1333, when they recaptured Gibraltar. From 1333 to 1339 Castilian forces besieged Gibraltar while Muslim troops harassed them. By 1339 Abū al-Ḥasan planned an all-out war against the Castilians. He destroyed most of the Castilian fleet in the Straits of Gibraltar in April 1340 and transferred the bulk of his troops to Algeciras and Gibraltar. After meeting Yūsuf at Algeciras in August they began the siege of Tarifa in September. The Castilians recognized the risk to their holdings and Alfonso XI convinced the kings of Portugal, Aragón, and France that the Benimerines posed a threat to the entire peninsula. Alfonso obtained a crusading tithe from Pope Benedict XII, but even so he had problems financing the campaign.

The size of medieval armies is notoriously inflated in the records of any encounter, although the sources indicate that the Muslim army was larger than the Christian army. Some of Alfonso XI's advisers suggested surrendering Tarifa, but Alfonso refused. By October a new Castilian fleet arrived off Tarifa. Alfonso XI and Afonso IV advanced on Tarifa by land, accompanied by militias from the southern towns as well as Basque, Leonese, and Asturian troops. The battle took place at the Salado River outside of Tarifa. The Castilians were able to smuggle some troops into Tarifa without the knowledge of the enemy the night before the battle. The Castilians took the ford of Salado and the main guard, but dispersed to loot the camp; the forces from Tarifa foiled a Muslim attack upon the Castilian rear. The Portuguese defeated the Granadan troops. Both Yūsuf and Abū al-Ḥasan retreated, but Alfonso XI lacked the provisions to pursue them to Algeciras. The booty from the battle was considerable; the amount of gold and silver captured readjusted the prices of the two metals in Europe. The victory at Salado not only relieved Tarifa but also prevented the Benimerines from penetrating into the peninsula.

THERESA M. VANN

Bibliography

Huici Miranda, A. *Las grandes batallas de la reconquista*. Madrid, 1956.

Lomax, D. W. *The Reconquest of Spain*. London, 1978.

SALAMANCA, CITY OF

Salamanca is on the north plateau of the Iberian Peninsula, with a Roman bridge that spans the Tormes River. By the sixth century the city was integrated into the Visigoth Kingdom of Toledo and had an episcopal see. After the Muslim conquest in 711, the Asturian kings transferred part of the southern population to the north. In the middle of the ninth century, King Ordoño I attacked the Muslim residents of the city and so contributed to the scattering of the small, disorganized Muslim population. In the tenth century Ramiro II tried to repopulate the city, but the final repopulation was directed by Raimundo of Burgundy in 1102. The settlers who came were mainly Franks, Portuguese, Highlanders, Mozarabs, and Castilians. The presence of Jews and Muslims was documented soon after. Bishop Jerome, mentioned in the *Cantar de Mio Cid*, was the first prelate, and by the middle of the twelfth century the construction of the cathedral was well underway. During the thirteenth century the city grew under the reign of Alfonso IX and it was through his initiative that the university came into being around 1218 from the conversion of the old cathedral school. However, the consolidation of the Salamanca *studium* did not take place until the middle of the thirteenth century, when Alfonso X endowed its faculties of civil law and canon law, arts, and medicine. Pope Alexander IV conferred on its graduates a *licentia ubique docendi*. The conflict for control of the city council and power over the land, and the repercussions from the general problems of the crown resulted in the division into two bands or factions, which were the cause of frequent fighting. By the end of the Middle Ages the city had a population of eighteen thousand inhabitants, and the university enrolled more than two thousand students.

At that time plans were being made for the construction of the new cathedral.

JOSÉ LUIS MARTÍN MARTÍN

Bibliography

González García, M. *Salamanca en la Baja Edad Media.* Salamanca, 1982.

Martín Martín, J. L. "Historiografía sobre Salamanca en la Edad Media." In *I Congreso de Historia de Salamanca.* Salamanca, 1992. 339–57.

SALIC LAW

Salic law was derived from a phrase extracted from the *Lex Salica*, a fifth-century code of the Salian Franks, which excluded women from the ownership of property: *De terra Salica nulla portio ad fœminam.* This tradition is also referred to as the Salic law of succession, to distinguish it from the law code from whence it took its name. It was adopted as the tradition of royal succession by several European kingdoms, most notably France, who used it to exclude all females from the throne and later, those males whose claim to rule was based on descent through a female. Until the sixteenth century, Salic law was not named as such, and was not discussed in law texts. Instead it existed as a part of royal tradition invoked during succession disputes at the end of the French Capetian dynasty in the early fourteenth century, and again at the end of the Valois dynasty in the late sixteenth century. Salic law was used to justify exclusion of Edward III of England from the French throne in 1328, thus prompting the Hundred Years' War.

In the Iberian Peninsula, Salic law played its most prominent role during the uniting of Castile and Aragón under the Catholic Monarchs (1474–1504). The succession tradition of Aragón followed the Salic law pattern, while that of Castile—whose history included many examples of female accession to the throne when a male heir was lacking—did not. In practical terms, the Salic law tradition of Aragón meant that, lacking a direct male heir to the throne, the brother of the king was preferred for succession over the daughter of the king. This trend was the opposite in Castile, where the king's direct descendant—regardless of sex—inherited above the claims of the collateral branch. During the negotiations for union of the two realms after the accession of Isabel and Fernando in 1474 at Segovia, the Aragónese claimed that Fernando, as male and husband, should be lord of Castile. Instead, Isabel was named *reina propietaria*, or Queen Proprietess, of Castile, and a compromise was reached whereby the governance of the united kingdoms would be shared. Afterward, during the reign of the Catholic Monarchs this same Salic law dispute came to the fore in the 1498 refusal of the Aragónese *cortes* (Parliament) to approve Isabel of Portugal as heir because of her sex. Extraterritorially, in 1483 and again in 1488 the struggle between the Spanish and French over control of Navarre revolved around the claims of a female heir, Catalina de Foix. Accession of a woman to the crown reappeared at the center of peninsular conflict in the nineteenth century, when Fernando VII repealed the promulgation of Salic law in Spain under the French Bourbon monarchs and proclaimed his daughter, the astutely named Isabel II, as his successor, thus creating the conflict that resulted in the Carlist wars after Fernando's death in 1833.

According to research in the history of French jurisprudence, Salic law was not originally based on the idea that women were unfit to rule. Instead, it was meant to ensure that during the minority of a king's son, or in the absence of a male heir, the females of the royal family would not compete for the crown and a more stable transition could be achieved. It was only in later interpretations of French tradition in the seventeenth century that the debate centered around womens' abilities. In foreign relations, Salic law was designed from the outset to protect local sovereignty from foreign investiture. Given the intermarriage between European royal families that was standard practice, exclusion of females from the throne was a method of preventing a loss of sovereignty to a foreign power. It was assumed that, once married, the native princess would be subject to her foreign husband's commands. This connection between sovereignty and female accession was explicitly recognized in Fernando del Pulgar's account of the Segovia Compromise of 1474. In his account, Isabel argues that her right to inherit the crown must be recognized so that future female heirs will not be in danger of losing control of the crown to a foreign prince.

In contrast to the original intention of Salic law in France, in the Iberian Peninsula the conflict over Salic law under the Catholic kings *can* be connected to the question of whether women were fit to rule. The Salic law conflict gives historical underpinning to the late fifteenth-century prominence of literature that employed the formulas of courtly love and misogyny, and the debate over gender roles, which became a constituent feature of such works as *Celestina* or the *novelas sentimentales*. Direct reference to succession tradition as a part of the gender debate was usually only made by historians. On the Aragónese side, Guaberte Fabricio de Vagad's *Corónica de Aragón* (1499) provided a defense of Salic law tradition, while Diego Rodríguez de Almela, in various *tratados* directed to members of the Isabelline court, defended the idea of female accession as fundamental to Castilian identity (1483–1484).

In English literature, the defense of French sovereignty by means of Salic law plays its most famous role in Shakespeare's *Henry V*, where the Archbishop of Canterbury justifies Henry's claim to the French throne by arguing that the Salic law does not apply to French territory, and that many French kings have founded their claim to the throne on the distaff side, as Henry V will attempt to do (I, ii, 33–95).

WENDELL SMITH

Bibliography

Cosandey, F. "De Lance en Quenouille: La place de la reine dans l'Etat moderne (14e–17e siècles)." *Annales Histoire, Sciences Sociales* 52, no. 4 (1997), 199–220.

Jordan, C. "Woman's Rule in Sixteenth-Century British Political Thought." *Renaissance Quarterly* 40, no. 3 (1987), 421–51.

Pulgar, F. del. *Crónica de los Reyes Católicos*. Ed. and intr. J. de Mata Carriazo. Madrid, 1943.

Rodríguez de Almela, D. *Cartas: (BL MS Egerton 1173)*. Ed. and intr. D. Mackenzie. Exeter, 1980.

Scalingi, P. L. "The Scepter or the Distaff: The Question of Female Sovereignty, 1516–1607." *Historian* 41, no. 1 (1978), 59–75.

Segura Graíño, C. "Participación de las mujeres en el poder político." *Anuario de Estudios Medievales* 25, no. 2 (1995), 449–61.

Vagad, G. F. de. *Corónica de Aragón*. Facsimile ed. Ed. and intr. María del Carmen Orcástegui Gros. Zaragoza, 1996.

SAMPIRO, BISHOP OF ASTORGA

Named to that position in 1034 by Sancho III Garcés, el Mayor (1000–1035) of Navarre, then temporarily master of the kingdom of León as well. Sampiro continued in the see until November 1042. He is probably the same person as the eponymous minor court figure and sometime royal notary of the courts of Vermudo II (984–999), Alfonso V (999–1028), and Vermudo III (1028–1037), all of León. It is also likely that he was native to the district of Bierzo, a part of the diocese of Astorga.

Sampiro is chiefly revealed to us in his sole known work rather than in his deeds. He stood in the chronicle tradition and continued the work of earlier compilers of the history of the kings of Asturias and León, adding accounts of those beginning with the reign of Alfonso III (866–910) and ending with the initiation of that of Alfonso V. There are no independent manuscripts of his work known but his account was included in the early twelfth-century *Historia Silense* and also in the collection of earlier chronicles compiled by Bishop Pelayo of Oviedo about the same time.

BERNARD F. REILLY

Bibliography

Pérez de Urbel, J. (ed.) *Sampiro: Su crónica y la monarquia leonésa en el siglo X*. Madrid, 1952.

Quintana Prieto, A. *El obispado de Astorga en el siglo XI*. Astorga, 1977.

SAMSON, ABBOT OF CÓRDOBA

Samson (d. 890) was appointed as abbot of Pinna Mellaria, a monastery on the outskirts of Córdoba, in 858. At this same time, two monks from Paris came to him looking for relics. Samson offered them the remains of some of the martyrs of Córdoba who had been buried at the monastery. Aside from the account of this translation of relics authored by the Parisian monk Aimoin, the only source for Samson's life is the *Apologeticus*, a treatise that he wrote in 864 to defend himself against the accusations of Bishop Hostigesis of Málaga and Count Servandus of Córdoba. The events that elicited this response can be reconstructed from the lengthy preface to the second book. Apparently Hostigesis had cajoled the bishops attending a council in 862 into condemning Samson for his views on the Trinity and Incarnation. He was exonerated a short time later and was named abbot of the church of St. Zoylus in Córdoba. In 863 the emir Muḥammad I drafted him to translate into Latin a letter directed to the Carolingian king, Charles the Bald. Count Servandus accused him of making the contents of the letter known to enemies of the government. Hostigesis and Servandus also accused Samson and the Córdoban bishop Valentius of encouraging Christians to blaspheme Muḥammad. They managed to organize another episcopal council in Córdoba at which Valentius was deposed and Samson denounced for holding an extreme view of divine omnipresence. Samson fled to Martos, near Jaén, where he composed the *Apologeticus*, which not only offered a statement of his own faith, but also took the offensive against Hostigesis and Servandus. He accused them of working closely with the emir to the detriment of the Christian community, on which they imposed tax increases. In addition, Samson attacked Hostigesis's own profession of faith as heretical in its own right.

KENNETH B. WOLF

Bibliography

Colbert, E. "The Martyrs of Córdoba (850–859): A Study of the Sources." Ph.D. Diss., Catholic University of America, 1962, 357–81.

Gil, J. ed. *Corpus scriptorum mozarabicorum*. vol. 2. Madrid, 1973, 506–658.

SAN JUAN DE LA PEÑA

Situated in the mountains some ten kilometers southwest of Jaca, San Juan de la Peña was for centuries the most renowned monastic center of Aragón. Upon his conquest of the Aragón valley in 920, Count Galindo Aznárez II established the monastery of Sts. Julián and Basilisa on a site long favored by local hermits. This community apparently declined as a result of the Muslim attacks of al-Manṣūr and ʿAbd al-Mālik, and was revived by King Ramiro I of Aragón shortly after 1054 as an almonry of the nearby monastery of San Juan of Ruesta.

In 1071 King Sancho Ramírez established the monastery of San Juan de la Peña on the site, populating it with Cluniac monks, and richly endowing what he planned as the royal pantheon of Aragón. On 22 March of that year the Roman liturgy was introduced into Spain at San Juan, replacing the traditional Mozarabic liturgy. The monastery was expanded, and the new church built atop the tenth-century Mozarabic structure was consecrated on 4 December 1094 in the presence of King Pedro I. San Juan lost much of its royal patronage with the transfer of the Aragónese capital to Huesca after 1096, and was forced thereafter to struggle to defend its patrimony and privileges against the bishops of Huesca, Zaragoza, and Pamplona.

Legend making and forged documents played a large role in this conflict, and San Juan long claimed an antiquity and importance that it had not in fact possessed. The *Vitae* of San Juan of Atarés, St. Voto and St. Felix; the "Donation of Abetito"; numerous charters; and the Aragónese portions of the fourteenth-century *Crónica de San Juan de la Peña* were composed by the monks of San Juan toward this end, but to no avail. The struggle ended in 1571, when the newly established independent diocese of Jaca was endowed with much of San Juan's property. On 21 February 1675 a disastrous fire destroyed much of the monastery, including its rich archives. The monks abandoned the ruins, and moved the community to a new monastery on the plains above the site. There they remained until the disestablishment of the monastery in 1835.

San Juan de la Peña is remarkable in a number of respects, not the least of which is its impressive location, as it is built into the side of a cliff. The old monastery, declared a national monument in 1889, presents a rich mixture of Mozarabic, Romanesque, Gothic, and neoclassic styles. Its Romanesque cloister preserves the sculptures of the so-called Master of Jaca; its numerous inscriptions provide excellent examples of medieval epigraphy; and its Pantheon of the Nobles is the most extensive such monument in Spain. Its movable treasures have been dispersed: its cartularies are found in the library of the faculty of law of the University of Zaragoza, and other documents of its archives are in the Archivo Histórico Nacional; its illuminated Mozarabic Bible is in the Biblioteca Nacional of Madrid; and the Holy Grail, claimed by the monks to have been guarded for centuries in the monastery, is now in the Cathedral of Valencia.

LYNN H. NELSON

Bibliography

Buesa Conde, D. *El Monasterio de San Juan de la Peña.* León, 1975.

Ubieto Arteta, A., ed. *Crónica de San Juan de la Peña.* Valencia, 1961.

SAN JULIÁN DE PEREIRO, ORDER OF

See MILITARY ORDERS

SAN PEDRO, DIEGO DE

The best-known writer of sentimental romance in Spain, Diego de San Pedro, ironically, exercised far more influence on the development of fictional genres outside the Iberian Peninsula than within. His expert development of the epistolary form found little resonance in Spain with the exception of one or two novelettes of the early sixteenth-century, but his two sentimental romances, *Tratado de amores de Arnalte y Lucenda* (1491) and *Cárcel de Amor* (1492), were translated into several languages and circulated widely, playing a part in the development of epistolary sentimental fiction in France, England, and Italy.

Diego de San Pedro's own life is clouded in some mystery. Whinnom has shown that he is unlikely to be the mid-fifteenth-century "teniente de Peñafiel" postulated by Emilio Cotarelo y Mori, but he may well have been another contemporary named Diego de San Pedro who appears in later documents, perhaps a younger relative who inherited the older man's position as well. Whinnom also challenged Cotarelo's documented evidence that San Pedro was a *converso* (convert from Judaism) although on balance this seems likely. He certainly was a courtier in the court of Queen Isabel and a vassal of the Telles Girón family, who fell out of favor when they backed Juana la Beltraneja in the civil wars. Some of San Pedro's writings seem to have been attempts to curry favor with the ladies of the new court; he was a deft practitioner of courtly verse. His earliest work is a long religious poem on the death of Christ, *La pasión trobada* (1470s), which was his most popular work in the peninsula, reprinted in inexpensive chapbooks until the nineteenth century. He also wrote a verse, *Desprecio de Fortuna* in old age, perhaps at the turn of the fifteenth century, in which he renounced the writings of his youth. It is however his sentimental romance *Cárcel de Amor* that has established his reputation as an important precursor both of *Celestina* and of the seventeenth-century novel in Spain. This is by no means a direct line of descent. *Celestina* parodies *Cárcel*'s courtly lover Leriano in the figure of Calisto, the young lover who has been driven mad by reading sentimental romance and courtly verse. The character of Don Quixote will similarly be driven mad by reading chivalresque romance, fiction that is contemporary to the sentimental romance but a different genre. *Don Quixote* will incorporate some material that can be considered to be descended from sentimental romance, but again the genre is marginalized and the epistolary form exerts no influence.

Tratado de amores de Arnalte y Lucenda is seen by Whinnom as a first draft of *Cárcel* and he has shown convincingly how San Pedro's rhetorical style, overdone in this earlier book, matured and was refined for *Cárcel*. *Arnalte*, however, is an astonishingly original piece when one considers its peninsular antecedents, Juan Rodriguez del Padrón's *Siervo libre de Amor* and Condestable Don Pedro de Portugal's *Sátyra de felice e infelice vida*. San Pedro borrows the pseudo-autobiographical frame and tragic story from these antecedents but must conform to Padrón's translation of Ovid's *Epistles* in the *Bursario*, for it is the epistolary form that is the important, although not the unigue method of telling the story. Aeneas Sylvius's *Historia de dos amantes (De duobus amantibus)* was probably also influential in what is essentially a bourgeois tale of unrequited love. Arnalte is, however, a thoroughly bad courtly lover who breaks all the most important tenets of the code, particularly secrecy, and goes through extraordinary machinations, including disguising himself as a woman, to importune Lucenda. Some critics have seen parody in this version of the courtly lover. Certainly Lucenda's ultimate rejection of Arnalte seems reasonable enough, in view of his having killed his best friend Ilierso in a duel because Ilierso took advantage of Arnalte's absence to marry Lucenda.

If Arnalte is a portrait of the inept courtly lover, then Leriano of *Cárcel* represents the extreme of courtly virtue, the lover as a Christ-figure whose martyrdom for his impossible love leads finally to death from hunger. In *Cárcel* we are back in the world of the chivalresque romance and Laureola is a princess, thus rendering Leriano's suit an impossible dream. Beside the amatory epistle, San Pedro provides a fine assortment of rhetorical tricks to tell his tale—allegory (the jail of love), letters of challenge, the judicial charge and its defense, the defense of women, the planctus or lament. His narrator is again himself as author, but he becomes integrated into the action carrying the love letters himself (in *Arnalte* the author had merely listened to the sad tale, and the go-between was the protagonist's sister). Leriano, imprisoned in the allegorical jail of love, has been freed by Laureola's favor, but this in turn has meant her captivity and condemnation. Leriano frees her but in the end, Leriano's love has hopelessly compromised Laureola's honor and she does not dare show him any favor, or the cycle of imprisonment and freedom may begin again.

Leriano has no choice but to die of unrequited love, but not without first heatedly defending the virtue of women against his misogynist friend Tefeo. Leriano's mother is left to utter the planctus, which is one of a number of important precedents for *Celestina*. Rojas will use this lamentation as a model for Pleberio's lament for the dead Melibea. The direct influence of *Cárcel* on *Celestina*, the only Spanish text quoted verbatim by Rojas, cannot be underestimated. Although the sentimental romance would soon run its course as a genre, its intertextual legacy would continue throughout the sixteenth century.

DOROTHY SHERMAN SEVERIN

Bibliography

San Pedro, Diego de. *Obras completas*. Ed. K. Whinnom Vol. 3 with D. S. Severin. 3 vols. Madrid, 1973, 1971, 1979.

Whinnom, K. *Diego de San Pedro*. New York, 1974.

———., (ed. and trans.) *Diego de San Pedro, Prison of Love 1492, together with the continuation by Nicolás Núñez, 1496*. Edinburgh, 1979.

SANZ, COUNT OF ROUSSILLON

Born around 1155, Sanz was named the count of Provence in place of his brother Alfonso I, count of Barcelona, in 1181. In 1185 he revolted against Alfonso, and made a pact with Genoa and the counts of Toulouse and Forcalquier. Sent back to the counties of Millau and Rousillon, he still laid claim to his former throne, as is shown by the help he gave to Guillaume IV of Forcalquier against Count Alfonso II of Provence in 1204. As early as 1209, on the death of the latter, he governed Provence with the agreement of Pedro II. This was his indemnity for having abandoned his Rouergate principalities in favor of Ramon VI of Toulouse, as surety for the crown's many debts in Aragón. Immediately after the Battle of Muret (1213), he was given the function of *procurador* of Aragón and Catalonia. He attempted to get the constitutions of peace and truce accepted by those factions of the Aragónese nobility who were in revolt; he also had to combat his nephew Fernando, Abbot of Montearagón. His men fought with Ramon VI in the retaking of Toulouse (1217), but against Simon of Montfort he failed to preserve the county of Bigorre from Catalan influence. The threat of excommunication made by Pope Honorius III made him withdraw from the Occitan political theater. In September 1218, he renounced his regency in favor of Jaime I at the *cortes* (parliament) of Lleida (Lérida). He died sometime between 1223 and 1225; he was probably buried at the house of the Hospitalers at Cavaillon.

MARTÍ AURELL I CARDONA

Bibliography

Aurell, M. *La vielle et l'épée: Troubadours et politique en Provence au XIIIe, siècle*. Paris, 1989.

Soldevila, F. *Història de Catalunya*. 2d ed. Barcelona, 1963.

SANCHEZ DE ARÉVALO, RODRIGO

Rodrigo Sánchez de Arévalo (1404–1470) achieved prominence as a jurist, diplomat, and man of letters. Born in Castile, possibly in the diocese of Segovia, he attributed his chance at a university education to Catherine of Lancaster, the mother of King Juan II. Arévalo studied arts, theology, and particularly law at the University of Salamanca. By 1431 he had become a servant of the crown. Sent to the Council of Basel to represent Castile, Arévalo faithfully reflected in the 1430s the proconciliar stance of Juan II and his ally, Charles VII of France. In 1438 Arévalo accompanied Alfonso of Cartagena on his mission to profer Juan's greetings to the new Holy Roman Emperor, Albert II of Habsburg.

By 1439 Juan II had grown unhappy with the Council of Basel and Arévalo became an active promoter of the interests of that assembly's foe, Pope Eugenius IV. Thus, in 1440, while Castile's ambassador to yet another Habsburg Holy Roman Emperor, Frederick III, Arévalo received a letter from Nicholas of Cusa expounding the issues of the day in the light of his doctrine of "learned ignorance." In the winter of 1440 Arévalo was sent to Italy, where most of his remaining years would be spent.

Most of that period, Arévalo lived in Rome, where he alternately served Castile as an ambassador and the papacy as an official. Thus, when Pope Paul II arrested the members of the Roman Academy in 1468, Arévalo, as keeper of Castel Sant'Angelo, became their jailer.

Arévalo had begun writing papist treatises while he was Castile's representative in the north. These he continued to produce into his last years, employing his legal erudition on behalf of Rome and its crusade against the Turks. He also wrote political treatises, a geography of Spain, a history of Spain, a *Speculum humanae vitae*, and a work on the education of children.

THOMAS M. IZBICKI

Bibliography

Laboa, J. M. *Rodrigo Sánchez de Arévalo, alcaide de Sant'Angelo*. Madrid, 1973.

Trame, R. *Rodrigo Sánchez de Arévalo 1404–1470: Spanish Diplomat and Champion of the Papacy*. Washington, D.C., 1958.

SÁNCHEZ DE VERCIAL, CLEMENTE

Archdeacon Clemente Sánchez of the diocese of León finished his *Libro de los exenplos por a.b.c.* between 1400 and 1421. It is the most copious collection of exempla in prose in the Spanish language, containing 548 such brief narratives. Even though it is divided into 438 sections, each headed by a maxim in Latin and all alphabetically arranged, some of the sections contain more than one story, hence the higher number given. After each maxim in Latin appears a couplet that translates the Latin into full rhyme. The stories range from a few lines to several pages in length and the longer ones are almost literal translations of Latin sources. Since Sánchez cited not only titles of Latin works, but often book and chapter, he provides a remarkably complete listing of works available. Careful comparison between the original Latin and Sánchez's translation proves that he used primary sources and did not rely upon secondary material.

Two manuscripts are extant—that of the Bibliothèque Nationale, Paris (MS 432), partially edited by F. Morel-Fatio in 1898; and that of the Biblioteca Nacional de Madrid (MS 1182), a truncated text in that its first 71 exempla are missing, edited by Pascual de Gayangos in 1800. A complete edition, containing all the exempla is that of John E. Keller, Madrid, 1961, whose Introduction contains virtually all that has been published about this *Libro*.

Sánchez dedicated the *Libro* to his son in baptism, Johan Alfonso de la Barbolla, canon of Sigüenza. In addressing the canon he gave the *Libro's* title as well as an unusual statement of intent at variance with his more obvious didactic intent: "te escrivi que proponia de copilar un libro de exenplos por a.b.c. e despues rreduzirle en rromance, por que non solamente a ti mas ahun a los que non saben latin fuese solaz." ["I wrote to you that I proposed to compile a book of exempla arranged by a.b.c. and then translate it into Romance, so that not only for you but for all who do not know Latin it would be enjoyable"]. He seems to reflect similar ideas, included by Alfonso el Sabio in his *Siete Partidas*, in which for the sake of mental health, and by extension physical, people are advised to read romances (romance novels), fables, and other fictions and should listen to songs and play games. Recreational and hygienic intents, then, should accompany didactic intent.

Sánchez's style is lucid and as good or better than any found in Spanish prose before his time. It reads clearly and well and excels even that of Don Juan Manuel's *El conde Lucanor*.

Sánchez's sources are myriad and among them are some of the world's best-known tales. He translated nearly all of Pedro Alfonso's *Disciplina clericalis*, the first known translation into Spanish; he translated some of the best tales of Valerius Maximus, Seneca, Augustine, and Bede, of the *Historia tripartita*, and Gregory the Great, of the *Vitae Patrum*, and of the miracles of the Virgin, to name but a few. Some of the stories have not been traced to literary origins and must be considered as borrowing from the oral lore of the times.

The composition of alphabeta had gone out of fashion long before Sánchez composed his anthology, revealing once again Ernst Robert Curtius's remarks about Spain's cultural belatedness.

JOHN E. KELLER

Bibliography

Krappe, A. H. "Les sources du *Libro de los Exemplos*," *Bulletin Hispanique* 39 (1937), 5–54.

Keller, J. "The *Libro de los exenplos por a.b.c.*," *Hispania* 40 (1957), 179–86.

SANCHO I, KING OF LEÓN

The second son of Ramiro II (930–51), Sancho I ruled the kingdom of León during a period of such turbulent dynastic politics that he spent most of his reign just trying to hold on to the lands he inherited. The civil discord that marked Sancho's reign seriously weakened Leonese defenses and left the king struggling between two powerful opposing forces: Fernán González, count of Castile, and ʿAbd-al Raḥmān III, the Umayyad caliph of Córdoba.

Even though Ramiro left two adult sons at the time of his death, the royal succession in León in the early Middle Ages was not yet clearly established and his death left the kingdom vulnerable to outside interference. Sancho's elder brother Ordoño III succeeded to the throne, but his father-in-law, Fernán González, joined in a conspiracy with King García I Sánchez of Pamplona to replace Ordoño with Sancho. The attempt failed, Fernán González was forced into exile in Castile, and his daughter was repudiated by Ordoño. When Ordoño died prematurely four years later, Sancho succeeded him.

Sancho, known as "the Fat" due to the obesity that made it difficult for him to walk, much less mount a horse to ride to battle, renounced the truce with ʿAbd al-Raḥmān made by Ordoño in 955. This led the nobles, guided by Sancho's erstwhile advocate Fernán González, to depose him and elect Ordoño IV, "the Bad," who ruled from 957 to 960.

In order to regain his throne, Sancho sought assistance from the Umayyads, who saw in the dynastic dispute an opportunity to strengthen their position with respect to the Christian kingdoms. Sancho lost weight with the assistance of ʿAbd al-Raḥmān's Jewish physician, Hasdai ibn Shaprut, but to conclude the military arrangements, Sancho and his grandmother, the queen of Navarre, had to make a humiliating journey to Córdoba. Newly slender and accompanied by a large Muslim army, Sancho returned to León in 960 and successfully recovered his kingdom.

Sancho's pact with ʿAbd al-Raḥmān made it impossible for him to raid Umayyad territory, so he focused instead on building an alliance with his Christian neighbors, García I of Navarre, Fernán González, and Borell II and Miró, the counts of Barcelona. Fortified by this alliance, Sancho refused to fulfill one of the conditions of his alliance with Córdoba, namely the cession of ten fortresses along the Duero River. The caliph retaliated and threw his support to Sancho's rival Ordoño IV, who had taken refuge in Córdoba. This second attempt to unseat Sancho failed when Ordoño died in 962. The caliph, undeterred, sent armies to León, Castile, and Navarre to persuade Sancho to fulfill his side of the bargain.

His ambitions thwarted in the south and northeast, Sancho turned his attentions to Galicia, where he attempted to restore his royal authority. In the course of negotiations there in 967 he was poisoned by Gonzalo, duke of Galicia, and left his kingdom in the hands of his five-year-old son Ramiro III (966–984) with Sancho's sister, Elvira, acting as regent.

THERESA EARENFIGHT

Bibliography

Collins, R. *Early Medieval Spain: Unity in Diversity, 400–1000*. London, 1983.

Glick, T. F. *Islamic and Christian Spain in the Early Middle Ages*. Princeton, N.J., 1979.

O'Callaghan, J. F. *A History of Medieval Spain*. Ithaca, N.Y., 1975.

SANCHO II, KING OF CASTILE

Sancho II (ca. 1038–1072), eldest son of Fernando I (r. 1035–1065), was a forceful and energetic prince who spent much of his reign in battle, but not against foreign armies. Rather, he fought his own brothers in an attempt to rectify what he considered a grave injustice—the provision of his father's will that left him with a truncated inheritance.

Fernando's will, announced at an assembly at León two years before his death, divided his dominions among his three sons: to Sancho would go the lands of Castile as far west as the Pisuerga River and the tributes owed by the king of Zaragoza; Alfonso would receive León and the tributes of Toledo; and García would inherit Galicia, Portugal, and the tributes of Badajoz and Seville. Sancho lodged a formal protest, arguing that his ancestors had agreed among themselves that the land should always be under one lord. His words went unheeded, and so he set out to defy his father's will and deprive his brothers of their share of the inheritance.

The three brothers maintained an uneasy truce until the death of their mother, Sancha, in 1067. In 1068 Alfonso campaigned near Badajoz, territory that was part of García's inheritance, and forced the local ruler to become his tributary. Alfonso's actions made it clear that he, too, refused to abide by his father's will and he thus provided Sancho with a convenient excuse for his later aggressions.

Sancho responded quickly. In 1068 he defeated Alfonso at Llantada, but gained no territory. When García had further troubles in Galicia—a revolt of the Galician nobles and the murder of the bishop of Santiago de Compostela during Lent in 1069—Alfonso, supported by García's rebellious nobles, invaded Galicia. To placate an irate Sancho, Alfonso offered him unchallenged dominion over Galicia. Sancho, realizing that his two kingdoms would be separated by Alfonso's, refused the offer.

In January 1072 Sancho attacked León, captured Alfonso at the battle of Golpejera, and crowned himself in León on 12 January 1072, thus reuniting León and Castile for the third, albeit very brief, time in less than a century. From León, he marched into García's old territories of Galicia and Portugal, and defeated García near Santarém.

Despite his military triumphs, Sancho could not negotiate a satisfactory political settlement. Opposition from both the nobles and clergy was so fierce that he was forced to crown himself because the bishop of León refused to do so. Sancho's reign as king of Castile, León, and Galicia was brief: he was assassinated in Zamora on 6 October 1072 by someone thought to be in the employ of his sister Urraca, who conspired to help Alfonso. García, too, fell victim to the extraordinarily bitter familial animosity. He fled to Seville, and in 1073 he was imprisoned for life by Alfonso and Urraca. Alfonso inherited the kingdom of León-Castile and ruled it until his death in 1109.

The murder of Sancho II has become the stuff of legend, in part due to the military exploits of his loyal standard-bearer, Rodrigo Díaz de Vivar, known as "el Cid." But Sancho's most enduring legacy was his assertion of his right to inherit intact the kingdom of his father. Whether or not he understood the theoretical notions implicit in his protest of his father's will, his fight to restore what he perceived to be the historical unity of Castile and León was in fact a clear rejection of older patrimonial notions of inheritance in favor of primogeniture as a basis for kingship.

THERESA EARENFIGHT

Bibliography

O'Callaghan, J. F. *A History of Medieval Spain.* Ithaca, N.Y., 1975.

Reilly, B. F. *The Contest of Christian and Muslim Spain, 1031–1157.* Cambridge, Mass., 1992.

———. *The Kingdom of León-Castilla under King Alfonso VI, 1065–1109.* Princeton, N.J., 1988.

SANCHO III, KING OF NAVARRE

The reign of Sancho III Garcés, known as "el Mayor" (1000–1035) was a pivotal one, not only for Navarre but for all of Christian Spain. Possessed with prodigious political talents, he brought his small kingdom of Navarre to its apogee in the Middle Ages. Because the decline of Muslim influence in the region left him relatively free to focus his attentions elsewhere, he made no serious efforts to continue the Reconquest. Instead, he set about unifying all the Christian states except Castile under his rule. His cultural and political influences were French, and by his outlook and his actions he helped draw Spain out of its isolation and incorporate it into the rest of Western Christendom.

His inheritance was small—little more than a string of tiny counties in the foothills of the Pyrenees—but by skillful manipulation of marriage alliances, Sancho was able to widen his domains by acquiring adjacent territories. An important factor in his success was the marriage of his sister Urraca to King Alfonso V of León. Through Urraca, Sancho III continued to be a real power in that kingdom even after Alfonso's death. While Urraca served as regent for her son, Vermudo, Sancho gained control of Aragón and the old Marches counties of Sobrarbe and Ribagorza to the east of Aragón.

From his base in León, Sancho extended his influence to Castillian affairs through his brother-in-law García Sanchez, the count of Castile. When García Sanchez was murdered in 1029, Sancho took possession of Castile in his sister's name and designated his own son, Fernando, as heir. The Navarrese dynasty was firmly established in Castile in 1032 when Fernando married his first cousin Sancha, sister of Vermudo III, whose dowry brought to Navarre the disputed lands between the Cea and Pisguerga rivers.

Not all of Sancho's attempts to bring the Pyrennean states under Navarrese hegemony were so fruitful. By holding out the prospect of a military alliance against the Muslims in the central Ebro basin, he forced the count of Barcelona, Ramón Berenguer I (1018–1035), to become his vassal, although neither party would benefit much from this coalition. He tried to press his rights to succession in the duchy of Gascony, but his attempt to link the two Basque-speaking regions under one banner ultimately failed.

His political strength remained in Spain, however, and the high point of his career took place in 1034 when he occupied of the city of León, unseating his nephew Vermudo. Finally, possessing a political authority that encompassed Navarre, León, Aragón, and Castile, he styled himself Emperor of Hispania ("rex Dei gratia Hispaniarum") and coined money in affirmation of his new imperial dignity, thereby laying claim to a peninsular supremacy that had previously been attributed to the king of León.

His imperial career was short-lived, however. He died suddenly the next year, and Vermudo III regained León, ruling it until 1037. Although he governed a unified kingdom, Sancho's adherence to the patrimonial concept of kingship, as was the custom in France, which declared royal domains heritable and divisible among his heirs, made any permanent union of these states impossible. In his will Sancho stipulated that his several realms be divided among his sons, all of whom eventually bore the title of king: Navarre was granted to García III Sánchez (1035–1054); Castile, to Fernando I (1035–1065); and Aragón, to Ramiro I (1035–1063). As a result, the new frontier kingdoms of Castile and Aragón attained the status of kingdoms, and ultimately would overshadow Navarre and León.

His permanent influence on medieval Spanish culture extended far beyond territorial expansion and royal inheritances, however. During his reign, feudal concepts of law and landholding current in France penetrated into the peninsula. Under his aegis, Romanesque artistic styles, especially in architecture, became well established in Spain. He encouraged the pilgrimage to Santiago de Compostela, a principle vehicle for transmission of French ideas. For the convenience of the pilgrims, he modified and improved the difficult route through Álava and the Cantabrian Mountains. And during his reign Cluniac reform was introduced into the monasteries of Oña, Lerie, and San Juan de la Peña.

THERESA EARENFIGHT

Bibliography

Lacarra, J. M. *Historia del reino de Navarra en la Edad Media*. Pamplona, 1975.

O'Callaghan, J. F. *A History of Medieval Spain*. Ithaca, N.Y., 1975.

Pérez de Urbel, J. *Sancho el Mayor de Navarra*. Madrid, 1950.

SANCHO IV, KING OF CASTILE

Sancho IV, the second son of Alfonso X and Queen Violante, was born on 12 May 1258 in Valladolid. His sobriquet, "el Bravo," referred to his strength of will and determination. After the sudden death of his older brother Fernando de la Cerda in 1275, Sancho, rejecting the claims of his nephew, Alfonso de la Cerda, and demanded recognition as heir to the throne. Although Alfonso X acknowledged him, continual pressure from France and the papacy led the king to propose giving a portion of his dominions to his grandsons, Alfonso and Fernando, known collectively as the Infantes de la Cerda. Breaking with his father, Sancho, with the consent of the estates of the realm assembled at Valladolid in 1282, assumed royal authority, though he did not take the crown. A desultory civil war followed until the death of Alfonso X on 4 April 1284. Unreconciled and disinherited by his father, Sancho IV, nevertheless, was acclaimed as king and crowned at Toledo.

His situation was exceedingly precarious. Not only did Alfonso de la Cerda, supported by France, dispute his claim to the throne, but the pope had excommunicated Sancho and placed an interdict on his kingdom. The pope also denied the legitimacy of his marriage to his cousin, María de Molina; thus, their children would be considered illegitimate and lack any claim to inherit the throne. By challenging his father and by making many promises that he was unable to to carry out, Sancho IV also weakened the authority of the crown.

Throughout his reign he was engaged in an intense struggle to gain control of the straits of Gibraltar in order to prevent any Moroccan invasion in the future. Immediately after his accession he had to provide for the defense of the southern frontier against a new challenge by Abū Yūsuf, the Merinid emir, Alfonso X's last ally. Landing at Tarifa in April 1285, he besieged Jerez while his troops devastated a broad zone from Medina Sidonia to Carmona, Écija, and Seville. While Sancho IV sent his Genoese admiral, Benedetto Zaccaria, to protect the mouth of the Guadalquivir, a Castilian fleet of about one hundred ships waited in the straits to relieve Jerez or to disrupt the emir's communications with Morocco. When Sancho IV marched southward from Seville to Jerez, Abū Yūsuf decided not to test his fortunes in battle, and retreated to the safety of Algeciras in August. Two months later Sancho IV made peace with the emir.

Meanwhile, after the failure of the French crusade against Aragón, Sancho IV, because of continuing concern over the claims of Alfonso de la Cerda, was under pressure to enter an alliance with either kingdom. On the one hand, Philippe IV of France was Alfonso's cousin while Alfonso III of Aragón had custody of the two Infantes de la Cerda. Lope Díaz de Haro, lord of Vizcaya, who had much to do with securing Sancho IV's recognition as heir to the Castilian throne, preferred the alliance with Aragón as a guarantee that Alfonso de la Cerda would not be free to press his claims. Lope was the most influential person in the realm because the king had given him control over the royal household and finances as well as custody of all royal strongholds. Other members of the royal council eventually convinced Sancho IV that he had entrusted Lope with far too much authority. Thus the king turned against him in 1288 and caused his death in a violent scene.

Now free to decide for himself, Sancho IV broke with Aragón and allied with France. He expected that the continual threat of French intervention on behalf of the Infantes de la Cerda and papal opposition to the legitimation of his marriage and his children would be eliminated. He also promised to give the Infantes joint rule over Murcia and Ciudad Real as an independent realm, provided they renounced all claims to Castile. At that, Alfonso III of Aragón liberated the Infantes and proclaimed Alfonso de la Cerda as king of Castile. Inconclusive border warfare followed until 1291, when the new king of Aragón, Jaime II, concerned about his capacity to retain the kingdom of Sicily against papal opposition, decided to make peace. Jaime II left the Infantes de la Cerda to fend for themselves and agreed with Sancho IV on zones of future exploitation and conquest in North Africa.

The conclusion of this treaty came at an opportune moment because the Merinids were preparing to resume hostilities as soon as the truce with Castile ran out. Although Benedetto Zaccaria, again in Castilian service, defeated the Moroccan fleet in August 1291, Abū Ya'qūb, the Merinid emir, invaded Spain soon after. In the spring of 1292, Sancho IV, aided by Muḥammad II of Granada (who feared the Merinids), besieged Tarifa, a port often used by Moroccan forces entering Spain. Sancho IV entered the town in triumph on 13 October 1292. The king of Granada, who had expected that Tarifa would be restored to him, now broke with Castile and joined the Moroccans in a new siege of Tarifa in 1294. Nevertheless, Alfonso Pérez de Guzmán, known thereafter as "el bueno," successfully defended Tarifa until a Castilian and Catalan fleet compelled the enemy to withdraw. The capture and subsequent defense of Tarifa was the first stage in closing the gates of the peninsula to future Moroccan invasions.

Not long after Sancho IV died on 25 April 1295, his wife María de Molina, whom he married at Toledo in July 1282, became regent for their son, Fernando IV. Sancho wrote a book of counsel titled *Castigos e documentos* for Fernando.

JOSEPH F. O'CALLAGHAN

Bibliography

Gaibrois de Ballesteros, M. *Historia del reinado de Sancho IV.* 3 vols. Madrid, 1922.

SANT JORDI, JORDI DE

Valencian knight and poet. His short life coincided with the early years of King Alfonso the Magnanimous's court, among whose members we find Andreu Febrer, and Íñigo López de Mendoza, the marqués of Santillana. As a personal servant, he benefited from his young lord's confidence and devotion to poetry, and fought bravely in Alfonso's expeditions to Corsica and Sardinia (1420) and the south of Italy. There, while imprisoned in Naples (1423), he addressed to the king a realistic but dignified poem claiming freedom on the grounds of the chivalric ethic (*Presoner*). On the whole, Sant Jordi's poetry, though having slighter Occitan features than his predecessors', is the brilliant result of the last stage of the troubadour revival: according to Santillana's admired recollections, Sant Jordi embodied the best of an ancient but lively tradition (he even used to compose the music) that deserved the same literary glory as Dante. His thirteen love poems focus on the element of suffering in *fin' amor*, yet strikingly relating true love to an honorable condition (mainly in his allegorical *Passio amoris secundum Ovidium*) and even chastity. Two of them, which evoke with some intimate love for a certain Isabel, contrast with the other nine addressed to the widow queen Margarida de Prades, a real *midons* who held a sort of literary court. In these, Sant Jordi used his rhetorical skill to best effect for the highest expression of his love (*Stramps*). Moreover, Sant Jordi wrote four satirical complaints mainly against the upside-down world. His witty sense of humor as well as his virtuosity remind us of Cerverí de Girona and account for his ability to draw both on literature (the *enueg*, the prestigious metrics of *lai*, Petrarch's *adynata*) and reality, while offering another view of courtly principles.

LOLA BADIA

Bibliography

Riquer M. de, and L. Badia. *Les poesies de Jordi de Sant Jordi, cavaller valencià del segle XV.* Valencia, 1984.

SANTA CRUZ, ALONSO DE

A prominent figure in the intellectual life of sixteenth-century Spain, Alonso de Santa Cruz contributed to the study of its medieval history in his *Chronicle of the Catholic Monarchs*. Born in Seville around 1505, he seems to have received his education while resident in the city's Alcazar: it is not known whether he ever attended a university. By the time of his death, on 6 November 1567, he had been *cosmógrafo mayor* to both Charles V and Philip II and had achieved a massive production of work on cartography, cosmography, astronomy, geography, genealogy and heraldry, economics and politics, philosophy and history. Unusually, in comparison with his scholarly compatriots in the Siglo de Oro, he apparently eschewed religion as a subject, being fired from his early years, spent in and near the Casa de Contratación in Seville, by enthusiasm for the discoveries then being made in the New World. His long years of academic preparation were developed into practical experience when he accompanied Sebastian Cabot on his expedition, supposedly to the Moluccas but arriving in New Spain, or Mexico, between 1526 and 1530. Even if Santa Cruz had never been a historian of Fernando and Isabel, he would still have been notable for his cosmographical works, such as his *Islario general*, a description, heavily influenced by classical sources, of the islands of the Mediterranean. His chronicle of the Catholic Monarchs (ca.1550) inevitably relies on earlier writers, such as Andrés Bernáldez, Fernando del Pulgar, and Lorenzo Galíndez de Carvajal, but it also includes documentary sources. He also wrote a history of the reign of Charles V.

John Edwards

Bibliography

Cuesta Domingo, M. *Alonso de Santa Cruz y su obra cosmográfica*. 2 vols. (Madrid, 1983) Contains an edition of the *Islario general*.

Santa Cruz, Al. de. *Crónica de los Reyes Católicos*. 2 vols. Ed. J. de Mata Carriazo. Seville, 1951.

SANTA FE, JERÓNIMO DE

Joshua ben Joseph ibn Vives al-Lorqi was a Jewish scholar of some renown, possibly the son of Joseph al-Lorqui, an important scientist. The family originated perhaps, from Murcia, but Joshua lived in Aragón. There is no evidence he was a "student" of Rabbi Solomon ha-Levy of Burgos, but when Solomon (Pablo de Santa María) converted (ca.1390), Joshua heard about it and wrote him a Hebrew letter asking the reasons for his conversion (part of Pablo's reply survives). Sometime thereafter, Joshua himself converted, taking the name Jerónimo de Santa Fe. He was baptized by Vicente Ferrer, the Dominican missionary who converted perhaps thousands of Jews (his later canonization was due in large part to his baptism of this important Jewish scholar). The zealous new convert played a major role in the Tortosa disputation and composed his major work, an anti-Jewish polemic, in Latin shortly after this (*Hebraeomastyx*). A Hebrew translation was made and circulated widely, arousing numerous Jewish responses. The work was largely based on Ramón Martí's *Pugio fidei*.

Norman Roth

Bibliography

Landau, L. *Das apologetische Schreiben des Josua Lorki*. Antwerp, 1906.

Poznánski, S. "Le colloque de Tortose et de San Mateo." *Revue des Études Juives* 74 (1922), esp. 18–22, 34–39, 160–64.

SANTA MARÍA DE CARTAGENA, ORDER OF

See MILITARY ORDERS

SANTIAGO DE COMPOSTELA

The major urban center of the province of Galicia in the northwest of Iberia during the Middle Ages, Santiago de Compostela is located between the Tambre and Ulla Rivers about thirty miles inland from the Atlantic Ocean. There is no evidence for a town there during the Roman period but archaeological remains indicate the existence of some sort of Christian shrine and cemetery that continued in use into the subsequent Suevic and Visigothic periods. Both the failure of the archaeological record and the subsequent history of the site suggest its abandonment during the late Visigothic period, the time of the Muslim occupation of Galicia in the first half of the eighth century, and the earliest period of the Christian recovery of the province.

The history of the town proper may be said to have begun with the purported discovery there of the relics of St. James the Great by Bishop Theodomir of Iria Flavia sometime around the year 830. Iria Flavia (modern Padrón) was a Roman port and bishopric by the Ulla River not far from where the latter flows into the Ria de Arosa and thence into the Atlantic. The discovery of the remains of the apostle was quickly reported to Alfonso II (791–842) of Asturias who had the first shrine-church built on the site. The bishops of Iria Flavia soon began to reside in Compostela at least periodically, a community of clerics was formed to serve at the shrine, and two monastic communities, San Pelayo de Antealtares and San Martín Pinario, also

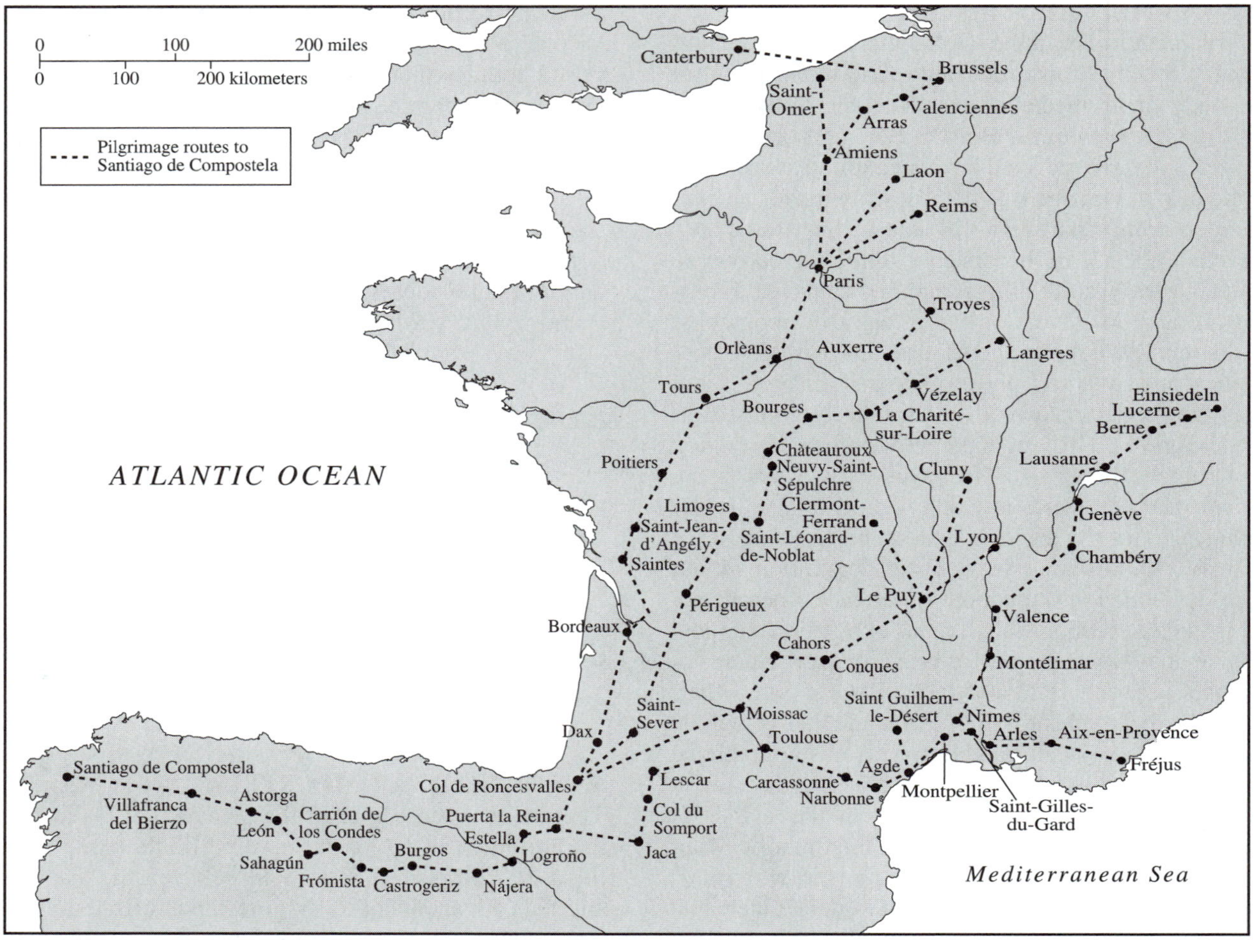

Pilgrimage Routes to Santiago de Compostela

came to cluster about the church. These clerical communities, and those who provisioned and waited on them, formed the first nucleus of the town.

The next major stage in the growth of the town resulted from the development of an international pilgrimage to Santiago de Compostela, after Rome itself the sole resting place of an apostle in the westen European world. During the ninth century Compostela seems to have been the object of a purely regional cult, gradually growing in importance. Alfonso III (866–910) of Asturias had the old church of Santiago torn down and rebuilt in a much grander style.

It is in the tenth century that the shrine began to attract pilgrims from beyond the Pyrenees and to figure occasionally in the records and letters of those who had visited the church or had at least heard of it. Compostela was of sufficient importance by the end of that time to merit the attentions of the great Muslim ruler of the south, Al-Manṣūr, who overran the town, sacking and burning it, in 997.

But Santiago de Compostela, like the remainder of Christian Iberia, seems to have recovered rapidly from the depradations of the Muslim chieftain. The pilgrimage from beyond the peninsula was swelling and the Christian rulers of León-Castile, into which the old kingdom of Asturias had grown, began to regard it in an ever more favorable light. The capture of Muslim Coimbra in 1064 by Fernando I (1037–1065) was credited to the favor of its saint who now began his long metamorphosis into "Santiago Matamoros," patron of the Reconquest and of Christian Spain. Bishop Diego Peláez (1071–1088) of Iria Flavia began, in 1076, the construction of a grand, new Romanesque church at the shrine. In 1095 Bishop Dalmatius of Iria Flavia returned to his native France to attend a papal council at Clermont. There he secured a bull from his

Facade. Cathedral, Santiago de Compostela, Spain. Copyright © Scala/Art Resource, NY.

fellow Frenchman, Pope Urban II, translating the see of Iria Flavia itself to Santiago de Compostela and exempting the translated see from its old subjection to the metropolitan of Braga and making it immediately dependent on Rome.

More directly than before the bishops now became, under the king, the civil as well as the ecclesiastical rulers of Santiago de Compostela. Under episcopal patronage and their management of the pilgrimage, the town prospered as the devout from as far away as Germany, Italy, France, England, and even the Scandinavias, traveled there to venerate the saint and incidentally to enrich the town's businessmen. In 1107 Alfonso VI (1065–1109) granted the bishops of Compostela the regalian right to mint coins in the town.

But the prosperity of the town and the authority of its bishops did not always sit well together. In 1116–1117 and 1135–1136 there were conspiracies eventuating in communal movements whose aim was to establish elected civil officials independent of their prelate to conduct the judicial and commercial business of the town. These conspirators were sufficiently influential to gain the ear of the the crown itself and both Queen Urraca (1109–1126) and Alfonso VII (1126–1157) were at times willing to cooperate with them for reasons both of politics and profit. These insurrections failed in their immediate objectives largely by reason of the violence to which they resorted. In 1117 an attempt to burn their prelate to death in a tower of his own cathedral narrowly failed and directly imperiled the life of Queen Urraca who was visiting with him at the time. Again in 1136 another attempt culminated in the stoning of their ordinary within the precincts of his own cathedral but again he escaped with his life and the perpetrators had to be disavowed by the crown.

Ironically these events coincided with the greatest period in the history of the town and of its church. In 1100 Diego Gelmírez, the scion of a local noble, became bishop. Under his direction the construction of the great Romanesque cathedral begun by Bishop Diego Peláez was carried much closer to completion. In 1120 Gelmírez was able to influence Pope Calixtus II to transfer the vacant metropolitan jurisdiction of Muslim-held Mérida to the shrine of the apostle and to concede to it the suffragan sees of Salamanca, Avila, and Coimbra. The now Archbishop Gelmírez was also to become papal legate for the ecclesiastical provinces of Santiago de Compostela and of Braga. He even attempted to move the papacy to transfer the primatial jurisdiction of the archbishopric of Toledo over the Iberian church to Compostela but was thwarted by the strong objections of the crown.

At the same time the prelate of Santiago was one of the greatest political figures of the realm. In 1107 he had become the guardian, along with Count Pedro Froílaz of the Galician line of the Trastámara, of the child who would become Alfonso VII in 1126. The guardianship made Gelmírez one of the most important allies and sometimes one of the most important opponents of the boy's mother, Queen Urraca, thoughout her reign. During the early years of the reign of Alfonso VII, he was one of the major advisers of his erstwhile ward, but after 1134 his influence waned and by his death in 1140 he was but a minor figure politically. No other archbishop of Santiago would loom so large in the politics of the Iberian Peninsula, for León-Castile was marching steadily southward as the Reconquest proceeded and the old primatial see of Toledo eclipsed Compostela in importance in the late twelfth century, as would Seville in the thirteenth. This process was delayed for a time when León-Castile was divided into two distinct realms after the death of Alfonso VII. That event magnified the importance of Compostela to Fernando II (1157–1188) and Alfonso IX (1188–1230), both of whom chose to be interred in the church of the Apostle. But the partial eclipse of the town resumed with the permanent reunion of the two kingdoms under Fernando III (1230–1252).

The enduring growth of the pilgrimage continued to underwrite the prosperity and growth of the town nevertheless. In 1181 Pope Alexander III conceded the priviledge of a Holy Year to the shrine in every year in which the feast-day of the apostle, 25 July, fell on a Sunday. During such a year the pilgrim to Compostela could secure the identical spiritual benefits as he might by a pilgrimage to Rome or to the Holy Land itself. Among a host of others, no less a personage than the great St. Francis of Assisi would make the journey to worship at this shrine. The potency of the apostle continued to swell the credit of Compostela with the popes of Rome as well and allowed it to build an ecclesiastical empire in the peninsula despite the opposition and claims of the archbishops of Braga and Toledo. Finally the suffragan bishops of Santiago came to number all of the Galician sees, once the suffragans of Braga; Lugo, Mondoñedo, Orense, and Túy, and then a series of bishoprics stretching south from Astorga through Zamora, Salamanca, Avila, Placentia, Ciudad Rodrigo, and Coria, even to Badajoz in the Guadiana River valley where it confronted the newly erected archbishopric of Seville.

The town continued to batten on the pilgrim trade. In particular the shops of its silversmiths just outside the cathedral itself became famous. But the patronage of the shrine supplied funds for the various building campaigns in and around its precincts that gave regular employment to the artisans and laborers of Compostela as well. Gelmírez had erected a new episcopal palace directly adjacent to the church in addition to carrying the cathedral itself as near to completion as medieval cathedrals ever were. The late twelfth century saw the construction of a new facade for the church, the famous Portico of Glory. In the early fourteenth century what later became the present clock tower was added. The fifteenth century saw major additions to the monastery of San Martín Pinario.

In law as well as in the economy Santiago de Compostela continued to be an ecclesiastical town. But the burghers of the city enjoyed a limited autonomy under the aegis of their own council, or *concejo*. Disputes continued to be frequent and, as before, involved appeals to the crown for support by one or the other party. Under Kings Fernando III and Alfonso X (1252–1284) they concerned the obligations of lands held by the townsmen in the countryside to episcopal officers, the rights of churchmen to dispose of the agricultural products of their rural properties in the city, the method of selection of the judges of the *concejo*, and of course the relative jurisdictions of these judges and the archiepiscopal judges in criminal and civil cases. Such disputes were complicated by the fact that the chief executive instrument of the archbishops themselves, the cathedral chapter, was composed largely of canons linked by birth to the burgher class of the town and to the local nobility of the countryside.

The fortunes of the town and its population were also affected, at least indirectly, by the success or failure of their prelate to collect Los Votos de Santiago. This annual tribute owed by each Christian household in the peninsula to the church of the Apostle was supposedly granted by Ramiro I (842–850) in gratitude for the assistance of Santiago in the defeat of the Muslims at the battle of Clavijo. The charter of Ramiro is actually a forgery of the early twelfth century. There may have been an earlier, more humble, local tribute paid to the shrine and its apostolic protector but the increasing attempts of its archbishops to widen its collection gave rise to strong resistance everywhere. Although the tribute was supposedly due from every Iberian Christian household, such attempts were concentrated in the growing ecclesiastical jurisdictions of the Compostelan archbishops in Galicia and their new suffragan sees of Extremadura. Usually such claims were settled by compromise that produced a lesser income from discrete properties in the area affected. The disputes engendered by the claim to Los Votos continued well into the modern period.

During the latter two centuries of the Middle Ages, Santiago de Compostela and its church shared in the congenital disorder and violence universal in western Europe. The Black Death and the Avignonese papacy of the fourteenth century, the Great Schism of the fifteenth, all had their toll in terms of absentee clerics and the growing importance of curial reservation and curial taxation in the governance of the local churches. In the secular sphere the spectacular collapse of the dynasty of Alfonso X (1252–1284) during the latter portion of his reign and the almost endemic civil war it engendered over the next two centuries brought the bloody disputes of the realm at large to sanction and embittered the old staples of Galician and Compostelan rivalries. The substantial growth of both papal and royal authority during the twelfth and thirteenth centuries and the consequent ability to project their power into hitherto relatively isolated areas of church and realm guaranteed that local problems would be linked to wider ones.

In 1317 Pope John XXII from Avignon appointed the French Berenguer of Landor, a general of the Dominican Order, as archbishop of Compostela in reaction to a contested election there. It took some four years of threats of war, diplomacy, and actual fighting before Berenguer was able to enter and rule his pontifical city in 1321. On 29 June 1366, Archbishop Suero Gómez was murdered in the streets of Compostela by royal agents while on his way to an interview with King Pedro I the Cruel (1350–1369) of Castile. Fully two-thirds of the archbishops of Santiago de Compostela during these centuries were strangers, imposed upon the city and church by the crown and the papacy. Frequently they were members of the great lineages of the realm such as the Lara archbishop Juan García Manrique (1383–1398) or Alfonso de Fonseca (1460–1506). Such prelates were often likely to reside at court for long periods, far from their city, and sometimes to die in the royal service while on campaign with their kings in the Muslim south.

What is most remarkable is that the pilgrimage, the foundation of the town's prosperity and even its existence seems to have endured with its attraction and reputation largely undiminished. Nevertheless the town could not escape the effects of that age in Iberia. From a population of perhaps fifteen hundred by the year 1000 it had reached an apogee by 1300 of roughly six thousand. As a result of the Black Death and the troubles, one suspects that its population dipped by at least a third and then, as was the usual European and Iberian experience, rebounded to something like its 1300 figure by 1500, when stability and prosperity returned under the Catholic Monarchs. But by that time the impending Protestant Reformation in northern Europe was about to deal a major blow to the veneration of saints generally and to the pious practice of pilgrimage in particular, and thereby to a town whose development had always depended more on religious factors than on geographical or economic ones.

BERNARD F. REILLY

Bibliography

López Alsina, F. *La ciudad de Santiago de Compostela en la Alta Edad Media*. Santiago de Compostela, 1988.

López Ferreiro, A. *Historia de la Santa Apostólica Metropolitana Iglesia de Santiago de Compostela*. 11 vols. Santiago de Compostela, 1898–1911.

Vázquez de Parga, L., J. M. Lacarra, and J. Uría Ríu (eds.) *Las peregrinaciones a Santiago de Compostela*. 3 vols. Madrid, 1948–49.

SANTIAGO, ORDER OF *See* MILITARY ORDERS

SÃO JORGE DA MINA

Castle, city, and important trading post established in 1482 by João II in Guinea, present-day Ghana. Its foundation followed closely the signing of the Treaty of Alcáçovas with Castile in 1479, which gave the Portuguese crown a free hand on the mainland of Africa (even though it recognized the Spanish as sovereign in the Canary Islands). Until its loss to the Dutch of the West India Company in 1637, it served as commercial center of trade with the entire region embracing the Malagueta, Gold, Ivory, and Slave Coasts, plus the islands of São Tomé and Príncipe. Undoubtedly the main reason for the castle itself was to ward off interlopers and protect the gold trade.

Its creation was remarkable for the time, for the castle, the most imposing trading fort ever constructed on the African mainland, was prefabricated in Portugal and shipped down in two *urcas*, or cargo vessels, along with one hundred workmen, all under the command of João II's councillor, Diogo de Azambuja. The date of departure from Lisbon is known: 12 December 1481, and the fleet consisted besides of ten caravels and five-hundred soldiers. Upon arrival, Azambuja first negotiated a location for his settlement with the local potentate, Caramansa—a village called Duas Partes. Thereafter, he lost no time in building a foundation and assembling the castle, the speed no doubt accelerated by local skirmishes with Caramansa's rivals. In 1486 João II accorded it the status of city. Its captains resided in the castle itself and served the usual three-year terms. Among them were Duarte Pacheco Pereira, Diego Lopes de Sequeira, Brás, the son of Afonso de Alburquerque, the chronicler João de Barros, and the heroic soldier of the Ethiopian campaign, Estevão da Gama.

Mina (also called Elmina) played an important part in the evolution of the Portuguese commercial system as well. Under Henrique, a customs, outfitting and warehousing establishment called the Casa de Guiné, had been created at Lagos to outfit and receive caravels on voyages to Africa and to collect the percentages of profits agreed upon in deals with authorized merchants. After the settlement at Mina, however, João II moved the operation at Lagos to Lisbon and paired it with the older *feitoria* at Arguin Island and the new and bigger one at Mina; it was then known as the Casa de Guiné e Mina. Until 1506 private and foreign merchants were allowed to invest their moneys in the African trade through its offices; its officials invested their moneys for them and distributed the profits.

GEORGE D. WINIUS

Bibliography

Blake, J. W. *European Beginnings in West Africa, 1454–1578*. London, 1937.

Lawrence, A. W. *Trade Castles and Forts of West Africa*. London, 1963.

SARAGOSSA *See* ZARAGOZA

SARAGOSSA, KINGDOM OF *See* BANŪ HŪD

SARMIENTO, PERO

Of minor nobility by origin, Pero Sarmiento was the chief butler (the honorary post of *repostero mayor*) to Juan II of Castile, and also became the king's *asistente* and *alcaide* in Toledo. His main claim to fame was the fact that he joined the rebel uprising in Toledo in 1449 and became its leader, widening popular grievances into a general attack on the court. The rebellion had begun as a popular reaction against tax collectors and *conversos*, (converts to Christianity), but Sarmiento redirected the movement into a broad-based attack on Alvaro de Luna, who was accused of subverting royal authority, fomenting corruption in municipal government, and being responsible for a decline in the economic fortunes of the greater and lesser nobility.

Of even greater significance, however, was the so-called *sentencia-estatuto*, which the Toledan rebels promulgated under Sarmiento's leadership on 5 June at the height of the uprising. This was specifically directed against the *conversos* who held office in Toledo and decreed their explusion from their posts. It has generally been accepted that Sarmiento's *sentencia-estatuto* marked the first decisive step in the formulation of the doctrine of *limpieza de sangre*. In theory the impediments and limitations imposed on the Jews had traditionally been based on religious grounds. The Jew as potential convert, therefore, was not irremediably wicked, and baptism, which made the Jew a New Christian or *converso*, was the crucial rite of transition that altered everything. This view was enshrined in the *Siete Partidas* of Alfonso X, and it was repeated during the Toledan crisis of 1449 by the *converso* and royal secretary Fernán Diáz de Toledo when he argued in his *Instrucción del Relator* that baptism turned the *converso* into a new person, and eliminated all previous sins and impediments. The *conversos*, therefore, could aspire to hold public offices in exactly the same way as the Old Christians, and many did so successfully. The view adopted by Sarmiento in his *Sentencia* was brutally simple: the *converso* remained a Jew despite his conversion and should therefore be barred from holding any public office.

Although the uprising failed, Sarmiento was allowed to leave Toledo and disappeared into obscurity into his northern siegnorial lands. Yet despite the fact that influential *conversos* like Fernán Diáz de Toledo and Bishop Alonso de Cartagena had openly written in defense of the *conversos* and against the absurd accusations of Sarmiento and the Toledan insurgents, the setting up of the Spanish Inquisition in 1478 in many ways confirmed that some of the views expressed in the *sentencia-estatudo* had been assimilated by official thinking.

ANGUS MACKAY

Bibliography

Benito Ruano, E. *Toledo en el siglo XV*. Madrid, 1961.

SAYAGÜÉS

Sayagüés was the name given to the speech of less articulate country folk as depicted mainly in sixteenth- and seventeenth-century Spanish plays. Misidentified with the town of Sayago in southwestern Zamora province, it was in reality based on *charro* (or *charruno*), the rustic Leonese dialect of the region around Salamanca. It was used most skillfully (and most authentically) by Juan del Encina (1468–1529) and, especially, Lucas Fernández (1474–1542), and less effectively by Gil Vicente and Bartolomé de Torres Naharro. Such later writers, as Quevedo, Lope de Vega, and Tirso de Molina, added Castilian archaisms and vulgarisms, pseudo-Latinisms, and apparent Lusisms to create a stylized and comical rustic parlance not traceable to any particular region. Cervantes, in the voice of Sancho Panza, opposed coarse *sayagüés* to refined Toledan speech.

Among characteristic features of *sayagüés* are (1) the palatalization of *l-* and *n-* (for example, *lladrón* "thief," *lluego* "then"; *ño* "no," and *ñuestro* "our"); (2) *r* for *l* in postconsonantal position (for example, *habrar* "to speak," *praze* "it pleases"); (3) aspiration of *f-* followed by *ue* (for example, *hu(e)* "he was," *huerte* "strong"); (4) monophthongal second-person plural endings (for example, *mandás* "you send," *traés* "you bring"; (5) second-person plural imperatives in *-ai/-ay* (for example, *miray* "look!"); (6) abundant apocope in verb forms (for example, *diz* "he says," *vien* "he comes"); (7) abuse of the prefix *per-* (for example, *percoger* "to gather," *pernotar* "to observe").

The term *sayagüés* ultimately came to designate not only rustic speech, but also uncouth behavior and customs of all sorts.

THOMAS J. WALSH

Bibliography

Fernández, L. *Farsas y églogas*. Ed. M. J. Canellada. Madrid, 1976, 27–59.

Lihani, J. *El lenguaje de Lucas Fernández: Estudio del dialecto sayagüés*. Bogotá, 1973.

SCHOOLS, CATHEDRAL

See EDUCATION, CHRISTIAN

SCIENCE, ANDALUSIAN

The period of Muslim occupation of the whole or a part of the Iberian Peninsula, which lasted between 711 and 1492, produced an important scientific development that did not have an equivalent in Christian Spain. This development affected, above all, astronomy, medicine, and pharmacology, agronomy (*Filāḥa*), and, to a lesser extent, mathematics, physics, and alchemy.

The Muslim conquerors of 711 were not cultivated people and the scientific knowledge they brought with them was limited to folk astronomy, practical rules concerning the orientation of mosques and the determination of the times of prayer, irrigation technologies for the construction of *qanāts*, and, perhaps, a kind of folk and religious medicine (*tibb al-Nabī*, "medicine of the Prophet"). This is why there is some evidence of the survival of a Latin scientific tradition in al-Andalus, especially until around 821 (beginning of the reign of ʿAbd al-Raḥmān II). The oldest extant astrological text (ca. 800) seems to be a translation of a lost Latin original and the Córdoban physician Ibn Juljul (b. 943), in his history of medicine, mentions six doctors for the period 852–912, of which five are Christians and practice medicine according to one of the books written by the Christians that had been translated into Arabic. This Latin tradition also affected agronomy: even if traditional theories concerning a direct transmission of the agronomical work of Iunius Moderatus Columela in al-Andalus seem to be discredited, scholars like Attié still defend the existence of Latin-Arabic translations of agronomical works and consider that the anonymous author of the *Kitāb tartīb awqāt al-ghirāsa wa-l-maghrūsāt* was a Christian. This should be combined with a very early development of an Islamic agronomy: ʿAbd al-Raḥmān I (756–788), the first Umayyad emir, founded the first botanical garden in the Ruṣāfa, near Córdoba, and made there the first attempts to grow plants brought from the Near East.

The period between the beginning of the reign of ʿAbd al-Raḥmān II (821–852) and the fall of the Umayyad Caliphate (1031) is characterized by the introduction of a new scientific culture developed in eastern Islam, since about 750, through the assimilation of the "sciences of the Ancients" (*ʿulūm al-awā'il*)—exact sciences, biology, medicine and pharmacology, physics, alchemy, mechanical technology, and philosophy—inherited from India, Iran, and especially, Greece. These new sciences reached al-Andalus as a result of *riḥla* (travel) made by young students in search of a higher education in Eastern capitals; the arrival in al-Andalus of the most important books published in the East due to the fact that the Umayyad emirs, since ʿAbd al-Raḥmān II, collected an important royal library, sent embassadors to the East and developed a network of commercial agents in order to acquire new publications; and in a few instances the arrival to Córdoba of Eastern scientists. Royal patronage fostered the development of two applied sciences that had practical applications for the emir: astrology—and this had an obvious influence in astronomy—and medicine. It is extremely difficult, due to the lack of sources, to follow the development of these sciences between about 821 and 950, although it seems that the introduction of Arabic versions of the works of Hippocrates and Galen started under ʿAbd al-Raḥmān II with the arrival of the Eastern physician Al-Ḥarrānī.

The situation changes toward the middle of the tenth century: the apparition of the mathematical and astronomical school of Maslama al-Majrīṭī (d. 1007) proves that Euclidean geometry, an arithmetic based on a mixture of Indian and Hellenistic methods, a new algebra, the Indian astronomy of the *Sindhind* tradition (introduced in al-Andalus around 850) and Ptolemaic astronomy had been fully introduced and maturely assimilated. During the reign of ʿAbd al-Raḥmān III (912–961) the physician Yaḥyā ibn Isḥāq, whose father was a Christian doctor, combines the Latin medical tradition with the writing of a book in which he summarizes all the Greek medicine known in his time. The works of Saʿīd ibn ʿAbd Rabbihi (d. 953 or 966), ʿArīb ibn Saʿīd (ca. 912–ca. 980)—the author of the first known handbook on gynecology and pediatrics—and Ibn Juljul show that the whole corpus of Hellenistic medicine has been fully assimilated and, thus, the situation is ready for the brilliant medical and surgical work of Abū al-Qāsim al-Zahrāwī (d. 1013). This is also the period in which we can place the birth of the Andalusian school of botany and pharmacology usually associated to the Córdoban revision of the Eastern Arabic translation, by Iṣṭīfan ibn Basīl, of Dioscorides's *Materia medica*. This was the standard Hellenistic compilation of "simple" drugs (mostly vegetal) but the Eastern translation had not identified most of the Greek names of the plants. Good diplomatic relations between Córdoba and Byzantium permitted the arrival in al-Andalus (ca. 948–ca. 951) of a good illustrated Greek codex of Dioscorides's work as well as of Nicholas, a Byzantine monk who was a good botanist. Nicholas was soon surrounded by a group of Córdoban physicians—among whom we find Ibn Juljul and the famous Jew Ḥasdai ibn Shapruṭ—who revised the translation and identified most of the simples described in it. In order to avoid further confusions the names of simples were given, since then, in all the languages in use at the time (Greek, classical and colloquial Arabic, Latin, and, often, several Romance dialects). Ibn Juljul, who seems to have played a central role in this job, formulated the program of research to be developed hereafter by Andalusian botanists: the identification of Dioscorides's simples had to be complemented with the identification, description, and classification of simples not mentioned by the Greek author and which could be found in both al-Andalus and the rest of the known world.

The fall of the caliphate in 1031 and the fragmentation of al-Andalus into multiple "petty kingdoms" (*mulūk al-tawā'if*) did not imply a scientific decay but rather the eclosion of a period of some fifty years (1031–1086) which could be considered "golden," during which Andalusian science reached its summit. The apparition of multiple centers of power had two important and contradictory consequences: on the one side these *ṭā'ifa* kings wanted to be surrounded by scientists in the same way as they also enjoyed the company of poets; on the other, none of them seems to have had enough economic capacity to continue the policy of a systematic acquisition of Oriental books that had been followed by the Umayyads. To this one should add that the high level reached by Andalusian scientists at that period implied that young students no longer needed travel to the East in order to complete their education. As a consequence the *ṭā'ifa* period marks a slowing down in the cultural relations with the Muslim East, the development of Andalusian science on its own basis, and, consequently, the fact that it reaches a high degree of originality in relation to its Eastern counterpart. The final result will be, however, that the end of this period also implies the beginning of the decay of an isolated Andalusian science.

During the *tā'ifa* period science is scattered in different centers that develop a certain degree of specialization: mathematics in Zaragoza, astronomy in Toledo, agronomy in Toledo and Seville. The development of the exact sciences can be followed. As for the rest one should remark the apparition of two important books on magic (*Ghāyat al-ḥakīm*, known as *Picatrix*) and alchemy (*Rutbat al-ḥakīm*) by the same author incorrectly identified with Maslama al-Majrīṭī. The *Rutbat* is one of the very rare alchemical Andalusian texts and it has the obvious interest of its careful descriptions of experiences done in the laboratory. The *Ghāya* is a treatise on talismanic magic, a discipline with obvious connections with astrology, and it insists on the role of the magician as a man who does not pretend—like the astrologer—to predict the future but who wants to alter and control nature. In other words, the magician appears as a predecessor of the engineer. This leads us to the very interesting recent (1977) discovery of the *Kitāb al-asrār fī natā'ij al-afkār* (Secrets of the Results of Thoughts), written by an otherwise unknown (Aḥma)d or (Muḥamma)d ibn Khalaf al-Murādī (fl. probably in Toledo, eleventh century), extant in a manuscript copied in Toledo during the reign of Alfonso X and in which we find the handwritten notes of Rabbi Isḥāq ben Sīd (*Rabiçag*), the most important of the Alfonsine scientists. This book is a treatise on mechanical engineering that includes descriptions of clepsidras with moving automats, toys, and war machines and it corresponds to a tradition completely different from the Eastern one.

Quite surprisingly, after the brilliant results obtained by medicine in the second half of the tenth century, we do not have medical texts of the *tā'ifa* period although pharmacology and botany continue along the lines marked by Ibn Juljul in the work of authors such as Ibn Wāfid (d. Toledo, 1075), Ibn Buklārish (d. beginning of the twelfth century) and others. With Ibn Buklārish a new subject of theoretical research appears: the determination of the degree of heat/cold, dryness/humidity of a compounded drug as a function of the degree of such qualities in the simples used to prepare it. Medicine and pharmacology have, on the other hand, an important influence in the development of a new scientific discipline, agronomy, the origins of which can be found, as we have seen, in the botanical garden founded in Córdoba in the eighth century. New botanical gardens appear in this period in Toledo, Seville, and Almería and a group of authors leave an important corpus of agronomical works in which we can discover the echoes of the best agronomical literature available (Greek, Latin, and Arabic) together with an interest for experimentation and observation of the techniques used by Andalusian peasants. The names to be quoted are Abū al-Khayr al-Ishbīlī (Seville), Ibn Baṣṣāl (Toledo and Seville), Ibn Ḥajjāj (fl. 1073, Seville), and Al-Ṭignarī (fl. 1075–1100, Seville and Almería). To the aforementioned list one should add the anonymous author of the *Kitāb tartīb awqāt al-ghirāsa wa-l-maghrūsāt*, whose chronology is not clear, and the agronomical work ascribed either to Ibn Wāfid or to the famous physician and surgeon Abū al-Qāsim al-Zahrāwī. Something should be remarked: most of these authors seem to have been physicians and/or pharmacologists and the Andalusian agronomical school is characterized by the creation of an agronomical theory and, consequently, an attempt to create a new science from agricultural practice. Such a theory is, basically, a transposition of the principles of Hippocratic and Galenic medicine in such a way that there is a perfect correspondence between the four elements of Empedocles, the four humours of the human body, and the four elements (*ʿanāṣir*) of agriculture: air, earth, water, and fertilizers (which occupy the place of fire).

After the brilliant period of the *mulūk al-ṭawā'if* al-Andalus—the extension of which had been considerably reduced due to the advance of the Christian conquests—would become, during a century and a half, a province of the Almoravid (1086–1145) and Almohad

(1145–1232) Maghribī empires. This obviously implies that the centers of power were beyond the straits of Gibraltar and, consequently, we begin to see migrations of Andalusian scientists toward North Africa. The intolerant character of the Almoravids did not favor the development of science and it probably explains why some scientists (Maimonides is a good example) abandoned al-Andalus and established themselves in the East: this is, perhaps, the moment in which some of the results of scientific research done in al-Andalus in the previous century became known in the Near and Middle East. The situation changes with the Almohads, who extended a certain patronage to physicians and, perhaps, astronomers. Concerning astronomy, the tradition of the schools of Maslama and Azarquiel continued in the work of Abū al-Ṣalt al-Dānī (ca. 1067–1134), Ibn al-Kammād (fl. ca. 1100–1150), and Ibn al-Hᶜim (fl. 1205), but there also appears a current of criticism of Ptolemaic astronomy in the works of Jābir ibn Aflaḥ (fl. 1250) and the members of the Aristotelian school of philosophers, especially Al-Biṭrūjī (fl. 1185–1192). This is also the only period in which we find a certain activity in the field of physics due to the work done by Abū Bakr ibn Zakarīyā (Avempace) (1070?–1138) whose research on Neoplatonic dynamics reappears in Italy in the sixteenth century and has an obvious influence on the work of Galileo in his Pisan period (1589–1591).

Pharmacology and botany seem to have reached a level of maturity requiring the compilation of new encyclopedias which would occupy the place of Dioscorides's *Materia medica* and such is the work of Aḥmad ibn Muḥammad al-Ghāfiqī (d. c.1150) and, especially, of ᶜAbd Allāh ibn Aḥmad ibn al-Bayṭār (c.1190–1248), whose role as the author of the greatest Andalusian botanical compilation is equivalent to that of Ibn al-ᶜAwwām (fl. 1170–1200) who wrote *Kitāb al-filāha* (On Agriculture), which summarizes all the efforts of his predecessors in agronomical research. These encyclopedic attempts are not, however, the only characteristic in the development of natural sciences in this period and we can also observe a very keen interest in botanical theory in an extremely important anonymous book, *ᶜUmdat al-ṭabīb fī maᶜrifat al-nabāt li-kull labīb* (Physician's Aid for the Knowledge of Plants that Can Be Used by Any Intelligent Person) which contains the first known attempt to classify plants into genera, species, and varieties before Andrea Cesalpino (1519–1603) and Georges Cuvier (1769–1832). A recent edition of this work (Rabat, 1990) ascribes it to the agronomer Abū al-Khayr al-Ishbīlī, mentioned above in the *ṭā'ifa* period.

Finally, the Almohad empire also saw a very important development of medicine that reaches, now, its second highest peak in the history of al-Andalus: the names to remember, here, are those of Abū Marwān ᶜAbd al-Malik ibn Zuhr (Avenzoar) (ca. 1092–1161) and that of the famous philosopher Abū al-Walīd ibn Rushd (Averroës) (1126–1198). Their attitudes toward medicine were entirely different: while Ibn Zuhr was a physician with an eminently practical spirit who aspired to give a solid background to the literature of the *kunnāsh* (collections of recipes often used by doctors that lacked a good theoretical preparation), Ibn Rushd appeared as the prototype of the *ḥakīm* (physician-philosopher) who—in his famous *Kulliyyāt fī-l-tibb* (*Colliget*, Generalities on Medicine)—pretended to integrate medicine into the general system of his thought, summarized Galen's works, and commented on them using the same methods he had applied to Aristotle while trying to reconcile his two authorities whenever he found a contradiction between them.

With the fall of the Almohad caliphate in 1232, al-Andalus had a long period (1232–1492) of pure agony. Its geographical extension was limited to the small Naṣrid kingdom of Granada. Contacts with Eastern Islam were rare and students usually completed their education in the Maghrib, where science had grown as a result of Andalusian seeds planted in the twelfth century. There was very little research done, and summaries and compilations were often the only scientific literature written. It is interesting, however, to remark that this period created two scientific institutions that were unknown until then in al-Andalus: the *madrasa* (the only institution of higher learning known in Islam, mainly dedicated to teaching law, but in which medicine and, perhaps, astronomy were occasionally taught), founded by Yūsuf I in Granada in 1349; the second institution is the *māristān* built in 1365–1367 by Muḥammad V, about which there is discussion on whether it was a hospital or an asylum for mentally ill patients.

On the whole there was a certain amount of uninterrupted scientific activity during the whole Naṣrid period that even affects mathematics: al-Qalaṣādī (c. 1412–1486 or 1506) plays an important local role in arithmetic and algebra. Astronomy is well represented by Ibn al-Raqqām (d. 1315)—author of an important book on the theory of sundials and of two sets of astronomical tables in the Zarqāllian tradition—and Ibn Bāṣo (d. 1316), who designed the last Andalusian universal astrolabe. There is reason to believe that there was astronomical activity until the very end: an astrolabe, with only one plate for the latitude of Granada, dated in 1481 has been recently published. The decay seems to be much stronger in the fields of botany, pharmacology, and agronomy: only the *urjūza* (a poem in *rajaz* meter) on agriculture written by Ibn Luyūn of

Almería (1282–1349) offers, once more, a compendium of Andalusian agronomy. A novelty in the period seems to be the interest in horses: five treatises dealing with hippology or hippiatrics are known. This is mainly due to the importance of these animals in warfare, a subject that, no doubt, interested the Naṣrids in Granada who used, in the siege of Huéscar (1324), a sort of gun loaded with gunpowder, probably for the first time in the history of medieval Spain.

Something should, finally, be said on the development of medicine, which was, without any doubt, the scientific discipline most cultivated in Granada. There are three names that deserve specific mention in this field: Muḥammad al-Shafra (d. 1360), Muḥammad al-Shaqūrī (b. 1327), and the famous polymath and politician Ibn al-Khaṭīb (1313–1375). Al-Shafra and al-Shaqūrī were practicing physicians whose works are full of references to their own experience especially in the case of the former, born in Crevillente, who studied surgery in Christian Valencia with a certain master Baznad (Bernat?) and who is never called *ṭabīb* (physician with a standard academic preparation) but rather *mutaṭabbib* (empyrical professional of medicine). Ibn al-Khaṭīb, on the contrary, is a pure scholar who probably never practiced medicine but who had read all the medical literature available to him and resumed it in his books on hygiene, embryology, and pathology. Ibn al-Khaṭīb was also one of the four Naṣrid authors who wrote on the famous Black Death of 1348 (Al-Shaqūrī was another), trying to establish its causes and the ways to prevent it: it is interesting to remark that the four of them agreed on contagion as the main cause for the spread of the epidemic. It is perhaps one of the last instances in which Andalusian science proved to be original.

JULIO SAMSÓ

Bibliography

Jayyussi, S. K. (ed.) *The Legacy of Muslim Spain*. 2 vols. Leiden, 1992.

Samsó, J. *Las ciencias de los antiguos en al-Andalus*. Madrid, 1992.

Vernet, J. *La ciencia en al-Andalus*. Seville, 1986.

Vernet, J., and J. Samsó (eds.) *El legado científico andalusí*. Madrid, 1992.

SCIENCE, CHRISTIAN

Guy Beaujouan once made the penetrating observation that science in medieval Spain was distinguished by four factors: its Muslim presence; the weakness of its universities; the early maturity of its languages; and the contribution of its Jews. This continues to remain a valuable characterization, though perhaps one might add a fifth factor he left implicit, the supportive role of its monarchs.

The coexistence of Muslim and Christian societies in the Iberian Peninsula made it a natural locus for intellectual transmission from very early times. From the second half of the tenth century, when Gerbert of Aurillac studied at Ripoll (whose MS 225 suggests the material available there) and brought back to France treatises on mathematics and astronomy, Spain was the principal center of Arabic-Latin translation; but the heyday of the translations was the twelfth century. Some of the translators (who often made use of a Jewish collaborator's knowledge of Arabic) were Spaniards—John of Seville (fl. 1140), for example, and Hugh of Santalla (fl. 1145). Others, like Hermann of Dalmatia or Robert of Chester, came from all over Europe and converged on the peninsula to engage in translation, as the fame of Arabic science grew. In the second half of the twelfth century translational activity centered on Toledo, where the Italian Gerard of Cremona was the most prolific figure: besides more than two dozen works on mathematics and astronomy (including the Toledan Tables of Azarquiel), Gerard rendered much of Aristotle's natural philosophical corpus into Latin, as well as medical writings of Galen, Rhazes, and Avicenna (the *Canon*). Michael Scot (Aristotle's *De animalibus*) in the first half of the thirteenth century and Arnau de Vilanova (works by Galen and Avicenna) in the second show how Spain continued to be a center of scientific translations for at least another century, though the rate of productivity fell off.

The new translations of Aristotle and Galen became the basis for scientific study in the new European universities of the thirteenth century—at Paris, Oxford, Bologna, and Montpellier, all of which were active intellectual centers before 1250. In contrast, Spain had only one important university in the thirteenth century: Salamanca, founded in 1227, which despite the two chairs in medicine given it by Alfonso X el Sabio of Castile remained primarily a school of law for its first two centuries of existence. The peninsula did give rise to some outstanding figures in thirteenth-century scientific thought, notably Peter of Spain (d. 1277) and Arnau de Vilanova (ca. 1250–1311), but both taught at foreign schools (Paris/Siena and Montpellier, respectively). The distinctive scientific philosophy or *ars* of Ramón Llull had a limited vogue in the later fourteenth century, but it was so peculiarly personal as to be incapable of full integration into European scholasticism. Lérida, the first university founded in the Crown of Aragón (1300), produced no scientific literature until a hundred years later, when Antoni Ricart developed some of Arnau's theories. Elsewhere in Spain cathedral schools did not soon develop into universities; their libraries show that the cathedrals found a practical use for scientific (particularly medical) knowledge but had no interest in elaborating or adding to it. The *Historia naturalis* of Juan Gil of Zamora (ca. 1275) at least proves that a Castilian Dominican could compile a scientific encyclopedia comparable to that of Thomas of Cantimpré or Vincent of Beauvais.

Rather than the university, the royal court would serve as a locus for scientific activity. In the third quarter of the thirteenth century Alfonso el Sabio instituted and supported a remarkable program of translation of Arabic works into Castilian, many united in the collection known as the *Libros del saber de astronomía*: it marks the first time that a Romance vernacular served as a medium for scientific thought. The Castilian texts had no circulation outside of Spain, however. One of them, the astronomical tables whose preparation the king had commanded—developed from the Toledan Tables but recalculated in 1272 on the basis of new observations—has long been supposed to have been the basis for the Latin Alfonsine Tables drawn up about 1327, but even this has recently been called into question.

It was the kings of Aragón-Catalonia who were the important patrons of Spanish science in the fourteenth century—most significantly Pedro IV the Ceremonious (r. 1336–1387). Pedro consciously emulated the achievements of Alfonso X in a variety of ways, and commissioned first Pere Gilbert and then Gilbert's disciple Dalmau ses Planes to make astronomical observations from 1361 to 1366, on the basis of which a set of tables for the meridian of Barcelona was finally completed by Jacob Corsino.

The work of Corsino, a Castilian Jew, is only one example of the contributions made to medieval science by the Spanish Jews, to an extent out of all proportion to their numerical presence in the population. They had often been indispensable linguistic mediators between Arabic scientific texts and Latin or Romance translations since the twelfth century, but they had an independent tradition of creative philosophical thought as well—as writers from Maimonides (born in Córdoba ca. 1135 and formed intellectually in Andalusia) to Hasdai Crescas (likely born in Barcelona, ca. 1340) reveal—that was definitively disrupted only with the Spanish pogroms of 1391. Patronized by the Christian monarchs, to whom they had more than linguistic skills to offer, it would be inappropriate to exclude them from an account of science within Christian society. Pedro IV's conquest of Mallorca (1343) brought the scientific accomplishments of the island's Jews to his attention: from the late 1350s men like Isaac Nafuci and Vidal and Bellshom Efraim produced for him not only treatises on astronomy and astrology but astronomical instruments (astrolabes, quadrants, compasses) and maps (as distinct from portolans), and the "Mallorcan school" of cartography helped provide the technical basis that made possible the fifteenth-century Age of Discovery.

Michael R. McVaugh

Bibliography

Beaujouan, G. *La science en Espagne aux XIVe et XVe siècles*. Paris, 1967.

———. *Science médiéval d'Espagne et d'alentour*. Aldershot, 1992.

Comes, M., R. Puig, and J. Samsó (eds.) *De astronomia Alphonsi Regis*. Barcelona, 1987.

García-Ballester, L. "Medical Science in Thirteenth-Century Castile: Problems and Prospects." *Bulletin of the History of Medicine* 61 (1987), 183–202.

Johannis Aegidii Zamorensis. *Historia naturalis*. Ed. A. Domínguez García and L. García Ballester. 3 vols. Salamanca, 1994.

Millás Vallicrosa, J. *Las tablas astronómicas del rey Don Pedro el Ceremonioso*. Madrid, 1962.

Poulle, E. "The Alfonsine Tables and Alfonso X of Castille." *Journal for the History of Astronomy* 19 (1988), 97–113.

Vernet, J. *La cultura hispanoárabe en Oriente y Occidente*. Barcelona, 1978.

———. (ed.) *Nuevos estudios sobre astronomía española en el siglo de Alfonso X*. Barcelona, 1983.

SCIENCE, JEWISH

Synopsis

Medieval Spain was the setting for an intense Jewish involvement in the scientific enterprise. Jews were active in just about every branch of science. Original scientific texts were composed in Hebrew and Arabic, and others were transcribed or translated into Hebrew. Scientific ideas penetrated into almost every branch of Jewish literature. Jews participated in several major projects sponsored by non-Jews, particularly the preparation of the astronomical tables associated with the names Al-Zarqāl, Alfonso X of Castille, and Pedro IV of Aragón. Hasdai ibn Shaprut minister to ʿAbd al-Raḥmān III (912–961), was instrumental in the translation into Arabic of Dioscorides's book on botany; in subsequent centuries, right up to the expulsion of 1492, many Jews served at the courts of Christian and Muslim rulers as physicians and astronomers. All in all, science seems to have been held in high esteem by Jews, and an acquaintance with its principal doctrines, if not a rather intimate knowledge, was requisite for anyone who desired intellectual recognition. Just about every philosophical treatise, including the mystical *Al-Hidāyah ilā farā'id al-qalūb* (*Duties of the Heart*) of

Baḥya ibn Paqudah as well as the Aristotelian *Emuna rama* (*High Faith*) of Abraham ibn Daūd, contain rather detailed, usually up-to-date and accurate, discussions of scientific import. Some works of poetry contain whole sections of exclusively scientific material; Ibn Gabirol's *Keter Malkhut* and Ibn Sahula's *Meshal ha-Qadmoni* are two examples. Many shorter poems, including liturgical hymns, take their theme from the sciences, especially astronomy. Exegetical writers frequently appealed to current scientific knowledge; the works of Moses Naḥmanides and Baḥya ben Asher, for instance, draw on a variety of sources in the sciences and pseudosciences. Abraham ibn Ezra criticized those who utilized biblical commentary as a forum for the display of scientific erudition. However, his own commentaries (which were composed after he left Spain) are not free of lengthy, cryptic excurses, and, in any event, the supercommentaries to his text, many of which were written in Spain in the fourteenth century, are a storehouse of medieval scientific and pseudoscientific lore.

The science that we are speaking of comprises, in general, the Aristotelian and Ptolemaic systems, whose ultimate harmonization with Judaism is the achievement of Maimonides, born in Spain but forced to flee at an early age. Certainly, however, Spanish Jews were exposed to a wide spectrum of scientific theories. Magic and pseudoscience were widely accepted, at least in theory. Some figures were attracted to far-out notions (for example, Ḥayyim Israeli, cousin of the famous fourteenth-century astronomer, who maintained that three-quarters of the earth's surface remains in primordial chaos).

On the other hand, Spain also witnessed the crystallization of sophisticated, fundamentally antiscientific religious perspectives that remain influential to the present day. The development of these quite complex viewpoints seems to be intimately related to the successful assimilation of science on the part of other Jewish thinkers and, in particular, to the perceived commonality of interest on the part of Jewish and non-Jewish intellectuals, something which at times proved stronger than the socioreligious barriers of that period and hence threatened the distinctiveness of the Jewish minority. Tensions are evident even before the Maimonidean controversies of the thirteenth and fourteenth centuries. Judah Halevi paid a good deal of attention to issues of science and Judaism in his *Kuzari*. His overriding concern is the uniqueness of the Jewish experience, and, in general, he has no objection to scientific investigations so long as they do not challenge the essential distinctiveness of the Jewish people. More complicated is the stance taken by Moses Naḥmanides of Girona (1194–1270). Although he espouses one half of the well-known *kalām* occasionalist doctrine—namely, the denial of any causality other than God's immediate will—he does not profess the other half (that is, atomism). The mixture of Aristotelianism, magic, and medicine that he accepts is indispensable for his biblical exegesis; and in his halakhic writings he decries the lack of anatomical observations on the part of his predecessors and offers some of his own. In short, Naḥmanides is rather eager to make use of the scientific knowledge of his day, but only after he has stripped science of any claim to be a self-sufficient explanatory system.

Survey

Several Jews composed encyclopedias. Abraham bar Ḥiyya's *Vesodei ha-Tevunah*, which survives only in part is a short work and concise. On the other hand, Judah ibn Mattka's *Midrash Ḥokhmah*, written in 1247, is a lengthy and comprehensive undertaking. Both these works emphasize the mathematical sciences, especially geometry and astronomy. By contrast, later endeavors contain little in the way of mathematics, highlighting instead natural philosophy, meteorology, and the description of terrestrial phenomena. Specimens are the *De'ot ha-Filosofim* of Shem Tov ibn Falaquera (d. ca. 1291), the *Shevilei Emunah* of Meir Aldabi (written in 1360), and a number of shorter works dating to the fourteenth century, such as *Ta'alumot Ḥokhmah* of Solomon ibn Gabbai and *Safer ha-Yesodot* of Joseph ben Joshua al-Lorqi.

The contribution of Jews to astronomy has been described elsewhere in this volume; it may be added that, in the medieval scheme, mathematical geography found its place in the astronomical literature, as did some mathematical topics, especially trigonometry. Turning to other branches of mathematics, we note Bar Ḥiyya's *Ḥibbur ha-Meshihah we-ha-Tishboret*, which contains an interesting derivation of the formula for the area of the circle; Plato of Tivoli's Latin translation of that work, *Liber embadorum*, was very influential. *Meyashsher ʿAqov*, which may have been written by the fourteenth-century apostate Abner of Burgos, contains an assortment of interesting material, for example, a construction of the asymptote to the conchoid. Isaac ben Moshe of Orihuela has left us a book on arithmetic. Finally, we must mention the valuable, as yet unstudied, compendium of one Aaron (fifteenth century); the unique copy is at Turin (MS A. V. 15). Medieval Jews do not display any keen interest in optics. A small section of Bar Ḥiyya's encyclopaedia treats this topic. The Arabic treatise of Aḥmad bin ʿIsa was transcribed into the Hebrew alphabet. The anatomy of the eye was discussed in the medical literature, and the psychology of perception was taken up in philosophical works.

We possess a very long list of Jewish physicians who served throughout the the Iberian Peninsula in the service of both Muslim and Christian rulers; only a few may be mentioned here. Isaac ibn Yashush, known also as Ibn Kastār (d. 1056), at Denia; Moses ha-Levy Abulafia (d. 1235) at Seville; in the service of the kings of Castile, Joseph ben Judah ibn Ezra, to Alfonso VII (1126–1257), Judah al-Fakhar (ca. 1235); Isaac and Abraham ibn Waqār to Sancho IV (1284–1295); and Moses ibn Zarzal and Meir Alguadix to Juan I (1371–1390); Isaac Hamon, who served at Granada, in 1375; and Crescas, the Jewish occulist who successfully treated the cataracts of Juan II of Aragón (1458–1479). Queen Juana of Navarre, on a visit to France in 1349, went to some effort to summon there her personal physician, Salomon of Tudela. Solomon Bytol received a remuneration from Queen Isabel in 1476.

Jewish physicians engaged also in private practice. Indeed, many if not most savants supported themselves from medicine. This is true not just of philosophers, poets, and astronomers, but also the early cabalist Isaac ibn Laṭif (d. ca. 1290), and many rabbis as well. Jews untrained in the standard curriculum also engaged in the healing arts; in 1337, a Jewish woman, convicted of being an untrained practitioner, was pardoned by Pedro IV of Aragón.

The church was not indifferent to the widespread penetration of Jews into medicine. Several councils (for example, Zamora, 1313; Valladolid, 1322; Salamanca, 1335) forbade Christians from seeking treatment at the hands of Jews, and Spanish monarchs were reproached by the pope for the same offense, for example, Alfonso VIII in 1205. On the other hand, a papal bull of 1422 confirmed the right of Spanish Jews to practice medicine. The popular perception that Jews dominated the medical profession was exploited by some preachers, including Ramon Llull (1235–1315).

Toward the end of the eleventh century, Ibn Buklarish of Almería composed a work on simple remedies, listing the technical terms in Arabic, Syriac, Persian, Greek, Spanish, and Berber; his book is known only through quotations by a later author. In the next century, the Barcelonan Joseph ben Meir ibn Zabara set down the facts of anatomy in a poem, *Battei ha-Nefesh*; and his *Sefer ha-Sha'ashuim*, though not a scientific work, contains much medical and ancillary material. In the second half of the thirteenth century, Natan ben Joel ibn Falaquera published a large compendium, *Ẓori la-Guf*. Avicenna's *Canon* seems to have been a particularly popular text. Joseph ben Joshua al-Lorqi translated and commented on part of that huge book sometime before 1402. Solomon ben Ya'ish of Seville (ca. 1280) Isaiah ben Isaac of Córdoba (ca. 1350), and Shem Tov ben Isaac ibn Shaprut of Tudela (ca. 1380–1400) also wrote commentaries to Avicenna. The apostate Johannes Hispalensis is perhaps the best known among the translators of medical works. Solomon ben David ibn Daūd, who translated Averroës *Canon* into Hebrew, was probably a Spaniard.

Y. TZVI LANGERMANN

Bibliography

Friedenwald, H. *The Jews and Medicine: Essays.* Baltimore, 1944.

Langermann, Y. T. "The Making of the Firmament: Ḥayyim Yisraeli, Isaac Israeli, and Maimonides," *Mehqerei Yerushalayim bi-Mahshevet Yisrael (S. Pines Festschrift)* 7, no. 1 (1988), 461–76; in Hebrew.

Vera, F. *Los judíos y su contribución a las ciernias exactas.* Buenos Aires, 1948.

SCULPTURE, GOTHIC, PORTUGAL

Gothic sculpture in Portugal spans the period from the mid-thirteenth century to the end of the fifteenth century. It incorporates, in order of importance, funerary art, devotional statues, and monumental sculpture, and displays influences from Spain, France, England, and to a lesser extent, Italy. The materials employed are directly related to the locale; thus, marble is used in Evora and Alemtejo, limestone in Coimbra and the surrounding areas, and granite in the north, where there were convenient connections with Galicia.

Three phases of funerary art can be discerned, the first of which corresponds to the latter part of the thirteenth century, with especially strong presence in Coimbra, Santarém, Lisbon, and Évora. The earliest preserved recumbent funerary monument is that of Rodrigo Sanches (d. 1245), created immediately following his death. In the Cathedral of Coimbra three interesting sepulchers of other bishops are preserved; particularly notable are the tombs of Tiburcio (d. 1246) and Egas Fafes (d. 1268), both especially dramatic expressions of the recumbent figure. After the mid-thirteenth century, the use of noble shields in the front part of the sarcophagus becomes popular.

The golden age of funerary sculpture covers the reigns of Dinis, Alfonso IV, Pedro I, and Fernando I, roughly from 1279 to 1383. The first of these rulers is buried in Odivelas. His tomb dates from about 1324 and displays the recumbent king on top of the sarcophagus, which is decorated with trilobate arches framed by gables, and with pairs of personages that participated in the king's funerary rites. In the same church, the empty tomb of María Alfonso (Dinis's illegitimate daughter) is preserved. The tomb of Leonor Alfonso, from around 1325, displays pairs of conversing figures beneath trilobate arches that evoke the Catalan sculpture of the time. In Évora, the cathedral is the center of funerary sculpture production, and the marble from Estremoz lends particular elegance to the works. One of the most outstanding is the tomb of Bishop Pedro (d. 1340), builder of the cloister and the funerary chapel.

Coimbra, however, was the most prosperous center of funerary art, beginning with the superb tomb of the queen, St. Isabel, wife of Dinis. Now located in the Convent of Santa Clara la Nueva, the work—like the tomb of the queen's granddaughter Isabel—originally resided in the Monastery of Santa Clara la Vieja, where Isabel requested to be buried. The sepulcher was carved before Isabel's death in 1336, and six lions serve as a foundation for the free-standing tomb. The four faces of the tomb are occupied by trilobate arches framed by gables, with figures of saints, martyrs, and bishops individually placed beneath each arch. Presiding over the ensemble are the Crucifixion and the Virgin, accompanied by angels and saints. The recumbent figure is extraordinary beneath a canopy, she is dressed as a queen and in the Franciscan habit commonly used for royal burial. At the head are two angels, with a small dog at the feet; below are several additional dogs, alternating with several shields. Stylistically, the work is related to Catalan sculpture, specifically to the royal tombs in Santes Creus, where Isabel's father Pedro III was buried.

Isabel's monument displays several similarities in both style and layout to the beautiful tomb of Bishop Gonzalo Pereira in the chapel of la Gloria, built in 1332 by Pereira himself for his burial in the cathedral of Braga. The master sculptors, Pedro de Coimbra and Tello García de Lisboa, contracted the work on 11 June 1334. It is a free-standing tomb, with figures of the Apostles and twelve deacons on the long sides, the Crucifixion and the lion and bull of St. Mark and St. Luke at the head, and the Virgin with Child at the feet. It is believed that the tomb is the work of Tello García and that the more accomplished recumbent statue, dressed in pontifical robes, is the work of Pedro, who has been considered a renovator of Portuguese Gothic sculpture, lending his figures a realistic touch, with faces embued with a sense of tranquility. Contemporary works include the tombs of Juan Gordo (1340–1350) in the cathedral of Oporto, Domingo Joanes and his wife in the chapel of the Ferreiros de Oliveira do Hospital, and doña Vataça in the cathedral of Coimbra.

In the region of upper Beira, a considerable number of granite sepulchers with hunting scenes were created; these are similar to Galician works of funerary sculpture like the tomb of Fernan Pérez de Andrade (finished before 1387), who built a large sepulchral chapel for his family in San Francisco de Betanzos.

The two most beautiful tombs of the Portuguese Gothic are clearly those of Pedro I and Inés de Castro, now found in the transept but originally in the hall of tombs at the Monastery of Alcobaça. Carved in limestone, the tombs were created in 1360 by unknown masters. They are free-standing works, with the king's tomb mounted on figures of lions, and that of doña Inés on sphinxes. The faces of each tomb is occupied by different figures, but the style and composition are similar, with the scenes of each tomb displayed beneath trilobate arches with small rose windows under gables. In the uppermost part the shields of each monarch alternate. The dimension and structure of the work, as well as the rose window that dominates the head of Pedro's tomb and the image of the Final Judgment at the head of Inés's tomb, all show a general dependence on architecture. The rose window, with scenes that are hard to interpret, seems to be identified with the Wheel of Fortune, an image frequently used in Gothic art and in the literature of the time. It also portrays the terrible history of the young Pedro, later king, and his wife Inés who, assassinated, will reign after death. The inscription A.E.A. FIM DO MUNDO refers to the anticipation of the end of the world, a theme that continues with the representation of the Final Judgment on Inés's tomb. Her sepulcher is a very detailed work, though it never loses its monumental character. The decoration of the tomb is filled with scenes from the life of Christ, with the Calvary at the head. Pedro's tomb is dedicated to the life of St. Bartholomew, his patron. The recumbent figures, particularly that of Inés, are handsome: both rest on pillows and are under the watch of groups of six angels, with a dog at the feet. This period of funerary sculpture concludes with the tomb of Fernando I (d. 1383), buried in the church of San Francisco de Santarém, where he executed important reforms in order to display his sepulcher in the new choir of the convent. The stigmatization of St. Francis connects the work with royal Neapolitan tombs of the same century, such as that of Catherine of Austria in S. Lorenzo Maggiore.

The last period, which brings about important sculptural renovations, begins with the Avís dynasty in 1385 and concludes with the reign of Manuel. Juan I and his wife Felipa of Lancaster were the founders of the Monastery of Batalha, and asked to be buried in a funerary chapel. The double tomb, which would give rise to a school of funerary sculpture including the tombs of Pedro de Meneses (ca. 1437), Fernando de Meneses and his wife doña Brites, and Pedro Esteves de Cogominho, was created before the king's death (1433). The significant English influence in the work came to Portugal through two channels: the queen, and the master builder of the monastery, Huguet, who worked at Batalha between 1402 and 1432. Both figures are sheltered by canopies. This layout will be repeated in the extraordinary tomb of Duarte Meneses, commissioned shortly after 1464 to contain the only remains—a tooth—of the deceased, killed in the battle of Alcácer Seghr. He was buried in San Francisco de Santarém and his tomb displays an appropriate heroic symbology.

Juan Alfonso's signature appears on the tomb of Fernán Gomes de Gois. The work employs a traditional structure repeated insistently throughout the fifteenth century, and is located in the church of Oliveira do Conde.

Several works of the last quarter of the fifteenth century are attributed to Diego Pires o Velho, including the tombs of Fernando Tellez de Meneses and the count of Ourem. The first work, located in the Convent of San Marcos de Coimbra, dates from 1481 and employs Venetian patterns in the sumptuous curtainry, and Castilian forms in the crowning of the arcosolio.

Another genre of interest is the devotional statue, which was particularly remarkable during the fourteenth and fifteenth centuries. These sculptures typically portray Christ, the Virgin, and the Saints. There are three notable crucifixes, of which the most important is the one found in the Museo Machado de Castro in Coimbra. This work is of the Gothic *doloroso* type, and is related to the Aragónese crucifixes of the fourteenth century. Like the Aragónese works, the Portuguese crucifix is of considerable size with a wide tunic typical of German-derived works.

Representations of the Virgin are the most numerous. Pedro de Coimbra, creator of the tomb of Gonzalo Pereira, was most likely the craftsman of a significant group of Virgin statues that are incorporated into Gonzalo's monument. These works display a softly curved body, and an oval face framed by wavy hair and almond eyes. The Virgen de la O in the Museo Machado de Castro, with a melancholic gaze, is particularly beautiful. This iconography may have extended into Galicia along with the angel of the Annunciation, which was highly esteemed in Spain: its first appearance is in the cathedral of León around 1300. A French influence with Hispanic elements is detected in a group of Virgins whose prototype is found in the cathedral of Braga: the later versions are in the chapel of the Ferreiros de Oliveira do Hospital, Nuestra Señora de las Nieves in the sanctuary of the Flor de Rosa in Crato, Seo de Oporto, and one in the Vilhena collection. The Virgin of the cloister of the cathedral of Évora, on a *mensula* (table) with two angels, recalls the same subject as it was interpreted in the Parisian workshops of the thirteenth century. It is one of the most beautiful works of Portuguese devotional imagery.

There are also interesting representations of saints, like that of Santa Agueda in the museum of Coimbra; and San Nicolás, Santiago, and San Pedro from the old Vilhena collection of Lisbon (now in the Museo de Arte Antiga). There is a Santa Clara in the same collection, and another in the Museo de Oporto. Other pieces of interest are the statue of St. George killing the dragon, in the hermitage of São Jorge de Aljubarrota in Calvaria de Cima, and a group of the Annunciation in granite in Carracedo de Montenegro. The sculpture in relief of the Nativity in the church of São Leonardo de Atouguía in Baleia displays a style clearly derived from fourteenth-century France. The placement of the Christ Child, seated—not like a newborn—with the terrestrial globe and receiving with the right hand the book that Mary offers him, is derived from the symbolism of Christ as both master/teacher and Lord of the world.

One of the most interesting works of Portuguese sculpture is the recumbent Christ, a classic piece in the bibliography of Portuguese art. In 1984, Bracons proposed its possible link to Catalan sculpture of the fourteenth century, a theory founded in the work's place of origin, the monastery of Santa Clara la Vieja in Coimbra, which was founded by the queen of Portugal, Isabel of Aragón. This Christ appears wrapped in a shroud, on top of the sepulchral slab with the sleeping soldiers below. The work dates to the late fourteenth century.

In the fifteenth century, João Alfonso de Oliveira do Conde is attributed with various Virgins and two statues of Santa Marina and Santa Catalina in the Vilhena collection; these works share stylistic similarities with the tomb signed by João Alfonso in Oliveira do Conde. These sculptures possess a lithe quality, with bodies inscribed in a curvacious pattern. There are works of a similar nature produced in the Mondego valley—São Gens de Boelhe, Tábua, Bobadela, Cantanhede, Sepins—among which a Santa Lucía (of Alhadas) and a São Miguel, now in the Museo Nacional de Arte Antiga in Lisbon, stand out.

The Corpo de Deus altarpiece, dated 1443 and now in the Museo Machado de Castro in Coimbra, recalls other contemporary works of Catalonia. This polychromatic work is of eucharistic nature, with two angels supporting a chalice with the host beneath three large canopies. The piece was commissioned by Alvaro Fernandez de Carvalho, and is stylistically similar to the São Pedro de Arouca, an image that was influential in the upper Beira region. Documents show that between 1473 and 1514 Diego Pires o Velho lived in

Coimbra, where he sculpted a statue of the Virgin for the church of Leça da Palmeira, commissioned by King Alfonso V. From this figure an interesting group of statues are derived.

In terms of architectural sculpture, interesting works include the capitals of the Monastery of Celas (consecrated in 1293), the facade of the cathedral of Évora, and the facade of the church at the Monastery of Batalha. The Évora facade dates from around the third decade of the fourteenth century, considering that the works were commissioned by Bishop Pedro between 1322 and 1340. In these pieces one can detect a French influence filtered through the Catalan style of the time. The Apostles are displayed in elegant form, with expressions reflecting a delicate melancholic touch. The main facade of the Monastery of Batalha, from the early fifteenth century, has undergone significant restoration, and some of its statues have been replaced. The group was inspired by the maestro Huguet, and exerted considerable influence on Portuguese sculpture of the fifteenth century. Other exemplary facades include the main facade of the Cathedral of Antuérpia and the episcopal facade of the Cathedral of Palencia.

ANGELA FRANCO MATA

Bibliography

Chicó, M. *A Arquitectura Gótica em Portugal*. 3d. ed. Lisbon, 1981.

———. *História da Arte em Portugal*. Vol. 2. Oporto, 1948. 135–176.

Dias, P. *História da Arte em Portugal*. Lisbon, 1986, 1111–37.

Dos Santos, R. *Oito Séculos de Arte Portuguesa*. Lisbon, n.d.

Junta de Castilla y León, Consejería de Cultura, *Relaciones artísticas entre Portugal y España*, Salamanca, 1986.

Rincón García, W. "Arte Medieval." In *Arte Portugués, Summa Artis* vol. 30. Madrid, 1986. 126–52.

SEGOVIA

City and diocesis capital in Old Castile. The region where the city is now located was populated as early as the Bronze and Iron Ages. Inexplicably, the Roman aqueduct built by Trajan or Nerva does not match the few other Roman ruins of the area.

In the mid-sixth century, the archbishop of Toledo, Montano, granted lifetime jurisdictional rights over Segovia to a cleric who had been named Bishop of Palencia without his consent. By 589, as the Council of Toledo shows, the diocese (which included Coca and Buitrago) had its own bishop.

In the Early Middle Ages, Segovia was located in the so-called Extramadura castellana. The theory of the Duero River valley depopulation in the latter part of the eighth century is well known. The scope of this phenomenon has been debated, but it was clearly a reality in Segovia, as is shown in the Christian repopulation efforts ordered by Alfonso VI and brought about by his son-in-law Raimundo de Borgoña in 1088. There are documents that describe the region previously as a barren land through which bears and wild boars roamed. Ilderedo recognized the existence of the new diocese of Simancas in 940, which was also the year of the repopulation of Sepúlveda. The new settlers in the area came initially from Burgos and la Rioja, then from Navarre, Aragón, and even Galicia and Portugal. There were also some French settlers, as one street referring to *gascos* (Gascons) attests.

The city and its surrounding villages constituted a district called a *Comunidad de villa y tierra*, which extended to the other side of the central mountain range, and still is in operation. The diocese, under the jurisdiction of Toledo, was restored in 1119, with the Cluniac Pedro de Agen as its first bishop. San Frutos, a hermit that had lived in the last years of the Visigothic era in the Duratón canyon in Sepúlveda (since 1076 the Benedictine convent of Silos), was adopted as patron saint of the diocese. During this period many Romanesque churchs were built, characterized by their atria.

The city militia participated in the reconquest of New Castile and Andalusia. Starting in the fourteenth century textile production developed; Salvador de Madariaga called Segovia the Manchester of its time, and the main cattle pathways (*cañadas*) of the *mesta* (sheep-herders' guild) passed through the region. The city played an important part in the dynastic and aristocratic conflicts of the fourteenth and fifteenth centuries. It was the favorite city of Enrique IV, who was almost a permanent resident. In 1474 Isabel la Católica was proclaimed Queen of Castile in the church of San Miguel.

ANTONIO LINAGE CONDE

Bibliography

Asenjo González, M. *Segovia. La ciudad y su tierra a fines del medievo*. Segovia, 1986.

Colmenares, D. *Historia de Segovia*, [1637]. Ed. Academia de San Quirce, Segovia, 1969.

SEPHARDIM *See* JEWS

SEPULCHRE, ORDER OF THE HOLY *See* MILITARY ORDERS

SERFDOM *See* FEUDALISM, PEASANTS

SERMONS

A sermon is a type of hortatory religious discourse, or homily, that traces its origins back to the first days of Christianity. The earliest form of sermons manifested itself principally as a running commentary on a biblical passage. By the thirteenth century, however, this had been displaced by a type of oration known as the university sermon, which was usually plotted out roughly in writing and delivered orally in Latin. It reflected scholasticism's interest in rhetoric and logic, requiring the use of elaborate formal divisions and distinctions. From about 1220 onward, in part moved forward by the recommendations of the Fourth Lateran Council (1215), the rules for composing these new sermons were codified in the *artes praedicandi*, extended theoretical treatises that dealt with everything from the formal aspects of the composition of sermons to their content and reception. The great majority of preserved medieval sermons are of the university type because some form of them was often committed to writing. Research has shown a close link between the sermon tradition, its use of *exempla*, or illustrative anecdotes, and the rise of imaginative vernacular literature in medieval Europe.

Until relatively recently, little was known, and little research had been carried out, on the vernacular sermon tradition in medieval Iberia. In the last twenty years, however, important new findings have emerged. Although very few sermons in relation to the number that daily must have been preached during the Middle Ages survive due to their oral delivery, current research has increased the number above the mere ten that originally were thought to have been preserved in Castilian or Aragónese. The greatest number of extant peninsular sermons are in Catalan, 160, of which 150 are by St. Vincent Ferrer. The rest, a little over 100 texts, is comprised of sermons in Latin. There are no known Portuguese sermons. A sum nearing three hundred is thus thought to be the total for the surviving vernacular sermons in all the Iberian languages, the vast majority of which remain unedited and in manuscripts. A very slim number is available in modern editions. As more and more Iberian libraries are systematically cataloged, however, references to sermons will doubtless continue to increase.

E. Michael Gerli

Bibliography

Cátedra, P. M. *Los sermones atribuidos a Pedro Marín*. Salamanca, 1990.

———. *Los sermones medievales en romance de la Real Colegiata de San Isidoro de León*. Salamanca, 2002.

———. *Sermón, sociedad y literatura en la Edad Media. San Vicente Ferrer en Castilla (1411–1414)*. Salamanca, 1994.

———. "Spanish Sermon Studies," *Medieval Sermon Studies Newsletter* 1 (1978), 18–19.

Deyermond, A. D. "The Sermon and Its Uses in Medieval Castilian Literature." *La Corónica* 8, no. 2 (1979–80) 127–45.

Rico, F. *Predicación y literatura en la España medieval*. Cádiz, 1977.

Sánchez Sánchez, M. A. *La primitiva predicación española medieval*. Salamanca, 2000.

SERRANILLA

A subgenre of lyric poetry characterized by the chance meeting in the countryside of a gentleman of the court with a rustic girl, and his ensuing attempt to seduce her, the *serranilla* seems to have its origins in the Provençal *pastourelle*, a learned form depicting such encounters whose earliest examples were parodies of courtly love. The Spanish version, however, is probably a hybrid of this courtly poetic form and medieval legends of dangerous mountain women that also appeared in popular song.

In the typical serranilla, the courtier recounts his travels through the sierra and his coincidental encounter with a shepherdess, whom he greets in a courtly manner that contrasts with her rustic character. It is at this point that poems of this genre begin to differ in the outcome of the initial conversation. Some peasant girls attempt to ward off the traveler with their rudeness; others, flattered by his courtly approach, immediately acquiesce to his desires. In the former case, the *caballero* (gentleman) will persevere in his persuasions with promises of gifts or a future life with him at the court, or further flattery. Possible resolutions include the seduction of the shepherdess, her continued rejection of his advances and subsequent departure from the scene, or an open denouement, in which the outcome of the episode is uncertain. Unlike some provençal examples, the Spanish pastoral lyric never depicts force used by the courtier in order to take by coercion what he is unable to obtain through persuasion, nor the arrival of peasant men to rescue the girl from possible violence.

An important element of the serranilla is its objective of contrasting the social classes of the protagonists; the "amorous" intentions of the gentleman never amount to more than licentious pursuit of a woman of humble birth who, by virtue of her low condition, is considered unworthy by him for the noble sentiments of courtly love. The serranilla was commonly recited to a court audience upon the return of a nobleman from a journey; thus the aristocratic public could share in the "humor" of a country lass's ingenuousness. The underlying note is, of course, one of disdain for the peasant class—particularly of its women—and the hypocrisy of the courtier in his veiled attempt to humiliate them.

There also exists a parodic version of the serranilla, notably in the *Libro de buen amor*. (Indeed, the first known pastourelle—written by the Provençal poet Marcabru in the twelfth century—is a mockery of courtly love and lovers.) In this variation, it is the shepherdess who initiates the ardent conversation; unlike the hypocritical man of the traditional form, she does not pretend to seek more than a brief, lascivious adventure. The female protagonist of the farcical model is normally of grotesque appearance contrived to be the antithesis of the era's concept of the ideal woman.

The most famous serranillas—and the best of this class of poetry—are the works of the Marqués de Santillana. It was he who first used the term "serranilla" to refer to these pieces, and his examples epitomize the genre. Santillana finds his inspiration in the classical *pastourelle* as well as the *Libro de buen amor*'s parody of it; unlike these predecessors, however, Santillana never allows the courtly lover to be scorned. A particular feature of these pastoral poems is their realism: the poet provides historical and geographical detail that allow the pieces to be dated and related to specific expeditions outside the court. As his ambition was to contribute in a significant way to the poetry of his era, Santillana takes advantage of a stock poetic context in order to provide variations on the theme: he changes meter, rhyme, the attitudes of the protagonists, and the outcome of the poetic moment to create a series of distinctly diverse serranillas. His treatment of this genre has never been equaled by those who preceded or followed him.

After the Marqués de Santillana, other poets attempted serranillas with varying success: The most notable among them was Carvajales, whose poetic production appears in the *Cancionero de Stúñiga*. Carvajales's pieces are characterized by the idealization of country life; indeed, he alters the traditional serranilla so that the rustic ambience becomes the salient feature, and replaces the shepherdess with a courtly lady. Other poets who composed serranillas are Pedro de Escavias, Fernando de la Torre, Francisco Bocanegra, Mendo de Campo, and Diego de San Pedro.

NANCY F. MARINO

Bibliography

Lapesa, R. "Las serranillas del Marqués de Santillana." In *El Comentario de textos*, 4th ed. Madrid, 1983, 243–76.

Marino, N. *La serranilla española: Notas para su historia e interpretación*. Potomac, Md., 1987.

SESMARIAS

Sesmarias were lands that the Portuguese medieval municipalities used to distribute to their inhabitants with the condition of their being cultivated within a certain time and thus satisfying *solving* the quitrents established by tradition or by the *forais* (privileges).

The need for settlement and colonization of many territories conquered by the Muslims during the eleventh to thirteenth centuries led to a number of forms of land grants for unused land. On the other hand, the general rise of population in western and southwestern Europe in the same period and afterward compelled the clearing of forests and fallow ground. In order to assure some discipline in land appropriation, municipal deputies, appointed by the king or elected among the aldermen, were in charge of granting all land that might be disposed of within the city limits. As there were usually six deputies in charge, each one was known as a *sesmeiro* (latin *seximus*, one-sixth), the land to be divided as a *sesmo* and the fraction distributed to each person as a *sesmaria*. Documented examples of *sesmarias* date from the early thirteenth to the late fifteenth centuries throughout most of Portugal and also in the new discovered islands of Madeira and the Azores, and in Brazil.

Being a form of land appropriation rather than a form of property, there were sesmarias granted in full property (*allodium*) as well as in long-term leases. Tilling the ground was always compulsory, although the stated periods varied from short terms (six months, one year) to indeterminate ones.

After 1348, the economic crisis aggravated by the Black Death and other plagues generated new interest in the sesmaria system. Several laws enacted by kings Afonso IV, Pedro I, Fernando I, and João I tried to make many lands productive that their holders had deserted, either by death or by emigration. They also forced rural and nonrural laborers to work for the same salaries and in the same way and place they always had. A system of passports was created to prevent open housing, and workers were apportioned among the proprietors. The law of 1375 (known as *Lei das Sesmarias*) went further in binding the workers to their traditional professions, preventing labor freedom, keeping wages low, and harassing the idle and the vagrant. In spite of this and other local regulations, enacted in the late fourteenth and early fifteenth centuries, the trend toward labor freedom, or at least greater labor freedom, continued. One hundred years later, a significant, if not a decisive, part of all labor was entirely free, and employment based on revocable and temporary hiring contracts.

A. H. OLIVEIRA MARQUES

Bibliography

Rau, V. *Sesmarias Medievais Portuguesas*. 2d ed. Lisbon, 1982.

Oliveira Marques, A. H. de. *History of Portugal*, 2d ed. New York, 1976.

SEVILLE, CITY OF

Seville is situated on the banks of the Guadalquivir River, to which it owes its existence and the role it has played throughout history as the center of an extensive hinterland and as a renowned port of call on the great international trading routes. Conquered by the Arabs in 712, it became the second city of al-Andalus and when the Umayyad caliphate was defeated, Seville became the capital of the most important kingdom to rise from its ruins. This position was maintained under the Almoravids and Almohads. Throughout these centuries a new city came into being, dominated by a local aristocracy that extended the perimeter of its city walls (287 hectares) and created a new city center that was consolidated in later centuries.

In 1248 Fernando III of Castile and León conquered the city. After a few decades of difficulties, natural conditions helped to make it one of the most important urban centers in the Iberian Peninsula, with more than three-thousand inhabitants at the end of the fourteenth century, increasing to some eight thousand in about 1500. The large perimeter of the city walls made an extension of these unnecessary, although districts grew up beyond the city walls for strategic and economic reasons. An urban structure, taking form around the cathedral and the Church of El Sạlvador, came about and remained for centuries. In this area, where the majority of the population was concentrated, administrative, religious, and economic centers were formed. The greatest part of the population (60 percent) was involved in craftwork and the maritime professions, serving a local and regional market; some 30 percent was involved in commerce and the service sector; around 6 percent made its living from agriculture and livestock. In the social order attention is drawn to the consolidation of an aristocracy, whose power is based on resources that come from their rural properties, and connected to trade at high levels, and a monopoly of local government; a numerous contingent of Franks (some fifteen hundred inhabitants in the fifteenth century); the presence of an influential foreign colony, above all Italian, that controlled trade at high levels; and a noteworthy Jewish community, most of whom after the pogroms of 1391 became converts.

La Giralda (ancient minaret of Seville mosque). Islamic, 12th century. Copyright © Giraudon/Art Resource, NY. Tower of Giralda, Seville, Spain.

ANTONIO COLLANTES DE TERÁN SÁNCHEZ

Bibliography

Boch Vilá, J. *Historia de Sevilla. La Sevilla islámica (712–1248)*. Seville, 1984.

Colantes de Terán Sánchez, A. *Sevilla en la Baja Edad Media: La ciudad y sus hombres*, Seville, 1984.

Ladero Quesada, M. A. *Historia de Sevilla: La ciudad medieval*, 3d ed. Seville, 1989.

SHAQUNDĪ, AL-

Abū-l-Walid Ismāʿīl Ibn Muḥammad al-Shaqundī, *qāḍi* (judge) in Baeza, Ubeda and Lorca, was born in Secunda near Córdoba and died in Seville (1231) a few years before the city was conquered by Ferdnando III of Castile. A poet in his own right, he is better known for his contribution to the genre of literary epistle. His *Risāla fi fadl al-andalus* (*Epistle on the Excellence of al-Andalus*) was considered of sufficient interest by the famous historian of al-Andalus, al-Maqqarī (d. 1631) as to be included in its entirety in his *Nafḥ at-ṭib*. The *Risāla* was conceived as a rejoinder to the praise of North Africa made by Abū Yaḥyā Muʿallim from Tangiers, with whom he had a learned discussion in the presence of the governor of Ceuta, A. Yaḥyā ibn Zakariyya. It was the governor who requested both to put their respective arguments in writing.

Al-Shaqundī's references to political figures, learned men and scientific achievements, famous poets and their compositions, cities and the artistic monuments by which they were known, which he summarized with exceptional sensitivity and good sense and expressed in a pleasant and elegant style, make this *risāla* a reliable source of information and a notable literary work. It is also of special interest for its unequivocal assertion of an Andalusian cultural identity and national conciousness against North African political, religious, and cultural imperialism in the Iberian Peninsula since the Almoravid invasion in the eleventh century.

VICENTE CANTARINO

Bibliography

García Gómez, E. *Al-Sequndi, Elogio del Islam Español*. Madrid and Granada, 1934.

Al-Maqqarī, *Nafḥ al-ṭib*. Ed. R. Dozy et al. Leiden, 1855–1860. 4:177–208.

SHEEP RAISING

The often sharply contrasting ecological patterns of the Iberian countryside, the frequent unsuitability for arable farming of extensive portions of the vast, elevated, mountain-strewn interior tableland of the *meseta* (plateau), and the manifest advantages during centuries of Reconquest warfare of mobile over fixed properties, all contributed to tilting medieval Spaniards and Portuguese in many regions toward a predominantly pastoral agrosystem atypical of western European mixed-crop and animal-husbandry agriculture. Roman Spain was already known for its superior wools; the *Leges Wisigothorum* show how on a drastically reduced commercial plane a pastoral economy persisted below the Pyrenees; and Islamic al-Andalus long possessed a flourishing sheep industry, producing milk for cheese, meat, and fleece for cloth making, an industry that was to bequeath some of its Berber pastoral vocabulary to the Christian north.

But it was the Luso-Hispanic states of the Middle Ages, commencing in the high Pyrenean and Cantabrian valleys, that were to advance far beyond such antecedents to create a dynamic complex of superior animals, skilled herdsmen (*pastores*), highly institutionalized forms and techniques, and an ever-expanding output of high-quality wools that by 1500 was to give Spain first place as supplier to the western European cloth markets and founder of even greater ovine empires in the New World.

The sheep upon which medieval Iberian pecuarialism rested were originally old native breeds of prehistoric origin such as the widespread, relatively coarse-fleeced, mottled-white churro; but this picture was radically altered by the introduction and rapid diffusion of the uniquely fine-fibered, heavy-fleeced North African merino breed, derived ultimately, as its name indicates, from the Merinid peoples of Atlantic Morocco. Just when this change began has been hotly contested; but so far as our known documentation goes, it did not antedate 1350 by much, and, after being perfected by Iberian Peninsular breeders, the merino swiftly became the lucrative staple insuring Spain's paramountcy in the European wool market.

A notable feature of peninsular sheep raising throughout the Middle Ages is its heavy dependence on transhumance, that is, the seasonal transfer of flocks from winter feeding grounds (*invernaderos*) to summer grazings (*agostaderos*) high in the mountains. This commonly operated within the boundaries of a single municipality or village community using the nearest sierra; but it could also take the form of more extensive highland foraging on the basis of intercommunal compacts, as with the Arago-Catalan *facerías* of the Pyrenees, Navarrese Salazar, and Rocal linkage with the Bárdenas Reales near Tudela, or the *hermandades* of the Castilian towns flanking the central Sierras. The long-distance transhumance of the *mesta* (sheep raisers guild) over the sheep highways (*cañadas*) between northern León-Castile and the southern meseta pasturages in Extremadura, New Castile (La Mancha), Murcia, and Andalusia are well known; others of lesser magnitude also existed in Portugal leading to the Serra da Estrêla, or in the Crown of Aragón running between the Pyrenees, the lower Ebro River valley, and the Valencian Maestrazgo.

Municipal *fueros* and *forais* (codes) show control over pastoral affairs normally retained by the town government; but in two areas there also arose partially self-governing local associations of sheepmen. After 1250 there appear in the Castilian kingdom between the central Sierras and Andalusia a certain number of municipal Mestas, with their own elected *alcaldes* and organized on the basis of a constitutional charter, the *ordenamiento de mesta*, commonly confirmed by the crown. Similarly after about 1250 *casas de ganaderos* developed in Aragón, notably that of Zaragoza and others are known for Arago-Catalan-Valencian lands as *ligallos* (or *lligallos*), under *jueces de ligallo* and ordinances.

Much is still to be learned regarding the life and practices of pastores, themselves often owners of small flocks; or about the lamb-sharing *partido* contracts between owners and chief herdsmen (*mayorales*, *rabadanes*), and the general cycle of the pastoral year from one San Juan to another. Shearing sheds, the baling of sheep clip, and cartage to commercial centers and ports also still await study.

C. JULIAN BISHKO

Bibliography

García Martín, P., and J. M. Sánchez Benito. *Contribución a la historia de la trashumancia en España*. Madrid, 1986.

Klein, J. *The Mesta*. Cambridge, Mass., 1920.

SHEM TOV OF CARRIÓN

Shem Tov Yiẓḥaq ben Arduti'el (ca. 1290–1360), Castilian rabbi and poet whose *Proverbios morales*, addressed to Pedro I and quoted in the Marqués de Santillana's *Prohemio e carta*, synthesizes Semitic poetics with the Spanish idiom in a permutation of a literary formula: the getting of wisdom. Its relative success has eclipsed Shem Tov's Hebrew compositions *Maʿaseh ha-rav*, a *maqáma* featuring a debate between pen and scissors; *Vam qohelet*, a *baqashah* consisting of two thousand words beginning with the letter *mem*; and, finally, *Ha-vidui ha-gadol*, a prayer of confession for Yom Kippur. This oeuvre provides a useful frame of reference for gauging the ethical, rhetorical, and philosophical dimensions of the *Proverbios morales*. Shem Tov also translated Yisra'el ha-Yisra'eli's liturgical treatise *Miẓvot zemaniyot* from Arabic into Hebrew; the authorship of other titles sometimes attributed to him is dubious. Excluding inferences from his work, the scant known biographical information is obtained from a *dīwán* (book of poetry) written by Shmu'el ben Yosef ben Sason, and places him in Carrión de los Condes in 1338.

Drawing on the language of paremiology, medieval philosophy, the Bible, Talmud, and Arabic wisdom anthologies, *Proverbios morales* examines the ostensible dilemma posed to the individual by the unpredictability of human existence and endorses adherence to the Aristotelian mean in ethical matters, recognition of circumstances in social conduct, and ultimate faith in the Creator. Here, all things exist in complementary opposition—night and day, loss and gain, and so on; therefore wealth is ephemeral, happiness is momentary, and power mere vanity. For the individual, successful negotiation of such a world requires the perspicacious appraisal of circumstance since an action once advantageous may now be disadvantageous, as Shem Tov shows in a paradox on speech and silence. For the monarch, God's representative, duty requires that he vouchsafe truth, justice, and peace, the foundations of political order.

The poem's language is consistent in its general phonetic, morphological, and syntactic features with medieval Castilian. Its distinctive traits include homoioteleuton rhyme, complex hyperbaton, phraseological parallelism, the prevalence of parataxis over hypotaxis, and the accumulation of grammatical functions in pleonastic pronouns.

The suggestion that the poem may be a vestige of a rabbinical *mester de clerecía* (clerical poetry) could ultimately establish its otherwise uncertain generic identity. The 725 alexandrine stanzas reveal a sustained tone of self-assurance in Shem Tov's poetic voice, equally adept at evoking poignancy, melancholy, or whimsy. The antonymic parallelism of his compositional technique, derived from Arabic and Hebrew poetics, sometimes interpreted as indicative of moral relativism, serves to enunciate extremes that define a center of equilibrium.

Each of the six extant manuscripts preserves multiple variants and stanza sequences, several suggest the complex social profile a single work may possess. One is redacted in Hebrew *aljamía* (Cambridge), another includes an anonymous prose prologue (Madrid), and a third records 219 stanzas written from memory and entered into evidence during proceedings for the crime of heresy (Cuenca). The first example implies genesis of the poem's main body for purposes of Jewish education. The latter pair allude to its essentially oral performance character; the commentator advocates memorizing the work, "que todo omne la deuiera decorar. Ca esta fue la entençio del sabio rraby que las fizo," ["that each person should memorize. That was the intention of the wise rabbi who made it"] and the defendant charged with heresy swears he recorded "quantas a la memoria me han venido" ["as many as have come to memory"].

That the *Proverbios morales* were presented to Pedro I for his edification seems apparent, but the assertion that it was written specifically for a Christian audience warrants appraisal. That hypothesis relies upon the poem's redaction in Castilian, an opening apostrophe and closing reference to Pedro I, and a *captatio benevolentiae* summarizing the Jewish poet's situation when addressing a Christian audience of superior social rank. The delivery of medieval Jewish sermons in a vernacular places a correlation between language choice and intended audience here in doubt. The use of the *V(os)* form of address, required for addressing a social superior, is limited to the poem's introductory and concluding passages, the main body prefers the *T(ú)* form suitable for an equal or inferior in status. It may be inferred therefore that Shem Tov composed the *Proverbios morales* for a destinatory of equal or inferior status—that is, the Jewish community, and redacted occassional material in order to accommodate the poem for presentation before a different audience.

A subtle poetic composition, *Proverbios morales* succeeds in incorporating the complexity of human existence into a persuasive discourse on ethics and philosophy that addresses the dynamic of the individual in society.

JOHN ZEMKE

Bibliography

Alarcos Llorach, E. "La lengua de los *Proverbios morales* de don Sem Tob," *Revisía de Filología Española* 35 (1951), 249–309.

Perry, T. A. *The "Moral Proverbs" of Santob de Carrion: Jewish Wisdom in Christian Spain*, Princeton, N.J., 1987.

Zemke, J. *Critical Approaches to the "Proverbios Morales" of Shem Tov de Carrión*. Newark, Del., 1997.

SHUSHTARĪ, AL-, ABŪ AL-ḤASAN

The medieval Hispano-Arabic mystical poet Abū al-Ḥasan al-Shushtarī (b. 1212), who was born and who lived most of his life in Muslim Spain, introduced the colloquial *zajal* to the field of Ṣūfi (Islamic mystical) poetry. The *zajal* is the well-known strophic poem that uses the colloquial as its medium—in this case, the Andalusian medieval dialect—and particularly originated in Muslim Spain during the Middle Ages. As a "popular" art form that had not been used before or thought appropriate for sublime Ṣūfi expression, the Hispano-Arabic zajal that existed at the time was especially perfected by another Andalusian poet, Ibn Quzmān, who mainly wrote satirical and courtly love zajals. There is today enough evidence that this type of zajal was performed, sometimes by means of choral singing. In the East, Ṣūfi poets like Ibn al-Farīd of Egypt (d. 577) had been using the classical form of the Arabic *qaṣīda*, with its traditional framework of monorhyme and monorhythm and with classical Arabic language to express Ṣūfi thoughts. In Spain, however, strophic poetry—namely the *muwashshaḥa* and the zajal—evolved in Andalusian Arabic verse, demonstrating the influence of Romance popular literature. In other words, the muwashshaḥa and the zajal in their inception in Arabic literature became uniquely associated with al-Andalus. But it was Al-Shushtarī who first chose the zajal for Ṣūfi purposes.

Therefore, most important about Al-Shushtarī in this context is that his strophic poetry forms a link between two areas of interest in the literature of Muslim Spain: the formal and esoteric, on the one hand (represented by the mystical philosophy of Ibn ʿArabī and Ibn Sabʿīn, two Ṣūfis whom Al-Shushtarī followed), and the "popular" aspect of the Hispano-Arabic literary world (represented by the informal zajal and its master, Ibn Quzmān) on the other. Through the unity of these two strands, Al-Shushtarī sought to interpret and make accessible mystical ideas and to propound an understanding of Ṣufism virtually synonymous with a vibrant, aesthetic perceptiveness. He therefore represents an important melding of the esoteric spirituality of Ṣūfism and a kind of emerging lay spirituality.

This yoking of a theological and an aesthetic perspective significantly illuminates the act and art of interpretation, which is the main area of concern in Al-Shushtarī's poetry. Ṣūfi scriptural (i.e., Qur'ānic) exegesis plays a fundamental role in this literary self-awareness that permeates the poetry. Consistent textual references such as "understanding" and "grasping allusions," "words," "terms," "symbols," or "signs" underline the concept of critical interpretation. Like all Ṣūfis, Al-Shushtarī did not deal with texts—scripture or otherwise—superficially. He constantly asked his audience to "untie symbols" and to "grasp ultimate meanings," urging them to think, to analyze, and to put parts of a poem together in the service of the whole, as if inviting them to join his Ṣūfi path by interpreting his songs. Hence, this literary self-consciousness ultimately reflects a mystical self-consciousness as well, while the Ṣūfi principle of Qur'ānic exegesis shaped the way Ṣūfi poets, such as Al-Shushtarī, composed poetry and the way they expected it to be interpreted.

Al-Shushtarī utilized the means provided by this mystical tradition for symbolic expression, but his innovation in the use of the zajal for such marks his contribution in the field. He could not merely depend on the techniques provided by traditional rhetoric to achieve a combination of artistry and mysticism. In al-Shushtarī, the concept of "interpretation" in itself becomes the main concern, and the poetry comes to express the interrelation between critical perceptiveness of text and mystical views. It is this integration that Al-Shushtarī's strophic poetry fully realizes.

This relationship between the lyrical and the mystical manifests itself in three main features that act as systems of reference and regulation that afford the audience effective ways of responding spiritually as well as aesthetically to the lyrics. These reference systems are regarded from the standpoint of their mystico-aesthetic correspondence to convey Al-Shushtarī's mystical and aesthetical philosophy simultaneously.

The first aspect is the idea of the multiple levels of meaning existing within the poems—that is, the symbolism. This feature directly translates into two areas of interest: the network of Ṣūfi doctrines and symbolic terminology as well as the literary self-conscious mode characterized by direct textual references. The major reference is that of *ramz* (symbol), hence underlying the symbolic composition of the poems and suggesting the application of symbolic interpretation in order to discern the text's binary dimension. In other words, Al-Shushtarī does not merely use symbols but calls attention to this use and to symbolic critical reading.

The second major area that also displays literary self-consciousness is structure—specifically ring composition and its relation to the theme of the "reflexive." The ring structure embodies a circular principle of interpretation, which is most appropriate to the Ṣūfi mode of perception and to the tradition of composing strophic poetry. Ṣūfi exegesis, called *ta'wī*, is the internal interpretation of the Qur'ān and seeks the inner level or primary meaning through returning the outward, literal plane of scripture to its original, hidden spiritual essence—hence a circular, reflexive movement. And in strophic poetry, the nature thereof allows the poet to utilize his strophes as movable structural units, which is more feasible than dealing with single lines in the more restrictive form of a classical qaṣida. Al-Shushtarī could also use the interplay between the different parts of the zajal or muwashshaḥa (such as the *matla*, the *qufl*, and the *kharja*) to solidify the ring composition. Moreover, the phenomena of borrowing and of composing a poem based on an already established kharja (the last line in the song)—that is, starting from the end—or based on an established prosodic pattern (contrafaction) are all typical compositional techniques that enhance the circular effect. Thus, Al-Shushtarī was very conscious of specific structural patterns and their significance to the art of critical interpretation.

The third manifestation of that general literary concern lies in the element of performance itself, which is naturally realized with the pioneering use of the zajal. Because this is a poem composed to be sung or performed in public (sometimes in a choral manner), it affords the audience or recipients interaction with the art presented. The active participation involved here is what distinguishes Al-Shushtarī's mystical work, adding a new dimension to Ṣūfi poetry in general, and invigorating the whole mystical experience. Ṣufi poetry here is thus no longer intellectually exclusive or highly theoretical and unreached, but a living part of the mystical existence. Al-Shushtarī even included within the lyrics themselves, and among his other created personalities, the persona of the *zajjal* (the zajal's composer) or singer—that is, the persona of the poet/artist.

The two other personae are the ascetic, pious *faqir* (epithet for Ṣūfi) and its symbolic counterpart, a wanton drunk. The first persona, the wandering, "ecstatic" Ṣūfi, seems to embody the character of Al-Shushtarī himself, a Ṣūfi faqir who wandered in various lands and took his zajal singing in the streets and marketplaces. At times, however, Al-Shushtarī adopts the Quzmāni wanton persona; as he says in his "Zajal 99," he literally puts on his defiant and unorthodox hat (exchanging his turban for a monk's hood). Of course, this device of putting on literary masks serves an important artistic purpose: the personalities ultimately join to form an underlying unity between literature and Ṣūfism.

As has been shown, the use of symbols and circular structure are ways of enhancing the concept of Ṣūfi exegesis and establishing the necessity of critical interpretation. In the same manner, drawing attention to performance and to various personae or voices further proves how Al-Shushtarī was aware that he presented a new art—not merely a Ṣūfi philosophical treatise or didactic poetry—and that he was interested in the intricate artistry of composition.

In the final analysis, the novel aesthetic position of Al-Shushtarī is that critical interpretation, from the Ṣūfi perspective, is a "circular" process in which an "essential," spiritual truth becomes a poem: then by means of interaction with an interpreting audience (through public performance) the poem is returned to its origins. The correspondence between the theological dimension and the aesthetic dimension has one purpose: to illuminate the nature of the process of interpretation when linked to religious hermeneutics. Al-Shushtarī's poetry illustrates his characteristic blend of appealing and melodic simplicity, on the one hand, and sophisticated and even enigmatic complexity on the other. He was able to make "perfect form" (i.e., (zajals and muwashshaḥas) in art indistinguishable from mystical pursuit.

Omaima Abou-Bakr

Bibliography

Corbin, H. *Creative Imagination in the Sufism of Ibn ʿArabī.* Trans. R. Manheim. Princeton, N.J., 1969.

Monroe, J. *Hispano-Arabic Poetry.* Berkeley, 1974.

"Prolegomena to the Study of Ibn Quzmān: The Poet as Jongleur." In *The Hispanic Ballad Today: History, Comparativism, Critical Bibliography.* Ed. S. G. Armistead, A. Sánchez-Romeralo, and D. Catalán. Madrid, 1979. 77–129.

Shushtarī, al-, A. al-Ḥasan. *Dīwān.* Ed. A. S. al-Nashshar. Cairo, 1960.

Stern, S. M. *Hispano-Arabic Strophic Poetry.* Ed. L. P. Harvey. Oxford, 1974.

SICILIAN VESPERS *See* SICILY

SICILY

Located at the maritime crossroads only a few days' sailing from the major Iberian and Levantine ports, Sicily played an important role in the political, commercial, and cultural development of the Mediterranean basin. While its strategic location made the island a natural port of call for merchant ships, offering its rulers considerable commercial advantages, it also made control of Sicily a unique political prize that was contested, at one time or another, by most of the major medieval powers. A parade of foreign invasions and temporary conquests dominate the political history: Romans, Vandals, Goths, Byzantines, Muslims, Normans, Hohenstaufens, Angevins, and Catalans all subjected Sicily to their authority. These conquests, while introducing fresh cultural influences, contributed to a xenophobic, pseudopatriotic belligerence among the populace that culminated in the bloody unrest of the fourteenth and fifteenth centuries. From the wreckage emerged an embryonic mafia, particularly in the island's rugged interior. Commercially, Sicily was an important center of agricultural production from Roman times, especially in cereals. The revival of trade in the tenth and eleventh centuries placed Sicily at the hub of Mediterranean commerce. With this advantage, the periods of Muslim and Norman rule enjoyed a singular prosperity that inspired a widespread and much-needed diversification of economic activity, including silk manufacture, the mining of alum, and the burgeoning trade in slaves.

Culturally, the royal court and coastal cities benefited from contacts with the other Mediterranean communities, whereas the inland territories experienced less foreign influence and less development. Contrary to her many mythologizing historians, Sicily's mixture of populations and cultures remained generally unmixed throughout the centuries, and the often-praised fusion of artistic styles in architecture and mosaics is evident in only a handful of examples, such as the magnificent cathedral at Monreale. The more common result was the stylistic chaos, interesting though unsuccessful, exemplified by the cathedral in Palermo. Nevertheless, Sicily was an important center for the translation of Greek philosophy and science, and the Sicilian school of poetry was influential in the development of the *dolce stil nuovo* of mainland poets like Guido Guinizelli and Dante.

Sicily became a frontier province of Byzantium in the early sixth century and was administered by military governors as a personal patrimony of the emperor. With its wealth of Latin and Greek ecclesiastical settlements, Sicily remained a principal contact point between Rome and Constantinople throughout the iconoclast era, and provided a refuge for many exiled iconodules, thus initiating the island's medieval tradition of offering asylum to dissident groups. The emperor Leo III (r. 717–741) reorganized the island into the thema system, mandated the registration of all male children for military service, imposed heavy new poll, or capitation, taxes, and transferred the Sicilian dioceses to the jurisdiction of the Eastern Church.

Muslim raids began in the early eighth century and continued sporadically until a beachhead was established at Mazara in 827. By 902, with the fall of Taormina, Muslim control was secured. Their rule brought a new vitality to Sicilian life, reflected by the introduction of new crops (citrus fruits, sugarcane, cotton) and Palermo's rapid rise as an international market. Efforts at Islamization, however, generally failed. The Christian populace, both Latin and Greek, as well as the small Jewish community, enjoyed the status of *dhimmis*, or protected minorities. While traders from throughout the Mediterranean transacted in her harbors, Sicily profited especially from the commerce between Muslim Spain and the Muslim East. But the dynastic struggles between the Aghlabids and the Fatimids in Northern Africa, and the subsequent transfer to Egypt of the hub of east-west trade, hurt the local economy and contributed to internal conflicts among the Sicilian emirs. The Norman conquest of the eleventh century capitalized on these tensions. Roger I's seizure of Palermo in 1072 marked the symbolic end of Muslim rule, but the Islamic community remained an important presence in cultural and economic life under the patronage of the royal court.

The Norman period is perhaps the most celebrated chapter in Sicily's history. Under a series of industrious rulers—Count Roger I (d. 1101), then kings Roger II (d. 1154), William I (d. 1166), and William II (d. 1189)—Sicily rose to prominence as a Mediterranean power, now controlling the peninsular territories of Calabria and Apulia as well. These monarchs drew upon several traditions to unite their disparate population. Elements of feudal monarchy, imported from the north, were combined with characteristics of Byzantine political theology and the mechanisms of a Muslim-styled central bureaucracy. The resulting administration was noted both for its efficiency and (toward the peninsular inhabitants especially, who were always eager to break away from the Sicilian court) its cruelty. The economy gained strength through continued diversification, such as the new manufacture of a sturdy, if unrefined, wool. A papal grant of legatine authority, though apparently intended only as an ad hoc arrangement to secure the interests of the Latin Church, gave the rulers broad powers to control the selection of bishops. Observance of the customary "personality of the law" provided separate Quʾrānic courts for the Muslim population and Byzantine justice for the Greeks. Laws and decrees were issued in Latin, Arabic, and Greek. Thus the realm enjoyed a considerable, and generally shared, prosperity, in which the various communities worked together and their cultures mingled in a series of notable artistic and scientific projects. Nevertheless it would be a mistake to exaggerate, as many have done, the beneficent tolerance of Norman-Sicilian society, for strong ethnic hatreds simmered beneath the surface. When Norman control collapsed, these burst into violence and became a hallmark of Sicilian life throughout the remaining medieval centuries.

The marriage of Princess Constance, aunt and heiress of William II, to Heinrich VI of Germany brought Hohenstaufen rule, and thus carried Sicily to the forefront of the papacy's political concerns. During the long minority of Frederick II (d. 1250), Pope Innocent III administered the realm with little success. Palace intrigues, Muslim revolts, and invasions from Genoa and Pisa impoverished the kingdom and caused the loss of most of the royal demesne. Aided by gifts from the coastal cities, Frederick assumed direct control of the government in 1208 and began his campaign to restore order. Although he succeeded, and while he made the Palermitan court once more into a cosmopolitan center of trade, science, and art, his rule was not popular. Increasingly, Sicily was viewed not as the center of an important Mediterranean state that included the mainland provinces, but as a power base and economic resource for political schemes elsewhere. Popular resentment against foreign rule grew throughout the thirteenth century, increasing dramatically when the pope installed an Angevin government to replace the Hohenstaufen after Frederick's death.

Angevin rule was harsh and hated. Charles I valued Sicily principally for what it could contribute to his larger aim to dominate peninsular Italy and the flagging Latin Empire of Constantinople. Needing to reward his supporters, he redistributed the inland estates and alienated several major urban centers. But the diminution of the royal demesne that this required cut deeply into royal revenues, for which loss he compensated by exacting heavy commercial taxes. These actions catalyzed antiforeign resentments among the Sicilians, displaced landholders and disgruntled traders alike. From 1282 to 1302 the War of the Sicilian Vespers engulfed the island. The French were driven off amid slaughter and their repeated attempts at reconquest successfully repulsed. But violent civil strife accompanied the larger struggle. Factions in favor of establishing an all-Sicilian republic battled pro-French enthusiasts, while the inland barons seized vast stretches of freeholds and of royal and ecclesiastical estates. Unable to form a stable government of their own, the Sicilians invited the ruling comital family in Barcelona to assume the throne in Palermo. The first Catalan kings—Pedro (d. 1285), Jaime (d. 1296), and Fadrique II (d. 1337)—achieved a modicum of order and prosperity, but at the expense of crippling concessions of economic privileges and grants of civil and criminal jurisdiction. The later monarchs fared even less well. The cry of "Morano li Catalani" called many rebellions to arms throughout the fourteenth century. Viewed increasingly as foreign opportunists, the Catalans secured their power by pulling Sicily ever closer to the Spanish orbit. Local landholders were displaced in favor of nobles from Iberia; trade privileges gave Catalan merchants an inordinate control of imports and exports. In 1409 Sicily passed by succession to the direct authority of the Aragónese kings, which brought a formal end to an independence that had in fact disappeared much earlier. Alfonso the Magnanimous's annexation of the mainland kingdom of Naples (1435) completed the process of subsuming the island into a larger Mediterranean polity that drew much of its strength from the resources it drained away from Sicily.

Despite its political woes, medieval Sicily recorded some signal achievements in art and science. Contact with Byzantium introduced a rich tradition of Basilian monasticism and the knowledge of seafaring, while Greek silkweavers, impressed into duty by Roger II's soldiers, established a noteworthy palace industry at Palermo. Mosaicists from the East produced the superb art at the Cefalù cathedral, the Cappella palatina, and the Martorana church in Palermo. Elements of Greek architecture are evident throughout the island, most beautifully in the monastery of San Giovanni degli Eremiti. Arab Sicily produced important translations of Greek philosophy and science, such as Galen's medical treatises and Euclid's astronomical writings, plus some valuable commentaries. Al-Idrīsī penned *Kitāb Rujār* (*King Roger's Book*), one of the greatest geographic works of the Middle Ages. Some good historical writing emerged after the eleventh century: Hugo Falcandus, Geoffrey Malaterra, and Peter of Eboli narrate the Norman period, while later centuries are described by Ramon Muntaner, Niccolò Speciale, and Michele da Piazza. A greater contribution lay in the further transmission of Greek and Arabic learning. Plato's *Phaedo*, Ptolemy's *Almagest*, and Euclid's *Optics*, among other works, arrived in the west via translations commissioned by the Sicilian court in the twelfth century. Frederick II's move to the mainland shifted the centers of literary and scientific study to cities like Naples and Salerno; Sicily itself acquired no university until the fifteenth century.

CLIFFORD BACKMAN

Bibliography

Amari, M. *La guerra del Vespro siciliano*. 9th ed. Milan, 1886. Reprt. Palermo, 1969.

Bresc, H. *Un monde méditerranéen: Économie et société en Sicile, 1300–1450*. 2 vols. Rome, 1986.

Chalandon, F. *Histoire de la domination normande en Italie et en Sicile*. 2 vols. Paris, 1907. Reprt., New York, 1969.

Romeo, R. (ed.) *Storia della Sicilia*. 10 vols. Naples 1977–81. Esp. vols. 3–4.

Wieruszowski, H. *Politics and Culture in Medieval Spain and Italy*. Rome, 1971.

SIETE PARTIDAS *See* ALFONSO X, AND LAW

SISEBUT

Of Sisebut's career prior to his election in 612 to succeed Gundemar (r. 610–612) nothing is known. He was possibly the most cultivated of all the Visigothic kings, and his accomplishments give some hint of the educational attainments of the Romano-Gothic aristocracy in this period. He composed a poetic epistle of sixty-one lines, which he dedicated to Isidore of Seville, on the subject of eclipses. This was in reply to Isidore's dedication to him of *De natura rerum*. This poem gives evidence of considerable reading on the king's part in the works of classical poets, including Lucretius and Manilius. Equally impressive is another probable composition of Sisebut: his *Life of St. Desiderius*, which recounts the career and death of the Bishop of Vienne who had been killed at the instigation of the Frankish rulers Brunechildis and Theoderic II in 607. Other evidence of his literary skill can be found in the small surviving group of letters attributed to him. These include an epistolary exchange with the leader of the Visigothic kingdom's principal enemies in the Iberian Peninsula, the Byzantine governor of Cartagena. Against the Byzantine enclave in the southwest Sisebut is reported by Isidore to have campaigned twice in person, and with some success. One of his generals and his successor as king, Suinthila (621–631), conquered one of the independent peoples of the northwest, the Ruccones. Sisebut's most controversial action would appear to have been his attempt early in the reign to impose conversion on the Jews. This was condemned after his death by the Spanish bishops. On his death in February 621 the throne passed briefly to his young son Reccared II, but the latter died within two months of causes that were never revealed.

ROGER COLLINS

Bibliography

Fontaine, J. "King Sisebut's 'Vita Desiderii' and the political function of Visigothic hagiography." In *Visigothic Spain: New Approaches*. Ed. E. James. Oxford, 1980, 93–129.

Gil, J., ed. *Miscellanea Wisigothica*. Seville, 1972.

Saitta, B. "I Giudei nella Spagna visigota: Da Recaredo a Sisebuto." In *Studi Visigotici*. Catania, 1983, 59–101.

SISNANDO DAVÍDIZ, COUNT

Mozarab count of the frontier district of Coimbra in the last quarter of the eleventh century. It has been asserted that he was initially installed there by Fernando I of León-Castile after the latter's conquest of that city in 1064, but the earliest document that would place him there dates only to 1070. He surely commanded that frontier during the reign of Alfonso VI until his own death on 25 August 1091. According to the contemporary Muslim historian Ibn Bassām, Sisnando negotiated the surrender of and then briefly became governor of Toledo after Alfonso VI had conquered it in 1085 and attempted without success to dissuade that monarch from converting the major mosque of the city to a Christian cathedral. Certainly the count held property in Toledo that subsequently passed to Alfonso's daughter, Urraca.

He is said, as well, to have been educated in Seville and to have fled from that city to Coimbra. There he is credited with defending the continued use of the Mozarabic rite against the introduction of the Roman rite and to have himself located a Mozarabic bishop to head that see. Unfortunately, many of the documents employed to establish his career are themselves objects of considerable suspicion.

BERNARD F. REILLY

Bibliography

García Gómez, E., and R. Menéndez Pidal. "El conde Mozárabe Sisnando." *Al-Andalus* 12 (1947), 27–41.

Pradalíe, G. "Les faux de la cathédrale et la crise à Coïmbre au début du XIIe siècle," *Mélanges de la Casa de Velázquez* 10 (1974), 77–98.

SLAVERY

Slavery in medieval Iberia was primarily an Andalusian phenomenon. The early Christian states could not afford to buy slaves. Captured Moors, like New World Indians later, made poor slaves, and most Moorish prisoners were more profitably traded for ransom. Andalusian conquests created an impoverished class of landless peasants, eager to work on any terms. In the late medieval period Moors captured at sea were used as slaves in Valencia and Mallorca, and Portuguese navigation provided access to a source of black slaves.

Even from al-Andalus, information on such a widespread institution is scant. Seldom do we know the names of slaves, and recorded words are rare. There was little if any discussion of slavery as an institution; it is in the sixteenth century, with Bartolomé de las Casas, that its legitimacy was first questioned. Existing sources are legislation regarding slaves, Muslim historical or literary works in which slaves appear, inferences backward from the (by comparison) abundant documentation on the fifteenth century and later, both within the Iberian Peninsula and in North Africa, and fragmentary information from Christian sources about Christian slaves.

Slavery in al-Andalus was quite different from the modern stereotype of the institution. While there was undoubtedly abuse and slaves were of course not free, they were on the whole better treated and had more rights, than did slaves in the American South. Many lived nearly as well as their masters and mistresses. Affection between slave and owner was not unusual. Slaves of the wealthy were sometimes pampered household favorites.

Slave women often led a better life than did free women. The concubine had freedom to go about the town, more access to education, and a richer emotional and sexual life, however deficient by today's standards. Slave concubines could manipulate their masters into giving rich gifts. Marriage between master and slave was also not uncommon.

Manumission, especially upon the owner's death, was frequent. The children of a free man with a slave woman were free, and the mother who bore a free man a son became free as well, contributing to the close bond between mother and son typical of later Hispanic culture. Slaves could own property, and some were able to purchase their liberty. Some slaves and freed slaves achieved influence and political power. Freed slaves found little racial discrimination and were easily absorbed into the society as a whole. As is often observed, this contributed to the reduced racial tensions in the Hispanic world today.

There was no prohibition on the education of slaves. As educated slaves were more valuable, an owner might educate a promising slave. A man might do office work, letter writing, and accounting. Women could be entertainers: musicians, dancers, and poets (a few names and works have been preserved). Mostly, however, slaves did the hard and dirty jobs: kitchen work, animal care, manual labor, sometimes soldiering and prostitution. Slaves customarily were found in urban household settings, rather than on rural plantations. Ownership of slaves gave the owner prestige; ownership of expensive slaves—eunuchs, educated, or white—even more so.

Slaves constituted some 10 to 20 percent of the population of al-Andalus. They were customarily imported rather than bred locally. A free man's offspring were free, and slave men, whose commercial value was low, were much less common than women. Those men there were had little interest in producing slave offspring, and the reproduction rate was low.

Slaves, therefore, were not just a significant demographic element but a source of continued ethnic and cultural mixing. Especially talented slaves were imported from Baghdad. The bulk of them were obtained through raids, as tribute from conquered kingdoms, or purchased in groups from native suppliers. Their origin changed considerably with changing external circumstances. In the first centuries of Islamic rule, most slaves came from eastern Europe; it was at this time that the word *slave* was split off from *Slav*. The well-developed industry was in the hands of the Jews, who brought caravans of slaves westward to the Andalusian slave markets, the largest of any contemporary Mediterranean country. Jewish doctors produced eunuchs, some of which were exported. When access to Slavic slaves was cut off by Christian development in France and Germany, black slaves came to replace them. These were transported by land across the Sahara. Mixture with them produced the dark skin of the Moors. Finally, there were Christian captives from northern Iberia. These were primarily women and children, the men having died in defending them. These scarce slaves were especially prized. Even if illiterate, they were better educated than blacks fresh from Africa. Also, their appearance was considered more attractive. They were favored as sexual partners, and were the mothers of nobles and rulers.

News of the sexual use of Christian women and children reached their homelands. The boy-martyr San Pelagio was a hero for resisting the amorous intentions of ʿAbd al-Raḥmān III, and the "Tribute of the Hundred Virgins" was an important Reconquest myth. The need to free Christian captives was frequently part of the call to arms. The existence of the captives was indeed convenient for Christian monarchs, and the issue was surely manipulated, just as in the sixteenth century the danger of Moorish pirates was used by the Castilian rulers to distract subjects from internal problems. All the same, the use of Christian women and children for sexual purposes, and the castration of Christian boys, were significant factors in solidifying Christian public opinion against Islam.

DANIEL EISENBERG

Bibliography

Verlinden, C. *L'esclavage dans l'Europe médiévale* Vol. 1, *Péninsule Ibérique-France*. Brugge, 1955.

———. "Les Radaniya et Verdun: À propos de la traite des esclaves slaves vers l'Espagne musulmane aux IXe et Xe siècles." In *Estudios en homenaje a Don Claudio Sánchez Albornoz en sus 90 años*. Vol. 2. Buenos Aires, 1983, 105–32.

SORT, STEVE DE

Catalonian composer (ca. 1340–ca. 1417). After distinguishing himself as a performer on the exaquier, rote, harp, and organ, he was recommended to Juan I of Aragón (1350–1396) in the most enthusiastic terms by Juan's ambassador at Avignon. In all likelihood trained at Avignon, he was already an Augustinian friar when hired 18 October 1394 as Juan I's chapel organist. Martín I retained him until Sort's resignation of his post of Aragónese royal chapel organist into the hands of his pupil, Antoni Sánchez, on 26 March 1407.

Composer of the Credo for three voices (triplum, contratenor, and tenor) of the so-called Mass of Barcelona (Biblioteca de Catalunya, MS 971, no. 3) that appears in more *Ars nova* manuscripts than any other portion of the Ordinary of the Mass, Sort hypothetically composed his Credo at the Toulouse Augustinian monastery, to which he belonged in early youth. Copied in eight manuscripts (from Ivrea, no. 60, dated about 1365 where it is identified as *de rege*, to Apt. 16 bis, no. 46, dated about 1417), his Credo may owe its widespread diffusion to the Valois dynasty of Charles V (1364–1380), who delighted in it.

Available in at least four modern editions, Sort's Credo divides into eighteen sections that tally with text incises. Triplum (the fast-moving upper texted part) is notated without accidental in the signature, contratenor and tenor with one-flat signature. Ranging over a tenth (B-d^1), the vivacious triplum is almost entirely syllabic, with no text repetition and with extended melisma only at the final Amen. Fourteen of the eighteen sections in this earliest Spanish polyphonic mass end on G-chords, three on A-chords, one on F (fifteen final chords lack thirds). The much slower untexted lower parts, usually made up of ligatured notes, were presumably assigned to instruments.

ROBERT STEVENSON

Bibliography

Gómez Muntané, M. del C. "Quelques remarques sur le répertorie sacré de l'*Ars nova* provenant de l'ancien royaume d'Aragón," *Acta Musicologica* 57, no. 2 (1985), 221–32.

Harder, H. "Die Messe von Toulouse," *Musica Disciplina* 7 (1953), 114–21.

Stevenson, R. "Iberian Musical Outreach before the Encounter with the New World," *Inter-American Music Review* 7, no. 2 (1987), 38–43.

SPAGNA

A courtly bassadanza (*dance*) that originated in mid-fifteenth century. The forty-six white semibreves that comprised the tune first appear with the title *Tenore del Re di spagna* in Antonio Cornazano's (ca. 1465) manuscript *Libro dell'arte del danzare* (Biblioteca Apostolica Vaticana, MS Capponiano No. 203), at folio 33^v. However, the first source to prescribe both the steps used in the dance and the dorian tune with a D-d octave compass bore the title *Casulle* [Castille] *la novele a xlvi notes a cincq mesures*. Published in Michel Toulouze's *S'ensuit l'art et instruction de bien dancer* (Paris, 1495/6), at folio A^v, this first printed version bore a name that changed with the dance's constant reappearance in various contexts to 1633 (*Alta, Le bail despaigne, La baixa de Castilla, Lo bas despagno, La basse dance de Spayn, El bayli de Spagna* and *Spanier Tantz* are examples).

The dorian tune itself, which begins with a downward leap of a fourth from A to E and ends on D, inspired some nine polyphonic settings before 1510. The Jewish dancing master Guglielmo Ebreo da Pesaro (ca. 1425–1480), who spent the years 1465 to 1468 at the Neapolitan court of Fernando of Aragón, led the way with a two-part version called *Falla con misuras* in Perugia MS G.26 and *La bassa castiglya* in Bologna, Civico Museo Bibliografico, Q 16, lviii verso-lix. Against the dance tenor the upper part moves in faster notes. The first Spanish setting is an instrumental three-voice *Alta* by Francisco de la Torre (who enrolled in Fernando V's choir 1 July 1483), copied at folio 223 in the *Cancionero musical de Palacio* (Madrid, Royal Palace Library). The Spagna tenor in Ottaviano Petrucci's *Canti C. N° cento cinquanta* (Venice, 1504), fols. 147^v–148, lacks a composer ascription but the *Novum et insigne opus musicum, sex, quingue et quatuor vocum* (Nuremberg, Hieronymus Formschneider for Johann Ott, 1537), number 6, credits Josquin des Prez (ca.1440–1521) with a four-voice setting entitled *Propter peccata quae peccatis*. Heinrich Isaac's *Missa la Spagna* (Petrucci, 1506) exploits the tune as a cantus firmus. The number of sixteenth-century instrumental settings by Antonio de Cabezón, Diego Ortiz, and others was multiplied by the use of the Spagna tune as a cantus firmus assigned to counterpoint students. The Roman composer Giovanni Maria Nanino left at least 157 counterpoints and canons utilizing the Spagna tune. Its pedagogical use continued into the seventeenth century among such Neapolitans as Antonio Mayone, Rocco Rodio, and Giovanni Maria Trabaci. In total at least 280 settings of the tune qualify the Spagna melody as the longest use of a *basse dance* tenor in musical history.

ROBERT STEVENSON

Bibliography

Bukofzer, M. "A Polyphonic Basse Dance of the Renaissance." in *Studies in Medieval and Renaissance Music*. New York, 1950.

Crane, F. *Materials for the Study of the Fifteenth Century Basse Dance*. Brooklyn, N.Y., 1968.

Gombosi, O. (ed.) *Compositione di Messer Vincenzo Capirola: Lute Book*. Neuilly-sur-Seine, 1955.

Meylan, R. *L'énigme de la musique des basses danses du quinzième siècle*. Berne, and 1968.

Stevenson, R. "Iberian Musical Outreach before the Encounter with the New World." *Inter-American Music Review*, 8, no. 2 (1987), 87–89.

SPANISH ERA *See* CALENDAR

SPANISH MARCH

The expression *Marca hispánica* has often been used to describe the area of northeastern Iberia that was taken into the Frankish Empire between 780 and 801 and that formed the core of what would subsequently be known as Catalonia. A "march" was a medieval frontier, and the term is preserved in the names of several other regions of Europe (the Welsh Marches, Marche, Steiermark). The Marca hispánica bordered Islamic Spain. From the Carolingian point of view this was a distant region at one limit of the empire. It is hard to know what else to call the eastern Pyrenees and the lands between the mountains and the Llobregat River when discussing the ninth to eleventh centuries. To refer to Catalonia is anachronistic as this is first found only in the twelfth century. Yet Marca hispánica is itself somewhat problematic by reason of its restricted appearance in contemporary sources and also because of the later tendentious implications of its use.

In the *Royal Frankish Annals* for the years 821 to 829, the term *Marca hispanica* appeared for the first time. In the official acts of the Carolingian rulers, however, the term was never employed. Rather, the region was identified as part of Spain (*Hispania*) or associated with Septimania as *Gothia*, and the inhabitants were called *Hispani* or *Gothi*. After 850, Marca hispánica drops out even in historical literature. It is notable that the so-called *Annales of Saint-Bertin* in their earlier redaction refer to the Spanish March (for the years 844, 849, and 850), but that references for later years are to *Gothia* or *Hispania*.

In the course of the ninth century several different counties were formed, of which the most durable would be those of Barcelona, Urgell, Roussillon, Empúries, and Pallars. By the latter part of the century, in a pattern found throughout the troubled Empire, the Pyrenean counties had little contact with the imperial court and were controlled by a local dynasty that split into several branches.

Late Carolingian precepts refer to these counties collectively as part of Gothia (along with Septimania), sometimes distinguishing it a "farthest part" of Gothia. Hispania had earlier referred either to Muslim Iberia or the Carolingian redoubt. Applied to the Spanish March, Hispania became more frequent in the tenth century, but there was never a consensus among learned chroniclers. The French historian Richer, writing near the year 1000, referred indiscriminately to "nearer Spain," "Iberia," and "Gothia." Absent completely from the late or post-Carolingian age was "Marca Hispanica."

In the mid- and late seventeenth century, in the aftermath of the Thirty Years War and the Revolt of the Catalans, Marca hispánica was revived by French historians arguing for the annexation of Catalonia or defending positions in the negotiations regarding the Treaty of the Pyrenees. Carolingian precedent was bought in to justify treating Catalonia as part of an original French state. Pierre de Marca, who was named *intendant* for Catalonia in 1644, collected and published documents showing the attachment of Catalonia to the Carolingian Empire and its successor. This exhaustive, partisan (and still very useful) book was published in 1688 under the title *Marca hispanica sive limes Hispanicus*, an erudite play on the author's name and sanctification of a locution implying dependence on France. The Spanish March here means a frontier beyond which lies Spain, not part of Spain itself.

Given this background, it is not surprising that historians now are inclined to avoid "Marca hispánica" or use it only to refer to the early years of Carolingian administration. Its convenience is outweighed by its misleading implications. As José Antonio Maravall has succinctly noted, "the Spanish March is not the name of a country." At the same time, as Catalan historians emphasize, a degree of self-consciousness, apart from both France and the rest of Iberia, already characterized the region by the tenth and eleventh centuries. The polemical implications of *Marca hispánica* are caught up in the destiny of the term *Catalonia*, a term with its own peculiar taxonomic history, first employed at the point when the County of Barcelona was uniting with the Kingdom of Aragón.

PAUL FREEDMAN

Bibliography

Abadal i de Vinyals, R. "Nota sobre la locucion 'Marca Hispanica,'" *Boletin de la Real Academia de Buenas Letras de Barcelona* 27 (1957–1958), 157–64.

Zimmermann, M. "Aux origines de la Catalogne. Géographie politique et affirmation nationale," *Le Moyen Age* 89 (1983), 5–40.

SUEVI *See* GERMANIC INVASIONS

ṢŪFISM

Ṣūfism, or *taṣawwuf* (from *suf*, wool) seems to have implied in its beginning a simpler ascetic way of life, with emphasis on poverty (*faqr*), and a life retired from the secular and luxurious ways of the new cities. It required a more personal approach to Islam, meditation of the Qurʾān, insistence on one's own spiritual purification, and the search for goodness and God. Only when this rightousness and conciousness was applied to society at large and to the social interpretation and observance of Islam did Muslim jurists (*fuqahā'*) begin to find this practice objectionable. In the doctrinal sense, primitive sufism soon involved itself in the Hellenistic ecclectic metaphysics used by the first philosophers, and thus the theologians, the *mutakallimūn*, opposed it too.

Andalusian Ṣūfism has its roots directly in the East. In al-Andalus, the majority of scholars (*ʿulamā'*) and jurists (*fuqahā'*) interpreted the Qurʾān and Muslim law according to the malikite school and based their interpretation of religious texts on the *thahir* (obvious), the literal sense. This created an unfavorable atmosphere for the more rationalistic interpretation of doctrine such as in *muʿtazilite* theology and to the individualistic ascetism or esoteric doctrines that ṣūfism was adopting in the East. In the late ninth and early tenth centuries some Andalusian travelers to the East came in contact with the great philosophical and sufi schools of Egypt and Syria. Even though it was not necessarily a rule, many of the mystics in the Iberian peninsula followed a cenobitic form of life, similar to that led by Christian monks in al-Andalus, but also by many sufi communities in the East. Notable were those near Almería, from where they spread to Seville, Córdoba, and Murcia.

One of the first known in al-Andalus was Ibn Masarra (931), also considered the first philosopher of the region. Nothing is extant of his writings, and what it is known of his doctrines has been gathered from references to his teachings made in the works of Muslim philosophers and mystics until well into the fourteenth century. After this initial generation, most of the Andalusian Ṣūfīs flourished after the conquests by the African Almoravids mid-eleventh century. And although they were a product of the philosophical and spiritual Andalusian world, most of them, as the case had been with Ibn Masarra, exerted their influence in northern Africa, to where many of them had been expelled or voluntarily emigrated to avoid the rigors of the Malikite rule predominant in al-Andalus. Of the Ṣūfis who spend their life in al-Andalus, many were seen as a political force often respected but never quite trusted by the orthodox exponents of Andalusian Islam. With the popularity given their spiritual masters in exile, they were often the cause of revolts, as the case was in Algarve with Abū-l-Qāsim ibn Qási and his novices, avowed followers of Al-ʿArif. In this sense they became socially important, although very little of their doctrine is known besides their claim to be disciples and followers of spiritual leaders of renown.

The first generation of prominence was that of Abū al-Abbās ibn al-ʿArif (1088–1141), born in Almería, already the center of a rather esoteric group of Ṣūfis. His method (*ṭarīqah*) attracted many students. Accused of heresy by the governor of Almería he was sent to respond to the Almoravid sultan in Marrakesh. Ibn al-ʿArif was released, but was poisoned by emissaries of the governor. He is held in great esteem because of his *Mahasin al-majalis* (*Book of Beautiful Seances*, perhaps in the sense of *states*). The book deals with the spiritual stages; written from the point of view of the mystic (*ʿarif*), everything, even virtues, are considered accidental and a means to an end, for the mystic only subsists in and with God.

Also persecuted and sent to Marrakesh with al-ʿArif were Muḥammed ibn al-Husain from Mallorca, who resided in Granada, and Abū al-Ḥakam ibn Barradjān from Seville, the famous author of a commentary on the Qurʾān and a book on the divine names.

These were followed in the next century by Abū Madyam of Seville and by the greatest of the Andalusian mystics, Muhyi ud-Dīn ibn ʿArabī (1165–1240). A prolific writer, Ibn ʿArabī known especially for his *Fusus al-hikma futuhat al-makkiyya* (*Meccan Revelations*), and a book of mystical poetry, *Tarjuman al ashwaq* (*Interpreter of Desires*), and its commentary. He was the first to formulate the doctrine of existentialist monism. For him the existence of the Creator is the very essence of the existence of all created things. This too is his explantion for his mystical poetry, for created beauty is essentially a reflected splendor of the divine.

In the same century, Ibn Sabʿīn of Murcia (1218–1269), a disciple of Ishaq ibn Daqn, emigrated to Ceuta where he led a Ṣūfi community. His practice of strict poverty and isolation aroused the fuqahā's suspicions and he was forced to emigrate; he died in Mecca. His main book is *Qutb ad-din* (*Axis of Religion*), while his most famous, *Sicilian Questions*, can only doubtfully be attributed to him.

It is difficult to give a summary of Ṣūfi doctrines. While many practices were adopted from Eastern Christian monasticism, the doctrinal body consists of eclectic elements of for the most part hellenistic, gnostic, neoplatonic, and some of Persian origin.

Ascetism is generally the beginning of the spiritual path: in the triumph over its attachment to the flesh the soul finds God. As the novice advances in his ascetic path (*ṭarīqa*) he receives spiritual graces, *fawaʿīd*, with their perception based on an experimental wisdom, *maʿarifa*, by stages, *maqāmāt*, or by steps, *aḥwal*, the soul reaches the ultimate goal, the divine, the only reality, *al-ḥaqq*.

The central theme of Ṣūfism is the mystical union, *fanā'*, which is normally explained in philosophical terms of mixed origin, always based on the notions of existence and knowledge. As there cannot be any reality besides God's, there cannot be existence besides His; as God cannot be dependent for His knowledge on what it is, He creates what he knows. This process of creative divine illumination leads on the one hand to the Aristotelian notion of the active intellect, but also to that of emanation, since reality, existence, and knowledge get easily confused.

Associated with the religious history of the peninsula is the dervish mystical order known as the *shadiliyya* movement, founded by Abū al-Ḥasan ash-Shadilī, born probably in Ceuta about 1197. Totally devoted to religious studies and mystical doctrines since his youth, he preached in Tunis and often visited Mecca. He died in Upper Egypt about 1258. As with many of the spiritual leaders, he did not write much, pronouncing his teachings in the form of spiritual sayings and admonitions, some of which were collected some fifty years later. Abū Madyan, who lived in northern Africa, and considered the cofounder of the sect, and Abū al-ʿAbbas al-Mursī (Murcia 1287), who led a secluded life in Alexandria, were both originally from Spain. Their well-deserved renown is based on their activities in the oral teaching of their novices (*murīdīn*), for neither seems to have written much. Their influence, especially in Tunisia and Algeria, determined the direction of the mystical trends in the following centuries. Principles (*uṣūl*) of the shadiliyya are fear of God, steadfast observance of the law (*sunna*) as the only rule (any revelation that conflicts with the sunna should be rejected), disdain of mankind, surrender to the will of Allah, and quest of God in sorrow and in joy. The spiritual union (*fana'*) is achieved through repetitive religious exercises. Ecstasy should not incapacitate one for the active life (if it is followed by sobriety).

The most important mystic of Andalusian origin associated with this school is Ibn ʿAbbad from Ronda (1332–1390). Born in Seville, he too spent most of his life in northern Africa. He is remembered for letters of spiritual direction and for his commentary on the sayings of the spiritual leader of the order, Ibn ʿAta' Allah (*Sharh li-l-hikam al-ʿata ʿiyya*).

Although some of the expressions used from Ibn Masarra to Al-ʿArif and Ibn ʿArabī can easily be understood as those of pantheism, others, who insist on God's inaccessibility and on the stages of the human soul on the way to the divine union, allow a metaphorical interpretation for even the most radical phrases. On the other hand for Ibn Masarra, and especially Ibn ʿArabī, by insisting on the unity of reality (*el-ḥaqq*) and the creative nature of divine illumination, both notions receive in Ṣūfism an ontological character, rather than a gnoseological one, and the mystic union *fanā'* that of substantial effacement of the self in God. For that reason emphasis on the esoteric interpretation of Ṣūfism lead even in the Islamic tradition to frequent accusations of pantheism.

Andalusian Ṣūfism could be characterized by its giving more importance to the Aristotelian, rather than Neoplatonic, analysis; by the relative absence of visionary aspects, even by the rejection of the charismatic graces and greater emphasis given to the ascetic path and to the psychological and pedagogical analysis of the several spiritual stages (Ibn al-ʿArif, Abū al-ʿAbbās of Murcia, Ibn ʿAbbād of Ronda).

After the Reconquest Ṣūfism suffered the same fate in the peninsula as Arabic culture and Muslim religion in general, showing its continuation in North Africa, while those Muslims remaining in the peninsula, the Moriscos, could not stop its rapid decline, and were able only to preserve religious traditions more as a ritual than as a doctrine.

For scholars of penisular spirituality the major challenge remains the study of the influence that Muslim mystic doctrine and practices may have had on the Christian mystics of the following centuries—specifically on the Carmelite school (Sts. John of the Cross and Teresa of Avila). The verification of documentary contacts between both has remained elusive. More plausible but equally as elusive to document has been the presumption of popular contacts.

VICENTE CANTARINO

Bibliography

Asín Palacios, M. *El Islam cristianizado, estudio del sufismo a través de las obras de Abenarabí de Murcia*. Madrid, 1932.

———. *Obras escogidas*. Vol. 1. Madrid, 1946.

Nicholson, R. A. *The Mystics of Islam*. New York, 1975.

SYNAGOGUES

The synagogue (Hebrew *bet ha-keneset*; Sp. *sinagoga*) dates in Spain probably to the very origins of known Jewish settlement (ca. 300), although the famous "synagogue" of Elche is now thought to be, in fact, a church. Few, if any, remains survive from that early period, therefore. In Muslim Spain, Jews tended to live (for unknown reasons) near the southwestern section of cities, usually near the mosque. Most of the synagogues in Muslim cities were located near one of the city walls. The major cities inhabited by Jews in the Muslim period included Córdoba, Seville, Granada, Málaga, Lucena, Toledo, Valencia, possibly Jaén, Tarragona, Burgos, Zaragoza, and Barcelona. No synagogues from the Muslim period survive.

One of the earliest references to a synagogue in Castile comes from the events of 1196 when, in violation of a treaty, Alfonso XI of León invaded Castile. Caught in the middle was the Jewish castle, Castro de los Judíos, which was attacked and destroyed, along with the synagogue.

Shortly after the conquest of Córdoba, Innocent IV complained (1250) to Fernando III that the Jews there had dared to rebuild their synagogue and add to its original height, contrary to canon law. The *Decretals*, composed by Ramón de Peñafort (ca. 1230), contain the ruling of Gregory I that Jews may not build any new synagogue, and that of Alexander III that a ruined synagogue may be rebuilt but not added to in any way. Fidel Fita was undoubtedly correct that once the increased height of the Córdoba synagogue was abandoned, the Jews were allowed to retain it and it was not destroyed. The present famous synagogue of Córdoba is certainly not this one, but a later building. It was made a national monument in 1885.

Interior of a former synagogue. S. Maria la Blanca, Toledo, Spain. Copyright © Scala/Art Resource, NY.

One way around the law of the *Decretals* was the creation of "private" synagogues in houses. Jaime I of Aragón-Catalonia, generally a good friend of Jews, granted such a right to a Jew of Barcelona in 1263, and ordered the *baile* to protect the synagogue and the Jews who came there. The *Siete Partidas*, composed for Alfonso X chiefly by Ramón de Peñafort, the same anti-Jewish canonist who wrote the *Decretals*, strictly prohibited the building of new synagogues (but noted that since the name of God is praised there, Christians are prohibited from defacing it, putting animals in it, or interfering with Jews worshiping there).

The two most famous synagogues extant in Spain today are, of course, those of Toledo. They are both national monuments, after having been converted into churches: Santa María la Blanca and El Tránsito (the latter now houses also the important Jewish museum). The former synagogue was constructed, supposedly, by Joseph Ibn Sūsan (d. 1205). However, careful examination of the present structure does not convince me that it is of so early a date, and it seems likely that it was either rebuilt later, or perhaps even constructed by another member of that illustrious family, not earlier than the thirteenth century. Little remains of what must have been the magnificent interior of this synagogue, but the impressive columns and remnants of the intricate engravings on the wall give some idea of its former glory.

The El Tránsito synagogue, near the home of El Greco (which was the house of the builder of the synagogue) was constructed by Samuel ha-Levy, the famous treasurer to Pedro I (ca. 1357). Its magnificent carved marble walls, intertwined with geometric and foliate designs and Hebrew inscriptions as well as the shields of Castile and León, have been repeatedly photographed and analyzed. A portion of the original tiled floor also remains.

There were numerous other synagogues in Toledo, including a later one (ca. 1380) which belonged to Samuel's son, Mayr.

In Seville, Alfonso X (1252) provided that three former mosques be given to the Jews to be used as synagogues. Others were soon constructed (in spite of canon law). The famous government official Yuçaf de Écija built another synagogue there sometime before 1339, and Alfonso XI requested permission from Clement VI at Avignon to allow the Jews to use this as a reward for their fighting together with Christians of the city against invading Muslims. In 1391, the notorious anti-Semitic archdeacon of Seville Ferrán Martínez, in stirring up the pogroms, complained of twenty-three synagogues in the city, but this is an obvious exaggeration. There were, however, at least six. Two were converted into churches (Santa Cruz and Santa María) and another remained a synagogue until the Expulsion, when it also became a church (San Bartolomé). Avila, another city with a very large Jewish population, also had several synagogues, most of which became churches.

In fact, since Jews lived in almost every city and small town in Spain, synagogues were found everywhere. Many churches in these towns are former synagogues. Important ones elsewhere in Castile were Burgos, Jerez, Jaén, Ocaña, Plasencia, Segovia, Huesca, Huete, and many others. Madrid, of course, had its synagogues, but they have long since disappeared. Similarly, throughout Aragón-Catalonia were those in Barcelona, Calatayud (at least six in the fourteenth century), Borja, Girona, Besalú, Lérida (earliest reference is 1173), and so on. Some interesting details include the bishop of Vic (1319) allowing Jews to relocate their synagogue in Tárrega; Jaime II (1326) permitting Jews of Burriana to build a new synagogue and cemetery; the infanta Violanta (1384), noting that Jews were widely scattered in the area and could not easily get to one synagogue, requested the bishop of Vic to allow a new synagogue in Cervera. The poet Samuel ibn Sason of Carrión wrote (ca. 1330–1340) that a Christian lady gave a house to the Jews to expand the synagogue of the ironsmiths.

Jews, like Christians, formed *cofradías* throughout Spain, either merchant or craft guilds or else charitable organizations. Hebrew sources confirm that many of these had their own synagogues. Women also, particularly in large cities, had their own separate synagogue. One of the most famous of these was in Zaragoza, which had numerous synagogues, including those of various cofradías (weavers, leatherworkers, visitors of the sick, etc.).

Women were not, however, always (usually?) separated from men in Spanish synagogues, as is obvious from manuscript illuminations, which are a major source for the interior of synagogues. In these illuminations may also be seen the large elevated platform, called *minbar* (never *almemar*, as modern authorities claim, and certainly not *anbol*), which is Arabic for a raised platform or pulpit in a mosque. From a desk on this platform the Torah would be read, which unlike Ashkenazic (European) synagogues was not kept in a large carved wooden ark, but rather enclosed in an elaborately decorated case (often of gold).

Another important fact to note is that, by Jewish law, a synagogue as such may only be used for services. Most of the synagogues in medieval Spain were, in fact, legally a *bet midrash* (house of study), where teaching and learning went on regularly. As such, they were also routinely used for public meetings of the communities. During the brief, horrible years (late thirteenth century) when Jews were compelled to listen to sermons by Dominican and Franciscan missionaries, synagogues were most commonly used for these.

Finally, unnoticed (remarkably) by all recent scholars is the fact that the palace of the Diputació General of Catalunya in Barcelona was constructed from Jewish houses, and that part of it is, in fact, the former "small synagogue" purchased from the Jews in 1416. The outer wall and windows still survive.

NORMAN ROTH

Bibliography

Cantera Burgos, F. *Sinagogas españolas*. Madrid, 1955.

Fita, F. "La sinagoga de Córdoba," *Boletín de la Real Academia de la Historia* 5 (1884), 361–99.

Halperin, D. *The Ancient Synagogues of the Iberian Peninsula*. Gainesville, Fla., 1969 (with caution).

Puig y Cadafalch, J. and J. Miret y Sans, "El Palau de la Diptació General de Cataluna," (Catalan) *Anuari de l'Institut d'Estudis Catalans* III (1909–10), 385–95.

T

TABLAS ALFONSÍES *See* ALFONSO X, KING OF CASTILE, ILLUMINATION

TAFUR, PERO

Pero Tafur was a courtier at the court of Juan II of Castile and the author of the *Andanças e viaje de Pero Tafur por diversas partes del mundo avidos*, a fifteenth-century book of travels. He was born at Seville in about 1413, where he was raised and educated until 1431. At the command of the master of the order of Calatrava, in 1437 Tafur undertook a journey to the Holy Land, described in his narrative. The entire trip took from that date until 1439. Embarking at San Lúcar de Barrameda on the Atlantic coast of the Iberian peninsula, Tafur's trajectory covered Italy, parts of North Africa, Judea, Cypress, Rhodes, Greece, the lands of the Tartars, Switzerland, Germany, Flanders, and Burgundy. In all his sojourns he encountered remarkable people and equally remarkable situations. He claims to have been grandly received most everywhere he went, especially in Germany where he was entertained by the emperor and in Italy by the pope.

The relation of Tafur's travels constitute a mesmerizing synthesis of both fact and fancy that competes easily with Marco Polo and Sir John Mandeville. Generally speaking they are comprised of both fact and fiction, reveal a fascination with wonder, and betray a close affinity to late Byzantine romance.

Upon returning to Castile, Tafur is said to have married a lady from Córdoba, had four children, and settled down to complete his memoirs in 1457. He died most likely in, or shortly before, 1484.

E. MICHAEL GERLI

Bibliography

Beltrán Llavador, R. "Tres itinerarios sobre el *Tratado de las andanças e viajes de Pero Tafur.*" *Monteolivete* 2 (1985), 17–34.

Meregalli, F. *Cronisti e viaggiatori castgliani del quattrocento.* Milan, 1957.

Ochoa Andón, J. A. "El viaje de Tafur por las costas griegas." *Erytheia* 8 (1987), 33–62.

Pérez Priego, M. A. "Estudios Literarios de los libros de viajes medievales." *Epos* 1 (1984), 217–39.

Vasiliev, A. "Pero Tafur: A Spanish Traveler of the Fifteenth Century." *Byzantion* 7 (1932), 75–122.

ṬĀ'IFA KINGDOMS

Muslim historians first used the term *ṭā'ifa* (Ar. *mulūk al-ṭawā'if*; Sp. *reyes de taifas*) in a pre-Islamic context, with reference to local Persian potentates who came to power after Alexander the Great's defeat of Darius III (333 B.C.). In Iberian terms, the taifa kings were those local rulers who emerged after the disintegration of the Umayyad Caliphate in 1009, in the tumultuous years that followed, both before and after the formal abolition of the Caliphate in 1031, and on through to the Almoravid invasions (1086+). In retrospect and with all due deference to significant geographic, ethnic, and political variations between the different taifa states, the *Memoirs* (*Al-Tibyān*) of the last Granadan taifa king, ʿAbd Allāh ibn Bulluggīn written around 1090, in exile at Aghmāt, in Morocco, after his deposition by the Almoravids, do not seem too far off the mark: "every military commander rose up in his own town and entrenched himself behind the walls of his own fortress, having first secured his own position, created his own army and amassed his own resources. These persons vied with one another for worldly power and each sought to subdue the other." Yet we should not consider all taifa leaders as tyrants or, in modern terms, as military dictators. In the absence of central authority, people urgently sought leadership wherever they could find it: members of prominent families, important landowners, lesser officials, *qāḍīs*, *wazīrs*, *faqīhs*, all were to contribute to the taifa governments. In ethnic terms, four different groups of rulers were to emerge: (1) *Andalusíes*; (2) "Old" Berbers; (3) "New" Berbers; and (4) *Ṣaqāliba* (sing. *ṣiqlabī*), Eastern European slaves. During the almost eighty-year duration of

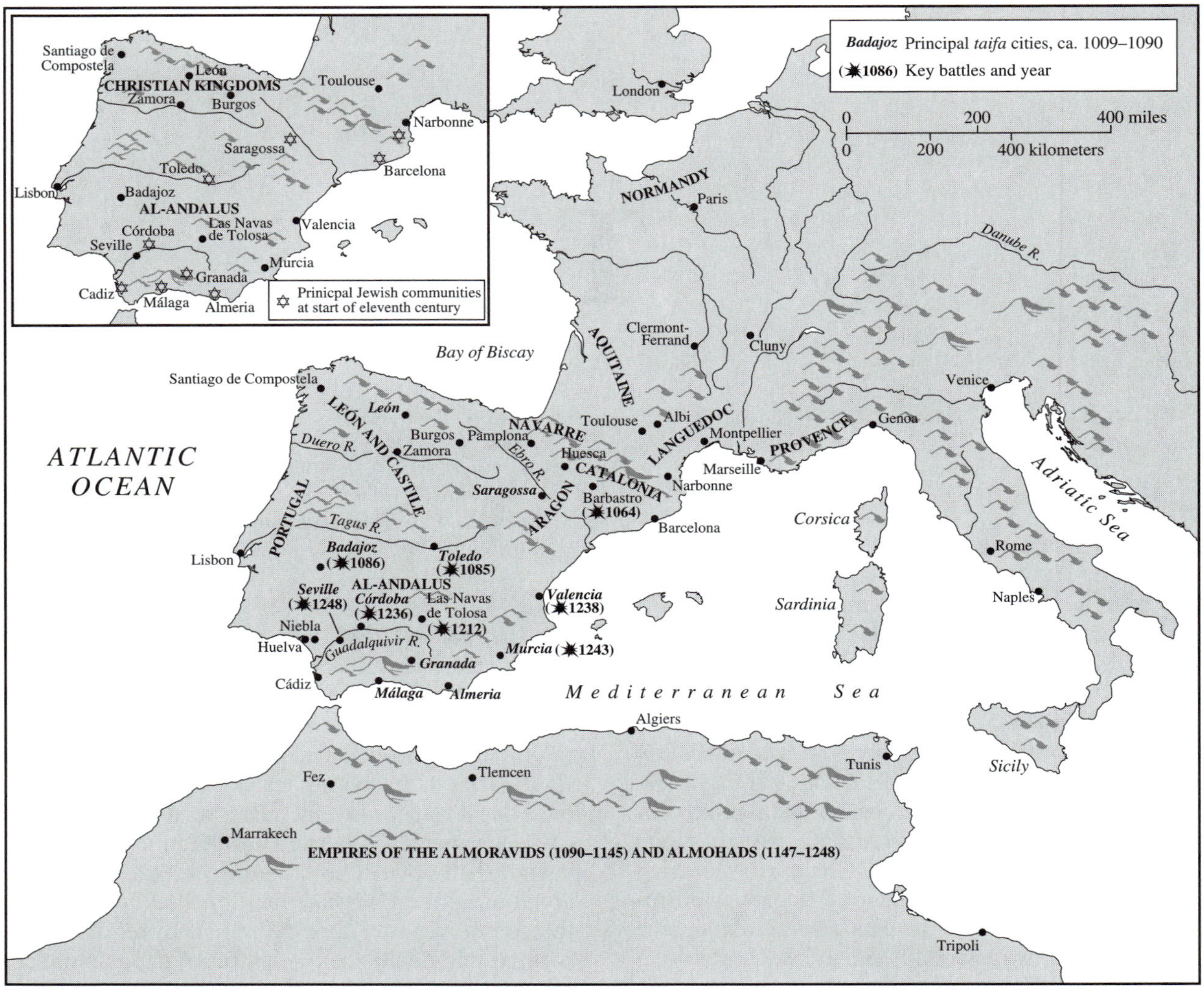

Tā'ifa Kingdoms

the taifa *fitna* (civil strife), the control and the frontiers of the approximately forty different taifa entities were in almost constant flux. Yet these four groups can, allowing for their shifting circumstances, also be identified in geographic terms.

1. The *Andalusíes* were acculturated, often patrician, descendants of early Arab invaders or, perhaps, also of early Hispano-Roman and Hispano-Gothic converts, who might eventually also pass as having "come over with the Mayflower." These Andalusians were to control large urban centers, such as Seville and Zaragoza, as well as some smaller taifas like Silves, Huelva, Niebla, and Murcia. Descendants of Hispanic converts (*muwalladūn*; *muladíes*) ruled in Murviedro (now known as Sagunto; Valencia Prov.) and Mértola (Baixo Alentejo). (For ongoing tensions between Old and New Muslims, see Monroe, *Shuʿūbiyya*.)
2. Berbers began settling in the Peninsula from the first years of the Muslim conquest. A descendant of one of these "Old" Berbers, ʿAbd Allāh ibn Muḥammad ibn al-Afṭas, was to gain control of Badajoz, taking the honorific title al-Muẓaffar (The Victorious). Following a pattern that was to evolve and prosper during the taifa period, Ibn al-Afṭas was a learned man, a noted poet, and a patron of the arts, forming a gigantic library and motivating the compilation of a now lost forty-volume encyclopedia: *Al-Muẓaffarī*. Other potentates of "Old" Berber extraction attained power in Toledo and in the towns of Alpuente (Valencia) and Albarracín (Teruel), the latter perpetuating the name of its taifa rulers, the Banū Razīn.

3. Like many another Muslim ruler, Al-Manṣūr had recruited numerous Berber troops from North Africa, to surround himself, as was the custom, with foreign mercenaries, who, initially at least, would be above local politics and on whose loyalty the sovereign could rely. (Compare the Egyptian Mameluks or the Moroccan sultan Mulay Ismā'īl's vast seventeenth- to eighteenth-century army of Senegalese slave soldiers [*ʿabīd*].) Some of these "New" Berbers were also to become taifa kings: notably in Granada and, for a time, also in Zaragoza and Toledo. Smaller Andalusian states were also ruled by "New" Berbers: Carmona, Morón [de la Frontera], Arcos, and Ronda.
4. Slavery was, of course, a thriving institution in al-Andalus. West African slaves reached Spain across the Sahara to Morocco, but there were also great numbers of Eastern European slaves (*ṣaqāliba*), many, but not all of them, Slavs, who were either sent overland through France and southward through the Ebro Valley, or by sea from Eastern Mediterranean ports. (Note the modern toponym *Ceclavín* [Cáceres] = Colloquial Hispano-Arabic plural *ṣiqlābīyīn* [Asín Palacios].) Most dealers were European, particularly Venetian, slave merchants. The word *ṣiqlabī* meant "slave," but it also came to mean "eunuch." Like other slaves in the Muslim world, some ṣaqāliba were able to reach positions of notable power. With the fall of the caliphate, many ṣaqāliba fled eastward to the Levant, where they established various taifas. The most impressive and most successful was the taifa of Denia, which extended far inland and also included the Balearic Islands. It was ruled by Mujāhid al-Ṣiqlabī, known as *al-rūmī* and probably of Sardinian origin. He maintained a substantial navy which he put to good use, even briefly invading his native island. Other taifas ruled by ṣaqāliba were Almería, Valencia, and Tortosa. Mujāhid left sons who held power in Denia and the Balearics long after their father's death in 1045, but other ṣaqāliba as eunuchs, obviously could not establish dynasties and their time in power tended to be relatively brief.

If the eight decades of taifa rule was a time of political weakness and chaos, it was also, by contrast, a time of dynamic and eminently successful cultural expansion. This was "the most intense and the most brilliant century of Arabic-Andalusian culture." Ṭā'ifa rulers, relatively powerless in politics and war, competed and outdid each other as patrons of the arts and sciences. As we have already seen, in the case of Ibn al-Afṭas in Badajoz, great libraries were formed and schools were established. The sciences flourished: mathematics, astronomy, pharmacology, engineering, agronomy. The Golden Age of Hispano-Arabic and of Hispano-Jewish literature was the age of the ṭā'ifas. The ṭā'ifas have also given us superb architectural monuments, carvings, metal work, and tapestries. But Christians from the Hispanic north, who themselves once held only diminutive ṭā'ifa-like kingdoms paying tribute to the Córdoban caliphs, could now turn the tables on Islamic Iberia and exact confiscatory payments (*parias*)—protection money—from their Muslim neighbors. Unrelenting Christian conquests of Muslim land, such as the brief, but disastrous taking of Barbastro by Frankish knights in 1064 or Alfonso VI's permanent capture of Toledo in 1085, brought ever greater pressure on the ṭā'ifa kings. Help, but help at great risk, was available in Africa. Al-Muʿtamid ibn ʿAbbād, the cultured poet-king of Seville, has left us a memorable one-liner with which to close the epoch of the taifa kings: "I would rather tend camels for the Almoravids than herd swine for the Christians." As the North African armies of Yūsuf ibn Tāshfīn swept northward, the elegant world of the taifas, with its refinement, its exquisite poetry, its luxury, and its tolerance, would come to an end and Al-Muʿtamid and his beloved Rumaykiyya would die in misery, as prisoners of the Almoravids at Aghmāt, in the Atlas Mountains.

SAMUEL G. ARMISTEAD

Bibliography

Asín Palacios, M. *Contribución a la toponimia árabe de España*. Madrid, 1944.

García Gómez, E. "A propósito de Ibn Ḥayyān." *Al-Andalus* 11 (1946), 21–30.

Guichard, P. "A propósito de los «Barbar al-andalus»." *Al-Qantara* 1 (1980), 92–110.

Kennedy, H. *Muslim Spain and Portugal*. London, 1998.

Lewis, B. *Race and Slavery in the Middle East*. Oxford, 1990.

Manzano Moreno, E. "Beréberes de al-Andalus." *Al-Qanṭara* 11 (1990), 13–60.

Menéndez Pidal, R. *La España del Cid*. 2 vols. Madrid, 1947.

Monroe, J. T. *The Shuʿūbiyya in al-Andalus*. Berkeley, 1970.

Pérès, H. *La poésie andalouse en arabe classique au XIe siècle*. Paris, 1953.

Sáenz-Badillos, A. *Literatura hebrea en la España Medieval*. Madrid, 1991.

Viguera Molins, M. J. *Los reinos de Taifas y las invasiones magrebíes*. Madrid, 1992.

Viguera Molins, M. J. et al. *Los reinos de Taifas*. Madrid, 1994.

———. *"Mulūk al-ṭawā'if." Encyclopaedia of Islam*. 2nd ed. Vol. 7. Leiden, 1993.

Wasserstein, D. *The Rise and Fall of the Party-Kings*. Princeton, 1985.

ṬĀ'IFA KINGDOMS: THE SECOND ṬĀ'IFAS

Some historians find it convenient to designate the relatively brief period of chaos (*fitna*) between the disintegration of Almoravid control and the Almohad conquest, as constituting a second *ṭā'ifa* epoch. Local governance was variously taken over by *qāḍīs* (judges), by military men, or by alternative religious leaders. *Ṣūfīs* ruled in Almería and the Algarve. Qāḍīs came to power, temporarily at least, in Córdoba, Jaén, Granada, and Málaga. Military leaders, who had previously served the Almoravids, won out in Zaragoza, Valencia, Murcia, Ronda, and Beja. Christians from the north eagerly took advantage of the new disorder in al-Andalus. Portuguese, with the help of northern European crusaders, took Lisbon in 1147; Castilians, allied with Navarre, Aragón, and Catalonia, and with Genoese and Pisan support on the sea, temporarily captured Almería, in that same year; the last Muslim strongholds in Catalonia—Lérida, Fraga, and Tortosa—were taken, with the help of Knights Templars, in 1148–1149. The most durable of the Second Tā'ifa military rulers was Abū ʿAbd Allāh Muḥammad ibn Saʿd ibn Mardanīsh (= Martínez?), doubtless a Muwallad of Christian extraction—though Arabic sources claim a Yemeni origin—who, based in Valencia and Murcia, controlled most of eastern al-Andalus, including Jaén, Úbeda, and Baeza, between 1147 and 1172, and who conquered Écija, Carmona, and Guadix, even laying siege to Córdoba and Seville and briefly taking Granada. Vigorous, irreligious, and overbearing—he increased his subjects' taxes—Ibn Mardanīsh was not averse to worldly pleasures, liked his wine, and, according to Ibn al-Khaṭīb, shared his roof with over two hundred slave girls. Especially after 1157, when the Almohads retook Almería, Ibn Mardanīsh—the *Rey Lobo* of Christian chroniclers—maintained and increased his contacts with the Castilians, who, along with Aragónese and Catalans, abundantly supplied him with mercenary soldiers. In 1169, Ibn Mardanīsh's ally and father-in-law, Abū al-Ḥasan ibn Hamushku ("the lop-eared"?; note Sp. *muesca* "ear markings of cattle"), the independent lord of Segura [de la Sierra] (Jaén), went over to the Almohads, dooming Ibn Mardanīsh's continued independence. He held out until 1172, when, at his death, his lands were taken over by the Almohads.

SAMUEL G. ARMISTEAD

Bibliography

Arié, R. *España musulmana (siglos VIII–XV)*. Barcelona, 1982.

Bosch-Vilá, J. "Ibn Mardanīsh." *Encyclopaedia of Islam*. 2d ed. Vol. 3. Leiden, 1971.

Hoenerbach, W. (trans.) *Islamische Geschichte Spaniens* (= Ibn al-Khaṭīb, *Aʿmāl al a'lām*). Zurich-Stuttgart, 1970.

Kennedy, H. *Muslim Spain and Portugal*. London, 1998.

Lacarra, J. M. "El Rey Lobo de Murcia . . . ," In *Estudios dedicados a Menéndez Pidal*. Vol. 3. Madrid, 1952, 102–08.

TAIO

Taio was Braulio's successor as bishop of Zaragoza. He took up his episcopal office in 651, and his signature is recorded among those of the bishops attending the Eighth and Ninth Councils of Toledo in 653 and 655. Little more is reported of his episcopate, nor is there any record of the date of his death. Indeed, the name of only one other bishop of Zaragoza has been preserved from the rest of the seventh and eighth centuries.

More is known of Taio's career in the period prior to his appointment to the episcopate, however. From two letters of Braulio, one of which is quite acrimonious, it may be deduced that Taio had been a priest and then the abbot of a monastery in or in the vicinity of Zaragoza. At some point in the 640s he was sent to Rome by the Visigothic king Chindasuinth (642–653) to find works of Pope Gregory the Great that were not then available in Spain. These would appear to have included some of the books of the *Moralia*. A legendary account of this visit, in which the whereabouts of the books were revealed to Taio in a vision, is contained in the Toledan *Chronicle of 754*. In 653/4 Taio produced a five-book collection of *Sententiae*, extracts from Pope Gregory's writings organized thematically, which he dedicated to Bishop Quiricus of Barcelona. Taio has also been attributed with six brief commentaries on the Books of Wisdom of the Old Testament, but this claim needs to be treated with skepticism.

ROGER COLLINS

Bibliography

España Sagrada. Vols. 30, 31 (text of the *Sententiae*), 56 (the commentaries).

Madoz, J. "Tajón de Zaragoza y su viaje a Roma." In *Mélanges J. de Ghellinck*. Vol. 1 Gembloux, 1951. 345–60.

TALAVERA, HERNANDO, DE ARCHBISHOP OF GRANADA

Born of *converso* (Christian convert) parents around 1430, Talavera studied and taught at the University of Salamanca and then rapidly rose through the ecclesiastical hierarchy, becoming Isabel the Catholic's favorite confessor and archbishop of Granada after its reconquest. He was almost certainly of Jewish origin, and his converso status was at one point investigated by the Inquisition; but he was also well connected to the nobility (the Álvarez de Toledo) and to influential clerics.

Talavera for a time taught classes of moral philosophy at the University of Salamanca before withdrawing to the Jeronymite house of Alba de Tormes. Later, his religious reputation persuaded Isabel the Catholic to invite him to the royal court, and by 1476 he was a member of the royal council and a political councillor of extraordinary influence, playing a strategic role in the financing of Columbus's "enterprise of the Indies," and above all taking charge of the religious fate of the population of reconquered Granada (1492). Talavera approached the problem of the defeated Muslims in an evangelical spirit, attempting to convert the defeated by persuasion and peaceful means. In this, however, he was thwarted by Jiménez de Cisneros who, rejecting Talavera's pastoral approach, used brutal force in order to convert or expel the Muslims.

Toward the end of his life, the saintly Talavera also had to undergo the indignity of having his family investigated by the Inquisition, on the grounds of heretical associations relating to a Jewish background. Although the notorious and sinister inquisitor Diego Rodríguez Lucero was dismissed from his charge by the pope, it was already too late for Talavera who, on his deathbed, entreated the Catholic Monarchs to intervene against the Inquisition. He died in May 1507. Talavera's concern with respect to the defeated Muslims of Granada damaged his reputation at the time but greatly enhanced it subsequently. By stressing teaching and persuasion rather than force, he anticipated later Counter-Reformation emphases of an evangelical nature. His reputation, even among the vanquished, was that of a truly religious man, even a saint.

ANGUS MACKAY

Bibliography

Azcona, T. de. *La Elección y reforma del episcopado español en tiempo de los Reyes Católicos*. Madrid, 1960.

TALMUD *See* RABBIS

TARIFA

City in Andalusia, province of Cádiz. The Romans knew it as Mellaria, important for its strategic location on the Mediterranean and for its role in Mediterranean commerce. It declined as a port under the Visigoths, but Muslim troops from Africa used the city as a beachhead for expeditions into the peninsula. Under Muslim rule, Tarifa also regained its economic importance. In July 710 Ṭarīf ibn Mallūq landed there with his forces and the city afterwards bore his name. After the decline of the emirate of Córdoba, Tarifa belonged first to Algeciras and then to the kingdom of Granada. Alfonso VI penetrated as far south as Tarifa in his raids on Seville in 1082. The Almohads captured Tarifa in 1146, and the Almohad general Al-Manṣūr used Tarifa from 1190 to 1195 to land his troops for the campaign that would culminate at Alarcos. In 1275, Muḥammad II of Granada gave Tarifa, Algeciras, and Gibraltar to Abū Yūsuf Yaʿqūb, sultan of Morocco, to use as a bridgehead to invade Castile. The Marinids established these cities as bases, which forced the Castilians to use naval power in the Straits of Gibraltar. The kings of Castile put pressure on the kings of Granada to surrender Tarifa, but Granada, fearing the loss of its link with Muslims in Africa, refused until Sancho IV captured Tarifa in 1292. Despite immediate efforts by the Granadans and the Moroccans to recapture the city, it remained Castilian, mostly due to the defense of the city by its *alcaide*, Alfonso Pérez de Gúzman (1256–1309). In April 1340 the combined armies of Granada and Morocco laid siege to Tarifa, but the siege was lifted by Alfonso XI of Castile and Afonso IV of Portugal in the Battle of Salado.

THERESA M. VANN

Bibliography

Fernández Barbera, T., and Col. D. Javier, *Historia de Tarifa*. Madrid, 1982.
Hillgarth, J. N. *The Spanish Kingdoms 1250–1516*. 2 vols. Oxford, 1976.
Lomax, D. W. *The Reconquest of Spain*. London, 1978.

ṬARĪQ IBN ZIYĀD

Of Berber origin, Ṭarīq was the freed former slave of the Arab governor of *Ifrīqiya* or North Africa, Mūṣā ibn Nusayr (ca. 700–712). He may have held regional authority under the latter in the area of the Tangiers Peninsula and the southern shore of the Straits of Gibraltar prior to the invasion of Spain. He is said to have commanded the main Arab and Berber army that carried out that invasion in 711 and defeated the Visigothic king Roderic (710–711) in what is often called the Battle of Guadalete. The Arab sources present Ṭarīq as turning what Mūṣā had intended to be an exploratory raid into a dramatic full-scale conquest in consequence of his victory. Mūṣā had to hasten across to Spain to take overall command of the operations to prevent his subordinate from winning all of the glory. In some accounts Mūṣā had Ṭarīq flogged for exceeding his instructions. The only early source for these events, the Christian *Chronicle of 754*, offers a subtly different version that commands greater credibility. According to this, civil war was raging in the Visigothic kingdom at the time of the invasion, and at least two Arab armies were involved, under the leadership of Mūṣā and of Ṭarīq, respectively. The latter won the victory over Roderic, but it was Mūṣā who took the

Visigothic capital Toledo. In the probably unreliable later Arab stories Mūṣā is said to have planned to kill Ṭarīq, but was prevented by the order of the caliph. Both men were summoned to Damascus (in 712), where Mūṣā fell into disgrace after the accession of the caliph Sulaymān in 715. After this nothing more is known of Ṭarīq.

ROGER COLLINS

Bibliography

Collins, R. *The Arab Conquest of Spain, 710–797.* Oxford, 1989.

Lévi-Provençal, E. *Histoire de l'Espagne musulmanne.* 3 vols. Leiden and Paris, 1950–51. Vol. 1.

TARRAGONA

Tarragona's prehistoric foundation is indicated by the popular attribution for its impressive "cyclopean" walls around its acropolis to mythical giants. The Romans used Tarraco as their main base of operation and developed the city as their provincial capital of Hispania Citerior, which was subsequently called the Tarraconensis. During the Middle Ages Tarragona was known, as it is today, for its vast Roman monuments and ruins: a forum; a circus, with its paleo-Christian basilica church at its center; harbor fortifications, and late antique and early Christian necropolises in the lower city; on the very visible acropolis with its walls and towers, a Roman temple and fortified *palatium* or castle-like residence for the Caesars; and outlying roads and bridges, triumphal arches, a quarry, and an aqueduct. It was also the old Romano-Visigothic metropolitan see of northeastern Spain connected by oral tradition to St. Paul's mission to western Mediterranean port cities. The see of Tarragona was hallowed during the Decian persecution by the blood of martyrs (Bishop Fructuosus and his deacons), commemorated by the hymns of Prudentius, and documented by papal decretals as early as A.D. 385, sixth-century conciliar acta, and historical and literary references in surviving classics.

When the Visigothic defense of the city collapsed in 718 before the Muslim onslaught, Prospero, the last Hispano-Roman archbishop of Tarragona, fled to Liguria with the church's precious relics and famous *Orational.* While Muslim forces pushed toward Barcelona and beyond, Tarragona was occupied through the tenth century as evidenced by repair to the walls and aqueduct, pottery and ceramic remains, and conversion of the temple into a mosque under ʿAbd al-Raḥmān III (912–963). The coastline was fortified up to the so-called Punta de la Mora where Tamarit Castle stands, and the Campo was dotted with small Muslim villages that retain their Arabic toponymy to this day. As the Muslim military occupation receded over the centuries, Tarragona became the focal point of a three-century contest for dominion.

The encroaching Christians by the eleventh century built a line of castles facing south from the march of Ausona to Barcelona's march of Olérdola between the coast and the Penedés, and above the Río Gayá along the northeastern edge of the Campo de Tarragona, while the Muslims built a juxtaposed hard-shell defense system in the mountains of the Priorat, the Muslim march of Ciurana with the Tarragona fortress as its vortex, to defend the Ebro borderland governed from Zaragoza and protected by Tortosa and Lleida. The Christians after the 970s attempted several reconstitutions of the ecclesiastical province and metropolitanate of Tarragona, unsuccessfully until Bishop Berenguer Llucanes of Vic in 1090, allied with the Gregorian Reform, became the archbishop *in partibus fidelium.* Count Ramón Berenguer I had even attempted in the 1050s a bold coup and occupation of the city of Tarragona with an enfeoffment to the marcher Lord Bernard Amat. But the real reconquest began in the contest with the African Almoravids and in reaction to their counterattacks after the fall of Balaguer in 1106 to Urgell and the Aragónese taking of Zaragoza in 1118, resulting in Muslim raids along the coastline above Tarragona, the defeat in 1124 of the Catalans outside Lleida at Corbins, the disaster at Fraga in 1134 that left the Aragónese routed and their king, Alfonso I, mortally wounded, and the whole frontier up for grabs.

Undaunted, the ambitious Count Ramón Berenguer III forged a grand pan-regnal alliance system stretching from Aragón to Pisa and Genoa, and crusade movement orchestrated by the famous bishop of Barcelona, Oleguer Bonestruga, who in 1118 became the archbishop of Tarragona. Ecclesiastical restoration and reconquest thereafter were coordinated. The prelate succeeded in recruiting Norman crusaders to take Tarragona; their leader, Robert Burdet, was made *princeps* of Tarragona in 1129. Tarragona city was reoccupied militarily but was not immediately repopulated. Although Christian settlers began to move onto the Campo and the Muslims withdrew to their highland march of Ciurana, the Almoravid counterthrust after 1118 through the 1130s meant that the frontier was still very dangerous. Archbishop Bernat Tort in 1146 called a provinical council to renew the crusade. The allies, with energies heightened by a daring raid on Almería in 1147, afterward set up a naval blockade from Salou southward with ships from Barcelona, Genoa, Pisa, and Montpellier. Christian forces attacked Tortosa, which fell in 1148, and Lleida capitulated the next year. It was only then that in an effort to attract more settlers to Tarragona, its inhabitants were granted a charter of freedoms. While the military orders and Arago-Catalan *hueste* (army) that subdued Lleida turned back toward Tarragona to outflank the Muslims in the Priorat, frontier barons from the Urgellian and Ausonan marches attacked from the north; Norman, English, and Catalan forces moved from Tarragona and Castelvel to secure the coast and southern defenses of the Ciuranan march. The Muslim castle of Ciurana fell in 1153, the campaign was largely over by 1155, and the spoils of war were mostly reallocated by 1158. Only then was the Campo de Tarragona really secure for Christian repopulation and the city safe for the permanent residence of the archbishop, who began building the see's new cathedral.

During the absence of the archbishops the Norman princes governed Tarragona semiautonomously, but with the formation of the Crown of Aragón, a separate principality there could not be tolerated by the house of Barcelona. Through their archbishops, beginning with Bernat Tort (1146–1163), pressure was applied to regain indirect secular authority over Tarragona. His successor, Hug de Cervelló (1163–1171), continued this policy of reimposition of archiepiscopal control over the Robert's sons, who revolted. A civil war ensued, during which the archbishop was assassinated in 1171. The Catalans united behind the new archbishop, Guillem de Torroja, and expelled the Normans, who were subsequently exiled to Mallorca. Thereafter archiepiscopal, abbatial, and baronial patronage sponsored a massive building program in the city, exemplified by commencement of a new cathedral, and throughout the Campo, especially at the Cistercian monasteries of Santes Creus and Poblet.

Tarragona as an ecclesiastical principality was reincorporated in 1173 into the Crown of Aragón by a concordat between Alfonso II and Archbishop Guillem for corule. This cooperation continued until 1391, when Juan I gave up all secular claim to the archbishops. Meanwhile, Tarragona was revived as a commercial center and naval base with its nearby port of Salou for operations against the Balearics and the southern coastal reconquest of Valencia (1238). Its lower industrial zone between the port and acropolis grew, a mercantile district developed below the fortress, the acropolis was repopulated, municipal government was expanded after reforms in 1231 finally to include three Jurats and a council, and outlying communities were incorported into the city. The Cistercians were the earliest arrivals, followed by the Carthusians much later, when they founded Scala Dei during the 1220s in the highlands; and within the city the Mercedarians were the first to arrive in 1224, the Poor Clares were next in 1256 with their confreres, the Franciscans coming later in 1274 at the same time as the Augustinians. Tarragona's prosperity was terminated by the Black Death of 1348 when a fourth of the population succumbed; the remaining suffered from intermittent civil strife, exorbitant royal taxation, and trade competition from Barcelona. Recovery was slow; Tarragona's urban renewal was postponed until after 1570.

LAWRENCE J. MCCRANK

Bibliography

McCrank, L. J. "Norman Intervention in the Catalan Reconquest: Robert Burdet and the Principality of Tarragona, 1129–1155," *Journal of Medieval History* 7, no. 1 (1980), 67–82.

———. *Restoration and Reconquest in Medieval Catalonia: The Church and Principality of Tarragona, 971–1177.* 2 vols. Charlottesville, Va., 1974.

Morera y Llauradó, E. *Tarragona cristiana. Historia del arzobispado de Tarragona.* 2 vols. Tarragona, 1889–99.

Recasens i Comes, J. M. *La Ciutat de Tarragona.* 2 vols. In *Enciclopèdia Catalunya. Biblioteca per el estudi de Catalunya, València i les Balears en tots els Aspectes*, vols. 35 and 39. Barcelona; 1966, 1975.

TÁRREGA, FRAY RAMÓN DE

Born of Jewish parents at Tárrega in the Catalan Urgell region (ca. 1335), he was baptized at age eleven, possibly upon the conversion of his parents. He entered the Dominican mendicant order at Cervera and studied at the Barcelona priory. At Palma in 1355 he taught logic, at Lérida from 1357, and theology at Cervera from 1365. His former teacher at Barcelona, the notoriously anti-Judaic Nicolau Eymerich, had in 1356 become inquisitor general of the Crown of Aragón; in 1368 he prosecuted Ramón for heresy for theological novelties. When Ramón refused to retract even under pressure from the Dominican master-general, Eymerich imprisoned him at the Santa Caterina priory in Barcelona.

Ramón's appeal on grounds of trial irregularities to the papal court at Avignon led to a papal commission of thirty theologians in 1371 to examine his writings. Ramón suddenly died on 20 September 1371, however, under circumstances suggesting murder or suicide; the metropolitan of Tarragona inaugurated a formal inquiry in 1371, no record of which has survived. Eymerich drew up twenty-two heretical propositions from Ramón's works; Pope Gregory XI condemned these in 1372. Sometimes called the Ramón Llull of Tárrega, his *Ars operativa* (also titled *De secretis* and *De quinta essentia*) is actually Llull's work. His *De invocatione daemonum* and *Conclusiones variae* are genuine.

ROBERT I. BURNS, S. J.

Bibliography

Robles, L. *Escritores dominicos de la corona de Aragón, siglos XIII–XV*. Salamanca, 1972.

Fort i Cogul, E. *Catalunya i la inquisició*. Barcelona, 1973.

TAXATION

The Roman tax system based on the *tributum soli*, or land tax, and the *capitatio humana*, or poll tax, continued in use in Visigothic Spain, though the distinction between them tended to be blurred. Regular evaluations of the land had been abandoned in the late imperial era so these tributes remained fixed amounts rather than variables depending on assessment. Other revenue sources included tolls on goods in transit, fines levied in court, confiscation, booty, and gifts. In Islamic Spain the principal legal impost was the *zakat*, or alms tax. Among other taxes were a land tax (*ushr, kharaj*), tolls, customs duties, sales taxes, tributes payable by Christians and Jews subject to Muslim rule, and tributes demanded of the Christian rulers.

In Christian Spain in the early medieval centuries the tax system was quite simple as the principal revenues continued to be drawn from sources fixed by custom. In general kings were able to manage quite well because their responsibilities were limited and so did not require a large bureaucracy; thus the expenses of the royal court were minimal. Nor did military operations entail substantial expenditures because royal armies were composed of individuals obligated to serve at their own cost. The expansion of the Christian kingdoms led to increases in the eleventh and twelfth centuries in both revenues and expenditures and the first appearance of an extraordinary tribute.

Customary tributes levied in the early medieval centuries included a land tax or rent (*functio, censum, tributum, infurción, quadragesima*; or, in Catalonia, *parata, usaticum, tasca*) of a seigneurial character payable by tenants on royal estates; this was also known as *marzadga* or *martiniega* because it was payable in kind, but later in money, either in March or at Martinmas (11 November). Tenants also owed the king labor services (*opera, sernas*), work on roads and bridges (*facendera*), payments for the use of pasturage (*herbaticum, herbazgo*) and woodland (*montaticum, montazgo*; in Catalonia, *forestatge*); inheritance dues (*nuntium, mortuarium, luctuosa*), hospitality (*hospicium, yantar, cena*), and provisions (*conductum, conducho*).

Also noteworthy were tolls (*portaticum, pedaticum, portazgo, pedazgo*) collected on goods and persons at the entrance to towns and at various points of transit. Among the important personal services required were guard duty (*anubda*; in Catalonia, *specula, mirall*), especially in frontier areas exposed to Muslim attack. Townspeople were also obliged to participate in military expeditions of one sort or another (*hueste, cabalgada*); failure to appear in the host or *fonsado* was punishable by a fine called *fonsadera*.

Regalian rights also enhanced the royal coffers, especially as the Reconquest moved below the Duero and the Tagus Rivers. The monarch claimed a monopoly of the profits of mines and salt pits, whose exploitation was leased to private persons. The distribution of salt was also controlled by the crown. Rental of shops, claims over strays, buried treasure, flotsam, and jetsam were also incidental sources of income.

In the middle years of the eleventh century the rulers of the Christian states were able to demand *parias*, or tributes, from the petty Muslim kingdoms (ṭawā'if) that replaced the caliphate of Córdoba. These sums were so substantial that Fernando I was able to pledge the payment annually of one thousand gold pieces to the monastery of Cluny; his son Alfonso VI doubled the amount, but the subjugation of the *tā'ifas* (party kingdoms) by the Almoravids brought that source of revenue to an end.

The invasion of Spain by the Almoravids, a sect of zealots from Morocco, raised the issue of extraordinary taxation for the first time. To meet the Moroccan challenge, in 1090 Alfonso VI asked for an extraordinary tax called a *petitum* or *pedido*, a name that describes its nature as a royal request. In time this seems to have become a regular levy collected without a prior request for it.

Royal needs expanded rapidly in the thirteenth century as greater funds were required to prosecute the Reconquest and to execute the more varied and complex functions of government. These tasks could not be carried out on the basis of the traditional imposts (*pechos*) of the past; though they continued to be levied, ever more frequent exemptions rendered many of them meaningless as sources of income for the crown. The expansion of government meant that chancery fees, fees charged by public notaries and scribes, and judicial fines (*calumnia, caloña*) were an increasing source of income that helped to pay the salaries and expenses of the personnel in the chancery and the courts. Military expenses could be met in part by the collection of fonsadera, as it was now often to the king's advantage to excuse people or communities from service in return for this payment. The king, in imitation of Islamic custom, also was entitled to a fifth (*quinto*) of the booty taken in war. The port towns along the Bay of Biscay were required from the thirteenth century onward to provide a certain number of ships for royal service or in lieu thereof a payment in coin.

Hospitality and provisions were two very important rights claimed by the monarch but they also aroused strong protest from the *cortes* (parliament). In 1284 Sancho IV set the amount of *yantar* due from the towns upon his personal visitation at six hundred *maravedís* for himself, two hundred for the queen, and three hundred for his son acting as his lieutenant. The cortes insisted that yantar was due only on a royal visit, but Alfonso XI declared that it should be paid even when he was engaged in military operations. The *adelantados* and *merinos mayores* responsible for territorial administration were also authorized to take an annual yantar of 150 maravedís. The cortes also charged that when royal officials took provisions, or *conducho*, they broke into houses, seizing food, drink, and animals, and often inflicted other damages without compensation.

In addition, the Mudéjars, or Muslims and Jews living under Christian rule, were subject to the payment of poll taxes whose importance rose as a consequence of expansion into Andalusia and Murcia in the thirteenth century. The Jewish communities in the towns were likely more well off than Mudéjars in rural areas and probably paid a more substantial amount. In 1280 Alfonso X compelled the Jews to increase their daily tribute from 6,000 to 12,000 maravedís, or from 2,190,000 to 4,380,000 annually. His son Sancho IV apparently reestablished the earlier amount.

As the Almohad regime disintegrated, Fernando III was able to impose an annual tribute on the kings of Granada, amounting to one-half the revenues of the kingdom, or 300,000 maravedís. In later times, whenever the king of Granada believed that he could do so with impunity, he refused payment, but he was usually compelled to resume it. This tribute was said to be one-fourth or one-fifth of the total revenue of the kingdom of Granada, which was estimated at about 560,000 *dinars* in the mid-fourteenth century, and at about one million silver *reales* in 1492.

The multiplicity of royal responsibilities required the development of extraordinary taxation. The problem was to find a suitable means. In the twelfth century the Christian rulers began to coin money for the first time and they quickly realized that one could profit by altering the content of coins while maintaining their face value. This practice evoked protest because of the resulting economic upheaval. Responding to such complaints, in 1202 Alfonso IX of León promised not to alter the coinage for seven years in return for the payment of one maravedí by each nonnoble freeman; this tribute came to be known as *moneta* or *moneda forera*. Three years later Pedro II of Aragón obtained a similar tribute called *monedatge*. The Portuguese cortes of 1254 also consented to the imposition of *monetágio* in return for Afonso III's pledge to maintain the coinage intact for seven years. In time moneda forera became a regular tax given to a new king at his accession.

Fernando III also discovered that the Reconquest of Andalusia could be financed in part by laying hands on the *tercias*, that third of the tithe destined for the upkeep of churches; when the clergy protested the king emphasized that he needed the money for the defense of Christendom and so the papacy finally authorized the crown to take it. In reality the *tercias reales* usually amounted to two-ninths of the total.

The development of extraordinary taxation was advanced greatly in the reign of Alfonso X, who introduced the *servicio y montazgo*, a tax on migratory flocks of sheep. The *montazgo*, a pasturage toll on migratory flocks of sheep collected by the municipalities, was effectively transferred to the crown in the cortes of 1261, when the sheepowners agreed to pay the king an annual *servicio*. After the king levied the *servicio de los ganados* on migratory flocks in the cortes of 1269, these two imposts came to be known henceforth as *servicio y montazgo*.

While the internal toll known as *portazgo* continued in existence, the crown derived little profit from it because of alienation and exemption. Much more valuable were customs duties (*diezmo, almojarifazgo*) levied on imports and exports. In 1268 Alfonso X organized the regular collection of customs duties at assigned ports along the Bay of Biscay, and in Andalusia and Murcia. Although the nobility protested, the collection of customs duties was never abandoned. The system was revised by Pedro I, Enrique III, and Juan II, who established a series of customs posts along the frontiers of Aragón and Navarre to regulate mercantile traffic. In the later medieval centuries *diezmos y aduanas* were collected in the bishoprics of Calahorra, Osma, Sigüenza, Cuenca, and Calahorra, bordering Navarre and Aragón; the *diezmo y medio diezmo de lo morisco* was levied along the frontier with Granada, while the *almojarifazgo*, an old Islamic duty, continued to be collected in the ports of Andalusia and Murcia; the *diezmos de la mar* were gathered in Galicia and the Bay of Biscay. Customs duties levied at frontier posts were one of the most lucrative sources of income.

The mounting financial needs also prompted kings to ask the cortes to consent to regular subsidies on income known as *servicios* (in Catalonia, *donatiu*). The royal obligation to ask for consent was affirmed many times. In justification of his request the king usually argued that the utility or necessity of the realm required it; in specific terms that often meant that money was needed for wars against the Muslims. Once the king offered an appropriate explanation the cortes was obliged t‹ ‑espond in a positive way. Thus the principle of conse‹ ıt to extraordinary taxation came to be firmly fixed. The servicio was at times a capitation tax payable at the same rate as moneda forera, but at other times it was a variable impost on movable goods. In Aragón and Catalonia the subsidy was often granted as a hearth tax (*fogatge*) or was based on customs duties.

Servicios voted by the Castilian *cortes* (parliaments) were usually collected from the townspeople, whose names and estimated wealth were recorded in registers (*padrones*) prepared for that purpose. Tax farmers (*arrendadores*) were ordinarily entrusted with collection, but their activities often provoked protest against their exorbitant demands or from those claiming exemption of one kind or another. In the cortes of 1387 Juan I tried to collect a *servicio* from everyone, but the nobles and clergy who were traditionally exempt complained and forced the king to back down.

Rising protests against the imposition of servicios caused the kings to look for still other ways of raising money. The *sisa*, varying from 1 percent to 3 percent, was a burden imposed on the consumer in the marketplace. An exceedingly unpopular tax levied initially by Sancho IV, it was abolished in 1295 after his death by his widow, who sought thereby to win support among the towns, but it was subsequently revised.

Under Alfonso XI, the *alcabala*, a sales tax of 5 percent falling on all consumers, whether clerics, nobles, townsmen, or peasants, came into general use. With the consent of various assemblies in 1342 and 1345 he was able to levy the alcabala to finance his military operations against the Moors. From the time of Enrique III, the alcabala, which increased to 10 percent in 1377, became a permanent tax levied annually without explicit authorization by the cortes and was the most important source of royal revenue.

In difficult times kings often resorted to the forced loan (*empréstito*) as a means of raising money. Fernando III was among the first to obtain such loans from the towns of Galicia in 1248. To allay protests, Alfonso X promised in 1255 to 1256 that he would not demand them, but the practice continued and Alfonso XI obtained loans of this kind in 1333 and 1337. Juan I in 1382 revealed that he had exhausted his income and intended to impose an empréstito; with that intention he indicated the specific sums that he expected several citizens of Murcia to pay. He assured them repayment of the moneda or alcabala in the next year, but he offered no guarantee that they would also receive interest.

The crown also borrowed money from domestic and foreign bankers but was often unable to promptly pay off these loans; thus a long-term debt made its appearance. In order to prosecute the war against Granada, Fernando and Isabel borrowed extensively, pledging repayment with an annual interest of 10 percent. As these certificates of indebtedness were held by *juro de heredad* that is, by hereditary right, they came to be known as *juros*. In time they were issued in such great numbers as to threaten the monarchy with financial catastrophe.

Throughout the high and late Middle Ages the monarchy was constantly in need of funds, partly because of the nearly constant alienation of revenue-producing lands, rights, and other sources, and partly because of the frequent exemption of clergy, nobles, and others best able to pay taxes. The collection of taxes was also often inefficient and did more to enrich the tax farmers than to fill the royal treasury.

JOSEPH F. O'CALLAGHAN

Bibliography

Gama Barros, H. da. *História da administração pública em Portugal nos séculos XII a XV*. 2d ed. 11 vols. Lisbon, 1945–54.

Ladero Quesada, M. A. *Fiscalidad y poder regio en Castilla (1252–1369)*. Madrid, 1993.

———. *La Hacienda Real de Castilla en el siglo XV*. La Laguna de Tenerife, 1973.

O'Callaghan, J. F. *A History of Medieval Spain*. Ithaca, N.Y., 1975.

TECHNOLOGY, ARABIC

Hydraulic technology was that area most developed in al-Andalus, and the one best studied. Recent investigations by medieval archeologists have focused not on the great peri-urban *huertas* that traditionally have been viewed as the outstanding monument to the hydraulic skills of the Arabs, but rather on smaller, mainly mountainous "mesosystems" that in all probability accounted for most of the irrigated development in the first two centuries or more of Muslim rule. This kind of irrigation, moreover, is associated with a distinctive pattern of rural settlement, largely undocumented, and which archeology has now revealed to us. This pattern, which can be characterized as the *hisn/qarya complex*, consisted of eight to ten villages (*alquerías*) grouped around a castle or *hisn* serving the area's peasants as a refuge in times of insecurity, and practicing irrigation agriculture. The alquerías were originally settled by clans or tribal segments, either Arab or Berber, but preeminently the latter.

Irrigation was accomplished by an array of associated techniques, all of which could be constructed by peasants or local artisans. Water was diverted from running streams by gravity flow in surface canals: both the diversion dam (*azud*, from *sadda*, "to close") and the canal (*acequia*, from *saqiya*) are known by Arabisms in Spanish. Water was also conducted to fields from wells, either by means of a lifting device, or through underground conduits. The lifting technique most used was the "Persian wheel," known as *naʿura* or *saniya* in Arabic (*naʿura* yields *noria* in Castilian, while in Catalonia, the same device is called *sénia*). This was a horizontal wheel moved by the traction of an animal, generally a burro or mule, that engages a vertical wheel on which is mounted an endless chain of pots (the noria pot, in Arabic *qadus*, became *arcaduz* in Castilian). In general, water was not delivered directly to the fields but stored in a holding tank (*birka*, yielding *alberca* in Castilian) and then released into the farmer's fields when most appropriate. The wells were made of stone- or brickwork, and some of them had stairways leading down to the surface of the water. Ibn al-ʿAwwām's suggestion that two wells be linked together below the surface of the water, thus delivering more water to the noria, was in fact put into practice.

The Arabs also introduced large, current-driven norias that were run on the main canals of irrigation systems or on special feeders diverted from rivers. The one at La Ñora on the Aljufia Canal in Murcia was famous, as were the wheels on the Tajo and Guadalquivir Rivers that lifted water to Toledo and Córdoba, respectively.

Another method of delivering water was the *qānāt*, also called a horizontal well. It too taps into the water table but rather than lift the water at the point of extraction, a tunnel is dug running along the surface of the water table, so that water filters into it along its entire length; hence the qānāt is also called a filtration gallery. In order to first dig and then service the tunnel, air holes are dug periodically (hence the qānāt is also called a "chain well," even though the holes in the chain are not wells). The qānāt has mainly been studied in Persia, where some of them reach great lengths and are true architectural masterpieces. Likewise, it was previously thought that Andalusian qānāts were typically the monumental ones bringing water to cities like Madrid, with its qānāt system in the Guadarrama Mountains. But recent archeological studies have demonstrated not only that qānāts were ubiquitous in al-Andalus, but that they were very modest, and were built with construction methods quite similar to those of wells. Thus in Mallorca, qānāts were typically between 1 and 1.5 meters in height with widths of between .45 and .9 meters. The modest nature of the Mallorcan qānāts can best be appreciated by their scant length. The longest of the thirteen studied are 196 and 299.9 meters, respectively. But most are much shorter: a qānāt of 24.5 meters, having but two ventilation shafts, and a mini-qānāt of 16 meters, with but one shaft, hardly the mighty channels like those bringing drinking water to Kirman or Madrid. Numerous place-names record the presence of qānāts: Canet (Mallorca), Puerto Lumbreras (Murcia), and Villacañas (Toledo) are examples.

Similar to the qānāt is the *cimbra*, a trench dug along the channel of a dry gulch in order to capture water by filtration, and then vaulted over. Tunnels carrying water underground but that have no filtration function are also known all over eastern Spain, where they are called *alcavóns*.

Water could also be lifted directly from a channel by a *swapes* or *shadufs*, known in al-Andalus as *aljataras* (as documented in the *Libros de Habices* of Granada).

We know a great deal about the incidence of hydraulic mills in Islamic Spain because many are listed in the *Libros de Repartimiento/Llibres de Repartiment*. The Repartiment of Mallorca lists numerous mills, some of them called *reha*, as in Reha Abenzeiar, from the Arabic *rāḥa*, meaning mill. Most of these mills were horizontal mills for grinding grain, run off of irrigation canals, and many, like the Molí de Cup, on the Canet Canal, were equipped with tanks called *cup* in Catalan, *cubo* in Castilian, so that water could be delivered to the paddle wheel under pressure. Thus there was ample power to drive multiple millstones in the same mill. The Repartiment of Valencia likewise lists more than one hundred mills. In rural areas, mills associated with irrigation systems were sited at the end of the canal system, whereas in Catalonia, the mill usually was sited near the head of the system with the irrigated fields downstream. In Mallorca, where the Arabs built very long sinuous canals winding through the mountains, each alquería's segment ended with a mill.

Inasmuch as horizontal mills were standard throughout the Mediterranean region, it is difficult to distinguish between those of Christian and Muslim construction; but one of the few mills still existing from before the conquest still stands, although ruined, on the Júcar River at Fortaleny.

Most industrial mills, such as fulling mills, forges, and some gristmills were vertical, powered by overshot or undershot wheels. Al-Qazwini describes an undershot mill on Mallorca that in times of water shortage could be converted to overshot. In Castile, the term *aceña* described a vertical mill—the famous aceñas lie on the Duero at Zamora—while *molino* implied a horizontal one. Paper, incidentally, was made entirely by hand in al-Andalus, although the Catalans later mechanized the process of macerating the paper.

THOMAS F. GLICK

Bibliography

Barceló, M., et al. *Les aigües cercades. Els qānāt(s) de l'Illa de Mallorca*. Palma de Mallorca, 1986.

Cressier, P. "Agua, fortificación y poblamiento: el aporte de la arqueología a los estudios sobre el sureste peninsular," *Aragón en la la Edad Media* 9 (1991), 403–27.

Glick, T. F. *Irrigation and Society in Medieval Valencia*. Cambridge, Mass., 1971.

González Tascón, I. *Fábricas hidráulicas españolas*. Madrid, 1987.

Schiøler, T. *Roman and Islamic Water-Lifting Wheels*. Copenhagen, 1973.

TECHNOLOGY, CHRISTIAN

T. F. Glick's work on Muslim technology in the Iberian Peninsula demonstrates clearly the gaps that the study of medieval Iberian technology presents, while also allowing an appreciation of the differences that exist between the emerging interest in the topic in its Islamic and Christian contexts.

As a result of Glicks work recently there has been a broadening of the technological approach to medieval research. Conferences like the fourth Congreso de Arqueología Medieval Española—along with other meetings of wider chronological focus, such as the conferences on irrigation and mining in Almería and Ripoll, respectively—are demonstrations of this emerging shift in attitude.

Two important points should be made, however. The first is that medieval Christian industry and technology has not been studied from a strictly technical perspective. There are certainly numerous historical, archaeological, and to a lesser extent, artistic studies centered on the subject, but these typically follow their own methodologies, making a true synthesis of the material difficult. The second point is that within the complex sphere of technology, only certain topics—the mill, irrigation, mining, and metallurgy—have attracted the attention of the scholar.

The broad chronology of the period is marked by a gradual increase in information and sources—written and material—that begins with St. Isidore's excessively generic reports and leads to the detailed legislation on technology found in the *fueros* and other municipal ordinances. At the same time, the almost complete lack of visual imagery representing technology is eventually replaced by multiple Romanesque and Gothic works depicting work scenes. Given the current state of things, scholars must take on the project of compiling all data pertinent to industrial processes, reading the ample existent documentation from a technical, and not just historical, perspective. We also need to revindicate the importance of those archaeological ruins associated with the acquisition, fabrication, and processing of products, as well as the transcendence of simple work tools and objects. Also fundamental is the need for the creation of an iconographic corpus, given that the integral form and use of medieval implements and tools can often be recuperated through historical images.

Finally, the study of medieval industry needs to move beyond a mere trend—this is apparent especially in the existence of "star topics"—and needs to widen its field of investigation to incorporate the whole range of topics associated with the subject.

Along with the unchanging nature of certain technological practices through periods of long duration, we must also emphasize the repercussions of economic factors as a counterpart to the continuity. Throughout periods of both economic prosperity and crisis, it is evident that the role of technology varies considerably. Parallel to these temporal variations, we should not lose sight of additional geographical variations; otherwise we risk mistaking what may be a local process for a widespread phenomenon of the Iberian Peninsula.

The complexity characteristic of the late Middle Ages is as much a product of the development of Christian society as it is a result of a greater abundance of available information. Therefore, it might be advisable to approach certain subjects going against the flow of time; that is, using an analysis of the abundant data provided in the late Middle Ages as a point of departure for a retrospective study of previous ages.

Excepting, in part, the topic of the mill, which generated an abundant historical bibliography starting in the 1970s, and a considerable group of archaeological studies in the 1980s, it is impossible to produce even a minimally coherent analysis of medieval Spanish technology. In fact, even with the mill there are still many loose ends that should be resolved in the future. For example, the differences among *rueda* (wheel), *molino* (a mill with a horizontal wheel), and *aceña* (a mill with a vertical wheel) need to be much better articulated, since several different types of mills often appear in the same place. Also, the meanings of these words within their regional and temporal contexts need to be better determined—in some occasions the aceña seems to be associated with irrigation as an element of water extraction. At the same time, the difference between molino and aceña should be distinguished, since the first was often transformed into the second. We also must differentiate between those molinos with intricate, costly infrastructures (barges, long canals, buckets) and those that lack a complex system of water transport and extraction.

The study of medieval agricultural industries can be approached and illuminated using both written texts and Romanesque and Gothic images, which until now have not been exploited to their full extent. It is perfectly possible to document certain characteristics and statistics relative to agriculture, including the number of plowshares used in a field of planted grain (documents of the Segovia cathedral chapter, late thirteenth century); the system for harvesting grain, whether through the use of a flail or a thresher (the *fueros* of León); or the terms of agreement and work conditions decided through the system of salaries and tithes (the *furs* of Catalonia), to cite a few examples. With respect to the first point, it is worth noting that in Zamora and Segovia—and possibly many other areas—documents as early as the eleventh and thirteenth centuries indicate the existence of a requirement to till the land four or five times, a date that anticipates considerably the same phenomenon in other parts of Europe. Using iconography and written documents allows us to show that the regions in which certain agricultural implements were used, such as the flail or the cart with moveable axle, were more extensive in the Middle Ages than in subsequent times, thus demonstrating the temporal mutability of certain industries that are usually deemed as unchanged throughout periods of time.

The study of Christian irrigation has only been approached by opposing it with its Islamic equivalent in order to see which Moorish traits remain or change (Glick studied this for the Valencian region). This type of analysis, however, has not focused on texts describing the northern zones of the peninsula, which do not have a strong link to the Islamic methods. The organization of hydraulic systems and water transport needs to be studied as a general process that includes the water mill, agricultural irrigation, fishing, and the thrashing mill, not only because these elements seem to be associated with the larger system, but also because the presence of one of these mechanisms often allows for the later development of others (as in the case of the mills, which are converted into aceñas or thrashing mills).

With respect to cattle raising, it is interesting that the practice has not drawn investigative attention as an industry; this is perhaps due to the lack of a significant material culture that accompanies it.

The hunt has been analyzed by studying municipal ordinances and iconography, which show a clear social duality in the hunt. In addition to the noble hunt connected to the courtly world and to war, there is another type of hunt practiced by the poorer sectors of the population. Laws reflect the varieties of techniques used by these lower classes—many of them prohibited in certain areas—and the complexity of situations associated with trespassing or with other places where hunting was not allowed. Though it has not been given the scholarly attention it deserves, fishing also takes on considerable importance in medieval life, as is reflected in the monastery's control of the practice, its association with the mill, and the regulation of fish sales in urban sectors.

Current research on mining or metallurgy in the Catalan Pyrenees or in the Cantabrian range will allow us to assess in the future the importance of the iron industry in the economy of neighboring areas and its influence on those industries in which the presence of metal is important.

The study of the handicraft industry is quite uneven; there are studies on the textile industry, the production of ceramics, etc., but we still lack studies on many other practices. We must keep in mind that in late urban documents, the craft industry is shown to have a high level of specialization.

From a social point of view, we must emphasize the fact that individuals in power—both in religious and secular positions—and members of the rural community played important roles as creators and guardians of industrial methods. This can be seen in various occasions in the clauses of agricultural contracts and in legislation in the fueros and municipal ordinances, and clearly takes shape in the specifications indicating what agricultural work needed to be performed and how such work should be realized, and in generic forms that required the work to be performed correctly. But the agricultural sphere is not the only sector where this occurs, as this attitude is also documented with respect to ironworks, breadmaking in the ovens of the nobility, and the mass-production of handmade works.

We cannot conclude without mentioning the importance of groups of "foreigners" in the development of certain technologies as evidence of the human mobility observable in the Middle Ages. A phenomenon like the Mozarabic migrations explains in part the spread of Islamic industrial methods in northern peninsular regions. In addition, the progressive conquest of zones in al-Andalus brings about the adoption of typically Moorish technological infrastructures that were not always well assimilated by Christian communities (on occasion the canal systems typical of irrigation-related industries show up in regions as far north as Catalonia *before* the conquest of Valencia or Andalusia). Other groups such as the Cistercian monks have affected the development of specific industries. Their relationship with the stress placed on mining and ironwork is well known; to a lesser extent, attention has also been drawn to the Cistercian influence on agriculture. In this brief summary, we should not forget the presence of an important collective of artisans from beyond the Pyrenees that spread their knowledge in Iberia.

José Luis Mingote Calderón

Bibliography

Caro Baroja, J. *Tecnología popular española*. Madrid, 1983.
Glick, T. F. *Tecnología, ciencia y cultura en la España medieval*. Madrid, 1992.
González Tascón, I. *Fábricas hidráulicas españolas*. Madrid, 1987.
Mingote Calderón, J. L. *Tecnología agrícola medieval en España. Una relación entre la etnología y la arqueología a través de los aperos agrícolas*. Madrid, 1995.
Various authors. *IV Congreso de Arqueología Medieval Española. Sociedades en transición*. 3 vols. Alicante, 1993–1994.

TÉLLEZ DE MENESES, LEONOR

A member of the Portuguese branch of the important Castilian Meneses family, Leonor was born circa 1350 in Trás-os-Montes. She became a lady-in-waiting to the Portuguese princess Beatriz, half-sister of King Fernando I (1367–1383). According to a 1371 treaty between Castile and Portugal, Fernando was to marry Leonor, daughter of Enrique II of Castile. He instead fell in love with Leonor Téllez, who was then married to João Lourenço da Cuhna. The king had their marriage annulled, and he wed Leonor himself in 1372. In spite of growing opposition from his subjects, Fernando empowered Leonor who, in rather unprecedented fashion, coruled with her husband and achieved extraordinary influence and power over the conduct of domestic and foreign affairs.

She established a long-lasting extramarital relationship with Juan Fernández Andeiro, a Castilian knight who had gone to serve the Duke of Lancaster in Gascony in 1371. When Fernando died in 1383, she was appointed regent with the power to govern until the majority of her daughter Beatriz who, in 1383, had married King Juan I of Castile with the stipulation that the child of this union would be future king of Portugal. When the queen's pro-Castilian policies became clear to the majority of the Portuguese and that this marriage virtually guaranteed the union of the two crowns, they rose against Leonor and her adviser and rallied around the figure of Fernando's illegitimate half-brother, João, master of the Order of Avis. The master arranged for the murder of the queen's favorite and prepared to resist the Castilian armies of Juan I summoned to Portugal by Leonor. She ceded the regency to the Castilian king but soon plotted to kill him. Juan ordered her taken to the nunnery of Santa Clara in Tordesillas, in Castile, where she died in 1386. Meanwhile, in the Battle of Aljubarrota, the Portuguese soundly defeated the Castilians, thus securing the throne for the House of Avis and averting the merger of the two kingdoms.

CLARA ESTOW

Bibliography

Lopes, F. *The English in Portugal 1367–87*. Trans. and ed. D. W. Lomax and R. J. Oakley. Warminster, England, 1988.

TEMPLE, ORDER OF THE *See* MILITARY ORDERS

TENORIO, PEDRO

Tenorio's date of birth is unknown; he died at Toledo, where he was archbishop, on 28 May 1399. Tenorio was a partisan of Enrique de Trastámara in the civil war leading to the murder of King Pedro I of Castile and the accession of the Trastámaran dynasty. Early on, as a result of his partisanship, he was forced into exile by Pedro I, first to France and then to Italy. While in Italy, he studied under the eminent canonist Baldo degli Ubaldi, taking a doctorate in canon law at Rome.

After the battle of Nájera, two of Tenorio's brothers were executed by Pedro I. Tenorio escaped the same fate thanks to the intervention of the papal legate, Guido da Bologna, in whose household he served. Tenorio went to Portugal and in 1371 was named archbishop of Coimbra. Pope Gregory XI named him archbishop of Toledo on 13 January 1377.

Tenorio is best known for his political and military activity. During the minorities of both Juan I and Enrique III, he exercised his authority and partisanship in advancing his personal interests as well as in the direction of the realm, becoming one of the most influential notables in the kingdom. In 1391, for example, after a controversy erupted over the will and intention of Juan I regarding the guardians of his son, Enrique II, a regency council under Tenorio's guidance was installed to direct the kingdom and watch over the boy during his minority. The arrangements lasted only into the first months of 1391, when deep divisions among the ambitious nobles who formed the membership emerged. Pero López de Ayala and his nephew Diego Hurtado de Mendoza figured in the latter group. The situation was immediately aggravated by a series of calamities that confronted the monarchy with a set of difficult decisions. Most important among those events was the anti-Semitic violence that broke out in Seville in the spring and spread throughout the kingdom during the rest of the summer. The council's internal divisions were resolved only by means of the actions of Enrique's aunt, Leonor, Queen of Navarra, who with the assistance of the papal legate, arranged for the disputing parties to accept, with some modifications, the original guardians Juan I had named for his son in his will. The following year was followed by trouble with the kingdom of Granada, and the Portuguese with whom a truce was finally reached in 1393. Despite all earlier efforts, discord among the members of the regency council continued and Tenorio, who threatened to resign, was taken prisoner and forced to turn over several fortifications under his protection.

E. MICHAEL GERLI

Bibliography

Diccionario de historia eclesiástica de España. 4 vols. Ed. Quintín Aldea Vaquero, et al. Madrid, 1972.

Suárez Fernández, L. "Don Pedro Tenorio, arzobispo de Toledo (1375–1399)." In *Estudios dedicados a Menéndez Pidal*. Vol. 4. Madrid, 1953. 139–48.

TERESA ALFÓNSEZ

The natural daughter of Alfonso VI of León-Castile, the first queen of an independent Portugal, and mother of the first king of Portugal, Afonso Henriques (1128–1185). Born about 1083 to a noblewoman of western Asturias, Jimena Munoz, she was married to the French Burgundian count Henry sometime before the fall of 1096. At that date the two were given the control of the county of Portugal by Alfonso VI. After the latter's death in 1109, Henry and Teresa attempted, without success, to displace Teresa's half-sister, Urraca, on the throne of León-Castile. In either 1109 or 1110 a son, Alfonso Enriquez, was born to the pair and in 1112 Count Henry died. From that point, Teresa ruled the county of Portugal, taking the title of queen in 1117. Her struggles with Urraca continued in the form of border disputes, and in the course of that rivalry she took the Galician noble, Fernando Pérez, first as lover and then as husband. This action led to a break with her son and in the Battle of San Mamed on 24 June 1128, the couple were defeated and forced to flee to Galicia, where Teresa died in November 1130. She also had a daughter, Sancha, by Count Fernando.

BERNARD F. REILLY

Bibliography

Reilly, B. F. *The Kingdom of Leon-Castilla under Queen Urraca, 1109–1126*. Princeton, N.J., 1982.

Soares, T. S. "O governo de Portugal pela Infante-Rainha D. Teresa." In *Colectânea de estudos im honra do Prof-Doutor Damião Peres*. Lisbon, 1974. 99–119.

TEXTILES

Textiles and textile fibers were important components of trade and industry in the Iberian Peninsula, both north and south, although Muslim Spain was more active in the production of luxury textiles for most of the medieval period. Andalusian textiles were widely

Detail of the so-called Gilgamesh motif on a silk weaving found in the tomb of Bishop Bemard Calvo of Vich. Moorish art, 12th c. An example of Islamic textiles which became treasures in Christian churches. Copyright © Werner Forman/Art Resource, NY. Cleveland Museum of Art, Cleveland, Ohio, U.S.A.

disseminated to Europe and the Islamic world from the ninth to the twelfth century. In the tenth century, the Muslim author Ibn Ḥawqal extolled the "precious garments of linen, cotton, and silk" available in Córdoba, and reported that Andalusian silks were sent to Egypt and even as far as Khurasan. References to luxurious "Spanish" textiles (probably of Andalusian manufacture since Christian Spain was not producing many fancy fabrics in this period) appear in European Latin texts by the ninth century. Later documents from the Muslim world, Europe, and Christian Spain show that Andalusian textiles were available in these regions. Within the peninsula, the 1162 *fuero* of Mos set a toll on "robes coming from the land of the Moors." Mozarabic wills from twelfth-century Toledo mentioned Andalusian articles of clothing, and Valencian fustians appear in an inventory of household effects from Zaragoza at the same period. In 1207, the Cortes of Toledo set tariffs on *cendal* imported from Murcia. Fabrics found in the royal tombs at Santa María la Real de las Huelgas in Burgos also testify to the diffusion of Almoravid, Almohad, and Naṣrid fabrics in the northern peninsula.

Silk was the most important fiber to the Andalusian textile industry, and silkworms probably reached the Iberian Peninsula in the eighth century. Three factors were necessary for the success of silk manufacturing. First, the mulberry trees on which to feed the silkworms; second, the human technical skills required to handle the silk; and third, sufficient numbers of people involved in the business to maintain viable levels of production. These requirements limited the silk industry geographically and rendered it susceptible to climatic and demographic fluctuations, but it thrived in southern Spain for most of the Muslim period. The industry reached its height under tā'ifa, Almoravid, and Almohad rule, and the Muslim geographer Al-Idrīsī counted three thousand farms raising silkworms in the mountains around Jaén in the middle of the twelfth century. Silk was also produced in Christian Spain by this century, particularly in Valencia, but this output was not competitive until the later Middle Ages.

We know most about the Muslim silk industry in Almería, where Al-Idrīsī reported eight hundred workshops devoted to the production of silks and brocades. Another twelfth-century geographer, Al-Zuhrī, reported that "nothing is hidden from any of the craftspeople here . . . in Almería, every type of elegant furnishing is manufactured, and everything is perfectly made. All the people here, men and women, work with their hands; the most frequent craft of women is spinning, which brings silk to its high price, and the most frequent craft among men is weaving." The high numbers cited here suggest that silk production was a cottage industry, both at the level of cultivation and later textile manufacture. Many people would have been involved, and even children were useful because their small fingers were better at unwinding the delicate filaments from the silk cocoons.

References to Andalusian raw silk and silk textiles decline after the early thirteenth century, and although the industry continued in Naṣrid Granada, it appears that Spanish silk no longer dominated western Mediterranean markets in the later Middle Ages. Demographic and political changes in the peninsula seem to have adversely affected the silk industry. Likewise, competition from silk ateliers in southern Italy and Sicily was a factor in the industry's decline, as was the increasing availability of other luxury fabrics. Whereas Muslim Spain had once exported silks to Europe, now Iberian consumers were eager for Flemish and Italian woolens and linens.

Beginning in the thirteenth century, the main centers of Iberian textile production moved to the northern peninsula, and there was a gradual shift in production so that wool, linen, and other fibers superseded silk by the later Middle Ages. An analysis of textile nomenclature in fifteenth-century Castilian documents indicates that the majority of textiles available in Christian Iberian markets were made of wool and fibers other than silk.

Sheep had been raised in the peninsula since Roman times, but Roman and Andalusian wools were inferior to the merino wool that became the standard Castilian export. There seems to have been a lag of roughly a century between the decay of Andalusian silk traffic and the full-fledged development of the wool industry. Already by 1253, however, the routes (*cañadas*) for the flocks had been established, and the incorporation of the Honorable Assembly of the Mesta of the Shepherds by Alfonso X in 1273 probably confirmed earlier royal grants (now lost). Small quantities of Iberian wool were imported to England by the 1260s, and a Bruges ordinance of 1304 also noted sales of Spanish wool. By the middle of the fourteenth century, exports of Iberian wool were well established and the wool trade would dominate the peninsula's commerce for the next two hundred years. It has been estimated that by 1467 the Castilian sheep population had reached 2,700,000 head, double what it had been in the thirteenth century.

The growth of Iberian wool production marked a dramatic reorientation of the peninsula's economy, since a textile industry and trade based on sheep, and on the long seasonal migrations of shepherds, was very different from the small, sedentary, family-based operations characteristic of silk cultivation. The development and success of the wool trade in the Iberian Peninsula may be attributed to several interrelated causes, among them the facts that the climate and terrain of Castile were well suited to migratory sheep herding (particularly in a period when military campaigns had disrupted agriculture in the central peninsula); that conquests and territorial expansion in the thirteenth century had thinned and redistributed the Castilian and Aragónese populations; and that foreign demand fostered traffic, and burgeoning textile industries in Flanders, France, and Italy provided a ready market for Spanish wool.

OLIVIA REMIE CONSTABLE

Bibliography

Alfau de Solalinde, J. *Nomenclatura de los tejidos españoles del siglo XIII*. Madrid, 1969.

Gual Camarena, M. "Orígenes y expansión de la industria lanera catalana en la Edad Media." In *Atti della seconda settimana di studio, Istituto F. Datini*. Florence, 1976. 511–23.

Iradiel Murugarren, P. *Evolución de la industria textil castellana en los siglos XIII–XVI*. Salamanca, 1974.

Lombard, M. *Les textiles dans le monde musulman*. Paris, 1978.

Martínez, M. *Los nombres de tejidos en castellano medieval*. Granada, 1989.

May, F. *Silk Textiles of Spain, 8th–15th Century*. New York, 1957.

Morral i Romeu, E., and A. Segura i Mas. *La seda en España: Leyenda, poder, y realidad*. Barcelona, 1991.

Partearroyo, C. "Almoravid and Almohad Textiles," In *Al-Andalus: The Art of Islamic Spain*. Ed. J. Dodds. New York, 1992. 105–13.

Riu, M. "The Woollen Industry in Catalonia in the Later Middle Ages." In *Cloth and Clothing in Medieval Europe: Essays in Memory of Professor E. M. Carus-Wilson*. London, 1983. 205–29.

THEATER

The conventional picture of medieval Iberia—particularly of central Spain and Portugal—as a theatrical desert is slowly yielding to a more balanced image of a region which, broadly speaking, engaged in the same ludic activities as other western European countries. The liturgical drama flourished in Catalonia, where the earliest texts are preserved in a tenth- or eleventh-century troper from the Benedictine monastery of Ripoll. One Easter drama, *Verses pascales de III M[ariis]*, boasts a highly developed apothecary scene. An extant fourteenth-century customary from Girona contains detailed staging instructions for eight plays, among them a sophisticated Easter drama, also *Repraesentatio Partus Beate Virginis* and *Processio prophetarum*. At the Cathedral of Vic, the *Cantus sibyllae* and *Quem queritis in presepe, pastores, dicite*? were chanted at Christmas but not the more developed European *Officium pastorum*.

Church documents from Lérida confirm that the cathedral mounted Christmas and Easter plays, also a spectacular Pentecostal *Devallament de la colometa*, which employed aerial machinery and a mechanical dove with firecrackers attached to its wings. Similar church dramas were staged in Valencia and Mallorca, although at Palma de Mallorca all the prophets, not just the Sibyl, appeared on Christmas Eve. Catalonia and Valencia were home to elaborate Assumption plays, with the Elche drama still an annual event. By the late fourteenth century the feast of Corpus Christi was celebrated with increasingly costly street processions that featured biblical pageants (ninety-nine in Barcelona by 1424). In Valencia some pageants evolved into genuine plays, three of which are extant.

Castile presents a somewhat different picture of liturgical drama with its two idiosyncratic eleventh-century Easter tropes from the Benedictine monastery of Silos. Richard Donovan argues that the overarching influence in Castile of Benedictine monks from Cluny accounts for the disappearance of liturgical drama after the eleventh century. This disappearance, however, appears to have been less than total and may be explained in part by the wanton destruction of monastic libraries. Early printed missals, with even earlier service books embedded in them, and allusions to church drama in heterogeneous documents strongly imply that, by the late fourteenth century, and possibly a hundred years earlier, Castile celebrated all the important feasts with plays in Latin and Spanish. Toledo records the *Cantus sibyllae* at Christmas Matins and *Pastores, dicite, quidnam vidistis?* at Lauds, with choir boys (*seises*) disguised as shepherds singing and dancing; also performances for Candlemas, Good Friday, Easter Sunday, and Pentecost. The *Auto de los Reyes Magos*, by far the most representational of the twelfth-century European vernacular plays, looms as an anomaly. Possibly of foreign provenance, it nonetheless survives in Mozarabic Spanish.

Elsewhere in central Spain there is evidence of the Sibylline chant in León, Easter drama in Zamora, the *Depositio crucis* and colorful *Procesión del pendón* in Palencia, the *Depositio crucis* and *Elevatio crucis* in Jaén, the *Quem quaeritis* in Zaragoza, and, after the Reconquest, the *Elevatio crucis*, *Visitatio sepulchri*, and *Procesión del pendón* in Guadix and Granada. Two early-fifteenth-century texts, one a Procession of Sibyls in Spanish and Latin, and a Latin *Planctus passionis*, are eminently actable. In the 1460s Gómez Manrique's Nativity play, composed for the Poor Clares of Calabazanos, features a traditional Joseph, who questions Mary's chastity and an Adoration scene in which the infant Jesus is presented with the instruments of his Passion. Manrique's passion play, with speaking parts for the Virgin, John, and Mary Magdalene, unfolds at the foot of the cross. Fr. Iñigo de Mendoza incorporated a stage-worthy Nativity play into his *Vita Christi*, while in 1487 in Zaragoza a spectacular Christmas song-drama, comparable to those mounted in Valencia, with a revolving heaven (*paraíso*), was performed for Fernando and Isabel.

The relatively late appearance in Castile of Corpus Christi pageants and plays is attributed to its late urbanization. Yet by the second half of the fifteenth century biblical *autos*, tracing the spiritual history of humankind and boasting speaking parts for the characters, were mounted on pageant-wagon stages in Toledo, and by the early sixteenth century in Salamanca, Seville, Zaragoza, and Madrid. Extant documents, however, make no allusion before the early sixteenth century to the uniquely Spanish *auto sacramental*.

In western Iberia records of church drama are even sketchier. In Galicia the *Visitatio sepulchri* satisfied European pilgrims visiting Santiago de Compostela at

Easter. In Portugal, however, no evidence has appeared yet of Latin Resurrection drama, but a Nativity tradition like that of Castile is recorded. On Christmas Eve 1500, choir boys disguised as shepherds entered the royal chapel, dancing and singing *Gloria in excelsis Deo*.

As early as the thirteenth century medieval chronicles record an Iberian court theater that included ostentatious pageants and mummings often accompanying royal receptions and banquets. In eastern Spain, among the most colorful ceremonies were the welcome of Alfonso X el Sabio to Valencia in 1269, and in Zaragoza the coronations of Aragónese monarchs Alfonso III in 1286, Sibila in 1381, Martín I in 1399, and Fernando de Antequera in 1414. Thus the ballroom of the Aljafería in Zaragoza, with its canopy depicting heaven, became the setting for an impressive series of allegorical pageants.

The Castilian kings, particularly Juan II, also relished the wooden castles, passages at arms, and allegorical *entremeses* that glorified the monarchy. The *Farsa de Avila* (Farce of Avila, 1465), conversely, enacted the mock deposition of Enrique IV. Also in the 1460s the court of Miguel Lucas de Iranzo, Condestable of Castile, became the center of a secular and religious theater including *invenciones*, *entremeses*, and *representaciones*. The condestable's Magi play claimed as its stage the streets of Jaén and interior of his palace. Two *momerías* (short, comical interludes) survive by Gómez Manrique, and one by Francisco Moner, while Francisco de Madrid's *Egloga* (1495) is a full-fledged political drama.

Portuguese mummings rivaling those of Castile accompanied royal weddings in 1387, 1429, 1451, 1486, and particularly December 1490, when the king appeared as the Knight of the Swan. There were also a *mourisca* (*festa de mouros*, or festival of Moors), wooden castles, and the familiar *paraiso*. The Christmas *momos* (interludes) of 1500 featured the Garden of Love in Ethiopia, which included a three-headed dragon, giant, a ship on wheels, and a large cast of performers that presage Gil Vicente's festival plays.

Medieval Iberia also witnessed popular expressions of festivity with theatrical overtones, but information about them is limited mainly to civil and ecclesiastical condemnations. Descendants of ancient mimes performed throughout Iberia in palaces, churches, and public squares. Minstrels sang, danced, played musical instruments, also blackened their faces or disguised themselves as devils, wild men, animals, and engaged in pantomime that smacked of paganism. Carnivalesque rejoicing is recorded both inside and outside the church. Under the vague, nondescript *juegos de escarnio*, (mocking games) Alfonso el Sabio attempted to outlaw from the churches cross-dressing and other excesses associated with the *festum stultorum* (feast of fools), but the proliferation of late fifteenth-century prohibitions attests to the resiliency of festive merrrymaking. The *fiesta del obispillo*, (feast of the little bishop) celebrated throughout Iberia by the late fifteenth century, also got out of hand and was repeatedly proscribed only to be reinstated by popular demand. Folk traditions like the *tarasca* (dragon in Corpus Christi play), *gigantes* (giants), and wild men eventually received official endorsement for Corpus Christi and other feasts. Church-sponsored biblical pageants reflected an attempt to curb spontaneously organized *juegos* in Spain, (*jogos* in Portugal), which included erotic scenes, mock battles, and cavorting devils. These shows, however, may contain the seeds of popular farce, whose first literary expression in Castile is the *Auto del repelón* (1509), attributed to Juan del Encina.

Evidence is stronger for a farcical tradition in medieval Portugal. Yet to be determined, however, is the extent to which the jogos and *arremedilhos* (imitations) helped shape Gil Vicente's and Anrique da Mota's farces, where comic medieval stereotypes like cuckolded husbands, scheming wives, pixilated clerics, incompetent judges, impoverished *hidalgos* (noblemen), avaricious Jews, loutish peasants, and conniving black servants appear in conventional farcical plots and speak a comic idiom that includes special dialects for peasants, blacks, and Jews. These farces satirize the political, social, and religious mores of their time.

Medieval definitions of ancient *theatrum*, *scaena*, *comoedia*, *tragoedia*, recorded already in Isidore of Seville's *Etymologiae*, were revived by fifteenth-century humanists. Enrique de Villena's description of *theatrum*, embedded in his annotated translation of Virgil's *Aeneid*, stands out as especially detailed and functional. Finally, Latin humanistic comedy shaped Fernando de Rojas's *Tragicomedia de Calisto y Melibea*, which was amenable to private as well as public reading with a single reader projecting all the roles, or with speaking parts assigned to a narrator and the action performed by mimes in accordance with medieval practice.

CHARLOTTE STERN

Bibliography

Alvarez Pellitero, A. *Teatro medieval*. Madrid, 1990.

Donovan, R. B. *The Liturgical Drama in Medieval Spain*. Toronto, 1958.

Gómez Moreno, A. *El teatro medieval castellano en su marco románico*. Madrid, 1991.

Stern, C. *The Medieval Theater in Castile*. Binghamton, N.Y. 1995.

Surtz, R. E. *Teatro medieval castellano*. Madrid, 1992.

THEODEMIR, COUNT OF MURCIA

In the wake of the Muslim invasion of 711, Theodemir came to terms with ʿAbd al-ʿAzīz, the son of Mūṣā ibn Nusayr, and retained control over Murcia as a tributary of the Muslim government. The pact (*dhimma*) worked out between the two has survived, providing historians of Spain with a rare, detailed look at the institution that allowed the Muslims to gain control over Spain so quickly. In it Theodemir—or Tudmir, as his name is transliterated in the Arabic document—agreed to recognize the overlordship of ʿAbd al-ʿAzīz and to pay tribute in the form of a yearly cash payment supplemented with specific agricultural products. In exchange, ʿAbd al-ʿAzīz promised to respect Theodemir's property and his dominion over the province.

An apparently interpolated passage in the *Mozarabic Chronicle of 754* provides more details about Theodemir. He had served under both Egica and Witiza, distinguishing himself in battle against Byzantine naval forces. The treaty that he negotiated with ʿAbd al-ʿAzīz was, according to the chronicle, respected by the caliphs in Damascus up to his death in 744. He was succeeded as lord of Murica by Athanagild, who may have been his son.

KENNETH B. WOLF

Bibliography

Collins, R. *The Arab Conquest of Spain, 710–797*. Oxford, 1989.

Simonet, F. *Historia de los mozárabes de España*. Madrid, 1903. 797–98.

Wolf, K. *Conquerors and Chroniclers of Early Medieval Spain*. Liverpool, 1990.

THEODOMIR, BISHOP OF IRIA FLAVIA

Theodomir (ca. 819–847) is the first of the medieval bishops of Iria Flavia, (now Padrón) on the northwest coast of Spain in Galicia, for whom we have secure historical evidence. That see had existed in the Visigothic period but the episcopal succession there was interrupted by the Muslim invasion after 711 and was only restored, probably, by Alfonso II of Asturias (791–842). Before the discovery of the inscribed cover to his coffin in this century it was possible to regard the bishop himself as an apocryphal figure.

Bishop Theodomir is famous largely as the prelate during whose pontificate the remains of St. James the Great were unearthed, sometime about the year 830, in the nearby location later to become known as Santiago de Compostela. The best-known source for the incident is the twelfth-century *Historia Compostelana*, which describes reports reaching the bishop of strange lights and angels that had begun to appear at night in a nearby forest. Investigating himself, the bishop found in the forest a small shrine and a marble tomb. He then reported the event to Alfonso II, who had the first of several churches erected over what was to become a shrine and pilgrimage center second only to Rome itself in the medieval western world. The bishop is also said to have moved the residence of the bishops of Iria Flavia to Santiago de Compostela.

The almost as famous but apocrypal grant of the *votos*, or annual tribute to be paid by all of Christian Spain to the shrine of Santiago, is actually dated during his pontificate, 25 May 834. But Theodomir is not mentioned in it and this purported diploma of Ramiro I (842–850) has largely ceased to have its defenders.

BERNARD F. REILLY

Bibliography

Fletcher, R. A. *Saint James' Catapult: The Life and Times of Diego Gelmírez of Santiago de Compostela*. Oxford, 1984.

Vázquez de Parga, L., J. M. Lacarra, and J. U. Ríu. *Las peregrinaciones a Santiago de Compostela*. 3 vols. Madrid, 1948–49. This is the magisterial work and the first volume covers the early sources for the shrine thoroughly.

THEODOSIAN CODE

The Theodosian Code was the first official codification of Roman law. It had been preceded in the late third century by two informal attempts at codifying existing imperial legislation, known as the Gregorian and Hermogenian Codes. This code was named after the emperor Theodosius II (402–450), under whose authority it was compiled. The work of codification was carried out by a commission headed by the former quaestor and prefect Antiochus. The code was promulgated in the year 438, and the text of its formal reception by the Senate in Rome has been preserved. The work was divided into sixteen books, each subdivided into titles. Each title contained, in chronological order, all of the laws relevant to its theme that had been issued in the form of imperial edicts or rescripts since the reign of the first Christian emperor, Constantine I (306–337). Because of the nature of the processes for the issuing of imperial law at this time, there was much contradiction and uncertainty as to the continuing validity of particular edicts, and thus the intention behind the codification was to produce an authoritative compilation that could be employed in the courts of the empire. In fulfilling this aspiration the Theodosian Code was only partly successful, and had to be replaced in the eastern half of the Roman Empire in 529 by the Code of Justinian. In the West, however, it remained influential and the Visigothic *Breviary of Alaric* and the Burgundian *Lex Romana Burgundionum* were derived from it.

ROGER COLLINS

Bibliography

Jones, A. H. M. *The Later Roman Empire*, 3 vols. Oxford, 1964. Vol. 1. 470–522.

Mommsen, T. (ed.) *Codex Theodosianus*. 3 vols. Berlin, 1905.

THEOLOGY

Despite the diversity of themes, methods, and questions in theological thought and practice in medieval Iberi from the sixth to the sixteenth century, two factors stand out during this period as common threads running through peninsular reflections on the divine and the relationship of the divine to the world. First, there really was no such thing at any time during this stretch as an Iberian theologian, a person whose main task it was to engage in theological speculation. Rather, we see a multitude of figures, be they monastic or lay reformers, bishops, abbots, friars, or canon lawyers, who wrote about theology as one part of their larger activities. Doctrinal formulation was not just inseparable from the more practical issues and questions about how to live as a Christian in the world, it emerged precisely out of seemingly mundane, in the literal sense, questions. Second, these very different figures are linked by the fact that they all habitually made use of the work of thinkers from outside the peninsula to respond to local issues and questions. What we see in Iberian theology is a host of creative people capable of taking ideas from others, defined in sometimes very different circumstances, and adopting and adapting them, whether in so-called original treatises or in works of compilation, to create new syntheses with Iberian problems and solutions in mind.

The conversion of the Visigothic kingdom from Arian to Catholic Christianity was the first problem requiring a theological component to its solution. The Visigothic Arians, who denied that the Son and Holy Spirit were coequal with the Father, had always been a minority among the Catholic Hispano-Roman subject population. King Reccared followed his personal conversion in 587 to Catholicism by formally converting the kingdom to orthodoxy at the Third Council of Toledo in 589, under the influence of Bishop Leander of Seville who had written works of anti-Arian polemic earlier in his career. The articles of the council, which were subscribed by eight formerly Arian bishops and five leading Visigothic nobles, among others, included a declaration of orthodoxy by Reccared that recalled the authority of the ecumenical church councils, cited the credal formulations of Nicaea (324), Constantinople (381), and Chalcedon (451), promulgated a new creed, and denounced Arian beliefs in a series of twenty-three anathemas that recapitulated Catholic doctrine. The theological formulations of this council bear the imprint of the North African theologians who were so influential in the Iberian Peninsula at this time. The council proposed three theological initiatives. It required the recitation of the Nicaean Creed during the Mass; it added to the Creed the *filioque* clause asserting that the Holy Spirit proceeded from the Son as well as from the Father; and, again under the influence of the African church, it ignored the condemnation of the Three Chapters by the Fifth Ecumenical Council of 553.

Later councils in the peninsula continued to dwell on questions of Trinitarianism and Christology. The Second Council of Seville included a discussion of the relationship between the divine and human natures in the single person of Christ that seems to bear the imprint of its presiding bishop, Isidore of Seville. Isidore is the most well-known author of the Visigothic period for his encyclopedic *Etymologies*, historical writings, works of exegesis, and his study of the liturgy, *On the Offices of the Church*. He was followed by other important authors, like the two bishops of Toledo, Ildefonsus, whose *On the Perpetual Virginity of the Virgin Mary* was an influential prod to Marian devotion in the West, and Julian, whose *Sign of the Future Life*, which exists in some 186 manuscripts, collects the teachings of Augustine, Jerome, Ambrose, Gregory the Great, and Isidore among others, on the origins of death, the fate of souls after death, and the resurrection of the body.

The peninsula was conquered by the Muslims in 711. The teachings known as Adoptionism of Elipandus of Toledo and Felix of Urgell, condemned by the Carolingian Synod of Frankfurt in 794, have often been seen as a response to the Muslim position that Jesus was simply a fully human prophet. Recent lines of argument see the controversy between the Adoptionists and their Iberian opponent, Beatus of Liébana, not as reflecting Eastern debates on Nestorianism and the positions taken by the Council of Chalcedon, but rather as differing interpretations of the Christological formulations of Western and African thinkers like Augustine, Tyconius, Leo, and Fulgentius. This reading sees the Adoptionists and Beatus as presenting different versions of a uniquely Iberian Christology. After the *Com-*

mentary on the Apocalypse of Beatus, we have very little original theological writing for several centuries, although theological ideas continue to be expressed in innovative ways through the media of the visual arts, in manuscripts, sculpture, and small objects.

From the thirteenth century, as Christian conquest of Muslim-held lands solidified, Christians had to come to terms for the first time with large populations of Muslims and Jews living in their midst. This fact reignited theological reflections of very different kinds including the emergence of a kind of theological school of thought in Toledo under the aegis of its archbishop, Rodrigo Jiménez de Rada. This school wedded together the neo-Platonic cosmology and mathematical speculations on the Trinity of thinkers associated with Chartres; ideas about divine grammar stemming from Gilbert of Poitiers and ultimately from Boethius; and a notion of the hierarchy of being deriving from Pseudo-Dionysius and John Scot Eriugena. Alain of Lille is the common denominator for much of this, and it is likely that Rodrigo, and possibly the other figures associated with this school, who include Michael Scot, Mauricio of Burgos, Mark of Toledo, and Diego García, chancellor of Castile, had contact with Alain at some point. Toledan thinkers shared an understanding of divine unity, of the relationship between divine unity and plurality, and of the cosmology of the universe as a hierarchy of being stemming from God and encompassing all creation. This understanding of the relationship between unity and plurality left a place for non-Christians to live, subordinated to the rule of the Christian Church. This theology justified a unified but not necessarily uniform Iberia.

Other thirteenth-century theological work is inseparable from joint projects to reform Christian life and to missionize to Muslims and Jews. We can place in this category the efforts of Ramon de Penyafort, canonist and general of the Dominican Order. Penyafort was a supporter of the mystic, missionary, and prolific author, Ramón Llull. Llull's goal was to provide convincing reasons for Muslims and Jews to convert by starting from principles acceptable to all, such as God's unity and goodness. Llull shows that the divine attributes, each of which is real and operates in a threefold mode of agent, patient, and action, are active and evident also in the created world. As expressed through his numerous polemical, contemplative, philosophical, and scientific works, Llull argues that the Christian mysteries, like the Trinity and the Incarnation, were part of the very structure of the universe. This is so he can prove the truth of these mysteries by showing that creation would be incomplete without them. Llull's system eliminates the gap between theology and philosophy or, indeed, any of the other sciences.

Beginning in the late twelfth and thirteenth centuries, the Iberian vernaculars come into their own as media for the transmission of theological thought, and the importance of these languages only increases in subsequent centuries. From the early period, we have Gonzalo de Berceo's *Sacrificio de la Missa* and his various Marian texts. Ramón Llull wrote many of his works in Catalan. Others wrote devotional texts like Arnaldo Pons's *Diálogos entre el alma y el Creador* and works on mental prayer, or catechetical works, as in those on the ten commandments. Notable is the thirteen-volume encyclopedia of Christianity, *Lo chrestià*, of the Franciscan, Francesc Eiximenis, and the work of Castilian poets like Ambrosio Montesino and Juan de Padilla.

In the fifteenth century we see a confluence of different streams of thought. Llullism, which had survived the fourteenth century attack on its perceived rationalism by Nicolás Eymeric, remained a potent force for its speculative and mystical theology. An indigenous Franciscan and Hieronymite Observantine tradition was joined by a Benedictine tradition infused by the Christian humanism of Naples and the reforming efforts of St. Justina of Padua. The Observantines share an emphasis on the humility and suffering of Christ, and the poverty and simplicity of their own lives. Finally, the Devotio Moderna tradition of northern Europe, which was to reach its culmination in the career of Erasmus, had an impact on the peninsula, with its nonmystical theology and devotion to the human Christ. The merging of these strands can be seen, for example, in the career and writings of García Jiménez de Cisneros, abbot of Montserrat and author of the *Exercises of the Spiritual Life*. These syntheses of the fifteenth century would go on to influence the creative geniuses of the sixteenth, Teresa of Ávila and Ignatius of Loyola.

Lucy K. Pick

Bibliography

Bonner, A. *Doctor Illuminatus: A Ramon Llull Reader*. Princeton, N.J., 1993.

Cavadini, J. C. *The Last Christology of the West: Adoptionism in Spain and Gaul, 785–820*. Philadelphia, 1993.

Fernández Conde, J. (ed.) *Historia de la Iglesia en España*, Vol. 2, parts 1 and 2. Madrid, 1982.

Fontaine, J. *Isidore de Séville: Genèse et originalité de la culture hispanique au temps des Wisigoths*. Turnhout, 2000

Melquiades, A. M. *La teología española en el siglo XVI*. Barcelona, 1970.

Pick, L. K. "Michael Scot in Toledo: *Natura naturans* and the Hierarchy of Being," *Traditio* 53 (1998), 93–116.

TIRANT LO BLANC

A fifteenth-century Catalan novel of chivalry written by the Valencian knight Joanot Martorell. The first edition (Valencia, 1490) bears a second author's name, Martí Joan de Galba, but it is difficult to know exactly what he contributed. A second edition (Barcelona, 1497) shows that *Tirant* was a best-seller of the fifteenth century. The plot has three parts. From chapters 1 to 116 Martorell describes the hero's education, which begins with the story of Guillem de Vàroic, the highest model for a Christian knight (chapters 1–27). Guillem is a character borrowed from the twelfth-century Anglo-Norman poem *Guy de Warwicke*, translated into Catalan by Martorell himself. Vàroic defeats the Muslim invaders of Great Britain and, after refusing all rewards for this great achievement, becomes a hermit. Tirant meets him in a lonely land during his journey to the king of England's marriage feasts and takes advice from him. On his way home, our hero and his cousin Diafebus tell Guillem about Tirant's great deeds (chapters 28–98), which made him the finest living knight in the world. In order to consecrate his military skill to the struggle against the unbelievers, Tirant decides to rescue the island of Rhodes, besieged by the Turks. During his visit to Sicily, Tirant arranges for the marriage of the heiress of that country to a younger son of the king of France. There Tirant receives a letter from the emperor of Constantinople asking for help. With his landing on Greek shores in chapter 117, the second part of the novel begins. From there to chapter 297 Martorell builds the best of his narrative on a mixture of romantic and military episodes. The hero falls passionately in love with the emperor's young daughter, Carmesina, and at the same time becomes the captain of all the Christian armies in Greece. The successful love stories between Diafebus and Estefania and Hipòlit and the empress, and the erotic games planned by the princess's friend Plaerdemavida are some of the most famous episodes of that part of the novel. Then Martorell describes the great victory of Tirant against his Muslim enemies and Greek adversaries and also his defeat in bed with Carmesina. In the following chapters the celebration of Christian victory is darkened by new Turkish aggressions. On the other hand, the Viuda Reposada, Carmesina's wicked nurse, manages to convince Tirant that his beloved has a repulsive black lover. The hero, in deep despair, decides to expose himself to death on the battlefield. The ship bringing him there sinks and the third part of the novel starts (chapters 298–487). Tirant reaches North African shores and begins a new period of military achievements; in the end he converts the entire local Muslim population to Christianity. The African king Escariano becomes Tirant's close friend and is one of the many allies that our hero gathers at the end of the book to rescue Constantinople from the Turks. Just when the emperor decides to make him his heir and the husband of Carmesina, Tirant dies of a bad cold, thus in turn causing his betrothed and her father to die of sorrow. Thanks to Tirant's deed, the new emperor rules a country free from Muslim danger, but he doesn't belong any more to the heroic lineage as his predecessors.

In spite of the variety of his sources (Ramon Llull, Muntaner, or Guillem de Torroella among Catalan writers, and John of Mandeville, Boccaccio, Petrarch, or Guido delle Colonne among Latin and Romance authors), Martorell was a very original literary creator who wrote an extraordinarily precise descriptive prose and endowed some of his characters with astonishing realistic features. But Martorell also filled his pages with long rhetorical digressions, often borrowed from other writers, which we assume were appreciated by contemporary readers.

LOLA BADÍA

Bibliography

Martorell, J., and M. J. Galba. *Tirant lo Blanc*. Trans. D. H. Rosenthal. New York, 1984.

———. *Tirant lo Blanc i altres escrits de Joanot Martorell*. Ed. M. de Riquer. Barcelona, 1979.

Riquer, M. de. *Aproximació al Tirant lo Blanc*. Barcelona, 1990.

TOLEDANO, EL *See* JIMÉNEZ DE RADA, RODRIGO

TOLEDO, CITY OF

The city of Toledo, the Toletum of pre-Roman origin, is situated almost at the geographical center of the Iberian Peninsula. Toledo rests on a granite hill surrounded on three sides by the Tajo River and, as such, until the modern age always enjoyed an ideal defensive position. Historically and culturally Toledo is one of the most important cities in Iberia. Early on it became an archiepiscopal see and, in the early Middle Ages, its archbishops became the primates of the Spains.

During the early Middle Ages, the Visigoths, who had invaded and conquered the Roman provinces of Hispania in the 470s, favored Toledo as their primary seat. Beginning in the sixth century, a distinguished series of archbishops of the see of Toledo presided over a succession of councils that issued important legislation for the early medieval Iberian Church. Toledo's greatest prosperity began under Islamic rule (712–1085), first as the seat of an emir and briefly after 1031 as the capital of an independent kingdom presided over by the Banū Dhū-l-Nūn, a Berber dy-

Toledo, Spain. Photograph of the medieval city. Copyright © Art Resource, NY.

nasty. Under its Islamic rulers, and later after its conquest in 1085 by the Christian king Alfonso VI of León and Castile, Toledo was the single most important crossroads of Jewish, Moslem, and Christian cultures in Europe. It was there that, almost immediately after the Christian conquest of the city, its new archbishop, Raimundus, inaugurated a vast project translating scientific, philosophical, and literary works from Arabic into Romance and then into Latin, for their subsequent diffusion in Europe. As a cultural and linguistic melting pot, it was always easy to find both the texts and the translators to render them into other languages prior to their dissemination. Azarquiel, the great Muslim astronomer, worked early on in Toledo; the *Ptolemaic Tables* (the so-called *Almagest* or *Tablas toledanas* were first translated there); and later the city attracted a distinguished host of scientists and men of letters ranging from Abelard of Bath, Michael Scot, Peter the Venerable, Gherardus of Cremona, and Hermannus Alemannus, to local savants like Dominicus Gundisalvus (Domingo González) and Juan Hispano, all hungry for knowledge and ready to exploit Toledo's universal reputation for learning. To be sure, Toledo's association with science and wonder won the city fame as a center of magic and the black arts throughout the Middle Ages.

E. Michael Gerli

Bibliography

Ferreiro Alemparte, J. "La escuela de nigromancia de Toledo." *Anuario de estuudios medievales* 13 (1983), 205–68.

Márquez Villanueva, F. "In *lingua tholetana* . . ." In *La escuela de traductores de Toledo*. Toledo, 1996.

Menéndez y Pelayo, M. *Historia de los heterodoxos de españoles*. Vol. 2. Madrid, 1909.

Vernet, J. *La cultura hispanoárabe en oriente y occidente*. Barcelona, 1978.

TOLEDO, COUNCILS OF

Introduction

The ancient Iberian Church deliberated matters of discipline largely through councils. Numerous episcopal assemblies were convoked in Spain, from the age of Diocletian (the council of Iliberis, ca. 306) until the Muslim invasion of the Iberian Peninsula in 711. These meetings were held in various Hispanic cities and under varying political conditions, both under the Roman Empire before and after the Edict of Milan (313) and under the Visigothic monarchy before and after the conversion of the barbarian populations to Christianity (589), all throughout a period of more than four hundred years. These assemblies, a large portion of whose acts have been preserved, created the institutional and disciplinary framework within which the activities of the Hispanic Church developed. The nature of the councils continued to evolve until the eighth century, when they gave shape to three types of conciliary assemblies: the diocesan synod, the provincial council, and the national council, which is known as the general council (*concilio general*) in historical sources. The majority were provincial councils, since the ecclesiastical laws in effect required all bishops in a given province to meet annually, though such ordinances were not always strictly obeyed. The most important councils, however, were the concilios generales, or national councils, of Toledo, convoked in the city that served both as capital of the monarchy and as the most important metropolitan seat of the Visigothic kingdom. These general councils constituted an innovation of the Hispanic Church.

The Number of Councils

Manuscript tradition has shown the existence of eighteen councils of Toledo. The first two were provincial Toledan councils that convened when Toledo was not yet the metropolitan seat of Cartagena. The first of the general councils was the Third Council of Toledo (589), held in the royal city to ratify the conversion of King Recared and the Visigothic people to Catholicism as well as their solemn abjuration of the Arian heresy. An additional interprovincial council in 597 and a Carthaginian episcopal assembly in 610, both convoked in Toledo, are not counted among the general councils nor anthologized in the *Colección Canónica Hispana*. The Ninth and Eleventh Councils of Toledo, held in

655 and 675 respectively, were also of a provincial nature. Although the Fourteenth Council of Toledo (684) was also of a provincial character, representatives of other ecclesiastical regions attended, making the assembly difficult to classify. The proceedings of the Eighteenth Council have not been preserved.

There were, then, twelve general Councils of Toledo: the Third (589), Fourth (633), Fifth (636), Sixth (638), Seventh (646), Eighth (653), Tenth (656), Twelfth (681), Thirteenth (683), Fifteenth (688), Sixteenth (693), and Seventeenth (694). As can be noted, these national councils were convoked in a highly irregular manner, responding to concrete necessities. Despite the evidently general nature of the Third Council (589), the institutional rules that regulated the concilio general were not elaborated until the Fourth Council of Toledo in 633.

Jurisdiction of the Councils

The seventh century saw the evolution and perfection of the organization and regulation of the provincial and general councils. These ordinances were expressed in an *ordo de celebrando concilio*, a ceremonial and canonic collection that was increasingly amplified starting with the Fourth Council of Toledo. While the provincial council took up ecclesiastical and civil matters in provincial areas and in principle met once a year, the general council was convoked whenever necessary to deal with general matters that affected the whole kingdom and to deliberate on problems of faith and of common interest, including political affairs. Therefore, the general council was designated as a superior deliberative body that decided both ecclesiastical and civil matters. In addition, it functioned as a judicial body in cases involving bishops: all prelates were subject to the council's jurisdiction, including the primate of Toledo. The general council's decisions became official legislation of the kingdom, after receiving royal sanction (*Lex in confirmatione concilii*). Because the Visigothic monarchy was chosen by election, at times serious conflicts arose concerning the legitimacy of certain kings who were helped to the throne via reproachable procedures: these aspirants to the monarchy sought justification through the protection of the general council. In doctrinal matters, the councils formulated a collection of theologically determined symbols of faith, always in concordance with the first four ecumenical councils, which were considered equivalent in authority to the four Gospels. The general Councils of Toledo also played the important role of serving as a unifying bond between the ecclesiastical community and the universal church.

The Nature of the Councils

Prelates in attendance at the councils were entrusted with responsibilities ranging from the ecclesiastical to the civil, the legislative to the judicial, and the fiscal to the dogmatic, depending on the circumstances. There was no clear demarcation of jurisdiction: the king and the Visigothic magnates possessed certain specific powers, but at the same time the council limited excessive civil authority in individual cases. As a result, the council was a sui generis institution that is difficult to comprehend through a modern lens. The peculiar collaboration and intersection of ecclesiastical and political powers was considered normal within the historical context, in which the monarchy declared itself Catholic and required the aid of the church in both matters of faith and of the state.

Following the ancient tradition of the ecumenical councils, the summoning of the council came from the king, who would then appear, advised by his counselors, at the commencement of the sessions in the hall where the assembly was gathered to deliver the *tomus regius*, which contained the day's schedule or the list of subjects around which the conciliary discussions would revolve. Once the council ended, the king generally sanctioned the assembly's proposals.

Naturally, the default members of the councils were the bishops, who could be represented by their vicars when necessary. The bishops always endorsed the conciliary proceedings and prepared the resulting canon laws. Titled members of the most important abbeys of the kingdoms also played important roles, but their signatures do not appear regularly until the councils of the latter part of the seventh century. Many councils were also attended by laymen from civil, administrative, and royal spheres, usually either as part of the king's entourage or as official attendees summoned by the conciliary fathers. As in the case of the abbots, the signatures of certain Visigothic magnates also began to appear in the late seventh century. The presence of these dignataries was petitioned because of the political nature of the subjects frequently debated in the councils.

Members of the lower clergy—priests and deacons, for example—were also known to attend certain sessions, always sitting behind the bishops. The bishops, in turn, were seated in order of precedence according to the date of their ordination. Complaints against bishops or others in power could be disclosed in the assembly.

Theological Contributions of the Councils

All general councils began with a three-day period of spiritual preparation dedicated to fasting and theological reflection on the mystery of the Trinity. This practice should probably be interpreted as an effort designed to eliminate any trace of Arianism, as well as a means of producing symbols of faith that would later prove useful in the formation and training of the clergy and in the catechistic indoctrination of the lay population. Some councils chose to manifest the assembly's faith following the confession of the Nicene-Constantinopolitan Creed, while others created their own formulas, many of which enjoyed considerable prestige because of their acceptance and diffusion throughout Christianity and their theological contribution to the church's growth. One of the most well-known contributions was the introduction of the *Filioque*, a dogmatic expression that would later provoke frequent difficulties with the Eastern Church.

Canon Law

The Councils of Toledo are the primary source of ecclesiastical legislation in the Hispanic Church. Canon law proceeding from the councils was incorporated in the *Liber Iudiciorum*; at the same time, royal decrees and orders were assumed by the councils. Based on these materials, with the addition of other non-Spanish councils and pontifical decretals, the *Colección Canónica Hispana* was created in the seventh century and adopted within the juridical world in the peninsula, which was governed *secundum legem gothicam et canonicam*. This collection of laws exerted great influence on the Carolingian collections and on Gratian's *Decretum*, through which the councils indirectly influenced the common law of the Latin Church.

RAMÓN GONZÁLVEZ RUIZ

Bibliography

Calpena y Avila, L. *Los concilios de Toledo*. Madrid, 1918.

Concilio III de Toledo. XIV Centenario. Toledo, 1991.

Diccionario de historia eclesiástica de España. Vol. 1. Ed. Q. Aldea Vaquero et al. Madrid, 1972. 566–73.

Garciá Villada, Z. *Historia eclesiástica de España*. Vol. 2. Madrid, 1932. 205–7.

Gams, P. B. *Die Kirchengeschichte von Spanien*. Vol. 2. Regensburg, 1874. 1–185.

Historia de los concilios de la España romana y visigoda. 1986.

Historia de la iglesia en España. Vol. 2. Ed. J. Fernández Conde. Madrid, 1979–1983. 440–75.

Martínez, G., and F. Rodríguez. *La Colección Canónica Hispana*, 5 vols. Madrid-Barcelona, 1966–1992.

Schwobel, H. *Synode und König im Westgotenreich. Grundlagen und Formen ihrer Beziehung*. Köln, 1982.

Vives, J. et al. *Concilios visigóticos e hispano-romanos*. Barcelona, 1963.

TOLEDO, VISIGOTHIC KINGDOM OF *See*

VISIGOTHIC KINGDOM, TOLEDO

TOMB CULTS

While the church and the faithful were clear about the special nature of sainthood, whether universally or only locally recognized, and honored the saints in calendars and special liturgies and images and relics, we find in many places in the Middle Ages cults of only slightly less veneration granted to secular persons of distinction when these persons had attracted legendary and especially literary fame. Monarchs and nobles alone seem to be candidates, and for a cult to arise it was essential that the person should be entombed, or believed to be entombed, in a prominent place inside a monastic or other church. Fictitious personages such as the epic heroes Bernardo del Carpio and the Siete Infantes de Lara could materialize out of folklore and vernacular epic and be provided with tombs—presumably containing bones—and then counted on an equal basis with heroes whose tombs were genuine. The medieval mind hardly concerned itself with questions of authenticity that so trouble us, and if a Christian or moral message for the faithful was created or enhanced by forgery of a tomb or of documents or objects—*pia fraus*—this was acceptable enough.

Burials of historical persons can be dated fairly precisely, though their tombs may often have been improved later, and the often important Latin verse epitaphs may not be contemporary with a first burial. Evidence for any cult is generally late and incomplete. The matter is important because while legendary accretions could occur at any time, literary texts about heroes had a point and date of creation and scholars try to determine these. On present evidence, whatever part monks and their documents played in literary creation by vernacular writers, the cult of a heroic tomb was the result of the propagation of a relevant literary text by oral or (more rarely) written means. Public interest was stimulated and the church then encouraged the cult. Both literary text and cult had ample models in France (e.g., poems and tombs relating to the stories of Roland and William of Orange) and were known in northern Iberia. The church's motivation was simple. Visitors to tombs gave money, important ones donated lands and legacies, and monarchs and nobles requested burial in churches already so distinguished, leaving more money so that masses should be said for their souls.

Aragónese, Leonese, and Portuguese lands seem to have had few such cults. Navarre was rich in Carolingian resonances (Roncesvalles, etc.), and Old Castile was prime territory for these cults as it was for heroic legend and epic verse (A.D. Deyermond has a helpful map and commentary in *Epic Poetry and the Clergy*. London, 1969, xviii). San Pedro de Arlanza claimed the tomb of its founder, Count Fernán González, and others connected with him; also of Mudarra, the avenging hero of the *Siete Infantes* story. San Salvador de Oña had a number of royal tombs, notably that of Sancho II of Castile who was killed before Zamora in 1072 in circumstances believed traitorous, and who was the subject of a Latin *Carmen* and a later vernacular epic; it is known that he twice promised his body to Oña (documents of 1066, 1070). San Pedro de Cardeña had the tomb of Count Garci Fernández (d. 995), reputed rebuilder of the monastery and victim-hero of the *Condesa traidora* story; also, and eventually of much greater importance, the tombs of the Cid Ruy Díaz de Bivar (d. 1099) and his wife Jimena. Aguilar de Campoo claimed the tomb of the fictitious epic hero Bernardo del Carpio. So valuable were these possessions in terms of prestige and income that competition developed (as for saintly relics): San Juan de la Peña in the Aragónese Pyrenees claimed the tomb of the Cid's Jimena (as it did possession of the Holy Grail); Oña and San Isidoro of León claimed the epic protagonist Infante García (d. 1029), both with convincing epitaphs; in the late 16th century Arlanza, San Millán de la Cogolla, and the parish church of Salas de los Infantes vied to claim diverse portions of personages from the epic *Siete Infantes de Lara*. Even villains might figure, presumably with tales of repentance Doña Sancha the *Condesa traidora* was at Oña, and prominent in its very foundation-legend. The two Infantes de Carrión from the Cid story were at Cornellana, west of Oviedo.

What form did a cult take? We do not know precisely. A tomb would have been shown at any time to visitors and improving tales told by a monk. On a special day in the year, a formal "anniversary," the community and local dignitaries might gather to give praise and hear readings. At Cardeña an immense pantheon of tombs was created for almost everyone associated with the Cid in life and literature, probably in the early fourteenth century; each tomb bore its heraldic device, important to local families and benefactors with proud genealogies. By 1272 the monks had confected a lengthy *Estoria del Cid* which mentioned these names while centering on the Cid's last pious weeks, death, and burial, adding details about objects displayed by the tomb: a chess-set, cups, a chest, the customary sword, spurs, and banner. Out in the courtyard the burial of his epic horse Babieca was shown too.

COLIN SMITH

Bibliography

Smith, C. "The Diffusion of the Cid Cult," *Journal of Medieval History* VI (1980), 37–60.

TORDESILLAS, TREATY OF

The Treaty (or more accurately, Treaties) of Tordesillas were signed between Castile and Portugal on 7 June 1494. The most important provision of the treaties was the agreement that Castile and Portugal would recognize a line of longitude running 370 leagues west of Cape Verde as separating their respective spheres of imperial activity.

Castilian and Portuguese traders and adventurers, often backed by members of the nobility, had competed for slaves, ransoms, and trading opportunities off the Atlantic coast of Morocco since the fourteenth century. Both kingdoms claimed sovereignty over the Canary Islands and initiated attempts to conquer and settle them. In the 1450s the papacy granted spiritual jurisdiction to the Portuguese Order of Christ, whose administrator was the Infante Dom Henrique (Henry the Navigator). After the outbreak of war in 1475, Castilian and Portuguese rivalry spread to the coast of Guinea, but in the Treaty of Alcaçovas in 1479 a preliminary demarcation of spheres of influence was agreed upon. Castile was to have sovereignty over the Canary Islands and Portugal was to have exclusive rights in Madeira, the Azores, and on the coast of Africa south of Cape Bojador.

King João II, who came to the throne in 1481, began the active search for a route to the East, sending exploratory expeditions down the African coast and rejecting Columbus's proposals for a western voyage in 1484. Although Africa was rounded in 1488, no route to the East had been opened when Columbus, by then in Castilian service, announced his discovery of islands to the west of the Azores in March 1493. João II at once claimed that these islands were in the Portuguese sphere but it was clear that the Treaty of Alcaçovas did not provide for these new discoveries. While Columbus prepared for his second voyage, Castilian diplomats at the papal court pressed the pope, the Spaniard Alexander VI, for bulls recognizing their sovereignty. Four bulls were issued between March and September 1493. By the second of these a line of demarcation was declared lying one hundred leagues west of the Azores, but the fourth bull declared that all the areas to be discovered in the East belonged to Castile unless they were already occupied by another Christian power.

Meanwhile Portugal had responded to Columbus's discoveries by threatening to intercept any further expedition and by initiating negotiations with Castile. An embassy went to Barcelona in April 1493 and proposed a demarcation line granting Castile all discoveries north and west of the Canaries while Portugal took the areas to the south of it. This was suggested on the mistaken assumption that Columbus's discoveries lay to the north as he himself had initially claimed. In August, after the publication of the second bull, the Portuguese sent another embassy, which had achieved nothing by the time the fourth bull was published in September. Further negotiations then took place at Lisbon and Medina del Campo during which the Portuguese accepted the principle of a line of longitude, as had been proposed in the second bull, but insisted that it be moved to 370 leagues west of Cape Verde (instead of 100 leagues). This was eventually accepted and incorporated in the treaty, which was signed in the Castilian frontier town of Tordesillas in June 1494.

It is remarkable that the two states should have adopted a line of longitude as the division since no one at that time could calculate longitude. The Portuguese insistence that the line be moved a further 270 leagues to the west has been taken as evidence that they already knew of the existence of Brazil, a significant part of which did indeed fall within their sphere under the Tordesillas agreement. An alternative suggestion is that the Portuguese already knew that the Atlantic wind systems circulated in a counterclockwise pattern and wanted to make sure that the seas that their ships would have to sail to reach the Orient fell within their jurisdiction.

The Tordesillas line only demarcated spheres of influence in the "Ocean Sea" (that is, the Atlantic) and was regularly featured on maps of the world after 1500. The Cantino Planisphere is the earliest Portuguese map to show the Tordesillas line. It was drawn in Lisbon in 1502 and was obtained for Ercole d'Este, Duke of Ferrara, by his agent, Alberto Cantino. The map is to be found in the Biblioteca Estense, Modena. A detailed account of the map is to be found in Cortesão A. and A. Teixeira da Mota. *Portugaliae Monumenta Cartographica*. 6 vols. Lisbon, 1960. Vol. 1, 7–13, and plate 4. The Tordesillas line proved remarkably successful in preventing quarrels between the two imperial powers, and no serious dispute took place between them in the Americas until the eighteenth century. The second Tordesillas agreement had covered North Africa and a further treaty in 1509 had defined the separate spheres of influence of the Castilians and Portuguese in that region. When Castilian ships under the renegade Portuguese, Magalhães (Magellan), reached the Moluccas in 1521 the threat of conflict in the spice islands led to an attempt to extend the Tordesillas line to the other side of the world. A new line was recognized at the Treaty of Zaragoza in 1529, which placed the Moluccas in the Portuguese "half" of the world but left the Spaniards free to exploit the Philippines.

MALYN NEWITT

Bibliography

Coimbra, C. "Os objectivos portugueses do Tratado de Tordesilhas." In *Actas, Proceedings of the International Colloquium on Luso-Brazilian Studies*. Vol. 2. Coimbra, 1965. 199–208.

Davenport, F. G. (ed.) *European Treaties Bearing on the History of the United States and Its Dependencies to 1648*. 4 vols. Washington, D.C., 1917–37.

"Linea de Demarcación." In *Diccionario de Historia de España*. Madrid, 1952.

Nowell, C. E. "The Treaty of Tordesillas and the Diplomatic Background of American History." In *Greater America*. Berkeley, 1945. 1–18.

TOROS DE GUISANDO *See* CATHOLIC MONARCHS; ENRIQUE IV, KING OF CASTILE, JUANA OF CASTILE

TORQUEMADA, JUAN DE

Juan de Torquemada (1388–1468) was the foremost papal apologist of his day. At an early age he entered the Dominican order at San Pablo de Valladolid. After attending the Council of Constance from 1416 to 1418, he studied theology at the University of Paris. Torquemada served as a prior in Castile before representing both his order and Juan II at the Council of Basel. In Basel, the friar joined the Reform Deputation, wrote in defense of orthodoxy, and composed his first papalist polemics. Eugenius IV rewarded Torquemada's efforts with the office of master of the Sacred Palace.

When Eugenius IV translated the council to Ferrara in 1437, Torquemada left Basel for Italy. He represented the pope in Germany in 1438 to 1439 before reaching the pope's council, then sitting at Florence. There the friar took part in the negotiations reuniting, briefly, the Greek and Latin churches. Then, when in 1439 Eugenius IV answered an effort by the Council of Basel to depose him with a bull of condemnation, he staged a debate between Cardinal Cesarini, defending conciliarism, and Torquemada, defending papalism. The Dominican theologian was absent in France representing the papacy when he learned of his promotion to the cardinalate.

After returning from France in 1440, Torquemada remained in the curia until his death in 1468. His one notable absence was his journey with Pius II to the Congress of Mantua (1459–1460), which attempted to organize a crusade against the Turks. Among the cardinal's writings from this period were an attack on

Islam, a defense of Jewish converts to Christianity, and tracts on apostolic poverty. Other writings were more devotional in nature; and one, his *Meditationes*, was the first illustrated book printed in Italy. The most important of Torquemada's writings were a commentary on Gratian's *Decretum*, reinterpreting key texts cited by the conciliarists in a papalist sense, and his *Summa de ecclesia* (1453). That monumental synthesis of medieval papalism defended the ecclesiastical institution against the doctrines of Wyclif and Hus, as well as attacking conciliarism. Torquemada's Thomist doctrine of papal supremacy argued that the power of jurisdiction, by which the church was governed, was given to lesser prelates by the papacy; but it claimed for the pope only an indirect role in temporal affairs, as a consequence of his spiritual responsibilities.

Torquemada also participated in the reform of individual religious houses; and he defended the interests of the Dominican order, particularly those of the Observant movement, at the curia. The cardinal also took an interest in art, employing Fra Angelico. His chief interests, however, remained theological. Torquemada is buried in the Annunciation Chapel at Santa Maria sopra Minerva in Rome. There he is depicted, in the habit of his order—not in a cardinal's robes—in a painting by Antonozzo Romano presenting to the Virgin of the Annunciation poor girls dowered by a guild he had founded in her name.

THOMAS M. IZBICKI

Bibliography

Izbicki, T. M. *Protector of the Faith: Cardinal Johannes de Turrecremata and the Defense of the Institutional Church*. Washington, D.C., 1981.

Torquemada, J. de. *A Disputation on the Authority of Pope and Council*. Trans. and intro. T. M. Izbicki. Oxford, 1988.

TORQUEMADA, TOMÁS DE

Born in the town from which he drew his surname, in the province of Palencia, in 1420. He was nephew to the no less famous Cardinal Juan de Torquemada, author of the *Tractatus contra Midianitas*, written in defense of the Jewish *conversos* (Christian converts) from whom he, and correspondingly Tomás, were said to have been descended. As a young man, Tomás entered the Order of St. Dominic in the priory of San Pablo in Valladolid, and resided as a friar in the convent at Piedrahita. He was later appointed prior of the convent of Santa Cruz in Segovia, a title he retained throughout his career; and at about the same time was chosen to be a confessor of Queen Isabel and King Fernando: it is in this role that he appears in the only painting that is believed to depict him faithfully, Berruguete's *Virgin of the Catholic Kings*, in the Prado.

On 11 February 1482 he was appointed by papal bull as one of seven new inquisitors to continue the work of the recently founded Inquisition (the first two inquisitors had been appointed in 1480). In 1483 a new central council, the Consejo de la Suprema y General Inquisición, was set up by the king and queen to govern the inquisition, and Torquemada was chosen to head it as inquisitor general. On 17 October 1483 another papal bull, which conceded control of the inquisitions of the Iberian Peninsula to the crown, also appointed Torquemada as joint inquisitor general of the three realms of Aragón, Catalonia, and Valencia. In this role, he was empowered to intervene in any part of the peninsula in a way that not even the crown was always able to. Torquemada subsequently played a key role in forcing through the introduction of the new inquisition in the realms of the Crown of Aragón, which still retained their old inquisitors from the medieval inquisition. In May 1484 Torquemada appointed new inquisitors for the eastern kingdoms, but faced enormous opposition, fundamentally because the new appointees were all Castilians and their tribunal was not subject to the laws of the kingdoms; in Aragón one of the appointees, Pedro Arbués, was murdered in 1485. To find a way out of the impasse, in February 1486 pope Innocent VIII sacked all the existing papal inquisitors in the Crown of Aragón, and secured the simultaneous withdrawal of the Castilian nominees. This left the way open for Torquemada to start again with new appointees.

The important contribution made by Torquemada to the new inquisition is confirmed by the fact that he wrote its first rule book, the *Instrucciones*, first drawn up in November 1484 and then later amplified in versions of 1485, 1488, and 1498. Together with additions made in 1500, these early rules were known as the *Instrucciones Antiguas*, and laid down all the procedures of the tribunal in its early period. Torquemada must not, however, be viewed as all-powerful. As inquisitor general he was no more than chairman of the Suprema and could be overruled by it; moreover, his commission, which came from the pope, could be revoked at any time. In 1491 and again in 1494, while Torquemada was still functioning, additional and temporary (until 1504) inquisitor generals were appointed to aid the work of the inquisition, proof that he did not hold unquestioned power.

No documentary proof whatsoever exists for attributing to Torquemada the evidently anti-Semitic philosophy of the early inquisition, or responsibility for the bloody excesses of the tribunal; but neither is there any reason to question the traditional view that sees him as the driving spirit behind its early years. It is unquestionable that he was a major force behind the expulsion of the Jews in 1492: King Fernando stated expressly, in a letter that he sent to several nobles, that "the Holy Office of the Inquisition has provided that the Jews be expelled from all our realms." A story of uncertain origin states that when the Jews tried to buy their way out of the expulsion, Torquemada burst into the presence of the king and queen and threw thirty pieces of silver on the table, demanding to know for what price Christ was to be sold again.

A strong supporter of religious reform, Torquemada in 1482 founded the beautiful monastery of Santo Tomás in Avila, where he died on 16 September 1498.

HENRY KAMEN

Bibliography

Kamen, H. *Historia de la Inquisición en España y América*. Madrid, 1984. Lea, H. C. *A History of the Inquisition of Spain*. 4 vols.

TORRE, ALFONSO DE LA

Theologian and writer in the vernacular active in the mid-fifteenth century, remembered nowadays as the author of the *Visión deleytable*, a philosophical dialogue and survey of the seven liberal arts, natural theology, and ethics. The work is in large part a cento of older texts, mostly unidentified and at times heavily amplified and supplemented by the author, and bound together by an allegorical dialogue. The *Visión* enjoyed a certain currency in its own century and in the two following. By the end of the seventeenth century it had undergone eleven printings, had been translated into Catalan and Italian and, unbelievably, back into Spanish.

What is most notable, indeed astonishing, about Torre's dialogue and the thought it expresses is the fundamentally Averroist and rationalist direction of its argument, especially of its theology. The main index to this tendency is, of course, the author's choice of sources, in some instances unremarkable, in others quite otherwise. Thus the passages on the liberal arts depend largely on Isidore of Seville and Al-Ghazāli. The pages on cosmology, on the influence of the spheres on the sublunary world, are from a source Torre calls simply "Hermes," but which is in fact the *Latin Asclepius*, very well known and influential in Western Christendom. But the matter on natural theology comes not from a Christian source, but from Maimonides's *Guide for the Perplexed*. This notable text brings to the *Visión* unaltered the Maimonidean teaching about the nature of God, eminently his existence, unity and incorporeity, but also his power, omniscience, and Providence. One should add that the passages in the *Guide* that express views at odds with what we could call common Christian theology—on providence, for example, or on the nature of evil—are preserved in the *Visión* without embarrassment. There is also in Torre's text, as we should note in fairness, a series of chapters that speak plain Christian language. But the author makes absolutely no effort to reconcile the sense of these pages with the rest of his argument, and one might indeed reasonably guess that this passage is a sop, a concession to the Christian reader, who elsewhere in the work is induced to accept views that at best are on the outer limits of orthodoxy.

The rationalist strain is sustained in the *Visión* in passages entirely separate from those directly and extensively dependent on the *Guide*. In a pair of lines early in the work Torre alludes hastily to Maimonides's theory of prophecy, roughly the view that God speaks to his prophets "mediante la lunbre yntelectual" (by means of intellectual enlightenment). In a second short passage he refers clearly to Maimonides's notion that the Bible speaks one language to the wise and learned and another to the vulgar, or in Leo Strauss's words, that Scripture "is an esoteric text, and that its esoteric teaching is akin to that of Aristotle." More important, perhaps, the *Visión*'s chapters on ethics make few significant allusions to Christianity, or indeed, even to the idea of rewards and punishments in the other world.

Torre at one point says that the will of God can be understood in two senses, as what he wills directly and as what he wills virtually as he foresees the consequences of his first decision. Significantly, this theme is not Maimonidean; it savors of Christian scholasticism, and is possibly of Scotist or nominalist tendency. In other words, Torre's rationalism is not an accident. When he presents unmodified Maimonidean teachings that are at variance with those of Christian theology, the choice of doctrine is not innocent; it is certainly not made in ignorance. Torre was, as we have seen, a legitimate theologian, a *bachiller en teología*, and the knowledge of Christian divinity revealed in details of the course of the *Visión* is fully professional. His choice of themes, therefore, must have been fully deliberate. What, then, are we to think of this strange book and its author? Was Torre a crypto-Jew? Perhaps; the case is interesting. One should note that the mixture in the *Visión* of Jewish authorities and Christian is in no way alien to later medieval Jewish Averroism; the conversion of Shlomo Halevy/Pablo de Santa María was due in great part to his early familiarity with Aquinas. Torre's final plea to the Infante don Carlos not to show his book to a third person is itself revealing. Maimonides himself lays it down firmly that high doctrine should not be revealed to the vulgar.

CHARLES FRAKER

Bibliography

Strauss, L. *How Fārābī Read Plato's Laws*. Damascus, 1957.

Torre, A. de la. *Visión deleytable*. 2 vols. Salamanca, 1991.

TORROELLAS, PERE

Poet of Catalan origin, born about 1410, who composed verse in both his native Catalan as well as in Castilian. Torroellas was closely tied to the court of Navarre and served as majordomo to Carlos, prince of Viana. In 1441 Torroellas fought as a partisan on the side of the Infantes de Aragón at Medina del Campo, where he was taken prisoner by don Alvaro de Luna. Ransomed by the Aragónese faction, he traveled to Naples in 1445 on a diplomatic mission for the Crown of Aragón. Between 1446 and 1450, Torroellas held the title of *oficial del cuchillo* (master of the knife) at the court of Navarre, returning to Naples in 1450, where he lived the life of a courtier and had occasion to come in contact with humanists like Giovanni Pontano. Upon the death of Alfonso V the Magnanimous, Torroellas returned to the Iberian Peninsula, where he led an intense political and literary life until his death in about 1486.

The period encompassing Torroellas's most concentrated literary activity ranges from 1440 to 1460. His *Maldezir de mugeres*, written sometime between these dates, circulated throughout the entire Iberian peninsula and lent him the reputation of the paradigmatic misogynist. Antón de Montoro, Gómez Manrique, and Suero de Ribera, among others, wrote verse responses to Torroellas's *Maldezir*, characterizing its author as the mortal enemy of womankind. In *Grisel y Mirabella*, a sentimental romance by Juan de Flores from the last quarter of the fifteenth century, Torroellas is portrayed as the arch-antifeminist who defends the qualities and virtues of men over women in a judicial debate with Braçayda, or Cressida of the legends of Troy. Braçayda is called to court to advocate the interests and virtue of women. After Torroellas's forensic triumph in the name of men, he attempts to seduce Braçayda, who—(along with other ladies of the court)—flails him alive.

E. MICHAEL GERLI

Bibliography

Bach y Rita, P. *The Works of Pere Torroellas, A Catalan Writer of the Fifteenth Century*. New York, 1930.

TORTOSA

The Roman city of Iulia Ilerga Dertosa named after Mercury as a place of commerce, situated along the Ebro River above its delta and the coastal thoroughfare from Valencia to Tarragona and Barcelona. The Romano-Visigothic city and its territory fell to Muslim dominion between 713 and 718, and after initial alliance with Valencia it more generally fell under Banū Hūd control from Zaragoza as the southernmost anchor of the Muslim march against the Christian northeast. Muslim Tortosa developed a sprawling residential and garden region beyond the walls of the old commercial district situated on a crowded shelf between the river and a fortified acropolis dominated by the castle of La Zuda. It grew increasingly autonomous after the civil war during the 1080s between the brothers Al-Mutʿamin and Al-Mundhir, as did the mountainous region between the Ebro and Tarragona. Its independence as a tā'ifa (party) kingdom ended in 1099 with the Almoravid invasion, and after the fall of Zaragoza in 1118 to the Aragónese and collapse of the Muslim alliance system, Tortosa became increasingly vulnerable to Christian reconquest.

In response to the Almoravid menace and in keeping with expansionist dynastic ambition after Count Ramón Berenguer IV's marriage to Petronila of Aragón, Barcelona initiated a panregnal program to absorb the entire Muslim march of the Ebro into the emerging Crown of Aragón. After helping his influential churchman, Bishop Oleguer of Barcelona, take and hold Tarragona in 1118 to 1128, Catalan forces began a systematic encroachment of the frontier between Tarragona and Tortosa. The Christian advance was slowed by its bifurcation between the Lleidan and Tortosan marches, the Muslim castle-dotted highland march of Ciurana, and Muslim naval supremacy on the Mediterranean. However, after 1146 the Christian grand alliance of Barcelona with Montpellier, Genoa, and Pisa that had been formed originally to take Tarragona, was renewed against Tortosa and its ally, Lleida. Preliminary land grants were promised in anticipation of victory and the Knights Templars moved into the borderlands. Armed with a crusade bull from Pope Eugenius II, comital forces penetrated the outlying Muslim defenses in 1147, laid seige to Tortosa on 1 July 1148, and entered the city at the very end of December. The major players were the Catalans from Barcelona, Ausona, and Urgell, led by Ramón Berenguer IV and the grand seneschal Guillem de Moncada; their new frontier baronage from Cervera, Castelvell, and Olérdola, and their castellans; churchmen led by Archbishop Bernard Tort, who would appoint the Augustinian Canon Ramon Gaufred from Saint Ruf in Avignon to the new see of Tortosa; the military orders, especially the Knights Templar from Barberá and Montblanc; a multistate naval blockade directed by consuls from Genoa; and even English and Norman mercenaries and crusaders who had participated in the subjugation of Lisbon and Tarragona.

Those Tortosan Muslims who did not leave for Valencia joined their countrymen outside the conquered city, which was divided largely into thirds as spoils of war: the Moncada would govern from La Zuda with rights to the old city where the church was also to make its claim; the port section went to Genoa; and the count took suburbia, while giving the Templars several outlying castles and a fifth of the revenues from the countryside to maintain the perimeter defenses. A separate Judería was established outside the walls. The Genoese occupied a merchant district, but by 1181 they abandoned their seignorial rights to the Templars. The bishopric reconstituted in 1150 by Pope Adrian IV was able to consecrate its cathedral by 1178. The southward advance of the Arago-Catalan reconquest slowed down to assimilate Tortosa, but in accord with Alfonso II's treaty of Cazola with Castile-León in 1179 the Christian drive south and across the Mediterranean to the Balearics was renewed in 1225 after the minority of Jaime I. The capture of Valencia in 1238 secured Christian Tortosa.

Tostosa grew like a boomtown as a regional commercial center and the major port between Tarragona and the war zone in Valencia. Trade routes with Naples and Sicily were especially lucrative. When the *Costums de Tortosa* developed between 1250 and 1260, the city fell increasingly to civilian control. By 1277 it was governed by three procurators, or municipal magistrates. It was reincorporated into Catalonia in 1295 by Jaime II, but its commercial heyday was eclipsed by post-reconquest Mallorca and Valencia. Tortosa lost population to intermittent plague and competing trade centers, and suffered from reccurring strife between its Christian majority and conversos, as attested by the famous Disputation of Tortosa convoked in 1413 by Pope Benedict XIII to debate Christian and Jewish polemics. Its Moriscos were finally expelled in 1610.

LAWRENCE J. MCCRANK

Bibliography

Bayerri y Bertoméu, E. *Historia de Tortosa y su comarca*. 8 vols. Tortosa: 1933–60.

Font Rius, J. M. "La comarca de Tortosa a raíz de la reconquista cristiana (1148), notas sobre su fisionomía político-social," *Cuadernos de Historia de España* 19 (1953), 104–28.

TOSTADO, EL

See MADRIGAL, ALFONSO DE

TOULOUSE, VISIGOTHIC KINGDOM OF

See VISIGOTHIC KINGDOM, TOLEDO, TOULOUSE

TOURNAMENTS

Strictly speaking, the tournament that developed in the countries between the Loire and the Rhine was not practiced in Iberian culture, although there were similar celebrations also incorporating horses and weapons. The history of the peninsular breed of tournament can be divided into two clearly distinct eras. Before the fourteenth century, they were indigenous Castilian traditions: *alancear tablados*, *bofordar*, and *correr toros*, for example, are mentioned in the history of the Infantes de Lara and in the *Siete Partidas*. These competitions are similar to the European competitions in which contestants display skill and strength through the control of their horse and the handling of their weapons, but lack other essential components of the tournament, particularly the one-on-one fight. Perhaps the most similar external feature was the formation of a team of bofordadores mounted *a la jineta*, on horses cloaked with heraldic emblems. Armed with the *bofordo*, a short projectile spear decorated with a pendant, the horsemen performed short equestrian exercises, throwing the bofordos into the air and catching them, or launching the spears at tablados, large wooden platforms, until they were destroyed. The atmosphere in these festivals was much more popular and traditional than the European tournament, and even the bofordadores belonged not to the nobility but to the middle class. Missing from these Castilian celebrations was the exaltation of the individual inherent in the chivalric spirit—the names of the bofordadores didn't matter much—as well as the marginal yet necessary rescue/ransom plots that provided a narrative (and often erotic) context for the tournament.

The traditions associated with the peninsular tournaments change during the fourteenth century, in part because of the effect of the growing Anglo-French cultural presence. At the same time, with the Reconquest's activity slowing down, knights no longer considered the fight against Islam an enterprise that justified their existence, and as a result began to perform feigned wars. Jousts, tournaments, and other knightly displays soon acquired social distinction and prestige, with participation reserved for the nobility. Accompanying these celebrations was the growing use of insignias, emblems, and other visual adornments, which became especially important for the aesthetic appeal and ambience of the event. Representations of tournaments in the plastic arts of the beginning of the fourteenth century, such as the ceiling work of the Cathedral of Teruel (portraying two Christians fighting each other) and the cloister of the Cathedral of Pamplona, attest to the popularity of the events. A short time later in 1335, Alfonso XI created the *Caballería de la Banda*, one of the first chivalric orders in Europe. Religious brotherhoods (*cofradías*) imitating these organizations, such as the Santiago de la Fuente in Burgos and Nuestra Señora de Salor in Cáceres, also began to appear, and also performed equestrian exercises.

The evolution of the Iberian tournament culminates in the first half of the fifteenth century, when a large number of jousts, tourneys, *juegos de cañas*, and displays of horsemanship take place. In those events, pomp, showiness, and dazzling—sometimes elaborate—stage scenery tend to overshadow the display of strength, skill, and valor.

FAUSTINO MENÉNDEZ PIDAL DE NAVASCUÉS

Bibliography

Andrés Díaz, R. "Las fiestas de la caballería en la Castilla de los Trastámara." In *En la España medieval*. Vol. 5. Madrid, 1986. 81–107.

Keen, M. *La caballería*. Barcelona, 1986.

TOWNS

The origins of towns in medieval Iberia have been the subject of a good deal of debate by historians. Most would now accept the thesis of Sánchez Albornoz that the Roman municipia atrophied in the wake of the late imperial economy and the taxation policies it engendered, declining yet further during the Germanic invasions. While urban life survived and even prospered in Muslim Spain, the Christian North endured what some have argued to be the near total disappearance of towns. While one might therefore offer a Pirennist model in Iberia, in fact Pirenne neither studied nor knew much about the Iberian peninsula during the post-Muslim invasion era. The Belgian scholar's influence is nonetheless felt, and Hispanic scholars have explored various decline and revival theories to explain the reappearance of towns in the northern territories. From these investigations, it is clear that no one model explains the growth of towns in Christian Hispania. Rather, historians have discovered a labyrinth of developmental paths affected by such variables as century of emergence, geographical location, economic opportunity, and military need. The availability of a coastline for commercial development dramatically influenced the evolution of many Asturian, Galician, Portuguese, and Catalan towns. On the other hand, the lack of sea access had a restrictive impact on León-Castile. The concentration of Roman and Muslim influences in the south and east affected municipal histories in those areas. As if geographical and cultural differences did not create sufficient complexities for the investigator, the relative paucity of source materials for much of the peninsula prior to the twelfth century limits our understanding yet more, especially in the case of León-Castile.

At least four major routes to the development of towns in Christian Hispania evolved. First, episcopal and archiepiscopal centers clearly generated concentrations of population that led to urban growth. Second, developing commercial and trading opportunities played a role, especially in Navarre and northern Castile, influenced by the growing importance of the pilgrimage to Santiago and in Catalonia, where land and seaborne trade developed by linkage to the Occitan and Provençal regions in France and to Genoa in Italy. Third, garrison theories find useful evidence of fortified areas on and behind the frontier that drew settlement through the provision of security. Finally, agrarian and pastoral settlements fostered by kings, nobles, and monasteries offered possibilities by means of the combination of group security and town-countryside regional trade. In most cases, some mix of these factors was at work to achieve a municipal concentration. Any of these routes could also provide the emergence of a sense of difference felt by the residents of these settlements that they were a class apart, members of a growing body of individuals we can call townsmen. To these categories of towns the Reconquest would provide the acquisition of larger Muslim settlements, especially Toledo (1085), Zaragoza (1118), Lisbon (1147), Córdoba (1236), Valencia (1238), Jaén (1246), and Seville (1248).

The best indications we have of the institutional development of peninsular towns survives in the charters they received, known as *fueros* or *cartas pueblas*. Some of these were granted at the time of settlement or conquest of a new site, others were awarded years or even decades subsequently. Such materials inform us as to the special legal status of the inhabitants, starting with a few exemptions or privileges in the eleventh and earlier twelfth centuries, then elaborating into full-scale law codes starting in the later twelfth century. During the thirteenth century, the kings began to explore the possibilities of revived Roman law, contributing to the issuance of large lists of customs for towns, especially in Portugal and Aragón. Attempts to establish such uniform statements by Alfonso X el Sabio in his granting of the *Fuero real* to a number of towns met with a sharp reaction by the older towns defending their traditional fueros, requiring Alfonso X to retreat from this policy later in his reign. These sources tell us that the various grantors, especially the kings, sought to attract settlers to these towns with attractive grants of freedom, an increased opportunity to elect their own local councils (*concejos*), elect their own executive officials (*jueces*, *alcaldes*, and *cónsules*), and establish their right to be independent of the local nobility. *Caballeros*, who maintained a horse and dwelled in such towns, enjoyed a tax exemption. From these towns the monarchs gained a settled populace in sometimes difficult frontier locations, and often a municipal militia to contribute to defense of the region as well as the campaigns of the king. The economic life in the Leonese-Castilian towns indicates a major dependency on livestock raising and warfare with its periodic infusion of booty. The wool they produced, enhanced by the addition of the merino breed from North Africa after the thirteenth century, fostered a respectable regional trade, and, at least in the case of Cuenca, actual manufacture of woolen cloth. Strengthened by their grants of freedoms and armed to meet their strategic situation, these Meseta towns would contest royal efforts to reestablish strong centrist government. The townsmen were aided in this effort by their participation in the meetings of the royal council (or *cortes*), occurring earlier in Spain than elsewhere in western Europe. The lesser aristocracy who dwelled in the municipalities, known as the *caballeros villanos*, increasingly came to dominate these towns by the late thirteenth century.

On the Atlantic and Mediterranean coasts, towns evolved somewhat differently. With more access to seaborne trade, especially on the Mediterranean, a more active commercial class developed on the Cantabrian coast, in parts of Portugal, and in Catalonia. Regarding institutional development, the towns of the upper Ebro in the kingdom of Aragón followed a pattern very like that of Castile. Exposed to Muslim assault but somewhat better protected by the Iberian Cordillera, the Aragónese towns received fueros like those of the center. Indeed, the *Fuero de Teruel* is very similar in content to that of Cuenca. Coastal Catalonia, on the other hand, while receiving royal grants of rights and obligations known as *cartas de franquicias*, *furs* and *costumbres* that were similar in format to the Castilian and Portuguese charters, reveals a wider variety of trading and commercial activity. The patrician wealthy class that developed in the larger towns like Barcelona and Valencia demonstrated strong resistance to royal authority as well as the countryside nobility. Italian influence was felt strongly in the Catalan towns in their maritime development and in art and architecture as well. By the late thirteenth century, however, the count-kings of Aragón pressed Roman-influenced law in the larger municipal codes like those of Valencia and Tortosa. The Crown of Aragón witnessed townsmen being invited to attend the royal cortes with the aristocrats at roughly the same time as Castile.

The conquest of the larger towns of Muslim Luso-Hispania by the Christian kingdoms presented the monarchs with problems not faced by their contemporaries to the north. Towns such as Toledo, Lisbon, Córdoba, Valencia, and Seville possessed well-developed economies and social structures, often more advanced than those of the municipalities of the conquering states. The Aragónese were more successful in maintaining these classes and structures in Valencia than was the case in Castile and Portugal, but at a cost of dealing with large Muslim populations that sometimes became sources of conflict for the newer Christian residents. Increasingly the Muslims and Jews were ghettoized, reducing the social contact needed to affect social interaction (*convivencia*). Seville and Córdoba, especially, saw their economies decline as the Muslims were driven to the countryside in the wake of urban revolts (1264–1266), and the links to the other Muslim states were atrophied. Valencia remained tied more closely to its former trading partners in the Mediterranean, and became for a time the most important town in the Crown of Aragón.

The towns engaged in an uneasy struggle with the peninsular monarchs during the later Middle Ages to retain their rights and privileges obtained during the earlier Reconquest. Occasionally the towns got the upper hand, wresting new privileges through insurrections, such as the Valencian Unión of 1348 or the alliances made by Barcelona with France in the fifteenth century. In Castile, Alfonso XI moved to constrain the growing power of the urban nobles, pressing royal officials (especially the *corregidores*) on the town governments, a movement set back by the civil war in the reign of Pedro the Cruel, then to be renewed by the Trastámaran kings. Fernando II of Aragón and Isabel I of Castile would intensify these efforts in the late fifteenth century in their respective realms, as Renaissance despotism defeated medieval municipal independence in all of the developed Western monarchies. Economically, the peninsular towns faced in turn the growing stagnation of the Western economies in the fourteenth century, followed by the devastations of the Black Death, that reached the east coast of Iberia in May 1348, striking the great port cities of Barcelona and Valencia and spreading throughout the peninsula by 1349. As with the remainder of Europe, Spain and Portugal experienced periodic later outbreaks of the Black Death, the worst years being 1384, 1415, and 1474–1479. In addition to the economic dislocations caused by these plagues, the social fabric of the towns was rent by the pogroms against the Jews by a fearful Christian population presuming God's wrath. Such disorders led to greater penetration of municipal government by the monarchs, and to the attitudes that resulted in the ultimate exile of Jews and then Muslims from Iberia.

JAMES POWERS

Bibliography

Font Rius, J. M. "Orígenes del régimen municipal de Cataluña," *Anuario de Historia del Derecho Español* 16 (1945), 389–529; 17 (1946), 229–585.

Gautier-Dalch, J. *Historia urbana de León y Castilla en la Edad Media*. Trans. E. Pérez Sedeño. Madrid, 1979.

Powers, J. F. *A Society Organized for War: The Iberian Municipal Militias in the Central Middle Ages, 1000–1284*. Berkeley, 1988.

Torres Balbás, L., et al. (eds.) *Resumen histórico del urbanismo*. 2d ed. Madrid, 1968.

Valdeavellano, L. G. de. *Orígenes de la burguesía en la España medieval*. Madrid, 1969.

TRADE, MUSLIM

From the Umayyad period until the early thirteenth century, the trade of al-Andalus was closely linked with markets elsewhere in the Muslim Mediterranean world. During these centuries, regular maritime traffic linked southern Spanish ports (particularly Seville, Málaga, and Almería) with trading centers in North Africa, Sicily, and Egypt. Some merchants traveled the entire length of the Mediterranean by sea, making stops along the way for trade and transhipment, while others made a shorter sea journey from Spain to North Africa, then continued their journeys overland by caravan.

International traffic was mainly limited to the port cities of Muslim Spain. Almería, the most important among these, was described by a twelfth-century Arab geographer as the "key" to Andalusian commerce, a city providing access to Iberian markets from the wider Mediterranean. Within the Iberian Peninsula, goods and merchants traveled by land with pack animals, or along rivers, to inland cities. For example, goods arriving by sea in Seville had to be transferred to smaller vessels for passage up the Guadalquivir River to Córdoba. Inland trade was probably handled by local merchants.

Muslim Spanish ports were also in contact with commercial centers in southwestern Europe, such as Genoa, Pisa, and Marseilles, by the late twelfth century. Genoese notarial documents, which survive from as early as the 1150s, show Genoese merchants trading with *Yspania* (the generic Latin term for Muslim Spain), the Balearics, Almería, Denia, Valencia, Seville, and other regions. After the middle of the thirteenth century, trade in southern Spain was dominated by Christian merchants, especially Catalans and Genoese. The latter gained special privileges in Seville (where Fernando III renewed earlier grants made to Genoese traders under Almohad rule), and in the ports of Naṣrid Granada. In the late Middle Ages, the opening of the Straits of Gibraltar to Christian shipping and the development of Atlantic routes allowed new commercial connections to grow up between ports in southern Spain and northern Europe.

Prior to this period, however, Andalusian trading interests focused almost exclusively on the Mediterranean and the Muslim world, and routes to and from Muslim Spain were controlled by Muslim and Jewish merchants. Some of these traders were based in Spain, and some had family ties in al-Andalus, while some came to the peninsula from other regions of the Muslim world. Many were affiliated with partnership networks stretching the length of the Mediterranean, and it would not have been unusual, in the eleventh or twelfth century, for merchants in Almería to correspond with partners in Tunis or Cairo about the price, quality, and availability of goods. Although Muslim and Jewish merchants controlled traffic between al-Andalus and other Muslim markets through the late twelfth century, these traders rarely visited Christian ports.

A wide variety of merchandise was bought and sold in Muslim Spanish markets, and all of the major commodities of general Mediterranean trade appear to have been available in the peninsula. Eastern "spices"—including dyestuffs such as indigo, lac, and brazilwood; spices such as pepper, ginger, cinnamon, and mastic; and aromatics such as musk, aloes, camphor, and spikenard—were all imported to Muslim Spain. A wide variety of woven textiles and textiles fibers also arrived (including Eastern rugs and vast quantities of Egyptian flax), together with metals, gemstones, foodstuffs, and ceramics. Muslim Spain also produced and exported an assortment of its own goods to balance these imports. These included Andalusian raw silk and silk textiles that were transported throughout the Mediterranean; "spices" such as *qīrmiz* (a dyestuff) and saffron; olive oil and dried fruits (especially figs); and Córdoban leather. Likewise, during certain periods, the peninsula served as a distribution point for commodities coming into the Muslim Mediterranean world from western Africa (gold) and northern Europe (slaves and furs).

Sources on Muslim Spanish trade are varied. Collections of Islamic legal rulings (*fatwas*), handbooks for market inspectors (*ḥisba* manuals), and biographical dictionaries provide data on merchants, commercial law, and commodities. Arabic geographical writings, travel accounts, and literature are also useful for their descriptions of Andalusian cities, markets, routes, and products. Documents from the Cairo Geniza, though mainly originating in Egypt, offer invaluable information on merchants and goods in the medieval Mediterranean world, including Muslim Spain. Although the Geniza letters were written to and from Jewish merchants, the data that they contain may be more generally applied. As noted above, Christian materials from northern Spain, France, and Italy are likewise useful.

OLIVIA REMIE CONSTABLE

Bibliography

Chalmeta G. P. *El señor del zoco en España. edades media y moderna, contribución al estudio de la historia del mercado*. Madrid, 1973.

Constable, O. R. *Trade and Traders in Muslim Spain. The Commercial Realignment of the Iberian Peninsula 900–1500*. Cambridge, 1994.

Goitein, S. D. "Judeo-Arabic Letters from Spain (Early 12th Century)." In *Orientalia Hispanica: Studies in Honor of F. M. Pareja*. Leiden, 1974. 331–50.

TRAGICOMEDIA DE CALISTO Y MELIBEA *See CELESTINA*

TRANSLATIONS, SCIENTIFIC, PHILOSOPHICAL, AND LITERARY (ARABIC)

In discussing translations in Iberia one is concerned primarily with translations from Arabic into Latin, and principally with scientific and philosophical texts. Not that there were no translations in the other direction, and from other languages. In Arabic Andalusia several Latin works—including portions of the Bible, Columella's book on agriculture, and Orosius's history were translated from Latin into Arabic. Moreover, Jewish scholars played an important part as interpreters for Christians and translated several Arabic texts into Hebrew for the Jewish communities in Spain. From the mid-thirteenth century, translations from Arabic into Castilian and Catalan began to be made. While Arabic tales and poetry undoubtedly influenced the Latin and Romance literature of the Middle Ages, the instances of a piece of Arabic literature being translated for its own sake are limited almost entirely to the field of exemplary tales, such as *Kalīla wa Dimna* ("The Tale of the Two Foxes").

The earliest known translations from Arabic in Iberia are in the fields of divination and astrology and those parts of mathematics that prepare the student for these subjects, such as geometry and astronomy. Divinatory techniques could at first have been picked up from Arabs by example rather than through texts. For instance, one could learn how to cast lines of dots randomly on the ground and join them together in pairs in order to form the figures used in "the science of the sand," which became known by the literary Latin term *geomancy*. Or one could learn how to turn the letters of the names of each of two protagonists in a battle or a contest into numbers to determine which of them would win. Or one could learn how to find out hidden things or predict the future by observing various marks on the shoulder blade of a sheep that had been slaughtered and boiled until the flesh had fallen from the bone. Most of these techniques could be learned with the aid of a good memory or, at most, a sheet of parchment giving the names and meanings of the sixteen geomantic figures, a list of the number-letter equivalents, or a plan of the shoulder blade with the significations of each of its areas written in.

At some stage, however, more detailed explanations were written down. Our earliest Latin text containing information from Arabic sources happens to be of this kind. It was written in the late tenth century, and is known variously as *Liber Alchandrei, Mathematica Alhandrei summi astrologi*, and *Mathematica Alexandri summi astrologi*—all these names implying some connection with Alexander the Great of Macedon. A large part of this text consists of "interrogations" posed by the client and "judgments" given by the astrologer on matters of everyday concern, such as marriage, business dealings, the sex of one's unborn child, and the outcome of an illness. The judgment is found by applying to the celestial "places," a number derived from the names of the client and of his mother. This form of judgment is distinctly Arabic, and survives to this day in North Africa. The *Liber Alchandrei* recalls the polyglot atmosphere of al-Andalus, for it includes, alongside Arabic names for the zodiac signs and the planets, Hebrew names for the same terms and for the letters in which the names of the client and his mother must be written and a letter of Petosiris to Nechepso, which was probably translated from Greek in the late classical period and was part of the surviving Latin culture in Spain.

At about the same time (late tenth century) we have our earliest examples of Arabic numerals, appearing in two Latin manuscripts of Isidore's *Etymologies* written in the monasteries of San Martín de Albelda and San Millán. The same Arabic numerals appear in early eleventh-century Latin texts on the abacus, in which they are used to differentiate between the nine different counters used for the nine digits. Toward the middle of the twelfth century the abacus began to be replaced by a method of calculation with Arabic numerals not marked on counters but written directly on a board thinly covered with sand, or on parchment. This was the algorism, in which the same Arabic numerals were used, and which had been taken, along with the method of calculation, from a single text by al-Khwārizmī—his *On Indian Calculation*.

The introduction of the algorism is symptomatic of the change in the process of transmission of Arabic science in the twelfth century. The transmission acquires a firm literary basis. This is hinted at in the injunction of Ibn ʿAbdūn, the jurist writing in Seville in the early years of the century who forbids the selling of books to Jews and Christians because they translate them and pass them off as their own compositions.

One of the earliest of these translators was Hugo of Santalla, working in Aragón under the patronage of Michael, who was bishop of Tarazona from the time of its reconquest (1119) until 1151. The subject matter of his translations is astronomy, astrology, the divinatory sciences, and a cosmology—*The Secrets of Nature*—that includes the earliest version of the alchemical "Emerald Table" of Hermes. A near Arabic neighbor of Bishop Michael was the last of the Banū Hūd Dynasty of Zaragoza, Saif al-Dawla. After the fall of Zaragoza to the Christians in 1118 the Banū Hūd took up residence in Rueda Jalón, some fifty-five kilometers from Tarazona. He had a library from which Bishop Michael was able to choose some works for Hugo to translate.

The Banū Hūd had a reputation for their patronage of learning. Two members of the dynasty themselves achieved reputations for their remarkable mathematical talents: Aḥmad al-Muqtadir bi-llāh (who ruled from 1046 to 1081) and his son Yūsuf al-Mu'taman ibn Hūd (1081–1085). The latter composed a comprehensive book on geometry known as "The Perfection" (*Al-Istikmāl*), which drew on a large number of sources, including Euclid's *Elements* and *Data*, the *Spherics* of Theodosius and Menelaus, the *Conics* of Apollonius, Archimedes's *On the Sphere and Cylinder*, Eutocius's commentary on this work, Thābit ibn Qurra's treatise on amicable numbers and Ibn al-Haitham's *Optics*. Probably during the reign of Aḥmad al-Muqtadir billāh, whose renown extended to astronomy and philosophy, Al-Qarmanī (d. 1065), a pupil of the best-known Andalusian mathematician of the Middle Ages, Maslamaal Al-Majrīṭī (tenth century), introduced the *Letters of the Brethren of Purity* into Zaragoza. It is likely that Al-Qarmanī also brought Maslama's revision of the tables of Al-Khwārizmī from Córdoba to Zaragoza.

Some idea of which texts remained in the library of the Banū Hūd when they moved to Rueda Jalón can be gauged from the evidence of Hugo's translations. In only one preface does he mention this library (*armarium Rotense*), but that is precisely his preface to a commentary on the tables of Al-Khwārizmī, which must have been known in Zaragoza. It was also translated by Abraham ibn Ezra, a Jewish scholar from neighboring Tudela, a town on the river Ebro with an important Jewish community.

The translators Hermann of Carinthia and Robert of Ketton are said to have been working in the region of the Ebro in 1141, and could well have been in Tudela; Robert was later canon of the church there. Hermann knew several of the same sources as Hugo, and perhaps also had access to the library of the Banū Hūd. For he knows the works of Theodosius and Archimedes, and made versions of Euclid's *Elements* and Al-Khwārizmī's astronomical tables, all of which were apparently in the Banū Hūd's possession. In his major original work, the cosmogony called *On the Essences* (*De essentiis*), Hermann cites the Emerald Tablet from the *The Secrets of Nature* (he is the only Latin scholar beside Hugo who appears to know the latter work), and refers to several other Hermetic works. Hugo's translations had a very limited diffusion. Hermann and Robert, on the other hand, advertised their work to the highest European authorities of the time. Robert promises to Peter the Venerable, abbot of Cluny, who was responsible for promoting the Cluniac reform of the Christian Church in Spain, "a celestial gift which embraces within itself the whole of science"—that is, a work on astronomy, whereas Hermann sent one of his translations (that of Ptolemy's *Planisphere*) to Thierry of Chartres, the foremost educator in France of the second quarter of the twelfth century. In the preface to this translation Hermann sketches a history of astronomy, refers to the basic textbooks on the subject, and advertises three of his own works and one of Robert's. Thierry was engaged in compiling an annotated "library" of texts on the seven liberal arts (the *Heptateuchon*), and included two translations from Arabic, which may be in Robert and Hermann's versions.

A decade or two after Robert and Hermann's project to translate and send to France texts on geometry and astronomy, an even more comprehensive program of translations was planned and undertaken, this time in Toledo. The motive force for this program seems to have been an archdeacon resident in Toledo called Dominicus Gundissalinus (Domingo González). He described each of the sciences in turn in his *On the Sciences*, drawing largely on the translation of Al-Fārābi's *Classification of the Sciences* made by Gerard of Cremona (d. 1187). Al-Fārābi's *Classification of the Sciences* provided a template for Gerard on which to pattern the program of his own translations, several of which were used in turn by Dominicus when he adapted Al-Fārābī's text into a comprehensive account of philosophy and its parts—*On the Division of Philosophy*—patterned on schemata developed by Thierry of Chartres and his pupils. With Dominicus and Gerard of Cremona we see not only a high public profile given to translations from Arabic, but also an expansion of the range of texts into medicine and philosophy. Gerard translated several of Aristotle's works and some commentaries on Aristotle by Arabic authors or Greek commentators whose work had been translated into Arabic. On the other hand, Dominicus and his associates Avendauth and Johannes Hispanus translated the works of Arabic and Jewish scholars who had summarized and reinterpreted Aristotle's philosophy in the light of Neoplatonic trends—for example, Ibn Sīnā, Ibn Gabirol, and Al-Ghazāli.

The thirteenth century witnessed a continuation of the translating activity. Two conspicuous elements about this activity should be noted: (1) The transmission of the results of the last flowering of philosophy in Islamic Spain; and (2) The rise of "official translation"—that is, translation as part of public policy, either to aggrandize the newly emerging Spanish nation, or to convert the Muslim.

Turning to the first of these, under the Almohads there occurred an Indian summer for philosophy in Islamic Spain. This took the form of a burst of "fundamentalist" Aristotelianism unparalleled elsewhere in the Arabic world. The central figure is Ibn Ṭufayl (d. 1185), the court physician of the Almohad leader in Córdoba and the composer of the philosophical novel *Ḥayy ibn Yaqẓān*, which inspired Daniel Defoe's *Robinson Crusoe*. Ibn Ṭufayl had introduced to the Almohad ruler the philosopher Ibn Rushd (Averroës, d. 1198), and inspired Al-Biṭrūjī (Alpetragius) to write his book on astronomy. This book, *On the Movements of the Heavens* (written ca 1200), was a revolutionary attempt to replace Ptolemy's astronomical system with a model that was compatible with Aristotelian physics. Averroës in his turn undertook the most ambitious project ever conceived for interpreting Aristotle: three levels of commentaries for the whole of Aristotle's works, to which a commentary on Plato's *Republic* was added. These consisted of summaries of the texts, paraphrases, and line-by-line exegeses.

Andalusian Aristotelianism appears to have had little influence on subsequent Arabic scholarship. Its influence on Latin and Hebrew philosophy and science was, on the other hand, immense. It was in this intellectual climate at Córdoba that the philosophy of Maimonides (1135–1204) was formed. And within a few years of their composition the works of both Al-Biṭrūjī and Ibn Rushd were being translated into Latin and Hebrew. The first translations were made in Spain. Michael Scot translated *On the Movements of the Heavens* in Toledo in 1217, five years after the defeat of the Almohads in the battle of Las Navas de Tolosa. To Michael Scot are also attributed the earliest translations of Averroës, which he probably began in Spain and continued when he moved to Italy in the 1220s.

The continuation of interest in Aristotelianism in Christian Spain in the thirteenth century is evident from the following facts: Álvaro of Toledo (fl. 1267–ca. 1286) copied out Michael Scot's translation of Al-Biṭūjī's *On the Movements of the Heavens* and wrote a commentry on Averroës's *On the Substance of the Globe*. He dedicated the latter to the archbishop of Toledo, Gonzalo García Gudiel, who himself had collected several manuscripts of the works of Aristotle, Avicenna, and Averroës by 1273. The archbishop commissioned a translation of those books on natural science in Avicenna's *Shifā'*, which had not been translated by Dominicus Gundissalinus.

With García Gudiel we come to the very end of the thirteenth century. If we retrace our steps we can follow the course of "official translations" through the century. The Battle of Las Navas de Tolosa (1212) and the subsequent capture of Seville and Córdoba, leaving as the only Islamic kingdom in Spain the vassal state of Granada, gave the Christian bishops and kings a great feeling of confidence. We see at least one archbishop and two kings who produce texts in their own names to further the Hispanisization and Christianization of the Iberian Peninsula.

Rodrigo Jiménez de Rada, archbishop of Toledo from 1210 to 1247, wrote the *Historia Gothica* and the *Historia Arabum*, both of which rely heavily on Arabic sources. A canon in his cathedral called Mark was asked by his archdeacon, Mauritius (whom we have mentioned before), to translate the Qur'ān and the Profession of Faith of the founder of the Almohad movement. Jaime the Conquerer, king of Aragón (d. 1276), was more a warrior than a cultural hero, and added Valencia, Murcia, and the Balearic Islands to his kingdom. But he also wrote a unique biography in Catalan—the *Llibre dels feyts*—and set up a school for training missionaries.

The most remarkable instance, however, is that of Alfonso X, el Sabio, king of León and Castile from 1252 until 1284. His nationalism is evident in his great law codes and histories (of Spain and of the world), which build on the earlier histories of Rodrigo Jiménez and even on the Islamic literature translated by Hermann of Carinthia and Robert of Ketton. Above all, it is evidenced by the fact that he chose to use Castilian as the literary language of his court. He was not so interested in Aristotle, but sponsored the translation of texts on magic, the science of the stars, entertaining stories, and games (including chess, draughts, and backgammon). Not only was the language of these translations Spanish, but also he made it seem that the authors themselves were Spanish, calling, for example, the author of the *Ghāyat al-ḥakīm* "Picatrix Hispanus." Of course, in a way, they were. The author of *Ghāyat al-ḥakīm*, though not Maslama al-Majrīṭī himself (as the Arabic attributions suggest), lived in al-Andalus in the eleventh century.

Latin-reading Europeans were interested in the texts for practical purposes or for making progress in mathematics or philosophy. The Arabs were not mere conduits of ancient Greek learning. Admittedly, translators were searching out Ancient Greek works and occasionally complained when they could only find an Arabic translation of a Greek work. This was the case with Eugene of Palermo (twelfth century), who reluctantly used the Arabic version of Ptolemy's *Optics*. The Greek version has yet to be found. Gerard of Cremona, Robert of Ketton, and Hermann of Carinthia were all aiming for the *Almagest* of Ptolemy, but they acknowledged that scholars writing in Arabic had developed, added to, or made more accessible the texts of antiquity. Understanding the *Almagest* may have been the aim of every aspiring astronomer, but most scholars in the Middle Ages, including Dante, found it easier to use the shorter *Elements of Astronomy* of Al-Farghānī. Ptolemy's *Tetrabiblos* was regarded as the fountainhead of teaching on astrology, yet the works of Abū Maʿshar and Al-Qabīṣī were much more frequently copied and cited. Avicenna's *Sufficiency* (*Shifā'*), as its title implied, provided a full curriculum in philosophy and, partly because it gave clear-cut answers rather than left questions hanging in the air, it was easier to manage than the several books of Aristotle's philosophy and was consequently popular. Averroes, on the other hand, with his three tiers of commentary to each of Aristotle's works, provided a thorough going method for a detailed study of Aristotle and a model for Latin commentaries from the mid-thirteenth century onwards.

The Arabs of the Middle Ages seem to have had a special flair for mathematics, and the Latin translations in this field provide only a dim reflection of the true splendor of the achievements of men like Al-Mu'taman ibn Hūd or Omar Khayyam. The translations did, however, introduce into the West calculation with Arabic numerals, algebra, trigonometry, and advanced geometry. In medicine, above all, Arabic works held sway in the Middle Ages. One need only mention the names that became familiar in the Latin forms of Avicenna (this time as author of the *Canon of Medicine*), Rhazes, Mesue, Isaac, and Abulcasim; these being Ibn Sinā, Al-Rāzī, Ibn al-Māsawaih, Isḥāq al-Isrā'īlī, and Abū-l-Qāsim, respectively.

Most of these texts had originally been translated in Spain. Many of them had been written by Muslims (or, to a lesser extent, Christians or Jews) resident in Spain. We have already mentioned Maslama al-Majrīṭī, Al-Biṭrūjī, Averroes—and Ibn Bājjah, whose views were known through the commentaries of Averroes. But there were others, such as ʿArīb ibn Sa'd, who contributed to the composition of the tenth-century Calendar of Córdoba; Abraham bar Ḥiyya (d. c. 1136), the author of a book on trigonometry translated by Plato of Tivoli under the title *Liber embadorum* ("Book of areas"); the eleventh-century mathematician and astronomer Ibn Muʿadh of Jaén whose works on atmospheric refraction (*De crepusculis*) and *Tables of Jaén* were translated by Gerard of Cremona; and Al-Zarqaluh, whose astronomical tables composed for Toledo in about 1070 became the standard tables in use in Latin translation in the West between the late twelfth and early fourteenth centuries. But Arabic texts also arrived in al-Andalus from the furthest parts of the Islamic world and this, in itself, testifies to the brilliance of the academic society in Islamic Spain. What Hugo of Santalla said of the subject of his own astrological translations would have been echoed by many of his fellow Latins: "It befits us to imitate the Arabs especially, for they are as it were our teachers and precursors in this art."

CHARLES BURNETT

Bibliography

Burnett, C. "Some Comments on the Translating of Works from Arabic into Latin in the Mid-Twelfth Century." In *Orientalische Kultur und europäisches Mittelalter*. Ed. A. Zimmermann. *Miscellanea Mediaevalia* 17. Berlin, 1985. 161–71.

———. "The Translating Activity in Medieval Spain." In *The Legacy of Muslim Spain*. Ed. S. K. Jayyusi. Leiden, 1992, 1036–58.

Burns, R. I. *Emperor of Culture: Alfonso X the Learned of Castile and His Thirteenth-Century Renaissance*. Philadelphia, 1990.

D'Alverny, M. T. "Les traductions à deux interprètes: D'arabe en langue vernaculaire et de langue vernaculaire en latin." In *Traductions et traducteurs au Moyen Âge*. Ed. G. Contamine. Paris, 1989. 193–206.

———. "Translations and Translators." In *Renaissance and Renewal in the Twelfth Century*. Ed. R. L. Benson and G. Constable. Oxford, 1982. 421–62.

Haskins, C. H. *Studies in the History of Mediaeval Science*. 2d ed. Cambridge, Mass., 1924.

Millàs Vallicrosa, J. M. *Estudios sobre historia de la cienci española*. Barcelona, 1949.

Vernet, J. *La cultura hispanoárabe en oriente y occidente*. Barcelona, 1978.

TRANSLATIONS, SCIENTIFIC, JEWISH

Jewish scientific and medical studies date at least to the Hellenistic period (if not earlier) and reached their first zenith in Babylon in the Talmudic era. The Muslim civilization brought increased knowledge, made available through Arabic translations, of all ancient science and mathematics. Jews played a major role in this, both as translators and as originators of scientific and medical knowledge. That tradition continued in Muslim Spain. There was as yet no need for translation, however, since all Jews knew Arabic. Only toward the end of the twelfth and throughout the thirteenth centuries do Hebrew and Spanish translations from Arabic texts appear.

It is at once necessary to dispel the old myth according to which Raimundo, the archbishop of Toledo (1125–1150), sponsored a "school of translators." There is not one shred of evidence to support this. This was even less true of Aragón-Catalonia, where writers talk about such a school under the patronage of Miguel, bishop of Tarrazona (1119–1152), or that of Barcelona with Plato of Tivoli (ca. 1116–1145) and which supposedly included the Jew Abraham bar Ḥiyya. In fact, the activity was mostly on an individual basis, and the present state of knowledge does not permit elaborate theories on the relationships between these translators.

The most problematic, and in many ways most important, of these Jewish translators was one who apparently converted (even this is far from certain), known as Juan ibn Daūd, or Johannes Avendauth, about whom much confused scholarship has been written. The only thing certain is that he worked in the latter part of the twelfth century with Domingo Gundisalvo (Domingo González). (There is certainly no reason to assume *two* Ibn Daūds, one a Jewish philosophical translator and the other a *converso* scientific translator; nor is he to be confused, as has been done, with Juan Hispalensis, bishop of Toledo.)

His translations into Latin, particularly of Arabic philosophical works, predate those of Domingo, and apparently even some works attributed to Domingo are actually Ibn Daūd's. Scientific works translated by him include *Qusṭā b. Lūqā,* various treatises of Ibn Sīnā, pseudo-Aristotle, *Liber de causis*, Maslama al-Majrīṭī of Córdoba's treatise on the astrolabe, and other works.

Far more important for science was the work of several Jewish translators and astronomers who collaborated in the scientific treatises sponsored by Alfonso X. Indeed, they wrote the majority of the works comprising the *Libros del saber de astronomía*, as well as the famous *Tablas Alfonsies*, and translated (into Spanish) many other works. Among these was the *Lapidario*, translated by Yehudah b. Moses ha-Kohen ("Mosca") and the *Azafeha* (*Ṣafīḥa*) of "Azarquiel" (Al-Zarqāllah) in Latin. He may also have played a part in the translation of the *Liber picatrix*. Yehudah was perhaps a physician of the king, possibly of the Ibn Sūsan family. Another more famous royal physician, Abraham Ibn Waqār (see Ibn Waqār Family), also was a translator for Alfonso, first of Sura 70 of the Qurʾān (*La escala de Mahoma*), then a cosmography of Ibn al-Haytham, and finally (1277) a new translation of *Azafeha*.

Another work translated by Yehudah ha-Kohen, not in the Alfonsine corpus, is an astronomical treatise of Al-Biṭrūjī of Seville, which was also translated by Moses Ibn Tibbon in Provence (1259).

The need for *Hebrew*, as opposed to Spanish or Latin, translations was most evident in Provence and parts of Catalonia, where few Jews knew Arabic. The earliest such translation was done by Abraham b. Hayya, himself a renowned philosopher and scientist (twelfth century). His scientific work itself contains summaries and excerpts from Arabic writings, but in Barcelona (1135–1136) he translated an astrological work of the famous Hali, as he became known to the Latin world (Aḥmad b. ʿAli al-ʿImrānī), and then worked with Plato of Tivoli on the Latin translation of a geometry book. (The translation work of another more famous Abraham, Ibn Ezra, is not considered here, because most of this work was done out of Spain.)

The Ibn Tibbon family of Provence was particularly famous in the field of translation. Moses Ibn Tibbon translated Aristotle's *Physics*, with a compendium of Ibn Rushd (Averroës), and also *De generatione et corruptione* (both published; the second only in a Latin translation), and the commentary of Ibn Rushd on *Parva naturalia* (all ca. 1250–1254). Later (1274) he translated Muḥammad Jābir Ibn Aflaʿḥ of Seville on astronomy, which was again translated by another famous member of the family, Jacob bar Makhir. Again, both Moses and Jacob made translations from the Arabic of the complete Euclid. Samuel Ibn Tibbon made a translation of Aristotle's *Meteora* for a patron in Toledo.

Zeraḥyah b. Isaac b. Shealtiel Gracian (Ḥen) was the most famous translator of Catalonia (Barcelona) in the thirteenth century. He was in Rome (1277–1290), where many of his scientific translations were done. Among these were Ibn Rushd's "Middle Commentary" on Aristotle's *Physics* (published), and on *De generatione et corruptione*, as well as a translation of the pseudo-Aristotelian *De causis*.

Medical works were, of course, also translated. The earliest is probably a work of Abū-l-Qāsim, translated by Shem Ṭov b. Isaac of Tortosa (b. 1196). Natan ha-Meʿaṭi also made a translation of this work, as well as other medical works (those of Galen, Hippocrates, et al.), some of which are actually named as being in the possession of a Jewish doctor in Fraga in 1381. The kings also employed Jews as official translators of Arabic, and at least one of these, Vidal Benvenist de Porta, was paid by Jaime II to translate Arabic medical works (1296). In Provence (fourteenth century) medical works were translated by Yehudah ben Solomon Natan and Abraham Avigdor, including chapters of Arnau de Villanova (all in manuscripts).

NORMAN ROTH

Bibliography

Alonso, M. Various articles in *Al-Andalus*, nos. 8–25.

Gil, J. *La escuela de traductores de Toledo y los colaboradores judíos*. Toledo, 1985.

Roth, N. "Jewish Collaborators in Alfonso's Scientific Work." In *Emperor of Culture*. Ed. R. I. Burns, Philadelphia, 1990. 59–71, 223–30.

TRASTÁMARA, HOUSE OF

The Trastámaran dynasty owed its origins to the civil wars of fourteenth-century Castile. When Alfonso XI (1312–1350) died, the succession fell to Pedro I (1350–1369), his legitimate son from his marriage to Mary of Portugal. The new king was violent and authoritarian by nature (hence his epithet, "the Cruel"), and he soon provoked the hostility of many nobles. Among the latter there were potential leaders of substantial power and influence, such as the children resulting from Alfonso XI's long liaison with his mistress Leonor de Guzmán, particularly Enrique of Trastámara, Pedro's illegitimate half-brother. But if in the early stages the civil wars represented a struggle between the authoritarian Pedro I and the coalition of nobles led by Enrique of Trastámara, both sides soon sought support from outside the kingdom, and Castile was drawn into the Hundred Years War, the French supporting Enrique and the English supporting Pedro. In 1365, the exiled Enrique invaded Castile and proclaimed himself king as Enrique II (1366). With the help of the English, Pedro mounted a counter invasion and defeated the Trastámarans at Nájera (1367). His triumph was temporary. In 1368, Charles V of France provided decisive military support for Enrique who yet again invaded Castile and finally defeated and murdered Pedro at Montiel (1369). Thereafter a succession of Trastámaran kings ruled in Castile: Enrique II himself (1369–1379); Juan I (1379–1390); Enrique III (1390–1406); Juan II (1406–1454); Enrique IV (1454–1474); and Isabel the Catholic (1474–1504).

But the Trastámaran dynasty also established itself in the Crown of Aragón and the kingdom of Navarre. In 1412, Enrique II of Castile's younger brother, Fernando of Antequera, succeeded in having himself elected as king of the Crown of Aragón at the Compromise of Caspe (Fernando I: 1412–1416) and was succeeded by other members of this Trastámaran line: Alfonso V (1416–1458); Juan II (1458–1479), who also became king of Navarre in 1425; and Fernando II the Catholic (1479–1516), who married Isabel the Catholic in 1469, both of them subsequently being known as the Catholic Monarchs and reigning in Castile from 1474 and in Aragón from 1479. With their respective deaths the Trastámaran dynasty came to an end and an imperfectly united Spain was ruled by the Hapsburg dynasty.

Were there any relatively consistent features that characterized the ruling members of the Trastámaran dynasty? At a rather pedestrian level it may well have been that a relatively regular policy of endogamous marriages produced what is frequently referred to as "the Hapsburg jaw," the pronounced jaw being very evident in the mortal remains of Enrique IV and perhaps inherited by the Hapsburgs from the Trastámaran dynasty.

But far more important were the evident concerns which at least some of the Trastámaran rulers felt both with respect to the legitimacy of their kingship and the need to reward those who had supported them. Enrique of Trastámara had depicted Pedro I as a tyrant who unjustly persecuted his subjects and was an enemy of Christ. These were grounds which might serve to justify rebellion, but they did not legitimize his own "illegitimate" claim to the throne. In order to do this he had to emphasise the elective nature of monarchy while at the same time trying to prevent the consequences that "election" might have on royal authority. He attempted to do this by arguing that there had not really been a rebellion against Pedro I; instead God had intervened to secure the tyrant's departure. Later, when facing the crisis posed by English military intervention in support of John of Gaunt's claim to the throne, derived by virtue of his marriage to Pedro I's daughter, Constanza, Juan I of Castile simply avoided the issue by blatantly asserting that the Trastámaran dynasty had the best hereditary right to the succession. Later Juan II was to go much further and make extensive use of what he referred to as his absolute royal power (*poder real absoluto*) in order to make new laws or ignore existing ones, but "elective" precedents were once again to surface as an issue when rebel nobles deposed the effigy of Enrique IV at Avila in 1465 and elected his half-brother Alfonso as king, justifying their actions by drawing upon precedents from as far back as the thirteenth century. Earlier, the Trastámaran dynasty in Aragón faced similar problems for the simple reason that Fernando of Antequera had been "elected" king at the Compromise of Caspe, a fact he attempted to ignore by stressing the role of divine intervention in the proceedings.

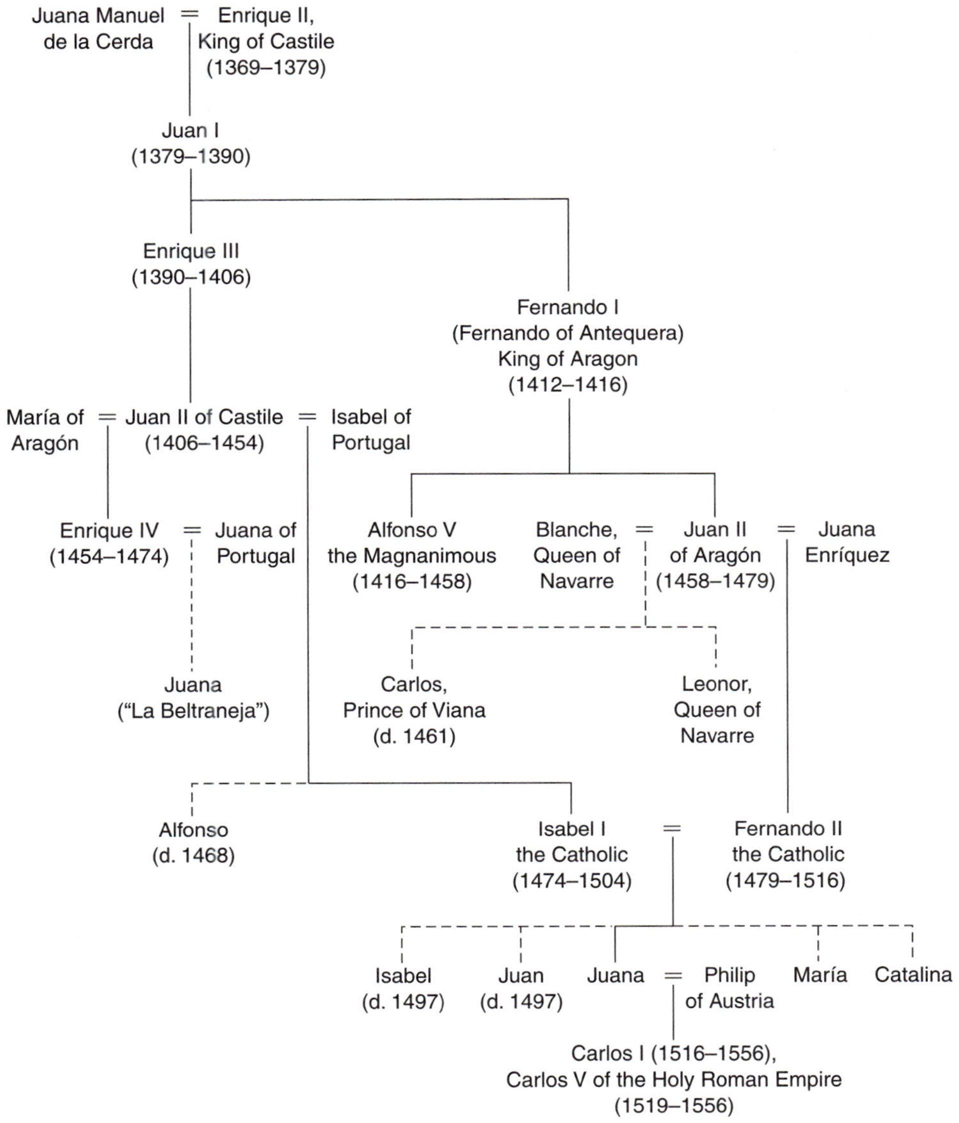

But how exactly did the divine intervention work? Another salient feature of the Trastámaran dynasty was its devotion to the Virgin Mary. Enrique II was devoted to the Virgin of Tobed, and the Trastámaran kings were particularly fond of the Heronymite monastery of Guadalupe, which was established in 1389 on the site where an image of the Virgin had been discovered. For his part, Fernando of Antequera went out of his way to stress that his "election" at Caspe was nothing less than a miracle, a predestined event arranged by the Virgin as a reward for his undoubted devotion to her. Poets predicted and celebrated the results with praise to the Virgin, and in an enormous altarpiece in the Prado, known as *El Retablo del arzobispo Sancho de Rojas*, the child Jesus, sitting comfortably on his mother's lap, leans down, blesses a kneeling Fernando of Antequera with one hand and places the royal crown on his head with the other (and, of course, not one elector is in sight).

The need to reward those who had supported them during a succession of serious crises posed enormous problems for the Trastámaran kings. The rewards may have been titles, lordships, privileges, the financing of mercenaries, or various forms of cash payments on a regular and recurring basis. Generally referred to as *mercedes*, they all ultimately involved money, either indirectly or directly. After all, did not these kings owe their power to French support, to soldiers of fortune like Bertrand du Guesclin who had led Free Companies of mercenaries in their support, and all those within Castile who had supported them? This financial crisis, moreover, was linked to another one of a more serious nature. In general, western Europe was in the grip of a famine of precious metals. Both silver and gold, the essential elements determining the content of minted coins, were in short supply due to factors affecting the sources of supply (Eastern Europe in the case of silver; trans-Saharan Africa in the case of gold). This "liquidity" crisis demanded solutions as urgently as did the political problems to which it was related. It is to the credit of their ingenuity and the skill of their councillors that the Trastámaran kings coped with such problems, although there were obvious and signally dismal exceptions, Enrique IV above all.

The first and most obvious way of dealing with these problems was debasement of the coinage, debasements that inevitably led to a devaluation of the Castilian money of account, the *maravadí*, an accounting money (not a real coin) used to calculate the sums involved. Devaluation of the maravadí inevitably entailed a reduction in the sums of money owed by the Trastámaran kings. Bertrand du Guesclin and other mercenaries were paid off in this way. Equally, the recipients of the famous mercedes within Castile were to find that the nominal values of their privileges were eroded in real terms. There were, however, exceptions. John of Gaunt insisted on being paid properly in international coins of a genuine fineness and weight, and in the course of time the recipients of mercedes within Castile realized that their privileges were being eroded in real terms and pressed for additional mercedes. The late fourteenth and fifteenth centuries (up to about 1485) were consequently affected by an alternating spiral of demands for monetary rewards by the nobility, royal debasements/devaluation of the coinage, and new demands for increments.

In the course of all these turbulent sociopolitical and economic fluctuations certain trends became clear. Plagued by internal problems (noble unrest, both real and potential) and by external obligations (Lancastrian debts; the need to honor the alliance with the French, at least morally), the Trastámaran kings could pay but scant attention to the traditional "manifest destiny" of Castile, the conquest of Granada. The result was that, with some infrequent but important exceptions (Fernando of Antequera above all), the task of reconquest was to be given up until the Catholic kings rescued it in the 1480s. On the whole, the pattern of relations between Trastámaran Castile and Muslim Granada was one of intermittent truces (never definitive peace treaties), the terms of which required that the Naṣrid rulers paid *parias* or tribute payments at fairly regular intervals to the kings of Castile in return for the temporary cessation of formal hostilities.

As far as the French were concerned, the early years of genuine partnership were largely over by the 1390s. French (and Burgundian) influences continued to be extremely important. The Castilians, for example, drew heavily on French experience when reforming their military institutions, and in literary, artistic, and architectural terms Franco-Burgundian patterns for long predominated over Italian ones. But in political and commercial terms, the Trastámaran monarchy concentrated on keeping vital trading routes open. When the French demanded privileges for their merchants, they found unexpected resistance from a Castile that was drawing closer to those whose trading interests were of mutual advantage, the Low Countries, Brittany, and even England.

The kings of the Trastámaran dynasty were, above all, opportunists. Despite appearances, their power was based on the principles of mutual self-interest: a sharing of power, wealth, and privileges with selected and loyal noble families (often newly promoted), a calculated policy of financial rewards to foreign and internal supporters, coupled with shrewd (but at times panicky) devaluations, and a foreign policy that paid lip service to ideals (the reconquest and support for the French against the English) without involving too many real sacrifices. Only with the Catholic kings, Fernando II and Isabel, were these patterns to change. By the time of their accession, the Trastámaran dynasty had been largely discredited, due above all to the miserable years of anarchy during the reign of Enrique IV.

ANGUS MACKAY

Bibliography

Hillgarth, J. N. *The Spanish Kingdoms, 1250–1516*. 2 vols. Oxford, 1976–78.

TRAVEL LITERATURE, CHRISTIAN

Travel literature may be defined as a narrative, presented as factual, in which the author relates his or her own journeys in foreign parts (as far as medieval texts are concerned, generally Asia). The features of such writing are, in varying degrees, curiosity (defined as a taste for the monstrous), piety, desire for knowledge, fakery, and a tension between personal experience and received tradition.

If the author's Galician nationality is accepted, the *Peregrinatio* of Aetheria (alias Egería), variously dated between the fourth and sixth centuries, is the earliest Hispanic travel book. It exemplifies the pilgrimage account, marked by piety and a greater interest in the past of the Holy Land as revealed in a set of monuments than in its contemporary human or economic geography. Also in the pilgrimage tradition is the Hebrew *itinerary* of Benjamin of Tudela (ca. 1161).

The *Libro del conoscimiento de todos los rregnos* (ca. 1350–1360) is, like the *Travels* of Sir John Mandeville, a fake, based not on the author's own travels, but more likely on a world map that, as was often the case, was copiously annotated. Its interest in heraldry, expressed in the inclusion of illuminated escutcheons in the manuscripts, classifies it as a work of political geography. The manuscripts also show the monstrous races, an iconographical theme that typifies the sixteenth-century printings of the Spanish translation of Mandeville.

Ramon de Perellòs visited St. Patrick's Purgatory circa 1396 in order to interrogate the soul of his master, Juan I of Aragón, who had died under suspicious circumstances. The *Viatge* combines a firsthand account of his journey to Ireland with a description of St. Patrick's Purgatory derived from written sources. The evidence of the manuscripts and the incunable edition suggests that early readers valued the latter, pious, element more highly. Ruy González de Clavijo, ambassador of Enrique III of Castile, led an embassy to Tamberlaine in 1401. The *Embajada a Tamorlán* is probably a group effort under the direction of Alfonso Páez de Santa María. Its descriptions are convincing firsthand accounts. Pero Tafur undertook his travels, written up as *Andanças e viajes*, circa 1453, in order to compare the political systems of various foreign states. The objective observations of Tafur and Clavijo distinguish them from earlier devotional or curious travelers.

The most successful medieval Hispanic travel book, with some 112 editions between 1515 and 1902, was the *Historia del infante don Pedro de Portugal*, attributed to one Gómez de Santisteban. It is, however, another fake.

The peninsula also produced medieval translations of other European travel books: Marco Polo (in an Aragónese version done for Juan Fernández de Heredia from Catalan), Prince Hayton (Heredian Aragónese), and Sir John Mandeville (Aragónese and a fragmentary Catalan version).

BARRY TAYLOR

Bibliography

Fick, B. W. *El libro de viajes en la España medieval*. Santiago de Chile, 1976.

Pérez Priego, M. A. "Estudio literario de los libros de viajes medievales," *Epos* 1 (1984), 217–39.

Rubio Tovar, J. (ed.) *Libros españoles de viajes medievales*. Madrid, 1986.

Taylor, B. "Los libros de viajes de la Edad Media hispánica: bibliografía y recepción." In *Actas do IV Congresso da Associaçao Hispanica de Literatura Medieval*. Vol. 1. Lisbon, 1991, 57–70.

TRAVEL LITERATURE, MUSLIM

Muslim travel literature is enormously rich and bridges both geographical writings and historiography. Here we will discuss some of the more important, representative authors and their works. As with other medieval Arabic literary genres, some early Hispano-Muslim travel writers are known only through brief quotations in secondary sources. Such is the case with Ibrāhīm ibn Aḥmad al-Ṭarṭūshī (from Tortosa, tenth century) and Aḥmad ibn ʿUmar al-ʿUdhrī (d. ca. 1083). Both traveled in northern Europe and both wrote detailed reports on France, England, Ireland, and the Baltic regions (Germanic, Old Prussian, and Slavic), noting local toponyms, customs, and other ethnographic data. Al-Ṭurṭūshī eloquently conveys his *dépaysement* in the face of Western singing: "Never have I heard more hateful singing than that of the people of Scheswig and it is a growling that comes out of their throats like the baying of dogs, but even more bestial." More amply documented, Abū Ḥāmid al-Gharnāṭī (from Granada) (ca. 1080–ca. 1169) lived most of his life in the East, made the pilgrimage to Mecca (1155), and traveled extensively in Asia and Europe and to Egypt, Syria, Iraq, Persia, Caspian regions, southern Russia, Rumania, and Hungary, reporting on cities, peoples, animals, and diverse marvels. Abū ʿAbdallāh al-Idrīsī, the great geographer (ca. 1100–1165), wrote under the patronage of the Norman king, Roger II of Sicily. His *Book of Roger* (*Kitāb al-Rujārī*) reflects extensive travels in Spain and the Maghrib and earns him a place of honor among the Hispano-Muslims, even though he was born south of the Straits. Abū-l-Ḥusayn Muḥammad ibn Jubayr (b. in Valencia, 1145) twice completed the pilgrimage and died at Alexandria during a third attempt (1217). He has left us a paradigmatic, colorful, day-by-day account of his first trip (1183–1185), a model for future *riḥla* literature (pilgrimage reports). Of particular interest to Hispanists are his pages on Christian-Muslim symbiosis at the court of William II of Sicily.

Prince and champion of Muslim travelers was the Moroccan Abū ʿAbdallāh ibn Baṭṭūṭa (1304–ca. 1368 or 1377), whose astounding *riḥla* was written down, edited, and supplemented (with frequent quotes from Ibn Jubayr and perhaps also personal recollections of al-Andalus) by the Hispano-Arabic scholar and poet, Abū ʿAbdallāh Muḥammad ibn Juzayy (b. in Granada, 1321–ca. 1355). Leaving Tangier in 1325, Ibn Baṭṭūṭa embarked on an epic journey, lasting almost thirty years, that would take him to the outermost reaches of the Islamic world, through North Africa, Egypt, Syria, Arabia, Iraq, Turkey, the Russian steppes, Persia, India, Bengal, and Sumatra, and onward to China and, after his return to Morocco in 1349, also to the city of Timbuktu, in Mali. There were four different visits to Mecca and innumerable side trips along the way: among the most memorable, to the city of Kilwa, in East Africa; to the Muslim Bulghars, on the Volga; to Constantinople, in the retinue of a Byzantine princess; to South India, with hairsbreadth escapes from death by shipwreck or at the hands of Hindu brigands; and to the Maldive Islands, off India, where Ibn Baṭṭūṭa married a total of six wives during his relatively brief sojourn. His visit to Islamic Spain (1350) is particularly interesting: Disembarking at Gibraltar, Ibn Baṭṭūṭa traveled by way of Ronda and Marbella—barely escaping capture by Christian pirates—through Málaga, Vélez, and Alhama, to Granada, which he characterizes as "the bride of the cities of al-Andalus" (anticipating, by almost a century, an exquisite metaphor in the famous ballad of *Abenámar*). A minor detail of the journey to Timbuktu eloquently evokes the cosmopolitan world of Muslim merchant-scholars, in which Ibn Baṭṭūṭa had come to move comfortably and to feel thoroughly at home: Waiting for the winter season, when caravans moved south across the Sahara, Ibn Baṭṭūṭa spent four months at the edge of the desert, in the Moroccan entrepôt of Sijilmāsa. His host was Muḥammad al-Bushrī, whose brother, Qiwām al-Dīn, had given Ibn Baṭṭūṭa lodging in the Chinese port of Qanjanfū, at the other end of the known world, just six years before.

Abū Isḥāq Ibrāhīm ibn al-Ḥājj al-Gharnāṭī (in ca. 1312–ca. 1367) twice made the pilgrimage, but his *riḥla* has only survived fragmentarily, in passages quoted by other authors. His travel notes on a trip through Morocco in 1344–1345 have, however, come down to us intact. The case of Leo Africanus (al-Ḥasan ibn Muḥammad al-Wazzān al-Zayyātī) is thoroughly exceptional. Born in Granada (ca. 1489–1495), his family took him to Morocco soon after the city's capture by the Christians (1492). Early on, the future Leo twice journeyed to Timbuktu and also traveled extensively throughout North Africa. He made two trips to Egypt and, on the second one (1517), completed the pilgrimage, but, on his way home, was captured by Sicilian pirates at Djerba, taken to Rome, and presented to Pope Leo X, Giovanni de Medici, who convinced him to be baptized (1520), taking the name of his patron, Johannis Leo de Medicis. In Italy, Leo became a renowned teacher and scholar. His *Descrittione dell'Africa*, reflecting his extensive travels, was written in Italian and translated into Latin and various modern European languages. Eventually, Leo was able to return to North Africa, where he died, a good Muslim, in Tunis, sometime before 1550.

The *Coplas* of an anonymous Morisco *alhichante* (pilgrim; Arabic, *al-hājj*), from the Aragónese town of Puey Monzón (now Pueyo de Santa Cruz), were written in *aljamía* (Spanish in Arabic letters) and are preserved in a unique manuscript, part of the secret personal library of a Muslim bookbinder who had hidden the volumes under the floorboards of his house, in the town of Almonacid de la Sierra, before going off into exile in 1609. The poem, only discovered in 1884, traces the pilgrim's adventures—departure from Valencia, a great sea storm off Libya, wonders of Cairo, Mecca, Medina, and Jerusalem, and the pilgrimage itself, with its sacred monuments, relics, and rituals. The *Coplas*, like other Morisco-Spanish texts, written in Arabic letters to disguise their content and, in this case, hidden away against religious persecution) conclude the record of Hispano-Muslim travelers on a note of sadness, fear, and deprivation.

SAMUEL G. ARMISTEAD

Bibliography

Del Casino, L. G. *Las Coplas del Alḥiĵante de Puey Monçon.* Ph.D. diss., Philadelphia, 1978.

Dozy, R., and M. J. de Goeje. *Description de l'Afrique et de l'Espagne par Edrîsî.* 2 vols. Leiden, 1866.

Dubler, C. E. *Abū Ḥāmid el Granadino.* Madrid, 1953.

Dunn, R. E. *The Adventures of Ibn Battuta.* Berkeley, 1986.

Épaulard, A. *Leo Africanus: Description de l'Afrique.* Paris, 1956.

Gribb, H. A. R. (trans.) *Travels of Ibn Baṭṭuta.* 3 vols. Cambridge, 1958–61.

Jacob, G. *Arabische Berichte von Gesandten an germanische Fürstenhöfe aus dem 9. und 10. Jahrhundert.* Berlin-Leipzig, 1927.

Premare, A.-L. de. *Maghreb et Andalousie au XIVe siècle.* Lyon, 1981.

TRINITY, ORDER OF THE

See CHURCH; RELIGIOUS ORDERS

TRISTE DELEYTACIÓN

Sentimental novel written in the third quarter of the fifteenth century by an anonymous author, perhaps Fray Artal de Claramunt (Riquer). The novel is an amatory fable with an unfavorable ending, with a preponderance of doctrinal discussions. Its schematically sketched characters are designated by acronyms. Narrated in both prose and verse, sometimes in first person, sometimes in third, the work plays with the status of the narrator and comments ironically on its own subject in several passages (Gerli, Blay Manzanera).

The novel consists of poems, letters, and debates that are in themselves complete literary works; an extensive versified ending narrates a journey to Love's Hell, Purgatory, and Paradise.

The only extant manuscript (Barcelona, Diputación, MS. 770) is described by Riquer. The linguistic problems and issues raised were not resolved in any of the existing editions (Gerli brings in errors; Rohland adds ambiguous graphical elements). The manuscript contains a Catalan lament as well as Catalan words, and was considered to be of Catalan origin until Goméz Fargas de Antolín defined these characteristics as Aragónese.

Certain autobiographical traits are reinforced by the presence of names of contemporary figures. Among its rich intertextualities are echoes of Boccaccio, Dante, Santillana, and Rodríguez de Padrón; poetic forms and techniques like the debate between the brain and the heart, the aedilic allegory, lamentations, the tomb of love, nonsense verse, and the journey to the afterlife; and names of literary characters. The work leaves behind the proposals of courtly love (which it addresses in discussing the theme of Andreas Capellanus's *De arte amandi*) and concludes instead that by observing certain "practical rules" (*normas prácticas*), the woman can and should *choose* her own lover, putting the fable's forewarned limitations to the test. According to Tudorica Impey, the text displays "una mentalidad nueva, vital y utilitaria, que descansa en un cambio de *mores* y valores (a new and lively utilitarian mentality based on a change of mores and values)".

REGULA ROHLAND DE LANGBEHN

Bibliography

Editions

Blay Manzanera Valencia, 1994.

Gerli, E. M. Washington, D.C., 1982 (excellent introduction).

Rohland de Langbehn, R. Morón, Argentina, 1983.

Criticism

Gómez Fargas, R. M. "Peculiaridades lingüísticas aragonesas en *Triste deleytación*," *Archivo de Filología Aragónesa* 42–43 (1989), 21–64.

Riquer, M. de "*Triste deleytación*, novela castellana del siglo XV," *Revista de Filología Española* 40, (1956), 33–65.

Tudorica Impey, O. "Un doctrinal para las doncellas enamoradas en la *Triste deleytación*," *Boletín de la Real Academia Española* 66 (1986), 191–234.

TROUBADOURS, CATALAN

Apart from geographical and linguistic connections, many historic events, starting with the reconquest of the northeast of Catalonia by the Franks, account for cultural, political, and religious links between this region and the Occitan territory. This northern perspective was highly developed politically in the twelfth century by the counts of the House of Barcelona (kings of Aragón since 1137) and finished dramatically at the Battle of Muret (ca. 1213), where King Pedro I the Catholic was defeated and killed when defending his Occitan vassals from the French army. Since then, the interests of the Crown of Aragón north of the Pyrenees were restricted to Rosselló and Montpellier, though, in the meantime, the troubadour lyric was so deeply rooted in the Catalan courts that they became not only a refuge but lively centers where this tradition, after Muret, underwent a decline.

The extant corpus of the Catalan contribution to the troubadour poetry is about two hundred poems, written by twenty-four poets, and roughly covers the first half of the twelfth century and the thirteenth. Apart from mere references to a certain Ot de Montcada and some other names, it starts with Guerau de Cabrera's *sirventes-ensenhamen* (poem of praise and blame), which contains a broad account of literary culture and mentions four troubadours of the second generation—his friend Marcabrun and Jaufré Rudel among them. Although controversial, Berenguer de Palol's production (nine *cansos* and four more of dubious attribution) should be placed between 1150 and 1164, and we know that the count-king Ramón Berenguer IV (d. in 1362) was alluded to in some passages from Marcabrun and Peire d'Alvernhe. All this points to earlier contacts, yet the very flourishing of troubadour lyric in the Catalan courts happened in the reign of Alfonso I the Chaste (1162–1196), *aquel que sabet trobar*, and his son Pere I (1196–1213). Alfonso's literary interest had much to do with politics. Through poetry, he tried to strengthen his rights to Provence by encouraging the troubadours to attend his court and even composing some poems himself: apart from one *canso*, we have a *partimen* with Guiraut de Bornelh, Alfonso's best propagandist. We find the best of the troubadours among those who write in his service (Folquet de Marselha, Arnaut Daniel, Peire Vidal, et al.) or against his expansionism (Bertran de Born) and, of course, there is mutual benefit from this literary exchange, as we can see in the case of Ponç de la Guàrdia (ca. 1140–ca. 1190), vassal of Alfonso whose rich love poetry seems to have been appreciated in Provence.

Guillem de Berguedà was the greatest Catalan troubadour of this period and also made use of poetry as a weapon, sometimes ironically, against Alfonso. He was endowed with a strong character and a sharp, often cruel sense of humor, which he never hesitated to use to ridicule his rivals. One can appreciate his poetical individuality in many of his thirty-one pieces, written from 1370 on, either when he combines ferocity with an apparent naivety of style, or in his sincere *planh* for one of his personal enemies' death. One can assign Guillem de Cabestany's life to a slightly later period, still hidden behind a sentimental legend that made him an archetype of the martyr of love. Contributing to this fame, his eight love poems are much on the sentimental side of the troubadour mainstream, such as *Lo doutz cossire*, a very synthesis of the delicacy of the *fin'amors*. Still in the second half of the twelfth century, the court of Huguet de Mataplana seems to have been another troubadour center. This nobleman, who died after being wounded at Muret, was delighted by holding poetical debates—once with Raimon de Miraval—in which he demonstrated a bizarre sense of humor, as when impersonating an evil apparition that visits an uncertain Blancasset. Furthermore, Huguet's literary environment was precisely evoked by Ramon Vidal de Besalú in his verse narrative *So fo el temps c'om era jais* (not after 1213). On the whole, Vidal's works reflect the transition from the Golden Age to the decline, since, insofar as he looks back to Alfonso's court (*Abrils issi'e mays intrava*, after 1199), he is putting an end to the former, whereas his courtly *fabliau*, the *Castia gilos* (after 1214), proves the vitality of the latter. Moreover, his grammatical treatise *Las rasos de trobar* (not after 1213), the earliest in a Romance language, is both a symptom of the decadence of Occitan and a personal reaction against its corruption.

The last great Catalan troubadour was Cerverí de Girona, who wrote 119 poems and a book of proverbs, signed as Guillem de Cervera. This impressive amount—the largest corpus extant—covers an astonishingly wide range of tones, though particular attention should be paid to Cerverí's virtuosity in the domain of the *trobar ric* (poetry with rare and difficult words and meanings) as well as to his popular style. This body of material leads us to the second half of the thirteenth century. In it, one can also place an unknown Guillem de Gironella and realize again how strongly poetry was linked to the royal family. Pédro II the Great (1276–1285) used to debate with his *joglars* (minstrels) Peironet and Pere Salvatge (perhaps the same person), and committed the latter and himself to writing verse propaganda against the French invaders. In addition, Jaime of Sicily, afterwards king of Aragón (1291–1327), composed a religious *dansa* (poem with dance rhythem) against the pope and, years after, his brother Frederic defended his rights to the island in a sirventes metrically modeled on Guillem de Berguedà, and answered, in turn, by Ponç Hug d'Empúries. Finally, apart from the poetry of an illegitimate member of the royal family, one should mention, still related to Jaime II, Amanieu de Sescars's ensenhamens and love verse epistles. However, what really gives an eye to the future is that Jaime himself ordered Jofre de Foixà to write the *Regles de trobar* (1289–1291), soon after followed by Berenguer d'Anoia's *Mirall de trobar* and other fourteenth-century language treatises: from then on, the gradual admixing of Catalan would be the key to the difference between troubadour and post-troubadour poetry.

LLUIS CABRÉ

Bibliography

Cluzel, I. "Princes et troubadours de la Maison Royale de Barcelone-Aragón," *Boletín de la Real Academia de Buenas Letras de Barcelona* 27 (1957–58), 321–73.

Riquer, M. de. "Els trobadors catalans." In *Història de la literatura catalana. Part Antiga*. Vol. 1. Barcelona, 1984. 21–196.

TUDENSE, EL *See* LUCAS OF TÚY

TURMEDA, ANSELM

Moralist born in Palma de Mallorca (ca. 1350) and died in Tunis (1430); wrote in Catalan and Arabic. He joined the Franciscan Order, and as a novice went off to study theology in Bologna in 1370. According to his supposed autobiography (later written in Arabic as the *Tuhfa*), Nicolau Martel, Turmeda's master in Bologna, taught him that Muḥammad, the prophet of Islam, was the Paraclete. In 1385 Turmeda, by then a friar, traveled to Tunis and solemnly abjured the Christian faith; he married a rich heiress and became ʿAbdallah al-Taryuman al Mayurquī, a high officer of the Tunisian customs service. Turmeda's *Tuhfa* (*The Present of the Believer against the Followers of the Cross*) contains true historical data and a traditionally Islamic refutation of Christian dogma, but it has been proven that the extant version from the seventeenth century has been considerably altered. The *Tuhfa* assured Turmeda a brilliant reputation among Muslims. On the other hand, writing Catalan works from a Christian point of view—while living in Tunis—Turmeda also attained great prestige in the Crown of Aragón: King Alfonso the Magnanimous asked him to return, and Pope Benedict XIII even assured him that he would be pardoned for his apostasy. The *Llibre dels bons amonestaments* (1398) is a Catalan verse translation of a popular catechism written in Italy in the thirteenth century to which Turmeda sometimes adds a bit of his own cynical advice. This work was later printed, and in Catalonia it was read as a children's schoolbook until the nineteenth century. The *Cobles de la divisió del regne de Mallorques* (1398) is a narrative strophic poem in which Turmeda explains the magical and astrological reasons for the internal conflicts among the citizens of Mallorca. The author presents himself as a wise man who has mastered the three religions. The *Disputa de l'ase* (1417–1418) is a prose work indebted to Arabic sources, whose Catalan original text has been lost. The extant sixteenth-century French version is in the form of a discussion between a speaking donkey and Turmeda about the dignity of humankind and animals. It is only because Christ was embodied in a man that Turmeda manages to defeat his opponent. At the end the donkey makes a prophecy about the future of the church.

Turmeda wrote some other prophetic works that were much appreciated by his contemporaries. The frequent colorful autobiographical allusions in Turmeda's writings made him a popular character and probably contributed to his legendary fame among both Christians and Muslims. ʿAbdallah's tomb in Tunis is still venerated.

LOLA BADÍA

Bibliography

Epalza, M. de. *La Tuhfa, autobiografía y polémica islámica contra el cristianismo de Abdallah al-Taryuman (fray Anselmo Turmeda).* Rome, 1971.

Turmeda, A. *Disputa de l'ase.* Barcelona, 1928.

———. *Obres menors.* Barcelona, 1926.

TÚY, LUCAS OF *See* LUCAS OF TÚY

U

ÚBEDA, BENEFICIADO DE

We know very little about the author of the rhymed version of the *Vida de San Ildefonso*, dated—by contradictory and ambiguous references—between 1303 and 1349.

In the oldest copy (found in a *flos sanctorum* from the fifteenth century) the poem consists of 279 stanzas, in which there can be apparently detected a tendency to the regularity of the canonic *cuaderna vía* (monorhymed Alexaudrime cuartets). The Beneficiado de Úbeda has been linked more often with Gonzalo de Berceo than with his contemporary authors, probably because of the metrics and his straightforward moralization. In fact, the characters and the structure serve the typical aim of hagiography, the exemplarity of the saint, though in a very particular sense here, since St. Ildefonso is above all a model of devotion and loyalty to the Virgin. However at least one other intention exists in the poem: the praise of the city of Toledo as cradle of saints, which might be interpreted as propaganda of the archdiocese of this town. It could be connected with a statement in stanza 276: the author had written a lost poem dealing with the Magdalen while being beneficiary of Úbeda, but he "lived in another status," probably in some ecclesiastic charge in Toledo, when he wrote the poem devoted to St. Ildefonso.

FERNANDO BAÑOS VALLEJO

Bibliography

Romero Tobar, L. "La Vida de San Ildefonso del Beneficiado de Úbeda: Dos versiones inéditas," *Revista de Filología Española* 60 (1978–80), 285–318.

Úbeda, B. de. *Vida de San Ildefonso*. Ed. M. A. Ezquerra. Bogotá, 1975.

ULFILAS, BISHOP *See* WULFILA, BISHOP

UMAYYAD DYNASTY

The Umayyads of Spain were a dynasty of Muslim emirs and caliphs who ruled from their capital in Córdoba from 756 to 1031. Their founder, ʿAbd al-Raḥmān I, was a grandson of one of the great Umayyad caliphs of Damascus, Hishām I. When the ʿAbbāsids overthrew the Umayyads in Syria in 750, they apparently killed all the members of the royal family except for ʿAbd al-Raḥmān, who escaped to North Africa. From there he entered Spain and took power from the local governor with the help of those still loyal to the Umayyad cause. His strength grew as Umayyad supporters from all parts of the Islamic world migrated to Spain; but ʿAbd al-Raḥmān and his descendants never gained enough power to seriously challenge the ʿAbbāsid caliphs in Baghdad.

ʿAbd al-Raḥmān I proclaimed himself emir of al-Andalus in 756 and ruled until 788. Although the general principle of Arab tribal culture is that any capable male from the agnate line can succeed to the throne, power in Muslim dynasties usually passes from father to son. ʿAbd al-Raḥmān I's son, Hishām I, ruled from 788 to 796 and was followed by his son, Al-Ḥakam I, who ruled from 796 to 822. His son, ʿAbd al-Raḥmān II, who ruled from 822 to 852, was the first to consolidate Umayyad power throughout the Muslim-held territories and to establish a court and culture in Córdoba that quickly rivaled any in the Islamic world at that time. He was followed by his son, Muḥammad I, who also had a relatively lengthy reign, 852–886. His son, Al-Mundhir, only ruled for two years, 886–888, before being killed in a battle with rebels in Bobastro. His brother ʿAbdallah, another son of Muḥammad I, ruled from 888 to 912.

ʿAbdallah's grandson, ʿAbd al-Raḥmān III, succeeded him as emir in 912. After fourteen years of consolidating power that had been lost to the provinces, in 926 ʿAbd al-Raḥmān III proclaimed himself caliph of al-Andalus, and commander of the faithful. Muslim Spain reached its zenith of political and economic stability, territorial expansion, and cultural flowering during his lengthy reign. This prosperity continued, especially in terms of cultural development,

Umayyad Dynasty

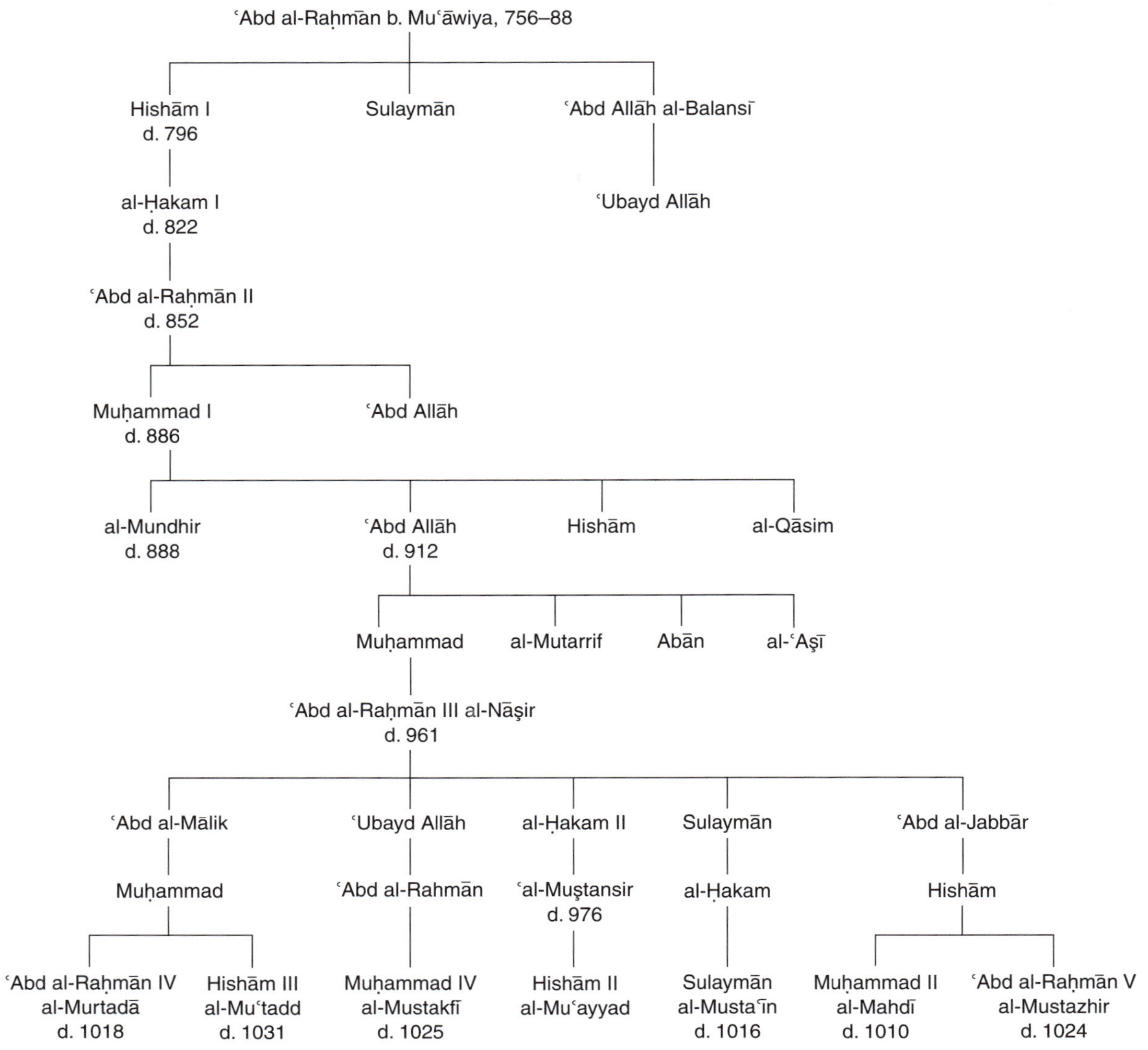

under the rule of his son, Al-Ḥakam II, who ruled from 961 to 976. Al-Ḥakam II was succeeded by his son Hishām II, who ruled from 976 to 1009, and it was during his rule that Umayyad power began to seriously decline. From 1009 until 1031 the caliphate changed hands many times. The powerful *ḥājib* (prime minister), Ibn ʿAbī ʿĀmir (also known as al-Manṣūr), and his sons ruled behind the scenes from 1009 to 1016, and after that, the various ethnic groups in and around Córdoba championed their respective pretenders to the throne. After 1031, political power dispersed among the various provincial powers, and the period known as the tā'ifa kingdoms began.

The Umayyads of Spain are known sometimes as the Marwānids (because of their descent from the caliph Marwān in Damascus). In addition to the titles of *emir* and *caliph*, they also used *mālik* (king) and *ibn alʿumaya* (son of the Umayyads).

MARILYN HIGBEE WALKER

Bibliography

Kennedy, H. *Muslim Spain and Portugal: A Political History of al-Andalus*. London, 1996.

Lévi-Provençal, E. *Histoire de l'Espagne musulmane*. 3 vols. Leiden, 1950–53.

UNIVERSITIES, CHRISTIAN

I. Introduction

I.1

The origin and evolution of the university is an essential cultural phenomenon of the Late Middle Ages in Europe. It is linked to the growth of urban culture and of commerce; to the industrial revolution responsible for the availability and reception between 1120 and 1250 of the works of Aristotle, Galen, Hippocrates, and Avicenna; to the Roman Church's interest in disseminating canon law as codified by Gratian; and to the monarchy's support in spreading Roman law, which was a crucial instrument of royal power.

Universities in the Iberian Peninsula reinforced the cultural tendencies of the urban and cathedral clergy, setting aside the ways of traditional monastic education. The university introduced new juridical programs and institutionalized medical knowledge (in the hands of Jewish and Arabic experts in Spanish kingdoms). Like other European institutions, Spanish universities were centers of higher education whose degrees were valid throughout all Christian lands by virtue of the special privileges conceded by the pope in the *licentia ubique docendii*. Besides this papal bull, there were other essential factors in the development and legitimization of the university. For one, royal and municipal leaders took special legal measures to provide benefits, tax exemptions, and jurisdictional protection that would attract students and professors to a particular institution; the good (and determined) will of those in powerful positions was also necessary in order to finance a *studium generale*. (Initially, *universitas* was a generic term applied to guilds of professors, scholars, businessmen, clergymen, etc., and until the fifteenth century was not used in the modern sense.) Strictly speaking, the only universities in medieval Iberia were: Lisbon-Coimbra in Portugal; Lérida and Huesca in Catalonia/Aragón, in addition to Perpignan; Palencia in Castile, and Salamanca in León (before the union of those two kingdoms); and Valladolid in the newly united kingdom of Castile and León.

Several different centers of higher education apart from the university operated during the Middle Ages. The church, which had renewed its efforts to control and educate its clergy after the Third and Fourth Lateran Councils of 1179 and 1215 (and after numerous provincial synods), responded to the growing presence of the university by either maintaining the cathedral schools of the twelfth century or creating new ones (such as Santiago de Compostela, Burgos, Sevilla, Toledo, Zaragoza, etc.). Interestingly, however, the constitutions of different thirteenth and fourteenth prelates allude to elementary studies of *grammatica* in these church schools: such studies likely incorporated some of the disciplines of the seven liberal arts (*trivium* and *quadrivium*) in the most accomplished institutions, like those in Santiago, Zaragoza, Valencia, and Seville. In other instances, the monarchy or municipal authorities mandated the organization of educational institutions: Alfonso X, for example, requested that Eastern languages be taught in Seville, while Barcelona, which took pride in its higher education in 1346, nourished the study of medicine and the arts. Nevertheless, these schools (and others like them that were administered by religious orders) had little to do with the studium generale, although some universities did have their roots in cathedral schools.

Many medieval centers of learning did not reach university status until the sixteenth century because they still lacked the papal document that would give their degrees recognition throughout Christianity. In other cases, the project failed due to lack of funding or to disagreement between those with vested interest in the institution: the monarchy, the papacy, the cathedral clergy, municipal leaders, and the university authorities themselves. Among other failed attempts that never materialized during the Middle Ages, the following deserve citation:

- Alcalá, which was granted foundational privileges by Sancho II at the end of the thirteenth century.
- Valencia, which received the papal *licentia* in 1246.
- Seville, which Alfonso X granted a letter of permission in 1254.
- Zaragoza, which had a prestigious cathedral school and received support from Pope Sixtus IV in 1476–1477.
- Girona, which received support from Alfonso V the Magnanimous in 1446.

Some cities were hesitant to allow communities like the university, over which municipal authorities had little control, in their midst. Barcelona, for example, rejected the offer made by Martín el Humano in 1398 to establish a university; despite this, the city changed its position and obtained privileges from Pope Nicholas V in 1450, but until 1498 the higher schools were still subordinate to the Chancellor of Medicine's authority.

I.2

Iberian universities share many characteristics with their European counterparts, including the organization of courses, the disciplines studied (except theology), the conferral of degrees, university government, the university community's love of autonomy, the struggle between, or collaboration of, different public authorities (the church, the crown, the urban middle class) to control the *estudio*, and the student lifestyle. The differences between Spanish and European universities are rooted largely in quantitative rather than qualitative aspects. There are, however, some significant differences: with the exception of Salamanca, peninsular universities are founded later than the European institutions they imitate; their scientific contributions were more limited; they are less cosmopolitan, with fewer foreign students and professors; finally, although all universities were burdened with economic problems, Hispanic estudios suffered especially, due to civil wars, the Reconquest, and the relative economic weakness of the urban bourgeoisie.

II. History

The earliest peninsular university was Palencia, which was linked to the city's cathedral school and was active at the end of the twelfth and beginning of the thirteenth century under Alfonso VIII of Castile; its biggest supporter was Bishop Tello. Among its students were likely Gonzalo de Berceo and, according to tradition, Santo Domingo de Guzmán; several Italian teachers were counted among its faculty. Palencia specialized in law, as did other subsequent Hispanic universities. The university had always struggled with scarce funds, among other problems; Pope Urban IV tried to revive the school in 1263, but it had been dormant for some time, and died out before the end of the thirteenth century.

The University of Salamanca was founded by Alfonso IX of León in 1218. In 1243, thirteen years after the union of Castile and León, Fernando III bestowed his protection on the students and professors of the estudio. Subsequent monarchs conferred tax exemptions and personal benefits and confirmed the university's juridical independence. Alfonso X was Salamanca's great protector: in 1254 he endowed chaired professorships, gave the university a foundational ordinance, and influenced Pope Alexander IV, who in 1255 approved Salamanca's licentia ubique docendi, giving the institution's degrees validity throughout all Christian lands except Paris and Bologna (a restriction that may have been lifted in the fourteenth century). As he had done with Bologna and Toulouse, in 1298 Pope Boniface VIII sent the university the *Liber sextus*, a collection of pontifical decretals and constitutions. Benedict XIII, another important supporter of Salamanca, authorized new constitutions (1381 and 1411), which were revised by Martin V in 1422. These served as groundwork for the splendor the university reached under Juan II (1406–1454), and for the educational stimulus put into effect by the Catholic Monarchs at the end of the century.

There are a few documents referring to an estudio at Valladolid at the end of the thirteenth century, likely connected to the Colegiata de Santa María. Municipal and royal interests were focused on Alfonso XI's petition to Clement VI, who converted the schools into a studium generale with a 1346 papal bull. Subsequent rulers granted privileges and exemptions for professors, and also set apart the necessary funds to assure the university's survival. Valladolid began to gain importance in the fifteenth century: Benedict XIII awarded it the Salamancan statutes in 1411, and Martin V authorized the conferral of theology degrees in 1418. At the end of the century the Colegio de Santa Cruz began to operate.

King Dinis supported the creation of the Portuguese university in Lisbon in 1290; the clergy had solicited papal support earlier in 1288. In 1308, however, the university was translocated to the more peaceful Coimbra. Dinis also conceded privileges of protection and jurisdiction to students and professors, showing special concern for student housing. In 1338 the university returned to Lisbon, only to relocate to Coimbra from 1354 to 1377. In 1384, João I promised not to move the institution from Lisbon, where it remained until the earthquake of 1531. In 1537 it settled in Coimbra for good. Like Castile, Portugal lacked a theology program at the beginning, and its degrees were not valid in Paris and Bologne.

After petitions from the citizens of Lérida, Jaime II established an estudio general in the city in 1300, due to the support of Pope Boniface VIII, who had also bestowed privileges on Toulouse in 1287. From the beginning the pope gave all members of the university community royal protection, tribute exemption, and rights to self-jurisdiction. The estudio settled into well-defined parishes (San Martín, San Andrés, San Lorenzo). In 1310 the cathedral chapter took part in university administration in exchange for its contributions to the institution's financial support, which was always lacking. In 1376 the Colegio Mayor de Santa María was founded; this was the first residence hall in the peninsula, preceding even the Colegio de Pan y Carbón in Salamanca. Early university statutes underwent significant reforms in 1399 (Martín I), 1432 (María de Aragón, wife of Alfonso V the Magnanimous), and 1447 (Bishop García Arnáez d'Anyon). Competition with Huesca, the civil war, and the siege of 1464 contributed to Lérida's decline. As with other peninsular universities, Lérida did not teach theology until the fifteenth century. The university's medical program, however, was superior to Salamanca's—among its distinguished faculty were Bernat Bonhora, of Jewish descent (1311); Juan Amel, a court physician from Montpellier (1313); and the famous

Jaime d'Agramunt (1345). In 1391 Juan I gave the university permission to perform autopsies.

Pedro IV established the University of Perpignan in 1349 to compete with Montpellier, where many of his subjects attended. However, its degrees were not recognized in the Christian world until Pope Clement VII gave them the proper documents in 1397. Degrees in art and theology were offered at Perpignan, though its most esteemed programs were law and medicine.

Pedro IV conferred the same privileges to Huesca in 1354 that had been granted to Lérida. The University of Huesca's theology program was noteworthy in the beginning, but financial difficulties soon brought about its downfall. In 1465 the university was reinvigorated with a papal bull from Paul II which confirmed the privileges granted by the king. Huesca functioned according to the Lérida model, and the government of the university was in the hands of the prior of Pilar and the abbots of Montearagón and San Juan de la Peña.

III. Institutionalization

III.1

Bologna served as a model for the government and administration of Iberian universities. In the Castilian schools, the intervention of the monarchy was important, though their power was tempered by the king's lack of resources: the approval of the pope, who was far away and delegated his participation to the local cathedral chapters, was crucial for financial support of the university. The balance of powers gave a certain level of autonomy to the members of the university community. In Portugal, on the other hand, royal intervention was much more pronounced. In spite of everything, though, Portuguese and Castilian universities flourished by the end of the fifteenth century, thanks to the protection offered by the monarchy, which tried to use the university as an instrument to their advantage. In this respect, the Catalan/Aragónese universities functioned quite differently: in Lérida and Huesca, and in later institutions in the region, local powers took on the responsibility for maintaining the estudio, participating decisively in its operation.

The balance of power in Bologna between different university groups was also imitated in Spain, with certain differences that are apparent in the pontifical constitutions of Salamanca in 1411 and 1422, the Coimbra privileges granted by Dinis in 1309, and the Lérida privileges of 1300.

In Salamanca, the pope was represented by the *maestrescuela*, a doctor or teacher of theology who held the authority to confer degrees and exercised jurisdiction over professors and students. At first, the maestrescuela was elected by the bishop and the cathedral chapter, but later the university was able to gain control of the election. In Lisbon, the bishop functioned as chancellor and was responsible for the conferral of degrees: jurisdiction was shared with two royal representatives. In Lérida the chancellor was the papal representative and the highest university authority; he was required to be a canon of la Seu (the cathedral), and his position was a lifetime appointment. Although he did award degrees, he did not hold jurisdictional rights.

Students were organized in *naciones* (nations). In Salamanca there were several such organizations (León; Galicia and Portugal; Castilla la Vieja and País Vasco; Castilla la Nueva, Toledo, and Andalucía). Every year, each nation elected two *consiliarios*—the elected representatives were responsible for electing the rector and the professors. The rector was the highest authority in the *escuelas* and was responsible for the selection and assignment of doctoral readings. Although the university administrator was appointed by the church, he answered to the rector and the consiliarios. In Portugal there were two rectors—both elected by the students—that governed the university. In Lérida, as in Salamanca, students were grouped into nations which took turns electing the rector. Unlike in Coimbra and Salamanca, in Lérida the rector had the responsibility of working with (and answering to) the king, the bishop, and city officials to assure that the university's privileges were observed. He also worked to resolve problems that arose between student groups, or with students' families. Normally, the requirements for the rectorate were quite general: the rector could not be a native of the city where the estudio was located, and once elected, he had to reside continually in that city (this condition, however, was often violated).

Professors' main responsibilities were to read their lectures and participate in exams. In Salamanca they were elected by the students, and in the fifteenth century they began to organize faculty meetings with the rector. Unique to Salamanca was a committee of *diputados*, created in 1422 to coordinate the different sectors of the university community and to direct everyday matters of university life. This committee was formed by the maestrescuela, the rector, ten students, and ten professors. In Lisbon professors were appointed by the king, with guidance from the university. In Lérida, unlike Salamanca and Portugal, the faculty was hired annually by the municipality, and had little say under the jurisdiction of the maestrescuela and the rector.

III.2

The estudio also required additional employees for its operation. In Portugal a *conservador real* shared jurisdiction with the chancellor. Salamanca also had *conservadores reales*, which represented the monarchy in university affairs. In Lérida the chancellor was the royal representative; the *clavarios*, university tax collectors, were important figures beginning in 1364. Two other important positions should be emphasized. The first is that of the *bedel* (porter), an essential employee in the Middle Ages, who also performed some secretarial functions. In Lérida the bedel was sometimes appointed by the university, and sometimes by the king. The second is that of the *estacionero*, bookseller of the university, who was responsible for the selling, lending, and copying of university texts.

III.3

Hispanic universities of the Middle Ages suffered an endemic scarcity of resources. Portuguese and Castilian institutions, impeled by the king, could pay their professors with the *tercias reales*, the two-ninths of the ecclesiastical tithe collected by the crown. Even though the monarchy granted permission for the establishment of the university, the financing of the institution depended on church funds, especially in Castile. Financial support from municipal authorities was minimal, except for the occasional gift of food or other goods during hard times. In Aragón, on the other hand, the city was responsible for the economic welfare of the estudio, even though it did not have sufficient funds. Consequently, from the beginning the king imposed several taxes on Lérida: the *lliura del vi* (a wine tax) in 1319, followed shortly by the *lliura de la carn* (a meat tax) and the *bancaje*, a tribute that students paid for seating. (Actually, this was a gratuity similar to the Bolognese *colecta* paid to the professor, which was in use at certain times in Salamanca and Portugal.) If the crises of the fifteenth century had especially harsh repercussions in Portugal, Salamanca, or Valladolid, the civil war almost destroyed the estudio at Lérida in 1464: between 1467 and 1472 the travails of the professors were so overwhelming that they refused to start courses.

Also among the setbacks and problems that medieval peninsular universities endured were the defects associated with classroom buildings, which were often either unfit or on loan. Salamanca, for example, did not have its own classrooms until the fifteenth century.

University students frequently took on minor ecclesiastical orders, and often financed their studies with the associated benefits. This system of ecclesiastical student benefits became essentially a kind of protectorate. Between the church's funds for professors and its benefits for students, it is not surprising that the papal bull ratifying the university was so important; nor should it be hard to believe that *Cánones* [canon law] was the largest university department of Castile until the eighteenth century, or that the layperson had little presence in the estudio until the end of the fourteenth century.

III.4

Most professors were of local origin—the peninsular university's low salaries and economic instability were not attractive to the great European teachers of the time. Whether they were appointed by the king (Portugal), chosen with the participation of the municipality (Lérida) or selected by student votes as designated by statutes (Salamanca), the election of professors was often accompanied by protests, scandals, and dissatisfaction. Whether they were hired annually (as in Lérida) or paid a fixed rate (as in Salamanca), professors received variable salaries, depending on the subject taught. The highest paid discipline was law, the lowest *Gramática*. Professors of medicine at Lérida were paid as high as law professors by the end of the fourteenth century.

The names of many Iberian professors are known: none were famous authors, excepting some of the medical professors of Lérida or the professors of canon law at Salamanca. University departments were filled with professors with insufficient training or with those that had other income. Graduates were often more attracted by the benefits of church or court positions, while those notable Hispanic academics in Bologna or Paris had either received training in foreign universities or had performed extraordinarily to receive their degrees.

III.5

Hispanic universities had fairly small, and mostly local, student populations (at the beginning of the fifteenth century, Salamanca had roughly 300 students, and Lérida 170). Contact and exchange between individual Iberian universities was sparse, excepting the few Portuguese that went to Salamanca. Those who left home preferred to settle in Paris, Bologna, or Avignon in search of work, or in Montpellier if they studied medicine. The first posters/announcements of student petition for papal benefits date from the end of the fourteenth century. These confirm that some students attended the university with exemptions; that generally students preferred pursuing professional activity to staying at the university; that the lay population was greater in Lérida than in Castile, though the presence of the layman in the latter would increase in the fifteenth century; and that in Catalonia/Aragón, more students graduated in *utroque* (both civil and canon law, simultaneously). In conclusion, the medieval university shaped and trained professionals who needed the church and the Crown, and students who relied more on positions and benefits than on knowledge.

IV. Academic Aspects

IV.1

There were few academic subjects until the fifteenth century, when they grew somewhat in number. In Salamanca, Alfonso X had endowed two professorships for law, logic, grammar, and physics, and one each for organ and decretals. Theology was introduced in the late fourteenth century. In Martin Pope V's statutes (1422), there are one professorship for theology, one for decretals; eight for law, four each for morning (*de prima*) and evening (*de víspera*) classes; one for a *licenciado* in Law (de vísperas); one (de vísperas) in medicine; one (de prima) in physics; two in grammar and one each for logic, natural philosophy, music, Hebrew, and Chaldean. The development of the quadrivium (the natural arts) was a European constant of the fifteenth century. In 1398 Valladolid had seven *cátedras*: decretals, canon law, law, natural philosophy, physics (medicine), and two for logic. After 1418, it also had a department of theology. In Lérida and Coimbra a similar development occurs—both are universities steeped in juridical tradition, though medicine in the Catalan/Aragónese kingdom is also important. Medicine begins to become more present in Salamanca in the fifteenth century, and enjoys a sort of symbiotic relationship with the arts (also witnessed earlier in Lérida) that lasts longer than the Middle Ages. As mentioned, the importance of each subject is reflected in the salary received by the corresponding professor, as is evident in Alfonso X's dispositions and in the statutes of Lérida (1300) and Salamanca (1422).

IV.2

Students entered the university with a convenient knowledge of Latin that was acquired in a cathedral, municipal or convent school, or with a private tutor. Although plenty of older students (often clergymen wishing to be promoted) and younger children enrolled in the university, the normal age for the entering student was fifteen or sixteen years old. Schoolwork, imitating other European universities, consisted in the professor's readings and glosses of texts chosen by the university, and in academic disputes.

University coursework required several successive steps:

1. All students had to enroll in the *Facultad de Artes* and attend (*oír*) classes of logic, natural philosophy, and moral philosophy. Initially the university mandated four or five years of coursework, but this requirement was frequently reduced to three years during the fifteenth century. After demonstrating that they had attended sufficient classes, students moved on to the next cycle. It was not necessary to obtain a *bachillerato* in *artes* as long as the student did not aspire to a *licenciatura* in the same department, although an initial degree did shorten the requirements for the licenciatura in other departments by one year.
2. To receive the degree of bachiller, the candidate moved up to a higher *facultad*. For a bachillerato in Law, the student attended six years of *corpus iuris* and *glossators*; for canon law, courses on gratian and the decretals of Gregory IX; for medicine, four years of Hippocrates, Galen, and Avicenna; for theology, three years of Peter Lombard (*Quatuor libri Sententiarum*) and two years of the Bible. The bachillerato was awarded in a simple ceremony: a *doctor* conferred the degree to the candidate and stated before the bedel and the rector that he had fulfilled the necessary requirements.
3. Finally, the student who pursued the licenciatura, (the *licentia docendi*) was required to lecture (*leer*) for several years in the corresponding department (either in *repetitio* or as a substitute). Medicine required four years of lecture, as well as four months of practice; arts required three years; canon law, five; theology, four.
4. The doctorate did not represent a higher level or degree than the licenciatura, but rather demonstrated that the candidate disposed of enough money to pay for the costly ceremony in which the doctoral insignias were conferred.

Not all universities required the same coursework. Salamanca registered complaints that Valladolid did not require sufficient years of study. Huesca and Lérida only required five years of coursework for the bachillerato in law, while Perpignan required more than the norm for medicine. On the other hand, the *rogue* with a degree was not an uncommon sight.

IV.3

One must turn to European sources and to the constitutions of Lérida (1300) or Salamanca (fifteenth century) to have some idea of university student life, which was a mixture of notable privileges and strict regulations (for clothing, housing, and behavior). Courses lasted from October to September, with numerous holidays throughout the school year. The academic schedule was cumbersome: one class first thing in the morning, followed by mass and breakfast; repetitions and debates until lunch; two more classes, new debates, dinner, and more repetitions. In addition, students had to order, study, and take care of their texts, which was no insignificant task, considering that they sat on the ground without heat or electricity during the cruel Iberian winter.

JUAN GUTIÉRREZ CUADRADO

Bibliography

Ajo y Zúñiga, C. M. *Historia de las Universidades Hispánicas. Origen y desarrollo desde su aparición hasta nuestros días*, 11 vols. Madrid, 1957–79.

Estudios sobre los orígenes de las universidades españolas: Homenaje de la Universidad de Valladolid a la Universidad de Bolonia en su IX Centenario. Valladolid, 1988.

García y García, A. "Consolidaciones del siglo XV." In *La Universidad de Salamanca*. Vol. 1, *Historia y Proyecciones*, ed. M. Fernández Alvarez, L. Robles Carcedo, E. Rodríguez San Pedro. Salamanca, 1989. 35–58.

———. "Los difíciles inicios (siglos XIII–XIV)." In *La Universidad de Salamanca*. Vol. 1, *Historia y Proyecciones*, ed, M. Fernández Alvarez, L. Robles Carcedo, E. Rodríguez San Pedro. Salamanca, 1989. 13–34.

Peset, M. "Interrelaciones entre las universidades españolas y portuguesas en los primeros siglos de su historia." In *Boletim da Faculdade de Diretio de Coimbra*, spec. ed., *Estudos em Homenagem aos Profs. Manuel Paul Merêa e Guilherme Braga da Cruz*. Coimbra, 1983.

Peset, M. and J. Gutiérrez Cuadrado. *Clérigos y juristas en la Baja Edad Media Castellano-leonesa*. Vigo, 1981.

Sánchez, E. "La época medieval." In *Historia de la Universidad de Valladolid*. Vol. 1. ed. L. A. Ribot. Valladolid, 1989. 25–71.

Valdeón, J. "La universidad medieval: Introducción." In *Historia de la Universidad de Valladolid*. Vol. 1. ed. L. A. Ribot. Valladolid, 1989. 17–23.

UNIVERSITIES, MUSLIM

For most of the history of al-Andalus, Muslim advanced education centered around the cathedral mosque. The most famous of these was the great mosque of Córdoba, founded in the middle of the eighth century and attaining its utmost level of splendor in the tenth century. In the post-caliphate period (after 1031), the central importance of this mosque declined and teaching mosques in Seville, Zaragoza, Denia, Granada, and other cities rose in prominence. In all of these mosques, students took specialized courses with individual teachers in specific areas of study. Curriculum centered on religious subjects, such as the various fields of Qurʾānic textual and exegetical study, prophetic tradition (*ḥadīth*), and Islamic law (*fiqh*). Nevertheless, coursework also included profane subjects that were regarded as necessary ancillaries to a well-rounded religious education, such as the Arabic grammar and lexicography, literature and poetics, history, and geography. Advanced study in other areas, including medicine, philosophy, the exact sciences, or in the scribal arts of the chancellery, occurred in private classes with experts in these fields. The most sophisticated level of education usually involved often lengthy apprenticeship with scholars in one's chosen field and frequently included extensive travel to study with famous scholars, whether in al-Andalus, North Africa, or the Eastern Islamic world.

In centering advanced education around the institution of the mosque, al-Andalus followed the educational pattern established from early times in the Muslim East. By the eleventh century, these institutional patterns in the East were changing. As a result, the teaching college, or madrasa, which was founded and sponsored by rulers and enriched through endowments known as *hubūs* or *waqf*, became increasingly significant. The madrasa system gradually made its way to the West and became influential in Morocco by the fourteenth century, when the Marīnids established prestigious and beautiful madrasas in Fez and Salé. Nevertheless, it remained of minor importance in al-Andalus, appearing only when the Naṣrid ruler Yūsuf I Abū ʿl-Ḥajjāj (d. 1354) founded his college in Granada in 1349.

A major advantage of the madrasa system and one reason for its general success outside of al-Andalus was that its endowment provided regular stipends for teachers and students alike. Prior to this, such support in al-Andalus was more informal. Compensation for instruction was essentially private; students paid individual fees to their teachers. Occasionally, a scholar received a royal or government stipend or was provided with a salary through the mosque in which he taught, but evidence suggests that such instances were not the rule, especially early on. Some teachers helped to support themselves by taking supplemental employment, becoming the *muezzin* or *imam* of a mosque, for example. Gradually, the tradition of dedicating religious bequests to mosques developed. One purpose of such donations was to provide regular stipends for faculty and advanced students, and as a result the level of institutional support increased.

In order to comprehend the rationale of the structure of Islamic education as practiced in al-Andalus, it is essential to grasp the centrality awarded to the process of oral transmission of knowledge. One way to do so is to examine the model of *ḥadīth*. In transmitting the accepted corpus of prophetic tradition, oral communication was more highly valued than merely studying written ḥadīth collections. Numerous written versions existed in plenty from the ninth century, but specialists in ḥadīth regarded these as secondary aids to commanding a store of information whose most valid form consisted of knowledge learned and memorized through oral instruction. In this way, specialists in ḥadīth transmitted the prophet Muḥammad's very words from one generation to the next without dilution or alteration. As such, the voice of the prophet echoed through the centuries to reach each new generation of Muslims with a force that replicated, to the extent possible, its original verbal authenticity and spiritual force.

Similar epistemological models existed in the other traditional sciences, whether linguistic, literary, or religious. For this reason, Muslim biographical dictionaries devoted to the lives of scholars focus on two areas: (1) the place the individual under consideration holds in this chain of transmission, (that is, the identities of his teachers and his students), and (2) the rank he holds in regard to his mastery of his fields of specialization. By knowing the identities of a particular scholar's teachers and his own professional reputation, readers are able to evaluate his trustworthiness as a transmitter of knowledge. Attestation of such competency was demonstrated by his receiving a certificate of mastery (*ijāza*) from a well-known teacher that testified that on the ideal, and often enough on the practical, level the scholar had committed the book studied to memory, and thus truly knew it.

Despite this ideal reliance on oral education, books were also plentiful. Booksellers abounded, and their markets served as meeting places for scholars. Other important venues for learned interchange were scholarly circles, assemblies, and soirees. These were regular meetings held in mosques or in private homes, sponsored by wealthy intellectuals or members of the court in which scholars from individual or diverse fields gathered to discuss and display their mastery. Although these groups might consist of friendly study groups and seminars in which social interaction was an important element, it was not unusual for professional competitiveness to infuse into them a strong degree of personal confrontation and disputational asperity.

Since scholars existed in a realm of private education in which it was normal for them to earn their livelihood from the fees paid to them by their students, social affluence played an important role in higher education. Most scholars and their students came from families wealthy enough to afford instructional fees and tuition. This meant that if the surplus social wealth that underpinned education decreased, so did the number of students and subsequently the number of teachers and scholars. It took decades for Andalusian society to establish the thriving network of rich and flourishing cities that was necessary to accumulate this wealth. Once achieved, however, the large number of important cities and their relative proximity to one another provided a firm base to support a rich intellectual and cultural tradition, even in the face of the political fractionalism and tumult of the tā'ifa, Almoravid, and Almohad periods. The loss of Muslim political control of much of al-Andalus to Christian states by the mid-thirteenth century, however, undercut the economic and social foundations of centers of learning. As a result, outside of Granada traditions of advanced education fell quickly into decline. Even in Granada, where a high level of sophistication of culture and knowledge was maintained, the small size of the Naṣrid territories was insufficient to provide a broad enough base for many significant new intellectual endeavors. As a result, the center of gravity for Muslim education moved to North Africa, while the focus of Jewish and Christian education moved to the increasingly important cultural centers of Christian Europe.

Finally, the importance in al-Andalus of classical Arabic as the universal linguistic medium of advanced educational and sophisticated cultural exchange deserves mention. Arabic was the primary language of educated individuals regardless of their ethnic allegiance or religious affiliation. It united the Muslim community, no matter whether they viewed themselves as Arab, Berber, or *muwallad*. And it was adopted by Andalusian Jews and Christians whenever they wanted to participate in common public cultural discourse in the realms of science and literature. Arabic also dictated where Andalusians pursued knowledge within the Islamic world; few Andalusian scholars sought knowledge in Muslim regions where Arabic was not the dominant language of culture (in Iran after the tenth century, for example). Eloquence in classical Arabic was a highly prestigious mark of cultural competency for educated individuals and remained an important cultural ideal for educated Muslim Andalusians throughout their history. Its loss of prestige among Christians and Jews after the thirteenth century is a striking indication of the decline of Muslim cultural dominance in Iberia.

PETER HEATH

Bibliography

Makdisi, G. *The Rise of the Colleges: Institutions of Learning in Islam and the West*. Edinburgh, 1981.

Pedersen, J., and G. Makdisi. "Madrasa." In *The Encyclopedia of Islam*. Ed. James Powell. 2d ed. Vol. 5, 1123–34.

Vernet, J. *La cultura hispanoárabe en Oriente y Occidente*. Barcelona, 1978.

URBANIZATION

Urbanization in the Iberian Peninsula during the Middle Ages was prolific due to different cultures that often succeeded in living together; the settlements founded were the base of the current urban network. Many vestiges of early urbanization still survive in the centers of Spanish cities. It is a rather difficult task to estimate the level of urbanization in the Middle Ages because of the lack of population records and because the urban settlements' extensive, nonurban lands were also included.

Up to the sixth century, urbanization was weak, although different stages can be differentiated. Before the sixth century urbanization was characterized by a relative continuity in the Roman urban settlements, mainly located in the peninsula's southern lands, Mediterranean coast, and the Ebro River valley, which had decayed during the Roman Low Empire.

In addition, the Barbarian invasions provoked the Hispano-Roman retreat to the cities that were assaulted. The Vandals ravaged Seville (425), and the Swabians attacked Mérida, Braga, Lisbon, and Coimbra. This trend changed with the establishment of Toledo (554) as the Visigothic realm capital and the foundation of new cities with military and residential functions such as Recópolis, Victoriacum, and Oligitis. Furthermore, the church built churches in the cities where councils were held or in those with episcopal sees.

In the eighth century Witiza promulgated a law that introduced an urban hierarchy differentiating from the administration concerns, *civitas*, *castellum*, and *vicus*. Leovigild created throughout his kingdom the city count figure (*comites civitates*). The urban settlement continuity was unequal in the peninsula. The most dynamic cities were those located in Baetica (Andalusia), Lusitania, and along the Mediterranean coast, that is, in the oldest settled regions.

Islamic civilization stressed urbanization contrasts. From the eighth to tenth centuries only the regions that had been occupied by the Muslims knew significant forms of urbanization. The peninsula showed a sharp contrast between the Christian rural north and the very urbanized Islamic southern lands. The Muslims transformed the seized cities' structures according to the Qur'ānic principles and organized economic, political, and religious urban life. They took up again the trade relationship with the Orient and were quite tolerant of Christians and Jews. They founded about twenty cities of military and commercial significance, such as Tudela on the river Ebro, Madrid protecting Toledo, and Almería, which served as the main harbor.

The main Islamic cities according to population size were Córdoba (100,000 inhabitants in the tenth century), and Seville, Toledo, Almería, Granada, Palma de Mallorca, Zaragoza, Málaga, and Valencia with more than 15,000 inhabitants. This situation continued during the ta'ifa period, and a century later Al-Idrīsī's *Geography* distinguished three types of cities according to their size.

In the Christian kingdoms urbanization started in the eleventh century, principally in cities such as León (1,500 inhabitants in 1000) and Burgos. Urban life was subjected to the Reconquest and its bases were demographic growth, market development, and fairs. Urban settlements were small and scarce up to the thirteenth century, but it is worthwhile mentioning León, Oviedo, Santiago, and the urban settlements located alongside the pilgrimage roads.

The frontier's advance toward the south and the intensification of the repopulation formed the urban network. Some cities had a defensive character while others were founded according to the laws of the frontier. A city's dynamism could be due to several factors: the extension of its boroughs (*alfoces*), its location on communication paths (Valladolid), or the grant of privileges (Cuenca). Furthermore, the consolidation of Christian kingdoms allowed the establishments of littoral urban settlements with important relationships beyond the Pyreneen lands. The Reconquest of the lands of the southern mountains system and the valley of the Ebro River led to the overlapping of Islamic and the Christian cities. Cities kept the Islamic urban structure and many economic features, but they were occupied by a new society, and the cities were organized according to distributions in quarters ruled by parishes, often located on the site of former mosques.

The Reconquest and further repopulation marked urban dynamism up to the thirteenth century. Afterward, the economy of urban settlements depended on the vanishing of the seignorial bond, the consolidation of citizen councils, and social specialization. The concept of the urban network was transformed from a legal character into a ranked socioeconomic one.

Blanca García Escalona

Bibliography

Carlé, María del Mar, et al. *La Sociedad hispano medieval: La ciudad*. 3 vols. Barcelona, Buenos Aires, 1984.

Dufourcq, Charles, and Jean Gautier-Dalché. *Historia económica y social de la España cristiana en la Edad Media*. Barcelona, 1983.

Vicens Vives, Jaime. *An economic history of Spain*. Trans. Frances M. López-Morillas. Princeton, 1969.

———. *Historia social y económica de España y América*. 4 vols. Barcelona, 1957–1966.

URGELL, COUNTY OF

The rural upland valley of Urgell formed by the upper Segre River constituted an outlying *comarca* of the larger Hispanic march of the Carolingians and was ruled from Carcassonne across the Pyrenees through

Andorra, and then by the mid-ninth century by the nascent dynasty of Aragón (Asnar I and Galí II, 820–ca. 838) and rival petty lords from neighboring comarcas: the Conflent, Osona, and Cerdanya. Its first cathedral, a modest Romanesque structure, was dedicated in 839. Count Guifré I's intervention from Ripoll brought Urgell into the sub-Pyrenean fold, but its natural isolation favored autonomy. Count Sunifred (897–948) consolidated the territory but failed to firmly establish his own dynasty. This awaited the intervention of Count Borrell II of Barcelona (942–992), the father of Count Ermengol I of Urgell (992–1018), who in 1010 participated in the daring Catalan raid against Córdoba. His dynasty continued through Countess Aurembaix (1209–1231), during which time Urgell played a major role in the Reconquest.

Although constrained by parallel southern expansions of Solsonna and Osona, Urgell pushed its borders past the Segre stronghold of Oliana to a string of frontier castles facing Muslim Lleida and the rugged steppes above Tarragona: Pons, Artesa de Segre, Cubells and Camarasa, Guissona, and Agramunt were all fortified between 1000 and 1050 under Counts Ermengol II (1018–1040) and III (1040–1065), and this frontier was resettled by their successors in league with the counts of Barcelona. Although the territory of Gerb was easily annexed, strongmen like Arnau Mirde Tost almost established semiautonomous domains in the frontier. Also influential was a viscomital line that can be traced from Miró I (d. 975) to the first Viscount of Castelbó, Pere I (d. 1150).

A more direct encroachment on Muslim lands began in the twelfth century, with Urgell by 1105 directing its effort at the walled city of Balaguer. Despite the fall of Zaragoza to the Aragónese in 1118, success beyond Balaguer was halted by the Almoravid intervention, and a Christian coalition including Urgellian troops was soundly defeated in 1124 outside the Muslim outpost of Corbins above Lleida. A second wave of sieges and castle rebuilding occurred thereafter, at Farfanya and Algerri in the 1130s, and again at Balaguer and Agramunt, in preparation for an allied assault on Lleida, which fell in 1149. Ermengol VI (1102–1183), whose long-lasting rule was responsible for this persistence, was awarded with a third of the reconquered city of Lleida.

The reconquest of this Ebro citadel brought Urgell into closer ties with Barcelona and an integral part of the Crown of Aragón. Urgell county proper consisted of 129 sites, but its influence continued to extend beyond the highlands. A scriptorium flourished at Seo d'Urgell, where short chronicles were compiled amid a much more impressive documentary production and a continuous development of cathedral archives. Cadet branches of the Ermengolian Dynasty, especially the Cabrera family, ruled during the interim (1220–1228) before a second comitial dynasty gained control in 1231 with the ascent of Ponc I. His line lasted until the death of Ermengol X (1267–1314), after which the inheritance passed to the royal family through Alfons the Benign, count of Urgell from 1314 who became Alfonso IV of Aragón-Catalonia (1328–1336). This third dynasty, descendants of the prince, Count Jaume I, and a subbranch of the family of Barcelona, governed through 1433 and had female descendants until 1455. Recognition of Urgell as an autonomous political entity blurred after the reign of King Jaime I (d. 1276), but because of the county's natural enclosure a separatism and regionalism continues to characterize its highland culture.

LAWRENCE J. MCCRANK

Bibliography

Baraut, C. *Els documents [dels segles IX–XII] conservats a l'Arxiu Capitular de la Seu d'Urgell*, published serially in *Urgellia: Anuari d'estudio históric desl antics Comtats de Cerdanya, Urgell, i Pallars, d'Andorra i la Vall d'Aran*. 1978– . Vol. 2, 7–145; Vol. 3, 7–166; Vol. 4, 7–186; Vol. 5, 7–158; Vol. 6, 7–243; Vol. 7, 7–218; Vol. 8, 7–149; Vol. 9, 7–312, cont'd.

———. *Les Actes de Consagracions d'esglésies de l'antic Bisbat d'Urgell (Segles IX–XII)*. La Seu d'Urgell, 1974.

Villanueva Estengo, J. *Memorias cronológicas de los Condes de Urgel*. Trans. C. Cortés. Ed. E. Corredera Gutierréz. Balaguer, 1976.

URRACA, QUEEN OF LEÓN AND CASTILE

Succeeded to the throne on 30 June 1109, upon the death of her father. The three major (interrelated) problems of her reign centered around the preservation of the integrity of the kingdom, swollen by the conquests of her grandfather, Fernando I, and her father. The first of these was due to her marriage in 1109 to Alfonso I el Batallador of Aragón. The marriage had been arranged by her father but was widely opposed by her subjects, some of whom secured its condemnation by Pope Paschal II in 1110 on the grounds that the couple shared the same great-grandfather, Sancho el Mayor of Navarra. The papal action, the failure of the queen to conceive an heir, and perhaps personal incompatibility led Urraca to abandon the marriage definitively in 1112. Yet Alfonso of Aragón continued to press his claims to the kingdom and actually held de facto control of large portions of it, including La Rioja, most of Castile, and a small area of León at the time of Urraca's death on 8 March 1126. The two had not been actively at odds since 1117 when a truce was arranged that was subsequently renewed at three-year intervals until her death.

The truce was desirable for Urraca because it freed her hands to deal with the ambitions of her half-sister, Teresa of Portugal (1096–1128). The latter was the natural daughter of Alfonso VI and a daughter of a noble of the Bierzo and had been married by her father to Count Henry of Burgundy, probably in 1096. The king then made them the administrators of the border county of Portugal. After Alfonso's death the two hoped themselves to succeed to the throne of León-Castile, and sometimes cooperated with Alfonso of Aragón in the early stages of the civil war there to achieve that end. After the death of Count Henry in 1112 Teresa could no longer pursue that policy actively. In 1117 she began to style herself "queen" in Portugal and to attempt to annex as large a portion of southern Galicia as possible. By constant struggle, Urraca was able to limit Teresa's gains to the lower valley of the Miño between 1117 and 1126.

The queen's third major problem arose from the use of her son by a previous marriage, the future Alfonso VII, against her by his guardians, Bishop-Archbishop Diego Gelmírez of Santiago de Compostela and Count Pedro Froílaz of the Trastámara family of Galicia. Urraca had been married about 1090 to Count Raymond of Burgundy, cousin of Count Henry, and the two had been entrusted with the administration of Galicia and Portugal by Alfonso VI about the same date. In 1105 a son, Alfonso Raimúndez, had been born to the pair. Then, in late 1107, Count Raymond had died and a royal council in León had provided that the boy would inherit the realm of Galicia should his mother subsequently remarry. In 1110 Gelmírez and Count Pedro would urge this claim against the Aragónese marriage and, at times, attempt to supplant Urraca entirely in favor of her son. From 1110, therefore, the queen had to cope with powerful, sometimes even rebellious, opposition in Galicia and the realm generally. In 1117 she recognized her son as eventual heir and then at least nominal sovereign of the territories to the south of Toledo, but her difficulties with the nobility of Galicia continued.

Fortunately, during her reign the power of the Almoravid empire in North Africa was beginning to fail and the "threat" of Islam in central Iberia was waning. In 1124 Urraca was able even to retake the fortress cities of Atienza and Sigüenza in the highlands northeast of Toledo from the Muslims.

BERNARD F. REILLY

Bibliography

Falque Rey, E. (ed.) *Historia Compostelana*. Turnholt, 1988.

Puyol y Alonso, J. (ed.) "Las crónicas anónimas de Sahagun," *Boletín de la Real Academia de la Historia* 76 (1920), 7–26, 111–22, 242–57, 339–56, 395–419, 512–19; and 77 (1921), 51–59 and 151–61.

Reilly, B. F. *The Kingdom of León-Castilla under Queen Urraca, 1109–1126*. Princeton, 1982.

USATGES DE BARCELONA

The *Usatges*, or usages of the court of Barcelona, is a twelfth-century hybrid compilation of discordant laws, customs, precedent-setting cases, interpretations and commentaries, and oral tradition that went through multiple revisions in a century-long attempt to form a coherent collection or code that accommodated written Roman law and, to a lesser extent, Visigothic law, and to create some continuity between local customs and past practice with new legislation and interpretations. Sources identified include the Justinian *Corpus Iuris Civilis*, possibly through Gratian's *Exceptiones legum Romanorum*, and the *Brevarium Alarici*; the *Lex Baiuvariorum*; the *Eytomologiae* of Isidore of Sevilla; legal fragments from the so-called *Book of Tübingen*; the Lombard *Consuetudines*; the Visigothic *Liber iudicorum* (*llei usuaria* or *Fuero juzgo*), which was being weeded by Catalan judges to retain Roman legal foundations but root out such practices as judgment by battle; canons from the Council of Clermont; canon law commentaries by Ivo of Chartres; pronouncements of the Peace and Truce of God; various collations or *repertoria* of baronial customs; and the overlaid royal constitutions of kings Alfons II, Pere II, and Jaume I.

The oldest extant manuscripts date to the early twelfth century, but because such compilation activity dealing with the old *Usalia* of Barcelona can be traced to more than a century earlier, the credit for the project's initiation is often given to Count Ramón Berenguer I and Countess Almodis, as it was by the authors of the *Gesta Comitum Barcinonensium*. However, the fuller promulgation of the *Usatges* can be placed more properly in the reign of Ramón Berenguer IV (1131–1162) in anticipation of the union between Catalonia and Aragón. Such work continued a tradition of *compendia* production, of which the *Caesaraugustana* was one of the most influential, that already attempted to blend Roman, Visigothic, Qu'rānic, and Canon law with various customals after the reconquest in 1118 of Zaragoza. The most systematic work at Barcelona for a comprehensive synthesis dates to the unified administration under Alfonso II (1162–1196), when scribes required a coherent, uniform law code to form a more durable bureaucracy. Their activity was commensurate with other codification and organization of records in formal archives. The *Usatges* appear in regional variations as the laws promulgated at Tarragona circa 1128; the *Costumes* of Girona, Lleida, Tortosa; and the *Furs* of Valencia. Ultimately Jaime I after 1243 refused the use of any other code in the Crown of Aragón courts. The main redaction dates from his reign, especially their codification after the cortes of 1251. Royal judges insured its widespread application thereafter. The *Usatges* thereby evolved into the law of the land, and ever since then have underpinned the Aragón–Catalan sense of regional autonomy and local freedoms.

LAWRENCE J. MCCRANK

Bibliography

Bastardas i Parera, J., T. Gracia, L. de Nadal, and P. Puig i Ustrell. (eds.) *Usatges de Barcelona. El codi a mitjani segle XII: establiment del text llatí i edici or de la verso o catalana del manuscrit del segle XIII de l'Arxiu de la Corona d'Aragó de Barcelona*. Barcelona, 1984.

Kagay, D. J. (trans.) *The Usatges of Barcelona: The Fundamental Law of Catalonia*. Philadelphia, 1995.

V

VALENCIA, KINGDOM AND CITY OF

The regions of Mediterranean Spain below the Tortosa region of the Ebro River delta and above the region of Murcia constituted the crusader kingdom of Valencia after its conquest from Islam by Jaime I of Aragón-Catalonia. In modern times Valencia comprised, from north to south, the Spanish provinces of Castellón, Valencia, and Alicante; currently it is one of Spain's "autonomies" as the Comunidad Valenciana, popularly also called the País Valencià. The mountain barrier at its back fairly isolates it from neighboring Aragón, Castile, and formerly Granada, facing it out to sea at its port cities. The strip of littoral and its hilly hinterland consequently had a north-south orientation and a maritime-international character. Its agriculture divided between intensely irrigated *huertas*, or mini-farm green zones, and dry-farming uplands of olive and vine, with transient as well as local flocks and stock raising on the larger estates of the north. Roughly the size and shape of the crusader Holy Land at the facing east of the Mediterranean, Valencia increased King Jaime's mainland holdings from 87,000 to over 104,000 square kilometers. Jaime wrote of almost fifty Islamic "castles," or strongholds and towers, defending it. In 1635 the Dutch mapmaker of Valencia described the realm as "about sixty leagues long, and seventeen wide at its widest point; it contains within its circuit four cities, sixty towns surrounded by walls, and a thousand villages; it is watered by thirty-five rivers, large and small [and] . . . it holds about 100,000 families."

Valencia's eighth-century conquest by Islam had broken radically the previous millennium of evolution, which had itself culminated in a Roman and then Visigothic-Roman civilization. Even a Mozarabic continuity was lacking after the Muslim conquest, since the bishop's flight and a fairly pagan countryside inhibited the development of semiautonomous *dhimma* status; northern immigrants and merchants did constitute some Christian presence until the harsh Almohad rule at the last. This distant eastern or Sharq al-Andalus frontier of Islamic Spain had an idiosyncratic development; its final and thorough Arabization and Islamization seems to have been engineered relatively late, as the central government's response to the Shiʿite Fāṭimid threat, both military and ideological. A current dispute, based largely on ambiguous toponymic and linguistic fragments, centers around the dominance of steady Berber immigration over the land, with its peculiar clannic and economic organization, as against a more cosmopolitan population with only Berber fringe-settlement and at the end the innovations of Almoravid-Almohad Berber dynasties.

At the time of Jaime's conquest, Valencia had remained a last outpost of Almohad rule in Spain under the *sayyid* Abū Zayd; but the adventurer Ibn Hūd was seeking to absorb Valencia from the south, while Zayyān internally had taken its central region and capital by civil war. Fending off Castilian ambitions of conquest here, Jaime joined Abū Zayd as ally and then replaced him, in a lengthy war of maneuver, negotiation, and surrender from 1232 to 1245, which left in place the Muslim majority as semiautonomous Mudéjars. The sieges of Burriana (1233) and Valencia city (1238), the pitched battle of Puig (1237), and the flanking naval operations were highlights, all described at lively length in Jaime's autobiographical *Llibre dels feyts*. Though historians see a series of post-conquest Mudéjar rebellions, with aid from Granada and North Africa, it is more exact to say that a crisis in Jaime's southern French realms forced him to patch up a truce in 1245 with the Muslim leader Al-Azraq and then renew his crusade from 1247 to 1258, coping with Mudéjar revolt mildly in the 1260s, and on a major scale in 1275 to 1278.

The second half of the thirteenth century witnessed the reconstruction or acculturative absorption of Valencia, complicated by the circumstance that Aragónese and Catalans imported different law codes, languages, administrative and institutional traditions, economic mechanisms, calendars, moneys, and mentalities. A monarchical-feudal, rural, and agricultural–stock-raising people confronted a comital-urban, maritime-commercial people. Jaime met the challenge by setting up a separate kingdom, with its new money (*solidi regalium*), parliament (*corts*), law code (*furs*), and enumeration of kings. He used the church to transform the public mood and perception: Gothic churches in the main cities, military and religious orders of every variety (Mendicants, Cistercians, ransomers, hospital groups), a papal university at the capital and proselytizing Dominican schools of Arabic at Valencia and Játiva, a tithe program, a network of parishes even where Christians were few, elaborate episcopal-chapter arrangements, and all the symbolic world of sight and sound, bells, and processions remembered from the settler's homelands.

Starting with his books of land division, the *Repartiment*, and continuing with a flood of charters, Jaime allotted farms, public monopolies from salt and baths to windmills and bakeries, merchant fonduks or caravansaries, rows and streets of shops, town markets, tax franchises, and notarial posts. He arranged for two dioceses: Valencia, the more southernly (over which he fought a protracted court battle against Castile), and Tortosa, which expanded over the north. He resisted with unequal success the intrusion of a Castilian enclave diocese at Segorbe. To these he appointed clerics high and low. Jaime kept nearly all the cities and much land for the crown, generously awarding lands to his nobles, burghers, Jews, the municipalities themselves, and religious groups. He expanded the irrigation network, built new bridges and roads, and reorganized the countryside into castle-and-town units, setting up the larger towns as semiautonomous communes with their elected jurates as executive, bailiff for taxes, council for legislation, and justiciar for judiciary. He converted the world-famous paper manufacturers of Játiva into a crown monopoly, and with the cheap paper began to amass the registers of outgoing charters so unique for their volume and variety.

In administering the kingdom as a whole, he used the Júcar River as the main division. (Jaime II at century's end would extend the southernmost boundary considerably [1304], encouraging a third division below the Jijona River.) Now and through the next two and even three centuries, the distinguishing characteristic and major problem of Valencia continued to be its uniquely large parallel society of Muslim communities, still pan-Islamic in sentiment, feared and restricted by the townsmen through crown and church but valued and protected by the rural lords. The Jews, whom Jaime recruited at home and abroad for his new kingdom, formed a large and important segment of the population, mostly artisans and merchants but with small consumer-loan activity to locals. Their main communities were at Alcira, Burriana-Castellón, Játiva, Murviedro (Sagunto), and Valencia city.

The fourteenth century was Valencia's *via dolorosa*, filled with war, plague, famine, and struggle. Agustín Rubio Vela divides this tragedy into three phases: "from expansion to crisis" (1304–1347), "difficult times" (1347–1375), and "slow recuperation" (1375–1410). Though stable and prosperous, unendingly receiving immigration, Valencia now suffered a mysterious agricultural crisis. Granadan invasions of 1304, 1331, and 1332; Moroccan attack in 1337; the Almería crusade of 1309; and endemic frontier banditry and sea piracy throughout the century evoked lasting paranoia against the Mudéjars, who now began large emigration. In this first period, however, Valencians played a major role in the Catalan conquest of Sardinia (1323–1324). The terrible middle period saw constant war with Castile (1356–1375), with six other nations joining in but with Valencia the main theater, occupied and ravaged. The Black Death, in recurrent waves, proved even more damaging. The "Union" crisis pitted townsmen against the crown's tendency to subordinate and provincialize the kingdom (1347–1348); bloodily suppressed, it nevertheless gained its point. (The Aragónese Union struggle had also gained a point for its nobles: Aragónese law could be used in Valencia for the diminishing minority who clung to it.)

In the recuperative phase of the century, commerce spectacularly expanded its international role, while production of rice, sugar, cereals, the ceramics of Manises, and especially textiles flourished. Anti-Semitism, however, burst out in the pogroms of 1391. During this tortured century, Valencians forged their identity as not merely Catalans but as a "nació valenciana" with a "Valencian" language (first reported respectively in 1391 and 1395). Notable Valencians of this era included Vincente Ferrer (1350–1419), arbiter of the Great Schism and contributor to Valencia's language and to its growing anti-Semitism; Joan Gilabert Jofre (1363–1417), creator of Europe's first psychiatric clinic and a modern approach to mental illness; and in letters, Francesc Eiximenis (1327–1409).

The fifteenth century was Valencia's apogee. Historians warn that the traditional contrast of fourteenth-century catastrophies with this century's triumphs is easily overdrawn. Plague and famine continued to be a problem; demographic stability was not the same everywhere, and the countryside suffered as a dispersed population of high mobility concentrated ever more in the capital and other nuclei. The demands of Alfonso the Magnanimous for his Italian wars and of the dynastic crisis and Catalan civil war at mid-century were onerous. And the fragmentation and instability of the nobility on their very small holdings destabilized society to a degree. Nevertheless Valencia became Spain's premier city in this century and a world emporium to rival Venice. Giddy affluence transformed it with mansions and churches.

The celebrated municipal bank, *Taula de Canvis*, was established (1407) and the merchants' exchange, or *Llotja*, constructed in its present splendor (1483–1498). In 1419 the kingdom was given its own archives. Agriculture became so speculative that most foodstuffs, especially wheat, had to be imported; municipal authorities subsidized foreign producers from Flanders to Sicily. A gulf opened between the famously hedonistic mercantile rich, with their tourneys and play at knighthood, and the moralistic lesser classes. Abroad Calixtus III sat the papal throne (1455–1458); and his "bad Borgia" relative, the future Alexander VI (1492–1503), was Valencia's archbishop. The 1456 sack of the *moreria* by mobs was one omen of trouble ahead. Even in piracy and privateering, large-scale entrepreneurs were forcing the small operators out of business by 1477. Surprisingly, Mudéjar merchants were fully integrated economically, and the reduced Jewish community still clung to its artisan and intermediary merchant activities. When protectionism failed as a policy, the municipality recruited German, Italian, and French immigrant communities, exploiting their skills and capturing their technologies. The Genoese, for example, revivified the flagging paper industry. The price of this policy was harm to local producers and such an increase in the number and affluence of the middle-merchant class as to pit them against aristocrats and artisans, causing electoral reforms, crises, crown arbitration, and an ominously unbalanced social structure.

This was Valencia's literary golden age. Antoni Ferrando conceptualizes the kingdom's literature as falling into a "national" period (1232–1383) and a "classic" era (1383–1523). The latter divides into "consolidation" (1383–1425), "plenitude" (1425–1497), and "crisis," or Renaissance frustrated (1497–1523). During the classic period all the elites converged to support letters, from crown and church to nobles and townsmen, while both French (Paris, papal Avignon) and Italian (Alfonso the Magnanimous's central court now at Naples) flowed in, with wide translating. In the troubadour contest of 1474, forty professionals contended. An aristocratic and a realistic-satirical current in letters moved parallel. Great names include Ausiàs March (1397–1459), Joan Roís de Corella (1433–1497), Jaume Roig (1434–1478), the novelists Joanot Martorell (1413–1468), Joan de Galba (ca. 1420–1490), and Isabel de Villena (1430–1490). Into this atmosphere was born the great humanist Joan Lluís Vives (1492–1540). Music culminated here in the theoretical treatises of Guillem de Puig (fl. 1480). But now an autocratic Fernando the Catholic was looming over urban administration (occasioning the 1502 revolt), while American gold and taxes for Italian wars would soon end Valencia's leadership.

Robert I. Burns, S. J.

Bibliography

Belenguer, E. (ed.) *Història del país valencià*. 5 vols. 2nd ed. Barcelona, 1988–90.

Burns, R. I. *The Crusader Kingdom of Valencia: Reconstruction on a Thirteenth-Century Frontier*. 2 vols. Cambridge, Mass., 1967.

———. *Medieval Colonialism: Postcrusade Exploitation of Islamic Valencia*. Princeton, N.J., 1975.

Guiral-Hadziiossif, J. *Valence, port méditerranéen au XVe siècle (1410–1525)*. Paris, 1986.

Sanchis Guarner, M. *La ciutat de València: Síntesi d'història de geografia urbana*. 2d ed. Valencia, 1976.

VALENCIA, UNION OF

To understand the relative success of the Valencian Union and the nature of the revolt that took place in 1347–1348, it is necessary to go back to the late thirteenth century. At that time the powerful Aragónese nobility had enlisted the support of the people from the surrounding *vilas* against the king, ostensibly to defend what they regarded as the erosion of their privileges. The main point at issue was a custom by which a monarch on accession to the throne, was required to take a separate oath of allegiance to Aragón and swear that he would uphold their rights and privileges. No occasion had arisen since the beginning of the fourteenth century to cause the nobles to assert their rights but in 1346–1347 Pedro III, who at that time had no male heir, tried to get his daughter, Constança, accepted as the heiress to the Crown of Aragón.

Using the question of the succession to the throne as a pretext, the Valencian nobles allied with the *Consell* enlisted the help of the king's brother, Jaime who, if Constança was accepted as queen, would himself be unable to succeed to the throne. He had allies among the Aragónese nobles, always ready to defend their privileges, and together with some four Aragónese towns they joined the Valencian Union. The union upheld the claims to the throne of Jaime of Urgell, the king's brother, against those of his daughter, Constança, and the death of Jaime in Barcelona in 1347 merely meant that the king's more formidable half-brother, Ferran, who could count on Castilian support, replaced him as the potential heir to the throne.

In 1348 civil war had spread throughout Aragón, and Pedro was forced to recognize Ferran as his heir and to go to Valencia where he remained a virtual prisoner from April until June of that year. The advent of the Black Death gave him an excuse to escape, not without ensuring that those who had been directly involved in the armed uprising, nobles and townsmen, were severely and cruelly punished. The loyalty of Catalonia to the crown, however, together with negotiations with Alfonso X1 and the military victory at Epila in July 1348, changed the situation. In October of the same year, at a meeting of the Cortes in Zaragosa, the Aragónese Union was destroyed. Two months later, a similar fate befell the Valencian Unionists and from then on Pedro III was obliged to respect the privileges of the kingdom of Aragón and Valencia. A general amnesty was finally granted, and in the Corts of Valencia in 1349 the privileges of the union were overturned thanks to the decision of the middle classes to reaffirm their allegiance to the king. In essence the Valencian Union succeeded in reaffirming the *furs* (codes) and forcing the king to respect their privileges.

JILL R. WEBSTER

Bibliography

Bisson, T. N. *The Medieval Crown of Aragón—A Short History*. Oxford, 1986.

Sanchis Guarner, M. *La ciutat de València*, Valencia, 1972. Reprt., 1989.

VALERA, DIEGO DE

According to Valera himself, he was born in 1412 and lived to a ripe old age, probably dying late in 1488. His father, Alonso Chirino de Guadalajara, was the chief royal physician to Juan II of Castile and author of at least two medical treatises, one of which was printed in Seville in 1506. In 1427 Valera joined the royal court at the age of fifteen and served as one of the *donceles* of Juan II, and then Prince Enrique (the future Enrique IV). He was present at the Christian victory of La Higueruela just outside the Naṣrid capital of Granada in 1431, and was made a knight at the conquest of Huelma.

In 1437 Valera began a series of travels and adventures throughout western Europe, being included by Fernando del Pulgar in his *Claros varones de Castilla* among a select list of famous knights errant "que con ánimo de cavalleros fueron por los reinos estraños a fazer armas con qualquier cavallero que quisiese fazerlas con ellos, e por ellas ganaron honrra para sí e fama de valientes e esforçados cavalleros para los fijosdalgos de Castilla." He was present at sieges, which Charles VII of France directed against the English, traveled to Prague, helped Albert V in his campaigns against the Hussites, and was rewarded by being made a member of several chivalrous orders. Returning to Castile, it was not long before Valera was on his travels again with the king's backing and accompanied by a royal herald, this time visiting Denmark, England, and Burgundy, taking part in a famous tournament near Dijon, and returning subsequently on yet another mission to the court of Charles VII of France.

Valera took part on the royal side at the battle of Olmedo in 1445, but he was soon to fall out of favor due to his habit of proferring unsolicited advice in letters addressed to Juan II and then, subsequently, to Enrique IV. As a result he passed into the service of the count of Plasencia, Pedro de Estúñiga, for several years. By his own detailed account in his final chapter of the *Crónica abreviada*, Valera played an important role in the downfall of Álvaro de Luna, who was beheaded in Valladolid in 1453.

Apart from short periods of judicial office in Palencia and Segovia as well as some service in the noble house of Medinaceli, Valera spent most of his later life in Puerto de Santa María, from where he continued to write letters of political and military advice, in particular to Fernando the Catholic.

Valera was a prolific author whose main interests were devoted to chronicles and short treatises of a chivalrous, political, or moral nature. Carriazo established a chronological list of his works as follows: *Arbol de las Batallas*, a translation of the famous French treatise on the laws of arms by Honoré Bonet, done for Álvaro de Luna (prior to 1441); *Espejo de Verdadero Nobleza*, a treatise on the origins and nature of nobility, dedicated to Juan II (ca. 1441); *Defensa de virtuosas mugeres*, dedicated to Queen María of Castile (prior to 1443); *Exhortación a la paz*, addressed to Juan II (ca. 1448); *Tratado de las armas*, for Afonso V of Portugal (ca. 1458–1467); *Providencia contra Fortuna*, dedicated to the marquis of Villena (ca. 1465); *Ceremonial de Príncipes*, also dedicated to the marquis of Villena (ca. 1462–1467); *Breviloquio de virtudes*, for Rodrigo Pimentel, count of Benavente; *Origen de Roma y Troya*, for Juan Hurtado de Mendoza; *Origen de la casa de Guzmán*; *Doctrinal de príncipes*, dedicated to Fernando the Catholic (ca. 1475–1476), perhaps one of Valera's more original works; *Preheminencias y cargos de los oficiales de armas*, for Fernando the Catholic; *Geneología de los Reyes de Francia*, dedicated to Juan Terrin; *Crónica abreviada de España* (1479–1481); *Memorial de diversas hazañas*; and *Crónica de los Reyes Católicos*.

In addition Carriazo listed another two works, a lost work on the Estúñiga family, and another of dubious attribution, also lost, on *Ilustres varones de Es-*

paña. In between all these works, the extraordinarily productive Valera also managed to write a considerable number of short poems of a moralistic or courtly love nature.

ANGUS MACKAY

Bibliography

Pulgar, F. del. *Claros varones de Castilla*. Ed. R. B. Tate. Oxford, 1971.

Valera, M. D. de. *Crónica de los Reyes Católicos*. Ed. J. de Mata Carriazo. Madrid, 1927.

———. *Memorial de diversas hazañas*. Ed. J. de Mata Carriazo. Madrid, 1941. This edition includes the *Crónica abbreviada* as well.

VALLADOLID, ALFONSO DE

Alfonso de Valladolid, originally known as Abner de Burgos, occupies a pivotal place in the history of medieval Jewish-Christian relations. As an especially able convert from Judaism to Christianity, he influenced not only his contemporaries but also successive generations with his philosophical treatises and polemical diatribes. Born around 1270, Abner/Alfonso wrestled with doubts regarding his faith for nearly twenty-five years. In the opening folios of his most important work, the still unedited *Mostrador de justicia* (*Teacher of Righteousness*), Alfonso provides a highly personal account of the circumstances ultimately leading to his conversion. Although hardly spontaneous, Alfonso's conversion appears to be genuine and unforced; nonetheless, some of his former coreligionists impugned the deed as mere opportunism. Alfonso subsequently served as sacristan in the cathedral of Valladolid. Toward the end of his life, Alfonso was instrumental in having King Alfonso XI proscribe putative insults against Christians in Jewish liturgy. Alfonso also inveighed against Jewish physicians, who, he claimed, sought to harm Christians. Until his death (ca. 1346), Alfonso was assiduous in his proselytizing efforts. In both Hebrew and Spanish treatises, he engaged in acrimonious polemics with the leading Jewish sages of his time, notably Isaac Polgar and Moses ben Joshua of Narbonne. Indeed, his writings continued to influence *converso* polemicists well into the fifteenth century. Alfonso's impact is perhaps most obvious in the widely diffused *Fortalitium fidei* (Fortress of Faith), where excerpts from Alfonso's nonextant *Milḥamot ha-Shem* (Wars of the Lord) aptly served Alonso de Espina's own polemical designs. There exist Spanish versions of a number of Alfonso's Hebrew works, including the *Minḥat Kena'oth* (Offering of Zeal), *Shalosh Iggarot* (Three Epistles), *Sefer Teshuvot ha-Meshuvot* (Reply to the Responses), and *Teshuvot la-Meḥaref* (Refutation of the Blasphemer). The following works have also been attributed to Alfonso: *Concordia de las leyes*, *Libro de las malldiciones de los judios*, *Contra los que dizen que ay fadas et ventura et oras menguadas*, and *Libro de las tres creencias*, often erroneously cited as *Libro de las tres gracias*.

DWAYNE E. CARPENTER

Bibliography

Baer, Y. *A History of the Jews in Christian Spain*. 2 vols. Trans. L. Schoffman. Philadelphia, 1978. 1:327–54.

Mettmann, W. *Die volkssprachliche apologetische Literatur auf der Iberischen Halbinsel im Mittelalter*. Opladen, 1987. 32–75.

VANDALS *See* GERMANIC INVASIONS

VARA DE JUDA

Title of the Amsterdam Spanish translation of a popular and influential work of Jewish history by Meir de León (first edition, 1640; printed "en casa de Emanuel Benbeniste" in a later edition in 1744). There is a later translation in Aljamía by David and Moses Alkalay (Belgrade, 1859). Subsequent Spanish quotations from the work and translations depend on these. The original seems to have been published no earlier than 1550. It is generally attributed to Solomon ibn Verga, a Castilian Jew who is documented in 1490 as having taken part in the redemption of the Jewish captives of Málaga.

Part of the book is divided into "eras of persecution," which extend from the period of the Second Temple to the Lisbon massacres of judeoconversos in 1506. Its distinctiveness from other Hebrew chronicles of persecution is immediately evident because of stylistic innovations that include the use of dialogue, stories, letters, and orations. This distinctiveness and its engaging tone have attracted the attention of a number of students of Jewish historiography who attempted to emphasize different aspects of the work and define it in various ways: as a repository of Jewish folklore (Loeb); as a work reflecting both the reactions to the problem of the Jewish diaspora in general in the wake of the Expulsion from Spain on the one hand and on the other the frivolity and humor of the Italian novellae that had influenced it (Baer); as a work of typically Renaissance ironic criticism of the Jewish counterpart of medieval scholasticism (Schohat); as an expression of the search for radically different, "modern" answers to the problems of Jewish history following the deep psychological impact of the Expulsion (Neuman); and as a vehicle for expressing a Jewish "aristocratic" social ideology with its positive appraisal of the role of the Christian monarchs in Jewish history (Yerushalmi).

Whereas the search for sources and analogues by Baer and certainly by De Prijs gave more prominence to general Jewish analogues or antecedents to ideas in the book, more recent research has tried to emphasize the book's context (Jewish, *converso* or Christian convert), and Christian-Hispanic mentality of the fifteenth and sixteenth centuries). It has been suggested that its stylistic strategies (the use of orations and dialogue, the care taken in dilating exempla into relatively well-developed stories, introducing historical individuals into the fictional universe of the book, quotations from nonexistent works), its ideas on wealth, lineage, the conversos, women, education, monsters, and its ambiguities (author's position on various issues as well as the putative unity of the authorial point of view versus editorial additions) all have contemporary Hispanic analogues, particularly in the works of Antonio de Guevara.

ELEAZAR GUTWIRTH

Bibliography

Gutwirth, E. "The Expulsion of the Jews from Spain and Jewish Historiography." In *Jewish History: Festschrift C. Abramsky*. Ed. A. Rapoport-Albert. London, 1988. 141–61, and the bibliography in the notes.

VASPASIANO

The legend of the destruction of Jerusalem by Vespasian in gratitude for his cure from leprosy by the image of Christ on St. Veronica's miraculous towel was widely diffused in medieval Iberia in a number of separate versions, in both prose and verse. The most common branch is that represented by the late "Estoria del noble Vaspasiano," the Castilian text of which (printed ca. 1491–1494, 1499, and later; a seventeenth-century manuscript) was the source of the Portuguese translation (printed 1496). These texts are close to, and may derive from, one of several variant Catalan prose manuscript versions of "La destrucción de Jherusalem," which contains an allegorical dream, based on "L'Estoire del Saint Graal," in which the mystery of the Virgin Birth is explained to Vespasian. "Vaspasiano" is customarily classed with Iberian Peninsular romances, often with the Arthurian cycle, by critics; in fact, it is, as some have noted, a popular religious narrative. One version was printed with other pious pseudepigrapha in Catalan and Castilian editions of "Gamaliel," while the Portuguese shipped one hundred copies to "Prester John" in Ethiopia in a consignment of religious books in 1515. The legend depicts a cruel revenge for the Crucifixion: Vespasian sells the Jews in batches of thirty for a penny; many are massacred, but enough are spared for future generations to revile. Pontius Pilate is tried, imprisoned, and dragged off to Hell by demons. Converts from Judaism, though, are favorably treated. The deliberate circulation of "Vaspasiano" in the context of the expulsions of Jews from Spain in 1492 and from Portugal in 1496 is a distinct probability.

DAVID HOOK

Bibliography

Hook, D. "The Legend of the Flavian Destruction of Jerusalem in Late Fifteenth-Century Spain and Portugal," *Bulletin of Hispanic Studies* 65 (1988), 113–28.

———. "Some Questions Concerning the Status of the Portuguese 'Estoria do muy nobre Vespesiano emperador de Roma.' " In *Studies Presented to Luís de Sousa Rebelo*. Ed. H. M. Macedo. London, 1991. 121–40.

VICENTE, GIL

Gil Vicente (ca. 1465–ca. 1536) is the first Portuguese dramatist whose plays have come down to us. Both the date and place of his birth are unknown, as are those of his death. We know only that for some thirty years he wrote and staged plays for the court of King Manuel the Fortunate (1469–1521; r. 1495–1521) and his son Juan II (1501–1557; r. 1521–1557). He has sometimes been identified with a goldsmith of the same name who worked for the court during the first two decades of the sixteenth century, but the identification of goldsmith with dramatist has not been accepted by all scholars.

Only one of Vicente's plays, the *Auto da Barca do Inferno* (*The Ship of Hell*), was printed in his lifetime (1518); it survives in a single copy, now in the Biblioteca Nacional in Madrid. Most of the others were first printed in the collected edition (*Copilaçam*) printed in Lisbon by João Alvarez in 1562, nearly thirty years after the playwright's death. The chronology of the plays cannot be established with certainty; the dates and places of first performances given in the *Copilaçam* are often demonstrably incorrect. The texts of the plays, too, are often unsatisfactory. I. S. Révah has argued that their deficiencies are due solely to the "carelessness, stupidity, and bad taste" of Vicente's son Luís, who prepared the *Copilaçam* for the press; others believe that Vicente's text was altered by the censors appointed by the Inquisition.

Eleven of Vicente's more than forty plays are entirely in Spanish while only fifteen are entirely in Portuguese; in the rest some characters use one language, some the other. Many other sixteenth-century Portuguese writers also composed much of their work in Spanish. Portuguese readers in this period read Spanish books more often than Portuguese ones, in part because there were more Spanish books to read. Many of Vicente's sources are Spanish. He draws upon the shepherds' plays of Encina and Fernández, together with the Spanish version of an Italian romance of chivalry for the *Auto de la sibila Casandra* (*The Play of the Sibyl Cassandra*) and on a Spanish romance of chivalry for *Don Duardos*. But Vicente is not just an imitator of foreign models. *Casandra* is richer and more subtle than any of its Spanish predecessors, while in *Don Duardos* a run-of-the-mill prose romance serves as a point of departure for one of his most original and most poetically satisfying works.

Almost all of Vicente's plays were intended for a single performance at court, often as only one element, perhaps a subordinate one, in some court entertainment. Some celebrate one of the great feasts of the liturgical year, like Easter or Epiphany, or, most often, Christmas. Others celebrate a particular occasion such as the birth of a prince or princess or a royal wedding. Many show similarities to the court masques of other countries, like those Ben Jonson wrote in collaboration with the scene designer Inigo Jones, though there are also important differences. Spectacular stage effects, so important in the English masques, play a much smaller role in Vicente's court entertainments. In the absence of the kind of stage machinery Jones employed to produce the "wonders" of the Stuart masques, Vicente had to rely on verbal description. The procession of courtiers and their ladies transformed into fishes and other sea creatures in *Cortes de Júpiter* (*Jupiter's Court*) was not staged but merely described; the description accounts for nearly half the total number of lines in the play.

The presence of popular elements in Vicente's plays, particularly the exquisite songs found in some of them, confirms rather than contradicts their essentially courtly character. Other contemporary poets and musicians who, like Vicente, depended on court patronage show a similar affection for folk songs. It is usually impossible to say whether a given song is Vicente's own creation or taken from popular tradition, perhaps with modifications to make it fit the dramatic action; Vicente often uses songs to advance the plot or reveal the personalities of the characters who sing them, as in the delightful and moving *Auto de la sibila Casandra*.

Thomas R. Hart

Bibliography

Hart, T. R. *Gil Vicente: "Casandra" and "Don Duardos."* London, 1981.

Teyssier, P. *Gil Vicente—o autor e a obra*. Lisbon, 1982.

VICENTIUS HISPANUS

Vicentius Hispanus was born in Portugal, though the exact place and date are unknown; he died in 1248. He probably arrived at Bologna as a student around 1200, and Silvestre Hispano, Lorenzo Hispano, and Juan Galense were likely his professors. In civil law he was a disciple of Azzo. From 1210 to 1215 he was a professor in the same institution where he studied, the University of Bologna. In one of the manuscripts of his works, the words *bonus et hilaris* (good and funny) appear next to his initials, which is in harmony with various passages of his works that demonstrate a fine sense of humor. He was archdeacon in Lisbon. The following are his known works:

1. Glosses to Gratian's *Decretum*
2. *Apparatus* to the *Compilatio prima antiqua*
3. *Apparatus* to the *Comilatio tertia antiqua*, which he worked on from 1210 to 1215
4. Isolated glosses to the *Compilatio secunda antiqua*
5. *Apparatus* to the constitutions of the fourth Lateran Council of 1215
6. *Casus* to the *Compilatio tertia antiqua*, which only consists of a few isolated titles
7. Possible authorship of some *Casus* to the fourth Lateran Council, which have recently been edited
8. *Casus* to the Decretals of Gregory IX
9. *Apparatus* or *Lectura* to the Decretals of Gregory IX
10. Glosses on the *arbores consanguinitatis et affinitatis* (trees of consanguinity and affinity)
11. *Summula* or *Quaestiones de exceptionibus*
12. *De discordia testium et de consonantia et qualiter debeant recipi et repelli.*

Antonio García y García

Bibliography

García y García, A. *Constitutiones Concilii quarti Lateranensis una cum commentariis glossatorum.* Vatican City, 1981.

———. "Glosas de Juan Teutónico, Vicente Hispano y Dámaso Húngaro a los *arbores consanguinitatis et affinitatis.*" *Zeitschrift der Savigny—Stiftung für Rechtsgeschichte* 68 (1982), 153–85.

Ochoa Sanz, J. *Vincentius Hispanus, canonista boloñés del s. XIII.* Rome, 1960.

VICH (VIC), CITY OF

Vich (or, as it is now officially spelled, "Vic"), is a small city lying inland, sixty kilometers north of Barcelona. It dominates a small, relatively fertile plain, a strategic point within the complicated landscape of hills and narrow valleys south of the Pyrenees. The Plain of Vich is bordered by Montseny near the coast and a series of hills to the west that separate it from the comarca of Bages. The valley formed part of an important route leading from Barcelona to Cerdanya, and through the Pyrenees to Foix and Languedoc. Vich was an important ecclesiastical and cultural center during the tenth and eleventh centuries, and a prosperous commercial and industrial town in the late Middle Ages.

In Roman and Visigothic times what is now Vic was known as Ausona (whence the name of the modern surrounding comarca of Osona). A Roman temple was built on a hill overlooking the Meder River. A bishop of Ausona is first mentioned in the early sixth century. In the aftermath of the Muslim invasions and only partially successful Carolingian reconquest, Ausona appears to have been largely deserted. After an anti-Frankish rebellion in 826 to 827, official attempts to resettle the district were abandoned until shortly before 886 when the diocese was reestablished. The new cathedral was built at some distance from the Roman town. As often would happen in medieval towns, two urban agglomerations existed next to each other, one military, one ecclesiastical. The remains of Roman Ausona were held from the count of Barcelona by a viscount of Ausona (first mentioned in 879), who fortified the temple ruins as a castle. A new episcopal town grew up around the cathedral, expanding rapidly, especially with the foundation of a market in the early eleventh century. The suburb or "vicus" of Ausona eclipsed the former center. The town was known for a time as the "vicus Ausonae" but by 1100 the entire complex was commonly referred to simply as "Vich."

A Romanesque cathedral was constructed in the eleventh century by Bishop Oliba. Its campanile and crypt survive. Vich was associated with the monastery of Ripoll and other cultural centers of Old Catalonia in the tenth and eleventh centuries, and with the Truce of God movement that culminated in the provincial and diocesan councils of the mid-eleventh century.

The bishop of Vich held extensive rights of secular lordship over the town from the tenth to fourteenth centuries. His judicial power and revenues from mints, tolls, and markets were supposedly based on a privilege from King Odo of France, dated 889, but this document contains substantial later interpolations. Counts of Barcelona tacitly or explicitly recognized episcopal powers during the tenth and eleventh centuries, but these came under increasing attack from the lords of the upper town who succeeded the defunct viscounts of Ausona. Under the family of the seneschals of the counts of Barcelona, who married into the Montcada lineage, episcopal lordship was challenged and its revenues often undermined or arrogated. Disputes often exploding into violent confrontation characterized the period shortly after 1200. A substantial class of merchants and other prominent townsmen took advantage of the weakening of ecclesiastical control. Although their movement to elect an independent municipal government was suppressed (ca. 1185), townsmen received a measure of immunity from taxation and arbitrary treatment shortly thereafter and formed guilds, charitable foundations, and other sources of power in the late Middle Ages.

King Jaime II bought out the secular lordship of the bishops of Vich over the town in 1315. The Montcadas and their successors, the counts of Béarn and Foix, continued to assert rights over their part of the city until they too were liquidated by the king in 1450.

PAUL H. FREEDMAN

Bibliography

Engels, O. "Die weltliche Herrschaft des Bischofs von Ausona-Vich (869–1315)," *Gesammelte Aufsätze zur Kulturgeschichte Spaniens* 24 (1968), 1–40.

Freedman, P. *The Diocese of Vic: Tradition and Regeneration in Medieval Catalonia.* New Brunswick, N.J., 1983.

Junyent, E. *La ciutat de Vic i la seva història.* Barcelona, 1976.

Ordeig i Mata, R. *Els Orígens històrics de Vic (segles VIII–X).* Vic, 1981.

VIDAL MAYOR

We have basically two works approved at the Huesca *cortes* (courts) in 1274: a shorter one, or *Compilatio minor*, and an enlarged one, or *Compilatio maior*.

From the last one there were at least two versions, one in Latin, another in Romance. The Latin version is named by the medieval forists as *Liber In excelsis, Fori Antiqui, Compilatio Domini Vitalis, Compilatio Magna*, and so forth. From this version—doubtless the original and already rare in the fifteenth century according to Miguel de Molino, 1513—we are not aware of manuscripts and only its prologue is known, preserved in MS 7391, Biblioteca Nacional, Madrid, and fragments preserved in quotations by Jaime de Hospital, Martín Díaz de Aux, Antich de Bages, Martín de Pertusa, Miguel de Molino, Jerónimo Blancas, and others.

The Romance version, known as *Vidal Mayor*, is preserved in a precious manuscript actually kept at the J. Paul Getty Museum, Santa Monica, California. Edited by G. Tilander in 1965 together with an introductory study and vocabulary, this manuscript has been recently reproduced in facsimile by the Diputacion Provincial and the Instituto de Estudios Altoaragoneses of Huesca, together with a volume of papers related to several aspects of the work. It is a copy made in the second half of the eighteenth century by the Navarrese notary Miguel López de Zandiu from a Romance version of the original Latin carried out by an individual not quite skilled in law who sometimes allows himself to interpolate the text explaining the meaning, in Romance, of some juridical terms. The work appears as a juridical body approved at the Huesca Cortes, 1247, whose redaction and division in nine books, commissioned by King Jaime, belongs to Vidal de Canellas. It was promulgated as the only legal code in the kingdom of Aragón, indicating to resort to the natural sense in case of legal loopholes. Looking at the transmitted manuscript we could imagine that it is partially mutilated. This Romance version could be basically coincidental with the original Latin version in spite of some disagreements between the Romance text and the Latin fragments preserved.

The *Compilatio minor* is a much shorter work, known also as *Fori novi*, which only covers the dispositive part of the *fueros*, leaving out the reasonings to which the *Compilatio maior* pays great attention. The Latin version has been transmitted in ten manuscripts (none original, not even from the thirteenth century) and eleven editions that do not seem to reflect its original stage, but the stage acquired around 1300 after some modifications that in the end became the official text for allegation in the courts. Four versions more or less complete are preserved in Romance, and two fragmentary ones. Some of them show an evolutive stage prior to the Latin version actually known.

ANTONIO PÉREZ MARTÍN

Bibliography

Pérez Martín, A. "La primera codificación oficial de los fueros aragoneses: las dos compilaciones de Vidal de Canellas," *Glossae Revista de Historia del Derecho Europeo* 2 (1989–90), 9–80.

Tilander, G. (ed.) *Vidal Mayor. Traducción aragonesa de la obra In excelsis Dei thesauris de Vidal de Canellas*. Vols. 1–3. Lund, 1956.

Ubieto Arteta, A. (ed.) *Vidal Mayor*. Vols. 1–2. Madrid, 1989.

VIKINGS

Both Christian and Muslim Spain suffered from Viking raids a number of times in the ninth and tenth centuries. The *Chronicle of Alfonso III* reports two attacks, one during the reign of Ramiro I (842–850) and the other during that of Ordoño I (850–866). According to the chronicler, Ramiro was able to repel this "pagan and extremely cruel people previously unknown to us" with his army near La Coruña. The account goes on to report that the Northmen subsequently headed south, where they attacked Seville and killed many Muslims. Apparently Ordoño was not as successful as Ramiro had been in defending Asturias: the chronicler simply noting that the Northmen ravaged the coasts of Spain with sword and fire, before heading for Morocco and then Greece.

Arabic sources corroborate these raids and allow us to pinpoint them to 844 (during the reign of ʿAbd al-Raḥmān II) and 859 (Muḥammad I). First sighted in Lisbon, the Vikings made their way south to the mouth of the Guadalquivir River, where they established a base on Isla Menor. From there they worked their way upriver to Seville, which they pillaged for an entire week. Many Muslims were killed and the principal mosque was put to the torch. From there the Vikings extended their raids on horseback until they were finally turned back by the emir's forces and forced out to sea. Some Arab histories (though significantly not the earliest ones) report that ʿAbd al-Raḥmān received a Viking embassy after the first attack and sent one of his own to the Danish king in turn. The second attack in 859 found the Muslim forces better prepared but still unable to defend Algeciras, where many of the inhabitants were slaughtered. From there the Vikings proceeded north, wintering on the southern coast of France and reportedly capturing and ransoming King García of Navarre.

Arabic sources indicate that there were two more Viking raids in the tenth century. In 966, they were repelled by an Andalusian fleet off of Lisbon, In 971, they seized Santiago de Compostela and were once again resisted by the Muslim fleet further south.

KENNETH B. WOLF

Bibliography

El-Hajji, A. "The Andalusian Diplomatic Relations with the Vikings during the Ummayad Period." *Hesperis Tamuda* 8 (1967), 67–110.

Wolf, K. *Conquerors and Chroniclers of Early Medieval Spain*. Liverpool, 1990.

VILANOVA, ARNAU DE

Arnau de Vilanova is a figure of unusual interest for his role in medieval intellectual history. Though he called himself "Catalanus" and grew up in Valencia, it seems likely that he came there with his parents from a village outside Daroca (in Aragón) during the Christian resettlement of the city after its reconquest in 1237/8. We can infer his medical training at the *studium* of Montpellier in the 1260s, but it is only with the 1280s that we can begin to reconstruct his biography in detail. During that decade he was in Barcelona in medical attendance on the kings of Aragón-Catalonia, first Pedro III el Gran and then Alfonso III. It was in this same period that his translation of Galen's *De rigore* from Arabic into Latin was finished (Barcelona, 1282); Arnau had presumably learned Arabic growing up in Aragón or Valencia. His other medical translations—of Avicenna's *De viribus cordis* and of Abulcasis's *De medicinis simplicibus*—though undated, may also have been completed in these years.

During the 1290s Arnau was apparently back at Montpellier, this time as a regent master, though occasionally he can also be found advising the new king, Jaime II, on his family's health. This was a period of great intellectual fruitfulness. Arnau composed a number of scientific works in these years, in which he developed aspects of medical theory. Simultaneously, his personal theological views were maturing along Joachimite lines; like the spiritual Franciscans with whom he was also beginning to establish close ties, he viewed the contemporary church, its institutions and orders, as corrupt, and he took that corruption to manifest the coming end of a historical age. When Jaime II sent him to Paris and to King Philip le Bel in 1300 to negotiate the status of the disputed Vall d'Aran, Arnau took the opportunity to defend these views as set out in his *De adventu antichristi* before the theologians of the Sorbonne: as a result, he was imprisoned as a heretic and released only at the intervention of the French monarch.

Seeking vindication, Arnau went now to Pope Boniface VIII, treating the pope successfully for the ailment of a stone and winning his agreement that Arnau's views, while rash, were not heterodox. With this assurance, Arnau renewed his attack on his adversaries, the scholastic theologians—Dominicans, in particular—whom he accused more harshly than ever of faithlessness, of having abandoned the study of the Bible for secular sciences. The installation of a friend as Pope Clement V in 1305 gave Arnau still more support and allowed him the calm to return to intellectual reflection and composition, in both his fields of activity. His most careful work on clinical medicinae, the *Regimen sanitatis* prepared for Jaime II, was written at this time, as was his *Speculum medicinae*, an ambitious attempt to draw current medical theory together synthetically. Yet simultaneously (1306) he was composing his *Expositio super antichristi*, doctrinally the most complex of his theological writings. He looked now to Clement as the authority destined to lead the reform of the church and society that would enable them to confront the Antichrist, and he believed that he had won over Jaime II and his brother Frederigo III of Sicily (Trinacria) to his program. But in 1309 Arnau went too far in his claims about Jaime, who thereupon broke completely with his former advisor and friend. Frederic, however, continued faithful, implementing Arnauldian spiritual principles in his kingdom even after Arnau's death in 1311.

On balance, Arnau enjoyed more success as a physician than as a theologian and reformer. A council at Tarragona condemned a dozen of his theological works in 1316, and most of the several Beguine communities inspired by his ideal of a lay spirituality dwindled away where they were not suppresssed outright. The taint of heterodoxy may have contributed to the later ascription to Arnau of many alchemical works, none with any verisimilitude. His genuine medical writings are numerous, however, and enjoyed great popularity down to the sixteenth century—particularly his *Regimen sanitatis* for Jaime II and the *Medicationis parabole* dedicated to Philip le Bel in 1300. Arnau's more abstract scientific writings are often original attempts to develop some particular aspect of medical theory and to imbed it within a broader naturophilosophical framework, and—like his *Aphorismi de gradibus*—they show considerable breadth of knowledge and imagination. Often harshly critical of his academic colleagues, he was particularly severe on their overdependence upon Avicenna's *Canon*, which had been the dominant authority behind the thirteenth-century schools. (To be sure, his own works are heavily marked by Avicennan problems and conclusions.) In 1309 he was one of three advisors who helped Clement V draw up a new curriculum for the medical faculty at Montpellier, one that made the works of Galen rather than Avicenna the core of medical instruction at that school. Attempts have been made to see his theological and medical positions as unified, but in many respects he seems to have been able to keep his two lives/passions compartmentalized.

MICHAEL MCVAUGH

Bibliography

Arnaldi de Villanova Opera Medica Omnia. vols. 2, 3, 4, 6.1, 15, 16, 18, 19 published to date. Barcelona, 1975– .

Crisciani, C. "Exemplum Christi e Sapere. Sull'epistemologia di Arnaldo da Villanova," *Archives Internationales d'Histoire des Sciences* 28 (1978), 245–92.

García Ballester, L. "Arnau de Vilanova (c. 1240–1311) y la reforma de los estudios médicos en Montpellier (1309)," *Dynamis* 2 (1982), 97–158.

Perarnau, J. *L'"Alia Informatio Beguinorum" d'Arnau de Vilanova*. Barcelona, 1978.

Santí, F. *Arnau de Vilanova: L'obra espiritual*. Valencia, 1987.

VILLENA, ISABEL DE

Elionor Manuel de Villena was born in 1430. She was the illegitimate daughter of the famous writer, Enrique de Villena, who died when she was a child. Her aunt, María of Castile, the queen of Aragón, raised her at the court in Valencia and probably encouraged her to become a nun in her teens. Taking the name Isabel, she entered the Trinidad of Valencia, an old monastery that the queen had just converted into a convent. Not without opposition, she became its abbess in her thirties. She died there in 1490 as a result of an epidemic of plague.

Isabel de Villena's only extant work is the *Vita Christi*, a lengthy book she left unfinished. Her successor as abbess, Aldonça de Montsoriu, had it printed in 1497, when Queen Isabel of Castile requested a copy. Isabel de Villena kept in touch with many important writers of her time, some of whom dedicated works to her. Scholars believe her book to be a response to the misogynist works of some of her contemporaries. Among the many feminist features mentioned are the great predominance of women characters and the defense of their moral superiority. This *Vita Christi* undoubtedly is unlike the other works of its kind.

In effect, the work begins with the immaculate conception of the Virgin and ends with her miraculous assumption to heaven, the life of Jesus being only its central part. Before and after the life of Jesus, there are lengthy allegorical scenes in which women play very important roles. During Jesus' life, Magdalene is presented as his true spiritual companion, the coprotagonist of this part of the work. The detailed description of their platonic love relationship is strikingly beautiful. Whereas other authors say Magdalene was frivolous, Isabel de Villena writes that common people always enjoy gossiping about rich women. Her passionate defense of Magdalene is perhaps a defense of her own mother and, ultimately, of herself. After all, Isabel apparently suffered due to the circumstances of her birth. Indeed, she probably was forced to become a nun, and had difficulties becoming an abbess, due to her irregular status. Like many other medieval women writers, Isabel de Villena invoked God's favor to strengthen a precarious position in an unfriendly world.

CRISTINA GONZÁLEZ

Bibliography

Hauf i Valls, Albert G. "La *Vita Christi* de Sor Isabel de Villena y la tradición de las *Vitae Christi* medievales," *Studia in honorem prof. M. de Riquer*. Vol. 2. ed. Carlos Alvar et al. Barcelona, 1987. 105–64.

Cantavella, Rosanna Introduction to *Protagonistes femenines a la "Vita Christi."* Ed. Rosanna Cantavella and Lluïsa Parra. Barcelona, 1987. vii–xxxi.

Villena, Isabel de. *Vita Christi*. Ed. R. Miquel i Planas. 3 vols, Barcelona, 1916.

VIOLANTE

Violante (1235–1300), wife of Alfonso X of Castile-León (1252–1284), daughter of Jaime I of Aragón (1213–1276) and Violante of Hungary. Violante's betrothal to Alfonso took place in 1243, but because of her age the marriage was not celebrated until 1249. Violante eventually bore Alfonso six sons and four daughters: Fernando, Sancho, Pedro, Juan, Jaime, Enrique, Berenguela, Isabel, Leonor, and Violante. She is better known for her intercessions into Castilian diplomacy. Violante played an active role in improving Alfonso's relations with Aragón during the unsuccessful 1254 revolt by the Infantes Enrique and Fadrique.

The Infantes and their allies, the Haros, had entered into an alliance with Jaime I that endured until Violante appeared before her father and begged for mercy for herself and her children. Jaime later claimed that consideration for the well-being of his daughter and grandchildren caused him to break the alliance. Violante strove to strengthen her family's position, and to this end she at first maintained political relations with her siblings and tried to arrange their marriages. As her children got older she served as an intermediary in their quarrels. At the *cortes* (parliament) of Seville in 1264 the towns of Extremadura petitioned her to intercede with the king over their taxes, which she accomplished successfully; at the cortes of Burgos in 1272 she was part of the committee that received noble and ecclesiastical petitions; and she negotiated peace between Alfonso and his brother, Felipe, after the latter's revolt in 1272 to 1273. During the crisis of succession caused by the death of her oldest son, Fernando de la Cerda, in 1275, Violante brought his children, known as the Infantes de la Cerda, and their mother, Blanche, out of Castile to her brother Pedro III of Aragón in January 1277, only returning to Castile at the request of Sancho in the summer of 1279. She abandoned Alfonso X during the 1282 civil war to support Sancho, and was present during the Cortes of Vallodolid in 1282 that degraded Alfonso and named Sancho ruler of Castile. Violante died while on pilgrimage to Rome at Roncesvaux in 1300.

THERESA M. VANN

Bibliography

Ballesteros Beretta, A. *Alfonso X El Sabio*. Barcelona, 1984.

Gonzalez, J. *Reinado y Diplomas de Fernando III*. 3 vols. Córdoba, 1980.

Hillgarth, J. N. *The Spanish Kingdoms 1250–1516*. 2 vols. Oxford, 1976.

O'Callaghan, J. F. *A History of Medieval Spain*. Ithaca, New York, 1975.

VISIGOTHIC KINGDOM, TOULOUSE AND TOLEDO

In 418 the Roman Empire, represented by the master of the soldiers and effective military dictator of the West, Constantius (d. 421), made a treaty with the Visigoths under their king, Wallia (r. 416–419). By this they were to be established as "federates" in the province of Aquitania Secunda, a region extending approximately from the Garonne to Carcassone, and to receive maintenance from the empire. Details of the nature and purpose of this arrangement remain uncertain and have generated much historiographical controversy recently. It has been argued that Aquitaine was chosen as the area of settlement to enable the Visigoths to defend western Gaul from the threat of the *Bagaudae*, peasant rebels and bandits who had been active north of the Loire until 417. Under the circumstances this is not entirely credible. Equally unclear is the nature of the system, known as *Hospitalitas*, by which the imperial government proposed to reward its new allies. Traditionally, this was seen as involving a redistribution of the estates, woodlands, and slaves of the principal Roman landowners of the region, with a third or more of the property being given to the German "guest." More recently and convincingly it has been argued that what was redistributed was not real estate but the tax revenue owed to the central government.

Wallia's successor, Theoderic I (r. 419–451), who established his capital at Toulouse, was less willing to cooperate with the empire than his two predecessors, and changes in the imperial government after 425 also led to an alteration in attitudes on the Roman side. Under the direction of the master of the soldiers, Aetius (d. 454), imperial armies tried to destroy the Visigothic kingdom. In 437 Toulouse was besieged, but the Roman commander Litorius was overconfident, and was defeated and killed. In 451, when the Huns under Attila invaded the western half of the empire, Aetius was forced to turn to the Visigoths for aid. They contributed most of the army that defeated Attila at the battle of the Catalaunian Plains. In this victory Theoderic I was killed, and was succeeded by his son Thorismund (r. 451–453). He soon fell victim to a conspiracy among his brothers.

Under Theoderic II (r. 453–466) the territory of the Visigothic kingdom rapidly expanded. His alliance with the new western military dictator Ricimer (d. 472), himself of Visigothic origin, led to an invasion of Spain in 456. The Suevic kingdom centered on Mérida was almost destroyed, and the southern provinces of Spain came under Visigothic rule. Theoderic's brother Euric (r. 466–484) completed the process in the 470s when his armies crossed the Pyrenees and conquered the remaining Roman territory in the northeast. Under this king, who had obtained the throne by murdering his brother, further territorial gains were also made in Gaul. The Auvergne, the last Gallic region under direct imperial rule, was ceded to the Visigoths in a treaty made with Emperor Julius Nepos in 475. By the time of Euric's death the Visigothic kingdom, still centered on Toulouse, extended from the valleys of the Loire and the Rhône to the southern coast of Spain. The only territory in this that was not under its rule, but subject to its influence, was the Suevic kingdom in the northwest of the peninsula.

Euric had been a committed Arian, and, like some of his predecessors, distrustful of the political loyalty of some of his principal Roman subjects. Under his son Alaric II (r. 484–507) a much closer integration between the two populations began to develop. In 506 a council representing the whole of the Catholic Church under Visigothic rule was held at Agde, and in the same year the king issued his *Breviary*, a substantial code of Roman law, which may have been intended to apply to all his subjects. However, the rise of the Merovingian Franks in northern Gaul in the 490s and 500s threatened the kingdom. Conflict broke out in 507, and in the Battle of Vouillé near Poitiers the Visigothic army was defeated and the king killed. In the aftermath virtually all of the Visigothic kingdom in Gaul except for Septimania, the Mediterranean coastal region in the southwest, fell into the hands of the Franks and their Burgundian allies.

According to a sixth-century chronicle, probably compiled in Zaragoza, the Visigoths had been establishing settlements in Spain in the 490s. This may help explain the ease of their eviction from Gaul and lack of resistance. Even so, many Visigoths may have remained in Gaul and passed under Frankish rule, in due course losing their Gothic identity. The numbers of Visigoths in Spain may in consequence have been quite limited. The center of royal government was moved from Toulouse to Narbonne, but after another defeat at the hands of the Burgundians in 511, which led to the overthrow of Alaric II's illegitimate son Gesalic (r. 507–511), it was transferred south of the Pyrenees to Barcelona.

The Visigothic kingdom was preserved at this point by the intervention of the powerful Ostrogothic ruler Theoderic the Great (ca. 454–526), whose kingdom in Italy dominated the western Mediterranean at this time. His armies intervened, and a regency was established for his infant grandson Amalaric, the son of Alaric II's marriage to Theoderic the Great's daughter Theodegotha. Little is recorded of this period of Ostrogothic domination, which remained centered on the northeast of Spain. Amalaric attained his majority in 526, the year of his grandfather's death, but he was probably murdered by his own men in 531 after yet another humiliating defeat at the hands of the Franks. Power was then taken by Theudis, one of the Ostrogothic generals who had previously dominated the kingdom.

For much of the sixth century, a poorly documented period in the Iberian Peninsula, there seems to have been little integration between Hispano-Romans and Goths. On the other hand, prior to the 580s there is not much evidence of the kind of mutual intolerance that had marked some of the late fifth century, and the Catholic Church was able to hold a number of provincial synods under Theudis. The decline of the Frankish threat in the middle of the sixth century seems to have led to more interest being paid by the kings to affairs in the south. Under Theudis the Visigoths established an enclave in North Africa centered on Ceuta, but were expelled from this by imperial forces around the year 546. Theudis's successor, Theudisclus (r. 548–549), set up his court in Seville prior to his murder in an act of private vengeance.

The difficulties of what was still rule by an army of occupation are very apparent in the next reign, that of Agila (r. 549–554), who so offended the citizens of Córdoba that they successfully rebelled against him, defeated his army, and captured his treasure. Following this humiliation he was overthrown in a civil war with Athanagild (r. 554–568). One or other of the two, the sources being divided on this, appealed to the emperor Justinian (527–565) for help. The imperial forces took control of a strip of land along the southeastern coast and set up an administration in Cartagena. From this they were not finally expelled until 626. Athanagild began the process of trying to recover this territory, and it was continued by his successor Leovigild (r. 569–586). It was also Athanagild who first established the center of royal government at Toledo in the very middle of the peninsula. Leovigild followed him in this, and it remained the capital until the fall of the kingdom in 711.

Leovigild transformed the standing of the Visigothic monarchy by a series of campaigns in the 570s that ended the rebellion of Córdoba (572) and brought virtually all of the north of the peninsula under his control. This was completed by the conquest of the tiny Suevic kingdom in 584. In the meantime Leovigild had had to face new problems in the south, with the revolt of his son Hermenegild in Seville in 580. This was crushed in 583 to 584, and the military unification of the peninsula under the Visigothic monarchy was virtually complete by the time of Leovigild's death.

His son Reccared (r. 586–601) added a crucial new dimension to this by his personal conversion to Catholicism in 587, and the holding of the Third Council of Toledo in 589, which formalized the rejection of Arianism throughout the kingdom. In consequence, a unitary church emerged that proved the most enthusiastic supporter of the Visigothic monarchy. It also became possible for remaining cultural conflicts between the Roman and Germanic elements in the kingdom to be resolved, and by the late seventh century there existed a real possibility that a new common ethnic identity was coming into being that would embrace all of the inhabitants of the realm. Thus Hispania could have turned into Gothia in the way that Gaul became Francia/France.

Although the evidence relating to personalities and events in seventh-century Spain is very limited, it is clear that the kingdom continued to develop, despite occasional periods of political instability. Military threats from beyond the frontier became fewer, and in consequence the general preparedness of the army to face invasion from Africa in 711 by Arab and Berber forces was not great. At the same time it seems probable that a civil war was raging in consequence of the unexpected death of King Wittiza in 710 and the contested seizure of power by Roderic (r. 710–711). With the defeat of the latter by the Arabs under Tarīq and the subsequent fall of Toledo, centralized resistance ended and the kingdom fell. Two last Visigothic kings, Achila (ca. 710–713) and Ardo (713–720), held out in Catalonia and Septimania until the Arab conquest of Spain was completed in 720. For all of its problems, though, the Visigothic period had created the idea of the unity of Spain, and many of the dominant features of its culture were revived in the Christian states in the north of the peninsula that emerged in the aftermath of the Arab conquest.

Roger Collins

Bibliography

Collins, R. *Early Medieval Spain: Unity in Diversity, 400–1000*. London, 1983.

Jiménez Garnica, A. M. *Orígenes y desarollo del Reino Visigodo de Toledo*. Valladolid, 1983.

Orlandis, J. *Historia del reino visigodo español*. Madrid, 1988.

Teillet, S. *Des Goths à la nation gothique*. Paris, 1984.

Thompson, E. A. *The Goths in Spain*. Oxford, 1969.

VISIGOTHIC KINGS

The institution of kingship was apparently unknown to the Visigoths prior to the election of Alaric in 395 as the leader of a large section of the people. The subsequent history of this group not only established the permanency of their separate ethnic identity, but also made the role of king central to their political organization. According to the historians—Roman in culture if not always in race—who wrote about the history of the people, Alaric and his family were Balts, descendants of a dominant lineage of the period prior to the Visigothic entry into the Roman Empire in 376. This claim needs to be treated with caution. Even if true, Alaric I (r. 395–410) was succeeded by his brother-in-law Ataulph (r. 410–416), and his successors Wallia (r. 416–419) and Theoderic I (r. 419–451) may have had no family relationship with the previous kings.

This was a continuous theme in the history of Visigothic kingship. For whatever reasons the first king of a new royal line was chosen, it was rare that his heirs were able to retain the throne for more than two or three generations. Thus the line of Theoderic I died out with his great-grandsons Gesalic (r. 507–511) and Amalaric (r. 526–531). The next dynasty, that founded by Liuva I (r. 568–573) and his brother Leovigild (r. 569–586), expired in the third generation with Liuva II (r. 601–603). In the seventh century Sisebut (r. 612–621) and Chintila (r. 636–639) passed the throne to infant sons, who were deposed or killed very rapidly. More successful were those who associated their sons as joint rulers during their own reign, as did Chindasuinth (r. 642–653) and Egica (r. 687–702), but their dynasties extended no further.

The problem was not one of political instability, in that, apart from the years 710 to 711, changes of dynasty were accomplished by palace coup and were not accompanied by civil war. The issue seems more to have been one of credibility. From its inception Visigothic kingship was related to war leadership. Children could not exercise this, and in consequence they were vulnerable to deposition. Although it is often said that Visigothic kingship was elective, and a formal elective process appears to have been carried out to validate royal successions, in practice this was no more than a ritual, and was functionally similar to the electoral procedure followed in the consecration of late Roman and Byzantine emperors. The vested interests of the supporters of the previous ruler normally guaranteed the succession of his heir, but in the event of weakness being displayed, due either to incompetence or mere youth, the king's own backers might conspire to remove him, to prevent more fundamental threats developing from opposition groups. A confrontational change of ruler might affect the economic standing and status of a wide body of office holders.

On occasion, though, a regionally based challenge to the central authority might develop. Thus the successful revolt of Sisenand (r. 631–636) against Suinthila (r. 621–631) began on the northeastern frontiers. Count Paul of Narbonne attempted to do the same in 672 against Wamba (r. 672–680), who had been chosen king by the court nobility. In 710 or 711 Achila II (r. 710–713) had made himself master of the same region in opposition to the centrally chosen Roderic. Other such regional rebels are not recorded in literary sources, of which there are few, but are known of from coins. Thus, a certain Ludila seems to have established a short-lived regime in Mérida and the South in the early 630s.

These coups and revolts have tended to make modern historians see the Visigothic kingdom as fundamentally unstable. However, far more striking is the fact that the kings preserved a unitary kingdom in the Iberian Peninsula from the sixth century to the Arab conquest. This is not true of the Franks, the Anglo-Saxons, or the Lombards. This achievement in forging and maintaining a politically united Hispania was unmatched in the West at this time. It also left an ideological legacy that later generations of Christian rulers in the Asturias, León, and Castile frequently attempted to manipulate.

The credit for much of this rests with the church. Following the Third Council of Toledo in 589, a relationship developed between the kings and the bishops that was unparalleled elsewhere in this period. A series of councils were held throughout the seventh century that dealt not only with matters of ecclesiastical observance and discipline, but also extended themselves into areas of government and law. In particular, a series of canons were issued by the Fifth (636) and Sixth (638) Councils of Toledo threatening the use of spiritual sanctions against those who plotted against the king, and also attempting to protect the interests of his supporters after his death. In practice, however, seizure of the throne by a coup, such as that of Chindasuinth in 642, did not lead to the threatened imposition of excommunication, as his success was proof of the new king's legitimacy and divine approval. Ecclesiastical censure was reserved for those who conspired and failed.

By the time of the Eighth Council of Toledo in 653 the church was going further by trying to mold the character of kingship and define the qualities needed in a ruler. The questions of legitimacy and opposition to regional attempts to subvert central authority were refined in the work of Bishop Julian of Toledo (680–690), who emphasized the need for formal procedures of investment, above all of anointing, to take place in Toledo. From the 680s until 710, succession was much more carefully managed within a framework of designation of the heir by the existing ruler and the formal preservation through intermarriage of dynastic continuity. This concern with consensus was disrupted by Roderic's seizure of power in defiance of the claims of his predecessor's family in 710.

It was also the church that developed and articulated the ideology of the *gens et patria* (people and homeland). This emphasis on the unity of the people and of the "country" underpinned the political reality of centralized rule of the kingdom on the part of the

Visigothic kings, and was intended to counteract the strongly centrifugal character of the society of the peninsula, which was the product of its geography and much of its history. In the upper levels of society at least a sense of common identity was actively being fostered at the time the kingdom came to its abrupt end.

A concomitant feature of this emphasis on unity centered on common adherence to the Catholic faith and a Gothic ethnic identity, and rule from Toledo by divinely selected kings was the rising persecution of the Jews in the kingdom. As religious uniformity was probably the strongest of the elements being used to express the unity and cultural cohesion of the kingdom, those who clearly could not conform in matters of faith also became subject to suspicion as to their political loyalty. Various kings attempted to remedy this, not always with the full support of the church. Sisebut (r. 612–621) attempted a conversion by force, which was deemed inappropriate. Conversion had to be genuine, though in practice later attempts at conversion were largely based on coercion and the imposition of legal liabilities on those who resisted. In the second half of the seventh century, kings and bishops came to doubt the genuineness of new converts' adherence to Christianity. What began as the persecution of a religion became increasingly that of a race. This culminated in the decree of King Egica (r. 687–702), enslaving most of the Jewish population of the kingdom. In part this measure may have been one prompted more by fiscal than by ideological motives. The enslaved Jews and what they themselves had owned became royal property.

The financial resources of the Visigothic monarchy may not have been sufficient for its needs at this time. Inadequate evidence survives relating to taxation in this period to make any firm pronouncements about it, but royal revenues may have derived primarily from land owned by the kings both by virtue of their office and by inheritance. A clear distinction was made in both secular and ecclesiastical legislation between royal lands and the family property of the king. The latter did not remain in the hands of the fisc after the ruler's death. Thus, nondynastic successions could present financial difficulties for a new ruler, and the solution was often the appropriation of the possessions of those who had supported the previous king. This certainly seems to have happened after Chindasuinth's seizure of power in 642.

Little is known about the mechanics of royal government, in that only a fragment of one document produced in a royal chancery has survived from the Visigothic kingdom. The existence in the major towns of royal officials, called counts, responsible for justice and maintenance of local order is certain. Other royal appointees held the office of "duke." There may have been only one of these for each of the six provinces, and their responsibilities were primarily military. They probably commanded the levies raised from local landowners. The king himself was surrounded by a permanent armed following, his *Comitatus*, which provided the nucleus for the royal army. The probable death of the king, the destruction of his *Comitatus*, and the rapid seizure of Toledo—the ritual and administrative center of the kingdom—explain the fatal paralysis that affected Visigothic Spain after the victory of the Arab invaders over Roderic in 711.

Roger Collins

Bibliography

Claude, D. *Adel, Kirche und Königtum im Westgotenreich.* Sigmaringen, 1971.

Collins, R. *The Arab Conquest of Spain.* Oxford, 1989. 6–22.

———. *Early Medieval Spain: Unity in Diversity, 400–1000.* London, 1983.

García Moreno, L. A. *Historia de España visigoda.* Madrid, 1989.

King, P. D. *Law and Society in the Visigothic Kingdom.* Cambridge, 1972.

VISIGOTHS

It is perhaps too easy to imagine the Visigoths as a unitary people, migrating over the course of half a millennium from an original home, located in the region of the southern Baltic, to a final one in the Iberian Peninsula. Older maps of the "Age of Migrations" link these two with a line of movement that takes the Visigoths from the Baltic to the steppes of southern Russia, across the Danube, around much of the Balkans, into and out of Italy, through France, and across the Pyrenees.

This implies a continuity in ethnic identity that is fallacious. Of the history of the already mixed body of population known up to the 370s as the *Theruingi* little is known, and that only from Roman sources. It is probably safer to say that a mixed confederacy of Germanic and Uralo-Altaic peoples established themselves in a region extending from the north shore of the Danube to the River Dnestr in the late third century. This lacked a unitary political structure, but the dominant cultural elements in it were of essentially Germanic origin. In the early 370s this society disintegrated, ostensibly as the result of attacks on it by the nomad confederacy of the Huns. This, though, should probably be seen as itself a symptom of significant ecological change in this region that made the maintenance of a settled agricultural economy less feasible.

In consequence, there occurred a large-scale movement of population out of this region and toward the frontier of the Roman Empire along the Danube. In 376 Emperor Valens (r. 364–378) permitted many of these refugees to enter the empire and settle themselves in the northeast of the Balkans. Ill-treatment at the hands of local Roman officials led to their revolt in 378, and the attempt by the government to suppress this led to disaster when the Roman army was defeated and Emperor Valens killed at the battle of Adrianople. The new emperor, Theodosius I (r. 379–395), who was of Spanish origin, was able to make a new agreement with the leaders of the rebels in 381, and for the rest of his reign they provided much of the military manpower that he used in his wars. In this period from 376 to 395 a new ethnic identity began to be forged, and the people thenceforth known as the Visigoths took shape. It was at this time that they converted as a group to Christianity, albeit of the then dominant Arian persuasion. With the death of Theodosius I a period of internal conflict and weakness developed in the empire, and a significant group of the Germanic soldiery united under the leadership of Alaric, the first king of the Visigoths. His confederacy, which was drawn from people of a wide range of tribal origins, was Gothic in that this was its predominant cultural component. However, it is important to note that other elements of population of Gothic origin remained behind in the Balkans when Alaric led his confederacy into Italy in 408. This event and the movement of this body of people through Italy, into Gaul, in 412, briefly into Spain in 416 through 418, and its establishment by treaty in southern Aquitaine in 418 really marked the decisive points in turning what could have been a short-lived and shifting confederacy into a coherent and self-conscious ethnic entity.

ROGER COLLINS

Bibliography

Collins, R. *Kingship, History and Ethnic Identity in the Early Middle Ages*. Alingsås, 1991.

Liebeschuetz, J. H. W. G. *Barbarians and Bishops: Army, Church and State in the Age of Arcadius and Chrysostom*. Oxford, 1990.

Wolfram, H. *History of the Goths*. Trans. C. J. Dunlap. Berkeley, 1988.

W

WALLĀDAH BINT AL-MUSTAFKI

Wallādah, who lived in Córdoba in the eleventh century, was the daughter of Caliph Muḥammad al-Mustakfi. Her house was a meeting place for writers. She had a tempestuous relationship with the famous poet Ibn Zaydūn, who dedicated many of his poems to her. Wallādah accused him of sleeping both with her slave and his own secretary, a man by the name of ʿAli. In turn, she had affairs with Muhya, a woman poet, and with the vizir. Her relationship with Ibn Zaydūn ended badly. Most of her nine extant poems are about him. Some are delicate love poems, such as: "Expect my visit at dusk, for I find that night is the best time to hide secrets. What I feel for you is such that by its side the sun would not shine, the moon would not rise and the stars would not begin their nocturnal journey." Some are obscene satirical poems: "You are called the hexagonous, a name that will endure beyond your life: faggot, buggerer, philanderer, fucker, cuckold, thief."

Although Wallādah's lifestyle was unconventional, her poetry was not. In addition to panegyrical poems, a genre she seems not to have cultivated, satirical and love poems were very popular among the poets of al-Andalus. The works of women poets, for the most part, took the form of a dialogue with their male counterparts. In accordance with this fashion, Wallādah's love and satirical poems consist of dialogues with Ibn Zaydūn. However, if she followed established genres, she did so with originality and flair. Wallādah held her own against the best male poets of her time. Indeed, she was considered brilliant.

It is said that Wallādah had the following two verses embroidered on her tunic: "By God, I was made for glory and I proudly follow my own path" and "I offer my cheek to whomever loves me and give a kiss to whomever desires me." She seems to have followed her mottos, because she became a legendary poet and lover who has excited the imagination of readers for centuries.

CRISTINA GONZÁLEZ

Bibliography

Garulo, T. *Diwan de las poetisas de al-Andalus*. Madrid, 1986.

Sobh, M. *Poetisas arábigo-andaluzas*. Granada, n.d.

WAMBA

Of Wamba's origins and early career nothing is known. He was elected king by the members of the court nobility assembled at Gerticos following the death of Recesvinth in September 672, and it is probable that he was one of their number. He was faced with opposition in the provinces of Narbonensis and Tarraconensis following his consecration at Toledo, a Count Paul was proclaimed king in Narbonne. After a brief campaign against the Basques in the upper Ebro River valley, Wamba crossed the Pyrenees and crushed Paul's revolt early in 673, capturing him at Nîmes. These early episodes are recorded in detail in Julian of Toledo's *Historia Wambae*, but the rest of the reign is less well documented. Wamba annoyed the church by a policy of establishing new dioceses, including one in the suburbs of the capital city, but no criticism was voiced in the Eleventh Council of Toledo of November 675, the only one held during his rule. From the inscriptions recorded in the *Chronicle of 754* it is clear that the walls of Toledo were restored by Wamba in 675. Other signs of military activity come from the law in the *Forum iudicum* attributed to Wamba, which lays down penalties for landowners, lay and clerical, who fail to turn out for army service. In 680 the king fell so ill that his death seemed inevitable, and he therefore assumed a penitential state, but he subsequently recovered. Bishop Julian of Toledo, doubtless with the support of some of the nobility, insisted that by canon law he could not resume his secular office, and forced him to retire to a monastery. A conspiracy between Julian and the new king, Ervig (680–687), has sometimes been suggested, and the Asturian chronicles see the latter's achievement of power as a usurpation. In the Roda version of the *Chronicle of Alfonso III*

Wamba, here said to be his uncle, is later made to advise King Egica to break free of his marriage to Ervig's daughter. However, it seems more probable that Wamba died before the holding of the Thirteenth Council of Toledo in November 683.

ROGER COLLINS

Bibliography

Orlandis, J. *Historia del reino visigodo español*. Madrid, 1988. 130–36

Thompson, E. A. *The Goths in Spain*. Oxford, 1969. 219–31.

WEIGHTS AND MEASURES

The ancient Roman system of weights and measures was likely introduced into Spain following the conquest initiated in the third century B.C. This system evidently remained operative in the Romanized parts of the Iberian Peninsula during the Visigothic era. In book 16, chapters 25–26 of his *Etymologies*, Isidore of Seville (ca. 560–636) discussed weights and measures. To some extent his purpose seems that of the antiquarian but the general import of what he says leads one to conclude that the ancient system was still in use.

The basic Roman weight was the *libra* (.722 of a pound) consisting of twelve Roman ounces. The subdivisions of the libra were: *sescunx* (1/8), *sextans* (1/6), *quadrans* (1/4), *trieme* (1/3), *quincunx* (5/12), *semis* (1/2), *septunx* (7/12), *bes* (2/3), *dodrans* (3/4), *dextans* (5/6), and *deunx* (11/12). The Roman ounce (*uncia*), 1/12 of a libra, or .96 ounces, was divided into *semuncia* (1/2), *duella* (1/3), *siculum* (1/4), *miliarum* (1/5), *solidus* (1/6), *semi-sextula* (1/12), *scripulum* (1/24), *obolus* (1/48), and *siliqua* (1/144). Measures of volume or capacity were the *sextarius* of .53 liters and its subdivisions: *quartarius* (1/4), *acetabulum* (1/8), *ligula* (1/48), and *hemina* (1/2). Multiples of a sextarius were *congius* (6), *modius* (16), *urna* (24), and *amphora* (48). Isidore mentioned many but not all of the weights and measures given above. The foot (*pes*) as a measure of length equalled 11.64 inches and was subdivided as follows: digit (*digitus*), 1/16 of a Roman foot, or .73 inches; inch (*uncia*), 1/12 of a Roman foot, or .97 inches; palm (*palmus*), 1/4 of a Roman foot, or 2.9 inches; *palmipes* of 14.5 inches; cubit (*cubitum*) of 17.4 inches; step (*gradus*), 29 inches; pace (*passus*), 5 Roman feet, or 58 inches; rod or pole (*decempeda*), 10 Roman, or 9.7 English feet; stade (*stadium*), 625 Roman, or 604 English, feet; mile (*mille passus*), 1000 paces, or .918 of a mile.

A major change transpired as a consequence of the Islamic invasion of Spain in the eighth century. The system of weights and measures devised during the first century of Islam was later imported into the peninsula. The standards for weight were the *ritl* (in Spanish, *arrelde*), or pound, consisting of 16 ounces (*ūkīya*). Multiples of the ritl were the qintār (in Spanish, *quintal*) of 100 pounds, and the *rub'* (in Spanish, *arroba*), a quarter of a qintār, or 25 pounds. Islamic sources do not always give the same values for each of these weights. For metals the weights were the *mithqāl* for gold (4.72 grams) and the *dirham* for silver; the *qirat* (in Spanish, *quilate*), or carat, was half a dirham. Dry measures of volume or capacity were the *mudd* (in Latin, *modius*; in Spanish, *almud*) of 15 ritl; the *sa'*, a quadruple of a mudd; the *qafīz* (in Spanish, *cahiz*) consisting of 60 ritl, 18 rub'; the *fanika* (in Spanish, *fanega*) was half a qafīz. The *kada*, a measure for wheat, was 15 to 30 pounds depending on the region. Liquid measures were the thumn, 1/8 of a rub' or 2 ritl; the *kulla* was 12 thumns; the kulaila, a small jug of 112 ounces; *khabiya*, a jar of 20 rub'. Measures of length included: the *dhirā'*, or cubit, of .71 meters; *shibr* of 237 millimeters; *qabda*, or palm, of 79 millimeters; the *kala* was seven cubits; the *kasaba* was 4 cubits. Distances were calculated in terms of a day's journey or *marhala*, and the *mil*, or mile, of 3000 cubits. The usual agrarian measure was the *mardja'* (in Spanish, *marjal*) of 25 square cubits and the *zawrj* of 1000 square cubits. This system continued after the collapse of the caliphate through the years of the kingdom of Granada.

In the course of time the Arabic system was largely adopted in Christian Spain. The *fueros* (municipal codes) of the eleventh and twelfth centuries indicate acceptance of such Arabic terminology as *arroba*, *cafiz*, and *quintal*. At the assembly of Jerez in 1268 Alfonso X attempted to establish uniformity by identifying specific weights and measures. For wheat he required the use of the cafiz of Toledo (about 18 bushels), consisting of 12 *fanegas* (about 1.60 bushels); each fanega contained 12 *celemines*, each subdivided into 12 *cucharas*, or tablespoons. The *arrelde* of Burgos (4 pounds) could also be used as a dry measure. The measure for wine was the *moyo* of Seville (258 liters, or 2.2. barrels), divided into sixteen *cántaras* (each about 4 gallons). The standard for weights was the *marco alfonsí* of 8 ounces. Two marcos equaled a *libra*, or pound (16 ounces), 25 libras an arroba, and 4 arrobas a quintal (100 pounds). The measurement for cloth was the *vara* (about 2.8 feet). Copies of these weights and measures were sent to each town where municipal inspectors were required to see that honest and true standards were maintained and to fine violators (*Fuero Real*, 3, 10, 1; *Partidas*, 7, .7, 7).

The usual land measurement was the *yugada* (in Latin, *juger*), the area that a yoke of oxen could plow in a day, or about 74 acres. In Andalusia vineyards, olive groves, and orchards were measured by the *aranzada*, about 1.23 acres.

Reiterating the need for uniformity, Alfonso XI laid down additional standards in the *Ordenamiento of Alcalá* (cap. 58) in 1348. He declared that coins should be weighed by the mark (*marco*) of Cologne (8 ounces). Other metals, liquids, and wool, sold by weight, should use the mark of Trier (8 ounces); 2 marcos equaled a libra; an arroba would be 25 libras; the quintal of oil in Seville would consist of 10 arrobas. Where the arrelde was in use, it would equal 4 libras. Wheat and wine and other things sold by measure would use the Toledan fanega (12 *celemines*) and the *cántara*, consisting of 8 *azumbres*. Cloth would be sold by the *vara*. At the close of the Middle Ages Fernando and Isabel once again required the use of uniform weights and measures.

JOSEPH F. O'CALLAGHAN

Bibliography

Arié, R. *L'Espagne musulmane au temps des Nasrides (1232–1492)*. Paris, 1973. 356–57.

O'Callaghan, J. F. *The Learned King: The Reign of Alfonso X of Castile*. Philadelphia, 1993. 123–24.

WHITE COMPANIES

Known also as the Great Companies and the Free Companies, these bands of mercenary soldiers provided valuable and professional military assistance to feudal lords and kings in times of war and lived off plunder and pillage in times of peace. The earliest medieval form of these professional armies-for-hire made its appearance in the mid-twelfth century, when international armed groups were assembled to assist in the crusading effort in the Holy Land. In spite of official attempts to disband them once the period of useful service was over—including a formal papal sanction in the thirteenth century—they remained a serious threat to safety and public order.

The frequent wars of the fourteenth century, especially the protracted conflict between England and France known as the Hundred Years' War, revitalized Western Europe's mercenary armies; increased their importance, number, and size; and resulted in serious threats to the safety and stability of many regions. When a truce or peace rendered them unemployed, they supported themselves by theft and pillage, generally choosing their victims from a kingdom's prosperous centers.

When the companies that had fought for the French against the English and the Navarrese in the 1360s found themselves at liberty, they became a serious nuisance to French authorities. In 1364, Pope Urban V excommunicated them; they were encamped on the ramparts of Villeneuve-lés-Avignon, near the papal residence, and they were both intimidating and embarrassing. At the same time, a series of political and military conflicts evolving in the Iberian Peninsula created a need for their military services.

Pedro I of Castile (r. 1350–1369) was pursuing an ambitious territorial war against neighboring Aragón whose king, Pedro IV, was unable to stop him without outside military help. Pedro's domestic policies, moreover, had alienated an important sector of the Castilian aristocracy, and they rallied around the claims of Pedro's half-brother, Enrique de Trastámara, to the Castilian throne. Enrique needed military support to unseat Pedro and looked for it in France, first from King Jean II, and after 1364, from his successor, Charles V.

The international situation also contributed to the company's deployment in Spain. Pedro, in a departure from his father's policy of relative neutrality in the Hundred Years' War, had antagonized the French, defied the Avignon papacy, and leaned toward a military alliance with the English. Pedro was a danger to France, thus their willingness to help Enrique, whose efforts—begun in 1362—came to fruition in 1365. Pope Urban, King Charles, and King Pedro of Aragón agreed to finance the companies' intervention in Castile with the ostensive purpose of helping Enrique take the throne. The French entrusted the task of removing the soldiers from Avignon and preparing them to cross into Spain to the accomplished mercenary captain Bertrand du Guesclin.

The companies, some ten thousand strong, entered Castile from Navarre, after crossing Aragón. They were an international group made up of French, Italian, German, English, and Gascon soldiers including such renowned captains as Hugh Calveley, Matthew Gournay, and William Elmham. They succeeded in forcing Pedro out of Castile in 1366 and went back to France. Pedro returned to Castile, assisted by the Black Prince and an army that included many of the English and Gascon mercenaries who had fought earlier for Enrique. Pedro and the English won at the Battle of Nájera in 1367 and Enrique fled, returning the following year with a new contingent of troops led by du Guesclin. By then Pedro's alliance with the English had collapsed. At the Battle of Montiel in 1369, Enrique's side prevailed; he killed Pedro and ruled as the uncontested king of Castile until 1379.

The companies returned to France when hostilities between the English and the French broke out again in 1369. They remained a problem for the French crown until the middle of the fifteenth century, when most of the mercenaries were incorporated into the royal military levy and the rest expelled from the country.

CLARA ESTOW

Bibliography

Delachenal, R. (ed.) *Chroniques des règnes de Jean II et de Charles* V. 4 vols. Paris, 1910–20.
Froissart, J. *Chroniques.* 11 vols. Paris, 1869–99.

WINE AND WINE PRODUCTION

Now nearly extinct in their sylvan state, grapes (*vitis vinifera*) grew throughout the ancient Mediterranean. In Italy, grape vines were cultivated both in the north by the Etruscans and in the south by Greek colonists. The earliest known work on wine and agriculture was written in Punic. After the destruction of Carthage in 146 B.C., the Roman Senate decreed that this treatise be translated into Latin, and it subsequently became an important source for all Roman writing on viticulture. Cato's *De agri cultura*, the earliest surviving work in Latin prose, provides the first comprehensive survey of Roman viticulture. In it, he discusses the production of wine on large slave-operated villa estates, which suggests the importance of vine cultivation in an agrarian economy that traditionally had been one of subsistence farming. By 154 B.C., according to Pliny, wine production in Italy was unsurpassed. By the time Pliny wrote, Iberia had also become an important producer of wine in the Mediterranean. That same year, the cultivation of vines was prohibited beyond the Alps in order to protect Roman viticulture. In his *Republic*, Cicero states that the Roman Senate banned wine production in Iberia so as to improve the export potential of the Italian Peninsula. For the first two centuries B.C. wine was exported to the provinces, especially to Gaul, in exchange for slaves whose labor was needed to cultivate the large estate vineyards. In part, the wine trade with Gaul and Iberia was so extensive because its inhabitants, according to Pliny, were besotted by wine, which was drunk undiluted and without moderation.

Roman taste leaned toward *mulsum*, a weak beverage. Mulsum was a cheap Roman wine sweetened with honey that was often freely distributed to the plebs at public events to solicit political support. By the first century A.D. the domestic market for it had became so demanding, however, that wine again had to be imported from Iberia and Gaul. Galen, a physician at a gladiatorial school in Pergamum before becoming the personal physician of Marcus Aurelius in A.D. 169, commented upon the medicinal uses of wine. He said he had used wine to bathe the wounds of gladiators and mixed potions of wine and theriacs (drugs) to protect the emperor from poisons.

Cultivation of the vinifera grape in ancient times was probably first introduced into Iberia by the Greeks. Wine growing held little importance for the Romans during the early years of the Republic, since they were busy fighting to expand their domination of the Iberian Peninsula. By the middle of the second century B.C., however, Rome controlled the Mediterranean, and there was wealth to be had in vineyards and in the wine trade from the provinces. Roman authors praised the quality of Spanish wines, especially those of the Ebro River valley and the southern part of the peninsula known as Betica. Most vineyards there were situated near the sea coast or along navigable rivers to facilitate transportation of the grapes and the wine produced from them.

Since the earliest times, vines were pruned and tended, and the grapes harvested and brought in baskets to be trodden or crushed in the wine press, which the Romans had developed and which could produce a second, inferior run of must or juice from the dregs. The must then underwent fermentation and maturation. Weaker wines were aged in large clay containers partially buried in the ground. The more full-bodied wines were fermented in the open air to promote the oxidation characteristic of a mature wine. The wine was then racked either for storage, sometimes in a warm, smoky loft to promote aging; or for transport, usually by sea since it was cheaper to ship wine from one end of the Mediterranean to the other than to haul it even short distances overland. The daily drink in the *taberna* or tavern, was usually red wine not more than a year old, drawn from supplies stored in skins and drunk from earthenware mugs.

Wine almost always was mixed with water for drinking. Drinking undiluted wine was considered provincial and even barbarous. The Romans usually mixed one part wine to two parts water (sometimes hot or even salted with sea water). The Greeks tended to dilute their wine with three or four parts water, which they always mixed by adding the wine. Many of these practices persist in the Mediterranean into modern times. Distillation was unknown in the ancient world and would not be discovered until the early Middle Ages. In Iberia in the thirteenth century, the Catalan physician, intellectual, and alchemist Arnau de Villanova commented on the distillation of wine in a treatise he wrote on the subject of flavoring of aqua vitae with various herbs and spices. He especially praised the restorative and life-giving properties of libations derived from distilled wine. Ramón Llull likewise asserted their vitality and believed their production by distillation was a divinely inspired gift from Heaven.

The cultivation of grape vines during the High Middle Ages became a cornerstone of Iberian Christian agricultural expansion into newly conquered territories. Their diffusion entailed a complicated interweaving of cultural, climatic, and economic processes. That the diffusion of the grape was intimately linked to that of monasticism is beyond doubt; the Benedictine rule specified that monks should drink approximately one liter of wine per day. During the Middle Ages, wine making was associated with practically all the monasteries of the Iberian Peninsula. In the Rioja region, for example, documents from the archives of San Millán de la Cogolla, San Martín de Albelda, San Prudencio de Monte Laturce, and other monastic houses, attest to the importance assigned to grape growing. Cultivation increased greatly during the high Middle Ages and plantings increased significantly with the gradual Christian conquest of the Muslim lands of the peninsula, although wine had been drunk and was sung about in Muslim Iberia from earliest times. Documentary references to vineyards in both La Rioja Alta and Baja abound from the second half of the eleventh century on. The cartularies make continuous references to specific vineyards and inventories, deeds of land, bequests, trades, and other transactions regarding wine.

One of the first monastic records to mention viticulture in the Iberian peninsula is the *Cartulario de Longares*, authorized by the Bishop of Nájera and the Prior and the monks of the Monastery of San Martín de Albelda in 1063. In it, the local population is obliged to dedicate two days per year to the monastery for the purpose of ploughing and tilling the land, pruning the vines, and harvesting the grapes. Additionally and in general, the transportation of grapes and wine to the lord's residence was a feudal obligation throughout Castile.

Some Castilian kings are known to have implemented sanctions to protect wine production. Sancho IV, his son, Fernando IV, and his grandson, Alfonso XI, for example, all forbade the importation of wine from Navarra and Álava. At one point, there were strong protests from the citizens of Vitoria who were enraged by the sight of carters transporting wine from Logroño. The sight of several of them was said to have provoked the angry protests of the citizens of Vitoria, who tore open the wineskins that were being transported and spilled their contents in the dust. Alarmed by the gravity of the offense, the town council of Logroño, petitioned help from the king in the form of a royal order that would suspend the actions of the offenders.

Until the end of the twelfth century, the growing demand for wine in Iberia resulted in the progressive conversion first of wasteland, then of cereal land, into vineyards. As grain production increased, the value of vineyards rose. Cultivation of grapes was especially attractive to the small free proprietor, who could work a vineyard without recourse to a plow and sell any surplus, placing him in better position to maintain his freedom than the small cereal farmer, who was dependent on others for tools and milling. Grapes became commonplace all over Iberia. The standard references to *vineas* in lists of appurtenances, however, frequently refer to backyard vines rather than to medium- to large-scale agricultural operations involving commercial crops. Nevertheless, more and more land was changed over to grapevines, as demand rose. In Castile-León vineyards were probably converted primarily from cereal-producing land. In Catalonia, where extensive terracing was practiced from the tenth century on, vineyards tended to spread over hilly country at the expense of wasteland. Because of limited transportation, the scant commercialization in a society with virtually no towns, and the unwillingness of peasants to invest in vineyards too close to the frontier, grapes were grown in many places where their cultivation ceased after the crop was commercialized: throughout León, where grapes were the most important crop, despite the acidity of the soil; in the Arlanzón-Upper Ebro region of Old Castile, where it is now considered too high and too cold for grapes, but where in the High Middle Ages they were grown anyway; in Catalonia, in the Pyrenaic foothills of the Upper Segre, the valley of Ribes, and the plain of Cerdaña, where in defiance of natural conditions they were grown for three hundred years. The spread of grape cultivation in Upper Aragón in the eleventh century is of particular interest, especially in view of the marginal climatic and soil conditions there, but most especially because of the highly reputed wines produced in the neighboring Islamic kingdom centered in Huesca. It may well have been the case that although the Muslims grew grapes in great supply, they produced only enough wine for the local trade, responding to what must have been a lower per capita consumption than was current among Christians. The abundance of contracts for new vineyards in Aragón between 1150 and 1180 could only have meant that wine was being exported.

Contrary to what might be expected given the Qur'ānic prohibitions against the consumption of wine, the spread of Islam not only failed to eradicate the grapevine, but in fact increased its cultivation owing to the inventiveness of Islamic horticulture. In spite of indications in the literature of *Repartimiento* that grapes were not widely grown in certain areas of southern Iberia where vineyards later flourished—Seville, for example—the Arabic sources indicate that grape-growing, wine production, and wine drinking were widespread. Although one may assume that wine production was attuned to a certain degree to the needs of the Christian and Jewish communities (in the time of al-Ḥakam I there was a state-operated wine market in the Secunda district of Córdoba, where many Christians lived), there was a tremendous market for grapes, raisins, and wine among Muslims as well. This is the result of Iraqi and not Christian influence. Abū Hanīfa's dictum declaring the legality of drinking date wine was extended by Andalusi jurists to include all wines. Widespread wine drinking was common during the wave of Iraqi cultural influence during the reign of ʿAbd al-Rahmān II and was said to have been introduced by Ziryāb, the famous singer and arbiter of style who is credited with the invention of toothpaste. Al-Shaqundī reports that in Málaga the vineyards stretched on over the countryside, and that in Úbeda (a place not associated with Christian minorities) grapes abounded to the point where there was no market in them. A well-known Andalusi variety was the *qanbanī* grape of the Córdoban campiña, perhaps the most productive dry-farming area in the country.

E. Michael Gerli

Bibliography

Allen, H. W. *A History of Wine*. New York, 1961.

Glick, T. *Islamic and Christian Spain in the Early Middle Ages*, Princeton, N. J., 1979.

Johnson, H. *Vintage: The Story of Wine*. New York, 1989.

P. McGovern, et al. (eds.) *The Origins and Ancient History of Wine*. Philadelphia, 1995.

Unwin, T. *Wine and the Vine: An Historical Geography of Viticulture and the Wine Trade*. New York, 1991.

WISDOM LITERATURE

Wisdom literature is the genre in Romance languages that gives advice on conduct in brief utterances (called *proverbios*, *exemplos*, *palabras*, *castigos*, *dichos*, *sentencias* and their cognates), paratactically arranged: the literal indicative *maxim* may be distinguished from the metaphorical *proverb* and the imperative *instruction*.

Ethos

Generally speaking, its ethos, like that of biblical wisdom and the *refranero*, is hardheaded and conservative, valuing silence and secrecy (*poridat*) over speech (typically hasty), testing over trusting, protecting over offering. Accordingly a strain of obscurantism is present. The quality it exalts is cunning (*buen/mucho seso*, *manera/maña*, *recabdo*), conceived of as a weapon of defense rather than offense, which heads a scale of values, with knowledge/learning in the middle rank and strength/riches/social status at the bottom: cunning is proof against fortune. Thus this is an intellectual, elitist, and ascetic genre. Revenge is positively presented, synonymous with righteous punishment. The attitude expressed toward flattery is ambiguous: it is recommended as preferable to force, but in others is regarded with suspicion.

Style

The corpus uses all the rhetorical figures of brevity (sometimes verging on the enigmatic) and certain forms typical of international aphoristic style (antithesis, paradox, "A better than B"). The choice of images is consistent within the corpus: wisdom is praised in luminous, medical, and architectural terms (wisdom is the cure, sin/folly the sickness; it is a wall, a fortification, a pillar, and a foundation); cause and effect are rendered by vegetable (root and branch, fruit) and spatial (road) images.

Sources

Its sources in the Iberian Peninsula are four.

ARABIC

Two translations of Arabic collections that derive from ancient Greek collections, possibly via Byzantine redactions: the *Libro de los buenos proverbios*, from the *Kitāb adab al-falāsifa* of Hunayn ibn Ishaq (809–873), and *Bocados de oro*, from the *Mukhtar al-hikam* (ca. 1048–1049) of Abū-al-Wafa' al-Mubashshir ibn Fatik. Although their Arabic originals are cited by Jewish writers in twelfth-century Aragón, *Buenos proverbios* and *Bocados* make their first Spanish appearance at the court of Alfonso X around 1260; they are then used in texts emanating from Castilian court circles: the work of Juan Manuel and the *Libro del consejo* by a "Maestre Pedro," probably Pedro Gómez Barroso.

In Catalonia, prose works such as Jafuda Bonsenyor's *Llibre de paraules e dits de savis e filosofs* (also available in Spanish translation in the *Cancionero de Ixar*), commissioned by Jaime II (r. 1291–1327), and the *Llibre de saviesa*, commissioned by a King Jaime (probably, Jaime II), are related to *Bocados* and *Buenos proverbios/Poridat*, respectively: but whether the Catalan texts use the Arabic directly and whether they influence or are influenced by the Castilian is unclear.

Also translated from Arabic is the *Historia de la Donzella Teodor*, a battle of wits in which the wise maiden confounds a team of male antagonists. (The Portuguese translations of the seventeenth and eighteenth centuries are a rare example of wisdom literature in Portugal.) The Catalan and Latin text "Ex proverbiis Arabum" (Tarragona, Biblioteca Pública, MS Santes Creus 108 [*olim* 201], ff. 107–117) includes some material of Oriental origin.

The *Libro de los doze sabios* (c. 1327) and *Flores de filosofía* (the only clue to its origin is its use in *Zifar*, III) are probably modeled on *Buenos proverbios* or *Bocados* rather than translated from lost Arabic sources.

CLASSICAL

The earliest Hispanic sapiential text to draw, albeit indirectly, on classical Latin material seems to be *Rams de flors*, commissioned by Juan Fernández de Heredia (1310–1396): its main source is a Catalan John of Wales.

The *Dichos de sabios e philosophos*, translated from a lost Catalan original in 1407 by Jacob Zadique de Uclés, is unusual in the Castilian corpus in that it uses classical sources (doubtless via florilegia) in broadly equal proportions with biblical matter: in this respect it shows its Catalan origins.

The fifteenth century sees translations from preexisting Latin florilegia. The *Proverbios de Séneca* were translated and glossed by Pedro Díaz de Toledo for Juan II. The fragmentary Portuguese Ps-Seneca, *Liber de moribus* and *Formula vitae honestae* (Braga, Arquivo Distrital, Pasta de Fragmentos [*olim* Caixa 287], n. 1]), is the only known vernacular Old Portuguese wisdom text. The *De vita et moribus antiquorum philosophorum* of Walter Burley (1275–1345?) in its Spanish version (not later than 1435) provided the prose sayings with which Santillana precedes his verse *Bias contra Fortuna* (ca. 1448). The *Floresta de los philosophos* (not before 1448), probably prepared for Fernán Pérez de Guzmán (d. 1460?), is abstracted entirely from vernacular versions. The *Dichos de Quinto Curcio*, attributed to Alfonso de Cartagena, may well have been translated from a Latin epitome.

BIBLICAL

Old Testament wisdom contributed the model for fatherly advice, as in the *Proverbis* (ca. 1180) of Cerverí de Girona, alias Guillem de Cervera, and Santillana's *Proverbios* (ca. 1437); Hebrew parallelism was not widely imitated. The most biblical of the Old Spanish corpus, in style and imagery, are the verse *Proverbios morales* of Santob de Carrión. Some biblical material is interpolated in *Buenos Proverbios* in MS Escorial h-III-1, f. 129. The verse *Proverbios de Salamón* and prose *Proverbis de Salamo* seem not to be drawn in full from the Bible.

The aphoristic works of Ramon Llull in Catalan and Latin, although they have no identified source, belong in the tradition of scripture-based ascetic florilegia typified by the *Sententiae*, alias *De summo bono*, of St. Isidore.

MEDIEVAL LATIN AND VERNACULAR

Castilian and Catalan (but apparently not Portuguese) also have their own translations of texts that were known throughout Europe: the Latin *Distichs of Cato* (a major source for Cerverí; several independent versions), the *Dialogue of Secundus and the Emperor Hadrian*, the Western counterpart of *Donzella Teodor* (one Castilian version was translated for Alfonso X from Vincent of Beauvais), *The Letter of Saint Bernard on the Care of the Household*, and the Italian *Fiori di virtù*. (There seems to be no Hispanic version of the Latin *Dialog of Solomon and Marcolf*.)

Arrangement

Bocados, *Buenos proverbios*, and *Bias* (following their sources) frame their aphorisms in the exemplary biographies of the sages (a Greek format). Thus contextualized, the occasional judgments and *obiter dicta* may characterize the sardonic, often crankily misogynistic and wisecracking sage. (The individualistic sage, pronouncer of practical rules, should be distinguished from the systematic philosopher who writes and founds a school: see Augustine, *The City of God*, VIII:2.) The contest of wits similarly forms the structure of *Teodor* and *Secundus*.

Floresta de philosophos, like many Latin compilations, follows the text order of its sources.

The predominant arrangement is by topic (Cerverí, *Libro del consejo*, Bonsenyor, *Flores*, Zadique de Uclés, Santillana): this is symptomatic of medieval mental schemata (virtues and vices, etc.) rather than an indication that these are reference tools.

Transmission

The most influential texts were *Bocados* and *Buenos proverbios* (fourteen and eight extant manuscripts, respectively): their utilization by authors up to the fifteenth century constitutes a rare example of a continuous vernacular prose tradition. (There are twelve extant manuscripts of the Latin translation of *Bocados* attributed to Giovanni da Procida.) Stylistic development is small or nil, largely because the rhetorical repertoire of wisdom is rigid between cultures and ages. In content, a tendency away from cynicism toward idealism may be detected. The medieval texts vary considerably in their periods of survival: leaving aside modern scholarly editions, some, like *Flores* or *Buenos proverbios*, were never printed; some made little incursion into the sixteenth century (*Bias* last printed 1511, in chapbook form); some were in print up to the end of the sixteenth century but not beyond (*Bocados*, ca. 1550; Santillana's *Proverbios*, 1594). Exceptionally, *Donzella Teodor* is found as a chapbook as late as the nineteenth century; an edition of 1833 was the basis for a number of translations into Mayan.

BARRY TAYLOR

Bibliography

Faraudo de Saint-Germain, L. "El texto de los *Mil proverbios* de Ramon Llull atribuído a Salamón en un códice valenciano del siglo XV." In *Homenatge Millàs Vallicrosa.* Vol. 1. Barcelona, 1954. 551–86.

Mettmann, W. "Spruchweisheit und Sprüchdichtung in der spanischen und katalanischen Literatur des Mittelalters," *Zeitschrift für Romanische Philologie* 76 (1960), 94–117.

Sola-Solé, J. M. "Las versiones castellanas y catalanas de la *Epistola de gubernatione rei familiaris*, atribuída a San Bernardo." In *Diakonia: Studies in Honor of Robert T. Meyer*. Ed. T. Halton and J. P. Williman. Washington, D.C., 1986. 261–78.

Taylor, B. "Old Spanish Wisdom Texts: Some Relationships." *La Corónica* 14 (1985–86), 71–85.

Walsh, J. K. (ed.) *El libro de los doze sabios, o Tractado de la nobleza y lealtad*. Madrid, 1975.

WITCHCRAFT

Witchcraft, like magic, is concerned with producing effects beyond the natural powers of human beings. Witchcraft, however, is distinguished from magic by the idea of a diabolical pact or at least an appeal to the intervention of evil spirits in order to produce these effects. In such cases, supernatural aid is usually invoked either to effect someone's death, awaken passion and desire in others, call up the dead, or bring calamity or impotence upon enemies, rivals, and oppressors. In traditional belief, witches or wizards who pursued these practices entered into a pact with Satan, renounced Christ and the Sacraments, observed "the witches' sabbath"—performing rites that often parody the mass or the offices of the church—or paid homage to the devil. In return, they received preternatural powers from the Prince of Darkness, such as the ability to leave their bodies and move through the air, transporting themselves magically over great distances in short periods of time, assuming different shapes at will, and tormenting chosen victims. Often an imp or "familiar spirit" was placed at the witch's disposal, able and willing to perform any service that might be needed to further the witch's nefarious purposes.

Belief in witchcraft and its practice has existed since the earliest recorded history. Since ancient Egypt and Babylon it has played a conspicuous part in the history of human spirituality. References to witchcraft in Scripture are frequent and usually in the form of proscriptions. It is strongly condemned in both the Old and New Testament (Exod. 22:18; Lev. 20:27; Deut. 18:11–12; Kings 28; Acts 8:9; 13:6; Gal. 5:20; and Apoc. 21:8; 22:15). Roman Imperial law also assumed the reality of magical powers, and Horace's frequent references to Canidia, the sorceress, permit us to see the fear witches could inspire in ancient Rome. Under the empire in the third century the punishment of burning alive was prescribed by the state for witches who plotted another person's death through enchantment. Early church legislation followed much the same course. In the Iberian Peninsula, as early as the Council of Elvira (306), the witholding of last holy communion was prescribed for anyone who had killed by spell (*per maleficium*) and adds that such a crime could not be committed "without idolatry," which implies without the aid of some material artifice or malevolent intervention, since devil worship and idolatry were considered synonymous. Later, during the reign of the Visigothic king Chindaswinth the law code known as the *Fuero juzgo* records several statutes that proscribe all practitioners of magic, including diviners, fortune-tellers, enchanters, and those who give poisons and herbs to others. It goes on to condemn those who use written or verbal spells and disturb minds by invoking the devil, and to denounce sorcerers and rainmakers who ruin the crops by means of curses and nocturnal sacrifices to the "evil one." Beyond these specific references, the early documentation for Iberia remains scant, although several practices and beliefs in Galicia and the Basque country, which have survived into the current day through folklore, must have existed in the Middle Ages as well. We know from other more copious sources, however, that witches abounded all over Europe in the high and low Middle Ages, especially in neighboring Gaul, where Charlemagne urged his subjects to forsake their superstitious beliefs and condemned all kinds of witchcraft. Later, Ivon of Chartres incorporated a canon against witches from the Council of Ancyra into his collection that can also be found in the *Decretum* of Gratian, a major legal authority for all of Christendom, while allusions to witchcraft can also be found in Vincent of Beauvais's *Speculum Morale*, and other works.

By the thirteenth century, among the heretical Cathars in the Rousillon, who had close ties to Catalonia and the Iberian Levant, we find the most reliable documents concerning witchcraft for this period. The Cathar's dualistic beliefs were instrumental in the development of the Inquisition and inquisitorial ideas about witchcraft, and they led to the crusade against the Albigensians (the group of Cathars centered at Albi). In their interrogations, the inquisitors outline the dualism of Albigensianism in such a way that its practitioners would today doubtless be referred to as sorcerers and witches. At any rate it was at Toulouse, a hotbed of Catharism, that in 1275 the earliest example of a witch burned to death after judicial sentence of an inquisitor is found. The woman had confessed to having given birth to a monster after intercourse with an evil spirit and to having nourished it with babies' flesh she procured during nocturnal expeditions. The possibility of carnal intercourse between human beings and demons was accepted by some of the great schoolmen of the age, St. Thomas Aquinas and St. Bonaventure among them.

In Iberia proper, Gonzalo de Berceo, a cleric at San Millán de la Cogolla in La Rioja, told the tale of Theophilus in his *Milagros de Nuestra Señora*, in which he relates how this character had a nocturnal encounter with the devil at a crossroads and entered into a pact with him and the *uest antigua*, (the host of the damned) to sell his soul. At about the same time, the *Fuero of Cuenca* states categorically that "a woman who is a witch or a sorceress shall either be burnt or saved by iron." Other legal documents of the thirteenth century show that enchantment practiced with good intentions could be considered respectable and even praiseworthy. This was the view of Alfonso X, who outlined the case for so-called white magic in his *Siete Partidas* just as he condemns and defines the black arts and its practitioners: "los que encantan los espíritus malos e hacen imágenes y otros echizos, o dan hierbas para enamoramiento de los ombres y de las mugeres," ["those who invoke bad spirits and make images and other talismans, or give herbs as love potions to men and women"].

By 1334 there was a large-scale witch trial carried out at Toulouse in which eight out of sixty-three persons accused of offenses were handed over to the secular arm to be burned and the rest were imprisoned either for long terms or life. Two of the condemned, both elderly women, after repeated torture, confessed that they had attended witches' sabbaths, worshiped the devil, had been guilty of indecencies with him and other persons present, and had eaten the flesh of infants whom they had carried off by night from their nurses. Later, the Catalan Dominican, Nicolas Eymerich (1320–1399) points to the existence of three types of witchcraft in his *Directorium inquisitorium* (ca. 1376): (1) Consorting with the devil; (2) devil worship without direct association; and (3) those who conjure the devil to assist them with malevolent plots and transformations. Shortly thereafter, in the first part of the fifteenth century, the polymath and intellectual, Enrique de Villena (1384–1434), was reputed to be a sorcerer on the basis of his interest in science and the preternatural. After his death, Juan II of Castile ordered Villena's confessor, Fray Lope de Barrientos, to burn Villena's library. Barrientos, who was not averse to Villena's interests, put the library to good use composing his *Tractado de especies y adivinanzas*.

By the end of the fifteenth century charges of witchcraft were often entertained by the Inquisition in Castile and Aragón in innumerable depositions, documents, and trials. However, it is a fictional character, Celestina, the main protagonist of the work of the same name by Fernando de Rojas (1499), who perhaps best exemplifies witchcraft in late medieval Iberia. She is an aged former prostitute whose beauty is spent and in later years has become a procuress. She oversees a small brothel in her home, watches over more exclusive courtesans, consorts with pimps, and makes cosmetics, perfumes, and other potions and philters in a laboratory in her attic, as well as practices minor surgery restoring lost maidenheads. Most importantly, she engages in erotic sorcery and conjures the devil through talismans to assist her in conquering others' objects of desire. While Celestina is a character from fiction, legal and inquisitorial documents from Toledo, Salamanca, and Seville from the period in which the work was first published show she was close to the real thing.

In conclusion, the evidence points to a sustained belief in Iberia and neighboring kingdoms during the Middle Ages that certain individuals, mostly women, could change themselves and others at will into animals; that they could fly through the air and enter secret places by leaving their body behind; that they could cast spells and make potions to inspire hate or desire in others; that they could conjure up storms, illnesses in humans and animals, and strike fear into enemies or mock them by playing terrifying jokes upon them.

E. Michael Gerli

Bibliography

Caro Baroja, J. "La magia en Castilla durante los siglos XVI y XVII." In *Algunos mitos españoles*. Madrid, 1944.

———. *The World of the Witches*. trans. Nigel Glendenning. Chicago, 1971.

Garrosa Resina, A. *Magia y superstición en la literatura castellana medieval*. Valladolid, 1987.

Homet, R. "Cultores de prácticas mágicas en Castilla medieval." *Cuadernos de Historia de España*, 63–64 (1980). 178–217.

Lea, C. H. *A History of the Inquisition of the Middle Ages*. Vol. 2. New York, 1955.

———. *A History of the Inquisition of Spain*. 3 vols. New York, 1966.

Severin, D. S. *Witchcraft in Celestina*. London, 1995.

WOMEN

Despite the Christian Church's assertion that a woman's claim to eternal salvation was the same as any man's, on earth women were nevertheless not considered equals. In medieval Iberia, their subordinate status is respected throughout the law codes of the different centuries and gave rise to laws clearly prejudicial to women.

In practical terms, women were nevertheless expected to be as strong and responsible as men. Men were the family members most often absent from the home and the nation. Women, especially wives, while physically less mobile, were capable of assuming continuous supervision over the family's possessions. In medieval Spain, women formed, along with the clerics, the more stable element of society, usually remaining behind to deal with, and bear responsibility for, the running of everyday life. Women administered estates, thereby allowing men the freedom, or obligation, to wage war; they raised children; cared for the sick and the destitute; and practiced crafts that helped keep the towns alive as centers of trade and commerce. Secure in the knowledge that they were in fact a much needed and appreciated segment of society, the somewhat destructive image of women left to literature was, no doubt, of little importance to women in the Middle Ages. They were not too concerned about the apparent inequalities of the law and the transparency of church dogma versus practice. They were too busy surviving.

As in all societies, every child born into the medieval world, aristocrat or peasant, male or female, Christian, Jew, or Muslim, received some form of instruction. In a threatened civilization, such as in medieval Spain, it was vital not only to maintain biological reproduction to assure physical survival but also to ensure cultural continuity. Each civilization and generation has to transmit its cultural identity to its young.

There were varying attitudes toward the formal education of women in medieval Europe. The *Siete Partidas* are quite clear in this regard, stating that girls be taught to read, to pray, and to sew. Early in life, the children of the nobility were put into the care of a tutor or governess after leaving the wet nurse. Approximately the first seven years of a boy's life were spent with women. Much attention was given to the choosing of a tutor for he would form and educate the boy, being his constant companion and adviser. No such requirements or guidance is given for the choice of a governess for a female child. Young noblewomen lived isolated from society, protected from the sight and sound of social evils. When the husband's duties called him away, the management of both the inner and outer economy of the estate fell to the wife. Herlihy has shown that in Spain between 700 and 1200, in comparison with the rest of Europe, a higher percentage of women and their heirs appear on documents as contiguous owners of land. Similarly, there is a higher percentage of women shown as principal alienators—donors or sellers—of land. This is no doubt due to the continued use in Spain of Visigothic laws and customs that permitted women—in contrast to the rest of Europe—to own land and to hold land for their minor children in their own names. It is also possible that, due to the husband's frequently long absences, and to avoid confusion and complication, conjugal lands were recorded in the wife's name only. Because a large part of the lands were sold or given to monasteries, this is also possibly indicative of more piety and generosity toward churches on the part of women in Spain.

The Arabs in Spain had schools for girls as well as for boys, with male and female teachers. The only limitation put upon female teachers was that they should be unmarried or, if married, be past the age of childbearing and rearing, such that they could be entirely dedicated to their students. The *Siete Partidas* contain many laws referring to instructors, schoolboys, and their studies, but there is not one reference to the presence of women as teachers or pupils. This is not to say that women were uneducated, or that they did not act as teachers. Queen Berenguela is referred to as the educating queen, since she taught not only her son Fernando III, but also her grandson Alfonso X. Alfonxo X in fact had two other tutors, García Fernández de Villademiro and his wife, María Arias. Most girls did not attend any kind of organized school; they were brought up at home, with a neighbor or relative. In fact, the extension of schooling for girls would not become common until the late eighteenth and early nineteenth centuries.

Women were not prevented in the Middle Ages from acting in a "masculine" fashion. Virility, in fact, was considered by many to be an enviable quality in a woman. All medieval women worked. Most women wove all the fabrics necessary to their households. Weaving was considered a very worthy occupation, even for the upper classes. Some wives living in a city helped their husbands sell goods at the markets and fairs, while others helped run shops. A literate wife was an essential asset to a merchant family, for the nascent capitalism of the Middle Ages could not afford to neglect the resources these capable women offered. In their husbands' absences, wives often ran family businesses, acting as agents. Others worked with their spouses as partners. Indeed, some women were trained by their fathers or husbands and themselves specialized in certain crafts. If the head of a family died prematurely, so as to guarantee the possession of the business to his heirs and to prevent a possibly tragic financial situation, women were allowed by the guilds to continue in their husbands' trade. They were given most of the prerogatives of master craftsmen. Most occupations open to women dealt with the cloth trade, clothing, jewelry, food preparation, and brewing. Usually working women founded their own all-women guilds. Before the thirteenth century, unmarried women could not become master craftsmen. After this time, provided they were over twenty years of age and had opened a shop or had the funds to do so, they were granted the privileges of a master and were allowed to hire journeymen and train apprentices. Peasant women worked in the fields beside their men. Like all working people in the Middle Ages, their lives were not idyllic; because they were vulnerable, women were perhaps exposed to more oppression than men.

For some children, religious vocation offered the chance to follow in paths quite different from those of their parents. The choice, though, was not always made by the child concerned. Technically, the practice of oblation became illegal in 1216. Nevertheless, in Spain children were put into convents, against their will at times, well before the mandatory age of fifteen. Monasteries were not only havens for those seeking to glorify God, but, not surprisingly, also served as places where parents could rid themselves of a crippled or burdensome child. The monastic ranks were replenished increasingly, not by individuals seeking perfection but by parents seeking a temporal vocation—similar to an apprenticeship—for their children. The incidence of religious calling among upper class women must have been quite high. Because girls were normally married at the age of fifteen or sixteen and widows were expected to remarry without undue delay, an unmarried woman was considered an anomaly in secular noble society. Great families felt bound to make provisions for girls unable or unwilling to marry and for those widows with important connections and an established place in society who could not be coerced into disposing of themselves and their property otherwise than as they wished. The convent served this purpose. This same refuge was sought by women whose marriages had been anulled and by repudiated wives. Convents then were apt to be exclusive, housing ladies and the daughters of the rich bourgeoisie. The poor and the low-born lived in the convents as servants. Unmarriageable rich girls were unproductive within their society and could easily be unburdened on convents, which required less dowry than a husband of their class. Poor girls, if unmarried, were still productive. They could stay at home and work in their brothers' homes and fields, or they could work outside the home as a domestic servant or in a trade. Convents also housed political prisoners, criminals, adulterous wives, unwanted mistresses, troublesome sisters, and the illegitimate offspring of nobles.

In the Middle Ages, one function that the monasteries and convents assumed was the operation of hospitals for the sick, the poor, the aged, and the destitute. Alfonso VIII of Castile recognized this need and founded such a hospital in Burgos. The women and men who cared for the sick there were probably nuns and monks from the nearby monastery as well as lay people. Working in a hospital must have been considered a form of penance for both lay and religious people. Many of the donations received by the religious orders were given with the proviso that the donor be cared for in old age. Before the separation of the sexes in the monasteries, elderly couples could both enter, either to care for the sick or to be cared for. Those with money received better treatment in the monasteries; those without means were given as much as possible in the hospitals. It would appear that these hospitals not only cared for the transients who became ill and for the chronically ill, but also for the majority of those rejected by society.

Women kept busy in many other walks of life. Certain "occupations" were not considered legitimate for men or for women. Minstrels, publicans, hagglers, and procuresses were considered *viles*. Some law codes demanded that female practitioners of certain "professions," such as herbalists, witches, and go-betweens, be burnt at the stake. There must have been a considerable number of these adventurers, both male and female, wandering the roads of the Iberan Peninsula, living off their wits, charity, or crime.

Abandoned or impoverished women formed the most vulnerable segment of society. These included women with or without children, family, or relatives willing to lodge and feed them; those unable to exercise a craft or art; and those ineligible or unwilling to enter a convent. In an effort to survive, many of these unfortunates became prostitutes.

As full participants, medieval women were expected and trained to be useful in the development of their society. Whether managerial, practical, or servile, their contributions were essential to the medieval world. In the castles, monasteries, shops, and fields of medieval Spain, women worked beside their men as equal partners.

MARJORIE RATCLIFFE

Bibliography

Alfonso X. *El Libro de las Siete Partidas*. 3 vols. Madrid, 1807.

Dillard, H. *Daughters of the Reconquest: Women in Castilian Town Society, 1100–1300*. Cambridge, 1984.

Herlihy, D. "Land, Family, and Women in Continental Europe, 701–1200," *Traditio* 18 (1962), 89–120.

WULFILA, BISHOP

Wulfila, or Ulfilas, was of mixed Gothic and Roman parentage, his grandparents on his mother's side being inhabitants of Cappadocia who were taken captive by the Goths in about A.D. 264. (He himself was born around the year 311.) He seems to have been one of a small number of Christians among the Goths in the early fourth century, and he devoted himself to evangelizing his people. In the early 340s he was made a bishop while on a mission to Constantinople, but was forced to flee to the Roman Empire in 348, when Athanaric began a persecution of Gothic Christians. He and other Gothic Christians were settled by Constantius II (r. 337–361) in the province of Moesia. Wulfila ruled this community as both bishop and political leader until his death in Constantinople, probably in 382. As during this period Arian theology was dominant in the imperial court and in many parts of the empire, it was this that Wulfila taught, and this contributed to the Visigoths accepting this form of Christian belief and converting *en masse* around the time of their entry into the empire in 376. At some unspecified stage in his career Wulfila translated a Greek version of the Gospels into Gothic. This is not preserved in full, in that the only substantial manuscript of the Gothic Gospels, the sixth-century *Codex Argenteus*, shows the influence on it of subsequent revisions based on Latin texts of the Bible. Gothic versions of the Epistles and of all or parts of the Old Testament are known only from fragments, but were probably not written before the fifth century.

ROGER COLLINS

Bibliography

Hunter, M. J. "The Gothic Bible." In *The Cambridge History of the Bible*. Vol. 2. Ed. G. W. H. Lampe. Cambridge, 1969. 338–62.

Thompson, E. A. *The Visigoths in the Time of Ulfila*. Oxford, 1966.

Y

YEHUDA ḤA-LEVĪ

Yehuda (Judah) ḥa-Levī (ca. 1075–1141), a physician and theologian, was chronologically the last of the four luminaries of the Andalusian school of Hebrew poets. He immigrated to al-Andalus from Christian Spain while a young man, but also spent considerable time in Toledo and in other towns along the fluctuating border between Islam and Christendom. Ḥa-Levī's brilliance as a lyric poet won him the acclaim and envy of Jewish literary intellectuals. By midlife he had become a highly respected communal leader. But after a glorious career as the darling of Jewish courtly society, Ḥa-Levī spent the last fifteen years of his life attempting to turn his back upon the culture and society that had nourished him. He began to formulate a plan to abandon Spain for a life of religious devotion in Palestine. After years of hesitation, and apparently against the counsel of his circle of friends, Ḥa-Levī finally set sail for Egypt in 1140, en route to Palestine, where he disembarked in 1141. He died shortly thereafter.

Ḥa-Levī's contribution to medieval Jewish religious thought is known as *The Kuzari*. This book of apologetics, the product of many years of work, underwent several revisions before its completion on the eve of Ḥa-Levī's departure for the East. Written for Jewish doubters, *The Kuzari* is the classic medieval defense of rabbinic Judaism against Christianity, Islam, Karaite Judaism, and, in particular, the Aristotelian philosophy that came into vogue in twelfth-century Muslim Spain. Constructed as a series of dialogues between a pagan king-turned-generic monotheist and representatives of philosophy, Christianity, Islam, and Judaism, *The Kuzari* endeavors to explain the apparent contradiction between the sociopolitical reality of the twelfth century and the claim of Judaism to be the supreme faith.

An unmistakable voice, a unique lyric sensibility, and vivid imagery characterize Ḥa-Levī's secular and liturgical verse. His masterful employment of quantitative meters to achieve poetic effects and his skill in cultivating the *muwashshaḥ* form earned him the reputation as the most gifted and adept poet of his age. Furthermore, Ḥa-Levī created new genres of Hebrew poetry and transfigured conventional motifs with his cycles of "sea poems" and "Zion poems." Early in his career he seemingly perfected the art of translating the worldly values of Andalusian courtly society into words of Hebrew poetry. Later, Hebrew verse became a vehicle for the expression of the poet's devotional longings and his religious disdain for Andalusian Jewish culture and society. The expressiveness and innovative content of Ḥa-Levī's poetry signal the beginnings of a break with many of the conventions of courtly tradition and the transition to the post-Andalusian age of Hispano-Hebrew poetry.

ROSS BRANN

Bibliography

Goitein, S. D. *A Mediterranean Society: The Jewish Communities of the Arab World as Portrayed in the Documents of the Cairo Genizah*. Vol. 5, *The Individual*. Berkeley, Calif., 1988, 448–68.

Schirmann, J. "The Life of Judah Ha-Levi." In *Studies in the History of Hebrew Poetry and Drama*. Jerusalem, 1979. Vol. 1, 250–341. (In Hebrew.)

YOSEF BEN MEIR IBN ZABARA

Yosef (Joseph) ibn Zabara (born ca. 1140) was a physician, Hebrew literary intellectual, and Jewish communal notable active in twelfth-century Barcelona. Little else is known about Ibn Zabara's life. He is principally known as the author of *The Book of Delight* (in Hebrew, *Sefer sha'ashu'im*), an artful and engaging book-length fantasy of self-discovery. In *The Book of Delight* a mysterious stranger lures Ibn Zabara's persona into traveling with him to distant and exotic lands. Along the way Yosef and the stranger experience unusual adventures and become locked in a battle of wisdom, wits, and will. They exchange information on an array of humanistic and scientific topics and entertain and test one another with countless poems, stories, anecdotes, parables, and maxims. At the end of their journey it becomes clear that the protagonist-stranger is actually Yosef's alter ego, with whom he must come to terms in order to return to his former life and station. There is some evidence to suggest that the idea for the story may have been based upon an event in Ibn Zabara's life.

Written in rhymed prose and interspersed with lines of poetry that enrich the narrative in various ways, *The Book of Delight* otherwise bears only the most superficial resemblance to Arabic and Hebrew *maqāma* literature. *The Book of Delight*'s frequent and extensive digressions and its incorporation of abundant miscellaneous scientific and literary material, much of it drawn from the corpus of international lore, on a wide array of subjects recalls the style of Arabic courtly prose literature (*adab*). On account of its rich and carefully plotted imaginative structure as well as its artistic quality, *The Book of Delight* stands out as a unique text in Hispano-Hebrew literary history.

Apart from *The Book of Delight*, Ibn Zabara appears to have authored several devotional poems and one or more works on medical topics. Since he is mentioned in a biblical commentary by the Narbonese exegete Joseph Qimhi, Ibn Zabara may have engaged in exegetical research as was common among Hispano-Hebrew literary intellectuals.

ROSS BRANN

Bibliography

Davidson, I. (ed.) *Sepher sha'shu'im le-r. Yosef ben Me'ir ben Zabara.* Berlin, 1925.
Dishon, J. *The Book of Delight by Joseph ben Meir Ibn Zabara* (Hebrew). Jerusalem, 1985.
Gonzàlez-Llubera, I. (trans.) *Llibre d'ensenyaments delectables.* Barcelona, 1931.

YSOPETE YSTORIADO

The earliest extant collections of Aesopic tales are in Latin verse (Phaedrus, 18 B.C.–A.D. 54), and in Greek prose (Babrius, first century A.D.). A series of recensions in Greek prose (Augustana) dating from the ninth century were printed by Bonius Accursius in 1474. The Accursian fable collection, sometimes also called the *Planudean* for Maximus Planudes (1260–1330), author of a Greek life of Aesop, were the source for Rinuccio Arezzo's (1380–1459) Latin translation of the folk biography and the tales. Relying on Rinuccio, Heinrich Steinhöwel prepared the first modern vernacular version, a German/Latin edition (Ulm, 1474). Translations based on Steinhöwel subsequently appeared in western Europe: Julien Macho (1480), William Caxton (1483), and three anonymous Spanish translations (Burgos, 1488; Zaragoza, 1489; Toulouse, 1496). Two Italian translations relied directly on Rinuccio: Francesco del Tuppo (1485), and Accio Zucco (manuscript, 1462; sixteen printed editions, 1479–1566).

The Spanish translations begin with the *Vida de Ysopo*, a folk narrative with ancient tales about the Babylonian Ahikar, the biblical Akyrios, and the Islamic Loqman that had adhered to the persona of Aesop, who was the prototypical clever slave. The first eighty tales, divided into four books, are based on medieval collections attributed to a fictional Romulus; seventeen tales thought to be Aesopic *Extravagantes*; seventeen attributed to Rinuccio (Remicio); twenty-seven from Avianus (end of fourth century, beginning of fifth); *Fábulas colectas* with fourteen tales from Petrus Alphonsi, eleven from Poggio Bracciolini (1488 edition). The 1489 and 1496 editions eliminate three Poggian tales; 1496 adds three from *Calila e Dimna*.

HARRIET GOLDBERG

Bibliography

Burrus, V., and H. Goldberg (eds.) *Esopete ystoriado (Toulouse 1488).* Madison, Wisc., 1990.
Cotarelo y Mori, E. (ed.) *Fábulas de Esopo: Reproducción en facsímil de la primera edición de 1489.* Madrid, 1929.

Z

ZAJAL *see* MUWASHSHAḤA

ZALLĀQAH, BATTLE OF

The opening engagement of a sixty-year-long struggle between León-Castile and the North African Berber Empire of the Almoravids for dominance in the Iberian Peninsula. It was fought on 23 October, 1086, on the plain north of Badajoz in that *tā'ifa* between the armies of the Almoravids commanded by the emir, Yūsuf ibn Tashf'in, and those of León-Castile led by its king, Alfonso VI. The Berber leader had the assistance of his Andalusian allies, chiefly the *tawā'if* of Seville, Málaga, Granada, Badajoz, and Murcia. Alfonso VI was assisted by a contingent from the kingdom of Aragón.

The battle lasted most of the day and both sides employed what were to remain their ordinary tactics. The Christians took the offensive with a frontal charge of heavy cavalry that failed to break the Muslim line of battle. The Muslims then began an attempt to envelop the Christian force, employing their superior numbers. Alfonso VI managed to fight free with a portion of his cavalry but his camp, foot soldiers, and perhaps 20 percent of his mounted warriors were lost in a running fight that lasted into the evening hours. He withdrew first to Coria and then to Toledo to prepare for a possible invasion of his own lands. But Yūsuf instead moved south to Seville and then returned to North Africa. He did not return to the peninsula until 1088.

BERNARD F. REILLY

Bibliography

Huici Miranda, A. *Las grandes batallas de la Reconquista durante las invasiones africanas*. Madrid, 1956.

Reilly, B. F. *The Kingdom of Leon-Castilla under King Alfonso VI, 1065–1109*. Princeton, N.J., 1988.

ZARAGOZA, CITY OF

Founded in 24 B.C. on the site of the Iberian settlement of Salduie, this veterans' colony received the name of Caesaraugusta and guarded a strategic bridge over the middle Ebro River. The capital of a *conventus* of the province of Tarraconensis, the city was an important center and, to judge by the remnants of its walls still standing, was strongly fortified. It was occupied by the Visigoths, and local uprisings in 496 and 506 were unsuccessful. Frankish attacks were directed against it in 541 and 621, and the city resisted forces of Froyla during his rebellion in 653. Although little is known of the Visigothic city, it appears to have been an important Christian center, and the church of Santa María la Mayor, popularly known as El Pilar, was already gaining fame.

Nevertheless, the city capitulated without resistance to the Muslim invaders in 714. Capital of a *waliate* (province) from 750 and chief city of the upper frontier, it was also the locale of numerous uprisings and civil strife, including that which led to Charlemagne's abortive attempt to seize the city in 778. It gained population and wealth under Muslim domination, profiting from its renowned textile manufacture, and became known as *Medina al-Baida*, the White City. In 1008, Zaragoza became an independent *tā'ifa* kingdom and entered an economic and intellectual golden age. Trade with Catalonia brought it wealth, and its rulers attracted poets, scientists, and scholars to their palace of the Aljafería, recently restored.

Muslim Zaragoza capitulated to Alfonso I of Aragón on 18 December 1118 after a siege of nine months and, in 1119, the Christian inhabitants were given the *fueros* of the *infanzones* of Aragón. Despite royal encouragement, the city was slow to recover from the exodus of Muslim craftsmen, scholars, and administrators. At the unexpected death of Alfonso of Aragón in 1134, Alfonso VII of Castile claimed sovereignty over the "Kingdom of Zaragoza," and the city was held by the Aragónese rulers in vassalage to Castile until 1162.

Zaragoza came to exercise many of the functions of capital of the Crown of Aragón. From 1276 onward, the kings were crowned there, with general *cortes* (parliament) in attendance. Under the union, cortes were held in the city annually, and, even after this requirement was rejected by the crown, Zaragoza remained the favorite site for convening such assemblies. The importance of the city as a manufacturing and commercial center grew slowly, reaching its height in the fifteenth century. It nevertheless remained a city of middle rank, with a population of about twenty thousand and dependent upon the export of agricultural products for its wealth. It failed to acquire a university, and its secular and ecclesiastical centers attracted relatively few intellectual or artistic leaders. Although the leading city of Aragón, it never achieved an importance comparable to the urban centers of Valencia and Barcelona.

LYNN H. NELSON

Bibliography

Beltrán Martínez, A. *Zaragoza: 2.000 años de historia*. Zaragoza, 1976.

Ledesma Rubio, M. L., and M. I. Falcón Pérez. *Zaragoza en la Baja Edad Media*. Zaragoza, 1977.

ZÉJEL *See* MUWASHSHAḤA

ZĪRIDS OF GRANADA, THE

The Zīrids were Berbers of the Ṣanhāja confederation in the tenth to twelfth centuries. The main branch was based at Qayrawān, but it was from the western branch, with its capital at Qalʿat Banī Ḥammād, that there sprang the Zīrids who intervened in the history of the Iberian Peninsula. In general, it was the policy of the ʿĀmirid *ḥājibs* to recruit troops from North Africa, but the historian Ibn Ḥayyān suggests that al-Manṣūr himself was unwilling to allow Zāwī (b. Zīrī) and his men to cross to al-Andalus because of Zāwī's reputation for shrewdness and cunning, and it was only under al-Manṣūr's son ʿAbd al-Malik, in 1002 or 1003, that they came. The caliphate was at this point descending rapidly into the Civil War of the Berbers (*al-fitna al-barbariyya*). In this, Zāwī backed the caliph Sulaymān (1009–1010, 1013–1016), and one explanation for the specific Zīrid connexion with Granada is that Sulaymān allocated Granada to them for services rendered. On the other hand the *Tibyān* [see below] has it that in the unsettled conditions then prevailing, the existing inhabitants of Elvira invited the Zīrids in to help them set up a more defensible stronghold on the Alhambra hill. (Perhaps the two stories may be reconcilable.) In 1019 Zāwī was able to beat off an attempt by one of the contenders for the caliphate, ʿAbd al-Raḥmān IV, to oust him from Granada, thus confirming the hold that the Zīrids had established there. But Zāwī was soon himself to return to North Africa (1020, or, according to García Gómez, 1025), leaving his nephew Ḥabūs (b. Māksan) in command. Ḥabūs styled himself only *ḥājib* (chief minister), and gave recognition to the caliphate of Yaḥyā (b. Ḥammūd) of Málaga, but with chaos all around, Ḥabūs kept his mountainous redoubt secure. The little state (*ṭā'ifa*) had many of the characteristics of tribal society, with much autonomy of action retained by clan chiefs, but in the circumstances of the day the formula worked well. Perhaps the most remarkable feature of this regime was the reliance it placed on Jewish administrators, in particular on Samuel (b. al-Nagrīlla) and his son, Joseph. The long reign of Ḥabūs's son Bādis (1038–1073) served further to consolidate Zīrid power, and there can be no doubt that the success of this little state was due to the administrative skills of its Jewish *wazīrs*. But the growing power of the Christians to the north to exert pressure and extract tribute (*parias*) meant that those responsible for raising the revenue (of necessity in excess of what was laid down in the Qur'ān, and thus unlawful) became deeply unpopular, and it was easy for the religious leadership to whip up anti-Jewish sentiment. In a pogrom in 1066 Joseph was killed (Samuel had died in 1055). The last of the Granadan Zīrids, ʿAbd Allah, 1073–1090, deprived of the services of this family of state servants, was ground down between the Christians, mainly the Castilians, and the rising power of the Almoravids, who became increasingly exasperated by what they saw as the ineffectual resistance that the various ṭā'ifas could offer to their infidel enemies. In 1090 ʿAbd Allah was forcibly removed from power, and shipped off to confinement in Agmāt in North Africa. It is to this circumstance that we owe a unique source of historical information. ʿAbd Allah in exile wrote his memoirs under the title of the *Kitāb al-tibyān* (Book of the Explanation), a far from straightforward account, but an invaluable one nevertheless. It brings out how the Ṣinhāja-based tribal solidarity on which Zīrid rule had at first rested disappeared in a welter of feuding and intrigue. Internal weaknesses might well have led to the collapse of the state had not the Almoravids come along first, and brought it to a sudden end.

L. PATRICK HARVEY

ZĪRĪDS OF GRANADA (CA. 1010–1090)

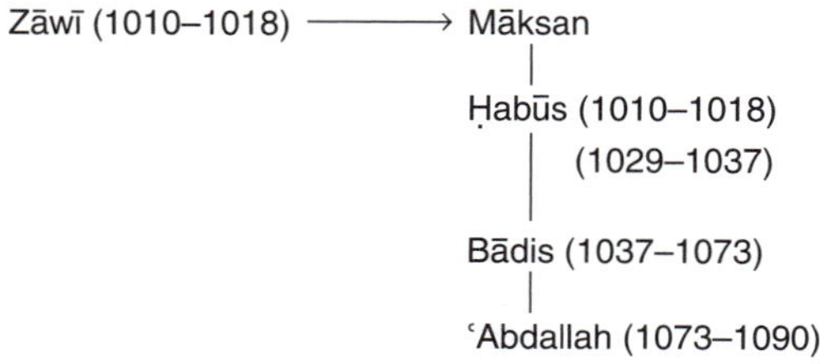

Bibliography

ʿAbd Allah (b. Buluggīn). *Kitāb al-tibyān*, Arabic text under the title *Mudhakkirāt al-amīr ʿAbd Allah* . . . Ed. E. Lévi-Provençal. Cairo 1955.

———. *El siglo XI en 1ª persona*. Trans. E. García Gómez. Madrid, 1980.

Idris, R. H. "Les Zirides d'Espagne," *Al-Andalus* 29 (1964), 39–137.

Peinado Santaella, R. G., and J. E. López de Coca Castañer. *Historia de Granada*. Vol. 2, *La época medieval: siglos VIII–XV*. Granada, 1987.

Tibi, A. *The Tibyān*. Leiden, 1986.

Wasserstein, D. *The Rise and Fall of the Party-Kings—Politics and Society in Islamic Spain 1002–1086*. Princeton, N.J., 1985.

Index